August 7-11, 2017
Shinjuku, Tokyo, Japan

Association for
Computing Machinery

Advancing Computing as a Science & Profession

SIGIR'17

Proceedings of the 40th International ACM SIGIR Conference on

Research and Development in Information Retrieval

Sponsored by:

ACM SIGIR

Supported by:

Yahoo Japan Corporation, Baidu, Alibaba Group, Amazon, Sogou, Rakuten, Wider Planet Inc., Microsoft Corporation, Yahoo Research, Google, IBM, eBay, NAVER Corporation, Huawei Technologies, Yandex, LINE Corporation, Hitachi Ltd., JASIST, FACEBOOK, Morgan & Claypool Publishers, Springer, NOW Publishers, Tokyo Metropolitan Government, NICT International Exchange Program, KDDI Foundation, The Association for Natural Language Processing, & National Institute of Informatics

Association for
Computing Machinery

Advancing Computing as a Science & Profession

The Association for Computing Machinery
2 Penn Plaza, Suite 701
New York, New York 10121-0701

Notice to Past Authors of ACM-Published Articles
ACM intends to create a complete electronic archive of all articles and/or other material previously published by ACM. If you have written a work that has been previously published by ACM in any journal or conference proceedings prior to 1978, or any SIG Newsletter at any time, and you do NOT want this work to appear in the ACM Digital Library, please inform permissions@acm.org, stating the title of the work, the author(s), and where and when published.

ISBN: 978-1-4503-5022-8 (Digital)

ISBN: 978-1-4503-5668-8 (Print)

Additional copies may be ordered prepaid from:

ACM Order Department
PO Box 30777
New York, NY 10087-0777, USA

Phone: 1-800-342-6626 (USA and Canada)
+1-212-626-0500 (Global)
Fax: +1-212-944-1318
E-mail: acmhelp@acm.org
Hours of Operation: 8:30 am – 4:30 pm ET

SIGIR 2017 Chairs' Welcome

Welcome to the 40th Annual International ACM SIGIR Conference on Research and Development in Information Retrieval (SIGIR 2017). SIGIR is the premier scientific conference in the broad area of information retrieval. We received a high-quality set of full-paper submissions to consider for inclusion in the conference program. We thank the 66 Senior Program Committee (SPC) members, 216 Program Committee (PC) members, and at least 70 additional reviewers for their contributions to paper selection. This pool of committed SIGIR volunteers was based in 33 countries and over 170 institutions, spanning academia, industry, and beyond. We recognized 8 SPC members and 29 PC members / additional reviewers whose contributions to the review process were outstanding.

We reviewed 362 papers for the full paper track, and accepted 78, for an acceptance rate of 22%. In total, there were 1056 authors from 42 countries: 299 from China, 232 from the United States, and 525 from the rest of the world. The countries (with at least 10 submissions) with the highest acceptance rates were the United Kingdom (42%), Italy (42%), Singapore (38%), Australia (27%), and the United States (24%). The most popular call-for-papers topics for accepted papers were ranking algorithms (19%), text representation (17%), behavioral analysis (15%), recommender systems (14%), and user studies (14%).

We made several modifications to the paper submission and review process for SIGIR 2017. We transitioned to EasyChair, one of three conference submission applications supported by ACM. We significantly updated the call for papers to broaden the range of topics considered in scope for the conference, and more accurately reflect current research trends. To boost diversity, we increased the number of women SPC members (24% this year, up from 15% last year) and increased the number of SPC members based in Asia (23% this year, up from 8% last year). To help improve review quality, we also required that PC members have at least one full paper at SIGIR and be active at the SIGIR conference in the past five years (some limited exceptions were permitted). The largest change was a modification to the role of the secondary SPC, with the goal of better utilizing their expertise and making better decisions for borderline papers. Each paper had a primary SPC member, who was responsible for writing the meta-review and making a recommendation regarding the paper's disposition. If they believed it was necessary, the primary SPC could request an additional review from a secondary SPC member, who did not see the other reviews or the discussion to date. Once they submitted the additional review, the secondary SPC member could see the other reviews and participate in the discussion. The additional SPC review informed discussion and helped the primary SPC make a recommendation. Overall, secondary SPC reviews were provided for 20% of full papers.

We ran an in-person SPC meeting at Microsoft in Redmond, WA. To allow more SPC members to take part, we enabled remote participation via video conference. Approximately half of the SPC participated, either in person or remotely. SPC members were asked to submit their full-paper recommendations prior to the meeting. During the meeting, we discussed papers flagged by SPCs as requiring discussion, as well as papers with "accept" and "reject" recommendations. Some of the papers marked as "reject" by SPC members before the meeting had strong support from at least one PC member. A subset of those full papers ended up being included in the conference program after a detailed discussion.

The short paper track received a record number of 398 submissions and accepted 121 (30%) of them. The track was chaired by Hui Fang, Mounia Lalmas and Yiqun Liu.

The demo paper track received 36 submissions and accepted 17 (47%) of them. The track was chaired by Gareth Jones and Takehiro Yamamoto.

The SIGIR Symposium on IR in Practice (SIRIP 2017) had seven invited talks and five accepted regular papers. The track was chaired by Sumio Fujita and Vanessa Murdock.

The doctoral consortium track received 14 submissions of which 9 (64%) were accepted. The track was chaired by Makoto P. Kato and Kira Radinsky.

The tutorial track received 14 proposals of which 8 (57%) were accepted. The track was chaired by Fernando Diaz and Adam Jatowt.

The workshop track received 12 proposals of which 8 (67%) were accepted. The track was chaired by Jaap Kamps and Grace Hui Yang.

We thank the above track chairs, their program committee members and reviewers for their hard work—including a small group of SIRIP PC members whom we have chosen not to disclose, as doing so would break the single blind review.

Hang Li
SIGIR'17 PC Co-chair
Huawei Noah's Ark Lab,
Hong Kong, PRC

Arjen P. de Vries
SIGIR'17 PC Co-chair
Radbound University,
The Netherlands

Ryen W. White
SIGIR'17 PC Co-chair
Microsoft Cortana,
USA

Noriko Kando
SIGIR'17 General Co-chair
National Institute of Informatics,
Japan

Tetsuya Sakai
SIGIR'17 General Co-chair
Waseda University,
Japan

Hideo Joho
SIGIR'17 General Co-chair
University of Tsukuba,
Japan

Table of Contents

Session 2A: Search Interaction 1

Session 2B: Filtering and Recommending 1

Session 2C: Other Applications and Specialized Domains

Session 3A: Search Interaction 2

Session 3B: Filtering and Recommending 2

Session 3C: Document Representation and Content Analysis 2

Session 4A: Evaluation 2

Session 4B: Retrieval Models and Ranking 2

Session 4C: Queries and Query Analysis

Session 5A: Retrieval Models and Ranking 3

Session 5B: Filtering and Recommending 3

Session 5C: Efficiency and Scalability

Session 6A: Personalization and Privacy

Session 6B: Conversations and Question Answering

Session 7A: Social

Session 7B: Entities

Short Research Papers

Short Resource Papers

Demonstration Papers

SIRIP 1: Start-Ups and Beyond

SIRIP 2: Start-Up Research and Academic Collaboration

SIRIP 3: Research at Large-scale Search Engines

Doctoral Consortium

Tutorials

Workshops

ACM SIGIR 2017 Conference Organization

General Chairs:	Noriko Kando, National Institute of Informatics Tetsuya Sakai, Waseda University Hideo Joho, University of Tsukuba
Program Chairs:	Hang Li, *Huawei Noah's Ark Lab* Arjen P. de Vries, Radboud University Ryen W. White, Microsoft Cortana
Short Paper Chairs:	Hui Fang, University of Delaware Mounia Lalmas, Yahoo! Yiqun Liu, Tsinghua University
Demonstration Paper Chairs:	Gareth Jones, Dublin City University Takehiro Yamamoto, Kyoto University
Best Paper Chair:	Douglas W. Oard, University of Maryland
SIRIP Chairs:	Sumio Fujita, Yahoo! JAPAN Vanessa Murdock, Microsoft
Publicity/Social Chairs:	Yukino Baba, Kyoto University Harumi Murakami, Osaka City University Falk Scholer, RMIT University
Tutorials Chairs:	Fernando Diaz, Spotify Adam Jatowt, Kyoto University
Doctoral Consortium Chairs:	Makoto P. Kato, Kyoto University Kira Radinsky, Technion
Workshops Chairs:	Jaap Kamps, University of Amsterdam Grace Hui Yang, Georgetown University
Proceedings Chairs:	Takuya Kida, Hokkaido University Masaharu Yoshioka, Hokkaido University
Sponsorship Chairs:	Tsuneaki Kato, The University of Tokyo Paraic Sheridan, Dublin City University
40th Anniversary Award Chair:	Diane Kelly, The University of Tennessee, Knoxville
Treasurers:	Akiko Aizawa, National Institute of Informatics Hiroaki Ohshima, University of Hyogo

Local Arrangements: Yuka Egusa, National Institute for Educational Policy Research
Emi Ishita, Kyushu University
Masao Takaku, University of Tsukuba

Student Volunteers Chair: Atsushi Keyaki, Tokyo Institute of Technology

Senior PC members: Eugene Agichtein, Emory University
James Allan, University of Massachusetts Amherst
Javed Aslam, Northeastern University
Leif Azzopardi, University of Strathclyde
Ricardo Baeza-Yates, NTENT / UPF / University of Chile
Peter Bailey, Microsoft
Timothy Baldwin, University of Melbourne
Krisztian Balog, University of Stavanger
Nicholas Belkin, Rutgers University
Michael Bendersky, Google
Paul Bennett, Microsoft Research
Peter Bruza, Queensland University of Technology
Jamie Callan, Carnegie Mellon University
David Carmel, Yahoo Research
Carlos Castillo, Eurecat
Yi Chang, Huawei
Kevyn Collins-Thompson, University of Michigan
Nick Craswell, Microsoft
Bruce Croft, University of Massachusetts Amherst
Brian Davison, Lehigh University
Maarten de Rijke, University of Amsterdam
David Elsweiler, University of Regensburg
Evgeniy Gabrilovich, Google
Julio Gonzalo, UNED
Jiyin He, Centrum Wiskunde & Informatica
Djoerd Hiemstra, University of Twente
Katja Hofmann, Microsoft Research
Xuanjing Huang, Fudan University
Grace Hui Yang, Georgetown University
Jaap Kamps, University of Amsterdam
Makoto P. Kato, Kyoto University
Diane Kelly, University of Tennessee
Oren Kurland, Technion, Israel Institute of Technology
Wai Lam, The Chinese University of Hong Kong
Matt Lease, University of Texas at Austin
Ee-Peng Lim, Singapore Management University
Christina Lioma, University of Copenhagen
Tie-Yan Liu, Microsoft Research Asia
Yiqun Liu, Tsinghua University
Yoelle Maarek, Yahoo Research
Qiaozhu Mei, University of Michigan
Donald Metzler, Google

Senior PC members (continued): Josiane Mothe, Universitŭ de Toulouse, Institut de Recherche en Informatique de Toulouse
Isabelle Moulinier, Thomson Reuters
Vanessa Murdock, Microsoft
Jian-Yun Nie, Universitŭ de Montrŭal
Douglas Oard, University of Maryland
Iadh Ounis, University of Glasgow
Benjamin Piwowarski, LIP6, Sorbonne Universitŭs/UPMC/CNRS
Barbara Poblete, University of Chile
Berthier Ribeiro-Neto, Google / Universidade Federal de Minas Gerais
Mark Sanderson, RMIT University
Chirag Shah, Rutgers University
Fabrizio Silvestri, Facebook
Mark Smucker, University of Waterloo
Ian Soboroff, National Institute of Standards and Technology
Ruihua Song, Microsoft Research Asia
Jaime Teevan, Microsoft Research
Andrew Trotman, University of Otago
Jun Wang, University College London
Jun Xu, Chinese Academy of Sciences
Emine Yilmaz, University College London
Chengxiang Zhai, University of Illinois at Urbana-Champaign
Min Zhang, Tsinghua University
Yi Zhang, University of California, Santa Cruz
Justin Zobel, University of Melbourne

PC Members: Mikhail Ageev, Moscow State University
Luca Maria Aiello, Bell Labs
Elif Aktolga, Apple
Omar Alonso, Microsoft
Ismail Sengor Altingovde, Middle East Technical University
Enrique Amigó, Universidad Nacional de Educaci: n
Massih-Reza Amini, Universitŭ Grenoble Alpes
Avi Arampatzis, Democritus University of Thrace
Ioannis Arapakis, Telefonica Research
Jaime Arguello, University of North Carolina at Chapel Hill
Xiao Bai, Yahoo Research
Zhifeng Bao, RMIT University
Gaurav Baruah, University of Waterloo
Klaus Berberich, Max Planck Institute for Informatics
Lidong Bing, Tencent
Roi Blanco, University of A Coru`a
Mohand Boughanem, Institut de Recherche en Informatique de Toulouse
Deng Cai, Zhejiang University
Iván Cantador, Universidad Aut: noma de Madrid
Robert Capra, University of North Carolina at Chapel Hill
James Caverlee, Texas A&M University
Kevin Chang, University of Illinois at Urbana-Champaign

PC Members (continued):

Hsin-Hsi Chen, National Taiwan University
Ruey-Cheng Chen, RMIT University
Zhumin Chen, Shandong University
Adrian-Gabriel Chifu, Aix-Marseille Universitŭ
Grzegorz Chrupala, Tilburg University
Tat-Seng Chua, National University of Singapore
Stephane Clinchant, Xerox Research Centre Europe
Michael Cole, LexisNexis
Gordon Cormack, University of Waterloo
Shane Culpepper, RMIT University
Tonya Custis, Thomson Reuters
Jeffrey Dalton, Google
Gianluca Demartini, University of Sheffield
Thomas Demeester, Ghent University
Dina Demner, National Institutes of Health
Hongbo Deng, Google
Laura Dietz, University of New Hampshire
B. Taner Dincer, University of Mugla
Shuai Ding, Google
Debora Donato, Mix Tech
Zhicheng Dou, Renmin University of China
Doug Downey, Northwestern University
George Drosatos, Democritus University of Thrace
Carsten Eickhoff, ETH ZΔrich
Tamer Elsayed, Qatar University
Yuan Fang, Institute for Infocomm Research
Yi Fang, Santa Clara University
Henry Feild, Endicott College
Nicola Ferro, University of Padua
Marcus Fontoura, Microsoft
Norbert Fuhr, University of Duisburg-Essen
Patrick Gallinari, Universitŭ Pierre et Marie Curie
Debasis Ganguly, IBM Research, Dublin
Bin Gao, Microsoft Research
Eric Gaussier, Joseph Fourier University
Shlomo Geva, Queensland University of Technology
Peter B. Golbus, Wayfair
Marcos Goncalves, Federal University of Minas Gerais
Roberto González-Ibáñez, Universidad de Santiago de Chile
David Graus, FD Mediagroep
Jiafeng Guo, Chinese Academy of Sciences
Ido Guy, eBay Research
Martin Halvey, University of Strathclyde
Allan Hanbury, TU Wien
Morgan Harvey, Northumbria University
Ahmed Hassan Awadallah, Microsoft Research
Claudia Hauff, Delft University of Technology
Ben He, Chinese Academy of Sciences

PC Members (continued): Qi He, LinkedIn
Xiangnan He, National University of Singapore
Daqing He, University of Pittsburgh
Chathra Hendahewa, Rutgers University
Liangjie Hong, Etsy
Frank Hopfgartner, University of Glasgow
Winston Hsu, National Taiwan University
Yuening Hu, Yahoo Research
Sam Huston, Google
Radu Tudor Ionescu, University of Bucharest
Shoaib Jameel, Cardiff University
Shen Jialie, Northumbria University
Jiepu Jiang, University of Massachusetts Amherst
Joemon Jose, University of Glasgow
Evangelos Kanoulas, University of Amsterdam
Jussi Karlgren, Gavagai / KTH Royal Institute of Technology
Enver Kayaaslan, NTENT Hispania
Heikki Keskustalo, University of Tampere
Evgeny Kharitonov, Criteo
Irwin King, The Chinese University of Hong Kong
Julia Kiseleva, Eindhoven University of Technology
Weize Kong, Google
Alexander Kotov, Wayne State University
Kriste Krstovski, Harvard-Smithsonian Center for Astrophysics
Udo Kruschwitz, University of Essex
Dmitry Lagun, Google
Will Lamond, Wayfair
Sylvain Lamprier, Universitŭ Pierre et Marie Curie
Yanyan Lan, Chinese Academy of Sciences
Ni Lao, Google
Léa Laporte, LIRIS
Birger Larsen, Aalborg University
Martha Larson, Radboud University
Chia-Jung Lee, Microsoft
Cheng-Te Li, National Cheng Kung University
Rui Li, University of Illinois at Urbana-Champaign
Cheng Li, University of Michigan
Chenliang Li, Wuhan University
Liangda Li, Yahoo Research
Shangsong Liang, University College London
Jimmy Lin, University of Waterloo
Huan Liu, Arizona State University
Xiaozhong Liu, Indiana University Bloomington
Chang Liu, Peking University
Bing Liu, University of Illinois at Chicago
Jingjing Liu, University of South Carolina
Claudio Lucchese, ISTI-CNR
Ping Luo, Chinese Academy of Sciences

PC Members (continued): Mihai Lupu, TU Wien
Yuanhua Lv, Microsoft Research
Hao Ma, Microsoft Research
Craig Macdonald, University of Glasgow
Joao Magalhaes, Universidade Nova de Lisboa
Ilya Markov, University of Amsterdam
Yosi Mass, IBM Research
Julian Mcauley, University of California, San Diego
Richard McCreadie, University of Glasgow
Rishabh Mehrotra, University College London
Tao Mei, Microsoft Research
Edgar Meij, Bloomberg
Massimo Melucci, University of Padua
Mandar Mitra, Indian Statistical Institute
Bhaskar Mitra, Microsoft
Alistair Moffat, University of Melbourne
Alessandro Moschitti, Qatar Computing Research Institute, HBKU
Yashar Moshfeghi, University of Glasgow
Franco Maria Nardini, ISTI-CNR
Liqiang Nie, National University of Singapore
Alexandros Ntoulas, LinkedIn
Salvatore Orlando, Universitō Cō Foscari Di Venezia
Jiaul Paik, Indian Institute of Technology Kharagpur
Laurence Park, Western Sydney University
Dae Hoon Park, Yahoo Research
Gabriella Pasi, University of Milano-Bicocca
Virgil Pavlu, Northeastern University
Jian Pei, Simon Fraser University
Raffaele Perego, ISTI-CNR
Vassilis Plachouras, Thomson Reuters
Pernilla Quarfordt, FX Palo Alto Laboratory
Kira Radinsky, eBay
Filip Radlinski, Google
Fiana Raiber, Yahoo Research
Karthik Raman, Google
Edie Rasmussen, University of British Columbia
Hadas Raviv, Technion, Israel Institute of Technology
Zhaochun Ren, JD.com
Xiang Ren, University of Illinois at Urbana-Champaign
Haggai Roitman, IBM Research
Oleg Rokhlenko, Amazon
Altigran S. Da Silva, Universidade Federal do Amazonas
Alan Said, University of Sk˚vde
Rodrygo Santos, Universidade Federal de Minas Gerais
Denis Savenkov, Facebook
Ralf Schenkel, Trier University
Pavel Serdyukov, Yandex
Huawei Shen, Chinese Academy of Sciences
Gianmaria Silvello, University of Padua

PC Members (continued): Marc Sloan, Context Scout
Aya Soffer, IBM
Alessandro Sordoni, Universitŭ Pierre et Marie Curie
Laure Soulier, Universitŭ Pierre et Marie Curie
Damiano Spina, RMIT University
Kazunari Sugiyama, National University of Singapore
Le Sun, Chinese Academy of Sciences
Aixin Sun, Nanyang Technological University
S.M.M. Tahaghoghi, Microsoft
Jiliang Tang, Michigan State University
Jie Tang, Tsinghua University
Paul Thomas, Microsoft
Nicola Tonellotto, ISTI-CNR
Christoph Trattner, MODUL University Vienna
Manos Tsagkias, 904 Labs
Andrew Turpin, University of Melbourne
Kazutoshi Umemoto, University of Tokyo
David Vallet, Google
Emre Velipasaoglu, Lightbend
Adriano Veloso, Universidade Federal de Minas Gerais
Rossano Venturini, University of Pisa
Vishwa Vinay, Adobe Research
Quan Wang, Chinese Academy of Sciences
Bin Wang, Chinese Academy of Sciences
Jian Wang, Google
Xuanhui Wang, Google
Meng Wang, Hefei University of Technology
Shuaiqiang Wang, University of Manchester
Lidan Wang, University of Maryland
Yue Wang, University of Michigan
Hongning Wang, University of Virginia
Ingmar Weber, Qatar Computing Research Institute
Gerhard Weikum, Max Planck Institute for Informatics
Ji-Rong Wen, Renmin University of China
Wei Wu, Microsoft Research Asia
Chenyan Xiong, Carnegie Mellon University
Makoto Yamada, RIKEN AIP
Ting Yao, Microsoft Research Asia
Zheng Ye, York University
Dawei Yin, JD.com
Xiaojun Yuan, University at Albany, State University of New York
Dell Zhang, Birkbeck, University of London
Qi Zhang, Fudan University
Weinan Zhang, Shanghai Jiao Tong University
Yongfeng Zhang, University of Massachusetts Amherst
Le Zhao, Houzz Inc.
Ke Zhou, University of Nottingham
Nivio Ziviani, Federal University of Minas Gerais
Guido Zuccon, Queensland University of Technology

Short Paper PC Members: Mikhail Ageev, Moscow State University
Dyaa Albakour, Signal Media
Omar Alonso, Microsoft
Ismail Sengor Altingovde, Middle East Technical University
Paavo Arvola, University of Tampere
Ashraf Bah Rabiou, University of Delaware
Rafael Banchs, I2R
Zhifeng Bao, RMIT University
Bodo Billerbeck, Bing
Gloria Bordogna, National Research Council of Italy - CNR
Arbi Bouchoucha, Yellow Pages Inc.
Mohand Boughanem, IRIT University Paul Sabatier Toulouse
Davide Buscaldi, LIPN, Universitŭ Paris 13, Sorbonne Paris Citŭ
Fidel Cacheda, Universidad de A Coru`a
Rui Cai, Microsoft Research, Asia
Fazli Can, Bilkent University
Cornelia Caragea, University of North Texas
Mark Carman, Monash University
Ben Carterette, University of Delaware
Praveen Chandar, IBM Research
Francine Chen, FX Palo Alto Laboratory
Hsin-Hsi Chen, National Taiwan University
Zhumin Chen, Shandong University
Stefano Cresci, National Research Council of Italy (IIT-CNR)
Bin Cui, Peking University
Sally Jo Cunningham, Waikato University
Emanuele Di Buccio, University of Padua
Giorgio Maria Di Nunzio, University of Padua
Laura Dietz, University of New Hampshire
Bekir Taner Dincer, University of Mugla
Carsten Eickhoff, ETH Zurich
Tamer Elsayed, Qatar University
Yi Fang, Santa Clara University
Katayoun Farrahi, Goldsmiths, University of London
Hakan Ferhatosmanoglu, Bilkent
Nicola Ferro, University of Padua
Luanne Freund, University of British Columbia
Ingo Frommholz, University of Bedfordshire
Patrick Gallinari, Sorbonne Universitŭs UPMC-LIP6
Debasis Ganguly, IBM Research, Dublin
Bin Gao, Microsoft Research
Wei Gao, Qatar Computing Research Institute, HBKU
Susan Gauch, University of Arkansas
Julio Gonzalo, UNED
Tatiana Gossen, Otto-von-Guericke University Magdeburg
Brigitte Grau, LIMSI, CNRS, ENSIIE, Universitŭ Paris-Saclay
David Graus, FD Mediagroep
Artem Grotov, University of Amsterdam

Short Paper PC Members (continued):

Xianpei Han, Chinese Academy of Science
Morgan Harvey, Northumbria University
Ben He, University of Chinese Academy of Sciences
Xiangnan He, National University of Singapore
Frank Hopfgartner, University of Glasgow
Adam Jatowt, Kyoto University
Gaya Jayasinghe, CSIRO
Shen Jialie, Northumbria University
Jiepu Jiang, University of Massachusetts Amherst
Joemon Jose, University of Glasgow
Marko Junkkari, University of Tampere
Nattiya Kanhabua, Aalborg University
Bahar Karaoğlan, Ege University
Makoto P. Kato, Kyoto University
Liadh Kelly, Dublin City University
Ashiqur Khudabukhsh, Carnegie Mellon University
Yubin Kim, Carnegie Mellon University
Julia Kiseleva, Eindhoven University of Technology
Alexander Kotov, Wayne State University
Kriste Krstovski, University of Massachusetts Amherst
Udo Kruschwitz, University of Essex
Sanna Kumpulainen, Tampere University of Technology
Yanyan Lan, Chinese Academy of Science
Chenliang Li, Wuhan University
Hui Li, The University of Hong Kong
Shuai Li, Cambridge University
Shangsong Liang, University College London
Christina Lioma, University of Copenhagen
Jiyun Luo, Georgetown University
Andrew Macfarlane, City University of London
Takuya Maekawa, Osaka University
Walid Magdy, University of Edinburgh
Maria Maistro, University of Padua
Thomas Mandl, University of Hildesheim
Ilya Markov, University of Amsterdam
Monica Marrero, Barcelona Supercomputing Center
Paul McNamee, Johns Hopkins University
Edgar Meij, Bloomberg L.P.
Aditya Mogadala, KIT
Alessandro Moschitti, Qatar Computing Research Institute, HBKU
Preslav Nakov, Qatar Computing Research Institute, HBKU
Michael Nelson, Old Dominion University
Dong Nguyen, Alan Turing Institute
Liqiang Nie, sdu
Neil O'Hare, Yahoo! Research
Alexandra Olteanu, IBM Research (US)
Jiaul Paik, IIT Kharagpur

Short Paper PC Members (continued):

Dipasree Pal, Abzooba India Infotech Private Limited
Filipa Peleja, Vodafone
Casper Petersen, University of Copenhagen (DIKU)
Karen Pinel-Sauvagnat, IRIT
Laura Po, UniversitŒdi Modena e Reggio Emilia
Filip Radlinski, Google
Zhaochun Ren, JD.com
Haggai Roitman, IBM Research Haifa
Paolo Rosso, Technical University of Valencia
Maya Sappelli, TNO
Michael Schuhmacher, Springer Nature
Jangwon Seo, Google Inc.
Gianmaria Silvello, University of Padua
Dandan Song, Beijing Institute of Technology
Yang Song, Google
Laure Soulier, Sorbonne Universitŭs UPMC-LIP6
Damiano Spina, RMIT University
Aixin Sun, Nanyang Technological University
Carla Teixeira-Lopes, Universidade do Porto
James A. Thom, RMIT University
Qi Tian, The University of Texas at San Antonio
Anastasios Tombros, Queen Mary University of London
Ricardo Torres, Institute of Computing, University of Campinas
Andrew Trotman, University of Otago
Hossein Vahabi, Pandora Media Inc.
Christophe Van Gysel, University of Amsterdam
Olga Vechtomova, University of Waterloo
Suzan Verberne, Institute for Computing and Information Sciences, Radboud University Nijmegen
Stephen Wan, CSIRO
Changhu Wang, Toutiao AI Lab
Hongning Wang, University of Virginia
Quan Wang, Institute of Information Engineering, Chinese Academy of Science
Wouter Weerkamp, 904Labs
Xing Wei, InMobi Inc.
Christa Womser-Hacker, University of Hildesheim
Hao Wu, University of Delaware
Liao Xiangwen, Fuzhou University
Chenyan Xiong, Carnegie Mellon University
Liu Xitong, Google Inc.
Ruifeng Xu, Harbin Institute of Technology
Tan Xu, AT&T Research
Takehiro Yamamoto, Kyoto University
Rui Yan, Peking University
Zheng Ye, StormorAI
Masaharu Yoshioka, Hokkaido Univeristy
Xiaojun Yuan, University at Albany, State University of New York
Mustafa Zengin, University of Delaware

Short Paper PC Members (continued):

Min Zhang, Tsinghua University
Peng Zhang, Tianjin University
Sicong Zhang, Georgetown University
Yongfeng Zhang, University of Massachusetts Amherst
Xin Zhao, Renmin University of China, School of Information
Wei Zheng, Google Inc.
Guido Zuccon, Queensland University of Technology

Demo Paper PC Members:

Omar Alonso, Microsoft
Krisztian Balog, University of Stavanger
Zhicheng Dou, Renmin University of China
Maria Eskevich, Radboud University
John Foley, University of Massachusetts Amherst
Sumio Fujita, Yahoo Japan Corporation
Debasis Ganguly,IBM Research, Dublin
Grant Ingersoll, Lucidworks
Sarvnaz Karimi, CSIRO
Udo Kruschwitz, University of Essex
Teerapong Leelanupab, King Mongkut's Institute of Technology Ladkrabang
Jochen L. Leidner, Thomson Reuters
Shuai Li, Cambridge University
Wei Li, Dublin City University
Javier Parapar, University of A Coru`a
Vassilis Plachouras, Thomson Reuters
Davood Rafiei, University of Alberta
Andrew Salway, Uni Research
Ruihua Song, Microsoft
Kazunari Sugiyama, National University of Singapore
Kazutoshi Umemoto, The University of Tokyo
Bin Wang, Institute of Information Engineering, Chinese Academy of Sciences
Guido Zuccon, Queensland University of Technology

Tutorials Selection Committee:

James Allan, UMass Amherst
Krisztian Balog, University of Stavanger
Michael Bendersky, Google, Inc.
Julio Gonzalo, UNED
Xuanjing Huang, Fudan University
Joemon Jose, University of Glasgow
Udo Kruschwitz, University of Essex
Josiane Mothe, Institut de Recherche en Informatique de Toulouse
Jian-Yun Nie, Universitŭ de Montrŭal
Benjamin Piwowarski, CNRS / University Pierre et Marie Curie
Mark Sanderson, RMIT University
Fabrizio Silvestri, Facebook
Andrew Trotman, University of Otago
Jun Xu, Institute of Computing Technology, Chinese Academy of Sciences

DC Selection Committee: Tat-Seng Chua, National University of Singapore
Kevyn Collins-Thompson, University of Michigan
Nick Craswell, Microsoft
Maarten de Rijke, University of Amsterdam
Susan Dumais, Microsoft Research
Claudia Hauff, Delft University of Technology
Jimmy Huang, York University
Jaap Kamps, University of Amsterdam
Oren Kurland, Technion, Israel Institute of Technology
Filip Radlinski, Google
Pavel Serdyukov, Yandex
Mark Smucker, University of Waterloo
Jaime Teevan, Microsoft Research
Ji-Rong Wen, Renmin University of China

Workshop Selection Committee: Cathal Gurrin, Dublin City University
Josiane Mothe, Institut de Recherche en Informatique de Toulouse
Hang Li, Huawei Technologies
Shlomo Geva, Queensland University of Technology
Ingo Frommholz, University of Bedfordshire
Parth Gupta, PRHLT Research Center, Universidad Politŭcnica de Valencia
Frank Hopfgartner, University of Glasgow
Gareth Jones, Dublin City University
Nicola Ferro, Department of Information Engineering - University of Padua
Norbert Fuhr, University of Duisburg-Essen
Aliaksei Severyn, Google
Omar Alonso, Microsoft

Additional Reviewers: Azad Abad, University of Trento
Qingyao Ai, University of Massachusetts Amherst
Saeid Balaneshinkordan, Wayne State University
Ghazaleh Beigi, Arizona State University
Daniele Bonadiman, University of Trento
Alexey Borisov, Yandex / University of Amsterdam
Wladmir Brandao, Pontificia Universidade Catolica de Minas Gerais
Sergio Canuto, Universidade Federal de Minas Gerais
Da Cao, Xiamen University
Alessandro Checco, University of Sheffield
Xixian Chen, The Chinese University of Hong Kong
Lingyang Chu, Simon Fraser University
Vittoria Cozza, University of Padua
Zhuoye Ding, JD.com
George Drosatos, Democritus University of Thrace
Pavlos Efraimidis, Democritus University of Thrace
Nicola Ferro, University of Padua
Bin Fu, Google
Linyun Fu, Twitter
Rafael Glater, Universidade Federal de Minas Gerais

Additional Reviewers (continued): Huan Gui, University of Illinois at Urbana-Champaign
Chun Guo, Indiana University Bloomington
Tahora H. Nazer, Arizona State University
Shuguang Han, University of Pittsburgh
Negar Hariri, Apple
Maram Hasanain, Qatar University
Zongcheng Ji, The University of Texas Health Science Center at Houston
Shan Jiang, University of Illinois at Urbana-Champaign
Zeng Jichuan, The Chinese University of Hong Kong
Vasileios Kandylas, Microsoft
Shubhra Kanti Karmaker, University of Illinois at Urbana-Champaign
Mucahid Kutlu, Qatar University
Anisio Lacerda, Centro Federal de Educacao de Minas
Alberto Laender, Universidade Federal de Minas Gerais
Peng Li, Chinese Academy of Sciences
Piji Li, The Chinese University of Hong Kong
Wenzhao Lian, Duke University
Aldo Lipani, TU Wien
Zhe Liu, IBM Research
Song Liu, Institute of Statistical Mathematics
Mirella M. Moro, Universidade Federal de Minas Gerais
Maria Maistro, University of Padua
Stefania Marrara, Universitō degli Studi di Milano-Bicocca
Flavio Martins, Universidade NOVA de Lisboa
Ahmed Mourad, RMIT University
Tanmoy Mukherjee, Queen Mary University of London
Massimo Nicosia, University of Trento
Zhen Qin, University of California, Riverside
Yongqin Qiu, Chinese Academy of Sciences
Navid Rekabsaz, TU Wien
Han Shao, The Chinese University of Hong Kong
Gianmaria Silvello, University of Padua
Andreas Spitz, Heidelberg University
Symeon Symeonidis, Democritus University of Thrace
Marwan Torki, Qatar University
Antonio Uva, University of Trento
Marco Viviani, Universitō degli Studi di Milano-Bicocca
Suhang Wang, Arizona State University
Yilin Wang, Arizona State University
Xiaolong Wang, Illinois Institute of Technology
Zhiwei Wang, Michigan State University
Ran Wolff, Yahoo Research
Liang Wu, Arizona State University
Shuai Xiao, Shanghai Jiao Tong University
Ruochen Xu, Carnegie Mellon University
Shiyan Yan, University of Michigan
Yu Yang, Simon Fraser University
Xiaotian Yu, The Chinese University of Hong Kong

Additional Reviewers (cont'd):	Ke Zhai, Microsoft Hongyi Zhang, The Chinese University of Hong Kong Tong Zhao, The Chinese University of Hong Kong Xiangyu Zhao, University of Science and Technology of China Guoqing Zheng, Carnegie Mellon University
Short Paper Additional Reviewer:	Rifat Ozcan, Independent Researcher
40th Anniversary Award Committee Members:	Leif Azzopardi, University of Strathclyde Fernando Diaz, Spotify Nicola Ferro, University of Padua Djoerd Hiemstra, University of Twente Birger Larsen, Aalborg University Thomas Mandl, *Universität Hildesheim* Andrew Turpin, University of Melbourne Mark D. Smucker, University of Waterloo

ACM SIGIR 2017 Sponsor & Supporters

Sponsor:

Supporters:

Institutional supporters

Forward to the Past:

Notes towards a Pre-history of Web Search

Stephen Robertson
stephenerobertson@hotmail.co.uk

ABSTRACT

To me, an awareness of history is a fundamental requirement for progress; and I believe that we in the field of information retrieval are currently ill-served in this domain, or at least not as aware as we should be. While it is true that a researcher in IR is expected to acquire some knowledge of what has gone before, this knowledge is typically fairly narrow in scope. There are some IR researchers who regard IR as a branch of computer science, for example, despite the fact that the field has a long and venerable history entirely outside the domain of computers, as well as a considerable current presence in academic departments well away from CSDs. Outside of our immediate community, there is a widespread belief that web search engines arose out of nothing, a totally new invention for the totally new world of the web.

This is unfortunate. It is true that there were huge changes in the information retrieval world in the second half of the twentieth century. The ideas, methods and systems that were around in 2000 (particularly the early web search engines, up to and including Google) seem at first glance to be completely different from the ideas, methods and systems that were around in 1950. But these developments involved in large measure the usual process of evolution rather than revolution, and the usual mix of steps large or small, forwards or backwards or sideways. Some of these steps were taken in the world of IR research, and some in the domain of practical commercial systems.

One of the real achievements of the web search engine world was to marry the basic technologies of large-scale inverted files and free-text indexing (which had been developed commercially over the previous two or three decades) with the ideas of natural language queries and search output ranking. These last had up to that point had been largely confined to research systems. However, it is important to be clear that the search engines did not invent (nor even re-invent) search output ranking they adapted and developed it, and added new evidence. I believe this fact is very clear to the IR research community, but not at all outside. But the histories of all three (free-text indexing, natural language queries, and ranking) are worth some further attention.

Another real advance was the discovery of web pages by crawling although spiders were not invented exclusively for web search, that was their major raison d'tre and the major stimulus to their development. This represents a necessary function that simply did not exist in most pre-web search environments. A third was the extraction of anchor text from incoming links, to improve the representation of the pointed-to page this, by contrast, represents an opportunity that did not really exist in other environments. (A fourth major advance, deriving from the exploitation of searcher behaviour as reflected in search logs, lies outside the scope of my pre-history.)

This talk is not a history: that would require a lot more gathering and reconciling of evidence than I am able to do. But I would like to put on record my understanding of this period of IR history (which I have lived through, been part of, and very much enjoyed), and provide some anecdotal evidence that may help a future historian. I will start by briefly reviewing two books which cover web search but which (in my opinion) have a too-limited view of the history.

Short Biography

Stephen Robertson has been researching in the field of information retrieval since 1968, and has been publishing since 1969. He is currently retired from full-time work, but remains Professor Emeritus at City University of London, Visiting Professor at University College London, and a Life Fellow at Girton College Cambridge. His previous employment includes five years at University College, twenty at City University, and fifteen at Microsoft Research Cambridge. In 1981 he received a Fulbright Award and spent some months at the University of California Berkeley. He won the Gerard Salton Award in 2000 and the Strix Award in 1998; he is an ACM Fellow. His main areas of research have been the evaluation of IR systems, particularly evaluation metrics, and probabilistic models. The latter led him in the early 1990s to invent the BM25 ranking function, which remains a benchmark for effective ranking of search results.

SIGIR '17, Shinjuku, Tokyo, Japan
 978-1-4503-5022-8/17/08...$15.00
DOI: http://dx.doi.org/10.1145/3077136.3080643

Mail Search: It's Getting Personal!

Yoelle Maarek
Yahoo Research
MATAM Park, Haifa 31905, Israel
yoelle@yahoo.com

ABSTRACT

Web Mail has significantly changed in the last decade. It keeps growing with 90% of its traffic being generated by automated scripts or "machines", [1]. At the same time, major mail services offer more and more free storage, ranging from 15GB for Gmail and Outlook.com to 1TB for Yahoo mail. As a result, we keep accumulating messages in our inbox, rarely deleting (and sometimes not even opening) many, [2]. Our inbox has become a big store mixing important information, such as e-tickets or bills, together with newsletters or promotions, from which we forgot to unsubscribe. Search is therefore a critical mechanism in order to retrieve the specific messages we need. Unfortunately, search in mail is far from being as trusted (and used) as in the Web today. Everything is personal and often private, from the content of the mailbox, to the search strategies, users' needs and queries, thus making traditional Web search techniques inapplicable "as is". Failure is evident when we can't find a message that we remember having read, and this increases our frustration. Most mail search services return sorted-by-time results in order for us to scan results chronologically and increase our perception of perfect recall. At the same time, the ranking mechanism drops less relevant results, in order to prevent them from being ranked first if recent. So in order to increase a (false) perception of recall, these systems actually hurt recall! Ranking results by mail-specific relevance would actually increase search success, [3] yet it is not widely adopted, with the exceptions of Inbox by Gmail and Yahoo Mail that show a few relevant results on top of traditional ranked-by-time results [4]. In addition, many of us still struggle with expressing our needs, typically issuing very short queries, like in the early days of the Web [5]. In this talk, I will first highlight the key characteristics of mail search and how they differ from Web search, in terms of searchers' needs and behavior [2,5]. I will then present recent progress in mail ranking [3,4] as well as in query assistance tools [5,6]. Finally, I will discuss directions for future research, and the need to revisit mail search and invent search mechanisms specifically tailored to the personal data store that our inbox has become.

BIOGRAPHY

Yoelle Maarek is Vice-President of Research at Yahoo. She holds an engineering degree from the Ecole des Ponts et Chaussees, a DEA in Computer Science from Paris VI university and a PhD in Computer Science from the Technion. Upon graduating, she joined IBM Research first in the US then in Israel, eventually becoming an IBM Distinguished Engineer. She later joined Google, as its first engineer in Israel and opened the Haifa engineering center. Her team there developed several notable features including Suggest, the Google query completion service. She returned to research, upon joining Yahoo, where she today serves as site manager of the Haifa office and guides the research organization of Yahoo worldwide. She has been serving in various senior roles at most of the recent SIGIR, WWW and WSDM conferences. She is a member of the Technion Board of Governors, and was inducted as an ACM Fellow in 2013.

SIGIR '17, August 07-11, 2017, Shinjuku, Tokyo, Japan.

ACM ISBN 978-1-4503-5022-8/17/08.
http://dx.doi.org/10.1145/3077136.3080642

REFERENCES

[1] Yoelle Maarek, Web Mail is not dead! It's just not human anymore. WWW'2017, Perth, Australia, April 2017.

[2] Dotan Di Castro, Zohar Karnin, Liane Lewin-Eytan, and Yoelle Maarek. You've got mail, and here is what you could do with it! Analyzing and predicting actions on email messages. WSDM'2016, San Francisco, CA, Feb 2016.

[3] David Carmel, Guy Halawi, Liane Lewin-Eytan, Yoelle Maarek and Ariel Raviv. Rank by time of by relevance? Revisiting Email Search. CIKM'2015, Melbourne Australia, Oct 2015.

[4] David Carmel, Liane Lewin-Eytan, Alex Libov, Yoelle Maarek, Ariel Raviv, Promoting Relevant Results in Time-Ranked Mail Search, WWW'2017, Perth, Australia, April 2017.

[5] David Carmel, Liane Lewin-Eytan, Alex Libov, Yoelle Maarek, Ariel Raviv, The Demographics of Mail Search and their Application to Query Suggestion, WWW'2017, Perth, Australia, April 2017.

[6] Michal Horovitz, Liane Lewin-Eytan, Alexander Libov, Yoelle Maarek and Ariel Raviv, Mailbox-Based vs. Log-Based Query Completion for Mail Search. SIGIR'2017, (short paper), Tokyo, Japan, August 2017.

Navigating Imprecision in Relevance Assessments on the Road to Total Recall: Roger and Me

Gordon V. Cormack
University of Waterloo
gvcormac@uwaterloo.ca

Maura R. Grossman
University of Waterloo
maura.grossman@uwaterloo.ca

ABSTRACT

Technology-assisted review ("TAR") systems seek to achieve "total recall"; that is, to approach, as nearly as possible, the ideal of 100% recall and 100% precision, while minimizing human review effort. The literature reports that TAR methods using relevance feedback can achieve considerably greater than the 65% recall and 65% precision reported by Voorhees as the "practical upper bound on retrieval performance . . . since that is the level at which humans agree with one another" (*Variations in Relevance Judgments and the Measurement of Retrieval Effectiveness*, 2000). This work argues that in order to build—as well as to, evaluate—TAR systems that approach 100% recall and 100% precision, it is necessary to model human assessment, not as absolute ground truth, but as an indirect indicator of the amorphous property known as "relevance." The choice of model impacts both the evaluation of system effectiveness, as well as the simulation of relevance feedback. Models are presented that better fit available data than the infallible ground-truth model. These models suggest ways to improve TAR-system effectiveness so that hybrid human-computer systems can improve on both the accuracy and efficiency of human review alone. This hypothesis is tested by simulating TAR using two datasets: the TREC 4 AdHoc collection, and a dataset consisting of 401,960 email messages that were manually reviewed and classified by a single individual, Roger, in his official capacity as Senior State Records Archivist. The results using the TREC 4 data show that TAR achieves higher recall and higher precision than the assessments by either of two independent NIST assessors, and blind adjudication of the email dataset, conducted by Roger, more than two years after his original review, shows that he could have achieved the same recall and better precision, while reviewing substantially fewer than 401,960 emails, had he employed TAR in place of exhaustive manual review.

1 INTRODUCTION

This study contributes to the body of empirical evidence showing that hybrid human-computer classification systems (known in the legal community as "technology-assisted review" or "TAR") can be more effective and more efficient than exhaustive manual review by experts, where effectiveness is measured with respect to an independent gold standard. The results amplify and extend our 2011 work, *Technology-Assisted Review in E-Discovery Can Be More Effective and More Efficient Than Exhaustive Manual Review* [14] in the following ways:

- We rigorously specify and evaluate a semi-automated process for human-in-the-loop classification in which the only human input is an initial query, followed by assessment of the documents selected for review by the system, until the system determines that high recall and precision have been achieved, and that the review process is complete;
- We extend the process with a quality-control ("QC") mechanism, in which the system suggests a subset of the documents for further adjudication, either by the user or another assessor, to mitigate the fallibility of the user's original assessments;
- We present a theory of information retrieval ("IR") system evaluation that extends the Cranfield method [30] to define the end-to-end effectiveness of an interactive IR process, and to model and control for dependencies between the assessments rendered by the human in the loop, and the assessments used to evaluate the result;
- Using the TREC 4 AdHoc collection and the alternate assessments used by Voorhees in *Variations in Relevance Judgments and the Measurement of Retrieval Effectiveness* [29], we provide evidence that our proposed TAR method achieves substantially better recall and precision than the the alternate NIST assessors would have achieved, had they reviewed the entire collection, with a small fraction of the effort;
- And finally, using a complete categorization of 401,960 email messages from the administration of Virginia Governor Tim Kaine, which was previously manually reviewed by Senior State Records Archivist Roger Christman ("Roger"), we show, using subsequent assessments rendered by Roger, that Roger could have achieved the same recall and higher precision, for a fraction of the effort, had he employed our TAR method to review the 401,960 email messages.

The following sections develop the theory of how to measure the end-to-end effectiveness of high-recall and high-precision IR efforts, how to simulate a human in the loop, our experimental design, and our results on the TREC 4 and Kaine email datasets.

SIGIR '17, August 07-11, 2017, Shinjuku, Tokyo, Japan

ACM ISBN 978-1-4503-5022-8/17/08.
https://doi.org/10.1145/3077136.3080812

2 THEORY

It is well understood that the notion of "relevance" is imprecise, and that different assessors—or even the same assessor at different times—may provide inconsistent relevance determinations for the same document, regardless of their knowledge and expertise, or the specificity with which "relevance" is defined. Nevertheless, it has been observed that relevance determinations by different assessors, while different, are essentially interchangeable as ground truth for the purposes of measuring the relative effectiveness of ad-hoc retrieval systems [3, 29]. In this work, we consider the problem of measuring the end-to-end effectiveness of "total-recall" methods, where the goal is to find substantially all relevant documents, and where the overall accuracy in determining relevance rivals that of the user, or any individual assessor. The model for a user is a "dedicated searcher, not a novice searcher," who is "willing to look at many documents" in order to find as much relevant information as possible (from TREC-1 [16]). This objective is shared by many critical applications, including electronic discovery in civil litigation, archiving of business or government records, patent search, and systematic review in evidence-based medicine. In 2015 and 2016, the TREC Total Recall Track [10, 15] addressed the total-recall problem, providing to participants a "Baseline Model Implementation" ("BMI"),[1] simulating a TAR method known as "continuous active learning" ("CAL") (*cf.* [9, 11]).

The ideal result of a "total-recall" IR effort is to identify *all* and *only* the relevant documents in a collection; that is, to achieve 100% recall and 100% precision. In practice, the ability to reach this goal is limited by the fallibility of human relevance assessment. Even if it were feasible to assess every document in the collection, a certain number of the resulting assessments would be incorrect, yielding less than 100% recall and less than 100% precision. Relevance assessments generated by a learned classifier would also be fallible, likewise falling short of 100% recall and precision. This article addresses the question: Can hybrid human-computer assessments yield higher recall and precision—with less effort—than human assessments alone?

To answer this question, it is necessary to estimate recall and precision, or another measure of how nearly all and only the relevant documents have been identified. The traditional Cranfield method for IR evaluation [30] offers limited insight because it relies on comparison with a "gold standard" for relevance, which itself relies on fallible assessments. At high levels of recall and precision, the Cranfield method tends to measure the ability of the method under test to reproduce the flaws in the gold standard, which—if the flaws are random—is impossible, and if the flaws are systematic—is possible only for methods with similar flaws.

Measuring the effectiveness of total recall is further complicated by the fact that most high-recall methods involve a human in the loop, and are influenced by that user's fallible assessments. In the simplest "ranked-retrieval" scenario, the system orders all documents in the collection by their likelihood of relevance, and the user examines them in order, until a sufficient number of relevant documents have been identified. In the "relevance-feedback" scenario, the user's assessment is communicated to the system, which uses this information to revise the ranking of the yet-to-be-examined documents. The "active-learning" or "uncertainty-sampling" scenario departs from relevance-feedback scenario in that the documents presented to the user are in the order most useful for machine learning, as opposed to likelihood of relevance, with the effect that the user is typically directed to the most marginally relevant documents to examine.

Regardless of the scenario, it is important to define precisely the circumstance under which a document is considered to be "identified" by the method. In the "*system-recall*" scenario, a document is deemed to be identified when it is presented to the user, regardless of the user's ultimate relevance assessment. In the "*end-to-end-recall*" scenario, a document is deemed to be identified only when it is presented to the user *and* the user judges it to be relevant. Where the user is fallible, system recall will generally be higher than end-to-end recall, while system precision will be lower. Which scenario is more apt depends on whether the role of the user is simply to provide guidance to the system, or to make the ultimate determination of whether a document is relevant or not.

Quality-control ("QC") procedures seek to mitigate the impact of fallible relevance assessments, using one or more supplemental assessments for some or all of the documents. In perhaps the easiest case, a second assessment might be rendered for each document. Where the assessments agree, it would be reasonable to assume that they are likely (but not certainly) both correct; where the assessments disagree, one is likely correct and the other is likely not—but how do we know which is which? One might defer to the second assessment, if it could be ascertained that it was more likely to be correct than the first, perhaps due to the application of additional care, or greater knowledge and skill on the part of the second assessor. One might defer to the "relevant" assessment if high recall were particularly important, and to the "not relevant" assessment if high precision were important. Alternatively, one might defer to a third assessment, effectively deeming the "majority vote" to be correct.

Majority-vote QC incurs overhead of $(1 + d)N$ additional assessments, where N is the number of documents in the collection, and d is the rate of discord between the first and second assessments. This overhead may be reduced by selecting a subset of $n \ll N$ documents for supplemental assessment. If the subset is a statistical sample, it is possible to quantify, but not to substantially mitigate, the fallibility of the first assessment. If a subset can be identified that includes many of the documents with discordant assessments, deferring to a third assessment for those particular documents can provide mitigation approaching that of majority vote, with considerably lower overhead.

This work distinguishes between *total-recall methods* and *search tools*. At the outset, TREC sought to measure the ease

[1] http://cormack.uwaterloo.ca/trecvm/.

with which *search tools* might be used within the context of a total-recall effort [16]:

> It should be assumed that the users need the ability to do both high precision and high recall searches, and are willing to look at many documents and repeatedly modify queries in order to get high recall. Obviously they would like a system that makes this as easy as possible.

To this end, relevance-based measures of search-tool effectiveness—notably, rank-based measures such as (mean) average precision ("(M)AP"), precision at a fixed cutoff ("P@k"), and R-precision ("P@R," where R is the number of relevant documents in the collection)—were used as proxies for ease of use [18]. With certain exceptions, primarily in the legal, intellectual property, and medical domains, interest within TREC and the IR community has generally shifted to more user-centric contexts, where the goal is to satisfy an ephemeral and user-specific information need, and search-tool effectiveness is quantified by proxy measures for user satisfaction, *cf.* [1].

Regardless of the context or proxy measure, evaluation efforts like those characterized by Voorhees [29, 30] have focused on search-tool (*i.e.*, "system") effectiveness, not the overall effectiveness of the user at using the tool to identify as nearly as practicable *all* and *only* the relevant documents, where "relevance" is defined by extrinsic criteria (*i.e.*, "end-to-end" effectiveness). The method of repeated ad-hoc search envisioned by TREC is commonly used, but is far from the only—or necessarily the most effective—total-recall method. In some domains, such as the curation of government archival records, exhaustive manual review by an expert constitutes the *de facto* standard of acceptable practice. In many contexts, a single query is used to identify the subset of the collection for manual review. In Boolean retrieval, the query specifies precisely the subset to be reviewed; in ranked retrieval, the query suggests the nature of relevance, the search tool ranks the documents by their likelihood of relevance, and the user assesses some number of the top-ranked documents. Traditionally, relevance feedback has been construed as a method to automate the query-formulation task envisioned by TREC: The user's assessment of the results from an initial query are provided to the search tool, which reformulates the query and presents a new set of results to the user, and so on. More recently, supervised machine-learning methods have been used to harness relevance feedback, with reported effectiveness apparently exceeding Voorhees' "practical upper bound," *see e.g.*, [6, 14, 25].

3 MODELING ASSESSMENT ERROR

3.1 Assessment Error in Measurement

For the purposes of this study, we assume that every document d is either "relevant" or "not relevant" in its own right ($r(d) \in \{rel, nrel\}$), but its relevance can be observed only indirectly by an assessment under conditions c yielding a positive or negative judgment ($j(c, d) \in \{+, -\}$). We use the abbreviations rel_d, $nrel_d$, $+_{cd}$, and $-_{cd}$ to denote $r(d) = rel$, $r(d) = nrel$, $j(c, d) = +$, and $j(c, d) = -$, respectively. We assume that for a random document D, a positive judgment is evidence of relevance: $\Pr[rel_D|+_{cD}] > \Pr[rel_D]$. It follows that a negative judgment is evidence of non-relevance: $\Pr[nrel_D|-_{cD}] > \Pr[nrel_D]$. One of the principal questions to be addressed by a model is: How strong is this evidence?

The Cranfield method generally assumes for the purpose of evaluation that human assessments are infallible ($\Pr[rel_D|+_{cD}] = 1$, $\Pr[rel_D|-_{cD}]) = 0$), where c is chosen carefully, considering the myriad of factors that influence relevance assessment.

Biased sampling and/or statistical sampling may be used to to reduce the cost of assessment. The pooling method [18] is the most prominent of a family of biased sampling methods that identify a subset of documents for human assessment, and render automatic judgments for the remaining documents. In the pooling method, each document d is either in the pool or not ($p(d) \in \{judged, unjudged\}$); documents in the pool are assessed, while documents not in the pool are summarily deemed not relevant. The pooling method can be viewed as a semi-automated assessment under conditions c' where $j(c', d) = \begin{cases} j(c, d) & (judged_d) \\ - & (unjudged_d) \end{cases}$. Biased sampling methods place further stress on the Cranfield assumption that $j(c', D)$ is infallible.

Statistical sampling may be used to estimate the proportion of relevant documents in particular subsets of the collection, as necessary to compute summary measures of effectiveness [2].

Multiple assessments per document may be used in place of a single assessment. The majority judgment of a n assessments under conditions $c_1 \ldots c_n$ will more closely approximate an infallible assessor, under the assumption that there is greater than 50% conditional probability that each judgment will be positive for a relevant document, and negative for a non-relevant document, notwithstanding the other judgments.

Where multiple fallible assessments are available, latent class analysis [21] may be used to infer the true positive rate $\Pr[+_{c_i D}|rel_D]$ and false positive rate $\Pr[+_{c_i D}|nrel_D]$ for each of the assessment conditions, as well as prevalence $\Pr[rel_D]$, under the assumption of pairwise conditional independence: $\Pr[+_{c_i D}|r(D)] = \Pr[+_{c_i D}|r(D), j(c_j, D)]$ for all $c_i \neq c_j$.

3.2 Assessment Error in Simulation

Total-recall methods may require relevance assessment for three purposes: (i) To train the system to rank or classify the remaining documents; (ii) to determine the ultimate disposition of each document presented to the user by the system (*e.g.*, produce or withhold in the context of electronic discovery in civil litigation, include or exclude in the context of systematic review in evidence-based medicine); and (iii) to inform the cost-benefit analysis inherent in determining when to stop the review process. For the purposes of this work, we aspire to emulate a user whose fallible assessments are conditionally independent of those used for evaluation. The fallible assessments used for evaluation, although they may closely emulate those of a user, would confound evaluation were they also to be used to simulate feedback, as they are not conditionally independent. Infallible assessments—if they existed—would be conditionally independent, but a poor emulation of a real user's feedback. In either case, it is desirable to use a separate set of assessments to emulate user feedback. Even so, it is well known that the order of presentation and the proportion of relevant documents can influence human assessment [24, 27, 28]; such influences are not easily controlled when simulating different total-recall methods. The quest for better models to emulate human assessment is met with a triple challenge: (i) determining the true relevance of a document; (ii) aptly modeling the user's response; and (iii) ensuring the model is conditionally independent of the model used for evaluation.

3.3 When to Stop?

An important but rarely studied issue in achieving total recall is when to stop. Blair and Maron [4] reported that users who terminated their searches when they believed they had achieved at least 75% recall, had in fact achieved 20% recall. Eliciting from the user a reliable judgment of when high recall has been achieved remains a vexing problem. Evaluations styled after the TREC AdHoc task have largely finessed this issue, reporting rank-based measures under the assumption that the user would know when to stop, perhaps after reading a fixed number of documents.

Automated methods show some promise, but have not previously been evaluated in terms of end-to-end recall with a human in the loop, where user feedback is independent of the assessments used for evaluation. Cormack and Grossman [6] have reported statistical and non-statistical methods for ensuring, with high probability, that their continuous active learning ("CAL") method achieves very high recall, at the expense of precision. The non-statistical "knee method" searches for an inflection point in the recall-effort curve—the "knee"—and continues well beyond that point. Empirical evidence, based on an assumption of infallible user feedback, suggests that their knee method can achieve system-level recall of over 90%, with more than 95% probability, with precision considerably less than 50%.

4 EXPERIMENTAL DESIGN

We conducted two experiments to test the hypothesis that total-recall systems with human assessors in the loop could achieve comparable—or higher—recall and precision, with a small fraction of the effort, than an expert assessor who examined every document in the collection. For this effect to be observable, it is necessary to depart from a model assuming infallible assessment, at least with respect to human assessors in the loop. For evaluation, it is necessary to have a source of reasonably authoritative assessments separate from those used for relevance feedback.

4.1 Datasets, Topics, and Assessments

Our first experiment simulated participation in the TREC 4 AdHoc Task, using the TREC 4 test collection consisting of 567,528 documents, 49 topics, and the official NIST gold standard of relevance [17]. For user feedback and QC, we used two alternate sets of judgments obtained by NIST, for the same topics, using assessors distinct from those who created the gold standard—the same set of alternate assessments studied by Voorhees [29].

Our second experiment reprised the exhaustive manual review of 401,960 email messages from the administration of former Virginia Governor Tim Kaine, which was undertaken by Senior State Archivist Roger Christman, prior to the publication, in 2014, of those he deemed to be "open records."[2] To simulate user feedback in our experiment, we used Roger's original assessments (the "Roger I" assessments). To simulate QC, Roger re-reviewed blind a stratified sample of 2,798 documents (the "Roger II" assessments). As the ultimate arbiter of truth, Roger reviewed blind, for a third time, all 901 cases of disagreement between Roger I and Roger II (the "Roger III" assessments).

4.2 Total-Recall Methods

Our simulation used the same TREC Total Recall Baseline Model Implementation ("BMI"), referenced above in Section 2, modified to read the dataset, topics, and simulated relevance assessments from local files, instead of a server, and to implement Cormack and Grossman's "knee-method" stopping criterion [6]. BMI runs autonomously and has no tunable parameters: Our input consisted of the datasets, topics, relevance assessments, and the knee method. Output from the BMI runs consisted of: a ranked list of documents, in the order presented to the simulated user, ending where the knee-method stopping criterion was met; and the inflection point ("knee") in the gain curve, determined retrospectively by the knee method.

The output from BMI was further manipulated to simulate three different result-selection strategies: (i) System-Determined, (ii) User-Determined, and (iii) Adjudicated. The end result of the *System-Determined* strategy was the entire ranked list returned by BMI. The end result of the *User-Determined* strategy was the subset of documents in the ranked list that the user judged to be relevant. The end result of the *Adjudicated* strategy was the subset of the ranked list consisting of those documents that the user *and* the knee method agreed were relevant, or, where the user and knee method disagreed, a second, auxiliary assessment deemed to be relevant. For the purposes of this work, we deemed the knee method to judge all documents in the ranked list before the knee to be relevant, and all documents after the knee to be non-relevant.

[2] *See* http://www.virginiamemory.com/collections/kaine/.

Strategy	Recall	Precision	F_1	Effort
Manual	0.57	0.69	0.63	567,528
System	0.94	0.06	0.10	**22,911**
User	0.55	0.81	0.62	**22,911**
Adjudicated	**0.64**	**0.82**	**0.69**	23,662
Adj. – Man.	0.07	0.13	0.06	543,866
p-value	0.0001	0.0002	0.0001	-

Table 1: Average Effectiveness Measures Over 98 Combinations of 49 TREC 4 Topics and Two Simulated Users. p was computed using a paired t-test.

4.3 Evaluation

For all strategies, we report recall, precision, and F_1 , as well as effort, as measured by the number of documents presented to the user for assessment. As a baseline, we used an *Exhaustive Manual Review* ("Manual Review") strategy, for which effort is simply the number of documents in the collection. For the System-Determined strategy, effort depends on the number of *relevant* documents in the collection, as well as the recall and precision achieved: For a given topic and recall level, effort is inversely proportional to precision. For the User-Determined and Adjudicated strategies, there is no direct relationship between effort and precision.

Only the System-Determined strategy returns a ranked list from which we can evaluate the recall-precision tradeoff. We can, however, plot recall and precision as a function of effort throughout the progress of a review. These curves illustrate the result that might have been achieved, had a different stopping criterion been applied. They also illustrate how quickly a substantial fraction of the relevant documents can be discovered and forwarded for further analysis or release, while the total-recall effort is still in progress.

4.4 Prediction and Rationale

Previously published results report recall-precision break-even scores on the order of 80% for BMI and related methods [7, 8, 11, 25]. With one notable exception (discussed below), these results were derived using simulated feedback from an assumed-infallible user, and evaluated with respect to the same assumed-infallible gold standard. On the one hand, the simulated feedback was conditionally dependent on the evaluation standard, and therefore possibly "too good to be true." On the other hand, the evaluation standard was assumed to be perfect, offering BMI no opportunity to better it. The experiments, by design, could not show whether or not BMI could achieve better recall and/or better precision than a fallible user.

There is no basis to assume that a hybrid human-computer system cannot exceed both the recall and precision of its human operator. The literature reports inter-assessor agreement results that are consistent with the hypothesis that a human assessor can achieve on the order of 70% recall and 70% precision [26, 29]. Are the higher results reported for BMI an artifact of too-perfect training, or is a system involving BMI and human assessment, combined, superior to human assessment alone?

Achieving a high recall-precision break-even score is irrelevant to the success of a total-recall effort, if the point at which this score is achieved is unknown to the user. Cormack and Grossman's knee-method stopping criterion sacrifices (System-Determined) precision to achieve very high recall, under the assumption that an infallible assessor would screen the results, and the only consequence of low precision would be increased effort. The User-Determined strategy has the (fallible) user act in this capacity.

The Adjudicated strategy has BMI and the user share the role of screening, deferring to a second (fallible) assessor the adjudication of cases of disagreement. We assume the inflection point calculated by the knee method to be a good approximation of the recall-precision break-even point; that documents before the knee are more likely to be relevant than not, and that documents after the knee are less likely to be so. This assumption motivates our choice to defer to a second assessor any document before the knee that is judged non-relevant by the user, and any document after the knee that is judged relevant by the user. This strategy makes no assumption that the second assessor is "better" than the user. As long as the second assessor is usually correct (as would certainly be the case for an assessor capable of achieving 70% recall and 70% precision), the Adjudicated strategy should achieve higher recall *and* higher precision than the User-Determined strategy.

As noted above, one strand of research has evaluated total-recall methods in the face of fallible users. The TREC Legal Track Interactive Task (*see*, *e.g.*, [19, 23]) assigned participating teams the task of finding all and only the relevant documents that were responsive to requests for production in a mock civil litigation. A subject matter expert (the "Topic Authority") was made available for consultation while the teams were conducting their reviews; the same Topic Authority adjudicated cases of disagreement, after the fact, between the teams and the human assessors who had created a provisional gold standard for evaluation. Teams were allowed to use any method of their choosing, with no restriction on the nature or quantity of human input. Two TAR methods—one rule-based and one substantially similar to BMI—achieved on the order of 80% recall and 80% precision [19]. In a subsequent analysis, Grossman and Cormack [14] estimated the recall and precision of the human assessments that comprised the provisional gold standard, on average, to have been 59.3% and 31.7%, respectively. While deferring a fuller discussion of these results to Section 5, we note that this work generated some criticism, *e.g.*, [12, 13, 31]; most notably, claims that: (i) the assessors were unskilled, poorly trained, poorly vetted, or poorly supervised; (ii) the assessors had a different "conception of relevance" from the Topic Authority; (iii) the participating teams devoted extraordinary skill or extraordinary resources to accomplishing the task; (iv) the gold standard, by virtue of the reconsideration process, was biased in favor of the participants; and (v) the gold standard, by

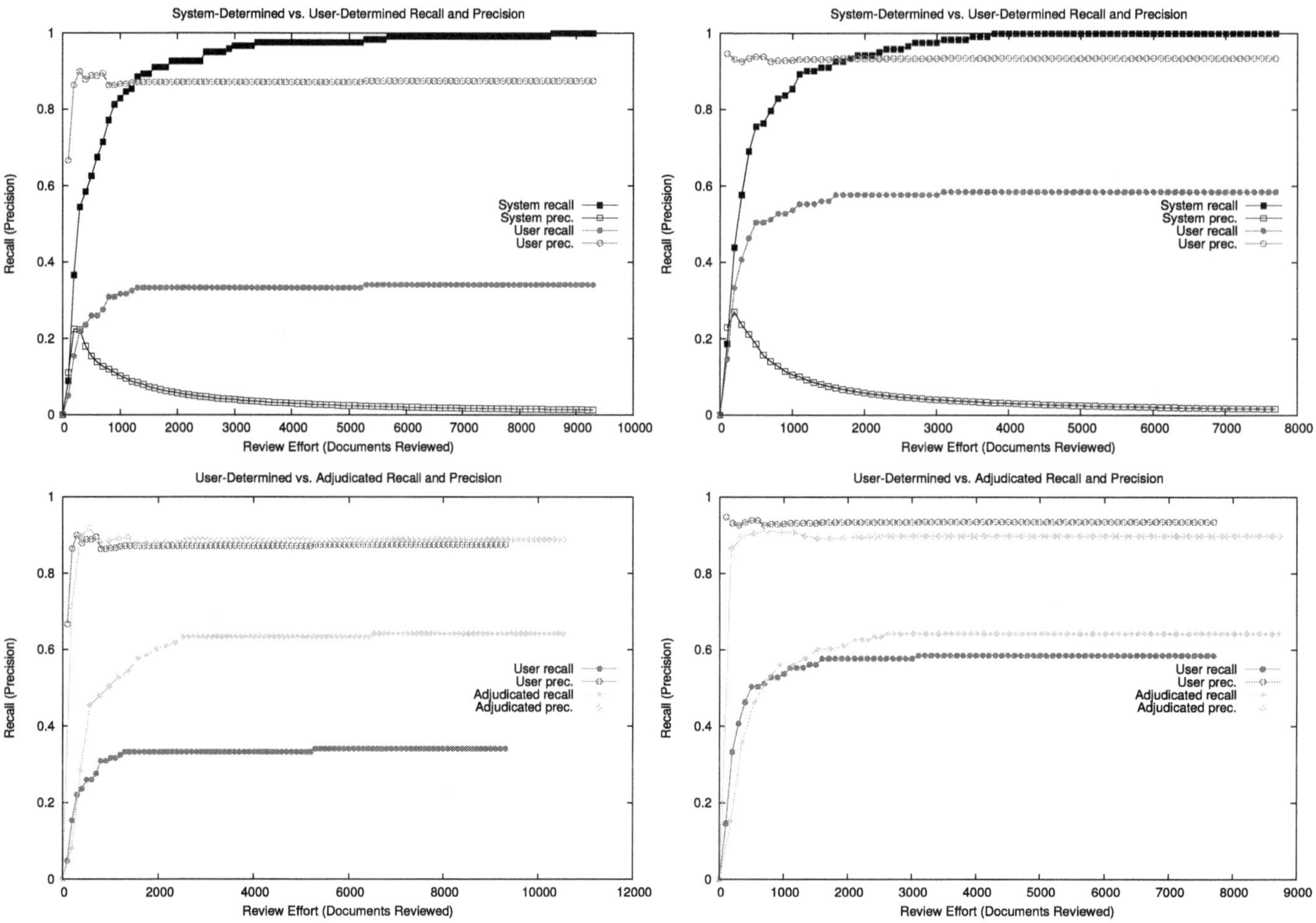

Figure 1: TREC 4 Topic 239 – Tradeoff Between Recall, Precision, and Effort. The top panels compare the System-Determined vs. User-Determined strategies; the bottom panels compare the User-Determined vs. Adjudicated strategies. For the left panels, the first alternate TREC assessor was the user, and the second alternate assessor was the adjudicator; for the right panels, the roles were reversed.

virtue of bias on the part of the Topic Authority and the lack of blinding of his or her review, was biased in favor of the participants.

This study controls for the skill, effort, and motivation of both users and assessors. The gold standard for the TREC 4 collection, as well as the alternate assessments, were fixed more than two decades ago. All of the NIST assessors were clearly skilled in their craft; most were former NSA analysts. The alternate assessors had no direct knowledge of the primary assessor's judgments. On the other hand, the simulated assessments for the Kaine email dataset were derived from an assessment of 401,960 documents, by the Virginia Senior State Records Archivist, in his official capacity. In forming the gold standard, the same archivist reviewed and then re-reviewed some of his own previous assessments, after wash-out periods of two years and then two months, respectively.

Our rationale predicted that: (i) BMI alone (the System-Determined strategy) would achieve superior recall to Manual Review, but inferior precision, for substantially less effort; (ii) the User-Determined strategy would achieve inferior recall, but superior precision, to the System-Determined strategy, for the same effort; and, (iii) the Adjudicated strategy would achieve superior recall and precision to all other strategies, for moderately higher effort than the System-Determined and User-Determined strategies, but still substantially less than Manual Review.

5 RESULTS

Figure 1 plots recall and precision for a representative TREC 4 topic as a function of effort for each of the BMI-derived methods, using each of the alternate assessors as the user, and the other assessor, as occasioned, for adjudication.[3] In comparison, the recall and precision of the Manual Review by

[3] Plots and raw results for the other 48 topics are available on request from the authors.

	Manual Review				Adjudicated			
Topic	Recall	Precision	F_1	Effort	Recall	Precision	F_1	Effort
Legal Hold	**0.97**	0.91	0.94	401,960	0.96	**0.96**	**0.96**	**40,522**
Archival	0.89	0.84	0.86	381,819	**0.90**	**0.89**	**0.89**	**332,410**
Restricted	**0.98**	0.75	0.84	146,594	0.95	**0.80**	**0.87**	**38,048**

Table 3: Individual Topic Effectiveness for the Kaine Email Dataset.

Roger I \ Roger II	rel	nrel
rel	16,640	1,736 1,765
nrel	474 227	381,065

Roger I \ Roger II	rel	nrel
rel	115,577	23,824 7,193
nrel	17,269 33,482	198,409

Roger I \ Roger II	rel	nrel
rel	23,050	3,661 296
nrel	1,135 7,536	130,821

Table 2: Agreement Among Roger I, Roger II, and Roger III on the Virginia Tech Legal Hold Emails. In split cells, numbers below the diagonal show agreement between Roger I and Roger III; numbers above the diagonal show agreement between Roger II and Roger III. The top panel shows Virginia Tech legal hold identification; the middle panel shows archival record identification; the bottom panel shows restricted record identification.

Strategy	Recall	Precision	F_1	Effort
Manual	**0.95**	0.83	0.88	310,196
Adjud.	0.93	**0.88**	**0.91**	**136,993**
Δ	-0.01	+0.05	+0.02	173,203
p-value	0.4	0.006	0.03	
95% *c.i.*	(−.05, .03)	(.03, .07)	(.004, .04)	

Table 4: Average Effectiveness Measures Over Three Topics for the Kaine Email Dataset. p was computed using a paired t-test.

	Legal Hold	Archival	Restricted
Roger I & Roger II	**80.6%**	60.2%	64.2%
System & Roger I	79.1%	**70.2%**	**67.9%**
System & Roger II	79.9%	62.1%	55.8%

Table 5: Pairwise Overlap (*i.e.*, Jaccard Index) Between the System, Roger I, and Roger II.

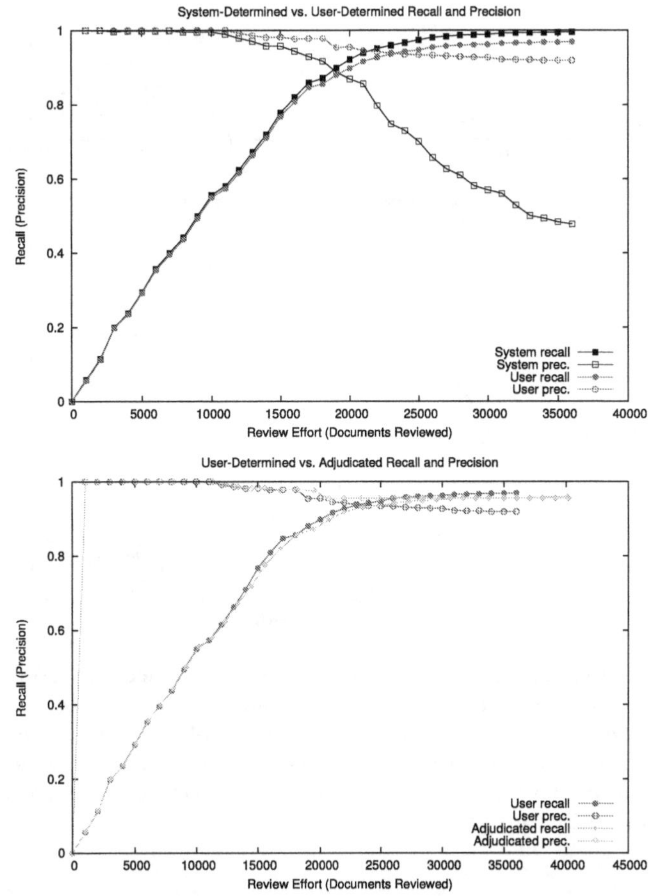

Figure 2: Identification of Kaine Administration Email Pertaining to the Virginia Tech Shooting for Legal Hold – Tradeoff Among Recall, Precision, and Effort. The top panel compares the System-Determined vs. User-Determined strategies; the bottom panel compares the User-Determined vs. Adjudicated strategies.

the two assessors were 0.34 and 0.88, and 0.59 and 0.94, respectively. Although the first assessor has substantially lower recall and precision than the second, the System-Determined recall curves are remarkably similar. The User-Determined recall curves are, as predicted, bounded by the recall of the respective users. On the other hand, the Adjudicated recall curves, like the System-Determined curves, are remarkably

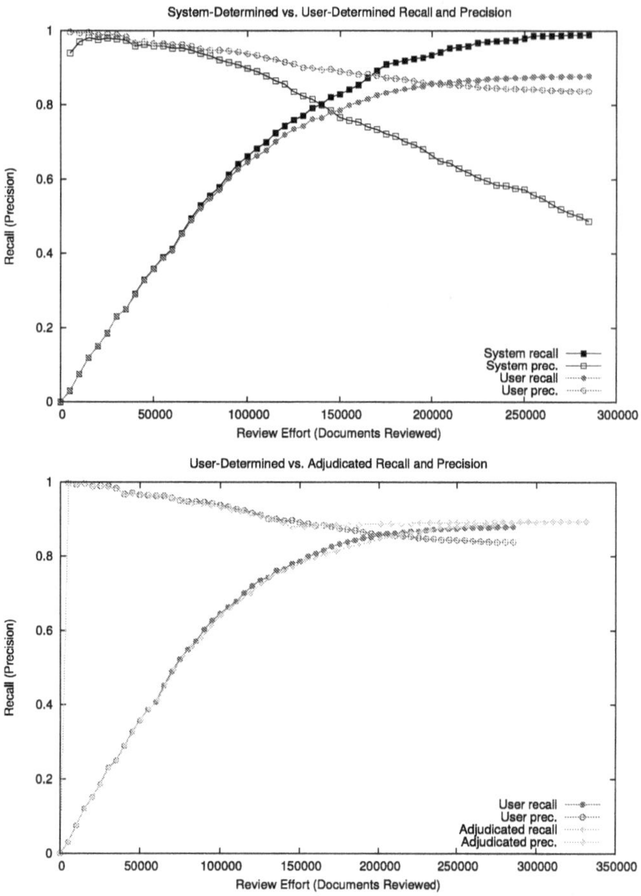

Figure 3: Identification of Archival Records from the Kaine Administration – Tradeoff Among Recall, Precision, and Effort. The top panel compares the System-Determined vs. User-Determined strategies; the bottom panel compares the User-Determined vs. Adjudicated strategies.

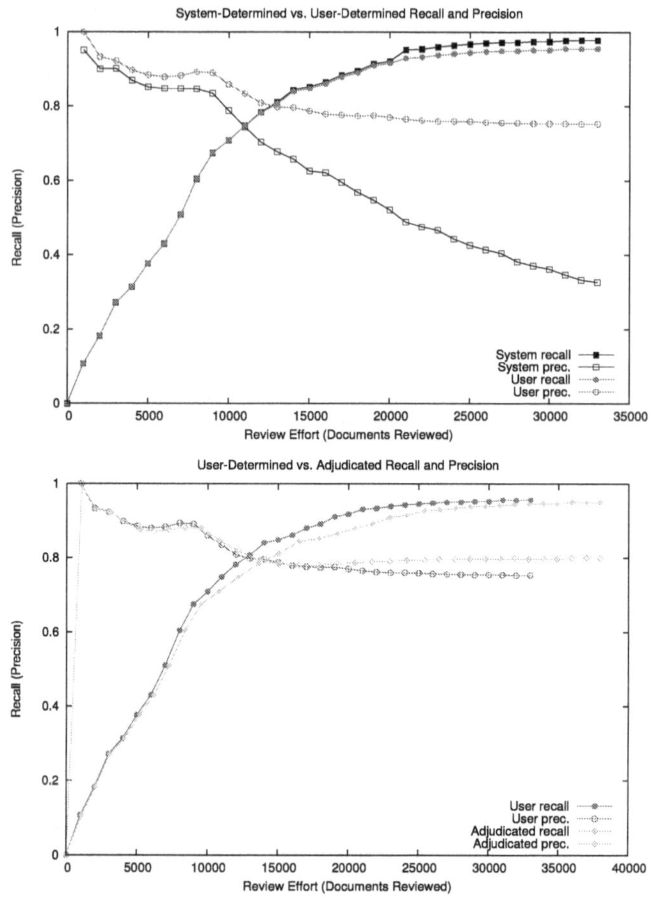

Figure 4: Identification of Restricted Archival Records from the Kaine Administration – Tradeoff Among Recall, Precision, and Effort. The top panel compares the System-Determined vs. User-Determined strategies; the bottom panel compares the User-Determined vs. Adjudicated strategies.

similar, but are superior to both the User-Determined curves. The System-Determined precision curve initially climbs and then declines with increased effort, as expected, while the User-Determined and Adjudicated precision curves are remarkably flat.

Table 1 shows average effectiveness and effort measures over 98 runs, comprising 49 topics and two simulated users. As predicted, the System-Determined strategy achieves very high recall on average, with 4% of the effort of Manual Review. The User-Determined strategy achieves slightly lower recall, but substantially higher precision than Manual Review, also with 4% of the effort. The Adjudicated strategy achieves substantially and significantly higher recall, and precision than Manual Review, with 4.2% of the effort.

The agreement between Roger I and Roger II, and Roger III's adjudication of their disagreements, is shown in Table 2.

Overall, Roger I and Roger II have overlap (*i.e.*, Jaccard index) of 80.6%, 60.2%, and 64.2% on each of three topics—higher than most reported results for separate assessors, but far from perfect. Roger III generally splits the difference between Roger I and Roger II, with a propensity to agree with the negative assessment. Roger, on completing the Roger III assessments, volunteered that "this was a challenging review," suggesting that the adjudication process had identified many hard-to-classify, as opposed to randomly misclassified, documents.

Roger I rendered these decisions for each of the three topics seriatim as follows: First, the Virginia Tech documents subject to a legal hold were identified; second, documents not subject to the hold were classified as either archival records or non-records; and finally, documents classified as archival records were categorized as restricted or open records. As a consequence, the document collection diminished for each subsequent topic. Roger II and Roger III employed the same protocol, resulting in a handful of anomalous judgments. For example, Roger I classified some records as records or non-records not subject to legal hold, while Roger II classified them as subject to legal hold. For these documents, we recorded the disagreement with respect to legal hold, and asked Roger II to specify whether the document would be an archival record or a non-record, were it not subject to legal hold. Roger III was asked in advance to consider all six combinations of: subject to legal hold or not, and open record, restricted record, or non-record. The appropriate hypothetical judgments were used as the gold standard for each topic.

The documents reviewed by Roger II formed a stratified sample of the dataset; measures using Roger II or Roger III were estimated using the Horvitz-Thompson estimator [20]. The strata were selected as follows: For each of the three topics and each of the four possible modes of disagreement, 200 documents were selected independently, at random. Because the documents were selected independently, there was some overlap among these strata, and the total number of unique documents was 2,398. After Roger II had commenced his review, it was discovered that one stratum had been repeated and one had been omitted due to a clerical error, so 200 documents from the omitted stratum were added, along with 200 randomly selected documents from outside the stratum, for a total sample size of 2,798. Inclusion probabilities were adjusted to account for the overlapping strata.

Figures 2, 3, and 4 show effectiveness versus effort for the Adjudication strategy, while Table 3 shows set-based measures for the three Kaine email topics, and Table 4 shows averages over the topics. The summary measures suggest that the Adjudication strategy achieves significantly better precision and F_1 than Roger I ($p < 0.05$), and no significant difference in recall. The gain in F_1 appears to come primarily from balancing recall and precision, which is consistent with the purpose of the Adjudication strategy. None of the differences is larger than 0.5%, suggesting that there is little to choose (in terms of effectiveness) between the Adjudication strategy and Manual Review. On the other hand, the Adjudication strategy offers a huge advantage in terms of efficiency.

Table 5 shows the pairwise overlap between the system's assessment (that was compared to Roger I's assessment in the Adjudication strategy), and Roger I and Roger II themselves. Collectively, the results indicate that, for all intents and purposes, there is little to choose between the system's judgments and Roger's, and that a second opinion—whether by a human or a bionic assessor—can be helpful.

The bootstrap method was used to determine the variance due to sampling in the Roger II and Roger III datasets, which showed all per-topic differences between the Adjudication strategy and Manual Review to be significant (with respect to sampling uncertainty).

DISCUSSION AND CONCLUSIONS

Effectiveness measures for total recall depend on who you ask, when you ask, and how often you ask. Even a small amount of error in gold-standard assessments can substantially depress recall, as evidenced by the provisional versus final recall estimates of the TREC 2009 Legal Track, where the estimated recall of the best submissions for four topics rose from less than 20% in the Notebook Draft, to about 80% in the Final Overview Paper [19, appendix]. While Webber et al. [32] attribute this difference to bias on the part of the assessors, it is equally well explained by a typical true positive rate $\Pr[+_D|rel_D > 0.7]$, and a typical false positive rate $\Pr[+_{cD}|nrel_D] \ll 0.01$. The difference between the Legal Track assessment and other TREC efforts is that the assessors reviewed a statistical sample of the entire collection, not just the pool of documents identified by the systems. As a consequence, a sample representing more than 700,000 non-relevant documents was reviewed; it is no surprise that examples representing several thousand of these non-relevant documents were incorrectly judged as relevant. Most of those false positives were identified by a process similar to the Adjudication strategy we evaluated, in which disagreements between the participating systems and the first assessor were adjudicated by a second assessor, the Topic Authority. It is not necessary to assume that the first assessor was incompetent, or that the Topic Authority was more competent than the first assessor, to explain the TREC 2009 results.

Our Adjudication strategy results on the Kaine email dataset are consistent with the superior results reported by Cormack and Mojdeh at TREC 2009 [5]; they "[re-]examined documents with high scores that were marked 'not relevant' and documents with low scores that were marked 'relevant.'" Our results are also entirely consistent with the results reported in our original 2011 study [14]. It is important to bear in mind that results measuring *system* recall, rather than *end-to-end* recall, cannot be compared to the results reported here, to those reported in the TREC 2009 Legal Track Overview [19], or to those reported by Grossman and Cormack [14]. Neither can such results be compared when the user assessments are the same as the evaluation assessments.

Our results do not support the mantra of "garbage in, garbage out," or that errors in user feedback are "amplified" by the use of a TAR method, as opposed to manual review. To the contrary, our results show that system effectiveness is hardly affected by inferior feedback, and that certain TAR methods can *mitigate* rather than *amplify* user error.

This study raises a number of questions that may be addressed by future work. It is well known—and reconfirmed by this study—that humans judge the same document differently under different circumstances, including the order of presentation. The effect of using a dynamically learned ranking on user feedback has yet to be studied. On the one hand, studies suggest that when assessors review a higher proportion of relevant documents, they are less likely to judge them relevant (*see, e.g.*, Roegiest [24]). Is this explained by a higher error rate, or by the general observation that higher prevalence or more experience with a review set can lead assessors to become more discriminating? Our results show that Roger III was less likely to judge documents relevant than Roger I or Roger II, perhaps because he exercised greater diligence, or maybe because he had become better informed through the course of examining borderline documents.

Roger II and Roger III were blind to the previous Rogers' assessments. While Roger II commented that he recalled several of the themes in the documents, it had been at least two years since he had previously reviewed them. Roger III, on the other hand, had seen the documents two months prior, and in the interim, had reviewed more than ten thousand emails from a different department of the Kaine administration. It is not apparent what effect Roger's memory may have had on the results. The impact of blind review with a wash-out period has yet to be studied; indeed, it is not clear whether the user should be blind, so as to reduce bias, or informed, so as to aid in deliberation, *cf.* [22]. At TREC 2009, Cormack and Mojdeh [5] appear to have achieved superior results without blinding and no discernible wash-out period, but more study is necessary to arrive at a definitive answer.

Overall, our results reconfirm the thesis that hybrid human-computer classification (*i.e.*, TAR) methods can achieve recall and precision that compare favorably with exhaustive manual review by experts, for much less effort. Where higher recall and precision is desired, additional resources are better spent re-reviewing documents that may have been misjudged by the user, than examining the ranked list to extraordinary depths, or sampling low-ranked documents. When recall and precision values approach 100%, it is essential to consider carefully both the accuracy and independence of the gold standard used for evaluation.

ACKNOWLEDGEMENT

We are very grateful for the enthusiasm and support we received from our colleagues at the Library of Virginia, most notably, Roger Christman, Susan Gray Page, Rebecca Morgan, and Kathy Jordan; without them, this work would not have been possible.

REFERENCES

[1] A. Al-Maskari and M. Sanderson. A review of factors influencing user satisfaction in information retrieval. *Journal of the American Society for Information Science and Technology*, 61(5):859–868, 2010.

[2] J. A. Aslam, V. Pavlu, and E. Yilmaz. A statistical method for system evaluation using incomplete judgments. In *SIGIR 2006*.

[3] P. Bailey, N. Craswell, I. Soboroff, P. Thomas, A. de Vries, and E. Yilmaz. Relevance assessment: are judges exchangeable and does it matter? In *SIGIR 2008*.

[4] D. Blair and M. E. Maron. An evaluation of retrieval effectiveness for a full-text document-retrieval system. *Communications of the ACM*, 28(3):289–299, 1985.

[5] G. Cormack and M. Mojdeh. Machine learning for information retrieval: TREC 2009 Web, Relevance Feedback and Legal Tracks. In *TREC 2009*.

[6] G. V. Cormack and M. R. Grossman. Engineering quality and reliability in technology-assisted review. In *SIGIR 2016*.

[7] G. V. Cormack and M. R. Grossman. Evaluation of machine-learning protocols for technology-assisted review in electronic discovery. In *SIGIR 2014*.

[8] G. V. Cormack and M. R. Grossman. Multi-faceted recall of continuous active learning for technology-assisted review. In *SIGIR 2015*.

[9] G. V. Cormack and M. R. Grossman. Scalability of continuous active learning for reliable high-recall text classification. In *CIKM 2016*.

[10] G. V. Cormack and M. R. Grossman. Waterloo (Cormack) participation in the TREC 2015 Total Recall Track. In *TREC 2015*.

[11] G. V. Cormack and M. R. Grossman. Autonomy and reliability of continuous active learning for technology-assisted review. *arXiv:1504.06868*, 2015.

[12] G. V. Cormack, M. D. Smucker, and C. L. Clarke. Efficient and effective spam filtering and re-ranking for large web datasets. *Information Retrieval*, 14(5):441–465, 2011.

[13] S. Green and M. Yacano. Computers vs. humans? Putting the TREC 2009 study in perspective. *New York Law Journal*, (Oct. 1), 2012.

[14] M. R. Grossman and G. V. Cormack. Technology-assisted review in e-discovery can be more effective and more efficient than exhaustive manual review. *Richmond Journal of Law & Technology*, 17(3), 2011.

[15] M. R. Grossman, G. V. Cormack, and A. Roegiest. TREC 2016 Total Recall Track Overview. In *TREC 2016*.

[16] D. Harman. Overview of the First Text REtrieval Conference (TREC-1). In *TREC 1*, 1992.

[17] D. Harman. Overview of the fourth text retrieval conference (trec-4). In *TREC 4*, 1996.

[18] D. K. Harman. The TREC ad hoc experiments. In E. M. Voorhees and D. K. Harman, editors, *TREC - Experiment and Evaluation in Information Retrieval*, chapter 4. MIT Press, 2005.

[19] B. Hedin, S. Tomlinson, J. R. Baron, and D. W. Oard. Overview of the TREC 2009 Legal Track. In *TREC 2009*.

[20] D. G. Horvitz and D. J. Thompson. A generalization of sampling without replacement from a finite universe. *Journal of the American Statistical Association*, 47(260):663–685, 1952.

[21] K. Krstovski. *Efficient Inference, Search and Evaluation for Latent Variable Models of Text with Applications to Information Retrieval and Machine Translation*. University of Massachusetts, 2016.

[22] T. McDonnell, M. Lease, T. Elsayad, and M. Kutlu. Why is that relevant? Collecting annotator rationales for relevance judgments. In *4th HCOMP*, 2016.

[23] D. W. Oard, B. Hedin, S. Tomlinson, and J. R. Baron. Overview of the TREC 2008 Legal Track. In *TREC 2008*.

[24] A. Roegiest and G. V. Cormack. Impact of review-set selection on human assessment for text classification. In *SIGIR 2016*.

[25] A. Roegiest, G. V. Cormack, M. R. Grossman, and C. L. A. Clarke. TREC 2015 Total Recall Track Overview. In *TREC 2015*.

[26] H. L. Roitblat, A. Kershaw, and P. Oot. Document categorization in legal electronic discovery: Computer classification vs. manual review. *Journal of the American Society for Information Science and Technology*, 61(1):70–80, 2010.

[27] M. Sanderson et al. Test collection based evaluation of information retrieval systems. *Foundations and Trends in Information Retrieval*, 4(4):247–375, 2010.

[28] L. Schamber. Relevance and information behavior. *Annual review of information science and technology (ARIST)*, 29:3–48, 1994.

[29] E. M. Voorhees. Variations in relevance judgments and the measurement of retrieval effectiveness. *Information Processing & Management*, 36(5), 2000.

[30] E. M. Voorhees. The philosophy of information retrieval evaluation. In *Workshop of the Cross-Language Evaluation Forum for European Languages*, pages 355–370. Springer, 2001.

[31] W. Webber. Re-examining the effectiveness of manual review. In *Proc. SIGIR Information Retrieval for E-Discovery Workshop*, 2011.

[32] W. Webber, D. W. Oard, F. Scholer, and B. Hedin. Assessor error in stratified evaluation. In *CIKM 2010*.

Meta-evaluation of Online and Offline Web Search Evaluation Metrics

Ye Chen[†], Ke Zhou[‡], Yiqun Liu[†*], Min Zhang[†], Shaoping Ma[†]
[†]Tsinghua National Laboratory for Information Science and Technology, Department of Computer Science & Technology, Tsinghua University, Beijing, China
[‡]University of Nottingham, Nottingham, U.K.
yiqunliu@tsinghua.edu.cn

ABSTRACT

As in most information retrieval (IR) studies, evaluation plays an essential part in Web search research. Both offline and online evaluation metrics are adopted in measuring the performance of search engines. Offline metrics are usually based on relevance judgments of query-document pairs from assessors while online metrics exploit the user behavior data, such as clicks, collected from search engines to compare search algorithms. Although both types of IR evaluation metrics have achieved success, to what extent can they predict user satisfaction still remains under-investigated. To shed light on this research question, we meta-evaluate a series of existing online and offline metrics to study how well they infer actual search user satisfaction in different search scenarios. We find that both types of evaluation metrics significantly correlate with user satisfaction while they reflect satisfaction from different perspectives for different search tasks. Offline metrics better align with user satisfaction in homogeneous search (i.e. ten blue links) whereas online metrics outperform when vertical results are federated. Finally, we also propose to incorporate mouse hover information into existing online evaluation metrics, and empirically show that they better align with search user satisfaction than click-based online metrics.

KEYWORDS

Search satisfaction, evaluation metrics, online evaluation

1 INTRODUCTION

Search engine evaluation is important in both academic and industrial IR research. The goal of IR researchers is to bulid search engine systems which can satisfy users' information needs. Both offline and online metrics have been adopted to measure how well the system serves real users. Offline metrics mainly originated from Cranfield approach [12] and are based on editorial judgments of the relevance of search results. Typical offline metrics include Average Precision (AP), Normalized Discounted Cumulative Gain (NDCG) and Rank-Biased Precision (RBP) [35]. These metrics are widely used to measure the quality of ranking algorithms [44] and are of great value in guiding search algorithm designing. However, although they may provide easily interpretable outcomes, offline search evaluation has encountered two major problems. The first one lies in that editorial judgments are often less credible when measuring actual user experience. Recent studies show that assessors' judgments may significantly differ from users' assessments [31]. The second problem is that the evaluation results based on offline metrics can be biased because they are usually generated with a small and incomplete dataset [13].

Rather than relying on offline metrics with relevance judgments, a popular contrasting approach is to use online metrics based on the simple fact that the interactions between users and search engines reflect the actual users' experiences in a natural usage environment. Such metrics are calculated based on practical users' behavior logs and can give us straightforward descriptions on how users interact with search engines. In addition, it is often cheap and fast to collect such data in modern search engines, making it particularly easy to scale up online evaluation. Typical online metrics include click-based metrics such as CTR (click through rate), UCTR [11] (binary value representing click) and PLC [9] (number of clicks divided by the position of the lowest click) as well as dwell time-based metrics such as query dwell time, average of click dwell time [21] and so on. Although easily scalable and arguably more truthful indication of operational IR effectiveness, online metrics can suffer from various biases present in typical search logs. Online behavior of users can be affected by many factors, with position bias being the most widely recognized effect, which requires de-biasing when inferring search success. In addition, online metrics may not be as reusable as offline metrics [42].

Both online and offline metrics have been widely used to measure search performance in the past years. Nonetheless, they are usually poorly correlated [11] because they measure IR systems from different perspectives. Which measures better reflect the ultimate actual user satisfaction remains an open research question. Therefore, in this work we investigate the relationship between offline/online metrics and actual user satisfaction, aiming to establish a thorough understanding of the effectiveness of those metrics in various search scenarios. We meta-evaluate a series of existing evaluation metrics based on two public datasets with more than two

*Corresponding author

This work was supported by Natural Science Foundation of China (Grant No. 61622208, 61532011, 61672311), Tsinghua University Initiative Scientific Research Program(2014Z21032), National Key Basic Research Program (2015CB358700).

SIGIR '17, August 07-11, 2017, Shinjuku, Tokyo, Japan
© 2017 ACM. ISBN 978-1-4503-5022-8/17/08...$15.00.
DOI: http://dx.doi.org/10.1145/3077136.3080804

thousand search sessions. Query-document relevance assessments, users' interaction behaviors and their explicit satisfaction feedback are all included in the datasets, which makes us able to compute most of the widely-used online and offline metrics. With more than thirty metrics, we calculate Pearson correlation and conduct concordance test [40] to study how well each metric infers actual search user satisfaction. We found that while online and offline metrics measure users' search experience from different perspectives, they generally both significantly correlate with actual user satisfaction.

To enable thorough meta-evaluation with different information needs, we categorize the search tasks according to two existing taxonomies, with respect to search goal types [5] and cognitive level [3]. We find that top-weighted offline metrics correlate extremely well with user satisfaction in *navigational* search while online metrics perform comparatively better in *informational* and *transactional* search tasks. Inspired by previous studies on federated search [10, 32], we also compare the performance of evaluation metrics in both homogeneous and heterogeneous search environment as users search behaviors as well as satisfaction perception may be affected by vertical results. We find that online metrics perform better than offline metrics in heterogeneous search environment. This is probably because offline metrics mainly rely on relevance assessments while the interaction-based online metrics may be more sensitive to the effect of vertical results. In addition, inspired by research on users' fine-grained interaction behaviors such as satisfied clicks [51] and mouse hovers [16], we also investigate the differences between online metrics calculated based on different interaction behavior signals (clicks, satisfied clicks, hovers). The results show that online metrics can better estimate user satisfaction when mouse hover information is incorporated.

Our contributions in this paper are three-folds: (1) We present a thorough meta-evaluation of online/offline metrics from the perspective of their relationship with user satisfaction for various types of information needs. The results provide insights for both evaluation metrics study and user satisfaction understanding. (2) We investigate the differences and applicabilities of different evaluation metrics in both homogeneous and heterogeneous search environment. We demonstrate that offline metrics work better in homogeneous search while online metrics outperform in heterogeneous search environment. (3) We propose to incorporate mouse hover information into existing online evaluation metrics and empirically demonstrate that they correlate better with user satisfaction.

2 RELATED WORK

Of particular interest to our research is the extensive body of work on (i) meta evaluation of IR metrics, and (ii) search satisfaction.

2.1 Meta Evaluation of IR Metrics

As evaluation serves as an important part in IR-related research, the meta-evaluation of evaluation metrics has also been widely studied in recent years and different criteria have been adopted to compare different evaluation metrics [33].

One widely-used method is to use "discriminative power" to measure evaluation metrics. Early in 2000, Buckley and Voorhees proposed to use error rate, which is the likely error of concluding "System A is better than system B", to compare between different metrics [6]. They also adopted "fuzziness value" to examine "the power of a measure to discriminate among systems". This idea was further formalized to be "discriminative power" by Sakai in 2006 [39]. He pointed out that mildly top-weighted metrics, such as AP, NDCG and RBP(0.95) usually have higher discrimination ratios than those strongly-weighted metrics, such as Prec@5 and RBP(0.5) [41]. In 2010, Yilmaz and Robertson compared AP and NDCG based on their statistical ability to predict outcomes on held-out data [50]. Another criteria to compare metrics is to calculate the correlations between the system orderings generated by different metrics. Correlation coefficients such as Kendall's τ and Spearman's ρ are widely used [42]. However, a weakness is that such coefficients introduce the same penalty for the discords at different ranking positions, whereas the top positions are usually more important in IR systems. To shed light on these considerations, Yilmaz et al. [49] introduced an AP-based correlation coefficient called τ_{ap} to achieve a top-weighted emphasis. Webber et al. [48] also proposed Rank Biased Overlap (RBO) to operate over indefinite and non-conjoint rankings. Other evaluation criteria including evaluation based on judgment cost [7, 8, 35, 49], coverage [38], inversions, interpretation and volatility matrix were also proposed in the past few years [33].

While A/B tests [27] and interleaving [23] as well as their variants [30, 43] are also widely-used approaches for search system evaluation [37], we choose user satisfaction as the ground truth for evaluating different evaluation metrics because satisfaction reflects users' search experience directly. Since the goal of IR systems is to satisfy users' information needs, it is important to investigate to what extent can existing evaluation metrics measure practical users' search experience. In this paper, we make a deep analysis of how different evaluation metrics correlate with user satisfaction. Because satisfaction has been regarded as the gold standard in search performance evaluation, we try to find metrics which can surrogate satisfaction, and introduce metrics which can better estimate user experience.

2.2 Search Satisfaction

Search satisfaction has become one of the major concerns in search evaluation studies. The concept of satisfaction was first proposed by Su et al. [45] and was defined as "the fulfillment of a specified desire or goal" by Kelly [25]. To evaluate a search system, satisfaction can be considered as regarding not only to the whole search experience but also to some specific aspects [46], such as the precision or completeness of search results, response time and so on. Since satisfaction is important for both search engine evaluation and optimization, a number of research studies have tried to quantify user satisfaction in both desktop search [20, 47] and mobile search [26, 28], and in both homogeneous [31] and heterogeneous search environment [10]. In recent years, a number of works (e.g, [21, 22]) have started using the benefit-cost framework to analyze the satisfaction judgement process of users. In this framework, both the benefit factors (document relevance) and cost factors (the effort users spend on examining search engine result pages (SERPs) and landing pages) are used to estimate satisfaction.

Although satisfaction can be regarded as the gold standard in search performance evaluation, as mentioned, it is not easy to be collected. This makes it urgent to find a reliable and reusable metric to estimate user satisfaction. However, as indicated by recent studies, relevance-based evaluation metrics, such as MAP and nDCG, may not be perfectly correlated with users' search experience [2, 20]. Recently, Mao et al. [34] further studied the relationship between relevance, usefulness and satisfaction and also suggested that traditional system-centric evaluation metrics are not well aligned with user satisfaction.

Different from these existing works, we study the relationships between user satisfaction and both offline and online evaluation metrics. Our work is complementary to those research on satisfaction understanding and prediction, but also provides additional insights from the evaluation measure perspective. We investigate how the existing metrics perform in different search scenarios and compare the applicabilities of different metrics in homogeneous and heterogeneous search environment. Meanwhile, we also investigate how mouse hover information can be incorporated into online metrics to obtain better alignment with user satisfaction. The major contribution of our work lies in that we comprehensively meta-evaluate over thirty most popular IR metrics for many search tasks. The obtained insights can be used for guiding search evaluation practitioners.

3 DATASET AND METHODOLOGY

In this section, we describe the datasets as well as the meta-evaluation methods used throughout this paper. We also perform an analysis of user satisfaction distribution according to the characteristics of the datasets.

3.1 Overview

Our study aims to meta-evaluate different metrics based on two datasets which we have made publicly available[1]. These two datasets contain more than 2400 search sessions collected under 56 search search tasks in total. The detailed statistics are shown in Table 1.

Table 1: Characteristics of Datasets

	# queries	# different rankings per query	# users	# sessions
Dataset #1	26	3	40	1038
Dataset #2	30	6~10	58	1397

These two datasets are generated under the same experimental process which is shown in Figure 1. Each participant completed a series of no more than 30 tasks in the datasets and they were required to perform two warm-up search tasks first to get familiar with the search process. Before each task, the participant was shown the search query and task explanations (see the card on the top right corner of Figure 1 as an example) first to avoid ambiguity. After that, the participant would be guided to search result page where the query is not allowed to change. Each participant was asked to examine the 10 fixed search results provided by the system and end the search session either if the search goal was completed or he/she was disappointed with the results. The provided search result lists were pre-crawled from commercial search engines and we made sure that the participant is able to complete the search goal as long as he/she examines all the provided search results. Each time the participant completed a search session, he/she was required to label a satisfaction score to reflect his/her search experience. Then they would be guided to continue to the next search task.

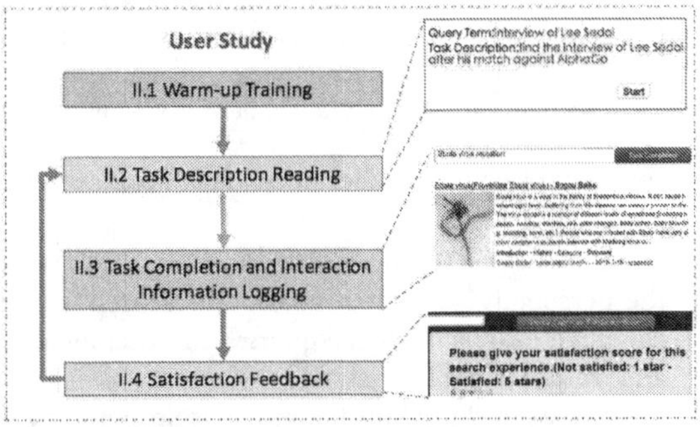

Figure 1: Data Collection Procedure

Note that no query reformulation are allowed and the number of search results are fixed to 10 for the consistency of result sets across users. Such data collection settings are similar to previous studies such as [36]. Meanwhile, we adopt SERP-level satisfaction rather than session-level satisfaction in this paper because most offline metrics are designed to measure the quality of only one search result page. While there may be ways to adjust or merge the metrics to measure session-level result quality, the metric adaptation may cause other uncontrollable effects and is out of the scope of this paper.

The search results in Dataset #1 are all organic search results and the ones in Dataset #2 are mainly federated search results. The vertical results included in Dataset #2 contain various types, including image, encyclopedia, news and download. The combination of Dataset #1 and Dataset #2 is consistent with real-life settings because not all SERPs provided by commercial search engines contain vertical results. Furthermore, such composition of our datasets also provides the advantage for us to evaluate how metrics perform differently in homogeneous and heterogeneous search environment (see section 4.4).

In these two datasets, each task is accompanied by several different search result pages provided by several ranking mechanisms with a same pre-specified query, which is to ensure that all users saw the same page under the same ranking mechanism. This makes it possible for us to meta-evaluate the performance of different evaluation metrics. Both datasets contain the following information for each search session: (1) Query and corresponding task descriptions. (2) Information of ranked search results as shown on SERPs. (3) 4-scaled relevance assessments of all search results. (4) 5-scaled user satisfaction annotations. (5) Users' interaction behaviors during the search process, including click-through, mouse hover and dwell time information.

With the rich information provided by the datasets, we can compute most widely-used offline / online metrics and hence meta-evaluate the relationship between these metrics and users' percieved satisfaction scores.

3.2 Search Task Taxonomy

To further evaluate the performance of different evaluation Metrics in different search scenarios, we classify the search sessions into different categories based on the query and corresponding task descriptions provided in the dataset. We organize the search sessions

[1] The link of the datasets and detailed data descriptions is https://1drv.ms/f/s!AqRbaaorUiT1avvHQdagVv9uOPM

Table 2: Examples of Search Queries and Corresponding Taxonomies

Query	Task Description	Search Goal	Cognitive Level
Meizu official website	find the official website of Meizu	Navigational	Remember
Stramaccioni	find a biographical sketch of Stramaccioni	Informational	Remember
interview of Lee Sedol	find the interview of Lee Sedol after his match against AlphaGo	Informational	Understand
yesterday once more	find the online audition of "yesterday once more" sung by carpenters	Transactional	Remember
dunk video	find online videos about dunking	Transactional	Understand

into the following two most widely-used task taxonomies in this paper:

- Search Goal [5]: This taxonomy classifies search tasks from the perspective of search goals. The search queries are classified into navigational queries, informational queries and transactional queries.
- Cognitive Level [3]: This taxonomy is proposed by Anderson and Krathwohl, which identifies six cognitive process dimensions: remember, understand, apply, analyze, evaluate and create.

Table 2 shows an example set of the search tasks and their corresponding taxonomies while Table 3 presents the numbers of search queries / sessions within different types of search tasks. Note that we only include a subset of all the task types described in the task taxonomies due to the composition of our dataset. With respect to the cognitive level taxonomy, we only classify search sessions as either "remember" or "understand" since it is difficult and unrealistic to classify the fixed 10 result based search sessions into the other four types of search tasks. The data size of the navigational search tasks is comparatively small. Although the meta-evaluation results may be potentially less reliable for this navigational search task, we believe this can still provide useful preliminary insights while the more thorough analysis with more data points are left for future work.

Table 3: Distribution of Queries and Sessions of Different Types of Search Tasks

	Navigational	Informational	Transactional
Queries	10	23	23
Sessions	400	1047	988

	Remember	Understand
Queries	31	25
Sessions	1325	1110

3.3 Analysis of User Satisfaction

In this section, we try to compare the satisfaction distribution across different search task taxonomies. Inspired by [25], which says satisfaction judgement may be quite subjective and different users may have different opinions, we regularize the satisfaction scores labelled by each user into Z-scores according to equation (1), where sat_i is one particular satisfaction score given by one user and $Avg(Sat)$ is the average of all satisfaction scores he/she labelled. $Var(Sat)$ in equation (1) refers to the variance of the satisfaction scores of this user.

$$Z\text{-}score_i = \frac{sat_i - Avg(Sat)}{Var(Sat)} \quad (1)$$

Figure 2 shows the distribution of quintiles in increasing Z-scores based on different search task taxonomies. Different colors show satisfaction scores from search sessions originated from different

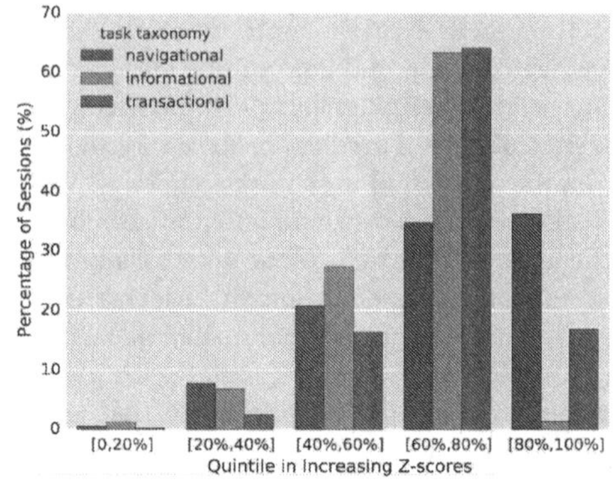

(a) Taxonomy I

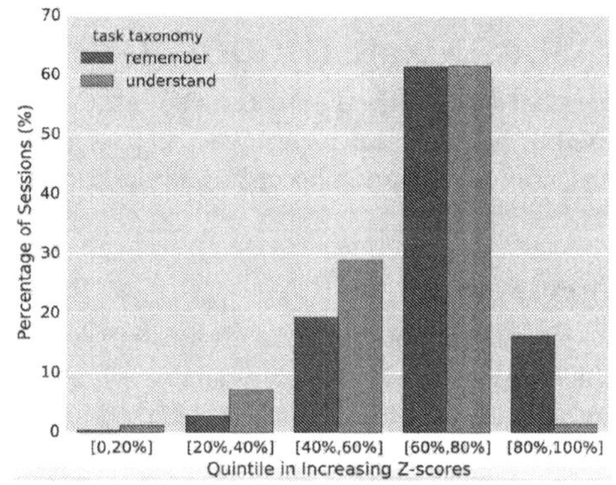

(b) Taxonomy II

Figure 2: Satisfaction Distribution Based on Different Search Task Taxonomies with Different Quintiles

task categories. We can see that in all types of search tasks, the general trend is that users tend to give a high satisfaction score in most cases, which indicates that commercial search engines generally provide promising results for these non-long-tailed search tasks.

With respect to the first taxonomy based on query intent, we can see that users tend to be the least satisfied if they are searching with informational queries because the percentage of sessions with lower Z-scores (less than 60%) is comparatively higher in the informational case (35.4%) than in navigational (29.0%) and transactional (18.9%) cases. Also, the percentage of sessions of the highest 20 percent of Z-scores is extremely low (1.3%) for informational search tasks compared with the other two types of search tasks. This is reasonable because in most navigational and transactional search tasks, users intended to find a specific website or information resource, which can often be satisfied with only one search result. While in the case of informational search tasks, users often have to read quite a number of search results to get a comprehensive understanding of the information need, which may be more difficult and time consuming.

$Total = 0; Correct_1 = 0; Correct_2 = 0;$
foreach *pair of search sessions* (s_1, s_2) **do**
  $Total + +;$
  $\delta M = M(s_1) - M(s_2);$
  $\delta M^* = M^*(s_1) - M^*(s_2);$
  if $(\delta M \times \delta M^*) > 0$ **then** // M and M^* positively agree
    $Correct_1 + +;$
  if $(\delta M \times \delta M^*) < 0$ **then** // M and M^* negatively agree
    $Correct_2 + +;$
  if $(\delta M = 0 \text{ and } \delta M^* = 0)$ **then** // M and M^* agree
    $Correct_1 + +;$
    $Correct_2 + +;$
$Correct = Max(Correct_1, Correct_2)$
$Concordance(M, M^*) = Correct/Total;$

Algorithm 1: Computing the concordance of metrics M and golden standard metric M^* (user satisfaction feedback) based on preference agreement.

From the perspective of the second task taxonomy based on task cognitive level, we can see that users give lower satisfaction scores in search tasks which belong to "understand" categories. This is in line with our expectation because search tasks identified as "understand" category are considered to be more difficult than those identified to be "remember" tasks. In general, from the results shown in Figure 2, we can see that users perceive different levels of satisfaction in different search scenarios, which inspires us to study the relationship between different evaluation metrics and satisfaction across different search task taxonomies.

3.4 Meta-Evaluation Methods

With satisfaction widely regarded as the gold standard of user-centric evaluation metrics, we analyze which metrics can better reflect user satisfaction based on the datasets described in this section. We do not consider session-based SAT in our work, rather we assume one SERP page interaction, which consists of most of the search sessions. With respect to the meta-evaluation methodology, we use both pearson correlation coefficient [4] and concordance test to compare different evaluation metrics. The idea of using concordance test is inspired by [40] and the method is described in Algorithm 1. We use s_1 and s_2 to denote different systems of the same task in our dataset and $M(s_i)$ to denote the averaged value of metric M computed on all sessions under s_i. The gold standard metric M^* is user satisfaction. Our algorithm differs from the algorithm used in [40] in that we take the possibility of both positive and negative correlation into consideration. Furthermore, we use strict $>$ and $<$ instead of $\geq$ and $\leq$ in the concordance test [40] because loose restrictions cannot work properly for two-valued metrics such as UCTR.

The number of data points for computing pearson correlation and data pairs for concordance test in different search scenarios are shown in Table 4. We should note that the size of data points/pairs of navigational search and homogeneous search (due to the limited ranking mechanisms of Dataset #1) is comparatively small, which may lead to the insignificant results in these two taxonomies.

Table 4: Numbers of data points / pairs for meta-evaluation

	# data points for Pearson Correlation	# data pairs for Concordance Test
All	291	744
Navigational	30	30
Informational	130	348
Transactional	131	366
Remember	152	378
Understand	139	366
Homogeneous	78	78
Heterogeneous	213	666

We believe our results (shown in Sec. 4) are still informative and evaluation on a larger dataset can be carried out in the future.

4 EXPERIMENTAL RESULTS

In this section, we meta-evaluate the performance of different evaluation metrics in different search scenarios based on the algorithm described in section 3.4 to obtain thorough insights into how different metrics perform according to different information needs. We first evaluate the performance of offline metrics and online metrics in section 4.1 and 4.2, respectively. In section 4.3, we take a deep insight into how some main offline/online metrics infer user satisfaction in different search scenarios. Finally, we incorporate mouse hover information into some existing online metrics and demonstrate its effectiveness in section 4.4.

4.1 Comparison Across Offline Metrics

Table 5: Comparison of Pearson Correlations / Concordance between Satisfaction and Offline Metrics (* indicates t-test statistical significance at $p < 0.01$ level)

	Pearson Correlation	Concordance
CG	0.354*	45.8%
DCG@3	0.356*	61.6%*
DCG@5	0.411*	65.7%*
DCG@10	0.421*	65.3%*
AP	0.396*	60.2%*
RBP(0.1)	0.389*	66.7%*
RBP(0.5)	0.438*	66.5%*
RBP(0.8)	**0.445***	65.7%*
RBP(0.95)	0.384*	63.4%*
ERR	0.433*	**66.8%***

Based on the search result relevance assessments provided by the datasets, we compute some widely-used traditional offline metrics and investigate how they align with user satisfaction, including cumulative gain (CG), discounted cumulative gain (DCG), average precision (AP) and rank-biased precision (RBP). For DCG, we compare the performance of the metric calculated at different ranking lengths to investigate the effect of evaluation depth. For RBP, we compare the metric performance when the persistence parameter p is set as 0.1, 0.5, 0.8 and 0.95, which is suggested to be appropriate for impatient, neutral, patient and extremely patient users [35], respectively. We also include expected reciprocal rank (ERR), which is based on the "cascade" user model and is suggested to better correlates with click-based metrics compared to DCG and other editorial metrics [9]. The pearson correlation coefficients and concordance test results between these metrics and user satisfaction are shown in Table 5. The best pearson correlation and concordance results are bolded.

We can see that ERR achieves the highest concordance with user satisfaction based on the results in Table 5, which is in line with the findings in [9]. This may be because the "cascade" user model utilized in ERR better models user behavior that capture satisfaction. RBP(0.8) achieves the highest pearson correlation among all the metrics, which may indicate that a patient (but not extremely patient) rank-biased user model can best describe the characteristic of the tested user group. From the perspective of DCG, we can see that DCG@10 correlates user satisfaction slightly better than DCG@3 and DCG@5, which probably indicates that metrics calculated based on a longer ranking length can capture more information and may have a better estimation of user satisfaction. Among all these offline metrics, CG has the lowest pearson correlation and concordance with user satisfaction. This is due to the fact that DCG, AP as well as ERR are all top-weighted metrics while CG is not. Relevant results placed at top positions may be much more important than those placed at bottom. Futhermore, we can note that the poor performance of CG is especially remarkable in the case of navigational search scenario (shown in Table 7) where one top-ranked relevant result is usually sufficient to complete the search goal.

Overall, we can observe that many offline metrics (DCG, RBP and ERR) have significant and moderate correlations (0.4 to 0.6 [14]) with user satisfaction.

4.2 Comparison Across Online Metrics

Table 6: Comparison of Pearson Correlations / Concordance between Satisfaction and Online Metrics (* indicates t-test statistical significance at $p < 0.01$ level)

	Pearson Correlation	Concordance
UCTR	-0.069	24.2%*
QCTR	-0.330*	57.9%*
PCTR@3	0.043	50.3%*
PCTR@5	-0.092	44.5%*
PCTR@10	-0.226*	33.5%*
MaxRR	0.095	50.1%*
MinRR	0.330*	**61.2%***
MeanRR	0.266*	59.5%*
PLC	0.222*	58.1%*
MaxScroll	**-0.519***	60.9%*
SumClickDwell	-0.417*	58.9%*
AvgClickDwell	-0.109	50.9%*
QueryDwellTime	**-0.559***	62.6%*
TimeToFirstClick	-0.432*	65.6%*
TimeToLastClick	-0.504*	**67.3%***
DsatClickCount	-0.170*	56.0%*
DsatClickRatio	-0.130*	52.3%*

While offline metrics are especially valuable when evaluating a system in prior to its deployment [13, 34], online metrics have been widely adopted for modern search engines because such metrics are calculated based on the interactions between practical users and systems. Inspired by previous research on metrics meta-evaluation [9, 11, 15, 19], we compare the evaluation performance of some most widely-used online metrics, including:

- Mouse-based (clicks or scroll) metrics
  - **UCTR** - Binary variable indicating whether there was a click or not in the session (the opposite of abandonment).
  - **QCTR** - Number of clicks in a session.
  - **PCTR** - Page click-through rate as defined in [51]. We use all clicks rather than satisfied clicks to calculate PCTR in Table 6, which is different from [51] where only satisfied clicks are used. Comparisons between metrics based on other user interaction signals (e.g. satisfied clicks) are further discussed in section 4.3.
  - **MaxRR, MinRR, MeanRR** - Respectively maximum, minimum and mean reciprocal ranks of the clicks. Zero if no clicks.
  - **PLC** - Number of clicks divided by the position of the lowest click.
  - **MaxScroll** - Maximum of scroll distance.
- Dwelltime-based metrics
  - **SumClickDwell, AvgClickDwell** - Respectively sum and average of click dwell time in a query.
  - **QueryDwellTime** - Query dwell time.
  - **TimeToFirstClick, TimeToLastClick** - Time delta between the start of search session and the first click and last click in the session, respectively.
  - **DsatClickCount, DsatClickRatio** - Previous studies divide clicks into satisfied clicks and dissatisfied clicks based on various dwell time thresholds [17, 21]. We tested different thresholds and choose to define clicks with a dwell time <15s as dissatisfied clicks because it performs the best on our dataset. Previous work [21] also analyzed the threshold of 15s to differentiate satisfied clicks. We calculate the number and ratio of dissatisfied clicks, respectively.

The online metrics we discuss in this section are mostly based on mouse (click and scroll) behaviors and dwell time information, which can be easily computed based on users' behavior logs. There are also several studies tried to utilize users' behavior information to quantify or predict user satisfaction (e.g. [1, 18]). We do not include these methods in our work because they are more complicated prediction models, rather than the simple and easy-to-interpret evaluation metrics of our interests. Meanwhile, we do not include the session-based metrics discussed in [17, 24] because there are no query reformulations included in the datasets.

The correlations / concordances between the online evaluation metrics and user satisfaction are shown in Table 6, whereas the highest correlation based on each interaction signals are shown in bolded terms. The results in reveal a number of interesting findings:

(1) In contrast to the positive correlation between offline metrics and user satisfaction, online metrics generally correlates with user satisfaction negatively. This is reasonable because the offline metrics measure the quality of search result page based on relevance assessments and users usually tend to feel more satisfied if the search results are of high quality [34]. On the contrary, the interactions signals which online metrics adopted usually reflects search effort and high search effort can reduce user satisfaction [10, 21]. MaxScroll also correlates with satisfaction negatively because a longer scroll distance may also indicate more search effort.

MaxRR, MinRR and MeanRR compute the reciprocal ranks of the clicked results and hence correlate with satisfaction positively. It is in line with the findings in previous studies that PLC correlates with satisfaction positively as PLC is regarded as approximately the precision of examined results [9].

(2) The metrics based on click behaviors in general correlates more weakly with user satisfaction, compared with dwelltime-based metrics. This may be because a clicked result does not always necessarily mean a high quality document hence the click-based metrics may fail. Meanwhile, previous studies [37, 43] pointed out that approximately one order of magnitude more online samples are required to match corresponding offline metrics' reliability, which may also explain the reason of the comparatively poor performance of click-based metrics. In contrast, some metrics based on scroll (MaxScroll) and dwelltime information (SumClickDwell, QueryDwellTime and TimeToLastClick) have stronger (moderate) negative correlation with user satisfaction, which means scrolls and dwelltime information are quite important behavior signals to infer user satisfaction.

(3) Among all these online metrics, TimeToLastClick has the best concordance with user satisfaction. The last click in a search session is usually considered as satisfied click [51] and therefore TimeToLastClick measures the time "wasted" before the user find a satisfactory document, which may account for the good performance of TimeToLastClick. We can also note that the concordance between TimeToLastClick and user satisfaction is even better than the offline metrics, which implies that online metrics can be as available as offline metrics even without offline relevance judgments. QueryDwellTime has the strongest (moderate) pearson correlation but relatively low concordance with user satisfaction. This may be because query dwell time has the largest value range among all these metrics, which may take an advantage during the computing process of pearson correlation.

(4) From the perspective of ranking length, we can observe that PCTR@10 correlates user satisfaction better than PCTR@3 and PCTR@5, which is consistent with the findings of DCG and further indicates that metrics calculated based on a longer ranking length can better estimate user satisfaction. We can also note that PCTR has very low concordance with user satisfaction compared with other metrics. This is because there are quite a number of SERPs with the same PCTR metric values in our dataset while there are minor changes within the satisfaction judgements. Therefore, this can result in discordance according to Algorithm 1.

(5) It is in line with our expectation that there is almost no correlation between user satisfaction and simple metrics such as UCTR. UCTR also has a very poor concordance with satisfaction, which is because it is a two-valued metric while we require strict $<$ or $>$ in Algorithm 1.

In general, we can observe that several online metrics (MaxScroll, QueryDwellTime,TimetoFirstClick and TimeToLastClick) maintain significant and moderate correlations (0.4 to 0.6) with satisfaction.

4.3 Online Metrics v.s. Offline Metrics

Based on the findings in section 4.1 and 4.2, we select out some well-behaved metrics and investigate their correlations with user satisfaction in different task taxonomies described in section 3.2 to make a more detailed comparison. The results are shown in Table 7. The highest correlation achieved by offline metrics/online metrics in each task taxonomy are in bolded terms.

The results in Table 7 show that generally online metrics have as good correlation and concordance as offline metrics, which further verifies the value of using online metrics in guiding search engine development because they achieve comparatively good performance without external relevance assessments. In most task scenarios, RBP and ERR perform the best among all offline metrics while TimeToLastClick along with QueryDwellTime perform the best among all online metrics, which is consistent with the findings in section 4.1 and 4.2.

From the search goal-based task taxonomy, we should note that top-weighted offline metrics correlate quite well with user satisfaction in navigational search tasks, especially for RBP(0.1) which models the search behavior of impatient users (strong pearson correlation, 0.6 to 0.8 [14]). While the concordance test results may be discrete and not so reliable due to the limited number of data pairs, the pearson correlation coefficients are extremely significant. This is because in navigational search scenario, where the user is usually required to reach a particular site [5], high quality results placed at the top positions are especially important. In contrast, online metrics perform slightly worse in navigational tasks than in informational and transactional tasks. This is probably because the search effort required in navigational search is usually less than that required in informational and transactional search, in which case the online metrics can hardly capture the differences of user's satisfaction perception.

We do not observe too much difference of the performance of different metrics from the perspective of cognitive level based taxonomy. The dwelltime based online metrics perform slightly better in "understand" search scenario but the difference is not remarkable. Such findings may suggest that users do not behave significantly different in such two types of search tasks. An analysis in tasks with more deep cognitive levels such as "analyze" and "create" [3] can be carried out in the future.

We also observe the poor concordance of PCTR. This is because the test is conducted within the same task across different SERPs generated by different ranking mechanisms. The results on different SERPs are the same in most cases while the rankings are different. Therefore, there might exist many identical metric PCTR values for the two SERPs of many data pairs while users' perceived satisfaction is different. According to Algorithm 1, such case will be regarded as discordance, which is the reason for the poor concordance of PCTR. While most of the results in Table 7 are informative, we must admit the comparatively small-scaled dataset in Navigational search scenarios is an inevitable limitation. A small number of data pairs for concordance test may result in discrete and unavailable results. We may need a larger dataset for more robust results in the future.

4.4 Metric Evaluation in Homogeneous / Heterogeneous Search

With data collected from both homogeneous search environment (Dataset #1) and heterogeneous search environment (Dataset #2), we investigate how different metrics perform in different search environments as shown in Table 8. The highest correlation achieved by different metrics in different search scenarios are bolded.

Table 7: Comparison of Pearson Correlations / Concordance between Satisfaction and Offline and Online Metrics in Different Search Scenarios(* indicates t-test statistical significance at $p < 0.01$ level)

	Search Goal			Cognitive Level	
	Navigational	Informational	Transactional	Remember	Understand
CG	0.335 / 53.3%	0.405* / 47.1%	0.354* / 44.0%*	0.414* / 44.7%*	0.389* / 47.0%*
DCG@10	0.543* / 76.7%*	0.454* / 64.1%*	0.403* / 65.6%*	0.475* / 67.5%*	0.437* / 63.1%*
RBP(0.1)	**0.653*** / **80.0%***	0.400* / 66.4%*	0.314* / **65.8%***	0.407* / **68.0%***	0.371* / 65.3%*
RBP(0.8)	0.566* / **80.0%***	**0.475*** / 65.8%*	**0.419*** / 64.5%*	**0.492*** / 66.7%*	**0.454*** / 64.8%*
ERR	0.625* / **80.0%***	0.451* / **66.7%***	0.348* / **65.8%***	0.432* / **68.0%***	0.430* / **65.6%***
QCTR	-0.187 / 53.3%	-0.345* / 58.0%*	-0.290* / 58.2%*	-0.272* / 58.2%*	-0.367* / 57.7%*
PCTR@10	-0.135 / 0.0%*	-0.358* / 33.9%*	0.018 / 35.8%*	-0.005 / 33.6%*	-0.392* / 33.3%*
MinRR	0.454* / **73.3%***	0.323* / 61.5%*	0.281* / 59.8%*	0.318* / 59.8%*	0.344* / 62.6%*
PLC	0.408* / 70.0%*	0.195* / 57.2%*	0.181* / 57.9%*	0.242* / 57.7%*	0.213* / 58.5%*
MaxScroll	**-0.477*** / **73.3%***	-0.577* / 59.2%*	-0.465* / 61.5%*	-0.471* / 63.2%*	-0.547* / 58.5%*
QueryDwellTime	-0.392* / 50.0%	**-0.600*** / 62.1%*	**-0.479*** / 64.2%*	**-0.485*** / 64.6%*	-0.572* / 60.7%*
TimeToLastClick	-0.351 / 50.0%	-0.525* / **68.1%***	-0.428* / **68.0%***	-0.445* / **67.5%***	**-0.551** / **67.2%***
DsatClickCount	-0.020 / 53.3%	-0.187 / 55.7%*	-0.145 / 56.6%*	-0.134 / 56.1%*	-0.223* / 56.0%*

Table 8: Comparison of Pearson Correlations / Concordance between Satisfaction and Offline and Online Metrics in Homogeneous and Heterogeneous Search Environment(* indicates t-test statistical significance at $p < 0.01$ level)

		homogeneous search		heterogeneous search	
		Pearson Correlation	Concordance	Pearson Correlation	Concordance
Offline Metrics	CG	0.483*	55.1%	0.321*	44.7%
	DCG@10	**0.535***	70.5%*	0.392*	64.7%*
	RBP(0.1)	0.433*	**71.8%***	0.383*	66.1%*
	RBP(0.8)	**0.535***	**71.8%***	0.418*	65.0%*
	ERR	0.462*	**71.8%***	**0.429***	**66.2%***
Online Metrics (Mouse-based)	QCTR	-0.137	55.1%	-0.401*	58.3%*
	PCTR@10	-0.062	2.6%*	-0.284*	37.4%*
	MinRR	0.417*	**64.1%***	0.325*	**60.8%***
	PLC	0.366*	61.5%*	0.176*	57.7%*
	MaxScroll	**-0.510***	**64.1%***	**-0.540***	60.5%*
Online Metrics (Dwelltime-based)	QueryDwellTime	-0.224*	**57.7%**	**-0.637***	65.0%*
	TimeToLastClick	**-0.235***	50.0%	-0.570*	**69.4%***
	DsatClickCount	-0.034	53.8%	-0.209*	56.3%*

Different metrics are categorized into three groups and it is obvious from Table 8 that different groups of metrics reveal different characteristics in different search environments. Offline metrics better align with user satisfaction in homogeneous search environment while in heterogeneous search tasks, online metrics, especially the dwelltime-based metrics perform much better. This is reasonable because most existing offline metrics do not take the effect of vertical results into consideration during the evaluation process. While both organic and vertical search results can provide relevant information, vertical results are presented in different styles and can help satisfy users' information need from various dimensions [10]. Offline metrics are solely based on relevance assessments and do not consider the effect of vertical results, which may account for their comparatively poor performance in heterogeneous search environment. Online metrics are mainly based on users' interaction behaviors, which may also be sensitive to the existence of vertical results. Therefore, the online metrics may be more effective in the heterogeneous search environment. Dwelltime-based metrics achieves a pearson correlation of around -0.6 (strong) in heterogeneous search while the best offline metrics is only moderately correlated (around 0.4). In addition, note that since high quality vertical results can provide users sufficient information to complete the search goal without a need to click (called "good abandonment" in previous work [29]), the number of clicks in heterogeneous search may not be sufficient and hence may lead to a drop of performance of click-based online metrics. In our datasets, there are on average 2.83 clicks in a homogeneous search session while only 1.81 clicks in a heterogeneous one. This may be the reason that click-based online metrics do not perform so well in heterogeneous search.

4.5 Click and Hover based Online Metrics

Previous research [10, 16] suggested that fine-grained user interaction information can help better model user behaviors and estimate user satisfaction. With the rich interaction informational provided by the datasets, we further investigate the performance of online metrics calculated based on the following four types of user interaction signals:

All click-based: This group of evaluation metrics are calculated based on all clicks in a search session, which is the same as the metrics used in the previous sections.

Satisfied click-based: Previous studies pointed out that sometimes clicks do not imply the high relevance of a result document in web search. This is because although the result snippet may appear to be relevant and attractive, the landing page may be of low quality. For example, a click is defined as a satisfied click if the user spent 30 seconds or more reading the clicked document or if it was the last click in the search session [51]. Satisfied click is widely regarded as the signal of a relevant document. For this group of metrics, we use satisfied clicks to replace the all clicks used in "all click-based" metrics.

Hover-based: Hovers are also regarded to be important behavior signal because there have been various types of results which do not require a click to provide users with necessary information [10, 29]. We use hovers to replace the all clicks used in "all click-based" metrics to achieve the "hover-based" metrics.

Click and Hover-based: We combine the click and hover information in this group of evaluation metrics. If a search results is either clicked or hovered on, then this result will be regarded as "clicked" as in the calculation process of "all click-based" metrics. In this way, we get the "click and hover-based" metrics.

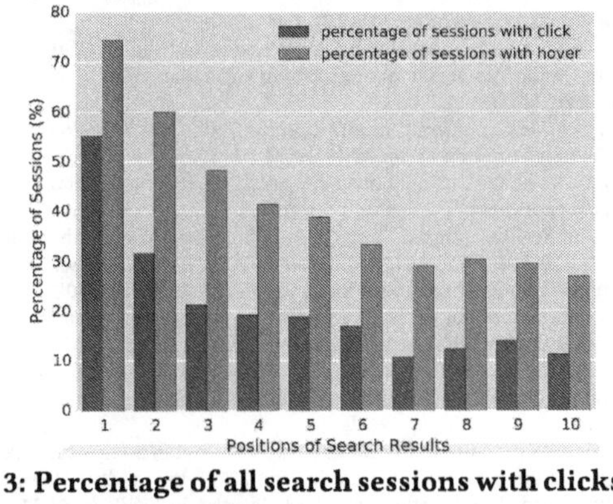

Figure 3: Percentage of all search sessions with clicks/hovers at different result positions

We use suffix "_ac", "_sc", "_h" and "_ch" to represent the "all click-based", "satisfied click-based", "hover-based" and "click and hover-based" metrics, respectively. We choose MinRR and PLC as examples because they correlate with user satisfaction better than other click-based metrics based on the findings in previous sections. The correlations between user satisfaction and metrics computed based on different information signals are shown in Table 9. The best correlation / concordance achieved by each metric in different search scenarios are bolded.

We can see from the results that in almost all search scenarios, both of these two click-based metrics can better estimate user satisfaction when hover information is incorporated. This is probably because in today's search engine, various types of results such as instant answers, verticals and even result snippets contain sufficient information to satisfy the users, which sometimes makes clicks unnecessary. In such case, hovers can help capture more information than clicks. It is not surprising that the performance of MinRR_h and MinRR_ch are the same because in most cases the clicked results are usually a subset of hovered results. Furthermore, we can see that the hover information is especially effective in heterogeneous search according to the performance of MinRR. When hover information is incorporated, the pearson correlation coefficient improves by 0.169(from 0.325 to 0.494) in heterogeneous search and only 0.025(from 0.417 to 0.442) in homogeneous search. The improvement of concordance test result is also larger in heterogeneous search environment. This is reasonable because sometimes users can accomplish their search tasks by interacting with the vertical results on heterogeneous SERPs. An example of the distribution differences between hovers and clicks are shown in Figure 3. For each rank position of search results, we compute the percentage of sessions with clicks and hovers respectively. It is apparent that there are more hovers than clicks in all positions, which may further help confirm that clicks solely may not be sufficient to capture users' interaction information. There appears to be at least 27% sessions with hovers in all positions while only the first two positions have a probability of more than 27% to be clicked. In this way, hovers may contain much more valuable information than clicks. From the perspective of MinRR and PLC, a metric which combines click and hover information may be the most reliable because neither click nor hover information alone (PLC_h) can achieve the best correlation with satisfaction.

5 CONCLUSIONS

Search engine evaluation is essential in both academic and industrial IR research. Both offline and online evaluation metrics are adopted to measure the performance of search engines. While search satisfaction is widely regarded as the gold standard in search performance evaluation, the relationship between different evaluation metrics and satisfaction remains under-investigated.

In this work, we meta-evaluate the performance of different offline/online evaluation metrics based on two datasets. We investigate how different metrics align with user satisfaction in different search scenarios using both pearson correlation and concordance test. We find that different types of evaluation metrics estimate user satisfaction from different perspectives. Offline metrics work better in homogeneous search environment while online metrics are more consistent with user satisfaction in heterogeneous search environment. We further compare the effectiveness of metrics calculated based on different user interaction signals. We propose to incorporate hover information into traditional click-based online metrics because they can help better estimate user satisfaction.

There are still some limitations of our work which we would like to list as our future work directions. Due to the nature of the utilized laboratory-based datasets, compared to the commercial search engine settings, online metrics are calculated based on relatively small-scale search sessions (from which our conclusions are drawn). Meanwhile, our datasets are based on a fixed search result page and no ability to reformulate the query, which may also affect users' interaction behaviors. While metrics calculated based on multi-query sessions can be developed, it will be another challenging research question. Our current aim is to meta-evaluate all the metrics on a single search page level, and we leave the session-level or even task-level evaluation as future work. Finally, all the participants within the datasets are undergraduate students. We think this may help reduce potential distractions and make the collected data more consistent. However, such specific age distribution may also cause potential bias. The study of large-scale online/offline metrics comparison, online metric sensitivity and more evaluation measures (such as interleaving) are left for future work.

REFERENCES

[1] Mikhail Ageev, Qi Guo, Dmitry Lagun, and Eugene Agichtein. 2011. Find it if you can: a game for modeling different types of web search success using interaction data. In *SIGIR'11*. ACM, 345–354.

[2] Azzah Al-Maskari, Mark Sanderson, and Paul Clough. 2007. The relationship between IR effectiveness measures and user satisfaction. In *SIGIR'07*. ACM, 773–774.

[3] Lorin W Anderson, David R Krathwohl, and Benjamin Samuel Bloom. 2001. *A taxonomy for learning, teaching, and assessing: A revision of Bloom's taxonomy of*

Table 9: Comparison of Pearson Correlations / Concordance between Satisfaction and Online Metrics Based on Different User Interaction Signals (* indicates t-test statistical significance at $p < 0.01$ level)

	Search Goal			Cognitive Level		Search Environment	
	Navigational	Informational	Transactional	Remember	Understand	Homogeneous	Heterogeneous
MinRR_ac	0.454* / 73.3%*	0.323* / 61.5%*	0.281* / 59.8%*	0.318* / 59.8%*	0.344* / 62.6%*	0.417*/64.1%*	0.325*/60.8%*
MinRR_sc	0.442* / **76.7%***	0.322* / **62.6%***	0.209* / 58.2%*	0.254* / 58.7%*	0.339* / **63.4%***	0.385*/**67.9%***	0.278*/60.2%*
MinRR_h	**0.464*** / 70.0%	**0.474*** / 61.8%*	**0.440* / 66.7%***	**0.462* / 67.5%***	**0.486*** / 61.5%*	**0.442***/65.4%*	**0.494*/64.4%***
MinRR_ch	**0.464*** / 70.0%	**0.474*** / 61.8%*	**0.440* / 66.7%***	**0.462* / 67.5%***	**0.486*** / 61.5%*	**0.442***/65.4%*	**0.494*/64.4%***
PLC_ac	0.408* / 70.0%*	0.195* / 57.2%*	0.181* / 57.9%*	0.242* / 57.7%*	0.213* / 58.5%*	0.366*/61.5%	0.176*/57.7%*
PLC_sc	0.416* / 73.3%*	0.198* / 56.9%*	0.119* / 57.1%*	0.190* / 57.7%*	0.215* / 58.5%*	0.360*/67.9%*	0.139/57.7%*
PLC_h	0.302 / 56.7%	0.113 / 48.0%	0.176 / 46.4%	0.198 / 47.6%	0.108 / 47.5%	0.179/51.3%	0.142/47/1%
PLC_ch	**0.444 / 80.0%***	**0.262* / 59.2%***	**0.302* / 61.7%***	**0.347* / 63.8%***	**0.271* / 58.7%***	**0.429*/69.2%***	**0.265*/60.4%***

educational objectives. Allyn & Bacon.

[4] Jacob Benesty, Jingdong Chen, Yiteng Huang, and Israel Cohen. 2009. Pearson correlation coefficient. In *Noise reduction in speech processing*. Springer, 1–4.

[5] Andrei Broder. 2002. A taxonomy of web search. In *ACM Sigir forum*, Vol. 36. ACM, 3–10.

[6] Chris Buckley and Ellen M Voorhees. 2000. Evaluating evaluation measure stability. In *SIGIR'00*. ACM, 33–40.

[7] Stefan Büttcher, Charles LA Clarke, Peter CK Yeung, and Ian Soboroff. 2007. Reliable information retrieval evaluation with incomplete and biased judgements. In *SIGIR'07*. ACM, 63–70.

[8] Ben Carterette, Evangelos Kanoulas, and Emine Yilmaz. 2010. Low cost evaluation in information retrieval. In *SIGIR'10*. ACM, 903–903.

[9] Olivier Chapelle, Donald Metlzer, Ya Zhang, and Pierre Grinspan. 2009. Expected reciprocal rank for graded relevance. In *CIKM'09*. ACM, 621–630.

[10] Ye Chen, Yiqun Liu, Ke Zhou, Meng Wang, Min Zhang, and Shaoping Ma. 2015. Does Vertical Bring more Satisfaction?: Predicting Search Satisfaction in a Heterogeneous Environment. In *CIKM'15*. ACM, 1581–1590.

[11] Aleksandr Chuklin, Pavel Serdyukov, and Maarten De Rijke. 2013. Click model-based information retrieval metrics. In *SIGIR'13*. ACM, 493–502.

[12] Cyril Cleverdon, Jack Mills, and Michael Keen. 1966. FACTORS DETERMINING THE PERFORMANCE OF INDEXING SYSTEMS VOLUME 1. DESIGN. (1966).

[13] Alex Deng and Xiaolin Shi. 2016. Data-Driven Metric Development for Online Controlled Experiments: Seven Lessons Learned. In *SIKDD'16*. ACM.

[14] Geoffrey Evans, Anthony Heath, and Mansur Lalljee. 1996. Measuring left-right and libertarian-authoritarian values in the British electorate. *British Journal of Sociology* (1996), 93–112.

[15] Steve Fox, Kuldeep Karnawat, Mark Mydland, Susan Dumais, and Thomas White. 2005. Evaluating implicit measures to improve web search. *TOIS'05* 23, 2 (2005), 147–168.

[16] Qi Guo, Dmitry Lagun, and Eugene Agichtein. 2012. Predicting web search success with fine-grained interaction data. In *CIKM'12*. ACM, 2050–2054.

[17] Ahmed Hassan, Xiaolin Shi, Nick Craswell, and Bill Ramsey. 2013. Beyond clicks: query reformulation as a predictor of search satisfaction. In *CIKM'13*. ACM, 2019–2028.

[18] Ahmed Hassan, Yang Song, and Li-wei He. 2011. A task level metric for measuring web search satisfaction and its application on improving relevance estimation. In *CIKM'11*. ACM, 125–134.

[19] Katja Hofmann, Lihong Li, Filip Radlinski, and others. 2016. Online evaluation for information retrieval. *Foundations and Trends® in Information Retrieval* 10, 1 (2016), 1–117.

[20] Scott B Huffman and Michael Hochster. 2007. How well does result relevance predict session satisfaction?. In *SIGIR'07*. ACM, 567–574.

[21] Jiepu Jiang, Ahmed Hassan Awadallah, Xiaolin Shi, and Ryen W White. 2015. Understanding and predicting graded search satisfaction. In *WSDM'15*. ACM, 57–66.

[22] Jiepu Jiang, Daqing He, and James Allan. 2014. Searching, browsing, and clicking in a search session: changes in user behavior by task and over time. In *SIGIR'14*. ACM, 607–616.

[23] Thorsten Joachims. 2002. Optimizing search engines using clickthrough data. In *SIGKDD'02*. ACM, 133–142.

[24] Evangelos Kanoulas, Ben Carterette, Paul D Clough, and Mark Sanderson. 2011. Evaluating multi-query sessions. In *SIGIR'11*. ACM, 1053–1062.

[25] Diane Kelly. 2009. Methods for evaluating interactive information retrieval systems with users. *Foundations and Trends in Information Retrieval* 3, 1fi!?2 (2009), 1–224.

[26] Julia Kiseleva, Kyle Williams, Jiepu Jiang, Ahmed Hassan Awadallah, Imed Zitouni, Aidan C Crook, and Tasos Anastasakos. 2016. Predicting User Satisfaction with Intelligent Assistants. In *SIGIR'16*. 495–505.

[27] Ron Kohavi, Roger Longbotham, Dan Sommerfield, and Randal M Henne. 2009. Controlled experiments on the web: survey and practical guide. *Data mining and knowledge discovery* 18, 1 (2009), 140–181.

[28] Dmitry Lagun, Chih-Hung Hsieh, Dale Webster, and Vidhya Navalpakkam. 2014. Towards better measurement of attention and satisfaction in mobile search. In *SIGIR'14*. ACM, 113–122.

[29] Jane Li, Scott Huffman, and Akihito Tokuda. 2009. Good abandonment in mobile and PC internet search. In *SIGIR'09*. ACM, 43–50.

[30] Lihong Li, Jin Young Kim, and Imed Zitouni. 2015. Toward predicting the outcome of an A/B experiment for search relevance. In *WSDM'15*. ACM, 37–46.

[31] Yiqun Liu, Ye Chen, Jinhui Tang, Jiashen Sun, Min Zhang, Shaoping Ma, and Xuan Zhu. 2015. Different users, different opinions: Predicting search satisfaction with mouse movement information. In *SIGIR'15*. ACM, 493–502.

[32] Zeyang Liu, Yiqun Liu, Ke Zhou, Min Zhang, and Shaoping Ma. 2015. Influence of vertical result in web search examination. In *SIGIR'15*. ACM, 193–202.

[33] Xiaolu Lu, Alistair Moffat, and J Shane Culpepper. 2016. The effect of pooling and evaluation depth on IR metrics. *Information Retrieval Journal* 19, 4 (2016), 416–445.

[34] Jiaxin Mao, Yiqun Liu, Ke Zhou, Jian-Yun Nie, Jingtao Song, Min Zhang, Shaoping Ma, Jiashen Sun, and Hengliang Luo. 2016. When does Relevance Mean Usefulness and User Satisfaction in Web Search?. In *SIGIR'16*. ACM.

[35] Alistair Moffat and Justin Zobel. 2008. Rank-biased precision for measurement of retrieval effectiveness. *TOIS'08* 27, 1 (2008), 2.

[36] Vidhya Navalpakkam, LaDawn Jentzsch, Rory Sayres, Sujith Ravi, Amr Ahmed, and Alex Smola. 2013. Measurement and modeling of eye-mouse behavior in the presence of nonlinear page layouts. In *WWW'13*. ACM, 953–964.

[37] Filip Radlinski and Nick Craswell. 2010. Comparing the sensitivity of information retrieval metrics. In *SIGIR'10*. ACM, 667–674.

[38] Sri Devi Ravana and Alistair Moffat. 2010. Score estimation, incomplete judgments, and significance testing in IR evaluation. In *AIRS'10*. Springer, 97–109.

[39] Tetsuya Sakai. 2006. Evaluating evaluation metrics based on the bootstrap. In *SIGIR'06*. ACM, 525–532.

[40] Tetsuya Sakai. 2013. How intuitive are diversified search metrics? Concordance test results for the diversity U-measures. In *AIRS'13*. Springer, 13–24.

[41] Tetsuya Sakai and Noriko Kando. 2008. On information retrieval metrics designed for evaluation with incomplete relevance assessments. *Information Retrieval* 11, 5 (2008), 447–470.

[42] Mark Sanderson. 2010. *Test collection based evaluation of information retrieval systems*. Now Publishers Inc.

[43] Anne Schuth, Katja Hofmann, and Filip Radlinski. 2015. Predicting search satisfaction metrics with interleaved comparisons. In *SIGIR'15*. ACM, 463–472.

[44] Hinrich Schütze. 2008. Introduction to Information Retrieval. In *Proceedings of the international communication of association for computing machinery conference*.

[45] Louise T Su. 1992. Evaluation measures for interactive information retrieval. *Information Processing & Management* 28, 4 (1992), 503–516.

[46] Louise T Su. 2003. A comprehensive and systematic model of user evaluation of Web search engines: II. An evaluation by undergraduates. *Journal of the American Society for Information Science and Technology* 54, 13 (2003), 1193–1223.

[47] Hongning Wang, Yang Song, Ming-Wei Chang, Xiaodong He, Ahmed Hassan, and Ryen W White. 2014. Modeling action-level satisfaction for search task satisfaction prediction. In *SIGIR'14*. ACM, 123–132.

[48] William Webber, Alistair Moffat, and Justin Zobel. 2010. A similarity measure for indefinite rankings. *TOIS'10* 28, 4 (2010), 20.

[49] Emine Yilmaz, Evangelos Kanoulas, and Javed A Aslam. 2008. A simple and efficient sampling method for estimating AP and NDCG. In *SIGIR'08*. ACM, 603–610.

[50] Emine Yilmaz and Stephen Robertson. 2010. On the choice of effectiveness measures for learning to rank. *Information Retrieval* 13, 3 (2010), 271–290.

[51] Masrour Zoghi, Tomáš Tunys, Lihong Li, Damien Jose, Junyan Chen, Chun Ming Chin, and Maarten de Rijke. 2016. Click-based Hot Fixes for Underperforming Torso Queries. SIGIR.

The Probability That Your Hypothesis Is Correct, Credible Intervals, and Effect Sizes for IR Evaluation

Tetsuya Sakai
Waseda University, Tokyo, Japan
tetsuyasakai@acm.org

ABSTRACT

Using classical statistical significance tests, researchers can only discuss $P(D^+|H)$, the probability of observing the data D at hand or something more extreme, under the assumption that the hypothesis H is true (i.e., the p-value). But what we usually want is $P(H|D)$, the probability that a hypothesis is true, given the data. If we use Bayesian statistics with state-of-the-art Markov Chain Monte Carlo (MCMC) methods for obtaining posterior distributions, this is no longer a problem. That is, instead of the classical p-values and 95% confidence intervals, which are often misinterpreted respectively as "probability that the hypothesis is (in)correct" and "probability that the true parameter value drops within the interval is 95%," we can easily obtain $P(H|D)$ and *credible intervals* which represent exactly the above. Moreover, with Bayesian tests, we can easily handle virtually any hypothesis, not just "equality of means," and obtain an Expected A Posteriori (EAP) value of any statistic that we are interested in. We provide simple tools to encourage the IR community to take up paired and unpaired Bayesian tests for comparing two systems. Using a variety of TREC and NTCIR data, we compare $P(H|D)$ with p-values, credible intervals with confidence intervals, and Bayesian EAP effect sizes with classical ones. Our results show that (a) p-values and confidence intervals can respectively be regarded as approximations of what we really want, namely, $P(H|D)$ and credible intervals; and (b) sample effect sizes from classical significance tests can differ considerably from the Bayesian EAP effect sizes, which suggests that the former can be poor estimates of population effect sizes. For both paired and unpaired tests, we propose that the IR community report the EAP, the credible interval, and the probability of hypothesis being true, not only for the raw difference in means but also for the effect size in terms of Glass's Δ.

CCS CONCEPTS

•Information systems → Retrieval effectiveness; Presentation of retrieval results;

SIGIR'17, August 7–11, 2017, Shinjuku, Tokyo, Japan.

978-1-4503-5022-8/17/08...$15.00
DOI: http://dx.doi.org/10.1145/3077136.3080766

KEYWORDS

Bayesian hypothesis tests; confidence intervals; credible intervals; effect sizes; Hamiltonian Monte Carlo; Markov Chain Monte Carlo; p-values; statistical significance

1 INTRODUCTION

In March 2016, the American Statistical Association (ASA) published an official statement about the limitations of classical significance tests and p-values, in response to their continued misuse and misinterpretations [33]. While ASA's main statement does not contain anything new (e.g., "*A p-value, or statistical significance, does not measure the size of an effect or the importance of a result*"), the document mentions some alternatives to classical significance tests, including *Bayesian methods.* It goes on to say: "*All these [alternative] measures and approaches rely on further assumptions, but they may more directly address the size of an effect (and its associated uncertainty) or whether the hypothesis is correct.*" In the IR community, similar warnings against classical significance tests have been given by Carterette [4] and Sakai [22], amongst others.

The above quotations from the ASA statement may be paraphrased as follows. Classical significance tests can only give us $P(D^+|H)$, the probability of observing the data D at hand or something more extreme under the assumption that the hypothesis H is true (i.e., the p-value). But what we usually want is $P(H|D)$, the probability that a hypothesis is true, given the data. Theoretically, the Bayesian framework proposed in the 18th century [2] can give us exactly this, but it was heavily criticised during the 19th and 20th centuries (See Section 2.1). However, with the recent advent of effective and efficient sampling algorithms for obtaining *posterior distributions* known as *Markov Chain Monte Carlo* (MCMC) methods [15], Bayesian approaches to statistical testing are rapidly gaining popularity among statisticians [30, 31]. Thus, as alternatives to the classical p-values and 95% confidence intervals which are often misinterpreted respectively as "probability that the hypothesis is (in)correct" and "probability that the true parameter value drops within the interval is 95%," we can employ Bayesian tests to easily obtain $P(H|D)$ and *credible intervals*, which represent exactly the above. Moreover, with Bayesian tests, we can easily handle virtually any hypothesis, not just "equality of means," as we shall demonstrate later.

We provide simple tools to encourage the IR community to take up paired and unpaired Bayesian tests for comparing two systems; our tools are based on a state-of-the-art MCMC method called *Hamiltonian Monte Carlo* and a recently-proposed variant called *No-U-Turn Sampler* [13]. Using a variety of TREC[1] and NTCIR[2]

[1] http://trec.nist.gov/
[2] http://research.nii.ac.jp/ntcir/

data, we compare $P(H|D)$ with p-values, credible intervals with confidence intervals, and Bayesian EAP effect sizes with classical ones. Our results show that (a) p-values and confidence intervals can respectively be regarded as approximations of what we really want, namely, $P(H|D)$ and credible intervals; and (b) sample effect sizes from classical significance tests can differ considerably from the Bayesian EAP effect sizes, which suggests that the former can be poor estimates of population effect sizes. For both paired and unpaired tests, we propose that the IR community report the EAP, the credible interval, and the probability of hypothesis being true, not only for the raw difference in means but also for the effect size in terms of Glass's Δ.

2 RELATED WORK

2.1 Frequentists Versus Bayesians

It is well known that Ronald A. Fisher heavily and persistently criticised the Bayesian statistics since the 1960s: "*the theory of inverse probability* [i.e., Bayesian statistics] *is founded upon an error, and must be wholly rejected*" [9] (p.9). During the 20th century, the de facto standard in statistical analysis was indeed the "frequentist" approach founded upon Fisher's views, and the Bayesian approach was largely neglected.

The Bayesian approach had two weaknesses. The first, which has not been resolved completely even to this day, is the fact that it relies on *prior probabilities* which nobody knows and therefore must be set based on researchers' *subjective* decisions or beliefs. However, given the lack of knowledge about priors, *noninformative priors* such as those that obey a uniform distribution can always be used, although this too is a subjective decision which may or may not reflect the true nature of the phenomenon under study[3]. In the present study, we simply follow the standard Bayesian practice of employing uniform distributions for obtaining priors.

The second weakness in the original Bayesian approach was that, despite the theoretical beauty of Bayes' Theorem, it was often difficult to obtain the posterior distributions as this often involves computationally infeasible integrations. However, this second problem has actually been solved, with the recent advent of effective and efficient sampling algorithms known as *Markov Chain Monte Carlo* (MCMC) methods [15]. Because of this, Bayesian statistics is now gaining popularity rapidly: for example, according to Toyoda [30], over one-half of *Biometrika*[4] papers published in 2014 utilised Bayesian statistics. In the present study, we utilise a state-of-the-art MCMC method called *Hamiltonian Monte Carlo* [17] and a recently-proposed variant called *No-U-Turn Sampler* [13], which come with easy-to-use implementations.

Meanwhile, the classical significance testing approach of the frequentists have also received many criticisms over the past decades (e.g. [12]). Some even consider significance tests to be harmful. First, the practice of using the significance criterion α instead of the p-value often leads to dichotomous thinking: "Is the difference statistically significant, or not?" Ziliak and McCloskey [35] hold Fisher responsible for this[5]. Second, even if the p-value is reported, this is a function not only of the *effect size* (the magnitude of the difference that we are interested in; See Section 3.6) but also the sample size. That is, a small p-value (i.e., a statistically highly significant result) may just reflect a large sample size (e.g., number of topics used for computing mean retrieval effectiveness scores) rather than a large effect size [22]. Moreover, as was mentioned in Section 1, the outcomes of classical significance tests are often misinterpreted. We believe that it is time for the IR community to start using Bayesian statistics regularly, perhaps along with classical significance tests if the community feels reluctant to let the latter go. Since the Bayesian approach is not only highly intuitive and flexible but now also computationally feasible, there really is no reason to reject it.

In the field of psychology, Kruschke [14] argues that the Bayesian approach is superior to the (unpaired) t-test: "*Some people may wonder which approach, Bayesian or NHST,*[6] *is more often correct. This question has limited applicability because in real research we never know the ground truth; all we have is a sample of data.* [...] *the relevant question is asking which method provides the richest, most informative, and meaningful results for any set of data. The answer is always Bayesian estimation.*" In the present study, we empirically demonstrate the relationships between paired/unpaired t-tests and the corresponding state-of-the-art Bayesian methods using a variety of real IR evaluation data.

2.2 Classical Significance Tests in IR

The limitations of classical significance tests have been pointed out in the field of IR as well. Carterette argues: "*we still believe p-values from paired t-tests provide a decent rough indicator that is useful for many of the purposes they are currently used for. We only argue that p-values and significance test results in general should be taken with a very large grain of salt, and in particular have an extremely limited effect on publication decisions and community-wide decisions about "interesting" research directions.*" Sakai [22] encourages IR researchers to report not only the p-values but also effect sizes and confidence intervals. However, Sakai's more recent examination of over 1,000 SIGIR and TOIS papers [23] shows that about 30% of the entire papers lack significance testing, while about 65% of the papers with significance testing neither report p-values nor test statistics.

While computer-based, distribution-free alternatives to classical significance tests, namely, the *bootstrap* [20] and the *randomisation test* [27], have been advocated for IR evaluation, they have not been used as widely as the classical tests [23]. Moreover, these tests address the same limited question as the classical tests: what is the p-value?

2.3 Bayesian Inferences for IR

We are already beginning to see Bayesian approaches to IR evaluation. Carterette [3, 5] have proposed to evaluate IR systems by modelling binary and graded relevance judgments directly instead

[3] In 2005, Efron remarked: "*What looks uninformative enough often turns out to subtly force answers in one direction or another*" while arguing that a combination of Bayesian and frequentist ideas is needed to handle modern problems [8].

[4] This is the journal in which William S. Gosset (or "Student") published the famous paper on the t-test in 1908 [29]. http://biomet.oxfordjournals.org/

[5] "*Ronald A. Fisher would say, "The potash manures are not statistically significant. Disregard them.* [...] *William S. Gosset would say,* "[...] *If you want to know about the potash manures you have to consider their pecuniary value compared to the barley you're trying to make money with*" [35].

[6] Null Hypothesis Significance Testing

of using evaluation measure scores as the atomic unit. Using three different TREC data sets, he compared t-test p-values with the posterior probabilities of his four Bayesian models to argue the advantages of the latter. Carterette uses JAGS (Just Another Gibbs Sampler), an open-source implementation of BUGS (Bayesian inference Using Gibbs Sampling) and its R interface `rjags` to conduct MCMC simulations.

Our present work is in a sense less ambitious than that of Carterette in that we are adhering to using evaluation measure scores as the atomic unit (just like Carterette's "Model 2"): we would like the IR community to take up the habit of using Bayesian approaches, and to do that, we believe that we need to move cautiously while clarifying how the transition from classical significance testing will affect our research findings. Carterette demonstrates that the t-test (i.e., his "Model 1") p-values and his Model 2 posterior probabilities are strinkingly similar; we generalise this in several ways, by using diverse data sets from NTCIR and TREC, and by comparing confidence intervals with credible intervals, and classical sample effect sizes with their Bayesian counterparts.

Zhang *et al.* [34] propose to replace the use of classical significance tests with Bayesian tests with probabilistic graphical models tailored to a specific problem in information retrieval, namely, text classification. Following Kruschke [14, 15], they propose to make a decision about two text classifers by comparing the *High Density Interval* (HDI) and the *Region of Practical Importance* (ROPE) of the performance difference δ. Zhang *et al.* use *Metropolis-Hastings* (MH) sampling for their MCMC simulations.

Regarding the implementation of MCMC, we employ the state-of-the-art Hamiltonian Monte Carlo (HMC) [17] and its variant No-U-Turn Sampler (NUTS) [13] using `stan` and its R interface `rstan`, which are gaining popularity. According to Hoffman and Gelman [13], HMC's features "*allow it to converge to high-dimentional target distributions much more quickly than simpler methods such as random walk Metropolis or Gibbs sampling*"; NUTS automatically sets a required parameter for HMC, namely the number of steps L for the *leap-frog method* (See Section 3.2). Also, according to Kruschke [15] (pp.399-400), "*HMC can be more effective than the various samplers in JAGS and BUGS, especially for large complex models. [...] However, Stan is not universally faster or better (at this stage in its development).*"

3 BAYESIAN TESTS

3.1 Bayesian Basics

To discuss Bayesian tests, let us start with the famous Bayes' rule:

$$f(\theta|x) = \frac{f(x|\theta)f(\theta)}{f(x)} = \frac{f(x|\theta)f(\theta)}{\int_{-\infty}^{+\infty} f(x|\theta)f(\theta)d\theta}, \quad (1)$$

where $f(\theta)$ is the *prior probability distribution* of a random variable θ (e.g., a population mean), $f(x|\theta)$ is the *likelihood* of data x given θ, and $f(\theta|x)$ is the *posterior probability distribution* of θ having observed x. Note that this view is already strikingly different from that of classical statistics: in classical significance testing, population parameters (θ's) are *constants*; in Bayesian statistics, they are *random variables* that form distributions. Since $f(\theta|x)$ is a probability distribution, $f(x)$ can be viewed as a *normalising constant* that ensures:

$$\int_{-\infty}^{+\infty} f(\theta|x)d\theta = \frac{1}{f(x)}\int_{-\infty}^{+\infty} f(x|\theta)f(\theta)d\theta = 1 . \quad (2)$$

Hence, Eq. 1 implies that the property of the posterior distribution $f(\theta|x)$ is governed by $f(x|\theta)f(\theta)$, i.e., the *kernel*.

If somehow the posterior distribution $f(\theta|x)$ has been obtained, a *point estimate* of the population parameter θ can be obtained as an *expected a posteriori* (EAP)[7]:

$$\hat{\theta}_{EAP} = E[\theta|x] = \int \theta f(\theta|x)d\theta = \int \theta\frac{f(x|\theta)f(\theta)}{f(x)}d\theta . \quad (3)$$

Moreover, how the random variable θ moves around $\hat{\theta}_{EAP}$ can be quantified by the *posterior variance* (or its square root, *posterior standard deviation*):

$$V[\theta|x] = E[(\theta - \hat{\theta}_{EAP})^2|x] = \int (\theta - \hat{\theta}_{EAP})^2 f(\theta|x)d\theta . \quad (4)$$

We can also obtain an *interval estimate* of θ by removing an $\alpha/2\%$ area from either side of $f(\theta|x)$. This is the $100(1-\alpha)\%$ *credible interval* (or *Bayesian confidence interval*), which is highly intuitive: the probability that the random variable θ lies within the interval is $100(1-\alpha)\%$. Recall that *confidence* intervals (CIs) used in classical statistics do *not* represent this probability: in the classical paradigm, θ is a *constant*, and when (say) 100 CIs are created from 100 different samples, $100(1-\alpha)\%$ of them are expected to contain that particular θ.

As we do not know $f(\theta)$, we employ a *non-informative* prior distribution to avoid subjectivity to the best of our ability. Our choice is to use a uniform distribution, in which case $f(\theta|x)$ is governed solely by the likelihood $f(x|\theta)$ in Eq. 1 and therefore the EAP reduces to the *maximum likelihood estimate* (MLE). That is, in our setting, the EAP of any parameter θ is *not* directly affected by our subjective choice of $f(\theta)$.

3.2 HMC and NUTS

In the above discussion, we assumed that $f(\theta|x)$ can be computed as defined in Eq. 1. However, in practice, it is usually not feasible to do this analytically. That is where MCMC methods, which try to sample θ repeatedly according to $f(\theta|x)$, come into play. MCMC methods construct Markov Chains of parameter values so that the underlying distribution eventually reaches a stationary distribution: after a *burn-in period* (B), all of the values in the chain obey the target distribution $f(\theta|x)$. Thus, if we collect T' values sequentially and throw away the intial B values, the remaining $T = T' - B$ values can be regarded as *realisations* of θ that obey $f(\theta|x)$. Suppose that we managed to obtain $T = 100,000$ realisations of θ; then, $\hat{\theta}_{EAP}$ (Eq. 3) can be obtained by simply averaging the T values. Similarly, the posterior variance (Eq. 4) can be obtained by averaging[8] the squared difference from $\hat{\theta}_{EAP}$. A 95% credible interval for θ can be obtained by sorting the T values in ascending order and then taking the 2,500th and 97,500th values as the lower and upper limits. The EAP values of other statistics such as effect sizes (See Section 3.6) can be computed similarly. Moreover, for virtually any hypothesis H (e.g., "mean 1 is higher than mean 2," "mean 1 is at least 0.2 points

[7] Alternatives would be a *maximum a posteriori* or a *posterior median*. These three estimates represent the mean, mode and median of the posterior distribution, respectively.
[8] Dividing by T suffices since T is large; there is no need for bias correction.

higher than mean 2," or "the effect size is greater than 0.5"), the probability that H is correct can be obtained by just counting the instances in which H holds among the T realisations. It is clear that this approach is more versatile than classical significance tests.

Hamiltonian Monte Carlo (HMC) [17] and its variant *No U-Turn Sampler* (NUTS) [13] are state-of-the-art MCMC methods which we utilise for obtaining realisations of θ from $f(\theta|x)$. For details of HMC, we refer the reader to recent books on this topic [15, 17]. However, it would help for us IR researchers to have a general idea about its basic principles. In physics, *Hamiltonian* is the sum of potential energy and kinetic energy; given a curved surface in an ideal physical world, any object would move on the surface while keeping the Hamiltonian constant. The path of the moving object is governed by *Hamilton's equations of motion*, which can be solved by the *leap-frog method* with parameters ϵ (stepsize) and L (leapfrog steps). To achieve sampling from a posterior distribution (which is our "curved surface"), an intuitive explanation of what HMC does is as follows: put an object somewhere on the surface and give it a push; after L units of time, let it halt and record its position; give it another push, and so on, until we have recorded T' positions.

Briefly, for a set of d parameters $\boldsymbol{\theta} = (\theta_1, \theta_2, \ldots, \theta_d)$, the HMC algorithm looks like this:

(1) Set $\boldsymbol{\theta}^{(1)}, \epsilon, L, T', B$ (where $T = T' - B$); Let $t = 1$;
(2) Generate d independent values $\boldsymbol{p}^{(t)} = (p_1^t, p_2^t, \ldots, p_d^t)$ from a standard normal distribution;
(3) Obtain candidates $\boldsymbol{\theta}^{(a)}, \boldsymbol{p}^{(a)}$ using the leap-frog method;
(4) Let $\boldsymbol{\theta}^{(t+1)} = \boldsymbol{\theta}^{(a)}$ (i.e., accept the transition candidate) with probability $\min(1, r)$; otherwise $\boldsymbol{\theta}^{(t+1)} = \boldsymbol{\theta}^{(t)}$ (i.e., reject the candidate and stay at the current position);
(5) End if $T' = t$; otherwise let $t = t + 1$ and go to Step 2.

The r in Step 4, which governs how often we can accept new candidates, is given by [30]:

$$r = \frac{f(\theta^{(a)}, p^{(a)}|x)}{f(\theta^{(t)}, p^{(t)}|x)}, \tag{5}$$

where $f(\theta, p|x)$ is a joint distribution of $f(\theta|x)$ and an independent standard normal distribution $f(p)$. One strength of HMC is that r is often close to one, and therefore we can achieve efficient sampling through many successful transitions in Step 4 while preserving the Hamiltonian.

NUTS is a variant of HMC that automatically determines an appropriate value of L [13]; both HMC and NUTS utilise an algorithm called *dual averaging* to automatically set ϵ [18]; hence, from the viewpoint of the users of HMC and NUTS for Bayesian tests, we do not have to worry about setting these parameters ourselves.

3.3 $\hat{R}$ and Effective Sample Size

For MCMC algorithms, methods for checking whether the values have converged to a stationary distribution and for measuring the sampling efficiency are available.

$\hat{R}$, a measure for checking convergence, assumes that the MCMC algorithm produces multiple Markov Chains, and compares the variance across the multiple chains with the variance within the chains[9]. According to Gelman [10], if $\hat{R}$ is less than 1.1 or 1.2, we can be assured that the chains have reached stationary distributions. MCMC produces Markov Chains and therefore the values in them are correlated to one another. If the chains produce very similar values repeatedly, then that is highly inefficient from the sampling point of view. *Effective Sample Size* (N_{eff}) is a measure available in `stan` for quantifying sampling efficiency, which means "you have obtained a sample of size T, but that is worth a sample of size (approximately) N_{eff} obtained when there is zero correlation within the chain." Hence, we should also check that N_{eff} is a large value. Both of the above measures are computed after removing the burn-in's from the chains. As our Bayesian test tools that we introduce in Section 3.7 rely on `stan` and its R interface `rstan`, the tools output $\hat{R}$ and N_{eff} on the R console. Since all experiments reported in the paper use sufficiently large sample sizes, namely $T = 100,000$, we do not discuss these indicators henceforth.

3.4 Classical versus Bayesian Tests for Comparing Two Means

As was discussed in Section 3.2, Bayesian tests are versatile. However, the present study focusses on the problems of comparing two means from paired and unpaired data, since these are the most common and basic problems in IR evaluation. While *two-sided* tests that ask "are the two systems equally effective or not?" are often recommended in classical significance tests given lack of prior knowledge as to which system might be better, this is not a very useful question from the Bayesian point of view, as two different systems are, by definition, different. What is more practical to consider is the probability that System 1 is better than System 2, $P(S1 > S2|D)$ (or, alternatively, $P(S1 < S2|D) = 1 - P(S1 > S2|D)$). Hence we compare Bayesian tests with classical *one-sided* tests. To be more specific, given two systems, we let $S2$ be the less effective system according to the sample data and consider $P(S1 < S2|D)$ (i.e., the probability of the less likely hypothesis) based on the Bayesian test, while setting the classical null and alternative hypotheses as $H_0 : S1 = S2$ and $H_1 : S1 > S2$ so that the p-value represents "$P(D^+|S1 = S2)$."

3.5 Statistical Models

For unpaired data, we assume that $S1$'s scores obey $N(\mu_1, \sigma_1^2)$, while $S2$'s scores obey $N(\mu_2, \sigma_2^2)$, for both Bayesian and classical tests. Hence, the classical test we employ is the *Welch's t*-test, which does *not* assume homoscedasticity (i.e., equal variances). It is known that Student's and Welch's t-tests yield virtually identical p-values when the two sample sizes are equal [16, 24]; the experiments reported in this paper satisifes this condition and therefore our classical test results can be regarded as representing both types of unpaired t-test.

For paired data, the classical test we apply is the paired t-test, which relies on the same normal assumptions as described above and therefore the score *differences* obey $N(\mu_1 - \mu_2, \sigma_1^2 + \sigma_2^2)$. As for the Bayesian test, we can easily consider a *bivariate* normal

[9]Zhang *et al.* [34] remark that "*it is perfectly right to do a single long sampling run and keep all samples.*" However, it is very easy to throw away burn-in's that may not yet obey the desired distribution and we prefer to do so. As for the number of chains, since $\hat{R}$ can be computed even for a single chain, by breaking it into multiple chains, we provide sample scripts for handling both multiple and single chains. The Bayesian test results are almost the same either way, but we report those based on multiple chains.

distribution [31]:

$$f(x_1, x_2|\mu_1, \mu_2, \sigma_1^2, \sigma_2^2, \rho) = \frac{1}{2\pi\sigma_1\sigma_2(1-\rho)} e^{-q/2}, \quad (6)$$

where

$$q = \frac{1}{1-\rho^2}[(\frac{x_1-\mu_1}{\sigma_1})^2 - 2\rho(\frac{x_1-\mu_1}{\sigma_1})(\frac{x_2-\mu_2}{\sigma_2}) + (\frac{x_2-\mu_2}{\sigma_2})^2]. \quad (7)$$

Here, ρ is the population correlation coefficient for x_1's and x_2's. Thus, for paired data, we can discuss hypotheses about the *correlation* between the two systems just as well as those about means and effect sizes if we are interested in that aspect.

3.6 Effect Sizes

Sakai [22] stresses the importance of reporting effect sizes and confidence intervals in the context of classical significance testing as a small p-value may just reflect a large sample size (See Section 2.2). When comparing two means, the effect size is usually given as the difference between the two measured in standard deviation units. We argue that Bayesian test results in IR should also be accompanied with effect sizes as well as *credible* intervals.

While there are several choices of effect sizes for comparing two means, we choose to avoid relying on the homoscedasticity assumption, to be consistent with the statistical models described in Section 3.5. One of the simplest effect size in such a case is Glass's Δ [19]. That is, if System 1 is taken as the baseline run (or "control group,") then its standard deviation is probably representative of an "ordinary world" before the advent of System 2, and therefore:

$$Glass\Delta_1 = \frac{\mu_1 - \mu_2}{\sigma_1}. \quad (8)$$

Thus, Glass's Δ measures the absolute difference in "ordinary" standard deviation units. Alternatively, if System 2 is taken as the baseline:

$$Glass\Delta_2 = \frac{\mu_1 - \mu_2}{\sigma_2}. \quad (9)$$

In our experiments, we focus on Eq. 9 since the second system is the less effective one (i.e., "baseline") according to the sample data. For convenience, we will hereafter refer to this version of effect size simply as "Glass2."

We can easily obtain the EAP and credible intervals for Glass2, as well as the probability of a hypothesis about the effect size being true, in exactly the same way as described in Section 3.2. For example, the EAP for Glass2 can be obtained by computing Eq. 9 T times using T realisations of μ_1, μ_2, σ_2 and then averaging them. Hence we propose that the IR community report the EAP, the credible interval and the probablity of hypothesis being true not only for the raw difference in means but also for effect sizes. Note that this is applicable to both paired and unpaired tests.

3.7 Implementation

Here, we briefly describe our Bayesian test tools for comparing two means. The sample R scripts are based on those developed by Hideki Toyoda [30][10]. We have sample scripts for generating both multiple and single chains but discuss only the former here. We have added a few shell scripts for postprocessing the Bayesian realisations, to encourage researchers to use credibile intervals not only for the raw difference in means but also for effect sizes. The scripts and sample data are available from our website[11]. R with the `rstan` package[12] and Rtools[13] must be installed first in order to use these scripts.

Figure 1 shows our sample R script for comparing paired data. It reads a stan file which describes the aforementioned bivariate normal distribution as well as *generated quantities* (the absolute difference and Glass's Δ's), and a system score file written in R, and generates five csv files that correspond to five Markov chains.

Figure 2 shows an output of our UNIX shell script that summarises the Bayesian test results by reading the csv files. Here, the first argument is "1032" because this is the line number in each csv file where the realisations start after the burn-in; the second argument is the number of realisations contained in the file (excluding the burn-in's); the third argument is the number of chains (i.e., number of csv files); the remaining arguments are the aforementioned Markov chain csv files. This script works for both multiple and single chains, by setting the arguments appropriately[14]. The screenshot provides the following information about the paired data from `run1` and `run2`:

- The EAP for the difference in means is 0.042, and the 95% credibile interval is [0.009, 0.074]. The probability that $\mu_1 - \mu_2$ is greater than the specified threshold (which is set to 0 by default within the script) is 99.4%;
- The EAP for Glass2 (with `run2` taken as the baseline) is 0.189 (i.e., about 19% of `run2`'s standard deviation), and the 95% credible interval is [0.043, 0.345]. The probability that this effect size is greater than the specified threshold (which is set to 0.2 by default) is 43.3%. Similar results with `run1` taken as the baseline are also presented.
- The EAP for the correlation (i.e., ρ in Eq. 6) between the scores of `run1` and `run2` is 0.857, and the 95% credible interval is [0.767, 0.920]. The probability that the correlation is greater than the specified threshold (which is set to 0.9 by default) is 12.2%.

Note that thresholds can be altered arbitrarily within the shell script according to researchers' practical needs.

Figures 3 and 4 provide similar screenshots of our scripts for comparing unpaired data.

4 EXPERIMENTS

To encourage IR researchers to transition comfortably from the classical significance test paradigm to the Bayesian one for comparison of means, we now report on experiments that compare Bayesian results against classifical test results using actual IR data. More specifically, we compare the probability that System X is better than System Y with p-values; credible intervals with classical confidence intervals, as well as effect sizes computed based on both approaches. We show that (a) p-values and confidence intervals can respectively be regarded as approximations of what we really want, namely, $P(H|D)$ and credible intervals; and (b) sample effect

[10] Toyoda's original scripts are available from http://www.asakura.co.jp/G_27_2.php?id=200. The present author is solely responsible for the modifications and any errors introduced thereby.

[11] http://www.f.waseda.jp/tetsuya/tools.html

[12] https://cran.r-project.org/

[13] https://cran.r-project.org/bin/windows/Rtools/

[14] By typing the command without arguments, suggested sets of arguments are displayed.

Table 1: IR data sets and evaluation measures used in this study

Data set name	year	track/task	language	measure	tool	#teams	#runs	#topics
NTCIR7IR4QA	2008	IR for question answering [25]	Chinese	Q-measure	NTCIREVAL	9	40 (20)	97
NTCIR9INTENT	2011	INTENT [28] (web diversity task)	Chinese	D♯-nDCG@10	NTCIREVAL	7	24 (20)	100
NTCIR12STC	2016	short text conversation [26] (tweet retrieval)	Chinese	nERR@10	NTCIREVAL	16	44 (20)	100
TREC03robust	2003	robust track [32]	English	nDCG@1000	NTCIREVAL	16	78 (20)	50
TREC11webD	2011	web track diversity task [7]	English	α-nDCG@10	ndeval	9	25 (20)	50
TREC15TS	2015	temporal summarisation track, task 2 [1]	English	$\mathcal{H}$	-	9	22 (20)	21

```
library(rstan)

scr <- "C:/work/R/modelPaired2.stan" #model written in Stan (see sample file)
par <- c( "mu", "Sigma", "rho", "delta", "glass" ) #mean, variances, correlation, delta,
glass's delta
war <- 1000 #burn-in
ite <- 21000 #iteration including burn-in
see <- 1234 #seed
dig <- 3 #significant digits
cha <- 5 #chains (number of trials = (ite-war)*cha)

source( "C:/work/R/run1_vs_run2.paired.R" ) #per-topic scores (see sample file)
outfile <- "C:/work/R/run1_vs_run2.NUTS.paired.csv" #output files
data <- list( N=N, x=x ) #sample size and per-topic scores

fit <- stan( file=scr, model_name=scr, data=data, pars=par, verbose=F, seed=see,
algorithm="NUTS", chains=cha, warmup=war, iter=ite, sample_file=outfile )
    # compile stan file and execute sampling (HMC may be used instead of NUTs)
print( fit, pars=par, digits_summary=dig )
```

Figure 1: A sample R script for comparing paired data.

```
BayesPairedSummary 1032 20000 5 run1_vs_run2.NUTS.paired_[1-5].csv
mu1-mu2 EAP: 0.042
mu1-mu2 95pct_cred_interval: 0.009 -- 0.074
P(mu1-mu2>0): 0.994
P(mu1-mu2<0): 0.006

glass1 EAP: 0.207
glass1 95pct_cred_interval: 0.047 -- 0.378
P(glass1>0.2): 0.522
P(glass1<0.2): 0.478
glass2 EAP: 0.189
glass2 95pct_cred_interval: 0.043 -- 0.345
P(glass2>0.2): 0.433
P(glass2<0.2): 0.567

rho EAP: 0.857
rho 95pct_cred_interval: 0.767 -- 0.920
P(rho>0.9): 0.122
P(rho<0.9): 0.878
```

Figure 2: A shell script for obtaining the EAP, credible intervals, and the probability that the hypothesis is correct (paired data) for the absolute difference, Glass's Δ, and correlation coefficient (paired data).

sizes from classical significance tests can differ considerably from the Bayesian EAP effect sizes, which suggests that the former can be poor estimates of population effect sizes.

Table 1 provides a brief summary of the six data sets we used for our experiments. To strengthen the generalisability of our experimental results, we tried to cover diverse IR tasks from both TREC and NTCIR. For each data set (i.e., test collection with its submitted runs), we chose one particular commonly-used evaluation measure: with the exception of TREC03robust[15], we chose from one of the

```
library(rstan)

scr <- "C:/work/R/modelUnpaired2.stan" #model written in Stan (see sample file)
par <- c( "mu1", "mu2", "sigma1", "sigma2", "delta", "glass" ) #means, s.d.'s, delta,
glass's delta
war <- 1000 #burn-in
ite <- 21000 #iteration including burn-in
see <- 1234 #seed
dig <- 3 #significant digits
cha <- 5 #chains (number of trials = (ite-war)*cha)

source( "C:/work/R/run1_vs_run2.unpaired.R" ) #per-topic scores (see sample file)
outfile <- "C:/work/R/run1_vs_run2.NUTS.unpaired.csv" #output files
data <- list( N1=N1, N2=N2, x1=x1, x2=x2 ) #sample sizes and per-topic scores

fit <- stan( file=scr, model_name=scr, data=data, pars=par, verbose=F, seed=see,
algorithm="NUTS", chains=cha, warmup=war, iter=ite, sample_file=outfile )
    # compile stan file and execute sampling (HMC may be used instead of NUTs)
print( fit, pars=par, digits_summary=dig )
```

Figure 3: A sample R script for comparing unpaired data.

```
BayesUnpairedSummary 1032 20000 5 run1_vs_run2.NUTS.unpaired_[1-5].csv
mu1-mu2 EAP: 0.042
mu1-mu2 95pct_cred_interval: -0.044 -- 0.127
P(mu1-mu2>0): 0.835
P(mu1-mu2<0): 0.165

glass1 EAP: 0.243
glass1 95pct_cred_interval: 0.011 -- 0.628
P(glass1>0.2): 0.534
P(glass1<0.2): 0.466
glass2 EAP: 0.222
glass2 95pct_cred_interval: 0.010 -- 0.575
P(glass2>0.2): 0.495
P(glass2<0.2): 0.505
```

Figure 4: A shell script for obtaining the EAP, credible intervals, and the probability that the hypothesis is correct (paired data) for the absolute difference, and Glass's Δ (unpaired data).

official measures of that track/task. Also, for each data set, we considered only the top 20 runs for pairwise comparisons as measured by that particular evaluation measure, which gives us 190 run pairs. For TREC11webD, α-nDCG was computed using their official evaluation script ndeval[16]; For TREC15TS, the values of $\mathcal{H}$ (which is basically like a nugget-based F-measure defined over a timeline [1]) were obtained from the official results of the track; other evaluation measures were computed using NTCIREVAL[17], with the exponential gain value setting (See, for example, [26]).

For each data set, we conducted Bayesian and classical tests for every system pair (where System 1 outperforms System 2 for the sample data), using both paired and unpaired tests. For classical paired and unpaired tests, *common* sample effect sizes were obtained by substituting sample means and System 2's sample standard deviations into Eq. 9. For Bayesian paired and unpaired tests, the EAP values of μ_1, μ_2, σ_2 were used with Eq. 9, under the two models described in Section 3.5, respectively.

[15] We chose nDCG rather than Average Precision (AP) for TREC03robust as AP cannot handle graded relevance even though the data set comes with graded relevance assessments.

[16] http://trec.nist.gov/data/web/11/ndeval.c

[17] http://research.nii.ac.jp/ntcir/tools/ntcireval-en.html

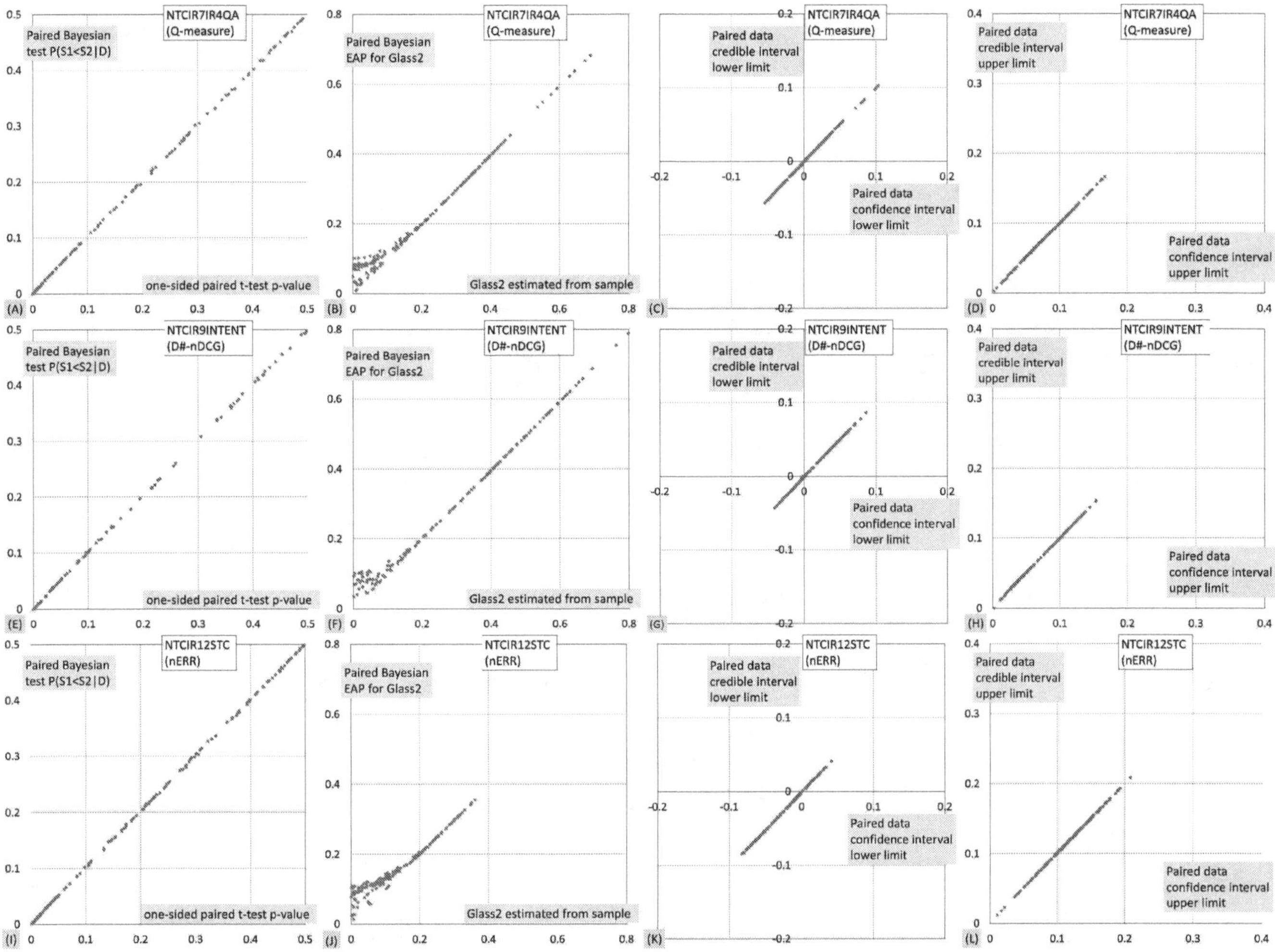

Figure 5: Paired Bayesian vs classical tests: comparisons with NTCIR data.

4.1 Paired Test Results

Here we compare the paired Bayesian test (based on NUTS) with the classical paired t-test. We compare: (I) the paired Bayesian $P(S1 < S2|D)$ (i.e., the probability of the less likely hypothesis) with the classical one-sided paired p-value (See Section 3.4); (II) the paired 95% credible interval with the classical paired 95% confidence interval; (III) the paired Bayesian EAP Glass2 with the classical Glass2 based on sample statistics. The margin of error for the classical paired 95% confidence interval is given by $t(n-1; 0.05)\sqrt{V/n}$, where n is the sample size, V is the sample variance of the score differences, and $t(\phi; \alpha)$ is the two-sided critical t value[18].

Figure 5 visualises the results of comparing the Bayesian and classical paradigms for paired data with NTCIR7IR4QA (graphs (A)-(D)), NTCIR9INTENT (graphs (E)-(H)), and NTCIR12STC (graphs (I)-(L)). Graphs (A), (E) and (I) (i.e., the leftmost column) compare the Bayesian $P(S1 < S2|D)$ with the p-value; graphs (B), (F), and (J) compare the Bayesian EAP Glass2 with the sample Glass2; graphs (C), (G) and (K) compare the Bayesian credible interval *lower* limit with the confidence interval lower limit; and graphs (D), (H) and (L) (i.e., the rightmost column) compare the Bayesian credible interval *upper* limit with the confidence interval upper limit. Figure 6 provides similar information for TREC03robust, TREC11webD, and TREC15TS.

With the exception of Figure 6(J), i.e., the effect size results for TREC15TS which we shall discuss in Section 4.3, the results in Figures 5 and 6 are highly consistent across the diverse NTCIR and TREC data sets and the messages are clear:

(1) Graphs (A), (E), and (I) in Figures 5 and 6 show that the Bayesian $P(S1 < S2|D)$ and the classical p-values are very highly correlated, echoing an earlier observation by Carterette [5] (See Section 2.3). Thus, while $P(S1 < S2|D)$ is what we usually want, it appears that the one-sided p-value, which represents $P(D^+|S1 = S2)$, can be considered as a reasonable approximation of $P(S1 < S2|D)$.

(2) Graphs (C), (D), (G), (H), (K), (L) in Figures 5 and 6 show that the Bayesian 95% credible intervals and the classical 95% confidence intervals are also very similar, despite the fundamental differences in what they represent. Thus, the confidence interval can be considered as an approximation to the credible interval, which is what we really want.

[18] T.INV.2T(P, α) with Microsoft Excel.

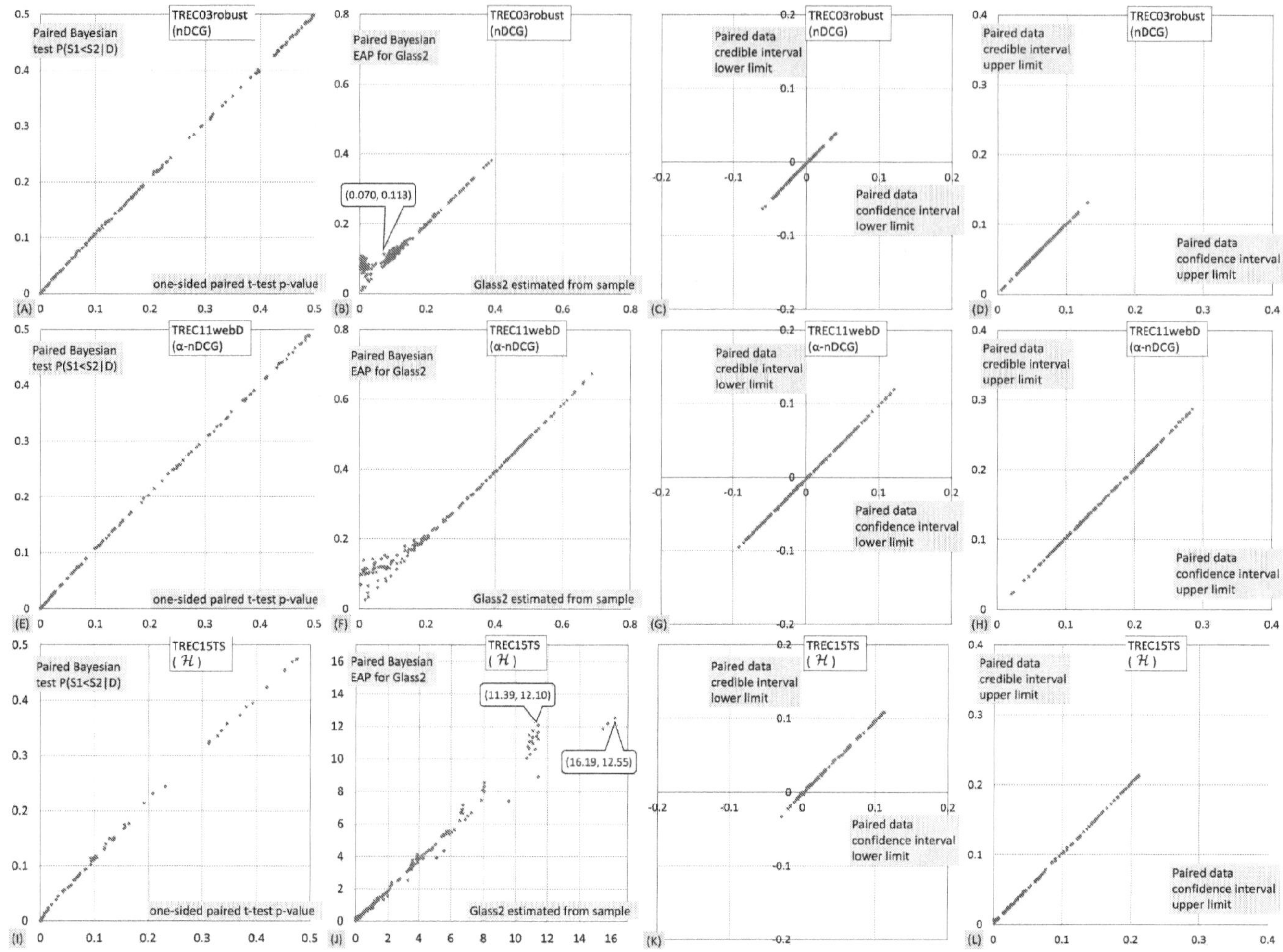

Figure 6: Paired Bayesian vs classical tests: comparisons with TREC data.

(3) Graphs (B) and (F) in Figures 5 and 6 suggest that, while the Bayesian EAP effect sizes generally align with the sample effect sizes (Glass2), if the sample effect size is small (e.g., less than 0.2), that may be an underestimation of the population effect size. For example, Figure 6(B) indicates an instance (with a baloon) where the sample effect size is 0.070 even though the Bayesian EAP effect size, which we believe to be more accurate, is 0.113.

Observations (1) and (2) suggest that, even though the IR community may have relied on p-values and confidence intervals for decades, sometimes with incorrect interpretations, switching to Bayesian approaches would not turn all the experimental results in the literature upside down. As for Observation 3, even though we lack the ground truth for population effect sizes, we would like to repeat Kruschke's argument [14]: "*the relevant question is asking which method provides the richest, most informative, and meaningful results for any set of data* [...]" (See Section 2.1).

4.2 Unpaired Test Results

Here we compare the unpaired Bayesian test (based on NUTS) with the classical Welch's t-test. We compare: (I) the unpaired Bayesian $P(S1 < S2|D)$ (i.e., the probability of the less likely hypothesis) with the classical one-sided unpaired p-value (See Section 3.4); (II) the unpaired 95% credible interval with the classical unpaired 95% confidence interval; (III) the unpaired Bayesian EAP Glass2 with the classical Glass2 based on sample statistics. The margin of error for the classical unpaired 95% confidence interval is given by $t(\phi^*; 0.05)\sqrt{V_1/n_1 + V_2/n_2}$, where n_1, n_2 are the sample sizes, V_1, V_2 are the sample variances, and the approximated degrees of freedom ϕ^* is given by [24]:

$$\phi^* = (\frac{V_1}{n_1} + \frac{V_2}{n_2})^2 / \{\frac{(V_1/n_1)^2}{n_1 - 1} + \frac{(V_2/n_2)^2}{n_2 - 1}\} . \quad (10)$$

In fact, since our unpaired test experiments merely regard the paired data from NTCIR and TREC (i.e., two systems evaluated with a common topic set) as unpaired data, $n_1 = n_2$ holds in our case.

Figure 7 visualises the results of comparing the Bayesian and classical paradigms for *unpaired* TREC data, similarly to Figure 6. The unpaired results with the NTCIR data, which look very much like the corresponding paired test results with the NTCIR data shown in Figure 5, are omitted in this paper due to lack of space.

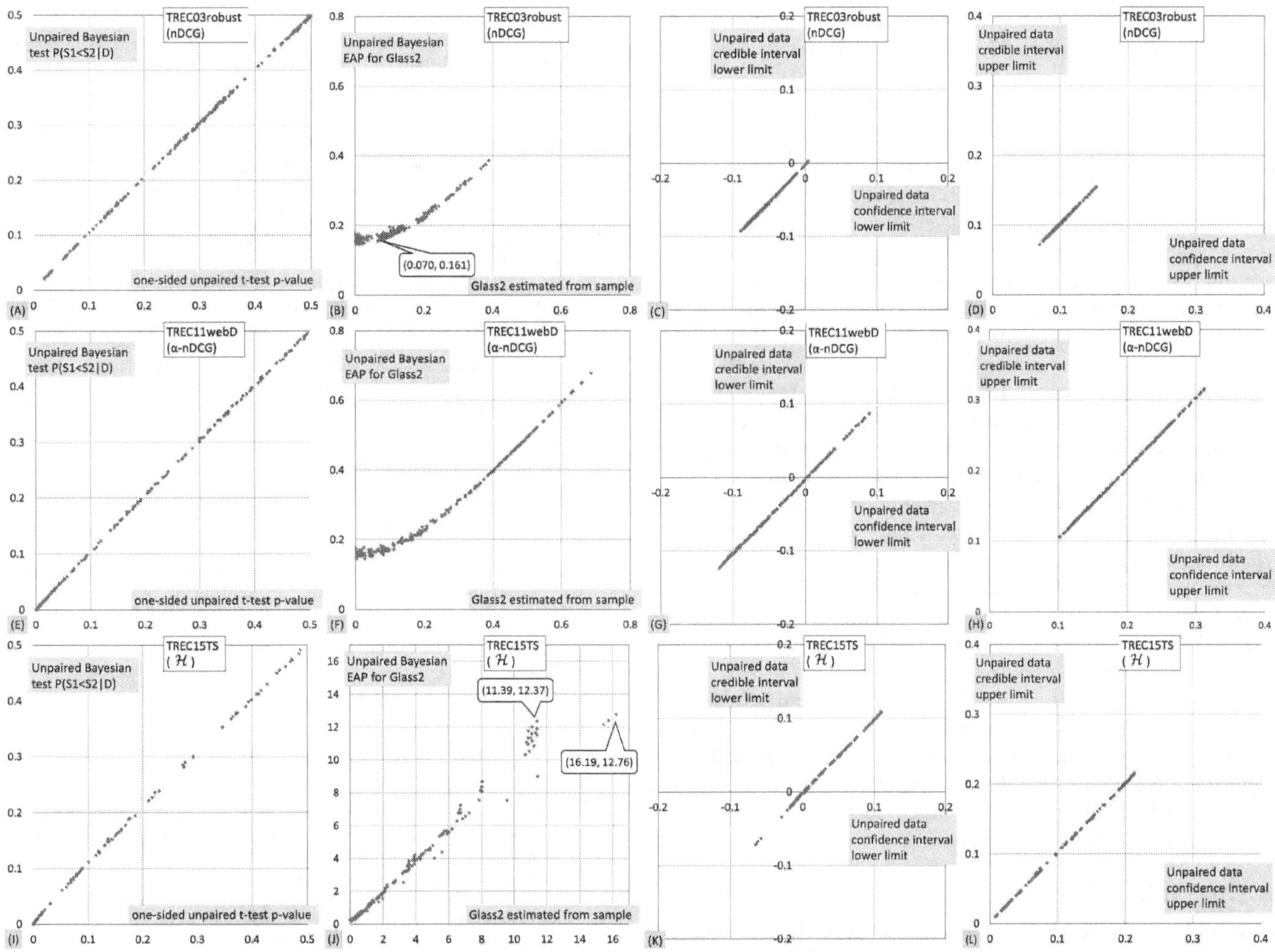

Figure 7: Unpaired Bayesian vs classical tests: comparisons with TREC data.

Note that the classical sample effect sizes used in Graphs (B), (F), and (J) are the same as the ones used in Figure 6. For example, we have observed from Figure 6(B) that while the sample effect size for a system pair was 0.070, the Bayesian paired model gives us an EAP Glass2 of 0.113; in contrast, Figure 7(B) indicates that the Bayesian unpaired model gives us an EAP Glass2 of 0.161 for the same system pair.

It is clear that Observations 1-3 listed up in Section 4.1 also hold for the unpaired tests as well, which further strengthens our findings. However, just like Figure 6(J), Figure 7(J) shows and anomalous result for TREC15TS: we therefore discuss these results separately in the next section.

4.3 On the Anomalous Behaviour of $\mathcal{H}$

The nugget-based $\mathcal{H}$ measure, the primary measure from the TREC 2015 Temporal Summarisation track, demonstrates a strange behaviour in Figure 6(J) and Figure 7(J), where the Bayesian EAP effect sizes and sample effect sizes are compared. The graphs look quite different from Graphs (B) and (F) of Figures 5-7. More specifically, for a small set of system pairs, EAP values are larger than sample effect sizes; for a few others, sample effect sizes are larger than EAPs. For example, for a system pair whose sample effect size is 11.39, the paired Bayesian EAP is 12.10 (Figure 6(J)), while the unpaired Bayesian EAP is 12.37 (Figure 7(J)), as indicated by baloons. Similarly, for a system pair whose sample effect size is 16.19, the paired Bayesian EAP is 12.55, while the unpaired Bayesian EAP is 12.76. This is in contrast to the aforementioned Observation 3 (Section 4.1) for the other data sets.

While the other evaluation measures used in our experiments have been studied quite extensively (e.g., [6, 20, 21]), we are not aware of any work in the literature that validated $\mathcal{H}$ in a similar way, and we believe that an investigation is in order. For example, while the actual nDCG scores from our `TREC03robust` data range between 0 and 0.9816 (i.e., almost fully covering the theoretical range of $[0, 1]$), the actual $\mathcal{H}$ scores from TREC15TS range between 0 and 0.4021: that is, the actual range width is about 0.4 rather than 1. Moreover, the standard deviations of $\mathcal{H}$ for each system are very low compared to the other measures, causing very large effect sizes (See Eq. 9): hence, note that the axis scales of Figure 6(J) and 7(J) are very different from the other effect size graphs. While studying the properties of a new measure is not the focus of this study, these anomalous results with $\mathcal{H}$ may deserve attention from other researchers such as the TREC track coordinators.

5 CONCLUSIONS AND FUTURE WORK

Using diverse data sets from TREC and NTCIR, we compared, under both paired and unpaired data settings, (I) the Bayesian $P(S1 < S2|D)$ (i.e., the probability of the less likely hypothesis) with the classical one-sided p-value; (II) the 95% credible interval with the classical 95% confidence interval; (III) the Bayesian EAP Glass2 with the classical Glass2 based on sample statistics. Our results showed that (a) p-values and confidence intervals can respectively be regarded as approximations of what we really want, namely, $P(H|D)$ and credible intervals; and (b) sample effect sizes from classical significance tests can differ considerably from the Bayesian EAP effect sizes, which suggests that the former can be poor estimates of population effect sizes. Fortunately, our results suggest that Bayesian statistics will not turn all experimental results in the IR literature upside down; however, we hope that these results, as well as our tools, will help IR researchers to take up Bayesian hypothesis testing approaches. For both paired and unpaired tests, we propose that the IR community report the EAP, the credible interval, and the probability of hypothesis being true, not only for the raw difference in means but also for Glass's Δ.

The present study focussed on the problem of comparing two systems, and did not address the *multiple comparison* and *familywise error rate* problems [11]. If a researcher is interested in the p-value of every system pair, one effective way to obtain them would be to employ the *randomised Tukey HSD test* [4, 22], which is completely distribution-free. In future work, we would like to explore Bayesian alternatives to this test and validate them.

ACKNOWLEDGEMENTS

We thank Professor Hideki Toyoda (Waseda University) for letting us modify his R code and distribute it, and Dr. Matthew Ekstrand-Abueg (Google) for providing the TREC temporal summarisation track results.

REFERENCES

[1] Javed Aslam, Fernando Diaz, Matthew Ekstrand-Abueg, Richard McCreadie, Virgil Pavlu, and Tetsuya Sakai. 2016. TREC 2015 Temporal Summarization Track. In *Proceedings of TREC 2015*.

[2] Thomas Bayes. 1763. An Essay towards Solving a Problem in the Doctrine of Chances. *Philosophical Transactions of the Royal Society of London* 53 (1763), 370–418.

[3] Ben Carterette. 2011. Model-Based Inference About IR Systems. In *Proceedings of ICTIR 2011 (LNCS 6931)*. 101–112.

[4] Ben Carterette. 2012. Multiple testing in statistical analysis of systems-based information retrieval experiments. *ACM TOIS* 30, 1 (2012).

[5] Ben Carterette. 2015. Bayesian Inference for Information Retrieval Evaluation. In *Proceedings of ACM ICTIR 2015*. 31–40.

[6] Charles L.A. Clarke, Nick Craswell, Ian Soboroff, and Azin Ashkan. 2011. A Comparative Analysis of Cascade Measures for Novelty and Diversity. In *Proceedings of ACM WSDM 2011*. 75–84.

[7] Clarles L. A. Clarke, Nick Craswell, Ian Soboroff, and Ellen M. Voorhees. 2012. Overview of the TREC 2011 Web Track. In *Proceedings of TREC 2011*.

[8] Bradley Efron. 2005. Bayesians, Frequentists, and Scientists. *J. Amer. Statist. Assoc.* 100, 469 (2005), 1–5.

[9] Ronald A. Fisher. 1970. *Statistical Methods for Research Workers (14th Edition)*. Oliver & Boyd.

[10] Andrew Gelman. 1996. Inference and Monitoring Convergence. In *Markov Chan Monte Carlo in Practice*, W. R. Gilks, S. Richardson, and D. J. Spiegelhalter (Eds.). Chapman & Hall/CRC, Chapter 8.

[11] Andrew Gelman, Jennifer Hill, and Masanao Yajima. 2008. *Why We (Usually) Don't Have to Worry about Multiple Comparisons*. Technical Report.

[12] Lisa L. Harlow, Stanley A. Mulaik, and James H. Steiger (Eds.). 2016. *What If There Were No Significance Tests (Classic Edition)*. Routledge.

[13] Matthew D. Hoffman and Andrew Gelman. 2014. The No-U-Turn Sampler: Adaptively Setting Path Lengths in Hamiltonian Monte Carlo. *Journal of Machine Learning Research* 15 (2014), 1351–1381.

[14] John K. Kruschke. 2013. Bayesian Estimation Supersedes the *t* test. *Journal of Experimental Psychology: General* 142, 2 (2013), 573–603.

[15] John K. Kruschke. 2015. *Doing Bayesian Data Analysis (Second Edition)*. Elsevier.

[16] Yasushi Nagata. 1996. *How to Understand Statistical Methods (in Japanese)*. Nikkagiren.

[17] Radford M. Neal. 2011. MCMC Using Hamiltonian Dynamics. In *Handbook of Markov Chain Monte Carlo*, Steve Brooks, Andrew Gelman, Galin L. Jones, and Xiao-Li Meng (Eds.). 113–162.

[18] Yurii Nesterov. 2009. Primal-Dual Subgradient Methods for Convex Problems. *Mathematical Programming* 120 (2009), 221–259.

[19] Matia Okubo and Kensuke Okada. 2012. *Psychological Statistics to Tell Your Story: Effect Size, Confidence Interval, and Power*. Keiso Shobo.

[20] Tetsuya Sakai. 2006. Evaluating Evaluation Metrics based on the Bootstrap. In *Proceedings of ACM SIGIR 2006*. 525–532.

[21] Tetsuya Sakai. 2011. Evaluating Diversified Search Results Using Per-Intent Graded Relevance. In *Proceedings of ACM SIGIR 2011*. 1043–1052.

[22] Tetsuya Sakai. 2014. Statistical Reform in Information Retrieval? *SIGIR Forum* 48, 1 (2014), 3–12.

[23] Tetsuya Sakai. 2016. Statistical Significance, Power, and Sample Sizes: A Systematic Review of SIGIR and TOIS, 2006-2015. *Proceedings of ACM SIGIR 2016* (2016), 5–14.

[24] Tetsuya Sakai. 2016. Two Sample T-tests for IR Evaluation: Student or Welch?. In *Proceedings of ACM SIGIR 2016*. 1045–1048.

[25] Tetsuya Sakai, Noriko Kando, Chuan-Jie Lin, Teruko Mitamura, Hideki Shima, Donghong Ji, Kuang-Hua Chen, and Eric Nyberg. 2008. Overview of the NTCIR-7 ACLIA IR4QA Task. In *Proceedings of NTCIR-7*. 77–114.

[26] Lifeng Shang, Tetsuya Sakai, Zhengdong Lu, Hang Li, Ryuichiro Higashinaka, and Yusuke Miyao. 2016. Overview of the NTCIR-12 Short Text Conversation Task. In *Proceedings of NTCIR-12*. 473–484.

[27] Mark D. Smucker, James Allan, and Ben Carterette. 2007. A Comparison of Statistical Significance Tests for Information Retrieval Evaluation. In *Proceedings of ACM CIKM 2007*. 623–632.

[28] Ruihua Song, Min Zhang, Tetsuya Sakai, Makoto P. Kato, Yiqun Liu, Miho Sugimoto, Qinglei Wang, and Naoki Orii. 2011. Overview of the NTCIR-9 INTENT Task. In *Proceedings of NTCIR-9*. 82–105.

[29] Student. 1908. The Probable Error of a Mean. *Biometrika* 6, 1 (1908), 1–25.

[30] Hideki Toyoda (Ed.). 2015. *Fundamentals of Bayesian statistics: Practical Getting Started by Hamiltonian Monte Carlo Method (in Japanese)*. Asakura Shoten.

[31] Hideki Toyoda. 2016. *An Introduction to Statistical Data Analysis: Bayesian Statistics for 'post p-value era' (in Japanese)*. Asakuha Shoten.

[32] Ellen M. Voorhees. 2004. Overview of the TREC 2003 Robust Retrieval Track. In *Proceedings of TREC 2003*.

[33] Ronald L. Wasserstein and Nicole A. Lazar. 2016. The ASA's Statement on P-values: Context, Process, and Purpose. *The American Statistician* (2016).

[34] Dell Zhang, Jun Wang, Emine Yilmaz, Xiaoling Wang, and Yuxin Zhou. 2016. Bayesian Performance Comparison of Text Classifiers. In *Proceedings of ACM SIGIR 2016*. 15–24.

[35] Stephen T. Ziliak and Deirdre N. McCloskey. 2008. *The Cult of Statistical Significance: How the Standard Error Costs Us Jobs, Justice, and Lives*. The University of Michigan Press.

Can Deep Effectiveness Metrics Be Evaluated Using Shallow Judgment Pools?

Xiaolu Lu
RMIT University
Melbourne, Australia

Alistair Moffat
The University of Melbourne
Melbourne, Australia

J. Shane Culpepper
RMIT University
Melbourne, Australia

ABSTRACT

Increasing test collection sizes and limited judgment budgets create measurement challenges for IR batch evaluations, challenges that are greater when using deep effectiveness metrics than when using shallow metrics, because of the increased likelihood that unjudged documents will be encountered. Here we study the problem of metric score adjustment, with the goal of accurately estimating system performance when using deep metrics and limited judgment sets, assuming that dynamic score adjustment is required per topic due to the variability in the number of relevant documents. We seek to induce system orderings that are as close as is possible to the orderings that would arise if full judgments were available.

Starting with depth-based pooling, and no prior knowledge of sampling probabilities, the first phase of our two-stage process computes a background gain for each document based on rank-level statistics. The second stage then accounts for the distributional variance of relevant documents. We also exploit the frequency statistics of pooled relevant documents in order to determine a threshold for dynamically determining the set of topics to be adjusted. Taken together, our results show that: (i) better score estimates can be achieved when compared to previous work; (ii) by setting a global threshold, we are able to adapt our methods to different collections; and (iii) the proposed estimation methods reliably approximate the system orderings achieved when many more relevance judgments are available. We also consider pools generated by a two-strata sampling approach.

KEYWORDS

Test collection; relevance assessment; pooling; shallow judgments.

1 INTRODUCTION

Batch evaluations are performed by calculating a metric score based on a set of judged documents. Despite five decades of success, this "Cranfield/TREC" paradigm also faces challenges. One of the key issues is that realistic collection sizes now greatly exceed the budget available to perform human judgments. "Pooling-to-depth-d" is one widely-used approach [25], in which documents in the union of the top-d lists returned from a set of contributing systems are judged, but other documents are not. The pooling depth d is ideally determined by the needs of the effectiveness metric to be used, but in reality is also constrained by the experimental budget. Although pooling has identified the majority of relevant documents in earlier collections [30], there is growing evidence that this is not true for the web collections that are now the norm [2, 11].

The uncertainty in effectiveness measurement in large collections is the key emphasis of our work here, focusing on how to estimate evaluation scores when reduced judgment sets are used. This is not a new problem, and a range of prediction mechanisms have been proposed [1, 22, 23, 27, 28], mainly focusing on predicting system orderings. We focus on prevailing pool-based test collection construction methods, as these best match our methodology, and on deep evaluation metrics, noting that pool depth has a lesser impact on shallow evaluation metrics such as ERR [6]. Alternative approaches using direct sampling exploit prior knowledge of the probability of each document being judged, and are applied during pool construction, on the assumption that all systems requiring measurement have been identified. But that process makes it difficult to infer scores for any new systems that get added later. On the other hand, pooling selects documents based on the assumption that top-ranked documents are both more likely to be relevant, and hence more influential in computing effectiveness scores. In this more general setting there is no *a priori* knowledge of the system scores, and while that means that regression cannot be applied, new systems can be considered. We also argue that the decision to apply score adjustment should be done on a per topic basis. Robertson [17] notes that topics vary in terms of the number of potential relevant documents, and that this can have a significant impact on evaluation scores. Dynamically identifying when to perform score adjustment is thus a second challenge that must be considered.

The end objective of an evaluation goes beyond the metric scores, of course; in the end we wish to be able to compare and choose between systems, meaning that it is also important that the score estimations are concordant with the system orderings that would arise if full knowledge were available. Since the latter is measured according to a reference point which may not be known, there is no clear optimization goal, another complication that we address. These various considerations lead to two questions:

Research Question 1: *For each topic, how can we estimate the evaluation score of a system using a shallow pooling depth?*

Research Question 2: *Can stable system rankings be achieved using the adjusted scores?*

In considering these two questions, we perform experiments using several different ad-hoc test collections and a range of modeled pool depths. Our results show that: (i) a two-stage optimization framework generates more accurate score estimations than previous approaches; (ii) topic-based adjustment thresholds identified using early TREC collections allow additional improvements in

SIGIR '17, August 07-11, 2017, Shinjuku, Tokyo, Japan

978-1-4503-5022-8/17/08...$15.00
DOI: http://dx.doi.org/10.1145/3077136.3080793

estimation accuracy; and (iii) the adjusted evaluation scores yield better approximations of the "true" system rankings than do the unadjusted scores. In addition to standard pooling methods, we also consider two-strata sampling [24].

2 RELATED WORK

Incomplete Judgments and Evaluation Bias. Two types of bias arise in batch evaluations: pooling depth bias [19] and system bias [20]. The first is caused by the use of shallow pools, and the second by performance underestimation for systems that did not contribute to the pool. Both are a result of documents appearing in the ranking for which judgments are not available. The simplest response to unjudged documents is to stipulate that anything not examined in the pooling process is not relevant. Zobel [30] challenged this notion using a series of leave-one-out experiments, and showed for several early TREC collections that while it was likely there were indeed further relevant documents that had not been identified, system bias was nevertheless within acceptable levels. However, on more recent web collections, there is growing evidence that this situation may not be assumed [2, 11].

Other responses to the issue of unjudged documents have been proposed. Buckley and Voorhees [3] describe BPref, which balances the rank positions of documents judged as non-relevant and relevant, and ignores unjudged documents. In a related approach, Sakai [18] considers *condensed lists*, which compute scores using a filtered ranking containing only judged documents, and finds that standard metrics give higher discriminative ratios than achieved by BPref. However, the condensed list methodology has not been shown to be stable when comparing relative system orderings using Kendall's τ or discrimination ratios [19, 20].

Score Estimation / Collection Construction. Documents without judgments are not distributed randomly in ranked result lists. Therefore, sample-based collection construction approaches have been suggested to support statistical inference [1, 22, 23, 27, 28]. Yilmaz and Aslam [27] present an inferred Average Precision (AP) metric that uses an expectation model, and can be coupled with a sampling process to select documents to be judged. Their InfAP metric uses uniform random sampling during collection construction. When compared with standard TREC-style pooling, the results produced by InfAP were strongly correlated with AP. However, this sampling process is random, and retrieval systems return documents in rank order, meaning that relevant documents are more likely to be returned at the top of the list if the system is effective.

The use of non-random sampling has also been explored. Yilmaz et al. [28] extended their previous work, proposing metrics XInfAP and XInfNDCG, based on a stratified sampling process. In contrast, Aslam et al. [1] consider the use of importance sampling for the same task, proposing statAP, which estimates the expectation of AP. The key difference between InfAP and statAP is that statAP is designed to generate the optimal distribution estimates using all of the contributing systems. Voorhees [24] further examines the effect of sampling methods on inferred metrics.

A recent study by Schnabel et al. [23] also used importance sampling, this time in conjunction with Discounted Cumulative Gain (DCG). The key idea in their approach was to use the probability of relevance with respect to rank information when determining the sample distribution. They provide an analysis on how to derive the optimal sampling distributions under different system comparison settings [22]. Using the proposed framework, any metric can be reformulated in the form of expectations and be estimated directly from the sampling process. Moffat et al. [14] had earlier examined targeted pooling and document judgment order in conjunction with the Rank-Biased Precision (RBP) metric.

Score Estimation Based on Pooling Methods. Estimation in traditional pooling techniques has also received considerable attention [4, 7, 9, 10, 16, 26]. Most existing techniques focus on adjusting the bias which exists between pooled and unpooled systems. Webber and Park [26] proposed two methods to perform score adjustment. The first uses an adjustment factor, which is computed from the contributing systems. Each contributing system has an error value assigned when it is left out of the training process, and the mean of those values is applied to any new system to be measured. The second approach requires a set of common topics with "complete judgments". A similar calculation is performed in order to obtain the adjustment factor, but restricted to the subset of common topics. To obtain additional adjustment accuracy, Webber and Park introduced randomization to build an unbiased estimator.

Recent work by Lipani et al. [9] using a precision metric outperformed the first method of Webber and Park. Their "anti-Precision" measurement is similar in spirit to the residual computed by RBP [15]. Lipani et al. [9] compute adjustment factors using the leave-one-run out methodology, and then improve their previous approach by computing an average distribution [10].

The closest work to our current approach is that of Ravana and Moffat [16]. They focus on pooling depth bias, proposing three methods to estimate the effect of unjudged documents, using the residual that can be computed for weighted-precision metrics [15]. Their first method uses a background estimation based on a static scaling factor; the second assumes that the percentage of relevant but unjudged documents can be derived directly from the known score component; and the third uses a parametric combination of the first two. Lu et al. [12] subsequently define the same problem in terms of the anticipated effectiveness gain as a function of ranking depth. Based on different assumptions derived from the underlying gain distributions, they propose several alternatives, and compare the estimates achieved. They empirically show that relatively simple models can be used to estimate gain values for unjudged documents.

An approach due to Büttcher et al. [4] directly predicts the relevance of unjudged documents, using two types of classifiers trained with the existing pool to predict the relevance of unjudged document in a new system. Although the effectiveness of the classifier is low, their results show that classification does help maintain similar system orderings when measured via Kendall's τ. Jayasinghe et al. [7] take a similar approach, and show that reliably predicting document relevance is often difficult.

3 PRELIMINARIES AND BASELINES

Pools. Figure 1 shows the construction of a pool for one topic, with $s_{j,i}$ (on the left) corresponding to the jth document in the run for system S_i, and with the corresponding documents (on the

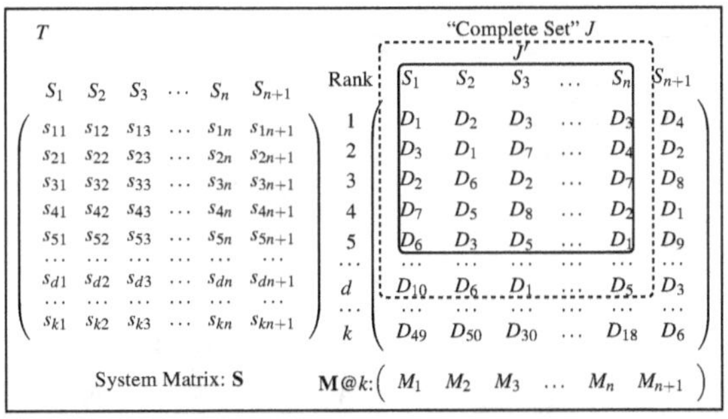

Figure 1: Pooling process for a topic T. The left matrix is a rank-based representation; the right one shows the equivalent document identifiers. The two boxes indicate two possible sets of pooled documents, the larger to depth d, and the smaller to some depth $d' < d$. The metric M is evaluated at some depth k, where k may or may not be less than or equal to d or d'.

right), each potentially retrieved by multiple systems at different rank positions. Hence, a document D can also be represented by its rank-position information, $\langle D, (\mathrm{p}_{D,1}, \mathrm{p}_{D,2}, \ldots, \mathrm{p}_{D,n})\rangle$, in which $\mathrm{p}_{D,i}$ is the rank returned for D by contributing system S_i. Metric evaluation to depth d for systems S_1 to S_n requires that the documents in the set $J = \{D \mid \min_{i=1}^{n} \mathrm{p}_{D,i} \leq d\}$ be judged. That is, both matrices can be further mapped to a matrix of relevance $\mathbf{R}_{d \times n}$ in which $r_{j,i}$ is a relevance, or *gain*, value.

If there is insufficient judgment volume available, a shallower pool J' might be formed, with documents D for which $\min_{i=1}^{n} \mathrm{p}_{D,i} > d'$ not judged, and elements in $\mathbf{R}_{d \times n}$ left without values. Unknown relevance labels may also arise for a new system S_{n+1}, regardless of the pooling and evaluation depths. In this framework, the first of the two research questions proposed in Section 1 can be split into two aspects: (1a) for each topic, how do we estimate the scores of a system using a set of shallow pooled judgments; and (1b) which topics may assume that unjudged documents are not relevant and which ones should not.

One method for dealing with missing data is to compute expected gains as a function of retrieval rank [12]. However, modeling relevance as a function of rank only considers the LHS representation in Figure 1, and ignores that documents can have multiple ranks. Addressing that limitation is a key part of our work here.

Metric Residuals. Suppose that for some topic T, a set of documents J results from pooling to depth d (Figure 1). Consider the ranked list returned by some system $S_i = (s_{1,i}, s_{2,i}, \ldots, s_{k,i})$ and let $r_{j,i}$ represent the gain of the document at rank j, normally (but not necessarily) a value in $[0, 1]$. The effectiveness M_i of S_i when computed to depth k by a weighted-precision metric M is:

$$\mathrm{M}_i = \mathrm{M}_{@k}(S_i, J) = \sum_{\substack{j=1 \\ s_{j,i} \in J}}^{k} r_{j,i} \cdot W_{\mathrm{M}}(j)\,, \tag{1}$$

where $W_{\mathrm{M}}(j)$ is the weight assigned by the metric at depth j, with $\sum_{j=1}^{\infty} W_{\mathrm{M}}(j) = 1$ [13, 15]; and where the restriction $s_{j,i} \in J$ is required to ensure that only defined values of $r_{j,i}$ are included. A corresponding residual Δ_i can then be computed, quantifying the metric weighting associated with the unjudged documents [15]:

$$\Delta_i = \sum_{\substack{j=1 \\ s_{j,i} \notin J}}^{k} r_{max} \cdot W_{\mathrm{M}}(j) + \sum_{j=k+1}^{\infty} r_{max} \cdot W_{\mathrm{M}}(j)\,, \tag{2}$$

where r_{max} is the maximum possible gain. Either term might be zero, depending on whether S_i contributed to the pool, on the relationship between the evaluation depth k and the pooling depth d, and on whether $W_{\mathrm{M}}(j) = 0$ when $j > k$, as occurs with truncated metrics.

There is a three-way tension between metric depth (quantified as the expected point reached in the ranking in the corresponding user model [13]); accuracy of measurement, captured by the residual; and the cost $|J|$ of performing the judgments. For example, in RBP the tail residual (the second component in Equation 2) is given by p^k, and if $p = 0.5$, $k \approx 10$ is sufficient. Similar calculations apply for ERR [6]. But in either case, the first term of Equation 2 might be non-zero for new runs. Furthermore, even the tail residuals might become large for deeper metrics, for example, RBP with $p = 0.95$. Truncated (that is, non-infinite) metrics such as Scaled DCG at depth 100, $\mathrm{SDCG}_{@100}$, also require deep pools if the residual is to be moderately bounded. The same requirement must apply by implication to other deep metrics such as Average Precision.

Problem Definition. Consider a set of n contributing systems $\{S_1, S_2, \ldots, S_n\}$. For one topic T, let d be a pooling depth at which it is believed that a majority of the relevant documents occurring in the runs of those systems have been identified. We refer to this set of judgments J as the "complete set". Let $d' < d$ be a shallower pooling depth, with judgments forming an incomplete set $J' \subseteq J$. Given a weighted precision metric M, the effectiveness score of S_i evaluated using M and J to depth d is denoted as $\mathrm{M}_i = \mathrm{M}_{@d}(S_i, J)$, with a residual of Δ_i. Similarly, an estimated metric score based on judgments to depth $d' < d$, is denoted as $\hat{\mathrm{M}}_i = E_d(\mathrm{M}_{@d'}(S_i, J'))$ where $E_d(\cdot)$ is an estimation function for the same metric at depth d. Following Lu et al. [12], the estimation error ϵ_i is then defined as:

$$\epsilon_i = \begin{cases} \mathrm{M}_i - \hat{\mathrm{M}}_i & \text{if } \hat{\mathrm{M}}_i < \mathrm{M}_i\,, \\ 0 & \text{if } \mathrm{M}_i \leq \hat{\mathrm{M}}_i \leq \mathrm{M}_i + \Delta_i\,, \\ \hat{\mathrm{M}}_i - (\mathrm{M}_i + \Delta_i) & \text{if } \hat{\mathrm{M}}_i > \mathrm{M}_i + \Delta_i\,. \end{cases} \tag{3}$$

This definition respects the residual range, and only gives non-zero values if the estimated effectiveness falls outside the score range arising from the use of J at depth d. The challenge is to develop a method $E_d(\cdot)$ that estimates the depth-d effectiveness score of a contributing system based on a subset J' of the judgments, and minimizes the average value of ϵ_i.

In the experiments in Section 6 we report the RMS aggregate of the ϵ_i values computed, across systems and topics; and, as a "percentage accurate", the fraction of those values that are zero.

Lower-Bound Estimation. A simple approach is to take $E_d(x) = x$, that is $\hat{\mathrm{M}}_i = \mathrm{M}'_i$, where M'_i is the score for system S_i when evaluated using J', and assert that documents outside J' do not alter the score. Taking unjudged documents to be not relevant is the normal default in batch evaluation, and is a valid estimator. But the estimation quality depends on the breadth of the pool, and whether a majority of relevant documents have been identified. When there

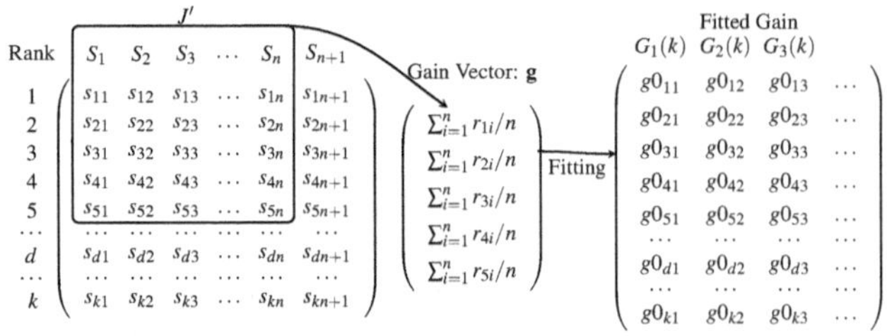

Figure 2: Overview of rank-based estimation for a single topic. The judgments J' are used to infer an observed gain vector g; each of a set of m functions $G_\ell(k)$ is then fitted to g.

are still many unjudged relevant documents, this estimator results in underestimation of system performance. Reasonably good rank correlation between the estimates and the true score over a set of systems can be obtained, but there is no guarantee that the performance of each of the systems has been accurately measured.

Interpolative Estimation. A second baseline is provided by the RM interpolative estimator proposed by Ravana and Moffat [16], who scale the metric score across the residual, assuming that unjudged documents are relevant at the same rate as judged ones:

$$\hat{\mathrm{M}}_i = \mathrm{M}'_i/(1-\Delta'_i)\,. \tag{4}$$

A collection-based background probability is used when $\Delta'_i = 1$. This estimator assumes that gain is accrued at the same rate across all of the documents retrieved by the system, both judged and unjudged. Although more robust than the LB estimator, it does not allow the likelihood of relevance to decrease as the pool is extended from d' to d.

Rank-Based Estimators. Lu et al. [12] introduce rank-based estimation, illustrated in Figure 2. The judgments J' are used to estimate expected gain as a function of rank on a per-topic basis. Those rank-based fractional gain predictions are then used for unjudged documents – interpolated at depths up to d', and extrapolated from d' to the metric evaluation depth k. Lu et al. explore alternative estimation functions, measuring the prediction error using the mechanism described in Equation 3, and find that while improvements are possible, no single estimator works consistently well across all collections and topics. Rank-based estimation also has the drawback of ignoring the fact that a document can appear at different ranks for different systems; and hence potentially assigns different gain estimates to the same document in different runs, a representational issue that usually leads to a biased estimation [29]. As a further drawback, an entire row in the system matrix S (see Figure 1) must be judged in order to compute the expected gain, limiting construction methods to pooling or sampling by rank, and possibly excluding stratified sampling processes.

Sampling-Based Estimation. Other sampling approaches can also be used when forming the judgment set. Voorhees [24] describes a two-strata sampling method, which consists of shallow pooled judgments J' to some depth d', and then 10% random sampling to depth d in a second set J_s. These judgments allow computation of inferred recall-based metrics, and also inferred versions of weighted-precision metrics, with $\hat{\mathrm{M}}_i$ for system i calculated as:

$$\hat{\mathrm{M}}_i = \sum_{\substack{j=1\\ s_{j,i}\in J'}}^{k} r_{j,i}\cdot W_{\mathrm{M}}(j) + \lambda\cdot \sum_{\substack{j=1\\ s_{j,i}\in J_s}}^{k} r_{j,i}\cdot W_{\mathrm{M}}(j)\,, \tag{5}$$

where

$$\lambda = \left(\sum_{\substack{j=1\\ s_{j,i}\notin J'}}^{k} W_{\mathrm{M}}(j)\right)\cdot\left(\sum_{\substack{j=1\\ s_{j,i}\in J_s}}^{k} W_{\mathrm{M}}(j)\right)^{-1}$$

and where the second term in Equation 5 estimates the total gain associated with documents contained in the second stratum. Here, λ is the interpolation estimator. Note that Equation 5 only adapts the RM method for sample based judgments.

4 TWO-STAGE ESTIMATION

Overview of the Framework. To compute score estimates, we propose a two-stage framework, guided by a unified optimization goal, and built on a set of $m \geq 1$ per-topic rank-level estimators. The overall structure of this mechanism is described in Algorithm 1. We omit the process of obtaining rank-level estimations, discussed briefly in the previous section, and in detail by Lu et al. [12]. That is, we assume as our starting point here that m different rank-based estimators have been generated, each derived from the judged documents $D \in J'$, and that values for a set of gain functions have been computed, with $g0_{j,\ell}$ the gain associated with an unjudged document that appears in the jth position of any of the n system

Algorithm 1 Estimation Framework

Input: System matrix $\mathrm{S}_{k\times n}$; partial relevance judgments J' with $g2[D]$ the gain associated with document D for $D \in J'$ and undefined otherwise; and a set of m rank-level background gain estimates, $g0_{j,\ell}$ for $1 \leq j \leq k$ and $1 \leq \ell \leq m$, with $g0_{*,\ell} \equiv \langle g0_{j,\ell} \mid 1 \leq j \leq k\rangle$ and $g1_*[D] \equiv \langle g1_\ell[D] \mid 1 \leq \ell \leq m\rangle$.
Output: Values $g2[D]$, gain estimates for the documents $D \in J \setminus J'$

```
for D ∈ J \ J' do g2[D] ← 0
γ ← ComputeCV(J', S)        // compute coefficient of variance
if γ > θ then               // adjust only if γ exceeds threshold
    for ℓ ← 1 to m do
        for D ∈ J' do g1_ℓ[D] ← 0
        w1_opt ← argmin_{w1∈[0,1]^n} L (h1(g0_{*,ℓ}, w1) | D ∈ J')
        for D ∈ J do
            g1_ℓ[D] ← h1 (g0_{*,ℓ}, w1_opt)
        end for
    end for
    w2_opt ← argmin_{w2∈[0,1]^m} L (h2(g1_*[D], w2) | D ∈ J')
    // get final per-document estimation
    for D ∈ J \ J' do
        g2[D] ← h2 (g1_*[D], w2_opt)
    end for
end if
return g2
```

rankings, as predicted by the ℓ th of the m different estimators. Prior to forming the new combined estimates, we first compute the coefficient of covariance γ from the judgment set [5], in order to determine whether to use a background "unjudged are not relevant" predictor. Estimation is computed by steps 4 to 15, with $h_1(\cdot)$ and $h_2(\cdot)$ two parametric combining functions, in which the parameters are obtained by minimizing a loss function $L(\cdot)$. We discuss the details of Algorithm 1, including the rationale behind the use of γ, in the next few paragraphs.

First Stage. As noted already, one problem with rank-based estimators is the potential inconsistency across runs of the gain attached to any particular document. As always, we assume that one topic is being addressed; the goal in the first stage is to aggregate the $m \times n$ per-document estimates across the m estimators and n systems into a smaller set of m estimates per document. That is, the m rank-level estimators are treated separately at first, in the loop at step 4, to obtain a consistent background gain for each document D for each model, denoted $g1_\ell[D]$. This is done via a combining function $h_1(\cdot)$ that maps a vector to a single value. Several options for $h_1(\cdot)$ are available, with the choice between them depending on assumptions about system quality and the degree to which the systems are correlated. For simplicity, we assume that the systems are independent and that they vary in quality. Therefore, for each document D, a natural combining function is to compute a weighted average, with h_1 (step 6) parameterized by an n-element weighting vector $\mathbf{w1}$ that is specific to the ℓ th estimator:

$$\forall D \in J',\ h_1(g0_{*,\ell}, \mathbf{w1} \mid D) = \sum_{i=1}^{n} g0_{\mathrm{p}_{D,i},\ell} \cdot \mathbf{w1}_i \qquad \text{with } \sum_{i=1}^{n} \mathbf{w1}_i = 1 \text{ and } \mathbf{w1}_i \in [0,1], \tag{6}$$

and where $g0_{\mathrm{p}_{D,i},\ell}$ applies the ℓ th estimator to the rank at which document D appears in the i th of the n runs. One practical issue is that a document may not be retrieved by all systems in their top-k ranked lists, where k is the maximum depth of lists returned. In such cases the rank-based background gain of that document for that system is set to the modeled gain at depth k.

To compute a value for $\mathbf{w1}$, we consider the aggregation process as an optimization problem, where the goal is to minimize the estimation error. The estimation error has two granularities: (i) the total error of system effectiveness score calculated using J'; and (ii) the total error of estimating the background gain of the labeled documents. From either perspective, we can formalize an objective function L and use it at step 6 of Algorithm 1. Consider the first case, with the system matrix as shown in Figure 1. We define L as:

$$L_a(\cdot) = \sqrt{\sum_{i=1}^{n}\left(\sum_{\substack{j=1\\ s_{j,i}\in J'}}^{k} \left(W_{\mathrm{M}}(j)\cdot(h_1(\cdot,\mathbf{w1}\mid s_{j,i}) - r_{j,i})\right)\right)^2}\,, \tag{7}$$

where $W_{\mathrm{M}}(j) \cdot h_1(\cdot, \mathbf{w1} \mid s_{j,i})$ is the estimated background gain for document $s_{j,i} \in J'$, and $r_{j,i}$ is the known relevance value of that same document. As noted, L_a minimizes the overall estimation error of the evaluation scores for the set of systems.

The second alternative uses the document-position representation $(\mathrm{p}_{D,1}, \mathrm{p}_{D,2}, \ldots, \mathrm{p}_{D,n})$:

$$L_b(\cdot) = \sum_{D\in J'} \sqrt{\sum_{i=1}^{n} \left(W_{\mathrm{M}}(\mathrm{p}_{D,i}) \cdot (h_1(\cdot,\mathbf{w1}\mid D) - r_D)\right)^2}\,, \tag{8}$$

in which r_D is the relevance value of document D and is included only once per document, rather than once per document-rank. When compared to Equation 7, which considers estimation errors at the system level, this loss function is focused at the per-document level, seeking to minimize the overall estimation error for the weighted gain of each document. Either Equation 7 or Equation 8 can be used at step 6 of Algorithm 1, with the combination function $h_1(\cdot)$ and constraints defined in Equation 6. The result is the computation of a sequence of $\mathbf{w1}_{\mathrm{opt}}$ vectors, one for each of the m different rank-level estimators.

Second Stage. Multiple fitting models have been proposed because different assumptions about the underlying relevance distributions across all systems are plausible, with a risk that no single model covers the true hypothesis space. Indeed, the limited non-random training data means that we may suffer from a high variance if only one model is considered. Therefore, a "meta" optimizer is also used, combining results from the first stage, as described by steps 11 to 15. A weighted average is used in this role too, considering each document D, together with the estimated background gains generated by the m previous computations, $g1_*[D]$. That combiner, $h_2(\cdot)$ (step 11), is defined via the m-vector $\mathbf{w2}$ as:

$$\forall D \in J',\ h_2(g1_*[D], \mathbf{w2}) = \sum_{\ell=1}^{m} g1_\ell[D] \cdot \mathbf{w2}_\ell\,, \qquad \text{with } \sum_{\ell=1}^{m} \mathbf{w2}_\ell = 1 \text{ and } \mathbf{w2}_\ell \in [0,1]. \tag{9}$$

Both L_a and L_b can be used in step 11, but may not necessarily be the same. Note that the m-vector $\mathbf{w2}_{\mathrm{opt}}$, computed at step 11 as the minimizing value for Equation 9, provides an indication of the importance of individual optimizers from the previous stage. Previous work has shown that the expected error of combining loss functions is smaller than the average error on results output by each optimizer in isolation from the first stage [29].

Computing the Coefficient of Variance. The score adjustment and estimation process has been presented on a per-topic basis, with an underlying assumption that a shallow judgment pool cannot identify a majority of the relevant documents. However, some topics may have only a small number of relevant documents, and a shallow depth may be sufficient to identify most of them, with adjustment unnecessary. Only if deeper pooling would identify further relevant documents can score adjustment have an effect on system effectiveness scores. Hence a coefficient of variance [5] is computed for the relevant documents in the shallow pool and used as an indicator, as described in step 2.

Pooling is treated as a sampling with replacement process, with an unknown probability of a relevant document being sampled. Although the final judgment process considers only the documents in the pool, a document returned by multiple systems has a selection frequency. The intuition behind γ is to make use of that frequency information to describe the sample coverage of relevant documents.

Consider the system matrix S in Figure 1 and a pooling depth d'. Each document $s_{j,i}$ ($1 \leq j \leq d'$, $1 \leq i \leq n$) has a multiplicity in $S_{d' \times n}$; we then group them by that frequency count. Let f_i be the number of relevant documents appearing i times in $S_{d' \times n}$, $R' = \sum_i f_i$ the number of relevant documents, and $C = \sum_i i \cdot f_i$ be the total occurrence count of relevant documents. For example, if only D_8 and D_1 in Figure 1 are identified as relevant documents, then we have $f_1 = 1, f_3 = 1$, and $R' = 2$ and $C = 4$. Based on these elements, the coefficient of variance, γ, is estimated via [5]:

$$\gamma^2 = \max \left\{ \frac{\frac{|R'|}{1 - f_1/C} \sum_i i \cdot (i-1) \cdot f_i}{C \cdot (C-1)} - 1, 0 \right\} . \tag{10}$$

When $\gamma = 0$, the probability of sampling a relevant document follows a uniform distribution; and when γ is high, the distribution is skewed, and it is likely that more relevant documents exist due to the low sampling coverage. Based on this, we have two hypotheses:

Hypothesis 1: *γ tends to decrease as pooling depth increases.*

Hypothesis 2: *There is a threshold θ, where if $\gamma < \theta$, then the existence of unjudged documents will only negligibly affect the estimate of the system performance, and they can be ignored.*

The first hypothesis is easy to understand, because increasing the pooling depth increases the sample size, and increases the sampling coverage. The second hypothesis assumes that the score can be dynamically adjusted based on a threshold. If this is correct, then a point at which the total estimation error is minimal can be observed. Otherwise, we must conclude that a shallow pool is not sufficient for finding relevant documents, and adjustment must be applied to all topics in all evaluations.

Discussion. We have described two possible realizations of loss functions, and one option for the combining functions $h_1(\cdot)$ and $h_2(\cdot)$. More sophisticated mechanisms are also possible. For example, the relationship between systems might be leveraged to derive a better $h_1(\cdot)$ and its constraint.

Note also that although our process targets the problem of estimating the effectiveness of runs that contribute to the pool, it is possible to apply the same process to estimate the score of a new system, and is demonstrated empirically in Section 6. Section 6 also shows that the framework can be applied to the judgments constructed using two-strata sampling [24], incorporating the additional information provided in the second stratum.

5 COMPARING SYSTEM RANKINGS

Section 3 already defined ϵ_i, a score-based evaluation criterion. But we are also interested in comparing system orderings as a measure of usefulness of an estimation regime.

Kendall's Distance. This distance metric is widely used to measure the similarity between ranked lists, and counts the number of inverted pairs between two n-item orderings. Let $\sigma_{i,j}$ represent the pairwise relationship between the effectiveness metric means $\bar{S_i}$ and $\bar{S_j}$ of systems S_i and S_j over a set of topics according to one measurement regime, with $\sigma_{i,j} \in \{-1, 0, 1\}$ indicating that $\bar{S_i} < \bar{S_j}$, that $\bar{S_i} = \bar{S_j}$, and that $\bar{S_i} > \bar{S_j}$, respectively; and let $\sigma'_{i,j}$ be the corresponding values for a second measurement regime and the system means that it induces, for example, using pooling to a different depth. Then Kendall's normalized τ distance is the number of pairs $1 \leq i < j \leq n$ in which $\sigma_{i,j} \cdot \sigma'_{i,j} < 0$, divided by $n(n-1)/2$ to bring it into the range $0 \leq \tau \leq 1$, with 0 meaning "identical".

Statistical Weighting. Paired t-tests are often used to quantify the strength of the relationship between two systems, and the values $\sigma_{i,j}$ and $\sigma'_{i,j}$ might be thought of as being continuous rather than ternary. Kumar and Vassilvitskii [8] describe a weighted τ distance that counts the strength of each discordant pair, focusing solely on cases where $\sigma_{i,j} \cdot \sigma'_{i,j} < 0$. In practice we are not only interested in the discordant pairs, but also in pairs that are deemed to be significantly different according to one of the measurement regimes but not the other, even if their overall relationship is concordant.

Suppose that $\bar{S_i} > \bar{S_j}$ according to the first measurement, and that a paired one-tail statistical test across topics yields $p_{i,j}$. Values of $p_{i,j}$ near zero indicate a significant superiority of S_i over S_j; values close to 0.5 indicate that it is by chance. If we define

$$\sigma_{i,j} = \begin{cases} 0.5 - p_{i,j} & \text{if } \bar{S_i} > \bar{S_j} \\ 0.0 & \text{if } \bar{S_i} = \bar{S_j} \\ p_{j,i} - 0.5 & \text{if } \bar{S_i} < \bar{S_j} , \end{cases}$$

then $-0.5 \leq \sigma_{i,j} \leq 0.5$ is a real-valued quantity that captures both the direction and strength of the relationship between the two systems according to the first measurement regime. We compute $\sigma'_{i,j}$ similarly using a second measurement approach, and then, to compare the alternative rankings of n systems induced by the two measurement techniques, calculate

$$dist = \sum_{1 \leq i < j \leq n} \alpha \cdot |\sigma'_{i,j} - \sigma_{i,j}| , \tag{11}$$

where $\alpha \geq 0$ is an additional scaling factor. For example, if $\alpha = |\sigma_{i,j}|$ then the strength of the relationship between S_i and S_j according to the first measurement regime also influences the measured distance. Overall, if $dist \approx 0$, then the two measurement regimes agree in terms of both the direction of each pairwise relationship S_i versus S_j, and also its strength. If $dist$ is substantially greater then zero, then the two measurement regimes give rise to many system pairs for which there are non-trivial disagreements (including in both discords and in concords) over the strength of the measured relationships. Compared with Kendall's τ distance, Equation 11 operates over continuous values, which makes it both resistant to inconclusive changes in rank position, and also sensitive to differences in which the direction of the relationship between S_i and S_j stays the same, but the statistical strength varies markedly.

6 EXPERIMENTS

The experiments described in this section include: (i) a post-hoc analysis for testing two hypotheses proposed in Section 4, and setting the threshold θ; (ii) evaluating prediction accuracy using RMSE and Acc% as defined by Lu et al. [12]; (iii) system ordering stability evaluation using the distance metric defined in Equation 11 with $\alpha = 1$, and using normalized τ distance; and (iv) a case study covering the ClueWeb 2010 (CW10) task.

Dataset	d	$\|S\|$	Judgments per topic				2-strata
			$d' = 10$	$d' = 20$	$d' = 30$	$d' = d$	
TREC5	100	76	272 (13)	512 (10)	747 (8)	2298 (4)	–
TREC9	100	59	174 (11)	322 (8)	462 (7)	1382 (4)	294 (7)
TREC10	100	54	182 (13)	335 (10)	480 (9)	1402 (5)	303 (9)
Rob04	100	42	75 (25)	139 (18)	206 (15)	710 (7)	134 (15)
TB04	80	33	164 (31)	313 (27)	453 (25)	1121 (19)	270 (25)
TB05	100	34	111 (41)	202 (36)	291 (33)	878 (25)	187 (33)
TB06	50	39	141 (31)	270 (26)	394 (23)	633 (19)	–
CW10	20	21	98 (30)	–	–	187 (28)	–

Table 1: Datasets used: d is the original pooling depth and provides the reference point for metric scores; d' is a notional pooling depth used our experimentation; and $|S|$ is the number of contributing runs. Only Adhoc Task runs are used. The middle four column pairs show the number of judgments averaged across topics at each pooling depth d', and the percentage of relevant documents. The last column shows the statistics when using two-strata sampling [24], averaged over topics and over ten random iterations.

Experimental Setup. The collections and configuration parameters used in our experiments are shown in Table 1. We also measured a range of behavior using the TREC7 and TREC8 collections, but do not include them here because those two collections were used as part of the post-hoc analysis and parameter setting. Scripts are available to reproduce all of the various results given here[1].

Pooling to different depths is simulated using the identified contributing systems, and the average number of judgments required per topic at different pool depths is also shown in Table 1, together with the corresponding percentage of documents identified as being relevant. In the experiments measuring rank stability, we also examine the two-strata sampling method described by Voorhees, and averages over ten runs for this randomized approach are included in the table. For the Robust04 task the last 49 topics are used, and judged to a depth of 100; for other tasks, we use all of the original topic set and judgments. Our goal in collection selection was to capture as much variety as possible. TREC5 and Rob04 use the NewsWire document collection, TREC9 and TREC10 use WT10G, a small web collection, and TB04/05/06 use the GOV2 web collection. The ClueWeb 2010 task (CW10) uses the largest web collection but also has fewer contributing systems and a shallow pool depth. It is representative of newer collections, which are large, and have more uncertainty associated with the judgment coverage – the core issue which motivated our investigation. We show results for this dataset as a practical application of our work, noting that a pooling depth of $d = 20$ cannot provide a ground truth for a deep metric [11].

We use RBP with $p = 0.95$ for training and for all testing, as a representative weighted-precision metric. RBP supports graded relevance (needed to make use of the estimated background gains we generate); allows residuals to be computed; and with $p = 0.95$ gives similar system orderings to AP and NDCG [15]. The estimated background gain of each document generated via training using RBP0.95 can also be used to compute other weighted-precision measures, such as the truncated metric SDCG$_{@k}$ when $k > d$.

[1]https://github.com/xiaolul/opt_est

We consider five methods for predicting effectiveness scores, three of which are baselines. The first baseline is the lower bound, LB, which assumes unjudged documents are not relevant; the second is the interpolative estimator of Ravana and Moffat [16] (Equation 4), denoted RM; and the third is the linear model Lin. that is the best of the rank-based approaches described by Lu et al. [12]. They are compared to the loss functions defined in Equations 7 and 8, denoted L_a and L_b respectively, with the same loss function used in both stages, and aggregation via Equations 6 and 9.

We use Linear, Zipf and Discrete Weibull models as initial rank-based estimators [12], and hence have $m = 3$. Two experiments explore rank stability, categorized by how the judgment set is constructed: (i) pooling based judgments; and (ii) two-strata sampling based judgments. Rank stability is measured using the approaches discussed in Section 5. The same baselines are used in the first rank stability evaluation. However, for the sample-based judgments, we consider the metrics InfRBP ($p = 0.95$) defined by Equation 5, and Yilmaz and Aslam's InfAP [27] as baselines. Throughout the experiments, the system scores (plus residuals) and system orderings computed using the same metric, but evaluated at the full pool depth (that is, at $k = d$), are taken as the "gold standard". The truncated metric AP$_{@d}$ is computed as described by Sakai [21].

Setting θ. We first test the two hypotheses in Section 4, with γ in Equation 10 normalized by the number of systems. Average (over topics) γ values are plotted against pool depth in the left-hand plot in Figure 3, showing that γ decreases as the pooling depth increases. This is as expected, since the increasing pooling depth results in a more complete judgment set. Among the plotted datasets the TB06 collection has the largest average γ, and corresponds to a high relevance rate (Table 1). TREC5 is a relatively complete test collection, and hence has the lowest γ among the datasets plotted.

The center pane in Figure 3 shows the distribution of γ across topics for $d' = 10$. Although γ is usually low for TREC5, there are still some topics that have high values. The same pattern is also observable for Rob04 and TREC10. Based on our hypothesis, this observation indicates that, on earlier TREC collections, not all topics necessarily require score adjustment even at $d' = 10$.

To set θ we use the earlier datasets TREC5, TREC7 and TREC8 and perform a post-hoc analysis, noting that the majority of relevant documents have been identified in these collections, and hence that the computed RMSE should be close to the true error. The right-hand pane in Figure 3 shows TREC5 outcomes, with three rank-based models plotted. Weibull (Wei.) may be an overestimate due to the shaping parameter, and Linear (Lin.) tends to provide low estimates due to the monotonically decreasing nature of the model [12]. At first, neither of the score estimation methods works better than the lower bound LB, but as θ increases, fewer topics need to be estimated, and when $\theta = 0.018$, both estimation methods outperform LB. Similar cross-overs occur for TREC7 and TREC8.

Prediction Accuracy. We then employed $\theta = 0.018$ for the other datasets, obtaining the results shown in Table 2. When $\theta = 0$ the L_b method outperforms all three baselines (LB, RM and Lin.) in terms of RMSE and Acc%, while the L_a approach has a higher RMSE than L_b and on earlier datasets (TREC9, TREC10) is slightly worse than the LB and Lin. baselines. That is, the loss function L_a provides poorer coverage of the true hypothesis space than does L_b. The RM

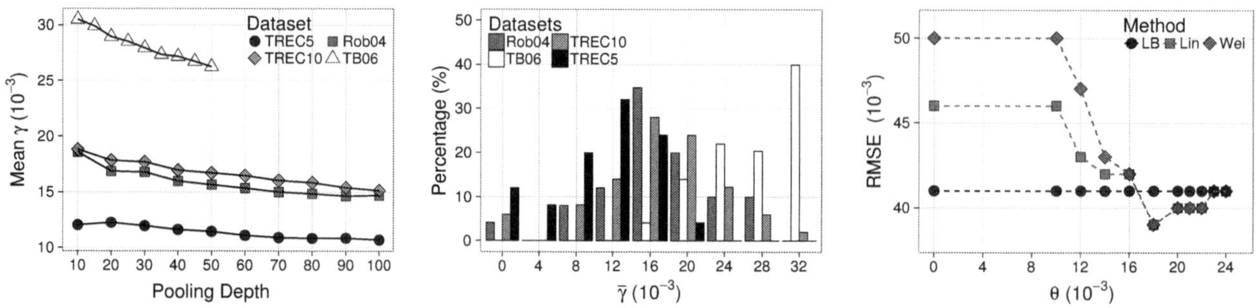

Figure 3: Left: γ relative to pooling depth d'. Middle: distribution of γ per topic when $d' = 10$. Right: impact of the threshold on the training set TREC5, with $d' = 10$.

Dataset	d'	LB	RM	Lin.		L_a		L_b	
				$\theta = 0$	$\theta = 0.018$	$\theta = 0$	$\theta = 0.018$	$\theta = 0$	$\theta = 0.018$
TREC9	10	0.031 (45)	0.056 (22)	0.037 (31)	0.031 (44)	0.038 (26)	**0.030** (44)	0.031 (41)	0.031 (**46**)
	20	0.012 (59)	0.025 (32)	0.013 (51)	0.012 (60)	0.013 (42)	0.012 (58)	**0.010** (**62**)	0.012 (61)
	30	0.006 (67)	0.012 (45)	0.006 (66)	0.006 (68)	**0.005** (63)	0.006 (68)	**0.005** (**71**)	0.006 (68)
TREC10	10	0.038 (**39**)	0.064 (16)	0.034 (25)	0.033 (31)	0.036 (13)	0.031 (27)	**0.027** (34)	0.028 (38)
	20	0.016 (53)	0.030 (25)	0.015 (45)	0.014 (51)	0.016 (36)	0.014 (50)	**0.012** (53)	**0.012** (**55**)
	30	0.007 (64)	0.015 (37)	0.007 (61)	0.007 (63)	0.007 (55)	0.007 (62)	**0.006** (**66**)	**0.006** (**66**)
Rob04	10	0.046 (**21**)	0.088 (5)	0.043 (**21**)	0.039 (20)	0.045 (9)	0.039 (17)	0.039 (20)	**0.035** (20)
	20	0.020 (34)	0.040 (9)	0.015 (33)	0.016 (34)	0.016 (26)	0.015 (32)	**0.013** (**38**)	0.016 (35)
	30	0.008 (49)	0.020 (14)	0.007 (49)	0.007 (52)	0.007 (47)	0.006 (53)	**0.005** (**59**)	0.006 (55)
TB04	10	0.117 (14)	0.082 (14)	0.082 (15)	0.087 (14)	**0.072** (15)	0.077 (15)	0.073 (**16**)	0.077 (**16**)
	20	0.053 (21)	0.039 (23)	0.039 (25)	0.041 (25)	0.035 (28)	0.037 (28)	**0.033** (**32**)	0.036 (31)
	30	0.026 (26)	0.020 (39)	0.018 (39)	0.019 (38)	**0.015** (**45**)	0.016 (44)	**0.015** (44)	0.016 (43)
TB05	10	0.125 (6)	0.080 (5)	0.085 (7)	0.085 (7)	0.070 (6)	0.070 (8)	**0.067** (7)	**0.067** (**9**)
	20	0.056 (10)	0.041 (10)	0.039 (13)	0.039 (13)	0.034 (14)	0.034 (14)	**0.033** (18)	**0.033** (**19**)
	30	0.028 (16)	0.022 (18)	0.021 (24)	0.021 (24)	0.018 (24)	0.018 (24)	**0.017** (**29**)	**0.017** (**29**)
TB06	10	0.089 (24)	0.065 (43)	0.059 (43)	0.059 (43)	**0.047** (**55**)	**0.047** (**55**)	0.053 (51)	0.053 (50)
	20	0.033 (40)	0.023 (68)	0.021 (66)	0.021 (66)	**0.013** (**81**)	**0.013** (**81**)	0.017 (73)	0.017 (73)
	30	0.013 (58)	0.007 (87)	0.006 (85)	0.006 (85)	**0.003** (**94**)	**0.003** (**94**)	0.005 (89)	0.005 (89)

Table 2: RMSE and Acc% scores for RBP0.95 for all estimation methods, with d' the depth of the reduced pool, and the reference depth d of each dataset as listed in Table 1. Bold numbers are the lowest RMSE and highest Acc% for that collection at that depth.

approach performs poorly on all of the earlier datasets, for which the assumption that unjudged documents are equivalent to judged ones is inappropriate. On the larger collections such as TB04/05/06, the gain decreases at a slower rate, making the assumptions in RM more appropriate. The LB approach has similar issues, seen in the TB04/05/06 collections. However, for TB06, smaller RMSE (and larger Acc%) values are achieved when compared to the other collections. This is because the reference depth $d = 50$ is smaller, resulting in larger residuals. As shown in Figure 3, some of the topics may not necessarily require a score adjustment process, especially in the earlier test collections. This explains why the LB estimator works well on those collections. As expected, applying a threshold θ improves the estimation for both L_a and for the Lin. model, on TREC9, TREC10 and Rob04 test collections. Unsurprisingly, on TB04/05/06, only minor score changes are observed when $\theta = 0.018$ is used, because the computed γ values are larger than the threshold, indicating low coverage of the relevant documents identified. The only unexpected observation occurs on the TB04 test collection, where the threshold falsely identifies Topic 734 as having a "sufficient" sampling of relevant documents, but around 48% in the final judged set are relevant, which increases the RMSE value. Table 3 shows the results for a leave-one-group-out experiment at $d' = 10$ (with $\theta = 0$), demonstrating the applicability of the framework in adjusting for both system and pooling depth bias.

System Ordering Stability on Pooling-Based Judgments. The system orderings derived from the score estimates when compared against the orderings at the reference depth of $k = d$ are shown in Figure 4. Kendall's τ correlation was also computed, but the closely-related τ distance is used here since it has a strictly positive value. In the first row, when normalized τ distance is measured, the estimation framework gives orderings close to the reference

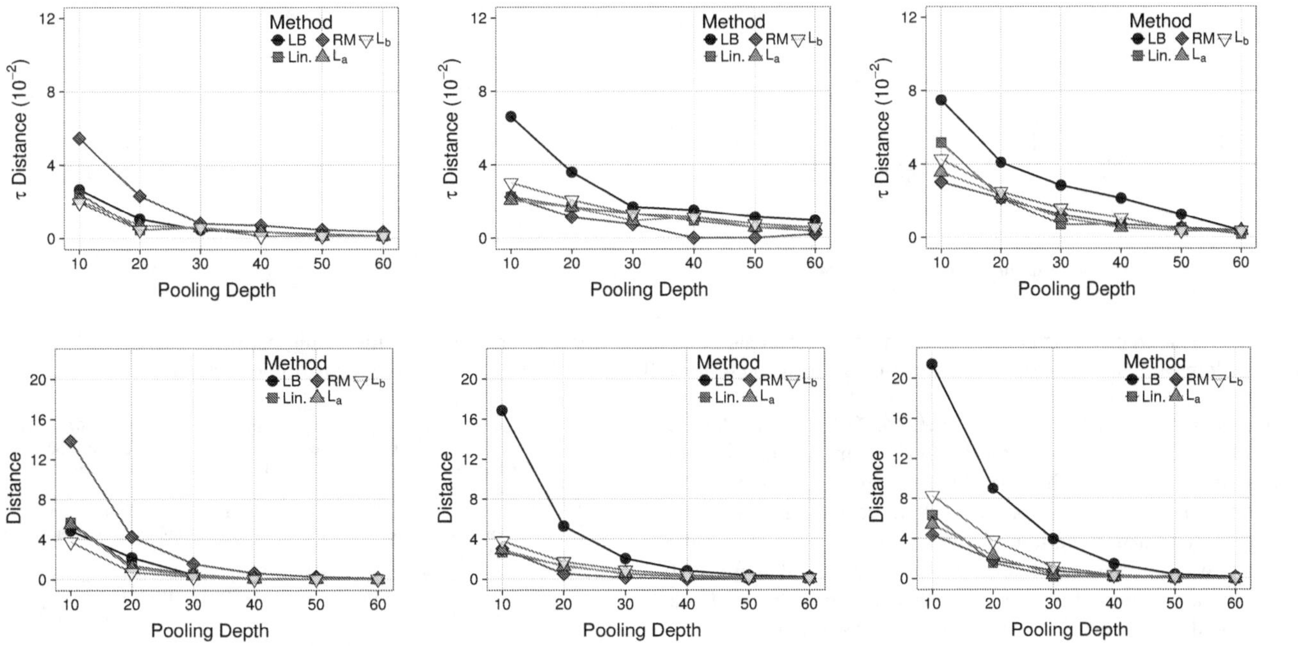

Figure 4: System ordering comparisons (RBP0.95) for five estimators. The first row uses normalized τ distance; the second row uses *dist* (Equation 11). The columns (from left) show Rob04, TB04, and TB05, with reference lists using LB at $d = 100$, $d = 80$ and $d = 100$, respectively.

Dataset	LB	RM	Lin.	L_a	L_b
Rob04	0.060 (**19**)	0.126 (4)	0.068 (11)	0.060 (9)	**0.050** (**19**)
TB04	0.181 (**11**)	0.202 (**11**)	0.131 (9)	**0.117** (**11**)	0.119 (**11**)
TB05	0.170 (**6**)	0.141 (5)	0.125 (4)	**0.110** (4)	**0.110** (5)
TB06	0.125 (22)	0.185 (32)	0.112 (35)	0.090 (**48**)	**0.086** (46)

Table 3: RMSE and Acc% for leave-out-one-group experiments with $d' = 10$ throughout, averages across groups assuming that each group in turn is omitted from pool construction (RBP0.95).

ordering across a range of nominal pool depths d'. The RM approach performs well on TB04/05, agreeing with the results in Table 2. However, as noted above, τ is sensitive to swaps that might be inconclusive. The bottom row of Figure 4 shows the *dist* measure of Equation 11. Overall, there are situations in which LB performs poorly, and situations in which RM performs poorly. The Lin., L_a, and L_b methods consistently provide the highest agreements.

We also carried out paired t-tests and calculated the discrimination ratio for a significance level $p = 0.05$, and compared against the original discrimination ratios. The Lin., L_a, and L_b estimation methods used with J' all have only a small effect on discrimination ratio when compared to the use of LB and J.

System Ordering Stability on Sample-Based Judgments. We also show the applicability of our methods on the judgment set constructed using a two-strata sampling method [24], which has been empirically shown to assist when computing inferred metrics. On this set of judgments we compute InfAP using trec_eval, and InfRBP as defined in Equation 5. Figure 6 shows that L_a, L_b and InfRBP give rise to stable system orderings, with normalized τ

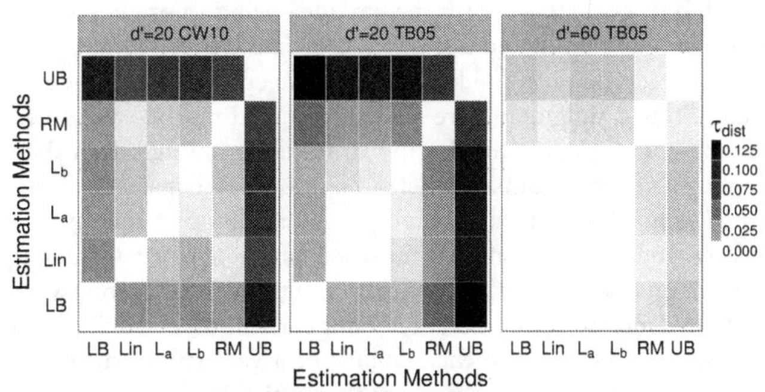

Figure 5: Normalized τ distance between system orderings generated by different estimation methods based on a pool of depth $d' = 20$, and on TB05 based on pool depths of $d' = 20$ and $d' = 60$.

distance scores below 0.05 across all collections. When *dist* is measured, L_a outperforms InfRBP on all collections but TREC9, while L_b outperforms InfRBP except on TB05. The slightly worse outcome for L_a on TREC9 is a consequence of the increase in the number of significantly different system pairs. Note the more variable outcomes generated when InfAP is used as the metric driving the system orderings.

Predictions in ClueWeb. As a final test of our approach, we examine the CW10 collection. It has a shallow pool depth ($d = 20$), meaning that validation is not possible, as there is no deep-pool reference ordering. Instead, we compute the normalized τ distance between each pair of estimation methods, and simply record how much the rankings differ, as shown in Figure 5. The UB estimator assumes that all unjudged documents are relevant. As a reference

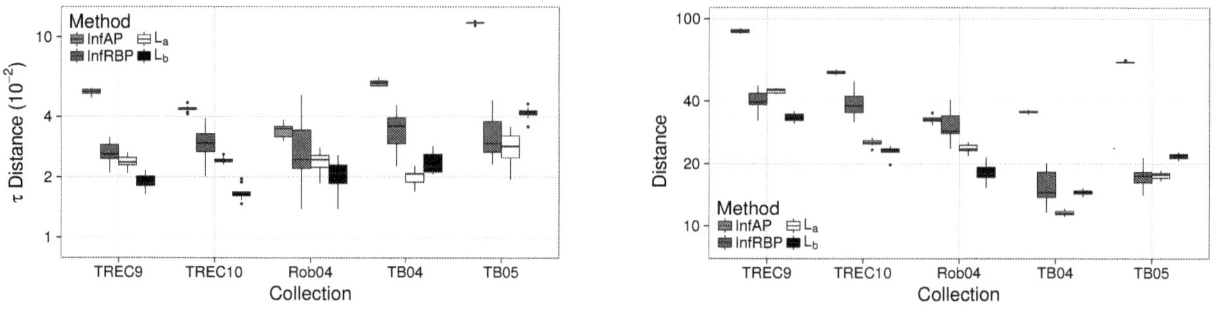

Figure 6: System ordering comparisons on a two-strata sampled judgment set, repeated ten times. Judgments are to depth $d' = 10$, plus a 10% random sample of remaining documents to depth 100 to form the second stratum. Note the logarithmic vertical scales.

point, we also compute the same values for TB05, at two depths, $d' = 20$ and $d' = 60$. At the latter depth all estimation approaches tend to agree with each other. On TB05, all of the estimation results, including UB, tend to agree on the system ordering. However, on CW10, there is clear uncertainty, confirming that $d = 60$ is a more robust pool depth for TB05 than is $d = 20$ on either TB05 or CW10 when seeking to apply RBP0.95 as an evaluation metric. Great caution should be exercised when the $d = 20$ CW10 judgments are used for anything other than shallow metrics.

7 CONCLUSIONS

We have presented new methods to improve system comparisons in batch IR evaluation, with the key idea being to predict a gain value for each unjudged document. We show that estimation is a viable technique to predict scores for deep evaluation metrics when limited judgments are available, including the case when the judgments are obtained using stratified sampling rather than pooling. One important aspect of our approach is to make decisions on *when* to adjust topics, instead of treating all topics equally.

A secondary contribution is the development of a new technique to more precisely compare system orderings. By focusing on swaps that are conclusive, our weighted rank correlation coefficient *dist* can be used to measure the stability of a variety of estimation techniques. Using *dist*, we show that estimation improves our ability to score and compare systems using limited judgments.

It must be noted, however, that the estimation is built on the m rank-based fitted models, each of which requires that when constructing the judgment set, documents up to some rank d' be fully judged. This means that for some sampling-based judgment approaches, the proposed method is not applicable. Second, while we show that our estimation methods can also account for system bias to some extent, outcomes might be further improved by introducing more randomization into the optimization framework. Hence, in answer to the question posed in the title, our answer remains a somewhat cautious "better than before", rather than a "yes".

Funding. This work was supported by the Australian Research Council's *Discovery Projects* Scheme (DP140103256 and DP170102231).

REFERENCES

[1] J. A. Aslam, V. Pavlu, and E. Yilmaz. 2006. A statistical method for system evaluation using incomplete judgments. In *Proc. SIGIR.* 541–548.
[2] C. Buckley, D. Dimmick, I. Soboroff, and E. M. Voorhees. 2007. Bias and the limits of pooling for large collections. *Inf. Retr.* 10, 6 (2007), 491–508.
[3] C. Buckley and E. M. Voorhees. 2004. Retrieval evaluation with incomplete information. In *Proc. SIGIR.* 25–32.
[4] S. Büttcher, C. L. A. Clarke, P. C. K. Yeung, and I. Soboroff. 2007. Reliable information retrieval evaluation with incomplete and biased judgements. In *Proc. SIGIR.* 63–70.
[5] A. Chao and S. Lee. 1992. Estimating the number of classes via sample coverage. *J. American Statistical Association* 87, 417 (1992), 210–217.
[6] O. Chapelle, D. Metlzer, Y. Zhang, and P. Grinspan. 2009. Expected reciprocal rank for graded relevance. In *Proc. CIKM.* 621–630.
[7] J. K. Jayasinghe, W. Webber, M. Sanderson, and J. S. Culpepper. 2014. Improving test collection pools with machine learning. In *Proc. Aust. Doc. Comp. Symp.* 2–9.
[8] R. Kumar and S. Vassilvitskii. 2010. Generalized distances between rankings. In *Proc. WWW.* 571–580.
[9] A. Lipani, M. Lupu, and A. Hanbury. 2015. Splitting water: Precision and anti-precision to reduce pool bias. In *Proc. SIGIR.* 103–112.
[10] A. Lipani, M. Lupu, E. Kanoulas, and A. Hanbury. 2016. The solitude of relevant documents in the pool. In *Proc. CIKM.* 1989–1992.
[11] X. Lu, A. Moffat, and J. S. Culpepper. 2016. The effect of pooling and evaluation depth on IR metrics. *Inf. Retr.* 19, 4 (2016), 416–445.
[12] X. Lu, A. Moffat, and J. S. Culpepper. 2016. Modeling relevance as a function of retrieval rank. In *Proc. AIRS.* 3–15.
[13] A. Moffat, P. Thomas, and F. Scholer. 2013. Users versus models: What observation tells us about effectiveness metrics. In *Proc. CIKM.* 659–668.
[14] A. Moffat, W. Webber, and J. Zobel. 2007. Strategic system comparisons via targeted relevance judgments. In *Proc. SIGIR.* 375–382.
[15] A. Moffat and J. Zobel. 2008. Rank-biased precision for measurement of retrieval effectiveness. *ACM Trans. Information Systems* 27, 1 (2008), 2:1–2:27.
[16] S. D. Ravana and A. Moffat. 2010. Score estimation, incomplete judgments, and significance testing in IR evaluation. In *Proc. AIRS.* 97–109.
[17] S. E. Robertson. 2007. On document populations and measures of IR effectiveness. In *Proc. ICTIR.* 9–22.
[18] T. Sakai. 2007. Alternatives to BPref. In *Proc. SIGIR.* 71–78.
[19] T. Sakai. 2008. Comparing metrics across TREC and NTCIR: The robustness to pool depth bias. In *Proc. SIGIR.* 691–692.
[20] T. Sakai. 2008. Comparing metrics across TREC and NTCIR: The robustness to system bias. In *Proc. CIKM.* 581–590.
[21] T. Sakai. 2014. Metrics, statistics, tests. In *Bridging Between Information Retrieval and Databases*, N. Ferro (Ed.). Springer, 116–163.
[22] T. Schnabel, A. Swaminathan, P. I. Frazier, and T. Joachims. 2016. Unbiased comparative evaluation of ranking functions. In *Proc. ICTIR.* 109–118.
[23] T. Schnabel, A. Swaminathan, and T. Joachims. 2015. Unbiased ranking evaluation on a budget. In *Proc. WWW.* 935–937.
[24] E. M. Voorhees. 2014. The effect of sampling strategy on inferred measures. In *Proc. SIGIR.* 1119–1122.
[25] E. M. Voorhees and D. K. Harman. 2005. *TREC: Experiment and Evaluation in Information Retrieval.* The MIT Press.
[26] W. Webber and L. A. F. Park. 2009. Score adjustment for correction of pooling bias. In *Proc. SIGIR.* 444–451.
[27] E. Yilmaz and J. A. Aslam. 2008. Estimating average precision when judgments are incomplete. *Knowledge and Information Systems* 16, 2 (2008), 173–211.
[28] E. Yilmaz, E. Kanoulas, and J. A. Aslam. 2008. A simple and efficient sampling method for estimating AP and NDCG. In *Proc. SIGIR.* 603–610.
[29] Z. Zhou. 2012. *Ensemble Methods: Foundations and Algorithms.* CRC press.
[30] J. Zobel. 1998. How reliable are the results of large-scale information retrieval experiments?. In *Proc. SIGIR.* 307–314.

Learning to Rank Using Localized Geometric Mean Metrics

Yuxin Su
Department of Computer Science and Engineering
The Chinese University of Hong Kong
Shatin, N.T., Hong Kong
yxsu@cse.cuhk.edu.hk

Irwin King
Department of Computer Science and Engineering
The Chinese University of Hong Kong
Shatin, N.T., Hong Kong
king@cse.cuhk.edu.hk

Michael Lyu
Department of Computer Science and Engineering
The Chinese University of Hong Kong
Shatin, N.T., Hong Kong
lyu@cse.cuhk.edu.hk

ABSTRACT

Many learning-to-rank (LtR) algorithms focus on query-independent model, in which query and document do not lie in the same feature space, and the rankers rely on the feature ensemble about query-document pair instead of the similarity between query instance and documents. However, existing algorithms do not consider local structures in query-document feature space, and are fragile to irrelevant noise features. In this paper, we propose a novel Riemannian metric learning algorithm to capture the local structures and develop a robust LtR algorithm. First, we design a concept called *ideal candidate document* to introduce metric learning algorithm to query-independent model. Previous metric learning algorithms aiming to find an optimal metric space are only suitable for query-dependent model, in which query instance and documents belong to the same feature space and the similarity is directly computed from the metric space. Then we extend the new and extremely fast global Geometric Mean Metric Learning (GMML) algorithm to develop a localized GMML, namely L-GMML. Based on the combination of local learned metrics, we employ the popular Normalized Discounted Cumulative Gain (NDCG) scorer and Weighted Approximate Rank Pairwise (WARP) loss to optimize the *ideal candidate document* for each query candidate set. Finally, we can quickly evaluate all candidates via the similarity between the *ideal candidate document* and other candidates. By leveraging the ability of metric learning algorithms to describe the complex structural information, our approach gives us a principled and efficient way to perform LtR tasks. The experiments on real-world datasets demonstrate that our proposed L-GMML algorithm outperforms the state-of-the-art metric learning to rank methods and the stylish query-independent LtR algorithms regarding accuracy and computational efficiency.

KEYWORDS

Learning to Rank, Distance Metric Learning, Local Metric Learning

ACM Reference format:
Yuxin Su, Irwin King, and Michael Lyu. 2017. Learning to Rank Using Localized Geometric Mean Metrics. In *Proceedings of SIGIR '17, August 07-11, 2017, Shinjuku, Tokyo, Japan*, , 10 pages.
DOI: http://dx.doi.org/10.1145/3077136.3080828

SIGIR '17, August 07-11, 2017, Shinjuku, Tokyo, Japan

DOI: http://dx.doi.org/10.1145/3077136.3080828

1 INTRODUCTION

In many information retrieval systems, especially Web search, users expect to obtain the most relevant documents according to users' query phrase or document. This task is technically formulated as a ranking problem. Most of the Web search engines exploit this ranking task based on learning-to-rank (LtR) techniques [21]. In the LtR framework, a machine learning algorithm is typically employed to derive a ranking model about document collection from a training subset of documents with labels or partial order. After the supervised or semi-supervised learning procedures, the ranking model is expected to retrieval top-k (ordered) relevant documents from the candidate collection when a query is given.

In practice, search engines develop the LtR model in two stages: (i) candidate retrieval and (ii) candidate re-ranking [22]. In the first stage, search engine retrieves from the inverted document repository a sufficiently large set of relevant candidate documents $\mathcal{D}_q$ matching a user's query. It is used to avoid applying the ranking model to all documents possibly matching a user's query. This stage usually requires that the size of candidate set is much larger than the number of the relevant URLs to be included in the returned page. Based on the candidate document set $\mathcal{D}_q$ obtained in the first stage, Web search engines reformulate the documents with features extracted from the query-document pair and hide query features, then employ the LtR model without the dependency of query instance to score and re-rank the document collection $\mathcal{D}_q$. Finally, search engines return the top-k documents to the user.

In Web search engine, the time-budget of this two-stage framework is usually limited. Therefore, strongly motivated by the time budget consideration, the current two most efficient and the state-of-the-art methods are based on the additive ensemble of regression trees, namely Gradient-Boosted Regression Tree (GBRT) [11] and λ-MART [4]. These two kinds of methods are capable of meeting the time requirement with acceptable accuracy even when thousands of regression tree are evaluated for each document. However, one of the drawbacks of this line of methods is that when the input samples contain an enormous amount of non-informative features, many methods fail to identify the most relevant features. Therefore, researchers are still trying to devise techniques and strategies to find a better way of combining features extracted from query-document pairs through discriminative training to accelerate the training process for document ranking without losing in quality [12, 35].

Another perspective to the ranking problem is to seek the best similarity measurement and develop the corresponding efficient algorithm. These approach aims to optimize the accuracy in the first stage to find candidate documents or even directly return the top-k documents with an order. Concerning accuracy, the similarity-based models for a ranking problem can be classified into three categories from the formulation of the loss function: pointwise, pairwise and listwise loss functions [3]. Practically, the pairwise loss function tends to be more efficient for training and have been widely adopted by large Web search engines [3].

The pairwise similarity motivates that how to apply the classical metric learning or similar learning methods to the ranking problem [7]. The metric learning algorithms aim to find a better distance metric than Euclidean metric to measure the pairwise similarity. The advantage of such metric-learning-to-rank [24] framework has two folds: (1) the metrics often preserves the nearest neighborhood information, which is the perfect structure to conduct ranking; (2) a proper metric containing the structural information of the document collections in the document space is useful for reducing the over-fitting and improving the robustness to noise features [16]. Therefore, the metric-learning-to-rank methods [18, 19, 25] typically enjoy higher accuracy. Nevertheless, unfortunately, the disadvantage of metric-learning-to-rank also has two folds: (1) many metric learning algorithms [8, 32] are degraded by its extremely high computational expense; (2) the similarity measurement is not suitable for LtR because we can not estimate the similarity between query and documents with features extracted from other domain knowledge.

In this paper, we focus on improving the ranking accuracy at the second stage in the search engine and attempt to provide a new query-independent model for LtR task. Different from the existing research on how to combine features extracted from other domains, we try to learn an optimal representation of these features via metric learning algorithm. To adopt query-dependent metric learning framework to a query-independent model, we propose a concept called *ideal candidate document*, which represents a perfect match for a given query. With the help of this concept, we can quickly evaluate all candidate documents and sort them by calculating the distance based on the optimal metric space between the *ideal candidate document* and other documents. Same with the query-dependent model, the shorter distance leads to a higher relevance to the query.

Since features from different domains generate local structure on the whole feature space, in order to preserve more local information and avoid overfitting, we develop a novel local metric learning framework for ranking with high efficiency and accuracy. Our localized metric learning algorithm extends from the state-of-the-art global metric learning algorithm called Geometric Mean Metric Learning (GMML) [36], and we apply Weighted Approximate Rank Pairwise (WARP) loss to optimize the metric space around the ideal document from the combination of several anchor documents.

We summarize our main contributions as follows:

- To the best of our knowledge, we are the first to extend geometric mean metric learning algorithm to a local metric learning approach in order to capture the local structures for LtR problem.
- We propose a novel *ideal candidate document* concept to transform metric-learning-to-rank framework from query-dependent model to query-independent model, which brings wider applications for metric learning and also improves the accuracy of classical LtR task.
- We conduct extensive experiments to reveal that our method outperforms the state-of-the-art query-dependent metric-learning-to-rank algorithms and query-independent LtR methods both in the accuracy and the computational complexity.

2 PRELIMINARIES AND RELATED WORK

Since our approach employs local metric learning algorithm to conduct the LtR task, two sets of previous work relate to our work:

2.1 Learning to Rank

In the information retrieval setting, a search engine maintains a collection of candidate examples $\mathcal{D}$. Given a query q, the search engine returns the top ranked subset of documents $\left\{p \in \mathbb{R}^d\right\} \subset \mathcal{D}_q \subset \mathcal{D}$ from the collection with order, ranked by a specific ranking model $f_q(p)$.

According to the formulation of the loss function, the LtR methods are categories into three folds: (1) pointwise loss approach, (2) pairwise loss approach and (3) listwise loss approach.

For pointwise loss function, Li et al. [17] cast the ranking problem to a multi-class classification problem. The training process relies on enough labeled information, which is not always easy to satisfy. Pairwise loss approach such as RankNet [2], RankBoost [10] focus on the relative order, which is capable of being adapted to classification problem. In the listwise loss approach, a relevance label l related with the query for ground truth is usually bound to the document p. Cao et al. [5] first propose to find the optimal permutation to minimize the listwise loss function. McFee [25] proposes a similar objective, but the different solution from the metric learning methods.

The majority of LtR methods follows listwise loss function. Currently, the most popular methods [4, 9, 11] come from the combination of an ensemble of trees like random forest and the boosting-like methods [10]. Based on multiple decision trees, this kind of methods gains an accepted level of accuracy.

2.2 Metric Learning

The (squared) Mahalanobis distance, an extension of Euclidean distance, measures the distance between two points lie on the special linear space. It is defined as

$$d_{\mathbf{M}}\left(p_1, p_2\right) = \left(p_1 - p_2\right)^T \mathbf{M} \left(p_1 - p_2\right), \tag{1}$$

where $p_1, p_2 \in \mathbb{R}^d$ are input examples, $\mathbf{M}$ is a symmetric and positive semi-definite $d \times d$ matrix. When $\mathbf{M} = \mathbf{I}$, the Mahalanobis distance is equivalent to the Euclidean distance.

There are plenty of algorithms aiming at learning such metric by solving a semidefinite or a quadratic program [29, 32, 34]. Almost all the metric learning algorithms try to constrain the similar data points and to scatter those dissimilar data points. Early work like [34] formulates this problem as an optimization problem on the second-order cone, which is costly solvable. Davis et al. [8], Weinberger et al. [32] and Shen et al. [29] formulate different kinds of optimization problems, namely ITML, LMNN, BoostMetric respectively. However, the common issue that their solutions are computationally expensive. Very recently, Zadeh et al. [36] propose a new objective function and give the closed-form solution from the geometric domain. It is the most promising global metric learning method because of the computational speed several orders of magnitude faster than the widely used ITML and LMNN methods.

There are two different roadmaps to conduct the LtR tasks from the metric learning perspective: (1), McFee [25] and Lim et al. [18, 19] learn global metric with Positive Semi-Definite (PSD) constraint on the metric parameter. They belong to the application of the standard metric learning algorithm. (2), Chechik et al. [7] and Liu et al. [20] remove PSD constraint and employ the bilinear model to measure the similarity between two data points. Usually, without PSD constraints, the bilinear model easily leads to over-fitting. However, PSD constraint brings a tremendous amount of computation.

In most cases, global metric learning relies on a learned PSD matrix, which is not only computational expensive in high-dimensional case but not reasonable for retrieval ranking problem. In the LtR framework, the local similarity is far more important than the dissimilar information because we aim at ranking the relevant documents around a user's query. Therefore, several important local metric learning approaches are related to our work. Wang et al. [31] parameterize the weight function of each data point. The approach enhances the model complexity but brings the extra computation. Hauberg et al. [13] provide the theoretical analysis about the optimal weight function. However, the calculation of the geodesics is extremely expensive.

3 OUR PROPOSED METHODOLOGY

In the LtR problem, a ranked list of the relevant documents is returned for a specific user's query. In this situation, we can assume without losing generality that all relevant documents should be closer to an unreal document than other irrelevant documents. This unreal document should be related to the query. Therefore, although the query instance is not accessible in the document feature space, we can still construct this unreal candidate document to represent the query in the feature space of the document. In our paper, this unreal but perfect-matching document is named as the *ideal candidate document*.

Usually, the indexed documents are assumed to be static, and the set of queries considered as input testing data is dynamic. This assumption allows us to transform the training documents to an another static representation, and model *ideal candidate documents* for each query to a dynamic combination of static documents.

In our paper, we assume the documents including candidate documents and ideal documents lie on the surface of a Riemannian manifold. Then, we attempt to build the similarity measurement between documents on the geodesic lines in the Riemannian manifold. Very often, a single linear metric $\mathbf{M}$ can not describe the whole surface of Riemannian manifold adequately. It reveals the inability of a single metric to model the complexity of the LtR problem. Furthermore, the discriminative features vary between different neighborhoods on the surface of the manifold. To address this limitation, researchers try to learn a set of local metrics representing the various regions of the surface. In most cases, local metric learning algorithms will generate a local metric for each learning example [26]. The whole parameters of these kinds of the algorithm are prohibitively huge when the number of examples becomes large.

In our approach, we follow [31] to learn a local metric for a part of the feature space of documents, in which case the number of learned metrics m can be considerably smaller than n, the size of the examples collection.

Suppose we have learned m local metrics $\{\mathbf{M}_1, \ldots, \mathbf{M}_m\}$ and the associated anchor points $\{p_1, \ldots p_r, \ldots p_m\}$. The choice of anchor points and the computation of local metrics are described in Subsection 3.1. Then the similarity model $f(q,p)$ between two documents p_i and p_j is extended from Eq. (1) as follows:

$$f(p_i,p_j) = d_{\mathbf{M}(p_i)}(p_i,p_j) \tag{2}$$

$$\mathbf{M}(p_i) = \sum_{r=1}^{m} w_r(p_i)\mathbf{M}_r, \tag{3}$$

where $w_r(p_i) \geq 0$ is the weight of document p_i for local metric $\mathbf{M}_r$. The PSD constraints of $\mathbf{M}(p)$ is automatically satisfied if all local metric $\mathbf{M}_r$ are PSD matrices. These formulation includes m anchor documents and p_i should be close to these anchor documents [27]. It is clear that the *ideal candidate document* should be close to several high relevant documents. Therefore, we can employ these high relevant documents as anchor documents to construct the local metric space around the *ideal candidate document*.

With the above assumption and observation, the task of information retrieval precedes in the following steps:

(1) Given a candidate collection $\mathcal{D}_q$ for query q , we employ high/low relevant documents to compute a $\mathbf{M}$ and find a anchor point p_r to maximize the ranking scorer under the metric $\mathbf{M}$ by computing $(p_i - p_r)\,\mathbf{M}\,(p_i - p_r)^\top$.
(2) After sampling m candidate collection to find m anchor documents and m associated metrics, we can construct the *ideal candidate document* based on a combination of m anchor documents.
(3) We can build an evaluation function to measure the similarity between candidate document and *ideal candidate document*, then, sort these documents via the similarity to *ideal candidate document*.

3.1 Computation of Basis Metrics

Before constructing the local metrics in Eq. (3), we need to learn m local metrics. With the assumption that each local metric $\mathbf{M}_r$ represents a part of feature space, we can employ the classical single metric learning algorithm associated with a subset of the triplets from a part of examples space.

In this paper, we extend the state-of-the-art global metric learning algorithm GMML [36] into local metric forms. The extension consists of two parts:

(1) The local basis metric associated with the triplets set $\mathcal{D}_r$ is computed by the original GMML.
(2) The smooth weighting function $w_r(p)$ is computed from Eq. (11).

Given a subset of the triplets $\mathcal{T}_r = (p_i, p_j, p_k)$ such that p_i is more similar to p_j than to p_k, we can extract the similarity set S_r and

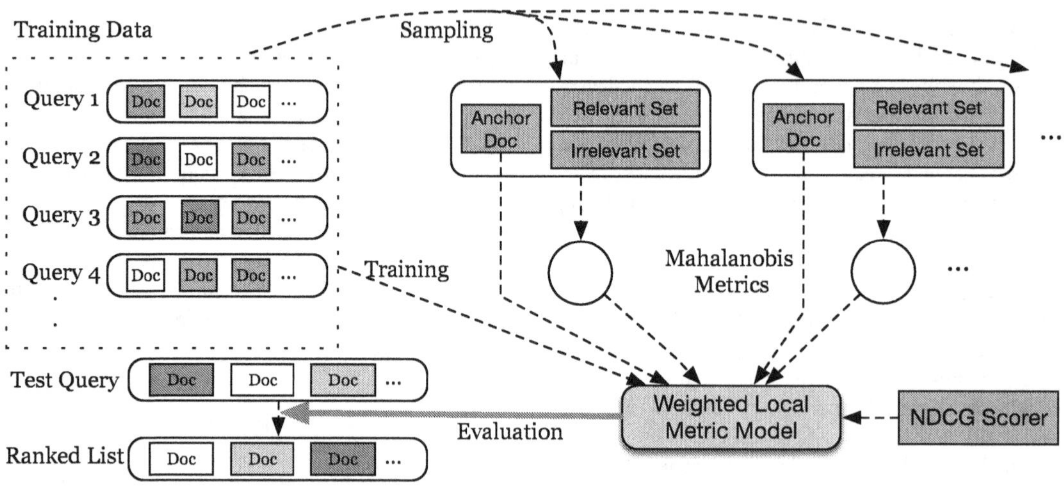

Figure 1: General framework of proposed L-GMML for ranking. Different gray levels in query test represent the relevant level of the document

the dissimilarity set D_r by following the instruction in Section 3.4. Then we construct two corresponding matrices:

$$\mathbf{S}_r = \sum_{(p_i,p_j)\in S_r} \left(p_i - p_j\right)\left(p_i - p_j\right)^\top \tag{4}$$

$$\mathbf{D}_r = \sum_{(p_i,p_k)\in D_r} \left(p_i - p_k\right)\left(p_i - p_k\right)^\top \tag{5}$$

Then, the basic optimization formulation of local metric $\mathbf{M}_r$ is defined as follows:

$$\min_{\mathbf{M}_r \succ 0} \quad h(\mathbf{M}_r) := \mathrm{tr}\left(\mathbf{M}_r\mathbf{S}_r\right) + \mathrm{tr}\left(\mathbf{M}_r^{-1}\mathbf{D}_r\right) \tag{6}$$

Equation (6) implies that GMML will return a single local metric $\mathbf{M}_r$ that minimize the sum of distances over all the similar pairs S_r and maximize the distance over all the dissimilar pairs D_r.

The closed-form solution of Eq. (6) is obtained by

$$\nabla h(\mathbf{M}_r) = \mathbf{S}_r - \mathbf{M}_r^{-1}\mathbf{D}_r\mathbf{M}_r^{-1} \tag{7}$$

Taking $\nabla h(\mathbf{M}_r) = 0$, we obtain:

$$\mathbf{M}_r\mathbf{S}_r\mathbf{M}_r = \mathbf{D}_r \tag{8}$$

Equation (8) is a Riccati equation whose unique solution is [36]

$$\mathbf{M}_r = \mathbf{S}_r^{-1/2}\left(\mathbf{S}_r^{1/2}\mathbf{D}_r\mathbf{S}_r^{1/2}\right)^{1/2}\mathbf{S}_r^{-1/2} \tag{9}$$

In experiments, $\mathbf{M}_r$ is efficiently computed from Cholesky-Schur method [14].

3.2 Smoothing Weight Functions

Lots of researchers try to provide the insights of their local metric learning approaches [13, 31] by modeling their methods from the perspective of Riemannian metric. An important property about the Riemannian metric is that a Riemannian metric $M(p)$ on a manifold $\mathcal{M}$ is a smoothly varying inner product $\langle x_i, x_j\rangle_p = x_i^T \mathbf{M}(p) x_j$ in the tangent space $\mathcal{T}_p\mathcal{M}$ of each point $p \in \mathcal{M}$. From Lemma 1 in [13], when the weight function $w_r(p)$ is smooth with p, Eq. (3) will be a well-studied Riemannian metric. Therefore, any well-designed local metric methods should provide a smooth weight function.

Another important issue is that the weight function $w_r(p)$ should reflect the fitness of the local metric $\mathbf{M}_r$. Suppose $(p, p_r) \in S_r$, it indicates that $\mathbf{M}_r$ is the best local metric to measure the similarity between p_r and other examples, which means that Eq. (8) should be robust against the additive similar pair (p, p_r). Therefore, the weight function $w_r(p)$ should be in the opposite to $\mathbf{M}_r(p-p_r)(p-p_r)^T\mathbf{M}_r$.

Take the limit as an example, if $\mathbf{M}_r(p-p_r)(p-p_r)^T\mathbf{M}_r = 0$, then,

$$\mathbf{M}_r\left(\mathbf{S}_r + (p-p_r)\right)\left(\mathbf{S}_r + (p-p_r)\right)^T\mathbf{M}_r = \mathbf{D}_r \tag{10}$$

The solution of Eq. (10) is the same with Eq. (9), which indicates that $\mathbf{M}_r(p-p_r)(p-p_r)^T\mathbf{M}_r$ is a proper measurement whether the $\mathbf{M}_r$ is the optimal local metric for the document p.

By taking consideration about the above observation, we propose the smoothing weight functions [1] as:

$$w_r(p) = \exp\left(-\frac{\rho}{2}\|p - p_r\|_{\mathbf{M}_r}\right), \tag{11}$$

where, $\|\cdot\|^2_{\mathbf{M}_r}$ is the L2 norm with the metric $\mathbf{M}_r$.

$$\|p - p_r\|^2_{\mathbf{M}_r} = \mathrm{tr}\left(\mathbf{M}_r(p-p_r)(p-p_r)^T\mathbf{M}_r\right) \tag{12}$$

From Eq. (12) and Eq. (10), we can easily know $\|p - p_r\|_{\mathbf{M}_r}$ is a proper measurement about the similarity between query p and the anchor point p_r associated with the local metric $\mathbf{M}_r$.

Therefore, our evaluation function is formulated as:

$$f_q(p, \Phi_q) = -\sum_{r=1}^{m} \Phi_q^{(r)} \cdot \exp\left(-\|p - p_r\|_{M_r}\right) \cdot \|p - p_r\|_{M_r}, \tag{13}$$

where, $\Phi_q \in \mathbb{R}^m$, $\Phi_q^{(r)} = \exp\left(\rho_q^{(r)}/2\right)$ is the key parameter we need to learn in order to find a better manifold structure. Higher $f_q(p, \Phi_q)$ means that p is closer to the *ideal candidate document.* In the next subsection, we will introduce our exploration to optimize Φ for a specific ranking problem.

3.3 Update of Φ

In the above subsection, we formulate a general local metric framework in Eq. (13) to represent the manifold structure. From the theoretical analysis in [27], the whole space of Φ keeps the learned manifold smooth. Therefore, we define our loss function under the popular Weighted Approximate Rank Pairwise (WARP) framework [33] and optimize the associated objective function to obtain an optimal solution for ranking task.

The WARP loss for a given set of candidate document $\mathcal{D}_q$ with query ID q is defined as:

$$\mathcal{L}(q) = \frac{1}{\left|\mathcal{D}_q^+\right|} \sum_{p \in \mathcal{D}_q^+} L\left(v_q\left(p^+\right)\right), \tag{14}$$

where $v_q(p^+)$ is the number of violators in $\mathcal{D}_q$ for positive p^+, defined as:

$$v_q(p^+) = \sum_{p^- \in \mathcal{D}_q^-} \mathrm{I}\left[f_q\left(p^-, \Phi_q\right) - f_q\left(p^+, \Phi_q\right)\right] \tag{15}$$

To obtain better NDCG score, $L(\cdot)$ is defined as:

$$L(k) = \sum_{i=1}^{k} \frac{1}{\log_2(i+1)} \tag{16}$$

In order to optimize Φ_q, we follows the methods in [18, 33] to approximate $L\left(v_q(p^+)\right)$ by a continuous formulation with hinge loss:

$$\sum_{p^- \in \mathcal{V}_{q,p^+}} L\left(\left|\mathcal{V}_{q,p^+}\right|\right) \frac{\left[\zeta - f_q\left(p^+, \Phi_q\right) + f_q\left(p^-, \Phi_q\right)\right]_+}{\left|\mathcal{V}_{q,p^+}\right|}, \tag{17}$$

where for a given q, p^+, ζ is the hinge loss margin. $\mathcal{V}_{q,p^+}$ is the set of violators with hinge loss:

$$\mathcal{V}_{q,p^+} = \left\{p^- \in \mathcal{X}_q^- \mid f_q(p^+, \Phi_q)\right\} \tag{18}$$

In order to obtain an unbiased estimation of the loss function in Eq. (17), we can randomly sample $q, p^+ \in \mathcal{D}_q$ and find an violator p^- such that $\zeta + f_q\left(p^-, \Phi_q\right) > f_q\left(p^+, \Phi_q\right)$. In this situation, the tuple of (q, p^+, p^-) has the following contribution to Eq. (17):

$$l\left(q, p^+, p^-\right) = L\left(\left|\mathcal{V}_{q,p^+}\right|\right)\left(\zeta - f_q\left(p^+, \Phi_q\right) + f_q\left(p^-, \Phi_q\right)\right) \tag{19}$$

From the WARP framework, $\left|\mathcal{V}_{q,p^+}\right|$ can be approximated by $\left\lfloor\left|\mathcal{D}_q^-\right| / N_q\right\rfloor$, where N_q is the number of less relevant documents p^- drawn with replacement from $\mathcal{D}_q^-$ until a violator is found.

Finally, the stochastic gradient descent for the parameter Φ can be easily conducted at iteration t as:

$$\begin{aligned}
&\Phi_q(t+1) \\
=&\Phi_q(t) - \mu \frac{\partial l\left(q, p^+, p^-\right)}{\partial \Phi_q(t)}, && (20) \\
=&\Phi_q(t) - \mu L\left(\left\lfloor\frac{\left|\mathcal{D}_q^-\right|}{N_q}\right\rfloor\right) \cdot \left[\frac{\partial f_q(p^-, \Phi_q(t))}{\partial \Phi_q(t)} - \frac{\partial f_q\left(p^+, \Phi_q(t)\right)}{\partial \Phi_q(t)}\right], && (21)
\end{aligned}$$

where $\frac{\partial f_q(p, \Phi_q)}{\partial \Phi_q} = \left[\frac{\partial f_q\left(p, \Phi_q^{(r)}\right)}{\partial \Phi_q^{(r)}}\right]_{r=1\ldots m}$. To avoid over-fitting, we project $\Phi_q^{(r)}$ to zero when Eq. (21) leads to negative value. We take derivation from Eq. (13) to obtain:

$$\frac{\partial f_q\left(p, \Phi_q^{(r)}\right)}{\partial \Phi_q^{(r)}} = \exp\left(-\|p - p_r\|_{M_r}\right) \cdot \|p - p_r\|_{M_r} \tag{22}$$

Overall, our proposed algorithm is illustrated in Figure 1 and summarized in Algorithm 2.

3.4 Sampling Strategy

Our approach will not iterate all triplets for $\mathcal{D}$ introduced in Section 3.1, because learning the global ranking model from all triplets is an NP-hard problem [23]. Hence, we choose to stochastically sample the triplets $\left(p_i, p_j, p_k\right)$ from candidate documents. p_i and p_j representing similar documents are sampled from high relevant documents, then p_k is sampled from the less relevant documents. In our implementation, we only sample p_k from the documents with zero relevant label.

For sampling procedure in Section 3.3, Φ_i and Φ_j are independent for two queries i and j. Therefore, the update can be computed in a highly parallel way.

ALGORITHM 1: Geometric Mean Metric Learning (GMML) [36]

Input: $\mathcal{D}^+$: positive set of documents, $\mathcal{D}^-$: negative set of documents, λ : regularization parameter

Output: $M \in \mathbb{S}_+^d$: Mahalanobis metric;

$\mathrm{S} = \lambda \mathrm{I} + \sum_{p_i \neq p_j, p_i \in \mathcal{D}^+, p_j \in \mathcal{D}^+} \left(p_i - p_j\right)\left(p_i - p_j\right)^\top$;

$\mathrm{D} = \lambda \mathrm{I} + \sum_{p_i \in \mathcal{D}^+, p_j \in \mathcal{D}^-} \left(p_i - p_j\right)\left(p_i - p_j\right)^\top$;

$\mathrm{M} = \mathrm{S}^{-1/2}\left(\mathrm{S}^{1/2}\mathrm{D}\mathrm{S}^{1/2}\right)^{1/2}\mathrm{S}^{-1/2}$

---

4 EVALUATION

In this section, we discuss the implementation of our approach for the LtR problem and display extensive experiments evaluating our methodology in comparison to the state-of-the-art (R-MLR, GBRT, and λ-MART). Our design on experiments tackle the following questions:

- Do we develop a correct localized extension to the global GMML? To answer this question, we generate varied scale synthetic datasets to evaluate the performance gain against global metric learning algorithm when a different number of local metrics invoke in our L-GMML approach to prove the correctness.

ALGORITHM 2: L-GMML to Rank

Input: Candidate set for c queries $\left\{\mathcal{D}_1, \mathcal{D}_2, \ldots, \mathcal{D}_q, \ldots, \mathcal{D}_c\right\}$, m : number of local metrics, T : number of iteration, μ : step size, ζ: hinge loss margin

Output: $\{(p_1, M_1), (p_2, M_2) \ldots, (p_m, M_m)\}$: set of local metrics and associated anchor points, $p \in \mathbb{R}^d$, $M \in \mathbb{S}^d_+$, $\Phi \in \mathbb{R}^{c \times m}$: weights for local metrics to model the *ideal candidate documents* for each queries

for $q \in [1, c]$ **do**
  Extract $\mathcal{D}_q^+$ and $\mathcal{D}_q^-$ from $\mathcal{D}_q$;
end
for $i \in [1, m]$ **do**
  Sample $\mathcal{D}_i^+$ and $\mathcal{D}_i^-$ from $\left\{\mathcal{D}_q\right\}_{q\in[1,c]}$;
  $M_i = \text{GMML}\left(\mathcal{D}_i^+, \mathcal{D}_i^-\right)$;
  for $p \in \mathcal{D}_i^+$ **do**
    $\Gamma_p^{(i)} \leftarrow$Sort $\mathcal{D}_i$ in ascending order by computing $\|p - d\|^2_{M_i}$ $\forall d \in \mathcal{D}_q$;
  end
  Find the anchor point p_r with maximum NDCG score of $\Gamma_{p_r}^{(i)}$;
end
for $t = 1$ *to* T **do**
  Sample a tuple (q, p^+, p^-) from $\left\{\mathcal{D}_q\right\}_{q\in[1,c]}$ such that $\zeta + f_q\left(p^+, \Phi_q(t)\right) > f_q\left(p^-, \Phi_q(t)\right)$;
  $N_q \leftarrow$ the number of less relevant documents drawn with replacement from $\mathcal{D}_q^-$ until p^- is found;
  $\Phi_q(t+1) = \left[\Phi_q(t) - \mu L\left(\left\lfloor \frac{|\mathcal{D}_q^-|}{N_q} \right\rfloor\right) \cdot \left[\frac{\partial f_q(p^-, \Phi_q(t))}{\partial \Phi_q(t)} - \frac{\partial f_q(p^+, \Phi_q(t))}{\partial \Phi_q(t)}\right]\right]_+$;
end

- Is our assumption on the existence of local structures reasonable? If reasonable, does our solution enjoy high computational efficiency and the good scalability for scaled datasets? We make comparisons with the state-of-the-art metric learning algorithms for ranking in the query-dependent model on scaled datasets. We attempt to demonstrate the improvements of our approach over other metric learning algorithms.
- Does our LtR algorithm have any amazing properties? We conduct experiments on real-world large-scale datasets to illustrate the enormous improvement of our approach on accuracy compared with the dominant ranking methods like GBRT and λ-MART in the query-independent framework.

4.1 Experiments Setting

In our experiments, we have implemented our local GMML (L-GMML) algorithm in Julia[1], the source code is released at Github[2]. To make a fair comparison against the state-of-the-art ranking methods, we also implement R-MLR, GBRT and λ-MART in Julia. We take RankLib[3], an open-source implementation of the GBRT and λ-MART algorithms and MLR[4] as references to implement these algorithms in Julia.

Our program is executed on an Ubuntu 14.04 LTS server with 12 Intel Xeon E5-2620 cores and 128GB main memory. All baseline methods and our method are performed in a parallel way to fully utilize the computational resources. Our R-MLR implementation is based on the parallel MLR-ADMM [19]. GBRT and λ-MART come from RankLib.

The statistical tests in the following experiments are computed over the values for Mean Average Precision (MAP) and Normalized Discounted Cumulative Gain (NDCG) [15] at the top k retrieved documents denoted as NDCG@k. These two metrics are the most important and frequently used in information retrieval community to evaluate a given permutation of a ranked list using binary and multi-relevance order.

Table 1: Different kinds of song representation

	# of features	# of songs
Audio	1,024	5,419
Lyrics-128	128	2000
Lyrics-256	256	2000

4.2 Datasets

For all real-world datasets, we split each of them into two components: 1), the training set is used to learn ranking models; 2), the test set is purely used to evaluate the performance of the learned ranking models.

All the datasets we use are freely available online for scientific purpose. Such datasets can be divided into two groups:

4.2.1 Query-dependent Dataset. We employ CAL10K [30] to make fair comparisons between our L-GMML and R-MLR. Because, in the original paper, R-MLR performs well on the CAL10K dataset. Following the experiments in [19], we use a subset of the CAL10K dataset, which is provided as ten 40/30/30 splits of a collection of 5419 songs.

4.2.2 Query-Independent Datasets. In this subsection, we employ two popular real-world large-scale datasets: Yahoo! and MSN to evaluate the competitive performance of proposed L-GMML against the state-of-the-art query-independent LtR methods.

Yahoo! datasets come from Yahoo! Learning to Rank Challenge [6]. The datasets consist of feature vectors extracted from query-url pairs along with relevance judgment labels.

In our experiments, we also employ the two set of MSN learning to rank[5] datasets: MSLR-10K and MSLS-30K, both of which consists of 136 features extracted from query-url pairs. The MSN datasets provide relevance judgment labels ranging from 0 (irrelevant) to 4 (perfect match). In experiments, each MSN dataset is partitioned into five subsets for five-fold cross validation.

The complete statistical information about these datasets are listed at Table 2.

[1]http://julialang.org/
[2]https://github.com/yxsu/LtR.jl
[3]http://sourceforge.net/p/lemur/wiki/RankLib/
[4]https://github.com/bmcfee/mlr
[5]https://www.microsoft.com/en-us/research/project/mslr/

Table 2: Characteristics of publicly available large-scale datasets for learning to rank

Name	# of Queries			# of Doc.			Rel. Levels	# of Features	Year
	Train	Vali.	Test	Train	Vali.	Test			
Yahoo! Set I	19,944	2,994	6,983	473,134	71,083	165,660	5	519	2010
Yahoo! Set II	1,266	1,266	3,798	34,815	34,881	103,174	5	596	2010
MSLR-WEB10K	6,000	2,000	2,000	723,412	235,259	235,259	5	136	2010
MSLR-WEB30K	31,531	6,306	6,306	3,771k	6,306	753k	5	136	2010

4.3 Evaluation of the Proposed Approach

In our L-GMML model, the most important hyper-parameter is the number of local metrics, which has significant influence on the overall model performance. We will evaluate the correction of our localized extension method from synthetic datasets, and reveal the impact of the metric numbers.

4.3.1 Global GMML vs Local GMML. In this subsection, we attempt to employ multi-class classification problem to verify the correction of the local metric learning algorithm. Because multi-class synthetic datasets certainly contain local structures around the center of each class. If the accuracy gain is observed, we can also address the objective that local metric learning approach is designed to extend the global metric learning method's ability of modeling complex data manifold.

We employ the normal distribution to generate synthetic datasets with multiple centers and 95% confidence interval. The datasets with {10,50,100} classes are denoted as Synthetic-10, Synthetic-50, Synthetic-100 respectively. In these synthetic datasets, we assign the index of class to the relevant label of the corresponding data point.

We report the performance gain of the proposed local GMML against the global GMML in Figure 2. We can easily find the fact that when the number of local metrics is approximate to the number of the real centers in Gaussian synthetic data distribution, the relative accuracy gain of local metrics is maximized. This observation meets the objective of local metric learning approach.

4.3.2 The Number of Local Metrics. In this subsection, we will evaluate the significance of the number of local metrics, which is typically the most important parameter in the field of local metric learning. A large number of local metrics will enhance the algorithm's ability to model the complex manifold structure. However the computational complexity increases linearly with the number of local metrics. In experiments, we need to carefully tune the number of local metrics to make the balance between model's ability and computational complexity.

Figure 3 displays the impact of the number of local metrics on all datasets used in our paper. For all datasets, localized method can compete with the corresponding global method with a single metric. This fact proves that our localized extension is reasonable. Another obvious observation is that the optimal number of local metrics varies dramatically among different datasets, since it is decided by the complexity of the manifold structure sealed in the data space.

4.3.3 Scalability. In our experiments, the synthetic datasets is primarily invoked to evaluate the scalability of our approach.

Due to the limited scalability of real-world datasets, we synthesize datasets with the feature dimensionality scaled from 10 to 1000. In this experiment, we fix the number of local metrics as 10 since we only concern about the computational complexity on different scaled dimensions instead of the optimal number of local metrics. Figure 4 illustrates the training time of our L-GMML on these datasets.

Compared with other local metric learning methods, the less training time come from two-fold issues: (1) the GMML in Algorithm 1 is very fast. (2) The update of weighting function in our approach is relatively simple and straightforward. It does not involve the huge computational resources to find the optimal form.

4.4 Comparison with R-MLR

The Robust Metric-Learning-to-Rank (R-MLR) [19] is the most competitive metric learning method for ranking. It retrieves relevant examples in response to a query instance. To make direct comparisons, we need to modify our approach by assigning all anchor points to the query instance. Because our approach is originally designed for the query-independent framework.

In this set of experiments, we evaluate our approach on the music similarity task, because the R-MLR method is verified to be successful in music similarity task compared with other metric-learning-to-rank methods such as MLR [25], $L1$-MLR [28]. For each song p_i, a relevant set $\mathcal{D}_i^+ \subset \mathcal{D}_{\text{train}}$ is defined as the subset of songs in the training set performed by the top 10 most similar artists to the performer of p_i, where the similarity between artists is measured by the number of shared users in a sample of collaborative filter data [24]. This top-10 thresholding results in the relevant sets in this data being asymmetric and non-transitive. Therefore, the traditional pairwise metric learning methods do not work in this situation. However, our approach based on the sampling on the relevant set is not necessary to obey the symmetric and transitive properties.

The experiments are conducted on two different kinds of song representation: audio and lyrics, whose details are listed in Table 1. We use recommended candidate hyper-parameters in the original paper to tune R-MLR on validation set and select the best parameter to evaluate the performance of the model.

Since the scalability of the original R-MLR is limited, the experiments of R-MLR employ the latent features compressed by PCA. Our approach has no such problem and is suitable to conduct the training process on the original 1,024 features.

Figure 5 illustrates the performance of three metric learning algorithms. We fix the number of local metrics in our L-GMML as 1 to obtain the global GMML algorithm. The motivation of making

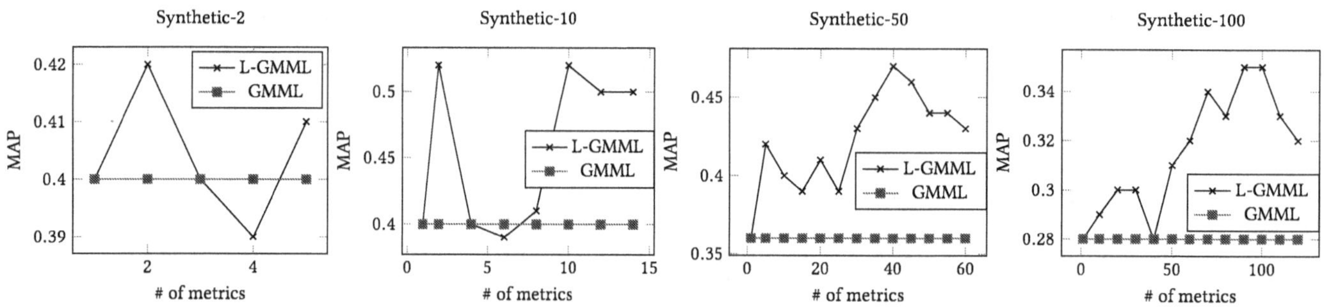

Figure 2: Comparisons between global GMML and local GMML on synthetic datasets. The performance is measured by MAP

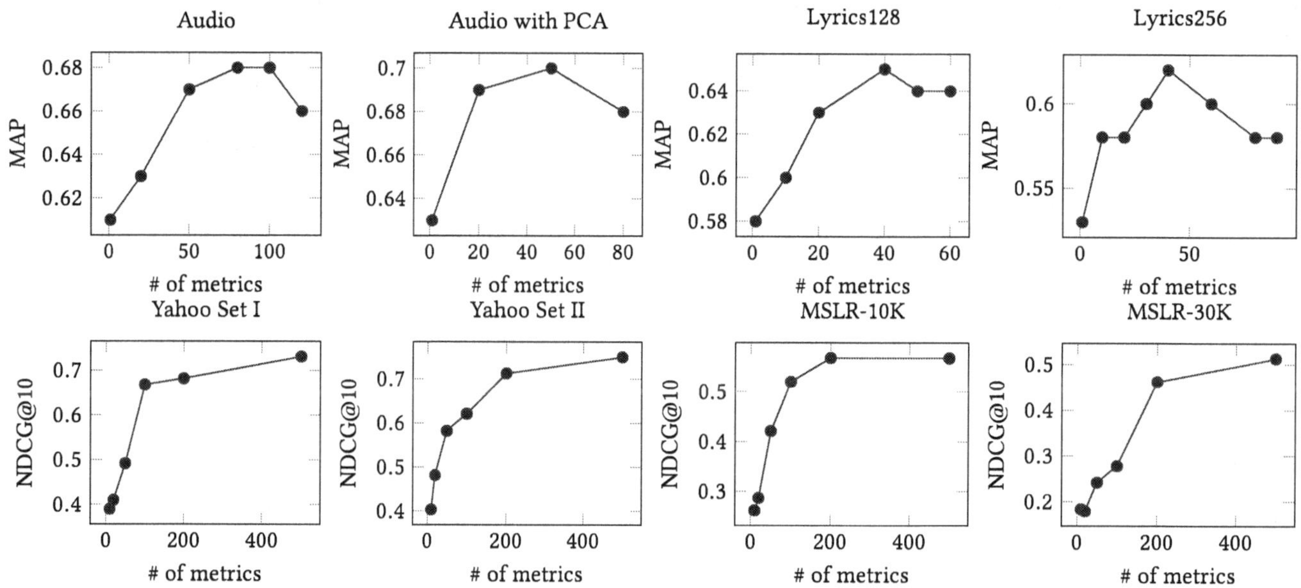

Figure 3: The variation of performance caused by different number of local metrics

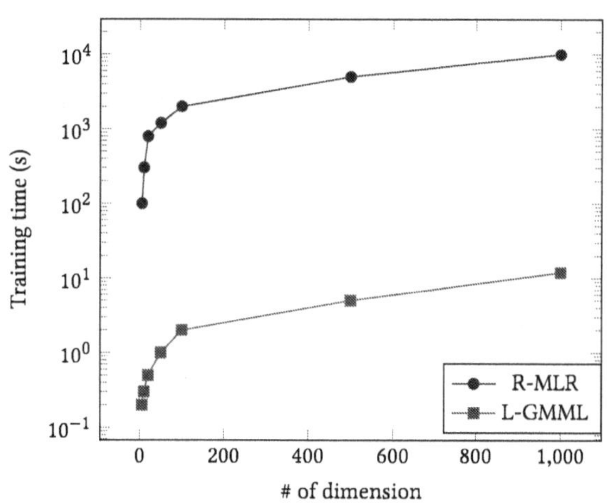

Figure 4: Training time of L-GMML on different scaled synthetic datasets

Table 3: Comparison on the training time of R-MLR and L-GMML. The number of local metrics in L-GMML is fixed as 50

Time (s)	R-MLR	L-GMML
Audio	N/A	38
Audio with PCA	607	4.7
Lyrics-128	302	2.6
Lyrics-256	1241	7.8

such comparison is that we attempt to demonstrate the different influence of the new GMML algorithm and our proposed L-GMML algorithm on the performance improvements.

Therefore, we can draw the conclusion from the experiments in this subsection that the proposed approach outperforms other metric learning algorithms for the ranking problem regarding accuracy and computational efficiency.

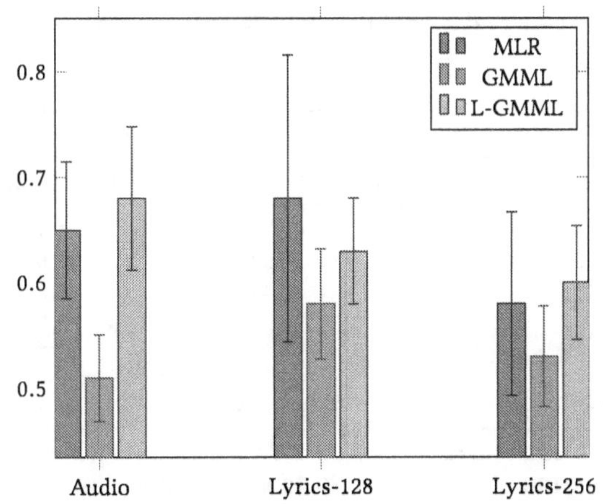

Figure 5: Music similarity performance of each algorithm on the three feature representation Audio, Lyrics-128 and Lyrics-256. Performance was measured by MAP and averaged across 10 folds.

4.5 Comparisons on Large-scale Real-world Datasets

We attempt to find amazing features of our method in the comparisons with two state-of-the-art ranking methods, Gradient-Boosted Regression Trees (GBRT) and λ-MART on Yahoo! Set I&II, MSLR-10K, and MSLR-30K. Because they have been proved to be the most effective in the Yahoo! learning to rank challenge and become the dominant methods in the LtR field.

For these four datasets, the feature domain varies dramatically. To avoid for challenging the floating point precision in complex mathematical computation, we preprocess these four datasets by normalizing each feature dimension with 2-norm. For the stochastic sampling procedure in Algorithm 2, to find the optimal model, we try different initial weight values $\Phi(1)$ ranging from 0.1 to 10, the hinge loss margin ζ ranging from 0.01 to 1.

The training time of GBRT and λ-MART is sensitive to the number of trees in both of the models. The number of local metrics also determines the training time of L-GMML. When we plan to make comparisons on the accuracy and training time of three methods, we fix the number of trees of GBRT and λ-MART as 5000 and the number of local metrics as 500. The motivation of these choices is that the performance of these two methods become stable on the four datasets. The comprehensive comparisons on a different measurement of the above three methods are illustrated in Table 4. From the table, we can draw a conclusion that our approach enjoys a huge advantage in accuracy compared with the state-of-the-art ranking methods.

Currently, the only disadvantage of our approach lies in scoring time. Table 5 displays the comparisons about the time of scoring documents. Our algorithm heavily relies on the scoring for each document in different stages, which is less efficient than GBRT and λ-MART. On the other hand, our approach is simple in structure, and GMML in the first stage is also efficient. Therefore, our method still has an advantage in computationally efficiency. The time-consuming comparison in Table 4 can prove this statement.

5 CONCLUSION

In this paper, we focus on improving the accuracy of LtR methods by utilizing the local structure of documents and degrading irrelevant features. We firstly developed a localized GMML algorithm for the query-independent ranking framework. Specifically, we proposed a concept called *ideal candidate document* to adopt metric learning for ranking algorithm from a query-dependent model to widely used query-independent model. In our approach, a well defined smooth weighting function is optimized by reducing the popular WARP loss, which is defined for the candidate document set of a given query. Then we can efficiently score document by calculating the distance between candidate documents and a nonexistent *ideal candidate document* from an optimized metric space. The experiments prove that our approach outperforms both of the state-of-the-art query-dependent algorithms and query-independent algorithms.

6 ACKNOWLEDGMENTS

We would like to thank the anonymous reviewers for their valuable comments and suggestions to improve the quality of the paper. The work described in this paper was partially supported by the Research Grants Council of the Hong Kong Special Administrative Region, China (No. CUHK 14208815 and No. CUHK 14234416 of the General Research Fund), and 2015 Microsoft Research Asia Collaborative Research Program (Project No. FY16- RES-THEME-005).

REFERENCES

[1] D. Broomhead, D. S. and Lowe. 1988. Multivariable Functional Interpolation and Adaptive Networks. *Complex Systems* 2 (1988), 321– 355.

[2] Chris Burges, Tal Shaked, Erin Renshaw, Ari Lazier, Matt Deeds, Nicole Hamilton, and Greg Hullender. 2005. Learning to rank using gradient descent. In *Proceedings of the 22nd international conference on Machine learning - ICML '05*. 89–96. DOI: http://dx.doi.org/10.1145/1102351.1102363

[3] Christopher J C Burges. 2010. From RankNet to LambdaRank to LambdaMART : An Overview. *Technical Report* (2010).

[4] Christopher J C Burges, Krysta M Svore, Paul N. Bennett, Andrzej Pastusiak, and Qiang Wu. 2011. Learning to Rank Using an Ensemble of Lambda-Gradient Models. *Journal of Machine Learning Research (JMLR): Workshop and Conference Proceedings* 14 (2011), 25–35.

[5] Zhe Cao, Tao Qin, Tie-Yan Liu, Ming-Feng Tsai, and Hang Li. 2007. Learning to rank. In *Proceedings of the 24th international conference on Machine learning - ICML '07*. ACM Press, New York, New York, USA, 129–136. DOI: http://dx.doi.org/10.1145/1273496.1273513

[6] Olivier Chapelle. 2011. Yahoo ! Learning to Rank Challenge Overview. *JMLR: Workshop and Conference Proceedings* 14 (2011), 1–24.

[7] Gal Chechik, Varun Sharma, Uri Shalit, and Samy Bengio. 2010. Large Scale Online Learning of Image Similarity Through Ranking. *The Journal of Machine Learning Research* 11 (3 2010), 1109–1135.

[8] Jason V Davis, Brian Kulis, Prateek Jain, Suvrit Sra, and Inderjit S Dhillon. 2007. Information-theoretic metric learning. In *Proceedings of the 24th international conference on Machine learning - ICML '07*. ACM Press, New York, New York, USA, 209–216. DOI: http://dx.doi.org/10.1145/1273496.1273523

[9] Clebson C.A. de Sá, Marcos A. Gonçalves, Daniel X. Sousa, and Thiago Salles. 2016. Generalized BROOF-L2R. In *Proceedings of the 39th International ACM SIGIR conference on Research and Development in Information Retrieval - SIGIR '16*. ACM Press, New York, New York, USA, 95–104. DOI: http://dx.doi.org/10.1145/2911451.2911540

[10] Yoav Freund, Raj Iyer, Robert E Schapire, and Yoram Singer. 2003. An Efficient Boosting Algorithm for Combining Preferences. *Journal of Machine Learning Research* 4 (2003), 933–969. DOI: http://dx.doi.org/10.1162/jmlr.2003.4.6.933

[11] Jerome H. Friedman. 2001. Greedy function approximation: A gradient boosting machine. *Annals of Statistics* 29, 5 (2001), 1189–1232. DOI: http://dx.doi.org/DOI10.1214/aos/1013203451 arXiv:arXiv:1011.1669v3

Table 4: Performance of GBRT, λ-MART and proposed L-GMML on large-scale real-world datasets. Results of MSLR-WEB10K and MSLR-WEB30K are averaged from the 5 folds in the datasets.

Dataset		GBRT		λ-MART		L-GMML	
		Test Set	Time (min.)	Test Set	Time (min.)	Test Set	Time (min.)
Yahoo! Set I	NDCG@5	0.6529	41.2	0.6567	46.5	**0.6698**	28.1
	NDCG@10	0.6824	43.3	**0.7060**	48.0	0.6715	28.9
	NDCG@20	0.6912	41.5	**0.7091**	46.9	0.6934	28.8
Yahoo! Set II	NDCG@5	0.6731	37.6	0.6791	43.1	**0.7096**	26.5
	NDCG@10	0.6817	36.8	0.7062	43.3	**0.7264**	26.6
	NDCG@20	0.6954	37.4	0.7087	43.8	**0.7219**	26.4
MSLR-WEB10K	NDCG@5	0.4019 ± **0.0083**	49.4 ± 5.2	0.4417 ± 0.0131	58.3 ± 2.8	**0.4771** ± 0.0951	19.7 ± 2.1
	NDCG@10	0.4342 ± 0.0219	48.3 ± 2.1	0.4513 ± **0.0196**	57.6 ± 3.8	**0.5390** ± 0.0812	19 ± 3.1
	NDCG@20	0.4512 ± 0.0279	48.8 ± 3.8	0.4634 ± **0.0257**	57.1 ± 5.2	**0.551** ± 0.0728	19 ± 2.8
MSLR-WEB30K	NDCG@5	0.409 ± 0.0312	167 ± 28.6	0.3812 ± **0.0297**	182 ± 19.8	**0.4837** ± 0.0715	71.7 ± 2.7
	NDCG@10	0.4146 ± 0.0327	177 ± 30.1	0.409 ± **0.0232**	183 ± 17.9	**0.4976** ± 0.0619	71.9 ± 3.9
	NDCG@20	0.421 ± 0.361	167 ± 27.3	0.4112 ± **0.0240**	181 ± 10.7	**0.5038** ± 0.0718	72.5 ± 5.3

Table 5: Per-document scoring time of GBRT, λ-MART and L-GMML on Yahoo! and MSLR datasets. The scoring time is united in *ms*

	GBRT	λ-MART	L-GMML
Yahoo! Set I	276	302	421
Yahoo! Set II	218	286	421
MSLR-WEB10K	73	92	158

[12] Yasser Ganjisaffar, Rich Caruana, and Cristina Videira Lopes. 2011. Bagging gradient-boosted trees for high precision, low variance ranking models. In *Proceedings of the 34th international ACM SIGIR conference on Research and development in Information - SIGIR '11*. ACM Press, New York, New York, USA, 85. DOI: http://dx.doi.org/10.1145/2009916.2009932

[13] SÃ¸ren Hauberg, Oren Freifeld, and Michael J. Black. 2012. A Geometric take on Metric Learning. In *Advances in Neural Information Processing Systems*. 2024–2032.

[14] Bruno Iannazzo. 2016. The geometric mean of two matrices from a computational viewpoint. *Numerical Linear Algebra with Applications* 23, 2 (3 2016), 208–229. DOI: http://dx.doi.org/10.1002/nla.2022

[15] Kalervo Järvelin and Jaana Kekäläinen. 2002. Cumulated gain-based evaluation of IR techniques. *ACM Trans. Inf. Syst.* 20, 4 (2002), 422–446. DOI: http://dx.doi.org/10.1145/582415.582418

[16] Brian Kulis. 2013. Metric Learning: A Survey. *Foundations and Trends® in Machine Learning* 5, 4 (2013), 287–364. DOI: http://dx.doi.org/10.1561/2200000019

[17] Ping Li, Qiang Wu, and Christopher J. Burges. 2008. McRank: Learning to Rank Using Multiple Classification and Gradient Boosting. In *Advances in Neural Information Processing Systems*. 897–904.

[18] Daryl Lim and Gert Lanckriet. 2014. Efficient Learning of Mahalanobis Metrics for Ranking. In *Proceedings of The 31st International Conference on Machine Learning*. 1980–1988.

[19] Daryl K H Lim, Brian Mcfee, and Gert Lanckriet. 2013. Robust Structural Metric Learning. *Proceeding of the 30th International Conference on Machine Learning (ICML '13)* 28 (2013), 615–623.

[20] Kuan Liu, AurÃ©lien Bellet, and Fei Sha. 2015. Similarity Learning for High-Dimensional Sparse Data. *Aistats* 38 (2015), 1–14.

[21] Tie-Yan Liu. 2009. Learning to Rank for Information Retrieval. *Foundations and Trends® in Information Retrieval* 3, 3 (6 2009), 225–331. DOI: http://dx.doi.org/10.1561/1500000016

[22] Claudio Lucchese, Franco Maria Nardini, Salvatore Orlando, Raffaele Perego, and Nicola Tonellotto. 2015. Speeding up Document Ranking with Rank-based Features. In *Proceedings of the 38th International ACM SIGIR Conference on Research and Development in Information Retrieval - SIGIR '15*. ACM Press, New York, New York, USA, 895–898. DOI: http://dx.doi.org/10.1145/2766462.2767776

[23] Brian McFee. 2012. *More like this: machine learning approaches to music similarity.* Ph.D. Dissertation.

[24] Brian McFee, Luke Barrington, and Gert Lanckriet. 2012. Learning content similarity for music recommendation. *IEEE Transactions on Audio, Speech and Language Processing* 20, 8 (2012), 2207–2218. DOI: http://dx.doi.org/10.1109/TASL.2012.2199109

[25] Brian McFee and Gert R Lanckriet. 2010. Metric learning to rank. *Proceedings of the 27th International Conference on Machine Learning (ICML-10)* (2010), 775–782.

[26] Yung-Kyun Noh, Byoung-Tak Zhang, and Daniel D Lee. 2010. Generative local metric learning for nearest neighbor classification. *Advances in Neural Information Processing Systems* 18 (2010), 417–424.

[27] Deva Ramanan and Simon Baker. 2011. Local Distance Functions A Taxonomy, New Algorithms, and an Evaluation. *IEEE Transactions on Pattern Analysis and Machine Intelligence* 33, 4 (2011), 794–806.

[28] Rómer Rosales and Glenn Fung. 2006. Learning sparse metrics via linear programming. In *Proceedings of the 12th ACM SIGKDD international conference on Knowledge discovery and data mining - KDD '06*. ACM Press, New York, New York, USA, 367. DOI: http://dx.doi.org/10.1145/1150402.1150444

[29] Chunhua Shen, Junae Kim, Lei Wang, and Anton van den Hengel. 2012. Positive Semidefinite Metric Learning Using Boosting-like Algorithms. *Journal of Machine Learning Research* 13 (2012), 1007–1036. http://dl.acm.org/citation.cfm?id=2343679

[30] Derek Tingle, Youngmoo E. Kim, and Douglas Turnbull. 2010. Exploring automatic music annotation with "acoustically-objective" tags. In *Proceedings of the international conference on Multimedia information retrieval - MIR '10*. ACM Press, New York, New York, USA, 55. DOI: http://dx.doi.org/10.1145/1743384.1743400

[31] Jun Wang, Alexandros Kalousis, and Adam Woznica. 2012. Parametric Local Metric Learning for Nearest Neighbor Classification. In *Advances in Neural Information Processing Systems*. 1601–1609.

[32] Kilian Q Weinberger and Lawrence K Saul. 2009. Distance Metric Learning for Large Margin Nearest Neighbor Classification. *Journal of Machine Learning Research* 10 (2009), 207–244. DOI: http://dx.doi.org/10.1126/science.277.5323.215

[33] Jason Weston, Samy Bengio, and Nicolas Usunier. 2010. Large scale image annotation: Learning to rank with joint word-image embeddings. *Machine Learning* 81, 1 (2010), 21–35. DOI: http://dx.doi.org/10.1007/s10994-010-5198-3

[34] Eric P. Xing, Michael I. Jordan, Stuart J. Russell, and Andrew Y. Ng. 2002. Distance Metric Learning with Application to Clustering with Side-Information. In *Advances in Neural Information Processing Systems*. 521–528.

[35] Zhixiang Eddie Xu, Kilian Q Weinberger, Olivier Chapelle, St Louis, and Olivier Chapelle Cc. 2012. The Greedy Miser: Learning under Test-time Budgets. In *Proceedings of the 29th International Conference on Machine Learning (ICML-12)*. 1175–1182.

[36] Pourya Habib Zadeh, Reshad Hosseini, and Suvrit Sra. 2016. Geometric mean metric learning. In *Proceedings of the 33rd International Conference on Machine Learning (ICML '16)*. 2464–2471.

End-to-End Neural Ad-hoc Ranking with Kernel Pooling

Chenyan Xiong*
Carnegie Mellon University
cx@cs.cmu.edu

Zhuyun Dai*
Carnegie Mellon University
zhuyund@cs.cmu.edu

Jamie Callan
Carnegie Mellon University
callan@cs.cmu.edu

Zhiyuan Liu
Tsinghua University
liuzy@tsinghua.edu.cn

Russell Power
Allen Institute for AI
russellp@allenai.org

ABSTRACT

This paper proposes K-NRM, a kernel based neural model for document ranking. Given a query and a set of documents, K-NRM uses a translation matrix that models word-level similarities via word embeddings, a new kernel-pooling technique that uses kernels to extract multi-level soft match features, and a learning-to-rank layer that combines those features into the final ranking score. The whole model is trained end-to-end. The ranking layer learns desired feature patterns from the pairwise ranking loss. The kernels transfer the feature patterns into soft-match targets at each similarity level and enforce them on the translation matrix. The word embeddings are tuned accordingly so that they can produce the desired soft matches. Experiments on a commercial search engine's query log demonstrate the improvements of K-NRM over prior feature-based and neural-based states-of-the-art, and explain the source of K-NRM's advantage: Its kernel-guided embedding encodes a similarity metric tailored for matching query words to document words, and provides effective multi-level soft matches.

KEYWORDS

Ranking, Neural IR, Kernel Pooling, Relevance Model, Embedding

1 INTRODUCTION

In traditional information retrieval, queries and documents are typically represented by discrete bags-of-words, the ranking is based on exact matches between query and document words, and trained ranking models rely heavily on feature engineering. In comparison, newer neural information retrieval (neural IR) methods use continuous text embeddings, model the query-document relevance via soft matches, and aim to learn feature representations automatically. With the successes of deep learning in many related areas, neural IR has the potential to redefine the boundaries of information retrieval; however, achieving that potential has been difficult so far.

*The first two authors contributed equally.

SIGIR '17, August 07-11, 2017, Shinjuku, Tokyo, Japan

DOI: http://dx.doi.org/10.1145/3077136.3080809

Many neural approaches use distributed representations (e.g., word2vec [17]), but in spite of many efforts, distributed representations have a limited history of success for document ranking. Exact match of query words to document words is a strong signal of relevance [8], whereas soft-match is a weaker signal that must be used carefully. Word2vec may consider 'pittsburgh' to be similar to 'boston', and 'hotel' to be similar to 'motel'. However, a person searching for 'pittsburgh hotel' may accept a document about 'pittsburgh motel', but probably will reject a document about 'boston hotel'. How to use these soft-match signals effectively and reliably is an open problem.

This work addresses these challenges with a kernel based neural ranking model (K-NRM). K-NRM uses distributed representations to represent query and document words. Their similarities are used to construct a translation model. Word pair similarities are combined by a new kernel-pooling layer that uses kernels to softly count the frequencies of word pairs at different similarity levels (soft-TF). The soft-TF signals are used as features in a ranking layer, which produces the final ranking score. All of these layers are differentiable and allow K-NRM to be optimized end-to-end.

The kernels are the key to K-NRM's capability. During learning, the kernels convert the learning-to-rank loss to requirements on soft-TF patterns, and adjust the word embeddings to produce a soft match that can better separate the relevant and irrelevant documents. This kernel-guided embedding learning encodes a similarity metric tailored for matching query and document. The tailored similarity metric is conveyed by the learned embeddings, which produces effective multi-level soft-matches for ad-hoc ranking.

Extensive experiments on a commercial search engine's query log demonstrate the significant and robust advantage of K-NRM. On different evaluation scenarios (in-domain, cross-domain and raw user clicks), and on different parts of the query log (head, torso, and tail), K-NRM outperforms both feature-based ranking and neural ranking states-of-the-art by as much as 65%. K-NRM's advantage is not from an unexplainable 'deep learning magic', but the long-desired soft match achieved by its kernel-guided embedding learning. In our analysis, if used without the multi-level soft match or the embedding learning, the advantage of K-NRM quickly diminishes; while with the kernel-guided embedding learning, K-NRM successfully learns relevance-focused soft matches using its embedding and ranking layers, and the memorized ranking preferences generalize well to different testing scenarios.

The next section discusses related work. Section 3 presents the kernel-based neural ranking model. Experimental methodology is discussed in Section 4 and evaluation results are presented in Section 5. Section 6 concludes.

2 RELATED WORK

Retrieval models such as query likelihood and BM25 are based on exact matching of query and document words, which limits the information available to the ranking model and may lead to problems such *vocabulary mismatch* [4]. *Statistical translation models* were an attempt to overcome this limitation. They model query-document relevance using a pre-computed *translation matrix* that describes the similarities between word pairs [1]. At query time, the ranking function considers the similarities of all query and document word pairs, allowing query words to be soft-matched to document words. The translation matrix can be calculated via mutual information in a corpus [12] or using user clicks [6].

Word pair interactions have also been modeled by *word embeddings*. Word embeddings trained from surrounding contexts, for example, word2vec [17], are considered to be the factorization of word pairs' PMI matrix [14]. Compared to word pair similarities which are hard to learn, word embeddings provide a smooth low-level approximation of word similarities that may improve translation models [8, 24].

Some research has questioned whether word embeddings based on surrounding context, such as word2vec, are suitable for ad hoc ranking. Instead, it customizes word embeddings for search tasks. Nalisnick et al. propose to match query and documents using both the input and output of the embedding model, instead of only using one side of them [19]. Diaz et al. find that word embeddings trained locally on pseudo relevance feedback documents are more related to the query's information needs, and can provide better query expansion terms [5].

Current neural ranking models fall into two groups: *representation* based and *interaction* based [8]. The earlier focus of neural IR was mainly on *representation* based models, in which the query and documents are first embedded into continuous vectors, and the ranking is calculated from their embeddings' similarity. For example, DSSM [11] and its convolutional version CDSSM [22] map words to letter-tri-grams, embed query and documents using neural networks built upon the letter-tri-grams, and rank documents using their embedding similarity with the query.

The *interaction* based neural models, on the other hand, learn query-document matching patterns from word-level interactions. For example, ARC-II [10] and MatchPyramid [20] build hierarchical Convolutional Neural Networks (CNN) on the interactions of two texts' word embeddings; they are effective in matching tweet-retweet and question-answers [10]. The Deep Relevance Matching Model (DRMM) uses pyramid pooling (histogram) [7] to summarize the word-level similarities into ranking signals [9]. The word level similarities are calculated from pre-trained word2vec embeddings, and the histogram counts the number of word pairs at different similarity levels. The counts are combined by a feed forward network to produce final ranking scores. *Interaction* based models and *representation* based models address the ranking task from different perspectives, and can be combined for further improvements [18].

This work builds upon the ideas of customizing word embeddings and the *interaction* based neural models: K-NRM ranks documents using soft matches from query-document word interactions, and learns to encode the relevance preferences using customized word embeddings at the same time, which is achieved by the kernels.

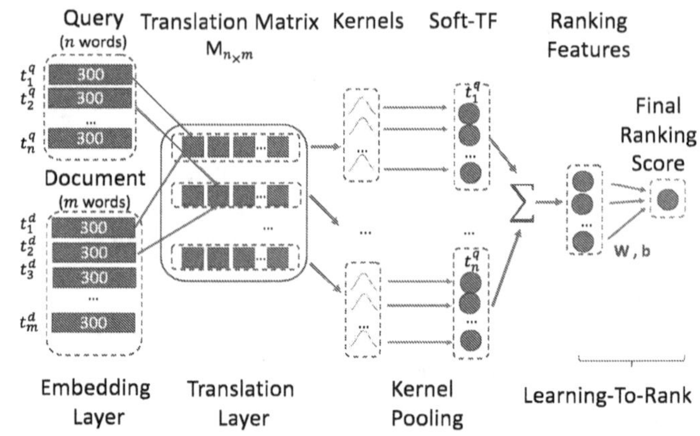

Figure 1: The Architecture of K-NRM. Given input query words and document words, the embedding layer maps them into distributed representations, the translation layer calculates the word-word similarities and forms the translation matrix, the kernel pooling layer generate soft-TF counts as ranking features, and the learning to rank layer combines the soft-TF to the final ranking score.

3 KERNEL BASED NEURAL RANKING

This section presents K-NRM, our kernel based neural ranking model. We first discuss how K-NRM produces the ranking score for a query-document pair with their words as the sole input (ranking from scratch). Then we derive how the ranking parameters and word embeddings in K-NRM are trained from ranking labels (learning end-to-end).

3.1 Ranking from Scratch

Given a query q and a document d, K-NRM aims to generate a ranking score $f(q, d)$ only using query words $q = \{t_1^q, ...t_i^q ..., t_n^q\}$ and document words $d = \{t_1^d, ...t_j^d ..., t_m^d\}$. As shown in Figure 1, K-NRM achieves this goal via three components: translation model, kernel-pooling, and learning to rank.

Translation Model: K-NRM first uses an `embedding layer` to map each word t to an L-dimension embedding $\vec{v}_t$:

$$t \Rightarrow \vec{v}_t.$$

Then a `translation layer` constructs a translation matrix M. Each element in M is the embedding similarity between a query word and a document word:

$$M_{ij} = \cos(\vec{v}_{t_i^q}, \vec{v}_{t_j^d}).$$

The translation model in K-NRM uses word embeddings to recover the word similarities instead of trying to learn one for each word pair. Doing so requires much fewer parameters to learn. For a vocabulary of size $|V|$ and the embedding dimension L, K-NRM's translation model includes $|V| \times L$ embedding parameters, much fewer than learning all pairwise similarities ($|V|^2$).

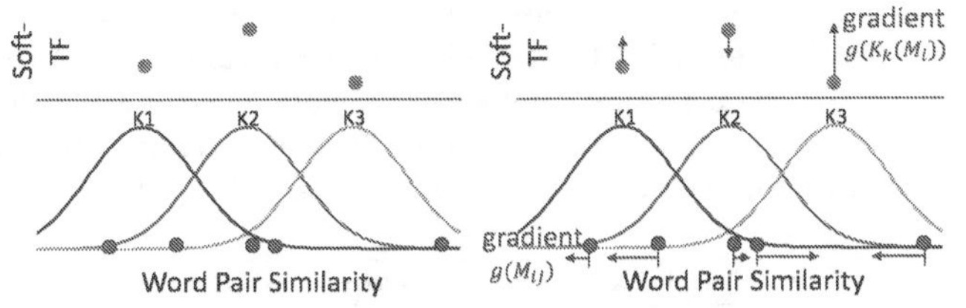

(a) Ranking (b) Learning

Figure 2: Illustration of kernels in the ranking (forward) process and learning (backward) process.

Kernel-Pooling: K-NRM then uses kernels to convert word-word interactions in the translation matrix M to query-document ranking features $\phi(M)$:

$$\phi(M) = \sum_{i=1}^{n} \log \vec{K}(M_i)$$
$$\vec{K}(M_i) = \{K_1(M_i), ..., K_K(M_i)\}$$

$\vec{K}(M_i)$ applies K kernels to the i-th query word's row of the translation matrix, summarizing (pooling) it into a K-dimensional feature vector. The log-sum of each query word's feature vector forms the query-document ranking feature vector ϕ.

The effect of $\vec{K}$ depends on the kernel used. This work uses the RBF kernel:

$$K_k(M_i) = \sum_j \exp(-\frac{(M_{ij} - \mu_k)^2}{2\sigma_k^2}).$$

As illustrated in Figure 2a, the RBF kernel K_k calculates how word pair similarities are distributed around it: the more word pairs with similarities closer to its mean μ_k, the higher its value. Kernel pooling with RBF kernels is a generalization of existing pooling techniques. As $\sigma \rightarrow \infty$, the kernel pooling function devolves to the mean pooling. $\mu = 1$ and $\sigma \rightarrow 0$ results in a kernel that only responds to exact matches, equivalent to the TF value from sparse models. Otherwise, the kernel functions as 'soft-TF'[1]. μ defines the similarity level that 'soft-TF' focuses on; for example, a kernel with $\mu = 0.5$ calculates the number of document words whose similarities to the query word are close to 0.5. σ defines the kernel width, or the range of its 'soft-TF' count.

Learning to Rank: The ranking features $\phi(M)$ are combined by a ranking layer to produce the final ranking score:

$$f(q, d) = \tanh(w^T \phi(M) + b).$$

w and b are the ranking parameters to learn. tanh() is the activation function. It controls the range of ranking score to facilitate the learning process. It is rank-equivalent to a typical linear learning to rank model.

[1]The RBF kernel is one of the most popular choices. Other kernels with similar density estimation effects can also be used, as long as they are differentiable. For example, polynomial kernel can be used, but histograms [9] cannot as they are not differentiable.

Putting every together, K-NRM is defined as:

$$f(q, d) = \tanh(w^T \phi(M) + b) \quad \text{Learning to Rank} \quad (1)$$
$$\phi(M) = \sum_{i=1}^{n} \log \vec{K}(M_i) \quad \text{Soft-TF Features} \quad (2)$$
$$\vec{K}(M_i) = \{K_1(M_i), ..., K_K(M_i)\} \quad \text{Kernel Pooling} \quad (3)$$
$$K_k(M_i) = \sum_j \exp(-\frac{(M_{ij} - \mu_k)^2}{2\sigma_k^2}) \quad \text{RBF Kernel} \quad (4)$$
$$M_{ij} = \cos(\vec{v}_{t_i^q}, \vec{v}_{t_j^d}) \quad \text{Translation Matrix} \quad (5)$$
$$t \Rightarrow \vec{v}_t. \quad \text{Word Embedding} \quad (6)$$

Eq. 5-6 embed query words and document words, and calculate the translation matrix. The kernels (Eq. 4) count the soft matches between query and document's word pairs at multiple levels, and generate K soft-TF ranking features (Eq. 2-3). Eq. 1 is the learning to rank model. The ranking of K-NRM requires no manual features. The only input used is the query and document words. The kernels extract soft-TF ranking features from word-word interactions automatically.

3.2 Learning End-to-End

The **training** of K-NRM uses the pairwise learning to rank loss:

$$l(w, b, \mathcal{V}) = \sum_q \sum_{d^+, d^- \in D_q^{+,-}} max(0, 1 - f(q, d^+) + f(q, d^-)). \quad (7)$$

$D_q^{+,-}$ are the pairwise preferences from the ground truth: d^+ ranks higher than d^-. The parameters to learn include the ranking parameters w, b, and the word embeddings $\mathcal{V}$.

The parameters are optimized using back propagation (BP) through the neural network. Starting from the ranking loss, the gradients are first propagated to the learning-to-rank part (Eq. 1) and update the ranking parameters (w, b), the kernels pass the gradients to the word similarities (Eq. 2-4), and then to the embeddings (Eq. 5).

Back propagations through the kernels: The embeddings contain millions of parameters $\mathcal{V}$ and are the main capacity of the model. The learning of the embeddings is guided by the kernels.

The back propagation first applies gradients from the loss function (Eq. 7) to the ranking score $f(q, d)$, to increase it (for d^+) or decrease it (for d^-); the gradients are propagated through Eq. 1 to the feature vector $\phi(M)$, and then through Eq. 2 to the the kernel scores $\vec{K}(M_i)$. The resulted $g(\vec{K}(M_i))$ is a K dimensional vector:

$$g(\vec{K}(M_i)) = \{g(K_1(M_i)), ..., g(K_K(M_i)\}.$$

Its each dimension $g(K_k(M_i))$ is jointly defined by the ranking score's gradients and the ranking parameters. It adjusts the corresponding kernel's score up or down to better separate the relevant document (d^+) from the irrelevant one (d^-).

The kernels spread the gradient to word similarities in the translation matrix M_{ij}, through Eq. 4:

$$g(M_{ij}) = \sum_{k=1}^{K} \frac{g(K_k(M_i)) \times \sigma_k^2}{(\mu_k - M_{ij}) \exp(\frac{(M_{ij} - \mu_k)^2}{-2\sigma_k^2})}. \quad (8)$$

The kernel-guided embedding learning process is illustrated in Figure 2b. A kernel pulls the word similarities closer to its μ to

Table 1: Training and testing dataset characteristics.

	Training	Testing
Queries	95,229	1,000
Documents Per Query	12.17	30.50
Search Sessions	31,201,876	4,103,230
Vocabulary Size	165,877	19,079

increase its soft-TF count, or pushes the word pairs away to reduce it, based on the gradients received in the back-propagation. The *strength* of the force also depends on the the kernel's width σ_k and the word pair's distance to μ_k: approximately, the wider the kernel is (bigger σ_k), and the closer the word pair's similarity to μ_k, the stronger the force is (Eq. 8). The gradient a word pair's similarity received, $g(M_{ij})$, is the combination of the forces from all K kernels.

The word embedding model receives $g(M_{ij})$ and updates the embeddings accordingly. Intuitively, the learned word embeddings are aligned to form multi-level soft-TF patterns that can separate the relevant documents from the irrelevant ones in training, and the learned embedding parameters $\mathcal{V}$ memorize this information. When testing, K-NRM extracts soft-TF features from the learned word embeddings using the kernels and produces the final ranking score using the ranking layer.

4 EXPERIMENTAL METHODOLOGY

This section describes our experimental methods and materials.

4.1 Dataset

Our experiments use a query log sampled from search logs of Sogou.com, a major Chinese commercial search engine. The sample contains 35 million search sessions with 96,229 distinct queries. The query log includes queries, displayed documents, user clicks, and dwell times. Each query has an average of 12 documents displayed. As the results come from a commercial search engine, the returned documents tend to be of very high quality.

The primary testing queries were 1,000 queries sampled from head queries that appeared more than 1,000 times in the query log. Most of our evaluation focuses on the head queries; we use tail query performance to evaluate model robustness. The remaining queries were used to train the neural models. Table 1 provides summary statistics for the training and testing portions of the search log.

The query log contains only document titles and URLs. The full texts of *testing* documents were crawled and parsed using Boilerpipe [13] for our word-based baselines (described in Section 4.3). Chinese text was segmented using the open source software ICTCLAS [23]. After segmentation, documents are treated as sequences of words (as with English documents).

4.2 Relevance Labels and Evaluation Scenarios

Neural models like K-NRM and CDSSM require a large amount of training data. Acquiring a sufficient number of manual training labels outside of a large organization would be cost-prohibitive. User click data, on the other hand, is easy to acquire and prior research has shown that it can accurately predict manual labels. For our experiments **training labels** were generated based on user clicks from the training sessions.

Table 2: Testing Scenarios. DCTR Scores are inferred by DCTR click model [3]. TACM Scores are inferred by TACM click model [15]. Raw Clicks use the sole click in a session as the positive label. The label distribution is the number of relevance labels from 0-4 from left to right, if applicable.

Condition	Label	Label Distribution
Testing-SAME	DCTR Scores	70%, 19.6%, 9.8%, 1.3%, 1.1%
Testing-DIFF	TACM Scores	79%, 14.7%, 4.6%, 0.9%, 0.9%
Testing-RAW	Raw Clicks	2,349,280 clicks

There is a large amount of prior research on building *click models* to model user behavior and to infer reliable relevance signals from clicks [3]. This work uses one of the simplest click models, DCTR, to generate relevance scores from user clicks [3]. DCTR calculates the relevance scores of a query-document pair based on their click through rates. Despite being extremely simple, it performs rather well and is a widely used baseline [3]. Relevance scores from DCTR are then used to generate preference pairs to train our models.

The **testing labels** were also estimated from the click log, as manual relevance judgments were not made available to us. *Note that there was no overlap between training queries and testing queries.*

Testing-SAME infers relevance labels using DCTR, the same click model used for training. This setting evaluates the ranking model's ability to fit user preferences (click through rates).

Testing-DIFF infers relevance scores using TACM [15], a state-of-the-art click model. TACM is a more sophisticated model and uses both clicks and dwell times. On an earlier sample of Sogou's query log, the TACM labels aligned extremely well with expert annotations: when evaluated against manual labels, TACM achieved an NDCG@5 of up to 0.97 [15]. This is substantially higher than the agreement between the manual labels generated by the authors for a sample of queries. This precision makes TACM's inferred scores a good approximation of expert labels, and Testing-DIFF is expected to produce evaluation results similar to expert labels.

Testing-RAW is the simplest click model. Following the cascade assumption [3], we treat the clicked document in each single-click session as a relevant document, and test whether the model can put it at the top of the ranking. Testing-Raw only uses single-click sessions (57% of the testing sessions are single-click sessions). Testing-RAW is a conservative setting that uses *raw* user feedback. It eliminates the influence of click models in testing, and evaluates the ranking model's ability to overcome possible disturbances from the click models.

The three testing scenarios are listed in Table 2. Following TREC methodology, the Testing-SAME and Testing-DIFF's inferred relevance scores were mapped to 5 relevance grades. Thresholds were chosen so that our relevance grades have the same distribution as TREC Web Track 2009-2012 qrels.

Search quality was measured using NDCG at depths $\{1, 3, 10\}$ for Testing-SAME and Testing-DIFF. We focused on early ranking positions that are more important for commercial search engines. Testing-RAW was evaluated by mean reciprocal rank (MRR) as there is only one relevant document per query. Statistical significance was tested using the permutation test with $p < 0.05$.

Table 3: The number of parameters and the word embeddings used by baselines and K-NRM. '–' indicates not applicable, e.g. unsupervised methods have no parameters, and word-based methods do not use embeddings.

Method	Number of Parameters	Embedding
Lm, BM25	–	–
RankSVM	21	–
Coor-Ascent	21	–
Trans	–	word2vec
DRMM	161	word2vec
CDSSM	10,877,657	–
K-NRM	49,763,110	end-to-end

4.3 Baselines

Our baselines include both traditional word-based ranking models as well as more recent neural ranking models.

Word-based baselines include BM25 and language models with Dirichlet smoothing (Lm). These unsupervised retrieval methods were applied on the full text of candidate documents, and used to re-rank them. We found that these methods performed better on full text than on titles. Full text default parameters were used.

Feature-based learning to rank baselines include RankSVM[2], a state-of-the-art pairwise ranker, and coordinate ascent [16] (Coor-Ascent[3]), a state-of-the-art listwise ranker. They use typical word-based features: Boolean AND; Boolean OR; Coordinate match; TF-IDF; BM25; language models with no smoothing, Dirichlet smoothing, JM smoothing and two-way smoothing; and bias. All features were applied to the document title and body. The parameters of the retrieval models used in feature extraction are kept default.

Neural ranking baselines include DRMM [9], CDSSM [21], and a simple embedding-based translation model, Trans.

DRMM is the state-of-the-art interaction based neural ranking model [9]. It performs histogram pooling on the embedding based translation matrix and uses the binned soft-TF as the input to a ranking neural network. The embeddings used are pre-trained via word2vec [17] because the histograms are not differentiable and prohibit end-to-end learning. We implemented the best variant, $\text{DRMM}_{\text{LCH}\times\text{IDF}}$. The pre-trained embeddings were obtained by applying the skip-gram method from word2vec on our training corpus (document titles displayed in training sessions).

CDSSM [22] is the convolutional version of DSSM [11]. CDSSM maps English words to letter-tri-grams using a word-hashing technique, and uses Convolutional Neural Networks to build representations of the query and document upon the letter-tri-grams. It is a state-of-the-art representation based neural ranking model. We implemented CDSSM in Chinese by convolving over Chinese characters. (Chinese characters can be considered as similar to English letter-tri-grams with respect to word meaning). CDSSM is also an end-to-end model, but uses discrete letter-tri-grams/Chinese characters instead of word embeddings.

Trans is an unsupervised embedding based translation model. Its translation matrix is calculated by the cosine similarity of word embeddings from the same word2vec used in DRMM, and then averaged to the query-document ranking score.

Baseline Settings: RankSVM uses a linear kernel and the hyper-parameter C was selected in the development fold of the cross validation from the range [0.0001, 10].

Recommended settings from RankLib were used for Coor-Ascent.

We obtained the body texts of testing documents from the new Sogou-T corpus [2] or crawled them directly. The body texts were used by all word-based baselines. Neural ranking baselines and K-NRM used only titles for training and testing, as the coverage of Sogou-T on the training documents is low and the training documents could not be crawled given resource constraints.

For all baselines, the most optimistic choices were made: feature-based methods (RankSVM and Coor-Ascent) were trained using 10-fold cross-validation on the *testing* set and use both document title and body texts. The neural models were trained on the training set with the same settings as K-NRM, and only use document titles (they still perform better than only using the testing data). Theoretically, this gives the sparse models a slight performance advantage as their training and testing data were drawn from the same distribution.

4.4 Implementation Details

This section describes the configurations of our K-NRM model.

Model training was done on the full training data as in Table 1, with training labels inferred by DCTR, as described in Section 4.2.

The **embedding layer** used 300 dimensions. The vocabulary size of our training data was 165, 877. The embedding layer was initialized with the word2vec trained on our training corpus.

The **kernel pooling layer** had $K = 11$ kernels. One kernel harvests exact matches, using $\mu_0 = 1.0$ and $\sigma = 10^{-3}$. μ of the other 10 kernels is spaced evenly in the range of $[-1, 1]$, that is $\mu_1 = 0.9, \mu_2 = 0.7, ..., \mu_{10} = -0.9$. These kernels can be viewed as 10 soft-TF bins. σ is set to 0.1. The effects of varying σ are studied in Section 5.6.

Model optimization used the Adam optimizer, with batch size 16, learning rate = 0.001 and $\epsilon = 1e-5$. Early stopping was used with a patience of 5 epochs. We implemented our model using TensorFlow. The model training took about 50 milliseconds per batch, and converged in 12 hours on an AWS GPU machine.

Table 3 summarizes the number of parameters used by the baselines and K-NRM. Word2vec refers to pre-trained word embeddings using skip-gram on the training corpus. End-to-end means that the embeddings were trained together with the ranking model.

CDSSM learns hundreds of convolution filters on Chinese *characters*, thus has millions of parameters. K-NRM's parameter space is even larger as it learns an embedding for every Chinese *word*. Models with more parameters in general are expected to fit better but may also require more training data to avoid overfitting.

5 EVALUATION RESULTS

Our experiments investigated K-NRM's effectiveness, as well as its behavior on tail queries, with less training data, and with different kernel widths.

[2]https://www.cs.cornell.edu/people/tj/svm_light/svm_rank.html

[3]https://sourceforge.net/p/lemur/wiki/RankLib/

Table 4: Ranking accuracy of K-NRM and baseline methods. Relative performances compared with Coor-Ascent are in percentages. Win/Tie/Loss are the number of queries improved, unchanged, or hurt, compared to Coor-Ascent on NDCG@10. †, ‡, §, ¶ indicate statistically significant improvements over Coor-Ascent†, Trans‡, DRMM§ and CDSSM¶, respectively.

(a) Testing-SAME. Testing labels are inferred by the same click model (DCTR) as the training labels used by neural models.

Method	NDCG@1		NDCG@3		NDCG@10		W/T/L
Lm	0.1261	−20.89%	0.1648	−26.46%	0.2821	−20.45%	293/116/498
BM25	0.1422	−10.79%	0.1757	−21.60%	0.2868	−10.14%	299/125/483
RankSVM	0.1457	−8.59%	0.1905	−14.99%	0.3087	−12.97%	371/151/385
Coor-Ascent	0.1594‡§¶	–	0.2241‡§¶	–	0.3547‡§¶	–	–/–/–
Trans	0.1347	−15.50%	0.1852	−17.36%	0.3147	−11.28%	318/140/449
DRMM	0.1366	−14.30%	0.1902	−15.13%	0.3150	−11.20%	318/132/457
CDSSM	0.1441	−9.59%	0.2014	−10.13%	0.3329‡§	−6.14%	341/149/417
K-NRM	**0.2642**†‡§¶	+65.75%	**0.3210**†‡§¶	+43.25%	**0.4277**†‡§¶	+20.58%	447/153/307

(b) Testing-DIFF. Testing labels are inferred by a different click model, TACM, which approximates expert labels very well [15].

Method	NDCG@1		NDCG@3		NDCG@10		W/T/L
Lm	0.1852	−11.34%	0.1989	−17.23%	0.3270	−13.38%	369/50/513
BM25	0.1631	−21.92%	0.1894	−21.18%	0.3254	−13.81%	349/53/530
RankSVM	0.1700	−18.62%	0.2036	−15.27%	0.3519	−6.78%	380/75/477
Coor-Ascent	0.2089‡¶	–	0.2403‡	–	0.3775‡¶	–	–/–/–
Trans	0.1874	−10.29%	0.2127	−11.50%	0.3454	−8.51%	385/68/479
DRMM	0.2068	−1.00%	0.2491‡	+3.67%	0.3809‡¶	+0.91%	430/66/436
CDSSM	0.1846	−10.77%	0.2358‡	−1.86%	0.3557	−5.79%	391/65/476
K-NRM	**0.2984**†‡§¶	+42.84%	**0.3092**†‡§¶	+28.26%	**0.4201**†‡§¶	+11.28%	474/63/395

Table 5: Ranking performance on Testing-RAW. MRR evaluates the mean reciprocal rank of clicked documents in single-click sessions. Relative performance in the percentages and W(in)/T(ie)/L(oss) are compared to Coor-Ascent. †, ‡, §, ¶ indicate statistically significant improvements over Coor-Ascent†, Trans‡, DRMM§ and CDSSM¶, respectively.

Method	MRR		W/T/L
Lm	0.2193	−9.19%	416/09/511
BM25	0.2280	−5.57%	456/07/473
RankSVM	0.2241	−7.20%	450/78/473
Coor-Ascent	0.2415‡	–	–/–/–
Trans	0.2181	−9.67%	406/08/522
DRMM	0.2335‡	−3.29%	419/12/505
CDSSM	0.2321‡	−3.90%	405/11/520
K-NRM	**0.3379**†‡§¶	+39.92%	507/05/424

5.1 Ranking Accuracy

Tables 4a, 4b and 5 show the ranking accuracy of K-NRM and our baselines under three conditions.

Testing-SAME (Table 4a) evaluates the model's ability to fit user preferences when trained and evaluated on labels generated by the same click model (DCTR). K-NRM outperforms word-based baselines by over 65% on NDCG@1, and over 20% on NDCG@10. The improvements over neural ranking models are even bigger: On NDCG@1 the margin between K-NRM and the next best neural model is 83%, and on NDCG@10 it is 28%.

Testing-DIFF (Table 4b) evaluates the model's relevance matching performance by testing on TACM inferred relevance labels, a good approximation of expert labels. Because the training and testing labels were generated by different click models, Testing-DIFF challenges each model's ability to fit the underlying relevance signals despite perturbations caused by differing click model biases. Neural models with larger parameter spaces tend to be more vulnerable to this domain difference: CDSSM actually performs worse than DRMM, despite using thousands times more parameters. However, K-NRM demonstrates its robustness and is able to outperform all baselines by more than 40% on NDCG@1 and 10% on NDCG@10.

Testing-RAW (Table 5) evaluates each model's effectiveness directly by user clicks. It tests how well the model ranks the most satisfying document (the only one clicked) in each session. K-NRM improves MRR from 0.2415 (Coor-Ascent) to 0.3379. This difference is equal to moving the clicked document's from rank 4 to rank 3. The MRR and NDCG@1 improvements demonstrate K-NRM's precision oriented property—its biggest advantage is on the earliest ranking positions. This characteristic aligns with K-NRM's potential role in web search engines: as a sophisticate re-ranker, K-NRM is most possibly used at the final ranking stage, in which the first relevant document's ranking position is the most important.

The two neural ranking baselines DRMM and CDSSM perform similarly in all three testing scenarios. The *interaction* based model, DRMM, is more robust to click model biases and performs slightly better on Testing-DIFF, while the *representation* based model, CDSSM, performs slightly better on Testing-SAME. However, the feature-based ranking model, Coor-Ascent, performs better than all neural

Table 6: The ranking performances of several K-NRM variants. Relative performances and statistical significances are all compared with K-NRM's full model. †, ‡, §, ¶, and ∗ indicate statistically significant improvements over K-NRM's variants of exact-match†, word2vec‡, click2vec§, max-pool¶, and mean-pool∗, respectively.

	Testing-SAME				Testing-DIFF				Testing-RAW	
K-NRM Variant	NDCG@1		NDCG@10		NDCG@1		NDCG@10		MRR	
exact-match	0.1351	−49%	0.2943	−31%	0.1788	−40%	0.3460¶	−18%	0.2147	−37%
word2vec	0.1529†	−42%	0.3223†¶	−24%	0.2160†¶	−27%	0.3811†¶	−10%	0.2427†¶	−28%
click2vec	0.1600	−39%	0.3790†‡¶	−11%	0.2314†¶	−23%	0.4002†‡¶∗	−4%	0.2667†‡¶	−21%
max-pool	0.1413	−47%	0.2979	−30%	0.1607	−46%	0.3334	−21%	0.2260	−33%
mean-pool	0.2297†‡§¶	−13%	0.3614†‡§¶	−16%	0.2424†¶	−19%	0.3787†¶	−10%	0.2714†‡¶	−20%
full model	**0.2642**†‡§¶∗	–	**0.4277**†‡§¶∗	–	**0.2984**†‡§¶∗	–	**0.4201**†‡¶∗	–	**0.3379**†‡§¶∗	–

baselines on all three testing scenarios. The differences can be as high as 15% and some are statistically significant. This holds even for Testing-SAME which is expected to favor deep models that access more in-domain training data. These results remind that no 'deep learning magic' can instantly provide significant gains for information retrieval tasks. The development of neural IR models also requires an understanding of the advantages of neural methods and how their advantages can be incorporated to meet the needs of information retrieval tasks.

Table 7: Examples of word matches in different kernels. Words in bold are those whose similarities with the query word fall into the corresponding kernel's range (μ).

μ	Query: 'Maserati' "
1.0	**Maserati** Ghibli black interior _ who knows
0.7	Maserati **Ghibli** black interior _ who knows
0.3	Maserati Ghibli **black** interior **_ who** knows
-0.1	Maserati Ghibli black interior _ who **knows**

5.2 Source of Effectiveness

K-NRM differs from previous ranking methods in several ways: multi-level soft matches, word embeddings learned directly from ranking labels, and the kernel-guided embedding learning. This experiment studies these effects by comparing the following variants of K-NRM.

K-NRM (exact-match) only uses the exact match kernel $(\mu, \sigma) = (1, 0.001)$. It is equivalent to TF.

K-NRM (word2vec) uses pre-trained word2vec, the same as DRMM. Word embedding is fixed; only the ranking part is learned.

K-NRM (click2vec) also uses pre-trained word embedding. But its word embeddings are trained on (query word, clicked title word) pairs. The embeddings are trained using skip-gram model with the same settings used to train word2vec. These embeddings are fixed during ranking.

K-NRM (max-pool) replaces kernel-pooling with max-pooling. Max-pooling finds the maximum similarities between document words and each query word; it is commonly used by neural network architectures. In our case, given the candidate documents' high quality, the maximum is almost always 1, thus it is similar to TF.

K-NRM (mean-pool) replaces kernel-pooling with mean-pooling. It is similar to Trans except that the embedding is trained by learning-to-rank.

All other settings are kept the same as K-NRM. Table 6 shows their evaluation results, together with the full model of K-NRM.

Soft match is essential. K-NRM (exact-match) performs similarly to Lm and BM25, as does K-NRM (max-pool). This is expected: without soft matches, the only signal for K-NRM to work with is effectively the TF score.

Ad-hoc ranking prefers relevance based word embedding. Using click2vec performs about 5-10% better than using word2vec. User clicks are expected to be a better fit as they represent user search preferences, instead of word usage in documents. The relevance-based word embedding is essential for neural models to outperform feature-based ranking. K-NRM (click2vec) consistently outperforms Coor-Ascent, but K-NRM (word2vec) does not.

Learning-to-rank trains better word embeddings. K-NRM with mean-pool performs much better than Trans. They both use average embedding similarities; the difference is that K-NRM (mean-pool) uses the ranking labels to tune the word embeddings, while Trans keeps the embeddings fixed. The trained embeddings improve the ranking accuracy, especially on top ranking positions.

Kernel-guided embedding learning provides better soft matches. K-NRM stably outperforms all of its variants. K-NRM (click2vec) uses the same ranking model, and its embeddings are trained on click contexts. K-NRM (mean-pool) also learns the word embeddings using learning-to-rank. The main difference is how the information from relevant labels is used when learning word embeddings. In KNRM (click2vec) and K-NRM (mean-pool), training signals from relevance labels are propagated *equally* to all query-document word pairs. In comparison, K-NRM uses kernels to enforce multi-level soft matches; query-document word pairs on different similarity levels are adjusted differently (see Section 3.2).

Table 7 shows an example of K-NRM's learned embeddings. The **bold** words in each row are those 'activated' by the corresponding kernel: their embedding similarities to the query word 'Maserati' fall closest to the kernel's μ. The example illustrates that the kernels recover different levels of relevance matching: $\mu = 1$ is exact match; $\mu = 0.7$ matches the car model with the brand; $\mu = 0.3$ is about the car color; $\mu = -0.1$ is background noise. The mean-pool and click2vec's uni-level training loss mix the matches at multiple levels, while the kernels provide more fine-grained training for the embeddings.

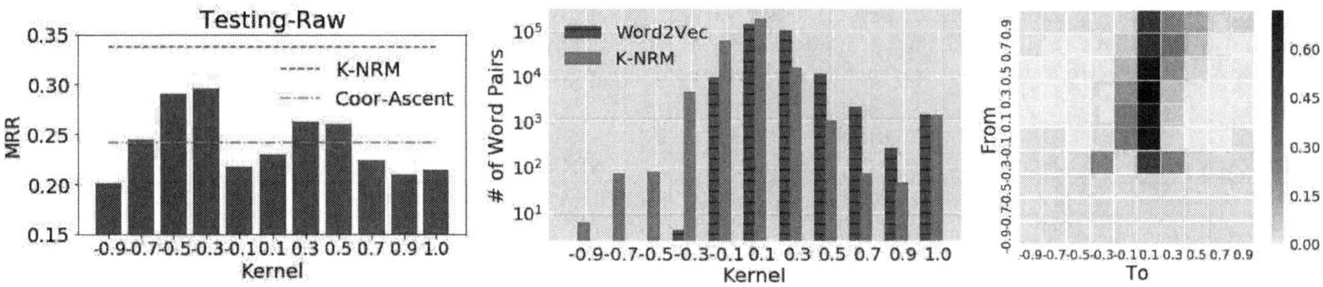

(a) Individual kernel's performance. (b) Kernel sizes before and after learning. (c) Word pair movements.

Figure 3: Kernel guided word embedding learning in K-NRM. Fig. 3a shows the performance of K-NRM when only one kernel is used in *testing*. Its X-axis is the μ of the used kernel. Its Y-axis is the MRR results. Fig. 3b shows the log number of word pairs that are closest to each kernel, before K-NRM learning (Word2Vec) and after. Its X-axis is the μ of kernels. Fig. 3c illustrates the word pairs' movements in K-NRM's learning. The heat map shows the fraction of word pairs from the row kernel (before learning, μ marked on the left) to the column kernel (after learning, μ at the bottom).

5.3 Kernel-Guided Word Embedding learning

In K-NRM, word embeddings are initialized by word2vec and trained by the kernels to provide effective soft-match patterns. This experiment studies how training affects the word embeddings, showing the responses of kernels in ranking, the word similarity distributions, and the word pair movements during learning.

Figure 3a shows the performance of K-NRM when only a single kernel is used during *testing*. The x-axis is the μ of the kernel. The results indicate the kernels' importance. The kernels on the far left (≤ -0.7), the far right (≥ 0.7), and in the middle ($\{-0.1, 0.1\}$) contribute little; the kernels on the middle left ($\{-0.3, -0.5\}$) contribute the most, followed by those on the middle right ($\{0.3, 0.5\}$). Higher μ does not necessarily mean higher importance or better soft matching. Each kernel focuses on a group of word pairs that fall into a certain similarity range; the importance of this similarity range is learned by the model.

Figure 3b shows the number of word pairs activated in each kernel before training (Word2Vec) and after (K-NRM). The X-axis is the kernel's μ. The Y-axis is the log number of word pairs activated (whose similarities are closest to corresponding kernel's μ). Most similarities fall into the range (-0.4, 0.6). These histograms help explain why the kernels on the far right and far left do not contribute much: because there are fewer word pairs in them.

Figure 3c shows the word movements during the embedding learning. Each cell in the matrix contains the word pairs whose similarities are moved from the kernel in the corresponding row (μ on the left) to the kernel in the corresponding column (μ at the bottom). The color indicates the fraction of the moved word pairs in the original kernel. Darker indicates a higher fraction. Several examples of word movements are listed in Table 8. Combining Figure 3 and Table 8, the following trends can be observed in the kernel-guided embedding learning process.

Many word pairs are decoupled. Most of the word movements are from other kernels to the 'white noise' kernels $\mu \in \{-0.1, 0.1\}$. These word pairs are considered related by word2vec but not by K-NRM. This is the most frequent effect in K-NRM's embedding learning. Only about 10% of word pairs with similarities ≥ 0.5 are kept. This implies that document ranking requires a stricter measure of soft match. For example, as shown in Table 8's first row, a person searching for 'China-Unicom', one of the major mobile carriers in China, is less likely interested in a document about 'China-Mobile', another carrier; in the second row, 'Maserati' and 'car' are decoupled as 'car' appears in almost all candidate documents' titles, so it does not provide much evidence for ranking.

New soft match patterns are discovered. K-NRM moved some word pairs from near zero similarities to important kernels. As shown in the third and fourth rows of Table 8, there are word pairs that less frequently appear in the same surrounding context, but convey possible search tasks, for example, 'the *search* for *MH370*'. K-NRM also discovers word pairs that convey strong 'irrelevant' signals, for example, people searching for 'BMW' are not interested in the 'contact us' page.

Different levels of soft matches are enforced. Some word pairs moved from one important kernel to another. This may reflect the different levels of soft matches K-NRM learned. Some examples are in the last two rows in Table 8. The -0.3 kernel is the most important one, and received word pairs that encode search tasks; the 0.5 kernel received synonyms, which are useful but not the most important, as exact match is not that important in our setting.

5.4 Required Training Data Size

This experiment studies K-NRM's performance with varying amounts of training data. Results are shown in Figure 4. The X-axis is the number of sessions used for training (e.g. $8K, 32K, \ldots$), and the coverage of testing vocabulary in the learned embedding (percentages). Sessions were randomly sampled from the training set. The Y-axis is the performance of the corresponding model. The straight and dotted lines are the performances of Coor-Ascent.

When only 2K training sessions are available, K-NRM performs worse than Coor-Ascent. Its word embeddings are mostly unchanged from word2vec as only 16% of the testing vocabulary are covered by the training sessions. K-NRM's accuracy grows rapidly with more training sessions. With only 32K (0.1%) training sessions and 50% coverage of the testing vocabulary, K-NRM surpasses Coor-Ascent on Testing-RAW. With 128K (0.4%) training sessions and 69% coverage on the testing vocabularies, K-NRM surpasses

Table 8: Examples of moved word pairs in K-NRM. From and To are the μ of the kernels the word pairs were in before learning (word2vec) and after (K-NRM). Values in parenthesis are the individual kernel's MRR on Testing-RAW, indicating the importance of the kernel. '+' and '–' mark the sign of the kernel weight w_k in the ranking layer; '+' means word pair appearances in the corresponding kernel are positively correlated with relevance; '–' means negatively correlated.

From	To	Word Pairs
$\mu = 0.9$ (0.20, –)	$\mu = 0.1$ (0.23, –)	(wife, husband), (son, daughter), (China-Unicom, China-Mobile)
$\mu = 0.5$ (0.26, –)	$\mu = 0.1$ (0.23, –)	(Maserati, car),(first, time) (website, homepage)
$\mu = 0.1$ (0.23, –)	$\mu = -0.3$ (0.30, +)	(MH370, search), (pdf, reader) (192.168.0.1, router)
$\mu = 0.1$ (0.23, –)	$\mu = 0.3$ (0.26, –)	(BMW, contact-us), (Win7, Ghost-XP)
$\mu = 0.5$ (0.26, –)	$\mu = -0.3$ (0.30, +)	(MH370, truth), (cloud, share) (HongKong, horse-racing)
$\mu = -0.3$ (0.30, +)	$\mu = 0.5$ (0.26, –)	(oppor9, OPPOR), (6080, 6080YY), (10086, www.10086.com)

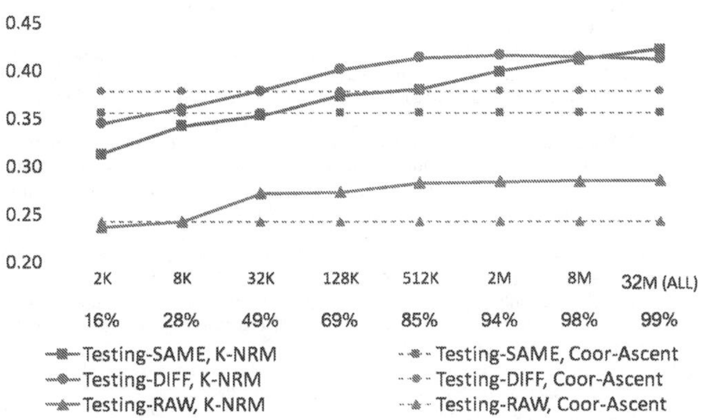

Figure 4: K-NRM's performances with different amounts of training data. X-axis: Number of sessions used for training, and the percentages of testing vocabulary covered (second row). Y-axis: NDCG@10 for Testing-SAME and Testing-DIFF, and MRR for Testing-RAW.

Coor-Ascent on Testing-SAME and Testing-DIFF. The increasing trends against Testing-SAME and Testing-RAW have not yet plateaued even with 31M training sessions, suggesting that K-NRM can utilize more training data. The performance on Testing-DIFF plateaus after 500K sessions, perhaps because the click models do not perfectly align with each other; more regularization of the K-NRM model might help under this condition.

5.5 Performance on Tail Queries

This experiment studies how K-NRM performs on less frequent queries. We split the queries in the query log into Tail (less than 50 appearances), Torso (50-1000 appearances), and Head (more than 1000 appearances). For each category, 1000 queries are randomly sampled as testing; the remaining queries are used for training. Following the same experimental settings, the ranking accuracies of K-NRM and Coor-Ascent are evaluated.

Table 9: Ranking accuracy on Tail (frequency < 50), Torso (frequency 50 – 1K) and Head (frequency > 1K) queries. † indicates statistically significant improvements of K-NRM over Coor-Ascent on Testing-RAW. Frac is the fraction of the corresponding queries in the search traffic. Cov is the fraction of testing query words covered by the training data.

	Frac	Cov	Testing-RAW, MRR		
			Coor-Ascent	K-NRM	
Tail	52%	85%	0.2977	0.3230†	+8.49%
Torso	20%	91%	0.3202	0.3768†	+17.68%
Head	28%	99%	0.2415	0.3379†	+39.92%

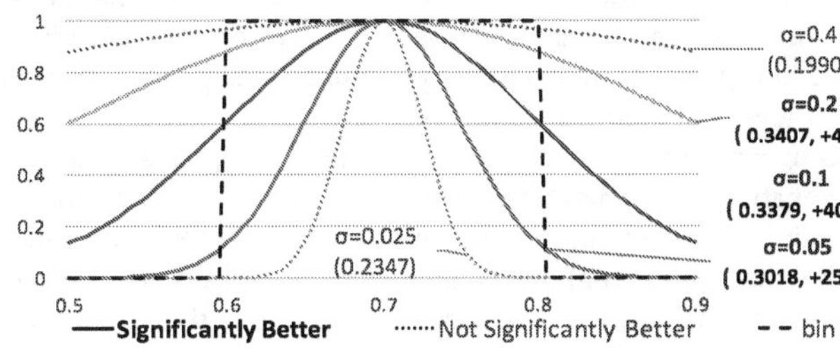

Figure 5: K-NRM's performance with different σ. MRR and relative gains over Coor-Ascent are shown in parenthesis. Kernels drawn in solid lines indicate statistically significant improvements over Coor-Ascent.

The results are shown in Table 9. Evaluation is only done using Testing-RAW as the tail queries do not provide enough clicks for DCTR and TACM to infer reliable relevance scores. The results show an expected decline of K-NRM's performance on rarer queries. K-NRM uses word embeddings to encode the relevance signals, and as tail queries' words appear less frequently in the training data, it is hard to generalize the embedded relevance signals through them. Nevertheless, even on queries that appear less than 50 times, K-NRM still outperforms Coor-Ascent by 8%.

5.6 Hyper Parameter Study

This experiment studies the influence of the kernel width (σ). We varied the σ used in K-NRM's kernels, kept everything else unchanged, and evaluated its performance. The shapes of the kernels with 5 different σ and the corresponding ranking accuracies are shown in Figure 5. Only Testing-RAW is shown due to limited space; the observation is the same on Testing-SAME and Testing-DIFF.

As shown in Figure 5, kernels too sharp or too flat either do not cover the similarity space well, or mixed the matches at different levels; they cannot provide reliable improvements. With σ between 0.05 and 0.2, K-NRM's improvements are stable.

We have also experimented with several other structures for K-NRM, for example, using more learning to rank layers, and using IDF to weight query words when combining their kernel-pooling results. However we have only observed similar or worse performances. Thus, we chose to present the simplest successful model to better illustrate the source of its effectiveness.

6 CONCLUSION

This paper presents K-NRM, a kernel based neural ranking model for ad-hoc search. The model captures word-level interactions using word embeddings, and ranks documents using a learning-to-rank layer. The center of the model is the new kernel-pooling technique. It uses kernels to softly count word matches at different similarity levels and provide soft-TF ranking features. The kernels are differentiable and support end-to-end learning. Supervised by ranking labels, the learning of word embeddings is guided by the kernels with the goal of providing soft-match signals that better separate relevant documents from irrelevant ones. The learned embeddings encode the relevance preferences and provide effective multi-level soft matches for ad-hoc ranking.

Our experiments on a commercial search engine's query log demonstrated K-NRM's advantages. On three testing scenarios (in-domain, cross-domain, and raw user clicks), K-NRM outperforms both feature based ranking baselines and neural ranking baselines by as much as 65%, and is extremely effective at the top ranking positions. The improvements are also robust: Stable gains are observed on head and tail queries, with fewer training data, a wide range of kernel widths, and a simple ranking layer.

Our analysis revealed that K-NRM's advantage is not from 'deep learning magic' but the long-desired soft match between query and documents, which is achieved by the kernel-guided embedding learning. Without it, K-NRM's advantage quickly diminishes: its variants with only exact match, pre-trained word2vec, or uni-level embedding training all perform significantly worse, and sometimes fail to outperform the simple feature based baselines.

Further analysis of the learned embeddings illustrated how K-NRM tailors them for ad-hoc ranking: More than 90% of word pairs that are mapped together in word2vec are decoupled, satisfying the stricter definition of soft match required in ad-hoc search. Word pairs that are less correlated in documents but convey frequent search tasks are discovered and mapped to certain similarity levels. The kernels also moved word pairs from one kernel to another based on their different roles in the learned soft match.

Our experiments and analysis not only demonstrated the effectiveness of K-NRM, but also provide useful intuitions about the advantages of neural methods and how they can be tailored for IR tasks. We hope our findings will be explored in many other IR tasks and will inspire more advances of neural IR research in the near future.

7 ACKNOWLEDGMENTS

This research was supported by National Science Foundation (NSF) grant IIS-1422676, a Google Faculty Research Award, and a fellowship from the Allen Institute for Artificial Intelligence. We thank Tie-Yan Liu for his insightful comments and Cheng Luo for helping us crawl the testing documents. Any opinions, findings, and conclusions in this paper are the authors' and do not necessarily reflect those of the sponsors.

REFERENCES

[1] A. Berger and J. Lafferty. Information retrieval as statistical translation. In *Proceedings of the 22nd Annual International ACM SIGIR Conference on Research and Development in Information Retrieval (SIGIR)*, pages 222–229. ACM, 1999.

[2] L. Cheng, Z. Yukun, L. Yiqun, X. Jingfang, Z. Min, and M. Shaoping. SogouT-16: A new web corpus to embrace ir research. In *Proceedings of the 40th International ACM SIGIR Conference on Research and Development in Information Retrieval (SIGIR)*, page To Appear. ACM, 2017.

[3] A. Chuklin, I. Markov, and M. d. Rijke. Click models for web search. *Synthesis Lectures on Information Concepts, Retrieval, and Services*, 7(3):1–115, 2015.

[4] W. B. Croft, D. Metzler, and T. Strohman. *Search Engines: Information Retrieval in Practice*. Addison-Wesley Reading, 2010.

[5] F. Diaz, B. Mitra, and N. Craswell. Query expansion with locally-trained word embeddings. In *Proceedings of the 54th Annual Meeting of the Association for Computational (ACL)*. ACL–Association for Computational Linguistics, 2016.

[6] J. Gao, X. He, and J.-Y. Nie. Clickthrough-based translation models for web search: from word models to phrase models. In *Proceedings of the 19th ACM international conference on Information and knowledge management (CIKM)*, pages 1139–1148. ACM, 2010.

[7] K. Grauman and T. Darrell. The pyramid match kernel: Discriminative classification with sets of image features. In *Tenth IEEE International Conference on Computer Vision (ICCV) Volume 1*, volume 2, pages 1458–1465. IEEE, 2005.

[8] J. Guo, Y. Fan, Q. Ai, and W. B. Croft. Semantic matching by non-linear word transportation for information retrieval. In *Proceedings of the 25th ACM International on Conference on Information and Knowledge Management (CIKM)*, pages 701–710. ACM, 2016.

[9] J. Guo, Y. Fan, A. Qingyao, and W. B. Croft. A deep relevance matching model for ad-hoc retrieval. In *Proceedings of the 25th ACM International on Conference on Information and Knowledge Management (CIKM)*, pages 55–64, year=2016, organization=ACM.

[10] B. Hu, Z. Lu, H. Li, and Q. Chen. Convolutional neural network architectures for matching natural language sentences. In *Advances in Neural Information Processing Systems (NIPS)*, pages 2042–2050, 2014.

[11] P.-S. Huang, X. He, J. Gao, L. Deng, A. Acero, and L. Heck. Learning deep structured semantic models for web search using clickthrough data. In *Proceedings of the 22nd ACM international conference on Conference on information & knowledge management (CIKM)*, pages 2333–2338. ACM, 2013.

[12] M. Karimzadehgan and C. Zhai. Estimation of statistical translation models based on mutual information for ad hoc information retrieval. In *Proceedings of the 33rd International ACM SIGIR Conference on Research and Development in Information Retrieval (SIGIR)*, pages 323–330. ACM, 2010.

[13] C. Kohlschütter, P. Fankhauser, and W. Nejdl. Boilerplate detection using shallow text features. In *Proceedings of the third ACM international conference on Web Search and Data Mining (WSDM)*, pages 441–450. ACM, 2010.

[14] O. Levy, Y. Goldberg, and I. Dagan. Improving distributional similarity with lessons learned from word embeddings. *Transactions of the Association for Computational Linguistics*, 3:211–225, 2015.

[15] Y. Liu, X. Xie, C. Wang, J.-Y. Nie, M. Zhang, and S. Ma. Time-aware click model. *ACM Transactions on Information Systems (TOIS)*, 35(3):16, 2016.

[16] D. Metzler and W. B. Croft. Linear feature-based models for information retrieval. *Information Retrieval*, 10(3):257–274, 2007.

[17] T. Mikolov, I. Sutskever, K. Chen, G. S. Corrado, and J. Dean. Distributed representations of words and phrases and their compositionality. In *Proceedings of the 2tth Advances in Neural Information Processing Systems 2013 (NIPS)*, pages 3111–3119, 2013.

[18] B. Mitra, F. Diaz, and N. Craswell. Learning to match using local and distributed representations of text for web search. In *Proceedings of the 25th International Conference on World Wide Web (WWW)*, pages 1291–1299. ACM, 2017.

[19] E. Nalisnick, B. Mitra, N. Craswell, and R. Caruana. Improving document ranking with dual word embeddings. In *Proceedings of the 25th International Conference on World Wide Web (WWW)*, pages 83–84. ACM, 2016.

[20] L. Pang, Y. Lan, J. Guo, J. Xu, S. Wan, and X. Cheng. Text matching as image recognition. In *Proceedings of the Thirtieth AAAI Conference on Artificial Intelligence*, AAAI, pages 2793–2799. AAAI Press, 2016.

[21] Y. Shen, X. He, J. Gao, L. Deng, and G. Mesnil. A latent semantic model with convolutional-pooling structure for information retrieval. In *Proceedings of the 23rd ACM International Conference on Conference on Information and Knowledge Management (CIKM)*, pages 101–110. ACM, 2014.

[22] Y. Shen, X. He, J. Gao, L. Deng, and G. Mesnil. Learning semantic representations using convolutional neural networks for web search. In *Proceedings of the 23rd International Conference on World Wide Web (WWW)*, pages 373–374. ACM, 2014.

[23] H.-P. Zhang, H.-K. Yu, D.-Y. Xiong, and Q. Liu. HHMM-based chinese lexical analyzer ICTCLAS. In *Proceedings of the second SIGHAN workshop on Chinese language processing*, pages 184–187. ACL, 2003.

[24] G. Zuccon, B. Koopman, P. Bruza, and L. Azzopardi. Integrating and evaluating neural word embeddings in information retrieval. In *Proceedings of the 20th Australasian Document Computing Symposium*, page 12. ACM, 2015.

Neural Ranking Models with Weak Supervision

Mostafa Dehghani*
University of Amsterdam
dehghani@uva.nl

Hamed Zamani
University of Massachusetts Amherst
zamani@cs.umass.edu

Aliaksei Severyn
Google Research
severyn@google.com

Jaap Kamps
University of Amsterdam
kamps@uva.nl

W. Bruce Croft
University of Massachusetts Amherst
croft@cs.umass.edu

ABSTRACT

Despite the impressive improvements achieved by *unsupervised* deep neural networks in computer vision and NLP tasks, such improvements have not yet been observed in ranking for information retrieval. The reason may be the complexity of the ranking problem, as it is not obvious how to learn from queries and documents when no supervised signal is available. Hence, in this paper, we propose to train a neural ranking model using *weak supervision*, where labels are obtained automatically without human annotators or any external resources (e.g., click data). To this aim, we use the output of an unsupervised ranking model, such as BM25, as a weak supervision signal. We further train a set of simple yet effective ranking models based on feed-forward neural networks. We study their effectiveness under various learning scenarios (point-wise and pair-wise models) and using different input representations (i.e., from encoding query-document pairs into dense/sparse vectors to using word embedding representation). We train our networks using tens of millions of training instances and evaluate it on two standard collections: a homogeneous news collection (Robust) and a heterogeneous large-scale web collection (ClueWeb). Our experiments indicate that employing proper objective functions and letting the networks to learn the input representation based on weakly supervised data leads to impressive performance, with over 13% and 35% MAP improvements over the BM25 model on the Robust and the ClueWeb collections. Our findings also suggest that supervised neural ranking models can greatly benefit from pre-training on large amounts of weakly labeled data that can be easily obtained from unsupervised IR models.

KEYWORDS Ranking model; weak supervision; deep neural network; deep learning; ad-hoc retrieval

1 INTRODUCTION

Learning state-of-the-art deep neural network models requires a large amounts of labeled data, which is not always readily available and can be expensive to obtain. To circumvent the lack of human-labeled training examples, unsupervised learning methods aim to model the underlying data distribution, thus learning powerful feature representations of the input data, which can be helpful for building more accurate discriminative models especially when little or even no supervised data is available.

A large group of unsupervised neural models seeks to exploit the implicit internal structure of the input data, which in turn requires customized formulation of the training objective (loss function), targeted network architectures and often non-trivial training setups. For example in NLP, various methods for learning distributed word representations, e.g., word2vec [27], GloVe [31], and sentence representations, e.g., paragraph vectors [23] and skip-thought [22] have been shown very useful to pre-train word embeddings that are then used for other tasks such as sentence classification, sentiment analysis, etc. Other generative approaches such as language modeling in NLP, and, more recently, various flavors of auto-encoders [2] and generative adversarial networks [13] in computer vision have shown a promise in building more accurate models.

Despite the advances in computer vision, speech recognition, and NLP tasks using unsupervised deep neural networks, such advances have not been observed in core information retrieval (IR) problems, such as ranking. A plausible explanation is the complexity of the ranking problem in IR, in the sense that it is not obvious how to learn a ranking model from queries and documents when no supervision in form of the relevance information is available. To overcome this issue, in this paper, we propose to leverage large amounts of unsupervised data to infer "noisy" or "weak" labels and use that signal for learning supervised models as if we had the ground truth labels. In particular, we use classic unsupervised IR models as a *weak supervision* signal for training deep neural ranking models. Weak supervision here refers to a learning approach that creates its own training data by heuristically retrieving documents for a large query set. This training data is created automatically, and thus it is possible to generate billions of training instances with almost no cost.[1] As training deep neural networks is an exceptionally data hungry process, the idea of pre-training on massive amount of weakly supervised data and then fine-tuning the model using a small amount of supervised data could improve the performance [11].

The main aim of this paper is *to study the impact of weak supervision on neural ranking models*, which we break down into the following concrete research questions:

RQ1 *Can labels from an unsupervised IR model such as BM25 be used as weak supervision signal to train an effective neural ranker?*

RQ2 *What input representation and learning objective is most suitable for learning in such a setting?*

*Work done while interning at Google Research.

[1] Although weak supervision may refer to using noisy data, in this paper, we assume that no external information, e.g., click-through data, is available.

SIGIR '17, August 07-11, 2017, Shinjuku, Tokyo, Japan
© 2017 Copyright held by the owner/author(s). 978-1-4503-5022-8/17/08.
DOI: 10.1145/3077136.3080832

RQ3 *Can a supervised learning model benefit from a weak supervision step, especially in cases when labeled data is limited?*

We examine various neural ranking models with different ranking architectures and objectives, i.e., point-wise and pair-wise, as well as different input representations, from encoding query-document pairs into dense/sparse vectors to learning query/document embedding representations. The models are trained on billions of training examples that are annotated by BM25, as the weak supervision signal. Interestingly, we observe that using just training data that are annotated by BM25 as the weak annotator, we can outperform BM25 itself on the test data. Based on our analysis, the achieved performance is generally indebted to three main factors: First, defining an objective function that aims to learn the ranking instead of calibrated scoring to relax the network from fitting to the imperfections in the weakly supervised training data. Second, letting the neural networks learn optimal query/document representations instead of feeding them with a representation based on predefined features. This is a key requirement to maximize the benefits from deep learning models with weak supervision as it enables them to generalize better. Third and last, the weak supervision setting makes it possible to train the network on a massive amount of training data.

We further thoroughly analyse the behavior of models to understand what they learn, what is the relationship among different models, and how much training data is needed to go beyond the weak supervision signal. We also study if employing deep neural networks may help in different situations. Finally, we examine the scenario of using the network trained on a weak supervision signal as a pre-training step. We demonstrate that, in the ranking problem, the performance of deep neural networks trained on a limited amount of supervised data significantly improves when they are initialized from a model pre-trained on weakly labeled data.

Our results have broad impact as the proposal to use unsupervised traditional methods as weak supervision signals is applicable to variety of IR tasks, such as filtering or classification, without the need for supervised data. More generally, our approach unifies the classic IR models with currently emerging data-driven approaches in an elegant way.

2 RELATED WORK

Deep neural networks have shown impressive performance in many computer vision, natural language processing, and speech recognition tasks [24]. Recently, several attempts have been made to study deep neural networks in IR applications, which can be generally partitioned into two categories [29, 46]. The first category includes approaches that use the results of trained (deep) neural networks in order to improve the performance in IR applications. Among these, distributed word representations or embeddings [27, 31] have attracted a lot of attention. Word embedding vectors have been applied to term re-weighting in IR models [32, 47], query expansion [10, 33, 43], query classification [25, 44], etc. The main shortcoming of most of the approaches in this category is that the objective of the trained neural network differs from the objective of these tasks. For instance, the word embedding vectors proposed in [27, 31] are trained based on term proximity in a large corpus, which is different from the objective in most IR tasks. To overcome this issue, some approaches try to learn representations in an end-to-end neural model for learning a specific task like entity ranking for expert finding [39] or product search [38]. Zamani and Croft [45] recently proposed relevance-based word embedding models for learning word representations based on the objectives that matter for IR applications.

The second category, which this paper belongs to, consists of the approaches that design and train a (deep) neural network for a specific task, e.g., question answering [6, 41], click models [4], context-aware ranking [42], etc. A number of the approaches in this category have been proposed for ranking documents in response to a given query. These approaches can be generally divided into two groups: *late combination models* and *early combination models* (or representation-focused and interaction-focused models according to [14]). The late combination models, following the idea of Siamese networks [5], independently learn a representation for each query and candidate document and then calculate the similarity between the two estimated representations via a similarity function. For example, Huang et al. [18] proposed DSSM, which is a feed forward neural network with a word hashing phase as the first layer to predict the click probability given a query string and a document title. The DSSM model was further improved by incorporating convolutional neural networks [35].

On the other hand, the early combination models are designed based on the interactions between the query and the candidate document as the input of network. For instance, DeepMatch [26] maps each text to a sequence of terms and trains a feed-forward network for computing the matching score. The deep relevance matching model for ad-hoc retrieval [14] is another example of an early combination model that feeds a neural network with the histogram-based features representing interactions between the query and document. Early combining enables the model to have an opportunity to capture various interactions between query and document(s), while with late combination approach, the model has only the chance of isolated observation of input elements. Recently, Mitra et al. [28] proposed to simultaneously learn local and distributional representations, which are early and late combination models respectively, to capture both exact term matching and semantic term matching.

Until now, all the proposed neural models for ranking are trained on either explicit relevance judgements or clickthrough logs. However, a massive amount of such training data is not always available.

In this paper, we propose to train neural ranking models using weak supervision, which is the most natural way to reuse the existing supervised learning models where the imperfect labels are treated as the ground truth. The basic assumption is that we can cheaply obtain labels (that are of lower quality than human-provided labels) by expressing the prior knowledge we have about the task at hand by specifying a set of heuristics, adapting existing ground truth data for a different but related task (this is often referred to distant supervision[2]), extracting supervision signal from external knowledge-bases or ontologies, crowd-sourcing partial annotations that are cheaper to get, etc. Weak supervision is a natural way to benefit from unsupervised data and it has been applied in NLP for various tasks including relation extraction [3, 15], knowledge-base completion [17], sentiment analysis [34], etc. There are also similar attempts in IR for automatically constructing test collections [1] and learning to rank using labeled features, i.e. features that an expert believes they are correlated with relevance [9]. In this paper, we make use of traditional IR models as the weak supervision signal to generate a large

[2]We do not distinguish between weak and distant supervision as the difference is subtle and both terms are often used interchangeably in the literature.

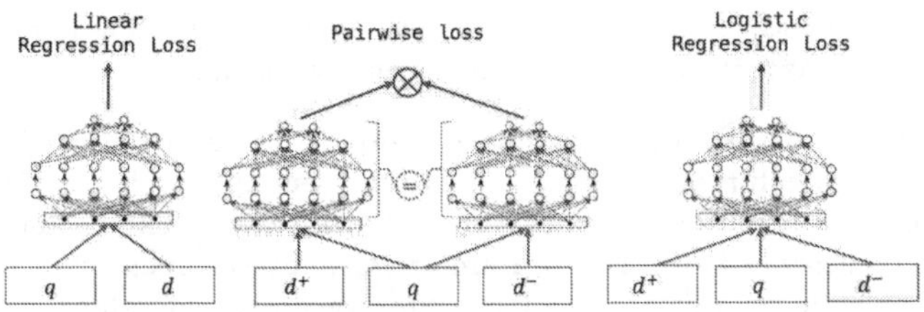

(a) Score model (b) Rank model (c) RankProb model

Figure 1: Different Ranking Architectures

amount of training data and train effective neural ranking models that outperform the baseline methods by a significant margin.

3 WEAK SUPERVISION FOR RANKING

Deep learning techniques have taken off in many fields, as they automate the onerous task of input representation and feature engineering. On the other hand, the more the neural networks become deep and complex, the more it is crucial for them to be trained on massive amounts of training data. In many applications, rich annotations are costly to obtain and task-specific training data is now a critical bottleneck. Hence, unsupervised learning is considered as a long standing goal for several applications. However, in a number of information retrieval tasks, such as ranking, it is not obvious how to train a model with large numbers of queries and documents with no relevance signal. To address this problem in an unsupervised fashion, we use the idea of "Pseudo-Labeling" by taking advantage of existing unsupervised methods for creating a weakly annotated set of training data and we propose to train a neural retrieval model with weak supervision signals we have generated. In general, weak supervision refers to learning from training data in which the labels are imprecise. In this paper, we refer to weak supervision as a learning approach that automatically creates its own training data using an existing unsupervised approach, which differs from imprecise data coming from external observations (e.g., click-through data) or noisy human-labeled data.

We focus on query-dependent ranking as a core IR task. To this aim, we take a well-performing existing unsupervised retrieval model, such as BM25. This model plays the role of "pseudo-labeler" in our learning scenario. In more detail, given a target collection and a large set of training queries (without relevance judgments), we make use of the pseudo-labeler to rank/score the documents for each query in the training query set. Note that we can generate as much as training data as we need with almost no cost. The goal is to train a ranking model given the scores/ranking generated by the pseudo-labeler as a weak supervision signal.

In the following section, we formally present a set of neural network-based ranking models that can leverage the given weak supervision signal in order to learn accurate representations and ranking for the ad-hoc retrieval task.

4 NEURAL RANKING MODELS

In this section, we first introduce our ranking models. Then, we describe the architecture of the base neural network model shared by different ranking models. Finally, we discuss the three input layer architectures used in our neural rankers to encode (query, candidate document) pairs.

4.1 Ranking Architectures

We define three different ranking models: one point-wise and two pair-wise models. We introduce the architecture of these models and explain how we train them using weak supervision signals.

Score model : This architecture models a point-wise ranking model that learns to predict retrieval scores for query-document pairs. More formally, the goal in this architecture is to learn a *scoring function* $\mathcal{S}(q,d;\theta)$ that determines the retrieval score of document d for query q, given a set of model parameters θ. In the training stage, we are given a training set comprising of training instances each a triple $\tau = (q,d,s_{q,d})$, where q is a query from training query set Q, d represents a retrieved document for the query q, and $s_{q,d}$ is the relevance score (calculated by a weak supervisor), which is acquired using a retrieval scoring function in our setup. We consider the mean squared error as the loss function for a given batch of training instances:

$$\mathcal{L}(b;\theta) = \frac{1}{|b|}\sum_{i=1}^{|b|}(\mathcal{S}(\{q,d\}_i;\theta) - s_{\{q,d\}_i})^2 \tag{1}$$

where $\{q,d\}_i$ denotes the query and the corresponding retrieved document in the ith training instance, i.e. τ_i in the batch b. The conceptual architecture of the model is illustrated in Figure 1a.

Rank model : In this model, similar to the previous one, the goal is to learn a scoring function $\mathcal{S}(q,d;\theta)$ for a given pair of query q and document d with the set of model parameters θ. However, unlike the previous model, we do not aim to learn a calibrated scoring function. In this model, as it is depicted in Figure 1b, we use a pair-wise scenario during training in which we have two point-wise networks that share parameters and we update their parameters to minimize a pair-wise loss. In this model, each training instance has five elements: $\tau = (q,d_1,d_2,s_{q,d_1},s_{q,d_2})$. During the inference, we treat the trained model as a point-wise scoring function to score query-document pairs.

We have tried different pair-wise loss functions and empirically found that the model learned based on the hinge loss (max-margin loss function) performs better than the others. Hinge loss is a linear loss that penalizes examples that violate the margin constraint. It is widely used in various learning to rank algorithms, such as Ranking SVM [16]. The hinge loss function for a batch of training instances is defined as follows:

$$\mathcal{L}(b;\theta) = \frac{1}{|b|}\sum_{i=1}^{|b|}\max\Big\{0, \varepsilon - \text{sign}(s_{\{q,d_1\}_i} - s_{\{q,d_2\}_i}) \\ (\mathcal{S}(\{q,d_1\}_i;\theta) - \mathcal{S}(\{q,d_2\}_i;\theta))\Big\}, \tag{2}$$

where ε is the parameter determining the margin of hinge loss. We found that as we compress the outputs to the range of $[-1,1]$, $\varepsilon = 1$ works well as the margin for the hinge loss function.

RankProb model : The third architecture is based on a pair-wise scenario during both training and inference (Figure 1c). This model learns a *ranking function* $\mathcal{R}(q,d_1,d_2;\theta)$ which predicts the probability of document d_1 to be ranked higher than d_2 given q. Similar to the *rank* model, each training instance has five elements: $\tau = (q,d_1,d_2,s_{q,d_1},s_{q,d_1})$. For a given batch of training instances, we define our loss function based on cross-entropy as follows:

$$\mathcal{L}(b;\theta) = -\frac{1}{|b|}\sum_{i=1}^{|b|} P_{\{q,d_1,d_2\}_i} \log(\mathcal{R}(\{q,d_1,d_2\}_i;\theta)) + (1-P_{\{q,d_1,d_2\}_i})\log(1-\mathcal{R}(\{q,d_1,d_2\}_i;\theta)) \tag{3}$$

where $P_{\{q,d_1,d_2\}_i}$ is the probability of document d_1 being ranked higher than d_2, based on the scores obtained from training instance τ_i:

$$P_{\{q,d_1,d_2\}_i} = \frac{s_{\{q,d_1\}_i}}{s_{\{q,d_1\}_i} + s_{\{q,d_2\}_i}} \tag{4}$$

It is notable that at inference time, we need a scalar score for each document. Therefore, we need to turn the model's pair-wise predictions into a score per document. To do so, for each document, we calculate the average of predictions against all other candidate documents, which has $O(n^2)$ time complexity and is not practical in real-world applications. There are some approximations could be applicable to decrease the time complexity at inference time [40].

4.2 Neural Network Architecture

As shown in Figure 1, all the described ranking architectures share a neural network module. We opted for a simple feed-forward neural network which is composed of: input layer z_0, $l-1$ hidden layers, and the output layer z_l. The input layer z_0 provides a mapping ψ to encode the input query and document(s) into a fixed-length vector. The exact specification of the input representation feature function ψ is given in the next subsection. Each hidden layer z_i is a fully-connected layer that computes the following transformation:

$$z_i = \alpha(W_i.z_{i-1} + b_i); 1 < i < l-1, \tag{5}$$

where W_i and b_i respectively denote the weight matrix and the bias term corresponding to the ith hidden layer, and $\alpha(.)$ is the activation function. We use the rectifier linear unit $ReLU(x) = \max(0,x)$ as the activation function, which is a common choice in the deep learning literature [24]. The output layer z_l is a fully-connected layer with a single continuous output. The activation function for the output layer depends on the ranking architecture that we use. For the *score* model architecture, we empirically found that a linear activation function works best, while *tanh* and the sigmoid functions are used for the *rank* model and *rankprob* model respectively.

Furthermore, to prevent feature co-adaptation, we use *dropout* [36] as the regularization technique in all the models. Dropout sets a portion of hidden units to zero during the forward phase when computing the activations which prevents overfitting.

4.3 Input Representations

We explore three definitions of the input layer representation z_0 captured by a feature function ψ that maps the input into a fixed-size vector which is further fed into the fully connected layers: (i) a conventional dense feature vector representation that contains various statistics describing the input query-document pair, (ii) a sparse vector containing bag-of-words representation, and (iii) bag-of-embeddings averaged with learned weights. These input representations define how much capacity is given to the network to extract discriminative signal from the training data and thus result in different generalization behavior of the networks. It is noteworthy that input representation of the networks in the *score* model and *rank* model is defined for a pair of the query and the document, while the network in the *rankprob* model needs to be fed by a triple of the query, the first document, and the second document.

Dense vector representation (Dense) : In this setting, we build a dense feature vector composed of features used by traditional IR methods, e.g., BM25. The goal here is to let the network fit the function described by the BM25 formula when it receives exactly the same inputs. In more detail, our input vector is a concatenation (||) of the following inputs: total number of documents in the collection (i.e., N), average length of documents in the collection (i.e., $avg(l_d)_D$), document length (i.e., l_d), frequency of each query term t_i in the document (i.e., $tf(t_i,d)$), and document frequency of each query term (i.e., $df(t_i)$). Therefore, for the point-wise setting, we have the following input vector:

$$\psi(q,d) = [N || avg(l_d)_D || l_d || \{df(t_i) || tf(t_i,d)\}_{1 \le i \le k}], \tag{6}$$

where k is set to a fixed value (5 in our experiments). We truncate longer queries and do zero padding for shorter queries. For the networks in the *rankprob* model, we consider a similar function with additional elements: the length of the second document and the frequency of query terms in the second document.

Sparse vector representation (Sparse) : Next, we move away from a fully featurized representation that contains only aggregated statistics and let the network performs feature extraction for us. In particular, we build a bag-of-words representation by extracting term frequency vectors of query (tfv_q), document (tfv_d), and the collection (tfv_c) and feed the network with concatenation of these three vectors. For the point-wise setting, we have the following input vector:

$$\psi(q,d) = [tfv_c || tfv_q || tfv_d] \tag{7}$$

For the network in *rankprob* model, we have a similar input vector with both tfv_{d_1} and tfv_{d_2}. Hence, the size of the input layer is $3 \times vocab\ size$ in the point-wise setting, and $4 \times vocab\ size$ in the pair-wise setting.

Embedding vector representation (Embed) : The major weakness of the previous input representation is that words are treated as discrete units, hence prohibiting the network from performing soft matching between semantically similar words in queries and documents. In this input representation paradigm, we rely on word embeddings to obtain more powerful representation of queries and documents that could bridge the lexical chasm. The representation function ψ consists of three components: an embedding function $\mathcal{E} : \mathcal{V} \to \mathbb{R}^m$ (where $\mathcal{V}$ denotes the vocabulary set and m is the embedding dimension), a weighting function $\mathcal{W} : \mathcal{V} \to \mathbb{R}$, and a compositionality function $\odot : (\mathbb{R}^m, \mathbb{R})^n \to \mathbb{R}^m$. More formally, the function ψ for the point-wise setting is defined as:

$$\psi(q,d) = [\odot_{i=1}^{|q|} (\mathcal{E}(t_i^q), \mathcal{W}(t_i^q)) || \odot_{i=1}^{|d|} (\mathcal{E}(t_i^d), \mathcal{W}(t_i^d))], \tag{8}$$

where t_i^q and t_i^d denote the ith term in query q and document d, respectively. For the network of the *rankprob* model, another similar term is concatenated with the above vector for the second document. The embedding function $\mathcal{E}$ transforms each term to a dense m-dimensional float vector as its representation, which is learned during the training phase. The weighting function $\mathcal{W}$ assigns a weight to each term in the vocabulary set, which is supposed to learn term global importance for the retrieval task. The compositionality function $\odot$ projects a set of n embedding and weighting pairs to an

m-dimensional representation, independent from the value of n. The compositionality function is given by:

$$\odot_{i=1}^{n}(\mathcal{E}(t_i),\mathcal{W}(t_i)) = \sum_{i=1}^{n}\widehat{\mathcal{W}}(t_i)\cdot\mathcal{E}(t_i), \tag{9}$$

which is the weighted element-wise sum of the terms' embedding vectors. $\widehat{\mathcal{W}}$ is the normalized weight that is learned for each term, given as follows:

$$\widehat{\mathcal{W}}(t_i) = \frac{\exp(\mathcal{W}(t_i))}{\sum_{j=1}^{n}\exp(\mathcal{W}(t_j))} \tag{10}$$

All combinations of different ranking architectures and different input representations presented in this section can be considered for developing ranking models.

5 EXPERIMENTAL DESIGN

In this section, we describe the train and evaluation data, metrics we report, and detailed experimental setup. Then we discuss the results.

5.1 Data

Collections. In our experiments, we used two standard TREC collections: The first collection (called *Robust04*) consists of over 500k news articles from different news agencies, that is available in TREC Disks 4 and 5 (excluding Congressional Records). This collection, which was used in TREC Robust Track 2004, is considered as a homogeneous collection, because of the nature and the quality of documents. The second collection (called *ClueWeb*) that we used is ClueWeb09 Category B, a large-scale web collection with over 50 million English documents, which is considered as a heterogeneous collection. This collection has been used in TREC Web Track, for several years. In our experiments with this collection, we filtered out the spam documents using the Waterloo spam scorer[3] [7] with the default threshold 70%. The statistics of these collections are reported in Table 1.

Training query set. To train our neural ranking models, we used the unique queries (only the query string) appearing in the AOL query logs [30]. This query set contains web queries initiated by real users in the AOL search engine that were sampled from a three-month period from March 1, 2006 to May 31, 2006. We filtered out a large volume of navigational queries containing URL substrings ("http", "www.", ".com", ".net", ".org", ".edu"). We also removed all non-alphanumeric characters from the queries. We made sure that no queries from the training set appear in our evaluation sets. For each dataset, we took queries that have at least ten hits in the target corpus using the pseudo-labeler method. Applying all these processes, we ended up with 6.15 million queries for the Robust04 dataset and 6.87 million queries for the ClueWeb dataset. In our experiments, we randomly selected 80% of the training queries as training set and the remaining 20% of the queries were chosen as validation set for hyper-parameter tuning. As the "pseudo-labeler" in our training data, we have used BM25 to score/rank documents in the collections given the queries in the training query set.

Evaluation query sets. We use the following query sets for evaluation that contain human-labeled judgements: a set of 250 queries (TREC topics 301–450 and 601–700) for the Robust04 collection that were previously used in TREC Robust Track 2004. A set of 200 queries (topics 1-200) were used for the experiments on the ClueWeb collection. These queries were used in TREC Web Track 2009–2012. We only used the title of topics as queries.

[3] http://plg.uwaterloo.ca/~gvcormac/clueweb09spam/

Table 1: Collections statistics.

Collection	Genre	Queries	# docs	length
Robust04	news	301-450,601-700	528k	254
ClueWeb	webpages	1-200	50m	1,506

5.2 Evaluation Metrics.

To evaluate retrieval effectiveness, we report three standard evaluation metrics: mean average precision (MAP) of the top-ranked 1000 documents, precision of the top 20 retrieved documents (P@20), and normalized discounted cumulative gain (nDCG) [19] calculated for the top 20 retrieved documents (nDCG@20). Statistically significant differences of MAP, P@20, and nDCG@20 values are determined using the two-tailed paired t-test with $p\_value < 0.05$, with Bonferroni correction.

5.3 Experimental Setup

All models described in Section 4 are implemented using TensorFlow [12, 37]. In all experiments, the parameters of the network are optimized employing the Adam optimizer [21] and using the computed gradient of the loss to perform the back-propagation algorithm. All model hyper-parameters were tuned on the respective validation set (see Section 5.1 for more detail) using batched GP bandits with an expected improvement acquisition function [8]. For each model, the size of hidden layers and the number of hidden layers were selected from [16,32,64,128,256,512,1024] and [1,2,3,4], respectively. The initial learning rate and the dropout parameter were selected from $[1E-3, 5E-4, 1E-4, 5E-5, 1E-5]$ and [0.0,0.1,0.2,0.5], respectively. For models with embedding vector representation, we considered embedding sizes of [100,300,500,1000]. As the training data, we take the top 1000 retrieved documents for each query from training query set Q, to prepare the training data. In total, we have $|Q|\times 1000$ ($\sim 6E10$ examples in our data) point-wise example and $\sim |Q|\times 1000^2$ ($\sim 6E13$ examples in our data) pair-wise examples. The batch size in our experiments was selected from [128,256,512]. At inference time, for each query, we take the top 2000 retrieved documents using BM25 as candidate documents and re-rank them by the trained models. In our experiments, we use the Indri[4] implementation of BM25 with the default parameters (i.e., $k_1 = 1.2$, $b = 0.75$, and $k_3 = 1000$).

6 RESULTS AND DISCUSSION

In the following, we evaluate our neural rankers trained with different learning approaches (Section 4) and different input representations (Section 4.3). We attempt to break down our research questions to several subquestions, and provide empirical answers along with the intuition and analysis behind each question:

How do the neural models with different training objectives and input representations compare? Table 2 presents the performance of all model combinations. Interestingly, combinations of the *rank* model and the *rankprob* model with embedding vector representation outperform BM25 by significant margins in both collections. For instance, the *rankprob* model with embedding vector representation that shows the best performance among the other methods,

[4] https://www.lemurproject.org/indri.php

Table 2: Performance of the different models on different datasets. ▲or ▽indicates that the improvements or degradations with respect to BM25 are statistically significant, at the 0.05 level using the paired two-tailed t-test.

Method	Robust04			ClueWeb		
	MAP	*P@20*	*nDCG@20*	*MAP*	*P@20*	*nDCG@20*
BM25	0.2503	0.3569	0.4102	0.1021	0.2418	0.2070
Score + Dense	0.1961▽	0.2787▽	0.3260▽	0.0689▽	0.1518▽	0.1430▽
Score + Sparse	0.2141▽	0.3180▽	0.3604▽	0.0701▽	0.1889▽	0.1495▽
Score + Embed	0.2423▽	0.3501	0.3999	0.1002	0.2513	0.2130
Rank + Dense	0.1940▽	0.2830▽	0.3317▽	0.0622▽	0.1516▽	0.1383▽
Rank + Sparse	0.2213▽	0.3216▽	0.3628▽	0.0776▽	0.1989▽	0.1816▽
Rank + Embed	**0.2811▲**	**0.3773▲**	**0.4302▲**	**0.1306▲**	**0.2839▲**	**0.2216▲**
RankProb + Dense	0.2192▽	0.2966▽	0.3278▽	0.0702▽	0.1711▽	0.1506▽
RankProb + Sparse	0.2246▽	0.3250▽	0.3763▽	0.0894▽	0.2109▽	0.1916
RankProb + Embed	**0.2837▲**	**0.3802▲**	**0.4389▲**	**0.1387▲**	**0.2967▲**	**0.2330▲**

surprisingly, improves BM25 by over 13% and 35% in Robust04 and ClueWeb collections respectively, in terms of MAP. Similar improvements can be observed for the other evaluation metrics.

Regarding the modeling architecture, in the *rank* model and the *rankprob* model, compared to the *score* model, we define objective functions that target to learn ranking instead of scoring. This is particularly important in weak supervision, as the scores are imperfect values—using the ranking objective alleviates this issue by forcing the model to learn a preference function rather than reproduce absolute scores. In other words, using the ranking objective instead of learning to predict calibrated scores allows the *rank* model and the *rankprob* model to learn to distinguish between examples whose scores are close. This way, some small amount of noise, which is a common problem in weak supervision, would not perturb the ranking as easily.

Regarding the input representations, embedding vector representation leads to better performance compared to the other ones in all models. Using embedding vector representation not only provides the network with more information, but also lets the network to learn proper representation capturing the needed elements for the next layers with better understanding of the interactions between query and documents. Providing the network with already engineered features would block it from going beyond the weak supervision signal and limit the ability of the models to learn latent features that are unattainable through feature engineering.

Note that although the *rankprob* model is more precise in terms of MAP, the *rank* model is much faster in the inference time ($O(n)$ compared to $O(n^2)$), which is a desirable property in real-life applications.

Why do dense vector representation and sparse vector representation fail to replicate the performance of BM25? Although neural networks are capable of approximating arbitrarily complex non-linear functions, we observe that the models with dense vector representation fail to replicate the BM25 performance, while they are given the same feature inputs as the BM25 components (e.g., TF, IDF, average document length, etc). To ensure that the training converges and there is no overfitting, we have looked into the training and validation loss values of different models during the training time. Figure 2 illustrates the loss curves for the training and validation sets (see Section 5.1) per training step for different models. As shown, in models with dense vector representation, the training losses drop quickly to values close to zero while this is not the case for the validation losses, which is an indicator of over-fitting on the training data. Although we have tried different regularization techniques, like l_2-regularization and dropout with various parameters, there is less chance for generalization when the networks are fed with the fully featurized input. Note that over-fitting would lead to poor performance, especially in weak supervision scenarios as the network learns to model imperfections from weak annotations. This phenomenon is also the case for models with the sparse vector representation, but with less impact. However, in the models with the embedding vector representation, the networks do not overfit, which helps it to go beyond the weak supervision signals in the training data.

How are the models related? To better understand the relationship of different neural models described above, we compare their performance across the query dimension following the approach in [28]. We assume that similar models should perform similarly for the same queries. Hence, we represent each model by a vector, called the performance vector, whose elements correspond to per query performance of the model, in terms of nDCG@20. The closer the performance vectors are, the more similar the models are in terms of query by query performance. For the sake of visualization, we reduce the vectors dimension by projecting them to a two-dimensional space, using t-Distributed Stochastic Neighbor Embedding (t-SNE)[5].

Figure 3 illustrates the proximity of different models in the Robust04 collection. Based on this plot, models with similar input representations (same color) have quite close performance vectors, which means that they perform similarly for same queries. This is not necessarily the case for models with similar architecture (same shape). This suggests that the amount and the way that we provide information to the networks are the key factors in the ranking performance.

We also observe that the *score* model with dense vector representation is the closest to BM25 which is expected. It is also interesting that models with embedding vector representation are placed far away from other models which shows they perform differently compared to the other input representations.

How meaningful are the compositionality weights learned in the embedding vector representation? In this experiment, we

[5]https://lvdmaaten.github.io/tsne/

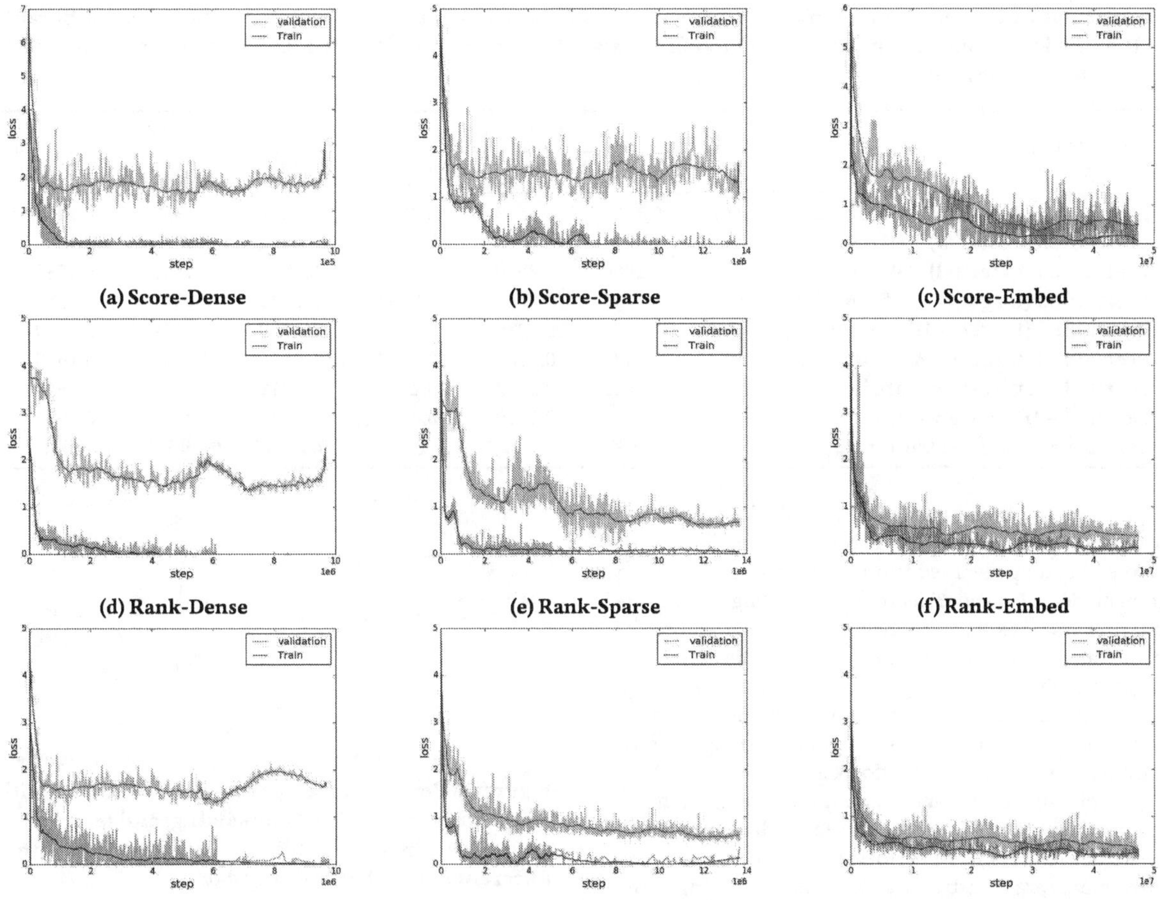

(a) Score-Dense (b) Score-Sparse (c) Score-Embed

(d) Rank-Dense (e) Rank-Sparse (f) Rank-Embed

(g) RankProb-Dense (h) RankProb-Sparse (i) RankProb-Embed

Figure 2: Training and validation loss curves for all combinations of different ranking architectures and feeding paradigms.

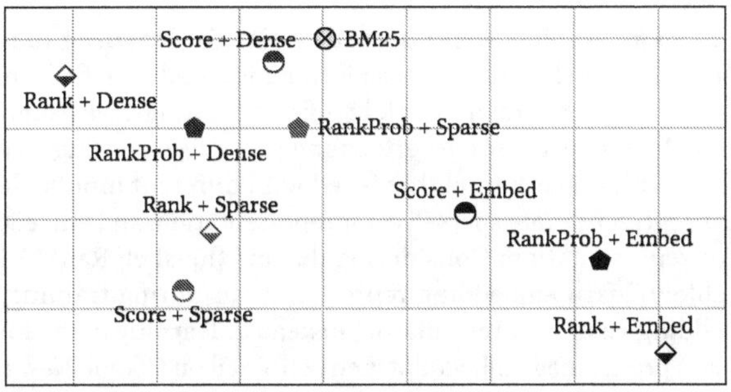

Figure 3: Proximity of different models in terms of query-by-query performance.

focus on the best performing combination, i.e., the *rankprob* model with embedding vector representation. To analyze what the network learns, we look into the weights $\mathcal{W}$ (see Section 4.3) learned by the network. Note that the weighting function $\mathcal{W}$ learns a global weight for each vocabulary term. We notice that in both collections there is a strong linear correlation between the learned weights and the inverse document frequency of terms. Figure 4 illustrates the scatter plots of the learned weight for each vocabulary term and its IDF, in both collections. This is an interesting observation as we do not provide any global corpus information to the network in training

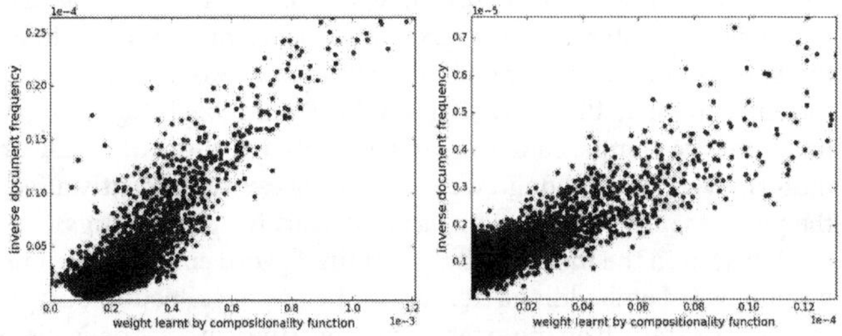

(a) Robust04 (Pearson Correlation: 0.8243) (b) ClueWeb (Pearson Correlation: 0.7014)

Figure 4: Strong linear correlation between weight learned by the compositionality function in the embedding vector representation and inverse document frequency.

and the network is able to infer such a global information by only observing individual training instances.

How well do other alternatives for the embedding and weighting functions in the embedding vector representation perform?

Considering embedding vector representation as the input representation, we have examined different alternatives for the embedding

Table 3: Performance of the *rankprob* model with variants of the embedding vector representation on different datasets. ▲indicates that the improvements over all other models are statistically significant, at the 0.05 level using the paired two-tailed t-test, with Bonferroni correction.

Embedding type	Robust04			ClueWeb		
	MAP	*P@20*	*nDCG@20*	*MAP*	*P@20*	*nDCG@20*
Pretrained (external) + Uniform weighting	0.1656	0.2543	0.3017	0.0612	0.1300	0.1401
Pretrained (external) + IDF weighting	0.1711	0.2755	0.3104	0.0712	0.1346	0.1469
Pretrained (external) + Weight learning	0.1880	0.2890	0.3413	0.0756	0.1344	0.1583
Pretrained (target) + Uniform weighting	0.1217	0.2009	0.2791	0.0679	0.1331	0.1587
Pretrained (target) + IDF weighting	0.1402	0.2230	0.2876	0.0779	0.1674	0.1540
Pretrained (target) + Weight learning	0.1477	0.2266	0.2804	0.0816	0.1729	0.1608
Learned + Uniform weighting	0.2612	0.3602	0.4180	0.0912	0.2216	0.1841
Learned + IDF weighting	0.2676	0.3619	0.4200	0.1032	0.2419	0.1922
Learned + Weight learning	**0.2837▲**	**0.3802▲**	**0.4389▲**	**0.1387▲**	**0.2967▲**	**0.2330▲**

function $\mathcal{E}$: (1) employing pre-trained word embeddings learned from an external corpus (we used Google News), (2) employing pre-trained word embeddings learned from the target corpus (using the skip-gram model [27]), and (3) learning embeddings during the network training as it is explained in Section 4.3. Furthermore, for the compositionality function $\odot$, we tried different alternatives: (1) uniform weighting (simple averaging which is a common approach in compositionality function), (2) using IDF as fixed weights instead of learning the weighting function $\mathcal{W}$, and (3) learning weights during the training as described in Section 4.3.

Table 3 presents the performance of all these combinations on both collections. We note that learning both embedding and weighting functions leads to the highest performance in both collections. These improvements are statistically significant. According to the results, regardless of the weighting approach, learning embeddings during training outperforms the models with fixed pre-trained embeddings. This supports the hypothesis that with the embedding vector representation the neural networks learn an embedding that is based on the interactions of query and documents that tends to be tuned better to the corresponding ranking task. Also, regardless of the embedding method, learning weights helps models to get better performance compared to the fixed weightings, with either IDF or uniform weights. Although weight learning can significantly affect the performance, it has less impact than learning embeddings.

Note that in the models with pre-trained word embeddings, employing word embeddings trained on the target collection outperforms those trained on the external corpus in the ClueWeb collection; while this is not the case for the Robust04 collection. The reason could be related to the collection size, since the ClueWeb is approximately 100 times larger than the Robust04.

In addition to the aforementioned experiments, we have also tried initializing the embedding matrix with a pre-trained word embedding trained on the Google News corpus, instead of random initialization. Figure 5 presents the learning curve of the models. According to this figure, the model initialized by a pre-trained embedding performs better than random initialization when a limited amount of training data is available. When enough training data is fed to the network, initializing with pre-trained embedding and random values converge to the same performance. An interesting observation here is that in both collections, these two initializations converge when the models exceed the performance of the weak supervision source, which is BM25 in our experiments. This suggests that the convergence occurs when accurate representations are learned by the networks, regardless of the initialization.

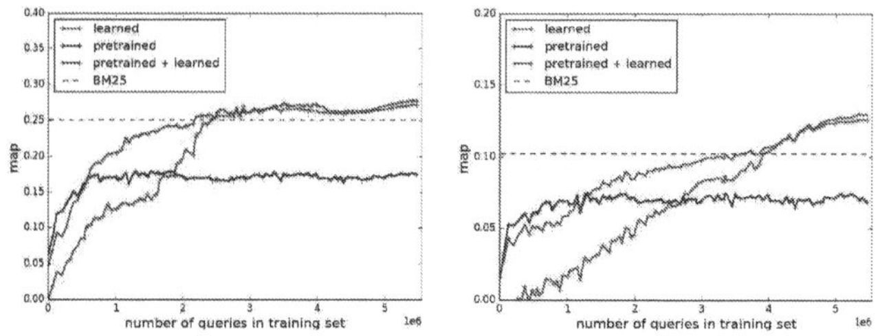

(a) Robust04 (b) ClueWeb

Figure 5: Performance of the *rankprob* model with learned embedding, pre-trained embedding, and learned embedding with pre-trained embedding as initialization, with respect to different amount of training data.

Are deep neural networks a good choice for learning to rank with weak supervision? To see if there is a real benefit from using a non-linear neural network in different settings, we examined RankSVM [20] as a strong-performing pair-wise learning to rank method with linear kernel that is fed with different inputs: dense vector representation, sparse vector representation, and embedding vector representation. Considering that off-the-shelf RankSVM is not able to learn embedding representations during training, for embedding vector representation, instead of learning embeddings we use a pre-trained embedding matrix trained on Google News and fixed IDF weights.

The results are reported in Table 4. As BM25 is not a linear function, RankSVM with linear kernel is not able to completely approximate it. However, surprisingly, for both dense vector representation and sparse vector representation, RankSVM works as well as neural networks (see Table 2). Also, compared to the corresponding experiment in Table 3, the performance of the neural network with an external pre-trained embedding and IDF weighting is not considerably better than RankSVM. This shows that having non-linearity in neural networks does not help that much when we do not have representation learning as part of the model. Note that all of these results are still lower than BM25, which shows that they are not good at learning from weak supervision signals for ranking.

Table 4: Performance of the linear RankSVM with different features.

Method	Robust04			ClueWeb		
	MAP	*P@20*	*nDCG@20*	*MAP*	*P@20*	*nDCG@20*
RankSVM + Dense	0.1983	0.2841	0.3375	0.0761	0.1840	0.1637
RankSVM + Sparse	0.2307	0.3260	0.3794	0.0862	0.2170	0.1939
RankSVM + (Pretrained (external) + IDF weighting)	0.1539	0.2121	0.1852	0.0633	0.1572	0.1494
Score (one layer with no nonlinearity) + Embed	0.2103	0.3986	0.3160	0.0645	0.1421	0.1322

Table 5: Performance of the *rankprob* model with embedding vector representation in fully supervised setting, weak supervised setting, and weak supervised plus supervision as fine tuning. ▲indicates that the improvements over all other models are statistically significant, at the 0.05 level using the paired two-tailed t-test, with Bonferroni correction.

Method	Robust04			ClueWeb		
	MAP	*P@20*	*nDCG@20*	*MAP*	*P@20*	*nDCG@20*
Weakly supervised	0.2837	0.3802	0.4389	0.1387	0.2967	0.2330
Fully supervised	0.1790	0.2863	0.3402	0.0680	0.1425	0.1652
Weakly supervised + Fully supervised	**0.2912▲**	**0.4126▲**	**0.4509▲**	**0.1520▲**	**0.3077▲**	**0.2461▲**

We have also examined the *score* model with a network with a single linear hidden layer, with the embedding vector representation, which is equivalent to a linear regression model with the ability of representation learning. Comparing the results of this experiment with Score-Embed in Table 2, we can see that with a single-linear network we are not able to achieve a performance that is as good as a deep neural network with non-linearity. This shows that the most important superiority of deep neural networks over other machine learning methods is their ability to learn an effective representation and take all the interactions between query and document(s) into consideration for approximating an effective ranking/scoring function. This can be achieved when we have a deep enough network with non-linear activations.

How useful is learning with weak supervision for supervised ranking? In this set of experiments, we investigate whether employing weak supervision as a pre-training step helps to improve the performance of supervised ranking, when a small amount of training data is available. Table 5 shows the performance of the *rankprob* model with the embedding vector representation in three situations: (1) when it is only trained on weakly supervised data (similar to the previous experiments), (2) when it is only trained on supervised data, i.e., relevance judgments, and (3) when the parameters of the network is pre-trained using the weakly supervised data and then fine tuned using relevance judgments. In all the supervised scenarios, we performed 5-fold cross-validation over the queries of each collection and in each step, we used the TREC relevance judgements of the training set as supervised signal. For each query with m relevant documents, we also randomly sampled m non-relevant documents as negative instances. Binary labels are used in the experiments: 1 for relevant documents and 0 for non-relevant ones.

The results in Table 5 suggest that pre-training the network with a weak supervision signal, significantly improves the performance of supervised ranking. The reason for the poor performance of the supervised model compared to the conventional learning to rank models is that the number of parameters are much larger, hence it needs much more data for training.

In situations when little supervised data is available, it is especially helpful to use unsupervised pre-training which acts as a network pre-conditioning that puts the parameter values in the appropriate range that renders the optimization process more effective for further supervised training [11].

With this experiment, we indicate that the idea of learning from weak supervision signals for neural ranking models, which is presented in this paper, not only enables us to learn neural ranking models when no supervised signal is available, but also has substantial positive effects on the supervised ranking models with limited amount of training data.

7 CONCLUSIONS

In this paper, we proposed to use traditional IR models such as BM25 as a weak supervision signal in order to generate large amounts of training data to train effective neural ranking models. We examine various neural ranking models with different ranking architectures and objectives, and different input representations.

We used over six million queries to train our models and evaluated them on Robust04 and ClueWeb 09-Category B collections, in an ad-hoc retrieval setting. The experiments showed that our best performing model significantly outperforms the BM25 model (our weak supervision signal) by over 13% and 35% MAP improvements in the Robust04 and ClueWeb collections, respectively. We also demonstrated that in the case of having a small amount of training data, we can improve the performance of supervised learning by pre-training the network on weakly supervised data.

Based on our results, there are three key ingredients in neural ranking models that lead to good performance with weak supervision: The first is the proper input representation. Providing the network with raw data and letting the network to learn the features that matter, gives the network a chance of learning how to ignore imperfection in the training data. The second ingredient is to target the right goal and define a proper objective function. In the case of having weakly annotated training data, by targeting some explicit labels from the data, we may end up with a model that learned to express the data very well, but is incapable of going beyond it. This is especially the case with deep neural networks where there are many parameters and it is easy to learn a model that overfits the data. The third ingredient is providing the network with a considerable amount of training examples. As an example, during the experiments we noticed that using the embedding vector representation, the network needs a lot of examples to learn embeddings that are more effective for retrieval compared to pre-trained embeddings. Thanks to weak supervision, we can generate as much training data as we need with almost no cost.

Several future directions can be pursued. An immediate task would be to study the performance of more expressive neural network architectures e.g., CNNs and LSTMs, with weak supervision setup. Other experiment is to leverage multiple weak supervision signals from different sources. For example, we have other unsupervised ranking signals such as query likelihood and PageRank and taking them into consideration might benefit the learning process. Other future work would be to investigate the boosting mechanism for the method we have in this paper. In other words, it would be interesting to study if it is possible to use the trained model on weakly supervised data to annotate data with more quality from original source of annotation and leverage the new data to train a better model. Finally, we can apply this idea to other information retrieval tasks, such as query/document classification and clustering.

ACKNOWLEDGMENTS

This research was supported in part by Netherlands Organization for Scientific Research through the *Exploratory Political Search* project (ExPoSe, NWO CI # 314.99.108), by the Digging into Data Challenge through the *Digging Into Linked Parliamentary Data* project (DiLiPaD, NWO Digging into Data # 600.006.014), and by the Center for Intelligent Information Retrieval. Any opinions, findings and conclusions or recommendations expressed in this material are those of the authors and do not necessarily reflect those of the sponsors.

REFERENCES

[1] Nima Asadi, Donald Metzler, Tamer Elsayed, and Jimmy Lin. 2011. Pseudo test collections for learning web search ranking functions. In *Proceedings of the 34th international ACM SIGIR conference on Research and development in Information Retrieval*. ACM, 1073–1082.

[2] Pierre Baldi. 2012. Autoencoders, unsupervised learning, and deep architectures. *ICML unsupervised and transfer learning* 27 (2012), 37–50.

[3] Lidong Bing, Sneha Chaudhari, Richard C Wang, and William W Cohen. 2015. Improving Distant Supervision for Information Extraction Using Label Propagation Through Lists. In *EMNLP '15*. 524–529.

[4] Alexey Borisov, Ilya Markov, Maarten de Rijke, and Pavel Serdyukov. 2016. A Neural Click Model for Web Search. In *WWW '16*. 531–541.

[5] Jane Bromley, Isabelle Guyon, Yann LeCun, Eduard Säckinger, and Roopak Shah. 1993. Signature Verification Using a "Siamese" Time Delay Neural Network. In *NIPS '93*. 737–744.

[6] Daniel Cohen and W. Bruce Croft. 2016. End to End Long Short Term Memory Networks for Non-Factoid Question Answering. In *ICTIR '16*. 143–146.

[7] Gordon V. Cormack, Mark D. Smucker, and Charles L. Clarke. 2011. Efficient and Effective Spam Filtering and Re-ranking for Large Web Datasets. *Inf. Retr.* 14, 5 (2011), 441–465.

[8] Thomas Desautels, Andreas Krause, and Joel W Burdick. 2014. Parallelizing exploration-exploitation tradeoffs in Gaussian process bandit optimization. *Journal of Machine Learning Research* 15, 1 (2014), 3873–3923.

[9] Fernando Diaz. 2016. Learning to Rank with Labeled Features. In *ICTIR '16*. 41–44.

[10] Fernando Diaz, Bhaskar Mitra, and Nick Craswell. 2016. Query Expansion with Locally-Trained Word Embeddings. In *ACL '16*.

[11] Dumitru Erhan, Yoshua Bengio, Aaron Courville, Pierre-Antoine Manzagol, Pascal Vincent, and Samy Bengio. 2010. Why does unsupervised pre-training help deep learning? *Journal of Machine Learning Research* 11 (2010), 625–660.

[12] Martín Abadi et al. 2015. TensorFlow: Large-Scale Machine Learning on Heterogeneous Systems. (2015). http://tensorflow.org/ Software available from tensorflow.org.

[13] Ian Goodfellow, Jean Pouget-Abadie, Mehdi Mirza, Bing Xu, David Warde-Farley, Sherjil Ozair, Aaron Courville, and Yoshua Bengio. 2014. Generative adversarial nets. In *NIPS*. 2672–2680.

[14] Jiafeng Guo, Yixing Fan, Qingyao Ai, and W. Bruce Croft. 2016. A Deep Relevance Matching Model for Ad-hoc Retrieval. In *CIKM '16*. 55–64.

[15] Xianpei Han and Le Sun. 2016. Global Distant Supervision for Relation Extraction. In *AAAI'16*. 2950–2956.

[16] Ralf Herbrich, Thore Graepel, and Klaus Obermayer. 1999. Support Vector Learning for Ordinal Regression. In *ICANN '99*. 97–102.

[17] Raphael Hoffmann, Congle Zhang, Xiao Ling, Luke Zettlemoyer, and Daniel S. Weld. 2011. Knowledge-based Weak Supervision for Information Extraction of Overlapping Relations. In *ACL '11*. 541–550.

[18] Po-Sen Huang, Xiaodong He, Jianfeng Gao, Li Deng, Alex Acero, and Larry Heck. 2013. Learning Deep Structured Semantic Models for Web Search Using Clickthrough Data. In *CIKM '13*. 2333–2338.

[19] Kalervo Järvelin and Jaana Kekäläinen. 2002. Cumulated Gain-based Evaluation of IR Techniques. *ACM Trans. Inf. Syst.* 20, 4 (Oct. 2002), 422–446.

[20] Thorsten Joachims. 2002. Optimizing Search Engines Using Clickthrough Data. In *KDD '02*. 133–142.

[21] Diederik Kingma and Jimmy Ba. 2014. Adam: A method for stochastic optimization. *arXiv preprint arXiv:1412.6980* (2014).

[22] Ryan Kiros, Yukun Zhu, Ruslan R Salakhutdinov, Richard Zemel, Raquel Urtasun, Antonio Torralba, and Sanja Fidler. 2015. Skip-thought vectors. In *NIPS '15*. 3294–3302.

[23] Quoc V Le and Tomas Mikolov. 2014. Distributed Representations of Sentences and Documents. In *ICML '14*, Vol. 14. 1188–1196.

[24] Yann LeCun, Yoshua Bengio, and Geoffrey Hinton. 2015. Deep Learning. *Nature* 521, 7553 (2015), 436–444.

[25] Xiaodong Liu, Jianfeng Gao, Xiaodong He, Li Deng, Kevin Duh, and Ye-yi Wang. 2015. Representation Learning Using Multi-Task Deep Neural Networks for Semantic Classification and Information Retrieval. In *NAACL '15*. 912–921.

[26] Zhengdong Lu and Hang Li. 2013. A Deep Architecture for Matching Short Texts. In *NIPS '13*. 1367–1375.

[27] Tomas Mikolov, Ilya Sutskever, Kai Chen, Greg S Corrado, and Jeff Dean. 2013. Distributed Representations of Words and Phrases and their Compositionality. In *NIPS '13*. 3111–3119.

[28] Bhaskar Mitra, Fernando Diaz, and Nick Craswell. 2017. Learning to Match Using Local and Distributed Representations of Text for Web Search. In *WWW '17*. 1291–1299.

[29] Kezban Dilek Onal, Ismail Sengor Altingovde, Pinar Karagoz, and Maarten de Rijke. 2016. Getting Started with Neural Models for Semantic Matching in Web Search. *arXiv preprint arXiv:1611.03305* (2016).

[30] Greg Pass, Abdur Chowdhury, and Cayley Torgeson. 2006. A Picture of Search. In *InfoScale '06*.

[31] Jeffrey Pennington, Richard Socher, and Christopher Manning. 2014. GloVe: Global Vectors for Word Representation. In *EMNLP '14*. 1532–1543.

[32] Navid Rekabsaz, Mihai Lupu, Allan Hanbury, and Hamed Zamani. 2017. Word Embedding Causes Topic Shifting; Exploit Global Context!. In *SIGIR'17*.

[33] Navid Rekabsaz, Mihai Lupu, Allan Hanbury, and Guido Zuccon. 2016. Generalizing translation models in the probabilistic relevance framework. In *Proceedings of the 25th ACM International on Conference on Information and Knowledge Management*. ACM, 711–720.

[34] Aliaksei Severyn and Alessandro Moschitti. 2015. Twitter Sentiment Analysis with Deep Convolutional Neural Networks. In *SIGIR '15*. 959–962.

[35] Yelong Shen, Xiaodong He, Jianfeng Gao, Li Deng, and Grégoire Mesnil. 2014. Learning Semantic Representations Using Convolutional Neural Networks for Web Search. In *WWW '14*. 373–374.

[36] Nitish Srivastava, Geoffrey Hinton, Alex Krizhevsky, Ilya Sutskever, and Ruslan Salakhutdinov. 2014. Dropout: A Simple Way to Prevent Neural Networks from Overfitting. *J. Mach. Learn. Res.* 15, 1 (2014), 1929–1958.

[37] Yuan Tang. 2016. TF.Learn: TensorFlow's High-level Module for Distributed Machine Learning. *arXiv preprint arXiv:1612.04251* (2016).

[38] Christophe Van Gysel, Maarten de Rijke, and Evangelos Kanoulas. 2016. Learning latent vector spaces for product search. In *CIKM'16*. 165–174.

[39] Christophe Van Gysel, Maarten de Rijke, and Marcel Worring. 2016. Unsupervised, efficient and semantic expertise retrieval. In *WWW'16*. 1069–1079.

[40] Fabian L. Wauthier, Michael I. Jordan, and Nebojsa Jojic. 2013. Efficient Ranking from Pairwise Comparisons. In *ICML'13*. 109–117.

[41] Liu Yang, Qingyao Ai, Jiafeng Guo, and W. Bruce Croft. 2016. aNMM: Ranking Short Answer Texts with Attention-Based Neural Matching Model. In *CIKM '16*. 287–296.

[42] Hamed Zamani, Michael Bendersky, Xuanhui Wang, and Mingyang Zhang. 2017. Situational Context for Ranking in Personal Search. In *WWW '17*. 1531–1540.

[43] Hamed Zamani and W. Bruce Croft. 2016. Embedding-based Query Language Models. In *ICTIR '16*. 147–156.

[44] Hamed Zamani and W. Bruce Croft. 2016. Estimating Embedding Vectors for Queries. In *ICTIR '16*. 123–132.

[45] Hamed Zamani and W. Bruce Croft. 2017. Relevance-based Word Embedding. In *SIGIR '17*.

[46] Ye Zhang, Md Mustafizur Rahman, Alex Braylan, Brandon Dang, Heng-Lu Chang, Henna Kim, Quinten McNamara, Aaron Angert, Edward Banner, Vivek Khetan, and others. 2016. Neural Information Retrieval: A Literature Review. *arXiv preprint arXiv:1611.06792* (2016).

[47] Guoqing Zheng and Jamie Callan. 2015. Learning to Reweight Terms with Distributed Representations. In *SIGIR '15*. 575–584.

Variational Deep Semantic Hashing for Text Documents

Suthee Chaidaroon
Department of Computer Engineering
Santa Clara University
Santa Clara, CA 95053, USA
schaidaroon@scu.edu

Yi Fang
Department of Computer Engineering
Santa Clara University
Santa Clara, CA 95053, USA
yfang@scu.edu

ABSTRACT

As the amount of textual data has been rapidly increasing over the past decade, efficient similarity search methods have become a crucial component of large-scale information retrieval systems. A popular strategy is to represent original data samples by compact binary codes through hashing. A spectrum of machine learning methods have been utilized, but they often lack expressiveness and flexibility in modeling to learn effective representations. The recent advances of deep learning in a wide range of applications has demonstrated its capability to learn robust and powerful feature representations for complex data. Especially, deep generative models naturally combine the expressiveness of probabilistic generative models with the high capacity of deep neural networks, which is very suitable for text modeling. However, little work has leveraged the recent progress in deep learning for text hashing.

In this paper, we propose a series of novel deep document generative models for text hashing. The first proposed model is unsupervised while the second one is supervised by utilizing document labels/tags for hashing. The third model further considers document-specific factors that affect the generation of words. The probabilistic generative formulation of the proposed models provides a principled framework for model extension, uncertainty estimation, simulation, and interpretability. Based on variational inference and reparameterization, the proposed models can be interpreted as encoder-decoder deep neural networks and thus they are capable of learning complex nonlinear distributed representations of the original documents. We conduct a comprehensive set of experiments on four public testbeds. The experimental results have demonstrated the effectiveness of the proposed supervised learning models for text hashing.

CCS CONCEPTS

•Information systems →Information retrieval; •Computing methodologies →Neural networks; Learning latent representations;

KEYWORDS

Semantic hashing; Variational autoencoder; Deep learning

SIGIR '17, August 07-11, 2017, Shinjuku, Tokyo, Japan

978-1-4503-5022-8/17/08...$15.00
DOI: http://dx.doi.org/10.1145/3077136.3080816

1 INTRODUCTION

The task of similarity search, also known as nearest neighbor search, proximity search, or close item search, is to find similar items given a query object [36]. It has many important information retrieval applications such as document clustering, content-based retrieval, and collaborative filtering [34]. The rapid growth of Internet has resulted in massive textual data in the recent decades. In addition to the cost of storage, searching for relevant content in gigantic databases is even more daunting. Traditional text similarity computations are conducted in the original vector space and could be prohibitive to use for large-scale corpora since these methods are involved with high cost of numerical computation in the high-dimensional spaces.

Many research efforts have been devoted to approximate similarity search that is shown to be useful for practical problems. Hashing [6, 29, 39] is an effective solution to accelerate similarity search by designing compact binary codes in a low-dimensional space so that semantically similar documents are mapped to similar codes. This approach is much more efficient in memory and computation. A binary representation of each document often only needs 4 or 8 bytes to store, and thus a large number of encoded documents can be directly loaded into the main memory. Computing similarity between two documents can be accomplished by using bitwise XOR operation which takes only one CPU instruction. A spectrum of machine learning methods have been utilized in hashing, but they often lack expressiveness and flexibility in modeling, which prevents them from learning compact and effective representations of text documents.

On the other hand, deep learning has made tremendous progress in the past decade and has demonstrated impressive successes in a variety of domains including speech recognition, computer vision, and natural language processing [19]. One of the main purposes of deep learning is to learn robust and powerful feature representations for complex data. Recently, deep generative models with variational inference [15, 28] have further boosted the expressiveness and flexibility for representation learning by integrating deep neural nets into the probabilistic generative framework. The seamless combination of generative modeling and deep learning makes them suitable for text hashing. However, to the best of our knowledge, no prior work has leveraged them for hashing tasks.

In this paper, we propose a series of novel deep document generative models for text hashing, inspired by variational autoencoder (VAE) [15, 28]. The proposed models are the marriage of deep learning and probabilistic generative models [1]. They enjoy the good properties of both learning paradigms. First, with the deep neural networks, the proposed models can learn flexible nonlinear distributed representations of the original high-dimensional documents. This allows individual codes to be fairly general and concise but their intersection to be much more precise. For example, nonlinear distributed representations allow the topics/codes "government," "mafia," and "playboy" to combine to give very high probability to the word "Berlusconi," which is not predicted nearly as strongly by each topic/code alone.

Meanwhile, the proposed models are probabilistic generative models and thus there exists an underlying data generation process characterizing each model. The probabilistic generative formulation provides a principled framework for model extensions such as incorporating supervisory signals and adding private variables. The first proposed model is unsupervised and can be interpreted as a variant of variational autoencoder for text documents. The other two models are supervised by utilizing the document label/tag information. The prior work in the literature [37] has demonstrated that the supervisory signals are crucial to boost the performance of semantic hashing for text documents. The third model further adds a private latent variable for documents to capture the information only concerned with the documents but irrelevant to the labels, which may help remove noises from document representations. Furthermore, specific constraints can be enforced by making explicit assumptions in the models. One desirable property of hash code is to ensure the bits are uncorrelated so that the next bit cannot be predicted based on the previous bits [39]. To achieve this property, we can just assume that the latent variable has a prior distribution with independent dimensions.

In sum, the probabilistic generative formulation provides a principled framework for model extensions, interpretability, uncertainty estimation, and simulation, which are often lacking in deep learning models but useful in text hashing. The main contributions of the paper can be summarized as follow:

- We proposed a series of unsupervised and supervised deep document generative models to learn compact representations for text documents. To the best of our knowledge, this is the first work that utilizes deep generative models with variational inference for text hashing.
- The proposed models enjoy both advantages of deep learning and probabilistic generative models. They can learn complex nonlinear distributed representations of the original high-dimensional documents while providing a principled framework for probabilistic reasoning.
- We derived tractable variational lowerbounds for the proposed models and reparameterize the models so that backpropagation can be applied for efficient parameter estimation.
- We conducted a comprehensive set of experiments on four public testbeds. The experimental results demonstrate significant improvements in our supervised models over several well-known semantic hashing baselines.

2 RELATED WORK

2.1 Hashing

Due to computational and storage efficiencies of compact binary codes, hashing methods have been widely used for similarity search, which is an essential component in a variety of large-scale information retrieval systems [34, 36]. Locality-Sensitive Hashing (LSH) [2] is one of the most popular hashing methods with interesting asymptotic theoretical properties leading to performance guarantees. While LSH is a data-independent hashing method, many hashing methods have been recently proposed to leverage machine learning techniques with the goal of learning data-dependent hash functions, ranging from unsupervised and supervised to semi-supervised settings. Unsupervised hashing methods attempt to integrate the data properties, such as distributions and manifold structures to design compact hash codes with improved accuracy. For instance, Spectral Hashing (SpH) [39] explores the data distribution by preserving the similarity between documents by forcing the balanced and uncorrelated constraints into the learned codes, which can be viewed as an extension of spectral clustering [26]. Graph hashing [22] utilizes the underlying manifold structure of data captured by a graph representation. Self Taught Hashing (STH) [42] is the state-of-the-art hashing method by decomposing the learning procedure into two steps: generating binary code and learning hash function.

Supervised hashing methods attempt to leverage label/tag information for hash function learning. It has attracted more and more attention in recent years. For example, Wang et al. [37] propose Semantic Hashing using Tags and Topic Modeling (SHTTM) to incorporate tags to obtain more effective hashing codes via a matrix factorization formulation. To utilize the pairwise supervision information in the hash function learning, Kernel-Based Supervised Hashing (KSH) proposed in [21] used a pairwise relationship between samples to achieve high-quality hashing. Binary Reconstructive Embedding (BRE) [16] was proposed to learn hash functions by minimizing the reconstructed error between the metric space and Hamming space. Moreover, there are also several works using the ranking order information to design hash functions. Ranking-based Supervised Hashing (RSH) [35] was proposed to leverage listwise supervision into the hash function learning framework. Semi-supervised learning paradigm was also employed to design hash functions by using both labeled and unlabeled data [33]. The hashing-code learning problem is essentially a discrete optimization problem which is difficult to solve. Most existing supervised hashing methods try to solve a relaxed continuous optimization problem and then threshold the continuous representation to obtain a binary code. Abundant related work, especially on image hashing, exists in the literature. Two recent surveys [34, 36] provide a comprehensive literature review.

2.2 Deep Learning

Deep learning has drawn increasing attention and research efforts in a variety of artificial intelligence areas including speech recognition, computer vision, and natural language processing. Since one main purpose of deep learning is to learn robust and powerful feature representations for complex data, it is very natural to leverage deep learning for exploring compact hash codes which can be regarded as binary representations of data. Most of the related work has focused on image data [4, 17, 20, 40] rather than text documents probably due to the effectiveness of the convolution neural networks (CNNs) to learn good low-dimensional representations of images. The typical deep learning architectures for hash function learning consist of CNNs layers for representation learning and hash function layers which then transform the representation to supervisory signals. The loss functions could be pointwise [20], pairwise [4], or listwise [17].

Some recent works have applied deep learning for several IR tasks such as ad-hoc retrieval [10], web search [12], and ranking pairs of short texts [30]. However, very few has investigated deep learning for text hashing. The representative work is semantic hashing [29]. It builds a stack of restricted Boltzmann machines (RBMs) [11] to discover hidden binary units which can model input text data (i.e., word-count vectors). After learning a multilayer RBM through pretraining and fine tuning on a collection of documents, the hash code of any document is acquired by simply thresholding the output of the deepest layer. A recent work [41] exploited convolutional neural network for text hashing, which relies on external features such as the GloVe word embeddings to construct text representations.

Recently, deep generative models have made impressive progress with the introduction of the variational autoencoders (VAEs) [15, 28] and Generative Adversarial Networks (GANs) [9]. VAEs are especially an appealing framework for generative modeling by coupling the approach of variational inference [32] with deep learning. As a result, they enjoy the advantages of both deep learning and probabilistic graphical models. Deep generative models parameterized by neural networks have achieved state-of-the-art performance in unsupervised and supervised learning [14, 15, 25]. To the best of our knowledge, our proposed models are the first work that utilizes variational inference with deep learning for text hashing. It is worth pointing out that both semantic hashing with stacked RBMs [29] and our models are deep generative models, but the former is undirected graphical models, and the latter is directed models. The underlying generative process of directed probabilistic models makes them easy to interpret and extend. The proposed models are very scalable since they are trained as deep neural networks by efficient backpropagation, while the stacked RBMs are often much harder to train [11].

3 VARIATIONAL DEEP SEMANTIC HASHING

This section presents three novel deep document generative models to learn low-dimensional semantic representations of documents for text hashing. In Section 3.1, we introduce the basic model which is essentially a variational autoencoder for text modeling. Section 3.2 extends the model to utilize label information to learn a more sensible representation. Section 3.3 further incorporates document private variables to model document-specific information. Based on the variational inference, all the three models can be viewed as having an encoder-decoder neural network architecture where the encoder compresses a high-dimensional document to a compact latent semantic vector and the decoder reconstructs the document (or the labels). Section 3.4 discusses two thresholding methods to convert the continues latent vector to a binary code for text hashing.

3.1 Unsupervised Learning (VDSH)

In this section, we present the basic variational deep semantic hashing (VDSH) model for the unsupervised learning setting. VDSH is a probabilistic generative model of text which aims to extract a continuous low-dimensional semantic representation $\boldsymbol{s} \in \mathbb{R}^K$ for each document. Let $\boldsymbol{d} \in \mathbb{R}^V$ be the bag-of-words representation of a document and $\boldsymbol{w}_i \in \{0,1\}^V$ be the one-hot vector representation of the ith word of the document where V is the vocabulary size. $\boldsymbol{d}$ could be represented by different term weighting schemes such as binary, TF, and TFIDF [24]. The document generative process can be described as follows:

- For each document $\boldsymbol{d}$,
  - Draw a latent semantic vector $\boldsymbol{s} \sim P(\boldsymbol{s})$ where $P(\boldsymbol{s}) = \mathcal{N}(\boldsymbol{0}, \boldsymbol{I})$ is the standard Gaussian distribution.
  - For the ith word in the document,
    - Draw $\boldsymbol{w}_i \sim P(\boldsymbol{w}_i | f(\boldsymbol{s};\theta))$.

The conditional probability over words $\boldsymbol{w}_i$ is modelled by multinomial logistic regression and shared across documents as below:

$$P(\boldsymbol{w}_i | f(\boldsymbol{s};\theta)) = \frac{\exp(\boldsymbol{w}_i^T f(\boldsymbol{s};\theta))}{\sum_{j=1}^{V} \exp(\boldsymbol{w}_j^T f(\boldsymbol{s};\theta))} \quad (1)$$

While $P(\boldsymbol{s})$ is a simple Gaussian distribution, any distribution can be generated by mapping the simple Gaussian through a sufficiently complicated function [3]. Thus, $f(\boldsymbol{s};\theta))$ is such a highly flexible function approximator usually a neural network. In other words, we can learn a function which maps our independent, normally-distributed $\boldsymbol{s}$ values to whatever latent semantic variables might be needed for the model, and then generate the word $\boldsymbol{w}_i$. However, introducing a highly nonlinear mapping from $\boldsymbol{s}$ to $\boldsymbol{w}_i$ results in intractable data likelihood $\int_{\boldsymbol{s}} P(\boldsymbol{d}|\boldsymbol{s})P(\boldsymbol{s})d\boldsymbol{s}$ and thus intractable posterior distribution $P(\boldsymbol{s}|\boldsymbol{d})$ [15]. Similar to VAE, we use an approximation $Q(\boldsymbol{s}|\boldsymbol{d};\phi)$ for the true posterior distribution. By applying the variational inference principle [32], we can obtain the following tractable lowerbound of the document log likelihood (see [15] and Appendix):

$$\mathcal{L}_1 = \mathbb{E}_Q\Big[\sum_{i=1}^{N} \log P(\boldsymbol{w}_i | f(\boldsymbol{s};\theta))\Big] - D_{KL}(Q(\boldsymbol{s}|\boldsymbol{d};\phi) \parallel P(\boldsymbol{s})) \quad (2)$$

where N is the number of words in the document and $D_{KL}(\ \|\ )$ is the Kullback-Leibler (KL) divergence between the approximate posterior distribution $Q(\boldsymbol{s}|\boldsymbol{d};\phi)$ and the prior $P(\boldsymbol{s})$. The variational distribution $Q(\boldsymbol{s}|\boldsymbol{d};\phi)$ acts as a proxy to the true posterior $P(\boldsymbol{s}|\boldsymbol{d})$. To enable a high capacity, it is assumed to be a Gaussian $\mathcal{N}(\boldsymbol{\mu}, \text{diag}(\boldsymbol{\sigma}^2))$ whose mean $\boldsymbol{\mu}$ and variance $\boldsymbol{\sigma}^2$ are the output of a highly nonlinear function of $\boldsymbol{d}$ denoted as $g(\boldsymbol{d};\phi)$ parameterized by ϕ, once again typically a neural network.

In training, the variational lowerbound in Eqn.(2) is maximized with respect to the model parameters. Since $P(\boldsymbol{s})$ is a standard Gaussian prior, the KL Divergence $D_{KL}(Q(\boldsymbol{s}|\boldsymbol{d};\phi) \parallel P(\boldsymbol{s}))$ in Eqn.(2) can be computed analytically. The first term $\mathbb{E}_Q$ can be viewed as an expected negative reconstruction error of the words in the document and it can be computed based on the Monte Carlo estimation [8].

Based on Eqn.(2), we can interpret VDSH as a variational autoencoder with discrete output: a feedforward neural network encoder $Q(\boldsymbol{s}|\boldsymbol{d};\phi)$ compresses document representations into continuous hidden vectors, i.e., $\boldsymbol{d} \rightarrow \boldsymbol{s}$; a softmax decoder $\sum_{i=1}^{N} P(\boldsymbol{w}_i | f(\boldsymbol{s};\theta))$ reconstructs the documents by independently generating the words $\boldsymbol{s} \rightarrow \{\boldsymbol{w}_i\}_{i=1}^{N}$. Figure 1(a) illustrates the architecture of VDSH. In

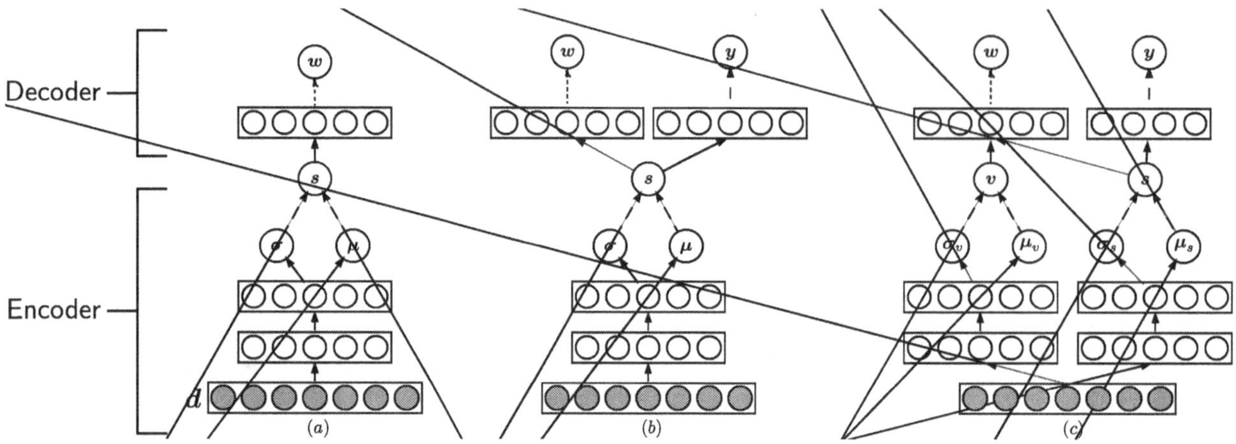

Figure 1: Architectures of (a) VDSH, (b) VDSH-S, and (c) VDSH-SP. The dashed line represents a stochastic layer.

the experiments, we use the following specific architecture for the encoder and decoder.

Encoder $Q(s|g(\boldsymbol{d};\phi))$:

$$t_1 = \text{ReLU}(W_1 \boldsymbol{d} + b_1)$$
$$t_2 = \text{ReLU}(W_2 t_1 + b_2)$$
$$\mu = W_3 t_2 + b_3$$
$$\log \sigma = W_4 t_2 + b_4$$
$$s \sim \mathcal{N}(\mu(\boldsymbol{d}), \text{diag}(\sigma^2(\boldsymbol{d})))$$

Decoder $P(w_i|f(s;\theta))$:

$$c_i = \exp(-s^T G w_i + b_{w_i})$$
$$P(w_i|s) = \frac{c_i}{\sum_{k=1}^{V} c_k}$$
$$P(\boldsymbol{d}|s) = \prod_{i=1}^{N} P(w_i|s)$$

This architecture is similar to the one presented in VAE [28] except that VDSH has the softmax layer to model discrete words while VAE is proposed to model images as continuous output. Here, the encoder has two Rectified Linear Unit (ReLU) [8] layers. ReLU generally does not face gradient vanishing problem as with other activation functions. Also, it has been shown that deep neural networks can be trained efficiently using ReLU even without pre-training [8].

In this architecture, there is a stochastic layer which is to sample s from a Gaussian distribution $\mathcal{N}(\mu(\boldsymbol{d}), \text{diag}(\sigma^2(\boldsymbol{d})))$, as represented by the dashed lines in the middle of the networks in Figure 1. Backpropagation cannot handle stochastic layer within the network. In practice, we can leverage the "location-scale" property of Gaussian distribution, and use the reparameterization trick [15] to turn the stochastic layer of s to be deterministic. As a result, the encoder $Q(s|\boldsymbol{d};\phi)$ and decoder $P(w_i|f(s;\theta))$ form an end-to-end neural network and are then trained jointly by maximizing the variational lowerbound in Eqn.(2) with respect to their parameters by the standard backpropagation algorithm [8].

3.2 Supervised Learning (VDSH-S)

In many real-world applications, documents are often associated with labels or tags which may provide useful guidance in learning effective hashing codes. Document content similarity in the original bag-of-word space may not fully reflect the semantic relationship between documents. For example, two documents in the same category may have low document content similarity due to the vocabulary gap, while their semantic similarity could be high. In this section, we extend VDSH to the supervised setting with the new model denoted as VDSH-S. The probabilistic generative process of a document with labels is as follows:

- For each document $\boldsymbol{d}$,
  - Draw a latent semantic vector $s \sim P(s)$ where $P(s) = \mathcal{N}(0, I)$ is the standard Gaussian distribution.
  - For the ith word in the document,
    - Draw $w_i \sim P(w_i|f(s;\theta))$.
  - For the jth label in the label set,
    - Draw $y_j \sim P(y|f(s;\tau))$.

where $y_j \in \{0,1\}^L$ is the one-hot representation of the label j in the label set and L is the total number of possible labels (the size of the label set). Let us use $Y \in \{0,1\}^L$ represent the bag-of-labels of the document (i.e., if the document has label j, the jth dimension of Y is 1; otherwise, it is 0). VDSH-S assumes that both words and labels are generated based on the same latent semantic vecotor.

We assume a general multi-label classification setting where each document could have multiple labels/tags. $P(y_j|f(s;\tau))$ can be modeled by the logistic function as follows:

$$P(y_j|f(s;\tau)) = \frac{1}{1 + \exp(-y_j^T f(s;\tau))} \quad (3)$$

Similar to VDSH, $f(s;\tau)$ is parameterized by a neural network with the parameter τ so that we can learn an effective mapping from the latent semantic vector to the labels. The lowerbound of the data log likelihood can be similarly derived and shown as follows:

$$\mathcal{L}_2 = \mathbb{E}_Q\Big[\sum_{i=1}^{N} \log P(w_i|f(s;\theta)) + \sum_{j=1}^{L} \log P(y_j|f(s;\tau))\Big] - D_{KL}(Q(s|\boldsymbol{d}, Y;\phi) \parallel P(s)) \quad (4)$$

Compared to Eqn.(2) in VDSH, this lowerbound has an extra term, $\mathbb{E}_Q\big[\sum_{j=1}^{L} \log P(y_j|f(s;\tau))\big]$, which can be computed in a similar way with $\mathbb{E}_Q\big[\sum_{i=1}^{N} \log P(w_i|f(s;\theta))\big]$ in Eqn.(2), by using the Monte Carlo estimation. In addition, we can drop the dependence on variable Y in the variational distribution $Q(s|\boldsymbol{d}, Y;\phi)$ since we may not have the label information available for new documents.

The architecture of the VDSH-S model is shown in Figure 1(b). It consists of a feedforward neural network encoder of a document $\boldsymbol{d} \rightarrow \boldsymbol{s}$ and a decoder of the words and labels of the document $\boldsymbol{s} \rightarrow \{\boldsymbol{w}_i\}_{i=1}^N; \{\boldsymbol{y}_j\}_{j=1}^L$. It is worth pointing out that the labels still affect the learning of latent semantic vector by their presence in the decoder despite their absence in the encoder. By using the reparameterization trick, the model becomes a deterministic deep neural network and the lowerbound in Eqn.(4) can be maximized by backpropagation (see Appendix).

3.3 Document-specific Modeling (VDSH-SP)

VDSH-S assumes both document and labels are generated by the same latent semantic vector $\boldsymbol{s}$. In some cases, this assumption may be restrictive. For example, the original document may contain information that is irrelevant to the labels. It could be difficult to find a common representation for both documents and labels. This observation motivates us to introduce a document private variable $\boldsymbol{v}$, which is not shared by the labels $\boldsymbol{Y}$. The generative process is described as follows:

- For each document $\boldsymbol{d}$,
  - Draw a latent semantic vector $\boldsymbol{s} \sim P(\boldsymbol{s})$ where $P(\boldsymbol{s}) = \mathcal{N}(0, \boldsymbol{I})$ is the standard Gaussian distribution.
  - Draw a latent private vector $\boldsymbol{v} \sim P(\boldsymbol{v})$ where $P(\boldsymbol{v}) = \mathcal{N}(0, \boldsymbol{I})$ is the standard Gaussian distribution.
  - For the ith word in the document,
    - Draw $\boldsymbol{w}_i \sim P(\boldsymbol{w}_i | f(\boldsymbol{s} + \boldsymbol{v}; \theta))$.
  - For the jth label in the label set,
    - Draw $\boldsymbol{y}_j \sim P(\boldsymbol{y} | f(\boldsymbol{s}; \tau))$.

As we can see, $\boldsymbol{s}$ models the shared information between document and labels while $\boldsymbol{v}$ only contains the document-specific information. We can view adding private variables as removing the noise from the original content that is irrelevant to the labels. With the added private variable, we denote this model as VDSH-SP. The tractable variational lowerbound of data likelihood can be derived as follows:

$$\mathcal{L}_3 = \mathbb{E}_Q \Big[\sum_{i=1}^{N} \log P(\boldsymbol{w}_i | f(\boldsymbol{s} + \boldsymbol{v}; \theta)) + \sum_{j=1}^{L} \log P(\boldsymbol{y}_j | f(\boldsymbol{s}; \tau)) \Big] \\ -D_{KL}(Q(\boldsymbol{s}|\boldsymbol{d}; \phi) \parallel P(\boldsymbol{s})) - D_{KL}(Q(\boldsymbol{v}|\boldsymbol{d}; \phi) \parallel P(\boldsymbol{v})) \quad (5)$$

Similar to the other two models, VDSH-SP can be viewed as a deep neural network by applying variational inference and reparametrization. The architecture is shown in Figure 1(c). The Appendix contains the detailed derivations of the model.

3.4 Binary Hash Code

Once a VDSH model has been trained, we can generate a compact continuous representation for any new document $\boldsymbol{d}_{new}$ by the encoder function $\mu_{new} = g(\boldsymbol{d}_{new}; \phi)$, which is the mean of the distribution $Q(\boldsymbol{s}|\boldsymbol{d}; \phi)$. The binary hashing code can then be obtained by thresholding μ_{new}. The most common method of thresholding for binary code is to take the median value of the latent semantic vector μ in the training data [37]. The rationale is based on the maximum entropy principle for efficiency which yields balanced partitioning of the whole dataset [39]. Thus, we set the threshold for binarizing the pth bit to be the median of the pth dimension of $\boldsymbol{s}$ in the training data. If the pth bit of document latent semantic vector μ_{new} is larger than the median, the pth binary code is set to 1; otherwise, it is set to -1. Another popular thresholding method is to use the Sign function on μ_{new}, i.e., if the pth bit of μ_{new} is nonnegative, the corresponding code is 1; otherwise, it is -1. Since the prior distribution of the latent semantic vector is zero mean, the Sign function is also a reasonable choice. We use the median thresholding as the default method in our experiments, while also investigate the Sign function in Section 5.3.

3.5 Discussions

The computational complexity of VDSH for a training document is $O(BD^2 + DSV)$. Here, $O(BK^2)$ is the cost of the encoder, where B is the number of the layers in the encoder network and D is the average dimension of these layers. $O(DNV)$ is the cost of the decoder, where S is the average length of the documents and V is the vocabulary size. The computational complexity of VDSH-S and VDSH-SP is $O(BD^2 + DS(V + L))$ where L is the size of the label set. The computational cost of the proposed models is at the same level as the deterministic autoencoder. Model learning could be quite efficient since the computations of all the models can be parallelized in GPUs, and only one sample is required during the training process.

The proposed deep generative model has a few desirable properties for text hashing. First of all, it has the capacity of deep neural networks to learn sophisticated semantic representations for text documents. Moreover, being generative models brings huge advantages over other deep learning models such as Convolutional Neural Network (CNN) because the underlying document generative process makes the model assumptions explicit. For example, as shown in [39], it is desirable to have independent feature dimensions in hash codes. To achieve this, our models just need to assume the latent semantic vector is drawn from a prior distribution with independent dimensions (e.g., standard Gaussian). The probabilistic approach also provides a principled framework for model extensions as evident in VDSH-S and VDSH-SP. Furthermore, instead of learning a particular latent semantic vector, our models learn probability distributions of the semantic vector. This can be viewed as finding a region instead of a fixed point in the latent space for document representation, which leads to more robust models. Compared with other deep generative models such as stacked RBMs and GANs, our models are computationally tractable and stable and can be estimated by the efficient backpropagation algorithm.

4 EXPERIMENTAL SETUP

4.1 Data Collections

We use the following four public document collections for evaluation. 1) *Reuters Corpus Volume I (RCV1)*. It is a large collection of manually labeled 800,000 newswire stories provided by Reuters. There are totally 103 classes. We use the full-topics version available at the LIBSVM website[1]. 2) *Reuters21578*[2]. A widely used text corpus for text classification. This collection has 10,788 documents with 90 categories and 7,164 unique words. 3) *20Newsgroups*[3].

[1] https://www.csie.ntu.edu.tw/~cjlin/libsvmtools/datasets/multilabel.html
[2] http://www.nltk.org/book/ch02.html
[3] http://ana.cachopo.org/datasets-for-single-label-text-categorization

	RCV1					*Reuters*				
Methods	8 bits	16 bits	32 bits	64 bits	128 bits	8 bits	16 bits	32 bits	64 bits	128 bits
LSH [2]	0.4180	0.4352	0.4716	0.5214	0.5877	0.2802	0.3215	0.3862	0.4667	0.5194
SpH [39]	0.5093	0.7121	0.7475	0.7559	0.7423	0.6080	0.6340	0.6513	0.6290	0.6045
STHs [42]	0.3975	0.4898	0.5592	0.5945	0.5946	0.6616	0.7351	0.7554	0.7350	0.6986
Stacked RBMs [29]	0.5106	0.5743	0.6130	0.6463	0.6531	0.5113	0.5740	0.6154	0.6177	0.6452
KSH [21]	0.9126	0.9146	0.9221	0.9333	0.9350	0.7840	0.8376	0.8480	0.8537	0.8620
SHTTM [37]	0.8820	0.9038	0.9258	0.9459	0.9447	0.7992	0.8520	0.8323	0.8271	0.8150
VDSH	0.7976	0.7944	0.8481	0.8951	0.8444	0.6859	0.7165	0.7753	0.7456	0.7318
VDSH-S	0.9652†	0.9749†	**0.9801**†	0.9804†	**0.9800**†	**0.9005**†	0.9121†	**0.9337**†	**0.9407**†	0.9299†
VDSH-SP	**0.9666**†	**0.9757**†	0.9788†	**0.9805**†	0.9794†	0.8890†	**0.9326**†	0.9283†	0.9286†	**0.9395**†
	20Newsgroups					*TMC*				
Methods	8 bits	16 bits	32 bits	64 bits	128 bits	8 bits	16 bits	32 bits	64 bits	128 bits
LSH [2]	0.0578	0.0597	0.0666	0.0770	0.0949	0.4388	0.4393	0.4514	0.4553	0.4773
SpH [39]	0.2545	0.3200	0.3709	0.3196	0.2716	0.5807	0.6055	0.6281	0.6143	0.5891
STH [42]	0.3664	0.5237	0.5860	0.5806	0.5443	0.3723	0.3947	0.4105	0.4181	0.4123
Stacked RBMs [29]	0.0594	0.0604	0.0533	0.0623	0.0642	0.4846	0.5108	0.5166	0.5190	0.5137
KSH [21]	0.4257	0.5559	0.6103	0.6488	0.6638	0.6608	0.6842	0.7047	0.7175	0.7243
SHTTM [37]	0.2690	0.3235	0.2357	0.1411	0.1299	0.6299	0.6571	0.6485	0.6893	0.6474
VDSH	0.3643	0.3904	0.4327	0.1731	0.0522	0.4330	0.6853	0.7108	0.4410	0.5847
VDSH-S	0.6586†	**0.6791**†	**0.7564**†	0.6850†	0.6916†	0.7387†	**0.7887**†	0.7883†	**0.7967**†	**0.8018**†
VDSH-SP	**0.6609**†	0.6551†	0.7125†	**0.7045**†	**0.7117**†	**0.7498**†	0.7798†	**0.7891**†	0.7888†	0.7970†

Table 1: Precision of the top 100 retrieved documents on four datasets with different numbers of hashing bits. The bold font denotes the best result at that number of bits. † denotes the improvement over the best result of the baselines is statistically significant based on the paired t-test (p-value < 0.01).

This dataset is a collection of 18,828 newsgroup posts, partitioned (nearly) evenly across 20 different newsgroups/categories. It has become a popular dataset for experiments in text applications of machine learning techniques. 4) *TMC*[4]. This dataset contains the air traffic reports provided by NASA and was used as part of the SIAM text mining competition. It has 22 labels, 21,519 training documents, 3,498 test documents, and 3,498 documents for the validation set. All the datasets are multi-label except *20Newsgroups*.

Each dataset was split into three subsets with roughly 80% for training, 10% for validation, and 10% for test. The training data is used to learn the mapping from document to hash code. Each document in the test set is used to retrieve similar documents based on the mapping, and the results are evaluated. The validation set is used to choose the hyperparameters. We removed the stopwords using SMART's list of 571 stopwords[5]. No stemming was performed. We use TFIDF [24] as the default term weighting scheme for the raw document representation (i.e., $\boldsymbol{d}$). We experiment with other term weighting schemes in Section 5.4.

4.2 Baselines and Settings

We compare the proposed models with the following six competitive baselines which have been extensively used for text hashing in the prior work [37]: Locality Sensitive Hashing (LSH)[6] [2], Spectral Hashing (SpH)[7] [39], Self-taught Hashing (STH)[8] [42], Stacked Restricted Boltzmann Machines (Stacked RBMs) [29], Supervised Hashing with Kernels (KSH) [21], and Semantic Hashing using Tags and Topic Modeling (SHTTM) [37]. We used the validation dataset to choose the hyperparameters for the baselines.

For our proposed models, we adopt the method in [7] for weight initialization. The Adam optimizer [13] with the step size 0.001 is used due to its fast convergence. Following the practice in [38], we use the dropout technique [31] with the keep probability of 0.8 in training to alleviate overfitting. The number of hidden nodes of the models is 1,500 for RCV1 and 1,000 for the other three smaller datasets. All the experiments were conducted on a server with 2 Intel E5-2630 CPUs and 4 GeForce GTX TITAN X GPUs. The proposed deep models were implemented on the Tensorflow[9] platform. For the VDSH model on the Reuters21578, 20Newsgroups, and TMC datasets, each epoch takes about 60 seconds, and each run takes 30 epochs to converge. For RCV1, it takes about 3,600 seconds per epoch and needs fewer epochs (about 15) to get satisfactory performance. Since RCV1 is much larger than the other three datasets, this shows that the proposed models are quite scalable. VDSH-S and VDSH-SP take slightly more time to train than VDSH does (about 40 minutes each on Reuters21578, 20Newsgroups, and TMC, and 20 hours on RCV1).

4.3 Evaluation Metrics

To evaluate the effectiveness of hashing code in similarity search, each document in the test set is used as a query document to search for similar documents based on the Hamming distance (i.e., number

[4]https://catalog.data.gov/dataset/siam-2007-text-mining-competition-dataset
[5]http://www.lextek.com/manuals/onix/stopwords2.html
[6]http://pixelogik.github.io/NearPy/
[7]http://www.cs.huji.ac.il/~yweiss/SpectralHashing/
[8]http://www.dcs.bbk.ac.uk/~dell/publications/dellzhang_sigir2010/sth_v1.zip
[9]https://www.tensorflow.org/

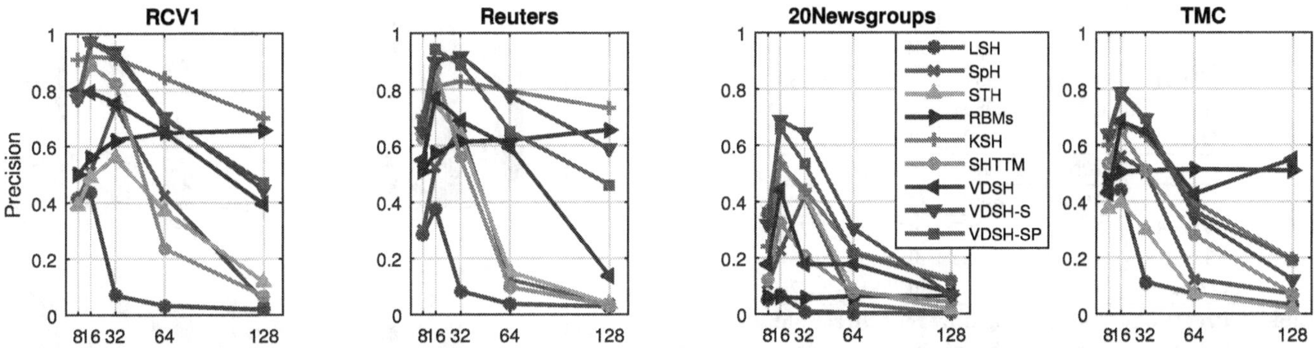

Figure 2: The Precision within the Hamming distance of 2 on four datasets with different hashing bits.

of different bits) between their hashing codes. Following the prior work in text hashing [37], the performance is measured by Precision, as the ratio of the number of retrieved relevant documents to the number of all retrieved documents. The results are averaged over all the test documents.

There exist various ways to determine whether a retrieved document is relevant to the given query document. In SpH [39], the K closest documents in the original feature space are considered as the relevant documents. This metric is not desirable since the similarity in the original feature space may not well reflect the document semantic similarity. Also, it is hard to determine a suitable K for the cutoff threshold. Instead, we adopt the methodology used in KSH [33], SHTTM [37] and other prior work [33], that is a retrieved document that shares any common test label with the query document is regarded as a relevant document.

5 EXPERIMENTAL RESULTS

5.1 Baseline Comparison

Table 1 shows the results of different methods over various numbers of bits on the four testbeds. We have several observations from the results. First of all, the best results at different bits are all achieved by VDSH-S or VDSH-SP. They consistently yield better results than all the baselines across all the different numbers of bits. All the improvements over the baselines are statistically significant based on the paired t-test (p-value < 0.01). VDSH-S and VDSH-SP produce comparable results between them. Adding private variables does not always help because it increases the model flexibility which may lead to overfitting to the training data. This probably explains why VDSH-SP generally yield better performance when the number of bits is 8 which corresponds to a simpler model.

Secondly, the supervised hashing techniques (i.e., VDSH-S, VDSH-SP, KSH) outperform the unsupervised methods on the four datasets across all the different bits. These results demonstrate the importance of utilizing supervisory signals for text hashing. However, the unsupervised model, STHs, outperforms SHTTM on the original 20 categories Newsgroups. One possible explanation is that SHTTM depends on LDA to learn an initial representation. But many categories in Newsgroup are correlated, LDA could assign similar topics to documents from related categories (i.e. Christian, Religion). Hence SHTTM may not effectively distinguish two related categories. Evidently, SHTTM and KSH deliver comparable results except on the 20Newsgroups testbed. It is worth noting that there exist substantial gaps between the supervised and unsupervised proposed models (VDSH-S and VDSH-SP vs VDSH) across all the datasets and configurations. The label information seems remarkably useful for guiding the deep generative models to learn effective representations. This is probably due to the high capacity of the neural network component which can learn subtle patterns from supervisory signals when available.

Thirdly, the performance does not always improve when the number of bits increases. This pattern seems quite consistent across all the compared methods and it is likely the result of model overfitting, which suggests that using a long hash code is not always helpful especially when training data is limited. Last but not least, the testbeds may affect the model performance. All the best results are obtained on the RCV1 dataset whose size is much larger than the other testbeds. These results illustrate the importance of using a large amount of data to train text hashing models.

It is worth noting that some of the baseline results are different from what were reported in the prior work. This is due to the data preprocessing. For example, [37] combined some categories in 20Newsgroup to form 6 broader categories in their experiments while we use all the original 20 categories for evaluation. [42] focused on single-label documents by discarding the documents appearing in more than one category while we use all the documents in the corpus.

5.2 Retrieval with Fixed Hamming Distance

In practice, IR systems may retrieve similar documents in a large corpus within a fixed Hamming distance radius to the query document. In this section, we evaluate the precision for the Hamming radius of 2. Figure 2 shows the results on four datasets with different numbers of hashing bits. We can see that the overall best performance among all nine hashing methods on each dataset is achieved by either VDSH-S or VDSH-SP at the 16-bit. In general, the precision of most of the methods decreases when the number of hashing bits increases from 32 to 128. This may be due to the fact that when using longer hashing bits, the Hamming space becomes increasingly sparse and very few documents fall within the Hamming distance of 2, resulting in more queries with precision 0. Similar behavior is also observed in the prior work such as KSH [21] and SHTTM [37]. A notable exception is Stacked RBMs whose

	RCV1		Reuters	
	Median	Sign	Median	Sign
VDSH	0.8481	0.8514	0.7753	0.7851
VDSH-S	0.9801	0.9804	0.9337	0.9284
VDSH-SP	0.9788	0.9794	0.9283	0.9346
	20Newsgroups		TMC	
	Median	Sign	Median	Sign
VDSH	0.4354	0.4267	0.7108	0.7162
VDSH-S	0.7564	0.7563	0.7883	0.7879
VDSH-SP	0.6913	0.6574	0.7891	0.7761

Table 2: Precision@100 of using different thresholding functions (Median vs Sign) for the proposed models on four testbeds with the 32-bit hash code

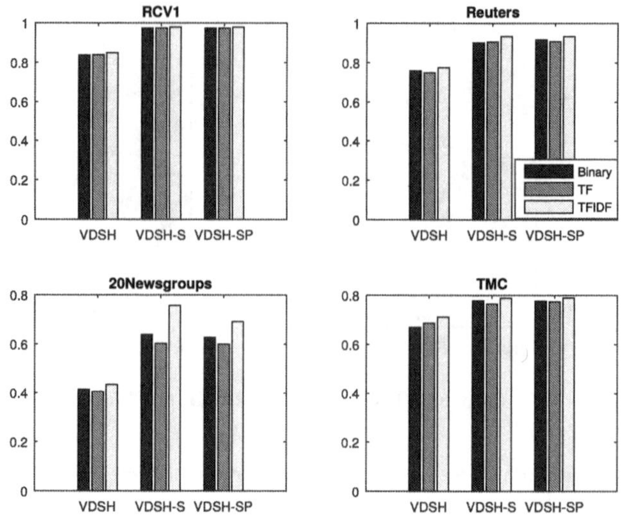

Figure 3: Precision@100 for different term weighting schemes on the proposed models with the 32-bit hash code.

performance is quite stable across different numbers of bits while lags behind the best performers.

5.3 Effect of Thresholding

Thresholding is an important step in hashing to transform a continuous document representation to a binary code. We investigate two popular thresholding functions: Median and Sign, which are introduced in Section 3.4. Table 2 contains the precision results of the proposed models with the 32-bit hash code on the four datasets. As we can see, the two thresholding functions generate quite similar results and their differences are not statistically significant, which indicates all the proposed models, whether being unsupervised or supervised, are not sensitive to the thresholding methods.

5.4 Effect of Term Weighting Schemes

In this section, we investigate the effect of term weighting schemes on the performance of the proposed models. Different term weights result in different bag-of-word representations of $\boldsymbol{d}$ as the input to the neural network. Specifically, we experiment with three term weighting representations for documents: Binary, Term Frequency (TF), Term Frequency and Inverse Document Frequency (TFIDF) [24]. Figure 3 illustrates the results of the proposed models with the 32-bit hash code on the four datasets. As we can see, the proposed models generally are not very sensitive to the underlying term weighting schemes. The TFIDF weighting always gives the best performance on all the four datasets. The improvement is more noticeable with VDSH-S and VDSH-SP on 20Newsgroups. The results indicate more sophisticated weighting schemes may capture more information about the original documents and thus lead to better hashing results. One the other hand, all the three models yield quite stable results on RCV1, which suggests that a large-scale dataset may help alleviate the shortcomings of the basic term weighting schemes.

5.5 Qualitative Analysis

In this section, we visualize the low-dimensional representations of the documents and see whether they can preserve the semantics of the original documents. Specifically, we use t-SNE[10] [23] to generate the scatter plots for the document latent semantic vectors in 32-dimensional space obtained by SHTTM and VDSH-S on the 20Newsgroup dataset. Figure 4 shows the results. Here, each data point represents a document which is associated with one of the 20 categories. Different colors represent different categories based on the ground truth.

As we can see in Figure (4)(b), VDSH-S generates well separated clusters with each corresponding to a true category (each number in the plot represents a category ID). On the other hand, the clustering structure from SHTTM shown in Figure (4)(a) is much less evident and recognizable. Some closeby clusters in Figure (4)(b) are also semantically related, e.g., Category 7 (Religion) and Category 11 (Atheism); Category 20 (Middle East) and Category 10 (Guns); Category 8 (WinX) and Category 5 (Graphics).

We further sampled some documents from the dataset and see where they are represented in the plots. Table 3 contains the DocIDs, categories, and subjects of the sample documents. Doc5780 discusses some trade rumor in NHL and Doc5773 is about NHL team leaders. Both documents belong to the category of Hockey and should be close to each other, which can be clearly observed in Figure (4)(b) by VDSH-S. However, these two documents are projected far away from each other by SHTTM as shown in Figure (4)(a). For another random pair of documents Doc3420 and Doc3412 in the plots, VDSH-S also puts them much closer to each other than SHTTM does. These results demonstrate the great effectiveness of VDSH-S in learning low-dimensional representations for text documents.

6 CONCLUSIONS AND FUTURE WORK

Text hashing has become an important component in many large-scale information retrieval systems. It attempts to map documents in a high-dimensional space into a low-dimensional compact representation, while preserving the semantic relationship of the documents as much as possible. Deep learning is a powerful representation learning approach and has demonstrated its effectiveness of

[10]https://lvdmaaten.github.io/tsne/

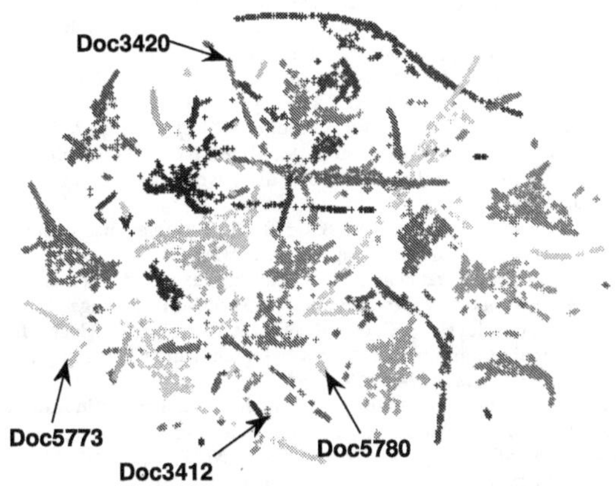

(a) SHTTM

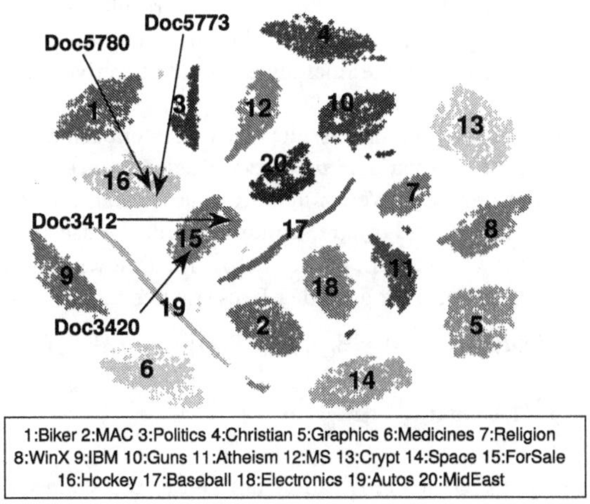

(b) VDSH-S

Figure 4: Visualization of the 32-dimensional document latent semantic vectors by SHTTM and VDSH-S on the 20Newsgroup dataset using t-SNE. Each point represents a document and different colors denote different categories based on the ground truth. In (b)VDSH-S, each number is a category ID and the corresponding categories are shown below the plot.

DocId	Category	Title/Subject
Doc5780	Hockey	Trade rumor: Montreal/Ottawa/Phillie
Doc5773	Hockey	NHL team leaders in +/-
Doc3420	ForSale	Books For Sale [Ann Arbor, MI]
Doc3412	ForSale	*** NeXTstation 8/105 For Sale ***

Table 3: The titles of the four sample documents in Figure 4

learning effective representations in a wide range of applications, but there is very little prior work on utilizing it for text hashing tasks. In this paper, we exploit the recent advances in variational autoencoder and propose a series of deep generative models for text hashing. The models enjoy the advantages of both deep learning and probabilistic generative models. They can learn subtle nonlinear semantic representation in a principled probabilistic framework, especially when supervisory signals are available. The experimental results on four public testbeds demonstrate that the proposed supervised models significantly outperform the competitive baselines.

This work is an initial step towards a promising research direction. The probabilistic formulation and deep learning architecture provide a flexible framework for model extensions. In future work, we will explore deeper and more sophisticated architectures such as Convolutional Neural Network (CNN), Recurrent Neural Network (RNN) [19], autoregressive neural network (NADE, MADE) [5, 18] for encoder and decoder. These more sophisticated models may be able to capture the local relations (by CNN) or sequential information (by RNN, NADE, MADE) in text. Moreover, we will utilize the probabilistic generative process to sample and simulate new text, which may facilitate the task of Natural Language Generation [27]. Last but not least, we will adapt the proposed models to hash other types of data such as images and videos.

APPENDIX

In this section, we show the derivations of the proposed models. Due to the page limit, we only focus on VDSH-SP, the most sophisticated one among the three models. The other two models can be similarly derived.

The likelihood of document d and labels Y is:

$$\log P(\boldsymbol{d}, Y) = \log \int_{\boldsymbol{s},\boldsymbol{v}} P(\boldsymbol{d}, Y, \boldsymbol{s}, \boldsymbol{v}) d\boldsymbol{s} d\boldsymbol{v}$$

$$= \log \int_{\boldsymbol{s},\boldsymbol{v}} Q(\boldsymbol{s}, \boldsymbol{v}|\boldsymbol{d}, Y) \frac{P(\boldsymbol{d}, Y, \boldsymbol{s}, \boldsymbol{v})}{Q(\boldsymbol{s}, \boldsymbol{v}|\boldsymbol{d}, Y)} d\boldsymbol{s} d\boldsymbol{v}$$

Based on the Jensen's Inequality [8],

$$\begin{aligned}
& \log P(\boldsymbol{d}, Y) \geq \mathbb{E}_{Q(\boldsymbol{s},\boldsymbol{v})}[\log P(\boldsymbol{d}, Y, \boldsymbol{s}, \boldsymbol{v}) - \log Q(\boldsymbol{s}, \boldsymbol{v}|\boldsymbol{d}, Y)] \\
= \; & \mathbb{E}_{Q(\boldsymbol{s},\boldsymbol{v})}[\log P(\boldsymbol{d}|\boldsymbol{s}, \boldsymbol{v})P(Y|\boldsymbol{s})] + \mathbb{E}_{Q(\boldsymbol{s},\boldsymbol{v})}[\log P(\boldsymbol{s}) \\
+ \; & \log P(\boldsymbol{v}) - \log Q(\boldsymbol{s}, \boldsymbol{v}|\boldsymbol{d}, Y)] \quad (6) \\
= \; & \mathbb{E}_{Q(\boldsymbol{s},\boldsymbol{v})}[\log P(\boldsymbol{d}|\boldsymbol{s}, \boldsymbol{v})P(Y|\boldsymbol{s})] + \mathbb{E}_{Q(\boldsymbol{s},\boldsymbol{v})}[\log P(\boldsymbol{s}) - \log Q(\boldsymbol{s}|\boldsymbol{d})] \\
+ \; & \mathbb{E}_{Q(\boldsymbol{s},\boldsymbol{v})}[\log P(\boldsymbol{v}) - \log Q(\boldsymbol{v}|\boldsymbol{d})] \quad (7) \\
= \; & \mathbb{E}_{Q(\boldsymbol{s},\boldsymbol{v})}[\log P(\boldsymbol{d}|\boldsymbol{s}, \boldsymbol{v})P(Y|\boldsymbol{s})] - D_{KL}(Q(\boldsymbol{s}|\boldsymbol{d}) \parallel P(\boldsymbol{s})) \\
- \; & D_{KL}(Q(\boldsymbol{v}|\boldsymbol{d}) \parallel P(\boldsymbol{v})) \quad (8) \\
= \; & \mathbb{E}_{Q(\boldsymbol{s},\boldsymbol{v})}[\log P(\boldsymbol{d}|\boldsymbol{s}, \boldsymbol{v})] + \mathbb{E}_{Q(\boldsymbol{s},\boldsymbol{v})}[\log P(Y|\boldsymbol{s})] \\
- \; & D_{KL}(Q(\boldsymbol{s}|\boldsymbol{d}) \parallel P(\boldsymbol{s})) - D_{KL}(Q(\boldsymbol{v}|\boldsymbol{d}) \parallel P(\boldsymbol{v})) \quad (9) \\
= \; & \mathbb{E}_{Q(\boldsymbol{s},\boldsymbol{v})}\Big[\sum_{i=1}^{N} \log P(\boldsymbol{w}_i|f(\boldsymbol{s}+\boldsymbol{v};\theta)) + \sum_{j=1}^{L} \log P(\boldsymbol{y}_j|f(\boldsymbol{s};\tau))\Big] \\
- \; & D_{KL}(Q(\boldsymbol{s}|\boldsymbol{d};\phi) \parallel P(\boldsymbol{s})) - D_{KL}(Q(\boldsymbol{v}|\boldsymbol{d};\phi) \parallel P(\boldsymbol{v})) \quad (10)
\end{aligned}$$

In Eqn.(6), we factorize the joint probability based on the generative process. Thus, $P(\boldsymbol{d}, Y, \boldsymbol{s}, \boldsymbol{v}) = P(\boldsymbol{d}|\boldsymbol{s}, \boldsymbol{v})P(Y|\boldsymbol{s})P(\boldsymbol{s})P(\boldsymbol{v})$. In Eqn.(7), the variational distribution, $Q(\boldsymbol{s}, \boldsymbol{v}|\boldsymbol{d}, Y)$ is equal to the product of $Q(\boldsymbol{s}|\boldsymbol{d})$ and $Q(\boldsymbol{v}|\boldsymbol{d})$ by assuming the conditional independence of $\boldsymbol{s}, \boldsymbol{v}, Y$ given $\boldsymbol{d}$. Eqn.(8) and Eqn.(9) are the results of rearranging and simplifying terms in Eqn.(7). Plugging the individual words and labels, we obtain the final lowerbound objective function in Eqn.(10) (also in Eqn.(5)).

Because of the Gaussian assumptions on latent semantic vector $\boldsymbol{s}$ and latent private variable $\boldsymbol{v}$, the two KL divergences in Eqn.(10) have analytic forms. We let $\boldsymbol{\mu}_s$ and $\boldsymbol{\sigma}_s$ are mean and standard deviation of $\boldsymbol{s}$. $\boldsymbol{\mu}_v$ and $\boldsymbol{\sigma}_v$ are similar defined. We use subscript k to denote the kth element of the vector. The following derivation is an analytical form for a single KL divergence term:

$$D_{KL}(Q(\boldsymbol{s}|\boldsymbol{d};\phi) \parallel P(\boldsymbol{s})) = \mathbb{E}_{Q(s)}[\log P(\boldsymbol{s})] - \mathbb{E}_{Q(s)}[\log Q(\boldsymbol{s}|\boldsymbol{d};\phi)]$$
$$= \frac{1}{2}\sum_{k=1}^{K}(1 + \log \sigma^2_{s,k} - \mu^2_{s,k} - \sigma^2_{s,k}) \quad (11)$$

$D_{KL}(Q(\boldsymbol{v}|\boldsymbol{d};\phi) \parallel P(\boldsymbol{v}))$ can be derived in the same way. The expectation terms in Eqn.(10) do not have a closed form solution, but we can approximate them by the Monte Carlo simulation as follows:

$$\mathbb{E}_{Q(\boldsymbol{s},\boldsymbol{v})}[\log P(\boldsymbol{d}|f(\boldsymbol{s}+\boldsymbol{v};\theta))] + \mathbb{E}_{Q(\boldsymbol{s},\boldsymbol{v})}[\log P(Y|\boldsymbol{s})]$$
$$= \frac{1}{M}\sum_{m=1}^{M}\left(\log P(\boldsymbol{d}|f(\boldsymbol{s}^{(m)}+\boldsymbol{v}^{(m)};\theta)) + \log P(Y|\boldsymbol{s}^{(m)})\right) \quad (12)$$

The superscript m denotes the mth sample. By shift and scale transformation, we have $\boldsymbol{s}^{(m)} = \boldsymbol{\epsilon}_s^{(m)} \odot \boldsymbol{\sigma}_s + \boldsymbol{\mu}_s$. We denote $\boldsymbol{\epsilon}_s$ as a sample drawn from a standard multivariate normal and $\odot$ is an element-wise multiplication. Also, $\boldsymbol{v}^{(m)}$ is obtained in the same way, $\boldsymbol{v}^{(m)} = \boldsymbol{\epsilon}_v^{(m)} \odot \boldsymbol{\sigma}_v + \boldsymbol{\mu}_v$. By using this trick, we can obtain multiple samples of $\boldsymbol{\epsilon}$ and feed them as the deterministic input to the neural network. The model becomes an end-to-end deterministic deep neural network with the following objective function:

$$\mathcal{L} = \frac{1}{M}\sum_{m=1}^{M}\left(\log P(\boldsymbol{d}|f(\boldsymbol{s}^{(m)}+\boldsymbol{v}^{(m)};\theta)) + \log P(Y|\boldsymbol{s}^{(m)})\right)$$
$$+ \frac{1}{2}\sum_{k=1}^{K}(2 + \log \sigma^2_{s,k} - \mu^2_{s,k} - \sigma^2_{s,k} + \log \sigma^2_{v,k} - \mu^2_{v,k} - \sigma^2_{v,k}) \quad (13)$$

ACKNOWLEDGMENTS

The authors would like to thank Mengwen Liu, for her many helpful comments and suggestions on the first draft, Travis Ebesu for his drawing of the model architectures in Figure 1, and anonymous reviewers for valuable comments and feedback.

REFERENCES

[1] D. M. Blei. Probabilistic topic models. *Communications of the ACM*, 55(4):77–84, 2012.

[2] M. Datar, N. Immorlica, P. Indyk, and V. S. Mirrokni. Locality-sensitive hashing scheme based on p-stable distributions. In *Proceedings of the twentieth annual symposium on Computational geometry*, pages 253–262. ACM, 2004.

[3] C. Doersch. Tutorial on variational autoencoders. *arXiv preprint arXiv:1606.05908*, 2016.

[4] V. Erin Liong, J. Lu, G. Wang, P. Moulin, and J. Zhou. Deep hashing for compact binary codes learning. In *CVPR*, pages 2475–2483, 2015.

[5] M. Germain, K. Gregor, I. Murray, and H. Larochelle. Made: Masked autoencoder for distribution estimation. In *ICML*, pages 881–889, 2015.

[6] A. Gionis, P. Indyk, R. Motwani, et al. Similarity search in high dimensions via hashing. In *VLDB*, volume 99, pages 518–529, 1999.

[7] X. Glorot and Y. Bengio. Understanding the difficulty of training deep feedforward neural networks. In *AISTATS*, pages 249–256, 2010.

[8] I. Goodfellow, Y. Bengio, and A. Courville. *Deep learning*. MIT Press, 2016.

[9] I. Goodfellow, J. Pouget-Abadie, M. Mirza, B. Xu, D. Warde-Farley, S. Ozair, A. Courville, and Y. Bengio. Generative adversarial nets. In *NIPS*, pages 2672–2680, 2014.

[10] J. Guo, Y. Fan, Q. Ai, and W. B. Croft. A deep relevance matching model for ad-hoc retrieval. In *CIKM*, pages 55–64. ACM, 2016.

[11] G. E. Hinton. A practical guide to training restricted boltzmann machines. In *Neural networks: Tricks of the trade*, pages 599–619. Springer, 2012.

[12] P.-S. Huang, X. He, J. Gao, L. Deng, A. Acero, and L. Heck. Learning deep structured semantic models for web search using clickthrough data. In *CIKM*, pages 2333–2338. ACM, 2013.

[13] D. Kingma and J. Ba. Adam: A method for stochastic optimization. *ICLR*, 2015.

[14] D. P. Kingma, S. Mohamed, D. J. Rezende, and M. Welling. Semi-supervised learning with deep generative models. In *NIPS*, pages 3581–3589, 2014.

[15] D. P. Kingma and M. Welling. Auto-encoding variational bayes. *ICLR*, 2014.

[16] B. Kulis and T. Darrell. Learning to hash with binary reconstructive embeddings. In *NIPS*, pages 1042–1050, 2009.

[17] H. Lai, Y. Pan, Y. Liu, and S. Yan. Simultaneous feature learning and hash coding with deep neural networks. In *CVPR*, pages 3270–3278, 2015.

[18] H. Larochelle and I. Murray. The neural autoregressive distribution estimator. In *AISTATS*, volume 1, page 2, 2011.

[19] Y. LeCun, Y. Bengio, and G. Hinton. Deep learning. *Nature*, 521(7553):436–444, 2015.

[20] K. Lin, H.-F. Yang, J.-H. Hsiao, and C.-S. Chen. Deep learning of binary hash codes for fast image retrieval. In *CVPR Workshops*, pages 27–35, 2015.

[21] W. Liu, J. Wang, R. Ji, Y.-G. Jiang, and S.-F. Chang. Supervised hashing with kernels. In *CVPR*, pages 2074–2081. IEEE, 2012.

[22] W. Liu, J. Wang, S. Kumar, and S.-F. Chang. Hashing with graphs. In *ICML*, pages 1–8, 2011.

[23] L. v. d. Maaten and G. Hinton. Visualizing data using t-sne. *JMLR*, 9(Nov):2579–2605, 2008.

[24] C. D. Manning, P. Raghavan, H. Schütze, et al. *Introduction to information retrieval*, volume 1. Cambridge: Cambridge university press, 2008.

[25] Y. Miao, L. Yu, and P. Blunsom. Neural variational inference for text processing. In *ICML*, 2016.

[26] A. Y. Ng, M. I. Jordan, Y. Weiss, et al. On spectral clustering: Analysis and an algorithm. In *NIPS*, volume 14, pages 849–856, 2001.

[27] E. Reiter, R. Dale, and Z. Feng. *Building natural language generation systems*, volume 33. Cambridge: Cambridge university Press, 2000.

[28] D. J. Rezende, S. Mohamed, and D. Wierstra. Stochastic backpropagation and approximate inference in deep generative models. *ICML*, 2014.

[29] R. Salakhutdinov and G. Hinton. Semantic hashing. *International Journal of Approximate Reasoning*, 50(7):969–978, 2009.

[30] A. Severyn and A. Moschitti. Learning to rank short text pairs with convolutional deep neural networks. In *SIGIR*, pages 373–382. ACM, 2015.

[31] N. Srivastava, G. E. Hinton, A. Krizhevsky, I. Sutskever, and R. Salakhutdinov. Dropout: a simple way to prevent neural networks from overfitting. *JMLR*, 15(1):1929–1958, 2014.

[32] M. J. Wainwright, M. I. Jordan, et al. Graphical models, exponential families, and variational inference. *Foundations and Trends® in Machine Learning*, 1(1–2):1–305, 2008.

[33] J. Wang, S. Kumar, and S.-F. Chang. Semi-supervised hashing for scalable image retrieval. In *CVPR*, pages 3424–3431. IEEE, 2010.

[34] J. Wang, W. Liu, S. Kumar, and S.-F. Chang. Learning to hash for indexing big data - a survey. *Proceedings of the IEEE*, 104(1):34–57, 2016.

[35] J. Wang, W. Liu, A. X. Sun, and Y.-G. Jiang. Learning hash codes with listwise supervision. In *ICCV*, pages 3032–3039, 2013.

[36] J. Wang, T. Zhang, J. Song, N. Sebe, and H. T. Shen. A survey on learning to hash. *TPAMI*, 2017.

[37] Q. Wang, D. Zhang, and L. Si. Semantic hashing using tags and topic modeling. In *SIGIR*, pages 213–222. ACM, 2013.

[38] W. Wang, H. Lee, and K. Livescu. Deep variational canonical correlation analysis. *arXiv preprint arXiv:1610.03454*, 2016.

[39] Y. Weiss, A. Torralba, and R. Fergus. Spectral hashing. In *NIPS*, pages 1753–1760, 2009.

[40] R. Xia, Y. Pan, H. Lai, C. Liu, and S. Yan. Supervised hashing for image retrieval via image representation learning. In *AAAI*, volume 1, page 2, 2014.

[41] J. Xu, P. Wang, G. Tian, B. Xu, J. Zhao, F. Wang, and H. Hao. Convolutional neural networks for text hashing. In *AAAI*, pages 1369–1375. AAAI Press, 2015.

[42] D. Zhang, J. Wang, D. Cai, and J. Lu. Self-taught hashing for fast similarity search. In *SIGIR*, pages 18–25. ACM, 2010.

ICE: Item Concept Embedding via Textual Information

Chuan-Ju Wang
Research Center for Information Technology Innovation, Academia Sinica
cjwang@citi.sinica.edu.tw

Ting-Hsiang Wang
Research Center for Information Technology Innovation, Academia Sinica
thwang@citi.sinica.edu.tw

Hsiu-Wei Yang
Research Center for Information Technology Innovation, Academia Sinica
leoyang@citi.sinica.edu.tw

Bo-Sin Chang
Department of Computer Science, National Chengchi University
105753001@nccu.edu.tw

Ming-Feng Tsai
Department of Computer Science, National Chengchi University
mftsai@nccu.edu.tw

ABSTRACT

This paper proposes an item concept embedding (ICE) framework to model item concepts via textual information. Specifically, in the proposed framework there are two stages: graph construction and embedding learning. In the first stage, we propose a generalized network construction method to build a network involving heterogeneous nodes and a mixture of both homogeneous and heterogeneous relations. The second stage leverages the concept of neighborhood proximity to learn the embeddings of both items and words. With the proposed carefully designed ICE networks, the resulting embedding facilitates both homogeneous and heterogeneous retrieval, including item-to-item and word-to-item retrieval. Moreover, as a distributed embedding approach, the proposed ICE approach not only generates related retrieval results but also delivers more diverse results than traditional keyword-matching-based approaches. As our experiments on two real-world datasets show, ICE encodes useful textual information and thus outperforms traditional methods in various item classification and retrieval tasks.

KEYWORDS

conceptual retrieval; concept embedding; textual information; information network

ACM Reference format:
Chuan-Ju Wang, Ting-Hsiang Wang, Hsiu-Wei Yang, Bo-Sin Chang, and Ming-Feng Tsai. 2017. ICE: Item Concept Embedding via Textual Information. In *Proceedings of SIGIR '17, August 07-11, 2017, Shinjuku, Tokyo, Japan, ,* 10 pages.
DOI: http://dx.doi.org/10.1145/3077136.3080807

1 INTRODUCTION

Learning meaningful and valuable representations of items is important for various applications where items that relate to information needs from a collection of information resources are to be obtained, such as item recommendation and entity retrieval. In traditional methods, each item is usually assumed to be independent of other items and is represented using a "one-hot" or "bag-of-objects" encoding format, for instance by representing a movie in terms of its genre or a song in terms of its listeners; this typically leads to difficulty with data sparsity, resulting in relatedness among items being simply ignored.

In recent years, distributed representations have been proposed to address the data sparsity problem in several fields, such as language modeling [1, 6–9] and information networks [2, 4, 10, 11, 14, 15]. The purpose of these approaches is to keep similar items (e.g., words, documents, or nodes) close to each other by embedding items as low-dimensional vectors. In [8], a skip-gram word embedding model is proposed to embed the target word to predict the embedding of each individual context word in a local window. Moreover, in [6] paragraph vectors are proposed to embed arbitrary pieces of text, e.g., sentences and documents. The fundamental idea behind these embedding approaches comes from the distributional hypothesis: "You shall know a word by the company it keeps" (Firth, J. R. 1957:11). In this quotation, Firth draws attention to the context-dependent nature of meaning with his notion of 'context of situation.' DeepWalk [10] further generalizes context dependency from sequences of words to graphs, and uses local information obtained from truncated random walks to learn latent representations of nodes in an information network. In addition, LINE [14] proposes an efficient edge-sampling method with carefully designed objective functions to learn latent representations in a large-scale information network. In comparison to classical approaches such as nearest neighbors that also utilize the distributional similarity of context, these embedding approaches have been proved to be effective and efficient, and scale to millions of nodes on a single machine.

Following the fruitful progress of these embedding approaches for information network modeling, several advanced embedding studies for more complex graphs or for specific applications have recently been proposed [3, 5, 13, 16, 17]. For example, HPE (heterogeneous preference embedding) [3] uses heterogeneous graphs (including users, tracks, albums, and artists) and encodes user preferences into low-dimensional vector spaces for music recommendations. Also following progress in LINE, which is mainly designed for homogeneous networks, the authors extend their previous work of unsupervised information network embedding and propose a

*The second author (Ting-Hsiang Wang) and the third author (Hsiu-Wei Yang) contributed equally.

978-1-4503-5022-8/17/08...$15.00
DOI: http://dx.doi.org/10.1145/3077136.3080807

semi-supervised predictive text embedding approach via heterogeneous text networks [13]. In these approaches, the learned vectors are used to make meaningful similarity comparisons only between homogeneous nodes and are thus appropriate for tasks involving only one type of entity, such as document classification and item-to-item retrieval. Despite that, in practice, various scenarios call for similarity comparisons between heterogeneous entities, e.g., using words to discover related songs for music recommendation. However, due to the essence of the complex graph structures designed in previous studies, comparison of heterogeneous nodes (e.g., heterogeneous search) is a difficult and complicated problem.

In this paper, we propose an item concept embedding (ICE) approach to model concepts of items via their associated textual information. We incorporate textual information because text is a coherent and readable set of symbols that transmits information, in which the learned low-dimension representations can easily be used to meet an information need in certain scenarios. In particular, there are two stages in our proposed approach: graph construction and embedding learning. In the first stage, a generalized network construction method is proposed by which we assemble a graph involving heterogeneous nodes (i.e., items and words) and a mixture of both homogeneous and heterogeneous relations. Here we leverage conceptual similarity between words and integrate these relations into the graph to better capture concepts behind both items and words. In the second stage, we leverage information about each node's neighbors to learn the embeddings of texts and items. The resulting embeddings are effective for both homogeneous and heterogeneous retrieval, including item-to-item and word-to-item retrieval. Moreover, as a distributed embedding approach, the proposed ICE approach provides not only related retrieval results but also delivers more diverse results than traditional keyword-matching-based approaches.

We conduct extensive experiments on two real-world datasets, including one movie dataset and one commercial music dataset. Experimental results show that the ICE network encodes useful textual information, outperforming traditional methods in various item classification and retrieval tasks. Most importantly, the proposed ICE approach is effectual for the tasks involving heterogeneous objects, such as word-to-item and item-to-word search. In summary, we make three major contributions in this paper:

(1) We propose a novel item concept embedding (ICE) approach to model concepts of items via their associated textual information.
(2) We propose a generalized network construction method to assemble a graph involving heterogeneous nodes and a mixture of both homogeneous and heterogeneous relations. The resulting ICE improves on the limitations of previous network embedding approaches and enhances the effectiveness of heterogeneous retrieval.
(3) We conduct extensive experiments on two real-world datasets. Experimental results attest the effectiveness of the proposed ICE approach. We also publish the IMDB dataset, which includes the textual descriptions of 36,586 movies.

The rest of this paper is organized as follows. In Section 2, we present the proposed ICE methodology in detail, including the formal definitions of the ICE problem, its related information network, graph construction, and embedding model learning. The results of empirical experiments are provided and discussed in Section 3.3. Section 4 concludes the paper.

2 METHODOLOGY

In Section 2.1, we define and formulate the item concept embedding (ICE) problem. We then describe in Section 2.2 how to construct the ICE network, and in Section 2.3 we show how to learn the ICE by leveraging neighborhood proximity, in the process briefly describing both model description and model optimization.

2.1 Problem Definition and Formulation

In this section we first define the ICE problem, and formulate it as a heterogeneous information network with entities and texts. The proposed ICE network is composed of two types of networks: entity-text networks and text-text networks. Below we define and describe in detail the two networks together with ICE networks.

Definition 2.1. **(Entity-Text Network)** An entity-text network, denoted as $G_{et} = (\mathcal{V} \cup \mathcal{T}, E_{et})$, is a *directed bipartite* graph with a *has-a* relation between items and words; $\mathcal{V}$ is a set of items, $\mathcal{T}$ is a set of words, and each edge $r \in E_{et}$ is associated with a positive weight reflecting the strength of the relation between an item and a word.

In an entity-text network, nodes and relations are both heterogeneous [12]. For such a network, entities can be different types of items, and the text can be any descriptive textual information associated with the item, depending on the real-world application. For example, for music recommendation, songs and the words in their lyrics form a typical entity-text bipartite network, where the weights of the edges can be either binary or any positive real number (e.g., the tf-idf value of a word in the lyrics). Note that in this paper we consider only positive network weights.

Definition 2.2. **(Text-Text Network)** A text-text network, denoted as $G_{tt} = (\mathcal{T}, E_{tt})$, is a *bidirected* graph with a *conceptually similar* relation between two words in $\mathcal{T}$, where $\mathcal{T}$ is a set of words, and each edge $r \in E_{tt}$ is associated with a positive weight reflecting the strength of the relation between two words.

By leveraging NLP resources (e.g., the pre-trained word2vec model [8] and ConceptNet[1]), a homogeneous text-text network can be built that illustrates the conceptual similarity between any two words in the network. For example, with a set of word2vec word vectors for words in a set T (denoted as $Q = (\vec{q}_{t_1}, \vec{q}_{t_2}, \ldots, \vec{q}_{t_{|T|}})$, where $\vec{q}_{t_i}$ denotes the low-dimensional vector of word t_i), one way to build such a network is to connect two words t_i and t_j if their cosine similarity is greater than a threshold h (i.e., $\cos(\vec{q}_{t_i}, \vec{q}_{t_j}) > h$); the weight of the connecting edge can be set to either one or the cosine distance. Note that in the text-text network, each node has a self-referencing bidirectional link (i.e., a self-loop), and the nodes and relations are all homogeneous [12].

In order to better model the item concept via textual information and facilitate heterogeneous retrieval, we further present the ICE network, a novel expanded entity-text-text network, the definition of which is below.

[1] http://conceptnet5.media.mit.edu

Definition 2.3. **(ICE Network)** The ICE network is an entity-text-text network denoted as $G_{ice} = (\mathcal{V} \cup \mathcal{T}, \overline{E}_{et} \cup E_{et} \cup E_{tt})$, where $\overline{E}_{et}$ denotes the expanded *has-a* relations between items and words.

Figure 1(a) is an example of the proposed ICE network, in which there exist heterogeneous nodes (items and words) and a mixture of both homogeneous (conceptually similar, purple lines) and heterogeneous (has-a, pink lines) relations. In the network, the expanded has-a relations $\overline{E}_{et}$ (the pink dashed lines in the figure) can be designed differently depending on the application. A general method of establishing such relations is described in Section 2.2.

Obtaining representative embeddings for such complex information networks is a vital but difficult problem; a solution for this would be of great use in a variety of retrieval and recommendation applications. In this paper, we aim to leverage the similarity of neighbor network structures of both items and words to describe each item and word via the corresponding low-dimensional vectors learned by our carefully designed ICE networks.

Definition 2.4. **(Neighborhood Proximity)** Given a graph $G = (\mathcal{V}, E)$, the *neighborhood proximity* of a pair of nodes (u, v) in the network is defined as the similarity between their neighborhood network structures. Mathematically, given the neighborhood structure of node b, denoted as $N_b = (u_{b1}, u_{b2}, \ldots, u_{b|\mathcal{V}|})$,[2] the neighborhood proximity between nodes u and v is decided by the similarity between the two vectors N_u and N_v. If there are no shared neighbors between u and v, the neighborhood proximity between them is 0.

In Figure 1, panels (b) and (c) illustrate the basic idea behind the ICE network, which can be seen as an alternative view of the original ICE network shown in panel (a). As shown in the figures, the neighbors of both items and words are of the same type (i.e., words), which means that both items and words are embedded via textual information. In this case, by quantifying neighborhood proximity, the resultant low-dimensional vectors of both items and words not only embed similar concepts illustrated with textual information but also facilitate homogeneous or heterogeneous retrieval. As an example, consider the second item (the music note with subscript 2) and the third word ($\mathbf{w}_3$) in Figure 1. These two heterogeneous nodes share the same neighborhood structure, i.e., $(\mathbf{w}_1, \mathbf{w}_2, \mathbf{w}_3)$, as illustrated in panel (c) of the figure; the learned representations of these two nodes are therefore close to each other.

2.2 ICE Network Construction

In this section, we describe a generalized network construction method for the proposed ICE network. Given an entity-text bipartite network $G_{et} = (\mathcal{V} \cup \mathcal{T}, E_{et})$ and a text-text bidirected network $G_{tt} = (\mathcal{T}, E_{tt})$ (see Definitions 2.1 and 2.2), we represent the two networks and their relations as matrices $M_{G_{et}}$ and $M_{G_{tt}}$ respectively:

- $M_{G_{et}} = (e_{ij})$ is a *biadjacency* matrix of size $|\mathcal{V}| \times |\mathcal{T}|$ such that each element e_{ij} is the weight of an edge for adjacent nodes and zero for nonadjacent nodes (see Figure 2(a)).

[2] The neighborhood structure of b can be represented by the first-order proximity of b to all the other nodes [14].

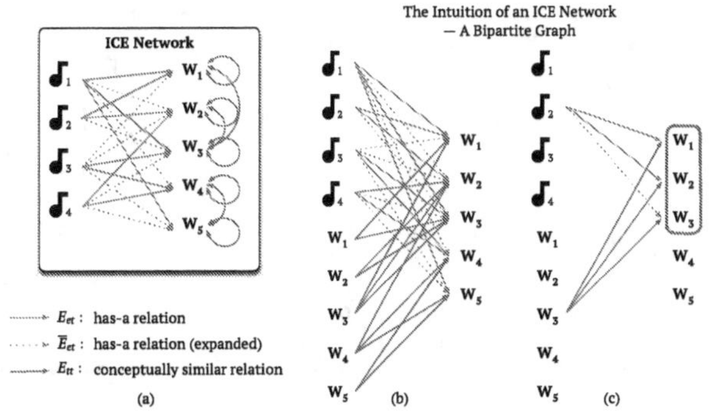

Figure 1: The basic idea behind the ICE network

- $M_{G_{tt}} = (t_{ij})$ is an *adjacency* matrix of size $|\mathcal{T}| \times |\mathcal{T}|$ such that each element t_{ij} is the weight of an edge for adjacent nodes and zero for nonadjacent nodes (see Figure 2(b)).

Note that since the conceptual similarity described by $M_{G_{tt}}$ is a homogeneous relation, rows and columns should not be permuted independently, but simultaneously, whereas $M_{G_{et}}$ relates to heterogeneous has-a relations, whose rows and columns can be permuted independently.

Establishing the expanded relations $\overline{E}_{et}$ between each item $i \in \mathcal{V}$ and each word $t \in \mathcal{T}$ is a way to better capture the concepts of items and words in the proposed ICE network. In this paper, we present a unified approach to construct these relations and construct the ICE network on the basis of the resulting relations. Assume for simplicity and demonstration purposes that both the entity-text bipartite network G_{et} and the text-text bidirected network G_{tt} are (0, 1)-graphs; i.e., each element in $M_{G_{et}}$ or $M_{G_{tt}}$, which represents the relation between nodes i and j, is one when there is a directed edge from node i to node j, and zero when there is no edge. Note that the diagonal elements of $M_{G_{tt}}$ are all set to one to represent the self-referencing links in the network G_{tt}. The inner product of the two matrices $M_{G_{et}}$ and $M_{G_{tt}}$ is defined as

$$A = (a_{ij}) = M_{G_{et}} \cdot M_{G_{tt}} \in \mathbb{R}^{|\mathcal{V}| \times |\mathcal{T}|}. \tag{1}$$

The intuition behind this operation is described as follows. Each element $a_{ij} \in A$ is the inner product of two vectors:

- $\vec{e}_i = (e_{i1}, e_{i2}, \ldots, e_{i|\mathcal{T}|})^\top \in \mathbb{R}^{|\mathcal{T}|}$ for item i, and
- $\vec{t}_j = (t_{1j}, t_{2j}, \ldots, t_{|\mathcal{T}|j})^\top \in \mathbb{R}^{|\mathcal{T}|}$ for word j.

There are two cases in which $a_{ij} > 0$:

- There is a directed edge from item i to word j;
- There is no directed edge from item i to word j, but there is at least one directed edge from item i to another word k and word j is bi-directionally connected to word k (the two words k and j are conceptually similar); i.e., $\exists k$ such that $k \neq j, e_{ik} = 1, t_{jk} = t_{kj} = 1$.

Given the two matrices $M_{G_{et}}$ and $M_{G_{tt}}$ associated with the two initial graphs G_{et} and G_{tt}, respectively, we define the transformation function $f(\cdot)$ to carry out the aforementioned operations together with a matrix augmenting operation to construct the ICE

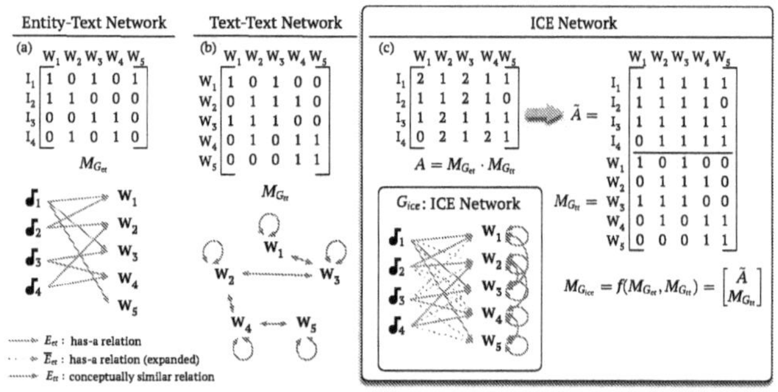

Figure 2: ICE network construction

network (the expanded entity-text-text network defined in Definition 2.3) as follows:

$$M_{G_{ice}} = f(M_{G_{et}}, M_{G_{tt}}) = \begin{bmatrix} \tilde{A} \\ M_{G_{tt}} \end{bmatrix} \in \mathbb{R}^{(|\mathcal{V}|+|\mathcal{T}|)\times|\mathcal{T}|}, \quad (2)$$

in which the matrix $\tilde{A}$ can be derived from matrix A in Equation (1). When building a (0, 1)-ICE-network, we have

$$\tilde{A} = (\tilde{a}_{ij}) = \left(\mathbb{1}_{\{a_{ij}>0\}}\right). \quad (3)$$

Although matrix $\tilde{A}$ can be designed in different ways (e.g., $\tilde{A} = A$ for weighted graphs), it is straightforward to apply our unified approach to different transformations. Finally, given the resulting matrix $M_{G_{ice}}$ (see Equation (2)), we obtain the ICE network, G_{ice}, treated as the input of the embedding learning algorithm (introduced in Section 2.3).

Figure 2 illustrates the ICE network construction method with an example (a (0,1)-graph), in which the matrix representations for the directed bipartite entity-text network G_{et} and the bidirected text-text network G_{tt} are shown in panels (a) and (b), respectively. As shown in panel (c), we obtain the expanded has-a relations by multiplying the two matrices $M_{G_{et}}$ and $M_{G_{tt}}$. For instance, there is no edge between the first item (the music note with subscript 1) and the second word ($\mathbf{w}_2$) in the original entity-text network; however, since the first item is linked to the third word ($\mathbf{w}_3$) and $\mathbf{w}_2$ and $\mathbf{w}_3$ are conceptually similar according to G_{tt} in panel (b), we have an expanded link between the first item and the second word (the pink dashed line) in panel (c).

2.3 Learning Embedding via Similarity of Neighborhood Network Structures

In a previous study [14], the LINE model was mainly proposed to learn the embeddings for homogeneous information networks, that is, graphs with the same type of vertices. In this paper we adopt *neighborhood proximity*, an essential idea from LINE as well as from various word embedding models, to manage the ICE networks, which are composed of heterogeneous nodes and a mixture of both homogeneous and heterogeneous relations. Neighborhood proximity presumes that nodes with similar neighborhood structures are similar and thus, when represented in a low-dimensional vector space, should be positioned close to each other.

To capture this proximity, each node in the graph plays two roles: the node itself and a specific "context" of other nodes. Although in an ICE network, both types of nodes (i.e., items and words) and relations (i.e., *has-a* and *conceptually similar* relations) are heterogeneous, the neighbors of each node are the same type: words; this reflects the careful design behind the ICE network, as introduced in Section 2.2.

Given an ICE network $G_{ice} = (\mathcal{V} \cup \mathcal{T}, \overline{E}_{et} \cup E_{et} \cup E_{tt})$, constructed via Equation (2), we introduce two vectors $\vec{v}_c$ and $\vec{v}'_c$, where $\vec{v}_c$ is the vector representation of node c when it plays the role of itself, whereas $\vec{v}'_c$ denotes node c's representation when it is taken as a specific context of other nodes. For each has-a relation between an item $n_i \in \mathcal{V}$ and a word $n_w \in \mathcal{T}$, the conditional probability of word n_w generated by item n_i is modeled as

$$P(n_w \mid n_i) = \frac{\exp\left(\vec{v}'^{\mathsf{T}}_{n_w} \cdot \vec{v}_{n_i}\right)}{\sum_{s\in\mathcal{T}} \exp\left(\vec{v}'^{\mathsf{T}}_{n_s} \cdot \vec{v}_{n_i}\right)}. \quad (4)$$

Similarly, for each conceptually similar relation between two words, $n_w \in \mathcal{T}$ and $n_{\check{w}} \in \mathcal{T}$, we have the conditional probability of word $\check{w}$ given word w as

$$P(n_{\check{w}} \mid n_w) = \frac{\exp\left(\vec{v}'^{\mathsf{T}}_{n_{\check{w}}} \cdot \vec{v}_{n_w}\right)}{\sum_{s\in\mathcal{T}} \exp\left(\vec{v}'^{\mathsf{T}}_{n_s} \cdot \vec{v}_{n_w}\right)}. \quad (5)$$

To model neighborhood structures via the item-word and word-word relations while preserving neighborhood proximity, for each node n_k, the conditional probabilities $P(\cdot \mid n_k)$ described by a set of low-dimensional representations should approximate the empirical probabilities $\hat{P}(\cdot \mid n_k)$. Here we follow the setting in [14] in setting the empirical probability for $\hat{P}(n_\ell \mid n_k)$ equal to $x_{k\ell}/d(n_k)$, in which $x_{k\ell}$ denotes the weight of the edge between nodes n_k and n_ℓ, and $d(n_k)$ is the out-degree of node n_k; that is, $d(n_k) = \sum_{n_g \in NB(n_k)} x_{kg}$, where $NB(n_k)$ is the set of the direct successors of node n_k. We proceed to minimize the following two objective functions O_E and O_T to learn the embeddings of items and words, respectively:

$$O_E = \sum_{n_i\in\mathcal{V}} d(n_i)\, D_{\mathrm{KL}}\left(\hat{P}(\cdot \mid n_i), P(\cdot \mid n_i)\right), \quad (6)$$

and

$$O_T = \sum_{n_w\in\mathcal{T}} d(n_w)\, D_{\mathrm{KL}}\left(\hat{P}(\cdot \mid n_w), P(\cdot \mid n_w)\right), \quad (7)$$

in which the Kullback-Leibler divergence $D_{\mathrm{KL}}(\cdot,\cdot)$ is adopted to measure the difference between the two distributions. By omitting some constants and adding O_E and O_T in Equations (6) and (7), the objective function becomes

$$O_{ice} = -\left(\sum_{(n_i,n_\ell)\in\tilde{E}_{et}} x_{i\ell} \log P(n_\ell \mid n_i) + \sum_{(n_w,n_\ell)\in E_{tt}} x_{w\ell} \log P(n_\ell \mid n_w)\right), \quad (8)$$

where $\tilde{E}_{et} = E_{et} \cup \overline{E}_{et}$. Equation (8) is minimized with stochastic gradient descent using edge sampling [14] and negative sampling [8], resulting in two sets of optimized representations $\{\vec{v}_c\}_{c\in\mathcal{V}\cup\mathcal{T}}$ and $\{\vec{v}'_c\}_{c\in\mathcal{V}\cup\mathcal{T}}$.

Table 1: Statistics of the two real-world datasets

	IMDB	KKBOX
# movies/songs	36,586	33,106
Average text length	65.0	215.24
Average # unique words	47.8	81.37
Vocabulary size	66,924	101,395
# single genres	28	-
# multi-label genres	915	-

3 EXPERIMENTS

We evaluate the performance of our proposed ICE approach on two real-world datasets. Section 3.1 first provides the details of the two datasets and the data processing conducted for the experiments. We then describe the experimental settings in Section 3.2, including the compared baselines and state-of-the-art methods, and the statistics of the constructed ICE information networks. Experimental results on various classification and retrieval tasks are provided in Section 3.3, where some interesting cases are also discussed.

3.1 Datasets and Data Preprocessing

In the experiments, two real-world datasets are used to assess the performance of the proposed ICE method, including one movie dataset (denoted as IMDB) and one music dataset (denoted as KKBOX, which is partially provided by a music-streaming company). Table 1 lists the statistics of the two data collections.

Below, we describe how we collect and process the datasets. The movie list of the IMDB dataset is that of the MovieLens 10/2016 *Full* datasets,[3] and we crawl the descriptions and genres of each movie from the IMDB website via the OMDB API.[4] Then, we filter out those movies without any descriptions, resulting in total 36,586 movies out of the 40,110 ones of the original MovieLens dataset; in average, the description of each movie contains around 65.0 words and 47.8 unique words. Moreover, there are 28 different single genres (e.g., horror and action) and 915 multi-label genres (e.g., horror-action-thriller) in total. For the KKBOX dataset, the music list is obtained from a commercial music-streaming company consisting of 33,106 Chinese songs, and we crawl the lyrics of each song for the following experiments. To process lyrics in the dataset, we use the Jieba Chinese segmentation toolkit[5] to conduct the word segmentation. After the procedure, there are in average 215.24 words and 81.37 unique words in each song, and there are in total 101,395 unique vocabularies, as shown in Table 1.

3.2 Experimental Setup

In our experiments, two different types of tasks are conducted to evaluate the performance of the proposed ICE approach, including classification task and retrieval task, the purpose of which is to verify the quality of the representations learned by ICE. Below, we describe the settings for each different task, respectively.

3.2.1 Settings for the Classification Task. For the classification task, we conduct a multi-label genre classification on the IMDB dataset. The classification model is trained via the LIBSVM toolkit,[6] and its input feature vectors are generated from 3 different types of document representation methods, which leverage the textual information of the movie descriptions:

(1) **BOW**: This is the traditional bag-of-words method for generating the word features for text classification. In specific, we use top tf-idf keywords of each movie description to represent a movie and train the classification models;
(2) **BPT**: This is the baseline embedding method for learning the representation of heterogeneous entities using a bipartite structure. In particular, we also use the top tf-idf keywords and movies to construct a simple entity-text bipartite network, as defined in Definition 2.1, and we use network embedding techniques to learn the representation of each movie for training the classification models;
(3) **ICE**: This is the proposed item concept embedding (ICE) method for learning the representations of heterogeneous entities. In specific, we also use the top tf-idf keywords and movies to construct the ICE network. However, different from the simple bipartite structure, the ICE network contains several careful designs, as described in Section 2.2, to better learn the representation of each movie for training the classification models.

For the experiments of this task, 5-fold cross validation is applied to verify the classification performance in terms of three measures: exact match ratio, micro-average and macro-average F-measures.

3.2.2 Settings for the Retrieval Tasks. For the retrieval tasks, there are two kinds of retrievals: homogeneous (i.e., word-to-word or item-to-item) and heterogeneous (i.e., item-to-word or word-to-item). In addition to the traditional keyword-based retrieval, we also conduct several methods based on embedding techniques for a comprehensive comparison. Below, we describe the settings of each retrieval method for the retrieval tasks:

(1) **RAND**: This is the baseline method which selects items or words randomly for each search task;
(2) **KBR**: This is the traditional keyword-based retrieval method for selecting items based on the given query. Note that the traditional keyword-based retrieval method can only be used for the word-to-item search task;
(3) **AVGEMB**: This is the method which represents entities using averaged word embeddings. In specific, we select top tf-idf words of each movie description or song lyric, and then average their word embeddings to represent the movie or song. In our experiments, the word embeddings used to represent entities in the IMDB dataset and the KKBOX dataset are trained on the Google News dataset[7] and the Chinese Wikipedia archive[8] using word2vec, respectively. The dimension of the word embedding vectors is set to 300;
(4) **BPT**: This is the baseline embedding method for learning the representation of heterogeneous entities using a bipartite structure. In particular, we also use the top tf-idf keywords and all items to construct a bipartite network, as defined in Definition 2.1, and apply network embedding

[3] https://grouplens.org/datasets/movielens/
[4] https://www.omdbapi.com
[5] https://github.com/fxsjy/jieba
[6] https://www.csie.ntu.edu.tw/~cjlin/libsvm/
[7] https://code.google.com/archive/p/word2vec/
[8] https://dumps.wikimedia.org/zhwiki/latest/zhwiki-latest-pages-articles.xml.bz2

Table 2: Statistics of IMDB information networks

	BPT		ICE (exp-3)		ICE (exp-5)	
$\|W\|$	10	20	10	20	10	20
$\|\mathcal{V}\|$	36,586	36,586	36,586	36,586	36,586	36,586
$\|\mathcal{T}\|$	62,066	65,036	84,990	87,222	113,820	116,630
$\|E_{et}\|$	358,160	622,004	358,160	622,004	358,160	622,004
$\|E_{tt}\|$	-	-	281,368	289,800	444,194	457,566
$\|\overline{E}_{et}\|$	-	-	942,633	1,696,638	1,569,753	2,823,767
$\overline{d}(\cdot)$	7.3	12.2	26.0	42.1	31.5	51.0

techniques to learn the representations of both items (i.e., movies or songs) and words;

(5) **ICE**: This is the proposed item concept embedding (ICE) method for learning the representation of heterogeneous entities. In specific, we also use the top tf-idf keywords and items to construct the ICE network. However, unlike the simple bipartite structure, the ICE network contains several careful designs, as described in Section 2.2, to better learn the representations of both items and words.

Note that, during the retrieval task, the above three embedding methods (i.e., AVGEMB, BPT, and ICE) will select the entities whose embeddings are the most similar to that of the user query in terms of the cosine similarity.

3.2.3 Information Networks. In the experiments, there are two types of information networks: the BPT and ICE networks. Table 2 and Table 3 tabulate the statistics of the two information networks. In these two tables, W denotes the set of the top tf-idf words of an item (e.g., movie descriptions or song lyrics) that is used to represent the item and to construct the information network; the "exp-n" in the parentheses denotes the number of expanded n words for each word. In the experiments, the expanded words for each given word are selected according to the cosine similarity of their pre-trained word embeddings, which are trained on the Google News dataset and the Chinese Wikipedia archive for the IMDB dataset and the KKBOX dataset using word2vec, respectively. For the IMDB dataset, the number of the top tf-idf words is set to 10 or 20 for each movie to construct the network, whereas for the KKBOX dataset, since songs are usually lyrically repetitive, the number is set to 1, 3, 5, 8, or 10 for each song to allow exploration for the optimal setting. Note that for the BPT networks, since there is only one type of relationship (has-a, described by E_{et} in the tables), the average degrees of nodes, $\overline{d}(\cdot)$, in such networks are smaller than those of the ICE networks.

3.2.4 Evaluation Metrics and Parameter Settings. In our experiments, the performance of multi-class classification is measured by three metrics: exact match ratio, micro-average F1, and macro-average F1, whereas that of retrieval is measured by precision and diversity. For the classification task, all the parameters are set to the LIBSVM's default values. For the network embedding approaches (BPT and ICE), the number of negative samples is set as 5, and the dimensionality of item and word vectors is set to 256 and 300 for the experiments on the IMDB and KKBOX datasets, respectively.

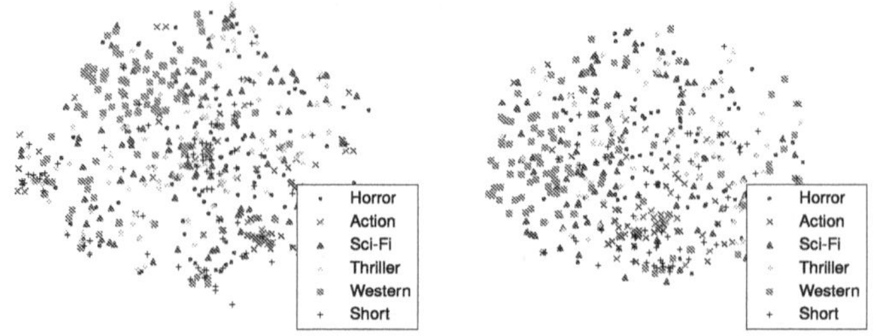

(a) BPT with $|W| = 20$ **(b) ICE (exp-5) with $|W| = 20$**

Figure 3: Visualization of the movies embeddings

3.3 Quantitative Results

3.3.1 Performance of the Classification Task. Table 4 lists the results of the three compared methods (i.e., BOW, BPT, and ICE) on the IMDB movie genre prediction, in which there are two sets of experiments, including $|W| = 10$ and $|W| = 20$. Note that, for this task, the testing items are all the same type (i.e., homogeneous). As shown in the table, increasing the number of words for representing a movie (i.e., $|W| = 10 \rightarrow |W| = 20$) clearly improves the classification performance of the three methods in terms of the three measures. Moreover, the two embedding-based methods (i.e., BPT and ICE) considerably outperform the BOW method, which suggests that the learned low-dimensional representations are indeed effective for such a classification task, as demonstrated in [13]. Furthermore, as observed in the table, the proposed ICE method yields comparable results with the BPT method; the result is anticipated due to the network constructions of both embedding-based methods are appropriate for the homogeneous classification task.

Figure 3 visualizes the learned representations of the movies from 6 different genres based on the BPT and ICE methods, in which 100 randomly picked movies for each genre are used for the visualization.[9] As shown in both figures, the movies of the same genre generally aggregate into one group, especially for western and action movies; the groups of thriller and horror movies overlap substantially with each other, which means that the usage of words in those movie descriptions are highly similar.

3.3.2 Performance of the Word-to-Movie Retrieval Task. We first conduct a heterogeneous retrieval task, i.e., *word-to-movie* retrieval task, on the IMDB dataset. The goal of this task is to use keywords to retrieve the movies with similar genre. In specific, we select the top 20 tf-idf words from all the movie descriptions in each genre as the query words, and then use the queries to retrieve the similar genre movies. For instance, the word "killer" is the top 1 tf-idf word from all thriller movie descriptions; therefore, we use "killer" as a query in an attempt to retrieve thriller movies.

Table 5 tabulates the retrieval results of the five compared methods in terms of precision@50 and precision@100. For the AVGEMB method, in addition to using top 20 tf-idf words of each movie description (i.e., $|W| = 20$), we also conduct an experiment of

[9]Each movie representation is a 256-dimensional real-valued embedding vector and transformed into two-dimensional space using t-distributed stochastic neighbor embedding (t-SNE), a technique for dimensionality reduction that is particularly well suited for the visualization of high-dimensional data.

Table 3: Statistics of KKBOX information networks

	BPT					ICE (exp-3)				
$\lvert W \rvert$	1	3	5	8	10	1	3	5	8	10
$\lvert \mathcal{V} \rvert$	33,106	33,074	32,999	32,603	31,527	33,106	33,074	32,999	32,603	31,527
$\lvert \mathcal{T} \rvert$	15,483	25,806	29,357	31,292	31,315	32,372	42,225	44,964	46,269	46,204
$\lvert E_{et} \rvert$	33,106	99,222	164,995	260,824	315,270	33,106	99,222	164,995	260,824	315,270
$\lvert E_{tt} \rvert$	-	-	-	-	-	120,368	184,133	204,942	215,861	215,780
$\lvert \overline{E}_{et} \rvert$	-	-	-	-	-	99,318	296,455	491,875	775,502	935,767
$\overline{d}(\cdot)$	1.4	3.4	5.3	8.2	10.0	7.7	15.4	22.1	31.8	37.7

Table 4: Movie genre classification task

	$\lvert W \rvert = 10$				$\lvert W \rvert = 20$			
	BOW	BPT	ICE (exp-3)	ICE (exp-5)	TF-IDF	BPT	ICE (exp-3)	ICE (exp-5)
Exact match ratio	0.136	**0.160**	0.156	0.157	0.162	**0.182**	**0.182**	0.181
Micro-average F-measure	0.365	0.401	0.408	**0.410**	0.415	**0.464**	0.462	0.463
Macro-average F-measure	0.087	0.166	**0.170**	**0.170**	0.156	**0.229**	0.223	0.222

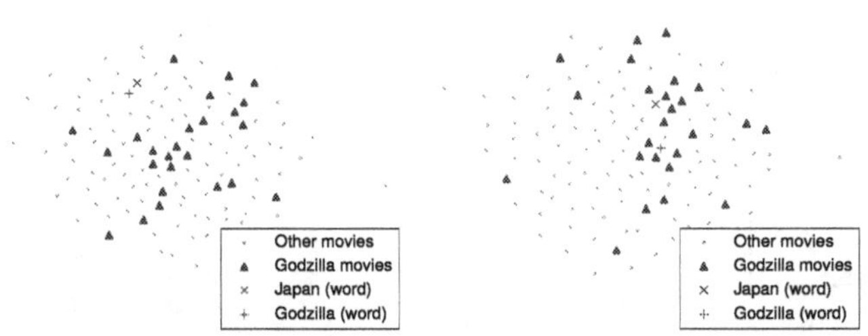

(a) BPT with $\lvert W \rvert = 20$ (b) ICE (exp-5) with $\lvert W \rvert = 20$

Figure 4: Visualization of the Representations of the Godzilla-related Movies and Two Related Keywords

AVGEMB (all) of averaging all word embeddings learned by word2vec, which can be considered another competitive baseline for this task. As shown in the table, in terms of average precision@50 and precision@100, the proposed ICE method can outperform all the compared baselines. Although, for some genres, the performance of ICE is only comparable with KBR and AVGEMB, for both action and short movies, the proposed ICE approach outperforms all of the baselines with a considerable amount. Note that for this heterogeneous word-to-movie retrieval task, BPT yields poor performance compared to our ICE approach; the result is due to the straightforward bipartite network is appropriate for the tasks involving only one type of entity, such as document classification and item-to-item retrieval, and fails for such a heterogeneous retrieval task.

Figure 4 visualizes an example to explain the phenomenon. In the figure, the red triangles represent Godzilla-related movies; the two selected words: Japan and Godzilla, which are highly related to the Godzilla-related movies, are denoted as cross and plus symbols, respectively. As shown in the figure, these two words are distant from all Godzilla-related movies with BPT, whereas the proposed ICE demonstrates an opposite outcome — the two words are close to the highly correlated movies, which again shows the superior ability of our ICE approach for the heterogeneous retrieval task.

3.3.3 Performance of the Word-to-Song Retrieval Task. We then conduct another heterogeneous retrieval task — *word-to-song* retrieval — on the KKBOX music dataset. In the experiments, three types of contextual keywords: mood, location, and time related keywords, are used as our queries; we select the top 5 tf-idf words for each category from our crawled song lyrics. Since we do not have a relevancy ground truth for this retrieval task, we consider a retrieved song as a relevant result on the following two conditions: (1) the lyrics of the retrieved song contains the query word, or (2) the song lyric contains at least one of the top k concept-similar words of the query. Note that each query case has its own set of relevant songs in our experiments.

Figures 5 and 6 report the results of the proposed ICE together with the four comparing models (i.e., RAND, KBR, AVGEMB, and BPT) with respect to the size of words used to describe a song ($\lvert W \rvert$). Overall, both ICE and AVGEMB improve their performance as $\lvert W \rvert$ increases; however, BPT hardly retrieve any songs containing the query word, which confirms again that the embeddings learned on the simple bipartite network is not appropriate for a heterogeneous retrieval. Note that in Figure 5, we do not compare the performance of these models with KBR because its performance is the upper bound of this task. For the case that songs with any of the top 3 concept-similar words are considered relevant, the proposed ICE approach generally outperforms the other four baseline methods, as shown in Figure 6. The experiments in these two figures suggest that the word embeddings learned by ICE are capable of retrieving the songs containing the given query and/or the query's concept-similar words, and thus the ICE method is effective for heterogeneous retrieval on the basis that the items and the query words are embedded by the textual information.

Table 6 tabulates the precision of each query word, in which there are five query words for each of the contexts. With Figures 5 and 6, we can observe some interesting phenomenon in the experiments. As shown in the table, for most of the queries, our ICE approach obtains much better precision than both AVGEMB and BPT; that is, in average, ICE achieves 0.533 and 0.201 for precision@100 in the keyword and concept-similar word retrieval tasks, surpassing

Table 5: Word-to-movie retrieval task

$\|W\| = 20$	Horror (3754/36586)	Thriller (4636/36586)	Western (751/36586)	Action (5029/36586)	Short (1094/36586)	Sci-Fi (2004/36586)	Average
				P@50			
RAND	0.080	0.080	0.060	0.080	0.000	0.120	0.070
KBR	0.324	**0.230**	**0.321**	0.418	0.062	0.373	0.288
AVGEMB	0.322	0.212	0.316	0.406	0.092	0.392	0.290
AVGEMB (all)	0.324	0.225	0.304	0.366	0.089	**0.401**	0.285
BPT	0.096	0.104	0.010	0.154	0.032	0.086	0.080
ICE (exp-5)	**0.354**	0.204	0.294	**0.444**	**0.142**	0.392	**0.305**
				P@100			
RAND	0.050	0.100	0.030	0.110	0.000	0.060	0.058
KBR	**0.327**	**0.224**	0.236	0.395	0.057	0.307	0.258
AVGEMB	0.324	0.215	0.266	0.385	0.074	0.372	0.273
AVGEMB (all)	0.314	0.208	**0.269**	0.376	0.074	**0.382**	0.270
BPT	0.088	0.116	0.012	0.156	0.034	0.086	0.082
ICE (exp-5)	0.321	0.193	0.264	**0.421**	**0.109**	0.362	**0.278**

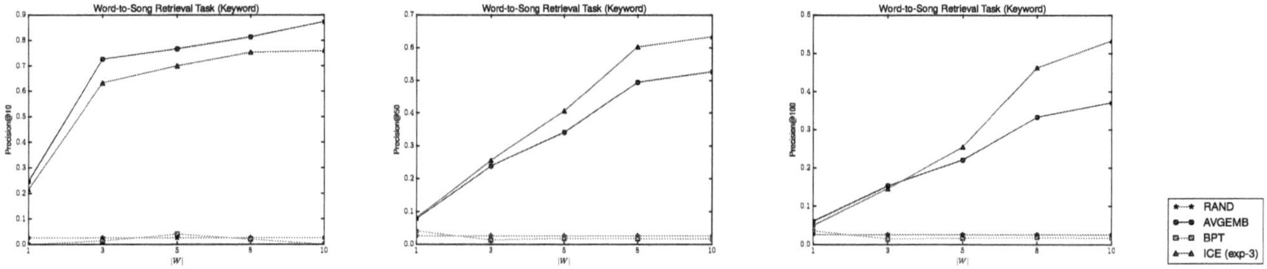

(a) (b) (c)

Figure 5: Word-to-song retrieval task (relevant songs: keyword included songs)

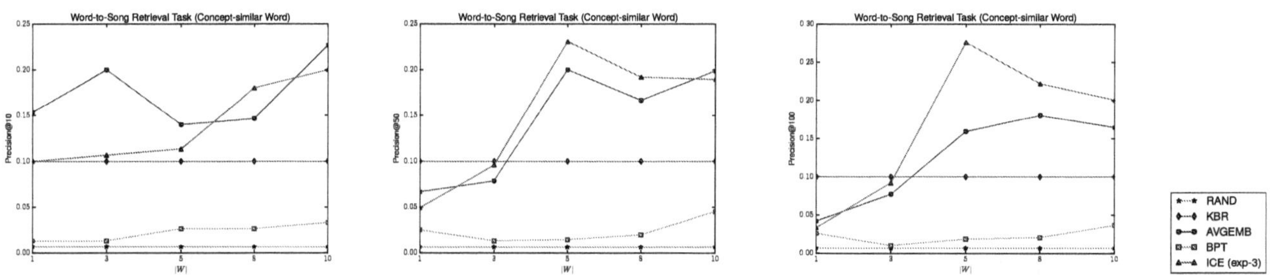

(a) (b) (c)

Figure 6: Word-to-song retrieval task (relevant songs: concept-similar words included songs)

those of the AVGEMB (0.239 and 0.186) and the BPT (0.017 and 0.037). Moreover, we can observe that it is relatively difficult for the location-based queries to retrieve songs containing the concept-similar words, which is due to the fact that few location-based songs exist in our datasets; for example, the query "房間 (room)" has 3 expanded words, "浴室 (bathroom)", "地下室 (basement)", and "臥室 (bedroom)", but only 28 songs contain any of these three concept-similar words in the KKBOX dataset.

Finally, we evaluate the proposed ICE in terms of precision and diversity using ConceptNet[10] (see Table 7). Given a keyword, we use ConceptNet, a human-labeled semantic knowledge graph, to obtain the keyword's concept-similar words.[11] On the basis of these obtained concept-similar words, we consider the songs that contain at least one concept-similar word relevant in our experiments; note

[10] http://conceptnet5.media.mit.edu

[11] In this experiments, we only selected 5 queries, whose corresponding concept-similar words are greater than 10 and less than 40, for consideration. Note that we also remove the one-character word in the set of concept-similar words.

Table 6: Performance comparison on the 15 keywords

$\|W\| = 10$		Keyword				Concept-similar word			
			P@100				P@100		
	Query	# keyword songs	BPT	AVGEMB	ICE (exp-3)	# concept-similar songs	BPT	AVGEMB	ICE (exp-3)
Mood	失落 (lost)	516	0.000	0.160	**0.470**	403	0.030	**0.120**	0.050
	心痛 (heartache)	824	0.050	0.080	**0.250**	4,075	0.170	0.500	**0.610**
	想念 (pining)	1,729	0.050	0.250	**0.700**	1,176	0.080	**0.180**	0.060
	深愛 (affectionate)	380	0.000	0.090	**0.550**	442	0.020	0.110	**0.250**
	難過 (sad)	1678	0.040	0.200	**0.530**	1,781	0.080	**0.320**	0.070
Location	回家 (home)	934	0.040	0.310	**0.900**	1,190	0.020	**0.340**	0.160
	房間 (room)	610	0.000	0.420	**0.510**	28	0.000	0.010	**0.060**
	海邊 (seaside)	264	0.000	0.230	**0.360**	91	0.000	0.070	**0.080**
	火車 (train)	151	0.010	0.330	**0.510**	20	0.000	**0.040**	0.020
	花園 (garden)	139	0.000	0.160	**0.390**	2	0.000	0.000	0.000
Time	夕陽 (dusk)	387	0.010	0.180	**0.360**	307	0.020	**0.100**	0.070
	日出 (sunrise)	240	0.000	0.290	**0.430**	390	0.060	0.380	**0.690**
	日落 (sunset)	226	0.030	0.380	**0.590**	407	0.010	0.270	**0.530**
	月亮 (moon)	598	0.000	0.360	**0.930**	1,608	0.030	0.320	**0.350**
	黑夜 (dark night)	1,189	0.030	0.140	**0.510**	279	**0.030**	**0.030**	0.010
	Total/Avg. P@100	9,865	0.017	0.239	**0.533**	12,199	0.037	0.186	**0.201**

Table 7: Performance evaluated by ConceptNet

$\|W\| = 10$		P@10		Diversity@10		P@100		Diversity@100	
Query	# words in ConceptNet	KBR	ICE (exp-3)	KBR	ICE (exp-3)	KBR	ICE (exp-3)	KBR	ICE (exp-3)
夕陽 (dusk)	11	0.00	**0.20**	0.00	0.00	**0.25**	0.08	0.00	**0.75**
房間 (room)	39	**0.60**	0.10	0.00	0.00	**0.36**	0.16	0.00	**0.69**
日出 (sunrise)	17	0.40	**1.00**	0.00	**0.70**	**0.30**	0.24	0.00	**0.75**
花園 (garden)	33	**0.30**	0.10	0.00	0.00	**0.34**	0.08	0.00	**0.50**
黑夜 (dark night)	17	0.50	**1.00**	0.00	0.00	0.50	**0.57**	0.00	**0.68**
Average	23.4	0.36	**0.48**	0.00	**0.14**	**0.35**	0.23	0.00	**0.67**

that, in this task, the songs containing the query word only are not considered as relevant songs. Then, we use the following measure to assess the diversity of the retrieved songs:

$$\text{Diversity@}n = \frac{|R \cap \bar{S}_k|}{|R|}, \tag{9}$$

where R denotes the set of relevant songs and S_k denotes the set of songs containing the given keyword k, from the retrieved n songs. Observing from the table, the proposed ICE outperforms the KBR method for the top 10 retrieval results, although the KBR method is naturally easy to achieve high precision in this task; that is because all songs retrieved by this method contain the given query word. Although the proposed ICE method cannot outperform the KBR method in terms of precision@100, our method provides more diverse retrieved results than the KBR approach does; that is, our ICE approach can retrieve the songs relevant in terms of similar concepts without resorting to keyword-matching, which is intractable for the classic KBR approach.

3.4 Case Study

This section provides several interesting case studies to demonstrate the capability of the proposed ICE in managing tasks which involve both homogeneous and heterogeneous entities. First, Table 8 gives an example for a movie-to-word retrieval task, in which the top 10 cosine-similar words in the given movie, *Toy Story (1995)*, are listed. As demonstrated in the table, while using the embeddings learned on BPT produces words unrelated to the given movie, our method provides much more reasonable results; for example, *Andy* is a major character and *Sid* is the main antagonist in the Toy Story.

Table 8: An example for movie-to-word retrieval

Query movie: Toy Story, 1995 (Animation, Adventure, Comedy)	
BPT	ICE (exp-5)
manias	andy
entraineuse	gave
taddeo	give
anuelo	sid
portico	tabbed
bep	robertson
meanness	Named
zanchi	stuffed_animals
sarti	toys
raffin	Toys

Table 9: An example for movie-to-movie retrieval

Movie query: The Avengers, 2012 (Action, Adventure, Sci-Fi)	
BPT	ICE (exp-5)
Justice League: War, 2014 (Animation, **Action**, **Adventure**)	Justice League: War, 2014 (Animation, **Action**, **Adventure**)
Lego DC Comics Super Heroes, 2015 (Animation, **Action**, **Adventure**)	A Cosmic Christmas, 1977 (Animation, Short, **Sci-Fi**)
Falling Skies, 2011-2015 (**Action**, **Adventure**, Drama)	Howard the Duck, 1986 (**Action**, **Adventure**, Comedy)
Marvel Super Hero Adventures: Frost Fight!, 2015 (Animation)	Hellboy II: The Golden Army, 2008 (**Action**, **Adventure**, Fantasy)
Doctor Mordrid, 1992 (**Action**, Fantasy, Horror)	The War in Space, 1977 (**Action**, **Adventure**, **Sci-Fi**)

Table 10: An example for word-to-movie retrieval

Word query: alien	
BPT	ICE (exp-5)
The Blue Lagoon, 1949 (Adventure, Drama, Romance)	Coneheads, 1993 (Comedy, **Sci-Fi**)
Turner & Hooch, 1989 (Comedy, Crime, Drama)	Without Warning, 1980 (**Sci-Fi**, Horror)
Only the Young, 2012 (Documentary, Comedy, Romance)	They Came from Beyond Space, 1967 (Adventure, **Sci-Fi**)
Brute Force, 1947 (Crime, Drama, Film-Noir)	Battle of the Stars, 1978 (**Sci-Fi**)
Home, 2015 (Animation, Adventure, Comedy)	Howard the Duck, 1986 (Action, Adventure, Comedy)

Table 9 tabulates the top 5 retrieved movies given the movie, *The Avengers (2012)*, as the query, which again demonstrates the fact that both BPT and ICE are effective for homogeneous retrieval. Finally, we use the word *alien* to search for the relevant movies (see Table 10). Clearly, the BPT approach fails on this task because of retrieving irrelevant movies in terms of genre, whereas 4, if not all, of the top 5 movies retrieved by the proposed ICE are highly correlated Sci-Fi movies.

4 CONCLUSION

This paper presents a novel item concept embedding approach called the "ICE," which aims to model item concepts via textual information. In this approach, we provide a generalized network construction method to build a network involving heterogeneous nodes and a mixture of both homogeneous and heterogeneous relations. We then leverage the concept of neighborhood proximity to learn the embeddings of both items and words. With the proposed carefully designed ICE networks, the resulting embedding facilitates both homogeneous and heterogeneous retrieval, including item-to-item and word-to-item search tasks. Experiments on two real-world datasets show that ICE encodes useful textual information and thus outperforms traditional methods in various item classification and retrieval tasks. In the future, we plan to investigate how to integrate the proposed ICE method into the recommender systems to advance contextual recommendation tasks.

5 ACKNOWLEDGEMENTS

The authors thank Chih-Ming Chen for his helpful comments and thank KKBOX Inc. for providing the music dataset for investigation. This research was partially supported by the Ministry of Science and Technology in Taiwan under the grants MOST 105-2221-E-001-035,104-2221-E-004-010, and 104-2420-H-004-033-MY3.

REFERENCES

[1] Yoshua Bengio, Réjean Ducharme, Pascal Vincent, and Christian Janvin. 2003. A neural probabilistic language model. *Journal of Machine Learning Research* 3 (2003), 1137–1155.

[2] Shaosheng Cao, Wei Lu, and Qiongkai Xu. 2015. GraRep: Learning graph representations with global structural information. In *Proceedings of the 24th ACM International on Conference on Information and Knowledge Management*. 891–900.

[3] Chih-Ming Chen, Ming-Feng Tsai, Yu-Ching Lin, and Yi-Hsuan Yang. 2016. Query-based music recommendations via preference embedding. In *Proceedings of the 10th ACM Conference on Recommender Systems*. 79–82.

[4] Aditya Grover and Jure Leskovec. 2016. node2vec: Scalable feature learning for networks. In *Proceedings of the 22nd ACM SIGKDD International Conference on Knowledge Discovery and Data Mining*. 855–864.

[5] H. Gui, J. Liu, F. Tao, M. Jiang, B. Norick, and J. Han. 2016. Large-Scale embedding learning in heterogeneous event data. In *Proceedings of IEEE 16th International Conference on Data Mining*. 907–912.

[6] Quoc V Le and Tomas Mikolov. 2014. Distributed representations of sentences and documents. In *Proceedings of the 31st International Conference on Machine Learning*. 1188–1196.

[7] Tomas Mikolov, Martin Karafiát, Lukas Burget, Jan Cernockỳ, and Sanjeev Khudanpur. 2010. Recurrent neural network based language model. In *Proceedings of Interspeech*. 1045–1048.

[8] Tomas Mikolov, Ilya Sutskever, Kai Chen, Greg S Corrado, and Jeff Dean. 2013. Distributed representations of words and phrases and their compositionality. In *Advances in Neural Information Processing Systems 26*. 3111–3119.

[9] Jeffrey Pennington, Richard Socher, and Christopher D Manning. 2014. Glove: Global vectors for word representation. In *Proceedings of Conference on Empirical Methods in Natural Language Processing*, Vol. 14. 1532–1543.

[10] Bryan Perozzi, Rami Al-Rfou, and Steven Skiena. 2014. DeepWalk: Online learning of social representations. In *Proceedings of the 20th ACM SIGKDD International Conference on Knowledge Discovery and Data Mining*. 701–710.

[11] Bryan Perozzi, Vivek Kulkarni, and Steven Skiena. 2016. Walklets: Multi-scale graph embeddings for interpretable network classification. *arXiv preprint arXiv:1605.02115* (2016).

[12] Gunther Schmidt. 2011. *Relational Mathematics*. Vol. 132. Cambridge University Press.

[13] Jian Tang, Meng Qu, and Qiaozhu Mei. 2015. PTE: Predictive text embedding through large-scale heterogeneous text networks. In *Proceedings of the 21th ACM SIGKDD International Conference on Knowledge Discovery and Data Mining*. 1165–1174.

[14] Jian Tang, Meng Qu, Mingzhe Wang, Ming Zhang, Jun Yan, and Qiaozhu Mei. 2015. Line: Large-scale information network embedding. In *Proceedings of the 24th International Conference on World Wide Web*. 1067–1077.

[15] Daixin Wang, Peng Cui, and Wenwu Zhu. 2016. Structural deep network embedding. In *Proceedings of the 22Nd ACM SIGKDD International Conference on Knowledge Discovery and Data Mining*. 1225–1234.

[16] Suhang Wang, Jiliang Tang, Charu Aggarwal, and Huan Liu. 2016. Linked document embedding for classification. In *Proceedings of the 25th ACM International on Conference on Information and Knowledge Management*. 115–124.

[17] Min Xie, Hongzhi Yin, Fanjiang Xu, Hao Wang, and Xiaofang Zhou. 2016. Graph-based metric embedding for next poi recommendation. In *Proceedings of International Conference on Web Information Systems Engineering*. 207–222.

Leveraging Contextual Sentence Relations for Extractive Summarization Using a Neural Attention Model

Pengjie Ren
jay.ren@outlook.com
Shandong University
Jinan, China

Zhumin Chen
chenzhumin@sdu.edu.cn
Shandong University
Jinan, China

Zhaochun Ren
renzhaochun@jd.com
Data Science Lab, JD.com
Beijing, China

Furu Wei
fuwei@microsoft.com
Microsoft Research Asia
Beijing, China

Jun Ma
majun@sdu.edu.cn
Shandong University
Jinan, China

Maarten de Rijke
derijke@uva.nl
University of Amsterdam
Amsterdam, The Netherlands

ABSTRACT

As a framework for extractive summarization, sentence regression has achieved state-of-the-art performance in several widely-used practical systems. The most challenging task within the sentence regression framework is to identify discriminative features to encode a sentence into a feature vector. So far, sentence regression approaches have neglected to use features that capture contextual relations among sentences.

We propose a neural network model, Contextual Relation-based Summarization (CRSum), to take advantage of contextual relations among sentences so as to improve the performance of sentence regression. Specifically, we first use sentence relations with a word-level attentive pooling convolutional neural network to construct sentence representations. Then, we use contextual relations with a sentence-level attentive pooling recurrent neural network to construct context representations. Finally, CRSum automatically learns useful contextual features by jointly learning representations of sentences and similarity scores between a sentence and sentences in its context. Using a two-level attention mechanism, CRSum is able to pay attention to important content, i.e., words and sentences, in the surrounding context of a given sentence.

We carry out extensive experiments on six benchmark datasets. CRSum alone can achieve comparable performance with state-of-the-art approaches; when combined with a few basic surface features, it significantly outperforms the state-of-the-art in terms of multiple ROUGE metrics.

CCS CONCEPTS

•Information systems →Summarization;

ACM Reference format:
Pengjie Ren, Zhumin Chen, Zhaochun Ren, Furu Wei, Jun Ma, and Maarten de Rijke. 2017. Leveraging Contextual Sentence Relations for Extractive Summarization Using a Neural Attention Model. In *Proceedings of SIGIR'17, August 07-11, 2017, Shinjuku, Tokyo, Japan*, , 10 pages.
DOI: http://dx.doi.org/10.1145/3077136.3080792

SIGIR'17, August 07-11, 2017, Shinjuku, Tokyo, Japan
© 2017 ACM. 978-1-4503-5022-8/17/08...$15.00
DOI: http://dx.doi.org/10.1145/3077136.3080792

1 INTRODUCTION

Extractive summarization aims to generate a short text summary for a document or a set of documents by selecting salient sentences in the document(s) [35]. In recent years, sentence regression has emerged as an extractive summarization framework that achieves state-of-the-art performance [3, 50]; it has been widely used in practical systems [16, 18, 40, 49]. There are two major components in sentence regression: *sentence scoring* and *sentence selection*. The former scores a sentence to measure its importance, and the latter chooses sentences to generate a summary by considering both the importance scores and redundancy.

Sentence scoring has been extensively investigated in extractive summarization. Many approaches [3, 33] directly measure the salience of sentences whereas others [13, 23] first rank words (or bi-grams) and then combine these scores to rank sentences. Traditional scoring methods incorporate feature engineering as a necessary but labor-intensive task. To the best of our knowledge, most features of these methods are surface features, such as sentence length, sentence position, TF-IDF based features, etc. In Table 1, we list the scores achieved by *t-SR* [40], a traditional feature engineering-based sentence regression method for extractive summarization that achieves state-of-the-art performance. We also list an upper bound for the performance of sentence regression, which is obtained by scoring the sentences against human written summaries. There is a sizable gap in performance between *t-SR* and the upper bound. We believe that the reason for this is that none of *t-SR*'s features tries to encode semantic information.

Recent neural network-based methods for *abstractive* summarization have addressed this matter [7, 31, 42]. Extracting semantic features via neural networks has received increased attention, also for extractive summarization [2, 3, 6]. Latent features learned by neural networks have been proven effective. PriorSum [3] is a recent example. To the best of our knowledge, PriorSum achieves the best performance on the three datasets listed in Table 1. But all methods, including PriorSum, extract latent features from standalone sentences. None considers their contextual relations.

Table 1: Multi-document summarization. ROUGE (%) of Sentence Regression (with greedy based sentence selection). Upper bounds are determined by scoring the sentences against human written summaries.

Dataset	Approach	ROUGE-1	ROUGE-2
	t-SR	34.82	7.76
DUC 2001	PriorSum	35.98	7.89
	Upper bound	40.82	14.76
	t-SR	37.33	8.98
DUC 2002	PriorSum	36.63	8.97
	Upper bound	43.78	15.97
	t-SR	37.74	9.60
DUC 2004	PriorSum	38.91	10.07
	Upper bound	41.75	13.73

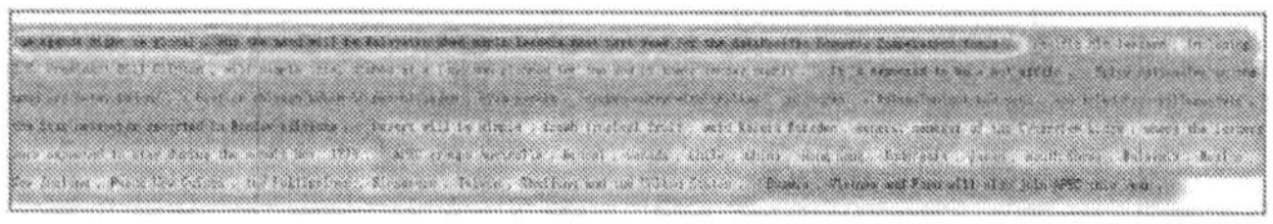

(a) General-to-specific

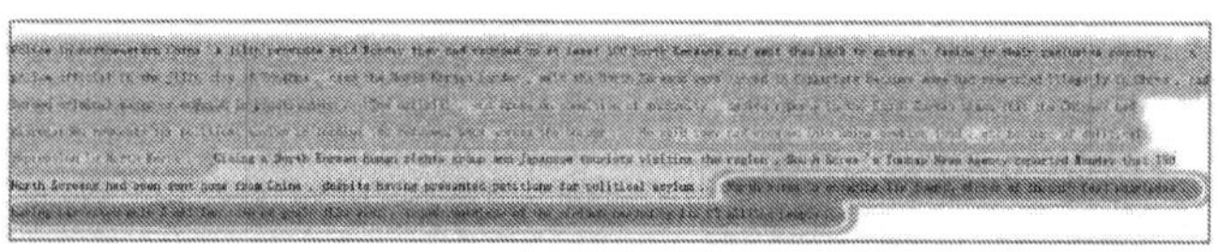

(b) Specific-to-general

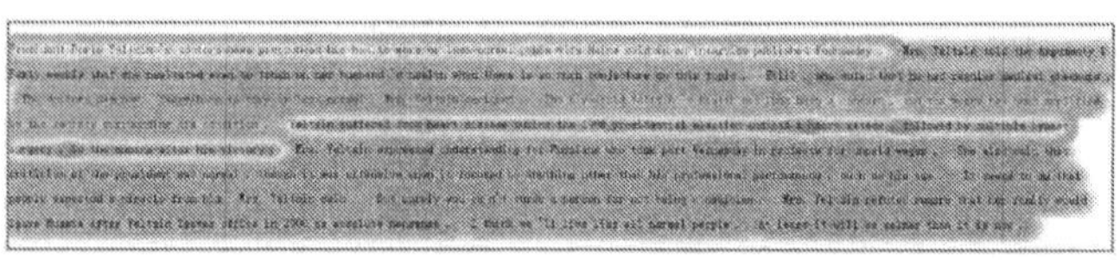

(c) Specific-to-general-to-specific

Figure 1: Sentence contexts in different instances from the DUC 2004 dataset. The color depth represents the importance of the sentence in terms of ROUGE-2 based on human written summaries. (Best viewed in color.)

We argue that sentence importance also depends on contextual relations, i.e., on relations of a sentence with its surrounding sentences. Figure 1(a) illustrates a general-to-specific paragraph structure, where the first sentence is a general summary of the event that is explained in detail by the following sentences. Figure 1(b) illustrates a specific-to-general paragraph structure, where the last sentence is a conclusion or reason of the event described by its preceding sentences. Figure 1(c) illustrates a specific-to-general-to-specific paragraph structure where the most important sentence is a connecting link between the preceding and the following context. So it summarizes both its preceding and following sentences.

We propose a hybrid neural model, namely Contextual Relation-based Summarization (CRSum), to automatically learn contextual relation features from data. CRSum applies a two-level attention mechanism (word-level and sentence-level) to attend differentially to more and less important content when constructing sentence/context representations. Specifically, we first leverage sentence relations using a convolutional neural network with word-level attentive pooling to construct sentence representations. Then, we leverage contextual relations using a recurrent neural network with sentence-level attentive pooling to construct context representations. With its two-level attention mechanism, CRSum can pay attention to more important content (words and sentences) in the surrounding context of a given sentence. Finally, CRSum jointly learns sentence/context representations as well as similarity scores between the sentence and its preceding/following context, which are regarded as the sentence's capacity to summarize its context.

We conduct extensive experiments on the DUC 2001, 2002, 2004 multi-document summarization datasets and the DUC 2005, 2006, 2007 query-focused multi-document summarization datasets. Our experimental results demonstrate that CRSum alone can achieve comparable performance to the state-of-the-art approaches. When combined with a few basic Surface Features (SF), CRSum+SF outperforms the state-of-the-art approaches in terms of ROUGE metrics.

To sum up, the main contributions in this paper are three-fold:

- We propose a neural model, CRSum, to take a sentence's contextual relations with its surrounding sentences into consideration for extractive summarization. CRSum jointly learns sentence and context representations as well as their similarity measurements. The measurements are used to estimate a sentence's ability to summarize its local context.
- We fuse contextual relations with a two-level attention mechanism in CRSum. With the mechanism, CRSum can learn to pay attention to important content (words and sentences) in the surrounding sentences of a given sentence.
- We carry out extensive experiments and analyses on six benchmark datasets. The results indicate that CRSum can significantly improve the performance of extractive summarization by modeling the contextual sentence relations.

2 RELATED WORK

We group related work on extractive summarization in three categories, which we discuss below.

2.1 Unsupervised techniques

In early studies on extractive summarization, sentences are scored by employing unsupervised techniques [37, 52]; centroid-based and Maximum Marginal Relevance (MMR)-based approaches are prominent examples. Centroid-based methods use sentence centrality as to indicate importance [29]. Radev et al. [37, 38] model cluster centroids in their summarization system, MEAD. LexRank (or TextRank) computes sentence importance based on eigenvector centrality in a graph of sentence similarities [10, 30]. Wan et al. [45–48] propose several centroid-based approaches for summarization. MMR-based methods consider a linear trade-off between relevance and redundancy [5]. Goldstein et al. [14] extend MMR to support extractive summarization by incorporating additional information about the document set and relations between the documents. McDonald [28] achieves good results by reformulating MMR as a knapsack packing problem and solving it using ILP. Later, Lin and Bilmes [26, 27] propose a variant of the MMR framework that maximizes an objective function that considers the linear trade-off between coverage and redundancy terms.

2.2 Feature engineering based techniques

Machine learning techniques have been used for better estimations of sentence importance. Kupiec et al. [22] train a Naive Bayes classifier to decide whether to include a sentence in the summary. Li et al. [24] evaluate sentence importance with support vector regression, after which a rule-based method is applied to remove redundant phrases. Gillick and Favre [13] evaluate bi-gram importance and use the scores to evaluate sentence importance and redundancy with a linear combination. Lin and Bilmes [26] propose a structural SVM learning approach to learn the weights of feature combinations using the MMR-like submodularity function proposed by Lin and Bilmes [26, 27]. Yan and Wan [51] propose the Deep Dependency Sub-Structure (DDSS) and topic-sensitive Multi-Task Learning (MTL) model. Given a document set, they parse all sentences into deep dependency structures with a Head-driven Phrase Structure Grammar parser and mine the frequent DDSSs after semantic normalization. They then employ MTL to learn the importance of these frequent DDSSs. Hu and Wan [19] propose PPSGen to automatically generate presentation slides by selecting and aligning key phrases and sentences. These methods all rely on human-engineered features. Most of the used features are surface features that do not take contextual relations into account.

2.3 Deep learning based techniques

Deep learning techniques have attracted considerable attention in the summarization literature, e.g., abstractive summarization [1, 7, 31], sentence summarization [11, 17, 42] and extractive summarization [2, 3, 6]. We focus on the use of deep learning techniques for extractive summarization. Kågebäck et al. [20] and Kobayashi et al. [21] use the sum of trained word embeddings to represent sentences or documents. They formalize the summarization task as the problem of maximizing a submodular function based on the similarities of the embeddings. Yin and Pei [53] propose CNNLM, a model based on convolutional neural networks, to project sentences into dense distributed representations, then model sentence redundancy by cosine similarity. Cao et al. [3] develop a summarization system called PriorSum, which applies enhanced convolutional neural networks to capture the summary prior features derived from length-variable phrases. In other work, the authors develop a ranking framework based on recursive neural networks (R2N2) to rank sentences for multi-document summarization. R2N2 formulates the ranking task as a hierarchical regression process that simultaneously measures the salience of a sentence and its constituents (e.g., phrases) in the parse tree [2]. Cheng and Lapata [6] treat single document summarization as a sequence labeling task and model it with recurrent neural networks. Their model is composed of a hierarchical document encoder and an attention-based extractor; the encoder derives the meaning representation of a document based on its sentences and their constituent words while the extractor adopts a variant of neural attention to extract sentences or words. Cao et al. [4] propose a system called AttSum for query-focused multi-document summarization that applies an attention mechanism to simulate the attentive reading of human behavior when a query is given.

A growing number of publications on extractive summarization focus on deep learning techniques. Unlike these publications, we propose a hybrid deep neural network that leverages the contextual information reflected by contextual sentence relations, which, to the best of our knowledge, are not considered in existing studies.

Table 2: Basic surface features used in this paper.

Feature	Description
$f_{len}(S_t)$	Length of S_t
$f_{pos}(S_t)$	Position of S_t in its document
$f_{tf}(S_t) = \frac{\sum_{w \in S_t} TF(w)}{f_{len}(S_t)}$	Average term frequency. $TF(w)$ is the term frequency of word w
$f_{df}(S_t) = \frac{\sum_{w \in S_t} DF(w)}{f_{len}(S_t)}$	Average document frequency. $DF(w)$ is the document frequency of word w

3 METHOD

3.1 Overview

There are two phases in our method to generate a summary: *sentence scoring* and *sentence selection.* In the sentence scoring phase, we learn a scoring function $f(S_t \mid \theta)$ for each sentence S_t to fit the ground truth ROUGE-2 score[1], i.e., ROUGE-2($S_t \mid S_{ref}$):

$$f(S_t \mid \theta) \sim \text{ROUGE-2}(S_t \mid S_{ref}) \tag{1}$$

where θ are the parameters; ROUGE-2($S_t \mid S_{ref}$) is the ground truth score of S_t in terms of ROUGE-2 based on human written summaries S_{ref} [25]. As with existing studies [3, 36, 40], we also use ROUGE-2 recall as the ground truth score. In §3.2, we detail how we model $f(S_t \mid \theta)$. During the sentence selection phase, we select a subset of sentences as the summary Ψ subject to a given length constraint l, i.e.,

$$\begin{aligned} \Psi^* &= \arg\max_{\Psi \subseteq D} \sum_{S_t \in \Psi} f(S_t \mid \theta) \\ &\text{such that} \sum_{S_t \in \Psi} |S_t| \leq l \text{ and } r(\Psi) \text{ hold,} \end{aligned} \tag{2}$$

where D is the set of sentences from one or more documents that belong to the same topic; $|S_t|$ is the length of S_t in words or bytes; $r(\Psi)$ is a constraint function to avoid redundancy in the final summary. Details of the algorithm are explained in §3.3.

3.2 Sentence scoring

Given a sentence S_t, we assume that its preceding context sentence sequence is $C_{pc} = \{S_{t-m}, \ldots, S_{t-c}, \ldots, S_{t-1} \mid 1 \leq c \leq m\}$ and that its following context sentence sequence is $C_{fc} = \{S_{t+1}, \ldots, S_{t+c}, \ldots, S_{t+n} \mid 1 \leq c \leq n\}$. Settings of m and n are discussed in §4 below. We use $f_{pc}(\mathrm{v}(S_t), \mathrm{v}_{pc}(S_t))$ to estimate the ability of S_t to summarize its preceding context:

$$f_{pc}(\mathrm{v}(S_t), \mathrm{v}_{pc}(S_t)) = \cos(\mathrm{v}(S_t), \mathrm{v}_{pc}(S_t)). \tag{3}$$

Similarly, $f_{fc}(\mathrm{v}(S_t), \mathrm{v}_{fc}(S_t))$ estimates the ability of S_t to summarize its following context:

$$f_{fc}(\mathrm{v}(S_t), \mathrm{v}_{fc}(S_t)) = \cos(\mathrm{v}(S_t), \mathrm{v}_{fc}(S_t)), \tag{4}$$

where $\mathrm{v}(S_t)$ is the sentence model of S_t; cos indicates the cosine similarity; $\mathrm{v}_{pc}(S_t)$ and $\mathrm{v}_{fc}(S_t)$ are the context models of C_{pc} and C_{fc}.

[1] http://www.berouge.com/Pages/default.aspx

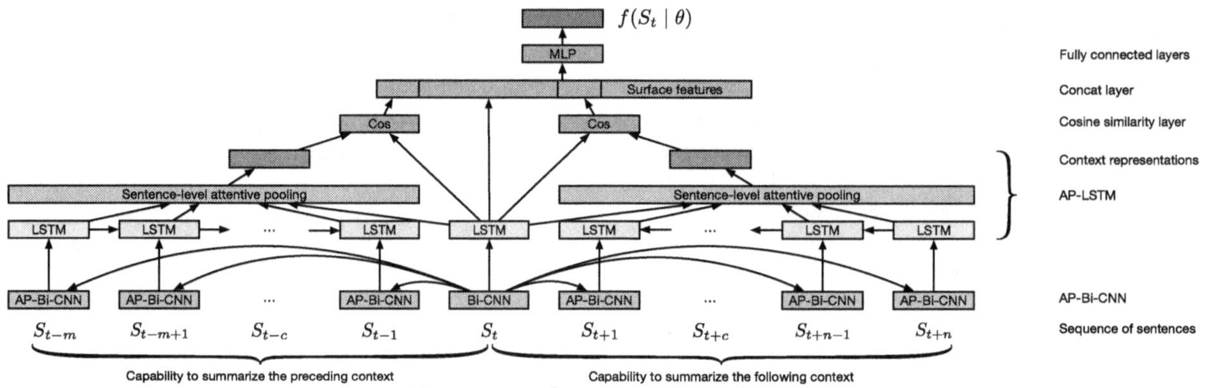

Figure 2: Architecture of CRSum+SF.

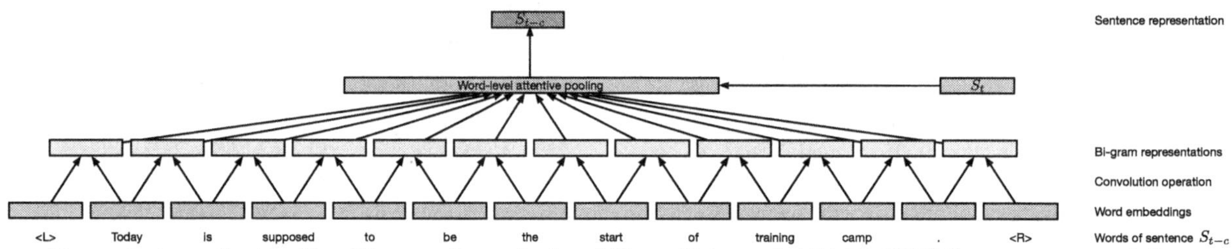

Figure 3: Attentive Pooling Bi-gram Convolutional Neural Network (AP-Bi-CNN) for sentence modeling.

Our model **CRSum+SF** is shown in Figure 2, where we combine $\mathrm{v}(S_t)$, $f_{pc}(\mathrm{v}(S_t), \mathrm{v}_{pc}(S_t))$ and $f_{fc}(\mathrm{v}(S_t), \mathrm{v}_{fc}(S_t))$ with four basic Surface Features (**SF**) listed in Table 2. Then we apply a MultiLayer Perceptron (MLP) [12, 41] as the decoder to transform the features into a single value as the final salience score to S_t, as shown in Eq. 5:

$$f(S_t \mid \theta) = \mathrm{MLP}\left(\begin{bmatrix} f_{pc}(\mathrm{v}(S_t), \mathrm{v}_{pc}(S_t)) \\ f_{fc}(\mathrm{v}(S_t), \mathrm{v}_{fc}(S_t)) \\ \mathrm{v}(S_t) \\ f_{len}(S_t) \\ f_{pos}(S_t) \\ f_{tf}(S_t) \\ f_{df}(S_t) \end{bmatrix}\right). \tag{5}$$

Here, θ are the parameters of the neural network. We use a 3 hidden layers MLP with tanh activation function; the sizes of the layers are 100, 50, and 1. Increasing the number and dimension size of layers has little influence on the performance according to our experiments. The model without the Surface Features (**SF**) in Table 2 is referred to as **CRSum**.

As with existing studies [2, 3, 40], we use the standard Mean Square Error (MSE) as the loss function to train CRSum (and CRSum+SF):

$$\begin{aligned} L(\theta) &= \frac{1}{|C| \cdot |D|} \sum_{D \in C} \sum_{S_t \in D} Err(S_t) \\ Err(S_t) &= \left(f(S_t \mid \theta) - \text{ROUGE-2}(S_t \mid S_{ref})\right)^2, \end{aligned} \tag{6}$$

where C is the set of all documents.

Sentence modeling: $\mathbf{v}(S_t)$. Since we conduct regression with respect to ROUGE-2, which is computed as the bi-gram overlap between the system generated summary and the human written summary, we use Bi-CNN [3] to model each sentence. We first concatenate adjacent words into bi-grams:

$$\mathrm{bi}(i, i+1) = \begin{bmatrix} \mathrm{v}_i \\ \mathrm{v}_{i+1} \end{bmatrix}, \tag{7}$$

where v_i is the word embedding for the i-th word of a sentence. After that, we perform convolutions on the bi-grams with a filter matrix:

$$\mathrm{v}_{bi}(i, i+1) = f(\mathrm{W}_c^T \cdot \mathrm{bi}(i, i+1) + b), \tag{8}$$

where $\mathrm{W}_c \in \mathbb{R}^{2|\mathrm{v}_i| \times |\mathrm{v}_i|}$ is the filter matrix; b is the bias; and $f(\cdot)$ is the activation function. We use the $\tanh(\cdot)$ function in our experiments.

Then we perform element-wise max pooling over the bi-gram representations $V_{bi}(S_t) = \{\mathrm{v}_{bi}(i, i+1) \mid 0 \le i \le |S_t|\}$ to get the sentence S_t's representation $\mathrm{v}(S_t)$:

$$\mathrm{v}(S_t) = \max_{\mathrm{v}_{bi}(i,i+1) \in V_{bi}(S_t)} \mathrm{v}_{bi}(i, i+1). \tag{9}$$

The function max chooses the maximum value of each dimension of the vectors in $V_{bi}(S_t)$.

In order to selectively encode the more important bi-grams into the sentence representations, an Attentive Pooling Convolutional Neural Network (AP-Bi-CNN) is applied, as shown in Figure 3. The difference with Bi-CNN is that we jointly learn a bi-gram weight $w_{bi}(i, i+1)$ when conducting pooling:

$$\mathrm{v}(S_{t-c}) = \max_{\mathrm{v}_{bi}(i,i+1) \in V_{bi}(S_{t-c})} w_{bi}(i, i+1) \cdot \mathrm{v}_{bi}(i, i+1). \tag{10}$$

Here, S_t is the sentence to conduct regression on; S_{t-c} is S_t's context sentence; and $w_{bi}(i, i+1)$ is the attention weight for the bigram vector $\mathrm{v}_{bi}(i, i+1)$.

Unlike existing attentive pooling techniques [8, 54], we use sentence relations to learn the pooling weights in Eq. 11:

$$\begin{bmatrix} w_{bi}(0,1) \\ \vdots \\ w_{bi}(i,i+1) \\ \vdots \\ w_{bi}(|S_{t-c}|, |S_{t-c}+1|) \end{bmatrix} = \text{softmax}\left(\begin{bmatrix} \cos(\mathrm{v}_{bi}(0,1), \mathrm{v}(S_t)) \\ \vdots \\ \cos(\mathrm{v}_{bi}(i,i+1), \mathrm{v}(S_t)) \\ \vdots \\ \cos(\mathrm{v}_{bi}(|S_{t-c}|, |S_{t-c}+1|), \mathrm{v}(S_t)) \end{bmatrix}\right). \tag{11}$$

We use the softmax function to normalize the weights. The index of w_{bi} starts from 0 and ends with $|S_{t-c}+1|$ because we add two padding words "<L>" (Left) and "<R>" (Right) to each sentence, as shown in Figure 3.

Context modeling: $\mathbf{v}_{pc}(S_t)$ and $\mathbf{v}_{fc}(S_t)$. In order to model the relations between a sentence and its context, we also need to encode the context sentences into a vector representation. Recurrent Neural Networks with a Long Short-Term Memory (LSTM) unit have been successfully applied to many sequence modeling tasks [11, 31, 42]. There are many variations of LSTM that differ in their connectivity structure and activation functions. The LSTM architecture we use is given by the following equations [15]:

$$\begin{aligned} &\text{LSTM} : \mathrm{h}_{t-1}, \mathrm{v}(S_t), c_{t-1} \rightarrow c_t, \mathrm{h}_t \\ &\mathrm{x}_t = \begin{bmatrix} \mathrm{h}_{t-1} \\ \mathrm{v}(S_t) \end{bmatrix} \\ &f_i = \text{sigm}(\mathrm{W}_i^T \cdot \mathrm{x}_t + b_i); \\ &f_f = \text{sigm}(\mathrm{W}_f^T \cdot \mathrm{x}_t + b_f) \\ &f_o = \text{sigm}(\mathrm{W}_o^T \cdot \mathrm{x}_t + b_o); \\ &f_g = \tanh(\mathrm{W}_g^T \cdot \mathrm{x}_t + b_g) \\ &c_t = f_f \odot c_{t-1} + f_i \odot f_g; \\ &\mathrm{h}_t = f_o \odot \tanh(c_t), \end{aligned} \tag{12}$$

where $\mathrm{W}_i, \mathrm{W}_f, \mathrm{W}_o, \mathrm{W}_g \in \mathbb{R}^{2|\mathrm{v}(S_t)| \times |\mathrm{v}(S_t)|}$ are the parameter matrices; b_i, b_f, b_o, b_g are the bias parameters; h_t is the hidden state with respective to the t-th time step input $\mathrm{v}(S_t)$; c_t is the memory cell vector of the t-th time step; and sigm and tanh are applied element-wise. LSTM has a complicated dynamics that allows it to easily "memorize" information for an extended number of timesteps. The "long term" memory is stored in a vector of memory cells c_t. LSTM can decide to overwrite the memory cell, retrieve it, or keep it for the next time step.

Given a sentence S_t, we recurrently apply the LSTM unit to its preceding context sentence sequence C_{pc} and following context sentence sequence C_{fc}. For each timestamp t, S_t is fed into the LSTM unit and a corresponding vector representation h_t is generated. Then, we have $V_{pc} = \{\mathrm{h}_{t-m}, \ldots, \mathrm{h}_{t-1}\}$ for C_{pc} and $V_{fc} = \{\mathrm{h}_{t+1}, \ldots, \mathrm{h}_{t+n}\}$ for C_{fc}. Finally, we encode V_{pc} and V_{fc} into vector representations with sentence-level attentive pooling which can attend differentially to more and less important sentences, as shown in Figure 2. The formula for S_t's preceding context is

$$\mathrm{v}_{pc}(S_t) = \max_{\mathrm{h}_{t-i} \in V_{pc}} w_{t-i} \cdot \mathrm{h}_{t-i}, \tag{13}$$

where w_{t-i} is the attention weight for the hidden context state h_{t-i}. The formula for S_t's following context is similar.

Unlike most existing attention mechanisms where the last hidden state of an LSTM is used to learn the attention weights [7, 42], here we apply contextual sentence relations to model attention weights:

$$\begin{bmatrix} w_{t-m} \\ \vdots \\ w_{t-i} \\ \vdots \\ w_{t-1} \end{bmatrix} = \text{softmax}\left(\begin{bmatrix} \cos(\mathrm{h}_{t-m}, \mathrm{h}_t) \\ \vdots \\ \cos(\mathrm{h}_{t-i}, \mathrm{h}_t) \\ \vdots \\ \cos(\mathrm{h}_{t-1}, \mathrm{h}_t) \end{bmatrix}\right). \tag{14}$$

3.3 Sentence selection

There are two branches of commonly used algorithms for sentence selection, namely Greedy and Integer Linear Programming (ILP). Greedy is a little less promising than ILP because it greedily maximizes a function which ILP exactly maximizes. However, it offers a nice trade-off between performance and computation cost. Besides, since the objective (Eq. 2) is submodular, maximizing it with Greedy has a mathematical guarantee on optimality [26, 27, 32]. Thus, we use Greedy as the sentence selection algorithm. The algorithm starts with the sentence of the highest score. In each step, a new sentence S_t is added to the summary Ψ if it satisfies the following two conditions:

(1) It has the highest score in the remaining sentences;
(2) $\frac{\textit{bi-gram-overlap}(S_t, \Psi)}{f_{len}(S_t)} \leq 1 - \lambda$, where $\textit{bi-gram-overlap}(S_t, \Psi)$ is the count of bi-gram overlap between sentence S_t and the current summary Ψ.

The algorithm terminates when the length constraint is reached. Settings of λ are discussed in §7.2 below.

4 EXPERIMENTAL SETUP

We list the datasets and metrics used in §4.1 and introduce the implementation details of our model in §4.2.

4.1 Datasets and evaluation metrics

For evaluation we use well-known corpora made available by the Document Understanding Conference (DUC).[2] The DUC 2001, 2002 and 2004 datasets are for multi-document summarization. The DUC 2005, 2006 and 2007 datasets are for query-focused multi-document summarization. The documents are from the news domain and grouped into thematic clusters. For each document cluster, we concatenate all articles and split them into sentences using the tool provided with the DUC 2003 dataset. We follow standard practice and train our models on two years of data and test on the third.

The ROUGE metrics are the official metrics of the DUC extractive summarization tasks [39]. We use the official ROUGE tool[3] [25] to evaluate the performance of the baselines as well as our approaches.

[2] http://duc.nist.gov/

[3] ROUGE-1.5.5 with options: -n 2 -m -u -c 95 -x -r 1000 -f A -p 0.5 -t 0.

The length constraint is "-l 100" for DUC 2001/2002, "-b 665" for DUC 2004 and "-l 250" for DUC 2005/2006/2007. We take ROUGE-2 recall as the main metric for comparison because Owczarzak et al. [36] show its effectiveness for evaluating automatic summarization systems. For significance testing we use a two-tailed paired Student's t-test with $p < 0.05$.

4.2 Implementation details

Stanford CoreNLP[4] is used to tokenize the sentences. The 50 dimensional GloVe[5] vectors are used to initialize the word embeddings. We replace a word that is not contained in the GloVe vocabulary as "<U>" (Unknown). The word embeddings are fine-tuned during training. Before feeding the word embeddings into the neural models, we perform the dropout operation that sets a random subset of its argument to zero. The dropout layer acts as a regularization method to reduce overfitting during training [44]. To learn the weights of our model, we apply the diagonal variant of AdaGrad [9] with mini-batches, whose size we set to 20. The parameters m and n that represent the number of context sentences are considered from 1 to 10. We found that there is no further improvement for $m, n > 5$, so we set $m, n = 5$ in our experiments. The best settings of the parameter λ are decided by presenting the ROUGE-2 performance with λ ranging from 0 to 0.9 with a step size of 0.05.

5 TWO EXAMPLES

We present two examples to illustrate our methods at work. The first is an instance from the DUC 2004 dataset. From top-left to bottom-right, Figure 4 shows the ground truth, SF, CRSum, and CRSum+SF, respectively. The depth of the color corresponds to the importance of the sentence given by ground truth or models. We can see that, SF cannot significantly distinguish the different importance of different sentences. It wrongly estimates which of the two is more important, the third sentence or the fourth. CRSum is better than SF, however its capability is still limited in distinguishing different degrees of importance compared to the ground truth. In contrast, when combining CRSum and SF, CRSum+SF can better fit the ground truth.

As a second example, we visualize the learned two-level attentive pooling weights of an instance, as shown in Figure 5. Figure 5(a) illustrates word-level attentive pooling. We can see that S_t helps to pick up the more important words of S_{t+1} when modeling S_{t+1} into a vector representation. Figure 5(b) illustrates sentence-level attentive pooling. As shown, the context sentences S_{t+1} to S_{t+5} are treated differently according to their relevance to S_t. The more relevant sentences have more effect on the final results.

6 RESULTS

In §6.1, we compare CRSum with several state-of-the-art methods on the DUC 2001, 2002 and 2004 multi-document summarization datasets. We confirm that modeling contextual sentence relations significantly improves the performance of extractive summarization. In §6.2 we evaluate the effectiveness of contextual features on the DUC 2005, 2006 and 2007 query-focused multi-document summarization datasets. Here, we show that modeling contextual

[4] http://stanfordnlp.github.io/CoreNLP/
[5] http://nlp.stanford.edu/projects/glove/

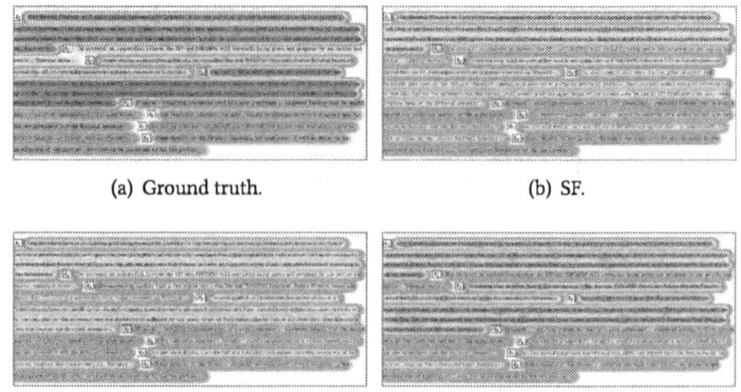

(a) Ground truth. (b) SF.

(c) CRSum. (d) CRSum+SF.

Figure 4: Visualization of sentence scoring. The depth of the color corresponds to the importance of the sentence given by groundtruth or models. The boxed characters S_i indicate sentence start. (Best viewed in color.)

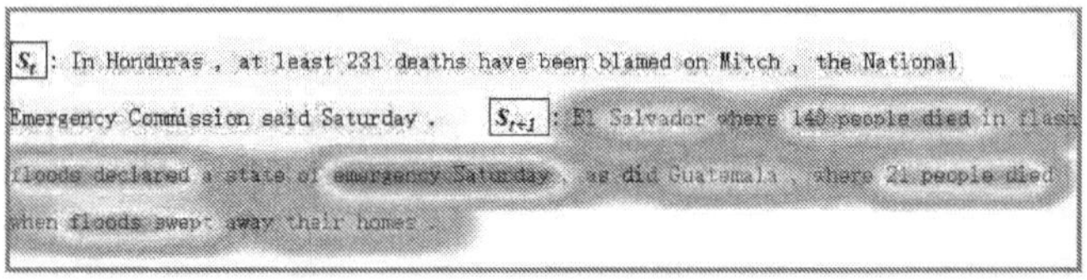

(a) Word-level attention. Color depth corresponds to the weight $w_{b_i}(i, i+1)$ (Eq. 11).

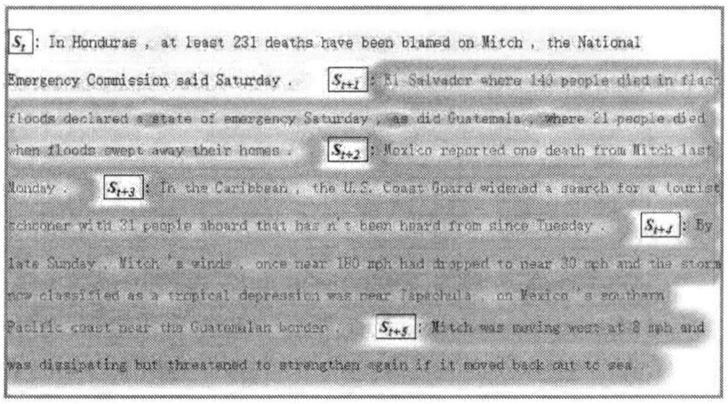

(b) Sentence-level attention. Color depth corresponds to the weight w_{t-i} (Eq. 14).

Figure 5: Visualization of word-level and sentence-level attention mechanisms. (Best viewed in color.)

sentence relations is also useful for query-focused summarization. We follow with further analyses of the results in §7.

6.1 Generic multi-document summarization

We first consider the generic multi-document summarization task. We list the methods compared against CRSum in Table 3. LexRank, ClusterHITS, ClusterCMRW are centroid-based methods; of these, ClusterHITS achieves the best ROUGE-1 score on DUC 2001. Lin is an MMR-based method. REGSUM, Ur, Sr, U+Sr and SF are feature engineering-based methods with different features. R2N2 uses an RNN to encode each sentence into a vector based on its parse tree, then performs sentence regression combined with 23 features. GA and ILP are greedy and ILP-based sentence selection algorithms,

Table 3: Methods considered for comparison in §6.1.

Acronym	Gloss	Reference
SF	Surface features with MLP as decoder	§3
CRSum	The proposed neural model in this paper	§3
CRSum (no attention)	CRSum without attention mechanism	§3
CRSum+SF	Combination of CRSum and SF	§3
Unsupervised methods		
LexRank	Centroid based method	[10]
ClusterHITS	Centroid based method	[48]
ClusterCMRW	Centroid based method	[48]
Lin	Maximal marginal relevance method	[27]
Feature engineering based methods		
REGSUM	Regression word saliency estimation	[2]
Ur	REGSUM with different features	[2]
Sr	SVR with 23 defined features	[2]
U+Sr	Combination of Ur and Sr	[2]
Deep learning based methods		
R2N2_GA	RNN with greedy sentence regression	[2]
R2N2_ILP	RNN with ILP sentence regression	[2]
PriorSum	REGSUM with different features	[3]

respectively. PriorSum uses a CNN to encode each sentence into a feature vector and then performs sentence regression combined with surface features.

The ROUGE scores of the methods listed in Table 3 on the DUC 2001, 2002 and 2004 datasets are presented in Table 4. For each metric, the best performance per dataset is indicated in bold face. Generally, CRSum+SF achieves the best performance in terms of both ROUGE-1 and ROUGE-2 on all three datasets. Although ClusterHITS achieves higher ROUGE-1 scores on DUC 2001, its ROUGE-2 scores are much lower. In contrast, CRSum+SF works quite stably across datasets. ClusterCMRW gets higher ROUGE-1 scores on DUC 2002 and its ROUGE-2 score is comparable with R2N2_GA, but CRSum+SF improves ClusterCMRW by over 1.6 percentage points (%pts) in terms of ROUGE-2.

The performance of CRSum is comparable to the state-of-the-art methods, R2N2_GA, R2N2_ILP and PriorSum. Note that CRSum is a pure neural network model while R2N2_GA, R2N2_ILP and PriorSum are combinations of neural models and dozens of hand-crafted features. The neural parts of R2N2_GA, R2N2_ILP and PriorSum model the standalone sentence, while CRSum further considers the local contextual relations.

When we combine CRSum with four basic surface features, there is a big improvement and CRSum+SF achieves the best performance. Specifically, CRSum+SF improves over PriorSum, the best method, in terms of ROUGE-2 by 1%pt on DUC 2001, 2002 and over 0.5%pt on DUC 2004. The improvements in terms of ROUGE-2 achieved on the three benchmark datasets are considered big [28, 39].

The main insight is that CRSum captures different factors than SF, which we will analyze in detail in §7.

6.2 Query-focused multi-document summarization

Next, we consider the performance of CRSum on the query-focused multi-document summarization task. We list the methods against which CRSum is compared in Table 6. LEAD simply selects the leading sentences to form a summary; it is often used as an official baseline of this task [4]. QUERY_SIM ranks sentences according to their TF-IDF cosine similarity to the query. MultiMR is a graph-based manifold ranking method. SVR and SF+QF are feature engineering-based methods. For the query-focused summarization task, the relevance of sentences to the query is an important feature, so we

Table 4: Multi-document summarization. ROUGE results (%) on DUC 2001, 2002, 2004 datasets. Per dataset, significant improvements over the underlined methods are marked with † (t-test, p < .05).

	Approach	ROUGE-1	ROUGE-2
DUC 2001	Peer T	33.03	7.86
	ClusterHITS*	**37.42**	6.81
	LexRank	<u>33.43</u>	<u>6.09</u>
	Ur*	34.28	6.66
	Sr*	34.06	6.65
	U+Sr*	33.98	6.54
	R2N2_GA*	35.88	7.64
	R2N2_ILP*	36.91	7.87
	PriorSum*	35.98	7.89
	SF	<u>34.82</u>	<u>7.76</u>
	CRSum	<u>35.36</u>	8.30
	CRSum+SF	36.54†	**8.75†**
DUC 2002	Peer 26	35.15	7.64
	ClusterCMRW*	38.55	8.65
	LexRank	<u>35.29</u>	<u>7.54</u>
	Ur*	34.16	7.66
	Sr*	34.23	7.81
	U+Sr*	35.13	8.02
	R2N2_GA*	36.84	8.52
	R2N2_ILP*	37.96	8.88
	PriorSum*	36.63	8.97
	SF	<u>37.33</u>	<u>8.98</u>
	CRSum	<u>37.10</u>	<u>9.29</u>
	CRSum+SF	**38.90†**	**10.28†**
DUC 2004	Peer 65	37.88	9.18
	REGSUM*	38.57	9.75
	LexRank	<u>37.87</u>	<u>8.88</u>
	Lin*	39.35	–
	Ur*	37.22	9.15
	Sr*	36.72	9.10
	U+Sr*	37.62	9.31
	R2N2_GA*	38.16	9.52
	R2N2_ILP*	38.78	9.86
	PriorSum*	38.91	10.07
	SF	<u>37.74</u>	<u>9.60</u>
	CRSum	<u>38.19</u>	<u>9.66</u>
	CRSum+SF	**39.53†**	**10.60†**

(Peer T, 26, 65 are the best performing participants at DUC 2001, 2002, 2004, respectively. Scores of the methods marked with * are taken from the corresponding references listed in Table 3.)

Table 5: Query Features (QF) used in this paper.

Feature	Description
$f_{q1}(S_t, S_q) = \cos(TF(S_t), TF(S_q))$	Cosine of TF vectors of sentence S_t and query S_q
$f_{q2}(S_t, S_q) = \cos(emb(S_t), emb(S_q))$	Cosine of average embedding vectors of S_t and S_q
$f_{q3}(S_t, S_q) = \frac{overlap(S_t, S_q)}{f_{len}(S_t)}$	Unigram overlap with respect to S_t
$f_{q4}(S_t, S_q) = \frac{overlap(S_t, S_q)}{f_{len}(S_q)}$	Unigram overlap with respect to S_q

Table 6: Methods considered for comparison in §6.2.

Acronym	Gloss	Reference
SF+QF	Surface features (Table 2+5) with MLP as decoder	§3
CRSum	The proposed neural model in this paper	§3
CRSum (no attention)	CRSum without attention mechanism	§3
CRSum+SF+QF	Combination of CRSum and SF	§3
Unsupervised methods		
LEAD	Select the leading sentences	[4]
QUERY_SIM	TF-IDF cosine similarity	[4]
MultiMR	Graph based manifold ranking method	[47]
Feature engineering based methods		
SVR	SVR with hand-crafted features	[34]
Deep learning based methods		
ISOLATION	Embedding and TF-IDF cosine similarity	[4]
DocEmb	Embedding distributions based summarization	[21]
AttSum	Neural attention summarization	[4]

combine the Surface Features (SF) in Table 2 and the Query Features (QF) in Table 5, using SF+QF to refer to the resulting method. ISOLATION contains two parts; sentence saliency is modeled as the cosine similarity between a sentence embedding and the document embedding; query relevance is modeled as the TF-IDF cosine similarity between a sentence and the query. DocEmb summarizes by asymptotically estimating KL-divergence based on document embedding distributions. AttSum learns distributed representations for sentences and the documents; it applies an attention mechanism to simulate human reading behavior.

The results on the query-focused multi-document summarization task on the DUC 2005, 2006 and 2007 datasets are presented in Table 7. Generally, CRSum alone is not enough for this task; it is outperformed by SF+QF. This is because CRSum does not consider relevance of a sentence given the queries; the relevance relation is captured by the features encoded in SF+QF. CRSum+SF+QF improves over SF+QF by 0.5%pt to 0.7%pt, which means that CRSum is also useful as a supplementary feature for the query-focused summarization task.

7 ANALYSIS

Having answered our main research questions in the previous section, we now analyze our experimental results and the impact of our modeling choices. We analyze the effectiveness of the learned contextual features compared to the surface features; we explore different settings of the threshold parameter λ in the greedy algorithm (sentence selection phase, §3.3) to determine the sensitivity of our method; and we analyze our attention mechanisms.

Table 7: Query-focused multi-document summarization. ROUGE results (%) on DUC 2005, 2006, 2007 datasets. Per dataset, significant improvements over the underlined methods are marked with † (t-test, p < .05).

	System	ROUGE-1	ROUGE-2
DUC 2005	Peer 15	37.52	7.25
	LEAD*	29.71	4.69
	QUERY_SIM*	32.95	5.91
	SVR*	36.91	7.04
	MultiMR*	35.58	6.81
	DocEmb*	30.59	4.69
	ISOLATION*	35.72	6.79
	AttSum*	37.01	6.99
	SF+QF	39.18	7.79
	CRSum	<u>36.96</u>	<u>7.01</u>
	CRSum+SF+QF	**39.52**†	**8.41**†
DUC 2006	Peer 24	41.11	9.56
	LEAD*	32.61	5.71
	QUERY_SIM*	35.52	7.10
	SVR*	39.24	8.87
	MultiMR*	38.57	7.75
	DocEmb*	32.77	5.61
	ISOLATION*	40.58	8.96
	AttSum*	40.90	9.40
	SF+QF	41.45	9.57
	CRSum	39.51	<u>9.19</u>
	CRSum+SF+QF	**41.70**	**10.03**†
DUC 2007	Peer 15	44.51	12.45
	LEAD*	36.14	8.12
	QUERY_SIM*	36.32	7.94
	SVR*	43.42	11.10
	MultiMR*	41.59	9.34
	DocEmb*	33.88	6.46
	ISOLATION*	42.76	10.79
	AttSum*	43.92	11.55
	SF+QF	44.29	11.73
	CRSum	<u>41.20</u>	<u>11.17</u>
	CRSum+SF+QF	**44.60**†	**12.48**†

(Peer 15, 24, 15 are the best performing participants at DUC 2005, 2006, 2007, respectively. Scores of the methods marked with * are taken from the corresponding references listed in Table 6.)

7.1 CRSum vs. the surface features

Pearson correlation coefficients can reflect the effectiveness of the feature to some extent. We examine correlations with the ground truth of the surface features in Table 2 and of CRSum, as shown in Table 8. CRSum achieves higher correlation scores than the surface features ($f_{len}(S_t)$, $f_{pos}(S_t)$, $f_{tf}(S_t)$ and $f_{df}(S_t)$) and comparable correlation scores with SF. The results also confirm that $f_{len}(S_t)$ and $f_{pos}(S_t)$ are important features for extractive summarization [2, 3, 49].

Pearson correlation coefficients only reflect linear correlations. Hence, we further visualize the relation between the feature space

Table 8: Pearson correlation coefficients of surface features and CRSum.

Features	DUC 2001	DUC 2002	DUC 2004
$f_{len}(S_t)$	0.31	0.31	0.37
$f_{pos}(S_t)$	0.28	0.31	0.40
$f_{tf}(S_t)$	0.14	0.20	0.24
$f_{df}(S_t)$	0.19	0.23	0.38
SF	0.45	**0.48**	**0.64**
CRSum	**0.46**	0.44	0.56

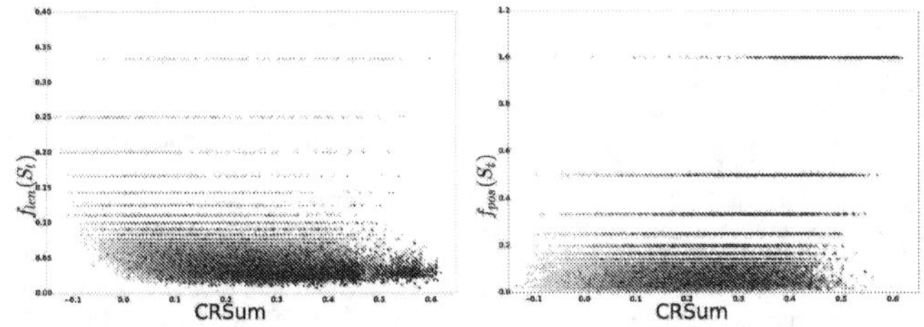

(a) CRSum vs. $f_{len}(S_t)$ (b) CRSum vs. $f_{pos}(S_t)$

(c) CRSum vs. $f_{tf}(S_t)$ (d) CRSum vs. $f_{df}(S_t)$

Figure 6: CRSum scores vs. surface feature scores. Each point represents a sentence. The color depth reflects the importance of the sentence according to the ground truth. (Best viewed in color.)

of CRSum and the surface features $f_{len}(S_t)$, $f_{pos}(S_t)$, $f_{tf}(S_t)$, and $f_{df}(S_t)$, as shown in Figure 6, by plotting CRSum scores against the feature values.[6] The color depth reflects the importance of a sentence according to the ground truth. Low CRSum scores mostly correspond to sentences with low ROUGE-2 scores, which means that CRSum can distinguish useless sentences effectively. Also, high CRSum scores mostly correspond to sentences with high ROUGE-2 scores, which means that CRSum can distinguish the most important sentences effectively. Obviously, this ability to identify the most important sentences is extremely useful, as a summary is usually short, containing just a few very important sentences; we should also note that this ability is still limited as there are low scoring and high scoring sentences mixed together.

7.2 Threshold parameter λ

Recall from §3.3 that after giving a salience score to each sentence, we greedily select the sentence with the highest score for inclusion in the final summary until the length constraint is reached. During the process, a parameter λ is used to avoid redundant sentences by discarding sentences whose bigram overlap with already selected

[6] The scores for CRSum range from -1 to 1 as its activation function is Tanh.

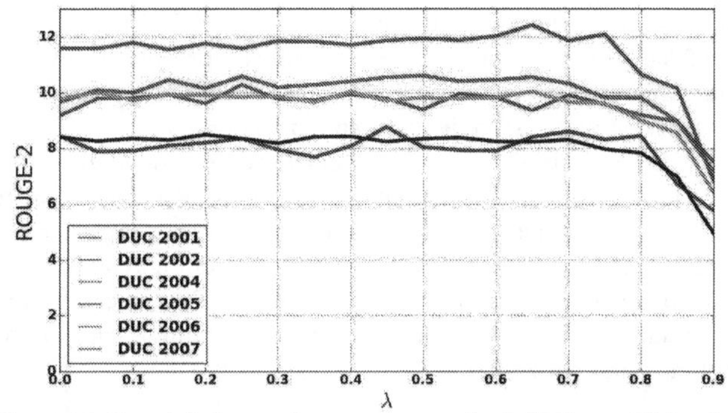

Figure 7: Sensitivity to the parameter λ of CRSum+SF during sentence selection.

sentences is larger than $1 - \lambda$. To investigate the sensitivity of our choice of λ, we examine the performance of CRSum+SF with the threshold parameter λ ranging from 0 to 0.9 with a step size of 0.05. The results are shown in Figure 7, where we plot performance in terms of ROUGE-2 against λ. Generally, the performance of CRSum+SF is not sensitive to the setting of λ for values less than 0.8, with the best performance achieved around 0.65 to 0.75.

7.3 Attention

We have illustrated our word and sentence level attention mechanisms with two examples in Figure 5. Here, we analyze the performance of these attention mechanisms in Table 9, using the same data as in §6.1. Generally, with two-level attentive pooling, CRSum gains around 0.3%pt–0.5%pt improvements in terms of ROUGE-2 over CRSum (without attention). The improvements are different on the three datasets with higher improvement on DUC 2001 and smaller improvement on DUC 2004. Interestingly, world-level and sentence-level attention yield comparable improvements over CRSum without attention. But their contribution is complementary as the combined attention mechanisms bring further improvements, on all metrics and datasets, demonstrating the need for both.

8 CONCLUSIONS & FUTURE WORK

This paper presents a novel neural network model, CRSum, to automatically learn features contained in sentences and in contextual relations between sentences. We have conducted extensive experiments on the DUC multi-document summarization datasets and query-focused multi-document summarization datasets. Without hand-crafted features, CRSum achieves a comparable performance with state-of-the-art methods. When combined with a few basic surface features, CRSum+SF significantly outperforms the baselines

Table 9: Analyzing attention mechanisms on the multi-document summarization task (%).

	DUC 2001	DUC 2002	DUC 2004
CRSum attention	ROUGE-1/2	ROUGE-1/2	ROUGE-1/2
without	34.33/7.81	36.18/8.91	37.76/9.32
word-level	34.54/7.95	36.31/9.09	37.80/9.37
sentence-level	34.57/8.01	36.29/9.07	37.82/9.41
two-level	**35.36/8.30**	**37.10/9.29**	**38.19/9.66**

and achieves the best published performance on the DUC 2001, 2002 and 2004 datasets. Based on our experimental results and subsequent analyses, we conclude that CRSum encodes supplementary information that surface features cannot capture.

We believe our work can be advanced and extended in several directions: CRSum can be enriched by introducing a mechanism to explicitly model fine-grained sentence relations, such as parallelism relations, progressive relations, inductive reasoning relations and deductive reasoning relations [43]. Variants of CRSum can be also extended to other tasks, such as abstractive summarization and sentence summarization.

9 ACKNOWLEDGMENTS

This work is supported by the Natural Science Foundation of China (61672322, 61672324), the Natural Science Foundation of Shandong province (2016ZRE27468), the Fundamental Research Funds of Shandong University, Ahold Delhaize, Amsterdam Data Science, the Bloomberg Research Grant program, the Dutch national program COMMIT, Elsevier, the European Community's Seventh Framework Programme (FP7/2007-2013) under grant agreement nr 312827 (VOX-Pol), the Microsoft Research Ph.D. program, the Netherlands Institute for Sound and Vision, the Netherlands Organisation for Scientific Research (NWO) under project nrs 612.001.116, HOR-11-10, CI-14-25, 652.002.001, 612.001.551, 652.001.003, and Yandex. All content represents the opinion of the authors, which is not necessarily shared or endorsed by their respective employers and/or sponsors.

REFERENCES

[1] L. Bing, P. Li, Y. Liao, W. Lam, W. Guo, and R. J. Passonneau. Abstractive multi-document summarization via phrase selection and merging. In *ACL*, 2015.

[2] Z. Cao, F. Wei, L. Dong, S. Li, and M. Zhou. Ranking with recursive neural networks and its application to multi-document summarization. In *AAAI*, 2015.

[3] Z. Cao, F. Wei, S. Li, W. Li, M. Zhou, and H. Wang. Learning summary prior representation for extractive summarization. In *ACL*, 2015.

[4] Z. Cao, W. Li, S. Li, and F. Wei. Attsum: Joint learning of focusing and summarization with neural attention. In *COLING*, 2016.

[5] J. Carbonell and J. Goldstein. The use of MMR, diversity-based reranking for reordering documents and producing summaries. In *SIGIR*, 1998.

[6] J. Cheng and M. Lapata. Neural summarization by extracting sentences and words. In *ACL*, 2016.

[7] S. Chopra, M. Auli, and A. M. Rush. Abstractive sentence summarization with attentive recurrent neural networks. In *NAACL-HLT*, 2016.

[8] C. N. dos Santos, M. Tan, B. Xiang, and B. Zhou. Attentive pooling networks. *CoRR*, 2016.

[9] J. Duchi, E. Hazan, and Y. Singer. Adaptive subgradient methods for online learning and stochastic optimization. *JMLR*, 12:2121–2159, 2011.

[10] G. Erkan and D. R. Radev. LexRank: Graph-based lexical centrality as salience in text summarization. *JAIR*, 22(1):457–479, 2004.

[11] K. Filippova, E. Alfonseca, C. A. Colmenares, L. Kaiser, and O. Vinyals. Sentence compression by deletion with LSTMs. In *EMNLP*, 2015.

[12] M. W. Gardner and S. Dorling. Artificial neural networks (the multilayer perceptron) – A review of applications in the atmospheric sciences. *Atmospheric environment*, 32(14):2627–2636, 1998.

[13] D. Gillick and B. Favre. A scalable global model for summarization. In *ILP-NLP*, 2009.

[14] J. Goldstein, V. Mittal, J. Carbonell, and M. Kantrowitz. Multi-document summarization by sentence extraction. In *NAACL-ANLP*, 2000.

[15] A. Graves, A. Mohamed, and G. E. Hinton. Speech recognition with deep recurrent neural networks. In *ICASSP*, 2013.

[16] K. Hong and A. Nenkova. Improving the estimation of word importance for news multi-document summarization. In *EACL*, 2014.

[17] B. Hu, Q. Chen, and F. Zhu. LCSTS: A large scale Chinese short text summarization dataset. In *EMNLP*, 2015.

[18] Y. Hu and X. Wan. PPSGen: Learning to generate presentation slides for academic papers. In *IJCAI*, 2013.

[19] Y. Hu and X. Wan. PPSGen: Learning-based presentation slides generation for academic papers. *TKDE*, 27(4):1085–1097, 2015.

[20] M. Kågebäck, O. Mogren, N. Tahmasebi, and D. Dubhashi. Extractive summarization using continuous vector space models. In *CVSC@ EACL*, 2014.

[21] H. Kobayashi, M. Noguchi, and T. Yatsuka. Summarization based on embedding distributions. In *EMNLP*, 2015.

[22] J. Kupiec, J. Pedersen, and F. Chen. A trainable document summarizer. In *SIGIR*, 1995.

[23] C. Li, X. Qian, and Y. Liu. Using supervised bigram-based ILP for extractive summarization. In *ACL*, 2013.

[24] S. Li, Y. Ouyang, W. Wang, and B. Sun. Multi-document summarization using support vector regression. In *DUC*, 2007.

[25] C.-Y. Lin. Rouge: A package for automatic evaluation of summaries. In *ACL*, 2004.

[26] H. Lin and J. Bilmes. Multi-document summarization via budgeted maximization of submodular functions. In *NAACL-HLT*, 2010.

[27] H. Lin and J. Bilmes. A class of submodular functions for document summarization. In *NAACL-HLT*, 2011.

[28] R. McDonald. A study of global inference algorithms in multi-document summarization. In *ECIR*, 2007.

[29] R. Mihalcea. Graph-based ranking algorithms for sentence extraction, applied to text summarization. In *ACL*, 2004.

[30] R. Mihalcea and P. Tarau. TextRank: Bringing order into texts. In *EMNLP*, 2004.

[31] R. Nallapati, B. Zhou, C. N. dos Santos, Ç. Gülçehre, and B. Xiang. Abstractive text summarization using sequence-to-sequence RNNs and beyond. In *CoNLL*, 2016.

[32] G. L. Nemhauser, L. A. Wolsey, and M. L. Fisher. An analysis of approximations for maximizing submodular set functions—i. *MATH PROGRAM*, 14(1):265–294, 1978.

[33] Y. Ouyang, S. Li, and W. Li. Developing learning strategies for topic-based summarization. In *CIKM*, 2007.

[34] Y. Ouyang, W. Li, S. Li, and Q. Lu. Applying regression models to query-focused multi-document summarization. *IPM*, 47(2):227–237, 2011.

[35] P. Over and J. Yen. Introduction to DUC-2001: An intrinsic evaluation of generic news text summarization systems. In *DUC*, 2004.

[36] K. Owczarzak, J. M. Conroy, H. T. Dang, and A. Nenkova. An assessment of the accuracy of automatic evaluation in summarization. In *NAACL-HLT*, 2012.

[37] D. R. Radev, H. Jing, and M. Budzikowska. Centroid-based summarization of multiple documents: Sentence extraction, utility-based evaluation, and user studies. In *NAACL-ANLP*, 2000.

[38] D. R. Radev, H. Jing, M. Styś, and D. Tam. Centroid-based summarization of multiple documents. *IPM*, 40(6):919–938, 2004.

[39] P. A. Rankel, J. M. Conroy, H. T. Dang, and A. Nenkova. A decade of automatic content evaluation of news summaries: Reassessing the state of the art. In *ACL*, 2013.

[40] P. Ren, F. Wei, Z. Chen, J. Ma, and M. Zhou. A redundancy-aware sentence regression framework for extractive summarization. In *COLING*, 2016.

[41] D. W. Ruck, S. K. Rogers, M. Kabrisky, M. E. Oxley, and B. W. Suter. The multilayer perceptron as an approximation to a bayes optimal discriminant function. *TNN*, 1(4):296–298, 1990.

[42] A. M. Rush, S. Chopra, and J. Weston. A neural attention model for abstractive sentence summarization. In *EMNLP*, 2015.

[43] W. Song, T. Liu, R. Fu, L. Liu, H. Wang, and T. Liu. Learning to identify sentence parallelism in student essays. In *COLING*, 2016.

[44] N. Srivastava, G. Hinton, A. Krizhevsky, I. Sutskever, and R. Salakhutdinov. Dropout: A simple way to prevent neural networks from overfitting. *JMLR*, 15 (1):1929–1958, 2014.

[45] X. Wan. An exploration of document impact on graph-based multi-document summarization. In *EMNLP*, 2008.

[46] X. Wan. Using bilingual information for cross-language document summarization. In *NAACL-HLT*, 2011.

[47] X. Wan and J. Xiao. Graph-based multi-modality learning for topic-focused multi-document summarization. In *IJCAI*, 2009.

[48] X. Wan and J. Yang. Multi-document summarization using cluster-based link analysis. In *SIGIR*, 2008.

[49] X. Wan and J. Zhang. CTSUM: extracting more certain summaries for news articles. In *SIGIR*, 2014.

[50] X. Wan, Z. Cao, F. Wei, S. Li, and M. Zhou. Multi-document summarization via discriminative summary reranking. *CoRR*, 2015.

[51] S. Yan and X. Wan. Deep dependency substructure-based learning for multidocument summarization. *ACM Transactions on Information Systems (TOIS)*, 34(1):3, 2015.

[52] C. yew Lin and E. Hovy. From single to multi-document summarization: A prototype system and its evaluation. In *ACL*, 2002.

[53] W. Yin and Y. Pei. Optimizing sentence modeling and selection for document summarization. In *IJCAI*, 2015.

[54] W. Yin, H. Schtze, B. Xiang, and B. Zhou. ABCNN: Attention-based convolutional neural network for modeling sentence pairs. *TACL*, 4(1):259–272, 2016.

Stacking Bagged and Boosted Forests for Effective Automated Classification*

Raphael Campos, Sérgio Canuto, Thiago Salles, Clebson C. A. de Sá and Marcos André Gonçalves
Federal University of Minas Gerais
Computer Science Department
Av. Antônio Carlos 6627 - ICEx
Belo Horizonte, Brazil
{rcampos,sergiodaniel,tsalles,clebsonc,mgoncalv}@dcc.ufmg.br

ABSTRACT

Random Forest (RF) is one of the most successful strategies for automated classification tasks. Motivated by the RF success, recently proposed RF-based classification approaches leverage the central RF idea of aggregating a large number of low-correlated trees, which are inherently parallelizable and provide exceptional generalization capabilities. In this context, this work brings several new contributions to this line of research. First, we propose a new RF-based strategy (BERT) that applies the boosting technique in bags of extremely randomized trees. Second, we empirically demonstrate that this new strategy, as well as the recently proposed BROOF and LazyNN_RF classifiers do complement each other, motivating us to stack them to produce an even more effective classifier. Up to our knowledge, this is the first strategy to effectively combine the three main ensemble strategies: stacking, bagging (the cornerstone of RFs) and boosting. Finally, we exploit the efficient and unbiased stacking strategy based on out-of-bag (OOB) samples to considerably speedup the very costly training process of the stacking procedure. Our experiments in several datasets covering two high-dimensional and noisy domains of topic and sentiment classification provide strong evidence in favor of the benefits of our RF-based solutions. We show that BERT is among the top performers in the vast majority of analyzed cases, while retaining the unique benefits of RF classifiers (explainability, parallelization, easiness of parameterization). We also show that stacking only the recently proposed RF-based classifiers and BERT using our OOB-based strategy is not only significantly faster than recently proposed stacking strategies (up to six times) but also much more effective, with gains up to 21% and 17% on MacroF_1 and MicroF_1, respectively, over the best base method, and of 5% and 6% over a stacking of traditional methods, performing no worse than a complete stacking of methods at a much lower computational effort.

*This work was partially funded by projects InWeb (grant MCT/CNPq 573871/20086) and MASWeb (grant FAPEMIG/PRONEX APQ-01400-14), and by the authors' individual grants from CNPq, FAPEMIG, Capes and Google Inc.

SIGIR '17, August 07-11, 2017, Shinjuku, Tokyo, Japan
© 2017 ACM. 978-1-4503-5022-8/17/08...$15.00
DOI: http://dx.doi.org/10.1145/3077136.3080815

KEYWORDS

Classification; Ensemble; Bagging; Boosting; Stacking

1 INTRODUCTION

Since the advent of the Web, the amount of data available has grown unprecedentedly. Thus, organizing and extracting useful information from this enormous amount of data has become an important (if not vital) task for industry and society. By using machine learning techniques to automatically associate documents with classes, Automatic Text Classification (ATC) provides means to organize information, allowing better comprehension and interpretation of the data [1]. Many important applications, such as topic categorization, sentiment analysis, spam filtering, language identification, recommender systems, among others, can be effectively and efficiently solved by automatic textual classifiers. Despite the wide applicability of ATC, text classification brings its own challenges, such as high dimensionality and the presence of noise [14]. Properly handling these issues is of great importance to guarantee high classification effectiveness. This is the central topic of this work.

Several machine learning techniques aimed at tackling the challenging ATC problem have been proposed. In particular, ensembles of classifiers have been shown to excel in this situation [4, 6, 23], enjoying high effectiveness in this domain. In particular, Random Forest (RF) is one of the most successful classifier ensembles in a wide variety of classification tasks [8]. Despite being a classifier with great generalization power, it has been shown that RF models may suffer from overfitting issues [24], having their effectiveness degraded in the presence of many irrelevant or noisy attributes—a characteristic of textual classification tasks. Recently, some RF-based classifiers were shown to achieve state-of-the-art results in text classification by exploiting distinct strategies to mitigate the overfitting issue faced by RF, namely, a lazy RF version called LazyNN_RF [22], and a boosted RF strategy named BROOF [23]. Both methods learn classification models focusing on specific subregions of the input space, hoping to filter out irrelevant attributes and data—the primary factors that contribute to RF's overfitting.

In this work, we advance the state-of-the-art in text classification by proposing a novel derivation of the RF classifier. More specifically, we propose a new boosted version of the RF classifier, based on some ideas explored by the BROOF classifier: the so-called Boosted Extremely Randomized Trees (BERT) classifier. While BROOF is able to mitigate the overfitting issue faced by the RF classifier when applied to high-dimensional noisy data, by avoiding the generation of overly complex trees, it offers limited capability of bias reduction (through the so-called selective out-of-bag based weight update strategy). Thus, bias may still pose as an important factor to contribute to the error rate. To tackle this potential issue, we here propose to introduce another source of randomization in the boosted strategy proposed in [23] in order to better control the learner's bias, by applying the BROOF-like strategies into the Extremely Randomized Trees (Extra-Trees) classifier [10]. This novel strategy has the following motivations: (*i*) we expect to avoid overly complex models (and thus mitigate overfitting) through the application of the BROOF-like strategies; (*ii*) to provide more control over the learner's bias through the additional randomization offered by the Extra-Trees classifier; and, finally, (*iii*) to exploit the fact that the Extremely Randomized was shown to be more robust to noise than the RF classifier. As we shall see, our proposed classifier outperforms the analyzed state-of-the-art classifiers, including SVM, kNN, Naïve Bayes, BROOF, and LazyNN_RF, often by large margins. This is the first main contribution of this work.

Moreover, motivated by the fact that distinct learning methods may complement each other, uncovering specific structures that underlie the input/output relationship of the data at hand, in this work we also propose to exploit the complementary characteristics of the recently proposed RF-based approaches and ours, by stacking them in order to learn an even more effective meta-classifier. As we shall see later, their level of disagreement is high, which motivates our idea. Up to our knowledge, this is the first attempt to combine the three main ensemble strategies: bagging, boosting and stacking. According to our experiments, the meta-classifier that exploits only RF-based techniques is able to achieve gains of up to 21% and 17% in MicroF_1 and MacroF_1, respectively, over the best base method, and of 5% and 6% over a stacking of traditional method, being the top performer in all analyzed cases. This is the second main contribution of this work.

Finally, when stacking classifiers, one usually relies on k fold cross-validation procedures to estimate the *a posteriori* class probabilities for each example, to serve as input for the meta-classifier. Based on these predicted *a posteriori* class distribution estimates, the meta-classifier induces a relationship between these predictions and the true class. However, such estimation strategy may be very costly and sometimes ineffective, since it depends on learning k different models to estimate the probability distributions that serve as input for the stacking procedure. In order to cope with this problem, we here propose to exploit the efficient and unbiased out-of-bag (OOB) error estimate, an out-of-the-box estimate naturally produced by the bootstrap procedure used in each RF-based learner. Thus, we avoid additional computation efforts to learn a stacked classifier. According to our findings, this strategy considerably speeds up the training process of stacking while preserving its high effectiveness. This is our third main contribution.

In summary, the main contributions of this work are: (*i*) the proposal of a novel RF-based classifier, named BERT, that is able to outperform state-of-the-art classifiers; (*ii*) the proposal of a new stacking classifier that exploits the complementary characteristics of BROOF, LazyNN_RF and BERT that is able to outperform all analyzed classification algorithms, including a stacking of traditional methods, often by large margins; (*iii*) the proposal of a new estimation strategy based on the exploitation of OOB for generating the input for the stacked meta-classifier that substantially reduces the computational effort/runtime of the stacking strategy while retaining its predictive power; and (iv) an extensive experimentation with 15 datasets in two domains – topic categorization and sentiment analysis; – against several baselines including traditional classifiers (to compare with BERT), several stacking combinations (to compare with the stacking of Forests) and several state-of-the-art stackers (to compare with our OOB-based approach).

Roadmap. Section 2 reviews some relevant literature related to this work. In Section 3 we detail our proposed BERT classifier, providing its motivations, learning strategy details, and extensive experimental evaluation. Section 4 details our proposed method to efficiently stack RF-based methods as well as its experimental evaluation and analysis. Finally, in Section 5 we conclude the paper, pointing out some possible directions for further investigation.

2 RELATED WORK

Ensembles of classifiers are an extensively studied machine learning technique [21]. Among several learning methods used in practice, ensembles are one of the most effective in several applications and can be divided into two groups: ensembles of homogeneous and heterogeneous classifiers. The former relies on learning many versions of the same classification technique, each one built by somehow disturbing the training set. Then, usually one averages the predictions in order to come up with final decisions with higher generalization capabilities. The latter combines a set of distinct learning methods trained with the same training set and then producing the final decisions according to the predictions made by these classifiers.

Regarding the text classification realm, in [7], the authors use what they call Moderated Asymmetric Naïve Bayes (MANB) as a base learner in their homogeneous ensemble configuration. Several homogeneous ensemble methods are contrasted, such as k-fold partitioning, bagging and boosting, as well as a heterogeneous ensemble method which combines SVM and NB learning algorithms. In [23], the authors combine two well-known homogeneous ensemble techniques, bagging and boosting, by exploiting Random Forests (RF) as "weak learners" in the boosting framework. The combination is achieved by means of "smoothly" updating the weights of only the out-of-bag instances. This combination mitigates the overfitting issue faced by RF models in textual classification tasks and leverages its generalization power. Recently, in [19] the authors empirically evaluate the effectiveness of ensemble learning methods on textual documents represented by keywords. They apply different keyword extraction strategies on the dataset. The authors evaluate five different homogeneous ensemble methods that use four different base classifiers. In [2, 4, 20], ensembles of heterogeneous classifiers are proposed, by combining classical text classification methods (e.g., SVM, kNN, NB and Rocchio). In all analyzed cases, significant improvements were observed when compared to the traditional classifiers. Furthermore, a combination of several distinct polarity classifiers for Twitter sentiment analysis is proposed in [13]. Unlike these works, we here aim at combining homogeneous and heterogeneous classifiers by stacking different RF-based methods in an original manner.

There are two common techniques to combine predictions of distinct classifiers, namely, fixed combining methods and trainable combining methods [18]. An advantage of applying fixed methods for ensemble systems is that there are no need to train a meta-classifier since they do not take into consideration the label information in the meta-level training set when combining the learners. Thus, they are less time-consuming than their counterparts. Many fixed combining methods can be found in literature, such as Sum, Product, Vote, and Average.

On the other hand, trainable combining methods work on meta-level data, in order to learn the prediction model. Although exploiting metal-level data to extract knowledge usually enhances classification effectiveness, it comes at the price of additional computational effort [18].

Perhaps, the most relevant studies about trainable combining methods are based on Stacking (a.k.a. Blending), which was originally conceived as "Stacked Generalization" by Wolpert [27]. In this case, a meta-level training set $\mathbb{D}_{meta}$ is generated by applying a **cross-validation** procedure, in which the original training set $\mathbb{D}_{train}$ is divided into T equally sized disjoint sets. Each base-level classifier is learned by considering $\mathbb{D}_{train} \setminus \mathbb{F}_t$ as training set and reserving $\mathbb{F}_t$ for testing. Formally, $\forall i = 1, ..., K : \forall t = 1, ..., T : C_i^t = L_i(\mathbb{D}_{train} \setminus \mathbb{F}_t)$. Subsequently, each learned classifier C_i^t produces a estimation for the posterior probability $p_i^t(c_m|x_j)$ that an observation x_j belongs to a class c_m; $\forall x_j \in F_t : C_i^t(x_j) = p_i^t(x_j) = (p_i^t(c_1|x_j), p_i^t(c_2|x_j), ..., p_i^t(c_M|x_j))$. The obtained meta-level training set $\mathbb{D}_{meta}$ is thus:

$$\begin{bmatrix} p_1(y_1|x_1) & \dots & p_1(y_M|x_1) & \dots & p_K(y_1|x_1) & \dots & p_K(y_M|x_1) \\ p_1(y_1|x_2) & \dots & p_1(y_M|x_2) & \dots & p_K(y_1|x_2) & \dots & p_K(y_M|x_2) \\ \vdots & \ddots & \vdots & \ddots & \vdots & \ddots & \vdots \\ p_1(y_1|x_N) & \dots & p_1(y_M|x_N) & \dots & p_K(y_1|x_N) & \dots & p_K(y_M|x_N) \end{bmatrix}$$

Finally, a combining classifier is trained on the meta-level training set and used to produce the final prediction.

Several methods have been designed to exploit label information in the meta-level training set. In one strategy, the predictions of classifiers are grouped according to the given classes and then a template associated with each label is built. Three methods using that strategy are Multiple Response Linear Regression (MLR) [25], Decision Template (DT) [15] and the recently proposed VIG [18]. MLR assumes that each classifier weights differently each class. In this case, the combining algorithm is based on the M linear combinations of the posterior class probabilities and the associated class weights. The predicted class is then decided by selecting the maximum value among these combinations. The Decision Template strategy [15] groups the meta-level training set according to the classes of each instance. Then, Decision Templates are built by averaging the meta-level instances observed in each class (forming centroids). Subsequently, the predicted class is decided by selecting the class label of the Decision Template that is more similar to the meta-data unlabeled observation. To this end, the authors propose eleven similarity functions based on fuzzy logic. Due to its simple computation, this method has low computational cost in both training and testing. In [17] a combination of Stacking, Correspondence Analysis (CA) and K-Nearest Neighbor (KNN) is proposed, in the form of a single learning algorithm called SCANN. The goal of such algorithm is to find the underlying relationship between the learning observations and the predictions of the base classifiers, by applying CA to an indicator matrix formed by the learned meta-level instances and their corresponding true labels. Then, a kNN procedure is employed to classify the unseen data in the new scaled space. Recently, Nguyen et al. [18] proposed a combining classifier based on the variational inference which is based on the assumption that instances belonging to a given class of the meta-level training set are drawn from a multivariate Gaussian distribution. Thus, M distributions are estimated by using Bayesian variational inference on the instances belonging to each class. The predicted class for a new unseen observation is given by selecting the label associated with maximum posterior probabilities computed by the M multivariate Gaussian models. All aforementioned methods are used as baselines in our stacking experiments.

Moreover, all those methods rely on the meta-level training sets obtained by costly procedures, such as cross-validation while combining bagging-based methods. In contrast, we here propose to take advantage of the out-of-bag (OOB) samples, naturally available by the bagging procedure, to yield an unbiased meta-level training set. This allows our solution to stack bagging-based methods with any other learning method without additional computational cost while using any combining methodology. In fact, some works attempt to improve the bagging procedure by utilizing stacking to combine the base classifiers [25, 26]. For instance, in [25] the authors propose a variant of bagging, where stacking rather than uniform majority voting is used to achieve the combination. The meta-level training set is obtained by the predictions of the each base learner over the original training set, which can lead the meta-classifier to overfit. In contrast to [25], in [26] the authors propose a linear combination in which the coefficients are estimated by the OOB error, thus generating a less biased combination. Those methods differ from ours since here we construct the meta-level data for bagging-based methods in a distinct manner, while also treating them as black-boxes when combining them with any other learning method.

3 THE BERT CLASSIFIER

In this section, we detail BERT, a boosted version of the RF classifier that aims at taking the advantages of BROOF while avoiding its potential bias tendency. As we detail in the following, BERT introduces an additional source of randomization to reduce bias, while, at the same time, exploiting the advantages of the boosting strategy, in order to achieve superior generalization. We start our discussion with a brief overview of the BROOF strategy. Then, we describe the key building block for the BERT strategy, namely, Extremely Randomized Trees. Finally, we describe BERT.

3.1 BROOF

Proposed in [23], the BROOF classifier combines boosting and bagging by exploiting RF as "weak learners" in a boosting framework. Boosting is a sequential meta-algorithm which trains several "weak learners" (that is, classifiers capable of yielding predictions better than random guessing) in order to generate a more precise model. For each iteration i of the boosting algorithm, let Δ^i be a probability distribution over the training set of size M. When $i = 0$, $\Delta^0(j) = \frac{1}{M}$, $\forall j|_{j=1}^{M}$. At iteration $i > 0$, for all examples in the training set x_j, if x_j is misclassified, its weight is incremented so that, in the succeeding iteration, an updated distribution Δ^{i+1} is considered, which emphasizes the misclassified instances (e.g, the hardest to classify ones). In contrast to AdaBoost [9], the update rule in BROOF uses the out-of-bag (OOB) samples, promptly generated by the RF classifier at training time, as an unbiased error estimate to drive the boosting iterations and "smoothly" reweights just the OOB instances.

In [23] the authors show that restricting the influence of training data to the hard-to-classify sub-regions of the input space, by means of a smooth combination of random forests and boosting, can mitigate the overfitting issue observed when learning decision trees composing the ensemble classifier, thus leveraging classification effectiveness on new unseen data. Also, the selective weight update strategy slows down boosting's tendency to focus on just a few hard-to-classify samples, thus offering some bias reduction capabilities. These ideias were even extended and generalized to realm of learning-to-rank (L2R) tasks [5].

However, although BROOF was shown to provide competitive results in text classification and L2R tasks, this can be mainly attributed to variance reduction, since its limited bias reduction capability may not be enough to fully mitigate its tendency to overly emphasize hard-to-classify examples, mainly in noisy environments. This has to do with the underlying boosting strategy adopted by BROOF and may compromise classification effectiveness. We here propose to tackle the potentially high bias faced by BROOF by means of an additional source of randomization, through the use of the so-called extremely randomized trees, described in the following.

3.2 Extremely Randomized Trees

Extremely Randomized Trees (a.k.a., Extra-Trees) [10] is an ensemble of trees similar to the RF. Unlike RFs, Extra-Trees do not bootstrap the training data when learning its composing trees. Instead, it uses the entire training set for doing so, relying on another more aggressive source of randomization to learn decorrelated trees. More specifically, while RF builds its trees by using bootstrapped samples from the training set, defining the decision nodes in order to optimize some information theoretic statistic (such as Information Gain, Chi Squared or Gini Index), the Extra-Trees classifier defines the decision nodes in a purely random fashion, thus guaranteeing reduced tree correlation in the ensemble.

The Extra-Trees classifier has some benefits when compared to RF classifiers. Besides yielding better classification effectiveness, it has been shown that Extra-Trees is more robust to noise than RFs. In this work, we take advantage of BROOF-like techniques and Extra-Trees, by proposing what we call BERT, a smooth combination of both, as detailed next.

3.3 Boosted Extremely Randomized Trees

Recall that boosting algorithms tend to overly emphasize hard-to-classify examples, mainly when applied to noisy data. Therefore, the undesired bias towards these hard-to-classify examples is minimized by BROOF by updating only the probabilities Δ^i related to out-of-bag samples as proposed in [23], hoping to decrease the misclassification rate when the "weak learner" is focused on hard-to-classify regions. Hence, by using a "weak learner" more robust to noisy data than Random Forests such as Extra-Trees [10], it is expected to achieve better performance when focused on hard-to-classify regions, thus, producing a model with higher generalization power. In fact, as we shall see, BERT is among the top performer classifiers in all tested datasets, outperforming the original BROOF in several cases

BERT combines boosting and Extra-Trees, by exploiting the following BROOF-like strategies: (*i*) to use the out-of-bag (OOB) error estimate as a less biased error estimation to drive the boosting algorithm; and (*ii*) to only update the weights of the out-of-bag instances during the boosting iterations. In order to smoothly combine these ideas to the Extremely Randomized Trees framework, we propose to introduce the bagging procedure into its training procedure, in order to allow proper OOB error estimation.

We argue that exploring these strategies through this novel classification framework brings two benefits: (i) it enables us to minimize variance (mitigating the overfitting problem faced by the trees composing the ensemble) and (ii) provide means to minimize bias, through the additional randomization source, leveraging the framework ability to avoid being stuck on a few hard-to-classify examples. We summarize the proposed method in Algorithm 1.

Algorithm 1 BERT Pseudo Code

function TRAIN($\mathbb{D}_{train} = \{(X_i, y_i)|_{i=1}^{N}\}, M, n_{trees}$)
  $L \leftarrow \emptyset$; $w_1 \leftarrow \frac{1}{|D_{train}|}$
  for each $m \in \{1, .., M\}$ **do**
    $(h_m^{XT}, (x, y, \hat{y})_i^{oob}) \leftarrow ExtraTrees(\mathbb{D}_{train}, n_{trees}, w_m)$
    $OOB_{err}^{w} \leftarrow \frac{\sum_{i \in \mathbb{O}} w_m^i I[y \neq \hat{y}]}{\sum_{i \in \mathbb{O}} w_m^i}$, where $\mathbb{O} = (x, y, \hat{y})_i^{oob}$
    $\alpha_m \leftarrow \log(\frac{1 - OOB_{err}^{w}}{OOB_{err}^{w}})$
    $w_{m+1}^i \leftarrow \frac{w_m^i \epsilon^{\alpha_m I[y \neq \hat{y}]}}{\mathbb{Z}}$, where $\mathbb{Z}$ is a normalizing constant
    $L \leftarrow L \cup \{(h_m^{XT}, \alpha_m)\}$
  end for
  return L
end function

3.4 Experimental Evaluation

We now report and discuss the conducted experimental evaluation regarding the proposed BERT classifier considering a set of datasets on topic categorization and sentiment analysis. We first detail the explored datasets and the experimental setup. Then, we discuss the obtained experimental results, comparing our proposal to state-of-the-art classifiers.

3.4.1 Experimental Setup and Parameterization. In order to evaluate the BERT classifier considering the textual classification domain, we consider five real-world topic categorization data sets as well as ten sentiment analysis ones, related to computer science articles (ACM), news (REUT), web pages (4UNI), medicine (MEDLINE), items reviews (Amazon), posts on social networks (Twitter, Debate), user comments (Youtube) and snippets of opinion news (NYT). Due to space restrictions, a detailed description of each dataset can be found in an online appendix[1]. In all cases, we performed a traditional preprocessing task that consists of removing stopwords (using the standard SMART list) and applying a simple feature selection procedure, removing terms with low "document

[1] homepages.dcc.ufmg.br/~rcampos/papers/sigir2017/appendix.pdf

frequency (DF)"[2]. Regarding term weighting, we tested TF, TF-IDF and L2 normalization schemes, choosing the best strategy for each classification approach. Particularly, we use TF for all classifiers based on RF and Naive Bayes, and TF-IDF with L2 normalization for both SVM and kNN. The explored classifiers were compared using two standard information retrieval measures: *micro averaged* F_1 (MicroF_1) and *macro averaged* F_1 (MacroF_1). While the MicroF_1 measures the classification effectiveness overall decisions (i.e., the pooled contingency tables of all classes), the MacroF_1 measures the classification effectiveness for each individual class and averages them. To compare the average results of our **5-fold** cross-validation experiments, we assess their statistical significance by applying a paired two-tailed t-test with 95% confidence and Bonferroni correction to account for multiple comparisons. This test assures that the best results, marked in **bold**, are statistically superior to others (up to the chosen confidence level).

We evaluate ten distinct learning algorithms. We use the scikit-learn implementation[3] of linear SVM, k-Nearest Neighbors (kNN), Multinomial Naïve Bayes (NB), Random Forests (RF) and Extremely Randomized Trees (Extra-Trees). We use our own implementation of the RF-based methods, namely, BROOF, the lazy version of the RF classifier (LAZY) and the lazy version of extra-trees (LXT), since there is no freely available implementation for these classifiers.

The free parameters of these classifiers include the cost C (for SVM), neighborhood size k (for KNN and LAZY) and the number of features considered in the split of a node on the RF-based approaches. These free parameters were set using 5-fold cross-validation within the training set. For the RF-based approaches, each tree is grown without pruning, as suggested in [12], and since the results obtained with 200, 300 and 500 trees are statistically tied (with 95% confidence), we adopted 200 trees due to the lower cost. Concerning the BROOF classifier, we use 8 weak learners, setting the maximum number of iterations to 200, as suggested in [23]. We use the same parameters for the proposed BERT method.

We would like to point out that some of the results obtained in some datasets may differ from the ones reported in other works for the same datasets. Such discrepancies may be due to several factors such as differences in dataset preparation[4], the use of different splits of the datasets (e.g., some datasets have "default splits" such as REUT and 20NG[5]). We would like to stress that we ran all alternatives under the same conditions in all datasets, using the best traditional feature weighting scheme, using standardized and well-accepted cross-validation procedures that optimize parameters for each of alternatives, and applying the proper statistical tools for the analysis of the results. Our datasets are available (for result replication and testing of new configurations) under request.

3.4.2 Results and Discussions. We now turn our attention to the obtained results regarding the described classifiers. We start by considering the effectiveness of each classifier in the topic categorization task (see Table 1). In this case, BERT presents statistically tied results with SVM on most datasets despite their fundamentally different classification paradigms. While BERT and other RF-based approaches are based on extracting specific association rules that relate different features, SVM measures the complexity of hypotheses based on the margin with which they separate the data, which is independent of the number of features. This characteristic makes the SVM as one of the best-known classification strategies to exploit discriminative evidence from high dimensional and sparse textual data. Even considering the specificities of each feature, BERT is capable of combining small pieces of evidence to build a general model with the same generalization power of SVM in scenarios which SVM traditionally works the best.

Despite SVM and BERT obtain statistically tied results in most datasets, BERT shows significantly superior results to SVM in the SPAM dataset. For this particular dataset, the BERT capability of identifying specific non-trivial relationships between individual words to the spam category grants superior effectiveness for BERT. On the other hand, the same SVM mechanism that captures good general patterns limits such classifier in finding specific pieces of evidence that relate individual features in more complex ways.

BERT is also superior to other RF-based approaches in most datasets, which provides evidence towards the benefits of the proposed strategy in mitigating the RF overfitting problem. Specifically, BERT presented significant improvements over RF on all datasets, with gains up to 7% and 30% on MicroF_1 and MacroF_1, respectively.

Other strategies designed to overcome the RF limitations also presented inferior results to BERT. The LAZY method is always inferior to BERT in terms of MacroF_1, indicating that LAZY has a hard time on discriminating minor classes. We argue that by trying to find discriminative patterns based on the neighborhood of documents, LAZY can bias its model towards the larger classes, since their documents are most likely to appear in the neighborhood of an arbitrary test document.

Another strategy aimed at improving RFs is the BROOF classifier. Our experimental results show that the proposed combination of boosting with extremly randomized trees can achieve better results than combining boosting with the original RFs. Although very competitive to BERT, BROOF is no match to our proposal in both the 20NG and ACM datasets.

Now we turn our attention to the classification results of the sentiment analysis task, presented in Table 2. The experimental results show that, overall, BERT outperforms or ties with the best classification method for each dataset. Specifically, BERT and BROOF achieved the best (and statistically tied) results in almost all datasets, which provides additional evidence towards the benefits of reducing the overfitting issues of RF-based methods using boosting. In the sentiment analysis context, both methods take advantage of being able to identify the presence of individual words that are highly correlated to a positive or negative sentiment. Their generalization capabilities of identifying noisy or irrelevant information provide improvements over the original RF, with 14% and 5% on MacroF_1 and MicroF_1, respectively.

In the sentiment analysis scenario, SVM is not always among the best approaches, since it does not have the ability to discriminate the fine-grained discriminative evidence present in individual words and non-linear relationships between words. Moreover, there is no clear winner between SVM and the simple NB classifier. In this scenario, NB has the advantage of learning how each word relates to

[2]We removed all terms that occur in less than six documents (i.e., DF<6).
[3]Available in http://scikit-learn.org/
[4]For instance, some works do exploit complex feature weighting schemes or feature selection mechanisms that do favor some algorithms in detriment to others.
[5]We believe that running experiments only in the default splits is not the best experimental procedure as it does not allow a proper statistical treatment of the results.

		20NG	4UNI	ACM	REUT90	SPAM	MED
BERT	microF1	**89.45 ± 0.46**	**84.61 ± 0.98**	**74.8 ± 0.59**	**67.33 ± 0.72**	**96.11 ± 0.52**	83.68 ± 0.32
	macroF1	**89.13 ± 0.58**	**73.61 ± 1.85**	**62.1 ± 0.99**	**29.24 ± 1.40**	**95.93 ± 0.55**	74.25 ± 0.37
SVM	microF1	**90.06 ± 0.43**	**83.48 ± 1.08**	**75.4 ± 0.66**	**68.19 ± 1.15**	92.55 ± 0.8	**86.19 ± 0.05**
	macroF1	**89.93 ± 0.43**	**73.39 ± 2.17**	**63.84 ± 0.55**	**31.95 ± 2.59**	92.12 ± 0.87	**78.46 ± 0.42**
BROOF	microF1	87.96 ± 0.24	**84.41 ± 1.07**	73.35 ± 0.79	**66.79 ± 0.97**	**96.09 ± 0.84**	83.05 ± 0.05
	macroF1	87.44 ± 0.28	**73.23 ± 1.10**	60.76 ± 0.8	**28.48 ± 2.17**	**95.9 ± 0.88**	73.25 ± 0.42
XGBOOST	microF1	81.88 ± 0.65	**85.52 ± 0.88**	73.78 ± 0.51	65.21 ± 0.84	**95.08 ± 0.52**	84.19 ± 0.05
	macroF1	81.38 ± 0.68	**74.44 ± 1.28**	**62.79 ± 1.38**	**29.06 ± 2.46**	**94.84 ± 0.54**	76.81 ± 0.21
LAZY	microF1	87.96 ± 0.37	**82.34 ± 0.61**	**74.02 ± 0.79**	**66.3 ± 1.07**	92.91 ± 0.68	84.88 ± 0.08
	macroF1	87.39 ± 0.37	68.33 ± 1.6	59.46 ± 1.35	26.61 ± 2.12	92.54 ± 0.71	72.90 ± 0.08
NB	microF1	**88.99 ± 0.54**	62.63 ± 1.7	73.54 ± 0.71	65.32 ± 1.13	79.27 ± 0.81	82.92 ± 0.14
	macroF1	**88.68 ± 0.55**	51.38 ± 3.19	58.03 ± 0.85	**27.86 ± 0.79**	78.18 ± 0.83	63.8 ± 0.43
KNN	microF1	87.53 ± 0.69	75.63 ± 0.94	70.99 ± 0.96	**68.07 ± 1.07**	83.31 ± 0.98	82.16 ± 0.08
	macroF1	87.22 ± 0.66	60.34 ± 1.36	55.85 ± 0.97	**29.93 ± 2.48**	82.91 ± 0.93	68.00 ± 0.34
Extra-Trees	microF1	87.03 ± 0.41	**82.87 ± 1.00**	73.08 ± 0.55	64.87 ± 0.81	**95.74 ± 0.55**	82.49 ± 0.07
	macroF1	86.65 ± 0.56	68.54 ± 2.60	58.71 ± 0.89	26.18 ± 2.55	**95.52 ± 0.58**	71.15 ± 0.31
LXT	microF1	88.39 ± 0.51	81.24 ± 0.71	69.63 ± 0.91	65.92 ± 0.82	92.42 ± 0.78	83.84 ± 0.11
	macroF1	88.05 ± 0.44	66.89 ± 1.23	57.33 ± 1.48	26.71 ± 2.53	92.05 ± 0.82	71.02 ± 0.23
RF	microF1	83.64 ± 0.29	81.52 ± 1	71.05 ± 0.31	63.92 ± 0.81	**95.46 ± 0.74**	81.61 ± 0.05
	macroF1	83.08 ± 0.35	65.44 ± 1.91	56.56 ± 0.45	24.36 ± 1.98	**95.22 ± 0.79**	70.41 ± 0.36

Table 1: Topic categorization - Obtained results for base classifiers.

		AMAZON	BBC	DEBATE	DIGG	MYSPACE	NYT	TWEETS	TWITTER	YELP	YOUTUBE
BERT	microF1	**75.76**	**86.04**	**79.38**	**75.7**	**86.46**	**68.14**	**88.3**	**76.15**	**94.26**	79.85
	macroF1	**74.16**	**53.78**	**77.24**	**63.03**	**67.35**	**67.01**	**85.49**	**74.71**	**94.26**	76.47
BROOF	microF1	74.52	86.17	**79.23**	**76.34**	**86.57**	**68.01**	**88.11**	**75.01**	**93.58**	79.69
	macroF1	**73.02**	**55.04**	**77.07**	**65.56**	**67.93**	**66.85**	**85.36**	**73.73**	**93.58**	76.18
NB	microF1	**74.68**	**86.84**	76	**76.09**	**85.5**	**67.1**	86.82	**74.88**	90.44	**83.43**
	macroF1	**73.32**	46.48	73.7	**64.38**	60.39	**66.06**	**84.4**	**73.89**	90.44	**80.3**
XT	microF1	73.88	**86.58**	**79.33**	**76.85**	**85.64**	**67.43**	86.46	**75.19**	91.74	79.65
	macroF1	72.1	**52.35**	**76.93**	60.84	**65.24**	**66.03**	83	**73.26**	91.73	76.22
SVM	microF1	74.24	86.43	**78.58**	**75.58**	**86.23**	66.34	86.87	**74.53**	92.94	**82.24**
	macroF1	72.84	50.34	**76.2**	60.96	**67.94**	65.48	**84.1**	**73.15**	92.94	77.99
RF	microF1	73.8	**86.84**	**78.53**	**75.31**	**85.74**	**67.43**	84.63	73.83	90.76	79.89
	macroF1	71.76	**52.4**	**75.79**	57.04	60.7	65.41	79.54	71.21	90.75	76.29
XGBOOST	microF1	71.49	**86.16**	75.89	74.29	**85.38**	61.06	84.24	72.47	90.84	74.74
	macroF1	69.98	**52.39**	73.01	57.46	63.57	60.08	80.11	69.01	90.83	68.13
LXT	microF1	72.22	**87.11**	**78.07**	**74.93**	85.26	64.41	82.36	71.91	90.82	77.22
	macroF1	69.24	49.36	74.98	56.91	55.64	61.5	75.35	68.51	90.82	67.56
LAZY	microF1	72.3	**87.37**	76.35	**76.21**	85.14	64.64	80.86	70.86	90.18	76.48
	macroF1	69	50.19	72.89	58.9	55.55	61.61	73.53	67.49	90.17	66.4
KNN	microF1	69.86	86.44	74.03	74.8	**85.49**	60.61	77.34	67.02	74.5	75.74
	macroF1	67.64	46.36	72.25	52.77	56.07	54.92	68.14	64.08	73.83	67.27

Table 2: Sentiment analysis - Obtained results for base classifiers.

a positive or negative sentiment, and they combine these pieces of evidence to determine the sentiment of a text document. However, unlike RF-based methods, there is no mechanism to identify noise or irrelevant words, which may affect its effectiveness results.

The methods KNN, LAZY, and LXT are usually associated with the worse results for the sentiment analysis task. Instead of focusing on individual words, these methods exploit the distribution of training examples among neighbors of a test example. This analysis of the neighborhood can be a potential source of noise since similar text documents can be associated with different sentiment labels.

Overall, according to the reported experimental results, the BERT classifier is the only approach consistently among the best results in both topic categorization and sentiment analysis. These results provide empirical evidence towards the benefits of improving the generalization power of random forests by using elaborated strategies to reduce overfitting.

Finally, for both sentiment analysis and topic classification, BERT is one of the most effective classification methods that combines discriminative pieces of evidence derived from exploring the complex sub-regions of the input space. Other classification approaches provide completely different strategies to exploit discriminative patterns, which motivates us to stack these different classification approaches to combine the potentially complementary information captured by each of them (see Section 4).

3.4.3 Effects of Extra-Trees as weak-learner. An important aspect to be further analyzed is the influence of the additional randomization enjoyed by BERT through the use of Extra-Trees (instead of traditional RFs, as done in BROOF). To this end, we analyze the effect of gradually increasing the number of Extra-Trees in the BROOF process over MicroF_1 and MacroF_1. Here, the number of iterations and trees were fixed to 200 and 8, respectively. Figure 2 shows the obtained results, where the x-axis represents the proportion of Extra-Trees composing the ensemble (0% means the absence of Extra-Trees, which degenerates to BROOF, and 100% represents the BERT classifier, composed entirely by Extra-Trees). There is a clear tendency of growth in MicroF_1 and MacroF_1 as we increase the proportion of Extra-Trees composing the ensemble. Thus, the additional randomization procedure employed in BERT plays an important role in improving the BROOF algorithm.

4 STACKING RF-BASED LEARNERS

Based upon the results reported in Section 3.4, one aspect should be clear by now: the analyzed RF-based classifiers do excel in both the explored text classification tasks. One question that naturally

$Dis_{i,j}^{norm}$	BROOF	LAZY	SVM	NB	KNN
BERT	0.12	0.29	0.30	0.32	0.33
BROOF	-	0.29	0.32	0.32	0.33
LAZY	-	-	0.31	0.32	0.19
SVM	-	-	-	0.27	0.30
NB	-	-	-	-	0.33

(a) 4UNI

$Dis_{i,j}^{norm}$	BROOF	LAZY	SVM	NB	KNN
BERT	0.07	0.18	0.23	0.32	0.25
BROOF	-	0.20	0.23	0.35	0.29
LAZY	-	-	0.25	0.32	0.23
SVM	-	-	-	0.29	0.25
NB	-	-	-	-	0.29

(b) ACM

$Dis_{i,j}^{norm}$	BROOF	LAZY	SVM	NB	KNN
BERT	0.15	0.23	0.28	0.39	0.35
BROOF	-	0.26	0.24	0.41	0.42
LAZY	-	-	0.29	0.43	0.38
SVM	-	-	-	0.37	0.36
NB	-	-	-	-	0.39

(c) 20NG

Table 3: Normalized Degree of Disagreement

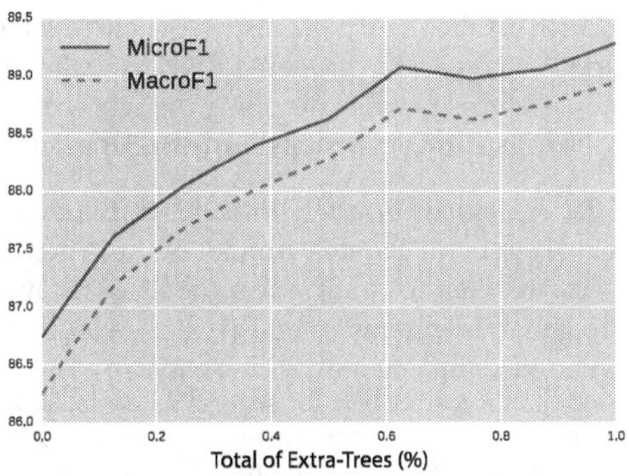

(a) 20NG

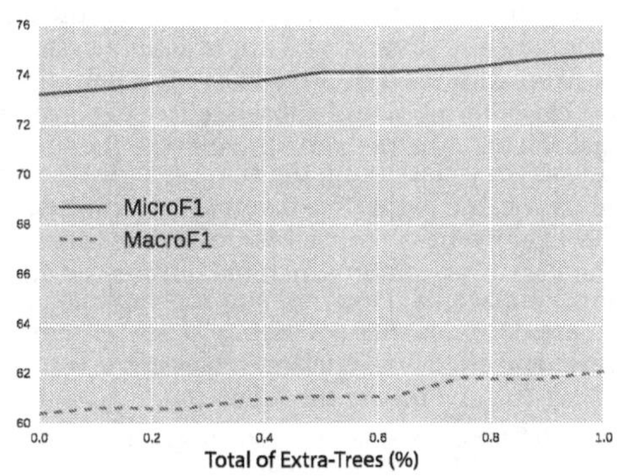

(b) ACM

Figure 2: Effect of Extra-Trees as weak-learner.

arises is: *can we explore these methods somehow in order to learn an even more effective classifier?* This is what we pursue in this section.

In order to combine RF-based classifiers, these classifiers should exhibit some degree of complementarity. In fact, each RF based classifier explore different learning strategies to come up with more effective predictions. However, it is still important to assess whether these distinct strategies do produce complementary information that could be explored to leverage classification effectiveness. To this end, we quantify such complementarity degree by means of the Degree of Disagreement [16] observed for a pair of classifiers. Let h_i and h_j be two classifiers, applied to examples from a validation set $\mathbb{D}_{valid}$ (e.g., a fold). Also, let $\mathbb{D}_{00}$ be the examples misclassified by both h_i and h_j ($n_{00} = |\mathbb{D}_{00}|$), $\mathbb{D}_{01}$ be the examples correctly classified just by h_i (($n_{01} = |\mathbb{D}_{01}|$)) and $\mathbb{D}_{10}$ be the examples correctly classified just by h_j (($n_{10} = |\mathbb{D}_{10}|$)). Finally, let $\mathbb{D}_{11}$ be the examples correctly classified by both learners (($n_{11} = |\mathbb{D}_{11}|$)). The Degree of Disagreement $\text{Dis}_{i,j}$ between h_i and h_j is given by:

$$\text{Dis}_{i,j} = \frac{n_{01} + n_{10}}{n_{00} + n_{01} + n_{10} + n_{11}} \quad (1)$$

This is a symmetric statistic that captures to what extent two classifiers disagree in terms of prediction. Classifiers with low disagreement degree tend to have similar behavior in terms of correctly or incorrectly classifying unseen examples and thus have low complementarity. In order to offer a more appropriate measure of disagreement degree between classifiers, however, one should also take into account their prediction capabilities. That way we guarantee a proper comparison between their behavior. For this purpose, we propose a normalized degree of disagreement metric. Recall that, in order to have minimal degree of disagreement, we must have $\mathbb{D}_{01} \subset \mathbb{D}_{10}$ or $\mathbb{D}_{10} \subset \mathbb{D}_{01}$. Also, we have that h_i accuracy can be expressed as $R_i = \frac{n_{01}+n_{11}}{\sum_{a,b \in 0,1} n_{a,b}}$, with R_j expressed analogously. It is straightforward to show that $\text{Dis}_{i,j}^{\min} = R_i + R_j - 2\min(R_i, R_j)$. Similarly, we maximize the degree of disagreement when n_{00} and n_{11} tend to 0. In that case, with some algebraic manipulation, one can show that $\text{Dis}_{i,j}^{\max} = 2 - R_i - R_j$. With such derivations in place, the normalized degree of disagreement metric is defined as

$$\text{Dis}_{i,j}^{norm} = \frac{\text{Dis}_{i,j} - \text{Dis}_{i,j}^{\min}}{\text{Dis}_{i,j}^{\max} - \text{Dis}_{i,j}^{\min}}. \quad (2)$$

The Degree of Disagreement values computed for the exemplified cases can be found on Table 3. This gives us some evidence that the explored learning methods, such as BROOF, LazyNN_RF and BERT do have some complementary information that can potentially be explored in order to come up with more effective learners. This is the main motivation to what we propose here: a novel strategy to stack RF based classifiers that, besides producing highly effective meta-learners, it also enjoys a significantly reduced runtime, guaranteeing its applicability on large classification problems.

We now introduce an efficient way of stacking bagging-based classifiers. Recall that bagging-based methods, such as Random Forests, typically yield models with higher generalization capabilities by controlling variance with the bootstrap procedure [3]. We rely on the out-of-bag samples produced by the bootstrap technique performed by these classifiers in order to estimate the *a posteriori* probability distributions for the training samples, thus producing the meta attributes to be fed to the stacked classifier. Since this information is promptly generated at training time by bagged classifiers, the meta learner can thus be built with negligible additional computational effort.

In details, recall that the bootstrap procedure (random sampling with replacement) generates samples $\mathbb{D}_{boot}$ comprising of approximately $1 - e^{-1} \approx 63\%$ of the original training set $\mathbb{D}_{train}$, with the remaining 36% samples being the so-called out-of-bag samples [12]. We here propose to use $\mathbb{D}_{oob} = \mathbb{D}_{train} \setminus \mathbb{D}_{boot}$ to estimate the class probability distribution at a point $x \in \mathbb{D}_{oob}$ to be used as meta attributes to train a stacked classifier. This comes at a very low cost, since the meta attributes can be efficiently computed during the training stage of bagged learners, without the needs to perform costly estimation strategies, such as cross-validation. Let M be the number of bootstrap iterations, $\mathbb{D}^i_{boot}|_{i=1}^M$ be the bootstrap samples and $h_i|_{i=1}^M$ the classifiers trained with the corresponding bootstrap samples. We compute the probability distribution estimates $p^{oob}(x)$ for each instance $x \in \mathbb{D}_{train}$ as follows:

$$p^{oob}(x) = \frac{1}{M}\sum_{j=1}^{M} p^{h_j}(x)I[x \in \mathbb{D}^j_{oob}], \tag{3}$$

where I denotes the indicator function, $p^{h_j}(x) = (p^{h_j}(c_1|x), p^{h_j}(c_2|x), \cdots, p^{h_j}(c_K|x))$, $\{c_1, ...c_K\}$ is the set of possible classes and $p^{h_j}(c_k|x)$ denotes the probability of x to belong to class c_k, according to learner h_j.

The estimated *a posteriori* probability $p^{oob}(x)$ can be naturally used in the traditional stacking framework as meta-features, along side the meta-features obtained by traditional means, in order to train any meta-learner as discussed in the Section 2. By doing so, one can stack bagged-based models efficiently either with bagged and non-bagged ones, thus, making feasible the applicability of such stacking systems in real world problems.

4.1 Experimental Evaluation

We now report our experimental evaluation of the proposed stacking model. To this end, we consider all the previously explored datasets regarding topic categorization and sentiment analysis (see Section 3.4.1). We contrast the proposed RF-based stacked classifier against traditional stacking of classical state-of-the-art methods in text categorization (e.g. SVM, kNN, Naïve Bayes). Then, we analyze our proposal in terms of runtime.

4.1.1 Results and Discussion. As we detail in the following, stacking RF-based classifiers brings substantial improvements in classification effectiveness over traditional methods and their combinations in both analyzed text classification tasks. The proposed RF-based stacking is even able to produce as good results as the combination of all evaluated classifiers in most analyzed datasets, at a much lower runtime, guaranteeing its applicability in text classification tasks.

The results regarding the topic categorization task can be found in Table 4. First, note that the combination of RF-based approaches *BERT* + *BROOF* + *LXT* + *LAZY* achieves better results over the two best base classifiers (BERT and SVM) in most datasets, with substantial gains of up to 17% and 21% in MacroF_1 and MicroF_1, respectively. In fact, stacking RF-based approaches clearly produces superior results when compared to the top-notch SVM and BERT classifiers. The combination *BERT* + *BROOF* + *LXT* + *LAZY* is also superior to the combination of classifiers *SVM*+*NB*+*KNN* in 4UNI and SPAM. These results provide evidence to our claim that stacking RF-based methods for text classification is a strong alternative to the stacking of traditional text classification approaches, since besides effective they are highly parallelizable, easily parameterized and efficiently combined by our OOB stacking proposal.

Furthermore, stacking RF-based methods also performs as well as the combination of all classification approaches (i.e., All_{stack}) in all but 20NG and MED datasets. This indicates that traditional classification methods may provide supplementary discriminative information for RF-based methods, which is the expected since they follow completely different classification paradigms.

Considering the sentiment analysis datasets, one can observe that most of the results regarding stacking different classifiers are statistically tied, as shown in Table 5. Moreover, BERT is not substantially improved when stacked with other classifiers. In fact, *BERT* ties with *BROOF* + *LAZY* + *BERT* + *LXT* in all datasets. Also, *BERT* also ties with All_{stack} in all datasets but one, YOUTUBE (in fact, due to the presence of the NB classifier in the All_{stack} ensemble). These results show that, despite the potential benefits of stacking various methods, the proposed *BERT* classifier remains as one of the top performers when detecting the sentiment of textual documents, being a strong candidate for consideration.

4.1.2 Effectiveness vs. diversity tradeoff. In the following, we perform an analysis of the Pareto's frontier of the generated ensembles. With this, we want to confirm that the RF-based methods are important to generate ensembles of classifiers with high generalization power and complementarity/diversity.

Figure 3 exhibits a scatter plot for several datasets, in which each point represents a stacking ensemble out of the possible ensembles generated by the combination of the nine base classifiers (number of classifiers composing the ensemble varies from 2 to 9). The x-axis represents the diversity metric *Double-Fault*, which was chosen because it is the pairwise metric that best represents the relationship between accuracy and diversity of an ensemble system[16]. The metric was originally used by [11] to form a pairwise diversity matrix for a classifier pool and subsequently to select classifiers that are least related. The metric estimates the likelihood of both classifiers incorrectly classifying the same sample (the smaller the value of the metric, the higher the diversity/complementarity). The y-axis is the effectiveness metric MacroF_1. For those points, we calculate the Pareto's frontier which maximizes the effectiveness metric and minimizes the Double-Fault metric (maximizes diversity), which are desirable characteristics of any ensemble method (highly diverse and effective). The ensembles in the frontier showed in Figures 3 (a), (b), and (c) are the following:

- (*LXT, NB*), (*LAZY, NB*), (*SVM, KNN*), (*LXT, SVM, NB*), (*LAZY, SVM, NB*), (*LXT, SVM, NB, KNN*), (*LXT, SVM, NB, KNN, XT*), (*LAZY, BERT, LXT, SVM, NB, KNN*), (*LAZY, LXT, SVM, NB, KNN, FA*)
- (*BERT, SVM*), (*BERT, LXT, SVM*), (*BROOF, BERT, SVM, KNN*), (*BERT, SVM, NB*)
- (*SVM, NB*), (*LAZY, SVM, NB*), (*BERT, SVM, NB*), (*LAZY, BERT, SVM, NB*), (*LAZY, BERT, LXT, SVM, NB*), (*LAZY, BERT, SVM, NB, KNN*), (*BROOF, LAZY, SVM, NB, KNN*), (*BERT, LXT, SVM, NB, AEA*), (*BROOF, BERT, LXT, SVM, NB, KNN*)

One can notice that as we go from left to right on the Pareto's frontier both, effectiveness and diversity[6] decreases. This implies that not necessarily a highly diverse combination will result in more accurate classifiers, but that there is a tradeoff between effectiveness and diversity of the base classifiers of the ensemble. By analyzing the Pareto's frontier, one can clearly notice that the RF extensions play an important role in providing a balance between diversity and generalization power in the most effective ensembles. It is also possible to note that the loss in diversity brought by the insertion of more similar methods into the ensemble (e.g., RF-based ones) is compensated by the high generalization power of those methods. These results along with the effectiveness analysis corroborate our hypothesis: by using RF-based algorithms in multi-classifier systems, it is possible to achieve higher effectiveness.

[6]In this Section, we will use the terms diversity and complementarity interchangeably.

		20NG	4UNI	ACM	REUT90	SPAM	MED
All_{stack}	microF1	**92.21 ± 0.44**	**86.85 ± 1.17**	**79.02 ± 0.72**	**80.76 ± 1.24**	**96.06 ± 0.78**	**88.76 ± 0.11**
	macroF1	**92.01 ± 0.42**	**79.43 ± 2.23**	**66.25 ± 1.01**	**39.28 ± 1.14**	**95.87 ± 0.82**	**81.62 ± 0.34**
BROOF+LAZY+BERT+LXT	microF1	90.63 ± 0.57	**86.79 ± 0.86**	**77.83 ± 0.80**	**80 ± 1.60**	**96.13 ± 0.86**	87.10 ± 0.07
	macroF1	90.4 ± 0.57	**79.63 ± 1.91**	**63.42 ± 0.92**	**38.66 ± 2.85**	**95.94 ± 0.90**	79.36 ± 0.59
SVM+NB+KNN	microF1	90.65 ± 0.45	84.95 ± 1.15	**77.78 ± 0.73**	**78.53 ± 1.09**	93.67 ± 0.34	87.96 ± 0.05
	macroF1	90.42 ± 0.44	75.86 ± 1.48	**65.08 ± 1.71**	37.10 ± 1.41	93.37 ± 0.34	80.33 ± 0.57
SVM+BERT	microF1	90.85 ± 0.50	**86.65 ± 1.05**	**77.25 ± 0.60**	**78.43 ± 1.33**	**95.91 ± 0.79**	87.65 ± 0.03
	macroF1	90.68 ± 0.50	**80.13 ± 2.49**	**66.29 ± 0.97**	36.8 ± 2.45	**95.72 ± 0.82**	80.55 ± 0.52
BERT	microF1	89.45 ± 0.46	84.61 ± 0.98	74.8 ± 0.59	67.33 ± 0.72	**96.11 ± 0.52**	83.68 ± 0.32
	macroF1	89.13 ± 0.58	73.61 ± 1.85	62.1 ± 0.99	29.24 ± 1.40	**95.93 ± 0.55**	74.25 ± 0.37
SVM	microF1	90.06 ± 0.43	83.48 ± 1.08	75.4 ± 0.66	68.19 ± 1.15	92.55 ± 0.8	86.19 ± 0.05
	macroF1	89.93 ± 0.43	73.39 ± 2.17	**63.84 ± 0.55**	31.95 ± 2.59	92.12 ± 0.87	78.46 ± 0.42

Table 4: Topic categorization - Obtained results for stacking and top-performer base classifiers.

		AMAZON	BBC	DEBATE	DIGG	MYSPACE	NYT	TWEETS	TWITTER	YELP	YOUTUBE
All_{stack}	microF1	**75.6**	**86.84**	**80.14**	**76.47**	**86.1**	**68.1**	**89.16**	**75.71**	**94.82**	**83.93**
	macroF1	**74.44**	**51.56**	**77.86**	**65.8**	**68.27**	**67.35**	**87.08**	**74.83**	**94.82**	**81.11**
BROOF+LAZY+BERT+LXT	microF1	**75.6**	**86.84**	**79.89**	**75.96**	**86.94**	**67.79**	**89.01**	**76.23**	**94.22**	81.5
	macroF1	**74.44**	50.03	**77.41**	**62.71**	**68.88**	**66.87**	**86.63**	**75.26**	**94.22**	77.63
SVM+NB+KNN	microF1	**75.37**	**86.7**	**78.83**	**77.5**	**86.09**	**67.41**	**88.35**	**75.32**	93.84	**84.13**
	macroF1	**74.14**	46.44	**76.71**	**64.84**	**65.98**	**66.53**	**86.07**	**74.24**	93.84	**81.05**
SVM+BERT	microF1	**75.96**	**86.7**	**79.99**	**76.46**	**86.11**	**67.73**	**88.25**	**75.89**	**94.64**	81.42
	macroF1	**74.85**	47.34	**77.88**	**63.05**	**67.14**	**66.92**	**85.81**	**74.79**	**94.64**	77.85
BERT	microF1	**75.76**	**86.04**	**79.38**	**75.7**	**86.46**	**68.14**	**88.3**	**76.15**	**94.26**	79.85
	macroF1	**74.16**	**53.78**	**77.24**	**63.03**	**67.35**	**67.01**	**85.49**	**74.71**	**94.26**	76.47
NB	microF1	74.68	**86.84**	76	**76.09**	85.5	**67.1**	86.82	**74.88**	90.44	**83.43**
	macroF1	73.32	46.48	73.7	**64.38**	60.39	66.06	84.4	**73.89**	90.44	**80.3**

Table 5: Sentiment analysis - Obtained results for stacking and top-performer base classifiers

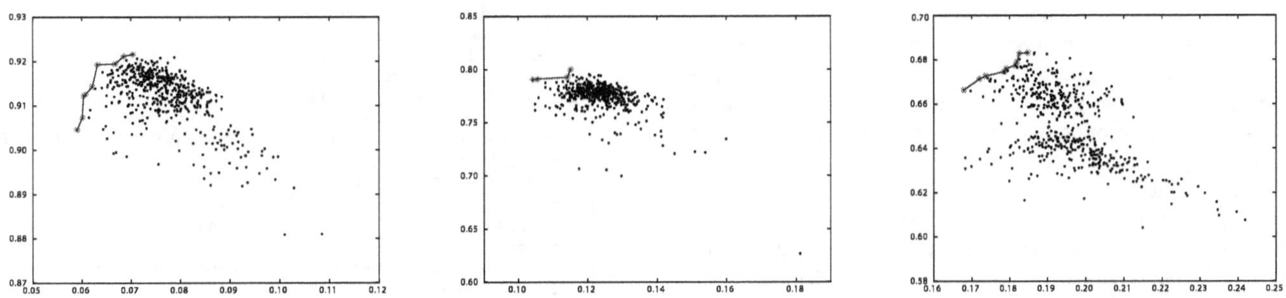

(a) 20NG (b) 4UNI (c) ACM

Figure 3: MacroF_1 vs. *Double-Fault* - each point represents a stacking out of all possible combination of the 9 base classifiers. The line connecting the highlighted points is the Pareto's frontier.

4.1.3 Computational Time and Effectiveness to Stack Bagging-based Methods. Table 6 shows the average time to combine all nine base learning algorithms using ours and the baseline stacking approaches, which generate the meta-level data by means of 5-fold cross-validation. We also contrast our proposed method with a fixed combination method (simple voting), which is the fastest possible combing strategy since it does not require training. As can be seen in Table 6, the stacking using our strategy based on Out-of-Bag (OOB) samples combined with RF as meta-level learner shows significant speedups in relation to all other stacking strategies, without degrading its predictive performance. Specifically, in the MEDLINE dataset, the stacking approaches using cross-validation were not able to handle the dataset in a suitable time. Moreover, one can notice that our approach is competitive regarding execution time when compared to a simple voting algorithm while excelling in effectiveness.

	20NG	4UNI	ACM	REUT90	MEDLINE
OOB-RF	**7244**	**2413**	**6762**	**13163**	**458013**
RF	20479	7358	17194	29256	-
MLR	21455	7334	17170	29131	-
DT	20448	7327	17163	27124	-
SCANN	21651	7330	17166	29007	-
VIG	20620	7499	17335	30296	-
Voting	2921	1046	2451	4017	375297

Table 6: Avg. time in seconds to combine (training + testing time) all 9 base learning algorithms with different stacking strategies. In the cases that a method was not able to handle a dataset, we marked the corresponding table cell with '-'.

Table 7 shows the effectiveness of different combination strategies, such as MLR, DT, SCANN and the recently proposed VIG in the largest datasets[7]. The results of these strategies are never superior to the use of RF as a meta-level combiner. Despite not being designed as a meta-level combiner, RF is capable of achieving

[7]This excludes the small SPAM dataset.

the best effectiveness results due to its capabilities of automatically identifying discriminative patterns on the relationship among classifier results. Moreover, the proposed usage of OOB can provide the same discriminative evidence as the output of the RF-based obtained by means of cross-validation, which eliminates the need for costly procedures to stack RF-based methods.

		20NG	4UNI	ACM	REUT90	MED
OOB-RF	microF1	**92.24**	**86.87**	**78.99**	**80.25**	**88.76**
	macroF1	**92.04**	**79.35**	65.75	**40.8**	**81.62**
RF	microF1	**92.21**	**86.85**	**79.02**	**80.76**	-
	macroF1	**92.01**	**79.43**	66.25	**39.28**	-
MLR	microF1	91.36	85.34	77.99	76.33	-
	macroF1	91.14	76.62	**68.26**	35.64	
DT	microF1	91.44	83.82	77.53	68.19	-
	macroF1	91.23	76.11	65.07	32.43	-
VOTING	microF1	91.55	84.27	77.7	66.71	86.91
	macroF1	91.29	72.2	64.31	28.89	77.41
SCANN	microF1	90.87	85.31	76.84	71.14	-
	macroF1	90.55	73.88	63.08	29.25	-
VIG	microF1	90.13	82.14	75.11	19.4	-
	macroF1	89.65	74.33	65.49	3.17	-

Table 7: Obtained results for different stacking strategies. In the cases that a method was not able to handle a dataset, we marked the corresponding table cell with '-'

5 CONCLUSIONS AND FUTURE WORK

In this work, we propose a boosted version of the extremely randomized trees classifier, named BERT, in order to leverage the learner's capability to minimize bias while maintaining high predictive power by properly reducing variance. As our experimental analysis reveal, our proposal enjoys top-notch classification effectiveness, being among the top performers in the vast majority of cases covering two challenging text classification tasks, namely, topic categorization and sentiment analysis. We also propose to stack the explored RF-based classifiers in order to exploit the complementarities observed among those classifiers. Unlike traditional stacking, that makes use of cross-validation procedures to learn the meta-features to be fed to the stacking procedure, we here rely on the out-of-bag samples obtained through bootstrapping the training set when learning the forests. More specifically, the out-of-bag samples are used to estimate the a posteriori class distributions used by the stacking procedure to learn the underlying input/output relationships. We show that such novel stacking approach is not only able to provide state-of-the-art classification effectiveness, but also at a significantly lower runtime.

Clearly, there is still room for improvements. For example, we plan to investigate if non-bagging strategies, such as the traditional kNN, Naïve Bayes and SVM classifier, could benefit from the bootstrap procedure in order to come up with a uniform stacking strategy that generalizes to any other classifier. Also, in the same vein of exploring the out-of-bag samples to estimate the a posteriori class distributions in our stacking approach, we could explore the out-of-bag error estimates in order to select the candidate features for decision nodes in order to improve both effectiveness and efficiency of the RF based classifiers, such as BERT, BROOF, LazyNN_RF, LXT and the traditional RF.

REFERENCES

[1] Ricardo A. Baeza-Yates and Berthier A. Ribeiro-Neto. 1999. *Modern Information Retrieval.* ACM Press / Addison-Wesley.

[2] Yaxin Bi, David Bell, Hui Wang, Gongde Guo, and Jiwen Guan. 2007. COMBINING MULTIPLE CLASSIFIERS USING DEMPSTER'S RULE FOR TEXT CATEGORIZATION. *Appl. Artif. Intell.* 21, 3 (March 2007), 211–239.

[3] Leo Breiman. 1996. Bagging Predictors. *Mach. Learn.* 24, 2 (Aug. 1996), 123–140.

[4] A. Danesh, B. Moshiri, and O. Fatemi. 2007. Improve text classification accuracy based on classifier fusion methods. In *Information Fusion, 2007 10th International Conference on.* IEEE, 1–6.

[5] Clebson C. A. de Sá, Marcos André Gonçalves, Daniel Xavier de Sousa, and Thiago Salles. 2016. Generalized BROOF-L2R: A General Framework for Learning to Rank Based on Boosting and Random Forests. In *Proceedings of the 39th International ACM SIGIR conference on Research and Development in Information Retrieval, SIGIR 2016, Pisa, Italy, July 17-21, 2016.* 95–104.

[6] Yan-Shi Dong and Ke-Song Han. 2004. A comparison of several ensemble methods for text categorization. In *Services Computing, 2004. (SCC 2004). Proceedings. 2004 IEEE International Conference on.* IEEE, 419–422.

[7] Yan-Shi Dong and Ke-Song Han. 2004. A Comparison of Several Ensemble Methods for Text Categorization. In *IEEE International Conference on Services Computing.* IEEE.

[8] Manuel Fernández-Delgado, Eva Cernadas, Senén Barro, and Dinani Amorim. 2014. Do We Need Hundreds of Classifiers to Solve Real World Classification Problems? *J. Mach. Learn. Res.* 15, 1 (Jan. 2014), 3133–3181.

[9] Yoav Freund and Robert E Schapire. 1997. A Decision-Theoretic Generalization of On-Line Learning and an Application to Boosting. *J. Comput. Syst. Sci.* 55, 1 (Aug. 1997), 119–139.

[10] Pierre Geurts, Damien Ernst, and Louis Wehenkel. 2006. Extremely randomized trees. *Machine Learning* 63, 1 (2006), 3–42.

[11] Giorgio Giancinto and Fabio Roli. 2001. Design of Effective Neural Network Ensembles for Image Classification Purposes. *IMAGE VISION AND COMPUTING JOURNAL* 19 (2001), 699–707.

[12] T. Hastie, R. Tibshirani, and J. H. Friedman. 2009. *The Elements of Statistical Learning.* Springer.

[13] Monisha Kanakaraj and Ram Mohana Reddy Guddeti. 2015. Performance analysis of Ensemble methods on Twitter sentiment analysis using NLP techniques. In *IEEE International Conference on Semantic Computing (ICSC).* IEEE.

[14] Aurangzeb Khan, Baharum Baharudin, Lam Hong Lee, Khairullah Khan, and Universiti Teknologi Petronas Tronoh. 2010. A Review of Machine Learning Algorithms for Text-Documents Classification. In *Journal of Advances In Information Technology.* Academy Publisher.

[15] Ludmila I. Kuncheva, James C. Bezdek, and Robert P. W. Duin. 2001. Decision templates for multiple classifier fusion: an experimental comparison. *Pattern Recognition* 34 (2001), 299–314.

[16] Ludmila I. Kuncheva and Christopher J. Whitaker. 2003. Measures of Diversity in Classifier Ensembles and Their Relationship with the Ensemble Accuracy. *Mach. Learn.* 51, 2 (May 2003), 181–207.

[17] Christopher J. Merz. 1999. Using Correspondence Analysis to Combine Classifiers. *Mach. Learn.* 36, 1-2 (July 1999), 33–58.

[18] Tien Thanh Nguyen, Thi Thu Thuy Nguyen, Xuan Cuong Pham, and Alan Wee-Chung Liew. 2016. A Novel Combining Classifier Method Based on Variational Inference. *Pattern Recogn.* 49, C (Jan. 2016), 198–212.

[19] Aytuğ Onan, Serdar Korukoğlu, and Hasan Bulut. 2016. Ensemble of Keyword Extraction Methods and Classifiers in Text Classification. *Expert Syst. Appl.* 57, C (Sept. 2016), 232–247.

[20] Gabriel Pui, Cheong Fung, Jeffrey Xu Yu, Haixun Wang, David W. Cheung, and Huan Liu. 2006. A Balanced Ensemble Approach to Weighting Classifiers for Text Classification. In *ICDM '06. Sixth International Conference on Data Mining.* IEEE.

[21] Lior Rokach. 2009. Taxonomy for characterizing ensemble methods in classification tasks: A review and annotated bibliography. In *Computational Statistics Data Analysis, In Press, Corrected Proof.*

[22] Thiago Salles, Marcos Gonçalves, and Leonardo Rocha. 2017. PhD Dissertation: Random Forest based Classifiers for Classification Tasks with Noisy Data. (2017). Federal University of Minas Gerais.

[23] Thiago Salles, Marcos Gonçalves, Victor Rodrigues, and Leonardo Rocha. 2015. BROOF: Exploiting Out-of-Bag Errors, Boosting and Random Forests for Effective Automated Classification. In *Proc. of the 38th International ACM SIGIR Conference on Inf. Retrieval.* ACM, 353–362.

[24] M. R. Segal. 2004. *Machine Learning Benchmarks and Random Forest Regression.* Technical Report. University of California.

[25] Kai Ming Ting and Ian H. Witten. 1997. Stacking Bagged and Dagged Models. In *Proceedings of the Fourteenth International Conference on Machine Learning (ICML '97).* Morgan Kaufmann Publishers Inc., San Francisco, CA, USA, 367–375.

[26] David Wolpert and William G. Macready. 1996. *Combining Stacking With Bagging To Improve A Learning Algorithm.* Technical Report.

[27] David H. Wolpert. 1992. Stacked Generalization. *Neural Networks* 5 (1992), 241–259.

Deep Learning for Extreme Multi-label Text Classification

Jingzhou Liu
Carnegie Mellon University
liujingzhou@cs.cmu.edu

Wei-Cheng Chang
Carnegie Mellon University
wchang2@andrew.cmu.edu

Yuexin Wu
Carnegie Mellon University
yuexinw@andrew.cmu.edu

Yiming Yang
Carnegie Mellon University
yiming@cs.cmu.edu

ABSTRACT

Extreme multi-label text classification (XMTC) refers to the problem of assigning to each document its most relevant subset of class labels from an extremely large label collection, where the number of labels could reach hundreds of thousands or millions. The huge label space raises research challenges such as data sparsity and scalability. Significant progress has been made in recent years by the development of new machine learning methods, such as tree induction with large-margin partitions of the instance spaces and label-vector embedding in the target space. However, deep learning has not been explored for XMTC, despite its big successes in other related areas. This paper presents the first attempt at applying deep learning to XMTC, with a family of new Convolutional Neural Network (CNN) models which are tailored for multi-label classification in particular. With a comparative evaluation of 7 state-of-the-art methods on 6 benchmark datasets where the number of labels is up to 670,000, we show that the proposed CNN approach successfully scaled to the largest datasets, and consistently produced the best or the second best results on all the datasets. On the Wikipedia dataset with over 2 million documents and 500,000 labels in particular, it outperformed the second best method by 11.7% ~ 15.3% in precision@K and by 11.5% ~ 11.7% in NDCG@K for K = 1,3,5.

1 INTRODUCTION

Extreme multi-label text classification (XMTC), the problem of finding each document its most relevant subset of labels from an extremely large space of categories, becomes increasingly important due to the fast growing of internet contents and the urgent needs for organizational views of big data. For example, Wikipedia has over a million of curator-generated category labels, and an article often has more than one relevant label: the web page of "potato" would be tagged with the class labels of "Solanum", "Root vegetables", "Crops originating from South America", etc. The classification system for Amazon shopping items, as another example, uses a large hierarchy of over one million categories for the organization of shopping items, and each item typically belongs to more than one relevant categories. Solving such multi-label classification problems in an extremely large scale presents open challenges for machine learning research.

Multi-label classification is fundamentally different from the traditional binary or multi-class classification problems which have been intensively studied in the machine learning literature. Binary classifiers treat class labels as independent target variables, which is clearly sub-optimal for multi-label classification as the dependencies among class labels cannot be leveraged. Multi-class classifiers rely on the mutually exclusive assumption about class labels (i.e., one document should have one and only one class label), which is wrong in multi-label settings. Addressing the limitations of those traditional classification methods by explicitly modeling the dependencies or correlations among class labels has been the major focus of multi-label classification research [7, 11, 13, 15, 42, 48]; however, scalable solutions for problems with hundreds of thousands or even millions of labels have become available only in the past few years[5, 36]. Part of the difficulty in solving XMTC problems is due to the extremely severe data sparsity issue. XMTC datasets typically exhibit a power-law distribution of labels, which means a substantial proportion of the labels have very few training instances associated with them. It is, therefore, difficult to learn the dependency patterns among labels reliably. Another significant challenge in XMTC is that the computational costs in both training and testing of mutually independent classifiers would be practically prohibiting when the number of labels reaches hundreds of thousands or even millions.

Significant progress has been made in XMTC recently. Several approaches have been proposed to deal with the huge label space and to address the scalability and data sparsity issues. Most of these approaches fall into two categories: target-embedding methods and tree-based ensemble methods. Let us briefly outline below the key ideas of these two categories and discuss the third category in addition, i.e., the deep learning methods which have made significant impact in multi-class classification problems but have not been explored in XMTC. Comparing the accomplishments and limitations of these three categories of work leads to the design of our proposed work in this paper and the aimed contributions.

1.1 Target-Embedding Methods

Target-embedding methods aim to address the data sparsity issue in training XMTC classifiers by finding a set of low-dimensional embeddings of the label vectors for training instances in the target space. Suppose the training data is given as n pairs of feature vectors and label vectors $\{(\boldsymbol{x}_i, \boldsymbol{y}_i)\}_{i=1}^n$ where $\boldsymbol{x}_i \in \mathbb{R}^D$ and $\boldsymbol{y}_i \in \{0,1\}^L$, D is the number of features and L is the number of labels. Notice

SIGIR '17, August 07-11, 2017, Shinjuku, Tokyo, Japan

DOI: http://dx.doi.org/10.1145/3077136.3080834

that L can be extremely large in XMTC, which means that learning a reliable mapping from arbitrary $\boldsymbol{x}$ to relevant $\boldsymbol{y}$ is difficult from limited training data. Instead, if we can effectively compress the label vectors from L-dimension to $\hat{L}$-dimension via a linear or nonlinear projection, then we can use standard classifiers (such as Support Vector Machines) to efficiently learn a reliable mapping from the feature space to the compressed label space. For classifying a new document we also need to project the predicted embedding of $\boldsymbol{y}$ back to the original high-dimensional space. The projection of target label vectors to their low-dimensional embeddings is called the compression process, and the projection back to the high-dimensional space is called the decompression process. Many variants of the target embedding methods have been proposed [3, 6, 9, 10, 14, 19, 20, 24, 40, 46, 50]. These methods mainly differ in their choices of compression and decompression techniques[36] such as compressed sensing[19, 24], Bloom filters[10], Singular Value Decomposition[39], landmark labels[3], output codes[50], etc. Among those methods, SLEEC [5] is considered representative as it outperformed competing methods on some benchmark datasets. We will provide more precise descriptions of this method in Section 2 as it is a strong baseline in our comparative evaluation (Section 4) in this paper.

1.2 Tree-based Ensemble Methods

Another category of efforts that has improved the state of the art of XMTC in recent years are the new variants of tree-based ensemble methods [1, 36, 41]. Similar to those in classical decision-tree learning, the new methods induce a tree structure which recursively partitions the instance space or sub-spaces at each non-leaf node, and has a base classifier at each leaf node which only focuses on a few active labels in that node. Different from traditional decision trees, on the other hand, the new methods learn a hyperplane (equivalent to using a weighted combination of all features) to split the current instance space at each node, instead of selecting a single feature based on information gain (as in classical decision trees) for the splitting. The hyperplane-based induction is much less greedy than the single-feature based induction of decision trees, and hence potentially more robust for extreme classification with a vast feature space. Another advantage of the tree-based methods is that the prediction time complexity is typically sublinear in the training-set size, and would be logarithmic (as the best case) if the induced tree is balanced. For enhancing the robustness of predictions, most tree-based methods learn an ensemble of trees, each of which is induced based on a randomly selected subset of features at each level of the tree. The top-performing method in this category is FastXML [36], for which we will provide a detailed description in Section 2 as it is a strong baseline in our comparative evaluation (Section 4).

1.3 Deep Learning for Text Classification

It should be noted that all the aforementioned methods are based on bag-of-word representations of documents. That is, words are treated as independent features out of context, which is a fundamental limitation of those methods. How to overcome such a limitation of existing XMTC methods is an open question that has not been studied in sufficient depth. Deep learning models, on the other hand, have achieved great successes recently in other related domains by automatically extracting context-sensitive features from raw text. Those areas include various tasks in natural language understanding [37], language modeling [33], machine translation[38], and more. In multi-class text classification in particular, which is closely related to multi-label classification but restricting each document to having only one label, deep learning approaches have recently outperformed linear predictors (e.g., linear SVM) with bag-of-word based features as input, and become the new state-of-the-art. The strong deep learning models in multi-class text classification include the convolutional neural network by [25] (CNN), the recurrent neural network by [27] (RNN), the combination of CNN and RNN by [49], the CNN with attention mechanism by [2, 43] and the Bow-CNN model by [21, 22]. Although some of those deep learning models were also evaluated on multi-label classification datasets [21], those methods are designed for multi-class settings, not taking multi-label settings into account in model optimization. We will provide more details about the CNN-Kim [25] and Bow-CNN [21] models in Section 2 as the representative deep learning models (which are applied to but not tailored for XMTC) in our comparative evaluation (Section 4).

The great successes of deep learning in multi-class classification and other related areas raise an important question for XMTC research, i.e., can we use deep learning to advance the state of the art in XMTC? Specifically, how can we make deep learning both effective and scalable when both the feature space and label space are extremely large? Existing work in XMTC has not offered the answer; only limited efforts have been reported in this direction, and the solutions have not scaled to extremely large problems [26, 34, 44, 47].

1.4 Our New Contributions

Our primary goal in this paper is to use deep learning to enhance the state of the art of XMTC. We accomplish this goal with the following contributions:

- We re-examine the state of the art of XMTC by conducting a comparative evaluation of 7 methods which are most representative in target-embedding, tree-based ensembling and deep learning approaches to XMTC, on 6 benchmark datasets where the label space sizes are up to 670,000.
- We propose a new deep learning method, namely XML-CNN, which combines the strengths of existing CNN models and goes beyond by taking multi-label co-occurrence patterns into account in both the optimization objective and the design of the neural network architecture, and scales successfully to the largest XMTC benchmark datasets.
- Our extensive experiments show that XML-CNN consistently produces the best or the second best results among all the competing methods on all of the 6 benchmark datasets. On the Wikipedia dataset with over 2 million documents and 500,000 labels in particular, our proposed method outperforms the second best method by 11.7%~15.3% in precision@K and by 11.5%~11.7% in NDCG@K for K = 1,3,5.

The rest of the paper is organized as follows. Section 2 outlines six existing competitive methods which will be used (together with our XML-CNN) in our comparative evaluation. Section 3 describes the new XML-CNN method. Section 4 reports our extensive experiments and results, followed by conclusion in Section 5.

2 EXISTING COMPETITIVE METHODS

We outline six methods, including the most representative methods in XMTC and some successful deep learning methods which are designed for mutli-class text classification but also applicable to XMTC with minor adaptations. Later in Section 4 we will compare those methods empirically against our proposed XML-CNN method (Section 3).

2.1 SLEEC

SLEEC [5] is most representative for target-embedding methods in XMTC. It consists of two steps of learning embeddings and kNN classification. SLEEC learns $\hat{L}$-dimensional embeddings $\boldsymbol{z}_i \in \mathbb{R}^{\hat{L}}$ for the original L-dimensional label vectors $\boldsymbol{y}_i \in \{0, 1\}^L$ that non-linearly capture label correlations by preserving pairwise distances between only closest label vectors, i.e. $d(\boldsymbol{z}_i, \boldsymbol{z}_j) \approx d(\boldsymbol{y}_i, \boldsymbol{y}_j)$ only if i is among j's k nearest neighbors under some distance metric $d(\cdot, \cdot)$. Then regressors $V \in \mathbb{R}^{\hat{L} \times D}$ are learned such that $V\boldsymbol{x}_i \approx \boldsymbol{z}_i$ with ℓ_1 regularization on $V\boldsymbol{x}_i$, which results in sparse solutions.

At prediction time, for a novel document $\boldsymbol{x}^* \in \mathbb{R}^D$ SLEEC performs a kNN search for its projection $z^* = V\boldsymbol{x}^*$in the $\hat{L}$-dimensional embedding space. To speed up the kNN search, SLEEC groups training data into many clusters, and learns embeddings for each separate cluster, then kNN search is performed only within the cluster this novel document belongs to. Since clustering high dimensional data is usually unstable, an ensemble of SLEEC models are induced with different clusterings to boost prediction accuracy.

2.2 FastXML

FastXML [36] is considered the state-of-the-art tree-based method for XMTC. It learns a hierarchy of training instances and optimizes an NDCG-based objective at each node of the hierarchy. Specifically, a hyperplane parameterized by $w \in \mathbb{R}^D$ is induced at each node, which splits the set of documents in the current node into two subsets; the ranking of the labels in each of the two subsets are jointly learned. The key idea is to have the documents in each subset sharing similar label distribution, and to characterize the distribution using a set-specific ranked list of labels. This is achieved by jointly maximizing NDCG scores of the ranked label lists in the two sibling subsets. In practice, an ensemble of multiple induced trees are learned to improve the robustness of predictions.

At prediction time, each test document is passed from the root to a leaf node in each induced tree, and the label distributions in all the reached leaves are aggregated for the test document. Suppose T trees are induced, H is the average height of the trees, and $\hat{L}$ is the average number of labels per leaf node. The prediction cost is approximately $O(TDH + T\hat{L} + \hat{L}\log\hat{L})$, which is dominated by $O(TDH)$ when $\hat{L}$ is small. If the trees are near balanced, then $H = \log N \approx \log L$, and prediction cost is approximately $O(TD\log L)$, which is logarithmic in the number of labels.

2.3 FastText

FastText [23] is a simple yet effective deep learning method for multi-class text classification. A document representation is constructed by averaging the embeddings of the words that appear in the document, upon which a softmax layer is applied to map the document representation to class labels. This approach was inspired by the recent work on efficient word representation learning, such as skip-gram and CBOW[32]. It ignores word order in the construction of document representations, and uses a linear softmax classifier. This simplicity makes FastText very efficient to train yet achieving state-of-the-art performances on several multi-class classification benchmarks, and often is several orders of magnitude faster than other competing methods [23]. However, simply averaging input word embeddings with the shallow architecture for document-to-label mapping might limit its success in XMTC, as in XMTC, document presentations need to capture much richer information for successfully predicting multiple correlated labels and discriminating them from enormous numbers of irrelevant labels.

2.4 CNN-Kim

CNN-Kim [25] is one of the first attempts of applying convolutional neural networks to text classification. CNN-Kim constructs a document vector with the concatenation of its word embeddings, and then t filters are applied to this concatenated vector in the convolution layer to produce t feature maps, which are in turn fed to a max-over-time pooling layer to construct a t-dimensional document representation. This is followed by a fully-connected layer with L softmax outputs, corresponding to L labels. In practice CNN-Kim has shown excellent performance in multi-class text classification, and is a strong baseline in our comparative evaluations.

2.5 Bow-CNN

Bow-CNN [21] (Bag-of-word CNN) is another strong method in multi-class classification. It represents each small text region (several consecutive words) using a bag-of-word indicator vector (called the one-hot vector). Denoting by D the size of the feature space (the vocabulary), a D-dimensional binary vector is constructed for each region, where the i-th entry is 1 iff the i-th word in the vocabulary appears in the that text region. The embeddings of all regions are passed through a convolutional layer, followed by a special dynamic pooling layer that aggregates the embedded regions into a document representation, and then fed to a softmax output layer.

2.6 PD-Sparse

PD-Sparse [45] is a recently proposed max-margin method designed for extreme multi-label classification. It does not fall into the three categories in Section 1 (target-embedding methods, tree-based methods, and deep learning methods). In PD-Sparse, a linear classifier is learned for each label with ℓ_1 and ℓ_2 penalties on the weight matrix associated with this label. This results in a solution extremely sparse in both the primal and dual spaces, which is desirable in terms of both time and memory efficiency in XMTC. PD-Sparse proposes a Fully-Corrective Block-Coordinate Frank-Wolfe training algorithm that exploits sparsity in the solution and achieves sub-linear training time w.r.t the number of primal and dual variables, but prediction time is still linear w.r.t the number of labels. [45] has shown that PD-Sparse outperforms 1-vs-all SVM and logistic regression on multi-label classification, with significantly reduced training time and model size.

3 PROPOSED METHOD

Our model architecture (XML-CNN), shown in Figure 1, is based on CNN-Kim [25], the CNN model for multi-class text classification described in 2.4.

Similar to other CNNs[21, 25], our model learns a rich number of feature representations by passing the document through various convolutional filters. The key attributes of our model lie in the following connected layers. Specifically, our model adopts a dynamic max pooling scheme that captures more fine-grained features from different regions of the document. We furthermore utilize a binary cross-entropy loss over sigmoid output that is more tailored for XMTC. An additional hidden bottleneck layer is inserted between pooling and output layer to learn compact document representations, which reduces model size as well as boosts model performance. In the following we describe our model in detail.

Let $\boldsymbol{e}_i \in \mathbb{R}^k$ be the k-dimensional word embedding corresponding to the i-th word in the current document, $i = 1, .., m$. The whole document is represented by the concatenation of its word embeddings $\boldsymbol{e}_{1:m} = [\boldsymbol{e}_1, .., \boldsymbol{e}_m] \in \mathbb{R}^{km}$. In general, the text region from the i-th word to the j-th word is represented by $\boldsymbol{e}_{i:j} = [\boldsymbol{e}_i, .., \boldsymbol{e}_j] \in \mathbb{R}^{k(j-i+1)}$. A convolution filter $\boldsymbol{v} \in \mathbb{R}^{kh}$ is applied to a text region of h words $\boldsymbol{e}_{i:i+h-1}$ to produce a new feature:

$$c_i = g_c(\boldsymbol{v}^T \boldsymbol{e}_{i:j+h-1})$$

where g_c is the nonlinear activation function for this convolution layer, such as sigmoid or ReLU. We omit all bias terms for simplicity. All c_i's together form a feature map $\boldsymbol{c} = [c_1, ..., c_m] \in \mathbb{R}^m$ associated with the applied filter $\boldsymbol{v}$. Here we pad the end of the document to obtain m features if the length is short. Multiple filters with different window sizes are used in a convolution layer to capture rich semantic information. Suppose t filters are used and the t resulting feature maps are $\boldsymbol{c}^{(1)}, .., \boldsymbol{c}^{(t)}$. Then a pooling operation $P(\cdot)$ is applied to each of these t feature maps to produce t p-dimensional vectors $P(\boldsymbol{c}^{(i)}) \in \mathbb{R}^p$. We will discuss the choice of $P(\cdot)$ in Section 3.1. The output of pooling layer is followed by a fully connected bottleneck layer with h hidden units and then an output layer with L units corresponding to the scores assigned to each label, denoted by $\boldsymbol{f} \in \mathbb{R}^L$:

$$\boldsymbol{f} = \boldsymbol{W}_o g_h(\boldsymbol{W}_h[P(\boldsymbol{c}^{(1)}), .., P(\boldsymbol{c}^{(t)})]) \quad (1)$$

Here $\boldsymbol{W}_h \in \mathbb{R}^{h \times tp}$ and $\boldsymbol{W}_o \in \mathbb{R}^{L \times h}$ are weight matrices associated with the bottleneck layer and output layer; g_h is the element-wise activation functions applied to the bottleneck layer. The key attributes that make our model especially suited for XMTC are the pooling operation, loss function, and the hidden bottleneck layer between pooling and output layer. We will verify that each of these three components contributes to performance improvement in XMTC through an ablation test in Section 4.4. In the remainder of this section, we introduce these three key attributes of our model.

3.1 Dynamic Max Pooling

In previous CNN models for text classification, including CNN-Kim, a max-over-time[12] pooling scheme is usually adopted. This simply means taking the maximum element of a feature map: $P(\boldsymbol{c}) = \hat{c} = \max\{\boldsymbol{c}\}$. The idea is to capture the most important feature, i.e. the entry with the largest value, in each feature map. Using max-over-time pooling, each filter generates a single feature, so the output of the pooling layer is $[P(\boldsymbol{c}^{(1)}), .., P(\boldsymbol{c}^{(t)})] = [\hat{c}^{(1)}, .., \hat{c}^{(t)}] \in \mathbb{R}^t$. However, one drawback of max-over-time pooling is that for each filter, only one value, i.e. the largest value in the feature map, is chosen to carry information to subsequent layers, which is especially problematic when the document is long. Moreover, this pooling scheme does not capture any information about the position of the largest value.

In our model, we adopt a dynamic max pooling scheme, which is similar to [8, 21]. Instead of generating only one feature per filter, p features are generated to capture richer information. For a document with m words, we evenly divide its m-dimensional feature map into p chunks, each chunk is pooled to a single feature by taking the largest value within that chunk, so that information about different parts of the document can be received by the top layers. Under this pooling scheme, each filter produces a p-dimensional feature (assuming m is dividable by p):

$$P(\boldsymbol{c}) = [\max\{\boldsymbol{c}_{1:\frac{m}{p}}\}, .., \max\{\boldsymbol{c}_{m-\frac{m}{p}+1:m}\}] \in \mathbb{R}^p$$

which captures both important features and position information about these important features.

3.2 Loss Function

The most straightforward adaptation from the mult-class classification problems to multi-label ones would be to extend the traditional cross-entropy loss. Specifically, [16–18, 25] consider the extended cross-entropy loss function as

$$\min_{\Theta} \quad -\frac{1}{n}\sum_{i=1}^{n}\sum_{j=1}^{L} y_{ij}\log(\hat{p}_{ij}) = -\frac{1}{n}\sum_{i=1}^{n}\sum_{j\in \boldsymbol{y}_i^+}\frac{1}{|\boldsymbol{y}_i^+|}\log(\hat{p}_{ij}),$$

where Θ denotes model parameters, $\boldsymbol{y}_i^+$ denotes the set of relevant labels of instance i and $\hat{p}_{ij}$ is the model prediction for instance i on label j , through a softmax activation:

$$\hat{p}_{ij} = \frac{\exp(f_j(\boldsymbol{x}_i))}{\sum_{j'=1}^{L}\exp(f_{j'}(\boldsymbol{x}_i))}.$$

Another intuitively reasonable objective for XMTC is rank loss [47] that minimizes the number of mis-ordered pairs of relevant and irrelevant labels, i.e. it aims to assign relevant labels with higher scores than irrelevant labels. However, rank loss has shown to be inferior to binary cross-entropy loss (BCE) over sigmoid activation when applied to multi-label classification datasets in a simple feed-forward neural network[34]. The binary cross-entropy objective can be formulated as:

$$\min_{\Theta} \quad -\frac{1}{n}\sum_{i=1}^{n}\sum_{j=1}^{L}\left[y_{ij}\log(\sigma(f_{ij})) + (1-y_{ij})\log(1-\sigma(f_{ij}))\right] \quad (2)$$

where σ is sigmoid function $\sigma(x) = \frac{1}{1+e^{-x}}$.

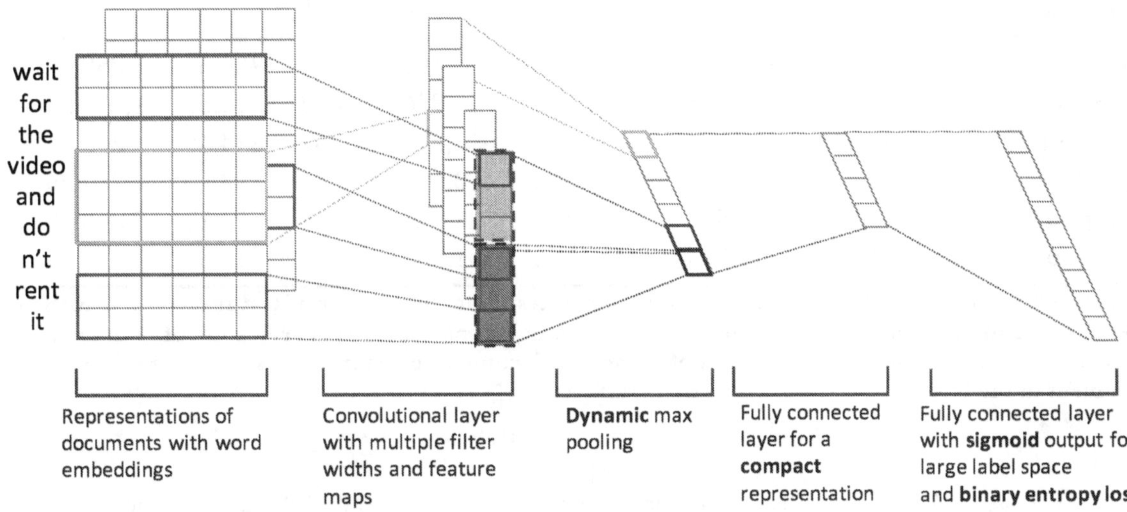

Figure 1: Proposed architecture XML-CNN with an example sentence.

We find that the BCE loss is more suited for multi-label problems and outperforms cross-entropy loss in our experiments (Section 4.4). Therefore, we adopt the BCE loss for our final model.

3.3 Hidden Bottleneck Layer

Unlike CNN-Kim [25] or Bow-CNN [21] where pooling layer and output layer are directly connected, we propose to add a fully-connected hidden layer with h units between pooling and output layer, referred to as the hidden bottleneck layer, as the number of its hidden units is far less than the pooling and output layer. The reason for this is two-fold. First, with pooling layer directly connected to output layer, the number of parameters between these two layers is $O(pt \times L)$. When the document is long, and the number of labels is large, more filters and more chunks in pooling operation are needed to obtain good document representations, and in XMTC setting, L can be up to millions, so model size of $O(pt \times L)$ might not fit into a common GPU memory. With an additional hidden bottleneck layer inserted between pooling and output layer, the number of parameters reduces to $O(h \times (pt + L))$, which can be an order of magnitude less than without this bottleneck layer. Second, without this hidden bottleneck layer, the model only has one hidden layer of non-linearity, which is not expressive enough to learn good document representations and classifiers. Experiments in Section 4 show that this hidden bottleneck layer does help to learn better document representations and improve prediction accuracy.

4 EXPERIMENTS

In this section we report our evaluation of the proposed method and the six competing methods introduced in Section 2 on XMTC benchmark datasets, and compare both the effectiveness and scalability of those methods. We also analyze the contribution of each component of our method via an ablation test.

4.1 Datasets

We used six benchmark datasets, including two small-scale datasets RCV1 [29] (103 labels) and EUR-Lex [31] (3865 labels), two medium-scale datasets Amazon-12K [30] (12,277 labels) and Wiki-30K [51] (29,947 labels), and two large-scale datasets Amazon-670K [28] (670,091 labels) and Wiki-500K[1] (501,069 labels). The dataset statistics are summarized in Table 1.

The TF-IDF features and the class labels for all of these datasets are available in the Extreme Classification Repository[1]. In our experiments, the non-deep learning methods (FastXML, SLEEC and PD-Sparse) used the vectors of TF-IDF features to represent input documents, while the deep learning methods (FastText, Bow-CNN and CNN-Kim and XML-CNN) require raw text of documents as input, which we obtained from the authors of the repository[1]. We removed words that do not have corresponding TF-IDF features from the raw text so that the feature set (vocabulary) of each dataset is the same in the experiments for both the deep learning and non-deep learning methods. Each dataset has an official training set and test set, which we used as they are. We reserved 25% of the training data as the validation set for model selection (i.e., for tuning hyper-parameters); the remaining 75% is used for training the models.

4.2 Evaluation Metrics

In extreme multi-label classification datasets, even though the label spaces are very large, each instance only has very few relevant labels (see Table 1). This means that it is important to present a short ranked list of potentially relevant labels for each test instance for user's attention, and to evaluate the quality of such ranked lists with an emphasis on the relevance of the top portion of each list. For these reasons rank-based evaluation metrics have been commonly used for comparing XMTC methods, including the precision at top K (P@K) and the Normalized Discounted Cummulated Gains

[1]https://manikvarma.github.io

datasets	N	M	D	L	$\bar{L}$	$\tilde{L}$	$\bar{W}$	$\hat{W}$
RCV1	23,149	781,265	47,236	103	3.18	729.67	259.47	269.23
EUR-Lex	15,449	3,865	171,120	3,956	5.32	15.59	1,225.20	1,248.07
Amazon-12K	490,310	152,981	135,895	12,277	5.37	214.45	230.25	224.67
Amazon-670K	490,449	153,025	135,895	670,091	5.45	3.99	230.20	224.62
Wiki-30K	12,959	5,992	100,819	29,947	18.74	8.11	2,246.58	2,210.10
Wiki-500K	1,646,302	711,542	2,381,304	501,069	4.87	16.33	750.64	751.42

Table 1: Data Statistics: N is the number of training instances, M is the number of test instances, D is the total number of features, L is the total number of class labels, $\bar{L}$ is the average number of label per document, $\tilde{L}$ is the average number of documents per label, $\bar{W}$ is the average number of words per document in the training set, $\hat{W}$ is the average number of words per document in the test set.

(NDCG@K) [1, 5, 36, 41, 45]. We follow such convention and use these two metrics in our evaluation in this paper, with $k = 1, 3, 5$. Denoting by $\boldsymbol{y} \in \{0, 1\}^L$ as the vector of true labels of an document, and $\hat{\boldsymbol{y}} \in \mathbb{R}^L$ as the system-predicted score vector for the same document, the metrics are defined as:

$$\text{P@}k = \frac{1}{k} \sum_{l \in r_k(\hat{\boldsymbol{y}})} y_l$$

$$\text{DCG@}k = \sum_{l \in r_k(\hat{\boldsymbol{y}})} \frac{y_l}{\log(l+1)}$$

$$\text{NDCG@}k = \frac{\text{DCG@}k}{\sum_{l=1}^{\min(k, \|\boldsymbol{y}\|_0)} \frac{1}{\log(l+1)}}$$

where $r_k(\hat{\boldsymbol{y}})$ is the set of rank indices of the truly relevant labels among the top-k portion of the system-predicted ranked list for a document, and $\|\boldsymbol{y}\|_0$ counts the number of relevant labels in the ground truth label vector $\boldsymbol{y}$. P@K and NDCG@K are calculated for each test document and then averaged over all the documents.

4.3 Main Results

The performance of all methods in P@K and NDCG@K on all six datasets are summarized in Tables 2 and 3. Each line compares all the methods on a specific dataset, where the best score is in boldface. We conducted paired t-tests to compared the performance score of each method against the best one in the same line, where the number of documents in each test set is the number of trials.

As we can see in Table 2, XML-CNN has the best scores in 11 out of the 18 lines in the table, and each of the 11 scores is statistically significantly better than the 2nd best score in the corresponding line. On the other hand, the target-embedding method SLEEC is the best in 4 lines, the deep learning method Bow-CNN is the best in 2 lines, and the tree-based ensemble method FastXML is the best in only 1 line. Similar observation can be found in Table 3 of the NDCG@K scores, where XML-CNN has the best results in 12 out of the 18 lines. On the Wiki-500K dataset with over 2 million documents and 500,000 labels in particular, XML-CNN outperformed the second best method by 11.7% ~ 15.3% in P@K and by 11.5% ~ 11.7% in NDCG@K for K = 1,3,5. In the lines XML-CNN does not have the best score, it has the 2nd best score.

Why did XML-CNN perform particularly strong on the datasets of RCV1, Amazon-12K and Wiki-500K? We notice that these datasets have a higher number of training instances per class than that in other datasets (see the column of $\tilde{L}$ in Table 1). This confirms our intuition about deep learning: it typically requires more training data in order to achieve advantageous performance than other methods, and XML-CNN successfully took this advantage on these datasets. As for why other deep learning methods especially CNN-Kim performed much worse on the other hand, we will analyze this via the ablation test in Section 4.4.

As for why SLEEC, the leading target-embedding method, had the strongest performance on EUR-Lex and Wiki-30K in particular, we notice that these two datasets have much longer documents than other datasets (see column of $\bar{W}$ in Table 1). In other words, the feature vectors of documents in these two datasets are denser and possibly information-richer than those in other datasets. As we described in Section 2, SLEEC uses a linear regression model to establish the mapping from documents to label vectors in a dimension reduced target space. But why such a relatively simple linear mapping should lead to better predictions for long documents than the more complex deep learning or tree-based models is not clear at this point – answering this question requires future research.

An interesting observation is that all the methods performed relatively well on RCV1, and each method has much stronger performance on this dataset than itself on other datasets. Notice that this dataset has a much smaller number of labels (103 only) than those of other datasets, and the smallest number of labels (3.18) per document. These means that this dataset is the least challenging one among the six included in this study.

Another interesting observation is that FastText and CNN-Kim had significantly worse results than other methods on Amazon-670K (with 670K labels) and Wiki-500K (with 500K labels). The extremely huge label spaces mean that the data sparsity issue would be severe, especially for the long tail of rare labels. Both FastText and CNN-Kim are designed for multi-class classification and not for modeling label correlations, and hence suffered significantly in XMTC when the label spaces are extremely large. Other models like PD-Sparse and Bow-CNN would have a similar weakness but we cannot examine them empirically as they failed to scale up on these two datasets.

4.4 Ablation Test

Given that CNN-Kim and XML-CNN are closely coupled in the sense that the latter is an extension of the former by adding a few components that especially suit XMTC, it would be informative to empirically examine the impact of each new component in XML-CNN via an ablation test. The results are shown in Figure 2, where CNN-Kim is the original model designed for multi-class problems; suffix v1 denotes the model obtained by replacing the original loss function of CNN-Kim by the binary cross-entropy loss over sigmoid output (Section 3.2); suffix v2 denotes the model obtained by inserting the hidden bottleneck layer to model v1; suffix v3 denotes the model obtained by adding the dynamic pooling layer to model v2. That is, v3 is the full version of our XML-CNN model. We show results on three representative datasets in terms of their category sizes (small, medium and large scale). Results on the other three datasets demonstrate similar trends and we omit them here due to space limit.

Overall, we can see that each of the three new components improved the performance of XML-CNN. First, the new loss function certainly is more suitable for dealing with multi-label problems. We also found that the hidden bottleneck layer not only consistently boosted the performance of XML-CNN, but also improved the scalability as it compresses the output of the pooling layer into a smaller one and makes XML-CNN scalable on the largest dataset. Last but not least, dynamic max-pooling layer plays a crucial role in our model, leading to significant improvement of XML-CNN over CNN-Kim, indicating its effectiveness in extracting richer information from the context of documents.

4.5 Efficiency and Scalability

The training and testing time in clock-time seconds for all the methods on the six benchmark datasets are summarized in Table 4. Notice that four of those methods (FastXML, SLEEC, PD-Sparse and FastText) are implemented for running on CPU, while the remaining deep learning methods (Bow-CNN, CNN-Kim and XML-CNN) were implemented for running on GPU. The left portion of Table 4 presents the time in seconds on CPU for the former group (running time using a single thread is reported), and the right portion presents the time in seconds on GPU for the latter group. Although the two groups are not directly comparable, they are informative in a practical sense. For the CPU runs we used Intel(R) Xeon(R) CPU E5-2630v3 2.40GHz with 192 GB memory, and for the GPU runs we used Nvidia GTX TITAN X.

In addition, we also ran all the methods on subsets of the Wiki-500K data, which were obtained by randomly sampling 1%, 5%, 10% and 25% of its 501,069 labels and corresponding documents. Figure 3 summarizes the training time on CPU or GPU in seconds, depending on the methods. Three methods (SLEEC, Bow-CNN and PD-Sparse) are not scalable to the fullset and the larger subsets of Wiki-500K because that their excessive memory requirements exceed the limits of our machines, and hence the early stop of their curves. In order to fill in the training-time slot for SLEEC in Table 4 on Wiki-500K, we had to reduce the feature space to 5000 instead of the full dimension of D=2,381,304; otherwise it could not fit into our memory. Thus the listed CPU seconds (209,735) in this table does not reflect the full complexity of SLEEC in training.

Combining Table 4 and Figure 3 we have the following points:

(1) For scalability comparison, time complexities on the largest datasets, e.g., Wiki-500K and Amazon-670K, are most informative. Only four methods, i.e., XML-CNN, CNN-Kim, FastXML and FastText successfully scaled to these extremely large problems; the remaining methods failed for memory issues;
(2) Both XML-CNN and FastXML (the 4th best method on average in this study) scaled well with both extremely large feature spaces and label spaces;
(3) SLEEC (the 2nd best method on average in this study) scaled well with extremely large label spaces (e.g., on Amazon-670K) but suffered from extremely large feature spaces (e.g., on Wiki-500K);
(4) CNN-Kim has comparable time complexities as XML-CNN in both training and testing, but CNN-Kim performed substantially worse on all of the datasets;
(5) FastText is less efficient on EUR-Lex, Wiki-30K as its training cost is proportional to document length on average;
(6) Bow-CNN is relatively fast in training if it were not running into memory issues. This is partly due to its implementation[2]; also, it has a dynamic pooling layer directly connected to output layer, resulting in $O(ptL)$ memory (as we discussed in Section 3.3), where t, p are the number of filters and pooling chunks, which can be an order of magnitude larger than that of XML-CNN ($O(h(pt + L))$) and CNN-Kim ($O(tL)$).

4.6 Experimental Details

In our proposed model XML-CNN, we used rectified linear units as activation functions, one-dimensional convolutional filters with the window sizes of 2, 4, 8; the number of feature maps for each filter was 128 for small datasets (RCV1, Wiki-30K, EUR-Lex, Amazon-12K) and 32 for large datasets (Wiki-500K, Amazon-670K), dropout rate was $p = 0.5$, and the number of hidden units of the bottleneck layer was 512. These hyper-parameters were fixed across all datasets.

For all the six baseline methods (Section 2) except for CNN-Kim, we used the author-provided implementations [123]; XML-CNN and CNN-Kim are implemented in THEANO[4]. For SLEEC, the number of learners was set to 15, embedding dimension was set to 100 for small datasets and 50 for large datasets as suggested in [5]. For FastXML, the number of trees was set to 50 and hyper-parameter $C_\delta = C_r = 1.0$ as suggested in [36]. For PD-Sparse, the tuning parameter C was set to 1.0. All other hyper-parameters of these methods were chosen on the validation set.

For word embeddings in deep learning models (except for Bow-CNN, which uses one-hot vectors as input) we used pre-trained 300-dimensional Glove vectors [35].

[2] http://riejohnson.com/cnn_download.html
[3] https://github.com/facebookresearch/fastText

Datasets	Metrics	FastXML	SLEEC	PD-Sparse	FastText	Bow-CNN	CNN-Kim	XML-CNN
RCV1	P@1	94.62	95.35	95.16	95.40	96.40	93.54	**96.86**
	P@3	78.40	79.51	79.46	79.96	**81.17**	76.15	81.11
	P@5	54.82	55.06	55.61	55.64	**56.74**	52.94	56.07
EUR-Lex	P@1	68.12	**78.21**	72.10	71.51	64.99	42.84	76.38
	P@3	57.93	**64.33**	57.74	60.37	51.68	34.92	62.81
	P@5	48.97	**52.47**	47.48	50.41	42.32	29.01	51.41
Amazon-12K	P@1	94.58	93.61	88.80	82.11	92.77	90.31	**95.06**
	P@3	78.69	79.13	70.69	71.94	69.85	74.34	**79.86**
	P@5	62.26	63.54	55.70	58.96	48.74	58.78	**63.91**
Amazon-670K	P@1	**35.59**	34.54	-	8.93	-	15.19	35.39
	P@3	31.87	30.89	-	9.07	-	13.78	**31.93**
	P@5	28.96	28.25	-	8.83	-	12.64	**29.32**
Wiki-30K	P@1	83.26	**85.96**	82.32	66.19	81.09	78.93	84.06
	P@3	68.74	73.13	66.96	55.44	50.64	55.48	**73.96**
	P@5	58.84	62.73	55.60	48.03	35.98	45.06	**64.11**
Wiki-500K	P@1	49.27	53.60	-	8.66	-	23.38	**59.85**
	P@3	33.30	34.51	-	7.32	-	11.95	**39.28**
	P@5	25.63	25.85	-	6.54	-	8.59	**29.81**

Table 2: Results in P@K – bold face indicates the best method in each line; * denotes the method (if any) whose score is not statistically significantly different from the best one; '-' denotes the methods which failed to scale due to memory issues.

Datasets	Metrics	FastXML	SLEEC	PD-Sparse	FastText	Bow-CNN	CNN-Kim	XML-CNN
RCV1	G@1	94.62	95.35	95.16	95.40	96.40	93.54	**96.88**
	G@3	89.21	90.45	90.29	90.95	92.04*	87.26	**92.22**
	G@5	90.27	90.97	91.29	91.68	**92.89**	88.20	92.63
EUR-Lex	G@1	68.12	**78.21**	72.10	71.51	64.99	42.84	76.38
	G@3	60.66	**67.86**	61.33	63.32	55.03	36.95	66.28
	G@5	56.42	**61.57**	55.93	58.56	49.92	33.83	60.32
Amazon-12K	G@1	94.58	93.61	88.80	82.11	92.77	90.31	**95.06**
	G@3	88.26	88.61	80.48	79.90	80.96	83.87	**89.48**
	G@5	84.89	86.46	77.81	79.36	73.01	81.21	**87.06**
Amazon-670K	G@1	**35.59**	34.54	-	8.93	-	15.19	35.39
	G@3	33.36	32.70	-	9.51	-	14.60	**33.74**
	G@5	31.76	31.54	-	9.74	-	14.12	**32.64**
Wiki-30K	G@1	83.26	**85.96**	82.32	66.19	81.09	78.93	84.06
	G@3	72.07	76.10*	70.54	57.87	57.26	60.52	**76.35**
	G@5	64.34	68.14	61.74	52.12	45.28	51.96	**68.94**
Wiki-500K	G@1	49.27	53.60	-	8.66	-	23.38	**59.85**
	G@3	41.64	43.64	-	8.43	-	15.45	**48.67**
	G@5	40.16	41.31	-	8.86	-	13.64	**46.12**

Table 3: Results in NDCG@K – bold face indicates the best method in each line; * denotes the method (if any) whose score is not statistically significantly different from the best one; '-' denotes the methods which failed to scale due to memory issues.

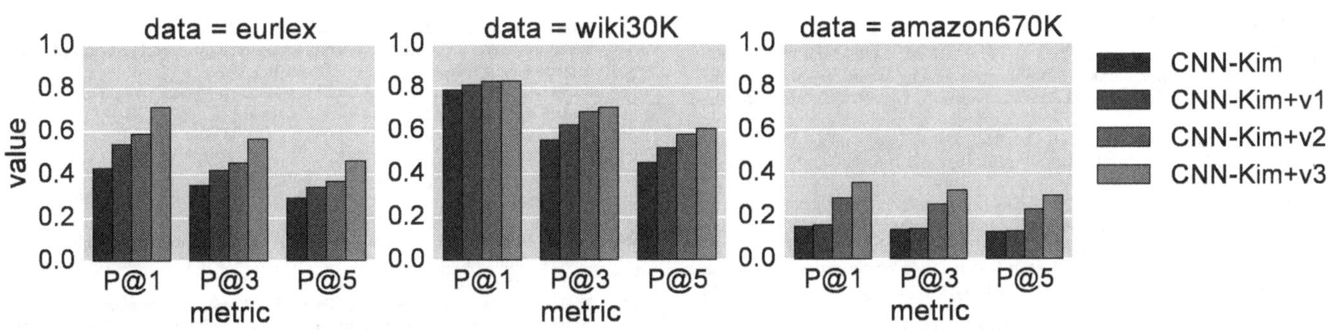

Figure 2: Result of the ablation test – v1 uses the new loss function for multi-label classification over CNN-Kim**; v2 denotes the insertion of the additional hidden layers over v1, and v3 denotes the insertion of the dynamic max pooling layer over v2 (hence the full version of** XML-CNN**).**

	CPU								GPU					
	FastXML		SLEEC		PD-Sparse		FastText		Bow-CNN		CNN-Kim		XML-CNN	
dataset	train	test	train	test	train	test	train	test	train	test	train	test	train	test
RCV1	552	615	888	1,764	20	15	858	184	804	85	3,720	92	2,340	89
EUR-Lex	756	55	4,617	16	322	0.4	19,518	7	1,665	4	660	0.6	1,020	0.7
Amazon-12K	27,949	1,015	90,925	2,506	2,399	15	20,790	499	11,097	135	41,460	34	48,000	45
Amazon-670K	47,342	1,300	63,991	2,856	-	-	19,353	26,746	-	-	138,060	889	188,040	2,476
Wiki-30K	2,047	21	2,646	0.6	238	60	6,354	20	2,377	20	1,020	3	5,280	9
Wiki-500K	192,741	8,972	209,735	20,002	-	-	721,444	84,442	-	-	494,400	4,534	422,040	16,511

Table 4: Training and testing time (seconds) of 7 methods on 6 datasets

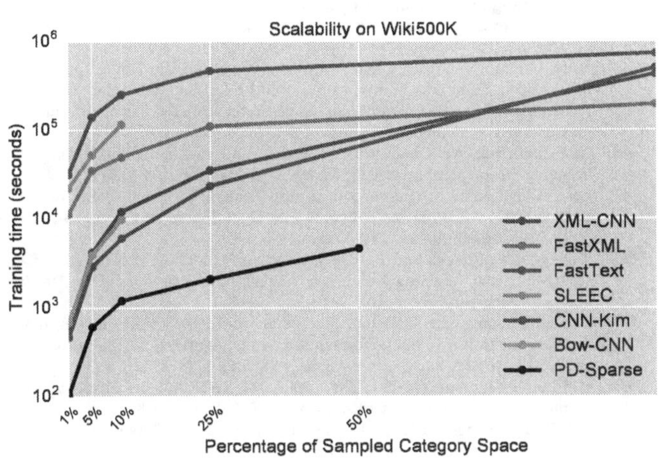

Figure 3: Scalability results on Wiki-500K**.**

5 CONCLUSION

This paper presented a new deep learning approach to extreme multi-label text classification, and evaluated the proposed method in comparison with other state-of-the-art methods on six benchmark datasets where the label-set sizes are up to 670K. Our proposed method XML-CNN goes beyond the deep learning methods for binary or multi-class classification by using a dynamic max pooling scheme that captures richer information from different regions of the document, a binary cross-entropy loss that is more suitable for multi-label problems, and a hidden bottleneck layer for better representations of documents as well as for reducing model size. The advantageous performance of XML-CNN over other competing methods is evident as it obtained the best or second best results on all the benchmark datasets in our comparative evaluation. We hope this study is informative for XMTC research.

ACKNOWLEDGMENTS

We thank the reviewers for their helpful comments. This work is supported in part by the National Science Foundation (NSF) under grant IIS-1546329.

REFERENCES

[1] Rahul Agrawal, Archit Gupta, Yashoteja Prabhu, and Manik Varma. 2013. Multi-label learning with millions of labels: Recommending advertiser bid phrases for web pages. In *Proceedings of the 22nd international conference on World Wide Web*. ACM, 13–24.

[2] Dzmitry Bahdanau, Kyunghyun Cho, and Yoshua Bengio. 2014. Neural machine translation by jointly learning to align and translate. *arXiv preprint arXiv:1409.0473* (2014).

[3] Krishnakumar Balasubramanian and Guy Lebanon. 2012. The landmark selection method for multiple output prediction. *arXiv preprint arXiv:1206.6479* (2012).

[4] James Bergstra, Olivier Breuleux, Frédéric Bastien, Pascal Lamblin, Razvan Pascanu, Guillaume Desjardins, Joseph Turian, David Warde-Farley, and Yoshua Bengio. 2010. Theano: A CPU and GPU math compiler in Python. In *Proc. 9th Python in Science Conf.* 1–7.

[5] Kush Bhatia, Himanshu Jain, Purushottam Kar, Manik Varma, and Prateek Jain. 2015. Sparse local embeddings for extreme multi-label classification. In *Advances in Neural Information Processing Systems*. 730–738.

[6] Wei Bi and James Tin-Yau Kwok. 2013. Efficient Multi-label Classification with Many Labels.. In *ICML (3)*. 405–413.

[7] Matthew R Boutell, Jiebo Luo, Xipeng Shen, and Christopher M Brown. 2004. Learning multi-label scene classification. *Pattern recognition* 37, 9 (2004), 1757–1771.

[8] Yubo Chen, Liheng Xu, Kang Liu, Daojian Zeng, and Jun Zhao. 2015. Event Extraction via Dynamic Multi-Pooling Convolutional Neural Networks.. In *ACL (1)*. 167–176.

[9] Yao-Nan Chen and Hsuan-Tien Lin. 2012. Feature-aware label space dimension reduction for multi-label classification. In *Advances in Neural Information Processing Systems*. 1529–1537.

[10] Moustapha M Cisse, Nicolas Usunier, Thierry Artieres, and Patrick Gallinari. 2013. Robust bloom filters for large multilabel classification tasks. In *Advances in Neural Information Processing Systems*. 1851–1859.

[11] Amanda Clare and Ross D King. 2001. Knowledge discovery in multi-label phenotype data. In *European Conference on Principles of Data Mining and Knowledge Discovery*. Springer, 42–53.

[12] Ronan Collobert, Jason Weston, Léon Bottou, Michael Karlen, Koray Kavukcuoglu, and Pavel Kuksa. 2011. Natural language processing (almost) from scratch. *Journal of Machine Learning Research* 12, Aug (2011), 2493–2537.

[13] André Elisseeff and Jason Weston. 2001. A kernel method for multi-labelled classification. In *Advances in neural information processing systems*. 681–687.

[14] Chun-Sung Ferng and Hsuan-Tien Lin. 2011. Multi-label Classification with Error-correcting Codes.. In *ACML*. 281–295.

[15] Johannes Fürnkranz, Eyke Hüllermeier, Eneldo Loza Mencía, and Klaus Brinker. 2008. Multilabel classification via calibrated label ranking. *Machine learning* 73, 2 (2008), 133–153.

[16] Sayan Ghosh, Eugene Laksana, Stefan Scherer, and Louis-Philippe Morency. 2015. A multi-label convolutional neural network approach to cross-domain action unit detection. In *Affective Computing and Intelligent Interaction (ACII), 2015 International Conference on*. IEEE, 609–615.

[17] Yunchao Gong, Yangqing Jia, Thomas Leung, Alexander Toshev, and Sergey Ioffe. 2013. Deep convolutional ranking for multilabel image annotation. *arXiv preprint arXiv:1312.4894* (2013).

[18] Matthieu Guillaumin, Thomas Mensink, Jakob Verbeek, and Cordelia Schmid. 2009. Tagprop: Discriminative metric learning in nearest neighbor models for image auto-annotation. In *Computer Vision, 2009 IEEE 12th International Conference on*. IEEE, 309–316.

[19] Daniel Hsu, Sham Kakade, John Langford, and Tong Zhang. 2009. Multi-Label Prediction via Compressed Sensing.. In *NIPS*, Vol. 22. 772–780.

[20] Shuiwang Ji, Lei Tang, Shipeng Yu, and Jieping Ye. 2008. Extracting shared subspace for multi-label classification. In *Proceedings of the 14th ACM SIGKDD international conference on Knowledge discovery and data mining*. ACM, 381–389.

[21] Rie Johnson and Tong Zhang. 2015. Effective use of word order for text categorization with convolutional neural networks. In *Proceedings of the 2015 Conference of the North American Chapter of the Association for Computational Linguistics: Human Language Technologie*. 103–112.

[22] Rie Johnson and Tong Zhang. 2015. Semi-supervised convolutional neural networks for text categorization via region embedding. In *Advances in neural information processing systems*. 919–927.

[23] Armand Joulin, Edouard Grave, Piotr Bojanowski, and Tomas Mikolov. 2016. Bag of tricks for efficient text classification. *arXiv preprint arXiv:1607.01759* (2016).

[24] Ashish Kapoor, Raajay Viswanathan, and Prateek Jain. 2012. Multilabel classification using bayesian compressed sensing. In *Advances in Neural Information Processing Systems*. 2645–2653.

[25] Yoon Kim. 2014. Convolutional neural networks for sentence classification. In *Proceedings of the 2014 Conference on Empirical Methods in Natural Language Processing (EMNLP)*. 1746–1751.

[26] Gakuto Kurata, Bing Xiang, and Bowen Zhou. 2016. Improved neural network-based multi-label classification with better initialization leveraging label co-occurrence. In *Proceedings of NAACL-HLT*. 521–526.

[27] Siwei Lai, Liheng Xu, Kang Liu, and Jun Zhao. 2015. Recurrent Convolutional Neural Networks for Text Classification.. In *AAAI*. 2267–2273.

[28] Jure Leskovec and Andrej Krevl. 2015. {SNAP Datasets}:{Stanford} Large Network Dataset Collection. (2015).

[29] David D Lewis, Yiming Yang, Tony G Rose, and Fan Li. 2004. Rcv1: A new benchmark collection for text categorization research. *Journal of machine learning research* 5, Apr (2004), 361–397.

[30] Julian McAuley and Jure Leskovec. 2013. Hidden factors and hidden topics: understanding rating dimensions with review text. In *Proceedings of the 7th ACM conference on Recommender systems*. ACM, 165–172.

[31] Eneldo Loza Mencia and Johannes Fürnkranz. 2008. Efficient pairwise multilabel classification for large-scale problems in the legal domain. In *Joint European Conference on Machine Learning and Knowledge Discovery in Databases*. Springer, 50–65.

[32] Tomas Mikolov, Kai Chen, Greg Corrado, and Jeffrey Dean. 2013. Efficient estimation of word representations in vector space. *arXiv preprint arXiv:1301.3781* (2013).

[33] Tomas Mikolov, Martin Karafiát, Lukas Burget, Jan Cernockỳ, and Sanjeev Khudanpur. 2010. Recurrent neural network based language model.. In *Interspeech*, Vol. 2. 3.

[34] Jinseok Nam, Jungi Kim, Eneldo Loza Mencía, Iryna Gurevych, and Johannes Fürnkranz. 2014. Large-scale multi-label text classificationfi!?revisiting neural networks. In *Joint European Conference on Machine Learning and Knowledge Discovery in Databases*. Springer, 437–452.

[35] Jeffrey Pennington, Richard Socher, and Christopher D Manning. 2014. Glove: Global Vectors for Word Representation.. In *EMNLP*, Vol. 14. 1532–1543.

[36] Yashoteja Prabhu and Manik Varma. 2014. Fastxml: A fast, accurate and stable tree-classifier for extreme multi-label learning. In *Proceedings of the 20th ACM SIGKDD international conference on Knowledge discovery and data mining*. ACM, 263–272.

[37] Richard Socher, Alex Perelygin, Jean Y Wu, Jason Chuang, Christopher D Manning, Andrew Y Ng, and Christopher Potts. 2013. Recursive deep models for semantic compositionality over a sentiment treebank. In *Proceedings of the conference on empirical methods in natural language processing (EMNLP)*, Vol. 1631. Citeseer, 1642.

[38] Ilya Sutskever, Oriol Vinyals, and Quoc V Le. 2014. Sequence to sequence learning with neural networks. In *Advances in neural information processing systems*. 3104–3112.

[39] Farbound Tai and Hsuan-Tien Lin. 2012. Multilabel classification with principal label space transformation. *Neural Computation* 24, 9 (2012), 2508–2542.

[40] Jason Weston, Samy Bengio, and Nicolas Usunier. 2011. Wsabie: Scaling up to large vocabulary image annotation. (2011).

[41] Jason Weston, Ameesh Makadia, and Hector Yee. 2013. Label Partitioning For Sublinear Ranking.. In *ICML (2)*. 181–189.

[42] Yiming Yang and Siddharth Gopal. 2012. Multilabel classification with meta-level features in a learning-to-rank framework. *Machine Learning* 88, 1-2 (2012), 47–68.

[43] Zichao Yang, Diyi Yang, Chris Dyer, Xiaodong He, Alex Smola, and Eduard Hovy. 2016. Hierarchical attention networks for document classification. In *Proceedings of the 2016 Conference of the North American Chapter of the Association for Computational Linguistics: Human Language Technologies*.

[44] Chih-Kuan Yeh, Wei-Chieh Wu, Wei-Jen Ko, and Yu-Chiang Frank Wang. 2017. Learning Deep Latent Spaces for Multi-Label Classification. (2017).

[45] Ian EH Yen, Xiangru Huang, Kai Zhong, Pradeep Ravikumar, and Inderjit S Dhillon. 2016. PD-Sparse: A Primal and Dual Sparse Approach to Extreme Multiclass and Multilabel Classification. (2016).

[46] Hsiang-Fu Yu, Prateek Jain, Purushottam Kar, and Inderjit S Dhillon. 2014. Large-scale Multi-label Learning with Missing Labels.. In *Proceedings of the 31th International Conference on Machine Learning*. 593–601.

[47] Min-Ling Zhang and Zhi-Hua Zhou. 2006. Multilabel neural networks with applications to functional genomics and text categorization. *IEEE transactions on Knowledge and Data Engineering* 18, 10 (2006), 1338–1351.

[48] Min-Ling Zhang and Zhi-Hua Zhou. 2007. ML-KNN: A lazy learning approach to multi-label learning. *Pattern recognition* 40, 7 (2007), 2038–2048.

[49] Rui Zhang, Honglak Lee, and Dragomir Radev. 2016. Dependency sensitive convolutional neural networks for modeling sentences and documents. *arXiv preprint arXiv:1611.02361* (2016).

[50] Yi Zhang and Jeff G Schneider. 2011. Multi-Label Output Codes using Canonical Correlation Analysis.. In *AISTATS*. 873–882.

[51] Arkaitz Zubiaga. 2012. Enhancing navigation on wikipedia with social tags. *arXiv preprint arXiv:1202.5469* (2012).

Engaged or Frustrated? Disambiguating Emotional State in Search

Ashlee Edwards
University of North Carolina at Chapel Hill
Chapel Hill, NC, USA
ashlee.a.edwards@gmail.com

Diane Kelly
University of Tennessee
Knoxville, TN, USA
dianek@utk.edu

ABSTRACT

One of the primary ways researchers have characterized engagement during information search is by increases in search behaviors, such as queries and clicks. However, studies have shown that frustration is also characterized by increases in these same behaviors. This research examines the differences in the search behaviors and physiologies of people who are engaged or frustrated during search. A 2x2 within-subject laboratory experiment was conducted with 40 participants. Engagement was induced by manipulating task interest and frustration was induced by manipulating the quality of the search results. Participants' interactions and physiological responses were recorded, and after they searched, they evaluated their levels of engagement, frustration and stress. Participants reported significantly greater levels of engagement when completing tasks that interested them and significantly less engagement during searches with poor results quality. For all search behaviors measured, only two significant differences were found according to task interest: participants had more scrolls and longer query intervals when searching for interesting tasks, suggesting greater interaction with content. Significant differences were found for nine behaviors according to results quality, including queries issued, number of SERPs displayed and number of SERP clicks, suggesting these are potentially better indicators of frustration rather than engagement. When presented with poor quality results, participants had significantly higher heart rates than when presented with normal quality results. Finally, participants had lower heart rates and greater skin conductance responses when conducting interesting tasks than when conducting uninteresting tasks. This research provides insight into the differences in search behaviors and physiologies of participants when they are engaged versus frustrated and presents techniques that can be used by those wishing to induce engagement and frustration during laboratory IIR studies.

SIGIR '17, August 07-11, 2017, Shinjuku, Tokyo, Japan
© 2017 Association for Computing Machinery.
ACM ISBN 978-1-4503-5022-8/17/08…$15.00
http://dx.doi.org/10.1145/3077136.3080818

CCS CONCEPTS

• Information systems → Information retrieval; Users and interactive retrieval

KEYWORDS

Interactive information retrieval, search behavior, emotion, engagement, frustration, physiological signals

ACM Reference format:

Ashlee Edwards and Diane Kelly. 2017. Engaged or Frustrated? Disambiguating Emotional State in Search. In Proceedings of ACM SIGIR conference, Tokyo, Japan, August 2017 (SIGIR'17), 10 pages.

DOI: http://dx.doi.org/10.1145/3077136.3080818

1 INTRODUCTION

The study of engagement in interactive information retrieval is one area where the integration of subjective experience and interaction measures is needed. To date, search engagement has been overwhelmingly characterized by a focus on behavioral signals as proxies for engagement [10, 19, 20]. These measures have primarily been frequency-focused: frequency of clicks and queries, as well as greater frequency in overall activity per session. While behavioral signals can be useful, other work has contradicted this frequency-based notion of engagement. For example, O'Brien and Lebow [24] investigated the relationship between engagement and search behavior and found participants who rated their engagement highest had the lowest reading times overall, lowest browsing times, and lowest total session times. Participants who rated their engagement highest also visited the fewest pages and used the least recommended links, suggesting that participants who were the most engaged had the least amount of search interaction [24]. This calls into question work that has suggested that engagement is signaled by an increase in interaction measures. One possibility is that instead of experiencing increased engagement, people who click and query frequently are actually frustrated. Feild, Allan and Jones [13], for example, found that frustrated participants also exhibit periods of high search activity.

Opportunities for disambiguating engagement and frustration during search may lie in linking behavioral signals with other measures, specifically physiological measures. It is well known that frustration generally produces higher stress responses [29]. However, there is conflicting evidence about how engagement manifests itself physiologically. Work in psychology has found that as engagement increases, stress hormones also linearly increase [23]. However, O’Brien and Lebow [24] found negative correlations between electrodermal activity, heart rate, and self-report engagement. In this work, we address the following research questions: 1) To what extent do search behaviors differ when people are engaged or frustrated? (2) To what extent do physiological signals help disambiguate engaging and frustrating search episodes?

2 PREVIOUS WORK

Historically, IR research has emphasized the functional aspects of search systems such as performance and usability; however, in recent years, there has been growing interest in creating engaging search experiences for searchers. O’Brien and Toms [25] define engagement as a “category of user experience characterized by attributes of challenge, positive affect, endurability, aesthetic and sensory appeal, attention, feedback, variety/novelty, interactivity, and perceived user control” (p.7).

Researchers in IR have primarily examined engagement by focusing on signals that can be extracted from search logs such as clicks and dwell time. Generally, the underlying assumption is greater frequency of certain behaviors, such as clicks and dwell times, indicates more engaged users. Lehmann and colleagues have completed an extensive body of research on engagement within the context of large-scale search logs [19, 20, 21]. Lehmann et al. [21] proposed and evaluated three interaction-based models of engagement: a general model, a time-based model and a user-based model. Their general model of engagement focused primarily on popularity and clicks on a site, while the time-based model was more focused on loyalty, and the user-based model was more focused on an individual user’s behavioral patterns. Lehmann et al. [19] continued this work by proposing the concept of networked user engagement, referring to engagement within a network of websites and later focused on user engagement during multitasking episodes using dwell time and page views [20]. These basic signals were transformed into metrics like attention shift, attention range, and cumulative actions. Dupret and Lalmas [10] investigated the usefulness of absence time, or the time between two user visits, as a metric of user engagement. This was based on the assumption that users who are engaged will return to a site sooner, meaning that their absence times will be shorter. Ortiz-Cordova and Jansen [27] sought to identify those who were more engaged with site content and advertisements, and defined engagement in terms of new visits, number of pages visited during the duration of the session, time spent on a site, click-through rate, ads clicked, ad impressions, and rate of return to the site.

On the other hand, there is evidence that searchers exhibit more search behaviors when they are frustrated or experiencing difficulties. For example, Feild, et al. [13] found that frustrated participants engaged in increased search behavior. Aula et al. [5] gave participants easy and difficult tasks and found that participants attempted longer queries and had more query reformulations when completing difficult tasks. Hassan, White, Dumais and Wang [15] classified search behaviors as either struggling or exploring, and found participants who were struggling tended to submit less diverse queries than participants who were exploring. They also found that dwell time was lower for participants who were struggling. Also in contrast to studies that have equated increased behavior with increased engagement is the work of O’Brien and Lebow [24] who found participants with the highest levels of engagement had the lowest display times overall, lowest browsing times, and lowest total session times. Participants who rated their engagement highest visited the fewest pages and used the least recommended links. Thus, the challenge is that increases (or decreases) in behavioral signals can be (and have been) used to indicate frustration, task difficulty, task interest, relevance, satisfaction and so forth. Though behavioral signals are useful in that they can potentially serve as indicators of what the user is thinking and feeling, using them alone to define engagement is problematic because what they indicate is often ambiguous.

One potential way to better determine if a person is engaged or frustrated during search is to ask them. Several of the studies described above, including Feild, et al. [13], Aula et al. [5] and O’Brien and Lebow [24] collected self-report data to better understand the user’s experiences. Another potential way is to use physiological measures. While the use of physiological measures is not widespread in IR, several recent papers have demonstrated their usefulness [22, 12, 6, 4] and a recent workshop at the 2015 SIGIR Conference called for more work integrating these measures with other standard IR measures[1]. Physiological measures include things such as skin conductance, heart rate, skin resistance, muscle tension and neuronal activity. One of the underlying motives for using such measures is they provide information about a person’s emotional experiences, including those that might be subconscious (and thus, unlikely to be reported by the person) [6].

In IR, physiological measures have been combined with other measures such as search behaviors and self-report measures to better understand the search process. Moshfeghi and Jose [22] combined facial expression, heart rate, galvanic skin response, and EEG signals with dwell time to predict relevance. Arapakis, Konstas, and Jose [4] combined galvanic skin response, heart rate, temperature, and facial expression analysis with machine learning to predict which documents or video snippets would be relevant. Arapakis, Jose, and Gray [2] linked facial expressions with subjective reports of emotions experienced and discovered that irritation and anxiety were linked to perceptions of difficulty and feelings of fatigue experienced during a task. Barreda-Angeles et al. [6] used physiological signals to examine the unconscious effects of response latency on participants, and found indications of physiological effects even at small increases in latency.

Physiological measures have also been used to better understand frustration [29], engagement with content [22, 4] and reactions to search interfaces [12]. Scheirer, Fernandez, Klein, and Picard [29] discriminated between frustrated and non-frustrated states by linking increases in galvanic skin response

[1] https://sites.google.com/site/neuroir2015/home

(GSR) and blood volume pressure (BVP) to frustration as a result of delayed mouse clicks. O佮rien and Lebow [24] found that in an online news context, participants who were more engaged had lower levels of electrodermal activity and electromyography (facial movement). Arapakis, Lalmas and Valkanas [3] investigated the usefulness of mouse gestures and gaze behavior as possible indicators of engagement with search results and found a correlation between gaze behavior and engagement, specifically, participants had more fixations when reading an interesting article and spent more time with the content.

The studies cited above focused on engagement or frustration, but did not attempt to distinguish between these two emotions. We found one study that attempted to use physiological measures to distinguish between these two states [14]. Grafsgaard, et al. [14] used facial expression and skin conductance to differentiate between engaging and frustrating episodes in the context of online tutoring. Students were given a modified version of the endurability sub-scale of O佮rien and Toms佮[26] User Engagement Scale (UES) and also completed portions of the NASA-TLX. Grafsgaard, et al. found that certain facial expressions could be used to distinguish between engagement and frustration. For example, endurability was predicted by more frequent inner brow raising and frustration by more frequent brow lowering. While this study provided interesting results regarding facial expression, it did not examine some of the other physiological measures reported in previous IR studies, which complicates cross-study comparisons.

Our review of the literature shows that while a number of studies have used increases in search behaviors such as clicking, querying and time spent as indicators of engagement, other work has found these same measures are associated with constructs such as frustration, and at least one study found that fewer (not more) search behaviors were associated with more engaging experiences. While there has been some work integrating physiological measures into the study of engagement and frustration, to our knowledge there has been no study which has examined how the combination of physiological signals, search behaviors and self-report measures can potentially be used to distinguish between engaging and frustrating search experiences. Moreover, none of the studies above examined frustration and engagement during a single study and within the same participant. In this work, we attempt to see if, for the same participant, we can distinguish between engaging and frustrating searches with respect to search behaviors and physiological responses.

3 METHOD

A laboratory experiment was conducted, with two within-subject experimental conditions, each with two levels. These conditions are described in more detail below. Unless otherwise reported, two-way repeated measures ANOVAs and Bonferroni佮 post-hoc tests were used for analyses. A total of 40 undergraduate participants were recruited through a university email list. Participants佮average age was 20.45 (SD=1.77), and most were female (n=31). Participants came from a variety of majors: the natural sciences (n=13), humanities (n=11), social sciences (n=8) and professional schools (n=7). Most participants reported having between 7-9 years of search experience, and reported conducting online searches for information more than 7 times a day. This study was approved by our university IRB (#15-0956).

3.1 Search Tasks

The tasks used in this study were based on tasks created and evaluated by Kelly, et al. [17]. Specifically, we modeled our tasks after those labeled as evaluative because participants in this previous study rated these types of tasks as engaging and spent about ten minutes completing them. The evaluate task type requires participants to search for information in order to evaluate several options, make a selection based on this information, and then justify the selection (Figure 1). A total of eight tasks were used (see http://bit.ly/2r6w5w2). Tasks were from four domains (health, science, technology and entertainment). Participants were asked to bookmark pages that helped them address the tasks. Participants were not given any task time limits.

> You recently heard a story on National Public Radio about the use of biomass as fuel. Biomass refers to material created from living organisms. What are different types of biomasses that are used as fuels and how are they created? How do biomass fuels compare with fossil fuels when it comes to environmental impact? Which do you think is better? Why?

Figure 1. Example search task in the science domain

3.2 Experimental Conditions

Our study rests on people being engaged while they search. Manipulating engagement during a laboratory study is not an easy task and there is little guidance in the IIR literature about how to do this. O佮rien and Toms [25], as well as researchers in other fields [29, 14] have shown that interest is a key component of engagement. Thus, in this study we attempt to induce engagement through task interest. To identify tasks that did and did not interest participants from the set of eight we created, we asked them to rank the tasks according to their interest the day before they completed the experiment using an online form. The presentation order of the topics was randomized to avoid selection bias. During the experiment, participants were given four tasks to complete: the two tasks they ranked as most interesting (ranks 1 and 2) and the two tasks they ranked as least interesting (ranks 7 and 8). Participants佮rankings of tasks can be found online at: http://bit.ly/2r6w5w2. Thus, in this study, task interest has two levels: interesting and uninteresting.

To induce frustration, we manipulated search engine results page (SERP) quality. This was accomplished by modifying the source code of the search system so that results were presented beginning at rank 500. During pilot testing, we tried other starting points (100, 200), but found we needed to start at 500 to ensure consistently poor result quality. Thus, in this study, SERP quality has two levels: normal and bad. In total, participants completed four search tasks: (1) interesting/normal SERP; (2) interesting/bad SERP; (3) uninteresting/normal SERP and (4) uninteresting/bad SERP. These combinations were counterbalanced.

3.3 Search System & Cover Story

We used a search system developed by members of our lab, which used the Bing API. The interface for this system was similar to a standard Web search interface although there were no advertisements. Participants were presented with a query box and a list of search results with snippets (10 per page). The search task was also printed at the top of the page just above the search box. Participants could perform normal activities such as querying, clicking and bookmarking pages. A cover story was used to keep participants from becoming suspicious of the poor results. Participants were told they were evaluating four different search systems. Participants were debriefed at the end of the experiment regarding the deception and manipulation.

3.4 Search Behaviors

Search behaviors were logged and we extracted queries, clicks, and time. These behaviors were chosen because they have been used in other work to examine engagement [24], to determine whether a user is struggling or exploring [15] and to study frustration during search [13].

3.5 Self-Report Measures

3.5.1 Task Evaluations: Interest and Difficulty

Participants completed pre-search questionnaires, which asked them about their prior knowledge and experience searching for the task topic, task relevance, their interest in the task (manipulation check) and how difficult they expect it will be to search. Participants completed post-task questionnaires after each task, which asked them about experienced difficulty and success, and their perceptions of their own skill, and the ability of the system to retrieve documents. All of these items were evaluated with 5-point scales and coded so that higher values indicated more of the construct being evaluated (e.g., more difficult, more success).

3.5.2 Engagement

Engagement was measured using the User Engagement Scale (UES) [26], and defined earlier in this paper. The scale used in [26], which is a specialized version of the UES designed for online search situations (namely Wikipedia), includes several subscales: aesthetics (5 items), perceived usability (8 items), felt involvement (3 items), novelty (2 items), endurability (5 items), and focused attention (5 items), for a total of 28 items. The aesthetics subscale was not used in this study because the interface was constant throughout. We also changed the term 佸Wikipedia,佅which was evaluated in the original study, to 佸search system.佅Finally, we dropped one item from the felt involvement subscale because it did not make sense in the context of our study. Thus, in total we had 22 items. All of these items were evaluated with a 5-point Likert scale, where 1=strongly disagree and 5=strongly agree. Responses were coded so that higher values indicated more of the construct being measured. Each subscale score represents an average of the items along each dimension.

3.5.3 Frustration & Stress

Frustration was defined in this study using Amsel佮[1] definition of primary frustration, or 佸temporary state that results when a response is nonreinforced in the presence of reward expectancy佅 (p. 2). Peters, O佮onnor and Rudolf佮[28] three-item scale was used to measure frustration. The scale contains 5-points, where 1=not at all and 5=extremely (higher values equal more frustration). An example item from this scale is 佸rying to complete this task was a frustrating experience.佅This measure served to verify that our manipulation of frustration (i.e., SERP quality) worked.

In addition to engagement and frustration, we also measured self-reported stress as a way to better understand physiological measures. Stress was defined as 佸 particular relationship between the person and environment that is appraised by the person as taxing or exceeding his or her resources佅[18] (p. 40). Stress was measured using the 24-item Short Stress State Questionnaire (SSSQ) [16]. The SSSQ has three factors: distress, worry, and engagement. Since we already had a scale in place to measure engagement, these items were removed from the questionnaire. Distress is a measure of negative affect, and contains items such as 佸 feel depressed佅or 佸 feel irritated.佅 Worry is a measure of self-perception, and contains items such as 佸 feel concerned about the impression I am making,佅and 佸 thought about how I would feel if I were told how I performed.佅 The scale contains 5-points, where 1=not at all and 5=extremely (higher values equal greater stress). Items were changed to reflect past tense and 佸his task佅was changed to 佸his search task.佅

3.6 Physiological Measures

Skin conductance and heart rate were measured using BioPac. Previous work has shown that these are useful signals of stress [7]. To measure skin conductance, electrodes were attached to the thenar and hypothenar eminences of each participants佮non-dominant palm. To measure heart rate, electrodes were attached to the collarbone and ribs of each participant. Braithwaite, et al. [8] offer recommendations for using the BioPac and accompanying software to perform electrodermal measurement, which we followed. After the electrodes were attached to participants, a three-minute resting period was observed for each participant before he/she was instructed to start the experiment.

Data was gathered at a rate of 1sample/msec. The electrodermal activity signal was recorded with a high band pass filter of 0Hz, and a low band pass filter of 35Hz, with a gain of 1000Hz. Skin conductance values are reported in microsiemens (μs). The electrocardiography signal was recorded with a high band pass filter set at 0.5 and a low band pass filter set at 35Hz, with a gain of 1000Hz. Heart rate was extracted from the raw ECG signal and is reported in beats per minute (bpm). Both the skin conductance and heart rate data were visually inspected for any errors or potential aberrant artifacts. A Shannon entropy analysis was conducted to look for aberrations or potential artifacts in the data, as was done in other work [4]. Both signals were examined for entropy values across conditions, and the differences were non-significant. The average entropy for skin conductance signals was 3.24, and the average entropy for heart rate data was 3.64. These values indicate very little aberrant fluctuation in either measure.

4 RESULTS

4.1 Self-Report Measures

We presented preliminary results regarding task interest in an earlier short paper [11]. This paper did not report results of the SERP quality manipulation and was instead focused on presenting the method we used to identify and assign search tasks that interested participants, since this is an important methodological concern for IIR researchers. Results show the interest manipulation was successful (Table 1): participants were significantly more interested in tasks they ranked as more interesting, reported significantly higher prior knowledge, relevance and search frequency, and expected these tasks to be significantly less difficult than tasks ranked as less interesting.

Table 1. Means, standard deviations, and paired-sample t-test results of pre-task evaluations, ***p<.001

	Interesting Tasks	Uninteresting Tasks	t-values df=79	Cohen’s d
Interest	4.01 (0.96)	2.77 (1.15)	7.39***	1.17
Prior Knowledge	3.00 (1.13)	2.20 (1.80)	5.27***	0.53
Relevance	3.61 (1.23)	2.24 (1.23)	7.06***	1.11
Search Frequency	2.44 (1.20)	1.64 (0.94)	4.69***	0.74
Difficulty	3.35 (1.15)	3.81 (0.93)	2.72***	0.44

Tables 2 and 3 show participants’ post-task evaluations. Although repeated measures ANOVAs were conducted, there were no significant interaction effects, so we present data in separate tables to simplify the presentation. There were significant main effects for SERP quality for all items lending support that our frustration manipulation was successful. When SERP quality was bad, participants rated tasks as significantly more difficult, rated their skills lower, rated system performance lower and reported less success. There were no significant main effects for task interest and no significant interaction effects.

Table 2. Means, standard deviations, and F-test results of post-task evaluations according to task interest

	Interesting Tasks	Uninteresting Tasks	F-values df=1, 39	η^2
Difficulty	3.61 (0.83)	3.38 (0.89)	1.76	0.04
Skill	3.85 (0.70)	3.62 (0.85)	2.47	0.06
System	3.49 (0.86)	3.35 (1.04)	0.07	<0.01
Success	3.77 (0.69)	3.80 (0.77)	0.03	<0.01

Table 3. Means, standard deviations, and F-test results of post-task evaluations according to SERP quality, ***p<.001

	Bad SERP Quality	Normal SERP Quality	F-values df=1, 39	η^2
Difficulty	3.33 (1.26)	1.66 (0.91)	56.27***	0.59
Skill	3.29 (1.02)	4.19 (0.84)	23.57***	0.37
System	2.49 (1.50)	4.26 (1.19)	43.31***	0.53
Success	3.14 (1.28)	4.44 (0.90)	32.99***	0.46

Participants reported significantly greater felt involvement, focused attention, and novelty when completing interesting tasks (Table 4). When SERP quality was bad, they reported significantly lower perceived usability, felt involvement, and endurability (Table 5). There were no interaction effects.

Table 4. Means, standard deviations, and F-test results of engagement according to task interest, *p<0.05; **p<0.01

	Interesting Tasks	Uninteresting Tasks	F-values df=1, 39	η^2
Perceived Usability	3.63 (0.60)	3.56 (0.79)	0.24	<0.01
Focused Attention	2.87 (0.79)	2.64 (0.66)	7.21**	0.16
Felt Involvement	3.61 (0.50)	3.27 (0.72)	5.35*	0.12
Endurability	3.41 (0.58)	3.20 (0.76)	3.41	0.08
Novelty	3.72 (0.67)	3.09 (0.90)	19.66**	0.34

Table 5. Means, standard deviations, and F-test results of engagement according to SERP quality, **p<0.01; ***p<0.001

	Bad SERP Quality	Normal SERP Quality	F-values df=1, 39	η^2
Perceived Usability	2.93 (1.05)	4.25 (0.82)	56.17***	0.59
Focused Attention	2.73 (0.82)	2.78 (0.85)	0.22	<0.01
Felt Involvement	3.16 (1.00)	3.72 (0.72)	19.87***	0.34
Endurability	2.83 (1.02)	3.78 (0.79)	36.26***	0.48
Novelty	3.15 (1.20)	3.66 (0.97)	8.65**	0.18

Tables 6 and 7 show the results of the frustration and stress scales according to task interest and SERP quality, respectively. There were no differences in participants’ reported frustration or stress according to task interest. Participants reported experiencing significantly more frustration when completing tasks where the SERP quality was bad, suggesting a successful manipulation of frustration. Participants also reported experiencing significantly more distress and overall stress when completing tasks where SERP quality was bad. There were no interaction effects.

Table 6. Means, standard deviations, and F-test results of frustration and stress according to task interest

	Interesting Tasks	Uninteresting Tasks	F-values df=1, 39	η^2
Frustration	2.42 (1.04)	2.52 (0.97)	0.02	0.01
Stress: Distress	1.56 (0.62)	1.60 (0.73)	0.26	0.01
Stress: Worry	1.52 (0.51)	1.50 (0.54)	0.16	<0.01
Stress: Overall	1.55 (0.45)	1.56 (0.53)	0.03	<0.01

Table 7. Means, standard deviations, and F-test results of frustration and stress according to SERP quality, ***p<.001

	Bad SERP Quality	Normal SERP Quality	F-values df=1, 39	η^2
Frustration	3.18 (1.10)	1.75 (0.94)	70.52***	0.97
Stress: Distress	1.58 (0.67)	1.27 (0.47)	34.54***	0.47
Stress: Worry	1.56 (0.56)	1.46 (0.48)	2.35	0.57
Stress: Overall	1.75 (0.50)	1.35 (0.39)	30.18***	0.44

4.2 Search Behaviors

There was no difference in the number of queries submitted by participants for interesting tasks, or in the length of these queries, or number of clicks made per query (Table 8). Participants displayed similar numbers of SERPs, clicked on a similar number of results and saved a similar number of results when completing interesting and uninteresting tasks. There were significantly more scrolls made to SERPs for interesting than uninteresting tasks.

Participants submitted significantly more queries when completing tasks when the SERP quality was bad (Table 9). These queries were significantly shorter and participants made significantly more clicks per query. When the quality was bad, participants displayed significantly more SERPs, clicked more SERPs, made more scrolls and saved fewer results.

Table 8. Means, standard deviations, and F-test results of search behaviors according to task interest, *p<.05

	Interesting Tasks	Uninteresting Tasks	F-values df=1, 39	η^2
Queries Issued	5.65 (4.45)	5.06 (4.13)	0.96	0.02
Query Length	3.50 (1.67)	3.65 (1.79)	0.73	0.02
Clicks per Query	7.77 (4.77)	6.79 (3.97)	2.09	0.05
SERPs Displayed	13.80 (9.16)	12.29 (7.88)	1.83	0.04
SERP Clicks	19.52 (14.30)	17.70 (13.75)	1.39	0.03
SERP Scrolls	31.78 (27.59)	23.02 (18.94)	5.91*	0.13
Pages Saved	3.60 (2.06)	3.42 (1.83)	0.41	0.01

Table 9. Means, standard deviations, and F-test results of search behaviors according to SERP quality, **p<.01, ***p<.001

	Bad SERP Quality	Normal SERP Quality	F-values df=1, 39	η^2
Queries Issued	7.51 (4.66)	3.20 (4.42)	57.18***	0.60
Query Length	3.53 (1.83)	3.62 (1.64)	52.07***	0.57
Clicks per Query	8.27 (5.03)	6.29 (3.42)	11.18***	0.22
SERPs Displayed	15.52 (9.87)	8.56 (5.90)	39.72***	0.50
SERP Clicks	23.04 (15.57)	14.19 (10.66)	21.15**	0.35
SERP Scrolls	41.15 (32.01)	13.66 (14.52)	54.45***	0.58
Pages Saved	3.14 (1.40)	3.88 (2.31)	7.53**	0.16

Participants spent similar amounts of time completing interesting and uninteresting tasks (Table 10). They also spent similar amounts of time per SERP and per document. When completing interesting tasks, participants had significantly greater query intervals, or time between subsequent queries. There were significant main effects for SERP quality for overall time spent and time per SERP (more time for bad SERP quality) (Table 11).

Table 10. Means, standard deviations, and F-test results of time according to task interest, ***p<.001

	Interesting Tasks	Uninterestin g Tasks	F-values df=1, 39	η^2
Time per Task	6.86 (3.84)	5.88 (3.06)	3.66	0.09
Time per SERP	2.04 (1.80)	1.74 (1.30)	2.00	0.05
Time per Doc	2.72 (2.25)	2.33 (1.79)	2.07	0.06
Query Interval	5.02 (3.70)	2.96 (3.57)	19.30***	0.33

Table 11. Means, standard deviations, and F-test results of time according to SERP quality, *p<.01, **p<.001

	Bad SERP Quality	Normal SERP Quality	F-values df=1, 39	η^2
Time per Task	7.11 (3.66)	5.63 (3.17)	7.26*	0.16
Time per SERP	2.71 (1.71)	1.08 (0.84)	56.13**	0.62
Time per Doc	2.66 (2.16)	2.40 (1.91)	0.63	0.02
Query Interval	4.36 (3.95)	3.62 (3.53)	2.91	0.07

4.3 Physiological Measures

Physiological data from 39 participants is reported because of a logging failure. The overall skin conductance values were similar for both task interest and SERP quality (Tables 12 and 13, rows 1 and 2). There were no significant main or interaction effects.

A window analysis was performed by splitting the data along ten-second intervals, and averaging those windows for each participant for each task in an effort to better capture any fluctuations that might happen over time (Tables 12 and 13, rows 3 and 4). This resulted in 42 ten-second-time windows for each task. These windows impose an artificial seven-minute length for each participant, although task times varied; this was done to compare participants for a given time period. There were no significant main effects for skin conductance according to task interest or SERP quality, but there was a significant interaction effect. Post-hoc tests showed participants had the highest skin conductance when conducting interesting tasks with normal SERP quality, the second highest when conducting uninteresting tasks with bad SERP quality. The lowest skin conductance was observed when participants completed uninteresting tasks with normal SERP quality. Participants had significantly higher heart rates for uninteresting tasks and for tasks where bad quality SERPs were presented. There were also significant interaction effects: participants completing interesting tasks with normal SERP quality experienced significantly lower heart rates than any other combination (Table 14, rows 1 and 2).

Skin conductance responses (SCRs) are characterized by an increase in electrodermal response followed by a decrease in response, usually involving an increase of one or more microsiemens [7]. Each participant had between 0 to 15 SCRs per task (Tables 12 and 13, row 5). Participants had significantly more SCRs when completing interesting tasks than uninteresting tasks. They also experienced significantly more SCRs when the SERP quality was bad. There were no interaction effects.

The data were also examined for changes within the first 60 seconds of the task, where the stimulus is likely to have the most dramatic effect [7] (Tables 12 and 13, rows 6 and 7). There was a significant effect for SERP quality, with those receiving normal SERP quality experiencing greater skin conductance. There was also a significant interaction effect, with the highest skin conductance being found for those completing interesting tasks with normal SERP quality and the lowest for those completing interesting tasks with bad SERP quality (Table 14, row 3).

Participants experienced similar heart rates during interesting and uninteresting tasks within the first 60 seconds (Tables 12 and 13, row 7). A significant main effect for SERP quality was found for heart rate in the first 60 seconds, with those experiencing normal SERP quality having slightly higher heart rates. There was also a significant interaction effect, with those completing interesting tasks with normal SERP quality having the highest heart rates and those completing interesting tasks with bad SERP quality the lowest (Table 14).

Table 12. Means, standard deviations, and F-test results of physiological measures according to task interest, *p<.05, ***p<0.001

	Interesting Tasks	Uninteresting Tasks	F-values	η^2
Skin Conduct. (SK)	7.19 (4.57)	7.15 (4.73)	0.02	<0.01
Heart Rate (HR)	79.57 (16.79)	79.88 (16.03)	0.24	0.01
Window SC	7.15 (0.47)	7.03 (0.60)	3.68	0.08
Window HR	77.70 (2.21)	79.36 (1.22)	35.97***	0.47
SK Responses	4.50 (4.18)	3.45 (2.99)	4.12*	0.10
First 60sec SC	7.38 (0.40)	7.39 (0.31)	0.59	0.01
First 60sec HR	80.43 (2.26)	80.17 (1.90)	2.63	0.04

Table 13. Means, standard deviations, and F-test results of physiological measures according to SERP quality, ***p<.001

	Bad SERP Quality	Normal SERP Quality	F-values	η^2
Skin Conduct. (SK)	7.22 (4.52)	7.12 (4.78)	0.12	<0.01
Heart Rate (HR)	79.38 (16.33)	80.07 (16.50)	2.93	0.07
Window SC	7.08 (0.33)	7.10 (0.70)	0.05	<0.01
Window HR	78.75 (1.45)	78.14 (2.33)	9.48***	0.19
SK Responses	4.79 (4.21)	2.91 (2.71)	16.40***	0.30
First 60sec SC	7.20 (0.37)	7.58 (0.40)	128.65***	0.69
First 60sec HR	79.78 (2.26)	80.82 (1.77)	27.56***	0.32

Table 14. Interaction effects for physiological measures, *p<0.05, ***p<.001

	SERP Quality	Interesting	Uninteresting	F-values (η^2)
Window SC	Bad	7.04 (0.37)	7.11 (0.28)	14.45***
	Normal	7.26 (0.53)	6.94 (0.80)	(0.26)
Window HR	Bad	78.42 (1.64)	79.34 (1.05)	29.12***
	Normal	76.97 (2.48)	79.37 (1.38)	(0.41)
First 60sec SC	Bad	6.96 (0.32)	7.43 (0.23)	156.41***
	Normal	7.80 (0.29)	7.36 (0.36)	(0.73)
First 60sec HR	Bad	80.14 (2.66)	79.42 (1.72)	4.26*
	Normal	80.72 (1.76)	80.92 (1.78)	(0.07)

4.3.1 Multilevel models of physiological data

A mixed-effects multilevel growth model was performed to further investigate the relationship and variation between skin conductance, heart rate, interest and frustration. Growth models are a type of multilevel modeling predicated on time-ordered data. These models are especially suited for modeling physiological data (such as the ones gathered in this experiment) over time [7]. In this experimental setup, interest, frustration, and task order are fixed effects, while task time is a random effect. The coefficients of these effects essentially represent values by which skin conductance and heart rate can be predicted. Tables 15 and 16 detail the models of skin conductance and heart rate, respectively. A log likelihood ratio, or "L-ratio" was computed for each model. Log likelihood refers to the log taken of the "likelihood" score produced by the model, which serves as an indication of the probability of the observed values given certain parameters. In multilevel modeling, log likelihood scores are compared to test for significant differences. Thus, the L-ratio represents a test statistic by which significance is determined.

The best fitting model for skin conductance was Model 3, which only had interest and frustration as fixed effects. Model 3, when examined, showed a significant effect for interest, while there was no significant effect for frustration. The best fitting model for heart rate was the model with interest, frustration, and task order (Table 16). In the 3rd and 4th models, interest was non-significant while frustration was significant, indicating that frustration contributed more to heart rate than interest. In the 4th model for heart rate, task order also significantly contributed to the model.

Table 15. Models of skin conductance data, *p<0.05

Model	Fixed Effects	Random Effects	Coefficients	L-ratio
1	Interest (I)	Task Time	-0.51	3.45
2	Frustration (F)		-0.10	
3	Interest + Frustration		I: -0.63* F: -0.26	4.59
4	Interest + Frustration + Task Order (TO)		I: -0.59 F: -0.26 TO: -0.19	3.56

Table 16. Models of heart rate data, *p<0.05

Model	Fixed Effects	Random Effect	Coefficients	L-ratio
1	Interest (I)	Task Time	0.32	0.61
2	Frustration (F)		-0.70	
3	Interest + Frustration		I: 0.15 F: -0.67*	1.20
4	Interest + Frustration + Task Order (TO)		I: 0.24 F: -0.72* TO: -1.08	4.89

5 DISCUSSION

The goal of this study was to investigate the differences in search behaviors and physiologies of participants when they are engaged or frustrated during online information search. This study was motivated by previous findings that seemingly contradicted one another: in some cases, increases in search behaviors such as clicking, querying and time spent, have been associated with engagement, while in other studies, these same measures have been associated with constructs such as frustration. While there has been some work integrating physiological measures into the study of engagement and frustration, to our knowledge there has been no study which has examined how the combination of physiological signals, search behaviors and self-report measures can potentially be used to distinguish between engaging and frustrating search experiences. This study was also novel in that it studied engagement and frustration simultaneously, and within the same participant. There were a number of significant results, which we summarize and discuss below. Importantly, many of the results had strong effect sizes.

Our study rested on our being able to induce engagement and frustration in a laboratory setting. Both the engagement and frustration manipulations were successful, and one contribution of this study is the method used to induce interest and frustration in the laboratory, which could be used by other IIR researchers. Participants reported significantly greater interest in, prior knowledge of, and relevance of tasks they ranked as more interesting than those they ranked as less interesting. They also indicated they had searched more frequently in the past for tasks they ranked as more interesting, and expected to experience significantly greater difficulty when completing less interesting tasks, although their post-search ratings showed no significant differences in experienced difficulty. There were also no differences in participants' post-search ratings of their own skills completing tasks, the system's ability to complete tasks, and their overall success with each task. These results provide support for the method used to induce interest and also show that participants' prior interest in a task may not have a strong impact on their perceived abilities to successfully complete the task in a laboratory setting. There were also no differences in the levels of frustration and stress reported by participants, which provides evidence that task interest may not be related to these affective components of search.

There were significant differences in participants' ratings of three of the five user engagement subscales, with participants reporting greater focused attention, felt involvement and novelty when searching for tasks they had previously ranked as more interesting. There were no differences in perceived usability, which is not surprising since the system components were stable (i.e., there were equal numbers of instances of poor and normal search quality for each of the interesting and uninteresting tasks). The lack of significant results regarding endurability suggest a person's lasting impression of a system might be more greatly impacted by factors other than task interest. Overall, however, these results support the idea that task interest is an important component of engagement, especially regarding dimensions that are more related to cognitive absorption, and that task interest can have a positive influence on the extent to which a person becomes engaged during search, which is consistent with, and extends, past research [9]. Researchers wishing to induce engagement in laboratory settings might continue to explore how interest can be exploited. Of course, one potential risk of allowing participates to pre-select tasks that interest them is a skew towards particular tasks. In this study, online communication was the most popular task, while vehicle purchasing and tattoo removal were the least popular tasks. The over- and under-representation of tasks can complicate data analysis and may impact the generalizability of the results.

Our manipulation of frustration was also successful. Participants reported significantly higher levels of frustration during search tasks with bad SERP quality, as well as significantly more distress and overall stress. There was no difference in the level of worry reported between groups, which suggests that while participants might have become frustrated and distressed during search episodes, they did not find their experiences worrisome. This could be a limitation of measuring these constructs in a laboratory setting – in real world search situations, a person might find bad SERP results more worrisome.

Other post-search ratings also provide evidence that the frustration manipulation was successful. When completing tasks where poor results were presented, participants rated the tasks as significantly more difficult, rated their skill and the system’s ability as significantly worse, and reported significantly less task success. Finally, the user engagement ratings provide evidence of how frustration impacts a participant’s experiences: felt involvement, perceived usability and endurability were all rated significantly lower when poor search results were presented.

There were no significant differences between interesting and uninteresting tasks for nearly all measures of search behavior, with the exception of scrolls on the SERP and query intervals. The increased amount of scrolling on SERPs when conducting interesting tasks could reflect increased scrutiny of the search results. The significant main effect for time between queries also suggests that participants cognitively, rather than physically, engaged more with search results for tasks they found interesting (this time includes both time viewing SERPs and time examining documents).

While participants generally issued more queries, made more clicks, displayed more SERPs, and spent longer amounts of time when completing tasks that interested them, most of these differences were not significant. These negative results potentially have implications for the design of IIR studies where search tasks are assigned. A typical concern when assigning search tasks is that participants might exhibit different amounts of effort depending on motivation and interest. In this study, interest did not have a huge impact on user effort, at least as measured by things such as clicks, queries and time. However, we did not explicitly measure motivation and it might be that this has a larger impact on effort than interest, and that the relationship among motivation, interest and effort in laboratory studies is complicated and in need of further study.

There were a number of significant differences in participant search behaviors based on the quality of the search results. When presented with bad SERP quality (when participants were frustrated), participants submitted significantly more queries, made more clicks per query, displayed more SERPs, made more clicks on the SERP, made more scrolls and saved fewer documents. Most of these differences were quite strong, suggesting that physical measures of effort might provide greater evidence of frustration, rather than engagement. Participants also spent significantly more time completing tasks and more time per SERP, but they did not spend more time per document or more time between queries, which continues to support the notion that these measures might be better indicators of engagement. These findings complement other work on engagement and frustration in that they support findings such as the relationship between engagement and dwell time [15] and Feild et al.’s [13] finding that frustrated participants exhibit periods of high search activity.

With respect to the physiological measures, there were no differences in overall skin conductance or heart rate according to whether the task was interesting or not, or according to the quality of the search results. However, an examination of the data at different levels of granularity (window analysis) and at different points in time (first 60 seconds) did reveal several interaction effects for both skin conductance and heart rate. Participants had the highest skin conductance when completing interesting tasks with normal SERP quality, which suggests participants experienced some positive arousal in this condition since they did not self-report frustration or stress during these tasks. Participants in this condition also experienced greater skin conductance in the first 60 seconds of the search. The lowest skin conductance was exhibited by participants conducting uninteresting tasks with normal SERP quality, which further shows that the participant’s level of task interest is what caused the positive arousal. Interestingly, the second highest skin conductance was exhibited by participants completing uninteresting tasks with poor SERP quality, which also suggests heightened arousal, only in this case it can be interpreted as negative when combined with the self-report data.

Participants completing uninteresting tasks had the highest heart rates, and those conducting interesting tasks with normal SERP quality has the lowest rates, which suggests that heart rate might be more associated with negative arousal, while skin conductance with positive arousal. The results of the multilevel modeling further support this: task interest provided the best predictor of variations in skin conductance, while frustration provided the best predictor of variations in heart rate.

6 CONCLUSIONS

This research offers insight into the utility of physiological signals in search evaluation, and provides evidence about the relationships between search behaviors, engagement and frustration. Specifically, it demonstrated the successful induction of engagement and frustration via experimental manipulation, as well as a novel approach to understanding competing emotional states present within the same participant. It also showed that physiological signals can be difficult to use as tools of disambiguation when examined during emotional states with high arousal. Lastly, it demonstrated that increased search behaviors were stronger indicators of frustration rather than interest. Other studies have characterized both engagement and frustration by an increase in search behaviors, and this research, through its linkage of subjective evaluation and search behaviors, clarifies some of the intricacies of these relationships.

This work is well situated among other work that has incorporated physiological signals in measuring subjective experience as well as objective measures such as search behavior [6]. It has confirmed that physiological signals can be useful as indicators of engagement, though their interpretation and application must be carefully handled. Other studies have characterized both engagement and frustration by an increase in search behaviors [15], and this research, through its linkage of subjective evaluation and search behaviors, helps clarify the intricacies of these relationships. The utility of the other physiological measures in discrimination is unclear, and it is also unclear how interest and frustration combine to produce particular levels of arousal. It is possible that task interest creates a more pronounced response early in the session, and then as a person becomes frustrated, responses associated with this emotion begin to dominate.

This work also poses several questions, in particular: what advantage does disambiguating engagement and frustration offer? Both states could signal a need for customized search experiences, so characterizing these states in the context of behavior and tasks is the first step in deciding whether to intervene. Future work could include trying to identify a threshold over which participants pass from being engaged to unengaged, or frustrated to not frustrated. There also may be other ways to disambiguate engagement and frustration, such as incorporating more physiological signals to create a more comprehensive model of user state, or encouraging greater engagement in the laboratory by having participants bring in genuine tasks.

ACKNOWLEDGMENTS

This work was conducted when the first author was a doctoral student at the University of North Carolina at Chapel Hill. The authors wish to thank Ioannis Arapakis, Jaime Arguello, Rob Capra and Heather O’Brien for their feedback on this work as members of the first author’s dissertation committee. The authors also wish to thank the School of Information and Library Science at UNC for its support of this research.

REFERENCES

[1] Abram Amsel. 1958. The role of frustrative nonreward in noncontinuous reward situations. Psychological bulletin, 55, 102-119.

[2] Ioannis Arapakis, Joemon Jose, and Phillip D. Gray. 2008. Affective feedback: an investigation into the role of emotions in the information seeking process. In Proceedings SIGIR, 395-402.

[3] Ioannis Arapakis, Mounia Lalmas, George Valkanas. 2014. Understanding within-content engagement through pattern analysis of mouse gestures. In Proceedings CIKM, 1439-1448.

[4] Ioannis Arapakis, Ioannis Konstas, and Joemon Jose. 2009. Using facial expressions and peripheral physiological signals as implicit indicators of topical relevance. In Proceedings of ACM Multimedia, 461-470.

[5] Anne Aula, R.M. Khan, Zhiwei Guan. 2010. How does search behavior change as search becomes more difficult? In Proceedings of SIGCHI, 35-44.

[6] Miguel Barreda-é ngeles, Ioannis Arapakis, I., Xiao Bai, B. Barla Cambazoglu, and Alexandre Pereda-Ba`os. 2015. Unconscious Physiological Effects of Search Latency on Users and Their Click Behaviour. In Proceedings of SIGIR, 203-212.

[7] Wolfram Boucsein. 2012. Electrodermal activity. Springer Science and Business Media.

[8] Jason J. Braithwaite, Derrick G. Watson, Robert Jones, Mickey Rowe. 2013. A Guide for Analysing Electrodermal Activity (EDA) & Skin Conductance Responses (SCRs) for Psychological Experiments. In Psychophysiology, 49, 1017-1034.

[9] Mihaly Csikszentmihalyi. 2014. Flow. In Flow and the Foundations of Positive Psychology, 227-238.

[10] Georges Dupret and Mounia Lalmas. 2013. Absence time and user engagement: evaluating ranking functions. In Proceedings of WSDM, 173-182.

[11] Ashlee Edwards and Diane Kelly. How does interest in a work task impact search behavior and engagement? 2016. In CHIIR 2016, 249-252.

[12] Ashlee Edwards, Diane Kelly, and Leif Azzopardi 2015. The impact of query interface design on stress, workload and performance. In Advances in Information Retrieval, 691-702.

[13] Henry A. Field, James Allan, and Rosie Jones. 2010. Predicting searcher frustration. In Proceedings of SIGIR, 34-41.

[14] Joseph F. Grafsgaard, Joseph B. Wiggins, Kristy Elizabeth Boyer, Eric N. Wiebe, and James Lester. 2013. Automatically recognizing facial expression: Predicting engagement and frustration. In Educational Data Mining 2013, 8 pages.

[15] Ahmed Hassan, Ryen W. White, Susan Dumais, and Yi-Min Wang. 2014. Struggling or exploring?: disambiguating long search sessions. In Proceedings of WSDM, 53-62.

[16] William S. Helton. 2004. Validation of a short stress state questionnaire. In Proceedings of the Human Factors and Ergonomics Society Annual Meeting, 1238-1242.

[17] Diane Kelly, Jaime Arguello, Ashlee Edwards, and Wan-Ching Wu. 2015. Development and evaluation of search tasks for IIR experiments using a cognitive complexity framework. In Proceedings of ICTIR, 101-110.

[18] Richard S. Lazarus and Susan Folkman. 1984. Stress, appraisal, and coping. New York: Springer Pub. Co.

[19] Janette Lehman, Mounia Lalmas, Ricardo Baeza-Yates, and Elad Yom-Tov. 2013. Networked user engagement. In Proceedings of the 1st Workshop on User Engagement Optimization, 7-10.

[20] Janette Lehmann, Mounia Lalmas, Georges Dupret, and Ricardo Baeza-Yates. 2013. Online multitasking and user engagement. In Proceedings of CIKM, 519-528.

[21] Janette Lehmann, Mounias Lalmas, Elad Yom-Tov, and Georges Dupret. 2012. Models of user engagement. In User Modeling, Adaptation, and Personalization, 164-175.

[22] Yashar Moshfeghi, and Joemon Jose. 2013. An effective implicit relevance feedback technique using affective, physiological and behavioural features. In Proceedings of SIGIR, 133-142.

[23] Lise Solberg Nes, Suzanne C. Segerstrom, and Sandra E. Sephton. 2005. Engagement and arousal: Optimism’s effects during a brief stressor. In Personality and Social Psychology Bulletin, 31, 111-120.

[24] Heather L. O’Brien and Maria Lebow. 2013. Mixed-methods approach to measuring user experience in online news interactions. In JASIST, 64, 1543-1556.

[25] Heather L. O’Brien and Elaine G. Toms. 2008. What is user engagement? A conceptual framework for defining user engagement with technology. In JASIST, 59, 938-955.

[26] Heather L. O’Brien and Elaine G. Toms. 2013. Examining the generalizability of the User Engagement Scale (UES) in exploratory search. In IP&M, 49, 1092-1107.

[27] Adan Ortiz-Cordova and Bernard J. Jansen. 2012. Classifying web search queries to identify high revenue generating customers. In JASIST, 63, 1426-1441.

[28] Lawrence H. Peters and Edward J O’Connor. 1980. Situational constraints and work outcomes: The influences of a frequently overlooked construct. In Academy of Management Review, 5, 391-397.

[29] Jocelyn Scheirer, Raul Fernandez, Jonathan Klein, Rosalind W. Picard. 2002. Frustrating the user on purpose: a step toward building an affective computer. In Interacting with Computers, 14, 93-118.

A Study of Snippet Length and Informativeness

Behaviour, Performance and User Experience

David Maxwell
School of Computing Science
University of Glasgow
Glasgow, Scotland
d.maxwell.1@research.gla.ac.uk

Leif Azzopardi
Computer & Information Sciences
University of Strathclyde
Glasgow, Scotland
leif.azzopardi@strath.ac.uk

Yashar Moshfeghi
School of Computing Science
University of Glasgow
Glasgow, Scotland
Yashar.Moshfeghi@glasgow.ac.uk

ABSTRACT

The design and presentation of a *Search Engine Results Page (SERP)* has been subject to much research. With many contemporary aspects of the SERP now under scrutiny, work still remains in investigating more traditional SERP components, such as the *result summary*. Prior studies have examined a variety of different aspects of result summaries, but in this paper we investigate the influence of result summary length on search behaviour, performance and user experience. To this end, we designed and conducted a within-subjects experiment using the *TREC AQUAINT* news collection with 53 participants. Using *Kullback-Leibler distance* as a measure of *information gain*, we examined result summaries of different lengths and selected four conditions where the change in information gain was the greatest: *(i)* title only; *(ii)* title plus one snippet; *(iii)* title plus two snippets; and *(iv)* title plus four snippets. Findings show that participants broadly preferred longer result summaries, as they were perceived to be more informative. However, their performance in terms of correctly identifying relevant documents was similar across all four conditions. Furthermore, while the participants felt that longer summaries were more informative, empirical observations suggest otherwise; while participants were more likely to click on relevant items given longer summaries, they also were more likely to click on non-relevant items. This shows that longer is not necessarily better, though participants perceived that to be the case – and second, they reveal a positive relationship between the length and informativeness of summaries and their attractiveness (i.e. clickthrough rates). These findings show that there are tensions between perception and performance when designing result summaries that need to be taken into account.

CCS CONCEPTS

•Information systems →Search interfaces;

ACM Reference format:
David Maxwell, Leif Azzopardi, and Yashar Moshfeghi. 2017. A Study of Snippet Length and Informativeness. In *Proceedings of SIGIR '17, August 07-11, 2017, Shinjuku, Tokyo, Japan*, , 10 pages.
DOI: http://dx.doi.org/10.1145/3077136.3080824

978-1-4503-5022-8/17/08...$15.00
DOI: http://dx.doi.org/10.1145/3077136.3080824

1 INTRODUCTION

Interactive Information Retrieval (IIR) is a complex, non-trivial process where a searcher undertakes a variety of different actions during a search session [16]. Core to their experience and success is the *Search Engine Results Page (SERP)*, with its presentation and design over the years having been subject to much research. With more complex components now becoming commonplace in modern day Web search engines (such as the *information card* [5, 36] or *social annotations* [35]), much work however still remains on examining how more traditional SERP components (such as *result summaries*) are designed and presented to end users.

Result summaries have traditionally been viewed as the *'ten blue links'* with the corresponding URL of the associated document, and one or more textual *snippets* of *keywords-in-context* from the document itself, approximately 130-150 characters (or two lines) in length [15]. Numerous researchers have explored result summaries in a variety of different ways, such as: examining their length [11, 19, 38]; the use of thumbnails [47, 52]; their attractiveness [9, 14]; and the generation of *query-biased snippets* [41, 48]. The performance of users has broadly been evaluated in a limited fashion (e.g. by examining task completion times). In this work, we are interested in how the length and information content of result summaries affects SERP interactions and a user's ability to select relevant over non-relevant items. Prior research has demonstrated that longer result summaries tend to lower completion times for informational tasks (where users need to find one relevant document) [11], but does this hold in other contexts, specifically for ad-hoc retrieval, where users need to find *several* relevant items? Furthermore, how does the length and information associated with longer result summaries affect the user's ability to discern the relevant from the non-relevant?

This work therefore serves as an investigation into the effects of search behaviour and search performance when we vary *(i)* result summary snippet lengths, and by doing so *(ii)* the information content within the summaries. To this end, a within-subjects crowdsourced experiment (n = 53) was designed and conducted. Under ad-hoc topic retrieval, participants used four different search interfaces, each with a different size of result summary. Findings allow us to address the two main research questions of this study. ***RQ1*** How does the value of information gain represented as snippet length affect behaviour, performance and user experience? ***RQ2*** Does information gain – again represented as snippet length – affect the decision making ability and accuracy (identifying relevant documents) of users? We hypothesise that longer and more informative snippets will enable users to make better quality decisions (i.e. higher degrees of accurately identifying relevant content).

2 RELATED WORK

As previously mentioned, the design and presentation of SERPs has been examined in depth. Researchers have examined various aspects of SERPs, and how the designs of such aspects influence the behaviour of users. Here, we provide a summary of the various aspects that have been investigated. Specifically, we focus upon: the layout of SERPs; the size of SERPs; how snippet text is generated; and how much text should be presented within each result summary – the latter being the main focus of this work.

2.1 SERP Layouts and Presentation

Early works regarding the presentation of result summaries [6, 12] examined approaches to automatically categorise result summaries for users, similar to the categorisation approach employed by early search engines. Chen and Dumais [6] developed an experimental system that automatically categorised result summaries on-the-fly as they were generated. For a query, associated categories were then listed as verticals, with associated document titles provided underneath each category header. Traditional result summaries were then made available when hovering over a document title. Subjects of a user study found the interface easier to use than the traditional 'ten blue links' approach - they were 50% faster at finding information displayed in categories. This work was then extended by Dumais et al. [12], where they explored the use of hover text to present additional details about search results based upon user interaction. Searching was found to be slower with hover text, perhaps due to the fact that explicit decisions about when to seek additional information (or not to) were required.

Alternatives to the traditional, linear list of result summaries have also been trialled (like grid-based layouts [8, 20, 40]). For example, Krammerer and Beinhaur [20] examined differences in user behaviour when interacting with a standard list interface, compared against a tabular interface (title, snippet and URL stacked horizontally in three columns for each result), and a grid-based layout (result summaries placed in three columns). Users of the grid layout spent more time examining result summaries. The approach demonstrated promise in overcoming issues such as *position bias* [10], as observed by Joachims et al. [17].

Marcos et al. [34] performed an eye-tracking user study examining the effect of user behaviour while interacting with SERPs – and whether the *richness* of result summaries provided on a SERP (i.e. result summaries enriched with metadata from corresponding pages) impacted upon the user's search experience. Enriched summaries were found to help capture a user's attention. Including both textual and visual representations of a document when presenting results could have a positive effect on relevance assessment and query reformulation [18]. Enriched summaries were also examined by Ali et al. [2] in the context of navigational tasks. Striking a good balance between textual and visual cues were shown to better support user tasks, and search completion time.

2.2 Generating Snippet Text

Users can be provided with an insight by result summaries as to whether a document is likely to be relevant or not [14]. Consequently, research has gone into examining different kinds of snippets, and how long a snippet should be. Work initially focused upon how these summaries should be generated [30, 31, 39, 48, 51]. These early works proposed the idea of summarising documents with respect to the query (query-biased summaries) or keywords-in-context – as opposed to simply extracting the representative or lead sentences from the document [29]. Tombros and Sanderson [48] showed that subjects of their study were likely to identify relevant documents more accurately when using query-biased summaries, compared to summaries simply generated from the first few sentences of a given document. Query-biased summaries have also been recently shown to be preferred on mobile devices [45].

When constructing snippets using query-biased summaries, Rose et al. [41] found that a user's perceptions of the result's quality were influenced by the snippets. If snippets contained truncated sentences or many fragmented sentences *(text choppiness)*, users perceived the quality of the results more negatively, regardless of length. Kanungo and Orr [21] found that poor readability also impacts upon how the resultant snippets are perceived. They maintain that readability is a crucial presentation attribute that needs to be considered when generating a query-biased summary. Clarke et al. [9] analysed thousands of pairs of snippets where result A appeared before result B, but result B received more clicks than result A. As an example, they found results with snippets which were very short (or missing entirely) had fewer query terms, were not as readable, and attracted fewer clicks. This led to the formulation of several heuristics relating to document surrogate features, designed to emphasise the relationship between the associated page and generated snippet. Heuristics included: *(i)* ensuring that all query terms in the generated snippet (where possible); *(ii)* withholding the repeating of query terms in the snippet if they were present in the page's title; and *(iii)* displaying (shortened) readable URLs.

Recent work has examined the generation of snippets from more complex angles – from manipulating underlying indexes [4, 49] to language modelling [14, 32], as well as using user search data to improve the generation process [1, 42]. Previous generation approaches also may not consider what parts of a document searchers actually find useful. Ageev et al. [1] incorporated into a new model post-click searcher behaviour data, such as mouse cursor movements and scrolling over documents, producing *behaviour-biased snippets*. Results showed a marked improvement over a strong text-based snippet generation baseline. Temporal aspects have also been considered – Svore et al. [46] conducted a user study, showing that users preferred snippet text with *trending* content in snippets when searching for trending queries, but not so for general queries.

2.3 Results per Page

Today, a multitude of devices are capable of accessing the *World Wide Web (WWW)* – along with a multitude of different screen resolutions and aspect ratios. The question of how many result summaries should be displayed per page – *or results per page (RPP)* – therefore becomes hugely important, yet increasingly difficult to answer. Examining behavioural effects on mobile devices when interacting with SERPs has attracted much research as of late (e.g. [24–26]), and with each device capable of displaying a different number of results *above-the-fold*, recent research has shown that the RPP value can influence the behaviour of searchers [17, 25]. Understanding this behaviour can help guide and inform those charged with designing contemporary user interfaces.

In a Google industry report, Linden [33] however stated that users desired more than 10RPP, despite the fact that increasing the RPP yielded a 20% drop in traffic; it was hypothesised that this was due to the extra time required to dispatch the longer SERPs. This drop however be attributed to other reasons. Oulasvirta et al. [37] discusses the *paradox of choice* [43] in the context of search, where more options (results) – particularly if highly relevant – will lead to poorer choice and degrade user satisfaction. In terms of user satisfaction, modern search engines can therefore be a victim of their own success, presenting users with *choice overload*. Oulasvirta et al. [37] found that presenting users with a six-item search result list was associated with higher degrees of satisfaction, confidence with choices and perceived carefulness than an a list of 24 items.

Kelly and Azzopardi [22] broadly agreed with the findings by Oulasvirta et al. [37]. Here, the authors conducted a between-subjects study with three conditions, where subjects were assigned to one of three interfaces - the baseline interface, showing 10RPP (the 'ten blue links'), and two interfaces displaying 3RPP and 6RPP respectively. Their findings showed that individuals using the 3RPP and 6RPP interfaces spent significantly longer examining top-ranking results and were more likely to click on higher ranked documents than those on the 10RPP interface. Findings also suggested that subjects using the interfaces showing fewer RPP found it comparatively easier to find relevant content than those using the 10RPP interface. However, no significant difference was found between the number of relevant items found across the interfaces. Currently, 10RPP is still considered the *de-facto* standard [15].

2.4 Snippet Lengths: Longer or Shorter?

Snippet lengths have been examined in a variety of ways. A user study by Paek et al. [38] compared a user's preference and usability against three different interfaces for displaying result summaries. With question answering tasks, the interfaces: displayed a *normal* SERP (i.e. a two line snippet for each summary, with a clickable link); an *instant* interface, where an expanded snippet was displayed upon clicking it; and a *dynamic* interface, where hovering the cursor would trigger the expanded snippet. The instant view was shown to allow users to complete the given tasks in less time than the normal baseline, with half of participants preferring this approach.

Seminal work by Cutrell and Guan [11] explored the effect of different snippet lengths (*short*: 1 line, *medium*: 2-3 lines; and *long*: 6-7 lines). They found that longer snippets significantly improved performance for *informational tasks* (e.g. `'Find the address for Newark Airport.'`). Users performed better for informational queries as snippet length increased. This work was followed up by Kaisser et al. [19]. They conducted two experiments that estimated the preferred snippet length according to answer type (e.g. finding a person, time, or place), and comparing the results of the preferred snippet lengths to users' preferences to see if this could be predicted. The preferred snippet length was shown to depend upon the type of answer expected, with greater user satisfaction shown for the snippet length predicted by their technique.

More contemporary work has begun to examine what snippet sizes are appropriate for mobile devices. Given smaller screen sizes, this is important – snippet text considered acceptable on a computer screen may involve considerable scrolling/swiping on a smaller screen. Kim et al. [27] found that subjects using longer snippets on mobile devices exhibited longer search times and similar search accuracy under informational tasks[1]. Longer reading times and frequent scrolling/swiping (with more viewport movements) were exhibited. Longer snippets did not therefore appear to be very useful on a small screen – an *instant* or *dynamic* snippet approach (as per Paek et al. [38]) may be useful for mobile search, too.

The presentation of result summaries has a strong effect on the ability of a user to judge relevancy [14]. Relevant documents may be overlooked due to uninformative summaries – but conversely, non-relevant documents may be examined due to a misleading summary. However, longer summaries also increase the examination cost, so there is likely a trade-off between informativeness/accuracy and length/cost. The current, widely accepted standard for result summaries are two query-based snippets/lines [15]. This work examines whether increasing and decreasing the length (and consequently the informativeness) of result summary snippets affects user accuracy and costs of relevance decisions in the context of ad-hoc topic search, where multiple relevant documents are sought.

3 EXPERIMENTAL METHOD

To address our two key research questions outlined in Section 1, we conducted a within-subjects experiment. This allowed us to explore the influence of snippet length and snippet informativeness on search behaviours, performance and user experience. Subjects used four different search interfaces, each of which varied the way in which result summaries were presented to them.

To decide the length and informativeness of the result summaries, we performed a preliminary analysis to determine the average length (in words) and informativeness (as calculated by the *Kullback-Leibler distance* [28] to measure *information gain*, or *relative entropy*) of result summaries with the title and varying numbers of snippet fragments (0–10). The closer the entropy value is to zero, the more information gained. Figure 1 plots the number of words, the information gain, and the information gain per word[2]. It is clear from the plot that a higher level of information gain was present in longer snippets. However, as the length increases with each additional snippet fragment added, the informativeness per word decreased. Consequently, for this study, we selected the four different interface conditions in the region where informativeness had the highest change, i.e. from zero to four. The conditions we selected for the study were therefore:

- ***T0*** where only the title for each result summary were presented;
- ***T1*** where for each result summary, a title and one query-biased snippet fragment were presented;
- ***T2*** where a title and two query-biased snippet fragments were presented; and
- ***T4*** where a title and four query-biased snippet fragments were presented,

where our independent variable is snippet informativeness, controlled by the length. Figure 2 provides an example of the different

[1]The tasks considered by Kim et al. [27] were similar to those defined by Cutrell and Guan [11], where a single relevant document was sought.

[2]To obtain these values, we submitted over 300 queries from a previous study (refer to Azzopardi et al. [3]) conducted on similar topics and on the same collection to the search system that we used.

result summaries in each condition. The remainder of this section details our methodology for this experiment, including a discussion of: the corpus, topics and system used (Subsection 3.1); how we generated snippets (Subsection 3.2); the behaviours we logged (Subsection 3.3); how we obtained the opinions of subjects regarding their experience (Subsection 3.4); and further details on our study, including measures taken for quality control (Subsection 3.5).

3.1 Corpus, Search Topics and System

For this experiment, we used the TREC AQUAINT test collection. Using a traditional test collection provided us with the ability to easily evaluate the performance of subjects. The collection contains over one million newspaper articles from the period 1996-2000. Articles were gathered from three newswires: the *Associated Press (AP)*; the *New York Times (NYT)*; and *Xinhua*.

We then selected a total of five topics from the *TREC 2005 Robust Track*, as detailed by Voorhees [50]. The topics selected were: № 341 *(Airport Security)*; № 347 *(Wildlife Extinction)*; № 367 *(Piracy)*; № 408 *(Tropical Storms)*; and № 435 *(Curbing Population Growth)*. We selected topic № 367 as a practice topic so that subjects could familiarise themselves with the system. These topics were chosen based upon evidence from a previous user study with a similar setup, where it was shown that the topics were of similar difficulty [23]. For each subject, the remaining four topics were assigned to an interface (one of ***T0***, ***T1***, ***T2*** or ***T4***) using a Latin-square rotation.

To ground the search tasks, subjects of the experiment were instructed to imagine that they were newspaper reporters, and were required to gather documents to write stories about the provided topics. Subjects were told to find as many relevant documents as they could during the allotted time, which was 10 minutes per topic – hereafter referred to as a *search session*. With the traditional components of a SERP, such as the query box and result summaries present (refer to Figure 3), subjects were instructed to mark documents they considered relevant by clicking on the `'Mark as Relevant'` button within the document view – accessed by clicking on a result summary he or she thought was relevant. Coupled with a two minute period to familiarise themselves with the system (using topic № 367), subjects spent approximately 45-50 minutes undertaking the complete experiment when pre- and post-task surveys were accounted for.

For the underlying search engine, we used the *Whoosh Information Retrieval (IR)* toolkit [3]. We used BM25 as the retrieval algorithm ($b = 0.75$), but with an implicit ANDing of query terms to restrict the set of retrieved documents to only those that contained all the query terms provided. This was chosen as most search systems implicitly AND terms together.

3.2 Snippet Generation

For interfaces ***T2*** and ***T4***, each result summary presented to the subjects required one or more textual snippets from the corresponding document. These snippet fragments were query-biased [48], and were generated by scoring sentences according to BM25 and selecting fragments from those sentences. Fragments were then extracted

[3]Whoosh can be accessed at https://pypi.python.org/pypi/Whoosh/.

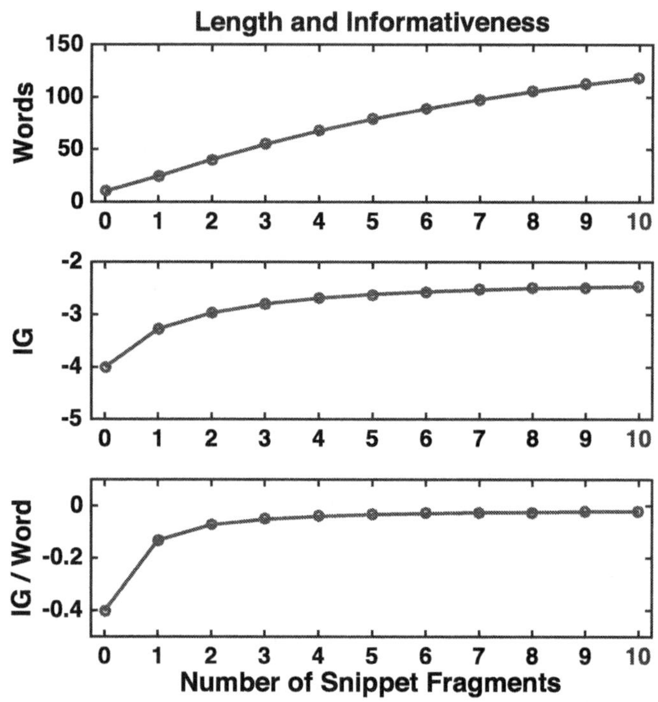

Figure 1: Plots showing the length (in words), informativeness (in information gain, *IG*) and the information gain *(IG)* per word for title, plus 0 to 10 snippets. The closer the value is to zero, the more information that is gained.

from the ordered series of sentences, by identifying query terms within those sentences with a window of 40 characters from either side of the term. Figure 2 provides a complete, rendered example of the result summaries generated by each of the four interfaces. Each result summary contains a document title, a newswire source (acting as a replacement for a document URL), and, if required, one or more textual snippets.

3.3 Behaviours Logged

In order for us to address our research questions, our experimental system was required to log a variety of behavioural attributes for each subject as they performed the variety of actions that take place during a search session. Search behaviours were operationalised over three types of measures: *(i)* interaction, *(ii)* performance, and *(iii)* the time spent undertaking various search activities. All behavioural data was extracted from the log data produced by our system, and from the TREC 2005 Robust Track QRELs [50]. All data was recorded with the interface and topic combination used by the subject at the given time.

Interaction measures included the number of queries issued, the number of documents viewed, the number of SERPs viewed, and the greatest depths in the SERPs to which subjects clicked on – and hovered over – result summaries.

Performance measures included a count of the documents marked as relevant by the subject, the number of documents marked that were also TREC relevant – as well as TREC non-relevant, and *P@k*

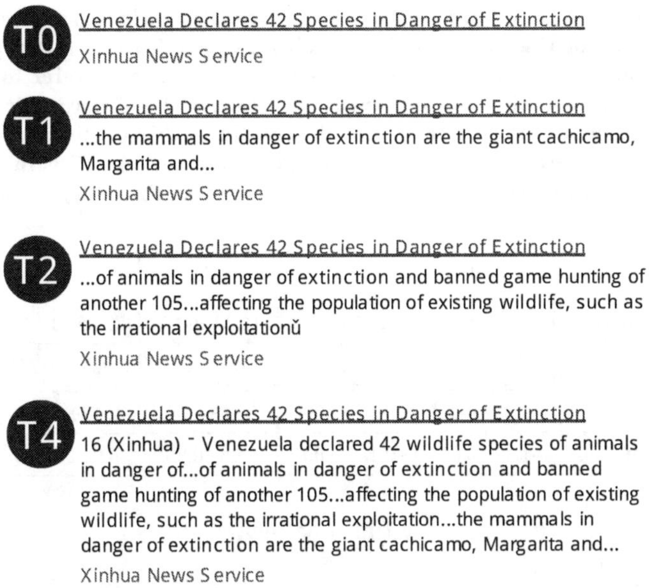

Figure 2: Examples of the result summaries generated by each of the four interfaces used in this study. The same document above is used – with the circle denoting what interface is being shown (of *T0*, *T1*, *T2* or *T4*). Each of the result summaries consists of a title (in blue, underlined), none, one or more snippet fragments (in black, with fragments separated by ellipses), and a newswire source (in green).

measurements for the performance of the subject's issued queries for a range of rankings.

Time-Based measures included the time spent issuing queries, examining SERPs – as well as examining result summaries[4] – and the time spent examining documents. All of these times added together yielded the total search session time, which elapsed once 10 minutes had been reached.

From this raw data, we could then produce summaries of a search session, producing summarising measures such as the number of documents examined by searchers per query that they issued. We could also calculate from the log data probabilities of interaction, including a given subject's probability of clicking a result summary link, given that it was TREC relevant ($P(C|R)$) or TREC non-relevant ($P(C|N)$) – or the probability of marking a document that was clicked, given it was either TREC relevant ($P(M|R)$) or TREC non-relevant ($P(M|N)$). Actions such as hover depth over result summaries were inferred from the movement of the mouse cursor, which in prior studies has been shown to correlate strongly with the user's gaze on the screen [7, 44].

3.4 Capturing User Experiences

To capture user experiences, we asked subjects to complete both pre- and post-task surveys for each of the four interface conditions.

[4]Result summary times were approximated by dividing the total recorded SERP time by the number of snippets hovered over with the mouse cursor. We believe this is a reasonable assumption to make – the timings of hover events proved to be unreliable due to occasional network latency issues beyond our control.

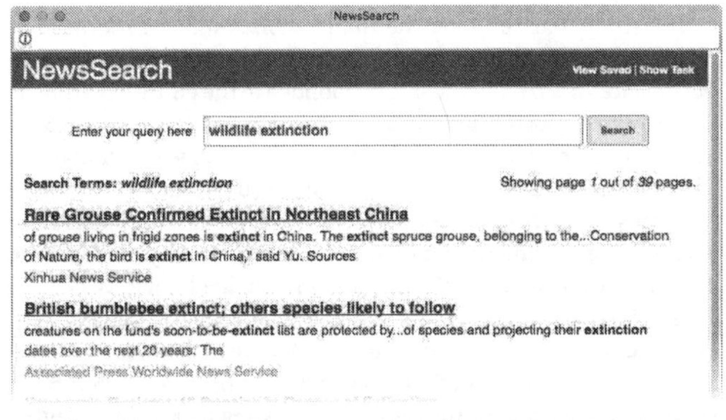

Figure 3: Screenshot of the experimental search interface, showing the SERP view, complete with query box (with query 'wildlife extinction') and the associated result summaries. In this example screenshot, interface *T2* – presenting two snippets per result summary – is shown.

Pre-task surveys consisted of five questions, each of which was on a seven-point Likert scale (7 – *strongly agree* to 1 – *strongly disagree*). Subjects were sought for their opinions on their: *(i)* prior knowledge of the topic; *(ii)* the relevancy of the topic to their lives; *(iii)* their desire to learn about the topic; *(iv)* whether they had searched on this topic before; and *(v)* the perceived difficulty to search for information on the topic.

The same Likert scale was used for post-task surveys, where subjects were asked to judge the following statements: ***(clarity)*** – the result summaries were clear and concise; ***(confidence)*** – the result summaries increased my confidence in my decisions; ***(informativeness)*** – the result summaries were informative; ***(relevance)*** – the results summaries help me judge the relevance of the document; ***(readable)*** – the result summaries were readable; and ***(size)*** – the result summaries were an appropriate size and length.

At the end of the experiment, subjects completed an exit survey. From five questions, they were asked to pick which of the four interfaces was the closest fit to their experience. We sought opinions on what interface: ***(most informative)*** – yielded the most informative result summaries; ***(least helpful)*** – provided the most unhelpful summaries; ***(easiest)*** – provided the easiest to understand summaries; ***(least useful)*** – provided the least useful result summaries; and ***(most preferred)*** – the subject's preferred choice for the tasks that they undertook.

3.5 Crowdsourced Subjects & Quality Control

As highlighted by Zuccon et al. [54], crowdsourcing provides an alternative means for capturing user interactions and search behaviours from traditional lab-based user studies. Greater volumes of data can be obtained from more heterogeneous workers at a lower cost – all within a shorter timeframe. Of course, pitfalls of a crowdsourced approach include the possibility of workers completing tasks as efficiently as possible, or submitting their tasks without performing the requested operations [13]. Despite these issues, it has been shown that there is little difference in the quality between crowdsourced and lab-based studies [54]. Nevertheless, quality control is a major component of a well-executed crowdsourced experiment [5]. Here, we detail our subjects and precautions taken.

The study was run over the *Amazon Mechanical Turk (MTurk)* platform. Workers from the platform performed a single *Human Intelligence Task (HIT)*, which corresponded to the entire experiment. Due to the expected length of completion for the study (45-50 minutes), subjects who completed the study in full were reimbursed for their time with US$9; a typically larger sum (and HIT duration) than most crowdsourced experiments. A total of 60 subjects took part in the experiment, which was run between July and August, 2016. However, seven subjects were omitted due to quality control constraints (see below). In all, of the 53 subjects who satisfied the expected conditions of the experiment, 28 were male, with 25 female. The average age of our subjects was 33.8 years ($min = 22$; $max = 48$; $stdev = 7.0$), with 19 of the subjects possessing a bachelor's degree or higher, and all expressing a high degree of search literacy, with all subjects stating that they conducted at least five searches for information online per week. With 53 subjects, each searching over four topics, this meant a total of 212 search sessions were logged.

We examined extra precautionary measures to ensure the integrity of the log data that was recorded. Precautions were taken from several angles. First, workers were only permitted to begin the experiment on the MTurk platform that: *(i)* were from the United States, and were native English speakers; *(ii)* had a HIT acceptance rate of at least 95%; and *(iii)* had at least 1000 HITs approved. Requiring *(ii)* and *(iii)* reduced the likelihood of recruiting individuals who would not complete the study in a satisfactory manner. Recruits were forewarned about the length of the HIT, which was considerably longer than other crowdsourced experiments.

We also ensured that the computer the subject was attempting the experiment on had a sufficiently large screen resolution (1024x768 or greater) so as to display all of the experimental interface on screen. With the experiment being conducted in a Web browser popup window of a fixed size, we wanted to ensure that all subjects would be able to see the same number of results on a SERP within the popup window's viewport. As the experiment was conducted via a Web browser, we wanted to ensure that only the controls provided by the experimental apparatus were used, meaning that the popup window had all other browser controls disabled to the best of our ability (i.e. history navigation, etc.). The experimental system was tested on several major Web browsers, across different operating systems. This gave us confidence that a similar experience would be had across different system configurations.

We also implemented a series of log post-processing scripts after completion of the study to further identify and capture individuals who did not perform the tasks as instructed. It was from here that we identified the seven subjects that did not complete the search tasks in a satisfactory way – spending less than three of the ten minutes searching. These subjects were excluded from the study, reducing the number of subjects reported from 60 to 53. Finally, results are reported based upon the first 360 seconds as some of the remaining subjects didn't fully use all 600 seconds.

4 RESULTS

Both search behaviour and user experience measures were analysed by each interface. To evaluate these data, ANOVAs were conducted using the interfaces as factors; main effects were examined with $\alpha = 0.05$. Bonferroni tests were used for post-hoc analysis. It should be noted that the error bars as shown in the plots for Figures 4 and 5 refer to the *standard error*.

Table 1: Characters, words and *Information Gain (IG)* across each of the four interface conditions. An ANOVA test reveals significant differences, with follow-up tests (refer to Section 4) showing that each condition is significantly different to others. There are clearly diminishing returns in information gain as snippet length increases. An IG value closer to zero denotes a higher level of IG. In the table, *IG/W.* denotes *IG per word.*

	T0	*T1*	*T2*	*T4*
Words	6.58±0.01*	25.21±0.06*	44.29±0.10*	77.06±0.13*
Chars.	37.37±0.05*	103.29±0.17*	168.36±0.23*	284.78±0.31*
IG	-6.35±0.01*	-3.59±0.00*	-3.00±0.00*	-2.67±0.00*
IG/W.	-1.17±0.00*	-0.18±0.00*	-0.08±0.00*	-0.04±0.00*

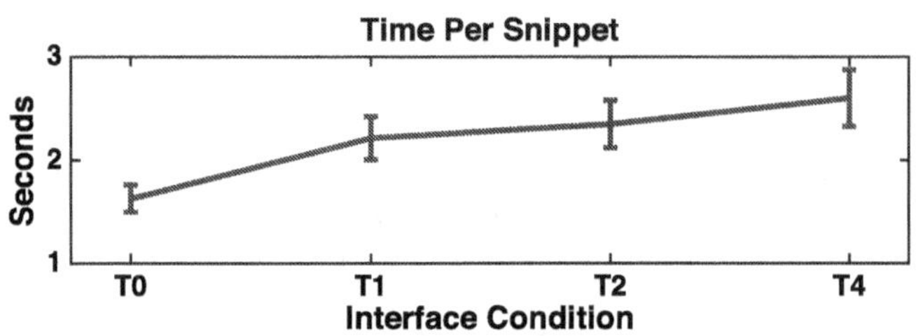

Figure 4: Plot showing the mean time spent examining result summaries across each of the four interfaces examined. Note the increasing mean examination time as the snippet length increases, from *T0*→*T4*.

To check whether the interfaces were different with respect to snippet length and information gain, we performed an analysis of the observed result summaries. Table 1 summarises the number of words and characters that result summaries contained on average. As expected, the table shows an increasing trend in words and characters as snippet lengths increase. Information gain for each snippet was then calculated using the Kullback-Leibler distance [28] to measure information gain (e.g. relative entropy). Statistical testing showed that the differences between snippet length ($F(3, 208) = 1.2x10^5, p < 0.001$) and information gain ($F(3, 208 = 2.6x10^5, p < 0.001)$) were significant. Follow up tests revealed that this was the case over all four interfaces, indicating that our conditions were different on these dimensions. These findings provide some justification for our choices for the number of snippet fragments present for each interface – a diminishing increase in information gain after four snippets suggested that there wouldn't be much point generating anything longer.

4.1 Search Behaviours

Interactions. Table 2 presents the mean (and standard deviations) of the number of queries issued, the number of SERPs viewed per query, documents clicked per query, and the click depth per query over each of the four interfaces examined. Across the four different interfaces, there were no significant differences reported between

Table 2: Summary table of both interaction and performance measures over each of the four interfaces evaluated. For each measure examined, no significant differences are reported across the four interfaces.

	T0	*T1*	*T2*	*T4*
Number of Queries	3.72± 0.34	3.19± 0.35	3.30± 0.35	3.28± 0.31
Number of SERP Pages per Query	2.87± 0.29	2.69± 0.23	2.43± 0.13	2.40± 0.20
Number of Docs Clicked per Query	4.23± 0.55	4.83± 0.54	5.14± 0.66	4.76± 0.62
Depth per Query	24.47± 2.96	22.87± 2.47	20.02± 1.46	19.40± 2.04
P@10	0.25± 0.02	0.23± 0.02	0.27± 0.02	0.25± 0.03
Number of Documents Marked Relevant	6.68± 0.66	7.00± 0.63	6.49± 0.58	7.60± 0.79
Number of TREC Rels Found	2.58± 0.34	2.28± 0.25	2.47± 0.28	2.66± 0.32
Number of Unjudged Docs Marked Relevant	1.85± 0.32	2.08± 0.29	1.98± 0.24	1.68± 0.32

Table 3: Summary table of times over each of the four interfaces evaluated. Significant differences exist between T0 and T4 (identified by the *, where $\alpha = 0.05$) on a follow-up Bonferroni test.

	T0	*T1*	*T2*	*T4*
Time per Query	8.29± 0.57	7.99± 0.57	9.42± 0.79	8.12± 0.48
Time per Document	17.31± 2.12	22.82± 6.03	17.19± 1.86	18.99± 2.13
Time per Result Summary*	1.63 ± 0.13*	2.21± 0.21	2.35± 0.23	2.60 ± 0.27*

any of these measures. The number of queries issued follows a slight downward trend as the length of result summaries increases (3.72 ± 0.34 for ***T0*** to 3.28 ± 0.31 for ***T4***), as too does the number of SERPs examined, and the number of documents examined per query. The depth to which subjects went to per query however follows a downward trend – as the length of snippets increases, subjects were likely to go to shallower depths when examining result summaries (24.47 ± 2.96 for ***T0*** to 19.4 ± 2.04 for ***T4***).

Interaction probabilities all showed an increasing trend as snippet length increased over the four interfaces, as shown in Table 4. Although no significant differences were observed over the four interfaces and the different probabilities examined, trends across all probabilities show an increase as the snippet length increases. An increase of both the probability of clicking result summaries on the SERP ($P(C)$) and marking the associated documents ($P(M)$) as relevant were observed. When these probabilities are examined in more detail by separating the result summaries clicked and documents marked by their TREC relevancy (through use of TREC QRELs), we see increasing trends for clicking and marking – both for TREC relevant ($P(C|R)$ and $P(M|R)$ for clicking and marking, respectively) and TREC non-relevant documents ($P(C|N)$ and $P(M|N)$). This interesting finding shows that an increase in snippet length does not necessarily improve the accuracy of subjects – simply the likelihood that they would consider documents as relevant.

Performance. Table 2 also reports a series of performance measures over the four conditions, averaged over the four topics examined. We report the mean performance of the queries issued with $P@10$, the number of documents marked relevant, and the number of documents marked relevant that were TREC relevant. Like the interaction measures above, no significant differences were observed over the four interfaces for each of the performance measures examined. The performance of queries issued by subjects was very similar across all four conditions ($P@10 \approx 0.25$), along with the number of documents identified by subjects as relevant (6.49 ± 0.58 for ***T2*** to 7.6 ± 0.79 for ***T4***), and the count of documents marked that were actually TREC relevant (2.28 ± 0.25 for ***T1*** to 2.66 ± 0.32 for ***T4***). We also examined the number of documents marked that were not assessed (unjudged) by the TREC assessors, in case one interface surfaced more novel documents. On average, subjects marked two such documents, but again there was no significant differences between interfaces.

Time-Based Measures. Table 3 reports a series of selected interaction times over each of the four evaluated interfaces. We include: the mean total query time per subject, per interface; the mean time per query; the mean time spent examining documents per query; and the mean time spent examining result summaries per query. No significant differences were found between the mean total query time, the time per query and the time per document. However, a significant difference did exist for the time spent per result summary. A clear upward trend in the time spent examining snippets can be seen in Figure 4 as result summaries progressively got longer, from 1.63 ± 0.13 for ***T0*** to 2.6 ± 0.27 for ***T4***, which was significantly different ($F(3, 208) = 3.6, p = 0.014$). A follow-up Bonferroni test showed that the significant difference existed between ***T0*** and ***T4***. This suggests that as result summary length increases, the amount of time spent examining result summaries also increases (an intuitive result). This also complies with trends observed regarding examination depths. When the length of result summaries increased, subjects were likely to examine result summaries to shallower depths.

Table 4: Table illustrating a summary of interaction probabilities over each of the four interfaces evaluated. Note the increasing trends for each probability from *T0* → *T4* (short to long snippets). Refer to Section 4.1 for an explanation of what each probability represents.

	T0	*T1*	*T2*	*T4*
P(C)	0.20± 0.02	0.25± 0.02	0.26± 0.03	0.28± 0.03
P(C|R)	0.28± 0.03	0.34± 0.03	0.35± 0.03	0.40± 0.04
P(C|N)	0.18± 0.02	0.23± 0.02	0.25± 0.03	0.24± 0.03
P(M)	0.61± 0.04	0.68± 0.04	0.65± 0.03	0.71± 0.03
P(M|R)	0.66± 0.06	0.69± 0.05	0.67± 0.05	0.66± 0.05
P(M|N)	0.55± 0.04	0.65± 0.04	0.58± 0.04	0.67± 0.04

Table 5: Summary table of the recorded observations for the post-task survey, indicating the preferences of subjects over six criteria and the four interfaces, where * indicates that T0 was significantly different from the other conditions. In the table, *Conf.* represents *Confidence, Read.* represents *Readability, Inform.* represents *Informativeness,* and *Rel.* represents *Relevancy.*

	T0	T1	T2	T4
Clarity	4.16± 0.27*	5.00± 0.21	5.06± 0.24	5.40± 0.20
Conf.	3.71± 0.26*	4.66± 0.26	4.75± 0.24	5.06± 0.25
Read.	5.18± 0.31*	6.32± 0.17	6.46± 0.14	6.36± 0.14
Inform.	4.20± 0.30*	5.38± 0.24	5.27± 0.24	5.62± 0.20
Rel.	3.84± 0.28*	4.89± 0.25	5.08± 0.24	5.36± 0.20
Size	4.00± 0.31*	4.94± 0.25	5.21± 0.22	5.36± 0.19

Table 6: Table presenting responses from the exit survey completed by subjects. The survey is discussed in Section 3.4.

	T0	T1	T2	T4
Most Informative	1	4	20	29
Least helpful	46	5	1	2
Easiest	4	4	24	22
Least Useful	49	4	0	1
Most Preferred	3	5	20	26

4.2 User Experience

Task Evaluations. Table 5 presents the mean set of results from subjects across the four interfaces, which were answered upon completion of each search task. The survey questions are detailed in Section 3.4. Using the seven-point Likert scale for their responses (with 7 indicating *strongly agree*, and 1 indicating *strongly disagree*), significant differences were found in all question responses (**clarity** $F(3, 208) = 5.22, p = 0.001$, **confidence** $F(3, 208) = 5.3, p = 0.001$, **readable** $F(3, 208) = 9.25, p < 0.001$, **informative** $F(3, 208) = 5.22, p = 0.001$, **relevance** $F(3, 208) = 6.44, p < 0.001$, and **size** $F(3, 208) = 7.28, p < 0.001$). Follow-up Bonferroni tests however showed that the significant difference existed only between ***T0*** and the remaining three interfaces, ***T1***, ***T2*** and ***T4***. A series of discernible trends can be observed throughout the responses, with subjects regarding longer snippets as more concise, and a higher degree of clarity (4.16±0.27 for ***T0*** to 5.4±0.2 for ***T4***). This perceived clarity also made subjects feel more confident that the longer result summaries helped them make better decisions as to whether they were relevant to the given topic – interaction results presented above however differ from this, where the overall probability of marking documents increased, regardless of the document/topic TREC relevancy judgement. Other notable trends observed from the results included an increase in how informative subjects perceived the result summaries to be – again, with longer summaries proving more informative. Subjects also reported a general increase in satisfaction of the length of the presented result summaries/snippets – although, as mentioned, no significant difference existed between the three interfaces that generated snippets (***T1***, ***T2*** and ***T4***).

System Evaluations. Upon completion of the study, subjects completed the exit survey as detailed in Section 3.4. Responses from the subjects are presented in Table 6. From the results, subjects found result summaries of longer lengths (i.e. those generated by interfaces ***T2*** and ***T4***) to be the most informative, and those generated by ***T0*** – without snippets – to be the least helpful and useful. The longer result summaries were also consistently favoured by subjects, who preferred them over the result summaries generated by interfaces ***T0*** and ***T1***. Subjects also found the result summaries of longer length easier to use to satisfy the given information need.

From the results, it is therefore clear that a majority of subjects preferred longer result summaries to be presented on SERPs, generated by interfaces ***T2*** and ***T4***. Figure 5 provides summary plots, showing general trends across the four interfaces, examining observed interactions and reported experiences.

5 DISCUSSION AND FUTURE WORK

In this paper, we investigated the influence of result summary length on search behaviour and performance. Using the Kullback-Leibler distance [28] as a measure of information gain, we examined result summaries of different lengths, selected a series of snippet lengths where there was a significant difference in information gain between them, which yielded the configurations for our four experimental conditions, ***T0***, ***T1***, ***T2*** and ***T4***. We conducted a crowd-sourced user study comprising of 53 subjects, each of whom undertook four search tasks, using each of the four interfaces.

Our work was focused around addressing our two research questions, which explored **RQ1** how the value of information gain (represented by snippet length) affected search behaviour and user experience; and **RQ2** whether information gain affected the decision making ability and accuracy of users. Addressing **RQ1** first in terms of search behaviour, there was little difference – but we did observe the following trends: as summary length increases, participants: issued fewer queries; examined fewer pages; but clicked more documents, i.e. they spent more of their time assessing documents at higher ranks. Second, our results show that in terms

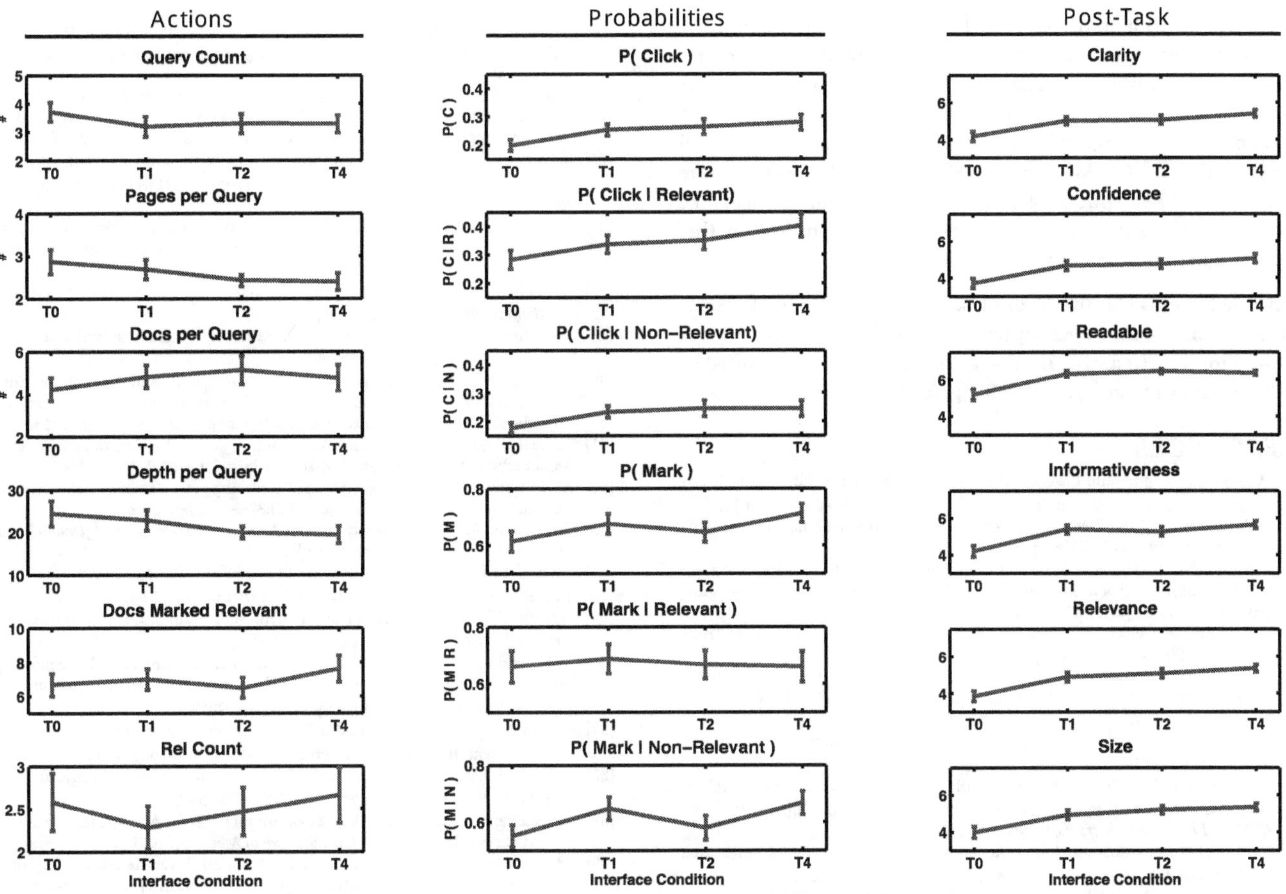

Figure 5: Plots, showing a variety of measures and survey results from subjects across the four interfaces examined. From left to right: actions associated with the subjects' search behaviours and performance; probabilities of interaction; and post-task survey responses, using a seven-point Likert scale (7 - *strongly agree* to 1 - *strongly disagree*).

of experience, subjects broadly preferred longer summaries. The participants felt that longer summaries were more clear, informative, readable – and interestingly – gave them more confidence in their relevance decisions. With respect to **RQ2**, we again observed little difference in subjects' decision making abilities and accuracy between the four interfaces. While subjects perceived longer snippets to help them infer relevance more accurately, our empirical evidence shows otherwise. In fact, it would appear that longer result summaries were more attractive, increasing the information scent of the SERP [53]. This may account for the increase in clicks on the early results, without the benefits, however: accuracy of our subjects did not improve with longer snippets; nor did they find more relevant documents. Increased confidence in the result summaries (from ***T0*** → ***T4***) may have led to a more relaxed approach at marking content as relevant – as can be seen by increasing click and mark probabilities for both relevant and non-relevant content. It is also possible that the *paradox of choice* [37] could play a role in shaping a user's preferences. For example, in the condition with longer result summaries (***T4***), users viewed fewer results/choices than on other conditions. This may have contributed to their feelings of greater satisfaction and increased confidence in their decisions.

These novel findings provide new insights into how users interact with result summaries in terms of their experiences and search behaviours. Previous work had only focused upon task completion times and accuracy of the first result while not considering their experiences (e.g. [11, 19]). Furthermore, these past works were performed in the context of Web search where the goal was to find one document. However, we acknowledge that our work also has limitations. Here, we examined out research questions – with respect to topic search within a news collection – to explore how behaviour and performance changes when searching for multiple relevant documents. It would be interesting to examine this in other search contexts, such as product search, for example. News article titles also can be crafted differently from documents in other domains. Summaries in this domain may perhaps be more important than in other domains, and so the effects and influences are likely to be larger. Furthermore, we only considered how behaviours changed on the desktop, rather than on other devices where users are more likely to be sensitive to such changes (e.g. [25, 27]). For example, during casual leisure search, multiple relevant documents on tablet devices are often found, and so it would be interesting to perform a follow up study in this area.

To conclude, our findings show that longer result summaries, while containing a greater amount of information content, are not necessarily better in terms of decision making – although subjects perceived this to be the case. We also show a positive relationship between the length and informativeness of result summaries and their attractiveness (clickthrough rates). These results show that the experience and perceptions of users – and the actual performance of those users – is different, and when designing interfaces, this needs be taken into account.

Acknowledgments Our thanks to Alastair Maxwell and Stuart Mackie for their comments, the 53 participants of this study, and the anonymous reviewers for their feedback. The lead author is financially supported by the UK Government through the EPSRC, grant №. 1367507.

REFERENCES

[1] M. Ageev, D. Lagun, and E. Agichtein. Improving search result summaries by using searcher behavior data. In *Proc. 35th ACM SIGIR*, pages 13–22, 2013.
[2] H. Ali, F. Scholer, J. A. Thom, and M. Wu. User interaction with novel web search interfaces. In *Proc. 21st OZCHI*, pages 301–304.
[3] L. Azzopardi, D. Kelly, and K. Brennan. How query cost affects search behavior. In *Proceedings of the 36th International ACM SIGIR Conference on Research and Development in IR*, pages 23–32, 2013.
[4] H. Bast and M. Celikik. Efficient index-based snippet generation. *ACM Trans. Inf. Syst.*, 32(2):6:1–6:24, Apr. 2014.
[5] H. Bota, K. Zhou, and J. M. Jose. Playing your cards right: The effect of entity cards on search behaviour and workload. In *Proc. 1st ACM CHIIR*, pages 131–140, 2016.
[6] H. Chen and S. Dumais. Bringing order to the web: Automatically categorizing search results. In *Proc. 18th ACM CHI*, pages 145–152, 2000.
[7] M. C. Chen, J. R. Anderson, and M. H. Sohn. What can a mouse cursor tell us more?: Correlation of eye/mouse movements on web browsing. In *Proc. 19th ACM CHI Extended Abstracts*, pages 281–282, 2001.
[8] F. Chierichetti, R. Kumar, and P. Raghavan. Optimizing two-dimensional search results presentation. In *Proc. 4th ACM WSDM*, pages 257–266, 2011.
[9] C. L. A. Clarke, E. Agichtein, S. Dumais, and R. W. White. The influence of caption features on clickthrough patterns in web search. In *Proc. 30th ACM SIGIR*, pages 135–142, 2007.
[10] N. Craswell, O. Zoeter, M. Taylor, and B. Ramsey. An experimental comparison of click position-bias models. In *Proc. 1st ACM WSDM*, pages 87–94, 2008.
[11] E. Cutrell and Z. Guan. What are you looking for?: an eye-tracking study of information usage in web search. In *Proc. 25th ACM CHI*, pages 407–416, 2007.
[12] S. Dumais, E. Cutrell, and H. Chen. Optimizing search by showing results in context. In *Proc. 19th ACM CHI*, pages 277–284, 2001.
[13] H. Feild, R. Jones, R. Miller, R. Nayak, E. Churchill, and E. Velipasaoglu. Logging the search self-efficacy of amazon mechanical turkers. In *Proc. CSE SIGIR Workshop*, pages 27–30, 2010.
[14] J. He, P. Duboue, and J.-Y. Nie. Bridging the gap between intrinsic and perceived relevance in snippet generation. In *Proc. of COLING 2012*, pages 1129–1146, 2012.
[15] M. Hearst. *Search user interfaces.* Cambridge University Press, 2009.
[16] P. Ingwersen and K. Järvelin. *The Turn: Integration of Information Seeking and Retrieval in Context.* 2005.
[17] T. Joachims, L. Granka, B. Pan, H. Hembrooke, and G. Gay. Accurately interpreting clickthrough data as implicit feedback. In *Proc. 28th ACM SIGIR*, pages 154–161, 2005.
[18] H. Joho and J. M. Jose. A comparative study of the effectiveness of search result presentation on the web. In *Proc. 28th ECIR*, pages 302–313, 2006.
[19] M. Kaisser, M. A. Hearst, and J. B. Lowe. Improving search results quality by customizing summary lengths. In *Proc. 46th ACL*, pages 701–709, 2008.
[20] Y. Kammerer and P. Gerjets. How the interface design influences users' spontaneous trustworthiness evaluations of web search results: comparing a list and a grid interface. In *Proc. of the Symp. on Eye-Tracking Research & Applications*, pages 299–306, 2010.
[21] T. Kanungo and D. Orr. Predicting the readability of short web summaries. In *Proc. 2nd ACM WSDM*, pages 202–211, 2009.
[22] D. Kelly and L. Azzopardi. How many results per page?: A study of serp size, search behavior and user experience. In *Proc. 38th ACM SIGIR*, pages 183–192, 2015.
[23] D. Kelly, K. Gyllstrom, and E. W. Bailey. A comparison of query and term suggestion features for interactive searching. In *Proc. 32nd ACM SIGIR*, pages 371–378, 2009.
[24] J. Kim, P. Thomas, R. Sankaranarayana, and T. Gedeon. Comparing scanning behaviour in web search on small and large screens. In *Proc. 17th ADCS*, pages 25–30, 2012.
[25] J. Kim, P. Thomas, R. Sankaranarayana, T. Gedeon, and H.-J. Yoon. Eye-tracking analysis of user behavior and performance in web search on large and small screens. *J. of the Assoc. for Information Science and Technology*, 2014.
[26] J. Kim, P. Thomas, R. Sankaranarayana, T. Gedeon, and H.-J. Yoon. Pagination versus scrolling in mobile web search. In *Proc. 25th ACM CIKM*, pages 751–760, 2016.
[27] J. Kim, P. Thomas, R. Sankaranarayana, T. Gedeon, and H.-J. Yoon. What snippet size is needed in mobile web search? In *Proc. 2nd ACM CHIIR*, pages 97–106, 2017.
[28] S. Kullback and R. A. Leibler. On information and sufficiency. *The Annals of Mathematical Statistics*, 22:79–86, 1951.
[29] J. Kupiec, J. Pedersen, and F. Chen. A trainable document summarizer. In *Proc. 18th ACM SIGIR*, pages 68–73, 1995.
[30] T. Landauer, D. Egan, J. Remde, M. Lesk, C. Lochbaum, and D. Ketchum. Enhancing the usability of text through computer delivery and formative evaluation: the superbook project. *Hypertext: A psychological perspective*, pages 71–136, 1993.
[31] L. Leal-Bando, F. Scholer, and A. Turpin. Query-biased summary generation assisted by query expansion. *J. Assoc. for Info. Sci. and Tech.*, 66(5):961–979, 2015.
[32] Q. Li and Y. P. Chen. Personalized text snippet extraction using statistical language models. *Pattern Recogn.*, 43(1):378–386, Jan. 2010.
[33] G. Linden. *Marissa mayer at web 2.0*, November 2006. *http://glinden.blogspot.com/2006/11/marissa-mayer-at-web-20.html.*
[34] Marcos, M-C. and Gavin, F. and Arapakis, I. Effect of snippets on user experience in web search. In *Proc. 16th Intl. Conf. on HCI*, pages 47:1–47:8, 2015.
[35] A. Muralidharan, Z. Gyongyi, and E. Chi. Social annotations in web search. In *Proc. 30th ACM CHI*, pages 1085–1094, 2012.
[36] V. Navalpakkam, L. Jentzsch, R. Sayres, S. Ravi, A. Ahmed, and A. Smola. Measurement and modeling of eye-mouse behavior in the presence of nonlinear page layouts. In *Proc. 22nd WWW*, pages 953–964, 2013.
[37] A. Oulasvirta, J. Hukkinen, and B. Schwartz. When more is less: The paradox of choice in search engine use. In *Proc. 32nd ACM SIGIR*, pages 516–523, 2009.
[38] T. Paek, S. Dumais, and R. Logan. Wavelens: A new view onto internet search results. In *Proc. 22nd ACM CHI*, pages 727–734, 2004.
[39] J. Pedersen, D. Cutting, J. Tukey, et al. Snippet search: A single phrase approach to text access. In *Proc. 1991 Joint Statistical Meetings*, 1991.
[40] M. L. Resnick, C. Maldonado, J. M. Santos, and R. Lergier. Modeling on-line search behavior using alternative output structures. In *Proc. Human Factors and Ergonomics Soc. Annual Meeting*, volume 45, pages 1166–1170, 2001.
[41] D. E. Rose, D. Orr, and R. G. P. Kantamneni. Summary attributes and perceived search quality. In *Proc. 16th WWW*, pages 1201–1202, 2007.
[42] D. Savenkov, P. Braslavski, and M. Lebedev. Search snippet evaluation at yandex: lessons learned and future directions. *Multilingual & Multimodal Information Access Evaluation*, pages 14–25, 2011.
[43] B. Schwartz. *The Paradox of Choice: Why More Is Less.* Harper Perennial, 2005.
[44] M. Smucker, X. Guo, and A. Toulis. Mouse movement during relevance judging: Implications for determining user attention. In *Proc. 37th ACM SIGIR*, pages 979–982, 2014.
[45] N. V. Spirin, A. S. Kotov, K. G. Karahalios, V. Mladenov, and P. A. Izhutov. A comparative study of query-biased and non-redundant snippets for structured search on mobile devices. In *Proc. 25th ACM CIKM*, pages 2389–2394, 2016.
[46] K. M. Svore, J. Teevan, S. T. Dumais, and A. Kulkarni. Creating temporally dynamic web search snippets. In *Proc. 35th ACM SIGIR*, pages 1045–1046, 2012.
[47] J. Teevan, E. Cutrell, D. Fisher, S. M. Drucker, G. Ramos, P. André, and C. Hu. Visual snippets: Summarizing web pages for search and revisitation. In *Proc. 27th ACM CHI*, pages 2023–2032, 2009.
[48] A. Tombros and M. Sanderson. Advantages of query biased summaries in information retrieval. In *Proc. 21st ACM SIGIR*, pages 2–10, 1998.
[49] A. Turpin, Y. Tsegay, D. Hawking, and H. E. Williams. Fast generation of result snippets in web search. In *Proc. 30th ACM SIGIR*, pages 127–134, 2007.
[50] E. M. Voorhees. Overview of the trec 2005 robust track. In *Proc. TREC-14*, 2006.
[51] R. W. White, J. M. Jose, and I. Ruthven. A task-oriented study on the influencing effects of query-biased summarisation in web searching. *Info. Processing & Management*, 39(5):707–733, 2003.
[52] A. Woodruff, R. Rosenholtz, J. B. Morrison, A. Faulring, and P. Pirolli. A comparison of the use of text summaries, plain thumbnails, and enhanced thumbnails for web search tasks. *J. Am. Soc. Inf. Sci. Technol.*, 53(2):172–185, 2002.
[53] Wu, W-C. and Kelly, D. and Sud, A. Using information scent and need for cognition to understand online search behavior. In *Proceedings of the 37th International ACM SIGIR Conference*, SIGIR '14, pages 557–566, 2014.
[54] G. Zuccon, T. Leelanupab, S. Whiting, E. Yilmaz, J. Jose, and L. Azzopardi. Crowdsourcing interactions: using crowdsourcing for evaluating interactive information retrieval systems. *Information Retrieval*, 16(2):267–305, 2013.

Improving Exploratory Search Experience through Hierarchical Knowledge Graphs

Bahareh Sarrafzadeh
Cheriton School of Computer Science
University of Waterloo, Canada
bsarrafz@uwaterloo.ca

Edward Lank
Cheriton School of Computer Science
University of Waterloo, Canada
CRIStAL, University of Lille, France
lank@uwaterloo.ca

ABSTRACT

In information retrieval and information visualization, hierarchies are a common tool to structure information into topics or facets, and network visualizations such as knowledge graphs link related concepts within a domain. In this paper, we explore a multi-layer extension to knowledge graphs, hierarchical knowledge graphs (HKGs), that combines hierarchical and network visualizations into a unified data representation. Through interaction logs, we show that HKGs preserve the benefits of single-layer knowledge graphs at conveying domain knowledge while incorporating the sense-making advantages of hierarchies for knowledge seeking tasks. Specially, this paper describes our algorithm to construct these visualizations, analyzes interaction logs to quantitatively demonstrate performance parity with networks and performance advantages over hierarchies, and synthesizes data from interaction logs, interviews, and thinkalouds on a testbed data set to demonstrate the utility of the unified hierarchy+network structure in our HKGs.

CCS CONCEPTS

•Information systems →Search interfaces;

KEYWORDS

Knowledge Graphs, Hierarchies, Exploratory Search, Information Seeking, Representations of Search Results

1 INTRODUCTION

Finding information on the Web is often difficult. There are two predominant paradigms for finding information on the Web: Searching (i.e, Search by query) and Browsing (i.e, Search by Navigation) [20, 31]. While current search engines, following a "search by query" paradigm, are generally sufficient when the information need is well-defined in the searcher's mind, examining search results remains a necessary step within a larger information seeking process [23, 25]. To elaborate, Searching requires the user to translate an information need into queries, while Browsing accommodates the knowledge gap between what the user is able to communicate and what the system requires to find the desired information. This knowledge gap (also formalized as an 'anomalous state of knowledge' by Belkin [5]) is more evident when information is sought to address broad curiosities, for learning and other complex mental activities [2, 43].

This paper focuses on the design of tools to support browsing. Researchers note that, while search interfaces must support query formulation and an effective ranking algorithm, browsing interfaces require effective representations of search results to accommodate searcher's 'state of knowledge' and provide 'information scent' to guide the user during navigation [31, 32]. Related to this observation of 'information scent' is the observation that information seekers often express a desire for a user interface that organizes search results into meaningful structures to facilitate browsing and understanding of the retrieved results [15].

The desire for browsing support via structure has given rise to interfaces that represent the structure of information. These structures typically exist in one of two forms: hierarchies and networks [11]. First, information can be presented into hierarchies based on categories. Included in this class of search results organizations are techniques such as faceted browsing or automatic clustering. Second, alongside hierarchies, entity relationship or network representations are also used. In these representations, rather than clustering objects into labeled categories, the connections between objects (people, places, things, etc.) in a document corpus represent a relationship between two items. These network representations include knowledge graphs [18] and concept maps [29].

Recent work has explored the relative benefits of hierarchies and networks and has noted that the benefits are largely complementary: hierarchies provide users with some understanding of central topics, allowing them to develop a better overview of information; whereas networks allow people to glean concrete information from the representation rather than needing to extensively read individual documents [39]. Given the complementary advantages of knowledge graphs and hierarchies, our main research question in this paper is that whether we can algorithmically generate a seamless data structure that combines the advantages of both hierarchies and networks into a single unified structure.

In this paper, we evaluate the efficacy of hierarchical knowledge graphs (HKGs) as a combined representation of low-level entity relationships and high-level central concepts. We generate these knowledge graphs automatically using a simple parsing algorithm [37], then extract hierarchies using a dynamic thresholding approach. We evaluate these HKGs using a mixed methods approach. Quantitative data argues that HKGs preserve the transparency advantages of knowledge graphs and structural advantages

SIGIR '17, August 07-11, 2017, Shinjuku, Tokyo, Japan
© 2017 ACM. 978-1-4503-5022-8/17/08...$15.00
DOI: http://dx.doi.org/10.1145/3077136.3080829

of hierarchies. Qualitative data triangulates with quantitative observations and provides additional insight into the advantages and disadvantages of both hierarchical and network visualizations.

2 RELATED WORK

In this section we survey related work in classifying and understanding web search and in techniques to augment search results.

2.1 Understanding web search

There exist several characterizations of web search queries [6–8, 35, 44]. Marchionini [24] focuses specifically on a process he terms *exploratory search*. Marchionini defines three categories of web search: Look-up, Learn, and Investigate and groups Learn and Investigate tasks under the umbrella of exploratory search.

Learn and Investigate tasks involve sensemaking [14, 36]. Sensemaking is the process of searching for a representation and encoding data in that representation to answer task-specific questions [36]. Russell et al. [36] present four main cognitive stages that are involved in sensemaking: an interaction between a bottom-up 'Search for representation' phase and a top-down representation instantiation phase, a phase of shifting representations to fit newly discovered data into the current representation, and an application of the representation to the user's specific task.

The top-level representation that results from sensemaking has many different names: a "holistic cognitive structure" [42], a mind-map, a concept map [29]. Regardless, the construction of this representation must be either provided explicitly by the interface or constructed implicitly by the user [36, 42] before the user can fully "make sense" of the retrieved information.

Alongside the distinction between "look-up" and exploratory search, there are also varying levels of complexity associated with exploratory search tasks [24]. At the simplest level, one might simply wish to read a document to understand a topic. However, consider tasks such as comparing two different diets to understand health benefits (e.g. oriental and Mediterranean), comparing two different political systems to understand relative authoritarianism (e.g. President of Russia versus Iran), or comparing two different educational systems to understand relative student success (e.g. British versus Canadian). All of these, as examples of exploratory search tasks, require both searching and browsing to identify information, acquire knowledge, and contrast related data across two contexts. As the complexity of comparison increases (three or more alternatives, more abstract concepts), the information seeking task continues to increase in complexity. Searching is highly effective at identifying relevant documents to guide basic exploratory search, but browsing and reformulating are needed to fully acquire and synthesize knowledge [23, 26]. Therefore, understanding both searching and browsing behaviors are of vital importance to design effective interactive information retrieval systems.

2.2 Organizing Search Results

Because of the importance of structure in search, there have been efforts to contrast strengths and weaknesses of different spatial representations and groupings of search results. A taxonomy of techniques for organizing search results was proposed by Wilson et al. [46]. They identify two main classes of approaches: (1) Coupling results with additional metadata and classifications such that searchers can interact and control the presentation of results. (e.g. faceted browsing or categories), or (2) providing alternative or complementary representations of search results (e.g, a network representation). Wilson et al. also present four common approaches to structured classification [46]: hierarchical classifications, faceted classifications, automated clustering, and social classifications.

Looking first at structured classification, early forays into the domain of structuring search results contrasted categories with automatic clustering to support search. Hearst [16] showed that categories, because they were more interpretable for the user, captured important information about the document but became unwieldy when the document corpus was too large. Clusters, by comparison, were highly variable with respect to quality and were often less meaningful for the user.

Given the lack of intuitiveness associated with clustering [17] and a desire for understandable hierarchies in which categories are presented at uniform levels of granularity [33, 34], alongside specified hierarchies such as tables-of-contents, researchers have explored faceted categories, i.e. categories that are semantically related to the search task of the user, to organize search results. These include systems that define faceted categories [48], research that studies the use of facets to support browsing [9], and research that identifies strengths and weaknesses of faceted browsers [45]. In terms of strengths and weaknesses, faceted browsing has proven beneficial for users already clear about their search task [45]; additional information on interactions between facets (e.g. inter-facet relationships) is helpful when users are unfamiliar with a domain and need 'sensemaking'. In other words, exploratory tasks (e.g.learning or investigating [24]) are precisely those tasks where interactions between facets are needed.

The need to represent relationships between facets or concepts has given rise to the use of network structures to depict relationships between concepts or entities in a corpus. These network structures include concept maps, knowledge graphs, and other entity-relationship diagrams. Concept mapping has been widely used in education as a method for knowledge examination, sharing, and browsing [10, 29]. Knowledge graphs have been popularized by Google to represent web-based information. One drawback to network structures is it is hard both to get an overview of an information network and to navigate through the network effectively: users are easily "lost" in these systems [12, 22, 31].

A final question within this space is how competing representations fare in presenting results for exploratory search tasks. While some past research has explored using questionnaires to determine the efficacy of different knowledge representations [30], or has evaluated the efficacy of hierarchies, networks, or concept maps with respect to ordered lists (e.g. [1, 9, 10, 27, 38]), we have found little research that directly compares networks to hierarchies to understand their competing affordances. The one exception to this is recent work by Sarrafzadeh et al. [39]; they find that networks eliminate the need for reading documents – users can glean information from the networks with statistically significantly less time spent reading – and that hierarchies particularly benefit low-knowledge participants by giving them an effective overview of the domain.

Given Sarrafzadeh et al.'s observation of the complementary benefits of hierarchies and networks, one question is whether studies have examined the use of hierarchies and networks as combined – synchronized and simultaneous – representations of search results. We have found little work that explores combined networks+hierarchies. Part of the challenge may arise from the complexity of seamlessly integrating both hierarchies and networks into a single unified structure. For example, hierarchies are typically best when the structure aligns well with the user's task, but, given this alignment, entities in networks may have many multiple 'parents' within the structure, yielding a many-to-many relationship within the hierarchy, i.e. a three-dimensional graph.

3 HIERARCHICAL KNOWLEDGE GRAPHS

In this section, we describe hierarchical knowledge graphs, an extension of knowledge graphs that include hierarchical information about the lower level graphical structures. The rationale behind our proposed approach for employing hierarchical knowledge graphs to represent search results is the complementary benefits [39] of hierarchies [17, 47] and network structures [2, 29, 38] to support exploratory browsing of search results. More specifically, hierarchies provide a breadth-first exploration of the information that allows the user to iteratively reduce confusion, obtain an overview, and slowly exploit detail. They thus provide a structured way to navigate from more general concepts to more fine grained data and are valuable when people feel a need to orient themselves. In contrast network structures allow users to glean more information from the representation (document reading time is reduced), are more engaging, yield more control over exploration at the lower level of inter-concept relationships [39], and are more similar to one's mental model [3, 11, 28, 39].

Given the complimentary benefit of networks and hierarchies, the next question is how to design a representation that can seamlessly merge these two representations. We take the approach that a knowledge graph will be an appropriate low-level representation and seek to incorporate a hierarchical view of this low-level representation of corpus content. To incorporate a hierarchical view into a knowledge graph, we need to find answers to the following three design questions (DQs):

(1) How do we integrate network and hierarchical views into a single, seamless data structure?
(2) How can both the global and the local view of a knowledge graph be co-visualized?
(3) How can transitions between views be designed to maximize visualization stability?

To answer these DQs, we first focus on DQ1 and describe the design of our data structure. Next, to address DQ2 and DQ3 we describe an interface that supports interaction with the data structure. Alongside our DQs, we add one additional constraint to our design. We want to ensure that both the low-level knowledge graph and the hierarchies gleaned from that knowledge graph can be automatically generated from a targeted search performed by the user.

3.1 Visualization Design and Creation

As noted above, given that we take the approach that a knowledge graph will constitute the lower-level visualization of our data, the task becomes creating a knowledge graph and creating a hierarchy that is gleaned from and corresponds directly to the underlying knowledge graph.

Figure 1 depicts the system architecture that supports the process of automatically generating the hierarchical knowledge graph representation. To simplify hierarchy generation, we create a 3-level hierarchy for any document corpus. Beyond the base layer knowledge graph, there is an intermediate layer of central concepts gleaned from the knowledge graph. Finally, at the top-level, the documents, themselves, represent the top level of the hierarchical knowledge graphs. In Figure 1, three main steps are depicted to generate hierarchical knowledge graphs: Document Retrieval (yielding the top-level of the hierarchy), Knowledge Graph Generation (yielding the bottom level of the hierarchy), and Hierarchy-from-graph Generation (yielding an intermediate view of an individual knowledge graph, which we dub a *minimap*[1]).

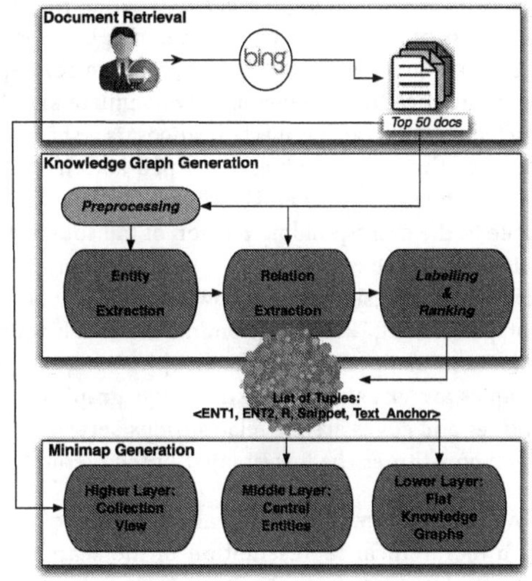

Figure 1: Generating Hierarchical Knowledge Graphs

3.1.1 Document Retrieval. The Document Retrieval component aims at creating an initial document collection based on a user's query. This collection will then be used as an input for the Knowledge Graph Generation component and will represent the top view of the target hierarchy.

To generate a document corpus, we use the Bing Search engine to retrieve the top n documents for a query while attempting to ensure a reasonable quality of information in the retrieved documents. By default, to ensure that retrieved documents are consistent in their credibility and coverage, we specify Wikipedia as the target domain. Furthermore, because it is known that searchers typically view only a few results [19] and rarely stray past the first page of results [4], we selected n=10 documents to generate collections. The target domain from which to glean documents (e.g. a user might specify webmd for medical documents, 'gov' for public policy documents, 'bbc' for news) and the size of the initial collection can be specified by the user at the time of query submission. Finally,

[1]The term minimap is drawn from the gaming literature. It represents a less detailed overview of a gaming world, allowing the user to orient themselves.

since most exploratory search tasks require multiple queries to retrieve documents for different aspects of the information need, this component assigns one partition per query so the user can narrow down the retrieved collection further.

3.1.2 Knowledge Graph Generation. Inspired by past work [37], we create knowledge graphs for an individual document or set of documents as follows. (1) Entity taggers [2] are used to extract entities from text. (2) Sentences that contain at least two entities are selected and parsed using the Stanford Dependency Parser. For each sentence, we extract meaningful relations between the entities by finding the shortest path in the corresponding parse tree. (3) Finally, labels are automatically generated for the extracted relations. The labeled relations are ranked based on relevance to the query and the informativeness of the extraction [37].

The outcome is a set of tuples in the form of <entity1, entity2, relation, snippet, document_anchor>. These tuples collectively correspond to a knowledge graph representation of retrieved documents where *entity* is usually a term or a noun phrase in text that corresponds to a concept in the domain, *relation* corresponds to a simplified sentence that is semantically complete and describes how entity1 and entity2 are connected, *snippet* is a short portion of text from which the corresponding entity pair and the relationship is derived, and *text_anchor* is an HTML anchor that links the extracted tuple to the corresponding portion of the source document in the collection. For example, from a paragraph on powers and responsibilities of a president the following tuple can be extracted: <president, parliament, "President nominates the Cabinet members to the Parliament", snippet, [URL][anchor]>.

These tuples are visualized as a knowledge graph where nodes are the entities and edges are the relationships between them. This visualization constitutes the lowest layer of the hierarchy.

3.1.3 Minimap Generation. The final component of this system generates a hierarchical representation of the search results by extracting a middle layer from the input Knowledge graph tuples and provides bidirectional mappings between all three layers. As noted earlier, we call this layer the minimap layer.

A natural result of the entity-relationship tuples extracted above is that some entities have a higher number of edges, i.e. are of higher degree. A higher edge count implies a larger number of connections to other entities in the graph; in other words, those entities with higher edge counts were more frequently linked with other entities in the document. We call these higher degree vertices *central concepts* and hypothesize that one alternative to hierarchical faceted structures is to consider a multi-level view of a knowledge graph around central concepts. The multilevel view focusing on central concepts simply introduces information seekers to those entities or objects that are most frequently linked to other entities within the corpus. Generating the hierarchy becomes a thresholding task to appropriately scope the intermediate level of the visualization. Algorithm 1 describes this process more formally.

3.2 Prototype Development

Given our hierarchical representation (DQ1), we must support mechanisms for viewing and interacting with the visualization

[2] https://cogcomp.cs.illinois.edu/page/software_view/NETagger

Algorithm 1 Extracting Central Concepts

Require: *Nodes*: array of nodes in the knowledge graph, *min_degree*: a pre-specified threshhold for the minimum degree of node to be considered as a central concept (starting value = 3), *max_count*: an experimentally derived threshold for the maximum number of Central Concepts to be included in the middle layer (default value = 15).

function ExtractCC(*Nodes*, *min_degree*, *max_count*)
    while true **do**
        CentralNodes ← []
        for all *node* in *Nodes* **do**
            if *node.degree* ≤ *min_degree* **then**
                CentralNodes.add(*node*)
        if *CentralNodes.size()* ≤ *max_count* **then**
            return *CentralNodes*
        min_degree++

(DQ2 and DQ3). In information retrieval, it is difficult to separate any visualization for representing search results from the interface that contains that visualization [17]. We iteratively designed an interface to support navigation of our hierarchical knowledge graphs via a series of pilot studies.

Based on established literature and pilot studies we found that knowledge graphs can become overwhelming or confusing for participants [12, 22, 31, 39]. The overwhelming nature of the full knowledge graph leads to a need to create filtered views of our graph. These filtered views draw inspiration from the "expand-from-known" paradigm in information visualization [41]. Specifically, at the top level of the full corpus, a user selects a document, then a central concept from the minimap visualization. While preserving the entire knowledge graph, we alpha-blend all nodes in the knowledge graph *except* those nodes directly related to the central concept from the minimap. Recall that the central concept is simply a high-degree vertex from the knowledge graph; therefore, the central concept and all its linked nodes are shown saturated. As a result, users can identify the central concept, linked entities, and can see closely related additional entities. Together, this focused detailed view seems to effectively support expand-from-known at the knowledge graph level.

As well, for the Hierarchical View, the biggest challenge to address was the disorientation among the participants during transitions between collection, minimap, and knowledge graph views, a common problem in interfaces that show multiple levels of abstraction. To address this disorientation (DQ3), we maintained the connection between the hierarchical view and the graph view in two ways. First, the user can move between the layers of Collection View and the Document View smoothly through a zooming functionality that changes the focus of the UI (see Figure 2). Second, the interplay between the Document View and the Detailed View is designed such that the overview of the document is present at all times, in terms of a callout on the left side of the screen, an actual *minimap* as in computer gaming, which allows the user to maintain a sense of where he or she is while manipulating the fine-grained nodes and edges in the Detailed View.

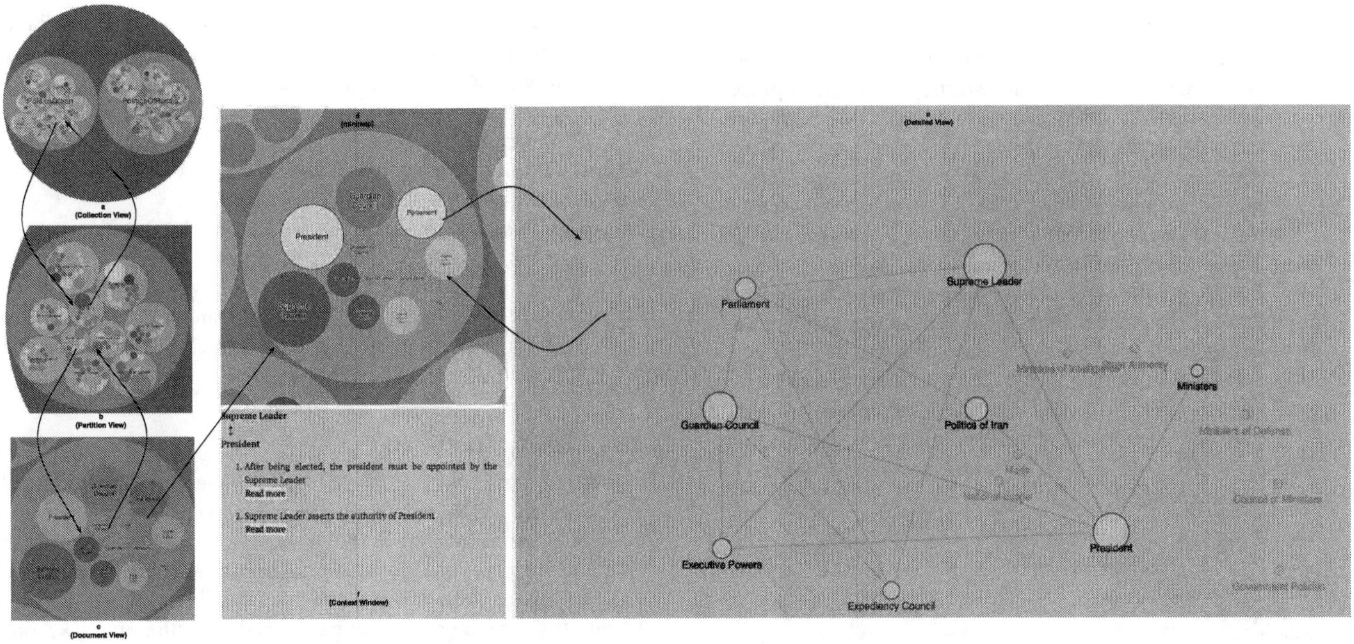

Figure 2: MultiLayer Graph Interface: (a) Collection View; (b) Partition View; (c) Document View; (d) Minimap (i.e. Global View); (e) Detailed View (Local View); (f) Snippet Window

The iterative process culminated in the final prototype shown in Figure 2.

In this interface, we see an initial overview, the Collection View that presents an overview of the underlying documents' structure in the collection (Figure 2-a). The collection view can potentially provide multiple partitions on the documents. Figure 2-b illustrates one partition of a collection. As an information seeker drills down on each document, the view is altered (Figure 2-c) such that an overview of the document is presented. The Document View provides a Global View of the corresponding document in terms of its central concepts. In this overview, the salient concepts in that article are visualized as circles of different sizes, where size indicates the frequency of occurrence in that article. We used force and pack layouts (as part of the D3 library[3]) to visualize the different layers of the knowledge graph representation.

The lowest layer of our representation is the Detailed View (Figure 2-e). This view is a knowledge graph that represents entities and relationships between them. The Detailed View, similar to Sarrafzadeh et al.'s graph interface [39], contains labeled nodes and unlabeled links between nodes. Nodes that represent entities with low frequency are hidden in the initial view, and only appear once a higher-frequency, connected node is clicked, ensuring that the graph does not become too cluttered. Once the user hovers over a node, that node and all connected nodes are highlighted, while the remainder of the graph is alpha-blended into the background. Clicking on a node can expand it by adding in its related nodes. Alternatively, clicking on a node can collapse its neighbours if they are expanded already. Nodes can also be dragged and placed at different parts of the canvas. This functionality can help with organizing the graph structure in a way that is more meaningful to the user and it can help with minimizing label overlap in the graph.

Edges can similarly be highlighted by hovering. By clicking on any edge, the user can see the relationship(s) between the two corresponding nodes (linked by this edge) in the context window located on the lower left side of the interface (Figure 2-f). For each relationship in the context region, a hyperlink allows users to view the corresponding web page.

[3]http://d3js.org/

4 EXPERIMENTAL DESIGN

Given that we have designed hierarchical knowledge graphs, a related question is how hierarchical knowledge graphs compare to hierarchies and/or knowledge graphs with respect to information seeking tasks. To evaluate this question, we need a set of control interfaces (reference interfaces that can be compared to hierarchical knowledge graphs, HKGs) and a reference data set. These can then be leveraged to design an experiment. As well, experimental design should replicate, as closely as possible, past work to ensure experimental validity.

In recent work, Sarrafzadeh et al. [39] developed two interfaces for exploratory search: one knowledge graph interface and one hierarchical tree interface. To preserve experimental validity, we use identical interfaces as control interfaces. We also leverage the identical data sets, ensuring that topic is eliminated as a confound. Finally, we use exactly the same experimental task, ensuring that performance numbers are representative between experiments.

4.1 Control Interfaces

- The first interface, a knowledge graph interface, functions as follows: As the interface starts, nodes that represent entities with low frequency are hidden in the initial view, and only appear once a higher-frequency, connected node is clicked. Users can also filter the knowledge graph by clicking on a node; when a user clicks on an edge, snippets and links associated with that edge are shown in a preview pane on the left side of the interface.
- The second interface utilized a hierarchy (or a tree) structure to organize headings and sub-headings of the articles, as observed in each page's table-of-contents. When the user launches the application, the user is presented with a fully expanded tree. By clicking on any node within the tree, that portion of the Wikipedia document corresponding to the node is presented in the preview area at the left of the interface.

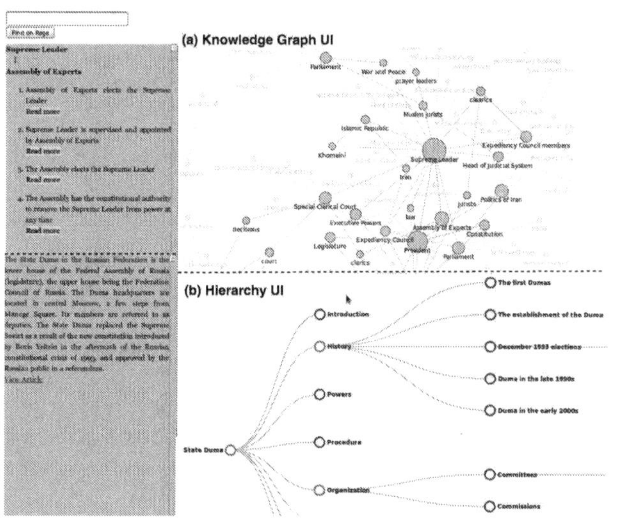

Figure 3: Control interfaces for Knowledge graph and Hierarchy. More details in Sarrafzadeh et al. [39].

Figure 3 depicts these two interfaces. Contrasting these interfaces with Figure 2 shows a similar preview pane for snippets. Links within the snippets function identically across all three interfaces.

4.2 Data Set

We leveraged the two data sets from Sarrafzadeh et al.'s previous study: A history data set, specifically a corpus of Wikipedia articles describing the historical locations of the capital city of Canada; And a global politics data set, a Wikipedia corpus representing governmental structures in Iran and Russia.

4.3 Search Tasks

We used the same two exploratory search tasks [24], a simple and a complex exploratory search task, as follows:

Simple Politics: What governmental body or bodies are involved in the impeachment of the President of Iran and of Russia? (sample question)

Complex Politics: Imagine you are a high school student who is going to write an essay on the Political Systems of Iran and Russia. Knowing little about the presidents of these two countries, you wish to determine which president has more power. Find at least 3 arguments to justify your answer.

Simple History: As a result of which act were Upper and Lower Canada formed? (sample question)

Complex History: Imagine you are a high school student who is going to write an essay on the History of Canada. Knowing little about Canadian History, you wish to know which cities have served as a capital for Canada. You would also like to understand the reasons behind moving the capital from one city to another.

4.4 Study Design

Our study design was a $3 \times 2 \times 2$ [interface, topic, complexity] mixed design. For Knowledge graph and hierarchy, we leverage the data set of Sarrafzadeh et al. [39], available from the researchers in anonymized form. We add additional participants for our HKGs to yield our mixed design as follows.

For HKGs, each participant performed two different tasks, one simple and one complex. The topic area (history or politics) differed for each of these tasks. More formally, for these participants, our design was a 2×2 full factorial mixed design, with topic and complexity as within subjects factors and complexity to topic assignment as a between subject factor. We counter-balanced the order in which the tasks were assigned to the participants.

Alongside the HKG participants, leveraging data from Sarrafazdeh et al. [39] adds two additional levels of Interface (hierarchical tree or knowledge graph) as a between subject factor. Combining the data sets yield the $3 \times 2 \times 2$ mixed design [interface, topic, complexity] with interface as a between subjects factor, and topic and complexity as within subjects factors.

4.5 Participants

In total we analyze data from forty seven participants. Twenty six participants, thirteen female, used hierarchies and knowledge graphs, the control interfaces. An additional twenty-one participants (4 female) used HKGs, the experimental condition, as a between subjects factor. All participants use the Internet on a regular basis to search for information. Participants were aged between 18 and 45 years old (62% were between 20 and 29 years old). Participants received a $15 incentive for their participation.

4.6 Procedure

After introducing the study, participants were presented with an experimental interface (populated with an unrelated data set), and were given time to familiarize themselves with the interface and data structure. Once participants had developed some comfort with the features of the interface ($\sim$ 3 minutes), participants completed a questionnaire assessing their familiarity with the topic used for the first task. They were then given the description of their task (see above), and were asked to complete the task using the interface (15 minutes per task). Participants completed a post-task questionnaire that evaluated the experience; we used questionnaires provided by

TREC-9 Interactive Searching track [4] modified to fit our experiment. The same process was repeated for the second task.

At the end of the second task, a semi-structured interview explored participants' experience using the interface. Interviews explored the conceptual usability of the visualization, the technical usability of the application and the efficacy of the interface for different types of search tasks. Feedback on competing interfaces was also collected from participants.

4.7 Data Collection

Alongside a mixed design of within subject and between subject factors, we perform a mixed methods analysis of both quantitative and qualitative data [13]. Data was captured as follows:

(a) The interface was instrumented with a logger which monitored movement on the computer screen and participants' interactions with the system. Interactions collected included node or edge clicks, snippets read, articles viewed, and time spent reading the articles. In HKGs, the transition between the layers and switches between the MiniMap and the knowledge graph were captured.

(b) Two assessors evaluated the quality of answers provided by the participants for each of the search tasks independently. Simple queries were rated as either correct or incorrect. Complex questions were rated on a scale. Scores for all queries were normalized to reflect a value in the range [0, 1]. Inter-assessor reliability was evaluated using Pearson coefficient and an overall value of 0.97 for simple queries and 0.94 for complex queries was found.

(c) We captured field notes during participant interactions, audio recorded all sessions, transcribed final interviews, and collected questionnaire data. This data was analyzed collectively using open coding to extract low-level themes and axial coding to identify thematic connections between elements. Coding was performed incrementally as each participant's data was collected, and saturation was found after coding qualitative data from field notes and transcripts for 15 of our 21 participants.

4.8 Hypotheses and Research Questions

Quantitative data allows us to test the following hypotheses:

- Hierarchical knowledge graphs result in fewer document views and less time spent reading documents than do hierarchical trees.
- Hierarchical knowledge graphs exhibit statistically similar behaviors to Knowledge Graphs.

Alongside hypothesis testing, our log data provides insight into whether hierarchies are used in hierarchical knowledge graphs and on whether task complexity affects the use of hierarchies. As well, to triangulate quantitative data, we leverage our qualitative data to compare and contrast the nature of the hierarchies between the tree interface and the hierarchical knowledge graphs and to understand whether the hierarchies provide similar affordances.

5 RESULTS

5.1 Quantitative Analysis

Scoring of participant responses by independent evaluators and log file analysis produced the quantitative measures in Table 1 for Hierarchical Knowledge Graphs (H. Graphs), Hierarchical Trees (H. Trees), and Knowledge Graphs (K. Graphs). Rows represent measures for Marks (MK), Nodes clicked (NK), Edges Clicked (EC), Document Views (V) and Document View Time (VT). We break each measurement out by two query levels, Simple and Complex, as described previously.

[4]www-nlpir.nist.gov/projects/t9i/qforms.html

		H. Graphs	H. Trees	K. Graphs
Simple	MK	0.43 (0.21)	0.32 (0.20)	0.37 (0.14)
	NC	11.4 (8.6)	19.0 (10.04)	11.38 (9.4)
	EC	18.3 (8.9)	NA	27.15 (12.9)
	V	**2.38 (1.61)**	**6.08 (2.49)**	**2.38 (3.00)**
	VT	**145.6 (153.7)**	**1430.9 (2302.8)**	**211.6 (228.0)**
Complex	MK	0.62 (0.18)	0.57 (0.28)	0.58 (0.16)
	NC	13.38 (9.2)	20.09 (17.7)	26.23 (19.12)
	EC	23.09 (12.7)	NA	41.07 (19.4)
	V	**2.15 (2.13)**	**4.38 (2.24)**	**4.38 (2.24)**
	VT	**103.4 (97.6)**	**985.38 (1848.3)**	**78.76 (131.5)**

Table 1: Hierarchical (H.) Graphs vs. Hierarchical Trees and Knowledge (K.) Graphs: Mean (Standard Deviation) values for marks (MK - average independent evaluator scores), clicks on nodes (NC) and edges (EC), document views (V), and document view time (VT). Bolded dependent variables exhibited significant differences in post-hoc testing.

5.1.1 Hypotheses Testing. Multivariate analysis of variance with respect to interface (tree versus graph versus hierarchical graph), topic (history versus politics), and task (simple versus complex) for Marks (MK), Views (V), and View Time (VT) shows a statistically significant effect of interface ($F_{6,172} = 7.126, p < 0.001, \eta^2 = 0.2$) and task ($F_{3,86} = 12.22, p < 0.001, \eta^2 = 0.3$) on dependent variables. Post-hoc factor analysis using Tukey correction indicates that the tree interface exhibited statistically significantly higher numbers of document views than both hierarchical graphs and knowledge graphs. As well, the tree exhibited statistically longer reading times than hierarchical graphs ($p < 0.05$), but not than knowledge graphs ($p = 0.064$) in our analysis. Hierarchical graphs and knowledge graphs did not differ significantly in their effects on any dependent variables. Task significantly impacted the marks but no other variables.

Clicks are not directly comparable between H. Trees, H.Graphs, and K.Graphs, as edges are not clickable in hierarchies (NA value in Table 1). Performing pairwise comparison between H.Graphs and K.Graphs, our analysis showed no statistically significant effect on dependent variables ($F_{3,30} = 0.752, p > 0.5, \eta^2 = 0.70$), including node click and edge click behavior.

Given the above analyses, we reject both null hypotheses and conclude that our hypotheses are supported by our data set. Hierarchical Knowledge Graphs preserve the advantages of Knowledge graphs over hierarchical trees in both reading time and in document views. Focusing specifically on our hierarchical graph, we find that our hierarchical graph has statistically lower document views (61% fewer document views, on average) and time reading (90% less time reading documents) than does hierarchical trees and that its behavior is statistically indistinguishable from the prior observations of knowledge graph interfaces. Furthermore, the effect size measures, η^2, are significantly above the threshold (0.14) typically considered to be a large effect, lending support to these differences being sufficiently large to be meaningful. In summary, our quantitative results support our hypothesis that our hierarchical knowledge graphs fully preserve the quantitative advantages identified by Sarrafzadeh et al [39] for knowledge graphs over hierarchies.

5.1.2 Additional Quantitative Analysis. Given the statistically indistinguishable nature of HKGs and Knowledge Graphs, one question is if (and whether) intermediate hierarchical representations are used. It is possible that Hierarchical Knowledge Graphs are indistinguisable from Knowledge Graphs because users ignore the hierarchy and simply leverage the knowledge graph.

	GlobalView	MiniMap	DetailedView
Simple Task	27.03%	14.61%	58.0%
Complex Task	23.83%	17.24%	58.90%

Table 2: Percentage of Time spent on each of Global View, Minimap and Detailed View

To specifically explore this question, we looked at how much time users spent on each of the provided views in our HKG interface. Overall, our data indicated that participants took advantage of all three layers relatively similarly across both Simple and Complex tasks. Further, while the the time spent on detailed view dominates other views (58% for the simple task and 59% for the complex task), over 40% of time was spent on additional views in the hierarchy (Table 2). Looking specifically at how participants spent their time in different layers of the hierarchy (i.e. utilizing different views of the data) for different tasks we see that the time spent at the detailed view is similar for both levels of complexity. On the other hand, participants seem to spend less time in MiniMap than Global for the simple task (Pairwise t-tests with Tukey correction yields statistical significance, $p < 0.01$). For Complex task, however, time in Global versus mid-level are not statistically different ($p > 0.1$). Essentially, in the complex task, sensemaking is split between global and minimap views of the hierarchy more equitably, i.e., the minimap is particularly useful during our complex tasks.

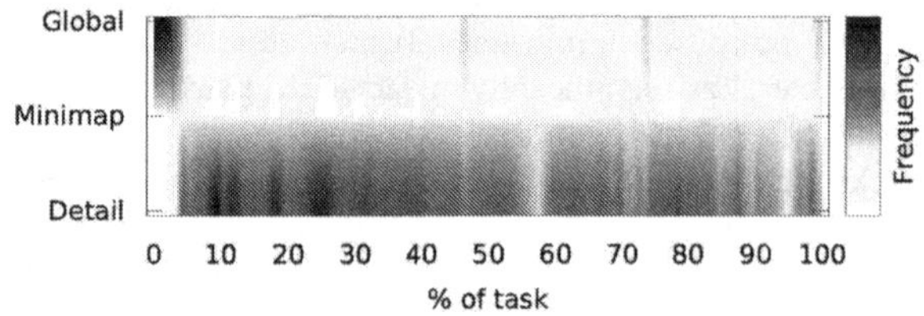

Figure 4: Heatmap visualizing the patterns of users navigating views in HKG for intervals of 1% of task length.

We also explored usage patterns of views. Figure 4 is a heatmap that visualizes use of different views for intervals of 1% of task length. Early in the task, we see frequent use of the global view. While difficult to see, MiniMap usage peaks just after the halfway point in the task, but there is no strong concentration of use. The hierarchy, and particularly the MiniMap visualization, seems to be used throughout the task.

5.2 Qualitative Analysis

The next question we explore involves participant perspectives on hierarchical knowledge graphs as a representation of search results. We were particularly interested in the overviews knowledge graphs provide for the information space and their contrast with Table-of-content-based hierarchies.

To address these questions, we performed open-coding of observations, transcripts, and questionnaire data. We coded incrementally, and saturation occurred after fifteen participants were coded. We coded all participants for completeness. Once open coding was complete, axial coding and thematic analysis was performed collaboratively by the researchers. We present three themes arising from our qualitative data analysis: Supporting Exploratory Search Tasks, Imposing a Structure versus Open Exploration and the Self-Orienting nature of HKGs.

5.2.1 Supporting Exploratory Search Tasks. As noted in our study design, we incorporate two exploratory information seeking tasks with different levels of complexity. In post-experiment interviews the participants were able to compare how different task complexities are supported by the assigned interface.

The hierarchical graph representation was found to provide more support for the Complex Task (i.e., more open ended and exploratory tasks such as essay writing or learning) versus Simple tasks (such as question answering and specific knowledge finding). This observation seems to be true for any multi-level structure which provides an overview and allows a gradual immersion into details: Finding a specific piece of information to satisfy a simple query is best done using a traditional search engine.

Looking specifically at HKGs and complex tasks, the overview allowed participants to identify the central concepts of a domain at a glance and the size of the circles indicates their prominence in the corresponding article. As many participants noted, 'relevance' or 'prominence' of a concept with respect to the main topic or the domain they are exploring is an important asset in Complex Search tasks. This qualitative observation may explain the more equitable use of the MiniMap representation for complex search tasks noted in our quantitative analysis. Complex tasks required synthesizing, rationalizing, and comparing, which seem to require more awareness of the entire data set.

This identification of central concepts was also linked to a perception of value of the MiniMap as a starting or entry point into the topic of the document being examined. Several participants articulated a belief that the overview provided by Central Concepts helped with "going from knowing nothing to having a plan", "learning terminology", "relevance, importance, or prominence", and "objectively learning about a domain". In particular, the *objective* nature of central concepts was cited by many participants as key to their utility.

As White and Roth [43] point out, exploratory search is motivated by complex information problems, poor understanding of terminology and information space structure, and often a 'desire to learn'. Vakkari [40] also argues "more support is needed in the initial stages of a task", when users have an unstructured mental model. Inspired by Kim [21], Sarrafzadeh et al. [39] found that hierarchical trees provide this benefit in unfamiliar domains. A strength of our design of hierarchical knowledge graphs is that it enables the user to engage in two alternative navigation paradigms. Users can exploit overview layers to explore the collection at a higher level followed by targeted immersion in the detailed view.

5.2.2 Imposing a Structure versus Open Exploration. While most participants were unanimous that the hierarchical representation imposes a [subjective] [rigid] structure onto the information space, their attitude towards this phenomenon varied. The level of domain knowledge and the complexity of the search tasks were found to be the major factors affecting their attitude.

When the searcher is dealing with a domain where he has limited knowledge, he is more open to accepting the structure that the representation imposes. Both hierarchical trees and hierarchical knowledge graphs incorporate imposed structures. Participants articulated a variety of advantages to structures: it was "easier to follow", "contained important aspects" that "simplified focus", and guided participants in "where to go" or "what steps to follow". With respect to hierarchical trees, some participants simply "trusted" the designer of the hierarchy (e.g. the author of an article) to be "logical" or "rational" in the way he broke down things. This was particularly true for participants with limited knowledge of a topic domain and replicates findings by Sarrafzadeh et al. [39] and Amadieu et al. [1] that low knowledge learners benefited from hierarchical structures in free recall performance and exhibited reduced disorientation.

In the case of higher domain knowledge, our participants were split in their preferences and attitudes. Some still trusted the logic behind the layout of a hierarchical trees and the fact that their knowledge of the domain can guide them to find what they want using this hierarchy. They trusted the designer to place items in close proximity to where the item should be. Other participants strongly opposed the rigid structure of a hierarchy, feeling it was "not the way I think", "based on the mindset of the author", or "did not match the domain structure".

One interesting perspective of the multi-layer graph representation which presents central concepts of a domain as an overview for each document is that it reflects the knowledge graph concepts. This reflection made it, for many participants, more flexible and exploratory, a window into the knowledge graph. Many participants commented on this phenomenon, noting it was "guiding but not imposting", "more open", "sparked interest" in the lower level structure, or was "visually appealing" and "fun".

5.2.3 Self-Orienting or Relative Positioning. One main advantage of a the Hierarchical Tree visualization in Sarrafzadeh et al. [39] was the explicit connections between nodes (categories or headings) in the representation. These edges help in two ways:

(1) At a glance, you can tell why a concept appeared in this overview, or in this domain. To whit, the hierarchical structure exists the way it does because of a human author's decision.
(2) The Path from the root to each of these nodes in the Tree Layout can provide useful information on where a concept is positioned relative to the topic.

Sarrafzadeh et al. [39] note that participants may perceive a domain to have a derivative/hierarchical structure or a multi-faceted structure. If salient relationships are viewed as derivative or hierarchical (e.g. 'is-a' relationships), then a tree can best capture this view of data, whereas if salient relationships are more heterogeneous and resist structure as a hierarchy, that disadvantages the hierarchies.

This is not the case in our MiniMap, where the connection between each of these main concepts and the main topic is unknown at first glance. Central concepts are simply extracted based on their high connectivity with other concepts within a specific document within a corpus. However, it is also true that it would be quite surprising if highly linked concepts were not, somehow, important components of any individual document. The more pervasively they link, the more they interconnect with other concepts, the more important it is to understand them and their relationship. In this way, HKGs become self-orienting for out participants.

6 LIMITATIONS

Any study has limitations. Because we leverage the research methodology and data sets of Sarrafzadeh et al. [39], we inherit the limitations of that study, including topic and implementation issues which may bias the study. Despite this, there is also a strength in replication: if interfaces are redesigned, data sets differ, and tasks are unique it becomes difficult to ensure a lack of confound in experimental design. We address this by preserving, to the limit possible, all aspects of a similar study within this space contrasting data structures.

Our mixed design of within and between subject factors is a particular strength to our study design. Because topic (history/politics) and task complexity are within-subject factors, they are controlled across participants. Because we are most interested in interface and it is a between subject factor, to observe statistical significance we need good separation of dependent variables between the two data sets, reducing the likelihood of a type-one error in our analysis.

7 CONCLUSION

The primary goal of our research was to explore whether we could combine benefits from both knowledge graphs and hierarchies into one data structure for visualizing search results. We note that our hierarchical graphs significantly reduce documents read and reading time as compared to hierarchical trees and perform on par with knowledge graphs. We also provide evidence that the hierarchy is used by participants via analysis of interaction logs.

Qualitative data from our participants does indicate that hierarchies grounded in tables-of-contents are more familiar, easier to follow, and more focused. This in turn helps users orient themselves in the data. The vetted nature of hierarchical tables-of-contents was also perceived to be an asset absent from our hierarchical knowledge graphs. The hierarchies in our knowledge graph were viewed slightly differently, as noted above, with a more quantitative perspective giving them a certain cachet with respect to the unbiased nature of topic selection.

A final issue to consider is whether any hierarchy might provide benefits. While it may, one advantage of the hierarchy in our HKGs is its tight connection to the entities contained in a knowledge graph and the ease of automatically extracting the hierarchy through thresholding. Another advantage is flexibility: while we currently leverage only three levels – corpus, central concept, and knowledge graph – it is easy to generalize the hierarchy to an arbitrary number of thresholds depending on the complexity of the domain. We do not generalize the hierarchy in this paper because, for a first experimental validation, there are a limited number of factors that can be assessed. However, future work can address more detailed inquiries into scalability to larger corpora, scalability to multi-level hierarchies, and contrasts with other hierarchies such as automatic clusters or user-specified facets.

In summary, we find that our hierarchical knowledge graphs preserve many of the previously observed advantages of traditional knowledge graphs, i.e. fewer document views and reduced reading time. Alongside this, hierarchical knowledge graphs introduce an effective hierarchical representation into knowledge graphs.

ACKNOWLEDGEMENTS

Funding for this research was provided by the Natural Science and Engineering Research Council of Canada (NSERC). Authors also thank Saeed Nejati for his contributions in implementing the interface.

REFERENCES

[1] Franck Amadieu, André Tricot, and Claudette Mariné. 2010. Interaction between prior knowledge and concept-map structure on hypertext comprehension, coherence of reading orders and disorientation. *Interacting with computers* 22, 2 (2010), 88–97.

[2] Anne Aula and Daniel M Russell. 2008. Complex and exploratory web search. In *Information Seeking Support Systems Workshop (ISSS 2008), Chapel Hill, NC, USA.*

[3] David Paul Ausubel, Joseph Donald Novak, Helen Hanesian, and others. 1968. Educational psychology: A cognitive view. (1968).

[4] Steven M Beitzel, Eric C Jensen, Abdur Chowdhury, David Grossman, and Ophir Frieder. 2004. Hourly analysis of a very large topically categorized web query log. In *Proceedings of the 27th annual international ACM SIGIR conference on Research and development in information retrieval.* ACM, 321–328.

[5] Nicholas J Belkin. 1980. Anomalous states of knowledge as a basis for information-retrieval. *Canadian Journal of Information Science-Revue Canadienne Des Sciences De L Information* 5, MAY (1980), 133–143.

[6] Andrei Broder. 2002. A taxonomy of web search. In *ACM Sigir forum*, Vol. 36. ACM, 3–10.

[7] Katriina Bystr̀Om. 2002. Information and information sources in tasks of varying complexity. *Journal of the American Society for information Science and Technology* 53, 7 (2002), 581–591.

[8] Donald J Campbell. 1988. Task complexity: A review and analysis. *Academy of management review* 13, 1 (1988), 40–52.

[9] Robert Capra, Gary Marchionini, Jung Sun Oh, Fred Stutzman, and Yan Zhang. 2007. Effects of structure and interaction style on distinct search tasks. In *Proceedings of the 7th ACM/IEEE-CS joint conference on Digital libraries.* ACM, 442–451.

[10] Mary Carnot, Paul Feltovich, Robert Hoffman, Joan Feltovich, and Joseph Novak. 2003. A summary of literature pertaining to the use of concept mapping techniques and technologies for education and performance support. (2003).

[11] Hsinchun Chen, Andrea L Houston, Robin R Sewell, and Bruce R Schatz. 1998. Internet browsing and searching: User evaluation of category map and concept space techniques. *Journal of the American Society for Information Science, Special Issue on AI Techniques for Emerging Information Systems Applications* (1998).

[12] Andy Cockburn and Steve Jones. 1996. Which way now? Analysing and easing inadequacies in WWW navigation. *International Journal of Human-Computer Studies* 45, 1 (1996), 105–129.

[13] John W Creswell. 2013. *Research design: Qualitative, quantitative, and mixed methods approaches.* Sage publications.

[14] Brenda Dervin. 1998. Sense-making theory and practice: an overview of user interests in knowledge seeking and use. *Journal of knowledge management* 2, 2 (1998), 36–46.

[15] Marti Hearst. 2009. *Search user interfaces.* Cambridge University Press.

[16] Marti A Hearst. 1999. The use of categories and clusters for organizing retrieval results. In *Natural language information retrieval.* Springer, 333–374.

[17] Marti A Hearst. 2006. Clustering versus faceted categories for information exploration. *CACM* 49, 4 (2006), 59–61.

[18] P James. 1991. Knowledge graphs. *Order* 501 (1991), 6439.

[19] Bernard J Jansen and Amanda Spink. 2003. An Analysis of Web Documents Retrieved and Viewed.. In *International Conference on Internet Computing.* Citeseer, 65–69.

[20] Sussane Jul and George W Furnas. 1997. Navigation in electronic worlds: a CHI 97 workshop. *SIGCHI bulletin* 29 (1997), 44–49.

[21] Kyung-Sun Kim. 1999. Searching the Web: Effects of Problem Solving Style on Information-Seeking Behavior. In *World Conference on Educational Multimedia, Hypermedia and Telecommunications*, Vol. 1999. 1541–1542.

[22] Anita Komlodi, Gary Marchionini, and Dagobert Soergel. 2007. Search history support for finding and using information: User interface design recommendations from a user study. *Information processing & management* 43, 1 (2007), 10–29.

[23] Bill Kules and Robert Capra. 2008. Creating exploratory tasks for a faceted search interface. *Proc. of HCIR 2008* (2008), 18–21.

[24] Gary Marchionini. 2006. Exploratory search: from finding to understanding. *CACM* 49, 4 (2006), 41–46.

[25] Gary Marchionini and Ben Shneiderman. 1988. Finding facts vs. browsing knowledge in hypertext systems. *Computer* 21, 1 (1988), 70–80.

[26] Gary Marchionini and Ben Shneiderman. 1993. 3.1 Finding facts vs. browsing knowledge in hypertext systems. *Sparks of innovation in human-computer interaction* (1993), 103.

[27] Kent L Norman and John P Chin. 1988. The effect of tree structure on search in a hierarchical menu selection system. *Behaviour & Information Technology* 7, 1 (1988), 51–65.

[28] Joseph D Novak. 1990. Concept mapping: A useful tool for science education. *Journal of research in science teaching* 27, 10 (1990), 937–949.

[29] Joseph D Novak and Alberto J Cañas. 2008. The theory underlying concept maps and how to construct and use them. *FIHM Fl* 284 (2008).

[30] Laura R Novick and Sean M Hurley. 2001. To matrix, network, or hierarchy: That is the question. *Cognitive Psychology* 42, 2 (2001), 158–216.

[31] Christopher Olston and Ed H Chi. 2003. ScentTrails: Integrating browsing and searching on the Web. *ACM Transactions on Computer-Human Interaction (TOCHI)* 10, 3 (2003), 177–197.

[32] Peter Pirolli, Stuart K Card, and Mija M Van Der Wege. 2000. The effect of information scent on searching information: visualizations of large tree structures. In *Proceedings of the working conference on Advanced visual interfaces.* ACM, 161–172.

[33] Wanda Pratt, Marti A Hearst, and Lawrence M Fagan. 1999. A Knowledge-Based Approach to Organizing Retrieved Documents.. In *AAAI/IAAI.* 80–85.

[34] Kerry Rodden, Wojciech Basalaj, David Sinclair, and Kenneth Wood. 2001. Does organisation by similarity assist image browsing?. In *Proceedings of the SIGCHI conference on Human factors in computing systems.* ACM, 190–197.

[35] Daniel E Rose and Danny Levinson. 2004. Understanding user goals in web search. In *Proceedings of the 13th international conference on World Wide Web.* ACM, 13–19.

[36] Daniel Russell, Mark Stefik, Peter Pirolli, and Stuart Card. 1993. The cost structure of sensemaking. In *Proc. of INTERACT'93 and CHI'93.* ACM, 269–276.

[37] Bahareh Sarrafzadeh, Rakesh Guttikonda, Kaheer Suleman, Jack Thomas, and Olga Vechtomova. March 2013. *Automatic discovery of related concepts.* Technical Report.

[38] Bahareh Sarrafzadeh, Olga Vechtomova, and Vlado Jokic. 2014. Exploring knowledge graphs for exploratory search. In *Proc. of IIiX.* ACM, 135–144.

[39] Bahareh Sarrafzadeh, Alexandra Vtyurina, Edward Lank, and Olga Vechtomova. 2016. Knowledge Graphs versus Hierarchies: An Analysis of User Behaviours and Perspectives in Information Seeking. In *Proc. of the 2016 ACM on Conference on Human Information Interaction and Retrieval.* ACM, 91–100.

[40] Pertti Vakkari. 2000. Relevance and contributing information types of searched documents in task performance. In *Proc. of SIGIR.* ACM, 2–9.

[41] Frank Van Ham and Adam Perer. 2009. "Search, Show Context, Expand on Demand": Supporting Large Graph Exploration with Degree-of-Interest. *Visualization and Computer Graphics, IEEE Transactions on* 15, 6 (2009), 953–960.

[42] Charles K West, James A Farmer, and Phillip M Wolff. 1991. *Instructional design: Implications from cognitive science.* Prentice Hall Englewood Cliffs, NJ.

[43] Ryen W White and Resa A Roth. 2009. Exploratory search: Beyond the query-response paradigm. *Synthesis Lectures on Information Concepts, Retrieval, and Services* 1, 1 (2009), 1–98.

[44] Barbara M Wildemuth and Luanne Freund. 2012. Assigning search tasks designed to elicit exploratory search behaviors. In *Proc. of HCIR 2012.* ACM, 4.

[45] Max L Wilson and others. 2009. The importance of conveying inter-facet relationships for making sense of unfamiliar domains. (2009).

[46] Max L Wilson, Bill Kules, Ben Shneiderman, and others. 2010. From keyword search to exploration: Designing future search interfaces for the web. *Foundations and Trends in Web Science* 2, 1 (2010), 1–97.

[47] Yi-fang Brook Wu, Latha Shankar, and Xin Chen. 2003. Finding more useful information faster from web search results. In *Proceedings of the twelfth international conference on Information and knowledge management.* ACM, 568–571.

[48] Ka-Ping Yee, Kirsten Swearingen, Kevin Li, and Marti Hearst. 2003. Faceted metadata for image search and browsing. In *Proc. of CHI.* ACM, 401–408.

Searching on the Go: The Effects of Fragmented Attention on Mobile Web Search Tasks

Morgan Harvey
CIS Department, Northumbria University
Newcastle upon Tyne, United Kingdom
morgan.harvey@northumbria.ac.uk

Matthew Pointon
CIS Department, Northumbria University
Newcastle upon Tyne, United Kingdom
m.pointon@northumbria.ac.uk

ABSTRACT

Smart phones and tablets are rapidly becoming our main method of accessing information and are frequently used to perform on-the-go search tasks. Mobile devices are commonly used in situations where attention must be divided, such as when walking down a street. Research suggests that this increases cognitive load and, therefore, may have an impact on performance. In this work we conducted a laboratory experiment with both device types in which we simulated everyday, common mobile situations that may cause fragmented attention, impact search performance and affect user perception.

Our results showed that the fragmented attention induced by the simulated conditions significantly affected both participants' objective and perceived search performance, as well as how hurried they felt and how engaged they were in the tasks. Furthermore, the type of device used also impacted how users felt about the search tasks, how well they performed and the amount of time they spent engaged in the tasks. These novel insights provide useful information to inform the design of future interfaces for mobile search and give us a greater understanding of how context and device size affect search behaviour and user experience.

CCS CONCEPTS

•**Information systems →Information retrieval;** *Users and interactive retrieval;* •**Human-centered computing →Empirical studies in ubiquitous and mobile computing;** *User studies;*

KEYWORDS

mobile search; fragmented attention; search experience; cognition; user study; experimentation

1 INTRODUCTION

Recent years have seen rapid growth in the sale and use of various mobile computing devices, giving people the ability to access the Internet away from the confines of a desk, and in many different environmental contexts. Over two-thirds of Americans own a smart phone and almost half own a, somewhat larger, tablet device. At the same time, the sales of desktop and laptop computers have begun to stagnate and even to fall [1]. Almost all smart phone owners (97%) use their devices to access the Internet, many of whom search for information, and to complete fairly complex retrieval tasks: 62% have used them to look up information about a health condition; 57% to do a search for real estate and 40% to look up government services [35].

People use mobile devices to search the web in a variety of different contexts - on public transport, while walking from place to place [17, 23, 33] or in social contexts, where the presence of others can cause distraction [8]. Interaction with such devices is achieved via touch screens upon which small "soft buttons" are drawn for users to select items and input text. Although these buttons may be easy to accurately press in an *ideal environment*, e.g. when seated, such small and non-tactile targets can be significantly more difficult to interact with in other situations [4]. While the ability to perform such tasks "on the go" can be of real benefit, hazards and other changes in the surroundings do necessitate the user's brain switching attention between the ambient environment and the device [11].

These distractions can preoccupy users [30], reducing their effectiveness in interacting with the UI [4, 23] and may even affect user perceptions of the environment and tasks [9]. The result is a larger number of misspelled queries and an attempt by users to shorten queries when searching [32, 33]. In fact, concentration on a mobile task while walking even has an effect on how we walk; to compensate the brain subtly (and subconsciously) alters stance and gait [34]. As such, using a mobile device whilst walking requires both cognitive and motor abilities and so users must divide their attention between the two tasks [21], meaning either an increase in cognitive load, a decrease in pace, a decrease in task performance or a combination of these [22]. The level of difficulty experienced may additionally be influenced by the device size and type and the amount of encumbrance it itself causes [5, 12].

Despite the popularity of mobile devices, their ubiquity in everyday life and the ability they give us to engage in complex search tasks, little is known about how using them on the go impacts upon search behaviour and search performance and whether or not device type and size is an important factor. With this in mind, we investigate whether the small behaviour changes identified in the literature for simple tasks (such as tapping on a highlighted button) result in significant behavioural changes, different perceptions of the task, and different task performance for relatively complex web search problems on both smart phone and tablet devices. Does the change in context impact on user *behaviour*, is this something that users themselves are aware of and does the type of device used matter? To ensure repeatability, we conducted our study in a lab

SIGIR'17, August 7–11, 2017, Shinjuku, Tokyo, Japan

978-1-4503-5022-8/17/08...$15.00
DOI: http://dx.doi.org/10.1145/3077136.3080770

using simulated contexts - walking on a treadmill, navigating an obstacle course and sitting still at a desk.

Our main research questions, therefore, are:

- Do common mobile situations that cause fragmented attention have an impact on:
  - *RQ1* Users' perceptions of the task and their own performance?
  - *RQ2* Objective measures of users' task performance and behaviour?
- *RQ3* What impact does the device type have on user performance and perception thereof?

The remainder of the paper is structured as follows: In section 2 we consider related work on the topics of mobile device use, fragmented attention and user distraction; section 3 describes the user studies we performed to investigate searching on the go; sections 4,5 and 6 describe the results of the user studies in detail; section 7 discusses how the results relate to the existing literature and suggests reasons and intuition behind them; and section 8 concludes the paper with suggestions for potential future work.

2 RELATED WORK

Improvements in mobile technologies in recent years have led to a dramatic change in how and when people access and use information, and has "a profound impact on how users address their daily information needs" [7]. Research shows that as the power of these devices - as well as the amount of screen space they afford - increases, the complexity of tasks people use them for also increases, with mobile search sessions becoming longer and less homogeneous [19]. Many people now use their smart devices in different contexts to find information, keep up to date with news or to alleviate boredom [35] and frequently use them whilst walking or on public transport. This relatively novel situation of interacting with a computing device when non-stationary can be distracting as attention must be shared (or "fragmented") between operating the device and maintaining motility, typically necessitating a change in posture, stance and gait [34].

A large body of work has investigated user contexts and how fragmented attention affects user input on mobile devices. Early work designed and evaluated forms of human computer interaction in fixed, non-fragmented contexts of use, in a single domain such as a lab [16]. As mobile research evolved, studies began to investigate situations in which attention is diverted from the interface. Oulasvirta et al. found that when following a pre-defined, but otherwise uncontrolled, route through a city users experienced significant impairment when compared with a "non-social laboratory condition" [30]. In a more controlled set of experiments, Lin et al. [23] demonstrated that error rates of stylus input significantly increased as the amount of distraction, and thus degree of attention fragmentation, increased. Similar effects were later demonstrated for touch-based input, with error rates increasing in line with walking speed [28].

Early investigations of reading comprehension and word search when walking [3] showed that contextual variations can have large effects on user behaviour, impairs performance and increases task workload. Mizobuchi et al. looked into mobile text entry and found additional workload effects when walking and identified walking speed as a secondary measure of mental workload [24]. They concluded that texting whilst walking results in either a reduction in input speed (but not accuracy) or a reduction in walking pace. Large-scale analysis of mobile search logs [18] has shown that the increase in time required for mobile searches deters some types of search behaviour, such as exploratory search, and causes search sessions to be considerably shorter than in desktop search. These lines of investigation concluded that times increased significantly when walking compared to a sitting condition, search behaviour altered whilst mobile and walking speed when texting reduces by a fixed amount independent of the level of input difficulty, which varied between participants. These types of investigative conditions create situational impairments which fragment a users' attention, exerting a range of effects on performance and creating compelling opportunities for research [20].

Interaction with such devices is commonly achieved via touch screens upon which relatively small "soft buttons" are drawn for users to select items and input text. The examination of soft buttons, hardware buttons, and surface gestures under conditions of medium and high distraction found that marking menus (i.e. directional gestures) activated along a smartphone's bevel provided the fastest response time [4, 26]. While these buttons may be easy to accurately press in an ideal environment, such as when seated, such small and non-tactile targets may be much more difficult to interact with in other distracting situations [4]. Other investigations assessed the effects of walking on performance with soft buttons, attempting to quantify the negative effects on use due to walking and exploring design changes that may improve a user's experience with a mobile device [20].

Screen real-estate on a mobile device also creates interaction difficulties as a user moves, combined with increasing complexity of mobile task, resulting in considerable obstacles [5, 6, 13]. The limited input modalities afforded by mobile devices have a negative effect on usability [13], a problem compounded by screen size and the device's reduced ability to present information and navigational cues [5, 6]. Small screens can easily become cluttered with information and widgets (buttons, menus, windows, etc.) and this presents a difficult challenge for interface designers [5]. Use of larger devices, such as tablets, which have correspondingly larger screens, may mitigate some of these issues and result in notably different modalities of use [25].

Research shows that smart phones and tablets are often used for different tasks [25, 31] and an analysis of query logs [36] suggests that querying behaviour differs between tablet and smart phone users. Furthermore, there may be a negative correlation between screen size and perceived task difficulty and experienced workload [12], although it has not been investigated when comparing smart phones and tablets and it is unknown what effect situational context has, if any. In general, little is known about the impact differences between the devices has on user behaviour, perceptions and performance on retrieval tasks and under varying mobile conditions.

Delays and time pressures, which may be induced by increased levels of distraction and input error rate, also have a significant impact on search behaviour and objective performance. A study by Crescenzi et al. [10] compared two groups of users on a number of search tasks: one group was given a per–task time limit of 5 minutes, while the other was given no limit. The results showed that users faced with time pressures experience increased (perceived) task difficulty and less satisfaction with their performance and felt an increased need to work fast and engage in more metacognitive monitoring. Earlier work [9] by the same authors showed that time pressure leads to more queries being issued, fewer documents being viewed and less focus on examination of documents and SERPs. Recent work [15] has demonstrated that users perceive a similar increase in search task difficulty and reduction in satisfaction of their own performance when put under more distracting experimental conditions. These effects are likely as a result of the increased cost of complex cognitive tasks under such conditions, leading to a modification in behaviour as explained by the search models and studies of Azzopardi et al. [2].

Indeed, distractions during walking, driving, and other real-world interactions can preoccupy users [30], reducing their effectiveness in interacting with the UI [4, 23] and resulting in a larger number of misspelled queries and an attempt by users to shorten queries [32, 33]. Walking whilst using a mobile device requires both cognitive and motor abilities and users must divide their attention between the two tasks [21]. This means either an increase in cognitive load, a decrease in pace, a decrease in task performance or a combination of these [22]. There are many examples of distracted input on smart phones where users must split their attention between the task of navigating their physical environment and navigating information on the smart phone screen [26]. It could even be interpreted that users are performing tasks inside a bubble, flipping back and forth between the information on the screen and the outside world [17]. Given that today's users are more likely to be mobile when they search for information online, a deeper understanding of their interactions and challenges whilst mobile will help understand situational search behaviour and the influences of these fragmentations on search.

3 METHOD

We conducted a laboratory experiment with 24 participants drawn from a large European University (a mixture of academic staff, support staff and post-graduate students), of whom 13 were male. Although participants were randomly assigned to one of the 3 conditions, there was a very equal spread of genders with no fewer than 3 of each gender assigned to all conditions (χ^2=0.59, p-value=0.75). Ages ranged from 18 to 60, with 2 modal age ranges of between 25 and 30 and between 31 and 40. Ages were also distributed between the experimental conditions with no significant differences (χ^2=5.13, p-value=0.74). 18 of the participants were native English speakers and the rest were completely fluent in the language.

There were two independent variables: the type of *device* (tablet or phone; a Huawei MediaPad M2 8" and Moto X Style respectively, both running Android version 5 with the Google Chrome web browser) and the level of *distraction*. The distraction level was varied by simulating 2 everyday situations experienced by mobile device users: walking quickly on a treadmill and navigating an environment with obstacles, as well as a baseline condition in which the participant was seated without any distractions. Participants were randomly allocated to one of the three conditions, resulting in 8 participants for each. Distraction level was a between-subjects variable, while device type was within-subjects.

Following the procedure of Lin et al. [23], participants on the treadmill were asked to select a comfortable walking pace using the increase and decrease belt speed buttons, which was then increased by 20% to induce a small amount of ambulatory distraction. The resulting speeds ranged between 2.2 MPH (3.5 KPH) and 3.8 MPH (6.1 KPH) with a mean of 2.9 MPH (4.7 KPH) and men choosing to walk, on average, 0.78 MPH faster than women. The obstacle course group was shown how to navigate a pre-defined layout (see Figure 1), were asked to maintain a normal walking pace and were prompted to speed up by the researchers if their pace began to noticeably decrease during the task.

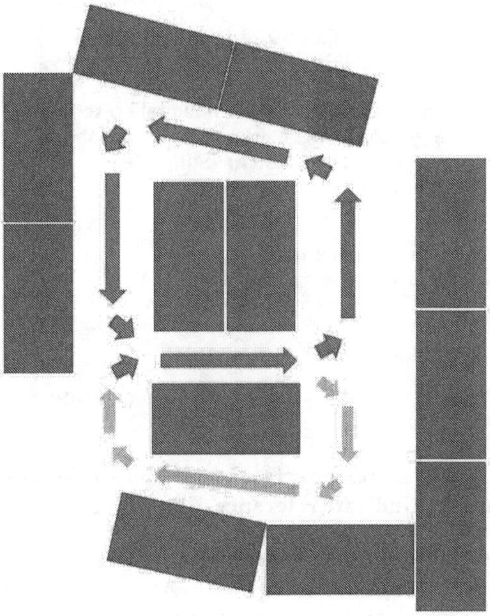

Figure 1: Plan view of obstacle course layout. Participants began at the orange arrow and followed the course in an anti-clockwise direction (green circle followed by yellow).

In order to ensure that we could control the search system and record interaction data we developed a simple mobile search interface named *zing*, shown in Figure 2. The zing interface mimics a standard search engine by showing the titles of 10 links in descending order of relevance together with snippets for each. The interface allowed participants to enter search terms and indicate (via checkboxes) which documents they thought were relevant. It showed the current task (TREC topic) at the bottom of the screen and allowed participants to progress to the next topic at any time. The interface also prompted users to fill in pre- and post-topic questionnaires to survey their perceptions about the task and their self-assessed post-task performance, satisfaction, perceived time pressure and focus/involvement on the task. Half of the participants completed their first 2 topics on a phone, moving on to the tablet for their final 2 topics, while the other half began with the tablet.

We used a standard test collection: AQUAINT, and removed duplicate documents in a pre-processing step to provide a better

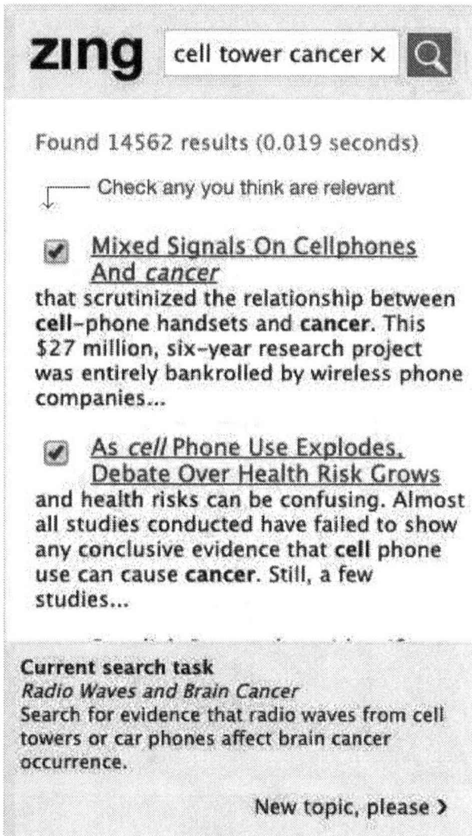

Figure 2: zing search interface on an Apple iPhone 5. Checkboxes used to indicate relevance.

#	Title	AP	Pre	Post
362	Human smuggling	0.29	2.83	2.75
367	Modern Piracy	0.26	2.79	2.25
638	Wrongful convictions	0.23	2.83	3
404	Ireland peace talks	0.28	3.25	2.79

Table 1: TREC topics used.

and more familiar user experience. To assess performance we made use of pre-defined TREC topics from the 2005 Robust track [37], of which we chose 4 at random from a subset of those which are neither too difficult nor too easy[1]. Table 1 shows the topics chosen as well as the average precision (AP) of their titles on the AQUAINT collection and the participants' perceptions of each topic's difficulty before (pre) and after (post) completing it.

Indexing, searching and snippet generation was provided by Apache SOLR[2]. Each participant was given the same 4 topics (tasks) in a random order with a per-task time limit of 15 minutes and alternated between the two *device* conditions by conducting the first two tasks on one device before switching to the other for the final 2 topics. The starting device for each user was allocated at random to prevent fatigue and/or learning effects from confusing the results. Participants were asked to imagine they wanted to learn more about the subject of each topic for a short report and were requested to select between two and four documents they thought were relevant for each topic and were told they could submit multiple queries per topic, if necessary. Participant actions and behaviour were recorded by means of a GoPro camera worn on the head, a wide-angle view of the obstacle course and by recording and logging interactions with the touchscreen and browser interface (Figure 3).

Figure 3: Example of data recorded via the cameras and screen recording software. Note that information from all 3 sources is temporally synced.

4 RESULTS

In the following we use t-tests to compare distributions that are normal (as well as results from Likert scales) and Wilcoxon sign-rank tests in cases of non-normal data (e.g. task duration and number of hits).

4.1 Pre-study questionnaire

Before being told anything about the experiment, participants were asked to fill in a short pre-study questionnaire asking them about their use of mobile devices and search engines as well as how difficult they would expect it to be to search on a phone or a tablet in various contexts.

All but two participants use a mobile device several times a day and all but three use a search engine to find information several times per day and all participants but one said they were either "confident" or"very confident" at using a search engine to find information. 19 use their mobile device at least once per day whilst walking, 9 use it daily on public transport and all but 3 use it to search the web on a daily basis. Participants expected that using both devices whilst walking on a treadmill, navigating an obstacle course or while sitting in a noisy pub or cafe would be significantly more difficult than when sitting still (see Figure 4). They expected using a mobile phone to be significantly more difficult when navigating an obstacle course compared with when walking

[1] After the method of Harvey et al. [14], whereby the difficulty of a topic is determined by the average precision of its title over the document collection.
[2] http://lucene.apache.org/solr/

on a treadmill (t=2.95, p-value=0.005) and expected, for both devices, that searching in a noisy pub or cafe would be significantly easier than in either of the other two conditions (all tests p-value $\ll 0.01$).

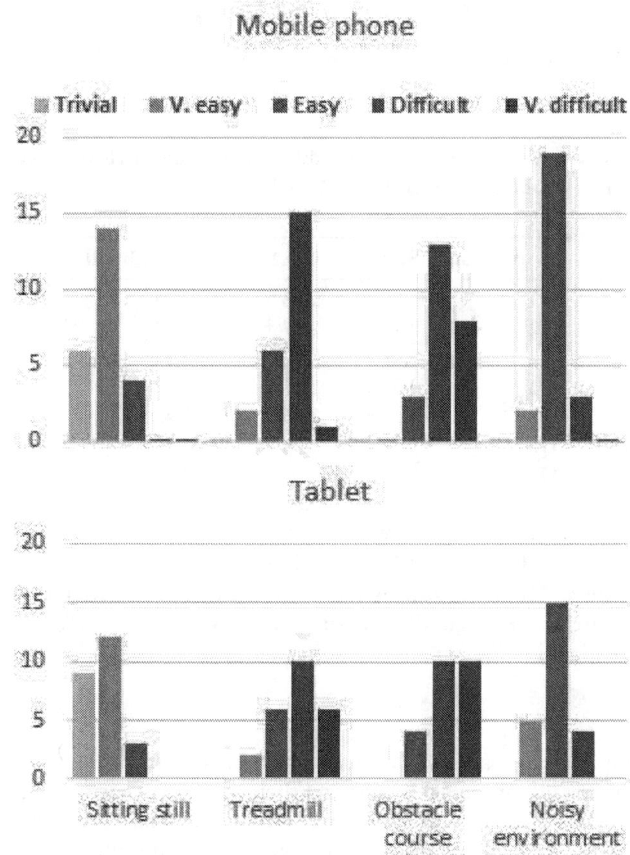

Figure 4: Expected difficulty of searching on mobile phones and tablets under various conditions.

As participant age increased, the expected difficulty of using either a mobile phone or a tablet on a treadmill (R-squared=0.27, p-value=0.005; R-squared= 0.17 p-value=0.028) and when navigating an obstacle course (R-squared=0.34, p-value=$\ll$0.01; R-squared= 0.29, p-value=0.004) increased, however this was not the case for use when sitting still or in a noisy pub or cafe. The more confident people were at using search engines in general, the easier they expected the task to be on the treadmill (R-squared=0.24, p-value=0.015) and the obstacle course (R-squared=0.2, p-value: 0.03) on both devices. However, this relationship only held for the tablet when imagining sitting still (R-squared=0.28, p-value=0.008). There was no significant relationship between search engine confidence and expected difficulty in the noisy pub environment. Surprisingly, the participants' familiarity of using mobile devices when walking or in noisy environments was not predictive of their expected difficulty of searching under the same conditions.

4.2 Pre-task perception

Before each task (TREC topic), the zing interface prompted participants to fill in a short questionnaire about their prior knowledge of the topic, their interest in it and how difficult they expected the task to be (overall difficulty, difficulty in finding relevant documents, and difficulty in knowing when to finish; see Figure 5). To aid them in doing so, the topic title and description were presented at the bottom of the screen. There was little variation in the responses between the topics with most people stating that they had fairly little prior knowledge and were moderately interested in the topics. Responses did indicate an expectation that topic 404 ("Ireland peace talks") would be the most difficult, although the difference was not significant. There were only two instances where a participant was unsure of how to complete the task and in only 14% of cases was a topic deemed to be either very difficult or very easy. As expected, responses to all 3 questions on perceived task difficulty were all significantly correlated with each other.

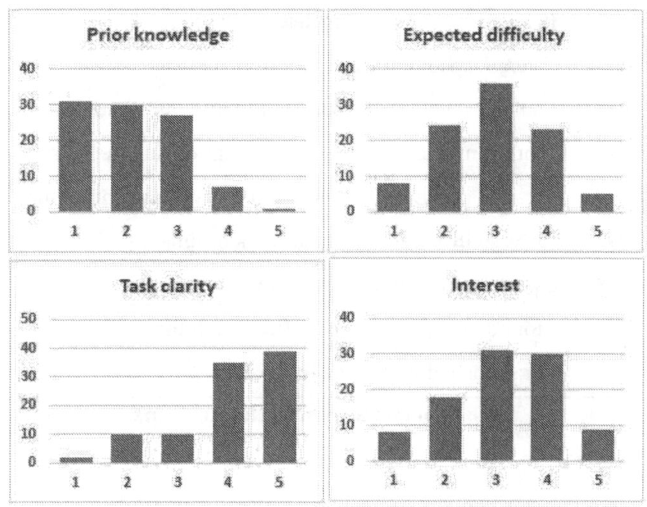

Figure 5: Results of pre-task questionnaire.

Condition	Sitting	Obstacles	Treadmill
Overall difficulty	2.21 ∗†	3.06	3.36
Finding rel. docs.	2.43 †	2.59 †	3.03
When to finish	2.79 †	3.06	3.58

Table 2: Mean responses about task difficulty from pre-task questionnaires by condition. ∗ = sig. diff. with Obstacles; † = sig. diff. with Treadmill

It seems that participants took experimental condition into account when estimating the difficulty of tasks as there were differences in the perceived difficulty of tasks, as shown in Table 2. Those who knew they would be sitting still expected the tasks to be significantly easier than those who were navigating the obstacle course (t=3.95; p-value $\ll$ 0.01) and those who were on the treadmill (t=5.08; p-value $\ll$ 0.01). Those who were sitting still and those on the obstacle course thought finding relevant documents would be equally easy (t=0.7, p-value=0.49), however those on the treadmill expected this to be significantly more difficult (t=2.58, p-value=0.012). The treadmill group thought that knowing when to finish the task (i.e. ascertaining when they'd found enough information) would be significantly more difficult than the baseline group (t=3.15, p-value=0.002). There were no significant differences in perceived task clarity between any of the groups, although those in the baseline group did claim to know more about the topics a priori than those in the other groups (compared to treadmill: t=2.22, p-value=0.031 ; compared to obstacle course: t=2.18, p-value=0.033).

4.3 Post-task perception

#	Question
Q1	I felt hurried or rushed when completing this task
Q2	It was important to complete this task quickly
Q3	Overall, I thought this was a difficult task
Q4	I am satisfied with steps I took to find information
Q5	I forgot my immediate surroundings during the task
Q6	I was so involved that I ignored everything around me
Q7	I was so involved that I lost track of time
Q8	I was absorbed in my search task
Q9	I found enough info. about the search topic
Q10	I am satisfied with the info. I found

Table 3: Selected post-task questions.

Immediately after each task participants filled in a post-task questionnaire, which included items from the *focused attention scale* of O'Brien et al. [29] as well as items from Crescenzi et al. [10] (see Table 3 for selected items). The questions were chosen to ascertain the participants' levels of perceived time pressure, self-assessed performance and involvement in the search task. There were significant differences in terms of perceived difficulty between the 4 topics with 2 topics scoring a median Q3 ("Overall, I thought this was a difficult task") agreement of 2, one at 3 and the most difficult scoring 4. There were, however, no significant differences between the 4 topics for the other questions. Interestingly, women reported feeling significantly less absorbed in the task (Q8; t=2.96; p-value=0.004) than men and felt less like they lost track of time (Q7; t=1.99; p-value=0.049).

As shown in Table 4, the different experimental conditions had a number of different effects on the participants' perceptions. Those on the treadmill felt significantly more rushed than in the other two conditions (Q1) and those sitting still felt significantly less pressure to complete the tasks quickly than the other 2 groups (Q2). It appears that those sitting still generally found the tasks easiest (Q3; see Figure 6) - significantly more so than those in the treadmill group - and were more satisfied with the steps they took to find relevant information (Q4). Those sitting and on the treadmill were significantly more likely to forget their immediate surroundings than those on the obstacle course (Q5) and felt more involved in the task (Q6). Although differences were not significant, there was a trend that those on the treadmill felt more involved in the task to the point where they lost track of time (Q7) and those on the obstacle course felt less absorbed in the search tasks (Q8). In terms of being able to find sufficient information to fulfill the task, those in the baseline and obstacle course conditions felt there significantly more able to find enough information (Q9) and were significantly more satisfied with what they found than those on the treadmill (Q10).

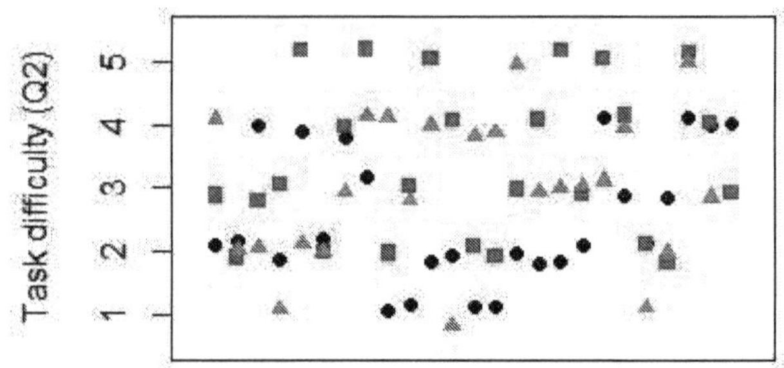

Figure 6: Perceived post-task difficulty by condition. • = sitting; ▲ = obstacle course; ■ = treadmill

Condition	Sitting	Obstacles	Treadmill
Q1	2.25 †	2.53 †	3.28
Q2	2.14 *†	2.87 †	3.44
Q3	2.43 †	3.0	3.31
Q4	3.86 †	3.47	3.03
Q5	3.64 *	3.16 †	3.42 *
Q6	3.53	3.03 †	3.47 *
Q7	3.39	3.09	3.52
Q8	3.96	3.56	3.81
Q9	3.39 †	3.75 †	2.91
Q10	3.46 †	3.56 †	2.8

Table 4: Mean responses from post-task questionnaires by condition. * = sig. diff. with Obstacles; † = sig. diff. with Treadmill

5 SEARCH PERFORMANCE

In order to objectively evaluate search performance, we rely on three main metrics: the average number of hits (relevant documents) returned per search query; the mean average precision attained; the number of documents bookmarked; the number of documents read; the ratio of relevant documents bookmarked relative to the total number bookmarked (to give an indication of how accurate users were with their bookmark choices); and the same ratio for documents read. Based on the results of linear models, the number of hits, mean average precision and number of documents read are all significant predictors of perceived success (Q9 and Q10 in the post-task questionnaire). We also consider a number of other proxies of overall search and task performance as well as metrics such as query length and search duration.

5.1 Performance by experimental condition

Condition	Sitting	Obstacles	Treadmill
# of queries/user	13	12	14
Hits/query	3.71 *†	2	1.75
MAP	0.104 *†	0.085	0.083
Bookmarks/query	1.32 †	1.74 †	1.03
(Ratio relevant)	0.55	0.47	0.49
Docs read/query	1.58 †	1.19	1.0
(Ratio relevant)	0.43	0.41	0.44
# of query terms	3.61 *	3.17	3.38
Query duration	39.5s *†	30.5s	35s

Table 5: Objective performance measures by condition. * = sig. diff. with Obstacles; † = sig. diff. with Treadmill

Table 5 shows how the objective performance measures varied by experimental condition. Most notably, the average number of hits per query achieved by the baseline users is significantly greater than those by either the treadmill (p-value=0.029) or obstacle course (p-value=0.023) groups, even though all groups submitted very similar numbers of queries (see Figure 7). This is also true for mean average precision. This suggests that those sitting were able to generate more accurate and precise queries than those in the other two groups. This may be because the queries they submitted were longer and more detailed (significantly longer than the obstacle course group: p-value=0.002) and because they spent significantly more time per query than the others - over 5 seconds longer on average per query (compared to treadmill: p-value=0.023; compared to obstacle course: p-value=0.005).

Those sitting and those on the obstacle course bookmarked significantly more documents than the treadmill group (p-values= 0.01 and 0.001 resp.). The participants on the obstacle course bookmarked the most often, however, as they bookmarked a larger number of non-relevant documents, they had the lowest ratio of relevant bookmarks. The baseline group read the largest number of documents on average, perhaps partially explaining their increased query durations, and read significantly more than those on the treadmill (W=7371, p-value= 0.015). This may be because sitting at a desk is a more comfortable environment for in-depth tasks such as reading, which requires concentration and may be disrupted by movements of the screen or eyes.

6 IMPACT OF DEVICE USED

To determine what impact device type has on search, half of the search tasks were completed on a smart phone and the other half were completed on a larger tablet device. As shown in Table 6, although the objective performance measures recorded for the different devices were almost identical (i.e. no significant differences), there was substantial variation in the participants' perceptions of searching on each device. In general, people found the smart phone to be much less useful for the tasks set than the tablet: They felt significantly more hurried and rushed when using the phone (t=2.25;

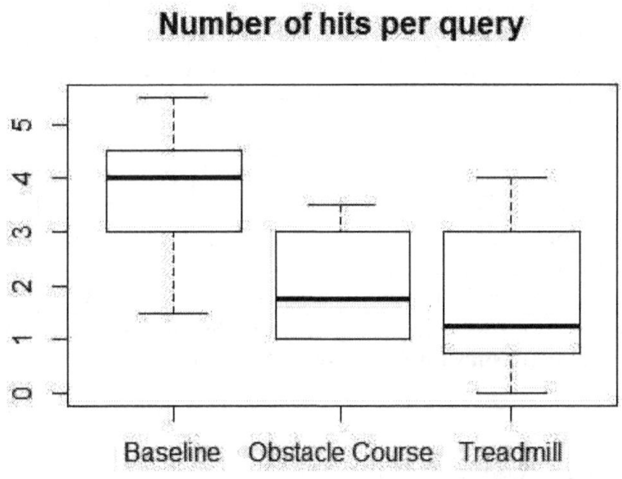

Figure 7: Number of hits (relevant documents) returned per query.

p-value=0.025) and found the tasks to be significantly more difficult (t=2.7; p-value=0.007). Although users felt equally satisfied on both devices about the steps they themselves had taken to find the necessary information (t=-0.45; p-value=0.65), when using the smart phone they were significantly less satisfied with the information they found (t=-3.14; p-value ≪ 0.01), suggesting that they placed the blame on the device and not on their own search behaviour.

Device type	Smart phone	Tablet
Hits/query	2.8	2.77
Bookmarks/query	1.48	1.2
# of query terms	3.39	3.4
Query duration	48.6	49.2
Q1 felt hurried/rushed	2.98 *	2.69
Q3 difficult task	3.49 *	3.12
Q4 satisfied with step taken	3.18	3.25
Q10 satisfied with info. found	2.77 *	3.22

Table 6: Objective and subjective performance measures by device type. * = sig. diff.

It seems the experimental condition had an impact on how users perceived differences between the devices (Table 7). Users in the baseline condition (sitting at a desk) actually performed better - in terms of number of hits - on the tablet than on the phone, albeit not significantly (W=977, p-value=0.121). This trend was, however, reversed under the other two experimental conditions with those on the phone seemingly performing better than those on the tablet. This was also reflected in the users' perception of flow/involvement in the task: Those sitting felt significantly less aware of their surroundings when using the tablet (Q5; t = 2.2, p-value=0.03) than the phone, while those in the other conditions had the opposite experience (Q5; t=-2.11, p-value=0.036); and those in the non-baseline conditions felt less aware of time passing when using the phone than the tablet (Q7; t=3.53, p-value=0.001). It's also notable that the baseline group spent longer on the tasks (*query duration*) when using the tablet than the phone, but the other groups actually spent longer when using the phone.

	Baseline		Other cond.	
	P	*T*	*P*	*T*
Hits/query	2.67	3.64	2.84	2.37
Query duration	59.1	64.1	44.2	42.2
Q5 forgot surroundings	3.17 *	3.7	3.53 *	3.18
Q7 lost track of time	2.98 *	3.42	3.73 *	3.1

Table 7: Performance and perception by condition and device type (P=smart phone, T=tablet). * = sig. diff.

7 DISCUSSION

This research set out three research questions aimed at exploring mobile searching and the effects of fragmented attention in common situations. The following discussion will consider each of the research questions in turn.

Do common mobile situations impact on users' perceptions of the task and their own performance? (RQ1)

Our results demonstrate that the different conditions had a number of fairly profound effects on user perceptions, both before and after completing the tasks. The pre-study questionnaire showed that participants expected using both devices whilst walking on a treadmill would be more difficult than sitting still and navigating an obstacle course. This is something that tallies with past research, which shows that situational impairments do exert a range of effects on performance, adding levels of difficulty as interaction with the device takes place [20]. The treadmill lessened their feeling of control, or lack of it, which reduced their perceived effectiveness as they interact with the UI [4, 23]. The older a participant was, the greater the expected difficulty of using a tablet on a treadmill, but this was not the case for phones or when sitting, perhaps because younger people are more familiar with such devices and may have more experience using them in mobile situations [1].

Post-task perception showed that different experimental conditions had a number of different effects on the participants' perceptions. Those on the treadmill felt significantly more rushed than in the other two conditions. Oulasvita et al. [30] pointed to the effect of a situation on the duration of continuous attention, finding that participants in their laboratory experiments were more focused on the tasks compared with participants on a busy street. In this study, those sitting and on the treadmill were significantly more likely to forget their immediate surroundings than those on the obstacle course and more involved in the task. This may be because there is an increased need to attend to the surrounding environment when walking, but with the treadmill this is not the case as the situation does not change [23].

Participants seemed to take the experimental conditions into account when estimating task difficulty, recording significant differences in perceived task difficulty. With the frequency of mobile use continuously on the increase, participants were likely to be aware of these potential challenges as they interacted. They expected these difficulties to increase their cognitive workload and the changes in mobility (i.e. walking) to influence not only their walking speed but mental workload during the tasks [24]. Those who knew they would be sitting still expected the tasks to be easier than the other conditions while those who were sitting still and those on the obstacle course thought finding relevant documents would be equally easy.

It is interesting that people expected the treadmill to be most difficult, despite the fact that it should require more cognitive effort to avoid the obstacles. This may be because these participants have control over the pace at which they are walking, while those on the treadmill are kept at a constant speed by the mechanism. Those on the obstacle course have the possibility to slow down while conducting demanding tasks, such as assessing document relevance, thereby reducing their overall cognitive load [21]. This may explain why Mizobuchi et al. [24] observed no reduction in input accuracy when walking and texting - the participants simply reduced their walking speed to prioritise text input.

Participants on the obstacle course felt less absorbed in the search tasks. This could be due to the fact that walking while using a smart phone requires both cognitive and motor abilities and appropriate division of attention to each [20]. The level of absorption in the search tasks is less due to the participant needing to be aware of their surroundings. The participants are walking and using the device, in doing so they take longer to complete a set route and, therefore, walk more slowly. There are two repercussions to this, they will slow down on the obstacle route (because they have control) and experience increased cognitive load on the treadmill (not being able to adjust their speed) [22].

Do common mobile situations impact on objective measures of users' task performance and behaviour? (RQ2)

Although the effects on objective performance were perhaps not quite as numerous or great as they were on perception, the different conditions did impact search behaviour and, consequently, performance. The most profound difference was found in the quality, in terms of number of hits and MAP, of the queries submitted - those sitting were able to generate significantly more accurate and precise queries than those in the other two groups. Perhaps this is because sitting evokes an environment more like desktop search, where users feel that they have more time to think carefully about the queries they enter [18]. This was also evidenced by the sitting group's queries being significantly longer (i.e. being comprised of more terms) and is in line with the studies of Kamvar et al. [18] and Schaller et al. [32, 33] and also corresponds with the results from the post-task questionnaire, which showed that the users on the treadmill and on the obstacle course felt more hurried and rushed and were more aware of time pressures.

Additionally, it seems the effects of time pressure on search behaviour highlighted in the studies of Crescenzi et al. [9, 10] are also relevant in this context, even though in the case of our study time pressures were perceived rather than enforced. Interestingly, though, we did not observe the same increase in querying frequency. [9]. A possible way to mitigate these issues might be to detect when users are walking (by using the device's motion sensors and gyroscopes) and to adapt the interface to offer more querying support and to present more concise snippets in such situations.

Participants on the treadmill bookmarked significantly fewer documents than the other two groups. A situation which is again likely because they felt more rushed, meaning they were less likely to explore the search results and to assess potentially relevant documents for relevance [9], tasks that will likely incur a higher "cost" [2] when input accuracy [26] and reading comprehension [3] is reduced. Similarly, participants in both of the non-baseline groups spent significantly less time on each SERP and, therefore, assessed significantly fewer documents for relevance.

What impact does the device type have on user performance and perception thereof? (RQ3)

There was substantial variation in the participants' perceptions of searching on each device, contradicting the objective performance observed on the devices, which were identical. We found that the device used influenced participants' perceptions of the search tasks and that the tablet was, on the whole, preferred, although this was somewhat dependent on experimental condition. People felt more hurried, found the tasks harder and were less satisfied with the information they had found when using the phone. The increased (perceived) difficulty on the phone may be because users have less screen space to work with, making interaction with the various UI controls more difficult, especially when interaction occurs in a distracting environment [4]. Since larger screens appear less cluttered with information, users may have felt less overwhelmed by the amount of information presented on the relatively more spacious tablet screen [5]. These findings are in line with those of Hancock et al. [12], however our results are novel as they demonstrate that this effect holds between smart phone and tablet devices and is in fact more profoundly felt in the context of mobile search.

In contrast to the results of Song et al. [36], we didn't find any difference in query length or query duration between the two devices, although there was notable interaction between the device type and experimental condition. Users in the baseline (seated) group performed better on the tablet than the phone, however, those in the other two groups performed rather better on the phone than the tablet. This may be because phones are more typically used as a handheld device at arm's length, while the larger, heavier tablets are more often used when propped up on a table or cradled in one arm [31] and rarely used out of the home [25]. This is also evidenced by the difference in perceived immersion/flow in the task - when seated, using the tablet resulted in a greater feeling of immersion than the phone, while this was reserved for the other two conditions. The extra heft of the tablet when walking may make the device too conspicuous, serving to pull the user out of flow, while the much lighter, less cumbersome phone does not prevent the users from becoming immersed.

The variation in the amount of time spent on tasks (baseline users spend longer on the tablet than the phone, with the situation reversed for the other conditions) is interesting and perhaps speaks to the difference in weight (and therefore experienced encumbrance) between the two devices. Increased encumbrance has been shown to result in reduced input accuracy and increased mental load [27] and may lead to users more rapidly becoming fatigued, which would explain their propensity to give up the tasks earlier on the tablet when walking. When choosing between devices for a given task, it may therefore be useful to consider whether or not the user is likely to be moving or seated.

8 CONCLUSIONS

The main aim of this study was to investigate how different mobile situational contexts and different mobile devices (i.e. phones and tablets) affect user performance and experience when performing web search tasks. We conducted a laboratory experiment with 24 participants in which three different conditions were simulated: sitting at a table (the baseline), walking on a treadmill and navigating an obstacle course. Analysis of subjective measures, derived from pre- and post-task questionnaires, as well as objective performance metrics showed that both the context and device variables had a number of effects on performance, both perceived and measured, as well as participants' feelings of immersion, satisfaction and urgency.

Our results provide useful insights to inform the design of future interfaces for mobile search and give us a greater understanding of how context and device size affect search behaviour and user experience. It is clear that some contexts have negative effects on user search experience and that this is additionally affected by device type. When seated, tablets are preferable for complex search tasks, however this is reversed in instances where the advantage of the device's extra screen space is offset by its additional weight (and therefore, the extra encumbrance experience by the user).

These insights suggest the need for more care to be taken when designing mobile search interfaces by considering the context in which the system will be used, as well as the type of device. Interfaces could be developed that adapt when a walking-like motion is detected to aid the user in generating queries and to present information in a terser, more focused manner to reduce mental load and simplify the information space. This work also has potential repercussions for IR and HCI researchers: When designing and evaluating mobile search systems, it is clear that whether the user is in motion and the combination of device size and weight and situational context have significant effects on perception. It is also clear from this work that a treadmill may not always be appropriate for simulating mobile search as in reality users adjust their walking speed to prioritise interaction with the device, something which is not possible under this condition. Therefore, practitioners should be aware of these factors to ensure that these insights are incorporated into study design and taken into account when assessing user performance so that results are in fact demonstrative of effects induced by the experimental conditions and not other unmeasured variables.

8.1 Future work

As future research in this area we plan to expand on this work by looking into user search behaviour in more detail using the additional qualitative sources of information we captured during the study. As noted earlier, we have recorded GoPro footage of each participant as well as screen recordings of their interactions which we plan to evaluate to identify patterns and behaviours unique to each experimental condition. Using the data from the GoPro we will be able to evaluate the participants' spatial awareness (especially on the predefined route) and their "attention-switches" away from the device in different situations. Using the 3 everyday situations we will be able to assess the levels of immersion with each task and compare the GoPro data to the pre-task perceptions - does their initial thinking match reality and can we confirm our suspicions that the tablet's weight and bulk is the main cause of the differences observed in this research? We intend to develop search interfaces that adapt to the user's situation (i.e. walking or not) and the device type and to investigate whether these changes can in fact aid users in fragmented contexts to query as well as those who are seated. We would also like to simulate other situations that induce attention fragmentation, such as a busy restaurant or bar, and determine whether or not this causes similar changes in user behaviour and performance.

REFERENCES

[1] Monica Anderson, *Technology device ownership, 2015*, Pew Research Center, 2015.
[2] Leif Azzopardi, Diane Kelly, and Kathy Brennan, *How query cost affects search behavior*, Proceedings of the 36th international ACM SIGIR conference on Research and development in information retrieval, ACM, 2013, pp. 23–32.
[3] Leon Barnard, Ji Soo Yi, Julie A Jacko, and Andrew Sears, *Capturing the effects of context on human performance in mobile computing systems*, Personal and Ubiquitous Computing **11** (2007), no. 2, 81–96.
[4] Andrew Bragdon, Eugene Nelson, Yang Li, and Ken Hinckley, *Experimental analysis of touch-screen gesture designs in mobile environments*, Proceedings of the SIGCHI Conference on Human Factors in Computing Systems, ACM, 2011, pp. 403–412.
[5] Stephen Brewster, *Overcoming the lack of screen space on mobile computers*, Personal and Ubiquitous Computing **6** (2002), no. 3, 188–205.
[6] Minhee Chae and Jinwoo Kim, *Do size and structure matter to mobile users? an empirical study of the effects of screen size, information structure, and task complexity on user activities with standard web phones*, Behaviour & information technology **23** (2004), no. 3, 165–181.
[7] Karen Church, Mauro Cherubini, and Nuria Oliver, *A large-scale study of daily information needs captured in situ*, ACM Transactions on Computer-Human Interaction (TOCHI) **21** (2014), no. 2, 10.
[8] Karen Church and Nuria Oliver, *Understanding mobile web and mobile search use in today's dynamic mobile landscape*, Proceedings of the 13th International Conference on Human Computer Interaction with Mobile Devices and Services, ACM, 2011, pp. 67–76.
[9] Anita Crescenzi, Diane Kelly, and Leif Azzopardi, *Time pressure and system delays in information search*, Proceedings of the 38th International ACM SIGIR Conference on Research and Development in Information Retrieval, ACM, 2015, pp. 767–770.
[10] ———, *Impacts of time constraints and system delays on user experience*, ACM CHI, ACM, 2016, pp. 141–150.
[11] Mark Dunlop and Stephen Brewster, *The challenge of mobile devices for human computer interaction*, Personal and ubiquitous computing **6** (2002), no. 4, 235–236.
[12] PA Hancock, BD Sawyer, and S Stafford, *The effects of display size on performance*, Ergonomics **58** (2015), no. 3, 337–354.
[13] Rachel Harrison, Derek Flood, and David Duce, *Usability of mobile applications: literature review and rationale for a new usability model*, Journal of Interaction Science **1** (2013), no. 1, 1.
[14] Morgan Harvey, Claudia Hauff, and David Elsweiler, *Learning by example: training users with high-quality query suggestions*, Proceedings of the 38th International ACM SIGIR Conference on Research and Development in Information Retrieval, ACM, 2015, pp. 133–142.
[15] Morgan Harvey and Matthew Pointon, *Perceptions of the effect of fragmented attention on mobile web search tasks*, ACM SIGIR Conference on Human Information Interaction & Retrieval (CHIIR), 2017.
[16] Peter Johnson, *Usability and mobility; interactions on the move*, Proceedings of the First Workshop on Human-Computer Interaction with Mobile Devices, 1998.
[17] Anne Kaikkonen, *Full or tailored mobile web-where and how do people browse on their mobiles?*, Mobility, ACM, 2008, p. 28.
[18] Maryam Kamvar and Shumeet Baluja, *A large scale study of wireless search behavior: Google mobile search*, Proceedings of the SIGCHI conference on Human Factors in computing systems, ACM, 2006, pp. 701–709.
[19] ———, *Deciphering trends in mobile search*, IEEE Computer **40** (2007), no. 8, 58–62.
[20] Shaun K Kane, Jacob O Wobbrock, and Ian E Smith, *Getting off the treadmill: evaluating walking user interfaces for mobile devices in public spaces*, Proceedings of the 10th international conference on Human computer interaction with mobile devices and services, ACM, 2008, pp. 109–118.
[21] Eric M Lamberg and Lisa M Muratori, *Cell phones change the way we walk*, Gait & posture **35** (2012), no. 4, 688–690.
[22] Sammy Licence, Robynne Smith, Miranda P McGuigan, and Conrad P Earnest, *Gait pattern alterations during walking, texting and walking and texting during cognitively distractive tasks while negotiating common pedestrian obstacles*, PLoS one **10** (2015), no. 7, e0133281.
[23] Min Lin, Rich Goldman, Kathleen J Price, Andrew Sears, and Julie Jacko, *How do people tap when walking? an empirical investigation of nomadic data entry*, International Journal of human-computer studies **65** (2007), no. 9, 759–769.
[24] Sachi Mizobuchi, Mark Chignell, and David Newton, *Mobile text entry: relationship between walking speed and text input task difficulty*, Proceedings of the 7th international conference on Human computer interaction with mobile devices & services, ACM, 2005, pp. 122–128.
[25] Hendrik Müller, Jennifer L. Gove, John S. Webb, and Aaron Cheang, *Understanding and comparing smartphone and tablet use: Insights from a large-scale diary study*, Proceedings of the Annual Meeting of the Australian Special Interest Group for Computer Human Interaction (New York, NY, USA), OzCHI '15, ACM, 2015, pp. 427–436.
[26] Matei Negulescu, Jaime Ruiz, Yang Li, and Edward Lank, *Tap, swipe, or move: attentional demands for distracted smartphone input*, Proceedings of the International Working Conference on Advanced Visual Interfaces, ACM, 2012, pp. 173–180.
[27] Alexander Ng, John Williamson, and Stephen Brewster, *The effects of encumbrance and mobility on touch-based gesture interactions for mobile phones*, Proceedings of the 17th International Conference on Human-Computer Interaction with Mobile Devices and Services, ACM, 2015, pp. 536–546.
[28] Hugo Nicolau and Joaquim Jorge, *Touch typing using thumbs: Understanding the effect of mobility and hand posture*, ACM CHI (New York, NY, USA), CHI '12, ACM, 2012, pp. 2683–2686.
[29] Heather L O'Brien and Elaine G Toms, *The development and evaluation of a survey to measure user engagement*, Journal of the American Society for Information Science and Technology **61** (2010), no. 1, 50–69.
[30] Antti Oulasvirta, Sakari Tamminen, Virpi Roto, and Jaana Kuorelahti, *Interaction in 4-second bursts: the fragmented nature of attentional resources in mobile hci*, ACM CHI, ACM, 2005, pp. 919–928.
[31] Tommaso Piazza, Morten Fjeld, Gonzalo Ramos, AsimEvren Yantac, and Shengdong Zhao, *Holy smartphones and tablets, batman!: mobile interaction's dynamic duo*, Proceedings of the 11th Asia Pacific Conference on Computer Human Interaction, ACM, 2013, pp. 63–72.
[32] Richard Schaller, Morgan Harvey, and David Elsweiler, *Entertainment on the go: finding things to do and see while visiting distributed events*, IIiX, ACM, 2012, pp. 90–99.
[33] ———, *Out and about on museums night: Investigating mobile search behaviour for leisure events*, Searching4Fun WS at ECIR, 2012.
[34] Kelly M Seymour, Christopher I Higginson, Kurt M DeGoede, Morgan K Bifano, Rachel Orr, and Jill S Higginson, *Cellular telephone dialing influences kinematic and spatiotemporal gait parameters in healthy adults*, Journal of Motor Behavior **48** (2016), no. 6, 535–541.
[35] Aaron Smith et al., *Us smartphone use in 2015*, Pew Research Center **1** (2015).
[36] Yang Song, Hao Ma, Hongning Wang, and Kuansan Wang, *Exploring and exploiting user search behavior on mobile and tablet devices to improve search relevance*, Proceedings of the 22nd international conference on World Wide Web, ACM, 2013, pp. 1201–1212.
[37] E.M. Voorhees, *The trec 2005 robust track*, SIGIR Forum **40** (2006), no. 1, 41–48.

User Interaction Sequences for Search Satisfaction Prediction

Rishabh Mehrotra*
University College London
London, United Kingdom
r.mehrotra@cs.ucl.ac.uk

Imed Zitouni[1], Ahmed Hassan Awadallah[2],
Ahmed El Kholy[1], Madian Khabsa[2]
[1]Microsoft, [2]Microsoft Research
Redmond, WA, USA
{izitouni,hassanam,ahkhol,makhab}@microsoft.com

ABSTRACT

Detecting and understanding implicit measures of user satisfaction are essential for meaningful experimentation aimed at enhancing web search quality. While most existing studies on satisfaction prediction rely on users' click activity and query reformulation behavior, often such signals are not available for all search sessions and as a result, not useful in predicting satisfaction. On the other hand, user interaction data (such as mouse cursor movement) is far richer than just click data and can provide useful signals for predicting user satisfaction. In this work, we focus on considering holistic view of user interaction with the search engine result page (SERP) and construct detailed *universal interaction sequences* of their activity. We propose novel ways of leveraging the universal interaction sequences to automatically extract informative, interpretable subsequences. In addition to extracting frequent, discriminatory and interleaved subsequences, we propose a Hawkes process model to incorporate temporal aspects of user interaction. Through extensive experimentation we show that encoding the extracted subsequences as features enables us to achieve significant improvements in predicting user satisfaction. We additionally present an analysis of the correlation between various subsequences and user satisfaction. Finally, we demonstrate the usefulness of the proposed approach in covering abandonment cases. Our findings provide a valuable tool for fine-grained analysis of user interaction behavior for metric development.

KEYWORDS

satisfaction; interaction sequences; subsequences; hawkes process

1 INTRODUCTION

As increasingly larger proportions of users rely on search engine interactions to satisfy their information needs and as retrieval systems advance, the need for good evaluation metrics increases. As such, developing better understanding of how users interact with search engines becomes increasingly important for improving user's search experience. Since obtaining explicit feedback from users is prohibitively expensive and challenging to implement in real-world retrieval systems, commercial search engines have exploited implicit feedback signals derived from user activity. While users interact with a search engine, they leave behind fine grained traces of interaction patterns. These interaction patterns contain valuable information, which could be useful for predicting user satisfaction as well as developing metrics for search engine evaluation to assist rapid experimentation.

Recent work has extensively studied implicit feedback measures (e.g., mouse scrolling, gaze tracking, physiological signals, etc.), and verified their effectiveness in predicting search satisfaction (or dissatisfaction) [11, 13, 21, 31]. Compared to coarser models of clicks alone, such user interactions provide additional insight into searchers' behavior. Despite recent progress in utilizing such implicit interaction signals, developing metrics around these signals often involves intensive manual effort [11, 20] to gain insights about the data, and to make use of it for practical applications. Also, existing models around utilizing detailed user interaction data are not interpretable and require deep investigation to extract meaningful insights. For example, popular approaches like visualizing areas of high cursor activity via heatmaps require manual inspection and lacks detail about sequences of user activity.

In this work, we focus on considering a holistic view of user interaction with the search engine result page (SERP) and construct detailed *universal interaction sequences* of their activity. We propose novel ways of leveraging the universal interaction timelines to automatically extract informative, interpretable subsequences. In addition to proposing ways to extract frequent and discriminative subsequences, we propose an interleaved subsequence extraction method which is able to jointly leverage discriminatory and frequent aspects of subsequences to extract subsequences which allow for noisy actions to interleave amidst more meaningful and informative signals.

Further, while the subsequences extracted are able to capture informative user interactions, they ignore the temporal spread of actions. To this end, we incorporate time in a principled manner when modeling user interaction sequences and leverage recent advancements in point process models to do so. We propose a Hawkes process formulation of interaction sequences which enables us to weigh the extracted subsequences based on the inter-activity times. We present a large scale evaluation of the proposed approach using crowdsourced judgments as well as weakly labeled data and demonstrate that including the proposed subsequences significantly improves user satisfaction prediction performance. We additionally show that the proposed techniques work in abandonment cases too and can be further explored to develop sophisticated methods for detecting and predicting good abandonment. Our findings provide a valuable tool for fine-grained analysis of user interaction behavior for developing metrics and gauging user satisfaction.

*Work conducted while at Microsoft Research.

SIGIR '17, August 07-11, 2017, Shinjuku, Tokyo, Japan
© 2017 ACM. 978-1-4503-5022-8/17/08...$15.00
DOI: 10.1145/3077136.3080833

2 RELATED WORK

As search systems become more sophisticated, developing techniques for evaluating their performance plays an increasingly pivotal role. The current research builds upon and advances research in three directions: (i) User Satisfaction prediction, (ii) Implicit feedback, and (iii) Subsequence mining.

User Satisfaction

The concept of satisfaction was first introduced in IR researches in 1970s according to Su et al. [38]. A recent definition states that "satisfaction can be understood as the fulfillment of a specified desire or goal" [24]. However, search satisfaction itself is a subjective construct and is difficult to measure. Some existing studies tried to collect satisfaction feedback from users directly. For example, Guo *et al.* 's work [13] on predicting Web search success and Feild et al.'s work [6] on predicting searcher frustration were both based on searchers' self-reported explicit judgments. Differently, other researchers employed external assessors to restore the users' search experience and make annotations according to their own opinions. For example, Guo et al.fis work [14] on predicting query performance was based on this kind of annotations. Recently, simplistic user feedback signals have been used to gauge user satisfaction. For instance, it has previously been shown that clicks followed by long dwell times are correlated with satisfaction [9]. Hassan et al. [16] propose to use query reformulation as a negative indicator of search success and thus satisfaction and show how an approach based on query features outperforms an approach based on click features, with the best performance being achieved by a combination of the two. Kim et al. [25] consider three measures of dwell time and evaluate their use in detecting search satisfaction. Lagun *et al.*[29] consider scroll and viewport features for predicting satisfaction in mobile search.

Subsequence & Timeseries mining

Sequential pattern mining was first introduced by Agrawal *et al.* [2] in the context of market basket analysis, which led to a number of other algorithms for frequent sequence mining. Frequent sequence mining suffers from pattern explosion: a huge number of highly redundant frequent sequences are retrieved if the given minimum support threshold is too low. We refer the interested reader to Chapter 11 of [1] for a survey of frequent sequence mining algorithms. There has also been some existing research on probabilistic models for sequences, especially using Markov models. Gwadera et al. [10] use a variable order Markov model to identify statistically significant sequences. More recently, Fowkes *et al.* [8] proposed a subsequence interleaving model based on a probabilistic model of the sequence database.

Gestures for Relevance & Satisfaction

Traditional evaluation techniques relied on classical methodologies that use query sets and relevance judgments. More recently, a number of different interaction behaviors have been taken into consideration in the prediction of search user satisfactions including both coarse-grained features (e.g. clickthrough based features in [14]) and fine-grained ones (e.g. cursor position and scrolling speed in [13]). Mouse movement information like scroll and hover have proven to be valuable signals in inferring user behavior and

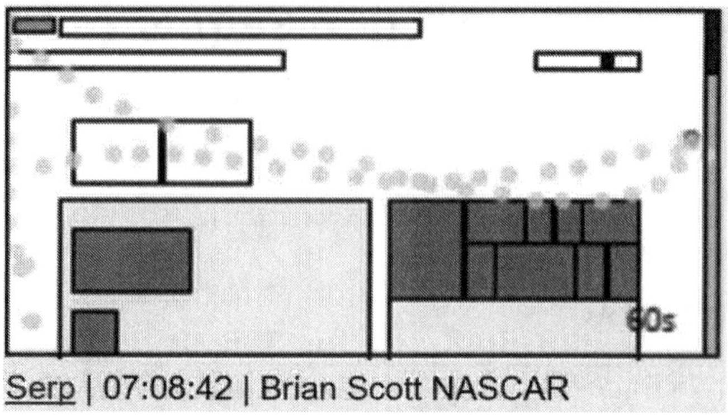

Figure 1: Example of user interaction with the SERP elements rendered for the query *Brian Scott NASCAR*. The sequence of green dots denotes the user's cursor position over a period of time.

preferences [11, 21, 35], search intent [12], search examination [32] and predicting result relevance [22]. However, none of these studies tried to extract mouse movement patterns and adopt them to predict search satisfaction. Arapakis et al. [3] extracted mouse gestures to measure within-content engagement. Lagun et al. [28] introduced the concept of frequent cursor subsequences (namely motifs) in the estimation of result relevance. Different from their work, we focus on how to extract informative subsequences from user interactions to help predict search satisfaction a search impression level instead of result level.

User action sequences have been used to predict user satisfaction [15], graded satisfaction [23] and to study search engine switching behavior [36, 39]. Sequential user actions have also been used to explore developing search trails composed of query sequences for enhancing search support [17, 37]. Our work differs from these works in two aspects. First, while past work considered only high-level actions, we consider more detailed fine-grained actions and in the process, propose few novel user actions. Second, most existing work uses the entire action sequences to make predictions while we focus on a slightly different problem of extracting meaningful subsequences which are most representative of user interaction and predictive of user satisfaction.

The closest work to ours is Liu *et al.* [31] which estimate the utilities of search results and the efforts in search sessions with motifs extracted from mouse movement data on search result pages (SERPs). Our work is different since we aim at a slightly different problem of extracting interpretable subsequences and focus on informative action sequences rather than mouse movement coordinates for predicting search satisfaction.

3 EXTRACTING USER INTERACTION SEQUENCES

Our goal in this work is to extract informative and interpretable subsequences from user interaction data which best predict user satisfaction. In this section, we define key concepts used throughout the paper (3.1), describe a way to first construct and then use the *Universal Timeline* of user interaction to extract interaction sequences (3.2), and finally analyse the interaction sequences (3.3) and characterize generic trends in user interaction with the SERP.

Action	Description
Click_algoX	Click on the X-th algorithmic result
Click_Ans	Click on any answer (non-image) result
Click_IMG	Click on any image result
MouseRead	horizontal line across a result snippet of length > 50px and duration > 100 ms that goes from left to right which starts and ends inside an algo-result, or advertisement or an answer result
Scroll	page scroll recorded on the search engine result page
Move	any cursor movement of length > 10px and duration greater than > 50 ms
pause	smallPause: no cursor movement on the SERP for time < 5 seconds mediumPause: no cursor movement on the SERP for 5s < time < 20s longPause: no cursor movement on the SERP for 20s < time < 40s veryLongPause: no cursor movement on the SERP for time > 40s
Resize	change in the size of the window/screen encompassing the result page
IssueQuery	user movement to the Search Box on the SERP and typing of text in the query box
dwellTime	smallDwellTime: dwell time on a clicked result URL with time spent < 10s mediumDwellTime: dwell time on a clicked result URL with 10s < time < 40s longDwellTime: dwell time on a clicked result URL with time spent > 40s
QuickBack	click on a SERP URL followed by returning back to the SERP within 5s

Table 1: Examples of actions considered along with their description used to create the user interaction sequence.

Example Sequences
Scroll → smallPause → Move → Move-algo-1 → smallPause → Move-algo-2 → Move-ans → Move → mediumPause → Move → Move-algo-2 → smallPause → Click-algo-2
smallPause → Move → Click-IMG → longDwellTime
mediumPause → Scroll → Move_algo9 → Move_algo8 → veryLongPause → Move → Click_algo3 → QuickBack → Move_algo3 → smallPause

Table 2: Example of sequences extracted.

3.1 Definitions

We first define what constitutes a sequence and use this definition to define subsequence.

Sequence: Given a search impression and a list of possible user actions, a sequence is defined as a time-ordered list of actions performed by the user when interacting with the search result page.

Subsequence: is a subset of continuous or interleaved actions extracted from the sequence.

Informative Subsequence: is a subsequence which helps a system predict user satisfaction with the search result page.

Interpretable Subsequence: is a human readable, comprehensible set of actions which are easy for system designers to understand and develop metrics around.

Such Informative and Interpretable subsequences represent common user- and query-invariant subsequences which would be difficult to identify or describe by manual inspection or feature engineering. Table 2 presents three examples of user interaction sequences extracted from real world search traffic. With this background, we formally define the problem of extracting subsequences as:

Subsequence Extraction: Given a labeled set of interaction sequences with satisfaction labels, our aim in this work is to infer a set of informative and interpretable subsequences which best predict user satisfaction with the search result page.

A robust subsequence extraction system helps us extract a set of meaningful patterns that are useful for helping a human analyst understand the important properties of user interaction, that is, subsequences should reflect the most important patterns in the interaction data, while being sufficiently concise and non-redundant that they are suitable for manual examination. These criteria are inherently qualitative, reflecting the fact that the goal of subsequence mining is to build human insight and understanding for subsequent metric development and satisfaction prediction.

3.2 Universal Timeline Creation

The richness of the result page rendered in response to a user query allows users to interact with SERPs in myriad ways, including clicking results, scrolling, expanding task panels, hovering over images, pausing to read and absorb content, among others. While most existing work has considered click based interaction signals or mouse movement features, these signals either lack coverage or are often abstracted at high SERP-level aggregates, which blinds the model to finer level user interaction signals. Our aim here is to analyze user interaction with the SERP (as depicted in Figure 1) and extract an interpretable interaction sequence (as shown in Table 2). To do so, we construct a universal action sequence timeline from the following three different timelines:

(1) **Viewport Timeline**: Viewport is defined as the position of the webpage that is visible at any given time to the user. Viewport timeline allows us to consider user actions concerning the viewport, for example, scroll on the result page and resize of the screen.
(2) **Cursor Timeline**: The cursor timeline provides us with all the cursor related user activity. Backend search logs record detailed user mouse activity which helps us track the mouse movement and link the corresponding cursor activity to the different elements on the SERP. Cursor timeline provides a major portion of the activities we consider in our work.

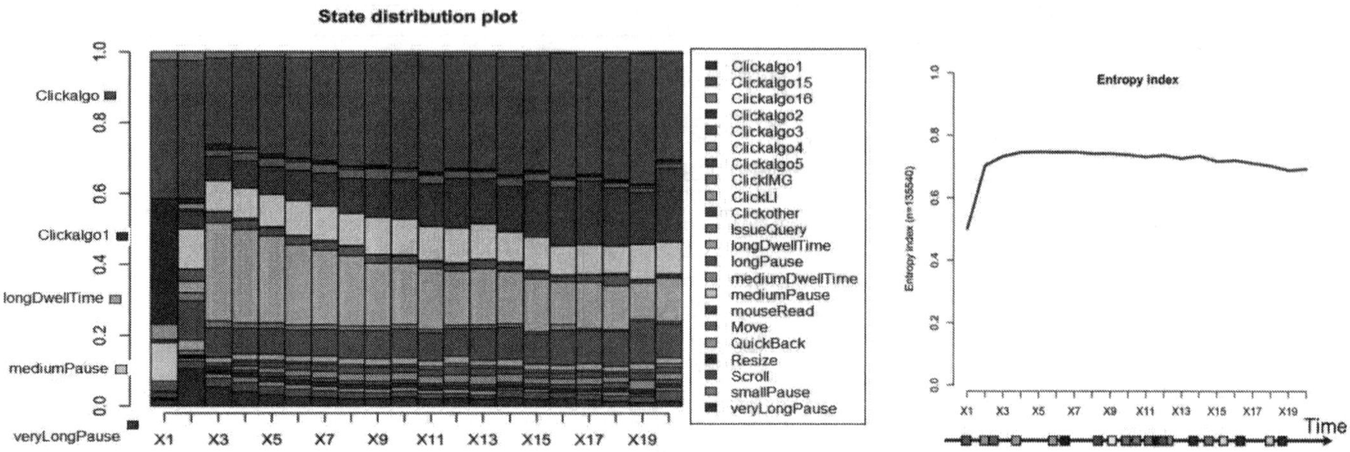

(a) State distribution plot of actions across positions

(b) The entropy plot of actions spread over positions in interaction sequence.

Figure 2: Analyzing the extracted sequences: (a) State distribution plot & (b) The entropy plot.

(3) **Keyboard Timeline**: The keyboard timeline records all keyboard related user activity (for example, text enter).

For each search impression, we log the three timelines with corresponding user actions along with the timestamp. Based on these three timelines, we generate one holistic universal action sequence timeline describing all user activity on the SERP by temporal sorting of individual timelines followed by stacking up the three timelines, and then interleaving them based on timestamps of the recorded actions. This provides us with a universal sequence of user interaction, examples of which are shown in Table 2. We next take a more detailed look at the actions considered to construct the timelines.

Actions Considered: In order to construct the three timelines, we considered a number of actions which includes different types of interactions performed by the users. For click based actions, we associate the cursor information with the corresponding element on the SERP and recorded the joint action-element pair as an action, for example, click_algo1 signified a click on algorithmic result at position 1. Beyond clicks, we considered a range of cursor movement actions ranging from simple Move (denoting a mouse movement across different SERP element) to more sophisticated and intentional cursor movements like a *MouseRead*. We define a *MouseRead* as a horizontal line across a result snippet of length > 50px and duration > 100 ms that goes from left to right which starts and ends inside an algo-result, or advertisement or an answer result. Beyond cursor movement actions, we considered inter-activity time as pauses and categorized a pause into one of three types based on the duration of the pause: (i) short pause (time), (ii) medium pause (time) and (iii) longPause (time). We additionally considered issuing query and scroll related activities. Table 1 lists the major actions considered.

3.3 Analyzing Interaction Sequences

As shown in Table 2, the set of actions and the total sequence length differs across the different sequences, which hints at an inherent diversity across the different sequences. While the dataset considered is described in detail in Sections 6.1 & 7, we consider a subset of user interactions from a major US commercial search engine and analyze the extracted interaction sequences based on a number of factors including sequence length, state distribution and state entropy.

3.3.1 Sequence Length. Sequence length counts the number of actions present in the sequence. To some extent, sequence length approximates user engagement with the SERP with longer sequences highlighting detailed and richer interaction with the result page. We observe that most sequences are between 2 - 10 actions long, with a strong peak at 4-5 actions, denoting that most sequences average 4-5 actions. The sequences of length 0 represent abandonment cases wherein the user didn't interact with the result page at all. We observe a low rate of abandonment in the data considered.

3.3.2 State Distribution. We next analyze the observed sequences in terms of the actions and the position in the sequence where the actions appear. Figure 2a shows the action distribution at each position of the sequence. For each position, we plot the proportion of sequences which contain a particular action at a particular position in the sequence. Indeed, as expected, certain actions are more likely to happen at the start of interaction, for example, click on the first algorithmic result is expected to happen at the start of the user interaction. *longDwellTime* is another action whose proportion drops significantly as we go to the right. As expected, long dwell time is positively correlated with search satisfaction. Since higher ranked documents result in more satisfying clicks, we notice the presence of *longDwellTime* earlier in the sequence. Additionally, we observe that the occurrence of certain actions decreases towards the right - which implies that certain actions are more likely to occur at later stages of user interaction than at the start. Finally, certain actions are equally likely throughout the sequence, for example, clicks on image results, *mediumPause* etc.

3.3.3 State Entropy. In order to measure the diversity of actions observed at different positions of interactions, we compute the

Shannon entropy of the action distribution at different positions. Letting p_i denote the proportion of sequences having action i at the considered time sequence position, the entropy is: $h(p_1, p_2, ..., p_n) = -\sum_{i=1}^{n} p_i log(p_i)$ where s is the size of the alphabet. The entropy is 0 when all sequences contain the same action and is maximal when the same proportion of sequences contain each action. The entropy can be seen as a measure of the diversity of states observed at the considered sequence position. Figure 2b presents the entropy scores across the different positions in the interaction sequence. Higher entropy implies more diversity in the user actions at that particular position in the action sequence. We observe lower entropy at the start of interaction sequences, which implies that there is low diversity at start of interactions; and the trend continues to exhibit high diversity at user interacts more. With lower entropy at the start, we expect low discriminability of the sequence.

4 EXTRACTING INFORMATIVE SUBSEQUENCES

So far we have looked at how to obtain detailed user interaction sequences from their interaction with the result page and looked at some analysis characterizing the observed sequences. Next, we leverage the interaction sequences to extract informative subsequences which are most predictive of user satisfaction. We next describe three ways of extracting the subsequences.

4.1 Frequent Subsequences

Our first method is based on frequent subsequence mining, which aims at capturing the most common subsequences present in the observed interaction sequences. The subsequences are generated by maintaining a sliding window of a given length and shifting it across the entire sequence for all the sequence. We considered subsequences with varying sizes from unigrams (individual actions) to 4-gram subsequences. Table 3 shows the top subsequences of size 2 and above.An advantage of considering frequent subsequences is the fact that most sequences would contain these subsequences and hence they don't suffer from low coverage. We use these extracted frequent subsequences along with most frequent actions and action bigrams as features when predicting user satisfaction.

4.2 Discriminative Subsequences

An important and desired characteristic of subsequences is their discriminatory power. Indeed, the more discriminatory a subsequence is, the better it helps us differentiate satisfying interactions from unsuccessful search interactions. To this end, we propose our second subsequence extraction method which, given a dataset of observed subsequences and their corresponding class labels (SAT/DSAT), aims at extracting the most discriminatory subsequences which help us best differentiate between SAT subsequences from DSAT subsequences.

Assuming that we are given a set of sequences with the corresponding satisfaction label (SAT/DSAT), we make use of the well-established chi-square test to compute the discriminatory power of a given subsequence. The Chi-square test calculates the probability of getting the experimental result on the basis that the null hypothesis is true. In our case, we state the Null and Alternative Hypothesis as follows:

Null Hypothesis (H0): there is no detectable difference between two classes
Alternative hypothesis (HA): there is a detectable difference between the two classes.

The statistical principle behind any discrimination test should be to reject a null hypothesis (H0) that states there is no detectable difference between two classes. Given the observed sequences and the corresponding class label (SAT/DSAT) as input, the Chi-Square test computes the residuals based on:

$$\chi^2 = \sum \left[\frac{(O-E)^2}{E} \right] \quad (1)$$

where O = observed frequency; E = expected frequency. Table 3 presents the top subsequences ordered by their discriminatory power for the set of sequences from a labeled dataset (described in detail in Section 6.1). We observe that a Click → *longDwellTime* is ranked high in terms of discriminatory power which confirms established notion that SAT interactions usually have a satisfying click, i.e., a click followed by a long dwell time. Additionally, we observe that the extracted discriminatory subsequences picks up new potentially SAT subsequences, for example: Scroll → *Mouseread* → *Move*. We also observe few potential DSAT interactions, as expressed by the interaction susequence: (*smallPause* → *Move* → *mediumPause* → *Move*) which highlights the user moving around on the SERP.

An important point to note here is that these discriminatory subsequences are not that popular - the Index column highlights the ranked index of the corresponding subsequences based on their frequency. This suggests that while these subsequences are discriminatory, they are not that popular and hence might not be more generally useful in discriminating SAT/DSAT interactions.

4.3 Interleaved Subsequences

One key limitation of the frequent and discriminative methods of extracting subsequences is that they only look at adjacent actions while extracting subsequences, while failing to consider interleaved subsequences. In this section, we introduce an alternate perspective on subsequence mining, in which we develop subsequences by interleaving a group of subsequences. We formulate the problem of identifying a set of *important* sequences that are useful for explaining the observed interaction sequences. We define *important* subsequence as those subsequences that best *explain* the observed sequences under an interleaved model of subsequences.

Quantifying Importance:
One can think of *importance* score as the weight of the subsequence in the model: the higher the score, the more supported sequences the subsequence explains. Thus importance score provides a more balanced measure than just frequency and discriminatory aspects alone, at the expense of missing some frequent subsequences that only explain some of the observed sequences they support. We jointly encode the notion of discriminability of the subsequence together with its support while defining the importance score of a

Frequent Subsequences		Discriminative Subsequences			
Subsequence	**Coverage**	**Subsequence**	**Index**	**Residual0**	**Residual1**
(Clickother → longDwellTime)	0.226767	(smallPause → Move → Click	138	-2.21152	2.123184
(Scroll → smallPause)	0.215066	(Scroll → Move → smallPause → Move → Click-algo3 → longDwellTime	735	-2.19005	2.102566
(Clickalgo1 → longDwellTime)	0.169337	(Clickalgo1 → longDwellTime)	15	-1.78004	1.708939
(smallPause → Clickother)	0.159562	(Move → smallPause → Move → mediumPause → Move)	265	1.950145	-1.87225
(smallPause → mediumPause)	0.131312	(Scroll → smallPause → Move → ClickLI)	569	-1.98225	1.903068
(smallPause → Clickother → longDwellTime	0.125173	(Move → Clickalgo1)	70	-1.84755	1.773754
(mediumPause → smallPause)	0.120038	(smallPause → mediumPause → Move)	105	1.861069	-1.78673
(smallPause → Clickalgo1)	0.114195	(Scroll → mouseRead → Move)	376	-1.9366	1.859247
(smallPause → mouseRead)	0.114129	(smallPause → Move → mouseRead → Move)	134	-1.68427	1.616994

Table 3: Frequent & Discriminative subsequences extracted. Coverage represents the fraction of sequences which contain the frequent subsequences. Index refers to the rank in terms of frequency of the subsequence, while Residual0 and Residual1 denote the discriminatory power of the subsequence for predicting DSAT and SAT respectively.

subsequence. More formally,

$$imp(S) = \varphi(S)\frac{\sum_{i=1}^{N}[z_S^i \geq 1]}{supp(S)} \quad (2)$$

where $\varphi(S)$ denotes the dsicriminability score of a subsequence obtained from Section 4.2, $\sum_{i=1}^{N}[z_S^i \geq 1]$ counts the number of sequences *explained* by the subsequence S and $supp(S)$ is the support of the subsequence S. The variable z_S^i counts the number of times the subsequence S appears in the i-th sequence in an interleaved manner. The primary intuition while selecting subsequences being to prefer subsequences which are discriminative while at the same time cover a larger number of observed sequences.

We next describe the approach for generating new candidate subsequences that are to be considered for inclusion in the set of *interleaved* subsequences. We initialize the set of *interleaved* subsequences with singleton actions along with their supports. We maintain a priority queue ordered by the importance score and sort the current set I by decreasing order of importance score. The algorithm then iteratively selects all ordered pairs $S_1, S_2 \in I$ and generates a new candidate $S = S_1S_2$ and adds the candidate to the priority queue. Finally, we pull the top-k highest ranked candidate based on their importance score to compose the set of interleaved subsequences.

An important information which we haven't utilized so far is the temporal aspect of the user interaction. We next describe a principled approach of incorporating time while using the extracted subsequences in the SAT prediction model.

5 INCORPORATING TIME VIA HAWKES PROCESS

While the subsequences extracted so far are able to capture informative user interactions, they ignore the temporal spread of actions. So far, time has been modeled in terms of few time-related aspects like pause and dwell time. In this section, we aim at incorporating time in a principled manner when modeling user interaction sequences. We leverage recent advancements in point process models and propose a Hawkes process formulation of interaction sequences. We first give a brief background on Hawkes process (5.1) and later describe how we use the Hawkes process model parameters for weighing the extracted subsequences (5.3).

5.1 Hawkes Process

A point process N is a random measure on a completely separable metric space S that takes values on $N \cup \{\infty\}$. A point process is typically characterized by prescribing its conditional intensity $\lambda(t)$, which represents the infinitesimal rate at which events are expected to occur around a particular time t, given the history of the process up to t, $H_t = t_i : t_i < t$ [33, 34] Thus, in a point process, $N(t)$ counts the number of points (i.e., occurrences of events) in $(-\infty, t]$, and the conditional intensity function $\lambda(t|H_t)$ denotes the expected instantaneous rate of future events at timestamp t depending on H_t, the history of events preceding t.

An important example of a point process is the Poisson process, which always has a deterministic conditional intensity $\lambda(t)$. We say that a point process N is self-exciting if

$$Cov[N(t_1, t_2), N(t_2, t_3)] > 0 \quad (3)$$

for any $t_1 < t_2 < t_3$. This means that if an event occurs, a successive event becomes more likely to occur locally in time and space. This is, however, not true for a Poisson process which has independent increments, hence $Cov[N(t_1, t_2), N(t_2, t_3)] = 0$.

The Hawkes process is a specific class of self- or mutually-exciting point process models [18, 19]. A univariate Hawkes process $\{N(t)\}$ is defined by its intensity function

$$\lambda(t) = \mu(t) + \int_{-\infty}^{t} \mu(t-s)dN(s) \quad (4)$$

where $\lambda_0 : \Re \rightarrow \Re^+$ is a deterministic base intensity, $\mu : \Re^+ \rightarrow R^+$ is a kernel function expressing the positive influence of past events on the current value of the intensity process. In terms of discrete time intervals, we can re-write the intensity function as:

$$\lambda(t) = \lambda_0(t) + \sum_{t_i < t} \mu(t-s) \quad (5)$$

The process is well known for its self-exciting property, which refers to the phenomenon that the occurrence of one event in the past increases the probability of events happening in the future. Such a self-exciting property can either exist between every pair of events, as assumed in a normal univariate Hawkes process, or only exist between limited pairs of events. We next formulate the extracted interaction sequence in a multi-variate version of Hawkes processes and later describe a way of weighing the subsequences using the Hawkes process parameters.

5.2 Modeling Sequences

Given a set of user interaction sequences composed of (maximum) M distinct actions, we model the sequences using a Multivariate Hawkes process model. A Multivariate Hawkes process can be defined as an d-dimensional Hawkes process wherein events can occur along any of the d-dimensions at any given time. Each one-dimensional Hawkes process can be influenced by the occurrence of events of other types. Without loss of generality, we will consider that these mutual excitations take place along the edges of an unweighted directed network G = (V, E) of d nodes and adjacency matrix $A \in \{0, 1\}^{d \times d}$. The intensity function in a d-dimensional multivariate Hawkes process can be defined as:

$$\lambda(t) = \lambda_m(t) + \sum_{m:t_m<t} A_{u_m u} \kappa_{u_m u}(t - t_m) \quad (6)$$

where $\lambda_m(t) \geq 0$ is the natural occurrence rate of events of type m (i.e. along that dimension) at time t, and the triggering kernel function evaluation $\kappa_{uv}(t - t_m) \geq 0$ determines the increase in the occurrence rate of events of type u at time t_i, caused by an event of type v at a past time.

In our case, the number of dimensions corresponds to the number of actions considered (M); the intensity function for each dimension can be interpreted as a rate at which that action occurs. The summation in the second term is over all the action events that have happened up to time t. $\lambda_m(t)$ describes the background rate of action occurrence that is time-independent, whereas the second term describes the mutual-excitation part, so that another action in the past increases the probability of observing this action in the (near) future. The natural occurrence rates and triggering kernels are usually inferred by means of log-likelihood maximization, the details of which are beyond the scope of the current work. We refer interested readers to Embrechts *et al.* [5].

5.3 Kernel Weighting of Subsequences

The Hawkes process model described above enables us to compute the base rates for each action ($\lambda_0(m)$) as well as the triggering kernel ($\kappa_{uv} \in R^{M \times M}$). The triggering kernel value (κ_{uv}) capture the mutually exciting property between the actions u and v. Intuitively, it captures the dynamics of influence of events occurred in the action v to the action u. As such, larger value of κ_{uv} indicates that action u is more likely to trigger an occurrence of action v. We propose to use the triggering kernel to score each subsequence extracted by the techniques proposed earlier. Hawkes kernel weighting of the subsequences allows us to incorporate temporal aspects of the interaction; thereby weighing temporally relevant subsequences more than others. Given a subsequence, we look at adjacent pair-wise actions in the subsequence, compute the kernel trigger score for the corresponding pair, and average it across all the adjacent action pair in the subsequence. We then use the obtained averaged kernel weight of the subsequence as a feature for SAT prediction experiment.

6 EXPERIMENTAL EVALUATION

Estimating user satisfaction from user behavior signals is of critical importance to web search engines. In this section, we demonstrate how automatically extracted subsequences can be used to improve estimation of user satisfaction. We conduct a number of experiments using crowdsourced judgments as well as real world search engine traffic and compare the proposed approach to a number of baselines.

6.1 Crowdsourced Judgments

Our data consists of a random sample of user sessions from a major US commercial search engine engine during a week in June 2016. We randomly sampled user sessions with substantial user activity, and included all queries and the search result page rendered for all search impressions from that user in the timeframe. Additionally, detailed user activity on the result page was logged for model development. Crowdsourced judgments have commonly been used to obtain labeled data [40, 41]. For each search impression, we obtained human labeled judgments on whether the user interaction was satisfying (labeled SAT) or not (labeled DSAT).

The labeling was conducted using an in-house micro-tasking platform that outsources crowd work to vendors, similar to CrowdFlower, and provides access to judges who regularly perform relevance judgment tasks. Workers were under NDA and all data containing personal identifiable information (PII), such as names, phone numbers, addresses, or social security numbers, were removed. The internal human annotation platform was used to design, publish and manage human annotation tasks.

Detailed guidelines were issued to the judges to describe the task and a number of examples were shown explaining how to judge for satisfaction. To ensure the quality of the judging results, we apply a series of quality control methods. One of the methods is creating 'gold hits' that you already know the answer of, then measure the judges by comparing how far off their answers are from the gold hits answers. We also measure the quality of the judgments with the amount of consensus reached which required overlap on the hits, i.e. the same hit to be judged by multiple judges.

In order to provide relevant information to the judges, we provided a detailed summary of user interaction with the SERP. The judges were provided a link to the SERP shown to the user alongside details like number of clicks, time spent on the SERP and scroll information. Additionally, for all the clicked documents, we provided URL level details which included the exact URL, the position on the SERP where it was shown and the total dwell time on each URL.

We randomly sampled over 2100 user sessions and over 450 judges provided judgments for about 6820 search impressions, resulting in over 20460 judgments. Among the first two judgments collected for each query, the judges agreed on the label 74% of the time. We measured inter-rater agreement using Fleiss' Kappa [7], which allows for any number of raters and for different raters rating different items. This makes it an appropriate measure of inter-rater agreement in our study since different judges provided labels for different items. A kappa value of 0 implies that any rater agreement is due to chance, whereas a kappa value of 1 implies perfect agreement. In our data, $\kappa = 0.64$, which, according to Landis and Locke [30], represents substantial agreement.

6.2 Baselines

We consider a number of baselines from recent published literature.

- Baseline 1 (click with dwell time): This baseline is based on the common approach in the literature as labeling satisfaction as occurring if a user clicks on a search result and then spends a minimum of t seconds on a page and does not follow the query up with a reformulation. Spending

Method	Accuracy	Pos P	Pos R	Neg P	Neg R
Baseline 1 (Clicks + DwellTime)	0.56	**0.99**	0.559	0	0
Baseline 2 (Click based actions)	0.59	0.58	**0.99**	0	0
Baseline 3 (Mouse Movement)	0.606	0.643	0.741	0.587	0.454
Baseline 4 (Scroll & Viewport)	0.586	0.679	0.703	0.521	0.364
Baseline 5 (Reading Pattern Signals)	0.596	0.652	0.771	0.564	0.415
All Actions	0.62*	0.653	0.775	0.562	0.414
Action Bigrams	0.582	0.594	0.93	0.521	0.096
Frequent Subsequences	0.603	0.626	0.811	0.52	0.29
Discriminative Subsequences	0.592	0.61	0.886	0.56	0.18
Interleaved Subsequences	0.613	0.631	0.862	0.572	0.22
Actions + Frequent + Discriminative Subsequences	0.622*	0.65	0.8	0.581	0.39
Hawkes weighted Actions	0.631*	0.663	0.781	0.57	**0.462***
Hawkes-weigthed-Actions + Hawkes-weigthed-Subsequences	**0.672***	0.677	0.86	**0.65***	0.37

Table 4: Measurements of prediction quality based on different methods on all user study data. * indicates statistical significant ($p \leq 0.05$) using paired t-tests compared to the corresponding best performing baseline.

a minimum amount of time on a webpage is known as a long dwell click and has been shown to be correlated with satisfaction [26]. In this study, we set t = 30 seconds.

- Baseline 2 (click based actions): This baseline is based on predicting satisfaction based on clickthrough based features [13].
- Baseline 3 (Mouse movement): This baseline is based on recent work aimed at predicting satisfaction using mouse movement patterns.
- Baseline 4 (Scroll & Viewport): This baseline is based on the recently proposed scrolling and viewport features [41]
- Baseline 5 (Reading pattern signals): This baseline is based on the reading pattern signals from Kiseleva *et al.*[27]

We additionally consider variants of the proposed techniques: (i) All Actions, (ii) action bigrams, (iii) the three different types of extracted subsequences, (iv) hawkes weighted actions and (v) combinations of different features.

6.3 SAT Prediction

Based on the obtained judgments, we aim at predicting user satisfaction for each impression. We used Gradient Boosted Decision Trees (GBDT) as the classifier with 5-fold cross-validation for all the results reported. Each extracted subsequence was used as a feature, first with a binary label marking its presence and then with the temporal Hawkes weights. We compare the proposed subsequence based features with a number of standard techniques used in state-of-the-art user satisfaction prediction systems. Table 4 presents the prediction results for the crowdsourced data.

6.3.1 Quantifying gains of detailed actions. We begin by investigating the gains obtained by considering fine-grained user actions over traditionally used clickbased and dwell time based features. Clicks and dwell times have been shown to accurately predict user satisfaction [26] and power a number of industrial experimentation metrics [42]. We observe a 6% increase in SAT prediction accuracy over dwell time based features and ~ 3% increase over click based actions. We also observe that considering all actions are more predictive than individual scroll based or mouse movement based signals. This suggests that adding fine grained user actions indeed helps improve prediction performance, and that other types of actions beyond clicks, are also informative and should be considered by developing metrics.

6.3.2 Comparing subsequences. Having shown the utility of considering fine grained actions beyond clicks, we investigate the performance of the various proposed subsequence extraction techniques. We observe that the action bigrams perform the worst among the extracted subsequences, with all three frequent, discriminatory and interleaved subsequences performing better. It is interesting to note that the discriminatory subsequences do not perform as well as the frequent ones, despite that the fact that they're discriminatory by definition. Such poor performance of discriminatory might stem from the fact that most of the discriminatory subsequences are ranked very low in terms of frequency; hence, despite them being helpful in discriminating the SAT interactions form DSAT ones, they may not always be present and hence impact the prediction accuracy to a less extent. Additionally, the joint encoding of discriminability and importance enables the Interleaved subsequences to perform the best among the extracted subsequences. Such subsequences, when combined with actions, results in over 6% improvement over click and dwell time baseline.

6.3.3 Quantifying Benefits of Incorporating Temporal Aspects. We observe that incorporating temporal aspects of user interaction helps. As can be seen from the improved performance of the Hawkes process weighted actions, the SAT prediction accuracy increases by ~ 5% over the action bigrams and performs slightly better than other subsequence extraction techniques as well as the best baseline performance. When the temporal aspects of all extracted subsequences are incorporated via Hawkes weighting scheme, we observe an improvement of over 12% in terms of prediction accuracy over traditionally used click and dwell time based signals. Indeed, time plays a major role in differentiating satisfying user interactions from DSAT interactions.

6.4 Feature Correlation Analysis

One major motivation for the current work is to extract meaningful informative and interpretable subsequences from user interactions

Top Positively Correlated		Top Negatively Correlated	
Subsequence	**Correlation**	**Subsequence**	**Correlation**
longDwellTime	0.213252	Scroll, mediumPause, smallPause	-0.05476
Clickalgo1	0.109037	smallPause, mediumPause, Move	-0.05183
Clickalgo1, longDwellTime	0.102703	Move, smallPause, mediumPause, Move	-0.03799
Move, Clickalgo1	0.102603	Move, IssueQuery	-0.03356
smallPause, Move, ClickLI, longDwellTime	0.053584	longPause, Move	-0.02571
smallPause, Move, mouseRead, Move	0.050649	IssueQuery	-0.02363

Table 5: Correlation analysis of the different subsequences.

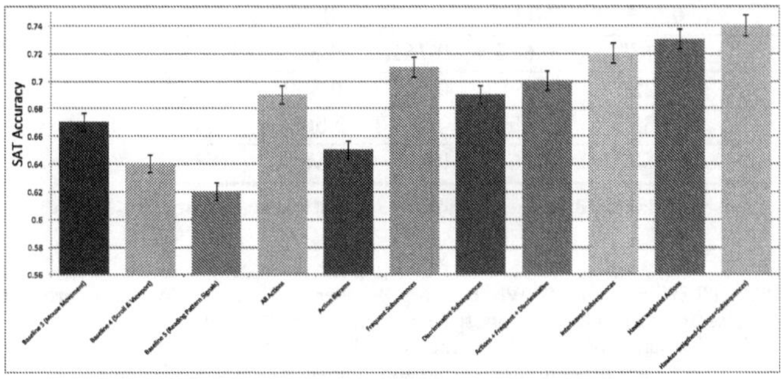

Figure 3: Impact on Abandonment Cases

for developing satisfaction metrics. To this end, we present the feature correlation analysis in Table 5 to gauge the impact of the different subsequences on predicting user satisfaction. We compute the Pearson correlation between the user SAT label and the subsequences and show the top most informative subsequences.

The correlation results re-establish known facts - clicks and long dwell time features are strongly correlated with predicting SAT. Beyond clicks and dwell time, we observe that frequent subsequences like Scroll → Move → Pause are also predictive of SAT label. The discriminatory subsequence: smallPause → Move → MouseRead → Move is strongly correlated with the satisfaction label. Additionally, subsequences highlighting general random user movement in the SERP, for example: Move → smallPause → mediumPause → Move, is negatively correlated with satisfaction. These correlation results could provide insight into which kind of interaction signals should be detected and used for gauging user satisfaction.

6.5 Impact on Abandonment Cases

Often, there are cases where a user may not click on any search result but still be satisfied. This scenario is referred to as good abandonment and presents a challenge for most approaches measuring search satisfaction, which are usually based on clicks and dwell time. As our final crowdsourcing experiment, we consider the utility of the proposed methods in the abandonment cases. We consider all impressions which had no click activity in the user interaction sequence and repeat the user satisfaction prediction experiment on the considered sequences. Figure 3 presents the results. We observe that the same approach works well in abandonment cases too. SAT prediction accuracy increases as we incorporate signals and actions beyond clicks and dwell time. We observe that a combination of different subsequences and temporal aspects via Hawkes process outperforms all other approaches and boosts the SAT prediction accuracy to over 74%. We leave the detailed exploration of interaction signals for good abandonment cases for future work.

7 LARGE SCALE PSEUDO-LABELLED DATA

Owing to the limited scale of experimentation possible with crowdsourced judgments as well as the differences in opinion of crowdsourced judges and actual users, we may have insufficient data and labels to reliably evaluate the performance of the proposed subsequence extraction techniques. To resolve this problem, we build a pseudo-labeled dataset comprised of large-scale query logs wherein we randomly extracted over 148000 query impressions from the query logs of the same search engine that provided the data for the crowd-sourced assessment. To assign pseudo satisfaction labels to search interactions, we assume that a click followed by a query reformulation is a dissatisfied click, while a click with a dwell time of ≥ 30 seconds not followed by a query reformulation is a satisfied click. A query reformulation is the act of submitting a follow up query to modify a previous search query in hope of retrieving better results. Post-click query reformulation is considered a strong DSAT predictor and has been used as a predictor of search satisfaction in previous work [16, 26]. The intuition here is that dissatisfied users will reformulate their queries, while satisfied users will not. This is a crude estimate of user satisfaction but it allows us to easily generate large numbers of pseudo labeled instances without leveraging any information about the click itself (which could lead to confounding).

To identify query reformulations we use a method similar to that described in Boldi *et al.*[4], where features of query similarity (e.g. edit distance, word overlap, etc.) and time between queries are used to identify query reformulations. Using these assumptions, we randomly collected 14,670 user sessions with 148561 search impressions from the search logs of the engine described earlier.

Table 6 presents measurement of prediction quality on this dataset. We observe a similar trend with respect to the relative performance of the actions and subsequences for satisfaction prediction. We find that fine grained actions perform better than the baseline methods, and the interleaved subsequences performing the best among the extracted subsequences. Finally, adding temporal aspect via Hawkes weighting scheme helps boost predictive power by over 7% compared to the best performing baseline.

8 DISCUSSION

Predicting user satisfaction plays an instrumental role in designing and experimenting with search systems. We adopted a novel way of considering user interactions, and constructed universal interaction sequences and leveraged them via three methods to extract informative subsequences which performed better than generic click and dwell time based action signals for predicting user satisfaction. Further, we proposed a Hawkes process model to incorporate temporal

Method	Accuracy	Pos P	Pos R	Neg P	Neg R
Baseline 1 (Clicks + DwellTime)	0.522	**0.965**	0.511	0.22	0.18
Baseline 2 (Click based actions)	0.59	0.602	0.3	0.531	**0.79**
Baseline 3 (Mouse Movement)	0.583	0.592	**0.92**	0.531	0.11
Baseline 4 (Scroll & Viewport)	0.605	0.61	0.81	0.51	0.28
Baseline 5 (Reading Pattern Signals)	0.563	0.581	0.742	0.54	0.13
All Actions	0.62	0.655	0.771	0.562	0.4
Action Bigrams	0.595	0.59	0.937	0.512	0.09
Frequent Subsequences	0.603	0.611	0.812	0.51	0.283
Discriminative Subsequences	0.591	0.6	0.88	0.55	0.17
Interleaved Subsequences	0.613*	0.645	0.761	0.572	0.32
Actions + Frequent + Discriminative Subsequences	0.622*	0.64	0.802	0.582	0.38
Hawkes weighted Actions	0.635*	0.657	0.77	0.565*	0.41
Hawkes-weigthed-Actions + Hawkes-weigthed-Subsequences	**0.667***	0.665	0.872	**0.656***	0.37

Table 6: Measurements of prediction quality based on different methods on large scale pseudo-labelled dataset. * indicates statistical significant ($p \leq 0.05$) using paired t-tests compared to the corresponding best performing baseline.

aspects of user interactions while modeling the extracted subsequences, which when combined with other signals, outperforms all the baselines considered.

The promising results call for deeper investigation into such detailed user activity. Our investigation suggests three concrete areas of further investigation: (i) the type of search result shown, (ii) user type analysis to detect user groups for personalized interaction modeling and (iii) development of sequential models around the extracted universal interaction sequences.

REFERENCES

[1] Charu C Aggarwal and Jiawei Han. 2014. *Frequent pattern mining*. Springer.
[2] Agrawal and Srikant. Mining sequential patterns. In *ICDE 1995*.
[3] Ioannis Arapakis, Mounia Lalmas, and George Valkanas. Understanding within-content engagement through pattern analysis of mouse gestures. In *CIKM 2014*.
[4] Paolo Boldi, Francesco Bonchi, Carlos, Debora, Aristides, and Sebastiano. The query-flow graph: model and applications. In *CIKM 2008*.
[5] Paul Embrechts, Thomas Liniger, Lu Lin, and others. 2011. Multivariate Hawkes processes: an application to financial data. *Journal of Applied Probability* (2011).
[6] Henry A Feild, James Allan, and Rosie Jones. Predicting searcher frustration. In *SIGIR 2010*.
[7] Joseph L Fleiss. 1971. Measuring nominal scale agreement among many raters. *Psychological bulletin* (1971).
[8] Jaroslav Fowkes and Charles Sutton. 2016. A Subsequence Interleaving Model for Sequential Pattern Mining. *arXiv preprint arXiv:1602.05012* (2016).
[9] Steve Fox, Kuldeep Karnawat, Mark Mydland, Susan Dumais, and Thomas White. 2005. Evaluating implicit measures to improve web search. *ACM TOIS* (2005).
[10] A Gaivoronski. 2005. Markov models for identification of significant episodes. (2005).
[11] Qi Guo and Agichtein. Beyond dwell time: estimating document relevance from cursor movements and other post-click searcher behavior. In *WWW 2012*.
[12] Qi Guo and Eugene Agichtein. Exploring mouse movements for inferring query intent. In *SIGIR 2008*.
[13] Qi Guo, Dmitry Lagun, and Eugene Agichtein. Predicting web search success with fine-grained interaction data. In *CIKM 2012*.
[14] Qi Guo, Ryen W White, Susan T Dumais, Jue Wang, and Blake Anderson. 2010. Predicting query performance using query, result, and user interaction features. In *Adaptivity, Personalization and Fusion of Heterogeneous Information*.
[15] Ahmed Hassan, Rosie Jones, and Kristina Lisa Klinkner. Beyond DCG: user behavior as a predictor of a successful search. In *WSDM 2010*.
[16] Ahmed Hassan, Xiaolin Shi, Nick Craswell, and Bill Ramsey. Beyond clicks: query reformulation as a predictor of search satisfaction. In *CIKM 2013*.
[17] Ahmed Hassan and Ryen W White. Task tours: helping users tackle complex search tasks. In *CIKM 2012*.
[18] Alan G Hawkes. 1971. Point spectra of some mutually exciting point processes. *JSTOR* (1971).
[19] Alan G Hawkes. 1971. Spectra of some self-exciting and mutually exciting point processes. *Biometrika* (1971).
[20] Jeff Huang, Ryen White, and Georg Buscher. User see, user point: gaze and cursor alignment in web search. In *CHI 2012*.
[21] Jeff Huang, Ryen W White, Georg Buscher, and Kuansan Wang. Improving searcher models using mouse cursor activity. In *SIGIR 2012*.
[22] Jeff Huang, Ryen W White, and Susan Dumais. No clicks, no problem: using cursor movements to understand and improve search. In *CHI 2011*.
[23] Jiepu Jiang, Ahmed Hassan Awadallah, Xiaolin Shi, and Ryen W White. Understanding and predicting graded search satisfaction. In *WSDM 2015*.
[24] Diane Kelly. 2009. Methods for evaluating interactive information retrieval systems with users. *Foundations and Trends in Information Retrieval* (2009).
[25] Youngho Kim, Ahmed Hassan, White, and Zitouni. Comparing client and server dwell time estimates for click-level satisfaction prediction. In *SIGIR 2014*.
[26] Youngho Kim, Ahmed Hassan, Ryen W White, and Imed Zitouni. Modeling dwell time to predict click-level satisfaction. In *WSDM 2014*.
[27] Julia Kiseleva, Kyle Williams, Hassan Awadallah, Crook, Zitouni, and Anastasakos. Predicting user satisfaction with intelligent assistants. In *SIGIR 2016*.
[28] Dmitry Lagun, Ageev, Qi Guo, and Agichtein. Discovering common motifs in cursor movement data for improving web search. In *WSDM 2014*.
[29] Dmitry Lagun, Chih-Hung Hsieh, Webster, and Navalpakkam. Towards better measurement of attention and satisfaction in mobile search. In *SIGIR 2014*.
[30] J Richard Landis and Gary G Koch. 1977. The measurement of observer agreement for categorical data. *Biometrics* (1977).
[31] Yiqun Liu, Ye Chen, Jinhui Tang, Jiashen Sun, Min Zhang, Shaoping Ma, and Xuan Zhu. Different users, different opinions: Predicting search satisfaction with mouse movement information. In *SIGIR 2015*.
[32] Yiqun Liu, Wang, Ke Zhou, Nie, Zhang, and Ma. From skimming to reading: A two-stage examination model for web search. In *CIKM 2014*.
[33] Yosihiko Ogata. 1988. Statistical models for earthquake occurrences and residual analysis for point processes. *Journal of the American Statistical association* (1988).
[34] Y Ogata. 1989. Statistical model for standard seismicity and detection of anomalies by residual analysis. *Tectonophysics* (1989).
[35] Kerry Rodden, Xin Fu, Anne Aula, and Ian Spiro. Eye-mouse coordination patterns on web search results pages. In *CHI 2008*.
[36] Denis Savenkov, Dmitry Lagun, and Liu. Search engine switching detection based on user personal preferences and behavior patterns. In *SIGIR 2013*.
[37] Adish Singla, Ryen White, and Jeff Huang. Studying trailfinding algorithms for enhanced web search. In *SIGIR 2010*.
[38] Louise T Su. 1992. Evaluation measures for interactive information retrieval. *Information Processing & Management* (1992).
[39] Ryen W White and Susan T Dumais. Characterizing and predicting search engine switching behavior. In *CIKM 2009*.
[40] Ryen W White, Matthew Richardson, and Wen-tau Yih. Questions vs. queries in informational search tasks. In *WWW 2015*.
[41] Kyle Williams, Julia Kiseleva, Aidan C Crook, Zitouni, Awadallah, and Khabsa. Detecting good abandonment in mobile search. In *WWW 2016*.
[42] Xing Yi, Liangjie Hong, Erheng Zhong, Nanthan Nan Liu, and Suju Rajan. Beyond clicks: dwell time for personalization. In *RecSys2014*.

Multi-site User Behavior Modeling and Its Application in Video Recommendation

Chunfeng Yang
The Chinese University of Hong Kong
Hong Kong, China
yc012@ie.cuhk.edu.hk

Huan Yan
Tsinghua University
Beijing, China
yanh14@mails.tsinghua.edu.cn

Donghan Yu
Tsinghua University
Beijing, China
yudh14@mails.tsinghua.edu.cn

Yong Li
Tsinghua University
Beijing, China
liyong07@tsinghua.edu.cn

Dah Ming Chiu
The Chinese University of Hong Kong
Hong Kong, China
dmchiu@ie.cuhk.edu.hk

ABSTRACT

As online video service continues to grow in popularity, video content providers compete hard for more eyeball engagement. Some users visit multiple video sites to enjoy videos of their interest while some visit exclusively one site. However, due to the isolation of data, mining and exploiting user behaviors in multiple video websites remain unexplored so far. In this work, we try to model user preferences in six popular video websites with user viewing records obtained from a large ISP in China. The empirical study shows that users exhibit both consistent cross-site interests as well as site-specific interests. To represent this dichotomous pattern of user preferences, we propose a generative model of Multi-site Probabilistic Factorization (**MPF**) to capture both the cross-site as well as site-specific preferences. Besides, we discuss the design principle of our model by analyzing the sources of the observed site-specific user preferences, namely, site peculiarity and data sparsity. Through conducting extensive recommendation validation, we show that our **MPF** model achieves the best results compared to several other state-of-the-art factorization models with significant improvements of F-measure by 12.96%, 8.24% and 6.88%, respectively. Our findings provide insights on the value of integrating user data from multiple sites, which stimulates collaboration between video service providers.

CCS CONCEPTS

•**Information systems → Collaborative filtering; Personalization;** *Decision support systems;*

KEYWORDS

Multi-site transfer learning, user modeling, recommender systems

SIGIR'17, August 7–11, 2017, Shinjuku, Tokyo, Japan.

DOI: http://dx.doi.org/10.1145/3077136.3080769

1 INTRODUCTION

Online video consumption has become one of the most popular Internet activities worldwide. This trend has created a few very popular video content providers (sites). For example, YouTube and Netflix are among the top websites around the world. Similarly, most users in China also look for videos to watch from a few top video sites. These video content providers compete hard for user eyeballs. In the current market equilibrium, these top websites all tend to have their specialization in video content, e.g. some focus more on movies, while others focus on TV shows, or musical shows. Besides, there are often some overlaps of video catalogs among different sites. Some users visit multiple video sites to find videos of their interest, while some exclusively visit one site.

Normally, each video content provider only has access to its own user-video viewing records. Due to our collaboration with a major ISP in China, we are provided with access to a dataset that includes records of user accessing all video websites in a big city for a window of time. This opens up the possibility for us to investigate various interesting questions about multi-site user modeling: What can we learn about users from multi-site data that is not possible from a single site? How much value is the multi-site data to any video content provider? The answers to these questions allow us to understand more global patterns of online video service, and the nature of competition between video service providers, and whether it makes sense for them to share information.

In the systems studied, the first challenge for accurate user modeling is data sparsity [9], which affects many applications, including personalized recommendation, customer relationship management, targeted advertising, etc., and can be alleviated with more data. In our dataset, more than half of the users are multi-homed (in more than one site's data) users, who view more videos in general than exclusive users. In addition, while the majority of videos are exclusive videos, multi-homed videos are much more popular on average and contribute a considerable proportion of views to the system. Due to the existence of multi-homed users and multi-homed videos, an additional impact of multiple-site data on recommender systems is that one site may recommend to a user some videos that have been viewed in another site by this user. However, in our dataset, a user rarely views a video multiple times, which means knowing multiple-site data can avoid making potential duplicate recommendation. This issue is referred to as information completeness in this paper.

One important finding from our analysis is that there are both cross-site commonality and site peculiarity. Specifically, the multi-homed videos or common types of videos among different sites contribute to the consistent cross-site user preferences, while the exclusive videos affect users' choices in each site, leading to different observed interests in each site. This is evident from the result of principle component analysis in the empirical study section. Because of site peculiarity, merging the multiple-site data as if it is a single merged site does not exploit the most value from the multi-site data. Thus, we propose a generative model of Multi-site Probabilistic Factorization (**MPF**) to capture both the cross-site as well as site-specific aspects of user preferences. Moreover, we illustrate the design principle of our model by analyzing the origins of the observed site-specific user preferences, namely, site peculiarity and data sparsity that also affect how much information should be transferred between sites. The **MPF** model tries to seek a balance between exploiting multi-site data for a smoothed model and capturing site-specific information with each site's data.

We further compare the performance of different factorization models via a variety of recommendation experiments, including experimentation of all six sites, pairs of two sites, different number of latent features, and various sparsity levels. The results show that our model achieves the best recommendation performance by accurately capturing multi-site user preferences. Our findings provide insights for data sharing between video service providers, that is, sharing user viewing data is beneficial for improving recommendation. The main contributions of this work are as follows.

- We measure the user viewing records in six popular video websites, which shows potential value of multiple-site data (alleviating data sparsity and avoiding potential duplicate recommendation) and consistent cross-site as well as site-specific aspects of user preferences.
- We propose a generative model of Multi-site Probabilistic Factorization (**MPF**) to capture the cross-site commonality and site peculiarity of user preferences, which describes how users select videos in multiple video websites.
- We summarize the design principle of our model by analyzing the sources of observed discrepancy of user preferences in multiple sites, i.e., site peculiarity and data sparsity are shown to co-exist and affect the optimal degree of transferring we can apply.
- We conduct various experiments of video recommendation to show that our model outperforms several other state-of-the-art factorization models with significant improvements of F-measure by 12.96%, 8.24% and 6.88%, respectively, which provides insights for win-win data sharing between video service providers.

The rest of this paper is organized as follows. We introduce the data collection with basic statistics in Sec. 2. The empirical study on the data and the motivation of our model are shown in Sec. 3. In Sec. 4, we describe and analyze the proposed model of **MPF**. Then, experimental results are illustrated in Sec. 5. Finally, we present the related work in Sec. 6 and conclude the paper in Sec. 7.

2 DATA COLLECTION AND DESCRIPTION

2.1 Data Collection

The dataset in our study is an anonymized viewing log of 8,062,857 users, which is collected by a major ISP's fixed network from Shanghai, one of the major metropolitan in China, between November 1 and December 31, 2014. There are over 205 million viewing logs of 6 most popular video websites, including Youku (YK), Iqiyi (IQI), Sohu Video (SH), Kankan (KK), LETV (LE), and Tencent (TC). Each log contains user ID, timestamp and request URL. By crawling and parsing the video URLs, we obtain video title, type and viewed website from the respective content providers. Specifically, we classify videos into 6 common video types including show, TV, user generated content (UGC), movie, cartoon, and news. Meanwhile, we find multi-homed videos via matching the video titles. To be specific, since different content providers have their own naming conventions of videos titles, we first manually identify the rules. For example, we observe that the content provider' name is embedded at the beginning of the video titles for some video websites. Then, with the identified naming conventions, we can preprocess the video titles from our dataset and distinguish multi-homed videos accurately and effectively.

2.2 General Statistics

The general statistics of our dataset, including the number of users, videos, viewing records in each site, etc., are shown in Table 1. Moreover, their distributions in terms of different video types are illustrated in Figure 1. We observe that TV dominates the video collections and contributes the largest part of the total eyeballs in each site. However, the view count of a video type is not necessarily proportional to their catalog volume. For example, in TC, a very small portion of news videos contribute considerable viewing records. We also compare the view count distributions of users and videos, as shown in Figure 2. Unlike the nearly power-law distribution of video popularity, the user activeness (view count per user) distribution is heavy-tailed due to that (1) most users are inactive; (2) individual users cannot view too many videos in a limited period of time.

We categorize users and videos into two types, i.e., exclusive (only in one site's data) and multi-homed (in more than one site's data), as per the number of associated sites. In our data, 50.3% of users are multi-homed users (to be specific, 20.3% in twos sites, 11.4% in three sites, 7.7% in four sites, 5.7% in five sites and 5.2% in all six sites), who view more videos (47 videos vs. 5 videos on average) in general than exclusive users. Moreover, while 97% of videos are exclusive videos, multi-homed videos are much more popular on average (956 views vs. 62 views) and contribute more than 25% of views to the system.

3 EMPIRICAL STUDY AND MOTIVATION

In our data collection, the first challenging issue for accurate user modeling is data sparsity [9]. As shown in Figure 2, around two thirds of the users have no more than 10 viewing records. Many applications are affected by this issue, such as personalized recommendation, customer relationship management, targeted advertising, etc.

Table 1: General Statistics

	YK	IQI	SH	KK	LE	TC
Total user count	4479428	3156249	3156351	1351640	2190856	2781976
Total video count	1936643	169889	174229	59041	111250	130240
Total view count	90647660	24721556	39927427	8455611	24091297	17883308

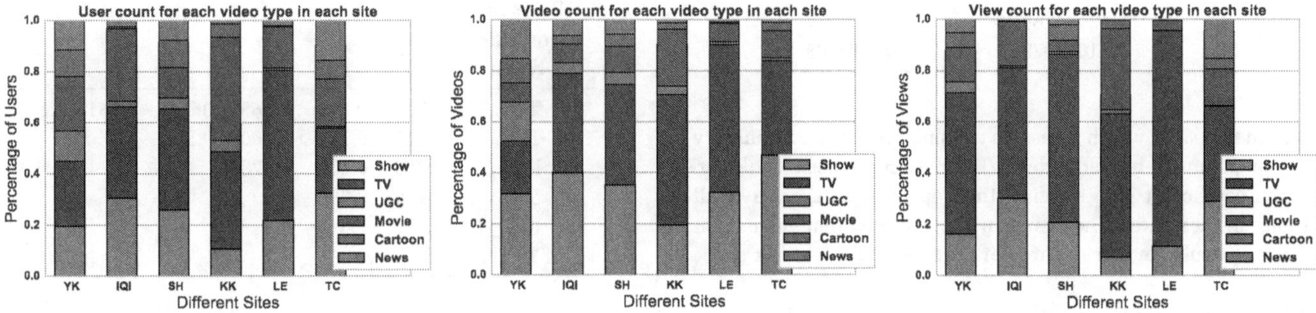

(a) (b) (c)

Figure 1: Number of users, videos, and viewing records of different video types in each site.

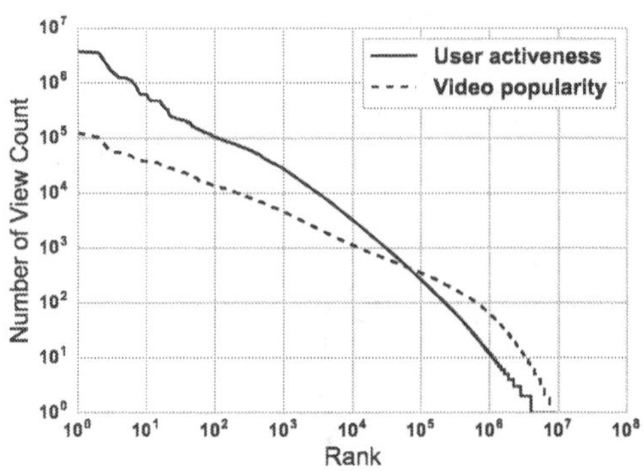

Figure 2: Distribution of user activeness and video popularity.

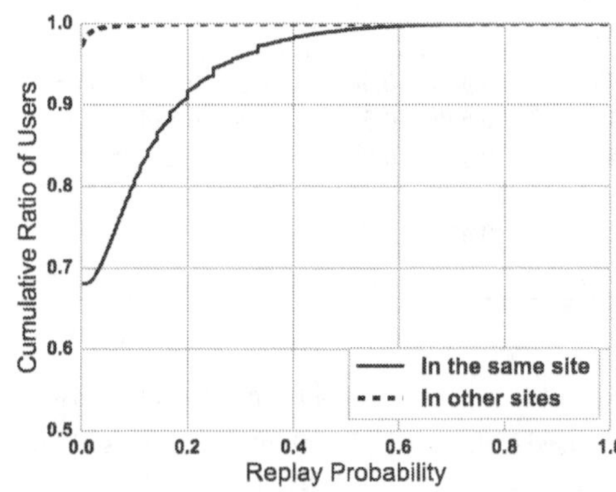

Figure 3: Cumulative distributions of users' replay probability in the same site and other sites.

Furthermore, since there are multi-homed users and multi-homed videos, it may happen that one site recommends to a user some videos that have been viewed in another site by this user. However, as shown in Figure 3, where replay probability of a user is defined as the ratio of views occurring on videos that have been viewed previously by her, users rarely replay videos watched before either in the same site[1] or in other sites, which means multiple-site data can help avoid making potential duplicate recommendation. This issue is referred to as information completeness. To show to what extent this issue exists, we define a potential duplicate recommendation for a certain site as that one of its multi-homed users viewed a video in another site while the same video also exists in the catalog of this site. Then we compare the amount of potential duplicate recommendation with the total view count in each site.

From the results shown in Table 2, we can observe that for most sites (especially IQI, LE and TC), the total amount of potential duplicate recommendation is quite large, which reflects a proprietary aspect of the global information's value.

Merging the multiple-site data can mitigate the data sparsity problem and eliminate the information completeness issue, which, however, may ignore the discrepancy between different sites. Intuitively, the exclusive videos affect users' choices in each site, leading to difference in observed user interest. To check whether site peculiarity exists, we conduct empirical studies from the perspectives of videos and users, respectively.

Video-based Discrepancy. We calculate the Spearman's rank correlation coefficient [13] between the popularity of multi-homed

[1]The true value of intra-site replay probability may be even smaller because the case that users spend multiple time periods to finish watching a video was also counted as replaying.

Table 2: Information Completeness

	Total potential duplicate recommendation	Total view count
YK	9056541	90647660
IQI	19762540	24721556
SH	12172228	39927427
KK	1826602	8455611
LE	12404769	24091297
TC	11048972	17883308

videos in two sites, which measures the similarity of the popularity order of the multi-homed videos. The reason we use a rank correlation coefficient is to alleviate the impact of different eyeball volumes in these sites. The results in Table 3 show that videos that are more popular in one site are not necessarily for another site.

Table 3: Spearman Correlation of Multi-homed Videos' Popularity in Two Sites (Significant at the 0.01 Level)

Spearman Correlation	YK	IQI	SH	KK	LE	TC
TC	0.460	0.543	0.353	0.242	0.656	1
LE	0.542	0.589	0.513	0.314	1	
KK	0.197	0.299	0.151	1		
SH	0.515	0.524	1			
IQI	0.471	1				
YK	1					

User-based Discrepancy. Considering the case of two sites, $u_i^{(1)}$ and $u_i^{(2)}$ are used to denote the latent interest factors in site 1 and site 2 for multi-homed user i. We use the Principal Component Analysis (PCA) to derive $u_i^{(1)}$ and $u_i^{(2)}$ for multi-homed users who have many viewing records[2] (more than 100 views), without distinguishing the sites of multi-homed videos. The number of principal components is set so that the proportion of explained variance is up to 95 percent. Then we measure the average Pearson product-moment correlation between $u_i^{(1)}$ and $u_i^{(2)}$ for those multi-homed users[3].

The results in Table 4 show that a user's interest in different sites is neither identical nor independent, validating the existence of both cross-site commonality and site peculiarity[4]. The discrepancy on the video basis as well as the user basis reflects site peculiarity from the aggregate level (videos) and the individual level (users), respectively. While the site peculiarity may stem from different sets of exclusive videos and featured videos (featured videos refer to those received more opportunities of impression or recommendation), the multi-homed videos or common types of videos among different sites contribute to the cross-site commonality of user preferences. The co-existence of cross-site and site-specific aspects of user preferences motivates the design of our transfer learning model.

Table 4: Average Pearson Correlation of Multi-homed Users' Latent Factors in Two Sites (Significant at the 0.01 Level)

Pearson Correlation	YK	IQI	SH	KK	LE	TC
TC	0.295	0.391	0.365	0.390	0.361	1
LE	0.281	0.374	0.300	0.331	1	
KK	0.223	0.334	0.378	1		
SH	0.190	0.396	1			
IQI	0.299	1				
YK	1					

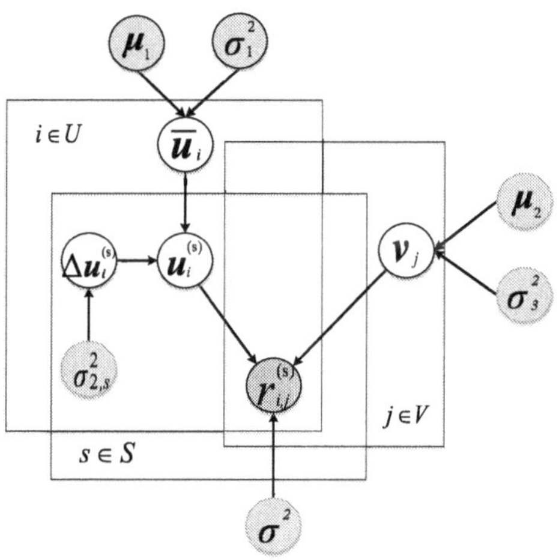

Figure 4: Graphical representation of MPF.

4 MODEL SPECIFICATION AND ANALYSIS

4.1 Model Specification

In this section, we propose a generative model of Multi-site Probabilistic Factorization (**MPF**) to capture the cross-site commonality and site peculiarity. The goal of the generative model is not just for solving the recommendation problem (predictive), but also for modeling multi-site user preferences that can be used to describe how users select videos so as to result roughly in the given distribution of users choosing the web sites as in the viewing records (descriptive).

We denote the set of sites in our study as S. The user set in all sites and in site s is denoted as U and $U^{(s)}$ with the size $|U|$ and $|U^{(s)}|$, respectively. The video set in all sites and in site s is represented as V and $V^{(s)}$ with the size $|V|$ and $|V^{(s)}|$, respectively. User i's viewing video set in site s is denoted as $V_i^{(s)}$. The set S_i is the sites where user i view videos. Thus, the multi-homed user

[2]To obtain more accurate latent interest of users.

[3]Other distance measures, such as Maximum Mean Discrepancy (MMD) can also be used.

[4]The specific values of correlation are not completely accurate due to finite user-video records, but they can still provide insights for the conclusion.

set is $\{i \in U \mid |S_i| > 1\}$. We use R to represent the user-video viewing matrix in all sites. Let $R^{(s)}$ be the $|U^{(s)}| \times |V^{(s)}|$ viewing matrix for site s, whose element $r^{(s)}_{i,j} = 1$ if $j \in V^{(s)}_i$, and $r^{(s)}_{i,j} = 0$, otherwise. Note that, since we only have the implicit feedback data, i.e., the videos viewed by users, which take up a very small portion of all the videos, in order to solve the one-class problem, we adopt the sampling-based approach proposed in [14] to balance the positive and negative samples, which will be discussed in the Sec. 5. Multiple viewing of the same video from a user is only counted as one, which seldomly happens since the replay probability is very low.

The basic idea of **MPF** is to model cross-site user preferences and site-specific user preferences simultaneously, where the cross-site common part is learned over multiple-site data together and the site-specific part is learned with each site's data separately. With user-video viewing records data, we use matrix factorization techniques to find a common latent representation for users and videos in these sites. Let $\mathbf{U}^{(s)} \in \mathbb{R}^{K\times|U^{(s)}|}$ and $\mathbf{V}^{(s)} \in \mathbb{R}^{K\times|V^{(s)}|}$ be the latent user and video feature matrices in site s, with column vectors $\mathbf{u}^{(s)}_i$ and $\mathbf{v}_j$ representing the K-dimensional user-specific latent feature vector of users i in site s and video-specific latent feature vector of video j, respectively. Note that, we assume that interest shown by viewing a certain video is independent of the specific site, thus it holds one set of features for multi-homed videos[5].

We define the conditional distribution over the whole viewing matrix as

$$p(R|\mathbf{U}, \mathbf{V}, \sigma^2) = \prod_{s\in S} p(R^{(s)}|\mathbf{U}^{(s)}, \mathbf{V}^{(s)}, \sigma^2) = \prod_{s\in S} \prod_{r^{(s)}_{i,j}\in R^{(s)}} \mathcal{N}(r^{(s)}_{i,j}|g\left((\mathbf{u}^{(s)}_i)^T \mathbf{v}_j\right), \sigma^2), \quad (1)$$

where $\mathbf{U}$ and $\mathbf{V}$ are the set of user and video latent feature vectors in all sites, respectively. $\mathcal{N}(x|\mu, \sigma^2)$ is the probability density function of the Gaussian distribution with mean μ and variance σ^2. The function $g(x)$ is the logistic function $g(x) = \frac{1}{(1+e^{-x})}$ to bound the range of $(\mathbf{u}^{(s)}_i)^T \mathbf{v}_j$ within $[0, 1]$, because our data is binary. For users in multiple sites, we decompose their latent feature vectors in each site into two parts, namely, common part and site-specific part: $\mathbf{u}^{(s)}_i = \overline{\mathbf{u}}_i + \Delta\mathbf{u}^{(s)}_i$. For exclusive user i in site s, $\mathbf{u}^{(s)}_i = \overline{\mathbf{u}}_i + \mathbf{0}$. The latent feature vector $\mathbf{v}_j$ of a video j is site-agnostic. We also place multivariate Gaussian priors on user and video feature vectors:

$$p(\mathbf{U}|\mu_1, \sigma_1^2, \sigma_{2,*}^2) = \prod_{i\in U}\left(\mathcal{N}(\overline{\mathbf{u}}_i|\mu_1, \sigma_1^2\mathbf{I}) \prod_{s\in S_i} \mathcal{N}(\Delta\mathbf{u}^{(s)}_i|\mathbf{0}, \sigma_{2,s}^2\mathbf{I})\right),$$
$$p(\mathbf{V}|\mu_2, \sigma_3^2) = \prod_{j\in V} \mathcal{N}(\mathbf{v}_j|\mu_2, \sigma_3^2\mathbf{I}), \quad (2)$$

where each site has a different prior for the site-specific part of users' latent feature vectors. The graphical representation of **MPF** is illustrated in Figure 4. The generative process of the proposed **MPF** model is as follows:

- For each user i,
  - draw the vector $\overline{\mathbf{u}}_i \sim \mathcal{N}(\mu_1, \sigma_1^2\mathbf{I})$;
  - for each site $s \in S_i$, sample $\Delta\mathbf{u}^{(s)}_i \sim \mathcal{N}(\mathbf{0}, \sigma_{2,s}^2\mathbf{I})$, and set the user latent vector as $\mathbf{u}^{(s)}_i = \overline{\mathbf{u}}_i + \Delta\mathbf{u}^{(s)}_i$.
- For each video j, draw the vector $\mathbf{v}_j \sim \mathcal{N}(\mu_2, \sigma_3^2\mathbf{I})$.
- For each user-video pair (i, j) in site s, draw the value $r^{(s)}_{i,j} \sim \mathcal{N}(g\left((\mathbf{u}^{(s)}_i)^T\mathbf{v}_j\right), \sigma^2)$.

Through a Bayesian inference, the posterior probability of the latent feature vector sets $\mathbf{U}$ and $\mathbf{V}$ can be obtained as follows:

$$\begin{aligned} &p(\mathbf{U}, \mathbf{V}|R, \mu_1, \mu_2, \sigma^2, \sigma_1^2, \sigma_{2,*}^2, \sigma_3^2) \\ &\quad \propto p(R|\mathbf{U}, \mathbf{V}, \sigma^2) p(\mathbf{U}|\mu_1, \sigma_1^2, \sigma_{2,*}^2) p(\mathbf{V}|\mu_2, \sigma_3^2) \\ &\quad = \prod_{s\in S} \prod_{r^{(s)}_{i,j}\in R^{(s)}} \mathcal{N}(r^{(s)}_{i,j}|g\left((\overline{\mathbf{u}}_i + \Delta\mathbf{u}^{(s)}_i)^T\mathbf{v}_j\right), \sigma^2) \\ &\quad \times \prod_{i\in U}\left(\mathcal{N}(\overline{\mathbf{u}}_i|\mu_1, \sigma_1^2\mathbf{I}) \prod_{s\in S_i} \mathcal{N}(\Delta\mathbf{u}^{(s)}_i|\mathbf{0}, \sigma_{2,s}^2\mathbf{I})\right) \\ &\quad \times \prod_{j\in V} \mathcal{N}(\mathbf{v}_j|\mu_2, \sigma_3^2\mathbf{I}). \end{aligned} \quad (3)$$

The log of the posterior distribution over the user and video latent features is calculated as

$$\begin{aligned} &\ln p(\mathbf{U}, \mathbf{V}|R, \mu_1, \mu_2, \sigma^2, \sigma_1^2, \sigma_{2,*}^2, \sigma_3^2) \\ &\quad = -\frac{1}{2\sigma^2} \sum_{s\in S} \sum_{r^{(s)}_{i,j}\in R^{(s)}} \left[r^{(s)}_{i,j} - g\left((\overline{\mathbf{u}}_i + \Delta\mathbf{u}^{(s)}_i)^T\mathbf{v}_j\right)\right]^2 \\ &\quad - \frac{1}{2\sigma_1^2} \sum_{i\in U} \|\overline{\mathbf{u}}_i - \mu_1\|_F^2 - \sum_{i\in U} \sum_{s\in S_i} \frac{1}{2\sigma_{2,s}^2} \left\|\Delta\mathbf{u}^{(s)}_i\right\|_F^2 \\ &\quad - \frac{1}{2\sigma_3^2} \sum_{j\in V} \left\|\mathbf{v}_j - \mu_2\right\|_F^2 \\ &\quad - \frac{1}{2} \sum_{s\in S} |U^{(s)}||V^{(s)}| \ln \sigma^2 + \frac{1}{2} K|U| \ln \sigma_1^2 \\ &\quad + \frac{1}{2} \sum_{s\in S} |U^{(s)}| \ln \sigma_{2,s}^2 + \frac{1}{2} K|V| \ln \sigma_3^2 + C \quad , \end{aligned} \quad (4)$$

where C is a constant that does not depend on the parameters. $\|\cdot\|_F^2$ denotes the Frobenius norm. Keeping the parameters, i.e., observation noise variance and prior variance, fixed, maximizing the log-posterior over latent features of users and videos is equivalent to minimizing the following objective function, which is a sum of squared errors with quadratic regularization terms:

$$\begin{aligned} &\mathcal{L}(R, \mathbf{U}, \mathbf{V}) \\ &= \frac{1}{2} \sum_{s\in S} \sum_{r^{(s)}_{i,j}\in R^{(s)}} \left[r^{(s)}_{i,j} - g\left((\overline{\mathbf{u}}_i + \Delta\mathbf{u}^{(s)}_i)^T\mathbf{v}_j\right)\right]^2 + \frac{\lambda_1}{2} \|\overline{\mathbf{u}}_i - \mu_1\|_F^2 \\ &+ \sum_{i\in U} \sum_{s\in S_i} \frac{\lambda_{2,s}}{2} \left\|\Delta\mathbf{u}^{(s)}_i\right\|_F^2 + \frac{\lambda_3}{2} \sum_{j\in V} \left\|\mathbf{v}_j - \mu_2\right\|_F^2, \end{aligned} \quad (5)$$

where $\lambda_1 = \frac{\sigma^2}{\sigma_1^2}, \lambda_{2,s} = \frac{\sigma^2}{\sigma_{2,s}^2}, \lambda_3 = \frac{\sigma^2}{\sigma_3^2}$. A local minimum of the objective function can be found by performing gradient descent on

[5]This is reasonable because videos are static and objective, while users are more dynamic and subjective.

$\overline{\mathbf{u}}_i$, $\Delta\mathbf{u}_i^{(s)}$, $\mathbf{v}_j$, μ_1 and μ_2 for all users and videos.

$$\frac{\partial \mathcal{L}}{\partial \overline{\mathbf{u}}_i} = \sum_{s\in S} \sum_{r_{i,j}^{(s)} \in R^{(s)}} \left[g\left((\overline{\mathbf{u}}_i + \Delta\mathbf{u}_i^{(s)})^T \mathbf{v}_j \right) - r_{i,j}^{(s)} \right] \times g'\left((\overline{\mathbf{u}}_i + \Delta\mathbf{u}_i^{(s)})^T \mathbf{v}_j \right) \mathbf{v}_j + \lambda_1(\overline{\mathbf{u}}_i - \mu_1), \quad (6)$$

$$\frac{\partial \mathcal{L}}{\partial \Delta\mathbf{u}_i^{(s)}} = \sum_{r_{i,j}^{(s)} \in R^{(s)}} \left[g\left((\overline{\mathbf{u}}_i + \Delta\mathbf{u}_i^{(s)})^T \mathbf{v}_j \right) - r_{i,j}^{(s)} \right] \times g'\left((\overline{\mathbf{u}}_i + \Delta\mathbf{u}_i^{(s)})^T \mathbf{v}_j \right) \mathbf{v}_j + \lambda_{2,s} \Delta\mathbf{u}_i^{(s)}, \quad (7)$$

$$\frac{\partial \mathcal{L}}{\partial \mathbf{v}_j} = \sum_{s\in S} \sum_{r_{i,j}^{(s)} \in R^{(s)}} \left[g\left((\overline{\mathbf{u}}_i + \Delta\mathbf{u}_i^{(s)})^T \mathbf{v}_j \right) - r_{i,j}^{(s)} \right] \times g'\left((\overline{\mathbf{u}}_i + \Delta\mathbf{u}_i^{(s)})^T \mathbf{v}_j \right) (\overline{\mathbf{u}}_i + \Delta\mathbf{u}_i^{(s)})^T + \lambda_3(\mathbf{v}_j - \mu_2), \quad (8)$$

$$\frac{\partial \mathcal{L}}{\partial \mu_1} = \frac{\sum_{i\in U} \overline{\mathbf{u}}_i}{|U|}, \quad (9)$$

$$\frac{\partial \mathcal{L}}{\partial \mu_2} = \frac{\sum_{j\in V} \mathbf{v}_j}{|V|}, \quad (10)$$

where $g'(x)$ is the derivative of the logistic function and $g'(x) = \frac{e^{-x}}{(1+e^{-x})^2}$.

To reduce the time complexity of model training, we adopted a mini-batch gradient descent approach to learn the parameters. With sampling, the cost of the gradient update no longer grows linearly in the number of matrix entries related to $\mathbf{u}_i^{(s)}$ and $\mathbf{v}_j$, but in the number of entries sampled. The hyper-parameters, i.e., the number of latent features, and regularization coefficients, are set by cross validation.

4.2 Model Analysis

On top of the multiple-site data, three other factorization models can be used. If no information is transferred between sites, the model is Separate Matrix Factorization (**SMF**) [19]. If we combine the user-video matrices of all sites directly and apply the matrix factorization to the merged data, the method is called Merged Matrix Factorization (**MMF**). The Collective Matrix Factorization (**CMF**) proposed in [20] assumes the latent features of multi-homed videos to be site-agnostic and learns the user preferences in each site independently. The difference of four factorization models is summarized in Table 5 and their graphical representations are illustrated in Figure 5.

Table 5: Comparison of Four Factorization Models

	SMF	MMF	CMF	MPF
Transfer user latent features?	No	Complete	No	Partially
Transfer video latent features?	No	Complete	Complete	Complete

If we observe non-identical interests in different sites for multi-homed users[6], the disparity mainly results from two factors: (1) site peculiarity; (2) data sparsity. The first factor stems from different video catalogs, i.e., exclusive videos, and different featured types of videos, etc., in these sites. If we assume users' global preferences exist, the intrinsic preferences are shaped by site peculiarity, leading to different observed interest in each site. The latter factor means that, with a small sample size, interest is partially exposed, and data sparsity will exaggerate the observed discrepancy of cross-site user preferences.

From the perspective of a model's generalization ability, the generalization risk (a.k.a., testing error) of a model is mainly comprised of estimation error (due to randomness of training data, that is, finite sample size and noise) and approximation error (due to restriction of the model space). If data sparsity is the only reason, we can merge the data, and apply single-task learning method to solve the problem. In this case, the estimation error can be reduced with more data, and MMF is suitable for this case. If site peculiarity dominates, and in the extreme case user preferences are independent across different sites, multi-homed users should be modeled separately to avoid negative transfer between tasks that are less related. Using MMF in this case will obtain a smoothed model and enlarge the approximation error because it restricts the model space of learning heterogeneous patterns in each site. Therefore, CMF is appropriate in this case.

By intuition, users' preferences are unlikely to change drastically from site to site, which means even site peculiarity really exists, users' preferences still share commonality across different sites, as validated in Table 4.[7] Besides, there are many users with very few records. Therefore, these two factors, namely, site peculiarity and site data sparsity[8] co-exist and affect the degree of transferring we can apply. For example, we can transfer more between sites with sparser data and less peculiarity. The degree of transferring is reflected by the hyper-parameter λ_1 and $\lambda_{2,s}$, which can be set heuristically by cross validation.

Compared with MMF and CMF, our model aims to mitigate the limitations of these two approaches by accounting for both cross-site commonality and site peculiarity. In other words, **MPF** tries to seek a balance between reducing the estimation error by exploiting multi-site data for a smoothed model and capturing site-specific information with each site's data. Therefore, **MPF** is superior to MMF and CMF in modeling multi-site user preferences.

5 EXPERIMENTAL DESIGN AND RESULTS

5.1 Experimental Design

In this section, we conduct extensive experiments to compare the recommendation capabilities of our proposed **MPF** model with several state-of-the-art factorization models. Our experiments aim at answering the following questions:

(1) What results can be achieved by different algorithms for each site using multiple-site data?
(2) How much one site's recommendation can be improved with each of the other site's data?

[6]The interest reflected by viewing a video is considered to be site-agnostic, thus we mainly analyze the discrepancy of users' interests in different sites.

[7]In the principle component analysis, we selected very active multi-homed users to reduce the impact of data sparsity.

[8]We can even consider individual level data sparsity, i.e., number of user's viewing records. In our work, we did not use distinct regularization parameters for each user since it may cause overfitting.

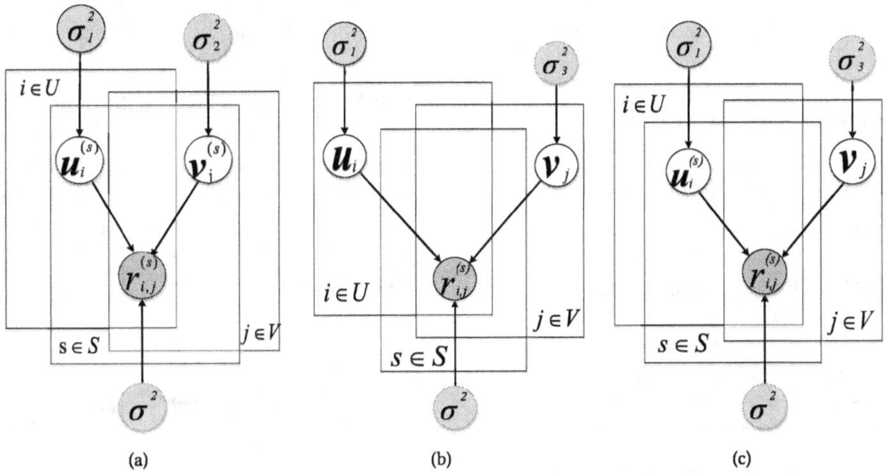

Figure 5: Graphical representation of SMF, MMF, and CMF.

(3) How does K (number of latent features) affect the performance of different approaches?
(4) How do different factorization models perform under various sparsity levels?

To evaluate the **MPF** model that describes how users select videos in different sites, we focus on multi-homed users. We remove videos with too few views (less than 100 views). Since there is no explicit rating data available, we use the implicit feedback data and make top-N recommendation instead of predicting ratings to validate the proposed model.

The generation of training set and test set is as follows. The viewing records data can be viewed as positive samples, which is split randomly into the positive training samples and the positive test samples with 70-30 proportions (this proportion holds for all experiments except for that on different sparsity levels). To balance the positive and negative samples in the training set, for each user, we draw the same number of negative samples as that of her positive training samples from the videos not viewed. Moreover, to avoid predicting all the user-video pairs in the evaluation, which is computationally challenging, we draw 10 times as many negative samples as the number of positive test samples for each user in the test set. Note that, in the test set we only keep users and videos that are also in the training set to make the prediction applicable.

In the model training, we perform 5-fold cross validation to set the hyper-parameters in our experiments. The top-N recommendation generation process for all the factorization models is as follow. For each user i in the test set, we predict a preference score $\hat{r}_{i,j}^{(s)}$ for each video j in the candidate set (union of positive test set and negative test set), where $\hat{r}_{i,j}^{(s)}$ is estimated as $(\mathbf{u}_i^{(s)})^T \mathbf{v}_j$ with different approaches to learn $\mathbf{u}_i^{(s)}$ and $\mathbf{v}_j$ in each factorization model[9]. The top-N recommendation list is obtained by sorting $\hat{r}_{i,j}^{(s)}$ in a descending order and keeping the first N videos.

[9]We did not use the logistic function since it's a monotonically increasing function which won't affect the ranking results.

In particular, since users differ in the number of viewed videos, we are not interested in the specific value of N. Therefore, we make N, namely, the number of videos recommended, equal to the number of her positive samples in the test set for each user. The ratio of negative samples and positive samples holds roughly the same for each user as described in the test set generation process.

Comparative Algorithms. To show the performance improvement of our **MPF** model, we use the three following state-of-the-art algorithms.

- **SMF** [19] This is the traditional matrix factorization approach that factorizes the user-video matrix of each site separately.
- **MMF** This approach combines the user-video matrix of all sites and applies the same factorization method as SMF to learn one set of user factors and video factors, irrespective of the specific site.
- **CMF** [20] This method uses one set of factors for multi-homed videos and learns the factors of users in each site separately.

Evaluation Metrics. With only binary ground truth data available, we adopt F-measure as the performance metrics. Since N is equal to the number of positive test samples for each user, the F-measure value is the same as the precision value as well as the recall value.

$$\text{F-measure} = \frac{\sum_{i \in U^{\text{test}}} \left|V_i^{\text{test}} \cap V_i^{\text{rec}}\right|}{\sum_{i \in U^{\text{test}}} \left|V_i^{\text{test}}\right|}, \tag{11}$$

where U^{test} is the set of users in the test set; V_i^{test} is the set positive test samples for user i; and V_i^{rec} is the set of top-N recommended videos for user i.

5.2 Experimental Results

5.2.1 Overall Performance with Multiple-site Data. The first question to investigate is how the overall recommendation performance of our approach compares with that of other state-of-the-art factorization models by virtue of multiple-site data. To achieve this, we train each factorization model based on the data of six sites, and apply the learned models into top-N recommendation of each site to test the performance.

Table 6: Performance with Data of All Sites

F-measure	SMF	MMF	CMF	MPF
YK	0.880	0.888	0.881	**0.911**
IQI	0.699	0.779	0.761	**0.829**
SH	0.771	0.808	0.806	**0.868**
KK	0.694	0.717	0.706	**0.788**
LE	0.800	0.837	0.833	**0.892**
TC	0.692	0.769	0.770	**0.834**
Overall	0.756	0.799	0.789	**0.854**

From Table 6, we can observe that our **MPF** model outperforms the other approaches. On average, it improves the F-measure by 12.96%, 8.24%, and 6.88% compared to SMF, CMF and MMF, respectively. The significant improvements show the promising benefit of our probabilistic factorization approach. The results demonstrate that multi-site data is valuable, however, blindly merging the data cannot make the best of the data. Moreover, all the experimental results in Sec. 5 are statistically significant.

5.2.2 Site-site Performance Improvement. We conduct a pairwise experiment to investigate how much the recommendation in one site can be improved by virtue of the data of another one. Specifically, we calculate the improved rate of F-measure achieved by **MPF** over that by SMF for each site when collaborating with one of the other sites. The results are shown in Table 7. Note when using one site's data, **MPF** degenerates to SMF, thus, this experiment is to justify the value of more data. The entry 1.10% in the table means **MPF** can improve 1.10% of F-measure for recommendation in site YK over SMF with the help of data from site IQI.

Table 7: Site-site Improved Rate of F-measure by MPF over SMF

Improved Rate	YK	IQI	SH	KK	LE	TC
YK	\	1.10%	4.35%	0.97%	11.3%	7.86%
IQI	9.70%	\	11.8%	13.0%	15.2%	23.7%
SH	1.93%	8.83%	\	9.35%	6.09%	17.2%
KK	3.18%	10.9%	9.50%	\	6.15%	13.2%
LE	0.45%	9.68%	6.08%	4.96%	\	11.6%
TC	9.01%	18.4%	13.1%	10.5%	11.9%	\

As observed in Table 7, the improved rate varies from one pair of sites to another. We further calculate the coefficient of multiple correlation [1] between the improved rate and two predictor variables, namely, site-site correlation of multi-homed users' latent factors shown in Table 4 and data sparsity of each site (i.e., proportion of unobserved entries in the user-video matrix). The multiple correlation coefficient is 0.716, which validates the analysis that data sparsity level and site peculiarity are two of the key factors affecting the optimal degree of transferring[10]. This also provides insights for tuning the hyper-parameters of regularization.

5.2.3 Impact of K. Intuitively, increasing K, i.e., number of latent features, will add more flexibility to the model. The results in Figure 6 for different values of K show that increasing K from the beginning improves the results. However, after reaching the peak, further increasing K lowers the performance, which may be caused by overfitting with redundant parameters. We obtain the overall performance of different algorithms using data from all sites by changing the value of K.

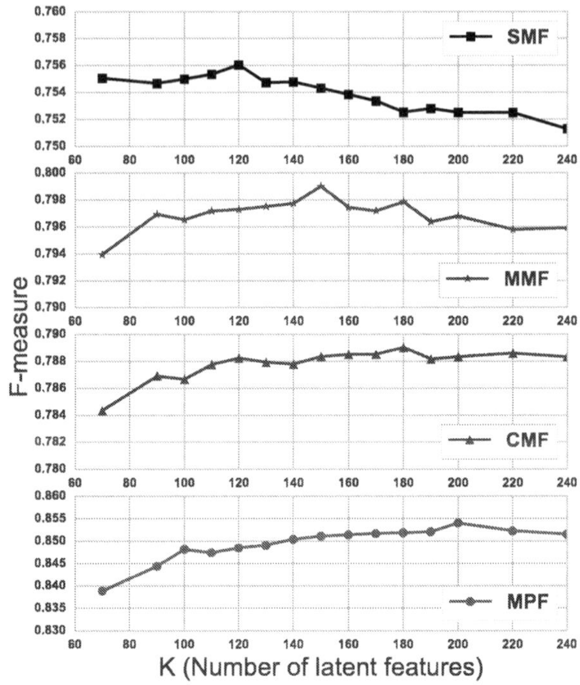

Figure 6: F-measure of each algorithm with different K.

The result in Figure 6 shows that the optimal value of K in this experiment is MPF > CMF > MMF > SMF. SMF fits users and videos in each site independently. Thus, the optimal number of latent features will not outnumber the largest number of topics in any of the sites. MMF fits users and videos in all sites as a whole and obtained smoothed results (unpopular topics may be overwhelmed). CMF fits videos in all sites, while user preferences are learned separately. **MPF** fits all sites jointly and can learn both the common topics and the site-specific topics. Compared with MMF and MPF, CMF does not need to smooth user preferences. However, with less data in each single site, some weak signals may be neglected. These results also imply that our model captures more of users' interest.

5.2.4 Different Levels of Sparsity. We try to explore how multiple site data can help recover the user-video matrix when the data is at different sparsity levels. Specifically, we use different ratios of training data (10%, 30%, 50%, 70%, and 90%) to test all the

[10]Other factors may include information completeness, data volume in each site, etc.

algorithms. Training data 90%, for example, means we randomly select 90% of the user-video data as the training data to predict the remaining 10% of data. The corresponding sparsity is 99.983%, 99.958%, 99.930%, 99.903% and 99.875%, respectively. The results are shown in Figure 7.

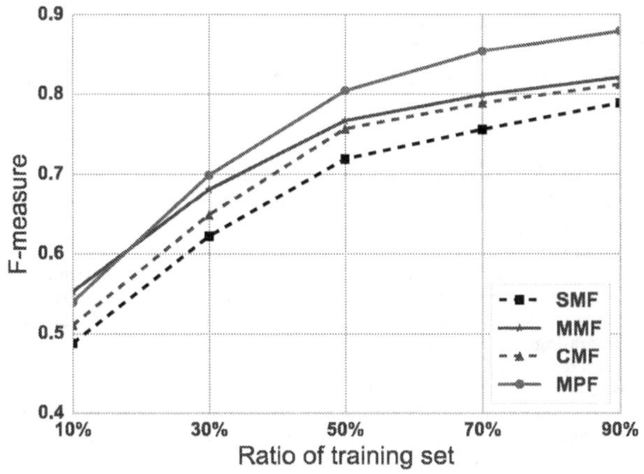

Figure 7: F-measure under different levels of data sparisty.

In summary, we have the following important observations:

- With the lowest ratio of training set, MMF performs best, while SMF is worst, where site data sparsity is a dominant factor.
- As data density increases, **MPF** outperforms the other three algorithms, which indicates that **MPF** needs moderate data to capture the site-specific user preferences.
- The gap between SMF and MMF reduces as the training data becomes denser, which means the impact of data sparsity decreases. Note that even when the ratio is 0.9, the data is still quite sparse.

In conclusion, when data sparsity is the main issue for cross-site user behavior modeling, multiple-site information is valuable and combining the user-video matrices of all sites directly (MMF) works well enough. When both data sparsity and site peculiarity matter, **MPF** performs best.

5.3 Discussion

The experimental results provide an insight that data sharing of multiple sites is win-win for each other. One concern is how to share the data safely and avoid malicious competition, which is not our focus. A potential strategy is to authorize a trusted third party to gather the multiple-site data and train the **MPF** model, and then distribute only the trained model rather than share the data to each of the sites.

The recommendation performance improvement we obtain from multiple-site data stems from three aspects: data sparsity, information completeness, and personalization. While the first two can be tackled by merging the multiple-site data directly, the last aspect requires the consideration of site peculiarity. **MPF** can control the degree of transferring which is affected by site peculiarity and data sparsity. Site peculiarity and data sparsity, on the other hand, are two major factors for the observed discrepancy of user preferences in multiple sites.

Instead of optimizing the recommendation performance for a certain site, we focus on modeling the multi-site user behaviors and show the benefit to each site with a unified model. However, it is not difficult to adjust our model into an adaptive transfer learning model [7] by adding weights W_s to the user-video matrix of each site s, and learning the optimal weights by cross validation to optimize the recommendation accuracy for a specified site. Another approach for adjustment is iteratively reweighting data samples in both the non-target sites and the target site, that is, increasing the weights of the misclassified data in the target site and reducing the weights of the misclassified data in the non-target sites, which is similar to the idea of TrAdaBoost (i.e., Transfer Adaboost) [5]. To conclude, we use a single model to investigate the problem that whether video websites can benefit from each other from the multi-task learning perspective. Additionally, adaptive transfer learning is more suitable for the case that data in the auxiliary domain is much more than that in the target domain.

6 RELATED WORK

In this section, we mainly review some related works on recommendation with implicit feedback and cross-domain collaborative filtering.

Explicit feedbacks, such as numerical ratings, are often unavailable in reality. Thus, recommendation is often based vast amounts of implicit user behaviors, such as views, clicks, purchases [2, 4]. Existing methods handling implicit feedback mainly fall into two categories [3], i.e., imputation-based methods and Bayesian personalized ranking. The basic idea of imputation-based approaches [8] is to convert the one-class data to a balanced dataset by artificially assigning values to some unobserved preferences. Bayesian Personalized Ranking (BPR) [18] utilizes Bayesian inference to train a pairwise ranking model from only positive feedback, based on the assumption that any observed action of a user on an item is an indication that the user should prefer this item to any other item on which she has not performed an action. In addition, with implicit feedback, several matrix factorization methods [10, 21]have been proposed for collaborative filtering, where user and item features are learned through low-rank approximations.

Cross-domain collaborative filtering (CF) is an emerging research topic in recommender systems. It aims to alleviate the sparsity problem in individual CF domains by transferring knowledge among related domains. Matrix factorization based methods are also the state-of-the-art in cross-domain collaborative recommendation because they are able to digest the sparse data well via learning latent variables and are also flexible to incorporate different types of auxiliary data. Some representative cross-domain collaborative filtering methods can categorized into adaptive knowledge transfer and collective knowledge transfer [15] where the former is a directional way exploiting information from a source domain to make recommendations in a target domain, while collective knowledge transfer jointly learns the shared knowledge and unshared effects of multiple domains simultaneously, similar to multi-task learning algorithms. CodeBook Transfer (CBT) [11] studies knowledge transfer ability between two distinct data domains in an adaptive style. Specifically, it transfers knowledge of cluster-level rating behavior from auxiliary data of movies to target data of books. Rating-Matrix Generative Model [12] extended this idea with a probabilistic model to solve collective transfer learning problems. The drawback of RMGM comes from its inability to handle binary feedback data for transferring. Coordinate System Transfer (CST) [17] is transfer learning method of collaborative filtering to transfer the latent features from auxiliary implicit feedbacks of browsing records to target explicit feedbacks of ratings in an adaptive way. The counterpart of CST with respect to collective knowledge transfer is Transfer by Collective Factorization (TCF) [16]. The defect of CST is that it can not be applied to the multiple domains (more than two). Moreover, the heterogeneity between different domains in our study does not lie in the rating scale. Another popular method for collective transfer of latent features is Collective Matrix Factorization (CMF) [20] which explores co-factorizing multiple matrices in the context of relational learning. Both MMF, as described in Sec. 4.2, and CMF merely capture one aspect of the dichotomous pattern of user preferences.

The method in this paper is a bit similar to that in [6] and [10]. However, the focus of [6] is multi-task SVM rather than multi-site collaborative filtering. Moreover, the focused matrix factorization model (FMF) proposed in [10] is an adaptive knowledge transfer approach that leverages information from non-targeted campaigns into targeted campaigns that are usually smaller, whereas our model is a generative probabilistic model that collectively learns user preferences in multiple sites and shows win-win benefits of data sharing between video service providers.

The main novelty of this work is summarized as follows: 1) No prior work focuses on mining user behaviors in multiple video websites due to the data privacy of different online video service providers; 2) There are multi-homed and exclusive users and videos in the studied system, and information completeness presents one unique value of multiple-site data; 3) We observe the cross-site commonality and site peculiarity and model multiple-homed users' preferences as the integration of the common part and site-specific part; 4) The proposed model can be applied to two or more sites to improve their recommendation performance, acting as the incentive of win-win data sharing for multiple sites.

7 CONCLUSION

In this work, with user viewing records obtained from a large ISP of China, we model user preferences in six popular video websites, which is unexplored before. Through real data analysis, we observe the dichotomous pattern of user preferences comprising both consistent cross-site interests as well as site-specific interests. To represent this pattern, we propose a generative model **MPF** to capture both the cross-site as well site-specific aspects of user preferences. The model parameters can be derived via matrix factorization based on our multi-site user video consumption data. The proposed **MPF** model helps address the data sparsity problem, information completeness issue, and personalization of user modeling, which exist in the systems we studied. We conduct a variety of top-N video recommendation experiments to validate the performance of our model in different scenarios of recommendation. The results show that **MPF** model performs best compared with three state-of-the-art factorization models. Our findings provides insights on the value of combining user data from multiple sites, which motivates win-win data sharing between video service providers.

ACKNOWLEDGEMENTS

We acknowledge the support of Hong Kong RGC GRF (grant No. 1420814).

REFERENCES

[1] Herve Abdi. 2007. Multiple correlation coefficient. *The University of Texas at Dallas* (2007).

[2] Nicola Barbieri and Giuseppe Manco. 2011. An analysis of probabilistic methods for top-n recommendation in collaborative filtering. In *Joint European Conference on Machine Learning and Knowledge Discovery in Databases*. Springer, 172–187.

[3] Haolan Chen, Di Niu, Kunfeng Lai, Yu Xu, and Masoud Ardakani. 2016. Separating-Plane Factorization Models: Scalable Recommendation from One-Class Implicit Feedback. In *Proceedings of the 25th ACM International on Conference on Information and Knowledge Management*. ACM, 669–678.

[4] Paolo Cremonesi, Yehuda Koren, and Roberto Turrin. 2010. Performance of recommender algorithms on top-n recommendation tasks. In *Proceedings of the fourth ACM conference on Recommender systems*. ACM, 39–46.

[5] Wenyuan Dai, Qiang Yang, Gui-Rong Xue, and Yong Yu. 2007. Boosting for transfer learning. In *Proceedings of the 24th international conference on Machine learning*. ACM, 193–200.

[6] Theodoros Evgeniou and Massimiliano Pontil. 2004. Regularized multi–task learning. In *Proceedings of the tenth ACM SIGKDD international conference on Knowledge discovery and data mining*. ACM, 109–117.

[7] Ignacio Fernández-Tobías, Iván Cantador, Marius Kaminskas, and Francesco Ricci. 2012. Cross-domain recommender systems: A survey of the state of the art. In *Spanish Conference on Information Retrieval*.

[8] Yifan Hu, Yehuda Koren, and Chris Volinsky. 2008. Collaborative filtering for implicit feedback datasets. In *2008 Eighth IEEE International Conference on Data Mining*. Ieee, 263–272.

[9] Dietmar Jannach, Markus Zanker, Alexander Felfernig, and Gerhard Friedrich. 2010. *Recommender systems: an introduction*. Cambridge University Press.

[10] Bhargav Kanagal, Amr Ahmed, Sandeep Pandey, Vanja Josifovski, Lluis Garcia-Pueyo, and Jeff Yuan. 2013. Focused matrix factorization for audience selection in display advertising. In *Data Engineering (ICDE), 2013 IEEE 29th International Conference on*. IEEE, 386–397.

[11] Bin Li, Qiang Yang, and Xiangyang Xue. 2009. Can Movies and Books Collaborate? Cross-Domain Collaborative Filtering for Sparsity Reduction.. In *IJCAI*, Vol. 9. 2052–2057.

[12] Bin Li, Qiang Yang, and Xiangyang Xue. 2009. Transfer learning for collaborative filtering via a rating-matrix generative model. In *Proceedings of the 26th annual international conference on machine learning*. ACM, 617–624.

[13] Jerome L Myers, Arnold Well, and Robert Frederick Lorch. 2010. *Research design and statistical analysis*. Routledge.

[14] Rong Pan, Yunhong Zhou, Bin Cao, Nathan N Liu, Rajan Lukose, Martin Scholz, and Qiang Yang. 2008. One-class collaborative filtering. In *2008 Eighth IEEE International Conference on Data Mining*. IEEE, 502–511.

[15] Weike Pan. 2016. A survey of transfer learning for collaborative recommendation with auxiliary data. *Neurocomputing* 177 (2016), 447–453.

[16] Weike Pan, Nathan N Liu, Evan W Xiang, and Qiang Yang. 2011. Transfer learning to predict missing ratings via heterogeneous user feedbacks. In *IJCAI Proceedings-International Joint Conference on Artificial Intelligence*, Vol. 22. 2318.

[17] Weike Pan, Evan Wei Xiang, Nathan Nan Liu, and Qiang Yang. 2010. Transfer Learning in Collaborative Filtering for Sparsity Reduction.. In *AAAI*, Vol. 10. 230–235.

[18] Steffen Rendle, Christoph Freudenthaler, Zeno Gantner, and Lars Schmidt-Thieme. 2009. BPR: Bayesian personalized ranking from implicit feedback. In *Proceedings of the twenty-fifth conference on uncertainty in artificial intelligence*. AUAI Press, 452–461.

[19] Ruslan Salakhutdinov and Andriy Mnih. 2011. Probabilistic matrix factorization. In *NIPS*, Vol. 20. 1–8.

[20] Ajit P Singh and Geoffrey J Gordon. 2008. Relational learning via collective matrix factorization. In *Proceedings of the 14th ACM SIGKDD international conference on Knowledge discovery and data mining*. ACM, 650–658.

[21] Quan Yuan, Li Chen, and Shiwan Zhao. 2011. Factorization vs. regularization: fusing heterogeneous social relationships in top-n recommendation. In *Proceedings of the fifth ACM conference on Recommender systems*. ACM, 245–252.

Item Silk Road: Recommending Items from Information Domains to Social Users

Xiang Wang
National University of Singapore
xiangwang@u.nus.edu

Xiangnan He*
National University of Singapore
xiangnanhe@gmail.com

Liqiang Nie
ShanDong University
nieliqiang@gmail.com

Tat-Seng Chua
National University of Singapore
dcscts@nus.edu.sg

ABSTRACT

Online platforms can be divided into information-oriented and social-oriented domains. The former refers to forums or E-commerce sites that emphasize user-item interactions, like Trip.com and Amazon; whereas the latter refers to social networking services (SNSs) that have rich user-user connections, such as Facebook and Twitter. Despite their heterogeneity, these two domains can be bridged by a few overlapping users, dubbed as *bridge users*. In this work, we address the problem of *cross-domain social recommendation, i.e.*, recommending relevant items of information domains to potential users of social networks. To our knowledge, this is a new problem that has rarely been studied before.

Existing cross-domain recommender systems are unsuitable for this task since they have either focused on homogeneous information domains or assumed that users are fully overlapped. Towards this end, we present a novel *Neural Social Collaborative Ranking* (NSCR) approach, which seamlessly sews up the user-item interactions in information domains and user-user connections in SNSs. In the information domain part, the attributes of users and items are leveraged to strengthen the embedding learning of users and items. In the SNS part, the embeddings of bridge users are propagated to learn the embeddings of other non-bridge users. Extensive experiments on two real-world datasets demonstrate the effectiveness and rationality of our NSCR method.

CCS CONCEPTS

•Information systems → Social recommendation; Retrieval models and ranking; Recommender systems;

KEYWORDS

Cross-domain Recommendation, Deep Collaborative Filtering, Neural Network, Deep Learning

*Xiangnan He is the corresponding author.

SIGIRfi17, August 7–11, 2017, Shinjuku, Tokyo, Japan
© 2017 ACM. 978-1-4503-5022-8/17/08...$15.00
DOI: http://dx.doi.org/10.1145/3077136.3080771

1 INTRODUCTION

Nowadays online platforms play a pivotal role in our daily life and encourage people to share experiences, exchange thoughts, and enjoy online services. Regardless of applications, we can roughly divide the existing platforms into information-oriented and social-oriented domains. The former typically refers to forums or E-Commerce sites that have thorough knowledge on items, such as point-of-interests in Trip.com, movies in IMDb, and products in Amazon. These sites have ample user-item interactions available in the form of users' reviews, ratings, along with various kinds of implicit feedback like views and clicks [1]. On the other hand, the social-oriented domains are mainly social network sites, which emphasize the social connections among users [15].

When adopting an item, besides consulting the information sites, a user usually gathers more detailed information from her experienced friends. This refers to *word-of-mouth marketing*, which is widely recognized as the most effective strategy for producing recommendation. As reported by Cognizant[1], more than 45% of travelers rely on social networks to seek advice from friends for travel. However, most existing SNSs, like Facebook and Twitter, are designed mainly for users to rebuild their real-world connections, rather than for seeking options regarding items. Though some item cues implying users' preference can be found in SNSs, they typically contain item names only with limited details. The sparse and weak user-item interactions greatly hinder the ability of SNSs to offer item recommendation services.

Fortunately, some users may be simultaneously involved in both SNSs and information-domain sites, who can act as a bridge to propagate user-item interactions across domains. For example, it is not unusual for a user to share her travel experiences in Trip.com; and if the user also holds a Facebook account, we can recommend her friends in Facebook with her liked items from Trip.com. In social circles, these bridge users are like the *silk road* to route relevant items from information domains to (non-bridge) users of social networks. As such, we formulate the task of *cross-domain social recommendation*, which aims to recommend relevant items of information domains to the users of social domains. Apparently, this task is related to the recently emerging topic — cross-domain recommendation [13]. However, we argue that existing efforts have either focused on homogeneous domains (*i.e.*, multiple sites of the information domain) [5], or unrealistically assumed that the users are fully overlapped [13, 30]. Our task to address is particularly challenging due to the following two practical considerations.

[1]https://www.cognizant.com.

- Insufficient bridge users. To gain a deep insight, we analyzed the overlapped users between Trip.com and Facebook/Twitter, finding that only 10.5% of 8,196 Facebook users and 6.9% of 7,233 Twitter users have public accounts in Trip.com. It is highly challenging to leverage history of such limited number of bridge users to provide quality recommendation for non-bridge users.
- Rich attributes. The users and items of an information domain are usually associated with rich attributes. For instance, Trip.com enables users to indicate their travel preference explicitly, and associates travel spots (*i.e.,* items) with specific travel modes, among other information. However, little attention has been paid to leverage these attributes to boost the performance of cross-domain recommendation.

In this work, we propose a novel solution named *Neural Social Collaborative Ranking* (NSCR) for the new task of cross-domain social recommendation. It is developed based on the recent advance of neural collaborative filtering (NCF) [11], which is further extended to model the cross-domain social relations by combining with the graph regularization technique [9]. We entail two key technical components of our NSCR as follows.

- For the modelling of information domain, we build an attribute-aware recommender based on the NCF framework. To fully exploit the interactions among a user, an item, and their attributes, we enhance NCF by plugging a *pairwise pooling* operation above the embedding vectors of user (item) ID and attributes. In contrast to the default average pooling used by NCF [11] and other recent neural recommenders [4], our use of pairwise pooling better captures feature interactions in the low level [10, 21], greatly facilitating the following deep layers to learn higher-order interactions among users, items and attributes.
- For the modelling of social domain, it is natural to guide the embedding learning of social users by using the embeddings of bridge users. As the embeddings of bridge users are optimized to predict user–item interactions (*e.g.,* ratings and purchases), propagating their embeddings to social users helps to bridge the heterogeneity gap between information domain and social domain. To implement such propagation effect, we employ the *smoothness* constraint (*i.e., graph Laplacian*) on the social network, which enforces close friends to have similar embedding so as to reflect their similar preferences.

To sum up, the key contributions of this work are three-fold:

(1) To our knowledge, we are the first to introduce the task of cross-domain social recommendation, which recommends relevant items of information domains to target users of social domains.
(2) We propose a novel solution that unifies the strengths of deep neural networks in modelling attributed user-item interactions and graph Laplacian in modelling user-user social relations.
(3) We construct two real-world benchmark datasets for exploring the new task of cross-domain social recommendation and extensively evaluate our proposed solution.

2 PRELIMINARY

We first formulate the task of cross-domain social recommendation, and then shortly recapitulate the matrix factorization model, highlighting its limitations for addressing the task.

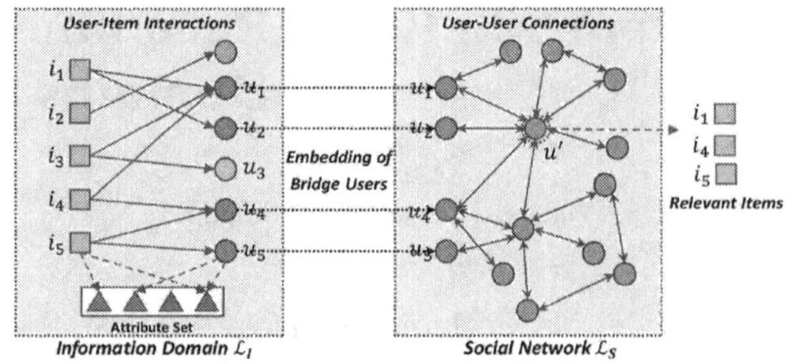

Figure 1: Illustration of the cross-domain social recommendation task.

2.1 Problem Formulation

Figure 1 illustrates the task of cross-domain social recommendation. In the information domain, we have the interaction data between users and items. Let u and $\mathcal{U}_1 = \{u_t\}_{t=1}^{M_1}$ denote a user and the whole user set of the information domain, respectively; similarly, we use i and $\mathcal{I} = \{i_t\}_{t=1}^{N}$ to denote an item and the whole item set, respectively. The edges between users and items denote their interactions, $\mathcal{Y} = \{y_{ui}\}$, which can be real-valued explicit ratings or binary 0/1 implicit feedback. Traditional collaborative filtering algorithms can then be performed on the user-item interaction data.

In addition to the ID that distinguishes a user or an item, most information-domain sites also associate them with abundant side information, which can help to capture users' preferences and item properties better. For example, in Trip.com, the user may choose the travel tastes of {*luxury travel, art lover*} in her profile; while, the item *Marina Bay Sands* is tagged most with travel modes {*luxury travel, family travel, nightlife*}. We term these associated information as *attributes*, most of which are discrete categorical variables for the web domain [10]. Formally, we denote g and $\mathcal{G} = \{g_t\}_{t=1}^{V}$ as an attribute and the whole attribute set, respectively; for a user u and an item i, we can then construct the associated attribute set as $\mathcal{G}_u = \{g_1^u, \cdots, g_{V_u}^u\} \subset \mathcal{G}$ and $\mathcal{G}_i = \{g_1^i, \cdots, g_{V_i}^i\} \subset \mathcal{G}$, respectively.

In the social domain, we have social connections between users, such as the undirected friendship or directed follower/followee relations. We denote a social user as u', all users of the social domain as $\mathcal{U}_2 = \{u_t'\}_{t=1}^{M_2}$, and all social connections as $\mathcal{S} = \{s_{u'u''}\}$. We define the bridge users as the overlapping users between the information domain and social domain. These bridge users can be expressed as $\mathcal{U} = \mathcal{U}_1 \cap \mathcal{U}_2$. In a social network, a user's behaviours and preferences can be propagated along the social connections to influence her friends. As such, these bridge users play a pivotal role in addressing the cross-domain social recommendation problem, which is formally defined as:

Input: An information domain with $\{\mathcal{U}_1, \mathcal{I}, \mathcal{Y}, \mathcal{G}_u, \mathcal{G}_i\}$; a social domain with $\{\mathcal{U}_2, \mathcal{S}\}$; and $\mathcal{U}_1 \cap \mathcal{U}_2$ is nonempty.

Output: A personalized ranking function for each user u' of the social domain $f_{u'} : \mathcal{I} \rightarrow \mathbb{R}$, which maps each item of the information domain to a real number.

It is noted that there indeed exist sparse and weak user-item interactions in SNSs as aforementioned. However, we simplify this scenario of cross-domain social recommendation by only emphasizing the social connections in SNSs and leaving the exploration of weak interactions as the future work.

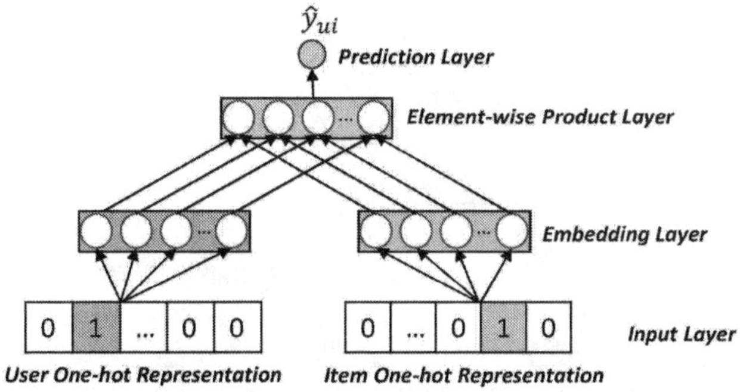

Figure 2: MF as a shallow neural network model.

2.2 Factorization Model

Collaborative filtering (CF) is the key technique for personalized recommendation systems. It exploits user-item interactions by assuming that similar users would have similar preference on items. Model-based CF approaches [1, 33] achieve this goal by describing the interaction data with an underlying model, for which the holistic goal is to build:

$$\widehat{y}_{ui} = f_\Theta(u, i), \tag{1}$$

where f denotes the underlying model with parameters Θ, and $\widehat{y}_{ui}$ denotes the predicted score for a user-item interaction y_{ui}. Matrix factorization (MF) is one of the simplest yet effective models for the recommendation task, which characterizes a user or an item with a latent vector, modelling a user-item interaction as the inner product of their latent vectors:

$$f_{MF}(u, i|\mathbf{p}_u, \mathbf{q}_i) = \mathbf{p}_u^\top \mathbf{q}_i = \sum_{k=1}^{K} p_{uk} q_{ik}, \tag{2}$$

where $\mathbf{p}_u \in \mathbb{R}^K$ and $\mathbf{q}_i \in \mathbb{R}^K$ are model parameters denoting the latent vector (*aka.* representation) for user u and item i, respectively.

Despite its effectiveness, we note that MF's expressiveness can be limited by the use of the inner product operation to model a user-item interaction. To illustrate this, we present a neural network view of the MF model. As shown in Figure 2, we feed the one-hot representation of user/item ID into the architecture, and project them with a fully connected embedding layer. By feeding the user/item embedding vectors into the element-wise product layer, we obtain a hidden vector $\mathbf{h} = \{p_{uk} q_{ik}\}$. If we directly project $\mathbf{h}$ into the output score, we can exactly recover the MF model. As such, MF can be deemed as a shallow neural network with one hidden layer only. Based on this connection, we argue that there are two key limitations of MF-based approaches for cross-domain social recommendation:

- First, MF only considers the simple two-way interaction between a user and an item, by assuming that their cross latent factors (*i.e.,* $\mathbf{p}_u$ and $\mathbf{q}_i$) are independent of each other. However, such an independence assumption can be insufficient to model real-world data, which usually have complex and non-linear underlying structures [10, 15].
- The case can be even worse if we take the attributes into account. A typical way to extend MF with side attributes is SVDfeature, *i.e.,* by summing attribute embedding vectors with user/item embedding vector. As a result, the rich correlations among users, items, and attributes are unintentionally ignored.

Our proposed NSCR solution addresses the above limitations of MF by 1) using a deep learning scheme to capture the higher-order correlations between user and item latent factors, and 2) devising a pairwise pooling operation to efficiently model the pair-wise correlations among users, items, and attributes.

3 OUR NSCR SOLUTION

The goal of cross-domain social recommendation is to select relevant items from the information domain for social users. Under the paradigm of embedding-based methods (*aka.* representation learning), the key for addressing the task is on how to project items (of the information domain) and users (of the social domain) into the same embedding space. A generic solution is the factorization machine (FM) [20, 21], which merges the data from the two domains by an early fusion; that is, constructing the predictive model by incorporating social users as the input features. While the solution sounds reasonable conceptually, the problem is that the training instances which can incorporate social users are only applicable to the bridge users, which can be very few for real-world applications. As such, the generic recommender solution FM can suffer severely from the problem of insufficient bridge users.

To address the challenge of insufficient bridge users, we propose a new framework that separates the embedding learning process of each domain. By enforcing the two learning processes to share the same embeddings for bridge users, we can ensure that items and social users are in the same embedding space. Formally, we devise the optimization framework as:

$$\mathcal{L} = \mathcal{L}_I(\Theta_I) + \mathcal{L}_S(\Theta_S), \tag{3}$$

where $\mathcal{L}_I$ (or $\mathcal{L}_S$) denotes the objective function of the information domain (or social domain) learning with parameters Θ_I (or Θ_S), and most importantly, $\Theta_I \cap \Theta_S$ are nonempty denoting the shared embeddings of bridge users.

By separating the learning process for two domains, we allow the design of each component to be more flexible. Specially, we can apply any collaborative filtering solution for $\mathcal{L}_I$ to learn from user-item interactions, and utilize any semi-supervised learning technique for $\mathcal{L}_S$ to propagate the embeddings of bridge users to non-bridge users. In the remainder of this section, we first present our novel neural collaborative ranking solution for $\mathcal{L}_I$, followed by the design of social learning component $\mathcal{L}_S$. Lastly, we discuss how to optimize the joint objective function.

3.1 Learning of Information Domain

To estimate the parameters for a CF model from user-item interaction data, two types of objective functions — point-wise [1, 11] and pair-wise [2, 21, 26] — are most commonly used. The point-wise objective functions aim to minimize the loss between the predicted score and its target value. Here, to tailor our solution for both implicit feedback and the personalized ranking task, we adopt the pair-wise ranking objective functions.

Formally, we denote an observed user-item interaction as $y_{ui} = 1$, otherwise $y_{ui} = 0$. Instead of forcing the prediction score $\hat{y}_{ui}$ to be close to y_{ui}, ranking-ware objective functions concern the relative order between the pairs of observed and unobserved interactions:

$$\mathcal{L}_I = \sum_{(u,i,j)\in O} \mathcal{L}(y_{uij}, \hat{y}_{uij}), \quad (4)$$

where $y_{uij} = y_{ui} - y_{uj}$ and $\hat{y}_{uij} = \hat{y}_{ui} - \hat{y}_{uj}$; O denotes the set of training triplets, each of which comprises of a user u, an item i of observed interactions (*i.e.*, $y_{ui} = 1$), and an item j of unobserved interactions (*i.e.*, $y_{ui} = 0$). An ideal model should rank all (i, j) item pairs correctly for every user. To implement the ranking hypotheses, we adopt the regression-based loss [26]:

$$\mathcal{L}_I = \sum_{(u,i,j)\in O} (y_{uij} - \hat{y}_{uij})^2 = \sum_{(u,i,j)\in O} (\hat{y}_{ui} - \hat{y}_{uj} - 1)^2. \quad (5)$$

Note that other pair-wise ranking functions can also be applied, such as the bayesian personalized ranking (BPR) [2, 21] and contrastive max-margin loss [23]. In this work, we use the regression-based ranking loss as a demonstration for our NSCR, and leave the exploration of other choices as the future work.

3.1.1 ***Attribute-aware Deep CF Model***. Having established the optimization function for learning from information domain, we now present our attribute-aware deep collaborative filtering model to estimate a user-item interaction $\hat{y}_{ui}$. Figure 3 illustrates its architecture, which is a multi-layered feed-forward neural network. We elaborate its design layer by layer.

Input Layer. The input to the model is a user u, an item i, and their associated attributes $\mathcal{G}_u$ and $\mathcal{G}_i$. We transform them into barbarized sparse vectors with one-hot encoding, where only the non-zero binary features are recorded.

Embedding Layer. The embedding layer maps each non-zero feature into a dense vector representation. As we have four types of features here, we differentiate them with different symbols: $\mathbf{u}$, $\mathbf{i}$, $\mathbf{g}_t^u$, and $\mathbf{g}_t^i$ denote the K-dimensional embedding vector for user u, item i, user attribute g_t^u, and item attribute g_t^i, respectively.

Pooling Layer. The output of the embedding layer is a set of embedding vectors to describe user u and item i, respectively. As different users (items) may have different number of attributes, the size of the embedding vector set may vary for different inputs. To train a neural network of fixed structure, it is essential to convert the set of variable-length vectors to a fixed-length vector, *i.e.*, the pooling operation.

The most commonly used pooling operations in neural network modelling are average pooling and max pooling. However, we argue that such simple operations are insufficient to capture the interaction between users/items and attributes. For example, the average pooling assumes a user and her attributes are linearly independent, which fails to encode any correlation between them in the embedding space. To tackle the problem, we consider to model the pairwise correlation between a user and her attributes, and all nested correlations among her attributes:

$$\mathbf{p}_u = \varphi_{pairwise}(\mathbf{u}, \{\mathbf{g}_t^u\}) = \sum_{t=1}^{V_u} \mathbf{u} \odot \mathbf{g}_t^u + \sum_{t=1}^{V_u}\sum_{t'=t+1}^{V_u} \mathbf{g}_t^u \odot \mathbf{g}_{t'}^u, \quad (6)$$

where $\odot$ denotes the element-wise product of two vectors. We term it as *pairwise pooling*, which is originally inspired from the design of factorization machines [10, 19]. By applying pairwise pooling on the item counterpart, we can similarly model the pair-wise correlation between an item and its attributes:

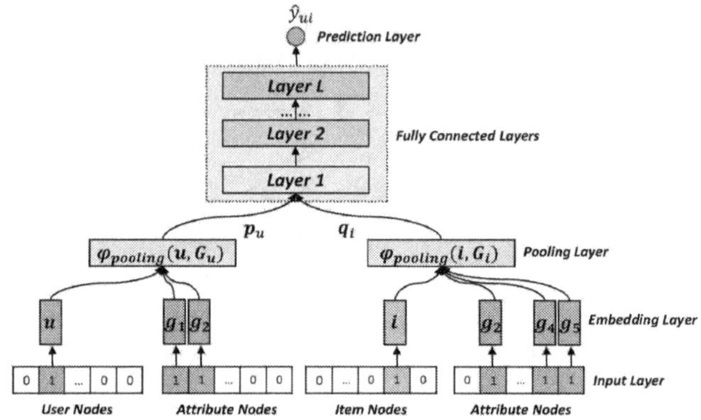

Figure 3: Illustration of our Attributed-aware Deep CF model for estimating an user-item interaction.

$$\mathbf{q}_i = \varphi_{pairwise}(\mathbf{i}, \{\mathbf{g}_t^i\}) = \sum_{t=1}^{V_i} \mathbf{i} \odot \mathbf{g}_t^i + \sum_{t=1}^{V_i}\sum_{t'=t+1}^{V_i} \mathbf{g}_t^i \odot \mathbf{g}_{t'}^i. \quad (7)$$

It is worth pointing out that although pairwise pooling models the correlation between each pair of features, it can be efficiently computed in linear time — the same time complexity with average/max pooling. To show the linear time complexity of evaluating pairwise pooling, we reformulate Eqn.(6) as,

$$\mathbf{p}_u = \frac{1}{2}\left[(\mathbf{u} + \sum_{t=1}^{V_u} \mathbf{g}_t^u) \odot (\mathbf{u} + \sum_{t=1}^{V_u} \mathbf{g}_t^u) - \mathbf{u} \odot \mathbf{u} - \sum_{t=1}^{V_u} \mathbf{g}_t^u \odot \mathbf{g}_t^u\right], \quad (8)$$

which can be computed in $O(KV_u)$ time. This is a very appealing property, meaning that the benefit of pairwise pooling in modelling all pair-wise correlations does not involve any additional cost, as compared to the average pooling that does not model any correlation between input features.

Hidden Layers: Above the pairwise pooling is a stack of full connected layers, which enable us to capture the nonlinear and higher-order correlations among users, items, and attributes. Inspired by the neural network view of matrix factorization (*cf.* Figure 2), we first merge user representation $\mathbf{p}_u$ and item representation $\mathbf{q}_i$ with an element-wise product, which models the two-way interaction between u and i. We then place a multi-layer perceptron (MLP) above the element-wise product. Formally, the hidden layers are defined as:

$$\begin{cases} \mathbf{e}_1 = \sigma_1(\mathbf{W}_1(\mathbf{p}_u \odot \mathbf{q}_i) + \mathbf{b}_1) \\ \mathbf{e}_2 = \sigma_2(\mathbf{W}_2\mathbf{e}_1 + \mathbf{b}_2) \\ \cdots\cdots \\ \mathbf{e}_L = \sigma_L(\mathbf{W}_L\mathbf{e}_{L-1} + \mathbf{b}_L) \end{cases}, \quad (9)$$

where $\mathbf{W}_l$, $\mathbf{b}_l$, σ_l, and $\mathbf{e}_l$ denote the weight matrix, bias vector, activation function, and output vector of the l-th hidden layers, respectively. As for the activation function in each hidden layer, we opt for Rectifier (ReLU) unit, which is more biologically plausible and proven to be non-saturated. Regarding the structure of hidden layers, common choices include the tower [4, 11], constant, and diamond, among others. In this work, we simply set all hidden layers have the same size, leaving the further tuning of the deep structure as the future work.

Prediction Layer: At last, the output vector of the last hidden layer $\mathbf{e}_L$ is transformed to the prediction score:

$$\hat{y}_{ui} = \mathbf{w}^\top \mathbf{e}_L, \tag{10}$$

where $\mathbf{w}$ represents the weight vector of the prediction layer.

Note that we have recently proposed a neural factorization machine (NFM) model [10], which similarly uses a pairwise pooling operation to model the interaction among features. We point out that the main architecture difference is in our separated treatment of the user and item channel, where each channel can essentially be seen as an application of NFM on the user/item ID and attributes.

3.2 Learning of Social Domain

With the above neural collaborative ranking solution, we obtain an attribute-aware representation $\mathbf{p}_u$ and $\mathbf{q}_i$ for each user and item, respectively. To predict the affinity score of a social user to an item of the information domain, we need to also learn an representation for the social user in the same latent space of the information domain. We achieve this goal by propagating $\mathbf{p}_u$ from bridge users to representations for non-bridge users of the social domain. The intuition for such representation propagation is that, if two users are strongly connected (*e.g.*, close friends with frequent interactions), it is likely that they have the similar preference on items; as such, they should have similar representations in the latent space. This suits well the paradigm of graph regularization [7, 9, 28, 29] (*aka.* semi-supervised learning on graph), which has two components:

Smoothness: The smoothness constraint implies the structural consistency — the nearby vertices of a graph should not vary much in their representations. Enforcing smoothness constraint in our context of social domain learning will propagate a user's representation to her neighbors, such that when a steady state reaches, all vertices should have been placed in the same latent space. The objective function for smoothness constraint is defined as:

$$\theta(\mathcal{U}_2) = \frac{1}{2} \sum_{u', u'' \in \mathcal{U}_2} s_{u'u''} \left\| \frac{\mathbf{p}_{u'}}{\sqrt{d_{u'}}} - \frac{\mathbf{p}_{u''}}{\sqrt{d_{u''}}} \right\|^2, \tag{11}$$

where $s_{u'u''}$ denotes the strength of social connection between u' and u'', and $d_{u'}$ (or $d_{u''}$) denotes the outdegree of u' (or u'') for normalization purpose. It is worth noting that the use of normalization is the key difference with the social regularization used by [16, 36], which does not apply any normalization on the smoothness constraint. As pointed out by He *et al.* [9], the use of normalization helps to suppress the impact of popular vertices, which can lead to more effective propagation. We empirically verify this point in Section 4.3.

Fitting: The fitting constraint implies the latent space consistency across two domains — the bridge users' representations should be invariant and act as the anchors across domains. Towards this end, we encourage the two representations of the same bridge users to be close to each other. The objective function for fitting constraint is defined as,

$$\theta(\mathcal{U}) = \frac{1}{2} \sum_{u' \in \mathcal{U}} \left\| \mathbf{p}_{u'} - \mathbf{p}_{u'}^{(0)} \right\|^2, \tag{12}$$

where for each bridge user u', $\mathbf{p}_{u'}$ (or $\mathbf{p}_{u'}^{(0)}$) is her representation of the SNS (or information domain). As such, the fitting constraint essentially acts as the bridges connecting the two latent spaces.

Lastly, we combine the smoothness constraint with the fitting constraint and obtain the objective function of the social domain learning as,

$$\mathcal{L}_S = \theta(\mathcal{U}_2) + \mu\theta(\mathcal{U}), \tag{13}$$

where μ is a positive parameter to control the tradeoff between two constraints.

3.2.1 ***Prediction for Social Users.*** With the representations of social users and items (*i.e.*, $\mathbf{p}_{u'}$ and $\mathbf{q}_i$) at hand, we can feed them into the fully connected layers as Eqn.(9) shows and utilize the prediction layer as Eqn.(10) displays. At last, we can obtain the predicted preference $\widehat{y}_{u'i}$, as follows,

$$\begin{cases} \mathbf{e}_1 = \sigma_1(\mathbf{W}_1(\mathbf{p}_{u'} \odot \mathbf{q}_i) + \mathbf{b}_1) \\ \cdots\cdots \\ \mathbf{e}_L = \sigma_L(\mathbf{W}_L \mathbf{e}_{L-1} + \mathbf{b}_L) \\ \widehat{y}_{u'i} = \mathbf{w}^\top \mathbf{e}_L \end{cases}. \tag{14}$$

3.3 Training

We adopt the alternative optimization strategy on Eqn.(3) since it can emphasize exclusive characteristics within individual domains. In the information domain, we employ stochastic gradient descent SGD) to train the attribute-aware NSCR in the mini-batch mode and update the corresponding model parameters. In particular, we first sample a batch of observed user-item interactions (u, i) and adopt negative sampling [11] to randomly select an unobserved item j for each (u, i). We then generate a triplet (u, i, j). Following that, we take a gradient step to optimize the loss function $\mathcal{L}_I$ in Eqn.(5). As such, we obtain the enhanced representations of users. In the SNS, we feed the enhanced representations of bridge users into our graph Laplacian to update all representations of social users. Towards this end , we can simplify the derivative of $\mathcal{L}_S$ regarding user representation $\mathbf{P}$ and then obtain the close-form solution as,

$$\mathbf{P} = \frac{\mu}{1+\mu} \left(\mathbf{I} - \frac{1}{1+\mu} \mathbf{D}^{-\frac{1}{2}} \mathbf{S} \mathbf{D}^{-\frac{1}{2}} \right)^{-1} \mathbf{P}^{(0)}, \tag{15}$$

where $\mathbf{P}^{(0)}$ is the embedding of social users, which includes the updated representations of bridge users from NSCR part; $\mathbf{S}$ and $\mathbf{D}$ are the similarity matrix and diagonal degree matrix of social users, respectively, whereinto $S_{u'u''} = s_{u'u''}$ and $D_{u'u'} = d_{u'}$. Thereafter, we view the newly updated representations of bridge users as the next initialization for the bridge users in NSCR. We repeat the above procedures to approximate the model parameter set Θ. As for the regularization term in Eqn.(3), we omit it since we utilize *dropout* technique in neural network modeling to avoid overfitting.

Dropout: Dropout is an effective solution to prevent deep neural networks from overfitting. The idea is to randomly drop part of neurons during training. As such, only part of the model parameters, which contribute to the final ranking, will be updated. In our neural CR model, we propose to adopt dropout on the pairwise pooling layer. In particular, we randomly drop ρ of $\mathbf{p}_u$ and $\mathbf{q}_i$, whereinto ρ is the dropout ratio. Analogous to the pooling layer, we also conduct dropout on each hidden layer.

4 EXPERIMENTS

To comprehensively evaluate our proposed method, we conducted experiments to answer the following research questions:

- **RQ1:** Can our NSCR approach outperform the state-of-the-art recommendation methods for the new cross-domain social recommendation task?
- **RQ2:** How do different hyper-parameter settings (*e.g.*, the dropout ratio and tradeoff parameters) affect NSCR?
- **RQ3:** Are deeper hidden layers helpful for learning from user-item interaction data and improving the performance of NSCR?

4.1 Data Description

To the best of our knowledge, there is no available public benchmark dataset that fits the task of cross-domain social recommendation. As such, we constructed the datasets by ourselves. We treated Trip.com as the information domain, Facebook and Twitter as the social domains. In Trip.com, we initially compiled 6,532 active users, who had at least 5 ratings over 2,952 items (*e.g., gardens by the bay* in Singapore and *eiffel tower* in Pairs). We transformed their 93,998 ratings into binary implicit feedback as ground truth, indicating whether the user has rated the item. Moreover, we collected 19 general categories regarding the travel mode (*e.g., adventure travel, business travel,* and *nightlife*) and used them as the attributes of users and items. Subsequently, we parsed the users' profiles to identify their aligned accounts in Facebook and Twitter, inspired by the methods in [17, 24]. We obtained 858 and 502 bridge users for Facebook and Twitter, respectively. Thereafter, we crawled the public friends or followers of each bridge user to reconstruct the social networks, resulting in 177,042 Facebook users and 106,049 Twitter users. However, the original social data are highly sparse, where most non-bridge users have only one friend, making it ineffective to propagate users' preferences. To ensure the quality of the social data, we performed a modest filtering on the data, retraining users with at least two friends. This results in a subset of the social data that contains 7,233 Twitter users with 42,494 social connections and 8,196 Facebook users with 49,156 social connections. The statistics of the datasets are summarized in Table 1.

4.2 Experimental Settings

Evaluation Protocols: Given a social user, each method generates an item ranking list for the user. To assess the ranking list, we adopted two popular IR metrics, *AUC* and *recall*, to measure the quality of preference ranking and top-*N* recommendation.

- **AUC:** Area under the curve (AUC) [12, 21] measures the probability that a recommender system ranks a positive user-item interaction higher than negative ones:

$$AUC = \frac{\sum_{i \in \mathcal{I}_u^+} \sum_{j \in \mathcal{I}_u^-} \delta(\widehat{y}_{uij} > 0)}{|\mathcal{I}_u^+||\mathcal{I}_u^-|}, \tag{16}$$

where $\mathcal{I}_u^+ = \{i|y_{ui} = 1\}$ and $\mathcal{I}_u^- = \{j|y_{uj} = 0\}$ denote the sets of relevant (observed) item i and irrelevant (unobserved) item j for user u, respectively; and δ is the count function returning 1 if $\widehat{y}_{uij} > 0$ and 0 otherwise. Below we report the averaged AUC for all testing users.

Table 1: Statistics of the complied datasets. The social user set includes the bridge users.

Information Domain	User#	Item#	Interaction#
Trip.com	6,532	2,952	93,998
SNSs	**Bridge User#**	**Social User#**	**Social Connection#**
Twitter	502	7,233	42,494
Facebook	858	8,196	49,156

- **R@K:** Recall@K considers the relevant items within the top K positions of the ranking list. A higher recall with lower K indicates a better recommender system, which can be defined as,

$$R@K = \frac{|\mathcal{I}_u^+ \cap \mathcal{R}_u|}{|\mathcal{I}_u^+|}, \tag{17}$$

where $\mathcal{R}_u$ denotes the set of the top-K ranked items for the given user u. Analogous to AUC, we report the average $R@5$ for all testing users.

By learning representations for social users and information-domain items together, our NSCR is capable of recommending items for both bridge and non-bridge users. However, due to the limitation of our static datasets, it is difficult for us to evaluate the recommendation quality for non-bridge users, since they have no interaction on the information-domain items. As such, we rely on the bridge users for evaluating the performance. Following the common practice in evaluating a recommender algorithm [11, 21], we holdout the latest 20% interactions of a bridge user as the test set. To tune hyper-parameters, we further randomly holdout 20% interactions from a bridge user's training data as the validation set. We feed the remaining bridge users, all the non-bridge users in SNSs, and the remaining user-item interactions in the information domains into our framework for training.

Baselines: To justify the effectiveness of our proposal, we study the performance of the following methods:

- **ItemPop:** This method ranks items base on their popularity, as judged by the number of interactions. It is a non-personalized method that benchmarks the performance of a personalized system [21].
- **MF:** This is the standard matrix factorization model that leverages only user–item interactions of the information domain for recommendation (*cf.* Eqn.(2)).
- **SFM:** Factorization machine [19] is a generic factorization model that is designed for recommendation with side information. We construct the input feature vector by using one-hot encoding on the ID and attributes of users and items. To adjust FM for modelling social relations, we further plug a (bridge) user's friends into the input feature vector, dubbed this enhanced model as Social-aware FM (SFM).
- **SR:** This [16] is a state-of-the-art factorization method for social recommendation. It leverages social relations to regularize the latent vectors of friends to be similar. To incorporate attributes into their method, we adjust the similarity of two users based on their attribute sets, which leads to better performance.

Note that for all model-based methods, we optimize them with the same pair-wise ranking function of Eqn.(5) for a fair comparison on the model's expressiveness. To explore the efficacy of attributes, we further explore variants that remove attribute modelling from SFM, SR, and NSCR, named as SFM-a, SR-a, and NSCR-a, respectively.

Table 2: Performance comparison between all the methods, when the embedding size= 64 and signifficance test is based on AUC.

Datasets	Twitter-Trip			Facebook-Trip		
Methods	AUC	R@5	p-value	AUC	R@5	p-value
ItemPop	0.7193	0.0164	3e-5	0.7439	0.0249	8e-6
MF	0.8285	0.0375	3e-4	0.8596	0.0821	1e-4
SFM	0.8832	0.0492	2e-3	0.8908	0.0856	1e-3
SR	0.9013	0.0747	9e-3	0.9267	0.1433	4e-2
NSCR	**0.9222**	**0.0807**	-	**0.9390**	**0.1466**	-

Parameter Settings: We implemented our proposed framework on the basis of Tensorflow[2], which will be made publicly available, as well as our datasets. For all the neural methods, we randomly initialized model parameters with a Gaussian distribution, whereinto the mean and standard deviation is 0 and 0.1, respectively. The mini-batch size and learning rate for all methods was searched in [128, 256, 512, 1024] and [0.0001, 0.0005, 0.001, 0.05, 0.1], respectively. We selected Adagrad as the optimizer. Moreover, we empirically set the size of hidden layer same as the embedding size (the dimension of the latent factor) and the activation function as ReLU. Without special mention, we employed two hidden layers for all the neural methods, including SFM, SR, and NSCR. We randomly generated ten different initializations and feed them into our NSCR. For other competitors, the initialization procedure is analogous to ensure the fair comparison. Thereafter, we performed paired t-test between our model and each of baselines over 10-round results.

4.3 Performance Comparison (RQ1)

We first compare the recommendation performance of all the methods. We then purpose to justify how the social modelling and the attribute modelling affect the recommendation performance.

Overall Comparison: Table 2 displays the performance comparison *w.r.t.* AUC and R@5 among the recommendation methods on Twitter-Trip and Facebook-Trip datasets, where the embedding size is 64 for all the methods. We have the following findings:

- ItemPop achieves the worst performance, indicating the necessity of modelling users' personalized preferences, rather than just recommending popular items to users. As for MF, its unsatisfied performance reflects that the independence assumption is insufficient to capture the complex and non-linear structure of user-item interactions.
- NSCR substantially outperforms the state-of-the-art methods, SFM and SR. We further conduct one-sample t-tests, verifying that all improvements are statistically significant with p-value < 0.05. It justifies the effectiveness of our proposed framework.
- The performance on Twitter-Trip clearly underperforms that of Facebook-Trip. It is reasonable since more bridge users are available in Facebook, which can lead to better embedding learning in SNSs. It again verifies the significance of the bridge users.

Effect of Social Modelling: To analyze the effect of social modelling, we only consider the variants, SFM-a, SR-a, and NSCR-a.

[2]https://www.tensorflow.org.

Figure 4 presents the performance comparison *w.r.t.* the number of latent factors on two datasets. We have the following observations.

- ItemPop and MF perform worst since neither of them considers the social connections from SNSs. It highlights the necessity of social modelling in cross-domain social recommendation.
- Clearly, NSCR-a significantly outperforms SFM-a and SR-a by a large margin. Formally, in terms of AUC, the relative improvement over SFM-a and SR-a, on average, is 3.19% and 1.01% respectively. While SFM-a considers modelling the social connections, it treats these connections as ordinary features, overlooking the exclusive characteristics of social networks. This leads to the poor expressiveness of the social users' embedding. On the contrary, SR-a and NSCR-a emphasizes the social modelling via the effective social regularization.
- Lastly, NSCR-a shows consistent improvements over SR-a, admitting the importance of the normalized graph Laplacian. It again verifies that the normalized graph Laplacian can suppress the popularity of friends and further prevent the social modelling from being dominated by popular social users.

Effect of Attribute Modelling: As Figure 5 demonstrates, we verify the substantial influence of attribute modelling and the effectiveness of our pairwise pooling operation. Due to the poor performance of ItemPop and MF, they are omitted. Jointly analyzing the performance of all the methods and their variants, we find that,

- For all methods, modelling user/item attributes can achieve significant improvements. By leveraging the similarity of users' attributes, SR enriches the pairwise similarity of any two users and strengthens their connections; meanwhile, SFM can model the correlations of user-attribute, item-attribute, and attribute-attribute, and accordingly enhances the user-item interactions. Benefiting from the pairwise pooling operation, NSCR can encode the second-order interactions between user/item and attributes and boost the representation learning. The significance of attribute is consistent with [34].
- Varying the embedding size, we can see that large embedding may cause overfitting and degrade the performance. In particular, the optimal embedding size is 64 and 32 for AUC and R@5, respectively. It indicates that the setting of embedding size can effect the expressiveness of our model.

4.4 Study of NSCR (RQ2)

In this subsection, we empirically study the convergence of NSCR and then purpose to analyse the influences of several factors, such as dropout ratio and tradeoff parameter, on our framework.

Convergence: We separately present the training loss and the performance w.r.t. AUC and R@5 of each iteration in Figures 6(a), 6(b), and 6(c). Jointly observing these Figures, we can see that training loss of NSCR gradually decreases with more iterations, whereas the performance is generally improved. This indicates the rationality of our learning framework. Moreover, the most effective updates occurs in the first 20 iterations, which indicates that effectiveness of our learning framework. As Figure 6(c) shows, the performance regarding R@5 fluctuates markedly over the iteration times, while that regarding AUC is quite stable. It is reasonable since R@5 only considers the top-5 results rather than the relative order as AUC defined.

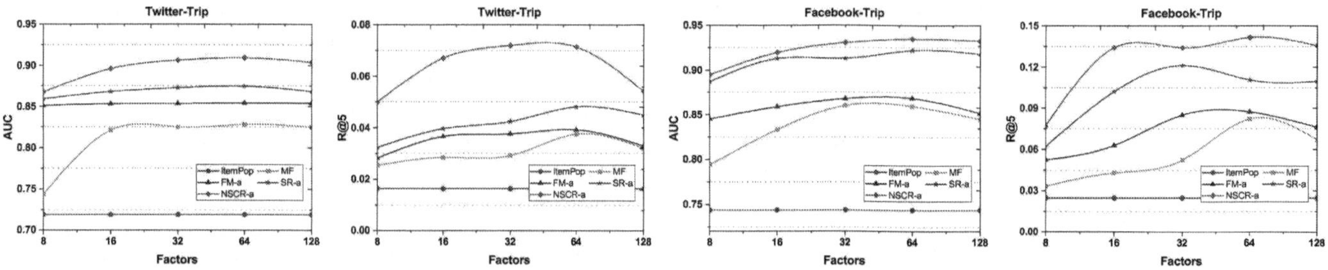

(a) AUC on Twitter-Trip (b) R@5 on Twitter-Trip (c) AUC on Facebook-Trip (d) R@5 on Facebook-Trip

Figure 4: Performance comparison of AUC and R@5 *w.r.t.* the embedding size on Twitter-Trip and Facebook-Trip datasets.

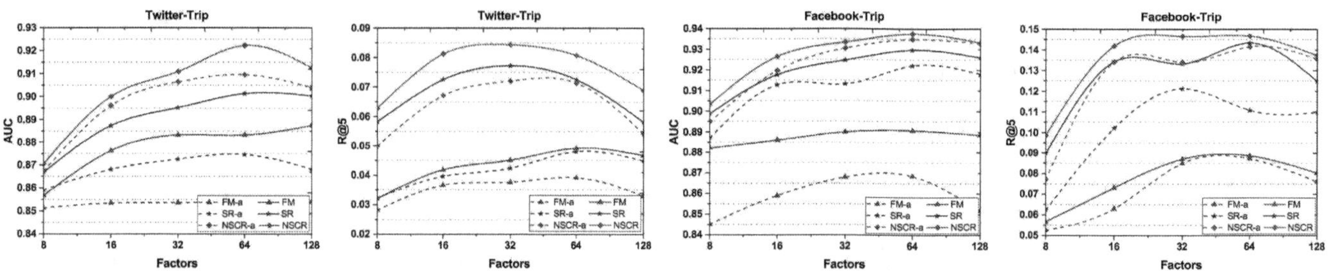

(a) AUC on Twitter-Trip (b) R@5 on Twitter-Trip (c) AUC on Facebook-Trip (d) R@5 on Facebook-Trip

Figure 5: Performance comparison of AUC and R@5 *w.r.t.* the embedding size on Twitter-Trip and Facebook-Trip datasets.

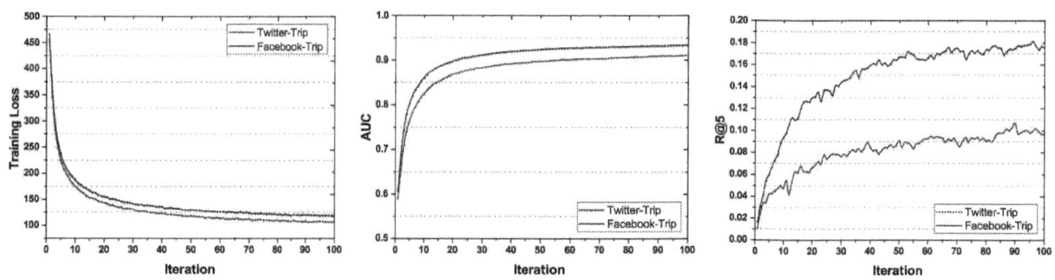

(a) Training Loss (b) AUC (c) R@5

Figure 6: Training loss and recommendation performance regarding AUC and R@5 *w.r.t.* the number of iterations.

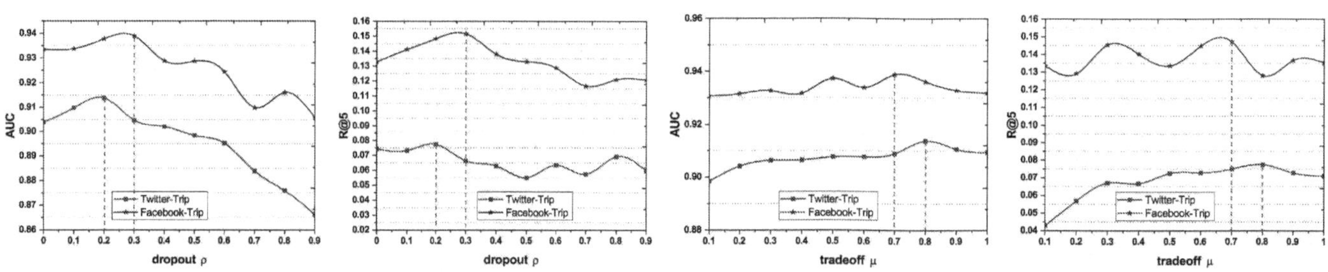

(a) AUC vs. dropout ratio ρ (b) R@5 vs. dropout ratio ρ (c) AUC vs. tradeoff parameter μ (d) R@5 vs. tradeoff parameter μ

Figure 7: Performance comparison of AUC and R@5 *w.r.t.* the dropout ratio ρ and tradeoff parameter μ on Twitter-Trip and Facebook-Trip datasets.

Impact of Dropout: We employ the dropout technique in NSCR to prevent our model from overfitting, instead of regularizing model parameters. Figures 7(a) and 7(b) present the performance *w.r.t.* AUC and R@5 of NSCR-0 by varying the dropout ratio ρ on the pairwise pooling layer, respectively. As we can see, when dropout ratio equals to 0, NSCR-0 suffers severely from overfitting. Moreover, using a dropout ratio of 0.3 and 0.2 leads to the best performance on Twitter-Trip and Facebook-Trip datasets, respectively. However, when the optimal dropout ratio exceeds the optimal settings, the performance of NSCR-0 greatly decreases, which suffers from insufficient information. This highlights the significance of using dropout, which can be seen as ensembling multiple sub-models [25].

Table 3: Recommendation performance of NSCR with different hidden layers.

Metrics	AUC			R@5		
Factors	NSCR-0	NSCR-1	NSCR-2	NSCR-0	NSCR-1	NSCR-2
Twitter-Trip						
8	0.8598	0.8630	**0.8704**	0.0585	0.0604	**0.0628**
16	0.8883	0.8984	**0.9026**	0.0738	0.0672	**0.0812**
32	0.9018	0.9056	**0.9109**	0.0723	0.0742	**0.0843**
64	0.9138	0.9175	**0.9222**	0.0717	0.0697	**0.0725**
128	0.9003	0.9034	**0.9125**	0.0519	0.0653	**0.0688**
Facebook-Trip						
8	0.8978	0.8922	**0.9034**	0.0860	0.0872	**0.0986**
16	0.9165	0.9197	**0.9265**	0.1048	0.1388	**0.1419**
32	0.9303	0.9322	**0.9335**	0.1441	**0.1486**	0.1465
64	0.9337	0.9376	**0.9390**	0.1353	0.1359	**0.1466**
128	0.9270	0.9310	**0.9332**	0.1168	0.1304	**0.1373**

Impact of Tradeoff Parameter: There is one positive parameter μ in the social modelling, which can capture the tradeoff between the fitting regularizer and the normalized graph Laplacian, as Eqn.(15) shows. Figures 7(c) and 7(d) present the performance *w.r.t.* . AUC and R@5, respectively. As we can see, setting μ of 0.8 and 0.7 can lead to the optimal performance on Twitter-Trip and Facebook-Trip datasets, respectively. And the performance of NSCR-0 changes within small ranges nearby the optimal settings. It justifies that our model is relatively insensitive to the parameter around its optimal configuration.

4.5 Impact of Hidden Layer (RQ3)

To capture the complex and non-linear inherent structure of user-item interactions, we employ the a deep neural network for our task. It is curious whether NSCR can benefit from the deep architecture. Towards this end, we further investigate NSCR with different number of hidden layers. As it is computationally expensive to tune the dropout ratio ρ for each hidden layer, we simply apply the same settings for all layers. The empirical results on two datasets are summarized in Table 3 whereinto NSCR-2 indicates the NSCR method with two hidden layers (besides the embedding layer and prediction layer), and similar notations for others. We have the following observations:

- In most cases, stacking more hidden layers is helpful for the recommendation performance. NSCR-2 and NSCR-1 achieve consistent improvement over NSCR-0, which has no hidden layers and directly projects the embedding to the prediction layer. We attributed the improvement to the high nonlinearity achieved by stacking more hidden layers. Our finding is consistent with [8] and again verifies the deep neural networks have strong generalization ability. However, it is worth mentioning that such a deep architecture needs more time to optimize our framework and easily leads to the overfitting due to the limited training data in our datasets.
- Increasing the width of hidden layers (*i.e.*, the embedding size) from 8 to 64 can improve the performance significantly, as that of increasing their depth. However, with the embedding size of 128, NSCR degrades the performance. It again verifies that using a large number of the embedding size has powerful representation ability [8], but may adversely hurt the generalization of the model (*e.g.*, overfitting the data) [8, 11].

5 RELATED WORK

5.1 Social Recommendation

Social recommendation aims to leverage users' social connections to enhance a recommender system [18, 32]. It works by modelling social influence, which refers to the fact that a user's decision can be affected by her friends' opinions and behaviours. Ma *et al.* [16] propose a social regularization term to enforce social constraints on traditional recommender systems. Based on a generative influence model, the work [31] exploits social influence from friends for item recommendation by leveraging information embedded in the user social network. The authors in [35] utilize social links as complementary data source to mine topic domains and employed domain-specific collaborative filtering to formulate users' interests. More recently, [13] represents a star-structured hybrid graph centered at a user domain, which connects with other item domains, and transfers knowledge on social networks.

It is worth noting that the aforementioned studies are all based on social network relations of an information domain. While in this work, we focus on how to distill useful signal from an external social network (*e.g.*, Facebook and Twitter), so as to improve the recommendation service of any information domain.

5.2 Cross-Domain Recommendation

Distinct from the traditional recommendation methods that focus on data within a single domain, cross-domain recommendation concerns data from multiple domains. A common setting is leveraging the user-item interaction of a related auxiliary domain to improve the recommendation of the target domain. However, existing cross-domain recommendation work has an underlying assumption that the target and auxiliary domains are homogeneous. Depending on [5, 6, 13], they can be divided into two directions. One is assuming that different domains share overlapped user or item sets. The work [22] augments ratings of movies and books for the shared users and accordingly conducts CF. Based on the shared users' latent space, the authors in [3] leveraged cluster-level tensor sharing as a social regularization to bridge the domains. One more step, the authors in [12] formulated a generalized triadic user-item-domain relation over the common users and accordingly to capture domain-specific user factors and item factors. More recently, the authors [5] proposed a multi-view deep learning recommendation system by using auxiliary rich features to represent users from different domains. Without aligned user or item, the other direction is on homogeneous data with the same rating scale. Codebook Transfer [14] represents cluster-level rating patterns between two rating matrices in two related domains. [27] introduces a topic model to recommend authors to collaborate from different research fields.

Despite the compelling success achieved by previous work, little attention has been paid to recommendation across heterogeneous domains. In our settings, the source domain is a social network with user-user relations only, while the target domain is an information domain with user-item interactions. Hence, the auxiliary information is the social friendship, rather than the conventional interaction data. As a result, existing approaches can be hardly applied to this new research problem.

6 CONCLUSION

In this work, we systematically investigated cross-domain social recommendation, a practical task that has rarely been studied previously. Towards this end, we proposed a generic neural social collaborative ranking (NSCR) solution, which seamlessly integrates user-item interactions of the information domain and user-user social relations of the social domain. To validate our solution, we constructed two real-world benchmarks of the travel domain, performing extensive experiments to demonstrate the effectiveness and rationality of our NSCR solution. The key finding of the work is that social signals contain useful cues about users' preference, even if the social signals are from social networks in a different domain. We achieved the goal by leveraging bridge users to unify the relevance signals from the two heterogeneous domains.

Due to our restricted resources in collecting cross-domain data, the result is preliminary. Here we discuss several limitations of the current work, and our plans to address them in future. First, in this work, we studied the recommendation performance of a travel-based information domain only, which is mainly for the ease of accessing the users' account on Facebook/Twitter. This results in a relatively small number of bridge users of our cross-domain datasets. As a future work, we will collect a larger-scale set of data from the more popular information domains, such as E-commence sites, to explore the generalization ability of our solution to other information domains. Second, due to the small number of bridge users, we forwent the study of user cold-start problem, as further holding out bridge users to simulate the cold-start scenario will pose challenge to the stability of evaluation. With a larger-scale cross-domain data, we will study the effectiveness of our solution for cold-start users, as well as the influence of the bridge users' percentage. Moreover, we restricted the SNSs by emphasizing only the social connections and omitting the weak user-item interactions in user-generated-contents. We will consider the weak user-item interaction in both domains to improve the recommendation performance.

Acknowledgement We would like to thank the anonymous reviewers for their valuable comments. NExT research is supported by the National Research Foundation, Prime Minister's Office, Singapore under its IRC@SG Funding Initiative.

REFERENCES

[1] Immanuel Bayer, Xiangnan He, Bhargav Kanagal, and Steffen Rendle. 2017. A Generic Coordinate Descent Framework for Learning from Implicit Feedback. In *WWW*. 1341–1350.

[2] Jingyuan Chen, Hanwang Zhang, Xiangnan He, Liqiang Nie and Wei Liu, and Tat-Seng Chua. 2017. Attentive Collaborative Filtering: Multimedia Recommendation with Item- and Component-Level Attention. In *SIGIR*.

[3] Wei Chen, Wynne Hsu, and Mong-Li Lee. 2013. Making recommendations from multiple domains. In *SIGKDD*. 892–900.

[4] Paul Covington, Jay Adams, and Emre Sargin. 2016. Deep Neural Networks for YouTube Recommendations. In *RecSys*. 191–198.

[5] Ali Mamdouh Elkahky, Yang Song, and Xiaodong He. 2015. A Multi-View Deep Learning Approach for Cross Domain User Modeling in Recommendation Systems. In *WWW*. 278–288.

[6] Aleksandr Farseev, Ivan Samborskii, Andrey Filchenkov, and Tat-Seng Chua. 2017. Cross-Domain Recommendation via Clustering on Multi-Layer Graphs. In *SIGIR*.

[7] Fuli Feng, Liqiang Nie, Xiang Wang, Richang Hong, and Tat-Seng Chua. 2017. Computational social indicators: a case study of Chinese university ranking. In *SIGIR*.

[8] Kaiming He, Xiangyu Zhang, Shaoqing Ren, and Jian Sun. 2016. Deep Residual Learning for Image Recognition. In *CVPR*. 770–778.

[9] Xiangnan He, Tao Chen, Min-Yen Kan, and Xiao Chen. 2015. TriRank: Review-aware Explainable Recommendation by Modeling Aspects. In *CIKM*. 1661–1670.

[10] Xiangnan He and Tat-Seng Chua. 2017. Neural Factorization Machines for Sparse Predictive Analytics. (2017).

[11] Xiangnan He, Lizi Liao, Hanwang Zhang, Liqiang Nie, Xia Hu, and Tat-Seng Chua. 2016. Neural Collaborative Filtering. In *WWW*. 173–182.

[12] Liang Hu, Jian Cao, Guandong Xu, Longbing Cao, Zhiping Gu, and Can Zhu. 2013. Personalized recommendation via cross-domain triadic factorization. In *WWW*. 595–606.

[13] Meng Jiang, Peng Cui, Xumin Chen, Fei Wang, Wenwu Zhu, and Shiqiang Yang. 2015. Social Recommendation with Cross-Domain Transferable Knowledge. *TKDE* 27, 11 (2015), 3084–3097.

[14] Bin Li, Qiang Yang, and Xiangyang Xue. 2009. Can Movies and Books Collaborate? Cross-Domain Collaborative Filtering for Sparsity Reduction. In *IJCAI*. 2052–2057.

[15] Lizi Liao, Xiangnan He, Hanwang Zhang, and Tat-Seng Chua. 2017. Attributed Social Network Embedding. *arXiv preprint arXiv:1705.04969* (2017).

[16] Hao Ma, Dengyong Zhou, Chao Liu, Michael R. Lyu, and Irwin King. 2011. Recommender systems with social regularization. In *WSDM*. 287–296.

[17] Liqiang Nie, Xuemeng Song, and Tat-Seng Chua. 2016. *Learning from Multiple Social Networks*. Morgan & Claypool Publishers.

[18] Zhaochun Ren, Shangsong Liang, Piji Li, Shuaiqiang Wang, and Maarten de Rijke. 2017. Social Collaborative Viewpoint Regression with Explainable Recommendations. In *WSDM*. 485–494.

[19] Steffen Rendle. 2010. Factorization Machines. In *ICDM*. 995–1000.

[20] Steffen Rendle. 2012. Factorization Machines with libFM. *TIST* 3, 3 (2012), 57:1–57:22.

[21] Steffen Rendle, Christoph Freudenthaler, Zeno Gantner, and Lars Schmidt-Thieme. 2009. BPR: Bayesian Personalized Ranking from Implicit Feedback. In *UAI*. 452–461.

[22] Shaghayegh Sahebi and Peter Brusilovsky. 2013. Cross-Domain Collaborative Recommendation in a Cold-Start Context: The Impact of User Profile Size on the Quality of Recommendation. In *UMAP*. 289–295.

[23] Richard Socher, Danqi Chen, Christopher D. Manning, and Andrew Y. Ng. 2013. Reasoning With Neural Tensor Networks for Knowledge Base Completion. In *NIPS*. 926–934.

[24] Xuemeng Song, Liqiang Nie, Luming Zhang, Mohammad Akbari, and Tat-Seng Chua. 2015. Multiple Social Network Learning and Its Application in Volunteerism Tendency Prediction. In *SIGIR*. 213–222.

[25] Nitish Srivastava, Geoffrey E. Hinton, Alex Krizhevsky, Ilya Sutskever, and Ruslan Salakhutdinov. 2014. Dropout: a simple way to prevent neural networks from overfitting. *JMLR* 15, 1 (2014), 1929–1958.

[26] Gábor Takács and Domonkos Tikk. 2012. Alternating Least Squares for Personalized Ranking. In *RecSys*. 83–90.

[27] Jie Tang, Sen Wu, Jimeng Sun, and Hang Su. 2012. Cross-domain collaboration recommendation. In *SIGKDD*. 1285–1293.

[28] Meng Wang, Weijie Fu, Shijie Hao, Hengchang Liu, and Xindong Wu. 2017. Learning on Big Graph: Label Inference and Regularization with Anchor Hierarchy. *TKDE* 29, 5 (2017), 1101–1114.

[29] Meng Wang, Weijie Fu, Shijie Hao, Dacheng Tao, and Xindong Wu. 2016. Scalable Semi-Supervised Learning by Efficient Anchor Graph Regularization. *TKDE* 28, 7 (2016), 1864–1877.

[30] Xiang Wang, Liqiang Nie, Xuemeng Song, Dongxiang Zhang, and Tat-Seng Chua. 2017. Unifying Virtual and Physical Worlds: Learning Toward Local and Global Consistency. *TOIS* 36, 1 (2017), 4.

[31] Mao Ye, Xingjie Liu, and Wang-Chien Lee. 2012. Exploring social influence for recommendation: a generative model approach. In *SIGIR*. 671–680.

[32] Chao Zhang, Keyang Zhang, Quan Yuan, Luming Zhang, Tim Hanratty, and Jiawei Han. 2016. GMove: Group-Level Mobility Modeling Using Geo-Tagged Social Media. In *SIGKDD*. 1305–1314.

[33] Hanwang Zhang, Fumin Shen, Wei Liu, Xiangnan He, Huanbo Luan, and Tat-Seng Chua. 2016. Discrete Collaborative Filtering. In *SIGIR*. 325–334.

[34] Hanwang Zhang, Zheng-Jun Zha, Yang Yang, Shuicheng Yan, Yue Gao, and Tat-Seng Chua. 2013. Attribute-augmented semantic hierarchy: towards bridging semantic gap and intention gap in image retrieval. In *MM*. 33–42.

[35] Xi Zhang, Jian Cheng, Ting Yuan, Biao Niu, and Hanqing Lu. 2013. TopRec: domain-specific recommendation through community topic mining in social network. In *WWW*. 1501–1510.

[36] Z. Zhao, H. Lu, D. Cai, X. He, and Y. Zhuang. 2016. User Preference Learning for Online Social Recommendation. *TKDE* 28, 9 (2016), 2522–2534.

Cross-Domain Recommendation via Clustering on Multi-Layer Graphs

Aleksandr Farseev*, Ivan Samborskii** *, Andrey Filchenkov**, Tat-Seng Chua*
*National University of Singapore, **ITMO University
farseev@u.nus.edu,samborskiy.ivan@gmail.com,afilchenkov@niuitmo.ru,chuats@nus.edu.sg

ABSTRACT

Venue category recommendation is an essential application for the tourism and advertisement industries, wherein it may suggest attractive localities within close proximity to users' current location. Considering that many adults use more than three social networks simultaneously, it is reasonable to leverage on this rapidly growing multi-source social media data to boost venue recommendation performance. Another approach to achieve higher recommendation results is to utilize group knowledge, which is able to diversify recommendation output. Taking into account these two aspects, we introduce a novel cross-network collaborative recommendation framework C^3R, which utilizes both individual and group knowledge, while being trained on data from multiple social media sources. Group knowledge is derived based on new cross-source user community detection approach, which utilizes both inter-source relationship and the ability of sources to complement each other. To fully utilize multi-source multi-view data, we process user-generated content by employing state-of-the-art text, image, and location processing techniques. Our experimental results demonstrate the superiority of our multi-source framework over state-of-the-art baselines and different data source combinations. In addition, we suggest a new approach for automatic construction of inter-network relationship graph based on the data, which eliminates the necessity of having pre-defined domain knowledge.

ACM Reference format:
Aleksandr Farseev*, Ivan Samborskii** *, Andrey Filchenkov**, Tat-Seng Chua*. 2017. Cross-Domain Recommendation via Clustering on Multi-Layer Graphs. In *Proceedings of SIGIR '17, Shinjuku, Tokyo, Japan, August 07-11, 2017,* 10 pages.
https://doi.org/10.1145/3077136.3080774

1 INTRODUCTION

There has been an exponential growth of publicly available data on the Web. This growth may be linked to users using multiple online social networks, such as that seen among many adult users, who were found to use three or more online social networks daily [8]. These social networks are inter-connected through the deployment of the so-called cross-linking functionality [10, 33], which offers information about the same users from different perspectives [9].

SIGIR '17, August 07-11, 2017, Shinjuku, Tokyo, Japan

ACM ISBN 978-1-4503-5022-8/17/08...$15.00
https://doi.org/10.1145/3077136.3080774

In an attempt to make sense of the overwhelming amount of multi-source data, various recommender systems were designed to extract relevant information from individual users. However, most of them utilize data from a single-source or of a single modality, while disregarding the potential of cross-source multi-modal recommendation. Another aspect which lacks research, and is worth exploring, is the role of personal and group knowledge integration in cross-source multi-modal recommendation. It has been established in an earlier study that effective recommendation can be achieved based on the combination of group and individual knowledge [7, 53]. While individual knowledge is useful for the incorporation of personal experience [48], group knowledge helps to improve the recommendation diversity [26].

Aiming to bridge these two research gaps, in this study, we focus on the problem of **recommendation across data sources** (also known as cross-domain recommendation) based on multi-view social media data. Specifically, this work is devoted to the emerging topic of venue category recommendation [4, 18, 49], where we recommend a ranked list of Foursquare venue categories to users with accounts in three social networks, namely Twitter, Instagram, and Foursquare [19]. By performing filtering based on venue categories of places around user's current location, our recommender system does not depend on any particular geographical area. This means that it can be used for many real-world scenarios, such as tourist route planning [32], facility arrangement [46], or interactive mobile assistance [20]. For example, based on one's venue category preferences, we could further recommend a particular venue (i.e. Chinese Restaurant, Movie Theatre, etc.) near his/her current location, rather than a similar place located far away, even if the venue located farther away may slightly better fit his/her preferences. Last but not least, the venue category recommendation (but not venue recommendation) also helps to overcome evaluation difficulty, which often arises due to location datasets' sparsity.

Despite its potential, we recognize the challenges of integrating cross-source venue category recommendation with individual and group knowledge. One challenge is **data integration**. Multiple data sources often describe distinct sides of users' activities. For example, Twitter may casually reveal users' daily life updates, while Instagram may uncover their visual preferences. At the same time, social media content comes in many forms (modalities), such as text, images or videos, which also exhibit different facets of users' online experiences. Such multi-source multi-modal data must be integrated into one recommendation framework in a mutually-consistent fashion, which is an open research problem. Another challenge pertains to **group representation learning**. Group representation can be naturally expressed in the form of user communities, which must be extracted from heterogeneous multi-source data. However, the detection of such user communities from multi-source multi-modal data is not an easy task due to the necessity of proper inter-source and intra-source relationship modeling.

Inspired by previous studies and the challenges above, we seek to address three research questions. First, to support the assumptions behind this study, it is important to answer: **(RQ1) Is it possible to improve the recommendation performance by integrating individual and group knowledge?** Second, even though the topic has been discussed with respect to some problems, it is still unclear if: **(RQ2) Inter-source relationship information enable us to find better user communities.** Finally, for further recommendation improvement, it is important to understand: **(RQ3) What the contribution is of each data source (modality) towards venue category recommendation.**

To answer these research questions, we introduce a novel recommender framework **C³R** that utilizes group and individual knowledge to perform **C**ross-Source User **C**ommunity-Based **C**ollaborative venue category **R**ecommendation. Individual knowledge is obtained from user's experience, which is modeled as the distribution among venue categories that a user has visited in past. To incorporate group knowledge, we detected cross-source user communities in a latent space, where the relationship between users is modeled as a multi-layer graph. The community detection approach incorporates inter-source relationships during the process of learning individual source representations and preserves inter-source consistency at the stage of learning latent sources' representation. The inter-source relationship graph is computed automatically from the data and further utilized via novel graph-constrained regularization. The experimental results show that our framework can achieve better recommendation performance in three geographical regions, as compared to state-of-the-art baselines and different data source combinations.

The main contributions of this paper are threefold: First, we present a **cross-source venue recommendation framework** that utilizes both individual and group knowledge; second, we propose a **novel cross-source user community detection approach** that utilizes both inter-source relationship and sources' ability to complement each other via efficient regularization; third, we suggest a **new approach for automatic construction of inter-source relationship graph** based on the data, which eliminates the necessity of having expert knowledge.

2 RELATED WORKS

Probably one of the first studies towards improving recommendation performance based on multi-source data was conducted by Abel et al. [1]. The authors aggregated user profiles from Flickr, Twitter, and Delicious to demonstrate that their cross-network user modeling strategies have a large impact on the recommendation quality in cold-start settings. At the same time, Tiroshi et al. [47] utilized network-related and domain-related features to perform user interest recommendation. Later on, Yan et al. [56] proposed a two-stage solution of cross-source video recommendation problem: first, user preferences were transferred from an auxiliary network by learning cross-network behavior correlations; next, the transferred preferences were integrated with the observed behaviors on target network in an adaptive fashion. Concurrently, Qian et al. [37] introduced a probabilistic framework that solved the problem of cross-domain recommendation by utilizing shared domain priors and modality priors for collaborative learning of a latent representation. Recently, Farseev et al. [18] performed cross-source venue category recommendation by implementing a recommender system based on their proposed Multi-Source re-Ranking approach, where the ranks of individual sources were obtained by performing nearest neighbor collaborative filtering. These works are related to our study regarding the cross-source approaches utilized. Finally, Farseev et al. [17] and Wang et al. [52] proposed cross-domain recommender systems, where inter-domain linking was implemented via the so-called "bridge" users (social media users who have accounts on two or more social networks). However, they do not incorporate both group and individual knowledge into recommendation, which our study is recommending, and is an essential aspect of our study.

At the same time, several works highlighted the potential of multi-source data to find better user communities. For example, Su et al. [45] demonstrated the usefulness of multi-source community discovery for various applications; Rhouma and Romdhane [40] proposed an approach for multi-source user community detection in partially-overlapping social network graphs; while Dong et al. [12] introduced a multi-source clustering approach, where the distance between different data sources was measured on Grassmann Manifolds. The works mentioned above are supportive of utilizing multi-source community detection strategies; however, they are limited because inter-source relationship was not incorporated during the community discovery process. This could potentially lead to sub-optimal results in real world settings.

There were also research efforts in studying the contribution of multiple data sources for different applications. For example, Farseev et al. [15, 16] proposed a multi-source multi-task learning frameworks that aim to combine multi-source multimodal data and data from wearable sensors for Body Mass Index inference; while Song et al. [44] and Akbari et al. [3] developed multi-task learning frameworks for user interests inference and wellness events categorization, respectively. In these four studies, the inference category relationship "weights" were automatically inferred from the data and used to guide the learning model, which can also be applied to solve our problem.

3 CROSS-SOURCE RECOMMENDATION

Strategic decision making is known to be influenced by external factors like personal experiences and public opinions [5]. The public opinion can be expressed by explicit and implicit user communities that are formed based on social relations and their data similarity, respectively. This phenomenon can be leveraged to enhance recommendation performance. To do so, we perform venue category recommendation based on both personal and group knowledge, which naturally models the impact of society on an individual's behavior during the selection of a new place to go. Formally, our proposed C^3R recommendation approach is defined as follows:

$$\text{rec(u)} = \text{sort}\left(\gamma \cdot vec_u + \theta \frac{\sum_{v \in C_u} vec_v}{|C_u|}\right) \quad (1)$$

where vec_u is the distribution of the user u among items (venue categories) **in u's past**, and $\frac{\sum_{v \in C_u} vec_v}{|C_u|}$ is the normalized (by the number of members in user community C_u) distribution of all community members among venue categories **in C_u's past**, γ controls the personal aspect of recommendation, while θ regulates the group experience impact of the user community C_u. Besides the benefits described earlier, incorporation of user communities reduces the search space during the recommendation process and provides better candidates to compare for further collaborative filtering [42]. While personal information (i.e. users' previous activity) is often available, in most of the cases user communities are not explicitly indicated, which gives rise to user community detection challenge.

4 USER COMMUNITY DETECTION

4.1 Similarity Graph Construction

The first step in finding representative user groups is the modeling of users' relationships in the form of a graph so that dense subgraphs of such graph can be treated as user communities. The graph can be constructed based on: (a) social connections between users (i.e. follower/followee relationship) that are often hidden behind the privacy settings; or (b) user-generated content (UGC), where similarity between users is estimated as a distance between data representations of users and each data source (modality) modeled as a layer in a multi-layer graph. In our work, we adopt the graph construction based on UGC to avoid privacy concerns and limitations in mining explicit user social relations. Specifically, for every graph node pair (i, j) from the m-th graph layer, the corresponding distance can be computed by applying *Heat* kernel:

$$d_{m_{i,j}} = e^{-\frac{||x_{m_i} - x_{m_j}||^2}{\sigma}},$$

where $||x_{m_i} - x_{m_j}||$ is the Euclidean norm, and σ is a graph sparsity-related parameter that could be found by grid search. There are certain benefits of such graph construction approach [14]. Firstly, it does not suffer from the lack of information about users' relationship, since the relations between users are simply modeled as distances between users based on UGC similarity. Secondly, it naturally solves the problem of cross-region recommendation, where the condition for related users to be explicitly connected in social networks is relaxed.

4.2 Problem Formulation

To simplify the reading process, we summarize all defined notations in Table 1.

One of the commonly used formulations of the community detection problem is its representation in a form of NCut formulation, which conditions the sum of graph edges' weights in each community to be minimized among all communities [43]. This simply means that all communities are formed by users that are most "similar" to each other. Such a definition is naturally applicable to our task of group representation learning based on users' interests. We thus adopt the NCut formulation in our study. The NCut definition is given below:

$$NCut(C_1, \ldots, C_k) = \sum_{i=1}^{k} \frac{W(C_i, \overline{C}_i)}{vol(C_i)} = \sum_{i=1}^{k} \frac{cut(C_i, \overline{C}_i)}{vol(C_i)},$$

where $vol(C_i)$ is the sum of weights of all edges attached to vertices in C_i.

Table 1: Notations summary

Symb.	Description
vec_u	Distribution of the user u among items (venue categories) in u's past
C_u	Community of the user u
γ	Parameter that controls personal aspect of rec-n
θ	Parameter that controls group aspect of rec-n
N	Number of users
M	Number of data sources (graph layers)
L_i	Laplacian matrix of the i-th layer
U_i	Eigendecomposition matrix of the i-th layer
$\hat{L_i}$	Inter-layer relationship regularized Laplacian of the i-th layer
$\hat{U_i}$	Inter-layer relationship regularized eigendecomposition matrix of the i-th layer
$\hat{L}_{mod}$	Sub-space regularized Laplacian matrix
W_R	Adjacency matrix of inter-layer similarity graph
k	Parameter that controls the number of clusters
α	Parameter that controls sub-space regularization
β_i	Parameter that controls inter-layer regularization for the layer i

However, the NCut problem is proven to be $\mathcal{NP}$-hard [51]. Fortunately, there exists a state-of-the-art approximation that is defined as a standard trace minimization (also known as *spectral clustering*) [50]:

$$\min_{U \in R^{n \times k}} \operatorname{tr}(U^{\top} L_{sym} U), \ s.t. \ U^{\top} U = I. \tag{2}$$

By the Rayleigh-Ritz theorem, the solution of the problem in Equation (2) is given by the first k eigenvectors of the normalized graph Laplacian $L_{sym} = I - D^{-\frac{1}{2}} W D^{-\frac{1}{2}}$, where W is adjacency matrix, and D is degree matrix [30]. The mapping of each user to a cluster can be further obtained by i.e. k-means clustering over the eigenvector space [50].

4.3 Spectral clustering on multi-layer graph

The well-known disadvantages of early fusion and late fusion data aggregation strategies [3] encourage us to perform joint clustering from all graph layers simultaneously. The final data representation (latent representation) must be consistent with all graph layers so that clustering will not be biased towards individual graph layers. One way to keep the latent representation consistent to all layers of the multi-layer graph is to apply regularization during the clustering process, which will keep graph layers "close" to the target representation. A well-adopted approach for measuring "closeness" between target latent space U and the space of each layer U_i is based on Grassman Manifolds [25], where the projected distance between two spaces S_1 and S_2 on Grassman Manifold is equal to [12]:

$$d^2_{Proj}(S_1, S_2) = \frac{1}{2} ||S_1 S_1^{\top} - S_2 S_2^{\top}||_F^2, \tag{3}$$

where $||A||_F$ is the Frobenius norm [22] of the matrix A.

Since mappings $S_1 S_1^{\top}$ and $S_2 S_2^{\top}$ preserve distinctness [12], we consider the projection distance as a distance measure between subspaces. The distance between target subspace S and all the other individual subspaces $\{S_i\}_{i=1}^{M}$ can thus be defined as the sum of squared projection distances between S and all individual subspaces $\{S_i\}_{i=1}^M$ [12]:

$$d^2_{Proj}(S, \{S_i\}_{i=1}^M) = kM - \sum_{i=1}^{M} \mathrm{tr}(SS^\top S_i S_i^\top). \tag{4}$$

By utilizing the Equation (4), the Equation (2) can be extended to introduce the subspace-regularized objective:

$$\min_{U\in\mathbb{R}^{n\times k}} \sum_{i=1}^{M} \mathrm{tr}(U^\top L_i U) + \alpha(kM - \sum_{i=1}^{M} \mathrm{tr}(UU^\top U_i U_i^\top)), \quad s.t.\ U^\top U = I, \tag{5}$$

where α controls sub-space regularization. We can rearrange Equation (4) to present it in a form of standard trace minimization problem [12]:

$$\begin{aligned} &\min_{U\in\mathbb{R}^{n\times k}} \sum_{i=1}^{M} \mathrm{tr}(U^\top L_i U) + \alpha(kM - \sum_{i=1}^{M} \mathrm{tr}(UU^\top U_i U_i^\top)) \\ &= \min_{U\in\mathbb{R}^{n\times k}} \mathrm{tr}(U^\top \sum_{i=1}^{M}(L_i - \alpha U_i U_i^\top)U), \end{aligned} \tag{6}$$

which, by the Rayleigh-Ritz theorem [30], can be solved as the first k eigenvectors of the modified Laplacian $L_{mod} = \sum_{i=1}^{M}(L_i - \alpha U_i U_i^\top)$. The eigen decomposition of the matrix L_{mod} is not in the scope of the paper, but can be efficiently computed by well-known algorithms [28].

4.4 Incorporating inter-layer relationship

Even though the subspace-regularized spectral clustering approach performed well on synthetic dataset [12], real world problems often require a consideration of inter-layer relationship (similarity) during the learning process. Such a requirement is caused by the difference between data modalities and the way they describe the users [18]. Specifically, for particular applications some data sources or modalities may be more informative than others. For example, Foursquare check-ins could be more useful for venue category recommendation than textual posts, while Twitter text data is of crucial importance for demographic profiling [19].

Inspired by previous works [6, 18, 54] and based on our observations, we take a step further in multi-layer clustering by introducing a novel model regularization schema that guides clustering process based on predefined inter-layer relationship graph. Given the multi-layer user relationship graph G, which is constructed as described in previous sections, let's assume that there exists a complete undirected inter-layer similarity graph R with the adjacency matrix W_R, where each value of the matrix $w_{i,j}$ represent the similarity between i-th and j-th layer of G. While W_R can be automatically computed from the data (see next section for details), we first describe our inter-layer regularized spectral clustering approach.

Essentially, our goal is to regularize the conventional spectral clustering in such a way that the representation of each layer $\hat{U}_i$ would be computed with respect to the inter-layer similarities $w_{i,j}$, which are taken from adjacency matrix of the inter-layer relationship graph R. Let's also note that the approach in Equation (6) relies on pre-computed layers' Laplacians $\{L_i\}_{i=1}^M$ and their spectral spaces $\{U_i\}_{i=1}^M$. In our work, we apply the inter-layer regularization on the process of computing the layers' spectral spaces, so that the final multi-layer spectral space is computed as in Equation (6). By using previously defined distance on Grassman manifold, we define the new objective function for the i-th layer as follows:

$$\min_{\hat{U}_i\in\mathbb{R}^{n\times k}} \mathrm{tr}(\hat{U}_i^\top L_i \hat{U}_i) + \beta_i(kM - \sum_{j=1, j\neq i}^{M} w_{i,j}\, \mathrm{tr}(\hat{U}_i \hat{U}_i^\top U_j U_j^\top)), \quad s.t.\ \hat{U}_i^\top \hat{U}_i = I, \tag{7}$$

where $\hat{U}_i^\top$ is the new spectral space of the i-th layer, β_i — parameter that controls inter-layer regularization for the layer i, $\{U_j\}_{j=1}^M$ — spectral spaces of all layers after standard spectral clustering, $w_{i,j}$ — similarity between layer i and layer j. The problem in Equation (7) can be then presented as a standard trace minimization:

$$\begin{aligned} &\min_{\hat{U}_i\in\mathbb{R}^{n\times k}} \mathrm{tr}(\hat{U}_i^\top L_i \hat{U}_i) + \beta_i(kM - \sum_{j=1, j\neq i}^{M} w_{i,j}\, \mathrm{tr}(\hat{U}_i \hat{U}_i^\top U_j U_j^\top)) \\ &= \min_{\hat{U}_i\in\mathbb{R}^{n\times k}} \mathrm{tr}(\hat{U}_i^\top (L_i - \beta_i \sum_{j=1, j\neq i}^{M} w_{i,j} U_j U_j^\top)\hat{U}_i), \end{aligned}$$

thus, by the Rayleigh-Ritz theorem, it can be solved as the first k eigenvectors of the regularized Laplacian $\hat{L}$:

$$\hat{L}_i := L_i - \beta_i \sum_{j=1, j\neq i}^{M} w_{i,j} U_j U_j^\top.$$

We now presented all necessary components to define our multi-layer clustering approach with the following objective function:

$$\begin{aligned} &\min_{U\in\mathbb{R}^{n\times k}} \sum_{i=1}^{M} \mathrm{tr}(U^\top \hat{L}_i U) + \alpha(kM - \sum_{i=1}^{M} \mathrm{tr}(UU^\top \hat{U}_i \hat{U}_i^\top)) \\ &= \min_{U\in\mathbb{R}^{n\times k}} \mathrm{tr}(U^\top \sum_{i=1}^{M}(\hat{L}_i - \alpha \hat{U}_i \hat{U}_i^\top)U), \quad s.t.\ U^\top U = I. \end{aligned} \tag{8}$$

To make the clustering procedure clear, we present the pseudocode as shown in Algorithm 1.

From the pseudocode, it can be seen that optimization of the Equation (8) and further clustering consists of four main steps: 1) Perform conventional spectral clustering on each layer to obtain L_i and U_i; 2) By incorporating inter-layer relationship graph R, perform inter-layer relationship regularized spectral clustering on each layer to obtain $\hat{L}_i$ and $\hat{U}_i$; 3) Execute subspace-regularized spectral clustering on each layer to obtain $\hat{L}_{mod}$ and U; 4) Normalize U to obtain U_{norm} and execute the x-means clustering over it [35].

The value of the subspace regularization parameter α and the inter-layer regularization parameters β_i can be found by grid search. In next section, we outline the construction of inter-layer similarity graph G.

4.5 Computing Inter-Layer Relationship

Intuitively, the inter-layer relationship graph R must represent the similarity between layers in terms of clustering results, summarized for different values of k. We thus define the similarity $sim(w, q)$ between graph layers q and w as a normalized difference between $N \times N$ k-clustering co-occurrence matrices $M_{q,k}$, $M_{w,k}$, in which each value $m_{i,j}$ is equal to 1 if user i is assigned to the same cluster as user j in both layers w and q, and 0 otherwise. The clustering co-occurrence matrices are obtained by performing single-layer spectral clustering on each layer of the multi-layer graph and for

Algorithm 1 C^3R clustering

```
function CLUSTER({W_i}_{i=1}^M, W_R, k, α, {β_i}_{i=1}^M)
    ▷ {W_i}_{i=1}^M are weighted adjacency matrices of layers {G_i}_{i=1}^M,
    W_R is adjacency matrix of inter-layer similarity graph,
    k is target number of clusters,
    α and {β_i}_{i=1}^M are regularization parameters

    for i ← [0; M − 1] do
        Compute L_i and U_i for G_i [50]
            ▷ L_i is the normalized Laplacian matrix of the layer i,
            U_i is subspace representation of the layer i,
            G_i is ith layer graph
        Compute L̂_i ← L_i − β_i Σ_{j=1,j≠i}^M w_{i,j} U_j U_j^T
            ▷ L̂_i is the regularized Laplacian matrix of ith layer
        Compute Û_i ∈ R^{N×k}
            ▷ Û_i is the the matrix of first k eigenvectors of L̂_i [28]
    end for
    Compute L̂_mod ← Σ_{i=1}^M (L̂_i − α Û_i Û_i^T)
        ▷ L̂_mod is the modified Laplacian matrix [12]
    Compute U ∈ R^{N×k}
        ▷ U is the matrix of first k eigenvectors [28] of L̂_mod
    Normalize rows of U to get U_norm
    {C}_{i=1}^k ← FINALCLUSTERING(U_norm)
        ▷ FINALCLUSTERING() is k-means or x-means clustering

    return {C}_{i=1}^k
        ▷ C_1, ..., C_k are cluster assignment
end function
```

different values of k ($k = 2..K$, where $K = \sqrt{N}$ [23]). We then take an average among relation values obtained for different k:

$$sim(w, q) = \left(\sum_{k=2}^{K} \left(1 - \frac{||M_{w,k} - M_{q,k}||}{\sqrt{N(N-1)}} \right) \right) / (K-1).$$

The above formulation is the modified and normalized version of the Partition Difference measurement [29]. Being averaged over different values of k, it is able to serve as a reliable indicator of the similarity between different social networks in terms of clustering results. We explicitly would like to mention that our-proposed inter-layer relationship graph construction approach is purely automated and does not require any expert knowledge. This suggests its further usage for other graph-constraint unsupervised learning approaches.

4.6 Computational time complexity analysis

To analyze the complexity of C^3R clustering, we need to estimate the complexity of each step of Algorithm 1. If N is the number of users, M the number of graph layers (data modalities), and k is the number of first eigenvectors to compute, C^3R time complexity can be estimated as $O(N^2(M^2k + MN + k^2))$. Below, we discuss the complexity in more details.

First, each Laplacian (L_i) and eigenvector matrix (U_i) computational complexity is $O(N^3)$, which sums up to $O(MN^3)$ for computing them for all graph layers. The computation of each $\hat{L_i}$ costs $O(MN^2k)$, which gives the computational complexity of $O(M^2N^2k)$. The total cost of $\hat{U_i}$ computation is $O(MN^3)$. $\hat{L}_{mod}$ can be computed in $O(MN^2k)$ time. The computation of matrix U takes $O(N^3)$ time, while the complexity of x-means clustering in space U_{norm} is $O(N^2k^2)$ [35]. The total C^3R time complexity, thus, is $O(M^2N^2k) + O(MN^3) + O(N^2k^2) = O(N^2(M^2k + MN + k^2))$, where $M, k \ll N$.

5 EVALUATION

5.1 On Community Detection Evaluation

There are two main approaches for evaluating community detection algorithms: direct evaluation and indirect evaluation. Direct evaluation uses a quality measure (e.g. Modularity) to compare community detection results achieved by different algorithms explicitly. However, there is no any widely accepted measure to quantify community detection results in the case of multi-source community discovery. Moreover, many of such quality estimation measures were found to be weakly related to the actual quality of the detected communities [21]. Indirect evaluation, in turn, compares results achieved by approaches from other application domains (e.g. Recommendation, Classification, etc.). Such approaches must be created based on earlier obtained communities. The latter conforms well with our study and allows for evaluating both our proposed cross-source recommendation approach and its backbone — multi-layer community detection approach. In this work, we thus perform the indirect evaluation.

5.2 Dataset

To answer our research questions, we evaluate the C^3R recommendation framework based on largest available multi-source multi-modal cross-region social dataset NUS-MSS [19]. The dataset is provided for three social networks (Twitter, Foursquare, and Instagram), and was collected during the period of *10 July 2014 – 20 Dec 2014* in Singapore, London, and New York [19]. Farseev et al. [19] first collected a set of active users, who have recently posted tweets through the cross-linking functionality of Instagram or Swarm mobile apps. Further, authors utilized Twitter REST API to perform the location-dependent tweets search in three geographical regions. Based on the active user list, Farseev et al. [19] crawled user generated contents for those users, who posted their activities from other social networks on Twitter. For example, each sampled Twitter cross-linking post (e.g. Foursquare check-in) contains a short link to the original check-in page, where the check-in details are available [15].

For every geographical region the following five feature types are provided:

Textual features (3 feature types combined in one vector): 70 LIWC distribution features [36], distribution over 50 LDA topics, and 14 writing style features [19] from Twitter posts, Instagram image captions, and Foursquare "shouts".

Location (Venue Category) Features: distribution over 764 venue categories.

Visual features: distribution over 1000 ImageNet [11] concepts, extracted from Instagram images.

Based on the data collection time frame, Farseev et al. [19] split NUS-MSS dataset into fixed training and test sets. In other words, **check-ins posted by the same users but in different time intervals were used to form training and testing sets.** The *training set* consists of the first 3 months of data, while the *testing set* consists of the last 2 months. Only users who contributed content to all three social networks during both train and test set time frames were included in the evaluation process[1]. This gives rise to 1801 users from Singapore, 813 users from London, and 1602 users from New York. The number of recommendation items (venue categories) in all three geographical regions equals to 764.

5.3 Additionally-Extracted Features

In addition to the features provided by NUS-MSS dataset, we extracted a 48-dimensional temporal feature and 4 mobility features. It is known that online activity of social-media users is tightly knit to temporal and mobility aspects [34], which makes it reasonable to incorporate such data into community detection process. Intuitively, users with similar mobility patterns (i.e. often co-located) and similar temporal patterns (i.e. often perform activities at similar time intervals) may have similar interests and can form an interests-based community. Below, we give a brief description of the mobility and temporal data features that we used to form mobility and temporal layers of user relationship graph.

The mobility features were computed based on users' *areas of interest (AOIs)* [38], which are geographical regions of user's high geo-location density (regardless the geo-location semantic meaning, which could be a geo-located tweet, geo-located Instagram image, or Foursquare check-in). AOIs were obtained by performing density-based clustering[2] [41] over the geo locations of each user and considering the convex hull of each cluster as a new AOI. ε was computed by analyzing the average distance between neighbors in MinPts-distance graph ($MinPts = 3$ was selected empirically) [13]. User's AOIs represent his/her geographical mobility patterns [34, 38] that can be related to user's lifestyle and interests. We extracted the following **Mobility And Temporal** features:

Average number of posts during each of the 8 daytime durations, where each time duration is 3 hours long. The temporal features were computed for each data source with respect to weekday/weekend factor. In total, there were $8 \times 3 \times 2 = 48$ temporal data dimensions computed. The temporal features indicate users' temporal online activity and related to their urban mobility [34].

Number of areas of interest (AOI). This feature reflects the mobility side of user's physical activity. For example, users with the higher number of AOIs may have a physically intense lifestyle. AOIs also represent users' frequent areas of activity (i.e. home, office, university/school) [38] and may indicate how far users are willing to travel on a daily basis.

Median size of user's AOIs[3], which indicates users' mobility inside each AOI. The feature is an indicator of users' traveling habits inside their main activity areas.

Normalized number of AOI outliers. The feature indicates how often users visit places that are not located inside their AOI, which may show how often users deviate from their regular mobility patterns.

Median distance between AOIs. This feature reflects users' mobility at intra-city/inter-city/international level. Specifically, it shows how often and how far users travel between their activity zones and can be useful to infer travel-related user communities.

5.4 Evaluation Measures

To evaluate our framework against competing systems, we chose the following two widely accepted measures:

Normalized Discounted Cumulative Gain (*NDCG*) measure, which is defined as:

$$NDCG@p = \frac{DCG@p}{IDCG@p}, \; DCG@p = \sum_{i=1}^{p} \frac{2^{rel_i}}{\log_2(i+1)}, \; rel_i = \frac{Cat_i}{N_{Cat}},$$

where *IDCG* is the maximum possible (Ideal) *DCG* for a given set of queries, rel_i is the graded relevance of the result at position i, Cat_i is number of times user checked-in at venue of category i, and $N_{Cat} = 764$ is the total number of Foursquare venue categories in the dataset.

Average Precision (*AP*), which is defined as:

$$AP@p = \frac{1}{\sum_{i=1}^{p} r_i} \sum_{i=1}^{p} r_i \left(\frac{\sum_{j=1}^{i} r_j}{i} \right), \; r_i = \begin{cases} 1, & \text{i is in top p visited cat.)} \\ 0, & \text{otherwise.} \end{cases}$$

In this section, we briefly describe competing recommendation approaches, and different C^3R modifications.

5.4.1 Recommender System Baselines.

Popular (POP) — performs recommendation only based on user's past experience (distribution on user's check-ins among 764 Location (Venue Category) features in past). To note, it is the special case of C^3R recommendation (Equation (1)), where $\theta = 0$.

Popular$_{All}$ (POP$_{All}$) — performs recommendation based on aggregated experience of all users, which produces user-independent recommendation output (764 Venue Category features were utilized).

Multi-Source Re-Ranking (MSRR) [18] — linearly combines recommendation results from all data modalities and determines source weights via Stochastic Hill Climbing With Random Restart (SHCR) (See Farseev et al. [19] for details): $w_{tw} = 0.42$, $w_{fsq} = 0.95$, $w_{isnt} = 0.36$, $w_{temp} = 0.65$, $w_{mob} = 0.02$.

Nearest Neighbor Collaborative Filtering (CF) [2] — produces recommendation based on top $k = 20$ (determined by SHCR) most similar users from the recommendation source (Foursquare, in our case) using a similarity measure (in our case, *Heat* distance) over 764 Venue Category features.

Early Fusion (EF) [55] — fuses multi-source data into a single feature vector (of dimension 1952) and performs recommendation via CF.

Implicit Feedback-Enhanced Singular Value Decomposition (SVD++) [27] — makes use of the "implicit feedback" information in factorization model (trained on 764 Venue Category features), where $\lambda = 0.67$, $\gamma = 0.06$, $k = 277$, $iter = 55$ are obtained by SHCR [19].

Factorization Machines (FM) [39] — brings together the advantages of different factorization-based models via regularization. In our study, we trained FM based on 764 Venue Category features, utilized the *MCMC* optimization technique [39] and the regression loss, where $k = 30$, $iter = 140$ are obtained by SHCR [19].

[1] The requirement of conducting evaluation based on users with data from all three social networks is dictated by the necessity to make a fair comparison of clustering performance on different data source combinations. Such comparison is only possible in case when the results were obtained based on fixed training and testing sets that consist of the same users.

[2] Most of NUS-MSS's check-ins belong to three geographical regions (Singapore, New York, London), which makes it possible to compute DBScan clusters for most of the NUS-MSS users

[3] Where AOI size is defined as the median distance between the center of mass and all points inside AOI.

5.4.2 **C³R** *And Its Modifications.*
In four **C³R** modifications below, recommendation was performed according to Equation 1, and community detection was performed over all 1952 features.

C³R — our proposed C^3R recommendation approach (Equation 1), where user communities are detected as minimization of Equation (8) via the Algorithm 1. The estimated parameters are: $k = 10$, $\alpha = 0.922$, $\beta_i = 1$ $(i = 1..M)$, $\gamma = 1$, $\theta = 0.248$, which are inferred by SHCR. The adjacency matrix W_R of the automatically constructed (See Section 4.5) inter-layer similarity graph is given below:

$W_R =$

	txt	**loc**	**vis**	**tmp**	**mob**
txt	1	0.632	0.621	0.643	0.561
loc	0.632	1	0.614	0.631	0.570
vis	0.621	0.614	1	0.621	0.551
tmp	0.643	0.631	0.621	1	0.560
mob	0.561	0.570	0.551	0.560	1

$\mathbf{C^3R_{-\hat{L}}}$ — C^3R recommendation without inter-layer regularization ($\beta_i = 0, i = 1..M$), where $k = 10$, $\alpha = 0.521$, $\gamma = 1$, $\theta = 0.1$ are obtained by SHCR [19].

$\mathbf{C^3R_{-\hat{L}-L_{mod}}}$ — C^3R recommendation without inter-layer regularization ($\beta_i = 0, i = 1..M$) and sub-space regularization ($\alpha = 0$), where $k = 22$, $\gamma = 1$, $\theta = 0.147$ are obtained by SHCR [19].

$\mathbf{C^3R_{-Comm}}$ — C^3R recommendation without user community extraction (all users are considered to be in the same community).

C³R (DBScan) — C^3R recommendation, where user communities are detected by Density-Based clustering (DBScan) [41]. The DBScan's $\varepsilon = 0.9$ and $MinPts = 6$ were obtained by grid search.

C³R (x-means) — C^3R recommendation, where user communities are detected by x-means clustering [35]

C³R (Hierarchical) — C^3R recommendation, where user communities are detected by Hierarchical Clustering. Parameter $k = 10$ and "single linkage" inter-cluster distance measure were obtained by grid search.

5.5 Comparing With Baselines

To answer **RQ1**[4], we evaluate C^3R framework against other recommender systems. The evaluation results are presented in Figure 1.

First, an interesting observation is the poor performance of the EF approach, regarding both *AP* and *NDCG* evaluation metrics, which, once again [18], suggests the necessity of using proper data fusion approaches for multi-source learning. On the other hand, the recommendation approach based on user's past items distribution (POP) produces comparably good recommendation output, especially for the small values of p. It means that Foursquare users tend to re-visit venue categories that they have already visited in past, which highlights the importance of individual knowledge for venue category recommendation and allows *POP* for achieving high recommendation performance. At the same time, the POP_{All} baseline (non-personalized popularity-based recommendation) outperforms FM and EF approaches concerning *NDCG* metric, which suggests the usefulness of group knowledge for recommendation purposes. Finally, it can be seen that the combination of individual and group knowledge in C^3R significantly outperforms other baselines in terms of both *AP* and *NDCG* evaluation metrics. This confidently confirms the necessity of individual and group knowledge integration and **positively answers RQ1**.

Let us also highlight the weak performance of the factorization-based models. For example, even after proper negative sampling [24], FM is not able to perform relevant recommendation in the head of the recommendation list, which explains its poor performance in terms of *NDCG* measure. At the same time, SVD++ fails to outperform others in terms of *Precision*, which could be explained by the limited applicability of the "implicit feedback" concept to the task of venue category recommendation. Specifically, the fact that some users did not visit a venue of a particular category does not necessarily mean that they do not appreciate such venue type. Alternatively, such behavior could be a result of the geographical [34] or social [31] constraints. Another interesting observation is the advance of popularity-based baseline (POP) over other recommendation approaches in New York region (regarding *AP*). The possible explanation is that Foursquare users often re-visit venues of the same category, which means that their corresponding training and test sets significantly overlap in many cases (regarding item distributions). The last is not typical for recommendation systems and may lead to the sub-optimal performance.

5.6 Comparing C³R Modifications

To answer **RQ2**[5], we compare different C^3R modifications, which include different variants of our proposed community detection approach as well as other state-of-the-art clustering approaches. The evaluation results are presented in Figure 2.

First, we note that the non-regularized version of the framework ($C^3R_{-\hat{L}-L_{mod}}$) performs the worst against its relatives and other clustering algorithms. This is due to the inability of such non-regularized clustering to build a consistent latent representation, which does not consider inter-network relationship and leads to poor recommendation performance. At the same time, the inter-layer regularized C^3R framework beat all the baselines in all three cities, which could not be achieved by its non-regularized versions ($C^3R_{-\hat{L}-L_{mod}}, C^3R_{-\hat{L}}, C^3R_{-Comm}$). The above observation suggests the importance of subspace regularization in combination with inter-source regularization for balanced user-community detection and, as a result, better recommendation performance. It also allows us to give a **positive response to RQ2**.

Let us also outline the good performance of other clustering approaches, where the recommendation based on x-means clustering (C^3R (x-means)) performs slightly better than other clustering baselines. The above is consistent with the previous study [17] and can be explained by algorithm's ability to automatically infer the parameter k (number of clusters), which allows for finding more distinctive (regarding Bayesian Information Criterion) user communities and, eventually, provide more relevant recommendation.

5.7 Comparing Data Source Combinations

To gain insight into the role of different data sources (modalities) for venue category recommendation and answer **RQ3**[6], we evaluate our framework trained on all data modalities against different

[4]Is it possible to improve the recommendation performance by integrating individual and group knowledge?

[5]Does inter-source relationship information enable us to find better user communities?

[6]What the contribution is of each data source (modality) towards venue category recommendation?

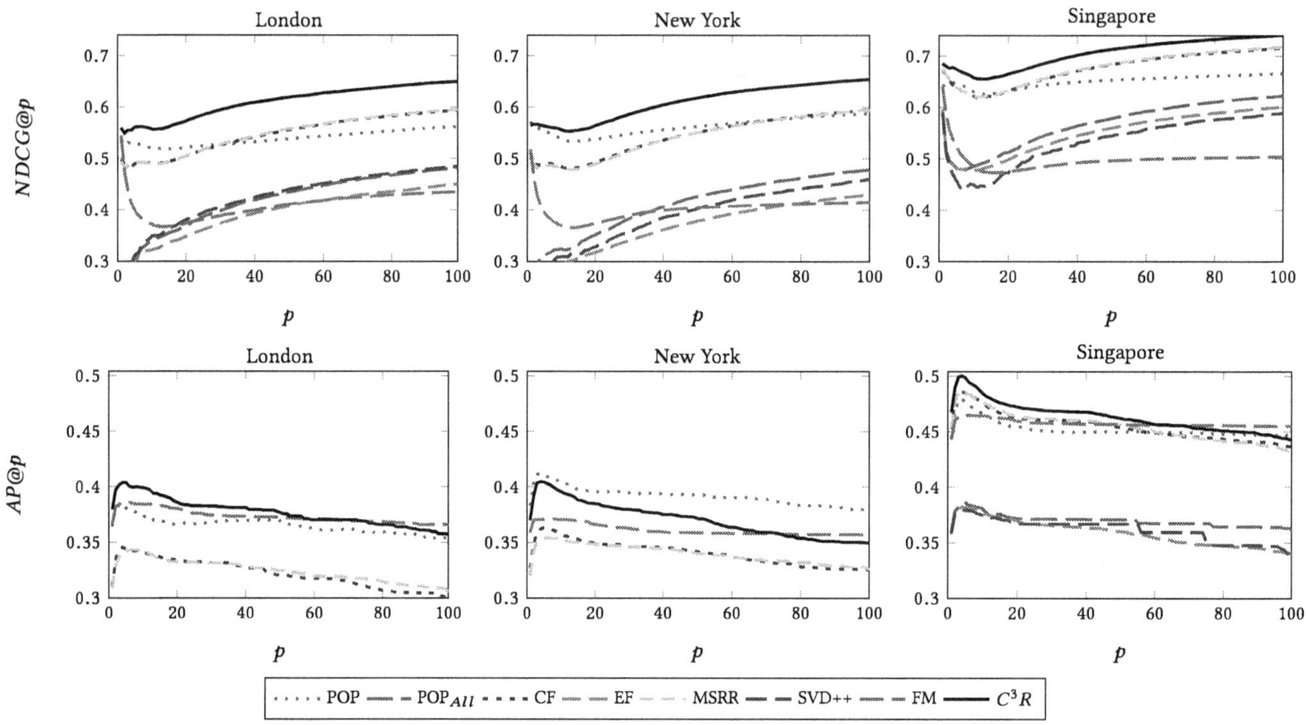

Figure 1: Evaluation of C^3R framework against other recommendation approaches ($NDCG@p$, $AP@p$)

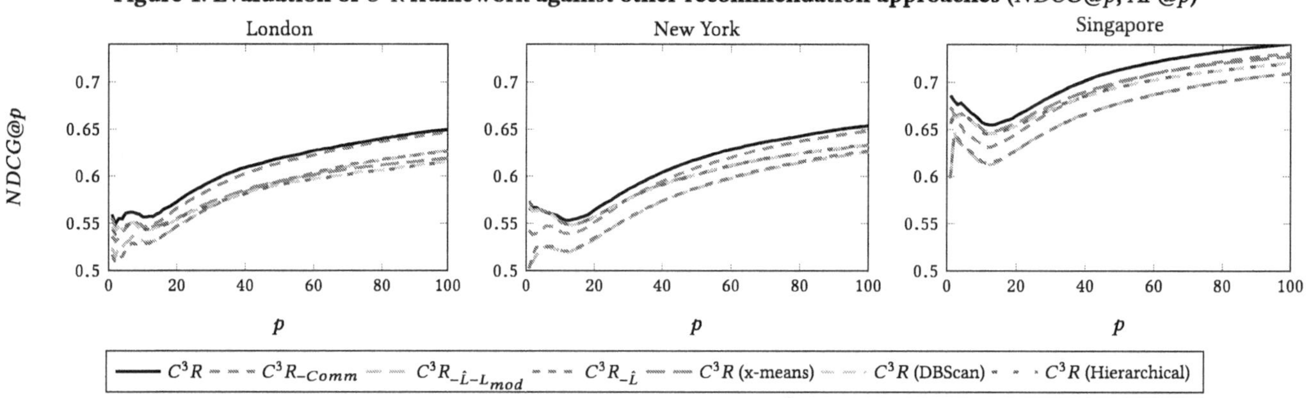

Figure 2: Recommendation performance of different modifications of C^3R framework (different clustering algorithms)

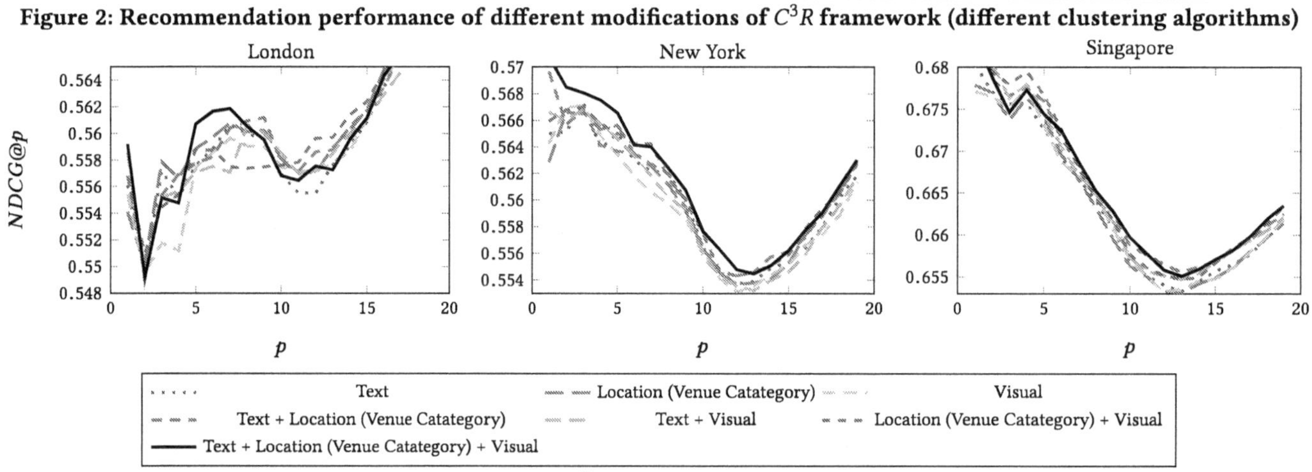

Figure 3: Recommendation performance of C^3R framework based on different data source combinations

data modality combinations. Due to space constraints, in Figure 3 we do not present all feature combinations (31 different combinations), but only show the combinations that include Temporal and Mobility features. For example, the combination "Text" includes Textual, Temporal, and Mobility features, while the combination "Text + Location (Venue Category)" includes Text, Location (Venue Category), Temporal, and Mobility features.

It is not surprising that the recommendation purely based on venue category distribution performs the best among all single-modal baselines in all three cities [18]. The reason is that the venue category data from Foursquare contains explicit knowledge about the distribution of recommendation items in the training set, and thus can forecast the distribution of items in the test set accurately. Bi-source combination results also provide for interesting observations. For example, the Location (Venue Category) + Text combination achieves the best recommendation performance in London and New York regions, but not in Singapore (where text from Twitter gives way to Instagram images). The possible reason is the differences in daily social media usage patterns in different geographical regions: London and New York users mainly post interest-related messages on Twitter, while Singapore users (where Twitter is not widely used) upload pictures of their interests on Instagram (i.e. pictures of food [31]). The above is also supported by the previous study [19], where image data plays a crucial role for the task of multi-source demographic profiling in Singapore. Lastly, we also notice that the combination of all data sources performs the best for all three geographical regions, where the maximum recommendation performance is achieved in Singapore. This could be possibly because of the fact that Singapore has the largest amount of available multi-source data, in comparison with New York and London [19]. Summarizing the above, we **answer the RQ3 by highlighting the importance of venue category, temporal and location-based data** as a major contributors towards recommendation performance. At the same time, depending on geographical region and users' posting behavior, **visual data and textual data may impact differently**, while the **combination of all data sources allows for achieving the best recommendation performance** in most of the cases.

5.8 Qualitative Evaluation

The key idea of our recommendation approach is the incorporation of group knowledge into recommendation via detecting relevant user communities from multiple social multimedia data sources. The evaluation against the baselines indirectly shows the ability of C^3R framework to detect important user communities. To support our answer to **RQ2** and demonstrate the community detection performance explicitly, in Table 2, we have listed the profiles of the 3 largest user communities detected in Singapore. User profiles are constructed as a "bag-of-words" over textual, visual, and location data modalities. From the table, it can be seen that most popular data representations ("words") in all data modalities are consistent with each other and represent distinct user communities. For example, the user community "Com1" is represented by words: "device", "launcher", "android"; visual concepts: "mouse", "digital clock", "hard disk"; and venue categories: "electronics store", "startup", "technology building". We thus named this community as "Gadgets". The distinctness of detected user communities allows C^3R to perform

Table 2: User communities profiles

Community	Bag of Words for different modalities		
	Text	Visual	Location
(Com1) "Gadgets" 832 users	device, launcher, android	mouse, digital clock, hard disc	electronics store, tech. building
(Com2) "Arts" 538 users	painting, landscape, reflection	obelisk, paint-brush, pencil box	arts & crafts store, arts & museum
(Com3) "Food" 446 users	dining, coffee, cooking	pineapple, microwave, frying pan	italian restaurant, pizzeria, restaurant

collaborative filtering based on those social media users, who are semantically "close" to the user of the recommendation system, which helps to boost the recommendation performance. The inter-modal consistency of the community profiles shows that C^3R can perform balanced clustering on a multi-layer graph, which is achieved via inter-layer regularization. The overall results suggest the applicability of the proposed techniques for a task of multi-source user community detection and encourage further research along these directions.

6 LIMITATIONS

Although C^3R outperforms the baselines, there are several limitations that we would like to highlight. First, our proposed multi-source clustering approach requires simultaneous availability of data from all three social networks. This does not allow for its usage in a cold-start settings. Such problem could be addressed by introducing multi-source data completion prior to clustering process, or by performing late model fusion [18]. Another limitation is the time complexity of the framework, which is introduced by the graph Laplacians computation. The issue could be potentially resolved via reformulating the spectral clustering problem in a smaller space [10]. Particularly, by replacing $N \times N$ graph Laplacians with $P \times P$ matrices ($P \ll N$), a solution of mathematically-equivalent problem in significantly reduced space could be obtained. The final clustering could be then recovered from the obtained solution, while P can be chosen to be much smaller than N so that the running time could grow almost linearly to N [10]. We plan to address the above limitations in our future work.

7 CONCLUSION

In this paper, we presented a study on cross-source collaborative recommendation. The proposed recommendation framework C^3R utilizes both individual and group knowledge to solve a task of venue category recommendation. Individual knowledge is modeled as the distribution among venue categories that user has visited in past, while group knowledge is modeled as the distribution of Foursquare venue categories among user community members. The user communities are detected based on novel regularized spectral clustering approach that is able to perform an efficient partitioning of multi-layer user relations graph. By performing comprehensive evaluation against the state-of-the-art baselines and different data source combinations, we demonstrated that our proposed user-community-empowered venue category recommendation framework can achieve superior recommendation performance. Additionally, we contributed a new fully-automated method for inter-network relationship graph construction, which eliminates the necessity of involving a pre-defined expert knowledge.

8 ACKNOWLEDGMENTS

NExT++ research center is supported by the National Research Foundation, Prime Minister's Office, Singapore under its IRC@SG Funding Initiative.

REFERENCES

[1] F. Abel, S. Araújo, Q. Gao, and G.-J. Houben. Analyzing cross-system user modeling on the social web. In *International Conference on Web Engineering*. Springer, 2011.
[2] G. Adomavicius and A. Tuzhilin. Toward the next generation of recommender systems: A survey of the state-of-the-art and possible extensions. *IEEE transactions on knowledge and data engineering*, 2005.
[3] M. Akbari, X. Hu, N. Liqiang, and T. Chua. From tweets to wellness: Wellness event detection from twitter streams. In *Proceedings of the Thirtieth AAAI Conference on Artificial Intelligence*, 2016.
[4] M.-D. Albakour, R. Deveaud, C. Macdonald, I. Ounis, et al. Diversifying contextual suggestions from location-based social networks. In *Proceedings of the 5th Information Interaction in Context Symposium*, pages 125–134. ACM, 2014.
[5] A. Ambrus, B. Greiner, P. Pathak, et al. Group versus individual decision-making: Is there a shift. *W. Paper 91*, 2009.
[6] K. Buraya, A. Farseev, A. Filchenkov, and T. Chua. Towards user personality profiling from multiple social networks. In *Proceedings of the Thirty-First AAAI Conference on Artificial Intelligence*, 2017.
[7] R. Burke. Integrating knowledge-based and collaborative-filtering recommender systems. In *Proceedings of the Workshop on AI and Electronic Commerce*, 1999.
[8] P. R. Center. Social networking fact sheet. http://www.pewinternet.org/fact-sheet/social-media.
[9] J. Chen, H. Zhang, X. He, L. Nie, W. Liu, and T. Chua. Attentive collaborative filtering: Multimedia recommendation with item- and component-level attention. In *Proceedings of the 40th ACM SIGIR Conference*. ACM, 2017.
[10] Y. Chen, C. Zhuang, Q. Cao, and P. Hui. Understanding cross-site linking in online social networks. In *Proceedings of the 8th Workshop on Soc. Net. Mining and Analysis*, 2014.
[11] J. Deng, W. Dong, R. Socher, L.-J. Li, K. Li, and L. Fei-Fei. Imagenet: A large-scale hierarchical image database. In *Computer Vision and Pattern Recognition, 2009. CVPR 2009. IEEE Conference on*. IEEE, 2009.
[12] X. Dong, P. Frossard, P. Vandergheynst, and N. Nefedov. Clustering on multi-layer graphs via subspace analysis on grassmann manifolds. *IEEE Transactions on Signal Processing*, 2014.
[13] D. Eppstein, M. S. Paterson, and F. F. Yao. On nearest-neighbor graphs. *Disc. & Comp. Geometry*, 1997.
[14] A. Farseev, M. Akbari, I. Samborskii, and T. Chua. 360° user profiling: past, future, and applications. *ACM SIGWEB Newsletter*, (Summer), 2016.
[15] A. Farseev and T. Chua. Tweet can be fit: Integrating data from wearable sensors and multiple social networks for wellness profile learning. *ACM Transactions on Information Systems (TOIS)*, 2017.
[16] A. Farseev and T. Chua. Tweetfit: Fusing multiple social media and sensor data for wellness profile learning. In *Proceedings of the Thirty-First AAAI Conference on Artificial Intelligence. AAAI*, 2017.
[17] A. Farseev, N. Gukov, I. Gossoudarev, and U. Zarichnyak. Cross-platform online venue and user community recommendation based upon social networks data mining. *Computer Instruments in Education*, 6:28–38, 2014.
[18] A. Farseev, D. Kotkov, A. Semenov, J. Veijalainen, and T. Chua. Cross-social network collaborative recommendation. *ACM International Conference on Web Science*, 2015.
[19] A. Farseev, L. Nie, M. Akbari, and T. Chua. Harvesting multiple sources for user profile learning: a big data study. In *Proceedings of the 5th ACM on International Conference on Multimedia Retrieval*, 2015.
[20] A. Farseev, I. Samborskii, and T. Chua. bbridge: A big data platform for social multimedia analytics. In *Proceedings of the 2016 ACM on Multimedia Conference*, pages 759–761. ACM, 2016.
[21] S. Fortunato. *Community detection in graphs*. Physics Reports, 2010.
[22] G. H. Golub and C. F. Van Loan. *Matrix computations*. 2012.
[23] J. A. Hartigan and M. A. Wong. Algorithm as 136: A k-means clustering algorithm. *Journal of the Royal Statistical Society. Series C (Applied Statistics)*, 1979.
[24] X. He, H. Zhang, M.-Y. Kan, and T. Chua. Fast matrix factorization for online recommendation with implicit feedback. In *Proceedings of the 39th ACM SIGIR Conference*, 2016.
[25] S. Helgason. The radon transform on euclidean spaces, compact two-point homogeneous spaces and grassmann manifolds. *Acta Mathematica*, 1965.
[26] R. Hu and P. Pu. Helping users perceive recommendation diversity. In *Proceedings of the Workshop on novelty and diversity in recommender systems.*, 2011.
[27] Y. Koren. Factorization meets the neighborhood: a multifaceted collaborative filtering model. In *Proceedings of the 14th ACM SIGKDD international conference on Knowledge discovery and data mining*. ACM, 2008.
[28] R. B. Lehoucq and D. C. Sorensen. Deflation techniques for an implicitly restarted arnoldi iteration. *SIAM Journal on Matrix Analysis and Applications*, 1996.
[29] T. Li, M. Ogihara, and S. Ma. On combining multiple clusterings. In *Proceedings of the 13th ACM international conference on Information and knowledge management*, 2004.
[30] H. Lutkepohl. Handbook of matrices. *Computational Statistics and Data Analysis*, 1997.
[31] Y. Mejova, H. Haddadi, A. Noulas, and I. Weber. # foodporn: Obesity patterns in culinary interactions. In *Proceedings of the 5th International Conference on Digital Health*, 2015.
[32] A. S. Niaraki and K. Kim. Ontology based personalized route planning system using a multi-criteria decision making approach. *Expert Systems with Applications*, 2009.
[33] L. Nie, L. Zhang, M. Wang, R. Hong, A. Farseev, and T.-S. Chua. Learning user attributes via mobile social multimedia analytics. *ACM Transactions on Intelligent Systems and Technology (TIST)*, 8(3):36, 2017.
[34] A. Noulas, S. Scellato, N. Lathia, and C. Mascolo. Mining user mobility features for next place prediction in location-based services. In *Proceedings of the Data mining (ICDM), 2012 IEEE 12th international conference on*, 2012.
[35] D. Pelleg, A. W. Moore, et al. X-means: Extending k-means with efficient estimation of the number of clusters. In *ICML*, volume 1, 2000.
[36] J. W. Pennebaker, M. E. Francis, and R. J. Booth. Linguistic inquiry and word count: Liwc 2001. *Mahway: Lawrence Erlbaum Associates*, 2001.
[37] S. Qian, T. Zhang, R. Hong, and C. Xu. Cross-domain collaborative learning in social multimedia. In *Proceedings of the 23rd Annual ACM Conference on Multimedia*, 2015.
[38] Y. Qu and J. Zhang. Trade area analysis using user generated mobile location data. In *Proceedings of the 22nd international conference on World Wide Web*, 2013.
[39] S. Rendle. Factorization machines with libFM. *ACM Trans. Intell. Syst. Technol.*, 3(3).
[40] D. Rhouma and L. B. Romdhane. An efficient algorithm for community mining with overlap in social networks. *Expert Systems with Applications*, 41(9), 2014.
[41] J. Sander, M. Ester, H.-P. Kriegel, and X. Xu. Density-based clustering in spatial databases: The algorithm gdbscan and its applications. *Data mining and knowledge discovery*, 1998.
[42] B. Sarwar, G. Karypis, J. Konstan, and J. Riedl. Item-based collaborative filtering recommendation algorithms. In *Proceedings of the 10th international conference on World Wide Web*, 2001.
[43] J. Shi and J. Malik. Normalized cuts and image segmentation. *Transactions on Patt. Anal. and M. Intelligence*, 2000.
[44] X. Song, L. Nie, L. Zhang, M. Liu, and T. Chua. Interest inference via structure-constrained multi-source multi-task learning. In *Proceedings of the International Joint Conference on Artificial Intelligence*, 2015.
[45] W.-C. Su. Integrating and mining virtual communities across multiple online social networks: Concepts, approaches and challenges. In *4th International Conference on digital Inf. and comm-n Tech. and it's App.* IEEE, 2014.
[46] J. C. Teixeira and A. P. Antunes. A hierarchical location model for public facility planning. *European Journal of Operational Research*, 2008.
[47] A. Tiroshi, S. Berkovsky, M. A. Kaafar, T. Chen, and T. Kuflik. Cross social networks interests predictions based ongraph features. In *Proceedings of the 7th ACM conference on Recommender systems*. ACM, 2013.
[48] S. Trewin. Knowledge-based recommender systems. *Encyclopedia of Library and Information Science: Volume 69-Supplement 32*, 2000.
[49] M. H. Veiga and C. Eickhoff. Privacy leakage through innocent content sharing in online social networks. *arXiv preprint arXiv:1607.02714*, 2016.
[50] U. Von Luxburg. A tutorial on spectral clustering. *Statistics and computing*, 2007.
[51] D. Wagner and F. Wagner. *Between min cut and graph bisection*. Springer, 1993.
[52] X. Wang, X. He, L. Nie, and T. Chua. Item silk road: Recommending items from information domains to social users. In *Proceedings of the 40th ACM SIGIR Conference*. ACM, 2017.
[53] X. Wang, L. Nie, X. Song, D. Zhang, and T. Chua. Unifying virtual and physical worlds: Learning toward local and global consistency. *ACM Transactions on Information Systems (TOIS)*, 36(1):4, 2017.
[54] X. Wang, Y.-L. Zhao, L. Nie, Y. Gao, W. Nie, Z.-J. Zha, and T. Chua. Semantic-based location recommendation with multimodal venue semantics. *Transactions on MM*, 2015.
[55] P. Winoto and T. Tang. If you like the devil wears prada the book, will you also enjoy the devil wears prada the movie? a study of cross-domain recommendations. *New Generation Computing*, 2008.
[56] M. Yan, J. Sang, and C. Xu. Unified youtube video recommendation via cross-network collaboration. In *Proceedings of the 5th ACM on International Conference on Multimedia Retrieval*, 2015.

Optimizing Trade-offs Among Stakeholders in Real-Time Bidding by Incorporating Multimedia Metrics

Xiang Chen
National University of Singapore
chxiang@comp.nus.edu.sg

Bowei Chen
University of Lincoln
bchen@lincoln.ac.uk

Mohan Kankanhalli
National University of Singapore
mohan@comp.nus.edu.sg

ABSTRACT

Displaying banner advertisements (in short, ads) on webpages has usually been discussed as an Internet economics topic where a publisher uses auction models to sell an online user's page view to advertisers and the one with the highest bid can have her ad displayed to the user. This is also called *real-time bidding* (RTB) and the ad displaying process ensures that the publisher's benefit is maximized or there is an equilibrium in ad auctions. However, the benefits of the other two stakeholders – the advertiser and the user – have been rarely discussed. In this paper, we propose a two-stage computational framework that selects a banner ad based on the optimized trade-offs among all stakeholders. The first stage is still auction based and the second stage re-ranks ads by considering the benefits of all stakeholders. Our metric variables are: the publisher's revenue, the advertiser's utility, the ad memorability, the ad click-through rate (CTR), the contextual relevance, and the visual saliency. To the best of our knowledge, this is the first work that optimizes trade-offs among all stakeholders in RTB by incorporating multimedia metrics. An algorithm is also proposed to determine the optimal weights of the metric variables. We use both ad auction datasets and multimedia datasets to validate the proposed framework. Our experimental results show that the publisher can significantly improve the other stakeholders' benefits by slightly reducing her revenue in the short-term. In the long run, advertisers and users will be more engaged, the increased demand of advertising and the increased supply of page views can then boost the publisher's revenue.

KEYWORDS

Display advertising; real-time bidding; ad recommendation; trade-offs optimization

ACM Reference format:
Xiang Chen, Bowei Chen, and Mohan Kankanhalli. 2017. Optimizing Trade-offs Among Stakeholders in Real-Time Bidding by Incorporating Multimedia Metrics. In *Proceedings of SIGIR'17, August 7–11, 2017, Shinjuku, Tokyo, Japan*, , 10 pages.
DOI: http://dx.doi.org/10.1145/3077136.3080802

SIGIR'17, August 7–11, 2017, Shinjuku, Tokyo, Japan

DOI: http://dx.doi.org/10.1145/3077136.3080802

1 INTRODUCTION

Over the last few years, a significant development in display advertising is the emergence of RTB. It is a non-guaranteed delivery system in which page views (also called *impressions*) are bought and sold via programmatic instantaneous auctions [15]. The success of RTB can be largely attributed to its user targeting and wide access. In RTB, advertisers bid for an impression from their targeted user and this impression can be from any webpage from any ad network or platform. If an advertiser wins the auction, her ad will be selected and be displayed to the user in almost real time.

RTB has two major limitations. The first limitation is that it can not provide guaranteed delivery to advertisers. Therefore, those who want to secure and access future impressions in advance will not be satisfied [29]. The solution is to develop a new system that enables time-dependent allocation and pricing of future impressions. Notable examples include the recently discussed programmatic guarantee and ad options [8–11, 41]. The second limitation of RTB is that those displayed ads may not fit their hosting webpages well due to user targeting. It can be: the ad content is irrelevant to the webpage content; the color of the ad image is too light or dark to sufficiently contrast with the webpage color scheme. Ill-fitting ads will affect the effectiveness of ad branding for the advertiser, or even worse annoy users, and potentially reduce the publisher's webpage visits and revenue. It should be noted that this limitation only exists in display advertising, since sponsored search ads are displayed in terms of textual links where visual effects are not very important and also these ads are keyword-based which are well matched with the user's search query. In display advertising, this limitation is worth investigating. Firstly, it has received surprisingly little attention in the recent studies. Secondly, it is an interesting topic that lies in the area combining the research of marketing, multimedia, recommendation, and Internet economics.

In this paper, we discuss a solution to the second limitation of RTB by proposing a computational framework that optimizes trade-offs among stakeholders. As shown in Fig. 1, the framework has two stages. The first stage is based on the existing ad auction model used in RTB; and the second stage re-ranks ads based on the optimal trade-offs. In the re-ranking, there are six metric variables: the publisher's revenue, the advertiser's utility, the ad memorability, the ad CTR, the contextual relevance and the visual saliency. Revenue is always the key concern for the publisher. From an advertiser's perspective, her utility is the short-term benefit and the ad memorability is the long-term benefit. The rest three metric variables represent the user's benefits. Under the proposed framework, we discuss an algorithm that determines the optimal weights of the metric variables. In the paper, we validate the proposed framework on several datasets, including ad auction datasets and multimedia datasets. The ground truth and possible weights combinations for

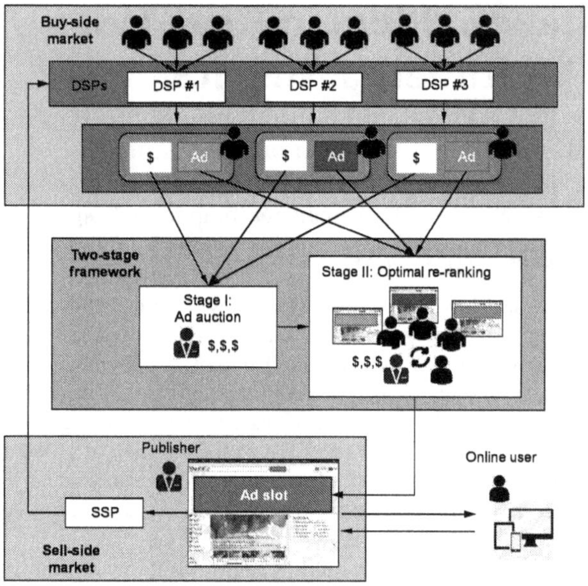

Figure 1: Schematic view of the two-stage framework.

re-ranking are discussed. Our experimental results show that a slight decrease in the publisher's revenue can increase the performance of other variables significantly in the short term, which will also improve the engagements of both advertisers and users in the long term, and further increase the publisher's revenue.

This paper has two major contributions. Firstly, the user's benefits have been taken into account. This is similar to the work of Bachrach et al. [3]. Compared to their work, we increase the dimension of benefits by discussing trade-offs among stakeholders' multiple benefits. The framework is also tailored to RTB rather than sponsored search. Our proposed model can be regarded as a generalized framework that non-guaranteedly deliveries banner ads in RTB. Secondly, multimedia metrics have been introduced to measure some stakeholders' benefits, such as the ad memorability, the contextual relevance, and the visual saliency. These metrics naturally fit display banner ads but have not yet been discussed along with auction models in previous studies. To the best of our knowledge, this is the first work that combines multimedia metrics and auction theory together.

The rest of the paper is organized as follows. Section 2 reviews the related literature. Section 3 discusses the proposed two-stage framework. Section 4 presents our experimental results, and Section 5 concludes the paper.

2 RELATED WORK

In online advertising, the generalized second-price (GSP) auction [14, 40] and the Vickrey-Clark-Groves (VCG) auction [32] have been widely used on different platforms, including display and search domains. Revenue maximization is always the key issue. Lahaie and Pennock [19] proposed to use a squashing parameter to increase revenue of GSP auctions in sponsored search, and then Lahaie and McAfee [18] showed that it can improve social welfare as well. Ostrovsky and Schwarz [30] investigated the effects of optimal reserve prices for GSP auctions on Yahoo's platform. Thompson and Leyton-Brown [39] studied a variety of ways of increasing revenue of GSP auctions, including reserve prices and squashing parameter. Furthermore, Yuan et al. [42] implemented a large scale experiment and empirically compared algorithms of setting reserve price for maximizing revenue in RTB.

Trade-offs among multiple objectives or stakeholders have been discussed in several works. Likhodedov and Sandholm [23] proposed a framework that linearly combines revenue and social welfare in a single-item auction. Radlinski et al. [34] investigated the optimization of relevance and revenue in sponsored search. Similarily, Liao et al. [22] combined revenue and relevance for video advertising. Lucier et al. [24] discussed the revenue of GSP auction at equilibrium, and demonstrated that revenue can be maximized at a non-envy-free equilibrium that also generates a socially inefficient allocation. Roberts et al. [36] discussed a new ranking algorithm for sponsored search auction that uses reserve prices to order the ads and discussed conditions under which revenue can be increased. Bachrach et al. [3] proposed a framework that linearly combines objectives relevant to the search engine (revenue), the advertiser (welfare), and the user (clicks).

Most related advertising research focuses on the economic benefits, little attention has been paid to the advertiser's branding effectiveness and user's experience. Therefore, we introduce several multimedia metrics in this paper. Literature in marketing and consumer psychology has already shown that the contextual relevance between the content of hosting webpage and the ads makes a large difference in their clickability [7], and it also has a leading effect on user's online experience [25]. There exists rich research on measuring the contextual relevance using textual information. Neto et al. [35] investigated ten strategies for a vector space model and evaluated their effectiveness individually. Although the vector space model is widely used, a more advanced matching strategy is required due to the vocabulary impedance problem among ads and webpages. Broder et al. [5] proposed an approach for contextual ad matching based on a combination of semantic and syntactic features. Li et al. [21] further measured the contextual relevance by introducing category relevance, keyword relevance, and style relevance. Category relevance measures whether the ad and webpage belong to the same category; keyword relevance measures the relevance between the keywords extracted from ads and webpage; and style relevance measures the style consistency between the ads and webpage. Zhang et al. [44] proposed an advertising keywords recommendation system for short-text webpages with the help of Wikipedia. Other than textual information, images and videos are more popular on the Internet. Chen et al. [13] allocated ads for images through image recognition techniques. To achieve better contextual relevance, Mei et al. [26, 27] and Guo et al. [16] proposed a multimodal approach which considered both textual and visual relevance for video and image advertising.

Although display banner ads appear on nearly every webpage, their effectiveness remains debatable. Through a series of eye-tracking experiments, recent research found that users tend to avoid ads in web search and surfing [4] and they intentionally avoid looking at such ads even when they are designed to be attention-grabbing [37]. This is also known as *ad overlook*. Moreover, Owen et al. [31] explored the relationship between ads location and the degree of blindness – the phenomenon of website users actively

Table 1: Notations.

Notation	Description
$Z, \tilde{Z}$	Set of auctions
N_z	Set of advertisers in auction z, $z \in Z$
K	Set of metric variables for Stage II re-ranking, $\|K\| = 6$
$b_{i,z}$	Bid price of advertiser i in auction z, $i \in N_z$, $z \in Z$
$b_{(i),z}$	ith highest bid in auction z, $i \in N_z$, $z \in Z$
$y_{i,j,z}$	Probability that advertiser i is allocated to slot j in auction z
$p_{i,z}(b_z)$	Payment of advertiser i in auction z, $b_z = (b_{1,z}, \cdots, b_{n_z,z})$
ω_k	Weight of metric variable k in the re-ranking, $k \in K$
$x_{k,*,z}$	Value of metric variable k for the selected advertiser in auction z by our proposed model
$x_{k,\neg,z}$	Value of metric variable k for the selected advertiser in auction z by the SP auction (the ground truth)
$\xi_{k,Z}$	Average change of metric variable k of auctions in set Z
θ_k	Threshold for the change of metric variable k
$rs_{i,z}$	Rank score of advertiser i in auction z
$rs_{*,z}$	Rank score of the selected advertiser in auction z by our proposed model
$rs_{\neg,z}$	Rank score of the selected advertiser in auction z by the SP auction (the ground truth)

ignore web banner ads – and found that users tend to ignore ads located on the bottom and right area. Intuitively, any ad that fails to capture an user's attention will be ineffective in delivering information. It has been recognized that there are five basic stages before a user accepts a message: attention, comprehension, yielding, retention and action [1]. Motivated by the above observation, in addition to the contextual relevance, we further introduce two other factors to increase user engagement towards banner ads: the visual saliency and the ad image memorability. The former increases the probability that an user will notice the displayed ad while the latter improves an user's brand perception after she sees the ad image.

3 THE TWO-STAGE FRAMEWORK

The proposed framework consists of two stages. The first stage is based on the second-price (SP) auction model. The second stage re-ranks ads based on the weighted linear combination of benefits of multiple stakeholders, which ensures the selected ad will optimize the trade-offs among them. For the reader's convenience, the key notations are summarized in Table 1.

3.1 Stage I: Ad Auction

In RTB, the SP auction model has been widely used. Consider auction $z \in Z$, a single impression is bidded by n_z advertisers, their cost-per-impression[1] bids are denoted by a bid vector $b_z = (b_{1,z}, \cdots, b_{n_z,z})$, and their true values are denoted by a value vector $v_z = (v_{1,z}, \cdots, v_{n_z,z})$. In the simplest scenario, the advertiser with the highest bid will be selected and her ad will be displayed to the user. When the ad is displayed, the advertiser then pays the publisher for this page view. In order to re-rank ads in the second stage, we need to know what would be the possible payments from other advertisers. To achieve this, $n_z - 1$ pseudo ad slots are created so that the payments from other advertisers can be estimated.

We denote the auction outcome by $\{y_{i,j,z}, p_{i,z}\}_{i \in N_z, j \in N_z, z \in Z}$, where $y_{i,j,z}$ is the probability that advertiser i is allocated to slot j in auction z, and $p_{i,z}$ is her payment. Note that slots are ranked so that slot $j \geq 2$ is the created pseudo slot. The auction outcome satisfies the following conditions:

$$0 \leq y_{i,j,z} \leq 1, \quad (1)$$

$$\sum_{i \in N_z} y_{i,j,z} \leq 1, \quad (2)$$

$$\sum_{j \in N_z} y_{i,j,z} \leq 1. \quad (3)$$

Let $b_{(i),z}$ be the ith highest bid in b_z, then

$$y_{i,j,z}(b_z) = \mathbb{I}_{\{b_{i,z} = b_{(j),z}\}}, \quad (4)$$

where $\mathbb{I}_{\{\cdot\}}$ is the indicator function. Then advertiser i's payment is

$$p_{i,z}(b_z) = \sum_{j \in N_z} b_{(j+1),z} y_{i,j,z}(b_z), \quad (5)$$

where $b_{(n_z+1),z}$ is equal to the reserve price, whose value can be set to be any value between 0 and $b_{(n_z),z}$.

3.2 Stage II: Optimal Re-Ranking

All advertisers are re-ranked in the second stage. The rank score of advertiser $i, i \in N_z$, is defined as follows:

$$rs_{i,z} = \sum_{k \in K} \omega_k x_{k,i,z}, \quad (6)$$

where $x_{k,i,z}$ is the input value of metric variable k, ω_k is its weight, and $k \in K = \{1, \cdots, 6\}$. Below we discuss what are these variables, how to obtain their input values and their weights in the re-ranking.

3.2.1 Specifications of Metric Variables. Table 2 specifies our metric variables in the re-ranking, including the publisher's revenue, the advertiser' utility, the ad memorability, the ad CTR, the contextual relevance, and the ad saliency. The input values of these metric variables in the second stage are denoted by $x_{k,i,z}, \forall k \in K$, respectively. They are the normalized values lying between 0 and 1 by using the min-max method for a set of auctions.

Revenue is always the key issue for the publisher. In rank score $rs_{i,z}$, it can be measured by advertiser i's (normalized) payment, whose value can be obtained from ad auction in Stage I.

For advertiser i, her benefit can be measured at short-term and long-term levels. The short-term benefit is her utility, which is defined as the difference between her value and payment. It shows the advertiser's cost saving. In the long run, the ad's memorability is an important metric, particularly, for branding purpose [28]. It shows how likely the user will remember the advertiser's ad a few weeks or months later. Here we employ the MemNet model [17] to predict visual memorability of ad image. It is a convolutional neural network (CNN) trained in an annotated image memorability dataset, where the input is an ad image and the output is a single real value which indicates the memorability of this image. The higher the value is, the more memorable is the image.

The user's benefit can be measured by her page view experience, including the ad CTR, the contextual relevance and the ad saliency [20]. The ad CTR is defined as the number of clicks on the advertiser's ad divided by the number of displays, whose value is

[1] In display advertising industry, the cost-per-impression is usually quoted in terms of cost-per-mille (CPM) which represents the price of 1000 impressions.

Table 2: Specifications of metric variables for Stage II.

Variable	Computation			Input for Stage II
	Method	Input	Output	
Publisher's revenue	Stage I	Bid	Payment	$x_{1,i,z}$ = normalized $p_{i,z}$
Advertiser's utility	Stage I	Bid, payment	Utility	$x_{2,i,z}$ = normalized $(v_{i,z} - p_{i,z})$
Ad memorability	MemNet [17]	Ad image	Memorability score	$x_{3,i,z}$ = normalized score
Ad CTR	Given by data	CTR	CTR	$x_{4,i,z}$ = normalized CTR
Contextual relevance	TakeLab [38]	Title, keywords, description	Semantic similarity score	$x_{5,i,z}$ = normalized score
Ad saliency	MBS [43]	Web page snapshot, ad image	Saliency map and ratio	$x_{6,i,z}$ = normalized ratio

usually given by data or can be estimated from historical advertising records. In essence, the ad CTR is an ad quality metric – a high CTR means that the advertiser's ad is attractive and also more relevant to the user's needs. The contextual relevance measures if the ad content is more or less relevant to its hosting webpage content. If an ad is more relevant, it will be less intrusiveness [27]. In the paper, we use the TakeLab system [38] to measure the semantic similarity of textual contents between the ad and the webpage. TakeLab uses a support vector regression model with multiple features measuring the word-overlap similarity and syntax similarity. The input is two textual sentences and the output is the semantic similarity score. The score ranges from 0 to 5, where 0 indicates irrelevant and 5 indicates totally relevant. We construct the textual information of the webpage and the ad by using the webpage title, keywords and description, etc. An advantage of TakeLab is that it has an outstanding performance in measuring the similarity between short text snippets, while most other algorithms focus on large documents. The ad saliency metric measures whether the ad image can be easily spotted within its hosting webpage. The more salient ads tend to draw more user's attention [12]. In the paper, we use the minimum barrier salient (MBS) object detection method [43] to calculate the saliency of the ad image. The input is image screenshots of ad and webpage, and the output is the corresponding saliency map. For each pair of webpage and ad candidate, we embed the ad into the webpage and use the MBS method to compute the saliency map and the saliency score is the mean value of each pixel within the ad area.

3.2.2 Determination of the Optimal Weights. The weights of variables in the rank score determine the optimal trade-offs. As described earlier, the publisher needs to sacrifice a certain amount of revenue in the short term in order to increase the benefits of other stakeholders. Let θ_1 be the maximum pre-determined loss rate of revenue and let $\theta_k, \forall k \in K\backslash\{1\}$, be the minimum increase rate of other variables. Given the maximum loss and the minimum increase targets, we can obtain the optimal weights from the training set $\widetilde{Z}$.

Our algorithm can be expressed as follows:

$$\max_{\omega_1,\cdots,\omega_6} \sum_{z\in\widetilde{Z}} rs_{*,z}, \tag{7}$$

$$\text{subject to } 0 \le \omega_k \le 1, \forall k \in K, \tag{8}$$

$$\sum_{k\in K} \omega_k = 1, \tag{9}$$

$$|\xi_{1,\widetilde{Z}}| \le |\theta_1|, \theta_1 \le 0, \tag{10}$$

$$\xi_{k,\widetilde{Z}} \ge \theta_k, \theta_k \ge 0, \forall k \in K\backslash\{1\}, \tag{11}$$

where $rs_{*,z}$ is the rank score of the selected advertiser in auction z by our proposed model, $\xi_{k,\widetilde{Z}}$ is the mean of changes of variable k between our proposed model and the ground truth, defined by

$$\xi_{k,\widetilde{Z}} = \frac{\sum_{z\in\widetilde{Z}}(x_{k,*,z} - x_{k,\neg,z})}{\sum_{z\in\widetilde{Z}} x_{k,\neg,z}}, \tag{12}$$

where $x_{k,*,z}$ is the input value of metric variable k for the selected advertiser in auction z by our proposed model, $x_{k,\neg,z}$ is the input value of metric variable k for the selected advertiser in auction z in the ground truth.

The optimal weights maximize the sum of rank scores of the select advertisers from all auctions in the training set. Eqs. (8)-(9) ensure each variable has an impact in the re-ranking but its impact has an upper bound. Eqs. (10)-(11) further specify the lower bounds of trade-offs where the maximum decrease of the publisher's revenue and the minimum increases for other variables.

3.3 Discussion

Display advertising is an interplay among different stakeholders. A vigorous and healthy advertising eco-system should consider the benefits of all stakeholders. Compared with the existing advertising systems that select ads mainly from the publisher's interest, our proposed framework select ads based on the optimized trade-offs among stakeholders. The incorporated multimedia metrics are computed by the state-of-the-art multimedia techniques, including the MemNet model for the ad image memorability [17], the TakeLab method for the semantic similarity [37], and the MBS method for the visual saliency [43]. Moreover, our framework can be extended with more metrics, such as ad interestingness and image aesthetic.

It should be also noted that the proposed two-stage framework does not ensure advertisers to be truth-telling in Stage I. If an advertiser is truth-telling, her utility can be obtained by computing the difference between her bid and payment. If she is not truth-telling, her value can be learnt from historical ad auctions in Stage I. Value estimation models were discussed by Athey and Nekipelov [2], and Pin and Key [33], respectively. Similarly, we can assume each advertiser is optimal – who maximizes her expected utility in the bidding – and then estimate her value from the training data, and the data should be obtained from the two-stage framework rather than the existing RTB campaigns. On the other hand, we think the proposed framework will not significantly affect an advertiser's truthfulness. Firstly, the three multimedia metric variables and the ad CTR are exogenous. They do not directly affect an advertiser's bidding behaviour. Secondly, advertisers' payments are computed by creating pseudo slots. If an advertiser is not the winning advertiser in the ground truth but she is selected after re-ranking, her

Table 3: Multimedia datasets.

Dataset	AOL	YouTube
Ad network	AOL ONE	Google AdSense
From	06 Sept 2016	06 Sept 2016
To	09 Sept 2016	09 Sept 2016
Location	Singapore	Singapore
# of unique webpages	5,243	7,173
# of unique ads	96	539

Table 4: Ad auction datasets.

Dataset	SSP	Microsoft
Ad type	Display	Search
Ad auction	SP (RTB)	GSP
Market	UK	US
From	08 Jan 2013	26 Dec 2011
To	14 Feb 2013	03 Mar 2012
# of ad slots	31	4,376
# of user tags	NA	NA
# of publishers	NA	1
# of advertisers	374	NA
# of auctions	6,646,643	35,550
# of bids	33,043,127	NA
Bid quote	GBP/CPM	GBP/CPC
Bids of each auction	√	NA
Winning bid	√	√
Winning payment	√	√
Estimated CTR	NA	√

Table 5: Summary of CTRs in the Microsoft dataset.

Position	Minimum of CTR	Maximum of CTR	Mean of CTR	Std. of CTR
1	0.00‰	333.30‰	13.97‰	28.49‰
2	0.00‰	200.00‰	7.97‰	15.30‰
3	0.00‰	750.00‰	5.66‰	12.47‰
4	0.00‰	90.90‰	4.53‰	9.68‰
5	0.00‰	76.90‰	1.53‰	3.58‰
6	0.00‰	333.30‰	1.11‰	3.62‰
7	0.00‰	1000.00‰	0.68‰	5.73‰
8	0.00‰	108.10‰	0.51‰	1.65‰

actual payment in the two-stage framework is equal to the payment from the SP auction without other advertisers who have higher bids than her. Since advertisers' bids are not disclosed, compared to the existing RTB, the winning advertiser has no further information to support her nontruth-telling biddings.

4 EXPERIMENTS

This section describes our datasets, experimental settings, variable analysis, sensitivity analysis, and overall results.

4.1 Datasets

Four distinct datasets are used in our experiments, including two multimedia datasets and two ad auction datasets. The two multimedia datasets contain the data collected from AOL and YouTube over the period from 06 September to 09 September in 2016. AOL is an article sharing website while YouTube is a video sharing website.

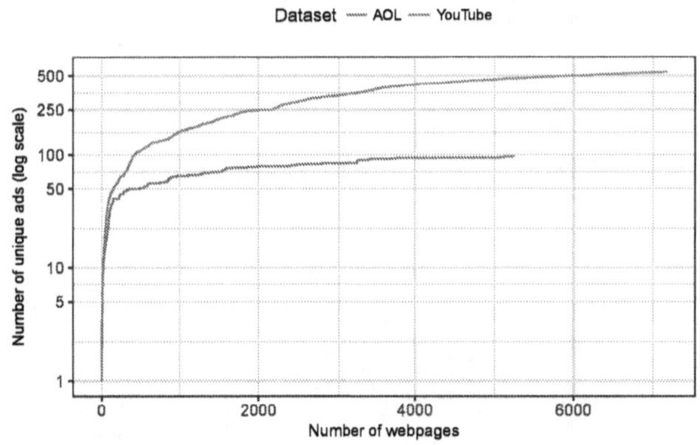

Figure 2: Unique ads in the multimedia datasets.

The two platforms use different ad networks: AOL uses AOL Advertising; YouTube uses Google AdSense. Both datasets were collected in Singapore. As we focus on the single slot ad displaying, each webpage in our datasets contains only one ad slot. We start collecting the data from a particular seed URL that contains multiple categories of content.[2] In this way, the diversity of webpages and banner ads can be ensured. In collecting the data, the web browser is set in the privacy mode, which disables browsing history, web cache and data storage in cookies so that the collected banner ads are not affected by the previous page views. In each dataset, we extract the ads from their webpages to create a set of banner ads and a set of webpages with blank ad slots. For each webpage, the collected data includes title, keywords, description, whole webpage snapshot, ad image. We also crawl title, keywords and description from the ad landing page (i.e., the delivered webpage if an ad is clicked by the visiting user). Note that we do not consider animation ads in our banner ads. When collecting text information about the webpage for YouTube, we also crawl video tags. All the collected text data can be viewed as a summary about the webpage, which can be used to measure the contextual relevance with ad candidates in experiments. Table 3 describes our multimedia datasets. We collect 5,243 unique webpages from AOL and 7,173 unique webpages from YouTube, and the number of their corresponding unique banner ads are 96 and 539, respectively. Fig. 2 shows the growth trends of unique ads on both platforms. Although there are a large number of impressions in the ad network, only a few ads are displayed. We find that some ads re-appear from time to time. The repetitive display strategy reinforces users' memory for branding but it also is a source of intrusiveness into users' online experience [6].

The two ad auction datasets contain campaign information for display advertising and sponsored search. Table 4 provides a brief summary of both datasets. For display advertising, the dataset reports 33,043,127 bids in 6,646,643 auctions over 31 ad slots from a medium-size supply-side platform (SSP) in the UK over the period from 08 January 2013 to 14 February 2013. This SSP dataset has also been used in several recent online advertising studies [8, 11, 42] and is used as the major dataset in our experiments. In the other ad

[2] AOL: `http://www.aol.com`
YouTube: `https://www.youtube.com/channels`

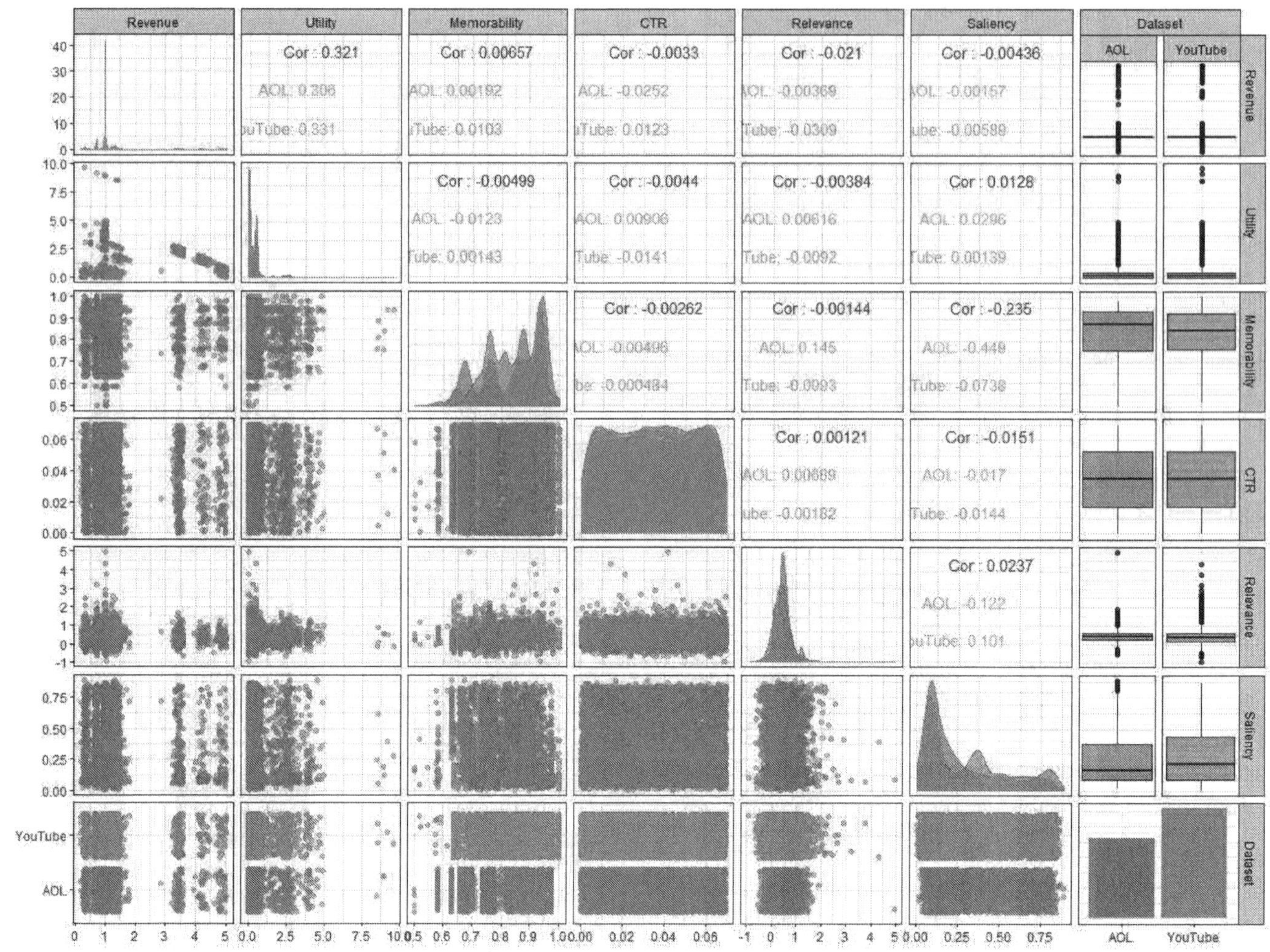

Figure 3: Relationship among variables in the ground truth data (before normalization).

auction dataset, the estimated campaign results of 547 keywords were crawled from Microsoft adCentre (now Bing Ads) over the period from 26 Dec 2011 to 03 Mar 2012. In adCentre, the targeted keywords, budget, and other settings like matching types were submitted to the system. It then returned a list of estimated statistics, including the estimated cost-per-click (CPC), clicks, and impressions based on 8 positions, which are ranked from top to bottom in the mainline paid listing and sidebar paid listing of search engine result pages. The Microsoft dataset provides information of CTRs, which is important in our proposed model but is not included in the SSP dataset. Table 5 summarizes CTRs across keywords in the Microsoft dataset. Since we focus on the single slot ad displaying, we use the CTR estimated from the first ad position from the mainline paid listing to simulate the CTR in our experiments.

4.2 Experimental Settings

As described in Section 4.1, each of our datasets only provides partial information: the SSP dataset provides advertisers' bids for each auction which can also be used for computing the revenue and the utility; the Microsoft dataset provides CTR distributions on different ad positions; the AOL and YouTube datasets contain screenshots of ads and webpages and their textual descriptions, which can be used to calculate the multimedia metrics such as ad image memorability, the contextual relevance, and the visual saliency. To simulate a real world display advertising environment, we randomly sample and match records and metrics to connect our auction datasets with the multimedia datasets so that each ad will have both bidding campaign records and multimedia metrics. Given a webpage from the multimedia datasets, we use the following five steps to reproduce its corresponding auction:

Step 1: Sampling an auction in RTB
We randomly sample an auction from the SSP dataset. The auction contains a set of advertisers and their bids.

Step 2: Creating the ground truth data
Since the given webpage has an ad displayed when it is web crawled. This original ad is considered as the ground truth.

Step 3: Sampling candidate ads
Let n denote the number of advertisers in the sampled auction in Step 1. We then randomly sample $n-1$ ads from the same

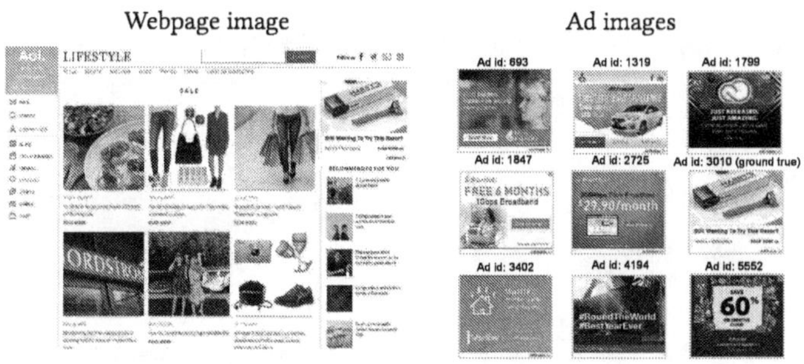

Variables for re-ranking (after normalization)

Ad id	x_1	x_2	x_3	x_4	x_5	x_6
693	0.1999	0.0000	0.7164	0.9387	0.1699	0.7286
1319	0.0400	0.0000	0.8277	0.4077	0.2187	0.1639
1799	0.0160	0.0264	0.5567	0.3353	0.3698	0.8360
1847	0.0000	0.0176	0.8971	0.3698	0.2671	0.1025
2725	0.0000	0.0000	0.9244	0.0712	0.2617	0.8763
3010	**0.1999**	**0.1101**	**0.9139**	**0.2596**	**0.2734**	**0.1059**
3402	0.1441	0.0614	0.8950	0.7269	0.2361	0.7804
4194	0.0400	0.0000	1.0000	0.0720	0.2163	0.2629
5552	0.0400	0.1148	0.5420	0.2836	0.3405	0.8823

(a)

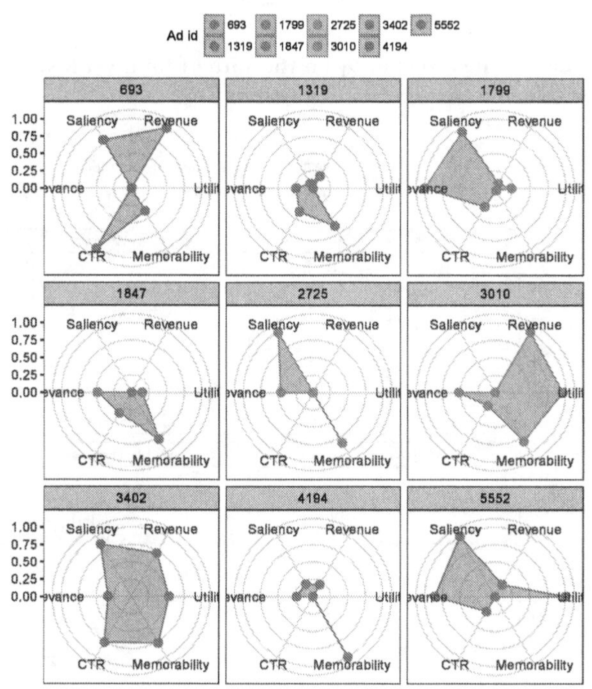

(b)

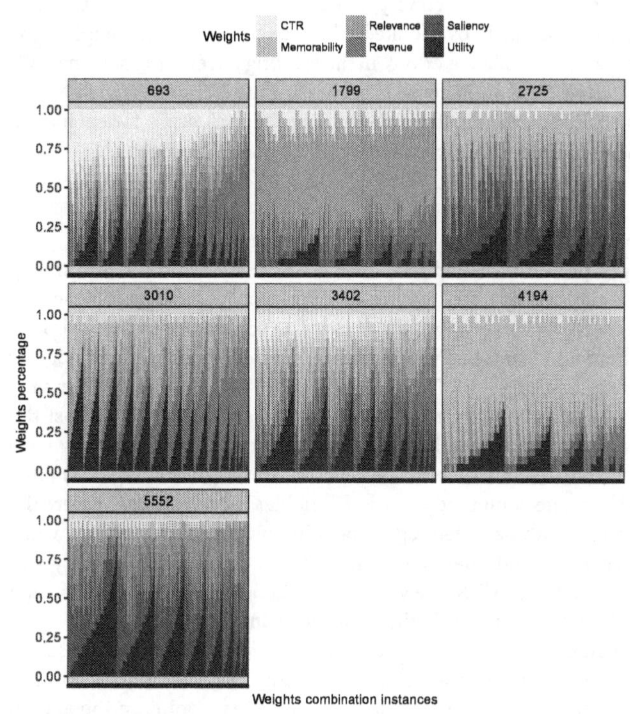

(c)

Figure 4: Empirical example of sensitivity analysis of re-ranking for an AOL page view: (a) the raw data in the auction where the ground truth has been highlighted in bold; (b) the comparison of the ground truth ad with other candidates; (c) sensitive analysis of weights in this auction.

multimedia dataset of the webpage. To ensure the uniqueness of each ad in the auction, we exclude the original ad when we sample $n-1$ ads from the multimedia dataset.

Step 4: Matching ads and bids

We match the n bids with n ads. Since the original ad is displayed, we consider it belongs to the winning advertiser in the auction and match it with the highest bid. The rest $n-1$ ads and $n-1$ bids are then randomly matched.

Step 5: Simulating CTRs

For each ad, we generate its CTR from a uniform distribution in the range of 0 and 13.97‰+ 1.96×28.49‰. This is based on the mean and std. of CTRs in the first position in the Microsoft dataset, as also shown in Table 5.

The above five steps allow us to have enough information to compute the mentioned six metric variables for each ad in each auction. We then re-rank ads based on the trade-offs preference, which is expressed in terms of weights. In experiments, we perform the 10-fold cross validation method to obtain the optimal weights as well as to provide the performance analysis.

4.3 Variable Analysis

The values of metric variables in the ground truth are examined – those ads which have been recommended to users under the SP auction model in RTB. For each impression, it contains the publisher's revenue, the advertiser's utility, the ad CTR, and the multimedia variables. Fig. 3 shows the descriptive statistics. The density plots along the diagonal show the distribution of each variable individually; the scatter plots lying in the lower triangular region show how much one variable is affected by another; and their linear correlations are given in the corresponding areas in the upper triangular part. The scatter plots lying on the bottom row shows the values of each variable under the two platforms and the right column show the variations and outliers of each variable. Note that relevance score ranges from 0 to 5, where 5 indicates most relevant and 0 indicates irrelevant, and the scores of memorability and saliency range from 0 to 1, respectively. Several findings are worth mentioning. Firstly, many displayed ads in the ground truth data are irrelevant to the contents of their hosting webpages, which will result in less user engagement. Secondly, most of displayed ads are not salient, thus can be easily overlooked. These two findings may explain the phenomenon of ad overlook in the existing advertising systems [37]. We also find that pairwise variables are independent, which allows using linear combination to calculate the rank score for each ad in the auction without considering the correlation matrix.

4.4 Sensitivity Analysis

Fig. 4 presents an empirical example of analysing trade-offs among stakeholders by investigating all advertisers' ads and possible weights of metric variables. Fig. 4(a) shows the screenshot of the webpage, where ad 3010 (i.e., the ground truth) is displayed on the side bar. Since the sampled RTB auction has 9 advertisers, we further sample 8 candidate ads from the AOL dataset. They have almost the same width and length as the ground truth ad. However, they have different contents, color themes, and descriptions. Fig. 4(a) table exhibits the computed values of variables for re-ranking, where the ground truth has been highlighted in bold. It has the highest value in revenue; and relatively high values in utility, memorability; but small values in CTR, relevance and saliency. Obviously, the ground truth is biased towards the publisher's interest.

Radar charts shown in Fig. 4(b) provide a clearer comparison of the ground truth ad with other ad candidates. Each radar chart has multiple axes and each variable is shown as a point on the axis. A point closer to the center on an axis indicates a lower value and vice versa. In radar charts, all values of variables are further normalized into the range between 0 and 1. If all the variables' values of an ad are less than another ad, we call it being *strictly dominated* because this ad will have no possibility to be selected in the second stage re-ranking. For example, ad 1319 is strictly dominated and its area in the radar chart can be fully covered by ad 3402.

Fig. 4(c) shows all possible combinations of the weights in the re-ranking. For each subplot, x-axis represents all the weights instances that make the ad win the auction, and y-axis represents the values of weights in each instance based on stack bars. Note that the subplots of ad 1319 and ad 1847 are empty, indicating that no matter what weights we choose, these two ads will never be selected in the auction. An ad can be selected if its high valued variables have large weights. Of course, the weights represent the preference of trade-offs and different numbers of weights combination instances of ads also tell that they do not have equal chances to be selected in the re-ranking. Although ad 1847 is not strictly dominated in radar charts, it is not been selected in all weights combinations. This is because most of its variables' values are relatively small and its highest variable value is still less than that of ad 3010. Therefore, even when the trade-offs preference is biased towards the ad memorability, the rank score of ad 1847 is still less than ad 3010. We simply call it to be *weakly dominated.*

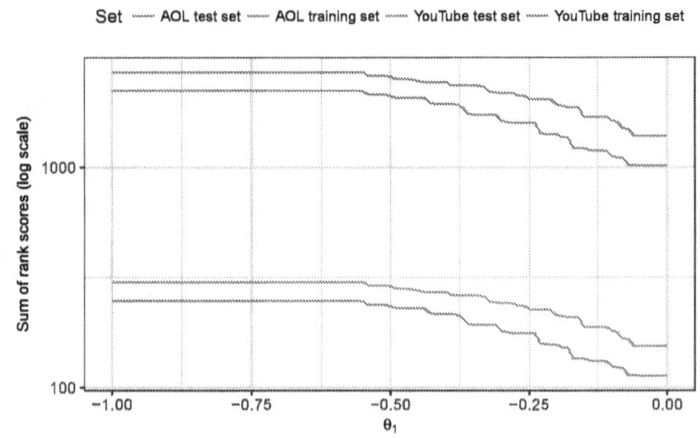

Figure 5: The effect of θ_1 on the sum of total rank scores of the selected advertisers in auctions.

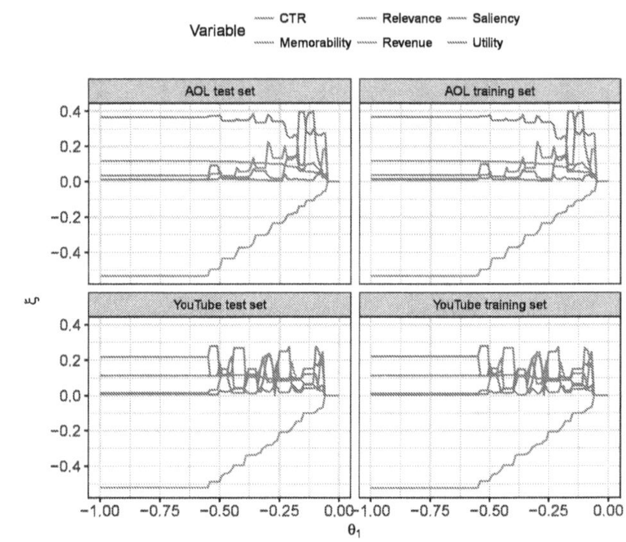

Figure 6: The effect of θ_1 on the changes of variables.

4.5 Overall Results

We validate the proposed framework by conducting the 10-fold cross validation on both AOL and YouTube datasets. The optimal weights are estimated from the training set; they are then used for re-ranking ads in the auctions in the test set. For simplicity but without lose of generality, the threshold value θ_k is set to be zero for any $k \in K \setminus \{1\}$ so that the effects of θ_1 can be examined explicitly. As described earlier, θ_1 is the maximum decrease of the publisher's revenue, which indicates how much the publisher would like to sacrifice in order to increase the benefits of the other two stakeholders. Therefore, θ_1 lies in the interval between -1 and 0.

Table 6: Summary of optimal trade-offs among stakeholders in the AOL dataset where $\theta_1 = -0.06$. Note that $\omega_i, i = 1, \ldots, 6$ represent the optimal weights obtained from training set, and $\xi_i, i = 1, \ldots, 6$ represent the changes of corresponding variables.

Fold	Optimal weight						Training set						Test set					
	ω_1	ω_2	ω_3	ω_4	ω_5	ω_6	ξ_1	ξ_2	ξ_3	ξ_4	ξ_5	ξ_6	ξ_1	ξ_2	ξ_3	ξ_4	ξ_5	ξ_6
1	0.45	0.30	0.05	0.05	0.15	0.00	-5.5%	2.3%	3.4%	26.7%	17.4%	4.4%	-5.8%	1.0%	4.0%	30.1%	23.7%	1.3%
2	0.45	0.30	0.05	0.05	0.15	0.00	-5.5%	2.5%	3.5%	26.7%	17.6%	4.1%	-5.7%	-0.7%	3.9%	30.6%	22.0%	3.7%
3	0.45	0.30	0.05	0.05	0.15	0.00	-5.5%	1.8%	3.6%	27.3%	18.2%	3.7%	-5.7%	6.3%	3.0%	25.3%	16.7%	7.6%
4	0.45	0.30	0.05	0.05	0.15	0.00	-5.5%	1.9%	3.5%	27.5%	17.8%	4.1%	-5.1%	4.8%	3.3%	23.4%	19.7%	4.3%
5	0.45	0.30	0.05	0.05	0.15	0.00	-5.5%	2.5%	3.4%	27.3%	18.0%	4.1%	-5.5%	0.1%	4.1%	25.4%	18.5%	3.8%
6	0.45	0.30	0.05	0.05	0.15	0.00	-5.6%	2.4%	3.6%	27.2%	18.2%	4.1%	-5.0%	0.9%	2.9%	26.3%	16.2%	4.2%
7	0.45	0.30	0.05	0.05	0.15	0.00	-5.5%	2.2%	3.5%	26.8%	18.2%	4.3%	-5.9%	2.5%	3.4%	29.3%	16.7%	2.4%
8	0.45	0.30	0.05	0.05	0.15	0.00	-5.6%	2.1%	3.6%	27.4%	18.4%	4.4%	-4.9%	3.4%	2.6%	24.2%	14.6%	1.5%
9	0.45	0.30	0.05	0.05	0.15	0.00	-5.5%	2.2%	3.5%	27.2%	18.3%	4.0%	-5.3%	2.7%	3.8%	25.7%	15.6%	4.7%
10	0.45	0.30	0.05	0.05	0.15	0.00	-5.4%	2.3%	3.5%	26.6%	18.1%	3.7%	-6.1%	1.3%	4.0%	30.8%	17.0%	8.0%
Mean	-	-	-	-	-	-	-5.5%	2.2%	3.5%	27.1%	18.0%	4.1%	-5.5%	2.2%	3.5%	27.1%	18.1%	4.1%
Std.	-	-	-	-	-	-	0.000	0.002	0.000	0.002	0.003	0.002	0.003	0.020	0.004	0.026	0.027	0.021

Table 7: Summary of optimal trade-offs among stakeholders in the YouTube dataset where $\theta_1 = -0.07$. Note that $\omega_i, i = 1, \ldots, 6$ represent the optimal weights obtained from training set, and $\xi_i, i = 1, \ldots, 6$ represent the changes of corresponding variables.

Fold	Optimal weight						Training set						Test set					
	ω_1	ω_2	ω_3	ω_4	ω_5	ω_6	ξ_1	ξ_2	ξ_3	ξ_4	ξ_5	ξ_6	ξ_1	ξ_2	ξ_3	ξ_4	ξ_5	ξ_6
1	0.45	0.25	0.10	0.00	0.15	0.05	-6.2%	0.3%	4.9%	0.0%	23.5%	17.9%	-6.2%	0.5%	4.7%	-2.7%	30.5%	18.2%
2	0.45	0.30	0.05	0.05	0.10	0.05	-6.9%	5.7%	2.2%	27.2%	14.7%	20.9%	-6.8%	7.2%	1.3%	27.4%	18.9%	21.8%
3	0.45	0.30	0.05	0.05	0.10	0.05	-6.9%	5.8%	2.1%	27.4%	14.6%	21.0%	-6.8%	6.8%	2.6%	25.7%	19.2%	21.1%
4	0.45	0.30	0.05	0.05	0.10	0.05	-6.8%	5.4%	2.1%	27.0%	15.4%	21.1%	-7.2%	9.5%	2.4%	29.1%	12.5%	20.1%
5	0.45	0.30	0.05	0.05	0.10	0.05	-6.8%	5.9%	2.1%	27.4%	15.4%	20.9%	-7.2%	5.9%	2.3%	24.9%	12.1%	22.5%
6	0.45	0.30	0.05	0.05	0.10	0.05	-6.9%	6.2%	2.2%	27.3%	15.4%	20.5%	-6.8%	3.4%	2.0%	25.7%	12.4%	25.8%
7	0.45	0.30	0.05	0.05	0.10	0.05	-6.8%	6.0%	2.1%	26.8%	15.1%	20.8%	-7.2%	4.2%	2.4%	30.7%	15.1%	23.1%
8	0.45	0.30	0.05	0.05	0.10	0.05	-6.8%	5.9%	2.1%	27.2%	15.2%	21.1%	-7.2%	5.4%	2.9%	26.6%	14.4%	20.8%
9	0.45	0.30	0.05	0.05	0.10	0.05	-6.9%	5.8%	2.2%	27.1%	14.9%	21.1%	-6.9%	6.3%	1.8%	27.8%	16.5%	20.3%
10	0.45	0.30	0.05	0.05	0.10	0.05	-6.9%	5.8%	2.2%	26.9%	15.3%	21.4%	-6.9%	6.5%	1.8%	30.3%	12.9%	17.7%
Mean	-	-	-	-	-	-	-6.8%	5.3%	2.4%	24.4%	16.0%	20.7%	-6.9%	5.6%	2.4%	24.5%	16.5%	21.1%
Std.	-	-	-	-	-	-	0.001	0.016	0.008	0.081	0.025	0.009	0.002	0.023	0.008	0.092	0.053	0.022

The smaller the value of θ_1, the more is the increase in the benefits of other stakeholders.

Fig. 5 presents the effect of θ_1 on the sum of rank scores of the selected advertisers in auctions. When θ_1 decreases, the sum of rank scores increases. This monotone decreasing pattern is because that the solution space of weights increases if θ_1 decreases (see Section 3.2.2). Also, in the 10-fold cross validation, the size of the training set is 9 times of the test set, the solution space of weights and the sum of rank scores in the training set are roughly 9 times of the test set. The effects of θ_1 on the changes of metric variables are examined in Fig. 6. In both AOL and YouTube datasets, the changes of variables in the training data follow the same patterns as those in the test data. If θ_1 is close to 0, the SP auction (the ground truth) is the optimal solution. This means that our model suggests that the publisher shouldn't sacrifice any revenue. If the publisher further decreases θ_1, the optimal weights change. There will be some growth in the variables of other stakeholders, and of course, the publisher's revenue starts to decrease. If θ_1 is small, the publisher's revenue will decrease significantly and she may find it unacceptable. As shown in Fig. 6, if θ_1 is less than -0.3, it reduces the publisher's revenue by almost 30%. There is no monotone increasing pattern in other variables. Analyzing the changes in variables will help the publisher to decide a proper θ_1. Tables 6-7 further present two special cases: $\theta_1 = -0.06$ for the AOL dataset; and $\theta_1 = -0.07$ for the YouTube dataset. Both cases show the results when the decrease in the publisher's revenue is close to the pre-specified threshold value θ_1. For example, there is about 5.5% decrease in the publisher's revenue in the AOL training set and other variables enjoy certain increases ranging from 2.2% to 27.1%.

5 CONCLUSION

This paper discusses a two-stage framework that optimizes trade-offs among stakeholders in display advertising. Different to many related studies which only focus on the publisher's revenue, we further consider the benefits of the advertiser and the user by incorporating multimedia metrics. The trade-offs optimization is based on a linear combination of all metric variables and their weights are learnt from data. Variable and sensitivity analysis are conducted to explore the solution space. Our experimental results validate the proposed framework and show that it is able to increase the benefits of other two stakeholders with just a slight decrease in the publisher's revenue. In the long run, better engagement of advertisers and users will increase the demand of advertising and supply of webpage visits, which can then boost the publisher's revenue. Future research can potentially discuss a framework which considers a generalised scenario where a webpage has multiple ad slots being separately auctioned off in RTB. The long-term effects of trade-offs optimization can also be further investigated and it would be very interesting if the framework can be tested over a live setting.

6 ACKNOWLEDGEMENT

This research is supported by the National Research Foundation, Prime Ministerfis Office, Singapore under its International Research Centre in Singapore Funding Initiative.

REFERENCES

[1] L. Alwitt and A. Mitchell. *Psychological processes and advertising effects.* Lawrence Erlbaum, 1985.

[2] S. Athey and D. Nekipelov. A structural model of sponsored search advertising auctions. In *6th Ad Auctions Workshop*, 2010.

[3] Y. Bachrach, S. Ceppi, I. Kash, P. Key, and D. Kurokawa. Optimising trade-offs among stakeholders in ad auctions. In *Proceedings of the 15th ACM Conference on Economics and Computation*, pages 75–92, 2014.

[4] A. Broder, P. Ciccolo, M. Fontoura, E. Gabrilovich, V. Josifovski, and L. Riedel. Search advertising using web relevance feedback. In *Proceedings of the 17th ACM Conference on Information and Knowledge Management*, pages 1013–1022, 2008.

[5] A. Broder, M. Fontoura, V. Josifovski, and L. Riedel. A semantic approach to contextual advertising. In *Proceedings of the 30th International ACM SIGIR Conference on Research and Development in Information Retrieval*, pages 559–566, 2007.

[6] D. Campbell and R. Wright. Shut-up I don't care: understanding the role of relevance and interactivity on customer attitudes toward repetitive online advertising. *Journal of Electronic Commerce Research*, 9(1):62, 2008.

[7] P. Chatterjee, D. Hoffman, and T. Novak. Modeling the clickstream: implications for web-based advertising efforts. *Marketing Science*, 22(4):520–541, 2003.

[8] B. Chen. Risk-aware dynamic reserve prices of programmatic guarantee in display advertising. In *Proceedings of the 16th IEEE International Conference on Data Mining Workshops*, pages 511–518, 2016.

[9] B. Chen and J. Wang. A lattice framework for pricing display advertisement options with the stochastic volatility underlying model. *Electronic Commerce Research and Applications*, 14:465–479, 2015.

[10] B. Chen, J. Wang, I. Cox, and M. Kankanhalli. Multi-keyword multi-click advertisement option contracts for sponsored search. *ACM Transactions on Intelligent Systems and Technology*, 7(5), 2015.

[11] B. Chen, S. Yuan, and J. Wang. A dynamic pricing model for unifying programmatic guarantee and real-time bidding in display advertising. In *Proceedings of the 8th International Workshop on Data Mining for Online Advertising*, pages 1–9, 2014.

[12] X. Chen, T. V. Nguyen, and M. Kankanhalli. Salad: A multimodal approach for contextual video advertising. In *2015 IEEE International Symposium on multimedia*, pages 211–216, 2015.

[13] Y. Chen, O. Jin, G. Xue, J. Chen, and Q. Yang. Visual contextual advertising: bringing textual advertisements to images. In *Proceedings of the 24th AAAI Conference on Artificial Intelligence*, pages 1314–1320, 2010.

[14] B. Edelman, M. Ostrovsky, and M. Schwarz. Internet advertising and the generalized second-price auction: selling billions of dollars worth of keywords. *American Economic Review*, 97(1):242–259, 2007.

[15] Google. The arrival of real-time bidding and what it means for media buyers. In *White Paper*, 2011.

[16] J. Guo, T. Mei, F. Liu, and X.-S. Hua. AdOn: an intelligent overlay video advertising system. In *Proceedings of the 32nd International ACM SIGIR Conference on Research and Development in Information Retrieval*, pages 628–629, 2009.

[17] A. Khosla, A. Raju, A. Torralba, and A. Oliva. Understanding and predicting image memorability at a large scale. In *Proceedings of the IEEE International Conference on Computer Vision*, pages 2390–2398, 2015.

[18] S. Lahaie and P. McAfee. Efficient ranking in sponsored search. In *Proceedings of the 7th International Conference on Internet and Network Economics*, pages 254–265, 2011.

[19] S. Lahaie and D. Pennock. Revenue analysis of a family of ranking rules for keyword auctions. In *Proceedings of the 8th ACM Conference on Electronic Commerce*, pages 50–60, 2007.

[20] J. Lehmann, M. Lalmas, E. Yom-Tov, and G. Dupret. Models of user engagement. In *Proceedings of the 20th International Conference on User Modeling, Adaptation, and Personalization*, pages 164–175, 2012.

[21] L. Li, T. Mei, X. Niu, and C. Ngo. PageSense: style-wise web page advertising. In *Proceedings of the 19th International Conference on World Wide Web*, pages 1273–1276, 2010.

[22] W. Liao, K. Chen, and W. Hsu. AdImage: video advertising by image matching and ad scheduling optimization. In *Proceedings of the 31st Annual International ACM SIGIR Conference on Research and Development in Information Retrieval*, pages 767–768, 2008.

[23] A. Likhodedov and T. Sandholm. Auction mechanism for optimally trading off revenue and efficiency. In *Proceedings of the 4th ACM Conference on Electronic Commerce*, pages 212–213, 2003.

[24] B. Lucier, R. Leme, and E. Tardos. On revenue in the generalized second price auction. In *Proceedings of the 21st International Conference on World Wide Web*, 2012.

[25] S. McCoy, A. Everard, P. Polak, and D. Galletta. The effects of online advertising. *Communications of the ACM*, 50(3):84–88, 2007.

[26] T. Mei, X. Hua, L. Yang, and S. Li. VideoSense: towards effective online video advertising. In *Proceedings of the 15th ACM International Conference on Multimedia*, pages 1075–1084, 2007.

[27] T. Mei, L. Li, X. Hua, and S. Li. ImageSense: towards contextual image advertising. *ACM Transactions on Multimedia Computing, Communications, and Applications*, 8(1):6, 2012.

[28] M. Neumeier. *The Brand Gap: How to Bridge the Distance Between Business Strategy and Design.* New Riders, 2005.

[29] OpenX. Programmatic + premium: current practices and future trends. Technical report, White Paper, 2013.

[30] M. Ostrovsky and M. Schwarz. Reserve prices in Internet advertising auctions: a field experiment. In *Proceedings of the 12th ACM Conference on Electronic Commerce*, pages 59–60, 2011.

[31] J. Owens, B. Chaparro, and E. Palmer. Text advertising blindness: the new banner blindness? *Journal of Usability Studies*, 6(3):172–197, 2011.

[32] D. Parkes. *Algorithmic Game Theory*, chapter Online Mechanisms. Cambridge University Press, 2007.

[33] F. Pin and P. Key. Stochastic variability in sponsored search auctions: observations and models. In *Proceedings of the 12th ACM Conference on Electronic Commerce*, pages 61–70, 2011.

[34] F. Radlinski, A. Broder, P. Ciccolo, E. Gabrilovich, V. Josifovski, and L. Riedel. Optimizing relevance and revenue in ad search: a query substitution approach. In *Proceedings of the 31st Annual International ACM SIGIR Conference on Research and Development in Information Retrieval*, pages 403–410, 2008.

[35] B. Ribeiro-Neto, M. Cristo, P. Golgher, and E. Silva de Moura. Impedance coupling in content-targeted advertising. In *Proceedings of the 28th Annual International ACM SIGIR Conference on Research and Development in Information Retrieval*, pages 496–503, 2005.

[36] B. Roberts, D. Gunawardena, I. Kash, and P. Key. Ranking and tradeoffs in sponsored search auctions. In *Proceedings of the 14th ACM Conference on Electronic Commerce*, pages 751–766, 2013.

[37] P. Sajjacholapunt and L. Ball. The influence of banner advertisements on attention and memory: human faces with averted gaze can enhance advertising effectiveness. *Frontiers in Psychology*, 5, 2014.

[38] F. Šarić, G. Glavaš, M. Karan, J. Šnajder, and B. Bašić. Takelab: systems for measuring semantic text similarity. In *Proceedings of the 1st Joint Conference on Lexical and Computational Semantics*, pages 441–448, 2012.

[39] D. Thompson and K. Leyton-Brown. Revenue optimization in the generalized second-price auction. In *Proceedings of the 14th ACM conference on Electronic Commerce*, pages 837–852, 2013.

[40] H. Varian. Position auctions. *International Journal of Industrial Organization*, 25(6):1163–1178, 2007.

[41] J. Wang and B. Chen. Selling futures online advertising slots via option contracts. In *Proceedings of the 21st International Conference on World Wide Web*, pages 627–628, 2012.

[42] S. Yuan, J. Wang, B. Chen, P. Mason, and S. Seljan. An empirical study of reserve price optimisation in real-time bidding. In *Proceedings of the 20th ACM SIGKDD Conference on Knowledge Discovery and Data Mining*, pages 1897–1906, 2014.

[43] J. Zhang, S. Sclaroff, Z. Lin, X. Shen, B. Price, and R. Mech. Minimum barrier salient object detection at 80 fps. In *Proceedings of the IEEE International Conference on Computer Vision*, pages 1404–1412, 2015.

[44] W. Zhang, D. Wang, G. Xue, and H. Zha. Advertising keywords recommendation for short-text web pages using Wikipedia. *ACM Transactions on Intelligent Systems and Technology*, 3(2):36, 2012.

A Probabilistic Reformulation of Memory-Based Collaborative Filtering – Implications on Popularity Biases

Rocío Cañamares
Universidad Autónoma de Madrid
C/ Fco. Tomás y Valiente 11, Madrid, Spain
rocio.cannamares@uam.es

Pablo Castells
Universidad Autónoma de Madrid
C/ Fco. Tomás y Valiente 11, Madrid, Spain
pablo.castells@uam.es

ABSTRACT

We develop a probabilistic formulation giving rise to a formal version of heuristic k nearest-neighbor (kNN) collaborative filtering. Different independence assumptions in our scheme lead to user-based, item-based, normalized and non-normalized variants that match in structure the traditional formulations, while showing equivalent empirical effectiveness. The probabilistic formulation provides a principled explanation why kNN is an effective recommendation strategy, and identifies a key condition for this to be the case. Moreover, a natural explanation arises for the bias of kNN towards recommending popular items. Thereupon the kNN variants are shown to fall into two groups with similar trends in behavior, corresponding to two different notions of item popularity. We show experiments where the comparative performance of the two groups of algorithms changes substantially, which suggests that the performance measurements and comparison may heavily depend on statistical properties of the input data sample.

CCS CONCEPTS

• Information systems → Recommender Systems; Collaborative Filtering; Probabilistic Retrieval Models; Evaluation of Retrieval Results

KEYWORDS

Recommender systems; collaborative filtering; probabilistic models; popularity; algorithmic bias; evaluation

ACM Reference format:

R. Cañamares and P. Castells. 2007 A Probabilistic Reformulation of Memory-Based Collaborative Filtering – Implications on Popularity Biases. In Proc. of International ACM SIGIR Conference on Research and Development in Information Retrieval, Tokyo, Japan, August 2017 (SIGIR 2017), 10 pages.

1 INTRODUCTION

Nearest-neighbor algorithms (kNN) are probably the most popular and widely-known approach to collaborative filtering (CF) [1,16]. They can be said to be the first technique to be explicitly documented as a strategy to implement a proper recommender system as we understand it today [17]. kNN was further popularized for being the core approach in the pioneering large-scale deployment of recommendation technologies in e-commerce by Amazon [15]. They have been shown to have competitive empirical effectiveness and are still widely used today. Newer CF approaches, notably ones based on matrix factorization [12], have been reported to outperform kNN in raw recommendation accuracy, yet neighbor-based methods closely follow the former in this task. Furthermore, the kNN approach provides tradeoff advantages such as easier-to-explain outputs to end-users, a straightforward easy-to-understand formulation scheme, and ease of implementation [16].

A current limitation of the kNN scheme is its heuristic nature –heuristic is in fact a name by which they are often referred to [1]. The kNN formulation was borrowed from classification and regression, but does not arise from a formal justification. Its use is supported by intuition ("users with similar behavior in the past should have similar behavior in the future") and empirical effectiveness, but the latter has not been explained in a principled way [14]. Furthermore, different variants of the kNN scheme have been used by different authors with often differing results, and there has not been a clear basis to decide upon which alternative is best or when, other than by practical comparative effectiveness [6].

In this paper we take on to develop a probabilistic formulation for nearest-neighbor recommendation. A probabilistic basis has obvious well-understood advantages for algorithm development, such as a design justification, a deeper understanding of the algorithm behavior and properties, and enabling variations and extensions of the scheme. The development we propose results in a formulation that closely matches the structure of traditional heuristic kNN. As we shall see, different independence assumptions in our scheme lead to user-based, item-based, normalized and non-normalized variants. We report experiments showing the probabilistic version is roughly equivalent in performance to the corresponding heuristic formulations. We further find the probabilistic basis enables explanations for some of the properties of the kNN approach, such as its effectiveness, the advantages of one variant over the other, and connections between kNN and popularity.

The rest of the paper is organized as follows. We start recalling the basics and notation for the recommendation task and the kNN approach. Then in section 3 we develop the proposed probabilistic formulation. We analyze the connections between kNN and popularity in section 4, after which in section 5 we contrast the theoretical analysis with empirical observations on different datasets. We discuss related work in the section following that, after which we end with a brief summary and some conclusions.

2 THE NEAREST NEIGHBOR COLLABORATIVE FILTERING APROACH

The recommendation task is widely known and needs little introduction today [18]. In summary, a recommender system receives

SIGIR '17, August 7-11, 2017, Shinjuku, Tokyo, Japan

ACM ISBN 978-1-4503-5022-8/17/08...$15.00
http://dx.doi.org/10.1145/3077136.3080836

as input data collected from observed user-item interactions, which can be abstracted to a set of user / item / timestamp records (for so-called implicit data directly obtained from natural user activity), or user / item / rating value (for so-called explicit preference feedback provided by users). Given this input, the recommender system's task is to predict unobserved user-item preferences, and thereupon deliver a set of ranked items (typically different for each user) that satisfy the needs of end-users. More detailed descriptions and discussion of the recommendation problem can be found elsewhere (see e.g. [1] for a popular introduction).

Following a common convention in recommender systems research, we shall denote by $r(u,i)$ the observed rating by a user u for an item i, and by $\hat{r}(u,i)$ the system score (which may or may not aim to be literally a rating prediction) by which an item is selected and ranked for recommendation to a user. We shall use the convention $r(u,i) = 0$ to indicate $r(u,i)$ is unknown to the system –note that by this we are implying 0 is not an allowed rating value; the reader may find this shall bring a slight simplification in notation along the way, with no generality loss. Finally, we shall use the symbols $\mathcal{U}$ and $\mathcal{I}$ to refer to, respectively, the set of users and the set of items involved in the recommendation problem.

The recommendation task can be refined in different ways [10], most notably including a) predicting rating values as accurately as possible, and b) delivering an item ranking that satisfies as much as possible the target users as viewed in an information retrieval perspective (i.e. returning as many relevant items as possible, as early as possible in the ranking). In this paper we take on the latter perspective, which is understood today to be more closely related to real recommendation scenarios [6].

The nearest-neighbor collaborative filtering strategy (also known as memory-based, or heuristic) is one among hundreds of solutions to the recommendation problem. It can be said to be the first proper approach envisioned for the task [17] and probably remains the most popular. It builds on the intuition that users with similar tastes in the past may enjoy similar choices in the future. The most common simple materialization of this principle has taken the following structure (see e.g. [16]):

$$\hat{r}(u,i) = C \sum_{v \in N_k[u]} sim(u,v) r(v,i) \tag{1}$$

where $sim(u,v)$ is a similarity function that estimates how much the tastes of two users look alike, $N_k[u]$ is a neighborhood of k users who are most "suitable" for contributing to the aggregated advice for u, and C is a normalizing constant. Neighborhood "suitability" is commonly defined as being among the k most similar users to u in terms of $sim(u,v)$, though neighbor selection is a modular problem open to alternative approaches aiming to improve the resulting recommendations.

By the partial symmetry of the item and user spaces it also makes sense to consider an item-based kNN variant based on the similarity between items:

$$\hat{r}(u,i) = C \sum_{j \in N_k[i]} sim(i,j) r(u,j) \tag{2}$$

The similarity functions can be defined in innumerous ways, the most popular being the cosine function and Pearson correlation. For instance, the cosine similarity can be defined as:

$$sim(u,v) = \frac{\sum_{j \in \mathcal{I}} r(u,j) r(v,j)}{\sqrt{\sum_{j \in \mathcal{I}} r(u,j)^2} \sqrt{\sum_{j \in \mathcal{I}} r(v,j)^2}} \tag{3}$$

$$sim(i,j) = \frac{\sum_{v \in \mathcal{U}} r(v,i) r(v,j)}{\sqrt{\sum_{v \in \mathcal{U}} r(v,i)^2} \sqrt{\sum_{v \in \mathcal{U}} r(v,j)^2}} \tag{4}$$

From this basic scheme many variations arise for which, again, we refer the reader e.g. to the survey in [16] for a good starting point. For the sake of our research, the above straightforward versions are sufficiently well-behaved and appropriately simple as a frame of reference for our proposed development.

A point of variation in the scheme will nonetheless get our attention, namely the normalizing constant C. Most of the literature (including popular surveys [1,16]) reports taking $C = 1/\sum_{v \in N_k[u] \wedge r(u,i)>0} |sim(u,v)|$ in order to make of equation 1 a weighted sum of ratings with weights adding to 1 (and analogously for equation 2). However it has been recently found that $C = 1$ is generally more effective at the item ranking task (see e.g. [2,6,22]). In this paper we will propose a formal basis for both options, and we will find that each of them leads to quite different theoretical and empirical implications, which we shall formally characterize.

3 PROBABILISTIC kNN

We derive a probabilistic formulation from a formalization of the user-item interaction dynamics as a random process in a sampling space, as follows. Along with the $\mathcal{U}$ and $\mathcal{I}$ spaces, let us consider the set $\mathcal{T}$ of all time instants where some user interacts with (consumes, purchases, rates, choses, etc.) some item. Taking the time points in $\mathcal{T}$ as (theoretically) fine-grained as needed (e.g. real numbers), we can assume there is only a user-item pair interaction at each $t \in \mathcal{T}$, that is, two users cannot access an item at the exact same time. This is just a condition that facilitates having well-defined probability distributions, as we shall see. Actually, assigning an arbitrary unique ID to each interaction would do as well for our purposes –time is just a convenient and particularly meaningful one. We consider $\mathcal{T}$ includes all interactions, both observed and non-observed by the system. We can also consider that $\mathcal{T}$ includes both past and future interactions. It is not a problem for us to introduce such an abstract construct, as it will just as well serve our theoretical purposes. We may also consider for a moment an ideal situation in which users have full omniscient knowledge of the whole item space and always choose items in full awareness of how much they would benefit (enjoy, gain, etc.) from each item, therefore choosing the item that maximizes their satisfaction at that time.

We consider the user choices are not deterministic and may depend on the occasion, therefore it makes sense to describe them by a probability distribution over items (for each user) to represent this uncertainty. For this purpose, over the set $\mathcal{T}$ we define two functions $U: \mathcal{T} \to \mathcal{U}$ and $I: \mathcal{T} \to \mathcal{I}$. For a given $t \in \mathcal{T}$, $U(t)$, which we shall abbreviate as U_t, is the user who had the interaction at time t, and $I(t)$, which we shall abbreviate as I_t, is the item that U_t interacted with. We can consider U and I as random variables for which $p(U_t = u)$ and $p(I_t = i)$ are well-defined (categorical) probability distributions over $u \in \mathcal{U}$ and $i \in \mathcal{I}$ respectively.

Now assume we have a target user u for whom we are to produce a recommendation. Say $t \in \mathcal{T}$ is the next time u will consume some item (either spontaneously by his own initiative, or induced by the system delivering a recommendation, or by any other means). Defining t this way means that $U_t = u$. Upon this formal scheme, we may define the recommendation task as estimating the probability for each item to be the one the user would choose at that time. That is, we wish to estimate $p(I_t = i|U_t = u)$. If we can do that, an optimal recommendation for u (which maximizes user satisfaction in expectation) is ranking items by decreasing value of this probability. In other words, we should take $p(I_t = i|U_t = u)$ as the ranking function (ranking score) for recommendation, to optimize the chance to satisfy a user who browses our recommendation top-down.

Upon this initial basis, we shall derive formulations of user-based and item-based kNN by introducing a second user (or, respectively, item) –the neighbor– as a second random variable over which we shall marginalize the ranking function, as we show next.

3.1 User-Based kNN

Let $t' < t$ be a time when the target item I_t (whichever that item happens to be) was interacted with by some other user v. Applying the law of total sum we can marginalize the objective function as follows:

$$p(I_t = i|U_t = u) \sim \sum_{v \in \mathcal{U}} p(I_{t'} = i|U_{t'} = v)p(U_{t'} = v|U_t = u, I_{t'} = I_t) \quad (5)$$

where we apply some independence assumptions: first, $p(I_t = i|U_t = u) \sim p(I_t = i|U_t = u, I_{t'} = I_t)$ considering that $I_{t'} = I_t$ does not provide much meaningful information in the absence of any further condition related to time t' –the equality just states a condition as vague as the fact that some undefined user chose item I_t at some undefined moment t' in the past. Second, given that we do not have any direct evidence of the preference of the target user u for target items i (otherwise we would not consider i for recommendation to u), and assuming we do have some direct observation of other users v interacting with i, we have removed $U_t = u$ from the conditional part of the first term in the summation:

$$\begin{aligned} p(I_t = i|U_t = u, U_{t'} = v, I_{t'} = I_t) &\sim p(I_t = i|U_{t'} = v, I_{t'} = I_t) \\ &= p(I_{t'} = i|U_{t'} = v, I_{t'} = I_t) \sim p(I_{t'} = i|U_{t'} = v) \end{aligned} \quad (6)$$

The second term in equation 5, $p(U_{t'} = v|U_t = u, I_{t'} = I_t)$, denotes the probability that v has chosen sometime an item that u will also pick. It can be rewritten as:

$$p(U_{t'} = v|U_t = u, I_{t'} = I_t) = \frac{p(U_{t'} = v, U_t = u, I_{t'} = I_t)}{\sum_{w \in \mathcal{U}} p(U_{t'} = w, U_t = u, I_{t'} = I_t)} \quad (7)$$

3.2 Estimation from Observed Data

Now let us neglect the variations in user tastes over time. This is a very strong assumption, but one that basic non context-sensitive recommender systems make to generate their predictions: user behavior consistency over time.

If we do that, then we may estimate the above distributions based on observed data as follows. Assume the observations we have are a set of recorded interactions between users and items. This can be represented as a sample of triples $\mathcal{F} \subset \mathcal{U} \times \mathcal{I} \times \mathcal{T}$ so that $(u, i, t) \in \mathcal{F}$ means that u has been observed consuming i at time t. We denote by $r(u, i) = |\{(u, i, t) \in \mathcal{F}\}|$ the number of times u has been observed to pick i. As a frequency, $r(u, i)$ follows a multinomial distribution resulting from the categorical probability that the user will pick the item in question at any given time, that is, in expected value:

$$r(u, i) \Big/ \sum_{j \in \mathcal{I}} r(u, j) \sim p(I_t = i|U_t = u) \quad (8)$$

which provides an estimate for the distribution in equation 6.

This scheme, and the derivations we will develop hereupon, can be generalized to $r(u, i)$ denoting explicit numeric ratings also, to the extent that it is reasonable to assume that rating values reflect (are a monotonically increasing function of, or more strictly, are proportional to) the expected frequency with which a user would pick an item. To that extent, we will henceforth occasionally (and intentionally) refer to $r(u, i)$ as a "rating".

As for equation 7, the chances that v and u pick the same item at any two (arbitrary) different points in time can be estimated by the number of times this was observed to occur in our sample $\mathcal{F}$:

$$\begin{aligned} p(U_{t'} = v, U_t = u, I_{t'} = I_t) &= \sum_{j \in \mathcal{I}} p(U_{t'} = v, U_t = u, I_{t'} = I_t = j) \\ &\sim \frac{1}{|\mathcal{F}|^2} \sum_{j \in \mathcal{I}} |\{(t_1, t_2) \in \mathcal{T}^2 | (u, j, t_1) \in \mathcal{F} \land (v, j, t_2) \in \mathcal{F}\}| \\ &= \frac{1}{|\mathcal{F}|^2} \sum_{j \in \mathcal{I}} |\{t_1 \in \mathcal{T} | (u, j, t_1) \in \mathcal{F}\}||\{t_2 \in \mathcal{T} | (v, j, t_2) \in \mathcal{F}\}| \\ &= \frac{\sum_{j \in \mathcal{I}} r(u, j) r(v, j)}{\left(\sum_{w \in \mathcal{U}} \sum_{j \in \mathcal{I}} r(w, j)\right)^2} \end{aligned} \quad (9)$$

Substituting equation 9 into 7 we get:

$$p(U_{t'} = v|U_t = u, I_{t'} = I_t) \sim \frac{\sum_{j \in \mathcal{I}} r(u, j) r(v, j)}{\sum_{w \in \mathcal{U}} \sum_{j \in \mathcal{I}} r(u, j) r(w, j)} \quad (10)$$

And finally, replacing equations 8 and 10 into 5 we have:

$$\begin{aligned} p(I_t = i|U_t = u) &\sim \frac{1}{\sum_{w \in \mathcal{U}} \sum_{j \in \mathcal{I}} r(u, j) r(w, j)} \sum_{v \in \mathcal{U}} \frac{\sum_{j \in \mathcal{I}} r(u, j) r(v, j)}{\sum_{j \in \mathcal{I}} r(v, j)} r(v, i) \\ &\propto \sum_{\substack{v \in \mathcal{U} \\ v \neq u}} \frac{\sum_{j \in \mathcal{I}} r(u, j) r(v, j)}{\sum_{j \in \mathcal{I}} r(u, j) \sum_{j \in \mathcal{I}} r(v, j)} r(v, i) \end{aligned} \quad (11)$$

where we have intentionally added $\sum_{j \in \mathcal{I}} r(u, j)$ in the denominator (as it is a constant for a fixed target user u, thus preserving the ranking) to make our point next. We also add the (redundant) condition $v \neq u$ because we should have $r(u, i) = 0$, i.e. no previous recorded interaction for any i we may consider as recommendation for u.

As we now can see, equation 11 defines a user-based kNN recommender where the similarity function looks quite like a cosine (as in equation 3), only using the L_1 norm instead of L_2 in the cosine similarity. We have thus just shown that the ranking function of a common user-based kNN algorithm can be described as the computation of a probability. The specific variant matches the heuristic kNN scheme defined by equations 1 plus 3 with $C = 1$, that is, no normalization [2,6,22].

We may now want to restrict the set of users v to a subset of neighbors, or not –this would just be an ad-hoc refinement of the probabilistic scheme. In our experiments, similarly to heuristic kNN, we shall consider neighbor selection based on the highest values of the weights in the rating sum in equation 11, which correspond to $p(U_t = u, I_{t'} = I_t | U_{t'} = v)$, for each target user u.

Moreover, we found in our experiments that smoothing the probability estimates slightly improves empirical results. Specifically we tested Dirichlet smoothing [25] on the equation 11 weights as estimates of $p(U_t = u, I_{t'} = I_t | U_{t'} = v)$, using $\sum_{w \in \mathcal{U}} \sum_{j \in \mathcal{I}} r(u,j) r(w,j) \,/\, \sum_{w \in \mathcal{U}} \sum_{j \in \mathcal{I}} r(w,j) \propto p(U_t = u, I_{t'} = I_t)$ as a Dirichlet prior estimate.

3.3 Normalized Variant

In equation 5, nothing prevents us from restricting the sum over users to essentially any condition on v, as far as the sum over v adds to one. In particular we can take the condition that v has been seen interacting with i in the system:

$$p(I_t = i | U_t = u) \sim \sum_{v \in \mathcal{U}} p(I_{t'} = i | U_{t'} = v, r(v,i) > 0) \; p(U_{t'} = v | U_t = u, I_{t'} = I_t, r(v,i) > 0)$$

With this variation, it is easy to see that equation 11 remains almost the same but, quite importantly, a constant C appears:

$$p(I_t = i | U_t = u) \sim C \sum_{v \in \mathcal{U}} \frac{\sum_{j \in \mathcal{I}} r(u,j) r(v,j)}{\sum_{j \in \mathcal{I}} r(u,j) \sum_{j \in \mathcal{I}} r(v,j)} r(v,i)$$

with $C = 1 / \sum_{w \in \mathcal{U}: r(w,i) > 0} \sum_{j \in \mathcal{I}} r(u,j) r(w,j)$. This is a normalized variant since the numerators of the weights in the sum of ratings $r(v,i)$ above now sum to 1, similar in structure to the heuristic normalized kNN [1,16] (except for $\sum_{j \in \mathcal{I}} r(v,j)$ in the denominator being left out of the normalization). Neighbor selection and smoothing can be introduced in a similar way as in the non-normalized variant.

3.4 Item-Based kNN

The analysis of user-based kNN can be developed in an item-oriented version as well. For this purpose, we marginalize $p(I_t = i | U_t = u)$ by neighbor items j, and we apply analogous developments to the ones detailed in section 3.2 for the user-based variant, only we start by inverting the target user and item in the initial ranking function:

$$\begin{aligned} p(I_t = i | U_t = u) &\propto_u p(I_t = i) p(U_t = u | I_t = i) \\ &\sim p(I_t = i) \sum_{j \in \mathcal{I}} p(I_{t'} = j | I_t = i, U_{t'} = U_t) \; p(U_t = u | I_t = i, I_{t'} = j, U_{t'} = U_t) \end{aligned} \quad (12)$$

Now similarly to the user-based version, we consider the independence assumption between target user and item for lack of observations:

$$p(U_t = u | I_t = i, I_{t'} = j, U_{t'} = U_t) \sim p(U_{t'} = u | I_{t'} = j)$$

We rewrite again the conditional pairwise item dependence as:

$$p(I_{t'} = j | I_t = i, U_{t'} = U_t) = \frac{p(I_{t'} = j, I_t = i, U_{t'} = U_t)}{\sum_{k \in \mathcal{I}} p(I_{t'} = k, I_t = i, U_{t'} = U_t)}$$

Applying equivalent model estimations on observed data, we get:

$$\begin{aligned} p(I_t = i | U_t = u) &\propto \left(\sum_{v \in \mathcal{U}} r(v,i) \right) \sum_{\substack{j \in \mathcal{I} \\ j \neq i}} \frac{\sum_{v \in \mathcal{U}} r(v,i) r(v,j)}{\sum_{k \in \mathcal{I}} \sum_{v \in \mathcal{U}} r(v,i) r(v,k)} \cdot \frac{r(u,j)}{\sum_{v \in \mathcal{U}} r(v,j)} \\ &\propto C \sum_{\substack{j \in \mathcal{I} \\ j \neq i}} \frac{\sum_{v \in \mathcal{U}} r(v,i) r(v,j)}{\sum_{v \in \mathcal{U}} r(v,j)} r(u,j) \end{aligned}$$

with $C = \sum_{v \in \mathcal{U}} r(v,i) / \sum_{j \in \mathcal{I}} \sum_{v \in \mathcal{U}} r(v,i) r(v,j)$.

Comparing this to equations 2 plus 4, we see we have obtained a formulation that has analogies to the heuristic item-based kNN. One difference is that the $\sum_{v \in \mathcal{U}} r(v,i)$ term is missing in the denominator here, and what is more, it is present in the numerator through C. We see on the other hand that the denominator in C somewhat balances this (for instance if $\sum_{j \in \mathcal{I}} r(v,j)$ were constant on v, then C would be constant on i).

On the other hand, as in user-based, we may consider the normalized version by conditioning on the observation of some interaction between the target user u and the neighbors j, which results in a refinement of the normalizing constant: $C = \sum_{v \in \mathcal{U}} r(v,i) / \sum_{j \in \mathcal{I}: r(u,j) > 0} \sum_{v \in \mathcal{U}} r(v,i) r(v,j)$. And neighborhoods and smoothing can be analogously introduced.

4 POPULARITY BIASES

Aiming to analyze the generic trends within the kNN formulations, we examine what course these algorithms follow when users' tastes (respectively item trends in the item-based variants) are pairwise independent.

4.1 User-Based Bias

In the user-based variant, user independence means $p(U_{t'} = v | U_t = u, I_{t'} = I_t) \sim p(U_{t'} = v)$ for all v and u, whereby equation 5 becomes:

$$\begin{aligned} p(I_t = i | U_t = u) &\sim \sum_{v \in \mathcal{U}} p(I_{t'} = i | U_{t'} = v) p(U_{t'} = v) \\ &= p(I_{t'} = i) \sim \frac{\sum_{v \in \mathcal{U}} r(v,i)}{\sum_{w \in \mathcal{U}} \sum_{j \in \mathcal{I}} r(w,j)} \propto \sum_{v \in \mathcal{U}} r(v,i) \end{aligned} \quad (13)$$

Thus by this independence assumption the ranking function $p(I_t = i | U_t = u)$ is estimated as proportional to the number (or the sum) of ratings of i, that is, the item's popularity. We also see that under this assumption we are approximating $(I_t = i | U_t = u) \sim p(I_{t'} = i)$, i.e. the probability that a random user picks the item i, which is a natural understanding of the notion of item popularity.

This means that whereas user-based kNN takes an exact decomposition of $p(I_t = i | U_t = u)$ by the law of total probability, popularity (as per equation 5) represents an inexact approximation to $p(I_t = i | U_t = u)$ by an additional independence assumption. To the extent that in some case we actually had $p(U_{t'} | U_t, I_{t'} = I_t) \sim p(U_{t'})$, popularity would start becoming a fair estimate for $p(I_t = i | U_t = u)$. In other words, kNN degrades to popularity-based recommendation when user tastes are independent from each other. In the absence of any particular pairwise bias in $p(U_{t'} | U_t, I_{t'} = I_t)$, user-based kNN simply ranks items by the number of ratings they have (or their sum).

If on the contrary user tastes are not pairwise independent, we have $p(U_{t'}|U_t, I_{t'} = I_t) \neq p(U_{t'})$, and equation 13 becomes a worse and worse approximation of equation 5 as the conditional distribution diverges from the user prior. In such situations kNN, as a more exact development of $p(I_t = i|U_t = u)$, should perform better than popularity, as the formal inaccuracy in the probabilistic development can be expected to translate into corresponding errors in the predictions thereupon.

Formal imprecisions are however not the only source of prediction inaccuracies. Another fundamental one is the approximate estimation of distributions from observed data. To this respect, popularity only uses the estimate $p(I_{t'} = i) \propto \sum_{v \in \mathcal{U}} r(v,i)$ as per equation 8, whereas kNN introduces, in addition, the estimations $p(I_{t'} = i|U_t = v) \propto r(v,i)$ by equation 8 and $p(U_{t'} = v|U_t = u, I_{t'} = I_t) \propto \sum_{j \in \mathcal{I}} r(u,j) r(v,j)$ by equation 10. If the estimates applied in kNN happen to be less reliable than the ones in popularity, then the estimation inaccuracy could outdo the formal accuracy to the point that kNN may perform worse than popularity. This might happen, as we shall see, in data sparsity situations, to which kNN appears to be more vulnerable than popularity. This is to be expected, since the estimation of popularity is one-dimensional (involving a single random variable i), whereas the estimates of kNN are two-dimensional (involving two variables v and i, u and v, respectively), and therefore more vulnerable to sparsity.

In sum, the probabilistic formulation thus shows why there is some degree of structural relation between kNN and popularity, and identifies a key factor (user dependence) for kNN to be (more) effective (than popularity).

4.2 Normalized Variant Bias

The pairwise user independence in the normalized version would mean $p(U_{t'} = v|U_t = u, I_{t'} = I_t, r(v,i) > 0) \sim p(U_{t'} = v| r(v,i) > 0)$, which for this variant yields:

$$
\begin{aligned}
p(I_t = i|U_t = u) \\
&\sim \sum_{v \in \mathcal{U}} p(I_{t'} = i|U_{t'} = v, r(v,i) > 0) p(U_{t'} = v|r(v,i) > 0) \\
&= \sum_{v \in \mathcal{U}} p(I_{t'} = i, U_{t'} = v|r(v,i) > 0) \\
&\sim \sum_{v \in \mathcal{U}} r(v,i) \Big/ \sum_{\substack{v \in \mathcal{U} \\ r(v,i)>0}} \sum_{j \in \mathcal{I}} r(v,j)
\end{aligned}
$$

If $\sum_{j \in \mathcal{I}} r(v,j)$ are not too different for the set of raters v of each item i (i.e. each item has a similar mix of highly an moderately active users), then $\sum_{v \in \mathcal{U}: r(v,i)>0} \sum_{j \in \mathcal{I}} r(v,j)$ is approximately proportional to the number of users who interacted with i, and $p(I_t = i|U_t = u)$ is then similar to the average rating of item i.

We thus remarkably see that the normalized user-based kNN becomes not similar to the sum of rating values of the target item, but to its average rating. This hints a potentially fundamental difference in the behavior of the normalized and non-normalized variants which can show up when the distribution of the sum and the average of item ratings diverge.

4.3 Item-Based Bias

If we assume pairwise item independence, i.e. $p(I_t|I_{t'}, U_{t'} = U_t) \sim p(I_t)$ then equation 12 becomes:

$$
p(I_t = i|U_t = u) \sim \sum_{j \in \mathcal{I}} p(I_t = i) p(I_{t'} = j|U_{t'} = u) = p(I_t = i)
$$

That is, item-based kNN becomes ranking by popularity, thus showing a similar popularity bias as in the user-based variant: item-based kNN degrades to popularity when the divergence of the inter-item distribution from the item prior is weak.

It is easy to see that the normalized item-based variant is equally related to popularity, and not to the average rating as its normalized user-based counterpart. This is because $p(I_t = i|r(u,j) > 0) \sim p(I_t = i)$, while $p(I_{t'} = j|U_{t'} = u, r(u,j) > 0)$ simply adds to 1 over j.

5 EMPIRICAL OBSERVATION

In order to test and quantify empirically the trends and theoretical analysis derived in the previous sections, we run a series of experiments on publicly available data. For this purpose we use data from the movie and music domains provided in the MovieLens 1M,[1] Netflix,[2] and Last.fm 1K[3] datasets. We show in Table 1 the volumetric details of the three datasets.

MovieLens is perhaps the most widely used dataset in the recommender systems research literature. It includes ratings for movies in a 1-5 scale by users of the MovieLens application. The Netflix dataset contains data of similar nature collected from Netflix subscriptors, and was released in 2006 in the Netflix Prize contest. The Last.fm dataset was collected by O. Celma [5] and includes records of music tracks played by users on Last.fm. The recorded data for each play action includes the user ID, track, artist and timestamp. For our experiments we just aggregate this data into user / artist / playcount triplets.

5.1 General Performance

The first question we aim to check is whether the probabilistic kNN formulations are as effective as the traditional versions. For this purpose we implement the probabilistic user-based (PUB), normalized user-based (nPUB), and item-based variants (PIB, nPIB) developed along the previous sections. We take the implementations of the heuristic kNN algorithms, as described by equations 1-4, provided in the RankSys[4] public library, including user-

Table 1: Dataset characteristics.

	Nr. users	Nr. items	Nr. ratings
MovieLens 1M	6,040	3,706	1,000,209
Netflix	480,189	17,770	100,480,507
Last.fm	992	174,091	898,073

Table 2: Neighborhood size k in the kNN configuration on each dataset ($k = \infty$ indicates all items are taken as neighbors).

	HUB	PUB	HIB	PIB	nHUB	nPUB	nHIB	nPIB
MovieLens 1M	50	50	100	100	10	20	10	40
Netflix	100	100	100	50	10	10	10	100
Last.fm	100	500	∞	∞	10	10	10	∞

[1] http://grouplens.org/datasets/movielens/1m
[2] http://www.netflixprize.com
[3] http://www.dtic.upf.edu/~ocelma/MusicRecommendationDataset/lastfm-1K.html
[4] http://ranksys.org

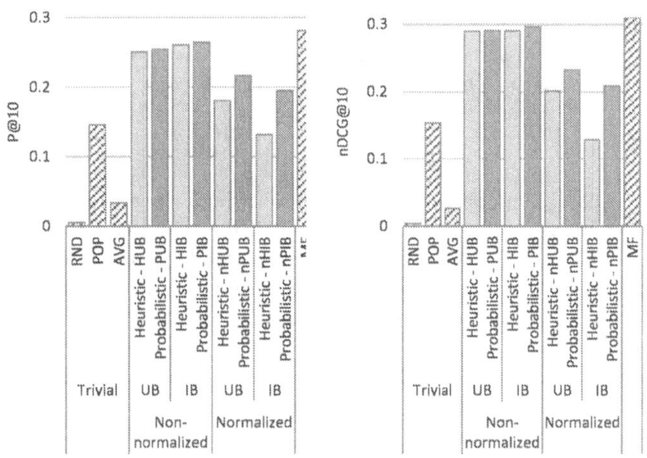

Figure 1: Comparative performance in the MovieLens 1M dataset. The metric value bars for heuristic and probabilistic versions of each variant are shown next to each other for ease of comparison. We use a darker color for the probabilistic versions, and a streaked color pattern for the algorithms other than kNN. The differences between the probabilistic and heuristic versions of non-normalized variants (PUB > HUB, PIB > HIB) are not statistically significant. All other pairwise comparisons are significant (**Student's two**-tailed t-test at $p < 0.001$).

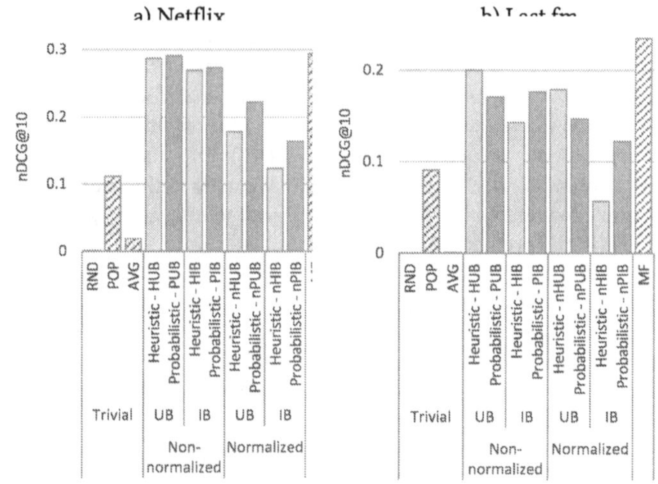

Figure 2: Comparative performance in the Netflix and Last.fm datasets. We use similar color codes as used in Fig. 1. All the pairwise comparisons are statistically significant (**Student's two**-tailed t-test at $p < 0.001$).

based (HUB), item-based (HIB), and normalized (nHUB, nHIB) variants as well. We shall show here the results with the overall most effective configuration of the heuristic variants, which uses the cosine similarity. We select the best neighborhood k for each kNN variant (in terms of P@10) by grid search starting with steps of 10 in the 10-100 interval, then steps of 100 in 100-1,000, and so forth. For all the normalized variants, we set a minimum number of 5 neighbor ratings for an item to be recommended to a target user. Table 2 shows the neighborhood size settings for each kNN variant on each dataset. We found Dirichlet smoothing [25] slightly improves the probabilistic algorithms on Netflix and MovieLens, with $\mu = 100$ on MovieLens and $\mu = 200$ on Netflix for PUB and nPUB; and $\mu = 200$ on MovieLens, $\mu = 20{,}000$ on Netflix for PIB and nPIB. We preprocess the rating values for all purposes by subtracting a relevance threshold (3 in MovieLens and Netflix, and 0 for Last.fm playcounts) and truncating the difference at zero.

As a frame of reference, we include trivial baseline recommendations: popularity-based (POP), average (AVG) and random (RND). In the datasets that consider rating values representing dislike (namely MovieLens and Netflix), we consider popularity defined as the sum of "positive" ratings (i.e. rating values above the relevance threshold), which provides a more effective and sensible recommendation than the total number of ratings (we obtain similar results with the number –instead of the sum– of positive ratings). For the average rating to work as a recommendation, one needs to smooth it, otherwise the top average values are taken up by items with very few ratings, which make for very poor recommendations. We have observed that a simple additive smoothing [25] is effective enough. Equivalently, in the results we report here, we simply require the items to have a minimum of 5 ratings to be recommended by average rating.

As a top-performing reference, we also include a matrix factorization approach (MF) proposed in [12] and implemented in RankSys, informally tuning the parameter values based on previously reported configurations [12,22] and our own experience with well-behaving values for this algorithm, finally taking $k = 20$ factors, $\alpha = 1$, and $\lambda = 0.1$, with 20 iterations on MovieLens and Last.fm, and 50 iterations on Netflix.

We test the effectiveness of the algorithms by splitting the rating data into training and test sets. Training ratings are given as input data for the recommendation algorithms, whereas positive ratings in the test set are taken as positive relevance judgments in the computation of the metrics. Test rating values indicating dislike (values below the relevance threshold) are taken as non-relevant judgments, and so are unrated items (as the equivalent of unjudged documents in IR tasks). In all three datasets we randomly sample 20% of the data for testing, and leave the remaining 80% for training.

Fig. 1 shows the results on the MovieLens dataset in terms of precision and nDCG. We can see that the probabilistic and heuristic non-normalized versions perform comparably well. PUB and PIB show slightly better results than their heuristic counterparts, but the differences are not statistically significant in this experiment. We also see that the normalized variants do not perform as well as the non-normalized ones. This goes along with the lower performance of average rating compared to popularity. Even though we are not aware of an explicit comparison and discussion on this point in the literature, we can assert that normalized kNN variants were devised for the rating value prediction task, to be evaluated with error metrics such as RMSE [10]. And this can account for their inferior performance at item ranking, a different task from the one they were originally designed for.

Matrix factorization shows to be the best system, confirming prior accounts that superior accuracy can be achieved by matrix factorization approaches [12]. But this is so by a rather small difference with respect to the best performing kNN algorithms. We also confirm the non-negligible effectiveness of recommendation by plain popularity reported in prior work [6], which in this experiment is as much as about half as effective as the best performing algorithm.

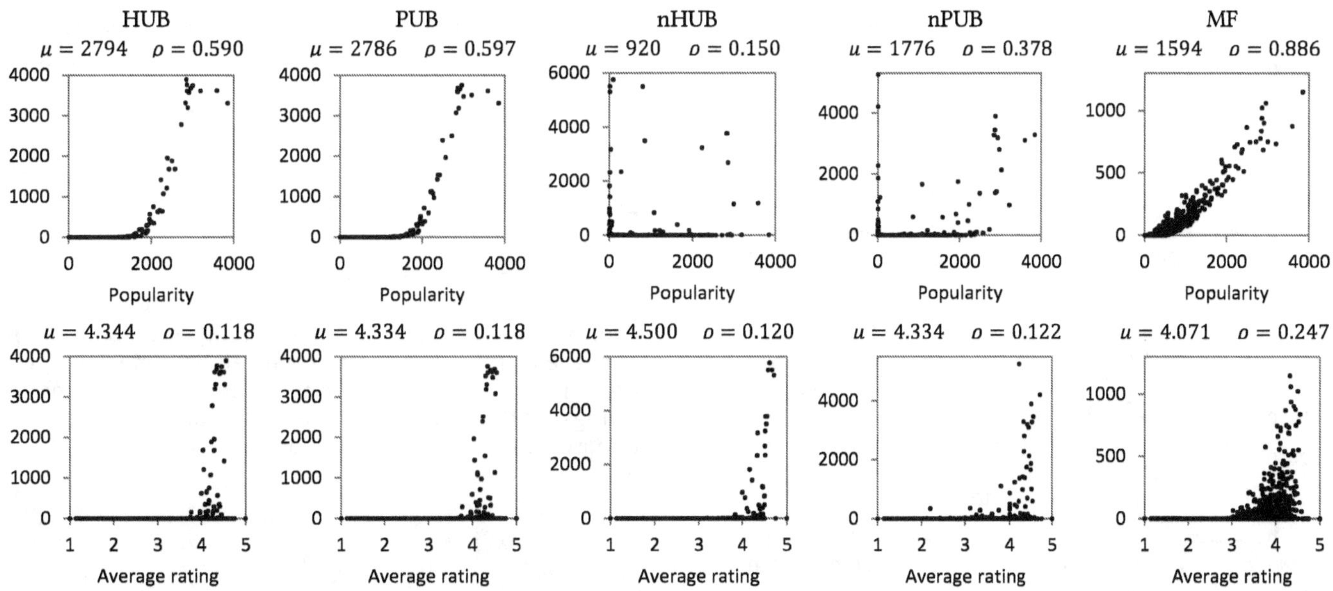

Figure 3: Popularity biases in recommendation algorithms on MovieLens 1M. Each point in the scatterplots corresponds to an item in the dataset; the x axis indicates its sum of positive ratings (top), and its average rating value (bottom); and the y axis indicates the number of users to whom the item is recommended in the top 10 by each algorithm. As further indication of the corresponding bias, on top of each plot we indicate a) as μ the global popularity –rounded to integers– (top) or rating value (bottom), averaged over the whole top 10 cutoff of each algorithm for all users, and b) the global Pearson correlation ρ between the x and y values. All kNN algorithms are shown here with $k = \infty$.

Complementing the MovieLens results, Fig. 2 shows similar trends on the two other datasets. For the sake of space we just show the nDCG results there (precision is very much in line with these). The comparison between the heuristic and probabilistic versions sometimes favors one and sometimes the other, by small differences, thus showing an overall equivalent empirical effectiveness. The generally better performance of the probabilistic version in the normalized variants on Netflix and MovieLens is partly achieved by the Dirichlet smoothing, though it brought no improvement on Last.fm. We lowered the minimum neighbor requirement to 2 for nHIB on Last.fm as it was suffering from too low coverage by the extremely long-tailed rating distribution over items. All in all, the normalized variants remain (with the exception of nHUB on Last.fm) systematically inferior to the non-normalized ones.

5.2 Popularity Biases

In order to check to what extent kNN looks alike or deviates from popularity, we visualize in Fig. 3 how much of each item popularity range is recommended in the top 10 of the ranking for each algorithm. The trends we show and discuss next are similar in the other two datasets. The details of the scatterplot display are described in the figure legend. To avoid the distorting effect of neighbor selection and show the biases more clearly, the plots are computed for the kNN algorithms taking all users (or items) as neighbors.

We see how HUB and PUB display a clear bias towards recommending popular items, confirming the trend formally analyzed in section 4. The bias may seem a trifle cleaner in the probabilistic version, as its structural connection to popularity is more direct. As context, the average popularity in the whole dataset is 261, and the global average rating is 3.581. The bias is clearly weaker in the normalized variants, which lean instead towards the average rating. We can see that the non-normalized variants also have a bias towards high average ratings, and even the normalized kNN have an, albeit weak, slight popularity bias. We can cast these as indirect biases, due to the correlation that actually exists in the dataset between the number of positive ratings and the average rating value. We show this in Fig. 7a, where we see that the average rating of the most popular items is very high. It has been hypothesized that this can be attributed to the propensity of people to rate items they like rather than ones they do not [4,19,20].

It is also interesting to see that the MF algorithm has a clear bias towards popular and highly rated items. This may hint that to some extent our analysis and findings on kNN could be generalized to other collaborative filtering approaches.

Finally, Fig. 4 confirms our theoretical findings regarding the popularity bias in item-based kNN, which in the non-normalized version is as strong as in the user-based counterpart. We also find a striking structural difference between the formal normalized item-based kNN and its heuristic counterpart. We confirm that – contrarily to the normalized user-based algorithm– the probabilistic item-based algorithms are indeed biased to popularity quite as much with or without normalization, while the normalization in nHIB completely does away with the popularity trend. This may also account for the somewhat worse performance of the heuristic normalized item-based variant we see in Fig. 1 and 2. The poor results of nHIB illustrate a weakness of heuristic compared to more principled approaches. Heuristics rely more heavily on trial, error and chance, and their success is hence harder to ensure beforehand.

5.3 A Second Look at Biases

Awareness of popularity biases in the data consumed by recommender systems and their evaluation has risen in the field in recent years. Researchers and practitioners have noticed the biases and are posing questions about it [3,4,8,13,19,20].

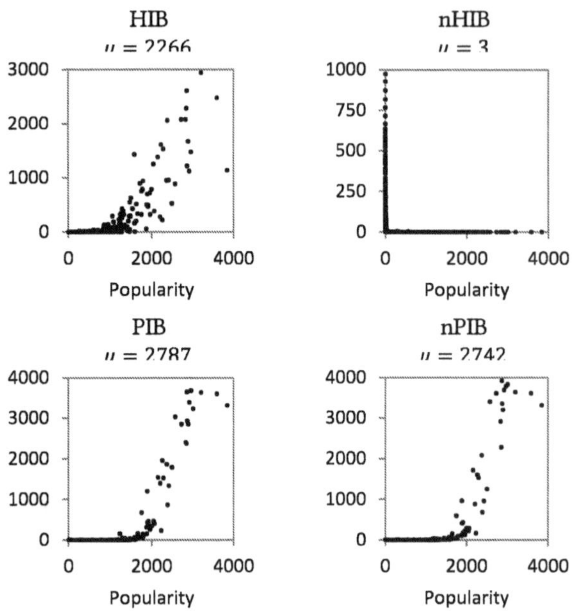

Figure 4: Popularity bias in item-based kNN on MovieLens 1M. The $\boldsymbol{x}$ and $\boldsymbol{y}$ axes and the $\boldsymbol{\mu}$ average have the same meaning as in Fig. 3.

We may say nonetheless that the effects of the popularity biases on offline experiments have not been thoroughly researched and understood yet. It is therefore legitimate to wonder whether a biased evaluation might be suffering from some sort of distortion on the comparison of biased algorithms. The factors that can be identified to generate popularity biases include discovery distributions (bias in the means by which items reach users –or viceversa), bias towards rating liked items (user behavior bias), and ultimately the actual user tastes (user preference bias), [4,19]. As a step in the direction of shedding light on this question, we set up to carry out an experiment with data missing at random where we remove the first two (artificial) sources of biases, isolating the true preference distribution as the only bias in the data.

For this purpose, we randomly sampled music tracks from a large database, Deezer,[5] containing over 30 million songs at the time of this experiment. Using this list of songs, we set up a survey on CrowdFlower[6] where we asked a number of users to rate 100 songs each, sampled uniformly at random from our set in such a way that each music track got around 100 ratings. The resulting dataset[7] includes 103,584 ratings by 1,054 users on 1,084 tracks.

A unique property of this dataset compared to all others available today is the absence of biases in the exposition of users to items. The discovery of items and the decision to rate them is forced rather than free. Even though the total number of ratings of each item is generated from a uniform distribution, the number of positive ratings is not uniform, as we show in Fig. 5, where we also see the rather flat distribution of the total number of ratings, in contrast to MovieLens (which is representative of the typical highly skewed distribution of the number of ratings over items in common datasets). In this dataset the kNN variants work best taking all neighbors (i.e. $k = \infty$) except $k = 200$ for nHIB. We use no

[5] https://www.deezer.com

[6] https://www.crowdflower.com

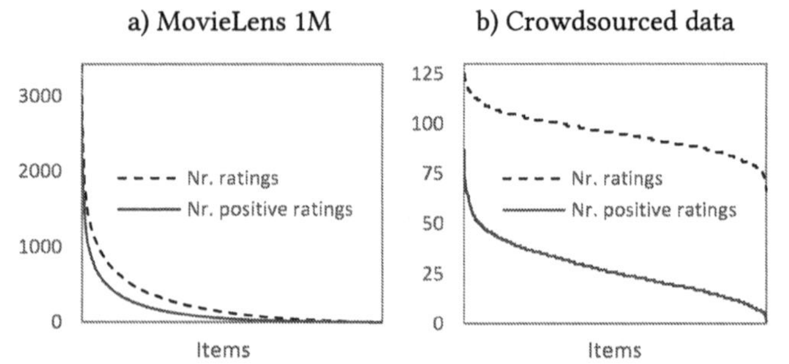

Figure 5: Total and positive rating distributions in MovieLens (left) vs. our crowdsourced dataset (right). The items in the $\boldsymbol{x}$ axis are ordered by decreasing number of ratings for the blue dashed line, and by decreasing number of positive ratings for the red continuous line.

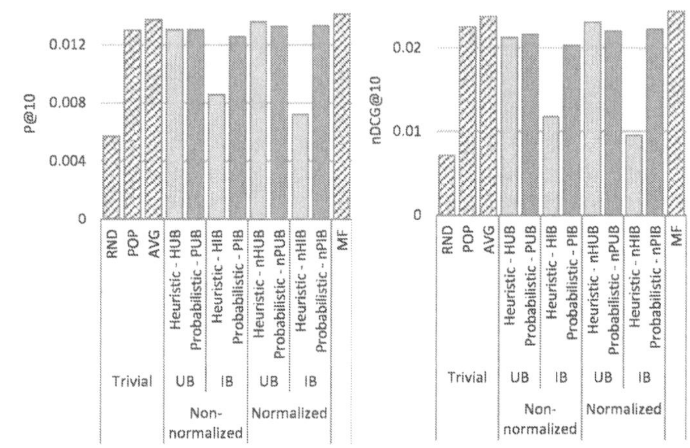

Figure 6: Comparative performance on the crowdsourced dataset. All pairwise comparisons between any two item-based variants are statistically significant (**Student's two-**tailed t-test at $\boldsymbol{p < 0.001}$), whereas they are not significant among user-based variants (except for nHUB > nPUB in nDCG@10).

Dirichlet smoothing and require no minimum number of neighbors in the normalized version, as we found these adjustments do not perceptibly improve the results on this dataset. We configure MF with $k = 5$, $\alpha = 10$, $\lambda = 500$, 20 iterations. To smooth the variance due to the smaller size of this dataset we average the metrics over 10 repetitions of the experiment (namely, of the random rating split, with 5-fold cross-validations each).

Fig. 6 shows the results. We see that the difference between all algorithms gets considerably reduced, including the random recommendation which performs at about 1/3 as well as the best recommender. This can be explained by the absence of bias in the total number of ratings over items. Yet the bias in the number of positive ratings (albeit less pronounced than in typical datasets) enables a better than random performance by popularity recommendation.

We also see that in these conditions popularity becomes a difficult baseline to overcome. We believe this may be due to the low "local" density of positive ratings. The total rating density of about 10% is higher than it is in all the other datasets we have reported results for (4.5% in MovieLens, 1.2% in Netflix, 0.5% in Last.fm), but

[7] The dataset is publicly available at http://ir.ii.uam.es/cm100k.

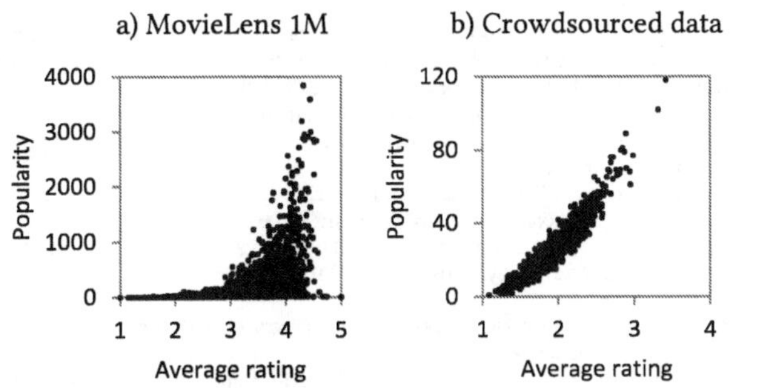

Figure 7: Average rating vs. popularity in MovieLens 1M (left), and the crowdsourced data (right). Each point in the scatterplot represents an item in dataset, the x axis is the average rating of the item, and the y value is the sum of positive rating values (popularity) of the item.

it is lower both in terms of positive preferences per user (~28 on average vs. e.g. ~95 in MovieLens) and per item (~27 vs. ~155 in MovieLens), and the resulting low pairwise overlapping between users and between items, further intensified by the uniform rating distribution. Still, we see several interesting phenomena. First, recommendation based on the average rating catches up in performance with the popularity-based recommendation. This makes sense, since in a uniform rating distribution, the number of positive ratings strongly correlates with the average rating value, as we see in Figure 7b. Yet it is quite a salient finding that in the absence of a bias in the number of ratings, the average rating is as effective as popularity, or more, in achieving decent recommendations.

On the other hand, following this trend, and quite remarkably, the normalized kNN variants, which we showed to go theoretically along with the average rating, now match or even slightly outperform their non-normalized counterparts. Fig. 8 further explains the good performance of the normalized algorithms: the normalized user-based versions retain a stronger popularity bias than they do on the biased datasets in section 5.2. In the absence of an item selection bias in the input data, popularity and average rating become almost equivalent signals, as we can see in Fig. 7b, and the normalized versions seem to more fully capture the remaining item popularity distribution as a meaningful and effective signal. We omit the plots for the item-based versions, but the pattern is similar to what we observed in MovieLens: the probabilistic variant retains its popularity bias in the normalized version, not so in the heuristic variant.

This qualitative disagreement in the comparative effectiveness of normalized vs. non-normalized variants with respect to the results we previously obtained in section 5.2 strike us as a hint that we should revise the observed results in offline experiments with the common biased datasets. The contrast in observations raises the question whether the low results of normalized kNN in common datasets is due to a truly poor performance, or to the bias in observations. The only definitive way to know for sure would be to obtain the missing relevance information in those datasets.

6 RELATED WORK

Many collaborative filtering methods have been proposed that build on a probabilistic basis [9,11] –and even on probabilistic IR models [21,23,24]–, but to the best of our knowledge none has

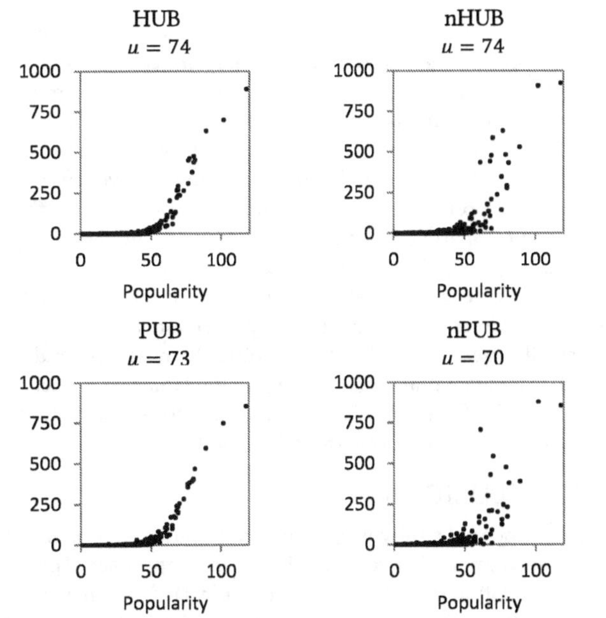

Figure 8: Popularity bias in user-based kNN on the crowdsourced dataset. The x and y axes and the μ average have the same meaning as in Fig. 3 and 4. As context, the global average popularity in this dataset is 26.

been proposed that explains or results in the structure of a kNN scheme through a fully probabilistic development.

Notably for our purpose nonetheless, Deshpande and Karypis [7] explored the use of conditional probabilities between users and items in the role of the similarity function in kNN, but this was otherwise an isolated probabilistic piece in a heuristic scheme for the rest of the formulation. Later on Aiolli [2] also tested conditional probability in place of cosine in a heuristic scheme, and hinted at the structural connection between the cosine similarity and conditional probabilities. More recently in this line, Valcarce et al. [21] apply more sophisticated probabilistic IR models to rank and select neighbors, but then follow on into a cosine-based ranking function similar to equations 1-4. Random walk models [9] and Markov chains have also been used to build solutions upon probabilistic inspiration, though they have been generally developed into a mix of formal and heuristic aspects (e.g. by a heuristic computation of the transition probabilities).

The concentration and popularity bias of collaborative filtering is a well-known issue that several researchers have pointed at and addressed in the field. To name a few, Fleder and Hosanagar [8] research the recursive dimension of the concentration biases of recommendations in their feedback loop. Cremonesi et al. [6] were to the best of our knowledge the first to report and discuss on the decent performance achieved by plain popularity-based recommendation. They proposed a simple trick to avoid it, consisting in excluding most popular items from the evaluation. Realizing the popularity biases that are commonly present in rating data streams, Steck [19,20] suggests biases are likely to lurk in the evaluation results drawn upon such conditions, and proposes new metrics aiming to cope with the biases, as well as modifications in collaborative filtering methods in the same direction. Bellogín et al. [3] similarly analyze the strong popularity biases that surface in IR evaluation methodologies when applied to recommendation. In prior work [4] we also addressed the question whether popularity reflects or contradicts the true distribution of user preference, and aimed to identify key factors that may determine the answer. Also recently, Jannach et al. [13] present a thorough study of concentration biases with respect to both the number of ratings and the average rating values. The reported study has a primary empirical orientation, testing and comparing different algorithms and configuration details, and proposing some bias-mitigating ideas.

Our work very much shares the concerns of such studies, which we address in a complementary direction: that of seeking theoretical explanations for the empirically observed and described phenomena, aiming to glimpse fundamental causes beneath them. We focus for this purpose on a narrower, specific recommender system approach, the kNN scheme.

7 CONCLUSIONS

We have proposed a fully probabilistic yet intuitive formalization for the nearest-neighbor collaborative filtering approach. The proposed formulation shows equivalent empirical effectiveness to the traditional heuristic formulations, and thus can serve to analyze properties of the kNN scheme on a more principled ground.

The probabilistic basis provides an explanation of the effectiveness of kNN at the same time that it relates the algorithm to popularity distributions, thus helping understand this well-known bias. The effectiveness of kNN relies on the pairwise statistical dependence between user behaviors, and can be expected to be most effective to the extent that the pairwise conditional distributions deviate from the prior collective behavior. Conversely, the more a user's tastes are as similar to any user as they are to the next, the more kNN behaves like a plain majority-based recommendation.

We further show that the theoretical characterizations align the algorithm variants along two fundamentally different trends: popularity and average rating. We report experiments showing that the comparison between algorithm variants (and normalized vs. non-normalized in particular) can change depending on statistical properties of the input data and the biases in the implicit or explicit item sampling in the data.

Our results suggest that further research would be needed to determine to what extent popularity biases are a helpful signal to produce effective recommendations, or a confounder that may distort offline results. Even a simple question as which of popularity and the average rating is a better signal would deserve further analysis at both the empirical and formal levels –further conclusions might be drawn on the corresponding kNN variants they are a trend within. The formal analysis of kNN we present here aims to be a step in this direction. Further research in this line might perhaps lead towards more generalized findings that are not exclusive of kNN but may be shared by collaborative filtering approaches.

ACKNOWLEDGMENTS

This work was supported by the national Spanish Government (grant nr. TIN2016-80630-P).

REFERENCES

[1] G. Adomavicius and A. Tuzhilin. 2005. Toward the next generation of recommender systems: A survey of the state-of-the-art and possible extensions. IEEE Transactions on Knowledge and Data Engineering 17, 6 (June 2005), 734–749.

[2] F. Aiolli. 2013. Efficient top-n recommendation for very large scale binary rated datasets. In Proceedings of the 7th ACM Conference on Recommender Systems (RecSys 2013). ACM, New York, NY, USA, 273–280.

[3] A. Bellogín, P. Castells, and I. Cantador. Statistical Biases in Information Retrieval Metrics for Recommender Systems. Information Retrieval. Springer, Netherlands, in press.

[4] R. Cañamares and P. Castells. 2014. Exploring social network effects on popularity biases in recommender systems. In Proceedings of the 6th Workshop on Recommender Systems and the Social Web (RSWeb 2014) at the 8th ACM Conference on Recommender Systems (RecSys 2014). Foster City, CA, USA, October 2014.

[5] O. Celma. 2010. Music Recommendation and Discovery in the Long Tail. Springer-Verlag Berlin Heidelberg.

[6] P. Cremonesi, Y. Koren, R. Turrin. 2010. Performance of recommender algorithms on top-n recommendation tasks. In Proedings of the 4th ACM Conference on Recommender Systems (RecSys 2010). ACM, New York, NY, USA, 39–46.

[7] M. Deshpande and G. Karypis. 2004. Item-based top-N recommendation algorithms. ACM Transactions on Information Systems 22, 1 (Jan 2004). ACM, New York, NY, USA, 143- 177.

[8] D. Fleder and K. Hosanagar. 2009. Blockbuster culture's next rise or fall: The impact of recommender systems on sales diversity. Management Science 55, 5 (May 2009). Informs, Catonsville, MD, USA, 697–712.

[9] F. Fouss, A. Pirotte, J-M. Renders, and M. Saerens. 2007. Random-Walk Computation of Similarities between Nodes of a Graph with Application to Collaborative Recommendation. IEEE Transactions on Knowledge and Data Engineering 19, 3 (March 2007). IEEE, Piscataway, NJ, USA, 355–369.

[10] J. L. Herlocker, J. A. Konstan, L. G. Terveen, and J. T. Riedl. 2004. Evaluating Collaborative Filtering .Recommender Systems. ACM Transactions on Information Systems 22, 1 (Jan. 2004). ACM, New York, NY, USA, 5–53.

[11] T. Hofmann. 2003. Collaborative filtering via Gaussian probabilistic latent semantic analysis. In Proceedings of the 26th Annual International ACM SIGIR Conference on Research and Development in Information Retrieval (SIGIR 2003). ACM, New York, NY, USA, 259–266.

[12] Y. Hu, Y. Koren, and C. Volinsky. 2008. Collaborative Filtering for Implicit Feedback Datasets. In Proceedings of the 8th IEEE International Conference on Data Mining (ICDM 2008). IEEE Computer Society, Washington, DC, USA, 15–19.

[13] D. Jannach, L. Lerche, I. Kamehkhosh, and M. Jugovac. 2015. What recommenders recommend: an analysis of recommendation biases and possible countermeasures. User Modeling and User-Adapted Interaction 25, 5 (Dec. 2015). Kluwer Academic Publishers Hingham, MA, USA, 427–491.

[14] Y. Koren. 2010. Factor in the neighbors: Scalable and accurate collaborative filtering. ACM Transactions on Knowledge Discovery from Data 4, 1 (Jan 2010), ACM, New York, NY, USA.

[15] G. Linden, B. Smith, and J. York. 2003. Amazon.com Recommendations: Item-to-Item Collaborative Filtering. IEEE Internet Computing 7, 1 (Jan. 2003). IEEE, Piscataway, NJ, USA, 76–80.

[16] X. Ning, C. Desrosiers, and G. Karypis. 2015. A Comprehensive Survey of Neighborhood-Based Recommendation Methods. In: Recommender Systems Handbook, 2nd ed., F. Ricci, L. Rokach, and B. Shapira (Eds.). Springer, New York, NY, USA, Chapter 2, 37–76.

[17] P. Resnick, N. Iacovou, M. Suchak, P. Bergstrom, and J. T. Riedl. 1994. Grouplens: An open architecture for collaborative filtering of netnews. In Proceedings of the ACM Conference on Computer Supported Cooperative Work (CSCW 1994). ACM, New York, NY, USA, 175–186.

[18] F. Ricci, L. Rokach, and B. Shapira (Eds.). 2015. Recommender Systems: Introduction and Challenges. In: Recommender Systems Handbook, 2nd ed., F. Ricci, L. Rokach, and B. Shapira (Eds.). Springer, New York, NY, USA, Chapter 2, 1–34.

[19] H. Steck. 2010. Training and testing of recommender systems on data missing not at random. In Proceedings of the 16th ACM SIGKDD International Conference on Knowledge Discovery and Data Mining (KDD 2010). ACM, New York, NY, USA, 713–722.

[20] H. Steck. 2011. Item popularity and recommendation accuracy. In Proceedings of the 5th ACM Conference on Recommender Systems (RecSys 2011). ACM, New York, NY, USA, 125–132.

[21] D. Valcarce, J. Parapar, and A. Barreiro. 2006. Language Models for Collaborative Filtering Neighbourhoods. In Proceedings of the 38th European Conference on Information Retrieval (ECIR 2016). LNCS Vol. 9626. Springer, Switzerland, 614–625.

[22] S. Vargas and P. Castells. 2014. Improving sales diversity by recommending users to items. In Proceedings of the 8th ACM Conference on Recommender Systems (RecSys 2014). ACM, New York, NY, USA, 145–152.

[23] J. Wang, S. Robertson, A. P. de Vries, and M. J. T. Reinders.2008. Probabilistic relevance ranking for collaborative filtering. Information Retrieval 11, 6 (Dec. 2008). Springer, Netherlands, 477–497.

[24] J. Wang, A. P. de Vries, M. J. T. Reinders. 2008. Unified relevance models for rating prediction in collaborative filtering. ACM Transactions on Information Systems 26, 3 (June 2008). ACM New York, NY, USA.

[25] C. Zhai and, J. D. Lafferty. 2004. A study of smoothing methods for language models applied to information retrieval. ACM Transactions on Information Systems 22, 2 (April 2004). ACM, New York, NY, USA, 179–14.

Deep Semantic Hashing with Generative Adversarial Networks*

Zhaofan Qiu
University of Science and Technology of China
Hefei, China
zhaofanqiu@gmail.com

Yingwei Pan
University of Science and Technology of China
Hefei, China
panyw.ustc@gmail.com

Ting Yao
Microsoft Research Asia
Beijing, China
tiyao@microsoft.com

Tao Mei
Microsoft Research Asia
Beijing, China
tmei@microsoft.com

ABSTRACT

Hashing has been a widely-adopted technique for nearest neighbor search in large-scale image retrieval tasks. Recent research has shown that leveraging supervised information can lead to high quality hashing. However, the cost of annotating data is often an obstacle when applying supervised hashing to a new domain. Moreover, the results can suffer from the robustness problem as the data at training and test stage may come from different distributions. This paper studies the exploration of generating synthetic data through semi-supervised generative adversarial networks (GANs), which leverages largely unlabeled and limited labeled training data to produce highly compelling data with intrinsic invariance and global coherence, for better understanding statistical structures of natural data. We demonstrate that the above two limitations can be well mitigated by applying the synthetic data for hashing. Specifically, a novel deep semantic hashing with GANs (DSH-GANs) is presented, which mainly consists of four components: a deep convolution neural networks (CNN) for learning image representations, an adversary stream to distinguish synthetic images from real ones, a hash stream for encoding image representations to hash codes and a classification stream. The whole architecture is trained end-to-end by jointly optimizing three losses, i.e., adversarial loss to correct label of synthetic or real for each sample, triplet ranking loss to preserve the relative similarity ordering in the input real-synthetic triplets and classification loss to classify each sample accurately. Extensive experiments conducted on both CIFAR-10 and NUS-WIDE image benchmarks validate the capability of exploiting synthetic images for hashing. Our framework also achieves superior results when compared to state-of-the-art deep hash models.

CCS CONCEPTS

• **Information systems** → **Similarity measures**; **Learning to rank**;

KEYWORDS

Hashing; Similarity Learning; GANs; CNN

*This work was performed at Microsoft Research Asia. The first two authors made equal contributions to the work.

SIGIR '17, August 07-11, 2017, Shinjuku, Tokyo, Japan

ACM ISBN 978-1-4503-5022-8/17/08... $15.00
https://doi.org/10.1145/3077136.3080842

1 INTRODUCTION

Accelerated by tremendous increase in Internet bandwidth and storage space, multimedia data have been generated, published and spread explosively. This has led to the surge of research activities in large scale visual search. One fundamental research problem is similarity search, i.e., nearest neighbor search, which attempts to identify similar instances according to a query example. The need to search for millions of visual examples in a high-dimensional feature space, however, makes the task computationally expensive and thus very challenging.

Hashing techniques, one direction of the most well-known Approximate Nearest Neighbor (ANN) search methods, have been studied extensively due to its great efficiency in gigantic data. The basic idea of hashing is to construct a series of hash functions to map each example into compact binary codes, making the Hamming distances on similar examples minimized and simultaneously maximized on dissimilar examples. In the literature, there have been several techniques, including traditional hashing models based on hand-crafted features [3, 4, 14, 25] and deep models [11, 13], being proposed for addressing the problem of hashing. The former seek hashing function on hand-crafted features, which separate the encoding of feature representations and their quantization to hash codes, resulting in sub-optimal solution. The latter jointly learn feature representations and projections from them to hash codes in a deep architecture. While encouraging performances are reported in the aforementioned approaches especially when supervised information is available, we are often facing the problems of applying these methods to new applications where there is only few labeled training data, not to mention that the distribution of training data may be even different with that in test stage.

We demonstrate in this paper that the above limitations can be mitigated by generating synthetic data for training through Generative Adversarial Networks (GANs). GANs is a new recently proposed framework for estimating generative models via an adversarial process. The spirit behind is a minimax two-player game, in which a generative model is to capture the data distribution and a discriminative model aims to estimate the probability that a sample is from the real training data rather than the generative model. The generative model and discriminative model are trained simultaneously and the learning of the generative model is to fool the discriminative model into making mistakes. Once the training is complete, GANs is capable of generating both diverse and discriminable training examples, which have a great potential to characterize the statistical structures of natural data.

By consolidating the idea of generating training data for boosting hashing, we present a novel Deep Semantic Hashing with GANs (DSH-GANs) architecture, as shown in Figure 1. Specifically, a semi-supervised GANs is first pre-trained on both labeled and unlabeled training data to produce synthetic examples conditioning on class labels. Then, we form a set of real-synthetic triplets and each tuple contains one real image as query image, one synthetic and semantically similar image and another synthetic but dissimilar image. A shared CNN is exploited to capture image representations, followed by importing into an adversary stream for differentiating the synthetic images from real ones, a hash stream to encode hash codes and a classification stream for measuring semantics. An adversarial loss is computed to correct the predicted labels (i.e., synthetic or real) of the images in adversary stream and a triplet ranking loss is devised to preserve relative similarities at the top of hash stream. Meanwhile, a classification error is formulated in classification stream. By jointly learning the three streams, our DSH-GANs is expected to offer a hashing model with high generalization ability and the generated hash codes could better reflect semantic relations between images. It is also worth noting that the whole architecture is trainable in an end-to-end fashion.

In summary, this paper makes the following contributions:

(1) We explore the problem of supervised hashing by exploiting the synthetic training data from GANs. To the best of our knowledge, this paper represents the first effort towards this target in the information retrieval research community.

(2) A novel hashing architecture, which combines adversary process, hash coding and classification, is proposed to enhance the generalization ability of hashing model and produce hash codes, which preserve not only relative similarity between images but also semantics of images.

(3) Extensive experiments on two widely used datasets demonstrate the advantages of our proposal over several state-of-the-art hashing techniques.

2 RELATED WORK

We briefly group the related works into two directions: hashing for image search and image synthesis with Generative Adversarial Networks (GANs). The former draws upon research in encoding visual images into compact binary codes for efficient image search, while the latter investigates synthesizing realistic images by utilizing GANs.

Hashing for Image Search. The research in this direction has proceeded along two dimensions: hand-crafted features based hashing and deep architectures for hashing.

There are three main categories on hand-crafted features based hashing: unsupervised hashing, semi-supervised hashing and supervised hashing. Unsupervised hashing [3, 4] refers to the setting when the label information is not available. Locality Sensitive Hashing (LSH) [3] is one of the most popular unsupervised hashing methods, which simply uses random linear projections to construct hash functions. This method is subsequently expanded to Kernelized and Multi-Kernel Locality Sensitive Hashing [10, 27]. Another effective method named Iterative Quantization (ITQ) [4] is proposed for better quantization rather than random projections. Semi-supervised hashing approaches attempt to improve the quality of hash codes by leveraging supervised information into learning procedure. For example, Wang *et al.* develop a Semi-Supervised Hashing (SSH) [25] which utilizes pairwise information on labeled samples to preserve semantic similarity. In another work [8], Semi-Supervised Discriminant Hashing (SSDH) learns hash codes based on Fisher's discriminant analysis to maximize separability between labeled data from different classes while the unlabeled data are exploited for regularization. When the label information is all available, we refer to the problem as supervised hashing. The representative in this category is Kernel-based Supervised Hashing (KSH) [14] which utilizes pairwise relationship between examples to achieve high quality hashing.

Inspired by recent advances in visual representation learning [9, 17, 19] by using deep convolutional neural networks, several deep architecture based hashing methods have been proposed. Semantic Hashing [23] is one of the early works to exploit deep learning techniques for hashing. It applies the stacked Restricted Boltzman Machine (RBM) [6] to learn binary hash codes for visual search. Recently, Xia *et al.* propose Convolutional Neural Networks Hashing (CNNH) [28] to decompose the hash learning process into a stage of learning approximate hash codes with the pairwise relationship and a following stage of simultaneously learning image feature and hash function. Later in [12], such a two-stage method with pairwise labels is further developed into an end-to-end system, Deep Pairwise-Supervised Hashing (DPSH), which performs simultaneous feature learning and hash encoding. Similar in spirit, Network In Network Hashing (NINH) [11] incorporates the supervised information among triplet labels into the feature learning based deep hashing architecture. More recently, Zhu *et al.* devise Deep Hashing Network (DHN) to simultaneously optimize the pairwise cross-entropy loss on

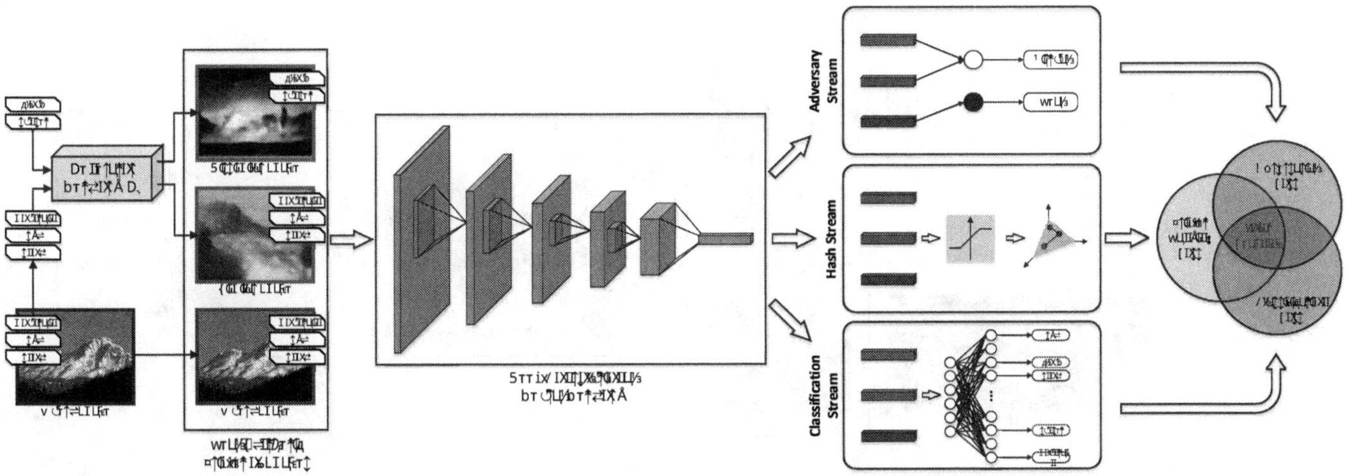

Figure 1: Deep Semantic Hashing with GANs (DSH-GANs) framework (better viewed in color). The input to DSH-GANs architecture is in the form of real-synthetic image triplets and each tuple consists of one real image as query image, one synthetic and similar image produced with same labels of query image through generator network G, and another synthetic but dissimilar image synthesized by G conditioning on different labels. A shared deep convolutional neural networks is exploited for learning image representations, followed by three streams, i.e., hash stream, adversary stream and classification stream. Hash stream is to encode each image into hash codes with relative similarity preservation measured by a triplet ranking loss. Adversary stream is to distinguish synthetic images from real ones trained with an adversarial loss. Classification stream is to characterize the semantic structures on image and softmax loss or cross entropy loss is computed for single label and multi-label classification, respectively. The whole architecture is jointly optimized in an end-to-end fashion.

semantically similar pairs and the pairwise quantization loss on compact hash codes for hashing in [30].

In summary, our work belongs to deep architecture based hashing. The aforementioned deep approaches often focus on leveraging supervised information for training CNNs. Our work in this paper contributes by not only exploring image semantic supervision for hash learning, but also preserving relative similarity between real and synthetic images which are generated through a semi-supervised GANs with intrinsic invariance and global coherence.

Image Synthesis with GANs. Synthesizing realistic images has been studied and analyzed widely in AI systems for characterizing the pixel level structure of natural images. Thanks to the recent development of Generative Adversarial Networks (GANs), researchers have strived to automatically synthesize image with GANs, which could be regarded as the generator network modules learnt with a two-player minimax game mechanism. Goodfellow *et al.* propose a theoretical framework of GANs and utilize GANs to generate images without any supervised information in [5]. Although the early GANs offer a distinct and promising direction for image synthesis, the results are somewhat noisy and blurry. Hence, Laplacian pyramid is further incorporated into GANs in [2] to produce high quality images. Later in [20], Radford *et al.* devise deep convolutional generative adversarial networks (DCGANs) for unsupervised representation learning.

The aforementioned three works mainly explore image synthesis task in an unconditioned manner that generates synthetic images without any supervised information. Another direction of image synthesis with GANs is to synthesize images by conditioning on supervised information (e.g., class labels or text descriptions). [15] is one of the works that develop a conditional version of GANs by additionally feeding class labels into both discriminator and generator of GANs. Later in [16], this model is further expended with a specialized cost function for classification, named auxiliary classifier GANs (AC-GANs), for generating synthetic images with global coherence and high diversity. Recently, Reed *et al.* utilize GANs for image synthesis based on given text descriptions in [21], enabling translation from character level to pixel level.

Most of the above approaches focus on leveraging GANs for image synthesis. Our work is different that we apply the synthetic images generated from GANs learnt on both largely unlabeled and limited labeled images for hash learning, leading to more effective and robust binary image representation for image retrieval task.

3 DEEP SEMANTIC HASHING WITH GANS (DSH-GANS)

In this section, we will present the proposed Deep Semantic Hashing with GANs (DSH-GANs) in detail. Figure 1 illustrates an overview of our architecture for hash learning, which consists of four components: a shared CNN for learning image representations, an adversary stream for distinguishing synthetic images from real ones, a hash stream for encoding each

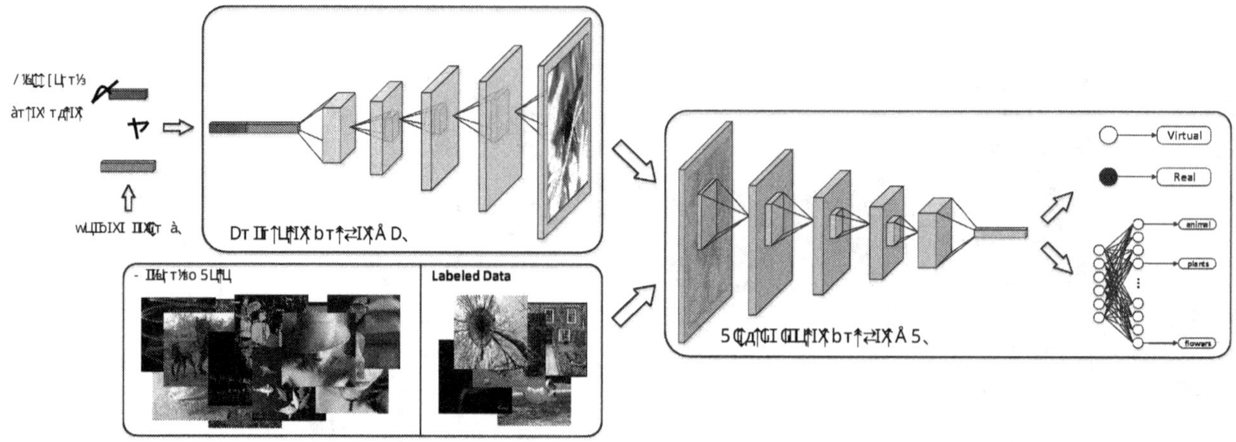

Figure 2: Our semi-supervised GANs framework mainly consists of a generator network G and a discriminator network D (better viewed in color). For the generator network G, it tries to synthesize realistic images with the concatenation input of the class label vector $\mathbf{C}$ and random noise vector $\mathbf{z}$. For the discriminator network D, it tries to simultaneously distinguish real images from synthetic ones and classify input images with correct class labels. The whole architecture is trained with the adversarial loss for assigning correct source and the classification loss for assigning correct class label in a two-player minimax game mechanism.

image into hash codes and a classification stream for leveraging semantic supervision. Specifically, a semi-supervised GANs is first devised to leverage both unlabeled and labeled images for producing synthetic images conditioning on class labels, followed by the three streams in our proposed DSH-GANs framework. In particular, hash stream is trained with the input real-synthetic triplets in a triplet-wise manner, adversary stream recognizes the label of synthetic or real for each image example while classification stream reinforces the hash learning to preserve semantic structures on both real and synthetic images. Finally, the whole optimization of DSH-GANs and hash codes generation for image retrieval are elaborated.

3.1 Notation

Suppose there are n images in the whole set, represented as: $\mathcal{X} = \{x_i | i = 1, \cdots, n\}$ and each image can be presented as x. Similarly, assume there are L ($L < n$) labeled images and the set of the labeled images are denoted as $\mathcal{X}_l = \{x_j | j = 1, \cdots, L\}$. The goal of image hashing is to learn a mapping $\mathcal{H} : x \to \{0, 1\}^K$, such that an input image x will be encoded into a K-bit binary code $\mathcal{H}(x)$.

3.2 Semi-supervised GANs

An unconditional generative adversarial networks (GANs) consists of two networks: a generator network G that captures the data distribution for synthesizing image and a discriminator network D that distinguishes real images from synthetic ones. In particular, the generator network G takes a random noise vector $\mathbf{z}$ as input and produces a synthetic image $x_{syn} = G(\mathbf{z})$. For the discriminator network D, it takes an image x as input stochastically chosen (with equal probability) from training real images or synthetic images through G and produces a probability distribution $P(S|x) = D(x)$ over the two image sources. As proposed in [5], the whole GANs can be trained in a two-player minimax game. Concretely, given an image sample x, the discriminator network D is trained to minimize the adversarial loss, i.e., maximizing the log-likelihood of assigning correct source to this sample:

$$l_a(x) = \begin{cases} -\log P(S = real|x), x \in \mathcal{X} \\ -\log P(S = synthetic|x), x \in \mathcal{X}_{syn} \end{cases}, \quad (1)$$

where $\mathcal{X}$ and $\mathcal{X}_{syn}$ denote the collections of real images in training and synthetic images produced by G, respectively. Meanwhile, the generator network G is trained to maximize the adversarial loss in Eq.(1), targeting for maximally fooling the discriminator network D with its generated synthetic images $\mathcal{X}_{syn}$.

To characterize the pixel level structure of both unlabeled and labeled natural images in one architecture elegantly, we take the inspiration from conditional GANs [15, 16] purely trained with supervised samples and devise a novel semi-supervised GANs architecture as shown in Figure 2. Similar to aforementioned architectures of unconditional GANs, our semi-supervised GANs consists of a generator network G for synthesizing images conditioning on class labels, and a discriminator network D that simultaneously distinguishes real images from synthetic ones and classify the input images with correct semantics. Specifically, given the whole image set $\mathcal{X}$ including L labeled images in c classes, the class label information of each labeled image is first encoded into a c-dimensional vector $\mathbf{C} \in \{0, 1\}^c$, whose element is a class label indicator. The indicator is 1 if the image contains this label otherwise the indictor is 0. As such, the class label vector $\mathbf{C}$ of each unlabeled image is set as zero vector $\mathbf{0}$. Then the generator network G takes the concatenation of the class label vector $\mathbf{C}$ and random noise vector $\mathbf{z} \in \mathcal{N}(0, 1)$ as the input for producing a synthetic image $x_{syn} = G(\mathbf{C}, \mathbf{z})$. The discriminator network D generates both a probability distribution over two sources and a probability distribution over all the c class labels, i.e., $\{P(S|x), P(C|x)\} = D(x)$, for each image example x from either real images or synthetic images through G. It is worth noting that both the unlabeled and labeled images are included in the real image selection pool of D for better understanding the statistical structures of natural data.

The overall objective function of our semi-supervised GANs is composed of two parts: the adversarial loss $l_a(x)$ in Eq.(1) for assigning correct source to the image example x, and the classification loss $l_c(x)$ for assigning correct class label to this image. The details of how to measure the classification loss for images with single label or multiple labels will be presented in Section 3.5. Accordingly, the discriminator network D is learnt to minimize $l_c(x) + l_a(x)$ for recognizing both correct source and class label, while the generator network G is trained to minimize $l_c(x) - l_a(x)$ for fooling D on source prediction and meanwhile preserving the correct class label. After training the whole semi-supervised GANs with unlabeled and labeled natural images, the learnt generator network G is directly utilized as the pre-trained generator network in our DSH-GANs architecture for synthesizing realistic images conditioning on class labels.

3.3 Hash Stream

In the traditional binary representation learning, the hash encoding of each image is always treated independently in point-wise hashing learning methods, regardless of the relationships of similar or dissimilar between images. More importantly, the relative similarity relations like "for query image x, it should be more similar to image x^+ than to image x^-," are reflected in the image class labels in view that image x and x^+ belong to the same class while image x^- comes from other categories. The utilization of these relative similarity relations has also been proved to be effective in hash coding [1, 11, 18, 29]. Inspired by the idea of preserving relative similarity in deep architecture [11], we propose a hash stream for encoding hash codes learnt in a triplet-wise manner, which aims to preserve the relative similarity ordering in the input real-synthetic triplets.

Specifically, we can easily obtain a set of real-synthetic triplets $\mathcal{T}$ based on image labels, where each tuple $(x, x^+_{syn}, x^-_{syn})$ consists of one real image x as query image, one synthetic and semantically similar image x^+_{syn}, and another synthetic but dissimilar image x^-_{syn}. Note that x^+_{syn} is synthesized by generator network G conditioning on the same class labels of query image x, while x^-_{syn} is produced through G conditioning on different labels of x. To preserve the similarity relations in the real-synthetic triplets, we aim to learn a hash mapping $\mathcal{H}(\cdot)$ which makes the compact code $\mathcal{H}(x)$ more similar to $\mathcal{H}(x^+_{syn})$ than to $\mathcal{H}(x^-_{syn})$. Hence, the triplet ranking loss is employed and defined as

$$\begin{aligned} &\hat{l}_{triplet}(x, x^+_{syn}, x^-_{syn}) \\ &= \max(0, 1 - \left\|\mathcal{H}(x) - \mathcal{H}(x^-_{syn})\right\|_H + \left\|\mathcal{H}(x) - \mathcal{H}(x^+_{syn})\right\|_H) \,, \\ &\quad s.t. \quad \mathcal{H}(x), \mathcal{H}(x^+_{syn}), \mathcal{H}(x^-_{syn}) \in \{0,1\}^K \end{aligned} \tag{2}$$

where $\|\cdot\|_H$ represents Hamming distance. For ease of optimization, natural relaxation tricks are utilized on Eq.(2) to change integer constraint to the range constraint and replace Hamming norm with l_2 norm. Then, the triplet ranking loss function is reformulated as

$$\begin{aligned} &\hat{l}_{triplet}(x, x^+_{syn}, x^-_{syn}) \\ &= \max(0, 1 - \left\|\mathcal{H}(x) - \mathcal{H}(x^-_{syn})\right\|_2^2 + \left\|\mathcal{H}(x) - \mathcal{H}(x^+_{syn})\right\|_2^2) \,. \\ &\quad s.t. \quad \mathcal{H}(x), \mathcal{H}(x^+_{syn}), \mathcal{H}(x^-_{syn}) \in [0,1]^K \end{aligned} \tag{3}$$

3.4 Adversary Stream

Noticing that the input real-synthetic triplets of aforementioned hash stream contain not only different semantics, but also are from distinctly different sources. As a result, we additionally devise an adversary stream to distinguish synthetic images from real ones within each real-synthetic triplet, targeting for exploiting the mutual but also fuzzy relationship between the hash codes learning and source discrimination in GANs. In particular, for the adversary stream, the shared CNN for learning image representation can be treated as the discriminator network D in GANs, followed by a cross entropy loss layer for source prediction. Thus, given the real-synthetic triplet $(x, x^+_{syn}, x^-_{syn})$, an adversarial loss is used to measure the correctness of the predicted source (i.e., real or synthetic) of all the three images:

$$\hat{l}_a(x, x^+_{syn}, x^-_{syn}) = \frac{1}{3}\left(l_a(x) + l_a(x^+_{syn}) + l_a(x^-_{syn})\right), \tag{4}$$

where $l_a(\cdot)$ denotes the log-likelihood adversarial loss for each image as in Eq.(1).

3.5 Classification Stream

Image labels not only provide knowledge in classification but also are useful supervised information for mining semantic structures in images. A valid question is how to leverage the semantic supervision into both hashing and GANs, and make the generated hash codes better reflecting semantic similarities between images. Hence, we propose a joint learning mechanism by combining hash stream, adversary stream and classification stream. In the classification stream, a classification error is measured based on the input real-synthetic triplets. Specifically, for the single label classification, we use softmax optimization method. Given an input image x, the softmax loss is then formulated as

$$l_c(x) = -\sum_{j=1}^{c} I_{(y=j)} log \frac{e^{\boldsymbol{\theta}_j^\top \mathbf{x}}}{\sum_{l=1}^{c} e^{\boldsymbol{\theta}_l^\top \mathbf{x}}}, \tag{5}$$

where $\mathbf{x}$ is the output image representation of the shared CNN for image x, $\boldsymbol{\theta}_j$ denotes the parameter matrix in a softmax layer and $y \in \{1, 2, ..., c\}$ represents image class label. The indicator function $I_{condition} = 1$ if *condition* is true; otherwise $I_{condition} = 0$.

If an image contains multiple class labels, we refer to this problem as multi-label classification. Cross entropy loss is then employed in this case. Similar to softmax loss, cross entropy loss is computed by

$$l_c(x) = -\sum_{j=1}^{c} \left[I_{(\mathbf{C}_j=1)} \log\left(P(\mathbf{C}_j = 1|\mathbf{x})\right) + \left(1 - I_{(\mathbf{C}_j=1)}\right) \log\left(1 - P(\mathbf{C}_j = 1|\mathbf{x})\right) \right], \quad (6)$$

$$P(\mathbf{C}_j = 1|\mathbf{x}) = \frac{1}{1 + e^{-\boldsymbol{\delta}_j^T \mathbf{x}}}$$

where $\mathbf{C}_j$ denotes the j-th element in class label vector $\mathbf{C}$ and $\boldsymbol{\delta}_j$ denotes the parameter matrix in a sigmoid layer.

Hence, given the real-synthetic triplet $(x, x^+_{syn}, x^-_{syn})$, the classification error is calculated on all the three examples by

$$\hat{l}_c(x, x^+_{syn}, x^-_{syn}) = \frac{1}{3}\left(l_c(x) + l_c(x^+_{syn}) + l_c(x^-_{syn})\right). \quad (7)$$

3.6 Optimization

The overall training objective of DSH-GANs integrates the triplet ranking loss in Eq.(3), adversarial loss in Eq.(4) and classification error in Eq.(7). As our DSH-GANs is a variant of GANs architecture which mainly consists of generator network G for image synthesis with labels and the shared CNN for image representation learning, we train the whole architecture in a two-player minimax game mechanism. In particular, for the shared CNN, we update its parameters according to the following overall loss:

$$\hat{l}_{CNN} = \sum_{\mathcal{T}} \left[\hat{l}_{triplet}(x, x^+_{syn}, x^-_{syn}) + \hat{l}_a(x, x^+_{syn}, x^-_{syn}) + \hat{l}_c(x, x^+_{syn}, x^-_{syn}) \right], \quad (8)$$

where $\mathcal{T}$ is the set of real-synthetic triplets. By minimizing this term, the shared CNN is trained to preserve the relative similarity ordering in the real-synthetic triplets and simultaneously recognize both correct sources and class labels of images in the triplets.

For the generator network G, its parameters are adjusted with the following loss:

$$\hat{l}_G = \sum_{\mathcal{T}} \left[\hat{l}_{triplet}(x, x^+_{syn}, x^-_{syn}) - \hat{l}_a(x, x^+_{syn}, x^-_{syn}) + \hat{l}_c(x, x^+_{syn}, x^-_{syn}) \right]. \quad (9)$$

Thus, the generator network G is trained to fool the shared CNN on source prediction and meanwhile preserve the relative similarity ordering and correct class labels of the real-synthetic triplets.

3.7 Image Retrieval

After the optimization of DSH-GANs, we can employ hash stream in the architecture followed by a sigmoid layer to generate K-bit hash codes for each input image. In this procedure, an image x is first encoded into a K-dimension feature vector $\mathbf{h} = \mathcal{H}(x)$. Then, a quantization operation $\mathbf{b} = \mathcal{Q}(\mathbf{h})$ is exploited to generate hash codes $\mathbf{b}$, where $\mathcal{Q}(\mathbf{h})$ is a sign function on vector $\mathbf{h}$ with $\mathcal{Q}(h_i) = 1$ if $h_i > 0.5$ and otherwise $\mathcal{Q}(h_i) = 0$. Given a query image, the retrieval list of images is produced by sorting the Hamming distances of hash codes between the query image and images in search pool.

4 EXPERIMENTS

We conducted extensive evaluations of our proposed architecture on two image datasets, i.e., CIFAR-10[1] which is a collection of tiny images and NUS-WIDE[2] of a large-scale Web image dataset.

4.1 Datasets

The **CIFAR-10** dataset consists of 60,000 real world tiny images (32×32 pixels), which can be divided into 10 categories and 6,000 images for each category. We randomly select 1,000 images (100 images per class) as the test query set. For the unsupervised setting, all the rest images are used as training samples. For the supervised setting, we additionally sample 500 images from each class in the training samples and constitute a subset of 5,000 labeled images for training. The rest training images are treated as the unlabeled data.

The **NUS-WIDE** dataset contains 269,648 images collected from Flickr. Each of these images is associated with one or multiple labels in 81 semantic concepts. For a fair comparison, we follow the settings in [11] to employ the subset of images associated with 21 most frequent labels, where each label associates with at least 5,000 images. Similar to the split in CIFAR-10, we randomly select 2,100 images (100 images per class) as the test query set. For the unsupervised setting, all the rest images are used as the training set. For the supervised setting, we uniformly sample 500 images from each class to construct the labeled subset for training and the rest training images are all treated as unlabeled data.

4.2 Experimental Settings

On both datasets, we utilize AlexNet [9] as our basic CNN architecture and take the outputs of fc6 layer from AlexNet as the image representation. The shared CNN architecture is pre-trained on ImageNet dataset [22] and the generator network G is pre-trained with our proposed semi-supervised GANs on each dataset.

We mainly implement our proposed method based on Caffe [7], which is one of the widely adopted deep learning frameworks. For the semi-supervised GANs, we follow the standard settings in [20] and train our GANs models on both datasets by utilizing Adam optimizer with a mini-batch size of 128. All weights are initialized from a zero-centered Normal distribution with standard deviation 0.02 and the slope of the leak is set to 0.2 in the LeakyReLU. We fix the learning rate and momentum to 0.0002 and 0.9, respectively. For our DSH-GANs architecture, it is trained by stochastic gradient descent with 0.9 momentum. The start learning rate is set to 0.0001, and we decrease it to 10% after 10,000 iterations on CIFAR-10 and after 40,000 iterations on NUS-WIDE, respectively. The mini-batch size of images is 64 and the weight decay parameter is 0.0005.

[1] http://www.cs.toronto.edu/ kriz/cifar.html
[2] http://lms.comp.nus.edu.sg/research/NUS-WIDE.htm

Table 1: Accuracy in terms of MAP. The best MAPs on each number of hash bits are shown in boldface. Note that the MAP performance is calculated on the top 5,000 returned images for NUS-WIDE dataset.

Method	CIFAR-10 (MAP)				NUS-WIDE (MAP)			
	12-bits	24-bits	32-bits	48-bits	12-bits	24-bits	32-bits	48-bits
DSH-GANs	**0.735**	**0.781**	**0.787**	**0.802**	**0.838**	**0.856**	**0.861**	**0.863**
DSH-GANs$^-$	0.726	0.769	0.772	0.783	0.823	0.847	0.845	0.854
DPSH	0.713	0.727	0.744	0.757	0.794	0.822	0.838	0.851
NINH	0.552	0.566	0.558	0.581	0.674	0.697	0.713	0.715
CNNH	0.439	0.476	0.472	0.489	0.611	0.618	0.625	0.608
KSH+CNN	0.446	0.502	0.518	0.516	0.746	0.774	0.765	0.749
ITQ+CNN	0.212	0.230	0.234	0.240	0.728	0.707	0.689	0.661
SH+CNN	0.158	0.157	0.154	0.151	0.620	0.611	0.620	0.591
LSH+CNN	0.134	0.157	0.173	0.185	0.438	0.586	0.571	0.507
KSH	0.303	0.337	0.346	0.356	0.556	0.572	0.581	0.588
ITQ	0.162	0.169	0.172	0.175	0.452	0.468	0.472	0.477
SH	0.127	0.128	0.126	0.129	0.454	0.406	0.405	0.400
LSH	0.121	0.126	0.120	0.120	0.403	0.421	0.426	0.441

4.3 Protocols and Baseline Methods

We follow four evaluation protocols, i.e., mean average precision (MAP), hash lookup, precision-recall curve, and precision curves w.r.t. different numbers of top returned samples, which are widely used in [4, 11, 14]. We compare the following approaches for performance evaluation:

(1) Locality Sensitive Hashing [3] (LSH) aims to map similar examples to the same bucket with high probability by using a Gaussian random projection matrix. The property of locality in the original space will be largely preserved in the Hamming space.

(2) Spectral Hashing [26] (SH) is based on quantizing the values of analytical eigenfunctions computed along PCA directions of the data.

(3) Iterative Quantization [4] (ITQ) learns similarity-preserving binary codes by directly minimizing the quantization error of mapping data to vertices of the binary hypercube.

(4) Kernel-based Supervised Hashing [14] (KSH) employs a kernel formulation for learning the hash functions to handle linearly inseparable data.

(5) Convolutional Neural Networks Hashing [28] (CNNH) firstly learns approximate hash codes with the supervised pairwise relationship and then trains CNN architecture with approximate hash codes and image tags.

(6) Network In Network Hashing [11] (NINH) utilizes a triplet ranking loss to preserve relative similarity and divide-and-encode modules to encode hash bits.

(7) Deep Pairwise-Supervised Hashing [12] (DPSH) performs simultaneous feature learning and hash learning by leveraging pairwise labels in an end-to-end system.

(8) Deep Semantic Hashing with Generative Adversarial Networks (DSH-GANs) is our proposal in this paper. A slightly different of this run is named as DSH-GANs$^-$, which is trained without classification stream.

Note that for the four hashing methods using hand-crafted features (i.e., LSH, SH, ITQ and KSH), each image in CIFAR-10 and NUS-WIDE is represented by a 512-dimensional GIST vector and an officially available 500-dimensional bag-of-words vector, respectively. For the deep hashing methods, we resize all images to be 224×224 pixels and then directly exploit the raw image pixels as input. Moreover, we also conduct the experiments by using the outputs of fc6 layer in AlexNet as image representation in the four traditional hashing approaches and name them as LSH+CNN, SH+CNN, ITQ+CNN and KSH+CNN, respectively.

4.4 Results on CIFAR-10 Dataset

The left half of Table 1 shows the MAP performance comparisons on CIFAR-10 dataset. Overall, the results across different number of hash bits indicate that our DSH-GANs consistently outperforms others. In particular, the MAP of DSH-GANs with 48-bits makes the relative improvement over the best traditional competitor KSH with GIST features or the outputs of fc6 layer in AlexNet, and deep model DPSH by 125.3%, 55.4% and 5.9%, respectively. Furthermore, traditional approaches with image representations extracted from CNN architecture lead to a large performance boost against these methods with GIST features, which is expected as deep CNN has demonstrated its high capability in generating image representations. Compared to the traditional models with deep image representations, deep hash models which benefit from the joint learning of image representations and hash coding exhibit better performances. DSH-GANs$^-$ outperforms DPSH and NINH. The result basically indicates the advantage of exploring synthetic images in hashing. DSH-GANs further improves DSH-GANs$^-$ with a relative increase of 1.2%∼2.4%, demonstrating the strength of boosting hashing by additionally preserving semantics of images through classification. In addition, when utilizing a deeper CNN architecture VGG-19 [24] networks as our basic CNN, the MAP performance of our DSH-GANs with 12-bits, 24-bits, 32-bits and 48bits will be boosted up to 86.1%, 88.1%, 87.9% and 88.4%, respectively.

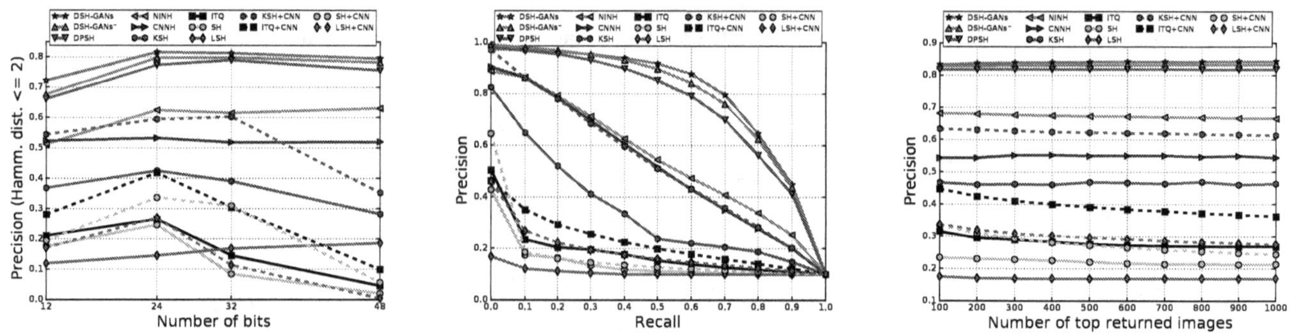

(a) (b) (c)

Figure 3: Comparisons with state-of-the-art approaches on CIFAR-10 dataset. (a) Precision within Hamming radius 2 using hash lookup. (b) Precision-Recall curves with 48-bits. (c) precision curves with 48-bits w.r.t. different number of top returned samples. Better viewed in original color pdf file.

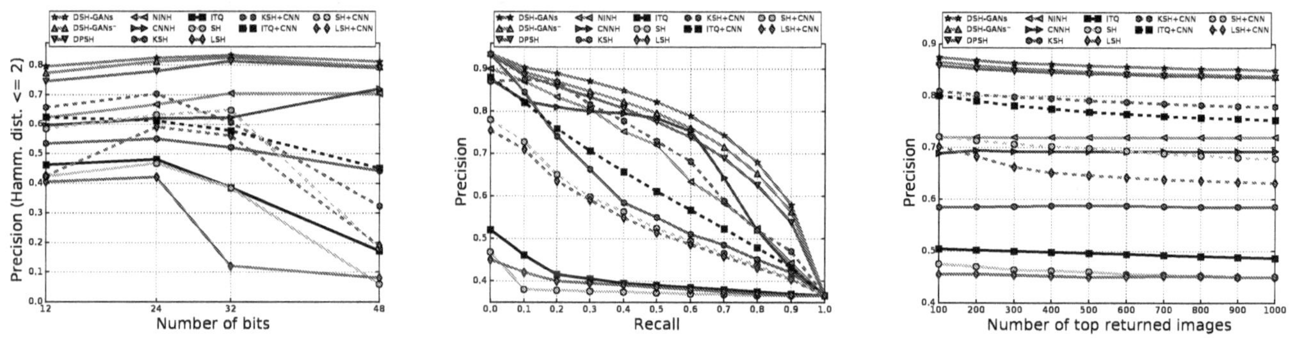

(a) (b) (c)

Figure 4: Comparisons with state-of-the-art approaches on NUS-WISE dataset. (a) Precision within Hamming radius 2 using hash lookup. (b) Precision-Recall curves with 48-bits. (c) precision curves with 48-bits w.r.t. different number of top returned samples. Better viewed in original color pdf file.

In the evaluation of hash lookup within Hamming radius 2 as shown in Figure 3(a), the precisions for most of the traditional methods drop when a longer size of hash codes is used (48 bits in our case). This is because the number of samples falling into a bucket decreases exponentially for longer sizes of hash codes. Therefore, for some query images, there are not even any neighbor in a Hamming ball of radius 2. Even in this case, the precision of our proposed DSH-GANs only has a slight decrease from 80.6% of 32 bits to 79.7% of 48 bits, indicating fewer failed queries for DSH-GANs. We further detail the precision-recall curves and precision curves with 48-bits w.r.t. different number of top returned samples in Figure 3(b) and 3(c). The results confirm the trends observed in Figure 3(a) and demonstrate performance improvements by our proposed DSH-GANs approach over other methods.

4.5 Results on NUS-WIDE Dataset

The right half of Table 1 lists the MAP performance comparisons on NUS-WIDE dataset. Precision with Hamming radius 2 using hash lookup, precision-recall curves with 48-bits and precision curves with 48-bits w.r.t. different number of top returned samples is given in Figure 4(a), 4(b) and 4(c), respectively. DSH-GANs constantly exhibits better performance than other baselines across different performance metrics. Specifically, the MAP performance and precision with Hamming radius 2 using hash lookup of DSH-GANs achieve 86.3% and 81.2% with 48-bits, which make the improvements over the best competitor DPSH by 1.4% and 2.7%, respectively. This again verifies the effectiveness of generating synthetic and discriminable training data through GANs for hashing. Furthermore, DSH-GANs is benefited from utilizing semantic supervision and thus shows a relative increase of 1.1%~1.9% over DSH-GANs$^-$ in terms of MAP.

Figure 5 further showcases the top ten image search results by different methods in response to two query images. We can see that the proposed DSH-GANs method achieves the most satisfying results and retrieves eight "excellent images" in the returned top ten images to each query image. It is worth noticing that "excellent images" here refer to images whose annotations completely contain all the labels of the query image (e.g., "water," "clouds," "ocean" and "beach" of the first image example). As a result, the images retrieved

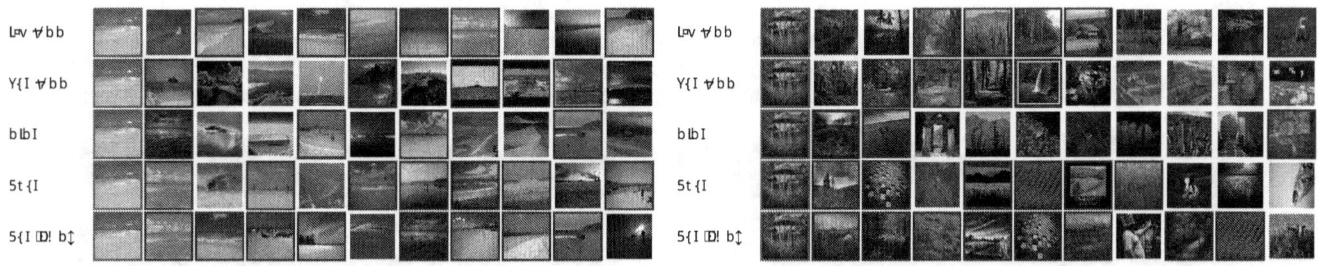

Figure 5: Examples showing the top 10 image retrieval results by different methods in response to two query images on NUS-WIDE dataset (better viewed in color). In each row, the first image with a red bounding box is the query image and the images whose annotations completely contain all the labels of the query image are regarded as excellent ones, which are enclosed in a blue bounding box.

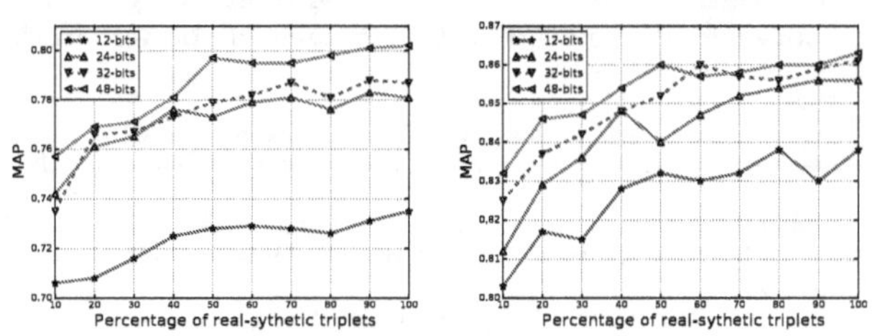

(a) CIFAR-10. (b) NUS-WIDE.

Figure 6: MAP performance comparison with different percentage of synthetic data in training triplets.

by our DSH-GANs approach are more similar in semantics with the query image.

4.6 Comparison between Synthetic and Real Examples for Hashing

In order to examine how performance is affected when exploiting synthetic examples in training triplets of different degree by DSH-GANs, we compare the MAP performances of using synthetic data with percentage ranging from 10% to 100%. In the previous experiments, the similar and dissimilar images in the training triplets are all synthetic images, which refers to 100% in this analysis. We control the ratio between real and synthetic data in training by replacing part of synthetic images with real ones. Figure 6 shows the results on both CIFA-10 and NUS-WIDE datasets across different hash bits. The results are encouraging in the way that involving more synthetic data tends to achieve better performance. This empirically validates our proposal of generating synthetic data through semi-supervised GANs which additionally leverages largely unlabeled data, making the generated examples more discriminable to characterize the structure of the data.

4.7 Visualization of Synthetic Images

Figure 7 illustrates image examples on CIFAR-10 dataset, which are both randomly selected from each class in the dataset (left half) and generated for each class through our semi-supervised GANs (right half). In general, the generated images are plausible and semantically relevant to each class.

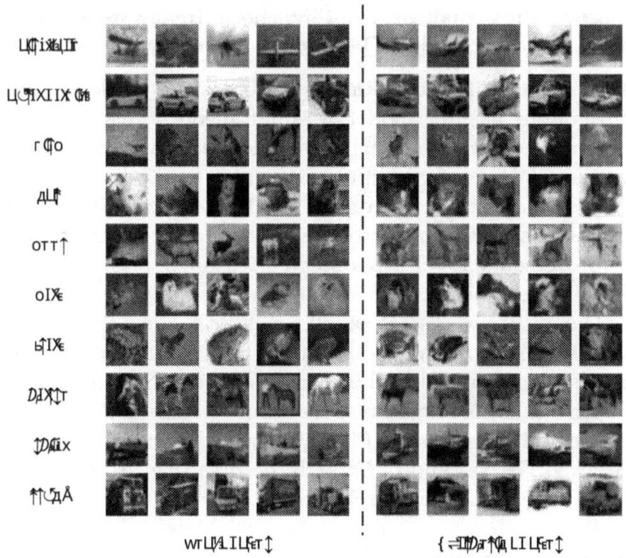

Figure 7: Visualization of image examples on CIFAR-10 dataset. Left half: images randomly selected from each class in the dataset; Right half: synthetic image examples for each class through our semi-supervised GANs.

Figure 8 further visualizes the synthetic image examples on NUS-WIDE dataset. The images in the right half of each row are semantically related to the images in the left half. Take the first row as an example, the images in the left half are generated with label "clouds," while the images in the right half are synthesized with labels "clouds" and "sunset." All the images look real and the generated images in the right part could clearly manifest the semantics of "sunset" and differentiate them from the images in the left part with only semantics of "clouds."

5 CONCLUSIONS

We have presented a Deep Semantic Hashing with Generative Adversarial Networks (DSH-GANs) architecture which explores semi-supervised GANs to generate synthetic training data for hashing. Particularly, a semi-supervised GANs is trained on both labeled and unlabeled data to produce compelling and discriminable examples conditioning on class

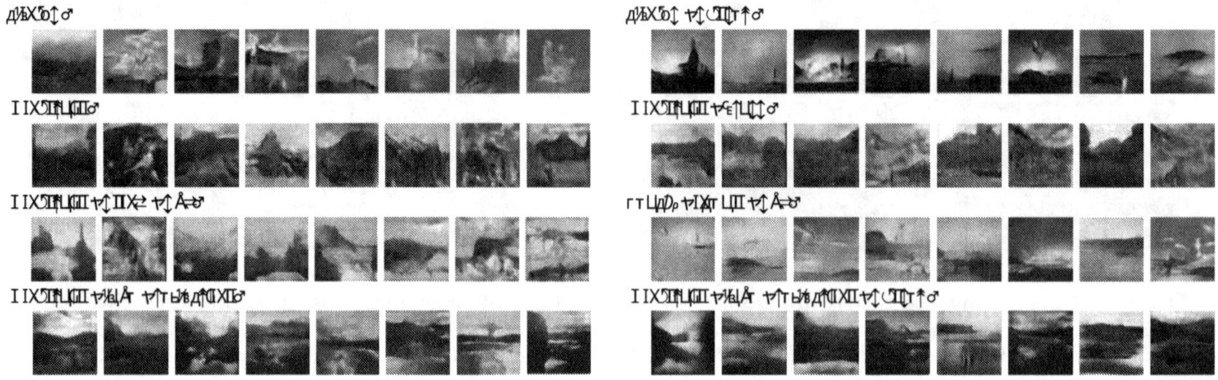

Figure 8: Visualization of synthetic image examples on NUS-WIDE dataset. All the image examples are generated with multiple labels. The images in the right half of each row are semantically related to the images in the left half.

labels. To verify our claim, we optimize the whole architecture of our hashing model by simultaneously distinguishing synthetic images from real ones and preserving not only relative similarity between images but also semantics of images. Experiments conducted on both CIFAR-10 and NUS-WIDE datasets validate our proposal and analysis. Performance improvements are clearly observed when comparing to other hashing techniques.

Our future works are as follows. First, as our architecture is a joint learning procedure, how the architecture performs on classification task will be further evaluated. Next, more in-depth studies of how to fuse the three streams in a principled way could be explored. Finally, more advanced GANs (e.g., Stacked GANs) and CNN architectures (e.g., ResNet) will be investigated in our architecture.

REFERENCES

[1] Qi Dai, Jianguo Li, Jingdong Wang, and Yu-Gang Jiang. 2016. Binary Optimized Hashing. In *ACM MM*.

[2] Emily Denton, Soumith Chintala, Arthur Szlam, and Rob Fergus. 2015. Deep Generative Image Models using a Laplacian Pyramid of Adversarial Networks. In *NIPS*.

[3] Aristides Gionis, Piotr Indyky, and Rajeev Motwaniz. 1999. Similarity search in high dimensions via hashing. In *VLDB*.

[4] Yunchao Gong, Svetlana Lazebnik, Albert Gordo, and Florent Perronnin. 2013. Iterative Quantization: A Procrustean Approach to Learning Binary Codes for Large-scale Image Retrieval. *IEEE Trans. Pattern Anal. Mach. Intell.* (2013).

[5] Ian Goodfellow, Jean Pouget-Abadie, Mehdi Mirza, Bing Xu, David Warde-Farley, Sherjil Ozair, Aaron Courville, and Yoshua Bengio. 2014. Generative adversarial nets. In *NIPS*.

[6] Geoffrey E Hinton and Ruslan R Salakhutdinov. 2006. Reducing the Dimensionality of Data with Neural Networks. *Science* (2006).

[7] Yangqing Jia, Evan Shelhamer, Jeff Donahue, Sergey Karayev, Jonathan Long, Ross Girshick, Sergio Guadarrama, and Trevor Darrell. 2014. Caffe: Convolutional architecture for fast feature embedding. In *ACM MM*.

[8] Saehoon Kim and Seungjin Choi. 2011. Semi-supervised Discriminant Hashing. In *ICDM*.

[9] Alex Krizhevsky, Ilya Sutskever, and Geoffrey E. Hinton. 2012. ImageNet Classification with Deep Convolutional Neural Networks. In *NIPS*.

[10] Brian Kulis and Kristen Grauman. 2012. Kernelized Locality-sensitive Hashing. *IEEE Trans. Pattern Anal. Mach. Intell.* (2012).

[11] Hanjiang Lai, Yan Pan, Ye Liu, and Shuicheng Yan. 2015. Simultaneous Feature Learning and Hash Coding with Deep Neural Networks. In *CVPR*.

[12] Wu-Jun Li, Sheng Wang, and Wang-Cheng Kang. 2016. Feature learning based deep supervised hashing with pairwise labels. In *IJCAI*.

[13] Venice Erin Liong, Jiwen Lu, Gang Wang, Pierre Moulin, and Jie Zhou. 2015. Deep Hashing for Compact Binary Codes Learning. In *CVPR*.

[14] Wei Liu, Jun Wang, Rongrong Ji, Yu-Gang Jiang, and Shih-Fu Chang. 2012. Supervised hashing with kernels. In *CVPR*.

[15] Mehdi Mirza and Simon Osindero. 2014. Conditional generative adversarial nets. *arXiv preprint arXiv:1411.1784* (2014).

[16] Augustus Odena, Christopher Olah, and Jonathon Shlens. 2016. Conditional Image Synthesis With Auxiliary Classifier GANs. *arXiv preprint arXiv:1610.09585* (2016).

[17] Yingwei Pan, Yehao Li, Ting Yao, Tao Mei, Houqiang Li, and Yong Rui. 2016. Learning deep intrinsic video representation by exploring temporal coherence and graph structure. IJCAI.

[18] Yingwei Pan, Ting Yao, Houqiang Li, Chong-Wah Ngo, and Tao Mei. 2015. Semi-supervised hashing with semantic confidence for large scale visual search. In *SIGIR*.

[19] Zhaofan Qiu, Ting Yao, and Tao Mei. 2017. Deep Quantization: Encoding Convolutional Activations with Deep Generative Model. In *CVPR*.

[20] Alec Radford, Luke Metz, and Soumith Chintala. 2016. Unsupervised representation learning with deep convolutional generative adversarial networks. In *ICLR*.

[21] Scott Reed, Zeynep Akata, Xinchen Yan, Lajanugen Logeswaran, Bernt Schiele, and Honglak Lee. 2016. Generative adversarial text to image synthesis. In *ICML*.

[22] Olga Russakovsky, Jia Deng, Hao Su, Jonathan Krause, Sanjeev Satheesh, Sean Ma, Zhiheng Huang, Andrej Karpathy, Aditya Khosla, Michael Bernstein, Alexander C. Berg, and Li Fei-Fei. 2015. ImageNet Large Scale Visual Recognition Challenge. *IJCV* (2015).

[23] Ruslan Salakhutdinov and Geoffrey Hinton. 2009. Semantic Hashing. *IJAR* (2009).

[24] Karen Simonyan and Andrew Zisserman. 2015. Very Deep Convolutioanl Networks for Large-scale Image Recognition. In *ICLR*.

[25] Jun Wang, Sanjiv Kumar, and Shih-Fu Chang. 2012. Semi-Supervised Hashing for Large-Scale Search. *IEEE Trans. Pattern Anal. Mach. Intell.* (2012).

[26] Y. Weiss, A. Torralba, and R. Fergus. 2008. Spectral hashing. In *NIPS*.

[27] Hao Xia, Pengcheng Wu, Steven CH Hoi, and Rong Jin. 2012. Boosting Multi-kernel Locality-sensitive Hashing for Scalable Image Retrieval. In *SIGIR*.

[28] Rongkai Xia, Yan Pan, Hanjiang Lai, Cong Liu, and Shuicheng Yan. 2014. Supervised Hashing for Image Retrieval via Image Representation Learning. In *AAAI*.

[29] Ting Yao, Fuchen Long, Tao Mei, and Yong Rui. 2016. Deep semantic-preserving and ranking-based hashing for image retrieval. In *IJCAI*.

[30] Han Zhu, Mingsheng Long, Jianmin Wang, and Yue Cao. 2016. Deep Hashing Network for Efficient Similarity Retrieval. In *AAAI*.

Characterizing and Predicting Enterprise Email Reply Behavior

Liu Yang[1] Susan T. Dumais[2] Paul N. Bennett[2] Ahmed Hassan Awadallah[2]
[1] Center for Intelligent Information Retrieval, University of Massachusetts Amherst, Amherst, MA, USA
[2] Microsoft Research, Redmond, WA, USA
lyang@cs.umass.edu,{sdumais,pauben,hassanam}@microsoft.com

ABSTRACT

Email is still among the most popular online activities. People spend a significant amount of time sending, reading and responding to email in order to communicate with others, manage tasks and archive personal information. Most previous research on email is based on either relatively small data samples from user surveys and interviews, or on consumer email accounts such as those from Yahoo! Mail or Gmail. Much less has been published on how people interact with enterprise email even though it contains less automatically generated commercial email and involves more organizational behavior than is evident in personal accounts. In this paper, we extend previous work on predicting email reply behavior by looking at enterprise settings and considering more than dyadic communications. We characterize the influence of various factors such as email content and metadata, historical interaction features and temporal features on email reply behavior. We also develop models to predict whether a recipient will reply to an email and how long it will take to do so. Experiments with the publicly-available Avocado email collection show that our methods outperform all baselines with large gains. We also analyze the importance of different features on reply behavior predictions. Our findings provide new insights about how people interact with enterprise email and have implications for the design of the next generation of email clients.

KEYWORDS

Email reply behavior; information overload; user behavior modeling

1 INTRODUCTION

Email remains one of the most popular online activities. Major email services such as Gmail, Outlook, and Yahoo! Mail have millions of monthly active users, many of whom perform frequent interactions like reading, replying to, or organizing emails. A recent survey shows that reading and answering emails takes up to 28% of enterprise workers' time, which is more than searching and gathering information (19%), communication and collaboration internally (14%), and second only to role specific tasks (39%) [6]. Understanding and characterizing email reply behaviors can

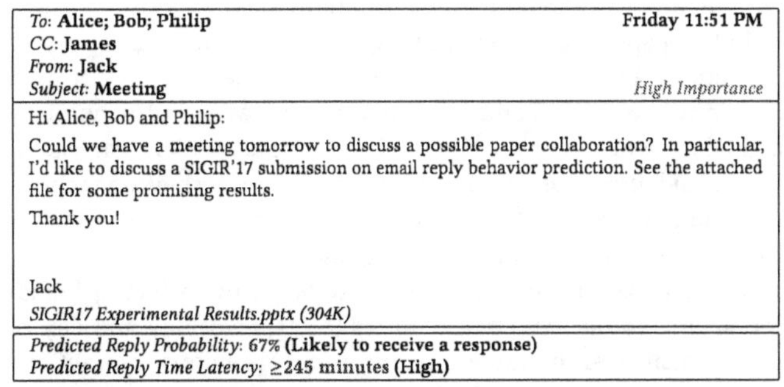

Figure 1: A motivational email example with predicted reply probability and reply time latency.

improve communication and productivity by providing insights for the design of the next generation of email tools.

By modeling user reply behaviors like reply rate and reply time, we can integrate machine intelligence into email systems to provide value for both email recipients and senders. For email recipients, reply predictions could help filter emails that need replies or fast replies, which can help reduce email overload [9]. For email senders, the reply behaviors could be predicted in advance during email composition. More generally, better reply strategies could lead to improved communication efficiency. Figure 1 shows a motivating email example with predicted reply probability and reply time latency shown in the bottom panel. Specific features could also be highlighted. For example, identifying a request in the email (*Could we have a meeting...*) could improve automated triage for the recipient by highlighting that a reply is needed; or alerting the sender that a reply is likely to take longer if it is sent late at night or over the weekend could improve communication efficiency.

Previous work investigated strategies that people use to organize, reply to, or delete email messages [9, 10, 22, 29]. However, those studies are based on relatively small surveys or interviews. Some recent research proposes frameworks for studying user actions on emails with large scale data [11, 20]. Both of these studies are based on consumer emails from Yahoo! Mail. Enterprise email has received little attention compared to consumer email even though several studies have shown that enterprise email usage is not the same as consumer email usage. For example, [25] reports that enterprise users send and receive twice as much emails as consumer users and [15] shows that consumer email is now dominated by machine-generated messages sent from business and social networking sites.

Perhaps the closest prior research to our work is the study on email reply behavior in Yahoo! Mail by Kooti et al. [20]. However, they focus on personal email and only consider a subset of email exchanges, specifically those from dyadic (one-to-one) email conversations for pairs of users who have exchanged more than 5 prior

Work primarily done during Liu Yang's internship at Microsoft Research.

SIGIR'17, August 7–11, 2017, Shinjuku, Tokyo, Japan

DOI: http://dx.doi.org/10.1145/3077136.3080782

emails in consumer email. Focusing only on dyadic email conversations is limiting, especially in the context of enterprise emails. In the enterprise email data that we study, 52.99% of emails are non-dyadic emails, that is, they are sent to more than one recipient other than the sender. Thus it is important and more realistic to study the more general setting of modeling email reply behavior including both dyadic emails and emails sent to a group of people, without any threshold on previous interactions.

In this paper, we address this gap by characterizing and predicting reply behaviors in enterprise emails, where we consider both dyadic conversations and group discussions. We use the publicly-available Avocado research email collection,[1] which consists of emails and attachments taken from a defunct information technology company referred to as "Avocado". There are 938, 035 emails from 279 accounts in this email collection.

We analyze and characterize various factors affecting email replies including: temporal features (e.g. time of day and day of week), historical interaction features (e.g., previous interactions between sender and recipients), properties of the content features (e.g. length of subject and email body), predictions based on textual content features (e.g., sentiment, contains a request), address features (e.g., recipients), and metadata features (e.g., attachments). We find several interesting patterns connecting these factors to reply behavior. For example, emails with requests or commitments get more but slower replies while longer emails tend to get fewer and slower replies. Based on this analysis, we used a variety of features to build models to predict whether an email will receive a reply and the corresponding reply time. We show that our proposed model outperforms all baselines with large gains. We also perform feature importance analysis to understand the role different features play in predicting user email reply behavior.

Our contributions can be summarized as follows:

(1) We introduce and formalize the task of reply behavior prediction in enterprise emails involving both one-to-one (dyadic) and one-to-many communication. Unlike previous work either on small user surveys and interviews [9, 10, 22, 29] or only for dyadic email conversations in consumer emails [20], our work is the first to model reply behavior in a more general setting including emails sent to groups of people as well as individuals for enterprise email.
(2) We analyze and characterize various factors affecting email replies. Compared to previous work, we study many novel factors including email textual content, request / commitment in emails, address features like internal/external emails, and number of email recipients.
(3) We extract 10 different classes of features and build models to predict email reply behaviors. We perform thorough experimental analysis with the publicly-available Avocado email collection and show that the proposed methods outperform all baselines with large gains. We also analyze the importance of each class of features in predicting email reply behavior.

[1] https://catalog.ldc.upenn.edu/LDC2015T03

2 RELATED WORK

Our work is related to several research areas, including modeling actions on email, email overload, email acts and intent analysis, email classification and mining.

Modeling Actions on Email. Our work is related to previous research on user behavior and email action modeling [10, 11, 20, 23, 24, 28]. Dabbish et al. [10] examined people's ratings of message importance and the actions they took on specific email messages with a survey of 121 people at a university. While this work provides insights on email usage and user actions on email messages, how well the results generalize to other user groups is not clear. DiCastro et al. [11] studied four common user actions on email (read, reply, delete, delete-withoutread) using an opt-in sample of more than 100k users of the Yahoo! Mail service. They proposed and evaluated a machine learning framework for predicting these four actions. Kooti et al. [20] also used Yahoo! Mail data to quantitatively characterize the reply behavior for pairs of users. They investigated the effects of increasing email overload on user behaviors and performed experiments on predicting reply time, reply length and whether the reply ends a conversion. Our work is inspired by the latter two studies but it differs in several important ways. These two studies looked at behavior in Yahoo! Mail, a consumer email collection, whereas we studied interaction in a enterprise setting using the Avocado collection. What's more, the study by Kooti et al. [20] only considers dyadic emails from a subset of people who had at least five previous email interactions. Our work considers a more general setting where we consider both dyadic emails and emails sent to a group of users. We allow cases where there is no previous interactions between the sender and receivers, which makes our prediction task a more challenging (and realistic) one. Our experimental data is also publicly available in the recently-released Avocado collection from LDC, whereas prior research used proprietary internal data. Last but not least, we analyzed several novel features including properties of the content like email subject and body length, predictions of whether the email contained a request or commitment, and address features like internal vs. external emails and showed that they are useful for building models to predict user email reply behavior.

Email Overload. Several research efforts have examined the *email overload* problem and proposed solutions to reduce it [2, 9, 12, 22, 29]. In their pioneering work, Whittaker and Sidner [29] explored how people manage their email and found that email was not only used for communication, but also for task management and maintaining a personal archive. A decade later, Fisher et al. [12] revisited the email overload problem by examining a sample of mailboxes from a high-tech company. They showed that some aspects of email dramatically changed, such as the size of archive and number of folders, but others, like the average inbox size remained more or less the same. Several researchers have proposed solutions to mitigate the email overload problem [1, 2, 13, 18]. Aberdeen et al. [1] proposed a per-user machine learning model to predict email "importance" and rank email by how likely the user is to act on that mail; this forms the the Priority Inbox feature of Gmail. Our work shares similar motivations for handling the email overload problem by modeling and predicting user reply behaviors on emails. We focused on email reply behaviors, specifically identifying emails

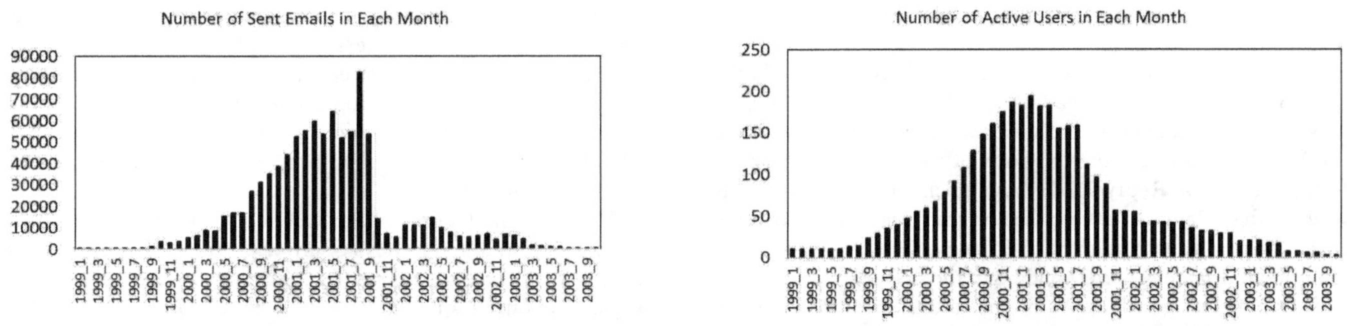

(a) The number of sent emails in each month.

(b) The number of active users in each month.

Figure 2: Temporal analysis of the number of sent emails and active users in each month of the Avocado email collection.

which receive replies and the reply latency. Their work looked at consumer emails, Gmail, whereas we focus on the enterprise email collection, Avocado.

Email Acts and Intent Analysis. Previous research studied email acts and email intent analysis [3, 7, 21, 26, 27]. Cohen et al. [7] proposed machine learning methods to classify emails according to an ontology of verbs and nouns, which describe the "email speech act" intended by the email sender. Follow-up work by Carvalho and Cohen [4] described a new text classification algorithm based on a dependency-network-based collective classification method and showed significant improvements over a bag-of-words baseline classifier. In a recent study using the Avocado collection, Sappelli et al. [26] studied email intent and tasks, and proposed a taxonomy of tasks in emails. They also studied predicting the number of tasks in emails. Our work extends previous research on email acts and intent by extracting requests and commitments from emails and using them as features for predicting user reply behavior.

Email Classification and Mining. We formalized the user email reply behavior prediction task as a classification task. There are many previous papers on email classification and mining [5, 14–16, 19]. Klimt and Yang [19] introduced the Enron corpus as a data set and used it to explore automated classification of email messages into folders. Graus et al. [14] studied the task of recipient recommendation. They also used enterprise email collections, but their collection was proprietary and their focus was on recipient recommendation, rather than reply behavior modeling.

To summarize, the research described in this paper extends previous research on email interaction in several ways. Using a recently released public enterprise email collection, we formalize the task of prediction whether an email will be responded to and how long it will take to do so. In contrast to earlier work on reply prediction, we study enterprise (vs. consumer) email behavior, consider both one-to-one (dyadic) and one-to-many emails, and develop several new types of features to characterize the email content and intent and study their importance in reply prediction.

3 DATA SET & TASK DEFINITION

Our data set is the Avocado research email collection from the Linguistic Data Consortium. This collection contains corporate emails from a defunct information technology company referred to as "Avocado". The collection contains the full content of emails, various meta information as well as attachments, folders, calendar entries, and contact details from Outlook mailboxes for 279 company employees.

The full collection contains 938, 035 emails and 325, 506 attachments. Since our goal is to study email reply behavior, we need to preprocess the data to figure out the reply relationships between emails. For emails that are replies, the email meta information includes a "reply_to" relationship field, containing the ID of the email that this email is replying to. We generate the email thread structure by parsing the "reply_to" relationship fields in email meta data. Specifically, we first use the "reply_to" relationship fields to collect sets of messages that are in the same thread. Then emails in the same thread are ordered by the sent time to generate their thread positions. We removed all the duplicated quoted "original messages" in the email text files to identify the unique body for each message. From the "reply_to" relationship fields and associated email sent time, we generate the ground truth for reply behavior including whether the email received a reply, and reply latency.

We first perform a temporal analysis of sent emails and active users in each month. Figure 2a and Figure 2b show the number of sent emails and the number of active people in this collection respectively. Emails are aggregated by the sent time into different months. Each person is represented by an interval based on the sent time of his/her first and last email. Then the number of active people in each month is the number of overlapping intervals during the month. We see that the number of active people increases to a peak in February 2001 and then decreases to under 50 after February 2002, as the company started laying off employees. The number of emails sent has a similar pattern over months. To ensure that our analysis and experimental results are built upon emails when the company was under normal operations, we select the emails from June 1st 2000 to June 1st 2001.

We further perform a few additional data cleaning and filtering steps. We focus on the reply behaviors toward the first message in each thread. Because replies towards the first messages and follow-up replies may have different properties and we want to focus on one phenomenon in this study. We filter out email threads where the first reply comes from the sender himself or herself and emails where the only recipient is the sender. After these filtering steps, we have 351, 532 emails left, which become the basis of our data analysis.[2]

The email behavior we study includes the reply action and reply time. We formally define the task as following. Given an email message m that user u_i sent to a user set $\{u_j\}$ at time t, we study: (1) **Reply Action**: whether any one of users in $\{u_j\}$ will reply to message m; (2) **Reply Time**: how quickly users in $\{u_j\}$ reply, which is the difference between the first response time and the start time t. If there are multiple replies from users in $\{u_j\}$, we consider only the time latency corresponding to the first reply.

Thus our setting includes both "one-to-one" and "one-to-many" emails, which is more general than [20] which only included dyadic emails between pairs of users with at least five previous emails.

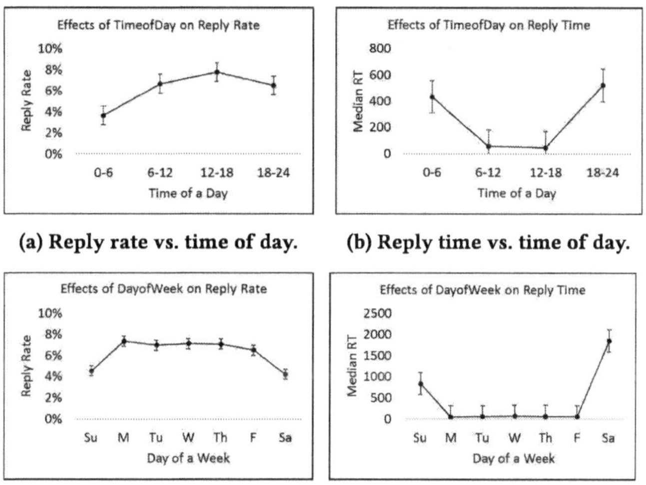

(a) Reply rate vs. time of day. **(b) Reply time vs. time of day.**

(c) Reply rate vs. day of week. **(d) Reply time vs. day of week.**

Figure 3: The effects of temporal features of the original sent emails on user email reply behavior. The median reply time denoted by Median RT is in minutes.

4 CHARACTERIZING REPLY BEHAVIOR

We characterize multiple factors affecting email reply action and reply time. For reply action, we compute the reply rate which is the percentage of emails that received replies. [3] In Section 5 we show that these factors enable us to learn models to predict user reply behavior.

4.1 Temporal Factors

We first study the impact of temporal factors on user replies. Figure 3a and Figure 3b show the reply rate and median reply time to emails sent at different times of the day. We partition the time of a day into Night (0 to 6), Morning (6 to 12), Afternoon (12 to 18) and Evening (18 to 24). Then we aggregate emails in each time range and compute the reply rate and median reply time. The unit of reply time is in minutes. We see that emails sent in morning and afternoon receive more and faster replies. For reply rate, emails sent in the afternoon have the highest reply rate (7.77%) and emails sent at night have the lowest reply rate (3.63%). For reply time, the median reply time for morning and afternoon is less than 1 hour, whereas reply time for mails sent in evening and night is more than 7 hours. This makes sense since users are more active during the day than night time.

Figure 3c and Figure 3d show the reply rate and reply time to emails sent on different days of a week. We see that emails sent on weekdays receive more and faster replies. The reply rate for emails sent on weekdays is around 7%, but that rate drops to 4% on weekends. For the median reply time, we see that emails sent on weekdays receive replies in less than 1 hour. However, emails sent on the weekend have 13 (for Sunday) or 30 (for Saturday) times longer reply latency. This is consistent with the fact that most people don't check or reply to emails as regularly on the weekend. Most emails sent over the weekend are replied to after Sunday.

4.2 Email Subject and Body

Next we study the effects of properties of the email content on user reply behavior. We start with the length of email subjects and email bodies. We remove punctuations and maintain stop words when counting the number of words. Figure 4a and Figure 4b show the effects of email subject length on user reply behavior. The reply rate decreases from 11.47% to 1.10% as the length of email subject increases from 1 to 29, which is an interesting phenomenon. Because we have access to the full content of emails in Avocado, we were able to examine emails that have long and short subjects to identify. We found that many long subjects include announcements in the subjects but no text in the body or some machine generated bug reports. Such email subjects are similar to "*[Bug 10001] Changed - Loop length not assigned correctly for xml file when extracted to a file and tested, works OK when tested from database.*". [4] Users don't need to reply to such emails, leading to lower reply rate.

In examining short subjects, we computed the reply rates for all unique subjects. Checking those that occur 20 times or more, we summarize those that have the highest reply rate. A large number of these are simply company names – these often indicate current contracts, customers, or sales leads that are being pursued. Other phrases such as "*expense report*", "*sales training*", "*meeting*", "*lunch*", and "*alerts*" indicate common activities that require approval, co-ordination, or action. Finally, a set of other phrase types such as "*hello*", "*hi*", "*hey*", etc. indicate recipient-sender familiarity (note that spam e-mail filters were in place before collection). We also find that reply time is influenced by subject length. The main trend is that the reply time decreases as the subject length increases.

We also analyze the impact of the email body length on reply behavior. Figure 4c and Figure 4d show the effects of email body length on reply behavior. We see that the reply rate initially increases from 4.65% to 9.64% words as the email length increases from 1 to 40 words and then decreases to 2.82% as the email body length increases to 500 words. Thus people are not likely to reply to emails with too few or too many words. The median reply time increases as the length of the email body increases. This may be

[2]The email IDs of the filtered subset can be downloaded from https://sites.google.com/site/lyangwww/code-data.

[3]For partitions of the data we compute the reply rate for each partition separately. For example, the reply rate to emails sent at night is the percentage of emails sent at night that receive a reply regardless of whether the reply is sent at night or day.

[4]We paraphrase this sentence due to data sensitivity.

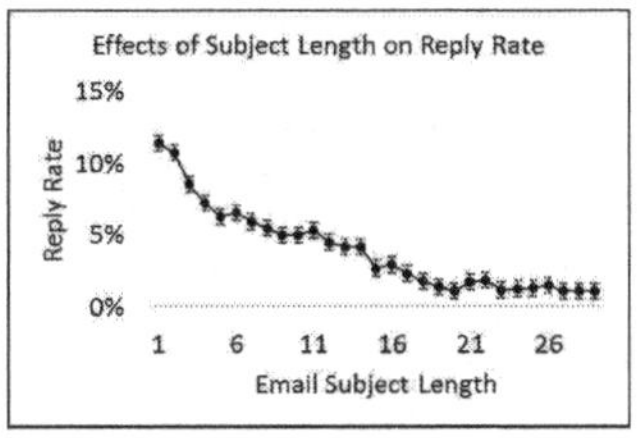

(a) Reply rate vs. subject length.

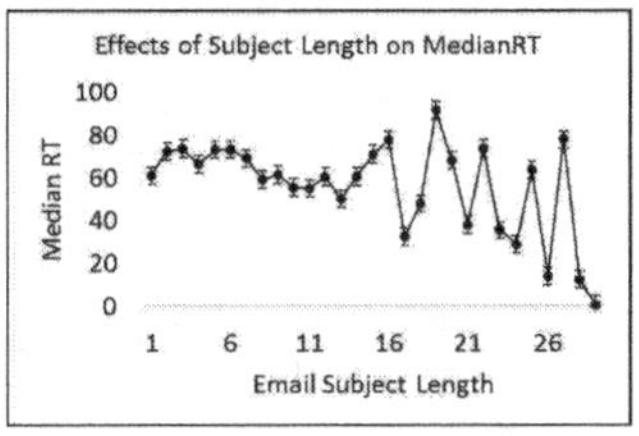

(b) Reply time vs. subject length.

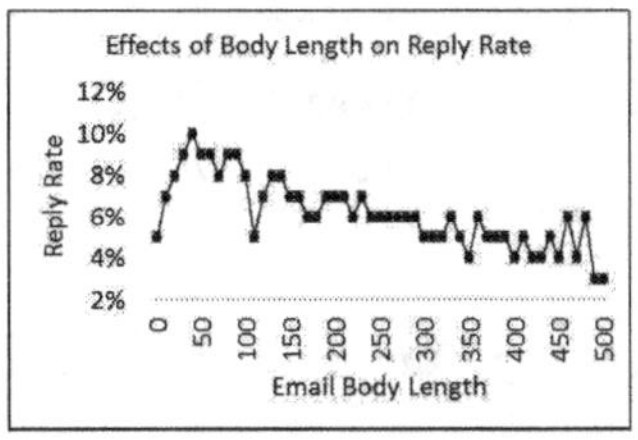

(c) Reply rate vs. body length.

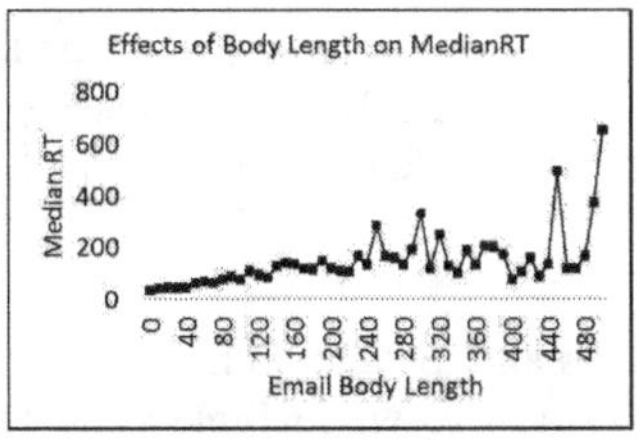

(d) Reply time vs. body length.

Figure 4: The effects of email subject length and email body length on reply rate and median reply time. The median reply time denoted by Median RT is in minutes.

Table 1: The effects of requests and commitments in emails on user reply behavior. The median reply time denoted by Median RT is in minutes.

Factor	Requests		Commitments	
Email Feature	HasReq	NoReq	HasCom	NoCom
Reply Rate	14.81%	7.45%	8.32%	8.78%
Median RT	81.13	54.51	86.71	60.60

because people need to spend more time reading and digesting the content of longer emails, thus increasing reply time.

4.3 Requests and Commitments in Emails

Previous work [3, 4, 7, 21] has studied "speech acts" in emails. Carvalho and Cohen [4] developed algorithms to classify email messages as to whether or not they contain certain "email acts", such as a request or a commitment. We classify emails into those with requests (e.g. "Send me the report.") or commitments (e.g. "I'll complete and send you the report.") and those without requests or commitments using an internally developed classifier inspired by previous work in this area [8].

Table 1 shows the effects of whether an email contains a request or commitment on reply rate and reply time. Emails that contain requests are almost twice as likely to receive replies as those that do not, 14.81% vs. 7.45% respectively. This is reasonable since intuitively people are more likely to reply to emails if the sender makes a request. In contrast, there is very little differences between the reply rate toward emails with and without commitments.

The median reply time toward emails with requests or commitments is longer, which may seem a bit counter-intuitive. However, this may be because such emails are associated with tasks, and therefore, people may need to do some work like searching information, reading or writing before they can reply to such a mail.

Table 2: The effects of email addresses and attachments on user reply behavior. The median reply time denoted by Median RT is in minutes.

Factor	Email Addresses		Attachments	
Email Feature	Internal	External	HasAttach	NoAttach
Reply Rate	7.76%	2.26%	8.08%	6.38%
Median RT	65.52	134.67	80.37	61.23

4.4 Internal / External Email Addresses

Next we investigate the impact of internal or external emails on reply rate and reply time. To do this, we adopt a heuristic method to classify the email addresses. For each receiver address, we check whether there is a "@" in it. If a receiver address contains "@" and does not contain "@avocadoit.com", this address is assigned an "external" label. If there is no "@" or only "@avocadoit.com" in a receiver address, we classify it as an internal address. Email addresses with "@avocadoit.com" are definitely internal addresses. However, a limitation of this method is that if email addresses with external domains are in the sender's contacts, they will be treated as internal addresses. In this sense, the internal email addresses in our analysis are those of Avocado employees or people who have frequent communications with Avocado employees and are stored in the contact books. Emails sent to at least one external address are labeled as external, otherwise they are treated as internal emails.

Table 2 shows the comparison of the reply rate/ reply time for internal emails and external emails. People are 3.4 times more likely to reply to internal emails (7.76%) than external emails (2.26%). In addition median reply time to internal emails is 2.1 times faster than to external emails, 66 vs. 135 minutes respectively. In our context, internal emails come from the colleagues or people in the sender's contacts, and are thus more likely to be quickly replied to.

4.5 Email Attachments

We further analyze the effects of email attachments on user reply behaviors. Table 2 shows that reply rates are higher for emails with attachments (8.08%) than emails without attachments (6.38%). This may be because the types of emails that contain attachments are more likely to require replies. The median reply time for emails with attachments is 23.81% longer than that for emails with no attachments. This result is consistent with the fact that people need to open the attachments and spend more time reading or replying to emails with attachments.

4.6 Number of Email Recipients

Unlike [20] who consider only dyadic emails, we also include emails sent to multiple recipients in our analysis. Figure 5 shows the comparisons of reply rate and reply time for emails with different number of recipients. Most emails are sent to 1 to 8 addresses. Emails sent to 3 to 5 addresses have the highest reply rates (approximately 10%). As the number of email recipients continues to increase, the reply rate begins to decrease. Thus more email recipients does not always mean a higher reply rate. There are at least two reasons for this: 1) some emails sent to many addresses are general announcements or reports which do not require replies; 2) when an email is

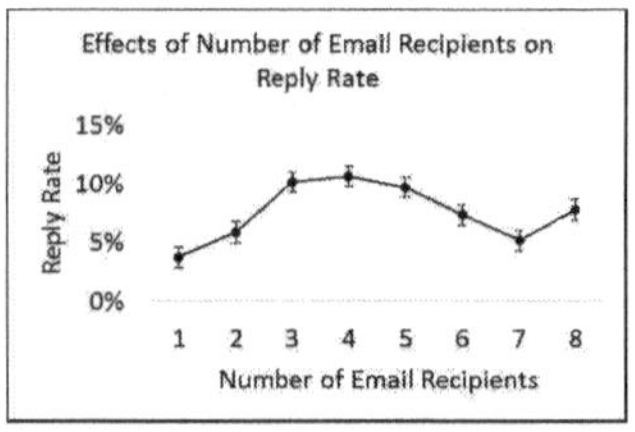

(a) Reply rate vs. the number of email recipients.

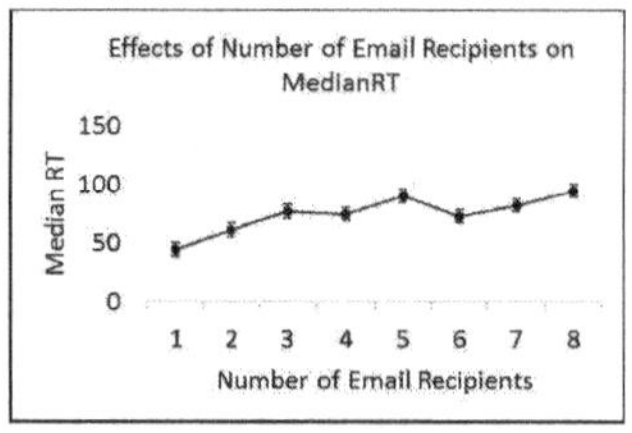

(b) Reply time vs. the number of email recipients.

Figure 5: The effects of the number of email recipients on reply rate and median reply time. The median reply time denoted by Median RT is in minutes.

sent to many recipients, it is more likely that no one will reply to it since people may think the other co-recipients will reply to it.

Median reply time increases from 44 minutes to 95 minutes as the number of email recipients increases from 1 to 8. Thus emails sent to more recipients get slower replies. When an email has many recipients, people may wait a while to see if others reply before they choose to do so, or it may be that emails that are sent to many people require some work to be accomplished before the reply.

5 PREDICTING REPLY BEHAVIOR

The results presented in Section 4 show that email reply behaviors are influenced by various factors such as time, email content, email addressees, email recipients and attachments. In this section, we use these insights to guide the development of features to train a supervised learning model to predict email reply behavior including reply time and reply action.

5.1 Data Overview and Methodology

Given the Avocado email collection described in Section 3, we split the data into training / testing partitions using the sent time of emails. Specifically, we use emails in 9 months from June 1st 2000 to February 28th 2001 for training and use emails in 3 months from March 1st 2001 to June 1st 2001 for testing. Because email is a temporally ordered collection, we used a split by time (rather than randomly) to ensure that we do not use future information to predict past reply behavior.

We formalize the reply action prediction task as a binary classification problem and the reply time prediction task as a multi-class classification problem. We follow the notations and task definitions presented in Section 3. Given an email message m that user u_i sent to a user set $\{u_j\}$ at time t, reply action prediction is to predict whether any user in $\{u_j\}$ will reply to message m. Thus the classified instances are emails with binary labels. For reply time prediction, we do not necessarily need to get the exact reply time latency. We follow a similar setting as previous related work [20], where we consider three classes of reply times: immediate replies that happen within 25 minutes (32.80% of the training data), quick replies that happen between 25 minutes and 245 minutes (32.84% of the training data), and slow replies that take longer than 245 minutes (34.36% of the training data). The ground truth labels can be directly extracted from the training/testing data based on the actual reply time and actions on emails. The statistics of the experimental

Table 3: Reply time prediction class distribution.

Class	Training Data		Testing Data	
1: ≤ 25min	5,143	32.80%	3,299	38.53%
2: 25-245min	5,150	32.84%	2,820	32.93%
3: ≥ 245min	5,389	34.36%	2,444	28.54%

Table 4: Reply action prediction class distribution.

Class	Training Data		Testing Data	
0: No Reply	224,605	93.47%	102,682	92.30%
1: Has Reply	15,682	6.53%	8,563	7.70%

data and the distribution of labels for reply time/action prediction task are shown in Table 3 and Table 4.

5.2 Learning Models and Evaluation Metrics

We experiment with a variety of machine learning algorithms including Logistic Regression, Neural Networks, RandomForest, AdaBoost [31] and Bagging algorithms. Since the focus of our work is on feature analysis, we only report the experimental results with a basic Logistic Regression (LR) model and the best model, AdaBoost. We used the sklearn[5] package for the implementation of LR and AdaBoost. We did multiple runs of hyper-parameter tuning by grid search to find the best setting for each model with cross validation on the training data.[6]

Since reply action prediction is highly imbalanced (see Table 4) and ranking quality is of importance for tasks like triage, we report Area Under the ROC Curve (AUC), which is a ranking metric insensitive to class imbalance, as the metric for reply action prediction. For reply time prediction, we report precision, recall, F-1 and accuracy (i.e., the percentage of correctly classified emails). The precision, recall, and F-1 are computed as weighted macro averages over all three classes.

5.3 Features

Our analysis in Section 4 identifies factors that impact email reply behaviors. Building on these observations we develop 10 classes of features that can be used to build models for predicting both reply time and reply action. The summary and description of the extracted features is provided in Table 5. In total, we extract 65 features and Bag-of-Words features in 10 feature groups. We normalize all features to be in the range of [0, 1] using min-max feature normalization.

Address Features (Address): These features include features derived from the email addresses such as whether the email is internal or external and the number of recipients.

[5] http://scikit-learn.org

[6] For reply time prediction with LR, we set $C = 1$, the maximum number of iterations as 500, tolerance for stopping criteria as 0.0001, penalization as l1 norm. For reply action prediction with LR, we set $C = 1$, the maximum number of iterations as 100, tolerance for stopping criteria as 0.0001, penalization as l1 norm. For reply time prediction with AdaBoost, we set the learning rate as 0.1, the maximum number of estimators as 800, boosting algorithm as $SAMME.R$. For the reply action prediction with AdaBoost, we set the learning rate as 1, the maximum number of estimators as 50, boosting algorithm as $SAMME.R$.

Table 5: The features extracted for predicting user email reply behaviors. The 10 feature groups Address, BOW, CPred, CProp, HistIndiv, HistPair, Meta, MetaAdded, Temporal, User stand for "Address Features", "Bag-of-Words", "Content Predictions", "Content Properties", "Historical Interaction-Individual", "Historical Interaction-Pairwise", "Metadata Properties", "Metadata Properties-Sender Added", "Temporal Features" and "User Features" respectively. Note that for the computation of features in User, HistIndiv and HistPair, we respect the temporal aspects of the data and only use the historical information before the sent time of the email instance.

Feature	Group	Description
IsInternalExternal	Address	1 binary feature indicating whether the email is internal or external
NumOfRecipients	Address	The number of recipients of the email
BagOfWords	BOW	The bag-of-words features indicating the TF-IDF weights of terms in the email body text
SentimentWords	CPred	2 integer features indicating the number of positive/negative sentiment words in the email body text
CommitmentScore	CPred	The commitment score of the email from an internal binary classifier
RequestScore	CPred	The request score of the email from an internal binary classifier
EmailSubLen	CProp	The length of the subject of the email
EmailBodyLen	CProp	The length of the body of the email
HistReplyRateGlobalUI	HistIndiv	The historical reply rate of the sender u_i towards all the other users
HistReplyNumGlobalUI	HistIndiv	The historical reply count of the sender u_i towards all the other users
HistRecEmailNumSTGlobalUI	HistIndiv	The historical number of received emails of the sender u_i as in sent to address from all the other users
HistRecEmailNumCCGlobalUI	HistIndiv	The historical number of received emails of the sender u_i as in CC address from all the other users
HistSentEmailNumGlobalUI	HistIndiv	The historical number of sent emails of sender u_i to all the other users
HistReplyTimeMeanGlobalUI	HistIndiv	The historical mean reply time of sender u_i to all the other users
HistReplyTimeMedianGlobalUI	HistIndiv	The historical median reply time of sender u_i to all the other users
HistGlobalUJ	HistIndiv	21 features indicating similar mean/min/max historical behavior statistics of recipients $\{u_j\}$ towards the other users
HistReplyNumLocal	HistPair	3 features indicating the historical mean, min, max reply count of the recipient $\{u_j\}$ to sender u_i
HistReplyTimeMeanLocal	HistPair	3 features indicating the historical mean, min, max of the mean reply time of the recipient $\{u_j\}$ towards sender u_i
HistReplyTimeMedianLocal	HistPair	3 features indicating the historical mean, min, max of the median reply time of the recipient $\{u_j\}$ towards sender u_i
HasAttachment	Meta	1 binary feature indicating whether the email has attachments
NumOfAttachment	Meta	1 integer feature indicating the number of attachment of the email
IsImportant	MetaAdded	1 binary feature indicating the importance of the email, which is a tag specified by u_i
IsPriority	MetaAdded	1 binary feature indicating the priority of the email, which is a tag specified by u_i
IsSensitivity	MetaAdded	1 binary feature indicating the sensitivity of the email, which is a tag specified by u_i
TimeOfDay	Temporal	4 binary features indicating the time of the day (0-6, 6-12, 12-18, 18-24)
DayOfWeek	Temporal	7 binary features indicating the day of week (Sun, Mon, ... , Sat)
WeekDayEnd	Temporal	2 binary feature indicating whether the day is a weekday or a weekend
UserDepartment	User	1 feature indicating the department of the email sender u_i.
UserJobTitle	User	1 feature indicating the job title of the email sender u_i.

Bag-of-Words (BOW): These features include the TF-IDF weights of non-stop terms in the email body text. The vocabulary size of our experimental data set is 554061.

Content Predictions (CPred): These features include some predictions like positive / negative sentiment words, commitment / request scores from email textual content. We count the number of positive sentiment words and negative sentiment words in email body text using a sentiment lexicon from a previous research [17]. We also include the commitment and request score of emails from an internal classier to infer the likelihood of whether an email contains a commitment or a request.

Content Properties (CProp): These features are content properties including the length of email subjects and email body text.

Historical Interaction-Individual (HistIndiv): These features characterize the historical email interactions related to each sender u_i and recipient in $\{u_j\}$ aggregated across all interactions. This feature group has two subgroups: global interaction features for the sender u_i and global interaction features for recipients $\{u_j\}$. The global interaction features for the sender u_i contain a set of features to capture the historical interactions between u_i with all the other users such as reply rate, reply count, number of received emails, number of sent emails, mean/median reply time, etc. For the global interaction features for recipients $\{u_j\}$, since there could be multiple recipients, we compute the mean/min/max of those statistics to capture the historical interactions between $\{u_j\}$ and all other users.

Historical Interaction-Pairwise (HistPair): These features characterize the local (pairwise) interactions between the sender u_i and the recipients $\{u_j\}$, which are statistics like number of replied emails, mean/median reply time from the historical interactions between the sender u_i and the recipients $\{u_j\}$. Note that for the computation of "HistIndiv" and "HistPair" features, we compute per day updated user profiles and only use the information before the email instance.

Metadata Properties (Meta): This feature group contains features derived from email attachments including whether the email has attachments and number of email attachments.

Metadata Properties-Sender Added (MetaAdded): These features include tags specified by the sender u_i to indicate the importance, priority or sensitivity of the sent email. In our data, less than 3% of emails have such tags. But they can still provide some clues to infer user reply behavior once they are set by the sender.

Temporal Features (Temporal): These features are generated based on the sent time of emails to capture the temporal factors on user email reply behaviors.

User Features (User): These features include the department and job title of the person.

Table 6: Summary of the prediction results for user email reply time and reply action. The Precision, Recall and F-1 scores are weighted averages by supports over all classes. The best performance is highlighted in boldface. Both LR and AdaBoost show significant improvements over all baseline methods with p < 0.01 measured by micro sign test [30].

	Action	Time			
Method	AUC	Prec	Rec	F1	Accuracy
Random	.5024	.3262	.3253	.3244	.3257
Majority Vote	.5000	.0815	.2854	.1267	.2854
Previous Reply	.5858	.3717	.3742	.3613	.3633
LR	.7036	.3952	.4098	.3791	.4098
AdaBoost	**.7208**	**.4561**	**.4591**	**.4476**	**.4591**

5.4 Baselines

We compare our method against three baselines as follows:

Random. This method randomly generates a predicted class from the label distribution in the training data.

Majority Vote. This method always predicts the largest class, which is class 0 (no reply) for reply action prediction and class 3 (> 245min) for reply time prediction.

Previous Reply. This method generates predictions according to the previous reply behaviors of the recipients $\{u_j\}$ towards the sender u_i before the sent time t of email m. For reply action, it predicts 0 (no reply) if there is no previous reply behavior from $\{u_j\}$ to u_i. For reply time, it predicts the majority class if there is no previous reply behavior from$\{u_j\}$ to u_i. If there are previous reply behaviors, it computes the median time of previous reply time as the predicted result. Note that this baseline is similar to the "Last Reply" baseline used in [20]. [7]

5.5 Experimental Results and Analysis

We now analyze the results of our proposed method compared with various baseline methods. Table 6 shows the prediction results for reply action and reply time. Figure 6 shows the ROC curves for all methods for reply action prediction. The baseline "Majority Vote", while accurate since 92.30% of emails are negative, achieves zero true positive rate (recall) and predicts no positive instances. Likewise "Random" falls nearly on the $x = y$ dashed line in red which indicates expected random performance (empirical variance leads to a slight bit of luck). As shown in Table 6, both LR and AdaBoost outperform all three baselines by AUC. The best model AdaBoost achieves large improvements of 44.16% comparing with "Majority Vote" and 23.05% comparing with "Previous Reply". AdaBoost achieves slightly better performance than LR. Examining the ROC curves, the most competitive baseline is "Previous Reply", which is still under the ROC curves of LR and AdaBoost. The AUC scores show that our methods outperform all baseline methods with a large margin.

For reply time prediction, both LR and AdaBoost models with the proposed features outperform all baseline methods with large gains. The differences are statistically significantly with $p < 0.01$ measured by a micro sign test [30]. The best method based on AdaBoost achieves large improvements of 23.89%, 26.36% for F-1 and accuracy comparing with "Previous Reply" and 253.18%, 60.85% for F-1, accuracy comparing with "Majority Vote". Comparing the two learning models, AdaBoost has better performance than LR in terms of both F-1 and accuracy. This shows the advantages of AdaBoost that can feed the relative "hardness" of each training sample into the tree growing algorithm such that later trees tend to focus on harder-to-classify instances.

[7] For the proposed method in [20], we can not reproduce their method since they don't disclose the details of the 83 features in their model and they also don't release the code and data due the proprietary nature of their work.

5.6 Feature Importance Analysis

Feature Group Analysis. We further perform analyses to understand the relative importance of different feature groups in predicting reply time. We consider two approaches: (1) Remove one feature group. We observe the change in performance when we remove any one of the 10 feature groups. (2) Only one feature group. We observe the change in performance when we classify emails only using one feature group. Table 7 and Table 8 show the results of these analyses for reply action prediction and reply time prediction using the AdaBoost model, which is the best method in our previous experiments.

Table 7 shows the performance when we use only one feature group. The classes are ordered by AUC scores on action prediction. The most important features are highlighted using a triangle. For reply action prediction, "HistIndiv" and "HistPair" show the best performance compared to other feature groups. Using only "HistIndiv" features results in 0.6924 for the AUC score, which is close to the performance with all feature groups. These results suggest that historical interactions are important features for reply action prediction. "CPred" features (i.e., algorithmic predictions of request, commitments and sentiment) are also important although somewhat less so than the historical interaction features. However, for reply time prediction we see a different story. "Temporal" features are the most important features for predicting reply time as highlighted in Table 7. Using only "Temporal" features results in good latency prediction accuracy of 0.4261, which is only slightly worse than the result from combining all feature groups. "HistIndiv" features which result in accuracy above 0.40 are also helpful in predicting latency. For reply actions, historical interaction features are the most important in indicating whether people will reply to the email eventually no matter the time latency. Given they will reply to an email, people seem to strongly prefer to reply during office hours on workdays, which explains why "Temporal" factors are so important for reply time prediction.

Another way of looking at the importance of features is to remove one class and look at the decrease in performance. Table 8) shows the results of removing one feature group. Performance decrease the most when we remove "HistIndiv" features for reply action prediction and "Temporal" features for reply time prediction. These results are consistent with the results when we only use one feature group. We also found some features are not very useful for reply behaviour prediction. For instance, when we remove "Meta" features which are derived from email attachments, both F-1 and accuracy increase slightly for reply time prediction. This suggests that there is still space for feature selection to further improve the

Table 7: Comparison of performance on predicting reply time and reply action when we only use one feature group. The learning model used is AdaBoost. The best performance is highlighted in boldface. ▲ indicates strong performance when only use one feature group. The feature settings are sorted by the AUC scores.

	Action	Time			
Feature Set	AUC	Prec	Rec	F-1	Accuracy
HistIndiv	.6924▲	.3891	.4104▲	.3642	.4104▲
HistPair	.6382▲	.3721	.3890	.3463	.3890
CPred	.5954	.3748	.3784	.3352	.3784
User	.5944	.3729	.3847	.3575	.3847
Address	.5912	.3790	.3641	.3038	.3641
Temporal	.5401	.4436▲	.4261▲	.4264▲	.4261▲
CProp	.5346	.3415	.3785	.3060	.3785
MetaAdded	.5291	.2524	.3877	.2672	.3877
Meta	.5247	.2398	.3670	.2866	.3670
BOW	.5106	.3744	.3976	.3391	.3976
AllFeat	**.7208**	**.4561**	**.4591**	**.4476**	**.4591**

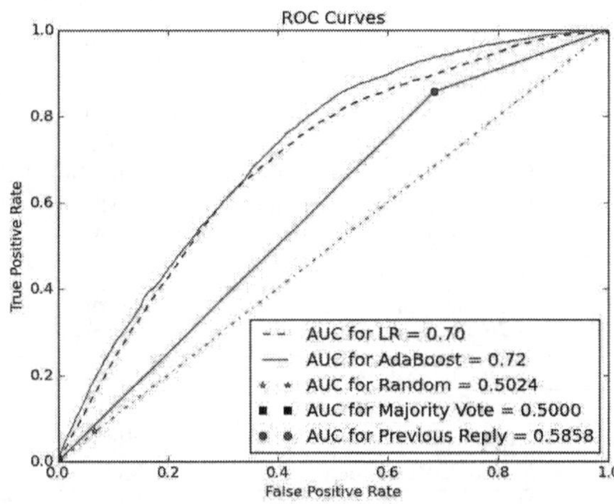

Figure 6: The ROC curves of different methods for the reply action prediction task.

Table 8: Comparison of performance on predicting reply time and reply action when we remove one feature group. The learning model used is AdaBoost. ▼ indicates large drops in performance when remove one feature group. The feature settings are sorted by the AUC scores.

	Action	Time			
Feature Set	AUC	Prec	Rec	F-1	Accuracy
–HistIndiv	.6620▼	.4453	.4481	.4409▼	.4481
–CProp	.7112	.4472	.4543	.4413	.4543
–Address	.7187	.4550	.4599	.4476	.4599
–MetaAdded	.7191	.4549	.4579	.4449	.4579
–HistPair	.7198	.4544	.4572	.4432	.4572
–Meta	.7216	.4573	.4604	.4515	.4604
–Temporal	.7218	.3841▼	.4056▼	.3800▼	.4056▼
–CPred	.7229	.4540	.4611	.4457	.4611
–BOW	.7237	.4539	.4573	.4503	.4573
–User	.7256	.4473	.4482	.4431	.4482
AllFeat	.7208	.4561	.4591	.4476	.4591

performance of reply behavior prediction. We leave the study of feature selection to future work.

Importance of Individual Features. AdaBoost [31] provides a mechanism for reporting the relative importance of each feature. By analyzing the relative importance, we gain insights into the importance of individual features for different email reply prediction tasks. Table 9 shows the most important features for predicting reply time and reply action with the relative feature importance learned by AdaBoost. The most important features for reply action prediction are historical interaction features including "HistReplyCountRecipientMax", "HistSentEmailCountSender", "HistReceiveEmailSTRecipientMin", content properties like the length of email subjects and email bodies, and address features like "NumOfReceivers", "IsInternalExternal" etc. On the other hand, temporal features like "TimeOfDay1Morning", "IsWeekDay", "DayOfWeek1Sunday", "TimeOfDay4Night" are among the most important features for reply time prediction. These interesting differences are also consistent with the results in the feature group analysis. Some features including historical interaction features and content properties like the length of email bodies are important for both reply action prediction and reply time prediction.

6 CONCLUSIONS AND FUTURE WORK

In this paper, we introduce and formalize the task of reply behavior prediction in a corporate email setting, using the publicly available Avocado collection. We characterize various factors affecting email reply behavior, showing that temporal features (time of day and day of week), content properties (such as the length of email subjects and email bodies) and prior interactions between the sender and recipients are related to reply behavior. We use these insights to extract 10 classes of features groups and build models to predict whether an email will be responded to and how long it will take to do so. We show that the proposed methods outperform all baselines with large gains. We further show that temporal, textual content properties, and historical interaction features are especially important in predicting reply behavior.

Our research represents an initial effort to understand email actions in a corporate setting. We examined email reply behavior in detail in one technology company, but is unclear how representative the company is. It is important to see how our findings generalize to different industry sectors and different demographic backgrounds of employees. Future work will consider more available email collections and more features that could be signals for user reply behavior prediction. Of special interest is the use of richer content features such as lexical, syntactic and semantic features. We shared the IDs of the emails that we consider in our research so that others can extend our research on the Avocado collection.

Table 9: The most important features for predicting reply time and reply action with relative feature importances in AdaBoost.

	Reply Action Prediction			Reply Time Prediction		
Rank	Feature Name	Group	Importance	Feature Name	Group	Importance
1	EmailSubjectLen	Cprop	1.0000	TimeOfDay1Morning	Temporal	1.0000
2	HistReplyCountRecipientMax	HistIndiv	0.5714	IsWeekDay	Temporal	0.8083
3	HistSentEmailCountSender	HistIndiv	0.4286	DayOfWeek1Sunday	Temporal	0.4946
4	HistReceiveEmailSTRecipientMin	HistIndiv	0.4286	EmailBodyLen	Cprop	0.3260
5	NumOfReceivers	Address	0.4286	TimeOfDay4Night	Temporal	0.3052
6	EmailBodyLen	Cprop	0.4286	HistRTMedianRecipientAvg	HistIndiv	0.1690
7	HistLocalMeanRTMin	HistPair	0.2857	HistRTMedianRecipientMin	HistIndiv	0.1563
8	IsInternalExternal	Address	0.2857	HistLocalReplyCountMax	HistPair	0.1125
9	UserJobTitleSender	User	0.2857	HistReceiveEmailSTSender	HistIndiv	0.1101
10	HistLocalReplyCountMin	HistPair	0.2857	IsPriority	MetaAdded	0.0951
11	NumoOfAttachment	Meta	0.2857	IsWeekEnd	Temporal	0.0909
12	HistReceiveEmailCCSender	HistIndiv	0.1429	HistLocalMedianRTMin	HistPair	0.0907
13	HistRTMeanSender	HistIndiv	0.1429	HistReceiveEmailCCSender	HistIndiv	0.0858
14	HistReplyCountRecipientAvg	HistIndiv	0.1429	IsSensitivity	MetaAdded	0.0759
15	HistLocalReplyCountMax	HistPair	0.1429	HistRTMeanRecipientAvg	HistIndiv	0.0674

7 ACKNOWLEDGMENTS

This work was supported in part by the Center for Intelligent Information Retrieval and in part by NSF grant #IIS-1419693. Any opinions, findings and conclusions or recommendations expressed in this material are those of the authors and do not necessarily reflect those of the sponsor.

REFERENCES

[1] Douglas Aberdeen, Ondrej Pacovsky, and Andrew Slater. The Learning behind Gmail Priority Inbox. In *NIPS 2010 Workshop on Learning on Cores, Clusters and Clouds*.

[2] Victoria Bellotti, Nicolas Ducheneaut, Mark Howard, and Ian Smith. Taking Email to Task: The Design and Evaluation of a Task Management Centered Email Tool. In *CHI '03*.

[3] Paul N. Bennett and Jaime Carbonell. Detecting Action-items in E-mail. In *SIGIR '05*.

[4] Vitor R. Carvalho and William W. Cohen. On the Collective Classification of Email "Speech Acts". In *SIGIR '05*.

[5] Marta E. Cecchinato, Abigail Sellen, Milad Shokouhi, and Gavin Smyth. Finding Email in a Multi-Account, Multi-Device World. In *CHI'16*.

[6] Michael Chui, James Manyika, Jacques Bughin, Richard Dobbs, Charles Roxburgh, Hugo Sarrazin, Geoffrey Sands, and Magdalena Westergren. 2012. The social economy: Unlocking value and productivity through social technologies. (2012). A report by McKinsey Global Institute.

[7] William W. Cohen, Vitor R. Carvalho, and Tom M. Mitchell. Learning to Classify Email into Speech Acts. In *EMNLP '04*.

[8] Simon Corston-Oliver, Eric Ringger, Michael Gamon, and Richard Campbell. Integration of Email and Task Lists. In *First Conference on Email and Anti-Spam*.

[9] Laura A. Dabbish and Robert E. Kraut. Email Overload at Work: An Analysis of Factors Associated with Email Strain. In *CSCW '06*.

[10] Laura A. Dabbish, Robert E. Kraut, Susan Fussell, and Sara Kiesler. Understanding Email Use: Predicting Action on a Message. In *CHI '05*.

[11] Dotan Di Castro, Zohar Karnin, Liane Lewin-Eytan, and Yoelle Maarek. You've Got Mail, and Here is What You Could Do With It!: Analyzing and Predicting Actions on Email Messages. In *WSDM '16*.

[12] Danyel Fisher, A. J. Brush, Eric Gleave, and Marc A. Smith. Revisiting Whittaker & Sidner's "Email Overload" Ten Years Later. In *CSCW '06*.

[13] Michael Freed, Jaime G. Carbonell, Geoffrey J. Gordon, Jordan Hayes, Brad A. Myers, Daniel P. Siewiorek, Stephen F. Smith, Aaron Steinfeld, and Anthony Tomasic. RADAR: A Personal Assistant that Learns to Reduce Email Overload. In *AAAI '08*.

[14] David Graus, David van Dijk, Manos Tsagkias, Wouter Weerkamp, and Maarten de Rijke. Recipient Recommendation in Enterprises Using Communication Graphs and Email Content. In *SIGIR '14*.

[15] Mihajlo Grbovic, Guy Halawi, Zohar Karnin, and Yoelle Maarek. How Many Folders Do You Really Need?: Classifying Email into a Handful of Categories. In *CIKM '14*.

[16] Ido Guy, Michal Jacovi, Noga Meshulam, Inbal Ronen, and Elad Shahar. Public vs. Private: Comparing Public Social Network Information with Email. In *CSCW '08*.

[17] Minqing Hu and Bing Liu. Mining and Summarizing Customer Reviews. In *KDD '04*.

[18] Anjuli Kannan, Karol Kurach, Sujith Ravi, Tobias Kaufmann, Andrew Tomkins, Balint Miklos, Greg Corrado, Laszlo Lukacs, Marina Ganea, Peter Young, and Vivek Ramavajjala. Smart Reply: Automated Response Suggestion for Email. In *KDD '16*.

[19] Bryan Klimt and Yiming Yang. The Enron Corpus: A New Dataset for Email Classification Research. In *ECML'04*.

[20] Farshad Kooti, Luca Maria Aiello, Mihajlo Grbovic, Kristina Lerman, and Amin Mantrach. Evolution of Conversations in the Age of Email Overload. In *WWW '15*.

[21] Andrew Lampert, Robert Dale, and Cecile Paris. Detecting Emails Containing Requests for Action. In *HLT '10*.

[22] Carman Neustaedter, A. J. Bernheim Brush, and Marc A. Smith. Beyond "From" and "Received": Exploring the Dynamics of Email Triage. In *CHI EA '05*.

[23] Byung-Won On, Ee-Peng Lim, Jing Jiang, Amruta Purandare, and Loo-Nin Teow. Mining Interaction Behaviors for Email Reply Order Prediction. In *ASONAM '10*.

[24] Ashequl Qadir, Michael Gamon, Patrick Pantel, and Ahmed Hassan Awadallah. Activity Modeling in Email. In *NAACL-HLT '16*.

[25] S. Radicati. 2014. Email statistics report, 2014-2018. (2014).

[26] Maya Sappelli, Gabriella Pasi, Suzan Verberne, Maaike de Boer, and Wessel Kraaij. 2016. Assessing E-mail intent and tasks in E-mail messages. *Inf. Sci.* 358-359 (2016), 1–17.

[27] Michael Gamon Richard Campbell Simon H. Corston-Oliver, Eric Ringger. Task-focused Summarization of Email. In *ACL'04*.

[28] Joshua R. Tyler and John C. Tang. When Can I Expect an Email Response? A Study of Rhythms in Email Usage. In *ECSCW'03*.

[29] Steve Whittaker and Candace Sidner. Email Overload: Exploring Personal Information Management of Email. In *CHI '96*.

[30] Yiming Yang and Xin Liu. A Re-examination of Text Categorization Methods. In *SIGIR '99*.

[31] Ji Zhu, Hui Zou, Saharon Rosset, and Trevor Hastie. 2009. Multi-class AdaBoost. *Statistics and Its Interface* (2009).

ReAct: Online Multimodal Embedding for Recency-Aware Spatiotemporal Activity Modeling

Chao Zhang[1], Keyang Zhang[1], Quan Yuan[1], Fangbo Tao[1], Luming Zhang[2], Tim Hanratty[3], and Jiawei Han[1]
[1]Computer Science Department, University of Illinois at Urbana-Champaign, Urbana, IL, USA
[2]Department of CSIE, Hefei University of Technology, China
[3]U.S. Army Research Laboratory, Adelphi, MD, USA
[1]{czhang82, kzhang53, qyuan, ftao2, hanj}@illinois.edu
[2]zglumg@gmail.com [3]timothy.p.hanratty@mail.mil

ABSTRACT

Spatiotemporal activity modeling is an important task for applications like tour recommendation and place search. The recently developed geographical topic models have demonstrated compelling results in using geo-tagged social media (GTSM) for spatiotemporal activity modeling. Nevertheless, they all operate in batch and cannot dynamically accommodate the latest information in the GTSM stream to reveal up-to-date spatiotemporal activities. We propose ReAct, a method that processes continuous GTSM streams and obtains *recency-aware* spatiotemporal activity models on the fly. Distinguished from existing topic-based methods, ReAct embeds all the regions, hours, and keywords into the same latent space to capture their correlations. To generate high-quality embeddings, it adopts a novel semi-supervised multimodal embedding paradigm that leverages the activity category information to guide the embedding process. Furthermore, as new records arrive continuously, it employs strategies to effectively incorporate the new information while preserving the knowledge encoded in previous embeddings. Our experiments on the geo-tagged tweet streams in two major cities have shown that ReAct significantly outperforms existing methods for location and activity retrieval tasks.

ACM Reference format:
Chao Zhang[1], Keyang Zhang[1], Quan Yuan[1], Fangbo Tao[1], Luming Zhang[2], Tim Hanratty[3], and Jiawei Han[1] . 2017. ReAct: Online Multimodal Embedding for Recency-Aware Spatiotemporal Activity Modeling. In *Proceedings of SIGIR '17, August 07-11, 2017, Shinjuku, Tokyo, Japan*, , 10 pages.
DOI: 10.1145/3077136.3080814

1 INTRODUCTION

Today's big cities pose big challenges when people try to find desired resources like places and activities. Consider a tourist in a metropolis like New York City. What are the popular activities in her neighborhood at the time being? Which regions should she stay if she cares much about quality food and accessible transportation around her hotel? With hundreds of thousands places in the city and the complex spatiotemporal dynamics, answering such questions is challenging not only for tourists, but even for local citizens who have lived in New York City for many years.

Years ago, developing data-driven approaches to model people's activities in the physical world was almost impossible due to the lack of reliable sources. Traditional approaches have resorted to human surveys to unveil land uses [31, 32], yet such knowledge is still too limited to support downstream activity retrieval applications. The recent proliferation of geo-tagged social media (abbreviated as GTSM onwards), however, sheds light on this problem. As every GTSM record (*e.g.*, geo-tagged tweet, Foursquare checkin) contains a location, a timestamp, and a text message, the massive GTSM data generated from various platforms serve as a result of crowd sensing — they contain rich information about spatiotemporal dynamics as people probe different regions as human sensors. With tens of millions of GTSM records being collected every day, it becomes possible to perform data-driven spatiotemporal activity modeling to address people's information needs.

The recent studies [13, 16, 24, 28, 34, 35] have demonstrated the potential of GTSM for modeling spatiotemporal activities. By incorporating the spatial information into classical topic models like LDA [5], their proposed geographical topic models can detect the activities in different regions, and vice versa. While compelling results have been obtained by those geographical topic models, they all assume the GTSM data is given as static. In practice, however, people's activities in the physical world are dynamically evolving in nature, and the end users often demand the *latest* knowledge. For example, consider the user who queries for popular activities around her. What she needs are the activities popular in recent months or even weeks, rather than the ones that were popular years ago but no longer popular now. As another example, when users seek for places for outdoor activities in summer time, beach-area attractions could be good answers to such queries. But when it comes to the fall time, beach-related activities become too chilly for most people, while other places like parks with hiking trails are more appropriate. Such information is readily available in GTSM streams. Unfortunately, existing geographical topic models all operate in batch and cannot capture the latest information about spatiotemporal activities.

In this paper, we learn *recency-aware* spatiotemporal activity models from dynamic GTSM streams. This task is challenging on account of the following issues. First, *integrating diverse data types is nontrivial.* GTSM involves three different data types: location, time, and text. Considering the totally different representations

SIGIR '17, August 07-11, 2017, Shinjuku, Tokyo, Japan
© 2017 ACM. 978-1-4503-5022-8/17/08...$15.00
DOI: 10.1145/3077136.3080814

of these data types and their complicated inter-type interactions, effectively fusing them into a unified model is a challenge. Second, *it is hard to capture activity semantics from short text.* In GTSM, the semantics of people's activities are expressed through short text messages instead of long documents. To build high-quality spatiotemporal activity models, it is important yet difficult to capture the semantics of such short text messages. Third, *recency-aware processing of massive streaming data is required.* We have to handle the online GTSM stream to build recency-aware spatiotemporal activity models. Nevertheless, it is challenging to effectively accommodate the new records without overfitting them. In addition, it is key to build an update-efficient model to process massive GTSM streams.

We propose a recency-aware spatiotemporal activity model named ReAct. The main technical contributions of ReAct are highlighted as follows:

(1) In ReAct, we directly embed all the regions, hours, and keywords into the same latent space to preserve their inter-type interactions. If two elements are highly correlated (*e.g.*, the JFK airport region and the keyword 'flight'), their representations in the latent space tend be close. Compared with geographical topic modeling methods, the multimodal embedding does not impose any distributional assumptions on people's activities, and incurs much lower computational cost in the learning process.
(2) We employ a novel semi-supervised paradigm in ReAct to generate high-quality embeddings. In a considerable number of records, the users explicitly specify the point-of-interest (POI) to indicate their activity categories (*e.g.*, outdoor, shop). The category information can serve as clean and well-structured knowledge, which allows us to better separate the elements with different semantics in the latent space. Hence, we adopt a semi-supervised paradigm that leverages the clean category information to guide the embedding process and generates better-quality embeddings.
(3) As new GTSM records arrive continuously, we design two strategies to update the embeddings and obtain recency-aware spatiotemporal activity models. The first imposes life-decaying weights on the records such that recent records are emphasized. The second treats previous embeddings as prior knowledge, and employs a constrained optimization procedure to obtain updated embeddings. With either strategy, ReAct effectively incorporates the information in the new records, while largely preserving the knowledge encoded in the previous embeddings to avoid overfitting.

To the best of our knowledge, ReAct represents the first work that can learn recency-aware spatiotemporal activity models from dynamic GTSM streams on the fly. We have performed extensive experiments on two million-scale geo-tagged tweet data sets collected from Los Angeles and New York City. We find that ReAct can generate spatiotemporal activity models in which the latest patterns of spatiotemporal activities are well captured. Across a variety of activity retrieval tasks, ReAct outperforms state-of-the-art methods significantly.

2 OVERVIEW

Problem Description. Let $\mathcal{R} = \{r_1, r_2, \dots, r_N, \dots\}$ be a stream of geo-tagged social media (GTSM) records. Each record $r \in \mathcal{R}$ is defined by a tuple $\langle t_r, l_r, m_r \rangle$ where: (1) l_r is a two-dimensional vector that represents the user's location when r is created; (2) t_r is the creating timestamp; and (3) m_r is a bag of keywords that represent the text message of r.

Our goal is to use the stream $\mathcal{R}$ to learn *recency-aware* spatiotemporal activity models. As there are three different attributes (*i.e.*, location, time, and text) that are intertwined, an effective spatiotemporal activity model should carefully capture their inter-type correlations. Further, to continuously incorporate the *latest* information in $\mathcal{R}$, the model should keep updating as new records arrive. At any time, the learnt model should be able to answer two types of queries: 1) *Spatial query.* Given a spatial location, what are the popular activities around it? and 2) *Textual query.* Given an activity query represented by a bunch of keywords, what are the suitable regions or places for such an activity? For both queries, the users can also specify a timestamp in their query. As such, the model can return time-specific results in response, *e.g.*, returning brunch places for the query 'food' issued in the morning and dining places for the same query issued in the afternoon.

Overview of ReAct. To model people's spatiotemporal activities, ReAct embeds all the spatial, temporal, and textual elements into the same latent space. While the keywords can serve as natural embedding elements for the textual part, it is infeasible to embed every location and timestamp as the space and time are continuous. We thus map each timestamp to some hour in a day and use the mapped hour as a basic temporal element, and hence have 24 possible temporal elements in total. Similarly, we partition the geographical space into equal-size regions and consider each region as a basic spatial element.

Meanwhile, we observe that a considerable number of records explicitly specify the points-of-interests (POIs), *e.g.*, many Foursquare users link their accounts with Twitter to *checkin* at different venues. The category information (*e.g.*, outdoor, shop) of those records, which is clean and well-structured, can serve as useful signals to understand people's activities. We thus regard those categories as labels, and design a semi-supervised paradigm to guide the learning of quality embeddings. At a high level, ReAct aims to learn the embeddings L, T, W, and C where: (1) L is the embeddings for regions; (2) T is the embeddings for hours; (3) W is the embeddings for keywords; and (4) C is the embeddings for categories. Take L as an example. Each element $\mathbf{v}_l \in L$ is a D-dimensional ($D > 0$) vector, which represents the embedding for region l.

Figure 1 shows the framework of ReAct. As shown, it adopts a semi-supervised paradigm for multimodal embedding. 1) For an unlabeled record r_u, we optimize the embeddings L, T, W for the task of recovering the attributes in r_u; and 2) For a labeled record r_l, we optimize the embeddings L, T, W, C for not only attribute recovery but also activity classification. In such a process, the embeddings of the regions, hours, and keywords are shared across the two tasks, while the category embeddings are specific to the activity classification task. In this way, the semantics of activity categories are propagated from labeled records to unlabeled ones, thereby better separating the elements with different semantics in the latent space.

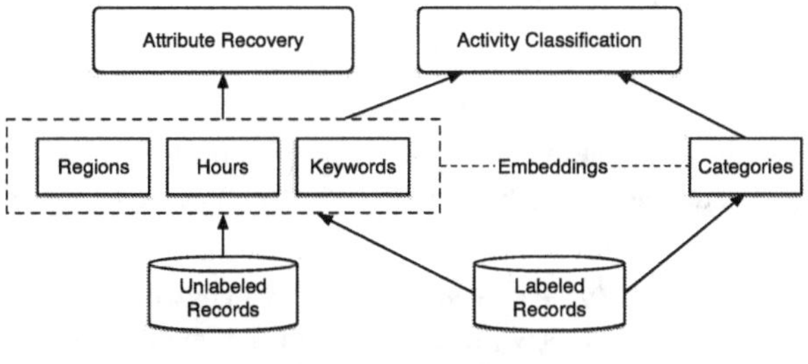

Figure 1: The semi-supervised multimodal embedding framework of ReAct.

The entire learning proceeds in an online manner. When a collection $\mathcal{R}_\Delta$ of new records arrive, our goal is to update the embeddings (L, T, W, C) to accommodate the information contained in $\mathcal{R}_\Delta$. While it is tempting to use $\mathcal{R}_\Delta$ to learn the embeddings from scratch, such an idea not only incurs unnecessary computational overhead, but also leads to overfitting of the new data. To address this issue, we propose an online learning procedure in Section 3, which effectively incorporates the new records while largely preserving the information encoded in the previous embeddings.

3 LEARNING THE REACT MODEL

In this section, we describe the learning procedures for ReAct. As aforementioned, given a collection of records $\mathcal{R}_\Delta$, for any record $r \in \mathcal{R}_\Delta$, either labeled or unlabeled, ReAct first takes the attribute recovery task, and updates the embeddings L, T, and W to correctly recover the attributes of r. If r is labeled, ReAct further leverages the category information as supervision, and updates L, T, W, and C such that r can be classified into the correct category.

The key problem in the above online learning framework is, how to update the embeddings with the goal of effectively incorporating the information in $\mathcal{R}_\Delta$ without overfitting it? We develop two different strategies for this problem: one is life-decaying learning, and the other is constraint-based learning. In what follows, we first describe the details of those two strategies in Section 3.1 and 3.2. Then we analyze their space and time complexities in Section 3.3.

3.1 Life-Decaying Learning

Our first strategy, called life-decaying learning, assigns different weights to the records in the GTSM stream such that more recent records receive higher weights. Specifically, for any record r that has appeared in the stream, we set its weight as:

$$w_r = e^{-\tau a_r},$$

where $\tau > 0$ is a decaying parameter, and a_r is r's age with regard to the current time. The general philosophy of such a weighing scheme is to emphasize the recent records and highlight the up-to-date observations of urban activities. On the other hand, the old records in the stream are not completely ignored, they have smaller weights but are still involved in model training to prevent overfitting.

Practically, it is infeasible to store all the records seen so far on account of the massive size of the GTSM stream. For tackling this issue, we maintain a continuously updating buffer $\mathcal{B}$, as shown in Figure 2. The buffer $\mathcal{B}$ consists of m buckets $B_0, B_1, \ldots, B_{m-1}$, where all the buckets have the same time span ΔT. For each bucket $B_i (0 \le i < m)$, we assign an exponentially decaying weight $e^{-\tau i}$ to it, where the weight represents the percentage of samples that we preserve for the respective time span. In other words, the most recent bucket B_0 holds the complete set of records within its time span, the next bucket B_1 holds $e^{-\tau}$ of the corresponding records, and so on. When a new collection of records $\mathcal{R}_\Delta$ arrive, the buffer $\mathcal{B}$ is updated to accommodate $\mathcal{R}_\Delta$. The new records $\mathcal{R}_\Delta$ are fully stored in the most recent bucket B_0. For each other bucket $B_i (i > 0)$, the records in its predecessor B_{i-1} are downsampled with rate $e^{-\tau}$ and then moved into B_i.

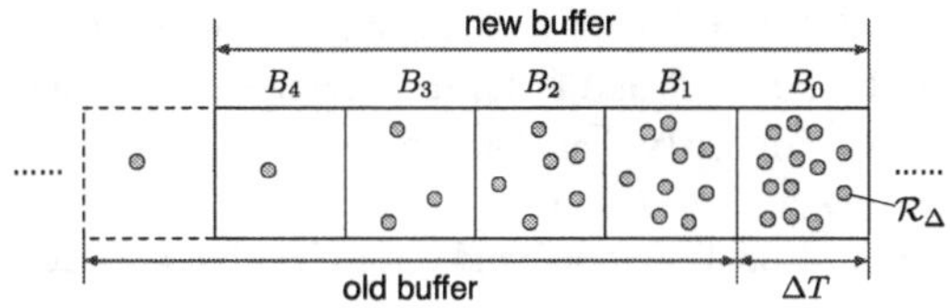

Figure 2: Maintaining a buffer $\mathcal{B}$ for life-decaying learning. For any bucket B_i, $e^{-\tau i}$ of the records falling in B_i's time span are preserved for model updating. When new records arrive, $\mathcal{B}$ is updated based on downsampling and shifting.

Algorithm 1 sketches the learning procedure of ReAct with the life-decaying strategy. As shown, when a collection $\mathcal{R}_\Delta$ of new records arrive, we first shift the records from B_{i-1} to B_i by downsampling (lines 1-2), and store $\mathcal{R}_\Delta$ into B_0 in full (lines 3). Once the buffer $\mathcal{B}$ is updated, we randomly sample records from $\mathcal{B}$ (line 4-7) to update the embeddings. First, for any record r, we consider the attribute recovery task and update the embeddings L, T, and W such that the attributes of r can be correctly recovered. Second, if r is labeled, we further update L, T, W, and C such that r can be classified into the correct activity category. Such a process is repeated over $\mathcal{R}_\cup$ for a number of epochs before the updated embeddings of L, T, W, and C are output. In the following, we detail the updating rules for attribute recovery (line 8) and activity classification (line 9), respectively.

3.1.1 *The Attribute Recovery Task.*

For attribute recovery, we optimize the embeddings L, T, W such that each attribute of a record r can be maximally recovered, assuming the other attributes of r are already observed. Given a record r, for any attribute $i \in r$ with type X (region, hour, or keyword), we model the likelihood of observing i as

$$p(i|r_{-i}) = \exp(s(i, r_{-i})) / \sum_{j \in X} \exp(s(j, r_{-i})),$$

where r_{-i} is the set of all the attributes in r except i, and $s(i, r_{-i})$ is the similarity score between i and r_{-i}.

In the above, the key is how to define $s(i, r_{-i})$. A natural idea is to average the embeddings of the attributes in r_{-i}, and compute $s(i, r_{-i})$ as $s(i, r_{-i}) = \mathbf{v}_i^{\mathrm{T}} \sum_{j \in r_{-i}} \mathbf{v}_j / |r_{-i}|$, where $\mathbf{v}_i$ is the embedding for attribute i. Nevertheless, such a simple definition fails to consider the continuities of the space and time. Take the spatial continuity as an example. Because of spatial locality, two regions

Algorithm 1: Life-decaying learning of ReAct.

Input: The previous embeddings L, T, W, and C.
A buffer of m buckets $\mathcal{B} = \{B_0, B_1, \ldots, B_{m-1}\}$.
A collection $\mathcal{R}_\Delta$ of new records.
Output: The updated buffer $\mathcal{B}$ and embeddings L, T, W, and C.
// Downsampling with rate $e^{-\tau}$.
for *i from 1 to n* **do**
  $B_i \leftarrow e^{-\tau}$-downsampled records from B_{i-1};
$B_0 \leftarrow \mathcal{R}_\Delta$;
$\mathcal{R}_\cup \leftarrow \mathcal{B}_{m-1} \cup \mathcal{B}_{m-2} \ldots \cup \mathcal{B}_0$;
for *epoch from 1 to N* **do**
  for *i from 1 to* $|\mathcal{R}_\Delta|$ **do**
    $r \leftarrow$ Randomly sample a record from $\mathcal{R}_\cup$;
    // for labeled and unlabeled records
    Update L, T, and W for recovering r's attributes;
    // for only labeled records
    if *r is labeled* **then**
      Update L, T, W, and C for classifying r's activity;
Return $\mathcal{B}$, L, T, W, and C;

that are close to each other should be considered correlated instead of independent. We thus introduce *spatial smoothing* and *temporal smoothing* to capture the spatiotemporal continuities. With the smoothing technique, ReAct not only maintains local consistency of neighboring regions and hours, but also alleviates data sparsity.

Figure 3 illustrates the spatial and temporal smoothing processes. As shown, for each region l, we introduce a pseudo region $\hat{l}$. The embedding of $\hat{l}$ is the weighted average of the embeddings of l and l's neighboring regions, namely

$$\mathbf{v}_{\hat{l}} = (\mathbf{v}_l + \alpha \sum_{l_n \in \mathcal{N}_l} \mathbf{v}_{l_n})/(1 + \alpha|\mathcal{N}_l|),$$

where $\mathcal{N}_l$ is the set of l's neighboring regions, and α is a constant for spatial smoothing. Similarly, for each hour t, we introduce a pseudo hour $\hat{t}$, whose embedding is the weighted average of the embeddings of t and t's neighboring hours:

$$\mathbf{v}_{\hat{t}} = (\mathbf{v}_t + \beta \sum_{t_n \in \mathcal{N}_t} \mathbf{v}_{t_n})/(1 + \beta|\mathcal{N}_t|),$$

where $\mathcal{N}_t$ is the set of t's neighboring hours, and β is a temporal smoothing constant. In practice, we find that setting $\alpha = 0.1$ and $\beta = 0.1$ usually leads to satisfactory performance of the model.

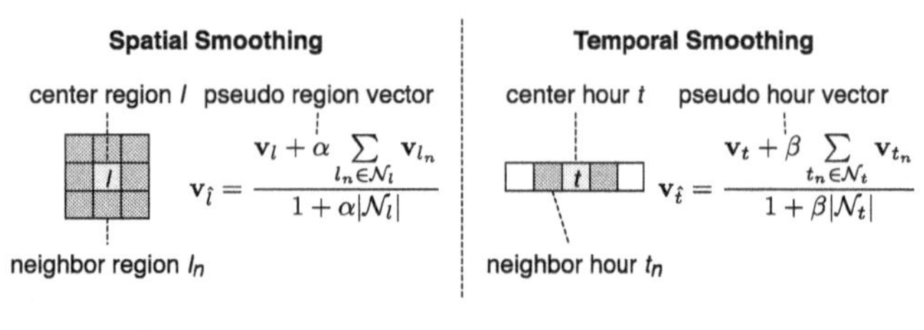

Figure 3: Spatial and temporal smoothing. For each region (hour), we combine it with its neighboring regions (hours) to generate a pseudo region (hour).

In addition to the above pseudo region and hour embeddings, we also introduce pseudo keyword embeddings for notational ease. Given r_{-i}, its pseudo keyword embedding is defined as:

$$\mathbf{v}_{\hat{w}} = \sum_{w \in \mathcal{N}_w} \mathbf{v}_w / |\mathcal{N}_w|,$$

where $\mathcal{N}_w$ is the set of keywords in r_{-i}. With these pseudo embeddings, we define a smoothed version of $s(i, r_{-i})$ as $s(i, r_{-i}) = \mathbf{v}_i^{\mathrm{T}} \mathbf{h}_i$, where

$$\mathbf{h}_i = \begin{cases} (\mathbf{v}_{\hat{l}} + \mathbf{v}_{\hat{t}} + \mathbf{v}_{\hat{w}})/3, & \text{if } i \text{ is a keyword,} \\ (\mathbf{v}_{\hat{t}} + \mathbf{v}_{\hat{w}})/2, & \text{if } i \text{ is a region,} \\ (\mathbf{v}_{\hat{l}} + \mathbf{v}_{\hat{w}})/2, & \text{if } i \text{ is an hour.} \end{cases}$$

Finally, the loss function for the attribute recovery task is simply the negative log-likelihood of observing all the attributes of the records in $\mathcal{R}_\cup$:

$$J_{\mathcal{R}_\cup} = -\sum_{r \in \mathcal{R}_\cup} \sum_{i \in r} \log p(i|r_{-i}). \quad (1)$$

To efficiently optimize the above objective, we use stochastic gradient descent (SGD) and negative sampling [22]. At each time, we use SGD to sample a record r and an attribute $i \in r$. With negative sampling, we randomly select K negative attributes that have the same type with i but do not appear in r, then the loss function for the selected samples becomes:

$$J_r = -\log \sigma(s(i, r_{-i})) - \sum_{k=1}^{K} \log \sigma(-s(k, r_{-i})),$$

where $\sigma(\cdot)$ is the sigmoid function. The updating rules for $\mathbf{v}_i$, $\mathbf{v}_k$ and $\mathbf{h}_i$ can be obtained by taking the derivatives of J_r:

$$\frac{\partial J_r}{\partial \mathbf{v}_i} = (\sigma(s(i, r_{-i})) - 1)\mathbf{h}_i,$$

$$\frac{\partial J_r}{\partial \mathbf{v}_k} = \sigma(s(i, r_{-i}))\mathbf{h}_i,$$

$$\frac{\partial J_r}{\partial \mathbf{h}_i} = (\sigma(s(i, r_{-i})) - 1)\mathbf{v}_i + \sum_{k=1}^{K} \sigma(s(k, r_{-i}))\mathbf{v}_k.$$

For any attribute j in $\mathbf{h}_i$, we have $\partial L/\partial \mathbf{v}_j = \partial L/\partial \mathbf{h}_i \cdot \partial \mathbf{h}_i/\partial \mathbf{v}_j$, as $\mathbf{h}_i$ is linear in j, the term $\partial \mathbf{h}_i/\partial \mathbf{v}_j$ is convenient to calculate.

3.1.2 The Activity Classification Task.

The objective of the activity classification task is to learn the embeddings such that the activity categories of those labeled records in $\mathcal{R}_\cup$ can be correctly predicted. Let r be a labeled record with category c. The basic intuition is to make c's embedding close to the constituent attributes in r. Based on this intuition, we model the probability of classifying r into category c as:

$$p(c|r) = \exp(s(c, r)) / \sum_{c' \in C} \exp(s(c', r)).$$

For the similarity score $s(c, r)$, we define it in a smoothed way similar to the attribute recovery task. That is, $s(c, r) = \mathbf{v}_c^{\mathrm{T}} \mathbf{h}_r$, where $\mathbf{h}_r = (\mathbf{v}_{\hat{l}} + \mathbf{v}_{\hat{t}} + \mathbf{v}_{\hat{w}})/3$.

The objective function of the activity classification task is then the negative log-likelihood of predicting the activities categories

Algorithm 2: Constraint-based learning of ReAct.

Input: The previous embeddings L, T, W, and C.
A collection $\mathcal{R}_\Delta$ of new records.
Output: The updated embeddings L, T, W, and C.

```
for epoch from 1 to N do
    Randomly shuffle the records in R_Δ;
    foreach r ∈ R_Δ do
        Update L, T, and W for constrained attribute recovery;
        if r is labeled then
            Update L, T, W, and C for constrained activity
            classification;
Return L, T, W, and C;
```

for the new records in $\mathcal{R}_\cup$:

$$J_{\mathcal{R}_\cup} = -\sum_{r \in \mathcal{R}_\cup} \log p(c|r). \quad (2)$$

We again use SGD and negative sampling to optimize the objective efficiently. In specific, given the labeled record r with the positive category c, we randomly pick a negative category c' satisfying $c' \neq c$. Then the loss function for r in the activity classification task becomes:

$$J_r = -\log \sigma(s(c, r)) - \log \sigma(-s(c', r)).$$

Similar to the derivation in the attribute recovery task, the updating rules of the attributes and categories can be easily obtained by taking the derivatives of J_r and then applying SGD.

3.2 Constraint-Based Learning

The life-decaying strategy relies on the buffer $\mathcal{B}$ to keep old records besides $\mathcal{R}_\Delta$, thereby incorporating the information in $\mathcal{R}_\Delta$ without overfitting. However, maintaining $\mathcal{B}$ could incur additional space and time overhead. To avoid such overhead, we propose our second strategy named constraint-based learning. The key is to to accommodate the new records $\mathcal{R}_\Delta$ by fine-tuning the previous embeddings. During the fine-turning process, we impose the constraint that the updated embeddings do not deviate much from the previous ones. In this way, ReAct generates embeddings that are optimized for $\mathcal{R}_\Delta$ while respecting the prior knowledge encoded in previous embeddings. Algorithm 2 sketches the constraint-based learning procedure of ReAct. As shown, when a collection $\mathcal{R}_\Delta$ of new records arrive, we directly use them to update the embeddings for a number of epochs, where the updating for both attribute recovery and activity classification is performed under constraints.

Let us first examine the constraint-based attribute recovery task. Given the new records $\mathcal{R}_\Delta$ and their attributes, our goal is still to recover the attributes of $\mathcal{R}_\Delta$, but now we add a regularization term in the objective to ensure the result embeddings can retain the previous embeddings. In formal, we design the objective function for attribute recovery as:

$$J_{\mathcal{R}_\Delta} = -\sum_{r \in \mathcal{R}_\Delta} \sum_{i \in r} \log p(i|r_{-i}) + \lambda \sum_{i \in L,T,W,C} \|\mathbf{v}_i - \mathbf{v}'_i\|^2,$$

where $\mathbf{v}_i$ is the updated embedding of attribute i, and $\mathbf{v}'_i$ is i's previous embedding learnt before the arrival of $\mathcal{R}_\Delta$. In the above objective function, it is important to note the regularization term $\sum_{i \in L,T,W,C} \|\mathbf{v}_i - \mathbf{v}'_i\|^2$. It prevents the updated embeddings from deviating drastically from the previous embeddings. The value of λ ($\lambda \geq 0$) plays an important role in controlling the regularization strength. When $\lambda = 0$, the embeddings are purely optimized for fitting $\mathcal{R}_\Delta$; when $\lambda = \infty$, the learning process completely ignore the new records and all the embeddings remain unchanged.

We still combine SGD and negative sampling to optimize the above objective function. Consider a record r and an attribute $i \in r$. With negative sampling, we randomly select a set of K negative attributes N_i^-, then the objective for the selected samples is:

$$J_r = -\log \sigma(s(i, r_{-i})) - \sum_{k \in N_i^-} \log \sigma(-s(k, r_{-i})) + \lambda \sum_{i \in \{r\} \cup N_i^-} \|\mathbf{v}_i - \mathbf{v}'_i\|^2.$$

The updating rules for different attributes can be easily obtained by taking the derivatives of J_r. Taking attribute i as an example, the corresponding derivative and updating rule are given by

$$\frac{\partial J_r}{\partial \mathbf{v}_i} = (\sigma(s(i, r_{-i})) - 1)\mathbf{h}_i + 2\lambda(\mathbf{v}_i - \mathbf{v}'_i),$$

$$\mathbf{v}_i \leftarrow \mathbf{v}_i + \eta(1 - \sigma(s(i, r_{-i})))\mathbf{h}_i - 2\eta\lambda(\mathbf{v}_i - \mathbf{v}'_i),$$

where η is the learning rate for SGD.

By examining the updating rule for i, we can see the constraint-based strategy enjoys two attractive properties: 1) It tries to make i's embedding close to the average embedding (*i.e.*, $\mathbf{h}_i$) of the other attributes in r. Especially when the current embeddings do not produce high similarity score between i and r_i, *i.e.*, $s(i, r_{-i})$ is small, the updating takes an aggressive step to push $\mathbf{v}_i$ close to $\mathbf{h}_i$; and 2) With the term $-2\eta\lambda(\mathbf{v}_i - \mathbf{v}'_i)$, the learnt embeddings are constrained to preserve the information encoded in the previous embeddings. In specific, if the learnt embedding $\mathbf{v}_i$ deviates from the previous embedding $\mathbf{v}'_i$ too much, the updating rule would subtract the difference to some extent and drag $\mathbf{v}_i$ towards $\mathbf{v}'_i$.

We proceed to examine the activity classification task under the constraint-based strategy. The overall objective is to maximize the log-likelihood of predicting the activities categories for $\mathcal{R}_\Delta$ while minimizing the deviation from the previous embeddings. Using SGD, for any record r with activity category c, we generate a negative category c', and then define the objective as

$$J_r = -\log \sigma(s(c, r)) - \log \sigma(-s(c', r)) + \lambda \sum_{c \in \{c, c'\}} \|\mathbf{v}_c - \mathbf{v}'_c\|^2.$$

Again, the updating rules for the different variables in the above objective can be easily obtained by taking the derivatives of J_r, we omit the details here to save space.

3.3 Complexity Analysis

Space complexity. With either life-decaying learning or constraint-based learning, we need to maintain the embeddings of all the regions, hours, keywords, and categories. Let D be the dimension of the latent space. Then the space cost for maintaining those embeddings is $O(D(|L| + |T| + |W| + |C|))$, where $|L|$, $|T|$, $|W|$, and $|C|$ are the numbers of regions, hours, keywords, and categories, respectively. In addition, both strategies need to keep a collection of training records. For the constraint-based learning, the space cost of this part is $O(|\mathcal{R}_{max}|)$ where $|\mathcal{R}_{max}|$ is the maximum number of new records that arrive at one time. The life-decaying learning strategy needs to keep the new records as well as some old ones. As it imposes exponentially decaying sampling rates on the buckets, the space cost for maintaining those records is

$$O(|\mathcal{R}_{max}|(1+e^{-\tau}+\ldots+e^{-(m-1)\tau}))=O(|\mathcal{R}_{max}|\frac{1-e^{-m\tau}}{1-e^{-\tau}}).$$

Time complexity. We first analyze the time complexity of the constraint-based learning strategy. Examining Algorithm 2, one can see that the constraint-based strategy needs to go over $\mathcal{R}_\Delta$ for N epochs and process every record in $\mathcal{R}_\Delta$ exactly once in each epoch. Hence, the time complexity is $O(NDM^2|\mathcal{R}_{max}|)$, where M is the maximum number of attributes in any record. Since N and D are fixed beforehand, and M is usually sufficiently small, ReAct scales roughly linearly with $\mathcal{R}_\Delta$. Similarly, the time complexity of the life-decaying strategy is derived as $O(NDM^2|\mathcal{R}_{max}|+|\mathcal{R}_\cup|)$, where $|\mathcal{R}_\cup|=|\mathcal{R}_{max}|(1-e^{-m\tau})/(1-e^{-\tau})$.

4 EXPERIMENTS

4.1 Experimental Setup

4.1.1 Data Sets. Our experiments are based on two real-life geo-tagged tweet data sets: LA and NY. The LA data set contains ~1.10 million geo-tagged tweets published in Los Angeles. We crawled the LA data set by monitoring the Twitter Streaming API[1] during 2014.08.01 – 2014.11.30 and continuously gathering the geo-tagged tweets in the bounding box of LA. In addition, we crawled all the POIs in LA through Foursquare's public API[2]. We are able to link ~0.11 million of the crawled tweets to the POI database and assign them to one of the following categories: Food, Shop & Service, Travel & Transport, College & University, Nightlife Spot, Residence, Outdoors & Recreation, Arts & Entertainment, Professional & Other Places. We preprocessed the raw data as follows. For the text part, we removed user mentions, URLs, stopwords, and the words that appear less than 100 times in the corpus. For the space and time, we partitioned the LA area into small grids with size 300m*300m, and broke the one-day period into 24 one-hour windows. The NY data set is also collected from Twitter and then linked with Foursquare. It consists of ~1.20 million geo-tagged tweets in New York City during 2014.08.01 - 2014.11.30, and we are able to link ~0.10 million of them with Foursquare POIs. The preprocessing steps are the same as LA.

4.1.2 Baselines. We compare our proposed ReAct model with the following baseline methods:

- LGTA [34] is a geographical topic model that assumes a number of latent spatial regions — each described by a Gaussian. Meanwhile, each region has a multinomial distribution over the latent topics that generate keywords.
- MGTM [16] is a state-of-the-art geographical topic model based on the multi-Dirichlet process. It is capable of finding geographical topics with non-Gaussian distributions, and does not require a pre-specified number of topics.
- Tensor [9] builds a 4-D tensor to encode the co-occurrences among location, time, text, and category. It then factorizes the tensor to obtain low-dimensional representations of all the elements.
- SVD first constructs the co-occurrence matrices between each pair of location, time, text, and category, and then performs Singular Value Decomposition on the matrices.
- TF-IDF constructs the co-occurrence matrices between each pair of location, time, text, and category. It then computes the tf-idf weight for each entry in the matrix by treating rows as documents and columns as words.

Similar to our ReAct method, Tensor, SVD, and TF-IDF also rely on space and time partitioning to obtain regions and time periods. We use the same partitioning granularity for those methods to ensure fair comparison. For the two different learning strategies of ReAct, we refer to the life-decaying one as RA-Decay, and the constraint-based one as RA-Cons. Besides them, we also implement two weakened variants of ReAct to validate the effectiveness of recency-ware learning and the semi-supervised paradigm: 1) RA-Base is a variant of ReAct that neither adopts recency-aware training, nor leverages the category information as supervision; and 2) RA-Semi is another variant, which uses the category information as supervision, but does not perform recency-aware training. Note that both RA-Base and RA-Semi perform training in batch instead of online, treating all the seen instances equally.

4.1.3 Parameter Settings. There are five common parameters for the life-decaying and constraint-based strategies: 1) the latent embedding dimension D; 2) the number of epochs N; 3) the SGD learning rate η; 4) the spatial smoothing constant α; and 5) the temporal smoothing constant β. By default, we set $D=300$, $N=50$, $\eta=0.01$, and $\alpha=\beta=0.1$. Meanwhile, the life-decaying strategy has its specific parameters, the decaying rate τ and the number of buckets m; and the constraint-based strategy also has its own parameter, the regularization strength λ. We set their default values to $\tau=0.01$, $m=500$, and $\lambda=0.3$.

In LGTA, there are two major parameters, the number of regions R, and the number of latent topics Z. After careful tuning, we set $R=300$ and $Z=10$. MGTM is a non-parametric method that involves several hyper-parameters. We set the hyper-parameters following the original paper [16]. For Tensor and SVD, we set the latent dimension as $D=300$ to compare with ReAct fairly.

4.1.4 Evaluation Tasks and Metrics. We use two types of activity retrieval tasks to evaluate the effectiveness of different models. The first is to *retrieve locations for a given activity*. Specifically, recall that each GTSM record reflects a user's activity with three attributes: a location l_r, a timestamp t_r, and a bag of keywords m_r. In the location retrieval task, the input is the timestamp t_r and the keywords m_r, and the goal is to accurately pinpoint the ground-truth location from a pool of candidates. We retrieve the location at two different granularities: 1) *coarse-grained region retrieval* is to retrieve the ground-truth region that r falls in; and 2) *fine-grained POI retrieval* is to retrieve the ground-truth POI that r corresponds to. Note that fine-grained POI retrieval is only evaluated on the tweets that have been linked with Foursquare. The second task is to *retrieve activities for a given location*. In this task, the input is the timestamp t_r and the location l_r, and the goal is to pinpoint the ground-truth activities at two different granularities: 1) *coarse-grained category retrieval* is to retrieve the ground-truth activity category of r. Again, such a coarse-grained activity retrieval is performed only on the

[1] https://dev.twitter.com/streaming/overview
[2] https://developer.foursquare.com/

tweets that have been linked with Foursquare; and 2) *fine-grained keyword retrieval* is to retrieve the ground-truth message m_r from a candidate pool of messages.

To summarize, we study four sub-tasks in total: 1) region retrieval; 2) POI retrieval; 3) category retrieval; and 4) keyword retrieval. For each retrieval task, we generate a candidate pool by mixing the ground truth with a set of M negative samples. Take region retrieval as an example. Given the ground-truth region l_r, we mix l_r with M randomly chosen regions. Then we try to pinpoint the ground truth from the size-$(M + 1)$ candidate pool by ranking all the candidates. Intuitively, the better a model captures the patterns underlying people's activities, the more likely it ranks the ground truth to top positions. We thus use Mean Reciprocal Rank (MRR) to quantify the effectiveness of a model. Given a set Q of queries, the MRR is defined as: $\text{MRR} = (\sum_{i=1}^{|Q|} 1/\text{rank}_i)/|Q|$, where rank_i is the ranking of the ground truth for the i-th query.

We describe the ranking procedures of different methods as follows. Again consider region retrieval as an example. For ReAct, we compute the average cosine similarity of each candidate region to the observed elements (hour and keywords), and rank them in the descending order of the similarity; for LGTA and MGTM, we compute the likelihood of observing each candidate given the keywords, and rank the candidates by likelihood; for Tensor and SVD, we use the decompositions to reconstruct densified co-occurrence tensor and matrices, and then retrieve the tensor/matrix entries to rank the candidates; for TF-IDF, we rank the candidates by computing average tf-idf similarities.

On each data set, we randomly generate 20 one-hour query windows in 2014.08.01 – 2014.11.30, and use all the tweets in those windows as test instances. Within those query windows, there are ~11 thousand test tweets in LA, and ~12 thousand test tweets in NY. We set the number of candidates to $M = 10$ for different retrieval tasks except for category retrieval (there are only nine categories in total). For each query window, we use the tweets that have arrived before the window start to train different models. All the methods except for ReAct work in a batch manner, hence we have to train them repeatedly for 20 times, with different training data for different query windows. As ReAct works online, we use a one-hour window to hold new records and update ReAct hourly. We ensure ReAct uses the same training data as other methods during the one-pass training process.

Table 1: The MRRs of different methods for location retrieval. For each test tweet, we assume its timestamp and keywords are observed, and perform location retrieval at two granularities: 1) *region retrieval* retrieves the ground-truth region; and 2) *POI retrieval* retrieves the ground-truth POI (for Foursquare-linked tweets).

Method	Region Retrieval		POI Retrieval	
	LA	NY	LA	NY
LGTA	0.3583	0.3544	0.5889	0.5674
MGTM	0.4007	0.391	0.5811	0.553
Tensor	0.3592	0.3641	0.6672	0.7399
SVD	0.3699	0.3604	0.6705	0.7443
TF-IDF	0.4114	0.4605	0.719	0.776
RA-Base	0.5373	0.5597	0.7845	0.8508
RA-Semi	0.5586	0.5632	0.8155	0.8712
RA-Cons	0.5714	0.5864	0.8311	**0.8896**
RA-Decay	**0.5802**	**0.5898**	**0.8473**	0.885

Table 2: The MRRs of different methods for activity retrieval. For each test tweet, we assume its location and timestamp are observed, and retrieve activities at two granularities: 1) *category retrieval* retrieves the ground-truth category (for Foursquare-linked tweets); and 2) *keyword retrieval* retrieves the ground-truth message.

Method	Category Retrieval		Keyword Retrieval	
	LA	NY	LA	NY
LGTA	0.4409	0.4527	0.3392	0.3425
MGTM	0.4587	0.464	0.3501	0.343
Tensor	0.8635	0.7988	0.4004	0.3744
SVD	0.8556	0.7826	0.4098	0.3728
TF-IDF	0.9137	0.8259	0.5236	0.4864
RA-Base	0.6225	0.5874	0.5693	0.5538
RA-Semi	0.9056	0.8993	0.5832	0.5793
RA-Cons	0.92	0.8964	0.6097	0.5887
RA-Decay	**0.9272**	**0.9026**	**0.6174**	**0.5928**

4.2 Effectiveness Comparison

4.2.1 Qualitative Results. We first use several examples to examine whether ReAct can capture the dynamic evolutions of spatiotemporal activities, as well as how well it models the correlations between location, time, and text. Specifically, we perform one-pass training of RA-Decay on LA and NY, and launch a bunch of queries at different stages. For each query, we retrieve the top-10 most similar elements with different types from the entire search space.

Textual Queries. Figure 4(a) shows the results when we query with the keyword 'beach' on LA. We find the results quite meaningful: the top regions fall along the coastline; the top POIs are famous beach attractions; and the top keywords well reflect people's activities on the beach (*e.g.*, 'sand', 'boardwalk'). Figure 4(b) and 4(c) show the results for the query 'outdoor + weekend' issued on NY for two different days. Interestingly, the results obtained for the two days both relate to 'outdoor', but exhibit clear evolutions. While the results for 2014.08.30 contain many swimming-related activities, those for 2014.10.30 are mostly fitness venues. Based on such phenomena, one can clearly see that ReAct captures not only the inter-type correlations between different attributes but also the temporal evolutions underlying spatiotemporal activities.

Spatial Queries. Figure 4(d) and 4(e) illustrate the evolutions of two spatial queries: 1) the Metlife Stadium; and 2) the Universal Studio. Again, we can see the results well match the query location and meanwhile reflect urban dynamics clearly. For the Metlife Stadium query, the top keywords evolve from concert-related ones to football-related ones. It is because the NFL season opens in early September, and people start visiting the stadium to watch the games of the Giants and the Jets. For the Universal Studio query, we intentionally include Halloween and Thanksgiving in the query days. In such a setting, we find the latter two lists contain holiday-specific keywords, verifying the capability of ReAct for capturing the most recent activity patterns.

POI	Keyword
The Big Vee on Venice	beach
Pacific Ocean	beachlife
Hermosa Beach	sand
Westin on The Long Beach	boardwalk
Port of Long Beach	long
It Yoga	venice
L@P Pool	breeze
Manhattan Beach Volleyball	ocean
Venice Coffee and Creamery	cruiser
Muscle Beach Juice Bar	wave

Region POI Keyword

(a) Query = 'beach' + 3pm (2014.08.30@LA)

POI	Keyword
Union Street Bridge	weekend
Hancock & Malcolm X	outdoor
Mccarren Pool Lap Swim	sunday
The Pool	saturday
The Rooftop at Rockrose	lovely
The Wave Pool	enjoy
William Playground	sundayfunday
Astoria Park	swimming
Shorefront	nofilter
Teardrop Park	pool

Region POI Keyword

(b) Query = 'outdoor + weekend' (2014.08.30@NY)

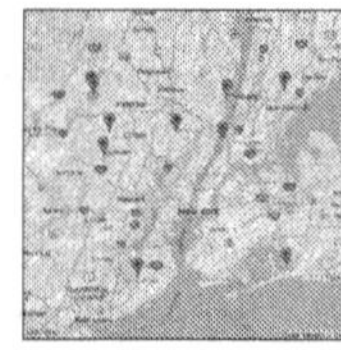

POI	Keyword
388 Greenwich St. Courtyard	weekend
King's Bay Basketball	outdoor
Yoga Vida	arrive
Ya Moms	urbanspacenyc
Elite Performance Training	visit
The Fitting Room	spooky
Downing St. Playground	rainy
Disco Teadance at Howl	winter
Temperance Fountain	workout
Tompkins Outdoor Gym	fabulous

Region POI Keyword

(c) Query = 'outdoor + weekend' (2014.10.30@NY)

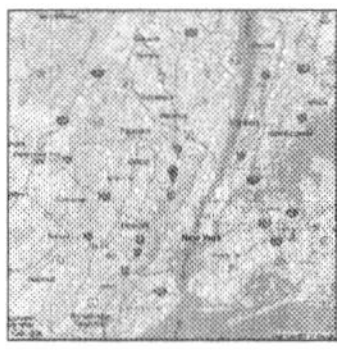

2014.08.30	2014.09.30	2014.11.30
sideline	nyjets	49ers
tour	touchdown	touchdown
concert	jet	jet
shady	giant	steelers
malice	hamstring	giant
monster	football	nyjets
vick	nygiants	nygiants
eminem	jetsnation	nfl
attractive	bigblue	fan
rooting	score	niner

Query Location 2014.08.30 ⟶ 2014.09.30 ⟶ 2014.11.30

(d) Query = '(40.8128, -74.0764)' (Metlife Stadium@NY)

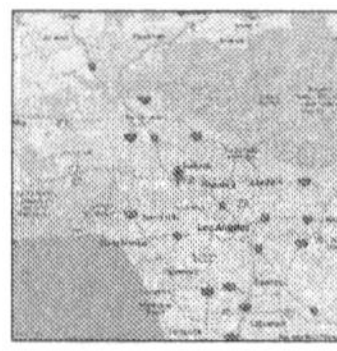

2014.08.30	2014.10.30	2014.11.27
universal	universal	universal
studio	studio	studio
minion	horrornights	sheraton
mummy	bates	thanksgiving
despicable	halloween	hollywood
unistudios	photo	tour
hollywood	night	holiday
thesimpsons	minion	dinner
globe	horror	transformer
jurassic	suvived	hackthon

Query Location 2014.08.30 ⟶ 2014.10.30 ⟶ 2014.11.27

(e) Query = '(34.1381, -118.3534)' (Universal Studio@LA)

Figure 4: Illustrative cases. Figure 4(a), 4(b), and 4(c) are textual queries issued on different days (*i.e.*, the dates in bracket). For each query, we use the trained model on the issuing day to retrieve ten most similar regions (the markers in the map denote the region centers), POIs, and keywords, based on cosine similarities of the embeddings. Figure 4(d) shows two spatial queries at the Metlife Stadium and Universal Studio. For each query, we retrieve ten most similar keywords on different days.

4.2.2 Quantitative Results. Table 1 and 2 report the quantitative results of different methods for location and activity retrievals, respectively. As shown, on all of the four sub-tasks, ReAct and its variants achieve much higher MRRs than the baseline methods. Compared with the two geographical topic models (LGTA and MGTM), ReAct yields as much as 62% performance improvement for location retrieval, and 83% for activity retrieval. There are three factors for explaining the performance gap: (1) Neither LGTA nor MGTM models the time factor, and thus fails to leverage the time information for prediction; (2) ReAct emphasizes recent records to capture up-to-date spatiotemporal activities, while LGTA and MGTM work in batch and treat all training instances equally; and (3) Instead of using generative models, ReAct directly maps different data types into a common space to capture their correlations more directly.

Tensor, SVD, and TF-IDF have better performance than LGTA and MGTM by modeling time and category, yet ReAct still outperforms them by large margins. Interestingly, TF-IDF turns out to be a strong baseline, demonstrating the effectiveness of the tf-idf similarity for the retrieval tasks. SVD and Tensor can effectively recover the co-occurrence matrices and tensor by filling in the missing values. However, the raw co-occurrence seems a less effective relatedness measure for location and activity retrieval.

Comparing the variants of ReAct, we see clear performance gaps between RA-Base and RA-Semi, particularly for the category retrieval task. The major difference between RA-Base and RA-Semi is that, RA-Base just treats category descriptions as keywords, while RA-Semi uses activity categories as labels to guide embedding. This phenomenon shows the semi-supervised paradigm indeed helps propagate structured category information into the embedding process to generate high-quality embeddings.

RA-Semi is inferior to RA-Decay and RA-Cons considerably. Although the three variants all use semi-supervised training, RA-Semi treats all the training instances equally whereas the other two work online and emphasize recent instances more. This fact verifies that there are notable evolutions underlying people's activities in the four-month time period, and the recency-aware nature of ReAct effectively captures such evolutions to better suit users' retrieval needs. Finally, examining the performance of RA-Decay and RA-Cons, we find that the life-decaying learning strategy performs slightly better than the constraint-based one in practice, but at the cost of extra space and time overhead.

4.3 Effects of Parameters

Lastly, we study the effects of different parameters on the performance of ReAct. Figure 5(a) and 5(b) show the effects of the latent dimension D and the number of epochs N. Since the trends are very similar for fine-grained and coarse-grained retrieval tasks, we omit the results for POI retrieval and category retrieval for clarity. As shown in Figure 5(a), the MRRs of both methods keep increasing with D and gradually converge. This phenomenon is expected because a larger D leads to a more expressive model that can capture latent semantics more accurately. From Figure 5(b), one can see as N increases, the performance of ReAct also increases first and finally becomes stable: when N is small, the updated embeddings do not incorporate the new information sufficiently; when N is large, both the life-decaying and constraint-based strategies can effectively prevent ReAct from overfitting the new records.

Figure 5(c) and 5(d) depict the effects of τ and λ on the performance of the two learning strategies, respectively. As shown, for life-decaying learning, its performance first increases with τ, then becomes stable, and finally deteriorates. The reason is two-fold: 1) a too small τ makes the buffer contain too many old records in the history, thus diluting the most recent information; and 2) a too large τ leads to a buffer that contains only recent records,

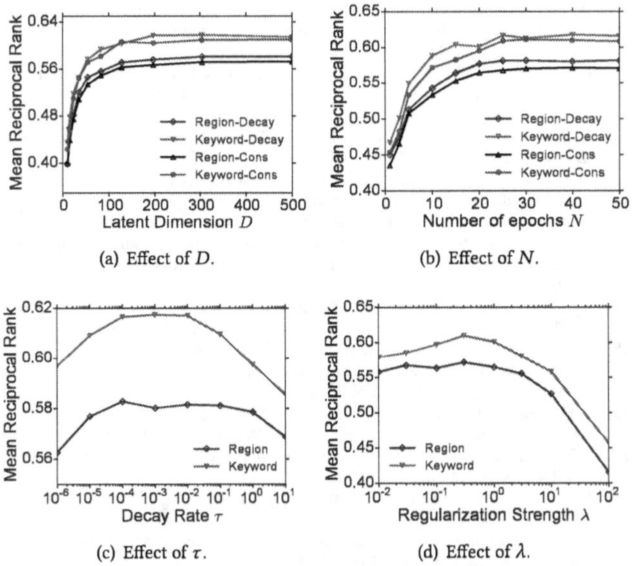

(a) Effect of D. (b) Effect of N.

(c) Effect of τ. (d) Effect of λ.

Figure 5: Parameter study on LA. Figure 5(a) and 5(b) show the effects of the latent dimension D and the number of epochs N on RA-Decay and RA-Cons. Figure 5(c) shows the effect of the decaying rate τ on RA-Decay. Figure 5(d) shows the effect of the regularization strength λ on RA-Cons.

making the result model suffer from overfitting. The effect of λ on the constraint-based learning is similar. A too large λ causes underfitting of the new records, while a too small λ causes overfitting. Besides the above parameters, we have also studied the effects of the smoothing parameters α and β, and found that the performance of ReAct varied no more than 3% when α and β are set to the range $[0.05, 0.5]$, thus we omit the results to save space.

5 RELATED WORK

Spatiotemporal Activity Modeling. Previous approaches to spatiotemporal activity modeling mostly rely on geographical topic modeling, which extends classical topic models to discover representative topics for different regions. Specifically, Sizov *et al.* [28] extend LDA [5] by assuming that each latent topic has a multinomial distribution over text, and two Gaussians over latitudes and longitudes. They later upgrade the model to find topics that have complex and non-Gaussian distributions [16]. Yin *et al.* [34] extend PLSA [12] by assuming that each region has a normal distribution that generates locations, as well as a multinomial distribution over the latent topics that generate text. While the above models are designed to detect crowd-level geographical topics, Hong *et al.* [13] and Yuan *et al.* [35] introduce the user factor in the modeling process to infer individual-level user preferences. Our work resembles the studies [16, 28, 34] more because we also model crowd-level activities instead of individual-level preferences. That said, ReAct differs from these methods notably. Instead of using latent states to indirectly bridge different data modalities, it jointly maps location, time, and text into the same space, which not only frees us from imposing distribution assumptions for different modalities, but also makes it scalable.

Representation learning techniques have been proposed for learning distributed representations for words [22], graph nodes [25, 29, 30], user-item interactions [10], multimedia data [23], *etc.*. Recently, Zhang *et al.* [38] propose CrossMap, a cross-modal representation learning method for spatiotemporal activity modeling. It first detects the hotspot regions and time periods underlying people's activities, and then jointly maps different regions, periods, and keywords into the same latent space. The key difference between ReAct and CrossMap is two-fold: (1) Instead of handling static data, ReAct processes continuous GTSM streams and learns recency-aware models online; and (2) while CrossMap learns cross-modal embeddings in an unsupervised way, ReAct adopts a semi-supervised framework, which is capable of leveraging activity category information to learn better-quality embeddings.

Spatiotemporal event detection. Several studies [1, 8, 15, 19, 20, 27, 40] use GTSM for spatiotemporal event detection. Sakaki *et al.* [27] train a classifier to judge whether an incoming tweet is related to an earthquake or not, and release an alarm when the number of earthquake-related tweets is large. Krumm *et al.* [19] monitor the spatiotemporal distributions of tweet streams, and detect spikes in the signal as interesting events. Zhang *et al.* [40] propose a method that achieves real-time local event detection from geo-tagged tweet streams. There is a clear difference between spatiotemporal event detection and spatiotemporal activity modeling. The former attempts to extract *unusual* activities bursted in local areas, whereas the latter aims at summarizing the *typical* activities at different locations and time.

Human mobility modeling. There have also been studies that leverage GTSM data to extract mobility patterns underlying people's activities. Cho *et al.* [7] collect large-scale checkin data and find that people's activities are usually centered around a few fixed locations, and exhibit strong periodicity. Yuan *et al.* [36] propose a Bayesian non-parametric model to automatically extract the regions that a user visits periodically. Zhang *et al.* [37] apply sequential pattern mining techniques to extract frequent movement sequences from check-in data. Later, Zhang *et al.* [39] apply the Hidden Markov Model to GTSM data, observing that there are latent states underlying people's daily activities and people move between them with strong regularity. Although these mobility modeling methods also models the time factor, they aim to understand the temporal transitions of human movements in the physical world, whereas we focus on the temporal evolution of global-level activities.

Temporal evolution modeling. A handful of studies [17, 26, 41] have investigated the temporal evolutions of spatiotemporal activities. Noulas *et al.* [24] analyze user activities with Foursquare checkins and find that the checkin data reveal meaningful spatiotemporal patterns. Zhang *et al.* [41] find people's activities exhibit temporal dynamics via analyzing the number of Foursquare checkins in different areas. Kling *et al.* [17] apply LDA to checkin data by treating hourly-aggregated checkins as documents. They show notable topical evolutions across different hours. Pozdnoukhov *et al.* [26] first apply online LDA to the streaming tweet data, and then analyze the spatiotemporal distributions of the extracted topics in a post-processing step. While these pioneering studies have clearly demonstrated that dynamic evolutions exist in urban activities, they do not address our problem of designing a unified model that dynamically captures the inter-type correlations among location, time, and text from GTSM streams.

Modeling the temporal evolutions in data streams has also been studied for classical tasks like classification [33], clustering [2, 6], topic modeling [3, 4, 14, 21], and recommendation [11, 18]. For instance, Blei *et al.* [4] propose the Dynamic Topic Model, which uses the Markovian assumption and state space models to capture dynamic topical evolutions. Distinguished from these studies, our problem is new in that we aim to capture the dynamic evolutions for spatiotemporal activity modeling. From the technical standpoint, we model the dynamic evolutions in a novel framework of semi-supervised embedding, rendering our method fundamentally different from existing techniques.

6 CONCLUSION

We proposed a recency-aware spatiotemporal activity model that learns from geo-tagged social media streams online. Our proposed model, ReAct, embeds all the regions, hours, and keywords into the same latent space with a novel semi-supervised multimodal embedding paradigm. ReAct employs two strategies to emphasize the information contained in newly arrive records without overfitting. Our empirical evaluations have shown that ReAct outperforms the existing spatiotemporal activity modeling methods significantly in location and activity retrieval tasks.

7 ACKNOWLEDGEMENTS

We would like to thank the reviewers for their insightful comments. This work was sponsored in part by the U.S. Army Research Lab. under Cooperative Agreement No. W911NF-09-2-0053 (NSCTA), National Science Foundation IIS-1017362, IIS-1320617, and IIS-1354329, HDTRA1-10-1-0120, and Grant 1U54GM114838 awarded by NIGMS through funds provided by the trans-NIH Big Data to Knowledge (BD2K) initiative (www.bd2k.nih.gov), and MIAS, a DHS-IDS Center for Multimodal Information Access and Synthesis at UIUC. Luming Zhang was supported in part by the National Natural Science Foundation of China (Grant no. 61572169, 61472266), the National University of Singapore (Suzhou) Research Institute, and the Fundamental Research Funds for the Central Universities. The views and conclusions contained in this document are those of the authors and should not be interpreted as representing any funding agencies.

REFERENCES

[1] H. Abdelhaq, C. Sengstock, and M. Gertz. Eventweet: Online localized event detection from twitter. *PVLDB*, 6(12):1326–1329, 2013.
[2] C. C. Aggarwal, J. Han, J. Wang, and P. S. Yu. A framework for clustering evolving data streams. In *VLDB*, pages 81–92, 2003.
[3] L. AlSumait, D. Barbará, and C. Domeniconi. On-line LDA: adaptive topic models for mining text streams with applications to topic detection and tracking. In *ICDM*, pages 3–12, 2008.
[4] D. M. Blei and J. D. Lafferty. Dynamic topic models. In *ICML*, pages 113–120, 2006.
[5] D. M. Blei, A. Y. Ng, and M. I. Jordan. Latent dirichlet allocation. *Journal of Machine Learning Research*, 3(1):993–1022, 2003.
[6] D. Chakrabarti, R. Kumar, and A. Tomkins. Evolutionary clustering. In *KDD*, pages 554–560, 2006.
[7] E. Cho, S. A. Myers, and J. Leskovec. Friendship and mobility: User movement in location-based social networks. In *KDD*, pages 1082–1090, 2011.
[8] W. Feng, C. Zhang, W. Zhang, J. Han, J. Wang, C. Aggarwal, and J. Huang. Streamcube: hierarchical spatio-temporal hashtag clustering for event exploration over the twitter stream. In *ICDE*, pages 1561–1572, 2015.
[9] R. A. Harshman. Foundations of the PARAFAC procedure: Models and conditions for an "explanatory" multi-modal factor analysis. *UCLA Working Papers in Phonetics*, 16(1):84, 1970.
[10] X. He, L. Liao, H. Zhang, L. Nie, X. Hu, and T. Chua. Neural collaborative filtering. In *WWW*, pages 173–182, 2017.
[11] X. He, H. Zhang, M. Kan, and T. Chua. Fast matrix factorization for online recommendation with implicit feedback. In *SIGIR*, pages 549–558, 2016.
[12] T. Hofmann. Probabilistic latent semantic indexing. In *SIGIR*, pages 50–57, 1999.
[13] L. Hong, A. Ahmed, S. Gurumurthy, A. J. Smola, and K. Tsioutsiouliklis. Discovering geographical topics in the twitter stream. In *WWW*, pages 769–778, 2012.
[14] L. Hong, D. Yin, J. Guo, and B. D. Davison. Tracking trends: incorporating term volume into temporal topic models. In *KDD*, pages 484–492, 2011.
[15] W. Kang, A. K. H. Tung, W. Chen, X. Li, Q. Song, C. Zhang, F. Zhao, and X. Zhou. Trendspedia: An internet observatory for analyzing and visualizing the evolving web. In *ICDE*, pages 1206–1209, 2014.
[16] C. C. Kling, J. Kunegis, S. Sizov, and S. Staab. Detecting non-gaussian geographical topics in tagged photo collections. In *WSDM*, pages 603–612, 2014.
[17] F. Kling and A. Pozdnoukhov. When a city tells a story: urban topic analysis. In *SIGSPATIAL*, pages 482–485, 2012.
[18] Y. Koren. Collaborative filtering with temporal dynamics. In *KDD*, pages 447–456, 2009.
[19] J. Krumm and E. Horvitz. Eyewitness: Identifying local events via space-time signals in twitter feeds. In *SIGSPATIAL*, 2015.
[20] R. Lee, S. Wakamiya, and K. Sumiya. Discovery of unusual regional social activities using geo-tagged microblogs. *World Wide Web*, 14(4):321–349, 2011.
[21] Q. Mei and C. Zhai. Discovering evolutionary theme patterns from text: an exploration of temporal text mining. In *KDD*, pages 198–207, 2005.
[22] T. Mikolov, I. Sutskever, K. Chen, G. S. Corrado, and J. Dean. Distributed representations of words and phrases and their compositionality. In *NIPS*, pages 3111–3119, 2013.
[23] J. Ngiam, A. Khosla, M. Kim, J. Nam, H. Lee, and A. Y. Ng. Multimodal deep learning. In *ICML*, pages 689–696, 2011.
[24] A. Noulas, S. Scellato, C. Mascolo, and M. Pontil. An empirical study of geographic user activity patterns in foursquare. In *ICWSM*, pages 570–573, 2011.
[25] B. Perozzi, R. Al-Rfou, and S. Skiena. Deepwalk: Online learning of social representations. In *KDD*, pages 701–710, 2014.
[26] A. Pozdnoukhov and C. Kaiser. Space-time dynamics of topics in streaming text. In *LBSN*, pages 1–8, 2011.
[27] T. Sakaki, M. Okazaki, and Y. Matsuo. Earthquake shakes twitter users: real-time event detection by social sensors. In *WWW*, pages 851–860, 2010.
[28] S. Sizov. Geofolk: latent spatial semantics in web 2.0 social media. In *WSDM*, pages 281–290, 2010.
[29] J. Tang, M. Qu, and Q. Mei. Pte: Predictive text embedding through large-scale heterogeneous text networks. In *KDD*, pages 1165–1174, 2015.
[30] J. Tang, M. Qu, M. Wang, M. Zhang, J. Yan, and Q. Mei. Line: Large-scale information network embedding. In *WWW*, pages 1067–1077, 2015.
[31] P. H. Verburg, P. P. Schot, M. J. Dijst, and A. Veldkamp. Land use change modelling: current practice and research priorities. *GeoJournal*, 61(4):309–324, 2004.
[32] P. Waddell. Urbansim: Modeling urban development for land use, transportation, and environmental planning. *Journal of the American Planning Association*, 68(3):297–314, 2002.
[33] H. Wang, W. Fan, P. S. Yu, and J. Han. Mining concept-drifting data streams using ensemble classifiers. In *KDD*, pages 226–235, 2003.
[34] Z. Yin, L. Cao, J. Han, C. Zhai, and T. S. Huang. Geographical topic discovery and comparison. In *WWW*, pages 247–256, 2011.
[35] Q. Yuan, G. Cong, Z. Ma, A. Sun, and N. M. Thalmann. Who, where, when and what: discover spatio-temporal topics for twitter users. In *KDD*, pages 605–613, 2013.
[36] Q. Yuan, W. Zhang, C. Zhang, X. Geng, G. Cong, and J. Han. Pred: Periodic region detection for mobility modeling of social media users. In *WSDM*, 2017.
[37] C. Zhang, J. Han, L. Shou, J. Lu, and T. F. L. Porta. Splitter: Mining fine-grained sequential patterns in semantic trajectories. *PVLDB*, 7(9):769–780, 2014.
[38] C. Zhang, K. Zhang, Q. Yuan, H. Peng, Y. Zheng, T. Hanratty, S. Wang, and J. Han. Regions, periods, activities: Uncovering urban dynamics via cross-modal representation learning. In *WWW*, pages 361–370, 2017.
[39] C. Zhang, K. Zhang, Q. Yuan, L. Zhang, T. Hanratty, and J. Han. Gmove: Group-level mobility modeling using geo-tagged social media. In *KDD*, pages 1305–1314, 2016.
[40] C. Zhang, G. Zhou, Q. Yuan, H. Zhuang, Y. Zheng, L. Kaplan, S. Wang, and J. Han. Geoburst: Real-time local event detection in geo-tagged tweet streams. In *SIGIR*, pages 513–522, 2016.
[41] K. Zhang, Q. Jin, K. Pelechrinis, and T. Lappas. On the importance of temporal dynamics in modeling urban activity. In *UrbComp*, 2013.

EntiTables: Smart Assistance for Entity-Focused Tables

Shuo Zhang
University of Stavanger
shuo.zhang@uis.no

Krisztian Balog
University of Stavanger
krisztian.balog@uis.no

ABSTRACT

Tables are among the most powerful and practical tools for organizing and working with data. Our motivation is to equip spreadsheet programs with smart assistance capabilities. We concentrate on one particular family of tables, namely, tables with an entity focus. We introduce and focus on two specific tasks: populating rows with additional instances (entities) and populating columns with new headings. We develop generative probabilistic models for both tasks. For estimating the components of these models, we consider a knowledge base as well as a large table corpus. Our experimental evaluation simulates the various stages of the user entering content into an actual table. A detailed analysis of the results shows that the models' components are complimentary and that our methods outperform existing approaches from the literature.

CCS CONCEPTS

•**Information systems** →**Environment-specific retrieval;** *Users and interactive retrieval; Recommender systems;* Probabilistic retrieval models;

KEYWORDS

Table completion; intelligent table assistance; semantic search

ACM Reference format:
Shuo Zhang and Krisztian Balog. 2017. EntiTables: Smart Assistance for Entity-Focused Tables. In *Proceedings of SIGIR'17, August 07–11, 2017, Shinjuku, Tokyo, Japan.*, , 10 pages.
DOI: http://dx.doi.org/10.1145/3077136.3080796

1 INTRODUCTION

Tables are one of the most effective and widely used tools for organizing and working with data. Spreadsheet programs are among the most commonly used desktop applications, both in business environments and in personal use, because of their ease of use and flexibility. The overall objective of this study is to develop an intelligent personal assistant that can offer smart assistance for people working with tables. It may be imagined as the infamous Office Clippy, albeit we prefer it to be less obtrusive. This study represents the first step towards this ambitious endeavor.

The scenario we consider in this paper is the following. We assume a user, working with a table, at some intermediate stage in the process. At this point, she has already set the caption of the table and entered some data into the table. The table is assumed to have a column header (located above the first content row), which identifies each column with a unique label. We further narrow the focus of our study to tables with an *entity focus*. It means that the leftmost column of the table contains entities. This can also be imagined as having a designated row heading, which may contain only (unique) entities. An entity in the context of this work is a specific object with a unique identifier. (We shall show later in the paper, in §6.2, that a significant portion of tables have an entity focus.) Against this setting, our objective is to aid the user by offering "smart suggestions," that is, recommending (i) additional entities (rows) and (ii) additional column headings, to be added to the table. We shall refer to these tasks as *row population* and *column population*, respectively. See Figure 1 for an illustration.

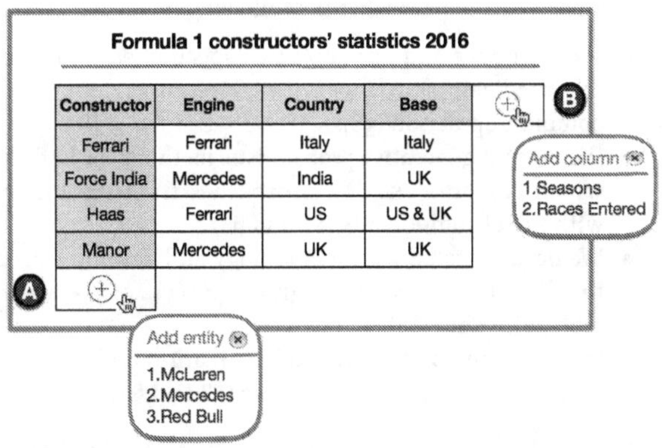

Figure 1: Envisioned user interface. Column headings and the leftmost column are marked with a grey background. The user can populate the table with (A) additional entities (rows) and (B) additional column headings. The suggestions in the pop-ups are updated dynamically as the content of the table changes.

Let us point out here that some elements of these tasks have been addressed in prior work. Our work, however, has not only a different overall motivation, but the specific tasks we tackle have not been addressed in these flavors before. We also introduce a number of innovative elements on the component level.

The task of row population relates to the task of *entity set expansion* [4, 8, 10, 16, 26, 29], where a given set of seed entities (examples) is to be completed with additional entities. We also have a seed set of entities from the leftmost table column. But, in addition to that, we can also make use of the column heading labels and the caption of the table. We show in our experiments, that utilizing these can lead to substantial improvements over using only the seed entities.

The second task, column population, shares similarities with the problem of *schema complement* [2, 8, 12, 30], where a seed table is to be complemented with related tables that can provide additional

SIGIR'17, August 07–11, 2017, Shinjuku, Tokyo, Japan.
© 2017 ACM. 978-1-4503-4887-4/17/08...$15.00
DOI: http://dx.doi.org/10.1145/3077136.3080796

columns. Many of these approaches utilize the full table content and also address the task of merging data into the seed table. Here, our focus is only on finding proper column headings, using the same sources as for row population (i.e., leftmost column, header row, and table caption). We show in our experiments that this task can be performed effectively.

In summary, this paper makes the following novel contributions:

- We introduce and formalize two specific tasks for providing intelligent assistance with tables: row population and column population (§3).
- We present generative probabilistic methods for both tasks, which combine existing approaches from the literature with novel components (§4 and §5).
- We design evaluation methodology and develop a process that simulates a user through the process of populating a table with data (§6).
- We perform an experimental evaluation and carry out a detailed analysis of performance (§7 and §8).

All resources developed within this study are made publicly available at http://bit.ly/sigir2017-table.

2 RELATED WORK

There is a growing body of work on web tables and spreadsheets, addressing a range of tasks, including table extension, table completion, table search, table mining, etc. The task of row population is also related to the problem of entity set completion.

Table Extension/Completion. Extending a local table with additional columns based on the corpus of tables is a relatively new research area. The Mannheim Search Joins Engine [12] operates on a corpus of web tables, searches for tabular data describing entities in the local table, and then picks relevant columns from the top-k candidate tables to merge. With a focus on Wikipedia tables, Bhagavatula et al. [2] target column-matched tables with the local table and perform correlation mining to find "interesting" numeric columns. InfoGather [30] is a table augmentation framework based on topic sensitive PageRank for matching the local table against web tables. The context surrounding the tables is leveraged in a machine learning framework, where the similarity between two tables is captured via a set of features. Related tables can be utilized not only for column extension, but for row extension as well. Methods to detect related tables are proposed for the relatedness capture framework in [8]. Two types of table relatedness are identified: entity complement and schema complement. Entity complement tables can be united to produce a meaningful table, and schema complement tables can provide additional meaningful columns. *Table completion* refers to the task of filling missing values in a local table. Ahmadov et al. [1] propose a hybrid data imputation approach, relying on the characteristics of missing values, in order to (i) look up missing values from web data, (ii) predict them using machine learning methods, or (iii) combine both to find the most appropriate values. To look up missing values, two keyword subqueries are created from the input table, to search entities and attributes separately. These resemble our row and column populating subtasks. However, Ahmadov et al. [1] have a different target and merge the two search results for table selection.

Table Search and Mining. There has been an increasing research interest in mining and searching table content, see, e.g., [5, 6, 15, 22, 25, 32]. Wikipedia's tables contain rich, semi-structured encyclopedic content that is hard to query. Muñoz et al. [18] extract factual content from Wikipedia tables in the form of RDF triples, contributing to recovering table semantic and discovering table relations. Apart from the factual content extraction from web tables, *table mining* also covers tasks like *table interpretation* [6, 18, 25] and *table recognition* [7, 33].

Cafarella et al. [6] extracted 14.1 billion HTML tables from a Google crawl, estimating that 154 million of them contain high-quality relational data. The relations extracted from these represent a valuable data resource. To disambiguate web tables, Zwicklbauer et al. [33] propose a methodology to annotate table headers with semantic type information based on the column's content. Similarly, Crestan and Pantel [7] present a supervised framework for classifying HTML tables into their taxonomy. In addition to factual content and relations, numeric attributes are present in a vast number of web tables. However, web tables are not systematic and cannot be used, e.g., for aggregation. To improve the usability of quantities in heterogenous web tables, a line of work aims at detecting quantity mention [9, 11, 14, 21, 24] and canonicalizing table quantities [3, 11, 13, 19]. Another line of work focuses on extracting and fusing numeric attribute values and numeric expressions in natural language text [9, 14, 21, 24].

Tables could be well searched and mined for question answering or for extending knowledge bases. Yin et al. [31] investigate the task of executing queries on knowledge base tables using Neural Enquirer, which is a fully neuralized DNNs model, both for query planning and for query execution. Sekhavat et al. [23] describe a probabilistic method that augments an exiting knowledge base (YAGO). In [28], a table search engine is applied to further expand and enrich Probase, which is a universal probabilistic taxonomy framework capable of understanding the entities, attributes and values in web tables. Knowledge Vault is created as a probabilistic knowledge base [9] by analyzing the extracted content from tabular data, along with other web resources.

Entity Set Completion. The problem of row population is related to the task of *set completion* or *list expansion*, which is to generate a ranked list of entities starting from a small set of seed entities [8]. Bron et al. [4] propose an approach that combines structure-based and text-based similarity between a candidate entity and the seed entities. The QBEES framework [16] is designed as an aspect-based entity model to find similar entities based on one or more example entities. He and Xin [10] focus on entity list data, by picking the top-k entities based on relevance between the candidate entity and seed entities, and then iteratively ranking them according to a combination of relevance and coherence. Similar iterative steps are conducted in [26, 29]. Wang and Cohen [29] use a random walk method for ranking during iterations. Wang et al. [26] focus on web tables, instead of entity lists, with the help of a web table search engine, called WTS.

3 PROBLEM STATEMENT

In this section, we provide a formal description of the tasks we propose to undertake. We refer to Table 1 for our notation.

Table 1: Notation used in this paper.

Symbol	Description
T	Table
c	Table caption
E	Seed entities $E = (e_1, \dots, e_n)$
L	Seed column labels $L^{(j)} = (l_1, \dots, l_m)$

Definition 1 (Table): *A table T is grid of cells, which hold values, arranged in $n+1$ rows and m columns. The top row is a special designated place, where the column headings reside. It is followed by n regular (content) rows. We let $L = (l_1, \dots, l_m)$ be the list of column heading labels. In addition to the grid content, the table also has a caption c.*

Definition 2 (Entity-Focused Table): *A table is said to be entity-focused, if its leftmost column contains only entities as values, and those entities are unique within the column. We let $E = (e_1, \dots, e_n)$ be the list of entities corresponding to the leftmost table column. I.e., the table takes the following shape:*

$$T = \begin{bmatrix} l_1 & l_2 & \dots & l_m \\ e_1 & v_{1,2} & \dots & v_{1,m} \\ e_2 & v_{2,2} & \dots & v_{2,m} \\ \vdots & \vdots & \ddots & \vdots \\ e_n & v_{n,2} & \dots & v_{n,m} \end{bmatrix},$$

where $v_{i,j}$ ($i \in [1..n], j \in [2..m]$) denote the cell values.

Our objective is to provide intelligent assistance for an user who is working on an entity-focused table. We shall refer to the table that is being edited by the user as *seed table*. We assume that the seed table has already been given a caption, and contains some heading labels (*seed labels*) in the top row and some entities (*seed entities*) in the leftmost column. Note that we do not make any assumptions about the values in the other table cells. Essentially, the $v_{i,j}$ values are immaterial, therefore, we omit them in the followings.[1] When we talk about a table containing entity e, we always mean the leftmost table column.

Our goal is to present suggestions for the user for extending the seed table with (i) additional entities, and (ii) additional column heading labels. Both tasks are approached as a ranking problem: given a seed table, generate a ranked list of entities (for row population) or column labels (for column population).

Definition 3 (Row Population): *Row population is the task of generating a ranked list of entities to be added to the leftmost column of a given seed table, as e_{n+1}.*

Definition 4 (Column Population): *Column population is the task of generating a ranked list of column labels to be added to the column headings of a given seed table, as l_{m+1}.*

[1] We note that the $v_{i,j}$ values may also be utilized for row/column population. However, this is left for future work.

In the following two sections, we present our approaches for row and column population. Following prior studies [1–3, 6–8, 12, 23, 25, 26, 28, 30, 31], we rely heavily on the availability of a large table corpus as an external resource (which, in our case, is extracted from Wikipedia). Additionally, we also exploit information stored about entities in a knowledge base (in our case, DBpedia). Further specifics about our data sources are provided in §6.1.

4 POPULATING ROWS

In this section, we address problem of row population using a two-step approach. We assume that a seed table is given, with a list of n seed entities E, a list of m seed column labels L, and a table caption c. The task is to generate a ranked list of suggestions for entity e_{n+1}, which may be added to the seed table as a new row. First, we identify a set of candidate entities (§4.1), and then rank them in a subsequent entity ranking step (§4.2).

4.1 Candidate Selection

We identify candidate entities using two sources: knowledge base (KB) and table corpus (TC). In the knowledge base, each entity e is described by a set of properties $\mathcal{P}_e$. We focus on two specific properties: types and categories. We discuss these notions in the context of DBpedia, but note that all knowledge bases employ some taxonomy of types. Types in DBpedia are assigned from a small ontology (the DBpedia Ontology, containing a few hundred classes). Categories originate from Wikipedia; these do not form a strict is-a hierarchy, and may be seen more like "semantic sets." Categories are in the order of several 100K. Intuitively, an entity e that has several types or categories overlapping with those of the seed entities represents a good candidate. Thus, we rank entities based on the overlap of these properties, and then take the top-k ones as the set of candidates:

$$score(e, E) = \left|\mathcal{P}_e \cap \left(\cup_{i=1}^{n} \mathcal{P}_{e_i} \right)\right| .$$

When using the table corpus, we search for tables that contain the seed entities or have a similar caption to that of the seed table. This can be efficiently performed using existing retrieval methods against an inverted index of tables. Specifically, we use either the seed table's caption or seed entities as the search query and rank tables using the BM25 retrieval algorithm.

4.2 Ranking Entities

We introduce a probabilistic formulation and rank candidate entities according to the multi-conditional probability $P(e|E, L, c)$. By applying Bayes's theorem and making a full independence assumption between table caption, seed entities, and seed column labels, we factor this probability as follows:

$$\begin{aligned} P(e|E, L, c) &= \frac{P(E, L, c|e)P(e)}{P(E, L, c)} \\ &= \frac{P(E|e)P(L|e)P(c|e)P(e)}{P(E)P(L)P(c)} \\ &\propto P(e|E)P(L|e)P(c|e) . \end{aligned} \quad (1)$$

In the last step, we rewrote $P(E|e)$ using Bayes' rule (which cancelled out $P(e)$ and $P(E)$). We further dropped the probabilities $P(L)$ and $P(c)$ from the denominator, since those are the same across all candidate entities and thus do not influence their ranking. Then, entities are ranked by multiplying (i) the posteriori probability $P(e|E)$ that expresses entity similarity, (ii) the column labels likelihood $P(L|e)$, and (iii) the caption likelihood $P(c|e)$. The reason for keeping the latter two probabilities conditioned on the candidate entity is that column labels and captions are very short. In those cases, the candidate entity offers a richer observation. Below, we discuss the estimation of each of these probabilities.

Note that entities may be ranked using any subset of the components in Eq. (1). We explore all possible combinations in our experimental section (§7). It is our expectation that using all three sources of evidence (seed entities, seed column labels, and table caption) would result in the best performance.

4.3 Entity Similarity

The estimation of $P(e|E)$ corresponds to the task of *entity list completion* (also known as *set/concept expansion* or *query by example*): given a small set of seed entities, complement this set with additional entities. The general idea is to measure the semantic similarity between the candidate entity and the set of seed entities. One line of prior work [4, 16] relies on a knowledge base for establishing this semantic similarity. Another family of approaches [8, 26, 29] leverages a large table corpus for collecting co-occurrence statistics. We combine both these sources in a single model:

$$P(e|E) = \lambda_E P_{KB}(e|E) + (1 - \lambda_E) P_{TC}(e|E) , \qquad (2)$$

where P_{KB} is based on the knowledge base and P_{TC} is the estimate based on the table corpus.

4.3.1 Estimation Using a Knowledge Base. Bron et al. [4] create a structured entity representation for each entity from the RDF triples describing that entity. The structured representation of an entity is comprised by the set of relations of the entity. Each relation r is modeled as a pair, by removing the entity itself from the triples. E.g., given the triple ⟨`dbr:Japan, dbo:capital, dbr:Tokyo`⟩ describing the entity Japan, the corresponding relation becomes ⟨`dbo:capital, dbr:Tokyo`⟩. We write $\hat{e}$ to denote the structured representation of entity e. Formally, given a set of subject-predicate-object (s, p, o) triples describing the entity (i.e., the entity stands either as subject or object):

$$\hat{e} = \{(p, o) : (s = e, p, o)\} \cup \{(s, p) : (s, p, o = e)\} .$$

Similarly, each seed entity is represented as a set of pairs: $\hat{e}_1, \ldots, \hat{e}_n$. The set of seed entities is modeled as a multinomial probability distribution θ_E over the set of relations. The probability $P(e|E)$ is then obtained by considering all relations that appear in the representation of the candidate entity:

$$P_{KB}(e|E) = \sum_{r \in \hat{e}} P(r|\theta_E) = \sum_{r \in \hat{e}} \frac{\sum_{i=1}^{n} \mathbb{1}(r, \hat{e}_i)}{|\theta_E|} ,$$

where $\mathbb{1}(r, \hat{e}_i)$ is a binary indicator function, which is 1 is r occurs in the representation of $\hat{e}_i$ and is 0 otherwise. The denominator is the representation length of the seed entities, i.e., the total number of relations of all seed entities: $|\theta_E| = \sum_{i=1}^{n} \sum_{r \in \hat{e}_i} \mathbb{1}(r, \hat{e}_i)$.

Instead of using a single model built for the set of seed entities, we also explore an alternative approach by taking the average pairwise similarity between the candidate and seed entities (similar in spirit to [8, 10]):

$$P_{KB}(e|E) \propto \frac{1}{n} \sum_{i=1}^{n} \text{sim}(e, e_i) ,$$

where $\text{sim}(e, e_i)$ is a similarity function. We consider two alternatives for this function. The first is the *Wikipedia Link-based Measure* (WLM) [17], which estimates the semantic relatedness between two entities based on other entities they link to:

$$\text{sim}_{WLM}(e, e_i) = 1 - \frac{\log(\max(|\mathcal{L}_e|, |\mathcal{L}_{e_i}|)) - \log(|\mathcal{L}_e \cap \mathcal{L}_{e_i}|)}{\log(|\mathcal{E}| - \log(\min(|\mathcal{L}_e|, |\mathcal{L}_{e_i}|)))} ,$$

where $\mathcal{L}_e$ is the set of outgoing links of e (i.e., entities e links to) and $|\mathcal{E}|$ is the total number of entities in the knowledge base. The second similarity function is the Jaccard coefficient, based on the overlap between the outgoing links of entities:

$$\text{sim}_{Jacc}(e, e_i) = \frac{|\mathcal{L}_e \cap \mathcal{L}_{e_i}|}{|\mathcal{L}_e \cup \mathcal{L}_{e_i}|} .$$

4.3.2 Estimation Using a Table Corpus. Another way of establishing the similarity between a candidate entity e and the set of seed entities E is to obtain co-occurrence statistics from a table corpus (as in [1, 8]). We employ a maximum likelihood estimator:

$$P_{TC}(e|E) = \frac{\#(e, E)}{\#(E)} ,$$

where $\#(e, E)$ is the number of tables that contain the candidate entity together with all seed entities, and $\#(E)$ is the number of tables that contain all seed entities. Provided that the table corpus is sufficiently large, we expect this simple method to provide an accurate estimate.

4.4 Column Labels Likelihood

For computing $P(L|e)$, we consider the tables from the table corpus where the entity appears in the leftmost column. We obtain and combine two different estimates. The first one is the representation of the entity in terms of the words of the column labels, i.e., an unigram language model (LM). The second one is a maximum likelihood estimate using exact label matching (EM), i.e., without breaking labels up to words. We consider each individual label l from the seed column labels and combine the above two estimates using a linear mixture:

$$P(L|e) = \sum_{l \in L} \Big(\lambda_L \Big(\prod_{t \in l} P_{LM}(t|\theta_e) \Big) + \frac{(1 - \lambda_L)}{|L|} P_{EM}(l|e) \Big) .$$

The first component is a Dirichlet-smoothed unigram language model, calculated using:

$$P_{LM}(t|\theta_e) = \frac{tf(t, e) + \mu P(t|\theta)}{|e| + \mu} ,$$

where $tf(t, e)$ is the total term frequency of t in column heading labels of the tables that include e in their leftmost column. One may think of it as concatenating all the column heading labels of the tables that include e, and then counting how many times t appears in there. The length of the entity $|e|$ is the sum of all term frequencies for the entity ($|e| = \sum_{t'} tf(t', e)$). The background language model $P(t|\theta)$ is built from the column heading labels of all tables in the corpus.

The exact label matching probability is estimated using:

$$P_{EM}(l|e) = \frac{\#(l,e)}{\#(e)} ,$$

where $\#(l,e)$ is the number of tables containing both e and l, and $\#(e)$ is the total number of tables containing e.

4.5 Caption Likelihood

To estimate the caption likelihood given an entity, $P(c|e)$, we combine two different term-based entity representations: one from the knowledge base and one from the table corpus. Formally:

$$P(c|e) = \prod_{t \in c} \left(\lambda_c P_{KB}(t|\theta_e) + (1-\lambda_c) P_{TC}(t|e)\right) .$$

The knowledge base entity representation is an unigram language model constructed from the entity's description (specifically, its abstract in DBpedia). Smoothing is done analogously to the column labels language model, but the components of the formula are computed differently:

$$P_{KB}(t|\theta_e) = \frac{tf(t,e) + \mu P(t|\theta)}{|e| + \mu} ,$$

where $tf(t,e)$ denotes the (raw) term frequency of t in the entity's description, $|e|$ is the length (number of terms) of that description, and $P(t|\theta)$ is a background language model (a maximum likelihood estimate from the descriptions of all entities in the KB).

To construct a term-based representation from the table corpus, we consider the captions of all tables that include entity e:

$$P_{TC}(t|e) = \frac{\#(t,e)}{\#(e)} ,$$

where $\#(t,e)$ denotes the number of tables that contain term t in the caption as well as entity e in the leftmost column. The denominator $\#(e)$ is the total number of tables containing e.[2]

5 POPULATING COLUMNS

In this section, we address the problem of column population using a two-step approach: we identify a set of candidate column heading labels (or *labels*, for short), and then subsequently rank them.

5.1 Candidate Selection

We use (i) the table caption, (ii) table entities, and (iii) seed column heading labels to search for similar tables. The searching method is the same as in §4.1, i.e., we use BM25 similarity using either of (i)–(iii) to get a ranking of tables from the table corpus. From these tables, we extract the column heading labels as candidates (excluding the seed column labels). When searching is done using the seed column labels as query, our method is equivalent to the FastJoin matcher [27] (which was also adopted in [12]).

5.2 Ranking Column Labels

We are interested in estimating the probability $P(l|E,c,L)$, given j seed labels, the table caption, and a set of entities from the rows.

[2]We also experimented with constructing a smoothed language model, similar to how it was done for the KB, but that gave inferior results.

5.2.1 *Baseline Approach.*

Das Sarma et al. [8] consider the "benefits" of additional columns. The benefit of adding l to table T is estimated as follows:

$$P(l|L) = LB(L,l) = \frac{1}{|L|} \sum_{l_1 \in L} cs(l_1, l_2) , \quad (3)$$

where L denotes column labels and cs is the AcsDB [6] (*Attribute Correlation Statistics Database*) schema frequency statistics, which is given in Eq. (4). It is more effective to derive the benefit measure by considering the co-occurrence of pairs of labels, rather than the entire set of labels [8]. Eq. (4) determines the consistency of adding a new label l_2 to an existing label l_1:

$$cs(l_1,l_2) = P(l_2|l_1) = \frac{\#(l_1,l_2)}{\#(l_1)} , \quad (4)$$

where $\#(l_1,l_2)$ is number of tables containing both l_1 and l_2, and $\#(l_1)$ is the number of tables containing l_1.

5.2.2 *Our Approach.*

Instead of estimating this probability directly, we use tables as a bridge. We search related tables sharing similar caption, labels, or entities with the seed table. Searching tables with only one aspect similarity is thought as a single method, e.g., searching tables with similar caption has the probability of $P(T|c)$. All these related tables are candidate tables acting as bridges. Each candidate table is weighted by considering its relevance with each candidate label, denoted as $P(l|T)$.

By applying the law of total probability, we get:

$$P(l|E,c,L) = \sum_T P(l|T)P(T|E,c,L) ,$$

where $P(l|T)$ is the label's likelihood given a candidate table (see §5.3), and $P(T|E,c,L)$ expresses that table's relevance (see §5.4).

5.3 Label Likelihood

Label likelihood, $P(l|T)$, may be seen as the importance of label l in a given table T. The simplest way of setting this probability is *uniformly* across the labels of the table:

$$P(l|T) = \begin{cases} 1, & \text{if } l \text{ appears in } T \\ 0, & \text{otherwise} . \end{cases}$$

5.4 Table Relevance Estimation

Table relevance expresses the degree of similarity between a candidate table and the seed table the user is working with. Tables with higher relevance are preferred. Specifically, we search for tables by considering the similarity of the set of entities, table caption, and column labels. The probability of a candidate table is factored as:

$$P(T|E,c,L) = \frac{P(T|E)P(T|c)P(T|L)}{P(T)^2} .$$

Notice that an independence assumption between E, c, and $L^{(j)}$ was made. Further, assuming that the prior probability of a table follows a uniform distribution, the denominator can be dropped. The components of this model are detailed below.

5.4.1 Entity Coverage. When selecting a candidate table, the coverage of the tables' entity set is a important factor [1, 8]. We compute the fraction of the seed table's entities covered by candidate table as:

$$P(T|E) = \frac{|T_E \cap E|}{|E|} .$$

We note that the same concept is used in [8], where it is referred to as *entity coverage.*

5.4.2 Caption Likelihood. Having similar captions is a strong indicator that two tables are likely to have similar contents. An effective way of calculating caption similarity is to use the seed table's caption as a query against a caption index of the table corpus. We can use any term-based retrieval model (like BM25 or language modeling) for measuring caption similarity:

$$P(T|c) \propto \text{sim}(T_c, c) .$$

5.4.3 Column Labels Likelihood. Finally, we estimate the column labels likelihood similar to Lehmberg et al. [12], who rank tables according to the number of overlapping labels:

$$P(T|L) = \frac{|T_L \cap L|}{|L|} .$$

6 EXPERIMENTAL DESIGN

We present the data sets we use in our experiments and our evaluation methodology. We develop an approach that simulates a user through the process of populating a seed table with data.

6.1 Data

We use the WikiTables corpus [3], which contains 1.6M tables extracted from Wikipedia. The knowledge base we use is DBpedia (version 2015-10). We restrict ourselves to entities which have an abstract (4.6M in total).

We preprocess the tables as follows. For each cell that contains a hyperlink we check if it points to an entity that is present in DBpedia. If yes, we use the DBpedia identifier of the linked entity as the cell's content (with redirects resolved); otherwise, we replace the link with the anchor text (i.e., treat it as a string).

6.2 Entity-Focused Tables

Recall that we defined an entity-focused table as one that contains only unique entities in its leftmost column (cf. §3). In addition to being an entity-focused table, we require that the table has at least 6 rows and at least additional 3 columns (excluding the entity column). We introduce these constraints so that we can simulate a real-world scenario with sufficient amount of content.

In Table 2, we report statistics based on what percentage of cells in the leftmost column contains entities. Let us note here that only those entities are recognized that have a corresponding Wikipedia article. Thus, the reported numbers should be treated as lower bound estimates. It is clear that many tables have an entity focus.

To be able to perform an automated evaluation without any human intervention, we apply the most strict conditions. Out of the tables that contain 100% unique entities in their leftmost column and have at least 6 rows and at least 4 columns (53 K in total), see Table 2, we randomly select 1000 tables as our validation set (used for parameter tuning) and another 1000 tables as our test set. We use a different random selection of validation/test tables for row and column population. The validation and test sets are excluded from the table corpus during training. It is important to note that we use all other tables from the corpus when computing statistics, and not only those that classify as entity-focused.

Table 2: Statistics of table corpus. Constraints mean having > 5 rows and > 3 columns.

leftmost column (X% are entities)	# tables total	# tables with constraints
Existing entity	726913	212923
60%	556644	139572
80%	483665	119166
100%	425236	78611
100% unique	376213	53354

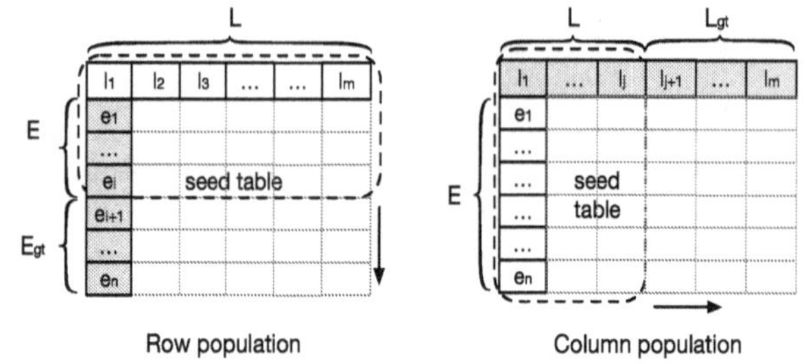

Figure 2: Illustration of our evaluation methodology. A part of an existing table is designated as seed table; the entities/column labels outside the seed table serve as ground truth. The arrows indicate the direction of the population.

6.3 Simulation Process

We evaluate row/column population by starting from an actual (complete) entity-focused table, with n content rows (with an entity in each) and m column headings. We simulate an user through the process of completing that table by starting with some seed rows/columns and iteratively adding one row/column at a time.

- For evaluating row population, we take entities from the first i rows ($i \in [1..5]$) as seed entities E, and use the entities from the remaining rows as ground truth, $\hat{E}$. We use all column heading labels.
- For evaluating column population, we take labels from the first j column ($j \in [1..3]$) as seed column labels L, and use the labels from the remaining columns as ground truth, $\hat{L}$. We use all entities from the table's rows.

See Figure 2 for an illustration. Notice that we are expanding in a single dimensions at a time; populating both rows and columns at the same time is left for future work.

6.4 Matching Column Labels

For the column population task, we are matching string labels (as opposed to unique identifiers). Let us consider `Date` as the ground truth column label. When the suggested labels are compared against this using strict string matching, then `date`, `Dates`, `date:`, etc. would not be accepted as correct, despite being semantically identical. Therefore, we apply some simple normalization steps, on both the ranked and ground truth column labels, before comparing them using strict string matching. When multiple ranked labels are normalized to the same form, only the one with the highest score is retained.

6.5 Evaluation Metrics

Given that the relevance judgments are binary, we use Mean Average Precision (MAP) as our main evaluation metric. In addition, we also report on Mean Reciprocal Rank (MRR). We measure statistical significance using a two-tailed paired t-test. To avoid cluttering the discussion, we report significance testing only for our main metric.

7 EVALUATION OF ROW POPULATION

This section presents the evaluation of row population.

7.1 Candidate Selection

In §4.1, we have introduced four individual methods to select candidates: entity category (A1) and entity type (A2) from the knowledge base, and table caption (B) and table entities (C) from the table corpus. These methods involve a cut-off threshold parameter k; the top-k entities are considered as candidates for the subsequent ranking step. A larger k value typically implies higher recall. At the same time, each of the candidate entities will need to be scored, which is a computationally expensive operation. Therefore, we wish to find a setting that ensures high recall, while keeping the number of candidate entities manageably low (to ensure reasonable response time). We use the validation set to explore a range of k values: 2^6, 2^8, 2^{10}, and 2^{12}. For each method, we select the k value that produces the best recall and candidate entity number ratio.

The results are reported in the top block of Table 3. We observe that more seed entities we have, the better recall gets. This is expected behavior. Out of the two entity properties from the knowledge base, categories and types, categories performs far better. For types, even with $k = 4096$, the recall is still unsatisfactory. This is because many of the DBpedia entities have no ontology type information assigned to them. Moreover, ontology types are more general than categories and result in too many candidates. The best individual method is (C) table entities; it is the most effective (achieves the highest recall) and the most efficient (produces the lowest number of candidates) at the same time.

To further enhance performance, we combine the individual methods. However, we exclude type (A2) from this combination, because of its low performance. We find that all combinations improve over the single methods. This means that they capture complimentary aspects. Combining all three methods (A1+B+C) leads to the best overall performance. The last two lines of Table 3 show the performance of this combination (A1+B+C) using two different k values. We find that with a high k value (4096), we are able to achieve close to perfect recall. The number of candidates, however, is a magnitude larger than with a low k (256). Motivated by efficiency considerations, we decided not to pay this price and chose to use $k = 256$, which still gives us very high recall.

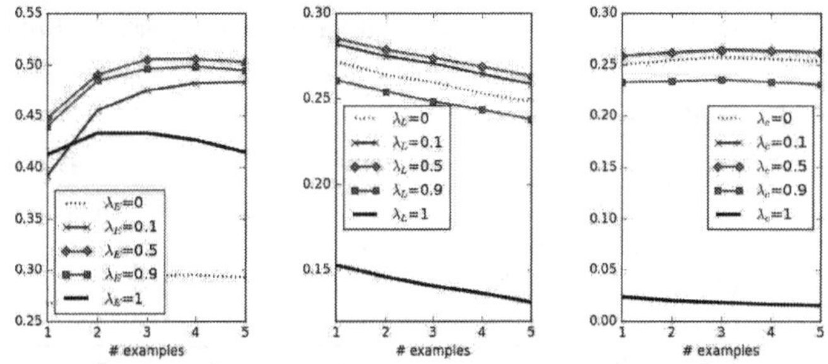

Figure 3: Effect of varying the interpolation parameters for $P(e|E)$ (Left), $P(L|e)$ (Middle), and $P(c|e)$ (Right). The plots show MAP scores measured on the validation set.

7.2 Entity Ranking

Our entity ranking model is comprised of three components: entity similarity ($P(e|E)$), column labels likelihood ($P(L|e)$), and caption likelihood ($P(c|e)$). Each of these methods involve an interpolation parameter (λ_E, λ_L, and λ_c, respectively). We train these parameters on the validation set, by performing a sweep in 0.1 steps over the [0..1] range. The effect of varying the parameter values is shown in Figure 3. It can be seen that the value 0.5 provides the best setting everywhere. We also found that there is very little difference in terms of performance when λ is in the 0.3..0.7 range (hence the choice of showing the 0.1 and 0.9 values on the plots).

We start by discussing the performance of individual components, reported in the top block of Table 4. The two-component entity similarity model combines estimated based on the knowledge base and the table corpus (cf. Eq. (2)). For the former, we compare three alternatives: using relations of entities, as in [4] (A1), and two similarity methods based on outgoing links of entities: WLM (A2), and Jaccard similarity (A3). Out of the three methods, (A1) Relations has the best performance. However, (A3) has only marginally lower retrieval performance, while being computationally much more efficient. Therefore, we choose (A3), when it comes to combining it with the other elements of the entity ranking model. Compared to entity similarity ($P(e|E)$), the other two components (B and C) have much lower performance. The differences (A3) vs. (B) and (A3) vs. (C) are highly significant ($p < 10^{-5}$). This means that the knowledge base contributes more.

Next, we combine the individual components to further enhance performance. The middle block of Table 4 reports results when two components are used. We find that these combinations improve significantly over the individual methods in all cases ($p < 10^{-5}$). It is interesting to note that while (C) caption likelihood outperforms (B) column labels likelihood in the individual comparison (significantly so for #1..#3 seed entities, $p < 0.001$), the two perform on a par when combined with (A3) entity similarity.

As expected, using all three component (A3 & B & C) results in the best performance. The differences between this vs. (A3 & C) and vs. (B & C) are significant for any number of seed entities ($p < 0.001$); regarding (A3 & B & C) vs. (A3 & B), the differences are significant only for seed entities #1 and #5 ($p < 0.05$). This means that combining information from the knowledge base with column

Table 3: Candidate selection performance for the row population task on the validation set. #cand refers to the number of candidate entities. Highest recall values are typeset in boldface.

Method	#Seed entities (|E|) 1		2		3		4		5	
	Recall	#cand	Recall	#cand	Recall	#cand	Recall	#cand	Recall	#cand
(A1) Categories (k=256)	0.6470	1721	0.6985	2772	0.7282	3678	0.7476	4507	0.7604	5224
(A2) Types (k=4096)	0.0553	7703	0.0577	8047	0.0585	8225	0.0605	8419	0.0600	8551
(B) Table caption (k=256)	0.3966	987	0.3961	987	0.3945	987	0.3938	987	0.3929	987
(C) Table entities (k=256)	0.6643	312	0.7212	458	0.7435	589	0.7564	689	0.7639	759
(B) & (C) (k=256)	0.7090	1250	0.7464	1383	0.7626	1505	0.7732	1599	0.7788	1664
(A1) & (B) (k=256)	0.7642	2671	0.7969	3711	0.8157	4610	0.8305	5434	0.8405	6145
(A1) & (C) (k=256)	0.8434	1962	0.8885	3118	0.9038	4117	0.9196	5014	0.9285	5773
(A1) & (B) & (C) (k=256)	0.8662	2880	0.8997	4018	0.9154	5005	0.9255	5894	0.9329	6645
(A1) & (B) & (C) (k=4096)	**0.9576**	28733	**0.9718**	40171	**0.9787**	49478	**0.9811**	58021	**0.9821**	65204

labels from the table corpus yields significant benefits; considering the captions of tables on top of that leads to little additional gain.

For baseline comparison, we employ the method by [4], which combines text-based and structure-based similarity. Note that we used only the structure-based part of their method earlier, as (A1); here, we use their approach in its entirety. It requires a keyword query, which we set to be the table caption. We find that our methods substantially and significantly ($p < 10^{-5}$) outperforms this baseline; see the bottom two rows in Table 4.

One final observation is that performance climbs when moving from a single to two and three seed entities; after that, however, it plateaus. This behavior is consistent across all methods, including the baseline. The phenomena is known from prior work [4, 16, 20].

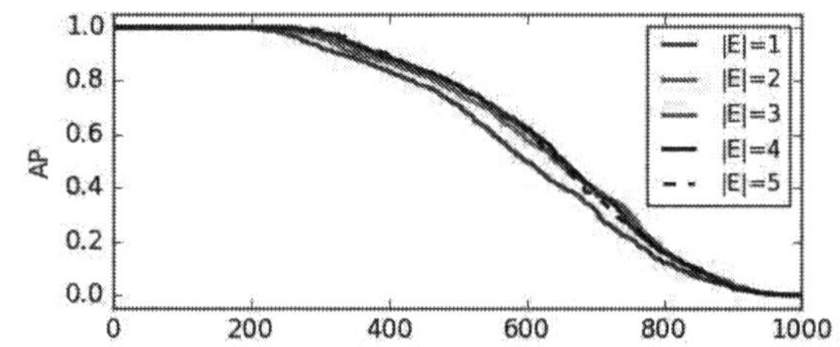

Figure 4: Performance of individual tables, ordered by decreasing Average Precision, for row population.

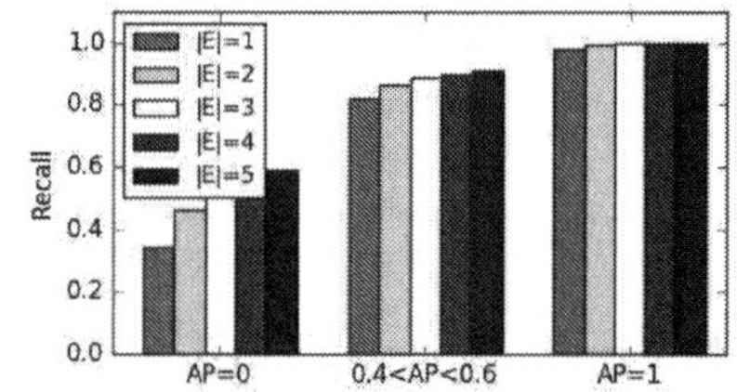

Figure 5: Recall of candidate selection against entity ranking performance, for row population.

7.3 Analysis

Now that we have presented our overall results, we perform further examination on the level of individual tables. Figure 4 shows the average precision (AP) scores for the 1000 test tables, ordered by decreasing score. Statistically, there are 285 tables having $AP = 1$, 193 tables having $0.4 < AP < 0.6$, and 42 tables having $AP = 0$. To understand the reasons behind this, we check the recall of the candidate selection step for these three categories; see Figure 5. In this figure, we can observe that higher recall generally leads to better AP. Delving deeper, we compute the average number of tables containing at least one ground truth entity, for each of the three groups. When $AP = 0$, the number is 18, for $0.4 < AP < 0.6$ it is 79, and for $AP = 1$ it is 127. It appears that we could provide excellent suggestions, when there were enough similar tables to the seed table in the table corpus. However, for tables that are "too unique," we would need alternative methods for suggestions.

8 EVALUATION OF COLUMN POPULATION

This section presents the evaluation of column population. This task relies only on the table corpus; the data set is exactly the same as for row population, see §6.1.

8.1 Candidate Selection

In §5.1, we have introduced three individual methods to select candidates: table caption (A), column heading labels (B) and table entities (C). Method (B) actually corresponds to the FastJoin matcher in [27]. These methods also involve a cut-off threshold parameter k, for the same reasons we already discussed in §7.1. The results are reported in the top block of Table 5. We observe that the more seed labels we have the better recall gets when using labels. We also explore combinations of pairs of methods as well as using all three. We find that all combinations improve over the single methods, and that combining all three methods leads to the best overall performance. Our selected method is the second to last in Table 5, motivated by efficiency considerations; for comparison, we also show the performance for $k = 4096$.

8.2 Column Label Ranking

Our column label ranking model is comprised of two components: table relevance and label likelihood. For estimating candidate table relevance, we have three individual methods, using table caption

Table 4: Entity ranking performance on the test set.

Method	#Seed entities ($\|E\|$) 1		2		3		4		5	
	MAP	MRR	MAP	MRR	MAP	MRR	MAP	MRR	MAP	MRR
(A1) $P(e\|E)$ Relations ($\lambda = 0.5$)	0.4962	0.6857	0.5469	0.7297	0.5687	0.7415	0.5734	0.7294	0.5693	0.7274
(A2) $P(e\|E)$ WLM ($\lambda = 0.5$)	0.4674	0.6246	0.5154	0.6901	0.5293	0.6930	0.5331	0.6861	0.5258	0.6789
(A3) $P(e\|E)$ Jaccard ($\lambda = 0.5$)	0.4905	0.6731	0.5427	0.7086	0.5617	0.7270	0.5662	0.7098	0.5609	0.7058
(B) $P(L\|e)$	0.2857	0.3558	0.2878	0.3518	0.2717	0.3463	0.2651	0.3365	0.2585	0.3336
(C) $P(c\|e)$	0.2348	0.2656	0.2366	0.2676	0.2371	0.2656	0.2350	0.2614	0.2343	0.2602
(A3) & (B)	0.5726	0.7593	0.6108	**0.8055**	0.6189	**0.7879**	0.6182	0.7755	0.6108	**0.7689**
(A3) & (C)	0.5743	0.7467	0.6108	0.7749	0.6221	0.7746	0.6211	0.7668	0.6156	0.7447
(B) & (C)	0.3677	0.4521	0.3715	0.4508	0.3712	0.4455	0.3688	0.4408	0.3667	0.4378
(A3) & (B) & (C)	**0.5922**	**0.7729**	**0.6260**	0.8000	**0.6339**	0.7849	**0.6348**	**0.7800**	**0.6310**	0.7630
Baseline [4]	0.3076	0.4967	0.3273	0.5156	0.3404	0.5326	0.3428	0.5290	0.3406	0.5202

Table 5: Candidate selection performance for the column population task on the validation set.

Method	#Seed column labels ($\|L\|$) 1		2		3	
	Recall	#cand	Recall	#cand	Recall	#cand
(A) Table caption (k=256)	0.7177	232	0.7115	232	0.7135	231
(B) Column labels (k=256)	0.2145	115	0.5247	235	0.7014	357
(C) Table entities (k=64)	0.7617	157	0.7544	156	0.7505	155
(A) (k=256) & (B) (k=256) & (C) (k=64)	0.8799	467	0.8961	572	0.9040	682
(A) (k=4096) & (B) (k=4096) & (C) (k=4096)	**0.9211**	2614	**0.9292**	3309	**0.9351**	3978

(A), column labels (B), and table entities (C). All methods use the same estimation of label likelihood (cf. §5.3).

We start by discussing the performance of individual methods, which is reported in the top block of Table 6. Of the three, method (C) outperforms the other two, and does significantly so ($p < 10^{-5}$). Looking at the tendency of MAP, the increasing number of seed column labels only contributes to method (B). When combining two of the methods, all combinations improve significantly over the individual methods ($p < 10^{-5}$). Out of the three, (B) & (C) performs best in terms of both *MAP* and *MRR*. In the end, putting together all three individual methods delivers the best results. Also, this combination (A & B & C) improves significantly over the combination of any two of the methods ($p < 10^{-5}$).

For baseline comparison, we employ the method by Das Sarma et al. [8]. They consider the "benefits" of adding additional columns, which expressed in Eq. (3). We find that our three-component method substantially and significantly ($p < 10^{-5}$) outperforms this baseline. It should be noted that the baseline in [8] uses our candidate selection method to make it comparable; this actually performs better than their original approach.

8.3 Analysis

Figure 6 plots the performance of individual (test) tables, in decreasing order of average precision score. We find that there are 427 tables having $AP = 1$, 122 tables having $0.4 < AP < 0.6$, and 186 tables having $AP = 0$. We examine these three table groups, based on performance, in terms of their corresponding recall values from the candidate selection step. Figure 7 shows these values (averaged over all tables that fall in the given performance group). Looking at the number of tables containing at least one ground truth column heading label, it is 204 for $AP = 0$, 403 for $0.4 < AP < 0.6$, and 1114 for $AP = 1$. We can draw similar conclusions here as we did for entity ranking.

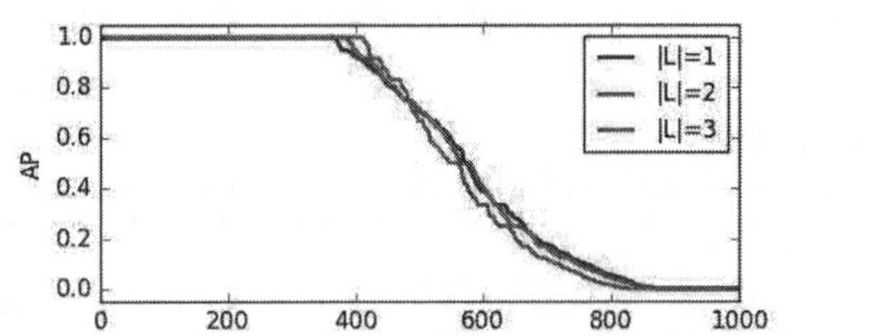

Figure 6: Performance of individual tables, ordered by decreasing Average Precision, for column population.

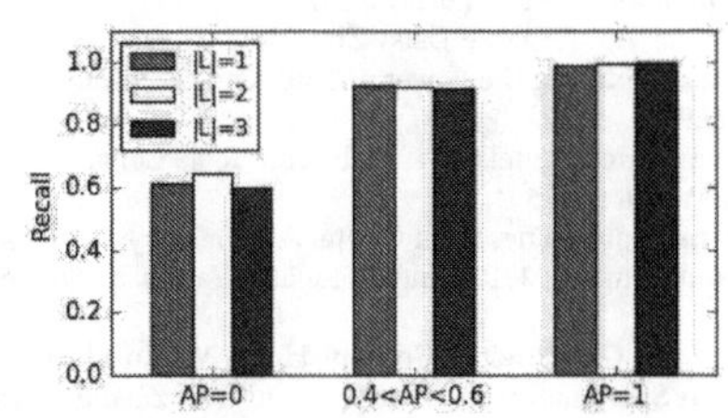

Figure 7: Recall of candidate selection against column label ranking performance, for column population.

Table 6: Column label ranking performance on the test set.

Method	#Seed column labels (|L|)					
	1		2		3	
	MAP	MRR	MAP	MRR	MAP	MRR
(A) Table caption	0.2584	0.3496	0.2404	0.2927	0.2161	0.2356
(B) Column labels	0.2463	0.3676	0.3145	0.4276	0.3528	0.4246
(C) Table entities	0.3878	0.4544	03714	0.4187	0.3475	0.3732
(A) & (B)	0.4824	0.5896	0.4929	0.5837	0.4826	0.5351
(A) & (C)	0.5032	0.5941	0.4909	0.5601	0.4724	0.5132
(B) & (C)	0.5060	0.5954	0.5410	0.6178	0.5323	0.5802
(A) & (B) & (C)	**0.5863**	**0.6854**	**0.5847**	**0.6690**	**0.5696**	**0.6201**
Baseline [8]	0.4413	0.5473	0.4640	0.5535	0.4535	0.5079

9 CONCLUSION

In this paper, we have introduced the idea of a smart table assistant and have taken the first steps towards its realization. Specifically, we have concentrated on tables with an entity focus, and investigated the tasks of row population and column population. We have devised methods for each task and showed experimentally how the different components all contribute to overall performance. For evaluation, we have developed a process that simulates a user through her work of populating a table with data. Our overall results are very promising and substantially outperform existing baselines.

In future work, we plan to extend the capabilities of our assistant to be able to populate data cells as well with values. Further along the road, we also wish to relax our requirement regarding the entity focus, and make our methods applicable to arbitrary tables.

REFERENCES

[1] Ahmad Ahmadov, Maik Thiele, Julian Eberius, Wolfgang Lehner, and Robert Wrembel. 2015. Towards a Hybrid Imputation Approach Using Web Tables.. In *Proc. of BDC '15*. 21–30.

[2] Chandra Sekhar Bhagavatula, Thanapon Noraset, and Doug Downey. 2013. Methods for Exploring and Mining Tables on Wikipedia. In *Proc. of IDEA '13*. 18–26.

[3] Chandra Sekhar Bhagavatula, Thanapon Noraset, and Doug Downey. 2015. TabEL: Entity Linking in Web Tables. In *Proc. of ISWC 2015*. 425–441.

[4] Marc Bron, Krisztian Balog, and Maarten de Rijke. 2013. Example Based Entity Search in the Web of Data. In *Proc. of ECIR'13*. 392–403.

[5] Michael J. Cafarella, Alon Halevy, and Jayant Madhavan. 2011. Structured Data on the Web. *Commun. ACM* 54 (2011), 72–79.

[6] Michael J. Cafarella, Alon Halevy, Daisy Zhe Wang, Eugene Wu, and Yang Zhang. 2008. WebTables: Exploring the Power of Tables on the Web. *Proc. VLDB Endow.* 1 (2008), 538–549.

[7] Eric Crestan and Patrick Pantel. 2011. Web-scale Table Census and Classification. In *Proc. of WSDM '11*. 545–554.

[8] Anish Das Sarma, Lujun Fang, Nitin Gupta, Alon Halevy, Hongrae Lee, Fei Wu, Reynold Xin, and Cong Yu. 2012. Finding Related Tables. In *Proc. of SIGMOD '12*. 817–828.

[9] Xin Dong, Evgeniy Gabrilovich, Geremy Heitz, Wilko Horn, Ni Lao, Kevin Murphy, Thomas Strohmann, Shaohua Sun, and Wei Zhang. 2014. Knowledge Vault: A Web-scale Approach to Probabilistic Knowledge Fusion. In *Proc. of KDD '14*. 601–610.

[10] Yeye He and Dong Xin. 2011. SEISA: set expansion by iterative similarity aggregation. In *Proc. of WWW '11*. 427–436.

[11] Yusra Ibrahim, Mirek Riedewald, and Gerhard Weikum. 2016. Making Sense of Entities and Quantities in Web Tables. In *Proc. of CIKM '16*. 1703–1712.

[12] Oliver Lehmberg, Dominique Ritze, Petar Ristoski, Robert Meusel, Heiko Paulheim, and Christian Bizer. 2015. The Mannheim Search Join Engine. *Web Semant.* 35 (2015), 159–166.

[13] Girija Limaye, Sunita Sarawagi, and Soumen Chakrabarti. 2010. Annotating and Searching Web Tables Using Entities, Types and Relationships. *Proc. of VLDB Endow.* 3 (2010), 1338–1347.

[14] Aman Madaan, Ashish Mittal, Mausam, Ganesh Ramakrishnan, and Sunita Sarawagi. 2016. Numerical Relation Extraction with Minimal Supervision. In *Proc. of AAAI'16*. 2764–2771.

[15] Jayant Madhavan, Loredana Afanasiev, Lyublena Antova, and Alon Y. Halevy. 2009. Harnessing the Deep Web: Present and Future. *CoRR* abs/0909.1785 (2009).

[16] Steffen Metzger, Ralf Schenkel, and Marcin Sydow. 2014. Aspect-Based Similar Entity Search in Semantic Knowledge Graphs with Diversity-Awareness and Relaxation. In *Proc. of WI-IAT '14*. 60–69.

[17] David Milne and Ian H. Witten. 2008. An Effective, Low-Cost Measure of Semantic Relatedness Obtained from Wikipedia Links. In *In Proc. of AAAI 2008*.

[18] Emir Muñoz, Aidan Hogan, and Alessandra Mileo. 2014. Using Linked Data to Mine RDF from Wikipedia's Tables. In *Proc. of WSDM '14*. 533–542.

[19] Varish Mulwad, Tim Finin, and Anupam Joshi. 2013. Semantic Message Passing for Generating Linked Data from Tables.. In *Proc. of ISWC 2013*. 363–378.

[20] Patrick Pantel, Eric Crestan, Arkady Borkovsky, Ana-Maria Popescu, and Vishnu Vyas. 2009. Web-scale Distributional Similarity and Entity Set Expansion. In *Proc. of EMNLP '09*. 938–947.

[21] S. Roy, T. Vieira, and D. Roth. 2015. Reasoning about Quantities in Natural Language. *Transactions of the Association for Computational Linguistics* 3 (2015).

[22] Sunita Sarawagi and Soumen Chakrabarti. 2014. Open-domain Quantity Queries on Web Tables: Annotation, Response, and Consensus Models. In *Proc. of KDD '14*. 711–720.

[23] Yoones A. Sekhavat, Francesco Di Paolo, Denilson Barbosa, and Paolo Merialdo. 2014. Knowledge Base Augmentation using Tabular Data. In *Proceedings of WWW'14)*.

[24] Thibault Sellam and Omar Alonso. 2015. Raimond: Quantitative Data Extraction from Twitter to Describe Events. In *Proc. of ICWE 2015*. 251–268.

[25] Petros Venetis, Alon Halevy, Jayant Madhavan, Marius Paşca, Warren Shen, Fei Wu, Gengxin Miao, and Chung Wu. 2011. Recovering Semantics of Tables on the Web. *Proc. VLDB Endow.* 4 (2011), 528–538.

[26] Chi Wang, Kaushik Chakrabarti, Yeye He, Kris Ganjam, Zhimin Chen, and Philip A. Bernstein. 2015. Concept Expansion Using Web Tables. In *Proc. of WWW '15*. 1198–1208.

[27] Jiannan Wang, Guoliang Li, and Jianhua Feng. 2014. Extending String Similarity Join to Tolerant Fuzzy Token Matching. *ACM Trans. Database Syst.* 39, 1 (2014), 1–45.

[28] Jingjing Wang, Haixun Wang, Zhongyuan Wang, and Kenny Q. Zhu. 2012. Understanding Tables on the Web. In *Proceedings of ER'12*. 141–155.

[29] Richard C. Wang and William W. Cohen. 2008. Iterative Set Expansion of Named Entities Using the Web. In *Proc. of ICDM '08*. 1091–1096.

[30] Mohamed Yakout, Kris Ganjam, Kaushik Chakrabarti, and Surajit Chaudhuri. 2012. InfoGather: Entity Augmentation and Attribute Discovery by Holistic Matching with Web Tables. In *Proc. of SIGMOD '12*. 97–108.

[31] Pengcheng Yin, Zhengdong Lu, Hang Li, and Ben Kao. 2016. Neural Enquirer: Learning to Query Tables in Natural Language. In *Proc. of IJCAI '16*. 2308–2314.

[32] Meihui Zhang and Kaushik Chakrabarti. 2013. InfoGather+: Semantic Matching and Annotation of Numeric and Time-varying Attributes in Web Tables. In *Proc. of SIGMOD '13*. 145–156.

[33] Stefan Zwicklbauer, Christoph Einsiedler, Michael Granitzer, and Christin Seifert. 2013. Towards Disambiguating Web Tables. In *Proc. of ISWC-PD'13*. 205–208.

Understanding and Modeling Success in Email Search

Jin Young Kim*
Snap Inc.
Venice, CA
jink@snap.com

Nick Craswell
Microsoft
Redmond, WA
nickcr@microsoft.com

Susan Dumais
Microsoft Research
Redmond, WA
sdumais@microsoft.com

Filip Radlinski
Microsoft
Redmond, WA
filrad@microsoft.com

Fang Liu
Microsoft
Redmond, WA
fangliu@microsoft.com

ABSTRACT

Email has been a dominant form of communication for many years, and email search is an important problem. In contrast to other search setting, such as web search, there have been few studies of user behavior and models of email search success. Research in email search is challenging for many reasons including the personal and private nature of the collection. Third party judges can not look at email search queries or email message content requiring new modeling techniques.

In this study, we built an opt-in client application which monitors a user's email search activity and then pops up an in-situ survey when a search session is finished. We then merged the survey data with server-side behavioral logs. This approach allows us to study the relationship between session-level outcome and user behavior, and then build a model to predict success for email search based on behavioral interaction patterns.

Our results show that generative models (MarkovChain) of success can predict the session-level success of email search better than baseline heuristics and discriminative models (RandomForest). The success model makes use of email-specific log activities such as reply, forward and move, as well as generic signals such as click with long dwell time. The learned model is highly interpretable, and reusable in that it can be applied to unlabeled interaction logs in the future.

CCS CONCEPTS

•Information systems → Evaluation of retrieval results;

1 INTRODUCTION

Email remains an important form of communication, with each email account becoming a private corpus of potentially highly personal or business-critical information. Email systems typically have a search interface that retrieves a list of messages matching the query, sorting the messages from newest to oldest. Some interfaces also offer a relevance ranking and multiple metadata-based sortings options, although users may seek out the date-sorted option even when it is not the default [10].

The role of relevance metrics in email search is to evaluate the quality of different ordering and interface options. Do users prefer a particular sort order, or a hybrid ordering with a short relevance-ranked list followed by a longer date-ordered one? Does the preferred sort order vary by query? By user? When there is relevance ranking, what ranking function is best? The matching function that is used to select messages could also be evaluated. Should it use stemming? What email fields should be matched and should there be measures in place to eliminate spurious matches from the list? Matching is be particularly important for date-ordered lists, since a large number of recent spurious matches has the effect of demoting older results that the user may be trying to find.

The metrics developed in this paper can be used to study these different choices. They can also be used to study different users, such as different levels of expertise, different types of information needs, which may lead to differences in desired system interface and results. Although it is important to develop evaluation metrics for email search, there are also challenges in doing so. Because of the sensitive nature of email corpora, it is usually impossible or undesirable to create a traditional test collection, with shared queries, message content and relevance judgments. A notable exception is Gord Cormack's work [9] on email spam detection in which they use an evaluation method that brings the model to private data.

In this work, we turn to server-side email search logs for building evaluation metrics. Modern email systems may operate in the web browser or in a client-server setup that allows the centralized collection of activity logs. For evaluating email search, these logs may be comparable to logs studied in web search.

However, there are some important differences between web and email search logs. Email search logs should be managed in a way that can preserve the privacy of users. The logs studied in this paper do not have any text from the user's query or messages, to maintain the privacy of users, unlike in web search logs where the content of queries and web pages are often studied. This adds extra challenges in finding signals that will be useful for evaluating email search logs.

On the other hand, email activity logs are richer than web search activity logs, because there are a wider range of activities. In web search the main activities are to enter a query and to click a search result, and unless the user returns to the search engine, the search

*Work done while this author was at Microsoft.

SIGIR'17, August 7–11, 2017, Shinjuku, Tokyo, Japan.
© 2017 ACM. ISBN 978-1-4503-5022-8/17/08...$15.00
DOI: http://dx.doi.org/10.1145/3077136.3080837

logs do not indicate how long the user spent on the clicked document before moving on or closing the browser. By contrast in email search the user remains in the system and their activities can be logged. For instance, after querying and selecting (clicking) a message, the timing and type of their next actions may indicate the relevance of the selected message. Perhaps reading a message for a long time is positive, but another signal of satisfaction would be whether they respond to the message. This may be true even for a short dwell time, in contrast to web search where a short dwell time tends to be a bad sign [12].

Given this availability of rich signals, the next challenge is finding a good interpretation of them, which is a nontrivial task due to the variety of signals (i.e., how would you characterize the value of 'message deletion' during a email search session) and the anonymity requirement for the log data. Our main approach here is to build a model that can predict the success (or failure) of a search session, which in turn can be used to characterize the performance of a search engine.

Building a model of success has been extensively studied in Web search settings [13], mostly relying on annotation of search sessions by human judges. To build such model for email search we need to switch from third party annotation of sessions to in-situ labeling by the searcher [12]. This allows us to understand email search with precision, because all our implicit and explicit data come from the same people in-situ. We develop a metric that can be used directly to evaluate success and effort in email search, and our insights can also be used as a comparison point for more traditional lab or test collection studies of email search.

Our in-situ collection of survey and behavior log data provides three main research contributions. First, we characterize the overall differences between successful and unsuccessful email search, at the user level, session level and the message level. Second, we characterize, for the variety of email actions (such as reply, forward, flag, delete), which actions are associated with successful rather than unsuccessful search sessions. Third, we develop predictive models to distinguish between successful and unsuccessful email search sessions. These insights and success models for email search are new, and should offer a useful comparison point in future email lab studies, test collections and real-world controlled experiments.

2 RELATED WORK

Several areas of prior research are relevant to our current paper, including different forms of offline and online information retrieval evaluation and the analysis of email management strategies and behavior.

Information retrieval evaluation. The dominant form of evaluation for information retrieval research is the test collection, comprising query topics, a corpus of content and relevance judgments [19]. The relevance judgments are usuallt made by third party judges rather than in-situ users as they interact with the search engine. The queries can come from search logs of a real system, but this raises the problem that the third party judge may not be able to understand the context of a real user, such as their real information need and the types of results they prefer. More critically, in our case we can not show email messages to third party judges for privacy reasons.

For this reason it is more desirable to build a behavior-based evaluation metric. In the Web this has been done by getting third party annotators to replay logged user sessions [13] and provide success annotations. Then Markov Chain models are built to characterize the relationship between logged activity and annotations. Later work [2, 3, 17] used web search data and labels collected from a browser toolbar or a game-like interface, and built more elaborate models. Recently the work was also extended to multi-level annotations [14]. Their best explanation for levels of satisfaction was a combination of the outcome of the session and the level of effort. We ask about both outcome and effort in our in-situ survey.

In this work we adapt models from [13] which have the advantage of simplicity and interpretability. However, unlike these studies, in our case we can not replay sessions for third party annotators for privacy reasons. In fact replay based on the server-side logs used in this study is impossible, because the logs do not contain message and query text. Our only source of query and message text (such as message subject) in this study is from the in-situ survey, not the logs.

Because of these privacy concerns, there is a hard tradeoff between having real users with real email and having third party relevance judging. It is not possible to have both, without violating user privacy. In this study we focus on the case with real email and without third party judges, although later it may be possible to validate the other approaches (third party judges with a public email corpus) against our findings. We now consider evaluation approaches that do not rely on third party judging. Table 1 summarizes characteristics of the users, types of labels collected and evaluation metrics for five studies.

In our setting it could be possible to use interleaving [8] to evaluate two retrieval systems, for example comparing query-message matching with and without stemming. We do not study interleaving here, but our findings about dwell time and email actions could inform the interleaving design. Interleaving makes use of implicit behavior to elicit a preference between rankers, and our findings indicate which of the many logged actions in email is associated with search success.

Interactive lab experiments could be a way of studying the effectiveness of email search [11]. Such an approach would usually require some simulated work tasks to be set up. This differs from our in-situ setup, where search is motivated by a real user rather than a simulated task. However, it would be interesting to use the analysis from this paper to interpret behavior in lab studies, and compare.

The approach used in this paper is closest to the curious browser developed by Fox et al. [12], an app which was deployed to hundreds of users. The app logs search behavior such as queries and clicks. It also regularly asks users in-situ for session-level satisfaction labels, as well as result-level labels, for both clicked results and a sample of skipped results. For predicting result-level satisfaction the most important implicit variables were dwell time, position of click and end action (back to SERP, close browser, timeout, address bar navigation, new query). For predicting session-level judgments the most important variables were the result-level judgments, the number of results visited and end action.

Since result-level judgments are not known in practice, removing them made average dwell time, number of results and end action the

Table 1: Different forms of evaluation and their characteristics. Q-D indicates a relevance label on a query-document pair. SAT indicates a satisfaction label at the overall session or task level.

	Real users	In-situ labels	3rd party labels	Metric Type
TREC ad hoc [19]	No	No	Q-D	Average precision
Hassan et al. [13]	Yes	No	Q-D, SAT	SAT predict via behavior
Interleaving [8]	Yes	No	No	Ranker preference via behavior
TREC interactive [11]	In-lab	Yes	No	SAT
Curious browser [12]	Yes	Q-D, SAT	No	SAT predict via behavior

most important signals. Judgments were on three levels: Satisfied, partially satisfied, and dissatisfied. Grouping together satisfied and partially satisfied into one 'positive' label, users were positive on 78% of result-level labels and 77% of session-level labels. Since Fox et al. studied web search rather than email search, the curious browser did not have access to the rich set of user signals studied in this paper such as reply, move, forward and delete.

Email management and retrieval. Email is method of exchanging digital messages online, where messages accumulate over time unless deleted. Besides its use for communication, email is also used for task and time management [16] as well as for personal archiving [21]. Email management strategies have been identified [21] according to the number of folders used and the frequency of their use. *No filers* do not use folders except to archive or delete messages every few months. *Frequent filers* use folders, making daily passes of move and delete actions. *Spring cleaners* do the same but every 1-3 months rather than daily. Cecchinato et al. [7] found that the same person can use different strategies for their personal and work accounts.

Email search may occur under any of the identified email management strategies. Narang et al. [18] performed a large-scale analysis of email search logs, finding that people who organize their email less tend to search more. A related study [1] found that people perform a variety of activities during search, including organization actions such as move and delete. That study used both search logs and a survey, but it was not an in-situ survey paired with the log data, so it was not possible to analyze whether users who organized their email during search would report that their search was successful. Such analysis is possible here (see Table 1).

Carmel et al. [6] used both logs and labeling to evaluate email ranking. The log-based evaluation was a retrospective experiment, considering the rank position of a message selected by the user and how that would change under offline reranking. The relevance labeling evaluation was carried out by judges searching their own email, who each invented 25 queries based on a pre-identifed set of common query patterns. In both cases, a machine learned ranker could outperform the default date-sorted list of email search results.

The ranking approach could be further validated using a controlled trial online, assigning users to different rankers at random and seeing which group has activities that look most successful according to one of our models such as MarkovChain(1). Unlike the log-based evaluation in [6], users would see the ranked list, so the test would take into account whether date sorting makes a results list easier and faster to scan. Unlike the relevance labeling evaluation, the test would involve real users with real information needs, in-situ. It would be based on behavior rather than gathering new labels.

3 DATA COLLECTION

In this section, we described the data collection process. We first describe the in-situ survey we ran for client-side data collection, followed by the description of server-side activity logs and the merging of client-side and server-side data.

3.1 In-situ Survey Methodology

We implemented an in-situ survey application to collect the outcome of each email search session. Once a user installs the app on their PC, the app monitors search activity in the user's email client. When the end of a search session is detected, the app pops up an interface for a short survey about the success and ease of the search session. We used the following two conditions to detect the end of a search session:

- Explicit ending: the user clears the query input control and results by navigating away from the search interface
- Implicit ending: the user abandons the email search interface, which we defined as 3 minutes of inactivity

These conditions are reasonable but not perfect. In both cases there is some chance that the user may reenter the search interface and start another query soon after. However, during the development of the survey app we found these conditions work well in most cases. Note that we chose 3 minutes threshold in implicit ending which is shorter than 10 minutes in sessionization threshold so that people can respond to survey while their memory is fresh.

Figure 1 shows the user interface for the survey app. The user first answers a question about the success of their search session which included the query (or queries) shown. If the user responded 'yes' to the first question, then they are asked to answer additional questions about effort and relevance of clicked messages. The first additional question is the ease of finding what they were looking for. The second question asks about the relevance of each email message that was clicked. Finally, there is an optional box for additional comments about the search.

Often an email search happens in the middle of a task, and responding to the survey may cause an unwanted interruption. In order to make the survey participation as unobtrusive as possible, we also allowed the user to skip the survey once (Skip), or the for the rest of the day (Skip & disable for the day). After the user responded to a survey or Skipped the survey, we did not show the survey for the next 30 minutes to avoid making two many requests.

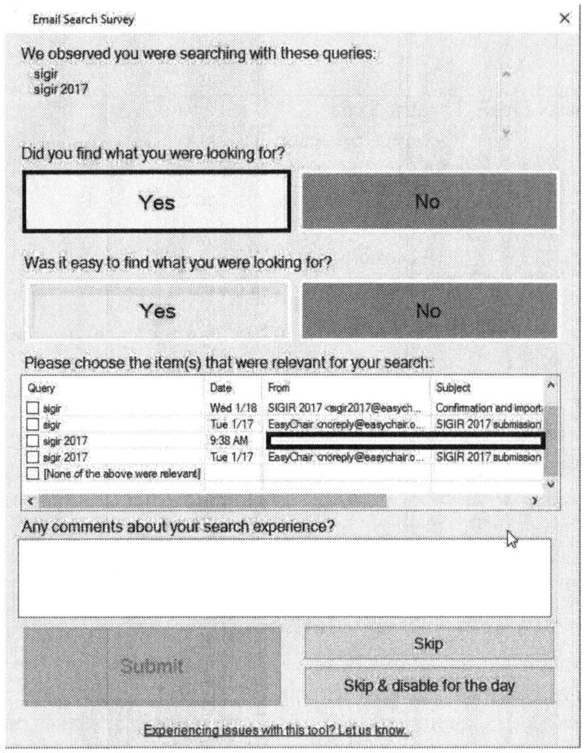

Figure 1: In-Situ Email search survey client interface. Some text has been removed for privacy reasons.

Once a survey is submitted, all the information *visible* in the survey pop-up window was sent to a remote database. This included the search queries, the subjects of clicked messages, and any textual comments they provided. For the search query and email reading activities, we also saved timestamps that were detected on the client. Participants were informed about the data being shared with researchers at the time of signing up for the study, and had the opportunity to opt out if they did not want to share this information. In addition, in the case of Skip, no information was sent to the server.

We ran the survey within our organization. The participants were recruited via internal mailing list, and we informed participants about the usage of the application and the data being shared with researchers. The participants were mostly IT professionals working in various locations in US and abroad. In order to keep the participation going, we also ran weekly raffle for a gift card throughout the duration of the study in which any active participant (i.e., those who kept the application running during the week) was eligible.

After 2 months, we had 1875 email search sessions collected from 65 users. Most people in our sample used the Microsoft Outlook email client application for their search, although some search sessions were from web email clients. Both the Outlook email application and the web email clients have standard email search capabilities, which includes: a search box at the top left corner of the interface, search results displayed in the middle of the screen and sorted by date by default, and the full-text email message in the right pane by default.

Table 2: Activities we captured in server-side log.

Activity	Remark
Send	Send a message
Move	Move a message
Reply	Reply to a message
Forward	Forward a message
Flag	Flag a message as a task
Mark	Mark a message as read/unread
Delete	Delete a message
Search	Issue a search query
ReadingLong	Read a message (dwell time >= 30 seconds)
ReadingShort	Read a message (dwell time < 30 seconds)
Create	Create a folder or message

Table 3: Summary of survey results for each outcome in overall (above) / after merging with activity log data (below).

	Failure	Success/Easy	Success/Hard
Survey Only	258(14%)	1534(82%)	83(4%)
Survey+Log	145(18%)	621(77%)	45(5%)

3.2 Activity Log Collection

In order to obtain a full view of users' search activities, we also collected the server-side log data from our organization's email server. For privacy reasons, the log data does not contain any textual information, yet it includes the activity user engaged in along with timestamp. The list of activities are shown in Table 2.

3.3 Data Processing

Our goal is to get a full picture of the users' email search including users' subjective impression along with activity records, therefore we merged the survey data with server-side activity logs. Since we had only the account owner information and timestamp for merging, we first aligned server-side (activity) and client-side (survey) data for each user by timestamp. We found that the server and client-side timestamp does not always align for various reasons, which resulted in some data loss.

Once we have the time-aligned merge data, we then split the data by session. We used the ten minutes of inactivity to sessionize the data, following the convention from previous studies [1]. Once we sessionized the data, the boundary for each search activity is detected within each session. We used the first search activity as the beginning of the session, and the user's submission of survey as the end of the session.

Table 3 summarizes the statistics of data before and after merging with the activity log. Note that the data decreased by 57% after the merging. We use the *Survey Only* data for the analyses in Section 4, and the *Survey+Log* data for predictive modeling in Section 5.

4 UNDERSTANDING SUCCESS IN EMAIL SEARCH

In this section, we analyze the in-situ survey data to better understand success and effort in email search. While the survey data does not have full activity logs, it has all the search and reading activities, along with timestamps. We first look at behavioral patterns associated with search session with different outcomes. We then look at the differences at the message-level.

4.1 Understanding User-level Success

The usage of email is personal in nature, and previous work [1] shows that there is wide variety in how people use email search. Some people seldom use search functionality, instead relying on various categorization mechanism provided by email clients or scanning the inbox, while other use search much more frequenty. A recent study[18] found this complementary nature of search and organization strategies for email. Among the people who tend to use search for email access, there may still be a wide range of difference in information needs and search strategies.

Our survey data provides a way to understand these individual differences in email search behavior and how they affect success in email search. We first compute six measures of search activity for each user and the look at the distribution across users. Figure 2 shows the distribution of six per-user session measures as box plots, where each plot presents the distribution of statistics aggregated for each user.

The first two plots show that the median number of queries per session is slightly less than 2 and the median number of read messages is about 3. The third plot shows that proportion of viewed messages that were relevant was slightly less than 50%. The fourth plot shows that the proportion of queries with advanced operators (e.g., from:) was approximately 20%, but the variance across users is large. The fifth plot shows that search success is high (median 90%) and there is little variance across users. The final plot shows the number of judgments submitted per user.

Email clients provide various search operators as shown in Table 4. Most query operators correspond to different email fields and are therefore self-explanatory, except for the 'Conversation:' operator which provides a way to find the messages in the same thread. This operator is automatically invoked in the interface by selecting a message and then a menu item called 'Find Related Messages in this Conversation'. How much are these operators used in practice? Figure 2 shows that 20% of queries had an operator in median, although the variability was quite high.

A recently study of email search log [1] found similar trends, showing that 18% of queries had the operator, and that the percentage of the *from:* operator is 75% and the *to:* operator is 13%, respectively.

We now consider the extent to which these per-user session measures are correlated. Table 5 presents the Pearson correlation coefficient across different user-level measures. The correlation is generally low, except for that between message count and query count, which is expected since if a person queries a lot they have more opportunity to view messages. There is an interesting correlation (0.25) between the usage of query operators and success rate, which seems to suggest that users who use query operator more are also more successful in their searches.

Table 4: Summary of query operators.

Query Operator	Count	Percentage
from:	704	72%
to:	123	13%
Conversation:	119	12%
subject:	14	1%
contents:	5	1%
hasattachments:	5	1%

4.2 Understanding Session-level Success

Table 6 summarizes the measures of session-level behavior. The table is grouped by sessions with different outcomes – success with low effort (*Success/Easy*), success with high effort (*Success/Hard*), and failure (*Failure*).

The results highlight the differences among sessions with different outcome. As for query counts, we find that *Success/Easy* sessions have the lowest number of queries. Interestingly, *Success/Hard* sessions had higher message count than *Failure* sessions. It is possible that the type of search tasks in *Success/Hard* sessions are very important, so users were willing to spend extra effort to complete the search compared to *Failure* sessions where they gave up.

Another measure of user effort is query length, which is also shown in the Table 6. Note that we removed all queries with operators from this calculation, since the query operators can be chosen from the menu instead of manually typing, thereby skewing the length measure. We can see that failure sessions have longer queries on average compared to successful sessions.

As we saw in the previous section, the usage rate of query operators is correlated with user-level success. The same trend holds true at session-level. From Table 6, we can see that the proportion of queries that contained query operators was highest in *Success/Easy* sessions in mean and median, followed by *Success/Hard* sessions.

Another angle to session-level behavior is the characteristics of messages read. In Table 6, the average number of messages read during a session is by far highest in *Success/Hard* sessions. *Failure* sessions have higher message count than *Success/Easy* sessions, yet the difference is small. This trend is consistent with those from the query counts.

We also looked at the ratio of messaged marked relevant by participants, and the ratio was 60% in *Success/Easy* sessions, which is more than twice as high as *Success/Hard* sessions. Since we did not ask people to judge the relevance of messages when they failed to find what they were looking for, this value is not available for *Failure* sessions.

Among the properties of messages read, message age is of particular interest. Message age is defined by the interval between when the email was sent or received and the time of search. The overall age of messages read during a search session could be affected by various factors.

Table 6 shows the comparison of median age for all messages and relevant messages across sessions with different outcomes. We

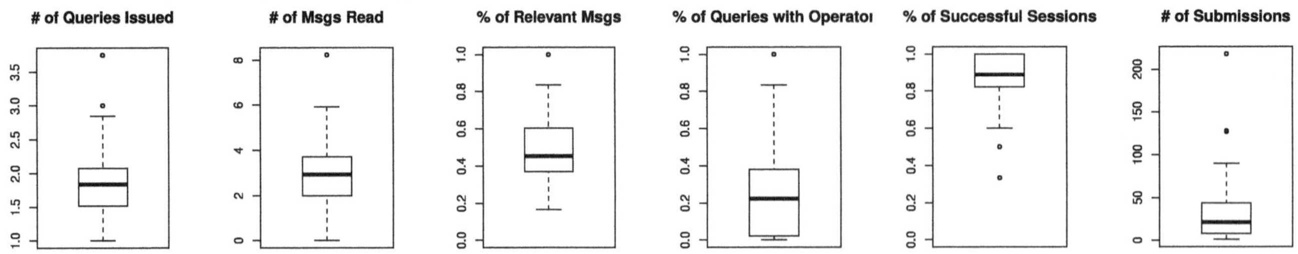

Figure 2: Distribution of per-user session statistics.

Table 5: Correlation among per-user session statistics. Statistics above 0.2 are boldfaced.

	AvgMsgCount	AvgQueryCount	SurveyCount	QueryOperator%
AvgQryCount	**0.60**			
SurveyCount	-0.11	-0.08		
QueryOperator%	0.13	**0.21**	0.19	
Success%	0.05	-0.03	-0.03	**0.25**

Table 6: Statistics of session-level behavior for sessions with different outcomes.

Session Outcome	Query Count	Query Length	QueryOperator %	MsgRead Count	RelevantMsg %	MedMsgAge (in Days)	MedRelevantMsg Age (in Days)	Survey Count
Success/Easy	1.71	1.40	32%	2.68	60%	3	3	1534
Success/Hard	2.87	1.47	21%	5.47	27%	12	10	83
Failure	2.20	1.59	17%	2.93	0%	9.5	NA	257

present the median instead of mean because the distribution of message age is heavily skewed toward right. Note that relevance labels are not available for successful sessions.

4.3 Understanding Message-level Success

In addition to session-level success labels, we also collected relevance labels for each message read. This allows us to understand success in email search at individual message level, which in turn can be valuable in collecting labels for training relevance-based ranking methods [6]. Here we delve into this, focusing on dwell time at each message, which is an important signal in understanding the users' engagement with individual messages [15].

Note that dwell time is reported for only non-last messages within each session because we do not have a reliable way to detect reading time for the last message is a session. Also, if a message is the last one read during a session, it is an important signal for relevance in and of itself. Table 7 confirms this intuition, where the ratio of relevant messages among last-read messages was 54%, compared to 24% for non-last read messages.

If being the last message read indicates relevance, what would the dwell time for non-last messages tell us about its relevance? Table 8 shows that the average dwell time for relevant messages is about 37 seconds, whereas the value is 22 seconds for non-relevant messages. Figure 3 shows the distribution of dwell time in the box plots, where the median dwell time for relevant vs. non-relevant messages are 12 and 6 seconds, respectively.

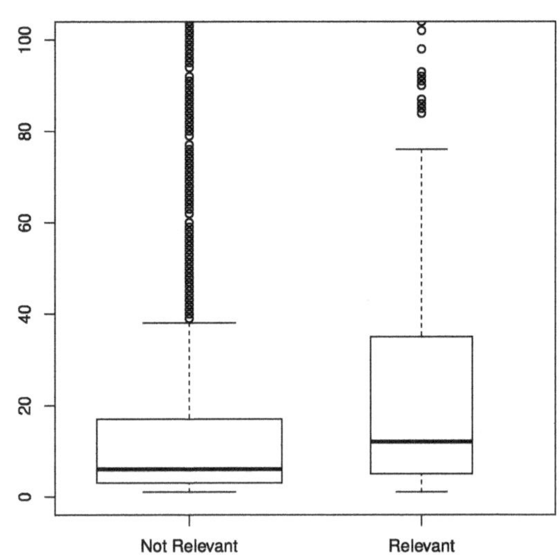

Figure 3: Comparison of dwell time among messages with different relevance labels.

Table 7: Cross-tabulation of the relevance label for each message read and whether the reading was the last activity.

Message Relevance	Last Activity	Non-Last Activity
Not Relevant	681	2468
Relevant	793	737
P(Relevant)	54%	24%

Table 8: Average dwell time for relevant vs. non-relevant reading activities.

MsgRelevance	DwellTime(mean)	SampleSize
Not Relevant	22.38	2468
Relevant	37.23	737

5 MODELING SUCCESS IN EMAIL SEARCH

In the previous section, we looked at the characteristics of success in email search at the user, session and message levels. While these are informative in and of themselves, it would be even more valuable if we could build a model that could predict the success of an email search. Such model would further contribute to our understanding of success in email search, and could be used to evaluate a new search method against baseline.

There are many approaches to building models for predicting search success, and here we provide the rationale for approaches taken in this work. First, one can model success at session-level vs. message-level, and we decided to model session-level success because that's the level at which we have cleanest labels and features. Second, the modeling choice can focus on multiple aspects, including prediction accuracy, interpretability and efficiency. We focused on interpretability in this work because the goal was to build a transparent model which provides insights about its outcome upon inspection.

5.1 Experimental Design

Here we describe the details of experiments we ran. We used the merged data set of the client-side survey and the server-side activity log as described in Section 3.3. The data contained the list of activities that occurred during each search session, along with various session-level properties and labels from the survey. Since the data was collected over 2 months, we used the data from the first month for training models and the data from the second month for evaluation. Using random sampling or k-fold cross validation would mean the that the future might be used to predict the past.

The evaluation setup is as follows: each model takes in various session-level features and calculates a score for session-level success. The score for each model is then compared against the ground truth session-level labels we obtained from the survey. This is a binary classification task which predicts the success vs. failure of a given session. Since reading time has previously been shown to be an important feature in predicting search success [13], we built every model with or without reading time.

Now we describe the evaluation metric and models we used. As a metric we used AUC (area under curve) of the ROC (receiver operating characteristic) curve [4]. There are a few reasons for

Table 9: Markov Chain models and activity examples.

	MarkovChain (0)	MarkovChain (1)
Activities	$P(Query_t)$ $P(Reading_t)$	$P(Reading_{t-1}, Query_t)$
Activities + Reading Time	$P(Query_t)$ $P(ReadingShort_t)$ $P(ReadingLong_t)$	$P(ReadingShort_{t-1}, Query_t)$ $P(ReadingLong_{t-1}, Query_t)$ ...

this choice: Since we employed different modeling approaches, the scores from each model are not necessarily comparable. Also, there is a skew in the distribution of target labels, which the ROC curve is known to be robust tp.

5.2 Models Compared

Here we compare a few approaches for predicting the success of email search. Each model combines different subsets of input features. Our first model is a heuristic baseline, which associates a subset of activities with session-level success, and outputs a positive label when any of these activities are found during a search session. The activities we considered as success for this baseline model includes 'Move','Reply', 'Forward', 'Flag', 'ReadingLong' (for the version that incorporates reading time).

While this simple approach takes into account the activities performed during a search session in order to make a prediction, it uses heuristics in assessing the contribution of each activity toward success. A more data-driven approach is to use the survey data we collected to determine the weights. Since we have a sequence of activities along with success label for each search session, a natural choice is a discrete Markov Chain of user behavior.

We experimented with Markov Chain models based on different Markov properties, where the zero-order Markov Chain assumes the independence among activities, and the first-order Markov Chain assumes that the present activity is dependent on the previous activity. The first-order Markov Model can potentially model the context in which an activity is triggered more carefully, although the expanded state space may result in sparsity in estimation.

The Markov Chain models we experimented with can be further distinguished based on whether reading time is considered or not. Previous work on modeling search success [13] notes that the time spent on reading is an important indicator of success, and here we decided to incorporate time by splitting the reading activities into short reading vs. long reading, where the short reading is defined by the reading activity with duration less than 30 seconds.

Table 9 shows the example activities for four varieties of Markov Chain model we experimented with. Note that the state space is defined by individual activity for the zero-order Markov Chain models (*Markov Model (0)*), whereas the state space is defined by activity pairs for the first-order Markov Chain models (*Markov Model (1)*). Also, the *Reading* activity is divided into *ReadingLong* and *ReadingShort* for Markov Chain models with reading time.

Now we focus on how we derive success score from models. Given the state space in Markov Chain as above, we can estimate two models (M_s and M_f) corresponding to successful sessions and failure sessions, respectively. We can calculate the chance of success for a new model using these two models. The detailed calculation varies depending on the type of Markov Chain used. $P_{M0}(S_i)$ represent the probability of observing the ith state in the sample space of activities for zero-order Markov Chain $M0$. $P_{M1}(S_i, S_{i-1})$ represent the probability of observing the transition from $i-1$th state to ith state in the sample space of activities for first-order Markov Chain $M1$.

$$L_{M0}(S) = \prod_{i=1}^{n} P_M(S_i) \tag{1}$$

$$L_{M1}(S) = \prod_{i=2}^{n} P_M(S_i|S_{i-1}) \tag{2}$$

Given a Markov Chain model M, we can calculate the likelihood of observing a sequence of activities for a new session $S = (S_1, S_2, ..., S_n)$ by multiplying the probability for each action pairs. Using the the likelihood values from model of success P_s and failure P_f, we can calculate the odds ratio of the likelihood from success model L_s over L_f. Finally, we take the log of the odds ratio to avoid numerical underflow. The equation below shows the overall calculation of log odds for zero-order Markov Chain (above) and first-order Markov Chain (below).

$$LogOdds_{M0}(S) = \sum_{i=1}^{n} log(P_s(S_i)) - \sum_{i=1}^{n} log(P_f(S_i)) \tag{3}$$

$$LogOdds_{M1}(S) = \sum_{i=2}^{n} log(P_s(S_i|S_{i-1})) - \sum_{i=2}^{n} log(P_f(S_i|S_{i-1})) \tag{4}$$

The Markov Chain approach described above can be considered as a generative model in that the scoring is based on the likelihood of a sequence generated from probabilistic models. Alternatively, one can think of a discriminative approach where the goal is to find a model which directly optimize for the classification performance.

We use RandomForest [5] for this reason, which is a discriminative model known to perform well out-of-the-box. We experiment with two models with Markov Chain features - activity counts from zero-order Markov Chain (RandomForest(0)), activity counts from first-order Markov Chain (RandomForest(1)). These are models based on the same set of features as Markov Chain models, except they they are fed into RandomForest model.

The third RandomForest model we tested employed session-level features along with activity counts from first-order Markov Chain (RandomForest(1+S)). Session-level features we used include the count of queries, count of messages, ratio of operators in session queries and average message age. Note that the Markov Chain model does not accommodate these features since they do not have a probabilistic interpretation.

The models we tested have distinctive characteristics. The baseline model has the simplest calculation procedure (i.e., whether the given set of activities exist in the new session or not), and does not require any training data in the form of activities and labels.

Markov Chain models have high interpretability in that the scores from individual activity contribute linearly to the final score. This means that we can also calculate the odds ratio at the level of individual activities, as we show in Section 5.4.

Table 10: Comparison of Area under ROC (AUC) values across models we evaluated.

	Activities	Activities + Reading Time
Baseline	0.602	0.659
MarkovChain(0)	0.659	0.693
MarkovChain(1)	0.719	0.753
RandomForest(0)	0.623	0.655
RandomForest(1)	0.681	0.709
RandomForest(1+S)	0.739	0.769

In contrast, the RandomForest models employ a large collection of decisions trees to produce a prediction, which makes the results harder to interpret. It has the advantage of being able to incorporate arbitrary features, as well as the ability to model complex and possibly non-linear interaction among features.

5.3 Experimental Results

Here we present the outcome of prediction for session-level satisfaction. Table 10 summarizes the Area under ROC values for the models we evaluated. Note that the results are grouped into 1) baseline 2) variants of Markov Chain models 3) variants of RandomForest, with the columns showing the results with or without taking into account the reading time.

The first overall trend from Table 10 is that both Markov Chain and RandomForest models are much better than the baseline and that the Markov Chain model is slightly better than the RandomForest model with the same feature set. Since RandomForest is a more powerful model, it may outperform Markov Model given enough training data.

In terms of feature sets used, it is also clear the first-order models that use activity pairs are always better than the zero-order models that consider each activity independently. In addition, it is clear that adding reading time provides a further boost in AUC in all cases. Finally, adding session-level features to RandomForest(1+S) model improves the performance as well.

Now, let's look at ROC curve for each model to interpret the results in more detail. An ROC curve characterizes the performance of a classifier by plotting Sensitivity (true positive rate) against Specificity (1 - false positive rate). We first compare the Markov Chain models against the baseline model. Figure 4 presents the ROC curve for two Markov Chain models, along with a baseline model. It shows that the use of activity pairs improves the sensitivity in all but the leftmost side of the plot (high specificity / low false positive rate region). This shows that the use of activity pairs provides additional evidence when the signal from individual activity is weak.

Next, we compare RandomForest models against the baseline model. Figure 5 presents the ROC curve for three RandomForest models, along with the baseline model. It shows that the use of activity pairs improves the true positive rate in all but the leftmost side of the plot (high specificity / low false positive rate region), as we saw in Markov Chain model. Also, the inclusion of session-level features improves the performance across the board.

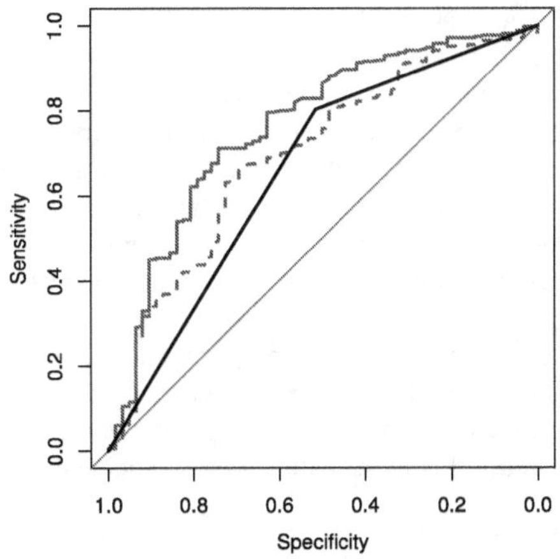

Figure 4: ROC curve for MarkovChain(1) (red solid line) vs. MarkovChain(0) (red dashed line) with reading time. Baseline model with reading time is shown in black solid line.

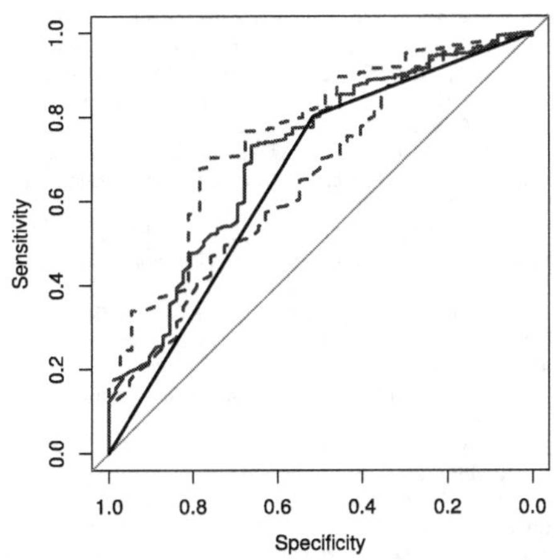

Figure 5: ROC curve for RandomForest(0) (blue dotted line) vs. RandomForest(1) (blue solid line) vs. RandomForest(1+S) (blue dashed line) models with reading time. Baseline model with reading time is shown in black solid line.

Finally, Figure 6 compares the ROC curve for MarkovChain(1) against RandomForest(1) model, along with the baseline. The Markov Chain model outperforms the RandomForest model in all but the leftmost side of the figure. This shows that the discriminative model is better at getting the first few instances right (i.e., high sensitivity at high specificity region) yet worse in overall.

5.4 Further Analysis

Here we present a few additional analyses to provide further insight into the results we presented in Section 5.3. These analyses are based on Markov Chain models, which provides a simple interpretation of session-level results in terms of individual activities.

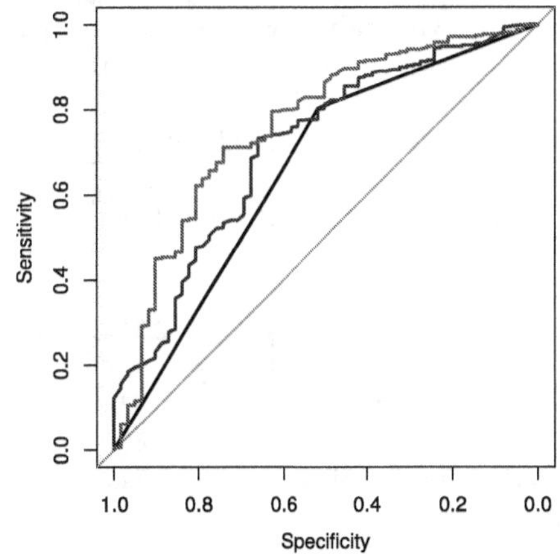

Figure 6: ROC curve for MarkovChain(1) (red solid line) against RandomForest(1) (blue solid line) model. Baseline model with reading time is shown in black solid line.

Table 11: Odds Ratio for Activities ($\frac{P_s(a)}{P_f(a)}$).

Activity	Odds Ratio	Sample Size
Send	2.87	324
Reply	1.99	194
Move	1.93	402
Forward	1.62	38
Delete	1.25	366
Mark	1.21	832
ReadingLong	1.13	1256
Flag	1.02	19
Search	0.94	3199
ReadingShort	0.88	5930
Create	0.24	75

Table 11 presents the odds ratio for each activity. The odds ratio is calculated as the probability of observing an activity in successful sessions divided by the probability in failure sessions. Note that top part of the table is dominated by typical message-level actions, which would be done for relevant message(s). Since *Search* and *ReadingShort* are two frequent activities with odds ratio less than one (and negative log odds ratio), any session with long sequences of search and short reading activities will be regarded as a failure.

Table 12 presents the odds ratio for each activity pair. The odds ratio is calculated in the same way as above, except with activity pairs instead of individual activities. Interestingly, we can see *ReadingShort* activity both at the top and bottom of the table, by which we can see that a short reading is positive when followed by reply or send activity, yet negative when it is found around search, delete, or another short reading activity. This result exemplifies the power of evaluating an activity in the context of other activities.

Table 12: Odds Ratio for Activity Pairs ($\frac{P_s(a_t|a_{t-1})}{P_f(a_t|a_{t-1})}$). Only top 5 and bottom 5 activity pairs are shown due to space limitations.

Activity Pair	Odds Ratio	Sample Size
Send → Reply	7.22	50
Move → Move	4.51	53
ReadingShort → Reply	3.38	89
ReadingShort → Send	3.09	160
Search → ReadingLong	2.51	170
...	...	...
Search → ReadingShort	0.82	888
Delete → ReadingShort	0.80	147
ReadingShort → ReadingShort	0.74	3540
ReadingShort → Search	0.58	350
Search → END	0.30	55

6 CONCLUSIONS

Unlike some other information retrieval applications such as web search where it is common to build a test collection using third party judges, email search occurs over a private corpus, so it is useful to develop new methods of analysis and evaluation. Here we employed an in-situ survey that is tightly coupled with user activity logs, to get both explicit and implicit data on search success for the same individuals.

This allows us to analyze general characteristics of email search success, which could be reused as a comparison point in other studies of email. In the survey, 20% of queries had an operator, with the most common operator being *from:*. Use of search operators was associated with a higher success rate, although we have no evidence of a causal link. Easy successful sessions were also associated with finding more recent messages, with fewer shorter queries, and fewer opened messages. High-effort successful sessions, while rare, had more queries and opened messages, and the opened messages were older, suggesting the need for better information retrieval support for such cases. Failed sessions were in between, perhaps indicating that the user gave up because the search was not all that important or they used other means for finding the relevant message.

At the message level, having a higher dwell time and being the last-selected message were both good success indicators, agreeing with findings from web search [12]. After joining with activity logs, a wide variety of activity types were found to be associated with session success. Specifically the following actions were all associated with search success: Reply, Move, Forward, Delete, Mark, ReadingLong and Flag. Short dwell selection (ReadingShort) was the only message-level negative indicator for overall success. Considering actions not tied to a new search result, sending a message was the most positive, and Search and Create were negative. The negative events may indicate that the user is still trying to find the information they need, via another search or by creating an email or meeting request, perhaps to ask someone else for some information that they failed to retrieve. These event-level insights could be used directly in future studies, rewarding and penalizing activities observed during an email search experiment. The insights could also be compared against findings from other email search interfaces and analysis methods.

Once the predictive models of search success have been learned, they can be applied to new log data without any new survey data. For example, MarkovChain(0) can be applied using only the data in Table 11 in equation (1). Future work could consider how to automatically optimize an email search system to yield these positive events and avoid the negative events. One approach would be to treat our predictive model as a utility function, then use a factored design as in [20].

As a future work, the proposed approach can be extended in many ways. More complex learning models can potentially improve the quality of prediction. New search experiences such as voice can be evaluated using this hybrid approach of label and log data.

REFERENCES

[1] Qingyao Ai, Susan T. Dumais, Nick Craswell, and Dan Liebling. 2017. Characterizing Email Search using Large-scale Behavioral Logs and Surveys. In *Proceedings of WWW'2017.* ACM.

[2] Ahmed Hassan Awadallah. 2012. A semi-supervised approach to modeling web search satisfaction. In *Proceedings of SIGIR 2012.* ACM.

[3] Ahmed Hassan Awadallah, Yang Song, and Li-wei He. 2011. A task level metric for measuring web search satisfaction and its application on improving relevance estimation. In *Proceedings CIKM 2011.* 125–134. DOI:http://dx.doi.org/10.1145/2063576.2063599

[4] Andrew P. Bradley. 1997. The Use of the Area Under the ROC Curve in the Evaluation of Machine Learning Algorithms. *Pattern Recogn.* 30, 7 (July 1997), 1145–1159. DOI:http://dx.doi.org/10.1016/S0031-3203(96)00142-2

[5] Leo Breiman. 2001. Random Forests. *Mach. Learn.* 45, 1 (Oct. 2001), 5–32. DOI:http://dx.doi.org/10.1023/A:1010933404324

[6] David Carmel, Guy Halawi, Liane Lewin-Eytan, Yoelle Maarek, and Ariel Raviv. 2015. Rank by Time or by Relevance?: Revisiting Email Search. In *Proceedings of the 24th CIKM.* ACM, 283–292.

[7] Marta E Cecchinato, Abigail Sellen, Milad Shokouhi, and Gavin Smyth. 2016. Finding email in a multi-account, multi-device world. In *CHI Conference on Human Factors in Computing Systems.* ACM, 1200–1210.

[8] Olivier Chapelle, Thorsten Joachims, Filip Radlinski, and Yisong Yue. 2012. Large-scale validation and analysis of interleaved search evaluation. *ACM Transactions on Information Systems (TOIS)* 30, 1 (2012), 6.

[9] Gordon V Cormack and Thomas R Lynam. 2005. Spam Corpus Creation for TREC.. In *CEAS.*

[10] Susan Dumais, Edward Cutrell, Jonathan J Cadiz, Gavin Jancke, Raman Sarin, and Daniel C Robbins. 2003. Stuff I've Seen: a system for personal information retrieval and re-use. In *Proceedings of the 26th SIGIR.* ACM, 72–79.

[11] Susan T Dumais and Nicholas J Belkin. 2005. The TREC interactive tracks: Putting the user into search. *TREC: Experiment and evaluation in information retrieval* (2005), 123–153.

[12] Steve Fox, Kuldeep Karnawat, Mark Mydland, Susan Dumais, and Thomas White. 2005. Evaluating implicit measures to improve web search. *ACM Transactions on Information Systems (TOIS)* 23, 2 (2005), 147–168.

[13] Ahmed Hassan, Rosie Jones, and Kristina Lisa Klinkner. 2010. Beyond DCG: user behavior as a predictor of a successful search. In *Proceedings of the WSDM 2010.* ACM, 221–230.

[14] Jiepu Jiang, Ahmed Hassan Awadallah, Xiaolin Shi, and Ryen W White. 2015. Understanding and predicting graded search satisfaction. In *Proceedings of the WSDM 2015.* ACM, 57–66.

[15] Youngho Kim, Ahmed Hassan, Ryen W. White, and Imed Zitouni. 2014. Modeling Dwell Time to Predict Click-level Satisfaction. In *Proceedings of the WSDM 2014 (WSDM '14).* ACM, New York, NY, USA, 193–202. DOI:http://dx.doi.org/10.1145/2556195.2556220

[16] Wendy E Mackay. 1988. Diversity in the use of electronic mail: A preliminary inquiry. *ACM TOIS* 6, 4 (1988), 380–397.

[17] Dmitry Lagun Mikhail Ageev, Qi Guo and Eugene Agichtein.

[18] Kanika Narang, Susan T. Dumais, Nick Craswell, and Dan Liebling. 2017. Analysis of Email Search and Org Strategies. In *Proceedings of CHIIR'2017.* ACM.

[19] Ellen M Voorhees and Donna K Harman. 2005. *TREC: Experiment and evaluation in information retrieval.* Vol. 1. MIT press Cambridge.

[20] Yue Wang, Dawei Yin, Luo Jie, Pengyuan Wang, Makoto Yamada, Yi Chang, and Qiaozhu Mei. 2016. Beyond ranking: Optimizing whole-page presentation. In *WSDM.* ACM, 103–112.

[21] Steve Whittaker and Candace Sidner. 1996. Email overload: exploring personal information management of email. In *Proceedings of the SIGCHI.* ACM, 276–283.

Investigating Examination Behavior of Image Search Users

Xiaohui Xie
DCST, Tsinghua University
xiexh_thu@163.com

Yiqun Liu
DCST, Tsinghua University
yiqunliu@tsinghua.edu.cn

Xiaochuan Wang
Sogou Incorporation
wxc@sogou-inc.com

Meng Wang
Hefei Institute of Technology
eric.mengwang@gmail.com

Zhijing Wu
DCST, Tsinghua University
wzjingzai@163.com

Yingying Wu
Department of Mathematics,
The University of Texas at Austin
ywu@math.utexas.edu

Min Zhang
DCST, Tsinghua University
z-m@tsinghua.edu.cn

Shaoping Ma
DCST, Tsinghua University
msp@tsinghua.edu.cn

ABSTRACT

Image search engines show results differently from general Web search engines in three key ways: (1) most Web-based image search engines adopt the two-dimensional result placement instead of the linear result list; (2) image searches show snapshots instead of snippets (query-dependent abstracts of landing pages) on search engine result pages (SERPs); and (3) pagination is usually not (explicitly) supported on image search SERPs, and users can view results without having to click on the "next page" button. Compared with the extensive study of user behavior in general Web search scenarios, there exists no thorough investigation how the different interaction mechanism of image search engines affects users' examination behavior. To shed light on this research question, we conducted an eye-tracking study to investigate users' examination behavior in image searches. We focus on the impacts of factors in examination including position, visual saliency, edge density, the existence of textual information, and human faces in result images. Three interesting findings indicate users' behavior biases: (1) instead of the traditional "Golden Triangle" phenomena in the user examination patterns of general Web search, we observe a middle-position bias, (2) besides the position factor, the content of image results (e.g., visual saliency) affects examination behavior, and (3) some popular behavior assumptions in general Web search (e.g., examination hypothesis) do not hold in image search scenarios. We predict users' examination behavior with different impact factors. Results show that combining position and visual content features can improve prediction in image searches.

CCS CONCEPTS

•**Information systems** → **Image search;** *Multimedia and multimodal retrieval;*

SIGIR '17, August 07-11, 2017, Shinjuku, Tokyo, Japan

DOI: http://dx.doi.org/10.1145/3077136.3080799

KEYWORDS

Image search; Eye-tracking; Examination behavior;

1 INTRODUCTION

Multimedia content (e.g., images, video) has been increasingly incorporated into search engine result pages (SERPs) to increase both user experience and engagement. However, the way to show results in image search engines differs greatly from that of general Web search engines. Take the SERP in Figure 1 for example; in image searches, results are placed in a two-dimensional panel rather than a sequential result list. Instead of the query-dependent abstract of the landing page, the image snapshot is shown together with some meta information of the image (sometimes the meta information is only available with a hover behavior on the result), highlighted in Figure 1 with a red rectangle. Further, since results are joined, users can view results by scrolling up and down instead of clicking on the "next page" button.

User behavior data has been successfully adopted to improve general Web searches in result ranking [1, 36], query suggestion [7, 35], query auto completion [16, 17], etc. We therefore believe that understanding user interaction behavior in these multimedia search scenarios will also provide valuable insight into the optimization of their performances.

There exist a number of studies on user behavior log analysis of image search engines [2, 11, 20, 24, 30]. Click-through behaviors, query reformulation patterns, and session characteristics are investigated in [23, 24]. A comparison with general Web search behaviors was also performed in [2, 11]. Some researchers [15, 20, 22] focus on extracting implicit feedback signals from image search user behavior to improve result ranking performance. However, compared with the research on general Web searches, little attention has been paid to the examination behavior of image search users.

Examination is one of the prime concerns in existing search behavior studies because it is closely related with a user's attention distribution mechanism. With a better understanding of examination behavior, we can make better use of existing click-through signals, designing better evaluation metrics and helping users achieve their information needs more effectively. Although much research exists on search examination behavior, most efforts are focused on the SERP layout containing a single column of search results

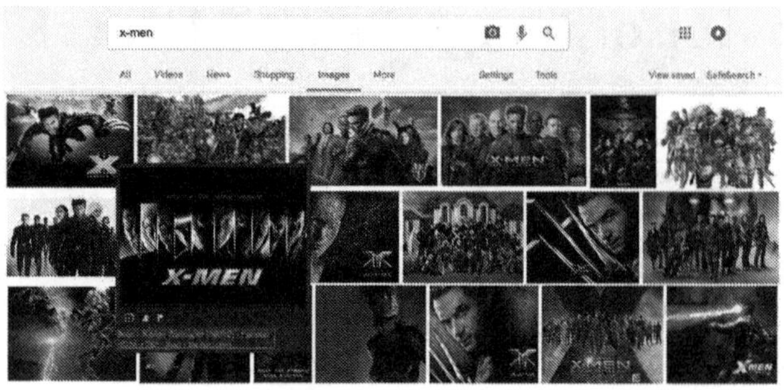

Figure 1: An example SERP in image search engine (The red box shows the meta information of the image while cursor hovering on the corresponding position)

[9, 19] or with some sidebar components such as knowledge graph [3, 34]. Considering that image SERPs usually present results in a two-dimensional placement style, whether the examination bias and hypothesis remain applicable becomes an open question.

As a preliminary attempt to model image search examination behavior, we perform a lab-based user study with the help of eye-tracking devices. We collect click-through, eye movement, mouse movement, and other behavior data during the search processes. The relevance scores of image results are also annotated to reveal its relationship with examination and click-through behaviors. We focus on the factors (behavior biases) that have impacts on user examination behavior and how to predict users' attention distribution using these factors. Specifically, this study addresses the following research questions:

- *RQ 1: How do positions of results affect user examination behaviors in image searches: are there also vertical position biases as in general Web searches? How do the horizontal positions of results affect user examination?*
- *RQ 2: How do the content of image search results affect user examination behaviors? Do content factors such as saliency, edge density, the existence of human faces, or textual information affect user examination during image searches?*
- *RQ 3: What are the relations between relevance, examination, and click in image searches? Does the examination hypothesis [8] still hold or there are new patterns?*
- *RQ 4: Can we predict examination behavior in image search? How can this prediction help us better understand users' examination behaviors?*

The paper is organized as follows. Section 2 reviews related work. Section 3 introduces our user-study settings. Sections 4-6 present findings from the user study. We report the experimental results of examination behavior prediction in Section 7. Finally, Section 8 discusses conclusions and future work.

2 RELATED WORK

We briefly summarize the related work in two categories: user behavior in image search and examination behavior of Web users. The former concentrates on analyzing large scale image search logs, and the latter employs eye-tracking devices to investigate user examination behavior in different settings.

2.1 User behavior in Image Search

With the high volume of traffic on Web search engines, the analysis of query logs becomes one of the most common approaches to understand user behavior. Previous works in image search also characterized the general user behaviors based on search logs [2, 11, 20, 24, 30]. Many features like query reformulation patterns, session length, and the number of viewed result pages are measured. Compared to general Web (text) search, image search leads to shorter queries, tends to be more exploratory, and requires more interactions. Park et al. [23] analyzed a large-scale query log from Yahoo Image Search to investigate user behavior toward different query types and identified important behavioral differences across them.

Interactive behaviors with image search result pages contain abundant implicit user feedback. Previous studies on multimedia search [14, 15, 22] explored user click-through data to bridge user intention gaps for image searches. O'Hare et al. [20] proposed a number of implicit relevance feedback features based on additional interactions including hover-through rate, converted-hover rate, and referral page click-through to improve image search result-ranking performance.

Most of the above works focused on mouse-based interactive behavior and tried to improve result ranking performance with corresponding features. Although Wang et al. [32] showed that understanding user examination behavior in Web searches provides powerful insight into user behavior modeling, little attention has been paid to examination behavior in multimedia searches.

2.2 Examination Behavior of Web Users

Understanding examination behavior is important for advertising, interaction design, and result ranking in Web search researches. Compared to techniques that rely on the explicit user actions (e.g., mouse clicks), eye-tracking yields more detailed moment-by-moment observations about how users interact with search information [13]. Cutrell et al. [9] used eye-tracking to explore the effects of changing in the presentation of search results. Pan et al. [21] and Buscher et al. [5] explored the determinants of ocular behavior on a single web page and tried to predict salient regions on Web pages. Tatler and Vincent [29] discovered that understanding eye-moving biases triggers gazing decisions in complex scenes. Underwood et al. [31] investigated how eye movements are affected by visual saliency and the semantic incongruence when inspecting pictures. The above works showed the effectiveness of eye-tracking in understanding examination behavior on images in different settings. In this study, we carry out an eye-tracking experiment to investigate the user examination behavior in image searches.

Click models also are used to model users' click and examination behavior in Web searches. Previous works on click models and search user's examination behavior patterns [8, 10, 32] were based on general search result pages with one-dimensional result lists. The major variables that most click models consider include examination, click, and relevance. They follow the examination hypothesis [8] that a clicked document should satisfy two independent conditions: it is examined and it is relevant. The cascade model [8] assumes that while a user examines the results from top to bottom sequentially, she/he immediately decides whether to click on a result. The partially observable Markov Model (POM) [33] treats

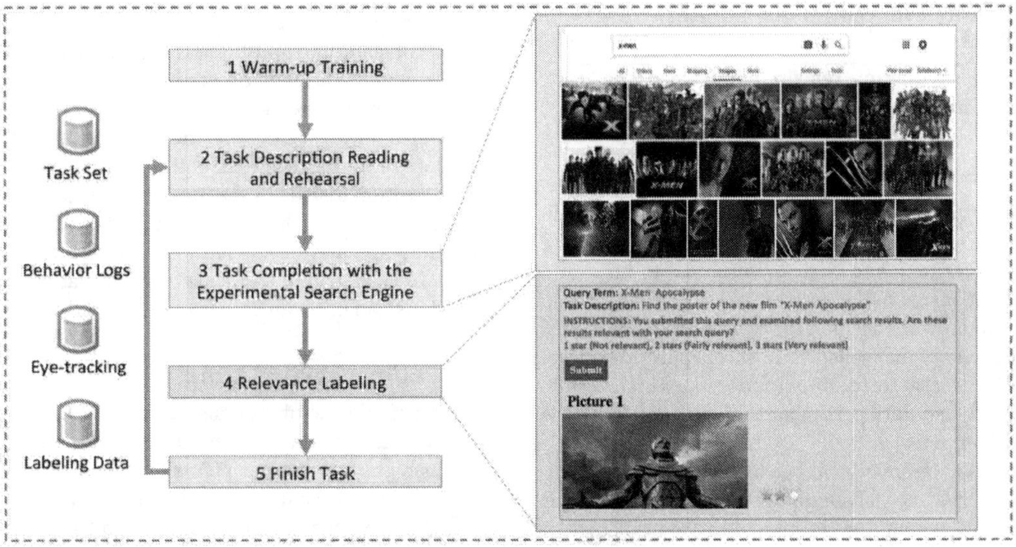

Figure 2: Data Collection Procedure

Table 1: Examples of Search Queries and Corresponding Taxonomies

Query Type [23]	#Query	Query Example (Task Description)
Specific	8	Doraemon (Find an image of Doraemon for your Wechat profile picture)
Generic	7 (1 for Warm-up Training)	New York (Find images about New York City's beautiful scenery)
Abstract	6	pleasant surprise (Find some images that express pleasant surprise to make a WeChat expression)

the user examination events as a partially observable stochastic process. Wang et al. [32] investigated the user's non-sequential examination behavior in ordinary search result pages and proposed a click model named PSCM (Partially Sequential Click Model) that captures this behavior. To the best of our knowledge, no existing click models are employed to model user examination behavior in image searches. Through our investigation in user examination behavior and its relation to clicks and relevance in two-dimensional result pages we may help design better click models that describes the interaction processes of image search users more precisely.

3 USER BEHAVIOR DATASET

3.1 Data Collection procedure

To conduct the tasks of our experiment , we sampled 21 intermediate frequency queries from the query log of a popular image commercial search engine[1]. Since search behaviors may be affected by different types of queries [23], we tried to design tasks to cover different query categories. We applied the Shatford-Panofsky approach [26] for image classification, like previous work in image search analysis has performed in [23]. In the sampled query set, eight queries are "Specific" (e.g., "Doraemon"), seven queries are "Generic" (e.g., "New York"), and six queries are "Abstract" (e.g., "pleasant surprise"). We also provided a task description for each query to make sure that users know exactly what results need to be looked for on the image SERPs. Table 1 shows a sample set of search queries and their corresponding descriptions. We crawled these queries' result pages from the commercial search engine and displayed them as SERPs in our experiment. The SERPs in the experiment contain 20 rows of image results to ensure a reasonable user study duration.

To investigate user's examination behavior during the search process, we carry out a laboratory study. The process is shown in Figure 2. Our user study consists of two stages. In the first stage, the participants perform several image search tasks, and meanwhile, their eye movement behaviors are collected. In the second stage, the participants are asked to annotate the relevance of each examined image search result. The dataset involves 46 undergraduate students majored in science, engineering and arts. All of them were frequent users of Web search engines. Because of calibration problems with the eye-tracking devices, not all participants' eye movement data were available, and 40 of them (female=16, male=24) were finally taken into account. Among the 40 participants, 20 performed the first stage of the experiment while the others took part in both stages, including recording eye-tracking data and labeling relevance.

At the beginning of the first stage, participants are given 21 search tasks, which include 1 warm-up task to familiarize them with the procedure and other 20 formal tasks. For each search task, participants were presented with an initial search query and a short description about the task. After reading the instructions, users click "start" button and a retrieved SERP containing 20 rows of pictures for this query is returned. Participants are instructed

[1]The data overs the period of June in the year of 2016, which we will release after the review process

Table 2: Relevance Labeling Dataset

#Images	#Images with same relevance judgement (66%)	
	#Relevant Images	#Irrelevant Images
1522	585	414

to examine the SERPs as they normally do. Like practical search scenario, they could scroll to move the page up and down, use the mouse to see hover text, and click a thumbnail to view and download the full-size image in the preview page. In the warm-up task, participants can browse and click the search results, and they can adjust the sensitivity of the mouse to the most appropriate level as well. We do not give any further instruction on which results to click on or when to end until participants are familiar with the experimental search engine.

The second stage is about relevance labeling. For each task, participants are given a relevance labeling page containing 20 images sampled from the images that they examined in the first stage in SERP. Users are asked to label each image with one of three levels (1-not relevant; 2-fairly relevant; 3-very relevant), consistent with previous works on query-image pairs relevance labeling[14, 37]. We deem the images to be relevant if their labels are score 2 or score 3. To further make sure the quality of the relevance judgment, we remove all images which participants have different opinions in their relevance and only retain the ones that different participants have the same opinions. The remaining annotated image set contains 999 images, in which 585 are relevant and 414 are irrelevant. Details about our relevance labeling dataset are shown in Table 2.

3.2 Data Collection System

In our study, we inject customized JavaScript into search result pages to log mouse activities on search pages when users perform search tasks. Considering that head-free eye trackers allow the collected interactions to be more natural and realistic, a Tobii X2-30 eye tracker is used to capture participants' eye movements. The search system is deployed on a 17-inch LCD monitor whose resolution is 1366 × 768. Google Chrome browser is used to display results of search system. To identify users' examination behavior, we detect fixations using built-in algorithms and all default parameters from Tobii Studio. All the collected data including the relevance judgments will be open to public after the double-blind review process.

4 POSITION BIAS AND EXAMINATION

With the user behavior data set described in Section 3, we look into the examination behavior of image search users and try to answer the four research questions in Section 1. Firstly, we focus on the influence of the position factor (*RQ*1).

4.1 Two-dimensional Placement of Results

As stated in previous sections, image search results are placed in a two-dimension manner. In the image search engine from which we collected SERPs, each result page contains 5 rows (row height = 200 px) and there are 3 to 7 images in each row (4 to 6 images in most cases). The users can scroll across different pages without having to click a "next page" button as in general Web search. Since we retain only the top 20 rows of results for each query, the SERP we collected each contains 4 "pages" of results (although the pages are only conceptional and there is only a page number shown on the SERP which is usually omitted by users).

Considering the fact that each row may contain different numbers of results (for example, the first row in the SERP from Figure 1 contains 6 images while the third contains 7), we decide to use absolute position instead of the border of images to segment the SERPs. Specifically, for each SERP, we equally divided it into 20 rows and 5 columns and use the median values of fixation duration/first arrival time in each grid to show users' examination patterns. Median is used instead of mean values here to reduce effects of outliers.

4.2 First arrival time

First arrival time of an image is the first time that a user gazes at the image. It is usually used to show user's examination sequence facing a given Web page. Figure 3(a) shows the heat map of the first arrival time of the images in the first result page, where the y-axis denotes the row number from 1 to 5. In Figure 3(b), we plot another heat map which represents the first arrival time of the images in page 1 to 4, with y-axis being the page number. The x-axis in Figure 3 indicates the column number as noted in Section 4.1. From Figure 3(a), we can see that the minimum first arrival time of the first row is at the position (1, 2), which is located around the middle position of the first row and highlighted by a black rectangular frame in the figure.

From both Figures 3(a) and 3(b), we can see that users generally follow a top-down pattern in the vertical direction of their examination sequences since the first row (in 3(a)) and the first page (in 3(b)) are both firstly fixated. However, in both of the first two rows in 3(a), the leftmost positions are not examined firstly. This is an interesting finding considering that the top-left position is usually regarded as the firstly-viewed position on a Web page [13]. In most current ranking strategies of image search engines, the most relevant image is usually placed at the top-left position (1, 1). However, according to our results, perhaps (1, 2) is a better choice since users pay attention firstly to this position (1, 2).

4.3 Examination duration

Examination duration of an image is defined as the dwell time during which a user examines the image. Dwell time has been regarded as an important implicit feedback for improving result ranking in search engines [21]. We calculate the examination duration for each image and plot users' examination duration distribution in Figure 4.

Similar with Figure 3, we also notice a middle position bias in the horizontal direction in both Figures 4(a) and 4(b). In 4(a), the position (1, 3) is fixated the most (as highlighted by a black rectangular frame), which is located around the middle position of the first row with a median fixation duration of 1.35 seconds. The left-most position (1,1) of the first row is fixated longer than the right-most position (1,5), but the duration is still shorter than the middle position (1,3). In 4(b), we also find that the middle position of the first page is fixated the most. In each page, it seems that the middle positions always draw more attention than the left-most or the right-most positions. This leads to a "T-shape" fixation distribution instead of the "F-shape" one (or "Golden Triangle") as described in most existing general Web search studies [13].

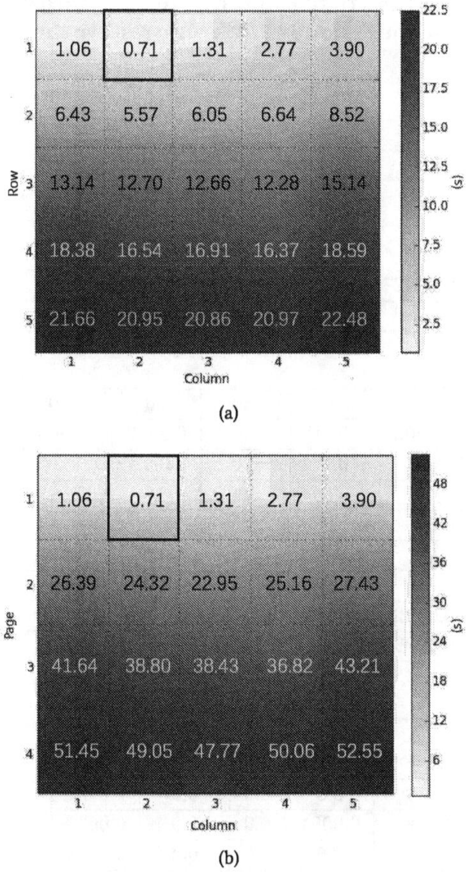

Figure 3: First arrival time distribution(s) in first page view (a) and global view (b)

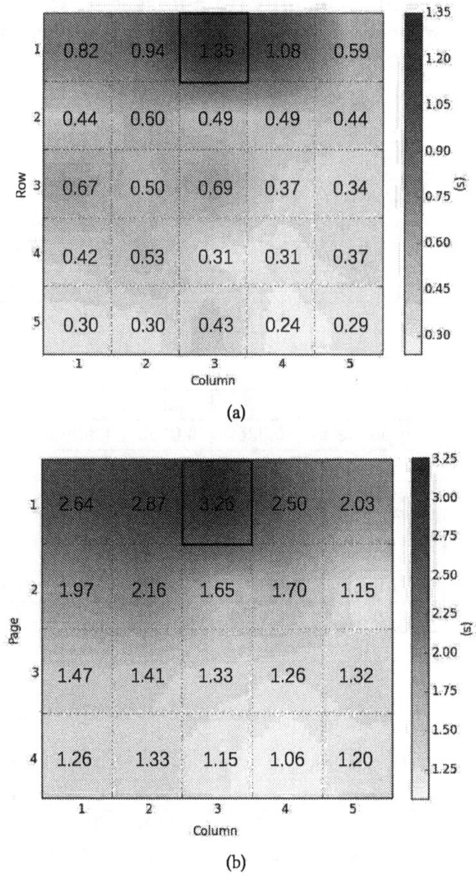

Figure 4: Examination duration distribution (s) in first page view (a) and global view(b)

In the vertical direction, we can see from Figures 4(a) and 4(b) that the first row and first page attract more user attention than the other positions. Generally, the fixation duration decreases with the row number or page number.

4.4 Statistical Modeling of Middle-position Bias

In this section, we statistically verify the observed middle-position bias in Figures 3 and 4 by analyzing the relation between the location of an image and gaze behaviors using a linear mixed model. The mixed model is a statistical model introduced by Bryk and Raudenbush [25]. The model contains both fixed effects and random effects, and they are particularly apt for multiple observations that are gathered over time on a set of people. The experiment was conducted with a set of 40 participants performing 20 search tasks, so we chose a linear mixed model, which is suitable for this data set size.

More specifically, we consider the effect of placing an image in the center columns (Columns 2, 3, and 4) on the first arrival time of the gaze. The dependent variable is "first arrival time," and the predictor variable is whether an image is placed in the center columns or on the sides (Columns 1 and 5). The random intercepts for both user and task are significant with $p < 2.2\times10^{-16}$ each. Therefore, we chose a linear mixed model with the user and task controlled as random effects. Testing the first arrival time with both the user and task controlled as random effects, the difference between the center columns and the sides is significant with $p < 2.2 \times 10^{-16}$. Hence the statistical model suggests that users tend to look first at pictures placed in the center columns and then at ones on the sides.

Similarly, we consider the effect on the fixation duration of gaze. The dependent variable is "fixation duration," and the predictor variable is whether an image is placed in the center columns or on the sides. The random intercepts for both user and task are significant with $p < 2.2 \times 10^{-16}$ each. Hence, we chose a linear mixed model with the user and task controlled as random effects as well. Testing the duration with both the user and task controlled as random effects, the difference is significant with $p < 2.2 \times 10^{-16}$. Therefore, the statistical model shows that the fixation duration tends to be longer for pictures placed in the center columns than for those on the sides.

In conclusion, eye gaze behaviors are related to the location of an image, and placing an image in the middle columns has a significant impact on both the first arrival time and the fixation

Table 3: Eye shift probability from images at Left column (a), middle column (b) and right column (c) to other images. Number 1 to 10 mean the distance (d) from image *i* to image *j* which defines according to the Equation 1. We only reserve the probability larger than 0.0001

(a)

	1	2	3	4	5	6	7	8	9	10	>10
Down	0.1137	0.0085	0.0006	0.0002	0.0001	0.0	0.0	0.0001	0.0	0.0	0.0044
Lower-right	0.0769	0.0693	0.0348	0.0101	0.0019	0.0	0.0001	0.0	0.0002	0.0	0.0334
Right	0.2187	0.1302	0.0685	0.0205	0.0043	0.0006	0.0	0.0	0.0	0.0	0.0001
Upper-right	0.0428	0.0458	0.0214	0.0093	0.0026	0.0005	0.0002	0.0001	0.0002	0.0001	0.0006
Up	0.0696	0.0060	0.0015	0.0010	0.0003	0.0003	0.0002	0.0	0.0003	0.0001	0.0001

(b)

	1	2	3	4	5	6	7	8	9	10	>10
Upper-left	0.0289	0.0150	0.0043	0.0012	0.0004	0.0004	0.0002	0.0001	0.0001	0.0002	0.0004
Left	0.1918	0.0497	0.0080	0.0013	0.0001	0.0	0.0	0.0	0.0	0.0	0.0
Lower-left	0.0567	0.0303	0.0074	0.0014	0.0002	0.0001	0.0	0.0	0.0001	0.0	0.0019
Down	0.0902	0.0128	0.0019	0.0004	0.0002	0.0	0.0001	0.0	0.0	0.0	0.0017
Lower-right	0.0518	0.0266	0.0060	0.0012	0.0001	0.0001	0.0	0.0	0.0	0.0	0.0021
Right	0.2143	0.0570	0.0095	0.0013	0.0001	0.0	0.0	0.0	0.0	0.0	0.0001
Upper-right	0.0296	0.0167	0.0049	0.0013	0.0003	0.0004	0.0002	0.0001	0.0001	0.0001	0.0003
Up	0.0541	0.0086	0.0024	0.0010	0.0007	0.0004	0.0003	0.0003	0.0002	0.0001	0.0003

(c)

	1	2	3	4	5	6	7	8	9	10	>10
Upper-left	0.0329	0.0337	0.0193	0.0066	0.0022	0.0008	0.0007	0.0001	0.0	0.0001	0.0009
Left	0.1966	0.1024	0.0662	0.0194	0.0030	0.0007	0.0	0.0	0.0	0.0	0.0
Lower-left	0.0978	0.1110	0.0641	0.0182	0.0052	0.0003	0.0001	0.0001	0.0	0.0	0.0039
Down	0.1139	0.0161	0.0016	0.0002	0.0001	0.0001	0.0	0.0	0.0	0.0001	0.0018
Up	0.0660	0.0082	0.0023	0.0004	0.0005	0.0009	0.0	0.0	0.0	0.0	0.0001

duration. These results agree with the observed middle-position bias in Section 4.2 and 4.3.

4.5 Transition Probabilities of Eye Fixation

Different from Web search results, the display of image search results is two-dimensional, so the transitions of fixation positions are in eight directions (upper left, up, upper right, right, lower right, down, lower left and left). To look into the eye movement patterns between different image search results, we show the transition probabilities for results in different directions and distances in Table 3. We also compare the differences of results in different positions (left-most column, right-most column and middle-column). Here, we define the distance (*d*) from image *i* to image *j* as:

$$d = max(abs[X_j - X_i], abs[Y_j - Y_i]) \quad (1)$$

Where X_i and X_j are row numbers of image *i* and image *i* while Y_i and Y_j are column numbers. The experimental data suggests the following findings.

- Most (44%) outgoing transitions from images located at the left column goes to the right while 23% goes lower right, 13% goes down, 12% goes upper right, and 8% goes up.
- Most (28%) outgoing transitions from images in the middle column goes to the right while 25% goes left, 11% goes down, 10% goes lower left, 10% goes lower right, 7% goes up, 5% goes upper right, and 4% goes upper left.
- Most (39%) outgoing transitions from images in the right column goes to the left, 30% goes lower left, 13% goes down, 10% goes upper left, and 8% goes up.
- In every direction, the transition probability decreases monotonically as the distance from the original image result increases.

From the transition probability, we infer that no matter where users' fixations are, eyes tend to move horizontally rather than vertically or diagonally. Results show a tendency toward a "near by principle" in which users prefer short-distance saccades than long-distance ones. These findings accord with existing researches in the mechanisms of eye movements [29].

5 IMAGE CONTENT AND EXAMINATION

Besides the position factor, we also want to investigate the influence of result content in examination. In many existing researchers, content of images have been shown to have impacts in people's attention allocation mechanisms. Therefore, we also want to look into the correlations between image content features and users' examination behavior including fixation duration and number of durations.

Table 4: Image content features

Feature Name	Feature Description
Saliency	Sum, mean and max of the given element.
Edge	Density of the given element.
Face	The number of human faces, the ratio of face areas.
Text	The number of texts, the ratio of text areas. (a Chinese character or an English word contributes for one text)

Table 5: Correlation between image content feature and examination behavior. *(or **) indicates the difference is significant at p < 0.05 (p < 0.01)

(coefficient, *p*-value)	Examination duration	Examination times
Sum Saliency	0.4842, **	0.5015, **
Mean Saliency	0.3442, **	0.3589, **
Max Saliency	0.2380,**	0.2583,**
Edge Density	0.1394,0.0532	0.1375,0.0566
Face num	0.0441,0.6731	0.0461,0.6589
The ratio of face areas	0.0324,0.7559	-0.0554,0.5956
Text num	0.1815,0.1889	0.0014,0.9919
The ratio of text areas	-0.0237,0.8648	-0.1801,0.1926

Image content features have been thoroughly surveyed in existing works. In [18], visual saliency features are demonstrated to significantly improve the success of examination prediction. Low-dimensional features like edge density are also found to be maximally informative features [4]. High-dimensional features like face and textual information are also widely used in image retrieval [27]. In this paper, we study four static image content features elaborated in Table 4. The GBVS algorithm [12] is applied to generate the visual saliency map. We use an edge detection algorithm introduced by Canny [6] to determine the boundaries of items (e.g., buildings) in the images. One of the authors manually labeled whether an image contains human face or textual information and use the labeling results as the features as well.

Given a list of image, we can extract static features from each image based on the method above. Further, each image's fixation duration and number of fixations are also collected by the eye-tracking devices. We use the Spearman's correlation coefficient which is a nonparametric measure of rank correlation used to assess the relation between image content features and users' examination behavior. The results are shown in Table 5 which shows that saliency has the highest correlation with fixation behavior in the sum, mean, and max of a given element, followed by the edge density feature. However, face features and the textual features are not closely related to the examination behavior. The reason why the high-dimensional features of faces and text have less influence on users' fixation may be that the number of faces and amount of text contained in image search results are limited, and sometimes they are auxiliary. For example, most texts in keyword-based image search results are watermarks rather than meaningful information.

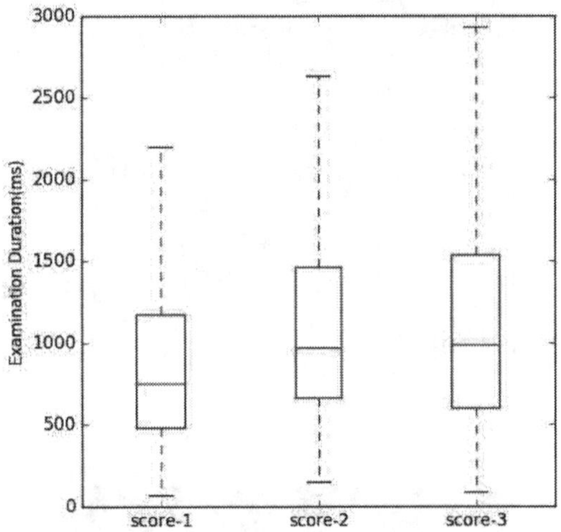

Figure 5: Examination duration boxplots for results with different relevance labeling scores

6 RELEVANCE, CLICK AND EXAMINATION

In the first stage of our experiment, we obtained participants' examination data and mouse behavior information including "click," "move," and "scroll" recorded by our built-in designed JavaScript. We conducted relevance labeling in the second stage. Thus, we obtained a feature space for selected images including examination duration, revisit behavior, click, and relevance score, which enabled us to investigate the relations between examination, click behavior, and relevance in our task. In this paper, We use pairwise T-test to verify the significance of differences between the different features and report the *p*-value.

6.1 Examination duration and Relevance

For each image in a task, we used a tuple with three elements (row, column, and duration) to describe it in an examination. An image has two or more tuples when there exist more than one fixations on it. We calculate the sum of examination duration for each image in the result panel if the image has two or more tuples. Based on the second stage of our experiment, we obtained a list of images with relevance scores. We draw a boxplot to illustrate the relation between examination duration and relevance in Figure 5, and perform a t-test between two of three image sets with different scores. Figure 5 shows that the mean examination duration of images with score 3 or score 2 is longer than images with score 1 (p-value < 0.01) while the difference between image set with score 2 and image set with score 3 is not significant. The above results show that when an image has a longer examination duration, it is more likely to be relevant, which may be labeled as "fairly relevant" or "very relevant". Thus, users' examination duration can be considered as a sign of image relevance, which implies that longer examination duration has a strong correlation with relevance.

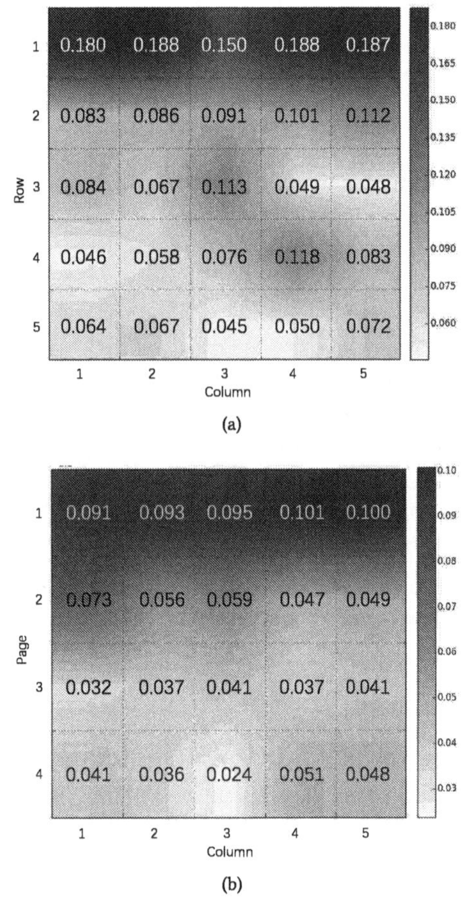

Figure 6: Click through rate distribution in first page view (a) and global view (b)

6.2 Revisit and Relevance

A revisit behavior in a task means that a user goes back to the previously examined image after examining another image. Here, we calculate the average scores of two groups of images (revisited and not revisited) The average score of revisited images in our task is 2.60 and higher than that of un-revisited ones (2.49). With paired two-tailed t-test, revisit behavior is significantly different between "relevant" and "irrelevant" (p-value < 0.05 for score 1 and score 2, and p-value < 0.01 for score 1 and score 3). This finding shares the same perspective in [36]. Xu et al. [36] shows that 50.2% of the revisited items in general web search have a high relevance.

6.3 Click and Relevance

Previous studies in image search [22, 28] indicate that image search click-through data is considerably more accurate in general than document-based search click-through data and can be used to boost the performance of an image search re-ranking system [15]. Therefore, based on the built-in JavaScript in our experimental platform, we investigate users' click behavior. Corresponding results are illustrated in Figure 6. Figure 6(a) shows the click-through rate for the first page. In contrast to the first arrival time and examination duration distribution, there is no noticeable middle-position bias on the first page. Furthermore, the four result pages overviewed in Figure 6(b) indicate that more clicks are observed on the first page and the left column of the second page, which is different from the middle position bias in examination behaviors shown in Figure 3(b) and Figure 4(b). Please be noted that if one of the images whose center positions are within the grid is clicked, then the grid receive one click.

The differences between click behavior and examination behavior (first arrival time, examination duration, and examination distribution) motivated us to further investigate the relation among click, examination, and relevance.

In this section, we address the two questions in *RQ*3: (1) Does examination hypothesis still hold in image search? (2) What is the relation between click, examination, and relevance? or will an image be clicked if it is examined and relevant with search target in image searches?

Examination hypothesis [8] assumes that a document being clicked ($C_i = 1$) accords with two conditions which are independent from each other: it is examined ($E_i = 1$) and it is relevant ($R_i = 1$). It is widely applied in Web search related studies such as click model constructions [10, 32]. Following this assumption, the probability of a document being clicked is determined as follows:

$$P(C_i = 1) = P(E_i = 1)P(R_i = 1) \quad (2)$$

According to the examination hypothesis, if an image in image searches is examined and relevant, then it will be clicked. We deem the images to be relevant if they obtain score 2 or score 3 and regard the images that have examination duration longer than 200ms as examined. If an image satisfies the examination hypothesis, it needs to satisfy any one of the following conditions: (1) it is relevant, examined and clicked; (2) it is not relevant and not clicked; (3) it is not examined and not clicked. Based on the experimental data, for each participant, we calculate the proportion of images that satisfy examination hypothesis. Result shows that 53% of images satisfy examination hypothesis while other 47% do not. Thus, in image search engine where results are shown in a completely different way with general Web search engines, examination hypothesis may not still hold.

To further investigate the relations among click, examination, and relevance, and to determine why the examination hypothesis is not applicable in image search, we calculated a confusion matrix that shows the relation between click (C) and relevance score, shown in Table 6. Because few images are not examined (6.7%), we only illustrate the results of examined images. We see that irrelevant images receive almost none click, which is consistent with the result in a general search. However, the probability of one relevant result being clicked is also very low ((4.08+4.84)%/(6.94+60.88)%=13.15%), which is not true according to Equation 2. This phenomenon may be caused by the fact that there are many similar images in the result panels in both the visual sense and content (for example, 4 out of 6 images in the first row of Figure 1 looks quite similar with each other). Sometimes there will be many relevant results. In contrast to general Web search results, image search results are self-contained, so that, users do not need to click the document as in a Web search to view the landing page in general. Instead, they can observe several images before deciding which ones to download or to click to see the larger version. Therefore, there is no need to

Table 6: Relation between click and relevance score given images are examined

E=1	C=1	C=0
Score=1	0.21%	26.72%
Score=2	4.08%	6.94%
Score=3	4.84%	60.88%

click each relevant image (many of them look quite similar with each other) to collect the required information and examination hypothesis doesn't hold any more here.

7 EXAMINATION BEHAVIOR PREDICTION

Through the eye-tracking study introduced in Sections 4-6, we obtained several interesting findings on user behavior biases including a middle-position bias in the user examination process and correlation biases between visual features and user examination behavior. As presented in Section 6, examination behavior can be an implicit feedback for content relevance. Therefore, predicting users' examination behavior based on static features that can be obtained offline is meaningful for search page optimization and UI evaluation.

7.1 Features and Model

As Table 5 illustrates, saliency and edge features play important roles in affecting the users' examination behavior. We extracted the visual saliency and edge density of images in our task into the feature space, which also contains image position (row, column) used to incorporate position bias into our prediction model. Because the first page receives more user examination as shown in Figure 4(b), the images in the first page are selected to construct our dataset which contains around 7,000 triples (participants,tasks and images). We set the input of the prediction model to be a combination of different features, and we compared the root mean square error (RMSE) of predictions by different feature combinations in Section 7.2. The prediction model outputs the probability of an image being examined, while the actual examination was obtained from the eye-tracking device as ground truth.

In this study, we compare different combinations of position and visual features. Our baseline feature group contains only the position feature (PF). Position bias is modeled in most existing click modeling efforts, so we use it as a reference to track how much improvement can be achieved by our method. Feature group SF involves only saliency features, and we use an index to mark which measurement (1-Sum, 2-Mean, 3-Max) it belongs. In feature group EF we only consider the edge density of images.

Given an image with a combination of features, our task is to predict its examination probability, which can be treated as a regression problem. In this paper, we apply a gradient boosting regression tree (GBRT) for the examination prediction tasks as in [18]. The prediction results of different combinations are compared with a 10-fold cross validation, and we report the average performance on the test folds.

Table 7: Examination prediction performance of different features groups

	RMSE	p-value
PF	0.1200	-
SF_1	0.1138	0.0904
$PF+SF_1$	0.1131	0.0279
$PF+SF_2$	0.1126	0.0296
$PF+SF_3$	0.1124	0.0070
PF+EF	0.1117	0.0332
PF+SF+EF	0.1098	0.0388

7.2 Prediction results and Discussions

We report RMSE for comparison, and a two-tailed t-test was performed to detect significant changes in the RMSE of prediction with position feature. Table 7 illustrates the corresponding results.

As Table 7 shows, adding visual saliency or edge information to a position-based feature (PF) can improve the RMSE of prediction. We find that $PF+SF_1$, $PF+SF_2$, $PF+SF_3$, and PF+EF significantly (with paired two-tailed t-test) outperform PF with p-value < 0.05 while $PF+SF_3$ has p-value < 0.01. Further, when we combine all features PF+SF+EF, the prediction model outperforms other combinations with p-value < 0.05. Thus, we can infer that combining position and visual features boosts the prediction performance in image searches. What is noteworthy is that as the features used in our prediction model are all static and can be calculated offline, they can be quite valuable for situations lacking users' behavior information.

8 CONCLUSIONS AND FUTURE WORK

In this paper, we carry out a lab-based user study with the help of eye-tracking devices in image search and obtain three interesting findings. (1) Based on first arrival time and examination duration analysis, We observe a middle-position bias of user's examination behavior, and we also apply a linear mixed model to justify the middle-position bias is significant statistically. Furthermore, we find that users are "lazy" in image search, they prefer small amplitude and short distance transitions between images. (2) Besides the position factor, visual features including saliency and edge density are demonstrated to have stronger correlation with user's examination behavior than high-dimensional features like the existences of human faces and textual features. (3) We investigate the relation between click, examination and relevance and find that examination duration is an useful implicit feedback for relevance of query-image pairs in image search. Also, as image results are self-contained, users do not need to click a document as in a Web search to view the landing page which results in the failure of examination hypothesis in image search scenarios.

Besides user study, we also perform an examination prediction experiment. Results show that combining position and visual features which can be calculated offline improves the prediction performance in image searches.

The research outputs of this paper are meaningful to inform the future image searches. For example, as there exists a middle-position bias of user's examination behavior, placing the most relevant results in the middle of each row rather than the leftmost positions may improve the users' satisfaction.

Our study makes a first step towards user's examination behavior analysis in image search. Interesting directions for future work include interaction behavior analysis result in preview pages (which is similar with but not completely the same as landing pages in general Web search). Moreover, we also plan to investigate user behavior in image searches on mobile devices and perform a comparison with PC based image searches.

ACKNOWLEDGMENTS

This work was supported by Natural Science Foundation of China (Grant No. 61622208, 61532011, 61672311), Tsinghua University Initiative Scientific Research Program(2014Z21032), National Key Basic Research Program (2015CB358700). Wu was supported in part by NIH grant 5U54CA193313.

REFERENCES

[1] Eugene Agichtein, Eric Brill, and Susan Dumais. 2006. Improving web search ranking by incorporating user behavior information. In *Proceedings of the 29th annual international ACM SIGIR conference on Research and development in information retrieval.* ACM, 19–26.

[2] Paul André, Edward Cutrell, Desney S Tan, and Greg Smith. 2009. Designing novel image search interfaces by understanding unique characteristics and usage. In *IFIP Conference on Human-Computer Interaction.* Springer, 340–353.

[3] Ioannis Arapakis and Luis A Leiva. 2016. Predicting user engagement with direct displays using mouse cursor information. In *Proceedings of the 39th International ACM SIGIR conference on Research and Development in Information Retrieval.* ACM, 599–608.

[4] Roland J Baddeley and Benjamin W Tatler. 2006. High frequency edges (but not contrast) predict where we fixate: A Bayesian system identification analysis. *Vision research* 46, 18 (2006), 2824–2833.

[5] Georg Buscher, Edward Cutrell, and Meredith Ringel Morris. 2009. What do you see when you're surfing?: using eye tracking to predict salient regions of web pages. In *Proceedings of the SIGCHI conference on human factors in computing systems.* ACM, 21–30.

[6] John Canny. 1986. A computational approach to edge detection. *IEEE Transactions on pattern analysis and machine intelligence* 6 (1986), 679–698.

[7] Huanhuan Cao, Daxin Jiang, Jian Pei, Qi He, Zhen Liao, Enhong Chen, and Hang Li. 2008. Context-aware query suggestion by mining click-through and session data. In *Proceedings of the 14th ACM SIGKDD international conference on Knowledge discovery and data mining.* ACM, 875–883.

[8] Nick Craswell, Onno Zoeter, Michael Taylor, and Bill Ramsey. 2008. An experimental comparison of click position-bias models. In *Proceedings of the 2008 International Conference on Web Search and Data Mining.* ACM, 87–94.

[9] Edward Cutrell and Zhiwei Guan. 2007. What are you looking for?: an eye-tracking study of information usage in web search. In *Proceedings of the SIGCHI conference on Human factors in computing systems.* ACM, 407–416.

[10] Georges E Dupret and Benjamin Piwowarski. 2008. A user browsing model to predict search engine click data from past observations.. In *Proceedings of the 31st annual international ACM SIGIR conference on Research and development in information retrieval.* ACM, 331–338.

[11] Abby Goodrum and Amanda Spink. 1999. Visual Information Seeking: A Study of Image Queries on the World Wide Web.. In *Proceedings of the ASIS Annual Meeting,* Vol. 36. ERIC, 665–74.

[12] Jonathan Harel, Christof Koch, and Pietro Perona. 2006. Graph-based visual saliency. In *Advances in neural information processing systems.* 545–552.

[13] Gord Hotchkiss, Steve Alston, and Greg Edwards. 2005. Eye tracking study. *Research white paper, Enquiro Search Solutions Inc* (2005).

[14] Xian-Sheng Hua, Linjun Yang, Jingdong Wang, Jing Wang, Ming Ye, Kuansan Wang, Yong Rui, and Jin Li. 2013. Clickage: towards bridging semantic and intent gaps via mining click logs of search engines. In *Proceedings of the 21st ACM international conference on Multimedia.* ACM, 243–252.

[15] Vidit Jain and Manik Varma. 2011. Learning to re-rank: query-dependent image re-ranking using click data. In *Proceedings of the 20th international conference on World wide web.* ACM, 277–286.

[16] Jyun-Yu Jiang, Yen-Yu Ke, Pao-Yu Chien, and Pu-Jen Cheng. 2014. Learning user reformulation behavior for query auto-completion. In *Proceedings of the 37th international ACM SIGIR conference on Research & development in information retrieval.* ACM, 445–454.

[17] Yanen Li, Anlei Dong, Hongning Wang, Hongbo Deng, Yi Chang, and ChengXiang Zhai. 2014. A two-dimensional click model for query auto-completion. In *Proceedings of the 37th international ACM SIGIR conference on Research & development in information retrieval.* ACM, 455–464.

[18] Yiqun Liu, Zeyang Liu, Ke Zhou, Meng Wang, Huanbo Luan, Chao Wang, Min Zhang, and Shaoping Ma. 2016. Predicting Search User Examination with Visual Saliency. In *Proceedings of the 39th International ACM SIGIR conference on Research and Development in Information Retrieval.* ACM, 619–628.

[19] Yiqun Liu, Chao Wang, Ke Zhou, Jianyun Nie, Min Zhang, and Shaoping Ma. 2014. From skimming to reading: A two-stage examination model for web search. In *Proceedings of the 23rd ACM International Conference on Conference on Information and Knowledge Management.* ACM, 849–858.

[20] Neil O'Hare, Paloma de Juan, Rossano Schifanella, Yunlong He, Dawei Yin, and Yi Chang. 2016. Leveraging user interaction signals for web image search. In *Proceedings of the 39th International ACM SIGIR conference on Research and Development in Information Retrieval.* ACM, 559–568.

[21] Bing Pan, Helene A Hembrooke, Geri K Gay, Laura A Granka, Matthew K Feusner, and Jill K Newman. 2004. The determinants of web page viewing behavior: an eye-tracking study. In *Proceedings of the 2004 symposium on Eye tracking research & applications.* ACM, 147–154.

[22] Yingwei Pan, Ting Yao, Tao Mei, Houqiang Li, Chong-Wah Ngo, and Yong Rui. 2014. Click-through-based cross-view learning for image search. In *Proceedings of the 37th international ACM SIGIR conference on Research & development in information retrieval.* ACM, 717–726.

[23] Jaimie Y Park, Neil O'Hare, Rossano Schifanella, Alejandro Jaimes, and Chin-Wan Chung. 2015. A large-scale study of user image search behavior on the web. In *Proceedings of the 33rd Annual ACM Conference on Human Factors in Computing Systems.* ACM, 985–994.

[24] Hsiao-Tieh Pu. 2005. A comparative analysis of web image and textual queries. *Online Information Review* 29, 5 (2005), 457–467.

[25] Stephen W Raudenbush and Anthony S Bryk. 2002. *Hierarchical linear models: Applications and data analysis methods.* Vol. 1.

[26] Sara Shatford. 1986. Analyzing the subject of a picture: a theoretical approach. *Cataloging & classification quarterly* 6, 3 (1986), 39–62.

[27] Arnold WM Smeulders, Marcel Worring, Simone Santini, Amarnath Gupta, and Ramesh Jain. 2000. Content-based image retrieval at the end of the early years. *IEEE Transactions on pattern analysis and machine intelligence* 22, 12 (2000), 1349–1380.

[28] Gavin Smith and Helen Ashman. 2009. Evaluating implicit judgements from image search interactions. (2009).

[29] Benjamin W Tatler and Benjamin T Vincent. 2009. The prominence of behavioural biases in eye guidance. *Visual Cognition* 17, 6-7 (2009), 1029–1054.

[30] Dian Tjondronegoro, Amanda Spink, and Bernard J Jansen. 2009. A study and comparison of multimedia Web searching: 1997–2006. *Journal of the American Society for Information Science and Technology* 60, 9 (2009), 1756–1768.

[31] Geoffrey Underwood and Tom Foulsham. 2006. Visual saliency and semantic incongruency influence eye movements when inspecting pictures. *The Quarterly journal of experimental psychology* 59, 11 (2006), 1931–1949.

[32] Chao Wang, Yiqun Liu, Meng Wang, Ke Zhou, Jian-yun Nie, and Shaoping Ma. 2015. Incorporating non-sequential behavior into click models. In *Proceedings of the 38th International ACM SIGIR Conference on Research and Development in Information Retrieval.* ACM, 283–292.

[33] Kuansan Wang, Nikolas Gloy, and Xiaolong Li. 2010. Inferring search behaviors using partially observable Markov (POM) model. In *Proceedings of the third ACM international conference on Web search and data mining.* ACM, 211–220.

[34] Yue Wang, Dawei Yin, Luo Jie, Pengyuan Wang, Makoto Yamada, Yi Chang, and Qiaozhu Mei. 2016. Beyond ranking: Optimizing whole-page presentation. In *Proceedings of the Ninth ACM International Conference on Web Search and Data Mining.* ACM, 103–112.

[35] Wei Wu, Hang Li, and Jun Xu. 2013. Learning query and document similarities from click-through bipartite graph with metadata. In *Proceedings of the sixth ACM international conference on Web search and data mining.* ACM, 687–696.

[36] Danqing Xu, Yiqun Liu, Min Zhang, Shaoping Ma, and Liyun Ru. 2012. Incorporating revisiting behaviors into click models. In *Proceedings of the fifth ACM international conference on Web search and data mining.* ACM, 303–312.

[37] Yongdong Zhang, Xiaopeng Yang, and Tao Mei. 2014. Image search reranking with query-dependent click-based relevance feedback. *IEEE transactions on image processing* 23, 10 (2014), 4448–4459.

Extracting Hierarchies of Search Tasks & Subtasks via a Bayesian Nonparametric Approach

Rishabh Mehrotra[†] and Emine Yilmaz[†*]
[†]University College London, London, United Kingdom
[*]The Alan Turing Institute, British Library, London, United Kingdom
{r.mehrotra,e.yilmaz}@cs.ucl.ac.uk

ABSTRACT

A significant amount of search queries originate from some real world information need or tasks [13]. In order to improve the search experience of the end users, it is important to have accurate representations of tasks. As a result, significant amount of research has been devoted to extracting proper representations of tasks in order to enable search systems to help users complete their tasks, as well as providing the end user with better query suggestions [9], for better recommendations [41], for satisfaction prediction [36] and for improved personalization in terms of tasks [24, 38]. Most existing task extraction methodologies focus on representing tasks as flat structures. However, tasks often tend to have multiple subtasks associated with them and a more naturalistic representation of tasks would be in terms of a hierarchy, where each task can be composed of multiple (sub)tasks. To this end, we propose an efficient Bayesian nonparametric model for extracting hierarchies of such tasks & subtasks. We evaluate our method based on real world query log data both through quantitative and crowdsourced experiments and highlight the importance of considering task/subtask hierarchies.

KEYWORDS

search tasks; bayesian non-parametrics; hierarchical model

ACM Reference format:
Rishabh Mehrotra[†] and Emine Yilmaz[†*]. 2017. Extracting Hierarchies of Search Tasks & Subtasks via a Bayesian Nonparametric Approach. In *Proceedings of SIGIR'17, August 7–11, 2017, Shinjuku, Tokyo, Japan*, , 10 pages.
DOI: http://dx.doi.org/10.1145/3077136.3080823

1 INTRODUCTION

The need for search often arises from a person's need to achieve a goal, or a task such as booking travels, buying a house, etc., which would lead to search processes that are often lengthy, iterative, and are characterized by distinct stages and shifting goals. [13]. Thus, identifying and representing these tasks properly is highly important for devising search systems that can help end users complete their tasks. It has previously been shown that these task representations can be used to provide users with better query suggestions [9], offer improved personalization [24, 38], provide better recommendations [41], help in satisfaction prediction [36] and search result re-ranking. Moreover, accurate representations of tasks could also be highly useful in aptly placing the user in the task-subtask space to contextually target the user in terms of better recommendations and advertisements, developing task specific ranking of documents, and developing task based evaluation metrics to model user satisfaction. Given the wide range of applications these tasks representations can be used for, significant amount of research has been devoted to task extraction and representation [12, 13, 15, 17, 21].

Task extraction is quite a challenging problem as search engines can be used to achieve very different tasks, and each task can be defined at different levels of granularity. A major limitation in existing task-extraction methods lies in their treatment of search tasks as flat structure-less clusters which inherently lack insights about the presence or demarcation of subtasks associated with individual search tasks. In reality, often search tasks tend to be hierarchical in nature. For example, a search task like planning a wedding involves subtasks like searching for dresses, browsing different hairstyles, looking for invitation card templates, finding planners, among others. Each of these subtasks (1) could themselves be composed of multiple subtasks, and (2) would warrant issuing different queries by users to accomplish them. Hence, in order to obtain more accurate representations of tasks, new methodologies for constructing hierarchies of tasks are needed.

As part of the proposed research, we consider the challenge of extracting hierarchies of search tasks and their associated subtasks from a search log given just the log data without the need of any manual annotation of any sort. In a recent poster we showed that Bayesian nonparametrics have the potential to extract a hierarchical representation of tasks [25]; we extend this model further to form more accurate representations of tasks.

We present an efficient Bayesian nonparametric model for discovering hierarchies and propose a tree based nonparametric model to discover this rich hierarchical structure of tasks/subtasks embedded in search logs. Most existing hierarchical clustering techniques result in binary tree structures with each node decomposed into two child nodes. Given that a complex task could be composed of an arbitrary number of subtasks, these techniques cannot directly be used to construct accurate representations of tasks. In contrast, our model is capable of identifying task structures that can be composed of an arbitrary number of children. We make use of a number of evaluation methodologies to evaluate the efficacy of the proposed task extraction methodology, including quantitative and qualitative analyses along with crowdsourced judgment studies

SIGIR'17, August 7–11, 2017, Shinjuku, Tokyo, Japan
© 2017 ACM. ISBN 978-1-4503-5022-8/17/08...$15.00
DOI: http://dx.doi.org/10.1145/3077136.3080823

specifically catered to evaluating the quality of the extracted task hierarchies. We contend that the techniques presented expand the scope for better recommendations and search personalization and opens up new avenues for recommendations specifically targeting users based on the tasks they involve in.

2 RELATED WORK

Web search logs provide explicit clues about the information seeking behavior of users and have been extensively studied to improve search experiences of users. We cover several areas of related work and discuss how our work relates to and extends prior work.

2.1 Task Extraction

There has been a large body of work focused on the problem of segmenting and organizing query logs into semantically coherent structures. Many such methods use the idea of a *timeout* cutoff between queries, where two consecutive queries are considered as two different sessions or tasks if the time interval between them exceeds a certain threshold [6, 10, 33]. Often a 30-minute timeout is used to segment sessions. However, experimental results of these methods indicate that the timeouts are of limited utility in predicting whether two queries belong to the same task, and unsuitable for identifying session boundaries.

More recent studies suggest that users often seek to complete multiple search tasks within a single search session [20, 23] with over 50% of search sessions having more than 2 tasks [23]. At the same time, certain tasks require significantly more effort, time and sessions to complete with almost 60% of complex information gathering tasks continued across sessions [1, 22]. There have been attempts to extract in-session tasks [13, 20, 35], and cross-session tasks [15, 37] from query sequences based on classification and clustering methods, as well as supporting users in accomplishing these tasks [9]. Prior work on identifying search-tasks focuses on task extraction from search sessions with the objective of segmenting a search session into disjoint sets of queries where each set represents a different task [12, 21].

Kotov et al. [15] and Agichtein et al. [1] studied the problem of cross-session task extraction via binary same-task classification, and found different types of tasks demonstrate different life spans. While such task extraction methods are good at linking a new query to an on-going task, often these query links form long chains which result in a task cluster containing queries from many potentially different tasks. With the realization that sessions are not enough to represent tasks, recent work has started exploring cross-section task extraction, which often results in complex non-homogeneous clusters of queries solving a number of related yet different tasks. Unfortunately, pairwise predictions alone cannot generate the partition of tasks efficiently and even with post-processing, the final task partitions obtained are not expressive enough to demarcate subtasks [18]. Finally, authors in [17] model query temporal patterns using a special class of point process called Hawkes processes, and combine topic model with Hawkes processes for simultaneously identifying and labeling search tasks.

Jones et al. [13] was the first work to consider the fact that there may be multiple subtasks associated with a user's information need and that these subtasks could be interleaved across different sessions. However, their method only focuses on the queries submitted by a single user and attempts to segment them based on whether they fall under the same information need. Hence, they only consider solving the task boundary identification and same task identification problem and cannot be used directly for task extraction. Our work alleviates the same user assumption and considers queries across different users for task extraction. Finally, in a recent poster [25], we proposed the idea of extracting task hierarchies and presented a basic tree extraction algorithm. Our current work extends the preliminary model in a number of dimensions including novel model of query affinities and task coherence based pruning strategy, which we observe gives substantial improvement in results. Unlike past work, we also present detailed derivation and evaluation of the extracted hierarchy and application on task extraction.

2.2 Supporting Complex Search Tasks

There has been a significant amount of work on task continuation assistance [1, 28], building task tours and trails [30, 34], query suggestions [2, 14, 27], predicting next search action [5] and notes taking when accomplishing complex tasks [8]. The quality of most of these methods depends on forming accurate representations of tasks, which is the problem we are addressing in this paper.

2.3 Hierarchical Models

Rich hierarchies are common in data across many domains, hence quite a few hierarchical clustering techniques have been proposed. The traditional methods for hierarchically clustering data are bottom-up agglomerative algorithms. Probabilistic methods of learning hierarchies have also been proposed [3, 19] along with hierarchical clustering based methods [7, 11]. Most algorithms for hierarchical clustering construct binary tree representations of data, where leaf nodes correspond to data points and internal nodes correspond to clusters. There are several limitations to existing hierarchy construction algorithms. The algorithms provide no guide to choosing the correct number of clusters or the level at which to prune the tree. It is often difficult to know which distance metric to choose. Additionally and more importantly, restriction of the hypothesis space to binary trees alone is undesirable in many situations - indeed, a task can have any number of subtasks, not necessarily two. Past work has also considered constructing task-specific taxonomies from document collections [39], browsing hierarchy construction [40], generating hierarchical summaries [16]. While most of these techniques work in supervised settings on document collections, our work instead focused on short text queries and offers an unsupervised method of constructing task hierarchies.

Finally, Bayesian Rose Trees and their extensions have been proposed [3, 4, 32] to model arbitrary branching trees. These algorithms naively cast relationships between objects as binary (0-1) associations while the query-query relationships in general are much richer in content and structure.

We consider a number of such existing methods as baselines and the various advantages of the proposed approach is highlighted in the evaluation section wherein the proposed approach in addition to being more expressive, performs better than state-of-the-art task extraction and hierarchical methods.

Symbol	Description
n_T	number of children of tree T
$ab\|c$	partition of set $\{a,b,c\}$ into disjoint sets $\{a,b\}$,$\{c\}$
ch(T)	children of T
$\phi(T)$	partition of tree T
$p(D_m\|T_m)$	likelihood of data D_m given the tree T_m
π_{T_m}	mixing proportions of partition of tree T
$f(D_m)$	marginal probability of the data D_m
$\mathbb{H}(T)$	set of all partitions of queries $Q = leaves(T)$
$f(Q)$	task affinity function for set of queries Q
$r^k_{q_i,q_j}$	the k-th inter-query affinity between q_i & q_j

Table 1: Table of symbols

3 DEFINING SEARCH TASKS

Jones et al. [13] was one of the first papers to point out the importance of task representations, where they defined a search task as:

Definition 3.1. A *search task* is an atomic information need resulting in one or more queries.

Ahmed et al. [9] later extended this definition to a more generic one, which can also capture task structures that could possibly consist of related subtasks, each of which could be complex tasks themselves or may finally split down into simpler tasks or atomic informational needs. Following Ahmed *et al.* [9], a complex search task can then be defined as:

Definition 3.2. A *complex search task* is a multi-aspect or a multi-step information need consisting of a set of related subtasks, each of which might recursively be complex.

The definition of complex tasks is much more generic, and captures all possible search tasks, that can be either complex or atomic (non-complex). Throughout this paper we adopt the definition provided in Definition 3.2 as the definition for a search task.

Hence, by definition a search task has a hierarchical nature, where each task can consist of an arbitrary number of, possibly complex subtasks. An effective task extraction system should be capable of accurately identifying and representing such hierarchical structures.

4 CONSTRUCTING TASK HIERARCHIES

While hierarchical clustering are widely used for clustering, they construct binary trees which may not be the best model to describe data's intrinsic structure in many applications, for example, the task-subtask structure in our case. To remedy this, multi-branch trees are developed. Currently there are few algorithms which generate multi-branch hierarchies. Blundel *et al.* [3, 4] adopt a simple, deterministic, agglomerative approach called BRTs (Bayesian Rose Trees) for constructing multi-branch hierarchies. In this work, we adapt BRT as a basic algorithm and extend it for constructing task hierarchies. We next describe the major steps of BRT approach.

4.1 Bayesian Rose Trees

BRTs [3, 4] are based on a greedy probabilistic agglomerative approach to construct multi-branch hierarchies. In the beginning,

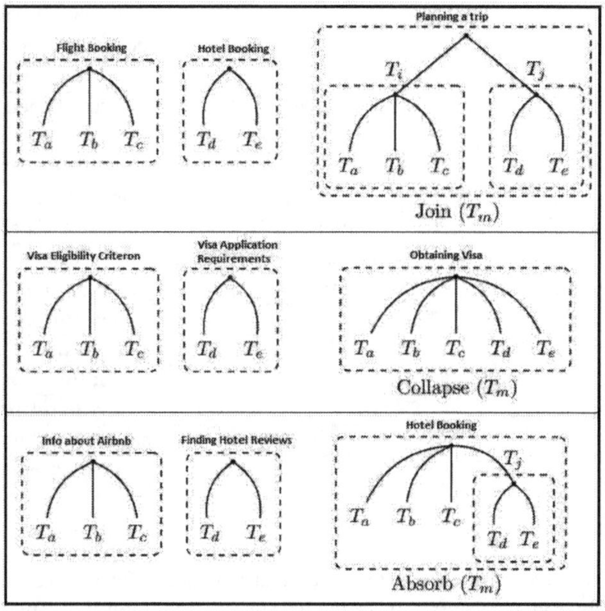

Figure 1: The different ways of merging trees which allows us to obtain tree structures which best explain the task-subtask structure.

each data point is regarded as a tree on its own: $T_i = \{x_i\}$ where x_i is the feature vector of i-th data. For each step, the algorithm selects two trees T_i and T_j and merges them into a new tree T_m. Unlike binary hierarchical clustering, BRT uses three possible merging operations, as shown in Figure 1:

- **Join**: $T_m = T_i, T_j$, such that the tree T_m has two children now
- **Absorb**: $T_m = children(T_i) \cup T_j$, i.e., the children of one tree gets absorbed into the other tree forming an absorbed tree with >2 children
- **Collapse**: $T_m = children(T_i) \cup children(T_j)$, all the children of both the subtrees get combined together at the same level.

Specifically, in each step, the algorithm greedily finds two trees T_i and T_j to merge which maximize the ratio of probability:

$$\frac{p(D_m|T_m)}{p(D_i|T_i)p(D_j|T_j)} \tag{1}$$

where $p(D_m|T_m)$ is the likelihood of data D_m given the tree T_m, D_m is all the leaf data of T_m, and $D_m = D_i \cup D_j$. The probability $p(D_m|T_m)$ is recursively defined on the children of T_m:

$$p(D_m|T_m) = \pi_{T_m} f(D_m) + (1 - \pi_{T_m}) \prod_{T_i \in ch(T_m)} p(D_i|T_i) \tag{2}$$

where $f(D_m)$ is the marginal probability of the data D_m and π_{T_m} is the "*mixing proportion*". Intuitively, π_{T_m} is the prior probability that all the data in T_m is kept in one cluster instead of partitioned into sub-trees. In BRT[4], π_{T_m} is defined as:

$$\pi_{T_m} = 1 - (1 - \gamma)^{n_{T_m} - 1} \tag{3}$$

where n_{T_m} is the number of children of T_m, and $0 \geq \gamma \leq 1$ is the hyperparameter to control the model. A larger γ leads to coarser

Query-Term Based Affinity (r^1)	
cosine	cosine similarity between the term sets of the queries
edit	norm edit distance between query strings
Jac	Jaccard coeff between the term sets of the queries
Term	proportion of common terms between the queries
URL Based Affinity (r^2)	
Min-edit-U	Minimum edit distance between all URL pairs from the queries
Avg-edit-U	Average edit distance between all URL pairs from the queries
Jac-U-min	Minimum Jaccard coefficient between all URL pairs from the queries
Jac-U-avg	Average Jaccard coefficient between all URL pairs from the queries
Session/User Based Affinity (r^3)	
Same-U	if the two queries belong to the same user
Same-S	if the two queries belong to the same session
Embedding Based Affinity (r^4)	
Embedding	cosine distance between embedding vectors of the two queries

Table 2: Query-Query Affinities.

partitions and a smaller γ leads to finer partitions. Table 1 provides an overview of notations & symbols used throughout the paper.

4.2 Building Task Hierarchies

We next describe our task hierarchy construction approach built on top of Bayesian Rose Trees. A tree node in our setting is comprised of a group of queries which potentially compose a search task, i.e. these are the set of queries that people tend to issue in order to achieve the task represented in the tree node.

We define the task-subtask hierarchy recursively: T is a task if either T contains all the queries at its node (an atomic search task) or if T splits into children trees as $T = \{T_1, T_2, ..., T_{n_T}\}$ where each of the children trees (T_i) are disjoint set of queries corresponding to the n_T subtasks associated with task T. This allows us to consider trees as a nested collection of sets of queries defining our task-subtask hierarchical relation.

To form nested hierarchies, we first need to model the query data. This corresponds to defining the marginal distribution of the data $f(D_m)$ as defined in Equation 2. The marginal distribution of the query data ($f(D_m)$) helps us encapsulate insights about task level interdependencies among queries, which aid in constructing better task representations. The original BRT approach [4] assumes that the data can be modeled by a set of binary features that follow the Bernoulli distribution. In other words, features (that represent the relationship/similarities between data points) are not weighted and can only be binary. Binary (0/1) relationships are too simplistic to model inter-query relationships; as a result, this major assumption fails to capture the semantic relationships between queries and is not suited for modeling query-task relations. To this end, we propose a novel query affinity model and to alleviate the binary feature assumption imposed by BRT, we propose a conjugate model of query affinities, which we describe next.

4.3 Conjugate Model of Query Affinities

A tree node in our setting is comprised of a group of queries which *potentially* belong to the same search task. The likelihood of a tree should encapsulate information about the different relationships which exists between queries. Our goal here is to make use of the rich information associated with queries and their result set available to compute the likelihood of a set of queries to belong to the same task. In order to do so, we propose a query affinity model which makes use of a number of different inter-query affinities to determine the tree likelihood function.

We next describe the technique used to compute four broad categories of inter-query affinity and later describe the Gamma-Poisson conjugate model which makes use of these affinities to compute the marginal distribution of the data.

Query-term based Affinity (r^1):
Search queries catering to the same or similar informational needs tend to have similar query terms. We make use of this insight and capture query level affinities between a pair of queries. We make use of cosine similarity between the query term sets, the normalized edit distances between queries and the Jaccard Coefficient between query term sets.

URL-based Affinity (r^2):
Users tackling similar tasks tend to issue queries (possibly different) which return similar URLs, thus encoding the URL level similarity between pairs of queries into the query affinity model helps in capturing another task-specific similarity between queries. Any query pair having high URL level similarity increase the possibility of the query pair originating from similar informational needs. We capture a number of URL-based signals including minimum and average edit distances between URL domains and jaccard coefficient between URLs.

User/Session based Affinity (r^3):
It is often the case that users issue related queries within a session so as to satisfy their informational need. We leverage this insight by making use of session level information (as a 0/1 binary feature) and user-level information (as a 0/1 binary feature) in our affinity model to identify queries issued in the same session and by the same user accordingly.

Query Embedding based Affinity (r^4):
Word embeddings capture lexico-semantic regularities in language, such that words with similar syntactic and semantic properties are found to be close to each other in the embedding space. We leverage this insight and propose a query-query affinity metric based on such embeddings. We train a skip-gram word embeddings model where a query term is used as an input to a log-linear classifier with continuous projection layer and words within a certain window before and after the words are predicted. To obtain a query's vector representation, we average the vector representations of each of its query terms and compute the cosine similarity between two queries' vector representations to quantify the embedding based affinity (r^4).

Table 2 summarizes all features considered to compute these affinities. Our goal is to capture information from all four affinities when defining the likelihood of the tree. We assume that the global affinity among a group of queries can be decomposed into a product of independent terms, each of which represent one of the four affinities from the query-group. For each query group Q, we take the normalized sum of the affinities from all pairs of queries in the group Q to form each of the affinity component (r^k, k=1,2,3,4).

Poisson models have been shown as effective query generation models for information retrieval tasks [26]. While these affinities could be used with a lot of distributions, in the interest of computational efficiency and to avoid approximate solutions, our model will use a hierarchical Gamma-Poisson distribution to encode the query-query affinities. We incorporate the gamma-Poisson conjugate distribution in our model under the assumptions that the query affinities are discretized and for a group of queries Q, the affinities can be decomposed to a product of independent terms, each of which represents contributions from the four different affinity types. Finally, for a tree (T_m) consisting of the data (D_m), i.e. the set of queries Q, we define the marginal likelihood as:

$$f(D_m) = f(Q) = \prod_{k=1}^{k=4} p\Big(\sum_{i \in 1 \cdots |Q|} \sum_{j \in 1 \cdots |Q|} r^k_{q_i, q_j} | \alpha_k, \beta_k \Big) \quad (4)$$

where α_k & β_k are respectively the shape parameter & the rate parameter of the four different affinities. Making use of the Poisson-Gamma conjugacy, the probability term in the above product can be written as:

$$p(r|\alpha, \beta) = \int_\lambda p(r|\lambda) p(\lambda|\alpha, \beta) d\lambda \quad (5)$$

$$= \left\{ \frac{\Gamma(\alpha + r)}{r! \, \Gamma(\alpha)} \left(\frac{\beta}{\beta + 1} \right)^\alpha \left(\frac{1}{\beta + 1} \right)^r \right\} \quad (6)$$

where λ is the Poisson mean rate parameter which gets eliminated from computations because of the Gamma-Poisson conjugacy and where r, α & β get replaced by affinity class specific values.

4.4 Task Coherence based Pruning

The search task extraction algorithm described above provides us a way of constructing a task hierarchy wherein as we go down the tree, nodes comprising of complex multi-aspect tasks split up to provide finer tasks which ideally should model user's fine grained information needs. One key problem with the hierarchy construction algorithm is the continuous splitting of nodes which results in singleton queries occupying the leave nodes. While splitting of nodes which represent complex tasks is important, the nodes representing simple search task queries corresponding to atomic informational needs should not be further split into children nodes. Our goal in this section is to provide a way of quantifying the task complexity of a particular node so as to prevent splitting up nodes representing atomic search task into further subsets of query nodes.

4.4.1 Identifying Atomic Tasks. We wish to identify nodes capturing search subtasks which represent atomic informational need. In order to do so, we introduce the notion of *Task Coherence*:

Definition 4.1. *Task Coherence* is a measure indicating the atomicity of the information need associated with the task. It is captured by the semantic closeness of the queries associated with the task.

By measuring Task Coherence, we intend to capture the semantic variability of queries within this task in an attempt to identify how complex or atomic a task is. For example, a tree node corresponding to a complex task like planning a vacation would involve queries from varied informational needs including flights, hotels, getaways, etc; while a tree node corresponding to a finer task representing an atomic informational need like finding discount coupons would involve less varied queries - all of which would be about discount coupons. Traditional research in topic modelling has looked into automatic evaluation of topic coherence [29] via Pointwise Mutual Information. We leverage the same insights to capture task coherence.

4.4.2 Pointwise Mutual Information. PMI has been studied variously in the context of collocation extraction [31] and is one measure of the statistical independence of observing two words in close proximity. We wish to compute PMI scores for each node of the tree. A tree node in our discussion so far has been represented by a collection of search queries. We split queries into terms and obtain a set of terms corresponding to each node, and calculate a node's PMI scores using the node's set of query terms.

More specifically, the PMI of a given pair of query terms (w_1 & w_2) is given by:

$$PMI(w_1, w_2) = log \frac{p(w_1, w_2)}{p(w_1) p(w_2)} \quad (7)$$

where the probabilities are determined from the empirical statistics of some full standard collection. We employ the AOL log query set for this and treat two query terms as co-occurring if both terms occur in the same session. For a given task node (Q), we measure task coherence as the average of PMI scores for all pairs of the search terms associated with the task node:

$$PMI - Score(Q) = \frac{1}{|w|} \sum_{i=1}^{|w|} \sum_{j=1}^{|w|} PMI(w_i, w_j) \quad (8)$$

where $|w|$ represents the total number of unique search terms associated with task node Q. The node's PMI-Score is used as the final measure of task coherence for the task represented via the corresponding node.

4.4.3 Tree Pruning. We use the task coherence score associated with each node of the task hierarchy constructed, and prune lower level nodes of the tree to avoid aggressive node splitting. The overall motivation here is to avoid splitting nodes which represent simple search tasks associated with atomic informational needs. We scan through all levels of the search task hierarchy obtained by the algorithm described above and for each node compute its task coherence score. If the task coherence score exceeds a specific threshold, it implies that all the queries in this particular node are aimed at solving the same or very similar informational need and hence, we prune off the sub-tree rooted at this particular node and ignore all further splits of this node.

4.5 Algorithmic Overview

We summarize the overall algorithm to construct the hierarchy by outlining the steps. The problem is treated as one of greedy model selection: each tree T is a different model, and we wish to find the model that best explains the search log data in terms of task-subtask structure.

Step 1: Forrest Initialization:
The tree is built in a bottom-up greedy agglomerative fashion, starting from a forest consisting of n (=$|Q|$) trivial trees, each corresponding to exactly one vertex. The algorithm maintains a forest F of trees, the likelihood $p(i) = p(D_i|T_i)$ of each tree $T_i \in F$ and the different query affinities. Each iteration then merges two of the trees in the forest. At each iteration, each vertex in the network is a leaf of exactly one tree in the forest. At each iteration a pair of trees in the forest F is chosen to be merged, resulting in forest $F*$.

Step 2: Merging Trees:
At each iteration, the best potential merge, say of trees X and Y resulting in tree I, is picked off the heap. Binary trees do not fit into representing search tasks since a task is likely to be composed of more than two subtasks. As a result, following [3] we consider three possible mergers of two trees T_i and T_j into T_m. T_m may be formed by joining T_i and T_j together using a new node, giving $T_m = \{T_i, T_j\}$. Alternatively T_m may be formed by absorbing T_i as a child of T_j, yielding $T_m = \{T_j\} \bigcup ch(T_i)$, or vice-versa, $T_m = \{T_i\} \bigcup ch(T_j)$. We explain the different possible merge operations in Figure 1. We obtain arbitrary shaped sub-trees (without restricting to binary tress) which are better at representing the varied task-subtask structures as observed in search logs with the structures themselves learnt from log data. Such expressive nature of our approach differentiates it from traditional agglomerative clustering approaches which necessarily result in binary trees.

Step 3: Model Selection:
Which pair of trees to merge, and how to merge these trees, is determined by considering which pair and type of merger yields the largest Bayes factor improvement over the current model. If the trees T_i and T_j are merged to form the tree M, then the Bayes factor score is:

$$SCORE(M; I, J) = \frac{p(D_M|F*)}{p(D_M|F)} \tag{9}$$

$$= \frac{p(D_M|M)}{p(D_i|T_i)p(D_j|T_j)} \tag{10}$$

where $p(D_i|T_i)$ and $p(D_j|T_j)$ are given by the dynamic programming equation mentioned above. After a successful merge, the statistics associated with the new tree are updated. Finally, potential mergers of the new tree with other trees in the forest are considered and added onto the heap.

The algorithm finishes when no further merging results in improvement in the Bayes Factor score. Note that the Bayes factor score is based on data local to the merge - i.e., by considering the probability of the connectivity data only among the leaves of the newly merged tree. This permits efficient local computations and makes the assumption that local community structure should depend only on the local connectivity structure.

Step 4: Tree Pruning:
After constructing the entire hierarchy, we perform the post-hoc tree pruning procedure described in Section 4.4 wherein we identify atomic task nodes via their task coherence estimates and prune all child nodes of the identified atomic nodes.

5 EXPERIMENTAL EVALUATION

We perform a number of experiments to evaluate the proposed task-subtask extraction method. First, we compare its performance with existing state-of-the-art task extraction systems on a manually labelled ground-truth dataset and report superior performance (5.1). Second, we perform a detailed crowd-sourced evaluation of extracted tasks and additionally validate the hierarchy using human labeled judgments (5.2). Third, we show a direct application of the extracted tasks by using the task hierarchy constructed for term prediction (5.3).

Parameter Setting:
Unless stated otherwise, we made use of the best performing hyperparameters for the baselines as reported by the authors. The query affinities in the proposed approach were computed from the specific query collection used in the dataset used for each of the three experiments reported below. While hyperparmeter optimization is beyond the scope of this work, we experimented with a range of the shape and inverse scale hyperparameters (α, β) used for the Poison Gamma conjugate model and used the ones which performed best on the validation set for the search task identification results reported in the next section. Additionally, for the tree pruning threshold, we empirically found that a threshold of 0.8 gave the best performance on our toy hierarchies, and was used for all future experiments.

5.1 Search Task Identification

To justify the effectiveness of the proposed model in identifying search tasks in query logs, we employ a commonly used AOL data subset with search tasks annotated which is a standard test dataset for evaluating task extraction systems. We used the task extraction dataset as provided by Lucchese *et al.*[20]. The dataset comprises of a sample of 1000 user sessions for which human assessors were asked to manually identify the optimal task-based query sessions, thus producing a ground-truth that can be used for evaluating automatic task-based session discovery methods. For further details on the dataset and the dataset access links, readers are directed to Lucchese *et al.*[20].

We compare our performance with a number of search task identification approaches:

- **Bestlink-SVM** [37]: This method identified search task using a semi-supervised clustering model based on the latent structural SVM framework.
- **QC-HTC/QC-WCC** [20]: This series of methods viewed search task identification as the problem of best approximating the manually annotated tasks, and proposed both clustering and heuristic algorithms to solve the problem.
- **LDA-Hawkes** [17]: a probabilistic method for identifying and labeling search tasks that model query temporal patterns using a special class of point process called Hawkes processes, and combine topic model with Hawkes processes for simultaneously identifying and labeling search tasks.
- **LDA Time-Window(TW)**: This model assumes queries belong to the same search task only if they lie in a fixed or flexible time window, and uses LDA to cluster queries into topics based on the query co-occurrences within the same time window. We tested time windows of various sizes and report results on the best performing window size.

5.1.1 Metrics. A commonly used evaluation metric for search task extraction is the pairwise F-measure computed based on pairwise precision/recall [13, 15] defined as,

$$p_{pair} = \frac{\Sigma_{i \leq j} \delta(y(q_i), y(q_j)) \delta(\hat{y}(q_i), \hat{y}(q_j))}{\delta(\hat{y}(q_i), \hat{y}(q_j))} \tag{11}$$

$$r_{pair} = \frac{\Sigma_{i \leq j} \delta(y(q_i), y(q_j)) \delta(\hat{y}(q_i), \hat{y}(q_j))}{\delta(y(q_i), y(q_j))} \tag{12}$$

where p_{pair} evaluates how many pairs of queries predicted in the same task, i.e., $\delta(\hat{y}(q_i), \hat{y}(q_j) = 1$, are actually annotated as in the same task, i.e., $\delta(y(q_i), y(q_j)) = 1$ and r_{pair} evaluates how many pairs annotated as in the same task are recovered by the algorithm. Thus, globally F-measure evaluates the extent to which a task contains only queries of a particular annotated task and all queries of that task. Given p_{pair} and r_{pair}, the F-measure is computed as:$F_1 = \frac{2 \times p_{pair} \times r_{pair}}{p_{pair} + r_{pair}}$.

5.1.2 Results & Discussion. Figure 2 compares the proposed model with alternative probabilistic models and state-of-the-art task identification approaches by F1 score. To make fair comparisons, we consider the last level of the pruned tree constructed as task clusters when computing pairwise precision/recall values. It is important to note that the labelled dataset has only flat tasks extracted on a per user basis; as a result, this dataset is not ideal for making fair comparisons of the proposed hierarchy extraction method with baselines. Nevertheless, the proposed approach manages to outperform existing task extraction baselines while having much greater expressive powers and providing the subdivision of tasks into subtasks. LDA-TW performs the worst since its assumptions on query relationship within the same search task are too strong. The advantage over QC-HTC and QC-WCC demonstrates that appropriate usage of query affinity information can even better reflect the semantic relationship between queries, rather than exploiting it in some collaborative knowledge.

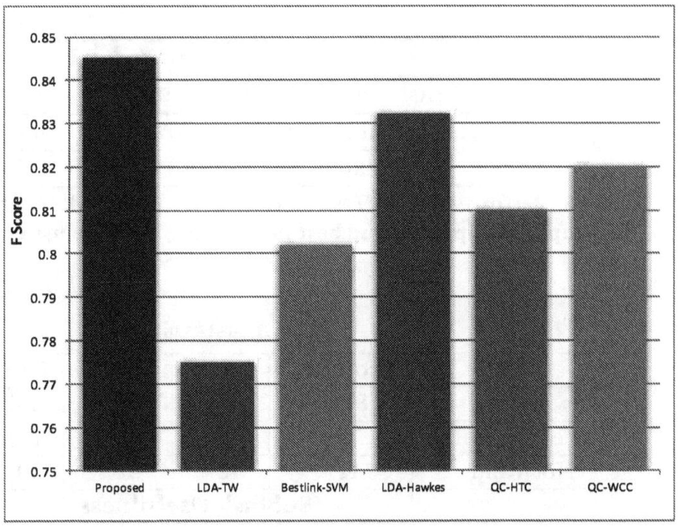

Figure 2: F1 score results on AOL tagged dataset

5.2 Evaluating the Hierarchy

While there are no gold standard datasets for evaluating hierarchies of tasks, we performed crowd-sourced assessments to assess the performance of our hierarchy extraction method. We separately evaluated the coherence and quality of the extracted hierarchies via two different set of judgements obtained via crowdsourcing.

Evaluation Setup

For the judgment study, we make use of the AOL search logs and randomly sampled entire query history of frequent users who had more than 1000 search queries. The AOL log is a very large and long-term collection consisting of about 20 million of Web queries issued by more than 657000 users over 3 months. We run the task extraction algorithms on the entire set of queries of the sampled users and collect judgments to assess the quality of the tasks extracted. Judgments were provided by over 40 judges who were recruited from the Amazon Mechanical Turk crowdsourcing service. We restricted annotators to those based in the US because the logs came from searchers based in the US. We also used hidden quality control questions to filter out poor-quality judges. The judges were provided with detailed guidelines describing the notion of search tasks and subtasks and were provided with several examples to help them better understand the judgement task.

Evaluating Task Coherence

In the first study, we evaluated the quality of the tasks extracted by the task extraction algorithms. In an ideal task extraction system, all the queries belonging to the same task cluster should ideally belong to the same task and hence have better task coherence. To this end, we evaluate the task coherence property of the tasks extracted by the different algorithms. For each of the baselines and the proposed algorithm, we select a task at random from the set of tasks extracted and randomly pick up two queries from the selected task. We then ask the human judges the following question:

	Task Relatedness				
	Proposed	**LDA-TW**	**QC-WCC**	**LDA-Hawkes**	**QC-HTC**
Task Related	**72%***	47%	60%	67%	61%
Somewhat Related	20%	14%	15%	13%	5%
Unrelated	**10%**	23%	25%	20%	34%

Table 3: Performance on Task Relatedness. The results highlighted with * signify statistically significant difference between the proposed approach and best performing baseline using χ^2 test with $p \leq 0.05$.

	Subtask Validity			
	Proposed	**Jones**	**BHCD**	**BAC**
Valid	**81%***	69%	51%	49%
Somewhat Valid	8%	19%	17%	21%
Not Valid	11%	12%	32%	30%
	Subtask Usefulness			
Useful	**67%***	52%	41%	43%
Somewhat Useful	8%	17%	19%	20%
Not Useful	25%	31%	40%	37%

Table 4: Performance on Subtask Validity and Subtask Usefulness. Results highlighted with * signify statistically significant difference between the proposed framework and best performing baseline using χ^2 test with $p \leq 0.05$.

RQ1: Task Relatedness: Are the given pairs of queries related to the same task? The possible options include (i) Task Related, (ii) Somewhat Task Related and (iii) Unrelated.

The task relatedness score provides an estimate of how coherent tasks are. Indeed, a task cluster containing queries from different tasks would score less in Task Relatedness score since if the task cluster is impure, there is a greater chance that the 2 randomly picked queries belong to different tasks and hence get judged Unrelated.

Evaluating the hierarchy

While there are no gold standard dataset to evaluate hierarchies, in our second crowd-sourced judgment study, we evaluate the quality of the hierarchy extracted. A valid task-subtask hierarchy would have the parent task representing a higher level task with its children tasks representing more focused subtasks, each of which help the user achieve the overall task identified by the parent task.

We evaluate the correctness of the hierarchy by validating parent-child task-subtask relationships. More specifically, we randomly select a parent node from the hierarchy and then randomly select a child node from the set of its immediate child nodes. Given such parent-child node pairs, we randomly pick 5 queries from the parent node and randomly pick 2 queries from the child node. We then show the human judges these parent and child queries and ask the following questions:

RQ2: Subtask Validity: Consider the set of queries representing the search task and the pair of queries representing the subtask. How valid is this subtask given the overall task?

The possible judge options include (i) Valid Subtask, (ii) Somewhat valid and (iii) Invalid. Answering this question helps us in analyzing the correctness of the parent-child task-subtask pairs.

RQ3: Subtask Usefulness: Consider the set of queries representing the search task and the pair of queries representing the subtask. Is the subtask useful in completing the overall search task?

The possible judge options include (i) Useful, (ii) Somewhat Useful and (iii) Not Useful. This helps us in evaluating the usefulness of task-subtask pairs by finding the proportion of subtasks which help users in completing the overall task described by the parent node. Overall, the RQ2 and RQ3 help in evaluating the correctness and usefulness of the hierarchy extracted.

Baselines

Since RQ1 evaluates task coherence without any notion of task-subtask structure, we compare against the top performing baselines from the task extraction setup described in section 5.1. On the other hand, RQ2 & RQ3 help in answering questions about the quality of hierarchy constructed. To make fair comparisons while evaluating the hierarchies, we introduce additional hierarchy extraction baselines:

- **Jones Hierarchies** [13]: A supervised learning approach for task boundary detection and same task identification. We train the classifier using the supervised Lucchese AOL task dataset and use it to extract tasks on the current dataset used in the judgment study.
- **BHCD** [3]: A state-of-the-art bayesian hierarchical community detection algorithm based on stochastic blockmodels and makes use of Beta-Bernoulli conjugate priors to define a network. We build a network of queries and apply BHCD algorithm to extract hierarchies of query communities.
- **Bayesian Agglomerative Clustering (BAC)** [11]: A standard agglomerative hierarchical clustering model based on Dirichlet process mixtures.

Results & Discussion

For the first judgment study, each HIT is composed of 20 query pairs per approach being judged for task relatedness. We had three judges work on every HIT. Overall, per method we obtained judgments for 60 query pairs to evaluate the performance on task-relatedness. From among the three judges judging each query-pair, we followed majority voting mechanism to finalize the label for the instance.

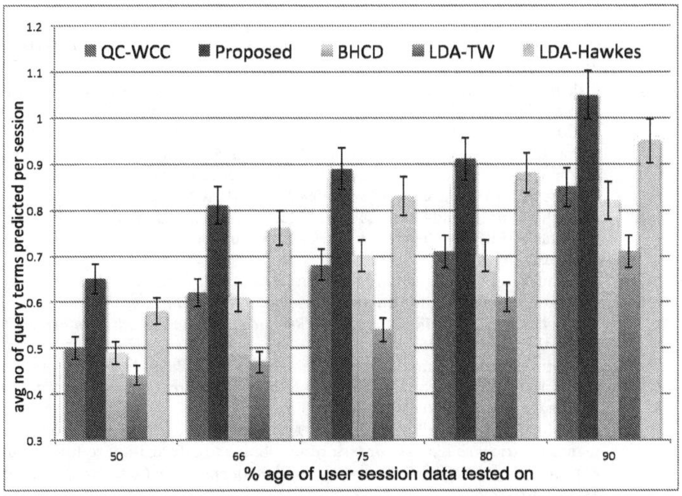

Figure 3: Term Prediction performance

Table 3 presents the proportions of query pairs judged as related. About 72% of query pairs were judged task-related for the proposed approach with LDA-Hawkes performing second best with 67%. Task relatedness measures how pure the task clusters obtained are, a higher score indicates that the queries belonging to the same task are indeed used for solving the same search task. The overall results indicate that the tasks extracted by the proposed task-subtask extraction algorithm are indeed better than those extracted by the baselines.

For the second judgment study used for evaluating the quality of the hierarchy, we show 10 pairs of parent-child questions in each HIT and ask the human annotators to judge the subtask validity and usefulness. Overall, per method we evaluate 300 such judgments resulting in over 1200 judgments and used maximum voting criterion from among the 3 judges to decide the final label for each instance. Table 4 compares the performance of the proposed hierarchy extraction method against other hierarchical baselines. The identified subtask was found useful in 67% cases with the best performing baseline being useful in 52% of judged instances. This highlights that the extracted hierarchy is indeed composed of better subtasks which are found to be useful in completing the overall task depicted by the parent task. It is interesting to note that for BHCD and BAC baselines, most often the subtasks were found to be invalid and not useful.

Since the same parent-child task-subtask was judged for validity and usefulness, it is expected that the proportion of task-subtasks judged useful would be less than the ones judged valid. Indeed, as can be seen from the Table 4, the relative proportions of tasks-subtasks found useful is much less than those found valid.

5.3 Term Prediction

In addition to task extraction and user study based evaluation, we chose to follow an indirect evaluation approach based on *Query Term Prediction* wherein given an initial set of queries, we predict future query terms the user may issue later in the session.This is in line with our goal of supporting users tackling complex search tasks since a task identification system which is capable of identifying "*good*" search tasks will indeed perform better in predicting the set of future query terms.

To evaluate the performance of the proposed task extraction method, we primarily work with the TREC Session Track 2014 [?] and AOL log data and constructed a new dataset consisting of user sessions from AOL logs concerned with Session Track queries. The session track data consists of over 1200 sessions while AOL logs consists of 20M search queries issued by over 657K users. We find the intersection of queries between the Session Track data and AOL logs to identify user sessions in AOL data trying to achieve similar task objectives. The Session Track dataset consists of 60 different ***topics***. For each of these 60 topics, we separately find user sessions from the entire AOL logs which contain query overlaps with these topics. For each topic, we iterate through the entire AOL logs and select any user session which contains query overlap with the current topic. As a result, we obtain a total of 14030 user sessions which contain around 6.4M queries.

Given the initial queries from a user session and a set of tasks extracted from Session Track data, we leverage queries from the identified task to predict future query terms. For each Session Track topic, we construct a task hierarchy and use the constructed task hierarchy to predict future query terms in the associated user sessions. More specifically, for each topic, we split each user session into two parts: (i) task matching and (ii) held-out evaluation part. We use queries from the task matching part of user sessions to obtain the right node in the task hierarchy from which we then recommend query terms. We pick the tree node which has the highest cosine similarity score based on all the query terms under consideration. We evaluate based on the absolute recall scores - the average number of recommended query terms which match with the query terms in the held-out evaluation part of user sessions.

We baseline against the top performing task extraction baselines from Section 5.1 as well as the top performing hierarchical algorithms from Section 5.2. To make fair comparisons, we consider nodes at the bottom most level of the pruned tree for task matching and term recommendation.

Figure 3 compares the performance on term prediction against the considered baselines. We plot the average number of query terms predicted against the proportion of user session data used. The proposed method is able to better predict future query terms than a standard task extraction baseline as well as a very recent hierarchy construction algorithm.

6 CONCLUSION

Search task hierarchies provide us with a more naturalistic view of considering complex tasks and representing the embedded task-subtask relationships. In this paper we first motivated the need for considering hierarchies of search tasks & subtasks and presented a novel bayesian nonparametric approach which extracts such hierarchies. We introduced a conjugate query affinity model to capture query affinities to help in task extraction. Finally, we propose the idea of Task Coherence and use it to identify atomic tasks. Our experiments demonstrated the benefits of considering search task hierarchies. Importantly, we were able to demonstrate competitive performance while at the same time outputting a richer and more expressive model of search tasks. This expands the scope for better task recommendation, better search personalization and opens up new avenues for recommendations specifically targeting users based on the tasks they are involved in.

REFERENCES

[1] Eugene Agichtein, Ryen W White, Susan T Dumais, and Paul N Bennet. 2012. Search, interrupted: understanding and predicting search task continuation. In *Proceedings of the 35th international ACM SIGIR conference on Research and development in information retrieval*. ACM, 315–324.

[2] Ricardo Baeza-Yates, Carlos Hurtado, and Marcelo Mendoza. 2004. Query recommendation using query logs in search engines. In *International Conference on Extending Database Technology*. Springer, 588–596.

[3] Charles Blundell and Yee Whye Teh. 2013. Bayesian hierarchical community discovery. In *Advances in Neural Information Processing Systems*. 1601–1609.

[4] Charles Blundell, Yee Whye Teh, and Katherine A Heller. 2012. Bayesian rose trees. *arXiv preprint arXiv:1203.3468* (2012).

[5] Huanhuan Cao, Daxin Jiang, Jian Pei, Enhong Chen, and Hang Li. 2009. Towards context-aware search by learning a very large variable length hidden markov model from search logs. In *Proceedings of the 18th international conference on World wide web*. ACM, 191–200.

[6] Lara D Catledge and James E Pitkow. 1995. Characterizing browsing strategies in the World-Wide Web. *Computer Networks and ISDN systems* 27, 6 (1995), 1065–1073.

[7] Shui-Lung Chuang and Lee-Feng Chien. 2002. Towards automatic generation of query taxonomy: A hierarchical query clustering approach. In *Data Mining, 2002. ICDM 2003. Proceedings. 2002 IEEE International Conference on*. IEEE, 75–82.

[8] Debora Donato, Francesco Bonchi, Tom Chi, and Yoelle Maarek. 2010. Do you want to take notes?: identifying research missions in Yahoo! search pad. In *Proceedings of the 19th international conference on World wide web*. ACM, 321–330.

[9] Ahmed Hassan Awadallah, Ryen W White, Patrick Pantel, Susan T Dumais, and Yi-Min Wang. 2014. Supporting complex search tasks. In *Proceedings of the 23rd ACM International Conference on Conference on Information and Knowledge Management*. ACM, 829–838.

[10] Daqing He, Ayşe Göker, and David J Harper. 2002. Combining evidence for automatic web session identification. *Information Processing & Management* 38, 5 (2002), 727–742.

[11] Katherine A Heller and Zoubin Ghahramani. 2005. Bayesian hierarchical clustering. In *Proceedings of the 22nd international conference on Machine learning*. ACM, 297–304.

[12] Wen Hua, Yangqiu Song, Haixun Wang, and Xiaofang Zhou. 2013. Identifying users' topical tasks in web search. In *Proceedings of the sixth ACM international conference on Web search and data mining*. ACM, 93–102.

[13] Rosie Jones and Kristina Lisa Klinkner. 2008. Beyond the session timeout: automatic hierarchical segmentation of search topics in query logs. In *Proceedings of the 17th ACM conference on Information and knowledge management*. ACM, 699–708.

[14] Rosie Jones, Benjamin Rey, Omid Madani, and Wiley Greiner. 2006. Generating query substitutions. In *Proceedings of the 15th international conference on World Wide Web*. ACM, 387–396.

[15] Alexander Kotov, Paul N Bennett, Ryen W White, Susan T Dumais, and Jaime Teevan. 2011. Modeling and analysis of cross-session search tasks. In *Proceedings of the 34th international ACM SIGIR conference on Research and development in Information Retrieval*. ACM, 5–14.

[16] Dawn J Lawrie and W Bruce Croft. 2003. Generating hierarchical summaries for web searches. In *Proceedings of the 26th annual international ACM SIGIR conference on Research and development in informaion retrieval*. ACM, 457–458.

[17] Liangda Li, Hongbo Deng, Anlei Dong, Yi Chang, and Hongyuan Zha. 2014. Identifying and labeling search tasks via query-based hawkes processes. In *Proceedings of the 20th ACM SIGKDD international conference on Knowledge discovery and data mining*. ACM, 731–740.

[18] Zhen Liao, Yang Song, Li-wei He, and Yalou Huang. 2012. Evaluating the effectiveness of search task trails. In *Proceedings of the 21st international conference on World Wide Web*. ACM, 489–498.

[19] Xueqing Liu, Yangqiu Song, Shixia Liu, and Haixun Wang. 2012. Automatic taxonomy construction from keywords. In *Proceedings of the 18th ACM SIGKDD international conference on Knowledge discovery and data mining*. ACM, 1433–1441.

[20] Claudio Lucchese, Salvatore Orlando, Raffaele Perego, Fabrizio Silvestri, and Gabriele Tolomei. 2011. Identifying task-based sessions in search engine query logs. In *Proceedings of the fourth ACM international conference on Web search and data mining*. ACM, 277–286.

[21] Claudio Lucchese, Salvatore Orlando, Raffaele Perego, Fabrizio Silvestri, and Gabriele Tolomei. 2013. Discovering tasks from search engine query logs. *ACM Transactions on Information Systems (TOIS)* 31, 3 (2013), 14.

[22] Bonnie Ma Kay and Carolyn Watters. 2008. Exploring multi-session web tasks. In *Proceedings of the SIGCHI Conference on Human Factors in Computing Systems*. ACM, 1187–1196.

[23] Rishabh Mehrotra, Prasanta Bhattacharya, and Emine Yilmaz. 2016. Characterizing users' multi-tasking behavior in web search. In *Proceedings of the 2016 ACM on Conference on Human Information Interaction and Retrieval*. ACM, 297–300.

[24] Rishabh Mehrotra and Emine Yilmaz. 2015. Terms, topics & tasks: Enhanced user modelling for better personalization. In *Proceedings of the 2015 International Conference on The Theory of Information Retrieval*. ACM, 131–140.

[25] Rishabh Mehrotra and Emine Yilmaz. 2015. Towards hierarchies of search tasks & subtasks. In *Proceedings of the 24th International Conference on World Wide Web*. ACM, 73–74.

[26] Qiaozhu Mei, Hui Fang, and ChengXiang Zhai. 2007. A study of Poisson query generation model for information retrieval. In *Proceedings of the 30th annual international ACM SIGIR conference on Research and development in information retrieval*. ACM, 319–326.

[27] Qiaozhu Mei, Dengyong Zhou, and Kenneth Church. 2008. Query suggestion using hitting time. In *Proceedings of the 17th ACM conference on Information and knowledge management*. ACM, 469–478.

[28] Dan Morris, Meredith Ringel Morris, and Gina Venolia. 2008. SearchBar: a search-centric web history for task resumption and information re-finding. In *Proceedings of the SIGCHI Conference on Human Factors in Computing Systems*. ACM, 1207–1216.

[29] David Newman, Jey Han Lau, Karl Grieser, and Timothy Baldwin. 2010. Automatic evaluation of topic coherence. In *Human Language Technologies: The 2010 Annual Conference of the North American Chapter of the Association for Computational Linguistics*. Association for Computational Linguistics, 100–108.

[30] Brendan O'Connor, Michel Krieger, and David Ahn. 2010. TweetMotif: Exploratory Search and Topic Summarization for Twitter.. In *ICWSM*. 384–385.

[31] Pavel Pecina. 2010. Lexical association measures and collocation extraction. *Language resources and evaluation* 44, 1-2 (2010), 137–158.

[32] Eran Segal and Daphne Koller. 2002. Probabilistic hierarchical clustering for biological data. In *Proceedings of the sixth annual international conference on Computational biology*. ACM, 273–280.

[33] Craig Silverstein, Hannes Marais, Monika Henzinger, and Michael Moricz. 1999. Analysis of a very large web search engine query log. In *ACm SIGIR Forum*, Vol. 33. ACM, 6–12.

[34] Adish Singla, Ryen White, and Jeff Huang. 2010. Studying trailfinding algorithms for enhanced web search. In *Proceedings of the 33rd international ACM SIGIR conference on Research and development in information retrieval*. ACM, 443–450.

[35] Amanda Spink, Sherry Koshman, Minsoo Park, Chris Field, and Bernard J Jansen. 2005. Multitasking web search on vivisimo. com. In *Information Technology: Coding and Computing, 2005. ITCC 2005. International Conference on*, Vol. 2. IEEE, 486–490.

[36] Hongning Wang, Yang Song, Ming-Wei Chang, Xiaodong He, Ahmed Hassan, and Ryen W White. 2014. Modeling action-level satisfaction for search task satisfaction prediction. In *Proceedings of the 37th international ACM SIGIR conference on Research & development in information retrieval*. ACM, 123–132.

[37] Hongning Wang, Yang Song, Ming-Wei Chang, Xiaodong He, Ryen W White, and Wei Chu. 2013. Learning to extract cross-session search tasks. In *Proceedings of the 22nd international conference on World Wide Web*. ACM, 1353–1364.

[38] Ryen W White, Wei Chu, Ahmed Hassan, Xiaodong He, Yang Song, and Hongning Wang. 2013. Enhancing personalized search by mining and modeling task behavior. In *Proceedings of the 22nd international conference on World Wide Web*. ACM, 1411–1420.

[39] Hui Yang. 2012. Constructing task-specific taxonomies for document collection browsing. In *Proceedings of the 2012 Joint Conference on Empirical Methods in Natural Language Processing and Computational Natural Language Learning*. Association for Computational Linguistics, 1278–1289.

[40] Hui Yang. 2015. Browsing hierarchy construction by minimum evolution. *ACM Transactions on Information Systems (TOIS)* 33, 3 (2015), 13.

[41] Yongfeng Zhang, Min Zhang, Yiqun Liu, Chua Tat-Seng, Yi Zhang, and Shaoping Ma. 2015. Task-based recommendation on a web-scale. In *Big Data (Big Data), 2015 IEEE International Conference on*. IEEE, 827–836.

Using Information Scent to Understand Mobile and Desktop Web Search Behavior

Kevin Ong
School of Science
RMIT University
kevin.ong@rmit.edu.au

Kalervo Järvelin
School of Information Science
University of Tampere
kalervo.jarvelin@uta.fi

Mark Sanderson
School of Science
RMIT University
mark.sanderson@rmit.edu.au

Falk Scholer
School of Science
RMIT University
falk.scholer@rmit.edu.au

ABSTRACT

This paper investigates if Information Foraging Theory can be used to understand differences in user behavior when searching on mobile and desktop web search systems. Two groups of thirty-six participants were recruited to carry out six identical web search tasks on desktop or on mobile. The search tasks were prepared with a different number and distribution of relevant documents on the first result page. Search behaviors on mobile and desktop were measurably different. Desktop participants viewed and clicked on more results but saved fewer as relevant, compared to mobile participants, when information scent level increased. Mobile participants achieved higher search accuracy than desktop participants for tasks with increasing numbers of relevant search results. Conversely, desktop participants were more accurate than mobile participants for tasks with an equal number of relevant results that were more distributed across the results page. Overall, both an increased number and better positioning of relevant search results improved the ability of participants to locate relevant results on both desktop and mobile. Participants spent more time and issued more queries on desktop, but abandoned less and saved more results for initial queries on mobile.

CCS CONCEPTS

•**Human-centered computing** → **HCI theory, concepts and models;** •**Information systems** → *Information retrieval query processing; Users and interactive retrieval;*

KEYWORDS

Information Foraging Theory; Search Process; Search Stopping

1 INTRODUCTION

Information Foraging Theory [24] (IFT) seeks to understand how information seekers behave when searching. The theory compares information seeking behavior to food-foraging strategies used by animals. It posits that information seekers will adapt their behavior and gravitate towards an equilibrium that optimizes valuable information gain per unit cost [24].

An Information Scent model has been proposed [6], which is a prediction model based on IFT. It suggests that information seekers will use visual cues to guide them towards relevant information sources. Such cues can come from the contents of a Search Engine Result Page (SERP), which contains information (e.g. title, URL, summary) about retrieved documents. Searchers can then make use of this information to help them decide if a document is relevant and if they will click on it. Researchers applied the Information Scent model to a study of desktop web search behavior by varying the number of relevant search results (*level*) and their distribution (*pattern*) [31]. They found that both features are predictive of some user behaviors. Searchers are more likely to abandon their search if: 1) fewer relevant search results are presented or 2) the relevant search results are in lower positions on a SERP.

It has been argued that the continual growth of mobile search has brought a paradigm shift in web search behavior. Searching on mobile and desktop can be considered as searching in different environments. Mobile is different from desktop in terms of timely access to information and differences in screen sizes [9]. The applicability of desktop-based interface research findings to mobile environments is not clear. It is therefore worth investigating whether different environments affect mobile and desktop search behavior differently.

We focus our efforts on understanding how differences between mobile and desktop affect search behavior. We investigate the effect of staying above the fold, a concept borrowed from print-newspaper terminology, on search behavior. *Above the fold* refers to the portion of the SERP that is immediately seen on screen; *below the fold* refers to the portion that needs to be scrolled to. Using IFT, we seek to understand the extent to which information scent may influence search behavior in different environments. We address the following research questions:

RQ1: To what degree can mobile and desktop web search behavior be explained by Information Scent Level (ISL)?
We vary the number of relevant information items in a SERP and measure searchers' behavior in mobile and desktop environments.

SIGIR '17, August 07-11, 2017, Shinjuku, Tokyo, Japan
© 2017 ACM. 978-1-4503-5022-8/17/08...$15.00
DOI: http://dx.doi.org/10.1145/3077136.3080817

RQ2: To what degree can mobile and desktop web search behavior be explained by Information Scent Pattern (ISP)? We vary the distribution of a fixed number of relevant search results in a SERP and measure searchers' behavior.

RQ3: How does search behavior differ as a result of different environments? Information visibility can influence search behavior [13]. We use different environments (desktop and mobile) as representatives of different folds to measure the differences in search behavior. We seek to understand how different levels of visibility may influence search behavior when users are given the same search tasks with identical ISL/ISP conditions but in different environments.

2 LITERATURE REVIEW

The development of search models is studied widely by the information science community [2, 24, 31]. In this section, we discuss research related to understanding search behavior.

2.1 Web Search Behavior

A wide range of observational studies have had been conducted on web search behavior on desktop [2, 8, 10, 13] and mobile [14, 15, 18, 20, 21, 26].

Desktop Web Search: *Granka et al.* [10] studied thirty-six users focusing on their actions before the selection of the first retrieved document. They found that the users tended to focus on URLs in particular, and the first and second search results in the SERP. *Joachims et al.* [13] found that users clicked on the first result regardless of the quality of subsequent results. They observed that users tended to perform a top-down search pattern and placed substantial trust in the search engine's ordering of documents. They also observed that the quality of retrieved results influenced clicking behavior. When the SERPs were made deliberately worse, users clicked on fewer relevant search results. *Cutrell and Guan* [8] studied twenty-two participants using an eye tracker while they conducted *informational* and *navigational* tasks [3]. They observed that users preferred longer snippets for informational tasks and shorter for navigational tasks. User's search accuracy (i.e. clicking on relevant search results) was improved for informational tasks but degraded for navigational tasks when snippet lengths were increased. Similar to previous work [13], the researchers ascertained that the ranking of relevant search results influenced user behavior. When relevant results were placed in lower positions in a SERP, users were less likely to locate those results. *Azzopardi et al.* [2] studied thirty-six undergraduate students. They associated *query cost* with the degree of difficulty in issuing search queries. An inverse relationship between query number and search depth was observed. They found that when search interfaces got more complicated, users issued fewer queries and increased search depth. *Maxwell et al.* [22] later proposed six search stopping strategies based on *disgust* and *frustration* point rules, to predict the moment when a user would stop searching. One strategy, stoppage after a certain fixed depth, was found to be accurate.

Searching on Mobile: Search behavior on mobile can be different from desktop [7, 9, 14, 15, 20]. *Jones et al.* [14] studied twenty computer science students and staff on two tasks using desktop screens and mobile (simulated) screens. Mobile participants were twice as likely to fail in finding relevant information and twice as likely to use the search functions, compared to desktop participants. Searchers would rather use the search function than attempt to locate the relevant information manually when it was harder to find on the page. However, it was noted that both groups were using actual physical keyboards, which might influence their preference for search functions for the mobile participants. Finding relevant information involves entering queries and examining results. When input was unhindered, search increased [14]. When given actual devices, however, searchers issued both shorter and fewer queries on mobile than on desktop [15]. In a study by *Kamvar and Baluja* [16], the average number of queries per session on mobile was two. A later comparative mobile study by *Song et al.* [28] found that the average length of users' issued queries increased but this was attributed to a better auto-completion feature on mobile. It was also observed that the number of query submissions per session on mobile was smaller than on desktop. *Ghose et al.* [9] observed that the ranking effects of results were greater on mobile than on desktop due to the limited number of results that can be displayed at once. Scrolling through more results incurs cognitive costs, as the searcher has to remember past results. *Lagun et al.* [20] studied mobile search behavior of thirty participants. Similar to past work [13], they observed that position bias affected user search accuracy when searching on mobile devices. However, they found users spent more time on second and third results compared to the first. *Ren et al.* [26] examined mobile search behavior in a large indoor retail space by analyzing ISP logs over a one-year period and found that mobile Web searching and browsing behavior was different. *Church et al.* [7] carried out a diary study over four weeks to study twenty users' mobile information needs. They found that mobile information needs differ significantly from general Web (i.e. desktop) needs. As users increasingly use mobile as their only device for search[1], mobile information needs and search deserve further attention.

2.2 Search Strategies

Considering search strategies, *Klöckner et al.* [19] observed two distinct approaches: breadth-first (skimming through a number of snippets first before clicking) and depth-first search (clicking each document sequentially before looking at new snippets). They observed that users who preferred depth-first search were significantly more likely to click a promising link before looking at others within the list. *Teevan et al.* [29] interviewed fifteen Computer Science graduates twice a day over five days, grouping them into *filers* (people who organized information using fixed structures) and *pilers* (people who maintained unstructured information organization). They observed that filers and pilers relied on two different search strategies. Filers relied more on keyword searches, while pilers were more likely to use site search engines (such as eBay site search) rather than generic search engines. *Aula et al.* [1] used an eye tracker to study twenty-eight users and also observed two types of search strategy patterns: *economic* and *exhaustive*. Similar

[1] https://storage.googleapis.com/think/docs/twg-how-people-use-their-devices-2016.pdf

to depth-first searchers [19], they found that *economic* users examined results sequentially from the top-down and clicked on the first relevant search result they saw, whereas *exhaustive* searchers examined all results before even considering which to click. *White and Drucker* [30] studied the extent of users' search behavior variability over a five month period. They concluded that information seekers can be classified into two broad categories: *Navigators* and *Explorers.* Navigators, like filers, employ a search strategy to organize information, with directed searches and topical coherence in the search trails. Explorers, similar to pilers, have information overlap (re-visits to multiple links) when searching for information. *Kim et al.* [17] investigated search examination strategies on different screen sizes with thirty-two participants using *Klöckner et al. [19]*'s taxonomy. They observed that users implemented more breadth-first and fewer depth-first strategies on a large screen than on a small screen, contrary to *Klöckner et al. [19]*'s findings. Apart from Kim et al. [17], these previous works looked at search strategies on the desktop and suggested that user factors and individual differences resulted in two distinct search strategies of interaction with search engines. *Li et al.* [21] discussed the concept of *good abandonment.* It was considered as good abandonment when a user's information need was already satisfied by information displayed on the SERP itself resulting in no result clicks. The good abandonment rate was found to be significantly higher on mobile than on desktop. In general, the ease of query inputs and the difficulty in finding relevant information would both encourage additional reformulations beyond the first queries.

2.3 Information Foraging

Information Foraging Theory (IFT) was proposed by *Pirolli and Card* [24] to understand web search behavior from an ecological standpoint. Information seekers, analogous to food foraging animals, will evolve over time to optimize their information seeking, gathering, and consumption behaviors. There are three derivative models from IFT: Diet Selection (factors that determine the preference for one type of information over another), Information Patch (factors to remain within sources of information) and Information Scent (factors that determine the value of information based on visual cues and metadata). The use of Information Scent [5] has been suggested to explain a user's web search behavior on SERPs [8, 31].

Card et al. [4] later developed the Web Behavior Graphs methodology using IFT, to illustrate search structures performed by users. They concluded that Information Scent played an important role in the methodology. *Cutrell and Guan* [8] found that positions of relevant search results influenced searcher's behavior and suggested the use of IFT for future work. *Wu et al.* [31] then conducted an IFT-based study to understand user behavior on the desktop. SERPs with different *levels* and *distributions* of Information Scent conditions were prepared. Participants viewed documents in lower positions when more relevant search results were present. They also abandoned their search earlier if relevant search results were only shown later on the SERPs. A cognitive scale, Need For Cognition (NFC) measures the extent to which a person enjoys tasks that require thinking. *Wu et al.* found that for users interacting with SERPs with a medium level of information scent, search behavior

	ISL			ISP		
Rank	ILL	ILM	ILH	IPB	IPP	IPD
1	**R**	**R**	**R**	–	**R**	**R**
2	–	**R**	**R**	–	**R**	**R**
3	–	**R**	**R**	–	–	**R**
Above the fold (mobile) ↑ *Below the fold (mobile)* ↓						
4	–	–	**R**	**R**	–	**R**
5	–	–	**R**	**R**	**R**	–
6	–	–	–	**R**	–	–
7	–	–	–	**R**	–	–
8	–	–	–	–	**R**	–
Above the fold (desktop) ↑ *Below the fold (desktop)* ↓						
9	–	–	–	–	–	–
10	–	–	–	–	–	–

Figure 1: SERP display following first query for each ISL/ISP condition. (R = relevant; – = not relevant). Eight and three results are above the fold (immediately seen without scrolling) on the desktop and mobile respectively.

was different depending on a user's NFC; users with higher NFC tended to ignore lower-ranked search results and to paginate less.

Past work has demonstrated the differences between desktop and mobile search behavior. Additionally, it has been shown that IFT can be used to understand search behavior better. However, we found no comparative work that discussed the influence of different environments on search behavior or search strategies using IFT.

3 EXPERIMENTAL SETUP

The experimental design is based on previous work by *Wu et al. [31]*, where users are asked to carry out searches with an experimental IR system modeled closely on a web search engine. Users are asked to mark the search results which they believe to be relevant to the current search topic. Our study has some modifications and one key difference. Instead of being required to view each search document and indicate the item as relevant, participants in the experiments save each result as relevant using a checkbox displayed next to each snippet directly on the search results page. We made it optional for participants to view actual documents. This is done so as to estimate the likelihood that users would only view a snippet to decide if a document is relevant. This is particularly important for mobile, due to higher good abandonment rate [21]. The study was run in two environments: searching on a desktop and on a mobile device. For both, participants were asked to find relevant search results for a provided task until they were satisfied. Six open-ended search topics and one demo topic were prepared beforehand for the user studies. The first search result page was fixed in content and layout so as to ensure particular levels and patterns of relevant and non-relevant documents were present in the SERP. Figure 1 shows the layout of retrieved documents for each of the ISL (Low, Medium, and High) and ISP (Bursting, Persistent, and Disrupted). ISL-Low (ILL), ISL-Medium (ILM), ISL-High (ILH) contained one, three and five relevant search results from the first position respectively. ISP-Bursting (IPB), ISP-Persistent (IPP), ISP-Disrupted (IPD) distributed four relevant search results on the first SERP. ISP showed zero, half and all relevant search results above the fold under IPB, IPP and IPD conditions on mobile.

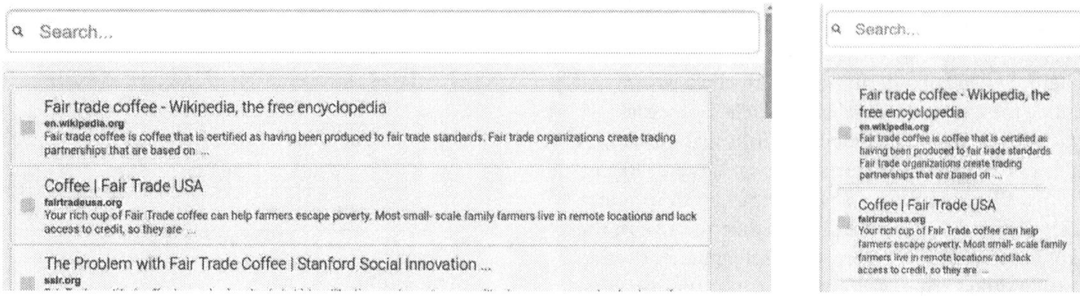

(a) desktop (b) mobile

Figure 2: Mockups of the search Interface used by participants for desktop and mobile search respectively

3.1 Participants

Seventy-two students from various disciplines, aged between 18 to 47, were recruited in a local campus library to participate in the user studies via opportunistic sampling. The study was reviewed and approved by the RMIT University Human Research Ethics Committee. All participants claimed to be English language and search engine proficient. They completed a total of 429 search tasks on both desktop and mobile, with our custom built search engine. We excluded 3 search tasks from 2 participants due to problems with logging and system stability issues.

3.2 Tasks

Participants were divided into two groups of thirty-six, to carry out their searches using either desktop or mobile devices. Each participant completed the same six search tasks. Half the tasks to investigate the influence of ISL and the remaining half on the influence of ISP. These were the same six informational tasks developed by *Wu et al.* [31]. Each task was presented to participants with a predefined topic description and participants were free to express their queries as they saw fit. However, for their first query for each task, the participants saw a predefined SERP drawn from one of the ISL/ISP conditions in Figure 1. Topics and Information Scent conditions were rotated and counter-balanced to avoid possible learning and ordering effects. Therefore, each task with identical ISL/ISP conditions was seen twelve times across all the participants, but in a random order.

All videos, images, maps, PDFs, and related links were removed so that all tasks showed the same text search results. All result pages for the first query for each topic were cached locally, and documents were shown should the participants chose to open any link. The topics were chosen to be relatively simple, which should take no more than 5–7 minutes to complete. Participants were told not to spend more than 45 minutes in total, but could freely allocate their time between topics. They were also free to leave the study at any time - though none did. At the end of the session, they were compensated with a $20 voucher for their participation.

Procedure. All participants were first introduced to the experiment and were asked to fill out a pre-task questionnaire on their search experience and expertise. They then performed a simple test to collect information on their typing behavior and were given the demo task for them to familiarize with the search interface, as well as to reinforce the perception that the search results were live. The search interface was created to have a similar feel to a commercial search engine (see Figure 2).

After reading each topic motivation and description, participants were free to type in any query into the interface and were asked to find as many relevant search results as possible until they were satisfied. Participants could save relevant results at any time by marking a checkbox next to each result in a SERP. After their first query for each task, the search results for subsequent reformulations were retrieved from a commercial search engine. We did not prepare the SERPs for additional reformulations according to ISL/ISP conditions because reformulation search behavior is different from initial search behavior [27].

SERP Construction. A set of relevant and non-relevant search results were constructed by issuing queries to a commercial search engine. We used the top issued queries from previous work [31] and submitted our own non-relevant search queries. We combined the relevant and non-relevant search results into a SERP according to the order dictated by Figure 1. Three assessors then evaluated the search result lists based on the topic statement. Results that were not agreed upon by all three assessors were discarded until enough search results were gathered to construct the SERP pages for all six topics. We also placed three relevant search results in the twelfth, fifteenth, and eighteenth positions on the second SERP. This was displayed to participants who choose to view results beyond the first ten search results, for all six result list patterns, so that participants would not find viewing the second page to be fruitless.

3.3 Apparatus

Desktop. Participants in this group completed the search tasks on a laptop with a 15” screen. We gathered information about their preferred device as the keyboard may not be the one they are familiar with. However, we found no correlation in regard to keyboard familiarity and typing behavior by the time they finished the demo task. Participants were also provided with a mouse to interact with the search results. However, they could choose to use the trackpad if they preferred. In the desktop environment, eight results are visible above the fold.

Table 1: Average Relevant Scent (ARS) values.

	ILL	ILM	ILH	IPB	IPP	IPD
ARS value	1.0	2.0	3.0	5.5	4.0	2.5

Mobile. Participants in this group could choose to use either an iPhone 6 or Samsung S6 to complete their task. The iPhone 6 display is 4.7" while the Samsung S6 display is 5.1". To account for the differences in screen size, the font sizes on both devices was calibrated as closely as possible to ensure that the number of characters across both screens were similar when viewing the SERP. Three results were visible above the fold on both devices.

3.4 Measurements

We record two types of search behavior: task level and initial query level.

Task level search behavior:

- **TimeTotal**: Total Time spent examining search results per task.
- **NumQuery**: Number of query submissions per task.

Initial query search behavior:

- **QueryAction**: The first action carried out after an *initial* query submission, apart from viewing/marking documents on the SERPs: (1) issuing a new query (*Reformulation* action), (2) viewing the second SERP (*Pagination* action) without reformulation or (3) ending the task after viewing the first SERP (*Stopping* action) without (1) and (2).
- **Time**: The time spent examining search results for the first query per task.
- **NumPage**: The number of SERP paginations per task.
- **NumClick**: The number of documents examined for each search result set.
- **DRC**: The lowest search result position among all clicked documents, 0 if no results were clicked.
- **DRV**: The lowest search result position that became visible on screen during a search, logged using a Javascript package. If the participant fetches the second page, search depth ranges from 11–20.
- **ROA**: Rate Of Abandonment is the rate of not clicking or saving any document as relevant, following the initial query submission for each task.
- **DRS**: The lowest position of search results on the first SERP saved as relevant per participant.
- **STotal**: The total number of search results on the first SERP saved as relevant per topic per participant.

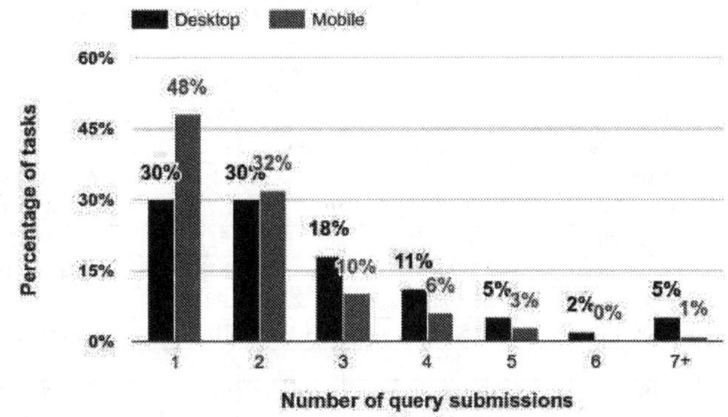

Figure 3: Number of query submissions per task.

- **SRele**: The total number of relevant search results on the first SERP (according to ISL/ISP relevance conditions) saved as relevant per topic per participant.
- **SRele%**: The percentage of saved relevant search results against the total number of relevant search results on the first SERP. A higher value indicates better search accuracy.

3.5 Calculating Average Relevant Scent (ARS)

We define Average Relevant Scent (ARS) as the average rank position of relevant documents on the first SERP:

$$ARS = \frac{\sum pos_d}{\sum doc} \quad (1)$$

where pos_d is the position of relevant document d on the first SERP and doc is the number of relevant documents on the first SERP. ARS attempts to summarize the depth to which participants are willing to examine documents on the first SERP based on the different information scent conditions. These values are given in Table 1.

4 RESULTS

Across the two groups of 36 participants and 429 search tasks, 414 mobile and 568 desktop queries were submitted over the study. The mean time taken for each task was less than 5 minutes. Shortest and longest time per task on the desktop was 81 seconds and 18.5 minutes; on mobile, 71 seconds and 15.4 minutes.

Figure 3 illustrates the distribution of query submissions across all the tasks. 60% and 80% of the tasks were completed with 1 to 2 query submissions on desktop and mobile environments respectively. The distribution of queries was more gradual on the desktop than mobile. Only 12% of desktop and 4% of mobile tasks exceeded 4 queries per topic.

Table 2: Search behavior at the environment level.

	TimeTotal (sec)	Time	NumQuery	NumPage	NumClick	DRC	DRV	ROA	DRS	STotal	SRele
Desktop	267****	64	2.67****	.46*	.58*	2.54*	14.15****	22%*	3.11*	1.81	1.70
Mobile	214****	61	1.92****	.35*	.42*	1.59*	11.81****	14%*	3.49*	1.94	1.77

Wilcoxon signed-rank test: *$p < .05$, **$p < .01$, ***$p < .001$, ****$p < .0001$

Table 3: Search behavior measures (M, SD) by Information Scent Level (ISL).

ISL	Desktop			Mobile		
Measures	**ILL**	**ILM**	**ILH**	ILL	ILM	ILH
TimeTotal#	265.58 (110.60)*	**280.20 (185.70)**	260.17 (143.99)	201.77 (95.04)*	214.26 (111.84)	**218.63 (146.65)**
Time#	47.92 (28.19)	57.37 (38.11)	**62.94 (39.85)**	43.06 (21.20)	**62.37 (44.21)**	53.91 (26.39)
NumQuery	**2.97 (2.17)***	2.74 (1.74)	2.94 (2.39)**	2.03 (1.06)*	**2.22 (2.13)**	1.89 (1.43)**
NumPage	.31 (.47)	.46 (.51)	**.49 (.51)**	.28 (.45)	**.31 (.47)**	**.31 (.47)**
NumClick	.39 (.49)	.40 (.81)	**.69 (1.16)***	.19 (.40)	**.56 (.91)**	.31 (.92)*
DRC	1.53 (3.88)****	**2.17 (5.08)******	2.00 (4.35)*	.50 (1.84)****	.75 (1.16)****	**1.31 (3.90)***
DRV	12.44 (5.18)*	14.17 (5.38)**	**14.34 (5.41)****	10.83 (5.60)*	11.17 (5.74)**	**11.69 (5.19)****
ROA[1]	39%	23%	**17%**	28%	**11%**	**11%**
DRS	.53 (.56)***	1.86 (1.44)	**3.17 (2.55)**	1.42 (2.13)***	2.42 (1.65)	**3.69 (2.45)**
STotal	.53 (.56)*	1.60 (1.33)	**2.37 (1.88)**	.92 (.91)*	1.86 (1.25)	**2.78 (1.74)**
SRele	.50 (.51)	1.49 (1.09)	**2.26 (1.80)**	.61 (.49)	1.64 (1.07)	**2.61 (1.55)**
SRele%	**50%**	49%	45%	**61%**	55%	52%

Mean and (standard deviation) values are shown. Significant differences are indicated for same ISL conditions across different environments.
[1] Lowest value for ROA were bold for higher user interaction.
- indicates Student's t-test, otherwise Chi-squared test. Note: $*p < .05$, $**p < .01$, $***p < .001$, $****p < .0001$.

Desktop Versus Mobile Search Behavior: General search behavior trends are reported in Table 2. The Wilcoxon signed-rank test is used to evaluate the significance of differences in distributions of values between the two environments: desktop and mobile. We report significant differences between both environments where $p < 0.05$. Participants spent significantly longer TimeTotal per task on desktops compared to mobiles ($p < .0001$). The participants submitted 2.67 and 1.92 queries on average, for desktop and mobile respectively ($p < .0001$). Participants on desktop issued more queries (NumQuery) and viewed lower rank positions (DRV) than on mobile ($p < .0001$). In addition, NumPage, NumClick, and DRC were significantly different between mobile and desktop ($p < .05$). DRS was lower ($p < .05$) on mobile for the first query. Overall, search behavior across desktops and mobiles was measurably different. While desktop participants searched and viewed more results, fewer results were saved for their first queries.

ISL & Search Behavior: Considering the influence of different Information Scent Level (ISL) conditions between desktop and mobile search behavior, Figure 4 shows the distribution of three main QueryActions across tasks for different ISL conditions. On the desktop, *R*eformulation decreased by 20% from 83.3% to 66.7% while both *P*agination and *S*topping increased by 75% and 148% respectively, when ISL increased from ILL to ILH. On the mobile, *R* decreased by 24% from 58.3% to 44.4% while both *P* and *S* increased by 14% and 50% respectively, when ISL increased from ILL to ILH conditions. Between ILL and ILM condition on mobile, *P* did not increase.

We test the significance of changes in search behavior due to ISL using the Chi-square test, with results reported in Table 3. Significant differences between different ISL conditions for $p < 0.05$ are reported. The critical values for X^2 across the ISL conditions for both desktop and mobile environments are reported separately in Table 5 (left side). There are significant differences between different ISL conditions for both desktop and mobile for DRS, STotal, and SRele ($p < .0001$). For mobile, NumClick ($p < .05$) and DRC ($p < .001$) were significantly different between conditions. These differences indicated that ISL manipulations influenced search behavior in different environments.

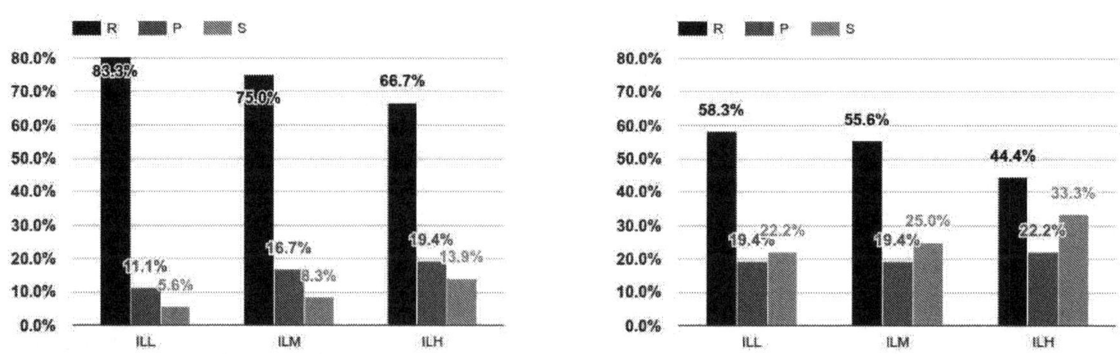

(a) Desktop (b) Mobile

Figure 4: Distribution of Search Behavior by QueryAction: Reformulation (R), Pagination (P) and Stopping (S) for the first query controlled by ISL conditions on both desktop and mobile.

Significant differences across different ISL conditions are reported for desktop, followed by mobile. The highest values, within the same environments, are denoted in bold. In the *Desktop* columns of Table 3, STotal (X^2 = 39.20, $p < .0001$) and SRele (X^2 = 37.62, $p < .0001$) increased with higher ISL. DRS are deeper with increasing ISL conditions (X^2 = 65.11, $p < .0001$). SRele% dropped by 10% from 50% to 45%, as ISL increased. We also observed that ROA reduced by 51% as ISL increased from ILL to ILH, from 39% to 17%. The deepest document click-through rate increased by 38% from ILL to ILM before dropping 8% in the ILH condition.

In the *Mobile* columns of Table 3 show that participants clicked on documents in lower positions (X^2 = 14.37, $p < .001$) as ISL increased. Similar to the desktop, both STotal ($X^2 = 33.67, p < .0001$) and SRele ($X^2 = 44.45, p < .0001$) register lower values under higher ISL conditions. Participants also tended to save documents in lower positions (DRS) with increased ISL ($X^2 = 37.40, p < .0001$). SRele% dropped 15% from 61% to 52% as the information scent increased. Time spent under ILM condition were 42% and 15% more, compared to the ILL and ILH conditions respectively ($X^2 = 113.19, p < .001$). NumClick was highest under ILM condition ($X^2 = 7.00, p < .05$). Therefore, higher ISL did not always contribute to higher NumClick. There was also no differences between the ILM and ILH conditions for ROA and NumPage. Therefore, search behavior measures did not consistently increase between ILM and ILH under mobile ISL conditions. In general, the measures for search behavior increased (while ROA decreased) as the ISL increased from Low to High on the desktop but not on mobile.

ISP & Search Behavior: Next, the impact of different ISP conditions on search behavior is considered. Figure 5 shows the three QueryActions for desktop and mobile. For the ISP conditions on the desktop, there was no consistent observable trend for the QueryActions. The Reformulation rate was consistently above 60%, while the Pagination rate dipped by 30% to 19.4% in the IPP condition before rising back to 27.8% under the IPD condition. Search stopping behavior on desktop showed a 34% increase from 8.3% to 11.1% from the IPB condition to both the IPP and IPD conditions. For mobile, search stopping behavior increased by 83% from 16.7% to 30.6% when the average positions of relevant search results moved into higher positions. Apart from Search Stopping behavior on mobile which increased when ARS improved, desktop and mobile ISP conditions did not show a consistent trend.

Changes in performance for search behavior are reported in Table 4 for ISP conditions. The critical values for X^2 across the ISP conditions within a single environment (desktop or mobile) are reported separately in Table 5 (right side). DRS between the different conditions within desktop ($X^2 = 17.12, p < .001$) and mobile ($X^2 = 25.08, p < .0001$) are significantly different. Time is different between desktop ISP conditions ($X^2 = 82.34, p < .0001$) and TimeTotal is different between mobile ISP conditions ($X^2 = 14.01, p < .001$). This indicates that, in general, the ISP manipulations do not heavily influence search behavior across the different ISP conditions in either environment.

In the *Desktop* columns of Table 4, document depth corresponded to the change in ISP conditions, DRS decreased from 5.06 to 3.17 as ISP changed from IPB to IPD conditions ($X^2 = 17.12, p < .001$). Time and NumClick also increased as ARS moved from 5.5 to 2.5 (IPB to IPD conditions). ROA also decreased by 50% from the IPB to IPD conditions. We observed that both STotal, SRele increased as relevant results are displayed earlier on the SERPs. Search accuracy improved by 22% from 45% to 55% as the ARS changed from 5.5 to 2.5. Overall, participants saved documents in higher positions and spent more time when the relevant search results were placed in higher positions.

In the *Mobile* columns of Table 4, similar to *Desktop*, show inconsistencies in the measures for search behavior. Participants saved documents in lower positions when relevant search results were placed lower ($X^2 = 25.08, p < .001$). We also observed that search performance improved by 24% from 42% to 52% as relevant search results were placed in higher positions from IPB to IPD conditions.

Environments & Search Behavior: Next, we examine the influence of different environments (*Desktop* and *Mobile*) on search behavior. Examining Table 3, the differences between the environments for search behavior measures can be determined. The p-values indicated on the tables are for the same conditions across

Table 4: Search behavior measures (M, SD) by Information Scent Pattern (ISP).

ISP	Desktop			Mobile		
Measures	**IPB**	**IPP**	**IPD**	**IPB**	**IPP**	**IPD**
TimeTotal#	268.22 (165.86)	**270.80 (162.70)**	259.22 (115.12)	211.91 (106.67)	211.86 (115.03)	**223.49 (162.83)**
Time#	72.67 (60.90)	62.57 (33.58)	**78.47 (49.12)**	**69.66 (50.05)**	67.49 (45.81)	67.54 (62.60)
NumQuery	**2.56 (2.10)***	2.51 (1.63)*	2.28 (1.83)	1.81 (.92)*	1.69 (.89)*	**1.86 (1.20)**
NumPage	**.56 (.50)**	.46 (.51)	.50 (.51)	**.44 (.50)**	.39 (.49)	.36 (.49)
NumClick	.50 (.94)	.60 (.88)	**.92 (1.32)**	.33 (.76)	.53 (.94)	**.58 (1.00)**
DRC	**3.53 (6.00)********	2.69 (4.96)	3.31 (5.42)**	1.86 (3.85)****	**2.56 (4.61)**	2.19 (4.57)**
DRV	**15.06 (5.29)****	14.17 (5.47)	14.75 (5.14)**	**12.64 (5.27)****	12.42 (5.59)	12.11 (5.46)**
ROA[1]	22%	17%	**11%**	19%	**8%**	**8%**
DRS	**5.06 (2.88)**	4.89 (3.62)	3.17 (2.29)	**5.50 (2.93)**	4.83 (3.30)	3.08 (1.66)
STotal	1.89 (1.47)	2.03 (1.42)	**2.44 (1.95)**	1.86 (1.31)	2.00 (1.29)	**2.19 (1.26)**
SRele	1.81 (1.43)	1.97 (1.42)	**2.19 (1.41)**	1.69 (1.33)	1.97 (1.23)	**2.08 (1.20)**
SRele%	45%	49%	**55%**	42%	49%	**52%**

Mean and (standard deviation) values are shown. Significant differences are indicated for same ISP conditions across different environments.

[1] Lowest value for ROA were bold for higher user interaction.

- indicates Student's t-test, otherwise Chi-squared test. Note: *$p < .05$, **$p < .01$, ***$p < .001$, ****$p < .0001$.

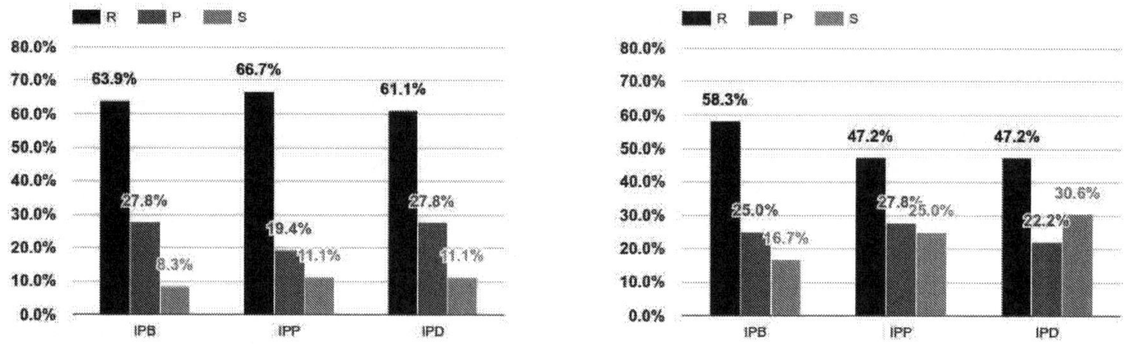

(a) Desktop (b) Mobile

Figure 5: Distribution of Search Behavior by QueryAction: Reformulation (R), Pagination (P) and Stopping (S) for the first query controlled by ISP conditions on both desktop and mobile.

Table 5: Results for ISL/ISP conditions (X^2 significance) comparing search behavior across ISL/ISP conditions within the same environment (desktop or mobile).

	ISL		ISP	
Measure	Desktop	Mobile	Desktop	Mobile
TimeTotal	26.65****	16.41***	5.55	14.01***
Time	58.38****	113.19****	82.34****	1.08
NumQuery	0.43	0.99	0.64	0.29
NumPage	1.41	0.63	0.44	0.33
NumClick	3.85	7.00*	5.25	2.58
DRC	3.49	14.37***	5.23	3.94
DRV	3.77	1.21	2.10	0.41
ROA	2.60	4.00	1.37	2.46
DRS	65.11****	37.40****	17.12***	25.08****
STotal	39.20****	33.67****	3.07	1
SRele	37.62****	44.45****	1.47	1.51

*$p < .05$, **$p < .01$, ***$p < .001$, ****$p < .0001$

the two environments. For example, NumQuery for ILL on desktop and mobile is $p < .05$. Document click-throughs (DRC) are significantly higher on desktop compared to mobile across all the ISL conditions, when ISL is low ($X^2 = 18.75, p < .0001$), medium ($X^2 = 23.31, p < .0001$) and high ($X^2 = 4.52, p < .05$). More snippets are viewed (DRV) on desktop compared to mobile across all the ISL conditions, when ISL is low ($X^2 = 4.01, p < .05$), medium ($X^2 = 10.04, p < .01$) and high ($X^2 = 7.11, p < .01$). Considering lowest position of documents saved (DRS), participants saved significantly deeper on mobile compared to desktop for low ISL ($X^2 = 14.63, p < .001$). Some moderately significant differences in search behavior measures were observed between desktop and mobile when SERPs were manipulated under ISL conditions. Generally, in terms of differences between desktop and mobile, we recorded 5 notable differences: (1) query submissions numbered higher on the desktop compared to mobile, significantly higher under ILL and ILH conditions. (2) Desktop participants significantly viewed more and (3) clicked on documents in lower positions. (4) Mobile participants saved significantly more results under ILL condition from the first queries and (5) more accurately throughout all ISL conditions, compared to the desktop participants.

Differences in search behavior measures between desktop and mobile environments, under the influence of ISP conditions, are reported in Table 4. Desktop query submissions are significantly higher in number when relevant search results are lower in positions (IPB) ($X^2 = 4.64, p < .05$) or distributed throughout the SERPs (IPP) ($X^2 = 4.89, p < .05$). Document click-throughs (DRC) are also lower in position under IPB ($X^2 = 18.56, p < .0001$) and IPD ($X^2 = 8.08, p < .01$) conditions on desktop. More search results snippets are viewed on desktop under IPB ($X^2 = 7.59, p < .0001$) and IPD ($X^2 = 8.08, p < .01$) conditions. In general, search behavior measures between desktop and mobile, under Information Scent Pattern conditions, were not able to show any differences consistently.

5 DISCUSSION

We investigated the extent to which Information Foraging Theory could be used to explain changes in search behavior measures in different search environments. For both desktop and mobile, the findings suggest that ISL was a better predictor of search behavior than ISP. Allowing items to be saved as relevant directly on the SERP, without requiring click-throughs, we made different observations from previous work [31].

RQ1: ISL and Search Behavior: In RQ1, we sought to understand "to what extent can desktop and mobile search behavior be explained by Information Scent Level (ISL)". We posited that if ISL influenced search behavior, then the measures should increase correspondingly, apart from NumQuery and ROA which should be reducing because having enough relevant information should mitigate additional reformulations.

On the desktop, apart from NumQuery, DRC and TimeTotal, there was a consistent increase in search behavior measures, when ISL increased from ILL to ILH. Documents saved (DRS, STotal and SRele) also significantly increased with ISL. We conclude that ISL was influential in desktop search behavior.

On the mobile, the changes in user behavior measures were mixed. Increasing ISL did not increase search behavior measures consistently. Measurements for saved documents (DRS, STotal, and SRele) and click depth (DRC) were significantly increased as ISL changed, but document click-throughs (NumClick) decreased from ILM to ILH. As documents saved (DRS, STotal, and SRele) are the only measures that reflect ISL conditions, we concluded that ISL was only partially influential on mobile search behavior.

RQ2: ISP and Search Behavior: RQ2 sought to address "to what extent can desktop and mobile search behavior be explained by Information Scent Pattern (ISP)". We refer to ISP conditions by their ARS values in this subsection, as scent centrality is useful to explain how search behavior changes over the different conditions (see Table 1). If ISP influenced search behavior, then as ARS increased from 5.5 to 2.5, we would expect changes in search behavior that reflect user interactions. In alignment with previous work [12], we would expect document click-throughs (NumClick) and/or the number of documents saved (STotal and SRele) to increase as the position of relevant documents were moved into higher positions. The rate of abandonment (ROA) and depth of document saved (DRS) were also be expected to decrease as it became easier to find relevant information [11]. We would also expect position-based measures (DRC, DRV, and DRS) to be lower. Similarly, we would expect participants to expend less effort to reformulate, resulting in fewer query submissions (NumQuery).

On the desktop, the identified search behavior measures mostly aligned with our hypothesized changes. As ARS improved from 5.5 to 2.5, NumClick, STotal, and SRele increased while NumQuery and ROA decreased as expected. Overall, ISP was moderately successful to explain search behavior on the desktop.

On the mobile, only some search behavior measures agreed with our initial hypothesis. As ARS improved, document click-throughs (NumClick) and saved (STotal and SRele) increased likewise. Position-based measures, such as DRS and DRV decreased likewise. While not significant, changes in NumQuery and DRC were unexpected. DRC should be highest when ARS is 5.5, however, it was the lowest. This indicated that there was a higher probability that users opted not to click on anything, which resulted in the lowest value. When given a choice not to view documents, participants would select documents based on snippets alone. This observation was mentioned by Li et al. [21], discussing the significantly higher abandonment rate on mobile. This anomalous behavior on mobile will be discussed later.

RQ3: Environments and Search Behavior: RQ3 sought to address "how does search behavior differ as a result of different environments". If environments influenced search behavior, then search behavior measured across environments under identical ISL/ISP conditions, would be different. Results from Table 2 illustrate that measures were generally different between mobile and desktop.

Search strategies can be classified into two categories: depth-focused and reformulation-focused where depth and reformulation are inversely related [2]. While both NumQuery and DRV are higher on the desktop than on mobile, the inverse is true for DRS (see Table 2). Mobile participants were more likely to find and save documents from the initial queries than desktop participants and avoid additional reformulations when possible. This behavior is also illustrated in Figures 4 and 5 where the Reformulation QueryAction was consistently lower across all ISL/ISP conditions on mobile than desktop. Search cost on mobile was thought to be higher because typing was harder.

The lower ROA on mobile than on desktop is consistent with previous work [21] as participants expend more effort to find relevant results within the first queries. Our user studies showed that under the ILH condition, mobile (but not the desktop) participants clicked on significantly fewer documents. Such a difference might suggest that information consumption satiety thresholds differ across the two environments.

We also observed that ranking affects search accuracy and confirmed *Guan and Cutrell*'s [11] findings. Search accuracy (SRele) increased for SERPs with more and higher ranked relevant results. The differences in search behavior on desktop and mobile were dependent on the type of Information Scent conditions. For tasks with an increasing number of relevant search results, mobile users had better search accuracy than desktop participants. Conversely, desktop users had better search accuracy than mobile participants for tasks with a distributed number of relevant search results. Overall, we found that different environments could affect changes in search behavior. The observation that NumClick was lower between ILM and ILH conditions only in the mobile environment may suggest a lower information need threshold, with the participants' information diet being restricted by the environment.

While visible search results above the fold influenced search behavior, having more relevant information below the fold should not make search behavior substantially different. Unlike Desktop, search measurements were not indicative that ILH had the highest information scent on mobile. Both NumPage and ROA were identical between the ILM and ILH conditions on mobile. ROA was also recorded as the same between the IPP and IPD conditions. A higher fold on mobile suggests a much-diminished gain for including more relevant information below the fold. Our study shows that user behavior on mobile is indeed different from desktop, similar to *Lagun et al. [20]*'s findings. However, the gap between mobile and desktop search is closing. It will be interesting to investigate how mobile search behavior continue to evolve.

Limitations. We acknowledged that an artificial time constraint of forty-five minutes might potentially reduce the total number of documents examined [25]. However, the timing was kept constant across both experiments. While we recognized the importance of cross-device search [23], we sought to understand web search behavior when searchers were restricted to single devices. Search results were limited to twenty retrieved documents, due to the low likelihood that users going beyond the first SERPs [31]. Participants spent less than five minutes per task on average and paginated similarly to previous experiment. We sought thirty-six participants for each user study and noted that other user studies had smaller [14, 18, 20] or similar [10, 31] numbers of participants. As SERPs were prepared beforehand, we recognized that participants might encounter SERPs that were not targeted to their initial query terms but there were strong merits to keep SERPs consistent to users. Participants were interviewed during the exit questionnaires, and apart from one user, no concerns were raised regarding the number of search results, total time given, and SERP manipulations. From this evidence, we conclude the experimental manipulations were not noticeable in general.

6 CONCLUSION AND FUTURE WORK

This research investigated how ISL and ISP can be used to measure differences in web search behavior in mobile and desktop environments. We found that desktop participants behaved in similar ways to those observed in past work [31] but not for mobile participants.

By allowing participants to save answer items directly on the SERP, without having to examine documents, we observed that document click-throughs were not an indicator of the strength of information scent level. This is relevant for mobile, because of previously observed higher good abandonment rate [21]. In general, participants in both environments tended to abandon SERPs when the number of relevant search results was fewer, or if found after non-relevant search results. Users were also more likely to click documents in lower positions when more relevant search results were present on the SERPs.

While participants consistently preferred SERPs with a higher number of relevant search results on the desktop, this preference was not apparent on the mobile. We conjectured that the higher fold on the mobile impaired their initial impression of differences in overall page quality since they were only able to see the first few items, but more research is required to fully understand this effect. Desktop participants submitted more queries and saved fewer documents in lower positions than their mobile counterparts. Differences in information scent and environments have been observed to change search behavior. The significant inverse relationship between NumQuery and DRS in different environments suggested that whether the search was carried out on the desktop or mobile, influenced their search strategies. These differences in preferences may also contribute to how information is consumed in different environments.

In conclusion, we conducted two comparative user studies using IFT and found differences between two environments. Increasing ISL generally increased search interactions under desktop ISL conditions. However, NumClick dropped when ISL was above ILM under mobile ISL conditions. A possible lower information need threshold in the mobile environment has been suggested. Similar to previous work, the results under ISP conditions for both environments were mixed. This suggests that search strategies might change, contingent on the environment. Our findings have implications for the design of search systems and suggest several areas for future work: 1) presenting more search results with shorter snippets above the fold, 2) techniques to make mobile query reformulation easier, and 3) using multi-touch approaches to examine SERPs with the ability to 'peek' at additional information via pop-ups when needed.

7 ACKNOWLEDGMENTS

This project is funded by ARC Discovery Grant, ref: DP140102655 and an APA scholarship. Travel funding is also provided by ACM SIGIR for the lead author to attend the conference. We thank Diane Kelly and Wan-Ching Wu for providing clarification as well as Bruce Croft, Doug Oard and the anonymous reviewers for their valuable feedback.

REFERENCES

[1] Anne Aula, Päivi Majaranta, and Kari-Jouko Räihä. 2005. Eye-Tracking Reveals the Personal Styles for Search Result Evaluation. In *Proceedings of INTERACT.* 1058–1061.

[2] Leif Azzopardi, Diane Kelly, and Kathy Brennan. 2013. How Query Cost Affects Search Behavior. In *Proceedings of SIGIR.* 23–32.

[3] Andrei Broder. 2002. A Taxonomy of Web Search. In *SIGIR Forum*, Vol. 36. 3–10.

[4] Stuart K. Card, Peter Pirolli, Mija Van Der Wege, Julie B. Morrison, Robert W. Reeder, Pamela K. Schraedley, and Jenea Boshart. 2001. Information Scent as a Driver of Web Behavior Graphs: Results of a Protocol Analysis Method for Web Usability. In *Proceedings of SIGCHI.* 498–505.

[5] Ed H. Chi, Peter Pirolli, Kim Chen, and James Pitkow. 2001. Using Information Scent to Model User Information Needs and Actions and the Web. In *Proceedings of SIGCHI.* 490–497.

[6] Ed H. Chi, Peter Pirolli, and James Pitkow. 2000. The Scent of a Site: A System for Analyzing and Predicting Information Scent, Usage, and Usability of a Web Site. In *Proceedings of SIGCHI.* 161–168.

[7] Karen Church and Barry Smyth. 2009. Understanding the Intent behind Mobile Information Needs. In *Proceedings of IUI.* 247–256.

[8] Edward Cutrell and Zhiwei Guan. 2007. What Are You Looking For?: An Eye-Tracking Study of Information Usage in Web Search. In *Proceedings of SIGCHI.* 407–416.

[9] Anindya Ghose, Avi Goldfarb, and Sang Pil Han. 2012. How Is the Mobile Internet Different? Search Costs and Local Activities. *Information Systems Research* 24, 3 (2012), 613–631.

[10] Laura A. Granka, Thorsten Joachims, and Geri Gay. 2004. Eye-Tracking Analysis of User Behavior in WWW Search. In *Proceedings of SIGIR.* 478–479.

[11] Zhiwei Guan and Edward Cutrell. 2007. An Eye Tracking Study of the Effect of Target Rank on Web Search. In *Proceedings of SIGCHI.* 417–420.

[12] Ahmed Hassan, Xiaolin Shi, Nick Craswell, and Bill Ramsey. 2013. Beyond Clicks: Query Reformulation as a Predictor of Search Satisfaction. In *Proceedings of CIKM.* 2019–2028.

[13] Thorsten Joachims, Laura Granka, Bing Pan, Helene Hembrooke, and Geri Gay. 2005. Accurately Interpreting Clickthrough Data as Implicit Feedback. In *Proceedings of SIGIR.* 154–161.

[14] Matt Jones, Gary Marsden, Norliza Mohd-Nasir, Kevin Boone, and George Buchanan. 1999. Improving Web Interaction on Small Displays. *Computer Networks* 31, 11 (1999), 1129–1137.

[15] Maryam Kamvar and Shumeet Baluja. 2006. A Large Scale Study of Wireless Search Behavior: Google Mobile Search. In *Proceedings of SIGCHI.* 701–709.

[16] Maryam Kamvar and Shumeet Baluja. 2007. Deciphering Trends in Mobile Search. *Computer* 40, 8 (2007), 58–62.

[17] Jaewon Kim, Paul Thomas, Ramesh Sankaranarayana, and Tom Gedeon. 2012. Comparing Scanning Behaviour in Web Search on Small and Large Screens. In *Proceedings of ADCS.* 25–30.

[18] Jaewon Kim, Paul Thomas, Ramesh Sankaranarayana, Tom Gedeon, and Hwan-Jin Yoon. 2015. Eye-Tracking Analysis of User Behavior and Performance in Web Search on Large and Small Screens. *JASIST* 66, 3 (2015), 526–544.

[19] Kerstin Klöckner, Nadine Wirschum, and Anthony Jameson. 2004. Depth-and Breadth-First Processing of Search Result Lists. In *Proccedings of CHI.* 1539–1539.

[20] Dmitry Lagun, Chih-Hung Hsieh, Dale Webster, and Vidhya Navalpakkam. 2014. Towards Better Measurement of Attention and Satisfaction in Mobile Search. In *Proceedings of SIGIR.* 113–122.

[21] Jane Li, Scott Huffman, and Akihito Tokuda. 2009. Good Abandonment in Mobile and PC Internet Search. In *Proceedings of SIGIR.* 43–50.

[22] David Maxwell, Leif Azzopardi, Kalervo Järvelin, and Heikki Keskustalo. 2015. Searching and Stopping: An Analysis of Stopping Rules and Strategies. In *Proceedings of CIKM.* 313–322.

[23] George D. Montanez, Ryen W. White, and Xiao Huang. 2014. Cross-Device Search. In *Proceedings of CIKM.* 1669–1678.

[24] Peter Pirolli and Stuart Card. 1999. Information Foraging. *Psychological Review* 106, 4 (1999), 643–675.

[25] Chandra Prabha, Lynn Silipigni Connaway, Lawrence Olszewski, and Lillie R. Jenkins. 2007. What Is Enough? Satisficing Information Needs. *Documentation* 63, 1 (2007), 74–89.

[26] Yongli Ren, Martin Tomko, Kevin Ong, and Mark Sanderson. 2014. How People Use the Web in Large Indoor Spaces. In *Proceedings of CIKM.* 1879–1882.

[27] Soo Young Rieh and others. 2006. Analysis of Multiple Query Reformulations on the Web: The Interactive Information Retrieval Context. *IP&M* 42, 3 (2006), 751–768.

[28] Yang Song, Hao Ma, Hongning Wang, and Kuansan Wang. 2013. Exploring and Exploiting User Search Behavior on Mobile and Tablet Devices to Improve Search Relevance. In *Proceedings of WWW.* 1201–1212.

[29] Jaime Teevan, Christine Alvarado, Mark S. Ackerman, and David R. Karger. 2004. The Perfect Search Engine Is Not Enough: A Study of Orienteering Behavior in Directed Search. In *Proceedings of SIGCHI.* 415–422.

[30] Ryen White and Steven M. Drucker. 2007. Investigating Behavioral Variability in Web Search. In *Proceedings of WWW.* 21–30.

[31] Wan-Ching Wu, Diane Kelly, and Avneesh Sud. 2014. Using Information Scent and Need for Cognition to Understand Online Search Behavior. In *Proceedings of SIGIR.* 557–566.

Deep Character-Level Click-Through Rate Prediction for Sponsored Search

Bora Edizel*
Pompeu Fabra University & Eurecat
Barcelona, Spain
bora.edizel@upf.edu

Amin Mantrach†
Criteo Labs
Palo Alto, California, U.S.A
a.mantrach@criteo.com

Xiao Bai
Yahoo Labs
Sunnyvale, California, U.S.A
xbai@yahoo-inc.com

ABSTRACT

Predicting the click-through rate of an advertisement is a critical component of online advertising platforms. In sponsored search, the click-through rate estimates the probability that a displayed advertisement is clicked by a user after she submits a query to the search engine. Commercial search engines typically rely on machine learning models trained with a large number of features to make such predictions. This inevitably requires a lot of engineering efforts to define, compute, and select the appropriate features. In this paper, we propose two novel approaches (one working at character level and the other working at word level) that use deep convolutional neural networks to predict the click-through rate of a query-advertisement pair. Specifically, the proposed architectures only consider the textual content appearing in a query-advertisement pair as input, and produce as output a click-through rate prediction. By comparing the character-level model with the word-level model, we show that language representation can be learnt from scratch at character level when trained on enough data. Through extensive experiments using billions of query-advertisement pairs of a popular commercial search engine, we demonstrate that both approaches significantly outperform a baseline model built on well-selected text features and a state-of-the-art word2vec-based approach. Finally, by combining the predictions of the deep models introduced in this study with the prediction of the model in production of the same commercial search engine, we significantly improve the accuracy and the calibration of the click-through rate prediction of the production system.

CCS CONCEPTS

•Computing methodologies →Machine learning; Natural language processing; •Computer systems organization →Neural networks;

*This work was done when the author interned at Yahoo.
†This work was done when the author was at Yahoo.

SIGIR '17, August 07-11, 2017, Shinjuku, Tokyo, Japan
© 2017 ACM. 978-1-4503-5022-8/17/08...$15.00.
DOI: http://dx.doi.org/10.1145/3077136.3080811

KEYWORDS

Deep Learning; NLP; Online Advertising; Sponsored Search; CTR Prediction

ACM Reference format:
Bora Edizel, Amin Mantrach, and Xiao Bai. 2017. Deep Character-Level Click-Through Rate Prediction for Sponsored Search. In *Proceedings of SIGIR '17, August 07-11, 2017, Shinjuku, Tokyo, Japan, ,* 10 pages.
DOI: http://dx.doi.org/10.1145/3077136.3080811

1 INTRODUCTION

Click-through rate (CTR) prediction is a critical component of any online advertising platform. For an advertisement, the value of the click-through rate can be estimated by the number of times it is clicked divided by the number of times it is shown, quantifying the extent to which an ad[1] is likely to be clicked in a specific context. In sponsored search, ad impressions are typically monetized on a pay-per-click basis through the generalized second price auction [9]. Given a query issued by a user, in order to foresee the potential revenue, a commercial search engine has to predict the probability that an ad is clicked by the user for this query (i.e., CTR) as accurately as possible. Over predicting the click-through rate tends to give an ad a higher ranking position in the search result page. If it is not clicked, the search engine does not only lose the expected revenue from this ad but also lose the opportunity of getting more revenue from ads ranked at lower positions due to the position bias affecting ad clicks [4]. On the other hand, under predicting the click-through rate may result in an ad being placed at a lower position or even not showing up in the search result page, decreasing the revenue that may be made from the ad.

The problem of click-through rate prediction has led to many research efforts in the past few years [14, 20], including those from leading search engine companies [5, 11, 24]. So far the most successful models across the industry rely on a large number of well designed features to predict the click-through rate. Despite of the prediction accuracy of such models, it has been noted that it is very challenging to select the right features [14], and to deal with feature sparsity and management at scale, etc. [24] in a complex dynamic system. Moreover, when facing a new context, e.g., new query, new ad, or new query-ad pair, such models may not be able to make accurate predictions [28]. For instance, the most predictive features of click prediction models are those capturing historical click information [14] as frequent clicks imply user preference for an ad in a specific context. However, new queries and ads may not

[1]In the remainder, ad(s) will be used to refer to advertisement(s)

have enough history to compute reliable features for accurate prediction. To alleviate this kind of cold-start problems, one may rely on hybrid approaches to learn patterns or latent representations from the observed data that generalize well to unobserved contexts, or may rely solely on content-based features that are independent of the click history (see [30] for a description of various cold-start solutions). For instance, the BM25 score of an ad relatively to a query [2] is an effective content-feature of this kind.

Most recently, following the advancements in deep learning, especially in natural language processing, new architectures have been proposed to learn word embeddings and text similarity between a query and a web page [17, 32], or between a query and an ad [34]. This alleviates the need of designing and implementing large amounts of features, even though maintaining and refreshing the learnt word embeddings still requires huge engineering efforts. Interestingly, the last aforementioned advancements in deep learning have not yet been applied to the click prediction problem. Indeed, state-of-the-art CTR prediction models are hybrid models relying on well designed historical, context and content-based features [14, 24].

In this work, we directly predict the click-through rate of a query-ad pair by solely relying on its textual content. Specifically, we present two novel deep convolutional neural networks that process the text appearing in a query-ad pair as input without any additional information, and output a CTR prediction. The first model learns directly from a binary encoding of the textual input in a bag-of-character space, and does not require any external dictionary. The second model exhibits a similar structure but takes as input pre-trained word vectors, and hence assumes a pre-existing word dictionary.

To the best of our knowledge, we are the first: (1) to learn meaningful textual similarity between two pieces of text (i.e., query and ad) from scratch, i.e., at character level, and (2) to directly predict the click-through rate in the context of sponsored search without any feature engineering. By directly learning and predicting CTR at character level and at word level, we naturally broaden the use of the click prediction model to cold-start (i.e., new) and long-tail (i.e., rare) queries and ads as the character-level model can be applied on any query-ad pair as far as their characters are part of the considered input alphabet (e.g., the 26 English letters plus a few punctuations). In fact, although the coverage of the word-level model may be slightly limited by the pre-computed word dictionary, as shown in our experiments, using word-level representation helps to bring external knowledge about the words to boost the prediction accuracy on tail queries and ads.

In this work, we aim at delivering an additional and generalizable signal to improve CTR prediction for sponsored search. We conduct a thorough experimental evaluation, using billions of query-ad pairs from a major commercial search engine, to address the following research questions:

(1) *Can we automatically learn representations from the query-ad content without any feature engineering in order to predict the CTR in sponsored search?* We show that the proposed character-level and word-level deep learning models can improve the AUC of a feature-engineered logistic regression model with 185 content-based features by up to 0.09 (Section 4.2). As the three models optimize for the same loss function on the same training data, this clearly shows that the proposed deep models can automatically learn more meaningful representations for predicting CTR of query-ad pairs than the feature-engineered model with well-selected features.

(2) *How does the performance of the character-level deep learning model differ from that of the word-level model for CTR prediction?* In Section 4.2, we show that learning query-ad similarity at character level reaches slightly better performance with an AUC of 0.862, than its word-level alternative that reaches an AUC of 0.859. This slight difference is statistically significative on 27M test points. Interestingly, character-level model outperforms word-level model when the models are trained with enough data (i.e., more than 1 billion query-ad pairs, Figure 5). This highlights one of the main findings of this work: language representation can be learnt from scratch, at character level, without the need of any precomputed dictionary. In addition, we observe that the word-level model outperforms the character-level model on tails (i.e., queries, ads, and query-ad pairs with low frequency) because it can benefit from the external knowledge provided by the pre-trained word vectors. On the other hand, the character-level model outperforms the word-level model on heads since it can benefit from the better representations of the domain learnt from scratch.

(3) *How do the introduced character-level and word-level deep learning models compare to the baseline models? What is the improvement of prediction accuracy on head, torso, and tail queries, ads, and query-ad pairs?* We show in Section 4.2 that the two proposed models improve the AUC of a baseline model built on well-selected content-based features by up to 0.090, and the AUC of a word2vec-based approach [12] by up to 0.082 (Table 1). Specially, the proposed models improve the AUC of the two baselines on head, torso, and tail by up to 0.088, 0.086, and 0.059 respectively (Table 2).

(4) *Can the proposed character-level and word-level deep learning models be leveraged to improve the CTR prediction model running in the production system of a popular commercial search engine?* In Section 4.2, we show that by combining the prediction of one of the deep models proposed in this work (i.e., character-level or word-level model) with the prediction of the production model, we can increase the AUC of the production system by up to 0.86%. Interestingly, when considering mobile devices, the improvement on AUC reaches 3.95% (Table 4).

2 RELATED WORK

In this work, we propose to use deep convolutional neural network to directly learn click-through rate from the characters and the words of query-ad pairs. We present in this section the state-of-the-art of the various domains covered by this research, and discuss how our contributions differ from the existing works. We first review the related work in CTR prediction. Then, we look at previous research on sentence similarity learning and matching using deep neural networks. Finally, we discuss previous deep models working at character level used for tasks different from ours.

2.1 CTR prediction

Computational advertisement, and more particularly sponsored search, has been a subject of study particularly active since the beginning of the century [25]. A large body of work discussing computational advertising is devoted to finding models and techniques that enable the most accurate prediction of the probability for an ad to be clicked when returned to a user for her query (i.e., CTR) [11, 15, 24, 28, 31, 33, 36]. Graepel *et al.* [11] describe the Bayesian online learning algorithm used in Bing's production system to predict CTR. This model relies on query features, ad features, context features, as well as the Cartesian product of these base features. McMahan *et al.* [24] discuss the CTR prediction algorithm used at Google, along with many practical insights to build a large-scale online learning system. This work particularly confirms the challenges in building CTR prediction model that requires computing, maintaining and serving a large number of sparse contextual and semantic features. In fact, even in the related domain of display advertising, machine learning models trained with a large number of features have so far been the mostly adopted. For instance, He *et al.* [14] present the CTR prediction model at Facebook and clearly point out that the most important challenge to reach accurate predictions is selecting good features, which however may not be trivial. There have been different efforts on building features, including text features [31], click features [28], psychology features [33], query segment features [15], to improve CTR prediction models for sponsored search. Most recently, deep neural networks have also been used for CTR prediction. Jiang *et al.* [19] proposed to use recurrent neural networks to learn features from queries, ads and clicks for a logistic regression model. Zhang *et al.* [36] relies on features extracted from user's sequential ad browsing behavior to train a recurrent neural network. Different from all these works, our model does not need any heavy feature engineering but only the textual content appearing in a query-ad pair suffice.

2.2 Deep Similarity Learning and Matching

Matching a search query to a number of ads that are likely to attract user clicks is central to any commercial search engine. With the pervasive success of deep learning, recent works start modeling the similarity between texts using deep network models [16] and exploring their use in web search [17, 32] and sponsored search [12, 34].

Grbovic. *et al.* [12] mine search sessions that include queries, clicks on ad and search links, dwell times and skipped ads to learn semantic embeddings for queries and ads, and use cosine similarity between the learnt embeddings to measure the similarity between a query and an ad. The main drawback of the approach is that the learning is done at full query level, and ad identifier level. This means that the approach can not exploit two queries with similar content except if they occur often in the same context in search sessions. The algorithm also suffers from the out-of-vocabulary problem as a significant fraction of search queries are new and advertisers are actively updating their ads. To solve this problem, Zhai *et al.* [34] propose to use an attention network on top of recurrent neural networks to map both queries and ads to real valued vectors, and then rely on cosine similarity between the query and ad vectors to measure their similarity. Unlike [12], they are directly working at word level and therefore are less sensitive to the out-of-vocabulary problem. In this work we actually propose to go down to character level and therefore inherently deal with any input of the considered alphabet. At the difference of [34], and [12] we are not learning (in a weakly supervised way) query vectors, and ad vectors to be used in a cosine similarity function but instead are learning (in a supervised way) a complex similarity function embedded in a neural network predicting directly the CTR of a query-ad pair.

In the context of web search, Huang *et al.* [17] introduce the letter n-gram based word hashing encoding. Compared with the one-hot vector encoding, word hashing allows to represent a query or a document using a vector with much lower dimensionality. However, when compared to character-level one-hot encodings, the dimension are much higher. Indeed, the character-level encoding dimensionality corresponds to the number of characters of the input times the size of the alphabet, which is much less than the dimensionality of vectors using letter trigrams. Furthermore, this encoding looses the sequence information at the opposite of the character-level one-hot encodings. Similarly, Shen *et al.* [32] use word-n-gram representations of queries and web pages in convolutional neural networks to learn query-document similarity. Different from [17], they project each raw word-n-gram in a low-dimensional feature vector and perform a max pooling operation to select the highest neuron activation value across all word-n-gram features at each dimension. This is similar to the word-level representation used in our deep model. However, our model does not rely on cosine similarity as [17] and [32] but uses the cross-convolutional operator [16] to capture query-ad similarity. Another difference between our work and the model proposed in [32] is that the latter uses negative sampling on search click logs while we directly use the not-clicked ads as negative samples.

Hu *et al.* [16] also propose to directly capture the similarity between two sentences without explicitly relying on semantic vector representations. As DeepWordMatch, this model works at word level, but is targeting matching task as: sentence completion, matching a response to a tweet, and paraphrase identification.

2.3 Deep Character-level Models

There are a number of works learning at character level for different natural language processing (NLP) tasks in recent years. Nogueira dos Santos *et al.* [7] are among the first to use character-level information for part-of-speech tagging. They propose to jointly use character-level representation and the more traditional word embedding in a deep neural network for this task. Later on, they propose to use a similar deep neural network with character-level and work-level representations to perform name entity recognition [29]. Unlike these early efforts, our character-level model does not use any word embedding as input.

Several following works [3, 6, 21, 35] demonstrate the power of character-level information alone in NLP tasks. Ballesteros *et al.* [3] discuss the benefits of replacing word-level representation by character-level representation in long short-term memory (LSTM) recurrent neural networks to improve transition-based parsing. Kim *et al.* [21] show in their work that character inputs are sufficient for modeling most of the languages, and their LSTM recurrent neural network language model processing character inputs is as good as the state-of-the-art models using word-level or morpheme-level inputs for English. Zhang *et al.* [35] explore the use of character-level convolutional networks for text classification and show that character-level convolutional networks achieve competitive results against traditional models and deep models such as word-based ConvNets [23]. Conneau *et al.* [6] further show that when using very deep networks of up to 29 convolutional layers, a model that operates directly at character level achieves significant improvements over the state-of-the-art on several public text classification tasks. Interestingly, in case of big datasets, they report good results using shallower neural networks.

Although character-level models have been successfully applied in so many different tasks, none of them is learning similarity between two pieces of text. This clearly motivates us to design our deep character-level model for click-through rate prediction.

3 DEEP CTR MODELING

In this section, we design two novel deep convolutional neural networks, namely DeepCharMatch and DeepWordMatch, to directly model the CTR of query-ad pairs based on their content at character level and at word level. We start by formalizing the general CTR prediction problem in the context of sponsored search. We then present the key components of our models. We finally provide details on the input representation and model architecture of the character-level model DeepCharMatch, and the word-level model DeepWordMatch respectively.

3.1 CTR Modeling

To model the CTR distribution of query-ad pairs, we have at our disposal a query-ad search log sampled from $\mathcal{QA} \subseteq \mathcal{Q} \times \mathcal{A}$, where $\mathcal{Q}$ is the set of all possible queries that users can submit on their devices (e.g., desktop and mobile), $\mathcal{A}$ is the set of all possible ads that advertisers can register into the advertising platform, and $\mathcal{QA}$ in the subset of all query-ad pairs that received at least one impression during a time period τ. Each query-ad pair, $q\_a \in \mathcal{QA}$ is associated to a binary click feedback variable $c_{q\_a} \in \{0, 1\}$, 1 meaning clicked and 0 meaning not clicked.

In order to obtain a well-calibrated CTR prediction, we build on the cross-entropy loss function [8]:

$$L = \sum_{q\_a:c_{q\_a}=1} \log p_{q\_a} + \sum_{q\_a:c_{q\_a}=0} \log(1 - p_{q\_a}) \quad (1)$$

where $p_{q\_a} = p(c_{q\_a} = 1 | q\_a; \theta)$ is the probability for a query-ad pair to be clicked (*i.e.*, the CTR), and θ represents the model parameters. In the remainder, we decompose θ as parameters of a deep convolutional neural network with the aim of modeling p_{q_a} directly from the sequence of characters that compose the query and the ad.

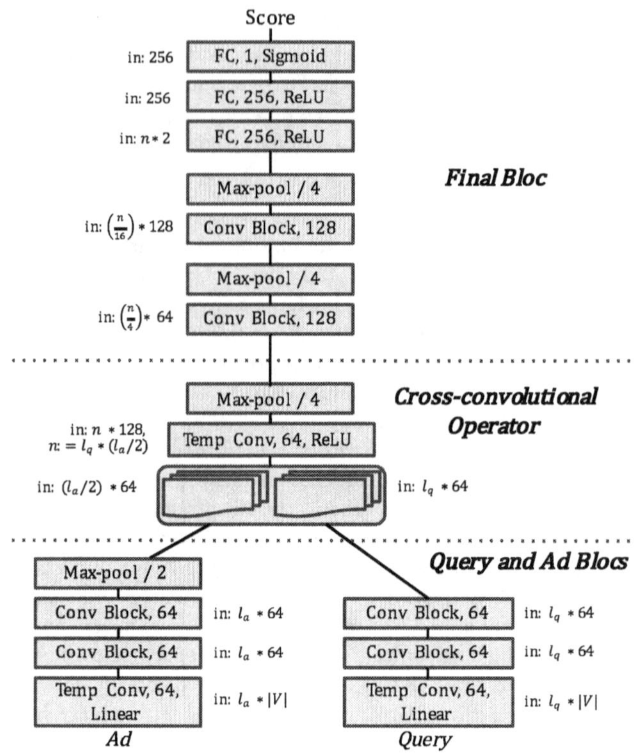

Figure 1: DeepCharMatch Model Architecture.

3.2 Key Components

Temporal Modules. In order to exploit the sequential nature of query and ad at character level, we build on the work of Zhang *et al.* [35] that introduces the key components to process character-level sequential input in convolutional neural networks. Since we are dealing with textual data which is one-dimensional and temporal, we make use of temporal convolution, temporal max-pooling and temporal batch normalization. These temporal modules work in the same way as their corresponding spatial modules used in images and the only difference is their input dimension.

The temporal convolutional module consists of a set of filters whose weights are learnt during the training. The module applies a convolution operation between its input and filters. Since the filter weights are shared across the input width, patterns can be learnt regardless of locality. For the module parameters, we use a fixed filter size of 3, a stride of 1 and we do not use zero paddings. In Figures 1 and 2, we represent convolutions by "*Temp Conv*, X, Y" where X corresponds to the number of filters and Y corresponds to the activation function.

Temporal max-pooling applies non-linear downsampling to its input in order to reduce dimensionality. The downsampling is done by applying a max filter to the non-overlapping partitioned sequences of the initial one-dimensional input. Throughout the paper, we refer to temporal max-pooling modules by "$Max{-}pool/X$" where X is the size of filter.

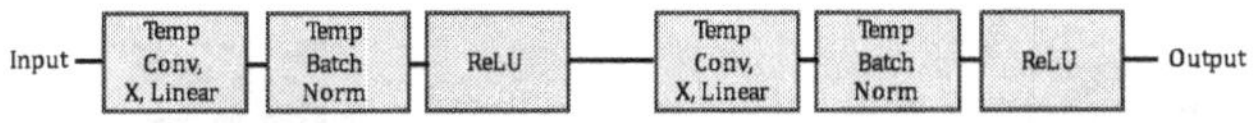

Figure 2: Convolutional Block.

Lastly, temporal batch normalization module normalizes its input. This accelerates the training obtaining an additional regularization effect [18].

Convolutional Block. For the ease of the notation, following [6], we make use of convolutional blocks (Conv Block). As presented in Figure 2, a convolutional block is composed of two consecutive sub-blocks where each sub-block is a sequence of a temporal convolution, a temporal batch normalization, and a ReLU activation function [10]. ReLU is a non-saturating activation function such that for an input x, it outputs $max(0, x)$.

Other functions. Additionally, we use fully connected layers. We refer to them by "FC, X, Y" where X is the number of neurons and Y is the activation function.

3.3 DeepCharMatch Model

The architecture of the character-level CTR prediction model is presented in Figure 1. We refer to this model by DeepCharMatch. Before exploring its architecture, we first explain how the input is represented at character level.

3.3.1 Input Representation. Considering an alphabet V, and fixed query length l_q, queries are represented with a matrix of one-hot-encodings (*i.e.*, binary) of size $l_q \times |V|$. More precisely, each character of the query sequence corresponds to a row of size $1 \times |V|$ in the input matrix. Each row contains only one unique entry that is set to 1 at the position corresponding to the dimension indicated by the considered character of the query while all the other entries of the same row are set to 0. Hence, the full query matrix has a number of 1 that corresponds to the length of the query, *i.e.*, l_q (and thus to number of rows of the matrix). By so doing, the ith row of the matrix encodes the ith character of the query. When the query length is smaller than l_q we use zero-paddings, *i.e.*, the remaining rows are fully padded with zeros entries. When the query length is larger than l_q, we simply ignore all the characters appearing after the l_q^{th} character of the query.

The same approach is used for representing ads. The three components of a textual ad, *i.e.*, ad title, ad description and ad display URL, are first concatenated in the aforementioned order in one unique sequence, and then encoded with a matrix of of one-hot-encodings of size $l_a \times |V|$.

3.3.2 Model Architecture. DeepCharMatch consists of two parallel deep architectures that are joined by a cross-convolutional operator followed by a final bloc that models the relationship between a query and an ad. We detail this architecture in the following.

Query and Ad Blocs. Query and ad blocs are two parallel structures that take as input a character-level one-hot encodings of the query and the ad respectively. Each bloc is a sequence of a temporal convolution, followed by 2 convolutional blocks whose output is a vector representation of the considered input (*i.e.*, the query or the ad). Learnt representations can be seen as a higher-level representation of the query and of the ad.

Cross-convolutional Operator. Cross-convolutional operator (as introduced in [16]) takes as input higher-level representations of the query and of the ad (outputs of query and ad blocs) and operates a convolution on the cross-product of the query and the ad. More precisely, let H_Q be the higher-level query matrix representation with dimensions $k \times l$ and H_A be the higher-level ad matrix representation with dimensions $m \times r$ and H_{AQ} be the cross product of H_Q and H_A with dimensions $(k * m) \times (l + r)$. Formally, each row of H_{AQ} is set to

$$H_{QA}[i, \cdot] := H_Q[\lceil i/m \rceil, \cdot]^\frown H_A[i - m * (\lceil i/m \rceil - 1), \cdot],$$

where $i \in \mathbb{N}$, $1 \leq i \leq k * m$ and $^\frown$ represents concatenation. With this operation, we aim to capture possible intra-word and intra-sentence relationships between the query and the ad. A temporal max-pooling is applied at the end of this operation.

Final Bloc. The final operations start with a sequence of two blocks, where each block is a convolutional block followed by a temporal max-pooling. Finally, the architecture is ended with three fully connected layers. The Final Bloc models the relationship between the ad and the query. The output of the final bloc is p_{q_a} which is the CTR prediction of DeepCharMatch for the query-ad pair q_a.

3.4 DeepWordMatch Model

We also propose a deep convolutional neural network using word-level input. We refer to this model as DeepWordMatch. DeepWordMatch is also trained to maximize the conditional log-likelihood of the clicked and non-clicked sponsored impressions, *i.e.*, ads (Equation 1), and hence outputs the CTR prediction of the considered query-ad pair q_a.

3.4.1 Input Representation. Different from DeepCharMatch, DeepWordMatch processes pre-trained, word vectors instead of one-hot character encodings as input. The word vectors can be learnt using either search logs or external sources like Wikipedia [26]. Devising the best way of training word vectors is an interesting open problem but is independent of the model we propose. Considering given word dictionary W, dimension of word vectors d_w, fixed query length d_q and fixed ad length d_a, queries are represented with a query matrix with dimension $d_q \times d_w$. Similarly, ads are represented with an ad matrix with dimension $d_a \times d_w$.

3.4.2 Model Architecture. The structure of the neural network is inspired from the matching algorithm for natural languages sentences introduced in [16]. It consists of a cross-convolution operator ended by a final block capturing the commonalities between the query and the ad. Ad and query matrixes consist of pre-trained word vectors directly feed into cross-convolution operator. In order to control dimensionality, kernel sizes of the temporal max-pooling operations are set to 2. Except those points, the architecture of DeepWordMatch is equivalent to the architecture of DeepCharMatch.

4 EXPERIMENTS

We evaluate the performance of the proposed CTR prediction models in this section. We first present how we collect the data set to conduct the experiments, the different baselines that are important to this study, and the metrics that are relevant to evaluate CTR

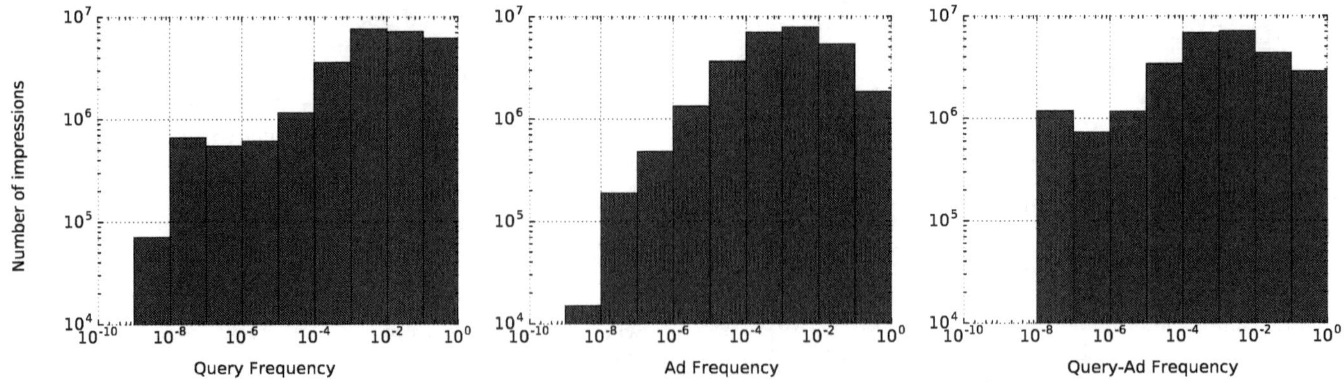

Figure 3: Distribution of impressions in the test set with respect to query, ad, and query-ad frequencies computed on six months (The frequencies are normalized by the maximum value in each subplot).

prediction models. We also describe the platform to run our experiments and the choice of parameters. We then dive into each research question raised in the introduction and discuss the results we obtain from the related experiments.

4.1 Experimental Setup

4.1.1 Dataset. In order to test our research hypotheses (Section 1) we randomly sample query-ad pairs served by a popular commercial search engine. More precisely, we randomly sample from the log the *training set* that consists of about 1.5 billion query-ad pairs served during the period going from August 6 to September 5, 2016. We only consider the sponsored ads that are shown in the north of the search result pages (*i.e.* above the algorithmic search results). Each sampled query-ad consists of the query, the ad title, the ad description and the displayed URL of the ad's landing page, in their canonical form, and a binary variable indicating if the ad is clicked or not. In the following 15 days from September 6 to September 20, 2016, We randomly sample the *test set* that consists of about 27 millions query-ad pairs without any page position restriction (*i.e.*, we also test for the ads displayed on the east and the south of search result pages).

In order to study the performance of our models on queries and ads with different popularity, we compute query frequency distribution, ad frequency distribution and query-ad frequency distribution of the queries and ads in our test set over a long period (*i.e.*, some consecutive months of 2016). Figure 3 reports the distributions of the total number of ad impressions related to the queries, ads or query-ad pairs following into each frequency bin. Notice that this period fully covers the periods in which our training and test sets are generated. Therefore, low frequency measures the coldness relative to the entire period.

4.1.2 Baselines. ***Feature-engineered logistic regression (FELR).*** Logistic regression is a state-of-the-art algorithm to predict CTR at massive scale [24]. Therefore, we implement a logistic regression model with content-based features as a baseline. Our objective is to test the hypotheses that DeepCharMatch and DeepWordMatch can learn directly from the textual input meaningful representations that are better than feature-engineered models.

Table 1: AUC of DeepCharMatch, DeepWordMatch, Search2Vec and FELR.

	All	Desktop	Mobile
DeepCharMatch	**0.862**	**0.870**	**0.828**
DeepWordMatch	0.859	0.867	0.827
Search2Vec	0.780	0.796	0.705
FELR	0.772	0.784	0.710

The logistic regression model optimizes the same cross-entropy loss function as DeepCharMatch and DeepWordMatch (Equation 1). In this case, θ is simply a parameter vector representing the weights to be learned for each feature along with the bias. We use the 185 state-of-the-art features designed to capture the pairwise relationship between a query and the three different components in a textual ad, *i.e.*, its title, description, and display URL. The full set of features consists of 12 common counts features, 12 Jaccard features, 10 length features, 4 cosine similarity features, 4 BM25 features, 8 Brand features, 4 LSI features, 3 semantic coherence features, and 128 hash embedding features. These features are explained in details in [1] and are achieving state-of-the-art results in relevance prediction for sponsored search. Most of these features are the state-of-the-art features in traditional search tasks as supervised ranking, semi-supervised ranking, and ranking aggregation [27].

Search2Vec. Our second baseline is a state-of-the-art word2vec-based approach, namely Search2Vec [12], which learns semantic embeddings for queries and ads from search sessions, and uses the cosine similarity between the learnt vectors to measure the textual similarity between a query and an ad. This approach leads to high-quality query-ad matching in sponsored search. Different from DeepCharMatch and DeepWordMatch, Search2Vec does not learn CTR directly. Instead, clicks are used indirectly in the session data as context of the surrounding queries and ads. Therefore, this approach is considered to be weakly-supervised. Another important difference is that Search2Vec works at query level and ad level, implying that it is more sensitive to the out-of-vocabulary problem.

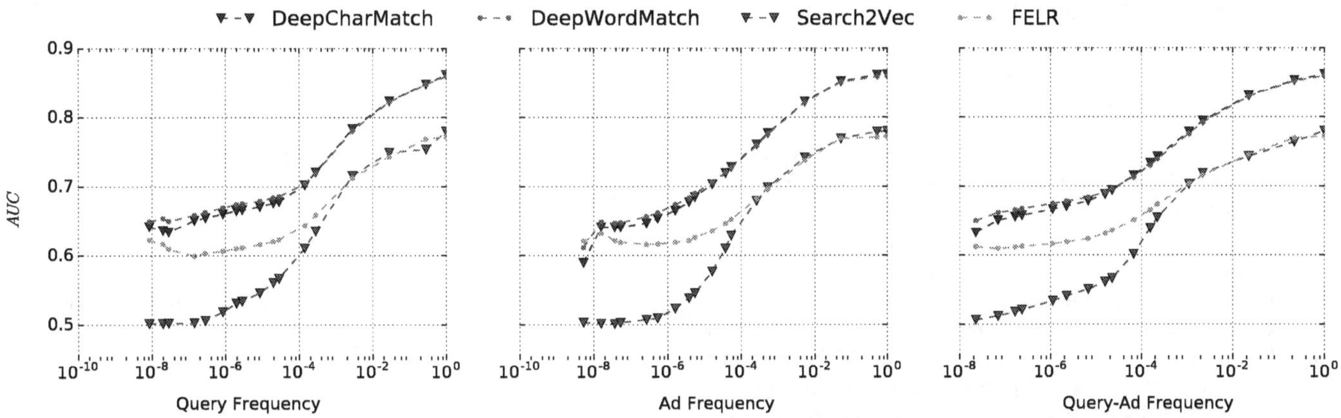

Figure 4: Cumulative AUC by query, ad, and query-ad frequency for DeepCharMatch, DeepWordMatch, Search2Vec and FELR. Frequencies are normalized by the maximum value in each subplot. For each bin, the number of impressions used to compute AUC is reported in Figure 3. Cumulative means that at x the plot reports AUC of points whose frequency is lower than x.

Table 2: AUC of DeepCharMatch, DeepWordMatch, Search2Vec and FELR, on *tail*, *torso*, and *head* of the query, ad, and query-ad frequency distributions. Tail stands for normalized frequency $nf < 10^{-6}$, torso for $10^{-6} \leq nf < 10^{-2}$, and head for $nf \geq 10^{-2}$.

	Query			Ad			Query-Ad		
	tail	*torso*	*head*	*tail*	*torso*	*head*	*tail*	*torso*	*head*
DeepCharMatch	0.661	**0.814**	**0.909**	0.659	**0.836**	**0.926**	0.665	**0.828**	**0.943**
DeepWordMatch	**0.670**	0.812	0.907	**0.668**	0.835	0.922	**0.674**	0.826	**0.943**
Search2Vec	0.521	0.739	0.817	0.516	0.753	0.844	0.532	0.740	0.854
FELR	0.606	0.733	0.821	0.618	0.751	0.830	0.615	0.742	0.879

Production model. As a very strong baseline, we are considering the CTR prediction model in the production system of a popular commercial search engine. This model is a machine learning model trained with a rich set of features, including click features, query features, ad features, query-ad pair features, vertical features, contextual features such as geolocation or time of the day, and user features. The learning algorithm is optimizing Equation 1 as well. This model involves great engineering efforts to design relevant features, especially those content-based features extracting the relationship between queries and ads. Our objective is to study what are the relative improvements one can expect in production when adding a deep learning content-based dimension (*i.e.*, DeepCharMatch or DeepWordMatch prediction) into this model. Therefore, we use a simple approach that averages the deep model CTR with the production model CTR. In the remainder we refer to these algorithms as DCP and DWP, for the combination of character-level model, and word-level model respectively with production. While these approaches are very simple, it suffices to demonstrate that a content-based deep learning approach can be leveraged to improve the model in production of a commercial search engine that is not learning automatically content-based query-ads representations.

4.1.3 Evaluation Metrics. We measure two standards metrics: (1) the area under the ROC curve (AUC), and (2) the calibration of the CTR [2].

AUC. For comparing the different baselines we use the AUC to evaluate the ability of the different methods to predict which ad impressions are going to be clicked. On ad impressions held out during learning, AUC measures whether the clicked ad impressions are ranked higher than the non-clicked ones. The perfect ranking has an AUC of 1.0, while the average AUC for random rankings is 0.5.

Calibration. The calibration is the ratio of the number of expected clicks to the number of actually observed clicks. Having a well calibrated prediction of CTR insures that advertisers are paying a fair price, and is thus critical for online adverting auction. The closer the calibration measure is to 1.0, the better the CTR prediction is [14].

4.1.4 Experimental Platform. We train DeepCharMatch, DeepWordMatch, and FELR using the same environment. We use the distributed Tensorflow platform[2] in an asynchronous fashion on multiple GPUs. Adam Optimizer [22] is used in order to optimize the cross-entropy loss function. To initialize the parameters, we use the initialization strategy described in [13]. The mini-batch size is set to 64. For DeepCharMatch, we fix the query length l_q to 35 characters, and ad length l_a to 140 characters. For DeepWordMatch, we fix the query word-length d_q to 7 and the ad word-length d_a to 40. The word vectors feeding the input of DeepWordMatch are publicly available[3] and consists of 50 dimension vectors obtained by running GloVe algorithm on Wikipedia and Gigaword5[4] [26].

[2]https://www.tensorflow.org/
[3]http://nlp.stanford.edu/data/glove.6B.zip
[4]https://catalog.ldc.upenn.edu/LDC2011T07

4.2 Experimental Results

We report in this section the performance of the proposed character-level and word-level CTR prediction models by answering the following research questions.

Research Question 1. Can we automatically learn representations from the query-ad content without any feature engineering in order to predict the CTR in sponsored search?

Our objective is to test the extent to which the representations learnt by the introduced deep models are more effective than the 185 engineered-features injected in a state-of-the-art algorithm for CTR prediction, *i.e.*, FELR. We show that DeepCharMatch and DeepWordMatch outperform FELR on Desktop and Mobile in terms of AUC by up to 0.086 and 0.118 respectively (Table 1). This confirms that both models can automatically learn more effective query-ad representations for predicting the CTR than the 185 engineered-features used by FELR. Notice that the improvements are larger on the head of the distributions where the frequency are the highest (Figure 4 and Table 2). This highlights that the automatically learnt representations generalize better than engineered features when queries, ads, and query-ads are more frequent.

Research Question 2. How does the performance of the character-level deep learning model differ from that of the word-level model for CTR prediction?

Here, we are interested to study the learning curve performance of the two proposed models. In other words, as we increase the number of training samples, what AUC can we expect on the same independent randomly sampled test set. We hypothesize that by learning at character level instead of word level, the model can fit the CTR distribution better. This hypothesis is based on the fact that the character-level model has a higher degree of freedom as it needs to learn 1,672,002 parameters, *i.e.*, 16.21% more than the word-level model (Table 3).

Table 3: Number of parameters per model

DeepCharMatch	DeepWordMatch	FELR
1,672,002	1,438,786	186

To answer this question, we conduct a parallel experiment between DeepCharMatch and DeepWordMatch. Both models are studied under exactly the same conditions, *i.e.*, learnt on the same training points and assessed on the same test points.

We show that as the number of training points goes over one billion, DeepCharMatch offers more flexibility than DeepWordMatch to learn the underlying query-ad matching. At 1.5 billion points the difference becomes significant: on the 27 millions test points, DeepCharMatch and DeepWordMatch reaches an AUC of 0.862 and 0.859 respectively (Figure 5 and Table 1). This confirms that, when provided with enough training points, DeepCharMatch learns the underlying representations from scratch without the need of a pre-computed dictionary (like the Wikipedia word vectors used by DeepWordMatch in this particular study). Interestingly, when looking at the differences in terms of heads and tails of the query, ad, and query-ad distributions, DeepCharMatch outperforms or equals to DeepWordMatch on the heads where the volume is the highest.

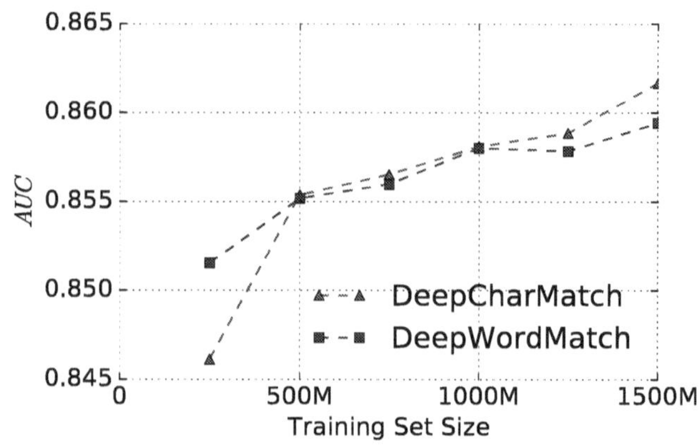

Figure 5: AUC of DeepCharMatch and DeepWordMatch by number of training points.

Inversely, DeepWordMatch outperforms DeepCharMatch on the tails (Table 2). Indeed, DeepWordMatch has an advantage on the tails as it benefits from pre-trained vectors that provide at cold-start an initial knowledge that the character-level model is ignorant of. On the other hand, when shifting towards the heads, DeepCharMatch benefits from its representations learnt from scratch to build a better understanding of the domain.

Research Question 3. How do the introduced character-level and word-level deep learning models compare to the baseline models? What is the improvement of prediction accuracy on head, torso, and tail queries, ads, and query-ad pairs?

Here we are interested to study how the proposed deep models compare to both baselines FELR and Search2Vec especially in different areas of the query, ad, and query-ad distributions. While globally Search2Vec outperforms FELR (Table 1), it appears to be a very poor baseline when it comes to tail queries, ads, and query-ads (Table 2). This emphasizes the fact that Search2Vec is working at query, and ad-identifier level. In other words, the approach cannot relate similar ads or queries based on their content, but only based on their occurrences in the same context. Both DeepCharMatch and DeepWordMatch consistently outperform the baselines from a minimum 0.041 of AUC on the tail of the ad distribution, to a maximum of 0.088 of AUC on the head of the queries distribution. Interestingly, the improvements over the baselines are more important for mobile devices (Table 1), which could indicate that the introduced deep models are less sensitive to the sampling bias (as our training data is by nature more populated with desktop impressions). We leave as further work a deeper analysis of the importance of the sampling on performance obtained by each device.

Research Question 4. Can the proposed character-level and word-level deep learning models be leveraged to improve the CTR prediction model running in the production system of a popular commercial search engine?

The current system in production is relying on engineering-efforts to design relevant content features extracting the relationship between queries and ads. Our objective is to study how much relative improvements one can expect in production in terms of

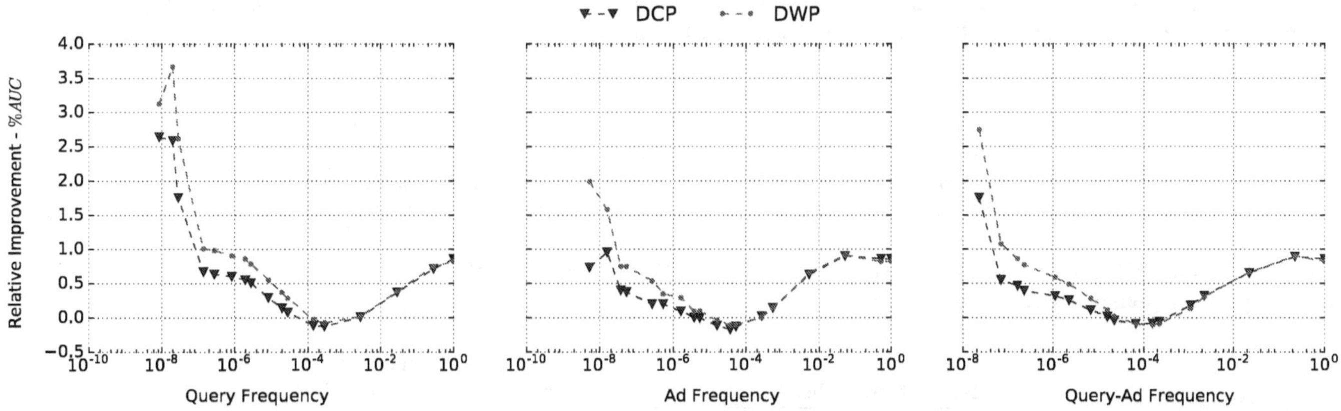

Figure 6: Cumulative relative improvements of DCP and DWP over Production model in terms of %*AUC*. Frequencies are normalized by the maximum value of each subplot. For each bin, the number of impressions used to compute AUC is reported in Figure 3. Cumulative means that at x the plot reports relative improvements of points whose frequency is lower than x.

Table 4: Relative AUC Improvement in % of DCP over Production model.

	All	Desktop	Mobile
DCP	**0.86**	**0.29**	3.76
DWP	0.82	0.23	**3.95**

Table 5: Relative Calibration Improvement in % of DCP over Production Model.

	All	Desktop	Mobile
DCP	**35.76**	**34.95**	**40.40**
DWP	32.21	30.85	38.50

AUC and calibration when adding a deep learning content-based dimension into the production model. We proceed this test using two simple approaches, DCP and DWP, which average respectively the character-level and word-level predicted CTR to the production predicted CTR (as explained in Section 4.2). We observe relative improvements of 0.86% of the production AUC when considering the complete test set, with very significant improvements of 3.75% of the production AUC when restricting to mobile devices (Table 4). Major gains are observed on the head of the distribution with improvements of up to 1.18% of the production AUC (Table 6). Interestingly, as observed previously, we observe higher improvements with the character-level model at the heads of the distributions, while the word-level model is more beneficial on the tails. This highlights that DeepWordMatch benefits more of its pre-trained vectors on tails, while on the heads the DeepCharMatch reaches a better understanding of the domain by learning directly its representations at character level.

For calibration analysis, let us consider the relative gain in calibration of model $\mathcal{M}$ over the Production model:

$$\frac{|1 - Calibration(Production)| - |1 - Calibration(\mathcal{M})|}{|1 - Calibration(Production)|}$$

This gain measures the relative decrease of the calibration error in production (*i.e.* —1-Calibration(Production)—) when using model $\mathcal{M}$. We observe an important relative calibration gain in production with DCP model and DWP model with up to 34.95% on Desktop and 40.40% on Mobile (Table 5). Finally, we observe that the calibration is better on the heads than on the tails especially with the character-level model (Table 7).

5 CONCLUSIONS

We present in this paper two new content-based click-though-rate prediction models for sponsored search. Both models are built on convolutional neural network architectures and learnt in a supervised way from clicked and non-clicked query-ad impressions sampled from the log of popular a commercial search engine. We demonstrate through large-scale experiments (with 1.5 billions query-ad training samples) that query-ad representations can be learnt from scratch, at character level, to predict the CTR, and the prediction is particularly accurate for frequent queries, ads and query-ad pairs. We also show that when using pre-trained word vectors, the proposed word-level model can make more accurate prediction on the tail of the query, ad and query-ad frequency distributions than the character-level model. One important contribution of this work is to show that predicting CTR of query-ad pairs directly at character level can outperform the traditional machine learning models trained with well-designed features. Particularly, when combining the CTR prediction of the proposed deep learning models with that of the machine learning model trained with a rich set of content-based and click-based features in the production system of a popular commercial search engine, we can significantly improve the accuracy and the calibration of the model in production.

REFERENCES

[1] Luca Maria Aiello, Ioannis Arapakis, Ricardo A. Baeza-Yates, Xiao Bai, Nicola Barbieri, Amin Mantrach, and Fabrizio Silvestri. 2016. The Role of Relevance in Sponsored Search. In *Proceedings of the 25th ACM CIKM*. 185–194.
[2] Ricardo A. Baeza-Yates and Berthier Ribeiro-Neto. 1999. *Modern Information Retrieval*. Addison-Wesley Longman Publishing Co., Inc., Boston, MA, USA.

Table 6: Relative AUC Improvements in % of DCP and DWP over Production on *tail*, *torso*, and *head* of the query, ad, and query-ad frequency distributions. Tail stands for normalized frequency $nf < 10^{-6}$, torso for $10^{-6} \leq nf < 10^{-2}$, and head for $nf \geq 10^{-2}$.

	Query			Ad			Query-Ad		
	tail	torso	head	tail	torso	head	tail	torso	head
DCP	0.593	0.205	**1.176**	0.127	0.793	**0.817**	0.322	**0.584**	1.010
DWP	**0.906**	**0.218**	1.096	**0.324**	**0.818**	0.723	**0.604**	0.571	**1.090**

Table 7: Relative Calibration Improvements in % of DCP and DWP over Production on *tail*, *torso*, and *head* of the query, ad, and query-ad frequency distributions.

	Query			Ad			Query-Ad		
	tail	torso	head	tail	torso	head	tail	torso	head
DCP	**31.44**	**33.62**	**38.02**	**32.82**	**35.01**	**38.38**	**30.28**	**34.30**	**42.64**
DWP	30.73	31.02	32.96	29.89	32.27	32.31	29.33	31.51	37.68

[3] Miguel Ballesteros, Chris Dyer, and Noah A Smith. 2015. Improved Transition-Based Parsing by Modeling Characters instead of Words with LSTMs. In *Proceedings of EMNLP.* 349–359.

[4] Ye Chen and Tak W Yan. 2012. Position-normalized click prediction in search advertising. In *Proceedings of the 18th ACM SIGKDD.* 795–803.

[5] Haibin Cheng and Erick Cantú-Paz. 2010. Personalized click prediction in sponsored search. In *Proceedings of the 3rd ACM WSDM.* ACM, 351–360.

[6] I Conneau, Holger Schwenk, Loïc Barrault, and Yann LeCun. 2016. Very Deep Convolutional Networks for Natural Language Processing. *CoRR* abs/1606.01781 (2016).

[7] Cicero Nogueira dos Santos and Bianca Zadrozny. 2014. Learning Character-level Representations for Part-of-Speech Tagging. In *Proceedings of the 31st ICML.* 1818–1826.

[8] Stephan Dreiseitl and Lucila Ohno-Machado. 2002. Logistic regression and artificial neural network classification models: a methodology review. *Journal of biomedical informatics* 35, 5 (2002), 352–359.

[9] Benjamin Edelman, Michael Ostrovsky, and Michael Schwarz. 2005. *Internet Advertising and the Generalized Second Price Auction: Selling Billions of Dollars Worth of Keywords.* Technical Report 11765. National Bureau of Economic Research.

[10] Xavier Glorot, Antoine Bordes, and Yoshua Bengio. 2011. Deep Sparse Rectifier Neural Networks. In *Proceedings of the 14th AISTAT,* Vol. 15. 315–323.

[11] Thore Graepel, Joaquin Q Candela, Thomas Borchert, and Ralf Herbrich. 2010. Web-scale bayesian click-through rate prediction for sponsored search advertising in Microsoft's Bing search engine. In *Proceedings of the 27th ICML.* 13–20.

[12] Mihajlo Grbovic, Nemanja Djuric, Vladan Radosavljevic, Fabrizio Silvestri, Ricardo Baeza-Yates, Andrew Feng, Erik Ordentlich, Lee Yang, and Gavin Owens. 2016. Scalable semantic matching of queries to ads in sponsored search advertising. In *Proceedings of the 39th ACM SIGIR.* 375–384.

[13] Kaiming He, Xiangyu Zhang, Shaoqing Ren, and Jian Sun. 2015. Delving deep into rectifiers: Surpassing human-level performance on imagenet classification. In *Proceedings of IEEE ICCV.*

[14] Xinran He, Junfeng Pan, Ou Jin, Tianbing Xu, Bo Liu, Tao Xu, Yanxin Shi, Antoine Atallah, Ralf Herbrich, Stuart Bowers, and others. 2014. Practical lessons from predicting clicks on ads at facebook. In *Proceedings of the 8th International Workshop on Data Mining for Online Advertising.* 1–9.

[15] Dustin Hillard, Eren Manavoglu, Hema Raghavan, Chris Leggetter, Erick Cantú-Paz, and Rukmini Iyer. 2011. The Sum of Its Parts: Reducing Sparsity in Click Estimation with Query Segments. *Information Retrieval* 14, 3 (June 2011), 315–336.

[16] Baotian Hu, Zhengdong Lu, Hang Li, and Qingcai Chen. 2014. Convolutional Neural Network Architectures for Matching Natural Language Sentences. In *Proceedings of the 27th NIPS.* 2042–2050.

[17] Po-Sen Huang, Xiaodong He, Jianfeng Gao, Li Deng, Alex Acero, and Larry Heck. 2013. Learning Deep Structured Semantic Models for Web Search Using Clickthrough Data. In *Proceedings of the 22nd ACM CIKM.* 2333–2338.

[18] Sergey Ioffe and Christian Szegedy. 2015. Batch Normalization: Accelerating Deep Network Training by Reducing Internal Covariate Shift. In *Proceedings of the 32nd ICML.* 448–456.

[19] Zilong Jiang, Shu Gao, and Wei Dai. 2016. Research on CTR Prediction for Contextual Advertising Based on Deep Architecture Model. *Journal of Control Engineering and Applied Informatics* 18, 1 (2016), 11–19.

[20] Yuchin Juan, Yong Zhuang, Wei-Sheng Chin, and Chih-Jen Lin. 2016. Field-aware factorization machines for CTR prediction. In *Proceedings of the 10th ACM RecSys.* 43–50.

[21] Yoon Kim, Yacine Jernite, David Sontag, and Alexander M Rush. 2016. Character-Aware Neural Language Models. In *Proceedings of the 13th AAAI.* 2741–2749.

[22] Diederik P. Kingma and Jimmy Ba. 2014. Adam: A Method for Stochastic Optimization. In *Proceedings of the 3rd ICLR.*

[23] Y. Lecun, L. Bottou, Y. Bengio, and P. Haffner. 1998. Gradient-based learning applied to document recognition. *Proc. IEEE* 86, 11 (1998), 2278–2324.

[24] H Brendan McMahan, Gary Holt, David Sculley, Michael Young, Dietmar Ebner, Julian Grady, Lan Nie, Todd Phillips, Eugene Davydov, Daniel Golovin, and others. 2013. Ad click prediction: a view from the trenches. In *Proceedings of the 19th ACM SIGKDD.* 1222–1230.

[25] Aranyak Mehta, Amin Saberi, Umesh Vazirani, and Vijay Vazirani. 2005. AdWords and Generalized On-line Matching. In *Proceedings of the 46th IEEE FOCS.* 264–273.

[26] Jeffrey Pennington, Richard Socher, and Christopher D. Manning. 2014. GloVe: Global Vectors for Word Representation. In *Proceedings of EMNLP.* 1532–1543.

[27] Tao Qin and Tie-Yan Liu. 2013. Introducing LETOR 4.0 Datasets. *CoRR* abs/1306.2597 (2013).

[28] Matthew Richardson, Ewa Dominowska, and Robert Ragno. 2007. Predicting clicks: estimating the click-through rate for new ads. In *Proceedings of the 16th WWW.* 521–530.

[29] Cicero Nogueira dos Santos and Victor Guimaraes. 2015. Boosting named entity recognition with neural character embeddings. *CoRR* abs/1505.05008 (2015).

[30] Martin Saveski and Amin Mantrach. 2014. Item cold-start recommendations: learning local collective embeddings. In *Proceedings of the 8th ACM RecSys.* 89–96.

[31] Benyah Shaparenko, Özgür Çetin, and Rukmini Iyer. 2009. Data-driven Text Features for Sponsored Search Click Prediction. In *Proceedings of the 3rd International Workshop on Data Mining and Audience Intelligence for Advertising.* 46–54.

[32] Yelong Shen, Xiaodong He, Jianfeng Gao, Li Deng, and Grégoire Mesnil. 2014. A latent semantic model with convolutional-pooling structure for information retrieval. In *Proceedings of the 23rd ACM CIKM.* 101–110.

[33] Taifeng Wang, Jiang Bian, Shusen Liu, Yuyu Zhang, and Tie-Yan Liu. 2013. Psychological Advertising: Exploring User Psychology for Click Prediction in Sponsored Search. In *Proceedings of the 19th ACM SIGKDD.* 563–571.

[34] Shuangfei Zhai, Keng-hao Chang, Ruofei Zhang, and Zhongfei (Mark) Zhang. 2016. DeepIntent: Learning Attentions for Online Advertising with Recurrent Neural Networks. In *Proceedings of the 22nd ACM SIGKDD.* 1295–1304.

[35] Xiang Zhang, Junbo Zhao, and Yann LeCun. 2015. Character-level Convolutional Networks for Text Classification. In *Proceedings of the 28th NIPS.* 649–657.

[36] Yuyu Zhang, Hanjun Dai, Chang Xu, Jun Feng, Taifeng Wang, Jiang Bian, Bin Wang, and Tie-Yan Liu. 2016. Sequential Click Prediction for Sponsored Search with Recurrent Neural Networks.. In *Proceedings of the 11th AAAI Conference.* 1369–1375.

Personalized Key Frame Recommendation

Xu Chen*
Tsinghua University
xu-ch14@mails.tsinghua.edu.cn

Yongfeng Zhang*
University of Massachusetts Amherst
zhangyf07@gmail.com

Qingyao Ai
University of Massachusetts Amherst
aiqy@cs.umass.edu

Hongteng Xu
Georgia Institute of Technology
hxu42@gatech.edu

Junchi Yan
East China Normal University
IBM Research -- China
jcyan@sei.ecnu.edu.cn

Zheng Qin†
Tsinghua University
qinzh@mails.tsinghua.edu.cn

ABSTRACT

Key frames are playing a very important role for many video applications, such as on-line movie preview and video information retrieval. Although a number of key frame selection methods have been proposed in the past, existing technologies mainly focus on how to precisely summarize the video content, but seldom take the user preferences into consideration. However, in real scenarios, people may cast diverse interests on the contents even for the same video, and thus they may be attracted by quite different key frames, which makes the selection of key frames an inherently personalized process. In this paper, we propose and investigate the problem of personalized key frame recommendation to bridge the above gap. To do so, we make use of video images and user time-synchronized comments to design a novel key frame recommender that can simultaneously model visual and textual features in a unified framework. By user personalization based on her/his previously reviewed frames and posted comments, we are able to encode different user interests in a unified multi-modal space, and can thus select key frames in a personalized manner, which, to the best of our knowledge, is the first time in the research field of video content analysis. Experimental results show that our method performs better than its competitors on various measures.

KEYWORDS

Key Frame; Personalization; Recommender Systems; Collaborative Filtering; Video Content Analysis

1 INTRODUCTION

All along, key frames are of fundamental importance for the video-based applications, for example, users in the on-line movie websites can readily preview a video under the help the exhibited key frames even without watching the whole content, video search engines can efficiently return the results by matching the queries with the key frames of the candidate items. Although key frame extraction methods [10, 22, 58] have been widely investigated in the past, the proposed technologies mostly aim to summarize the video content, but seldom consider user preferences on the extracted key frames. However, in many applications, different people may be interested in various video contents, and thus may be attracted by quite different key frames. Without the guidance of tailored key frames, users may easily miss their potentially favorite videos. Therefore, in this paper, we would like to ask "whether it is possible to design an effective model to select and recommend personalized key frames according to users' different tastes."

In real scenarios, the main challenge to answer the above question is the lack of users' personalized interaction information that reveals their "frame-level" viewing preferences. Fortunately, the emerging of video sharing websites such as Niconico[1], BiliBili[2], and AcFun[3] may shed light on this problem, where users are allowed to express opinions directly to the frames of interest by time-synchronized comments (or TSCs, first introduced in [49], see Figure 1) in a real-time manner. Intuitively, the user behaviors of commenting on a frame can be regarded as implicit feedback reflecting the *frame-level preference*, while the image features of the reviewed frame and the text features in the posted time-synchronized comment can further help to model the *user specific (or finer-grained) preference* from different perspectives. For example in Figure 1, user A expresses her preference on a frame with time-synchronized comment "*... I like his overcoat, it looks cool and also must be very comfortable with good quality*". On one hand, from the content of the time-synchronized comment we can indicate that the user express a positive sentiment on this frame, and the particular aspect that attracts her attention is the quality of the clothes. On the other hand, from the frame image, we can further infer the visual features of her interests, such as clothing texture, which are usually difficult to describe with text. By leveraging all the historical implicit feedback as well as the features (image and text) of users' interest, we can collaboratively match a target user with her potentially favorite frames.

Based on the above motivation and intuition, we describe and analyze a novel **K**ey **F**rame **R**ecommender by modeling user time-synchronized **C**omments and the key frame **I**mages simultaneously (called **KFRCI**). The main building block of our proposed method is to integrate the power of model-based collaborative filtering and

* Both authors contributed equally to this work.
† Corresponding author.

SIGIR '17, August 7–11, 2017, Shinjuku, Tokyo, Japan

978-1-4503-5022-8/17/08...$15.00
DOI: http://dx.doi.org/10.1145/3077136.3080776

[1]http://www.nicovideo.jp
[2]http://www.bilibili.com
[3]http://www.acfun.cn

long-short term memory network. The carefully designed collaborative filtering component aims to capture user preferences based on image features, while the modified long-short term memory network component aims to model user time-synchronized comments to excavate her personalized opinions toward different frames. Furthermore, by integrating these two components, we build a unified framework that can encode user preference in a multi-modal space so as to facilitate comprehensive user profiling and accurate key frame recommendation.

Compared with previous works, the main contributions of our paper are as follows:

- We propose and investigate the problem of personalized key frame recommendation, and to the best of our knowledge, this is the first work to select video key frames based on users' personalized preferences.
- For better addressing the above novel problem, we present a novel neural architecture that combines collaborative filtering and long-short term memory network together to jointly model user time-synchronized comments and video key frame images.
- We conduct extensive experiments to demonstrate the effectiveness of our proposed models, and also we present detailed analysis on the parameters as well as the effects of different information sources (image and text) in our framework.

In the rest of the paper, we first introduce the related work in section 2, and then formally define our problem in section 3. Our framework is illustrated in section 4. In section 5, we verify the effectiveness of our method with experimental results. Conclusions and outlooks of this work are presented in section 6.

2 RELATED WORK

2.1 Review-based Recommendation

Recommender system is a well studied field with many effective models proposed [5, 7, 17, 19, 35, 39]. Recently, for better capturing user preferences, user reviews has attracted more and more research interest [3, 42, 43], and many review-based models have been proposed to improve the recommendation performance [2, 4, 9, 11, 29, 31, 37, 41, 45, 46, 51, 56] or enhance the interpretability [16, 38, 50, 50, 57].

According to the review processing methods, these models can be generally classified into two categories. On one hand, some methods leverage the review text on document- or review-level, which take every piece of user review as a whole for global analysis. Specifically, [31, 41] link the latent factors in rating data with the topics in the textual review to generate more accurate recommendations, and [9, 51] propose to leverage probabilistic graphical method to include more flexible prior knowledge for review modeling. To better capture the local semantic information in user reviews, [56] combine traditional matrix factorization technology with word2vec [34] for more precise review modeling and recommendation.,

On the other hand, some approaches try to leverage textual reviews on a feature- or aspect-level, which first extract product features and user sentiments from user reviews, and then represent the unstructured free-text reviews as structured feature-opinion

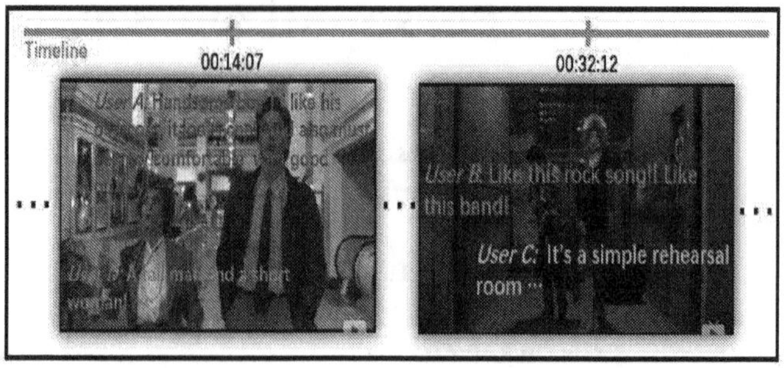

Figure 1: A simple example of TSC. Different users may express real-time opinions directly upon their interested frames. The comments are manually translated into English by the authors.

pairs to facilitate finer-grained user preference modeling. Particularly, [57] use multi-matrix factorization to generate explainable recommendations based on the extracted product features. [4] further captures user favorite product features in a learning to rank manner.

Compared with the aforementioned methods, we leverage long-short term memory network in our model to capture the word sequential properties mirrored in the time-synchronized comments, which has mostly been ignore by the previous works.

2.2 Image-based Recommendation

Recently, there is a trend to incorporate visual features into the research of personalized recommendation [8, 15, 32]. Specifically, [15] infuses the image features into the traditional ranking-based method to improve the performance of Top-N recommendation. [8] combines the product images and item descriptions together to make dynamic predictions. [32] leverages visual features to discover different relationships between items.

Generally, these methods aim to take advantage of image features to boost the performance of traditional item recommendation, such as product recommendation in E-commerce. Instead, we aim at a very different task of key frame (which itself is an image) recommendation, where image is not a side information but the target to process. Besides, previous works did not capture user preference from the time-synchronized comments, which is another main difference when compared with our model.

2.3 Time-synchronized Comments

Time-Synchronized Comments (TSC) is first introduced in [49] for automatic video shot tagging, where the authors proposed a novel method to extract time-synchronized video tags by automatically exploiting crowd-sourcing comments. [52] further leverages TSC to extract highlight shots for a video with a frequency-based method. However, the extracted highlight shots are static and could not provide tailed key frames for different users, which is the inherent difference from the personalized key frame recommendation task targeted in our work.

2.4 Key Frame Extraction

A similar research direction to our work is key frame extraction (or video summarization), it has attracted much research interest and many models have been proposed in the past. Early works [13, 28] usually extract visual features of frames at first, and then cluster frames accordingly to generate key frames. To improve the performance, other types of information beyond visual features are considered in recent work, including the viewer attention [30, 53, 54], audio signal [23], subtitles [27], etc. Moreover, semantic information has also been exploited to summarize videos, including special events [47, 48], key people and objects [24, 26], and story-lines [25]. Compared with these models, our work essentially make a further step forward by distinguishing user preferences on the extracted key frames.

3 PRELIMINARIES AND PROBLEM DEFINITION

3.1 Dataset Inspection

The data used in our work is crawled from a well-known video sharing website Bilibili[4]. We obtained the time-synchronized comments from the movie category till December 10th, 2015. To better understand the insights of this dataset, we conducted preliminary statistic analyses, which are listed as Table 1 and Figure 2.

Table 1: Overall statistics of the time-synchronized comment (TSC) dataset.

Total number of users (#users)	1,133,750
Total number of movies (#movies)	7,166
Total number of TSCs (#TSCs)	11,842,166
Ave. TSCs per movie	1,652.5
Ave. users per movie	465.9
Ave. TSCs per user	10.4
Max/Min number of TSCs for a movie	8,028/101
Max/Min number of users for a movie	3,370/1
Max/Min number of TSCs for a user	68,236/1

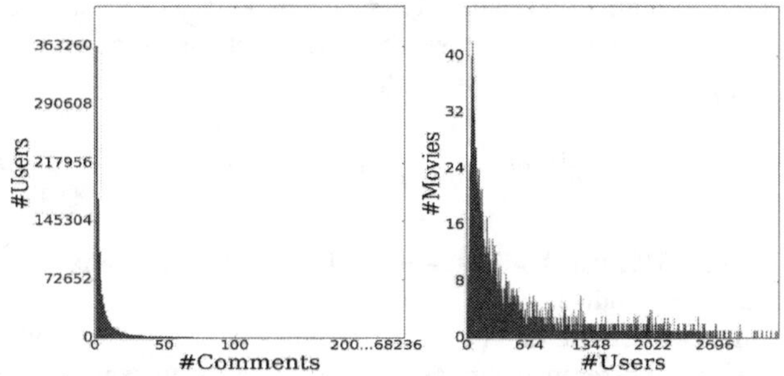

Figure 2: On the left is the relation between the number of comments and users, while on the right is the relation between the number of users and movies.

[4]http://www.bilibili.com

As can be seen in Figure 2, the quantity of active users is relatively small, and most users only sent a small number of TSCs, which conforms to the "long tail" theory that is frequently observed in user behavior analysis. Similar results can also be found between the number of users and movies.

3.2 Problem Formalization

Suppose there are N users $\boldsymbol{u} = \{u_1, u_2, ..., u_N\}$ and M videos $\boldsymbol{v} = \{v_1, v_2, ..., v_M\}$. We first segment each movie $v_i \in \boldsymbol{v}$ into L shots $\boldsymbol{l}_{v_i} = \{l^1_{v_i}, l^2_{v_i}, ..., l^L_{v_i}\}$, and then generate key frames correspondingly leveraging existing methods such as [33, 36]. The key frame in shot $l^j_{v_i}$ is defined as $k^j_{v_i}$, and $\boldsymbol{K}$ represents the whole set of key frames among all the videos.

Suppose the visual features of key frame k is defined as $\boldsymbol{vsl}_k$, and let user u's time-synchronized comment on key frame k be tsc_{uk} with sentiment polarity $\boldsymbol{pol}_{uk}$, which is determined by the Stanford sentiment analysis toolkit[5]. The word list in tsc_{uk} is defined as $\boldsymbol{w}_{tsc_{uk}} = \{w^0_{tsc_{uk}}, w^1_{tsc_{uk}}, ..., w^{s_{uk}-1}_{tsc_{uk}}\}$, where s_{uk} is the length of the comment.

Given all the visual features $\boldsymbol{VSL} = \{\boldsymbol{vsl}_k | k \in \boldsymbol{K}\}$ as well as users' historical time-synchronized comments $\boldsymbol{W} = \{\boldsymbol{w}_{tsc_{uk}} | u \in \boldsymbol{u}, k \in \boldsymbol{K}\}$ and their corresponding sentiments $\boldsymbol{POL} = \{pol_{uk} | u \in \boldsymbol{u}, k \in \boldsymbol{K}\}$, for a target user u and one of her unseen movie $v_i \in V$ with preselected key frames $\{k^1_{v_i}, k^2_{v_i}, ...k^L_{v_i}\}$, our task is to find a function $g(\cdot)$ to re-rank these key frames according to $u's$ interest, that is, $g(\{k^1_{v_i}, k^2_{v_i}, ..., k^L_{v_i}\} | u, \boldsymbol{W}, \boldsymbol{POL}, \boldsymbol{VSL}) = \{k^{o1}_{v_i}, k^{o2}_{v_i}, ...k^{oL}_{v_i}\}$, where $\{o1, o2, ..., oL\}$ is an ordering of $\{1, 2, ..., L\}$. The top n key frames among the final results are at last recommended (shown) to user u. To make more clear presentation, we list the notations used throughout the paper in Table 2.

4 KEY FRAME RECOMMENDER

We first propose an improved collaborative filtering method to capture users' frame-level preference by making use of image visual features. Then to model the textual features mirrored in time-synchronized comments, we modify the long short term memory network by infusing per-user personalization information. Lastly, we design a unified framework to jointly model frame images as well as time-synchronized comments.

For clarity and integrality, we first re-describe the widely used matrix factorization (MF) model as a neural network. Formally, let $\boldsymbol{p_u}$ and $\boldsymbol{q_k}$ represent the latent factors of user u and item k, then the likeness (or score) of u to k can be predicted as $\hat{y}_{uk} = \boldsymbol{p}^T_{\boldsymbol{u}} \boldsymbol{q_k}$. In the context of neural network (see Figure 3), the user/item IDs with one-hot format can be seen as inputs fed into the architecture, then the embedding layer projects these sparse representations into denser vectors, which can be regarded as the latent factors in matrix factorization models. At last, the final result $\hat{y}_{uk}$ is computed as the vector inner product between $\boldsymbol{p_u}$ and $\boldsymbol{q_k}$.

4.1 Image-based Model

To capture user preference from frame images, we fuse the visual features into the above framework. Specifically, our principled design is shown in Figure 4. Suppose the dimension of the user/frame

[5]https://nlp.stanford.edu/sentiment/

Table 2: Notations and descriptions.

Notations	Descriptions
$\boldsymbol{u}$	The set of N users $\{u_1, u_2, ..., u_N\}$.
$\boldsymbol{v}$	The set of M movies $\{v_1, v_2, ..., v_M\}$.
l_{v_i}	The set of L shots $\{l^1_{v_i}, l^2_{v_i}, ...l^L_{v_i}\}$ for movie v_i.
$k, k^j_{v_i}, K$	An arbitrary key frame, the key frame of shot $l^j_{v_i}$, and the set of all key frames.
$\boldsymbol{vsl}_k, VSL$	The preprocessed visual feature of frame k, and the set of all visual features.
tsc_{uk}, pol_{uk}	u's time-synchronized comment on key frame k, and the polarity of tsc_{uk}
$w_{tsc_{uk}}, W$	The word list $\{w^0_{tsc_{uk}}, w^1_{tsc_{uk}}, ...w^{s_{uk}-1}_{tsc_{uk}}\}$ in tsc_{uk}, and the set of all time-synchronized comments.
$\boldsymbol{p}_u, \boldsymbol{q}_k$	Latent factors of user u and frame k.
O^+, O^-	The set of positive, and sampled negative feedbacks.
K^{neg}	Number of negative instances.
N^{word}	Size of the word vocabulary.
$\boldsymbol{h}_t$	The hidden state in LSTM at iteration t
D	The number of non-linear layers.
$\boldsymbol{e}^{pre_0}_{uk}, \boldsymbol{e}^{pre_1}_{uk}, ..., \boldsymbol{e}^{pre_D}_{uk}$	Preference embeddings of u on k.
$\boldsymbol{W}^{image}, \boldsymbol{W}^{i}, \boldsymbol{w}^{output}$	Weighting matrix that maps $\boldsymbol{vsl}_k$ into a K dimensional vector, the coefficient matrix used to weight $\boldsymbol{e}^{pre_{i-1}}_{uk}$, and a vector that maps $\boldsymbol{e}^{pre_D}_{uk}$ into a scalar.
$MERGE(), LOGISTIC(), LSTM()$	The merge function, logistic function, and LSTM network.
$\hat{y}^{image}_{uk}, \hat{y}^{TSC}_{uk}, \hat{y}^{integrated}_{uk}$	User u's predicted likeness score to frame k when using image, TSC, and integrated information.

latent factors (embedding) is d, then each visual feature is first mapped into a d dimensional vector, which is then merged with the frame latent factor to generate a new embedding (blue circle in the figure). Lastly, the user latent factors together with the newly generated embedding are fed into the inner product layer to compute the final prediction.

Image enhanced key frame representation. Again, let $\boldsymbol{p}_u$ and $\boldsymbol{q}_k$ be the latent factors of user u and key frame k, respectively. We first use Caffe deep learning framework [21] to generate visual features from the original frame images, where we adopted the Caffe reference model with 5 convolutional layers followed by 3 fully-connected layers that has been pre-trained on 1.2 million ImageNet (ILSVRC2010) images. For frame k, we use the output of FC7, namely, the second fully-connected layer, as the final visual feature $\boldsymbol{vsl}_k$, which is a feature vector of length 4096.

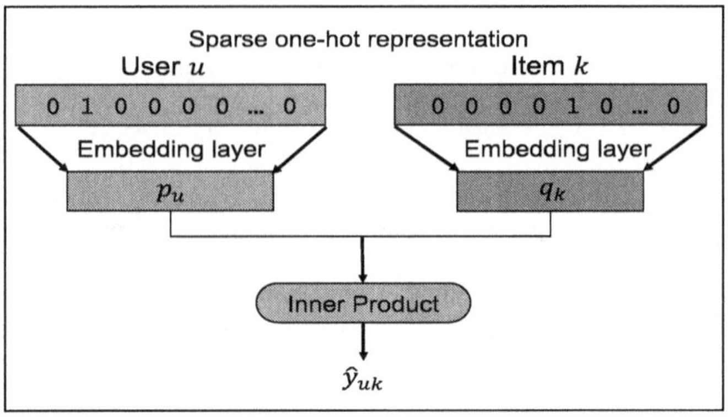

Figure 3: Matrix Factorization as Neural Network.

Let $\boldsymbol{W}^{image} \in R^{d \times 4096}$ be the weighting matrix that maps $\boldsymbol{vsl}_k$ into a d dimensional vector, then the new key frame representation can be derived as:

$$\boldsymbol{q}^*_k = MERGE(\boldsymbol{q}_k, \boldsymbol{W}^{image} \cdot \boldsymbol{vsl}_k) \tag{1}$$

where $MERGE : R^d \times R^d \rightarrow R^d$ is a function that merges two d dimension vectors into one. The particular choice of $MERGE$ in our model is a simple element-wise multiplication, i.e.,

$$MERGE\Big((a_1, a_2, ..., a_K), (b_1, b_2, ..., b_K)\Big) = (a_1 b_1, a_2 b_2, ..., a_K b_K) \tag{2}$$

however, it is not necessarily restricted to this function and many choices can be used in practice according to the specific application scenario.

Sentiment-based user preference modeling. Intuitively, users would comment on their favorite frames with positive sentiment. Therefore, we first determine the polarity of each time-synchronized comment by the Stanford Sentiment analysis toolkit[6], and then for simplicity, we set the polarity of tsc_{uk} – i.e., pol_{uk} – as 1 if the result is *very positive*, *positive*, *or neutral*, and 0 otherwise.

In our framework, we take the prediction of a user's likeness to a frame as a binary classification problem, where 1 means a user likes a frame, and 0 otherwise; the likeness of user u to frame k – i.e., $\hat{y}^{image}_{uk} \in [0, 1]$ – can be predicted as:

$$\hat{y}^{image}_{uk} = LOGISTIC(\boldsymbol{p}_u \cdot \boldsymbol{q}^*_k). \tag{3}$$

where $LOGISTIC(x) = \frac{1}{1+e^{-x}}$ is the logistic function, and "$\cdot$" denotes inner product.

Then we use the binary cross-entropy as our loss function to model user preference, whose superiority has been explored and demonstrated in [18], and the final objective function to be maximized is:

[6] https://nlp.stanford.edu/sentiment/

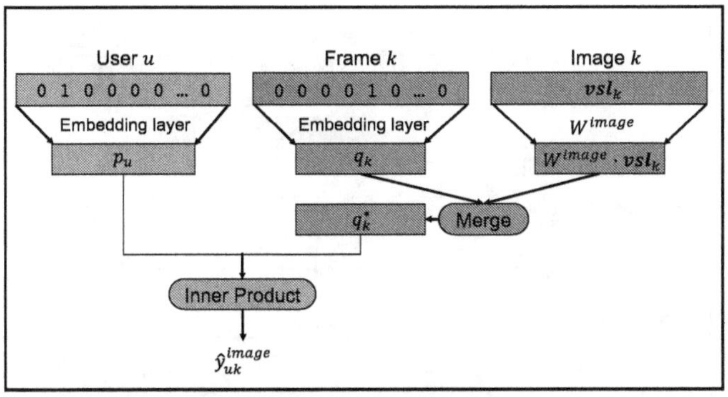

Figure 4: The framework of image-based model. The preprocessed image feature is merged with frame latent factors to derive a new embedding, which is then multiplied by the user latent factors to generate the prediction.

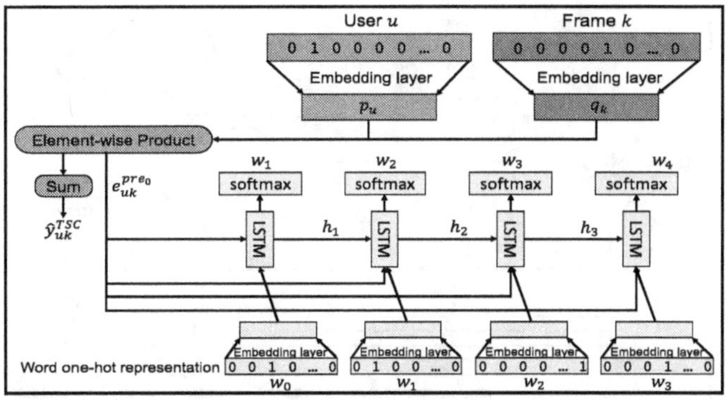

Figure 5: The framework of text-based model. The preference embedding $e_{uk}^{pre_0}$ is fed as an extra input to LSTM at each step. The likeness score of user u to frame k can be simply predicted by applying logistic function to the inner product between p_u and q_k.

$$
\begin{aligned}
L_1 &= log \prod_{(u,k)} (\hat{y}_{uk}^{image})^{y_{uk}} (1-\hat{y}_{uk}^{image})^{1-y_{uk}} \\
&= log \prod_{(u,k)\in O^+} \hat{y}_{uk}^{image} \prod_{(u,k)\in O^-} (1-\hat{y}_{uk}^{image}) \\
&= \sum_{(u,k)\in O^+} log\, \hat{y}_{uk}^{image} + \sum_{(u,k)\in O^-} log\,(1-\hat{y}_{uk}^{image})
\end{aligned} \tag{4}
$$

where y_{uk} is the ground truth that would be 1 if u has commented on k with $pol_{uk} = 1$, and 0 otherwise. O^+ is the set of positive feedbacks, i.e., $O^+ = \{(u,k)|u\ has\ commented\ on\ k, pol_{uk} = 1\}$, while O^- is the set of sampled negative feedback, namely, $O^- \subseteq O^{neg} \cup O^*$, where $O^{neg} = \{(u,k)|u\ has\ commented\ on\ k, pol_{uk} = 0\}$, and $O^* = \{(u,k)|u\ has\ not\ commented\ on\ k\}$. In the training phase, for each positive feedback (u,k), we uniformly sample K^{neg} negative instances, and the parameters can be learned via stochastic gradient descent (SGD).

4.2 Text-based Model

Existing review-based recommendation methods mostly consider the words in a comment as independent elements, and they usually ignore the word sequential information – which is yet very important for understanding the semantic of a comment. In Figure 1 for example, user D wrote the review "*A tall man and a short woman*", where if we leave out the consideration of word sequential information, it would be computationally identical to "*A tall woman and a short man*", which obviously expresses a completely opposite meaning.

To capture the word sequential information, we make use of the long short term memory (LSTM) [20] network, which has been successfully applied to a number of sequence modeling tasks such as machine translation [1], image caption [44], and video classification [55].

Preference-aware LSTM. Intuitively, the content of a time-synchronized comment on a frame is influenced by both the user preference and the frame itself. When it comes to our model, as a result, the word generation process in LSTM should be influenced by both the user and the frame latent factors. So in our framework as shown in Figure 5, we first merge the user and frame latent factors into a preference embedding using element-wise vector multiplication, and then feed it as an extra input to LSTM at each step.

An alternative strategy is to only use the preference embedding as the "Zero State" of LSTM. However, we have empirically verified that this approach leads to unfavored performance for the task of personalized key frame recommendation.

Formally, suppose the time-synchronized comment of user u on frame k is tsc_{uk} with words $\boldsymbol{w}_{tsc_{uk}} = \{w_{tsc_{uk}}^0, w_{tsc_{uk}}^1, ...w_{tsc_{uk}}^{s_{uk}-1}\}$, where s_{uk} is the length of the comment, and the size of the word vocabulary is defined as N^{word}. We formalize our architecture into an encoder-decoder framework similar to [6, 40].

More specifically, the user embedding and the frame embedding are first encoded into a joint preference embedding $\boldsymbol{e}_{uk}^{pre_0} = \boldsymbol{p}_u \odot \boldsymbol{q}_k$, where $\odot$ is element-wise multiplication. Then, given $\boldsymbol{e}_{uk}^{pre_0}$ and all the previously predicted words, the decoder predicts each word at iteration step t by a conditional distribution:

$$\boldsymbol{h}_1 = LSTM(w_{tsc_{uk}}^0, \boldsymbol{e}_{uk}^{pre_0}) \tag{5}$$

$$\boldsymbol{h}_t = LSTM(\boldsymbol{h}_{t-1}, w_{tsc_{uk}}^{t-1}, \boldsymbol{e}_{uk}^{pre_0})\ t \in \{2,3,...s_{uk}\} \tag{6}$$

$$p(w_{tsc_{uk}}^t | \boldsymbol{e}_{uk}^{pre_0}, \boldsymbol{w}_{tsc_{uk}}^{0:t-1}) = SOFTMAX(\boldsymbol{h}_t) \tag{7}$$

where $SOFTMAX()$ is an N^{word}-way softmax, $\boldsymbol{h}_t$ is the hidden state in LSTM at iteration t, $\boldsymbol{w}_{tsc_{uk}}^{0:t-1} = \{w_{tsc_{uk}}^{t-1}, w_{tsc_{uk}}^{t-2}, ..., w_{tsc_{uk}}^0\}$ is the set of all previous words before iteration t, $LSTM()$ is the long short term memory (LSTM) net. At last, by simultaneously predicting users' likeness and time-synchronized comments, our final objective function to be maximized is:

$$
\begin{aligned}
L_2 = &\sum_{(u,k)\in O^+ \bigcup O^-} \sum_{t=1}^{s_{uk}-1} log\, p(w_{tsc_{uk}}^t | \boldsymbol{e}_{uk}^{pre_0}, \boldsymbol{w}_{tsc_{uk}}^{0:t-1}) \\
&+ \sum_{(u,k)\in O^+} log\, \hat{y}_{uk}^{TSC} + \sum_{(u,k)\in O^-} log\,(1-\hat{y}_{uk}^{TSC})
\end{aligned} \tag{8}
$$

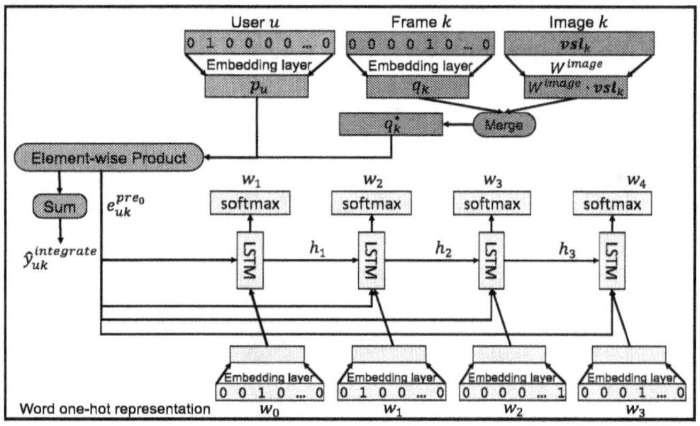

Figure 6: A model that directly combines the methods proposed in section 4.1 and 4.2. The output of the linear element-wise multiplication layer is directly used as an input of LSTM and to generate $\hat{y}_{uk}^{integrated}$.

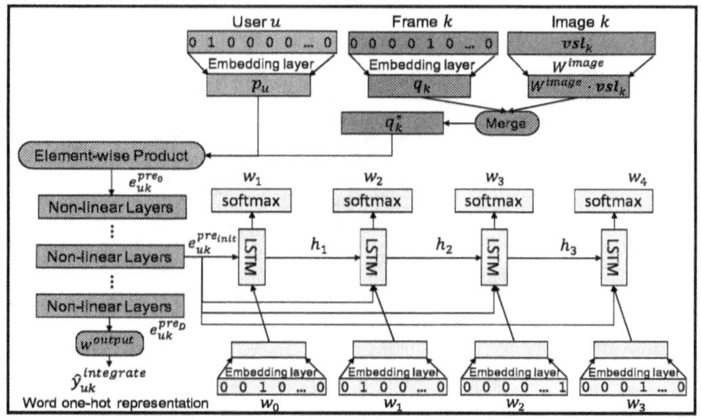

Figure 7: Our integrated recommender. D fully connected layers are introduced to capture the non-linear relationship between image and text features. Either the output of linear element-wise multiplication layer or the results from a non-linear layer can be used to initialize LSTM. $\hat{y}_{uk}^{integrated}$ is generated from the last non-linear layer.

where $\hat{y}_{uk}^{TSC} = LOGISTIC(\boldsymbol{p_u} \cdot \boldsymbol{q_k})$ is the prediction of user u's likeness score on frame k.

4.3 Integrated Recommender

In this subsection, we propose to jointly model frame image and time-synchronized comment in a unified framework.

Deep feature adapting. Intuitively, we may directly combine the above two models for user preference learning, which is shown in Figure 6. However, as image and text features come from quite different and heterogeneous information sources, the linear element-wise multiplication layer (see Figure 6) can be extremely biased when directly adapting such different information. To overcome this weakness, we stack several fully connected layers on top of the element-wise multiplication layer to capture the non-linear relationship among different features.

Formally, suppose the output of the element-wise multiplication layer is: $\boldsymbol{e}_{uk}^{pre_0}$, and there are totally D non-linear layers. Then the output of each non-linear layer and the final output can be derived as:

$$\boldsymbol{e}_{uk}^{pre_0} = \boldsymbol{p_u} \odot \boldsymbol{q}_k^* \tag{9}$$

$$\boldsymbol{e}_{uk}^{pre_i} = g^{nl}(\boldsymbol{W}^i \cdot \boldsymbol{e}_{uk}^{pre_{i-1}}) \; i \in \{1, 2, ...D\} \tag{10}$$

$$\hat{y}_{uk}^{integrated} = LOGISTIC(\boldsymbol{w}^{output} \cdot \boldsymbol{e}_{uk}^{pre_D}) \tag{11}$$

where g^{nl} is the active function, where we select Rectifier (ReLU) in our model because (1) it is practically more reasonable from a biological perspective [12], and (2) it can usually prevent deep models from over-fitting. $\boldsymbol{e}_{uk}^{pre_i}$ is the output of the i-th non-linear layer, $\boldsymbol{W}^i$ is the coefficient matrix used to weight $\boldsymbol{e}_{uk}^{pre_{i-1}}$, and $\boldsymbol{w}^{output}$ is a vector that maps $\boldsymbol{e}_{uk}^{pre_D}$ into a scalar so as to conduct logistic. Note that $\boldsymbol{w}^{output}$ is a parameter that needs to be learned by the model.

For now, we have described the key components (image modeling, text modeling and the D non-linear layers) of our final framework, and we further fuse them together (see Figure 7). Careful readers might have found that, except for the original preference embedding $\boldsymbol{e}_{uk}^{pre_0}$, any one of $\{\boldsymbol{e}_{uk}^{pre_1}, \boldsymbol{e}_{uk}^{pre_2}, ...\boldsymbol{e}_{uk}^{pre_D}\}$ can be used as the extra input of LSTM at each step, suppose we use $\boldsymbol{e}_{uk}^{pre_{init}}$ as the extra input, where $init \in \{0, 1, 2, ...D\}$ is a pre-defined constant. Our final framework can be learned by maximizing the following objective function:

$$L_3 = \alpha \sum_{(u,k) \in O^+ \bigcup O^-} \sum_{t=1}^{s_{uk}-1} log\, p\left(w_{tsc_{uk}}^t | \boldsymbol{e}_{uk}^{pre_{init}}, \boldsymbol{w}_{tsc_{uk}}^{0:t-1}\right) +$$
$$(1-\alpha)\left(\sum_{(u,k) \in O^+} log\, \hat{y}_{uk}^{integrated} + \sum_{(u,k) \in O^-} log\left(1 - \hat{y}_{uk}^{integrated}\right)\right) \tag{12}$$

where α is a weighting parameter that balances the effects of different optimization objectives. Once the model has been learned, for a user u and a key frame k with visual feature $\boldsymbol{vsl_k}$, we can readily predict the likeness score of u to k by Equation (11), according to which we can further recommend u with the key frames that the user is most likely interested in.

5 EXPERIMENTS

In this section, we evaluate our proposed models focusing on the following three key research questions:

RQ 1: What is the performance of our final framework for the task of personalized key frame recommendation?
RQ 2: What are the effects of different types of information for personalized key frame recommendation?
RQ 3: Can the stacked non-linear layers promote the performance of personalized key frame recommendation?

We begin by introducing the experimental setup, and then report and analyze the experimental results to answer these research questions.

5.1 Experimental Setup

Dataset preprocess. The raw comments are generally pre-preprocessed (word segmentation and stop-word filtering) by an open-source Chinese natural language processing toolbox Jieba[7]. After that, we conduct more detailed pre-processing according to the special inherent characteristics of time-synchronized comments, and this is conducted on two aspects: on one hand, we manually remove the meaningless reviews, e.g., the ones at the beginning of the movies that are generally not relevant to the movie content; on the other hand, we map the slangs that express the same meaning (e.g., 2333..., namely, several 3's following a 2, which means "happiness" in online language environment) into a unified word (e.g., wonderful[8]) for more accurate modeling.

In our crawled dataset, the time stamp is recorded when a user sent an edited comment, however, the actual favored frame should be the one corresponding to the time when he/she began to type the comment, rather than the frame when the comment was posted out. As a result, we revise the time stamp by subtracting the time of typing according to the length of the comment and a person's general typewriting speed (approximately 40 words/minute). We pre-segment each movie as 1000 shots, and use the first frame as a shot's key frame. Because the frames in a shot are always very similar, all the commenting behaviors in a shot are seen as reviewing on its key frame, and we do not deliberately distinguish a shot from its key frame in the rest of the paper. To avoid "cold-start" problem, we remove those users with less than 100 time-synchronized comments, and finally sample a smaller dataset containing 40 users' 29,137 comments (20,312 positive ($pol_{uk} = 1$) and 8,825 negative ($pol_{uk} = 0$)) on 11,000 key frames.

Baselines. To demonstrate the effectiveness of our models, we adopt the following methods as baselines for performance comparison:

- **MostPopular:** This is a non-personalized static method utilizing user reviews, where for each user it just selects the most popularly positive key frames as the final results.
- **PMF:** The Probabilistic Matrix Factorization method proposed in [35], which is a frequently used state-of-the-art approach for rating-based optimization and prediction. We set the score of user u to key frame k as 1, if u commented on k with $pol_{uk} = 1$, and 0 otherwise.
- **BPR:** This is a well known ranking-based method [39] for user implicit feedback modeling, the preference pairs are constructed between the positively commented key frames and the other ones. In our experiments, we randomly sample one negative instance for each positive feedback.
- **HFT:** This is a stat-of-the-art method in terms of making rating prediction with textual reviews [31], as the rating information is absent in our dataset. We set the ratings of one's positively commented key frames as 1, and 0 otherwise for each user.
- **VBPR:** This is a stat-of-the-art visual-based recommendation method [15]. Similar to [15], the image features are pre-generated from the original key frame pictures using the Caffe deep learning framework [21].
- **KFRI:** This is a **K**ey **F**rame **R**ecommender based only on **I**mage features, which is proposed in section 4.1 with L_1 as its objective function.
- **KFRC:** This is a **K**ey **F**rame **R**ecommender based only on **C**omments, which is proposed in section 4.2 with L_2 as its objective function.

Evaluation method. If a user comments on a key frame with positive sentiment ($pol_{uk} = 1$), then this frame would be the one that attracts her, so the empirical experiments are conducted by comparing the predicted key frames with the true positive ones ($pol_{uk} = 1$). 30% of each user's positive key frames ($pol_{uk} = 1$) are selected as the test dataset, while the others are used for training. We adapt F_1-score and normalized discounted cumulative gain (NDCG) to evaluate the performance of the baselines and our proposed models.

Parameter settings. The hyper-parameters in our frameworks are tuned by conducting 5-fold cross validation, while the model parameters are first randomly initialized according to a uniform distribution in the range of $(0, 1)$, and then updated by conducting stochastic gradient descent (SGD). The learning rate of SGD is determined by grid searching in the range of $\{1, 0.1, 0.01, 0.001, 0.0001\}$. We set the number of non-linear layers as $D = 3$, and to learn more abstractive features, their dimensions are empirically set as $\{40, 20, 10\}$ to form a tower structure [14].

We evaluate different number of latent factors K in the range of $\{50, 100, 150, 200, 250, 300\}$ for both user and frame vector representations. The number of negative samples K^{neg} is empirically set as 5, while the weighting parameter α is set as 0.5 to make different optimization parts equally contribute to the final results. For better performance, we leverage grid search technology to determine the batch size in the range of $\{64, 128, 256, 512, 1024\}$. When implementing the baselines, 5-fold cross validation and grid search technology are used to determine the parameters. Our experiments are conducted by predicting Top-5,10, and 20 favorite key frames respectively. All the models are repeated for 10 times, and we report the average as well as bound values as the final results for clear illustration.

5.2 Performance of Our Models (RQ1)

Different models (except **MostPopular**) may reach their best performance at various number of latent factors, so for each baseline, we implement it by setting the dimension as 50,100,150,200,250 and 300 respectively, and the best result is finally reported. From Figure 8, we can see: KFRCI achieves the best performance on both F_1 and $NDCG$ when recommending different number of key frames. It can on average enhance the performance by about 7.8% and 6.7% upon F_1-score and $NDCG$ respectively when compared with VBPR, which performs best among all the methods. Paired t-tests on the results also verify that the improvements are statistically significant

[7] https://github.com/fxsjy/jieba/tree/jieba3k

[8] Manually translated into English by the authors

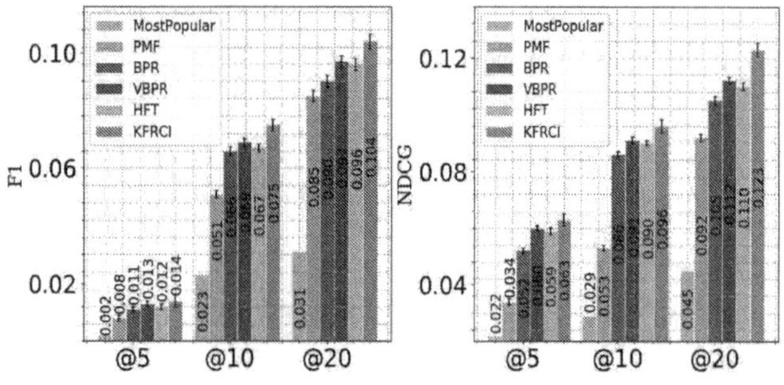

Figure 8: Comparison between our method and baseline methods. The values on the bar indicate the average performance of the corresponding models.

on 0.01 level. Among the baselines, PMF, as expected, performs better than MostPopular due to the consideration of diverse personalities. By directly optimizing the ranking objective, BPR shows better effectiveness compared with PMF on both F_1 and *NDCG*, which is consistent with the observations in [39]. By introducing textual or visual features, HFT/VBPR on average outperforms BPR by about 3.5%/5.4% on F_1 and 8.6%/6.1% on *NDCG* respectively.

5.3 Effects of Different Information (RQ2)

For capturing more comprehensive user preference, frame images and time-synchronized comments are combined together in our final framework for joint modeling. However, different information sources may play different roles, in this section, we would like to study the influence of diverse information for our task of personalized key frame recommendation. To begin with, we compare our final framework KFRCI with KFRI and KFRC, which only use image or text information in their modeling processes. For fair comparison and to avoid disturbance of the deep architecture, we do not use any non-linear layers in KFRCI. The other parameters follow the above settings. From the results shown in Figure 10, we can see:

1. All the models can reach their best performance when the dimension falls in the range of [100, 150], while additional dimensions do not help promoting the performance. The reason may be that too many latent factors can lead to the over-fitting problem, which would weaken our models' generalization ability on the test dataset.

2. KFRI performs slightly better than KFRC in most cases, which tells us that, in our dataset, image features maybe more important compared with time-synchronized comments for the task of personalized key frame recommendation. This may be of the reason that although time-synchronized comments are helpful, they are too diverse and may include too much noise for capturing user inherent preference.

3. It is highly encouraging that although we did not use any non-linear layer, KFRCI exhibits higher performance compared with both KFRC and KFRI across all the dimensions. This observation demonstrates that the integration of visual and textual features can indeed help excavate more accurate user preference, which is in line with our intuition in Section 1.

Weighting parameter α. In this section, we study how the performance of KFRCI changes as the weighting parameter α increases from 0.1 to 0.9. In this experiment, the number of user/frame latent factors is fixed as 100, while the other parameters follow the settings in section 5.1. We predict Top-20 user favorite key frames, the results are shown in Figure 9, from which we can see: the performance (F_1@20) of KFRCI continues to rise until α reaches around 0.3, then after hovering approximately stable in the range of [0.3, 0.5], it begins to drop rapidly with the increase of α. This observation indicates that we should make a suitable balance between the two components in our final framework. Besides, similar results can be observed on *NDCG*@20.

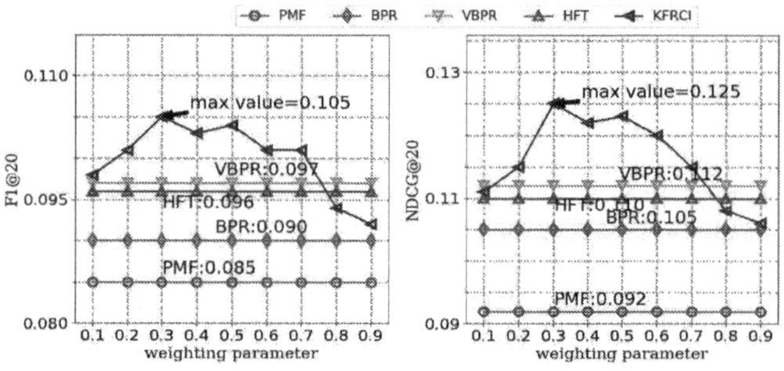

Figure 9: The influence of weighting parameter α. For clear comparison, we also list the performances of the other models, although they don't change with α. MostPopular is not listed herein because its performance is much lower.

5.4 Promotion of the Deep Architecture (RQ3)

In this section, we would like to test whether deep architectures are helpful to our task. To do so, we evaluate the performance of our final model KFRCI based on F_1 and *NDCG* by changing the number of non-linear layers. Note that when there is no non-linear layer, we are actually evaluating the straightforward model as shown in Figure 6. In this experiment, the dimensions of the non-linear layers from the first layer to the output layer are set as {40, 20, 10, 5}, and the number of user/frame latent factors is fixed as 100. The output non-linear layer is used to link LSTM. All the other parameters follow the above settings.

The results are shown in Table 3, from which we can see that our model can reach its best performance when there are two or three non-linear layers, and introducing more non-linear layers does not bring positive effects. These observations indicate that deep model may be helpful for personalized key frame recommendation, however, only relatively small number of non-linear layers are required to capture the complex relationship among heterogeneous features.

"Extra input" of LSTM. When there are multiple non-linear layers, an obvious problem is that, which output should be selected as the "Extra input" of LSTM. So we further evaluate our model by using different layers' output $e_{uk}^{pre_{init}}$ as the LSTM "Extra input". Note that $init = 0$ means directly linking the output of element-wise

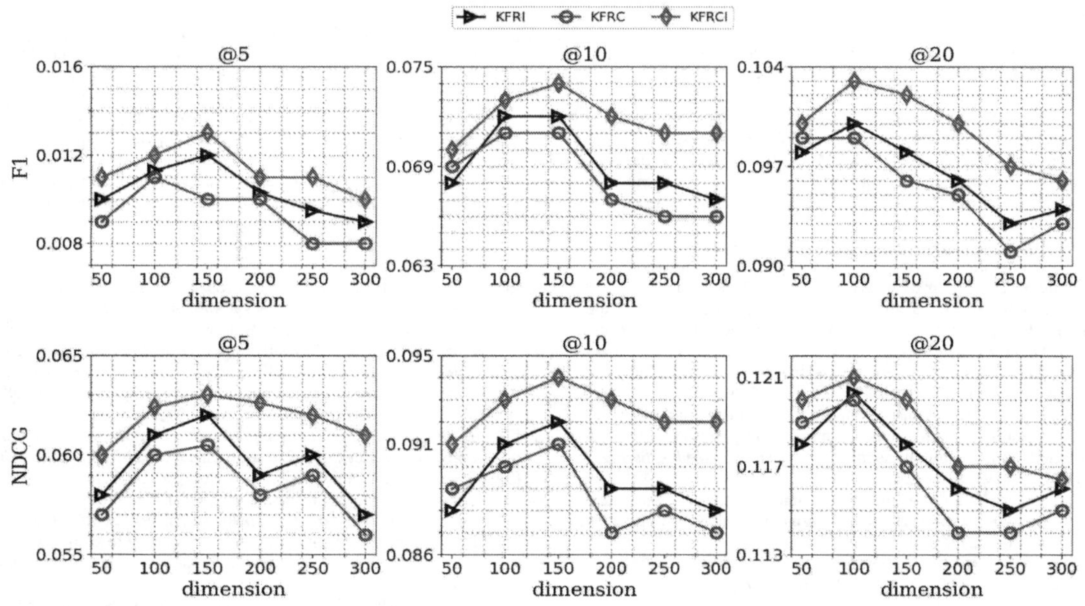

Figure 10: Evaluating the performances of our models when using different features. The dimension of the latent factors ranging from 50 to 300.

Table 3: The effect of deep architecture.

number of layers	0	1	2	3	4
$F_1@5$	0.012	0.014	**0.015**	0.014	0.013
NDCG@5	0.060	0.064	**0.065**	0.063	0.062
$F_1@10$	0.071	0.073	0.074	**0.075**	0.072
NDCG@10	0.092	0.094	0.095	**0.096**	0.091
$F_1@20$	0.103	0.104	**0.106**	0.104	0.103
NDCG@20	0.120	0.123	**0.124**	0.123	0.121

multiplication layer to the LSTM. In this experiment, we use 3 nonlinear layers with the dimensions of $\{40, 20, 10\}$, other parameters follow the above settings.

From the results on $F_1@20$ and $NDCG@20$ shown in Table 4, we see that it can lead to improved performance when $init = 1, 2$ *or* 3 compared with $init = 0$, which manifests that introducing nonlinear operations is important for better adapting the user/frame latent factors with the underlying motivations for generating time-synchronized comments.

Table 4: The effects of different LSTM "Extra inputs".

init	0	1	2	3
$F_1@20$	0.103	0.104	**0.105**	0.104
NDCG@20	0.121	0.122	**0.124**	0.123

6 CONCLUSIONS AND OUTLOOK

In the paper, we propose the problem of personalized key frame recommendation for the first time. To do so, we propose to leverage the rich time-synchronized comment information in video sharing websites, and further design a novel framework that combines model-based collaborative filtering and long-short term memory network together to model user commented key frames and time-synchronized comments simultaneously. Comprehensive evaluation verified the effectiveness of our framework.

This is a first step towards our goal in personalized key frame recommendation, and there is much room for further improvements. For example, more other information (e.g. audio features) can be included to capture more comprehensive user preference, which may also bring us more inspiring insights on the inherent natures of the user preference patterns upon video key frames. Beyond personalized key frame recommendation, our work also points to promising future directions in personalized video summarization, personalized image captioning, and personalized story telling based on images or videos.

ACKNOWLEDGMENT

This work was supported in part by the Center for Intelligent Information Retrieval and in part by NSF IIS-1160894, NSFC 61602176 and NSFC 61672231. Any opinions, findings and conclusions or recommendations expressed in this material are those of the authors and do not necessarily reflect those of the sponsor.

REFERENCES

[1] D. Bahdanau, K. Cho, and Y. Bengio. Neural machine translation by jointly learning to align and translate. *arXiv preprint arXiv:1409.0473*, 2014.

[2] Y. Bao, H. Fang, and J. Zhang. Topicmf: Simultaneously exploiting ratings and reviews for recommendation. In *AAAI*, pages 2–8, 2014.
[3] Y. Cao, J. Li, X. Guo, S. Bai, H. Ji, and J. Tang. Name list only? target entity disambiguation in short texts. In *EMNLP*, pages 654–664, 2015.
[4] X. Chen, Z. Qin, Y. Zhang, and T. Xu. Learning to rank features for recommendation over multiple categories. In *Proceedings of the 39th International ACM SIGIR conference on Research & development in information retrieval*. ACM, 2016.
[5] X. Chen, P. Wang, Z. Qin, and Y. Zhang. Hlbpr: A hybrid local bayesian personal ranking method. In *Proceedings of the 25th International Conference Companion on World Wide Web*, pages 21–22. International World Wide Web Conferences Steering Committee, 2016.
[6] K. Cho, B. Van Merriënboer, C. Gulcehre, D. Bahdanau, F. Bougares, H. Schwenk, and Y. Bengio. Learning phrase representations using rnn encoder-decoder for statistical machine translation. *arXiv preprint arXiv:1406.1078*, 2014.
[7] P. Covington, J. Adams, and E. Sargin. Deep neural networks for youtube recommendations. In *Proceedings of the 10th ACM Conference on Recommender Systems*, pages 191–198. ACM, 2016.
[8] Q. Cui, S. Wu, Q. Liu, and L. Wang. A visual and textual recurrent neural network for sequential prediction. *arXiv preprint arXiv:1611.06668*, 2016.
[9] Q. Diao, M. Qiu, C.-Y. Wu, A. J. Smola, J. Jiang, and C. Wang. Jointly modeling aspects, ratings and sentiments for movie recommendation (jmars). In *Proceedings of the 20th ACM SIGKDD international conference on Knowledge discovery and data mining*, pages 193–202. ACM, 2014.
[10] N. Ejaz, T. B. Tariq, and S. W. Baik. Adaptive key frame extraction for video summarization using an aggregation mechanism. *Journal of Visual Communication and Image Representation*, 23(7):1031–1040, 2012.
[11] G. Ganu, N. Elhadad, and A. Marian. Beyond the stars: Improving rating predictions using review text content. In *WebDB*, volume 9, pages 1–6. Citeseer, 2009.
[12] X. Glorot, A. Bordes, and Y. Bengio. Deep sparse rectifier neural networks. In *Aistats*, volume 15, page 275, 2011.
[13] Y. Gong and X. Liu. Video summarization using singular value decomposition. In *Computer Vision and Pattern Recognition, 2000. Proceedings. IEEE Conference on*, volume 2, pages 174–180. IEEE, 2000.
[14] K. He, X. Zhang, S. Ren, and J. Sun. Deep residual learning for image recognition. *arXiv preprint arXiv:1512.03385*, 2015.
[15] R. He and J. McAuley. Vbpr: visual bayesian personalized ranking from implicit feedback. *arXiv preprint arXiv:1510.01784*, 2015.
[16] X. He, T. Chen, M.-Y. Kan, and X. Chen. Trirank: Review-aware explainable recommendation by modeling aspects. In *Proceedings of the 24th ACM International on Conference on Information and Knowledge Management*, pages 1661–1670. ACM, 2015.
[17] X. He, M. Gao, M.-Y. Kan, and D. Wang. Birank: Towards ranking on bipartite graphs. *IEEE Transactions on Knowledge and Data Engineering*, 29(1):57–71, 2017.
[18] X. He, L. Liao, H. Zhang, L. Nie, X. Hu, and T.-S. Chua. Neural collaborative filtering. In *Proceedings of the 26th International Conference Companion on World Wide Web (WWW)*, pages 173–182. International World Wide Web Conferences Steering Committee, 2017.
[19] X. He, H. Zhang, M.-Y. Kan, and T.-S. Chua. Fast matrix factorization for online recommendation with implicit feedback. In *Proceedings of the 39th International ACM SIGIR conference on Research and Development in Information Retrieval*, pages 549–558. ACM, 2016.
[20] S. Hochreiter and J. Schmidhuber. Long short-term memory. *Neural computation*, 9(8):1735–1780, 1997.
[21] Y. Jia, E. Shelhamer, J. Donahue, S. Karayev, J. Long, R. Girshick, S. Guadarrama, and T. Darrell. Caffe: Convolutional architecture for fast feature embedding. In *Proceedings of the 22nd ACM international conference on Multimedia*, pages 675–678. ACM, 2014.
[22] R. M. Jiang, A. H. Sadka, and D. Crookes. Advances in video summarization and skimming. In *Recent Advances in Multimedia Signal Processing and Communications*, pages 27–50. Springer, 2009.
[23] W. Jiang, C. Cotton, and A. C. Loui. Automatic consumer video summarization by audio and visual analysis. In *ICME*, pages 1–6, 2011.
[24] A. Khosla, R. Hamid, C.-J. Lin, and N. Sundaresan. Large-scale video summarization using web-image priors. In *CVPR*, pages 2698–2705, 2013.
[25] G. Kim, L. Sigal, and E. P. Xing. Joint summarization of large-scale collections of web images and videos for storyline reconstruction. In *CVPR*, 2014.
[26] Y. J. Lee, J. Ghosh, and K. Grauman. Discovering important people and objects for egocentric video summarization. In *CVPR*, pages 1346–1353, 2012.
[27] L. Li, K. Zhou, G.-R. Xue, H. Zha, and Y. Yu. Video summarization via transferrable structured learning. In *WWW*, pages 287–296. ACM, 2011.
[28] Y. Li, T. Zhang, and D. Tretter. An overview of video abstraction techniques. Technical report, Technical Report HPL-2001-191, HP Laboratory, 2001.
[29] H. Liu, J. He, T. Wang, W. Song, and X. Du. Combining user preferences and user opinions for accurate recommendation. *Electronic Commerce Research and Applications*, 12(1):14–23, 2013.
[30] Y.-F. Ma, X.-S. Hua, L. Lu, and H.-J. Zhang. A generic framework of user attention model and its application in video summarization. *IEEE transactions on multimedia*, 7(5):907–919, 2005.
[31] J. McAuley and J. Leskovec. Hidden factors and hidden topics: understanding rating dimensions with review text. In *Proceedings of the 7th ACM conference on Recommender systems*, pages 165–172. ACM, 2013.
[32] J. McAuley, C. Targett, Q. Shi, and A. van den Hengel. Image-based recommendations on styles and substitutes. In *Proceedings of the 38th International ACM SIGIR Conference on Research and Development in Information Retrieval*, pages 43–52. ACM, 2015.
[33] E. Mendi and C. Bayrak. Shot boundary detection and key frame extraction using salient region detection and structural similarity. In *Proceedings of the 48th Annual Southeast Regional Conference*, pages 66–67, 2010.
[34] T. Mikolov, K. Chen, G. Corrado, and J. Dean. Efficient estimation of word representations in vector space. *arXiv preprint arXiv:1301.3781*, 2013.
[35] A. Mnih and R. Salakhutdinov. Probabilistic matrix factorization. In *Advances in neural information processing systems*, pages 1257–1264, 2007.
[36] A. Nagasaka and Y. Tanaka. Automatic video indexing and full-video search for object appearances. *Journal of Information Processing*, 15(2):316, 1992.
[37] J. Peng, Y. Zhai, and J. Qiu. Learning latent factor from review text and rating for recommendation. In *2015 7th International Conference on Modelling, Identification and Control (ICMIC)*, pages 1–6. IEEE, 2015.
[38] Z. Ren, S. Liang, P. Li, S. Wang, and M. de Rijke. Social collaborative viewpoint regression with explainable recommendations. *Under submission*, page 10, 2016.
[39] S. Rendle, C. Freudenthaler, Z. Gantner, and L. Schmidt-Thieme. Bpr: Bayesian personalized ranking from implicit feedback. In *Proceedings of the 25th Conference on Uncertainty in Artificial Intelligence*, pages 452–461. AUAI Press, 2009.
[40] I. Sutskever, O. Vinyals, and Q. V. Le. Sequence to sequence learning with neural networks. In *Advances in neural information processing systems*, pages 3104–3112, 2014.
[41] Y. Tan, M. Zhang, Y. Liu, and S. Ma. Rating-boosted latent topics: Understanding users and items with ratings and reviews. In *IJCAI*. AAAI, 2016.
[42] D. Tang, B. Qin, and T. Liu. Learning semantic representations of users and products for document level sentiment classification. In *ACL*, pages 1014–1023, 2015.
[43] D. Tang, B. Qin, T. Liu, and Y. Yang. User modeling with neural network for review rating prediction. In *IJCAI*, pages 1340–1346, 2015.
[44] O. Vinyals, A. Toshev, S. Bengio, and D. Erhan. Show and tell: A neural image caption generator. In *Proceedings of the IEEE Conference on Computer Vision and Pattern Recognition*, pages 3156–3164, 2015.
[45] H. Wang, N. Wang, and D.-Y. Yeung. Collaborative deep learning for recommender systems. In *SIGKDD*, pages 1235–1244, 2015.
[46] H. Wang, S. Xingjian, and D.-Y. Yeung. Collaborative recurrent autoencoder: Recommend while learning to fill in the blanks. In *NIPS*, pages 415–423, 2016.
[47] M. Wang, R. Hong, G. Li, Z.-J. Zha, S. Yan, and T.-S. Chua. Event driven web video summarization by tag localization and key-shot identification. *Multimedia, IEEE Transactions on*, 14(4):975–985, 2012.
[48] Z. Wang, M. Kumar, J. Luo, and B. Li. Sequence-kernel based sparse representation for amateur video summarization. In *Proceedings of the 2011 joint ACM workshop on Modeling and representing events*, pages 31–36, 2011.
[49] B. Wu, E. Zhong, B. Tan, A. Horner, and Q. Yang. Crowdsourced time-sync video tagging using temporal and personalized topic modeling. In *SIGKDD*, pages 721–730, 2014.
[50] C.-Y. Wu, A. Beutel, A. Ahmed, and A. J. Smola. Explaining reviews and ratings with paco: Poisson additive co-clustering. In *Proceedings of the 25th International Conference Companion on World Wide Web*, pages 127–128. International World Wide Web Conferences Steering Committee, 2016.
[51] Y. Wu and M. Ester. Flame: A probabilistic model combining aspect based opinion mining and collaborative filtering. In *WSDM*, pages 199–208. ACM, 2015.
[52] Y. Xian, J. Li, C. Zhang, and Z. Liao. Video highlight shot extraction with time-sync comment. In *Workshop on Hot Topics in Planet-scale mobile computing and online Social networking*, pages 31–36, 2015.
[53] H. Xu, Y. Zhen, and H. Zha. Trailer generation via a point process-based visual attractiveness model. In *IJCAI*, pages 2198–2204, 2015.
[54] J. You, G. Liu, L. Sun, and H. Li. A multiple visual models based perceptive analysis framework for multilevel video summarization. *CSVT, IEEE Transactions on*, 17(3):273–285, 2007.
[55] J. Yue-Hei Ng, M. Hausknecht, S. Vijayanarasimhan, O. Vinyals, R. Monga, and G. Toderici. Beyond short snippets: Deep networks for video classification. In *Proceedings of the IEEE Conference on Computer Vision and Pattern Recognition*, pages 4694–4702, 2015.
[56] W. Zhang, Q. Yuan, J. Han, and J. Wang. Collaborative multi-level embedding learning from reviews for rating prediction. In *IJCAI*. ACM, 2016.
[57] Y. Zhang, G. Lai, M. Zhang, Y. Zhang, Y. Liu, and S. Ma. Explicit factor models for explainable recommendation based on phrase-level sentiment analysis. In *Proceedings of the 37th international ACM SIGIR conference on Research & development in information retrieval*, pages 83–92. ACM, 2014.
[58] Y. Zhuang, Y. Rui, T. S. Huang, and S. Mehrotra. Adaptive key frame extraction using unsupervised clustering. In *Image Processing, 1998. ICIP 98. Proceedings. 1998 International Conference on*, volume 1, pages 866–870. IEEE, 1998.

Personalized Itinerary Recommendation with Queuing Time Awareness

Kwan Hui Lim
The University of Melbourne, Australia
Data61, CSIRO, Australia
limk2@student.unimelb.edu.au

Jeffrey Chan
RMIT University, Australia
The University of Melbourne, Australia
jeffrey.chan@rmit.edu.au

Shanika Karunasekera
Christopher Leckie
The University of Melbourne, Australia
{karus,caleckie}@unimelb.edu.au

ABSTRACT

Personalized itinerary recommendation is a complex and time-consuming problem, due to the need to recommend popular attractions that are aligned to the interest preferences of a tourist, and to plan these attraction visits as an itinerary that has to be completed within a specific time limit. Furthermore, many existing itinerary recommendation systems do not automatically determine and consider queuing times at attractions in the recommended itinerary, which varies based on the time of visit to the attraction, e.g., longer queuing times at peak hours. To solve these challenges, we propose the PersQ algorithm for recommending personalized itineraries that take into consideration attraction popularity, user interests and queuing times. We also implement a framework that utilizes geo-tagged photos to derive attraction popularity, user interests and queuing times, which PersQ uses to recommend personalized and queue-aware itineraries. We demonstrate the effectiveness of PersQ in the context of five major theme parks, based on a Flickr dataset spanning nine years. Experimental results show that PersQ outperforms various state-of-the-art baselines, in terms of various queuing-time related metrics, itinerary popularity, user interest alignment, recall, precision and F1-score.

CCS CONCEPTS

• **Information systems → Personalization; Recommender systems**; *Location based services*; *Data mining*; Web applications;

KEYWORDS

Tour Recommendations; Trip Planning; Personalization; User Interests

ACM Reference format:
Kwan Hui Lim, Jeffrey Chan, Shanika Karunasekera, and Christopher Leckie. 2017. Personalized Itinerary Recommendation with Queuing Time Awareness. In *Proceedings of SIGIR '17, Shinjuku, Tokyo, Japan, August 07-11, 2017,* 10 pages.
https://doi.org/http://dx.doi.org/10.1145/3077136.3080778

SIGIR '17, August 07-11, 2017, Shinjuku, Tokyo, Japan

ACM ISBN 978-1-4503-5022-8/17/08...$15.00
https://doi.org/http://dx.doi.org/10.1145/3077136.3080778

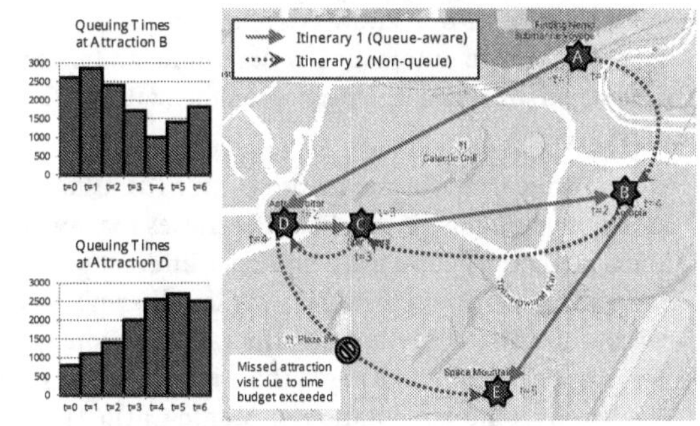

Figure 1: Example of itinerary recommendation with queue time consideration

1 INTRODUCTION

Touring and travelling are popular leisure activities for many people, as shown by the 1.18 billion annual tourists in 2015 [39]. A critical task for any tourist is to plan a trip itinerary that comprises popular and interesting attractions, which can be completed within a specific time limit. This task is especially complex and challenging due to: (i) the need to identify a set of popular attractions that are also aligned with the traveller's interests; (ii) the need to organize these attractions in the form of an itinerary with the constraints of a starting/ending place (e.g., near a traveller's hotel) and limited time for touring; and (iii) the need to plan for travelling, visiting and queuing times at the attractions, where queuing times are dependent on the time of attraction visit. In particular, neglecting to account for queuing times can create a frustrating experience for travellers as they spend an unnecessarily long time queuing instead of enjoying the attractions, and possibly miss attraction visits in their itineraries due to these queuing times exceeding their available touring time.

Figure 1 illustrates the importance of queuing time awareness in itinerary recommendation. Itinerary 2 (dotted blue line) does not consider queuing time and recommends an attraction visit sequence of $A \rightarrow B \rightarrow C \rightarrow D \rightarrow E$. However, this itinerary is unable to complete the visit to Attraction E, due to excessive queuing times at Attractions B and D that causes the time budget to be exceeded. Moreover, Itinerary 2 schedules visits to Attractions B and D at the peak (longest) of their queuing times. In contrast, Itinerary 1 (solid green line) considers queuing time and recommends that attractions be visited in the sequence of $A \rightarrow D \rightarrow C \rightarrow B \rightarrow E$, as Attraction D has a lower queuing time at $t = 2$, compared to Attraction B at the same time. By the time Itinerary 1 visits Attraction B (at $t = 4$), its queuing time has shortened drastically, compared to earlier at $t = 2$. In addition, Itinerary 1 schedules visits to Attractions B and D when queues are the shortest, thus making the itinerary more enjoyable with less time wasted on queuing. In real-life, itinerary recommendation is even more complex due to: (i) the need to consider attraction popularity and user interest preferences; and (ii) since queuing times are time-dependent, itinerary recommenders need to also consider the time of visit to attractions and their queuing times.

In this work, we aim to address these issues and propose the PersQ algorithm for recommending itineraries that are popular, personalized to user interests, and minimize queuing times at attractions. To the best of our knowledge, our work is the first to use geo-tagged photos to automatically determine and incorporate queuing time in personalized itinerary recommendations. Our main contributions are:

- We introduce and formulate the QueueTourRec problem for recommending personalized itineraries that aim to maximize attraction popularity and user interest preferences and minimize queuing times, while adhering to a time constraint for completing the itinerary (Section 3).
- We propose the PersQ algorithm, where we have developed a novel implementation of Monte Carlo Tree Search (MCTS) for the domain of personalized itinerary recommendation with queuing time awareness (Section 5).
- We implement a framework for automatically extracting attraction popularity, user interests and queuing time from geo-tagged photos (Section 6). Using this framework, we have collected a dataset of user visits in five major theme parks across nine years, which is made publicly available at https://sites.google.com/site/limkwanhui/datacode#sigir17 (Section 7.1).
- We introduce various queuing-related evaluation metrics and compare PersQ against various state-of-the-art baselines. The results show that PersQ recommends itineraries with the lowest ratio of queuing time to total touring time, and schedules visits to popular attractions at times with the shortest queues. In addition, PersQ offered the best overall performance in terms of itinerary popularity, user interest, precision, recall and F1-scores (Sections 7 and 8).

For the rest of our paper, Section 2 discusses related work in itinerary recommendation, while Section 4 provides some background on MCTS.

2 RELATED WORK

General Itinerary Recommendation. Many early works on itinerary recommendation [10, 11, 19, 26] are based on the Orienteering problem [17, 38, 41], where the main objective is to recommend an itinerary that maximizes a global profit/reward and can be completed within a specific budget. Attraction popularity is frequently used as a global profit/reward in the context of recommending and planning an itinerary in touristic cities [10, 11, 19, 26] or theme parks [18, 24, 42]. While these are interesting works in itinerary recommendations, the use of a global profit/reward is common among all users and thus provides no personalization for user interest preferences. In recent years, more researchers have incorporated user interests and/or specific preferences to personalize such itinerary recommendations and we discuss these works next.

Table 1: Description of Key Notations

Notation	Description
A	The set of all attractions
a_x	A specific attraction, where $a_x \in A$
Cat_{a_x}	The category of attraction a_x
Dur_{a_x}	The visit duration at attraction a_x
$Trav_{a_x,a_y}$	Travelling time from a_x to a_y
$t^a_{a_x}$	The arrival time at attraction a_x
$t^d_{a_x}$	The departure time from attraction a_x
V_x	An user-attraction visit, $V_x = (a_x, t^a_{a_x}, t^d_{a_x})$
$Pop(a_x)$	The popularity of attraction a_x
$Int_u(c)$	The interest of user u in attraction a_x
$Queue^t(a_x)$	The queuing time at attraction a_x at time t

Personalized Itinerary Recommendation. Many recent works aim to recommend itineraries that are personalized to users based on their interest preferences [40] or personalized requirements such as a specific attraction visit sequence [15], mandatory attraction categories [8, 28], group interest satisfaction [14, 30], among others. For example, [49, 50] implemented a heuristic approximation algorithm to construct personalized itineraries that optimize for a heuristic of attraction popularity and user interests relative to the travelled distance, while [43] utilized a modified Ant Colony System [13] to recommend personalized itineraries that comprise less crowded attractions. Others such as [29, 31] modelled the personalized itinerary recommendation problem as an integer program with the objectives of recommending popular attractions and tailoring the attraction visit duration based on user interest. Similarly, [3, 5] aim to first identify a set of interesting and popular attractions, then construct an itinerary comprising these attractions using a variant of the Travelling Salesman Problem [32]. In addition, there have been many websites and applications [4, 8, 34, 44] developed for itinerary recommendations based on variants of the above-mentioned research.

Top-k POI Recommendation. An adjacent research area to itinerary recommendation are works on top-k POI recommendation, which has been extensively studied by the Information Retrieval community [25, 27, 46–48]. Most of these works are based on matrix factorization or collaborative filtering approaches and their main objective is to recommend a ranked list of top-k POIs to a user. To achieve this purpose, they utilize various sources of information such as social links [46], acitivity/user types [25], geographical/temporal aspects of POIs [27, 47, 48]. Although these works propose interesting uses of various POI information, the task of top-k POI recommendation is distinctly different from itinerary recommendation, which encompasses the added complexity of constructing a set of relevant POIs as a time-constrained connected itinerary with the consideration of travelling time and POI visit durations, among others.

Discussion of Related Work. While these earlier works are the state-of-the-art in itinerary and POI recommendation, our work differs from these earlier works in several important aspects, namely: (i) our QueueTourRec problem optimizes for attraction popularity, user interest preferences and queuing times distribution, which is automatically constructed based on geo-tagged photos and then included as part of the travelling cost along with transport time and attraction visit duration; (ii) unlike top-k POI recommendations, our QueueTourRec problem involves recommending a set of POIs and planning it as a connected itinerary with the associated time constraints of travelling between POIs, visiting POIs and completing the itinerary within a time budget; and (iii) while MCTS is typically used for board game playing [6, 12][1], we propose a novel and non-trivial adaptation of MCTS (denoted the PersQ algorithm) for solving the QueueTourRec problem.

3 BACKGROUND AND PROBLEM DEFINITION

Table 1 highlights the key notations used in our work, which we elaborate more in the next section.

3.1 Preliminaries

For each theme park, there are are m attractions, and we represent this set of attractions as $A = \{a_1, ..., a_m\}$. Each attraction a_x is also associated with its latitude/longitude coordinates, category Cat_{a_x} (e.g., roller coaster, water rides, indoor), and the duration Dur_{a_x} needed to visit that attraction (e.g., 10 minutes for a roller coaster). For itinerary recommendation in theme parks, the primary mode of transportation is by walking. Thus, we use $Trav_{a_x,a_y}$ to denote the amount of time taken to walk from attractions a_x to a_y, which is derived from a leisure walking speed of 5km/hour [7] to cover the distance between attractions a_x and a_y.

While we define our problem in the context of a theme park, these definitions and problem formulation are generalizable to any general path planning related context. For example, in the context of a city, there are also various attractions that a tourist can visit, where each attraction is also associated with a specific category (e.g., shopping, beach, park) and visit duration. The travelling speed $Trav_{a_x,a_y}$ can also modified to reflect the transport modes of walking, cycling or driving. Similarly, in the context of a museum, the attractions would be in the form of an artifact or painting, each also associated with a specific category (e.g., classical, modern, gothic) and visit duration.

Definition 1: Attraction Visits. For a user u who has visited n attractions, we represent each visited attraction a_x as a tuple, $V_x = (a_x, t^a_{a_x}, t^d_{a_x})$. In this tuple, a_x denotes the visited attraction, while $t^a_{a_x}$ and $t^d_{a_x}$ denote the time that user u arrived at and departed from attraction a_x, respectively. Given $t^a_{a_x}$ and $t^d_{a_x}$, we can then derive the amount of time that user u spent at attraction a_x, by calculating the difference between the arrival and departure times, i.e., $t^a_{a_x}$ and $t^d_{a_x}$. Note that this time spent includes both the queuing time at attraction a_x and its visiting duration Dur_{a_x}. We later describe (in Definition 5) how these queuing times can be calculated.

Definition 2: Visit Sequence. Given the set of visited attractions (i.e., multiple tuples of $V_x = (a_x, t^a_{a_x}, t^d_{a_x})$) by a user u, we can construct his/her visit sequence by joining consecutive attraction visits to form a chronologically-ordered sequence, $S_u = (V_1, V_2, ..., V_n)$. A visit sequence is split into two separate visit sequences if two consecutive attraction visits take place more than 8 hours apart, i.e., $t^d_{a_x} - t^a_{a_{x+1}} > 8\ hours$. Other researchers have adopted a similar approach to divide such visit sequences based on an interval of 8 hours [10, 29, 31]. This list of visit sequences subsequently serves as the ground truth of real-life theme park visits, which is used as part of our experimentation and evaluation of the various algorithms and baselines.

Definition 3: Popularity of Attractions. Many earlier itinerary recommendation works [5, 10, 30] represent the popularity of a Point of Interest (POI) based on the number of visits that this POI has received. In our work, we employ a similar measure of popularity for each attraction based on the number of times this attraction has been visited, which is defined as:

$$Pop(a) = \sum_{u \in U} \sum_{a_x \in S_u} \delta(a_x = a),\ \forall\ a \in A \tag{1}$$

where $\delta(a_x{=}a) = 1$ if attraction a_x is the same as attraction a, and $\delta(a_x{=}a) = 0$ otherwise.

Definition 4: User-Attraction Interest Relevance. While attraction popularity is the same for all users, the interest relevance of an attraction differs from user to user, i.e., each user will have their own unique interest preferences. Given that C represents the set of all attraction categories and P the set of photos taken by user u, we define the interest level of user u in category c as:

$$Int_u(c) = \frac{1}{|P|} \sum_{p \in P} \delta(p = c),\ \forall\ c \in C \tag{2}$$

where $\delta(p = c) = 1$ if photo p is of an attraction that belongs to category c, and $\delta(p = c) = 0$ otherwise. In short, the interest level of a user u in attraction category c is based on the number of photos of attractions that belong to category c, relative to the total number of photos taken. The intuition behind this definition is that a user is more likely to take more photos of an attraction (category) that interests him/her, and less photos otherwise.

Definition 5: Queuing Times of Attractions. In general, each attraction is also associated with a certain queuing time before a user can visit the attraction, e.g., queuing to ride a roller coaster or to buy tickets for a show. Given that V_a is the set of visits to attraction a and t is the visiting time, we represent the queuing times at an attraction a as:

$$Queue^t(a) = \frac{1}{|V_a|} \sum_{u \in U} \sum_{a_x \in S_u} \delta(a_x = a)\big((t^d_{a_x} - t^a_{a_x}) - Dur_{a_x}\big) \tag{3}$$

where $\delta(a_x{=}a) = 1$ if attraction a_x is the same as attraction a, and $\delta(a_x{=}a) = 0$ otherwise. In short, we calculate the queuing time at an attraction a based on the total time spent at an attraction (which includes queuing time and visit duration), subtracted by its attraction visit duration (e.g., 10 minutes for a roller coaster). We derive this total time spent based on the departure time $t^d_{a_x}$ and arrival time $t^a_{a_x}$, which we then subtract by the attraction visiting time Dur_{a_x}. For simplicity, we consider the time t of $Queue^t(a)$ in terms of the hour of visit and use the average visit duration of attraction a at a time t to derive its queuing time at time t.[2]

[1]More background on MCTS is provided later in Section 4.

[2]Although we consider t in terms of the hour of visit, t can be easily generalized to smaller or larger units of time (e.g., 30 min or 2-hourly blocks)

3.2 Problem Definition

We first define the problem of recommending a personalized itinerary to a single user, with the main objectives of maximizing the popularity and interest relevance of recommended attractions in this itinerary, while minimizing the queuing times at these attractions. We denote this problem as the QueueTourRec problem. Our formulation of QueueTourRec is modelled based on a variant of the Orienteering problem [38, 41].

Given the set of attractions A, a time budget B, a starting point a_1 and destination point a_N, our objective is to recommend an itinerary $I = (a_1, ..., a_N)$ that maximizes the total reward $Rwrd(I)$ accumulated from the recommended itinerary I, while ensuring that the itinerary is completed within the time budget B. The reward function $Rwrd(I)$ is calculated based on the popularity, interest relevance and queuing times of the attractions $a_x \in A$ recommended in itinerary I, as denoted by $Pop(a_x)$, $Int(Cat_{a_x})$ and $Queue(a_x)$, respectively. The time budget B is calculated using the function $Cost(a_x, a_y) = Trav(a_x, a_y) + Dur(a_y) + Queue^t(a_y)$, i.e., considering for travelling time, attraction/ride duration and queuing time at $time = t$.

Unlike earlier works that do not automatically determine and consider queuing times, our work differs in the following ways: (i) we derive a queuing time distribution for each attraction (i.e., expected queuing duration at specific times), based on past tourist visits; (ii) we incorporate these queuing times into the itinerary based on the proposed visit time at each attraction; (iii) we recommend an itinerary that optimizes for attraction popularity, user interests and queuing times; and (iv) in contrast to the Orienteering problem with fixed costs, QueueTourRec includes a time-dependent cost that affects the chosen attractions and queuing times, thus we cannot utilize traditional algorithms designed for the former.

In essence, our main goal is to plan an itinerary $I = (a_1, ..., a_N)$ that maximizes the following objective function:

$$\max \sum_{a_i \in I} \sum_{a_j \in I, a_i \neq a_j} Path^t_{a_i,a_j} \left(\frac{Int(Cat_{a_i}) + Pop(a_i)}{Queue^t(a_i)} \right) \quad (4)$$

where $Path^t_{a_i,a_j} = 1$ if a path from attraction a_i to a_j is taken at time t (i.e., we visit attractions a_i and a_j in sequence), and $Path^t_{a_i,a_j} = 0$ otherwise.

Following which, we then attempt to solve for Eqn. 4, subject to the following constraints:

$$\sum_{a_i \in I, i \neq 1} Path^t_{a_1,a_i} = \sum_{a_j \in I, j \neq N} Path^{t+d}_{a_j,a_N} = 1 \quad (5)$$

$$\sum_{a_i \in I, k \neq N} Path^t_{a_i,a_k} = \sum_{a_j \in I, k \neq 1} Path^{t+d}_{a_k,a_j} \leq 1 \quad (6)$$

$$\sum_{a_i \in I} \sum_{a_j \in I, a_i \neq a_j} Path^t_{a_i,a_j} Cost^t(a_i, a_j) \leq B \quad (7)$$

where the cost function used in Equation 7 is defined as:

$$Cost(a_i, a_j) = Trav_{a_i,a_j} + Dur_{a_j} + Queue^t(a_j) \quad (8)$$

Equation 4 is a multi-objective function that aims to recommend attractions in an itinerary I that maximizes the popularity and interest relevance of all visited attractions, while minimizing the queuing times at these attractions. Equation 4 can also be enhanced with different weights for $Int(Cat_{a_i})$, $Pop(a_i)$ and $Queue^t(a_i)$ to provide varying levels of emphasis on each component. The optimization of Equation 4 is also subjected to Constraints 5 to 7. Constraint 5 ensures that the recommended itinerary begins from a specific attraction a_1, while terminating at attraction a_N.[3] Thereafter, Constraint 6 ensures that all paths in the recommended itinerary are connected and no attractions are visited multiple times. Constraint 7 ensures that the recommended itinerary can be completed within the time budget B. Specifically, the function $Cost(a_x, a_y)$ (i.e., Equation 8) is applied to all visited attractions to obtain the total time taken for the itinerary, which includes the consideration for travelling time $Trav_{a_i,a_j}$, attraction/ride duration Dur_{a_j} and queuing time $Queue^t(a_j)$.

The QueueTourRec problem formulation is based on a variant of the Orienteering problem, which has been shown to be NP-hard as the Orienteering problem is a specialized instance of the Travelling Salesman Problem [38, 41].[4] Furthermore, this problem formulation incorporates a time-dependent cost function $Cost^t(a_x, a_y)$, which adds to the complexity of this problem. Due to this NP-hard complexity, solving the QueueTourRec problem optimally is not feasible. To overcome these problems, we propose the PersQ algorithm for solving the QueueTourRec problem of recommending personalized and queue-aware itineraries. In the following sections, we provide some background on Monte Carlo Tree Search (MCTS) before describing our PersQ algorithm, which is partially based on the MCTS algorithm.

4 MONTE CARLO TREE SEARCH

MCTS is a popular search algorithm that has been successfully applied to many board games such as Chess, Go, Othello, among others [6, 12]. We first provide some background information on the MCTS algorithm in its typical application to board games. MCTS approaches the task of board game playing as a tree search problem, where nodes of the tree represent a specific board position and leaf nodes represent a terminal game state, i.e., a win or loss. Thus, moving from a node to a child node corresponds to making a game move that results in a new board position. The main objective is to perform a tree search that results in a set of optimal moves (nodes) leading to a win state. In the MCTS algorithm, the basic idea is that game play initially commences with iterations of random node selection to explore moves, and recording the outcome of choosing those moves. Thereafter, at subsequent game plays, MCTS departs from random moves and progressively builds upon previous successes by converging to moves that result in win states.

The MCTS algorithm typically runs for a fixed number of iterations (e.g., run for 100 iterations) or repeats the iterations for a specific running time (e.g., run as many iterations in 10 seconds). At each iteration, MCTS operates with four main steps:

[3]For a more general itinerary recommendation task, such as in a city, a_1 and a_N can be defined as the hotel that the tourist is residing in, and thus any recommended itinerary will start and end at the tourist's hotel.

[4]The QueueTourRec problem is also NP-hard as it can be generalized to the Orienteering problem, by using attraction popularity $Pop(a_i)$ as a global reward in Equation 4 and setting the queuing times $Queue^t(a_i)$ to be uniform. For a more detailed proof on the NP-hardness of the Orienteering problem, please refer to [2, 16].

(1) ***Selection.*** MCTS starts at the root node r and recursively *selects* a child node c to expand based on a certain strategy, until reaching either a leaf/terminal node or an unvisited/unexpanded node. Thus, the root node r corresponds to the start state of the board, while the child node c corresponds to a move that results in a new board position.

(2) ***Expansion.*** If the selected node c is not a leaf node (i.e., a terminal game condition leading to a win or loss), expand node c and randomly select one of its unvisited child nodes.

(3) ***Simulation.*** Steps 1 and 2 are then continuously *simulated* (repeated) until reaching the end of the game, i.e., a leaf/terminal node.

(4) ***Back-propagation.*** At this stage, the game would have ended, resulting in a win or loss to the player. The results of this game is then *back-propagated* to all the traversed nodes (board positions) during this iteration.

Steps 1 to 4 are considered one iteration of MCTS, which are repeated for a fixed number of iterations or for a specific running time. Each node (board position) will be labelled with the number of wins/losses (1/0) and the number of times it has been visited. Step 1 typically employs a selection strategy that exploits nodes with a high win-to-visited ratio, while Step 2 uses a random exploration strategy for previously unvisited nodes. Steps 3 and 4 then simulate the game play to the end and back-propagate the results to all the visited nodes, incrementing their win count (if game was won) and visited count by 1.

4.1 Motivations of MCTS for Itinerary Recommendation

Monte Carlo based methods have also been applied to various routing problems, such as variants of the Travelling Salesman Problem [33] and Vehicle Routing Problem [20], with the main purpose of identifying an appropriate next node to visit in the route. Although it is possible to solve such routing-related problems optimally as an Integer Linear Program, the problem complexity increases exponentially with the number of nodes (attractions). In the case of the QueueTourRec problem, there is the added complexity of a time-variable in the form of queuing times at attractions. More importantly, real-life applications typically require that solutions be generated in a short time-frame (minutes rather than hours). MCTS is well-poised for solving our QueueTourRec problem due to two main reasons [6]: (i) Instead of traversing the entire search tree, MCTS allows us to explore a smaller, more promising region of the solution space, thus leading to a shorter running time; and (ii) MCTS can be adapted to run only for a fixed amount of time, thus making it very suitable for real-life application;

However, the direct application of MCTS to the QueueTourRec problem is non-trivial for several reasons: (i) in board games, each move from a node to a child node has a uniform cost of 1, whereas this cost is variable for itinerary recommendation and can be based on distance or travel times; (ii) furthermore, this cost is time-dependent in the QueueTourRec problem, due to different queuing times at the same attraction based on the visit time; and (iii) each win/lose state in a board game corresponds to a binary reward of 1 or 0, which leads to a simple back-propagation strategy (Step 4). In contrast, itinerary recommendation results in a complex reward structure that is based on the attractions recommended and their corresponding popularity, interest relevance and queuing times. In the following sections, we describe our proposed PersQ algorithm, which is an adaptation of MCTS for the QueueTourRec problem, and we evaluate the effectiveness of PersQ against various state-of-the-art methods for personalized tour recommendations.

Algorithm 1: PersQ - Overview of Algorithm

input : $a_1 \in A$: Starting attraction, $a_N \in A$: Ending attraction, S: Starting time of itinerary, B: Total time budget, *maxLoop*: Number of iterations.

output : $I = (a_1, ..., a_N)$: Recommended itinerary.

1 **begin**
2 Initialize T_{visits} as a tree of visit count;
3 Initialize T_{reward} as a tree of reward collected;
4 Initialize I_{list} as a list of itineraries;
5 **for** *iterations* $\leftarrow$ 1 **to** *maxLoop* **do**
6 Initialize I_{temp} as a list of attraction visits;
7 Append attraction a_1 to I_{temp};
8 $a_i \leftarrow a_1$;
9 $a_j \leftarrow \emptyset$;
10 $totalCost \leftarrow 0$;
11 **while** $totalCost < B$ **do**
12 $a_j \leftarrow SelectNextNode(a_i, T_{visits}, T_{reward})$;
13 Append attraction a_j to itinerary I_{temp};
14 $totalCost \leftarrow totalCost + Trav_{a_i,a_j} + Dur_{a_j} + Queue^t(a_j)$;
15 **if** $a_j == a_N$ **then**
16 Break loop;
17 $a_i \leftarrow a_j$;
18 $BackpropC(I_{temp}, T_{visits})$;
19 **if** $a_j == a_N$ **then**
20 $R \leftarrow Simulate(I_{temp})$;
21 $BackpropR(I_{temp}, T_{reward}, R)$;
22 Append itinerary I_{temp} to itinerary list I_{list};
23 Return best itinerary I from I_{list};

5 OVERVIEW OF PERSQ ALGORITHM

Algorithm 1 gives an overview of our proposed PersQ algorithm, which takes as input a desired starting attraction a_1, ending attraction a_N, starting time S and time budget B for completing the itinerary. The output is in the form of a recommended itinerary $I = (a_1, ..., a_N)$, which starts from attraction a_1 at time S and finishes at attraction a_N by time $S + B$.

At the start of Algorithm 1 (Lines 2 and 3), two similar trees are initialized with the root node n_1 as the starting attraction a_1, with its child nodes as the set of attractions $a_i \in A$, up to a depth of $|A|$ (the number of attractions in the theme park). Thus, the traversal of nodes in this tree is equivalent to an itinerary $I = (a_1, ..., a_N)$, with a_1 as the node selected at $depth = 1$, a_2 at $depth = 2$ and so on, until a_N at $depth = N$. The two above-mentioned trees differ in terms of the values associated with each node, T_{visits} contains

Algorithm 2: PersQ - SelectNextNode()

```
input  : a_i ∈ A: Current attraction; I = (a_1, ...): Current
         itinerary; T_visits; Tree of visit counts; T_reward: Tree
         of accumulated reward.
output : a_n ∈ A: Next attraction.
1  begin
2      visitCount_{a_i} ← GetVisitCount(a_i, T_visits);
3      a_n ← ∅;
4      UCT_max ← 0;
5      for a_j ∈ A and a_j ∉ I do
6          visitCount_{a_j} ← GetVisitCount(a_j, T_visits);
7          totalReward_{a_j} ← GetTotalReward(a_j, T_reward);
8          exploit_{a_j} ←
           totalReward_{a_j} / visitCount_{a_j} + (Int(Cat_{a_j})+Pop(a_j)) / (Trav_{a_i,a_j}+Dur_{a_j}+Queue^t(a_j));
9          explore_{a_j} ← 2C_p sqrt(2 ln visitCount_{a_i} / visitCount_{a_j});
10         UCT_{a_j} ← exploit_{a_j} + explore_{a_j};
11         if UCT_{a_j} > UCT_max then
12             a_n ← a_j;
13     Return a_n;
```

the number of times a specific node has been selected (Lines 2), while T_{reward} contains the total reward accumulated by a specific node (Lines 3). Line 4 initializes I_{list}, which will contain a list of explored itineraries $I_{list} = (I_1, I_2, ..., I_{maxLoop})$ at the conclusion of our algorithm.

Algorithm 1 then runs for a fixed number of iterations *maxLoop* (Line 5) and we set $maxLoop = 1,000$ as this value allows the algorithm to complete in reasonable time (< 3 minutes). Each iteration (Lines 5 to 22) is equivalent to a single run of MCTS. At the start of each iteration, Lines 6 and 7 initialize an itinerary $I_{temp} = (a_1)$ as an ordered list with a_1 as the first attraction to be visited. Following which, Lines 11 to 17 construct an itinerary that can be completed within the time budget B based on travelling time, ride duration and queuing times (Line 14). This itinerary is constructed by iteratively calling the *SelectNextNode*() method (Line 12) and appending the next recommended attraction to I_{temp} (Line 13). The *SelectNextNode*() method reflects the Selection and Expansion stages of traditional MCTS and is discussed further in Section 5.1. Attractions are continuously appended to I_{temp} until either the time budget B is exceeded (Line 11) or the destination attraction a_N is reached (Line 15). After which, *BackpropC*() (Line 18) updates/increments the visit count of visited nodes in T_{visits} based on the recommended attractions in itinerary I_{temp}. If itinerary I_{temp} ends at attraction a_N (Line 19), we calculate the reward gained from I_{temp} (Line 20), update the accumulated rewards of visited nodes in T_{reward} accordingly (Line 21), and append I_{temp} to I_{list}. The calculation of reward and back-propagation of visit counts/rewards are described in more detail in Section 5.2. At the end of all iterations (Line 23), we examine all explored itineraries $I \in I_{list}$ and return the itinerary with the highest reward.

5.1 Selection and Expansion

Algorithm 2 describes the *SelectNextNode*() method, which is used for selecting the next attraction (node) to visit based on a current attraction a_i, visit count tree T_{visits}, and reward tree T_{reward}. Instead of examining all possible neighbours of attraction a_i, Line 5 focuses the search on attractions that have not been visited. Lines 6 to 10 are a variant of the Upper Confidence Bound [1] applied to Trees, commonly denoted as UCT [21]. The main aim of UCT is to choose a next attraction (node) a_j to visit, that maximizes:

$$UCT_{a_j}^{Orig} = \frac{totalReward_{a_j}}{visitCount_{a_j}} + 2C_p\sqrt{\frac{2\ln visitCount_{a_i}}{visitCount_{a_j}}} \quad (9)$$

In Equation 9, the first term $\frac{totalReward_{a_j}}{visitCount_{a_j}}$ controls for the *exploitation* of attractions (nodes) that results in itineraries with high rewards, relative to the number of times these nodes were chosen. The second term $2C_p\sqrt{\frac{2\ln visitCount_{a_i}}{visitCount_{a_j}}}$ controls for the *exploration* of nodes (attractions) that have not been previously selected, thus ensuring that different attractions (and hence, itineraries) are considered. The parameter C_p determines the emphasis to give to the *exploration* of nodes and we set $C_p = \frac{1}{\sqrt{2}}$, which Kocsis and Szepesvári [22] has proved to be the best value as it statisfies Hoeffding's inequality.

Our proposed PersQ algorithm improves upon the original UCT (Equation 9) by including an additional heuristic for next node (attraction) selection. Our version of UCT is defined as:

$$\begin{aligned} UCT_{a_j}^{PersQ} = & \frac{Int(Cat_{a_j}) + Pop(a_j)}{Trav_{a_i,a_j} + Dur_{a_j} + Queue^t(a_j)} \\ & + \frac{totalReward_{a_j}}{visitCount_{a_j}} + 2C_p\sqrt{\frac{2\ln visitCount_{a_i}}{visitCount_{a_j}}} \end{aligned} \quad (10)$$

Unlike the original MCTS that considers uniform cost (i.e., board games where each move has a cost of 1), the cost in itinerary recommendation is variable based on the selected next node (attraction). Thus, the addition of the heuristic $\frac{Int(Cat_{a_j})+Pop(a_j)}{Trav_{a_i,a_j}+Dur_{a_j}+Queue^t(a_j)}$ favours attractions with a higher interest relevance and popularity but with lower associated travelling and queuing time.

5.2 Simulation and Back-propagation

In traditional MCTS for game play, the simulation stage simulates a run from the root node to a terminal node and calculates the reward, which is either a 1 for a win or a 0 for a loss. For the purposes of itinerary recommendation, a simple binary value of 1 and 0 does not accurately reflect the rewards associated with different itineraries. Thus, we chose a reward that reflects the attraction popularity, user interest and queuing times associated with each itinerary, which is defined as:

$$Reward = \sum_{a \in I_{temp}} \left(\frac{Int(Cat_a) + Pop(a)}{Queue^t(a)} \right) \quad (11)$$

In Algorithm 1, this reward value is calculated in Line 20 after every iteration of itinerary generation, and subsequently back-propagated to our reward tree T_{reward} in Line 21. Specifically, this reward is back-propagated to all visited nodes only if the itinerary ends at attraction a_N as specified in Constraint 5. The reason for this is so that we do not unnecessarily favour itineraries that do not satisfy our destination attraction constraint. On the other hand, we back-propagate the visit count (i.e., increment by one) to our visit tree T_{visits} (Line 18), regardless of whether the itinerary ends at our desired destination attraction a_N. As a result, nodes that are frequently visited but with low/no reward are less likely to be chosen based on our $UCT_{a_j}^{PersQ}$ formulation (Equation 10), due to the high denominator of total visit count.

6 ITINERARY RECOMMENDATION FRAMEWORK

Our framework for itinerary recommendation utilizes geo-tagged photos to derive attraction-related statistics and our PersQ algorithm for planning a personalized itinerary. This framework comprises the following steps:

(1) **Crawling of Geo-tagged Photos**. For each theme park, we used the Flickr API [45] to retrieve all geo-tagged photos that were taken within the theme park. The photos are tagged with 16 levels of geo-location accuracy and we only consider photos with the highest accuracy level of 16. Each of these photos is also tagged with the user ID of the taker, timestamp, and latitude/longitude geo-coordinates.

(2) **Mapping of Photos to Attractions**. Based on the geo-coordinates of the photos and theme park attractions, we map each photo to an attraction if they differ by <100m according to the Haversine formula [36]. If a photo is near to multiple attractions, we map this photo to the nearest attraction. At the end of this step, we have a set of attraction visits of all users to a theme park, as described in Definition 2 of Section 3.1.

(3) **Constructing Visit Sequences**. Following which, we chronologically order and join all attraction visits (from Step 2) of a single user to obtain the visit sequence of this user, as described in Definition 2 of Section 3.1.

(4) **Calculating Attraction Popularity, User Interests and Queuing Times**. Using the visit sequences from Step 3, we calculate the attraction popularity, user interests and queuing times according to Definitions 3, 4 and 5 of Section 3.1, respectively.

(5) **Recommending Personalized Itineraries With Queuing Time**. At the conclusion of Steps 1 to 4, we use the computed visit sequences, attraction popularity, user interests and queuing times to generate an itinerary recommendation based on our proposed PersQ algorithm, as described in Section 5.

One limitation of this framework is potential noise in the geo-tagged photos, which could affect the calculation of visit sequences and queuing times. An alternative is to use proprietary trajectory data from actual theme park operators, which are typically obtained via tracking devices issued to theme park visitors to monitor their trajectories (via sensors located throughout the theme park). While such datasets have high accuracy, these proprietary datasets are often not publicly available for researchers and furthermore, to construct a similar dataset for another theme park requires the installation of sensors and explicitly tracking visitors in the new theme park. As such, we utilized the above-mentioned framework that is built upon open-source data, i.e., publicly available geo-tagged photos, and can be easily extended for other theme parks or cities.

Table 2: Dataset description

Theme Park	No. of Photos	No. of Users	Attraction Visits	# Visit Sequences
Disneyland	181,735	3,704	119,987	11,758
Disney Epcot	90,435	2,725	38,950	5,816
California Adv.	193,069	2,593	57,177	6,907
Hollywood	57,426	1,972	41,983	3,858
Magic Kingdom	133,221	3,342	73,994	8,126

7 EXPERIMENTAL METHODOLOGY

7.1 Dataset

Our dataset comprises nine years of geo-tagged photos that were taken in five theme parks from Aug 2007 to Aug 2016. The five theme parks are Disneyland, Epcot, California Adventure, Disney Hollywood and Magic Kindgom. This dataset was collected using the Flickr API [45], then mapped to attraction visits and visit sequences, as described in Steps 1 to 3 of Section 6. Each attraction a_x is also assigned a category Cat_{a_x} (e.g., roller coaster, water rides, etc) based on its corresponding Wikipedia page. Similarly, each attraction a_x is also associated with a ride duration Dur_{a_x}, which can also be found on that attraction's Wikipedia page or a website like [37]. While earlier works have constructed datasets from geo-tagged photos, our dataset is the first that includes the queuing time distribution at each attraction based on these geo-tagged photos. The descriptive statistics of this dataset are shown in Table 2.

7.2 Baseline Algorithms

As there is no existing work that considers all three components of queuing time, attraction popularity and user interest, we select various state-of-the-art baselines that consider both attraction popularity and user interest for recommending personalized itineraries. These baselines are as follows:

- **Iterative Heuristic Approximation (IHA)**. A heuristic algorithm proposed in [49, 50] that commences with an itinerary from the starting attraction a_1 to destination attraction a_N and iteratively adds a new attraction between the current and destination attractions, until the budget is reached. The attraction selected to be added is the one with the maximum heuristic value of $\frac{Int(Cat_{a_j})+Pop(a_j)}{Trav_{a_i,a_j}+Dur_{a_j}}$, i.e., the next attraction with the highest profit relative to its travelling cost.
- **User Based Collaborative Filtering for Itineraries (UBCF-I)**. A variant of the popular User Based Collaborative Filtering (UCBF) [35, 47, 48] that utilizes user interest similarities (based on their ratings on items) to recommend a set of top-k items for another user. In our adaptation to itinerary recommendations, we define user ratings based on the number of posted photos on a specific attraction, hence more photos represent a higher rating. Thereafter,

we take the ranked top-k items (attractions) and iteratively add them to the starting attraction a_1 until the budget is reached, resulting in the recommended itinerary.

- **Personalized Tour Recommender (PersTour).** An Integer Programming based algorithm proposed in [29, 31] is used, which recommends personalized itineraries that consider attraction popularity and user interest, with a variable visit duration to attractions based on a user's interest preferences. The PersTour algorithm defines user interest levels based on the length of time a user stays at attractions, relative to the average user.
- **Tour Recommendation With Interest Category (TourInt).** The TourInt algorithm [28] formulates the tour recommendation problem with a mandatory category, which has to be visited at least once in the recommended itinerary. To personalize the recommended itinerary, TourInt defines this mandatory category as the attraction category that has been most frequently visited in the user's other visit sequences.
- **Trip Builder (TripBuild).** We adapted the problem formulation in [3, 5] to fit our QueueTourRec problem, by adding in constraints of start and destination attractions. TripBuild recommends personalized itineraries that optimize for attraction popularity and user interest, where user interest is based on the number of times a user has visited attractions of a certain category, relative to his/her total attraction visits.

7.3 Evaluation

Like many recent itinerary recommendation works [5, 9, 29, 31, 43], our experimental evaluation uses the visit sequences of users as the ground truth of real-life visits by these users. Each visit sequence corresponds to the real-life attraction visits of users in a specific theme park, e.g., *Attraction* $a_4 \longrightarrow a_{12} \longrightarrow a_7 \longrightarrow a_{23}$. To ensure a fair comparison with the baselines, which consider user interest, we perform our evaluation only on users with at least two visit sequences. Using these travel sequences, we then apply leave-one-out evaluation [23], where we use one visit sequence for evaluation and the other visit sequences to determine the interest preferences of this user. For each visit sequence, we use the first and last attraction of each visit sequence as input to PersQ and the baselines, along with the actual time spent in the visit sequence as the time budget. In addition, we also incorporate queuing time into the evaluation and thus attractions may be dropped from recommended itineraries due to the additional queuing time. We repeat the evaluation for all travel sequences in our dataset and compare PersQ against the various baselines using the following evaluation metrics:

(1) **Maximum Queue-time** (MQ_I). The queuing times at attractions recommended in itinerary I, relative to their max. queuing time, defined as: $MQ_I = \frac{1}{|I|} \sum_{a \in I} \frac{Queue^t(a)}{Max_{t \in T}(Queue^t(a))}$.

(2) **Queue:Cost Ratio** (QC_I). The average ratio of queuing time to itinerary (time) cost of an itinerary I, defined as: $QC_I = \frac{1}{|I|} \sum_{a_i \in I, i \neq 1} \frac{Queue^t(a)}{Trav_{a_{i-1},a_i} + Dur_{a_i} + Queue^t(a_i)}$.

(3) **Queue:Popularity Ratio** (QP_I). The average ratio of queuing time to attraction popularity of an itinerary I, defined as: $QP_I = \frac{1}{|I|} \sum_{a \in I} \frac{Queue^t(a)}{Pop(a)}$.

(4) **Popularity** (Pop_I). The total popularity based on all attractions in an itinerary I, defined as: $Pop_I = \sum_{a \in I} Pop(a)$.

(5) **Interest** (Int_I). The total interest alignment (to a user u) based on all attractions in an itinerary I, defined as: $Int_I^u = \sum_{a \in I} Int_u(Cat_a)$.

(6) **Recall:** R_I. The ratio of attraction visits in a user's real-life visit sequence that also exist in the recommended itinerary I. Given that A_r is the set of attractions in the recommended itinerary I and A_v is the set of attraction visits in the real-life travel sequence, we define recall as: $R_I = \frac{|A_r \cap A_v|}{|A_v|}$.

(7) **Precision:** P_I. The ratio of attractions in the recommended itinerary I that also exist in a user's real-life visit sequence. Using the same notations for A_r and A_v, we define precision as: $P_I = \frac{|A_r \cap A_v|}{|A_r|}$.

(8) **F-score** (F_I). The harmonic mean of the precision P_I and recall R_I of an itinerary I, defined as: $F_I = \frac{2 \times P_I \times R_I}{P_I + R_I}$.

Metric 1 allows us to determine the extent to which an itinerary schedules visits to attractions at their maximum (longest) queuing times (MQ_I=1) or at their minimum (MQ_I=0), where a smaller value of MQ_I is preferred as it means we avoided attractions at their busiest time. Metric 2 measures the ratio of queuing time to the total time spent travelling to, queuing at and visiting/riding attractions, where a smaller QC_I value shows that the user spends less time queuing as part of the itinerary. Metric 3 measures the ratio of queuing time to the attraction popularity, and allows us to better differentiate between popular attractions (which are more likely to have longer queuing times) and unpopular ones with shorter queuing times. Similarly for Metric 3, a smaller value of QP_I is preferred as it indicates short queuing times at popular attractions. Metrics 4 and 5 are standard measures of itinerary popularity (Pop_I) and user-interest alignment (Int_I), respectively, while Metrics 6, 7 and 8 measure how well a recommended itinerary reflects the real-life attraction visits of a user.

8 RESULTS AND DISCUSSION

Queue-time Metrics. Table 3 gives an overview of the experimental results, in terms of the six evaluation metrics introduced in Section 7.3. PersQ outperforms all baselines with the lowest Maximum Queue-time (MQ_I), Queue:Cost Ratio (QC_I), Queue:Popularity Ratio (QP_I). In relative terms, PersQ out-performed all baselines with a reduction of 8.5% to 65.9% in Maximum Queue-time, 9.0% to 24.6% in Queue:Cost Ratio, and 21.6% to 45.1% in Queue:Popularity Ratio. These results indicate that PersQ recommends visits to popular attractions at times with the shortest queues, and constructs itineraries that include minimal time spent queuing at attractions.

Recall, Precision, F1-score. In terms of Recall (R_I) and F1-score (F_I), PersQ also out-performs all baselines for all datasets, with relative improvements of 24.2% to 45.5% for Recall, and 15.3% to 19.1% for F1-score. In terms of Precision (P_I), PersQ out-performs all baselines in 24 out of 25 cases, with a relative improvement

Table 3: Comparison between PersQ and various baselines, in terms of the mean and standard errors of Maximum Queue-time (MQ_I), Queue:Cost Ratio (QC_I), Queue:Popularity Ratio (QP_I), Popularity (Pop_I), Interest (Int_I), Recall (R_I), Precision (P_I) and F1-score (F_I). Lower values of MQ_I, QC_I and QP_I are preferred, while higher values of Pop_I, Int_I, R_I, P_I and F_I are better. The bold/blue numbers indicate the best result for each metric.

	Algorithm	Maximum Queue-time	Queue:Cost Ratio	Queue:Pop Ratio	Popularity	Interest	Recall	Precision	F1-score
Cali. Adv.	PersQ	**0.059±.002**	**0.257±.007**	**2515±121**	**1.794±.055**	**3.704±.105**	**0.483±.010**	**0.307±.007**	**0.338±.007**
	IHA	0.173±.006	0.346±.009	7669±904	1.394±.043	3.425±.083	0.332±.006	0.296±.006	0.287±.005
	UBCF-I	0.196±.007	0.330±.009	15679±1665	0.636±.025	1.530±.048	0.258±.005	0.282±.006	0.244±.004
	PersTour	0.188±.008	0.330±.011	5583±917	0.902±.033	1.423±.055	0.227±.007	0.223±.007	0.204±.006
	TourInt	0.188±.007	0.339±.011	4583±319	0.910±.033	1.444±.057	0.228±.007	0.225±.007	0.206±.006
	TripBuild	0.197±.008	0.321±.011	5182±360	0.871±.033	1.469±.055	0.225±.006	0.223±.007	0.205±.006
Hollywood	PersQ	**0.184±.005**	**0.298±.011**	**3585±335**	1.28±.053	**2.12±.088**	**0.482±.015**	**0.439±.014**	**0.431±.013**
	IHA	0.283±.009	0.423±.015	4570±223	**1.29±.044**	1.85±.070	0.367±.010	0.417±.012	0.371±.010
	UBCF-I	0.320±.012	0.410±.012	17493±1270	0.62±.029	1.09±.045	0.297±.008	0.370±.010	0.313±.008
	PersTour	0.263±.010	0.402±.013	10287±931	0.82±.033	1.23±.058	0.305±.009	0.367±.012	0.317±.010
	TourInt	0.256±.010	0.395±.013	9543±861	0.81±.033	1.22±.058	0.302±.010	0.364±.012	0.314±.010
	TripBuild	0.272±.011	0.412±.014	12144±1071	0.77±.034	1.24±.058	0.309±.010	0.374±.012	0.322±.009
Epcot	PersQ	**0.113±.004**	**0.284±.008**	**4088±152**	**0.891±.031**	2.407±.086	**0.472±.012**	**0.413±.012**	**0.407±.010**
	IHA	0.279±.006	0.344±.010	6861±285	0.852±.025	**2.511±.069**	0.380±.008	0.368±.008	0.353±.007
	UBCF-I	0.212±.007	0.331±.010	11664±823	0.500±.017	1.232±.044	0.291±.007	0.314±.008	0.283±.006
	PersTour	0.250±.008	0.356±.011	8034±360	0.604±.021	1.490±.060	0.310±.008	0.322±.009	0.297±.007
	TourInt	0.252±.007	0.352±.011	8112±340	0.599±.021	1.459±.058	0.317±.008	0.327±.009	0.303±.007
	TripBuild	0.246±.008	0.342±.011	8208±386	0.584±.021	1.561±.060	0.300±.008	0.312±.009	0.287±.008
Disneyland	PersQ	**0.161±.004**	**0.263±.005**	**5673±263**	**0.731±.017**	2.287±.055	**0.332±.006**	0.295±.006	**0.289±.005**
	IHA	0.198±.004	0.332±.006	13437±419	0.690±.020	**3.531±.068**	0.267±.004	0.270±.004	0.249±.003
	UBCF-I	0.176±.004	0.378±.007	14986±1072	0.495±.012	1.567±.037	0.235±.004	**0.296±.005**	0.240±.004
	PersTour	0.177±.005	0.322±.008	8255±579	0.623±.017	1.523±.045	0.190±.004	0.201±.005	0.180±.004
	TourInt	0.193±.005	0.313±.008	10267±1324	0.612±.017	1.498±.044	0.188±.004	0.200±.005	0.179±.004
	TripBuild	0.193±.005	0.289±.008	10601±1634	0.580±.017	1.454±.043	0.176±.004	0.181±.005	0.165±.004
Magic King.	PersQ	**0.132±.003**	**0.244±.005**	**4275±133**	**0.901±.025**	**3.330±.088**	**0.440±.008**	**0.326±.007**	**0.343±.006**
	IHA	0.240±.004	0.321±.008	6885±329	0.772±.017	3.159±.064	0.305±.005	0.312±.006	0.288±.004
	UBCF-I	0.206±.005	0.323±.007	11328±424	0.474±.012	1.389±.038	0.265±.004	0.304±.006	0.261±.004
	PersTour	0.208±.006	0.303±.010	8822±494	0.486±.016	1.305±.047	0.202±.005	0.201±.006	0.186±.005
	TourInt	0.195±.006	0.316±.010	9410±531	0.490±.017	1.311±.048	0.200±.005	0.200±.006	0.185±.005
	TripBuild	0.191±.006	0.287±.009	9074±456	0.479±.017	1.393±.048	0.193±.005	0.189±.006	0.177±.005

of up to 5.3%. The only exception is for the Disneyland dataset, where PersQ out-performs all baselines but under-performs UBCF-I by less than 0.34% in terms of Precision. Moreover, we are more interested in the F1-score, as it considers both precision and recall, and PersQ out-performs all baselines by at least 15.3% in terms of F1-score. These results indicate that itineraries recommended by PersQ are highly representative of the real-life visits of these users.

Popularity and Interests. In terms of Attraction Popularity (Pop_I) and User Interests (Int_I), PersQ also offers the best overall performance, while IHA offers the second best performance. PersQ has the highest Popularity scores for four of five theme parks and the highest Interest scores in three of five theme parks, while IHA leads in Popularity and Interest for one and two theme parks, respectively.

Discussion. The superior performance of PersQ is due to its three-fold consideration of attraction popularity, user interests and queuing times, which is automatically determined from geo-tagged photos. In contrast, the various baselines only consider attraction popularity and user interests, and hence may recommend visits to attractions that are popular and interesting but with excessive queuing times. This excessive queuing time consumes a large portion of the touring time, as indicated by the high QC_I scores, thus causing attractions later in the itinerary to be missed. Apart from PersQ, IHA is also able to offer a relatively good performance in terms of attraction popularity and user interests due to its use of the profit (popularity and interest) over cost (travelling time) heuristic.

9 CONCLUSION AND FUTURE WORK

In this paper, we proposed the QueueTourRec problem of recommending personalized itineraries of popular and interesting attractions, while minimizing queuing times. QueueTourRec is an NP-hard problem that includes time-dependent queuing times, which we then solve using our proposed PersQ algorithm that is adapted from MCTS. For determining queuing times, we also implemented a framework that utilizes geo-tagged photos to determine the distribution of queuing times at each attraction, as well as the attraction popularity and user interest preferences. We evaluated PersQ on a dataset of five major theme parks and show that PersQ out-performs the state-of-the-art in terms of maximum queuing times, queuing time to itinerary cost ratio, queuing time to attraction popularity ratio, attraction popularity, user interest alignment, recall, precision and F1-score.

In future, we intend to address other aspects of the QueueTourRec problem, such as: (i) addressing the cold-start problem by using social ties of users to solicit user interest; (ii) accounting for the effects of holidays, special events, weather and other uncertainties on attraction operations; (iii) developing a game-theoretic approach to itinerary recommendation that optimizes for global queuing times and crowdedness for the entire population of theme park visitors; (iv) incorporating a strict attraction category constraint for various user demographics (e.g., no dark rides for kids).

Acknowledgments. This work was supported in part by Data61, a Google PhD Fellowship in Machine Learning, a Google PhD Travel Scholarship and an ACM SIGIR Student Travel Grant. The authors thank the anonymous reviewers for their useful comments.

REFERENCES

[1] Peter Auer, Nicolo Cesa-Bianchi, and Paul Fischer. 2002. Finite-time analysis of the multiarmed bandit problem. *Machine Learning* 47, 2-3 (2002), 235–256.
[2] Avrim Blum, Shuchi Chawla, David R. Karger, Terran Lane, Adam Meyerson, and Maria Minkoff. 2007. Approximation algorithms for orienteering and discounted-reward TSP. *SIAM J. Comput.* 37, 2 (2007), 653–670.
[3] Igo Brilhante, Jose Antonio Macedo, Franco Maria Nardini, Raffaele Perego, and Chiara Renso. 2013. Where shall we go today? Planning touristic tours with TripBuilder. In *Proc. of CIKM'13.* 757–762.
[4] Igo Brilhante, Jose Antonio Macedo, Franco Maria Nardini, Raffaele Perego, and Chiara Renso. 2014. TripBuilder: A Tool for Recommending Sightseeing Tours. In *Proc. of ECIR'14.* 771–774.
[5] Igo Ramalho Brilhante, Jose Antonio Macedo, Franco Maria Nardini, Raffaele Perego, and Chiara Renso. 2015. On planning sightseeing tours with TripBuilder. *Information Processing & Management* 51, 2 (2015), 1–15.
[6] Cameron B. Browne, Edward Powley, Daniel Whitehouse, Simon M. Lucas, Peter I. Cowling, Philipp Rohlfshagen, Stephen Tavener, Diego Perez, Spyridon Samothrakis, and Simon Colton. 2012. A survey of monte carlo tree search methods. *IEEE Trans. on Computational Intel. and AI in Games* 4, 1 (2012), 1–43.
[7] Raymond C. Browning, Emily A. Baker, Jessica A. Herron, and Rodger Kram. 2006. Effects of obesity and sex on the energetic cost and preferred speed of walking. *Journal of Applied Physiology* 100, 2 (2006), 390–398.
[8] Luis Castillo, Eva Armengol, Eva Onaindía, Laura Sebastiá, Jesús González-Boticario, Antonio Rodríguez, Susana Fernández, Juan D. Arias, and Daniel Borrajo. 2008. SAMAP: An user-oriented adaptive system for planning tourist visits. *Expert Systems with Applications* 34, 2 (2008), 1318–1332.
[9] Dawei Chen, Cheng Soon Ong, and Lexing Xie. 2016. Learning Points and Routes to Recommend Trajectories. In *Proc. of CIKM'16.* 2227–2232.
[10] Munmun De Choudhury, Moran Feldman, Sihem Amer-Yahia, Nadav Golbandi, Ronny Lempel, and Cong Yu. 2010. Automatic construction of travel itineraries using social breadcrumbs. In *Proc. of HT'10.* 35–44.
[11] Munmun De Choudhury, Moran Feldman, Sihem Amer-Yahia, Nadav Golbandi, Ronny Lempel, and Cong Yu. 2010. Constructing travel itineraries from tagged geo-temporal breadcrumbs. In *Proc. of WWW'10.* 1083–1084.
[12] Rémi Coulom. 2006. Efficient selectivity and backup operators in Monte-Carlo tree search. In *Proc. of CCG'06.* 72–83.
[13] Marco Dorigo, Mauro Birattari, and Thomas Stützle. 2006. Ant colony optimization. *IEEE Computational Intelligence Magazine* 1, 4 (2006), 28–39.
[14] Inma Garcia, Laura Sebastia, and Eva Onaindia. 2011. On the design of individual and group recommender systems for tourism. *Expert Systems with Applications* 38, 6 (2011), 7683–7692.
[15] Aristides Gionis, Theodoros Lappas, Konstantinos Pelechrinis, and Evimaria Terzi. 2014. Customized tour recommendations in urban areas. In *Proc. of WSDM'14.* 313–322.
[16] Bruce L. Golden, Larry Levy, and Rakesh Vohra. 1987. The Orienteering problem. *Naval Research Logistics* 34, 3 (1987), 307–318.
[17] Aldy Gunawan, Hoong Chuin Lau, and Pieter Vansteenwegen. 2016. Orienteering Problem: A survey of recent variants, solution approaches and applications. *European Journal of Operational Research* 255, 2 (2016), 315–332.
[18] Aldy Gunawan, Zhi Yuan, and Hoong Chuin Lau. 2014. A Mathematical Model and Metaheuristics for Time Dependent Orienteering Problem. In *Proc. of PATAT'14.* 202–217.
[19] Hsun-Ping Hsieh, Cheng-Te Li, and Shou-De Lin. 2012. TripRec: recommending trip routes from large scale check-in data. In *Proc. of WWW'12.* 529–530.
[20] Astrid S. Kenyon and David P. Morton. 2003. Stochastic vehicle routing with random travel times. *Transportation Science* 37, 1 (2003), 69–8.
[21] Levente Kocsis and Csaba Szepesvári. 2006. Bandit based monte-carlo planning. In *Proc. of ECML'06.* 282–293.
[22] Levente Kocsis, Csaba Szepesvári, and Jan Willemson. 2006. *Improved monte-carlo search.* Technical Report. University of Tartu, Institute of Computer Science.
[23] Ron Kohavi. 1995. A study of cross-validation and bootstrap for accuracy estimation and model selection. In *Proc. of IJCAI'95.* 1137–1145.
[24] Hoong Chuin Lau, William Yeoh, Pradeep Varakantham, Duc Thien Nguyen, and Huaxing Chen. 2012. Dynamic Stochastic Orienteering Problems for Risk-Aware Applications. In *Proc. of UAI'12.* 448–458.
[25] Kenneth Wai-Ting Leung, Dik Lun Lee, and Wang-Chien Lee. 2011. CLR: a collaborative location recommendation framework based on co-clustering. In *Proc. of SIGIR'11.* 305–314.
[26] Xun Li. 2013. Multi-day and multi-stay travel planning using geo-tagged photos. In *Proc. of GeoCrowd'13.* 1–8.
[27] Xutao Li, Gao Cong, Xiao-Li Li, Tuan-Anh Nguyen Pham, and Shonali Krishnaswamy. 2015. Rank-GeoFM: a ranking based geographical factorization method for point of interest recommendation. In *Proc. of SIGIR'15.* 433–442.
[28] Kwan Hui Lim. 2015. Recommending Tours and Places-of-Interest based on User Interests from Geo-tagged Photos. In *Proc. of SIGMOD'15 PhD Symposium.* 33–38.
[29] Kwan Hui Lim, Jeffrey Chan, Christopher Leckie, and Shanika Karunasekera. 2015. Personalized Tour Recommendation based on User Interests and Points of Interest Visit Durations. In *Proc. of IJCAI'15.* 1778–1784.
[30] Kwan Hui Lim, Jeffrey Chan, Christopher Leckie, and Shanika Karunasekera. 2016. Towards Next Generation Touring: Personalized Group Tours. In *Proc. of ICAPS'16.* 412–420.
[31] Kwan Hui Lim, Jeffrey Chan, Christopher Leckie, and Shanika Karunasekera. 2017. Personalized Trip Recommendation for Tourists based on User Interests, Points of Interest Visit Durations and Visit Recency. *Knowledge and Information Systems* (2017), In Press.
[32] Clair E. Miller, Albert W. Tucker, and Richard A. Zemlin. 1960. Integer programming formulation of traveling salesman problems. *J. ACM* 7, 4 (1960), 326–329.
[33] Edward J. Powley, Daniel Whitehouse, and Peter I. Cowling. 2013. Monte Carlo tree search with macro-actions and heuristic route planning for the multiobjective physical travelling salesman problem. In *Proc. of CIG'13.* 1–8.
[34] Ioannis Refanidis, Christos Emmanouilidis, Ilias Sakellariou, Anastasios Alexiadis, Remous-Aris Koutsiamanis, Konstantinos Agnantis, Aimilia Tasidou, Fotios Kokkoras, and Pavlos S. Efraimidis. 2014. myVisitPlanner GR: Personalized Itinerary Planning System for Tourism. In *Proc. of SETN'14.* 615–629.
[35] Paul Resnick, Neophytos Iacovou, Mitesh Suchak, Peter Bergstrom, and John Riedl. 1994. GroupLens: an open architecture for collaborative filtering of netnews. In *Proc. of the CSCW'94.* 175–186.
[36] Roger W. Sinnott. 1984. Virtues of the Haversine. *Sky and Telescope* 68, 158 (1984).
[37] TouringPlans.com. 2016. Disney's Hollywood Studios Attraction Durations. (2016). https://touringplans.com/hollywood-studios/attractions/duration.
[38] Theodore Tsiligirides. 1984. Heuristic methods applied to Orienteering. *Journal of the Operational Research Society* 35, 9 (1984), 797–809.
[39] UNWTO. 2016. United Nations World Tourism Organization (UNWTO) Annual Report 2015. (2016). http://www2.unwto.org/annual-reports.
[40] Pieter Vansteenwegen, Wouter Souffriau, Greet Vanden Berghe, and Dirk Van Oudheusden. 2011. The city trip planner: An expert system for tourists. *Expert Systems with Applications* 38, 6 (2011), 6540–6546.
[41] Pieter Vansteenwegen, Wouter Souffriau, and Dirk Van Oudheusden. 2011. The Orienteering problem: A survey. *Euro. J. of Operational Rsch.* 209, 1 (2011), 1–10.
[42] Pradeep Varakantham and Akshat Kumar. 2013. Optimization approaches for solving chance constrained stochastic orienteering problems. In *Proc. of ADT'13.*
[43] Xiaoting Wang, Christopher Leckie, Jeffery Chan, Kwan Hui Lim, and Tharshan Vaithianathan. 2016. Improving Personalized Trip Recommendation to Avoid Crowds Using Pedestrian Sensor Data. In *Proc. of CIKM'16.*
[44] Wolfgang Wörndl and Alexander Hefele. 2016. Generating Paths Through Discovered Places-of-Interests for City Trip Planning. In *Information and Communication Technologies in Tourism.* Springer International Publishing, 441–453.
[45] Yahoo. 2016. Flickr API. (2016). https://www.flickr.com/services/api/.
[46] Lina Yao, Quan Z. Sheng, Yongrui Qin, Xianzhi Wang, Ali Shemshadi, and Qi He. 2015. Context-aware Point-of-Interest Recommendation Using Tensor Factorization with Social Regularization. In *Proc. of SIGIR'15.* 1007–1010.
[47] Mao Ye, Peifeng Yin, Wang-Chien Lee, and Dik-Lun Lee. 2011. Exploiting geographical influence for collaborative point-of-interest recommendation. In *Proc. of SIGIR'11.* 325–334.
[48] Quan Yuan, Gao Cong, Zongyang Ma, Aixin Sun, and Nadia Magnenat Thalmann. 2013. Time-aware point-of-interest recommendation. In *Proc. of SIGIR'13.*
[49] Chenyi Zhang, Hongwei Liang, and Ke Wang. 2016. Trip Recommendation Meets Real-World Constraints: POI Availability, Diversity, and Traveling Time Uncertainty. *ACM Transactions on Information Systems* 35, 1 (2016), 5.
[50] Chenyi Zhang, Hongwei Liang, Ke Wang, and Jianling Sun. 2015. Personalized Trip Recommendation with POI Availability and Uncertain Traveling Time. In *Proc. of CIKM'15.* 911–920.

Attentive Collaborative Filtering: Multimedia Recommendation with Item- and Component-Level Attention

Jingyuan Chen
National University of Singapore
jingyuanchen91@gmail.com

Hanwang Zhang
Columbia University
hanwangzhang@gmail.com

Xiangnan He*
National University of Singapore
xiangnanhe@gmail.com

Liqiang Nie
ShanDong University
nieliqiang@gmail.com

Wei Liu
Tencent AI Lab
wliu@ee.columbia.edu

Tat-Seng Chua
National University of Singapore
dcscts@nus.edu.sg

ABSTRACT

Multimedia content is dominating today's Web information. The nature of multimedia user-item interactions is 1/0 binary implicit feedback (*e.g.*, photo likes, video views, song downloads, *etc.*), which can be collected at a larger scale with a much lower cost than explicit feedback (*e.g.*, product ratings). However, the majority of existing collaborative filtering (CF) systems are not well-designed for multimedia recommendation, since they ignore the implicitness in users' interactions with multimedia content. We argue that, in multimedia recommendation, there exists *item-* and *component-level* implicitness which blurs the underlying users' preferences. The item-level implicitness means that users' preferences on items (*e.g.*, photos, videos, songs, *etc.*) are unknown, while the component-level implicitness means that inside each item users' preferences on different components (*e.g.*, regions in an image, frames of a video, *etc.*) are unknown. For example, a "view" on a video does not provide any specific information about how the user likes the video (*i.e.*, item-level) and which parts of the video the user is interested in (*i.e.*, component-level). In this paper, we introduce a novel *attention* mechanism in CF to address the challenging item- and component-level implicit feedback in multimedia recommendation, dubbed Attentive Collaborative Filtering (ACF). Specifically, our attention model is a neural network that consists of two attention modules: the component-level attention module, starting from any content feature extraction network (*e.g.*, CNN for images/videos), which learns to select informative components of multimedia items, and the item-level attention module, which learns to score the item preferences. ACF can be seamlessly incorporated into classic CF models with implicit feedback, such as BPR and SVD++, and efficiently trained using SGD. Through extensive experiments on two real-world multimedia Web services: Vine and Pinterest, we show that ACF significantly outperforms state-of-the-art CF methods.

*Xiangnan He is the corresponding author.

SIGIR'17, August 7–11, 2017, Shinjuku, Tokyo, Japan.

DOI: http://dx.doi.org/10.1145/3077136.3080797

CCS CONCEPTS

•**Information systems** →**Multimedia information systems;**

KEYWORDS

Collaborative Filtering, Implicit Feedback, Attention, Multimedia Recommendation

1 INTRODUCTION

As we log into a multimedia Web service, *e.g.*, Youtube, just like other billions of users, we have billions of contents online ready to view and share. Meanwhile, due to the advance of mobile devices, millions of new images and videos are streaming into these websites. Take Snapchat, one of the most popular video-based social App, as an example. During the time of reading this paragraph, around 50 thousand video snippets are shared and 2.4 million videos are viewed. Without a doubt, the dominating Web multimedia content requires modern recommender systems, in particular those based on Collaborative Filtering (CF), to sift through massive multimedia contents for users in a highly dynamic environment.

CF analyzes relationships between users and interdependencies among items, in order to identify new user-*item* associations [21, 23, 37]. In the context of multimedia recommendation, *item* refers to different kinds of multimedia contents consumed by users, such as a video, a photo or a song. Most CF systems rely on explicit user interests as input, *e.g.*, star ratings of products, which provide *explicit feedback* [19, 25, 38]. However, explicit ratings are not always available in many applications. Due to the large-scale and extreme diversity of multimedia contents [15], inherent user-item interactions in multimedia recommendation systems are mostly based on *implicit feedback*, such as "view" of a video, "like" of a photo, "play" of a song, *etc.* As implicit feedback lacks substantial evidence on which items user dislike (*i.e.*, negative feedback), existing CF methods [20, 21, 30] with implicit feedback generally focus on how to tap the missing user-item interactions into preference modeling. However, few methods deeply explore the implicitness of users' preferences. In particular, we argue that there are two levels of implicit feedback in multimedia recommendation, which have been neglected by most existing CF methods.

Item-Level Implicit Feedback. Each user is associated with a set of items (*i.e.*, positive feedback) via tracking their consumption habits. However, a positive set of user feedback does not necessarily indicate equal item preferences. This phenomenon is extremely prevailing in multimedia services as most of them are social-oriented. For example, some images clicked as "like" may be only due to the fact that they are taken by friends but are not of users' real interests. Even though for images consistent with users' real interests, users' preferences on them are not the same. Such cases that the preference information on each item is not provided are named as *item-level implicitness*. To better characterize users' preference profile, the implicit feedback in the item-level requires different attentions on the set of items. However, to the best of our knowledge, existing CF models generally resort to either a constant weight [23] or pre-defined heuristic weights [21], and thus the conventional neighborhood context obtained by such a weighted sum fails to model the item-level implicit feedback.

Component-Level Implicit Feedback. Feedback on multimedia content is typically at the whole item level. However, multimedia content usually contains diverse semantics and multiple components. We use *component-level implicitness* to denote cases that feedback for each component is not available. Take a video about a basketball match as an example, the whole video contains multiple players and abundant actions. A "play" feedback from a user on this video does not necessarily indicate that the user likes the whole content of the video, while it may be triggered by his interest in the last part of the video which is about the final scores in the match. Therefore, unlike traditional content-based CF methods that only consider multimedia content as a whole [4, 12], we should model user preferences with lower-level content components, *e.g.*, image features in different locations [39] and video features of various frames [6, 10, 41].

However, directly modeling the item-level and component-level implicit feedback to facilitate recommendation is non-trivial since the ground-truth for the implicitness in each level is not available. To address this problem, we propose a novel CF framework dubbed Attentive Collaborative Filtering (ACF) for multimedia recommendation, which can automatically assign weights to the two levels of feedback in a distant supervised manner. ACF draws on the latent factor model, by transforming both items and users to the same latent factor space to make them directly comparable. To incorporate the two levels of implicit feedback, a neighborhood-based model is integrated to characterize users' interest profile through their historical behavior which is a weighted sum of items. The influence of two levels feedbacks is reflected by the weights of items in the neighborhood model. Specifically, in order to model the item-level feedback, we propose a weighting function which is a multi-layer neural network and takes the characteristics of both user and item, as well as the multimedia content feature as input (cf. Section 4.2). The multimedia content feature in the item-level is actually generated by assembling multiple components of the item with attentive weights. In particular, the component-level attention is also a multi-layer neural network that takes user and component features as input. Then, all the attentive components together compose a content feature vector, which is one of the input of the item-level attention (cf. Section 4.3). ACF can be efficiently trained using Stochastic Gradient Decent (SGD) on large user-item interactions of both images and videos (cf. Section 4.4). We evaluate ACF extensively on two real-world datasets that represent a spectrum of different media: Pinterest (images) and Vine (videos). Experimental results show that ACF consistently outperforms competing methods ranging from CF-based methods, content-based methods [28, 35] and hybrid methods [9, 33] (cf. Section 5).

Our contributions are summarized as follows:

- We propose a novel CF framework named Attentive Collaborative Filtering (ACF) to employ attention modeling in CF with implicit feedback. To the best of our knowledge, this is the first framework that is designed to tackle the implicit feedback in multimedia recommendation.
- To address two levels of implicit feedback, we introduce two attention modules, each is a neural network that can be seamlessly incorporated into any neighborhood models with efficient end-to-end SGD training.
- Through extensive experiments conducted on two real-world datasets, we show that ACF consistently outperforms several state-of-the-art CF methods with implicit feedback.

2 RELATED WORK

2.1 Implicit Feedback

Recommendation with implicit feedback is also called the one-class problem [27] because of the lack of negative feedback, where only positive feedback (*e.g.*, click, view) is available. Apart from the positive feedback, the remaining data is a mixture of real negative feedback and missing values. Therefore, it is hard to reliably infer which item a user did not like from implicit feedback.

To cope with the problem of missing negative samples, several approaches have been proposed which can be roughly classified into two categories: sample based learning [20, 27, 30] and whole-data based learning [21, 23]. The former samples negative feedback from the missing data, while the latter treats all the missing data as negative. Therefore, sample-based approaches are more effective while whole-data based approaches provide higher coverage.

Traditional whole-data based methods assume that all unobserved events are negative samples and are equally weighted [23]. However, this may not be realistic, due to the fact that the unobserved data may contain missing values which are false negative. Towards this end, several recent efforts [21, 27] focus on the weighting scheme, taking the confidence whether the unobserved samples are indeed negative ones into consideration. For example, certain nonuniform weighting schemes on the negative samples, such as user-oriented [27] and item popularity-oriented [21], have been proposed and proven to be more effective than the uniform weighting scheme. However, one major limitation of the non-uniform weighting method is that the weighting schemes are defined based on assumptions proposed by the authors, which may not be correct in the real data.

As can be seen, most of the existing efforts till now focused on the negative feedback sampling or weighting schemes to tackle the problem of no negative feedback, while no much attention has been paid on the two levels of implicit feedback—item-level attention and component-level attention—which can be seen as the weighting strategy on positive samples. To fill up the empty in positive sample weighting, we propose a novel attention mechanism to weight positive implicit signal automatically based on the user-item interaction matrix and the content of the item.

2.2 Multimedia Recommendation

The significance of multimedia recommendation has led to the great attention from both the industry and academia [8, 16, 32, 36]. Most of the current state-of-the-art multimedia recommendation techniques are based on the CF analysis [2, 4]. Although these approaches work well for popular and frequently watched contents, they are less applicable to fresh contents or tail contents with few views, due to the sparsity of the data. Therefore, for these items, CF analysis based solely on user-item interaction matrix or co-views information may yield either low-quality suggestions or no suggestions at all. To address the problem of tail contents, researchers have developed hybrid approaches [33] that incorporate the context and content of multimedia items with the CF model for recommendation. For example, several efforts have been dedicated to conduct the video recommendation utilizing different context information, such as the multi-modal relevance [26, 34], cross-domain knowledge [11, 14] and latent attributes feature [12, 44]. Moreover, [3, 4] have proposed hybrid approaches to video recommendation, which combines the video content (topics mined from video metadata, related queries, *etc.*) with the co-view information. Another widely used strategy is using a latent factor model for recommendation, and further predicting the latent factors from multimedia contents to handle the cold start scenario [15, 33]. However, most of the exisitng methods failed to pay attention to the two levels of implicitness in the multimedia recommendation, which is the major concern of our work.

2.3 Attention Mechanism

Attention mechanism has been shown effective in various machine learning tasks such as image/video captioning [7, 39, 40] and machine translation [1]. Its success is mainly due to the reasonable assumption that human recognition does not tend to process a whole signal in its entirety at once; instead, one only focuses on selective parts of the whole perception space when and where as needed. Our component-level attention adopts the soft spatial attention model in [39] for images and the soft temporal attention model in [40] for videos. The key idea of soft attention is to learn to assign attentive weights (normalized by sum to 1) for a set of features: higher (lower) weights indicate that the corresponding features are informative (less informative) for the end task.

In fact, the attention assumption is reasonable in many real-world situations, not just in the domain of computer vision and natural language processing. To the best of our knowledge, ACF is the first attention-based CF model in the area of recommender systems.

3 PRELIMINARIES

We begin with some notations. We denote a user-item interaction matrix as $\mathbf{R} \in \mathbb{R}^{M \times N}$, where M and N denote the number of users and items, respectively. Specifically, we use R_{ij} to represent the (i, j)-th entry of $\mathbf{R}$. As for implicit feedback, $R_{ij} = 1$ indicates that the i-th user has interacted with the j-th item and $R_{ij} = 0$ indicates that there is no interaction between user i and item j in the observed data. We use $\mathcal{R} = \{(i, j) | R_{ij} = 1\}$ to denote the set of user-item pairs where there exist implicit interactions. The goal of a CF model with implicit feedback is to exploit the entire $\mathbf{R}$ to estimate $\hat{R}_{ij}$ for the unobserved interactions.

3.1 Latent Factor Models

Latent factor models map both users and items to a joint low-dimensional latent space where the user-item preference score is estimated by vector inner product. We will focus on models that are induced by Singular Value Decomposition (SVD) on the user-item ratings matrix. We denote user latent vectors as $\mathbf{U} = [\mathbf{u}_1, ..., \mathbf{u}_M] \in \mathbb{R}^{D \times M}$ and item latent vectors as $\mathbf{V} = [\mathbf{v}_1, ..., \mathbf{v}_N] \in \mathbb{R}^{D \times N}$, where $D \ll min(M, N)$ is the latent feature dimension. The preference score R_{ij} is estimated as:

$$\hat{R}_{ij} =< \mathbf{u}_i, \mathbf{v}_j >= \mathbf{u}_i^T \mathbf{v}_j. \tag{1}$$

The objective is to minimize the following regularized squared loss on observed ratings:

$$\arg\min_{\mathbf{U},\mathbf{V}} \sum_{(i,j) \in \mathcal{R}} (R_{ij} - \hat{R}_{ij})^2 + \lambda(||\mathbf{U}||^2 + ||\mathbf{V}||^2), \tag{2}$$

where λ controls the strength of regularization, which is usually an L_2 norm to prevent overfitting. After we obtain the optimized user and item vectors, recommendation is then reduced to a ranking problem according to the estimated scores $\hat{R}_{ij}$.

However, applying SVD in implicit feedback domain raises difficulties due to the high portion of unobservable data. Carelessly treating the unobserved entries as negative samples in SVD may introduce false negative samples in the training data.

3.2 Bayesian Personalized Ranking (BPR)

BPR is a well-known framework for addressing the implicitness in CF [30]. Instead of point-wise learning as in SVD, BPR models a triplet of one user and two items, where one of the items is observed and the other one is not. Specifically, from the user-item matrix $\mathbf{R}$, if an item j has been viewed by user i, then it is assumed that the user prefers this item over all the other unobserved items.

The optimization objective for BPR is based on the maximum posterior estimator. In particular, by applying the above latent factor models, a widely used BPR model is given as:

$$\arg\min_{\mathbf{U},\mathbf{V}} \sum_{(i,j,k) \in \mathcal{R}_B} - \ln \sigma(\hat{R}_{ij} - \hat{R}_{ik}) + \lambda(||\mathbf{U}||^2 + ||\mathbf{V}||^2), \tag{3}$$

where σ is the logistic sigmoid function and λ is regularization parameter. The training data $\mathcal{R}_B$ is generated as:

$$\mathcal{R}_B = \{(i, j, k) | j \in \mathcal{R}(i) \wedge k \in \mathcal{I} \backslash \mathcal{R}(i)\}, \tag{4}$$

where $\mathcal{I}$ denotes the set of all items in the dataset and $\mathcal{R}(i)$ represents the set of items that are interacted by the i-th user. The semantics of $(i, j, k) \in \mathcal{R}_B$ is that user i is assumed to prefer item j over k.

In this work, we use BPR as our basic learning model because of its effectiveness in exploiting the unobserved user-item feedback.

4 ATTENTIVE COLLABORATIVE FILTERING

In this section, we will introduce our Attentive Collaborative Filtering (ACF) model in detail. First, we present the general ACF framework, elaborating the motivation of the model. We then show the detailed formulations of the proposed item-level and component-level attentions. Note that in the following sections, "item-" means video or image, and "component-" means the frame in video or space region in images. Lastly we will go through the optimization details of ACF.

4.1 General Framework

ACF is a hierarchical neural network that models user's preference score with respect to the item in *item*-level and content in *component*-level. Given a user i, an item l and the m-th component in item l, we use $\alpha(i,l)$ to denote user i's preference degree in item l and further $\beta(i,l,m)$ to denote user i's preference degree in the m-th component of item l. We use two attention sub-networks to learn these two preference scores jointly. Specifically, we employ component-level module to generate content representations for each item and item-level module to obtain user representation.

Objective Function. In addition to explicitly parameterizing each user i with $\mathbf{u}_i$, ACF also models users based on the set of items $\mathcal{R}(i)$ that they interacted with. Therefore, each item l is associated with two factor vectors. One is denoted by $\mathbf{v}_l$, which is the basic item vector in latent factor model. The other one, denoted by $\mathbf{p}_l$, is the auxiliary item vector which is used to characterize users based on the set of items they interacted with. The representation of a user i is through the sum: $\mathbf{u}_i + \sum_{l \in \mathcal{R}(i)} \alpha(i,l)\mathbf{p}_l$.

ACF is optimized in the BPR pairwise learning objective [30]: optimizing the pairwise ranking between the positive and non-observable items:

$$\arg\min_{\mathbf{U},\mathbf{V},\mathbf{P},\Theta} \sum_{(i,j,k)\in\mathcal{R}_B} -\ln\sigma\left\{\left(\mathbf{u}_i + \sum_{l\in\mathcal{R}(i)} \alpha(i,l)\mathbf{p}_l\right)^T \mathbf{v}_j - \left(\mathbf{u}_i + \sum_{l\in\mathcal{R}(i)} \alpha(i,l)\mathbf{p}_l\right)^T \mathbf{v}_k\right\} + \lambda(||\mathbf{U}||^2 + ||\mathbf{V}||^2 + ||\mathbf{P}||^2), \tag{5}$$

where set $\mathcal{R}(i)$ denotes the set of items that are interacted by the i-th user and Θ is the parameters in attention network. $\alpha(i,l)$ is the item-level attention module, which measures the preference degree of user i to item l. Note that the component-level attention module is also integrated into $\alpha(i,l)$.

Inference. After we obtain the optimized user, item and auxiliary item vectors, *i.e.*, U, V and P, as well as the parameters of the attention networks, recommendation is then reduced to a ranking problem among all the items in the dataset based on estimated score $\hat{R}_{ij}$:

$$\hat{R}_{ij} = \left(\mathbf{u}_i + \sum_{l\in\mathcal{R}(i)} \alpha(i,l)\mathbf{p}_l\right)^T \mathbf{v}_j. \tag{6}$$

Relations to Neighborhood Models. Note that if we rewrite Eqn. (6) as:

$$\hat{R}_{ij} = \overbrace{\mathbf{u}_i^T\mathbf{v}_j}^{latent\ factor\ model} + \underbrace{\sum_{l\in\mathcal{R}(i)} \alpha(i,l)\mathbf{p}_l^T\mathbf{v}_j}_{neighborhood\ model}, \tag{7}$$

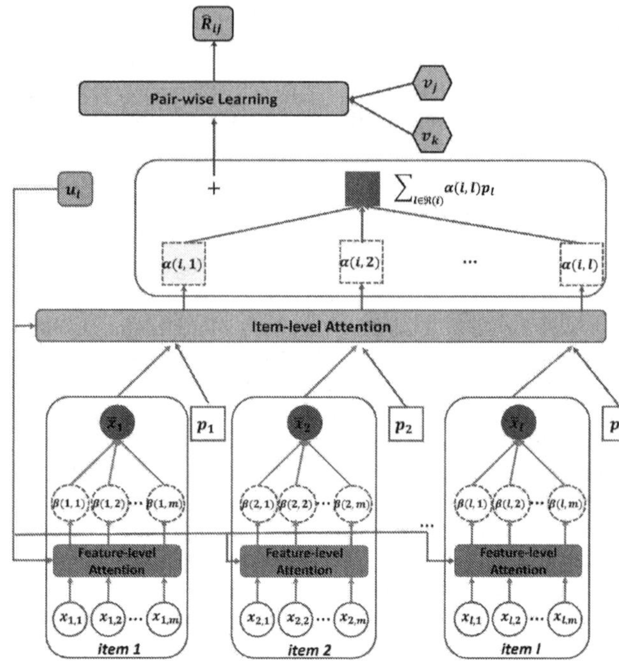

Figure 1: The architecture of our proposed Attentive Collaborative Filtering framework. Our attention model contains two level modules: component-level attention and item-level attention (cf. Section 4.1).

where $\mathbf{p}_l^T\mathbf{v}_j$ can be viewed as the similarity measure function between items in the neighborhood-based collaborative filtering [24]. The first part of Eqn. (7) corresponds to the latent factor model and the second part corresponds to the neighborhood model. Specifically, if we replace the attention weight $\alpha(i,l)$ with a normalized weight $\frac{1}{|\mathcal{R}(i)|}$, our ACF model will degenerate into SVD++ [25]; or, the weight is a heuristic function, ACF is similar to FISM [24]. However, they failed to consider the two levels of implicit feedback in recommendation, where a fixed weight assumes that all the items contribute equally to the prediction. In fact, the weights should be highly dependent to the user and the item content as we will introduce in Section 4.2 and Section 4.3.

Figure 1 illustrates the workflow of ACF. We start from the set of items that are liked by the i-th user. First, for each item l, we access the set of component features $\{\mathbf{x}_{lm}\}$ (blue solid circles), where $\mathbf{x}_{lm}$ could be the image region feature at the m-th spatial location [39] or the frame feature of the m-th frame in a video [41]. Then, the component-level attention module, which is a sub-network, takes the user latent vector $\mathbf{u}_i$ and the feature $\mathbf{x}_{lm}$ as input and output the component-level attentive weight $\beta(l,m)$ for the m-th component (dashed blue circles). Thus, the final representation of the l-th item content $\bar{\mathbf{x}}_l$ is calculated by the weighted sum $\sum\beta(l,m)\mathbf{x}_{lm}$ (filled blue circles). After we have obtained $\bar{\mathbf{x}}_l$, we can use the item-level attention module by taking user latent vector $\mathbf{u}_i$, item latent vector $\mathbf{v}_l$, auxiliary item latent vector $\mathbf{p}_l$, and the content feature $\bar{\mathbf{x}}_l$ to calculate the item-level attentive weight $\alpha(i,l)$ for each neighborhood item (dashed green squares). Then, similar to the component-level attentions, we obtain the final neighborhood vectors for user i by the weighted sum $\sum\alpha(i,l)\mathbf{p}_l$ (filled green

Algorithm 1: Attentive Collaborative Filtering

Input: User-item interaction matrix $\mathbf{R}$. Each item l is represented by a set of component features $\{x_{l*}\}$.
Output: Latent feature matrix $\mathbf{U}$, $\mathbf{V}$, $\mathbf{P}$ and parameters in attention model Θ

1: Initialize $\mathbf{U}$, $\mathbf{V}$ and $\mathbf{P}$ with Gaussian distribution. Initialize Θ with xavier [17].
2: **repeat**
3: draw (i, j, k) from $\mathcal{R}_B$
4: For each item l in $\mathcal{R}(i)$:
5: For each component m in $\{\mathbf{x}_{l*}\}$:
6: Compute $\beta(i, l, m)$ according to Eqns. (10) and (11)
7: Compute $\overline{\mathbf{x}}_l$ according to Eqn. (12)
8: Compute $\alpha(i, l)$ according to Eqns. (8) and (9)
9: $\mathbf{u}'_i \leftarrow \mathbf{u}_i + \sum_{l \in \mathcal{R}(i)} \alpha(i, l)\mathbf{p}_l$
10: $\hat{R}_{ijk} \leftarrow \mathbf{u}'_i \mathbf{v}_j - \mathbf{u}'_i \mathbf{v}_k$
11: For each parameter θ in $\{\mathbf{U}, \mathbf{V}, \mathbf{P}, \Theta\}$:
12: Update $\theta \leftarrow \theta + \eta \cdot (\frac{\exp^{-\hat{R}_{ijk}}}{1+\exp^{-\hat{R}_{ijk}}} \cdot \frac{\partial \hat{R}_{ijk}}{\partial \theta} + \lambda \cdot \theta)$.
13: **until** convergence
14: return $\mathbf{U}$, $\mathbf{V}$, $\mathbf{P}$ and Θ.

squares). Lastly, combined with the basic user latent vector, we can use stochastic gradient descent to optimize the BPR pairwise learning objective (cf Eqn. (5)).

4.2 Item-Level Attention

The goal of the item-level attention is to select items that are representative to users' preferences and then aggregate the representation of informative items to characterize users. Given the basic user latent representation $\mathbf{u}_i$, the neighborhood item latent vector $\mathbf{v}_l$, the neighborhood auxiliary item vector $\mathbf{p}_l$, and the item content feature $\overline{\mathbf{x}}_l$ (detailed in the next section), we use a two-layer network to compute the attention score $a(i, l)$ as,

$$a(i, l) = \mathbf{w}_1^T \phi(\mathbf{W}_{1u}\mathbf{u}_i + \mathbf{W}_{1v}\mathbf{v}_l + \mathbf{W}_{1p}\mathbf{p}_l + \mathbf{W}_{1x}\overline{\mathbf{x}}_l + \mathbf{b}_1) + \mathbf{c}_1. \quad (8)$$

where the matrices $\mathbf{W}_{1*}$ and bias $\mathbf{b}_1$ are the first layer parameters, and the vector $\mathbf{w}_1$ and bias $\mathbf{c}_1$ are the second layer parameters; $\phi(x) = max(0, x)$ is the ReLU function, which was found better than a single layer perceptron with a hyperbolic tangent nonlinearity.

The final item-level weights are obtained by normalizing the above attentive scores using Softmax, which can be interpreted as the contribution of the item l to the preference profile of user i:

$$\alpha(i, l) = \frac{exp\,(a(i, l))}{\sum_{n \in \mathcal{R}(i)} exp\,(a(i, n))}. \quad (9)$$

4.3 Component-Level Attention

Multimedia items contain complex information while different users may like different parts of contents in the same multimedia item. Each multimedia item l may be encoded into a variable-sized set of component features $\{\mathbf{x}_{l*}\}$. We use $|\{\mathbf{x}_{l*}\}|$ to denote the size of the set and $\mathbf{x}_{lm}$ to denote the feature of the m-th component in the set. Unlike conventional content-based CF models that generally adopt average pooling [6, 33] for extracting a unified representation, the goal of component-level attention is to assign components attentive weights that are consistent with user preference, and then apply the weighted sum to construct the content representation.

Similar to the item-level attention, the component-level attention score for the m-th component $\mathbf{x}_{lm}$ of item l from user i is also a two-layer network:

$$b(i, l, m) = \mathbf{w}_2^T \phi(\mathbf{W}_{2u}\mathbf{u}_i + \mathbf{W}_{2x}\mathbf{x}_{lm} + \mathbf{b}_2) + \mathbf{c}_2, \quad (10)$$

where the matrices $\mathbf{W}_{2*}$ and bias $\mathbf{b}_2$ are the first layer parameters, and the vector $\mathbf{w}_2$ and bias $\mathbf{c}_2$ are the second layer parameters; $\phi(x) = max(0, x)$ is the ReLU function. Then, the final component-level attention is normalized as:

$$\beta(i, l, m) = \frac{exp\,(b(i, l, m))}{\sum_{n=1}^{|\{\mathbf{x}_{l*}\}|} exp\,(b(i, l, n))}. \quad (11)$$

After we obtain the component-level attention $\beta(i, l, m)$, the content representation of item l with the encoded preference of user i is calculated as the following weighted sum:

$$\overline{\mathbf{x}}_l = \sum_{m=1}^{|\{\mathbf{x}_{l*}\}|} \beta(i, l, m) \cdot \mathbf{x}_{lm}, \quad (12)$$

4.4 Algorithm

A stochastic gradient descent algorithm based on bootstrap sampling of training triples is proposed to solve the network. The steps for training the model are summarized in Algorithm 1.

For notational simplicity, we divide ACF into three steps: 1) subroutine ACFcomp runs from Line 5 to Line 7. Note that the component can be image region features for image or video frame feature for video; 2) subroutine ACFitem runs from Line 4 to Line 9; and 3) subroutine BPR-OPT runs back propagation with respect to Eqn. (5). Due to space limit, we use Θ to denote the set of parameters in item-level attention and component-level attention, and $\hat{R}_{ijk}$ to denote $\hat{R}_{ij} - \hat{R}_{ik}$. Note that Line 12 are the gradients of the model parameters updated using chain rules. To optimize the objective function, we employ stochastic gradient descent (SGD) – a universal solver for optimizing neural network models. At each time, it randomly selects a training instance and updates each model parameter towards the direction of its negative gradient.

Note that if more computational resources are available, we can also achieve end-to-end CNN module fine-tuning. We will investigate whether we can train more powerful visual features using user-item implicit feedback in future.

5 EXPERIMENTS

In this section, we will conduct experiments to answer the following research questions:

- **RQ1** Does ACF outperform state-of-the-art recommendation methods?
- **RQ2** How do the proposed item-level and component-level attentions perform?

We will first present the experimental settings, follow by answering the above two research questions, and end with some illustrative examples.

5.1 Experimental Settings

Datasets. We experimented with two publicly accessible datasets: Pinterest[1] and Vine [5]. The characteristics of the two datasets are summarized in Table 1.

Table 1: Statistics of the evaluation datasets.

Dataset	Interaction#	Item#	User#	Sparsity
Pinterest	1,091,733	14,965	50,000	99.85%
Vine	125,089	16,243	18,017	99.96%

1. Pinterest. This implicit feedback dataset is constructed by [15] for evaluating image recommendation. Due to the large volume and high sparsity of this dataset, for instance, over 20% of users have only one pin, we filter the dataset by retaining the top 15,000 popular images and sampling 50,000 users who have interactions on the 15,000 images. This results in a subset of data that contains 50,000 users, 14,965 images and 1,091,733 interactions. Each interaction denotes whether the user has pinned the image to his/her own board.

2. Vine. This video dataset [6, 45] is crawled from Vine, a micro-video sharing social network. The crawling starts with a set of active users. Then the breadth-first crawling strategy is adopted to expand the seed users by crawling their followers. Totally, the dataset contains 98,166 users and their interactions on 1,303,242 micro-videos. An interaction denotes whether the user has posted or re-posted the video. To evaluate the recommendation task, we filtered the dataset by retaining users with at least 4 interactions. This results in a subset of data that contains 18,017 users, 16,243 videos and 125,089 interactions.

Evaluation Protocols. To evaluate the performance of item recommendation, we adopted the leave-one-out evaluation, which has been widely used in literature [21, 30]. For each user, we held-out his/her latest interaction as the test set and utilized the remaining data for training. As we mentioned in Section 3.1, the recommendation task is reduced to a ranking problem based on the estimated score. To assess the ranked list with the ground-truth item that user has actually consumed, we adopt Hit Ratio (HR) and Normalized Discounted Cumulative Gain (NDCG) [13], where HR measures whether the ground truth item is present on the ranked list and NDCG accounts for the position of hit [19]. We report the average score for all test users. If not specifically specified, we truncate the ranked list at 100 among all the items for both metrics.

Baselines. We compared ACF with the following methods. Note that all model-based CF models are learned by optimizing the same pairwise ranking loss of BPR (cf Eqn. (3)) for a fair comparison.

CF-based Methods:

- **UCF [46].** User-based collaborative filtering analyzes the user-item matrix to compute the similarities between users and then recommends items to people with similar tastes and preference.
- **ItemKNN [31].** This is a standard item-based CF for which we adopted Cosine similarity to measure the similarity among items and followed the setting of [23] to adapt it for implicit data.
- **BPR [30].** This method optimizes the latent factor model with a pairwise ranking loss, which is tailored to learn from implicit feedback. It is a highly competitive baseline for item recommendation, which is also the basic learning scheme of our model (cf. Section 3.2).
- **SVD++ [25].** SVD++ is a merged model of latent factor and neighborhood models, in which a second set of item factors is added, to model the item-item similarity, which is also a special case of our model when the item-level attention scheme is replaced by the average pooling.

Content-based Methods:

- **CBF [28].** Content-based filtering generates a user feature vector by averaging all the item features interacted with the user and then recommend items based on the similarity between the item features and the user features.

Hybrid Methods:

- **SVDFeature [9].** SVDFeature is a generic model for feature-based collaborative filtering, which incorporates different features that directly affect users' preferences over items with CF. In this paper we use the item visual feature as raw features to feed into SVDFeature.
- **Deep Hybrid [33].** Deep content-based method decomposes the user-item matrix into latent user and item vectors by matrix factorization (MF) and uses convolution neural network to regress multimedia content to the item latent vectors. In this paper, we use the SVD++ framework to learn the latent vectors for a fair comparison and use CNN [18] to regress the visual representations of multimedia items to the latent vectors.

Feature Extraction. We adopted the widely-used architectures ResNet-152 [18] to extract visual features for both images and frames of videos.

- **Image.** As we mentioned before, different users may be interested in different parts/components of the same image; in the context of image recommendation, the "components" of an image is considered in spatial level as the "regions" of the image. We use the *res5c* layer feature map in the ResNet-152 architecture to construct the component-level features. Specifically, for each image, the $7 \times 7 \times 2048$ feature map can be seen as 49 feature vectors of 2048-D for the 49 different regions in the image.
- **Video.** For each video, the component-level visual features are decomposed into the frame level. The frame feature can be obtained through the same way as that for the image feature based on the feature map. To simplify the process, we use the output of *pool5* layer in ResNet-152, which is actually the mean pooling of the feature maps, as the feature vector for each frame.

Parameter Settings. For models that are based on MF, we randomly initialized model parameters with a Gaussian distribution (with a mean of 0 and standard deviation of 0.01), optimizing the model with stochastic gradient descent (SGD). We tested the batch size of [256, 512], the latent feature dimension of [32,64,128], the learning rate of [0.001, 0.005, 0.01, 0.05, 0.1] and the regularizer of [0.00001, 0.0001, 0.001, 0.01, 0.1, 0]. As the findings are consistent across the dimension of latent vectors, if not specified, we only show the results of $D = 128$, a relatively large number that returns good accuracy.

[1] https://goo.gl/LjMoYa

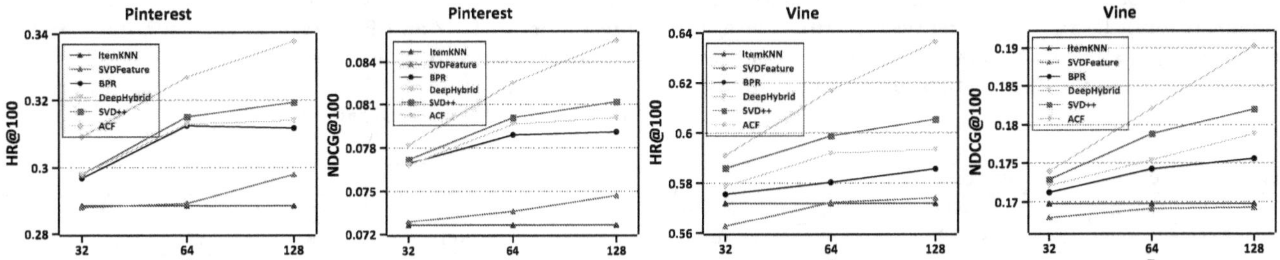

(a) Pinterest-HR@100 (b) Pinterest-NDCG@100 (c) Vine-HR@100 (d) Vine-NDCG@100

Figure 2: Performance of HR@100 and NDCG@100 w.r.t. the number of predictive factors on two datasets.

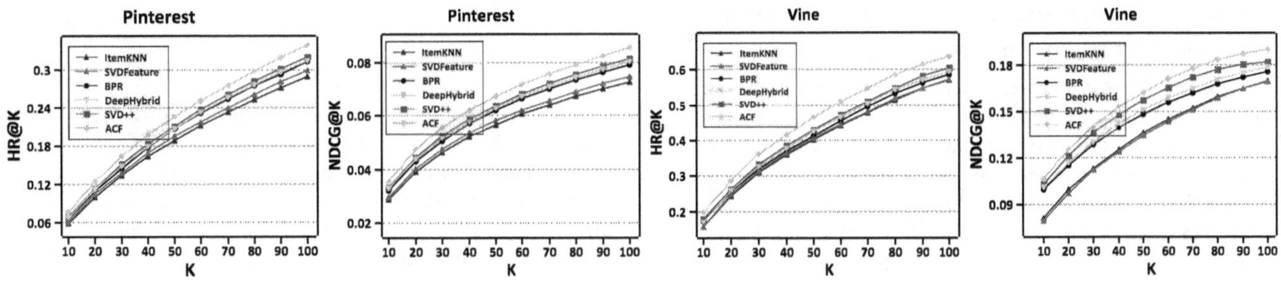

(a) Pinterest-HR@K (b) Pinterest-NDCG@K (c) Vine-HR@K (d) Vine-NDCG@K

Figure 3: Performance of Top-K item recommendation where K ranges from 10 to 100 on two datasets.

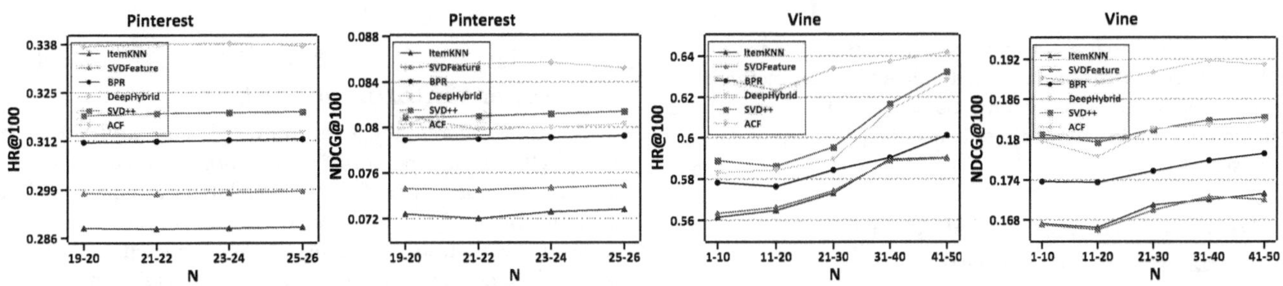

(a) Pinterest-HR@100 (b) Pinterest-NDCG@100 (c) Vine-HR@100 (d) Vine-NDCG@100

Figure 4: Performance of HR@100 and NDCG@100 w.r.t. the number of items per user on two datasets.

5.2 Model Comparison (RQ1)

Figure 2 shows the performance of HR@100 and NDCG@100 with respect to the number of latent factors. Due to the poor performance of UCF and CBF, they are omitted in Figure 2 to better highlight the performance differences among the rest of methods. From the figure, we can observe that:

(1) Our proposed method achieves the best performance on both datasets, significantly outperforming the state-of-the-art MF and Hybrid methods (on average, the relative improvement over the best baseline SVD++ is 5.19%).

(2) Although the Vine dataset is more sparse than Pinterest, the performance is much better. The reason may be that the set of videos and users in Vine is constructed from the set of densely connected users, in which the user-item pattern is more strong. This is also the reason why the performance of ItemKNN on Vine is closer to that of the other MF methods, since the neighborhood CF method, such as ItemKNN, could achieve acceptable performance based on the strong pattern.

(3) With the increase of the number of latent factors, the performance improvement of ACF compared with other baseline methods also increases. The reason may be that the visual features are more informative, which require relatively larger hidden dimension to incorporate the visual information.

Figure 3 shows the performance of Top-K recommended lists where the ranking position K ranges from 10 to 100. As can be seen, ACF demonstrates consistent improvements over other methods across all positions, and we further conducted the one-sample paired t-tests, to verify that all improvements are statistically significant for $p < 0.05$.

Table 2: Effect of attention mechanism on item and component (comp) level. AVG represents the average pooling strategy and ATT represents the attention mechanism. * denotes the statistical significance for $p < 0.05$.

Model	Level		Pinterest		Vine	
	Item	Comp	HR	NDCG	HR	NDCG
ACF	AVG	–	31.95%	8.12%	60.54%	18.20%
	ATT	AVG	33.21%	8.42%	62.81%	18.75%
	ATT	ATT	**33.78%***	**8.55%***	**63.65%***	**19.03%***

Table 3: Effect of user, item and content attention mechanisms. U, V and P represents the user, item, and the auxiliary item information in Eqn. (5) respectively, and X indicates the content information of the item in Eqn. (8). * denotes the statistical significance for $p < 0.05$.

Model	Attention Type	Pinterest		Vine	
		HR	NDCG	HR	NDCG
ACF	None	31.95%	8.12%	60.54%	18.20%
	U+V	32.17%	8.31%	61.68%	18.36%
	U+P	32.69%	8.34%	62.37%	18.65%
	U+V+P	32.96%	8.32%	62.60%	18.71%
	U+V+P+X	**33.78%***	**8.55%***	**63.65%***	**19.03%***

5.3 Model Analysis: Performance over Users of Different Sparsity Levels (RQ1)

Recall that our model characterizes each user based on the set of items the user has interacted with. To investigate the performance of our model over users of different sparsity levels, we show the performance with respect to the number of items a user has in Figure 4. Note that we did not re-train the model with different sets of users, instead we divide the test set into different groups by the number of items per user. From Figure 4, we observe that:

(1) Our model ACF with attention mechanisms of item- and component-level information consistently outperforms other baseline methods for all the number of item settings. It demonstrates the robustness and flexibility of ACF on different datasets.

(2) We also found that when the number of items per user is relatively small, ACF performs much better than the other methods, which indicates that the attention mechanism could improve the recommendation quality when there is insufficient training data for each user.

5.4 Model Ablation: Effect of Attention Mechanisms at Item- and Component-Level (RQ2)

To get a better understanding of the proposed ACF model, we further evaluate the key components of ACF — attention mechanism at item and component level. Table 2 shows the effect of attention mechanism at item- or component-level respectively. Note that (1) when we do not consider both the two levels of attentions, which means a normalized constant weight is used for neighborhood nodes in Eqn. (7), our model degenerates to SVD++ and (2) when we consider only the item-level attention, the item content feature at the item-level attention is the whole image/video feature which is the average of component features in the item. From the table, we can observe that:

(1) When the attention mechanism is applied at both the item- and the component-level, the performance for multimedia recommendation is improved as compared with utilizing average pooling in each level. The good performance of attention mechanism shows that the characteristics of users, items and visual contents are reflected at both levels. The contribution of collaborative information of users and items and the visual content will be evaluated in the next section.

(2) The attention mechanism at item-level contributes more for our model as compared to that at component-level. This may be due to the fact that the item-level attention mechanism can capture the representative items among all user's interactions, while the component-level attention mechanism may only work in complex items with rich contents. For example, as for some micro-videos on Vine, the visual content is highly related to a single theme and the difference among frames is not significant. In such situation, the component-level attentive network could give similar weights to frames, which may weaken the effect of component-level attention.

5.5 Model Ablation: Effect of User, Item and Content Information (RQ2)

Recall that to generate the attention weights α and β in Eqn. (8) and Eqn. (10), we incorporate different information sources, such as collaborative information of users (U) and items (V and P), and the visual content (X). To evaluate the contribution of each information source to the attention mechanism, we conducted experiments based on different combination of these sources as shown in Table 3. Note that since the number of all combinations is too large, we omit the ones without user information, which perform the worst among all combinations. From the table, we can observe that:

(1) The information of both user and item contributes to our model as compared to a constant weight model. It demonstrates that our attention mechanism can utilize the characteristics of each user and item to improve the performance of the recommendation task.

(2) The information of users is more effective than the items to improve recommendation performance. Hence, the discrimination of user preference is more discriminative than item characteristics, which is consistent with the previous finding that item-level attention is more important than component-level attention. Another interesting finding is that the auxiliary item latent vector **P** is more effective than **V**. This may be due to the different functions of the two vectors, that **V** is used to represent the item itself while **P** is proposed to characterize the user from the perspective of items. Therefore, when combining with user vector **U** to calculate the attention weight, **P** performs better since they are in the same domain.

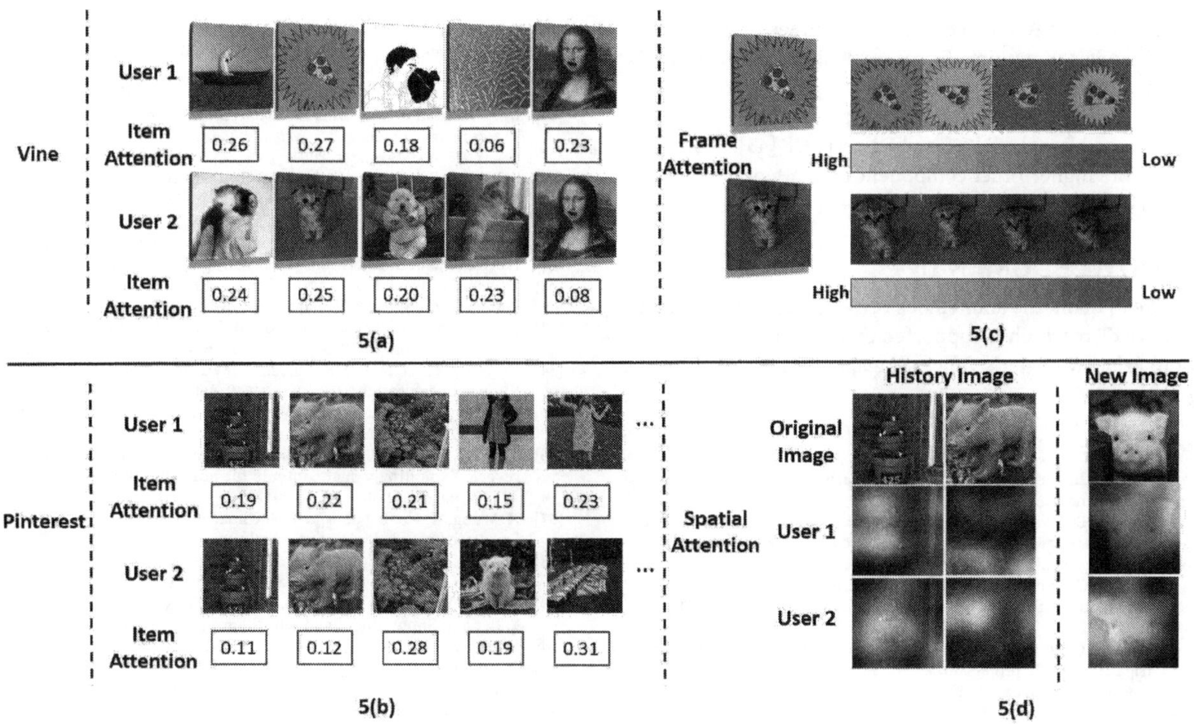

Figure 5: Visualization results on item-level attention and component-level attention from each dataset. For the item-level, the value under each item represents the attention weight of the item. While for the component-level, we use a heat map to represent the attention value, in which the darker the color is, the lower its represented attention value is (cf. Section 5.6).

5.6 Attention Visualization

We provide qualitative examples in Figure 5 for the better understanding of our attention model. In particular, Figure 5(a) and 5(b) show the item-level attention weights with respect to the items users liked in Vine and Pinsterest datasets, respectively. As can be seen from Figure 5(a), user 1 seems to have a preference for "cartoon" videos as he/she liked four related videos (except the 4-th one), while user 2 tends to prefer videos about "animals". Accordingly, we observe that the corresponding item-level attention weights depict these facts well. Specifically, the item-level attention weights of user 1 of the "cartoon" videos are much higher compared to that of the 4-th video. In addition, we find that for the same user, similar videos would share close attention weights, as the first 4 videos liked by user 2 are all about "animals" and hence share similar weights. These observations suggest that our model is able to capture user preferences via the item-level attention.

In addition, we also investigate the component-level attention visualization on both datasets. Figure 5(c) shows users' frame attention over videos from Vine and Figure 5(d) presents users' spatial attention over images from Pinterest. As shown in Figure 5(c), users can show different interest in different frames of the same videos. This may be affected by the content of the frame and the taste of the user. However, for each video example in Figure 5(c), the attention weights of frames are not that different since there is no much visual difference among them. For the spatial attention shown in Figure 5(d), we observe that users 1 and 2 share much similar attention pattern for the first image, which only contains a simple object (i.e., the "potted landscape"). From the second image that generally consists of two objects—a "pig" and a pair of red "boots"—we can see that users 1 and 2 are then attracted by different parts, *i.e.*, the "boots" and the "pig" parts. This implies that users can be interested in different regions of images with rich semantics. User 1 gives high attention weight to the "boots" part may due to the fact that she has liked many fashion-related images that contain red "boots". To further validate this point, we took a new image as an testing sample and visualized users 1 and 2's attentions. As can be seen, user 1 focuses more on the red flowers while user 2 is more interested in the "pig".

6 CONCLUSIONS

In this paper, we have proposed an Attentive Collaborative Filtering (ACF) model to address the implicit feedback in multimedia recommendation. We argue that there are two types of implicit feedback: item-level and component-level, which are usually neglected in conventional methods. To this end, we introduced the item- and component-level attention model to assign attentive weights for inferring the underlying users' preferences encoded in the implicit user feedback. ACF can be efficiently trained by employing SGD. To the best of our knowledge, ACF is the first model that exploits an attention mechanism in CF with implicit feedback. We conducted the extensive experiments on two real-world multimedia social networks: Vine and Pinterest, and demonstrated that ACF can consistently outperform the state-of-the-art CF models in multimedia recommendation. Since ACF is a generic attention-based CF framework, we plan to extend ACF in various CF models such as factorization machines [29], and the recently proposed Neural CF [20] and Discrete CF [43]. Moreover, we would explore higher-order component-level attentions such as relationships between objects [22, 42].

7 ACKNOWLEDGMENTS

We would like to thank the anonymous reviewers for their valuable comments. NExT research is supported by the National Research Foundation, Prime Minister's Office, Singapore under its IRC@SG Funding Initiative.

REFERENCES

[1] D. Bahdanau, K. Cho, and Y. Bengio. Neural machine translation by jointly learning to align and translate. In *ICLR*, 2014.
[2] S. Baluja, R. Seth, D. Sivakumar, Y. Jing, J. Yagnik, S. Kumar, D. Ravichandran, and M. Aly. Video suggestion and discovery for youtube: taking random walks through the view graph. In *WWW*, pages 895–904. ACM, 2008.
[3] M. Bendersky, L. G. Pueyo, J. J. Harmsen, V. Josifovski, and D. Lepikhin. Up next: retrieval methods for large scale related video suggestion. In *KDD*, pages 1769–1778. ACM, 2014.
[4] B. Chen, J. Wang, Q. Huang, and T. Mei. Personalized video recommendation through tripartite graph propagation. In *Proceedings of the International Conference on Multimedia*, pages 1133–1136. ACM, 2012.
[5] J. Chen. Multi-modal learning: Study on A large-scale micro-video data collection. In *Proceedings of the 2016 ACM Conference on Multimedia Conference, MM 2016, Amsterdam, The Netherlands, October 15-19, 2016*, pages 1454–1458. ACM, 2016.
[6] J. Chen, X. Song, L. Nie, X. Wang, H. Zhang, and T. Chua. Micro tells macro: Predicting the popularity of micro-videos via a transductive model. In *MM*, pages 898–907. ACM, 2016.
[7] L. Chen, H. Zhang, J. Xiao, L. Nie, J. Shao, W. Liu, and T.-S. Chua. Sca-cnn: Spatial and channel-wise attention in convolutional networks for image captioning. In *CVPR*. IEEE, 2017.
[8] T. Chen, X. He, and M.-Y. Kan. Context-aware image tweet modelling and recommendation. In *MM*, pages 1018–1027. ACM, 2016.
[9] T. Chen, W. Zhang, Q. Lu, K. Chen, Z. Zheng, and Y. Yu. Svdfeature: a toolkit for feature-based collaborative filtering. *JMLR*, 13:3619–3622, 2012.
[10] X. Chen, Y. Zhang, H. X. Qingyao Ai, J. Yan, and Z. Qin. Personalized key frame recommendation. In *SIGIR*. ACM, 2017.
[11] Z. Cheng and J. Shen. On effective location-aware music recommendation. *TOIS*, 34(2):13:1–13:32, 2016.
[12] P. Cui, Z. Wang, and Z. Su. What videos are similar with you?: Learning a common attributed representation for video recommendation. In *MM*, pages 597–606. ACM, 2014.
[13] A. Farseev, I. Samborskii, A. Filchenkov, and T.-S. Chua. Cross-domain recommendation via clustering on multi-layer graphs. In *SIGIR*. ACM, 2017.
[14] F. Feng, L. Nie, X. Wang, R. Hong, and C. Tat-Seng. Computational social indicators: a case study of chinese university ranking. In *SIGIR*. ACM, 2017.
[15] X. Geng, H. Zhang, J. Bian, and T. Chua. Learning image and user features for recommendation in social networks. In *ICCV*, pages 4274–4282. IEEE, 2015.
[16] X. Geng, H. Zhang, Z. Song, Y. Yang, H. Luan, and T. Chua. One of a kind: User profiling by social curation. In *MM*, pages 567–576. ACM, 2014.
[17] X. Glorot and Y. Bengio. Understanding the difficulty of training deep feedforward neural networks. In *JMLR*, pages 249–256. JMLR.org, 2010.
[18] K. He, X. Zhang, S. Ren, and J. Sun. Deep residual learning for image recognition. In *CVPR*, pages 770–778. IEEE, 2016.
[19] X. He, M. Gao, M.-Y. Kan, and D. Wang. Birank: Towards ranking on bipartite graphs. *TKDE*, 29(1):57–71, 2017.
[20] X. He, L. Liao, H. Zhang, L. Nie, X. Hu, and T.-S. Chua. Neural collaborative filtering. In *WWW*, pages 173–182. ACM, 2017.
[21] X. He, H. Zhang, M. Kan, and T. Chua. Fast matrix factorization for online recommendation with implicit feedback. In *SIGIR*, pages 549–558. ACM, 2016.
[22] R. Hu, M. Rohrbach, J. Andreas, T. Darrell, and K. Saenko. Modeling relationships in referential expressions with compositional modular networks. In *CVPR*, 2016.
[23] Y. Hu, Y. Koren, and C. Volinsky. Collaborative filtering for implicit feedback datasets. In *ICDM*, pages 263–272. IEEE, 2008.
[24] S. Kabbur, X. Ning, and G. Karypis. FISM: factored item similarity models for top-n recommender systems. In *KDD*, pages 659–667. ACM, 2013.
[25] Y. Koren. Factorization meets the neighborhood: a multifaceted collaborative filtering model. In *KDD*, pages 426–434. ACM, 2008.
[26] T. Mei, B. Yang, X. Hua, L. Yang, S. Yang, and S. Li. Videoreach: an online video recommendation system. In *SIGIR*, pages 767–768. ACM, 2007.
[27] R. Pan, Y. Zhou, B. Cao, N. N. Liu, R. M. Lukose, M. Scholz, and Q. Yang. One-class collaborative filtering. In *ICDM*, pages 502–511. IEEE, 2008.
[28] M. J. Pazzani and D. Billsus. Content-based recommendation systems. In *Proceedings of the Adaptive Web, Methods and Strategies of Web Personalization*, pages 325–341. Springer, 2007.
[29] S. Rendle. Factorization machines. In *ICDM*, pages 995–1000. IEEE, 2010.
[30] S. Rendle, C. Freudenthaler, Z. Gantner, and L. Schmidt-Thieme. BPR: bayesian personalized ranking from implicit feedback. In *UAI*, pages 452–461. IEEE, 2009.
[31] B. Sarwar, G. Karypis, J. Konstan, and J. Riedl. Item-based collaborative filtering recommendation algorithms. In *WWW*, pages 285–295. ACM, 2001.
[32] J. Shen, M. Wang, S. Yan, and P. Cui. Multimedia recommendation: technology and techniques. In *SIGIR*, page 1131. ACM, 2013.
[33] A. van den Oord, S. Dieleman, and B. Schrauwen. Deep content-based music recommendation. In *NIPS*, pages 2643–2651. NIPS Foundation, 2013.
[34] M. Wang, H. Li, D. Tao, K. Lu, and X. Wu. Multimodal graph-based reranking for web image search. *TIP*, 21(11):4649–4661, 2012.
[35] M. Wang, X. Liu, and X. Wu. Visual classification by l1-hypergraph modeling. *TKDE*, 27(9):2564–2574, 2015.
[36] S. Wang, Y. Wang, J. Tang, K. Shu, S. Ranganath, and H. Liu. What your images reveal: Exploiting visual contents for point-of-interest recommendation. In *WWW*, pages 391–400. ACM, 2017.
[37] X. Wang, X. He, L. Nie, and T.-S. Chua. Item silk road: Recommending items from information domains to social users. In *SIGIR*. ACM, 2017.
[38] X. Wang, L. Nie, X. Song, D. Zhang, and T.-S. Chua. Unifying virtual and physical worlds: Learning toward local and global consistency. *TOIS*, 36(1):4, 2017.
[39] K. Xu, J. Ba, R. Kiros, K. Cho, A. C. Courville, R. Salakhutdinov, R. S. Zemel, and Y. Bengio. Show, attend and tell: Neural image caption generation with visual attention. In *ICML*, pages 2048–2057. JMLR.org, 2015.
[40] Q. You, H. Jin, Z. Wang, C. Fang, and J. Luo. Image captioning with semantic attention. In *CVPR*, pages 4651–4659. IEEE, 2016.
[41] M. Zanfir, E. Marinoiu, and C. Sminchisescu. Spatio-temporal attention models for grounded video captioning. In *ACCV*, pages 104–119. Springer, 2016.
[42] H. Zhang, Z. Kyaw, S.-F. Chang, and T.-S. Chua. Visual translation embedding network for visual relation detection. In *CVPR*, 2017.
[43] H. Zhang, F. Shen, W. Liu, X. He, H. Luan, and T. Chua. Discrete collaborative filtering. In *SIGIR*, pages 325–334. ACM, 2016.
[44] H. Zhang, Z. Zha, Y. Yang, S. Yan, Y. Gao, and T. Chua. Attribute-augmented semantic hierarchy: towards bridging semantic gap and intention gap in image retrieval. In *MM*, pages 33–42. ACM, 2013.
[45] J. Zhang, L. Nie, X. Wang, X. He, X. Huang, and T. Chua. Shorter-is-better: Venue category estimation from micro-video. In *MM*, pages 1415–1424. ACM, 2016.
[46] Z. Zhao and M. Shang. User-based collaborative-filtering recommendation algorithms on hadoop. In *KDD*, pages 478–481. ACM, 2010.

Neural Rating Regression with Abstractive Tips Generation for Recommendation*

Piji Li
Department of Systems Engineering and Engineering Management,
The Chinese University of Hong Kong.
pjli@se.cuhk.edu.hk

Zihao Wang
Department of Systems Engineering and Engineering Management,
The Chinese University of Hong Kong.
zhwang@se.cuhk.edu.hk

Zhaochun Ren
Data Science Lab, JD.com,
North Star Century Center,
Beijing, China
renzhaochun@jd.com

Lidong Bing
AI Lab, Tencent Inc.
Hi-tech Park, Nanshan District,
Shenzhen, China
lyndonbing@tencent.com

Wai Lam
Department of Systems Engineering and Engineering Management,
The Chinese University of Hong Kong.
wlam@se.cuhk.edu.hk

ABSTRACT

Recently, some E-commerce sites launch a new interaction box called Tips on their mobile apps. Users can express their experience and feelings or provide suggestions using short texts typically several words or one sentence. In essence, writing some tips and giving a numerical rating are two facets of a user's product assessment action, expressing the user experience and feelings. Jointly modeling these two facets is helpful for designing a better recommendation system. While some existing models integrate text information such as item specifications or user reviews into user and item latent factors for improving the rating prediction, no existing works consider tips for improving recommendation quality. We propose a deep learning based framework named **NRT** which can simultaneously predict precise ratings and generate abstractive tips with good linguistic quality simulating user experience and feelings. For abstractive tips generation, gated recurrent neural networks are employed to "translate" user and item latent representations into a concise sentence. Extensive experiments on benchmark datasets from different domains show that NRT achieves significant improvements over the state-of-the-art methods. Moreover, the generated tips can vividly predict the user experience and feelings.

CCS CONCEPTS

• **Information systems → Information retrieval; Recommender systems;** *Collaborative filtering;*

*The work described in this paper is substantially supported by grants from the Research Grant Council of the Hong Kong Special Administrative Region, China (Project Code: 14203414) and the Microsoft Research Asia Urban Informatics Grant FY14-RES-Sponsor-057. This work is also affiliated with the CUHK MoE-Microsoft Key Laboratory of Human-centric Computing and Interface Technologies.

SIGIR '17, August 07-11, 2017, Shinjuku, Tokyo, Japan

ACM ISBN 978-1-4503-5022-8/17/08...$15.00
https://doi.org/10.1145/3077136.3080822

Figure 1: Examples of reviews and tips selected from the restaurant "Gary Danko" on Yelp. Tips are more concise than reviews and can reveal user experience, feelings, and suggestions with only a few words. Users will get conclusions about this restaurant immediately after scanning the tips with their mobile phones.

KEYWORDS

Rating Prediction; Tips Generation; Deep Learning.

1 INTRODUCTION

With the explosive growth of Internet information, recommendation systems have been playing an increasingly important role in on-line E-commerce and applications in a variety of areas, including music streaming service such as Spotify[1] and Apple Music, movie rating such as IMDB[2], video streaming service such as Netflix and Youtube, job recommendation such as LinkedIn[3], and product recommendation such as Amazon. Many recommendation methods are based on Collaborative Filtering (CF) which mainly makes use

[1] http://www.spotify.com
[2] http://www.imdb.com
[3] http://www.linkedin.com

of historical ratings [14, 15, 18, 22, 31, 33, 35]. Recently, some approaches also consider text information in addition to the rating data [1, 21, 23, 26, 40, 49]. After some investigations, we observe that the text information in most recommendation tasks can be generally classified into two types: item specifications [40–42] and user reviews [1, 21, 23, 26, 46, 47, 49]. Item specifications are the text information for describing the attributes or properties of the items. For example, in article recommendation such as CiteULike[4], it refers to titles and abstracts of papers. In product recommendation such as Amazon, it refers to product descriptions and technical specification information. The second type is user reviews which are written by users to explain why they like or dislike an item based on their usage experiences. Multi-faceted information can be extracted from reviews and used as user preferences or item features, which otherwise cannot be obtained from the overall ratings [5]. Although both types of text data are found to be useful for the recommendation task, they have some inherent limitations. Concretely, the former cannot reflect users' experience and preference, and the latter is usually too long and suffers from noise.

Recently, some E-commerce sites such as Yelp[5] launch a new interaction box called **Tips** on their mobile platforms. As shown in Figure 1, the left column is a review from the user "Monica H.", and tips from several other users are shown on the right column. In the review text, Monica first generally introduced the restaurant, and then narrated her dining experience in detail. In the tips text, users expressed their experience and feelings plainly using short texts, such as "The risotto was excellent. Amazing service.". They also provide some suggestions to other people directly in several words, such as "You have to make reservations much in advance." In contrast to item specifications and user reviews, tips have several characteristics: (1) tips are typically single-topic nuggets of information, and shorter than reviews with a length of about 10 words on average; (2) tips can express user experience, feelings, and suggestions directly; (3) tips can give other people quick insights, saving the time of reading long reviews. In essence, writing some tips and giving a numerical rating are two facets of a user's product assessment action, expressing the user experience and feelings. Jointly modeling these two facets is helpful for designing a better recommendation system.

Existing models only integrate text information such as item specifications [40–42] and user reviews [1, 21, 23, 26, 46, 47, 49] to enhance the performance of latent factor modeling and rating prediction. To our best knowledge, we are the first to consider tips for improving the recommendation quality. We aim at developing a model that is capable of conducting the latent factor modeling and rating prediction, and more importantly, it can generate tips based on the learnt latent factors. We do not just extract some existing sentences and regard them as tips. Conversely, we investigate the task of automatically construing a concise sentence as tips, such capability can be treated as simulating how users write tips in order to express their experience and feelings, just as if they have bought and consumed the item. Therefore, we named this task *abstractive tips generation*, where "abstractive" is a terminology from the research of text summarization [3].

[4]http://www.citeulike.org
[5]http://www.yelp.com

Generating abstractive tips only based on user latent factors and item latent factors is a challenging task. Recently, gated recurrent neural networks such as Long Short-Term Memory (LSTM) [12] and Gated Recurrent Unit (GRU) [6] demonstrate high capability in text generation related tasks [2, 30]. Moreover, inspired by [11, 41], neural network based models can help learn more effective latent factors when conducting rating prediction and improve the performance of collaborative filtering. We employ deep learning techniques for latent factor modeling, rating prediction, and abstractive tips generation. For abstractive tips generation, gated recurrent neural networks are employed to "translate" a user latent factor and an item latent factor into a concise sentence to express user experience and feelings. For neural rating regression, a multilayer perceptron network [28] is employed to project user latent factors and item latent factors into ratings. All the neural parameters in the gated recurrent neural networks and the multilayer perceptron network as well as the latent factors for users and items are learnt by a multi-task learning approach in an end-to-end training paradigm.

The main contributions of our framework are summarized below:

- We propose a deep learning based framework named NRT which can simultaneously predict precise ratings and generate abstractive tips with good linguistic quality simulating user experience and feelings. All the neural parameters as well as the latent factors for users and items are learnt by a multi-task learning approach in an end-to-end training paradigm.
- We are the first to explore using tips information to improve the recommendation quality. In essence, writing some tips and giving a numerical rating are two facets of a user's product assessment action, expressing the user experience and feelings. Jointly modeling these two facets is helpful for designing a better recommendation system.
- Experimental results on benchmark datasets show that our framework achieves better performance than the state-of-the-art models on both tasks of rating prediction and abstractive tips generation.

2 RELATED WORKS

Collaborative filtering (CF) has been studied for a long time and has achieved some success in recommendation systems [27, 37]. Latent Factor Models (LFM) based on Matrix Factorization (MF) [15] play an important role for rating prediction. Various MF algorithms have been proposed, such as Singular Value Decomposition (SVD) and SVD++ [14], Non-negative Matrix Factorization (NMF) [18], and Probabilistic Matrix Factorization (PMF) [31]. These methods map users and items into a shared latent factor space, and use a vector of latent features as the representation for users and items respectively. Then the inner product of their latent factor vectors can reflect the interactions between users and items.

The recommendation performance will degrade significantly when the rating matrix is very sparse. Therefore, some works consider text information for improving the rating prediction. Both item specifications and user reviews have been investigated. In order to use the item specifications, CTR [40] integrates PMF [31] and Latent Dirichlet Allocation (LDA) [4] into a single framework and employs LDA to model the text. Collaborative Deep Learning (CDL)

[41] employs a hierarchical Bayesian model which jointly performs deep representation learning for the specification text content and collaborative filtering for the rating matrix. For user review texts, some research works, such as HFT [23], RMR [21], TriRank [10], and sCVR [26], integrate topic models in their frameworks to generate the latent factors for users and items incorporating review texts. Moreover, TriRank and sCVR have been explicitly claimed that they can provide explanations for recommendations. However, one common limitation of them is that their explanations are simple extractions of words or phrases from the texts. In contrast, we aim at generating concise sentences representing tips, which express the feeling of users while they are reviewing an item.

Deep Learning (DL) techniques have achieved significant success in the fields of computer vision, speech recognition, and natural language processing [8]. In the field of recommendation systems, researchers have made some attempts by combining different neural network structures with collaborative filtering to improve the recommendation performance. Salakhutdinov et al. [32] employ a class of two-layer Restricted Boltzmann Machines (RBM) with an efficient learning algorithm to model user interactions and perform collaborative filtering. Considering that the training procedure of Auto-Encoders [25] is more straightforward, some research works employ auto-encoders to tackle the latent factor modeling and rating prediction [34, 39, 44]. Recently, He et al. [11] combine generalized matrix factorization and multi-layer perceptions to find better latent structures from the user interactions for improving the performance of collaborative filtering. To model the temporal dynamic information in the user interactions, Wu et al. [43] propose a recurrent recommender network which is able to predict future behavioral trajectories.

3 FRAMEWORK DESCRIPTION

3.1 Overview

The goal of recommendation, similar to collaborative filtering, is to predict a rating given a user and an item. Additionally, in our proposed task, our model also generates abstractive tips in the form of a concise sentence. At the operational stage, only a user and an item are given. There is no given review texts and obviously no tips texts.

At the training stage, the training data consists of users, items, tips texts, and review content. Table 1 depicts the notations and key concepts used in our paper. We denote the whole training corpus by $\mathcal{X} = \{\mathcal{U}, \mathcal{I}, \mathcal{R}, \mathcal{C}, \mathcal{S}\}$, where $\mathcal{U}$ and $\mathcal{I}$ are the sets of users and items respectively, $\mathcal{R}$ is the set of ratings, $\mathcal{C}$ is the set of review documents, and $\mathcal{S}$ is the set of tips sentences. As shown in Figure 2, our framework contains two major components: neural rating regression on the left and abstractive tips generation on the right. There are two crucial latent variables : user latent factors $\mathbf{U} \in \mathbb{R}^{k_u \times m}$ and item latent factors $\mathbf{V} \in \mathbb{R}^{k_v \times n}$, where m is the number of users, and n is the number of items. k_u and k_v are the latent factor dimension for users and items respectively. For neural rating regression, given the user latent factor $\mathbf{u}$ and the item latent factor $\mathbf{v}$, a multi-layer perceptron network based regression model is employed to project $\mathbf{u}$ and $\mathbf{v}$ to a real value via several layers of non-linear transformations.

Table 1: Glossary.

Symbol	Description
$\mathcal{X}$	training set
$\mathcal{V}$	vocabulary
$\mathcal{U}$	set of users
$\mathcal{I}$	set of items
$\mathcal{R}$	set of ratings
$\mathcal{C}$	set of reviews
$\mathcal{S}$	set of tips
C_{ctx}	context for tips decoder
$\mathbf{U}$	user latent factors
$\mathbf{V}$	item latent factors
$\mathbf{E}$	word embeddings
$\mathbf{H}$	neural hidden states
$\mathbf{u}$	user latent factor
$\mathbf{v}$	item latent factor
$\mathbf{W}$	mapping matrix
$\mathbf{b}$	bias item
$\mathbf{\Theta}$	set of neural parameters
$r_{u,i}$	rating of user u to item j
σ	sigmoid function
ς	softmax function
$tanh$	hyperbolic tangent function

For abstractive tips generation, we design a sequence decoding model based on a gated recurrent neural network called Gated Recurrent Unit (GRU) [6] to "translate" the combination of a user latent factor $\mathbf{u}$ and an item latent factor $\mathbf{v}$ into a sequence of words, representing tips. Moreover, two kinds of context information generated based on $\mathbf{u}$ and $\mathbf{v}$ are also fed into the sequence decoder model. One is the hidden variable from the rating regression component, which is used as sentiment context information. The other is the hidden output of a generative model for review texts. At the operational or testing stage, we use a beam search algorithm [13] for decoding and generating the best tips given a trained model. All the neural parameters and the latent factors for users, items, and words are learnt by a multi-task learning approach. The model can be trained efficiently by an end-to-end paradigm using back-propagation algorithms [29].

3.2 Neural Rating Regression

The aim of the neural rating regression component is to conduct representation learning for the user factor $\mathbf{u}$ and the item factor $\mathbf{v}$ mentioned above. In order to predict a rating, we need to design a model that can learn the function $f_r(\cdot)$ which can project $\mathbf{u}$ and $\mathbf{v}$ to a real-valued rating $\hat{r}$:

$$\hat{r} = f_r(\mathbf{u}, \mathbf{v}) \tag{1}$$

In most of the existing latent factor models, $f_r(\cdot)$ is represented by the inner product of $\mathbf{u}$ and $\mathbf{v}$, or adds a bias item for the corresponding user and item respectively:

$$\hat{r} = \mathbf{u}^T \mathbf{v} + b_u + b_v + b \tag{2}$$

It is obvious that the rating is calculated by a linear combination of user latent factors, item latent factors, and bias. The learnt latent

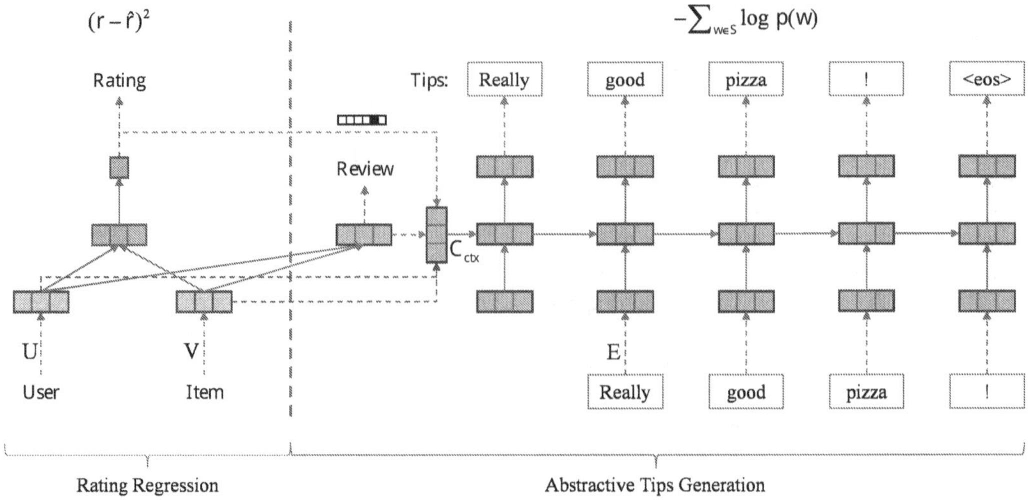

Figure 2: Our proposed framework NRT for rating regression and abstractive tips generation.

factors may not capture the complex structure implied in the user historical interactions. Recently, some research works on representation learning from different fields, such as computer vision [9, 16], natural language processing [17, 24], and knowledge base completion [36], demonstrate that non-linear transformations will enhance the representation ability. Moreover, most latent factor models assume that users and items or even text information are in the same vector space and share the same latent factors. Actually, user, item, and text information are different kinds of objects with different characteristics. Modeling them in the same vector space would lead to limitations.

As shown in left part in Figure 2, we let user latent factors $\mathbf{U} \in \mathbb{R}^{k_u \times m}$ and item latent factors $\mathbf{V} \in \mathbb{R}^{k_v \times n}$ in different vector space, where k_u and k_v are the latent factor dimension for users and items respectively. m and n are the number of users and items respectively. In order to model the relationship between users and items, one may consider to use a neural tensor network [36] to describe the interactions between users and items, such as $\mathbf{u}^T\mathbf{W}\mathbf{v}$, where $\mathbf{W} \in \mathbb{R}^{k_u \times d \times k_v}$. However, our investigation shows that such tensor network has too many parameters resulting in difficulty for handling large-scale datasets commonly found in recommendation applications. Therefore, we employ a multi-layer perceptron network to model the interactions between users and items, and map user latent factors and item latent factors into real-valued ratings.

Specifically, we first map latent factors to a shared hidden space:

$$\mathbf{h}^r = \sigma(\mathbf{W}^r_{uh}\mathbf{u} + \mathbf{W}^r_{vh}\mathbf{v} + \mathbf{b}^r_h) \quad (3)$$

where $\mathbf{W}^r_{uh} \in \mathbb{R}^{d \times k_u}$ and $\mathbf{W}^r_{vh} \in \mathbb{R}^{d \times k_v}$ are the mapping matrices for user latent factors and item latent factors respectively. $\mathbf{b}^r_h \in \mathbb{R}^d$ is the bias term. d is the dimension of the hidden vector $\mathbf{h}^r$. The superscript r refers to variables related to the rating prediction component. $\sigma(\cdot)$ is the sigmoid activation function:

$$\sigma(x) = \frac{1}{1+e^{-x}} \quad (4)$$

This non-linear transformation can improve the performance of the rating prediction. For better performance, we can add more layers of non-linear transformations into our model:

$$\mathbf{h}^r_l = \sigma(\mathbf{W}^r_{hh_l}\mathbf{h}^r_{l-1} + \mathbf{b}^r_{h_l}) \quad (5)$$

where $\mathbf{W}^r_{hh_l} \in \mathbb{R}^{d \times d}$ is the mapping matrix for the variables in the hidden layers. l is the index of a hidden layer. Assume that $\mathbf{h}^r_L$ is the output of the last hidden layer. The output layer transforms $\mathbf{h}^r_L$ into a real-valued rating $\hat{r}$:

$$\hat{r} = \mathbf{W}^r_{hr}\mathbf{h}^r_L + b^r \quad (6)$$

where $\mathbf{W}^r_{hr} \in \mathbb{R}^d$ and $b^r \in \mathbb{R}$.

In order to optimize the latent factors $\mathbf{U}$ and $\mathbf{V}$, as well as all the neural parameters Θ, we formulate it as a regression problem and the loss function is formulated as:

$$\mathcal{L}^r = \frac{1}{2|\mathcal{X}|}\sum_{u \in \mathcal{U}, i \in \mathcal{I}} (\hat{r}_{u,i} - r_{u,i})^2 \quad (7)$$

where $\mathcal{X}$ represents the training set. $r_{u,i}$ is the ground truth rating assigned by the user u to the item i.

3.3 Neural Abstractive Tips Generation

Generating abstractive tips only based on user latent factors and item latent factors is a challenging task. As mentioned above, abstractive tips generation is different from review content summarization and explainable topic words extraction. At the operational stage, the input only consists of a user and an item, but without any text information. After obtaining the user latent factor $\mathbf{u}$ and the item latent factor $\mathbf{v}$ from the matrices $\mathbf{U}$ and $\mathbf{V}$, we should design a strategy to "translate" these two latent vectors into a fluent sequence of words. Recently, gated recurrent neural networks such as Long Short-Term Memory (LSTM) [12] and Gated Recurrent Unit (GRU) [6] demonstrate high capability in text generation related tasks [2, 30]. Inspired by these works and considering that GRU has comparable performance but with less parameters and more efficient computation, we employ GRU as the basic model in our sequence modeling framework. The right part of Figure 2 depicts our tips generation model.

The major idea of sequence modeling for tips generation can be expressed as follows:

$$p(s_t|s_1, s_2, \ldots, s_{t-1}, C_{ctx}) = \varsigma(\mathbf{h}_t^s) \tag{8}$$

where s_t is the t-th word of the tips s. C_{ctx} denotes the context information which will be described in the following sections. $\varsigma(\cdot)$ is the softmax function and defined as follows:

$$\varsigma(\mathbf{x}^{(i)}) = \frac{e^{\mathbf{x}^{(i)}}}{\sum_{k=1}^{K} e^{\mathbf{x}^{(k)}}} \tag{9}$$

$\mathbf{h}_t^s$ is the sequence hidden state at the time t and it depends on the input at the time t and the previous hidden state $\mathbf{h}_{t-1}^s$:

$$\mathbf{h}_t^s = f(\mathbf{h}_{t-1}^s, s_t) \tag{10}$$

Here $f(\cdot)$ can be the vanilla RNN, LSTM, or GRU. In the case of GRU, the state updates are processed according to the following operations:

$$\begin{aligned} \mathbf{r}_t^s &= \sigma(\mathbf{W}_{sr}^s \mathbf{s}_t + \mathbf{W}_{hr}^s \mathbf{h}_{t-1}^s + \mathbf{b}_r^s) \\ \mathbf{z}_t^s &= \sigma(\mathbf{W}_{sz}^s \mathbf{s}_t + \mathbf{W}_{hz}^s \mathbf{h}_{t-1}^s + \mathbf{b}_z^s) \\ \mathbf{g}_t^s &= \tanh(\mathbf{W}_{sh}^s \mathbf{s}_t + \mathbf{W}_{hh}^s (\mathbf{r}_t^s \odot \mathbf{h}_{t-1}^s) + \mathbf{b}_h^s) \\ \mathbf{h}_t^s &= \mathbf{z}_t^s \odot \mathbf{h}_{t-1}^s + (1 - \mathbf{z}_t^s) \odot \mathbf{g}_t^s \end{aligned} \tag{11}$$

where $\mathbf{s}_t \in \mathbf{E}$ is the embedding vector for the word s_t of the tips and the vector is also learnt from our framework. $\mathbf{r}_t^s$ is the reset gate, $\mathbf{z}_t^s$ is the update gate. $\odot$ denotes element-wise multiplication. *tanh* is the hyperbolic tangent activation function.

As shown in Figure 2, when $t = 1$, the sequence model has no input information. Therefore, we utilize the context information C_{ctx} to initialize $\mathbf{h}_0^s$. Context information is very crucial in a sequence decoding framework, which will directly affect the performance of sequence generation. In the field of neural machine translation [45], context information includes the encoding information of the source input and the decoding attention information from the source. In the field of neural summarization [19, 30], the context is the encoded document information. In our framework, the corresponding user u and item i are the input from which we design two kinds of context information for tips generation: predicted rating $\hat{r}_{u,i}$ and the generated hidden variable for the review text $\mathbf{h}_L^c$.

For the input, we just find the user latent factor and the item latent factor from the matrices U and V:

$$\mathbf{u} = \mathbf{U}(:, u), \mathbf{v} = \mathbf{V}(:, i) \tag{12}$$

For the context of rating information, we can employ the output of the rating regression component in Section 3.2. Specifically, after getting the predicted rating $\hat{r}_{u,i}$, for example, $\hat{r}_{u,i} = 4.321$, we cast it into an integer 4, and add a step of vectorization. Then we get the vector representation of rating $\hat{r}_{u,i}$. If the rating range is $[0, 5]$, we will get the rating vector $\hat{\mathbf{r}}_{u,i}$:

$$\hat{\mathbf{r}}_{u,i} = (0, 0, 0, 0, 1, 0)^T \tag{13}$$

$\hat{\mathbf{r}}_{u,i}$ is used as the context information to control the sentiment of the generated tips.

Another context information is from review texts. One should note that review texts cannot be used as the input directly. The reason is that at the testing state, there are no review information. We only make use of reviews to enhance the representation ability of the latent vectors U and V. We develop a standard generative model for review texts based on a multi-layer perceptron. For review content $c_{u,i}$ written by the user u to the item i, the generative process is defined as follows. We first map the user latent vector u and the item latent factor v into a hidden space:

$$\mathbf{h}^c = \sigma(\mathbf{W}_{uh}^c \mathbf{u} + \mathbf{W}_{vh}^c \mathbf{v} + \mathbf{b}_h^c) \tag{14}$$

It is obvious that we can also add more layers of non-linear transformation into the generative hidden layers. Assume that $\mathbf{h}_L^c$ is the output of the last hidden layer. We add the final generative layer to map $\mathbf{h}_L^c$ into a $|\mathcal{V}|$-size vector $\hat{\mathbf{c}}$, where $\mathcal{V}$ is the vocabulary of words in the reviews and the tips:

$$\hat{\mathbf{c}} = \varsigma(\mathbf{W}_{hc}^c \mathbf{h}_L^c + \mathbf{b}^c) \tag{15}$$

where $\mathbf{W}_{hc}^c \in \mathbb{R}^{|\mathcal{V}| \times d}$ and $\mathbf{b}^c \in \mathbb{R}^{|\mathcal{V}|}$. $\varsigma(\cdot)$ is the softmax function defined in Equation 9. In fact we can regard $\hat{\mathbf{c}}$ as a multinomial distribution defined on $\mathcal{V}$. Therefore, we can draw some words from $\hat{\mathbf{c}}$ and generate the content of the review $c_{u,i}$. We let c be the ground truth of $c_{u,i}$. $\mathbf{c}^{(k)}$ is the term frequency of the word k in $c_{u,i}$. We employ the likelihood to evaluate the performance of this generative process. For convenience, we use the Negative Log-Likelihood (NLL) as the loss function:

$$\mathcal{L}^c = -\sum_{k=1}^{|\mathcal{V}|} \mathbf{c}^{(k)} \log \hat{\mathbf{c}}^{(k)} \tag{16}$$

One characteristic of the design of our model is that both the rating and review texts are generated from the same user latent factors U and item latent factors V, i.e., U and V are shared by the subtasks of rating prediction and review text generation. Thus, in the training stage, both of U and V receive the feedback from all the subtasks, which improves the representation ability of the latent factors.

After obtaining all the context information $C_{ctx} = \{\hat{\mathbf{r}}, \mathbf{h}_L^c\}$, we integrate them into the initial decoding hidden state $\mathbf{h}_0^s$ using a non-linear transformation:

$$\mathbf{h}_0^s = tanh(\mathbf{W}_{uh}^s \mathbf{u} + \mathbf{W}_{vh}^s \mathbf{v} + \mathbf{W}_{rh}^s \hat{\mathbf{r}} + \mathbf{W}_{ch}^s \mathbf{h}_L^c + \mathbf{b}_c^s) \tag{17}$$

where u is the user latent factor, v is the item latent factor, $\hat{\mathbf{r}}$ is the vectorization for the predicted rating $\hat{r}$, and $\mathbf{h}_L^c$ is the generated hidden variable from the review text. Then GRU can conduct the sequence decoding progress. After getting all the sequence hidden states, we feed them to the final output layer to predict the word sequence in tips.

$$\hat{\mathbf{s}}_{t+1} = \varsigma(\mathbf{W}_{hs}^s \mathbf{h}_t^s + \mathbf{b}^s) \tag{18}$$

where $\mathbf{W}_{hs}^s \in \mathbb{R}^{d \times |\mathcal{V}|}$ and $\mathbf{b}^s \in \mathbb{R}^{|\mathcal{V}|}$. $\varsigma(\cdot)$ is the softmax function defined in Equation 9. Then the word with the largest probability is the decoding result for the step $t + 1$:

$$w_{t+1}^* = \arg\max_{w_i \in \mathcal{V}} \hat{\mathbf{s}}_{t+1}^{(w_i)} \tag{19}$$

At the training stage, we also use NLL as the loss function, where I_w is the vocabulary index of the word w:

$$\mathcal{L}^s = -\sum_{w \in Tips} \log \hat{\mathbf{s}}^{(I_w)} \tag{20}$$

Algorithm 1 Beam search for abstractive tips generation

Input: Beam size β, maximum length η, user id u, item id v, and tips generation model $\mathcal{G}$.
Output: β best candidate tips.
Initialize $\Pi = \emptyset$, $\pi[0:\beta-1] = \mathbf{0}$, $\Pi_p = \emptyset$, $\pi_p = \mathbf{0}$, $t = 0$;
Get user latent factor and item latent factor:
  $\mathbf{u} = \mathbf{U}(:, u)$ and $\mathbf{v} = \mathbf{V}(:, v)$
while $t < \eta$ **do**
  Generate β new states based on Π: $\{\hat{\mathbf{s}}_t\}_0^{\beta-1} = \mathcal{G}(\Pi)$
  for i from 0 to β **do**
    Uncompleted sequence $s_i \leftarrow \Pi(i)$
    Top-β words $\{w_0, w_1, \ldots, w_{\beta-1}\} \leftarrow \beta\text{-}\arg\max_{w_i \in \mathcal{V}} \hat{\mathbf{s}}_{t_i}^{(w_i)}$
    for each word w_j **do**
      Concatenation: $\Pi_p.inseart(s_i + w_j)$
      Likelihood: $\pi_p.inseart(\pi[i] + \log \hat{\mathbf{s}}_{t_i}^{(w_j)})$
    end for
  end for
  Get the top-β sequences with largest likelihood:
    $\{s\}_0^{\beta-1}, \{l\}_0^{\beta-1} = \beta\text{-} \arg\max_{s \in \Pi_p, l \in \pi_p} l$
  $\Pi \leftarrow \{s\}_0^{\beta-1}$, $\pi \leftarrow \{l\}_0^{\beta-1}$, $\Pi_p = \emptyset$, $\pi_p = \mathbf{0}$
  $t \leftarrow t + 1$
end while
return Π, π.

At the testing stage, given a trained model, we employ the beam search algorithm to find the best sequence s^* having the maximum log-likelihood.

$$s^* = \arg\max_{s \in \mathcal{S}} \sum_{w \in s} \log \hat{\mathbf{s}}^{(I_w)} \tag{21}$$

The details of the beam search algorithm is shown in Algorithm 1.

3.4 Multi-task Learning

We integrate all the subtasks of rating prediction and abstractive tips generation into a unified multi-task learning framework whose objective function is:

$$\mathcal{J} = \min_{\mathbf{U},\mathbf{V},\mathbf{E},\Theta} (\lambda_r \mathcal{L}^r + \lambda_c \mathcal{L}^c + \lambda_s \mathcal{L}^s + \lambda_n (\|\mathbf{U}\|_2^2 + \|\mathbf{V}\|_2^2 + \|\Theta\|_2^2)) \tag{22}$$

where $\mathcal{L}^r$ is the rating regression loss from Equation 7, $\mathcal{L}^c$ is the review text generation loss from Equation 16, and $\mathcal{L}^r$ is the tips generation loss from Equation 20. Θ is the set of neural parameters. λ_r, λ_c, λ_s, and λ_n are the weight proportion of each term. The whole framework can be efficiently trained using back-propagation in an end-to-end paradigm.

4 EXPERIMENTAL SETUP

4.1 Research Questions

We list the research questions we want to investigate in this paper:

- **RQ1**: What is the performance of NRT in rating prediction tasks? Does it outperform the state-of-the-art models? (See Section 5.1.)
- **RQ2**: What is the performance of NRT in abstractive tips generation? Can the generated tips express user experience and feelings? (See Section 5.2)
- **RQ3**: What is the relationship between predicted ratings and the sentiment of generated tips? (See Section 5.3)

We conduct extensive experiments to investigate the above research questions.

Table 2: Overview of the datasets.

	Books	Electronics	Movies&TV	Yelp-2016
users	603,668	192,403	123,960	684,295
items	367,982	63,001	50,052	85,533
reviews	8,887,781	1,684,779	1,697,533	2,346,227
$\|\mathcal{V}\|$	258,190	70,294	119,530	111,102

4.2 Datasets

In our experiments, we use four standard benchmark datasets from different domains to evaluate our model. The ratings of these datasets are integers in the range of $[0, 5]$. There are three datasets from Amazon 5-core[6]: **Books**, **Electronics**, and **Movies & TV**. "Books" is the largest dataset among all the domains. It contains 603,668 users, 367,982 items, and 8,887,781 reviews. We regard the field "summary" as tips, and the number of tips texts is same with the number of reviews.

Another dataset is from **Yelp** Challenge 2016[7]. It is also a large-scale dataset consisting of restaurant reviews and tips. The number of users is 684,295, which is the largest among all the datasets. Therefore this dataset is also the most sparse one. Tips are included in the dataset. For samples without tips, the first sentence of review texts is extracted and regarded as tips.

We filter out the words with low term frequency in the tips and review texts, and build a vocabulary $\mathcal{V}$ for each dataset. We show the statistics of our datasets in Table 2.

4.3 Evaluation Metrics

For the evaluation of rating prediction, we employ two metrics: Mean Absolute Error (*MAE*) and Root Mean Square Error (*RMSE*). Both of them are widely used for rating prediction in recommender systems. Given a predicted rating $\hat{r}_{u,i}$ and a ground-truth rating $r_{u,i}$ from the user u for the item i, the RMSE is calculated as:

$$RMSE = \sqrt{\frac{1}{N} \sum_{u,i} (r_{u,i} - \hat{r}_{u,i})^2} \tag{23}$$

where N indicates the number of ratings between users and items. Similarly, MAE is calculated as follows:

$$MAE = \frac{1}{N} \sum_{u,i} |r_{u,i} - \hat{r}_{u,i}| \tag{24}$$

For the evaluation of abstractive tips generation, the ground truth s_h is the tips written by the user for the item. We use *ROUGE* [20] as our evaluation metric with standard options[8]. It is a classical

[6] http://jmcauley.ucsd.edu/data/amazon
[7] https://www.yelp.com/dataset_challenge
[8] ROUGE-1.5.5.pl -n 4 -w 1.2 -m -2 4 -u -c 95 -r 1000 -f A -p 0.5 -t 0

evaluation metric in the field of text summarization [3, 20]. It counts the number of overlapping units between the generated tips and the ground truth written by users. Assuming that s is the generated tips, g_n is n-gram, $C(g_n)$ is the number of n-grams in $\tilde{s}$ (s_h or s), $C_m(g_n)$ is the number of n-grams co-occurring in s and s_h, then the ROUGE-N score for s is defined as follows:

$$ROUGE\text{-}N(s) = \sum_{g_n \in s_h} C_m(g_n) / \sum_{g_n \in \tilde{s}} C(g_n) \tag{25}$$

When $\tilde{s} = s_h$, we can get $ROUGE_{recall}$, and when $\tilde{s} = s$, we get $ROUGE_{presicion}$. We use Recall, Precision, and F-measure of ROUGE-1 (R-1), ROUGE-2 (R-2), ROUGE-L (R-L), and ROUGE-SU4 (R-SU4) to evaluate the quality of the generated tips.

4.4 Comparative Methods

To evaluate the performance of rating prediction, we compare our model with the following methods:

- **RMR**: **R**atings **M**eet **R**eviews [21]. It utilizes a topic modeling technique to model the review texts and achieves significant improvements compared with other strong topic modeling based methods.
- **CTR**: **C**ollaborative **T**opic **R**egression [40]. It is a popular method for scientific articles recommendation by solving a one-class collaborative filtering problem. Note that CTR uses both ratings and item specifications.
- **NMF**: **N**on-negative **M**atrix **F**actorization [18]. It only uses the rating matrix as the input.
- **PMF**: **P**robabilistic **M**atrix **F**actorization [31]. Gaussian distribution is introduced to model the latent factors for users and items.
- **LRMF**: **L**earning to **R**ank with **M**atrix **F**actorization [35]. It combines a list-wise learning-to-rank algorithm with matrix factorization to improve recommendation.
- **SVD++**: It extends **S**ingular **V**alue **D**ecomposition by considering implicit feedback information for latent factor modeling [14].
- **URP**: **U**ser **R**ating **P**rofile modeling [22]. Topic models are employed to model the user preference from a generative perspective. It still only uses the rating matrix as input.

For abstractive tips generation, we find that no existing works can generate abstractive tips purely based on latent factors of users and items. In order to evaluate the performance and conduct comparison with some baselines, we refine some existing methods to make them capable of extracting sentences for tips generation as follows.

LexRank [7] is a classical method in the field of text summarization. We add a preprocessing procedure to prepare the input texts for LexRank, which consists of the following steps: (1) Retrieval: For the user u, we first retrieve all her reviews C_u from the training set. For the item i, we use the same method to get C_i. (2) Filtering: Assuming that the ground truth rating for u and i is $r_{u,i}$, then we remove all the reviews from C_u and C_i whose ratings are not equal to $r_{u,i}$. The reviews whose words only appear in one set are also removed. (3) Tips extraction: We first merge C_u and C_i to get $C_{u,i}$, then the problem can be regarded as a multi-document summarization problem. LexRank can extract a sentence from $C_{u,i}$ as the final tips. Note that we give an advantage of this method since the ground truth ratings are used.

Table 3: Baselines and methods used for comparison.

Acronym	Gloss	Reference
NRT	Neural rating and tips generation	Section 3
Rating prediction		
RMR	Ratings meet reviews model	[21]
CTR	Collaborative topic regression model	[40]
NMF	Non-negative matrix factorization	[18]
PMF	Probabilistic matrix factorization	[31]
LRMF	List-wise learning to rank for item ranking	[35]
SVD++	Factorization meets the neighborhood	[14]
URP	User rating profile modeling using LDA	[22]
Tips generation		
LexRank	Pagerank for summarization	[7]
CTR_t	CTR for tips topic extraction	[40]
RMR_t	RMR for tips topic extraction	[21]

CTR contains a topic model component and it can generate topics for items. So the topic related variables are employed to extract tips: (1) We first get the latent factor θ_i for item i, and draw the topic z with the largest probability from θ_i. Then from ϕ_z, which is a multinomial distribution of z on $\mathcal{V}$, we select the top-50 words with the largest probability. (2) The most similar sentence from $C_{u,i}$ is extracted as the tips. This baseline is named $\mathbf{CTR}_t$. Another baseline method $\mathbf{RMR}_t$ is designed in the same way.

Finally, we list all the methods and baselines in Table 3.

4.5 Experimental Settings

Each dataset is divided into three subsets: 80%, 10%, and 10%, for training, validation, and testing, receptively. All the parameters of our model are tuned with the validation set. After the tuning process, we set the number of latent factors $k = 10$ for LRMF, NMF, PMF, and SVD++. We set the number of topics $K = 50$ for the methods using topic models. In our model NRT, we set $K = 300$ for user latent factors, item latent factors, and word latent factors. The dimension of the hidden size is 400. The number of layers for the rating regression model is 4, and for the tips generation model is 1. We set the beam size $\beta = 4$, and the maximum length $\eta = 20$. For the optimization objective, we let the weight parameters $\lambda_r = \lambda_c = \lambda_s = 1$, and $\lambda_n = 0.0001$. The batch size for mini-batch training is 200.

All the neural matrix parameters in hidden layers and RNN layers are initialized from a uniform distribution between $[-0.1, 0.1]$. Adadelta [48] is used for gradient based optimization. Our framework is implemented with Theano [38] on a single Tesla K80 GPU.

5 RESULTS AND DISCUSSIONS

5.1 Rating Prediction (RQ1)

The rating prediction results of our framework NRT and comparative models on all datasets are given in Table 4. It shows that our model consistently outperforms all comparative methods under both MAE and RMSE metrics on all datasets. From the comparison,

Table 4: MAE and RMSE values for rating prediction.

	Books		Electronics		Movies		Yelp-2016	
	MAE	RMSE	MAE	RMSE	MAE	RMSE	MAE	RMSE
LRMF	1.939	2.153	2.005	2.203	1.977	2.189	1.809	2.038
PMF	0.882	1.219	1.220	1.612	0.927	1.290	1.320	1.752
NMF	0.731	1.035	0.904	1.297	0.794	1.135	1.062	1.454
SVD++	0.686	0.967	0.847	1.194	0.745	1.049	1.020	1.349
URP	0.704	0.945	0.860	1.126	0.764	1.006	1.030	1.286
CTR	0.736	0.961	0.903	1.154	0.854	1.069	1.174	1.392
RMR	0.681	0.933	0.822	1.123	0.741	1.005	0.994	1.286
NRT	**0.667***	**0.927***	**0.806***	**1.107***	**0.702***	**0.985***	**0.985***	**1.277***

*Statistical significance tests show that our method is better than RMR [21].

we notice that the topic modeling based methods CTR and RMR are much better than LRMF, NMF, PMF, and SVD++. The reason is that CTR and RMR consider text information such as item specifications and user reviews to improve the representation quality of latent factors, while the traditional CF-based models (e.g. LRMF, NMF, PMF, and SVD++) only consider the rating matrix as the input. Statistical significance of differences between the performance of NRT and RMR, the best comparison method, is tested using a two-tailed paired t-test. The result shows that NRT is significantly better than RMR.

Except jointly learning the tips decoder, we did not apply any sophisticated linguistic operations on the texts of reviews and tips. Jointly modeling the tips information is already very helpful for recommendation performance. In fact, tips and its corresponding rating are two facets of product assessment by a user on an item, namely, the qualitative facet and the quantitative facet. Our framework NRT elegantly captures this information with its multi-task learning model. Therefore the learnt latent factors are more effective.

5.2 Abstractive Tips Generation (RQ2)

Our NRT model can not only solve the rating prediction problem, but also generate abstractive tips simulating how users express their experience and feelings. The evaluation results of tips generation of our model and the comparative methods are given in Table 5~Table 8. In order to capture more details, we report Recall, Precision, and F-measure (in percentage) of ROUGE-1, ROUGE-2, ROUGE-L, and ROUGE-SU4. Our model achieves the best performance in the metrics of Precision and F1-measure among all the four datasets. On the dataset of Movies&TV, NRT also achieves the best Recall for all ROUGE metrics.

For most of the datasets, our NRT model does not outperform the baselines on Recall. There are several reasons: (1) The ground truth tips used in the training set are very short, only about 10-word length on average. Naturally, the model trained using this dataset cannot generate long sentence. (2) The mechanism of typical beam search algorithm makes the model favor short sentences. (3) The comparison models are extraction-based approaches and these models favor to extract long sentence, although we add a length (i.e., 20 words) restriction on them.

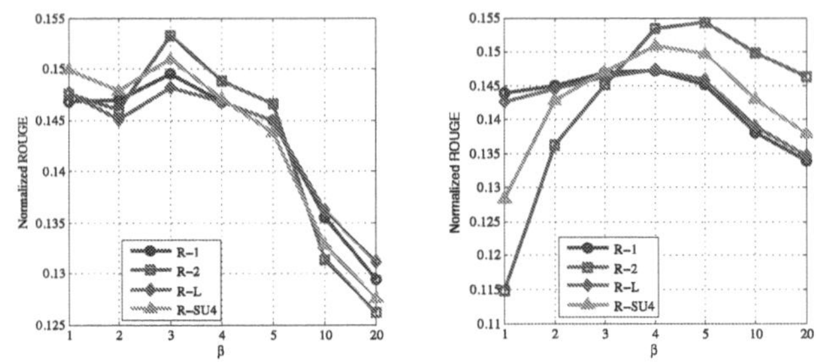

(a) Electronics. **(b) Movies&TV.**

Figure 3: Effectiveness of beam size β on the validation set.

We investigate the performance of different beam size β used in the beam search algorithm. The relationship between ROUGE and β on two validation sets of Electronics and Movies&TV is shown in Figure 3. We test $\beta \sim \{1 \sim 5, 10, 20\}$ and find that when $\beta = 3 \sim 5$ our model can achieve the best performance of tips generation.

Inspired by [45], we make use of Length-Normalization (LN) to adjust the log-probability in the beam search algorithm to make the beam search algorithm also consider long sentences:

$$LN(s) = \frac{(n + |s|)^{\alpha}}{(n + 1)^{\alpha}} \tag{26}$$

where s is the decoded sequence, $n = 2$, and $\alpha = 0.6$. We conduct several experiments to verify the effectiveness of LN. The comparison results are shown in Table 9, where F1-measures of ROUGE evaluation metrics are reported. It is obvious that our model NRT with LN is much better than the one without LN.

5.3 Case Analysis (RQ3)

For the purpose of analyzing the linguistic quality and the sentiment correlation between the predicted ratings and the generated tips, we selected some real cases form different domains. The results are listed in Table 10. Although our model generates tips in an abstractive way, tips' linguistic quality is quite good.

For the sentiment correlation analysis, we also choose some generated tips with negative sentiment. Take the tips "Not as good as i expected." as an example, our model predicts a rating of 2.25, which clearly shows the consistent sentiment. The ground truth

Table 5: ROUGE evaluation on dataset Books.

Methods	ROUGE-1			ROUGE-2			ROUGE-L			ROUGE-SU4		
	R	P	F1	R	P	F1	R	P	F1	R	P	F1
LexRank	12.94	12.02	12.18	2.26	2.29	2.23	11.72	10.89	11.02	4.13	4.15	4.02
RMR_t	13.80	11.69	12.43	1.79	1.57	1.64	12.54	10.55	11.25	4.49	3.54	3.80
CTR_t	14.06	11.85	12.62	2.03	1.80	1.87	12.68	10.64	11.35	4.71	3.71	3.99
NRT	10.30	**19.28**	**12.67**	1.91	**3.76**	**2.36**	9.71	**17.92**	**11.88**	3.24	**8.03**	**4.13**

Table 6: ROUGE evaluation on dataset Electronics.

Methods	ROUGE-1			ROUGE-2			ROUGE-L			ROUGE-SU4		
	R	P	F1	R	P	F1	R	P	F1	R	P	F1
LexRank	13.42	13.48	12.08	1.90	2.04	1.83	11.72	11.48	10.44	4.57	4.51	3.88
RMR_t	15.68	11.32	12.30	2.52	2.04	2.15	13.37	9.61	10.45	5.41	3.72	3.97
CTR_t	15.81	11.37	12.38	2.49	1.92	2.05	13.45	9.62	10.50	5.39	3.63	3.89
NRT	13.08	**17.72**	**13.95**	**2.59**	**3.36**	**2.72**	11.93	**16.01**	**12.67**	4.51	**6.69**	**4.68**

Table 7: ROUGE evaluation on dataset Movies&TV.

Methods	ROUGE-1			ROUGE-2			ROUGE-L			ROUGE-SU4		
	R	P	F1	R	P	F1	R	P	F1	R	P	F1
LexRank	13.62	14.11	12.37	1.92	2.09	1.81	11.69	11.74	10.47	4.47	4.53	3.75
RMR_t	14.64	10.26	11.33	1.78	1.36	1.46	12.62	8.72	9.67	4.63	3.00	3.28
CTR_t	15.13	10.37	11.57	1.90	1.42	1.54	13.02	8.77	9.85	4.88	3.03	3.36
NRT	**15.17**	**20.22**	**16.20**	**4.25**	**5.72**	**4.56**	**13.82**	**18.36**	**14.73**	**6.04**	**8.76**	**6.33**

Table 8: ROUGE evaluation on dataset Yelp-2016.

Methods	ROUGE-1			ROUGE-2			ROUGE-L			ROUGE-SU4		
	R	P	F1	R	P	F1	R	P	F1	R	P	F1
LexRank	11.32	11.16	11.04	1.32	1.34	1.31	10.33	10.16	10.06	3.41	3.38	3.26
RMR_t	11.17	10.25	10.54	2.25	2.16	2.19	10.22	9.39	9.65	3.88	3.66	3.72
CTR_t	10.74	9.95	10.19	2.21	2.14	2.15	9.91	9.19	9.41	3.96	3.64	3.70
NRT	9.39	**17.75**	**11.64**	1.83	**3.39**	**2.22**	8.70	**16.27**	**10.74**	3.01	**7.06**	**3.78**

Table 9: Effectiveness of Length-Normalization (LN). R-* refers to ROUGE-*.

Dataset	Method	R-1	R-2	R-L	R-SU4
Electronics	NRT w/o LN	13.36	2.65	12.34	4.56
	NRT	**13.72**	**2.68**	**12.57**	**4.66**
Movies&TV	NRT w/o LN	14.86	3.72	13.76	5.46
	NRT	**15.21**	**4.00**	**13.90**	**5.71**

tips of this example is "Jack of all trades master of none. ", which also conveys a negative sentiment. One interesting observation is that its ground truth rating is the full mark 5, which we guess, may be clicked by a fat finger. Nevertheless, our model can generate a consistent sentiment between this case's rating and tips. Another generated tips "What a waste of time and money." with a negative predicted rating of 1.46 also demonstrates this property.

There are also some bad cases. For example, the predicted rating of the generated tips "Not bad for the price." is 4.34, which is a positive polarity. But the sentiment of the generated tips is neutral, consistent with the ground truth. Generally speaking, our model can achieve satisfactory performance on both rating prediction and abstractive tips generation.

6 CONCLUSIONS

We propose a deep learning based framework named **NRT** which can simultaneously predict precise ratings and generate abstractive tips with good linguistic quality simulating user experience and feelings. For abstractive tips generation, GRU with context information is employed to "translate" user and item latent factors into a concise sentence. All the neural parameters as well as the latent factors for users and items are learnt by a multi-task learning approach in an end-to-end training paradigm. Experimental results on benchmark datasets show that NRT achieves better performance than the state-of-the-art models on both tasks of rating prediction and abstractive tips generation. The generated tips can vividly predict the user experience and feelings.

Table 10: Examples of the predicted ratings and the generated tips. The first line of each group shows the generated rating and tips. The second line shows the ground truth.

Rating	Tips
4.64	***This is a great product for a great price.***
5	Great product at a great price.
4.87	***I purchased this as a replacement and it is a perfect fit and the sound is excellent.***
5	Amazing sound.
4.69	***I have been using these for a couple of months.***
4	Plenty of wire gets signals and power to my amp just fine quality wise.
4.87	***One of my favorite movies.***
5	This is a movie that is not to be missed.
4.07	***Why do people hate this film.***
4	Universal why didnt your company release this edition in 1999.
2.25	***Not as good as i expected.***
5	Jack of all trades master of none.
1.46	***What a waste of time and money.***
1	The coen brothers are two sick bastards.
4.34	***Not bad for the price.***
3	Ended up altering it to get rid of ripples.

REFERENCES

[1] Amjad Almahairi, Kyle Kastner, Kyunghyun Cho, and Aaron Courville. 2015. Learning distributed representations from reviews for collaborative filtering. In *RecSys*. ACM, 147–154.

[2] Dzmitry Bahdanau, Kyunghyun Cho, and Yoshua Bengio. 2015. Neural machine translation by jointly learning to align and translate. In *ICLR*.

[3] Lidong Bing, Piji Li, Yi Liao, Wai Lam, Weiwei Guo, and Rebecca Passonneau. 2015. Abstractive Multi-Document Summarization via Phrase Selection and Merging. In *ACL*. 1587–1597.

[4] David M Blei, Andrew Y Ng, and Michael I Jordan. 2003. Latent dirichlet allocation. *JMLR* 3, Jan (2003), 993–1022.

[5] Li Chen, Guanliang Chen, and Feng Wang. 2015. Recommender systems based on user reviews: the state of the art. *User Modeling and User-Adapted Interaction* 25, 2 (2015), 99–154.

[6] Kyunghyun Cho, Bart van Merriënboer Caglar Gulcehre, Dzmitry Bahdanau, Fethi Bougares Holger Schwenk, and Yoshua Bengio. 2014. Learning Phrase Representations using RNN Encoder–Decoder for Statistical Machine Translation. *EMNLP* (2014), 1724–1734.

[7] Günes Erkan and Dragomir R Radev. 2004. Lexrank: Graph-based lexical centrality as salience in text summarization. *JAIR* 22 (2004), 457–479.

[8] Ian Goodfellow, Yoshua Bengio, and Aaron Courville. 2016. *Deep Learning*. MIT Press. http://www.deeplearningbook.org.

[9] Ian Goodfellow, Jean Pouget-Abadie, Mehdi Mirza, Bing Xu, David Warde-Farley, Sherjil Ozair, Aaron Courville, and Yoshua Bengio. 2014. Generative adversarial nets. In *NIPS*. 2672–2680.

[10] Xiangnan He, Tao Chen, Min-Yen Kan, and Xiao Chen. 2015. Trirank: Review-aware explainable recommendation by modeling aspects. In *CIKM*. ACM, 1661–1670.

[11] Xiangnan He, Lizi Liao, Hanwang Zhang, Liqiang Nie, Xia Hu, and Tat-Seng Chua. 2017. Neural Collaborative Filtering. In *WWW*. 173–182.

[12] Sepp Hochreiter and Jürgen Schmidhuber. 1997. Long short-term memory. *Neural computation* 9, 8 (1997), 1735–1780.

[13] Philipp Koehn. 2004. Pharaoh: a beam search decoder for phrase-based statistical machine translation models. In *Conference of the Association for Machine Translation in the Americas*. Springer, 115–124.

[14] Yehuda Koren. 2008. Factorization meets the neighborhood: a multifaceted collaborative filtering model. In *KDD*. ACM, 426–434.

[15] Yehuda Koren, Robert Bell, Chris Volinsky, and others. 2009. Matrix factorization techniques for recommender systems. *Computer* 42, 8 (2009), 30–37.

[16] Alex Krizhevsky, Ilya Sutskever, and Geoffrey E Hinton. 2012. Imagenet classification with deep convolutional neural networks. In *NIPS*. 1097–1105.

[17] Quoc V Le and Tomas Mikolov. 2014. Distributed Representations of Sentences and Documents.. In *ICML*. 1188–1196.

[18] Daniel D Lee and H Sebastian Seung. 2001. Algorithms for non-negative matrix factorization. In *NIPS*. 556–562.

[19] Piji Li, Zihao Wang, Wai Lam, Zhaochun Ren, and Lidong Bing. 2017. Salience Estimation via Variational Auto-Encoders for Multi-Document Summarization. In *AAAI*. 3497–3503.

[20] Chin-Yew Lin. 2004. Rouge: A package for automatic evaluation of summaries. In *ACL Workshop*, Vol. 8.

[21] Guang Ling, Michael R Lyu, and Irwin King. 2014. Ratings meet reviews, a combined approach to recommend. In *RecSys*. 105–112.

[22] Benjamin M Marlin. 2003. Modeling user rating profiles for collaborative filtering. In *NIPS*. 627–634.

[23] Julian McAuley and Jure Leskovec. 2013. Hidden factors and hidden topics: understanding rating dimensions with review text. In *RecSys*. ACM, 165–172.

[24] Tomas Mikolov, Ilya Sutskever, Kai Chen, Greg S Corrado, and Jeff Dean. 2013. Distributed representations of words and phrases and their compositionality. In *NIPS*. 3111–3119.

[25] Andrew Ng. 2011. Sparse autoencoder. *CS294A Lecture notes* 72 (2011), 1–19.

[26] Zhaochun Ren, Shangsong Liang, Piji Li, Shuaiqiang Wang, and Maarten de Rijke. 2017. Social collaborative viewpoint regression with explainable recommendations. In *WSDM*.

[27] Francesco Ricci, Lior Rokach, and Bracha Shapira. 2011. *Introduction to recommender systems handbook*. Springer.

[28] Frank Rosenblatt. 1961. *Principles of neurodynamics. perceptrons and the theory of brain mechanisms*. Technical Report. DTIC Document.

[29] David E Rumelhart, Geoffrey E Hinton, and Ronald J Williams. 1988. Learning representations by back-propagating errors. *Cognitive modeling* 5, 3 (1988), 1.

[30] Alexander M Rush, Sumit Chopra, and Jason Weston. 2015. A neural attention model for abstractive sentence summarization. In *EMNLP*.

[31] Ruslan Salakhutdinov and Andriy Mnih. 2007. Probabilistic Matrix Factorization.. In *NIPS*. 1–8.

[32] Ruslan Salakhutdinov, Andriy Mnih, and Geoffrey Hinton. 2007. Restricted Boltzmann machines for collaborative filtering. In *ICML*. ACM, 791–798.

[33] Badrul Sarwar, George Karypis, Joseph Konstan, and John Riedl. 2001. Item-based collaborative filtering recommendation algorithms. In *WWW*. ACM, 285–295.

[34] Suvash Sedhain, Aditya Krishna Menon, Scott Sanner, and Lexing Xie. 2015. Autorec: Autoencoders meet collaborative filtering. In *WWW*. ACM, 111–112.

[35] Yue Shi, Martha Larson, and Alan Hanjalic. 2010. List-wise learning to rank with matrix factorization for collaborative filtering. In *RecSys*. 269–272.

[36] Richard Socher, Danqi Chen, Christopher D Manning, and Andrew Ng. 2013. Reasoning with neural tensor networks for knowledge base completion. In *NIPS*. 926–934.

[37] Xiaoyuan Su and Taghi M Khoshgoftaar. 2009. A survey of collaborative filtering techniques. *Advances in artificial intelligence* 2009 (2009), 4.

[38] Theano Development Team. 2016. Theano: A Python framework for fast computation of mathematical expressions. *arXiv e-prints* abs/1605.02688 (2016).

[39] Pascal Vincent, Hugo Larochelle, Isabelle Lajoie, Yoshua Bengio, and Pierre-Antoine Manzagol. 2010. Stacked denoising autoencoders: Learning useful representations in a deep network with a local denoising criterion. *JMLR* 11 (2010), 3371–3408.

[40] Chong Wang and David M Blei. 2011. Collaborative topic modeling for recommending scientific articles. In *KDD*. ACM, 448–456.

[41] Hao Wang, Naiyan Wang, and Dit-Yan Yeung. 2015. Collaborative deep learning for recommender systems. In *KDD*. ACM, 1235–1244.

[42] Hao Wang, SHI Xingjian, and Dit-Yan Yeung. 2016. Collaborative recurrent autoencoder: Recommend while learning to fill in the blanks. In *NIPS*. 415–423.

[43] Chao-Yuan Wu, Amr Ahmed, Alex Beutel, Alexander J Smola, and How Jing. 2017. Recurrent Recommender Networks. In *WSDM*. 495–503.

[44] Yao Wu, Christopher DuBois, Alice X Zheng, and Martin Ester. 2016. Collaborative denoising auto-encoders for top-n recommender systems. In *WSDM*. ACM, 153–162.

[45] Yonghui Wu, Mike Schuster, Zhifeng Chen, Quoc V Le, Mohammad Norouzi, Wolfgang Macherey, Maxim Krikun, Yuan Cao, Qin Gao, Klaus Macherey, and others. 2016. Google's Neural Machine Translation System: Bridging the Gap between Human and Machine Translation. *arXiv preprint arXiv:1609.08144* (2016).

[46] Yinqing Xu, Wai Lam, and Tianyi Lin. 2014. Collaborative filtering incorporating review text and co-clusters of hidden user communities and item groups. In *CIKM*. ACM, 251–260.

[47] Yinqing Xu, Bei Shi, Wentao Tian, and Wai Lam. 2015. A Unified Model for Unsupervised Opinion Spamming Detection Incorporating Text Generality. In *IJCAI*. 725–731.

[48] Matthew D Zeiler. 2012. ADADELTA: an adaptive learning rate method. *arXiv preprint arXiv:1212.5701* (2012).

[49] Lei Zheng, Vahid Noroozi, and Philip S Yu. 2017. Joint deep modeling of users and items using reviews for recommendation. In *WSDM*. ACM, 425–434.

Neural Factorization Machines for Sparse Predictive Analytics*

Xiangnan He
School of Computing
National University of Singapore
Singapore 117417
dcshex@nus.edu.sg

Tat-Seng Chua
School of Computing
National University of Singapore
Singapore 117417
dcscts@nus.edu.sg

ABSTRACT

Many predictive tasks of web applications need to model categorical variables, such as user IDs and demographics like genders and occupations. To apply standard machine learning techniques, these categorical predictors are always converted to a set of binary features via one-hot encoding, making the resultant feature vector highly sparse. To learn from such sparse data effectively, it is crucial to account for the interactions between features.

Factorization Machines (FMs) are a popular solution for efficiently using the second-order feature interactions. However, FM models feature interactions in a linear way, which can be insufficient for capturing the non-linear and complex inherent structure of real-world data. While deep neural networks have recently been applied to learn non-linear feature interactions in industry, such as the *Wide&Deep* by Google and *DeepCross* by Microsoft, the deep structure meanwhile makes them difficult to train.

In this paper, we propose a novel model *Neural Factorization Machine* (NFM) for prediction under sparse settings. NFM seamlessly combines the linearity of FM in modelling second-order feature interactions and the non-linearity of neural network in modelling higher-order feature interactions. Conceptually, NFM is more expressive than FM since FM can be seen as a special case of NFM without hidden layers. Empirical results on two regression tasks show that with one hidden layer only, NFM significantly outperforms FM with a 7.3% relative improvement. Compared to the recent deep learning methods Wide&Deep and DeepCross, our NFM uses a shallower structure but offers better performance, being much easier to train and tune in practice.

CCS CONCEPTS

•Information systems → Information retrieval; Recommender systems; •Computing methodologies → Neural networks; Factorization methods;

KEYWORDS

Factorization Machines, Neural Networks, Deep Learning, Sparse Data, Regression, Recommendation

*NExT research is supported by the National Research Foundation, Prime Minister's Office, Singapore under its IRC@SG Funding Initiative.

SIGIR'17, August 7–11, 2017, Shinjuku, Tokyo, Japan
© 2017 ACM. 978-1-4503-5022-8/17/08...$15.00
DOI: http://dx.doi.org/10.1145/3077136.3080777

1 INTRODUCTION

Predictive analytics is one of the most important techniques for many information retrieval (IR) and data mining (DM) tasks, ranging from recommendation systems [2, 16], targeted advertising [21], to search ranking [19, 39], visual analysis [35], and event detection [40]. Typically, a predictive task is formulated as estimating a function that maps predictor variables to some target, for example, real valued target for regression and categorical target for classification. Distinct from continuous predictor variables that are naturally found in images and audios, such as raw features, the predictor variables for web applications are mostly discrete and categorical. For example, in online advertising, we need to predict *how likely* (target) a *user* (first predictor variable) of a particular *occupation* (second predictor variable) will click on an *ad* (third predictor variable). To build predictive models with these categorical predictor variables, a common solution is to convert them to a set of binary features (*a.k.a.* feature vector) via one-hot encoding [2, 9, 16, 30, 31]. Thereafter, standard machine learning (ML) techniques such as logistic regression and support vector machines can be applied.

Depending on the possible values of categorical predictor variables, the generated feature vector can be of very high dimension but sparse. To build effective ML models with such sparse data, it is crucial to account for the interactions between features [4, 23, 31]. Many successful solutions in both industry and academia largely rely on manually crafting combinatorial features [9], *i.e.*, constructing new features by combining multiple predictor variables, also known as *cross features*. For example, we can cross variable $occupation = \{banker, doctor\}$ with $gender = \{M, F\}$ and get a new $occupation\_gender = \{banker\_M, banker\_F, doctor\_M, doctor\_F\}$. It is well known that top data scientists are usually masters of crafting combinatorial features, which play a key role in their winning formulas [31]. However, the power of such features comes at a high cost, since it requires heavy engineering efforts and useful domain knowledge to design effective features. Thus these solutions can be difficult to generalize to new problems or domains.

Instead of augmenting feature vectors manually, another solution is to design a ML model to learn feature interactions from raw data automatically. A popular approach is factorization machines (FMs) [27], which embeds features into a latent space and models the interactions between features via inner product of their embedding vectors. While FM has yielded great promise[1] in many prediction tasks [2, 8, 21, 24], we argue that its performance can be limited by its linearity, as well as the modelling of pairwise (*i.e.*, second-order) feature interactions only. Specifically, for real-world data

[1] https://securityintelligence.com/factorization-machines-a-new-way-of-looking-at-machine-learning

that have complex and non-linear underlying structure, FM may not be expressive enough. Although higher-order FMs have been proposed [27], they still belong to the family of linear models and are claimed to be difficult to estimate [28]. Moreover, they are known to have only marginal improvements over FM, which we suspect the reason might be due to the modelling of higher-order interactions in a linear way.

In this work, we propose a novel model for sparse data prediction named *Neural Factorization Machines* (NFMs), which enhances FMs by modelling higher-order and non-linear feature interactions. By devising a new operation in neural network modelling — *Bilinear Interaction* (Bi-Interaction) pooling — we subsume FM under the neural network framework for the first time. Through stacking non-linear layers above the Bi-Interaction layer, we are able to deepen the shallow linear FM, modelling higher-order and non-linear feature interactions effectively to improve FM's expressiveness. In contrast to traditional deep learning methods that simply concatenate [9, 31, 44] or average [16, 36] embedding vectors in the low level, our use of Bi-Interaction pooling encodes more informative feature interactions, greatly facilitating the following "deep" layers to learn meaningful information. We conduct extensive experiments on two public benchmarks for context-aware prediction and personalized tag recommendation. With one hidden layer only, our NFM significantly outperforms FM (the official LibFM [28] implementation) with a 7.3% improvement. Compared to the state-of-the-art deep learning methods — the 3-layer Wide&Deep [9] and 10-layer DeepCross [31] — our 1-layer NFM shows consistent improvements with a much simpler structure and fewer model parameters. Our implementation is available at: https://github.com/hexiangnan/neural_factorization_machine.

The main contributions of this work are summarized as follows.

(1) To the best of our knowledge, we are the first to introduce the Bi-Interaction pooling operation in neural network modelling, and present a new neural network view for FM.
(2) Based on this new view, we develop a novel NFM model to deepen FM under the neural network framework for learning higher-order and non-linear feature interactions.
(3) We conduct extensive experiments on two real-world tasks to study the Bi-Interaction pooling and NFM model, demonstrating the effectiveness of NFM and great promise in using neural networks for prediction under sparse settings.

2 MODELLING FEATURE INTERACTIONS

Due to the large space of combinatorial features, traditional solutions typically rely on manual feature engineering efforts or feature selection techniques like boosted decision trees to select important feature interactions. One limitation of such solutions is that they cannot generalize to combinatorial features that have not appeared in the training data. In recent years, embedding-based methods become increasingly popular, which try to learn feature interactions from raw data [9, 18, 24, 30, 31, 44]. By embedding high-dimensional sparse features into a low-dimensional latent space, the model can generalize to unseen feature combinations. Regardless of domain, we can categorize the approaches into two types: 1) factorization machine-based linear models, and 2) neural network-based non-linear models. In what follows, we shortly recapitulate the two representative techniques.

2.1 Factorization Machines

Factorization machines are originally proposed for collaborative recommendation [27, 30]. Given a real valued feature vector $\mathbf{x} \in \mathbb{R}^n$, FM estimates the target by modelling all interactions between each pair of features via factorized interaction parameters:

$$\hat{y}_{FM}(\mathbf{x}) = w_0 + \sum_{i=1}^{n} w_i x_i + \sum_{i=1}^{n}\sum_{j=i+1}^{n} \mathbf{v}_i^T \mathbf{v}_j \cdot x_i x_j, \tag{1}$$

where w_0 is the global bias, w_i models the interaction of the i-th feature to the target. The $\mathbf{v}_i^T \mathbf{v}_j$ term denotes the factorized interaction, where $\mathbf{v}_i \in \mathbb{R}^k$ denotes the embedding vector for feature i, and k is the size of embedding vector, also termed as *number of latent factors* in literature. Note that due to the coefficient $x_i x_j$, only interactions of non-zero features are considered.

One main power of FM stems from its generality — in contrast to matrix factorization (MF) that models the relation of two entities only [17], FM is a general predictor working with any real valued feature vector for supervised learning. Clearly, it enhances linear/logistic regression (LR) using the second-order factorized interactions between features. By specifying input features, Rendle [27] showed that FM can mimic many specific factorization models such as the standard MF, parallel factor analysis, and SVD++ [22], Owing to such genericity, FM has been recognized as one of the most effective embedding methods for sparse data prediction. It has been successfully applied to many predictive tasks, ranging from online advertising [21], microblog retrieval [26], to open relation extraction [25].

2.1.1 *Expressiveness Limitation of FM.*

Despite effectiveness, we point out that FM still belongs to the family of (multivariate) linear models. In other words, the predicted target $\hat{y}(\mathbf{x})$ is linear *w.r.t.* each model parameter [28]. Formally, for each model parameter $\theta \in \{w_0, \{w_i\}, \{v_{if}\}\}$, we can have $\hat{y}(\mathbf{x}) = g + h\theta$, where g and h are expressions independent of θ. Unfortunately, the underlying structure of real-world data is often highly non-linear and cannot be accurately approximated by linear models [12]. As such, FM may suffer from insufficient representation ability for modelling real data with complex inherent structure and regularities.

In terms of methodology, many variants [18, 21, 24, 38] of FM have been developed. For example, Hong *et al.* [18] proposed Co-FMs to learn from multi-view data; Oentaryo *et al.* [24] encoded prior knowledge of features to FM by designing a hierarchical regularizer; and Lin *et al.* [21] proposed field-aware FM, which learned multiple embedding vectors for a feature to differentiate its interaction with features of different fields. More recently, Xiao *et al.* [38] proposed attentional FM, using an attention network [7, 39] to learn the importance of each feature interaction. However, these variants are all linear extensions of FM and model the second-order feature interactions only. As such, they can suffer from the same expressiveness issue for modelling real-world data.

In this work, we contribute improvements on the expressiveness of FM by endowing it the ability of non-linearity modelling. The idea is to perform non-linear transformation on the latent space

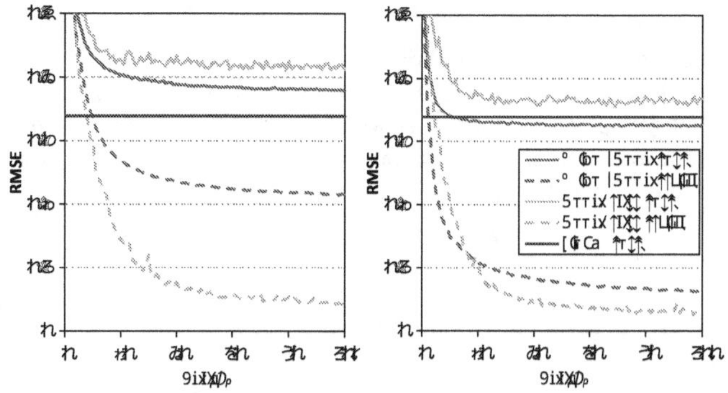

(a) Random initialization (b) FM as pre-training

Figure 1: Training and test error of each epoch of Wide&Deep and DeepCross on Frappe. Random initialization of embeddings leads to poor performance, worse than LibFM (a). Initializing using the embeddings learned by FM improves the performance significantly (b). This reveals optimization difficulties for training deep neural networks.

of the second-order feature interactions; meanwhile, higher-order feature interactions can be captured.

2.2 Deep Neural Networks

In recent five years, deep neural networks (DNNs) have achieved immense success and have been widely used on speech recognition, computer vision and natural language processing. However, the use of DNNs is not as widespread among the IR and DM community. In our view, we think one reason might be that most data of IR and DM tasks are naturally sparse, such as user behaviors, documents/queries and various features converted from categorical variables. Although DNNs have exhibited strong ability to learn patterns from dense data [14], the use of DNNs on sparse data has received less scrutiny, and it is unclear how to employ DNNs for effectively learning feature interactions under sparse settings.

Until very recently, some work [6, 9, 16, 31, 44] started to explore DNNs for some scenarios of sparse predictive analytics. In [16], He *et al.* presented a neural collaborative filtering (NCF) framework to learn interactions between users and items. Later, the NCF framework was extended to model attribute interactions for attribute-aware CF [37]. However, their methods are only applicable to learn interactions between two entities and do not directly support the general setting of supervised learning. Zhang *et al.* [44] developed a FM-supported Neural Network (FNN), which uses the feature embeddings learned by FM to initialize DNNs. Cheng *et al.* [9] proposed Wide&Deep for App recommendation, where the deep part is a multi-layer perceptron (MLP) on the concatenation of feature embedding vectors to learn feature interactions. Shan *et al.* [31] proposed DeepCross for ads prediction, which shares a similar framework with Wide&Deep by replacing the MLP with the state-of-the-art residual network [14].

2.2.1 ***Optimization Difficulties of DNN.*** It is worthwhile to mention the common structure of these neural network-based approaches, *i.e.,* stacking multiple layers above the concatenation of embedding vectors to learn feature interactions. The expectation is that the multiple layers can learn combinatorial features of arbitrary orders in an implicit way [31]. However, we find a key weakness of such an architecture is that simply concatenating feature embedding vectors carries too little information about feature interactions in the low level. An empirical evidence is from He *et al.*'s recent work [16], which shows that simply concatenating user and item embedding vectors leads to very poor results for collaborative filtering. To remedy this, one has to rely on the following deep layers to learn meaningful interaction function. While it is claimed that multiple non-linear layers are able to learn feature interactions well [9, 31], such a deep architecture can be difficult to optimize in practice due to the notorious problems of vanishing/exploding gradients, overfitting, degradation, among others [14].

To demonstrate optimization difficulties of DNNs empirically, we plot the training and test error of each epoch of Wide&Deep and DeepCross on the Frappe data in Figure 1. We use the same architecture and parameters as reported in their papers, where Wide&Deep applies a 3-layer tower structure and DeepCross uses a 10-layer residual network with successively decreasing hidden units. From Figure 1a, we can see that training the two models from scratch leads to a performance much worse than the shallow FM model. For Wide&Deep, the training error is relatively high, which is likely because of the degradation problem [14]. For DeepCross, the very low training error but high test error implies that the model is overfitting. Inspired by FNN [44], we further explore the use of feature embeddings learned by FM to initialize DNNs, which can be seen as a pre-training step. As can be seen from Figure 1b, both models achieve much better performance (over 11% improvements). For Wide&Deep, the degradation problem is well addressed, evidenced by the much lower training error, and the test performance is better than LibFM. However for the 10-layer DeepCross, it still suffers from severe overfitting and underperforms LibFM. These relatively negative results reveal optimization difficulties for training DNNs.

In this work, we present a new paradigm of neural networks for sparse data prediction. Instead of concatenating feature embedding vectors, we propose a new Bi-Interaction operation that models the second-order feature interactions. This results in a much more informative representation in the low level, greatly helping the subsequent non-linear layers to learn higher-order interactions.

3 NEURAL FACTORIZATION MACHINES

We first present the NFM model that unifies the strengths of FMs and neural networks for sparse data modelling. We then discuss the learning procedure and how to employ some useful techniques in neural networks — dropout and batch normalization — for NFM.

3.1 The NFM Model

Similar to factorization machine, NFM is a general machine learner working with any real valued feature vector. Given a sparse vector $\mathbf{x} \in \mathbb{R}^n$ as input, where a feature value $x_i = 0$ means the i-th feature does not exist in the instance, NFM estimates the target as:

$$\hat{y}_{NFM}(\mathbf{x}) = w_0 + \sum_{i=1}^{n} w_i x_i + f(\mathbf{x}), \tag{2}$$

where the first and second terms are the linear regression part similar to that for FM, which models global bias of data and weight

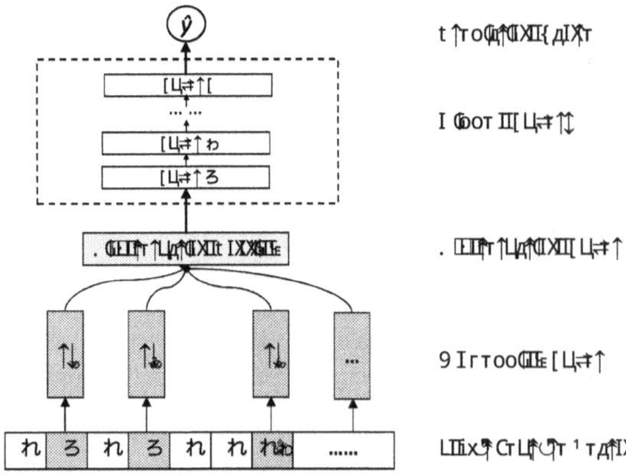

Figure 2: Neural Factorization Machines model (the first-order linear regression part is not shown for clarity).

of features. The third term $f(\mathbf{x})$ is the core component of NFM for modelling feature interactions, which is a multi-layered feed-forward neural network as shown in Figure 2. In what follows, we elaborate the design of $f(\mathbf{x})$ layer by layer.

Embedding Layer. The embedding layer is a fully connected layer that projects each feature to a dense vector representation. Formally, let $\mathbf{v}_i \in \mathbb{R}^k$ be the embedding vector for the i-th feature. After embedding, we obtain a set of embedding vectors $\mathcal{V}_x = \{x_1\mathbf{v}_1, ..., x_n\mathbf{v}_n\}$ to represent the input feature vector $\mathbf{x}$. Owing to sparse representation of $\mathbf{x}$, we only need to include the embedding vectors for non-zero features, *i.e.*, $\mathcal{V}_x = \{x_i\mathbf{v}_i\}$ where $x_i \neq 0$. Note that we have rescaled an embedding vector by its input feature value, rather than simply an embedding table lookup, so as to account for the real valued features [27].

Bi-Interaction Layer. We then feed the embedding set $\mathcal{V}_x$ into the Bi-Interaction layer, which is a pooling operation that converts a set of embedding vectors to one vector:

$$f_{BI}(\mathcal{V}_x) = \sum_{i=1}^{n}\sum_{j=i+1}^{n} x_i\mathbf{v}_i \odot x_j\mathbf{v}_j, \tag{3}$$

where $\odot$ denotes the element-wise product of two vectors, that is, $(\mathbf{v}_i \odot \mathbf{v}_j)_k = v_{ik}v_{jk}$. Clearly, the output of Bi-Interaction pooling is a k-dimension vector that encodes the second-order interactions between features in the embedding space.

It is worth pointing out that our proposal of Bi-Interaction pooling does not introduce extra model parameter, and more importantly, it can be efficiently computed in linear time. This property is the same with average/max pooling and concatenation that are rather simple but commonly used in neural network approaches [16, 31, 36]. To show the linear time complexity of evaluating Bi-Interaction pooling, we reformulate Equation (3) as:

$$f_{BI}(\mathcal{V}_x) = \frac{1}{2}\left[(\sum_{i=1}^{n} x_i\mathbf{v}_i)^2 - \sum_{i=1}^{n}(x_i\mathbf{v}_i)^2\right], \tag{4}$$

where we use the symbol $\mathbf{v}^2$ to denote $\mathbf{v} \odot \mathbf{v}$. By considering the sparsity of $\mathbf{x}$, we can actually perform Bi-Interaction pooling in $O(kN_x)$ time, where N_x denotes the number of non-zero entries in $\mathbf{x}$. This is a very appealing property, meaning that the benefit of Bi-Interaction pooling in modelling pairwise feature interactions does not involve any additional cost.

Hidden Layers. Above the Bi-Interaction pooling layer is a stack of fully connected layers, which are capable of learning higher-order interactions between features [31]. Formally, the definition of fully connected layers is as follows:

$$\begin{aligned}
\mathbf{z}_1 &= \sigma_1(\mathbf{W}_1 f_{BI}(\mathcal{V}_x) + \mathbf{b}_1),\\
\mathbf{z}_2 &= \sigma_2(\mathbf{W}_2\mathbf{z}_1 + \mathbf{b}_2),\\
&\cdots\cdots\\
\mathbf{z}_L &= \sigma_L(\mathbf{W}_L\mathbf{z}_{L-1} + \mathbf{b}_L),
\end{aligned} \tag{5}$$

where L denotes the number of hidden layers, $\mathbf{W}_l$, $\mathbf{b}_l$ and σ_l denote the weight matrix, bias vector and activation function for the l-th layer, respectively. By specifying non-linear activation functions, such as sigmoid, hyperbolic tangent (tanh), and Rectifier (ReLU), we allow the model to learn higher-order feature interactions in a non-linear way. This is advantageous to existing methods for higher-order interaction learning, such as higher-Order FM [3] and Exponential Machines [23], which only support the learning of higher-order interactions in a linear way. As for the structure of fully connected layers (*i.e.*, size of each layer), one can freely choose tower [9, 16], constant [31], and diamond [44], among others.

Prediction Layer. At last, the output vector of the last hidden layer $\mathbf{z}_L$ is transformed to the final prediction score:

$$f(\mathbf{x}) = \mathbf{h}^T\mathbf{z}_L, \tag{6}$$

where vector $\mathbf{h}$ denotes the neuron weights of the prediction layer.

To summarize, we give the formulation NFM's predictive model as:

$$\begin{aligned}
\hat{y}_{NFM}(\mathbf{x}) &= w_0 + \sum_{i=1}^{n} w_i x_i\\
&+ \mathbf{h}^T\sigma_L(\mathbf{W}_L(...\sigma_1(\mathbf{W}_1 f_{BI}(\mathcal{V}_x) + \mathbf{b}_1)...) + \mathbf{b}_L),
\end{aligned} \tag{7}$$

with all model parameters $\Theta = \{w_0, \{w_i, \mathbf{v}_i\}, \mathbf{h}, \{\mathbf{W}_l, \mathbf{b}_l\}\}$. Compared to FM, the additional model parameters of NFM are mainly $\{\mathbf{W}_l, \mathbf{b}_l\}$, which are used for learning higher-order interactions between features. In remainder of this subsection, we first show how NFM generalizes FM and discuss the connection of NFM between existing deep learning methods; we then analyze the time complexity of evaluating NFM model.

3.1.1 ***NFM Generalizes FM.*** FM is a shallow and linear model, which can be seen as a special case of NFM with no hidden layer. To show this, we set L to zero and directly project the output of Bi-Interaction pooling to prediction score. We term this simplified model as NFM-0, which is formulated as:

$$\begin{aligned}
\hat{y}_{NFM-0} &= w_0 + \sum_{i=1}^{n} w_i x_i + \mathbf{h}^T\sum_{i=1}^{n}\sum_{j=i+1}^{n} x_i\mathbf{v}_i \odot x_j\mathbf{v}_j\\
&= w_0 + \sum_{i=1}^{n} w_i x_i + \sum_{i=1}^{n}\sum_{j=i+1}^{n}\sum_{f=1}^{k} h_f v_{if} v_{jf} \cdot x_i x_j.
\end{aligned} \tag{8}$$

As can be seen, by fixing $\mathbf{h}$ to a constant vector of $(1, ..., 1)$, we can exactly recover the FM model[2].

[2]Note that for NFM-0, a trainable $\mathbf{h}$ can not improve the expressiveness of FM, since its impact on prediction can be absorbed into feature embeddings.

It is worth pointing out that, to our knowledge, this is the first time FM has been expressed under the neural network framework. While a recent work by Blondel *et al.* [4] has unified FM and Polynomial network via kernelization, their kernel view of FM only provides a new training algorithm and does not provide insight for improving the FM model. Our new view of FM is highly instructive and provides more insight for improving FM. Particularly, we allow the use of various neural network techniques on FM to improve its learning and generalization ability. For example, we can use dropout [33] — a well-known technique in deep learning community to prevent overfitting — on the Bi-Interaction layer as a way to regularize FM, which we find can be even more effective than the conventional L_2 regularization (see Figure 3 of Section 4).

3.1.2 ***Relation to Wide&Deep and DeepCross.*** NFM has a similar multi-layered neural architecture with several existing deep learning solutions [9, 16, 31]. The key difference is in the Bi-Interaction pooling component, which is uniquely used in NFM. Specifically, if we replace the Bi-Interaction pooling with concatenation and apply a tower-structure MLP (or residual units [14]) to hidden layers, we can recover the Wide&Deep (or DeepCross) model. An obvious limitation of the concatenation operation is that it does not account for any interaction between features. As such, these deep learning approaches have to rely entirely on the following deep layers to learn meaningful feature interactions, which unfortunately can be difficult to train in practice (*cf.* Section 2.2.1). Our use of Bi-Interaction pooling captures second-order feature interactions in the low level, which is more informative than the concatenation operation. This greatly facilitates the subsequent hidden layers of NFM to learn useful higher-order feature interactions in a much easier way.

3.1.3 ***Time Complexity Analysis.*** We have shown in Equation (4) that Bi-Interaction pooling can be efficiently computed in $O(kN_x)$ time, which is the same as FM. Then the additional costs are caused by the hidden layers. For hidden layer l, the matrix-vector multiplication is the main operation which can be done in $O(d_{l-1}d_l)$, where d_l denotes the dimension of the l-th hidden layer and $d_0 = k$. The prediction layer only involves inner product of two vectors, for which the complexity is $O(d_L)$. As such, the overall time complexity for evaluating a NFM model is $O(kN_x + \sum_{l=1}^{L} d_{l-1}d_l)$, which is the same as that of Wide&Deep and DeepCross.

3.2 Learning

NFM can be applied to a variety of prediction tasks, including regression, classification and ranking. To estimate model parameters of NFM, we need to specify an objective function to optimize. For regression, a commonly used objective function is the squared loss:

$$L_{reg} = \sum_{\mathbf{x} \in \mathcal{X}} (\hat{y}(\mathbf{x}) - y(\mathbf{x}))^2, \tag{9}$$

where $\mathcal{X}$ denotes the set of instances for training, and $y(\mathbf{x})$ denotes the target of instance $\mathbf{x}$. The regularization terms are optional and omitted here, since we found that some techniques in neural network modelling such as dropout can well prevent NFM from overfitting. For classification task, we can optimize the hinge loss or log loss [16]. For ranking task, we can optimize pairwise personalized ranking loss [29, 37] or contrastive max-margin loss [43]. In this work, we focus on the regression task and optimize the squared loss of Equation (9). The optimization for ranking/classification tasks can be done in the same way.

Stochastic gradient descent (SGD) is a universal solver for optimizing neural network models. It iteratively updates the parameters until convergence. In each time, it randomly selects a training instance $\mathbf{x}$, updating each model parameter towards the direction of its negative gradient:

$$\theta = \theta - \eta \cdot 2(\hat{y}(\mathbf{x}) - y(\mathbf{x}))\frac{d\hat{y}(\mathbf{x})}{d\theta}, \tag{10}$$

where $\theta \in \Theta$ is a trainable model parameter, and $\eta > 0$ is the learning rate that controls the step size of gradient descent. As NFM is a multi-layered neural network model, the gradient of $\hat{y}(\mathbf{x})$ *w.r.t.* to each model parameter can be derived using the chain rule. Here we give only the differentiation of the Bi-Interaction pooling layer, since other layers are just standard operations in neural network modelling and have been widely implemented in ML toolkits like TensorFlow and Keras.

$$\frac{df_{BI}(\mathcal{V}_x)}{d\mathbf{v}_i} = (\sum_{j=1}^{n} x_j\mathbf{v}_j)x_i - x_i^2\mathbf{v}_i = \sum_{j=1, j\neq i}^{n} x_i x_j \mathbf{v}_j. \tag{11}$$

As such, for end-to-end neural methods, upon plugging in the Bi-Interaction pooling layer, they can still be learned end-to-end. To leverage the vectorization and parallelism speedup of modern computing platforms, mini-batch SGD is more widely used in practice, which samples a batch of training instances and updates model parameters based on the batch. In our implementation, we use mini-batch Adagrad [10] as the optimizer, rather than the vanilla SGD. Its main advantage is that the learning rate can be self adapted during the training phase, which eases the pain of choosing a proper learning rate and leads to faster convergence than the vanilla SGD.

3.2.1 ***Dropout.*** While neural network models have strong representation ability, they are also easy to overfit the training data. Dropout [33] is a regularization technique for neural networks to prevent overfitting. The idea is to randomly drop neurons (along with their connections) of the neural network during training. That is, in each parameter update, only part of the model parameters that contributes to the prediction of $\hat{y}(\mathbf{x})$ will be updated. Through this process, it can prevent complex co-adaptations of neurons on training data. It is important to note that in the testing phase, dropout must be disabled and the whole network is used for estimating $\hat{y}(\mathbf{x})$. As such, dropout can also be seen as performing model averaging with smaller neural networks [33].

In NFM, to avoid feature embeddings co-adapt to each other and overfit the data, we propose to adopt dropout on the Bi-Interaction layer. Specifically, after obtaining $f_{BI}(\mathcal{V}_x)$ which is a k-dimensional vector of latent factors, we randomly drop ρ percent of latent factors, where ρ is termed as the dropout ratio. Since NFM with no hidden layer degrades to the FM model, it can be seen as a new way to regularize FM. Moreover, we also apply dropout on each hidden layer of NFM to prevent the learning of higher-order feature interactions from co-adaptations and overfitting.

3.2.2 ***Batch Normalization.*** One difficulty of training multi-layered neural networks is caused by the fact of covariance shift [20]. It means that the distribution of each layer's inputs changes during training, as the parameters of the previous layers change. As a result, the later layer needs to adapt to these changes (which are often noisy) when updating its parameters, which adversely slows down the training. To address the problem, Ioffe and Szegedy [20] proposed *batch normalization* (BN), which normalizes layer inputs to a zero-mean unit-variance Gaussian distribution for each training mini-batch. It has been shown that BN leads to faster convergence and better performance in several computer vision tasks [14, 42].

Formally, let the input vector to a layer be $\mathbf{x}_i \in \mathbb{R}^d$ and all input vectors to the layer of the mini-batch be $\mathcal{B} = \{\mathbf{x}_i\}$, then BN normalizes $\mathbf{x}_i$ as:

$$BN(\mathbf{x}_i) = \gamma \odot (\frac{\mathbf{x}_i - \mu_B}{\sigma_B}) + \beta, \tag{12}$$

where $\mu_B = \frac{1}{|\mathcal{B}|}\sum_{i\in\mathcal{B}}\mathbf{x}_i$ denotes the mini-batch mean, $\sigma_B^2 = \frac{1}{|\mathcal{B}|}\sum_{i\in\mathcal{B}}(\mathbf{x}_i - \mu_B)^2$ denotes the mini-batch variance, and γ and β are trainable parameters (vectors) to scale and shift the normalized value to restore the representation power of the network. Note that in testing, BN also needs to be applied, where μ_B and σ_B are estimated from the whole training data.

In NFM, to avoid the update of feature embeddings changing the input distribution to hidden layers or prediction layer, we perform BN on the output of the Bi-Interaction pooling. For each successive hidden layer, the BN is also applied.

4 EXPERIMENTS

As the key contributions of this work are on Bi-Interaction pooling in neural network modelling and the design of NFM for sparse data prediction, we conduct experiments to answer the following research questions:

- **RQ1** Can Bi-Interaction pooling effectively capture the second-order feature interactions? How does dropout and batch normalization work for Bi-Interaction pooling?
- **RQ2** Are hidden layers of NFM useful for capturing higher-order interactions between features and improving the expressiveness of FM?
- **RQ3** How does NFM perform as compared to higher-order FM and the state-of-the-art deep learning methods Wide&Deep and DeepCross?

In what follows, we first present the experimental settings, followed by answering the above research questions one by one.

4.1 Experimental Settings

4.1.1 ***Datasets.*** We experimented with two publicly accessible datasets: Frappe[3] and MovieLens[4]:

1. Frappe. Frappé is a context-aware app discovery tool. This dataset is constructed by Baltrunas *et al.* [1]. It contains 96, 203 app usage logs of users under different contexts. Besides user ID and app ID, each log contains 8 context variables, including weather, city and daytime (*e.g.*, morning or afternoon). We converted each log (*i.e.*, user ID, app ID and all context variables) to a feature vector using one-hot encoding, resulting in 5, 382 features in total. A target value of 1 means the user has used the app under the context.

[3] http://baltrunas.info/research-menu/frappe

[4] http://grouplens.org/datasets/movielens/latest

Table 1: Statistics of the evaluation datasets.

Dataset	Instance#	Feature#	User#	Item#
Frappe	288,609	5, 382	957	4,082
MovieLens	2,006,859	90, 445	17,045	23,743

2. MovieLens. This is the *Full* version of the latest MovieLens data published by GroupLens [13]. As this work concerns higher-order interactions between features, we study the task of personalized tag recommendation rather than collaborative filtering [16] that considers the second-order interactions only. The tagging part of the data includes 668, 953 tag applications of 17, 045 users on 23, 743 items with 49, 657 distinct tags. We converted each tag application (*i.e.*, user ID, movie ID and tag) to a feature vector, resulting in 90, 445 features in total. A target value of 1 means the user has assigned the tag to the movie.

As both original datasets contain positive instances only (*i.e.*, all instances have target value 1), we sampled two negative instances to pair with one positive instance to ensure the generalization of the predictive model. For each log of Frappe, we randomly sampled two apps that the user has not used in the context; for each tag application of MovieLens, we randomly sampled two tags that the user has not assigned to the movie. Each negative instance is assigned to a target value of −1. Table 1 summarizes the statistics of the final evaluation datasets.

4.1.2 ***Evaluation Protocols.*** We randomly split the dataset into training (70%), validation (20%), and test (10%) sets. The validation set was used for tuning hyper-parameters and the final performance comparison was conducted on the test set. The study of NFM properties (*i.e.*, the answering of RQ1 and RQ2) was performed on the validation set, which can also reflect how we choose the optimal hyper-parameters. To evaluate the performance, we adopted *root mean square error* (RMSE), where a lower RMSE score indicates a better performance. Note that RMSE has been widely used for evaluating regression tasks such as recommendation with explicit ratings [5, 30] and click-through rate prediction [24]. We rounded up the prediction of each model to 1 or −1 if it was out of the range. The one-sample paired t-test was performed to judge the statistical significance where necessary.

4.1.3 ***Baselines.*** We implemented NFM using TensorFlow[5]. We compared with the following competitive embedding-based models that are specifically designed for sparse data prediction:

- **LibFM** [28]. This is the official implementation[6] of FM released by Rendle. It has shown strong performance for personalized tag recommendation and context-aware prediction [30]. We used the SGD learner for a fair comparison with other methods which were all optimized with SGD (or its variants).

- **HOFM**. This is the TensorFlow implementation[7] of higher-order FM, as described in [27]. We experimented with order size 3, since the MovieLens data concerns the ternary relationship between users, movies and tags.

- **Wide&Deep** [9]. As introduced in Section 2.2, the deep part first concatenates feature embeddings, followed by a MLP to model

[5] Codes are available at https://github.com/hexiangnan/neural_factorization_machine

[6] http://www.libfm.org/

[7] https://github.com/geffy/tffm

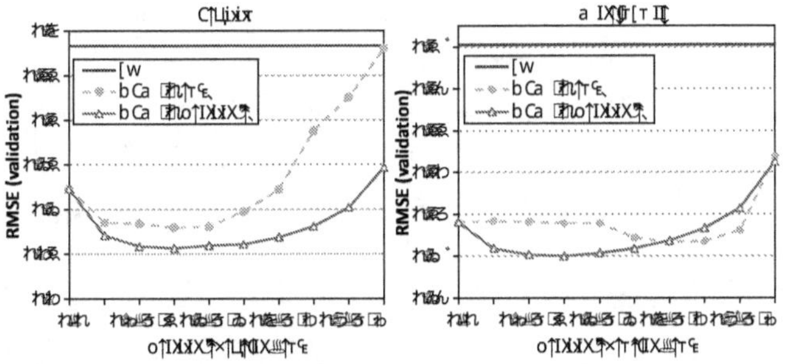

Figure 3: Validation error of NFM-0 *w.r.t.* dropout on the Bi-Interaction layer and L_2 regularization on embeddings.

feature interactions. As the structure of a DNN is difficult to be fully tuned, we used the same structure as reported in their paper, which has three layers with size 1024, 512 and 256, respectively. While the wide part (which is a linear regression model) is subjected to design to incorporate cross features, we used the raw features only for a fair comparison with FM and NFM.

- **DeepCross** [31]. It applies a multi-layered residual network on the concatenation of feature embeddings for learning feature interactions. We used the same structure as reported in their paper, which stacks 5 residual units (each unit has two layers) with the hidden dimension 512, 512, 256, 128 and 64, respectively.

4.1.4 ***Parameter Settings.*** To fairly compare models' capability, we learned all models by optimizing the square loss (Equation (9)). The learning rate was searched in [0.005, 0.01, 0.02, 0.05] for all methods. To prevent overfitting, we tuned the L_2 regularization for linear models LibFM and HOFM in $[1e^{-6}, 5e^{-6}, 1e^{-5}, ..., 1e^{-1}]$, and the dropout ratio for neural network models Wide&Deep, DeepCross and NFM in $[0, 0.1, 0.2, ..., 0.9]$. Note that we found that dropout can well regularize the hidden layers of Wide&Deep and NFM; however it did not work well for the residual units of DeepCross. Besides LibFM that optimized FM with the vanilla SGD, all other methods were optimized with mini-batch Adagrad [10], where the batch size was set to 128 for Frappe and 4096 for MovieLens. Note that the batch size was selected by considering both training time and convergence rate, as a larger batch size usually led to faster training per epoch but slower convergence. For all methods, the early stopping strategy was performed, where we stopped training if the RMSE on validation set increased for 4 successive epochs. Without special mention, we show the results of embedding size 64, and more results of larger embedding sizes are shown in Section 4.4.

4.2 Study of Bi-Interaction Pooling (RQ1)

We empirically study the Bi-Interaction pooling operation. To avoid other components (*e.g.*, hidden layers) affecting the analysis, we study the NFM-0 model that directly projects the output of Bi-Interaction pooling to prediction score with no hidden layer. As discussed in Section 3.1.1, NFM-0 is identical to FM as the trainable **h** does not impact model's expressiveness. We first compare dropout with traditional L_2 regularization for preventing model overfitting, and then explore the impact of batch normalization.

4.2.1 ***Dropout Improves Generalization.*** Figure 3 shows the validation error of NFM-0 *w.r.t.* dropout ratio on the Bi-Interaction layer and L_2 regularization on feature embeddings. The performance of linear regression (LR) is also shown for benchmarking the performance of prediction that does not consider feature interactions. First, LR leads to very poor performance, highlighting the importance of modelling interactions between sparse features for prediction. Second, we see that both L_2 regularization and dropout can well prevent overfitting and improve NFM-0's generalization to unseen data. Between the two strategies, dropout offers better performance. Specifically, on Frappe, using a dropout ratio of 0.3 leads to a lowest validation error of 0.3562, which is significantly better than that of L_2 regularization 0.3799. One reason might be that enforcing L_2 regularization only suppresses the values of parameters in each update numerically, while using dropout can be seen as ensembling multiple sub-models [33], which can be more effective. Considering the genericity of FM that subsumes many factorization models, we believe this is a new interesting finding, meaning that dropout can also be an effective strategy to address overfitting of linear latent-factor models.

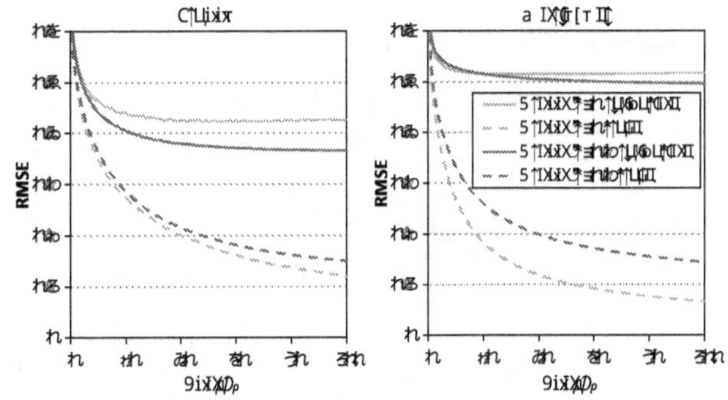

Figure 4: Training and validation error of each epoch of NFM-0 with and without dropout on Bi-Interaction layer.

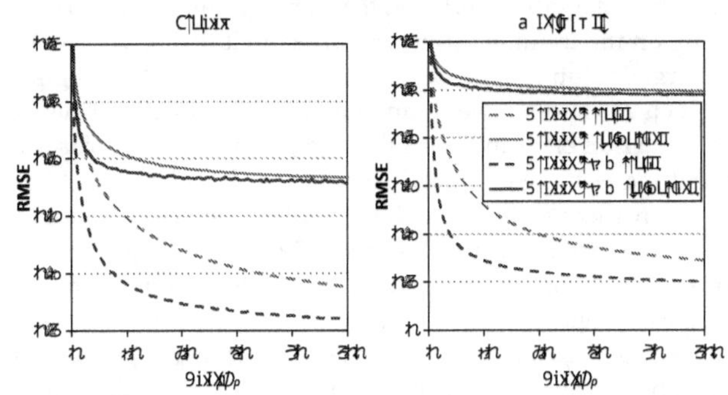

Figure 5: Training and validation error of each epoch of NFM-0 with and without BN on the Bi-Interaction layer.

To be more clear about the effect of dropout, we show the training and validation error of each epoch of NFM-0 with and without dropout in Figure 4. Both datasets show that with a dropout ratio of 0.3, although the training error is higher, the validation error becomes lower. This demonstrates the ability of dropout in preventing overfitting and as such, better generalization can be achieved.

4.2.2 ***Batch Normalization Speeds up Training.*** Figure 5 shows the training and validation error of each epoch of NFM-0 with and without BN on the Bi-Interaction layer. The dropout is

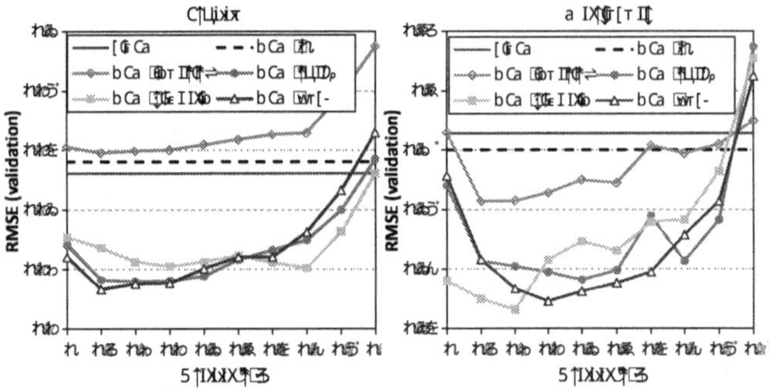

Figure 6: Validation error of LibFM, NFM-0 and NFM with different activation functions on the first hidden layer.

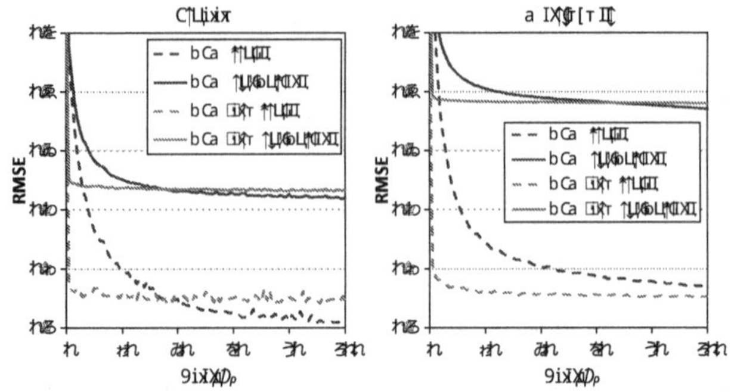

Figure 7: Training and validation error of each epoch of NFM-1 with and without pre-training.

enabled with a ratio of 0.3, and the learning rate is set to 0.02. Focusing on the training error, we can see that BN leads to a faster convergence; on Frappe, when BN is applied, the training error of epoch 20 is even lower than that of epoch 60 without BN; and the validation error indicates that the lower training error is not overfitting — in fact, [14, 20] showed that by addressing the internal covariate shift with BN, the model's generalization ability can be improved. Our result also verifies this point, where using BN leads to slight improvement (although the improvement is not statistically significant). Furthermore, we notice that BN makes the learning less stable, as evidenced by the larger performance fluctuation of blue lines. This is caused by our use of dropout and BN together, as randomly dropping neurons can change the input distribution normalized by BN. It is an interesting direction to effectively combine BN and dropout.

4.3 Impact of Hidden Layers (RQ2)

The hidden layers of NFM play a pivotal role in capturing higher-order interactions between features. To explore the impact, we first add one hidden layer above the Bi-Interaction layer and slightly overuse the name NFM to indicate this specific model. To ensure the same model capability with NFM-0, we set the size of hidden layer the same as the embedding size.

Figure 6 shows the validation error of NFM *w.r.t.* different activation functions and dropout ratios for the hidden layer. The performance of LibFM and NFM-0 are also shown for benchmarking purposes. First and foremost, we observe that by using non-linear activations, NFM's performance is improved with a large margin — compared to NFM-0 which has a similar performance with LibFM, the relative improvement is 11.3% and 5.2% for Frappe and MovieLens, respectively. This highlights the importance of modelling higher-order feature interactions for quality prediction. Among the different non-linear activation functions, there is no obvious winner. Second, when we use the identity function as the activation function, *i.e.*, the hidden layer performs a linear transformation, NFM does not perform that well. This provides evidence to the necessity of learning higher-order feature interactions with non-linear functions.

To see whether a deeper NFM can further improve the performance, we stack more ReLU layers above the Bi-Interaction layer. As it is computationally expensive to tune the size and dropout ratio for each hidden layer separately, we use the same setting for all layers and tune them the same way as NFM-1. As can be seen from Table 2, when we stack more layers, the performance is not further improved, and best performance is when we use one hidden layer only. We have also explored other designs for hidden layers, such as the tower structure and residual units, however, the performance is still not improved. We think the reason is because the Bi-Interaction layer has encoded informative second-order feature interactions, and based on which, a simple non-linear function is sufficient to capture higher-order interactions. To verify this, we replaced the Bi-Interaction layer with concatenation (which leads to the same architecture as Wide&Deep), and found that the performance can be gradually improved with more hidden layers (up to three); however, the best performance achievable is still inferior to that of NFM-1. This demonstrates the value of using a more informative operation for low-level layers, which can ease the burden of higher-level layers for learning meaningful information. As a result, a deep structure becomes not necessarily required.

Table 2: NFM *w.r.t.* different number of hidden layers.

Methods	Frappe	MovieLens
NFM-0	0.3562	0.4901
NFM-1	**0.3133**	**0.4646**
NFM-2	0.3193	0.4681
NFM-3	0.3219	0.4752
NFM-4	0.3202	0.4703

4.3.1 ***Pre-training Speeds up Training.*** It is known that parameter initialization can greatly affect the convergence and performance of DNNs [11, 16], since gradient-based methods can only find local optima for DNNs. As have been shown in Section 2.2.1, initializing with feature embeddings learned by FM can significantly enhance Wide&Deep and DeepCross. Now the question arises, how does pre-training impact NFM?

Figure 7 shows the state of each epoch of NFM-1 with and without pre-training. First, we can see that by using FM embeddings as pre-training, NFM exhibits extremely fast convergence — on both datasets, with 5 epochs only, the performance is on par with 40 epochs of NFM that is trained from scratch (with BN enabled). Second, we find that pre-training does not improve NFM's final performance, and a random initialization can achieve a result that is slightly better than that with pre-training. This demonstrates the robustness of NFM, which is relatively insensitive to parameter initialization. In contrast to the huge impact of pre-training on Wide&Deep and DeepCross (*cf.* Figure 1) that improves both their convergence and final performance, we draw the conclusion that

Table 3: Test error and number of trainable parameters for different methods on latent factors 128 and 256. M denotes "million"; * and ** denote the statistical significance for $p < 0.05$ and $p < 0.01$, respectively, compared to the best baseline.

	Frappe				MovieLens			
	Factors=128		Factors=256		Factors=128		Factors=256	
Method	Param#	RMSE	Param#	RMSE	Param#	RMSE	Param#	RMSE
LibFM [28]	0.69M	0.3437	1.38M	0.3385	11.67M	0.4793	23.24M	0.4735
HOFM	1.38M	0.3405	2.76M	0.3331	23.24M	0.4752	46.40M	0.4636
Wide&Deep [9]	2.66M	0.3621	4.66M	0.3661	12.72M	0.5323	24.69M	0.5313
Wide&Deep (pre-train)	2.66M	0.3311	4.66M	0.3246	12.72M	0.4595	24.69M	0.4512
DeepCross [31]	4.47M	0.4025	8.93M	0.4071	12.71M	0.5885	25.42M	0.5907
DeepCross (pre-train)	4.47M	0.3388	8.93M	0.3548	12.71M	0.5084	25.42M	0.5130
NFM	**0.71M**	**0.3127****	**1.45M**	**0.3095****	**11.68M**	**0.4557***	**23.31M**	**0.4443***

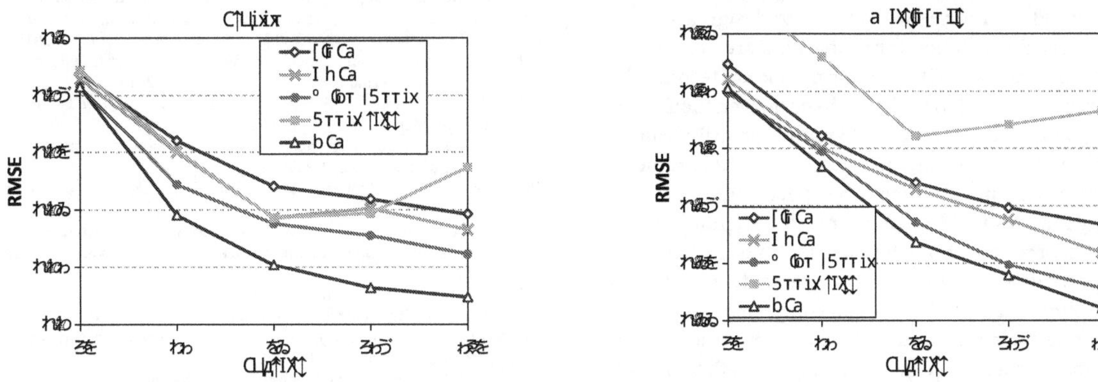

Figure 8: Performance comparison on the test set *w.r.t.* different embedding sizes. LibFM, HOFM and HOFM are trained from random initialization; Wide&Deep and DeepCross are pre-trained with FM feature embeddings.

NFM is much easier to train and optimize, which is due largely to the informative and effective Bi-Interaction pooling operation.

4.4 Performance Comparison (RQ3)

We now compare with state-of-the-art methods. For NFM, we use one hidden layer with ReLU as the activation function, since the baselines DeepCross and Wide&Deep also choose ReLU in their original papers. Note that the most important hyper-parameter for NFM is the dropout ratio, which we use 0.5 for the Bi-Interaction layer and tune the value for the hidden layer.

Figure 8 plots the test RMSE *w.r.t.* different number of latent factors (*i.e.,* embedding sizes), where Wide&Deep and DeepCross are pre-trained with FM to better explore the two methods. Table 3 shows the concrete scores obtained on factors 128 and 256, and the number of model parameters of each method. The scores of Wide&Deep and DeepCross without pre-training are also shown. We have the following three key observations.

First and foremost, NFM consistently achieves the best performance on both datasets with the fewest model parameters besides FM. This demonstrates the effectiveness and rationality of NFM in modelling higher-order and non-linear feature interactions for prediction with sparse data. The performance is followed by Wide&Deep, which uses a 3-layer MLP to learn feature interactions. We have also tried deeper layers for Wide&Deep, however the performance has not been improved. This further verifies the utility of using the informative Bi-Interaction pooling in the low level.

Second, we observe that HOFM shows slight improvement over FM with 1.45% and 1.04% average improvement on Frappe and MovieLens, respectively. This sheds light on the limitation of FM that models only the second-order feature interactions, and thus the usefulness of modelling higher-order interactions. Meanwhile, the large performance gap between HOFM and NFM reflects the value of modelling higher-order interactions in a non-linear way, since HOFM models higher-order interactions linearly and uses much more parameters than NFM.

Lastly, the relatively weak performance of DeepCross reveals that deeper learnings are not always better, as DeepCross is the deepest method among all baselines that utilizes a 10-layer network. On Frappe, DeepCross only achieves a comparable performance with the shallow FM model, while it underperforms FM significantly on MovieLens. We believe that the reasons are due to optimization difficulties and overfitting (as evidenced by the worse performance on factors 128 and 256).

5 CONCLUSION AND FUTURE WORK

In this work, we proposed a novel neural network model NFM, which brings together the effectiveness of linear factorization machines with the strong representation ability of non-linear neural networks for sparse predictive analytics. The key of NFM's architecture is the newly proposed Bi-Interaction operation, based on which we allow a neural network model to learn more informative feature interactions at the lower level. Extensive experiments on two real-world datasets show that with one hidden layer only, NFM significantly outperforms FM, higher-order FM, and state-of-the-art deep learning approaches Wide&Deep and DeepCross.

The work represents the first step towards bridging the gap between linear models and deep learning. Linear models, such as various factorization methods, have shown to be effective for many IR and DM tasks and are easy to interpret. However, their limited expressiveness may hinder the performance when modelling real-world data with complex inherent patterns. While deep learning models have exhibited great expressive power and yielded immense success on speech processing and computer vision, their performance is still unsatisfactory for IR tasks, such as collaborative filtering [16]. In our view, one reason is that most data of IR and DM tasks are naturally sparse; and to date, there still lacks effective deep learning solutions for prediction with sparse data. By connecting neural networks with FM — one of the most powerful linear models for supervised learning — we are able to design a simple yet effective deep learning solution for sparse data prediction.

With recent developments on GPU platforms, it is not technically difficult to build very deep models with hundreds or even thousands of layers [14]. However, deeper models do not necessarily lead to better results, since deeper models are less transparent and more difficult to optimize and tune. As such, we expect future research on deep learning for IR should focus more on designing better neural components or architectures for specific tasks, rather than relying on deeper models for minor improvements. Our proposed Bi-Interaction pooling is an effective neural component for sparse feature modelling, reducing the demand for deeper structure for quality prediction. In future, we will improve the efficiency of NFM by resorting to hashing techniques [32, 41] to make it more suitable for large-scale applications and study its performance for other IR tasks, such as search ranking and targeted advertising. While this work endows FM with non-linearities from predictive model perspective, another viable solution for incorporating non-linearities is to extend the objective function with regularizers like the graph Laplacian [15, 34]. Lastly, we are interested in exploring the Bi-Interaction pooling for recurrent neural networks (RNNs) for sequential data modelling.

REFERENCES

[1] L. Baltrunas, K. Church, A. Karatzoglou, and N. Oliver. Frappe: Understanding the usage and perception of mobile app recommendations in-the-wild. *CoRR*, abs/1505.03014, 2015.

[2] I. Bayer, X. He, B. Kanagal, and S. Rendle. A generic coordinate descent framework for learning from implicit feedback. In *WWW*, 2017.

[3] M. Blondel, A. Fujino, N. Ueda, and M. Ishihata. Higher-order factorization machines. In *NIPS*, 2016.

[4] M. Blondel, M. Ishihata, A. Fujino, and N. Ueda. Polynomial networks and factorization machines: New insights and efficient training algorithms. In *ICML*, 2016.

[5] D. Cao, X. He, L. Nie, X. Wei, X. Hu, S. Wu, and T.-S. Chua. Cross-platform app recommendation by jointly modeling ratings and texts. *ACM TOIS*, 2017.

[6] J. Chen, B. Sun, H. Li, H. Lu, and X.-S. Hua. Deep ctr prediction in display advertising. In *MM*, 2016.

[7] J. Chen, H. Zhang, X. He, L. Nie, W. Liu, and T.-S. Chua. Attentive collaborative filtering: Multimedia recommendation with feature- and item-level attention. In *SIGIR*, 2017.

[8] T. Chen, X. He, and M.-Y. Kan. Context-aware image tweets modelling and recommendation. In *MM*, 2016.

[9] H.-T. Cheng, L. Koc, J. Harmsen, T. Shaked, T. Chandra, H. Aradhye, G. Anderson, G. Corrado, W. Chai, M. Ispir, R. Anil, Z. Haque, L. Hong, V. Jain, X. Liu, and H. Shah. Wide & deep learning for recommender systems. In *DLRS*, 2016.

[10] J. Duchi, E. Hazan, and Y. Singer. Adaptive subgradient methods for online learning and stochastic optimization. *Journal of Machine Learning Research*, 2011.

[11] D. Erhan, Y. Bengio, A. Courville, P.-A. Manzagol, P. Vincent, and S. Bengio. Why does unsupervised pre-training help deep learning? *Journal of Machine Learning Research*, 2010.

[12] M. Genzel and G. Kutyniok. A mathematical framework for feature selection from real-world data with non-linear observations. *arXiv preprint arXiv:1608.08852*, 2016.

[13] F. M. Harper and J. A. Konstan. The movielens datasets: History and context. *ACM Transactions on Interactive Intelligent Systems*, 2015.

[14] K. He, X. Zhang, S. Ren, and J. Sun. Deep residual learning for image recognition. In *CVPR*, 2016.

[15] X. He, M. Gao, M.-Y. Kan, Y. Liu, and K. Sugiyama. Predicting the popularity of web 2.0 items based on user comments. In *SIGIR*, 2014.

[16] X. He, L. Liao, H. Zhang, L. Nie, X. Hu, and T.-S. Chua. Neural collaborative filtering. In *WWW*, 2017.

[17] X. He, H. Zhang, M.-Y. Kan, and T.-S. Chua. Fast matrix factorization for online recommendation with implicit feedback. In *SIGIR*, 2016.

[18] L. Hong, A. S. Doumith, and B. D. Davison. Co-factorization machines: Modeling user interests and predicting individual decisions in twitter. In *WSDM*, 2013.

[19] R. Hong, Y. Yang, M. Wang, and X.-S. Hua. Learning visual semantic relationships for efficient visual retrieval. *IEEE Transactions on Big Data*, 2015.

[20] S. Ioffe and C. Szegedy. Batch normalization: Accelerating deep network training by reducing internal covariate shift. In *ICML*, 2015.

[21] Y. Juan, Y. Zhuang, W.-S. Chin, and C.-J. Lin. Field-aware factorization machines for ctr prediction. In *RecSys*, 2016.

[22] Y. Koren. Factorization meets the neighborhood: A multifaceted collaborative filtering model. In *KDD*, 2008.

[23] A. Novikov, M. Trofimov, and I. Oseledets. Exponential machines. In *ICLR Workshop*, 2017.

[24] R. J. Oentaryo, E.-P. Lim, J.-W. Low, D. Lo, and M. Finegold. Predicting response in mobile advertising with hierarchical importance-aware factorization machine. In *WSDM*, 2014.

[25] F. Petroni, L. Del Corro, and R. Gemulla. Core: Context-aware open relation extraction with factorization machines. In *EMNLP*, 2015.

[26] R. Qiang, F. Liang, and J. Yang. Exploiting ranking factorization machines for microblog retrieval. In *CIKM*, 2013.

[27] S. Rendle. Factorization machines. In *ICDM*, 2010.

[28] S. Rendle. Factorization machines with libfm. *ACM Transactions on Intelligent Systems and Technology*, 2012.

[29] S. Rendle, C. Freudenthaler, Z. Gantner, and L. Schmidt-Thieme. Bpr: Bayesian personalized ranking from implicit feedback. In *UAI*, 2009.

[30] S. Rendle, Z. Gantner, C. Freudenthaler, and L. Schmidt-Thieme. Fast context-aware recommendations with factorization machines. In *SIGIR*, 2011.

[31] Y. Shan, T. R. Hoens, J. Jiao, H. Wang, D. Yu, and J. Mao. Deep crossing: Web-scale modeling without manually crafted combinatorial features. In *KDD*, 2016.

[32] F. Shen, Y. Mu, Y. Yang, W. Liu, L. Liu, J. Song, and H. T. Shen. Classification by retrieval: Binarizing data and classifier. In *SIGIR*, 2017.

[33] N. Srivastava, G. E. Hinton, A. Krizhevsky, I. Sutskever, and R. Salakhutdinov. Dropout: a simple way to prevent neural networks from overfitting. *Journal of Machine Learning Research*, 2014.

[34] M. Wang, W. Fu, S. Hao, D. Tao, and X. Wu. Scalable semi-supervised learning by efficient anchor graph regularization. *IEEE Transaction on Knowledge and Data Engineering*, 2016.

[35] M. Wang, X. Liu, and X. Wu. Visual classification by l1-hypergraph modeling. *IEEE Transaction on Knowledge and Data Engineering*, 2015.

[36] P. Wang, J. Guo, Y. Lan, J. Xu, S. Wan, and X. Cheng. Learning hierarchical representation model for nextbasket recommendation. In *SIGIR*, 2015.

[37] X. Wang, X. He, L. Nie, and T.-S. Chua. Item silk road: Recommending items from information domains to social users. In *SIGIR*, 2017.

[38] J. Xiao, H. Ye, X. He, H. Zhang, F. Wu, and T.-S. Chua. Attentional factorization machines: Learning the weight of feature interactions via attention networks. In *IJCAI*, 2017.

[39] C. Xiong, J. Callan, and T.-Y. Liu. Learning to attend and to rank with word-entity duets. In *SIGIR*, 2017.

[40] C. Zhang, G. Zhou, Q. Yuan, H. Zhuang, Y. Zheng, L. Kaplan, S. Wang, and J. Han. Geoburst: Real-time local event detection in geo-tagged tweet streams. In *SIGIR*, 2016.

[41] H. Zhang, F. Shen, W. Liu, X. He, H. Luan, and T.-S. Chua. Discrete collaborative filtering. In *SIGIR*, 2016.

[42] H. Zhang, M. Wang, R. Hong, and T.-S. Chua. Play and rewind: Optimizing binary representations of videos by self-supervised temporal hashing. In *MM*, 2016.

[43] H. Zhang, Z.-J. Zha, Y. Yang, S. Yan, Y. Gao, and T.-S. Chua. Attribute-augmented semantic hierarchy: Towards bridging semantic gap and intention gap in image retrieval. In *MM*, 2013.

[44] W. Zhang, T. Du, and J. Wang. Deep learning over multi-field categorical data. In *ECIR*, 2016.

Accounting for the Correspondence in Commented Data

Renqin Cai
rc7ne@virginia.edu
University of Virginia
Department of Computer Science
Charlottesville, VA 22904, USA

Chi Wang
chiw@microsoft.com
Microsoft Research
Redmond, WA 98052, USA

Hongning Wang
hw5x@virginia.edu
University of Virginia
Department of Computer Science
Charlottesville, VA 22904, USA

ABSTRACT

One important way for people to make their voice heard is to comment on the articles they have read online, such as news reports and blogs. The user-generated comments together with the commented documents form a unique *correspondence* structure. Properly modeling the dependency in such data is thus vital for one to obtain accurate insight of people's opinions and attention.

In this work, we develop a Commented Correspondence Topic Model to model correspondence in commented text data. We focus on two levels of correspondence. First, to capture topic-level correspondence, we treat the topic assignments in commented documents as the prior to their comments' topic proportions. This captures the thematic dependency between commented documents and their comments. Second, to capture word-level correspondence, we utilize the Dirichlet compound multinomial distribution to model topics. This captures the word repetition patterns within the commented data. By integrating these two aspects, our model demonstrated encouraging performance in capturing the correspondence structure, which provides improved results in modeling user-generated content, spam comment detection, and sentence-based comment retrieval compared with state-of-the-art topic model solutions for correspondence modeling.

CCS CONCEPTS

•**Information systems** →**Document topic models;** *Web mining;* •**Computing methodologies** →*Learning in probabilistic graphical models;*

KEYWORDS

Topic models; text correspondence modeling; social media; user comments

ACM Reference format:
Renqin Cai, Chi Wang, and Hongning Wang. 2017. Accounting for the Correspondence in Commented Data. In *Proceedings of SIGIR'17, August 7-11, 2017, Shinjuku, Tokyo, Japan.*, 10 pages.
DOI: http://dx.doi.org/10.1145/3077136.3080781

1 INTRODUCTION

Modern news media websites provide commenting facilities for their readers to openly express their attention and opinions on news events. Because of readers' active participation, the user-generated commenting content shapes the general public's opinions by supplementing the news stories with contextual information and new perspectives [21, 27]. However, oftentimes, a popular news article can easily accumulate thousands of comments within a short period of time, which makes it difficult for interested users to access and digest information in such data [17, 26]. Therefore, modeling the user-generated comments with respect to the commented news articles and automatically gaining the insight of readers' opinions and attention on the news event becomes an important research topic in web data mining [7, 11, 24].

SpaceX makes a successful return to flight
ArsTechnica 1/14/2017
Today SpaceX will attempt to launch its Falcon 9 rocket ... The instantaneous launch window for Saturday's attempt opens at 12:54pm ET (17:54pm UK), with liftoff occurring from Space Launch Complex 4E at Vandenberg Air Force Base in California.......Saturday's launch will boost 10 Iridium NEXT satellites to a 625-km orbit. These are the first 10 of 70 next generation satellites that SpaceX will launch for Iridium and its mobile voice and data satellite communications network. After boosting the satellites into space, the first stage of Falcon 9 will attempt a return on the *Just Read the Instructions* droneship in the Pacific Ocean. The webcast should begin about 20 minutes before Saturday's launch window opens.

Comment 1: Those sats are going into polar orbit (in this case I think, it is 89.4 degrees inclination) - so in order to get into right plane, launch has to happen when this orbital plane is passing by launch site (well, a bit earlier to be precise). Otherwise you would need a lot of delta-V to correct for that. That's why launch window is so short.

Comment 2: Usually I watch those webcasts online, but this Saturday, at that time, I will be sailing on SF bay. Internet reception is spotty on a sailboat.

Comment 3: The landing is just good old GPS. The ship holds a position, and the booster heads for the same position. The error in both is of the order of a few metres, which matches with what we see from very slightly off-centre landed rockets.

Figure 1: An example thread of user comments on a news article about SpaceX's rocket launch.

The key to a successful understanding of such user-generated commented data is its intrinsic *correspondence* structure, i.e., readers choose the part of their most interest to comment on, and pass along some perspectives, topics or words from the news articles to their comments. Figure 1 illustrates the correspondence structure in a typical discussion thread of users' comments on a news article. The news article covers details of the rocket's launch (in red color) and return (in blue color), the satellite's orbit and mission, and webcast of the launch. Two concrete examples of correspondence are highlighted in the first and third comment in red and blue respectively. The first user comment provides detailed explanation about why the launch window is so specific and short, and the third comment explains the technique behind rocket return. We can observe that a news article may emphasize some general or objective aspects of an event, while user comments may express more specific, subjective, and supplementary information. If such

SIGIR'17, August 7-11, 2017, Shinjuku, Tokyo, Japan.
© 2017 ACM. 978-1-4503-4887-4/17/08...$15.00
DOI: http://dx.doi.org/10.1145/3077136.3080781

correspondence structure can be automatically identified, it would help users easily retrieve comments related to a particular topic in the article, filter out irrelevant or spam comments, summarize the others' focus and opinions on the news article, and many more.

However, several challenges make the correspondence structure difficult to detect. First, there are salient stylistic and organizational distinctions between these two types of content: news articles are typically well-written and fact-oriented long stories by journalists or professionals, while comments are mostly personalized, more opinionated, and free-style short posts by average readers. The *vocabulary gap* between the news articles and user comments obscures correspondence modeling. For instance, the third comment in Figure 1 talks about the technique of rocket return, but it has almost no word overlapping with the article, as it keeps using the word "land" to explain the rocket "return" technique. Second, readers read the article before making comments, so that the background or context of their commenting content is often enclosed in the article but omitted in the comments. This further enlarges the vocabulary gap. Third, the existence of irrelevant comments further complicates correspondence modeling. For example, in Figure 1, the second comment is barely related to the main theme of the article. It is necessary to distinguish them from other relevant comments.

Researchers have attempted to resolve the first challenge using probabilistic topic modeling technique.

The basic idea of existing solutions roots in the correspondence LDA model (CorrLDA) [3], which was originally designed to model the correspondence between images and their captions. Follow-up work adopted this model as building blocks to capture the correspondence between news articles and comments [7, 17]. However, the CorrLDA-like models do not address the other two challenges discussed above. First, they assume comments' topics are a subset of the article's. This assumption generally holds in image-caption data, as a caption should be a concise summarization of the image. But in article-comment data, comments often cover topics missing in the news article, without mentioning the existence of irrelevant and spam comments. Second, existing solutions postulate that all article-comment threads share a common set of topic-word distributions. Such treatment has limited capability in capturing salient correspondence patterns which vary across threads. For example, in Figure 1, the phrase "*launch window*" from the article repeating in the first comment is a strong signal of topical correspondence, although they may not be the most typical words of that topic in the whole corpus.

In this work, we propose to address these limitations from two perspectives. At the topic level, we generate topic distributions in user comments from an article-specific Dirichlet prior. The prior consists of two parts. One part is from a common hyperparameter shared by all comments, and the other is from the topic distribution of the commented news article. This allows our model to capture the content of comments on both covered and uncovered topics of the article, while accounting for the correspondence. The impact of this prior is naturally adjusted due to the conjugacy between Dirichlet and multinomial distributions, i.e., topic assignments in shorter comments tend to get more influenced from the article, while longer comments tend to develop their own themes.

At the word level, we explicitly model the "burstiness" of word occurrences between article and comments to capture the thread-specific correspondence pattern, i.e., words from the articles repeat in their comments more often than just by chance. To the best of our knowledge, it is the first time that this phenomenon is confirmed in commented data. In particular, we choose the Dirichlet compound multinomial (DCM) distribution [9] to represent topics, capturing the tendency that the same topic manifests itself with different word distributions in different article-comment threads. Since DCM draws multinomial distributions for each article-comment thread from a corpus-wise shared Dirichlet distribution, the local word co-occurrence patterns are still connected to the global topic-word distributions.

Integrating these two new components, we develop Commented Correspondence Topic Model (CCTM). Extensive experiments on two large news archives with user comments confirm the effectiveness of our model: it provides improved results in predicting unseen comments, spam comment detection, and sentence-based comment retrieval compared with state-of-the-art topic model solutions.

2 RELATED WORK

The blooming of social media enables the public to freely express their opinions on various topics [15, 23]. And one typical way is to comment on the online articles. A rich body of research has been done to discover useful knowledge buried in such user-generated commented data for facilitating various information retrieval tasks, including document retrieval, classification, summarization, and so on. Hu et al. [14] selected sentences from articles by computing their similarities to the comments for generating comment-driven news summarization. Tholpadi et al. [25] studied multi-lingual commented data to cluster comments about the same news event across different languages. Park et al. [20] utilized commented app review data to improve app retrieval performance. In general, learning accurate representations of commented data has broad potential to facilitate these information retrieval tasks.

Probabilistic topic models like LDA have achieved great success in modeling unstructured text documents [2]. Formally, a topic is modeled as a probability distribution over terms in a shared vocabulary, and a document is concisely modeled as a mixture over the topics [4, 13]. In standard topic models, the dependency among documents is loosely governed by a globally shared prior over topic distributions, e.g., Dirichlet prior. The correspondence in commented data, such as between news articles and their comments, is not considered in such models.

As an extension to LDA, CorrLDA is desinged to model the correspondence in annotated image data [3]. CorrLDA captures the correspondence structure by enforcing the topics of captions to be uniformly sampled from the topics of the corresponding images. As a result, the topic distributions in these two types of data become dependent. Follow-up research extends this modeling approach to capture correspondence among different types of text documents [10, 17]. In [7], the specific correspondence topic model (SCTM) is proposed, which introduces Dirichlet Process prior [1] into CorrLDA to fit the correspondence between news articles and user comments. However, as restricted by the inherited design from CorrLDA of uniform sampling of topics from news articles to user comments, the choices of topics in comments are strongly

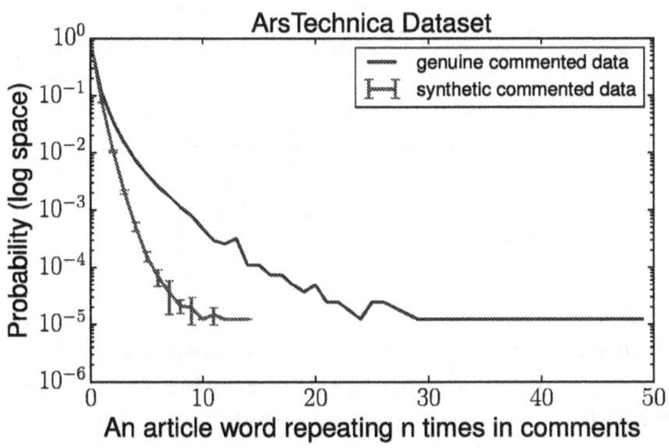

(a) ArshTechinica dataset

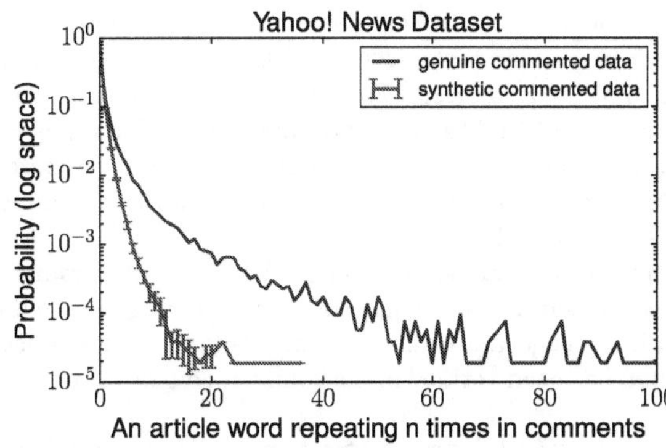

(b) Yahoo! News dataset

Figure 2: Burstiness in commented data. Synthetic comments are sampled from a unigram language model estimated via a maximum likelihood estimator on genuine comments in each data set. The x-axis denotes the frequency of a word in an article's comments if it is observed in the article, and the y-axis denotes the corresponding the probability in log space.

constrained by the existing topics in the articles. To relax this restriction, we consider topic distributions in news articles only as a prior to topic distributions in the corresponding user comments. New topics can therefore be sampled in user comments if there is support. Similar idea has been explored in [20], but they merged all comments into a single document when modeling the correspondence, which loses fine-grained understanding in an individual comment. Furthermore, in all aforementioned solutions, the topics are globally shared among all documents, such that possible vocabulary gap and local correspondence structure cannot be recognized. In our work, we introduce Dirichlet compound multinomial (DCM) distribution [18], replacing the multinomial distribution, to model the topics and capture detailed correspondence in a thread of article and comments.

[6, 16] noticed that the first occurrence of a term in a document increases the probability of its repeated appearances in the same document. This linguistic characteristics is referred as "burstiness." To capture burstiness in a text document, DCM assumes each document is generated from a document-specific multinomial distribution of words, which is drawn from a corpus-wise Dirichlet prior. Intuitively, it postulates a "bag-of-bags-of-words" generative process for documents. DCMLDA [8] extends this modeling approach to model a document as a mixture of DCM. In this work, we further extend the concept of burstiness beyond a single document: we verified that if a word is used once in a news article, it is more likely to be used again in the corresponding user comments. This helps us model local correspondence and align it with global topic distributions. This proves to be important in spam comment detection and sentence-based comment retrieval.

3 METHODOLOGY

In this section, we first state and verify our hypothesis about burstiness of word occurrences in commented news data, and then describe the detailed design of our proposed solution, which explicitly models the topic-level and word-level correspondence. An efficient Gibbs sampler is developed to perform posterior inference, and a stochastic Expectation Maximization algorithm is utilized to estimate the model parameters.

3.1 Burstiness in Commented Data

One of our most important observations in the commented news data is that words appearing in a news article are likely to re-occur in its comments, as users quote from the news articles after reading them. It is analogous to the burstiness of word occurrences in a single document observed in prior research [6, 16]. Importantly, the burstiness of a word and its informativeness are positively correlated: more informative words are more bursty [18].

Formally, we hypothesize that the probability of a word from an article appearing multiple times in its comments is significantly larger than the probability of this word appearing in the comments with the same frequency independently. We verify this hypothesis by the following statistical test. We count the frequency of words in a given commented news corpus to estimate the probability of a word from an article appearing n times in its comments (i.e., maximum likelihood estimation). To estimate the probability of a word from an article *independently* appearing n times in comments, we generate synthetic comments. We first estimate a unigram language model based on all comments in the corpus, and generate synthetic comments for each article by sampling from the language model. In particular, we enforce the synthetic comments to have the same length as the genuine comments. As the words are drawn from a unigram language model, they are independent from each other in the synthetic comments. Then we use the same maximum likelihood estimator to estimate the probability of an article word appearing n times in its synthetic comments. Note that we only count words *already observed* in the articles, and therefore if burstiness exists, it is about the repetition pattern of words from articles in its corresponding comments.

We tested our hypothesis on two large real-world commented corpora, Yahoo! News and ArsTechnica Science blog data set. The detailed descriptions about these two datasets and our preprocessing procedures can be found in the experiment section. We repeated the synthetic data generation procedure for ten times and reported the mean and standard deviation of the estimated probabilities in Figure 2. As we can clearly observe from the results, the probability of a word occurring multiple times in the genuine commented data is significantly larger than that in the synthetic data. Moreover, the maximum frequency of a word repeated in the genuine commented data is much larger than that in synthetic data. These observations indicate the repeated occurrences of words in the commented data are *not* independent, and thus our hypothesis about burstiness of words holds in such data. We should note that we only generated synthetic comments while keeping the genuine news articles intact in both cases for probability estimation.

In addition, as the comments are generally short, the burstiness of article words within each single comment is negligible. To the best of our knowledge, this is the first time that the word burstiness phenomenon has been verified in the commented text data.

3.2 Commented Correspondence Topic Model

In this section, we describe the details about our Commented Correspondence Topic Model (CCTM). As motivated in Section 1, our model integrates two main ideas: topic-level and word-level correspondence modeling.

At the topic level, both articles and comments are modeled as mixtures over K topics, where the mixing proportion θ^a in article a and θ^c in comment c are drawn from their corresponding Dirichlet priors. Accordingly, the topic assignments of words in articles and comments are drawn from those mixing proportions, i.e., $z^a \sim Mul(\theta^a)$ and $z^c \sim Mul(\theta^c)$. The prior distribution for θ^a is shared across all articles in the corpus, i.e., $\theta^a \sim Dir(\alpha^A)$; but CCTM differs from previous models in how θ^c is generated. As we discussed before, the model needs to account for both relevant and irrelevant comments to the article, and allow for both covered and uncovered topics in the article to appear in the comment. For this reason,

we postulate an article-specific Dirichlet prior for θ^c, which takes the topic assignments from the corresponding article as the parameter,

$$\theta^c \sim Dir(\bar{z}^a + \alpha^C) \tag{1}$$

where $\bar{z}^a = \frac{1}{N}\sum_{n=1}^{N} z_n^a$, z_n^a is the topic assignment for n-th word in article a, and α^C is a hyperparameter vector shared by all comments in the corpus. We choose $\bar{z}^a$ rather than θ^a as the parameter for topic prior of comments, because $\bar{z}^a$ represents the actual topics observed in the article, which is presumably more accurate to capture the article's theme. Due to this prior design, the posterior topic distribution θ^c in each comment of an article is not only determined by the shared context specified in $\bar{z}^a + \alpha^C$, but also by the observed words in comments. Consequently, comments on the same article tend to have similar topic distributions, but can also have different topic choices if there is support.

At the word level, each word w in an article or a comment is generated from a multinomial distribution parameterized by ϕ^z after its topic assignment z is determined. CCTM also differs from previous models in how ϕ^z is generated. To model both the thread-specific burstiness of words and the global word co-occurrence patterns, we leverage Dirichlet compound multinomial (DCM) distribution [18] when generating ϕ^z, and enforce an article and its comments to share the same set of thread-specific topics.

Specifically, for each article-comment thread, the DCM distribution draws a set of multinomial distributions $\left\{p(w|\phi_j)\right\}_{j=1}^{K}$, which are drawn from a set of Dirichlet priors parametrized by $\{\beta_j\}_{j=1}^{K}$:

$$\phi_j \sim Dir(\beta_j), j = 1, 2, ..., K.$$

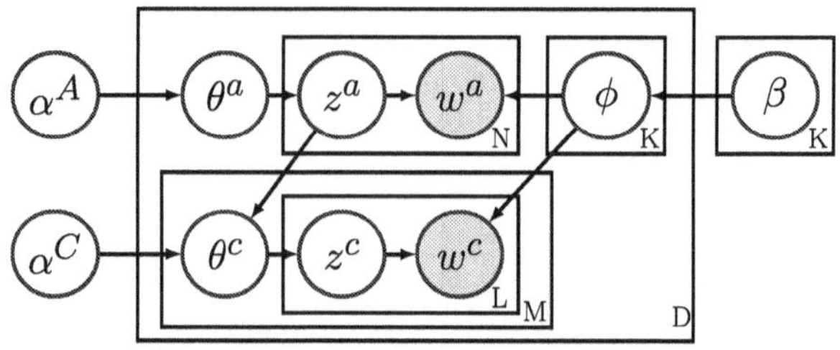

Figure 3: Graphical model representation of CCTM. Dark and light circles represent observable and latent random variables, and plates denote repetitions. Arrows encode dependency relation among the random variables.

The Dirichlet priors are shared in the corpus. Under this modeling assumption, an article-comment thread can have its own word distribution for each topic, and these local word distributions are loosely related across the article-comment threads by the commonly shared Dirichlet priors.

To be explicit, given the topic assignment of a word, the conditional probability of this word in a corpus is computed as,

$$\begin{aligned} p(w|z = k, \beta) &= \int p(w|\phi_k)p(\phi_k|\beta_k)d\phi_k \\ &= \prod_{d}^{D} \frac{\Gamma(A_{wkd}^{WKD} + \beta_{wk})}{\Gamma(\beta_{wk})} \frac{\Gamma(\sum_w \beta_{wk})}{\Gamma(\sum_w A_{wkd}^{WKD} + \beta_{wk})} \end{aligned} \tag{2}$$

where A_{wkd}^{WKD} denotes the number of times word w in the article-comment thread d is assigned to topic k. From Eq. (2), we can observe the probability of a word drawing a particular topic in an article-comment thread is *conditionally independent* from other article-comment threads given Dirichlet parameters $\{\beta_j\}_{j=1}^{K}$ in our model. Therefore, the repetition of words between an article and its comments becomes a very strong signal of content correspondence, even if this word is not globally representative of the topic.

Integrating these two model specifications, the generative process of the commented data in CCTM can be described as follows:

For each article a_d, $1 \le d \le D$,

1. For each topic k, $1 \le k \le K$, sample the word distribution $\phi_k^d \sim Dir(\beta_k)$;
2. Sample topic proportion $\theta^{a_d} \sim Dir(\alpha^A)$;
3. For each word $w_n^{a_d}$, $1 \le n \le N$ in a_d,
   I. Sample topic $z_n^{a_d} \sim Multi(\theta^{a_d})$;
   II. Sample word $w_n^{a_d} \sim Multi(\phi^d_{z_n^{a_d}})$;

   For each comment c_{dm}, $1 \le m \le M_{a_d}$ of a_d,
   1. Sample topic proportion $\theta^{c_{dm}} \sim Dir(\alpha^C + \bar{z}^{a_d})$;
   2. For each word $w_l^{c_{dm}}$, $1 \le l \le L_{c_{dm}}$ in c_{dm},
      I. Sample topic $z_l^{c_{dm}} \sim Multi(\theta^{c_{dm}})$;
      II. draw word $w_l^{c_{dm}} \sim Multi(\phi^d_{z_l^{c_{dm}}})$.

where D is the number of articles, N is the number of words in the article a_d, M_{a_d} is the number of comments associating with the article a_d, and $L_{c_{dm}}$ is the number of words in the comment c_{dm}. Using the language of graphical models, this generative process can be depicted in Figure 3.

3.3 Inference & Parameter Estimation

In CCTM, the latent variables of interest are the topic assignments $\{z_n^a\}_{n=1}^N$ for each article a, $\{z_l^c\}_{l=1}^L$ for each comment c, and $\{\phi_k\}_{k=1}^K$ for each article-comment thread. The discrete topic assignments represent articles and comments in a concise topic space and reflect the correspondence between these two types of documents. And the topic-word distributions $\{\phi_k\}_{k=1}^K$ reveal the instantiation of topics in each article-comment thread. However, exact inference of these random variables in CCTM is computationally intractable. Thanks to the conjugacy between Dirichlet and multinomial distributions, we develop an efficient collapsed Gibbs sampler to perform posterior inference of these random variables in each article and comment.

In traditional topic models, the corpus-level hyperparameters are usually set manually [12]. In CCTM, the hyperparameters, i.e., $\{\alpha^A, \alpha^C, \beta_{k=1:K}\}$ convey important semantics. Since DCM is used for modeling topics, $\{\beta_k\}_{k=1}^K$ represent K global topics. α^A and α^C reflect the topical focus in news articles and comments respectively. Manually tuning them is difficult, and we propose to estimate them from data. Our estimation is based on the maximization of complete data likelihood $p(\boldsymbol{w}, \boldsymbol{z}|\alpha^A, \alpha^C, \beta_{k=1:K})$ [5]. Specifically, we adopt the Monte Carlo Expectation Maximization algorithm. In E-step, we fix the hyperparameters, and perform posterior inference of the topic assignments in articles and comments. In M-step, we fix the topic assignments and maximize the complete data likelihood. To collect independent samples from the sampling chain, we only keep samples every five iterations, i.e., thinning the sampling chain. Besides, samples from the beginning of the sampling chain (i.e., the burn-in period) may not accurately represent the desired distribution. We only keep the posterior samples after the burn-in period (in our experiment, we discarded the first 20% of samples).

In the following, we provide the detailed inference and parameter estimation procedures in E-step and M-step.

• **E-step**. Due to the Dirichlet-multinomial conjugacy, the latent variables of θ^a, θ^c and $\{\phi_k\}_{k=1}^K$ can be marginalized out in the resulting posterior distribution in each article-comment thread. This leaves us an efficient collapsed Gibbs sampler to infer the topic assignments $\{z_n^a\}_{n=1}^N$ in article a and $\{z_l^c\}_{l=1}^L$ in comment c.

In the following derivation, we define a set of sufficient statistics to simplify our description of conditional probabilities for sampling. A_{wkd}^{WKD} represents the count of word w assigned to topic k in the article a_d and all its comments $\left\{c_{dm}\right\}_{m=1}^{M_{a_d}}$. A_{kd}^{KD} denotes the number of words assigned to topic k in the article a_d, and C_{kmd}^{KMD} denotes the number of words assigned to topic k in article a_d's comment c_{dm}. The special symbol '$-n$' denotes the word w_n is excluded when computing the corresponding sufficient statistics for sampling.

$$\begin{aligned} p(z_n^{a_d} &= j|w_n^{a_d}, z_{-n}^{a_d}, w_{-n}^{a_d}, \boldsymbol{z}^{c_d}, \boldsymbol{w}^{c_d}, \alpha^A, \alpha^C, \boldsymbol{\beta}) \\ &\propto \frac{\beta_{w_n^{a_d} j} + A_{wjd,-n}^{WKD}}{\sum_{w'}(\beta_{w'j} + A_{w'jd,-n}^{WKD})}(\alpha_j^A + A_{jd,-n}^{KD}) \\ &\times \prod_{m=1}^{M_{a_d}} \prod_{k=1}^{K} \frac{\Gamma\left(\alpha_k^C + \frac{A_{kd,-n}^{KD}{}^{+1(k=j)}}{\sum_k A_{kd}^{KD}} + C_{kmd}^{KMD}\right)}{\Gamma\left(\alpha_k^C + \frac{A_{kd,-n}^{KD}{}^{+1(k=j)}}{\sum_k A_{kd}^{KD}}\right)} \end{aligned} \tag{3}$$

Based on these notations, the conditional probability of assigning topic j to word $w_n^{a_d}$ in article a_d is computed as Eq.(3), where $\boldsymbol{w}^{c_d}$ and $\boldsymbol{z}^{c_d}$ represent the words and corresponding topic assignments in all comments associated with article a_d. And the conditional probability of assigning topic j to word $w_l^{c_{dm}}$ in comment c_{dm} is,

$$\begin{aligned} p(z_l^{c_{dm}} &= j|w_l^{c_{dm}}, z_{-l}^c, w_{-l}^c, z^a, w^a, \alpha^A, \alpha^C, \beta) \\ &\propto \frac{\beta_{w_l^{c_{dm}} j} + A_{wjd}^{WKD}}{\sum_{w'}(\beta_{w'j} + A_{w'jd,-l}^{WKD})} \frac{\alpha_j^C + \frac{A_{jd}^{KD}}{\sum_k A_{kd}^{KD}} + C_{jmd,-l}^{KMD}}{1 + \sum_k(\alpha_k^C + C_{kmd,-l}^{KMD})} \end{aligned} \tag{4}$$

The topic-level correspondence between an article and its comments is clearly depicted in the above sampling equations. As stated in Eq. (3), the topic assignments in an article are determined by not only the words in this article, but also words in all its comments (specified by the Gamma ratio function). Especially, this Gamma ratio function encourages the topic that is frequently mentioned in the comments (as we have C_{kmd}^{KMD} on the numerator) to be observed in the article. And this relation is more clearly encoded in the second part of Eq. (4): the topic assignments in the article serve as pseudo count in each comment's topic proportion, which promotes major topics of the article in their comments.

The word-level correspondence is also reflected in the sampling equations. As denoted in the first part of Eq. (3) and (4), the conditional probability of word w sampled from topic j depends on the word-topic allocation in the current article a_d, its comments $\{c_{dm}\}_{m=1}^{M_{a_d}}$, and the global Dirichlet prior. This promotes the local co-occurrence patterns of words, which might not be necessarily frequent in the whole corpus, and encourages assigning the same topic to the repeated words, i.e., capturing burstiness.

Once the sampling chain converges in each article-comment thread, we can easily estimate other latent variables as follows,

$$\theta_k^{a_d} \propto \alpha_k^A + A_{kd}^{KD} \tag{5}$$

$$\theta_k^{c_{dm}} \propto \alpha_k^C + \frac{A_{kd}^{KD}}{\sum_k A_{kd}^{KD}} + C_{kmd}^{KMD} \tag{6}$$

$$\phi_{wk}^d \propto \beta_{wk} + A_{wkd}^{WKD} \tag{7}$$

We should note that as $\{\phi_k\}_{k=1}^K$ are article-specific, the above sampling procedures can be readily parallelized with respect to the articles. This enables CCTM to easily scale to large collections of commented data.

• **M-step.** Based on the posterior inference results in each article-comment thread, the maximum likelihood estimation of the hyperparameters $\{\alpha^A, \alpha^C, \beta_{k=1:K}\}$ can be independently performed over the complete data log-likelihood function. We only illustrate the estimation procedure for $\{\beta_k\}_{k=1}^K$, as the same approach directly applies to α^A and α^C.

Specifically, we estimate $\{\beta_k\}_{k=1}^K$ by maximizing the complete log-likelihood function of CCTM,

$$\begin{aligned} L(\beta) = &\sum_{d,w,k} \left(\log\Gamma(A_{wkd}^{WKD} + \beta_{wk}) - \log\Gamma(\beta_{wk})\right) \\ &+ \sum_{d,k} \left(\log\Gamma(\sum_w \beta_{wk}) - \log\Gamma(\sum_w A_{wkd}^{WKD} + \beta_{wk})\right) \end{aligned}$$

This complete log-likelihood function indicates that the updates of $\{\beta_k\}_{k=1}^K$ are independent across K topics, and thus we can update these parameters in parallel. As no closed-form solution exists for the above optimization problem, we appeal to the fixed point iteration method to iteratively optimize it [19]. The update equation of β_{wk} is:

$$\beta_{wk}^{new} = \beta_{wk}^{old} \frac{\sum_d \left(\psi(A_{wkd}^{WKD} + \beta_{wk}^{old}) - \psi(\beta_{wk}^{old})\right)}{\sum_d \left(\psi(\sum_w A_{wkd}^{wKD} + \sum_w \beta_{wk}^{old}) - \psi(\sum_w \beta_{wk}^{old})\right)}$$

where β_{wk}^{old} is the value obtained in last M-step and $\psi(\cdot)$ is the first order derivative of the log Gamma function. The update of $\{\beta_k\}_{k=1}^K$ helps recondition global topics from the inferred local topics. Importantly, such an iterative solution is guaranteed to converge to a stationary point of the complete log likelihood function [19]; and for the Dirichlet distribution, the global maximum is the only stationary point.

4 EXPERIMENTAL EVALUATIONS

Our evaluation is conducted in multiple ways. First, we present case study in Section 4.1 to investigate the quality of inferred topics from CCTM. Second, we use perplexity to compare the capability of our model with several topic model based solutions in predicting unseen commented data in Section 4.2. Third, we study two important applications based on the inferred correspondence structure, namely spam comment detection and targeted comment retrieval in Section 4.3 and 4.4 respectively.

We used ArsTechnica Science [1] technical blog dataset and the Yahoo! News dataset provided in [7] as our evaluation corpus. In the ArsTechnica dataset, comments are manually annotated with their corresponding sentences in the articles. The annotations serve as ground-truth for us to evaluate the learned correspondence by different solutions. The Yahoo! News dataset was originally unannotated. We used crowd sourcing to annotate a set of pooled correspondence mappings between articles and comments based on different algorithms' inference results. Standard text preprocessing steps were performed on these two datasets, including stopword removal, stemming and normalization. We removed articles and comments whose length is shorter than 5 words after the pre-processing. The basic statistics of the two evaluation datasets after these pre-processing steps are shown in Table 1.

Table 1: Evaluation Corpus Statistics.

DataSet	ArsTechnica	Yahoo! News
#Articles	501	651
#Comments	2897	32285
#Words	216769	476497
Vocalbulary Size	6053	8755

In our evaluation, we include the following three topic model based solutions for correspondence modeling as our baselines.

• Latent Dirichlet Allocation (LDA) [4]. Each article and comment are modeled as independent documents.

• Correspondence LDA (CorrLDA) [3]. It is an extension of LDA model, where topics in comments are uniformly drawn from topics in the corresponding article.

• Specific Correspondence Topic Model (SCTM) [7]. It is a state-of-the-art model on capturing correspondence in commented data. In this model, each article is split into sentences, and the topics of words in comments are uniformly drawn from topic assignments in the selected sentences.

[1] http://arstechnica.com/

Besides these three existing models, we also include two variations of CCTM to evaluate the impact of the two main ingredients of CCTM: topic-level prior setting for flexible topic modeling, and word-level DCM for thread-specific topic-word distributions.

• CCTM-. It removes the DCM component from CCTM, i.e., using one shared set of multinomial distributions to represent topics for the entire corpus like the standard topic models.

• CorrLDA+. It adds the DCM component to CorrLDA, but the topics in comments are still uniformly sampled from topic assignments in the corresponding article.

4.1 Case Study

We first investigate the quality of topic-word distributions learned in CCTM, and then study the inferred topical representation of articles and comments. As similar results were obtained in Yahoo! News dataset, we only discuss the results obtained in ArsTechnica dataset in this section.

CCTM learns two levels of topics. The Dirichlet prior parameters $\{\beta_k\}_{k=1}^K$ in CCTM represent global topics, and $\{\phi_k\}_{k=1}^K$ in each article-comment thread represent thread-specific instantiation of global topics. Figure 4 visualizes three example global topics and corresponding local topics from two different article-comment threads, using a tree structure representation. The root nodes of the trees represent the words selected by $\{\beta_k\}_{k=1}^K$ from three global topics, and the leaf nodes of each tree represent the corresponding topics from two randomly selected article-comment threads, where the words are selected by the thread-specific topic-word distribution $\{\phi_k\}_{k=1}^K$. Article title corresponding to each leaf node is shown under the node. In each topic node, top 10 words are shown.

Take "topic 3" in Figure 4 as an example. The top words from β_3 indicate that it is a health-related topic, while the top words from the two threads' corresponding topic ϕ_3^1 and ϕ_3^2 are also related to health but with different emphases. The first thread concentrates on "*antibiotics*" and "*bacteria*", and the second focuses on "*HIV infection*" and "*HIV treatment*". And these topical words are all strongly related to the title of these two articles and the corresponding discussion content in the articles and comments. Due to space limit, we cannot display full articles' and comments' content, but we used word clouds to highlight the keywords in the article and two selected comments for two article-comment threads. Similar observations can also be found in other randomly selected topics and threads in the figure. This result suggests that the local and global topics extracted by CCTM are meaningful, especially the local topics capture fine grained variations of topic-word distributions. The learned relation between global topics and thread-specific topics is meaningful in the commented data.

We further visualize the content of two selected article-comment threads (thread 2 and 6) using word clouds and illustrate the corresponding topic distributions in Figure 4. The content of article 2 is mostly about "virus, hiv, infection", which match top words in ϕ_3^2. Consistently, the inferred topic distribution of article 2 shows that topic 3 occupies the main body of that article. Likewise, the topic distribution of comment 2_2 suggests that this comment talks

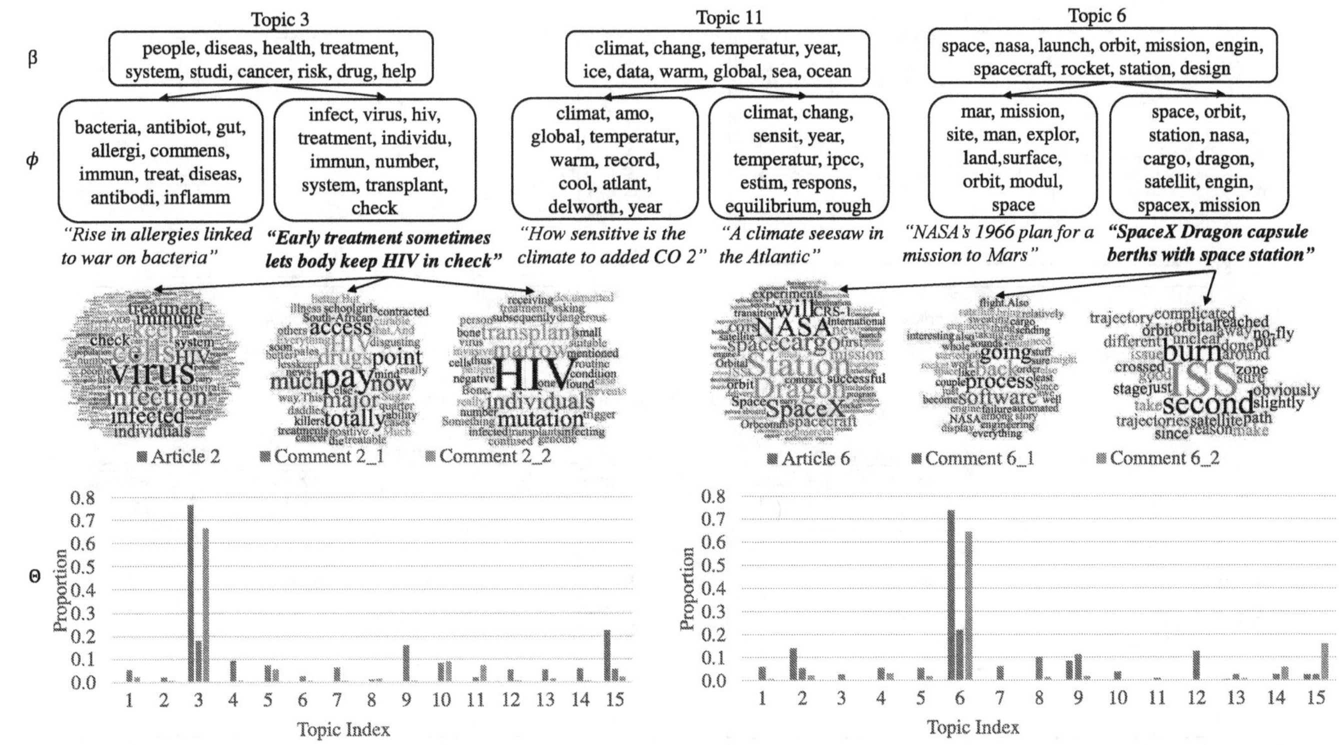

Figure 4: Illustration of the topics learned by CCTM in ArsTechnica dataset. In each box of the first level, top 10 words are selected from a global topic encoded by β_k; and in the second level, top 10 words from six randomly selected article-comment threads by ϕ_k accordingly. The article's title is labeled under each leaf node. Word clouds are used to to highlight the content of selected articles and comments on the second level. The inferred topic distributions in articles and comments are shown at the bottom of this figure.

about the same topic, which can be confirmed from its word content "HIV, mutation, transplant" highligted in the word cloud. On the other hand, comment 2_1 has fewer words related to "health, HIV", but its content spreads out on words like "pay," "access," and "point". Consistently, the inferred topic distribution of comment 2_1 is less concentrated on topic 3. This comment actually covers topics that are rarely mentioned in article 2, such as topic 4 and 9. These observations confirm that CCTM is able to identify diverse topic compositions in comments by not restricting the topics in comments as a subset of those in articles, but only treating topics in articles as a prior to the topics in comments.

4.2 Perplexity

Perplexity is a standard metric evaluating the predictive power of a probabilistic model, and it is computed as the exponentiation of the model's entropy on held-out data. A low perplexity indicates the model is good at predicting unseen data.

To compute perplexity in the commented data, we preserve a portion of article-comment threads as training data for estimating the model parameters, such as $\{\alpha^A, \alpha^C, \beta_{k=1:K}\}$ in CCTM. Then we apply the learned model on the rest part of collection for topic inference and likelihood computation. We varied the number of topics, performed ten-fold cross validation in each train/test separation, and reported the resulting perplexity on both evaluation datasets in Figure 5. One important parameter in all topic model based solutions is the number of topics. In our experiment, we varied the number of topics in all models and used perplexity as the metric to select the optimal settings. We found in most of cases, this setting did not affect the relative comparison of these models' perplexity results too much in both of our evaluation datasets. Consequently, we set the topic size to 15 in ArsTechnica dataset and set it to 80 in Yahoo! News dataset for all models in all our reported experiments.

From the results, we can observe that CCTM outperformed all baselines. The major reason of this low perplexity is that CCTM utilizes the DCM distribution to model topics, which provides sufficient flexibility for the article-comment thread specific topics to exploit local word co-occurrence patterns. But all the other topic models (except CorrLDA+) have to use globally shared topics in modeling the articles and their comments, which limits their ability to model unseen data. This conclusion can be further confirmed by CorrLDA+, where DCM distribution replaces the global multinomial distribution to model topics. Its perplexity is significantly lower than other baselines.

However, this standard definition of perplexity does not consider the whole story about correspondence modeling in the commented data: in such held-out testing data, the whole article-comment thread is available for topic inference. A good correspondence modeling method should be able to better predict the unseen document, immediately when some portion of the document becomes available. To make a more comprehensive comparison, we utilize partial perplexity [22, 29] to measure the performance of these models.

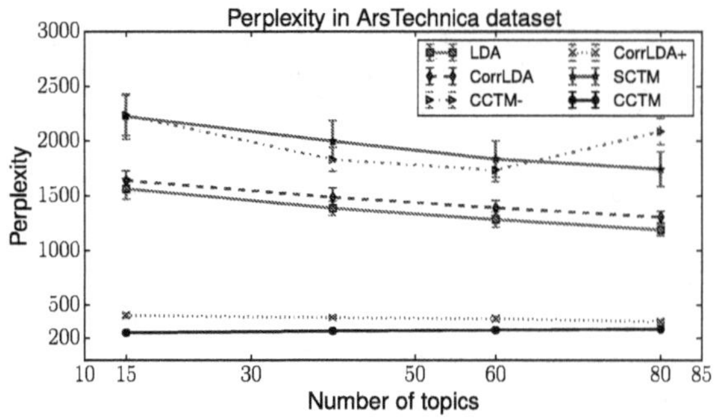

(a) ArshTechinica dataset

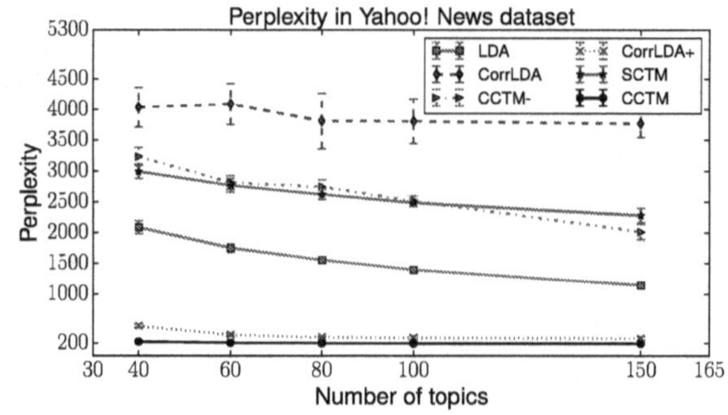

(b) Yahoo! News dataset

Figure 5: Perplexity on ArshTechinica and Yahoo! News datasets.

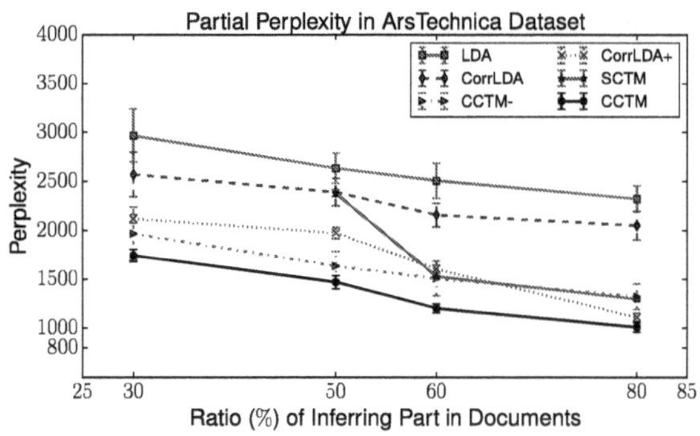

(a) ArshTechinica dataset

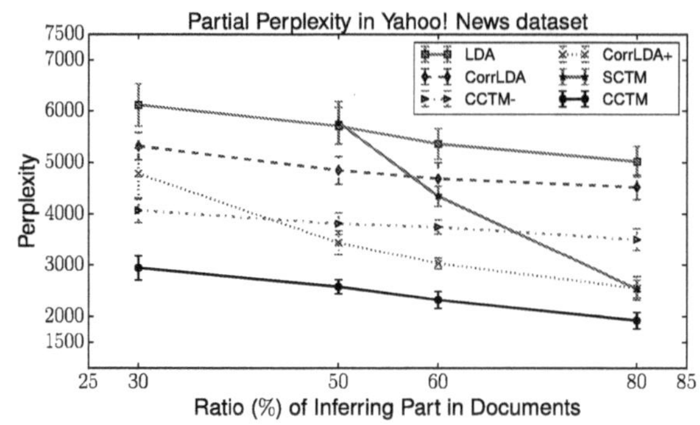

(b) Yahoo! News dataset

Figure 6: Partial Perplexity on ArshTechinica and Yahoo! News datasets.

To calculate partial perplexity, we further divide each article and comment in the test set into two parts. One part is used to infer the topic proportion of the document, a.k.a. *inferring part*, and the other part is used to compute the perplexity, a.k.a. *perplexity part*. This metric can avoid overfitting the test data, because the perplexity part is not used for inference.

We vary the ratio of inferring part to have a thorough insight about the performance of these models. At each ratio setting, perplexity is obtained via a ten-fold cross validation in each model. The results are shown in Figure 6.

Again CCTM achieved the best predictive capability against all baselines. It implies that our model characterizes the commented data more accurately due to better modeling of the correspondence structure. In addition, there is a clear gap between CCTM and its two simplified variants: CCTM- and CorrLDA+. That suggests both topic-level prior design and word-level DCM design account for the improvement over existing approaches. We can also notice that the impact of these two designs varies with respect to the ratio of inferring part. For example, on Yahoo! News dataset, when 30% of document content (including both article and comment) is used to infer the topic distribution, the gap between CorrLDA and CorrLDA+ is smaller than the gap between CorrLDA+ and CCTM, and the perplexity of CorrLDA+ is worse than CCTM-. That means the topic-level prior design plays a more important role than the local topic-word distribution design when only a few words are observed. This is expected that with fewer observations, the local word repetition pattern cannot be fully observed, and the topic assignment in comments gets more influence from the article, as the articles tend to be longer than comments in general. On the other hand, when 80% of document content is used to infer the topic distribution, the gap between CorrLDA and CorrLDA+ becomes larger than that between CorrLDA+ and CCTM, and the perplexity of CorrLDA+ is better than CCTM-. It means that when sufficient amount of words are observed, the thread-specific word burstiness pattern becomes more prominent, and thus the influence of DCM on perplexity is enhanced. The same conclusion can be drawn from both ArsTechnica and Yahoo! News datasets.

4.3 Detecting spam comments

Accurately filtering spam comments is an important task in assisting users digest the commented data. In ArsTechnica dataset, comments are exhaustively annotated with the corresponding sentences in the articles. As a result, we treat the comments without any aligned sentence in the article as irrelevant to the discussion thread, or spam comments. We assume spam comments should be more distinct from the article than the normal ones in terms of topical relatedness.

We adopt cosine similarity to measure the distance between the topic distribution in a comment and that in an article. The smaller the cosine similarity is, the more likely a comment is a spam. To study the performance of spam detection under different similarity thresholds, we report the precision and recall curve of each model in Figure 7, where ten-fold cross validation is performed.

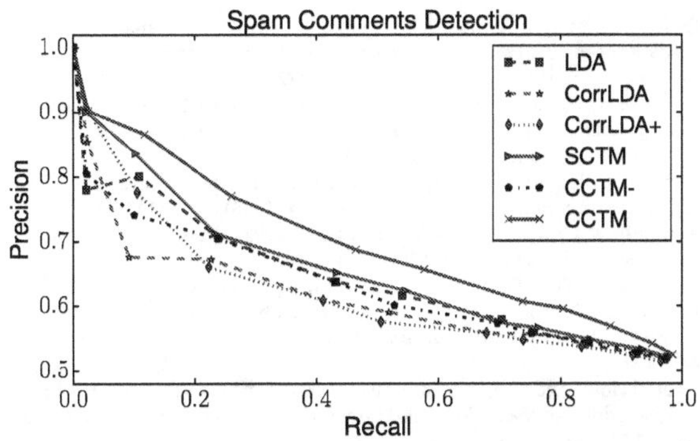

Figure 7: Performance of spam comment detection.

In this dataset, 1483 of 2897 comments are not aligned with any sentence in the article, and therefore are considered as spams. We can observe that at every recall level, CCTM achieved improved precision against all other models. CorrLDA restricts the topics of comments only to the existing topics in articles; but with the existence of spam comments, this restriction undermines the quality of learned topic distribution in comments and makes it difficult to recognize the spam comments. LDA independently models articles and comments, so that it can hardly capture the correspondence in commented data due to the vocabulary gap. Both CCTM- and CorrLDA+ performed worse than CCTM. CCTM- does not utilize the local word burstiness pattern, so that it cannot recognize the comments that use globally less popular words to describe the same topic in the articles. As a result, its precision tends to be lower at the same recall level. CorrLDA+ fails to assign unseen topics in an article to its comments although CorrLDA+ is able to capture the local topics with globally less popular words, and thus fails to detect spams as well.

SCTM is the best alternative model, which has a background topic to accommodate irrelevant comments [7]. However, as topics are globally shared in SCTM, it cannot leverage the thread-specific word-level correspondence and thus performed worse than CCTM. In addition, we can notice that SCTM has competitive precision when the recall is low, but the precision drops very quickly with increasing recall. Its precision gap to our CCTM model increases quickly too. When higher recall is required, the difficulty in detecting spam comments increases. A slower decrease in precision of our model means it outperforms other models not only on detecting obvious spam comments, but also on subtle ones via learning more accurate topical representation of comments and articles.

4.4 Retrieving comments for targeted sentences in articles

Retrieving relevant comments for a given sentence in a news article helps readers to track others' opinions and acquire complementary information about the article content. We consider a sentence from an article as a query and rank all the associated comments by the likelihood of generating this sentence given the inferred topics in comments [28]. We believe better correspondence modeling leads to better retrieval performance. In order to verify this, we employed three standard ranking metrics, Mean Average Precision (MAP), Normalized Discounted Cumulative Gain (NDCG), and Precision at 3 (P@3), to measure the retrieval performance of different models.

Table 2: Retrieval performance in ArsTechnica dataset.

Model	MAP	NDCG	P@3
LDA	0.605	0.708	0.295
CorrLDA	0.592	0.698	0.288
CCTM-	0.600	0.704	0.290
CorrLDA+	0.598	0.703	0.290
SCTM	0.616	0.716	0.296
CCTM	0.632*	0.728*	0.312*

* p-value<0.05

Table 3: Retrieval performance in Yahoo! News dataset.

Model	MAP	NDCG	P@3
LDA	0.639	0.782	0.520
CorrLDA	0.643	0.799	0.541
CCTM-	0.662	0.793	0.555
CorrLDA+	0.613	0.764	0.486
SCTM	0.587	0.753	0.486
CCTM	0.678*	0.816*	0.590*

* p-value<0.05

Specifically, the likelihood of generating a sentence s from a comment c can be computed as $p(s|c) = \prod_{w \in s} \sum_z p(w|z)p(z|c)$, where $p(z|c)$ represents the posterior topic distribution in the comment and $p(w|z)$ represents the word distribution of topic z. For LDA, CorrLDA, CCTM- and SCTM, $p(w|z)$ is obtained from word distributions in global topics. And for CorrLDA+ and CCTM, $p(w|z)$ is obtained from the word distributions in local topics.

In ArsTechnica dataset, we used existing annotations as ground-truth for relevance judgment. After removing sentences which are not annotated with any relevant comments, we have 2193 annotated sentences as queries. The results are reported in Table 2 and paired t-test is performed between the best and second best performing algorithms under each performance metric.

For the Yahoo! News dataset, there was no annotation. We used Amazon Mechanical Turk to obtain the relevance judgment of comments to sentences in a set of randomly selected news articles (as this data set is too large to perform exhaustive annotation). In particular, we chose the annotation candidates by pooling different algorithms' inferred correspondence pairs between a sentence and a comment. Each algorithm picks top 5 comments for 56 selected sentences from 19 news articles. To make the selected sentences representative, we kept the first sentence of the selected article selected as it usually serves as an abstract of the news report. And we also included the sentence that was associated with the largest pooled comment set. This indicated the models disagreed on the mapping for this sentence; and therefore it best differentiated different algorithms' ranking quality. Crowd sourcing workers were asked to give relevance label of each sentence-comment pair in five levels including (1) bad - totally irrelevant; (2) fair - not quite relevant; (3) good - somehow relevant; (4) excellent - relevant; and (5) perfect - exact match. Then we treat "bad" and "fair" as irrelevant while regarding the rest as relevant in relevance based ranking metrics (i.e., MAP and P@3). For each comment-sentence pair, we required at least three out of five workers to agree on the judged relevance, otherwise we would ignore the annotated pair. Majority vote was used to determine whether a comment is relevant to the sentence. As a result, we obtained 786 valid annotations for 428 comments with respect to 48 sentences. In average each sentence was ranked against 9 comments. The ranking performance of models is reported in Table 3, and the same t-test was performed to confirm the statistical significance of the comparison.

From the results, we can observe that CCTM achieves the best ranking performance under these three metrics on both datasets. SCTM performs the 2nd best in ArcTechnica dataset, and CCTM-is the runner-up in Yahoo! News dataset. Both of them underperformed CCTM due to their inability to leverage the local word burstiness patterns. In detail, we can find that CorrLDA was penalized in this retrieval evaluation, because of its overly restricted correspondence assumption between articles and comments. Since LDA model does not model the correspondence structure, it ranked comments solely based on the globally shared topic distribution and thus performed worse than CCTM.

5 CONCLUSION

In this paper, we developed a Commented Correspondence Topic Model to model correspondence structure in commented data. Both topic-level and word-level correspondence are explicitly captured by introducing the topic assignments in commented articles as the prior to their comments' topic proportions and utilizing Dirichlet compound multinomial distribution to capture the local word repetition patterns. And, for the first time, we performed hypothesis test to verify the phenomena of word burstiness also exists in the commented data. Empirical evaluations on two large text corpora confirmed the effectiveness of the proposed model in correspondence modeling, and its utility in mining such user-generated comments. Although we took commented news data as case study, the developed model can be potentially applied to many other types of text data with correspondence structure, such as forum discussions, social media comments and product reviews.

Currently, our model does not directly model the relationship among comments, which are not independent in practice as users might form groups and discuss via commenting on each other's posts. It is necessary to capture the correspondence at this level as well. In addition, our solution does not model sentences in articles, which limits its resolution in recognizing fine-grained correspondence between articles and comments. In our future work, we will add sentence structure into correspondence modeling. Furthermore, our empirical evaluation in this work mostly focused on commented news data; but the developed solution is not limited to such data. It is necessary to explore its applicability in other types of user-generated commented data, and identify new insights of correspondence structure there.

6 ACKNOWLEDGMENTS

We thank the anonymous reviewers for their insightful comments. This paper is based upon work supported by the National Science Foundation under grant IIS-1553568.

REFERENCES

[1] Charles E Antoniak. 1974. Mixtures of Dirichlet processes with applications to Bayesian nonparametric problems. *The annals of statistics* (1974), 1152–1174.

[2] David M Blei. 2012. Probabilistic topic models. *Commun. ACM* 55, 4 (2012), 77–84.

[3] David M Blei and Michael I Jordan. 2003. Modeling annotated data. In *Proceedings of the 26th annual international ACM SIGIR conference on Research and development in informaion retrieval.* ACM, 127–134.

[4] David M Blei, Andrew Y Ng, and Michael I Jordan. 2003. Latent dirichlet allocation. *Journal of machine Learning research* 3, Jan (2003), 993–1022.

[5] Gilles Celeux, Didier Chauveau, and Jean Diebolt. 1996. Stochastic versions of the EM algorithm: an experimental study in the mixture case. *Journal of Statistical Computation and Simulation* 55, 4 (1996), 287–314.

[6] Kenneth W Church and William A Gale. 1995. Poisson mixtures. *Natural Language Engineering* 1, 02 (1995), 163–190.

[7] Mrinal Kanti Das, Trapit Bansal, and Chiranjib Bhattacharyya. 2014. Going beyond Corr-LDA for detecting specific comments on news & blogs. In *Proceedings of the 7th ACM international conference on Web search and data mining.* ACM, 483–492.

[8] Gabriel Doyle and Charles Elkan. 2009. Accounting for burstiness in topic models. In *Proceedings of the 26th Annual International Conference on Machine Learning.* ACM, 281–288.

[9] Charles Elkan. 2006. Clustering documents with an exponential-family approximation of the Dirichlet compound multinomial distribution. In *Proceedings of the 23rd international conference on Machine learning.* ACM, 289–296.

[10] Kosuke Fukumasu, Koji Eguchi, and Eric P Xing. 2012. Symmetric correspondence topic models for multilingual text analysis. In *Advances in Neural Information Processing Systems.* 1286–1294.

[11] Giorgos Giannopoulos, Ingmar Weber, Alejandro Jaimes, and Timos Sellis. 2012. Diversifying user comments on news articles. In *International Conference on Web Information Systems Engineering.* Springer, 100–113.

[12] Thomas L Griffiths and Mark Steyvers. 2004. Finding scientific topics. *Proceedings of the National academy of Sciences* 101, suppl 1 (2004), 5228–5235.

[13] Thomas Hofmann. 1999. Probabilistic latent semantic indexing. In *Proceedings of the 22nd annual international ACM SIGIR conference on Research and development in information retrieval.* ACM, 50–57.

[14] Meishan Hu, Aixin Sun, and Ee-Peng Lim. 2008. Comments-oriented document summarization: understanding documents with readers' feedback. In *Proceedings of the 31st annual international ACM SIGIR conference on Research and development in information retrieval.* ACM, 291–298.

[15] Andreas M Kaplan and Michael Haenlein. 2010. Users of the world, unite! The challenges and opportunities of Social Media. *Business horizons* 53, 1 (2010), 59–68.

[16] Slava M Katz. 1996. Distribution of content words and phrases in text and language modelling. *Natural Language Engineering* 2, 01 (1996), 15–59.

[17] Zongyang Ma, Aixin Sun, Quan Yuan, and Gao Cong. 2012. Topic-driven reader comments summarization. In *Proceedings of the 21st ACM international conference on Information and knowledge management.* ACM, 265–274.

[18] Rasmus E Madsen, David Kauchak, and Charles Elkan. 2005. Modeling word burstiness using the Dirichlet distribution. In *Proceedings of the 22nd international conference on Machine learning.* ACM, 545–552.

[19] Thomas Minka. 2000. Estimating a Dirichlet distribution. (2000).

[20] Dae Hoon Park, Mengwen Liu, ChengXiang Zhai, and Haohong Wang. 2015. Leveraging user reviews to improve accuracy for mobile app retrieval. In *Proceedings of the 38th International ACM SIGIR Conference on Research and Development in Information Retrieval.* ACM, 533–542.

[21] Kristen Purcell, Lee Rainie, Amy Mitchell, Tom Rosenstiel, and Kenny Olmstead. 2010. Understanding the participatory news consumer: How Internet and cell phone users have turned news into a social experience. Pew Internet & American Life Project. (2010).

[22] Michal Rosen-Zvi, Thomas Griffiths, Mark Steyvers, and Padhraic Smyth. 2004. The author-topic model for authors and documents. In *Proceedings of the 20th conference on Uncertainty in artificial intelligence.* AUAI Press, 487–494.

[23] Clay Shirky. 2011. The political power of social media: Technology, the public sphere, and political change. *Foreign affairs* (2011), 28–41.

[24] Alexandru Tatar, Jérémie Leguay, Panayotis Antoniadis, Arnaud Limbourg, Marcelo Dias de Amorim, and Serge Fdida. 2011. Predicting the popularity of online articles based on user comments. In *Proceedings of the International Conference on Web Intelligence, Mining and Semantics.* ACM, 67.

[25] Goutham Tholpadi, Mrinal Kanti Das, Trapit Bansal, and Chiranjib Bhattacharyya. 2015. Relating Romanized Comments to News Articles by Inferring Multi-Glyphic Topical Correspondence.. In *AAAI.* 311–317.

[26] Manos Tsagkias, Wouter Weerkamp, and Maarten De Rijke. 2009. Predicting the volume of comments on online news stories. In *Proceedings of the 18th ACM conference on Information and knowledge management.* ACM, 1765–1768.

[27] Manos Tsagkias, Wouter Weerkamp, and Maarten De Rijke. 2010. News comments: Exploring, modeling, and online prediction. In *European Conference on Information Retrieval.* Springer, 191–203.

[28] Xing Wei and W Bruce Croft. 2006. LDA-based document models for ad-hoc retrieval. In *Proceedings of the 29th annual international ACM SIGIR conference on Research and development in information retrieval.* ACM, 178–185.

[29] Aonan Zhang, Jun Zhu, and Bo Zhang. 2013. Sparse online topic models. In *Proceedings of the 22nd international conference on World Wide Web.* ACM, 1489–1500.

Jointly Learning Word Embeddings and Latent Topics

Bei Shi
Department of Systems Engineering and Engineering Management
The Chinese University of Hong Kong
Hong Kong
bshi@se.cuhk.edu.hk

Wai Lam
Department of Systems Engineering and Engineering Management
The Chinese University of Hong Kong
Hong Kong
wlam@se.cuhk.edu.hk

Shoaib Jameel
School of Computer Science and Informatics
Cardiff University
Cardiff, UK
JameelS1@cardiff.ac.uk

Steven Schockaert
School of Computer Science and Informatics
Cardiff University
Cardiff, UK
SchockaertS1@cardiff.ac.uk

Kwun Ping Lai
Department of Systems Engineering and Engineering Management
The Chinese University of Hong Kong
Hong Kong
kplai@se.cuhk.edu.hk

ABSTRACT

Word embedding models such as Skip-gram learn a vector-space representation for each word, based on the local word collocation patterns that are observed in a text corpus. Latent topic models, on the other hand, take a more global view, looking at the word distributions across the corpus to assign a topic to each word occurrence. These two paradigms are complementary in how they represent the meaning of word occurrences. While some previous works have already looked at using word embeddings for improving the quality of latent topics, and conversely, at using latent topics for improving word embeddings, such "two-step" methods cannot capture the mutual interaction between the two paradigms. In this paper, we propose STE, a framework which can learn word embeddings and latent topics in a unified manner. STE naturally obtains topic-specific word embeddings, and thus addresses the issue of polysemy. At the same time, it also learns the term distributions of the topics, and the topic distributions of the documents. Our experimental results demonstrate that the STE model can indeed generate useful topic-specific word embeddings and coherent latent topics in an effective and efficient way.

CCS CONCEPTS

•**Information systems** → **Document representation;** *Document topic models;* •**Computing methodologies** → Topic modeling;

KEYWORDS

word embedding; topic model; document modeling

The work described in this paper is substantially supported by grants from the Research Grant Council of the Hong Kong Special Administrative Region, China (Project Code: 14203414) and the Microsoft Research Asia Urban Informatics Grant FY14-RES-Sponsor-057. Steven Schockaert and Shoaib Jameel are supported by ERC Starting Grant 637277.

SIGIR '17, August 07-11, 2017, Shinjuku, Tokyo, Japan

DOI: http://dx.doi.org/10.1145/3077136.3080806

ACM Reference format:
Bei Shi, Wai Lam, Shoaib Jameel, Steven Schockaert, and Kwun Ping Lai. 2017. Jointly Learning Word Embeddings and Latent Topics. In *Proceedings of SIGIR '17, August 07-11, 2017, Shinjuku, Tokyo, Japan*, , 10 pages.
DOI: http://dx.doi.org/10.1145/3077136.3080806

1 INTRODUCTION

Word embeddings, also known as distributed word representations, are a popular way of representing words in Natural Language Processing (NLP) and Information Retrieval (IR) applications [7, 22, 27, 35, 39]. Essentially, the idea is to represent each word as a vector in a low-dimensional space, in a way which reflects the semantic, and sometimes also syntactic, relationships between the words. One natural requirement is that the vectors of similar words are themselves also similar (e.g. in terms of cosine similarity or Euclidean distance). In addition, in some models, several kinds of linear regularities are observed. For example, in Skip-gram [21], one of the most commonly used word embedding models, analogous word pairs tend to form parallelograms in the space, a notable example being vec("man") - vec("king") ≈ vec("woman") - vec("queen"). Most word embedding models rely on statistics about how often each word occurs within a local context window of another word, either implicitly [22] or explicitly [27, 39].

Topic models, such as Latent Dirichlet Allocation (LDA) [5], assign a discrete topic to each word occurrence in a corpus. These topics can be seen as groups of semantically related words. In this sense, like word embeddings, topic models can be viewed as models for capturing the meaning of the words in a corpus. However, there are several key differences between word embeddings and topic models, which make them complementary to each other. First, word embeddings are continuous representations, whereas topic assignments are discrete. Second, word embeddings are learned from local context windows, whereas topic models take a more global view, in the sense that the topic which is assigned to a given word occurrence (in the case of LDA) equally depends on all the other words that appear in the same document. Several researchers have already exploited this complementary representation between word embeddings and topic models.

On the one hand, topic models can be used to improve word embeddings, by addressing the problem of polysemous words. Standard word embedding models essentially ignore ambiguity, meaning that the representation of a word such as "apple" is essentially a weighted average of a vector that would intuitively represent the fruit and a vector that would intuitively represent the company. A natural solution, studied in Liu et al. [19], is to learn different word embeddings for each word-topic combination. In particular, they propose a model called Topical Word Embeddings (TWE), which first employs the standard LDA model to obtain word-topic assignments. Regarding each topic as a pseudo-word, they then learn embeddings for both words and topics. Finally, a given word-topic combination is represented as the concatenation of the word vector and the topic vector.

On the other hand, word embeddings can also be used to improve topic models. For example, Nguyen et al. [26] suggest to model topics as mixtures of the usual Dirichlet multinomial model and a word embedding component. It is shown that the top words associated with the resulting topics are semantically more coherent. Word embeddings can also be used to help with identifying topics for short texts or small collections. For example, Li et al. [16] propose a model which can promote semantically related words, identified by the word embedding, by using the generalized Polya urn model during the sampling process for a given topic. In this way, the external knowledge about semantic relatedness that is captured by the word embedding is exploited to alleviate sparsity problems.

While combining word embeddings and topic models is clearly beneficial, existing approaches merely apply a pipeline approach, where either a standard word embedding is used to improve a topic model, or a standard topic model is used to learn better word embeddings. Such two-step approaches cannot capture the mutual reinforcement between the two types of models. For example, knowing that "apple" occurs in two topics can help us to learn better word embeddings, which can in turn help us to learn better topic assignments, etc. The research question which we address in this paper is whether a unified framework, in which topic assignments and word embeddings are jointly learned, can yield better results than the existing two-step approaches. The unified framework we propose, named STE, can learn different topic-specific word embeddings, and thus addresses the problem of polysemy, while at the same time generating the term distributions of topics and topic distributions of documents. Our hypothesis is that this will lead both to more meaningful embeddings and more coherent topics, compared to the current state-of-the-art.

From a technical point of view, there are two challenges that need to be addressed. The first challenge concerns the representation of topics with embedding vectors, and the mechanism by which words are generated from such topics. Clearly, the commonly used multinomial distribution is inappropriate in our setting. The second challenge is to obtain the embedding vectors efficiently. Because of the huge amount of parameters, the traditional Skip-gram model exploits the Hierarchical Softmax Tree [23] or Negative Sampling method to maximize the likelihood. When latent topics are considered, however, this alone does not lead to a sufficiently efficient method.

To address the first challenge, we use a generating function that can predict surrounding words, given a target word and its topic. The probability that a given word is generated is based on the inner product of a topic-specific embedding of that word and a topic-specific embedding of the target word. This generating function also allows us to identify the top-ranked words for each topic, which is important for the interpretability of the model. To address the second challenge, we design a scalable EM-Negative Sampling method. This inference method iterates over every skip-gram (i.e. each local context window), each time sampling the corresponding negative instances. In the E-step, we evaluate the posterior topic distribution for each skip-gram. In the M-step, we update the topic-specific embeddings and the topic distribution of the documents. We consider two variants of our model, which make different assumptions on the consistency of topics among the word pairs in a skip-gram.

We compare our model with existing hybrid models and perform extensive experiments on the quality of the word embeddings and latent topics. We also evaluate our performance on the downstream application of document classification. The experimental results demonstrate that our model can generate better word embeddings and more coherent topics than the state-of-the-art models.

2 RELATED WORK

In traditional vector space models, individual words are encoded using the so-called one-hot representation, i.e. a high-dimensional vector with all zeroes except in one component, corresponding to that word [1]. Such representations suffer from the curse of dimensionality, as there are as many components in these vectors as there are words in the vocabulary. Another important drawback is that semantic relatedness of words cannot be modelled using such representations. To address these shortcomings, Rumelhart et al. [32] propose to use distributed word representation instead, i.e., word embeddings. Several techniques for generating such representations have been investigated. For example, Bengio et al. [3, 4] propose a neural network architecture for this purpose. Later, Mikolov et al. [21] propose two methods that are considerably more efficient, namely Skip-gram and CBOW. This has made it possible to learn word embeddings from large data sets, which has led to the current popularity of word embeddings. Word embedding models have been applied to many tasks, such as named entity recognition [38], word sense disambiguation [8, 13], parsing [31], and information retrieval [29].

Basic word embedding methods perform poorly for polysemous words such as "apple" and "bank", as the vectors for such words intuitively correspond to a weighted average of the vectors that would normally be associated with each of the individual senses. Several approaches have been proposed to address this limitation, by learning multiple vectors for each word, one corresponding to each sense [28, 30, 33]. For example, Huang et al. [12] exploit global properties such as term frequency and document frequency to learn multiple embeddings via neural networks. Tian et al. [37] introduce a latent variable to denote the distribution of multiple prototypes for each word in a probabilistic manner. Neelakantan et al. [24] propose a non-parametric way to evaluate the number of senses for each word. Bartunov et al. [2] also propose a non-parametric Bayesian method to learn the required number of representations.

Note that our model is different from these models. First, the aforementioned models consider the prototype vectors for each word in isolation, intuitively by clustering the local contexts of each word. This means that these models are limited in how they can model the correlations between the multiple senses of different words. Second, these models do not capture the correlations between the prototypes of words and topics of documents. While there are some word embedding models that do consider topics, to the best of our knowledge no approaches have been studied that exploit the mutual reinforcement between latent topics and word embeddings. For example, Liu et al. [19] concatenate pre-trained topic vectors with the word vectors to represent word prototypes. Building on this idea, Liu et al. [18] combine topic vectors and word vectors via a neural network.

In traditional topic models, such as LDA [5] and PLSA [11], a document is represented as a multinomial distribution of topics, and the topic assignment of a word only depends on that multinomial distribution. In the Bi-gram Topic Model [40, 41], the topic of a given word additionally depends on the topic of the preceding word. Our model is related to this bi-gram model, in the sense that the objective functions of both models are based on a similar idea.

Nguyen et al. [26] propose a topic model named LFTM, which generates vectors from a pre-trained word embedding, instead of words. In this way, the model can benefit from the semantic relationships between words to generate better topics. The Gaussian LDA model from Das et al. [9], similarly associates with each topic a Gaussian in the word embedding, from which individual word vectors are sampled. Li et al. [16] propose a model which can promote semantically related words (given a word embedding) within any given topic. Note that the above models all rely on a pre-trained word embedding. Li et al [17] propose a model which learns an embedding link function to connect the word vectors and topics. However, their model mainly focuses on the distributed representation of each topic, instead of words, and generates topics as an abstract vector, thus losing the interpretability of topics.

3 MODEL DESCRIPTION

In this section, we present the details of our model, which we call Skip-gram Topical word Embedding (STE).

3.1 Representing Topics and Embeddings

Each word w is associated with an input matrix U_w and an output matrix V_w, both of which have dimension $K \times s$, with K the number of topics and s the number of dimensions in the word embedding. The fact that U_w and V_w are matrices, rather than vectors, reflects our modelling assumption that a word w may have a different representation under each topic.

As in standard topic models, a document will correspond to a probability distribution over topics. In contrast to standard topics models, however, topics in our case are more than probability distributions over words. In particular, for a document d and some central word w_t under consideration, the probability of predicting a surrounding word w_{t+j} depends on the topic of the word w_t. For example, suppose that the central word is "apple"; if its topic relates to technology, words such as "technology" might be predicted with high probability, whereas if its topic relates to fruit, words such as "juice" might instead be predicted. In particular, we assume that the probability of predicting the word w_{t+j} given the word w_t under the topic z is evaluated as follows:

$$p(w_{t+j}|w_t, d) = \sum_z p(w_{t+j}|w_t, z)p(z|d) \tag{1}$$

where the summation is over the set of all K topics, $p(.|d)$ is the topic distribution of the document d, and we assume that j is within the window size.

We consider two variants, which differ in how the probability $p(w_{t+j}|w_t, z)$ is evaluated. In the first variant, called STE-Same, we assume that for each skip-gram $\langle w_{t+j}, w_t \rangle$, the words w_{t+j} and w_t belong to the same topic z:

$$p(w_{t+j}|w_t, z) = \frac{\exp(V_{w_{t+j},z} \cdot U_{w_t,z})}{\sum_{w' \in \Lambda} \exp(V_{w',z} \cdot U_{w_t,z})} \tag{2}$$

where Λ is the vocabulary of the whole corpus. Computing the value $p(w_{t+j}|w_t, z)$ based on Eq. 2 is not feasible in practice, given that the computational cost is proportional to the size of Λ. However, similar as for the standard Skip-gram model, we can rely on negative sampling to address this (see Section 3.2).

In the second variant, called STE-Diff, we assume that for each skip-gram $\langle w_{t+j}, w_t \rangle$, the topic assignment z_{t+j} of word w_{t+j} is independent of the topic assignment z_t of word w_t. We then have:

$$\begin{aligned} p(w_{t+j}|w_t, d) &= \sum_{z_t=1}^{K} \sum_{z_{t+j}=1}^{K} p(w_{t+j}|w_t, z_t, z_{t+j})p(z_t, z_{t+j}|d) \\ &= \sum_{z_t=1}^{K} \sum_{z_{t+j}=1}^{K} p(w_{t+j}|w_t, z_t, z_{t+j})p(z_t|d)p(z_{t+j}|d) \end{aligned} \tag{3}$$

The probability that the word w_{t+j} is generated, given the central word w_t and the topic assignments z_{t+j} and z_t is then evaluated as follows:

$$p(w_{t+j}|w_t, z_t, z_{t+j}) = \frac{\exp(V_{w_{t+j},z_{t+j}} \cdot U_{w_t,z_t})}{\sum_{w' \in \Lambda} \exp(V_{w',z_{t+j}} \cdot U_{w_t,z_t})} \tag{4}$$

Clearly, both variants have complementary advantages and drawbacks. The STE-Same model will lead to more coherent topics, but it will not allow us to measure the similarity between words across different topics. The STE-Diff model, on the other hand, does allow us to evaluate such inter-topic similarities, but the resulting topics may be less coherent. In practice, we could of course also consider intermediate approaches, where $z_{t+j} = z_j$ is assumed to hold with a high probability, rather than being imposed as a hard constraint.

3.2 Algorithm Design

We need an inference method that can learn, given a corpus, the values of the model parameters, i.e. the word embeddings $U_{w,z}$ and $V_{w,z}$ corresponding to each topic z, as well as the topic distribution $p(z|d)$ for each document d. Our inference framework combines the Expectation-Maximization (EM) method with the negative sampling scheme. It is summarized for the STE-Same variant in Algorithm 1. The inference method for STE-Diff is analogous. In each iteration of this algorithm, we update the word embeddings and then evaluate the topic distribution $p(z|d)$ of each document. To update the word embeddings, we iterate over each skip-gram, sample several negative instances and then compute the posterior

Algorithm 1 EM negative sampling for STE-Same

```
Initialize U, V, p(z|d)
for out_iter = 1 to Max_Out_iter do
    for each document d in 𝒟 do
        for each skip-gram ⟨w_{t+j}, w_t⟩ in d do
            Sample negative instances from the distribution P.
            Update p(w_{t+j}|w_t, z), p(z_k|d, w_{t+j}, w_t) by Eq. 9
            and Eq. 6 respectively.
            for in_iter = 1 to Max_In_iter do
                Update U, V using the gradient decent method
                with Eq. 10 and Eq. 11
            end for
        end for
        Update p(z|d) using Eq. 8
    end for
end for
```

topic distribution for the skip-gram. Then we use the EM algorithm to optimize the log-likelihood of the skip-grams in the document. In the E-step, we use the Bayes rule to evaluate the posterior topic distribution and derive the objective function. In the M-step, we maximize the objective function with the gradient descent method and update the corresponding embeddings U_w and V_w.

The overall training objective measures how well we can predict surrounding words, taking into account the topic distributions of the documents. For each document d, given a sequence of words $w_1, w_2, \cdots, w_{T_d}$, the log-likelihood $\mathcal{L}_d$ is defined as follows.

$$\mathcal{L}_d = \sum_{t=1}^{T_d} \sum_{\substack{-c \leq j \leq c \\ j \neq 0}} \log p(w_{t+j}|w_t, d) \tag{5}$$

where c is the size of the training windows. The overall log-likelihood is then given by $\mathcal{L} = \sum_d \mathcal{L}_d$.

In the E-step, the topic distribution for each skip-gram in d can be evaluated using the Bayes rule as:

$$p(z'_k|d, w_t, w_{t+j}) = \frac{p(w_{t+j}|z'_k, w_t)p(z'_k|d)}{\sum_z p(w_{t+j}|z, w_j)p(z|d)} \tag{6}$$

In the M-step, given the posterior topic distribution Eq. 6, the goal is to maximize the following Q function:

$$\begin{aligned} Q &= \sum_d \sum_{t=1}^{T_d} \sum_{\substack{-c \leq j \leq c \\ j \neq 0}} \sum_z p(z|d, w_t, w_{t+j}) log(p(z|d)p(w_{t+j}|z, w_t)) \\ &= \sum_d \sum_{\{w_t, w_{t+j}\} \in P_d} n(d, w_t, w_{t+j}) \sum_z p(z|d, w_t, w_{t+j}) \\ &[\log(z|d) + \log(p(w_{t+j}|z, w_t))] \end{aligned} \tag{7}$$

where P_d is the set of the skip-grams in d. $n(d, w_t, w_{t+j})$ denotes the number of the skip-gram $\langle w_t, w_{t+j} \rangle$ in d. Using the Lagrange multiplier, we can obtain the update rule of $p(z|d)$, satisfying the normalization constrains that $\sum_z p(z|d) = 1$ for each document d:

$$p(z|d) = \frac{\sum_{\{w_t, w_{t+j}\} \in P_d} n(d, w_t, w_{t+j})p(z|d, w_t, w_{t+j})}{\sum_{\{w_t, w_{t+j}\} \in P_d} n(d, w_t, w_{t+j})} \tag{8}$$

As already mentioned, it is not feasible to directly optimize $U_{w,z}$ and $V_{w,z}$ due to the term $\sum_{w \in \Lambda} exp(V_{w,z} \cdot U_{w,z})$. Inspired by the negative sampling scheme, we therefore estimate the probability of predicting the context word $p(w_{t+j}|w_t, z)$ as follows:

$$\begin{aligned} \log p(w_{t+j}|w_t, z) &\propto \log \sigma(V_{w_{t+j},z} \cdot U_{w_t,z}) \\ &+ \sum_{i=1}^{n} \mathbb{E}_{w_i \sim P}[\log \sigma(-V_{w_i,z} \cdot U_{w_t,z})] \end{aligned} \tag{9}$$

where $\sigma(x) = 1/(1 + \exp(-x))$ and w_i is a negative instance which is sampled from the distribution $P(.)$. Mikolov et al. [21] have investigated many choices for $P(w)$ and found that the best $P(w)$ is equal to the unigram distribution $Unigram(w)$ raised to the $3/4rd$ power. We exploit the same setting of $P(w)$ in [21]. Evaluating $\log p(w_{t+j}|w_t, z)$ for each term in the overall objective function, we obtain the following gradients: Therefore, the gradients of the objective function with respect to U and V can be formulated as follows:

$$\frac{\partial \mathcal{L}}{U_{w_t,z}} = -(\xi_{w'w_t} - \sigma(V_{w',z} \cdot U_{w_t,z})) \cdot V_{w',z} \cdot P(z|d, w_t, w') \tag{10}$$

$$\frac{\partial \mathcal{L}}{V_{w',z}} = -(\xi_{w'w_t} - \sigma(V_{w',z} \cdot U_{w_t,z})) \cdot U_{w_t,z} \cdot P(z|d, w_t, w') \tag{11}$$

where

$$\xi_{w'w_t} = \begin{cases} 1, & \text{if } w' \text{is a word in the context window of } w_t \\ 0, & \text{otherwise} \end{cases} \tag{12}$$

The difference between the updated rules of U and V and those in the original Skip-gram model is that we maximize $P(z_k|d, w_t, w_{t+j}) \cdot \log P(w_{t+j}|w_t, z)$ instead of $\log P(w_{t+j}|w_t)$ for each skip-gram. This is in accordance with the fact that our model uses the topic distribution to predict context words.

$$\mathcal{L}_{BTM} = \sum_d \sum_{t=1}^{T_d} \log p(w_{t+1}|w_t, d) \tag{13}$$

Comparing the original likelihood of Bi-gram Topic Model (BTM) [40] in Eq. 13 with ours, we can see the connection between our STE model and BTM. Specifically the objective functions in Eq. 5 and Eq. 13 share similar form. Both of them are related to the product of conditional probabilities which predict the next word given the preceding word no matter skip-gram or bi-gram. Such connection provides an insight for our model indicating that it is capable of discovering good topics and identifying high-quality word embedding vectors jointly.

3.3 Topic Generation

One important aspect of topic models is their interpretability, where the semantic meaning of a topic can be naturally perceived by examining the top ranked words. In standard topic models, these top-ranked words are simply those that maximize $P(w|z)$ for the multinomial distribution associated with the considered topic z. In our model, on the other hand, we can evaluate the probability of $p(w_{t+j}|z, w_t)$ for each skip-gram $\langle w_t, w_{t+j} \rangle$. Therefore, we represent each topic as the ranked list of bi-grams. Each bi-gram is sorted using Eq. 9 and the top-ranked bi-grams are selected from the ranking list. The original time complexity of calculating $p(w_{t+1}|z, w_t)$ is $|\Lambda|^2 \times K$, where $|\Lambda|$ is the size of the vocabulary, i.e., around 10^5. To make it more efficient, we first collect all the bi-grams in the corpus and evaluate the corresponding probability $p(w_{t+1}|z, w_t)$. Then the time complexity is reduced to be linear to the number of bi-grams. Note that in Eq. 9, we do not need to consider the part related to the sampled negative instances for each bi-gram, i.e., the summation expression, as we can assume it to be constant.

3.4 Folding-in for New Documents

Given a new document d', our algorithm can infer the topic distribution of d'. Given U and V learned from the training process, we fix the values of U and V, and then only update $p(z|d')$ using Algorithm 1.

For each word w in d', the posterior topic distribution of w, $p(z|w, d')$ can also be inferred. We consider that the topic distribution of w is related to not only its context words but also the topic distribution of d'. Therefore, using the Bayes rule, we have:

$$\log p(z|w, c_w, d') \propto \log p(z|d') + \log p(c_w|z, w, d') \quad (14)$$

where c_w is the set of the context words of w. The likelihood term $\log p(c_w|z, w, d')$ can be defined as the sum of $\log p(w_{t+j}|w_t, z)$, where w_{t+j} belongs to the context words. The probability $p(w_{t+j}|w_t, z)$ can be computed in Eq. 9. The term $p(z|d')$ is the corresponding prior probability.

4 EXPERIMENTS

In this section, we present a detailed analysis of the performance of our method. We first present a qualitative analysis of the learned topic-specific embeddings. We then focus on evaluating the quality of the word embedding on a standard word similarity benchmark. Subsequently, we evaluate the quality of the identified topics, focusing in particular on their coherence. Finally, as an example of a downstream task, we analyze the performance of our model in a document classification task.

4.1 Qualitative Analysis

To illustrate the interactions between word embeddings and latent topics, we visualize the results of our STE-Same and STE-Diff models in Figures 1a and 1b respectively. For this figure, and in the following experiments, we have used the Wikipedia dump from April 2010 [34], which has previously been used for other word embedding models [12]. We have chosen the number of topics $K = 10$. The number of outer iterations and inner iterations are both set to 15. The dimension of the embedding vectors was chosen as 400, in accordance with [19]. For each skip-gram, we set the window size to 10 and sample 8 negative instances following [37]. To generate the visualization in Figure 1, we have used the t-SNE algorithm [20], applied to the vectors of the 500 most frequent words.

In Figure 1, each node denotes a topic-specific word vector. To illustrate how polysemy is handled, we show labels for the word "party", as an example of a polysemous word, and for the word "government", as an example of a monosemous word. The labels show both the word and topic index, separated by "#". In Figure 1a, we can observe that our STE-Same model divides the whole space into K disjoint subspaces, with each subspace representing a topic. Within each subspace the words with similar meanings are close. Note that the similarity of the words "government" and "party" depend on the considered sense for the latter word. Accordingly, we see that "government" and "party" are close to each other in some subspaces, but far apart in others. For example, in the subspace of Topic 0, the position of the word "party" is far from the position of the word "government", which suggests that the meaning of "party" under Topic 0 is not related to a political party. In contrast, for Topics 4, 6 and 8, the vectors for "party" and "government" are similar, suggesting that "party" in these spaces is regarded as a political organization.

On the other hand, Figure 1b illustrates how STE-Diff generates a more universal space in which word embeddings from different topics co-exist in this shared space. Words from different topics with a similar meaning are represented using similar vectors. In particular, for monosemous words such as "government" the word vectors are approximately the same. For the word "party", on the other hand, we see three clearly distinct representations, only one of which (party#2) is close to the vectors for "government". Moreover, we found that "party#3" represents the semantic sense of community because it is close to the word "organization" and the word "group". The representations of the word "party" from the other topics are approximately the same. They are close to the representations of the word "summer" and the word "shout". It indicates that the word "party" represents the meaning about the concept of human activity.

From the comparison between Figure 1a and Figure 1b, the STE-Same model and the STE-Diff model can be regarded as two different paradigms derived from the treatment of topic consistency in a skip-gram. The advantage of the STE-Diff model over the STE-Same model is that the STE-Diff model can support better the evaluation of the similarity of words from different topics. For example, the senses of "party" under Topics 4 and 6 are very close to "government" in the STE-Same model. However, when we evaluate the similarity between "party#4" and "government#6", we find that the distance cannot reflect very well the word similarity. Nevertheless, this STE-Same model can still achieve comparable performance with existing models in the quantitative word embedding evaluation experiment as presented in the next subsection. On the other hand, our STE-Diff model can handle very well the evaluation of the similarity of words from different topics. The reason is that it represents every sense in a more universal shared space without gaps between different topics.

Table 1: The most similar words identified by the original Skip-gram model and our STE-Diff model.

Model	Words	Similar Words
Skip-gram	apple	macintosh, ios, juice
STE-Diff	apple#1	peach, orange, juice
	apple#2	macintosh, ipod, windows
Skip-gram	java	sumatra, html, somalia
STE-Diff	java#1	sumatra, somalia, sudan
	java#2	html, lisp, jde
Skip-gram	cell	phones, viral, biology
STE-Diff	cell#1	phones, technology, scanner
	cell#2	viral, tumor, embryonic

Table 1 shows the nearest neighbours of some polysemous words, according to the Skip-gram model and our STE-Diff model (using cosine similarity in both cases). We observe that these nearest neighbours for Skip-gram mix different senses of the given words, which is expected since Skip-gram does not address polysemy. For

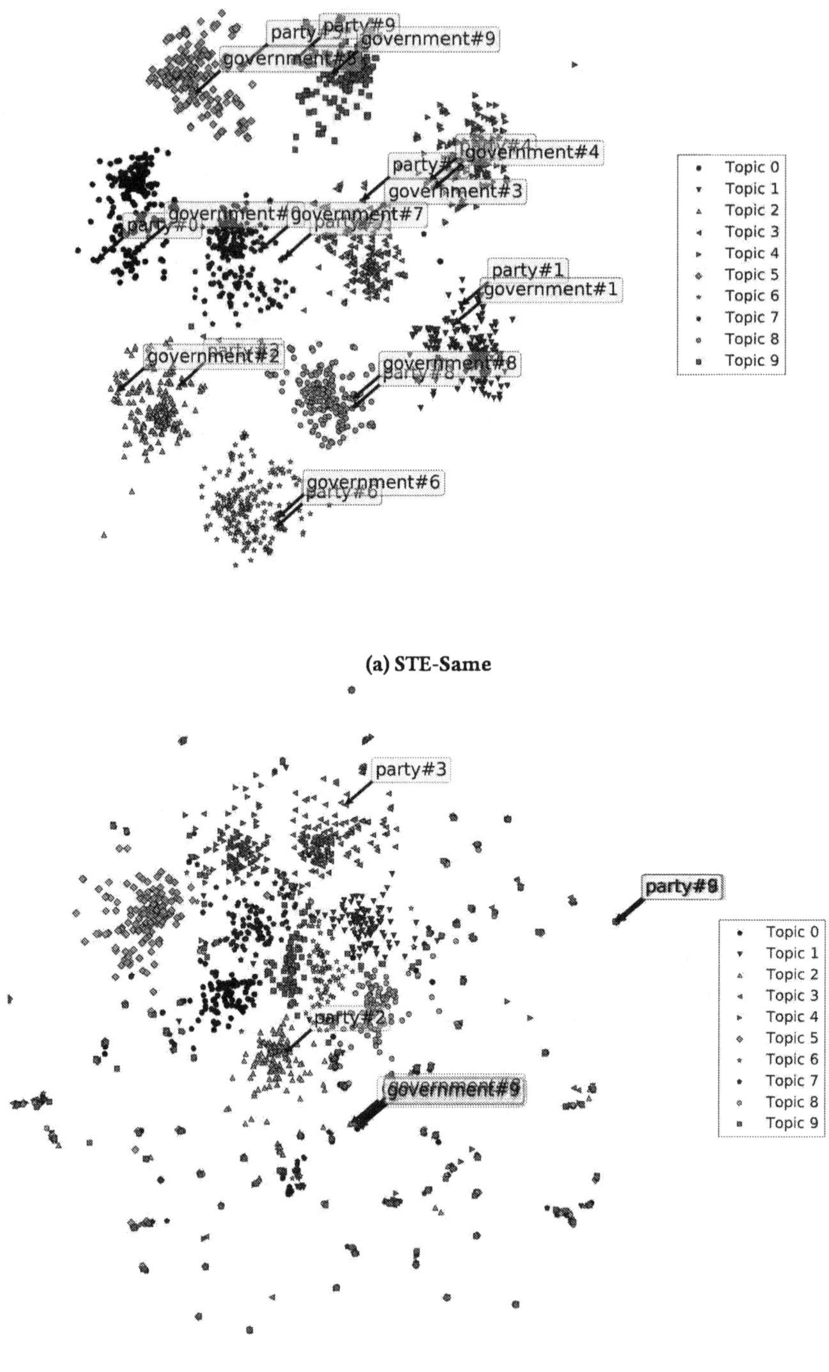

(a) STE-Same

(b) STE-Diff

Figure 1: Visualization of the word embeddings learned using STE-Same and STE-Diff with 10 topics. The polysemous word "party" and the monosemous word "government" are highlighted for the comparison.

example, the nearest neighbours of "apple" are given as "macintosh", "ios", and "juice", indicating the "company" and "fruit" interpretations of the word "apple" are mixed. In contrast, our STE-Diff model can distinguish different prototypes of polysemous words via the latent topics. For example, the most similar words of "apple" under Topic 1 are "peach", "orange" and "juice", which clearly corresponds to the fruit interpretation. Under Topic 2, they are "macintosh", "ipod" and "windows", clearly referring to the company interpretation.

4.2 Word Embedding Evaluation

The most common approach for evaluating word embeddings is to assess how well the similarity scores they produce correlate with human judgments of similarity. Although there are several word similarity benchmark datasets, most do not provide any context information for the words, and are therefore not appropriate for evaluating models of similarity for polysemous words. Huang et al. [12] prepared a data set, named Stanford's Contextual Word Similarity (SCWS) data set, which includes 2003 word pairs together with their context sentences. The ground truth similarity score with the range $[0, 10]$ was labeled by humans, according to the semantic meaning of the words in the given contexts. We adopt this benchmark data set for evaluating the quality of our word embeddings.

We compare our results with the following baselines and state-of-the-art methods, reporting the previously published results from their papers.

TFIDF We consider two variants, TFIDF and Pruned TFIDF. The TFIDF method represents each word as a vector, capturing the context words with which it co-occurs in a 10-word window. Each context word is presented by the one-hot representation and weighted via TF-IDF learned from the training set. The Pruned TFIDF method proposed by [28] improves the original TFIDF model by pruning the context words with low TF-IDF scores.

Word embedding These baselines include the C&W method proposed by [7] and the Skip-gram model [21]. Note that since neither of these methods considers polysemy, word similarity is evaluated without regarding the context sentences.

Topic models The first model, named LDA-S, represents each word w in a document d as the posterior topic distribution, namely, $p(z|w)$ where $p(z|w) \propto p(w|z)p(z|d)$. The second model, named LDA-C, additionally considers the posterior topic distribution of the surrounding context words, as follows:

$$p(z|w, c) \propto p(w|z)p(z|d) \prod_{w' \in c} p(w'|z) \tag{15}$$

where c is the set of the context words of w.

Multiple prototype models These methods represent each word sense as a fixed length vector. One representative work, proposed by Huang et al. [12], exploits global properties of the corpus such as term frequency to learn multiple embeddings via neural networks. Tian et al. [37] introduce a latent variable to denote the distribution of multiple prototypes for each word in a probabilistic manner. Liu et al. [19] propose a model called TWE, which concatenates the pre-trained topics with the word embeddings for representing each prototype.

We present the related parameter settings as reported in the previous papers [12, 19, 37]. For Pruned TFIDF, top 200 words with the highest scores are preserved. For the model in [37], each word is assumed with 10 prototypes. Following [19], the number of topics of LDA-S, LDA-C and TWE is 400. Note that the size of each embedding vector in TWE is 800 [19], which consists of 400-dimension word embedding and 400-dimension topic embedding. The parameter setting of our STE model is the same as described in Section 4.1.

For all the different representations, the word similarity is evaluated using cosine similarity. However, for the multiple prototype based methods, as well as for our STE model, two different variants are considered:

AvgSimC Given a word w and its associated context words c_w, we can infer the posterior topic distribution $p(z|w, c_w, d)$ according to Eq. 14. Then the averaged similarity between two words (w_i, w_j) over the assignments of topics is computed as:

$$AvgSimC(w_i, w_j) = \sum_{z_i} \sum_{z_j} p(z_i|w_i, c_{w_i})p(z_j|w_j, c_{w_j}) \times \cos(U_{w_i,z_i}, U_{w_j,z_j})$$

where $U(w_i, z_i)$ is the embedding vector of w_i under the topic z_i and $\cos(\cdot)$ is the cosine similarity.

MaxSimC In this case, we instead evaluate the similarity between the most probable vectors of each word. It is defined as:

$$MaxSimC(w_i, w_j) = Sim(U_{w_i,z_i}, U_{w_j,z_j})$$

where $z = \arg\max_z(p(z|w, c))$.

Following previous work, we use the Spearman correlation coefficient as the evaluation metric. The results are shown in Table 2. The STE model performs comparably to the state-of-the-art TWE model, and outperforms the baseline methods. TWE also exploits both topics and embeddings. However, the vectors in the TWE model have twice as many dimensions as those in our model, since each word is represented as the concatenation of a word vector and a topic vector. The STE-Diff variant outperforms STE-Same, for both the *AvgSimC* and *MaxSimC* ranking measures. While STE-Same can generate more coherent topics as indicated in Section 4.3, this comes at the price of slightly less accurate word vectors, which is not unexpected.

It is interesting to note that the original Skip-gram model can still achieve satisfactory performance. We observe that the words in the SCWS data set are mostly monosemous words. Particularly, among 2003 word pairs in this data set, there are 241 word pairs containing the same word within a word pair. One may expect that such identical words have different senses leading to a low ground truth similarity score. However, only 50 of them have the ground truth similarity score less than 5.0. It indicates that the proportion of the challenging polysemous words in this data set is quite small.

Table 2: Spearman correlation $\rho \times 100$ for the SCWS data set.

Model	Similarity Metrics	$\rho \times 100$
C&W	Cosine Similarity	57.0
Skip-gram	Cosine Similarity	65.7
TFIDF	Cosine Similarity	26.3
Pruned TFIDF	Cosine Similarity	62.5
LDA-S	Cosine Similarity	56.9
LDA-C	Cosine Similarity	50.4
Tian	$AvgSimC$	65.4
Tian	$MaxSimC$	63.6
Huang	$AvgSimC$	65.3
Huang	$AvgSimC$	58.6
TWE	$AvgSimC$	68.1
TWE	$MaxSimC$	67.3
STE-Same	$AvgSimC$	66.7
STE-Same	$MaxSimC$	65.5
STE-Diff	$AvgSimC$	68.0
STE-Diff	$MaxSimC$	67.7

4.3 Topic Coherence

In our model, topics can be interpreted by looking at the top-ranked bi-grams according to Eq. 9. To evaluate how coherent these topics are, we have applied our model to the training set of the 20Newsgroups corpus. The 20Newsgroups corpus[1] is a collection of 19,997 newsgroup documents. The documents are sorted by date and split into training set (60%) and test set (40%). The data is organized, almost evenly, into 20 different newsgroups, each corresponding to a different topic. Some of the newsgroups are very closely related to each other, however. The categories of this corpus, partitioned according to subject matter. are shown in Table 3. As text preprocessing, we have removed punctuations and stop words, and all words were lowercased.

Table 3: The categories of the 20Newsgroups corpus.

comp.graphics comp.os.ms-windows.misc comp.sys.ibm.pc.hardware comp.sys.mac.hardware comp.windows.x	rec.autos rec.motorcycles rec.sport.baseball rec.sport.hockey	sci.crypt sci.electronics sci.med sci.space
misc.forsale	talk.politics.misc talk.politics.guns talk.politics.mideast talk.religion.misc	alt.atheism soc.religion.christian

To evaluate the generated topics, we use a common topic coherence metric which measures the relatedness between the top-ranked words [6, 36]. The intuition is that topics where the top-ranked words are all closely semantically related are easy to interpret, and in this sense semantically coherent. Following Lau et al. [14, 25], we use the pointwise mutual information (PMI) score as our topic coherence metric. PMI has been found to strongly correlate with human annotations of topic coherence. For a topic z, given the top-ranked T words, namely, $w_1, w_2, \cdots, w_T$, the PMI score of the topic z can be calculated as follows:

Table 4: Topic coherence evaluation using the PMI metric with different numbers of top words.

	$T = 5$	T = 10	T = 15	T = 20
BTM	0.014	0.036	0.041	0.048
STE-Same	0.180	0.110	0.107	0.102
STE-Diff	0.015	0.067	0.058	0.054

$$\text{PMI-Score}(z) = \sum_{1 \le i \le j \le T} \log \frac{P(w_i, w_j)}{P(w_i)P(w_j)} \tag{16}$$

where $P(w_i, w_j)$ represents the probability that words w_i and w_j co-occur and $P(w_i) = \sum_w P(w_i, w)$. We compute the average PMI score of word pairs in each topic using Eq. 16. The average score of all the topics is computed. The higher the value, the better is the coherence. Newman et al. [25] observed that it is important to use another data set to evaluate the PMI based measure. Therefore, we use a 10-word sliding window in Wikipedia [34] to estimate the probabilities $P(w_i, w_j)$.

We compare our STE model with the Bi-gram Topic Model (BTM) [40] which predicts the next word given the topic assignments as well as the current word. Note that our STE model and LDA are not directly comparable because LDA can only output unigrams as topics.

All models are trained on the training set of the 20newsgroups corpus. The number of topics was set to 20 for all models, which is the same as the number of categories in the 20Newsgroups corpus. For our model, 400-dimensional word vectors were used. To extract the top-ranked words, we first learn the topic-specific word embeddings U_w and V_w and then use Eq. 9. Only bi-grams with frequency greater than 5 are considered. For the BTM model, we use the default setting of hyper-parameters provided by the package [2], i.e., $\alpha = 50.0$, $\beta = 0.01$, and $\gamma = 0.01$.

The average PMI scores with different numbers of top-ranked words are shown in Table 4. We can see that our STE model generally improves the coherence of the learned topics. Compared with BTM, our STE model incorporates the semantic relationship between words which is learned from word embeddings to improve the quality of topics. Compared with the variant STE-Diff, the STE-Same model can produce more coherent topics as presented in Figure 1.

Table 5 shows the top 10 bi-grams of the topics identified by the STE-Same model. We can observe that many topics are corresponding to categories from Table 3. For example, the top-ranked bi-grams of Topic 1, such as the terminology phrase "remote sensing" and the name of the company, "mcdonnell douglas", indicate that Topic 1 is related to the category "sci.space". Similarly, most of the top-ranked bi-grams of Topic 5 are medical terms, such as "mucus membrane" and "amino acids". The top-ranked bi-grams of Topic 6 are the names of some famous baseball and hockey players, such as "brind amour"[3] and "garry galley"[4], indicating that Topic 6 is associated to the categories "rec.sport.baseball" and "rec.sport.hockey". Among others, we also observe a connection between Topic 4 and

[1] http://qwone.com/ jason/20Newsgroups/

[2] http://mallet.cs.umass.edu/topics.php

[3] https://en.wikipedia.org/wiki/Rod_Brind'Amour

[4] https://en.wikipedia.org/wiki/Garry_Galley

"talk.politics", Topic 7 and "comp.sys.ibm.pc.hardware", as well as Topic 8 and "soc.religion.christian". These correspondences further illustrate that our model can identify latent topics effectively.

Another interesting observation is that most of top-ranked bi-grams are person names and domain-specific terms. This arises because we rank the bi-grams according to the probability $p(w_{i+1}|w_i, z)$, which indicates that the words w_{i+1} and w_i should have strong connections under the topic z. The name of famous people and domain-specific terms can satisfy this requirement.

4.4 Document Classification

We also analyze the suitability of our model for representing documents. To this end, we consider the task of document classification, using again the 20Newsgroup corpus. We have used the original splits into training (60%) and testing (40%) data. For our STE model, as before, we set the number of topics as 20 and the dimensionality of the vector space as 400. To apply our model to document representation, we first infer the posterior topic distribution of each word in the test set using Eq. 14, and then represent each document as the average of the word vectors in the document, weighted by the TF-IDF score of each word. In particular, each word vector is given by:

$$\mathrm{Vec}_w = TFIDF_w \times \sum_{z=1}^{K} p(z|w, c) U_{w,z} \tag{17}$$

where $TFIDF_w$ is the TF-IDF score of w in the document. To perform document classification, we use a linear SVM classifier using the package from [10].

We compare our approach with several other methods for representing documents, including bag-of-words, vector-space embeddings and latent topics. BOW is the standard bag-of-words model, which represents each document by weighting terms using the TFIDF score. As a form of feature selection, we only consider the 50,000 most frequent words in the bag-of-words representation. The embedding-based methods include the word embedding method Skip-gram, a document embedding method called the Paragraph Vector model (PV) [15], and the TWE model which also considers topics. For the Skip-gram model, we set the number of dimension to 400. We represent each document as the average of word vectors weighted by TFIDF scores. The PV model proposed by [15] represents each document directly as a vector. We use the doc2vec implementation [5] for PV. For TWE, we report the experimental results published in [19]. The topic based methods include LDA, LFTM [26], and GPU-DMM [16]. These models represent each document via the posterior topic distributions. For LFTM, we reported the experimental result published in [26]. Only F-measure of LFTM is provided. The number of topics for LFTM is 80, as that value was reported to lead to the best performance in [26]. The GPU-DMM model promotes semantically related words learned from pre-trained word embeddings by using the generalized Polya urn model. We use the default parameter setting in the GPU-DMM model. We use a number of standard evaluation metrics for classification tasks, namely accuracy, precision, recall and F1 measure.

[5] http://github.com/ccri/gensim

The results of the document classification task are presented in Table 6, showing that our STE-Diff model achieves the best results. Good results are also obtained for the TWE model, which suggests that the quality of document representations can clearly benefit from combining topics models with word embeddings. Nevertheless, compared to TWE, our model can take advantage of the interaction between topics and word embeddings to improve both, and is thus able to outperform the TWE model. The performance of GPU-DMM is not as good as expected. One reason is that this model is proposed for handling short texts [16]. Unfortunately, the documents in 20Newsgroups are not short texts.

5 CONCLUSIONS

We have proposed a model that jointly learns word embeddings and latent topics. Compared to standard word embedding models, an important advantage of incorporating topics is that polysemous words can be modeled in a more principled manner. Compared to standard topic models, using word embeddings can achieve superiority because more coherent topics can be obtained. While some previous works have already considered combinations of word embedding and topic models, these works have relied on a two-step approach, where either a standard word embedding was used as input to an improved topic model, or a standard topic model was used as input to an improved word embedding. In contrast, we jointly learn both word embeddings and latent topics, allowing our model to better exploit the mutual reinforcement between them. We have conducted a wide range of experiments, which demonstrate the advantages of our approach.

REFERENCES

[1] Ricardo Baeza-Yates, Berthier Ribeiro-Neto, and others. 1999. *Modern information retrieval*. Vol. 463.

[2] Sergey Bartunov, Dmitry Kondrashkin, Anton Osokin, and Dmitry Vetrov. 2015. Breaking Sticks and Ambiguities with Adaptive Skip-gram. *arXiv preprint arXiv:1502.07257* (2015).

[3] Yoshua Bengio. 2009. Learning deep architectures for AI. *Foundations and Trends® in Machine Learning* 2, 1 (2009), 1–127.

[4] Yoshua Bengio, Réjean Ducharme, Pascal Vincent, and Christian Jauvin. 2003. A neural probabilistic language model. *Journal of Machine Learning Research* 3 (2003), 1137–1155.

[5] David M Blei, Andrew Y Ng, and Michael I Jordan. 2003. Latent dirichlet allocation. *Journal of Machine Learning Research* 3 (2003), 993–1022.

[6] Jonathan Chang, Sean Gerrish, Chong Wang, Jordan L Boyd-Graber, and David M Blei. 2009. Reading tea leaves: How humans interpret topic models. In *Proceedings of NIPS*. 288–296.

[7] Ronan Collobert and Jason Weston. 2008. A unified architecture for natural language processing: Deep neural networks with multitask learning. In *Proceedings of ICML*. 160–167.

[8] Ronan Collobert, Jason Weston, Léon Bottou, Michael Karlen, Koray Kavukcuoglu, and Pavel Kuksa. 2011. Natural language processing (almost) from scratch. *Journal of Machine Learning Research* 12 (2011), 2493–2537.

[9] Rajarshi Das, Manzil Zaheer, and Chris Dyer. 2015. Gaussian lda for topic models with word embeddings. In *Proceedings of ACL*. 795–804.

[10] Rong-En Fan, Kai-Wei Chang, Cho-Jui Hsieh, Xiang-Rui Wang, and Chih-Jen Lin. 2008. LIBLINEAR: A library for large linear classification. *Journal of Machine Learning Research* 9 (2008), 1871–1874.

[11] Thomas Hofmann. 1999. Probabilistic latent semantic indexing. In *Proceedings of SIGIR*. 50–57.

[12] Eric H Huang, Richard Socher, Christopher D Manning, and Andrew Y Ng. 2012. Improving word representations via global context and multiple word prototypes. In *Proceedings of ACL*. 873–882.

[13] Ignacio Iacobacci, Mohammad Taher Pilehvar, and Roberto Navigli. 2016. Embeddings for word sense disambiguation: An evaluation study. In *Proceedings of ACL*. 897–907.

[14] Jey Han Lau, David Newman, and Timothy Baldwin. 2014. Machine Reading Tea Leaves: Automatically Evaluating Topic Coherence and Topic Model Quality.. In

Table 5: Top 10 bi-grams of the generated topics from the 20Newsgroups data set.

Topic 1	Topic 2	Topic 3	Topic 4
mcdonnell douglas	graphlib inria	carpal tunnel	deir yassin
remote sensing	inria graphlib	blaine gardner	ottoman empire
southern hemisphere	rainer klute	vernor vinge	bedouin negev
northern hemisphere	burkhard neidecker	thermal recalibration	negev bedouin
ozone layer	renderman pixar	syndrome carpal	ermeni mezalimi
cosmic rays	pixar renderman	tunnel syndrome	ishtar easter
orthodox physicists	spine dinks	mudder disciples	eighth graders
black holes	reflections shadows	lance hartmann	prime minister
ames dryden	marching cubes	hartmann lance	nagorno karabakh
sounding rockets	liquid fueled	blgardne javelin	lieutenant colonel
circular orbit	gravity assist	evans sutherland	democracy corps
Topic 5	**Topic 6**	**Topic 7**	**Topic 8**
mucus membrane	spring training	setjmp longjmp	saint aloysius
amino acids	brett hull	xtaddtimeout xtaddworkproc	empty tomb
kidney stones	cape breton	xtaddinput xtaddtimeout	respiratory papillomatosis
anti fungal	garry galley	bname pname	zaurak kamsarakan
candida albicans	brind amour	babak sehari	biblical contradictions
oxalic acid	bobby clarke	infoname uuname	recurrent respiratory
kirlian photography	cheap shot	uuname infoname	ohanus appressian
kidney stone	wade boggs	physicist dewey	archbishop lefebvre
glide jubilee	wayne komets	richardd hoskyns	joseph smith
penev venezia	tommy soderstrom	arithmetic coding	serdar argic
vaginal tract	chris chelios	mcdonnell douglas	rodney king

Table 6: Document classification results.

Model	Accuracy	Precision	Recall	F-measure
BOW	79.7	79.5	79.0	79.0
Skip-Gram	75.4	75.1	74.3	74.2
TWE	81.5	81.2	80.6	80.6
PV	75.4	74.9	74.3	74.3
LDA	72.2	70.8	70.7	70.0
LFTM	-	-	-	76.8
GPU-DMM	48.0	56.8	46.9	47.3
STE-Same	80.4	80.3	80.4	80.2
STE-Diff	**82.9**	**82.5**	**82.3**	**82.5**

Proceedings of EACL. 530–539.

[15] Quoc V Le and Tomas Mikolov. 2014. Distributed Representations of Sentences and Documents.. In *Proceedings of ICML.* 1188–1196.

[16] Chenliang Li, Haoran Wang, Zhiqian Zhang, Aixin Sun, and Zongyang Ma. 2016. Topic Modeling for Short Texts with Auxiliary Word Embeddings. In *Proceedings of SIGIR.* 165–174.

[17] Shaohua Li, Tat-Seng Chua, Jun Zhu, and Chunyan Miao. 2016. Generative topic embedding: a continuous representation of documents. In *Proceedings of ACL.* 666–675.

[18] Pengfei Liu, Xipeng Qiu, and Xuanjing Huang. 2015. Learning context-sensitive word embeddings with neural tensor skip-gram model. In *Proceedings of IJCAI.* 1284–1290.

[19] Yang Liu, Zhiyuan Liu, Tat-Seng Chua, and Maosong Sun. 2015. Topical Word Embeddings.. In *Proceedings of AAAI.* 2418–2424.

[20] Laurens van der Maaten and Geoffrey Hinton. 2008. Visualizing data using t-SNE. *Journal of Machine Learning Research* 9 (2008), 2579–2605.

[21] Tomas Mikolov, Ilya Sutskever, Kai Chen, Greg S Corrado, and Jeff Dean. 2013. Distributed representations of words and phrases and their compositionality. In *Advances in Neural Information Processing Systems.* 3111–3119.

[22] Tomas Mikolov, Wen-tau Yih, and Geoffrey Zweig. 2013. Linguistic Regularities in Continuous Space Word Representations.. In *Proceedings of NAACL.* 746–751.

[23] Frederic Morin and Yoshua Bengio. 2005. Hierarchical Probabilistic Neural Network Language Model. *Proceedings of AISTATS* (2005), 246.

[24] Arvind Neelakantan, Jeevan Shankar, Alexandre Passos, and Andrew McCallum. 2015. Efficient non-parametric estimation of multiple embeddings per word in vector space. In *Proceedings of EMNLP.* 1059–1069.

[25] David Newman, Jey Han Lau, Karl Grieser, and Timothy Baldwin. 2010. Automatic evaluation of topic coherence. In *Proceedings of NAACL.* 100–108.

[26] Dat Quoc Nguyen, Richard Billingsley, Lan Du, and Mark Johnson. 2015. Improving Topic Models with Latent Feature Word Representations. *TACL* 3 (2015), 299–313.

[27] Jeffrey Pennington, Richard Socher, and Christopher D. Manning. 2014. Glove: Global Vectors for Word Representation. In *Proceedings of EMNLP.* 1532–1543.

[28] Joseph Reisinger and Raymond J Mooney. 2010. Multi-prototype vector-space models of word meaning. In *Proceedings of NAACL.* 109–117.

[29] Navid Rekabsaz. 2016. Enhancing Information Retrieval with Adapted Word Embedding. In *Proceedings of SIGIR.* 1169–1169.

[30] Yafeng Ren, Yue Zhang, Meishan Zhang, and Donghong Ji. 2016. Improving Twitter Sentiment Classification Using Topic-Enriched Multi-Prototype Word Embeddings.. In *Proceedings of AAAI.* 3038–3044.

[31] Michael Roth and Mirella Lapata. 2016. Neural semantic role labeling with dependency path embeddings. (2016), 1192–1202.

[32] David E Rumelhart, Geoffrey E Hinton, and Ronald J Williams. 1988. Learning representations by back-propagating errors. *Cognitive modeling* 5, 3 (1988), 1.

[33] Bahar Salehi, Paul Cook, and Timothy Baldwin. 2015. A Word Embedding Approach to Predicting the Compositionality of Multiword Expressions.. In *Proceedings of NAACL.* 977–983.

[34] Cyrus Shaoul. 2010. The westbury lab wikipedia corpus. *Edmonton, AB: University of Alberta* (2010).

[35] Richard Socher, Cliff C Lin, Chris Manning, and Andrew Y Ng. 2011. Parsing natural scenes and natural language with recursive neural networks. In *Proceedings of ICML.* 129–136.

[36] Keith Stevens, Philip Kegelmeyer, David Andrzejewski, and David Buttler. 2012. Exploring topic coherence over many models and many topics. In *Proceedings of EMNLP.* 952–961.

[37] Fei Tian, Hanjun Dai, Jiang Bian, Bin Gao, Rui Zhang, Enhong Chen, and Tie-Yan Liu. 2014. A Probabilistic Model for Learning Multi-Prototype Word Embeddings.. In *Proceedings of COLING.* 151–160.

[38] Joseph Turian, Lev Ratinov, and Yoshua Bengio. 2010. Word representations: a simple and general method for semi-supervised learning. In *Proceedings of ACL.* 384–394.

[39] Peter D Turney, Patrick Pantel, and others. 2010. From frequency to meaning: Vector space models of semantics. *Journal of Artificial Intelligence Research* 37, 1 (2010), 141–188.

[40] Hanna M Wallach. 2006. Topic modeling: beyond bag-of-words. In *Proceedings of ICML.* 977–984.

[41] Xuerui Wang, Andrew McCallum, and Xing Wei. 2007. Topical n-grams: Phrase and topic discovery, with an application to information retrieval. In *Proceedings of ICDM.* 697–702.

On the Power Laws of Language: Word Frequency Distributions

Flavio Chierichetti*
Sapienza University
Rome, Italy
flavio@di.uniroma1.it

Ravi Kumar
Google
Mountain View, CA, USA
ravi.k53@gmail.com

Bo Pang
Google
Mountain View, CA, USA
bopang42@gmail.com

ABSTRACT

About eight decades ago, Zipf postulated that the word frequency distribution of languages is a *power law*, i.e., it is a straight line on a log-log plot. Over the years, this phenomenon has been documented and studied extensively. For many corpora, however, the empirical distribution barely resembles a power law: when plotted on a log-log scale, the distribution is concave and appears to be composed of two differently sloped straight lines joined by a smooth curve. A simple generative model is proposed to capture this phenomenon. The word frequency distributions produced by this model are shown to match the observations both analytically and empirically.

1 INTRODUCTION

The distribution of word frequencies is a fundamental phenotype of a language. Word frequency distributions have been studied by statisticians and linguists since the statistics of word usage yield valuable insights into the language, its construction, and its evolution. These distributions have been long-studied outside of statistics and linguistics as well. In information retrieval, word frequency distributions (and sometimes the ranks of word frequency) are directly used by many algorithms for many tasks, e.g., weighting the significance of documents and query terms [2, 36], text classification [6, 26], topic distillation [7, 13, 38], latent semantic analysis [24, 25], and so on. The word frequency distribution plays a central role in determining the size of inverted indices [14, 30], the compression ratio of natural texts [11, 12].

In his pioneering work, Zipf postulated that the frequency of any word in the language is inversely proportional to a power of its rank [44, 45]. On a log-log plot, with the x-axis representing the rank, and the y-axis representing the frequency, the distribution would thus appear as a straight line with a negative slope. Subsequent studies have confirmed similar phenomena on different corpora and genre. Even though the actual parameters can depend on the corpus, the power-law phenomenon itself was shown to be pervasive and robust. There have been many attempts to explain and refine Zipf's law [10, 15, 19, 20, 28, 29, 31, 34, 40, 41]. Additionally, Zipf's law has been considered in the context of document retrieval by IR systems [1–3, 8, 9].

In large-scale empirical studies, however, the rank-vs-frequency distributions do not appear as straight lines on a log-log plot. Instead, they exhibit a bend that makes the curve look concave; we call the rank value at which the bend occurs as the *knee*. Interestingly, the bend is consistent with Zipf's original plot: the maximum rank in his plots is close to 10^3, whereas the knee is usually observed at a rank that is an order of magnitude higher. It is likely that the lack of computing power and automated tools made it infeasible for Zipf to move to a rank significantly larger than 10^3. This concavity-in-the-tail phenomenon has been noted empirically [23].

In this work we focus on the concavity phenomenon of the word frequency distribution. We postulate that the concavity arises from a seamless fusion of two power laws around the knee; this fusion is the byproduct of a natural corpus generative model that we introduce. To validate our model, we examine a variety of corpora, ranging from novels to news articles, and fit the functional form that comes out of our process to their word frequency distributions. The fit is surprisingly accurate, at the head, the tail, and the knee of the distributions.

Informally stated, our model works in two stages. In the first stage, a vocabulary for the corpus is generated by choosing the words from a power law distribution on the language. In the second stage, the corpus is generated by sampling the vocabulary words according to the same or another power law distribution. We show that this two-stage process gives rise to a distribution that is made up of two fused power laws. We validate this model by showing that the distortion between the distributions produced by our model and the empirical distributions is quite small. We also argue that a double Pareto distribution, which is a natural candidate to explain two fused power laws, would not be able to produce such a small distortion. The use of a two-stage process is convenient for modeling corpora obtained from different topics (e.g., sports, politics), where the first stage selects the topic vocabulary. Latent factor models [24, 25] also use a two-level process for text generation; however, each word in the text is determined by a mixture of topics rather than a single topic.

We then turn our attention to the distribution of k-grams, which has also been studied [17, 21]. It has been observed for some English and Chinese corpora that the distribution becomes flatter as k increases [22, 23]. However, to the best of our knowledge, no work has tried to explain this phenomenon. We prove analytically that the k-gram distributions become flatter as k increases, under the simple assumption that the head of the word frequency distribution is a power law.

*Supported in part by the ERC Starting Grant DMAP 680153, by a Google Focused Research Award, and by the SIR Grant RBSI14Q743.

SIGIR '17, August 07-11, 2017, Shinjuku, Tokyo, Japan

978-1-4503-5022-8/17/08...$15.00
DOI: http://dx.doi.org/10.1145/3077136.3080821

2 RELATED WORK

Power laws, also known as Pareto distributions or Zipf's laws, have been observed in a broad range of settings, i.e., city populations, sizes of earthquakes, number of citations received by papers, sales of books, number of hits on webpages, etc. [33]. According to Mitzenmacher [32], "The first known attribution of the power law distribution of word frequencies appears to be due to Estoup [18], although generally the idea (and its elucidation) are attributed to Zipf [44–46]."

The power law, as stated by Zipf [46] ($y = Kx^{-\alpha}$), appears as a straight line on a log-log plot. Mandelbrot [29] extended this form to $y = K(B + x)^{-\alpha}$ to obtain a more accurate fit for high-frequency words. On the other hand, Simon [41] developed a stochastic process based on the work of Yule [43]. Sichel [40] studied empirical fit of word frequencies with compound Poisson distribution. Baayen [5] compared different statistical models proposed in previous work for word frequency distribution. These early papers used small-scale datasets (by today's standards) and therefore do not necessarily provide a good fit to the tail of large datasets. Ha et al. [23] noted that on large-scale datasets, the word frequency distribution clearly has a concavity when plotted on the log-log scale. That is, the curve bends away from the single straight line predicted by Zipf's law. This phenomenon was more pronounced when they looked at the distribution of Chinese characters. Ha et al. [23] did not attempt to explain the form of the curves. The double Pareto distribution, which approximates the concavity with two straight lines, has also been considered for approximating word frequency distributions [14]; the fit achieved by our model is significantly more accurate than the one achievable by double Pareto distributions (see Section 5.3). Baayen [4] studied similarity relations between words and word frequency distribution. He also noted that function words straighten out the head of the distribution and complex words straighten the tail. Samuelsson [37] related Zipf's law to Turing's local re-estimation formula and van Leijenhorst and van der Weide [42] related Zipf's law to Heap's law.

There has been some work on studying the distribution of k-grams as well. Ha et al. [22, 23] studied k-grams in English and Chinese and observed that the distribution became flatter as k increased. Character k-grams and k-tuple distributions were also studied in [17] and [21]. None of these works attempted to explain these phenomena; in our work, we analytically establish the form of the k-gram distributions and show these become flatter as k increases.

Various generative models have been proposed for producing power laws. Zipf [46] hypothesized that the power law is the result of the "principle of least effort"; this was re-examined later by Mandelbrot [29], Ferrer i Cancho and Sole [20], and Ferrer i Cancho et al. [19], who developed arguments for deriving power law distributions based on information-theoretic considerations. In another line of research, people have argued that preferential attachment can lead to power laws. The general argument can be traced back to Yule [43], and a generalization was proposed by Simon [41]. Perc [34] proposes a preferential attachment process for the evolution of a language, and uses it to derive the Zipf's law. Power laws can also be obtained through the "monkeys typing randomly" (or "not-so-randomly") processes [15, 28, 31]. None of these works attempted to explain the concavity in the tail of the word frequency distribution. Mitzenmacher [32] provides a good survey on the topic of power laws.

3 EMPIRICAL ANALYSIS

We first study if the concavity in word frequency distribution is pervasive and robust, i.e., does it exist over a broad range of datasets and does it exist even when we restrict the data to a specific genre or topic? A plausible hypothesis for observing the concavity could be that for a collection of text restricted to a given genre or a given topic, the distribution would be straighter; and mixing such distributions leads to the concavity. To test this hypothesis, we constructed different datasets that can be split by different criteria. What we observe is that the concavity exists for each sub-sample.

3.1 Datasets

We conducted our empirical studies over the following four datasets. The first is `Gutenberg`, which is a mixed-genre, multi-topic, multi-lingual, and multi-author corpus of electronic books that are in the public domain from the Gutenberg project. We use the average of the birth and death years of the author as the approximation for the publication year of the book. We took the subset of 16,797 books that were written in English and has a publication year between the 17th century and the 20th century, and grouped them into four disjoint time periods (by century). The vocabulary sizes range from 100K words to over 800K words, and corpus sizes from 10 million to over 500 million tokens. In addition, we can also sample this dataset by authors.

The second dataset is News, which is a large-scale collection of news articles on two topics, namely, sports and politics. The third dataset is ANC (American National Corpus), which is a collection of American English, with written texts of different genres and transcripts of spoken data produced post 1990. The fourth dataset is `Europarl`, which is a multilingual collection of European Parliament proceedings [27]. It includes semantically equivalent content in 21 European languages. The size of the text in each language ranges from 10 million to 50 million tokens. This allows us to examine the word frequency distribution in multiple languages without having to worry whether differences were due to differences in topics or genres.

All datasets went through the same preprocessing, where all punctuation marks were removed, and all remaining tokens lower-cased. Table 1 shows the main statistics of each of these four datasets.

dataset	vocabulary size (# types)	corpus size (# tokens)
`Gutenberg` 19th	400,876	185M
News (politics)	256,758	31M
ANC (written)	115,806	8.6M
`Europarl`	87,554	56M

Table 1: Details of the four datasets

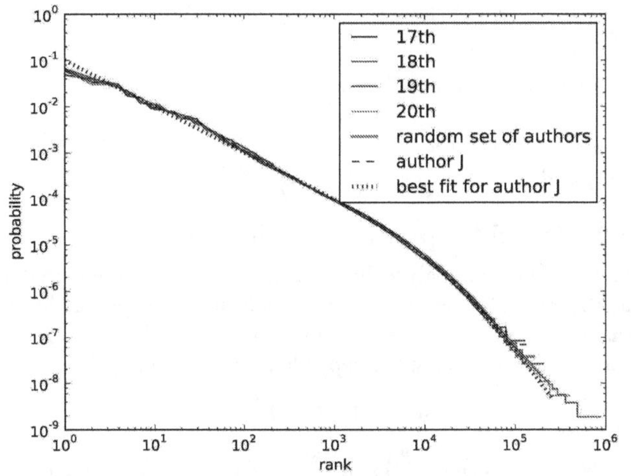

Figure 1: Word frequency distribution in the Gutenberg datasets: books in different time period (centuries), as well as a random subset of authors, and the subset of authors whose names begin with "J".

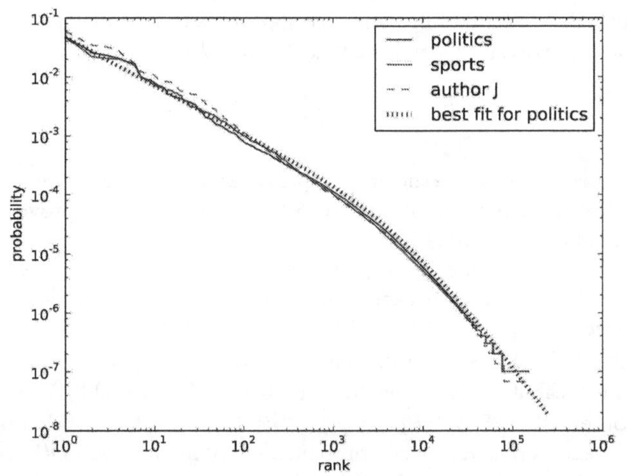

Figure 2: Word frequency distribution in news articles: politics vs sports

3.2 Word frequency distribution

First, we plot the empirical observations of word frequency distributions in different datasets on a log-log scale. We observe a clear concave shape over a broad range of corpora (Figures 1–3). Figure 1 shows word frequency distributions for different time periods in the `Gutenberg` dataset. As we can see, while the time periods (and vocabulary sizes) differ greatly, all curves closely resemble each other. In fact, the curve for `AuthorJ` (authors whose names begin with "J") largely follows the same shape. In subsequent plots, we include the `AuthorJ` curve as a reference point.

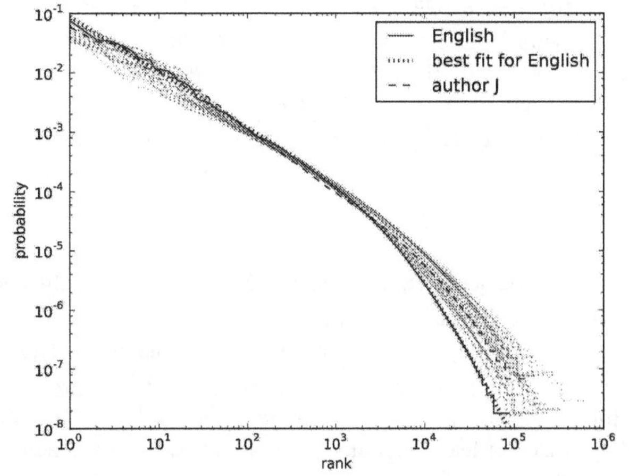

Figure 3: Word frequency distribution in 21 European languages. English is shown in blue solid line, other languages shown in dotted lines

Figure 2 shows word frequency distributions for two different topics (politics vs sports) in `News`. We observe a similar concave shape for both of them as `AuthorJ`. Figure 3 shows that the concave shape exists in a broad range of (21 European) languages. Furthermore, one could have hypothesized that smaller vocabulary leads to a straighter line (given previous studies with smaller datasets that focused on the straight-line Zipf distribution); but note the curve for English exhibits a more concave shape than that for `AuthorJ`, even though it is a smaller corpus and arguable over a more focused range of topics with less variations in styles.

3.3 k-gram frequency distribution

Figure 7 plots the empirical distribution of k-grams for $k = 1$ up to 5. Given the space constraints, we include only the plot for the `Europarl` data (where the unigram frequency distribution exhibits the highest degree of concavity). As observed in [22, 23] for some English and Chinese corpora, the lines get flatter as k grows.

4 MODEL

We define a simple and natural stochastic process for generating a corpus in a language. The process takes place in two stages. In the first stage, a *founding text* for the topic is written by choosing words from the language; the set of distinct words used in the founding text will form the *vocabulary* of the topic. In the second stage, the corpus itself is generated using the words in the vocabulary.

Let the parameters $\alpha, \beta \in (0,1)$, $\gamma > 0$, and a positive integer n, be given. Here, α is the exponent of the power law $P^{(\alpha)}_{|U|}$ defined over the universe of words U; n will be length of the founding text; β determines the position of *knee* (which will be located around n^{β}). The parameter γ is not necessary, but lends more flexibility to our model as we will see below.

We set $N = \left\lceil n^{\frac{1-\alpha\beta}{1-\alpha}} \right\rceil = |U|$, i.e., N is the number of words in the language. The distribution on the language will be the power law

corpus	α	β	γ	n
Gutenberg 19th	0.618	0.795	1.034	400,876
News (politics)	0.569	0.725	0.898	256,758
ANC (written)	0.595	0.866	0.996	115,806
Europarl	0.691	0.800	0.986	87,554

Table 2: Fitted parameters for various corpora.

$P_N^{(\alpha)}$. As we will see later, this choice of N guarantees that the knee will be positioned close to the rank n^β.

(i) In the first stage, we choose n words independently from U according to the power law $P_N^{(\alpha)}$ to produce the founding text of the topic. The vocabulary V of the topic will be the set of words that appeared at least once in the founding text. As we will see below, with high probability we will have $|V| \approx n$.

(ii) In the second stage, we use a second power law $P_N^{(\gamma)}$ over the language, possibly but not necessarily different from $P_N^{(\alpha)}$. A *corpus* for the topic is generated by choosing words independently from $P_N^{(\gamma)}$ restricted to the vocabulary (i.e., support) V.

The use of a two-stage process is convenient to model corpora belonging to different topics (e.g., sports, politics): the first stage effectively determines the vocabulary of the topic. The assumption of choosing words from V according to the original power law $P_N^{(\alpha)}$ has been made before; see, for example [40].

In our model, the parameter γ gives additional flexibility, since one is not forced to use the same power law exponent α to choose words from the vocabulary. If we insist on model parsimony, the γ parameter can be removed by choosing γ as a function of α.

Figure 5 shows the best fit of our model (formalized in the next Section) to four empirical corpora. Note that the fit from our model traces the empirical distribution quite accurately (we discuss this in Section 5.4). We include the parameters for each fit in Table 2.

5 THEORETICAL ANALYSIS

We prove in this section that, while having a very small number of parameters, our model is able to generate curves that match the empirically observed curves. We then study the distribution of k-grams and prove that the distribution gets flatter as a function of k, which matches the empirical observation as well.

All the proofs missing from this section can be found in the Appendix.

5.1 Preliminaries

We begin with some basic notation. Let the upper incomplete *Gamma function* be given by $\Gamma(a,b) = \int_b^\infty x^{a-1}e^{-x}dx$; let $\Gamma(a) = \Gamma(a,0)$. The function $\Gamma(a,b)$ is well-defined for every real a if $b > 0$ and is well-defined for every $a > 0$ if $b = 0$. For each integer $k \geq 1$, we have $\Gamma(k) = (k-1)!$.

Let $\zeta(\alpha) = \sum_{i=1}^\infty i^{-\alpha}$ be the value of the *Riemann Zeta* function at $\alpha > 1$. For $\alpha > 0$, and an integer $N \geq 1$, let $\zeta_N(\alpha) = \sum_{i=1}^N i^{-\alpha}$.

Suppose that $\alpha > 1$, and let $P^\alpha(i) = i^{-\alpha}/\zeta(\alpha)$ for each integer $i \geq 1$. Then, $P^{(\alpha)}$ is the *power law distribution* with exponent α, defined on the universe $U = \{1, 2, \ldots\} = \mathbb{N}$.

Also, let $[N] = \{1, 2, \ldots, N\}$. For $\alpha > 0$, if we let $U = [N]$, we have that the truncated power law distribution on U is given by $P_N^{(\alpha)}(i) = i^{-\alpha}/\zeta_N(\alpha)$, for $i \in U$.

We first obtain some bounds on $\zeta_N(\alpha)$ and $P_N^{(\alpha)}(i)$.

Lemma 5.1. *For each $0 < \alpha < 1$, it holds that $\zeta_N(\alpha) = \frac{N^{1-\alpha}}{1-\alpha} \pm O(1)$ and $P_N^{(\alpha)}(i) = \left(1 \pm O\left(N^{\alpha-1}\right)\right) i^{-\alpha}\frac{1-\alpha}{N^{1-\alpha}}$.*

5.2 Word frequency distribution

In this section we analyze the word frequency distribution produced by the generative model. We proceed to study the probability $R(i)$ that the ith word, $1 \leq i \leq N$, appears in the vocabulary V. Since V was constructed using n independent samples, we have

$$R(i) = 1 - (1 - P_N^{(\alpha)}(i))^n.$$

By $N = \left(1 + O\left(n^{-\frac{1-\alpha\beta}{1-\alpha}}\right)\right) \cdot n^{\frac{1-\alpha\beta}{1-\alpha}}$, and by Lemma 5.1, we have

$$P_N^{(\alpha)}(i) = \frac{1-\alpha}{i^\alpha n^{1-\alpha\beta}} - O\left(i^{-\alpha}n^{2\alpha\beta-2}\right).$$

That is,

$$P_N^{(\alpha)}(i) = \left(1 - O\left(n^{\alpha\beta-1}\right)\right)\frac{1-\alpha}{i^\alpha n^{1-\alpha\beta}}.$$

Since $0 < \alpha, \beta < 1$ the multiplier is no worse than $1 - o(1)$.

Our analysis begins by showing that $R(i)$ — that is, the probability that the ith term of the language appears in the vocabulary — can be expressed by a simple exponential term.

Lemma 5.2. $R(i) = (1 \pm o(1))\left(1 - e^{-(1-\alpha)\frac{n^{\alpha\beta}}{i^\alpha}}\right)$.

Lemma 5.2 can be shown by approximating $P_N^{(\alpha)}(i)$ as in Lemma 5.1, since the error term in Lemma 5.1 is small enough to prove the statement of Lemma 5.2.

We then use the new expression of $R(i)$ to compute the expected number of terms with rank at most k that appears in the vocabulary. Specifically, let $U_k \subseteq U$ be the set of words that have rank at most k in $P_N^{(\alpha)}$. We focus on the number of words in U_k that make it to the vocabulary V. I.e., we focus on the random variable $|V \cap U_k|$. Observe that $E[|V \cap U_k|] = \sum_{i=1}^k R(i)$. Lemma 5.3 shows that this expectation is very well approximated by the function $D(k)$ (we use this notation as a shorthand for $D_{\alpha,n^\beta}(k)$):

$$D(k) = k - \frac{(1-\alpha)^{1/\alpha}}{\alpha}n^\beta\Gamma\left(-\frac{1}{\alpha}, (1-\alpha)\left(\frac{n^\beta}{k}\right)^\alpha\right).$$

Lemma 5.3. $E[|V \cap U_k|] = (1 \pm o(1))D(k)$.

The above lemma can be shown by integrating the expression of $R(i)$ that we obtained in Lemma 5.2, and by controlling the error term.

The next step of the proof is showing that $D(k)$ behaves like a simple polynomial in the ranges $k < o(n^\beta)$ and $k > \omega(n^\beta)$, i.e., for all k far enough from the knee. This will be key for proving that the head and the tail of the final distribution will be power laws.

Lemma 5.4. *If $k < o\left(n^\beta\right)$, then $D(k) = (1 \pm o(1))k$. If $k > \omega\left(n^\beta\right)$, then $D(k) = (1 \pm o(1))n^{\alpha\beta}k^{1-\alpha}$.*

The proof of Lemma 5.4 is relatively simple. We just have to use the approximations of the $R(i)$'s given by Lemma 5.2, i.e., $R(i) = 1 - o(1)$ if $i < o\left(n^{\beta}\right)$, and $R(i) = (1 \pm o(1))n^{\alpha\beta}\frac{1-\alpha}{i^{\alpha}}$ if $i > \omega\left(n^{\beta}\right)$. Then, the linearity of expectation, and Lemma 5.2, directly entail the claim.

Negative dependence can be used to prove the next Lemma, which simply states that with high probability for each $k \in [N]$, the random variable $|V \cap U_k|$ will be quite close to its expectation $E[|V \cap U_k|]$; by Lemma 5.3, that random variable will then be very close to the function $D(k)$ itself.

LEMMA 5.5. *With probability* $1 - o(1)$, *we will have that for each* $k \in [N]$,

$$|V \cap U_k| = (1 \pm o(1)) \cdot D(k).$$

Lemma 5.5 allows us to get an expression for the frequency curve of the corpus. For $k \geq 1$, the frequency curve can be expressed parametrically as

$$x(k) = D(k), \quad \text{and} \quad y(k) = W \cdot k^{-\gamma},$$

where W is the normalization factor. In other words, the abscissa $x(y)$ that one has to associate to a given ordinate y is equal to $x(y) = D\left(\left(\frac{W}{y}\right)^{1/\gamma}\right)$.

Finally, we can state our main result about the word frequency distribution of the generative model. It follows as a corollary from Lemma 5.4 and Lemma 5.5.

THEOREM 5.6. *With probability* $1 - o(1)$, *we will have:*
(i) $|V| = (1 \pm o(1))n$, *and*
(ii) for each rank $1 \leq k \leq |V|$, *the probability associated to the word of rank* k *in* V *will be proportional to*

$$\begin{array}{ll} (1 \pm o(1)) \cdot k^{-\gamma}, & \text{if } k = o\left(n^{\beta}\right), \\ (1 \pm o(1)) \cdot \left(\frac{k}{n^{\alpha\beta}}\right)^{-\frac{\gamma}{1-\alpha}}, & \text{if } k = \omega\left(n^{\beta}\right). \end{array}$$

Theorem 5.6 states the main properties of the word frequency distribution: the model produces a vocabulary of size close to n, the head of the vocabulary frequency curve follows a power law with exponent $-\gamma$, and the tail follows a power law with exponent $-\gamma/(1-\alpha)$. Moreover, our parametric definition of the curve gives a precise description of how the two power laws merge in one another. This is important for us since we want to precisely fit the curve to the datasets we have. Figure 4 shows the word frequency distribution produced by our model. Observe that our model produces two power laws that are joined around the knee at n^{β}, as expected.

5.3 Relation with double Pareto

One might wonder why we did not use a simple double Pareto curve (as in [14]) to model the distributions. The main reason is that the ratio of the probability at the rank $i \simeq n^{\beta}$ of the double Pareto curve (with the correct power laws, and the correct knee) and of our curve at the same i is quite large. We will show in this section that (i) the multiplicative distortion is at least $\left(\frac{e}{e-1}\right)^{\gamma} = (1.5819\ldots)^{\gamma}$ for $\alpha \to 0$, and (ii) the distortion diverges exponentially to ∞ as α approaches 1. Moreover, we numerically obtain that at $\alpha = 0.6$ (close to empirical numbers; see Table 2), the distortion becomes $(3.0270\ldots)^{\gamma}$. Later in Section 5.4, we empirically analyze the distortion in two of our corpora.

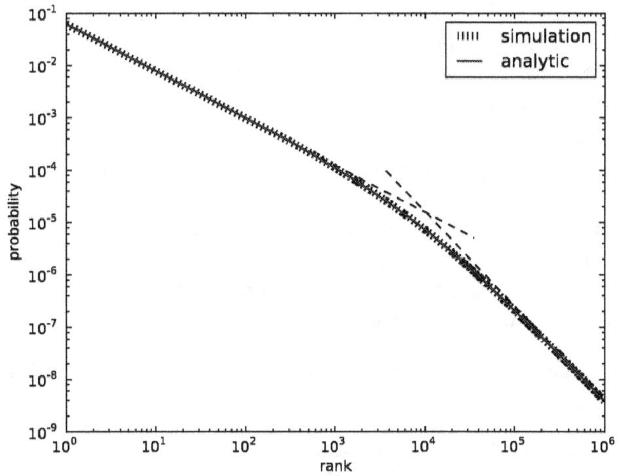

Figure 4: The result of an execution of the stochastic process with $\alpha = \frac{1}{2}, \beta = \frac{2}{3}, \gamma = \frac{9}{10}, n = 10^6$ and $N = n^{\frac{1-\alpha\beta}{1-\alpha}} = 10^8$. In this execution, the vocabulary V ended up with a cardinality of $|V| = 984328$, i.e., so many distinct words were randomly selected in the first stage of the process. The curve represents the probability distribution of the vocabulary. The head of the curve follows a power law with exponent $-\gamma = -0.9$ and the tail of the curve follows a power law with exponent $-\frac{\gamma}{1-\alpha} = -1.8$. Observe that the two power laws cross at an abscissa value close to $n^{\beta} = 10^4$.

We now show how this distortion can be computed, and obtain its limiting values at $\alpha = 0, 1$. First, for a given α, let k_{α} be the minimum integer such that $D(k_{\alpha}) \geq n^{\beta}$. Observe that $k_{\alpha} \geq n^{\beta}$. The probability of the $\left\lceil n^{\beta}\right\rceil$th word in our model's dictionary will then be $(1 \pm o(1)) \cdot W \cdot k_{\alpha}^{-\gamma}$ for some normalizing factor W.

Consider the double Pareto curve having the same head and tail power laws of our curve, and the same knee n^{β}. The value of this double Pareto curve at the $\left\lceil n^{\beta}\right\rceil$th word will be $(1 \pm o(1)) \cdot W \cdot n^{-\beta\gamma}$. Therefore, the distortion of the two curves at the $\left\lceil n^{\beta}\right\rceil$th word (i.e., at the knee) for a given α, as n tends to infinity, is at least $(d_{\alpha})^{\gamma}$, where

$$d_{\alpha} = \liminf_{n \to \infty} \frac{k_{\alpha}}{n^{\beta}}.$$

We show in Lemma 5.7 that $\lim_{\alpha \to 0^+} d_{\alpha} = \frac{e}{e-1}$ Moreover, we will show in Lemma 5.8 that, as α converges to 1, d_{α} diverges at least as fast as $c^{1/(1-\alpha)}$ for some constant $c > 1$.

We state the two Lemmas, and briefly comment on how they can be proved.

LEMMA 5.7. *For* $0 < \alpha < \frac{1}{2}$, *we have*

$$k_{\alpha} = \left(\frac{e}{e-1} \pm O\left(\alpha \ln 1/\alpha\right)\right) \cdot n^{\beta}.$$

A heuristic proof of the above statement would argue that, if $\alpha = 0$, then all the terms are equally likely to be chosen, i.e., they have probability N^{-1}, with $N = n^{\frac{1-\alpha\beta}{1-\alpha}} = n$. In other words, the vocabulary is constructed by throwing n balls (the words in the founding text), into $N = n$ bins (the words of the language). By the Chernoff bound, any given set of $t \gg 1$ bins will be hit by approximately t balls with high probability. Moreover, by classic balls-in-bins arguments, the $\frac{e}{e-1} \cdot n^\beta$ balls that hit the first $\frac{e}{e-1} \cdot n^\beta$ bins will be distributed across approximately n^β distinct bins with high probability (essentially because of the Poissonian approximation of the binomial distribution). Hence, $k_\alpha \approx \frac{e}{e-1} \cdot n^\beta$.

The above reasoning can be made formal, so that it can be applied to small $\alpha > 0$.

Finally, we show that in the opposite regime, $\alpha = 1 - \epsilon$, d_α diverges to infinity at an exponential rate.

Lemma 5.8. *There exists a constant $c > 1$ such that, for all $\frac{1}{2} < \alpha < 1$, we have*

$$k_\alpha \geq c^{\frac{1}{1-\alpha}} \cdot n^\beta.$$

The above statement can be proven by partitioning the set of words of index up to $c^{\frac{1}{1-\alpha}} \cdot n^\beta$ into buckets in such a way that words in a given bucket have roughly the same probability of being selected in the vocabulary. The bucketing makes it easy to compute the expected number of words per bucket that end up in the vocabulary. Finally, adding up these expected numbers gives the above lower bound.

5.4 Fitting

The parameters of the fitting were obtained by minimizing the Kullback-Leibler divergence $D_{\mathrm{KL}}(P||E)$ of our model's frequency distribution P from the empirical distribution E. I.e., given E, we searched for the P that minimizes $D_{\mathrm{KL}}(P||E) = \sum_i \left(P(i) \cdot \ln \frac{P(i)}{E(i)}\right)$.

More precisely, if the empirical distribution E was over n distinct words then, given a triple of parameters (α, β, γ), we computed a candidate distribution $P = P_{n,\alpha,\beta,\gamma}$ by letting, for each $i = 1, \ldots, n$, $P(i)$ be proportional to $k_i^{-\gamma}$ with k_i equal to the solution of $i = D_{\alpha,n^\beta}(k_i)$.

We used a brute-force approach to guess the optimal fitting parameters α, β, γ. The results are reported in Table 2. The empirical curves, and their fittings, are shown in Figure 5. To show how much better our curve's fits are (with respect to the double Pareto fits), we plot in Figure 6 the ratios between the probabilities given by our curve and the actual distribution, and those given by double Pareto and the actual distribution, for the `Gutenberg` and `News` corpora.

6 *K*-GRAM FREQUENCY DISTRIBUTION

Let $P^{(\alpha)}$ be the power law distribution with exponent $\alpha > 1$ over an infinite language $U = \mathbb{N}$. Given an integer $k \geq 1$, let $P^{(\alpha,k)}$ be the probability distribution on k-tuples $\langle u_1, \ldots, u_k \rangle$, where $u_1, \ldots, u_k \in U$ are chosen independently from $P^{(\alpha)}$. We now show analytically that (i) the distribution of $P^{(\alpha,k)}$ will be close to the original power law $P^{(\alpha)}$ and (ii) the curves corresponding to k-grams will become flatter as k increases, when plotted on a log-log scale; this phenomenon can be observed empirically in Figure 7.

Theorem 6.1. *If we sort the k-tuples decreasingly by their probabilities in $P^{(\alpha,k)}$, then the probability of the rth k-tuple will be equal*

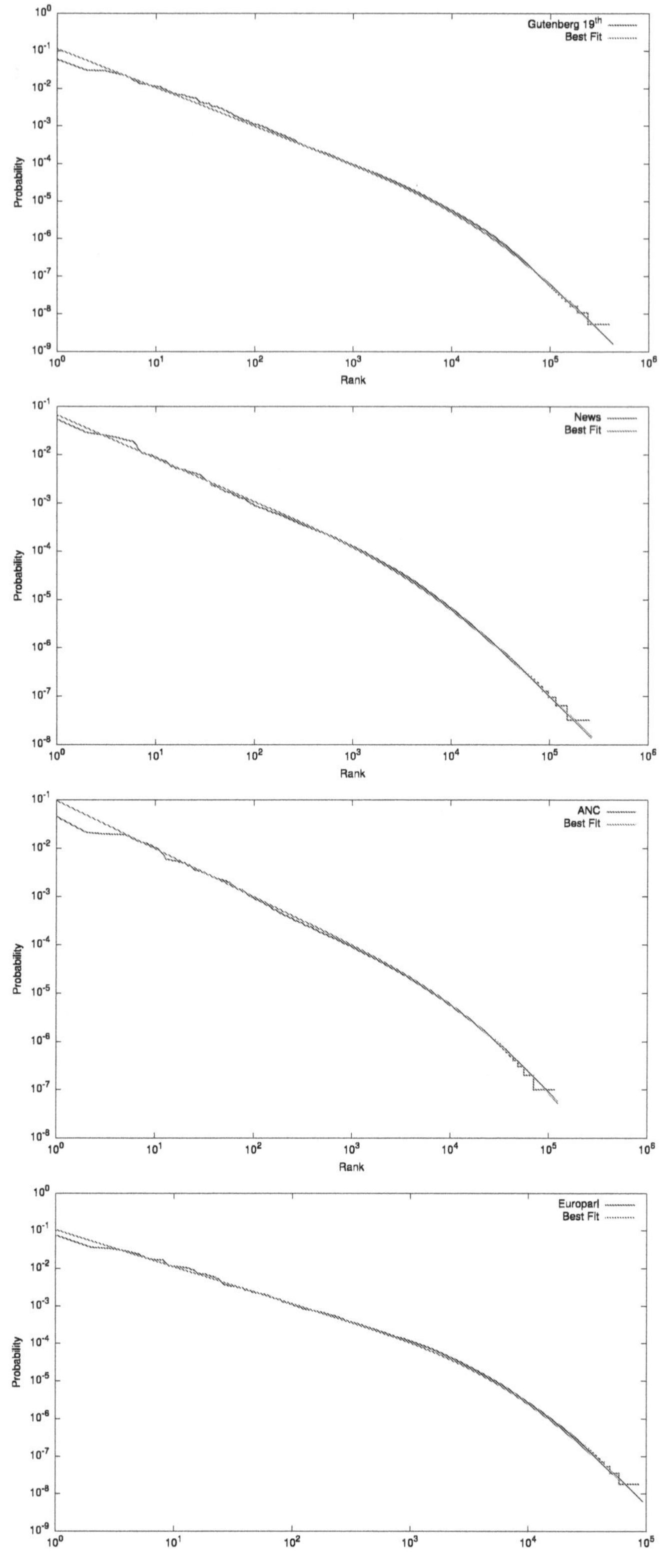

Figure 5: The empirical and the (fitted) theoretical curves of four corpora.

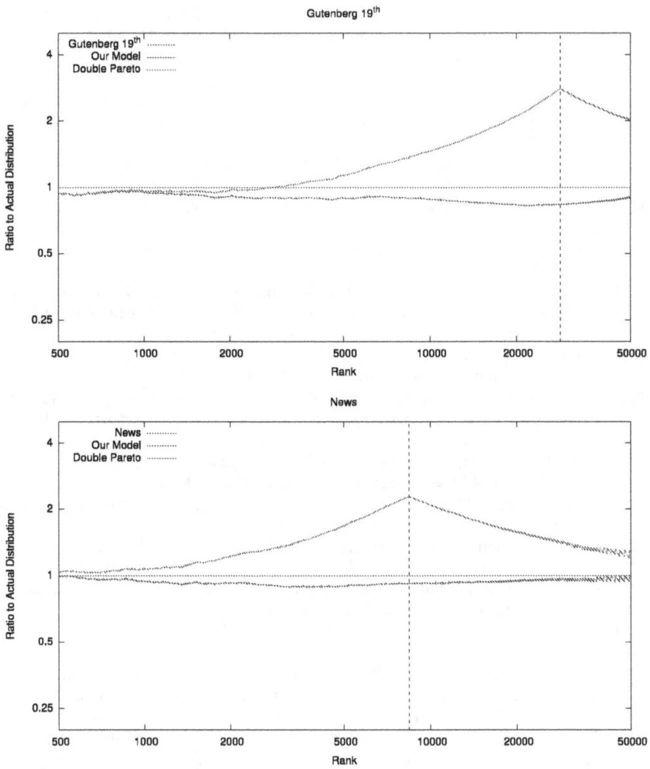

Figure 6: A log-log plot of the ratios between our fitted curve (resp., the Double Pareto curve) and the empirical curve, at word ranks 500 to 50000 (that is, around the knee). The vertical dashed line represents the position of the Double Pareto knee. Our curve is a very good multiplicative approximation of the empirical curve (the ratios induced by our curve are quite close to 1), and generally a much better approximation than Double Pareto; the maximum ratios, or distortions (see Section 5.3), incurred by Double Pareto happen around the knees: the ratios, there, are close to 2.8 in the Gutenberg corpus, and to 2.3 in the News corpus.

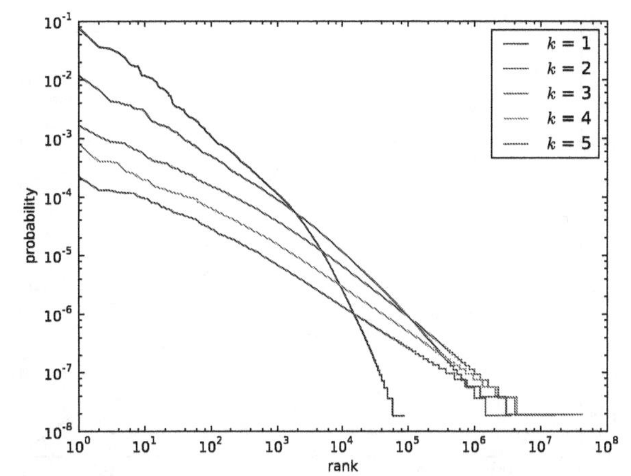

Figure 7: k-grams frequency distribution for the Europarl dataset (English).

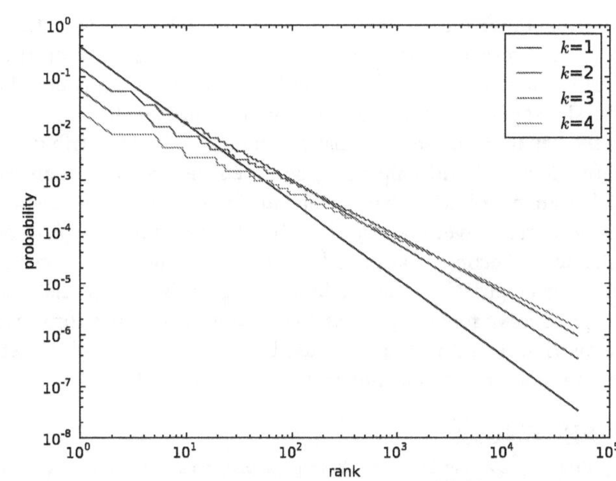

Figure 8: Computed k-gram distribution, $\alpha = 1.5$.

to

$$(1 \pm o_r(1)) \cdot \zeta(\alpha)^{-k} \cdot \Gamma(k)^{-\alpha} \cdot \left(\frac{\ln^{k-1} r}{r}\right)^{\alpha}.$$

Proof. Our goal is to compute the position (or rank) $r_{i_1,\ldots,i_k}$ of the product $P^{(\alpha)}(i_1) \cdots P^{(\alpha)}(i_k)$ in the ordered multiset

$$\left\{P^{(\alpha)}(j_1) \cdots P^{(\alpha)}(j_k) \mid j_1, \ldots, j_k \in \mathbf{Z}^+\right\}.$$

In other words, we aim to compute the number of tuples $\langle j_1, \ldots, j_k \rangle$ such that $P^{(\alpha)}(i_1) \cdots P^{(\alpha)}(i_k) < P^{(\alpha)}(j_1) \cdots P^{(\alpha)}(j_k)$. Rewriting this condition using the fact $p(i) \propto i^{-\alpha}$ and letting $n = i_1 \cdots i_k$, we get

$$\begin{aligned} r = r_n &= |\{\langle j_1, \ldots, j_k \rangle \mid j_1 \cdots j_k < n\}| \\ &= \frac{n \ln^{k-1} n}{\Gamma(k)} + O(n \ln^{k-2} n), \end{aligned}$$

which follows from [35, 39]. Inverting this, we obtain

$$n = (1 + o_r(1))\Gamma(k)\frac{r}{\ln^{k-1} r}.$$

The proof is concluded by recalling that the probability of the tuple $\langle i_1, \ldots, i_k \rangle$ is

$$P^{(\alpha)}(i_1) \cdots P^{(\alpha)}(i_k) = \zeta(\alpha)^{-k} n^{-\alpha}. \quad \square$$

Observe that our Theorem gives sharp bounds on the probability of the rth k-gram, as r diverges. Figure 8 shows the k-gram distribution computed with a synthetic power law distribution with $\alpha = 1.5$; Figure 9 shows the curves predicted by Theorem 6.1. We can see that the empirical curves agree asymptotically with the theoretical estimates.

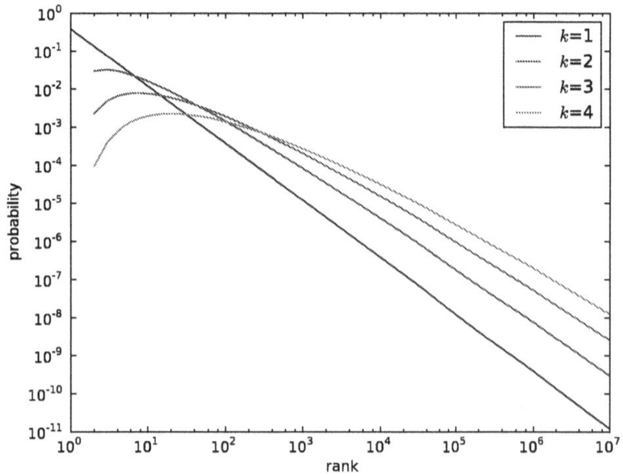

Figure 9: k-grams distribution using Theorem 6.1, $\alpha = 1.5$.

7 CONCLUSIONS

In this paper we took a closer look at the word frequency distribution. We observed a knee, leading to a concavity, in the empirical distributions of many different kinds of corpora, and proposed a natural text generation model to explain the knee and the concavity. We then analytically showed that our model produces distributions nearly identical to the empirically observed ones. We also analyzed the k-gram distribution that one obtains by picking words independently from a power law distribution. We proved that the k-gram distribution becomes flatter as k increases; this phenomenon had only been empirically observed in the literature but never analyzed. Our generative model opens up many interesting questions: can the distributions it produces be used in applications such as text compression, translation, and information retrieval?

REFERENCES

[1] IJsbrand Jan Aalbersberg. 1991. Posting compression in dynamic retrieval environments. In *SIGIR*. 72–81.

[2] IJsbrand Jan Aalbersberg. 1994. A document retrieval model based on term frequency ranks. In *SIGIR*. 163–172.

[3] Leif Azzopardi. 2009. Query Side Evaluation: An empirical analysis of effectiveness and effort. In *SIGIR*. 556–563.

[4] Harald Baayen. 1991. A stochastic process for word frequency distributions. In *ACL*. 271–278.

[5] Harald Baayen. 1992. Statistical models for word frequency distributions: A linguistic evaluation. *Computers and the Humanities* 26, 5 (1992), 347–363.

[6] L. Douglas Baker and Andrew Kachites McCallum. 1998. Distributional clustering of words for text classification. In *SIGIR*. 96–103.

[7] Krishna Bharat and Monika R. Henzinger. 1998. Improved algorithms for topic distillation in a hyperlinked environment. In *SIGIR*. 104–111.

[8] David C Blair. 1990. *Language and Representation in Information Retrieval.* Elsevier Science Publishers.

[9] David C. Blair. 2002. The challenge of commercial document retrieval, Part I: Major issues, and a framework based on search exhaustivity, determinacy of representation and document collection size. *Information Processing & Management* 38, 2 (2002), 273–291.

[10] Andrew D Booth. 1967. A "Law" of occurrences for words of low frequency. *Information and Control* 10, 4 (1967), 386–393.

[11] Nieves R. Brisaboa, Antonio Fariña, Susana Ladra, and Gonzalo Navarro. 2008. Reorganizing compressed text. In *SIGIR*. 139–146.

[12] Nieves R. Brisaboa, Antonio Fariña, Gonzalo Navarro, and José R. Paramá. 2007. Lightweight Natural Language Text Compression. *Information Retrieval* 10, 1 (2007), 1–33.

[13] Soumen Chakrabarti, Mukul Joshi, and Vivek Tawde. 2001. Enhanced topic distillation using text, markup tags, and hyperlinks. In *SIGIR*. 208–216.

[14] Flavio Chierichetti, Ravi Kumar, and Prabhakar Raghavan. 2009. Compressed web indexes. In *WWW*. 451–460.

[15] Brian Conrad and Michael Mitzenmacher. 2004. Power laws for monkeys typing randomly: The case of unequal probabilities. *IEEE Transactions on Information Theory* 50, 7 (2004), 1403–1414.

[16] Devdatt Dubhashi and Alessandro Panconesi. 2009. *Concentration of Measure for the Analysis of Randomized Algorithms.* Cambridge University Press.

[17] Leo Egghe. 2004. The distribution of N-grams. *Scientometrics* 47, 2 (2004), 237–252.

[18] Jean-Baptiste Estoup. 1916. *Gammes Sténographiques.* Institut Stenographique de France.

[19] Ramon Ferrer i Cancho, Oliver Riordan, and Béla Bollobás. 2005. The consequences of Zipf's law for syntax and symbolic reference. *Proceedings of the Royal Society B: Biological Sciences* 272, 1562 (2005), 561–565.

[20] Ramon Ferrer i Cancho and Ricard V. Sole. 2003. Least effort and the origins of scaling in human language. *PNAS* 100, 3 (2003), 788–791.

[21] Xiaocong Gan, Dahui Wang, and Zhangang Han. 2009. *N-tuple Zipf analysis and modeling for language, computer program and DNA.* Technical Report 0908.0500v1. arXiv.

[22] Le Q Ha, P Hanna, D W Stewart, and F J Smith. 2006. Reduced n-gram models for English and Chinese corpora. In *COLING-ACL*. 309–315.

[23] Le Quan Ha, E. I. Sicilia-Garcia, Ji Ming, and F. J. Smith. 2002. Extension of Zipf's law to words and phrases. In *COLING*. 1–6.

[24] Thomas Hofmann. 1999. Probabilistic Latent Semantic Analysis. In *UAI*. 289–296.

[25] Thomas Hofmann. 1999. Probabilistic Latent Semantic Indexing. In *SIGIR*. 50–57.

[26] Thorsten Joachims. 2001. A statistical learning model of text classification for support vector machines. In *SIGIR*. 128–136.

[27] Philipp Koehn. 2005. Europarl: A parallel corpus for statistical machine translation. MT summit. (2005).

[28] Andreas Krause and Andreas Zollmann. 2002. Not so randomly typing monkeys–Rank-frequency behavior of natural and artificial languages. Algorithms for Information Networks–Project Report. (2002).

[29] Benoit Mandelbrot. 1953. An informational theory of the statistical structure of language. In *Communication Theory*, W. Jackson (Ed.). Butterworths, London, 486–502.

[30] Christopher D. Manning, Prabhakar Raghavan, and Hinrich Schütze. 2008. *Introduction to Information Retrieval.* Cambridge University Press, New York.

[31] George A Miller. 1957. Some effects of intermittent silence. *The American Journal of Psychology* 70, 2 (1957), 311–314.

[32] Michael Mitzenmacher. 2004. A brief history of generative models for power law and lognormal distributions. *Internet Mathematics* 1, 2 (2004), 226–251.

[33] Mark EJ Newman. 2005. Power laws, Pareto distributions and Zipf's law. *Contemporary Physics* 46, 5 (2005), 323–351.

[34] Matja Perc. 2012. Evolution of the most common English words and phrases over the centuries. *Journal of The Royal Society Interface* 9, 77 (2012), 3323–33238.

[35] Adolf Piltz. 1881. *Über das Gesetz, nach welchem die mittlere Darstellbarkeit der natürlichen Zahlen als Produkte einer gegebenen Anzahl Faktoren mit der Grösse der Zahlen wächst.* Ph.D. Dissertation. University of Berlin.

[36] Gerard Salton and Christopher Buckley. 1988. Term-weighting approaches in automatic text retrieval. *Information Processing & Management* 24, 5 (1988), 513–523.

[37] Christer Samuelsson. 1996. Relating Turing's Formula and Zipf's Law. In *Proceedings of the 4th Workshop on Very Large Corpora*. 70–78.

[38] Issei Sato and Hiroshi Nakagawa. 2010. Topic Models with power-law using Pitman-Yor process. In *KDD*. 673–682.

[39] Atle Selberg. 1954. Note on a paper by L. G. Sathe. *J. Indian Math. Soc., N. Ser.* 18 (1954), 83–87.

[40] Herbert S Sichel. 1975. On a distribution law for word frequencies. *J. Amer. Statist. Assoc.* 70, 351a (1975), 542–547.

[41] Herbert A Simon. 1955. On a class of skew distribution functions. *Biometrika* 42, 3/4 (1955), 425–440.

[42] D.C. van Leijenhorst and Th.P. van der Weide. 2005. A formal derivation of Heaps' law. *Information Sciences* 170 (2005), 263–272.

[43] G Udny Yule. 1925. A mathematical theory of evolution, based on the conclusions of Dr. JC Willis, FRS. *Philosophical Transactions of the Royal Society of London. Series B, Containing Papers of a Biological Character* 213 (1925), 21–87.

[44] George K. Zipf. 1932. *Selective Studies and the Principle of Relative Frequency in Language.* Harvard University Press.

[45] George K. Zipf. 1935. *The Psycho-Biology of Language: An Introduction to Dynamic Philology.* Houghton Mifflin Company.

[46] George K. Zipf. 1949. *Human Behavior and the Principle of Least Effort.* Addison-Wesley Press.

APPENDIX

Proof of Lemma 5.1

First we upper bound $\zeta_N(\alpha)$ with one (the first term of its sum) plus the area under $x^{-\alpha}$ in the interval $[1, N]$,

$$\zeta_N(\alpha) \leq 1 + \int_1^N x^{-\alpha}\, dx = \frac{N^{1-\alpha} - \alpha}{1-\alpha}.$$

Analogously, a lower bound is given by the area under $(x+1)^{-\alpha}$ in the interval $[0, N]$,

$$\zeta_N(\alpha) \geq \int_0^N (x+1)^{-\alpha}\, dx \geq \frac{N^{1-\alpha} - 1}{1-\alpha}.$$

If $\alpha < 1$, using the expression for $P_N^{(\alpha)}(i)$, we get

$$i^{-\alpha}\frac{1-\alpha}{N^{1-\alpha}-\alpha} \leq P_N^{(\alpha)}(i) \leq i^{-\alpha}\frac{1-\alpha}{N^{1-\alpha}-1}. \quad \square$$

Proof of Lemma 5.2

If $i < o(n^\beta)$, then observe that, by $R(i) = 1 - (1 - P_N^{(\alpha)}(i))^n$ and $P_N^{(\alpha)}(i) = \left(1 - O\left(n^{\alpha\beta-1}\right)\right)\frac{1-\alpha}{i^\alpha n^{1-\alpha\beta}}$, we have

$$R(i) = 1 - o(1). \quad (1)$$

The right-hand expression in our claim simplifies to:

$$(1 \pm o(1))\left(1 - e^{-\omega(1)}\right) = 1 \pm o(1).$$

The claim is thus proved.

Next assume that i is a positive integer such that $i > \omega(n^{2\beta-1/\alpha})$. Observe that, by $\alpha, \beta < 1$, this case includes all the i's that are not part of the previous case.

For $0 < a < \frac{1}{2}$, and $b > 0$, it holds that

$$e^{-ab} \geq (1-a)^b \geq e^{-ab-2a^2b}.$$

Recall that $1 - R(i) = (1 - P_N^{(\alpha)}(i))^n$. Then, we bound the following quantities, using (5.2):

(1) $nP_N^{(\alpha)}(i) = (1-\alpha)n^{\alpha\beta}i^{-\alpha} + O\left(\frac{n^{\alpha\beta}}{i^\alpha}n^{\alpha\beta-1}\right)$. Observe that the error term is $o(1)$ for each i in our range.

(2) $2n\left(P_N^{(\alpha)}(i)\right)^2 = \Theta\left(\left(nP_N^{(\alpha)}(i)\right)P_N^{(\alpha)}(i)\right) = O\left(\frac{n^{\alpha\beta}}{i^\alpha}n^{\alpha\beta-1}\right)$, since $P_N^{(\alpha)}(i) = O\left(n^{\alpha\beta-1}\right)$ for each $i \geq 1$.

It follows that

$$1 - R(i) = e^{-(1-\alpha)n^{\alpha\beta}i^{-\alpha} \pm O\left(\frac{n^{\alpha\beta}}{i^\alpha}n^{\alpha\beta-1}\right)}$$
$$= \left(1 \pm O\left(\frac{n^{\alpha\beta}}{i^\alpha}n^{\alpha\beta-1}\right)\right)e^{-(1-\alpha)n^{\alpha\beta}i^{-\alpha}}.$$

Moreover, since $0 \leq e^{-(1-\alpha)n^{\alpha\beta}i^{-\alpha}} \leq 1$, we have

$$R(i) = 1 - e^{-(1-\alpha)n^{\alpha\beta}i^{-\alpha}} \pm O\left(\frac{n^{\alpha\beta}}{i^\alpha}n^{\alpha\beta-1}\right)$$

Observe that, if $i \leq n^\beta$, then we have $1 - e^{-(1-\alpha)n^{\alpha\beta}i^{-\alpha}} \geq 1 - e^{-1+\alpha} = \Theta(1)$, while $O\left(\frac{n^{\alpha\beta}}{i^\alpha}n^{\alpha\beta-1}\right) \leq O\left(n^{\alpha\beta-1}\right)$. That is, $R(i) = (1 \pm o(1))\left(1 - e^{-(1-\alpha)n^{\alpha\beta}i^{-\alpha}}\right)$.

On the other hand, if $i \geq n^\beta$, then if we let x be the exponent of the exponential term, we have $0 \leq x \leq 1$. For this range of x's, it holds $e^{-x} \leq 1 - \frac{x}{2}$ — equivalently, $1 - e^{-x} \geq \frac{x}{2}$. Therefore, $1 - e^{-(1-\alpha)n^{\alpha\beta}i^{-\alpha}} \geq \frac{1}{2}(1-\alpha)n^{\alpha\beta}i^{-\alpha}$. Therefore, even for $i \geq n^\beta$, we have

$$R(i) = (1 \pm o(1))\left(1 - e^{-(1-\alpha)n^{\alpha\beta}i^{-\alpha}}\right). \quad \square$$

Proof of Lemma 5.3

For each integer $k \geq 1$ and for each non-decreasing and non-negative function $f(x)$ admitting a finite integral in $[0, k+1]$, we have

$$F_L = \int_0^k f(x)dx \leq \sum_{i=1}^k f(i) \leq \int_1^{k+1} f(x)dx = F_U.$$

Suppose that $0 \leq f(x) \leq 1$. Then,

$$F_U - F_L = \int_k^{k+1} f(x)dx - \int_0^1 f(x)dx \leq 1,$$

and hence $\sum_{i=1}^k f(i) = F_L + \xi$ for some $\xi \in [0, 1]$.

Observe that for all $q > 0$ and $\alpha \in (0, 1)$, the function $f(x) = e^{-qx^{-\alpha}}$ satisfies the above conditions. We also have

$$\int f(x)dx = \frac{1}{\alpha}q^{1/\alpha}\Gamma\left(-\frac{1}{\alpha}, qx^{-\alpha}\right) + c,$$

where c is a constant. By choosing $q = (1-\alpha)n^{\alpha\beta}$, we get $e^{-(1-\alpha)\frac{n^{\alpha\beta}}{i^\alpha}} = f(i)$. Now,

$$F_L = \sum_{i=1}^k e^{-(1-\alpha)\frac{n^{\alpha\beta}}{i^\alpha}} - \xi =$$

$$\lim_{\epsilon\to 0^+}\left[\frac{\left((1-\alpha)n^{\alpha\beta}\right)^{1/\alpha}}{\alpha}\Gamma\left(-\frac{1}{\alpha}, \frac{(1-\alpha)n^{\alpha\beta}}{x^\alpha}\right)\right]_{x=\epsilon}^k =$$

$$n^\beta\frac{(1-\alpha)^{1/\alpha}}{\alpha}\Gamma\left(-\frac{1}{\alpha}, (1-\alpha)\cdot\left(\frac{n^\beta}{k}\right)^\alpha\right),$$

since by definition $\lim_{x\to\infty}\Gamma(a, x) = 0$. Thus, we have

$$\sum_{i=1}^k\left(1 - e^{-(1-\alpha)\frac{n^{\alpha\beta}}{i^\alpha}}\right) = D(k) - \xi. \quad (2)$$

Now, consider the first $o(n^\beta)$ terms of the LHS sum in (2). The exponent of e in each of them is $\omega(1)$, and therefore each of them has value $1 - o(1)$. It follows that the LHS of (2) has value $\omega(1)$. Since $0 \leq \xi \leq 1$, we have

$$(1 \pm o(1))\sum_{i=1}^k\left(1 - e^{-(1-\alpha)\frac{n^{\alpha\beta}}{i^\alpha}}\right) = D(k).$$

The claim then follows from Lemma 5.2 and the linearity of expectation. $\square$

Proof of Lemma 5.4

The first part is implied directly by (1) and Lemma 5.3. Hence, let $k = \omega\left(n^\beta\right)$. Let us define $g = \left\lceil\sqrt{n^\beta k}\right\rceil$ to be the ceiling of the geometric mean of n^β and k. Observe that $\omega\left(n^\beta\right) < g < o(k)$.

Since $R(i) \leq 1$, we have

$$\sum_{i=g+1}^{k} R(i) \leq E[|V \cap U_k|] \leq g + \sum_{i=g+1}^{k} R(i).$$

By Lemma 5.2, we have that $R(i) = (1 \pm o(1)) \cdot n^{\alpha\beta} \frac{1-\alpha}{i^\alpha}$ whenever $i > g$, since $g > \omega\left(n^\beta\right)$. Then, we can write:

$$\sum_{i=g+1}^{k} R(i) = (1 \pm o(1))(1-\alpha)n^{\alpha\beta} \sum_{i=g+1}^{k} i^{-\alpha}$$
$$= (1 \pm o(1))(1-\alpha)n^{\alpha\beta}\left(\zeta_k(\alpha) - \zeta_g(\alpha)\right)$$
$$= (1 \pm o(1))n^{\alpha\beta}k^{1-\alpha},$$

where the last step follows from Lemma 5.1. The value of the sum is $\Theta\left(n^{\alpha\beta}k^{1-\alpha}\right) = \omega\left(n^\beta\right)$, since $k > \omega\left(n^\beta\right)$. Therefore,

$$E[|V \cap U_k|] = (1 \pm o(1)) \cdot n^{\alpha\beta}k^{1-\alpha}.$$

Lemma 5.3 completes the proof. □

Proof of Lemma 5.5

Observe that, by Lemma 5.3, it is sufficient to prove that, with probability $1-o(1)$, it will happen that, for each $k \in [N]$, $|V \cap U_k| = (1 \pm o(1))E\left[|V \cap U_k|\right]$.

Let us define $X = n^\beta \log^{-\frac{1}{\alpha}} n$. We will use two arguments for proving the claim: one that holds if $k < o(X)$, and one that holds if $k > \omega\left(X^{1-\epsilon}\right)$, for any constant $0 < \epsilon < \frac{\beta}{4}$.

First, consider $k < o(X)$. Recall that we have $P_N^{(\alpha)}(i) = \Theta\left(\frac{1}{n}\left(\frac{n^\beta}{i}\right)^\alpha\right)$. Therefore, for $i < o(X)$, we have $P_N^{(\alpha)}(i) > \omega\left(\frac{\log n}{n}\right)$. For the same i's, therefore, we have

$$R(i) \geq 1 - \left(1 - \omega\left(\frac{\log n}{n}\right)\right)^n \geq 1 - n^{-\omega(1)}.$$

By the union bound, the probability that at least one of the terms of rank $i < o(X)$ in U does not end up in V is $n^{-\omega(1)}$. The claim is then proved for each $k < o(X)$.

Now consider $k > \omega\left(X^{1-\epsilon}\right)$. Let $Y_{i,j}$ be the indicator random variable of the event "the jth term of the founding text happened to be the ith term of the language". Then, for each j, the variables $Y_{1,j}, Y_{2,j}, \ldots, Y_{N,j}$ are negatively associated (see Chapter 3 of [16]). Moreover, by closure under product, the variables $Y_{i,j}$, for each $i \in [N], j \in [n]$ are as a whole negatively associated. Finally, since max is a monotone non-decreasing function the variables $Y_i = \max_{j=1,\ldots,n} Y_{i,j}$, $i \in [N]$, are also negatively associated — the Chernoff bound can then be applied to their sum, that is, to $\sum_{i=1}^{k} Y_i = |V \cap U_k|$. Thus, for each $0 < \delta < 1$,

$$\Pr\left[\left||V \cap U_k| - E\left[|V \cap U_k|\right]\right| \geq \delta E\left[|V \cap U_k|\right]\right]$$
$$\leq 2e^{-\frac{\delta^2}{3}E[|V \cap U_k|]}.$$

Since $k > \omega\left(X^{1-\epsilon}\right)$, we have $E[|V \cap U_k|] > \omega\left(n^{\beta-2\epsilon}\right)$. If we choose $\delta = n^{-\frac{1}{2}\beta+2\epsilon}$, we get:

$$\Pr\left[|V \cap U_k| = (1 \pm 2\delta) \cdot E\left[|V \cap U_k|\right]\right] \leq e^{-\Omega(n^{2\epsilon})}.$$

By the union bound, the claim is then proved for each $k > \omega\left(X^{1-\epsilon}\right)$. □.

Proof of Lemma 5.7

Suppose that $i = x \cdot n^\beta$. Then,

$$R(i) = (1 \pm o(1))\left(1 - e^{-(1-\alpha)x^{-\alpha}}\right).$$

Observe that, if $x \geq \alpha$, then $x^{-\alpha} \leq \alpha^{-\alpha} = e^{\alpha \ln \frac{1}{\alpha}} = 1 + O\left(\alpha \ln \frac{1}{\alpha}\right)$. Moreover, if $x \leq e$ then, $x^{-\alpha} \geq e^{-\alpha} = 1 - O(\alpha)$.

By the monotonicity of $x^{-\alpha}$ we thus obtain that $x^{-\alpha} = 1 \pm O\left(\alpha \ln \frac{1}{\alpha}\right)$ for all $x \in [\alpha, e]$.

For all $\alpha n^\beta \leq i \leq e n^\beta$, we then have

$$R(i) = (1 \pm O(\alpha \ln 1/\alpha)) \cdot \left(1 - e^{-1}\right).$$

For $i < \alpha n^\beta$, we have $R(i) \leq 1$. Therefore, for $\sum_{i=1}^{k_\alpha} R(i)$ to be at least n^β, we need

$$\frac{k_\alpha}{n^\beta} \geq \frac{1}{1-e^{-1}} - O(\alpha \ln 1/\alpha).$$

Moreover, for the inequality to hold, it suffices to have

$$\frac{k_\alpha}{n^\beta} \leq \frac{1}{1-e^{-1}} + O(\alpha \ln 1/\alpha). \quad \square$$

Proof of Lemma 5.8

Let us define $\epsilon = 1 - \alpha$. Recall that $E[|V \cap U_k|] = \sum_{i=1}^{k} R(i)$. Let $1 = t_0 < t_1 < \ldots < t_r = k$ be integers and, for $0 \leq j \leq r-1$, let p_j be any real number such that $p_j \geq R(t_j)$. Then, by the monotonicity of the $R(i)$'s, we have $p_j \geq R(i)$ for $1 \leq i \leq t_j$. Therefore,

$$E[|V \cap U_k|] = \sum_{j=1}^{r} \sum_{i=t_{j-1}}^{t_j} R(i) \leq \sum_{j=1}^{r} \sum_{i=t_{j-1}}^{t_j} R(t_{j-1})$$
$$\leq \sum_{j=1}^{r} \left(t_j \cdot p_{j-1}\right).$$

We set $t_0 = 1$ and, for $j \geq 1$, let $t_j = \left\lceil 2^{\frac{j-2}{\alpha}} \cdot n^\beta \right\rceil$. We let r be unspecified for now. Also, let $p_0 = 1$, and, for $j \geq 1$,

$$p_j = 1 - e^{-(1-\alpha)n^{\alpha\beta}t_j^{-\alpha}} = 1 - e^{-\epsilon 2^{2-j}} \leq O\left(\epsilon 2^{-j}\right).$$

We have that $\frac{1}{\alpha} - 1 = \frac{1}{1-\epsilon} - 1 \leq O(\epsilon)$. For $j = 1$, we have $t_j p_{j-1} = t_1 \leq \left\lceil \frac{n^\beta}{2} \right\rceil$. Moreover, for $j \geq 2$,

$$t_j \cdot p_{j-1} \leq O\left(\epsilon n^\beta 2^{j\left(\frac{1}{\alpha}-1\right)}\right) = \epsilon n^\beta 2^{O(j\epsilon)}.$$

As $j \leq O(1/\epsilon)$, the latter is at most $O(\epsilon n^\beta)$. In fact, there exists a constant $b > 0$ such that if we let $r = \lceil b/\epsilon \rceil$, we have

$$E[|V \cap U_k|] \leq \left\lceil \frac{n^\beta}{2} \right\rceil + \sum_{j=2}^{r} O\left(\epsilon n^\beta\right) < \frac{3}{4} \cdot n^\beta.$$

Lemma 5.3 shows that $D(k) = (1 \pm o(1))E[|V \cap U_k|]$. With our choice of r, k equals

$$k = t_r = \left\lceil 2^{\frac{r-2}{\alpha}} \cdot n^\beta \right\rceil \geq c^{1/\epsilon} \cdot n^\beta,$$

for some constant $c > 1$.

Therefore, $D\left(c^{1/\epsilon} \cdot n^\beta\right) \leq (1 \pm o(1))\frac{3}{4}n^\beta$. By the latter, and by the monotonicity in k of $E[|V \cap U_k|]$, we have that $k_\alpha \geq c^{1/\epsilon} \cdot n^\beta$. □

Retrieval Consistency in the Presence of Query Variations

Peter Bailey
Microsoft
Canberra, Australia

Alistair Moffat
The University of Melbourne
Melbourne, Australia

Falk Scholer
RMIT University
Melbourne, Australia

Paul Thomas
Microsoft
Canberra, Australia

ABSTRACT

A search engine that can return the ideal results for a person's information need, independent of the specific query that is used to express that need, would be preferable to one that is overly swayed by the individual terms used; search engines should be *consistent* in the presence of syntactic query variations responding to the same information need. In this paper we examine the retrieval consistency of a set of five systems responding to syntactic query variations over one hundred topics, working with the UQV100 test collection, and using Rank-Biased Overlap (RBO) relative to a centroid ranking over the query variations per topic as a measure of consistency. We also introduce a new data fusion algorithm, Rank-Biased Centroid (RBC), for constructing a centroid ranking over a set of rankings from query variations for a topic. RBC is compared with alternative data fusion algorithms.

Our results indicate that consistency is positively correlated to a moderate degree with "deep" relevance measures. However, it is only weakly correlated with "shallow" relevance measures, as well as measures of topic complexity and variety in query expression. These findings support the notion that consistency is an independent property of a search engine's retrieval effectiveness.

CCS CONCEPTS

•Information systems →Retrieval effectiveness; Test collections;

KEYWORDS

Test collections, retrieval consistency, semantic effectiveness

1 INTRODUCTION

Evaluating search effectiveness has several aspects. One aspect that has been especially popular is calculating average scores according to some relevance measure (such as NDCG or AP) over a set of topics and associated queries for some common corpus of information. In the batch evaluation methodology, different systems are compared using the same measure, and statistical tests are applied to determine whether the difference in performance is likely due to factors other than chance. Alternative methods for determining relevance include user studies, online interleaving, and A/B testing. What is important to note is that retrieval effectiveness encompasses more than just relevance.

Batch evaluation has typically used only a single query per topic, although a number of researchers working on early test collections advocated and explored the effect of using multiple queries per topic (see work by Spärck Jones and van Rijsbergen [35], Belkin et al. [5] and Buckley and Walz [7] among others). Recent work by Bailey et al. [3] and Koopman and Zuccon [22] has returned to this theme, resulting in new test collections with large numbers of query variations responding to each topic's information need.

The availability of such test collections allows us to consider a new dimension in assessing the retrieval effectiveness of search engines – namely, how *consistent* they are when returning results in response to query variations that address the same information need. The importance of consistency can be understood when we consider simple examples like mis-spellings. For example *"facebook"*, *"facebok"*, and *"faecbook"* pretty clearly all want to find the Facebook home page. Consistency also applies to more complex examples involving synonyms (for example, *"health benefits of vitamin c"* and *"health benefits of ascorbic acid"*) or entirely rephrased needs (for example, *"how much does a raspberry pi cost"* and *"price of raspberry pi computer"*). In each of these cases, we can contemplate that there exists an ideal ranked set of relevant results drawn from the corpus. Test collections are premised on this principle, where the ideal set for a topic is discovered through judging a document pool formed from different rankings. An ideal search engine would return (only) this set of results given a query for a topic, and the difference in relevance from what is actually returned and this ideal ranking is captured by a relevance measure. Equally, given a set of syntactic query variations, an ideal search engine would return this ideal ranking of results, independent of the query variation.

Indeed, much research in information retrieval seeks to tackle exactly this problem of finding an ideal set of results without relying solely on the original query's syntactic expression. For instance, query re-writing techniques such as spelling correction [11], term stemming [24], query expansion [33], and query substitutions [19] are used to manipulate the user-entered query and thereby extract a better set of documents from the index. Stemming and stopword removal [23, 25] may also be used in indexing processes or within the matching algorithms at query execution time.

Two strands of research have investigated how to combine rankings to improve relevance effectiveness: data fusion (for example,

SIGIR '17, August 07-11, 2017, Shinjuku, Tokyo, Japan

978-1-4503-5022-8/17/08...$15.00
DOI: http://dx.doi.org/10.1145/3077136.3080839

Belkin et al. [6]), which merges rankings from different query representations; and distributed information retrieval or meta-search (for example, Callan [8]), which merges rankings from different underlying search engines or indexes. These techniques have been assessed principally from the standpoint of improving relevance overall, as measured by the relevance score of the resulting ranking.

People use many different expressions to describe the same information need (see, for example, Furnas et al. [15]). Even when refinding a single information resource, the same person may use different queries [37]. Bailey et al. [2] give evidence that the effect of query variation on relevance scores dwarfs that of system and topic effects. We believe that these findings make it important to consider new approaches to characterizing effectiveness, including ones that address query variation for a single information need.

We propose that the *consistency* in rankings of a system when faced with many different query variations for a single topic can be one such measure. The Rank-Biased Overlap measure developed by Webber et al. [38] is adopted to characterize consistency, and used with the UQV100 test collection [3] to investigate consistency across a set of five systems. Due to the scale of variations within UQV100 (19–101 unique query variations per topic, for 100 topics), each individual topic has a similar number of queries as might be found in an entire query-only processed test collection like the TREC 2014 Web track [10].

To determine relative consistency for a single system and topic combination, RBO requires us to declare some reference ranking against which the individual rankings for each query variation can be compared. We develop a new fusion algorithm, the Rank-Biased Centroid (RBC), drawing inspiration from both RBO and Rank-Biased Precision [27], to determine this reference ranking.

We consider these research questions in regard to RBC fusion:

- **RQ-F1** Do RBC rankings outperform the initial query rankings for a system?
- **RQ-F2** How does RBC compare to other data fusion algorithms in relevance effectiveness?
- **RQ-F3** Does combining both query variations and systems for RBC outperform query variations-only RBC?

Then, in connection with consistency, we ask:

- **RQ-C1** Do topics vary in consistency?
- **RQ-C2** Does consistency vary with the number of query variations or with changes in topic complexity?
- **RQ-C3** Do systems vary in consistency?
- **RQ-C4** Are increases in per-topic consistency for a system independent of increases in relevance for a system?

2 RELATED WORK

2.1 Data fusion

Data fusion – combining evidence from different sources – is a widely-studied problem. In IR fusion is typically applied when evidence from multiple ranked answer lists needs to be combined into a single ranked list, for example in meta-search, where results from multiple independent search systems are combined into a single ranking [1], and in multi-lingual retrieval, where results from searches across collections in different languages are combined into a single answer list [16].

Data fusion approaches can be broadly grouped into those that use the ranker's score (that is, the value assigned by a ranking function) of each document in a results list, and those that make use only of the rank position of each document in the answer list. Perhaps the most well-known approaches in the former category are by Fox and Shaw [13], including CombMAX, where the final score of a document is the maximum of the ranker scores that it received in any input ranked list; CombSUM, where the final document score is the total of the ranker's scores that it received in the input lists; and CombMNZ, where the final document score is calculated as in CombSUM but further multiplied by the number of input lists in which the document appears, thereby promoting those documents that were retrieved in multiple lists. The document ranker scores in the input ranked lists may also be normalized in different ways, including linear re-scaling into a chosen range [39], or by controlling an upper bound based on the sum or variance of the input scores [28].

For fusion based only on rank information, techniques from social choice theory such as the Borda count and Condorcet criterion have been applied. In the Borda count [1], each candidate (document) receives a score determined by how many other candidates were ranked lower, with these scores summed across all ballots (input lists). The Condorcet criterion instead determines an outcome based on which candidate achieves the highest number of wins based on pairwise comparisons with all other candidates [12, 29]

The impact of data fusion techniques on effectiveness can vary from case to case, leading Wu and McClean [40] to investigate approaches for predicting the performance impact of applying fusion. Their results showed that the selective application of fusion, based on features such as the number of component result lists and the overlap of items in these lists, can further enhance the positive impact on final retrieval effectiveness.

Prior work that has specifically considered data fusion in the context of multiple queries for the same underlying information need was carried out by Belkin et al. [5], who investigated the effects of combining five independent Boolean query formulations for ten TREC topics, and demonstrated that fusing results can substantially boost performance. Subsequent work using the TREC-2 collection further demonstrated that good methods for fusing the results of multiple queries can lead to results that are better than those of the best single query [6]. Pickens et al. [30] also confirmed that combining multiple queries for the same intent boosts effectiveness.

2.2 Measuring consistency

In IR, as in many other domains, it can be important to compare the similarity, or consistency, of groups of things. These groups may be conjoint (consisting of the same items) or disjoint (one group may include items that do not occur in the other group), and may be set-based (where there is no known or inferred ordering of the items) or ordered (where the sequence in which the items occur matters). Typical examples where one might wish to compare groups include measuring the similarity of the answer lists returned by two search engines in response to the same query; or the similarity of the effectiveness ranking of a set of several different retrieval systems, when evaluated over two different test collections. A wide range of list similarity measures have been proposed and applied.

One of the similarity measures most commonly used in IR is Kendall's τ, a rank correlation coefficient that calculates the normalized number of concordant pairs (items that are ordered the same in two rankings) minus discordant pairs (items that are ordered differently in the two rankings), resulting in a score between 1 (perfect agreement between the two rankings) and −1 (perfect disagreement) [9]. Kendall's τ is a measure that assumes conjoint ranked lists, that is, the lists are permutations of the same set of items; it is also an unweighted measure, where each pair contributes equally to the outcome, wherever it occurs in the ranking. However, when comparing ranked answer lists, items that are higher in the ranking are more important (users pay more attention to top-ranked results); similarly, when comparing rankings of system effectiveness scores, differences between the top systems are generally of greater interest than differences between systems that perform less well. TauAP [41] addresses a number of these weaknesses, while Rank-Biased Overlap (RBO) [38] addresses even more. RBO is a generalized measure of similarity between rankings based on a probabilistic user model, and readily handles non-conjoint lists. It applies a geometric sequence of weights to items in the lists; with the emphasis of the weighting adjustable via a user persistence parameter ϕ, which also determines the probability that the user will reach a certain rank. Inspired by RBO, Tan and Clarke [36] define a family of Maximized Effectiveness Difference (MED) measures, each based on an IR effectiveness metric (and hence a different underlying user model).

Jiang et al. [18] examine ranking consistency in web search from the basis of finding similar classes of queries (based on sharing common entity types in a knowledge base), and preserving the relative ordering of URL domains in the rankings for queries belonging to the same class, for example, people who are professional basketballers but also appear in movies. Large scale web log click data is used to derive their models of class similarity, based on URL patterns. Jiang et al. develop a consistency measure based on Kendall's τ across all pairs of queries belonging to the same class.

Finally, Zuccon et al. [43] present an evaluation framework using mean variance analysis over retrieval effectiveness, for both inter-topic and intra-topic sources of variation. Systems are preferred, all other things being equal, when one system is more stable than another in the presence of such variation.

3 RANK-BIASED CENTROIDS

As noted in the previous section, a range of methods have been proposed for constructing fused rankings, given an initial set of same-basis source rankings. In this section we introduce a further approach: the *rank-biased centroid*, or RBC.

3.1 User model for Borda fusion

To motivate the discussion, consider the four alternative rankings R1, R2, R3, and R4 shown in the left side of Figure 1, with each of the elements denoted by a letter of the alphabet. One run has ordered all of the seven different elements, while the other three are truncated and omit one or more of the items – a typical situation. Moreover, note that even if they are all of the same length, the runs might contain different subsets of a larger group of elements – they need not be permutations of each other. Finally, note that in the

Rank	R1	R2	R3	R4	$\phi = 0.6$	$\phi = 0.8$	$\phi = 0.9$
1	A	B	A	G	A (0.89)	D (0.61)	D (0.35)
2	D	D	B	D	D (0.86)	A (0.50)	C (0.28)
3	B	E	D	E	B (0.78)	B (0.49)	A (0.27)
4	C	C	C	A	G (0.50)	C (0.37)	B (0.27)
5	G	–	G	F	E (0.31)	G (0.37)	G (0.23)
6	F	–	F	C	C (0.29)	E (0.31)	E (0.22)
7	–	–	E	–	F (0.11)	F (0.21)	F (0.18)

Figure 1: Example of RBC fusion: four example rankings (left); and three different fused orderings (right). Note that the RBC weights are shown to two decimal places only, and there are no score ties.

most general scenario, there are situations in which the provided rankings are prefixes of longer lists, themselves of unknown (and perhaps even infinite) length.

The Borda scoring process assigns a weight to item A of $7+7+4 = 18$ (note that A does not appear in ranking R2), tying it with B, and placing it behind item D, which gets $6 + 6 + 6 + 5 = 23$ points. The overall Borda ordering is D, A=B, C, G, E, F. In the Borda regime, swapping the two adjacent items at any pair of consecutive ranks gives one of the items a +1 score change, and the other item a −1 change. This occurs regardless of whether the swap takes place at rank 1, at rank 10, or at rank 100. That is, all binary item preferences as expressed in the visible input rankings are regarded as being of equal merit; and any preferences that may not have been surfaced (in the case that the provided rankings are prefixes) are ignored.

To create a user model that captures this behavior we can imagine a universe of agents, each of whom acts independently of the others, but follows the same simple rule: they randomly pick a depth d according to some probability distribution, they examine all of the input rankings to depth d (at most – but less if the rankings are shorter), and they sort the pool of items according to decreasing order of the number of times they saw each item in their set of length-d prefixes. The final fused ranking is then a probabilistic expectation over all agents of the orderings that were constructed.

Given this overall probabilistic structure, the Borda ordering is derived when the probability distribution used by the agents is taken to be $P(d = x) = 1/n$; that is, each agent is equally likely to select a prefix of any length between 1 and n, where n is the number of items. The Borda score for an item is then proportional to the expected value of the total number of times it was observed in the individual top-d sets of the probabilistic universe of agents.

3.2 An alternative weighting regime

Because there are many situations in which the supplied rankings are assumed to be prefixes of arbitrary-length ones, we contend that swaps near the heads of each of the rankings are somehow more indicative of preference than swaps deeper in the rankings. In the example shown in the left side of Figure 1, swapping A and D in ranking R1 has the same net effect on A's Borda score as does swapping A and F in ranking R4, but the latter swap might seem to be somewhat less damaging to A, since in R4 it has already been deprecated by the person or system that generated that ordering.

Instead of assigning a Borda weight of $(n - x + 1)/n$ (in a normalized sense) to each item at rank $1 \leq x \leq n$ when the rankings are over n items, we suggest that a geometrically decaying weight function be employed, with the distribution of d over depths x given not by $1/n$, but instead by $(1 - \phi)\phi^{x-1}$ for some value $0 \leq \phi \leq 1$ determined by considering the purpose for which the fused ranking is being constructed. The parameter ϕ is the *persistence*, or *patience* of the imagined universe of probabilistic agents; and use of a geometric sequence models the same behavior as is embedded in the effectiveness metric RBP [27] and in the rank correlation coefficient RBO [38] – namely, that the person examining the rankings always examines the first item in each, and thereafter proceeds from the i th to the $i + 1$ st with conditional probability ϕ, and ends their search at the i th with conditional probability $(1 - \phi)$. In an implementation the fused ranking is determined by assigning a weight of $(1 - \phi)\phi^{i-1}$ to each item at depth i in any of the rankings, and then summing over items and sorting by total weight.

There are a number of benefits of this proposed approach:

- as already motivated, greater emphasis is placed on the earlier preferences than on deeper ones in each ranking;
- an upper bound on the lengths of the rankings is not required, nor are the rankings required to be the same length (the Borda method shares this flexibility, albeit somewhat awkwardly);
- if further items are added at the tail of any of the rankings, the resultant item scores converge smoothly.

As extreme values, consider $\phi = 0$ and $\phi = 1$. When $\phi = 0$, the agents only ever examine the first item in each of the input rankings, and the fused output is by decreasing score of first preference; this is somewhat akin to a first-past-the-post election regime. When $\phi = 1$, each agent examines the whole of every list, and the fused ordering is determined by the number of lists that contain each item – a kind of "popularity count" of each item across the input sets. In between these extremes, the expected depth reached by the agents viewing the rankings is given by $1/(1 - \phi)$. For example, when $\phi = 0.9$, on average the first 10 items in each ranking are being used to contribute to the fused ordering; of course, in aggregate, across the whole universe of agents, all of the items in every ranking contribute to the overall outcome.

In practice, what this means is that different values of ϕ between 0 and 1 give rise to different fused orderings, balancing top-weightedness and exhaustivity. The right side of Figure 1 shows the orderings generated for the rankings R1, R2, R3, and R4, discussed earlier, for three different values of ϕ. The total weight associated with each item (to two decimals) is also shown. Note how item A is top-ranked when the ranking agents are relatively impatient, and (on average) abandon the ranking early ($\phi = 0.6$), but that if the fused ranking is assembled on a more patient basis ($\phi = 0.8$ and $\phi = 0.9$), items D and C become preferred, and A is demoted.

As with Borda fusion, unanimous preferences are respected: in the example, because C is below D in all of the four input rankings, it must also fall below D in the fused ranking, regardless of the value of ϕ. The differences that arise as ϕ varies are limited only to the elements where there is disagreement in the input rankings as to their respective ordering. These are, arguably, exactly the elements that we might be interested in focusing on.

3.3 Discussion

We have defined RBC in terms of a one-state user model [27]. Another way of looking at it is as an estimation of the normalized document scores used in CombMNZ and CombSUM. By assigning decreasingly small weights to documents further down the ranking, RBC can be viewed as seeking to approximate the long tail of document-query similarity scores generated by disjunctive ranked retrieval systems. Functions other than the geometric sequence might also be suitable for use, for example, Zipfian weightings.

4 FUSION OVER QUERY VARIATIONS

This section explores the practical benefit of fusing over query variations, and also shows that fusion over systems retains some of its power even after query variations have been incorporated.

4.1 The UQV100 collection

The UQV100 test collection is made up of 100 topics and associated information need statements, with approximately 100 individual query variations per topic; 10,835 in total [3]. When spelling correction and normalization are applied there are between 19 and 101 unique query variations per topic; 5,765 in total. There are also 55,587 relevance judgments available in regard to those 100 topics, covering ClueWeb12-CatB documents pooled from five systems, spanning three separate search engine code bases, and five different ranking algorithms [26]. We again employ the runs for those five contributing systems, anonymized here as Systems 1, 2, 3, 4, and 5. Due to some processing anomalies we observed in the run data, the overlapping set of unique query variations processed by all five systems contains 5,736 queries. Each system run contains a ranking of length 200 for each of those distinct queries. For definiteness we ordered the set of queries for each topic by decreasing frequency according to crowd-based process used to originally collect them [2], with ties broken randomly.

4.2 Fusion over query variations

Table 1 provides a detailed evaluation of approaches for fusion as applied to query variations. Each pane of the table gives results for one effectiveness metric, and within each pane the columns represent increasing numbers of query variations v (note that for $v \geq 20$, the legend $v = x$ indicates that as many as x query variations were used – some topics had fewer than the listed number of variations). Note that $v = 1$ makes use of the most frequently-suggested query for each of the UQV100 topics; $v = 2$ adds the second most frequently suggested one; and so on. Stepping across each row thus involves more and more input runs being used to form each output run, and as can be seen, effectiveness scores (with a few exceptions) increase. Many of the fusion methods give very similar effectiveness. Even so, there are some notable patterns:

- using as few as $v = 2$ query variations gives improved effectiveness (relative to the $v = 1$ baseline) for all metrics and all fusion methods;
- for all of the metrics, RBC with high values of p provides good fused outcomes, comparable with or better than those achieved by CombMNZ and Borda;
- for the two recall-based metrics, RBC-based fusion provides markedly better outcomes than Borda and CombMNZ;

Fusion	Number of variations per query					
	$v = 2$	$v = 4$	$v = 10$	$v = 20$	$v = 40$	$v = all$
RBC, $\phi = 0.9$	0.491	0.490	0.510	0.516	0.524	0.522
RBC, $\phi = 0.95$	0.497	0.504	0.516	0.526	0.529	0.526
RBC, $\phi = 0.98$	0.505	0.511	0.522	**0.535**	**0.533**	0.532
RBC, $\phi = 0.99$	**0.511**	0.520	0.525	**0.534**	**0.533**	**0.534**
Borda	0.511	**0.522**	**0.527**	0.534	0.532	**0.535**
CombMNZ	**0.513**	**0.521**	**0.527**	0.534	0.532	0.531

(a) RBP0.85, common baseline 0.474

Fusion	Number of variations per query					
	$v = 2$	$v = 4$	$v = 10$	$v = 20$	$v = 40$	$v = all$
RBC, $\phi = 0.9$	0.490	0.490	0.506	0.516	0.523	0.522
RBC, $\phi = 0.95$	0.496	0.504	0.514	0.526	0.528	0.527
RBC, $\phi = 0.98$	0.503	0.510	0.519	**0.533**	**0.533**	0.532
RBC, $\phi = 0.99$	**0.508**	**0.519**	0.523	**0.532**	**0.531**	**0.532**
Borda	0.507	**0.520**	**0.525**	0.530	0.528	**0.532**
CombMNZ	**0.509**	0.517	**0.524**	0.531	0.528	0.528

(b) INST, common baseline 0.471

Fusion	Number of variations per query					
	$v = 2$	$v = 4$	$v = 10$	$v = 20$	$v = 40$	$v = all$
RBC, $\phi = 0.9$	0.222	0.230	0.248	0.265	**0.288†**	**0.299†**
RBC, $\phi = 0.95$	0.223	0.234	**0.256**	**0.280†**	**0.297†**	**0.303†**
RBC, $\phi = 0.98$	0.225	0.239	**0.260†**	**0.275†**	0.281†	0.284†
RBC, $\phi = 0.99$	**0.226†**	**0.241†**	0.254†	0.264†	0.266†	0.270†
Borda	0.226	0.239	0.251	0.260	0.262	0.267
CombMNZ	**0.227**	**0.240**	0.252	0.260	0.273	0.266

(c) AP, common baseline 0.204

Fusion	Number of variations per query					
	$v = 2$	$v = 4$	$v = 10$	$v = 20$	$v = 40$	$v = all$
RBC, $\phi = 0.9$	0.437	0.454	0.484	0.505†	**0.539†**	**0.553†**
RBC, $\phi = 0.95$	0.438	0.458	**0.489†**	**0.519†**	**0.545†**	**0.554†**
RBC, $\phi = 0.98$	0.440	0.462	**0.492†**	**0.510†**	0.521†	0.525†
RBC, $\phi = 0.99$	**0.442**	**0.464**	0.481†	0.494†	0.499†	0.505†
Borda	0.442	**0.464**	0.478	0.489	0.493	0.502
CombMNZ	**0.442**	0.463	0.479	0.490	0.494	0.500

(d) NDCG, common baseline 0.409

Table 1: Fusion over query variations, average effectiveness across 100 UQV topics for runs generated from different numbers of query variations and according to different fusion approaches for System 1: (a) RBP0.85 scores; (b) INST scores; (c) AP scores; (d) NDCG scores. Query variations are sorted in decreasing order of occurrence frequency in the UQV100 collection. The baseline scores for $v = 1$ (that is, executing the single most popular query variation) are shown under each table. So that patterns of behavior can be seen, the two largest values in each column are highlighted in bold. Daggers indicate arrangements in which the RBC-based system was significantly better than the corresponding Borda run (one-sided paired t-tests with $p < 0.05$). No significant differences were detected for CombMNZ fusion, or using RBP0.85 or INST. Similar behavior was observed for other combinations of system and metric (not shown here).

Fusion	Metric			
	RBP0.85	INST	AP	NDCG
RBC, $\phi = 0.9$	0.503	0.501	0.217	0.441
RBC, $\phi = 0.95$	**0.508**	**0.506**	**0.219†**	0.442
RBC, $\phi = 0.98$	**0.506**	0.504	**0.220†**	**0.443†**
RBC, $\phi = 0.99$	0.505†	0.502	0.217†	0.440
Borda	0.503	0.500	0.215	0.440
CombMNZ	0.506	**0.505**	0.219†	**0.442†**

Table 2: Fusion over five different retrieval systems, based on one query variation ($v = 1$). All numbers are average effectiveness scores over the 100 topics in the UQV100 collection. Single-system scores for the four metrics are shown in the first two columns of Table 3. The largest two entries in each column are shown in bold. Daggers represent significance relative to Borda fusion ($p < 0.05$).

Metric	Initial, $v = 1$		Fused, $v = all$		Fused^2, $s = 5$	
	mean	max	mean	max	mean	gain
RBP0.85	0.474	0.487	0.530	0.557	0.559	+18%
INST	0.470	0.481	0.532	0.558	0.563	+20%
AP	0.190	0.204	0.268	0.303	0.303	+59%
NDCG	0.400	0.411	0.517	0.554	0.561	+41%

Table 3: Summary of effectiveness gains achieved by fusing first over query variations, and then second over systems. The first four data columns are mean and maximum average scores over five systems; the "gain" is relative to the initial system average in the first column. All fusion is carried out using RBC0.95.

- moreover, the greater the number of query variations being fused, the smaller the value of ϕ needed to obtain those outcomes.

We also explored round-robin fusion and CombSUM fusion; the former was never competitive (and effectiveness decreased as query variations were added); and CombSUM typically gave performance slightly inferior to CombMNZ.

4.3 Fusion over systems

Table 2 shows the outcome of applying fusion across the five systems used in our experiments. A single query is used in each input run ($v = 1$), and fusion applied to the five rankings for each topic. In this setting, all methods give comparable improvements in effectiveness, with Borda fusion marginally the worst of them.

4.4 Double fusion

Table 3 provides an overall summary of the effectiveness gains that can be achieved by fusing over query variations and then over systems, with RBC0.95 used at all fusing steps. Starting on the left, five systems each execute one query variation ($v = 1$) for each of the

Description	RBP0.85	INST	AP	NDCG
All queries ($v = all$)	0.405	0.394	0.151	0.336
First queries ($v = 1$)	0.474	0.471	0.204	0.409
Best query per topic	0.712	0.718	0.271	0.503

Table 4: Average metric scores for all queries per topic; for the most popular query per topic; and for per-metric per-topic "omniscient" query selections. System 1 is used throughout. These scores can be directly compared with those shown in the four panes of Table 1.

UQV100 topics; this can be regarded as being the starting baseline condition (no fusion performed) for both this table and Table 2. The five-way mean "average over 100 topics" and five-way maximum "average over 100 topics" values show typical behavior for five good retrieval systems when measured using a single query per topic. If each of those five systems is given more query variations, and generates a single fused run for each of the 100 topics as its output, the values in the middle pair of columns arise. Substantial performance improvements can be observed, and the means of the five "fusion over query variations" systems handsomely exceeds the best average score of the five original systems.

The third pair of columns in Table 3 then shows the outcome of fusing the five system runs generated after the query variations have been folded in. The mean scores shown (now with just a single ranking for each of the 100 topics) exceed the previous maximum scores in three of four cases, and exceed the middle-column mean scores in all four cases. The final column shows the end-to-end gain in effectiveness that has been achieved by the compound fusing ("initial mean" to "fused^2 mean"). That is, fusing first over query variations, and then over systems, gives rise to average effectiveness gains of 18% and higher. In terms of statistical significance, and looking at the various relativities summarized in Table 3:

- across the five systems and four metrics (twenty paired runs in total), the largest p-value computed by a two-tailed paired Student's t-test comparing the corresponding $v = 1$ and $v = all$ conditions was less than 0.005;
- when the five $v = all$ fused runs are compared with the final "fused^2" run, each metric yields one relatively large p-value, arising when the system that happens to be the "max" is compared with the final fused run ($p \approx 0.8$, 0.7, 0.9, and 0.3 respectively across the four metrics, with two different systems represented twice each as the "max" one), and a range of other smaller p-values, the largest of which was 0.059 (INST, comparing System 2 with $v = all$ against the final fused run), and the remainder of which were 0.01 or smaller.

That is, we are highly confident that fusion over queries helps retrieval effectiveness regardless of system and regardless of metric; and also confident that additional fusion across systems is also beneficial, helping ensure that the outcomes are as good as, or better than, what would have been attained if by chance we were already working with the best system for that metric.

4.5 An unrealistic target?

Hindsight is a wonderful guide, a fact that is also true in IR. Table 4 shows the result of a post-hoc evaluation of the runs generated for System 1. The first row shows the (unweighted) average metric scores across all of the UQV100 topics, and for each topic across the (approximately, on average) 55 distinct query variations. The second row shows the baseline effectiveness scores used in Table 1, arrived at by selecting the most popular of the query variations for each topic. The third row then shows results for four "oracle" query subsets, one for each metric, each incorporating (based post hoc on the relevance judgments and the computed metric scores) the "best" query variation for each of the UQV100 topics.

Comparing the first and second rows, the most frequently posed query generated by the crowd-workers for each topic obtains notably better effectiveness than the average of the variations. That difference is why we ordered the query variations as we did (Section 4.1). Comparing the second and third rows reveals a substantial further gap – for each of the topics and each of the metrics there are highly effective queries available within the sets created by the crowd-workers. For two of the metrics the single-query oracle runs are outperformed by the best of the fused approaches (Table 1), but for two metrics they are considerably better. Also worth noting is that the oracle runs have non-trivial differences, with different best queries arising for different metrics in many cases. Across the four metrics, a total of 193 best queries were identified.

5 CONSISTENCY DEFINED

5.1 Definition

As discussed in Section 2, Rank-Biased Overlap (RBO) [38] measures the top-weighted rank similarity between two non-conjoint indefinite rankings. As the rankings increase in similarity, especially towards the start of the rankings, the value of RBO trends towards 1.0. Due to the geometric sum of weights, governed by parameter ϕ, the total overlap score is bounded, ranging from 0.0 (no overlap) to 1.0 (total overlap).

To use RBO to measure consistency across query variations for a topic, we first select a common reference or objective ranking (the *centroid*) for each system-topic pair, making use of the RBC algorithm described in the previous sections. The persistence factor ϕ for RBC is set to 0.90, to mirror a user whose expected depth of examination into a ranked list is 10, a reasonably deep level of examination relative to standard web search; also, the UQV100 pooling ensured at least depth-10 judging for each query from each system. Different persistence factors could be selected, which would emphasize shallower or deeper probabilities of inspection of the lists forming the centroid or the depth of overlap. The centroid for all-systems might also have been considered; however we sought to measure a system's self-consistency, rather than with respect to a centroid that requires knowledge of other systems.

Given a centroid, we compute the RBO score for every query variation, using the same value of $\phi = 0.90$. Computation of RBO provides both a point-estimate, and a minimum, residual, and maximum value. Since system runs typically report 200 or more documents, when $\phi = 0.90$ the residual is less than 10^{-10}, and the point value is essentially equivalent to the minimum and maximum.

Formally, given a set of query variations $V_i = \{v_{i.1}, v_{i.2}, \ldots, v_{i.k}\}$ for a topic $t_i \in T = \{t_1, t_2, ..., t_n\}$, given a system S and its rankings for this set of variations $D_i = \{d_{v_{i.1}}, d_{v_{i.2}}, ..., d_{v_{i.k}}\}$, and given the corresponding RBC ranking for S and topic t_i, denoted $d_{i.\text{rbc}}$, we measure *topic consistency* C_{t_i} with respect to S as

$$C_{t_i} = \frac{\sum_{q=1}^{k} \text{RBO}(d_{v_{i,q}}, d_{i.\text{rbc}})}{k}, \quad (1)$$

and the *collection consistency* C_T as the average topic consistency over the set of topics T, again with respect to S, as

$$C_T = \frac{\sum_{i=1}^{n} C_{t_i}}{n}. \quad (2)$$

That is, consistency is the average RBO score relative to the per-topic centroids generated for the system, expressed either as a set of per-topic scores, or aggregated over topics for a per-collection score, but always with regard to a system S. We can also speak of a *system's* consistency, which is simply topic (or collection) consistency for a particular system. Note that the near-zero RBO residual means that issues of averaging over RBO scores with different residuals can be ignored. We choose the average of averages for C_T because the number of variations per topic may vary, and topics with large numbers of unique variations should not unduly bias final scores.

Unlike for RBC, where we explored the consequence of adding more variations and thus needed an ordering, for consistency we use all unique query expressions without repeats (unweighted). In UQV100, each topic typically has a small number of commonly chosen variations which occur multiple times, and a large number of variations that occur only once. We wished to avoid biasing the consistency measure unduly by counting the contribution of the more popular variations multiple times. The choice of unweighted query variations also reinforces the decision to compute average of averages for C_T; in UQV100 the number of unique query variations per topic ranges from 19 to 101, so double averaging helps avoid undue influence from the topics with more diverse variations.

5.2 Why this definition of consistency?

Test collection-based evaluation reduces many sources of variance that occur in information seeking in the wild to a level that is tractable from the standpoint of statistical analysis. Our definition of consistency is predicated on having test collections that embody some plausible set of query variations per information need. We do not claim that it can address all possible sources of, or needs for, desirable consistency (or inconsistency) in information seeking.

Our definition of consistency might be brought into question by queries that exhibit extrinsic diversity [31] or intrinsic diversity [32] or searching as learning [14]. Extrinsic diversity occurs when a query has many different information needs that might be associated with it, while intrinsic diversity addresses cases where there are multiple sub-tasks associated in satisfying the information need. Searching as learning involves evolving query expression throughout a session. For cases involving extrinsic diversity, test collections without query variations typically declare one information need and judge relevance with respect to that information need; other plausible information needs are ignored. From the standpoint of assessing consistency, our approach is the same and has the same flaw of ignoring other information needs. For cases involving intrinsic diversity and searching as learning, approaches have been developed that target aspects of such complex evaluation situations, including TREC's Web track's Diversity task [10] and the Session [20] and Tasks [42] tracks. For assessing just consistency, we suggest that test collections should involve more narrow information needs, with an emphasis on developing specific unambiguous topic statements. Despite this, we believe that consistency is also important for systems that are able to accurately detect and respond to intrinsic diversity queries, and just as with narrower information needs, there will be a wide range of query variations for an information need that is intrinsically diverse.

One more question the reader might have is why measure consistency at all, and why not just go straight to average relevance. Two issues arise: first, relevance judgments are a substantially more expensive resource to accumulate, particularly when dealing with test collections with thousands of query variations. Second, although two rankings may have identical relevance scores, they may be completely different. Consider an information need such as "*You are worried about the prevalence of fake news, and decide to find authoritative newspapers to read instead, just like people did last century.*" Now consider two rankings in response to two query variations, one of which lists [theguardian.com, zeit.de, ft.com, washingtonpost.com] and one of which lists [wsj.com, lemonde.fr, nytimes.com, theglobeandmail.com]. From a relevance standpoint, these rankings are effectively identical, but from a consistency perspective, they share nothing. If we accept that a searcher cares about refinding the same information for an information need, even if they forget the precise query variation they used previously [37], then it is clear that being able to quantify consistency in rankings is not captured by relevance equivalence alone.

6 ANALYSIS OF CONSISTENCY

6.1 Consistency and topics

We address **RQ-C1** by assessing C_{t_i} over the five contributed runs described in Section 4.1. **RQ-C1** asks whether topics vary in consistency, and to do this we plot the average and standard deviation of C_{t_i} against all 100 topics of UQV100, sorted by increasing C_{t_i}. We characterize this in two ways: Figure 2 shows the results for System 1 (where standard deviation is of the RBO scores per variation for the topic), while Figure 3 shows the results when aggregating over the C_{t_i} scores obtained from the five systems. Even with the large standard deviations that can be observed in both plots (while being clearly smaller in the second), we can conclude that different topics have different consistency. For persistence $\phi = 0.9$, approximately 25% of topics have consistency under 0.25, while around 12% have consistency greater than 0.5. We also observe that some topics have great variation in their consistency scores, and others much less; and, overall, that consistency does indeed vary across topics.

6.2 Consistency and topic attributes

In the first part of **RQ-C2** we ask whether there is a relationship between the number of query variations per topic t_i and corresponding consistency scores C_{t_i}. Intuitively, we might expect that the more unique query variations there are for a topic, the lower the consistency scores. We address this aspect through a correlation analysis, using Spearman's ρ, a non-parametric rank correlation statistic. Unlike Pearson's product-moment coefficient statistic, this does not rely on the data having equal variance or having few to no outliers. A scatter plot, not shown, demonstrated that these

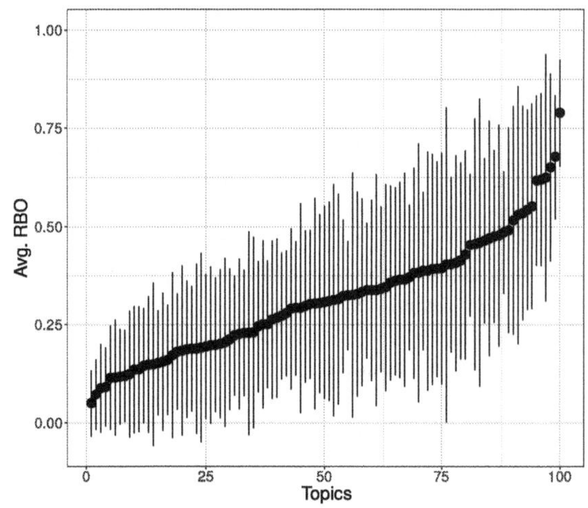

Figure 2: Consistency scores C_{t_i} for System 1, ordered by score, for 100 topics. Bars are ± 1 s.d. of the underlying RBO values.

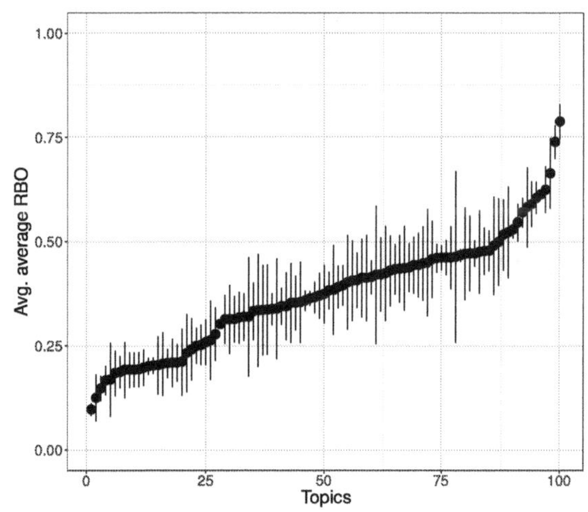

Figure 3: Average consistency scores C_{t_i} from five systems, ordered by increasing score, for 100 topics. Bars are ± 1 s.d. Note that the topics may not be in the same order as in Figure 2.

System	(a) Num. variations	(b) Est. docs	(c) Est. queries
1	−0.35‡	−0.30‡	−0.43‡
2	−0.43‡	−0.27‡	−0.43‡
3	−0.42‡	−0.35‡	−0.45‡
4	−0.36‡	−0.25‡	−0.39‡
5	−0.37‡	−0.36‡	−0.43‡

Table 5: Correlation measured using Spearman's ρ between C_{t_i} and: (a) number of unique query variations per topic; (b) average estimated useful documents per topic; and (c) average estimated useful queries per topic, for each (system, topic) pair. In all cases, $p < 0.01$(‡).

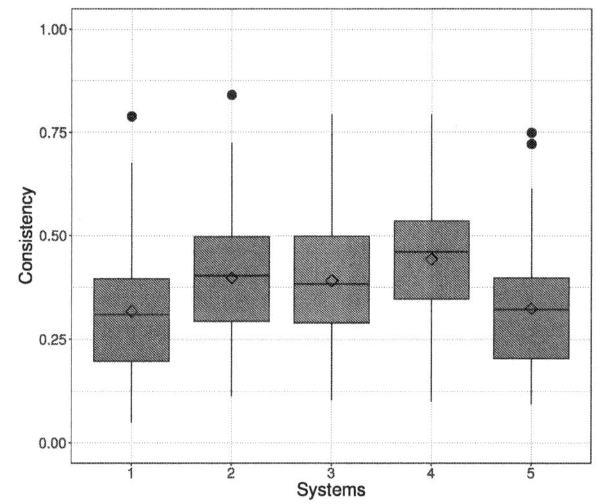

Figure 4: Consistency scores C_{t_i} for five systems and 100 topics. The diamond marks the median, and the horizontal line marks C_T.

requirements might not hold. In Table 5(a), we show the results for all systems. As expected, the direction of the association is negative (C_{t_i} goes down when the number of query variations goes up). However, the correlations are relatively weak weak magnitude ($0.3 < \rho < 0.5$) so although there is an association, it is not something we can reliably anticipate. The corresponding scatter plot of values is not shown for space reasons, but confirms that there is a broad range of consistency scores as the number of query variations per topic changes. These outcomes are a little surprising, suggesting that the causes of increased consistency are complex.

In the second part of **RQ-C2** we ask whether there is a relationship between the estimated topic complexity and corresponding consistency scores. Estimated topic complexity is available as the average of the estimates of the number of useful documents (and the number of queries) expected by each person providing a query variation for a topic description in UQV100. More complex topics have higher values for these two averaged estimates. Again, intuitively we might expect that the more complex a topic is, the lower the consistency score. As above, we assess the relationship using Spearman's ρ, for both the average estimated documents and average estimated queries per topic t_i and corresponding consistency scores C_{t_i}. Results are shown in Table 5(b) and (c), and just as before indicate a negative association, as surmised. However, once again the correlations are weak at best, at best of weak magnitude, meaning that increases in estimated topic complexity are only loosely associated with decreases in consistency. Interestingly, the estimates of the required number of queries all have a stronger correlation than the corresponding estimates of the required number of useful documents. This outcome might in part arise because the complexity estimate providers may be better at estimating changes in small numbers than in larger ones, but there are other possible explanations.

System	2	3	4	5
1	−9.756‡	−10.497‡	−14.362‡	−1.030
2		−0.930	−6.821‡	9.107‡
3			−8.035‡	8.490‡
4				12.330‡

Table 6: System differences measured using a paired Student's t-test between all pairs of systems over the corresponding C_{t_i} per topic. Values reported are the t statistic, $df = 99$ in all cases, and significant differences at $p < 0.05$ (†) and $p < 0.01$ (‡).

6.3 Consistency and systems

If consistency was identical across different retrieval systems, then it would be uninteresting when selecting an effective system. In **RQ-C3**, we examine the relationship between collection consistency C_T and the five systems which contributed to UQV100. In Figure 4 we report on the consistency scores for each system, using boxplots to show the spread of values. From this we can observe that Systems 1 and 5 are very similar to each other ($C_T \simeq 0.32$); Systems 2 and 3 are very similar to each other and more consistent ($C_T \simeq 0.40$), and System 4 is different and yet more consistent ($C_T = 0.44$). Using a two-tailed paired Student's t-test, we also assessed each pair of systems; Table 6 confirms our observations.

Another way of understanding the relationship between consistency and systems is to treat each topic as an "assessor" and each system as the "subject" being assessed with regards to its degree of consistency. Since topics in UQV100 contain a similar number of query variations (average of 55 per topic) as many existing test collections have queries, and past practice has been to examine rank order correlation of systems by comparing sets of systems across two or more collections, we will adopt a similar method here. We assess how similar the relative ordering of systems is using one-way Intraclass Correlation [4], Kendall's Coefficient of Concordance [21] (commonly written as Kendall's W), and Krippendorff's α [17]. All of these measures address inter-assessor agreement, for three or more assessors, and can accommodate ordinal data (and for ICC and α, interval or ratio data). In Table 7, we report the results for these measures of rank agreement, where the score is the topic consistency C_{t_i}. We use these measures rather than pair-wise comparisons of topics using Kendall's τ, since we have 100 topic "assessors" involved, and the measures allow us to consider multiple "assessors" with a single test statistic, while Kendall's τ only supports two "assessors". Due to the differences between ICC and Kendall's W, it is expected that ICC scores may be lower than Kendall's W scores over the same data, since it considers not just relative rank order but also the magnitude of differences, as discussed by Sheskin [34]. In all three measures, 1 indicates perfect agreement among the assessors, and 0 indicates no agreement beyond what would be expected by chance. Both ICC and α can report small negative values, which also signify no agreement. The values from ICC and Krippendorff's α both indicate there is a very low degree of inter-assessor agreement in rank ordering the systems by consistency; and although Kendall's W is 0.491 for C_{t_i}, this is still a relatively low degree of agreement.

From these two analyses, we conclude that although these systems do have different overall collection consistency C_T, they are not systematically ordered on the basis of topic consistency C_{t_i}. That is, for one topic a particular system may have high consistency, while for another topic a completely different system may have high consistency, and the earlier system may have low consistency.

Agreement	(a) ICC	(b) Kendall's W	(c) Krippendorff's α
C_{t_i}	0.111‡	0.491‡	0.090
NDCG	−0.002	0.169‡	−0.003
INST	−0.005	0.033†	−0.006

Table 7: Rank agreement over all five systems measured using (a) Intraclass Correlation; (b) Kendall's W; and (c) Krippendorff's α. For ICC and W, significance is reported as $p < 0.05$(†), and $p < 0.01$(‡); for α it is not reported. The top row uses C_{t_i} as the ranking score for each system; the bottom two rows use NDCG and INST (averaged by topic, as for C_{t_i}).

System	AP	NDCG	Q	RBP	INST
1	0.61‡	0.68‡	0.56‡	0.32‡	0.35‡
2	0.62‡	0.70‡	0.58‡	0.33‡	0.37‡
3	0.55‡	0.62‡	0.53‡	0.32‡	0.36‡
4	0.59‡	0.65‡	0.55‡	0.39‡	0.40‡
5	0.59‡	0.65‡	0.53‡	0.25†	0.30‡

Table 8: Correlation measured using Spearman's ρ between topic consistency C_{t_i} and corresponding relevance measures (AP, NDCG, Q measure, RBP0.85, and INST), for each (system, topic) pair. In all cases, there is a significant correlation, with $p < 0.01$ (‡), except for System 5 and RBP, significant only at $p < 0.05$ (†).

6.4 Consistency and relevance

Our last investigation, addressing **RQ-C4**, concerns the relationship between consistency and relevance. The construction of UQV100 guaranteed relevance judgments to at least depth 10 for all query variations for the five systems being analyzed. Thus we are able to explore the degree of correlation between consistency and relevance, across a range of relevance measures, including AP, NDCG, Q measure, RBP0.85, and INST. The results, calculated using Spearman's ρ, are displayed in Table 8. While there is moderate correlation for the "deep" relevance measures (AP, NDCG, and Q), there is only weak correlation for the "shallow" relevance measures (RBP0.85 and INST). Scatter plots of the data, not shown, indicate considerable spread of scores for all measures as C_{t_i} increases.

As a comparison with consistency, we repeat the topics-as-"assessors" inter-assessor agreement analysis, with results reported for average-by-topic NDCG and INST scores in rows two and three of Table 7. While any degree of agreement was only just observable for consistency, with these relevance measures, any agreement on the ordering of systems by relevance is effectively random.

7 CONCLUSIONS

Consistency – the ability to give similar results for a topic even when presented with different queries – is desirable for search engines in a variety of circumstances. We have defined a consistency measure and explored it across a set of 5,736 query variations across 100 topics, using a novel relevance-based centroid algorithm.

The RBC algorithm for fusing rankings has the benefit of incorporating a persistence parameter that allows modeling of different depths of attention into rankings, and adds another strand to the "RB-" family. RBC is competitive or better than existing algorithms, and like Borda count has no reliance on system scores. We confirmed previous findings that data fusion over queries and over systems is beneficial, and fusion over both is even better. With the oracle runs we have also demonstrated that substantially better effectiveness performance is possible, at least hypothetically.

Based on the various analyses, we can also state that the consistency measure informs us about something different to existing measures. Consistency varies by topic and by system, tends to decrease as topic complexity and the number of query variations increases, and has weak-to-moderate correlations with several relevance measures. However, in no circumstance is consistency strongly correlated with any of these existing test collection dimensions, confirming that it measures a different property altogether. Neither the measures of consistency nor relevance reliably order the five systems over the UQV100 topics, indicating there are no clear system winners or losers for this test collection on these dimensions of effectiveness when examined topic by topic.

More investigation is required into the nature of consistency and its effect on perceptions of the retrieval effectiveness of search systems. Such work might include user studies, low-level analysis of the root causes of variable ranking within one or more systems, and broadening the current analysis to similar test collections with multiple query variations per topic.

Acknowledgment This work was supported by the Australian Research Council's *Discovery Projects* Scheme (projects DP110101934 and DP140102655). Matt Crane, Xiaolu Lu, David Maxwell, and Andrew Trotman assisted greatly, providing the system runs that were analyzed. The UQV100 judgments were generated using resources provided by Microsoft.

REFERENCES

[1] J. A. Aslam and M. Montague. 2001. Models for metasearch. In *Proc. SIGIR.* ACM, 276–284.

[2] P. Bailey, A. Moffat, F. Scholer, and P. Thomas. 2015. User variability and IR system evaluation. In *Proc. SIGIR.* 625–634.

[3] P. Bailey, A. Moffat, F. Scholer, and P. Thomas. 2016. UQV100: A test collection with query variability. In *Proc. SIGIR.* 725–728. Public data: http://dx.doi.org/10.4225/49/5726E597B8376.

[4] J. J. Bartko. 1966. The intraclass correlation coefficient as a measure of reliability. *Psychological Reports* 19, 1 (1966), 3–11.

[5] N. J. Belkin, C. Cool, W. B. Croft, and J. P. Callan. 1993. The effect of multiple query representations on information retrieval system performance. In *Proc. SIGIR.* 339–346.

[6] N. J. Belkin, P. Kantor, E. A. Fox, and J. A. Shaw. 1995. Combining the evidence of multiple query representations for information retrieval. *Inf. Proc. & Man.* 31, 3 (1995), 431–448.

[7] C. Buckley and J. Walz. 1999. The TREC-8 query track. In *Proc. TREC.*

[8] J. Callan. 2002. Distributed information retrieval. In *Advances in Information Retrieval.* Springer, 127–150.

[9] B. Carterette. 2009. On rank correlation and the distance between rankings. In *Proc. SIGIR.* 436–443.

[10] K. Collins-Thompson, C. Macdonald, P. N. Bennett, F. Diaz, and E. M. Voorhees. 2014. TREC 2014 web track overview. In *Proc. TREC.*

[11] S. Cucerzan and E. Brill. 2004. Spelling correction as an iterative process that exploits the collective knowledge of web users. In *Proc. EMNLP.* 293–300.

[12] C. Dwork, R. Kumar, M. Naor, and D. Sivakumar. 2001. Rank aggregation methods for the web. In *Proc. WWW.* 613–622.

[13] E. A. Fox and J. Shaw. 1993. Combination of multiple searches. In *Proc. TREC.* 243–252.

[14] L. Freund, H. O'Brien, and R. Kopak. 2014. Getting the big picture: Supporting comprehension and learning in search. In *Proc. Searching As Learning (SAL) Workshop.*

[15] G. W. Furnas, T. K. Landauer, L. M. Gomez, and S. T. Dumais. 1987. The vocabulary problem in human-system communication. *Comm. ACM* 30, 11 (1987), 964–971.

[16] F. C. Gey, N. Kando, and C. Peters. 2005. Cross-language information retrieval: The way ahead. *Inf. Proc. & Man.* 41, 3 (2005), 415–431.

[17] A. F. Hayes and K. Krippendorff. 2007. Answering the call for a standard reliability measure for coding data. *Commun. Methods and Measures* 1, 1 (2007), 77–89.

[18] J.-Y. Jiang, J. Liu, C.-Y. Lin, and P.-J. Cheng. 2015. Improving ranking consistency for web search by leveraging a knowledge base and search logs. In *Proc. CIKM.* 1441–1450.

[19] R. Jones, B. Rey, O. Madani, and W. Greiner. 2006. Generating query substitutions. In *Proc. WWW.* 387–396.

[20] E. Kanoulas, B. Carterette, M. Hall, P. Clough, and M. Sanderson. 2011. Overview of the TREC 2011 session track. In *Proc. TREC.*

[21] M. G. Kendall and B. B. Smith. 1939. The problem of *m* rankings. *Annals of Mathematical Statistics* 10, 3 (1939), 275–287.

[22] B. Koopman and G. Zuccon. 2016. A test collection for matching patients to clinical trials. In *Proc. SIGIR.* 669–672.

[23] R. T.-W. Lo, B. He, and I. Ounis. 2005. Automatically building a stopword list for an information retrieval system. *J. Dig. Inf. Man.* 3, 1 (2005), 3–8.

[24] J. B. Lovins. 1968. *Development of a stemming algorithm.* MIT Information Processing Group, Electronic Systems Laboratory Cambridge.

[25] H. P. Luhn. 1957. A statistical approach to mechanized encoding and searching of literary information. *IBM J. Res. Dev.* 1, 4 (1957), 309–317.

[26] A. Moffat. 2016. Judgment pool effects caused by query variations. In *Proc. Aust. Doc. Comp. Symp.* 65–68.

[27] A. Moffat and J. Zobel. 2008. Rank-biased precision for measurement of retrieval effectiveness. *ACM Trans. Inf. Sys.* 27, 1 (2008), 2.1–2.27.

[28] M. Montague and J. A. Aslam. 2001. Relevance score normalization for metasearch. In *Proc. CIKM.* 427–433.

[29] M. Montague and J. A. Aslam. 2002. Condorcet fusion for improved retrieval. In *Proc. CIKM.* 538–548.

[30] J. Pickens, G. Golovchinsky, C. Shah, P. Qvarfordt, and M. Back. 2008. Algorithmic mediation for collaborative exploratory search. In *Proc. SIGIR.* 315–322.

[31] F. Radlinski, P. N. Bennett, B. Carterette, and T. Joachims. 2009. Redundancy, diversity and interdependent document relevance. *SIGIR Forum* 43, 2 (2009), 46–52.

[32] K. Raman, P. N. Bennett, and K. Collins-Thompson. 2013. Toward whole-session relevance: Exploring intrinsic diversity in web search. In *Proc. SIGIR.* 463–472.

[33] S. E. Robertson. 1990. On term selection for query expansion. *J. Documentation* 46, 4 (1990), 359–364.

[34] D. J. Sheskin. 2003. *Handbook of Parametric and Nonparametric Statistical Procedures.* CRC Press.

[35] K. Spärck Jones and C. J. van Rijsbergen. 1975. *Report on the need for and the provision of an "ideal" information retrieval test collection.* Technical Report 5266. Computer Laboratory, University of Cambridge. British Library Research and Development Report.

[36] L. Tan and C. L. A. Clarke. 2015. A family of rank similarity measures based on maximized effectiveness difference. *IEEE Trans. Know. Data Eng.* 27, 11 (2015), 2865–2877.

[37] J. Teevan, E. Adar, R. Jones, and M. A. S. Potts. 2007. Information re-retrieval: Repeat queries in Yahoo's logs. In *Proc. SIGIR.* 151–158.

[38] W. Webber, A. Moffat, and J. Zobel. 2010. A similarity measure for indefinite rankings. *ACM Trans. Inf. Sys.* 28, 4 (2010), 20.1–20.38.

[39] M. Wu, D. Hawking, A. Turpin, and F. Scholer. 2012. Using anchor text for homepage and topic distillation search tasks. *JASIST* 63, 6 (2012), 1235–1255.

[40] S. Wu and S. McClean. 2006. Performance prediction of data fusion for information retrieval. *Inf. Proc. & Man.* 42 (2006), 899–915.

[41] E. Yilmaz, J. A. Aslam, and S. Robertson. 2008. A new rank correlation coefficient for information retrieval. In *Proc. SIGIR.* 587–594.

[42] E. Yilmaz, M. Verma, R. Mehrotra, E. Kanoulas, B. Carterette, and N. Craswell. 2015. Overview of the TREC 2015 tasks track. In *Proc. TREC.*

[43] G. Zuccon, J. Palotti, and A. Hanbury. 2016. Query variations and their effect on comparing information retrieval systems. In *Proc. CIKM.* 691–700.

Comparing In Situ and Multidimensional Relevance Judgments

Jiepu Jiang
Center for Intelligent Information Retrieval, University of Massachusetts Amherst
jpjiang@cs.umass.edu

Daqing He
School of Computing and Information, University of Pittsburgh
dah44@pitt.edu

James Allan
Center for Intelligent Information Retrieval, University of Massachusetts Amherst
allan@cs.umass.edu

ABSTRACT

To address concerns of TREC-style relevance judgments, we explore two improvements. The first one seeks to make relevance judgments contextual, collecting in situ feedback of users in an interactive search session and embracing usefulness as the primary judgment criterion. The second one collects multidimensional assessments to complement relevance or usefulness judgments, with four distinct alternative aspects examined in this paper—novelty, understandability, reliability, and effort.

We evaluate different types of judgments by correlating them with six user experience measures collected from a lab user study. Results show that switching from TREC-style relevance criteria to usefulness is fruitful, but in situ judgments do not exhibit clear benefits over the judgments collected without context. In contrast, combining relevance or usefulness with the four alternative judgments consistently improves the correlation with user experience measures, suggesting future IR systems should adopt multi-aspect search result judgments in development and evaluation.

We further examine implicit feedback techniques for predicting these judgments. We find that click dwell time, a popular indicator of search result quality, is able to predict some but not all dimensions of the judgments. We enrich the current implicit feedback methods using post-click user interaction in a search session and achieve better prediction for all six dimensions of judgments.

KEYWORDS

Relevance judgment; search experience; implicit feedback.

1 INTRODUCTION

Test collection-based IR evaluation relies on human assessments of search result quality. The most popular method is the Cranfield-style relevance judgments [9], such as the approach used in TREC [10], where assessors (usually trained experts) judge a preassigned set of search results one after another using criteria that focus on topical relevance. This method had achieved great success but also attracted criticism such as focusing solely on topical relevance and ignoring real users' perceptions of the usefulness of results in a particular search context. We examine two directions to improve this status quo.

SIGIR '17, August 07-11, 2017, Shinjuku, Tokyo, Japan
© 2017 ACM. 978-1-4503-5022-8/17/08...$15.00
DOI: 10.1145/3077136.3080840

One direction is to incorporate context into assessments. That is, the value of a search result depends on the scenario and context of accessing the result. Belkin et al. [5] proposed to evaluate interactive search systems by the usefulness of each interaction for accomplishing a search task. We can apply this model to search result judgments—to assess the usefulness of a click (the perceived usefulness of a clicked result). This intrinsically requires us to switch from relevance to usefulness as the primary judgment criteria, and to collect in situ judgments to take into account the particular time and context of accessing a search result.

Two recent efforts [25, 36] examined this direction. Kim et al. [25] collected users' in situ feedback of clicked results after they had finished examining the results. However, they restricted the in situ feedback to "thumbs-up" or "thumbs-down". Mao et al. [36] asked users to assess the usefulness of the clicked results after a search session without considering the particular context. Both studies reported improved correlations with search experience measures comparing to TREC-style relevance judgments *by external assessors*. However, neither study excluded the influence of the difference between searchers and external assessors on relevance judgments.

The other direction is to use a combination of multiple aspects of judgments. Many previous studies tried to complement relevance with seemingly reasonable dimensions, such as novelty [6, 55], understandability [41, 56], credibility [39, 46, 51, 53], readability [42, 49], effort [20, 50, 54], freshness [11], etc. Multidimensional judgments are also popular approaches used in user-centric evaluation models [19, 27, 52]. However, most previous IR studies had only examined one particular alternative dimension to relevance, and they had not verified the value of multidimensional judgments by correlating with user experience measures.

We evaluate and compare these two directions. We collected users' search result judgments from six dimensions (relevance, usefulness, novelty, understandability, reliability, and effort) in two settings—an in situ one that happened right after users had finished examining a clicked search result (called *in situ judgments*), and a context-independent one collected after a search session (called *post-session judgments*). We evaluate the two types of judgments on six dimensions by correlating with six search experience measures collected from a laboratory user study. We also examined implicit feedback methods for predicting these judgments.

We examine the following questions in the rest of this article:

- Do in situ judgments better correlate with search experience measures than context-independent (post-session) ones? Do multiple dimensions of judgments help relevance/usefulness judgments better correlate with search experience measures? Which dimensions of judgments should we collect to improve a particular user experience measure? Section 3 seeks answers to these questions.

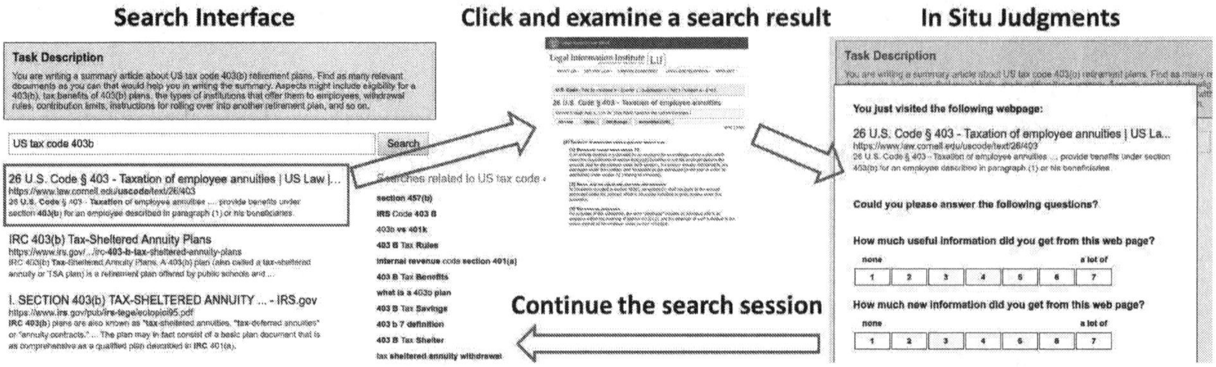

Figure 1: A screenshot of the search interface and the in situ judgments interface.

- Can we effectively predict different search result judgments using implicit feedback signals? Section 4 and Section 5 examine techniques for addressing this challenge.

2 USER STUDY

We designed a user study to collect search result judgments. The user study asked participants to work on different tasks in an experimental search system. We recorded users' search behavior and collected their in situ and post-session search result judgments.

2.1 Experiment Design

The user study employed a 2×2 within-subject design to balance different types of search tasks. The tasks come from the TREC session tracks [7] and were categorized into four types by the targeted task product and goal based on Li and Belkin's faceted classification framework [28]. The targeted task product is either *factual* (to locate facts) or *intellectual* (to enhance the user's understanding of a topic). The goal of a task is either *specific* (clear and fully developed) or *amorphous* (an ill-defined or unclear goal that may evolve along with the user's exploration).

We divided participants into groups of four. Participants in the same group worked on the same four tasks (one task for each type) but using a different sequence (rotated using a Latin square). We assigned different tasks to different groups to increase task diversity.

For each task, the participants went through two stages:

- **Search stage (10 minutes)**. The participants performed an interactive search session to address the task. They could submit and reformulate any queries and click on any search results. After clicking on a result's link, the participants switched to the result webpage in a new browser tab. When they had finished examining the result and turned back to the SERP, the participant needed to provide in situ judgments on the clicked results before they could resume the search session. Figure 1 shows the screenshots of the search interface and the in situ judgments.
- **Judgment stage (about 10 minutes)**. The participants rated their search experience in the session and finished post-session judgments on each result they visited in the session. Section 2.2 introduces details of the in situ and post-session judgments.

As Figure 1 shows, the interface of the experimental system is similar to popular web search engines. The system redirected users' queries to Google and returned filtered Google search results. The system only showed the "10-blue links", vertical search results (except image verticals), and related queries. Other SERP elements were removed to simplify the user study. The system displayed results in the same way they would appear on Google. The main difference between our system and Google in SERP design was that our system showed task description on the top of a SERP (to help participants recall task requirements) and we showed related searches on the right side of a SERP.

The participants spent about 100 minutes to finish an experiment. First, they worked on a training task (including all the steps) for 10 minutes. Then, they worked on four formal tasks, spending about 20 minutes on each task. We required the participants to take a 5-minute break after two formal tasks to reduce fatigue.

2.2 Collecting Search Result Judgments

We collected search result judgments in two different scenarios:

- **In situ judgments** – participants assessed a clicked result when they had finished examining it and turned back to the SERP.
- **Post-session judgments** – the judgments collected after a search session (in the judgment stage).

The in situ judgments measure the participants' perceptions of the clicked result at (roughly) the same time and contexts they visit the result. The approach is similar to Kim et al. [25], except that we adopted different measures to assess search results. In the search stage, we instructed the participants to examine results as they would normally do when using a search engine in their daily lives. For example, they did not need to fully read a result and they could abandon examining. Particularly, they were instructed that during the in situ judgments, they should not revisit the result for the purpose of answering the judgment questions (and we did not offer a link for revisiting in the in situ judgment interface). This is to ensure that the in situ judgments only measure participants' perceptions of the latest click activity.

The post-session judgments resemble the TREC-style relevance judgments, where the assessors judge results without a particular search context and in a random order—they are asked to judge a set of results one after another in detail. In our post-session judgments, the assessors are real searchers. We asked them to judge the set of results they visited in the session. We instructed them to examine the results in a better detail in the post-session judgments. The system also required participants to revisit each clicked result and spend at least 30 seconds to judge a result.

Table 1: Questions for collecting search result judgments and users' search experience.

Search Result Judgments	Question & Options
Topical Relevance (TRel)	How relevant is this webpage? • *Key* (3): this page or site is dedicated to the topic; authoritative and comprehensive; it is worthy of being a top result. • *Highly Relevant* (2): the content of this page provides substantial information on the topic. • *Relevant* (1): the content of this page provides some information on the topic, which may be minimal. • *Not Relevant* or *Spam* (0).
Usefulness (Usef)	**In Situ**: How much useful information did you get from this web page? From 1 (none) to 7 (a lot of). **Post-session**: How much useful information did this web page provide for the task? From 1 (none) to 7 (a lot of).
Novelty (Nov)	How much new information did you get from this web page? From 1 (none) to 7 (a lot of).
Effort (Effort)	How much effort did you spend on this web page? From 1 (none) to 7 (a lot of).
Understandability (Under)	How difficult was it for you to follow the content of this web page? From 1 (very difficult) to 7 (very easy).
Reliability (Relia)	How trustworthy is the information in this web page? From 1 (not at all trustworthy) to 7 (very trustworthy).

Search Experience Measures	Question & Options
Satisfaction (Sat)	How satisfied were you with your search experience? From 1 (very unsatisfied) to 7 (very satisfied).
Frustration (Frus)	How frustrated were you with this task? From 1 (not frustrated) to 7 (very frustrated).
System Helpfulness (Help)	How well did the system help you in this task? From 1 (very badly) to 7 (very well).
Goal Success (Succ)	How well did you fulfill the goal of this task? From 1 (very badly) to 7 (very well).
Session Effort (S.Eff)	How much effort did this task take? From 1 (minimum) to 7 (a lot of).
Difficulty (Diff)	How diffcult was this task? From 1 (very easy) to 7 (very difficult).

We collected users' in situ and post-session judgments of six different measures. Table 1 shows the detailed questions and options.

- **TREC relevance (TRel)** – the de facto standard of relevance judgments due to the popularity of TREC test collections. We collected TRel using the criteria of the latest TREC web track [10]. As Table 1 shows, the criteria focus on topical relevance. We excluded the relevance level *Nav* (the correct homepage of a navigational query) from the original TREC criteria because our search tasks do not include navigational search.
- **Usefulness (Usef)** – Following Belkin et al.'s model [5] and Mao et al.'s study [36], we collected users' perceptions regarding the usefulness of the clicked results.
- **Novelty (Nov)** – Novelty was often assessed algorithmically in previous studies based on sub-topic or "nugget" level relevance judgments [8, 40, 43, 55]. In contrast, we collect users' explicit novelty judgments.
- **Understandability (Under)** – the easiness of understanding the content of the result. Recent studies incorporated understandability into search result ranking [41] and evaluation [56].
- **Reliability (Relia)** – the reliability, credibility, and trustworthy of the information presented in the result [39, 46, 51] (here we do not distinguish the three constructs).
- **Effort** – Yilmaz et al. [54] and Verma et al. [50] examined effort as a dimension of evaluating search result.

The following table summarizes the measures collected in in situ and post-session judgments. We only collected TRel in post-session judgments because the TREC criteria do not consider context. We only collected Nov and Effort during in situ judgments because the participants of a pilot study reported confusions assessing the two measures twice. In the rest of this paper, we will use .i and .p suffixes to denote in situ and post-session judgments, respectively. For example, Usef.i denotes users' in situ usefulness judgments.

Except for TRel, we collected judgments using a 7-point Likert scale, because a previous study [48] showed that assessors approximate the optimal level of confidence when using a 7-point scale for relevance judgments. TRel used a different scale so that it is

	In Situ (.i)	Post-session (.p)
TREC relevance (TRel)		✓
Usefulness (Usef)	✓	✓
Novelty (Nov)	✓	
Effort (Effort)	✓	
Understandability (Under)	✓	✓
Reliability (Relia)	✓	✓

consistent with the TREC web track (as a representative example of the state-of-the-art relevance judgment methods).

2.3 Search Experience Measures

In the judgment stage, participants rated their search experience in a session. We collected six representative user experience measures used in previous studies of information retrieval and recommender systems—satisfaction (Sat) [17, 21, 26, 35, 36, 45], goal success (Succ) [1, 18], frustration (Frus) [12, 13], task difficulty (Diff) [4, 15, 29, 31, 32], the helpfulness of the system (Help) [19] and the total effort spent (S.Eff) [27]. Table 1 includes the questions.

2.4 Rationale of Experiment Design

The way we balance different types of tasks is similar to previous studies [22, 24, 30, 33, 36]. However, we acknowledge that the selected tasks cannot cover all varieties. It is also worth noting that the TREC session track tasks [7] are more complex than regular web search requests such as navigational search.

Our study aims to collect both in situ judgments and user behaviors related to the clicked results. This poses challenges to the experiment design. On the one hand, we hope to collect accurate in situ judgments, which often requires multi-item measurements [27, 52]. On the other hand, interrupting participants for in situ judgments breaks the flow of search session and can affect their subsequent search behaviors. To balance between the two purposes, we made a few compromises in experiment design, e.g., we only collected six popular dimensions of judgments, and we simply used one question to measure each dimension.

Table 2: Spearman's correlation (ρ) matrix of different judgments for the 727 unique clicks.

		In Situ Judgments					Post-session Judgments		
		Usef.i	Novelty	Effort	Under.i	Relia.i	TRel	Usef.p	Under.p
In Situ	Novelty	0.67	-	-	-	-	-	-	-
	Effort	0.22	0.24	-	-	-	-	-	-
	Understandability	0.20	0.14	−0.45	-	-	-	-	-
	Reliability	0.42	0.37	0.05	0.26	-	-	-	-
Post-session	Topical Relevance	0.63	0.46	0.16	0.14	0.42	-	-	-
	Usefulness	0.72	0.52	0.16	0.18	0.43	0.83	-	-
	Understandability	0.20	0.18	−0.36	0.68	0.29	0.18	0.24	-
	Reliability	0.43	0.38	0.04	0.22	0.82	0.48	0.51	0.31

The reported values are estimated from 1000 bootstrap samples (we used stratified sampling to balance user and task dependency).

While examining search behaviors, we excluded the time spent on answering in situ judgments from dwell time. On average the participants spent 57.1 seconds on a clicked result and 12.1 seconds to answer the five in situ judgment questions.

2.5 Collected Data

We recruited 28 participants (16 are female) through fliers posted on the campuses of two universities in the United States. We required participants to be English native speakers to exclude the influence of language fluency on relevance judgments [16]. All the participants were undergraduate or graduate students studying different fields. They were reimbursed $15 per hour.

We collected 112 sessions by 28 participants on 28 tasks. Each participant worked on four unique tasks and each task was performed by four unique users. In total, we collected 537 queries (4.8 per session) and 736 clicks (6.6 per session) on 727 unique session-URL pairs (9 cases of revisiting). We exclude the 9 cases of revisiting from the analysis (about 1% of the data) to simply the analysis.

3 IN SITU VS. POST-SESSION JUDGMENTS

3.1 Correlation of Different Judgments

Table 2 reports the correlation of different judgments, which are generally consistent with previous studies. For example, relevance and usefulness positively correlate with novelty and reliability [52], understandability negatively correlates with effort [50], etc. We examined the relationship of the judgments in another article [23].

Note that Mao et al. [36] reported a weak correlation (0.332) of *searchers'* post-session usefulness judgments and *external assessors'* relevance judgments. However, Table 2 shows that TRel and Usef.p are strongly correlated ($\rho = 0.83$) when both of them are assessed by searchers. This suggests that the low correlation reported by Mao et al. [36] may be mostly due to the disparity between searchers and external assessors, rather than the difference between using relevance or usefulness as the judgment criteria.

3.2 Correlating with User Experience

We evaluate different search result judgments by correlating with (regressing) users' search experience measures in a session. This is based on the assumption that the "quality" of the clicked results in a session can influence users' search experience in that session—thus, a reasonable search result judgment (assumed to indicate certain "quality"), or a reasonable set of judgments, should also correlate with users' search experience in a session.

3.2.1 Regression Analysis. We use multilevel regression analysis to examine the relationship between the judgments of the clicked results and users' search experience in a session. The dependent variables (DVs) are each of the six search experience measures. The independent variables (IVs) include the statistics of judgments regarding the clicked results in a session (such as the mean, maximum, and minimum ratings). For TRel, Usef.i, and Usef.p, we include the mean, maximum, and minimum ratings of the clicked results in a session as IVs in the regression analysis. For other search result judgments, we only include the maximum and minimum ratings of the clicked results as IVs. This is because the mean ratings of the other measures often highly correlate with those of TRel and Usef, causing multicollinearity issues for regression analysis.

For each user experience measure (the DV), we examine six different models that include different judgments as IVs.

- **Unidimensional & Context-independent** – Model ① and ② only include context-independent search result judgments from a single dimension—Model ① includes the statistics of TRel and Model ② includes those of Usef.p.
- **Unidimensional & In Situ** – Model ③ includes in situ judgments from a single dimension (the statistics of Usef.i) as IVs.
- **Multidimensional & Context-independent** – Model ④ and ⑤ extend Model ① and ② to include other dimensions of judgments (the statistics of Under.p, Relia.p, Nov, and Effort). Note that Model ④ and ⑤ include two in situ judgments (Nov and Effort) because we did not collect post-session judgments on these two dimensions (as discussed in § 2.2).
- **Multidimensional & In Situ** – Model ⑥ extends Model ③ to include other dimensions of judgments (the statistics of Under.i, Relia.i, Nov, and Effort).

	Context-independent	In Situ
Unidimensional	① TRel only ② Usef.p only	③ Usef.i only
Multidimensional	④ TRel + others ⑤ Usef.p + others	⑥ Usef + others

All six models also include the same set of control variables, including: gender (*Male* or *Female*), age (four levels; 0 for *18–24*, 1 for *25–30*, 2 for *31–40*, and 3 for *Over 40*), highest degree obtained or expected (*Undergraduate* or *Graduate*), the expertise of using web search engines (SE Expertise) rated using a Likert scale from 1 (*very badly*) to 5 (*very well*), task product and goal, user's familiarity with the topic of the task (Topic Familiarity) rated using a Likert scale from 1 (*very unfamiliar*) to 7 (*very familiar*), and the number of clicks (# clicks) and queries (# queries) in the session.

Table 3: The adjusted R^2 of different regression models.

Models	Sat	Frus	Succ	S.Eff	Help	Diff
Base (control only)	0.12	0.06	0.11	0.06	0.11	0.03
① TRel	0.23	0.09	0.18	0.10	0.16	0.09
② Usef.p	0.25	0.15	0.36	0.17	0.18	0.18
③ Usef.i	0.29	0.14	0.35	0.16	0.22	0.22
④ TRel + others	0.31	0.25	0.33	0.33	0.31	0.21
④ vs. ①	**	**	**	**	**	**
⑤ Usef.p + others	0.30	0.26	0.42	0.37	0.31	0.26
⑤ vs. ②	**	**	**	**	**	**
⑥ Usef.i + others	0.30	0.27	0.34	0.37	0.27	0.33
⑥ vs. ③		**		**	*	**

* and ** indicate $p < 0.05$ and $p < 0.01$ by F-test.

We examine multicollinearity between variables using variance inflation factor (VIF). The IVs of all models satisfy VIF < 4, the commonly suggested threshold (4–10) for concerns of multicollinearity issues [37]. Table 3 reports the adjusted R^2 of the six models for regressing the six dimensions of search experience.

3.2.2 TREC Relevance vs. Usefulness. We first compare TREC relevance criteria (TRel) and post-session usefulness judgments (Usef.p). This is a revisit of Mao et al.'s study [36], which compared searchers' usefulness judgments and external assessors' relevance judgments. Here we collected both judgments from real searchers, removing the influence caused by the difference between searchers and external annotators in relevance judgments. The regression analysis suggest that switching from TREC relevance to usefulness is fruitful, consistently enhancing the ability of the regression models to correlate with user experience (by adjusted R^2).

Models ① and ② include the mean, maximum, and minimum TRel or Usef.p ratings of the clicked results. Model ② consistently explains the six search experience measures better than Model ① (by adjusted R^2). We note that usefulness (Usef.p) seems to be particularly better than TREC relevance (TRel) in terms of correlating with goal success (Succ), with adjusted $R^2 = 0.36$ vs 0.18.

Models ④ and ⑤ further include other dimensions of judgments as IVs. This helps compare TRel and Usef.p judgments with other search result judgments as controls. Still, we consistently observe that Model ⑤ explains the six search experience measures better than or as well as model ④. These results verify that usefulness is indeed a better criteria of relevance judgments than TREC-style relevance (in terms of correlating with users' search experience).

3.2.3 In Situ vs. Context-independent (Post-session) Judgments. We further compare in situ and post-session judgments in both unidimensional and multidimensional settings. Results suggest in situ usefulness judgments have better correlations with a few (but not all) user experience measures than post-session usefulness judgments. However, after combining search result judgments from different dimensions, in situ judgments show limited advantages over post-session ones.

Models ③ and ② include the mean, maximum, and minimum Usef.i or Usef.p ratings of the clicked results as IVs. Results show Model ③ explains satisfaction (Sat), helpfulness (Help), and task difficulty (Diff) slightly better than Model ②, with about 0.04 difference in adjusted R^2.

We further compare in situ and post-session judgments in a multidimensional setting, using a combination of Usef.p/Usef.i and other four judgments as IVs (Models ⑤ and ⑥). Results show that the post-session multidimensional model (⑤) better correlates with search success (Succ) than the in situ one (adjusted R^2 0.42 vs 0.34), but the latter also better correlates with task difficulty (adjusted R^2 0.26 vs. 0.21). Overall, no evidence suggests either model is *consistently* better than another in terms of correlating with users' search experience measures.

Even though Model ③ (Usef.i only) performs slightly better than Model ② (Usef.p only), results suggest limited advantages of in situ judgments over post-session ones in terms of correlating with search experience measures. We suspect a possible reason is that a 10-minute session is not long enough to trigger sufficient differences between in situ and post-session judgments. Although we expect to observe a greater difference between in situ and post-session judgments in longer sessions, we believe a substantial proportion of web search sessions are no longer than 10 minutes, which may not benefit much from in situ judgments. In addition, it also requires a more complex experiment design to collect in situ judgments.

3.2.4 Unidimensional vs. Multidimensional Judgments. We further compare models using a combination of multiple aspects of judgments (Models ④, ⑤, and ⑥) with those using a single dimension (Models ①, ②, and ③). Results suggest that it is almost always helpful (enhancing the correlation with most of the six search experience measures significantly) to complement either relevance or usefulness with the alternative dimensions.

Models ④ and ⑤ explain all six dimensions of search experience measures significantly better than Models ① and ②, suggesting that multidimensional judgments are almost always helpful for TREC-style relevance judgments (TRel) and post-session usefulness judgments (Usef.p). We also note that in situ usefulness judgments (Usef.i) worked particularly well for correlating with users' satisfaction (Sat) and goal success (Succ), such that combining with more dimensions of judgments adds little to the model.

Results demonstrate that multidimensional search result judgments are helpful, complementing unidimensional judgments and yielding better correlation with search experience measures. This also suggests the advantages of multidimensional search result judgments over the in situ one—the former can consistently improve relevance/usefulness to better correlate with almost all user experience measures, while the latter shows limited advantages.

3.3 Which Dimensions To Judge?

A crucial issue of information retrieval is deciding which criteria to use to rank search results. We come to initial answers by looking into the standardized coefficients (β) of Model ⑤ (Table 4) as an example due to its superiority over other models. The standardized coefficient β stands for the magnitude of change in the DV (relative to its standard deviation) caused by one-unit change in the IV (relative to the IV's standard deviation) while other variables being equal. The coefficients of the model indicate how changes in the "quality" of the clicked results will (theoretically) affect users' search experience in a session. Table 4 suggests that:

- To enhance user **satisfaction**, a search system should present useful and novel results—both Usef.p (mean) and Nov (max) show significant positive effects on Sat in Model ⑤.

Table 4: Multilevel regression: standardized coefficients (β) of independent variables for Model ⑤ – `Usef.p + others`.

Independent Variables	DV: session-level search experience Sat	Frus	Succ	S.Eff	Help	Diff
Gender: *Male*	0.10	0.19	0.09	0.06	0.00	0.16
Age	−0.05	0.00	−0.03	−0.02	−0.11	0.00
Degree: *Graduate*	−0.03	0.05	0.01	0.13	−0.08	0.23
SE Expertise	0.12	0.04	0.08	0.01	0.12	−0.00
Product: *Factual*	0.02	−0.02	−0.06	−0.09	−0.00	0.02
Goal: *Specific*	0.02	−0.07	0.04	0.05	0.07	0.01
Topic Familiarity	0.10	−0.23	0.17	−0.20	0.19	−0.24
# clicks	0.20	−0.12	0.17	−0.07	0.18	−0.01
# queries	−0.36	0.17	−0.25	0.16	−0.35	−0.02
† Usef.p (mean)	0.23	−0.38	0.36	−0.36	0.08	−0.43
† Usef.p (max)	0.16	0.09	0.22	−0.07	0.11	−0.08
† Usef.p (min)	0.01	0.19	−0.04	0.19	0.01	0.18
† Nov (max)	0.24	−0.10	0.18	−0.09	0.25	−0.11
† Nov (min)	−0.01	−0.20	−0.08	−0.06	0.07	−0.00
† Under.p (max)	0.09	−0.27	0.30	−0.15	0.14	−0.22
† Under.p (min)	0.16	−0.08	0.14	−0.26	0.29	−0.27
† Relia.p (max)	−0.13	−0.08	0.01	0.05	−0.03	0.06
† Relia.p (min)	0.06	0.01	−0.05	0.08	−0.07	0.04
† Effort (max)	−0.12	0.16	0.08	0.28	−0.13	0.02
† Effort (min)	0.21	0.04	0.12	0.01	0.25	0.02
Adjusted R^2	0.30	0.26	0.42	0.37	0.31	0.26

Light and dark shadings indicate $p < 0.05$ and 0.01, respectively.

- To reduce user **frustration**, a search system should offer results that are useful and easy-to-understand—both `Usef.p` (mean) and `Under.p` (max) show significant negative effects on `Frus`.
- To help users **success**fully reach the goal (`Succ`), a search system should retrieve useful, novel, and easy-to-understand results—`Usef.p` (mean), `Nov` (max), and `Under.p` (max) show significant positive effects on `Succ`.
- To reduce the **total effort** of a search session, the system should retrieve easy-to-understand results and avoid those requiring too much effort—`Under.p` (min) shows a significant negative effect on `S.Eff` and `Effort` (max) shows a positive one.
- To better help users in a session (enhance the **helpfulness** of the system), a system should retrieve novel and easy-to-understand results—both `Nov` (max) and `Under.p` (max) show significant positive effects on `Help`.
- To reduce the perceived **task difficulty**, we need to retrieve useful and easy-to-understand results—both `Usef.p` (mean) and `Under.p` (min) show significant negative effects on `Diff`.

The coefficients suggest that the mean usefulness of the clicked results is helpful for explaining all six search experience measures (has statistically significant coefficients). In addition, novelty, understandability, and effort also significantly relate to many different search experience measures, suggesting they are useful complements to usefulness in search result judgments. In contrast, reliability shows no significant effect on any of the six user experience measures in Model ⑤. However, we suspect this is because the top-ranked results returned by Google are mostly reliable ones, which makes reliability a less important judgment measure among the clicked results.

Table 5: Statistics of the absolute difference of two users' ratings on the same results ($|\Delta|$).

	$|\Delta|$ mean (SD)	$|\Delta| = 0$	$|\Delta| \leq 1$	$|\Delta| \leq 2$
Usef.i	1.55 (1.45)	25.9%	58.2%	79.1%
Effort	1.52 (1.25)	22.9%	57.7%	76.1%
Nov	1.60 (1.47)	26.4%	54.2%	78.1%
Relia.i	1.23 (1.21)	31.3%	67.2%	86.1%
Under.i	1.18 (1.23)	34.8%	68.2%	88.1%
TRel	0.63 (0.68)	48.3%	89.1%	100.0%
Usef.p	1.53 (1.54)	29.9%	60.7%	77.6%
Relia.p	1.38 (1.35)	30.8%	62.2%	81.1%
Under.p	1.08 (1.31)	38.8%	76.6%	90.5%

3.4 Variability of Judgments

We further examine the variability of judgments among different searchers, because in many practical scenarios we may have to train and evaluate retrieval systems based on relevance judgments made by external assessors. We suspect different users may have a greater degree of inconsistencies in their in situ judgments than their post-session ones (due to the contextual nature of the former). However, results do not support this conjecture well.

We examine the absolute difference of two users' ratings on the same result. Table 5 reports the mean absolute difference and the distribution. The mean absolute difference for in situ and post-session usefulness judgments (`Usef.i` and `Usef.p`) are very close (1.55 vs. 1.53). The mean absolute difference of post-session reliability judgments (`Relia.p`) is slightly higher than that for in situ ones (`Relia.i`) (1.38 vs. 1.23), but that for post-session understandability judgments (`Under.p`) is also slightly lower than the in situ ones (`Under.i`, 1.08 vs. 1.18). Overall, no evidence suggests that either in situ or post-session judgments is more or less consistent than the other across different users.

Further, we note that different users' reliability and understandability judgments seem more consistent than those for usefulness, effort, and novelty judgments, regardless of performed in an in situ setting or a post-session one. This suggests that usefulness, effort, and novelty judgments may suffer from inter-rate consistency by a greater extent, while inter-rate agreement is less likely a concern for understandability and reliability judgments. However, since users judged `TRel` by a different scale, it remains unclear how do the other five judgments compare with standard TREC relevance judgments in terms of inter-rate consistency.

3.5 Summary

To sum up, this section discloses both opportunities and challenges for future search result judgments.

- **Opportunity** – Since a combination of multidimensional judgments explains user experience measures better than using relevance or usefulness alone, we expect that an appropriate ranking of search results by multiple criteria may potentially yield better user experience as well. The results in Table 4 also help select ranking criteria according to a targeted user experience measure.
- **Challenge** – Extending current judgments from a single dimension to multiple aspects largely increases the cost of judgments. This is a crucial issue for the scalability of multidimensional judgments. The following sections address this concern by predicting multidimensional judgments using implicit feedback techniques.

Table 6: Implicit feedback features and their correlation with different search result quality measures.

			Pearson's r with search result judgments					
	Click Dwell Time Features	**Note**	**TRel**	**Usef.p**	**Nov**	**Effort**	**Under.p**	**Relia.p**
T1	Click dwell time (log).		0.38	0.43	0.41	0.36	0.12	0.34
T2	$(t-\mu)/\sigma$. t is the result's dwell time; μ is average click dwell time; σ is the standard deviation of click dwell time. T3-5 are based on personalized versions of μ and σ.	all clicks	0.31	0.34	0.30	0.32	0.06	0.24
T3		by user	0.31	0.36	0.38	0.32	0.09	0.24
T4		by task	0.31	0.35	0.30	0.32	0.06	0.24
T5		by length	0.29	0.33	0.29	0.31	0.06	0.24
	Follow-up Query Features		**TRel**	**Usef.p**	**Nov**	**Effort**	**Under.p**	**Relia.p**
Q1	The number of terms in the next query found in the URL/title/body of the result.	URL	−0.04	0.03	−0.01	−0.02	−0.02	0.03
Q2		title	−0.03	−0.00	−0.00	0.01	−0.00	−0.02
Q3		body	−0.03	−0.03	0.10	0.06	0.03	−0.02
Q4	The percentage of terms in the next query found in the URL/title/body of the result.	URL	0.02	0.09	0.02	−0.04	0.01	0.08
Q5		title	0.07	0.10	0.06	−0.00	0.05	0.07
Q6		body	0.17	0.18	0.21	0.04	0.13	0.18
Q7	The number of newly added query terms in the next query reformulation found in the URL/title/body of the result.	URL	0.03	−0.01	−0.03	−0.06	0.02	0.02
Q8		title	0.07	0.04	0.00	−0.07	0.01	−0.00
Q9		body	0.07	0.07	0.13	−0.04	0.04	−0.02
Q10	The number of removed query terms in the next query reformulation found in the URL/title/body of the result.	URL	0.01	0.01	−0.00	−0.07	−0.04	−0.12
Q11		title	0.06	0.09	0.06	−0.09	0.03	−0.06
Q12		body	0.08	0.07	0.06	0.01	−0.09	−0.04
Q13	The mean/max/min log likelihood scores between the full content of the result and follow-up queries.	mean	0.22	0.23	0.22	−0.03	0.19	0.23
Q14		max	0.22	0.23	0.21	−0.03	0.17	0.18
Q15		min	0.15	0.19	0.19	−0.01	0.17	0.19
	Follow-up Click Features		**TRel**	**Usef.p**	**Nov**	**Effort**	**Under.p**	**Relia.p**
C1	The mean/max/min similarity between the title of the result and the titles of clicked results in follow-up searches.	mean	0.04	0.05	0.12	0.02	0.04	0.01
C2		max	0.05	0.04	0.09	0.00	0.06	0.00
C3		min	0.06	0.08	0.10	0.01	−0.01	0.03
C4	The mean/max/min similarity between the snippet of the result and the snippets of clicked results in follow-up searches.	mean	−0.00	0.01	0.01	0.04	0.02	0.03
C5		max	−0.04	−0.06	−0.06	−0.05	0.01	−0.04
C6		min	0.08	0.11	0.10	0.07	0.06	0.09
C7	The mean/max/min similarity between the full content of the result and the full contents of SAT clicks (dwell time > 30s) in follow-up searches.	mean	0.19	0.23	0.09	0.01	−0.02	0.10
C8		max	0.20	0.20	0.05	−0.00	0.00	0.08
C9		min	0.12	0.17	0.07	−0.00	−0.01	0.07
C10	The mean/max/min similarity between the title of the result and the titles of skipped results in follow-up searches.	mean	0.09	0.11	0.11	0.02	0.05	0.05
C11		max	0.11	0.09	0.06	−0.01	0.05	0.02
C12		min	0.09	0.13	0.13	−0.05	0.00	0.05
C13	The mean/max/min similarity between the snippet of the result and the snippets of skipped results in follow-up searches.	mean	0.01	0.03	0.03	0.11	−0.05	0.03
C14		max	0.02	0.01	−0.01	−0.00	0.02	−0.02
C15		min	0.10	0.12	0.12	0.13	−0.05	0.11

Light and dark shadings indicate the correlation is significant at 0.05 and 0.01 levels, respectively.

4 PREDICTION

This section introduces our techniques for predicting multidimensional judgments of clicked results from search logs. We model the prediction task as a regression problem—the input is features related to a target click, the output is the predicted judgment score of the clicked result. We use gradient boosted regression trees (GBRT) for prediction. Table 6 lists the prediction features. Due to the limited space, we only report results for predicting `TRel` and the judgments included in Model ⑤—`Usef.p`, `Nov`, `Effort`, `Under.p`, and `Relia.p`. However, the described approach can also effectively predict other search result judgments as well.

4.1 Click Dwell Time Features

Click dwell time (T1) is one of the most widely used implicit feedback measure. As Table 6 shows, T1 does not correlate much with understandability, but it still has 0.3–0.4 correlations (significant at 0.01 level) with other measures.

T2–T5 measure the deviation of a click's dwell time from the mean dwell time (μ) of a group of clicks (normalized by the standard deviation σ). T2 computes μ and σ based on all clicks in the training sets. T3 is based on clicks by the same user. T4 is based on clicks in sessions with the same task type. T5 is based on clicks on documents with similar length (we divide the clicked results into ten bins by length and compute μ and σ of a click based on its bin).

4.2 Follow-up Query Features

Follow-up query features are based on the intuition that a clicked result may influence follow-up query reformulation in a session. Thus, we can infer the quality of a click from queries issued after the clicked result in the same session.

Q1–Q6 match the terms in the immediate follow-up query with the target click. Q7–Q12 match the newly added and removed terms in the immediate follow-up query reformulation with the target click. Q13–Q15 match the target click with all follow-up queries.

Many of the follow-up query features (such as Q6 and Q13–Q15) have significant correlations with the search result quality measures, confirming that the intuition is reasonable. We also note that Q6 and Q13–Q15 have stronger correlations with understandability than click dwell time features.

4.3 Follow-up Click Features

Similar to follow-up query features, we may also infer the quality of a target click based on follow-up clicks in a session.

C1–C6 measure the similarity between the target click and follow-up clicks. C7–C9 measure the similarity with follow-up satisfactory (SAT) clicks. C10–C15 measure the similarity with follow-up skipped results (unclicked results ranked higher than a clicked result). Some features have significant correlations with the search result quality measures, suggesting they may be useful predictors.

4.4 Prior-to-click Features (Baseline)

Prior-to-click features include the existing techniques that predict search result quality measures using information available before users clicking on the result. In this paper, they serve as the baseline for the implicit feedback features. We include a full list of prior-to-click features in an online appendix[1].

We incorporate different prior-to-click features for predicting different measures. The shared features for all six measures include the rank of the result by Google search, ad hoc search models (QL, BM25, DFR [3], and SDM [38]), and session search models [14, 47]. The unique features for predicting each measure are:

- `TRel` – a subset of LETOR features [34].
- `Usef.p` – a subset of LETOR features [34] and a subset of the usefulness features by Mao et al. [36] that do not rely on post-click information.
- `Nov` – the similarity of the click with previous clicks and higher ranked results in the same SERP (motivated by previous work on novelty-based search result diversification [6, 43, 44, 55]).
- `Effort` – Yilmaz et al. [54] and Verma et al. [50].
- `Under.p` – Palotti et al. [41, 42].
- `Relia.p` – Olteanu et al. [39] and Wawer et al. [51].

Our prior-to-click features are representatives of the state-of-the-art techniques for predicting each dimension of judgments without using implicit feedback. However, we did not include features that we do not have the resource to calculate, which include link structure based features and social media popularity features such as Twitter mention. Note this may reduce the effectiveness of predicting reliability since the excluded features take about 1/3 of the features by Olteanu et al. [39] and Wawer et al. [51].

5 EVALUATION

5.1 Experiment Settings

We evaluate prediction (regression) by the Pearson's correlation between the predicted values and actual judgments (prediction correlation) and the root mean square error (RMSE) of the predicted values. Note that the RMSE for predicting different measures is not comparable—first, TREC relevance ranges from 0–3 while others from 1–7; second, their distributions vary a lot. Here we only report prediction correlation for its easy interpretability. The results of RMSE is highly consistent with that using prediction correlation.

The dataset for evaluation includes multidimensional judgments on the 727 unique clicked results. We use 10-fold cross validation for evaluation (using eight folds for training, one for validation, and one for testing). We randomly shuffle the dataset 10 times and apply 10-fold cross-validation for each random shuffling of the whole dataset—this generates prediction results on $10 \times 10 = 100$ test folds in total (note that we are not using a 100-fold cross validation). We report the mean and standard deviation (SD) of prediction correlation on the test folds. We note that the prediction correlation reported in this section is different from and cannot be compared with the correlation in Table 6, which are computed for the whole dataset without cross validation.

5.2 Click Dwell Time Features

Current techniques for inferring search result quality from logs rely on click dwell time. Results (① in Table 7) suggest the click dwell time features work reasonably well for predicting usefulness, novelty, and effort, but they have difficulties inferring the understandability and reliability of results.

The click dwell time features (①) are effective predictors for usefulness, novelty, and effort. For these three measures, the predicted values have about 0.3–0.4 mean Pearson's correlation with the actual judgments, which is comparable to that for predicting TREC relevance (mean $r = 0.35$). However, the click dwell time features perform much worse for predicting understandability and reliability. On average the predicted and actual judgments have only 0.10 and 0.22 correlation, suggesting it is necessary to incorporate new implicit feedback signals.

5.3 Follow-up Query and Click Features

We extend click dwell time to include signals from follow-up search activities. Results suggest the new features are helpful.

The follow-up query (②) and click features (③) alone have limited prediction capability. However, combining them with the click dwell time features (④) consistently produces better prediction than using click dwell time features alone (①): except for effort, the prediction correlation for the other five measures using feature set ④ is significantly better than that for click dwell time features (①). This indicates that follow-up queries and clicks indeed provide useful implicit feedback that are complementary to click dwell time.

The follow-up query and click features are particularly helpful for predicting reliability. Combining them with the click dwell time features improves the mean correlation of prediction from 0.22 to 0.36. The new features are also helpful for predicting TREC relevance and usefulness as well. This partly confirms our intuition—the quality of a clicked result may influence follow-up search activities, making it possible to infer the quality of a clicked result based on what happened afterward in the session.

The new features also improved the mean prediction correlation for understandability from 0.10 to 0.20. However, we note the combination of all implicit feedback features still does not work well for predicting understandability (mean $r = 0.20$). This suggests that, compared with other judgments, it is more challenging to predict understandability based on the implicit feedback information.

[1] http://ciir.cs.umass.edu/downloads/mdrel/

Table 7: The effectiveness of different features for predicting multidimensional search result judgments.

		Mean (SD) Pearson's r between true and predicted judgments over the test folds					
	Features	TRel	Usef.p	Nov	Effort	Under.p	Relia.p
①	Click Dwell Time	0.35 (0.11)	0.40 (0.11)	0.42 (0.11)	0.31 (0.10)	0.10 (0.14)	0.22 (0.13)
②	Follow-up Query	0.19 (0.11)	0.17 (0.14)	0.13 (0.13)	0.12 (0.11)	0.14 (0.12)	0.19 (0.12)
③	Follow-up Click	0.15 (0.12)	0.20 (0.11)	0.11 (0.12)	0.14 (0.11)	0.11 (0.12)	0.17 (0.12)
④	All (①+②+③)	**0.39** (0.09)	**0.46** (0.08)	**0.45** (0.09)	**0.33** (0.11)	**0.20** (0.13)	**0.36** (0.12)
	① vs. ④	**	**	*		**	**
⑤	Prior-to-click	0.36 (0.10)	0.29 (0.10)	0.28 (0.11)	0.13 (0.12)	0.20 (0.14)	0.18 (0.13)
	④ vs. ⑤	**	**	**	**		**
⑥	All+Prior-to-click	**0.45** (0.08)	**0.49** (0.09)	**0.47** (0.09)	**0.39** (0.09)	**0.26** (0.12)	**0.40** (0.11)
	⑤ vs. ⑥	**	**	**	**	**	**

* and ** indicate the difference is statistically significant at 0.05 and 0.01 levels by two-tail paired t -test.

5.4 Comparing to Prior-to-click Features

An important application of implicit feedback techniques is to infer relevance labels from search logs. Aggregating inferred relevance labels or implicit feedback signals from past search logs may help rank search results in the future [2]. We examine whether or not implicit feedback techniques can serve a similar purpose for multidimensional judgments.

The combination of the implicit feedback features and the prior-to-click features (⑥) generated significantly better prediction results on all the six judgments than using the prior-to-click features alone (⑤). This suggests that the implicit feedback features are indeed helpful and complementary to the prior-to-click features for predicting these judgments. We also note that the improvements in mean prediction correlation can be as large as over 0.2 (such as for predicting reliability and effort). However, even combining the two sets of features still cannot adequately predict understandability (mean $r = 0.26$).

6 DISCUSSION AND CONCLUSION

A crucial issue of information retrieval is deciding which criteria to use to rank search results. We compared two seemingly reasonable directions for improving current TREC-style relevance judgments. One direction is to collect in situ search result judgments. The other one is to complement a single dimension of judgments (such as relevance or usefulness) by combining with other aspects. We found that the latter direction seems more effective and versatile—using a combination of different dimensions of judgments, we can almost always improve correlation with user experience measures.

We envision future search engines should rank results by multiple aspects. We also offered initial suggestions on which criteria to adopt and when to adopt them. We further examined and improved implicit feedback techniques for predicting multiple judgments, addressing the scalability concern of applying multidimensional judgments in real web search applications.

Our study makes the following contributions:

- We evaluated and compared in situ usefulness judgments with regular relevance/usefulness judgments by searchers. We show that using usefulness as the judgment criteria is fruitful, but in situ judgments do not show clear benefits over regular ones.
- We evaluate multidimensional search result judgments considering four alternative aspects other than relevance/usefulness. We show that multidimensional judgments better correlate with user experience measures than using relevance/usefulness judgments alone. We also note that multidimensional judgments is a better direction for improving TREC-style relevance judgments.
- Our study also discloses the connections between different user experience measures and various dimensions of search result judgments. This offers practical suggestions for system design, such as the appropriate dimensions to judge search results for the purpose of improving a particular user experience measure.
- We successfully generalize implicit feedback signals to include follow-up searches and clicks in a search session to help click dwell time better predict multidimensional judgments. To the best of our knowledge, we are also the first to examine the effectiveness of implicit feedback approaches for predicting novelty, understandability, reliability, and effort.

Our work also sheds lights on a few critical areas for exploration in the future:

An important line of future work is to provide more accurate criteria for search result ranking and evaluation. Based on a regression analysis, we have already offered initial suggestions on what criteria to use and when to use them, as discussed in Section 3.3. We note that, with a sufficiently large dataset, one can possibly learn a prediction model for search experience measures by taking multidimensional judgments of results as input. Such a model can further address issues such as what are the proper weights to put on different aspects when ranking search results. It may also solve the discrepancy between offline evaluation measures and user experience measures, and ultimately serve as a better objective function for training ranking models.

Another important application is to perform multidimensional ranking of search results based on implicit feedback signals and other information. We have already demonstrated that implicit feedback approaches can infer judgments of usefulness, novelty, effort, and reliability with reasonable accuracy comparing to those for relevance labels. Aggregating such inferred judgments from past search logs may serve as useful features for performing multidimensional search result ranking in the future. However, we also note that our current technique needs to be improved to better infer understandability of results from search logs.

We do admit certain limitations in our current study. First, our analysis and experiments are solely based on data collected from one laboratory user study, which is limited in both scale and representativeness. We suggest that further studies employ larger datasets to verify our findings. Second, it is worth noting that our way of collecting in situ judgments influenced users' natural search behaviors. We observed in our log that users spent on average 12.1 seconds to finish the in situ judgments. Thus some particular user behavior patterns may vary when applied to another scenario (without interrupting users for in situ judgments). Third, we also note that we only collected search result judgments for the clicked results, while it remains unclear to which extent the findings can be generalized to the unclicked ones. Last but not least, the collected post-session judgments are more or less influenced by the search session and the in situ judgments (although we meant to collect context-independent judgments such as to compare with contextual ones). It is also worth noting that our post-session judgments are not fully representative of the existing TREC-style approach.

7 ACKNOWLEDGMENT

This work was supported in part by the Center for Intelligent Information Retrieval. Any opinions, findings and conclusions or recommendations expressed in this material are those of the authors and do not necessarily reflect those of the sponsor.

REFERENCES

[1] M. Ageev, Q. Guo, D. Lagun, and E. Agichtein. Find it if you can: A game for modeling different types of web search success using interaction data. In *SIGIR '11*, pages 345–354, 2011.

[2] E. Agichtein, E. Brill, and S. Dumais. Improving web search ranking by incorporating user behavior information. In *SIGIR '06*, pages 19–26, 2006.

[3] G. Amati and C. J. Van Rijsbergen. Probabilistic models of information retrieval based on measuring the divergence from randomness. *ACM Trans. Inf. Syst.*, 20(4):357–389, 2002.

[4] J. Arguello. Predicting search task difficulty. In *ECIR '14*, pages 88–99, 2014.

[5] N. J. Belkin, M. J. Cole, and J. Liu. A model for evaluation of interactive information retrieval. In *Proceedings of the SIGIR 2009 Workshop on the Future of IR Evaluation*, 2009.

[6] J. Carbonell and J. Goldstein. The use of MMR, diversity-based reranking for reordering documents and producing summaries. In *SIGIR '98*, pages 335–336, 1998.

[7] B. Carterette, P. Clough, M. Hall, E. Kanoulas, and M. Sanderson. Evaluating retrieval over sessions: The TREC session track 2011-2014. In *SIGIR '16*, pages 685–688, 2016.

[8] C. L. Clarke, M. Kolla, G. V. Cormack, O. Vechtomova, A. Ashkan, S. Büttcher, and I. MacKinnon. Novelty and diversity in information retrieval evaluation. In *SIGIR '08*, pages 659–666, 2008.

[9] C. W. Cleverdon. The evaluation of systems used in information retrieval. In *Proceedings of the International Conference on Scientific Information*, pages 687–698, 1959.

[10] K. Collins-Thompson, C. Macdonald, P. Bennett, F. Diaz, and E. Voorhees. TREC 2014 web track overview. In *TREC 2014*, 2014.

[11] N. Dai, M. Shokouhi, and B. D. Davison. Learning to rank for freshness and relevance. In *SIGIR '11*, pages 95–104, 2011.

[12] H. A. Feild and J. Allan. Modeling searcher frustration. In *HCIR '09*, pages 5–8, 2009.

[13] H. A. Feild, J. Allan, and R. Jones. Predicting searcher frustration. In *SIGIR '10*, pages 34–41, 2010.

[14] D. Guan, S. Zhang, and H. Yang. Utilizing query change for session search. In *SIGIR '13*, pages 453–462, 2013.

[15] J. Gwizdka. Revisiting search task difficulty: Behavioral and individual difference measures. In *ASIS&T '08*, 2008.

[16] P. Hansen and J. Karlgren. Effects of foreign language and task scenario on relevance assessment. *J. Doc.*, 61(5):623–639, 2005.

[17] A. Hassan. A semi-supervised approach to modeling web search satisfaction. In *SIGIR '12*, pages 275–284, 2012.

[18] A. Hassan, R. Jones, and K. L. Klinkner. Beyond DCG: User behavior as a predictor of a successful search. In *WSDM '10*, pages 221–230, 2010.

[19] R. Hu and P. Pu. A study on user perception of personality-based recommender systems. In *UMAP '10*, pages 291–302, 2010.

[20] J. Jiang and J. Allan. Adaptive effort for search evaluation metrics. In *ECIR '16*, pages 187–199, 2016.

[21] J. Jiang, A. Hassan Awadallah, X. Shi, and R. W. White. Understanding and predicting graded search satisfaction. In *WSDM '15*, pages 57–66, 2015.

[22] J. Jiang, D. He, and J. Allan. Searching, browsing, and clicking in a search session: Changes in user behavior by task and over time. In *SIGIR '14*, pages 607–616, 2014.

[23] J. Jiang, D. He, D. Kelly, and J. Allan. Understanding ephemeral state of relevance. In *CHIIR '17*, pages 137–146, 2017.

[24] D. Kelly, J. Arguello, A. Edwards, and W.-c. Wu. Development and evaluation of search tasks for IIR experiments using a cognitive complexity framework. In *ICTIR '15*, pages 101–110, 2015.

[25] J. Y. Kim, J. Teevan, and N. Craswell. Explicit in situ user feedback for web search results. In *SIGIR '16*, pages 829–832, 2016.

[26] J. Kiseleva, E. Crestan, R. Brigo, and R. Dittel. Modelling and detecting changes in user satisfaction. In *CIKM '14*, pages 1449–1458, 2014.

[27] B. P. Knijnenburg, M. C. Willemsen, Z. Gantner, H. Soncu, and C. Newell. Explaining the user experience of recommender systems. *User Modeling and User-Adapted Interaction*, 22(4-5):441–504, 2012.

[28] Y. Li and N. J. Belkin. A faceted approach to conceptualizing tasks in information seeking. *Inf. Process. Manage.*, 44(6):1822–1837, 2008.

[29] C. Liu, J. Liu, and N. J. Belkin. Predicting search task difficulty at different search stages. In *CIKM '14*, pages 569–578, 2014.

[30] J. Liu, J. Gwizdka, C. Liu, and N. J. Belkin. Predicting task difficulty for different task types. In *ASIS&T '10*, 2010.

[31] J. Liu, C. Liu, M. Cole, N. J. Belkin, and X. Zhang. Exploring and predicting search task difficulty. In *CIKM '12*, pages 1313–1322, 2012.

[32] J. Liu, C. Liu, J. Gwizdka, and N. J. Belkin. Can search systems detect users' task difficulty?: Some behavioral signals. In *SIGIR '10*, pages 845–846, 2010.

[33] J. Liu, C. Liu, X. Yuan, and N. J. Belkin. Understanding searchers' perception of task difficulty: Relationships with task type. In *ASIS&T '11*, 2011.

[34] T.-Y. Liu, J. Xu, T. Qin, W. Xiong, and H. Li. LETOR: Benchmark dataset for research on learning to rank for information retrieval. In *SIGIR 2007 workshop on learning to rank for information retrieval*, pages 3–10, 2007.

[35] Y. Liu, Y. Chen, J. Tang, J. Sun, M. Zhang, S. Ma, and X. Zhu. Different users, different opinions: Predicting search satisfaction with mouse movement information. In *SIGIR '15*, pages 493–502, 2015.

[36] J. Mao, Y. Liu, K. Zhou, J.-Y. Nie, J. Song, M. Zhang, S. Ma, J. Sun, and H. Luo. When does relevance mean usefulness and user satisfaction in web search? In *SIGIR '16*, pages 463–472, 2016.

[37] S. Menard. *Applied Logistic Regression Analysis*. Sage, 1997.

[38] D. Metzler and W. B. Croft. A markov random field model for term dependencies. In *SIGIR '05*, pages 472–479, 2005.

[39] A. Olteanu, S. Peshterliev, X. Liu, and K. Aberer. Web credibility: Features exploration and credibility prediction. In *ECIR '13*, pages 557–568, 2013.

[40] P. Over. The TREC interactive track: An annotated bibliography. *Inf. Process. Manage.*, 37(3):369–381, 2001.

[41] J. Palotti, L. Goeuriot, G. Zuccon, and A. Hanbury. Ranking health web pages with relevance and understandability. In *SIGIR '16*, pages 965–968, 2016.

[42] J. Palotti, G. Zuccon, and A. Hanbury. The influence of pre-processing on the estimation of readability of web documents. In *CIKM '15*, pages 1763–1766, 2015.

[43] D. Rafiei, K. Bharat, and A. Shukla. Diversifying web search results. In *WWW '10*, pages 781–790, 2010.

[44] R. L. Santos, C. Macdonald, and I. Ounis. On the role of novelty for search result diversification. *Inf. Retr.*, 15(5):478–502, 2012.

[45] A. Schuth, K. Hofmann, and F. Radlinski. Predicting search satisfaction metrics with interleaved comparisons. In *SIGIR '15*, pages 463–472, 2015.

[46] J. Schwarz and M. Morris. Augmenting web pages and search results to support credibility assessment. In *CHI '11*, pages 1245–1254, 2011.

[47] X. Shen, B. Tan, and C. Zhai. Context-sensitive information retrieval using implicit feedback. In *SIGIR '05*, pages 43–50, 2005.

[48] R. Tang, W. M. Shaw, Jr., and J. L. Vevea. Towards the identification of the optimal number of relevance categories. *J. Am. Soc. Inf. Sci.*, 50(3):254–264, 1999.

[49] J. van Doorn, D. Odijk, D. M. Roijers, and M. de Rijke. Balancing relevance criteria through multi-objective optimization. In *SIGIR '16*, pages 769–772, 2016.

[50] M. Verma, E. Yilmaz, and N. Craswell. On obtaining effort based judgements for information retrieval. In *WSDM '16*, pages 277–286, 2016.

[51] A. Wawer, R. Nielek, and A. Wierzbicki. Predicting webpage credibility using linguistic features. In *WWW '14 Companion*, pages 1135–1140, 2014.

[52] Y. Xu and Z. Chen. Relevance judgment: What do information users consider beyond topicality? *J. Am. Soc. Inf. Sci. Technol.*, 57(7):961–973, 2006.

[53] Y. Yamamoto and K. Tanaka. Enhancing credibility judgment of web search results. In *CHI '11*, pages 1235–1244, 2011.

[54] E. Yilmaz, M. Verma, N. Craswell, F. Radlinski, and P. Bailey. Relevance and effort: An analysis of document utility. In *CIKM '14*, pages 91–100, 2014.

[55] C. X. Zhai, W. W. Cohen, and J. Lafferty. Beyond independent relevance: Methods and evaluation metrics for subtopic retrieval. In *SIGIR '03*, pages 10–17, 2003.

[56] G. Zuccon. Understandability biased evaluation for information retrieval. In *ECIR '16*, pages 280–292, 2016.

Online In-Situ Interleaved Evaluation of Real-Time Push Notification Systems

Adam Roegiest, Luchen Tan, and Jimmy Lin
David R. Cheriton School of Computer Science
University of Waterloo, Ontario, Canada
{aroegies,luchen.tan,jimmylin}@uwaterloo.ca

ABSTRACT

Real-time push notification systems monitor continuous document streams such as social media posts and alert users to relevant content directly on their mobile devices. We describe a user study of such systems in the context of the TREC 2016 Real-Time Summarization Track, where system updates are immediately delivered as push notifications to the mobile devices of a cohort of users. Our study represents, to our knowledge, the first deployment of an interleaved evaluation framework for prospective information needs, and also provides an opportunity to examine user behavior in a realistic setting. Results of our online in-situ evaluation are correlated against the results a more traditional post-hoc batch evaluation. We observe substantial correlations between many online and batch evaluation metrics, especially for those that share the same basic design (e.g., are utility-based). For some metrics, we observe little correlation, but are able to identify the volume of messages that a system pushes as one major source of differences.

1 INTRODUCTION

There is growing interest in systems that address prospective information needs against continuous document streams, exemplified by social media services such as Twitter. We might imagine a user having some number of "interest profiles" representing prospective information needs, and the system's task is to automatically monitor the stream of documents to keep the user up to date on topics of interest. For example, a journalist might be interested in collisions involving autonomous vehicles and wishes to receive updates whenever such an event occurs. Although there are a number of ways such updates can be delivered, we consider the case where they are immediately pushed to the user's mobile device as notifications. At a high level, these push notifications must be relevant, novel, and timely.

To date, there have been two formal evaluations of the push notification problem, at the TREC 2015 Microblog Track [15] and the TREC 2016 Real-Time Summarization (RTS) Track [16]. Despite the obvious real-time nature of this problem, systems have been assessed with a post-hoc batch evaluation methodology. It seems obvious that the push notification task should be evaluated in an online manner that better matches how content is actually delivered in operational settings.

We describe a user study of real-time push notification systems in the context of the TREC 2016 RTS Track, in which systems' notifications are delivered to users' mobile devices as soon as they are generated. This evaluation is *online*, in contrast to post-hoc batch evaluations, and *in-situ*, in that the users are going about their daily activities and are interrupted by the systems' output. Since the RTS Track deployed both this online in-situ methodology and a more traditional batch methodology, the setup provided us with an opportunity to compare the results of both.

Contributions. We view our work as having two main contributions: First, we describe, to our knowledge, the first user study and actual deployment of an interleaved evaluation for prospective notifications. Our work is based on a previously-proposed interleaving framework [18] that has only been examined in simulation. We present an analysis of user behavior in such an evaluation methodology and demonstrate that it is workable in practice.

Second, we compare results of our online methodology to a more traditional batch methodology in the same evaluation. A number of metrics for assessing push notification systems have been proposed: we observe substantial correlations between many online and batch metrics, particularly those that share the same basic design (e.g., are utility-based). This is a non-obvious finding, since all judgments in our online methodology are sparse and made locally, with respect to one tweet at a time, whereas the batch evaluation methodology takes into account all relevant tweets via a global clustering process. There are two interpretations of this finding:

- If one believes in the primacy of user-centered evaluations, our results suggest that established batch evaluation metrics are able to capture user preferences.
- On the other hand, our online evaluation methodology is less mature than the batch evaluation methodology, which has been extensively examined over the past several years; its core ideas date back at least a decade. If one takes this perspective and believes in the primacy of the established approach, then our results suggest a cheaper way to conduct evaluation of push notifications systems that yield similar conclusions.

Despite substantial correlations between many online and batch metrics, there are some metrics that exhibit no meaningful correlation. We observe that systems vary widely in the volume of messages they push, and that this is the biggest source of metric disagreement. We do not believe that the proper role of message volume in evaluating push notification systems is fully understood, but this paper elucidates key issues as an important first step.

SIGIR'17, August 7–11, 2017, Shinjuku, Tokyo, Japan

978-1-4503-5022-8/17/08...$15.00
DOI: http://dx.doi.org/10.1145/3077136.3080808

2 BACKGROUND AND RELATED WORK

Work on prospective information needs against document streams dates back at least a few decades and is closely related to *ad hoc* document retrieval [6]. Major initiatives in the 1990s include the TREC Filtering Tracks, which ran from 1995 [13] to 2002 [21], and the research program commonly known as topic detection and tracking (TDT) [2]. The TREC Filtering Tracks are best understood as binary classification on *every* document in the collection with respect to standing queries, and TDT is similarly concerned with identifying *all* documents related to a particular event—with an intelligence analyst in mind. In contrast, we are focused on identifying a small set of the most relevant updates to deliver to users—any more than a handful of notifications per day would surely be annoying. Furthermore, in both TREC Filtering and TDT, systems must make online decisions as soon as documents arrive. In the case of push notifications, systems can choose to push older content, thus giving rise to the possibility of algorithms operating on bounded buffers. Latency is one aspect of the evaluation, allowing systems to trade off output quality with timeliness.

More recently, Guo et al. [8] introduced the temporal summarization task, whose goal is to generate concise update summaries from news sources about unexpected events as they develop. This has been operationalized in the TREC Temporal Summarization (TS) Tracks from 2013 to 2015 [4]. The task is closely related to the push notification problem that we study, and in fact the TREC Real-Time Summarization Track, which provides the context for our work, represents a merger of the TS and Microblog Tracks. However, nearly all previous evaluations, including TDT, TREC Filtering, and Temporal Summarization, merely *simulated* the streaming nature of the document collection, whereas in RTS the participants were required to build working systems that operated on tweets posted in real time (more details in Section 3).

Our online in-situ evaluation framework builds on growing interest in so-called Living Labs [22, 24] and related Evaluation-as-a-Service (EaaS) [9] approaches that attempt to better align evaluation methodologies with user task models and real-world constraints to increase the fidelity of research experiments. In this respect, our comparison between user-oriented and batch evaluations ties into a long history of research that examines the correlation between effectiveness metrics from system-oriented evaluations and metrics from user-oriented evaluations [1, 3, 10, 23, 26, 29–31]. There is, however, one important difference: all of these cited papers, with one exception [31], focus on *ad hoc* retrieval, which has received much attention over the years. Although there have been previous user studies on push notifications from the HCI perspective (e.g., [17]), there is relatively little empirical work on prospective information needs that we can draw from.

The final thread of relevant work concerns interleaved evaluations [7, 11, 19, 20, 25], which have emerged as the preferred approach to evaluating web search engines over traditional A/B testing [12]. Our work departs from this large body of literature because these papers all focus on web search ranking, whereas we tackle the push notification problem: in our task, systems must take into account temporality and redundancy, both of which are less important in web search. The length of system output (i.e., volume of pushed messages) is another major difference between our task and web ranking. These issues were explored in a recent paper by Qian et al. [18], who extended the interleaved evaluation methodology to retrospective and prospective information needs on document streams. However, their proposed approach was only validated in simulation. We take the next step by deploying an adapted version of their proposed technique in a live user study.

3 EVALUATION METHODOLOGY

Although the push notification problem is applicable to document streams in general, we focus on social media posts: the public nature of Twitter makes tweets the ideal source for shared evaluations. In particular, Twitter provides a streaming API through which clients can obtain a sample (approximately 1%) of public tweets—this level of access is available to anyone who signs up for an account. In order to evaluate push notification systems in a realistic setting, the TREC 2016 RTS Track defined an official evaluation period during which all participants "listened" to the tweet sample stream to identify relevant and novel tweets with respect to users' interest profiles in a timely manner. The evaluation period began Tuesday, August 2, 2016 00:00:00 UTC and lasted until Thursday, August 11, 2016 23:59:59 UTC.

Interest profiles, which represent users' information needs, followed the standard TREC *ad hoc* topic format of "title", "description", and "narrative". These were made available to all participants a few weeks prior to the beginning of the evaluation period. Given the prospective nature of the profiles, it is difficult to anticipate what topics will be discussed during the evaluation period and what events will be "interesting". Instead, the organizers adopted the strategy of "overgenerate and cull": in total, 203 interest profiles were provided to the participants, more than there were resources available for assessment, with the anticipation of letting users decide what profiles should be assessed (more details below).

3.1 Online Evaluation Setup

The TREC 2016 RTS Track contained two separate tasks: push notifications (so-called "Scenario A") and email digests (so-called "Scenario B"). In this paper we are only concerned with push notifications, but for more details we refer the reader to the track overview [16].

The overall evaluation framework is shown in Figure 1. Before the evaluation period, participants "registered" their systems with the evaluation broker to request unique tokens (via a REST API), which are used in subsequent requests to associate submitted tweets with specific systems.[1] During the evaluation period, whenever a system identified a relevant tweet with respect to an interest profile, the system submitted the tweet id to the evaluation broker (also via a REST API), which recorded the submission time. Each system was allowed to push at most ten tweets per interest profile per day; this limit represents an attempt to model user fatigue.

Once the evaluation broker recorded a system's submission, the tweet was *immediately* delivered to the mobile devices of a group of users, where it was rendered as a push notification containing both the text of the tweet and the corresponding interest profile.

[1] As is standard in TREC, each participant was permitted to submit multiple "runs" (usually system variants), but for the purposes of this discussion we refer to them as different systems.

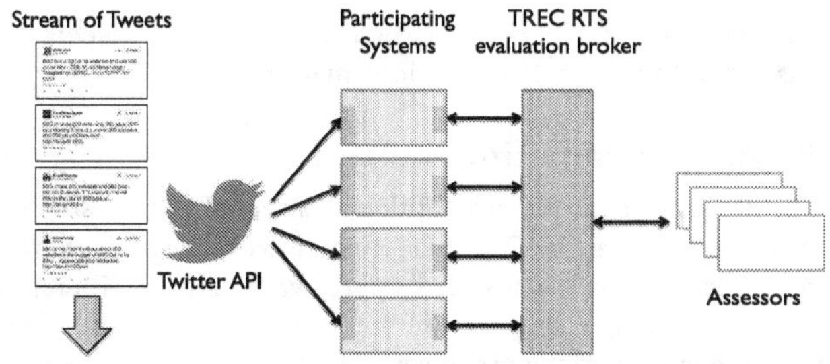

Figure 1: Evaluation setup for push notifications: systems "listen" to the live Twitter sample stream and send results to the evaluation broker, which then delivers push notifications to users.

The user may choose to attend to the tweet immediately, or if it arrived at an inopportune time, to ignore it. Either way, the tweet is added to a queue in a custom app on the user's mobile device, which she can access at any time to examine the queue of accumulated tweets. For each tweet, the user can make one of three judgments with respect to the associated interest profile: *relevant*, if the tweet contains relevant and novel information; *redundant*, if the tweet contains relevant information, but is substantively similar to another tweet that the user had already seen; *not relevant*, if the tweet does not contain relevant information. As the user provides judgments, results are relayed back to the evaluation broker and recorded. Users have the option of logging out of the app, at which point they will cease to receive notifications completely (until they log back in).

Our setup has two distinct characteristics: First, judgments happen online as systems generate output, as opposed to traditional batch post-hoc evaluation methodologies, which consider the documents some time (typically, weeks) after they have been generated by the systems. Note that although the push notifications are delivered in real-time, it is not necessarily the case that judgments are provided in real time since users can ignore the notifications and come back to them later. Second, our judgments are *in situ*, in the sense that the users are going about their daily activities (and are thus interrupted by the notifications). This aspect of the design accurately mirrors the intended use of push notification systems. Furthermore, from the evaluation perspective, we believe that this setup yields more situationally-accurate assessments, particularly for rapidly developing events. With post-hoc batch evaluations, there is always a bit of disconnect as the assessor needs to "imagine" herself at the time the update was pushed. With our evaluation framework, we remove this disconnect.

Our entire evaluation was framed as a user study (with appropriate ethics review and approval). A few weeks prior to the beginning of the evaluation period, we recruited users from the undergraduate and graduate student population at the University of Waterloo, via posts on various email lists as well as paper flyers on bulletin boards. The users were compensated $5 to install the mobile assessment app and then $1 per 20 judgments provided.

As part of the training process, users installed the custom app described above on their mobile devices. In addition, they subscribed, using an online form, to receive notifications for interest profiles they were interested in, selecting from the complete list of 203 interest profiles provided to all systems. To encourage diversity, we did not allow more than three users to select the same profile (on a first come, first served basis).

The evaluation broker followed the temporal interleaving strategy proposed by Qian et al. [18], which meant that tweets were pushed to users as soon as the broker received the submitted tweets from the systems. Although Qian et al. only discussed interleaving the output of two systems, it is straightforward to extend their strategy to multiple systems. The broker made sure that each tweet was only pushed once (per profile), in the case where the same tweet was submitted by multiple systems at different times. Although one can imagine different "routing" algorithms for pushing tweets to different users that have subscribed to a profile, we implemented the simplest possible algorithm where the tweet was pushed to *all* users that had subscribed to the profile. This meant that the broker might receive more than one judgment per tweet.

3.2 Online Metrics

The output of our online in-situ evaluation is a sequence of judgments, which need further aggregation before we can use the results to compare the effectiveness of different systems. Note that this aggregation is more complicated than a similar process in interleaved evaluations for web search because systems can vary widely in tweet volume (i.e., how many tweets they push). In standard interleaving techniques for evaluating web search, both variant algorithms being tested contribute to the final ranking for *all* queries—thus, it usually suffices to count the number (or fraction) of clicks to determine the winner (e.g., [7, 24]). However, in our case, there isn't a query that lends itself to a natural paired comparison. Some systems are quite profligate in dispatching notifications, while other systems are very quiet.

Another implication of our interleaved evaluation setup is that a user will encounter tweets from different systems, which makes the proper interpretation of "redundant" judgments more complex. A tweet might only be redundant because the same information was contained in a tweet pushed earlier by another system (and thus not the "fault" of the particular system that pushed the tweet). In other words, the interleaving itself was directly responsible for introducing the redundancy. This observation was made by Qian et al. [18], who proposed a heuristic for more accurate credit assignment when interleaving two systems. However, we decided to adopt a much simpler approach (explained below), which is justified by our experimental results (more details later).

Recognizing the issues discussed above, we computed two aggregate metrics based on user judgments:

Online Precision. A simple and intuitive metric is to measure precision, or the fraction of relevant judgments:

$$\frac{\text{relevant}}{\text{relevant} + \text{redundant} + \text{not relevant}} \quad (1)$$

We term this "strict" precision because systems don't get credit for redundant judgments. As an alternative, we could compute "lenient" precision, where the numerator includes redundant judgments. Extending this further, redundant judgments could in principle be assigned fractional credit, but as we discuss later, such schemes do not appear to have any impact on our overall findings.

Two minor details are worth mentioning for the proper interpretation of this metric: First, tweets may be judged multiple times since a tweet is pushed to all users who had subscribed to the profile. For simplicity, all judgments are included in our calculation. Second, our precision computation represents a micro-average (and *not* an average across per-profile precision). This choice was made due to the sparsity of judgments: macro-averaging would magnify the effects of profiles with few judgments.

Online Utility. As an alternative to online precision, we could take a utility-based perspective and measure the total gain received by the user. The simplest method would be to compute the following:

$$\text{relevant} - \text{redundant} - \text{not relevant} \tag{2}$$

which we refer to as the "strict" variant of online utility. Paralleling the precision variants above, we define a "lenient" version of the metric as follows:

$$(\text{relevant} + \text{redundant}) - \text{not relevant} \tag{3}$$

Of course, we could further generalize with weights for each type of judgment. However, we lack the empirical basis for setting the weights. Furthermore, experimental analyses show that our findings are insensitive to weight settings.

To summarize: from user judgments, we compute two aggregate metrics—online precision and online utility. Note that there is no good way to compute a recall-oriented metric since we have no control over when and how frequently user judgments are provided. This is a fundamental limitation of this type of user study.

3.3 Batch Evaluation Setup

In order to mitigate the risk inherent in any new evaluation methodology, the TREC 2016 RTS Track also deployed a more traditional post-hoc batch evaluation methodology—specifically, the approach developed for the Tweet Timeline Generation (TTG) task at the TREC 2014 Microblog Track [14], which was also used in 2015 [15]. The methodology has been externally validated [31] and can be considered mature due to its deployment in multiple formal evaluations. The assessment workflow proceeded in two major stages: relevance assessment and semantic clustering. Here we provide only a brief overview, referring the reader to the cited papers above for additional details.

Tweets returned by participating systems were judged for relevance by NIST assessors via pooling. Note that this occurred after the live evaluation period ended, so it was possible to gather all tweets pushed by all participating systems. NIST assessors began a few days after the end of the evaluation period to minimize the "staleness" of tweets. Each tweet was assigned one of three judgments: not relevant, relevant, or highly-relevant. After the relevance assessment process, the NIST assessors proceeded to perform semantic clustering on only the relevant and highly-relevant tweets. Using a custom interface, they grouped tweets into clusters in which tweets share substantively similar content, or more colloquially, "say the same thing". The interpretation of what this means operationally was left to the discretion of the assessor. In particular, they were not given a particular target number of clusters to form; rather, they were asked to use their judgment, considering both the interest profile and the actual tweets. The output of the cluster annotation process is a list of tweet clusters; each cluster contains tweets that are assumed to convey the same information.

3.4 Batch Evaluation Metrics

As previously discussed, push notifications should be relevant, non-redundant, and timely. One challenge, however, is that there is little empirical work on how users perceive timeliness. Therefore, instead of devising a single-point metric that tries to combine all three characteristics, the organizers decided to separately capture output quality (relevance and redundancy) and timeliness (latency). In this paper, we only focus on output quality metrics. In short, RTS batch evaluation metrics attempt to capture precision, recall, and overall utility. We elaborate below:

Expected Gain (EG) for an interest profile on a particular day is defined as $\frac{1}{N}\sum G(t)$, where N is the number of tweets returned and $G(t)$ is the gain of each tweet: not relevant tweets receive a gain of 0; relevant tweets receive a gain of 0.5; highly-relevant tweets receive a gain of 1.0. Once a tweet from a cluster is retrieved, all other tweets from the same cluster automatically become not relevant. This penalizes systems for returning redundant information. Expected gain can be interpreted as a precision metric.

Normalized Cumulative Gain (nCG) for an interest profile on a particular day is defined as $\frac{1}{\mathcal{Z}}\sum G(t)$, where $\mathcal{Z}$ is the maximum possible gain (given the ten tweet per day limit). The gain of each individual tweet is computed in the same way as above. Note that gain is not discounted (as in nDCG) because the notion of document ranks is not meaningful in this context. We can interpret nCG as a recall-like metric.

The score for a run is the average over scores for each day over all interest profiles. An interesting question is how scores should be computed for days in which there are no relevant tweets: for rhetorical convenience, we call days in which there are no relevant tweets for a particular interest profile (in the pool) "silent days", in contrast to "eventful days" (when there are relevant tweets). In the EG-1 and nCG-1 variants of the metrics, on a silent day, the system receives a score of one (i.e., a perfect score) if it does not push any tweets, or a score of zero otherwise. In the EG-0 and nCG-0 variants of the metrics, for a silent day, all systems receive a gain of zero no matter what they do. For more details about this distinction, see Tan et al. [28].

Therefore, under EG-1 and nCG-1, systems are rewarded for recognizing that there are no relevant tweets for an interest profile on a particular day and remaining silent (i.e., the system does not push any tweets). The EG-0 and nCG-0 variants of the metrics do not reward recognizing silent days: that is, it never hurts to push tweets. We show later in our analyses that EG-0 and nCG-0 are poorly-formulated metrics.

Gain Minus Pain (GMP) is defined as $\alpha \cdot \sum G - (1-\alpha) \cdot P$, where G (gain) is computed in the same manner as above, pain P is the number of non-relevant tweets that the system pushed, and α controls the balance of weights between the two. We investigated three α settings: 0.33, 0.50, and 0.66. Note that this metric is the same as the linear utility metrics used in the TREC Filtering [13, 21] and Microblog [27] Tracks, although our formulation takes a slightly different mathematical form.

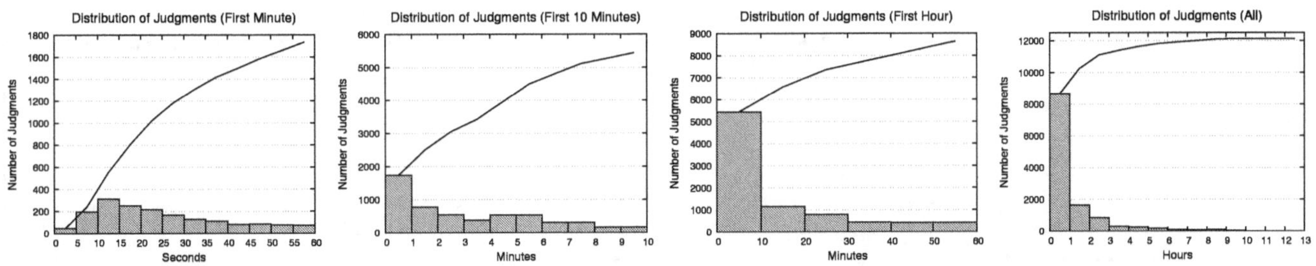

Figure 2: Distribution of response times over the first minute (14.3%), first ten minutes (44.9%), first hour (71.3%), and across the entire evaluation period. Percentages in parentheses show how many judgments were received in the corresponding period.

User	Judgments	Profiles	Messages	Response
1	53	4	1619	3.27%
2	3305	10	7141	46.28%
3	136	10	5860	2.32%
4	327	8	3795	8.62%
5	949	12	6330	14.99%
6	28	12	7211	0.39%
7	281	10	4162	6.75%
8	1908	15	7754	24.61%
9	3791	33	16654	22.76%
10	680	16	7257	9.37%
11	107	43	22676	0.47%
12	324	2	938	34.54%
13	226	12	7058	3.20%

Table 1: User statistics. For each user, columns show the number of judgments provided, the number of interest profiles subscribed to, the maximum number of push notifications received, and the response rate.

To summarize: we have multiple batch metrics for evaluating push notification systems: EG-1 and EG-0 (both of which measure precision), nCG-1 and nCG-0 (both of which measure recall), and GMP with $\alpha = \{0.33, 0.50, 0.66\}$ (which capture utility).

4 USER BEHAVIOR

The evaluation methodology for push notifications detailed above was deployed in the TREC 2016 Real-Time Summarization Track. In total, 18 groups from around the world participated, submitting a total of 41 systems (runs). Over the evaluation period, these runs pushed a total of 161,726 tweets, or 95,113 unique tweets after de-duplicating within profiles.

To simplify app development, we only targeted users of Android devices. For our evaluation, we recruited a total of 18 users, 13 of whom ultimately provided judgments. Of these, 11 were either graduates or undergraduate students at the University of Waterloo. In total, we received 12,115 judgments over the assessment period, with a minimum of 28 and a maximum of 3,791 by an individual user. Overall, 122 interest profiles received at least one judgment; 93 received at least 10 judgments; 67 received at least 50 judgments; 44 received at least 100 judgments.

We begin with descriptive characterizations of user behavior: a breakdown is shown in Table 1. The second column lists the number of judgments each user provided and the third column shows

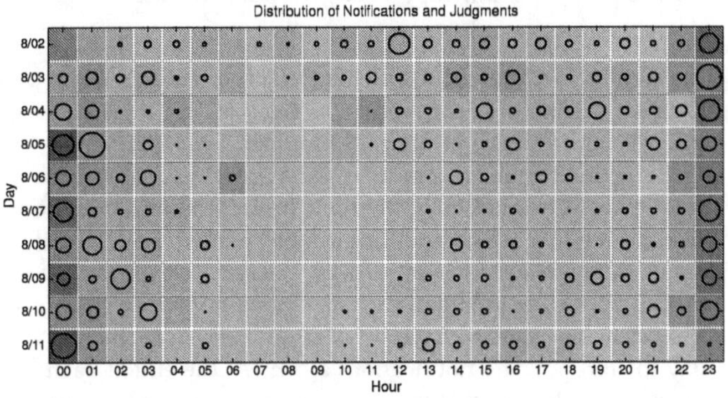

Figure 3: Heatmap showing the volume of push notifications, overlaid with circles whose areas are proportional to the number of received judgments.

the number of profiles that each user subscribed to. The fourth column shows the sum of all push notifications for the profiles that each user subscribed to: this count captures the maximum number of push notifications that the user *could have received* during the evaluation period. Note that we do not have the *actual* number of notifications each user received because the user could have logged out during some periods of time or otherwise adjusted the local device settings (e.g., to disable notifications). The final column shows the response rate, computed as the fraction between the second and fourth columns (which is a lower-bound estimate). From this table, we see that some users are quite diligent in providing judgments, while others provide judgments more sporadically.

How quickly do users provide judgments? The plots in Figure 2 answer this question, showing the distribution of response times over the first minute, first ten minutes, first hour, and across the entire evaluation period. The bars show bucketed counts, while the line graph shows cumulative counts. Normalizing, we find that 14.3% of judgments arrive within the first minute after the push notification has been delivered, 44.9% of judgments arrive in the first ten minutes, and 71.3% of judgments arrive in the first hour. We find that users are quite responsive to interruptions!

Finally, Figure 3 provides an overview of the entire evaluation period. In the heatmap, each box represents one hour across the ten-day evaluation period: the color reflects the total number of pushed tweets by all systems across all profiles that at least one user subscribed to. A deeper red indicates more tweets pushed. The overlaid circles represent judgments received from all users, where

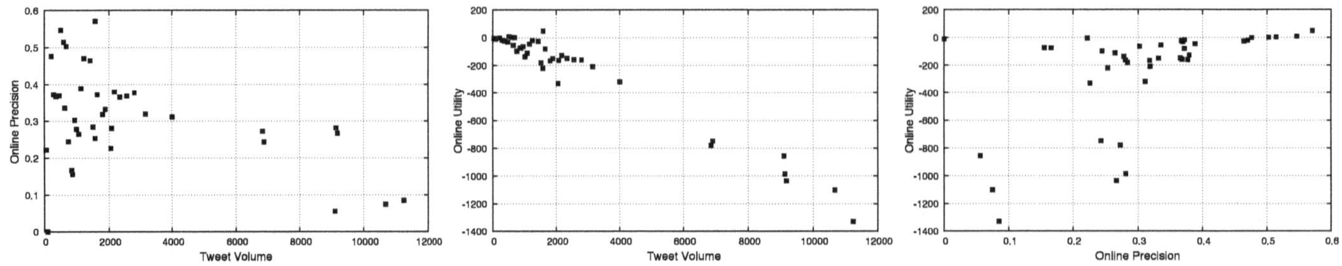

Figure 4: Analyses of online metrics. The left and middle plots show tweet volume vs. online precision and online utility. The right plot shows almost no correlation between online precision and online utility because systems with roughly the same online precision can vary widely in push volume.

the area is proportional to the number of judgments. Note that time is given in UTC; for reference, 00:00:00 UTC translates into 20:00:00 in the local time zone of the users.

A few interesting observations follow: we find that relatively more tweets are pushed by systems in the first and final hours of each day. We believe that this is mostly an evaluation artifact: recall that each system receives a quota of ten tweets per day per profile. At the beginning of each day (hour 00), the quota resets—thus allowing systems that have used up their quota the previous day to start pushing notifications again. At the end of each day (hour 23), we believe that the rise in tweets corresponds to systems "using up" the remainder of their quota.

Looking at the circles, which represent the volume of judgments, we see that they mostly line up with the push volume. That is, darker red cells generally have larger circles—the more tweets systems push, the more judgments we receive. However, there are some deviations, which represent delayed judgments—for example, a burst of tweets that wasn't examined until some time later. It is also interesting to note that with the exception of night time when users are asleep, there does not appear to be a consistent diurnal cycle across our population of users. The users are exposed to a pretty constant stream of push notifications throughout the day (and indeed during sleeping hours also), but there doesn't appear to be a time of the day when we consistently receive more judgments.

5 ANALYSIS

By design, the TREC 2016 RTS Track employed both the online in-situ interleaved evaluation methodology as well as the more traditional post-hoc batch evaluation methodology. This means that for the same systems and interest profiles, we have independently-derived metrics from two very different approaches. For the batch metrics, NIST assessors fully judged 56 interest profiles (relevance judgments and clusters). Section 3.3 and Section 3.4 provide an overview, but since this is not the focus of our work, we refer the reader to details provided in the track overview [16].

We begin by presenting separate analyses of online and batch metrics, and then describe results of correlation analyses between them. In particular, comparing online and batch metrics allows us to explore two questions: From the perspective of the user, do user preferences correlate with batch metrics? From the perspective of system-centered evaluations, can unreliable online judgments replace high-quality NIST assessors?

In considering the online metrics, there is a question regarding which metric to use—the "strict" or "lenient" variant of online precision and online utility (see Section 3.2). We performed analyses with both: All plots look very similar, except for systematic shifts due to the metric variants; for example, all the absolute precision values increase from "strict" to "lenient" precision, but the overall relationships between the points remain largely unchanged. Therefore, we only report the "strict" variants here for brevity. This also suggests that the credit assignment heuristic of Qian et al. [18], which lies somewhere between the strict and lenient variants, is also unlikely to alter our findings.

5.1 Online Metrics

Three different analyses of the online metrics are shown in Figure 4. We organize our findings around two themes:

Precision is an intrinsic metric of push notification quality, while utility is a convenient composite metric. Online precision computes the fraction of relevant user judgments, but does not factor in the volume of tweets that a system pushes. Online utility implies a particular precision target with volume as a scaling factor, and thus serves as a convenient composite metric. To see why this is so, consider a system that achieves a precision of 0.5: setting aside relevance grades for now, the expected utility per tweet is zero (for $\alpha = 0.5$) and the overall expected utility is also zero, regardless of how many tweets the system pushes. A system with lower precision has a negative expected utility per tweet, and the total expected utility is simply that value multiplied by the volume of tweets. Since the precision of most systems in the evaluation falls below 0.5, we observe a strong negative correlation between tweet volume and utility: this can be clearly seen in the middle plot in Figure 4, which shows tweet volume against online utility. Here, volume is measured as the number of tweets pushed by the system for all interest profiles that received at least one judgment.

Our argument can be generalized to other ways of computing utility. Of course, one could assign different weights to non-relevant tweets, but for every weighting scheme, there is an implied precision at which the expected utility per tweet is zero. Only systems that have higher precision can provide positive utility; otherwise, negative utility is directly proportional to push volume. The same idea can be straightforwardly extended to relevance grades: all utility-based metrics encode (at least implicitly) a breakeven point between "good" results and "bad" results.

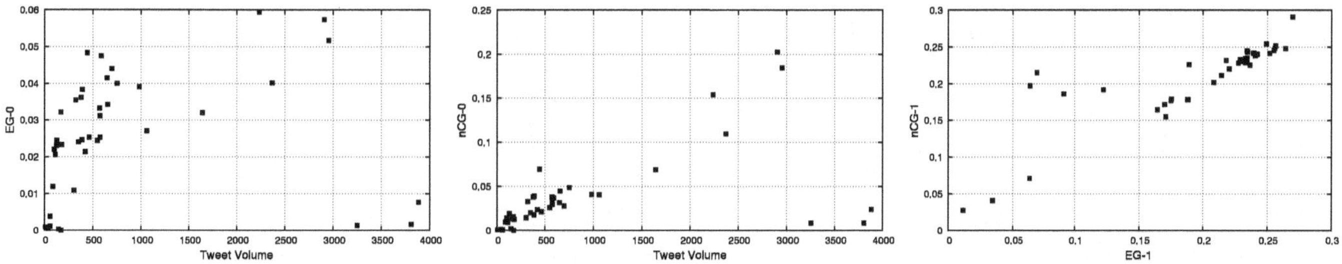

Figure 5: Analyses of batch metrics. The left and middle plots show tweet volume vs. EG-0 and nCG-0, illustrating the dominant effect of tweet volume, which is a major flaw in those metrics. The right plot shows a strong correlation between EG-1 and nCG-1 (with the exception of a few outliers).

Tweet volume is an independent and important measure of system output. Building on the previous observation, the independence of tweet volume and precision can be clearly seen in the right plot of Figure 4, where we observe almost no relationship between online precision and online utility. This is further reinforced in the left plot, which shows tweet volume vs. online precision. Although we observe a negative correlation overall, the effect is primarily due to outliers. If we focus only on systems with tweet volume under 2000, there is little correlation between online precision and volume. In particular, in the band from 0.3 to 0.4 precision, systems vary widely in volume. This leads to the wide spread of precision values for systems that have similar utility in the right plot. Thus, from the user perspective, we believe that online precision and tweet volume are the two fundamental inputs to metrics for measuring system effectiveness.

5.2 Batch Metrics

Analyses of batch metrics are shown in Figure 5. Our two main findings are as follows:

EG-0 and nCG-0 are flawed metrics. Recall that these variants do not reward systems for recognizing that there is no relevant information and staying silent, and thus it never hurts to push notifications. As a result, these two metrics reward systems that push a large volume of tweets without necessarily differentiating the quality of those tweets. This is most evident in the middle plot in Figure 5, which shows tweet volume against nCG-0. Tweet volume here is measured as the total number of tweets pushed across the interest profiles that were evaluated by NIST assessors. Due to the much more involved batch evaluation methodology, the NIST assessors considered a smaller set of interest profiles than users in the online evaluation, and thus the plots report smaller tweet volumes. While it is possible to push a large number of non-relevant tweets (bottom right corner of the middle plot), in general, the more tweets a system pushes, the higher its nCG-0 score.

We note a similar effect for EG-0, although less pronounced, from the left plot in Figure 5, which shows tweet volume against EG-0. Once again, disregarding the outliers in the bottom right corner, higher tweet volumes correlate with higher EG-0 scores. Since under EG-0 all systems receive EG scores of zero for silent days when there are no relevant tweets, it never hurts to "guess" by pushing tweets. Thus, we believe that EG-0 and nCG-0 are flawed metrics since it is unlikely that users desire high-volume systems that push tweets of questionable quality. We advocate that these metrics be dropped in future evaluations, and we remove EG-0 and nCG-0 from subsequent analyses in this paper.

EG-1 and nCG-1 are highly correlated. This correlation can be seen in the right plot in Figure 5. In contrast to EG-0 and nCG-0, these metrics reward systems for remaining silent on days when there is no relevant content. The plot shows that systems with higher gain (utility) also tend to achieve higher precision.

It is interesting to observe that such a strong correlation exists between EG-1 and nCG-1, since EG is quite similar to precision and nCG is recall-like: in principle, systems could make tradeoffs along these two dimensions independently. However, this might simply be a statement about the current state of push notification techniques. Nevertheless, we do observe some outliers: the group of runs around 0.06 in EG-1 and around 0.2 in nCG-1 are those that push a high volume of tweets. What they lack in the overall quality of individual tweets, they make up in volume, leading to higher nCG-1 than their EG-1 scores would otherwise suggest (i.e., the points lie above the trend).

5.3 Online vs. Batch Metrics

Scatter plots correlating various batch metrics against online utility and online precision are shown in Figure 6. In the top row we show correlations between EG-1, nCG-1, and GMP ($\alpha = 0.50$) against online utility; in the bottom row, the same metrics against online precision. Note that we removed EG-0 and nCG-0 from consideration given the discussion above. For GMP, the choice of α does not change the shape of the plots and does not affect our conclusions, so for brevity we omit GMP with $\alpha = \{0.33, 0.66\}$.

When performing correlational studies on retrieval experiments, outlier runs may have a disproportional influence on the results. For example, poor performing systems are easy to distinguish, and most metrics can easily identify poor systems. Therefore, including such systems tends to increase correlations in ways that are not particularly helpful in discriminating systems that are not outliers. The outliers in our case are systems that push a large volume of tweets and those that push very few tweets. From Figure 4 and Figure 5 we can identify the outliers as those runs that push more than 4000 tweets in the online evaluation and more than 1500 tweets in the batch evaluation. There are eight such systems and both criteria identify exactly the same systems. On the whole, these are systems that perform poorly. In the plots, we identify

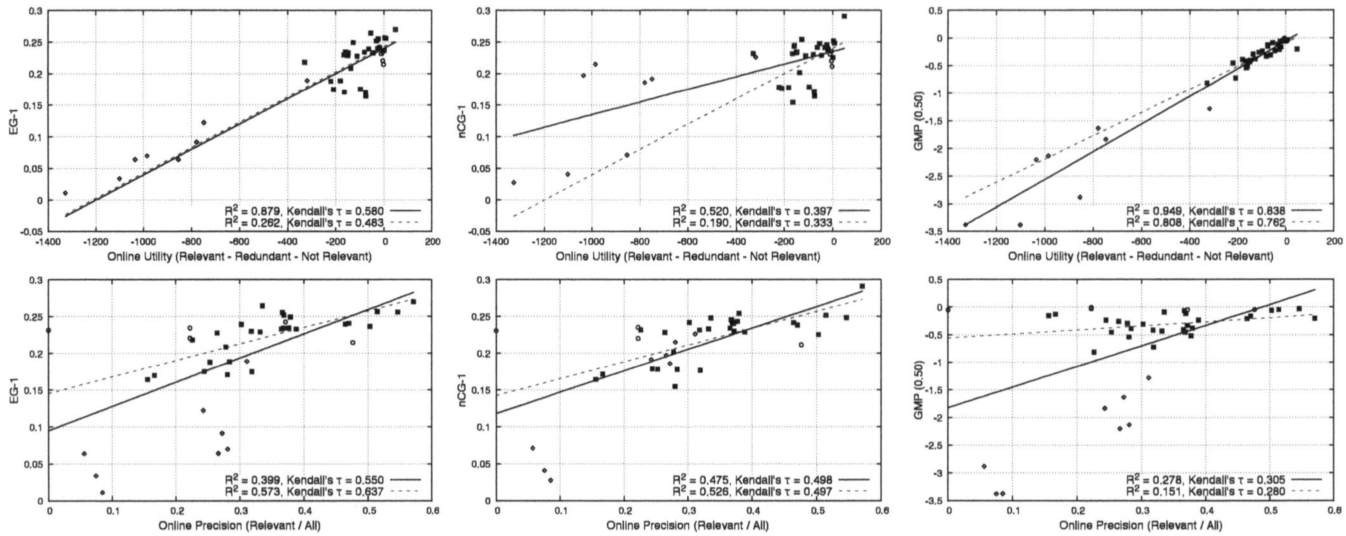

Figure 6: Scatter plots comparing EG-1, nCG-1, and GMP (α = 0.50) to online utility (top row) and to online precision (bottom row). High-volume systems are represented by empty diamonds and low-volume systems are represented by empty circles. Solid lines denote best fit lines with all points; dotted lines denote best fit lines discarding high- and low-volume systems.

these runs separately as empty diamonds. At the other end of the spectrum, we have runs that push very few tweets. We arbitrarily set this threshold to be less than 100 tweets pushed based on the batch evaluation. Since the batch evaluation considered 56 interest profiles spanning 10 days, this translates into less than two tweets per interest profile (over the entire span), which is close to a system that basically does nothing. There are five such runs, identified as empty circles in the plots. This leaves us with 28 systems (runs) whose tweet volumes fall somewhere in the middle, identified by the solid squares in the plots.

For each analysis, we considered two separate conditions: First, with *all* runs. The results of linear regressions are shown as solid lines. Second, we discarded high- and low-volume systems (as described above); the results of linear regressions in these cases are shown as dotted lines. The second condition attempts to remove the influence of these outliers: in some cases, it affects the findings, but in other cases, not. For both conditions, alongside the coefficient of determination for the linear regression shown in the legend, we also report rank correlation in terms of Kendall's τ, the standard metric of rank stability in information retrieval experiments.

There is a lot to unpack in our results, and so we organize our findings around several major themes:

Online utility is highly correlated with GMP. Our strongest finding is a high correlation between online utility and GMP (see Figure 6, top row, right plot). The correlation weakens slightly if we discard the high-volume and low-volume systems, but is still substantial. Because there are many points packed in the top right corner of the plot, the Kendall's τ we observe is a bit lower compared to the coefficient of determination, but still solidly in the range that would be considered good agreement for retrieval experiments.

At first glance, this might seem like an obvious finding since online utility and GMP are both utility-based metrics, but this is a non-obvious result for several reasons: GMP is computed over cluster judgments from pooled tweets and therefore represents a global view over tweets from all systems. In particular, tweets are grouped into clusters and systems do not get credit for pushing tweets that say the same thing. In contrast, online utility captures only a local view of content—users are making decisions about each tweet pushed to them, and the redundant judgments are subjected to the fallacies of human memory (i.e., users may have forgotten having seen similar tweets).

In addition, GMP is computed using "dense" judgments over a smaller set of profiles gathered by pooling, whereas online utility is computed from sparse judgments over uncontrolled samples, since we have no control over when and how frequently users provide judgments. It is surprising that sporadic, unpredictable, in-situ judgments from a multitude of users yield results that are highly-correlated with the careful deliberations of professional NIST assessors.

Online precision exhibits moderate correlations with EG-1 and nCG-1. This is shown in Figure 6, bottom row, left and center plots. Since the definition of EG-1 shares similarities with online precision, one might expect this, and since EG-1 and nCG-1 are correlated (right plot, Figure 5), it is no surprise to find that online precision also correlates with nCG-1. As with GMP above, we emphasize that online precision is computed from tweets evaluated in isolation, whereas EG-1 and nCG-1 are based on cluster annotations, which take into account the global cluster structure of tweets relevant to the interest profile.

In both cases, the correlation strengthens if we discard high- and low-volume systems (although for nCG-1, Kendall's τ is essentially unchanged). An empty run (i.e., a system that does nothing) would receive a score of 0.2339 for EG-1 and nCG-1, which is simply the fraction of silent days when there are no relevant tweets. Therefore, low-volume systems receive scores that are close to the score of an empty run, and this throws off the correlation.

Online utility exhibits at best a weak correlation with EG-1 and nCG-1. This is shown in Figure 6, top row, left and center plots. In both these cases, the correlation weakens substantially if we remove the high- and low-volume systems. Therefore, outliers are giving the impression of a stronger correlation than one that actually exists. In a sense, it is not surprising that we observe little correlation between a utility metric vs. precision-oriented and recall-like metrics.

Online precision exhibits almost no correlation with GMP. This is shown in Figure 6, bottom row, right plot. This finding is consistent with what we see in Figure 4. Precision doesn't capture tweet volume, whereas tweet volume has a substantial impact on utility, as previously discussed.

6 DISCUSSION AND LIMITATIONS

One potential objection to our evaluation methodology is our reliance on explicit user judgments. This, of course, stands in contrast to web ranking, which benefits from a tremendous amount of implicit judgments that are collected as a byproduct of users searching. However, we argue that explicit judgments are an important component of push notifications since they, by definition, interrupt the user. Given that the interruption has already occurred (if the user has chosen to attend to the notification), allowing the user an opportunity to provide feedback seems like good design. Thus, we argue that our evaluation setup is realistic, mirroring how a production push notification system might be deployed. For example, in some implementations today, notifications already appear with a "dismiss" option for users to take explicit action; adding options for quality feedback would incur minimal extra cost.

At a high-level, our work supports three findings: First, that online in-situ interleaved evaluations of push notifications systems are workable in practice. It is indeed possible to recruit users and they are willing to provide sufficient judgments (quite diligently, in fact) to meaningfully evaluate systems. This seems consistent with our arguments above regarding the role of explicit judgments in push notification systems. Second, we observe substantial correlations between online and batch evaluation metrics that share the same design (e.g., are precision-oriented or utility-based). Third, the volume of messages that a system pushes is an important aspect of system evaluation, but its role is not fully understood.

With respect to the second finding—the substantial correlation between online and batch metrics—this is by no means obvious, given the large body of literature that has shown divergences between user- and system-oriented metrics (see Section 2). We have touched on some of the main differences between the online and batch methodologies, but they bear additional emphasis:

- The batch evaluation considered all tweets that all systems pushed during the evaluation period. That is, all push notifications were included in the pool and so the judgments are exhaustive from the perspective of the participants. This stands in contrast to the online judgments, which are best characterized as a small convenience sample by users (see response rates in Table 1). We have no control over when and how many judgments are provided—and whether there are any systematic biases, for example, a user who only marks relevant tweets but ignores non-relevant tweets (i.e., a bias against explicit negative judgments).
- The batch metrics all operate at the level of semantic clusters, taking into account redundancy. These clusters are formed from the pool and therefore contain a "global" view of tweets pushed by all systems. Accordingly, systems are penalized for retrieving multiple tweets that say that same thing. In contrast, user judgments occur tweet-by-tweet and represent a "local" view—our users assess only the tweets in front of them. Furthermore, redundant judgments are made with respect only to tweets the users had previously assessed, and are subject to the effects of imperfect memory. Another consequence of this setup is that from batch judgments we can characterize silent days (at least within the limitations of pooling), whereas with online judgments there is no way for the user to obtain this information. Thus, it is not possible for an online metric to reward systems for "staying quiet". Finally, high-volume systems (which tend to have lower precision) are disproportionately represented.
- The batch evaluation used professional NIST assessors, many with decades of experience. They have become the gold standard against which human judgments are compared [5]. Contrast this with our users: since they are simply going about their daily lives (which is indeed the point), we have no idea in what context they are assessing tweets—were they alone in a quiet setting considering tweets with care or hurriedly skimming tweets while multi-tasking? We assume our users were acting in good faith and judging the tweets to the best of their ability (and we have no reason to suspect otherwise), but the overall fidelity and quality of judgments are likely to be lower than the NIST assessors who operated in a carefully-controlled environment.

These differences considered, we find the correlations between online and batch metrics non-obvious and interesting. There are two different interpretations to these results:

If one believes in the primacy of user-centered evaluations, our findings suggest that established batch evaluation metrics are able to capture user preferences. That is, the batch metrics are capturing aspects of what users care about in *useful* systems. This result nicely complements the findings of Wang et al. [31], who validated batch metrics for the related task of retrospective timeline summarization over tweet streams.

On the other hand, one might put more faith in a mature batch evaluation methodology that has been through the gauntlet of multiple deployments, and whose core ideas date back at least a decade. If one takes this perspective and believes in the primacy of the established approach, then our results suggest a cheaper way to conduct evaluations of push notification systems that yield similar conclusions. Of course, these two perspectives are not necessarily conflicting. Instead, they point to more work that is necessary to fully align user- and system-oriented perspectives to assessing push notification systems.

It makes sense to discuss some of the limitations of this work. Our users are compensated for their participation in the study and thus can be assumed to operate under certain social norms. One might argue that their behavior would be different had they "organically" discovered an app for push notifications. While this is certainly a legitimate criticism, it could be leveled against any user study that involves compensation—potential differences between paid subjects and "real users" are beyond the scope of this study.

A closely-related issue is the fact that our users subscribed to interest profiles that were not "their own", i.e., they did not come up with the information needs themselves. This concern, however, is mitigated by having users select from a broad range of profiles (a couple hundred) to match their interests. Therefore, our evaluation is less likely to have suffered from user indifference.

Another limitation of our study is that it captures only a snapshot of current technology. This, of course, is an implicit qualification of any evaluation, not just our work. For example, consider attempts to control the volume of push notifications and to recognize when there is no relevant content: such techniques are nascent at best, since the community is just beginning to understand the nuances of systems "learning when to shut up". We have found that these issues are confounding variables when trying to correlate online and batch metrics, but as the technology evolves and matures, the nature of the confound might change. As another example, we empirically observe that EG-1 and nCG-1 are correlated, even though in principle systems can operate in a tradeoff space in which the measures are not correlated. Nevertheless, we are unable to speculate on future developments that have yet to happen—we can only draw conclusions based on the data at hand. The only way to address this limitation is a follow-up study that considers systems once push notification techniques have substantially progressed.

7 CONCLUSIONS

This paper describes a formal user study of push notification systems with two distinct characteristics: tweets are assessed *online* and *in-situ*. As the infrastructure for conducting our evaluation can be reused (all software deployed in this study is open source), future iterations will take less effort. Therefore, we hope to see more of these evaluations as the methodology becomes "just another hammer" in the toolbox of information retrieval researchers and practitioners.

As an outstanding issue, we believe that the proper role of notification volume in evaluating systems is not yet fully understood. As we have empirically observed, systems with the same precision can vary widely in the volume of notifications they push. However, the question remains: how much content should a system actually push? Even assuming that systems can achieve high precision—let's say, 90% or greater—are more notifications really better? Intuitively, one would expect that, at some point, user fatigue sets in, even for a stream of high-quality tweets. We might imagine the user having access to a "volume dial" to provide feedback: "yes, these are all good tweets, but too many!" As we have shown, tweet volume is not directly captured in existing metrics, but the problem lies deeper: our understanding of how users perceive notifications in response to prospective information needs remains quite poor, especially when factoring in the cost of interruptions. More work on fundamental issues along these lines is needed.

8 ACKNOWLEDGMENTS

This work was supported by the Natural Sciences and Engineering Research Council (NSERC) of Canada, with additional contributions from the U.S. National Science Foundation under IIS-1218043 and CNS-1405688. Any findings, conclusions, or recommendations expressed do not necessarily reflect the views of the sponsors.

REFERENCES

[1] Azzah Al-Maskari, Mark Sanderson, Paul Clough, and Eija Airio. 2008. The Good and the Bad System: Does the Test Collection Predict Users' Effectiveness? In *SIGIR*. 59–66.

[2] James Allan. 2002. *Topic Detection and Tracking: Event-Based Information Organization*. Kluwer Academic Publishers, Dordrecht, The Netherlands.

[3] James Allan, Ben Carterette, and Joshua Lewis. 2005. When Will Information Retrieval Be "Good Enough"? User Effectiveness as a Function of Retrieval Accuracy. In *SIGIR*. 433–440.

[4] Javed Aslam, Fernando Diaz, Matthew Ekstrand-Abueg, Richard McCreadie, Virgil Pavlu, and Tetsuya Sakai. 2015. TREC 2015 Temporal Summarization Track Overview. In *TREC*.

[5] Peter Bailey, Nick Craswell, Ian Soboroff, Paul Thomas, Arjen P. de Vries, and Emine Yilmaz. 2008. Relevance Assessment: Are Judges Exchangeable and Does it Matter? In *SIGIR*. 667–674.

[6] Nicholas J. Belkin and W. Bruce Croft. 1992. Information Filtering and Information Retrieval: Two Sides of the Same Coin? *CACM* 35, 12 (1992), 29–38.

[7] Olivier Chapelle, Thorsten Joachims, Filip Radlinski, and Yisong Yue. 2012. Large-Scale Validation and Analysis of Interleaved Search Evaluation. *ACM TOIS* 30, 1 (2012), Article 6.

[8] Qi Guo, Fernando Diaz, and Elad Yom-Tov. 2013. Updating Users about Time Critical Events. In *ECIR*. 483–494.

[9] Allan Hanbury, Henning Müller, Krisztian Balog, Torben Brodt, Gordon V. Cormack, Ivan Eggel, Tim Gollub, Frank Hopfgartner, Jayashree Kalpathy-Cramer, Noriko Kando, Anastasia Krithara, Jimmy Lin, Simon Mercer, and Martin Potthast. 2015. Evaluation-as-a-Service: Overview and Outlook. *arXiv:1512.07454*.

[10] William Hersh, Andrew Turpin, Susan Price, Benjamin Chan, Dale Kramer, Lynetta Sacherek, and Daniel Olson. 2000. Do Batch and User Evaluations Give the Same Results? In *SIGIR*. 17–24.

[11] Katja Hofmann, Shimon Whiteson, and Maarten de Rijke. 2011. A Probabilistic Method for Inferring Preferences from Clicks. In *CIKM*. 249–258.

[12] Ron Kohavi, Randal M. Henne, and Dan Sommerfield. 2007. Practical Guide to Controlled Experiments on the Web: Listen to Your Customers not to the HiPPO. In *KDD*. 959–967.

[13] David D. Lewis. 1995. The TREC-4 Filtering Track. In *TREC*. 165–180.

[14] Jimmy Lin, Miles Efron, Yulu Wang, and Garrick Sherman. 2014. Overview of the TREC-2014 Microblog Track. In *TREC*.

[15] Jimmy Lin, Miles Efron, Yulu Wang, Garrick Sherman, and Ellen Voorhees. 2015. Overview of the TREC-2015 Microblog Track. In *TREC*.

[16] Jimmy Lin, Adam Roegiest, Luchen Tan, Richard McCreadie, Ellen Voorhees, and Fernando Diaz. 2016. Overview of the TREC 2016 Real-Time Summarization Track. In *TREC*.

[17] Abhinav Mehrotra, Veljko Pejovic, Jo Vermeulen, Robert Hendley, and Mirco Musolesi. 2016. My Phone and Me: Understanding People's Receptivity to Mobile Notifications. In *CHI*. 1021–1032.

[18] Xin Qian, Jimmy Lin, and Adam Roegiest. 2016. Interleaved Evaluation for Retrospective Summarization and Prospective Notification on Document Streams. In *SIGIR*. 175–184.

[19] Filip Radlinski and Nick Craswell. 2010. Comparing the Sensitivity of Information Retrieval Metrics. In *SIGIR*. 667–674.

[20] Filip Radlinski and Nick Craswell. 2013. Optimized Interleaving for Online Retrieval Evaluation. In *WSDM*. 245–254.

[21] Stephen Robertson and Ian Soboroff. 2002. The TREC 2002 Filtering Track Report. In *TREC*.

[22] Alan Said, Jimmy Lin, Alejandro Bellogín, and Arjen P. de Vries. 2013. A Month in the Life of a Production News Recommender System. In *CIKM Workshop on Living Labs for Information Retrieval Evaluation*. 7–10.

[23] Mark Sanderson, Monica Paramita, Paul Clough, and Evangelos Kanoulas. 2010. Do User Preferences and Evaluation Measures Line Up? In *SIGIR*. 555–562.

[24] Anne Schuth, Krisztian Balog, and Liadh Kelly. 2015. Overview of the Living Labs for Information Retrieval Evaluation (LL4IR) CLEF Lab 2015. In *CLEF*.

[25] Anne Schuth, Katja Hofmann, and Filip Radlinski. 2015. Predicting Search Satisfaction Metrics with Interleaved Comparisons. In *SIGIR*. 463–472.

[26] Mark Smucker and Chandra Jethani. 2010. Human Performance and Retrieval Precision Revisited. In *SIGIR*. 595–602.

[27] Ian Soboroff, Iadh Ounis, Craig Macdonald, and Jimmy Lin. 2012. Overview of the TREC-2012 Microblog Track. In *TREC*.

[28] Luchen Tan, Adam Roegiest, Jimmy Lin, and Charles L. A. Clarke. 2016. An Exploration of Evaluation Metrics for Mobile Push Notifications. In *SIGIR*. 741–744.

[29] Andrew Turpin and William R. Hersh. 2001. Why Batch and User Evaluations Do Not Give the Same Results. In *SIGIR*. 225–231.

[30] Andrew Turpin and Falk Scholer. 2006. User Performance versus Precision Measures for Simple Search Tasks. In *SIGIR*. 11–18.

[31] Yulu Wang, Garrick Sherman, Jimmy Lin, and Miles Efron. 2015. Assessor Differences and User Preferences in Tweet Timeline Generation. In *SIGIR*. 615–624.

Evaluating Web Search with a Bejeweled Player Model

Fan Zhang
DCST, Tsinghua University
Beijing, China
frankyzf94@gmail.com

Yiqun Liu*
DCST, Tsinghua University
Beijing, China
yiqunliu@tsinghua.edu.cn

Xin Li
DCST, Tsinghua University
Beijing, China
x-l08@163.com

Min Zhang
DCST, Tsinghua University
Beijing, China
z-m@tsinghua.edu.cn

Yinghui Xu
Alibaba Group
Hangzhou, China
renji.xyh@taobao.com

Shaoping Ma
DCST, Tsinghua University
Beijing, China
msp@tsinghua.edu.cn

ABSTRACT

The design of a Web search evaluation metric is closely related with how the user's interaction process is modeled. Each behavioral model results in a different metric used to evaluate search performance. In these models and the user behavior assumptions behind them, when a user ends a search session is one of the prime concerns because it is highly related to both benefit and cost estimation. Existing metric design usually adopts some simplified criteria to decide the stopping time point: (1) upper limit for benefit (e.g. RR, AP); (2) upper limit for cost (e.g. Precision@N, DCG@N). However, in many practical search sessions (e.g. exploratory search), the stopping criterion is more complex than the simplified case. Analyzing benefit and cost of actual users' search sessions, we find that the stopping criteria vary with search tasks and are usually combination effects of both benefit and cost factors. Inspired by a popular computer game named Bejeweled, we propose a Bejeweled Player Model (BPM) to simulate users' search interaction processes and evaluate their search performances. In the BPM, a user stops when he/she either has found sufficient useful information or has no more patience to continue. Given this assumption, a new evaluation framework based on upper limits (either fixed or changeable as search proceeds) for both benefit and cost is proposed. We show how to derive a new metric from the framework and demonstrate that it can be adopted to revise traditional metrics like Discounted Cumulative Gain (DCG), Expected Reciprocal Rank (ERR) and Average Precision (AP). To show effectiveness of the proposed framework, we compare it with a number of existing metrics in terms of correlation between user satisfaction and the metrics based on a dataset that collects users' explicit satisfaction feedbacks and assessors' relevance judgements. Experiment results show that the framework is better correlated with user satisfaction feedbacks.

*Corresponding author

SIGIR '17, August 07-11, 2017, Shinjuku, Tokyo, Japan

DOI: http://dx.doi.org/10.1145/3077136.3080841

CCS CONCEPTS

•Information systems → Evaluation of retrieval results;

KEYWORDS

Benefit and Cost; Evaluation Metrics; User Model

1 INTRODUCTION

System-oriented tests and user-oriented studies are currently two complementary approaches to Web search evaluation. A system-oriented test, which is known as Cranfield approach [15], typically develops a set of relevance judgments to compare the quality of ranked lists returned by different systems in response to a fixed set of queries. On the contrary, a user-oriented study makes use of actual user behaviors during interactive retrieval sessions to measure effectiveness of systems. For instance, *A/B testing* and *interleaving* method [24] are widely used by commercial search engines.

One of the main advantages of user-oriented studies is that they are designed to reflect users' opinions in the realistic search process. However, they are more costly and harder to reproduce than system-oriented tests. On the other hand, although a system-oriented test is inexpensive and reproducible, it cannot capture search activities of users. To tackle this challenge, most Web search evaluation metrics have been built on top of different user models. In these models, when user ends a search session is one of the prime concerns because it is highly related to both benefit and cost estimation.

Benefit, also referred to as *gain* or *utility* in some researches, has been discussed and introduced in a variety of ways. For example, utility is deemed to be associated with relevance [17], in the sense that one can receive benefit or gain from relevant documents. In terms of relevance, what constitutes it is subject to much interpretation [28]. *Cost* is considered as temporal efforts or cognitive efforts in processing, reading and understanding documents in many related works [2, 34, 38, 39]. In this paper, we use the terms *benefit* and *cost*, although many other equivalent terms are also used in existing researches.

Regarding benefit and cost, underlying user models of existing metrics usually adopt some simplified criteria to decide the stopping time point. For instance, user model of *Reciprocal Rank* (RR) assumes that a user will stop once he/she finds a perfect document. That is, when users stop only depends on when they get the benefit that they expected. We refer to this kind of stopping criterion as

upper limit for benefit. In contrast, *Precision@N* measures the percentage of relevant documents in top-N results, which means that users will scan a ranked list from top to bottom and stop at the N-th document. This kind of stopping criterion is called **upper limit for cost**. The user models of other metrics like *Discounted Cumulative Gain* (DCG) [23], *Expected Reciprocal Rank* (ERR) [12] and *Average Precision* (AP) are more complex, since user variety and stopping probability distribution at different ranked results are considered. Nevertheless, the stopping criteria of these user models still focus on only one aspect of upper limits for benefit or cost, as we show in Section 3.2. However, in many practical search sessions (e.g. exploratory search), the stopping criterion should be usually combination effects of both benefit and cost factors.

Figure 1 shows two search sessions collected from an experimental user study in [27]. Figure 1(a) shows a session where the user was seeking information on *ice-breaking games*. In this session, the user issued four queries and clicked four results. The usefulness feedbacks provided by the user indicated that the user judged all the clicked results to be "highly useful". The user was also "highly satisfied" with the session according to the satisfaction feedback. Therefore, we suppose that the user ended this session because he/she has received enough benefits from clicked results. It was upper limit for benefit that affected the stopping criterion. On the contrary, in Figure 1(b), we see a session where the user was exploring different aspects of a topic *"Fixed Gear Bicycle"*. In this session, the user issued seven queries and clicked eight results, while only one result is thought to be "fairly useful". The last result he clicked was "useless" and then he ended the session in spite that he was "somewhat satisfied". So we assume that the user stopped with no more patience. It seems to be the upper limit for cost that stopped the user.

Comparing the sessions, we find that the stopping criterion for a search session may be either upper limit for benefit or cost in difference circumstances. To take this a bit complex criterion into consideration, inspired by a popular computer game named *Bejeweled*, we propose a *Bejeweled Player Model* (BPM) to simulate users' search interaction processes and evaluate their search performances. In *Action Mode* on *Bejeweled*[1], the game starts with the timer bar at the bottom half full, which will start to decrease every second. The player must match gems to add more seconds, with bigger moves getting more time. The player will advance to the next level when the bar is full. However, if the bar completely empties, the player lose the game. When no more moves can be made, the game reshuffles the gems. Overall, the stopping criterion of the game may be the bar is either empty (i.e. *Game Over*) or full (i.e. *Level Up*). Similar to the game, frustration and satisfaction are two final states of Web search. Many related works [11, 19, 21] have worked on predicting these two states and tell the difference between them. However, to the best of our knowledge, there is no research that incorporates the difference between frustration and satisfaction into the design of evaluation framework. Inspired by the game, we assume that frustration often means that users have invested too much cost and run out their patience (i.e. the bar is empty) while satisfaction is usually due to the fulfillment of their benefits (i.e. the bar is full), so we propose the BPM to describe the stopping criterion for Web search. To be emphasized, unlike the

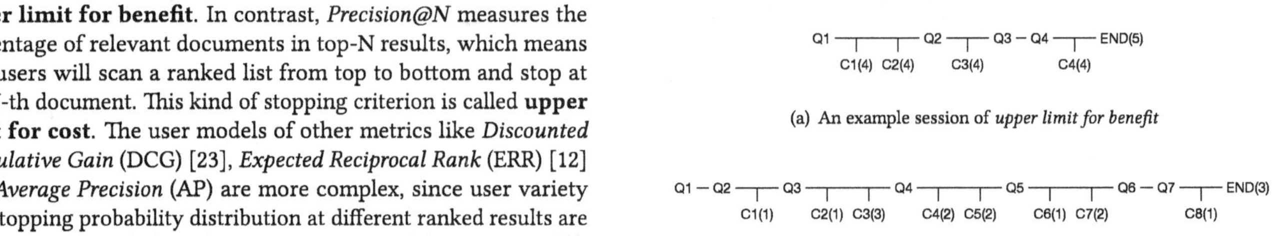

(a) An example session of *upper limit for benefit*

(b) An example session of *upper limit for cost*

Figure 1: Sessions showing different stopping criteria. Q: issuing a query; C: clicking a result. The number in brackets after a click is its usefulness level (4 point scale where 4 means the most useful) and that after the *END* is the session's satisfaction level (5 point scale where 5 means the most satisfied).

game where costs and scores are both represented as time in the same bar, we consider users' benefits and costs separately in the BPM. That is to say, benefits and costs are accumulated in two bars and there is an upper limit for each bar. The stopping criterion for a session is either the benefit bar is full or the cost bar is full.

As described above, in the BPM, a user stops when he/she either has found sufficient useful information or has no more patience to continue. Given this assumption, we propose a new evaluation framework based on upper limits (either fixed or evolving as search session proceeds) for both benefit and cost. To apply this framework to Web search evaluation, we show how to derive metrics from it. As mentioned previously, the stopping criteria of user models behind some metrics such as DCG, ERR and AP focus on only one aspect of upper limits for benefit or cost. Therefore, we demonstrate that these metrics can be derived from the framework considering one-sided case of the stopping criterion. Finally, to show effectiveness of the proposed framework, we compare it with a number of existing metrics in terms of the correlation between user satisfaction and the metrics.

In summary, we make the following contributions in our work:

- We introduce a *Bejeweled Player Model* to simulate users' search interaction processes and explain the stopping criterion for search sessions.
- Based on the BPM, we propose a new unified framework for Web search evaluation and demonstrate that some existing metrics can be derived from the framework considering one-sided case of the stopping criterion.
- Based on a dataset that collect users' explicit satisfaction feedbacks and assessors' relevance judgements, we show effectiveness of our proposed framework by comparing it with a number of existing metrics in terms of correlation between user satisfaction and the metrics.

The remainder of this paper is organized as follows. In Section 2, we introduce our proposed evaluation framework based on the BPM. Section 3 shows how to instantiate a metric from the framework and how it can be adapted to existing metrics. Then we show effectiveness of the framework by comparing it with existing metrics in terms of correlation between user satisfaction and the metrics in

[1] http://bejeweled.wikia.com/wiki/Action_mode

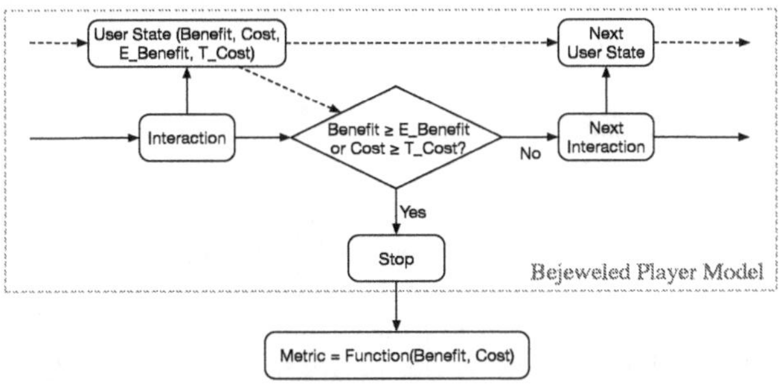

Figure 2: Evaluation framework based on the BPM

Section 4. We review related researches in Section 5 and conclude in Section 6.

2 EVALUATION FRAMEWORK

Figure 2 shows our proposed evaluation framework based on the *Bejeweled Player Model* (BPM). In a session described by the BPM, a user will interact with the system to satisfy her information need. At each round of *interaction*, the user will pay some costs and obtain some benefits simultaneously. As a result, she changes the *user state* with benefit and cost. Benefits and costs are accumulated with interactions and we use *Benefit* and *Cost* to denote them. The BPM supposes that the benefits that the user expects to obtain and the costs that she is willing to pay are limited, which are denoted as *Expected Benefit* (*E_Benefit*) and *Tolerated Cost* (*T_Cost*). Based on upper limits for both benefit and cost, a user stops when either she has found sufficient useful information (reach upper limit for benefit, i.e. $Benefit \geq E\_Benefit$) or she has no more patience to continue searching (reach upper limit for cost, i.e. $Cost \geq T\_Cost$). To be emphasized, *E_Benefit* and *T_Cost* may change with interactions, so we incorporate them into the *user state* with *Benefit* and *Cost* as well.

Note that in the BPM introduced above, we mainly focus on upper limits for both benefit and cost that determine when the user stops, rather than specific interactions. We believe that the BPM is an intrinsic user model which simulates users' search interaction processes and explains the stopping criterion for search sessions. We assume that user satisfaction can be represented by benefit and cost factors. Therefore, based on the BPM, we propose an evaluation framework by combining it with a metric function of *Benefit* and *Cost* at the end of the session. The function is defined to evaluate users' search performances. Given the framework, *interactions*, *Benefit* and *Cost*, *E_Benefit* and *T_Cost*, as well as *metric function* are important components for evaluation. Therefore, before we apply this conceptual framework to Web search evaluation, we should talk more about these components.

2.1 Interactions

In our proposed framework, user behaviors are represented as a sequence of interactions. These interactions are associated with user models. For example, the interactions are examining results one-by-one for user models behind most rank-based retrieval metrics such as DCG [23], ERR [12] and AP. While for click model-based information retrieval metrics [14, 37], the interactions would be examining snippets or click results. Sakai and Dou [33] proposed U-measure to evaluate Web search based on the concept *trailtexts*, where the interactions would be handling *trailtexts* of course. Though we do not focus on how to define interactions in this paper, we believe that interactions that are closer to user behaviors lead to more effective metrics.

2.2 Benefit and Cost

As suggested by Azzopardi et al. [5], benefits and costs are associated with interactions. They provide a summary of different benefits and costs for various interactions. For most traditional metrics that take examining results as interactions, the *benefit* of interaction is considered to be associated with relevance. Binary and graded relevance are two most common ways to model it.

As for the *cost*, most metrics assume that the cost of processing each document is the same. Recently, *cost* has been considered from a variety of angles. For instance, Smucker and Clarke [34] use the time spent by the user as a proxy for *cost* and propose Time Biased Gain (TBG). In addition, the *cost* involved in processing a document in terms of readability and understandability has been explicitly included in other measures (e.g., [2, 38, 39]).

In this paper, we will use $benefit_k$ and $cost_k$ to denote the benefit and the cost of the k-th *interaction*, while *Benefit* and *Cost* denote the benefits and costs accumulated on interactions. Unlike metrics that accumulate benefits or costs with a discount function for different interactions (e.g., DCG [23], TBG [34], U-measure [33] for benefit and ERR [12] for cost), we accumulate them with no discounts. Inspired by Carterette [10] and Moffat et al. [29], we argue that the discount function is the result of user variety and stopping probability distribution at different ranked results. This will be discussed further in Section 3.2.

2.3 E_Benefit and T_Cost

In this paper, we focus on upper limits for benefit and cost that determine when the user stops. *E_Benefit* denotes the benefit that the user expects to obtain (upper limit for benefit), which should be in the same unit with *Benefit*. For example, Moffat et al. [29] use a parameter T to denote the target number of relevant documents the user wishes to identify. *T_Cost* denotes the cost that the user is willing to pay (upper limit for cost), which should be in the same unit with *Cost*. For example, in TBG [34], *T_Cost* can be expressed as the time that the user is willing to use for search.

Motivated by [29], we argue that *E_Benefit* and *T_Cost* should be user-specrific and task-specrific. That is, for different users or different tasks, the values of *E_Benefit* and *T_Cost* are different. For instance, Broder [9] groups Web queries into informational, navigational and transactional categories. Given that informational queries often require more information than navigational or transactional queries to satisfy the information need, we assume that the value of *E_Benefit* will be larger for informational queries. On the other hand, for users who have more patience to search, the value of *T_Cost* will be larger as well, just like the persistence parameter p associated with RBP [30]. In [6], Bailey et al. reveal that searchers display substantial individual variation in the numbers of documents and queries they anticipate needing to issue, and there are underlying significant differences in these numbers in line with increasing task complexity levels. Therefore, we can consider different $E\_Benefit$ and T_Cost for different users and different tasks to design more sensitive evaluation metrics.

For further thinking, we suggest that *E_Benefit* and *T_Cost* should also be dynamic. Fuhr [20] proposes the Interactive Probability Ranking Principle (iPRP), an extension to the well known Probability Ranking Principle [32]. When developing the iPRP, one of the main requirements is allowing for the information need to change through the course of interaction. Motivated by this point, we assume that *E_Benefit* and *T_Cost* will also involve with interactions, thus incorporated into the *user state* with *Benefit* and *Cost*.

It is also important to note that interactions are affected by *user states*. In [4], Azzopardi et al. examine three theories of Information Seeking and Retrieval. They enumerate a list of hypotheses about search behavior, and show that these theories make similar predictions. Their work indicates that searchers will change their search behavior based on their context. Nevertheless, in this paper, we focus on independent interactions that users scan ranked results one-by-one from top to bottom.

2.4 Metric Function

This function is defined to instantiate a metric from the framework and measure user satisfaction when the user stops. In previous metrics, some focus on *Benefit* (e.g. DCG), some focus on *Cost* (e.g. ERR) while others focus on $Average\ Utility$ which means *Benefit* devided by *Cost* (e.g. AP). Therefore, we assume that the metric should be a function of *Benefit* and *Cost*. In this paper, however, we do not discuss the form what the *metric function* should be. We just compare three choices mentioned above, i.e. *Benefit*, *reciprocal Cost*, and *Benefit* devided by *Cost*.

3 METRICS

In Section 2, we proposed an evaluation framework based on the BPM. Now we will show how to instantiate a metric from the framework and how it can be adapted to existing metrics.

3.1 Metric Based on The BPM

For simplicity, in this paper we take *interactions* as scaning down ranked results one-by-one before the user stops. This simple interaction process is usually regarded as a cascade assumption [18] and accepted by many existing user behavior models. Given the k-th interaction (i.e. examining the k-th result), its benefit and cost will be $benefit_k$ and $cost_k$. In [10], Carterette compares different utility accumulation models that describe how a user accumulates utility in the course of browsing. For simplicity, here we assume *Benefit* or *Cost* accumulated with interactions to be the sum of $benefit_k$ or $cost_k$. Then in the k-th *user state* after the k-th interaction, *Benefit* and *Cost* can be represented as follow:

$$Benefit_k = \sum_{i=1}^{k} benefit_i, \quad Cost_k = \sum_{i=1}^{k} cost_i \tag{1}$$

As mentioned in Section 2.3, *E_Benefit* and *T_Cost* will change with interactions, thus represented as:

$$E\_Benefit_k = E\_Benefit_0 + \sum_{i=1}^{k} \Delta E\_Benefit_i \tag{2}$$

$$T\_Cost_k = T\_Cost_0 + \sum_{i=1}^{k} \Delta T\_Cost_i \tag{3}$$

where $E\_Benefit_0$ and T_Cost_0 are the initial values when the user starts searching. The increments, $\Delta E\_Benefit_i$ and ΔT_Cost_i, may depend on all the interactions and user states up to the i-th *user state*.

Considering the probability that the user stops at rank k:

$$P(k) = P(\geq k) - P(\geq k+1) \tag{4}$$

where $P(\geq k)$ denotes the probability that the stopping rank is not less than k. In our proposed framework, we assume that a user stops only when $Benefit \geq E\_Benefit$ or $Cost \geq T\_Cost$. So $P(\geq k)$ can be represented as follow:

$$P(Benefit_i < E\_Benefit_i, Cost_i < T\_Cost_i : i = 1, ..., k-1) \tag{5}$$

Then we can get the metric:

$$M = \sum_{k=1}^{\infty} Function(Benefit_k,\ Cost_k) * P(k) \tag{6}$$

Note that different users may stop at different ranks. Therefore, considering user variety, the metric is represented as the expectation of the metric function. For a system-oriented test, given definitions of $benefit_i$, $cost_i$, $\Delta E\_Benefit_i$, ΔT_Cost_i and the *metric function*, we can derive a specific metric from the framework.

3.2 Existing Metrics

Equation 6 shows how to instantiate a metric from our proposed framework based on the BPM. Given that the stopping criteria of user models behind some metrics such as DCG, ERR and AP focus on only one aspect of upper limits for benefit or cost, we assume that the framework can be applied to derive these metrics when considering their underlying user models. Therefore, in this part, we take DCG as an example to show how it can be derived from the framework.

Note that DCG is based on an assumption that the user scans down the ranked list one-by-one and the cost of processing each document is the same, so we define $cost_i$ as *one unit* for them, thus $Cost_k$ equals to k *units*. As described in [23], for DCG, $benefit_i$ is defined as $2^{rel_i} - 1$, where rel_i is the relevance level of $document_i$. Since DCG assumes that the probability that the lower-ranked documents are examined is smaller, which leads to a discount function $1/log_2(i+1)$, we explain it with different values of *T_Cost* for different users. To be specific, the proportion of users willing to examining at least i results is $1/log_2(i+1)$. Therefore, the probability that T_Cost_k equals to i is:

$$P(T\_Cost_k = i) = 1/log_2(i+1) - 1/log_2(i+2) \tag{7}$$

Note that T_Cost_k is independent of k, which means that *T_Cost* is static for each user and will not change with interactions. However, for DCG, benefit is not limited, which means *E_Benefit* is infinite.

Therefore, the probability that the stopping rank is not less than k can be written as:

$$\begin{aligned} P(\geq k) =& P(Cost_j < T\_Cost_j : j = 1, ..., k-1) \\ =& \sum_{i=1}^{\infty} P(j < i : j = 1, ..., k-1) \cdot P(T\_Cost_j = i) \\ =& \sum_{i=k}^{\infty} \left(\frac{1}{log_2(i+1)} - \frac{1}{log_2(i+2)} \right) = \frac{1}{log_2(k+1)} \end{aligned} \tag{8}$$

According to the Equation 4, the probability that the user stops at rank k equals to $1/log_2(k+1) - 1/log_2(k+2)$.

Since DCG focuses on cumulative gain, we define the *metric function* as:

$$Function(Benefit_k, Cost_k) = Benefit_k = \sum_{i=1}^{k} benefit_i \tag{9}$$

Then the form of DCG is:

$$\begin{aligned} DCG =& \sum_{k=1}^{\infty} Function(Benefit_k, Cost_k) * P(k) \\ =& \sum_{k=1}^{\infty} P(k) \sum_{i=1}^{k} benefit_i = \sum_{k=1}^{\infty} benefit_k \sum_{i=k}^{\infty} P(i) \\ =& \sum_{k=1}^{\infty} \left(2^{rel_k} - 1\right) \sum_{i=k}^{\infty} \left(\frac{1}{log_2(i+1)} - \frac{1}{log_2(i+2)} \right) \\ =& \sum_{k=1}^{\infty} \frac{2^{rel_k} - 1}{log_2(k+1)} \end{aligned} \tag{10}$$

Considering a truncate depth K, it reduced to the form that introduced in [23]. Note that the transition at line 2 in Equation 10 shows two ways to compute the expectation. $\sum_{i=1}^{k} benefit_i$ is the benefit cumulated from rank 1 to rank k and $P(k)$ is the probability that the user stops at rank k. Therefore, the left side of the transition should be denoted as *expected cumulated benefit*. On the other hand, $benefit_k$ is the benefit at rank k, and $\sum_{i=k}^{\infty} P(i)$ is equivalent to $P(\geq k)$. It is the probability that the stopping rank is not less than k, which also means the probability that the k-th result will be examined. Consequently, the right side of the transition should be denoted as *cumulated expected benefit*.

Similar to DCG, most existing metrics involve summing over the product of a discount function of ranks and a benefit function mapping relevance assessments to numeric utility values, i.e.

$$M = \sum_{k=1}^{K} benefit(rel_k) \cdot discount(k) \tag{11}$$

Based on the example described above, we can clearly see that the $discount(k)$ can be regarded as the probability that the k-th document is examined when a user scans a ranked list from top to bottom. Note that the k-th document being examined means that the user does not stop before rank k. So the discount function is the result of user variety and stopping probability distribution at different ranked results, as we mentioned in Section 2.2.

Here we should state that besides DCG, most other metrics including ERR, AP, RBP, TBG, U-measure etc. can also be derived from the framework given different definitions of $benefit_i$, $cost_i$, $E\_Benefit_k$, T_Cost_k and the *metric function*. Due to space limitations, we will not discuss all of them in detail. Table 1 shows the definitions for them. For simplicity, here we take *interactions* as examining results before the user stops, thus the benefit and cost are calculated based on rank. Although some metrics such as TBG and U-measure focus on time or trailtext rather than rank, we think the simplified cases can explain underlying user models of these metrics from the perspective of benefit and cost to some extent. However, we find that these metrics focus on only one aspect of upper limits for benefit or cost. That is, either *E_Benefit* or *T_Cost* is infinite. On the other hand, these metrics do not consider the situation where *E_Benefit* and *T_Cost* change with interactions. In this paper, we mainly focus on these two points to instantiate metrics from the framework to show its effectiveness.

3.3 Upper Limits for Both Benefit and Cost

In Section 3.2, we show that many existing metrics can be derived from our proposed framework based on the BPM while these metrics focus on only one aspect of upper limits for benefit or cost. However, according to the examples in Figure 1, we find that the stopping criteria vary with search tasks and are usually combinational effects of both benefit and cost factors, which indicates that upper limits for both benefit and cost exist simultaneously. In this section, at first, we consider a simple case where upper limits for both benefit and cost are independent of users and their interactions. In other words, $E\_Benefit_k$ and T_Cost_k are static values, thus denoted as E_B and T_C in this section. Therefore, Equation 5 can be written as:

$$P(\geq k) = P(Benefit_i < E\_B, Cost_i < T\_C : i = 1, ..., k-1) \tag{12}$$

Following a number of metrics like DCG, we adopt a graded $benefit_i$ associated with relevance level of $document_i$ and a $cost_i$ defined as one unit, which means that:

$$benefit_i = 2^{rel_i} - 1, \quad cost_i = 1 \tag{13}$$

Given E_B and T_C are static, we define them as follows:

$$E\_B = \alpha_B * (2^{rel_{max}} - 1), \quad T\_C = \alpha_C * 1 \tag{14}$$

where α_B and α_C are positive parameters for *Expected Benefit* and *Tolerated Cost* and rel_{max} is the maximum relevance level (e.g. $rel_{max} = 3$ if a 4 point scale is used). Approximately, α_B can be regarded as the number of highly relevant documents that a user expects to find, while α_C is the number of documents that the user is willing to examine. Though we do not know the optimal values of α_B and α_C, we suppose that they would be different for different tasks and compare different values of α_B and α_C. As we mentioned before, a *metric function* should be defined to instantiate a metric for evaluation. In this paper, the metrics defined above are called *Static BPM Metrics* and denoted as $SBPM_f(\alpha_B, \alpha_C)$, where α_B and α_C are parameters, while f is the *metric function*. Referring to the existing metrics, we adopt three forms of *metric function*, which are *Benefit* (B), *reciprocal Cost* (1/C) and *Average Benefit* (B/C, i.e. *Benefit* devided by *Cost*), and compare effectiveness of them.

Given the values of α_B and α_C, and the form of *metric function*, we can calculate the value of a *Static BPM Metric* for a ranked list where relevance judgements of top-N results are provided. Algorithm 1 shows the calculation process for *Static BPM Metrics*.

Table 1: Definitions of different components for different metrics. See more details in related researches [12, 30, 33, 34] . Note that here we consider TBG and U-measure as offline metrics given their associated parameters.

	$benefit_i$	$cost_i$	$E\_Benefit$	T_Cost	$P(k)$	$metric\ function$
ERR	$P(benefit_i = 1) = \frac{2^{rel_i - 1}}{2^{rel_{max}}}$	1	1	∞	$\prod_{j=1}^{k-1}\left(1 - \frac{2^{rel_j - 1}}{2^{rel_{max}}}\right)\frac{2^{rel_k - 1}}{2^{rel_{max}}}$	$1/Cost_k$
AP	rel_i	1	$P(E\_Benefit = j) = 1/m,\ j \in [1, 2, \ldots, m]$	∞	$\frac{1}{m}I(rel_k)$	$Benefit_k/Cost_k$

	$benefit_i$	$cost_i$	$E\_Benefit$	T_Cost	$P(k)$	$metric\ function$
DCG	$2^{rel_i} - 1$	1	∞	$P(T\_Cost = j) = \frac{1}{log_2(j+1)} - \frac{1}{log_2(j+2)},\ j \in [1, 2, \ldots, \infty)$	$\frac{1}{log_2(k+1)} - \frac{1}{log_2(k+2)}$	$Benefit_k$
RBP	rel_i	1	∞	$P(T\_Cost = j) = (1-p)p^{j-1},\ j \in [1, 2, \ldots, \infty)$	$(1-p)p^{k-1}$	$Benefit_k * (1-p)$
TBG	$b_{TBG}(i)$	$c_{TBG}(i)$	∞	$P(T\_Cost \le t) = F(t) = 1 - e^{-t\frac{ln2}{h}},\ t \in [0, \infty)$	$F(\sum_{i=1}^{k} cost_i) - F(\sum_{i=1}^{k-1} cost_i)$	$Benefit_k$
U-measure	$gv_l(s_i)$	$\|s_i\|$	∞	$P(T\_Cost = j) = 1/L,\ j \in [1, 2, \ldots, L]$	$\frac{min\{pos(s_k), L\} - min\{pos(s_{k-1}), L\}}{L}$	$Benefit_k$

Note: $b_{TBG}(i) = I(rel_i)P(C = 1|R = 1)P(S = 1|R = 1)$, $c_{TBG}(i) = T_S + T_D(L_i)P(C = 1|R = rel_i)$

Algorithm 1 Calculation process for *Static BPM Metrics.*

Require: $\alpha_B, \alpha_C, f(Benefit, Cost); rel_{max}, rel_i$: $i \in [1, N]$.
Ensure: $SBPM_f(\alpha_B, \alpha_C)$

$E\_B \leftarrow \alpha_B * (2^{rel_{max}} - 1), T\_C \leftarrow \alpha_C * 1;$
$B \leftarrow 0, C \leftarrow 0, i \leftarrow 1$
while $B < E\_B$ **and** $C < T\_C$ **and** $i < N$ **do**
  $i \leftarrow i + 1$
  $B \leftarrow B + (2^{rel_i} - 1), C \leftarrow C + 1$
end while
$SBPM_f(\alpha_B, \alpha_C) = f(B, C)$

Regarding *Static BPM Metrics*, we examine the following research questions based on a test collection (described in Section 4.1) containing user's explicit satisfaction feedbacks and external assessor's relevance judgments:

- **RQ1** Given proper upper limits for benefit and cost and forms of metric function, will *Static BPM Metrics* have a better correlation with user satisfaction feedbacks than existing metrics?
- **RQ2** Are there differences in optimal upper limits for benefit and cost between different taxonomies of queries (e.g. informational queries and navigational queries)?
- **RQ3** Are there differences in optimal forms of *metric function* between different taxonomies of queries?

3.4 Dynamic E_Benefit and T_Cost

As we mentioned before, upper limits for benefit and cost may evolve with the search interaction processes. Therefore, in this section, we will consider a situation where $E\_Benefit_k$ and T_Cost_k are dynamic values depending on interactions. They are described by Equation 2 and Equation 3.

Regarding $E\_Benefit_k$, we assume that when a user finds a relevant document, she may expect to find more relevant documents because she becomes more interested in this query topic and wants to learn more. On the contrary, if a user finds an irrelevant document, the number of relevant documents she expects to find may decrease. Given this assumption, we define a simple linear function for the increment $\Delta E\_Benefit_i$ in Equation 2 as follows:

$$\Delta E\_Benefit_i = h_B * (benefit_i - benefit_{median}) \quad (15)$$

where h_B is a sensitivity parameter for $E\_Benefit$ increment ($h_B > 0$). The larger h_B is, the more likely it is that a user will stop after finding an irrelevant document. As for $benefit_{median}$, it can be written as:

$$benefit_{median} = 2^{rel_{median}} - 1 \quad (16)$$

where rel_{median} is the median relevance level (e.g. $rel_{median} = 1.5$ if a 4 point scale is used).

On the other hand, in terms of T_Cost_k, our hypothesis is that when a user finds a relevant document, she may be willing to examine more documents since the user is more confident to find useful information in the remaining documents. In contrast, if a user finds an irrelevant document, the number of documents she is willing to examine may decrease. Given this assumption, we also define a simple linear function for the increment ΔT_Cost_i in Equation 3 as follows:

$$\Delta T\_Cost_i = h_C * (benefit_i / benefit_{median} - 1) \quad (17)$$

where h_C is a sensitivity parameter for T_Cost increment ($h_C > 0$). Similar to h_B, the larger h_C is, the more likely it is that a user will stop after finding an irrelevant document.

In addition, the initial values of upper limits for benefit and cost are defined in the same way as E_B and T_C:

$$E\_B_0 = \alpha_B * (2^{rel_{max}} - 1), \quad T\_C_0 = \alpha_C * 1 \quad (18)$$

Therefore, compared with *Static BPM Metrics*, the values of *Dynamic BPM Metrics*, which are denoted as $DBPM_f(h_B, h_C, \alpha_B, \alpha_C)$, based on dynamic upper limits for benefit and cost defined above can be calculated by Algorithm 2.

Regarding *Dynamic BPM Metrics*, we want to answer the following research question:

- **RQ4** Do our hypotheses about dynamic upper limits for benefit and cost hold? In other words, given proper values of h_B and h_C, will *Dynamic BPM Metrics* have a better correlation with user satisfaction feedbacks than *Static BPM Metrics*?

4 EXPERIMENTS

Kelly [25] stated that satisfaction can be understood as the fulfillment of a specified desire or goal. Satisfaction is used to reflect users' actual feelings about the system, thus becoming an important criterion in the user-centric evaluation for Web search engines [1, 22]. To show effectiveness of our proposed framework and answer the

Algorithm 2 A calculation process for *Dynamic BPM Metrics.*

```
Require: h_B, h_C; α_B, α_C, f(Benefit, Cost);
    rel_median, rel_max, rel_i: i ∈ [1, N].
Ensure: DBPM_f(h_B, h_C, α_B, α_C)
E_B ← α_B * (2^{rel_max} − 1), T_C ← α_C * 1;
    B ← 0, C ← 0, i ← 1
while B < E_B and C < T_C and i < N do
    i ← i + 1
    B ← B + (2^{rel_i} − 1), C ← C + 1
    E_B ← E_B + h_B * [(2^{rel_i} − 1) − (2^{rel_median} − 1)]
    T_C ← T_C + h_C * [(2^{rel_i} − 1)/(2^{rel_median} − 1) − 1]
end while
DBPM_f(h_B, h_C, α_B, α_C) = f(B, C)
```

Table 2: Statistics of the test collection

#tasks	#SERPs	#participants	#sessions
65	300	98	2685

research questions, we compare *Static BPM Metrics* and *Dynamic BPM Metrics* with a number of existing metrics in terms of correlation between user satisfaction and the metrics based on a test collection containing users' explicit satisfaction feedbacks and assessors' relevance judgements. We will briefly introduce the test collection in Section 4.1 and the results of our experiments will be shown and discussed in Section 4.2.

4.1 Test Collection

In our experiment, the test collection is based on experimental user studies conducted in our previous works [13, 26]. In the user studies, each participant was asked to complete 30 search tasks within about an hour. For each task, after understanding corresponding information need, the participant would be guided to pre-designed search result pages (SERPs) where the query and search results are fixed. The participant was asked to examine the results provided on the SERP and end the search session either if the information need was satisfied or he/she was disappointed with the results. Each time they ended a search session, they were required to provide a five point scaled satisfaction feedback to the session where 5 means the most satisfactory and 1 means the least. Then they would be guided to continue to the next search task. In addition, we invited three professional assessors from a commercial search engine company to label four point scaled relevance scores for all query-result pairs in the experiment. The KAPPA coefficient of their annotation is about 0.7, which can be characterized as a substantial agreement. There are 65 tasks in total, which contains 27 informational queries and 38 navigational queries. The specific statistics of the test collection are shown in Table 2.

4.2 Results

Following Chen et al. [13], considering that satisfaction feedback may be quite subjective, we regularize the satisfaction scores by each participant to Z-scores. For each session, given relevance judgements, we can compute the value of different metrics. In this paper, we use DCG@10, RBP-0.8 (0.8 is the value of the persistence parameter), AP and ERR as representatives of existing metrics. Since we assume that effectiveness of metrics based on the BPM may be affected by different taxonomies of queries, we compare different groups of queries. One group contains 27 informational queries in the test collection, while the other group contains 38 navigational queries.

Table 3: Pearson's Correlations between *Satisfaction Feedbacks* and *Existing Metrics.*

	informational queries	navigational queries
DCG@10	0.493	0.321
RBP-0.8	0.490	0.323
AP	0.400	0.326
ERR	0.393	0.313

4.2.1 Static BPM Metrics. In order to examine **RQ1**, **RQ2** and **RQ3**, first we compute Pearson's correlations between satisfaction feedbacks and existing metrics. The correlations are shown in Table 3. For informational queries, we can see that DCG@10 and RBP-0.8 have better correlations with satisfaction than AP and ERR. However, for navigational queries, all these metrics have similar correlations. Therefore, we use DCG@10 as a baseline to be compared with metrics based on the BPM in the following experiments. Then we compute Pearson's correlations between satisfaction feedbacks and *Static BPM Metrics.* Given that we should tune parameters α_B and α_C for *Static BPM Metrics*, to avoid overfitting and unfair comparison with the baseline, we randomly divide the test collection into two halves. The first half is the training set which containing 620 sessions of informational queries and 723 sessions of navigational queries for tuning parameters, while the other half is the test set which containing 620 sessions of informational queries and 722 sessions of navigational queries for comparing different metrics.

First we try different values of parameters α_B and α_C and different *metric functions* for *Static BPM Metrics* on the training set. The results are shown in Table 4. In order to compare two correlation coefficients (rs), we construct a t-statistic to test the significance of the difference between dependent r's [16]. Note that as long as $\alpha_B > \alpha_C = k$, after examining k documents, $Cost_k$ is equal to T_Cost_k while $Benefit_k$ is smaller than $E\_Benefit_k$. Then users will always stop at rank k, which is the same as the case where $\alpha_B = \alpha_C = k$. Therefore, we omit all the results for the cases where $\alpha_B > \alpha_C$. In addition, if the form of *metric function* is *reciprocal Cost* (i.e. $1/Cost$) and $\alpha_B = \alpha_C = k$, the *metrics* will have the same values (i.e. $1/k$) for all sessions. Then the correlations between satisfaction feedbacks and metrics will make no sense, thus omitted as well.

From the results, we can determine the parameters and the metric function. For informational queries, if we define *metric function* as *Benefit*, when $\alpha_B = 5$ and $\alpha_C = 8$ *or* 9, we can get the best correlation (0.520 or 0.521), which is significantly larger than DCG@10 (0.482) on the training set. For navigational queries, if we define *metric function* as *reciprocal Cost*, when $\alpha_B = 1$ and $\alpha_C = 5$, we can get the best correlation (0.365), which is significantly larger than DCG@10 (0.312) on the training set.

Table 4: Pearson's Correlation between *Satisfaction Feedbacks* and *Static BPM Metrics* for informational and navigitional queries. The first column is the form of *metric function*. Numbers in the second column are values of α_B, while numbers in the second row are values of α_C. * indicates the difference of correlation between the *Static BPM Metric* and *DCG@10* is significant at $p < 0.05$ when the *Static BPM Metric* has a better correlation with *Satisfaction*.

$f(B, C)$		*informational queries*										*navigational queries*									
		1	2	3	4	5	6	7	8	9	10	1	2	3	4	5	6	7	8	9	10
Benefit	1	0.345	0.338	0.279	0.242	0.170	0.029	-0.033	-0.068	-0.102	-0.122	0.335	0.248	0.166	0.088	-0.019	-0.100	-0.179	-0.198	-0.204	-0.225
	2	-	0.385	0.398	0.413	0.419	0.374	0.312	0.283	0.214	0.100	-	0.309	0.329	0.296	0.257	0.211	0.086	0.049	0.006	-0.032
	3	-	-	0.409	0.437	0.468	0.490	0.469	0.481	0.450	0.416	-	-	0.321	0.324	0.319	0.289	0.235	0.188	0.157	0.102
	4	-	-	-	0.433	0.462	0.490	0.501	0.521	0.510	0.502	-	-	-	0.308	0.322	0.309	0.277	0.254	0.228	0.204
	5	-	-	-	-	0.454	0.477	0.488	**0.520***	**0.521***	0.523	-	-	-	-	0.312	0.305	0.284	0.264	0.253	0.238
	6	-	-	-	-	-	0.469	0.475	0.497	0.502	0.502	-	-	-	-	-	0.299	0.279	0.266	0.258	0.247
	7	-	-	-	-	-	-	0.475	0.484	0.491	0.488	-	-	-	-	-	-	0.277	0.266	0.258	0.245
	8	-	-	-	-	-	-	-	0.483	0.478	0.477	-	-	-	-	-	-	-	0.264	0.256	0.246
	9	-	-	-	-	-	-	-	-	0.475	0.468	-	-	-	-	-	-	-	-	0.254	0.244
	10	-	-	-	-	-	-	-	-	-	0.465	-	-	-	-	-	-	-	-	-	0.242
$\frac{1}{Cost}$	1	-	0.313	0.332	0.343	0.353	0.360	0.365	0.365	0.366	0.366	-	0.351	0.355	0.362	**0.365***	0.364	0.363	0.363	0.363	0.363
	2	-	-	0.305	0.329	0.358	0.379	0.393	0.403	0.410	0.415	-	-	0.227	0.250	0.273	0.285	0.293	0.295	0.293	0.293
	3	-	-	-	0.303	0.326	0.350	0.369	0.385	0.400	0.410	-	-	-	0.182	0.213	0.234	0.251	0.263	0.270	0.275
	4	-	-	-	-	0.288	0.318	0.332	0.349	0.370	0.386	-	-	-	-	0.134	0.163	0.190	0.206	0.221	0.231
	5	-	-	-	-	-	0.252	0.293	0.319	0.337	0.355	-	-	-	-	-	0.106	0.119	0.169	0.191	0.207
	6	-	-	-	-	-	-	0.218	0.257	0.299	0.326	-	-	-	-	-	-	0.102	0.117	0.143	0.164
	7	-	-	-	-	-	-	-	0.180	0.198	0.222	-	-	-	-	-	-	-	0.061	0.100	0.120
	8	-	-	-	-	-	-	-	-	0.162	0.158	-	-	-	-	-	-	-	-	0.061	0.100
	9	-	-	-	-	-	-	-	-	-	0.162	-	-	-	-	-	-	-	-	-	0.061
	10	-	-	-	-	-	-	-	-	-	-	-	-	-	-	-	-	-	-	-	-
$\frac{Benefit}{Cost}$	1	0.345	0.363	0.370	0.378	0.391	0.393	0.392	0.392	0.392	0.391	0.335	0.339	0.353	0.354	0.355	0.355	0.353	0.353	0.353	0.353
	2	-	0.385	0.397	0.419	0.445	0.463	0.463	0.466	0.463	0.458	-	0.309	0.319	0.315	0.316	0.312	0.299	0.297	0.300	0.299
	3	-	-	0.409	0.432	0.450	0.465	0.463	0.471	0.466	0.460	-	-	0.321	0.313	0.313	0.302	0.286	0.281	0.280	0.280
	4	-	-	-	0.433	0.449	0.462	0.459	0.469	0.468	0.465	-	-	-	0.308	0.306	0.292	0.271	0.261	0.257	0.255
	5	-	-	-	-	0.454	0.465	0.465	0.475	0.473	0.468	-	-	-	-	0.312	0.296	0.272	0.259	0.254	0.252
	6	-	-	-	-	-	0.469	0.469	0.476	0.473	0.468	-	-	-	-	-	0.299	0.277	0.262	0.253	0.244
	7	-	-	-	-	-	-	0.475	0.483	0.475	0.464	-	-	-	-	-	-	0.277	0.264	0.254	0.240
	8	-	-	-	-	-	-	-	0.483	0.475	0.463	-	-	-	-	-	-	-	0.264	0.254	0.242
	9	-	-	-	-	-	-	-	-	0.475	0.465	-	-	-	-	-	-	-	-	0.254	0.242
	10	-	-	-	-	-	-	-	-	-	0.465	-	-	-	-	-	-	-	-	-	0.242

To answer **RQ1**, we examine correlations with satisfaction on the test set. For informational queries, we set $\alpha_B = 5$ and $\alpha_C = 8$ and choose *Benefit* as *metric function*. The Pearson's correlation between *Static BPM Metric* and satisfaction is 0.553, which is significantly larger than DCG@10 (0.503, $p < 0.01$). For navigational queries, we set $\alpha_B = 1$ and $\alpha_C = 5$ and choose *reciprocal Cost* as *metric function*. The Pearson's correlation is 0.298, which is smaller than DCG@10 (0.329). Based on these results, we can infer that for informational queries, *Static BPM Metrics* can have a better correlation with user satisfaction feedbacks than existing metrics given proper upper limits for benefit and cost and forms of metric function. However, for navigational queries, *Static BPM Metrics* has poor performance.

In terms of α_B, α_C and forms of *metric function*, we can see that there are differences between informational queries and navigational queries. For informational queries, *Benefit* is a good form of *metric function*, while *reciprocal Cost* is better for navigational queries. We suppose that it is because users are usually willing to pay more costs to get more information for informational queries than navigational queries, thus focusing more on *Benefit* for informational queries and *Cost* for navigational queries. In fact, for informational queries, 4-6 are proper values of α_B while 8-10 are proper values of α_C, which indicates that users may examine the whole result list to find a number of relevant documents for informational queries. However, for navigational queries, 1 is the best value of α_B. It suggests that users want to find just an exactly relevant document for navigational queries, which is consistent with the definition of navigational queries in [9]. Note that values of α_C have little effect on correlations between satisfaction and metrics. Our explanation is that the result lists for navigational queries are usually not bad. As a result, users often stop at lower ranks, which are smaller than upper limit for *Cost*.

Now we can answer **RQ2** and **RQ3**. Based on our results, there are differences in optimal upper limits and forms of *metric function* between informational queries and navigational queries. Users are usually willing to pay more costs and expect to obtain more benefits for informational queries than navigational queries. In other words, users searching for informational queries may have higher upper limits for benefit and cost. On the other hand, since users are willing to pay a lot of costs and expect to obtain a great many benefits for informational queries, they will focus on benefit rather than cost. However, for navigational queries, what users want to find is fixed, so they will focus more on their costs. These differences can guide us to choose proper *metric functions* and upper limits for different queries when we use metrics based on the BPM.

4.2.2 Dynamic BPM Metrics. Regarding **RQ4**, we compare effectiveness of *Dynamic BPM Metrics* with *Static BPM Metrics*. Specifically, we compute Pearson's correlations between satisfaction and *Dynamic BPM Metrics*. Here we focus on informational queries because our results shown in Section 4.2.1 suggest that *Static BPM Metrics* have a significantly better correlation with user satisfaction than existing metrics especially for informational queries. Inspired by the results, we define *metric function* as *Benefit*. Note that here we mainly focus on whether dynamic upper limit for benefit or cost affects effectiveness of *BPM Metrics*, rather than how it works. Therefore, we fixed one of them as zero and try different values of the other one from 0 to 1 with a step of 0.1. Based on our results, Table 5 shows two suboptimal cases for correlations between satisfaction and *Dynamic BPM Metrics*. Further analysis of parameters are not discussed and leaved for future work.

First, we examine effectiveness of dynamic upper limit for benefit based on the case where $h_B = 0.2$ and $h_C = 0$. From the results, we can see that when $\alpha_B = 3$ and $\alpha_C = 9$, we can get the best correlation (0.552), which is significantly larger than the optimal

Table 5: Pearson's Correlation between *Satisfaction Feedbacks* and *Dynamic BPM Metrics* for informational queries. The first column is the form of *metric function*. Numbers in the second column are values of α_B, while numbers in the second row are values of α_C. * (or **) indicates the difference of correlation between the *Dynamic BPM Metric* and the *Static BPM Metric* ($\alpha_B = 5, \alpha_C = 8$) is significant at $p < 0.05$ (or $p < 0.01$) when the *Dynamic BPM Metric* has a better correlation with *Satisfaction*.

$f(B, C)$		$h_B = 0.2, h_C = 0$										$h_B = 0, h_C = 0.3$									
		1	2	3	4	5	6	7	8	9	10	1	2	3	4	5	6	7	8	9	10
Benefit	1	0.349	0.393	0.384	0.390	0.420	0.400	0.379	0.376	0.372	0.372	0.367	0.330	0.275	0.243	0.160	0.090	0.027	0.012	-0.021	-0.053
	2	-	0.393	0.414	0.441	0.482	0.512	0.502	0.523	0.502	0.476	-	0.409	0.399	0.391	0.358	0.368	0.341	0.333	0.326	0.246
	3	-	-	0.414	0.444	0.477	0.521	0.529	0.550**	0.552**	0.543	-	-	0.423	0.434	0.454	0.480	0.477	0.492	0.481	0.453
	4	-	-	-	0.444	0.469	0.495	0.509	0.542*	0.539	0.541	-	-	-	0.446	0.484	0.498	0.507	0.525	0.526	0.516
	5	-	-	-	-	0.469	0.485	0.492	0.519	0.522	0.518	-	-	-	-	0.489	0.502	0.522	0.543	0.548	0.540
	6	-	-	-	-	-	0.485	0.488	0.497	0.508	0.507	-	-	-	-	-	0.489	0.513	0.532	0.535	0.527
	7	-	-	-	-	-	-	0.488	0.497	0.490	0.485	-	-	-	-	-	-	0.505	0.522	0.523	0.514
	8	-	-	-	-	-	-	-	0.497	0.490	0.479	-	-	-	-	-	-	-	0.511	0.511	0.502
	9	-	-	-	-	-	-	-	-	0.490	0.479	-	-	-	-	-	-	-	-	0.501	0.492
	10	-	-	-	-	-	-	-	-	-	0.479	-	-	-	-	-	-	-	-	-	0.487

Static BPM Metric (0.537) where $\alpha_B = 5$ and $\alpha_C = 8$. This may indicate that dynamic upper limit for benefit is effective to describe some aspects that *Static BPM Metrics* do not consider. When a user start search, she wants to get some useful information. If the user finds a relevant document, she may expect to find more relevant documents. However, if the user find an irrelevant document, the benefits she expects may decrease. We explain it with change of task difficulty perceived by the user. Then, we examine effectiveness of dynamic upper limit for cost based on the case where $h_B = 0$ and $h_C = 0.3$. There are no significant differences of correlations between *Dynamic BPM Metrics* and the optimal *Static BPM Metric*, which suggests that the costs users are willing to pay may not be affected by the relevances of documents they have examined before. We think it is due to the fact that in the experimental user studies, queries and SERPs are fixed and not allowed to change. Participants are usually willing to examine all the results if needed, thus have relatively static upper limits for cost. Based on the results, our answer for **RQ4** is that our hypotheses about dynamic upper limits for benefit and cost partially hold. Considering dynamic upper limit for benefit, effectiveness of *Dynamic BPM Metrics* can be improved. However, participants in experimental user studies usually have static upper limits for cost. We may have to leave further analysis in practical user behavior data set for future work.

5 RELATED WORK

In order to evaluate user satisfaction of Web search, many evaluation metrics are designed with different user models. In these models, when a user ends a search session is one of the prime concerns because it is highly related to both benefit and cost estimation.

The simple model of RBP [30] assumes that users progress from one result in the ranked list to the next with *persistence p* and end their examination with probability *1 - p*. The cascade model proposed by Craswell [18] assumes that a user views search results from top to bottom and has a certain probability of being satisfied at each position. Once the user is satisfied with a document, he/she terminates the search. Based on this model, ERR [12] defines the probability that a user is satisfied with a document to be related with relevance of the document. Considering realistic user behavior, some works [14, 37] combine evaluation metrics with click models, and estimate the probability of leaving a search session given the relevance of the clicked document from click logs. In [29], Moffat et al. explore the link between user models and metrics and use a function $C_M(i)$ to describe the conditional probability that users proceed to depth $i+1$ once they have reached depth i in the ranking. They analyze different forms of $C_M(i)$ for different user models. However, these models lack insights into factors which affect when users stop search sessions.

Some theories of search and search behavior are proposed to describe how users interact with search systems. A well known conceptual model of information seeking is the Berry Picker model proposed by Bates [7], which draws an analogy between a searcher and a forager. Based on this model, Information Foraging Theory (IFT) [31] predicts how long a forager should stay in a patch before moving on to the next patch. IFT assumes that foragers wish to maximize their gain per unit of time. More recently, Fuhr [20] extendes the PRP [32] to consider a series of interactions in the interactive Probability Ranking Principle (iPRP), which accounts for the different costs and benefits associated with particular choices when ranking documents. In [8], Birchler and Butler explain how Stigler's theory [35] can be applied to search in order to predict when a user should stop examining results in a ranked list. However, they did not conduct any empirical study to verify whether the theory was consistent with users' actual behavior. Then Azzopardi suggests that Production Theory [36] could be used to model the search process instead and proposes Search Economic Theory (SET) [3] to model ad-hoc topic retrieval. In [4], Azzopardi et al. examine three theories and show that the models are complementary to each other but operate at different levels. Given these theories, it is possible to explain why users behave the way they do. However, these theories are not applied to developing Web search evaluation.

6 CONCLUSION AND FUTURE WORK

In summary, in this work, we introduce a *Bejeweled Player Model* to simulate users' search interaction processes and explain the complex stopping criterion for search sessions. In the BPM, we suppose that a user stops when he/she either has found sufficient useful information or has no more patience to continue. Given this assumption, we propose a new evaluation framework based on upper limits for both benefit and cost. Then we show how to instantiate a metric from the framework and demonstrate that some existing metrics can be derived from the framework considering one-sided case of the stopping criterion. To show effectiveness of our proposed framework, we compare *Static BPM Metrics* and *Dynamic BPM Metrics* with a number of existing metrics in terms of correlation between user satisfaction and the metrics based on a test collection containing users' explicit satisfaction feedbacks and assessors' relevance judgements. The results show that, given proper upper limits for benefit and cost and forms of metric function, *Static*

BPM Metrics and *Dynamic BPM Metrics* have a better correlation with user satisfaction feedbacks than existing metrics, especially for informational queries. In addition, there are differences in optimal upper limits and forms of metric function between informational queries and navigational queries. We also compare effectiveness of *Static BPM Metrics* and *Dynamic BPM Metrics*, and we find that considering dynamic upper limit for benefit may further improve effectiveness of *BPM Metrics*.

Our work has a few limitations: (1) We make some simplified assumptions for *Static BPM Metrics* and *Dynamic BPM Metrics*. In the future work, we plan to explore more complex situations for them. For instance, we can consider upper limits as latent variables and estimate them with large scale user logs. (2) Our test collection is based on an experimental user study where users examine results on fixed SERPs. In fact, there is a natural upper limit for cost (i.e. 10 results for each SERP), which constrains effectiveness of upper limit for cost in our framework. We would like to use realistic user logs in the future. (3) We only measure correlation with user satisfaction to show effectiveness of the framework, but the usual comparison in IR is to see how well we can determine the quality of one retrieval system versus another. We will apply the framework to this comparison to see the performance of the metrics.

ACKNOWLEDGMENTS

This work is supported by Natural Science Foundation of China (Grant No. 61622208, 61532011, 61672311) and National Key Basic Research Program (2015CB358700).

REFERENCES

[1] Azzah Al-Maskari, Mark Sanderson, and Paul Clough. 2007. The relationship between IR effectiveness measures and user satisfaction. In *Proceedings of the 30th annual international ACM SIGIR conference on Research and development in information retrieval*. ACM, 773–774.
[2] Paavo Arvola, Jaana Kekäläinen, and Marko Junkkari. 2010. Expected reading effort in focused retrieval evaluation. *Information Retrieval* 13, 5 (2010), 460–484.
[3] Leif Azzopardi. 2011. The economics in interactive information retrieval. In *Proceedings of the 34th international ACM SIGIR conference on Research and development in Information Retrieval*. ACM, 15–24.
[4] Leif Azzopardi and Guido Zuccon. 2015. An analysis of theories of search and search behavior. In *Proceedings of the 2015 International Conference on The Theory of Information Retrieval*. ACM, 81–90.
[5] Leif Azzopardi and Guido Zuccon. 2016. An analysis of the cost and benefit of search interactions. In *Proceedings of the 2016 ACM on International Conference on the Theory of Information Retrieval*. ACM, 59–68.
[6] Peter Bailey, Alistair Moffat, Falk Scholer, and Paul Thomas. 2015. User variability and IR system evaluation. In *Proceedings of the 38th International ACM SIGIR Conference on Research and Development in Information Retrieval*. ACM, 625–634.
[7] Marcia J Bates. 1989. The design of browsing and berrypicking techniques for the online search interface. *Online review* 13, 5 (1989), 407–424.
[8] Urs Birchler and Monika Bütler. 2007. *Information economics*. Routledge.
[9] Andrei Broder. 2002. A taxonomy of web search. In *ACM Sigir forum*, Vol. 36. ACM, 3–10.
[10] Ben Carterette. 2011. System effectiveness, user models, and user utility: a conceptual framework for investigation. In *Proceedings of the 34th international ACM SIGIR conference on Research and development in Information Retrieval*. ACM, 903–912.
[11] Irina Ceaparu, Jonathan Lazar, Katie Bessiere, John Robinson, and Ben Shneiderman. 2004. Determining causes and severity of end-user frustration. *International journal of human-computer interaction* 17, 3 (2004), 333–356.
[12] Olivier Chapelle, Donald Metlzer, Ya Zhang, and Pierre Grinspan. 2009. Expected reciprocal rank for graded relevance. In *Proceedings of the 18th ACM conference on Information and knowledge management*. ACM, 621–630.
[13] Ye Chen, Yiqun Liu, Ke Zhou, Meng Wang, Min Zhang, and Shaoping Ma. 2015. Does vertical bring more satisfaction?: Predicting search satisfaction in a heterogeneous environment. In *Proceedings of the 24th ACM International on Conference on Information and Knowledge Management*. ACM, 1581–1590.
[14] Aleksandr Chuklin, Pavel Serdyukov, and Maarten De Rijke. 2013. Click model-based information retrieval metrics. In *Proceedings of the 36th international ACM SIGIR conference on Research and development in information retrieval*. ACM, 493–502.
[15] Cyril W Cleverdon, Jack Mills, and Michael Keen. 1966. Factors determining the performance of indexing systems. (1966).
[16] Jacob Cohen, Patricia Cohen, Stephen G West, and Leona S Aiken. 2013. *Applied multiple regression/correlation analysis for the behavioral sciences*. Routledge.
[17] William S Cooper. 1973. On selecting a measure of retrieval effectiveness. *Journal of the American Society for Information Science* 24, 2 (1973), 87–100.
[18] Nick Craswell, Onno Zoeter, Michael Taylor, and Bill Ramsey. 2008. An experimental comparison of click position-bias models. In *Proceedings of the 2008 International Conference on Web Search and Data Mining*. ACM, 87–94.
[19] Steve Fox, Kuldeep Karnawat, Mark Mydland, Susan Dumais, and Thomas White. 2005. Evaluating implicit measures to improve web search. *ACM Transactions on Information Systems (TOIS)* 23, 2 (2005), 147–168.
[20] Norbert Fuhr. 2008. A probability ranking principle for interactive information retrieval. *Information Retrieval* 11, 3 (2008), 251–265.
[21] Ahmed Hassan, Ryen W White, Susan T Dumais, and Yi-Min Wang. 2014. Struggling or exploring?: disambiguating long search sessions. In *Proceedings of the 7th ACM international conference on Web search and data mining*. ACM, 53–62.
[22] Scott B Huffman and Michael Hochster. 2007. How well does result relevance predict session satisfaction?. In *Proceedings of the 30th annual international ACM SIGIR conference on Research and development in information retrieval*. ACM, 567–574.
[23] Kalervo Järvelin and Jaana Kekäläinen. 2002. Cumulated gain-based evaluation of IR techniques. *ACM Transactions on Information Systems (TOIS)* 20, 4 (2002), 422–446.
[24] Thorsten Joachims. 2002. Optimizing search engines using clickthrough data. In *Proceedings of the eighth ACM SIGKDD international conference on Knowledge discovery and data mining*. ACM, 133–142.
[25] Diane Kelly and others. 2009. Methods for evaluating interactive information retrieval systems with users. *Foundations and Trends® in Information Retrieval* 3, 1–2 (2009), 1–224.
[26] Yiqun Liu, Ye Chen, Jinhui Tang, Jiashen Sun, Min Zhang, Shaoping Ma, and Xuan Zhu. 2015. Different users, different opinions: Predicting search satisfaction with mouse movement information. In *Proceedings of the 38th International ACM SIGIR Conference on Research and Development in Information Retrieval*. ACM, 493–502.
[27] Jiaxin Mao, Yiqun Liu, Ke Zhou, Jian-Yun Nie, Jingtao Song, Min Zhang, Shaoping Ma, Jiashen Sun, and Hengliang Luo. 2016. When does Relevance Mean Usefulness and User Satisfaction in Web Search?. In *Proceedings of the 39th International ACM SIGIR conference on Research and Development in Information Retrieval*. ACM, 463–472.
[28] Stefano Mizzaro. 1997. Relevance: The whole history. *JASIS* 48, 9 (1997), 810–832.
[29] Alistair Moffat, Paul Thomas, and Falk Scholer. 2013. Users versus models: What observation tells us about effectiveness metrics. In *Proceedings of the 22nd ACM international conference on Information & Knowledge Management*. ACM, 659–668.
[30] Alistair Moffat and Justin Zobel. 2008. Rank-biased precision for measurement of retrieval effectiveness. *ACM Transactions on Information Systems (TOIS)* 27, 1 (2008), 2.
[31] Peter Pirolli and Stuart Card. 1999. Information foraging. *Psychological review* 106, 4 (1999), 643.
[32] Stephen E Robertson. 1977. The probability ranking principle in IR. *Journal of documentation* 33, 4 (1977), 294–304.
[33] Tetsuya Sakai and Zhicheng Dou. 2013. Summaries, ranked retrieval and sessions: A unified framework for information access evaluation. In *Proceedings of the 36th international ACM SIGIR conference on Research and development in information retrieval*. ACM, 473–482.
[34] Mark D Smucker and Charles LA Clarke. 2012. Time-based calibration of effectiveness measures. In *Proceedings of the 35th international ACM SIGIR conference on Research and development in information retrieval*. ACM, 95–104.
[35] George J Stigler. 1961. The economics of information. *Journal of political economy* 69, 3 (1961), 213–225.
[36] Hal R Varian and Jack Repcheck. 2010. *Intermediate microeconomics: a modern approach*. Vol. 6. WW Norton & Company New York.
[37] Emine Yilmaz, Milad Shokouhi, Nick Craswell, and Stephen Robertson. 2010. Expected browsing utility for web search evaluation. In *Proceedings of the 19th ACM international conference on Information and knowledge management*. ACM, 1561–1564.
[38] Yinglong Zhang, Jin Zhang, Matthew Lease, and Jacek Gwizdka. 2014. Multidimensional relevance modeling via psychometrics and crowdsourcing. In *Proceedings of the 37th international ACM SIGIR conference on Research & development in information retrieval*. ACM, 435–444.
[39] Guido Zuccon. 2016. Understandability biased evaluation for information retrieval. In *European Conference on Information Retrieval*. Springer, 280–292.

Evaluating Mobile Search with Height-Biased Gain

Cheng Luo
luochengleo@gmail.com
DCST, Tsinghua University
Beijing, China

Yiqun Liu*
yiqunliu@tsinghua.edu.cn
DCST, Tsinghua University
Beijing, China

Tetsuya Sakai
tetsuyasakai@acm.org
Waseda University
Tokyo, Japan

Fan Zhang
franky94@gmail.com
DCST, Tsinghua University
Beijing, China

Min Zhang
z-m@tsinghua.edu.cn
DCST, Tsinghua University
Beijing, China

Shaoping Ma
msp@tsinghua.edu.cn
DCST, Tsinghua University
Beijing, China

ABSTRACT

Mobile search engine result pages (SERPs) are becoming highly visual and heterogenous. Unlike the traditional ten-blue-link SERPs for desktop search, different verticals and cards occupy different amounts of space within the small screen. Hence, traditional retrieval measures that regard the SERP as a ranked list of homogeneous items are not adequate for evaluating the overall quality of mobile SERPs. Specifically, we address the following new problems in mobile search evaluation: (1) Different retrieved items have different heights within the scrollable SERP, unlike a ten-blue-link SERP in which results have similar heights with each other. Therefore, the traditional rank-based decaying functions are not adequate for mobile search metrics. (2) For some types of verticals and cards, the information that the user seeks is already embedded in the snippet, which makes clicking on those items to access the landing page unnecessary. (3) For some results with complex sub-components (and usually a large height), the total gain of the results cannot be obtained if users only read part of their contents. The benefit brought by the result is affected by user's reading behavior and the internal gain distribution (over the height) should be modeled to get a more accurate estimation. To tackle these problems, we conduct a lab-based user study to construct suitable user behavior model for mobile search evaluation. From the results, we find that the geometric heights of user's browsing trails can be adopted as a good signal of user effort. Based on these findings, we propose a new evaluation metric, Height-Biased Gain, which is calculated by summing up the product of gain distribution and discount factors that are both modeled in terms of result height. To evaluate the effectiveness of the proposed metric, we compare the agreement of evaluation metrics with side-by-side user preferences on a test collection composed of four mobile search engines. Experimental results show that HBG agrees with user preferences 85.33% of the time, which is better than all existing metrics.

*Corresponding Author

SIGIR'17, , August 07-11, 2017, Shinjuku, Tokyo, Japan.

ACM ISBN 978-1-4503-5022-8/17/08...$15.00
http://dx.doi.org/10.1145/3077136.3080795

CCS CONCEPTS

• **Information systems → Evaluation of retrieval results**; *Retrieval on mobile devices*; *Environment-specific retrieval*;

KEYWORDS

evaluation metric; mobile search; user behavior

1 INTRODUCTION

With the rapid growth of mobile device usage, search engine users are able to take action to address their information needs almost anytime and anywhere, particularly with smartphones. The massive shift in search engine consumers' behavior [1] forces both industry and academia to redesign existing technologies in the context of mobile search.

Search evaluation sits at the center of Information Retrieval (IR) researches. It helps researchers measure the quality of search results and the search users' experiences. Compared to *user-oriented* evaluation methods which directly model key aspects of users' interaction process, we believe that *system-oriented* evaluation is still a necessity due to its simplicity and repeatability. In the Cranfield-style evaluation paradigm [8], once the relevance judgment is done, it can be easily reused. The evaluation metrics can be calculated with little effort and time. While user-oriented evaluation based on user study or online A/B test may take a few days or weeks, system-oriented evaluation might be more appropriate for iterative development of search engines.

Mobile search is different from desktop search in several aspects: First, the distribution of query categories is different [3, 14, 34]. Second, compared with desktop screens, mobile devices present much less content at once due to the limited screen size. Thus mobile users have to incur a higher interaction cost in order to access the same amount of information. On the other hand, modern mobile devices are usually equipped with mobile touch interactions (MTIs) [9], which provides opportunities to model users' rich interactions during search.

For both mobile and desktop search, today's search engines return far richer results than a *ten-blue-link* SERP. The results may be retrieved from various vertical information resources including news, shopping, images, knowledge cards, etc. and then federated together with traditional organic results to serve the search users. For example, Figure 1 presents the search engine result page of query *"fantastic beasts and where to find them"* (a 2016 movie) from a mobile search engine, we can see the first result of the SERP looks like a card and it includes the basic profile of the film, cast, introduction, reviews from online communities and etc. The snippet of this result is quite different from a traditional textual result, which usually contains a title, a URL and a document summary of one or two sentences. Compared with a traditional result, it occupies a much large area. The vertical results with rich information would help the user find relevant information on SERPs with minimal effort. Modern search engines often provide "direct answers" in response to head queries, so that the user will not have to click on it to access the landing page.

Figure 1: An example of SERP including multiple vertical results (Query: *"fantastic beasts and where to find them"*).

Due to these differences brought by "mobile v.s. desktop" and "ten-blue-links v.s. heterogenous results", traditional system-oriented evaluation method is facing a few serious challenges on mobile platforms:

Challenge 1 In mobile search, the results are heterogeneous in nature and presented in different styles. The results may occupy different percentages of the screen size, which probably means that the user's effort in examining the results varies accordingly. This poses a direct challenge to traditional rank-based evaluation measures, since the basic assumption behind them is that the ranked items and the effort spent on inspecting them are homogeneous. For mobile SERPs that include visual and heterogeneous contents, considering the height of each ranked item may be necessary.

Challenge 2 Compared with desktop search, verticals and cards are more frequently federated into mobile SERPs. In many circumstances, these results contain enough information for users' information needs. Therefore, there is no need to visit the corresponding landing pages and the effort to access useful information is reduced. However, most existing metrics do not take this factor into consideration.

Challenge 3 The internal structures of many vertical and card results are much more complex than traditional ten-blue-link results. The information contained in these complex results is also distributed among different sub-components. Therefore, it is not reasonable to assume that a user will obtain all the gain brought by the complex result once she reads one or a few sub-components. However, most existing metrics do not take the distribution of benefit/cost within results into consideration.

In the present study, we tackle the above three challenges by proposing a new evaluation metric for mobile search environment, named Height-Biased Gain (HBG). Basically, HBG follows the framework similar to Normalized Discounted Cumulative Gain (nDCG) [12], Rank Biased Precision (RBP) [24], Expected Reciprocal Rank (ERR) [6] and Q-measure [27]. It can be expressed as cumulated gain over the browsing trail of a ranked list.

With HBG, we try to address the problem of mobile search evaluation by making the following contributions:

(1) We propose to use the height of a *user browsing trail*, to estimate users' effort when they are involved in mobile search. The geometric height naturally takes both textual and non-textual contents into consideration and is therefore more appropriate to deal with heterogeneous results in mobile search (**Challenge 1**).

(2) We propose to consider a new variable, *Click Necessity* to model the cases in which users do not need to visit landing pages to derive relevant information (**Challenge 2**). We show with a labeling experiment that Click Necessity can be easily annotated with minimal effort. It can then be incorporated into HBG to improve mobile search evaluation.

(3) We investigate the internal gain distribution within complex search results and find that users' reading behavior in these results can be modeled with an inverse Gaussian distribution. It is then possible for HBG to model the benefit/cost within complex results (**Challenge 3**).

The remainder of this paper is organized as follows. We introduce our proposed metric, HBG, in Section 2. We calibrate a series of parameters in our model by conducting a small scale of user study in Section 3. Then we compare the performance of HBG and traditional rank-based metrics in predicting user performance on a test collection in Section 4. Before concluding this paper, we review related studies in Section 5.

2 HEIGHT-BIASED GAIN

2.1 A generic framework of metrics

A number of traditional evaluation metrics such as nDCG [12], RBG [24], Q-measure [27], TBG [33], U-measure [30] etc. can be expressed in a generic framework [4, 40] as:

$$\frac{1}{N}\sum_{k=1}^{\infty} g_k d_k \tag{1}$$

where N is a normalization factor. g_k denotes the utility that the user derives from the k-th result and it is usually calculated by mapping the binary/multi-graded relevance assessment to a numeric value. d_k indicates the discount factor of the k-th result, which is often viewed as the probability that a user scans down a ranked list, growing less interested, and stops at rank k.

Our proposed metric basically follows this framework. As suggested by Carterette [4], model-based measures are actually composed from the following three underlying models:

1. *Browsing Model*, which describes how a user interacts with a ranked result list;
2. *Document Utility Model*, describing how a user derives utility from individual relevant documents;
3. *Utility Accumulation Model*, which describes how a user accumulates utility in the course of browsing.

In the following parts of this section, we introduce our proposed metric, Height-Biased Gain (HBG), by describing the above three underlying models.

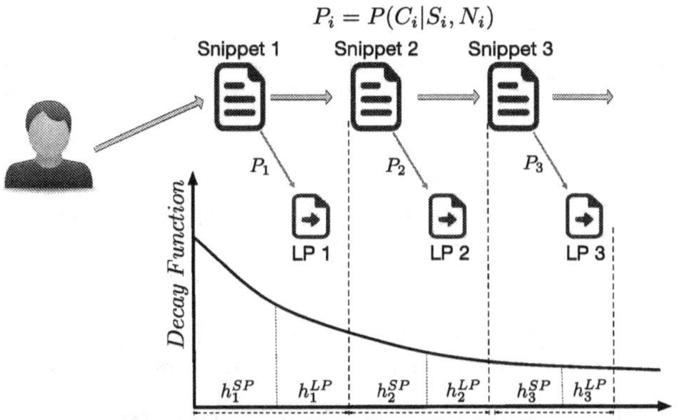

Figure 2: An illustration of user model: a user works her way down, and the value of relevant information decays with the cumulated height of viewed contents.

2.2 Browsing Model

In this study, we adopt a simple browsing model: as shown in Figure 2, the user starts at the first result of the ranking list and works her way down. For each result, the user first examines the snippet on SERP, which occupies a height of h_i^{SP} on her screen. Based on the *Snippet Relevance* (S_i) and *Click Necessity* (N_i) of the result (see Section 2.2.1), the user clicks (C_i) the hyperlink with a probability $P(C_i|S_i, N_i)$ to get more information. Otherwise, she can directly continue to examine the snippet of the next result. For the visit on the landing page of the i-th result, the user may view only part of, or the entire landing page, which is as high as h_i^{LP} on the user's screen. Eventually, the user will stop when she feels satisfied or exhausted.

2.2.1 *Click Necessity.*

In previous evaluation metrics such as TBG [33], EBU [39], U-measure [30] and ERR [6], the probability of click is assumed to only depend on the relevance of document (R_i). We argue that for a heterogeneous result, the snippet contains much more information than a traditional textual summary. The probability of click may also be related to the presentation of a result. For example, Figure 3 presents several results of a query *"iphone 7 plus specs"* from a commercial search engine on both mobile device and desktop. Consider the first and the second result on mobile screen: the first result presents much more detailed information to satisfy the user directly. However, it is more likely that users will not click the first result's URL as much as the second result's.

To solve the problem in **Challenge 2**, we formally introduce a new variable, *Click Necessity*, to model the impact of result presentation on clicks. *Click Necessity* is defined as follows:

Definition 2.1. Click Necessity means, given the presentation of a retrieved item, how necessary it is to click it and visit the landing page to collect relevant information.

Document Relevance and Click Necessity describe different perspectives on a certain result: *Document Relevance* puts the emphasis on how appropriate the content of the result is for the query, while *Click Necessity* addresses the ability that the presentation of the result could fulfill users' information needs within the SERP.

With *Click Necessity*, we model the probability of click as $P(C_i|S_i, N_i)$. Following the Yilmaz et al.'s approach [39] we replace the relevance of snippet (S_i) with the relevance of document (R_i), because previous work suggests that the probability of clicks is highly correlated with the relevance of corresponding document.

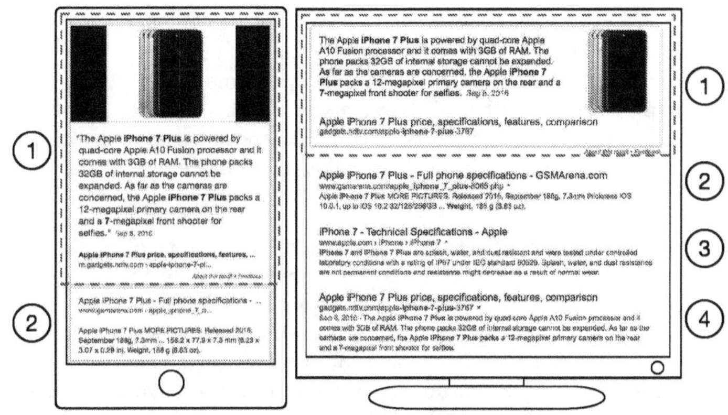

Figure 3: Results of different click necessities on mobile device and desktop (Query: "iphone 7 plus specs")

$$P(C_i|S_i, N_i) \approx P(C_i|R_i, N_i) \tag{2}$$

In our experiment, we collected multi-level click necessity judgments following similar settings of relevance judgment in TREC [36]. Experimental results demonstrate that the click necessity could be assessed offline with relatively high inner-consistency. Details will follow in Section 3.3.

2.2.2 *User Browsing Trail.*

Recall that our model implicitly assumes that a user scans the ranked list from top to bottom until she stops at a certain position [5]. This assumption, named *linear traversal*, forms the basis of virtually most existing evaluation metrics. Unlike rank-based evaluation metrics, TBG pays attention to the fact that the time spent at each rank differs, depending especially on document length and users' reading speed [33]. U-measure proposed by Sakai and Dou [30] used the concept of *trailtext* as a simple concatenation of the text read by users, for example, `''Snippet1 Ad2 Snippet3 Fulltext3''`. This measure does not rely on the linear traversal assumption.

Inspired by the idea of *trailtext*, we introduce *user browsing trail* in our framework. Suppose that we have observed that the user has viewed a series of contents in a search task. We can then define the user browsing trail as a simple concatenation of these contents. For example, if the user examined the first snippet, the second snippet and then visited the landing page of the second result, her browsing trail could be organized as `''Snippet1 Snippet2 LandingPage2''`. The height of each item in this trail, as shown in the mobile screen, can then be accumulated.

We use the geometric height of each viewed item as the basis for designing our evaluation measure based on the following considerations: First, although modern websites provide automatic screen adjustments for mobile users, reading a lot of contents on mobile screen is still difficult. If a user wants to read a document, she has to move the contents to the center of her viewport by pressing navigation buttons or scrolling on screen with fingers. This kind of "locate and read" would be done over and over again since the visible area on screen is quite small. In Figure 3, on mobile device there are only two results and the first one occupies about 3/4 of the viewport. The desktop actually presents the same list of results but the viewport accommodates four results and the first one only occupies about 1/3 of the screen area. Hence, geometric height may be a better indicator of the user's effort on mobile devices than the rank. Second, the trailtext of U-measure can only handle textual information. To accommodate the evaluation of SERPs that contain highly visual and other non-texual (as well as textual) contents, the height of each item seems a natural choice for replacing the U-measure's "number of characters/words read." Third, compared with time in TBG, heights of contents are not user specific and can be estimated offline. This makes HBG more appropriate for system-oriented evaluation.

2.2.3 Discount Factor. In the generic framework of evaluation metrics (Equation 1), the discount factor d_k could be viewed as the probability that the user stops at a specific rank.

In traditional evaluation metrics, some discount functions depend dynamically on relevance of previously viewed documents (ERR [6] and the Sakai/Robertson *Rank-Biased Normalized Cumulative Utility* measure [31]): whenever a relevant document is found, the value of another relevant document found later is discounted. This property is recognized as *diminishing return* [5], which is in contrast with some other metrics such as nDCG and Q-measure that adopt a static discount factor based on the rank.

TBG [33] is an evaluation metric based on time rather than ranks. The discount factor in TBG is modeled as the probability that the user continues until a specific time. In M-measure [15] and U-measure [30], the discount factor is a linear function based on the length of trailtext and the offset within trailtext.

In this study, we assume that the value of a relevant information unit decays with the cumulated height of the contents the user has viewed. Hence we propose a discount function expressed in terms of *height*, $D(h)$, where h indicates the offset in *user browsing trail*. $D(h)$ could be viewed as the probability that the user continues until the cumulated height of her viewed content is as high as h. Thus, $D(0) = 1$ and when $h \longrightarrow \infty$, $D(h)$ decreases to 0 monotonically.

$D(h)$ takes the difference in results' heights into consideration (**Challenge 1**). If the height of a snippet become larger, its height in the user browsing trail would probably grow, then the value of the information after this result would be discounted more. This is in line with our intuition, because it is more likely that a user would get bored or tired after reading a longer snippet, compared to a shorter one. We will provide estimations of $D(h)$ based on the the users' behavior in our user study (see Section 3).

2.3 Document Utility Model of HBG

In previous rank-based metrics, the utility (gain) of a document is usually treated as an atomic unit. That is to say, the assumption behind the evaluation metrics is that the user will get all the utility of the document once she reaches it.

While the general definition of TBG accumulates gain over time, the actual instantiation of it considered by Smucker and Clarke [33] takes the following form:

$$\frac{1}{N}\sum_{k=1}^{\infty} g_k D(T(k)) \tag{3}$$

where g_k denotes the gain of the k-th result and $T(k)$ is modeled as the time to reach the result. That is, TBG assumes that, whenever the user accesses the k-th result, he acquires the gain of the entire result. However, as was discussed in **Challenge 3**, this is too strong an assumption especially for mobile devices with a small screen, in which heterogeneous contents may be presented. It is possible that the user actually obtains information from some parts of the result. This was the motivation for us to consider an internal gain distribution over the snippet and landing page.

In our framework, we assume that the utility of a certain result is distributed over its user browsing trail, including both the snippet and the landing page. The distribution is denoted as $G_k(h)$, then

$$\int_0^{h_k} G_k(h)\,dh = g_k \tag{4}$$

where g_k is the gain value of the k-th result, h_k denotes the height of the k-th results within the user browsing trail.

In practical application, h_k could be estimated with the heights of the snippet and landing page. The overall utility value, g_k, could be presented as a relevance score [4]. Our proposed Document Utility Model is able to handle different assumptions of utility distribution.

2.4 Utility Accumulation Model of HBG

Based on our Browsing Model and Document Utility Model, we introduce the proposed evaluation metric, Height-Biased Gain (HBG), by cumulating the utility over a user browsing trail.

Consider a user working her way down, with both gain and discount factors expressed in terms of height. An equivalent of Equation 1 could be expressed as:

$$\frac{1}{N}\int_0^{\infty}\frac{dG(h)}{dh} * D(h)dh \tag{5}$$

where $G(h)$ denotes the cumulative gain experienced by the user at height h. Note that we accumulate the gains over heights, in contrast to TBG which accumulates them over time [33].

If we look at the gain collected on each result, let dg_k be the discounted gain of the k-th result, the metric could be written as:

$$\frac{1}{N}\sum_{k=1}^{\infty} dg_k \tag{6}$$

Here, the discounted gain at rank k is given by:

$$dg_k = \int_{start_k}^{start_k+h_k} G_k(h - start_k) * D(h)dh \tag{7}$$

where $start_k$ and h_k denotes the offset of the result in user browsing trail and the height of the k-th result respectively.

3 CALIBRATION

3.1 Estimation of user browsing trail

The central idea of HBG is to cumulate document utility over a user browsing trail, where both the gain and the discount factor are expressed in terms of height.

Our Browsing Model assumes that a user works down a ranked result list in order. The *user browsing trail* is a concatenation of all the content she has viewed. If we have observations about the user's behavior, for example, eye movement recorded by eyetrackers, or mobile touch interactions (MTIs) collected on SERP, the user's browsing trail could be easily constructed by summing up the segments viewed by user. An alternative method is inferring user browsing trail based on querylogs from online users.

However, in practice, user behavior information may be unavailable. Therefore, we introduce a method to estimate the height of the user browsing trail.

Consider a user examine the k-th result on a SERP. The *expected viewed height* (evh_k) of this result in user browsing trail could be represented as:

$$evh_k = f^{SP}\left(h_k^{SP}\right) + P(C_k|R_k, N_k) * f^{LP}\left(h_k^{LP}\right) \tag{8}$$

where h_k^{SP} and h_k^{LP} denotes the height of the snippet and landing page respectively. $f^{SP}(h)$ and $f^{LP}(h)$ are the examining models of the user on the snippet and landing page, which enable us to handle different user behavior assumptions. For example, if we assume that the user would only examine at most the first viewport of the landing page, the browsing model on Landing Page is

$$f^{LP}\left(h_k^{LP}\right) = \min\left(H_{viewport}, h_k^{LP}\right) \quad (9)$$

where $H_{viewport}$ is the height of the viewport.

The evh_k could be interpreted as the sum of two parts: we assume that the user would first examine the snippet on SERP, the expected viewed height $evh_k^{SP} = f^{SP}\left(h_k^{SP}\right)$. Then she may visit the landing page with a probability $P(C_k|R_k, N_k)$ and the expected viewed height on landing page is $evh_k^{LP} = P(C_k|R_k, N_k) * f^{LP}\left(h_k^{LP}\right)$.

Based on evh_k, the offset of each result in user browsing trail (see Section 2.4) could be estimated by summing up the expected viewed heights of the previous $k-1$ results.

$$start_k = \sum_{i=1}^{k-1} evh_i \quad (10)$$

Following previous work [33], we adopt an idealized user model representing an average user and provide a method to estimate the height of users' browsing trail. Going beyond the traditional assumption that the probability of click depends on the relevance of the document, we want to investigate whether and how the click necessity influences click behavior together with document relevance.

While traditional discount functions are based on rank or the time to reach the result, our proposed decaying function, $D(h)$, is actually defined as the probability a user continues when her browsing trail is as high as h. We need to estimate $D(h)$ based on actual user behavior.

Next, we explain how we calibrate our metric based on a laboratory user study.

3.2 User Study

To investigate users' behavior on mobile devices, we designed and conducted a laboratory user study with 20 search tasks. While this approach cannot give us a lot of data in the way search engine logs can, it enables us to collect very rich user interactions. The procedure of the experiment is shown in Figure 4.

Experiment Procedure. In our user study, the participants need to perform 20 ad-hoc search tasks on a mobile device. As shown in Figure 4, (I) Before the experiment, the participants need to complete a demographic questionnaire, which investigates their age, gender, major and familiarity with both search engines and smartphones. (II) Then they are required to watch an introduction video, which would ensure that the participants receive identical instruction. In the video, we introduce the procedure of the experiment by completing a training task. Then the participants are instructed to go through a training task to get familiar with our experimental system. (III) For each formal task, the participants are first presented with the search query (III-a). We also provide a brief explanation of the topic to make sure that the participants have the same interpretations about the information need. Then they are required to search with the query using a mobile phone in our system (III-b). More specifically, they are instructed as: *"Assume you have an information need described in the explanation. Please search with this query in our system as you are using an ordinal mobile search engine."*. A pre-defined SERP will be presented to the participants and we will explain how we generate and manipulate the SERP later. After search, a post-task questionnaire will collect their perceived quality and satisfaction during searching (III-c). While no time limits are imposed, the participants usually take about two hour to complete the 20 tasks assigned to them. Finally, they are directed to an exit-questionnaire (IV), which investigates their overall experiences in this study, for example, interest, fatigue level and etc. After collecting user behavior data from all the subjects, the relevance and click necessity of all the documents which have been presented (V) are assessed by third-party judges (see Section 3.3).

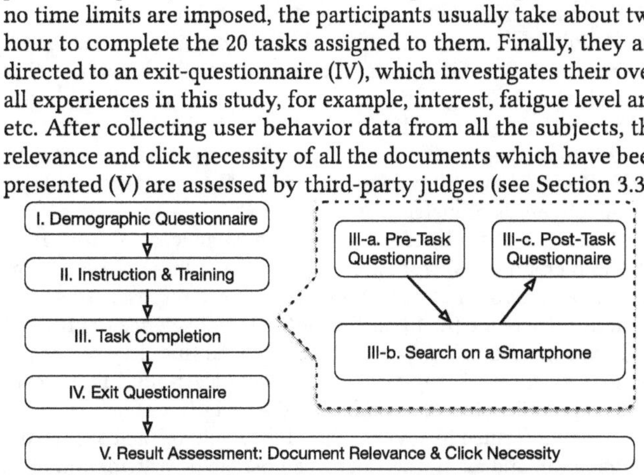

Figure 4: Experiment procedure of our user study.

Experimental System and Platform. The procedure mentioned before was conducted on an Android smart phone. It is equipped with a 5 inch screen and the resolution is 1280×720 pixels, representing one of the mainstream smartphone specifications in the year of 2016. The experiment was carried out via a Web-based system. We developed a mobile browser with Android SDK which could record the content of Webpage, MTIs (tapping, scrolling, flying and etc.) and click-throughs. All the behavior was logged by a back-end database.

Result Manipulation For each task, we have four SERPs from four major commercial search engines. Their results represent the most common search environment experienced by the majority of users. Although the presentation styles of different search engines are not exactly the same, basically the results are presented in a similar way: each result contains two parts. The first part is the a snippet on the SERP, which is intended to help the user decide if the full document should be visited or skipped. The second part is the full document itself. Due to the fact that the width of mobile devices is much smaller than that of a desktop display, the results are still ranked linearly.

To make sure that the SERPs are all adjusted for the smartphone, we crawled the search results from these four search engines by simulating a visit from the mobile device. We removed the ads, sponsored search and query suggestions to control variability and focused on the user behavior in browsing search results. All the SERPs were collected in one day of October, 2016. In this study, we focus on the user behavior on individual queries. To control variability we only present the results of the first page (about 11 results, Mean=11.48, SD=1.52) to the participants. Pagination and query reformulation was not allowed.

We then explain how we manipulate the SERPs presented to participants. The 20 tasks were divided into four groups (#1 to #5, #6 to #10 and etc.). For each participant, the queries in group was served with the SERPs from one the four search engines respectively. The user behavior data on the SERPs of 4 search engines is basically balanced, i.e. for each SERP from a certain search engine, it was presented to 11 or 12 participants. To avoid presentation order bias, the 20 tasks were rotated using a Latin Square.

Tasks and Participants The queries were sampled from query-logs of a mobile search engine. We further checked what vertical search engines these query would trigger. We found that these queries covered several major vertical result types by counting the number of tasks in each category: QA (n=10), Video (n=5), News (n=6), Image (n=6) and Knowledge (n=9). It should be noted that a task will be counted only if the SERPs from all the four search engines have presented at least one result of the corresponding vertical type. Although this taxonomy does not cover all the potential vertical types, we believe that the results belonging to these categories can represent the majority of the verticals' presentation styles. To avoid overfitting, we did not use these queries to evaluate the effectiveness of metrics (see Section 4).

We invited 43 students (20 female and 23 male, aged from 19 to 23, the median is 20) from a university via email, online forums and social networks. A variety of majors were represented across the natural science (n=13 participants), social science (n=10) and engineering (n=20). The participants reported that they were very familiar with search engine (Mean=5.68 in a 7-point Likert scale, from not familiar to very familiar) and smart phones (Mean=5.79). They were informed in advance that they would be paid $20 for the participation and all of them signed a post facto participation form revealing the content of the experiment.

3.3 Result Assessment

In our experiment, we have 80 SERPs from 4 different search engines and 918 results. On each SERP, there are 2.78 clicks on average (SD=1.70, Min=0, Max=10). In total, there are 2391 click-throughs observed.

After collecting interactions from our participants, we further assessed the results in terms of *Document Relevance* and *Click Necessity* with the help of several trained judges. The judges are graduate students whose research areas are information retrieval studies.

To make sure the assessors and the participants have similar experiences, all the assessments were done using the same type of smartphone that the participants used.

For *Document Relevance*, we used the typical four-level relevance criteria: irrelevant (R=1), marginally relevant (R=2), relevant (R=3) and highly relevant (R=4) following the TREC definition [36]. Each time only one result was shown to the assessors and the appearance of result was the same as what was shown to the participants. Assessors were required to visit the landing page before making their decisions. All the results were annotated by three assessors. The Fleiss' κ is 0.388. If there is a disagreement between judges, we use the median as the relevance of the result.

For *Click Necessity*, we adopt similar paradigm as *Document Relevance* and an independent group of assessors were hired. The difference is that we only showed the snippet on SEPR to the assessors and visiting landing page was not allowed. Then we asked them to make a decision by answering the following question with the options we provided.

Question: Assume we have an ideal document or information resource, which is presented in the same style as this result. Do you think it is necessary for the user to visit the landing page after examining the snippet?

- **Definitely Necessary (N=1)**: The snippet cannot present sufficient information and users need to visit the full document.
- **Possibly Necessary (N=2)**: The snippet could present some useful information. Some of the users may be satisfied while some others will visit the full document.
- **Not Necessary (N=3)**: The snippet is able to present sufficient information and most of the users could get enough information on the SERP. Visiting landing page is not a necessity.

Similar to *Document Relevance*, each result was assessed by three judges. The median was considered if there is a disagreement. The Fleiss' κ is 0.475, which shows that our proposed variable, *Click Necessity* could be assessed offline with a relatively high agreement.

3.4 Probability of Clicking

Based on the collected actual behavior and the assessments of results, we are able to examine how the document relevance and click necessity together impact users' clicks.

Given a SERP where the lowest clicked rank is k, we assume that the user examines all the snippets from ranks 1 through k. Thus, we are able to know all the examined snippets and clicked results in users' sessions. For every combination of Document Relevance level and Click Necessity level obtained from the judges, we computed the probability of click based on the user behavior data collected from the assessors. The probabilities are calculated by averaging #Click/#Examination over all the results. The possibilities are shown in Table 1.

Table 1: Probability of clicking given the Document Relevance (*R*) and Click Necessity (*N*).

$P(C\|R, N)$ (#Results)	N=1	N=2	N=3
R=1	0.403 (82)	0.067 (4)	0.093 (46)
R=2	0.438 (130)	0.313 (17)	0.040 (26)
R=3	0.607 (135)	0.500 (41)	0.147 (29)
R=4	0.884 (252)	0.757 (104)	0.647 (51)

We can see that the probability of clicking has a positive correlation with document relevance and a negative correlation with click necessity. An exception happens when $R = 1$, $P(C|R = 1, N = 3)$ is slightly larger than $P(C|R = 1, N = 2)$. A potential explanation is the data sparsity: in our dataset, only 4 results are labeled as $R = 1, N = 2$.

We find that even a result is highly relevant, if its click necessity score is 3, i.e. the snippet contains rich information to fulfill users' information needs, users are less likely to visit its landing page. This observation is in line with our assumption: the probability is affected by not only the relevance of the document but also the presentation on the SERP.

3.5 Modeling Browsing Behavior

Another goal of our user study is to calibrate our decay function according to the behavior of users. Our model provides no guidance regarding the form of the decay function. One of the possibilities is standard exponential decay which is used by some previous studies [10, 33, 40]. We present this decay function in terms of height h.

$$D_{Exp}(h) = e^{-h \frac{\ln 2}{half}} \tag{11}$$

where $half$ is a parameter and it is usually recognized as the "half-life" of users, i.e. the height (or time in TBG) at which half of the users have stopped browsing the results.

An alternative form of decay function is provided by Luo et al. [23]. They model users' behavior in browsing hedonic contents (e.g. mobile apps for video, music, news, jokes, pictures, social net- works etc.) as a stochastic process. Although their scenario is not exactly the same as mobile search, they do have something in common: e.g. the information items are organized in a ranked sequence. The exogenous factors which would drive the user to continue or leave are also similar, for instance, content quality, visit time and etc.

Luo et al. found that the distribution over browsing length for a visit can be described by the inverse Gaussian form with high precision. We further express $D(h)$ in this form.

$$D_{IG}(h) = 1 - \Phi\left(\sqrt{\frac{\lambda}{h}}\left(\frac{h}{\mu} - 1\right)\right) - \exp\left(\frac{2\lambda}{\mu}\right)\Phi\left(-\sqrt{\frac{\lambda}{h}}\left(\frac{h}{\mu} + 1\right)\right) \tag{12}$$

where Φ is the cumulative distribution function of a standard Gaussian distribution. μ denotes the mean of the original inverse Gaussian distribution, which determines the shape of $D(h)$ together with a shape parameter λ.

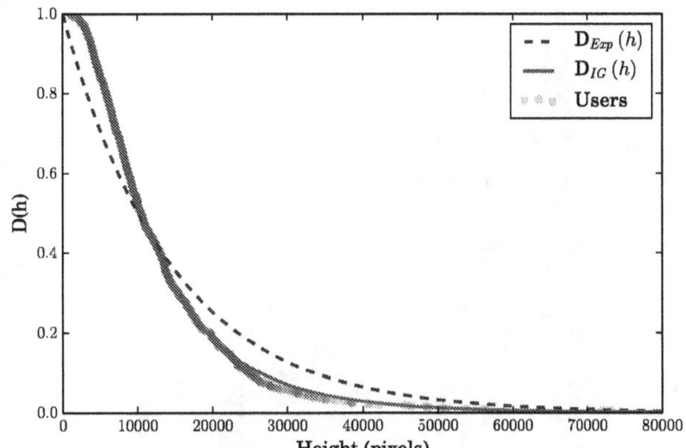

Figure 5: Decay curves with different functions.

Based on the collected MTIs, we are able to construct the browsing trail of users by concatenating all the contents they have viewed in each task. Then we fit the above two decay functions to our observations. The heights of users' browsing trail were recorded by the browser of our experimental system (see Section 3.2).

To compare the decay functions fairly, both of the decay functions were tuned to their best with the object of $L1$-norm. The optimal parameter of exponential decay is *half = 10069* while in the inverse Gaussian decay μ and λ equals to 13510 and 23070 respectively. The decay curves of these two functions are shown in Figure 5. We test the quality of the fits by the sum of the error over all the observations. The error of exponential decay is 63.08, compared to 5.57 of inverse Gaussian decay. This means the inverse Gaussian distribution describes the probability of users' browsing behavior more accurately.

4 EXPERIMENTAL RESULTS

In this section, we first introduce the detailed parameter settings of HBG and the test collection we used. The remaining parts discuss the following two research questions:

- **RQ1:** Whether and how does HBG correlate with traditional rank-based evaluation metrics in discriminating the performances of different systems?
- **RQ2:** Is HBG consistent with side-by-side user preference?

4.1 Parameter Settings of HBG

In HBG, there are several parameters and user models. Here we explain the detailed settings in our experiment.

Decay function $D(h)$: we consider the two decay functions, exponential decay ($D_{Exp}(h)$) and inverse Gaussian decay ($D_{IG}(h)$) introduced in Section 3.5, which further leads to two versions of HBG: HBG_ed and HBG_igd respectively.

Gain distribution $G_k(h)$: The benefit located at different parts in a result is difficult to measure. In this work, we only consider the difference between the snippet and the full document. We assume that the gain of the document distributes uniformly on the expected viewed height of snippet and landing page. An illustration is presented in Figure 6. For each result that has a snippet and a landing page, we assume that 40% of its gain is distributed over the snippet, while the other 60% is distributed over the landing page (Figure 6(a)). This ratio is based on Lorigo et al.'s finding that users usually spend 40% of their time looking at the snippet and the remainder elsewhere [22]. For each result that does not have a hyperlink pointing to a landing page (Figure 6(b)), we assume that all of its gain is distributed on the snippet. We can estimate more precise gain distribution by analyzing users' behavior on different types of results. We would like to explore this in our future work.

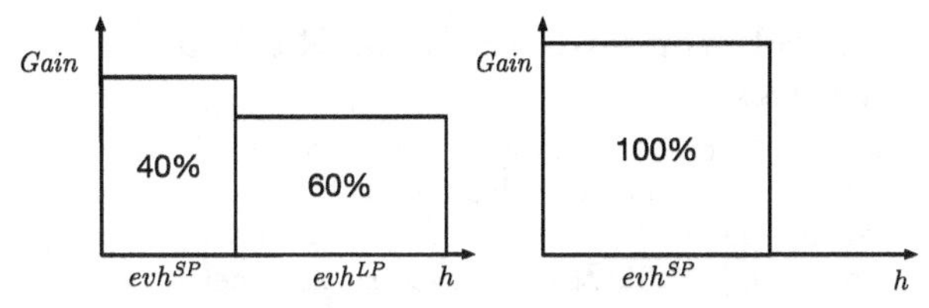

(a) $G(h)$ w/ landing page (b) $G(h)$ w/o landing page

Figure 6: An illustration of gain distribution in HBG.

Click Probability $P(C_i|R_i, N_i)$: we used the probabilities we estimated based on our user study. It should be noted that this probability may vary with search environment, enrolled ranking systems and etc. We may need to recalibrate it when the application scenario changes.

Browsing Model on SERP and landing page $f^{SP}\left(h_k^{SP}\right), f^{LP}\left(h_k^{LP}\right)$: in this study, we just use a simple browsing model $f^{SP}\left(h_k^{SP}\right) = h_k^{SP}$, $f^{LP}\left(h_k^{LP}\right) = h_k^{LP}$, indicating that users would browse the entire snippet and landing page of a result. A more fine-grained browsing model will be left for future work.

Normalization $\mathcal{N}$: Our metric is defined on the user browsing trail, which is affected by both relevance and clicked necessity. At this moment we do not see an easy way to construct an ideal result list. Therefore, following other metrics such as ERR, RBG, TBG and U-measure, we chose not to normalize our metric [29].

With these parameters and models, HBG is equipped with the ability to handle different user behavior assumptions. It is closely related to user behavior to bridge offline evaluation with real users' experiences.

4.2 Test Collection

In our study, we use SERPs from 4 mobile search engines, referred to as **A**, **B**, **C** and **D**. Our test collection was constructed by one of the four search engine companies, denoted as **A**. In the test collection, there are 50 queries. For each query, there are four mobile SERPs, among which one of them is from **A** the others belong to the other three companies respectively. To avoid overfitting, there is no overlap between this queryset and the queries we used for the user study.

For all the SERPs, the top 5 results are assessed by the professional assessors from Search Quality Department of **A**. They adopted the same 4-level relevance criteria as TREC [36]. They also annotated side-by-side user preference between their results and the other competitors'. The assessors were given two SERPs for a given query, one from **A** and the other from **B**, **C** or **D**. The SERP pairs were presented in parallel on two smartphones and the assessors were instructed to give a confidence score according to their satisfaction with the two SERPs in a 5-point scale (−2 to +2, from much worser to much better). Each SERP pair was annotated by 7 assessors. If there is a disagreement between assessors, following Zhou et al. [41], we adopted the majority of assessors' preferences.

The click necessity of these results were assessed by the same group of judges who had annotated the results in our user study (see Section 3.3), to make sure that all the decisions are made under the same criterion.

Thus, we have 50 queries, 4 runs and their relevance and click necessity annotations. We also have 150 user preference observations between one search engine and the other three.

4.3 Correlation with Tradition Rank-based Metrics

To answer **RQ1**, here we investigate the relationship between HBG and the other ranked-based evaluation metrics.

We calculated the ranked-based metrics with the help of an open evaluation tool, NTCIREVAL[1]. We used several metrics available in NTCIREVAL, including Precision, Hit, MSnDCG [12][2], ERR [6], nERR [7], P-plus [28], Q-measure [27], AP [36], RR [35], RBP [24] and two NCU metrics [31].

For the evaluation metrics which need a cutoff, we only report the results when cutoff equals 3, since the first viewport of mobile SERP usually accommodates about 3 results, which have the largest impact on users' experiences.

In our experiment, we do not compare our metric with TBG since the instantiation of TBG reported in their paper [33] is calibrated based on a particular user study. The scenario of their user study is a traditional Web search task and its appropriateness for heterogeneous mobile search environment is unknown.

The consistency between evaluation metrics are measured by the average kendall's τ. More specifically, given two evaluation metrics, M_A and M_B, the consistency between M_A and M_B is measured by the average of kendall's τ over all the queries:

$$avg\text{-}\tau\,(M_A, M_B) = \frac{\sum_q \tau\left(R_{q,A}, R_{q,B}\right)}{\#queries} \tag{13}$$

where $R_{q,A}$ and $R_{q,B}$ are the rankings of different systems according to M_A and M_B respectively.

The $avg\text{-}\tau$ between all the metric pairs is presented in Figure 7, in which darker grids denote higher agreements between the corresponding metrics. It is not surprising that the metrics from the same family are more likely to be consistent with each other, for example, the nERR@3 and ERR@3 since there are only minor differences between these metrics (cutoff, decay function, normalization and etc.). The high agreement usually indicates that the metrics are sharing similar underlying user models. For example, we find that Q@3 is closely related to MSnDCG@3. The interpretation is that both Q-measure and nDCG are top-heavy metrics suitable for informational search intents, as they have been designed to consider a lot of relevant documents.

Our proposed metrics, HBG_idg and HBG_ed have a high inner-correlation (0.968) because the only difference between these two metrics is the decay function. They have a moderate correlation with the other rank-based evaluation metrics (0.637 to 0.789) indicating that HBG could get similar performance in discriminating the performance of different mobile search engines.

The correlations between HBG_igd and Hit@3 (0.637), RR (0.659) are relatively lower than other metrics. We believe that simple binary-relevance measures such as Hit and RR are clearly not adequate for our purpose.

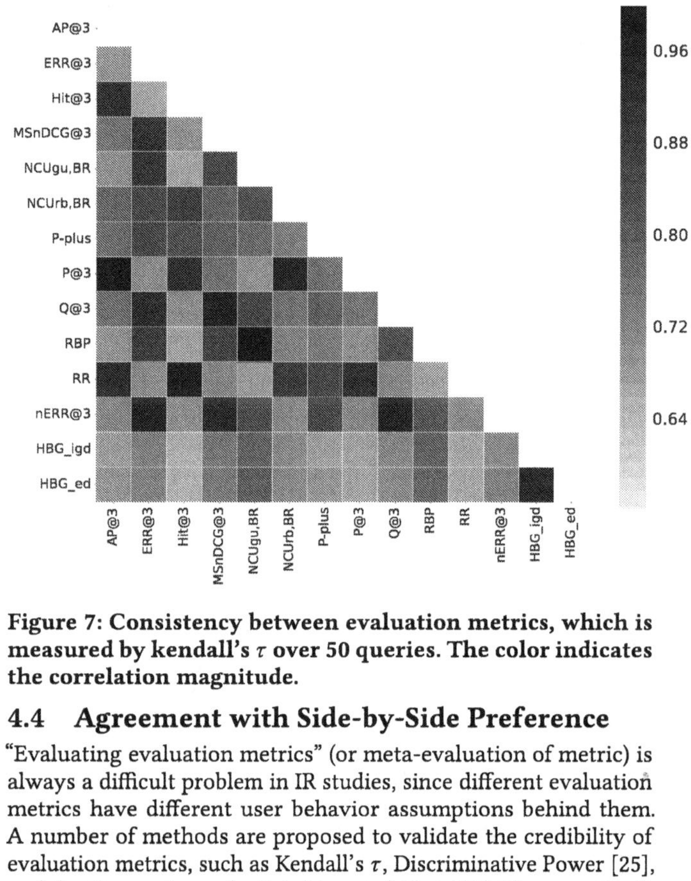

Figure 7: Consistency between evaluation metrics, which is measured by kendall's τ over 50 queries. The color indicates the correlation magnitude.

4.4 Agreement with Side-by-Side Preference

"Evaluating evaluation metrics" (or meta-evaluation of metric) is always a difficult problem in IR studies, since different evaluation metrics have different user behavior assumptions behind them. A number of methods are proposed to validate the credibility of evaluation metrics, such as Kendall's τ, Discriminative Power [25], and the Concordance (or Intuitiveness) Test [26]. These methods have been widely adopted and have aided us in gaining much insight into the effectiveness of evaluation metrics. However, they also follow certain types of user models or statistical assumptions and do not take the actual users' experiences into consideration.

Based on the user preference judgments, we look into the reliability of metrics by comparing the agreement between metrics and user preference judgments (**RQ2**). Similar approach has been adopted in a series evaluation studies to test whether the metrics line up with users' experiences [21, 32, 41]. We believe that the power to predict user preference is one of the key abilities of effectiveness measures since high agreement usually indicates that the measure is able to reflect real users' experiences.

Recall that our user preference test was conducted in a 5-point scale. We first folded them into 3 classes: Worse (−2, −1), Tie (0)

[1] http://research.nii.ac.jp/ntcir/tools/ntcireval-en.html
[2] MSnDCG is a Microsoft version of nDCG.

and Better (+1, +2). Consider the evaluation metrics, we assume if the difference between SERPs is small than a threshold δ, it should be interpreted as that there is a tie for the two SERPs in terms of result quality. More specifically, for two SERPs A and B measured by a evaluation metric m, there is a tie if $|m_A - m_B| < \delta$ when m is guaranteed to be between 0 and 1. Otherwise, we adopt $|m_A - m_B| < \delta * \max(m_A, m_B)$. In our experiment, we use $\delta = 0.05$, indicating that the difference is smaller than 5%. Then we can calculate the agreements between metrics and user preferences by counting the consistent instances. The results are presented in Table 2.

HBG_igd achieves an agreement of 85.33% while HBG_ed reaches an agreement of 80.00%, which is better than all the rank-based evaluation metrics. HBG_igd is better than HBG_ed probably due to the fact the inverse Gaussian decay function can better describe the users' leaving probabilities.

Both HBG_igd and HBG_ed outperform traditional rank-based evaluation metrics in terms of predicting user preference. We find that a potential reason is that HBG can discriminate the SERPs whose qualities are very close. For example, suppose we have two SERPs and all of their top five results are highly relevant. HBG is able to capture the impact of result presentation to user effort, while traditional rank-based metrics would probably get identical scores for the two SERPs.

We can see that among the traditional measures, Q@3 and other measures such as NCUrb,BR achieve 61-75% agreement. The next best group of traditional measures consists of NCUrb,BR, AP@3 and P@3: they achieve 47-48% agreement. The agreements for RR, RBP and Hit@3 are below 40%.

Table 2: Agreements between evaluation metrics and side-by-side user preference (Agr. and denotes #Agreements and #Disagreements respectively).

Metric	Agr.	Dis.	Rate	Metric	Agr.	Dis.	Rate
HBG_igd	128	22	85.33%	**NCUgu,BR**	100	50	66.67%
HBG_ed	120	30	80.00%	**NCUrb,BR**	92	58	61.33%
Q@3	113	37	75.33%	**AP@3**	71	79	47.33%
MSnDCG@3	111	39	74.00%	**P@3**	70	80	46.67%
nERR@3	109	41	72.67%	**RR**	58	92	38.67%
ERR@3	102	48	68.00%	**RBP**	56	94	37.33%
P-plus	101	49	67.33%	**Hit@3**	48	102	32.00%

To summarize, in this section we compare our proposed HBG and several rank-based evaluation metrics on a test collection from the following aspects: (1) We find a moderate correlation between HBG and rank-based metrics. (2) We compare the agreements between metrics and side-by-side user preference, HBG_igd achieves the highest agreement, 85.33%. (3) HBG_igd outperforms HBG_ed in terms of correlating with user preference. A possible explanation is the decay function of HBG_igd are more accurate than that of HBG_ed in describing users' reading behavior.

5 RELATED WORK

5.1 Web Search on Mobile Devices

Mobile search is different from desktop search in many aspects. According to several studies based on query logs of commercial search engine companies: Bing [34], Google [14] and Yahoo! [3, 38], the distributions of query categories on desktop/mobile devices are different. People are more likely to search for image, adult and entertainment information with mobile devices.

Compared with desktop screens, mobile devices accommodate much less content on their screens. Thus mobile users have to incur a higher interaction cost to access the same amount of information. Jones et al. found that information retrieval tasks will be harder to complete on devices with small screens [13]. Kim et al. [16, 17] conducted eye-tracking analysis of Web search users on both large and small screens. They found that with smaller screens, users exhibited less eye movement, and were slower to complete tasks.

A number of studies aim to improve users' experiences on mobile devices. Guo et al. [9] investigated mobile touch interactions (MTIs) during web search by comparing with interactions on desktop searches. They found that touch behaviors on mobile devices are significantly correlated with the document relevance. Lagun et al. [18] studied the effect of relevance in answer-like results on a mobile device. Their results indicated that users were less satisfied and tend to more time below the answer-like results. Another user study by Lagun et al. [19] put the emphasis on understanding searchers' attention with rich Ads formats on mobile devices during search sessions.

All of the aforementioned studies have aided us in gaining much insight into the users' behavior on mobile platforms and they can provide a good foundation and rationale for the construction our user behavior model.

5.2 Search Evaluation

Search evaluation is usually adopted in two ways: *System-oriented* approaches introduced a way to evaluate ranking systems with a document collection, a fixed set of queries, and relevance assessments from assessors, which is referred to as the Cranfield framework [8]. Ranking systems are evaluated with metrics, such as Precision, Recall, nDCG etc. This line of evaluation methods has the advantage that relevance annotations on query-document pairs can be reused. Beyond the Cranfield framework, IR community strives to make evaluation to correlate with real users' experiences more closely. The *user-oriented* evaluation methods, observing user behavior in their natural task procedures offer great promise in this regard. Similar evaluation protocols have also been adopted in other areas [11].

The proposed HBG is initially inspired by TBG [33] and U-measure [30]. What sets HBG apart from previous metrics is that: (1) We adopt the height of *user browsing trail* as the discount factor, instead of the integral rank in rank-based metrics, time in Time-Biased Gain (TBG) [33] and text length in U-measure [30] and M-measure [15]. (2) In HBG, we explicitly take the *Click Necessity* into consideration. The difference in click necessity may have an impact on user behavior, which further leads to various users' effort. (3) HBG takes the internal gain distribution within results into consideration while traditional rank-based evaluation metrics simply assume that users would get all the utility at a time.

Another line of research which is related to mobile search evaluation is evaluating aggregated search [41, 42]. Zhou et al. developed several metrics by extending traditional rank-based metrics (DCG, RBG, ERR and etc.) [41] and they also compared the performance of effectiveness metrics with user preferences. In the present study, we focus on evaluation in the context of mobile search, considering the impact of result presentation on users' behavior.

Recently, there have been a number of studies focusing on the "Good Abandonment" problem on both mobile and desktop searches. Given the rich presentation formats of heterogeneous results, search users may not have to click on result URLs to obtain the necessary information. A number of studies [2, 20, 37] have attempted to detect this kind of "Good Abandonment" in both desktop and mobile search environments. However, to the best of our knowledge, we are among the first to define the variable of click necessity and take this "Good Abandonment" phenomena into consideration in search evaluation studies.

6 CONCLUSIONS AND FUTURE WORK

In summary, in this paper, we proposed a new evaluation metric, Height-Biased Gain to tackle the challenges raised in the mobile search. We proposed to use the geometric height of a user browsing trail to estimate users' effort of interactions on small screens. The height can handle both textual and non-textual contents and is able to take results with different heights into consideration. Given the snippets with rich information, we propose to consider a new variable, Click Necessity to model the cases in which users do not need to visit landing pages to obtain useful information. Also, we adopted an internal gain distribution to describe a fine-grained utility derivation course within complex search results. Based on a lab-study with 43 participants, we calibrated our metric and found that the users' reading behavior can be modeled accurately with an inverse Gaussian distribution. The effectiveness of our proposed metric was evaluated on a proprietary test collections, which contains results from 4 mobile search engines. We found that HBG could achieve a better agreement with side-by-side user preference than existing evaluation metrics. Our study has a few limitations: (1) The parameters in our metrics are learnt from a small scale behavior dataset collected from university students. In the future, we plan to validate its appropriateness via a large scale practical log analysis. (2) In our test collection there are only 4 runs and 6 run pairs. We would like to examine the statistical properties (e.g., Discriminative Power) of HBG in the future, using more runs from a shared task.

7 ACKNOWLEDGMENTS

This work was supported by Natural Science Foundation (61622208, 61532011, 61472206) of China and National Key Basic Research Program (2015CB358700).

REFERENCES

[1] 2015. Mobile Search Tops at Google. http://blogs.wsj.com/digits/2015/10/08/google-says-mobile-searches-surpass-those-on-pcs/. (2015). Online; Accessed: 2016-12-20.
[2] Olga Arkhipova and Lidia Grauer. [n. d.]. Evaluating mobile web search performance by taking good abandonment into account. In *SIGIR '14*.
[3] Ricardo Baeza-Yates, Georges Dupret, and Javier Velasco. [n. d.]. A study of mobile search queries in Japan. In *WWW '07*.
[4] Ben Carterette. [n. d.]. System Effectiveness, User Models, and User Utility: A Conceptual Framework for Investigation. In *SIGIR '11*.
[5] Olivier Chapelle, Shihao Ji, Ciya Liao, Emre Velipasaoglu, Larry Lai, and Su-Lin Wu. 2011. Intent-based diversification of web search results: metrics and algorithms. *Information Retrieval* 14, 6 (2011), 572–592.
[6] Olivier Chapelle, Donald Metlzer, Ya Zhang, and Pierre Grinspan. [n. d.]. Expected Reciprocal Rank for Graded Relevance. In *CIKM '09*.
[7] Charles LA Clarke, Nick Craswell, Ian Soboroff, and Azin Ashkan. [n. d.]. A comparative analysis of cascade measures for novelty and diversity. In *WSDM '11*.
[8] Cyril W Cleverdon and Michael Keen. 1966. Aslib Cranfield research project-Factors determining the performance of indexing systems; Volume 2, Test results. (1966).
[9] Qi Guo, Haojian Jin, Dmitry Lagun, Shuai Yuan, and Eugene Agichtein. [n. d.]. Mining Touch Interaction Data on Mobile Devices to Predict Web Search Result Relevance. In *SIGIR '13*.
[10] Qi Guo and Yang Song. [n. d.]. Large-Scale Analysis of Viewing Behavior: Towards Measuring Satisfaction with Mobile Proactive Systems. In *CIKM '16*.
[11] Xiangnan He, Hanwang Zhang, Min-Yen Kan, and Tat-Seng Chua. [n. d.]. Fast matrix factorization for online recommendation with implicit feedback. In *SIGIR '16*.
[12] Kalervo Järvelin and Jaana Kekäläinen. 2002. Cumulated Gain-based Evaluation of IR Techniques. *ACM Trans. Inf. Syst.* 20, 4 (2002).
[13] Matt Jones, Gary Marsden, Norliza Mohd-Nasir, Kevin Boone, and George Buchanan. 1999. Improving Web interaction on small displays. *Computer Networks* 31, 11 (1999), 1129–1137.
[14] Maryam Kamvar, Melanie Kellar, Rajan Patel, and Ya Xu. [n. d.]. Computers and Iphones and Mobile Phones, Oh My!: A Logs-based Comparison of Search Users on Different Devices. In *WWW '09*.
[15] Makoto P Kato, Virgil Pavlu, Tetsuya Sakai, Takehiro Yamamoto, and Hajime Morita. [n. d.]. Two-layered Summaries for Mobile Search: Does the Evaluation Measure Reflect User Preferences?. In *EVIA '16*.
[16] Jaewon Kim, Paul Thomas, Ramesh Sankaranarayana, Tom Gedeon, and Hwan-Jin Yoon. 2015. Eye-tracking analysis of user behavior and performance in web search on large and small screens. *Journal of the Association for Information Science and Technology* 66, 3 (2015), 526–544.
[17] Jaewon Kim, Paul Thomas, Ramesh Sankaranarayana, Tom Gedeon, and Hwan-Jin Yoon. 2016. Understanding eye movements on mobile devices for better presentation of search results. *Journal of the Association for Information Science and Technology* (2016).
[18] Dmitry Lagun, Chih-Hung Hsieh, Dale Webster, and Vidhya Navalpakkam. [n. d.]. Towards better measurement of attention and satisfaction in mobile search. In *SIGIR '14*.
[19] Dmitry Lagun, Donal McMahon, and Vidhya Navalpakkam. [n. d.]. Understanding Mobile Searcher Attention with Rich Ad Formats. In *CIKM '16*.
[20] Jane Li, Scott Huffman, and Akihito Tokuda. [n. d.]. Good abandonment in mobile and PC internet search. In *SIGIR '09*.
[21] Yiqun Liu, Ruihua Song, Min Zhang, Zhicheng Dou, Takehiro Yamamoto, Makoto P Kato, Hiroaki Ohshima, and Ke Zhou. 2014. Overview of the NTCIR-11 IMine Task. In *NTCIR '12*.
[22] Lori Lorigo, Maya Haridasan, Hrönn Brynjarsdóttir, Ling Xia, Thorsten Joachims, Geri Gay, Laura Granka, Fabio Pellacini, and Bing Pan. 2008. Eye Tracking and Online Search: Lessons Learned and Challenges Ahead. *J. Am. Soc. Inf. Sci. Technol.* 59, 7 (2008).
[23] Ping Luo, Ganbin Zhou, Jiaxi Tang, Rui Chen, Zhongjie Yu, and Qing He. [n. d.]. Browsing Regularities in Hedonic Content Systems. In *IJCAI '16*.
[24] Alistair Moffat and Justin Zobel. 2008. Rank-biased Precision for Measurement of Retrieval Effectiveness. *ACM Trans. Inf. Syst.* 27, 1 (2008).
[25] Tetsuya Sakai. [n. d.]. Evaluating Evaluation Metrics Based on the Bootstrap. In *SIGIR '06*.
[26] Tetsuya Sakai. [n. d.]. Evaluation with Informational and Navigational Intents. In *WWW '12*.
[27] Tetsuya Sakai. [n. d.]. New Performance Metrics Based on Multigrade Relevance: Their Application to Question Answering.. In *NTCIR '04*.
[28] Tetsuya Sakai. 2007. On the properties of evaluation metrics for finding one highly relevant document. *Information and Media Technologies* 2, 4 (2007), 1163–1180.
[29] Tetsuya Sakai. 2014. *Metrics, Statistics, Tests.* Springer Berlin Heidelberg, Berlin, Heidelberg, 116–163.
[30] Tetsuya Sakai and Zhicheng Dou. [n. d.]. Summaries, Ranked Retrieval and Sessions: A Unified Framework for Information Access Evaluation. In *SIGIR '13*.
[31] Tetsuya Sakai and Stephen Robertson. 2008. Modelling A User Population for Designing Information Retrieval Metrics.. In *EVIA '08*.
[32] Mark Sanderson, Monica Lestari Paramita, Paul Clough, and Evangelos Kanoulas. [n. d.]. Do User Preferences and Evaluation Measures Line Up?. In *SIGIR '10*.
[33] Mark D. Smucker and Charles L.A. Clarke. [n. d.]. Time-based Calibration of Effectiveness Measures. In *SIGIR '12*.
[34] Yang Song, Hao Ma, Hongning Wang, and Kuansan Wang. [n. d.]. Exploring and Exploiting User Search Behavior on Mobile and Tablet Devices to Improve Search Relevance. In *WWW '13*.
[35] Ellen M Voorhees et al. 1999. The TREC-8 Question Answering Track Report.. In *Trec*, Vol. 99. 77–82.
[36] Ellen M. Voorhees and Donna K. Harman. 2005. *TREC: Experiment and Evaluation in Information Retrieval.* The MIT Press.
[37] Kyle Williams, Julia Kiseleva, Aidan C Crook, Imed Zitouni, Ahmed Hassan Awadallah, and Madian Khabsa. [n. d.]. Is This Your Final Answer?: Evaluating the Effect of Answers on Good Abandonment in Mobile Search. In *SIGIR '16*.
[38] Jeonghee Yi, Farzin Maghoul, and Jan Pedersen. [n. d.]. Deciphering mobile search patterns: a study of yahoo! mobile search queries. In *WWW '08*.
[39] Emine Yilmaz, Milad Shokouhi, Nick Craswell, and Stephen Robertson. [n. d.]. Expected Browsing Utility for Web Search Evaluation. In *CIKM '10*.
[40] Yuye Zhang, Laurence A. F. Park, and Alistair Moffat. 2010. Click-based evidence for decaying weight distributions in search effectiveness metrics. *Information Retrieval* 13, 1 (2010), 46–69.
[41] Ke Zhou, Ronan Cummins, Mounia Lalmas, and Joemon M. Jose. [n. d.]. Evaluating Aggregated Search Pages. In *SIGIR '12*.
[42] Ke Zhou, Ronan Cummins, Mounia Lalmas, and Joemon M Jose. [n. d.]. Evaluating reward and risk for vertical selection. In *CIKM '12*.

Efficient Cost-Aware Cascade Ranking in Multi-Stage Retrieval

Ruey-Cheng Chen
RMIT University
Melbourne, Australia

Luke Gallagher
RMIT University
Melbourne, Australia

Roi Blanco
RMIT University
Melbourne, Australia

J. Shane Culpepper
RMIT University
Melbourne, Australia

ABSTRACT

Complex machine learning models are now an integral part of modern, large-scale retrieval systems. However, collection size growth continues to outpace advances in efficiency improvements in the learning models which achieve the highest effectiveness. In this paper, we re-examine the importance of tightly integrating feature costs into multi-stage learning-to-rank (LTR) IR systems. We present a novel approach to optimizing cascaded ranking models which can directly leverage a variety of different state-of-the-art LTR rankers such as LambdaMART and Gradient Boosted Decision Trees. Using our cascade model, we conclusively show that feature costs and the number of documents being re-ranked in each stage of the cascade can be balanced to maximize both efficiency and effectiveness. Finally, we also demonstrate that our cascade model can easily be deployed on commonly used collections to achieve state-of-the-art effectiveness results while only using a subset of the features required by the full model.

1 INTRODUCTION

Learning-to-Rank (LTR) systems are now commonly deployed by major search engine companies and they have been repeatedly shown to be highly effective for a variety of search related problems [6, 15, 26, 30].Th ere has been a growing body of recent work which focuses on improving the efficiency of multi-stage LTR systems using several different techniques: improving tree traversal [19], cascaded ranking [36], tree pruning [18, 38, 39], and minimizing sample sizes in stages [11, 22].

In this paper we revisit the idea of cascaded ranking in order to provide more control over efficiency and effectiveness tradeoffs in large scale search systems. A cascade ranking model [36] is a sequence of learning-to-rank models (called *stages*) chained together to collectively rank a set of documents for a query.The main assumption behind cascaded ranking is that full inspection of the content, which would presumably require generating expensive features is not required for every incoming document as only a small fraction of all documents will be relevant.Th erefore, LTR models in a cascade can be deployed in an ascending order of model complexity, and only a fraction of documents in each stage will advance to the next stage. Generally, early-stage rankers are cheaper to run, and usually focus on executing an early-exit strategy, such asfi ltering out non-relevant documents as quickly as possible. Ranking models in later stages are usually more accurate but require more resources.

When discussing system performance, it is important to consider both ranking effectiveness and system throughput within the same framework. Wang et al. [36] used a modified AdaRank algorithm to incorporate the costs of individual rankers, in terms of execution time for each single-feature weak learner used in the training procedure.Th is cascade model, however, cannot be used with gradient-boosted tree models, which are now widely believed to be state-of-the art for web search ranking algorithms [25, 30].

Conceptually, the making of a tree-based cascade model can be reasonably separated into two steps, which are *cascade construction* and *model deployment*. In thefi rst step, a learning algorithm takes into account the effectiveness of features and the cost of feature extraction, makes the best tradeoffs by following the direction from cascade designer, and automatically trains a cascade of ranking models.Th e learned cascade can then be deployed in the second step, focusing on optimizing low-level system performance. In this paper, we develop a new approach to constructing a cost-aware cascade. A considerable amount of recent research effort has been invested in the space of optimizing the run-time performance of gradient-boosted tree models [3, 14, 19, 20], which can be directly leveraged by our new cascading approach.

Research Goals. In this work, we revisit the problem of integrating feature costs into learning-to-rank models. In particular, we focus on how best to balance feature importance and feature costs in multi-stage cascade ranking models. Our overarching goal is to devise a generic framework which can be used with *any* state-of-the-art LTR algorithm, and allows more control over balancing efficiency and effectiveness in the entire re-ranking process. In order to achieve these goals, we focus on two related research problems:

ResearchQu estion (RQ1): *When designing multi-stage retrieval systems, what approaches provide the best balance between extraction/runtime costs and feature importance when using cascaded LTR algorithms?*

ResearchQu estion (RQ2): *Can we build multi-stage ranking models that require substantially less costs than a full cost-insensitive model, and still achieve overall effectiveness close to the full model?*

SIGIR '17, August 07-11, 2017, Shinjuku, Tokyo, Japan

978-1-4503-5022-8/17/08...$15.00
DOI: http://dx.doi.org/10.1145/3077136.3080819

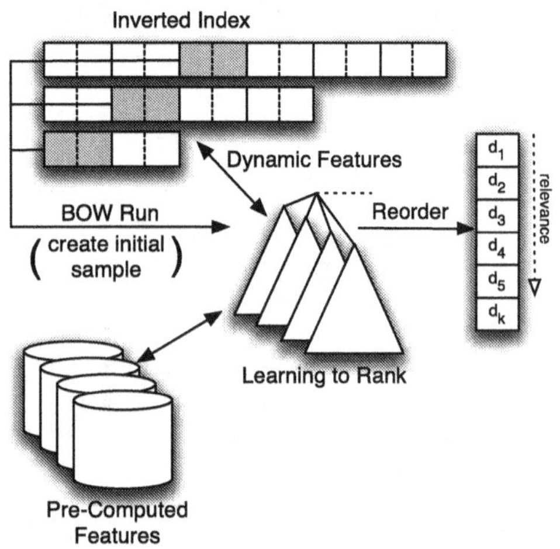

Figure 1: A typical learning-to-rank system configuration is composed of an inverted index which is used to generate an initial candidate set (sample) of s documents.Th is set of documents is then re-ordered using one or more rounds of machine learning algorithms.Th e number of documents can be pruned in each round, or iteratively smaller subsets of the highest ranking documents in the initial sample s are re-ordered. Afi nal top-k set of documents are then returned from the system in relevance order.

2 BACKGROUND AND RELATED WORK

Learning to rank. A significant body of prior work exists in the area of learning-to-rank (LTR) [15].Th e majority of research advances in LTR have focused on ways to improve the effectiveness of the systems, with several document collections released to test their performance. A recent study by Tax et al. [30] compare 87 learning to rank methods using 20 different test collections.

However, one common problem with these test collections is that the features used by the models are often not fully defined, making it very difficult to implement them using commonly used IR test collections.Th is in turn prevents easily transferring the advances made into working end-to-end search systems. While many different publicly available search engines [32] are commonly used by researchers and practitioners, only `Terrier 4.x` [23] currently supports end-to-end multi-stage retrieval on commonly used IR document collections with little or no manual intervention. So the chasm between academic research and large search engine companies on provably good system architectures remains relatively wide. Figure 1 shows the architecture of a complete LTR system consisting of at least two stages. Every aspect of this architecture should be considered when building effective and efficient search systems. Macdonald et al. [22] were among thefi rst to consider all of the different angles when building an LTR system for adhoc search.

Improving Efficiency in LTR Algorithms. A critical aspect of LTR must be considered when translating these powerful models into working search engines which must index internet-scale document collections – efficiency. Efficiency concerns may be strictly algorithmic [3, 7, 14, 19, 20], they may explicitly focus on feature costs [1, 6, 23, 35–37, 39], or they may perform post-learning optimizations to reduce the size of the tree ensembles [18, 38, 39].

Another related line of research is to focus on the importance of balancing efficiency and effectiveness in LTR systems, which is directly aligned with our current work. Perhaps the most comprehensive study on this problem is the recent work of Capannini et al. [7]. A less obvious trade-off concern is how to construct the "sample" of documents that are used for training and for scoring at runtime for new queries coming into the system [10, 22].This issue can have an important impact on both training and runtime scoring in multi-stage systems, and a problem that we revisit in the context of cascaded ranking. Finally, the cost of model training can also be an important problem [2, 22], but is not explored further in this work.

Cascade Ranking. Raykar et al. [28] described an approach to jointly train a cascade of classifiers to support clinical decision making, with the expected cost of feature acquisition taken into account.Th is approach does not attempt to address the issues of cascade design, such as the number of cascade stages and the design of cutoffs.Th e closest work to our own are the cascade models previously explored by Wang et al. [36] and Xu et al. [39]. Wang et al. proposed a cascade learning algorithm based on an additive ranking model AdaRank.Th e algorithm produces a cascade by incrementally incorporating weaker rankers in the ascending order of cost efficiency. In each stage only one weak ranker is incorporated. The document scores are accumulative, so conceptually all the previously selected features are involved in the scoring. However, more recent improvements in GBRT-based LTR algorithms has made this approach less competitive than state-of-the-art learning models.

Xu et al. [39] proposed an algorithm that takes a trained GBDT model and produces a cascade by reweighting the trees in the full model.Th e effectiveness of the cascade is roughly the same as a full GBDT model.Th ey use a monolithic cost function which accounts for several variables such as: model loss, tree evaluation costs, and feature cost. However, optimization of this loss function is quite complex, and their approach do not address the design issues pointed out in this paper, such as the effect of cascade structures on thefi nal retrieval effectiveness of the cascade model.

3 APPROACH

Stage-wise cascades arefl exible models that allow for a number of architectural decisions, such as: the number of stages used, the number of documents forwarded to the next stage, and so on.The choice of features involved in each stage is a critical factor in balancing efficiency and effectiveness in the end-to-end system.This trade-off is further elucidated by the following observations:

- A cascade may choose to defer the use of expensive features to later cascade stages as feature extraction on fewer documents is necessary, and will be more *cost efficient.*
- A cascade may choose to include useful features early on, since features extracted in earlier stages can be re-used in all remaining stages without incurring additional costs.The reusability of key features can make the cascade more *effective.*

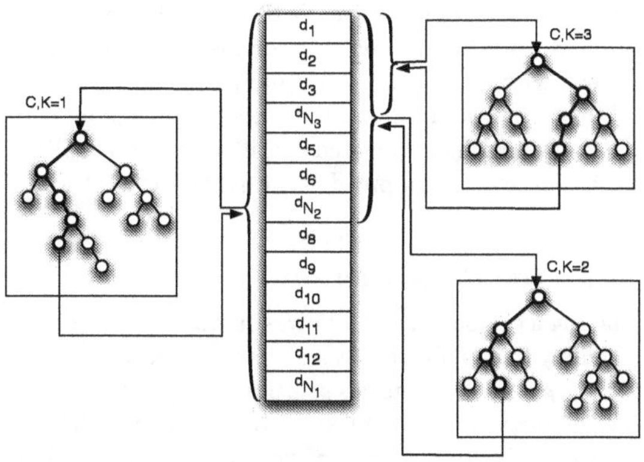

Figure 2: A three level cascade which initially takes d_s documents as the sample input. In Round 1, $C, K = 1$ reorders all d_{N_1} documents. In Round 2, a subset of the d_{N_2} documents are reordered by $C, K = 2$. In thefi nal round, d_{N_3} documents are reordered. Up to d_N documents total can be returned from thefi nal level.

Our general approach to cascade construction is tofi rst assign feature sets to different stages using a set of predefined heuristics (c.f. Sec. 4), and then perform automatic feature selection for every stage of the cascade, while jointly optimizing ranking effectiveness and efficiency. Ideally, the procedure should maintain performance comparable to a complete feature set model while at the same time accounting for feature costs. We now describe a theoretical framework for *model regularization* that reuses well-known solutions in the machine learningfi eld in order to achieve both objectives. Even though the goal of regularization is to minimize the effect of *overfitting*, in this paper we show how it can also be used to produce compact models that are feature extraction cost aware.

3.1 Cost-Aware Feature Selection

Regularization. Supervised machine learning algorithms are exposed to a training set of pairs $\{(\mathbf{x}_i, y_i)\}^n$ with the goal offinding an approximation to the function h, mapping y to $\mathbf{x}$ that minimizes the expected value of a predefined loss function $\mathcal{L}(y, h(\mathbf{x}))$ over the joint distribution of all $(\mathbf{x}, y)$ values:

$$h^* = \underset{h \in H}{\operatorname{argmin}}\, E_{y,\mathbf{x}}[\mathcal{L}(y, h(\mathbf{x}))] = \underset{h \in H}{\operatorname{argmin}}\, E_{\mathbf{x}}[E_y[\mathcal{L}(y, h(\mathbf{x}))]|\mathbf{x}]. \quad (1)$$

The choice of loss function depends on the type of problems being learned (classification, regression, pairwise, listwise). It is common practice to incorporate a regularization term $R(h)$ in the loss function to prevent overfitting. Regularization usually leads to improved effectiveness because sparsity is enforced in model training and, as a result, the learned model is less likely to overfit the training set.Th e most common type of regularizers apply a penalty on the complexity, shrinking the value of the parameters in order to reduce overfitting. For instance, if $h(\mathbf{x}) = \mathbf{w}^T\mathbf{x}$ is a linear model with its parameters represented by a weight vector $w \in R^d$, a widely-used regularizer is the L_2 norm of the weight vector. Given a training set of n instances, the model would minimize the following expression:

$$h^* = \underset{h \in H}{\operatorname{argmin}} \sum_{i=1}^{n} \mathcal{L}(y, h_{\mathbf{w}}(\mathbf{x})) + \beta \|\mathbf{w}\|_2^2 , \quad (2)$$

where in this case h functionally depends on $\mathbf{w}$. For instance $h(\mathbf{x}) = \mathbf{w}^T\phi(\mathbf{x})$, where ϕ is a kernel feature mapping.

Cost-Aware L_1 regularization. One problem with Equation 2 is that the learning algorithm is agnostic to feature costs. In order to minimize costs, one would like to reduce the number of features (covariates) that are used by the model, weighted by their cost, and at the same time maximize the performance.Th is problem is closely related to feature selection, and has a close connection with regularization. In fact, Equation 2 tries to bring down the contribution (weight) of each feature as much as possible while also minimizing the loss. In our case, however, having a non-zero weight for a particular feature implies that we have to pay *the whole* cost of extracting it, no matter how small it is.

Let $\mathbf{c} \in R^d$ be the feature-cost vector, in which each entry represents the normalized cost for extracting the feature. In the case of a linear model, we want to minimize $\mathbf{c}^T \mathcal{I}_{>0}(\mathbf{w})$, where $\mathcal{I}_{>0}$ is the component-wise indicator function, which is 1 if the weight is over zero, and 0 otherwise.Th is penalty factor would be included in the formulation of Equation 2. In practice, this means we need a procedure for controlling the amount of covariates included in thefi nal model automatically. To do this, we allow the learner to perform automatic feature selection by adding a L_1 penalty to the loss function (Eq. 2).Th is penalty is the L_1 norm of the weight vector weighted by the feature costs $\mathbf{c}$.

Conventionally, L_1 regularized regression models with a least square loss function are also known as LASSO (least absolute shrinkage and selection operator) and were originally designed to perform covariate selection, and help to make the model more interpretable. Lasso is able to achieve this by forcing the sum of the absolute value of the regression coefficients to be less than afi xed value, which in practice forces certain coefficients to be set to zero, effectively choosing a simpler model that does not include those coefficients [31]. In our case, we will exploit this property to generate less expensive models in terms of feature extraction time.

To sum up, the ranker would minimize the expression:

$$h^* = \underset{h \in H}{\operatorname{argmin}} \sum_{i=1}^{n} \mathcal{L}(y, h_{\mathbf{w}}(\mathbf{x})) + \beta \|\mathbf{w}\|_2^2 + \lambda \|\mathbf{c} \circ \mathbf{w}\| , \quad (3)$$

where β and λ are parameters that control the trade-off between the loss and regularization penalty, and $\circ$ is the component-wise product.Th erefore, the main idea is to learn a model using Equation 3, and then select the features that have a $\mathbf{w}_i > 0$, either directly in a linear model (we would use $h_{\mathbf{w}}$ for ranking), or as an input to other LTR methods (which would learn a model using only the subset of parameters selected).

There are several options for learning the parameters $\mathbf{w}$ of such a model. An effective method is to use stochastic gradient descent and update $\mathbf{w}$ one example at a time; in this case the training update for a sample $(\mathbf{x}_j, y_j)$ is as follows:

$$\mathbf{w}^{t+1} = \mathbf{w}^t - \eta^t \frac{\partial}{\partial \mathbf{w}} \left(\mathcal{L}(y, h_{\mathbf{w}}(\mathbf{x})) + \frac{\lambda}{n} \sum_i \mathbf{c}_i |\mathbf{w}_i| \right) , \quad (4)$$

where η^t is the learning rate, which may depend on t, the number of iterations so far. Note that the L_2 regularizer in Eq (3) is omitted here for clarity.

Strictly speaking, the L_1 norm is not differentiable (at $\mathbf{w} = 0$). However, methods that rely on subgradients can be used to solve minimization problems that involve L_1 regularized objective functions, which in this particular case, boils down to replacing the partial derivative of the regularizer with its sign, which for each feature i results in:

$$\mathbf{w}_i^{t+1} = \mathbf{w}_i^t - \eta^t \frac{\partial \mathcal{L}(y, h_\mathbf{w}(\mathbf{x}))}{\partial w_i} - \eta^t \frac{\lambda}{n} \text{sign}(\mathbf{w}_i^k) \tag{5}$$

One drawback of this formulation is that it may not produce a compact model, because the weight of a feature does not become zero unless it happens to be exactly zero, which is rare in practice. To overcome this limitation, we use a variant of a proximal method proposed by Tsuruoka et al. [33] which works well with the Stochastic Gradient Descent (SGD) optimization procedure, and has been shown empirically to produce very compact models.The main motivation is to smooth out thefl uctuation of the gradients through multiple iterations, which can be high when using SGD as it approximates the true gradient, and is computed using the whole sample, one example at a time.Th e original method, named SGD-cumulative, approximates the loss gradient using the following update rules:

$$\hat{\mathbf{w}}_\mathrm{i}{}^{t+1} = \mathbf{w}_\mathrm{i}{}^t - \eta^t \frac{\partial \mathcal{L}(y, h_\mathbf{w}(\mathbf{x}))}{\partial \mathbf{w}_\mathrm{i}}\bigg|_{\mathbf{w}=\mathbf{w}^t}, \tag{6}$$

$$u^t = \frac{\lambda}{n} \sum_{j=1}^{t} \eta^j, \tag{7}$$

$$q_i^t = \sum_{j=1}^{t} \left(\mathbf{w}_\mathrm{i}{}^{j+1} - \hat{\mathbf{w}}_\mathrm{i}{}^{j+1} \right), \tag{8}$$

andfinally

$$\mathbf{w}_\mathrm{i}{}^{t+1} = \begin{cases} \max(0, \hat{\mathbf{w}}_i{}^{t+1} - (u^t + q^{t-1})), & \hat{\mathbf{w}}_i{}^{t+1} > 0 \\ \min(0, \hat{\mathbf{w}}_i{}^{t+1} + (u^t - q^{t-1})), & \hat{\mathbf{w}}_i{}^{t+1} \le 0 \end{cases} \tag{9}$$

In order to introduce the per-feature cost c_i, we create one u_i^t variable per feature as $u_i^t = c_i \frac{\lambda}{n} \sum_{j=1}^{t} \eta^j$ which is then used to update $\mathbf{w}_\mathrm{i}{}^{t+1}$. It is important to note that the method is able to select a subset of features that can be used to further retrain any arbitrary model, and thus it can be used in combination with state of the art non-linear rankers such as the ones commonly used in production systems (GBRT or LambdaMART for example). Henceforth, we will use a least squares loss function, and simple linear regression for h:

$$\mathcal{L}(y, h_\mathbf{w}(\mathbf{x})) = \frac{1}{2} \left(y - \mathbf{w}^T \mathbf{x} \right)^2 \tag{10}$$

This proved to be empirically effective in our setup, while also converging quickly in fewer epochs.

There are several alternative feature selection methods, that in general are based on an optimality criteria metrics such as Bayesian information criterion, or Minimum Description Length. In this work, we also make further use of GBRT's feature importance [12],[1] as it intrinsically captures interdependencies between covariates. In short, the process learns a set of decision trees, where each node splits the data using one feature. With each split, the tree outputs are modified, and the training squared loss varies.Th en, once an ensemble is learned, the non-terminal nodes of the trees can be iterated through to compute the reduction of squared loss for every feature, and the results aggregated for different feature splits. Lastly, thefi nal importance is computed as the average over all of the trees.

[1] An equivalent process exists for the case of multi-class classification.

3.2 Cascade Construction

Constructing a cascade model involves setting a number of parameters, including the number of cascade stages K, the cutoff thresholds $\langle c_1, c_2, \ldots, c_K \rangle$, and the features sets used in each stage $\langle F_1, \ldots F_K \rangle$. As one might expect, the design space of a cascade model is humongous.Th e complexity of exploring the entire space of all possible parameter combinations and feature allocations is prohibitively large, and interdependencies between features can affect both the effectiveness and computational costs significantly.

Randomized Search. To tackle this problem, randomized search [4] is performed in this study to select the cascade configuration. This is done by randomly sampling a large number of cascade configurations from this space, followed by a seletion step that maximizes the cascade effectiveness on validation data. Ideally, this approach can explore any search space fairly efficiently within a relatively small number of rounds, but when feature allocation is involved many feature combinations it explores will not be effective. Randomized search does not work well when good configurations are difficult to reach.

The cost-aware L_1 regularization algorithm, as described in Sec. 3.1, was developed to mitigate this issue and simplify the search. It turns the search problem in a combinatorial space (that covers all possible ways of feature allocation) into a simple line search, making it possible to "sift through" the feature allocation space efficiently by tweaking λ. In our formulation, the coefficient λ controls the desired level of effectiveness-efficiency tradeoff, so when a different tradeoff is given a different subset of features that reflects this change will be selected. Practically speaking, a small λ leads to a gently reduced feature set with slightly decreased effectiveness compared to the full model; a large λ, on the other hand, will prune the feature set fairly aggressively and result in a compact model that uses only couples of features, which is ideal as an early stage model. Using this algorithm, a cascade can then be constructed by feeding in a sequence of decreasing λ values (from early to late) to generate cascade stages.

More details about the use of randomized search will be described in later sections. In thefi rst two experiments, we use a set of predefined cascade configurations to simplify the experimental setup and serve as the experimental control. Further investigations onfi ne-tuning cascade configurations is carried out using GOV2 with the best-performing cascade methods discussed in Sec. 4.3.

Feature Availability. We also experimented with a number of feature availability settings, and assume that the availability of a feature may change across cascade stages. In a production search system, some features might arrive much later than the others for various reasons, such as that they are expensive to run or their generation being deferred due to the design of the feature extraction procedure. To simulate this effect, our approach is to have certain models subdivide the full feature set into K equal-sized partitions and assign feature partitions to the respective cascade stages. The rationale behind this approach is that, by presenting a limited choice of features, which is $1/K$ of the full set, a feature extraction pipeline can be simulated to work in parallel with the ranking models, serving features in an order based on a pre-defined criteria. Each cascade stage has access to all features extracted in the previous stages without incurring additional costs. In this paper, we explored three different feature availability settings:

(1) **Cost-biased allocation (C)**: Features are first sorted in ascending order of unit cost and partitioned into K stages. This setting is a close approximation to the scenario where cheap features are available to the ranking model earlier than expensive ones.
(2) **Cost-efficiency-biased allocation (E)**: The features are first sorted in descending order of cost efficiency and partitioned into K stages. The cost efficiency of a feature is defined as the importance score divided by its unit cost, where importance is computed from a ground-truth tree model as described in Sec. 3.1. This setting simulates having a dedicated extraction pipeline for more cost-efficient features.
(3) **Full allocation (F)**: All features are accessible from individual cascade stages. This setting represents the scenario where the choice of extracted feature is unrestricted, providing the greatest flexibility to the underlying cost-aware feature selection algorithm.

After applying one of these settings, cost-aware L_1 regularization is performed to each cascade stage separately with a sequence of decreasing λ values. The algorithm (Sec. 3.1) will reach the desired level of feature size in 10–20 epochs. Running this procedure for more iterations does not change the results. We also set a constant decaying learning rate $\eta = 0.1$ across the board.

4 EXPERIMENTS

We now evaluate the impact of our approaches on reducing costs in cascade learners in two different settings, one large but shallow LTR dataset, and a standard TREC benchmark with 150 queries but a large number of documents to be ranked per query.

Experimental Setup. All experiments were executed on a 24-core Intel Xeon E5-2630 with 256 GB of RAM hosting RedHat RHEL v7.2, and baselines generated using Indri[2], Krovetz stemming, and dependency models generated using Metzler's MRF configuration[3]. All LTR algorithms were implemented in Python using `scikit-learn`[4] `0.18.1` and `xgboost` [5] `0.6a2`. Source code, configuration files, and detailed explanations for all experiments can be found in the GitHub repository for this paper[6].

Two different test collections were used for the experiments. The first collection is the C14 Webscope Yahoo Learning To Rank dataset [7] [9]. The dataset contains two subsets designed for different purposes and used different feature sets. We use only Set 1 (Y!S1) which contains 519 features (out of 700 in total) with an associated feature cost, and has 19,944 training queries, 1,266 validation queries, and 3,798 test queries. The original cost estimates included with the data were used without modification in our experiments. All features used in Set 1 have extraction costs between 1 and 200. Our second collection is the TREC GOV2 test collection (GOV2) using queries 701–850 in a 5-fold cross validated configuration. We created 425 features for this collection as described next in Section 4.2. For all queries, we created the initial sample by running BM25 with $k_1 = 0.9$ and $b = 0.4$ to an initial depth of 5,000. A summary of the two benchmark collections are shown in Table 1.

Table 1: Summary of the key properties of the two benchmark collections used in this study.

	#Queries	# Total Docs	# Features
Y!S1	6,983	165,660	519
GOV2	150	1,500,000	425

Learning Algorithms. Table 2 summarizes all of the baselines, as well as all of the new cascade model configurations tested on the two collections. We used a broad range of different learning algorithms in our experiments. These ranking models can be divided into the following three categories:

(1) **Ground Truth Models**: We compare with ranking models executed in a non-cascade setting, where the full set of features is used in training and prediction. Three ranking models are employed: Gradient-Boosted Decision Trees (GBDT) [12], Gradient-Boosted Regression Trees (GBRT) [12], and LambdaMART [5]. Our implementations of these ranking models are based on `xgboost`.
(2) **Baselines**: We use several baseline methods, such as QL [40], BM25 [29], and SDM [24], on GOV2 to verify the gain in effectiveness relative to a standard retrieval setting. These baseline methods are however not available for Y!S1.
(3) **Cascade Baselines**: We implemented the cascade ranking algorithm described in Wang et al. [36], using the suggested setting $\gamma = 0.1$. Note that setting a smaller γ does not improve its effectiveness. We also implemented early stopping on training effectiveness to avoid explicitly setting the number of cascade iterations.

Model hyperparameters (number of trees, depth, learning rate) were trained with the provided independent validation set for Y!S1, and using 5-fold cross-validation on GOV2. For ease of experimentation, some cascade parameters, such as the number of stages K, and cutoff thresholds $\langle c_1, c_2, \ldots, c_K \rangle$, were fixed in the first two experiments. Other parameters, such as λ, were tuned on the validation data using randomized search. Tree cascade parameters were tuned differently on the two datasets, as previous parameters for the ground truth models did not always generalize well on the learned cascades. We also empirically found that the linear cascades work better with the L_2 regularization turned off (i.e., $\beta = 0$), making the SGD optimizations more stable. Further experimental details are described in Sections 4.1 and 4.2.

[2] http://www.lemurproject.org/indri.php
[3] http://ciir.cs.umass.edu/~metzler/dm.pl
[4] http://scikit-learn.org/stable/
[5] https://github.com/dmlc/xgboost
[6] https://github.com/rmit-ir/LTR_Cascade
[7] https://webscope.sandbox.yahoo.com/catalog.php?datatype=c

Table 2: Summary of the baselines and new cascading methods used.

Method Name	Parameters	Description
GBDT-BL	Y!S1/GOV2: 1,000/525 trees, 16/16 nodes	GBDT [12] (**xgboost**), $\eta = 0.05$, subsample rate 0.8.
GBRT-BL	Y!S1/GOV2: 1,000/525 trees, 16/16 nodes	GBRT[12] (**xgboost**), $\eta = 0.05$, subsample rate 0.8.
LambdaMART-BL	Y!S1/GOV2: 1,000/525 trees, 16/32 nodes	LambdaMART [5] (**xgboost**), $\eta = 0.05$, subsample rate 0.8.
QL-BL, BM25-BL, SDM-BL	Default Indri settings	Commonly used single-pass retrieval runs to depth 1,000 usingQu ery likelihood with Dirichlet priors smoothing, BM25, and a Sequential Dependency Model (SDM). Note that while SDM is a strong effectiveness baseline, it has well-known efficiency limitations when used on large document collection [17].
WLM-BL	Y!S1: $\gamma = 0.1$, GOV2: $\gamma = 0.1$	Reimplementation of the linear cascade model by Wang et al. [36], with early stopping on training NDCG.
LM-C3-*X*		Three level cascade using linear model under the elected feature availability setting *X*, trained using Stochastic Gradient Descent (SGD) with batch size set to 50 and $\eta = 0.1$.Th e setting *X* could be **C/E/F**.
GBDT-C3-*X*	Y!S1: 1,000 trees, 16 nodes GOV2: adaptive (Sec. 4.2)	Three level cascade using GBDT under the elected feature availability setting *X*, using the same SGD configuration as LM-C3-*X*.
GBRT-C3-*X*	Y!S1: 1,000 trees, 16 nodes GOV2: adaptive (Sec. 4.2)	Three level cascade using GBRT under the elected feature availability setting *X*, using the same SGD configuration as LM-C3-*X*.
LambdaMART-C3-*X*	Y!S1: 1,000 trees, 16 nodes GOV2: adaptive (Sec. 4.2)	Three level cascade using LambdaMART under the elected feature availability setting *X*, using the same SGD configuration as LM-C3-*X*.

Evaluation Metrics. For retrieval effectiveness, we used standard early precision evaluation metrics: Expected Reciprocal Rank (ERR), Normalized Discounted Cumulative Gain (NDCG), and Precision (P), with three cutoffs (5, 10, and 20). We use **gdeval**[8] to compute ERR and NDCG, and **trec_eval**[9] to compute the precision to ensure that reported numbers are easily reproducible.

In this work, we focus on early precision improvements only, but if deeper metrics are desirable, our cascade approach can be tuned to support it.Th e cost of a cascade is given by the following formula:

$$\frac{1}{N}\sum_{i=1}^{K}\sum_{f\in F_i} N_i\, C(f),$$

where $C(f)$ denotes the unit cost of feature f, N_i denotes the number of documents that enter cascade level i, and N denotes the total number of documents that enter the cascade.

4.1 Experiments on the Y!S1 Collection

In thefi rst experiment, we tested the effectiveness of the proposed cascade ranking algorithm on the Y!S1 collection. As a significant number of queries in this data have less than 40 retrieved documents, there is relatively littlefl exibility in the design of cascade stages and cutoffs. In our initial investigation, we chose to utilize afi xed configuration to simplify the experimental design.Th e cascade is configured to contain only 3 stages, withfi xed cutoffs $\langle 20, 10\rangle$ between stages.

The λ values for the linear cascade models were derived using randomized search and NDCG on the validation data (cf. Table 3). For simplicity, all of the tree cascades in this experiment were trained with the same parameter setting as their ground truth counterparts. Note that tuning the number of trees/nodes in the tree cascades can further improve the performance, and this approach is explored further in Sec. 4.2.

Main Results. Th e main results for the Y!S1 experiments are presented in Table 3. In the table, the results are divided into three sections. From top to bottom they are: ground truth models, the cascade baseline, and the proposed cascade ranking models. Ground truth models, such as GBDT-BL or GBRT-BL, provide the best effectiveness in general, but the feature extraction costs are also significantly higher. Interestingly, these models already perform their own kind of feature selection as some of the input features are never used in thefi nal trees, and therefore incur different costs.

When comparing cascading models, the cascade baseline WLM-BL spends far less (0.62% of the cost incurred by GBDT-BL) on feature extraction than full models, at the cost of degraded effectiveness. Cascade models LM-C3-C, LM-C3-E, and LM-C3-F performed relatively poorly in terms of ERR@k and NDCG@k with respect to ground truth models, but in general their effectiveness is better than the WLM-BL baseline.Th e tree-based cascade models are more competitive than their linear model counterparts. Among all cascading models, LambdaMART-based cascades appear to provide the best tradeoff.Th e best-performing cascade LambdaMART-C3-F significantly outperformed WLM-BL on all 9 tested metrics, but is still less efficient that all three ground truth models, leaving a noticeable gap of 0.01–0.02 in ERR@k, 0.04–0.05 in NDCG@k, and 0.01–0.03 in P@k.

4.2 Experiments on the GOV2 Collection

In the second experiment, we investigate the use of the cascade ranking models on a commonly used web test collection, GOV2, where documents and features are to be processed and extracted by ourselves. To prepare the data for the cascade ranking experiment, for each query we retrieved 5,000 documents using BM25, and for each retrieved document 425 query or non-query features were

[8] http://trec.nist.gov/data/web/10/gdeval.pl
[9] http://trec.nist.gov/trec_eval/

Table 3: Main results on Yahoo! Learning-to-Rank Challenge data. For the proposed cascade models, significant improvements over WLM-BL are indicated by * for $p < 0.05$ and ** for $p < 0.01$ in a paired t-test.

	ERR@k			NDCG@k			P@k			
System	@5	@10	@20	@5	@10	@20	@5	@10	@20	Cost
Ground Truth Models										
GBDT-BL	**0.4605**	**0.4751**	**0.4789**	**0.7448**	**0.7872**	**0.8279**	0.8323	**0.7577**	**0.5967**	15988
GBRT-BL	0.4598	0.4744	0.4782	0.7420	0.7852	0.8264	0.8322	0.7562	0.5962	15876
LambdaMART-BL	0.4526	0.4674	0.4712	0.7314	0.7768	0.8203	**0.8330**	0.7564	0.5964	15856
Cascade Models (including Baseline) [a]										
WLM-BL	0.3679	0.3876	0.3933	0.5886	0.6506	0.7088	0.7832	0.7171	0.5673	99
LM-C3-C	0.3950	0.4127	0.4175	0.6461	0.7067	0.7638	0.8086**	0.7364**	0.5856**	1871
LM-C3-E	0.3871	0.4039	0.4089	0.6503	0.7033	0.7618	0.8192**	0.7413**	0.5885**	1580
LM-C3-F	0.3876	0.4047	0.4093	0.6541	0.7113	0.7666	**0.8226****	**0.7483****	**0.5915****	5278
GBDT-C3-C	0.4191	0.4357	0.4405	0.6535	0.7100	0.7631	0.7878*	0.7245**	0.5781**	1760
GBDT-C3-E	0.4264	0.4419	0.4466	0.6721	0.7180	0.7703	0.7942**	0.7241**	0.5778**	1535
GBDT-C3-F	0.4178	0.4350	0.4395	0.6554	0.7163	0.7672	0.7866	0.7310**	0.5819**	4953
GBRT-C3-C	0.4025	0.4203	0.4254	0.6304	0.6931	0.7488	0.7743	0.7168	0.5737**	1760
GBRT-C3-E	0.4100	0.4260	0.4313	0.6380	0.6867	0.7431	0.7697	0.7009	0.5637**	1535
GBRT-C3-F	0.4158	0.4332	0.4378	0.6479	0.7094	0.7612	0.7862	0.7294**	0.5802**	4949
LambdaMART-C3-C	0.4163	0.4332	0.4379	0.6577	0.7145	0.7673	0.7994**	0.7328**	0.5820**	1760
LambdaMART-C3-E	0.4183	0.4346	0.4394	0.6629	0.7133	0.7671	0.7968**	0.7268**	0.5786**	1535
LambdaMART-C3-F	**0.4353**	**0.4513**	**0.4557**	**0.6847**	**0.7354**	**0.7851**	0.8060**	0.7379**	0.5847**	4929

[a] All -C models set λ values ⟨100000, 30000, 500⟩, -E models use ⟨8000, 8000, 3000⟩, and -F models use ⟨5000, 800, 300⟩.

extracted. All 425 of the features implemented depend on either: the query; the query and term statistics from the indexed postings; the query, document and bigram statistics from ephemeral postings; the query and the document; or, the document. Table 5 shows a summary of these features. The majority of these features were derived from prior work within the LTR literature [15, 22, 23].

LTR Features. For all experiments, with GOV2, a total of 425 features were used. For each feature, several timing experiments were ran to compute the *relative* feature costs. We then normalized the costs based on the cheapest and most expensive features used in the experiments. Table 5 shows the complete feature breakdown based on the two main categories of features used.

The first set of features are a large collection of pre-retrieval features commonly used for predicting query difficulty [8], and more recently within LTR [21, 34] were gathered. These features draw on statistical information contained within the query alone or on simple scoring methods that require postings list access. As such they are reasonably efficient to compute on-the-fly at query time. The most important point about these features is that they are *query specific*, but must only be computed once using pre-computed unigram scores. This makes it relatively difficult to properly account for their true costs as LTR systems use SVM formatted inputfiles, which implicitly have a *per document* feature cost in the model. Therefore, we divide these one-off pre-retrieval feature costs by the number of documents produced in the initial retrieval stage, resulting in an amortized unit cost of 1. All other costs are computed relative to this cost.

The second set of features are *per document* costs. While the cost of a single Document Prior lookup is very fast in practice, it must be done for every document in the current stage, and therefore more expensive than the one-off cost of the aggregate pre-retrieval feature scores. Likewise, all models incorporating bigrams are more expensive than their unigram counterparts. The bigram costs include a one-off cost to generate an ephemeral posting for the bigram [16], that can be reused to compute all of the bigram pre-retrieval features, and also used on the fly for per document bigram scoring. This amortized cost is reflected in the final unit costs used for our experiments. Alternative indexing approaches [13, 27] have been proposed to improve the efficiency of n-gram scoring in recent years, but feature-specific performance enhancements are beyond the scope of this work.

Due to space constraints, we cannot describe all of the features or costs. A detailed description for all of the features as well as how costs (both estimated and real) can be found in the GitHub repository for the paper. The main point we want to make is that Table 5 provides realistic relative costs for both one-off and per-document features, and takes into account the relative complexity of each.

Main Results. In our initial investigation, the cascade is configured to 3 stages with cutoffs ⟨1000, 100⟩. In this basic configuration, the cutoff thresholds are selected from widely used cutoffvalues in adhoc retrieval experiments. The experiment is conducted in a 5-fold cross-validated setting, so fixing the cascade configuration can considerably speed up the search, with the caveat of achieving

Table 4: Main results on the GOV2 collection using 5-fold cross validation. For the proposed cascade models, significant improvements over QL-BL/WLM-BL are indicated by $^{*}/^{\dagger}$ for $p < 0.05$ ($^{**}/^{\ddagger}$ for $p < 0.01$) in a paired t-test.

	ERR@k			NDCG@k			P@k			
System	@5	@10	@20	@5	@10	@20	@5	@10	@20	Cost
Baseline Bag-of-Words and Term Dependency Models										
QL-BL	0.3937	0.4131	0.4218	0.3839	0.3826	0.3950	0.5275	0.5007	0.5000	–
BM25-BL	0.3781	0.3980	0.4062	0.3796	0.3806	0.3814	0.5114	0.4893	0.4705	–
SDM-BL	0.4453	0.4632	0.4702	0.4396	0.4346	0.4345	0.6013	0.5711	0.5443	(High)
Ground Truth LTR Models										
GBDT-BL	0.4361	0.4590	0.4652	0.4441	0.4473	0.4411	0.6255	0.6027	0.5487	213683
GBRT-BL	0.4501	0.4678	0.4745	0.4546	0.4446	0.4345	0.6161	0.5805	0.5305	211640
LambdaMART-BL	**0.4590**	**0.4802**	**0.4849**	**0.4684**	**0.4692**	**0.4593**	**0.6470**	**0.6215**	**0.5641**	213482
Cascade Models (cost ≤ 5000)										
WLM-BL	0.4221	0.4422	0.4485	0.4204	0.4177	0.4132	0.5919*	0.5664**	0.5242	1249
LM-C3-C	0.4297*	0.4454*	0.4537*	**0.4453****	0.4328**	0.4314	0.5933*	0.5624	0.5312	4013
LM-C3-E	0.4298**	0.4465**	0.4545**	0.4418**	0.4315**	0.4294**	0.5946**	0.5624**	0.5285*	11
LM-C3-F	0.4366*	0.4537*	0.4608*	0.4435**	0.4440**	**0.4509****‡	0.6161**	0.5779**	0.5601**‡	4717
Cascade Models (cost ~ 1/2 full model cost)										
LM-C3-F	0.4332*	0.4508*	0.4566*	0.4419**	0.4452**	0.4442**‡	0.6174**	0.5872**	0.5517**†	145693
LambdaMART-C3-F ^{a}	**0.4396***	**0.4578***	**0.4647***	0.4373*	0.4333**	0.4208	0.6094**	0.5732**	0.5181	129529
LM-C3-F, adaptive ^{b}	0.4295*	0.4469*	0.4530*	0.4435**	**0.4492****†	0.4501**‡	**0.6242****	**0.5926****	**0.5611****‡	110473

^{a} With 650 trees and 32 nodes ^{b} With λ values ⟨800, 0.1, 0.05⟩ and cutoffs ⟨2500, 700⟩

Table 5: Summary of all features used in this work.

Description	Unit Cost	# Features
Pre-Retrieval Features		
Query Dependent (Unigram)	1	159
Query Dependent (Bigram)	100	147
Document Dependent Features		
Stage 0 Score	1	1
Static Document Priors	500	9
Score (Unigram)	2,000	107
Score (Bigram)	8,000	2
Total		425

limited improvement on retrieval effectiveness.Th is issue is briefly investigated in this experiment by including a run that also optimizes the cutoff thresholds. In Sec 4.3, we explore various cascade configurations and investigate the effect of cascade parameters on retrieval effectiveness.

Using a randomized search-based approach, the cascade models LM-C3-C, LM-C3-E, and LM-C3-F are selected by maximizing the unbounded NDCG score on the validation folds. In a 5-fold cross validated setting, this metric is averaged across 5 folds on the respective validation sets.Th e unbounded NDCG is not specific to any cutoff threshold, so essentially it can be used to optimize any cascade stage. Similarly behaved recall-oriented metrics (such as Mean Average Precision) could also be used.

The main results for GOV2 are presented in Table 4. In contrast to the Y!S1 collection in the previous experiment, more than 72% of the features used on GOV2 are query dependent pre-retrieval features. The presence of query specific features poses a serious challenge to all cascade models.Qu ery features are usually cheaper to compute, and more likely to be selected (by cost-biased strategy, for example) in early cascade stages. GBDT and LambdaMART can effectively use these query features, but for other ranking models the query features are not as useful. As a result, cascading models that do not effectively utilize query features often see reduced effectiveness in the early cascade stages.

Ground truth models, as expected, give the best effectiveness among all baselines but also incurred the most feature extraction cost, around 210, 000–220, 000 unit cost. When compared with GBDT-BL and GBRT-BL, LambdaMART-BL achieves the best effectiveness.Th e cascade baseline WLM-BL spends far less on feature extraction, requiring only 0.58% of the full model cost, but at the cost of effectiveness.

A range of cascade models that spend less than 1/20 of the full model cost arefi rst selected using the LM-C3-C, LM-C3-E, and LM-C3-F approaches. All three linear cascades outperform the WLM-BL baseline in nearly all metrics with the exception of P@10. Compared to WLM-BL, LM-C3-F significantly improves NDCG@20 by 0.037, and P@20 by 0.035, spending three times more on feature extraction. All three selected models behave differently than in the

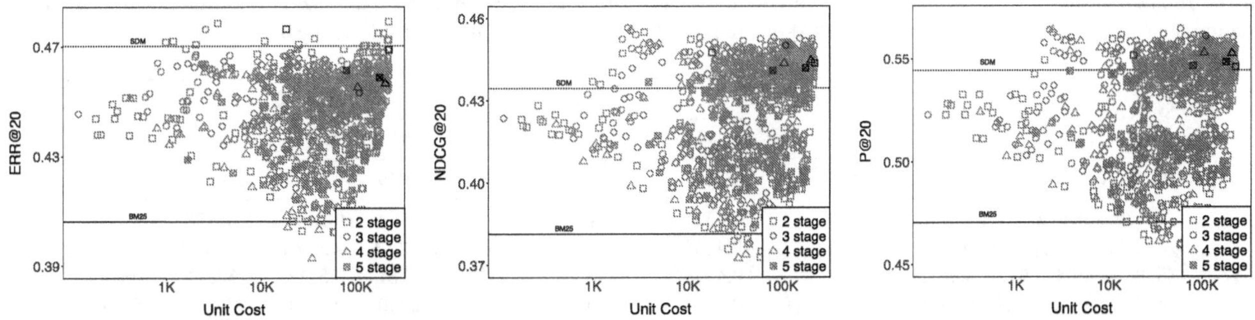

(a) ERR@20 (b) NDCG@20 (c) P@20

Figure 3: Effectiveness versus Cascade Cost in the GOV2 collection using the LM-C*-F models.Th e solid line at the bottom represents the effectiveness of a BM25 BOW run, the dotted line is a Sequential Dependency Model run which represents a competitive baseline on the collection, and the dots represent different LTR configurations and their respective trade-offs. Based on the validation data, the highlighted dots in black signify the most effective runs overall, while the highlighted dots in blue are the best cost-effective runs.

previous experiment. Both LM-C3-F and LM-C3-C are of comparable costs roughly in the range of 4, 000–4, 800. LM-C3-E tends to select extremely compact feature sets and results in a greatly reduced cascade model that uses only the cheapest features. In general, the order of the three models in terms of effectiveness (in descending order) is LM-C3-F, LM-C3-E, and LM-C3-C, despite the fact that LM-C3-E actually costs much less than LM-C3-C. Other cascading models which require 1/2 of the full model cost are also shown in the table. None of the configurations from LM-C3-C and LM-C3-E fall into this range.Th e best-scoring LM-C3-F model (in terms of validation set NDCG) achieves comparable performance to the same model selected in the previous group, but requires much more feature extraction resources. A LambdaMART-C3-F model trained byfitt ing the selected feature sets in LM-C3-F does slightly better on ERR@k but sees degraded performance on NDCG@k and P@k. Note that, unlike the Y!S1 experiment, the parameters used in training LambdaMART-BL do not generalize over LambdaMART-C3-F. Another round of randomized search is needed tofi nd the configuration that maximizes the tradeoff.

Finally, a LM-C3-F run that simultaneously optimizes the λ values and cutoff thresholds is also presented.Th is model is generally the most effective cascade model in terms of NDCG@k and P@k. It significantly outperforms the WLM-BL model on P@10 by 0.03, on P@20 by 0.035, and on NDCG@20 by 0.035.Th is result suggests that jointly optimizing feature allocation and cascade configuration can lead to further improvements.Th is issue is investigated further in the next experiment.

4.3 Effect of Cascade Configuration

In the third experiment, we investigate the effect of cascade configurations on retrieval effectiveness and cascade cost. We relax two variables that were heldfi xed in the previous experiments – the number of cascade stages, K, and the cutoffs $\langle c_1, c_2, \ldots, c_K \rangle$ – and jointly optimize these parameters together with λ values in a combined random search-based framework. As these configurations are more expensive to tune, the exploration was deferred until the influence of other variables was better understood.Th is experiment was carried out using the GOV2 collection. Our exploration starts by executing a full-range randomized search over the entire cascade design space.

We used predefined grids of each variable to ensure that the explored data points were not too densely packed [10]. We then iterated from $K = 2$ to 5, which indicates the number of cascade stages, and for each setting of K, sampled a set of feasible cutoffs and λ values from the aforementioned settings. In the experiment, each setting of K produced more than 200 configurations.

The effectiveness versus cascade cost for each explored combination were then plotted and shown in Figure 3, in which points from different settings of K are plotted in different colors and shapes. For each K setting, the best configuration (with cost < 1/2 full model cost) found by using NDCG validation is plotted as a black dot.Th ese "best" configurations are summarized in Table 6.

Figure 3 shows that a wide range of low cost but effective models can be found regardless of the choice of K. For ERR@20, two stage cascades are often quite effective, but can also be among the most expensive. For NDCG@20 and P@20, three stage cascades consistently provided the most effective configurations. Among all settings of K, three level cascades consistently provided the best trade-off between effectiveness and efficiency. We intend to investigate these trade-offs further in future work.

5 CONCLUSION

In this work, we have presented a new approach to cascaded ranking which can be used with any commonly used LTR algorithms. We make direct comparisons to several state-of-the-art approaches, and conclusively show that our approach can consistently achieve better trade-offs than other cascade ranking systems such as WLM-BL. In the experiments, we have presented several effective feature allocation strategies that have not previously been explored, and are thefi rst to directly explore the relationship between the number

[10]The range of λ searched was {0.01, 0.03, 0.05, 0.08, 0.1, 0.3, 0.5, 0.8, 1, 3, 5, 8, 10, 30, 50, 80, 100, 300, 500, 800 }; the range of the cutoff threshold is the union of the three sets: {20, 30, ..., 100}, {100, 200, ..., 1000}, and {2000, 2500, 3000, ..., 5000}.

Table 6: The best configuration for the K-stage LM-C3-F cascade (for $K = 2, 3, 4, 5$) found by maximizing the unbounded NDCG on the validation data. Significant improvements over WLM-BL are indicated by */** for $p < 0.05/p < 0.01$ in a paired t-test.

System (λ values; cutoffs)	NDCG@k			P@k			Cost
	@5	@10	@20	@5	@10	@20	
WLM-BL	0.4204	0.4177	0.4132	0.5919	0.5664	0.5242	1249
$\langle 800, 0.01\rangle; \langle 400\rangle$	**0.4529**	**0.4511***	0.4476**	0.6094	0.5866	0.5517*	18297
$\langle 800, 0.1, 0.05\rangle; \langle 2500, 700\rangle$	0.4435	0.4492*	**0.4501****	**0.6242**	**0.5926**	**0.5611***	110472
$\langle 500, 10, 0.03, 0.01\rangle; \langle 3000, 2000, 700\rangle$	0.4446	0.4446	0.4435**	0.6161	0.5913	0.5530*	106465
$\langle 800, 0.5, 0.1, 0.08, 0.05\rangle; \langle 2000, 800, 500, 80\rangle$	0.4343	0.4340	0.4408*	0.6040	0.5691	0.5466	80612

of cascades stages and document sample sizes on performance trade-offs.

In future work we wish to more closely explore the relationship between feature costs and feature importance weighting at different levels of the cascade. Our current approach to parameter selection is largely empirical, and is quite costly when using hundreds of features and large scale document collections, resulting in several strong Linear Models, which are currently needed before generalizing to gradient boosted tree models.Th erefore, an appealing next step in this work is tofi nd more principled approaches to dynamically select the best cascade configuration on a per-query basis, and to further explore the best configurations for a wider variety of LTR ranking algorithms

Funding Statement. Th is work was supported by the Australian Research Council's *Discovery Projects* Scheme (DP140103256 and DP170102231).

REFERENCES

[1] N. Asadi and J. Lin. 2013. Document Vector Representations for Feature Extraction in Multi-Stage Document Ranking. *Inf. Retr.* 16, 6 (2013), 747–768.

[2] N. Asadi and J. Lin. 2013. Training efficient tree-based models for document ranking. In *Proc. ECIR.* 146–157.

[3] N. Asadi, J. Lin, and A. P. De Vries. 2014. Runtime optimizations for tree-based machine learning models. *Trans. on Know. and Data Eng.* 26, 9 (2014), 2281–2292.

[4] James Bergstra and Yoshua Bengio. 2012. Random search for hyper-parameter optimization. *Journal of Machine Learning Research* 13, Feb (2012), 281–305.

[5] C. Burges. 2010. From ranknet to lambdarank to lambdamart: An overview. *Learning* 11, 23-581 (2010), 81.

[6] B. B. Cambazoglu, H. Zaragoza, O. Chapelle, J. Chen, C. Liao, Z. Zheng, and J. Degenhardt. 2010. Early Exit Optimizations for Additive Machine Learned Ranking Systems.. In *Proc. WSDM.* 411–420.

[7] G. Capannini, C. Lucchese, F. M. Nardini, S. Orlando, R. Perego, and N. Tonellotto. 2016.Qu ality versus efficiency in document scoring with learning-to-rank models. *Inf. Proc. & Man.* 52, 6 (2016), 1161–1177.

[8] D. Carmel and E. Yom-Tov. 2010. *Estimating theQu ery Difficulty for Information Retrieval.* Morgan & Claypool.

[9] O. Chapelle and Y. Chang. 2011. Yahoo! Learning to Rank Challenge Overview. 14 (2011), 1–24.

[10] C. L. A. Clarke, J. S. Culpepper, and A. Moffat. 2016. Assessing efficiency–effectiveness tradeoffs in multi-stage retrieval systems without using relevance judgments. *Inf. Retr.* 19, 4 (2016), 351–377.

[11] J. S. Culpepper, C. L. A. Clarke, and J. Lin. 2016. Dynamic Cutoff Prediction in Multi-Stage Retrieval Systems. In *Proc. ADCS.* 17–24.

[12] J. Friedman. 2001. Greedy function approximation: a gradient boosting machine. *Annals of statistics* (2001), 1189–1232.

[13] S. Huston, J. S. Culpepper, and W. B. Croft. 2014. Indexing Word-Sequences for Ranked Retrieval. *ACM Trans. Information Systems* 32, 1 (2014), 3.1–3.26.

[14] X. Jin, T. Yang, and X. Tang. 2016. A Comparison of Cache Blocking Methods for Fast Execution of Ensemble-based Score Computation. In *Proc. SIGIR.* 629–638.

[15] T.-Y. Liu. 2009. Learning to Rank for Information Retrieval. *Foundations and Trends in Information Retrieval* 3, 3 (2009), 225–331.

[16] X. Lu, A. Moffat, and J. S. Culpepper. 2015. On the Cost of Extracting Proximity Features for Term-Dependency Models. In *Proc. CIKM.* 293–302.

[17] X. Lu, A. Moffat, and J. S. Culpepper. 2016. Efficient and Effective Higher Order Proximity Modeling. In *Proc. ICTIR.* 21–30.

[18] C. Lucchese, F. M. Nardini, S. Orlando, R. Perego, F. Silvestri, and S. Trani. 2016. Post-learning optimization of tree ensembles for efficient ranking. In *Proc. SIGIR.* 949–952.

[19] C. Lucchese, F. M. Nardini, S. Orlando, R. Perego, N. Tonellotto, and R. Venturini. 2015.Qu ickScorer: A Fast Algorithm to Rank Documents with Additive Ensembles of Regression Trees. In *Proc. SIGIR.* 73–82.

[20] C. Lucchese, F. M. Nardini, S. Orlando, R. Perego, N. Tonellotto, and R. Venturini. 2016. Exploiting CPU SIMD extensions to speed-up document scoring with tree ensembles. In *Proc. SIGIR.* 833–836.

[21] C. Macdonald, R. L. T. Santos, and I. Ounis. 2012. On the Usefulness ofQu ery Features for Learning to Rank. In *Proc. CIKM.* 2559–2562.

[22] C. Macdonald, R. L. T. Santos, and I. Ounis. 2013.Th e whens and hows of learning to rank for web search. *Inf. Retr.* 16, 5 (2013), 584–628.

[23] C. Macdonald, R. L. T. Santos, I. Ounis, and B. He. 2013. About learning models with multiple query-dependent features. *ACM Trans. Information Systems* 31, 3 (2013), 11:1–11:39.

[24] D. Metzler and W. B. Croft. 2005. A Markov randomfi eld model for term dependencies.. In *Proc. SIGIR.* 472–479.

[25] A. Mohan, Z. Chen, and K. Q. Weinberger. 2011. Web-Search Ranking with Initialized Gradient Boosted Regression Trees. *Journal of Machine Learning Research* 14 (2011), 77–89.

[26] J. Pedersen. 2010.Qu ery understanding at Bing. *Invited talk, SIGIR* (2010).

[27] M. Petri, A. Moffat, and J. S. Culpepper. 2014. Score-safe term dependency processing with hybrid indexes. In *Proc. SIGIR.* 899–902.

[28] V. C. Raykar, B. Krishnapuram, and S. Yu. 2010. Designing efficient cascaded classifiers: tradeoff between accuracy and cost. In *Proc. KDD.* 853–860.

[29] S. E. Robertson, S. Walker, S. Jones, M. Hancock-Beaulieu, and M. Gatford. 1994. Okapi at TREC-3.. In *Proc. TREC-3.*

[30] N. Tax, S. Bockting, and D. Hiemstra. 2015. A cross-benchmark comparison of 87 learning to rank methods. *Inf. Proc. & Man.* 51, 6 (2015), 757–772.

[31] R. Tibshirani. 1994. Regression Shrinkage and Selection Via the Lasso. *Journal of the Royal Statistical Society, Series B* 58 (1994), 267–288.

[32] A. Trotman, C. L. A. Clarke, I. Ounis, J. S. Culpepper, M.-A. Cartright, and S. Geva. 2012. Open source information retrieval: a report on the SIGIR 2012 workshop. *SIGIR Forum* 46, 2 (2012), 95–101.

[33] Y. Tsuruoka, J. Tsujii, and S. Ananiadou. 2009. Stochastic Gradient Descent Training for L1-regularized Log-linear Models with Cumulative Penalty. In *Proc. ACL.* 477–485.

[34] S. Tyree, K. Q. Weinberger, K. Agrawal, and J. Paykin. 2011. Parallel Boosted Regression Trees for Web Search Ranking. In *Proc. WWW.* 387–396.

[35] L. Wang, J. Lin, and D. Metzler. 2010. Learning to efficiently rank. In *Proc. SIGIR.* 138–145.

[36] L. Wang, J. Lin, and D. Metzler. 2011. A Cascade Ranking Model for Efficient Ranked Retrieval. In *Proc. SIGIR.* 105–114.

[37] L. Wang, J. Lin, D. Metzler, and J. Han. 2014. Learning to efficiently rank on big data. In *Proc. WWW (Companion Volume).* 209–210.

[38] Z. Xu, M. J. Kusner, K. Q. Weinberger, and M. Chen. 2013. Cost-Sensitive Tree of Classifiers.. In *Proc. ICML.* 133–141.

[39] Z. Xu, M. J. Kusner, K. Q. Weinberger, M. Chen, and O. Chapelle. 2014. Classifier Cascades and Trees for Minimizing Feature Evaluation Cost. *Journal of Machine Learning Research* 15 (2014), 2113–2144.

[40] C. Zhai and J. Lafferty. 2004. A Study of Smoothing Methods for Language Models Applied to Information Retrieval. *ACM Trans. Information Systems* 22, 2 (April 2004), 179–214.

Computational Social Indicators: A Case Study of Chinese University Ranking

Fuli Feng
National University of Singapore
fulifeng93@gmail.com

Liqiang Nie
Shandong University
nieliqiang@gmail.com

Xiang Wang
National University of Singapore
xiangwang@u.nus.edu

Richang Hong
Hefei University of Technology
hongrc.hfut@gmail.com

Tat-Seng Chua
National University of Singapore
dcscts@nus.edu.sg

ABSTRACT

Many professional organizations produce regular reports of social indicators to monitor social progress. Despite their reasonable results and societal value, early efforts on social indicator computing suffer from three problems: 1) labor-intensive data gathering, 2) insufficient data, and 3) expert-relied data fusion. Towards this end, we present a novel graph-based multi-channel ranking scheme for social indicator computation by exploring the rich multi-channel Web data. For each channel, this scheme presents the semi-structured and unstructured data with simple graphs and hypergraphs, respectively. It then groups the channels into different clusters according to their correlations. After that, it uses a unified model to learn the cluster-wise common spaces, perform ranking separately upon each space, and fuse these rankings to produce the final one. We take Chinese university ranking as a case study and validate our scheme over a real-world dataset. It is worth emphasizing that our scheme is applicable to computation of other social indicators, such as Educational attainment.

CCS CONCEPTS

•**Information systems** → *Web mining; Information retrieval; Retrieval models and ranking;*

KEYWORDS

Computational Social Indicators, University Ranking

ACM Reference format:

Fuli Feng, Liqiang Nie, Xiang Wang, Richang Hong, and Tat-Seng Chua. 2017. Computational Social Indicators: A Case Study of Chinese University Ranking. In *Proceedings of SIGIR17, August 7–11, 2017, Shinjuku, Tokyo, Japan*, , 10 pages.
DOI: http://dx.doi.org/10.1145/3077136.3080773

SIGIR17, August 7–11, 2017, Shinjuku, Tokyo, Japan

DOI: http://dx.doi.org/10.1145/3077136.3080773

1 INTRODUCTION

Social indicators are defined as statistical measures and analytics that describe social trends and conditions that would impact social well-being [14]. A social indicator is usually in the form of a ranking list that orders the entities of interests according to some pre-defined rules. In the past few decades, professional organizations, such as mass media, academic institutes, and government agencies, have calculated and released hundreds of social indicators on different facets of our society, including cost of living [7], health expenditure [17], happiness index [35], and university quality [23]. Generally, social indicators have some key functions, spanning from providing information for decision-makers, monitoring and evaluating policies, to searching for a common good [3]. For instance, university ranking plays a pivotal role in selecting universities for high school students. Meanwhile, university rankings are mirrors for university themselves to improve their education and research quality. Therefore, the accuracy and timely creation of these indicators are extremely useful to a wide variety of users and applications, including the formulation of government policies and planning of social services.

Most of the released social indicators are typically computed in two steps: given a set of entities to be ranked, they first calculate the scores of these entities according to several factors related to the desired social indicator and then fuse the scores using hand-crafted weights to rank the entities. For instance, universities in QS World University Ranking 2016/17 are ranked by scores weighted upon six factors: academic reputation, employer reputation, student-to-faculty ratio, citations per faculty, international student ratio, and international faculty ratio[1]. However, such computation process usually suffers from the following problems: 1) Labor-intensive data collection. Data used to calculate social indicators usually rely heavily on user studies like questionnaire, especially, for subjective factors, such as the academic and employment reputation in the QS Ranking. It thus requires a lot of human resources and the collected data can hardly be applied to compute other social indicators. 2) Data insufficiency. Existing social indicators usually only cover a small fraction of target entities. For example, there indeed exist 2,553 universities in China[2], while most university rankings involve only less than 800 universities. That is because it is non-trivial to carry out a large-scale user study to gather comprehensive information for each target entity. 3) Expert-relied data fusion.

[1]http://tinyurl.com/zj9vgnj/.
[2]http://tinyurl.com/zcbumn3/.

Factor weighting policies rely heavily on experts and different weighting policies may lead to distinct social indicator results. Although we believe that we can find the outstanding experts and generate reasonable social indicator results, it is extremely resource-consuming.

With the fast development of Internet, we are able to collect large-scale and multi-facet data to describe any given entities from the Web, such as interactions and opinions shared in social networking services (SNSs), timely news reports in online mass media, and purchase history in e-commerce platforms. In a sense, the publicly accessible online data enable us to alleviate the aforementioned data collection and scarcity problems, and save human labors. Considering the university ranking as an example, rich data from multiple channels can be gathered to comprehensively describe each university: 1) Official statistics about students and teachers are available in platforms of the Ministry of Education (MOE) and various educational organizations. 2) Important events related to universities are updated on the website of mass media in real time. 3) Academic records are accessible through online bibliographic database like Microsoft Academic[3]. 4) Employment status of graduate students are shared in business and employment-oriented SNSs, such as LinkedIn[4]. 5) University-related comments and opinions from general users are shared in the mainstream social media like Twitter[5].

Much related works have been conducted to rank entities with multi-channel data. For example: 1) Early fusion, which concatenates all the extracted features from different channels into a single feature vector before feeding it into ranking models [9]; 2) Late fusion, which analyzes data from each channel separately and then aggregates their ranking results [13]; 3) Joint learning that simultaneously learns ranking from each channel and encourages the rankings to be consistent with others [16]; 4) Subspace learning, which derives compact latent representations by taking advantage of inherent structures and relations across multiple channels before ranking the entities based upon the latent representations [10, 28, 36]. However, none of these methods is suitable to compute social indicators, since social indicator computation has the following characteristics: 1) Complex channel relations. The correlation may be strong among some channels, while it may be very weak among others. Therefore, it will cause information loss if all channels are equivalently projected into the same space. 2) Data heterogeneity. There are both semi-structured and unstructured data on the Web. For instance, the tables and statistics in webpages are semi-structured; whereas, texts, images, and videos in mass media reports and social media posts are unstructured. 3) Ranking smoothness. Generally speaking, the latest social indicator is consistent with the last update to some extents, because the target entities in the ranking progress relatively slowly during a short duration. 4) Insufficiency and block-wise missing data for entities. It is not unusual that a social indicator involves up to only hundreds of entities, which constraints the usability of complicated methods relying on large-scale training samples, such as deep learning models. Besides, some channel data may be missing for some entities. For example, in university ranking, academic records of some unpopular universities, such as the Taishan University[6], may not be available, as they seldom publish papers in international conferences or journals.

To address the aforementioned problems, we present a novel graph-based multi-channel ranking scheme (GMR). In particular, we first collect multi-channel Web data corresponding to the given social indicator and extract a set of features from each channel to represent the candidates. For each channel, we construct a simple graph and a hypergraph on its features from semi-structured and unstructured data, respectively. Following that, we calculate the graph Laplacian for each graph, and cluster all the graphs into groups based on the correlations between their Laplacian matrices[7]. Thus, the involved channels in each cluster are strongly correlated. In the light of this, we derive a common space for each cluster and perform a graph-based ranking upon this common space. It is worth mentioning that we differ the entities with all channel data from those with block-wise missing data, when learning the cluster-wise common space. This strategy can avoid baised common representations caused by data incompletion [42]. Simultaneously, we fuse ranking results learned from different clusters to produce the final one. To enforce ranking smoothness, the aggregated result over different clusters is further regularized by the historical rankings. In this work, we apply the proposed generic scheme to address the Chinese university ranking problem, as shown in Figure 1. In particular, this scheme first collects multi-channel Web data, ranging from official data, mass media reports, academic records, employment status of graduate students, to public comments. It then extracts a rich set of features from each channel to comprehensively represent the universities and then feeds the features into the model of GMR to generate the university ranking. Extensive experiments have well-verified our approach. It is worthwhile highlighting that our ranking scheme is extendable to other social indicator computation, such as the cost of living.

The main contributions of this paper are threefold:

- We present a novel graph-based multi-channel ranking scheme towards social indicator computation. It inherits the advantages of late fusion and subspace learning by performing ranking in the cluster-wise common space.
- We successfully take the Chinese university ranking as a case study of social indicator computation.
- We released the involved codes and our constructed data to facilitate the research community[8].

The remainder of this paper is structured as follows. Section 2 reviews the related work. In Section 3, we introduce our proposed scheme. In Section 4, we apply our scheme to Chinese university ranking. Experimental settings and results are reported in Section 5, followed by conclusion and future work in Section 6.

2 RELATED WORK

Our work is related to recent studies on multi-view subspace learning, unsupervised ranking, and university ranking.

[3]https://academic.microsoft.com/.
[4]https://www.linkedin.com/.
[5]https://twitter.com/.
[6]http://www2.tsu.edu.cn/www/ywbtsu/.
[7]It is worth emphasizing that some channels may be placed into two clusters since they have one simple graph and one hypergraph Laplacian matrices. This is reasonable since semi-structured and unstructured data may convey different topics and hence may have different correlations with others.
[8]https://github.com/hennande/cur/.

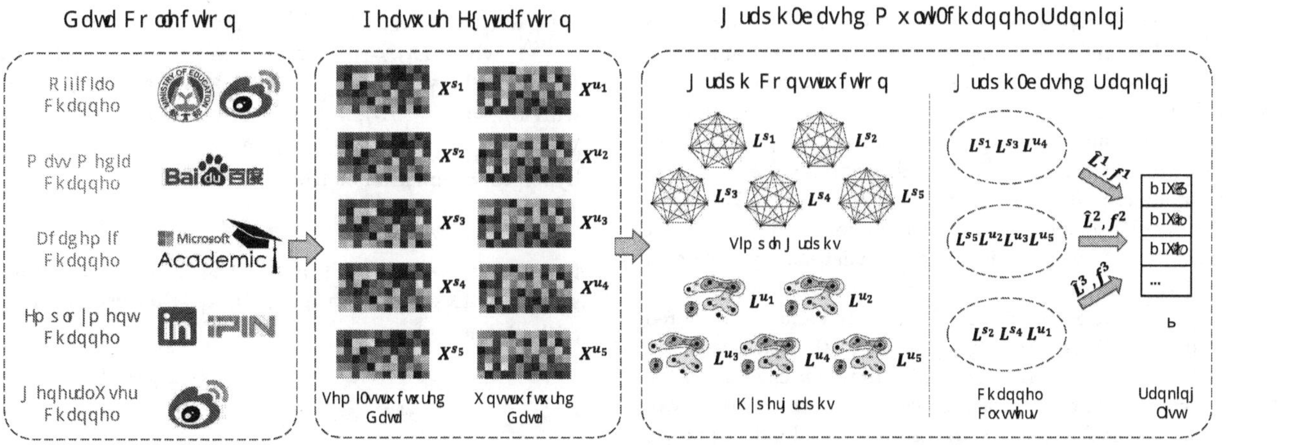

Figure 1: Schematic illustration of social indicator computing and a case study of Chinese university ranking.

2.1 Multi-view Subspace learning

Subspace learning is a widely explored technique to analyze multi-view data. It aims to obtain compact latent representations by leveraging underlying structures and relations across multiple views. Typically, multiple views are mapped into a common space by different algorithms [40], including canonical correlation analysis [15], dictionary learning [4], matrix factorization [20, 29, 41]. In addition, the latent representations are further regularized to be sparse with different norms [34]. Apart from the shallow learning methods, subspace learning is also explored with deep learning models, such as deep restricted Boltzmann machines [31], deep feedforward networks [2, 43], and deep autoencoders [39]. In summary, although great success has been achieved by these models, few of them simultaneously consider the difference between unstructured and semi-structured data, let alone block-wise data missing.

2.2 Unsupervised Ranking

Unsupervised ranking is a popular technique to produce permutation of entities without labled data. Studies on unsupervised ranking are roughly separated into two categories based on whether the entities have direct linkages: 1) Linkage-based ranking. These methods infer rank of entities from the link structure information. For example, PageRank [33] and HITS [24] estimate the importance of webpages from the hyperlinks jumping to the given page. Standing on the shoulder of them, a couple of improvements have been presented. For instance, PopRank [32] further handles Web spam and heterogeneous graphs. BrowseRank [27] integrates the metadata of user behaviors. BiRank [19] expanded it to the bipartite graph. And 2) similarity-based ranking. Similarity-based ranking algorithms enforce that similar entities obtain close ranks. For example, Agarwal [1] constructed a graph, where vertices and edges respectively represent entities and similarity between them, and derived rankings from the Laplacian of the graph. Zhou et al. [44] replaced the conventional graph Laplacian with an iterated and unnormalized one to improve the robustness. Cheng et al. [11] further considered the entity redundancy with sink points in the Laplacian. In addition, Bu et al. [9] utilized the hypergraph instead of the simple one to represent the entities. Yet, most of the aforementioned methods are designed to process single view data.

2.3 University Ranking

Traditional university rankings, such as the U.S.News & World Report[9], Times Higher Education[10], and QS[11], usually measure the qualities of universities with a few pre-defined factors, such as research reputation and academic reputation. These factors are then fused with human designated weights to obtain the final ranking scores. In China, several university rankings are calculated in a similar process by distinct organizations like the Chinese Universities Alumni Association (CUAA)[12], Research Center for China Science Evaluation (RCCSE)[13], and Chinese Academy of Management Science (CAMS)[14]. It is clear that the performance of these ranking systems highly depends on these pre-defined factors and heuristic weights.

Instead of heuristic weights, some researchers attempted to fuse factors with statistical methods. Guarino et al. [18] applied the Bayesian latent variable analysis to learn the weights. Dobrota et al. [12] used I-distance values to estimate the weights based on data from previous years. In addition, some attempts have been done to rank universities with new factors. Lages et al. [25] ranked universities by the importance of their corresponding Wikipedia pages. Kapur et al. [23] utilized LinkedIn Economic Graph data to rank universities by employment of graduates. To sum up, these aforementioned ranking methods pay more attention to weight tuning or calculating specific factors. With the multi-channel Web data, our ranking method explores multi-facets of universities and thus ranks the university precisely.

3 METHODOLOGY

We first define some notations. In particular, we use bold capital letters (e.g., $\mathbf{X}$) and bold lowercase letters (e.g., $\mathbf{x}$) to denote matrices

[9] http://www.usnews.com/rankings.
[10] https://www.timeshighereducation.com/.
[11] http://www.qs.com/.
[12] http://www.cuaa.net/cur/.
[13] http://www.nseac.com/html/168/.
[14] http://edu.sina.com.cn/gaokao/wushulian/.

and vectors, respectively. We employ non-bold letters (e.g., x) to represent scalars, and Greek letters (e.g., λ) to represent parameters. In addition, $tr(\mathbf{X})$ denotes the trace of $\mathbf{X}$. If not clarified, all vectors are in column forms.

The social indicator computation is formalized as: given a list of N entities, a historical ranking list of all the entities $\mathbf{y} \in \mathbb{R}^N$, and the latest entity descriptions from M channels, $\{[\mathbf{X}^{\mathbf{s}_1}, \mathbf{X}^{\mathbf{u}_1}], [\mathbf{X}^{\mathbf{s}_2}, \mathbf{X}^{\mathbf{u}_2}], \cdots, [\mathbf{X}^{\mathbf{s}_M}, \mathbf{X}^{\mathbf{u}_M}]\}$, social indicator computation is to learn a new ranking list $\mathbf{f} \in \mathbb{R}^N$ by harvesting the current data and the historical ranking list. Thereinto, $\mathbf{X}^{\mathbf{s}_m} \in \mathbb{R}^{N \times D^{sm}}$ and $\mathbf{X}^{\mathbf{u}_m} \in \mathbb{R}^{N \times D^{um}}$ are the features extracted from semi-structured and unstructured data from the m-th channel; and $\mathbf{y}$ refers to the latest released social indicator by professional organizations. For example, if the desired social indicator is Chinese university ranking in 2017, $\mathbf{y}$ will be the ranking results in 2016. To compute social indicators, we present a novel graph-based multi-channel ranking framework: 1) We first construct a simple graph on the semi-structured data and a hypergraph on the unstructured data for each channel. 2) We then cluster all the graphs into groups based on the correlation of their Laplacian matrices. 3) We ultimately learn a cluster-wise ranking list and fuse them together within a tailored objective function.

3.1 Graph Construction

In some channels, there indeed exist both semi-structured and unstructured data to describe the given entities. Semi-structured ones are of higher quality and thus more discriminative. On the contrary, the unstructured data are more noisy. As their distinct structures and features, we refuse to naively merge the semi-structured and unstructured data. Inspired by that simple graph is sensitive to the data noise; whereas the hypergraph is typically more robust but less discriminative than the simple one [15], we leverage the simple graph and hypergraph to represent the entities and their relations. For each channel, we construct a simple graph over the semi-structured data and a hypergraph over the unstructured ones so that we neither sacrifice the discrimination of semi-structured data nor be affected by the noisy unstructured ones.

3.1.1 Simple Graph Construction. In a simple graph, vertices represent entities and edges refer to their pairwise similarities. A simple graph with N vertices is represented by an incidence matrix, $\mathbf{W} \in \mathbb{R}^{N \times N}$ and a diagonal vertex degree matrix, $\mathbf{D} \in \mathbb{R}^{N \times N}$, where W_{ij} is the similarity between the i-th and j-th vertices; $D_{ii} = \sum_{j=1}^{N} W_{ij}$ is the degree of the i-th vertex. Given $\mathbf{X}^{\mathbf{s}_m}$, $\mathbf{W}$ is estimated as,

$$W_{ij} = \begin{cases} exp(-\|\mathbf{x}_i^{\mathbf{s}_m} - \mathbf{x}_j^{\mathbf{s}_m}\|^2/2\sigma^2), & \text{if } i \neq j, \\ 0, & \text{otherwise,} \end{cases} \quad (1)$$

where the radius parameter σ is simply set as the median of the Euclidean distances of all pairs. Following [1], we then calculate the normalized graph Laplacian matrix as,

$$\mathbf{L}^{\mathbf{s}_m} = \mathbf{D}^{-1/2}(\mathbf{D} - \mathbf{W})\mathbf{D}^{-1/2}. \quad (2)$$

3.1.2 Hypergraph Construction. Generalized from a simple graph where an edge links pairwise vertices, an edge in a hypergraph connects a set of vertices to represent the finitary relations. A hypergraph with N vertices and P edges is represented by an incidence matrix $\mathbf{H} \in \mathbb{R}^{N \times P}$, edge degree matrix $\mathbf{E} \in \mathbb{R}^{P \times P}$, edge weight matrix $\mathbf{W} \in \mathbb{R}^{P \times P}$, and vertex degree matrix $\mathbf{V} \in \mathbb{R}^{N \times N}$, where $H_{ij} = 1$ if the i-th vertex is connected by the j-th edge, otherwise $H_{ij} = 0$; $\mathbf{E}$, $\mathbf{W}$, and $\mathbf{V}$ are diagonal matrices with $E_{jj} = \sum_{i=1}^{N} H_{ij}$, W_{jj} as the weight of the j-th edge, and $V_{ii} = \sum_{j=1}^{P} W_{jj} H_{ij}$. Following [9], given $\mathbf{X}^{\mathbf{u}_m}$, we calculate the hypergraph Laplacian matrix with,

$$\mathbf{L}^{\mathbf{u}_m} = \mathbf{V}^{-1/2}(\mathbf{V} - \mathbf{H}\mathbf{W}\mathbf{E}^{-1}\mathbf{H}^T)\mathbf{V}^{-1/2}. \quad (3)$$

In particular, we construct the j-th edge by connecting the k-most similar vertices to the j-th vertex $\mathcal{N}_j(\mathbf{x}_j^{\mathbf{u}_m})$ and estimate the weight of the j-th edge by,

$$W_{jj} = \sum_{\mathbf{x}_i^{\mathbf{u}_m} \in \mathcal{N}_j(\mathbf{x}_j^{\mathbf{u}_m})} exp(-\|\mathbf{x}_i^{\mathbf{u}_m} - \mathbf{x}_j^{\mathbf{u}_m}\|^2/2\sigma^2). \quad (4)$$

3.2 Channel Clustering

After graph construction, the original multi-channel descriptions $\{[\mathbf{X}^{\mathbf{s}_1}, \mathbf{X}^{\mathbf{u}_1}], [\mathbf{X}^{\mathbf{s}_2}, \mathbf{X}^{\mathbf{u}_2}], \cdots, [\mathbf{X}^{\mathbf{s}_M}, \mathbf{X}^{\mathbf{u}_M}]\}$ are mapped to the Laplacian representations $\{[\mathbf{L}^{\mathbf{s}_1}, \mathbf{L}^{\mathbf{u}_1}], [\mathbf{L}^{\mathbf{s}_2}, \mathbf{L}^{\mathbf{u}_2}], \cdots, [\mathbf{L}^{\mathbf{s}_M}, \mathbf{L}^{\mathbf{u}_M}]\}$. It is not wise to directly fuse all graphs by conventional multi-view ranking techniques, because the correlation among some channels may be very strong, and it may be very weak among others. Therefore, some information may be lost if they are indiscriminately projected to a common space. Towards this end, we first divide all the graphs into groups based on the correlations between their Laplacian matrices with spectral clustering [37]. During the clustering, the distance between two Laplacian matrices is estimated by Hilbert-Schmidt Independence Criterion (HSIC),

$$dis(\mathbf{L}^{\mathbf{i}}, \mathbf{L}^{\mathbf{j}}) = HSIC(\mathbf{L}^{\mathbf{i}}, \mathbf{L}^{\mathbf{j}}, \phi, \varphi) = (N-1)^2/tr(\mathbf{PHQH}), \quad (5)$$

where ϕ and φ are the kernel functions of the i-th and j-th matrices; $\mathbf{P}$ and $\mathbf{Q} \in \mathbb{R}^{N \times N}$ are the Gram matrices with $P_{mn} = \phi(\mathbf{l}_m^{\mathbf{i}}, \mathbf{l}_n^{\mathbf{i}})$ and $Q_{mn} = \varphi(\mathbf{l}_m^{\mathbf{j}}, \mathbf{l}_n^{\mathbf{j}})$; $\mathbf{H} = \mathbf{I} - N^{-2}\mathbf{I}^1 \in \mathbb{R}^{N \times N}$ centers the Gram matrix to have zero mean, where $\mathbf{I}$ and $\mathbf{I}^1$ respectively denote identity and all-one matrices.

3.3 Objective Function

Given the historical ranking list $\mathbf{y}$ and the clustered Laplacian matrices in K groups, $\{\{\mathbf{L}^{1_1}, \cdots, \mathbf{L}^{1_{s^1}}\}, \cdots, \{\mathbf{L}^{K_1}, \cdots, \mathbf{L}^{K_{s^K}}\}\}$, where S^k denotes the number of matrices in the k-th cluster. The desired ranking list $\mathbf{f}$ is learned via the following function:

$$\Gamma = \min_{\hat{\mathbf{L}}^k, \mathbf{f}, \mathbf{f}^k} \frac{1}{2} \sum_{k=1}^{K} l_{intra}(\hat{\mathbf{L}}^k, \{\mathbf{L}^{k_1}, \cdots, \mathbf{L}^{k_{s^k}}\}) + \frac{\lambda_1}{2} \sum_{k=1}^{K} l_{man}(\hat{\mathbf{L}}^k, \mathbf{f}^k) + \frac{\lambda_2}{2} l_{inter}(\mathbf{f}, \mathbf{y}, \{\mathbf{f}^1, \cdots, \mathbf{f}^k\}), \quad (6)$$

where l_{intra}, l_{man}, and l_{inter} respectively denote the loss of: 1) intra-group fusion, 2) manifold ranking, and 3) inter-group fusion. The intra-group fusion aims to learn a common Laplacian matrix $\hat{\mathbf{L}}^k \in \mathbb{R}^{N \times N}$ to fuse the Laplacian matrices $\{\mathbf{L}^{k_1}, \cdots, \mathbf{L}^{k_{s^k}}\}$ in the k-th group. Upon the k-th common Laplacian matrix, the manifold ranking learns a ranking list $\mathbf{f}^k \in \mathbb{R}^N$. Inter-group fusion combines rankings from different groups into the final ranking $\mathbf{f}$. $\mathbf{f}$ is further regularized by the historical ranking result $\mathbf{y}$ so that it satisfies the ranking smoothness. λ_1 and λ_2 are hyper-parameters to balance the three kinds of loss.

3.3.1 Intra-group Fusion. The intra-group fusion leans a common Laplacian matrix $\hat{\mathbf{L}}^{\mathbf{k}}$ to fuse the Laplacian matrices in the k-th group $\{\mathbf{L}^{\mathbf{k}_1}, \cdots, \mathbf{L}^{\mathbf{k}_{S^k}}\}$ by minimizing l_{intra},

$$\frac{1}{2}\sum_{i=1}^{S^k} tr\left((\hat{\mathbf{L}}^{\mathbf{k}} - \mathbf{L}^{\mathbf{k_i}})^T \mathbf{S}^{\mathbf{k_i}}(\hat{\mathbf{L}}^{\mathbf{k}} - \mathbf{L}^{\mathbf{k_i}})\right). \quad (7)$$

Thereinto, $\mathbf{S}^{\mathbf{k_i}} \in \mathbb{R}^{N\times N}$ is a diagonal matrix with,

$$S_{jj}^{k_i} = \begin{cases} 0, & \text{if the } j\text{-th entity misses the } i\text{-th channel,} \\ 1, & \text{otherwise.} \end{cases} \quad (8)$$

It is a selector to avoid the biases in the common Laplacian caused by data missing. A toy example with two graphs shown in Figure 2 illustrates the effects of the selector. In the example, data of the n-th entity in the k_1-th graph are missing. Thus, $\mathbf{S}^{\mathbf{k}_1}$ and $\mathbf{S}^{\mathbf{k}_2}$ are set as $\mathbf{I} \in \mathbb{R}^{N\times N}$ except $S_{nn}^{k_1} = 0$. So entries related to the n-th entity in the common Laplacian learned by the intra-group fusion are the same as those in $\mathbf{L}^{\mathbf{k}_2}$. However, those entries could be bias towards zero if there is no selectors in the intra-group fusion. This is why we claim by integrating selectors, our intra-group fusion alleviates the impacts of data missing.

3.3.2 Manifold Ranking. Given a common Laplacian matrix $\hat{\mathbf{L}}^{\mathbf{k}}$, manifold ranking learns a ranking list $\mathbf{f}^{\mathbf{k}}$, where similar entities obtain close ranks, via,

$$\min_{\mathbf{f}^{\mathbf{k}}} l_{man}(\hat{\mathbf{L}}^{\mathbf{k}}, \mathbf{f}^{\mathbf{k}}) = \mathbf{f}^{\mathbf{k}T}\hat{\mathbf{L}}^{\mathbf{k}}\mathbf{f}^{\mathbf{k}}. \quad (9)$$

3.3.3 Inter-group Fusion. As aforementioned, different local ranking lists are learned from different clusters, i.e., we have $\{\mathbf{f}^1, \mathbf{f}^2, \cdots, \mathbf{f}^K\}$. The inter-group fusion learns a set of weights $\mathbf{b} = [b_1, b_2, \cdots, b_K] \in \mathbb{R}^K$ to get the desired ranking $\mathbf{f} = \sum_{k=1}^{K} b_k \mathbf{f}^{\mathbf{k}}$ and regulates the fused ranking to be smooth with the historical one by minimizing l_{inter},

$$(\sum_{k=1}^{K} b_k\mathbf{f}^{\mathbf{k}} - \mathbf{y})^T \mathbf{C}(\sum_{k=1}^{K} b_k\mathbf{f}^{\mathbf{k}} - \mathbf{y}),\ s.t.\ \sum_{k=1}^{K} b_k = 1, \quad (10)$$

where $\mathbf{C} \in \mathbb{R}^{N\times N}$ is diagonal matrix with $C_{jj} = c_j$. c_j is the pre-calculated weight of the j-th entity controlling the entity-aware ranking smoothness. Taking university ranking as an example, c_j is large for top universities while small for bottom ones.

3.4 Optimization

We adopt the alternating strategy to optimize the proposed model, until it converges.

3.4.1 Computing $\hat{\mathbf{L}}^{\mathbf{k}}$. To ease the optimization of $\hat{\mathbf{L}}^{\mathbf{k}}$, we set each common Laplacian as,

$$\hat{\mathbf{L}}^{\mathbf{k}} = \sum_{i=1}^{S^k} a_i^k \mathbf{L}^{\mathbf{k_i}},\ s.t.\ \sum_{i=1}^{S^k} a_i^k = 1, \quad (11)$$

and optimize each $\hat{\mathbf{L}}^{\mathbf{k}}$ independently keeping $\mathbf{f}$ and $\mathbf{b}$ fixed. After removing the fixed parts and substituting the constraint $\sum_{i=1}^{S^k} a_i = 1$ with Lagrange multipier δ, the objective function is rewritten as,

$$\min_{\mathbf{a}^{\mathbf{k}}} \frac{1}{2}\sum_{i=1}^{S^k} tr\left((\sum_{j=1}^{S^k} a_j^k\mathbf{L}^{\mathbf{k_j}} - \mathbf{L}^{\mathbf{k_i}})^T\mathbf{S}^{\mathbf{k_i}}(\sum_{j=1}^{S^k} a_j^k\mathbf{L}^{\mathbf{k_j}} - \mathbf{L}^{\mathbf{k_i}})\right) + \frac{\lambda_1}{2}\mathbf{f}^{\mathbf{k}T}\sum_{i=1}^{S^k} a_i^k\mathbf{L}^{\mathbf{k_i}}\mathbf{f}^{\mathbf{k}} + \delta(1 - \mathbf{e}^T\mathbf{a}^{\mathbf{k}}), \quad (12)$$

where $\mathbf{e} = [1, 1, \cdots, 1]^T \in \mathbb{R}^{S^k}$. We then take the derivative of Eqn.(12) regarding a_i^k, as follows,

$$\sum_{j=1}^{S^k}(a_j^k S^k - 1)tr\left(\mathbf{L}^{\mathbf{k_i}}\mathbf{S}^{\mathbf{k_i}}\mathbf{L}^{\mathbf{k_j}}\right) + \frac{\lambda_1}{2}\mathbf{f}^{\mathbf{k}T}\mathbf{L}^{\mathbf{k_i}}\mathbf{f}^{\mathbf{k}} - \delta. \quad (13)$$

Setting it to zero and rearranging the terms, all a_i^k's and δ can be learned by solving the following linear system,

$$\mathbf{M}\widehat{\mathbf{a}^{\mathbf{k}}} = \mathbf{u}, \quad (14)$$

where $\widehat{\mathbf{a}^{\mathbf{k}}} = [a_1^k, a_2^k, \cdots, a_{S^k}^k, \delta]^T \in \mathbb{R}^{S^k+1}$, $\mathbf{u} = [u_1, u_2, \cdots, u_{S^k}, 1]^T \in \mathbb{R}^{S^k+1}$, and $\mathbf{M} \in \mathbb{R}^{(S^k+1)\times(S^k+1)}$. M_{ij} and u_i are defined as follows,

$$\begin{cases} M_{ij} = S^k tr\left(\mathbf{L}^{\mathbf{k_i}}\mathbf{S}^{\mathbf{k_i}}\mathbf{L}^{\mathbf{k_j}}\right), & i,j \neq S^k + 1, \\ M_{ii} = 0, & i = S^k + 1, \\ M_{ij} = 1, & \text{otherwise,} \\ u_i = \sum_{j=1}^{S^k} tr\left(\mathbf{L}^{\mathbf{k_i}}\mathbf{S}^{\mathbf{k_i}}\mathbf{L}^{\mathbf{k_j}}\right) - \frac{\lambda_1}{2}\mathbf{f}^{\mathbf{k}T}\mathbf{L}^{\mathbf{k_i}}\mathbf{f}^{\mathbf{k}}. \end{cases} \quad (15)$$

3.4.2 Computing $\mathbf{f}$. By fixing $\hat{\mathbf{L}}^{\mathbf{k}}$'s and $\mathbf{b}$, we take the derivative of Eqn.(6) regarding $\mathbf{f}^{\mathbf{k}}$ and then reach the following linear system,

$$\mathbf{W}\widehat{\mathbf{f}} = \mathbf{t}, \quad (16)$$

which can be restated as,

$$\begin{bmatrix} \mathbf{W}_{11} & \mathbf{W}_{12} & \dots & \mathbf{W}_{1K} \\ \vdots & \vdots & \ddots & \vdots \\ \mathbf{W}_{K1} & \mathbf{W}_{K2} & \dots & \mathbf{W}_{KK} \end{bmatrix} \begin{bmatrix} \mathbf{f}^1 \\ \vdots \\ \mathbf{f}^K \end{bmatrix} = \begin{bmatrix} \mathbf{t}_1 \\ \vdots \\ \mathbf{t}_K \end{bmatrix}, \quad (17)$$

where $\mathbf{W} \in \mathbb{R}^{KN\times KN}$ is a block matrix with $K \times K$ blocks; $\widehat{\mathbf{f}} = [\mathbf{f}^{1T}, \mathbf{f}^{2T}, \cdots, \mathbf{f}^{ST}]^T \in \mathbb{R}^{KN}$ and $\mathbf{t} = [\mathbf{t_1}^T, \mathbf{t_2}^T, \cdots, \mathbf{t_K}^T]^T \in \mathbb{R}^{KN}$ are both block vectors with K blocks; $\mathbf{W_{kj}}$ and $\mathbf{t_k}$ are defined as follows,

$$\begin{cases} \mathbf{W_{kk}} = \lambda_1\mathbf{L}^{\mathbf{k}} + \lambda_2 b_k^2\mathbf{C}, & k = j, \\ \mathbf{W_{kj}} = \lambda_2 b_k b_j\mathbf{C}, & \text{otherwise,} \\ \mathbf{t_k} = \lambda_2 b_k\mathbf{C}\mathbf{y}. \end{cases} \quad (18)$$

As $\mathbf{t}$ can be treated as a constant vector as $\mathbf{b}$ is fixed, $\mathbf{W}$ is apparently invertible. We thus can derive the closed-form solution of $\widehat{\mathbf{f}}$ as,

$$\widehat{\mathbf{f}} = \mathbf{W}^{-1}\mathbf{t}. \quad (19)$$

Finally, $\mathbf{f}$ is updated based on the solved $\widehat{\mathbf{f}}$ as,

$$\mathbf{f} = \sum_{k=1}^{K} b_k\mathbf{f}^{\mathbf{k}}. \quad (20)$$

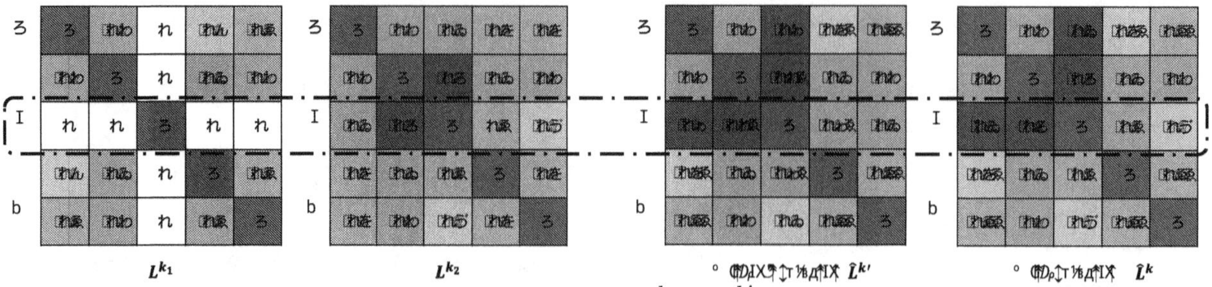

Figure 2: A toy example to illustrate the impact of missing data. L^k and $L^{k'}$ are the common Laplacian learned by the intra-group fusion with and without selectors.

Table 1: Statistics of the collected multi-channel data.

Channels	Sources	#Universities	#Items	Duration
Official Channel	MOE	743	96,551	13.06-15.06
	Sina Weibo	721	10,912,234	15.01-16.05
Mass Media Channel	Baidu News	743	508,851	15.01-16.05
Academic Channel	Microsoft Academic	456	1,211,102	11.01-16.03
Employment Channel	LinkedIn	411	411	-
	iPIN	722	722	-
General User Channel	Sina Weibo	573	2,025,777	15.01-16.05

3.4.3 Computing b. We first fix $\hat{\mathbf{L}}^{\mathbf{k}}$'s and $\mathbf{f}^{\mathbf{k}}$'s, and then substitute the constraint $\sum_{k=1}^{K} b_k = 1$ into the objective function with Lagrange multiplier δ and rewrite it without fixed part as,

$$\min_{\mathbf{b}} \frac{\lambda_2}{2}(\sum_{k=1}^{K} b_k \mathbf{f^k} - \mathbf{y})^T \mathbf{C}(\sum_{k=1}^{K} b_k \mathbf{f^k} - \mathbf{y}) + \delta(1 - \mathbf{e}^T \mathbf{b}), \quad (21)$$

where $\mathbf{e} = [1, 1, \cdots, 1]^T \in \mathbb{R}^K$. We then take the derivative of Eqn.(21) regarding b_k and obtain,

$$\mathbf{M}\widehat{\mathbf{b}} = \mathbf{u}, \quad (22)$$

where $\widehat{\mathbf{b}} = [b_1, b_2, \cdots, b_K, \delta]^T \in \mathbb{R}^{K+1}$, $\mathbf{u} = [\lambda_2 \mathbf{f^1}^T \mathbf{C}\mathbf{y}, \lambda_2 \mathbf{f^2}^T \mathbf{C}\mathbf{y}, \cdots, \lambda_2 \mathbf{f^K}^T \mathbf{C}\mathbf{y}, 1]^T \in \mathbb{R}^{K+1}$, and $\mathbf{M} \in \mathbb{R}^{(K+1)\times(K+1)}$ with M_{kj}, as follows,

$$\begin{cases} M_{kj} = \lambda_2 \mathbf{f^k}^T \mathbf{C}\mathbf{f^j}, & k, j \neq S+1, \\ M_{kk} = 0, & k = S+1, \\ M_{kj} = 1, & \text{otherwise}. \end{cases} \quad (23)$$

4 CHINESE UNIVERSITY RANKING

4.1 Data Collection

In this work, we take the Chinese university ranking as a case study of social indicator computation. For each university, we first collected Web data from five channels. They are the official, mass media, academic, employment, and general user channels. The statistics of the collected data are summarized in Table 1.

4.1.1 Official Channel. Official channel contains the primary information of universities, such as student quality, official activities, and development plans, which plays a pivotal role in inferring university quality. Data in official channel are usually released by government agencies and university themselves. They includes: 1) MOE[15]. From the platform of MOE, we collected university profiles, such as location and category, and the enrollment score of universities from 2013-2015[16]. 2) Sina Weibo[17]. Sina Weibo is one of the most popular SNSs in China. Most Chinese universities publicize their official activities and announcements through their official Sina Weibo accounts. We thus crawled the historical posts from such accounts.

4.1.2 Mass Media Channel. It contains insights of mass media which uncovers the hot topics, events, discoveries, and even criticisms related to universities. News reports from mass media are usually formalized by professional journalists with incisiveness of arguments, and hence their opinions are objective. To take full advantages of such opinions, we collected news reports mentioned the universities of interest from Baidu News[18].

4.1.3 Academic Channel. This channel contains academic records of universities showing their academic contributions and influences. Such records are available from online bibliographic databases. In this work, given a university, we collected papers whose authors' affiliation is the given university and papers' citations from Microsoft Academic.

4.1.4 Employment Channel. Employment channel contains employment status of universities' graduate students. This is one of the key factors related to university quality, because most of students pursue higher education for better employment. The employment data are accessible through employment-oriented SNSs and third party data analysis companies. They include: 1) iPIN[19]. We collected employment data of the university's graduate students, including average salary, working location distribution, and male-female ratio, from its homepage in iPIN, a data analysis company in China. 2) LinkedIn. We collected *People also viewed* information from universities' homepage in LinkedIn to infer employment similarity among universities.

[15]http://gaokao.chsi.com.cn/.
[16]In China, last year high school students first take part in the National College Entrance Examination (NCEE). They then apply for universities based on their NCEE scores. Regarding applications from students, the university selects students by their scores from high to low. The lowest score of the selected students is released as the enrollment score of the university.
[17]http://weibo.com/.
[18]http://news.baidu.com/.
[19]http://www.ipin.com/.

Table 2: Features extracted from the multi-channel data.

Channels	Semi-structured Data	Dimension	Unstructured Data	Dimension
Official Channel	NCEE_enrollment_line, category, is_985, is_211, key_subjects_count, city, fans_count, followers_count, posts_count, comments_count, likes_count, etc.	78	topics	56
Mass Media Channel	monthly_reports_count	16	topics, sentiment	95
Academic Channel	papers_count, first_author_papers_count, cooperated_papers_count, authors_count, citations_count, citations_author, citations_paper	13	-	0
Employment Channel	average_sallary, average_sallary_top5_subjects, working_city, male_female_ratio, similar_universities	443	-	0
General User Channel	posts_count, reposted_count, likes_count, comments_count,	4	topics, sentiment	81

4.1.5 General User Channel. It contains public impressions, attitudes, and sentiment polarities of universities shared in SNSs posts, signaling the reputation of universities. We hence collected posts mentioning the given university from Sina Weibo.

4.1.6 Historical Ranking Result. The historical ranking result y is estimated from three most popular Chinese university rankings: CUAA, RCCSE, and CAMS (Wu Shulian). To generate a relatively objective historical ranking list, we averagely fused ranking results in 2015 of these three traditional rankings. It should be noted, in the future, the historical ranking result can be obtained from our previous release rather than the result of traditional rankings.

4.2 Feature Extraction

Regarding the collected multi-channel data, we extracted three types of features to describe each university: 1) Sentiment features. We noticed that data in mass media and general user channels convey the attitude and sentiment of users [26]. We thus utilized the Chinese microblog sentiment analysis tool [22] to judge the polarity of contents from the mass media and general user channels. For each given input, this tool would generate a three dimension distribution to denote its probability to be negative, neutral, and positive. 2) Topic features. According to our observation, contents in the official, mass media, or general user channel about similar universities are likely to express similar topics. For instance, reports from mass media may have a higher probability to report the topics of "research achievements" and "technologies" for top universities. Inspired by this, we explored the topic distributions over official, mass media, and general user channel. In particular, we generated topic distributions using Latent Dirichlet Allocation [6], which has been widely used in topic modeling. 3) Statistic features. Quality of universities are directly reflected by the volume of statistics, for instance, the average salary of graduate students, the number of publications, and the NCEE enrollment scores. Together with the sentiment and topic features, the statistical features are summarized in Table 2.

5 EXPERIMENT

5.1 Experimental Settings

5.1.1 Entity-aware Ranking Smoothness. As our historical ranking y is estimated from CUAA, RCCSE, and CAMS, the ranking smoothness weight of the i-th univeristy C_{ii} in Eqn.(6) is assigned as the ratio of ranking lists containing the i-th university among CUAA, RCCSE, and CAMS.

Table 3: Statistics of the ground truth.

Universities	University Pairs			
	Label 1	Label 0	Label -1	All
640	178,342	48,448	178,342	405,132

5.1.2 Ground Truth. Establishing the ground truth for university ranking from scratch by ourselves is extremely resource consuming and not reliable. We thus turn to justify the 2016 university ranking results by our model in a pair-wise fashion. In particular, although the traditional university ranking results of CUAA, RCCSE, and CAMS are time- and resource-consuming, they were generated by experts with sufficient domain knowledge. They are hence remarkably reasonable. We established the pair-wise ground truth upon their 2016 results. Given a pair of universities $< u_i, u_j >$, if all CUAA, RCCSE, and CAMS rank u_i as better or worse than u_j, then the pair is labeled as 1 or -1, respectively. Otherwise, it is labeled as 0, meaning u_i and u_j are not distinguished. The statistics of the constructed ground truth are shown in Table 3.

5.1.3 Evaluation Metrics. The performance of our model and the baselines was measured by Cohen's kappa coefficient (κ) [30], macro-averaged precision (Pre), macro-averaged recall (Rec), macro-averaged F1 score (F1), and micro-averaged F1[20] [5]. We also carried out the significance test and reported the p-values.

5.1.4 University Pair Tagging. Regarding the learned ranking list f, the label of the i-th and j-th universities was set as,

$$\begin{cases} sign(f_i - f_j), & \text{if } |f_i - f_j| > \theta, \\ 0, & \text{otherwise.} \end{cases} \tag{24}$$

θ was set as 0.004, as it outperformed the others in $\{0.001, 0.002, \cdots, 0.01\}$ during our preliminary experiments.

5.1.5 Compared Methods. To show the effectiveness of our scheme, we compared it with the following state-of-the-art methods,

- **Historical Ranking (HR)**: It takes the historical ranking list y as current ranking, i.e., f = y.

[20]Regarding our ground truth, the micro-averaged Pre, Rec, and F1 are equal, we thus only reported the F1.

- **NCEE Enrollment Scores (NES)**: It ranks universities with higher average NCEE enrollment scores in the front.
- **Early Fusion (EF)**: It first concatenates features of all channels, constructs a simple graph as described in Section 3.1.1, and then performs manifold ranking with the simple graph [21].
- **Late Fusion (LF)**: It separately performs simple graph construction and manifold ranking upon each channel, and then averagely combines the generated ranking lists [8].
- **Joint Learning (JL)**: **JL** constructs simple graph on each channel and then learns a common ranking list by jointly regulating it on simple graph Laplacian matrices of all channels [38].
- **Subspace Learning (SL)**: It first maps multi-channel data to subspaces with the same dimension by dictionary learning [4]. Based on the representations in subspaces, it then performs ranking via **JL**.

It should be noted that **EF**, **lF**, **JL**, and **SL** also encourage the final ranking results to be close to the initial ranking one.

5.2 Parameter Tuning and Sensitivity Analysis

In the proposed **GMR**, we have two implicit parameters and two explicit parameters. They are the number of nearest neighbors k in hypergraph construction, the number of clusters K, λ_1 and λ_2. During the experiments, we heuristically set k as 5 based on our observation on the data. The optimal values of the remaining parameters were carefully tuned on the development set. In particular, in each round of the 5-fold cross-validation, we divided our dataset into two parts: 80% of the universities pairs were used for tuning, 20% were used for testing. We employed grid search to select the optimal parameters with a small but adaptive step size. The search ranges for λ_1, λ_2, and K are $[0.1, 100]$, $[10, 10,000]$, and $[1, 8]$. The parameters corresponding to the largest micro-averaged F1 were used to report the final results. For other compared methods, the procedures of parameter tuning are the same to ensure fair comparison.

Take the tuning procedure of one round in the 5-fold cross validation as an example, we observed that our model reached the optimal performance when $K = 3$, $\lambda_1 = 9$, $\lambda_2 = 500$. Figure 3 illustrates the performance of our model with respect to these three parameters. This was accomplished by varying one and fixing the others with optimal values.

5.3 Performance Comparison

The comparison results between our proposed **GMR** and baselines are summarized in Table 4. From this table, we have the following observations: 1) **NES** and **HR** perform worse than the others. This tells us that the graph-based ranking methods successfully leverage the multi-channel Web data and hence improve the ranking performance. 2) **LF** performs worse than the other multi-channel ranking methods. This is because it equally fuses channels instead of distinguishing them with different confidences. 3) **GMR** shows superior performance to the others. This justifies the importance of integrating the block-wise data completion, cluster-wise ranking, and ranking results fusion within a unified model. 4) All the p-values of the pairwise significance t-test based on 5-fold evaluation are greatly much than 0.05. This demonstrates that the performance improvements achieved by our model over the baselines are statistically significant.

5.4 Component-wise Comparison

We also carried out experiments to justify the effectiveness of each component in the proposed **GMR**. In particular, we compared the following methods by disabling some terms of our objective function in Eqn.(6).

- **GMR-HRC**: We set **C** to an identity matrix to ignore the historical ranking confidence. **GMR-MD**: We set all $\mathbf{S}^{\mathbf{k}_i}$'s to identity matrices to ignore the missing data problem.
- **GMR-DH**: In this method, the semi-structured and unstructured data from one channel are directly concatenated and used to construct the simple graph.
- **GMR-CC**: It learns a common space from all channels and then performs ranking on the common representations to ignore inter-group fusion.

Table 5 displays the performance of the above methods. From this table, we observed that: 1) **GMR** performs better than the remaining methods. It confirms the effectiveness of jointly considering of the block-wise data completion, cluster-wise ranking, and ranking results fusion. 2) **GMR-HRC** performs much worse than **GMR**. It shows the importance of carefully setting entity-aware ranking smoothness, and hence assigning identical ranking smoothness to all the entities may lead to suboptimal performance. 3) It is interesting to see that **GMR-DH** achieves better macro-averaged Rec since it predicts more university pairs to be 0, a relatively rare class. **GMR** fails to identify such pairs since the similarity between entities in the pair is carved by their nearest neighbors. Although sacrificing such pairs, **GMR** successfully recalls more pairs in total, and hence verifies the robustness of hypergraph.

5.5 Channel Comparison

To measure the representation ability of each channel, we held one channel out and fed the others into our **GMR** model. The experimental results are displayed in Table 6. We observed: 1) The performance of **GMR** decreases more when the official channel is not fed into. This suggests that the official channel provides more informative and important cues for university ranking. 2) With all channels fed into, **GMR** performs best, which indicates that universities can be comprehensively described by more channels. 3) All the p-values of the pairwise significance t-test are greatly smaller than 0.05, which verifies the significance of performance improvements.

5.6 Development Set Comparison

Parameter tuning of our **GMR** relies on the development set. Towards the whole ranking list generation in 2016, it is arbitrary to directly tune parameters with the ground truth. We thus constructed a new development set (DS2015) from the ranking results of CUAA, RCCSE, and CAMS in 2015 for whole ranking list generation task. University pairs in DS2015 were labeled in the same way as the ground truth. To uncover the effectiveness of the constructed development set, we compared it with arbitrarily tuning parameters based on ground truth (GT). Corresponding performances are shown in Table 7. As can be seen, the performance

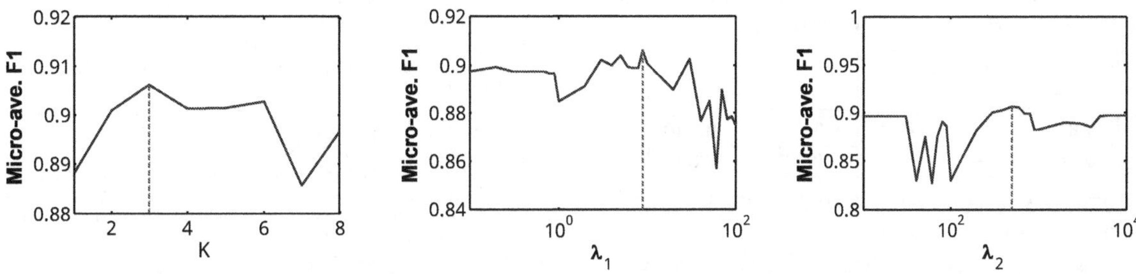

Figure 3: Procedure of parameter tuning by varying one and fixing others. The red dotted line marked the optimal settings.

Table 4: Performance comparison between our method and baselines.

Methods	Macro Averaged				Micro Averaged		κ	p-value@κ
	Pre	Rec	F1	p-value@F1	F1	p-value@F1		
NES	0.507±3e-7	0.576±4e-7	0.540±3e-7	8e-10	0.761±7e-1	4e-9	0.572±2e-6	3e-9
HR	0.776±4e-4	0.658±2e-7	0.618±2e-7	1e-9	0.868±3e-7	2e-7	0.764±1e-6	8e-8
EF	0.833±5e-6	0.786±4e-6	0.801±3e-6	1e-5	0.896±5e-7	2e-6	0.823±1e-6	2e-6
LF	**0.844±6e-5**	0.692±2e-6	0.684±6e-6	2e-8	0.878±7e-7	4e-7	0.784±2e-6	2e-7
JL	0.826±1e-5	0.789±6e-6	0.802±7e-6	2e-4	0.894±3e-6	1e-5	0.820±8e-6	1e-5
SL	0.822±1e-5	0.788±2e-6	0.800±4e-6	8e-5	0.893±2e-6	6e-6	0.818±6e-6	6e-6
GMR	0.841±1e-5	**0.797±4e-6**	**0.812±4e-6**	-	**0.906±2e-6**	-	**0.840±4e-6**	-

Table 5: Performance comparison among components in our GMR model.

Methods	Macro Averaged				Micro Averaged		κ	p-value@κ
	Pre	Rec	F1	p-value@F1	F1	p-value@F1		
GMR-HRC	0.838±9e-6	0.783±2e-6	0.800±2e-6	2e-6	0.898±8e-7	2e-6	0.825±2e-6	2e-6
GMR-MD	0.834±8e-6	0.794±5e-6	0.809±5e-6	8e-4	0.902±1e-6	3e-5	0.834±3e-6	3e-5
GMR-DH	0.833±3e-6	**0.798±7e-6**	0.811±5e-6	9e-2	0.903±8e-7	6e-4	0.835±2e-6	1e-3
GMR-CC	0.839±1e-5	0.786±2e-5	0.802±2e-5	5e-4	0.903±3e-6	4e-3	0.834±8e-6	3e-3
GMR	**0.841±1e-5**	0.797±4e-6	**0.812±4e-6**	-	**0.906±2e-6**	-	**0.840±4e-6**	-

Table 6: Performance comparison among channels with our GMR model. Official, Media, Academic, Employ, Crowd respectively denote the official, mass media, academic, employment, and general user channels.

Methods	Macro Averaged				Micro Averaged		κ	p-value@κ
	Pre	Rec	F1	p-value@F1	F1	p-value@F1		
No-Official	0.784±5e-6	0.807±7e-6	0.791±6e-6	7e-6	0.867±4e-6	9e-8	0.783±9e-6	1e-7
No-Media	0.810±2e-6	0.800±3e-6	0.805±2e-6	6e-5	0.893±6e-7	6e-7	0.820±2e-6	9e-7
No-Academic	0.828±1e-5	0.809±8e-6	**0.817±9e-6**	1e-3	0.902±3e-6	2e-4	0.835±9e-6	6e-4
No-Employ	0.831±9e-6	0.780±3e-6	0.795±4e-6	6e-5	0.900±1e-6	3e-4	0.829±3e-6	2e-4
No-Crowd	0.815±1e-5	**0.812±8e-6**	0.814±1e-5	8e-2	0.895±4e-6	1e-5	0.825±1e-5	3e-5
All	**0.841±1e-5**	0.797±4e-6	0.812±4e-6	-	**0.906±2e-6**	-	**0.840±4e-6**	-

of DS2015 is comparable to that of GT, which indicates that our scheme is truly usable and works appropriately without the latest ranking results of CUAA, RCCSE, and CAMS.

5.7 User Study

To further investigate the effectiveness of our scheme, we invited 17 volunteers[21] to evaluate our generated ranking list and the ranking results of RCCSM, CAMS, and CUAA in 2016. Each volunteer was presented the top-30 of each ranking list and was required to assign one of eleven scores (ranging from 0 to 10) according to their subjective opinions. These scores represent the strength of the volunteer's agreement with the given ranking list. The volunteer would assign score s to a ranking list, if the number of universities whose ranks are consensus with the expectations of the volunteer belongs to the range $(3(s-1), 3s]$. For instance, if the volunteer thinks that 20 of the top-30 universities are ranked as exepected, then he/she will assign 7 to the given ranking list. The user study results are summarized in Table 8. As can be seen, our ranking achieves higher average score than traditional rankings. Besides, over half of the volunteers assign highest score to our result among all the given rankings. It shows that our ranking results are comparable to those traditional rankings and further verifies the usability of our scheme.

[21] The volunteers are graduate students, research fellows, and visiting professors in different majors of National University of Singapore, coming from mainland China.

Table 7: Performance comparison between development sets towards the whole ranking list generation.

Methods	Macro Averaged			Micro Ave.	κ
	Pre	Rec	F1	F1	
GT	**0.841**	**0.797**	**0.812**	**0.906**	**0.840**
DS2015	**0.841**	0.793	0.809	0.905	0.837

Table 8: Performance comparison among our ranking and traditional Chinese university rankings.

Ranking Results	Ours	RCCSE	CAMS	CUAA
Average Scores	**8.12±0.99**	7.59±1.51	7.71±1.35	8.06±0.81
Highest Score Percentage	53%	18%	35%	**59%**

6 CONCLUSION AND FUTURE WORK

This paper presented a novel and automatic scheme for social indicator computation by exploring multi-channel Web data. This scheme integrates the block-wise data completion, cluster-wise ranking, and ranking results fusion within a unified model. The scheme is successfully applied to Chinese university ranking, a case study of social indicator. We observed that: 1) the official channel dominates the university ranking performance; and 2) the generated ranking results are comparable to the traditional Chinese university rankings, which demonstrates the effectiveness and rationality of our scheme.

In future, we plan to apply our scheme to other social indicator applications and consider the complementary relatedness among channels instead of simple correlations.

Acknowledgements We would like to thank the anonymous reviewers for their valuable comments. NExT research is supported by the National Research Foundation, Prime Ministers Office, Singapore under its IRC@SG Funding Initiative.

REFERENCES

[1] S. Agarwal. 2006. Ranking on graph data. In *ICML*. ACM, 25–32.
[2] G. Andrew, R. Arora, J. A. Bilmes, and K. Livescu. 2013. Deep canonical correlation analysis.. In *ICML*. 1247–1255.
[3] A. Armstrong, R. Francis, M. Bourne, and I. Dussuyer. 2002. *Difficulties of developing and using social indicators to evaluate government programs: a critical review*. Ph.D. Dissertation.
[4] S. Bahrampour, N. M. Nasrabadi, A. Ray, and W. K. Jenkins. 2016. Multimodal task-driven dictionary learning for image classification. *TIP* 25, 1 (2016), 24–38.
[5] P. N. Bennett and N. Nguyen. 2009. Refined experts: improving classification in large taxonomies. In *SIGIR*. ACM, 11–18.
[6] D. M. Blei, A. Y. Ng, and M. I. Jordan. 2003. Latent dirichlet allocation. *JMLR* 3, Jan (2003), 993–1022.
[7] M. J. Boskin. 2008. Consumer price indexes. *Concise Encyclopedia of Economics* (2008).
[8] E. Bruno and M. M. Stephane. 2009. Multiview clustering: a late fusion approach using latent models. In *SIGIR*. ACM, 736–737.
[9] J. Bu, S. Tan, C. Chen, C. Wang, H. Wu, L. Zhang, and X. He. 2010. Music recommendation by unified hypergraph: combining social media information and music content. In *MM*. ACM, 391–400.
[10] J. Chen, X. Song, L. Nie, X. Wang, H. Zhang, and T. Chua. 2016. Micro Tells Macro: Predicting the Popularity of Micro-Videos via a Transductive Model. In *MM*. ACM, 898–907.
[11] X. Q. Cheng, P. Du, J. Guo, X. Zhu, and Y. Chen. 2013. Ranking on Data Manifold with Sink Points. *TKDE* 25, 1 (Jan 2013), 177–191.
[12] M. Dobrota, M. Bulajic, L. Bornmann, and V. Jeremic. 2016. A new approach to the QS university ranking using the composite I-distance indicator: Uncertainty and sensitivity analyses. *Journal of the Association for Information Science and Technology* 67, 1 (2016), 200–211.
[13] C. Dwork, R. Kumar, M. Naor, and D. Sivakumar. 2001. Rank aggregation methods for the Web. In *WWW*. ACM, 613–622.
[14] Organisation for Economic Co-operation and Development. 1976. *Measuring social well-being: a progress report on the development of social indicators*. OECD Publications Center.
[15] Y. Fu, T. M. Hospedales, T. Xiang, and S. Gong. 2015. Transductive multi-view zero-shot learning. *TPAMI* 37, 11 (2015), 2332–2345.
[16] W. Gao and P. Yang. 2014. Democracy is good for ranking: towards multi-view rank learning and adaptation in web search. In *WSDM*. ACM, 63–72.
[17] U. Gerdtham and B. Jönsson. 2000. International comparisons of health expenditure: theory, data and econometric analysis. *Handbook of Health Economics* 1 (2000), 11–53.
[18] C. Guarino, G. Ridgeway, M. Chun, and R. Buddin. 2005. Latent variable analysis: a new approach to university ranking. *Higher Education in Europe* 30, 2 (2005), 147–165.
[19] X. He, M. Gao, M. Y. Kan, and D. Wang. 2017. BiRank: Towards Ranking on Bipartite Graphs. *TKDE* 29 (2017), 57–71.
[20] X. He, M. Kan, P. Xie, and X. Chen. 2014. Comment-based Multi-view Clustering of Web 2.0 Items. In *WWW*. ACM, 771–782.
[21] J. Jeon, V. Lavrenko, and R. Manmatha. 2003. Automatic image annotation and retrieval using cross-media relevance models. In *SIGIR*. ACM, 119–126.
[22] F. Jiang, Y. Liu, H. Luan, M. Zhang, and S. Ma. 2014. Microblog sentiment analysis with emoticon space model. In *Chinese National Conference on Social Media Processing*. Springer, 76–87.
[23] N. Kapur, N. Lytkin, B. Chen, D. Agarwal, and I. Perisic. 2016. Ranking universities based on career outcomes of graduates. In *SIGKDD*. ACM, 137–144.
[24] J. M. Kleinberg. 1999. Authoritative sources in a hyperlinked environment. *J. ACM* 46, 5 (1999), 604–632.
[25] J. Lages, A. Patt, and D. L. Shepelyansky. 2016. Wikipedia ranking of world universities. *The European Physical Journal B* 89, 3 (2016), 1–12.
[26] L. Liao, X. He, Z. Ren, L. Nie, X. Huan, and T. Chua. 2017. Representativeness-aware Aspect Analysis for Brand Monitoring in Social Media. In *IJCAI*.
[27] Y. Liu, B. Gao, T. Liu, Y. Zhang, Z. Ma, S. He, and H. Li. 2008. BrowseRank: letting Web users vote for page importance. In *SIGIR*. ACM, 451–458.
[28] X. Lu, F. Wu, S. Tang, Z. Zhang, X. He, and Y. Zhuang. 2013. A low rank structural large margin method for cross-modal ranking. In *SIGIR*. ACM, 433–442.
[29] H. Ma, T. C. Zhou, M. R. Lyu, and I. King. 2011. Improving recommender systems by incorporating social contextual information. *TOIS* 29, 2 (2011), 9:1–9:23.
[30] O. Megorskaya, V. Kukushkin, and P. Serdyukov. 2015. On the relation between assessor's agreement and accuracy in gamified relevance assessment. In *SIGIR*. ACM, 605–614.
[31] J. Ngiam, A. Khosla, M. Kim, J. Nam, H. Lee, and A. Y. Ng. 2011. Multimodal deep learning. In *ICML*. 689–696.
[32] Z. Nie, Y. Zhang, J. Wen, and W. Ma. 2005. Object-level ranking: bringing order to Web objects. In *WWW*. ACM, 567–574.
[33] L. Page, S. Brin, R. Motwani, and T. Winograd. 1999. *The PageRank citation ranking: bringing order to the Web*. Technical Report 66.
[34] S. Shekhar, V. M. Patel, N. M. Nasrabadi, and R. Chellappa. 2014. Joint sparse representation for robust multimodal biometrics recognition. *TPAMI* 36, 1 (2014), 113–126.
[35] K. Ura, S. Alkire, and T. Zangmo. 2012. A short guide to gross national happiness index. (2012).
[36] D. Wang, S. C. Hoi, P. Wu, J. Zhu, Y. He, and C. Miao. 2013. Learning to name faces: a multimodal learning scheme for search-based face annotation. In *SIGIR*. ACM, 443–452.
[37] D. Wang, T. Li, S. Zhu, and C. Ding. 2008. Multi-document summarization via sentence-level semantic analysis and symmetric matrix factorization. In *SIGIR*. ACM, 307–314.
[38] M. Wang, H. Li, D. Tao, K. Lu, and X. Wu. 2012. Multimodal graph-based reranking for web image search. *TIP* 21, 11 (2012), 4649–4661.
[39] W. Wang, R. Arora, K. Livescu, and J. Bilmes. 2015. On deep multi-view representation learning. In *ICML*. 1083–1092.
[40] X. Wang, L. Nie, X. Song, D. Zhang, and T. Chua. 2017. Unifying Virtual and Physical Worlds: Learning Toward Local and Global Consistency. *TOIS* 36 (2017), 4:1–4:26.
[41] W. Xu, X. Liu, and Y. Gong. 2003. Document clustering based on non-negative matrix factorization. In *SIGIR*. ACM, 267–273.
[42] Q. Yin, S. Wu, and L. Wang. 2015. Incomplete multi-view clustering via subspace learning. In *CIKM*. ACM, 383–392.
[43] H. Zhang, X. Shang, H. Luan, M. Wang, and T. Chua. 2017. Learning from Collective Intelligence: Feature Learning Using Social Images and Tags. *TOMCCAP* 13 (2017), 1:1–1:23.
[44] X. Zhou, M. Belkin, and N. Srebro. 2011. An iterated graph Laplacian approach for ranking on manifolds. In *SIGKDD*. ACM, 877–885.

Information Retrieval Meets Game Theory: The Ranking Competition Between Documents' Authors

Nimrod Raifer
Technion, Israel
nimo@campus.technion.ac.il

Fiana Raiber*
Yahoo Research, Israel
fiana@yahoo-inc.com

Moshe Tennenholtz
Technion, Israel
moshet@ie.technion.ac.il

Oren Kurland
Technion, Israel
kurland@ie.technion.ac.il

ABSTRACT

In competitive search settings as the Web, there is an ongoing *ranking competition* between document authors (publishers) for certain queries. The goal is to have documents highly ranked, and the means is document manipulation applied in response to rankings. Existing retrieval models, and their theoretical underpinnings (e.g., the probability ranking principle), do not account for post-ranking corpus dynamics driven by this strategic behavior of publishers. However, the dynamics has major effect on retrieval effectiveness since it affects content availability in the corpus. Furthermore, while manipulation strategies observed over the Web were reported in past literature, they were not analyzed as ongoing, and changing, post-ranking response strategies, nor were they connected to the foundations of classical ad hoc retrieval models (e.g., content-based document-query surface level similarities and document relevance priors). We present a novel theoretical and empirical analysis of the strategic behavior of publishers using these foundations. Empirical analysis of controlled ranking competitions that we organized reveals a key strategy of publishers: making their documents (gradually) become similar to documents ranked the highest in previous rankings. Our theoretical analysis of the ranking competition as a *repeated game*, and its *minmax regret equilibrium*, yields a result that supports the merits of this publishing strategy. We further show that it can be predicted with high accuracy, and without explicit knowledge of the ranking function, whether documents will be promoted to the highest rank in our competitions. The prediction utilizes very few features which quantify changes of documents, specifically with respect to those previously ranked the highest.

KEYWORDS

ad hoc retrieval; game theory; ranking competition

*The paper is based on work done while the author was at the Technion.

SIGIR '17, August 07-11, 2017, Shinjuku, Tokyo, Japan
© 2017 ACM. 978-1-4503-5022-8/17/08...$15.00
DOI: http://dx.doi.org/10.1145/3077136.3080785

1 INTRODUCTION

Ad hoc document retrieval models are often based on the assumption of a fixed document corpus — i.e., corpus dynamics is not accounted for. The core challenge is estimating the relevance of a document to the query. The probability ranking principle (PRP) [25] is the theoretical foundation of this practice: to maximize user utility, documents should be ranked by their relevance probabilities.

In practice, document corpora are not static as documents are changed, created or removed. Some of the corpus dynamics, specifically, in competitive search settings (e.g., the Web), results from *ranking incentives* of document authors, henceforth referred to as *publishers*. That is, publishers might modify documents to promote them in rankings induced for queries of interest. These modifications are referred to as search engine optimization (SEO) [16]. Spam filtering, and more generally, using document quality measures as features in learning-to-rank methods [4], are examples of approaches for rank-penalizing documents that have gone through unwarranted modifications (a.k.a., black-hat SEO [16]).

However, existing retrieval approaches, and their theoretical foundations, do not account for future corpus dynamics driven by rankings. For example, it was recently shown that the PRP is sub-optimal in competitive retrieval settings [3] as it can lead to decreased content breadth in the corpus, among other issues.

To estimate post-ranking corpus dynamics, specifically, that caused by responses of publishers to rankings (i.e., document modifications), analysis of the *strategic behavior* of publishers is called for. While types and techniques of SEO strategies were discussed in past work [16], these were not studied as response strategies with respect to rankings induced for specific queries. Rather, they were presented as general actions observed on the Web (e.g., keyword stuffing and content copying).

Furthermore, there are no studies, to the best of our knowledge, that analyze publishers' strategies with respect to retrieval models and their foundations; namely, the effect, over time, on features used for ranking. Such analysis is important for incorporating strategy predictions (estimates) in, and addressing their effects on, retrieval approaches. A case in point, it was shown that if the actual writing quality of publishers for topics is known, then this information can be used in non-deterministic retrieval models to promote content breadth in the corpus, and therefore improve search effectiveness along time [3]. More generally, analysis of the strategic behavior of publishers is crucial for setting theoretical foundations for handling post-ranking corpus dynamics. The same way user modeling is important for interactive information retrieval models [30], modeling the strategic behavior of publishers in response to induced rankings is important for addressing post-ranking corpus dynamics in retrieval models.

We present a novel initial theoretical and empirical analysis of the (temporal) strategic behavior of publishers in terms of changes they introduce to documents in response to induced rankings. The analysis is performed in the context of classical ad hoc retrieval models in two respects. First, we focus on content-based retrieval and accordingly content manipulation. Analyzing post-ranking strategies of changing hypertext, hyperlinks and affecting clicks or any additional signal that can be used for relevance estimation is outside the scope of this paper. Nevertheless, we note that (i) content-based relevance estimates (e.g., Okapi BM25 and language-model-based estimates) are among the most important ones used in learning-to-rank approaches applied over Web data [20]; (ii) content manipulation techniques are quite pervasive, specifically, over the Web [16]; and, (iii) for experiments we use a state-of-the-art learning-to-rank approach applied with content-based estimates. Second, we empirically study content manipulation in terms of the building blocks of classical, content-based, retrieval methods. These include document-query surface-level similarities [14] and query-independent document relevance priors [4].

Performing empirical analysis of the "ranking competition" between publishers whose incentive is to have their documents ranked high, even if assuming the availability of a large-scale log of a search engine, is a major challenge due to the numerous dynamic aspects that affect this competition. Over the Web, pages emerge and disappear, the search engine's index coverage changes rapidly, the ranking function, as well as estimates it utilizes, change throughout time and across sets of users and queries. Furthermore, different publishers cannot necessarily employ the same document modifications, and many modifications are not content-based as the ranking function also considers non content-based relevance signals.

Given that our goal, as described above, is to study the strategic behavior of publishers in the scope of the foundations of classical content-based retrieval models, we performed controlled empirical analysis by organizing ranking competitions between students in a course. Two basic conditions were set in these competitions. First, the students were not aware of the ranking function, nor of the actual features it used. Second, the students were incentivized to write quality documents that would be ranked high by the ranking function. As shown below, the dataset allowed to gain interesting and important observations about potential strategic behavior of publishers in a ranking competition.

An important observation that emerged in the competition analysis that we present is that publishers were gradually making their documents become more similar, in several respects, to those most highly ranked in previous rankings[1]. An interesting fundamental question that follows is whether this competing strategy can be theoretically justified given the information available to publishers: observations of past rankings and little to no knowledge of the ranking function. To address this question, we present a novel game theoretic analysis of the ranking competition as a *repeated game* [1]. Our main theoretical result with respect to the minmax regret equilibrium of the game [17] provides formal support to the merits of this publishing (competing) strategy.

In addition to analyzing the ranking competition theoretically and empirically, we set as a goal to predict whether a document would be ranked the highest given that this was not the case in the previous ranking; the predictor does not have explicit knowledge of the ranking function. Interestingly, relying on very few features that quantify the extent to which the document was changed and became similar to a document previously ranked the highest can yield high accuracy prediction. These features are inspired by the *cluster hypothesis* [18], and more specifically, one of the important operational premises that it gave rise to: "similar documents should receive similar retrieval scores" [9]. Thus, in lack of knowledge of the ranking function, the predictor essentially uses inter-document similarities as proxies for retrieval score similarities.

Our contributions can be summarized as follows.

- We present the first dataset of query-based ranking competitions between publishers. The focus is on content manipulation.
- We present an empirical analysis of publishers' strategies employed in the competitions.
- We present a novel game theoretic analysis of the ranking competition as a repeated game. The main result of analyzing the minmax equilibrium of the game provides formal support to the merits of a key strategy employed by publishers in our games.
- We show that, in our setting, it is possible to predict with high accuracy whether a document will be promoted to the highest rank in the next ranking. The prediction is based on very few features and does not rely on explicit knowledge of the ranking function.

2 RELATED WORK

There is much work on identifying, characterizing and addressing unwarranted (a.k.a. black-hat SEO [16]) actions of publishers [6]. In contrast, we focus on the strategic behavior of publishers when applying legitimate content-based manipulations.

Studies of the dynamic aspects of interactive retrieval focus on changes of queries and the ranking function (e.g., [15, 27, 30, 31]). Changes of clickthrough patterns were also studied [27]. The dynamics of the collection as a result of the ranking competition, which is our focus, was not addressed.

There has been work on studying and predicting the dynamics of the Web collection (e.g., [23, 26]), where the main operational goals were improving crawling policies and personalizing content delivery. Past versions of a Web page were used to improve its representation for ranking [13]. However, in contrast to our work, the dynamics has not been studied with respect to the ranking competition between publishers.

Recently, the publishers' ranking competition was analyzed using a game theoretic approach [3]. In contrast to our work, the assumption was that publishers have full knowledge of the ranking function, the competition was not analyzed as a repeated game, and no empirical analysis was presented.

[1] This strategy is conceptually reminiscent of the black-hat weaving and stitching content-based SEO techniques applied over the Web [6, 16] where content from legitimate pages is copied to spam pages so as to promote them.

The merits of non-deterministic ranking functions from [3] were argued using a *simulation* of a ranking competition between publishers who stuff query terms in documents [2]. In contrast with our work, publishers were assumed to know the basic (Okapi BM25) ranking function, there was no theoretical analysis of the competition and no analysis of non-simulated (real) ranking competitions.

A game theoretic approach was used to devise query-based ranking mechanisms that (i) maximize social welfare for ambiguous queries, by diversifying search results that are assumed to be scanned using random sequential search [12]; and (ii) balance relevance and monetization [11]. In contrast to our work, the competition between documents' authors (publishers) was not studied.

Game theoretical analysis has also been applied for adversarial classification [8, 10] and for optimizing learning-to-rank functions in non-adversarial retrieval settings [28]. We address the competitive (adversarial) ad hoc retrieval setting using different theoretical and empirical analyses.

3 GAME THEORETIC ANALYSIS

We analyze the ranking competition as a *repeated game* [1]. Analyzing the minmax regret equilibrium of the game yields a formal result that helps to explain a key strategy employed by publishers in the ranking competitions we organized as described in Section 5.

In what follows we assume that a query q, and some document ranking function (details below), have been fixed. Let $N = \{1, 2, \ldots, n\}$ be a set of n publishers (documents' authors) that would like to have their documents ranked high for q. Let D_i be a finite set of documents that publisher i can (or might) write to convey the information she wants to share. For ease of presentation, and to avoid technical tie-breaking issues, assume $D_i \cap D_j = \emptyset$ for any $i, j \in N, i \neq j$. Let $D = \cup_{i=1}^{n} D_i$ be the set of all documents that can be written by the publishers.

We assume a complete linear ordering over D, denoted $<$. Such ordering can be based, for example, on a single (numeric) feature in a document representation[2]. Alternatively, the distance, under some representation, to a document which serves as a reference point (e.g., a document ranked the highest at some point) can serve to induce the ordering. Thus, for ease of exposition we can associate D with elements in the interval $[0, 1]$. A document ranking function for q is a mapping $r : D \longrightarrow \Re_{+}$. For simplicity (and avoiding tie-breaking), we assume $r(d_i) \neq r(d_j)$ for any $d_i, d_j \in D$.

Definition 3.1. $RSP(D_1, \ldots, D_n) = RSP(D)$ denotes the single peak ranking functions. These are functions r defined over D, such that for no $d \in D$, there are $d_i, d_j \in D$, $d_i < d < d_j$ such that $r(d_i) > r(d)$ and $r(d_j) > r(d)$.

For example, linear learning-to-rank functions [20] are single peak with respect to each feature. The negative KL divergence used in the language modeling framework [19] is a single peak function over the multinomial distributions in the simplex by the virtue of being a concave function. However, the most effective ranking functions (e.g., those utilizing non-linear learning-to-rank methods) are not single peak. Nevertheless, it is important to keep in mind that we analyze the dynamics from the point of view of publishers who have no information about the ranking function except for that inferred by observing induced rankings. That is, publishers may assume, and act based on the belief, that the ranking function is single peak. Indeed, as shown in Section 5, the participants (publishers) in our ranking competitions can be viewed as searching for the structure of a single-peak ranking function for various features, although the ranking function is not single-peak.

Below we care only about the relative ranking of documents in D; thereby, we consider the possible total ordering induced by the ranking function over D; there are finitely many such orderings. With a slight abuse of notation we will therefore refer to $RSP(D)$ as the set of possible single-peak orderings of documents in D.

Let $D^0 = \{d_1^0, \ldots, d_n^0\}$ be an initial set of documents where $d_i^0 \in D_i$ is the initial document published by publisher i. We assume that each $i \in N$ possess no information at the beginning about the function $r \in RSP(D)$, beyond knowing it is a single-peak ordering. Consider t rounds, $l = 1, 2, \ldots, t$, in each of which each player i chooses a document $d_i \in D_i$, and obtains a utility of 1 if d_i is ranked first and 0 otherwise. Herein, a publisher or her document is called "winner" if the document was the highest ranked; all other publishers and their documents are called "losers". Let $TO(D)$ be the set of possible total ordering over D. Notice that selecting $d_i \in D_i$ for every $i \in N$ determines an ordering over the selected documents by the single-peak function $r \in RSP(D)$. The *strategy* of i at round l is defined as a function from the history of previously selected actions and outcomes (i.e., orderings) of all publishers, to the document selected by publisher i. The outcome at each round can be associated with a subset $R \subseteq RSP(D)$ of the possible single peak functions, as it rules out particular orderings. Henceforth, R is referred to as the *knowledge state*, as it captures the set of currently possible single peak orderings based on the observations received.

The *publishers ranking game* just described is a *repeated game* [1]. In a repeated game, the same game is repeatedly played in rounds (iterations). Specifically, at each round a publisher publishes a document, but a strategy in each round may relate to all information observed so far; e.g., the documents published and rankings induced in previous iterations. Accordingly, given the initial document set D^0, and the total number of rounds t, the set of possible strategies for player i is denoted $S_i(t, d_i^0)$.[3] The utility $U_i(t, d_i^0, s_1, \ldots, s_n)$, where $s_j \in S_j(t, d_j^0)$ for every $j \in N$, is the sum of utilities of player i in rounds $1, 2, \ldots, t$ given the corresponding strategies.

We now introduce a slight modification to the utility obtained by player i in a round to capture the cost of modifying documents. This cost reflects both the actual effort involved in changing a document and the "penalty" incurred by potentially drifting from the actual document i planned to publish. Assume there is some negligible cost C, i.e., $C|D| < 1$, where $eC > 0$ is the cost for changing document d to document d' in distance e (assume standard distance on $[0, 1]$) in a single round. Formally, the utility of publisher i in round l will be based on its ranking (either first or not) minus the cost of changing the document written in round $l - 1$.

Given the game described above, a major challenge is to define an appropriate solution concept which predicts behavior in the game. The classical solution concept in game theory is the celebrated Nash

[2] In this case, the analysis below applies to each feature in a document representation assuming that the values of others were fixed.

[3] $S_i(t, d^0)$ encodes all possible documents published by i at any round of the game given the previous potential orderings.

equilibrium, which is a strategy profile, one for each player, for which unilateral deviations are not beneficial (i.e., any single player cannot gain by deviating from her strategy assuming the others stick to their strategies). This solution concept always exists in finite games with complete information if players are allowed to use mixed strategies, and has been also extended to games with incomplete information where there are Bayesian assumptions about the actual game being played. However, our setting does not exhibit such stylized assumptions, and we need to appeal to other solution concepts. In particular, in a minmax regret equilibrium [17], we consider strategy profiles such that each player (publisher) minimizes her regret when compared to the best response she could have played had she known the exact environment state (e.g., the exact ranking function) assuming others stick to their strategies; and this holds for all players simultaneously.

Given a strategy profile $s = (s_1, \ldots, s_n)$ the regret of i is $max_x U_i(t, d_i^0, x, s_{-i}) - U_i(t, d_i^0, s)$; s_{-i} denotes the strategy profile applied by all players except for i. A strategy profile $s = (s_1, \ldots, s_n)$ is *minmax regret equilibrium* if for every i, s_i minimizes regret given s_{-i} [17]. Given the defined publishers game we can now show that:

THEOREM 3.2. *Any publishers game has a minmax regret equilibrium.*

PROOF. We construct the following equilibrium. Let R be the knowledge state at the beginning of a given round l. At the beginning of round 1 all ranking functions in $RSP(D)$ are possible, while at each following round the knowledge state can only shrink in terms of the number of ranking functions it contains. Let $V_l \subseteq [0, 1]$ be the set of documents which correspond to possible peaks of the functions in the knowledge state R; let d_i^{l-1} be the most recent document published by i. Let $v_i^l \in D_i \cap V_l$ such that $|v_i^l - d_i^{l-1}|$ is minimal; if two documents have this minimal distance one is arbitrarily selected. The document published by i in round l would be v_i^l. (In the first round it is d_i^0.) We now prove that this strategy of i minimizes its regret.

Let V_t be the knowledge state at the beginning of the last round t; V_t may result from arbitrary publishers' behavior in rounds $1, 2, \ldots, t-1$. No publisher $j \neq i$ will publish a document not in V_t as otherwise she cannot win (i.e., this strategy would be dominated). Hence, i's publishing a document out of V_t is dominated by publishing the previous document. (This has no cost, and publishing out of V_t cannot result in a win.) On the other hand, since any $v \in V_t$ can be a winner, the worst regret would be for not publishing v_i^t as defined above. This is because v_i^t might be the winner from this point on, by the virtue of being in V_t, but it incurs minimal cost. Thus, minimizing regret in the last round is achieved by selecting v_i^t as prescribed. By induction, using the argument from above results in i's strategy minimizing regret in every round. □

Two corollaries follow the proof:

COROLLARY 3.3. *The above constructed equilibrium is also a subgame perfect equilibrium.*

Namely, if an arbitrary sequence of documents has been selected up to round $l < t$, then in the remaining game, given the information provided so far on the potential peaks, following each player's strategy in the remaining rounds is still a minmax regret equilibrium.

COROLLARY 3.4. *Losers at round $l-1$ will publish in round l documents that become closer to (i.e., more similar) to that of the winner from round $l-1$.*

PROOF. Assume wlog that a publisher who lost round $l-1$ published $d_j \in [0, 1]$ that satisfies $d_j < d_w$ where $d_w \in [0, 1]$ was the winning document. As selecting any $d_{j'} < d_j$ is dominated given the knowledge state gathered, and the regret for publishing $d_{j'''} > d_w$ is higher than that of publishing $d_{j''}$ such that $d_w > d_{j''} > d_j$, we get the corresponding phenomenon. Notice that this will also imply that current winners will not change their documents. □

Thus, Corollary 3.4 helps to explain a key strategy employed by publishers in the competitions we organized as we show below; namely, mimicking the winners.

4 DATA

As discussed in Section 1, our goal is to analyze content-based ranking competitions so as to shed light on the strategic behavior of publishers. Since there are no publicly available datasets that can be used to that end, we organized repeated ranking competitions. The resulting dataset is available at https://github.com/asrcdataset/asrc. (See details in Appendix A.) We next describe the essentials of the competition.

Fifty two senior-undergrad and grad students in an information retrieval course were the publishers. The competition included 31 different repeated matches, each of which was with respect to a different TREC's ClueWeb09 query. Each student participated in three matches. Five students competed against each other in all matches except for one in which six students competed.

The competition was run for eight rounds; i.e., there were eight matches per query. Before the first round, an example of a relevant document was provided for each match (query). Students were incentivized by course-grade rewards to edit their documents along the rounds so as to have them ranked as high as possible.[4] As from the second round, students participating in a match were presented with the ranking of documents submitted in the previous round by all competitors in the same match.

All documents were unstructured plain text of up to 150 terms. The document ranking model was based on the state-of-the-art LambdaMART [29] learning-to-rank approach integrating three classes of features. The first are query-dependent features, such as **QueryTermsRatio** (ratio of query terms appearing in a document) and **LMIR.DIR** (language-model-based similarity of a document to the query). The second class of features are query-independent document quality measures [4, 21], including **Entropy** (entropy of the term distribution in a document) and **StopwordsRatio** (stopwords to non-stopwords ratio in a document). Increased entropy and occurrence of stopwords attest to content breadth and hence to high prior probability of relevance [4].

The feature in the third class, **SimInit**, was used to incentivize students to write documents that drift from the initial relevant document shared by all students competing in the same match: it is

[4] Students were assigned with unique IDs and all data was anonymized.

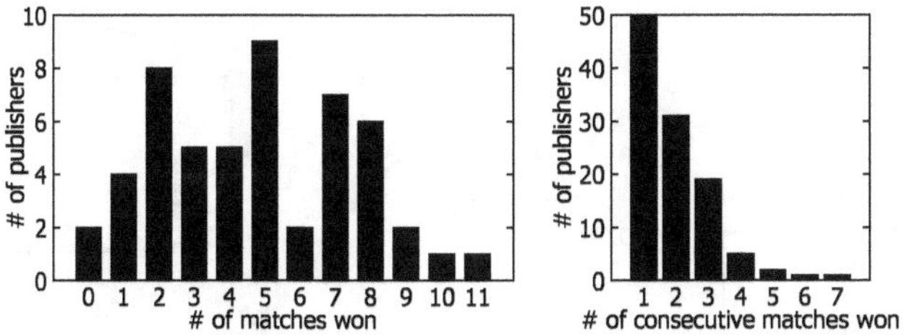

Figure 1: The number of (consecutive) matches won (x-axis) by a given number of publishers (y-axis).

based on the language-model similarity of a document to the initial relevant document. We note that in practical scenarios, publishers would rarely change their documents so they will not include the information originally intended for sharing. Indeed, in the theoretical analysis presented in Section 3, a cost was assigned to changes of documents. Yet, as we show below, the conclusions we draw about strategies are aligned with our theoretical results.

Documents (manually) classified as keyword stuffed were penalized in the ranking. Information about the ranking function and the features it utilizes was not disclosed to students. The resulting collection contains (i) 1279 documents: 31 initial relevant documents and 1248 documents created by students, 897 of which are unique[5]; (ii) keyword stuffing annotations; and (iii) exhaustive relevance judgments. Appendix A provides additional details of the collection and ranking model.

5 EMPIRICAL ANALYSIS

In the following analysis, winner (loser) is a document (or publisher thereof) which was (not) ranked first in a match.

5.1 Analysis of wins

Figure 1 (left) presents the number of matches won by a given number of publishers (students). The competition included 248 distinct matches (8 rounds × 31 matches per round). Each student was assigned with exactly 3 queries; hence, the maximum number of matches a student could win is 24. We see that only two of the students did not win even a single match, attesting to the students' engagement in the competition. The maximum number of matches won was 11, less than half of the maximal possible number of wins, indicating that the competition was dynamic.

Figure 1 (right) presents the number of consecutive matches won by a given number of students; the maximum is the number of rounds (eight). We see that most students could retain the first rank for at most three rounds. Only a small number of students retained the first rank in more than four rounds. This finding further attests to the strong competition held between the students.

5.2 Analysis of strategies

By Corollary 3.4, to win matches, losers in previous rounds will publish documents that become similar to that of the winner from the preceding round. Accordingly, we next analyze the similarity of documents that did not win a match (losers) to the winner over a series of rounds in which these documents remained losers. The similarity to the winner is estimated with respect to some of the features used to rank documents which were presented in Section 4.

The QueryTermsRatio and LMIR.DIR features quantify the query-document match; LMIR.DIR is a representative query-document surface-level similarity estimate [14]. The Entropy and StopwordsRatio features are among the most effective query independent content-based document relevance priors reported in the literature [4]. Hence, the analysis of the strategic behavior of publishers we present next relies on estimates that constitute the foundations of classical content-based ad hoc retrieval approaches.

Figure 2 depicts the average values of the features for documents that were losers in at least four consecutive rounds before winning a match[6]. We distinguish between documents whose feature value four rounds before winning a match was lower than or equal to that of the winner (**L≤W**) and those whose feature value was higher than that of the winner (**L>W**). We also present the average feature values of winners (**W**).

We see in Figure 2 that the average feature values of winners remain relatively stable along the competition; thus, winner documents, often written by different publishers, tend to be quite similar along a few dimensions (features).

Figure 2 also shows that, in general, Entropy often decreases along rounds and QueryTermsRatio increases. This attests to high content repetition in winner documents that might result from high occurrence of query terms. SimInit decreases which is potentially due to our rewarding diversification with respect to the initial relevant document.

More generally, we observe a clear trend throughout the competition: feature values of loser documents which became winners were becoming closer, often gradually converging, to those of winners from previous rounds regardless of their initial values. That is, in lack of knowledge of features used for document ranking, losers were mimicking winners and thereby indirectly affecting these features. This finding is in accordance with Corollary 3.4.

6 PREDICTING WINNERS

Given that loser publishers apply the strategy of mimicking the winners, an interesting challenge rises: leveraging aspects of this strategy to predict, without using explicit knowledge of the ranking function, which loser publisher in round $l-1$ will win round l assuming that a previous loser indeed wins this round.[7]

For prediction, we represent each document as a feature vector and define two sets of features (details below) that quantify the extent to which the document becomes more similar to the winner of the previous round. The features in the first set are estimates of this similarity on a *macro* level, where documents are treated as

[5]Several students submitted the same document over a few rounds; e.g., if the document was the highest ranked in a previous round.

[6]Similar trends were observed for other features used by the ranking model and for losers that lost in at least three or five consecutive rounds. These results are omitted as they convey no further insight.

[7]Predicting which publisher will win round l *regardless* if it won round $l-1$ is a challenge for future work. As stated in the proof of Corollary 3.4, and as observed in the competitions, winners did not tend to change their documents. This is a fundamental difference with the dynamics of loser documents which makes this prediction task challenging. For example, many of the dynamics-based features defined below for predicting whether a loser will turn to a winner are degenerated for winner documents which do not change.

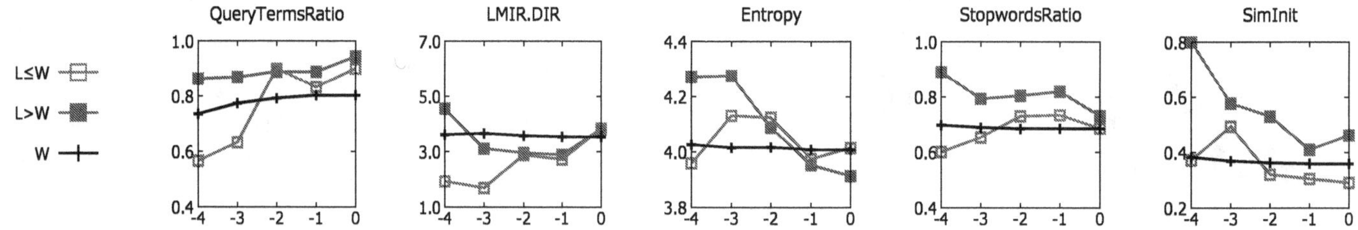

Figure 2: Averaged feature values of documents that were losers in at least four consecutive rounds before becoming winners, and whose feature values four rounds before winning were either lower or equal ('L≤W') or higher ('L>W') than those of the winner. 'W': averaged feature value of the corresponding winners. x-axis: (minus) number of rounds before a document won a match. The values of LMIR.DIR are scaled by 100.

whole units. The features in the second set are *micro* level similarity estimates that allow to analyze the potential actions taken by publishers to make their documents similar to the winner.

6.1 Features

The features in the first set, henceforth **Macro** features, are estimates of the bag-of-terms textual similarities (denoted SIM) between the document in round l (**D**), the document written by the same publisher in the previous round $l-1$ (**PD**) and the winner of the previous round $l-1$ (**PW**). The Cosine between tf.idf vector representations of documents is the similarity estimate. Three estimates are used: **SIM(D,PD)**, **SIM(D,PW)** and **SIM(PD,PW)**.

Using these inter-document similarity measures is inspired by the *cluster hypothesis* [18] which states that "closely associated documents tend to be relevant to the same requests". More specifically, an important operational manifestation of the cluster hypothesis is the premise that effective retrieval methods should assign similar documents with similar retrieval scores [9]. Based on the premise, given that the predictor we devise has no explicit knowledge of the ranking method used, inter-document similarities can potentially serve as proxies for similarities between retrieval scores.

The features in the second set, henceforth **Micro** features, focus on potential actions of publishers to make their documents similar to PW, the winner of the previous round. A document becomes similar to the winner, based on a bag-of-terms representation, if terms from the winner are added and terms not in the winner are removed. Accordingly, given a set $\mathcal{S}$ of terms, **ADD(PW)** and **RMV(PW)** are the number of unique terms $t \in \mathcal{S}$ used in PW that were added to, or removed from, the document, respectively. Similarly, **ADD(¬PW)** and **RMV(¬PW)** are the number of unique terms $t \in \mathcal{S}$ *not* used in PW that were added to or removed from the document, respectively. We define three term sets $\mathcal{S}$: (i) query terms (**Query**), (ii) frequent terms, specifically, stopwords (**Stopwords**), and (iii) non-frequent terms not in the query (**¬Query¬Stopwords**).[8]

Overall, we use 15 features: 3 Macro (SIM(D,PD), SIM(D,PW), SIM(PD,PW)) and 12 Micro ({ADD(PW), RMV(PW), ADD(¬PW), RMV(¬PW) } × {Query, Stopwords, ¬Query¬Stopwords}).

The Macro features, which quantify temporal inter-document similarity changes, are ranking-model agnostic. The Micro features are based on temporal changes of addition/deletion of terms. While term-based information (e.g., query-terms occurrence) would be used by any reasonable ranker, the prediction model uses no explicit knowledge about how this information is used by the non-linear ranker applied in the competition, nor about other features used for ranking.

6.2 Prediction setup

In each round of the competition, queries for which the winner of the previous round remained the winner were discarded, as our goal is to predict which *loser* publisher in a previous round will win the current round. Thus, the number of queries considered in each round ranges from 6 to 26 (out of all 31 queries).

We used the features[9] from Section 6.1 for binary classification with logistic regression (**LReg**), linear SVM (**LSVM**), polynomial SVM (**PSVM**) and random forests (**RForest**) via the scikit-learn library [22]; the two classes are winner and loser. To train the classifiers and set hyper-parameter values, we used leave-one-out cross validation over rounds. The documents submitted by students with respect to all considered queries in a round served for testing; those submitted in the remaining six rounds, excluding the first, served for training. Prediction was performed per query: the document in the current round which was written by a loser publisher from the previous round and which was assigned the highest classification score was predicted the winner; all other documents were predicted to be losers.

Prediction effectiveness is measured using **Accuracy**: the percentage of documents correctly predicted as winners or losers, and **F1**: harmonic mean of Precision and Recall.[10] Values are averaged over queries and test folds. Statistically significant effectiveness differences are determined using the two-tailed paired t-test with $p \leq 0.05$ applied over queries.

The hyper-parameter values of the classifiers were selected to optimize Accuracy over the train set. For LReg, LSVM and PSVM, the value of the regularization parameter is in $\{1, 10, 50, 100\}$.[11] The degree of the polynomial SVM (PSVM) was in $\{2, 3, 4, 5\}$. The number of trees and leaves for RForest were selected from $\{10, 50,$

[8]A term is considered a stopword if it is among the 100 most frequent alphanumeric terms in the ClueWeb09 Category B corpus.

[9]Feature values were min-max normalized per query.

[10] Precision is the fraction of correctly predicted winners out of all documents predicted to be winners. Recall is the fraction of winners correctly predicted as winners.

[11]LReg, LSVM and PSVM were trained with L1 regularization.

Table 1: Prediction effectiveness of the four classifiers (LReg, LSVM, PSVM, RForest) and the baselines. The performance differences between each of the classifiers and each of the baselines are statistically significant. All the differences with RForest are statistically significant. Bold: the best result in a row. Note: F1 of AllLosers is 0 due to zero Recall.

	Random	Majority	AllWinners	AllLosers	LReg	LSVM	PSVM	RForest
Accuracy	0.627	0.685	0.247	0.753	0.849	0.859	0.867	**0.878**
F1	0.242	0.363	0.396	0.000	0.695	0.712	0.730	**0.752**

100, 500} and {10, 20, 30}, respectively. All other hyper-parameters were set to their default values [22].

6.3 Prediction effectiveness

Main result. We compare the prediction effectiveness of the aforementioned classifiers with that of four baselines. All prediction algorithms predict as winner(s) documents whose publishers lost the previous round. (i) **Random**: a single winner is randomly selected; (ii) **Majority**: the document whose publisher won the majority of past rounds for the query is predicted the winner (ties are broken arbitrarily); (iii) **AllWinners**: all documents are predicted winners, in which case only one document per query is correctly predicted; and, (iv) **AllLosers**: all documents are predicted losers, in which case all but one of the documents are correctly predicted as losers. The results are presented in Table 1. Although the four classifiers (LReg, LSVM, PSVM and RForest) utilize no knowledge of the ranking model, they predict with high effectiveness the winner of the current round. Moreover, the differences in prediction effectiveness between each of the classifiers and each of the four baselines are substantial and statistically significant. These findings attest to the ability to predict winners from previous losers in our competitions based on macro-level and micro-level manipulation strategies of publishers.

Among the four classifiers, the lowest performance is posted by LReg, while the highest is posted by RForest. Hence, in the analysis to follow we focus on RForest.

Feature analysis. We next study the relative effectiveness of the *sets* of features used in RForest. Recall that the 15 features belong to two sets: Macro and Micro. The Micro features belong to three subsets: Query, Stopwords and ¬Query¬Stopwords. In Table 2 we compare the prediction effectiveness of training RForest using different combinations of these (sub)sets of features. We present for reference the effectiveness of the Majority, AllWinners and AllLosers baselines. We see that using even a single (sub)set of features yields prediction effectiveness that statistically significantly surpasses that of the baselines. Among the three subsets of Micro features, the query-term-based features (Query) are the most effective. Integrating all three subsets leads to prediction effectiveness that always statistically significantly surpasses that of using either one or two of the subsets. We also see that using Micro features alone leads to slightly higher effectiveness than using only Macro features; the difference is not statistically significant. Yet, combining both sets yields the highest prediction effectiveness. These findings suggest that the Micro and Macro features, as well as the three subsets of Micro features, are complementary to some extent.

Table 2: Using subsets of features for prediction. All differences with respect to Majority, AllWinners, AllLosers and Macro+Micro are statistically significant. Bold: best result in a column.

	Accuracy	F1
Majority	0.685	0.363
AllWinners	0.247	0.396
AllLosers	0.753	0.000
Query	0.821	0.635
Stopwords	0.809	0.594
¬Query¬Stopwords	0.796	0.587
Query+Stopwords	0.826	0.650
Query+¬Query¬Stopwords	0.825	0.648
Stopwords+¬Query¬Stopwords	0.813	0.617
Micro = Query+ Stopwords+¬Query¬Stopwords	0.837	0.673
Macro	0.836	0.671
Macro+Query	0.851	0.702
Macro+Stopwords	0.849	0.694
Macro+¬Query¬Stopwords	0.847	0.692
Macro+Micro (all features)	**0.878**	**0.752**

We next study the effectiveness of *individual* features. Table 3 presents the Accuracy of ablation tests performed upon RForest.[12] We also report **ΔMRR**: the mean difference between the reciprocal ranks of the *actual winner* when documents are ranked in descending and ascending order of individual feature values. We first see that removing any single feature statistically significantly hurts Accuracy. This attests to the complementary nature of the features.

The negative ΔMRR of SIM(D,PD) indicates, as expected, that to win a match, a loser publisher should change her document with respect to the previous round. The positive ΔMRR of SIM(PD,PW) and SIM(D,PW) suggest that the document should be similar to the winner (from the previous round) in the previous and current rounds so as to win the match. This finding is aligned with Corollary 3.4.

The ΔMRR of features in the Query and Stopwords subsets indicate that adding (removing) query terms is always good (bad) practice for becoming the winner, regardless of whether these terms were used by the winner. This finding is further supported by the observations about QueryTermsRatio in Section 5.2. In contrast, removing (adding) frequent terms, i.e., stopwords, is always good (bad) practice, regardless of the use of stopwords by the winner. The ΔMRR of features in the ¬Query¬Stopwords subset, which refers to terms that are neither query terms nor stopwords, imply that to

[12] Similar patterns were observed for F1. These results are omitted as they convey no additional insight.

Table 3: Ablation tests: Accuracy of RForest when trained without one feature. RForest's Accuracy with all features is 0.878. All differences with RForest are statistically significant. ΔMRR: the mean reciprocal ranks difference of the winner when ranking documents in descending and ascending order of feature values.

Macro Features			Micro Features						
				Query		Stopwords		¬Query¬Stopwords	
Feature	Ablation	ΔMRR	Feature	Ablation	ΔMRR	Ablation	ΔMRR	Ablation	ΔMRR
SIM(D,PD)	0.829	−0.136	ADD(PW)	0.844	0.130	0.840	−0.219	0.841	0.183
SIM(D,PW)	0.837	0.168	RMV(PW)	0.851	−0.043	0.843	0.043	0.857	−0.081
SIM(PD,PW)	0.820	0.184	ADD(¬PW)	0.840	0.104	0.856	−0.023	0.849	−0.053
			RMV(¬PW)	0.834	−0.620	0.847	0.060	0.837	0.029

win a match a document should become more similar to the winner by adding and not removing terms that were used by the winner (positive ΔMRR of ADD(PW) and negative ΔMRR of RMV(PW)), as well as removing and not adding terms that were not used by the winner (positive ΔMRR of RMV(¬PW) and negative ΔMRR of ADD(¬PW)). These manipulations which do not directly affect the query-document similarity estimates affect other features used by the ranking model (e.g., Entropy).

7 CONCLUSIONS

We presented an initial theoretical and empirical study of the strategic behavior of publishers (documents' authors) in query-based ranking competitions. The publishers' goal is promoting their documents in rankings using little available information, mainly about past rankings. Analysis of ranking competitions that we organized revealed that to achieve their goal, publishers were making their documents similar to those ranked the highest in previous rounds. A game theoretic analysis of the competition yielded a result that provides formal support to the merits of this strategy. We also showed that high accuracy prediction of whether a document will be promoted to the first rank in our competitions can be achieved using very few features which quantify document changes.

Acknowledgments We thank the reviewers for their comments. This work was supported in part by a Google Faculty Research Award.

A THE RANKING COMPETITIONS

We next discuss the competition guidelines provided to students (Section A.1), the incentives for participating in the competition (Section A.2), the queries and examples of relevant documents (Section A.3) and the ranking function used (Section A.4).

A.1 Guidelines

To alleviate the task for students, and to increase their engagement in the competition, the length of *all* documents was limited to 150 terms. Students were instructed to write unstructured plain text documents.

Duplication of other documents (determined based on a bag-of-terms comparison) resulted in the duplicate document being ranked last. The students were permitted to copy parts of other documents from the competition or the Web. Students were guided to write documents of the highest quality avoiding slang and informal language. The use of black hat SEO techniques [16], such as keyword stuffing, was discouraged by telling the students that the ranking function will penalize low quality documents, partly based on human annotations. We informed the students that they could use the provided examples of relevant documents, but that the documents they create need not necessarily be relevant.

A.2 Incentives

The incentive for participating in the competition was earning extra credit points for the exam. For each query, a student earned two thirds of a point if her document was ranked first for a query in a match. A third of a point was given to all other students competing with respect to the same query (i.e., the same match).

In the first half of the competition many students did not (significantly) update their documents even if these were not ranked first. Therefore, we further incentivized the students by changing the reward mechanism as from the fifth round. The student whose document was ranked first for a query was reworded one point. Students whose documents were ranked second and third were rewarded two thirds and third of a point, respectively. Students whose documents were ranked lower did not receive any credit.

A.3 Queries and initial relevant documents

We used the titles of 31 topics selected from 1-200 from TREC 2009-2012 as queries. The preference was selecting queries with clear commercial intent, since they were more likely to stir up competition as is the case on the Web. That is, having a document ranked high (first) with respect to these queries should lead to increased (monetary) profits to the document's publisher on the Web. The selected queries focused mostly on topics related to products or services. Examples include "used car parts", "cheap internet" and "gmat prep classes". The queries were randomly assigned to students ensuring that two students will not compete against each other in more than two different matches; the assignments were not changed throughout the competition.

As already noted, for each query we provided a single example of a relevant document. The goal was to provide the students with information regarding the underlying information need as the queries are very short. To produce these relevant documents, we first used the TREC topic description as a query in a commercial search engine. We extracted from the highly ranked documents

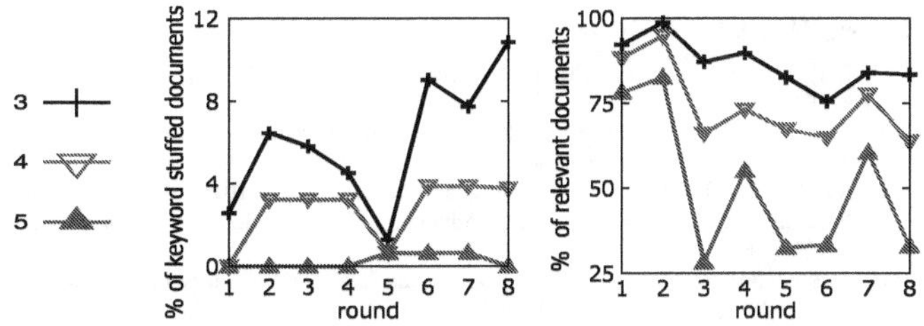

Figure 3: The percentage of documents annotated as keyword stuffed (left) and relevant (right) by at least 3, 4 or 5 annotators, averaged over queries per each of the eight competition rounds.

candidate window passages of up to 150 terms. The passages were annotated for relevance by four annotators. We kept extracting passages for each query until a passage was judged relevant by at least three annotators. This passage then served as the initial relevant document example for all students competing for the query.

A.4 Ranking model

We next describe the ranking model used for all queries in each round of every match in the competition.

A.4.1 Learning-to-rank. We used a learning-to-rank (LTR) approach with 25 features to rank the documents. Most of the features (22) were all those used in Microsoft's learning-to-rank datasets[13] for the "whole document" except for the Boolean Model, Vector Space Model and LMIR.ABS features. As noted above, the documents in our competition are unstructured plain text. Thus, all the features are computed only for the entire document. Since documents in our competitive setting are prone to manipulation, we used three additional features which were shown to be highly effective for spam classification [21] and Web retrieval [4]: (i) the ratio between the number of stopwords and non-stopwords in a document, (ii) the percentage of stopwords in a stopword list that appear in the document, and (iii) the entropy of the term distribution in a document [4]. For the two stopword-based features, the list of stopwords was composed of the 100 most frequent alphanumeric terms in the ClueWeb09 Category B corpus [21].

The ClueWeb09 category B dataset with queries 1-200 was used to learn the LTR model. Specifically, the model was applied upon the 1000 documents most highly ranked by using LMIR.DIR, i.e., the negative cross entropy between the unsmoothed and Dirichlet-smoothed (with $\mu = 1000$) unigram language models induced from the query and documents, respectively[14]. We used LambdaMART [29] via the RankLib library[15] to integrate the different features. The number of trees and leaves were selected from $\{100, 250, 500, 750, 1000\}$ and $\{10, 25, 50\}$, respectively. NDCG@5 served for optimization when learning the model. In each round of the competition, we added the (unjudged) documents submitted by students in all matches to the ClueWeb09 Category B corpus to have more updated values of corpus statistics, e.g., inverse document frequency (idf). Yet, we did not re-train the ranker. The Indri toolkit was used for indexing and retrieval[16]. We applied Krovetz stemming upon queries and documents and removed stopwords on the INQUERY list only from queries. The LMIR.JM feature was used with $\lambda = 0.1$; for BM25, we set $k1 = 1.2$ and $b = 0.75$.

A.4.2 Results diversification. To encourage students to considerably change their documents rather than introduce minor modifications to the initially provided relevant document, starting from the second round, they were advised to diversify their documents with respect to the relevant document. To further encourage diversification, we applied the MMR method [5] with respect to the initial relevant document d_{init}. Accordingly, the score assigned to document d with respect to query q is $score(q, d) \stackrel{def}{=} \lambda rank(d, LTR) - (1 - \lambda) rank(d, d_{\text{init}})$, where $\lambda = 0.5$, $rank(d, LTR)$ is the rank of d in a ranking of all the documents in a match induced by the LTR method and $rank(d, d_{\text{init}})$ is the rank of d in a ranking created based on the similarity with d_{init}; here, the rank of the lowest ranked document is 1. The similarity with d_{init} was computed using LMIR.DIR treating d as the query.

A.4.3 Keyword stuffing. Keyword stuffing [16], specifically of query terms, is one of the most applicable manipulation approaches the students could employ to promote their unstructured plain text documents in rankings. To avoid rewarding excessive keyword stuffing, and to encourage writing of high quality documents, each document was manually classified as keyword stuffed or not[17]. The annotation was performed via CrowdFlower[18]; each document was judged by five annotators from English speaking countries[19]. The inter-annotator agreement for keyword stuffing, computed using the free-marginal multi-rater kappa measure [24], is 0.88. A document classified as keyword stuffed by at least four annotators was rank-penalized: with probability 0.5 it was swapped with the next document in the ranking. If several consecutively ranked documents were keyword stuffed, then only the lowest ranked document was penalized.

In Figure 3 (left) we present for each round the percentage of documents classified as keyword stuffed by at least three, four or five annotators averaged over queries. We can see a mostly downward trend until the fifth round. In the fifth round we observe the lowest percentage of keyword stuffed documents. Starting from the fifth round the percentage of keyword stuffed documents gradually increases. We hypothesis that in the first half of the competition students' engagement gradually decreased. In the second half, as from the fifth round in which the rewards for having a document ranked high substantially increased, students started using manipulated texts even more so as to have their documents ranked high. In the fifth round, there might have been some confusion due to the introduction of a new reward mechanism.

[13] www.research.microsoft.com/en-us/projects/mslr

[14] We deliberately did not remove suspected spam documents from the initial document ranking, e.g., using Waterloo's spam classifier [7]. This practice allows learning a model using low quality (e.g., spam) documents.

[15] www.lemurproject.org/ranklib.ph

[16] www.lemurproject.org/indri

[17] A document was annotated as keyword stuffed if it contained excessive repetition of words which seemed unnatural or artificially introduced.

[18] www.crowdflower.com

[19] Annotators were also instructed to classify documents as spam if they were hard to understand, non-cohesive, did not make any sense or were useless to anyone seeking information. Yet, none of the documents was classified as spam.

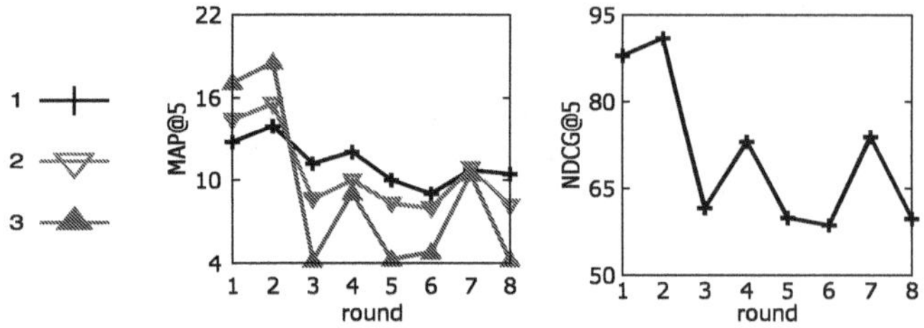

Figure 4: The MAP@5 (left) and NDCG@5 (right) performance of the ranking induced by the retrieval method in each round. Binary relevance judgments were induced for computing MAP@5 by considering a document relevant if its relevance grade was at least 1, 2 **or** 3.

A.5 Ranking effectiveness

All documents in the collection were judged for relevance. Annotators were presented with both the title and description of each TREC topic, and were asked to classify a document as relevant if it satisfied the information need stated in the description. As was the case with keyword stuffing annotation, each document was judged by five annotators from English speaking countries via CrowdFlower. The inter-annotator agreement rate, computed using the free-marginal multi-rater kappa measure [24], was 0.67. Four-scale graded relevance judgments were generated using the annotations as follows. A document judged relevant by less than three annotators was labeled as non-relevant (0). Documents judged relevant by at least three, four or five annotators were labeled as marginally relevant (1), fairly relevant (2) and highly relevant (3), respectively.

As noted above, to address the potential manipulation of documents by students, the retrieval method used in the competition (i) was based on a learning-to-rank approach with multiple features, (ii) incorporated highly effective document-quality measures and (iii) penalized keyword stuffed documents. Figure 3 (right) presents the percentage of documents classified relevant by at least three, four or five annotators per round averaged over queries. We see that, in general, the percentage of relevant documents decreased over the course of the competition. While many of the documents were judged relevant by at least three annotators, far fewer documents were judged relevant by at least four or five annotators. This finding attests to the negative effects of SEO.

In Figure 4 we present the MAP@5 and NDCG@5 effectiveness of the document ranking induced by the retrieval method in each of the eight competition rounds. We see that the effectiveness of the ranking has gradually decreased over rounds, which can be partially attributed to the fact that fewer relevant documents were generated by students as seen in Figure 3. We also see that in the first two rounds the effectiveness of the ranking was much higher than that in the rounds to follow. We found that in the first two rounds students used the initially provided relevant documents without significantly changing them. After the second round, in which the retrieval method was changed by applying diversification with respect to the given relevant document (see Section A.4.2), students started diversifying their documents by introducing noise, using non-relevant information and applying content manipulation.

REFERENCES

[1] R. Aumann and M. Maschler. 1995. *Repeated Games with Incomplete Information.* MIT Press.

[2] Ran Ben-Basat and Elad Kravi. 2016. The ranking game. In *Proceedings of the 19th International Workshop on Web and Databases*. 7.

[3] Ran Ben-Basat, Moshe Tennenholtz, and Oren Kurland. 2015. The Probability Ranking Principle is Not Optimal in Adversarial Retrieval Settings. In *Proceedings of ICTIR.* 51–60.

[4] Michael Bendersky, W. Bruce Croft, and Yanlei Diao. 2011. Quality-biased ranking of web documents. In *Proceedings of WSDM.* 95–104.

[5] Jaime G. Carbonell and Jade Goldstein. 1998. The Use of MMR, Diversity-Based Reranking for Reordering Documents and Producing Summaries. In *Proceedings of SIGIR.* 335–336.

[6] Carlos Castillo and Brian D. Davison. 2010. Adversarial Web Search. *Foundations and Trends in Information Retrieval* 4, 5 (2010), 377–486.

[7] Gordon V. Cormack, Mark D. Smucker, and Charles L. A. Clarke. 2011. Efficient and effective spam filtering and re-ranking for large web datasets. *Informaltiom Retrieval Journal* 14, 5 (2011), 441–465.

[8] Nilesh Dalvi, Pedro Domingos, Mausam, Sumit Sanghai, and Deepak Verma. 2004. Adversarial Classification. In *Proceedings of KDD.* 99–108.

[9] Fernando Diaz. 2005. Regularizing Ad Hoc Retrieval Scores. In *Proceedings of CIKM.* 672–679.

[10] Ran El-Yaniv and Mordechai Nisenson. 2010. On the Foundations of Adversarial Single-Class Classification. *CoRR* (2010).

[11] Kfir Eliaz and Ran Spiegler. 2011. A simple model of search engine pricing. *The Economic Journal* 121, 556 (2011), F329–F339.

[12] Kfir Eliaz and Ran Spiegler. 2016. Search design and broad matching. *American Economic Review* 106, 3 (2016), 563–586.

[13] Jonathan L. Elsas and Susan T. Dumais. 2010. Leveraging temporal dynamics of document content in relevance ranking. In *Proceedings of WSDM.* 1–10.

[14] Hui Fang, Tao Tao, and ChengXiang Zhai. 2004. A formal study of information retrieval heuristics. In *Proceedings of SIGIR.* 49–56.

[15] Norbert Fuhr. 2008. A probability ranking principle for interactive information retrieval. *Information Retrieval* 11, 3 (2008), 251–265.

[16] Zoltán Gyöngyi and Hector Garcia-Molina. 2005. Web Spam Taxonomy. In *Proceedings of AIRWeb 2005, First International Workshop on Adversarial Information Retrieval on the Web.* 39–47.

[17] Nathanael Hyafil and Craig Boutilier. 2004. Regret Minimizing Equilibria and Mechanisms for Games with Strict Type Uncertainty. In *Proceedings of UAI.* 268–277.

[18] N. Jardine and C. J. van Rijsbergen. 1971. The use of hierarchic clustering in information retrieval. *Information Storage and Retrieval* 7, 5 (1971), 217–240.

[19] John D. Lafferty and Chengxiang Zhai. 2001. Document language models, query models, and risk minimization for information retrieval. In *Proceedings of SIGIR.* 111–119.

[20] Tie-Yan Liu. 2011. *Learning to Rank for Information Retrieval.* Springer. I–XVII, 1–285 pages.

[21] Alexandros Ntoulas, Marc Najork, Mark Manasse, and Dennis Fetterly. 2006. Detecting spam web pages through content analysis. In *Proceedings of WWW.* 83–92.

[22] Fabian Pedregosa, Gaël Varoquaux, Alexandre Gramfort, Vincent Michel, Bertrand Thirion, Olivier Grisel, Mathieu Blondel, Peter Prettenhofer, Ron Weiss, Vincent Dubourg, Jake VanderPlas, Alexandre Passos, David Cournapeau, Matthieu Brucher, Matthieu Perrot, and Edouard Duchesnay. 2011. Scikit-learn: Machine Learning in Python. *Journal of Machine Learning Research* 12 (2011), 2825–2830.

[23] Kira Radinsky and Paul N. Bennett. 2013. Predicting content change on the web. In *Proceedings of WSDM.* 415–424.

[24] Justus J. Randolph. 2016. Online Kappa Calculator (2008). Retrieved February 6, http://justus.randolph.name/kappa. (2016).

[25] Stephen E. Robertson. 1977. The Probability Ranking Principle in IR. *Journal of Documentation* (1977), 294–304. Reprinted in K. Sparck Jones and P. Willett (eds), *Readings in Information Retrieval*, pp. 281–286, 1997.

[26] Aécio S. R. Santos, Bruno Pasini, and Juliana Freire. 2016. A First Study on Temporal Dynamics of Topics on the Web. In *Proceedings of WWW.* 849–854.

[27] Marc Sloan and Jun Wang. 2012. Dynamical information retrieval modelling: a portfolio-armed bandit machine approach. In *Proceedings WWW.* 603–604.

[28] Hong Wang, Wei Xing, Kaiser Asif, and Brian D. Ziebart. 2015. Adversarial Prediction Games for Multivariate Losses. In *Proceedings of NIPS.* 2728–2736.

[29] Qiang Wu, Christopher J. C. Burges, Krysta Marie Svore, and Jianfeng Gao. 2010. Adapting boosting for information retrieval measures. *Information Retrieval* 13, 3 (2010), 254–270.

[30] Grace Hui Yang, Marc Sloan, and Jun Wang. 2016. *Dynamic Information Retrieval Modeling.* Morgan & Claypool Publishers.

[31] Yinan Zhang and Chengxiang Zhai. 2015. Information Retrieval as Card Playing: A Formal Model for Optimizing Interactive Retrieval Interface. In *Proceedings of SIGIR.* 685–694.

On Application of Learning to Rank for E-Commerce Search

Shubhra Kanti Karmaker Santu
University of Illinois
Urbana-Champaign (UIUC)
karmake2@illinois.edu

Parikshit Sondhi
WalmartLabs
psondhi@walmartlabs.com

ChengXiang Zhai
University of Illinois
Urbana-Champaign (UIUC)
czhai@illinois.edu

ABSTRACT

E-Commerce (E-Com) search is an emerging important new application of information retrieval. Learning to Rank (LETOR) is a general effective strategy for optimizing search engines, and is thus also a key technology for E-Com search. While the use of LETOR for web search has been well studied, its use for E-Com search has not yet been well explored. In this paper, we discuss the practical challenges in applying learning to rank methods to E-Com search, including the challenges in feature representation, obtaining reliable relevance judgments, and optimally exploiting multiple user feedback signals such as click rates, add-to-cart ratios, order rates, and revenue. We study these new challenges using experiments on industry data sets and report several interesting findings that can provide guidance on how to optimally apply LETOR to E-Com search: First, popularity-based features defined solely on product items are very useful and LETOR methods were able to effectively optimize their combination with relevance-based features. Second, query attribute sparsity raises challenges for LETOR, and selecting features to reduce/avoid sparsity is beneficial. Third, while crowdsourcing is often useful for obtaining relevance judgments for Web search, it does not work as well for E-Com search due to difficulty in eliciting sufficiently fine grained relevance judgments. Finally, among the multiple feedback signals, the order rate is found to be the most robust training objective, followed by click rate, while add-to-cart ratio seems least robust, suggesting that an effective practical strategy may be to initially use click rates for training and gradually shift to using order rates as they become available.

ACM Reference format:
Shubhra Kanti Karmaker Santu, Parikshit Sondhi, and ChengXiang Zhai. 2017. On Application of Learning to Rank for E-Commerce Search. In *Proceedings of SIGIR '17, August 7–11, 2017, Shinjuku, Tokyo, Japan,* , 10 pages.
DOI: http://dx.doi.org/10.1145/3077136.3080838

1 INTRODUCTION

E-Commerce (E-Com) search is an important emerging new application of information retrieval. Virtually all major retailers have their own product search engines, with popular engines processing millions of query requests per day. As E-shopping becomes increasingly popular, optimization of their search quality is increasingly important since an improved E-Com search engine can potentially save all users' time while increasing their satisfaction.

Due to its importance, E-Com search has recently attracted increasing attention and has been studied from multiple perspectives [9, 10, 17, 21, 31, 32, 36] (See Section 5 for a more detailed review of all the major work). However, one of the most central questions in E-Com search: How to optimally apply learning to rank (LETOR) methods for ranking of products, has attracted little attention.

Over the past decade, Learning to Rank (LETOR) methods, which involve applying machine learning techniques on ranking problems, have proven to be very successful in optimizing search engines; specifically, they have been extensively studied in the context of Web search [3, 7, 18, 30] to combine multiple features to optimize ranking. Thus, not surprisingly, learning to rank is also the backbone technique for optimizing the ranking of products in product search.

While there has been much progress made in research on learning to rank and many LETOR methods have been proposed (see, e.g., [18, 20]), applications of these methods to any search engine optimization would still face many practical challenges, notably how to define features, how to convert the search log data into effective training sets, how to obtain relevance judgments including both explicit judgments by humans and implicit judgments based on search log, and what objective functions to optimize for specific applications. Compared with the vast amount of work on improving algorithms and models for learning to rank, there has been little work on studying these practical challenges; yet they must be tackled in order to effectively deploy a LETOR method for E-Com search applications.

In this paper, we study these practical challenges in applying LETOR to E-Com search with a focus on addressing research questions related to 1) Effective feature representation; 2) Effectiveness of crowdsourcing relevance judgments; and 3) Exploitation of multiple feedback signals. As no previous work has reported results on comparing the major LETOR methods for E-Com search, we first compare multiple representative major LETOR methods on an industry data set to see how well they perform for E-Com search; our results show that LambdaMART, one of the best performing methods for Web search, has also performed very well for E-Com search, outperforming all the other methods that we evaluated. Next, using LambdaMART as our LETOR method, we explore various issues related to feature representation, including particularly the effectiveness of popularity-based features and the issue of query attribute sparsity. Our results show that popularity-based features, despite their independence of queries, are clearly effective and LambdaMART is able to optimize their combination with relevance-based features. The sparsity of query attribute features, however,

SIGIR '17, August 7–11, 2017, Shinjuku, Tokyo, Japan
© 2017 ACM. 978-1-4503-5022-8/17/08...$15.00
DOI: http://dx.doi.org/10.1145/3077136.3080838

poses challenges for LETOR methods, and avoiding to use sparse attributes via feature selection is found to be beneficial.

Next, we study the reliability of using crowdsourcing to obtain relevance judgments for E-Com search. Since the power of LETOR mainly comes from high-quality training examples, how to obtain reliable relevance judgements is an important question. Crowdsourcing is a commonly used approach to obtain relevance judgments in an affordable way [2] and has been working well for Web search [15], but due to the fact that the relevance criterion in E-Com search tends to be more complex than Web search (users of an E-Com search engine have very strict preferences for the products that they would eventually want to buy), it is questionable whether we can reliably obtain useful relevance judgments for E-Com search via crowdsourcing. To address this question, we analyze the quality of the relevance judgments created via crowdsourcing by leveraging the search log data. The results indeed show that the quality of crowdsourced judgments is low with a significant number of the products of the highest-level relevance with zero or just one click according to the search log data, even though they have been presented to users many times, suggesting that although crowdsourcing has been useful for obtaining relevance judgments for training LETOR methods in Web search, it does not work as well for E-Com search.

Finally, we study how to best exploit the different feedback signals that we discussed above for LETOR by using LambdaMart as the learning algorithm and varying the combinations of these feedback signals for training and testing. Our experiment results show that among all the user feedback signals, click rates appear to be the easiest to predict, while add-to-cart ratios the hardest. Training to optimize order rates is found to be most robust (followed by click through rates) in predicting various other objectives (i.e., click rates, add-to-cart-ratios, and revenues), often delivering the best or near-the-best performance indistinguishable from training on the target signal itself. The closely related revenue, however, behaves less robustly. These findings suggest that a reasonable simple strategy for an E-Com search engine is to use click rate based models for query segments where sufficient order data is not available, but switch to order rate based models once it is.

In summary, our paper conducts the first systematic study of challenges in applying LETOR methods to E-Com search and makes the following contributions:

(1) We introduce and study multiple new challenges in applying LETOR to E-Com search, including relevance vs. popularity features, query attribute sparsity, difficulty in accurately eliciting human relevance judgments, complexity in optimal exploitation of multiple feedback signals.
(2) We show that popularity-based features are very effective despite their independence of queries and LETOR methods can effectively optimize their combination with other relevance-based features.
(3) We show that the sparsity of query attributes poses challenges for LETOR and selecting features to avoid or alleviate sparsity is beneficial.
(4) We show that while effective for Web search, crowdsourcing is not very effective for obtaining relevance judgments for E-Com search.
(5) We show that among all the feedback signals, order rate is the most robust (followed by clickthroughs), suggesting that an effective practical strategy may be to initially use click rates for training (due to their availability) and gradually shift to using order rates as they become available.

2 LEARNING TO RANK FOR E-COM SEARCH

In this Section, we provide some background on learning to rank for E-Com search to motivate our work and provide a context for the research questions that we study in this paper. We first give a general introduction to LETOR and then discuss multiple practical challenges in applying LETOR to E-Com search.

2.1 Overview of LETOR

Optimization of ranking of products is the primary goal of an E-Com search engine. As in other retrieval system applications, traditional retrieval models, such as BM25 and language modeling approaches, play an important role in E-Com search to enable matching of the queries from users with product descriptions in the product collection. However, content matching, while very important, is not the only signal for ranking products, and it is desirable to bring in many other potentially useful signals to improve ranking. Specifically, an E-Com search engine would be able to naturally accumulate large amounts of user interaction data, including particularly user queries, clickthroughs, add-to-carts, order rates, revenue information, which can all be leveraged to improve ranking. Learning to rank methods provide a principled way to combine a large number of features optimally and have been proven very effective for Web search [18, 20].

The basic idea of all these LETOR methods is to assume that given a query, the scoring of items to be ranked is a parameterized function of multiple features computed based on the query, the items and any other relevant information where the parameters are generally to control the weights (contributions) of different features. These parameters can then be learned by optimizing the performance of the parameterized ranking function on a training data set where we not only have queries and items, but also relevance judgments to indicate which items should have been ranked high for a query. Once the parameters are learned, the ranking function (now with parameter values that have been learned from a training set) can be applied to any future query to rank the items with respect the query. The traditional retrieval functions such as BM25 are generally the most elementary building blocks (features) in these LETOR methods, but LETOR enables us to use many more different kinds of features.

2.2 Application of LETOR to E-Com Search

Successful application of learning to rank methods for E-Com search requires us to optimize multiple practical decisions. The first is to choose a good LETOR model. Given the same data, is it better to learn a single model across the board, or train multiple models for different segments? How do well known learning to rank models perform for the task? In particular, are LambdaMART models, which perform very well for Web search, still the best?

Next there are important decisions regarding training dataset creation (e.g. feature representation, source of relevance judgments etc.) and model learning (e.g. objective to be optimized, model to use etc.). In particular the trained models should be capable of generalizing to:

(1) Previously unseen queries not in the training set
(2) Previously unseen documents to be ranked for queries seen in the training set

Note that, we use the term document/product interchangeably throughout the paper. Below we discuss the various challenges associated with achieving these modes of generalization, and highlight the relevant research questions that we will focus in our study.

2.2.1 Feature Representation: Successful application of LETOR methods often depend upon the construction of useful features. We can organize ranking features into three groups:

(1) Query Features: These features are purely query properties. Eg. Query length, expected product category etc.
(2) Document Features: These features are purely document properties. Eg. Title length, User Ratings, Total sales, department etc.
(3) Query-Document Features: These features are properties of a query-document pair. Eg. BM25F text match score, Whether document belongs to the department predicted for the query etc.

Query: blue iPhone 6 case

Query Attributes: { Color: Blue, Product Category: Phone Case}

Query-Document Features	 Color: Blue Cat.: Phone Case	 Color: Black Cat.: Phone Case	 Color: NULL Cat.: Book
q.color!=NULL & d.color!=NULL	1	1	0
q.color=d.color	1	0	0
q.Product Cat.= d.Product Cat.	1	1	0

Figure 1: Features in an E-com query

A key aspect of E-Com search is the presence of a large number of product and query attributes, around which ranking features need to be constructed. Product attributes are properties of products such as Brand, Rating, Category etc. present in the catalog either manually provided by the merchant or automatically extracted from the description. Query attributes are defined as the attributes expected by the query in the products. Macdonald et. al. investigated which types of query attributes are useful to improve learned models [22]. These query features are typically obtained by either parsing the query directly, analyzing search log data, or training an attribute predictor for the query. For example a query like *blue iPhone 6 case* expects products with attribute "Color: Blue" and "Category: Phone Cases". We refer to these as query attributes. These are then matched with document attributes to generate query-document features. An example is shown in Figure 1.

There are three specific challenges related to feature representation as we will discuss below.

1. Balancing of Relevance and Popularity: Figure 1 highlights two scenarios of challenges in optimizing the combination of features related to the balancing of relevance and popularity:

(1) Catalog has several "blue" iPhone cases. In which case the ranker should be able to rank more popular matching products higher. Popularity/ratings/sales etc. are purely document properties which now become important.
(2) Catalog has several "black" iPhone cases which are more popular than the "blue" iPhone cases. Apart from popularity, the black and blue iPhone cases differ only in 1 feature, i.e., the color. Document specific features which are primarily meant to resolve among equally relevant products, should not be allowed to promote irrelevant products.

More importantly certain query attributes may be more critical than others. The user may be open to buying a more popular "black" iPhone case even on a "blue iPhone case" query, but certainly would not be willing to buy an iPhone. Thus while in some cases allowing popularity to dominate over color match related features may be acceptable, letting it dominate over category match is certainly unacceptable.

Thus an interesting question here is whether LETOR methods can optimize the balancing of relevance and popularity and whether the popularity-based features are effective for E-Com search. The relevance vs popularity problem is especially severe in linear rankers, and we study whether a non-linear ranker such as LambdaMART can do better.

2. Query attribute sparsity: While a given product will typically have < 100 attributes associated with it, due to substantial diversity in the types of products in an E-Com catalog, one can easily expect 1000s of unique attributes to be present in the catalog. The number of attributes predicted for a query tend to be even smaller. This can cause problems for unseen queries. It is quite possible that an unseen query has a set of attributes rarely observed in the training set. To what extent does the sparsity negatively impact the performance? How can we train our models to still work well for these queries? One option is to try to gather more data on these queries, but this is generally expensive. More importantly there are always going to be unseen queries. An alternate option is to train a separate segmented ranker for such queries on a subset of overlapping features. We explore the conditions under which such a segmentation would make sense. We compare whether its better to use the same ranker or train a different one based on the intersection of attributes.

3. Engagement features: Engagement signals such as clicks, cart-adds, orders etc. are computed based on user interactions. As we discuss in the next section, they also serve as surrogates of relevance judgments. Due to this strong correlation, they tend to cause overfitting, and therefore we do not use them as features in our experiments.

2.2.2 Relevance judgments: One common challenge in applying LETOR is to obtain reliable relevance judgments so that one can create high-quality training data sets for training a LETOR method. The effectiveness of LETOR clearly depends on the quality of training data. Standardized web search test collections are based on query-document relevance ratings elicited from human experts and crowdsourcing [25]. This is not a viable option in the E-Com domain, where the relevance ratings need to reflect the utility of a product to the user rather than merely text relevance or intent match with the query. Utility is typically a complex function of a product not only matching the query intent, but also the product's brand, price, quality, value for money, associated warranty, availability etc. For example for a query like *14 inch laptop*, there are typically 100s of matching laptops which are all equally relevant from a human rater's perspective. However the likelihood of a user purchasing them varies significantly from one to the other, based on brand, quality, hardware specs, operating system, reviews, battery life, price, warranty etc [1], making it challenging to make relevance judgments; indeed, in such cases human judgments are not sufficient to provide a fine grained ground truth ordering of products for the query unless we have users to make judgements for their own queries.

In the absence of human judgements, we must turn to relevance feedback signals available from search logs for ground truth creation. In contrast with web search which only has clicks, E-Com search logs contain four prominent relevance feedback signals: clicks, cart-adds, orders and revenue. They represent potentially different training objectives as explained below. Formal equations for their computation are provided in section 3.1.

(1) **Perceived utility of search results (Click through rate):** Function of users' perceived utility of a product, assessed based on the resulting snippet, typically title, image, price and ratings etc. Computed as the ratio of clicks a product receives for a query and its impressions (number of times shown to the user) for the query. This is closest to a typical web search setting. It especially makes sense for E-Com search engines which are relatively nascent or when churn in product or query distributions is high, so sufficient order/add-to-cart data is not available.

(2) **Perceived utility of the product page (Add-to-cart ratio):** A function of users' perceived utility of a product, assessed based on the product's webpage containing comprehensive information such as detailed description, attributes, multiple images/videos and availability etc. Computed as the ratio of add-to-carts a product receives for a query and its number of clicks for the query. In case of high spam especially in online market places, this is a more suitable objective.

(3) **Overall user satisfaction (Order rate):** A function of users' overall satisfaction with a product. Computed as the ratio of orders a product receives for a query and its impressions for the query. It encompasses users' perceived utility based on both result page and item page information. Order data while being a stronger signal of user satisfaction, tends to be sparser compared to clicks and add-to-carts.

(4) **Business value (Revenue rate):** Based not only on user satisfaction metrics like the previous three, but also the revenue obtained from a product's purchases. Computed as the ratio of revenue generated by a product for a query and its impressions for the query. It has the same level of sparsity as order rate.

Choosing the right objective however is non-trivial. Clearly increasing available training data improves model quality, but high-quality signals tend to be sparse, leading to a tradeoff between the quantity and quality of training data. Understanding this trade-off is crucial to generating training datasets. To the best of our knowledge, no prior works have studied this question in E-Com domain.

One can also choose arbitrary combinations of these engagement metrics to define a target [29]. This is non-trivial and is often done based on several online experiments. For this work, we will focus more on the relationship between these objectives. We will systematically examine these different types of feedback signals and experimentally study how to best use them.

3 EXPERIMENT DESIGN

The main goal of our experiments is to study the new challenges in applying LETOR to E-Com search as we discussed in section 2.2. Below we will describe the data set we used, the implementation of LETOR methods, and our experiment procedure for each of the research questions we study.

3.1 Dataset

Our E-Com data set consists of $2.8K$ randomly selected product search queries, and a catalog of $5M$ product/documents[1]. For each query, we retrieved top 120 products using a $BM25F$[26] based retrieval algorithm. For each query-document pair (q, d), we then collected statistics on impressions[2] ($imp(q, d)$), clicks ($clicks(q, d)$), add-to-carts ($atc(q, d)$), orders ($orders(q, d)$) and revenue ($rev(q, d)$) from search logs. Based on these statistics, we then assigned relevance ratings as follows.

For each query, we eliminated products for which less than 100 impressions were observed in the search log, to reduce variance in rate estimates. One can also use alternate smoothing strategies here [13], but since these have not previously been tested on E-Com data and we had sufficient data available, we decided to simply drop the low impression products/documents. Post the filtering step, we had on average 94.2 documents per query. Each <query, document> pair is considered as a single training instance to the LETOR methods.

Let D_q be the set of documents selected for a query q after the first step. Then the click/order/revenue rates and add-to-cart ratios for q and $d \in D_q$ were computed as follows:

$$ctr(q, d) = \frac{clicks(q, d)}{imp(q, d)} \quad , \quad or(q, d) = \frac{orders(q, d)}{imp(q, d)}$$

$$revr(q, d) = \frac{revenue(q, d)}{imp(q, d)} \quad , \quad atcr(q, d) = \frac{atc(q, d)}{clicks(q, d)}$$

Finally, ground truth relevance ratings based on the above objectives were computed for all products in D_q by normalizing and discretizing to a 5 point integer scale $(0 - 4)$. For example, the formula for the ground truth relevance ratings in case of objective click rate, i.e., ctr, is presented below:

$$rel_{ctr}(q, d) = ceil\left(4.\frac{ctr(q, d)}{\max_{d \in D_q} ctr(q, d)}\right) \tag{1}$$

For each query, documents with the highest ctr always received a rating of 4, while documents with no clicks received 0. Ground truth relevance ratings based on other objectives ($rel_{atcr}, rel_{or}, rel_{revr}$) were computed similarly.

[1] A subset obtained from www.walmart.com product catalog. We use the term "product"/"document" interchangeably throughout the paper.

[2] Number of times a product was shown to the user for a query

Note that *atcr* unlike other rates is obtained by normalizing with *clicks* instead of *impressions*. Consistent with our second objective of product page utility, it represents the empirical probability of a user being satisfied by a product after the user has clicked on it and reviewed its product page.

The resulting distribution of relevance labels per query for the objective "click rate" is shown in Figure 2. Other relevance distributions look similar and have been omitted in the interest of space. One observes from the figure that there is a significant drop in the number of documents as we move from relevance rating 0 to 4. It suggests that most queries have a small number of best selling products which dominate in terms of clicks, cart-adds, orders etc. This characteristic can result from several reasons such as query specificity, competitive pricing, faster/free shipping, higher/better number of reviews and ratings, better value for money, brand loyalty etc. However, one does observe sufficient number of products associated with each relevance bucket implying that while some products tend to attract the most attention, there are indeed several products that users engage with and purchase.

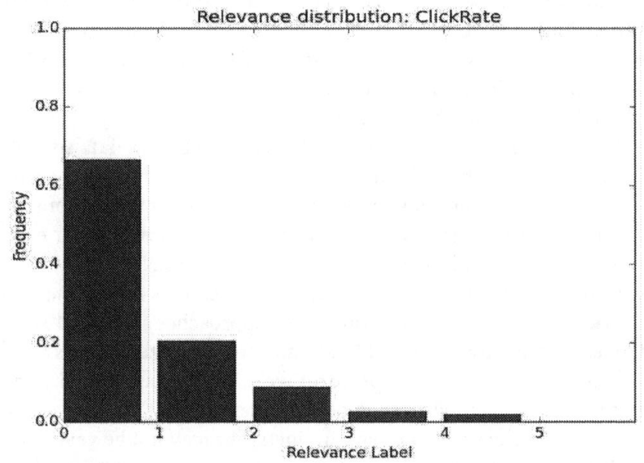

Figure 2: Relevance label distribution for the objective "click rate". Relevance labels are on a scale of 0-4. Average number of products per query was 94.2. Frequencies are normalized in the scale [0,1] for each query and the average of 2.8K queries are reported in the figure.

Our feature set consists of 562 features comprising various query specific, product specific and both query-product specific features. Below we highlight some of the prominent feature groups. We avoid a full list of features due to lack of space.

Text match: query - product BM25F[24] score, computed by matching the query with various text fields (eg. Brand, Title, Description, Department etc.) present in a semi-structured product specification document.

Product attributes: Overall product sales, rating, number of reviews, expected demand, brand, price etc.

Query-Document attribute match: Whether an attribute that takes a non-null value for the query, also takes a non-null value in the document. Similar to the first sample feature shown in Figure 1.

Query-Document attribute value match: Whether the predicted query attribute value matches the document attribute value. Similar to the second and third sample features shown in Figure 1. One feature for each type of attribute (eg. Category, Brand, Price, Color, Size etc.) available in the product catalog.

Note that both attribute match and attribute value match features were real valued. The value of the feature was the same as the prediction probability of the query attribute or attribute-value.

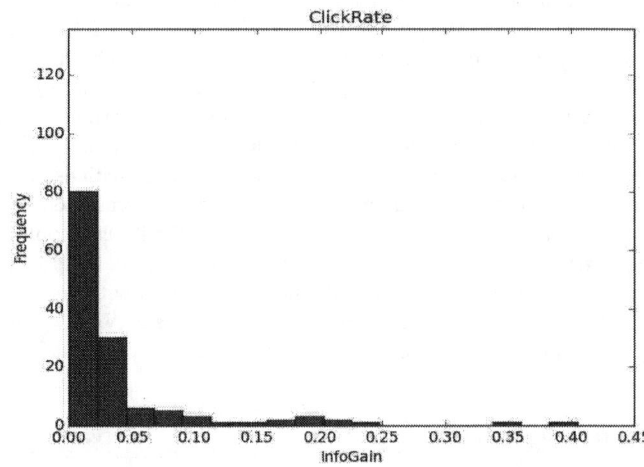

Figure 3: Feature Info-Gain Distribution

To give a deeper insight into the informativeness of our features, Figure 3 provides a histogram of information gain values w.r.t click rate based relevance rating (rel_{ctr}). It is evident that most of our features provide a moderate to low information gain w.r.t. the objective click rate, however, a few of them provide a high information gain w.r.t. the same objective. The relationships between these features and the other objectives are also similar and hence, omitted due to the lack of space. Note that we did not use any click, cart-add or order based features, in order to ensure our models generalize to previously unseen query-document pairs.

3.2 Implementation of LETOR methods

Algorithm	Short form
RankNet [5]	RNet
RankBoost [12]	RBoost
AdaRank [34]	ARank
Random Forest [4]	RF
LambdaMART [6]	LMART
Logistic Regression (L1 regularized) [11, 16]	L1LR
Logistic Regression (L2 regularized) [11, 19]	L2LR
SVM Classifier (L1 regularized, L2 Loss) [11, 28]	L1L2SVMC
SVM Classifier (L2 regularized, L1 Loss) [11, 28]	L2L1SVMC
SVM Regressor (L2 regularized, L2 Loss) [11, 27]	L2L2SVMR
SVM Regressor (L2 regularized, L1 Loss) [11, 27]	L2L1SVMR

Table 1: Popular learning to rank algorithms

There are many LETOR methods proposed. Table 1 lists the popular LETOR approaches along with popular classification and regression methods that have also been used for ranking applications. For notational convenience, we assign abbreviations to each method which is used throughout the rest of the paper.

Our study is more focused on studying some unique new challenges in applying any LETOR method to E-Com search, thus in our experiments, we have primarily used LambdaMART as our learning-to-rank model because it has been shown to work very well in Web search. However, since there does not yet exist any comparison of these popular LETOR methods on an E-Com data set, we also compare all the popular LETOR methods that we discussed above, mostly as a sanity check to see whether LambdaMART is also the best performing method for E-Com search. (As will be shown later, LambdaMART indeed outperforms all the other methods.) In these experiments, we used three different toolkits to experiment with learning to rank algorithms. For RankNet, Random Forest, AdaRank and RankBoost we used the RankLib toolkit [3] with default parameter settings. For LambdaMART, we used the jForests toolkit [4]. All LambdaMART models were trained using the jforests config properties shown in table 2. For Logistic regression and Support Vector Machines we used the LibLinear toolkit [11] with default parameter settings. In each case, we report average *NDCG@10* [14] computed using 5 fold cross validation, as the performance metric.

parameter name	value
trees.num-leaves	7
trees.min-instance-percentage-per-leaf	0.25
boosting.learning-rate	0.05
boosting.sub-sampling	0.3
trees.feature-sampling	0.3
boosting.num-trees	2000
learning.algorithm	LambdaMART-RegressionTree
learning.evaluation-metric	NDCG
params.print-intermediate-valid-measurements	true

Table 2: Parameter settings for LambdaMART

3.3 Research Questions and Experiment Procedure

We will study the following research questions in this paper; for each question, we briefly describe the experiment procedure.

(1) How well can LETOR methods optimize the combination of relevance-scoring features and static document-based features such as popularity features? Are popularity features useful? We can address these questions by experimenting with using only relevance-scoring features and using both relevance features and popularity features.
(2) How well can LETOR methods handle sparse query attributes? Would it be beneficial to select features to avoid sparse attributes? We can address these questions by varying the features used and comparing using all the features (more features, but causing sparsity) and using fewer features (losing some information, but avoiding sparsity).
(3) How reliable is crowdsourcing relevance judgments for E-Com search? How is the utility of such relevance judgments compared with using naturally available user feedback signals such as clicking data, add-to-cart ratio, and order rates? We address these questions by obtaining relevance judgements through crowdsourcing and analyzing it against the user behavior signals from the activity log data.
(4) What's the best way to exploit the multiple feedback signals? Increasing available training data improves model quality, but high-quality signals tend to be sparse, leading to a trade-off between the quantity and quality of training data. How does this tradeoff impact performance? Can we train a model to optimize one objective, e.g., click rate, for which sufficient data is available easily and then apply the model to predict some different objective, e.g., order rate? We address these questions by combining different feedback signals for training and testing respectively.

[3]http://www.lemurproject.org/
[4]https://github.com/yasserg/jforests

4 EXPERIMENT RESULTS

In this section, we discuss our experiment results.

4.1 Comparison of LETOR methods

As no previous work has compared the major LETOR methods for E-Com search, we first make such a comparison to help us determine the best-performing method for further study of other research questions that we discussed earlier.

Table 3 presents the summary of the results of applying different state-of-the-art LETOR algorithms on the E-com data set. We hypothesized that LambdaMART would be the best based on its superior performance in Web search, and the results indeed confirm this hypothesis; it achieves the highest test performance for each target objective, followed by AdaRank and RankNet. This observation is consistent with prior benchmark studies on web search dataset [30]. Linear classification based approaches such as L1 regularized Logistic Regression (L1LR) and L1 Regularized L2 loss SVM Classifier (L1L2SVM) also perform well. This is explained by the fact that these methods do a good job of separating the irrelevant (0 rated) from relevant (1-4 rated) products, but may not be very good with correctly ordering the relevant documents among themselves. Still, since a large percentage of documents in E-com dataset are 0 rated (Figure 2) and our raw features are sufficiently informative, the "simple" linear models are able to achieve reasonable ranking performance. Finally, we observe that if a method does well on one objective, it tends to do well on others as well.

4.2 Feature Representation

With LambdaMART selected as the LETOR method for further experiments, we now turn to the questions about feature representation, particularly the effectiveness of popularity-based attributes as features and the impact of query attribute sparsity, to be discussed below, respectively.

4.2.1 Results on popularity based attributes: As discussed earlier, due to the risk of the potential dominance of popularity-based features over relevance features, we cannot assume that popularity-based features are definitely effective. We thus setup an experiment to verify the usefulness of popularity based attributes in capturing the target objective. Without loss of generality, we set "order rate", which is also the highest quality feedback available form the user activity logs, as the optimization objective. We created two different

Algorithm	Click Rate		Cart Add Rate		Order Rate		Revenue	
	Train	Test	Train	Test	Train	Test	Train	Test
RNet	0.6857	0.6855	0.4399	0.4402	0.7158	0.7142	0.7577	0.7578
RBoost	0.5899	0.5904	0.4073	0.4043	0.5007	0.4994	0.5663	0.5639
ARank	0.6877	0.6857	0.4464	0.4401	0.7334	0.7349	0.757	0.7566
RF	0.6378	0.6125	0.4588	0.4296	0.5707	0.5288	0.6463	0.5959
LMART	0.8426	**0.8291**	0.7664	**0.7324**	0.7728	**0.7687**	0.8183	**0.7998**
L1LR	0.6284	0.6272	0.4274	0.4252	0.6677	0.6632	0.6873	0.6822
L2LR	0.5889	0.5866	0.4066	0.4025	0.5045	0.4983	0.5751	0.5675
L1L2SVMC	0.6366	0.6317	0.4348	0.4331	0.6870	0.6794	0.7105	0.7059
L2L1SVMC	0.4596	0.4594	0.3274	0.3219	0.4281	0.4289	0.4503	0.4462
L2L2SVMR	0.2358	0.2341	0.1909	0.1914	0.2100	0.2087	0.2030	0.2027
L2L1SVMR	0.2876	0.2865	0.2110	0.2096	0.2078	0.2038	0.2093	0.2121

Table 3: Comparison of ranking algorithms in terms of NDCG@10 for target variable "Click Rate", "Cart Add Rate", "Order Rate" and "Revenue"

sets of training sets which vary only in the set of features that they contain. The first training set contains all the 562 features available in the dataset, while the second one discards the popularity based features from the first training set. For each training set, we then trained a separate LambdaMART model and tested over the same testing set for both trained models. This whole process constitutes one out of the 5 folds in 5-fold cross validation, thus, we repeated this process four more times with different partitions of the data as testing data. We report the average results of the 5-fold cross validation experiment in Table 4. This table highlights that product popularity related features which are purely document attributes are indeed useful for ranking and suggests that LambdaMART was able to learn appropriate weights to balance relevance-based and popularity-based features. Both training and testing NDCG@10 drops significantly when we remove popularity features such as total sales, reviews, ratings etc.

Feature Set	Training	Testing
Without Popularity	0.71053	0.70415
With Popularity	0.7728	0.7687

Table 4: Effect of popularity attributes in predicting the target: "order rate"

4.2.2 Results on query attribute sparsity: We now examine the impact of query attribute sparsity on LETOR results and test the idea of selectively using only features that help avoiding the sparsity. Specifically, for this experiment, we randomly sampled 10 departments out of a total of 26 in the dataset. For each department, we did the following: we first removed all queries belonging to that department and used them to create a test set. Of the remaining queries in the dataset, we created a training set first by a) using all available attribute features and b) using only attribute features that appear in the test set i.e. the intersection set. We again chose "order rate" as the target objective as this is the highest quality feedback available from the user activity logs. For each training set, we trained a separate LambdaMART model and tested it on the testing set created as described above. Table 5 presents the summary of these results [5]. It clearly shows that using the intersection set

Dept.	Training <q,d> pairs	Testing <q,d> pairs	NDCG@10 All features	NDCG@10 Intersected Features	% increase
A	189602	44207	0.7712	0.8504	10.2570
B	233109	700	0.6940	0.7533	08.5443
C	226971	6838	0.7692	0.8675	12.7748
D	193615	40194	0.7859	0.8501	08.1733
E	210327	23482	0.7827	0.8732	11.5662
F	229258	4551	0.6986	0.7923	13.4090
G	214854	18955	0.7626	0.8512	11.6248
H	222374	11435	0.8236	0.8908	08.1598
I	225416	8393	0.8434	0.9496	12.5904
J	222300	11509	0.7903	0.8896	12.5765

Table 5: Results on Attribute Sparsity

leads to improved results. For example, using the intersection set of features improves LambdaMART testing NDCG@10 by almost 12% for the queries of department "C" , around 13.4% for the queries of department "F" etc. The number of query-document pairs available in the test and train sets are also listed. These results suggest that there is great potential to apply transfer learning and domain adaptation to LETOR for E-Com search, which should be a very interesting future direction for further study.

4.3 Results on crowdsourcing

In this experiment, we study the reliability of the relevance judgements provided by the crowd workers for e-commerce queries. We first randomly selected a query. For this query, workers were shown a product image, title and price along with the query. Different products were shown to the workers for the same query. They were then asked to rate the relevance of the product on a 0-4 rating scale. There were well defined guidelines on what each level means with 4 being ideal and 0 being non-relevant.

After the workers have provided their relevance judgements; for each query, we filtered out the products that were rated as 4, i.e., ideal, by the workers. Next, for all these products that were marked as ideal by the workers, we looked at the user activity log to find out their actual number of clicks and impressions for that query. What we found out is that even though the crowd-workers rated all these products with the ideal rating, i.e., 4, the actual number

[5] Departments refer to typical departments found on a generic eCommerce site. Actual names have been removed for confidentiality.

query	No of clicks	No of items	Impressions (top 2 ranks)		
			mean	median	max
Neutrogena	0	44	165.11	104.5	982
	5 or more	16	4866.56	999.5	21901
Vacuum Cleaner	0	28	84.46	56.5	277
	5 or more	13	3040.76	620	17799
Monster High Dolls	0	13	292.61	231	759
	5 or more	24	3492.66	1806.5	30460
Water Bottles	0	8	187.5	38.0	884
	5 or more	13	6107.07	1580	44044
Outdoor Furnitures	0	8	107.37	120.5	229
	5 or more	8	3254.125	841.0	18733

Table 6: Variation in relevance judgments obtained from click data for products rated as 4 (ideal) by the crowd.

of clicks the products received varied widely given that each item had a sufficiently large number of impressions in top 2 ranks.

Table 6 shows our findings for five example queries, i.e., "Neutrogena", "Vacuum Cleaner", "Monster High Dolls", "Water Bottles" and "Outdoor Furnitures". For each query, Table 6 bins products with respect to the actual number of clicks they received. For example, the first row of Table 6 shows that 44 items that were rated as ideal by crowd-workers with respect to query "Neutrogena" received no clicks from real users. To easily distinguish the wide variance in the number of clicks that these products received, we report the results for the two bins, i.e., 1) products with zero clicks and 2) products with five or more clicks. To demonstrate that all these items received sufficient impressions, we show the mean, median and maximum of the number of impressions (only in top 2 ranks) that the products in each bucket received. This indeed shows that, even if the crowd-workers judged all these items to be ideal with respect to the query, user click counts suggests the actual utility of the product varied significantly across different products. Thus we conclude that crowdsourcing fails to provide reliable relevance judgements for E-commerce queries. This also supports the findings of the study by Alonso et. al. [1] where they suggested that when users are interested in buying products, they apply different criteria when deciding relevance. This is often hard to judge by the crowd workers.

4.4 Cross Objective Learning Experiments

According to [35], the target metric is not always the best (most informative) metric for training a LETOR method. We thus would like to experimentally understand how to best exploit the multiple training objectives available in E-Com search. To achieve this goal, we evaluated the performance of LambdaMART models trained using one training objective on test datasets based on other objectives. The results are shown in Table 7, where each row corresponds to training with a different objective (e.g., the first row with numerical values is training on click rate), and each column corresponds to testing with a different objective (e.g., the first column with numerical values is testing with click rate as the objective).

We observe that the best performance on a given test objective is indeed not always achieved by models trained on the same objective. Specifically, Table 8 highlights optimal training objectives that lead to statistically significantly better models for a given test objective, compared to the sub-optimal objectives. For example, both *ctr* and *or* based models were found to perform significantly better in predicting click rates than *atcr* and *revr* based models. Also in each case, we did not observe any statistically significant improvements when comparing the optimal objectives among themselves.

Overall, for each test objective, order rate *or* turned out to be consistently optimal, while *atcr* turns out to be consistently sub-optimal. This highlights the importance of using order rate as a robust training objective. In general for any given query segment, one can initially build models trained on *ctr* (which is optimal for objectives *or*, *ctr* and is available easily in a significant amount) since order rates are pretty sparse on initial stages and then switch to *or* based models once sufficient order data is available.

5 RELATED WORK

E-Com search has recently attracted increasing attention and has been studied from multiple perspectives, including e.g., economic theory-based model [17], adaptation of traditional retrieval models for product search [10], applying representation learning to product search [31], facet selection for product search [32], beyond relevance ranking [21] and diversification of product search results [9, 36].

Several methods have been proposed to solve the Learning to Rank problem for web search. The best-performing methods include RankNet, LambdaMART, AdaRank and RankBoost etc. [18, 20]. Researchers have conducted comprehensive studies to compare the performance of popular LETOR approaches on benchmark web data-sets [7, 30]. In particular, LambdaMART [7, 30] and RankNet [30] are known to perform particularly well. In our work, we also compared many of these methods and confirmed that LambdaMART is very effective, outperforming all the other methods that we compared with.

Macdonald et. al. [23] proposed general guidelines on best practices for deploying LETOR methods. Specifically, they provided three important general observations critical to the deployment of LETOR models. First, the smallest effective sample for LETOR varies according to several factors: the information need, the evaluation measure used to test the models, and the presence of anchor text in the document representation used for sampling. Second, the choice of the learning evaluation measure can indeed have an impact upon the effectiveness of the resulting learned model. Third, the importance of different classes of features within a learned model are dependent on both the sample size and the rank cutoff of the learning evaluation measure. Our work extends this line of contributions by adding additional findings related to unique challenges in using LETOR for E-Com search, especially the effectiveness of popularity-based features, the effectiveness of selecting features to avoid query attribute sparsity, and findings about how to best exploit the multiple feedback signals. In other related works, Chapelle et. al. [8] lay out open challenges in Learning to rank for web search. Some prominent open challenges they mentioned include sample selection bias in training, efficiency and scalability of large scale learning to rank, transfer learning to rank, online learning to rank etc. Our results on query attribute sparsity clearly suggest the importance of some of these techniques, particularly transfer learning to rank.

	Test data objective			
Training data objective	**Click rate**	**Order rate**	**Revenue rate**	**Cart Add ratio**
click rate	0.8291	0.7680	0.7943	0.7175
Order Rate	0.8258	0.7687	0.8006	0.7252
Revenue	0.8206	0.7694	0.7998	0.7186
Cart Add Ratio	0.8061	0.7564	0.7701	0.7234

Table 7: Results for Cross Target Learning

Test objective objective	Optimal training objectives	Sub-optimal training objectives
Click Rate	*ctr, or*	*atcr, revr*
Order Rate	*or, revr, ctr*	*atcr*
Revenue	*revr, or*	*ctr, atcr*
Cart Add Ratio	*actr, or*	*ctr, revr*

Table 8: Suitable training objectives based on stat. significant improvements (Wilcoxon's signed rank test [33] at level 0.05)

Our exploration of crowdsourcing is related to the previous work on this topic [1] which discussed the different relevance criteria in E-Com, which may provide an explanation of our finding that crowdsourcing is not reliable for E-Com search.

6 CONCLUSIONS AND FUTURE WORK

Learning to rank for E-Commerce (E-Com) search is an emerging important problem whose study is still in its infancy with many interesting new challenges to be solved. This paper presents a systematic experimental study of the application of state of the art LETOR methods to E-Com search using an industry data set. Below we summarize our experimental findings and discuss multiple interesting future research directions related to LETOR for E-Com search motivated by our study and observations.

First, the relative performance of different learning to rank methods on our product search data set is mostly consistent with past observations on web data sets, confirming that LambdaMART is the best performing method, and can thus be recommended for use in E-Com application systems and as a reasonable baseline for further research on learning to rank for E-Com search.

Second, the popularity-based features are very effective; despite the potential risk of imbalanced weighting of popularity-based features and relevance-based features, LETOR methods can learn to balance this weighting appropriately. However, query attribute sparsity raises challenges for LambdaMART and selectively using a subset of features to avoid sparsity is beneficial.

Third, while useful for annotating Web search data sets, crowdsourcing is shown to generate mostly unreliable judgments for E-Com search.

Finally, when using LambdaMART, among all the user feedback signals, click rates appear to be the easiest to predict, while the add-to-cart ratios the hardest. Training to optimize order rates is found to be most robust (followed by click through rates) in predicting various other objectives (i.e., click rates, add-to-cart-ratios, and revenues), often delivering the best or near-the-best performance indistinguishable from training on the target signal itself. The closely related revenue, however, behaves less robustly. These findings suggest that a reasonable simple strategy for an E-Com search engine is to use click rate based models for query segments where sufficient order data is not available, but switch to order rate based models once it is.

As in the case of all experimental studies of retrieval systems, it is important to use more test collections to further verify our findings, which would be an important future work. It is also very interesting to further study what is the best way to use different feedback signals, a unique challenge specific to product search (not present in Web search). For example, given that training on the same signal as the target of prediction may not be as good as training on another correlated signal, can we intelligently combine various feedback signals to obtain a more robust effective ranker? How can we optimally combine them? There are clearly multiple possibilities, such as combining them as features vs. using each to train a different model and then combining multiple models. It would really be interesting to develop a method that can switch from click-rate to order-rate, or even better, a model that can combine both and adapt based on the amount of data that is available.

Another interesting direction is the following: since a lot of queries in E-com domain are category-related queries, e.g., show me "tv sets" or "sofas", this hints that there is a general tendency of exploratory-like search behavior in E-com. With this in mind, it would make sense to separate/classify queries into different classes, e.g., "product" and "category". Each class may require a different model and/or different evaluation measures. nDCG may be good for "focused" queries because these are more precision-oriented, but recall (or other measures) may be better for more abstract queries, like "tv sets" or "sofas". Finally, the unique challenges we identified in Section 2 can serve as a roadmap to help us identify potentially many interesting new research problems about using LETOR for E-Com search for future research. In particular, exploration of adaptive cutoff in NDCG that is sensitive to a query would be interesting given the high variance in browsing depth in E-Com search.

Our work has also revealed a number of interesting novel challenges for future research on LETOR in general which we briefly discuss below:

(1) Presence of Uncertain (engagement related) features: sales/ ratings/ reviews etc. related features are heavily dependent upon the age of the product in the catalog and the number of impressions a product has received. Products newly added in the catalog, typically have zero values associated with these features, and consequently get artificially penalized by the ranker. In future we intend to explore learning to rank methods capable of handling such uncertainties in feature values.

(2) Correlated features: clicks, cart-adds and orders are clearly understood to be closely related and hence ignored from the feature set. Hidden relationships may however still exist between these engagement signals and other features. Especially in context of industry setting where several engineers may be generating 1000s of features and the data scientists training the models may not know how exactly each was generated. Existence of such hidden relationships can lead to artificially high performance on the train/test set being used. Thus their detection is an important challenge.

(3) Data quality issues: Since the data is often entered by vendors or inferred automatically, there are always issues with data quality in terms of missing attributes or incorrect attributes etc.

(4) Query sparsity: Transfer learning to rank problems become particularly important when the goal is to generalize to unseen queries and solve some of the attribute sparsity challenges mentioned in the paper. Specially, having thousands of attribute values in products poses challenges in learning. How can we reduce the dimensionality and how much data do we need for this, is an interesting open problem. Ideas from deep neural networks may be useful here.

(5) Query-specific variable cutoff for NDCG measure to accommodate variable browsing depth of users: It is worth elaborating this point further. Typical web search studies have reported NDCG@10. We have very different K requirements for different queries in product search since there tend to be high variances in the browsing depth. Indeed, generic product queries such as *tv, desk, office chair* etc. constitute a substantial fraction of product search traffic. Such queries usually represent exploratory intents with 1000s of relevant products in the catalog. Depending upon the expenditure involved, a user may want to review several products, well beyond the top 10, before making a purchase decision. From a search quality perspective, this requires the search engine to maintain a high $NDCG@K$ for $K >> 10$. Thus while in Web search, people generally only pay attention to the first page of results, users have much higher variances in their browsing depth in E-Com search, making it questionable whether optimizing a metric such as NDCG at a fixed cutoff of 10 remains an appropriate strategy. We hypothesize that it might be beneficial to use query-specific variable cutoffs when computing NDCG (which affects the objective functions used for training LETOR methods), which would be a very interesting future research direction.

7 ACKNOWLEDGMENTS

We thank WalmartLabs search team, particularly Esteban Arcaute and Pranam Kolari, for providing the necessary funding and support for this work. We also thank the anonymous reviewers for their useful comments, which helped improving the quality of the paper significantly.

REFERENCES

[1] Omar Alonso and Stefano Mizzaro. 2009. Relevance criteria for e-commerce: a crowdsourcing-based experimental analysis. In *Proceedings of the 32nd international ACM SIGIR conference on Research and development in information retrieval.* ACM, 760–761.

[2] Omar Alonso, Daniel E Rose, and Benjamin Stewart. 2008. Crowdsourcing for relevance evaluation. In *ACM SigIR Forum*, Vol. 42. ACM, 9–15.

[3] Leif Azzopardi and Guido Zuccon. 2016. Advances in Formal Models of Search and Search Behaviour. In *Proceedings of the 2016 ACM on International Conference on the Theory of Information Retrieval.* ACM, 1–4.

[4] Leo Breiman. 2001. Random forests. *Machine learning* 45, 1 (2001), 5–32.

[5] Chris Burges, Tal Shaked, Erin Renshaw, Ari Lazier, Matt Deeds, Nicole Hamilton, and Greg Hullender. 2005. Learning to rank using gradient descent. In *Proceedings of the 22nd international conference on Machine learning.* ACM, 89–96.

[6] Christopher JC Burges. 2010. From ranknet to lambdarank to lambdamart: An overview. *Learning* 11 (2010), 23–581.

[7] Olivier Chapelle and Yi Chang. 2011. Yahoo! Learning to Rank Challenge Overview.. In *Yahoo! Learning to Rank Challenge.* 1–24.

[8] Olivier Chapelle, Yi Chang, and Tie-Yan Liu. 2011. Future directions in learning to rank.. In *Yahoo! Learning to Rank Challenge.* 91–100.

[9] Xiangru Chen, Haofen Wang, Xinruo Sun, Junfeng Pan, and Yong Yu. 2011. Diversifying Product Search Results. In *Proceedings of the 34th International ACM SIGIR Conference on Research and Development in Information Retrieval (SIGIR '11).* ACM, New York, NY, USA, 1093–1094.

[10] Huizhong Duan, ChengXiang Zhai, Jinxing Cheng, and Abhishek Gattani. 2013. Supporting Keyword Search in Product Database: A Probabilistic Approach. *Proc. VLDB Endow.* 6, 14 (Sept. 2013), 1786–1797.

[11] Rong-En Fan, Kai-Wei Chang, Cho-Jui Hsieh, Xiang-Rui Wang, and Chih-Jen Lin. 2008. LIBLINEAR: A library for large linear classification. *The Journal of Machine Learning Research* 9 (2008), 1871–1874.

[12] Yoav Freund, Raj Iyer, Robert E Schapire, and Yoram Singer. 2003. An efficient boosting algorithm for combining preferences. *The Journal of machine learning research* 4 (2003), 933–969.

[13] Wolfgang Härdle. 2012. *Smoothing techniques: with implementation in S.* Springer Science & Business Media.

[14] Kalervo Järvelin and Jaana Kekäläinen. 2002. Cumulated gain-based evaluation of IR techniques. *ACM Transactions on Information Systems (TOIS)* 20, 4 (2002), 422–446.

[15] John Le, Andy Edmonds, Vaughn Hester, and Lukas Biewald. 2010. Ensuring quality in crowdsourced search relevance evaluation: The effects of training question distribution. In *SIGIR 2010 workshop on crowdsourcing for search evaluation.* 21–26.

[16] Su-In Lee, Honglak Lee, Pieter Abbeel, and Andrew Y Ng. 2006. Efficient l1 regularized logistic regression. In *Proceedings of the National Conference on Artificial Intelligence*, Vol. 21. 401.

[17] Beibei Li, Anindya Ghose, and Panagiotis G. Ipeirotis. 2011. Towards a Theory Model for Product Search. In *Proceedings of the 20th International Conference on World Wide Web (WWW '11).* ACM, New York, NY, USA, 327–336.

[18] Hang Li. 2014. Learning to rank for information retrieval and natural language processing. *Synthesis Lectures on Human Language Technologies* 7, 3 (2014), 1–121.

[19] Chih-Jen Lin, Ruby C Weng, and S Sathiya Keerthi. 2008. Trust region newton method for logistic regression. *The Journal of Machine Learning Research* 9 (2008), 627–650.

[20] Tie-Yan Liu. 2009. Learning to rank for information retrieval. *Foundations and Trends in Information Retrieval* 3, 3 (2009), 225–331.

[21] Bo Long, Jiang Bian, Anlei Dong, and Yi Chang. 2012. Enhancing Product Search by Best-selling Prediction in e-Commerce. In *CIKM '12 (CIKM '12).* ACM, New York, NY, USA, 2479–2482. DOI: http://dx.doi.org/10.1145/2396761.2398671

[22] Craig Macdonald, Rodrygo LT Santos, and Iadh Ounis. 2012. On the usefulness of query features for learning to rank. In *Proceedings of the 21st ACM international conference on Information and knowledge management.* ACM, 2559–2562.

[23] Craig Macdonald, Rodrygo LT Santos, and Iadh Ounis. 2013. The whens and hows of learning to rank for web search. *Information Retrieval* 16, 5 (2013), 584–628.

[24] José R Pérez-Agüera, Javier Arroyo, Jane Greenberg, Joaquin Perez Iglesias, and Victor Fresno. 2010. Using BM25F for semantic search. In *Proceedings of the 3rd international semantic search workshop.* ACM, 2.

[25] Tao Qin and Tie-Yan Liu. 2013. Introducing LETOR 4.0 Datasets. *CoRR* abs/1306.2597 (2013). http://arxiv.org/abs/1306.2597

[26] Stephen E Robertson, Steve Walker, Susan Jones, Micheline M Hancock-Beaulieu, Mike Gatford, and others. 1995. Okapi at TREC-3. *NIST SPECIAL PUBLICATION SP* 109 (1995), 109.

[27] Alex Smola and Vladimir Vapnik. 1997. Support vector regression machines. *Advances in neural information processing systems* 9 (1997), 155–161.

[28] Johan AK Suykens and Joos Vandewalle. 1999. Least squares support vector machine classifiers. *Neural processing letters* 9, 3 (1999), 293–300.

[29] Liang Tang, Bo Long, Bee-Chung Chen, and Deepak Agarwal. 2016. An Empirical Study on Recommendation with Multiple Types of Feedback. In *Proceedings of the 22nd ACM SIGKDD International Conference on Knowledge Discovery and Data Mining.* ACM, 283–292.

[30] Niek Tax, Sander Bockting, and Djoerd Hiemstra. 2015. A cross-benchmark comparison of 87 learning to rank methods. *Information processing & management* 51, 6 (2015), 757–772.

[31] Christophe Van Gysel, Maarten de Rijke, and Evangelos Kanoulas. 2016. Learning Latent Vector Spaces for Product Search. In *Proceedings of the 25th ACM CIKM '16.* ACM, New York, NY, USA, 165–174.

[32] Damir Vandic, Flavius Frasincar, and Uzay Kaymak. 2013. Facet Selection Algorithms for Web Product Search. In *Proceedings of the 22Nd ACM International Conference on Information & Knowledge Management (CIKM '13).* ACM, New York, NY, USA, 2327–2332. DOI: http://dx.doi.org/10.1145/2505515.2505664

[33] Frank Wilcoxon. 1945. Individual comparisons by ranking methods. *Biometrics bulletin* 1, 6 (1945), 80–83.

[34] Jun Xu and Hang Li. 2007. Adarank: a boosting algorithm for information retrieval. In *ACM SIGIR.* ACM, 391–398.

[35] Emine Yilmaz and Stephen Robertson. 2010. On the Choice of Effectiveness Measures for Learning to Rank. *Inf. Retr.* 13, 3 (June 2010), 271–290.

[36] Jun Yu, Sunil Mohan, Duangmanee (Pew) Putthividhya, and Weng-Keen Wong. 2014. Latent Dirichlet Allocation Based Diversified Retrieval for e-Commerce Search. In *WSDM '14.* New York, NY, USA, 463–472.

Intent-Aware Semantic Query Annotation

Rafael Glater
CS Dept, UFMG
Belo Horizonte, MG, Brazil
rafaelglater@dcc.ufmg.br

Rodrygo L. T. Santos
CS Dept, UFMG
Belo Horizonte, MG, Brazil
rodrygo@dcc.ufmg.br

Nivio Ziviani
CS Dept, UFMG & Kunumi
Belo Horizonte, MG, Brazil
nivio@dcc.ufmg.br

ABSTRACT

Query understanding is a challenging task primarily due to the inherent ambiguity of natural language. A common strategy for improving the understanding of natural language queries is to annotate them with semantic information mined from a knowledge base. Nevertheless, queries with different intents may arguably benefit from specialized annotation strategies. For instance, some queries could be effectively annotated with a single entity or an entity attribute, others could be better represented by a list of entities of a single type or by entities of multiple distinct types, and others may be simply ambiguous. In this paper, we propose a framework for learning semantic query annotations suitable to the target intent of each individual query. Thorough experiments on a publicly available benchmark show that our proposed approach can significantly improve state-of-the-art intent-agnostic approaches based on Markov random fields and learning to rank. Our results further demonstrate the consistent effectiveness of our approach for queries of various target intents, lengths, and difficulty levels, as well as its robustness to noise in intent detection.

CCS CONCEPTS

•Information systems →Retrieval effectiveness;

KEYWORDS

Semantic query annotation; Learning to rank; Intent-aware;

ACM Reference format:
Rafael Glater, Rodrygo L. T. Santos, and Nivio Ziviani. 2017. Intent-Aware Semantic Query Annotation. In *Proceedings of SIGIR'17, August 7–11, 2017, Shinjuku, Tokyo, Japan*, , 10 pages.
DOI: http://dx.doi.org/10.1145/3077136.3080825

1 INTRODUCTION

A user's search query has traditionally been treated a short, underspecified representation of his or her information need [22]. Despite the trend towards verbosity brought by the popularization of voice queries in modern mobile search and personal assistant interfaces [20], query understanding remains a challenging yet crucial task for the success of search systems. One particularly effective strategy for improving the understanding of a query is to annotate it with semantic information mined from a knowledge base, such as DBPedia.[1] In particular, previous analysis has shown that over 70% of all queries contain a semantic resource (a named entity, an entity type, relation, or attribute), whereas almost 60% have a semantic resource as their primary target [32].

State-of-the-art semantic query annotation approaches leverage features extracted from the descriptive content of candidate semantic resources (e.g., the various textual fields in the description of an entity [28, 44]) or their structural properties (e.g., related semantic resources [39]) in a knowledge base. In common, these approaches treat every query uniformly, regardless of its target intent.[2] In contrast, we hypothesize that queries with different intents may benefit from specialized annotation strategies. For instance, some queries could be effectively annotated with a single entity (e.g., "*us president*") or an entity attribute (e.g., "*us president salary*"). Other queries could be better represented by a list of entities of a single type (e.g., "*us presidents*") or of mixed types (e.g., "*us foreign affairs*"). Finally, some queries may be simply ambiguous and demand annotations suitable for disambiguation (e.g., "*us*").

In this paper, we propose a framework for learning semantic annotations suitable to the target intent of each individual query. Our framework comprises three main components: (i) intent-specific learning to rank, aimed to produce ranking models optimized for different intents; (ii) query intent classification, aimed to estimate the probability of each query conveying each possible intent; and (iii) intent-aware ranking adaptation, aimed to promote the most relevant annotations given the detected intents. To demonstrate the applicability of our framework, we experiment with a state-of-the-art learning to rank algorithm for intent-specific learning, multiple classification approaches for intent classification, and two adaptive strategies for annotation ranking. Thorough experiments using a publicly available semantic annotation test collection comprising queries with different intents show that our proposed framework is effective and significantly improves state-of-the-art intent-agnostic approaches from the literature. Moreover, a breakdown analysis further reveals the consistency of the observed gains for queries of various target intents, lengths, and difficulty levels, as well as the robustness of the framework to noise in intent detection.

In summary, our main contributions are three-fold:

- An intent-aware framework for learning semantic query annotations from structured knowledge bases.
- An analysis of the specificity of several content and structural features for different query intents.
- A thorough validation of the proposed framework in terms of annotation effectiveness and robustness.

SIGIR'17, August 7–11, 2017, Shinjuku, Tokyo, Japan
© 2017 ACM. 978-1-4503-5022-8/17/08...$15.00
DOI: http://dx.doi.org/10.1145/3077136.3080825

[1] http://wiki.dbpedia.org/

[2] While the word "intent" has been used as a synonym of "information need" in some contexts, here we adopt the more traditional definition of intent as the type (or class) of an information need, such as informational or navigational [9].

In the remainder of this paper, Section 2 discusses related work on semantic query annotation and intent-aware information retrieval. Section 3 describes the various components of our proposed framework and their instantiation. Sections 4 and 5 describe the setup and the results of our empirical evaluation. Finally, Section 6 provides our conclusions and directions for future research.

2 RELATED WORK

In this section, we provide an overview of related work on semantic query annotation using knowledge bases. In addition, we discuss related attempts to exploit query intents in different search tasks.

2.1 Semantic Query Annotation

Semantic search approaches [4] have been extensively researched in recent years, motivated by a series of related workshops and evaluation campaigns [1, 2, 15]. While some research has been devoted to semantic search on the open Web [2, 10, 37], particularly relevant to this paper are approaches focused on ranking semantic resources (e.g., named entities) mined from a structured domain, such as a knowledge base. The top ranked resources can be used directly to enrich a search engine's results page with structured semantic information [5] or indirectly to annotate the user's query for further processing for improved search quality.

Search in knowledge bases is typically performed using structured query languages such as SPARQL.[3] However, producing structured queries requires some expertise from the user, which limits the applicability of this approach in a broader scenario. To support unstructured querying, most previous semantic search approaches adapt traditional IR techniques to find, in the knowledge base, resources that match the user's query. For instance, some related works have used standard bag-of-words models, like BM25 [3, 31, 39] and language models (LM) [16, 17, 21, 27, 43]. Extending traditional bag-of-words models, multi-fielded approaches have been proposed to appropriately weight information present in different fields describing a semantic resource. For instance, approaches based on BM25F [6, 7, 12, 18, 31, 39] permit the combination of the BM25 scores of different fields into the final retrieval score. Multi-fielded approaches based on a mixture of language models have also been proposed [11, 29], which linearly combine query likelihood estimates obtained from multiple fields.

Also contrasting with bag-of-words models, recent approaches have exploited dependencies among query term occurrences in the descriptive content of a semantic resource. Building upon the framework of Markov random fields (MRF) [26], these approaches construct a graph of dependencies among the query terms, which is used to estimate the relevance of each retrieved semantic resource. In particular, Zhiltsov et al. [44] introduced a multi-fielded extension of MRF, called FSDM, which estimates the weight of each field with respect to three types of query concept: unigram, ordered bigram, and unordered bigram. FSDM was later extended by Nikolaev et al. [28], who proposed to estimate field weights with respect to individual query concepts. To cope with the explosive number of concepts (i.e., every possible unigram, ordered, and unordered bigram), they instead learn field weights with respect to a fixed set of concept features (e.g., the probability of occurrence of the concept in a field). In contrast to both of these approaches, we propose to learn the appropriateness of intent-specific feature-based ranking models for each individual query, by automatically predicting the target intent of this query. In Section 5, we compare our approach to FSDM as a representative of the current state-of-the-art.

In addition to exploiting the descriptive content of semantic resources, other researchers have adopted a hybrid approach [11, 17, 21, 34, 39], leveraging structural properties of the knowledge base. In these approaches, an initial ranking of semantic resources is either re-ranked or expanded using the knowledge base structure to find related resources, which can be done through structured graph traversals [39] or random walks [34]. For instance, Tonon et al. [39] exploited entities initially retrieved using BM25 as seeds in the graph from which related entities could be reached. Bron et al. [11] proposed a method that makes a linear combination of the scores of a content-based approach using language models and a structure-based approach, which captures statistics from candidate entities represented according to their relations with other entities, expressed in RDF triples. Relatedly, Elbassouni et al. [17] proposed a language modeling approach to rank the results of exact, relaxed, and keyword-augmented graph-pattern queries over RDF triples into multiple subgraphs. The Kullback-Leibler divergence between the query language model and the language models induced by the resulting subgraphs was then used to produce the final ranking. While our main focus is on learning strategies rather than on specific features, to demonstrate the flexibility of our proposed framework, we exploit multiple structural properties of each semantic resource as additional features. In particular, these features are used for both detecting the intent of a query as well as for ranking semantic resources in response to this query.

2.2 Exploiting Query Intents

The intent underlying a user's search query has been subject of intense research in the context of web search. Broder [9] proposed a well-known intent taxonomy, classifying web search queries into informational, navigational and transactional. Rose and Levinson [35] later extended this taxonomy to consider more fine-grained classes. In the context of semantic search, Pound et al. [32] categorized queries into four major intents: entity queries, which target a single entity; type queries, which target multiple entities of a single type; attribute queries, which target values of a particular entity attribute; and relation queries, which aim to find how two or more entities or types are related. Entity queries and type queries accounted for more than 50% of a query log sampled in their study, whereas attribute and relation queries accounted for just over 5%. Other works focused on more specific intents, such as a question intent [40], which targets answers to the question expressed in the query. In our experiments, we use an intent taxonomy comprising the three major classes described in these studies, namely, entity, type, and question queries, as well as an additional class including less represented intents, such as attribute and relation queries.

In addition to detecting query intents, several approaches have attempted to adapt the ranking produced for a query in light of some identified query property, such as its intent. For instance, Yom-Tov et al. [42] proposed to adaptively expand a query depending on its predicted difficulty. Kang and Kim [23] proposed to apply

[3]https://www.w3.org/TR/rdf-sparql-query/

different hand-crafted ranking models for queries with a predicted informational, navigational, or transactional intent. However, such a hard intent classification may eventually harm the effectiveness of an adaptive approach, when queries of different intents benefit from a single ranking model [14]. To mitigate this effect, instance-based classification approaches have been used to identify similar queries (as opposed to queries with the same predicted intent) for training a ranking model. For example, Geng et al. [19] resorted to nearest neighbor classification for building training sets for a given test query. Relatedly, Peng et al. [30] proposed to estimate the benefit of multiple candidate ranking models for a given query by examining training queries that are affected by these models in a similar manner. In the context of search result diversification, Santos et al. proposed adaptive approaches for estimating the coverage of different query aspects given their predicted intent [38] as well as for estimating when to diversify given the predicted ambiguity of the query [36]. Our proposed approach resembles these adaptive ranking approaches as we also resort to query intent classification as a trigger for ranking adaptation. Nonetheless, to the best of our knowledge, our approach is the first attempt to produce adaptive learning to rank models for a semantic search task.

3 INTENT-AWARE RANKING ADAPTATION FOR SEMANTIC QUERY ANNOTATION

Annotating queries with semantic information is an important step towards an improved query understanding [1]. Given a query, our goal is to automatically annotate it with semantic resources mined from a knowledge base, including named entities, attributes, relations, etc. For instance, the query "*us president*" could be annotated with arguably relevant semantic resources including "Donald Trump", "Federal Government", "White House." In this paper, we hypothesize that the relevance of a semantic resource given a query depends on the intent underlying this query. For the previous example, knowing that the query "*us president*" targets information around a single entity could promote alternative semantic resources including "Inauguration", "First 100 days", and "Controversies".

In this section, we propose an intent-aware framework for learning to rank semantic query annotations. In particular, we posit that the probability $P(r|q)$ that a given semantic resource r satisfies the user's query q should be estimated in light of the possible intents $i \in \mathcal{I}$ underlying this query. Formally, we define:

$$P(r|q) = \sum_{i \in \mathcal{I}} P(i|q)\, P(r|q, i), \tag{1}$$

where $P(i|q)$ is the probability that query q conveys an intent i, with $\sum_{i \in \mathcal{I}} P(i|q) = 1$, and $P(r|q, i)$ is the probability of observing semantic resource r given the query and this particular intent.

In Figure 1, we describe the three core components of our framework. In particular, the *query intent classification* and the *intent-specific learning to rank* components rely on supervised learning approaches to estimate $P(i|q)$ and $P(r|q, i)$, respectively, for each intent $i \in \mathcal{I}$. In turn, the *intent-aware ranking adaptation* component implements two alternative policies to suit the final ranking to the detected intents of each individual query.

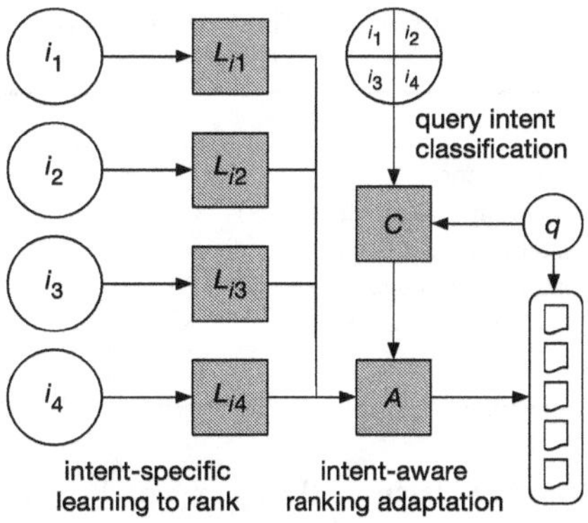

Figure 1: Intent-aware semantic query annotation. Each intent-specific ranking model L_i is learned on a query set comprising only queries with intent i. The query intent classification model C is learned on a set comprising queries of various intents. The intent-aware ranking adaptation strategy A uses the query intent classification outcome to decide on how to leverage the intent-specific ranking models.

3.1 Query Intent Classification

The first component of our framework is responsible for predicting the possible intents underlying a query [8]. For this task, we adopt a standard multi-class classification approach. In particular, we aim to learn a query classification model $C : \mathcal{X} \rightarrow \mathcal{Y}$ mapping the input space $\mathcal{X}$ into the output space $\mathcal{Y}$. Our input space $\mathcal{X}$ comprises m learning instances $\{\vec{x}_j\}_{j=1}^m$, where $\vec{x}_j = \Phi(q_j)$ is a feature vector representation of query q_j as produced by a feature extractor Φ. In turn, our output space $\mathcal{Y}$ comprises m labels $\{y_j\}_{j=1}^m$, where y_j corresponds to one of the target intents $i \in \mathcal{I}$ assigned to query q_j by a human annotator. To learn an effective classifier C, we experiment with several classification algorithms in Section 5.2.

Table 1 presents the features we use to represent a query for intent classification. We use a total of 31 simple features, including both lexical as well as semantic ones. Lexical features like number of query terms and mean query term size can help detect, for example, natural language queries, which are usually longer than others. In addition, part-of-speech tags can help identify question queries, indicating the presence of wh-pronouns (e.g., what, where, why, when). Lastly, semantic features include the number of categories and number of ontology classes returned when using the query to search a knowledge base. Our intuition is that queries seeking for a specific entity will probably return fewer categories or ontology classes than queries seeking for a list of entities. For instance, the query "*eiffel*" returns only 5 categories, while the query "*list of films from the surrealist category*" returns more than 103,000.

3.2 Intent-Specific Learning to Rank

The second component of our framework aims to produce multiple ranking models, each one optimized for a specific query intent $i \in \mathcal{I}$. To this end, we resort to learning to rank [24]. Analogously to our query intent classification models in Section 3.1, our goal is to learn an intent-specific ranking model $L_i : \mathcal{V} \rightarrow \mathcal{W}$ mapping the input space $\mathcal{V}$ into the output space $\mathcal{W}$. Our input space

Table 1: Query features for intent classification.

#	Feature	Qty
1	No. of query terms	1
2	Avg. query term size (in characters)	1
3	No. of matched categories in DBPedia	1
4	No. of matched ontology classes in DBPedia	1
5	No. of POS tags of different types	27
	TOTAL	31

includes n learning instances $\{\vec{V}_j\}_{j=1}^n$, where $\vec{V}_j = \Omega(q_j, \mathcal{R}_j)$ is a feature matrix representation (produced by some feature extractor Ω) of a sample of semantic resources $r \in \mathcal{R}_j$ retrieved for query q_j annotated with intent i. In our experiments, $\mathcal{R}_j$ is produced using BM25 [33], although any unsupervised ranking technique could have been used for this purpose. Our output space $\mathcal{W}$ comprises n label vectors $\{\vec{W}_j\}_{j=1}^n$, where $\vec{W}_j$ provides relevance labels for each semantic resource $r \in \mathcal{R}_j$. To learn an effective ranking model L_i for each intent $i \in \mathcal{I}$, we use LambdaMART [41], which represents the current state-of-the-art in learning to rank [13].

Table 2 lists all 216 features used to represent each semantic resource $r \in \mathcal{R}_j$. Features #1-#6 are content-based features commonly used in the learning to rank literature [24], such as number of tokens, BM25, coordination level matching (CLM), TF, and IDF scores. These are computed in a total of 8 descriptive fields of r, such as name, attributes, categories (see Section 4.1 for a full description). Since TF and IDF are defined on a term-level, query-level scores are computed using multiple summary statistics (sum, min, max, avg, var). Finally, CLM, TF, IDF, and TF-IDF are computed for both unigrams and bigrams. Next, features #7-#14 are semantic features derived from a knowledge base. For instance, feature #7 indicates whether r is an entity directly mentioned in the query, while feature #8 considers the number of direct connections between r and all entities mentioned in the query. As an example of the latter feature, in the query "*songs composed by michael jackson*", the candidate resource "Thriller" will be directly related to the entity "Michael Jackson" (present in the query). For both features, we use DBPedia Spotlight[4] for entity recognition in queries. Features #9-#14 are query-independent features quantifying the connectivity of each candidate resource r with respect to other resources in the knowledge base (e.g., entities, categories, ontology classes).

To keep our approach general, instead of handpicking features more likely to be useful for a particular intent, we use the same 216 available features when learning every intent-specific model L_i. To ensure that the learned model L_i is indeed optimized to its target intent i, intent-specific learning is achieved by using one training query set per intent, as illustrated in Figure 1.

3.3 Intent-Aware Ranking Adaptation

Sections 3.1 and 3.2 described supervised approaches for learning a query intent classification model C as well as multiple intent-specific ranking models L_i for all $i \in \mathcal{I}$. Importantly, all of these models are learned offline. When an unseen query q is submitted online, we must be able to return a ranking of semantic resources

[4]http://spotlight.dbpedia.org/

Table 2: Semantic resource features for learning to rank. Features marked as 'Bi' are computed also for bigrams.

#	Feature	Bi	Qty
1	No. of tokens (per-field)		8
2	BM25 (per-field)		8
3	CLM (per-field)	✔	16
4	TF (per-field sum, min, max, avg, var)	✔	80
5	IDF (per-field sum)	✔	16
6	TF-IDF (per-field sum, min, max, avg, var)	✔	80
7	Matching entity		1
8	No. of direct relations with query entities		1
9	No. of matched relations with query terms		1
10	No. of inlinks		1
11	No. of outlinks		1
12	No. of linked ontology classes		1
13	No. of linked categories		1
14	No. of linked entities		1
	TOTAL		216

well suited to the target intent of q. Because we tackle query intent classification as a multi-class problem, we can actually estimate the probability $P(i|q)$ of different intents $i \in \mathcal{I}$ given the query q.

To exploit this possibility, we devise two strategies to adapt the ranking produced for a query q to the target intent(s) of this query. Our first strategy, called *intent-aware switching*, assigns each query a single intent, namely, the most likely one as predicted by the intent classification model C. For instance, for a target set of intents $\mathcal{I} = \{i_1, i_2, i_3\}$ of which i_1 is predicted as the most likely for q, we could instantiate Equation (1) with $P(i_1|q) = 1$, $P(i_2|q) = 0$, and $P(i_3|q) = 0$. As a result, only $P(r|q, i_1)$ (estimated via ranking model L_1) would have an impact on the final ranking, such that:

$$P(r|q) = P(r|q, i_1).$$

Some queries may have no clear winning intent. Other queries may prove simply difficult to classify correctly. To cope with uncertainty in intent classification, we propose a second ranking adaptation strategy, called *intent-aware mixing*. In this strategy, we use the full probability distribution over intents predicted by the classification model C to produce the final ranking for q. In the aforementioned example, suppose the predicted intent distribution is $P(i_1|q) = 0.7$, $P(i_2|q) = 0.2$, and $P(i_3|q) = 0.1$. Leveraging this distribution directly in Equation (1), we have a mixture of intent-specific ranking models contributing to the final ranking:

$$\begin{aligned} P(r|q) &= 0.7 \times P(r|q, i_1) \\ &+ 0.2 \times P(r|q, i_2) \\ &+ 0.1 \times P(r|q, i_3). \end{aligned}$$

To assess the effectiveness of our proposed intent-aware ranking adaptation strategies for semantic query annotation, in the next section, we compare these strategies to each other as well as to state-of-the-art intent-agnostic approaches from the literature.

4 EXPERIMENTAL SETUP

In this section, we detail the experimental setup that supports the evaluation of our proposed intent-aware semantic query annotation approach introduced in Section 3. In particular, our experiments aim to answer the following research questions:

Q1. Do different intents benefit from different ranking models?
Q2. How accurately can we predict the intent of each query?
Q3. How effective is our semantic query annotation approach?
Q4. What queries are improved the most and the least?

In the following, we describe the knowledge base, queries, relevance judgments, and intent taxonomy used in our experiments. We also describe the baselines used for comparison and the procedure undertaken to train and test them as well as our own models.

4.1 Knowledge Base

The knowledge base used in our experiments is the English portion of DBPedia 3.7,[5] which comprises RDF triples extracted from Wikipedia dumps generated in late July 2011. This version of DBPedia contains information on more than 3.6 million entities organized in over 170,000 categories and 320 ontology classes in a 6-level deep hierarchy. We indexed this knowledge base using Elasticsearch 1.7.5[6] for textual content and Titan 0.5.4[7] for the underlying graph structure. RDF triples were parsed to created a fielded content representation. Following Zhiltsov et al. [44], we indexed the *Names*, *Attributes*, *Categories*, *Similar entity names* and *Related entity names* fields. In addition, we included three other fields: *Ontology classes*, *URL* and a special field *All*, concatenating the available content from all fields. Indexed terms were lower-cased, stemmed using Krovetz stemmer and standard stopwords were removed.

4.2 Queries, Relevance Judgments, and Intents

We use a publicly available benchmark[8] built on top of DBPedia 3.7, which comprises a total of 485 queries from past semantic search evaluation campaigns [3]. In total, there are 13,090 positive relevance judgments available. While some of these include graded labels, for a homogeneous treatment of all queries, we consider relevance as binary. The benchmark covers a wide variety of query intents, including entity, type, relation and attribute queries, as well as queries with a question intent. Following past research [3, 28, 44], we organize these queries into four intent-specific query sets, the salient statistics of which are described in Table 3:

- *E*: entity queries (e.g., "*orlando florida*");
- *T*: type queries (e.g., "*continents in the world*");
- *Q*: question queries (e.g., "*who created wikipedia?*");
- *O*: queries with other intents, including less represented ones, such as relation queries and attribute queries.

4.3 Retrieval Baselines

We compare our approach to multiple intent-agnostic baselines from the literature. As a vanilla ad-hoc search baseline, we consider BM25 with standard parameter settings ($k_1 = 1.2$, $b = 0.8$). To assess the effectiveness of our intent-aware ranking adaptation strategies introduced in Section 3.3, we further contrast them to two intent-agnostic strategies, which consistently apply a single ranking model for all queries, regardless of their target intent. As illustrated in Table 4, the *fixed* strategy applies a model L_i learned on one intent-specific query set, whereas the *oblivious* strategy applies a model L_R learned on a set of random queries. For a fair comparison, both of these baseline strategies as well as our own intent-aware switching and mixing strategies use the same learning algorithm (LambdaMART) and ranking features (all 216 features in Table 2). Lastly, we further contrast our approach to FSDM [44] (see Section 2.1) as a representative of the current state-of-the-art.

[5] http://wiki.dbpedia.org/data-set-37
[6] https://www.elastic.co/products/elasticsearch
[7] http://titan.thinkaurelius.com
[8] http://bit.ly/dbpedia-entity

Table 3: Statistics of the intent-specific query sets used in our evaluation. Length and qrels denote per-query averages of query length and positive judgements in each set.

Set	Campaign [3]	Queries	Length	Qrels
E	SemSearch ES	130	2.7	8.7
T	INEX-XER, SemSearch LS, TREC Entity	115	5.8	18.4
Q	QALD-2	140	7.9	41.5
O	INEX-LD	100	4.8	37.6
TOTAL		485	5.3	26.55

4.4 Training and Test Procedure

For a fair comparison between our intent-aware semantic query annotation approach and the intent-agnostic baselines described in Section 4.3, we randomly downsample all query sets in Table 3 until they reach 100 queries each (i.e., the number of queries in the smallest query set, namely, *O*). This procedure ensures the learning process is not biased towards any particular intent. To learn an intent-specific model L_i for each intent $i \in \mathcal{I} = \{E, T, Q, O\}$, we perform a 5-fold cross validation in the corresponding query set from Table 3. For the oblivious strategy, the intent-agnostic model L_R is also learned via 5-fold cross validation on a set of 100 queries sampled uniformly at random from the four intent-specific query sets after downsampling. This multi-intent query set is also used to tune the parameters of FSDM [44] for different concepts (unigrams, ordered, an unordered bigrams) and each of the fields listed in Section 4.1. In each cross-validation round, we use three partitions (60 queries) for training, one partition (20 queries) for validation, and one partition (20 queries) for testing.

Learning to rank is performed using the LambdaMART implementation in RankLib 2.7,[9] optimizing for normalized discounted cumulative gain at the top 100 results (nDCG@100). LambdaMART is deployed with default hyperparameter settings,[10] with 1,000 trees with 10 leaves each, minimum leaf support 1, unlimited threshold candidates for tree splitting, learning rate 0.1, and early stopping after 100 non-improving iterations. All results are reported as averages of all test queries across the five cross-validation rounds. In particular, we report nDCG@10, precision at 10 (P@10), and mean average precision (MAP). All evaluation metrics are calculated on the top 100 results returned by each approach. To check for statistically significant differences among them, we use a two-tailed paired

[9] https://sourceforge.net/p/lemur/wiki/RankLib%20How%20to%20use/
[10] Hyperparameter tuning on validation data showed no significant improvements in our preliminary tests.

Table 4: Example application of intent-agnostic (baseline) and intent-aware ranking adaptation strategies.

	intent-agnostic					intent-aware	
i	fixed-E	fixed-T	fixed-Q	fixed-O	oblivious	switching	mixing
E	L_E	L_T	L_Q	L_O	L_R	L_E	$\sum_i w_i L_i$
T	L_E	L_T	L_Q	L_O	L_R	L_T	$\sum_i w_i L_i$
Q	L_E	L_T	L_Q	L_O	L_R	L_Q	$\sum_i w_i L_i$
O	L_E	L_T	L_Q	L_O	L_R	L_O	$\sum_i w_i L_i$

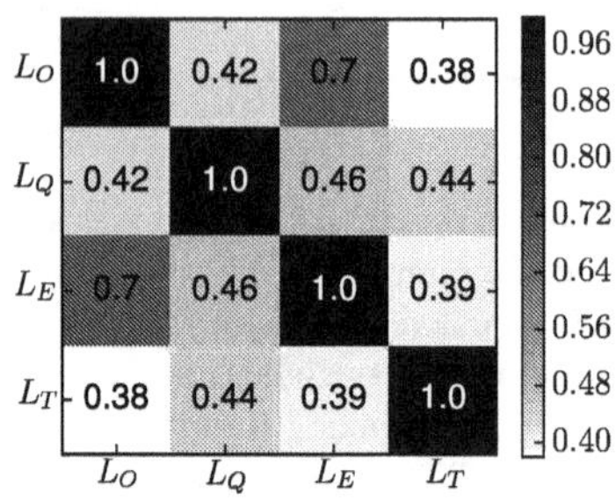

Figure 2: Spearman's correlation coefficient for feature importance across pairs of intent-specific ranking models.

t-test and write △ (▽) and ▲ (▼) to denote significant increases (decreases) at the 0.05 and 0.01 levels, respectively. A further symbol ∘ is used to denote no significant difference.

5 EXPERIMENTAL EVALUATION

In this section, we empirically evaluate our approach in order to answer the four research questions stated in Section 4. In the following, we address each of these questions in turn.

5.1 Intent Specificity

The core hypothesis of our proposal is that different queries may benefit from a ranking model optimized to their intent. To verify this hypothesis, we address *Q1*, by assessing the specificity of ranking models optimized to the four intents described in Table 3. To this end, Figure 2 correlates the importance assigned to all 216 features by each intent-specific ranking model L_i, for $i \in \mathcal{I} = \{E, T, Q, O\}$. Feature importance is quantified using the least square improvement criterion proposed by Lucchese et al. [25] for gradient boosted regression tree learners, such as LambdaMART. From Figure 2, we observe a generally low correlation ($\rho < 0.5$) between models, except for the L_E and L_O models, with $\rho \approx 0.7$.

Table 5 lists the five most important features for each intent-specific model. The entity-oriented L_E model gives importance to features related to the occurrence of bigrams in the name and similar entities fields. For instance, the query "*martin luther king*" expects semantic resources named "Martin Luther King III" and "Martin Luther King High School." While the type-oriented L_T model considers a variety of distinct features, two features related to the categories field are present in the top 5, which are useful for queries like "*state capitals of the united states of america.*" The question-oriented L_Q model gives importance to features describing the relation between entities and ontology classes, derived from both content fields as well as the graph structure underlying the knowledge base. These can help identify relevant resources linked to an entity in the query through qualified relations, as in the query "*who was the successor of john f. kennedy?*" Lastly, the L_O model, which is optimized on a set comprising queries of various intents, strongly favors content-based features, which are arguably effective for broad queries such as "*einstein relativity theory.*" Recalling question *Q1*, these results provide a strong indication of the specificity of different models to queries of different intents.

Table 5: Top 5 features per ranking model.

	#	Feature
L_E	1	TF-IDF sum of bigrams in *similar entities*
	2	Matching entity
	3	TF sum of bigrams in *similar entities*
	4	TF avg of bigrams in *similar entities*
	5	TF-IDF max of bigrams in *similar entities*
L_T	1	CLM in *categories*
	2	CLM in *all content*
	3	No. of inlinks
	4	No. of tokens in *similar entities*
	5	TF-IDF sum of bigrams in *categories*
L_Q	1	BM25 in *ontology classes*
	2	No. of matched relations with query terms
	3	No. of direct relations with query entities
	4	No. of inlinks
	5	TF-IDF max of unigrams in *ontology classes*
L_O	1	TF sum of bigrams in *name*
	2	BM25 in *name*
	3	TF-IDF max of unigrams in *categories*
	4	TF-IDF max of bigrams in *name*
	5	TF-IDF var of bigrams in *all content*

5.2 Intent Classification Accuracy

The results in the previous experiment suggest that exploiting the specificity of different query intents may result in more effective ranking models. Before investigating whether this is indeed the case, in this section, we address *Q2*, with the aim of establishing what level of query intent detection accuracy can be attained in practice. To this end, we experiment with a range of traditional classification algorithms implemented in Scikit-learn 0.17.1,[11] optimized via 5-fold cross validation using the same partitions leveraged for learning to rank, as detailed in Section 4.4. Table 6 reports

[11] http://scikit-learn.org/

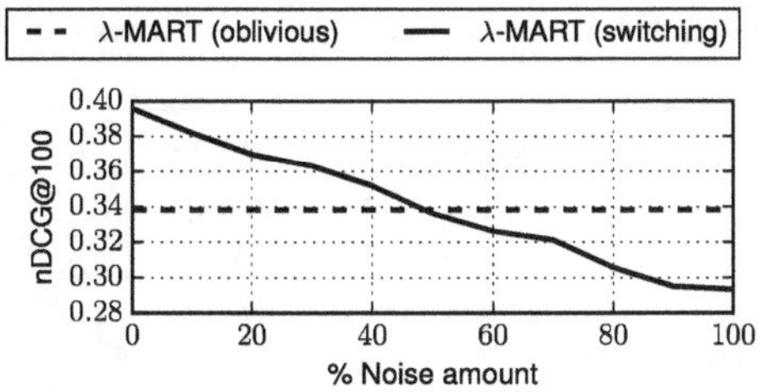

Figure 3: Semantic query annotation robustness for simulated intent classifiers of a range of accuracy levels.

intent classification accuracy averaged across test queries in all cross-validation rounds. As shown in the table, the most accurate intent classifier is learned via stochastic gradient descent with a log loss, which performs an incremental logistic regression. As a result, we will use this classifier in the remainder of our experiments. Other effective classification algorithms include random forest and bagging, while AdaBoost has the lowest accuracy.

Table 6: Query intent classification accuracy.

Algorithm	Accuracy
AdaBoost	67.00%
Support Vector Machines	74.00%
Gradient Boosting	75.75%
Bagging	76.00%
Random Forest	76.50%
Logistic Regression	**77.00%**

The top performing classifier in Table 6 still leaves room for further improvement in intent classification accuracy. An interesting question here is whether this level of accuracy is enough for an effective deployment of our proposed intent-aware semantic query annotation approach. To further investigate the role of the intent classification component in our approach, we measure the impact of a range of simulated intent classifiers on the effectiveness of the produced ranking of semantic annotations. In particular, starting from a perfect intent classifier (i.e., an oracle), we gradually introduce noise in the classification outcome by replacing the correct intent with a random one, up to the point where the classification itself becomes a random guess of the four available intents (i.e., *E*, *T*, *Q*, and *O*). As shown in Figure 3, our intent-aware switching strategy can outperform the intent-agnostic oblivious strategy with up to 50% of random noise in intent classification, which is a remarkable result. Recalling *Q2*, the experiments in this section demonstrate that accurate intent classification is feasible, and that the overall ranking annotation performance is robust to a considerable amount of noise in the predicted intents.

5.3 Annotation Effectiveness

Section 5.1 showed the promise of leveraging intent-specific ranking models, while Section 5.2 demonstrated that achieving this promise is feasible with reasonably accurate query intent classifiers. In this section, we address *Q3*, by assessing the effectiveness of our intent-aware semantic query annotation approach in contrast to the various baselines described in Section 4.3. These include BM25 as a vanilla ad-hoc search baseline, FSDM as a representative of the current state-of-the-art, and multiple deployments of LambdaMART using baseline intent-agnostic ranking adaptation strategies (fixed and oblivious) as well as our proposed intent-aware strategies (switching and mixing). Table 7 summarizes the results of this investigation in terms of P@10, nDCG@10, and MAP averaged across all 400 test queries from the four query sets in Table 3.[12] In each row describing baseline results (the top half of the table), a first of the symbols introduced in Section 4.4 denotes a statistically significant difference (or lack thereof) with respect to LambdaMART (switching), whereas a second symbol denotes potential differences with respect to LambdaMART (mixing). A further symbol is shown alongside LambdaMART (switching) to denote a significant difference (or lack thereof) with respect to LambdaMART (mixing).

Table 7: Comparison of intent-agnostic (BM25, FSDM, LambdaMART fixed and oblivious) and intent-aware (LambdaMART switching and mixing) semantic query annotation.

	P@10	nDCG@10	MAP
BM25	0.181▼▼	0.250▼▼	0.163▼▼
FSDM	0.204▼▼	0.289▼▼	0.195▼▼
LambdaMART			
(fixed-E)	0.178▼▼	0.244▼▼	0.162▼▼
(fixed-T)	0.202▼▼	0.275▼▼	0.172▼▼
(fixed-Q)	0.152▼▼	0.215▼▼	0.139▼▼
(fixed-O)	0.188▼▼	0.260▼▼	0.163▼▼
(oblivious)	0.192▼▼	0.276▼▼	0.178▼▼
(switching)	0.227▼	0.329▼	0.219▼
(mixing)	**0.243**	**0.346**	**0.229**

From Table 7, we first observe that FSDM performs strongly, outperforming all intent-agnostic variants deployed with LambdaMART, which confirms its effectiveness as a representative of the state-of-the-art. Also of note is the fact that a single model trained on a set of multiple intents using the oblivious strategy cannot consistently improve upon the best performing intent-specific model, produced by the fixed-T strategy. In contrast, both of our intent-aware ranking adaptation strategies are able to consistently leverage the best characteristics of each individual intent, significantly outperforming all intent-agnostic baselines in all settings. In particular, compared to FSDM, our switching strategy improves by up to 11% in P@10, 14% in nDCG@10, and 12% in MAP. Compared to the best performing intent-agnostic strategy under LambdaMART (fixed-T), gains are as high as 12% in P@10, 20% in nDCG@10, and 27% in MAP. Lastly, we also note that our mixing strategy further significantly improves upon the switching strategy. This result suggests that merging multiple intent-specific models (the mixing strategy) can be safer than applying a single model associated with the most likely query intent (the switching strategy). Recalling *Q3*, these results attest the effectiveness of our intent-aware ranking adaptation for semantic query annotation.

[12] Effectiveness breakdown analyses per query intent and various other query characteristics are presented in Section 5.4.

5.4 Breakdown Analyses

The previous analysis demonstrated the effectiveness of our approach on the entire set of 400 queries. To further shed light on the reasons behind such an effective performance, we address question *Q4*, by analyzing the improvements brought by our approach for queries with different intents, lengths, and difficulty.

5.4.1 Analysis by Query Intent. Table 8 breaks down the results in Table 7 according to the target intent of each query. For brevity, only the best among the fixed strategy variants is shown. Note that while our approach aims to predict the correct intent of each query, there is no guarantee that a perfect intent classification will be achieved, as discussed in Section 5.2. Hence, it is important to understand how well our approach performs on queries of each target intent. From Table 7, as expected, the best fixed strategy for each group of queries is that optimized for the group itself (e.g., fixed-E is the best fixed strategy for entity queries—the *E* group). Nonetheless, our intent-aware mixing strategy is the most consistent across all groups, with effectiveness on a par with the best fixed strategy for each group. Compared to our switching strategy, the mixing strategy is particularly effective for type queries (the *T* group), with statistical ties for all other groups. Regarding performance differences across the target intents, we note that all approaches achieve their best absolute performance on *E* queries followed by queries with other intents (the *O* group), which also includes entity queries. The effective results attained even by the simple BM25 baseline suggest that queries with these intents are well handled by content-based approaches.

Compared to the intent-agnostic FSDM baseline, our largest improvements are observed for type queries (the *T* group) and question queries (the *Q* group). For *T* queries, the structure-based features exploited by our learning to rank approach bring only small improvements, as observed by contrasting LambdaMART (oblivious) with FSDM. However, with our proposed intent-aware ranking adaptation strategies, further marked improvements are observed, with the mixing strategy significantly improving upon the oblivious strategy by up to 25% in P@10, 35% in nDCG@10, and 44% in MAP. For *Q* queries, both the extra features exploited via learning to rank as well as our ranking adaptation strategies help, with the switching strategy improving even further compared to the oblivious one by up to 56% in P@10, 51% in nDCG@10, and 50% in MAP. Figure 4 further illustrates the consistent improvements in terms of nDCG@100 attained by our intent-aware strategies (here represented by the mixing strategy) compared to the intent-agnostic oblivious baseline. Indeed, not only does mixing improve more queries than it hurts compared to oblivious, but it also shows larger increases and smaller decreases throughout queries of all four intents. Analyzing each intent separately, the most noticeable difference can be observed for *Q* queries, with mixing performing better for 50% of the queries and losing in only 10%. For *E* and *T* queries, the differences in nDCG are not as high, but mixing is still superior for 60% of the queries. The smallest gap between the two strategies appears in *O* queries, although once again mixing performs better for 60% the queries.

5.4.2 Analysis by Query Length. Continuing our detailed analysis, Table 9 breaks down the results from Table 7 according to the length of each query. In particular, we consider three groups of queries: short queries, with 1 or 2 terms (74 queries); medium queries, with 3 or 4 terms (193 queries); and long queries, with 5 or more terms (133 queries). From Table 9, we observe relatively higher performances of all approaches on short queries compared to those of other lengths. FSDM delivers a particularly strong performance on this group, with only a small gap from our mixing strategy, which is the overall best. This can be explained by FSDM's previously discussed effectiveness on *E* queries, which have only 2.7 terms on average. Compared to the oblivious strategy, mixing brings substantial and significant improvements, once again demonstrating the benefits of an intent-aware ranking adaptation. For medium and long queries (5 or more terms), both of our intent-aware strategies bring even more pronounced improvements compared to all intent-agnostic baselines, with the top performing mixing strategy outperforming the oblivious strategy by up to 32% in P@10, 30% in nDCG@10, and 36% in MAP. This tendency is somewhat expected given the effective performance observed

Table 8: Effectiveness breakdown by query intent.

	P@10	nDCG@10	MAP
	***E* queries (100 queries)**		
BM25	0.240▼▼	0.416▼▼	0.320▼▼
FSDM	0.286°°	0.499°°	0.396°°
LambdaMART			
(fixed-E)	0.293△°	0.498°°	0.387°°
(oblivious)	0.239▼▼	0.434▼▼	0.329▼▼
(switching)	0.282°	0.486°	0.377°
(mixing)	**0.297**	**0.502**	**0.390**
	***T* queries (100 queries)**		
BM25	0.190▽▼	0.193▼▼	0.141▼▼
FSDM	0.211°▼	0.223°▼	0.167°▼
LambdaMART			
(fixed-T)	**0.289**▲°	**0.327**▲°	**0.219**▲°
(oblivious)	0.216°▼	0.225°▼	0.146▼▼
(switching)	0.232▼	0.260▼	0.185▼
(mixing)	0.271	0.303	0.210
	***Q* queries (100 queries)**		
BM25	0.060▼▼	0.108▼▼	0.077▼▼
FSDM	0.061▼▼	0.127▼▼	0.098▼▼
LambdaMART			
(fixed-Q)	**0.143**°°	**0.273**°°	**0.203**°°
(oblivious)	0.091▼▼	0.177▼▼	0.132▼▼
(switching)	0.142°	0.267°	0.198°
(mixing)	0.141	0.266	0.194
	***O* queries (100 queries)**		
BM25	0.235°▼	0.282°▽	0.113°°
FSDM	0.258°°	0.308°°	0.119°°
LambdaMART			
(fixed-O)	0.259°°	0.304°°	0.113°▽
(oblivious)	0.221▼▼	0.267▽▼	0.105°▼
(switching)	0.254°	0.305°	0.116°
(mixing)	**0.264**	**0.312**	**0.123**

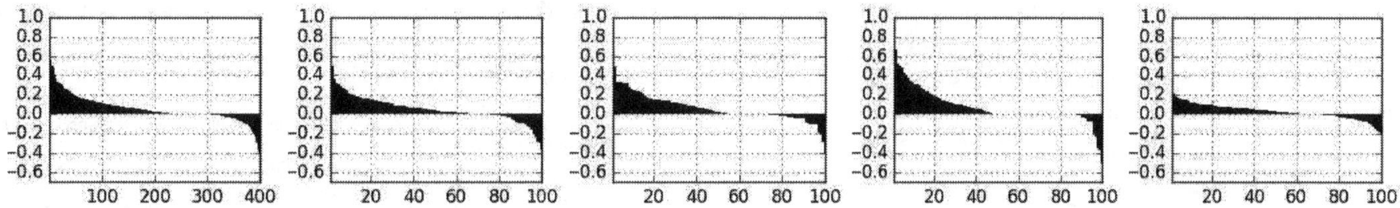

(a) All queries (b) *E* queries (c) *T* queries (d) *Q* queries (e) *O* queries

Figure 4: Differences in nDCG@100 between LambdaMART (mixing) and LambdaMART (oblivious) across: (a) all queries; (b) *E* queries; (c) *T* queries; (d) *Q* queries; (e) *O* queries. Positive values indicate mixing is better.

in Table 9 for the proposed intent-aware strategies on *Q* queries, which are typically longer (8 terms on average).

Table 9: Effectiveness breakdown by query length.

	P@10	nDCG@10	MAP
1 or 2 terms (74 queries)			
BM25	0.253▼▼	0.363▼▼	0.268▼▼
FSDM	0.323°°	0.456°°	0.331°°
LambdaMART			
(fixed-E)	0.324°°	0.453°°	0.327°°
(oblivious)	0.276▼▼	0.394▼▼	0.278▼▼
(switching)	0.324°	0.455°	0.324°
(mixing)	**0.337**	**0.465**	**0.332**
3 or 4 terms (193 queries)			
BM25	0.196▼▼	0.264▼▼	0.161▼▼
FSDM	0.221°▼	0.308▽▼	0.198▽▼
LambdaMART			
(fixed-T)	0.234°▼	0.307▽▼	0.182▼▼
(oblivious)	0.208▼▼	0.296▼▼	0.183▼▼
(switching)	0.240▼	0.349▼	0.227°
(mixing)	**0.265**	**0.376**	**0.239**
5 or more terms (133 queries)			
BM25	0.119▼▼	0.167▼▼	0.106▼▼
FSDM	0.114▼▼	0.171▼▼	0.115▽▼
LambdaMART			
(fixed-T)	0.141°▼	0.206°▽	0.134°▽
(oblivious)	0.121▼▼	0.181▼▼	0.116▼▼
(switching)	0.156°	0.230°	0.150▽
(mixing)	**0.160**	**0.236**	**0.158**

5.4.3 Analysis by Query Difficulty. To complete our breakdown analysis, we regroup all 400 queries in our investigation according to their difficulty. In particular, we consider three groups: difficult queries, with 3 or less relevant results in the ground-truth (108 queries); moderate queries, with 4 to 20 relevant results (184 queries); and easy queries, with more than 20 relevant results (108 queries). The results of this investigation are shown in Table 10. From the table, we note as expected that difficult queries generally incur in reduced precision at early ranks (as measured by both P@10 and nDCG@10), while easy queries tend to penalize recall at lower ranks (as measured by MAP). Nevertheless, our intent-aware adaptation strategies are once again the most effective across all groups of queries, with the mixing strategy consistently providing the overall best results. For difficult queries (3 or less relevant results), compared to the oblivious strategy, mixing improves by up to 19% in P@10, 24% in nDCG@10, and 26% in MAP. For easy queries (21 or more relevant results), improvements are as high as 24% in P@10, 27% in nDCG@10, and 39% in MAP.

Table 10: Effectiveness breakdown by query difficulty.

	P@10	nDCG@10	MAP
Difficult: 3 or less relevant results (108 queries)			
BM25	0.059°▼	0.224▼▼	0.179▼▼
FSDM	0.064°°	0.256▽▼	0.214°▽
LambdaMART			
(fixed-T)	0.062°▽	0.230▽▼	0.180▼▼
(oblivious)	0.063°▽	0.259▽▼	0.213▽▼
(switching)	0.069°	0.308°	0.260°
(mixing)	**0.075**	**0.322**	**0.268**
Moderate: 4 to 20 relevant results (184 queries)			
BM25	0.210▼▼	0.260▼▼	0.194▼▼
FSDM	0.245°▼	0.308°▼	0.235°▽
LambdaMART			
(fixed-O)	0.218▼▼	0.274▼▼	0.195▼▼
(oblivious)	0.214▼▼	0.276▼▼	0.202▼▼
(switching)	0.261▼	0.329▼	0.245▼
(mixing)	**0.279**	**0.345**	**0.257**
Easy: 21 or more relevant results (108 queries)			
BM25	0.255▼▼	0.259▼▼	0.094▼▼
FSDM	0.275▽▼	0.292▼▼	0.107▼▼
LambdaMART			
(fixed-T)	0.328°°	0.338°°	0.125°▼
(oblivious)	0.283▼▼	0.292▼▼	0.103▼▼
(switching)	0.328▽	0.352▽	0.134▼
(mixing)	**0.350**	**0.371**	**0.143**

Recalling *Q4*, the results in this section demonstrate the consistency of our intent-aware ranking adaptation strategies for semantic query annotation. Overall, both the switching and the mixing strategies achieve generally improved results for queries of different target intents, lengths, and difficulty levels, often significantly. Particularly, question-oriented queries (the Q intent), long queries (queries with 5 or more terms), and moderate to easy queries (queries with 4 or more relevant results) are the ones that benefit the most from our intent-aware approach.

6 CONCLUSIONS

We presented a framework for learning to rank semantic annotations suitable to the intent of each individual query. Our approach predicts the intent of a target query and adapts the ranking produced for this query using one of two strategies: *switching*, which applies a ranking model trained on queries of the same intent as predicted for the target query, or *mixing*, which combines the results of multiple intent-specific ranking models according to their predicted likelihood for the target query. Extensive experiments on a publicly available benchmark demonstrated the effectiveness of our approach for semantic query annotation, with significant improvements compared to state-of-the-art intent-agnostic approaches. The results also attested the consistency of the observed improvements for queries of different intents, lengths, and difficulty levels.

In the future, we plan to assess the impact of intent-aware learning on frameworks other than learning to rank. Preliminary results in this direction show that the FSDM baseline, which is based on the Markov random fields framework, can be improved with an intent-aware approach to hyperparameter tuning, although with less marked gains compared to the ones observed in our experiments with feature-based models using learning to rank. Another direction for future investigation includes evaluating our approach with a larger intent taxonomy, including more queries with less common intents such as attribute and relation queries.

ACKNOWLEDGMENTS

This work was partially funded by projects InWeb (MCT/ CNPq 573871/2008-6) and MASWeb (FAPEMIG/PRONEX APQ-01400-14), and by the authors' individual grants from CNPq and FAPEMIG.

REFERENCES

[1] Omar Alonso and Hugo Zaragoza. 2008. Exploiting semantic annotations in information retrieval: ESAIR '08. *SIGIR Forum* 42, 1 (2008), 55–58.

[2] Kriztian Balog, Arien P. de Vries, Pavel Serdyukov, Paul Thomas, and Thijs Westerveld. 2009. Overview of the TREC 2009 Entity track. In *TREC*.

[3] Krisztian Balog and Robert Neumayer. 2013. A Test Collection for Entity Search in DBpedia. In *Proc. of SIGIR*. 737–740.

[4] Hannah Bast, Björn Buchhold, Elmar Haussmann, and others. 2016. Semantic Search on Text and Knowledge Bases. *Foundations and Trends in Information Retrieval* 10, 2-3 (2016), 119–271.

[5] Bin Bi, Hao Ma, Bo-June (Paul) Hsu, Wei Chu, Kuansan Wang, and Junghoo Cho. 2015. Learning to Recommend Related Entities to Search Users. In *Proc. of WSDM*. 139–148.

[6] Roi Blanco, Peter Mika, and Sebastian Vigna. 2011. Effective and Efficient Entity Search in RDF Data. In *Proc. of ISWC*. 83–97.

[7] Roi Blanco, Peter Mika, and Hugo Zaragoza. 2010. Entity Search Track Submission by Yahoo! Research Barcelona. In *Proc. of Entity Search Track*.

[8] David J. Brenes, Daniel Gayo-Avello, and Kilian Pérez-González. 2009. Survey and Evaluation of Query Intent Detection Methods. In *Proc. of WSCD*. 1–7.

[9] Andrei Broder. 2002. A Taxonomy of Web Search. *SIGIR Forum* 36, 2 (2002), 3–10.

[10] Marc Bron, Krisztian Balog, and Maarten de Rijke. 2010. Ranking related entities: components and analyses. In *Proc. of CIKM*. 1079–1088.

[11] Marc Bron, Krisztian Balog, and Maarten De Rijke. 2013. Example Based Entity Search in the Web of Data. In *Proc. of ECIR*. 392–403.

[12] Stéphane Campinas, Renaud Delbru, Nur Aini Rakhmawati, Diego Ceccarelli, and Giovanni Tummarello. 2011. Sindice BM25F at SemSearch 2011. In *Proc. of SemSearch*.

[13] Olivier Chapelle and Yi Chang. 2011. Yahoo! learning to rank challenge overview.. In *Yahoo! Learning to Rank Challenge*. 1–24.

[14] Nick Craswell and David Hawking. 2004. Overview of the TREC 2004 Web track. In *Proc. of TREC*.

[15] Arjen P. de Vries, Anne-Marie Vercoustre, James A. Thom, Nick Craswell, and Mounia Lalmas. 2007. Overview of the INEX 2007 Entity Ranking track. In *Proc. of INEX*. 245–251.

[16] Shady Elbassuoni and Roi Blanco. 2011. Keyword Search over RDF Graphs. In *Proc. of CIKM*. 237–242.

[17] Shady Elbassuoni, Maya Ramanath, Ralf Schenkel, Marcin Sydow, and Gerhard Weikum. 2009. Language-Model-Based Ranking for Queries on RDF-Graphs. In *Proc. of CIKM*. 977–986.

[18] Besnik Fetahu, Ujwal Gadiraju, and Stefan Dietze. 2015. Improving entity retrieval on structured data. In *Proc. of ISWC*. 474–491.

[19] Xiubo Geng, Tie-Yan Liu, Tao Qin, Andrew Arnold, Hang Li, and Heung-Yeung Shum. 2008. Query dependent ranking using k-nearest neighbor. In *Proc. of SIGIR*. 115–122.

[20] Ido Guy. 2016. Searching by Talking: Analysis of Voice Queries on Mobile Web Search. In *Proc. of SIGIR*. 35–44.

[21] Daniel M Herzig, Peter Mika, Roi Blanco, and Thanh Tran. 2013. Federated Entity Search Using On-the-fly Consolidation. In *Proc. of ISWC*. 167–183.

[22] Bernard J. Jansen, Amanda Spink, and Tefko Saracevic. 2000. Real Life, Real Users, and Real Needs: A Study and Analysis of User Queries on the Web. *Information Processing and Management* 36, 2 (2000), 207–227.

[23] In-Ho Kang and GilChang Kim. 2003. Query type classification for Web document retrieval. In *Proc. of SIGIR*. 64–71.

[24] Tie-Yan Liu and others. 2009. Learning to rank for information retrieval. *Foundations and Trends® in Information Retrieval* 3, 3 (2009), 225–331.

[25] Claudio Lucchese, Franco Maria Nardini, Salvatore Orlando, Raffaele Perego, and Nicola Tonellotto. 2015. Speeding Up Document Ranking with Rank-based Features. In *Proc. of SIGIR*. 895–898.

[26] Donald Metzler and W. Bruce Croft. 2005. A Markov Random Field Model for Term Dependencies. In *Proc. of SIGIR*. 472–479.

[27] Robert Neumayer, Krisztian Balog, and Kjetil Nørvåg. 2012. On the Modeling of Entities for Ad-Hoc Entity Search in the Web of Data. In *Proc. of ECIR*. 133–145.

[28] Fedor Nikolaev, Alexander Kotov, and Nikita Zhiltsov. 2016. Parameterized Fielded Term Dependence Models for Ad-hoc Entity Retrieval from Knowledge Graph. In *Proc. of SIGIR*. 435–444.

[29] Paul Ogilvie and Jamie Callan. 2003. Combining Document Representations for Known-item Search. In *Proc. of SIGIR*. 143–150.

[30] Jie Peng, Craig Macdonald, and Iadh Ounis. 2010. Learning to select a ranking function. In *Proc. of ECIR*. 114–126.

[31] José R Pérez-Agüera, Javier Arroyo, Jane Greenberg, Joaquin Perez Iglesias, and Victor Fresno. 2010. Using BM25F for semantic search. In *Proc. of SemSearch*. 2.

[32] Jeffrey Pound, Peter Mika, and Hugo Zaragoza. 2010. Ad-hoc Object Retrieval in the Web of Data. In *Proc. of WWW*. 771–780.

[33] Stephen E. Robertson, Steve Walker, Micheline Hancock-Beaulieu, Mike Gatford, and A. Payne. 1995. Okapi at TREC-4. In *Proc. of TREC*.

[34] Cristiano Rocha, Daniel Schwabe, and Marcus Poggi Aragao. 2004. A Hybrid Approach for Searching in the Semantic Web. In *Proc. of WWW*. 374–383.

[35] Daniel E. Rose and Danny Levinson. 2004. Understanding User Goals in Web Search. In *Proc. of WWW*. 13–19.

[36] Rodrygo L. T. Santos, Craig Macdonald, and Iadh Ounis. 2010. Selectively diversifying web search results. In *Proc. of CIKM*. 1179–1188.

[37] Rodrygo L. T. Santos, Craig Macdonald, and Iadh Ounis. 2010. Voting for related entities. In *Proc. of RIAO*. 1–8.

[38] Rodrygo L. T. Santos, Craig Macdonald, and Iadh Ounis. 2011. Intent-aware Search Result Diversification. In *Proc. of SIGIR*. 595–604.

[39] Alberto Tonon, Gianluca Demartini, and Philippe Cudré-Mauroux. 2012. Combining Inverted Indices and Structured Search for Ad-hoc Object Retrieval. In *Proc. of SIGIR*. 125–134.

[40] Gilad Tsur, Yuval Pinter, Idan Szpektor, and David Carmel. 2016. Identifying Web Queries with Question Intent. In *Proc. of WWW*. 783–793.

[41] Qiang Wu, Chris JC Burges, Krysta M Svore, and Jianfeng Gao. 2008. *Ranking, boosting, and model adaptation.* Technical Report. Technical report, Microsoft Research.

[42] Elad Yom-Tov, Shai Fine, David Carmel, and Adam Darlow. 2005. Learning to estimate query difficulty: including applications to missing content detection and distributed information retrieval. In *Proc. of SIGIR*. 512–519.

[43] Nikita Zhiltsov and Eugene Agichtein. 2013. Improving Entity Search over Linked Data by Modeling Latent Semantics. In *Proc. of CIKM*. 1253–1256.

[44] Nikita Zhiltsov, Alexander Kotov, and Fedor Nikolaev. 2015. Fielded Sequential Dependence Model for Ad-Hoc Entity Retrieval in the Web of Data. In *Proc. of SIGIR*. 253–262.

Efficient & Effective Selective Query Rewriting with Efficiency Predictions

Craig Macdonald
University of Glasgow
Glasgow, Scotland, UK
craig.macdonald@glasgow.ac.uk

Nicola Tonellotto
ISTI-CNR
Pisa, Italy
nicola.tonellotto@isti.cnr.it

Iadh Ounis
University of Glasgow
Glasgow, Scotland, UK
iadh.ounis@glasgow.ac.uk

ABSTRACT

To enhance effectiveness, a user's query can be rewritten internally by the search engine in many ways, for example by applying proximity, or by expanding the query with related terms. However, approaches that benefit effectiveness often have a negative impact on efficiency, which has impacts upon the user satisfaction, if the query is excessively slow. In this paper, we propose a novel framework for using the predicted execution time of various query rewritings to select between alternatives on a per-query basis, in a manner that ensures both effectiveness and efficiency. In particular, we propose the prediction of the execution time of *ephemeral* (e.g., proximity) posting lists generated from uni-gram inverted index posting lists, which are used in establishing the permissible query rewriting alternatives that may execute in the allowed time. Experiments examining both the effectiveness and efficiency of the proposed approach demonstrate that a 49% decrease in mean response time (and 62% decrease in 95th-percentile response time) can be attained without significantly hindering the effectiveness of the search engine.

ACM Reference format:
Craig Macdonald, Nicola Tonellotto, and Iadh Ounis. 2017. Efficient & Effective Selective Query Rewriting with Efficiency Predictions. In *Proceedings of SIGIR '17, August 07-11, 2017, Shinjuku, Tokyo, Japan*, , 10 pages.
DOI: http://dx.doi.org/10.1145/3077136.3080827

1 INTRODUCTION

Search engines, such as those for the Web, are required to be effective at answering users' queries but yet also efficient. In particular, while the relevance of the results are important for users' satisfaction, users are in general not willing to wait long for the results to arrive [36]. While search engines are operated in distributed retrieval settings that can be scaled horizontally to reduce response times, the ramification of this is increased cost (in terms of both capital outlay and running, e.g., for power) for the search engine infrastructure. This being the case, the efficiency of the search engine is key to providing effective results without excessive financial burden. Typically, the infrastructure is designed to maintain a service level, where high percentile response time (the so-called "tail latencies" [16, 19]) should not exceed a given target. Indeed, for the Bing search engine, the target is reported to be that 99% percentile response time should not exceed 100 ms [19].

SIGIR '17, August 07-11, 2017, Shinjuku, Tokyo, Japan

DOI: http://dx.doi.org/10.1145/3077136.3080827

Table 1: Example rewrites for the query 'poker tournament'.

Original query:	poker tournament
Stemming:	poker #syn(tournaments tournament)
Proximity:	poker tournament #1(poker tournament)∧0.1 #uw8(poker tournament)∧0.1
Stemming and Proximity:	poker #syn(tournaments tournament) #1(poker #syn(tournaments tournament))∧0.1 #uw8(poker #syn(tournaments tournament))∧0.1

On the other hand, techniques that benefit the effectiveness of a search engine may hinder efficiency [41], due to their complex nature. For example, in a modern search engine deploying learning-to-rank approaches, the number of features to be computed and the learned models both contribute complexity, and have been the subject of recent studies (e.g., [25]). However, the time to traverse the inverted index's posting lists for the query terms, to identify the top K documents — which are then re-ranked by the learned approach — takes significant time [14].

Often the query submitted by the user is internally *rewritten* by the search engine to improve the quality of the search results [20, 33]. For instance, traditional pseudo-relevance feedback approaches typically results in a much larger query, with significant negative impact on efficiency. More recently, less aggressive query rewriting approaches such as term proximity [30], query substitutions [20] and query-time stemming [34] have been deployed by search engines. Each query rewriting approaches can lead to a query with additional terms, resulting in prolonged execution times.

Table 1 shows three possible rewritings of the query 'poker tournament', based on application of combinations of stemming [34] and sequential dependence (proximity) [30]. In the rewritten examples using an Indri-like query language, *complex query operators* [37] denote additional postings lists that must be traversed during retrieval, namely: #syn, which combines the constituent terms into a single posting list; #1 creates a posting list representing an exact occurrence of an n-gram; and #uwλ creates a posting list that provides the number of times a n-gram appears in an unordered window of size λ [37]. While the search engine may have indexed posting lists for some n-grams, not all possible query operators may have existing posting lists, and hence *ephemeral* posting lists are required, which need to be created on-the-fly from the constituent terms. Moreover, statistics such as the total number of postings in an ephemeral posting list are unknown, and hence the number of postings to be processed and the resulting execution time of a query containing complex operators cannot be known in advance.

Indeed, while recent work in query efficiency prediction has shown the possibility of estimating the execution time of a query prior to its processing [19, 21, 29, 38], none of the existing work

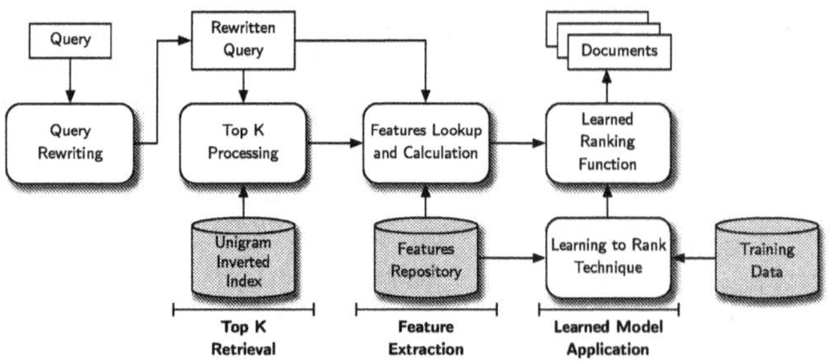

Figure 1: A pictorial representation of the reference web search engine architecture that we consider in this work.

has considered the execution time of queries containing query operators that generate ephemeral posting lists, such as #syn, or #1. This makes it difficult to select among query rewriting strategies that use such operators, as their likely execution time is unknown. Hence, in this work, we study the cost of scoring ephemeral posting lists, and use these observations to define accurate query efficiency predictions for advanced query operators. Furthermore, we use these query efficiency predictions to instantiate a novel mechanism that selects the best strategy among alternative query rewritings, to improve efficiency, while minimising impact on effectiveness.

Our conducted experiments to measure the efficiency of our proposed selective mechanism upon TREC Web track test collections show that a 49% decrease in mean response time, and 62% decrease in tail (95th-percentile) response time, can be attained without significantly hindering the effectiveness of the search engine. The contributions of this work are as follows: we show how to make query efficiency predictions for ephemeral posting lists created by complex operators such as #syn and #1; we use these advanced query efficiency predictions to propose a selector mechanism that permits the query to be rewritten in an effective manner while considering a target response time that the search engine should aim to meet.

The remainder of this paper is structured as follows: Section 2 provides an overview of a reference search engine architecture, describing the necessary background; Section 3 positions our contributions with respect to existing work; Section 4 describes our mechanism for selecting among query rewrites; Section 5 proposes new query efficiency predictors suitable for application to complex query operators. Our experimental setup and results follow in Sections 6 & 7. Finally, we provide concluding remarks in Section 8.

2 PRELIMINARIES

In this section, we provide some essential background on index organisation and query processing in search engines. In doing so, we follow the reference architecture for a search engine depicted by Figure 1. The following section summarises and discusses the state-of-the-art query rewriting techniques and approaches addressing efficient but effective retrieval.

Index Organisation. Given a collection $\mathcal{D}$ of documents, each document is identified by a non-negative integer called *document identifier*, or *docid* d_i. A *posting list* I_t is associated to each *term* t appearing in the collection, containing the list of the docids of all the documents in which the term occurs at least once. The collection of the posting lists for all of the terms is called the *inverted index* of $\mathcal{D}$, while the set of the terms is usually referred to as the *lexicon*. For each term t, the lexicon stores a pointer to its posting list as well as additional information on the statistics of the term in the collection, such as its *document frequency* N_t, i.e., the length of its posting list, and the total number of occurrences of the term in the collection F_t. Each *posting* in a posting list typically contains additional information about the term's occurrences in the document, such as the number of occurrences $f_{t,d}$, and the set of *positions*, $p_{t,d}$, where the term t occurs [13]. This position information facilitates phrasal retrieval without resort to large n-gram index data structures.

The docids in a posting list can be sorted in increasing order enabling the use of efficient compression algorithms and query processing [31]; or the posting lists can be frequency-sorted [39] or impact-sorted [2], allowing for good compression rates, but also presenting practical disadvantages such as their difficulty of use for phrasal queries [22, 37]. As such, in this paper, we focus on the more common search scenario of docid-sorted index layouts [15].

Query Processing. The top K ranked retrieval stage identifies the K highest scored documents in the collection, where the *relevance score* is a function of the query-document pair. Multi-stage retrieval systems have become the dominant model for efficient and effective web search engines [14]. In such systems (see Figure 1), a first "top K" stage retrieves from the inverted index a relatively small set of K possibly-relevant documents matching the user query, focusing on optimising recall. Subsequent stages compute additional query dependent (e.g., fields [28], proximity) and query independent features, before applying a learning-to-rank technique to re-rank the K documents coming from the first stage, aiming to maximise measures like NDCG [25]. The inverted index posting lists are processed in the first stage only, to produce a small set of candidate documents, that will be re-ranked in the subsequent stage(s).

Documents are typically scored in the first stage retrieval by the (weighted) linear combinations of weighting model (e.g., BM25, language models) functions computed for each term-document pair. Such weighting models are usually monotonically increasing in the number of occurrences of the term in the document $f_{t,d}$. An obvious way to compute the top K scored documents is to exhaustively apply the weighting model to all the documents that match at least one query term in the inverted index. As such an exhaustive method is very expensive for large collections, several *dynamic pruning* techniques have been proposed in the last few years. Dynamic pruning makes use of the inverted index, augmented with additional data structures, to skip documents that cannot reach a sufficient score to enter the top K. Thus, the final result is the same as an exhaustive evaluation, but obtained with significantly less work. These techniques include MaxScore [39], WAND [6], and BMW [17]. In this paper, we focus our attention on the WAND strategy, since we deal with (rewritten) queries that can have a large number of terms (i.e., long queries). Indeed, several previous studies have confirmed that MaxScore performs better than WAND for short queries while the opposite happens for long queries [18, 31] while, as we will discuss in Sec. 5, the BMW techniques are not suitable for processing rewritten queries.

WAND augments the posting list of each term t with an *upper bound* σ_t on the maximum score of that term among all documents in the list. While processing the query by iterating on the posting lists of its terms, it records the top K scores among the documents evaluated thus far. To enter the top K, a new document needs to have a larger score than the current K-th score, which we call the *min score*. WAND maintains the posting list iterators sorted by increasing docid; at every step, it sums up the maximum scores of the lists in increasing order, until the min score is reached. It can be seen that the current docid of the first list that exceeds the min score is the first docid that can reach a score higher than the min score, so the other iterators can safely skip all the documents up to that docid. The alignment of the posting lists during WAND processing is achieved by means of a $\mathrm{next}_t(d)$ method upon the posting list iterators, which returns the smallest docid in the posting list I_t that is greater than or equal to d. This functionality significantly enhances the retrieval speed exhibited by WAND, by skipping docids that would never be retrieved in the top K, and hence avoiding their decompression and scoring. Indeed, smaller values of K allow for more skipping, since the threshold is in general larger for small values of K than for large values, resulting in smaller query processing times, as reported, for example, in [38].

3 RELATED WORK

In the following, we survey existing work in query rewriting and in query efficiency predictions, and position our work accordingly.

Query Rewriting. There are a number of related works across the areas of query rewriting and efficient yet effective retrieval. The internal rewriting of a user's query within an IR system has a long history, including pseudo-relevance feedback in the form of automatic query expansion, first deployed by the SMART system in TREC-3 [7], while others considered the correction of spelling errors or the application of ontologies to identify related concepts [13, Ch. 6]. Indeed, query expansion, which adds additional terms to the query based upon their appearance in the top ranked documents, has been shown to be effective for adhoc retrieval tasks in evaluation forums such as TREC [42]. For web search, the significantly longer generated queries, as well as the need to conduct two retrieval phases, make pseudo-relevance feedback approaches infeasible for efficient retrieval. A further risk is the possibility that the topic of the expanded query can drift from the intent of the initial query.

Instead, some of the techniques widely deployed in web search have focused on rewriting the query based on the large amounts of user interaction data available to a web search engine. For instance Jones et al. [20] describe a way to mine common query reformulation patterns, based on log likelihood ratio, that can be automatically applied to refine a new query. Random walks on the query-click graph [12] offer similar possibilities for identifying common paraphrasing queries.

Rewriting the query to include common variants of the original query terms can have an important effectiveness benefit in addressing the word mismatch problem. Indeed, a query-side approach to stemming has a marked advantage of index-time stemming, in that the other words within the query can be taken into account to decide if the stemming is appropriate for a given word. For instance, Peng et al. [34] describe a context-sensitive stemming approach where *query segments*[1] are carefully considered for stemming, by comparing the language model generation probability of both the original and the replacement segments. Naturally, adding additional terms to the query can have a marked negative impact on efficiency, hence, as noted by Peng et al., it is not desirable to rewrite queries unnecessarily. In our work in this paper, query rewriting by application of stemming is one of the query rewriting techniques that we consider.

One method of query rewriting that has gained significant benefits in effectiveness is the application of term dependence (proximity) operators, to boost the retrieval of documents where the query terms occur close together [30, 35]. In particular, Metzler & Croft's Markov Random Field *sequential dependence model* makes use of the Indri complex query operators #1 and #uwλ formed from adjacent pairs of query terms, added to the original query terms with low weights (typically [0.05,0.1]). However, such rewritten queries have a negative efficiency impact, in that more posting lists must be traversed, while if the index only has unigram posting lists, ephemeral posting lists must be created to handle the #1 and #uwλ operators[2]. Another variant, the *full dependence model* – which adds complex query operators for each pair of query terms – is generally considered too inefficient for common retrieval use [4, 30]. Hence, for large-scale environments, there has to be a perceived benefit in deploying such a term dependence model, due to its inherent negative efficiency impact. For this reason, we note various works that extract term dependence proximity features at the re-ranking stage [28, 38] – an approach that we deploy within our baseline retrieval system in this paper.

On the other hand, motivated by the inefficiencies in deploying sequential dependence, Wang et al. [41] proposed an efficient variant where the weights for bi-gram operators were adjusted to jointly optimise combinations of effectiveness and efficiency, and bi-grams predicted not to be useful were eliminated. In this way, the work of Wang et al. is one of the closest to our work. However, their features for estimating the cost of the #1 and #uwλ bi-gram complex operators assumed the existence of bi-gram index statistics, something that our approach does not require; Moreover, their experiments did not consider deployment under a dynamic pruning strategy, where the efficiency cost of additional complex proximity operators, – which have low weighting in the query (see Table 1) – may be markedly reduced by the pruning. Finally, as we consider more than just proximity rewriting, our work is more general than that of Wang et al. [41].

Efficiency Predictions. Using a docid-sorted index layout, the time taken for a query to execute is correlated with the length of the posting lists of the query's constituent terms, as these posting lists must be traversed during execution. Dynamic pruning techniques such as WAND and BMW offer some relief as they offer the potential to safely skip the decompression of postings and the scoring of documents that cannot make the current top K. This makes the exact response time of a query difficult to predict, as not every posting in the postings lists will be decompressed and scored. Nevertheless recent work has considered making accurate predictions on the efficiency of a query, either in terms of absolute response time [29], or in terms of those queries with response times exceeding a threshold [19, 21].

Efficiency predictions facilitate a number of applications for ensuring efficient yet effective retrieval - for instance, routing queries

[1] N-gram subsequences of queries that demonstrate the underlying grammatical structure, usually determined by dividing longer sequences to maximise n-gram language model probabilities.

[2] For instance, according to the recent IR system reproducibility effort [23], Indri's average response time is decreased by a factor of 6 on deploying sequential dependence on the Gov2 corpus.

among busy replicated query shard servers [29]; selectively deploying multiple CPU cores for slow queries [19, 21]; or adjusting the pruning aggressiveness or size of K for different queries [5, 14, 38]. Of these, the work of Tonellotto et al. [38] is among the most similar to ours, in that they vary the number of documents to be retrieved, K, as well as the pruning aggressiveness, before passing to a learning-to-rank re-ranking phase, based on the predicted execution time of the query. Similarly, in a very recently published work, Culpepper et al. [14] defined an approach for training the rank cutoff in a multi-stage ranking system based on closeness in overlap to a "reference" system. However, their approach has a key disadvantage in that they use a simple reference system, and hence would not demonstrate the benefit in going beyond that system, for instance in deploying advanced query rewrites.

Indeed, differently from [14] & [38], in this paper, we go further by considering a prediction of the execution time of possible rewritings of the users' original queries. This is made possible by the novel prediction of the execution time of complex query operators such as #syn and #uwλ. In the following, we firstly define the problem and introduce our selection mechanism (Section 4), before defining how to obtain query efficiency predictions for queries involving complex operators in Section 5.

4 SELECTING AMONG QUERY REWRITINGS

4.1 Problem Statement

This work considers the efficient yet effective rewriting of a given query q. Indeed, the search engine may consider several possible ways to reformulate the query into a refined instance q', for instance, by splitting compound words, adding alternative words identified using stemming algorithms or common query reformulations approaches, or adding proximity terms such as #1. Some such query rewritings can result in a longer query formulation, hindering its efficiency compared to the original query [33].

Reformulating the query in a multi-stage ranking system – such as one deploying learning to rank – can be seen as aiming to improve the recall of the K documents retrieved in the Top K Retrieval stage. This ensures that when re-ranking the documents by the application of the learned model, the search engine has a high chance of identifying the most relevant documents for promotion to the top of the ranked list for presentation to the user. Naturally, improving the formulation of the query may also increase the high precision of these K documents – i.e., by retrieving more relevant documents towards the top of that initial list. This suggests that some rewritten queries only need a smaller $K' < K$. Moreover, as mentioned above, the efficiency of dynamic pruning techniques like WAND is benefited by smaller K.

Hence, with various different rewriting techniques available, a natural question arises: for a given query q, which possible rewritings are appropriate to be applied to the query, $q'_1 \dots q'_n$, such that effectiveness may be improved, and/or, K reduced to improve efficiency, without significantly damaging the overall effectiveness.

4.2 Selection Mechanism

To achieve this, we make use of query efficiency predictions that estimate the execution time of different rewritings of the query, before one is selected and executed. A particular challenge in doing so is making accurate estimations of the execution times of rewritten queries that use operators such as #syn, #1 and #uwλ. We discuss this further in Section 5.

Firstly, we generate all possible rewritings $\{q'_1 \dots q'_n\}$ of the original query q. We note that the size of this set varies for each query q, as not all rewritings are applicable to each query – for instance, no term dependence can be applied to a query with only a single term, or no stemming may be applicable for each query term. At the very least, the original query will always be present.

We also consider m different K values for the number of documents to retrieve in the first retrieval phase, which will then be re-ranked by application of the learned model, namely $K_1 \dots K_m$. In doing so, our intuition is that for some queries, simply identifying $K = 20$ documents will be sufficient to identify enough relevant documents, leading to marked efficiency benefits, particularly if the rewritten query permits higher recall of relevant documents within the top K. A possible *plan* for executing a query can be denoted as the tuple $\langle q'_i, K_j \rangle$. All possible query plans, denoted $\mathcal{P}(q)$, for executing the query can be generated from the Cartesian product:

$$\mathcal{P}(q) = \left\{ \langle q'_i, K_j \rangle \right\} = \{q'_1 \dots q'_n\} \times \{K_1 \dots K_m\} \tag{1}$$

The aim is then to rank and eliminate plans $\langle q'_i, K_j \rangle$ based on their predicted efficiency and expected effectiveness. While the number of possible rewrites for each query varies, $|\mathcal{P}(q)| \geq m$.

Consider that the search engine has a service level agreement in place [19], which aims to maximise the number of queries answered in time τ. Some plans for queries may exceed τ. We use query efficiency predictions, denoted $\widehat{t}(\langle q'_i, K_j \rangle)$ to eliminate such plans:

$$\mathcal{EP}(q, \tau) = \left\{ \langle q'_i, K_j \rangle \in \mathcal{P}(q) \mid \widehat{t}(\langle q'_i, K_j \rangle) \leq \tau \right\} \tag{2}$$

Naturally, plans will vary in effectiveness. One possible approach to select among the feasible plans $\mathcal{EP}(q, \tau)$ would be to try to predict the effectiveness of a given rewriting of a query. However, Tonellotto et al. [38] examined the usefulness of query performance (effectiveness) predictors within their selective pruning mechanism, and found them to have little correlation with maintaining effectiveness while enhancing efficiency. Moreover, we are not aware of any existing works that make effectiveness predictions in the presence of complex operators used by some rewritings.

Instead, to determine the likely effectiveness of a plan $\langle q'_i, K_j \rangle$, we measure the expectation of the effectiveness for some measure μ (e.g., NDCG) of that given rewriting upon a set of training queries Q^{tr}. Denoting with $\langle Q^{\text{tr}}_i, K_j \rangle$ the set of query plans for the rewritten queries according to the i-th rewriting, we compute the expected effectiveness of measure μ over all such query plans, $E_\mu(\langle Q^{\text{tr}}_i, K_j \rangle)$. However, due to excessively long posting lists, some queries may not have any plans that can be executed in time τ, i.e., $|\mathcal{EP}(q, \tau)| = 0$. For this reason, for such queries, we resort to a best attempt, by selecting the plan with the fastest predicted execution time. The final selection mechanism to identify the best plan $\mathcal{FP}(q, \tau)$ for executing the (possibly rewritten) query q in time τ is as follows:

$$\mathcal{FP}(q, \tau) = \begin{cases} \underset{\langle q'_i, K_j \rangle \in \mathcal{EP}(q, \tau)}{\operatorname{argmax}} \quad E_\mu(\langle Q^{\text{tr}}_i, K_j \rangle) & \text{if } |\mathcal{EP}(q, \tau)| > 0 \\ \underset{\langle q'_i, K_j \rangle \in \mathcal{EP}(q, \tau)}{\operatorname{argmin}} \quad \widehat{t}(\langle q'_i, K_j \rangle) & \text{otherwise} \end{cases} \tag{3}$$

The usefulness of this mechanism is driven by the need to have accurate estimation of the time to execute a given query plan, namely $\widehat{t}(\langle q'_i, K_j \rangle)$. Moreover, as mentioned above, the estimation of the

Table 2: Complex operators summary table.

Complex operator	Complex term	Ephemeral posting list
#syn	#syn(car, cars)	Disjunctive/OR
#1	#1(new, york)	Conjunctive/AND
#uwλ	#uw8(divx, codec)	Conjunctive/AND

execution time of complex query operators, particularly under dynamic pruning strategies such as WAND, have not previously been addressed. In the next section, we propose a novel method to address this problem, by using machine-learned models to predict the execution times of query plans that use complex operators.

5 EFFICIENCY PREDICTION FOR COMPLEX OPERATORS

The complex operators involved in stemming and proximity rewritings are summarised in Table 2. Such complex operators can be applied to two or more uni-gram terms, as well as other complex operators, i.e., complex operators can be nested. Complex operators, such as #1, generate complex terms once instantiated, such as #1(new, york). In the following, we discuss how the posting lists for such complex terms are generated (Section 5.1) and how they can be processed together with the original terms in the WAND strategy (Section 5.2). Section 5.3 presents our approach for predicting the query processing time of queries containing complex terms.

5.1 Complex terms and ephemeral posting lists

While posting lists for simple (e.g., uni-gram) terms are stored in the inverted index, it is not feasible to pre-compute statistics and posting lists for complex terms, since their space occupancy will quickly become unmanageable, particularly if complex operators can be nested. Hence, for a complex term $\#\mathsf{op}(t_1, \ldots, \#\mathsf{op}_1, \ldots)$, its posting list and statistics must be generated on-the-fly, such that it can be processed together with other simple and complex terms. Such *ephemeral posting lists* are materialised as required, depending on the complex operator and the involved terms. We consider two types of ephemeral posting lists: disjunctive/OR-based lists and conjunctive/AND-based lists (see Table 2). OR-based posting lists are used with #syn operators, where the posting lists of two or more terms are merged into a single posting list containing all docids appearing in at least one of the terms' posting lists. AND-based posting lists are used with #1 and #uwλ operators, where two or more terms' posting lists must be intersected, i.e., a posting appears in the ephemeral posting list only if it is present in all of the involved posting lists.

The involved complex operator defines how to merge postings into ephemeral posting lists. In OR-based ephemeral posting lists, when the postings of two different terms that refer to the same docid are merged, their term frequencies in a document must be added, and the positions arrays must be merged. Similarly, while the terms' frequencies in the collection (F_t) must be summed, we cannot know in advance the document frequencies (N_t) of the resulting ephemeral posting list, as the number of docids in common between the two posting lists is unknown. In AND-based ephemeral posting lists, there is no general way to merge term frequencies in documents, while term positions must be stored separately and processed depending on the semantics of the complex operator [24]. Again, the document frequency N_t of the resulting ephemeral posting list, i.e., its length, cannot be known in advance.

5.2 Query Processing

Given a user query q composed of *simple terms*, let us assume it is rewritten into a query composed of simple terms and *complex terms*, collectively denoted by q'. Complex terms are obtained by applying complex operators – summarised in Table 2 – to simple or other complex terms, in a nested fashion. The score of a document d w.r.t. the rewritten query q' can be expressed as follows:

$$s(q', d) = \sum_{t \in q \cap d} w_t \, s_{t,d} + \sum_{t' \in (q' \setminus q) \cap d} w_{t'} \, s_{t',d}, \tag{4}$$

where w_t (resp. $w_{t'}$) denotes the simple (resp. complex) terms weights (see Table 1), while $s_{t,d}$ and $s_{t',d}$ are weighting models for simple and complex terms respectively. The linearity of Eq. (4) makes it easily usable in any exhaustive query processing algorithm, by exploiting ephemeral posting lists as normal posting lists.

Conversely, dynamic pruning techniques are not directly usable, since they rely on the maximum score σ_t of each query term, calculated among all documents in the respective posting lists, i.e., $\sigma_t = w_t \cdot \max_{d \in I_t} s_{t,d}$. These maximum scores can be computed offline by taking the score value of the top document of a single term query stored in the lexicon. However, since ephemeral posting lists are materialised on-the-fly, such a computation cannot be performed offline, hence we must resort to a runtime estimation for upper bounds on these maximum scores. In [26], the authors proposed a general framework to approximate the term upper bounds for proximity weighting models that monotonically increase with respect to the frequency variable, called MaxTF. In that framework, the upper bound σ_t for a term t is computed by using the maximum term frequency $f_{\max}(t)$ that appears in the term's posting list as input for the scoring model, i.e.,

$$\sigma_t = w_t \, s_{t,d}\Big(f_{\max}(t)\Big), \text{ where } f_{\max}(t) = \max_{d \in I_t} f_{t,d}. \tag{5}$$

In our experiments, we exploit the DLH13 weighting model [1] for #syn operators and simple terms, and the pBiL dependence weighting model [35] for #uwλ and #1 operators[3]. Both models are a generalisation of the parameter-free hypergeometric DFR model in a binomial case, DLH13 for simple terms while pBiL for n-grams, and both are monotonically increasing with respect to the frequency variable $f_{t,d}$. Hence, given a complex term, we can compute a term upper bound by using the maximum term/n-gram frequency computed from the corresponding ephemeral posting list, as in the MaxTF framework. Unfortunately, even computing these maximum frequencies is impossible without a complete view of the posting lists, hence we must resort to a further upper bound on those frequencies, easily computed as follows:

$$\begin{aligned} f_{\max}\Big(\#\mathsf{syn}(t_1, t_2)\Big) &= f_{\max}(t_1) + f_{\max}(t_2), \\ f_{\max}\Big(\#1(t_1, t_2)\Big) &= \min\Big\{f_{\max}(t_1), f_{\max}(t_2)\Big\}, \\ f_{\max}\Big(\#\mathsf{uw}\lambda(t_1, t_2)\Big) &= \min\Big\{f_{\max}(t_1), f_{\max}(t_2)\Big\}. \end{aligned} \tag{6}$$

[3] We use these models as they are parameter free, and their MaxTF upper-bound approximations were proven in [26]; However, the method we describe here is equally applicable for scoring simple and complex terms using Dirichlet language modelling. BM25 cannot be applied, as N_t is not available while scoring complex terms.

For instance, consider an AND-based ephemeral posting list (such as #1): no document can have more occurrences of the n-gram than the *minimum* of the maximum frequencies of the involved terms that has been observed in their posting lists. For the OR-based #syn operator, the worst-case maximum frequency would occur if a single document had the maximum frequencies of the constituent terms. Hence, the maximum frequency within a #syn ephemeral posting list cannot be greater than the sum of the maximum observed frequencies of the respective constituent posting lists.

Such term upper bounds, computed by substituting Equations (6) into Equation (5) as required, can be used in dynamic pruning strategies such as MaxScore and WAND, which leverage *global* upper bounds on each term, both simple and complex. Conversely, query processing strategies such as BMW leverage *local* term upper bounds: each posting list is split into consecutive blocks of constant size, e.g., 128 postings per block, and, for each block, a score upper bound is computed and stored, together with largest docid of each block. This cannot be done with ephemeral posting lists, since their sequences of postings is not known in advance. Hence, no block score upper bounds can be computed or stored.

5.3 Predicting Complex Operator Efficiency

The time spent processing a query in dynamic pruning strategies depends on several factors, the most important being: (i) the number of terms to be processed, (ii) the total number of postings to be processed and (iii) the relative importance of terms, i.e., their score contribution to the overall relevance of a document [29]. As shown in [19, 21, 29, 38], by using statistics derived from terms and queries it is possible to estimate the query processing time. However, since we must deal with ephemeral posting lists, most of the statistics used in prior research are not applicable. For example, the mean scores of postings (used in [29]) cannot be precomputed for an ephemeral posting list, since the postings and their statistics for all possible n-grams cannot feasibly be computed offline. Hence, we must resort to "estimators" of the quantities of interest, in particular for the total number to be processed, i.e., the simple and ephemeral posting list lengths, and the corresponding term upper bounds.

To provide an upper bound approximation to the number of postings in an ephemeral posting list, consider a generic complex term #op(t_1, t_2), where t_1 and t_2 can be simple or (nested) complex terms. If #op corresponds to an OR-based posting list such as #syn, then the size of its posting list cannot be greater than the sum of the document frequencies of its constituent terms. If #op corresponds to an AND-based posting list, then the total size of its postings list cannot be greater than the minimum of the document frequencies of its constituent terms, i.e., the smallest constituent posting list.

For term scores upper bound approximations, we leverage the MaxTF framework, adapted to complex operators, as summarised in Eq. (6). Upper bound approximations are scaled according to the term-specific weight resulting from query rewriting (see Table 1).

We adopt a machine-learned approach to predict the processing times of complex queries, i.e., $\widehat{t}(\langle q_i', K_j \rangle)$, for different values of K. As we use the WAND dynamic pruning strategy (as justified in Section 2), the response times heavily depend on the K number of documents to be retrieved. Hence, we train a different model for each value of K, but all models share the same set of statistics. All previous works on query processing time prediction use of query statistics and aggregations (max, min, mean etc.) of term-based

Table 3: Prediction statistics, projectors and aggregators.

	Statistics
1.	Number of terms (query-based)
2.	Document frequency (term-based)
3.	Score upper bound (term-based)
	Projectors
1.	Global
2.	Original-only terms
3.	#syn-only terms
4.	#1-only terms
5-...	#uwλ-only terms, one per different λ
	Aggregators
1–2.	Minimum, Maximum
3–5.	Arithmetic, Harmonic, Geometric Means

statistics across the query terms, as reported in Table 3. However, different complex operators acting on the same set of terms can have very different impacts on the running time of a query. Hence, we propose an additional, intermediate step between statistics generation and aggregation, namely *projection*. In this step, all query- and term-based statistics are divided into subsets, whose elements are grouped depending on the nature of the term. Thus we have several statistics projections, one for every complex operator, one for simple terms and one considering all terms globally. Term-based aggregators are then applied to these subsets of statistics. Note that, due to the different nature of AND- and OR-based posting lists, we do not consider the sum and variance operators, while we include the minimum operator, as suggested by [19]. In our experiments, we use #uw8 and #uw12 operators, hence we have 6 query-based features and 2×6×5 term-based features, for a total of 66 features. Section 7.1 provides the details and parameters of the learning algorithm using these feature to predict the processing times of complex queries.

6 EXPERIMENTAL SETUP

6.1 Research Questions

In the following, we experiment to address two research questions:

- RQ1: How accurate are our query efficiency predictions for queries with complex operators? (Section 7.1)
- RQ2: Can we maintain effectiveness while reducing response time when selectively rewriting queries? (Section 7.2)

In the remainder of this section, we define the experimental setup under which our experiments are conducted.

6.2 Datasets & Retrieval System

Our experiments address both efficiency and effectiveness, and hence require diverse setups to ensure accurate conclusions can be drawn for both types of measures. All of our experiments are conducted on the TREC ClueWeb09 category B corpus[4], which consists of 50M Web documents. For testing effectiveness, we use the 197 queries from the TREC Web tracks 2009-2012 that have corresponding relevance assessments on a 4-point scale [9], and denote this as WT. For testing efficiency, we follow best practices in

[4] http://lemurproject.org/clueweb09/

sampling a significant number of queries from a real search engine, namely 1,956 successive queries from the MSN 2006 query log[5] [11].

We index all 50M documents of the ClueWeb09 corpus using the Terrier IR platform [32], including also the anchor text of incoming hyperlinks to each document. Position information is recorded for each term. Our index is compressed using Elias-Fano encoding provided in [40], widely considered to be the state-of-the-art in terms of fast decompression.

For retrieval, we conduct efficiency timings using a machine equipped with an AMD Opteron Processor 6276 with 6 MB L3 cache and 128 GB RAM. The entire index is loaded in memory. All experiments are performed on a single core. While the resulting retrieval times using a single machine for retrieval are marginally higher than would be expected for interactive retrieval in a deployed Web search engine, following previous work [41], this does not detract from the generality of the findings, and avoids the complexities of performing experiments in a distributed retrieval environment.

Finally, in our timing experiments, we do not include the time to rewrite the query, calculate efficiency predictions, nor to apply the learned model. Each of these stages is comparatively cheap: for instance, the rewriting approaches discussed below are commonly deployed in search engines; query efficiency predictions can be calculated quickly using only term statistics from the lexicon [19, 29]; and the application of a learned model is also relatively less expensive than the top-K retrieval [38].

6.3 Query Plans

Besides the None strategy, where the original queries are not rewritten, we deploy the following rewriting approaches:

MRF. To encapsulate proximity in rewriting a query, we deploy sequential dependence [30] proximity, by considering #1, #uw8 and #uw12 query operators for adjacent query terms.

Naïve. To address word mismatch, we rewrite the query by adding alternatives to query terms within a #syn query operator[6]. Inspired by Peng et al. [34], who noted corpus analysis as being a suitable method to determine similar words (based on which words they co-occur with). We select alternative terms for a given term t that each have the same stem as t based on Porter's stemmer, and which are among the M most similar terms to t within a word embedding space. We use Deeplearning4j's word2vec tool and word embeddings vectors trained on Wikipedia and the Gigaword corpus[7] and select words with common stems in the top $M = 20$ for each query term t. This results in a less aggressive stemming than either index-time stemming or the equivalent query-side stemming using all alternatives identified by a Porter stemmer.

NaïveMRF. Finally, we mix Naïve and MRF rewritings to create a final strategy of generating time-expensive query plans.

Table 4 reports the statistics of each query set, incl. the number of simple and complex terms generated by each rewriting approach. Finally, with regards to the value of K, i.e., the number of documents retrieved by WAND during the top K retrieval, we select 4 values, namely 20, 100, 1000 and 5000. This gives us a total of 16 query plans to be plugged into our selective mechanism, and for which we need to train and test our efficiency predictors.

[5] From a sample of 2000 queries, 44 queries had no matching terms in our collection, so were removed. [6] Initial experiments using the context-sensitive approach of [34] showed no effectiveness benefit over this simpler Naïve stemming. [7] Available from http://nlp.stanford.edu/projects/glove/

Table 4: Query sets statistics per rewriting.

Dataset	Queries	Rewriting	simple	#syn	#1	#uw8	#uw12
Train	978	NaïveMRF	1458	1125	1133	1133	0
		MRF	2556	0	1578	1578	781
		Naïve	1458	1125	0	0	0
		None	2556	0	0	0	0
Test	978	NaïveMRF	1452	1028	1185	1185	0
		MRF	2468	0	1491	1491	768
		Naïve	1452	1028	0	0	0
		None	2468	0	0	0	0
WT	197	NaïveMRF	121	126	113	113	0
		MRF	244	0	146	146	82
		Naïve	121	126	0	0	0
		None	244	0	0	0	0

Table 5: Query-dependent (QD) & -independent (QI) ranking features within our experiments.

QD	DLH13, Coordinate Level	2
QD	pBiL (term dependence)	2
QI	Inlinks, Outlinks, PageRank	3
QI	URL features	6
QI	Content quality [3]	4
QI	Spam score	1
Total		18

6.4 Ranking features

As mentioned in Section 5, in the top K retrieval phase, we use the DLH13 term weighting model [1] from the Divergence from Randomness framework for weighting simple and #syn terms; For #1 and #uwλ terms, we use the DFR pBiL model [35]. Next, Table 5 lists the 18 features used for re-ranking the top K results during the application of the learned model. Note, that regardless of whether term dependency complex operators are deployed as a rewritten query, we include the score for the term dependency operators in the feature set. This allows the learner to consider the term dependence features separately from the score used in the initial ranking phase.

For learning and ranking, we use the Jforests implementation[8] of LambdaMART [8], a gradient-boosted decision tree learning-to-rank technique. Effectiveness experiments on the 197 TREC Web track queries (denoted WT in Table 4) use a 5-fold cross validation, where each fold has 60% training, 20% validation and 20% test queries. We report NDCG@20.

7 RESULTS

In the following, we report the results and analysis addressing our two research questions concerning the accuracy of our efficiency predictions for queries with complex operators (Section 7.1), and the application of the selective rewriting mechanism based upon those efficiency predictions (Section 7.2).

[8] https://github.com/yasserg/jforests/

Table 6: Pearson correlation on the test query set, per rewriting and K value, of the baseline (Base) and the proposed predictors (Pred). Statistically significant improvements over the baseline are denoted in bold.

Rewriting	K							
	20		100		1000		5000	
	Base	Pred	Base	Pred	Base	Pred	Base	Pred
NaïveMRF	0.639	**0.833**	0.722	**0.840**	0.827	**0.881**	0.861	0.868
MRF	0.612	**0.803**	0.697	**0.813**	0.788	**0.870**	0.790	**0.884**
Naïve	0.620	**0.848**	0.735	**0.878**	0.828	**0.915**	0.886	**0.935**
None	0.548	**0.738**	0.691	**0.842**	0.802	**0.907**	0.884	**0.952**

7.1 RQ1: Efficiency Prediction

We use the 66 efficiency prediction features derived from statistics, projectors and aggregators summarised in Table 3 to train a machine-learned model on the 978 training queries (see Table 4), for every combination of rewriting and K value. The regression algorithm employed is gradient boosted regression trees, as provided by the `scikit-learn` toolbox. Denoting the 978 train queries as Q^{tr}, we perform a 5-fold cross validation to train each $\langle Q_i^{tr}, K_j\rangle$ model. Each model was trained with 20 trees, learning rate of 0.1, max depth of 5, and the least square loss function. To evaluate the accuracy of each model, we then used the 978 test queries Q^{te} to compute the Pearson correlation, reported in Table 6. We compare each of our models (denoted Pred) with a linear regressor trained using the sum of number of postings per each simple term in the original terms and complex operators (Base). Our models perform very well, with correlations always higher than 0.8, and almost always significantly improving over the Base baseline predictor (according to a Fisher Z-transform, $p < 0.05$). To further assess the quality of our predictors, in Table 7, we compare the mean actual query times and the mean predicted query times for each model. Our models incur a mean prediction error no greater than 13%, even if they tend to underestimate the actual processing time, in particular for the models using the original queries (None).

Moreover, since we use the trained model to compare the predicted execution times of query plans versus a given time τ, in Table 8 we report the precision/recall measures of our models when classifying queries with a predicted execution time greater than 0.750 seconds. As can be observed from the table, the recall of our models is close or above 0.9 for NaïveMRF, MRF and Naïve rewritings. The smaller recall value for None is not problematic, since very few queries exhibit an execution time greater than 0.750 seconds.

Finally, we use the feature importance metric within gradient boosted trees to assess the contribution of the 66 prediction features. To combine the feature importances across various models, for each model we rank features by decreasing importance, and measure mean reciprocal ranks (Mean RR) across models. Table 9 shows the top features across all trained models (reported features attained Mean RR greater than 0.1). All proposed statistics and aggregators appear in the top features, with the exception of geometric mean (which appears, but it is not reported, as next in the list). Notably, also the minimum document frequency across all terms is in the list, validating the assumption that the minimum aggregator is useful when processing AND-based posting lists. Moreover, all projectors appear in the top features list, with the notable exception of #uw12. We explain this by observing that, according to Table 4, the corresponding complex operator occurs infrequently in the processed queries compared with the frequency of other complex operators.

Hence, in addressing RQ1, we have experimentally evaluated the accuracy of our predictions at estimating the execution times of rewritten queries processed using WAND for different K. Overall, with correlations > 0.8 for all tested rewritings and values of K, we conclude that our efficiency predictions are indeed accurate.

Table 7: Average actual and predicted query processing times on the test query set (in ms), per rewriting and K value, with relative errors (in %).

Rewriting	K			
	20	100	1000	5000
	Actual times			
NaïveMRF	2718	3272	4244	5090
MRF	1438	1757	2618	3310
Naïve	992	1373	1893	2381
None	374	551	802	1042
	Predicted times			
NaïveMRF	2618 (−3.65)	3087 (−5.63)	4109 (−3.18)	4608 (−9.46)
MRF	1511 (5.12)	1762 (0.29)	2655 (1.44)	3101 (−6.31)
Naïve	953 (−3.92)	1261 (−8.16)	1866 (−1.42)	2339 (−1.78)
None	369 (−1.19)	485 (−12.13)	829 (−3.38)	1029 (−1.29)

Table 8: Precision/Recall accuracy to classify queries taking more than 750 milliseconds to process.

Rewriting	K							
	20		100		1000		5000	
	P	R	P	R	P	R	P	R
NaïveMRF	0.752	0.978	0.790	0.991	0.767	1.000	0.828	1.000
MRF	0.831	0.936	0.843	0.984	0.819	0.996	0.858	1.000
Naïve	0.769	0.908	0.813	0.935	0.843	0.979	0.867	0.998
None	0.800	0.520	0.839	0.719	0.836	0.881	0.783	0.963

Table 9: Top features ranked by the mean reciprocal rank of importance across all trained models.

Aggregator	Feature	Projector	Mean RR
Arithmetic mean	Document frequency	global	0.404
Maximum	Document frequency	#syn	0.350
Arithmetic mean	Score upper bound	global	0.306
Maximum	Document frequency	original	0.257
Maximum	Document frequency	#uw8	0.243
Maximum	Document frequency	global	0.215
Harmonic mean	Document frequency	global	0.185
–	Number of terms	global	0.171
Maximum	Document frequency	#1	0.152
Arithmetic mean	Document frequency	original	0.129
Minimum	Document frequency	global	0.109

7.2 RQ2: Selective Rewriting

In this section, we experiment to determine the levels of efficiency and effectiveness obtainable when using the selective mechanism proposed in Section 4, and using the predictors for complex operators evaluated in the preceding section. In terms of setup, our selective mechanism ranks the query plans by measuring μ = NDCG based on the validation set for each fold of the WT queries.

We consider the uniform application of ⟨None, K = 5000⟩ to all queries as the baseline that we compare to in terms of effectiveness. In particular, the use of K = 5000 for retrieving on ClueWeb09 has been used by various previous work on the same test collection [10, 28] and empirically verified in [27]. We denote the uniform application of this query plan as "Default". In our experiments, we aim to be more efficient than Default, while not experiencing a significant decrease in effectiveness. In addition to Default, we also report the efficiency and effectiveness of the uniform application of the Fastest, Slowest and Most Effective plans.

Table 10 provides the main findings of the efficiency and effectiveness of the uniform query plans. Note that, as discussed in Section 6, we use different query sets for measuring efficiency and effectiveness; in particular, we report mean and 95th percentile (or "tail") response times in milliseconds (MRT & TRT, respectively) on the 978 test queries from the MSN 2006 query log; for effectiveness, we report NDCG@20 for the 197 TREC Web track queries. The first group of rows reports efficiency and effectiveness for the Uniform plans, while the lower group reports the results for the Selection mechanism as threshold τ is varied. Finally, for each row, Rw denotes the percentage of queries rewritten from None.

On inspection of the uniform plan in the top half of Table 10, we note that the MRF and NaïveMRF uniform plans result in very high response times (up to 4.86 *times* slower than Default). In terms of effectiveness, deploying MRF to increase the recall in the sample results in a marked (but not statistically significant) increase in NDCG effectiveness of the system (0.1877→0.2001), however, this comes at the cost of retrieval that is 3.2 times slower than Default.

Next, we consider the selective mechanism in the bottom half of Table 10. As expected, as τ is varied we note changes in both effectiveness and efficiency. In particular, for τ = 500, we find that a mean response time of 537 ms can be achieved (49% decrease in mean response time, and 62% decrease in tail response time, compared to Default), without significantly degrading effectiveness (0.1877 → 0.1751). For this setting, 8-10% of queries are being rewritten. With higher levels of τ, we observe similar increases in effectiveness and observed response times, and with more queries being rewritten. Finally, we note that the selection mechanism does not strictly observe the τ threshold, as can be observed by the tail response times – this is expected, as the selection mechanism expressed in Equation (3) will default to the predicted fastest plan available (usually ⟨None, K = 20⟩) if no plans can be executed within τ.

To provide a graphical illustration of the efficiency/effectiveness tradeoff, Figure 2 presents mean response times and mean NDCG. Lines are provided for both our selective mechanism, Full, denoted by a solid line, as well as the same selective mechanism where the candidate plans are restricted only to those involving None (i.e., with K = {20, 100, 1000, 5000}), denoted None-only, and indicated by a dashed line. For most thresholds, the Full selective mechanism can be observed to offer the best tradeoff, with points closer to the upper left hand corner. For low mean response times (e.g., < 400 ms), the None-only line rises above Full, as only None plans can be deployed to achieve such low response times. On the other hand, for larger mean response times (e.g., > 650 ms), the Full line is more effective; this supports a central tenet of our work, i.e., when time allows, appropriate rewriting of queries results in increased effectiveness. Moreover, as indicated by the ▿ points of the None-only

Table 10: Efficiency/effectiveness results using the selective mechanism. * denotes NDCG values that significantly differ from that of ⟨None, K = 5000⟩ (paired t-test, $p < 0.05$). TRT denotes the tail response time (95%-th percentile), Rw denotes the % of queries rewritten from None. Times are in ms.

Strategy	Efficiency (Test)			Effectiveness (WT)	
	MRT	TRT	Rw	NDCG@20	Rw
Uniform Plans					
Default (⟨None, K = 5000⟩)	1037	5281	0	0.1877	0
Fastest (⟨None, K = 20⟩)	376	1779	0	0.1375*	0
Slowest (⟨NaïveMRF, K = 5000⟩)	5045	17994	100	0.1755	100
Most Effective (⟨MRF, K = 5000⟩)	3281	12099	100	0.2001	100
Selective Mechanism					
τ = 200	449	1986	1	0.1642*	0
τ = 300	472	1986	1	0.1670*	1
τ = 400	495	1986	4	0.1711*	6
τ = 500	537	2004	8	0.1751	10
τ = 600	577	2023	13	0.1762	14
τ = 700	606	2060	19	0.1782	18
τ = 750	617	2060	21	0.1779	19
τ = 800	639	2128	22	0.1807	19
τ = 900	691	2226	27	0.1825	21
τ = 1000	733	2256	30	0.1828	21

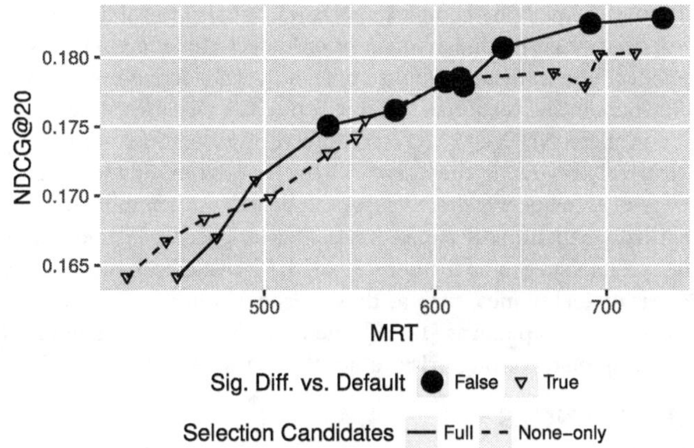

Figure 2: Efficiency/effectiveness tradeoff. The best tradeoff occurs for points closest to the upper left corner. Points denoted with ▿ are significantly less effective than ⟨None, K = 5000⟩ (paired t-test, $p < 0.05$).

line in Figure 2, to achieve the response times savings without selectively rewriting the query, we would be forced to accept significant degradations in effectiveness compared to the Default baseline.

Finally, to give a flavour of the impact of our selective mechanism, we inspect the queries rewritten for $\tau = 500$ and select the query 'disneyland hotel'. This query was rewritten to use the plan ⟨MRF, $K = 100$⟩ (as per the proximity example in Table 1), which had a predicted execution time of 486 ms, due to the relatively informative term disneyland (which only appears in $N_t = 78422$ documents). Hence, the more effective MRF rewrite was applied, which resulted in a 14% increase in NDCG@20 compared the Default plan (which had a predicted execution time of 542 ms).

Overall, in addressing RQ2 we have determined that our selective mechanism can achieve a 49% decrease in mean response time, and 62% decrease in tail (95th-percentile) response time without significant degradations in effectiveness.

8 CONCLUSIONS

This work has considered the selective rewriting of web search queries, with the aim of attaining efficient retrieval without hindering the system's effectiveness. In particular, we showed that it is possible to accurately measure the response time of a search engine in answering a query with complex operators such as #syn and #1, even when using the WAND dynamic pruning strategy. Our detailed experimental setup involved experiments upon the open TREC ClueWeb09 dataset, using TREC Web track queries for measuring effectiveness in terms of NDCG@20, and real search engine user queries for measuring efficiency. Moreover, we deployed three strategies to rewrite each query. Our experiments showed not only the accuracy of the newly proposed query efficiency predictions for queries involving complex operators, but also the ability of our proposed selective mechanism to enhance efficiency benefits (a 49% decrease in mean response time, and 62% decrease in tail, i.e., 95th-percentile, response time) without any significant degradation in mean NDCG@20. Overall, our results demonstrate that by selectively rewriting the query (when there is the time to execute the rewritten query), effectiveness can be at least maintained while markedly benefiting response times. Our proposed selective rewriting mechanism can be further extended, for instance to more query rewriting techniques, such as those based on query reformulation and query-click patterns [12, 20], and modelling the effectiveness of rewriting plans through risk rather than mean effectiveness alone.

REFERENCES

[1] Gianni Amati. 2006. Frequentist and Bayesian Approach to IR. In *ECIR*. 13–24.
[2] Vo Ngoc Anh, Owen de Kretser, and Alistair Moffat. 2001. Vector-space ranking with effective early termination. In *SIGIR*. 35–42.
[3] Michael Bendersky, W. Bruce Croft, and Yanlei Diao. 2011. Quality-biased ranking of web documents. In *WSDM*. 95–104.
[4] Michael Bendersky, Donald Metzler, and W. Bruce Croft. 2010. Learning Concept Importance Using a Weighted Dependence Model. In *WSDM*. 31–40.
[5] Daniele Broccolo, Craig Macdonald, Salvatore Orlando, Iadh Ounis, Raffaele Perego, Fabrizio Silvestri, and Nicola Tonellotto. 2013. Load-sensitive Selective Pruning for Distributed Search. In *CIKM*. 379–388.
[6] Andrei Z. Broder, David Carmel, Michael Herscovici, Aya Soffer, and Jason Y. Zien. 2003. Efficient query evaluation using a two-level retrieval process. In *CIKM*. 426–434.
[7] Chris Buckley, Gerard Salton, James Allan, and Amit Singhal. 1995. Automatic query expansion using SMART: TREC 3. In *TREC 3*. 69–80.
[8] Christopher J.C. Burges. 2010. *From RankNet to LambdaRank to LambdaMART: An Overview*. Technical Report MSR-TR-2010-82.
[9] Charles L. A. Clarke, Nick Craswell, and Ellen M. Voorhees. 2012. Overview of the TREC 2012 Web Track. In *TREC*.
[10] Nick Craswell, Dennis Fetterly, Marc Najork, Stephen Robertson, and Emine Yilmaz. 2010. Microsoft Research at TREC 2009. In *TREC*.
[11] Nick Craswell, Rosie Jones, Georges Dupret, and Evelyne Viegas (Eds.). 2009. *Proceedings of the Web Search Click Data Workshop at WSDM 2009*.
[12] Nick Craswell and Martin Szummer. 2007. Random walks on the click graph. In *SIGIR*. 239–246.
[13] W. Bruce Croft, Donald Metzler, and Trevor Strohman. 2009. *Search Engines: Information Retrieval in Practice*. Addison-Wesley Publishing Company.
[14] J. Shane Culpepper, Charles L. A. Clarke, and Jimmy Lin. 2016. Dynamic Cutoff Prediction in Multi-Stage Retrieval Systems. In *ADCS*. 17–24.
[15] Jeffrey Dean. 2009. Challenges in building large-scale information retrieval systems: invited talk. In *WSDM*.
[16] Jeffrey Dean and Luiz Andr Barroso. 2013. The Tail at Scale. *Commun. ACM* 56 (2013), 74–80.
[17] Shuai Ding and Torsten Suel. 2011. Faster top-k document retrieval using block-max indexes. In *SIGIR*. 993–1002.
[18] Marcus Fontoura, Vanja Josifovski, Jinhui Liu, Srihari Venkatesan, Xiangfei Zhu, and Jason Y. Zien. 2011. Evaluation Strategies for Top-k Queries over Memory-Resident Inverted Indexes. *PVLDB* 4, 12 (2011), 1213–1224.
[19] Myeongjae Jeon, Saehoon Kim, Seung-won Hwang, Yuxiong He, Sameh Elnikety, Alan L. Cox, and Scott Rixner. 2014. Predictive Parallelization: Taming Tail Latencies in Web Search. In *SIGIR*. 253–262.
[20] Rosie Jones, Benjamin Rey, Omid Madani, and Wiley Greiner. 2006. Generating Query Substitutions. In *WWW*. 387–396.
[21] Saehoon Kim, Yuxiong He, Seung-won Hwang, Sameh Elnikety, and Seungjin Choi. 2015. Delayed-Dynamic-Selective (DDS) Prediction for Reducing Extreme Tail Latency in Web Search. In *WSDM*. 7–16.
[22] Nicholas Lester, Alistair Moffat, William Webber, and Justin Zobel. 2005. Space-Limited Ranked Query Evaluation Using Adaptive Pruning. In *WISE*. 470–477.
[23] Jimmy Lin, Matt Crane, Andrew Trotman, Jamie Callan, Ishan Chattopadhyaya, John Foley, Grant Ingersoll, Craig Macdonald, and Sebastiano Vigna. 2016. Toward Reproducible Baselines: The Open-Source IR Reproducibility Challenge. In *ECIR*. 408–420.
[24] Xiaolu Lu, Alistair Moffat, and J. Shane Culpepper. 2015. On the Cost of Extracting Proximity Features for Term-Dependency Models. In *CIKM*. 293–302.
[25] Claudio Lucchese, Franco Maria Nardini, Salvatore Orlando, Raffaele Perego, Nicola Tonellotto, and Rossano Venturini. 2015. QuickScorer: A Fast Algorithm to Rank Documents with Additive Ensembles of Regression Trees. In *SIGIR*. 73–82.
[26] Craig Macdonald, Iadh Ounis, and Nicola Tonellotto. 2011. Upper-bound Approximations for Dynamic Pruning. *ACM Trans. Inf. Syst.* 29, 4 (2011), 17:1–17:28.
[27] Craig Macdonald, Rodrygo LT Santos, and Iadh Ounis. 2013. The whens and hows of learning to rank for web search. *Information Retrieval* 16, 5 (2013), 584–628.
[28] Craig Macdonald, Rodrygo L.T. Santos, Iadh Ounis, and Ben He. 2013. About Learning Models with Multiple Query-dependent Features . *ACM Trans. Inf. Syst.* 31, 3 (2013), 11:1–11:39.
[29] Craig Macdonald, Nicola Tonellotto, and Iadh Ounis. 2012. Learning to predict response times for online query scheduling. In *SIGIR*. 621–630.
[30] Donald Metzler and W. Bruce Croft. 2005. A Markov Random Field Model for Term Dependencies. In *SIGIR*. 472–479.
[31] Giuseppe Ottaviano, Nicola Tonellotto, and Rossano Venturini. 2015. Optimal Space-time Tradeoffs for Inverted Indexes. In *WSDM*. 47–56.
[32] Iadh Ounis, Gianni Amati, Vassilis Plachouras, Ben He, Craig Macdonald, and Christina Lioma. 2006. Terrier: A High Performance & Scalable IR Platform. In *OSIR*.
[33] Jan Pederson. 2010. Query Understanding at Bing. In *Invited Talk, SIGIR 2010 Industry Day*.
[34] Fuchun Peng, Nawaaz Ahmed, Xin Li, and Yumao Lu. 2007. Context Sensitive Stemming for Web Search. In *SIGIR*. 639–646.
[35] Jie Peng, Craig Macdonald, Ben He, Vassilis Plachouras, and Iadh Ounis. 2007. Incorporating Term Dependency in the DFR Framework. In *SIGIR*. 843–844.
[36] Eric Shurman and Jake Brutlag. 2009. Performance related changes and their user impacts. In *Velocity: Web Performance and Operations Conference*.
[37] Trevor Strohman, Howard Turtle, and W. Bruce Croft. 2005. Optimization Strategies for Complex Queries. In *SIGIR*. 219–225.
[38] Nicola Tonellotto, Craig Macdonald, and Iadh Ounis. 2013. Efficient and Effective Retrieval Using Selective Pruning. In *WSDM*. 63–72.
[39] Howard Turtle and James Flood. 1995. Query evaluation: Strategies and optimizations. *Information Processing & Management* 31, 6 (1995), 831 – 850.
[40] Sebastiano Vigna. 2013. Quasi-succinct indices. In *WSDM*. 83–92.
[41] Lidan Wang, Jimmy Lin, and Donald Metzler. 2010. Learning to Efficiently Rank. In *SIGIR*. 138–145.
[42] Jinxi Xu and W. Bruce Croft. 1996. Query Expansion Using Local and Global Document Analysis. In *SIGIR*. 4–11.

Relevance-based Word Embedding

Hamed Zamani
Center for Intelligent Information Retrieval
College of Information and Computer Sciences
University of Massachusetts Amherst
Amherst, MA 01003
zamani@cs.umass.edu

W. Bruce Croft
Center for Intelligent Information Retrieval
College of Information and Computer Sciences
University of Massachusetts Amherst
Amherst, MA 01003
croft@cs.umass.edu

ABSTRACT

Learning a high-dimensional dense representation for vocabulary terms, also known as a word embedding, has recently attracted much attention in natural language processing and information retrieval tasks. The embedding vectors are typically learned based on term proximity in a large corpus. This means that the objective in well-known word embedding algorithms, e.g., word2vec, is to accurately predict adjacent word(s) for a given word or context. However, this objective is not necessarily equivalent to the goal of many information retrieval (IR) tasks. The primary objective in various IR tasks is to capture *relevance* instead of term proximity, syntactic, or even semantic similarity. This is the motivation for developing unsupervised relevance-based word embedding models that learn word representations based on query-document relevance information. In this paper, we propose two learning models with different objective functions; one learns a relevance distribution over the vocabulary set for each query, and the other classifies each term as belonging to the relevant or non-relevant class for each query. To train our models, we used over six million unique queries and the top ranked documents retrieved in response to each query, which are assumed to be relevant to the query. We extrinsically evaluate our learned word representation models using two IR tasks: query expansion and query classification. Both query expansion experiments on four TREC collections and query classification experiments on the KDD Cup 2005 dataset suggest that the relevance-based word embedding models significantly outperform state-of-the-art proximity-based embedding models, such as word2vec and GloVe.

KEYWORDS

Word representation, neural network, embedding vector, query expansion, query classification

ACM Reference format:
Hamed Zamani and W. Bruce Croft. 2017. Relevance-based Word Embedding. In *Proceedings of SIGIR '17, August 07-11, 2017, Shinjuku, Tokyo, Japan,* , 10 pages.
DOI: http://dx.doi.org/10.1145/3077136.3080831

SIGIR '17, August 07-11, 2017, Shinjuku, Tokyo, Japan
© 2017 ACM. 978-1-4503-5022-8/17/08...$15.00
DOI: http://dx.doi.org/10.1145/3077136.3080831

1 INTRODUCTION

Representation learning is a long-standing problem in natural language processing (NLP) and information retrieval (IR). The main motivation is to abstract away from the surface forms of a piece of text, e.g., words, sentences, and documents, in order to alleviate sparsity and learn meaningful similarities, e.g., semantic or syntactic similarities, between two different pieces of text. Learning representations for words as the atomic components of a language, also known as word embedding, has recently attracted much attention in the NLP and IR communities.

A popular model for learning word representation is neural network-based language models. For instance, the word2vec model proposed by Mikolov et al. [24] is an embedding model that learns word vectors via a neural network with a single hidden layer. Continuous bag of words (CBOW) and skip-gram are two implementations of the word2vec model. Another successful trend in learning semantic word representations is employing global matrix factorization over word-word matrices. GloVe [28] is an example of such methods. A theoretical relation has been discovered between embedding models based on neural network and matrix factorization in [21]. These models have been demonstrated to be effective in a number of IR tasks, including query expansion [11, 17, 40], query classification [23, 41], short text similarity [15], and document model estimation [2, 31].

The aforementioned embedding models are typically trained based on term proximity in a large corpus. For instance, the word2vec model's objective is to predict adjacent word(s) given a word or context, i.e., a context window around the target word. This idea aims to capture semantic and syntactic similarities between terms, since semantically/syntactically similar words often share similar contexts. However, this objective is not necessarily equivalent to the main objective of many IR tasks. The primary objective in many IR methods is to model the notion of *relevance* [20, 34, 43]. In this paper, we revisit the underlying assumption of typical word embedding methods, as follows:

The objective is to predict the words observed in the documents relevant to a particular information need.

This objective has been previously considered for developing relevance models [20], a state-of-the-art (pseudo-) relevance feedback approach. Relevance models try to optimize this objective given a set of relevant documents for a given query as the indicator of user's information need. In the absence of relevance information, the top ranked documents retrieved in response to the query are assumed to be relevant. Therefore, relevance models, and in general all pseudo-relevance feedback models, use an online setting to obtain training data: retrieving documents for the query and then using the top retrieved documents in order to estimate the relevance distribution. Although relevance models have been proved to be effective in many IR tasks [19, 20], having a retrieval run for each query to obtain the training data for estimating the relevance distribution is not always practical in real-world search engines. We, in this paper, optimize a similar objective in an offline setting, which enables us to predict the relevance distribution without any retrieval runs during the test time. To do so, we consider the top retrieved documents for millions of training queries as a training set and learn embedding vectors for each term in order to predict the words observed in the top retrieved documents for each query. We develop two relevance-based word embedding models. The first one, the relevance likelihood maximization model (RLM), aims to model the relevance distribution over the vocabulary terms for each query, while the second one, the relevance posterior estimation model (RPE), classifies each term as relevant or non-relevant to each query. We provide efficient learning algorithms to train these models on large amounts of training data. Note that our models are unsupervised and the training data is generated automatically.

To evaluate our models, we performed two sets of extrinsic evaluations. In the first set, we focus on the query expansion task for ad-hoc retrieval. In this set of experiments, we consider four TREC collections, including two newswire collections (AP and Robust) and two large-scale web collections (GOV2 and ClueWeb09 - Cat. B). Our results suggest that the relevance-based embedding models outperform state-of-the-art word embedding algorithms. The RLM model shows better performance compared to RPE in the context of query expansion, since the goal is to estimate the probability of each term given a query and this distribution is not directly learned by the RPE model. In the second set of experiments, we focus on the query classification task using the KDD Cup 2005 [22] dataset. In this extrinsic evaluation, the relevance-based embedding models again perform better than the baselines. Interestingly, the query classification results demonstrate that the RPE model outperforms the RLM model, for the reason that in this task, unlike the query expansion task, the goal is to compute the similarity between two query vectors, and RPE can learn more accurate embedding vectors with less training data.

2 RELATED WORK

Learning a semantic representation for text has been studied for many years. Latent semantic indexing (LSI) [8] can be considered as early work in this area that tries to map each text to a semantic space using singular value decomposition (SVD), a well-known matrix factorization algorithm. Subsequently, Clinchant and Perronnin [5] proposed Fisher Vector (FV), a document representation framework based on continuous word embeddings, which aggregates a non-linear mapping of word vectors into a document-level representation. However, a number of popular IR models, such as BM25 and language models, often significantly outperform the models that are based on semantic similarities. Recently, extremely efficient word embedding algorithms have been proposed to model semantic similarly between words.

Word embedding, also known as distributed representation of words, refers to a set of machine learning algorithms that learn high-dimensional real-valued dense vector representation $\vec{w} \in \mathbb{R}^d$ for each vocabulary term w, where d denotes the embedding dimensionality. GloVe [28] and word2vec [24] are two well-known word embedding algorithms that learn embedding vectors based on the same idea, but using different machine learning techniques. The idea is that the words that often appear in similar contexts are similar to each other. To do so, these algorithms try to accurately predict the adjacent word(s) given a word or a context (i.e., a few words appeared in the same context window). Recently, Rekabsaz et al. [30] proposed to exploit global context in word embeddings in order to avoid topic shifting.

Word embedding representations can be also learned as a set of parameters in an end-to-end neural network model. For instance, Zamani et al. [39] trained a context-aware ranking model in which the embedding vectors of frequent n-grams are learned using click data. More recently, Dehghani et al. [9] trained neural ranking models with weak supervision data (i.e., a set of noisy training data automatically generated by an existing unsupervised model) that learn word representations in an end-to-end ranking scenario.

Word embedding vectors have been successfully employed in several NLP and IR tasks. Kusner et al. [16] proposed word mover's distance (WMD), a function for calculating semantic distance between two documents, which measures the minimum traveling distance from the embedded vectors of individual words in one document to the other one. Zhou et al. [47] introduced an embedding-based method for question retrieval in the context of community question answering. Vulić and Moens [37] proposed a model to learn bilingual word embedding vectors from document-aligned comparable corpora. Zheng and Callan [46] presented a supervised embedding-based technique to re-weight terms in the existing IR models, e.g., BM25. Based on the well-defined structure of language modeling framework in information retrieval, a number of methods have been introduced to employ word embedding vectors within this framework in order to improve the performance in IR tasks. For instance, Zamani and Croft [40] presented a set of embedding-based query language models using the query expansion and pseudo-relevance feedback techniques that benefit from the word embedding vectors. Query expansion using word embedding has been also studied in [11, 17, 35]. All of these approaches are based on word embeddings learned based on term proximity information. PhraseFinder [14] is an early work using term proximity information for query expansion. Mapping vocabulary terms to HAL space, a low-dimensional space compared to vocabulary size, has been used in [4] for query modeling.

As is widely known in the information retrieval literature [11, 38], there is a big difference between the unigram distribution of words on sub-topics of a collection and the unigram distribution estimated from the whole collection. Given this phenomenon, Diaz et al. [11] recently proposed to train word embedding vectors on the top retrieved documents for each query. However, this model, called local embedding, is not always practical in real-word applications, since the embedding vectors need to be trained during the query time. Furthermore, the objective function in local embedding is based on term proximity in pseudo-relevant documents.

In this paper, we propose two models for learning word embedding vectors, that are specifically designed for information retrieval needs. All the aforementioned tasks in this section can potentially benefit from the vectors learned by the proposed models.

3 RELEVANCE-BASED EMBEDDING

Typical word embedding algorithms, such as word2vec [24] and GloVe [28], learn high-dimensional real-valued embedding vectors based on the proximity of terms in a training corpus, i.e., co-occurrence of terms in the same context window. Although these approaches could be useful for learning the embedding vectors that can capture semantic and syntactic similarities between vocabulary terms and have shown to be useful in many NLP and IR tasks, there is a large gap between their learning objective (i.e., term proximity) and what is needed in many information retrieval tasks. For example, consider the query expansion task and assume that a user submitted the query "dangerous vehicles". One of the most similar terms to this query based on the typical word embedding algorithms (e.g., word2vec and GloVe) is "safe", and thus it would get a high weight in the expanded query model. The reason is that the words "dangerous" and "safe" often share similar contexts. However, expanding the query with the word "safe" could lead to poor retrieval performance, since it changes the meaning and the intent of the query.

This example together with many others have motivated us to revisit the objective used in the learning process of word embedding algorithms in order to obtain the word vectors that better match with the needs in IR tasks. The primary objective in many IR tasks is to model the notion of *relevance*. Several approaches, such as the relevance models proposed by Lavrenko and Croft [20], have been proposed to model relevance. Given the successes achieved by these models, we propose to learn word embedding vectors based on an objective that matters in information retrieval. The objective is to accurately predict the terms that are observed in a set of relevant documents to a particular information need.

In the following subsections, we first describe our neural network architecture, and then explain how to build a training set for learning relevance-based word embeddings. We further introduce two models, relevance likelihood maximization (RLM) and relevance posterior estimation (RPE), with different objectives using the described neural network.

3.1 Neural Network Architecture

We use a simple yet effective feed-forward neural network with a single linear hidden layer. The architecture of our neural network is shown in Figure 1. The input of the model is a sparse query vector $\vec{q}_s$ with the length of N, where N denotes the total number of vocabulary terms. This vector can be obtained by a projection function given the vectors corresponding to individual query terms. In this paper, we simply consider average as the projection function. Hence, $\vec{q}_s = \frac{1}{|q|} \sum_{w \in q} \vec{e}_w$, where $\vec{e}_w$ and $|q|$ denote the one-hot vector representation of term w and the query length, respectively. The hidden layer in this network maps the given query sparse vector to a query embedding vector $\vec{q}$, as follows:

$$\vec{q} = \vec{q}_s \times \mathcal{W}_Q \tag{1}$$

where $\mathcal{W}_Q \in \mathbb{R}^{N \times d}$ is a weight matrix for estimating query embedding vectors and d denotes the embedding dimensionality. The output layer of the network is a fully-connected layer given by:

$$\sigma(\vec{q} \times \mathcal{W}_w + b_w) \tag{2}$$

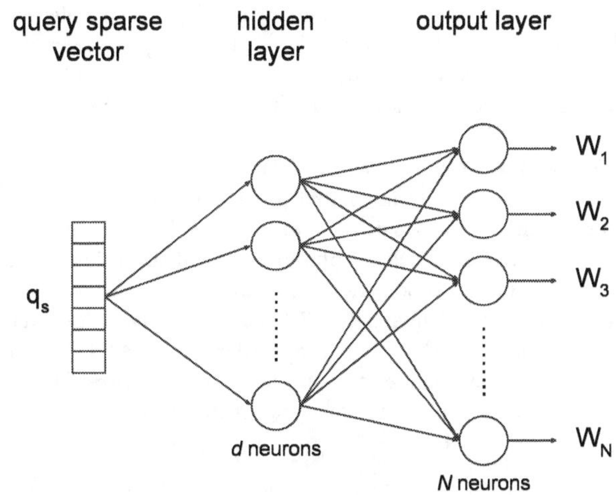

Figure 1: The relevance-based word embedding architecture. The objective is to learn d-dimensional distributed representation for words based on the notion of relevance, instead of term proximity. N denotes the total number of vocabulary terms.

where $\mathcal{W}_w \in \mathbb{R}^{d \times N}$ and $b_w \in \mathbb{R}^{1 \times N}$ are the weight and the bias matrices for estimating the probability of each term. σ is the activation function which is discussed in Sections 3.3 and 3.4.

To summarize, our network contains two sets of embedding parameters, $\mathcal{W}_Q$ and $\mathcal{W}_w$. The former aims to map the query into the "query embedding space", while the latter is used to estimate the weights of individual terms.

3.2 Modeling Relevance for Training

Relevance feedback has been shown to be highly effective in improving retrieval performance [7, 32]. In relevance feedback, a set of relevant documents to a given query is considered for estimating accurate query models. Since explicit relevance signals for a given query are not always available, pseudo-relevance feedback (PRF) assumes that the top retrieved documents in response to the given query are relevant to the query and uses these documents in order to estimate better query models. The effectiveness of PRF in various retrieval scenarios indicates that useful information can be captured from the top retrieved documents [19, 20, 44]. In this paper, we make use of this well-known assumption to train our model. It should be noted that there is a significant difference between PRF and the proposed models: In PRF, the feedback model is estimated from the top retrieved documents of the given query in an online setting. In other words, PRF retrieves the documents for the initial query and then estimates the feedback model using the top retrieved documents. In this paper, we propose to train the model in an offline setting. Moving from the online to the offline setting would lead to substantial improvements in efficiency, because an extra retrieval run is not needed in the offline setting. To learn a model in an offline setting, we consider a fixed-length dense vector for each vocabulary term and estimate these vectors based on the information extracted from the top retrieved documents for large numbers of training queries. Note that our models are unsupervised. However, if explicit relevance data is available, such as click data, without loss of generality, both the explicit or implicit relevant documents can be considered for training our models. We leave studying the vectors learned based on supervised signals for future work.

To formally describe our training data, let $T = \{(q_1, \mathcal{R}_1), (q_2, \mathcal{R}_2), \cdots, (q_m, \mathcal{R}_m)\}$ be a training set with m training queries. The ith element of this set is a pair of query q_i and the corresponding pseudo-relevance feedback distribution. These distributions are estimated based on the top k retrieved documents (in our experiments, we set k to 10) for each query. The distributions can be estimated using any PRF model, such as those proposed in [20, 36, 42, 44]. In this paper, we only focus on the relevance model [20], a state-of-the-art PRF model, that estimates the relevance distribution as:

$$p(w|\mathcal{R}_i) \propto \sum_{d \in F_i} p(w|d) \prod_{w' \in q_i} p(w'|d) \tag{3}$$

where F_i denotes a set of top retrieved documents for query q_i. Note that the probability of terms that do not appear in the top retrieved documents is equal to zero.

3.3 Relevance Likelihood Maximization Model

In this model, the goal is to learn the relevance distribution $\mathcal{R}$. Given a set of training data, we aim to find a set of parameters $\theta_{\mathcal{R}}$ in order to maximize the likelihood of generating relevance model probabilities for the whole training set. The likelihood function is defined as follows:

$$\prod_{i=1}^{m} \prod_{w \in V_i} \widehat{p}(w|q_i; \theta_{\mathcal{R}})^{p(w|\mathcal{R}_i)} \tag{4}$$

where $\widehat{p}$ is the relevance distribution that can be obtained given the learning parameters $\theta_{\mathcal{R}}$ and $p(w|\mathcal{R}_i)$ denotes the relevance model distribution estimated for the ith query in the training set (see Section 3.2 for more detail). V_i denotes a subset of vocabulary terms that appeared in the top ranked documents retrieved for the query q_i. The reason for iterating over the terms that appeared in this set instead of the whole vocabulary set V is that the probability $p(w|\mathcal{R}_i)$ is equal to zero for all terms $w \in V - V_i$.

In this method, we model the probability distribution $\widehat{p}$ using the softmax function (i.e., the function σ in Equation (2)) as follows:[1]

$$\widehat{p}(w|q; \theta_{\mathcal{R}}) = \frac{\exp(\vec{w}^T \vec{q})}{\sum_{w' \in V} \exp(\vec{w'}^T \vec{q})} \tag{5}$$

where $\vec{w}$ denotes the learned embedding vector for term w and $\vec{q}$ is the query vector came from the output of the hidden layer in our network (see Section 3.1). According to the softmax modeling and the log-likelihood function, we have the following objective:

$$\arg\max_{\theta_{\mathcal{R}}} \sum_{i=1}^{m} \sum_{w \in V_i} p(w|\mathcal{R}_i) \left(\log \exp(\vec{w}^T \vec{q_i}) - \log \sum_{w' \in V} \exp(\vec{w'}^T \vec{q_i}) \right) \tag{6}$$

Computing this objective function and its derivatives would be computationally expensive (due to the presence of the normalization factor $\sum_{w' \in V} \exp(\vec{w'}^T \vec{q})$ in the objective function). Since all the word embedding vectors as well as the query vector are changed during the optimization process, we cannot simply omit the normalization term as is done in [41] for estimating query embedding vectors based on pre-trained word embedding vectors. To make the computations more tractable, we consider a hierarchical approximation of the softmax function, which was introduced by Morin and Bengio [26] in the context of neural network language models and then successfully employed by Mikolov et al. [24] in the word2vec model.

The hierarchical softmax approximation uses a binary tree structure to represent the vocabulary terms, where each leaf corresponds to a unique word. There exists a unique path from the root to each leaf, and this path is used for estimating the probability of the word representing by the leaf. Therefore, the complexity of calculating softmax probabilities goes down from $O(|V|)$ to $O(\log(|V|))$ which is the height of the tree. This leads to a huge improvement in computational complexity. We refer the reader to [25, 26] for the details of calculating the hierarchical softmax approximation.

3.4 Relevance Posterior Estimation Model

As an alternative to maximum likelihood estimation, we can estimate the relevance posterior probability. In the context of pseudo-relevance feedback, Zhai and Laffery [44] assumed that the language model of the top retrieved documents is estimated based on a mixture model. In other words, it is assumed that there are two language models for the feedback set: the relevance language model[2] and a background noisy language model. They used an expectation-maximization algorithm to estimate the relevance language model. In this model, we make use of this assumption in order to cast the problem of estimating the relevance distribution $\mathcal{R}$ as a classification task: *Given a pair of word w and query q, does w come from the relevance distribution of the query q?* Instead of $p(w|\mathcal{R})$, this model estimates $p(R = 1|w, q; \theta_{\mathcal{R}})$ where R is a Boolean variable and $R = 1$ means that the given term-query pair (w, q) comes from the relevance distribution $\mathcal{R}$. $\theta_{\mathcal{R}}$ is a set of parameters that is going to be learned during the training phase.

Therefore, the problem is cast as a binary classification task that can be modeled by logistic regression (which means the function σ in Equation (2) is the sigmoid function):

$$\widehat{p}(R = 1|\vec{w}, \vec{q}; \theta_{\mathcal{R}}) = \frac{1}{1 + e^{(-\vec{w}^T \vec{q})}} \tag{7}$$

where $\vec{w}$ is the relevance-based word embedding vector for term w. Similar to the previous model, $\vec{q}$ is the output of the hidden layer of the network, representing the query embedding vector.

In order to address this binary classification problem, we consider a cross-entropy loss function. In theory, for each training query, our model should learn to model relevance for the terms appearing in the corresponding pseudo-relevant set and non-relevance for all the other vocabulary terms, which could be impractical, due to the large number of vocabulary terms. Similar to [24], we propose to use the noise contrastive estimation (NCE) [12] which hypothesizes that we can achieve a good model by only differentiating the data from noise via a logistic regression model. The main concept in NCE is similar to those proposed in the divergence from randomness model [3] and the divergence minimization feedback model [44].

[1] For simplicity, we drop the bias term in these equations.

[2] The phrase "topical language model" was used in the original work [44]. We call it "relevance language model" to have consistent definitions in our both models.

Based on the NCE hypothesis, we define the following negative cross-entropy objective function for training our model:

$$\arg\max_{\theta_{\mathcal{R}}} \sum_{i=1}^{m} \left[\sum_{j=1}^{\eta^+} \mathbb{E}_{w_j \sim p(w|\mathcal{R}_i)} \left[\log \widehat{p}(R = 1|\vec{w_j}, \vec{q_i}; \theta_{\mathcal{R}}) \right] + \sum_{j=1}^{\eta^-} \mathbb{E}_{w_j \sim p_n(w)} \left[\log \widehat{p}(R = 0|\vec{w_j}, \vec{q_i}; \theta_{\mathcal{R}}) \right] \right] \quad (8)$$

where $p_n(w)$ denotes a noise distribution and $\eta = (\eta^+, \eta^-)$ is a pair of hyper-parameters to control the number of positive and negative instances per query, respectively. We can easily calculate $\widehat{p}(R = 0|\vec{w_j}, \vec{q_i}) = 1 - \widehat{p}(R = 1|\vec{w_j}, \vec{q_i})$. The noise distribution $p_n(w)$ can be estimated using a function of unigram distribution $U(w)$ in the whole training set. Similar to [24], we use $p_n(w) \propto U(w)^{3/4}$ which has been empirically shown to work effectively for negative sampling.

It is notable that although this model learns embedding vectors for both queries and words, it is not obvious how to calculate the probability of each term given a query; because Equation 7 only gives us a classification probability and we cannot simply use the Bayes rule here (since, not all probability components are known). This model can perform well when computing the similarity between two terms or two queries, but not a query and a term. However, we can use the model presented in [41] to estimate the query model using the word embedding vectors (not the ones learned for query vectors) and then calculate the similarity between a query and a term.

4 EXPERIMENTS

In this section, we first describe how we train the relevance-based word embedding models. We further extrinsically evaluate the learned embeddings using two IR tasks: query expansion and query classification. Note that the main aim here is to compare the proposed models with the existing word embedding algorithms, not with the state-of-the-art query expansion and query classification models.

4.1 Training

In order to train relevance-based word embeddings, we obtained millions of unique queries from the publicly available AOL query logs [27]. This dataset contains a sample of web search queries from real users submitted to the AOL search engine within a three-month period from March 1, 2006 to May 31, 2006. We only used query strings and no session and click information was obtained from this dataset. We filtered out the navigational queries containing URL substrings, i.e., "http", "www.", ".com", ".net", ".org", ".edu". All non-alphanumeric characters were removed from all queries. Applying all these constraints leads to over 6 millions unique queries as our training query set. To estimate the relevance model distributions in the training set, we considered top 10 retrieved documents in a target collection in response to each query using the Galago[3] implementation of the query likelihood retrieval model [29] with Dirichlet prior smoothing ($\mu = 1500$) [45].

We implemented and trained our models using TensorFlow[4]. The networks are trained based on the stochastic gradient descent optimizer using the back-propagation algorithm [33] to compute the gradients. All model hyper-parameters were tuned on the training set (the hyper-parameters with the smallest training loss value were selected). For each model, the learning rate and the batch size were selected from [0.001, 0.01, 0.1, 1] and [64, 128, 256], respectively. For RPE , we also tuned the number of positive and negative instances (i.e., η^+ and η^-). The value of η^+ was swept between [20, 50, 100, 200] and the parameter η^- was selected from $[5\eta^+, 10\eta^+, 20\eta^+]$. As suggested in [40], in all the experiments (unless otherwise stated) the embedding dimensionality was set to 300, for all models including the baselines.

4.2 Evaluation via Query Expansion

In this subsection, we evaluate the embedding models in the context of query expansion for the ad-hoc retrieval task. In the following, we first describe the retrieval collections used in our experiments. We further explain our experimental setup as well as the evaluation metrics. We finally report and discuss the query expansion results.

4.2.1 Data. We use four standard test collections in our experiments. The first two collections (AP and Robust) consist of thousands of news articles and are considered as homogeneous collections. AP and Robust were previously used in TREC 1-3 Ad-Hoc Track and TREC 2004 Robust Track, respectively. The second two collections (GOV2 and ClueWeb) are large-scale web collections containing heterogeneous documents. GOV2 consists of the ".gov" domain web pages, crawled in 2004. ClueWeb (i.e., ClueWeb09-Category B) is a common web crawl collection that only contains English web pages. GOV2 and ClueWeb were previously used in TREC 2004-2006 Terabyte Track and TREC 2009-2012 Web Track, respectively. The statistics of these collections as well as the corresponding TREC topics are reported in Table 1. We only used the title of topics as queries.

4.2.2 Experimental Setup. We cleaned the ClueWeb collection by filtering out the spam documents. The spam filtering phase was done using the Waterloo spam scorer[5] [6] with the threshold of 60%. Stopwords were removed from all collections using the standard INQUERY stopword list and no stemming were performed.

For the purpose of query expansion, we consider the language modeling framework [29] and estimate a query language model based on a given set of word embedding vectors. The expanded query language model $p(w|\theta_q^*)$ is estimated as:

$$p(w|\theta_q^*) = \alpha p_{ML}(w|q) + (1 - \alpha)p(\vec{w}|\vec{q}) \quad (9)$$

where $p_{ML}(w|q)$ denotes maximum likelihood estimation of the original query and α is a free hyper-parameter that controls the weight of original query model in the expanded model. The probability $p(\vec{w}|\vec{q})$ is calculated based on the trained word embedding vectors. In our first model, this probability can be estimated using Equation (5); while in the second model, we should simply use the Bayes rule given Equation (7) to estimate this probability. However, since we do not have any information about the probability of each

[3] http://www.lemurproject.org/galago.php

[4] http://tensorflow.org/

[5] http://plg.uwaterloo.ca/~gvcormac/clueweb09spam/

Table 1: Collections statistics.

ID	collection	queries (title only)	#docs	avg doc length	#qrels
AP	Associated Press 88-89	TREC 1-3 Ad-Hoc Track, topics 51-200	165k	287	15,838
Robust	TREC Disks 4 & 5 minus Congressional Record	TREC 2004 Robust Track, topics 301-450 & 601-700	528k	254	17,412
GOV2	2004 crawl of .gov domains	TREC 2004-2006 Terabyte Track, topics 701-850	25m	648	26,917
ClueWeb	ClueWeb 09 - Category B	TREC 2009-2012 Web Track topics 1-200	50m	1506	18,771

Table 2: Evaluating relevance-based word embeddings in the context of query expansion. The superscripts 0/1/2/3/4 denote that the MAP improvements over MLE/word2vec-external/word2vec-target/GloVe-external/GloVe-target are statistically significant. The highest value in each row is marked in bold.

Collection	Metric	MLE	word2vec		GloVe		Rel.-based Embedding	
			external	target	external	target	RLM	RPE
AP	MAP	0.2197	0.2399	0.2420	0.2319	0.2389	**0.2580**^{01234}	0.2543^{01234}
	P@20	0.3503	0.3688	0.3738	0.3581	0.3631	**0.3886**^{01234}	0.3812^{034}
	NDCG@20	0.3924	0.4030	0.4181	0.4025	0.4098	**0.4242**^{01234}	0.4226^{01234}
Robust	MAP	0.2149	0.2218	0.2215	0.2209	0.2172	**0.2450**^{01234}	0.2372^{01234}
	P@20	0.3319	0.3357	0.3337	0.3345	0.3281	**0.3476**^{01234}	0.3409^{024}
	NDCG@20	0.3863	0.3918	0.3881	0.3918	0.3844	**0.3982**^{01234}	0.3955^{0}
GOV2	MAP	0.2702	0.2740	0.2723	0.2718	0.2709	**0.2867**^{01234}	0.2855^{01234}
	P@20	0.5132	0.5257	0.5172	0.5186	0.5128	**0.5367**^{01234}	0.5358^{01234}
	NDCG@20	0.4482	0.4571	0.4509	0.4539	0.4485	**0.4576**^{0234}	0.4557^{024}
ClueWeb	MAP	0.1028	0.1033	0.1033	0.1029	0.1026	**0.1066**^{01234}	0.1031
	P@20	0.3025	0.3040	0.3053	0.3033	0.3048	**0.3073**	0.3030
	NDCG@20	0.2237	0.2235	0.2252	0.2244	0.2244	**0.2273**^{01}	0.2241

term given a query, we use the uniform distribution. For other word embedding models (i.e., word2vec and GloVe), we use the standard method described in [11]. For all the models, we ignore the terms whose embedding vectors are not available.

We retrieve the documents for the expanded query language model using the KL-divergence formula [18] with Dirichlet prior smoothing ($\mu = 1500$) [45]. All the retrieval experiments were carried out using the Galago toolkit [7].

In all the experiments, the parameters α (the linear interpolation coefficient) and m (the number of expansion terms) were set using 2-fold cross-validation over the queries in each collection. We selected the parameter α from $\{0.1, \ldots, 0.9\}$ and the parameter m from $\{10, 20, ..., 100\}$.

4.2.3 Evaluation Metrics. To evaluate the effectiveness of query expansion models, we report three standard evaluation metrics: mean average precision (MAP) of the top ranked 1000 documents, precision of the top 20 retrieved documents (P@20), and normalized discounted cumulative gain [13] calculated for the top 20 retrieved documents (nDCG@20). Statistically significant differences of MAP, P@20, and nDCG@20 values based on the two-tailed paired t-test are computed at a 95% confidence level (i.e., $p\_value < 0.05$).

4.2.4 Results and Discussion. To evaluate our models, we consider the following baselines: *(i)* the standard maximum likelihood estimation (MLE) of the query model without query expansion, *(ii)* two sets of embedding vectors (one trained on Google News as a large external corpus and one trained on the target retrieval collection) learned by the word2vec model[6] [24], and *(iii)* two sets of embedding vectors (one trained on Wikipedia 2004 plus Gigawords 5 as a large external corpus[7] and the other on the target retrieval collection) learned by the GloVe model [28].

Table 2 reports the results achieved by the proposed models and the baselines. According to this table, all the query expansion models outperform the MLE baseline in nearly all cases, which indicates the effectiveness of employing high-dimensional word representations for query expansion. Similar observations have been made in [11, 17, 40, 41]. According to the results, although word2vec performs slightly better than GloVe, no significant differences can be observed between their performances. According to Table 2, both relevance-based embedding models outperform all the baselines in all the collections, which shows the importance of taking relevance into account for training embedding vectors. These improvements are often statistically significant compared to all the baselines. The relevance likelihood maximization model (RLM) performs better than the relevance posterior estimation model (RPE) in all cases and the reason is related to their objective function. RLM learns the relevance distribution for all terms, while RPE learns the classification probability of being relevance for vocabulary terms (see Equations (5) and (7)).

[6] We use the CBOW implementation of the word2vec model. The skip-gram model also performs similarly.

[7] Available at http://nlp.stanford.edu/projects/glove/.

Table 3: Top 10 expansion terms obtained by the word2vec and the relevance-based word embedding models for two sample queries "indian american museum" and "tibet protesters".

query: "indian american museum"				query: "tibet protesters"			
word2vec		Rel.-based Embedding		word2vec		Rel.-based Embedding	
external	target	RLM	RPE	external	target	RLM	RPE
history	powwows	chumash	heye	demonstrators	tibetan	tibetan	tibetan
art	smithsonian	heye	collection	protestors	lhasa	lama	tibetans
culture	afro	artifacts	chumash	tibetan	demonstrators	tibetans	lama
british	mesoamerica	smithsonian	smithsonian	protests	tibetans	lhasa	independence
heritage	smithsonians	collection	york	tibetans	marchers	dalai	lhasa
society	native	washington	new	protest	lhasas	independence	dalai
states	heye	institution	apa	activists	jokhang	protest	open
contemporary	hopi	york	native	protesting	demonstrations	open	protest
part	mayas	native	americans	lhasa	dissidents	zone	zone
united	cimam	apa	history	demonstrations	barkhor	followers	jokhang

To get a sense of what is learned by each of the embedding models[8], in Table 3 we report the top 10 expansion terms for two sample queries from the Robust collection. According to this table, the terms added to the query by the word2vec model are syntactically or semantically related to individual query terms, which is expected. For the query "indian american museum" as an example, the terms "history", "art", and "culture" are related to the query term "museum", while the terms "united" and "states" are related to the query term "american". In contrast, looking at the expansion terms obtained by the relevance-based word embeddings, we can see that some relevant terms to the whole query were selected. For instance, "chumash" (a group of native americans)[9], "heye" (the national museum of the American Indian in New York), "smithsonian" (the national museum of the American Indian in Washington DC), and "apa" (the American Psychological Association that actively promotes American Indian museums). A similar observation can be made for the other sample query (i.e., "tibet protesters"). For example, the word "independence" is related to the whole query that was only selected by the relevance-based word embedding models, while the terms "protestors", "protests", "protest", and "protesting" that are syntactically similar to the query term "protesters" were considered by the word2vec model. We believe that these differences are due to the learning objective of the models. Interestingly, the expansion terms added to each query by the two relevance-based models look very similar, but according to Table 2, their performances are quite different. The reason is related to the weights given to each term by the two models. The weights given to the expansion terms by RPE are very close to each other because its objective is to just classify each term and all of these terms are classified with a high probability as "relevant".

In the next set of experiments, we consider the methods that use the top retrieved documents for query expansion: the relevance model (RM3) [1, 20] as a state-of-the-art pseudo-relevance feedback model, and the local embedding approach recently proposed by Diaz et al. [11] with the general idea of training word embedding models on the top ranked documents retrieved in response to a given query. Similar to [11], we use the word2vec model to train word embedding vectors on top 1000 documents. The results are reported in Table 4. In this table, ERM refers to the embedding-based relevance model recently proposed by Zamani and Croft [40] in order to make use of semantic similarities estimated based on the word embedding vectors in a pseudo-relevance feedback scenario. According to Table 4, the ERM model that uses the relevance-based word embedding (RLM[10]) outperforms all the other methods. These improvements are statistically significant in most cases. By comparing the results obtained by local embedding and those reported in Table 2, it can be observed that there are no substantial differences between the results for local embedding and word2vec. This is similar to what is reported by Diaz et al. [11] when the embedding vectors are trained on the top documents in the target collection, similar to our setting. Note that the relevance-based model was also trained on the target collection.

Table 4: Evaluating relevance-based word embedding in pseudo-relevance feedback scenario. The superscripts 1/2/3 denote that the MAP improvements over RM3/Local Embedding/ERM with Local Embedding are statistically significant. The highest value in each row is marked in bold.

Collection	Metric	RM3	Local Emb.	ERM Local	ERM RLM
AP	MAP	0.2927	0.2412	0.3047	**0.3119**^{12}
	P@20	0.4034	0.3742	0.4105	**0.4233**^{12}
	NDCG@20	0.4368	0.4173	0.4411	**0.4495**^{123}
Robust	MAP	0.2593	0.2235	0.2643	**0.2761**^{123}
	P@20	0.3486	0.3366	0.3498	**0.3605**^{123}
	NDCG@20	0.4011	0.3868	0.4080	**0.4173**^{123}
GOV2	MAP	0.2863	0.2748	0.2924	**0.2986**^{123}
	P@20	0.5318	0.5271	0.5379	**0.5417**^{12}
	NDCG@20	0.4503	0.4576	0.4584	**0.4603**^{123}
ClueWeb	MAP	0.1079	0.1041	0.1094	**0.1121**^{12}
	P@20	0.3111	0.3062	0.3145	**0.3168**
	NDCG@20	0.2309	0.2261	0.2328	**0.2360**^{2}

[8]For the sake of space, we only report the expanded terms estimated by the word2vec model and the proposed models.

[9]see https://en.wikipedia.org/wiki/Chumash_people

[10]For the sake of space, we only consider RLM which shows better performance compared to RPE in query expansion.

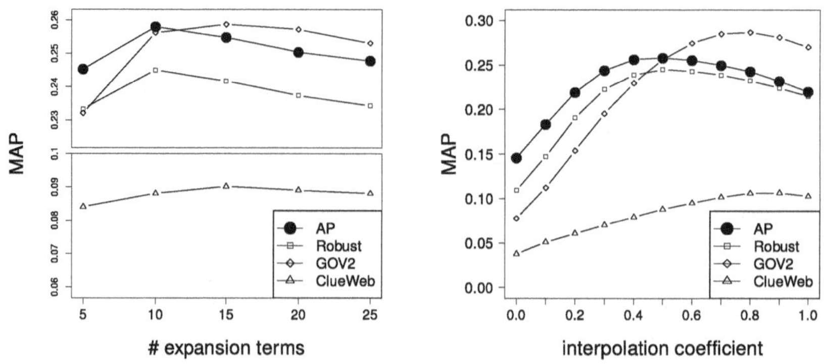

(a) # expansion terms (b) interpolation coefficient

Figure 2: Sensitivity of RLM to the number of expansion terms and the interpolation coefficient (α), in terms of MAP.

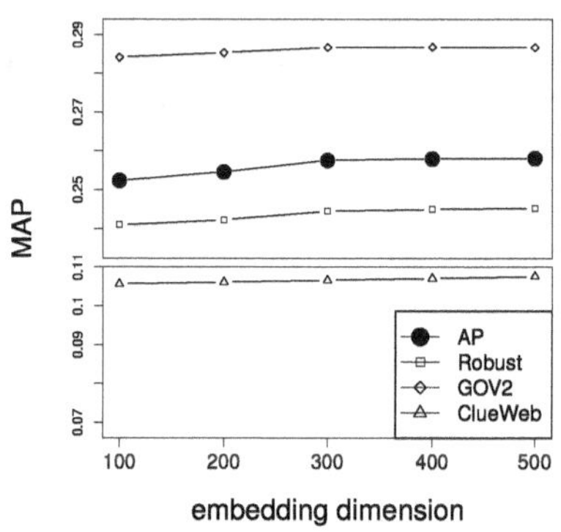

Figure 3: Sensitivity of RLM to the dimension of embedding vectors, in terms of MAP.

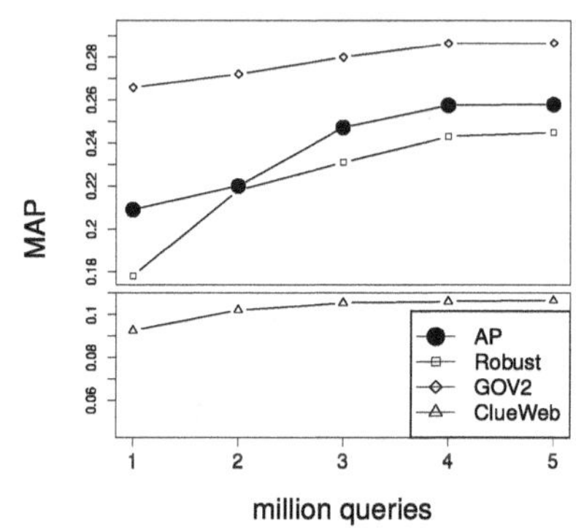

Figure 4: The Performance of RLM with respect to different amount of training data (training queries), in terms of MAP.

An interesting observation from Tables 2 and 4 is that the RLM performance (without using pseudo-relevant documents) in Robust and GOV2 is very close to the RM3 performance, and is slightly better in the GOV2 collection. Note that RM3 needs two retrieval runs[11] and uses top retrieved documents, while RLM only needs one retrieval run. This is an important issue in many real-world applications, since the efficiency constraints do not always allow them to have two retrieval runs per query.

Parameter Sensitivity. In the next set of experiments, we study the sensitivity of RLM as the best performing word embedding model in Table 2 to the expansion parameters. Figure 2a plots the sensitivity of RLM to the number of expansion terms where the parameter α is set to 0.5. According to this figure, in both newswire collections, the method shows its best performance when the queries are expanded with only 10 words. In the GOV2 collection, 15 words are needed for the method to show its best performance.

Figure 2b plots the sensitivity of the methods to the interpolation coefficient α (see Equation 9) where the number of expansion terms is set to 10. According to the curves correspond to AP and Robust, the original query language model needs to be interpolated with the model estimated using relevance-based word embeddings with equal weights (i.e., $\alpha = 0.5$). This shows the quality of the estimated distribution via the learned embedding vectors. In the GOV2 collection, a higher weight should be given to the original query model, which indicates that the original query plays a key role in achieving good retrieval performance in this collection.

We also study the performance of RLM as the best performing word embedding model for query expansion with respect to the embedding dimensionality. The results are shown in Figure 3, where the query expansion performance generally improves as we increase the embedding dimensionality. The performances become stable when the dimension is larger than 300. This experiment suggests that 400 dimensions would be enough for the relevance-based embedding model.

Due to the large number of parameters in the neural networks, they can require large amounts of training data to achieve good performance. In the next set of experiments, we study how much training data is needed for training our best model. The results are plotted in Figure 4. According to this figure, by increasing the number of training queries from one million to four million queries, the performance significantly increases, and becomes more stable after four million queries.

4.3 Evaluation via Query Classification

In this subsection, we evaluate the proposed embedding models in the context of query classification. In this task, each query is

[11] Diaz [10] showed that for precision-oriented tasks, the second retrieval run can be restricted to the initial rank list for improving the efficiency of PRF models. However, for recall-oriented metrics, e.g., MAP, the second retrieval helps a lot.

Table 5: Evaluating embedding algorithms via query classification. The superscripts 1/2 denote that the improvements over word2vec/GloVe are significant. The highest value in each column is marked in bold.

Method	Precision	F1-measure
word2vec	0.3712	0.4008
GloVe	0.3643	0.3912
Rel.-based Embedding - RLM	0.3943[12]	0.4267[12]
Rel.-based Embedding - RPE	**0.3961**[12]	**0.4294**[12]

assigned to a number of labels (categories) which are pre-defined and a few training queries are available for each label. This is a supervised multi-label classification task with little training data.

4.3.1 Data. We consider the dataset that was introduced in KDD Cup 2005 [22] for the internet user search query categorization task and was previously used in [41] for evaluating query embedding vectors. This dataset contains 800 web queries submitted by real users randomly collected from the MSN search logs. The queries do not contain "junk" text or non-English terms. The queries were labelled by three human editors. 67 categories were pre-defined and up to 5 labels were selected for each query by each editor.

4.3.2 Experimental Setup. In our experiments, we performed 5-fold cross-validation over the queries and the reported results are the average of those obtained over the test folds. In all experiments, the spelling errors in queries were corrected in a pre-processing phase, the stopwords were removed from queries (using the INQUERY stopword list), and no stemming was performed.

To classify each query, we consider a very simple kNN-based approach proposed in [41]. We first compute the probability of each category/label given each query q and then select the top t categories with the highest probabilities. The probability $p(C_i|q)$ is computed as follows:

$$p(C_i|q) = \frac{\delta(\vec{C_i}, \vec{q})}{\sum_j \delta(\vec{C_j}, \vec{q})} \propto \delta(\vec{C_i}, \vec{q}) \tag{10}$$

where C_i denotes the ith category. $\vec{C_i}$ is the centroid vector of all query embedding vectors with the label of C_i in the training set. We ignore the query terms whose embedding vectors are not available. The number of labels assigned to each query was tuned on the training set from $\{1, 2, 3, 4, 5\}$. In the query classification experiments, we trained relevance-based word embedding using Robust as the collection.

4.3.3 Evaluation Metrics. We consider two evaluation metrics that were also used in KDD Cup 2005 [22]: precision and F1-measure. Since the labels assigned by the three human editors differ in some cases, all the label sets should be taken into account. These metrics are computed in the same way as what is described in [22] for evaluating the KDD Cup 2005 submitted runs. Statistically significant differences are determined using the two-tailed paired t-test computed at a 95% confidence level ($p - value < 0.05$).

4.3.4 Results and Discussion. We compare our models against the word2vec and GloVe methods trained on the external collections that are described in the query expansion experiments. The results are reported in Table 5, where the relevance-based embedding models significantly outperform the baselines in terms of both metrics. An interesting observation here is that contrary to the query expansion experiments, RPE performs better than RLM in query classification. The reason is that in query expansion the weight of each term is considered in order to generate the expanded query language model. Therefore, in addition to the order of terms, their weights should be also effective for improving the retrieval performance with query expansion. In query classification, we only assign a few categories to each query, and thus as long as the order of categories is correct, the similarity values between the queries and the categories do not matter.

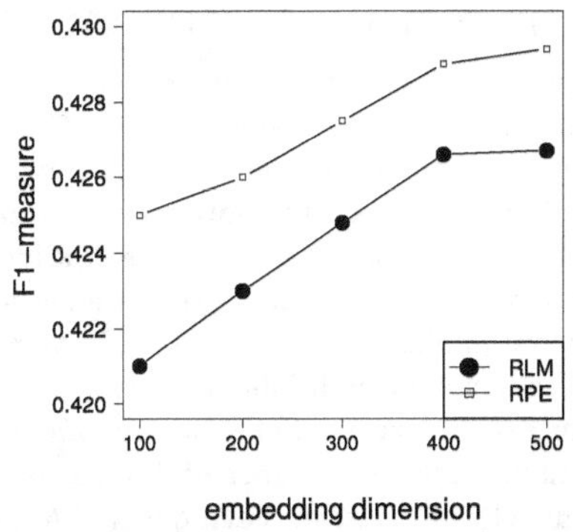

Figure 5: Sensitivity of the relevance-based embedding models to the embedding dimensionality, in terms of F1-measure.

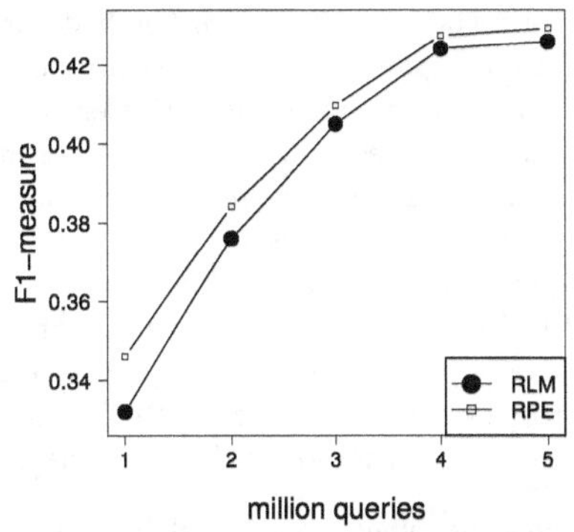

Figure 6: The Performance of relevance-based embedding models with respect to different amount of training data (training queries), in terms of F1-measure.

In the next set of experiments, we study the performance of our relevance-based word embedding models with respect to the embedding dimensionality. The results are plotted in Figure 5. According to this figure, the performance is generally improved by increasing the embedding dimensionality, and becomes stable when the dimension is greater than 400. This is similar to our observation in the query expansion experiments. We also study the amount of data needed for training our models in Figure 6. According to this figure, at least 4 million queries are needed in order to learn accurate relevance-based word embeddings. It can be seen from Figure 6 that RLM needs more training data compared to RPE in order to perform well, because by increasing the amount of training data the learning curves of these two models get closer.

5 CONCLUSIONS AND FUTURE WORK

In this paper, we revisited the underlying assumption in typical word embedding models, such as word2vec and GloVe. Instead of learning embedding vectors based on term proximity, we proposed learning embeddings based on the notion of relevance, which is the primary objective in many IR tasks. We developed two neural network-based models for learning relevance-based word embeddings. The first model, the relevance likelihood maximization model, aims to estimate the probability of each word in a relevance distribution for each query, while the second one, the relevance posterior estimation model, classifies each term as belonging to relevant or non-relevant class for each query. We evaluated our models using two sets of extrinsic evaluation: query expansion and query classification. The query expansion experiments using four standard TREC collections, two newswire and two large-scale web collections, suggested that the relevance-based word embedding models outperform state-of-the-art word embedding algorithms. We showed that the expansion terms chosen by our models are related to the whole query, while those chosen by typical word embedding models are related to individual query terms. The query classification experiments also validated these findings and investigated the effectiveness of our models.

In the future, we intend to evaluate the learned embedding models in other IR tasks, such as query reformulation, query intent prediction, etc. We can also achieve more accurate relevance-based embedding vectors by considering the clicked documents for training query, instead of or in addition to the top retrieved documents.

Acknowledgements. The authors thank Daniel Cohen, Mostafa Dehghani, and Qingyao Ai for their invaluable comments. This work was supported in part by the Center for Intelligent Information Retrieval. Any opinions, findings and conclusions or recommendations expressed in this material are those of the authors and do not necessarily reflect those of the sponsor.

REFERENCES

[1] Nasreen Abdul-jaleel, James Allan, W. Bruce Croft, Fernando Diaz, Leah Larkey, Xiaoyan Li, Donald Metzler, Mark D. Smucker, Trevor Strohman, Howard Turtle, and Courtney Wade. 2004. UMass at TREC 2004: Novelty and HARD. In *TREC '04*.

[2] Qingyao Ai, Liu Yang, Jiafeng Guo, and W. Bruce Croft. 2016. Analysis of the Paragraph Vector Model for Information Retrieval. In *ICTIR '16*. 133–142.

[3] Gianni Amati and Cornelis Joost Van Rijsbergen. 2002. Probabilistic Models of Information Retrieval Based on Measuring the Divergence from Randomness. *ACM Trans. Inf. Syst.* 20, 4 (2002), 357–389.

[4] P. D. Bruza and D. Song. 2002. Inferring Query Models by Computing Information Flow. In *CIKM '02*. 260–269.

[5] Stephane Clinchant and Florent Perronnin. 2013. Aggregating Continuous Word Embeddings for Information Retrieval. In *CVSC@ACL '13*. 100–109.

[6] Gordon V. Cormack, Mark D. Smucker, and Charles L. Clarke. 2011. Efficient and Effective Spam Filtering and Re-ranking for Large Web Datasets. *Inf. Retr.* 14, 5 (2011), 441–465.

[7] Bruce Croft, Donald Metzler, and Trevor Strohman. 2009. *Search Engines: Information Retrieval in Practice* (1st ed.). Addison-Wesley Publishing Company.

[8] Scott Deerwester, Susan T. Dumais, George W. Furnas, Thomas K. Landauer, and Richard Harshman. 1990. Indexing by Latent Semantic Analysis. 41, 6 (1990), 391–407.

[9] Mostafa Dehghani, Hamed Zamani, Aliaksei Severyn, Jaap Kamps, and W. Bruce Croft. 2017. Neural Ranking Models with Weak Supervision. In *SIGIR '17*.

[10] Fernando Diaz. 2015. Condensed List Relevance Models. In *ICTIR '15*. 313–316.

[11] Fernando Diaz, Bhaskar Mitra, and Nick Craswell. 2016. Query Expansion with Locally-Trained Word Embeddings. In *ACL '16*.

[12] Michael U. Gutmann and Aapo Hyvärinen. 2012. Noise-contrastive Estimation of Unnormalized Statistical Models, with Applications to Natural Image Statistics. *J. Mach. Learn. Res.* 13, 1 (2012), 307–361.

[13] Kalervo Järvelin and Jaana Kekäläinen. 2002. Cumulated Gain-based Evaluation of IR Techniques. *ACM Trans. Inf. Syst.* 20, 4 (Oct. 2002), 422–446.

[14] Yufeng Jing and W. Bruce Croft. 1994. An Association Thesaurus for Information Retrieval. In *RIAO '94*. 146–160.

[15] Tom Kenter and Maarten de Rijke. 2015. Short Text Similarity with Word Embeddings. In *CIKM '15*. 1411–1420.

[16] Matt J. Kusner, Yu Sun, Nicholas I. Kolkin, and Kilian Q. Weinberger. 2015. From Word Embeddings to Document Distances. In *ICML '15*. 957–966.

[17] Saar Kuzi, Anna Shtok, and Oren Kurland. 2016. Query Expansion Using Word Embeddings. In *CIKM '16*. 1929–1932.

[18] John Lafferty and Chengxiang Zhai. 2001. Document Language Models, Query Models, and Risk Minimization for Information Retrieval. In *SIGIR '01*. 111–119.

[19] Victor Lavrenko, Martin Choquette, and W. Bruce Croft. 2002. Cross-lingual Relevance Models. In *SIGIR '02*. 175–182.

[20] Victor Lavrenko and W. Bruce Croft. 2001. Relevance Based Language Models. In *SIGIR '01*. 120–127.

[21] Omer Levy and Yoav Goldberg. 2014. Neural Word Embedding as Implicit Matrix Factorization. In *NIPS '14*. 2177–2185.

[22] Ying Li, Zijian Zheng, and Honghua (Kathy) Dai. 2005. KDD CUP-2005 Report: Facing a Great Challenge. *SIGKDD Explor. Newsl.* 7, 2 (2005), 91–99.

[23] Xiaodong Liu, Jianfeng Gao, Xiaodong He, Li Deng, Kevin Duh, and Ye-yi Wang. 2015. Representation Learning Using Multi-Task Deep Neural Networks for Semantic Classification and Information Retrieval. In *NAACL '15*. 912–921.

[24] Tomas Mikolov, Ilya Sutskever, Kai Chen, Greg S Corrado, and Jeff Dean. 2013. Distributed Representations of Words and Phrases and their Compositionality. In *NIPS '13*. 3111–3119.

[25] Andriy Mnih and Geoffrey E Hinton. 2009. A Scalable Hierarchical Distributed Language Model. In *NIPS '09*. 1081–1088.

[26] Frederic Morin and Yoshua Bengio. 2005. Hierarchical Probabilistic Neural Network Language Model. In *AISTATS '05*. 246–252.

[27] Greg Pass, Abdur Chowdhury, and Cayley Torgeson. 2006. A Picture of Search. In *InfoScale '06*.

[28] Jeffrey Pennington, Richard Socher, and Christopher Manning. 2014. GloVe: Global Vectors for Word Representation. In *EMNLP '14*. 1532–1543.

[29] Jay M. Ponte and W. Bruce Croft. 1998. A Language Modeling Approach to Information Retrieval. In *SIGIR '98*. 275–281.

[30] Navid Rekabsaz, Mihai Lupu, Allan Hanbury, and Hamed Zamani. 2017. Word Embedding Causes Topic Shifting; Exploit Global Context!. In *SIGIR '17*.

[31] Navid Rekabsaz, Mihai Lupu, Allan Hanbury, and Guido Zuccon. 2016. Generalizing Translation Models in the Probabilistic Relevance Framework. In *CIKM '16*. 711–720.

[32] J. J. Rocchio. 1971. Relevance Feedback in Information Retrieval. In *The SMART Retrieval System: Experiments in Automatic Document Processing*. 313–323.

[33] D. E. Rumelhart, G. E. Hinton, and R. J. Williams. 1986. Learning representations by back-propagating errors. *Nature* 323 (Oct. 1986), 533–536.

[34] T. Saracevic. 2016. *The Notion of Relevance in Information Science: Everybody knows what relevance is. But, what is it really?* Morgan & Claypool Publishers.

[35] Alessandro Sordoni, Yoshua Bengio, and Jian-Yun Nie. 2014. Learning Concept Embeddings for Query Expansion by Quantum Entropy Minimization. In *AAAI '14*. 1586–1592.

[36] Tao Tao and ChengXiang Zhai. 2006. Regularized Estimation of Mixture Models for Robust Pseudo-relevance Feedback. In *SIGIR '06*. 162–169.

[37] Ivan Vulić and Marie-Francine Moens. 2015. Monolingual and Cross-Lingual Information Retrieval Models Based on (Bilingual) Word Embeddings. In *SIGIR '15*. 363–372.

[38] Jinxi Xu and W. Bruce Croft. 1996. Query Expansion Using Local and Global Document Analysis. In *SIGIR '96*. 4–11.

[39] Hamed Zamani, Michael Bendersky, Xuanhui Wang, and Mingyang Zhang. 2017. Situational Context for Ranking in Personal Search. In *WWW '17*. 1531–1540.

[40] Hamed Zamani and W. Bruce Croft. 2016. Embedding-based Query Language Models. In *ICTIR '16*. 147–156.

[41] Hamed Zamani and W. Bruce Croft. 2016. Estimating Embedding Vectors for Queries. In *ICTIR '16*. 123–132.

[42] Hamed Zamani, Javid Dadashkarimi, Azadeh Shakery, and W. Bruce Croft. 2016. Pseudo-Relevance Feedback Based on Matrix Factorization. In *CIKM '16*. 1483–1492.

[43] ChengXiang Zhai, William W. Cohen, and John Lafferty. 2003. Beyond Independent Relevance: Methods and Evaluation Metrics for Subtopic Retrieval. In *SIGIR '03*. 10–17.

[44] Chengxiang Zhai and John Lafferty. 2001. Model-based Feedback in the Language Modeling Approach to Information Retrieval. In *CIKM '01*. 403–410.

[45] Chengxiang Zhai and John Lafferty. 2004. A Study of Smoothing Methods for Language Models Applied to Information Retrieval. *ACM Trans. Inf. Syst.* 22, 2 (2004), 179–214.

[46] Guoqing Zheng and Jamie Callan. 2015. Learning to Reweight Terms with Distributed Representations. In *SIGIR '15*. 575–584.

[47] Guangyou Zhou, Tingting He, Jun Zhao, and Po Hu. 2015. Learning Continuous Word Embedding with Metadata for Question Retrieval in Community Question Answering. In *ACL '15*. 250–259.

IRGAN: A Minimax Game for Unifying Generative and Discriminative Information Retrieval Models

Jun Wang
University College London
j.wang@cs.ucl.ac.uk

Lantao Yu, Weinan Zhang*
Shanghai Jiao Tong University
wnzhang@sjtu.edu.cn

Yu Gong, Yinghui Xu
Alibaba Group
renji.xyh@taobao.com

Benyou Wang, Peng Zhang
Tianjin University
pzhang@tju.edu.cn

Dell Zhang
Birkbeck, University of London
dell.z@ieee.org

ABSTRACT

This paper provides a unified account of two schools of thinking in information retrieval modelling: the generative retrieval focusing on predicting relevant documents given a query, and the discriminative retrieval focusing on predicting relevancy given a query-document pair. We propose a game theoretical *minimax game* to iteratively optimise both models. On one hand, the discriminative model, aiming to mine signals from labelled and unlabelled data, provides guidance to train the generative model towards fitting the underlying relevance distribution over documents given the query. On the other hand, the generative model, acting as an attacker to the current discriminative model, generates difficult examples for the discriminative model in an adversarial way by minimising its discrimination objective. With the competition between these two models, we show that the unified framework takes advantage of both schools of thinking: (i) the generative model learns to fit the relevance distribution over documents via the signals from the discriminative model, and (ii) the discriminative model is able to exploit the unlabelled data selected by the generative model to achieve a better estimation for document ranking. Our experimental results have demonstrated significant performance gains as much as 23.96% on Precision@5 and 15.50% on MAP over strong baselines in a variety of applications including web search, item recommendation, and question answering.

1 INTRODUCTION

A typical formulation of information retrieval (IR) is to provide a (rank) list of documents given a query. It has a wide range of applications from text retrieval [1] and web search [3, 19] to recommender systems [21, 34], question answering [9], and personalised advertising [27], to name just a few. There are, arguably, two major schools of thinking when coming to IR theory and modelling [1].

The classic school of thinking is to assume that there is an underlying stochastic **generative** process between documents and information needs (clued by a query) [22]. In text retrieval, the classic relevance model of information retrieval is focused on describing how a (relevant) document is generated from a given information need: $q \longrightarrow d$, where q is the query (e.g., keywords, user profiles, questions, depending on the specific IR application), d is its corresponding document (e.g., textual documents, information items, answers), and the arrow indicates the direction of generation. Notable examples include Robertson and Sparck Jones's Binary Independence Model, of which each word token is independently generated to form a relevant document [35]. Statistical language models of text retrieval consider a reverse generative process from a document to a query: $d \longrightarrow q$, typically generating query terms from a document (i.e., the query likelihood function) [32, 48]. In the related work of word embedding, word tokens are generated from their context words [28]. In the application of recommender systems, we also see that a recommended target item (in the original document identifier space) can be generated/selected from known context items [2].

The modern school of thinking in IR recognises the strength of machine learning and shifts to a **discriminative** (classification) solution learned from labelled relevant judgements or their proxies such as clicks or ratings. It considers documents and queries jointly as features and predicts their relevancy or rank order labels from a large amount of training data: $q+d \longrightarrow r$, where r denotes relevance and symbol + denotes the combining of features. A significant development in web search is learning to rank (LTR) [3, 19], a family of machine learning techniques where the training objective is to provide the right ranking order of a list of documents (or items) for a given query (or context) [24]. Three major paradigms of learning to rank are pointwise, pairwise, and listwise. Pointwise methods learn to approximate the relevance estimation of each document to the human rating [23, 31]. Pairwise methods aim to identify the more-relevant document from any document pair [3]. Listwise methods learn to optimise the (smoothed) loss function defined over the whole ranking list for each query [4, 6]. Besides, a recent advance in recommender systems is matrix factorisation, where the interactive patterns of user features and item features are exploited via vector inner product to make the prediction of relevancy [21, 34, 46].

While the generative models of information retrieval are theoretically sound and very successful in modelling features (e.g., text statistics, distribution over document identifier space), they suffer from the difficulty in leveraging relevancy signals from other channels such as links, clicks etc., which are largely observable in Internet-based applications. While the discriminative models of information retrieval such as learning to rank are able to learn

*The corresponding authors: J. Wang and W. Zhang.

SIGIR'17, August 7–11, 2017, Shinjuku, Tokyo, Japan

DOI: http://dx.doi.org/10.1145/3077136.3080786

a retrieval ranking function implicitly from a large amount of labelled/unlabelled data, they currently lack a principled way of obtaining useful features or gathering helpful signals from the massive unlabelled data available, in particular, from text statistics (derived from both documents and queries) or the distribution of relevant documents in the collection.

In this paper, we consider the generative and discriminative retrieval models as two sides of the same coin. Inspired by Generative Adversarial Nets (GANs) in machine learning [13], we propose a game theoretical *minimax game* to combine the above mentioned two schools of thinking. Specifically, we define a common retrieval function (e.g., discrimination-based objective function) for both models. On one hand, the discriminative model $p_\phi(r|q,d)$ aims to maximise the objective function by learning from labelled data. It naturally provides alternative guidance to the generative retrieval model beyond traditional log-likelihood. On the other hand, the generative retrieval model $p_\theta(d|q,r)$ acts as a challenger who constantly pushes the discriminator to its limit. Iteratively it provides the most difficult cases for the discriminator to retrain itself by adversarially minimising the objective function. In such a way, the two types of IR models act as two players in a minimax game, and each of them strikes to improve itself to 'beat' the other one at every round of this competition. Note that our minimax game based approach is fundamentally different from the existing game-theoretic IR methods [26, 47], in the sense that the existing approaches generally try to model the interaction between user and system, whereas our approach aims to unify generative and discriminative IR models.

Empirically, we have realised the proposed minimax retrieval framework in three typical IR applications: web search, item recommendation, and question answering. In our experiments, we found that the minimax game arrives at different equilibria and thus different effects of unification in different settings. With the pointwise adversarial training, the generative retrieval model can be significantly boosted by the training rewards from the discriminative retrieval model. The resulting model outperforms several strong baselines by 22.56% in web search and 14.38% in item recommendation on Precesion@5. We also found that with new pairwise adversarial training, the discriminative retrieval model is largely boosted by examples selected by the generative retrieval model and outperforms the compared strong algorithms by 23.96% on Precision@5 in web search and 2.38% on Precision@1 in question answering.

2 IRGAN FORMULATION

In this section, we take the inspiration from GANs and build a unified framework for fusing generative and discriminative IR in an adversarial setting; we call it IRGAN, and its application to concrete IR problems will be given in the next section.

2.1 A Minimax Retrieval Framework

Without loss of generality, let us consider the following information retrieval problem. We have a set of queries $\{q_1, ..., q_N\}$ and a set of documents $\{d_1, ..., d_M\}$. In a general setting, a query is any specific form of the user's information need such as search keywords, a user profile, or a question, while documents could be textual documents, information items, or answers, depending on the specific retrieval task. For a given query q_n, we have a set of relevant documents labelled, the size of which is much smaller than the total number of documents M.

The underlying *true* relevance distribution can be expressed as conditional probability $p_{\text{true}}(d|q,r)$, which depicts the (user's) relevance preference distribution over the candidate documents with respect to her submitted query. Given a set of samples from $p_{\text{true}}(d|q,r)$ observed as the training data, we can try to construct two types of IR models:

Generative retrieval model $p_\theta(d|q,r)$, which tries to generate (or select) relevant documents, from the candidate pool for the given query q, as specified later in Eq. (8); in other words, its goal is to approximate the true relevance distribution over documents $p_{\text{true}}(d|q,r)$ as much as possible.

Discriminative retrieval model $f_\phi(q,d)$, which, in contrary, tries to discriminate well-matched query-document tuples (q,d) from ill-matched ones, where the goodness of matching given by $f_\phi(q,d)$ depends on the relevance of d to q; in other words, its goal is to distinguish between relevant documents and non-relevant documents for the query q as accurately as possible. It is in fact simply a binary classifier, and we could use 1 as the class label for the query-document tuples that truly match (positive examples) while 0 as the class label for those that do not really match (negative examples).

2.1.1 Overall Objective. Thus, inspired by the idea of GAN, we aim to unify these two different types of IR models by letting them play a minimax game: the generative retrieval model would try to generate (or select) relevant documents that look like the ground-truth relevant documents and therefore could fool the discriminative retrieval model, whereas the discriminative retrieval model would try to draw a clear distinction between the ground-truth relevant documents and the generated ones made by its opponent generative retrieval model. Formally, we have:

$$J^{G^*,D^*} = \min_\theta \max_\phi \sum_{n=1}^{N} \Big(\mathbb{E}_{d\sim p_{\text{true}}(d|q_n,r)} \left[\log D(d|q_n)\right] + \mathbb{E}_{d\sim p_\theta(d|q_n,r)} \left[\log(1 - D(d|q_n))\right] \Big), \tag{1}$$

where the generative retrieval model G is written as $p_\theta(d|q_n,r)$, directly and the discriminative retrieval D estimates the probability of document d being relevant to query q, which is given by the sigmoid function of the discriminator score

$$D(d|q) = \sigma(f_\phi(d,q)) = \frac{\exp(f_\phi(d,q))}{1+\exp(f_\phi(d,q))}. \tag{2}$$

Let us leave the specific parametrisation of $f_\phi(d,q)$ to the next section when we discuss three specific IR tasks. From Eq. (1), we can see that the optimal parameters of the generative retrieval model and the discriminative retrieval model can be learned iteratively by maximising and minimising the same objective function, respectively.

2.1.2 Optimising Discriminative Retrieval. The objective for the discriminator is to *maximise* the log-likelihood of correctly distinguishing the true and generated relevant documents. With the observed relevant documents, and the ones sampled from the current optimal generative model $p_{\theta^*}(d|q,r)$, one can then obtain the optimal parameters for the discriminative retrieval model:

$$\phi^* = \arg\max_{\phi} \sum_{n=1}^{N} \Big(\mathbb{E}_{d\sim p_{\text{true}}(d|q_n,r)} \left[\log(\sigma(f_\phi(d,q_n))\right] + \mathbb{E}_{d\sim p_{\theta^*}(d|q_n,r)} \left[\log(1-\sigma(f_\phi(d,q_n)))\right] \Big), \quad (3)$$

where if the function f_ϕ is differentiable with respect to ϕ, the above is solved typically by stochastic gradient descent.

2.1.3 Optimising Generative Retrieval. By contrast, the generative retrieval model $p_\theta(d|q,r)$ intends to *minimise* the objective; it fits the underlying relevance distribution over documents $p_{\text{true}}(d|q,r)$ and based on that, randomly samples documents from the whole document set in order to *fool* the discriminative retrieval model.

It is worth mentioning that unlike GAN [13, 18], we design the generative model to directly generate known documents (in the document identifier space) not their features, because our work here intends to select relevant documents from a given document pool. Note that it is feasible to generate new documents (features, such as the value of BM25) by IRGAN, but to stay focused, we leave it for future investigation.

Specifically, while keeping the discriminator $f_\phi(q,d)$ fixed after its maximisation in Eq. (1), we learn the generative model via performing its minimisation:

$$\begin{aligned}\theta^* &= \arg\min_{\theta} \sum_{n=1}^{N} \Big(\mathbb{E}_{d\sim p_{\text{true}}(d|q_n,r)} \left[\log \sigma(f_\phi(d,q_n))\right] + \mathbb{E}_{d\sim p_\theta(d|q_n,r)} \left[\log(1-\sigma(f_\phi(d,q_n)))\right] \Big) \\ &= \arg\max_{\theta} \sum_{n=1}^{N} \underbrace{\mathbb{E}_{d\sim p_\theta(d|q_n,r)} \left[\log(1+\exp(f_\phi(d,q_n)))\right]}_{\text{denoted as } J^G(q_n)}, \quad (4)\end{aligned}$$

where for each query q_n we denote the objective function of the generator as $J^G(q_n)$[1].

As the sampling of d is discrete, it cannot be directly optimised by gradient descent as in the original GAN formulation. A common approach is to use policy gradient based reinforcement learning (REINFORCE) [42, 44]. Its gradient is derived as follows:

$$\begin{aligned}&\nabla_\theta J^G(q_n) \\ &= \nabla_\theta \mathbb{E}_{d\sim p_\theta(d|q_n,r)} \left[\log(1+\exp(f_\phi(d,q_n)))\right] \\ &= \sum_{i=1}^{M} \nabla_\theta p_\theta(d_i|q_n,r) \log(1+\exp(f_\phi(d_i,q_n))) \\ &= \sum_{i=1}^{M} p_\theta(d_i|q_n,r) \nabla_\theta \log p_\theta(d_i|q_n,r) \log(1+\exp(f_\phi(d_i,q_n))) \\ &= \mathbb{E}_{d\sim p_\theta(d|q_n,r)} \left[\nabla_\theta \log p_\theta(d|q_n,r) \log(1+\exp(f_\phi(d,q_n)))\right] \\ &\simeq \frac{1}{K} \sum_{k=1}^{K} \nabla_\theta \log p_\theta(d_k|q_n,r) \log(1+\exp(f_\phi(d_k,q_n))), \quad (5)\end{aligned}$$

where we perform a sampling approximation in the last step in which d_k is the k-th document sampled from the current version of generator $p_\theta(d|q_n,r)$. With reinforcement learning terminology, the term $\log(1+\exp(f_\phi(d,q_n)))$ acts as the reward for the policy $p_\theta(d|q_n,r)$ taking an action d in the environment q_n [38].

In order to reduce variance during the REINFORCE learning, we also replace the reward term $\log(1+\exp(f_\phi(d,q_n)))$ by its advantage function:

$$\log(1+\exp(f_\phi(d,q_n))) - \mathbb{E}_{d\sim p_\theta(d|q_n,r)} \left[\log(1+\exp(f_\phi(d,q_n)))\right],$$

where the term $\mathbb{E}_{d\sim p_\theta(d|q_n,r)} \left[\log(1+\exp(f_\phi(d,q_n)))\right]$ acts as the baseline function in policy gradient [38].

The overall logic of our proposed IRGAN solution is summarised in Algorithm 1. Before the adversarial training, the generator and discriminator can be initialised by their conventional models. Then during the adversarial training stage, the generator and discriminator are trained alternatively via Eqs. (5) and (3).

Algorithm 1 Minimax Game for IR (a.k.a IRGAN)

Input: generator $p_\theta(d|q,r)$; discriminator $f_\phi(\mathbf{x}_i^q)$;
training dataset $\mathcal{S} = \{\mathbf{x}\}$
Initialise $p_\theta(d|q,r)$, $f_\phi(q,d)$ with random weights θ, ϕ.
Pre-train $p_\theta(d|q,r)$, $f_\phi(q,d)$ using $\mathcal{S}$
repeat
  for g-steps **do**
    $p_\theta(d|q,r)$ generates K documents for each query q
    Update generator parameters via policy gradient Eq. (5)
  end for
  for d-steps **do**
    Use current $p_\theta(d|q,r)$ to generate negative examples and combine with given positive examples $\mathcal{S}$
    Train discriminator $f_\phi(q,d)$ by Eq. (3)
  end for
until IRGAN converges

2.2 Extension to Pairwise Case

In many IR problems, it is common that the labelled training data available for learning to rank are not a set of relevant documents but a set of ordered document pairs for each query, as it is often easier to capture users' relative preference judgements on a pair of documents than their absolute relevance judgements on individual documents (e.g., from a search engine's click-through log) [19]. Furthermore, if we use graded relevance scales (indicating a varying degree of match between each document and the corresponding query) rather than binary relevance, the training data could also be represented naturally as ordered document pairs.

Here we show that our proposed IRGAN framework would also work in such a pairwise setting for learning to rank. For each query q_n, we have a set of labelled document pairs $R_n = \{\langle d_i, d_j\rangle | d_i \succ d_j\}$ where $d_i \succ d_j$ means that d_i is more relevant to q_n than d_j. As in Section 2.1, we let $p_\theta(d|q,r)$ and $f_\phi(q,d)$ denote the generative retrieval model and the discriminative retrieval model respectively.

The generator G would try to generate document pairs that are similar to those in R_n, i.e., with the correct ranking. The discriminator D would try to distinguish such generated document pairs from those real document pairs. The probability that a document pair $\langle d_u, d_v\rangle$ being correctly ranked can be estimated by the discriminative retrieval model through a sigmoid function:

$$\begin{aligned}D(\langle d_u, d_v\rangle|q) &= \sigma(f_\phi(d_u,q) - f_\phi(d_v,q)) \\ &= \frac{\exp(f_\phi(d_u,q) - f_\phi(d_v,q))}{1+\exp(f_\phi(d_u,q) - f_\phi(d_v,q))} = \frac{1}{1+\exp(-z)}, \quad (6)\end{aligned}$$

[1] Following [13], $\mathbb{E}_{d\sim p_\theta(d|q_n,r)}[\log(\sigma(f_\phi(d,q_n)))]$ is normally used instead for maximisation, which keeps the same fixed point but provides more sufficient gradient for the generative model.

where $z = f_\phi(d_u, q) - f_\phi(d_v, q)$. Note that $-\log D(\langle d_u, d_v \rangle | q) = \log(1 + \exp(-z))$ is exactly the pairwise ranking loss function used by the learning to rank algorithm RankNet [3]. In addition to the logistic function $\log(1 + \exp(-z))$, it is possible to make use of other pairwise ranking loss functions [7], such as the hinge function $(1 - z)_+$ (as used in Ranking SVM [16]) and the exponential function $\exp(-z)$ (as used in RankBoost [11]), to define the probability $D(\langle d_u, d_v \rangle | q)$.

If we use the standard cross entropy cost for this binary classifier as before, we have the following minimax game:

$$J^{G^*, D^*} = \min_\theta \max_\phi \sum_{n=1}^{N} \Big(\mathbb{E}_{\mathbf{o} \sim p_{\text{true}}(\mathbf{o}|q_n)} \left[\log D(\mathbf{o}|q_n)\right] + \mathbb{E}_{\mathbf{o}' \sim p_\theta(\mathbf{o}'|q_n)} \left[\log(1 - D(\mathbf{o}'|q_n))\right] \Big), \quad (7)$$

where $\mathbf{o} = \langle d_u, d_v \rangle$ and $\mathbf{o}' = \langle d'_u, d'_v \rangle$ are true and generated document pairs for query q_n respectively.

In practice, to generate a document pair through generator G, we first pick a document pair $\langle d_i, d_j \rangle$ from R_n, take the lower ranked document d_j, and then pair it with a document d_k selected from the unlabelled data to make a new document pair $\langle d_k, d_j \rangle$. The underlying rationale is that we are more interested in identifying the documents similar to higher ranked document d_i as such documents are more likely to be relevant to the query q_n. The selection of the document d_k is based on the criterion that d_k should be more relevant than d_j according to the current generative model $p_\theta(d|q, r)$. In other words, we would like to select d_k from the whole document set to generate a document pair $\langle d_k, d_j \rangle$ which can imitate the document pair $\langle d_i, d_j \rangle \in R_n$.

Suppose that the generative model $p_\theta(d|q, r)$ is given by a softmax function (which is indeed used throughout Section 3, as we shall see later)

$$p_\theta(d_k|q, r) = \frac{\exp(g_\theta(q, d_k))}{\sum_d \exp(g_\theta(q, d))}, \quad (8)$$

where $g_\theta(q, d)$ is a task-specific real-valued function reflecting the chance of d being generated from q. The probability of choosing a particular document d_k could then be given by another softmax function:

$$G(\langle d_k, d_j \rangle | q) = p_\theta(\mathbf{o}'|q) = \frac{\exp\left(g_\theta(d_k, q) - g_\theta(d_j, q)\right)}{\sum_d \exp\left(g_\theta(d, q) - g_\theta(d_j, q)\right)} = \frac{\exp\left(g_\theta(d_k, q)\right)}{\sum_d \exp\left(g_\theta(d, q)\right)} = p_\theta(d_k|q, r). \quad (9)$$

In this special case, $G(\langle d_k, d_j \rangle | q)$ happens to be equal to $p_\theta(d_k|q, r)$, which is simple and reasonable. In general, the calculation of $G(\langle d_k, d_j \rangle | q)$ probably involves both $p_\theta(d_k|q, r)$ and $p_\theta(d_j|q, r)$. For example, one alternative way is to sample d_k only from the documents more relevant to the query than d_j, and let $G(\langle d_k, d_j \rangle | q)$ be directly proportional to $\max(p_\theta(d_k|q, r) - p_\theta(d_j|q, r), 0)$.

This generative model $p_\theta(d|q, r)$ could be trained by the REINFORCE algorithm [42, 44] in the same fashion as we have explained in Section 2.1.

2.3 Discussion

It can be proved that when we know the true relevance distribution exactly, the above minimax game of IRGAN, both pointwise and pairwise, has a Nash equilibrium in which the generator perfectly fits the distribution of true relevant documents (i.e., $p_\theta(d|q, r) = p_{\text{true}}(d|q, r)$ in the pointwise case and $p_\theta(\mathbf{o}'|q) = p_{\text{true}}(\mathbf{o}|q)$ in the pairwise case), while the discriminator cannot distinguish generated relevant documents from the true ones (i.e., the probability of d being relevant to q, $D(d|q)$ in the pointwise case or $D(\mathbf{o}'|q)$ in the pairwise case, is always $\frac{1}{2}$) [13]. However, in practice, the true distribution of relevant documents is unknown, and in such a situation, how the generative/discriminative retrieval models converge to achieve such an equilibrium is still an open problem in the current research literature [13, 14]. In our empirical study of IRGAN, we have found that depending on the specific task, the generative and discriminative retrieval models may reach different levels of performance; and at least one of them would be significantly improved in comparison to the corresponding original model without adversarial training.

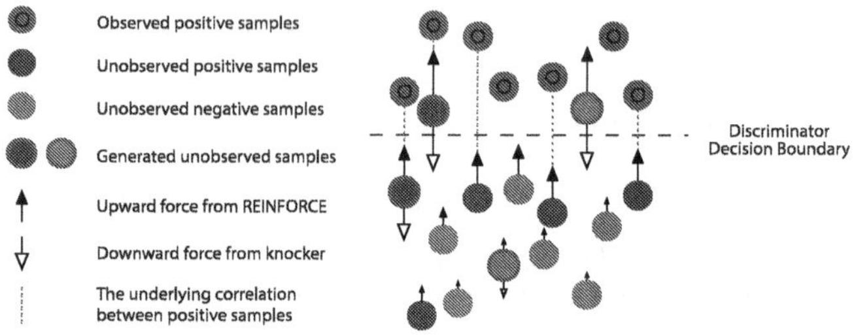

Figure 1: An illustration of IRGAN training.

How do the discriminator and the generator help each other? For the positive documents, observed or not, their relevance scores given by the discriminator $f_\phi(q, d)$ and the conditional probabilistic density $p_\theta(d|q, r)$ are likely to be somewhat positively correlated. In each epoch of training, the generator tries to generate samples close to the discriminator's decision boundary to confuse its training next round, while the discriminator tries to score down the generated samples. Since there exists positive correlations between the positive but unobserved (i.e., the true-positive) samples and (part of) the observed positive samples, the generator should be able to learn to push upwards these positive but unobserved samples faster than other samples with the signal from the discriminator.

To understand this process further, let us draw an analogy with a knocker kicking the floating soap in the water, as illustrated in Figure 1. There exist linking lines (i.e. positive correlations) between the unobserved positive soaps to the observed positive soaps that keep floating on the water surface (i.e. decision boundary of the discriminator) permanently. The discriminator acts as the knocker that kicks down the floating-up soaps, while the generator acts as the water that *selectively* floats the soaps up to the water surface. Even if the generator cannot perfectly fit the conditional data distribution, there could be still a dynamic equilibrium, which is obtained when the distribution of the positive and negative unobserved soaps get stable at different depth of the water. Since the unobserved positive soaps are linked to those observed positive soaps staying on the water surface, overall they should be able to reach higher positions than the (unobserved) negative soaps in the end.

Just like other GANs [12, 13, 44], the complexity of IRGAN training highly depends on the number of GAN iterations, each of which is of linear complexity $O(NKM)$ with respect to the number of candidate documents M. Such a complexity can largely be reduced to $O(NK \log M)$ by applying hierarchical softmax [28] in the sampling process of the generator.

2.4 Links to Existing Work

Let us continue our discussion on related work started in Section 1 and make comparisons with existing techniques in a greater scope.

2.4.1 Generative Adversarial Nets. Generative Adversarial Nets [13] were originally proposed to generate continuous data such as images. Our work is different in the following three aspects. First, the generative retrieval process is stochastic sampling over discrete data, i.e., the candidate documents, which is different from the deterministic generation based on the sampled noise signal in the original GAN. Specifically, as shown in Eq. (4), for each query q_n, the objective of the generative retrieval model is to minimise the expectation of the reward signal from the discriminative retrieval over the generated document distribution, while in the original GAN, the reward signal is solely dependent on a single generated instance. Second, our learning process of the generative retrieval model is based on the REINFORCE algorithm, a stochastic policy gradient technique in the field of reinforcement learning [44]. In IRGAN, the generative retrieval model can be regarded as an actor which takes an action of selecting a candidate document in a given environment of the query; the discriminative retrieval model can be regarded as a critic which performs a judgement whether the query-document pair is relevant enough. Third, during training, the conflict between ground-truth documents and generated documents is quite common, because documents are discrete and the candidate set is finite, which departs from the continuous (infinite) space for images or the extremely huge discrete (nearly infinite) space for text sequences [44]. Fourth, we also propose a pairwise discriminative objective, which is unique for IR problems.

Our work is also related to conditional GAN [29] as our generative and discriminative models are both conditional on the query.

2.4.2 MLE based Retrieval Models. For unsupervised learning problems that estimate the data p.d.f. $p(\boldsymbol{x})$ and supervised learning problems that estimate the conditional p.d.f. $p(y|\boldsymbol{x})$, maximum likelihood estimation (MLE) plays as the standard learning solution [30]. In IR, MLE is also widely used as an estimation method for many relevance features or retrieval models [1], such as Term Frequency (TF), Mixture Model (MM) [49], and Probabilistic Latent Semantic Indexing (PLSI) [17]. In this paper, we provide an alternative way of training and fusing retrieval models. First, the generative process is designed to fit the underlying true conditional distribution $p_{\text{true}}(d|q,r)$ via minimising the Jensen-Shannon divergence (as explained in [13]). Thus, it is natural to leverage GAN to distil a generative retrieval model to fit such an unknown conditional distribution using the observed user feedback data. Second, the unified training scheme of two schools of IR models offers the potential of getting better retrieval models, because (i) the generative retrieval adaptively provides different negative samples to the discriminative retrieval training, which is strategically diverse compared with static negative sampling [3, 34] or dynamic negative sampling using the discriminative retrieval model itself [4, 50, 51]; and (ii) the reward signal from the discriminative retrieval model provides strategic guidance on training the generative retrieval model, which is unavailable in traditional generative retrieval model training. From the generative retrieval's perspective, IRGAN is superior to traditional maximum likelihood estimation [18]. From the discriminative retrieval's perspective, IRGAN is able to exploit unlabelled data to achieve the effect of semi-supervised learning [36]. The advantages of employing two models working together have received more and more attention in recent research; one of the variations is *dual learning* [43] proposed for two-agent co-learning in machine translation etc.

It is also worth comparing IRGAN with pseudo relevance feedback [39, 45, 50], where the top retrieved documents are selected to refine the ranking result. The two techniques are quite different as (i) in pseudo relevance feedback the top retrieved documents are regarded as positive samples to train the ranker while in IRGAN the generator-picked documents are regarded as negative samples to train the ranker; (ii) in pseudo relevance feedback there is usually no further iterations while IRGAN involves many iterations of adversarial training.

2.4.3 Noise-Contrastive Estimation. Our work is also related to noise-contrastive estimation (NCE) that aims to correctly distinguish the true data $(y,\boldsymbol{x}) \sim p_{\text{data}}(y|\boldsymbol{x})$ from known noise samples $(y_n,\boldsymbol{x}) \sim p_{\text{noise}}(y_n|\boldsymbol{x})$. NCE is proved to be equivalent with MLE when noise samples are abundant [15]. With finite noise samples for contrastive learning, NCE is usually leveraged as an efficient approximation to MLE when the latter is inefficient, for example when the p.d.f is built by large-scale softmax modelling.

Furthermore, self-contrastive estimation (SCE) [14], a special case of NCE when the noise is directly sampled from the current (or a very recent) version of the model. It is proved that the gradient of SCE matches that of MLE with no prerequisite of infinite noise samples, which is a very attractive property of SCE learning. Dynamic negative item sampling [46, 51] in top-N item recommendation with implicit feedback turns out to be a practical use case of SCE, with specific solution of efficient sampling strategies.

The emergence of GANs [13], including our proposed IRGAN, opens a door to learning generative and discriminative retrieval models simultaneously. Compared to NCE and SCE, the GAN paradigm enables two models to learn together in an adversarial fashion, i.e. the discriminator learns to distinguish the true samples from the generated (faked) ones while the generator learns to generate high-quality samples to fool the discriminator.

3 APPLICATIONS

In this section, we apply our IRGAN framework to three specific IR scenarios: (i) web search with learning to rank, (ii) item recommendation, and (iii) question answering.

As formulated in Section 2, the generator's conditional distribution $p_\theta(d_i|q,r) = \exp(g_\theta(q,d_i))/\sum_{d_j}\exp(g_\theta(q,d_j))$, i.e., Eq. (8), fully depends on the scoring function $g_\theta(q,d)$. In the sampling stage, the temperature parameter τ is incorporated in Eq. (8) as

$$p_\theta(d|q,r) = \frac{\exp\left(g_\theta(q,d)/\tau\right)}{\sum_{j\in\mathcal{I}}\exp\left(g_\theta(q,d)/\tau\right)}, \quad (10)$$

where a lower temperature would make the sampling focus more on top-ranked documents. A special case is when the temperature is set to 0, which implies that the entropy of the generator is 0. In this situation, the generator simply ranks the documents in descending order and selects the top ones. More detailed study of τ will be given in Section 4.

The discriminator's ranking of documents, i.e., Eq. (2) for the pointwise setting and Eq. (6) for the pairwise setting, is fully determined by the scoring function $f_\phi(q,d)$.

The implementation of these two scoring functions, $g_\theta(q,d)$ and $f_\phi(q,d)$, are task-specific. Although there could be various implementations of $f_\phi(q,d)$ and $g_\theta(q,d)$ (e.g., $f_\phi(q,d)$ is implemented as a three-layer neural work while $g_\theta(q,d)$ is implemented as a factorisation machine [33]), to focus more on adversarial training, in this section we choose to implement them using the same function (with different sets of parameters)[2]:

$$g_\theta(q,d) = s_\theta(q,d) \quad \text{and} \quad f_\phi(q,d) = s_\phi(q,d) \ , \tag{11}$$

and in the following subsections we will discuss the implementation of the relevance scoring function $s(q,d)$ for those three chosen IR scenarios.

3.1 Web Search

Generally speaking, there are three types of loss functions designed for learning to rank in web search, namely, pointwise [31], pairwise [3] and listwise [6]. To our knowledge, the listwise approaches with a loss defined on document pairs and a list-aware weight added on document pairs, e.g., LambdaRank [5] and LambdaMART [4], often can achieve the best performance across various learning to rank tasks. Despite the variety of ranking loss functions, almost every learning to rank solution boils down to a scoring function $s(q,d)$.

In the web search scenario, each query-document pair (q,d) can be represented by a vector $\boldsymbol{x}_{q,d} \in \mathbb{R}^k$, where each dimension represents some statistical value of the query-document pair or either part of it, such as BM25, PageRank, TFIDF, language model score etc. We follow the work of RankNet [3] to implement a two-layer neural network for the score function:

$$s(q,d) = \boldsymbol{w}_2^\top \tanh(\boldsymbol{W}_1 \boldsymbol{x}_{q,d} + \boldsymbol{b}_1) + w_0 \ , \tag{12}$$

where $\boldsymbol{W}_1 \in \mathbb{R}^{l \times k}$ is the fully-connected matrix for the first layer, $\boldsymbol{b}_1 \in \mathbb{R}^l$ is the bias vector for the hidden layer, $\boldsymbol{w}_2 \in \mathbb{R}^l$ and w_0 are the weights for the output layer.

3.2 Item Recommendation

Item recommendation is a popular data mining task that can be regarded as a generalised information retrieval problem, where the query is the user profile constructed from their past item consumption. One of the most important methodologies for recommender systems is collaborative filtering which explores underlying user-user or item-item similarity and based on which performs personalised recommendations [41]. In collaborative filtering, a widely adopted model is matrix factorisation [21], following which we define our scoring function for the preference of user u (i.e. the query) to item i (i.e. the document) as

$$s(u,i) = b_i + \boldsymbol{v}_u^\top \boldsymbol{v}_i \ , \tag{13}$$

where b_i is the bias term for item i, $\boldsymbol{v}_u, \boldsymbol{v}_i \in \mathbb{R}^k$ are the latent vectors of user u and item i respectively defined in a k-dimensional continuous space. Here we omit the global bias and the user bias as they are reduced in the task of top-N item recommendation for each user[3].

To keep our discussion uncluttered, we have chosen a basic matrix factorisation model to implement, and it would be straightforward to replace it with more sophisticated models such as factorisation machines [33] or neural networks [8], whenever needed.

[2]We will, however, conduct a dedicated experiment on the interplay between these two players using the scoring functions of different model complexity, in Section 4.1.
[3]The user bias could be taken as a good baseline function for the advantage function in policy gradient (Eq. (5)) to reduce the learning volatility [38].

3.3 Question Answering

In question answering (QA) tasks [9], a question q or an answer a is represented as a sequence of words. Typical QA solutions aim to understand the natural language question first and then select/generate one or more answers which best match the question [9]. Among various QA tasks, the document-based QA task cab be regarded as a ranking process based on the matching score between two pieces of texts (for question and answer, respectively) [9]. Recently, end-to-end approaches to predicting the match of short text pairs have been proposed, by utilising neural networks, such as convolutional neural network (CNN) [9, 37] or long short-term memory neural network (LSTM) [40].

For any question-answer pair (q,a), we can define a relevance score. Specifically, one can leverage a convolutional neural networks (CNN) to learn the representation of word sequences [20], where each word is embedded as a vector in $\mathbb{R}^k$. By aligning the word vectors, an l-word sentence can be considered as a matrix in $\mathbb{R}^{l \times k}$. Then, a representation vector of the current sentence is obtained through a max-pooling-over-time strategy after a convolution operation over the matrix of aligned embedding vectors, yielding $\boldsymbol{v}_q$ and $\boldsymbol{v}_a \in \mathbb{R}^z$, where z is the number of convolutional kernels. The relevance score of such a question-answer pair can be defined as their cosine similarity, i.e.,

$$s(q,a) = \cos(\boldsymbol{v}_q, \boldsymbol{v}_a) = \frac{\boldsymbol{v}_q^\top \boldsymbol{v}_a}{|\boldsymbol{v}_q| \cdot |\boldsymbol{v}_a|} \ . \tag{14}$$

With the sentence representation and the scoring function defined above, the question answering problem is transformed into a query-document scoring problem in IR [37].

4 EXPERIMENTS

We have conducted our experiments[4] corresponding to the three real-world applications of our proposed IRGAN as discussed, i.e., web search, item recommendation, and question answering. As each of the three applications has its own background and baseline algorithms, this section about experiments is split into three self-contained subsections. We first test both the IRGAN-pointwise and IRGAN-pairwise formulations within a single task, web search; and then IRGAN-pointwise is further investigated in the item recommendation task where the rank bias is less critical, while IRGAN-pairwise is examined in the question answering task where the rank bias is more critical (usually only one answer is correct).

4.1 Web Search

4.1.1 Experiment Setup. Web search is an important problem in the IR field. Here we make use of the well-known benchmark dataset LETOR (LEarning TO Rank) [25] for webpage ranking to conduct our experiments.

Although standard learning to rank tasks assume explicit expert ratings for all training query-document pairs, implicit feedback from user interaction (such as the clicks information) is much more common in practical applications. This implies that we are usually faced with a relatively small amount of labelled data inferred from implicit feedback and a large amount of unlabelled data. In the unlabelled data, there could exist some hidden positive examples that have not been discovered yet. Thus, we choose to do experiments in a semi-supervised setting on the MQ2008-semi (Million Query

[4]The experiment code is provided at: https://github.com/geek-ai/irgan

track) collection in LETOR 4.0: other than the labelled data (judged query-document pairs), this collection also contains a large amount of unlabelled data (unjudged query-document pairs), which can be effectively exploited by our IRGAN framework.

Each query-document pair in the dataset is given a relevance level (-1, 0, 1 or 2). The higher the relevance level, the more relevant the query-document pair, except that -1 means "unknown". Each query-document pair is represented by a 46-dimensional vector of features (such as BM25 and LMIR). To evaluate our proposed IRGAN in the context of implicit feedback, we consider all the query-document pairs with relevance level higher than 0 as positive examples, and all the other query-document pairs (with relevance level -1 or 0) as unlabelled examples. According to our statistics, there are 784 unique queries in this dataset; on average each query is associated with about 5 positive documents and about 1,000 unlabelled documents. To construct the training and test sets, we perform a 4:1 random splitting. Both pointwise and pairwise IRGANs are evaluated based on this dataset.

Similar to RankNet [3], we adopt a neural network model with one hidden layer and tanh activation to learn the query-document matching score, where the size of the hidden layer equals to the size of features. Besides, both the generator and discriminator are trained from scratch.

In the experiments, we compare the generative retrieval model in our IRGAN framework with simple RankNet [3], LambdaRank [5], and the strong baseline LambdaMART [4] for which we use the RankLib[5] implementation. For the evaluation of those compared algorithms, we use standard ranking performance measures [7] such as Precision@N, Normalised Discounted Cumulative Gain (NDCG@N), Mean Average Precision (MAP) and Mean Reciprocal Ranking (MRR).

4.1.2 Results and Discussions. First, we provide the overall performance of all the compared learning to rank algorithms on the MQ2008-semi dataset in Table 1. In our IRGAN framework, we use the generative retrieval model to predict the distribution of the user preferred documents given a query and then carry out the ranking, which is identical to performing the softmax sampling with the temperature parameter set very close to 0. From the experimental results we can see clear performance improvements brought by our IRGAN approach on all the metrics.

Specifically, IRGAN-pairwise works better than IRGAN-pointwise on the metrics of Precision@3, NDCG@3 that focus on a few webpages at the very top of the ranked list, whereas IRGAN-pointwise performs better than IRGAN-pairwise on the metrics of Precision@10, NDCG@10 and MAP that take into account more webpages high in the ranked list. A possible explanation is that IRGAN-pointwise is targeted for the conditional distribution $p_{\text{true}}(d|q, r)$ which only concerns whether an individual document is relevant to the query, whereas IRGAN-pairwise cares about the whole ranking of the documents given the query.

It is worth mentioning that the dataset studied in our experiments comes with implicit feedback, which is common in real life applications including web search and online advertising. Traditional learning to rank methods like LambdaMART are not particularly effective in this type of semi-supervised setting, which may be due to its reliance on the ΔNDCG scoring for each document pair [5].

[5]https://sourceforge.net/p/lemur/wiki/RankLib/

Table 1: Webpage ranking performance comparison on the MQ2008-semi dataset, where $*$ means a significant improvement according to the Wilcoxon signed-rank test.

	P@3	P@5	P@10	MAP
MLE	0.1556	0.1295	0.1029	0.1604
RankNet [3]	0.1619	0.1219	0.1010	0.1517
LambdaRank [5]	0.1651	0.1352	0.1076	0.1658
LambdaMART [4]	0.1368	0.1026	0.0846	0.1288
IRGAN-pointwise	0.1714	0.1657	**0.1257**	**0.1915**
IRGAN-pairwise	**0.2000**	**0.1676**	0.1248	0.1816
Impv-pointwise	3.82%	22.56%*	16.82%*	15.50%*
Impv-pairwise	21.14%*	23.96%*	15.98%	9.53%
	NDCG@3	**NDCG@5**	**NDCG@10**	**MRR**
MLE	0.1893	0.1854	0.2054	0.3194
RankNet [3]	0.1801	0.1709	0.1943	0.3062
LambdaRank [5]	0.1926	0.1920	0.2093	0.3242
LambdaMART [4]	0.1573	0.1456	0.1627	0.2696
IRGAN-pointwise	0.2065	**0.2225**	**0.2483**	**0.3508**
IRGAN-pairwise	**0.2148**	0.2154	0.2380	0.3322
Impv-pointwise	7.22%	15.89%	18.63%	8.20%
Impv-pairwise	11.53%	12.19%	13.71%	2.47%

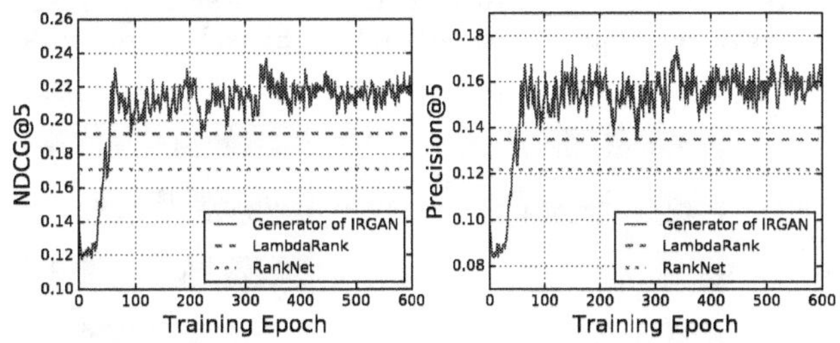

Figure 2: Learning curves of the pointwise IRGAN on the web search task.

Moreover, since adversarial training is widely regarded as an effective but unstable technique, we further investigate the learning trend of our proposed approach. Figures 2 and 3 show the typical learning curves of the generative/discriminative retrieval models in IRGAN-pointwise and IRGAN-pairwise respectively. Here we only show the performance measured by Precision@5 and NDCG@5 for discussion; the other metrics exhibit a similar trend. We can observe that after about 150 epoches for IRGAN-pointwise and 60 epoches for IRGAN-pairwise of adversarial training, both Precision@5 and NDCG@5 converge and the winner player consistently outperforms the best baseline LambdaRank.

Figure 4 shows how the ranking performance varies over the temperature parameter in Eq. (10) used by the generative retrieval model to sample negative query-document pairs for the discriminative retrieval model. We find the empirically optimal sampling temperature to be 0.2. The ranking performance increases when the temperature is tuned from 0 to the optimal value and then drops down afterwards, which indicates that *properly* increasing the aggressiveness (i.e. the tendency to focus on the top-ranked documents) of the generative retrieval model is important.

Furthermore, we study the impact of the model complexity of $f_\phi(q, d)$ and $g_\theta(q, d)$ upon the interplay between them. In Figure 5 we have compared different combinations of generative and discriminative model implementations (i.e., linear model and two-layer NN) under IRGAN-pointwise and IRGAN-pairwise, respectively. We observe that (i) for IRGAN-pointwise, the NN implemented generator

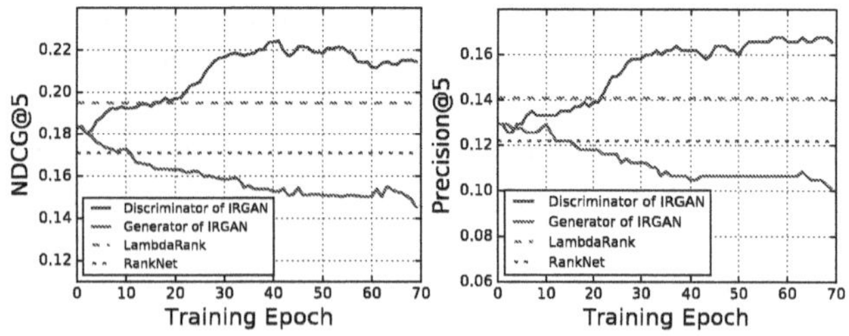

Figure 3: Learning curves of the pairwise IRGAN on the web search task.

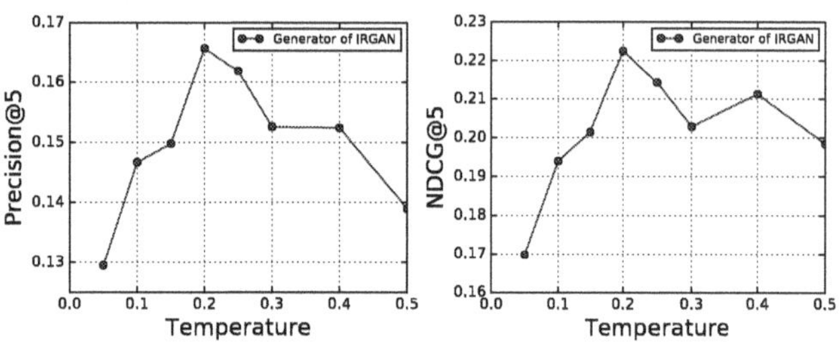

Figure 4: Ranking performance with different sampling temperatures of pointwise IRGAN on the web search task.

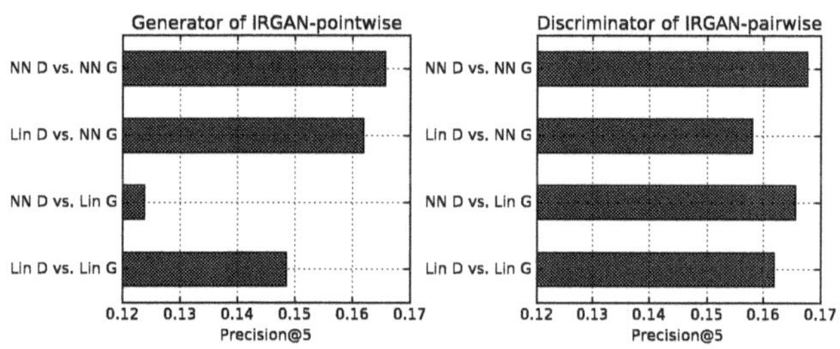

Figure 5: Ranking performance for IRGAN with different generator and discriminator scoring functions.

Table 2: Characteristics of the datasets.

Dataset	Users	Items	Ratings
Movielens	943	1,683	100,000
Netflix	480,189	17,770	100,480,507

works better than its linear version, while the NN implemented discriminator may not offer a good guidance if the generator has lower model complexity (i.e. linear); (ii) for IRGAN-pairwise, the NN implemented discriminator outperforms its linear version. This suggests that the model used for making the prediction (the generator in IRGAN-pointwise or the discriminator in IRGAN-pairwise) should be implemented with a capacity not lower than its opponent.

4.2 Item Recommendation

4.2.1 Experiment Setup. We conduct our experiments on two widely used collaborative filtering datasets: Movielens (100k) and Netflix. Their details are shown in Table 2. Following the experimental setting of [51], we regard the 5-star ratings in Netflix and both 4-star and 5-star ratings in Movielens as positive feedback and treat all other entries as unknown feedback, because we mainly focus on the implicit feedbacks problem. For training and test data splitting, we apply a 4:1 random splitting on both datasets as in [51]. The factor numbers for matrix factorisation are 5 and 16 for Movielens and Netflix respectively.

Table 3: Item recommendation results (Movielens).

	P@3	P@5	P@10	MAP
MLE	0.3369	0.3013	0.2559	0.2005
BPR [34]	0.3289	0.3044	0.2656	0.2009
LambdaFM [46]	0.3845	0.3474	0.2967	0.2222
IRGAN-pointwise	0.4072	0.3750	0.3140	0.2418
Impv-pointwise	5.90%*	7.94%*	5.83%*	8.82%*
	NDCG@3	**NDCG@5**	**NDCG@10**	**MRR**
MLE	0.3461	0.3236	0.3017	0.5264
BPR [34]	0.3410	0.3245	0.3076	0.5290
LambdaFM [46]	0.3986	0.3749	0.3518	0.5797
IRGAN-pointwise	0.4222	0.4009	0.3723	0.6082
Impv-pointwise	5.92%*	6.94%*	5.83%*	4.92%*

Table 4: Item recommendation results (Netflix).

	P@3	P@5	P@10	MAP
MLE	0.2941	0.2945	0.2777	0.0957
BPR [34]	0.3040	0.2933	0.2774	0.0935
LambdaFM [46]	0.3901	0.3790	0.3489	0.1672
IRGAN-pointwise	0.4456	0.4335	0.3923	0.1720
Impv-pointwise	14.23%*	14.38%*	12.44%*	2.87%*
	NDCG@3	**NDCG@5**	**NDCG@10**	**MRR**
MLE	0.3032	0.3011	0.2878	0.5085
BPR [34]	0.3077	0.2993	0.2866	0.5040
LambdaFM [46]	0.3942	0.3854	0.3624	0.5857
IRGAN-pointwise	0.4498	0.4404	0.4097	0.6371
Impv-pointwise	14.10%*	14.27%*	13.05%*	8.78%*

Specifically, to help train the discriminative retrieval model, the generative retrieval model is leveraged to sample negative items (in the same number of positive items) for each user via Eq. (10) with the temperature parameter set to 0.2, which to some extent pushes the item sampling to the top ones. Then the training of the discriminative retrieval model is dictated by Eq. (3). On the other side of the game, the training of the generative retrieval model is performed by REINFORCE as in Eq. (5), which is normally implemented by the policy gradient on the sampled K items from $p_\theta(d|q_n, r)$. In such a case, if the item set size is huge (e.g., more than 10^4) compared with K, it is more practical to leverage importance sampling to force the generative retrieval model to sample (some) positive examples $d \in R_n$, so that the positive reward can be observed from REINFORCE and the generative retrieval model can be learned properly.

In the experiments, we compare IRGAN with Bayesian Personalised Ranking (BPR) [34] and a state-of-the-art LambdaRank based collaborative filtering (LambdaFM) [46] for top-N item recommendation tasks [46, 51]. Similar to the web search task, the performance measures are Precision@N, NDCG@N, MAP and MRR.

4.2.2 Results and Discussion. First, the overall performance of the compared approaches on the two datasets is shown in Tables 3 and 4. From the experimental results, we can observe that IRGAN achieves statistically significant improvements across all the evaluation metrics and all the datasets. Note that the generative retrieval model in IRGAN does not explicitly learn to optimise the final ranking measures like what LambdaFM does, it still performs consistently better than LambdaFM. Our explanation is that the adversarial training provides both models a higher learning flexibility than the single-model training of LambdaFM or BPR.

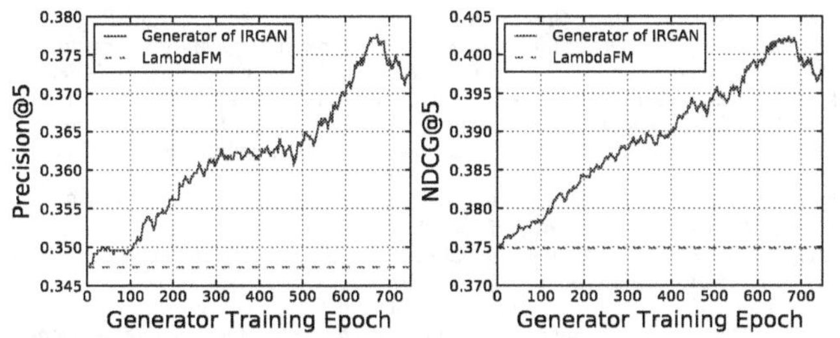

Figure 6: Learning curve of precision and NDCG of the generative retrieval model for the top-5 item recommendation task on the Movielens dataset.

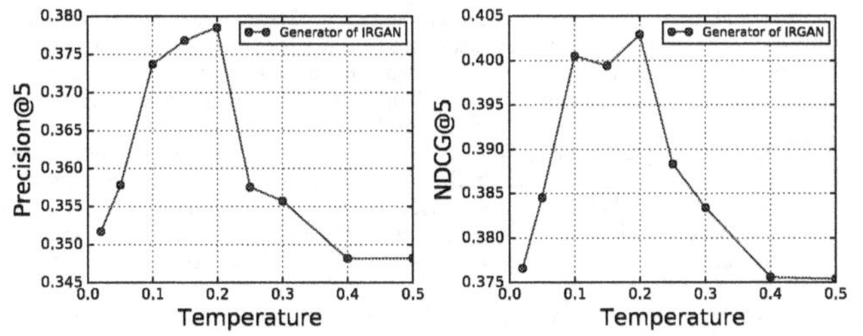

Figure 7: Ranking performance with different sampling temperatures on the Movielens dataset.

We further investigate the learning trend of the proposed approach. The learning curves are shown in Figure 6 for Precision@5 and NDCG@5. The experimental results demonstrate a reliable training process where IRGAN owns a consistent superiority over the baseline LambdaFM from the beginning of adversarial training. As for this case the curves are not as stable as those in web search (Figure 3), one can adopt the early stopping strategy based on a validation set.

In addition, as shown in Figure 7, we also investigate how the performance varies w.r.t. the sampling temperature in Eq. (10), which is consistent with our observations in the web search task.

4.3 Question Answering

4.3.1 Experiment Setup. InsuranceQA [10] is one of the most studied question-answering dataset. Its questions are submitted from real users and the high-quality answers are composed by professionals with good domain knowledge. So the candidate answers are usually randomly sampled from the whole answers pool (whereas other QA datasets may have a small-size fixed candidate answers for each single question). Thus InsuranceQA is suitable for testing our sampling/generating strategy. There are a training set, a development set, and two test sets (test-1 and test-2) in the published corpus. 12,887 questions are included in the training set with correct answers, while the development set have 1,000 unseen question-answer pairs and the two test sets consist of 1,800 pairs. The system is expected to find the *one and only* real answer from 500 candidate answers under the Precision@1 metric. As we have found from the web search task that IRGAN-pairwise works better for top-ranked documents, we concentrate on the former in the QA task experiments.

To focus on evaluating the effectiveness of IRGAN, we use a simple convolutional layer on the basic embedding matrix of a question sentence or an answer sentence. A representation vector of the current sentence is distilled from a max-pooling strategy after convolution [20], yielding $\boldsymbol{v}_q$ and $\boldsymbol{v}_a$ in Eq. (14). The matching probability of such a question-answer pair is given by the cosine distance, which is similar to the basic QA-CNN model [9].

In detail, the embedding of each word is initialised as a 100-dimension random vector. In the convolutional layer, the window size of the convolution kernel is set to $(1, 2, 3, 5)$. After the convolutional layer, the max-pooling-over-time strategy is adopted [20], where each feature map will be pooled as a scalar since its convolution kernel width is the same as the embedding vector. The performance on the test set is calculated by the model in the epoch with the best performance evaluated on the development set. Our IRGAN solution would load pre-trained models as the initial parameters for both generator and discriminator. A question with multiple answers are considered as multiple questions each with a single corresponding answer, which means that for each question-answer pair only the feeding positive answer is observed by the current discriminator but the other positive answers are not.

Table 5: The Precision@1 of InsuranceQA.

	test-1	test-2
QA-CNN [9]	0.6133	0.5689
LambdaCNN [9, 51]	0.6294	0.6006
IRGAN-pairwise	0.6444	0.6111
Impv-pairwise	2.38%*	1.75%

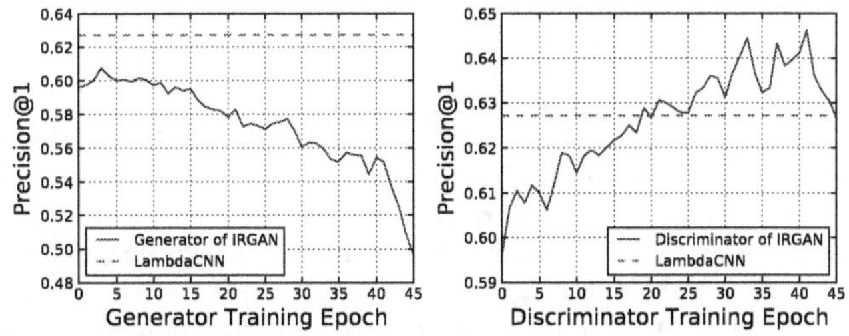

Figure 8: The experimental results in QA task.

4.3.2 Results and Discussion. As shown in Table 5, IRGAN outperforms both the basic CNN model with a random sampling strategy (QA-CNN) and the enhanced CNN model with a dynamic negative sampling strategy (LambdaCNN) [9, 51]. The learning curves of the two models are shown in Figure 8, which is evaluated on the test-1 set. The performance of the discriminative retrieval model in IRGAN-pairwise is better than LambdaCNN while the generative retrieval model tends to perform less effectively during the pairwise adversarial training. A reason for the worse generator could be the sparsity of the answers distribution, i.e., each question usually has only one correct answer and many more weak negative answers. Due to such a sparsity, the generator may fail to get a positive feedback from the discriminator. An inspection of the sampled answers from LambdaCNN and IRGAN has revealed that about 1/3 of their samples are different. This suggests the effectiveness of independently modelling the negative generator.

5 CONCLUSIONS

In this paper, we have proposed the IRGAN framework that unifies two schools of information retrieval methodologies, i.e., generative models and discriminative models, via adversarial training in a minimax game. Such an adversarial training framework takes advantages from both schools of methodologies: (i) the generative retrieval model is guided by the signals obtained from the discriminative retrieval model, which makes it more favourable than the non-learning methods or the maximum likelihood estimation scheme; (ii) the discriminative retrieval model could be enhanced to rank top documents better via strategic negative sampling from the generator. Overall, IRGAN provides a more flexible and principled training environment that combines these two kinds of retrieval models. Extensive experiments were conducted on four real-world datasets in three typical IR tasks, namely web search, item recommendation, and question answering. Significant performance gains were observed in each set of experiments.

Despite the great empirical success of GAN [13], there are still many questions with regard to its theoretical foundation remaining to be answered by the research community. For example, it is "not entirely clear" why GAN can generate sharper realistic images than alternative techniques [12]. Our exploration of adversarial training for information retrieval in the proposed IRGAN framework has suggested that different equilibria could be reached in the end depending on the task and setting. In the pointwise version of IRGAN, the generative retrieval model gets improved more than the discriminative retrieval model, but we have an opposite observation in the pairwise case. This phenomenon certainly warrants further investigation.

For future work, further experiments on more real-world datasets will be conducted. We also plan to extend our framework and test it over the generation of word tokens. One possible direction is to delve into the word weighting schemes such as [32, 35, 48] learned from the IRGAN generative retrieval model and then derive new ranking features on that basis. Furthermore, the language models could be re-defined along with GAN training, where new useful word patterns might emerge.

Acknowledgement We thank Geek.AI for hosting this collaborative project. The work done by SJTU is financially supported by NSFC (61632017) and Shanghai Sailing Program (17YF1428200).

REFERENCES

[1] Ricardo Baeza-Yates, Berthier Ribeiro-Neto, and others. 1999. *Modern information retrieval.*

[2] Oren Barkan and Noam Koenigstein. 2016. Item2vec: neural item embedding for collaborative filtering. In *MLSP Workshop.*

[3] Chris Burges, Tal Shaked, Erin Renshaw, Ari Lazier, Matt Deeds, Nicole Hamilton, and Greg Hullender. 2005. Learning to Rank Using Gradient Descent. In *ICML.*

[4] Christopher JC Burges. 2010. From RankNet to LambdaRank to LambdaMART: An Overview. *Learning* (2010).

[5] Christopher JC Burges, Robert Ragno, and Quoc Viet Le. 2006. Learning to Rank with Nonsmooth Cost Functions. In *NIPS.*

[6] Zhe Cao, Tao Qin, Tie-Yan Liu, Ming-Feng Tsai, and Hang Li. 2007. Learning to rank: from pairwise approach to listwise approach. In *ICML.*

[7] Wei Chen, Tie-Yan Liu, Yanyan Lan, Zhi-Ming Ma, and Hang Li. 2009. Ranking Measures and Loss Functions in Learning to Rank. In *NIPS.* 315–323.

[8] Paul Covington, Jay Adams, and Emre Sargin. 2016. Deep neural networks for youtube recommendations. In *RecSys.*

[9] Cícero Nogueira dos Santos, Ming Tan, Bing Xiang, and Bowen Zhou. 2016. Attentive Pooling Networks. *CoRR* (2016).

[10] Minwei Feng, Bing Xiang, Michael R Glass, Lidan Wang, and Bowen Zhou. 2015. Applying deep learning to answer selection: A study and an open task. In *ASRU Workshop.*

[11] Yoav Freund, Raj Iyer, Robert E Schapire, and Yoram Singer. 2003. An Efficient Boosting Algorithm for Combining Preferences. *JMLR* (2003).

[12] Ian Goodfellow. 2016. NIPS 2016 Tutorial: Generative Adversarial Networks. *arXiv preprint arXiv:1701.00160* (2016).

[13] Ian Goodfellow, Jean Pouget-Abadie, Mehdi Mirza, Bing Xu, David Warde-Farley, Sherjil Ozair, Aaron Courville, and Yoshua Bengio. 2014. Generative Adversarial Nets. In *NIPS.*

[14] Ian J Goodfellow. 2014. On Distinguishability Criteria for Estimating Generative Models. *arXiv:1412.6515* (2014).

[15] Michael Gutmann and Aapo Hyvärinen. 2010. Noise-contrastive estimation: A new estimation principle for unnormalized statistical models. In *AISTATS.*

[16] Ralf Herbrich, Thore Graepel, and Klaus Obermayer. 2000. Large Margin Rank Boundaries for Ordinal Regression. In *Advances in Large Margin Classifiers.*

[17] Thomas Hofmann. 1999. Probabilistic Latent Semantic Indexing. In *SIGIR.*

[18] Ferenc Huszár. 2015. How (not) to Train your Generative Model: Scheduled Sampling, Likelihood, Adversary? *arXiv preprint arXiv:1511.05101* (2015).

[19] Thorsten Joachims. 2002. Optimizing search engines using clickthrough data. In *KDD.*

[20] Yoon Kim. 2014. Convolutional Neural Networks for Sentence Classification. *arXiv preprint arXiv:1408.5882* (2014).

[21] Yehuda Koren, Robert Bell, and Chris Volinsky. 2009. Matrix factorization techniques for recommender systems. *Computer* (2009).

[22] John Lafferty and Chengxiang Zhai. 2002. Probabilistic Relevance Models Based on Document and Query Generation. In *Language Modeling and Information Retrieval.*

[23] Ping Li, Christopher JC Burges, Qiang Wu, JC Platt, D Koller, Y Singer, and S Roweis. 2007. McRank: Learning to Rank Using Multiple Classification and Gradient Boosting.. In *NIPS.*

[24] Tie-Yan Liu. 2009. Learning to rank for information retrieval. *Foundations and Trends in Information Retrieval* (2009).

[25] Tie-Yan Liu, Jun Xu, Tao Qin, Wenying Xiong, and Hang Li. 2007. LETOR: Benchmark Dataset for Research on Learning to Rank for Information Retrieval. In *Proceedings of SIGIR 2007 Workshop on Learning to Rank for Information Retrieval.*

[26] Jiyun Luo, Sicong Zhang, and Hui Yang. 2014. Win-win search: dual-agent stochastic game in session search. In *SIGIR.*

[27] H Brendan McMahan, Gary Holt, David Sculley, Michael Young, Dietmar Ebner, Julian Grady, Lan Nie, Todd Phillips, Eugene Davydov, Daniel Golovin, and others. 2013. Ad click prediction: a view from the trenches. In *KDD.*

[28] Tomas Mikolov, Ilya Sutskever, Kai Chen, Greg S Corrado, and Jeff Dean. 2013. Distributed representations of words and phrases and their compositionality. In *NIPS.*

[29] Mehdi Mirza and Simon Osindero. 2014. Conditional Generative Adversarial Nets. *arXiv preprint arXiv:1411.1784* (2014).

[30] In Jae Myung. 2003. Tutorial on maximum likelihood estimation. *Journal of mathematical Psychology* (2003).

[31] Ramesh Nallapati. 2004. Discriminative Models for Information Retrieval. In *SIGIR.*

[32] Jay M Ponte and W Bruce Croft. 1998. A language modeling approach to information retrieval. In *SIGIR.*

[33] Steffen Rendle. 2010. Factorization machines. In *ICDM.*

[34] Steffen Rendle, Christoph Freudenthaler, Zeno Gantner, and Lars Schmidt-Thieme. 2009. BPR: Bayesian personalized ranking from implicit feedback. In *UAI.*

[35] Stephen E Robertson and K Sparck Jones. 1976. Relevance weighting of search terms. *Journal of the American Society for Information science* (1976).

[36] Tim Salimans, Ian Goodfellow, Wojciech Zaremba, Vicki Cheung, Alec Radford, and Xi Chen. 2016. Improved Techniques for Training GANs. In *NIPS.*

[37] Aliaksei Severyn and Alessandro Moschitti. 2015. Learning to rank short text pairs with convolutional deep neural networks. In *SIGIR.*

[38] Richard S Sutton, David A McAllester, Satinder P Singh, Yishay Mansour, and others. 1999. Policy Gradient Methods for Reinforcement Learning with Function Approximation. In *NIPS.*

[39] Tao Tao and ChengXiang Zhai. 2006. Regularized estimation of mixture models for robust pseudo-relevance feedback. In *SIGIR.* ACM, 162–169.

[40] Di Wang and Eric Nyberg. 2015. A Long Short-Term Memory Model for Answer Sentence Selection in Question Answering. In *ACL.*

[41] Jun Wang, Arjen P De Vries, and Marcel JT Reinders. 2006. Unifying user-based and item-based collaborative filtering approaches by similarity fusion. In *SIGIR.*

[42] Ronald J Williams. 1992. Simple statistical gradient-following algorithms for connectionist reinforcement learning. *Machine learning* (1992).

[43] Yingce Xia, Di He, Tao Qin, Liwei Wang, Nenghai Yu, Tie-Yan Liu, and Wei-Ying Ma. 2016. Dual Learning for Machine Translation. In *NIPS.*

[44] Lantao Yu, Weinan Zhang, Jun Wang, and Yong Yu. 2017. SeqGAN: Sequence Generative Adversarial Nets with Policy Gradient. In *AAAI.*

[45] Shipeng Yu, Deng Cai, Ji-Rong Wen, and Wei-Ying Ma. 2003. Improving pseudo-relevance feedback in web information retrieval using web page segmentation. In *WWW.* ACM, 11–18.

[46] Fajie Yuan, Guibing Guo, Joemon M Jose, Long Chen, Haitao Yu, and Weinan Zhang. 2016. Lambdafm: learning optimal ranking with factorization machines using lambda surrogates. In *CIKM.*

[47] ChengXiang Zhai. 2016. Towards a game-theoretic framework for text data retrieval. *IEEE Data Eng. Bull.* (2016).

[48] Chengxiang Zhai and John Lafferty. 2004. A study of smoothing methods for language models applied to information retrieval. *TOIS* (2004).

[49] ChengXiang Zhai and John D. Lafferty. 2001. Model-based Feedback in the Language Modeling Approach to Information Retrieval. In *CIKM.*

[50] Peng Zhang, Qian Yu, Yuexian Hou, Dawei Song, Jingfei Li, and Bin Hu. 2017. A Distribution Separation Method Using Irrelevance Feedback Data for Information Retrieval. *ACM TIST* (2017).

[51] Weinan Zhang, Tianqi Chen, Jun Wang, and Yong Yu. 2013. Optimizing top-n collaborative filtering via dynamic negative item sampling. In *SIGIR.*

Personalized PageRank in Uncertain Graphs with Mutually Exclusive Edges*

Jung Hyun Kim
Arizona State University
Tempe, AZ 85287
jkim294@asu.edu

Mao-Lin Li
Arizona State University
Tempe, AZ, USA 85287
maolinli@asu.edu

K. Selçuk Candan
Arizona State University
Tempe, AZ, USA 85287
candan@asu.edu

Maria Luisa Sapino
University of Torino
I-10149 Torino, Italy
mlsapino@di.unito.it

ABSTRACT

Measures of node ranking, such as personalized PageRank, are utilized in many web and social-network based prediction and recommendation applications. Despite their effectiveness when the underlying graph is certain, however, these measures become difficult to apply in the presence of uncertainties, as they are not designed for graphs that include uncertain information, such as edges that mutually exclude each other. While there are several ways to naively extend existing techniques (such as trying to encode uncertainties as edge weights or computing all possible scenarios), as we discuss in this paper, these either lead to large degrees of errors or are very expensive to compute, as the number of possible worlds can grow exponentially with the amount of uncertainty. To tackle with this challenge, in this paper, we propose an efficient *Uncertain Personalized PageRank (UPPR)* algorithm to approximately compute personalized PageRank values on an uncertain graph with edge uncertainties. *UPPR* avoids enumeration of all possible worlds, yet it is able to achieve comparable accuracy by carefully encoding edge uncertainties in a data structure that leads to fast approximations. Experimental results show that *UPPR* is very efficient in terms of execution time and its accuracy is comparable or better than more costly alternatives.

1 INTRODUCTION

Measures of node ranking are used in many web and social media based prediction and recommendation applications [6, 24, 27]. There are several ways to rank nodes in a graph ranking, including the well known personalized PageRank (PPR) measure [9, 18], which weights the nodes in a given graph based on their positions relative to a given seed set of nodes (Section 2).

*This work has been funded by NSF grants #1339835, #1318788, #1610282, #1633381, and the EU-H2020 grant #690817.

SIGIR '17, August 07-11, 2017, Shinjuku, Tokyo, Japan
© 2017 ACM. 978-1-4503-5022-8/17/08...$15.00
DOI: 10.1145/3077136.3080794

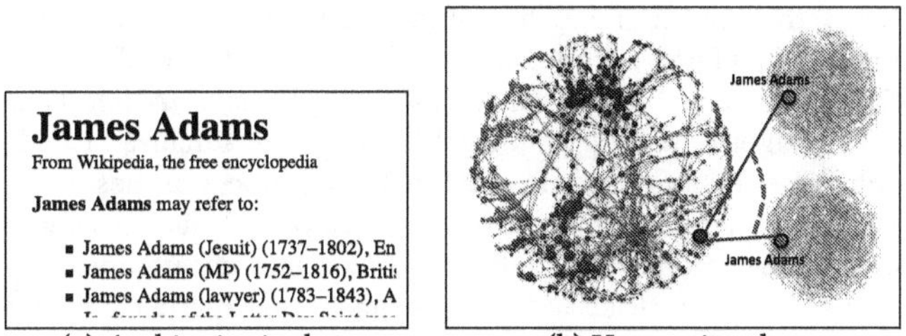

(a) Ambiguity in data (b) Uncertain edge

Figure 1: Ambiguity in Wikipedia and its potential impact on the proximity/cluster analysis

Despite their effectiveness when the underlying graph is certain, these measures become difficult to apply in the presence of graph uncertainties, as they are not designed for graphs that include uncertain information. Unfortunately, in many real world web and social-network based applications, it may not be possible to obtain a perfect and complete structure of the underlying knowledge graph for various reasons: This may be due to lack of information, noise in data collection, or privacy concerns [17].

Most existing works on graph uncertainty consider *existence uncertainty*, where a given edge exists probabilistically and the existence probabilities of the individual edges are assumed to be independent from each other [2, 10, 16, 20, 26, 29]. In practice, however, this assumption does not always hold: we may be aware of the existence of an edge, but we may not know between which pairs of nodes the edge exists. For example, we may be able to deduce that one of the several friends of an individual in a social network may be his/her father, but we may not know which friend. As another example, we may know that a name referred to in a web document is one of the many named entities in a knowledge base, but we may not know which one is the correct entity (Figure 1(a)).

In this paper, we propose an *uncertain edge model with mutual exclusion* that can handle such general forms of uncertainty[1] and consider the node ranking problem in the presence of such edges. Obtaining node rankings in such a graph is difficult because addition or removal of one single edge can have a drastic effect on proximity [11]: e.g., addition of just one edge may be sufficient to

[1]For relational data, this type of uncertainty is also known as "partial maybe null", where one is not sure if the attribute has a value or not, but if the value exists, then it must be within a specified set[1, 7]

link two otherwise distant node clusters, thereby significantly altering the proximities of a large number of pairs of nodes in the graph (Figure 1(b)). A naive way to deal with this would be to measure *expected node proximities* by taking into account the likelihoods of different interpretations and the node proximity measurements corresponding to each interpretation: one can

(1) first enumerate all possible interpretations (or possible worlds) of the uncertain graph, where each interpretation is a possible certain graph;
(2) compute node proximity under each possible world; and
(3) finally, combine all these node proximity measurements into a single *expected proximity* value.

It is, however, easy to see that an exhaustive enumeration based approach will quickly become intractable since (as we see in Section 3) the number of possible worlds can grow exponentially with the amount of uncertainty in the graph. To tackle this challenge, in this paper, we propose an efficient *Uncertain Personalized PageRank (UPPR)* algorithm to approximately compute personalized PageRank values on an uncertain graph with edge uncertainties. *UPPR* avoids enumeration of all possible worlds, yet it is able to achieve comparable accuracy by carefully encoding edge uncertainties in a data structure that leads to fast approximations. Experiment results show that *UPPR* is very efficient in terms of execution time (multiple orders faster than other algorithms with similar accuracy) and its accuracy is close to perfect.

In the next section, we discuss the related literature. In Section 3, we introduce the uncertain graph model. In Section 4, we discuss alternative "naive" techniques and discuss their individual shortcomings. Then, in Section 5, we present the proposed efficient and effective *uncertain personalized PageRank (UPPR)* technique. We evaluate the various techniques discussed in the paper in Section 6 using several data sets and conclude in Section 8.

2 RELATED WORKS

2.1 Graphs with Uncertainty

Uncertain graphs are common in many applications. For example, in biological protein interaction networks, uncertainty may be introduced when the existence of certain interactions are often only statistically probable [16, 20]. In communication networks, possibility of link failure needs to be accounted for in finding stable and reliable paths for packet delivery with minimum cost: this involves taking into account several forms of uncertainty, including *existence uncertainty, ambiguity*, and *confusion* on edges [10].

In web-based applications, such as social networks, uncertainties may exist due to inherent lack of prior knowledge regarding the existence of friendship or influence flow among the users in the underlying network [17] and it may be critical to take into account such forms of uncertainty in predicting which nodes are likely to be connected to which other nodes [24]. Other graph analysis operations that are affected from graph uncertainty include shortest paths, reachability analysis, and subgraph searching. A common challenge is that, in the presence of uncertainty, (already expensive) graph operations becomes more expensive. [8] presented an interval labeled edge model and discussed efficient computation of minimum paths and trees on such uncertain graphs without having to enumerate all possible worlds. [26] and [29] also focused on shortest paths, but on graphs where edges have probabilistic interpretations for existence in uncertain graphs. Given edges that are accompanied with the probability of existence, [16, 20] propose ways to compute reliability and reachability efficiently through Monte-Carlo sampling. [30] proposed pruning techniques to reduce the complexity of subgraph searching and subgraph pattern mining in uncertain graphs by avoiding enumeration of all possible worlds of the uncertain graph.

2.2 Node Ranking in Uncertain Graphs

PageRank is a widely-used measure to compute node importance / significance in a graph [5]. It takes into account the connectivity of nodes in the graph by defining the score of the node $v_i \in V$ as the amount of time spent on v_i in a sufficiently long random walk on the graph. The personalized PageRank (PPR) [9, 18] technique extends this in a way that takes into account the context defined by a given set of *important* nodes: given a set of seed nodes $S \subseteq V$, the PPR scores can be represented as a vector $\overrightarrow{r}$, where $\overrightarrow{r} = \alpha \mathrm{T} \overrightarrow{r} + (1-\alpha)\overrightarrow{s}$, where $\overrightarrow{s}[i] = \frac{1}{\|S\|}$ if $v_i \in S$ and $\overrightarrow{s}[i] = 0$, otherwise. Intuitively, given a set of nodes $S \subseteq V$, instead of jumping to a random node in V with probability $(1-\alpha)$, the random walk jumps to one of the nodes in the seed set, S. Since we constrain the teleportation jumps from any node in the graph to only the given set of important seed nodes, then the random-walk spends more time on nodes that are close to the seeds and, thus, those nodes are declared more significant based on the context defined by the seed nodes. Due to the cost of obtaining exact PPR scores, non-exact solutions (based on low rank decomposition [28] or Monte Carlo methods [22]) have been proposed.

Several works considered the problem of ranking on graphs with different forms of uncertainties. [13] considered PageRank when web graphs contain erroneous link information and proposed an approximate solution using interval matrices – the proposed approach captures the PageRank scores of the nodes affected by fragile links in terms of lower and upper bounds of PageRank values. A different node-centric uncertain graph model and node ranking approach are presented in [23]: in particular, [23] collapses the uncertain parts of a graph into a *cloud* graph, where the end of every undetected link is connected to this cloud graph and computes PageRank scores on this transformed graph. [12] considered uncertain graphs, where edges are annotated with existence probabilities and extended the SimRank measure [14] under probabilistic interpretations of edge existence and transition matrices.

In this paper, we propose a more general uncertainty model (of which the *existence* uncertainty considered by the works listed above is special case) and discuss efficient ways to compute PPR under this more powerful model.

3 PROBLEM FORMULATION

Let $G = (V, E)$ be a directed graph with a set, V, of nodes and a set, E, of edges. Conventionally, each edge $e \in E$ is defined using two nodes in the graph: a source node $source(e) \in V$ and a target node $target(e) \in V$. In this paper, on the other hand, we divide the graph edges into *certain* and *uncertain* edges.

Definition 3.1 (Certain edges). A certain edge $e_+ \in E$ has well defined source and target nodes, v_{source} and v_{dest}. We denote

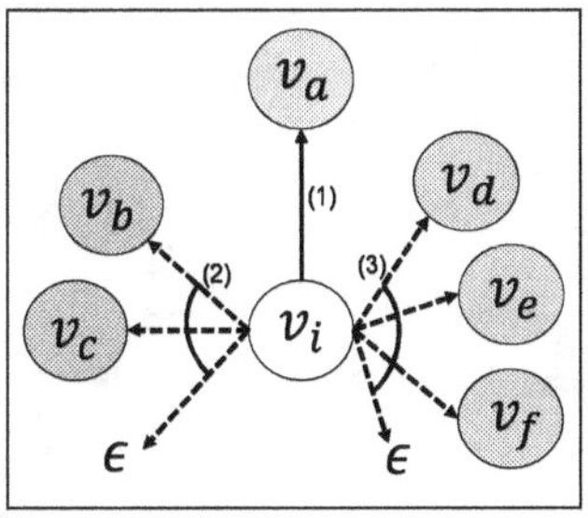

Figure 2: A graph with certain and uncertain edges

this with $source(e_+) = \{v_{source}\}$ and $target(e_+) = \{v_{dest}\}$. We denote the subset of E consisting of E's certain edges as E_+. ⋄

In Figure 2, $e_{+(1)} = \{\langle v_i, v_a\rangle\}$ is a certain edge from v_i to v_a. Note that, since $\|source(e_+)\| = \|target(e_+)\| = 1$, this edge type does not include any uncertain information. In this paper, we refer to this certainty as having a unique possible world. Each uncertain edge, on the other hand, can represent multiple possible worlds:

Definition 3.2 (Uncertain Edges). An uncertain edge $e_- \in E$ has a well defined source node but does not have a well defined target node.[2] More specifically, we have

- $source(e_-) \subseteq V$,
- $target(e_-) \subseteq V \cup \{\epsilon\}$ and $target(e_-) \neq \{\epsilon\}$, and
- $\|source(e_-)\| = 1$ and $\|target(e_-)\| > 1$.

Above ϵ denotes a non-existing node. We denote the subset of E consisting of all of E's uncertain edges as E_-. ⋄

Figure 2 includes two uncertain edges, $e_{-(2)}$ and $e_{-(3)}$ with different degrees. The uncertain edge $e_{-(3)}$ captures a form of *uncertainty with mutual exclusion* among the edges from v_i to v_d, v_e, or v_f. This uncertainty, however, is independent from the existence uncertainty of $e_{-(2)}$. Therefore, the proposed model allows as a special case the *independent existence uncertainty* model considered by many of the existing works [2, 10, 16, 20, 26, 29].

3.1 Possible Worlds of an Uncertain Edge

Each uncertain edge implicitly defines multiple possible worlds in which different interpretations are valid:

Definition 3.3 (Possible Worlds of an Edge under Mutual Exclusion Semantics). Let $e \in E$ be an edge. Let $source(e)$ denote a source node of the edge and let $target(e) \subseteq V \cup \{\epsilon\}$ denote the potential targets of the edge. Given this edge, we define *all possible worlds covered by this edge under mutual exclusion semantics* as

$$pw_{unique}(e) \quad = \quad \Big\{\langle v_i, v_j\rangle \mid (v_i = source(e)) \wedge (v_j \in target(e))\Big\}$$

The possible worlds covered by an uncertain edge consist of all combinations of target nodes; if a target node is potentially non-existent, then it is also a possible world. $\|pw_{unique}(e)\| = \|target(e)\|$ is the number of possible worlds on the edge, e ⋄

[2] Due to space constraints, in this paper we only deal with the case of uncertainty in the target nodes, while we consider the edges' source nodes as given.

In the example visualized in Figure 2, there are three possible worlds defined by $e_{-(2)}$ $(= \{\langle v_i, v_b\rangle, \langle v_i, v_c\rangle, \langle v_i, \epsilon\rangle\}$ – the last one implying that this edge does not exist) and four possible worlds defined by $e_{-(3)}$ $(= \{\langle v_i, v_d\rangle, \langle v_i, v_e\rangle, \langle v_i, v_f\rangle, \langle v_i, \epsilon\rangle\}$ – again the last one implying that this edge does not exist).

Note that under a more general interpretation, more than one of the potential combinations, implied by the uncertainty encoded in the edge, may be possible in the real world.

Definition 3.4 (Possible Worlds of an Edge under Multiple Edge Semantics). Let $e \in E$ be a certain or uncertain edge and $pw_{unique}(e)$ be the corresponding possible worlds covered by this edge under mutual exclusion semantics. Given this edge, we define *all possible worlds covered by this edge under multiple edge semantics* as all possible non-empty subsets of its target set[3]. Note that, since a possible world containing ϵ is equivalent to the world where ϵ has been removed, we have

$$\|pw_{multiple}(e)\| = \begin{cases} 2^{(\|pw_{unique}(e)\|-1)}, & \epsilon \in \text{target(e)} \\ 2^{\|(pw_{unique}(e)\|)} - 1, & \text{otherwise} \end{cases}$$ ⋄

Under these semantics, in the example in Figure 2, there would be $2^{(3-1)} = 4$ possible worlds defined by the uncertain edge $e_{-(2)}$ and $2^{(4-1)} = 8$ possible worlds defined by $e_{-(3)}$. For the certain edge $e_{(1)}$, this gives $2^{(1-1)} = 1$ possible world.

3.2 Possible Worlds of a Graph

Given the above definitions, we can now define the possible worlds of a graph with uncertainty:

Definition 3.5 (Possible Worlds of a Graph). Let $G = (V, E)$ be a directed graph which has a set of nodes V and a set of edges E. For all $e \in E$, let $pw(e)$ denote the possible worlds (under mutual exclusion or multiple edge semantics) of the edge e. We define *all possible worlds covered by this graph* as the Cartesian product of the possible worlds of edges: $pw(G) = \times_{e \in E}\, pw(e)$. ⋄

If we reconsider Figure 2, under mutual exclusion semantics, this graph would have $1 \times 3 \times 4 = 12$ possible worlds. In contrast, under the multiple edge semantics, the graph would have $1 \times 4 \times 8 = 32$ possible worlds. Since uncertain edges have ≥ 2 possible worlds, it is easy to see that the size of the $pw(G)$ grows exponentially in the number of uncertain edges; i.e., $\|pw(G)\|$ is $O(2^{\|E_-\|})$.

3.3 PPR under Uncertainty

We now define personalized PageRank under uncertainty.

Definition 3.6 (Personalized PageRank under Uncertainty). Let $G(V, E)$ be an uncertain graph. Given a seed set, S, of nodes we can define the personalized PageRank vector, $\vec{r}$, for G as follows:

$$\vec{r} = \underset{G_i \in pw(G)}{AVG} PPR(G_i, S),$$

where G_i denotes a possible world implied by the uncertain graph G and $PPR(G_i, S)$ returns a personalized PageRank vector, $\vec{r}_i$, corresponding to G_i and seed set S. ⋄

[3] This can be extended to the case where there is a constraint in the number of real edges an edge can potentially represent.

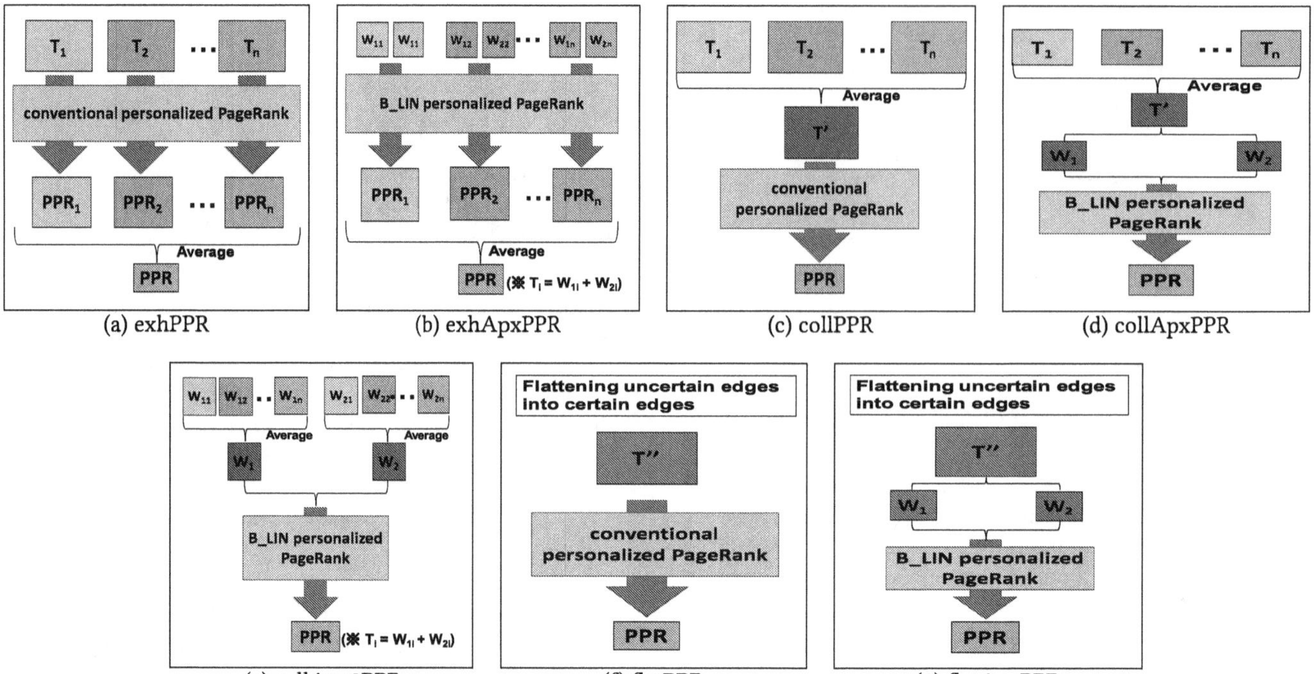

(a) exhPPR (b) exhApxPPR (c) collPPR (d) collApxPPR

(e) collApx2PPR (f) flatPPR (g) flatApxPPR

Figure 3: Alternative (naive) approaches for computing PPR values on an uncertain graph

Intuitively, under the assumption that all possible worlds are equally likely, the above definition of personalized PageRank corresponds to the *expected*[4] values of the node scores.

4 "NAIVE" APPROACHES

In this section, we present several (naive) approaches for computing PPR values on an uncertain graph (Figure 3):

4.1 Exhaustive Approaches

The most straightforward way to obtain the PPR values on an uncertain graph is to exhaustively enumerate all possible worlds, compute the PPRs for each possible world, and combine (i.e., average) the results. Obviously this exhaustive approach (exhPPR), visualized in Figure 3(a), is likely to be very expensive as it involves potentially exponential number of PPR computations.

One way to alleviate this cost is to rely on a fast approximate PPR technique (such as *B_LIN* [28], which partitions the given graph into subgraphs and pre-processes intra-partition edges, W_1, and inter-partition edges, W_2, on these subgraphs in a post-processing phase) to obtain PPR scores for each possible world (Figure 3(b)). Note that, while this exhaustive approximate approach, which we refer to as exhApxPPR, is likely to be faster than the basic approach, since it involves exponential number of (approximate) PPR computations, it is still likely to be prohibitively expensive.

4.2 Collapsing-based Approaches

Since the major cost of the exhaustive approach is the number of exhaustive PPR computations, one way to reduce the cost would be to enumerate all possible transition matrices corresponding to all possible worlds of the uncertain graph and then *collapse* these transition matrices into a single transition matrix by taking their average. After this, we can obtain the final PPR scores either by solving an exact PPR (collPPR, Figure 3(c)) or approximate PPR (collApxPPR, Figure 3(d)) problem.

Another alternative is to first partition each individual transition matrix of each possible world, G_i, and then *collapse* the intra-partition, W_{1i}, and inter-partition, W_{2i}, transition matrices for all possible worlds into an inter-partition and an intra-partition matrix to be processed using *B_LIN*[28] and combined in a post-processing phase. In Figure 3(e), we refer to this pre-partitioning based alternative approach as collApx2PPR.

Accuracy Problem with Collapsing: The collapsing based approach can lead to relatively large errors when uncertainty is concentrated around nodes with large PPR scores: Let G be an uncertain graph with two possible worlds with transition matrices, T_1 and T_2, respectively. Given these, we can compute the expected PPR scores as defined in the previous section as

$$\vec{r} = (\vec{r}_1 + \vec{r}_2)/2 = \left(\alpha\left(T_1\vec{r}_1 + T_2\vec{r}_2\right)\right)/2 + (1-\alpha)\vec{s},$$

where $\vec{s}$ is the teleportation vector for the seeds. In contrast, when using the collapsing based approach we instead compute

$$\vec{r}' = \alpha\left((T_1 + T_2)/2\right)\vec{r}' + (1-\alpha)\vec{s}.$$

Given these, the error term, $\vec{e} = \vec{r} - \vec{r}'$ can be obtained as

$$\vec{e} = \left(\alpha\left(T_1\vec{r}_1 + T_2\vec{r}_2\right)\right)/2 - \alpha\left((T_1 + T_2)/2\right)\vec{r}'.$$

[4] This can be extended to cases where each possible world has a different likelihood.

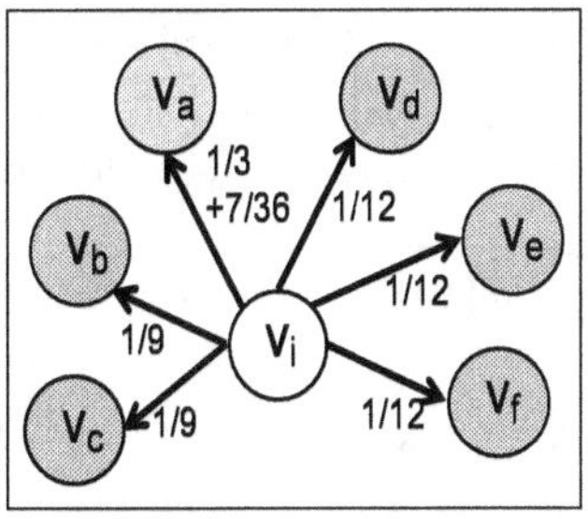

Figure 4: Flattening of the uncertain graph in Figure 2 into an (approximate) certain graph

Assuming that this error term is relatively small; i.e., $\vec{r} \sim \vec{r}'$, we can replace $\vec{r}'$ with $\vec{r} = (\vec{r}_1 + \vec{r}_2)/2$, to obtain

$$\begin{aligned} \vec{e} &\sim (\alpha (T_1\vec{r}_1 + T_2\vec{r}_2))/2 - \alpha((T_1 + T_2)/2)((\vec{r}_1 + \vec{r}_2)/2) \\ &\sim ((T1 - T2)/4)\vec{r}_1 + ((T2 - T1)/4)\vec{r}_2. \end{aligned}$$

In other words, the error term is especially large when the uncertainties (i.e., differences between the transition matrices of the possible worlds) are concentrated around nodes with large PPR scores.

Execution Time Problem with Collapsing: Since they reduce the number of PPR computations to just one, the collapsing based approaches are likely to be much faster than the exhaustive approach. Nevertheless, since it involves the enumeration of all possible worlds before obtaining the collapsed transition matrix, the cost is still exponential in the number of uncertain edges.

4.3 Flattening-based Approaches

An alternative approach to avoid the enumeration cost of collapsing is to approximate the collapsed transition matrix by constructing it directly from the uncertain graph G by flattening each uncertain edge into certain edges. Let v_i be a node with c outgoing certain edges and u outgoing uncertain edges. To flatten the outgoing edges of a node v_i, we do the following:

(1) Each outgoing certain edge is associated with $1/(c+u)$ transition probability.
(2) Let e_- be an outgoing uncertain edge, with t targets
   (a) each non-ϵ target of e_- is given a transition probability of $(1/t) \times (1/(c+u))$
   (b) if ϵ is a target for e_-, then the corresponding $(1/t) \times 1/(c+u)$ transition probability is distributed among the c certain edges of v_i; if the vertex does not have any outgoing certain edges, then the probability is re-distributed among all the nodes in the graph.

See [19] for details. For instance, in the example visualized in Figure 2, since there are three outgoing edges, the probabilities of outgoing edges for v_i would be set as $\frac{1}{3}$ on the edge going to v_a, $\frac{1}{3} \times \frac{1}{3} = \frac{1}{9}$ on the edge going to v_b and v_c, and $\frac{1}{3} \times \frac{1}{4} = \frac{1}{12}$ on the edge going to v_d, v_e, and v_f. Note that, when ϵ is selected for any of the outgoing edges, the only available traversal direction is towards v_a. Therefore, this would lead to an additional transition probability of $\frac{1}{9} + \frac{1}{12} (= \frac{7}{36})$ towards v_a. This is visualized in Figure 4.

Once the flattened transition matrix is obtained, we can solve the final PPR scores either using an exact PPR (flatPPR, Figure 3(f)) or an approximate PPR (flatApxPPR, Figure 3(g)) technique. Note that, while they are likely to be faster than both exhaustive and collapsing-based approaches, flattening-based solutions further compound the accuracy problems.

5 UPPR: PROPOSED APPROACH

We propose an efficient and effective *Uncertain Personalized PageRank (UPPR)* algorithm to approximately compute personalized PageRank values on an uncertain graph with edge uncertainties. In particular, *UPPR* avoids enumeration of all possible worlds, yet is able to achieve high accuracy by carefully encoding edge uncertainties in a data structure that leads to good approximations.

5.1 Special Case: Two Possible Worlds

Let $G(V,E)$ be an edge uncertain graph, Let us split $G(V,E)$ into two subgraphs: a subgraph, $G_c(V,E_c)$, consisting of certain edges, and a subgraph, $G_u(V,E_u)$, consisting of uncertain edges. Let us first consider the special case where $G_u(V,E_u)$ defines only two possible worlds. In Section 5.2, we will generalize this to the case where there may be more than two possible worlds.

Let T_1 and T_2 be transition matrices corresponding to two possible worlds of G. The personalized PageRank values $\vec{r_1}$ and $\vec{r_2}$ for T_1 and T_2 for seed set, S, are defined in Section 2.2 as

$$\vec{r_1} = \alpha T_1 \vec{r_1} + (1-\alpha)\vec{s}, \quad \text{and} \quad \vec{r_2} = \alpha T_2 \vec{r_2} + (1-\alpha)\vec{s},$$

where α is a *residual probability parameter* and $\vec{s}$ is a *re-seeding* vector such that if a node $v_i \in S$, then $\vec{s}[i] = \frac{1}{\|S\|}$ and $\vec{s}[i] = 0$, otherwise. It is easy to see that these two equations can be rewritten as follows to solve for $\vec{r_1}$ and $\vec{r_2}$:

$$\vec{r_1} = (1-\alpha)(I - \alpha T_1)^{-1}\vec{s} \quad \text{and} \quad \vec{r_2} = (1-\alpha)(I - \alpha T_2)^{-1}\vec{s}.$$

Given these, as defined in Section 3.3, we can compute the *expected* PPR values for the edge uncertain graph as

$$\vec{r} = \frac{1}{2}(\vec{r_1} + \vec{r_2}) = \frac{1-\alpha}{2}((I - \alpha T_1)^{-1} + (I - \alpha T_2)^{-1})\vec{s}.$$

Let us split both T_1 and T_2 into three parts:

$$T_1 = T_{BL} + T_X + P_1 \text{ and } T_2 = T_{BL} + T_X + P_2,$$

where $T_{BL} + T_X$ corresponds to the certain parts of the graph and P_1 and P_2 correspond to the uncertain edges in the two possible worlds. Let T_{BL} be the block-diagonal matrix, obtained by partitioning the graph into blocks (for example using *METIS* [15]), and T_X represent (certain) transitions across these partitions.

Note that, in general, we have $|T_{BL}| \gg |T_X|$. As we will see shortly, in this section, we further assume[5] that $|T_X| \gg |P_1|$ and $|T_X| \gg |P_2|$. As proposed in [28], assuming that the blocks are sufficiently small, we can efficiently compute $Q_{BL}^{-1} = (I - \alpha T_{BL})^{-1}$ by first computing the inverse matrices of each block and then combining these inverse matrices to obtain Q_{BL}^{-1}, which itself is in block-diagonal form. Moreover, since T_X, P_1, and P_2 are all sparse, we can also efficiently decompose the $T_X + P_1$ and $T_X + P_2$ into

$$T_X + P_1 \simeq U_1 S_1 V_1 \text{ and } T_X + P_2 \simeq U_2 S_2 V_2, \tag{1}$$

[5] While this is a common assumption in related work [2], in Section 5.5, we discuss how to relax this assumption in cases where the number of uncertain edges involved in each possible world is large.

using a sparse approximate decomposition algorithm, such as [3]. Given these, we can rewrite $\vec{r} = \vec{r} = \frac{1}{2}(\vec{r_1} + \vec{r_2})$ as

$$\simeq \frac{1-\alpha}{2}\left(\left(I-\alpha(T_{BL}+U_1S_1V_1)\right)^{-1} + \left(I-\alpha(T_{BL}+U_2S_2V_2)\right)^{-1}\right)\vec{s}.$$

Then, by applying the well-known Sherman-Morrison lemma [25] on the term $(I-\alpha(T_{BL}+U_iS_iV_i))^{-1}$, we can reformulate the above equation to obtain[6]

$$\vec{r} \simeq \frac{1-\alpha}{2}\Big(Q_{BL}^{-1} + \alpha Q_{BL}^{-1}U_1(S_1^{-1} - \alpha V_1Q_{BL}^{-1}U_1)^{-1}V_1Q_{BL}^{-1} + Q_{BL}^{-1} + \alpha Q_{BL}^{-1}U_2(S_2^{-1} - \alpha V_2Q_{BL}^{-1}U_2)^{-1}V_2Q_{BL}^{-1}\Big)\vec{s}.$$

When we further apply the Sherman-Morrison lemma on the term $(S_1^{-1} - \alpha V_1Q_{BL}^{-1}U_1)^{-1}$ in the above equation, we obtain

$$(1-\alpha)Q_{BL}^{-1}\vec{s} + \frac{\alpha(1-\alpha)}{2}Q_{BL}^{-1}\Big(U_1(S_1+\alpha S_1V_1(Q_{BL}-\alpha U_1S_1V_1)^{-1}U_1S_1)V_1 + U_2(S_2+\alpha S_2V_2(Q_{BL}-\alpha U_2S_2V_2)^{-1}U_2S_2)V_2\Big)Q_{BL}^{-1}\vec{s}.$$

This equation can be simplified by introducing the terms $M_1 = U_1S_1V_1$ and $M_2 = U_2S_2V_2$ (where $M_1 \simeq T_X + P_1$ and $M_2 \simeq T_X + P_2$):

$$\vec{r} \simeq (1-\alpha)\left(I + \frac{\alpha}{2}Q_{BL}^{-1}\Big((M_1+M_2) + \alpha\big(M_1(Q_{BL}-\alpha M_1)^{-1}M_1 + M_2(Q_{BL}-\alpha M_2)^{-1}M_2\big)\Big)\right)Q_{BL}^{-1}\vec{s}. \quad (2)$$

Relying on the assumption that $|T_{BL}| \gg |T_X| + |P_1|$ and $|T_{BL}| \gg |T_X|+|P_2|$, we can ignore the terms αM_1 and αM_2 in $(Q_{BL}-\alpha M_1)^{-1}$ and $(Q_{BL}-\alpha M_2)^{-1}$ in the above equation and rewrite the rest as

$$\vec{r} \simeq (1-\alpha)\left(I + \frac{\alpha}{2}Q_{BL}^{-1}\Big((2T_X+P_1+P_2) + \alpha\big(2T_XQ_{BL}^{-1}T_X + (P_1+P_2)Q_{BL}^{-1}T_X + T_XQ_{BL}^{-1}(P_1+P_2) + P_1Q_{BL}^{-1}P_1 + P_2Q_{BL}^{-1}P_2\big)\Big)\right)Q_{BL}^{-1}\vec{s}. \quad (3)$$

Furthermore, again relying on the assumption that $|T_{BL}| \gg |T_X| \gg |P_1|, |P_2|$, the term $P_1Q_{BL}^{-1}P_1 + P_2Q_{BL}^{-1}P_2$ will be negligible next to $(P_1+P_2)Q_{BL}^{-1}T_X + T_XQ_{BL}^{-1}(P_1+P_2)$ and thus can be ignored and $\vec{r}$ can be approximately computed as

$$(1-\alpha)\left(I + \frac{\alpha}{2}Q_{BL}^{-1}\Big((2T_X+(P_1+P_2)) + \alpha\big(2T_XQ_{BL}^{-1}T_X + (P_1+P_2)Q_{BL}^{-1}T_X + T_XQ_{BL}^{-1}(P_1+P_2)\big)\Big)\right)Q_{BL}^{-1}\vec{s}. \quad (4)$$

Summary and Key Advantages: First of all, assuming that the blocks are sufficiently small and Q_{BL}^{-1} can be efficiently computed, once Q_{BL}^{-1} is at hand, solving for $\vec{r}$ using the above equation involves very sparse matrix multiplications (involving T_X and P_1+P_2) and thus can be processed very efficiently (see Section 6). A second advantage of the above formulation is that it can be easily extended to any number of possible worlds.

[6]For space considerations, we do not provide the complete sequence of algebraic operations in each step.

5.2 General Case: > 2 Possible Worlds

When we have n possible worlds (i.e., $\vec{r} = \frac{1}{n}(\vec{r_1} + ... + \vec{r_n})$), the UPPR equation (Equation 4) can be generalized as

$$\simeq(1-\alpha)\left(I + \frac{\alpha}{n}Q_{BL}^{-1}\Big((nT_X+(P_1+...+P_n)) + \alpha\big(nT_XQ_{BL}^{-1}T_X + (P_1+...+P_n)Q_{BL}^{-1}T_X + T_XQ_{BL}^{-1}(P_1+...+P_n)\big)\Big)\right)Q_{BL}^{-1}\vec{s}. \quad (5)$$

As we see in Section 6, this formulation leads to efficient execution plans, especially because the term $\frac{1}{n}(P_1+...+P_n)$ in Equation 5 can be obtained (without having to enumerate all possible worlds) directly by computing the ratio of the number of possible worlds in which a given edge exists.

Under *mutual exclusion* semantics: As we have seen in Section 3.1, the possible worlds covered by an uncertain edge consist of all combinations of its target nodes. Under mutual exclusion semantics, only one of the edges implied by the uncertain edge can be valid in the real world. Let v_i be a node which has c outgoing certain edges and u outgoing uncertain edges. If, in a given possible world, some of the u outgoing uncertain edges map to ϵ, then in that possible world, the transition probabilities for the remaining certain and uncertain edges will be higher. We can use this observation to compute $P_{avg} = \frac{1}{n}(P_1+...+P_n)$ as follows:

Let v_j be a target node of an uncertain edge, e_-, with $\|target(e_-)\| = k$. The value of $P_{avg}(j,i)$ can be computed as[7]

$$\frac{1}{k}\times\Big(\sum_{h=0}^{u-1}\Big(\frac{1}{c+u-h}\Big)\text{(ratio of worlds s.t. } h \text{ of other unc.edges are } \epsilon)\Big).$$

Here, $p()$ denotes the probability of a given event.

Note that, if e_- has ϵ as a target, then the corresponding transition probability has to be redistributed among the outgoing certain edges of the node and, if none exists, then it needs to be redistributed among all nodes in the graph. Let e_+ be an outgoing certain edge from v_i and let us denote its target as v_j. The transition probability, for e_+, taking into account ϵ transition for the uncertain edges, can be computed as

$$\sum_{h=0}^{u}\Big(\frac{1}{c+u-h}\Big)\text{(ratio of worlds s.t. } h \text{ of unc.edges are } \epsilon).$$

However, since e_+ is a certain edge, it belongs to either intra-partition or cross-partition certain edges. Therefore, when we compute the $P_{avg}(j,i)$, we need to compensate for the portion of the transition probability already accounted in T_{BL} or T_X. Let $C(j,i)$ denote $T_{BL}(j,i) + T_X(j,i)$; then, the cell $[j,i]$ in P_{avg} has the compensated value

$$\Big(\sum_{h=0}^{u}\Big(\frac{1}{c+u-h}\Big)\text{(ratio of worlds s.t. } h \text{ of unc.edges are } \epsilon)\Big) - C(j,i).$$

If v_i does not have any certain edges, the transition probability is distributed among all nodes in the graph. See [19] for details.

In both cases, to compute, P_{avg}, we need to compute the probability that for h out of a given number of uncertain edges, ϵ will

[7]Note that, if v_j is a target for multiple outgoing edges from v_i, all transition probabilities to v_j need to be aggregated (see [19]).

be selected as the target. Let us be given $m = (m_0 + m_1)$ uncertain edges, such that m_0 many do not contain ϵ in the target set and m_1 many do. Let the maximum target size for this latter set of nodes be *max_target*. Then, we can group the m_1 uncertain edges to *max_target* many groups where, each group, g_l, consists of uncertain edges with target size l; i.e., $\|g_1\| + \|g_2\| + \ldots + \|g_{max\_target}\| = m_1$. Note that, by definition, any uncertain edge which contains ϵ as a target must also have at least one other node in its target set, $\|g_1\| = 0$.

Given this, we can compute the probability that h out of m uncertain edges will be ϵ as

$$p(h_2 + h_3 + \ldots + h_{max\_target} = h \text{ s.t. } \forall_{2 \le l \le max\_target}\ h_l \text{ in } \|g_l\| \text{ edges select } \epsilon).$$

The probability $p(h_l \text{ in } \|g_l\| \text{ edges select } \epsilon)$ is binomially distributed with $B(\|g_l\|, 1/l)$ – i.e., there are $\|g_l\|$ uncertain edges, each serving as an independent trial with $1/l$ success rate for the selection of ϵ among the available targets. Consequently, the probability that h out of m uncertain edges select ϵ as their targets is distributed as a summation of the binomial distributions $B(\|g_2\|, 1/2) + \ldots + B(\|g_{max\_target}\|, 1/max\_target)$. Algorithms to efficiently compute summation of binomial distributions are presented in [4]. See [19] for details.

Under *multiple edge* semantics: In this case, several of the edges implied by a given uncertain edge can be simultaneously valid. Let v_i be a node with c outgoing certain edges and u outgoing uncertain edges. Let v_j be a target node of an outgoing edge, e, from v_i. The value of $P_{avg}(j, i)$ can be computed as[8]

$$\sum_{h=0}^{total\_out} \left(\frac{1}{c+h}\right) \times p\left(\sum_{e \in U} num\_selected\_target\_nodes(e) = h\right),$$

where $total\_out = \sum_{e \in U} \|target(e)/\{\epsilon\}\|$ and $num\_selected\_target\_nodes(e)$ is the number of nodes selected as outgoing targets for e in a given possible world (if ϵ is the only target selected, then $num\_selected\_target\_nodes(e) = 0$).

Note that, similarly with the case of mutual exclusion semantics, for certain edges, we need to compensate for transition probabilities already accounted in T_{BL} or T_X. Also, if v_i does not have any certain edges, the transition probability for the case where all uncertain edges select ϵ as target needs to be distributed among all nodes. See [19] for details.

To compute P_{avg} using the above equation, we need to compute the probability $p\left(\sum_{e \in U} num\_selected\_target\_nodes(e) = h\right)$. Once again, this can be achieved by representing the distribution as a sum of binomial-like distributions: intuitively, if e is an uncertain edge with ϵ, then the probability that t many non-ϵ targets are selected can be represented in the form of a binomial with $\|target(e)\| - 1$ many trials and $1/2$ success rate. If, on the other hand, e is an uncertain edge without ϵ, the probability that t many targets are selected can be represented in the form of a binomial with $target(e)$ many trials and $1/2$ success rate. In the latter case, however, we need to correct for the situation where $t = 0$. This is because, under multiple edge semantics, for an uncertain edge without ϵ, the selected target nodes must include at least one node in the graph; thus, t cannot take the value of 0. See [19] for details.

[8] Again, all v_i to v_j transitions need to be aggregated.

5.3 Accuracy of UPPR

The UPPR equation (Equation 5) captures the underlying uncertainty in a way that leads to minimal approximation errors under the assumption $|T_{BL}| \gg |T_X| \gg |P_*|$. In particular, the UPPR process has three specific sources for potential errors, each of which is minimized under these, generally valid, assumptions:

The first source of error is the decomposition of $T_X + P_*$ into $U_* S_* V_*$ using an approximate algorithm, such as [3], that relies on the sparsity of the edges that cross partitions and of the uncertain edges (see Equation 1). The second source of error is the assumption that the terms αM_1 and αM_2 are negligible relative to the rest of the terms in Equation 2; this relies on the assumption that T_X and P_* that contribute to M_* are both sparse matrices. The third source of error is the assumption that the term $P_1 Q_{BL}^{-1} P_1 + P_2 Q_{BL}^{-1} P_2$ in Equation 3 is negligible relative to $(P_1 + P_2) Q_{BL}^{-1} T_X + T_X Q_{BL}^{-1} (P_1 + P_2)$.

Note that all three potential sources of error are minimized when $|T_{BL}| \gg |T_X| \gg |P_*|$. While the fact that whether $|T_{BL}| \gg |T_X|$ holds or not depends on the type of graph and the partitioning algorithm used, whether $|T_X| \gg |P_*|$ or not depends on the amount of uncertain edges in the graph. In Section 5.5, we discuss how to relax the assumption, $|T_X| \gg |P_*|$, in cases where there are significant number of uncertain edges in the graph rendering $|P_*|$ relatively dense, using a hybrid strategy.

5.4 Efficient Computation of UPPR Scores

Let us partition Equation 5 into 6 subcomponents:

$$\begin{aligned}
\vec{r} = \frac{1}{n}(\vec{r_1} + \ldots + \vec{r_n}) \simeq\ & \underbrace{(1-\alpha) Q_{BL}^{-1} \vec{s}}_{(1)} + \underbrace{\alpha(1-\alpha) Q_{BL}^{-1} T_X Q_{BL}^{-1} \vec{s}}_{(2)} \\
& + \underbrace{\frac{\alpha(1-\alpha)}{n} Q_{BL}^{-1} (P_1 + \ldots + P_n) Q_{BL}^{-1} \vec{s}}_{(3)} \\
& + \underbrace{\alpha^2 (1-\alpha) Q_{BL}^{-1} T_X Q_{BL}^{-1} T_X Q_{BL}^{-1} \vec{s}}_{(4)} \\
& + \underbrace{\frac{\alpha^2(1-\alpha)}{n} Q_{BL}^{-1} (P_1 + \ldots + P_n) Q_{BL}^{-1} T_X Q_{BL}^{-1} \vec{s}}_{(5)} \\
& + \underbrace{\frac{\alpha^2(1-\alpha)}{n} Q_{BL}^{-1} T_X Q_{BL}^{-1} (P_1 + \ldots + P_n) Q_{BL}^{-1} \vec{s}}_{(6)}.
\end{aligned}$$

Each of the six subcomponents above contains an extremely sparse re-seeding vector $\vec{s}$. Moreover, Q_{BL}^{-1} is a block diagonal matrix and T_X and P_* are all sparse. Consequently, each of the terms can be computed, right to left, through efficient vector-matrix multiplications. For example, the subcomponent (2) can be computed from right to left with the following sequence of efficient operations:

$$\underbrace{Q_{BL}^{-1}}_{|V|\times|V|} \underbrace{\vec{s}}_{|V|\times 1} \rightarrow \underbrace{T_X}_{|V|\times|V|} \underbrace{Q_{BL}^{-1} \vec{s}}_{|V|\times 1} \rightarrow \underbrace{Q_{BL}^{-1}}_{|V|\times|V|} \underbrace{T_X Q_{BL}^{-1} \vec{s}}_{|V|\times 1} \rightarrow \alpha(1-\alpha) \underbrace{Q_{BL}^{-1} T_X Q_{BL}^{-1} \vec{s}}_{|V|\times 1}.$$

Data	# of nodes	# of edges	# of partitions
ego-Facebook	4,039	88,234	3
Wiki-Vote	7,115	103,689	3
web-NotreDame	325,729	1,497,134	50
web-BerkStan	685,230	7,600,595	500

Table 1: Data sets

	# of uncertain edges	degree of edge uncertainty	edge semantics	# of possible worlds
different # of uncertain edges	2	4	mut.excl. (multiple)	16-64
	4			256-4,096
	6			4,096-262,144
	8(7)			65,536-2,097,152
different degree of edge uncertainty	4	2	mut.excl. (multiple)	16-16
		4		256-4,096
		6(5)		1,296-65,536
		8(6)		4,096-1,048,576
		10		10,000

Table 2: Uncertainty scenarios

Moreover, since the terms $(P_1 + ... + P_n)$, $Q_{BL}^{-1}\vec{s}$, $T_X Q_{BL}^{-1}\vec{s}$, and $Q_{BL}^{-1}T_X Q_{BL}^{-1}\vec{s}$ occur in multiple subcomponents, they can be cached and reused – once these terms are cached, the rest of the computations for the six subcomponents can be executed in parallel. Note further that several of the terms above can be cached and reused for the same uncertain graph with different seed vectors or even graphs with the same certain, but different uncertain components (to carry out hypothetical, if-then analyses).

5.5 Hybrid Computation in the Presence of Large Numbers of Uncertain Edges

As we have discussed in the previous section, the accuracy of the proposed UPPR technique relies on the assumption that $|T_{BL}| \gg |T_X| \gg |P_*|$. In particular, whether $|T_X| \gg |P_*|$ or not depends on the amount of uncertain edges in the graph: UPPR is likely to be highly effective and efficient if the number of uncertain edges in the graph is relatively small. In contrast, as we have seen in Section 4.2, the collapsing (and similarly flattening) based techniques may lead to large errors if the uncertain edges are concentrated around nodes with large PPR scores. We can leverage these two observations to deal with graphs with large numbers of uncertain edges: The idea is to eliminate uncertain edges in the graph, relying on the highly efficient *flattening* technique, away from the seed nodes of the graph (which are likely to have large PPR scores) and only maintain uncertain edges in the neighborhoods of the seed nodes. Consequently, errors due to flattening are minimized as this technique is utilized only in regions with less likelihood of producing high PPR scores; UPPR errors are also minimized, especially in large graphs, as the numbers ($|P_*|$) of uncertain edges in possible worlds that UPPR has to deal with have been reduced relative to the rest of the graph.

6 EXPERIMENTS

6.1 Datasets and Setup

We ran experiments on a 16-core CPU Nehalem Node with 64 GB RAM. All codes were implemented in Matlab and run using Matlab R2013b. Table 1 provides an overview of the four data sets [21], with different numbers of nodes and edges, and graph partitions, considered in the experiments (the partitions are obtained using METIS [15]). Table 2 details the volumes of uncertainty we have experimented with for the results reported in this section. Here, the "*degree of uncertainty*" refers to the number of target nodes on each uncertain edge it represents and the "*edge semantics*" describes "mutual exclusion" and "multiple edge" semantics. These together define the number of possible worlds corresponding to a given uncertain edge. To obtain uncertain graphs with the specifications in the table, we select random edges in the original graph and render them uncertain by augmenting destinations with random nodes. We further assume that the uncertain edges are located on the seeds (as discussed in Sections 4.2 and 5.5, uncertain edges away from the seeds can be flattened into certain edges).

6.2 Alternative Approaches

In this section, in addition to UPPR (presented in Section 5), we considered all alternative approaches discussed in Section 4. As a further baseline, we also consider a Monte Carlo-based solution (which starts from the seed nodes, and samples random walks of a given length) and *BEAR* [27], a recent PPR computation algorithm, which originally does not take uncertainty into account. For uncertainty, we use the flattened transition matrix for the transition matrix and compute PPR values. In the experiments, without loss of generality, we set the residual probability parameter, α to 0.85. To compare different algorithms, we consider both efficiency (i.e., PPR computation time) and accuracy (in terms of the correlations of PPR rankings for the nodes that are ranked top-50 by the exhaustive technique, exhPPR).

7 RESULTS AND DISCUSSIONS

We start the discussion of the results by considering efficiency and accuracy of the various algorithms on the Facebook data set, for different degrees of uncertainty in the graph.

Impact of the Degree of Uncertainty. Figures 5(a) and (b) show the execution times of different algorithms, as the overall number of uncertain edges and degree of uncertainty in the graph are increased. As we see in the figure 5, exhaustive and collapsing-based approaches (which need to enumerate the possible worlds) quickly become infeasible as the number of possible worlds increases. While flattening-based approaches are reasonably fast and scale better than the exhaustive and collapsing-based approaches, they are 1 or 2 order slower than UPPR. *BEAR* takes less time than *UPPR* for PPR computation but the difference between them is negligible. Figures 5(c) and (d) confirm that execution time savings on *UPPR* do not come with any drop in accuracy – *UPPR* provides similar (or in some cases better) accuracy to the two collapsing- and flattening-based approaches, collPPR and flatPPR, that rely on direct computation of PPR from the transition matrix, even though it uses an approximate solution for PPR. As expected, the accuracy of *BEAR* is very poor compared to *UPPR* and the accuracy is not stable and affected by the amount of uncertainty. Other techniques such as collApxPPR, collApx2PPR, and flatApxPPR that similarly solve PPR approximately, relying on a sparse approximation method, all have significantly degraded accuracies. This indicates that, by carefully accounting for the sources of errors, UPPR is able to achieve high

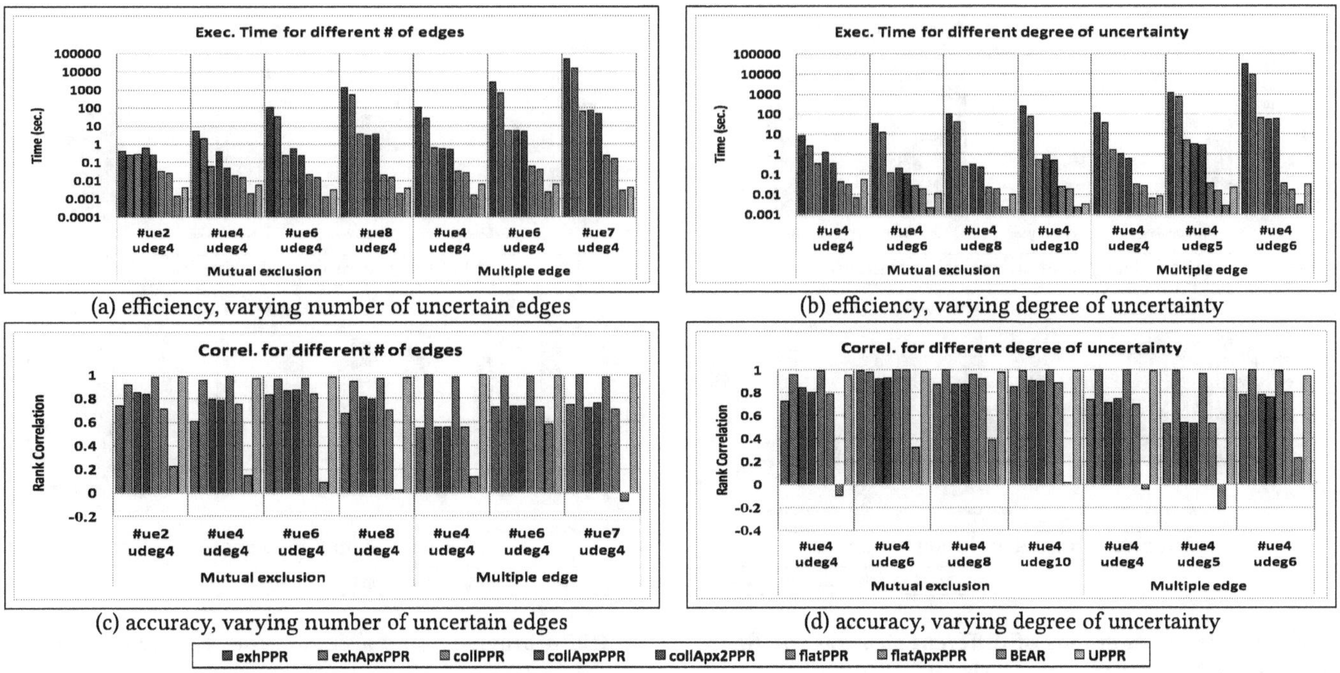

(a) efficiency, varying number of uncertain edges (b) efficiency, varying degree of uncertainty

(c) accuracy, varying number of uncertain edges (d) accuracy, varying degree of uncertainty

Figure 5: Results on the Facebook data set, for different amount of uncertainty with different edge semantics: UPPR provides almost perfect accuracy and its execution time is not affected by the amount of uncertainty

accuracies (~1.0) efficiently (~0.01 seconds) and avoids accuracy pitfalls that other schemes are not able to handle effectively.

UPPR vs. Monte Carlo Method. Additionally, we consider a Monte Carlo (MC) based alternative to UPPR. [22] notes that (in regular graphs) for estimating PPR values close to a desired threshold δ (where δ is the expected PPR score; i.e., $1/|V|$, where $|V|$ is the number of nodes), a Monte Carlo based algorithm would need $O(1/(\delta \times \rho^2)) = O(|V|/\rho^2)$, samples of length, $geometric(\frac{1}{1-\alpha})$, where ρ is the relative error and $1-\alpha$ is the teleportation rate. This means that, when we seek high accuracy, Monte Carlo based solutions may be *prohibitive* [22]. Indeed, for the Facebook data set, with ~ 4000 nodes, to have 95% accuracy, we would need $4000/0.05^2 = 1,600,000$ random walk samples (of length $\geq \lceil \frac{1}{0.15} \rceil = 7$, since we set α to 0.85).

In Table 3, we report the accuracy comparison for a more modest target error rate of 0.15, which leads to $\sim$ 150K, random walks – note that, even in this modest case, taking 150K random walk samples is more expensive (65 seconds in Matlab) to compute than UPPR (~0.01 seconds). In the table, we see that for top-100 to top-500 results, Monte Carlo, is able to match the target accuracy in the presence if mutual exclusion semantics; but fails to do so when all nodes are considered. In the presence of multiple edge semantics, MC is able to match the target error rate only when top-500 results are considered and the results are very poor for top-100 nodes, even with larger number of samples, with longer lengths. Note that UPPR is able to achieve significantly higher accuracy (for top-100, top-500, as well as for all nodes), very cheaply ($\sim$ 0.01 seconds for this data set as shown in Figure 5).

Different Data Sets and the Impact of the Graph Size. In the experiments reported in Figure 6, we compare the efficiency and effectiveness of the various algorithms we presented in the paper for graphs of different sizes. The figure reports results for two sample uncertainty complexities: Figures 6(a) and (c) report execution time and rank correlation for a scenario with mutual exclusion semantics, whereas Figures 6(b) and (d) consider a scenario with multiple edge semantics. As we see in this figure, the proposed UPPR method is scalable, not only in terms of the possible worlds of the graph, but also the graph size. While the closest algorithms to UPPR in terms of efficiency and scalability, flatApxPPR and BEAR, suffer significantly from accuracy degradations, UPPR provides very high (mostly close to perfect) accuracy in all cases considered in this section.

Here, we do not present the accuracy results for the largest Berk-Stan data set as the cost of performing the exhaustive enumeration needed to obtain the accuracy ground-truth is prohibitive on this data set. However, the results show that *UPPR* provides very good accuracy, while its execution time is minimally effected by graph size. In fact, on the largest data set, *UPPR* is even faster than the *BEAR* baseline, while providing significantly better accuracy.

8 CONCLUSIONS

In this paper, we presented an uncertain edge model with mutual exclusion and shown that, while there are several ways to naively extend existing personalized PageRank computation techniques to graphs with uncertain edges, these either lead to large degrees of errors or are very expensive to compute in practice. We therefore proposed a novel *Uncertain Personalized PageRank (UPPR)* algorithm to approximately compute personalized PageRank values on such graphs. Experiments confirmed that the proposed technique has very high accuracy and is multiple-orders faster than available algorithms that can provide comparable accuracy.

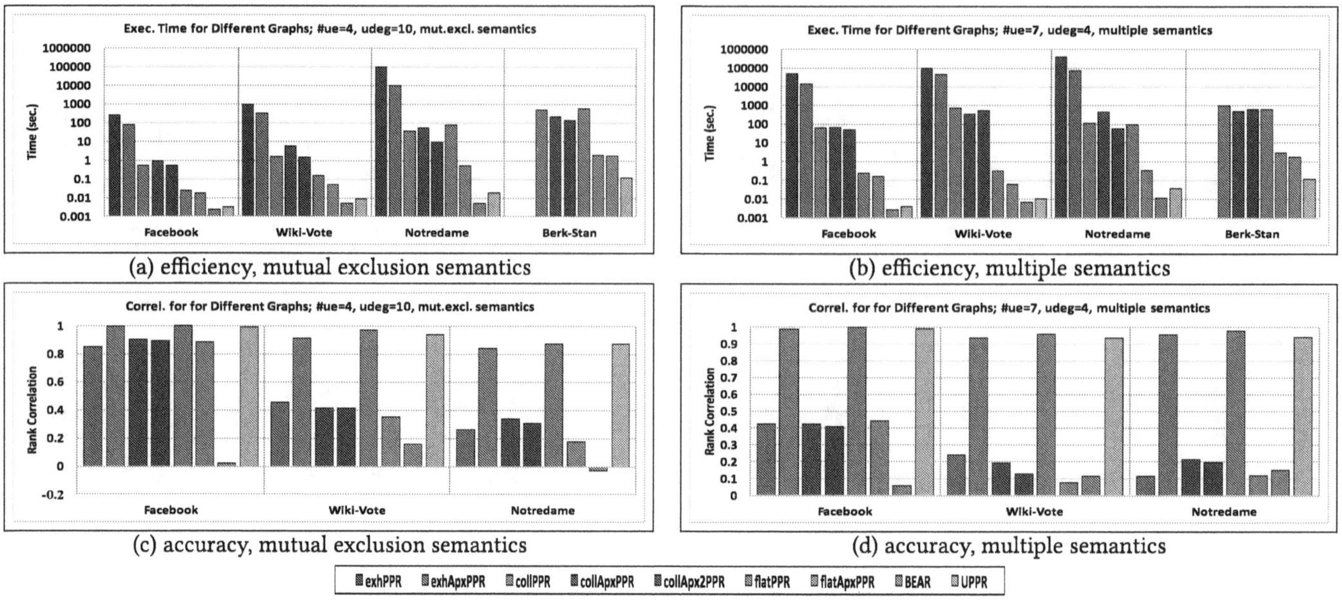

(a) efficiency, mutual exclusion semantics

(b) efficiency, multiple semantics

(c) accuracy, mutual exclusion semantics

(d) accuracy, multiple semantics

Figure 6: Results in graphs of different sizes: as the figures show, UPPR provides good accuracy and its execution time is minimally effected by the graph size

Edge type	# of random walks	Length of random walks	Top 100 acc.	Top 500 acc.	All nodes acc.
Mutual exclusion semantics (#ue=4, #udeg=10)	UPPR		**0.952**	**0.981**	**0.997**
	150K Monte Carlo	8	0.782	0.881	0.525
		10	0.816	0.919	0.583
		20	0.841	0.920	0.519
		30	0.834	0.908	0.533
	300K Monte Carlo	8	0.814	0.911	0.584
		10	0.845	0.927	0.545
		20	0.858	0.924	0.588
		30	0.813	0.913	0.571
Multiple edge semantics (#ue=7, #udeg=4)	UPPR		**0.998**	**0.989**	**0.997**
	150K Monte Carlo	8	0.193	0.878	0.571
		10	0.145	0.900	0.656
		20	0.258	0.969	0.658
		30	0.269	0.937	0.696
	300K Monte Carlo	8	0.193	0.945	0.649
		10	0.163	0.912	0.667
		20	0.148	0.905	0.660
		30	0.155	0.901	0.670

Table 3: UPPR vs. MC method on the Facebook graph

REFERENCES

[1] S. Adali, M.L. Sapino, and B. Marshall, A rank algebra to support multimedia mining applications, MDM'07, 2007

[2] P. Boldi, F. Bonchi, A. Gionis, and T. Tassa. Injecting Uncertainty in Graphs for Identity Obfuscation, PVLDB'12, 2012.

[3] M. Brand. Fast online svd revisions for lightweight recommender systems. SDM, pp 37–46. SIAM, 2003.

[4] K. Butler and M. Stephens. The distribution of a sum of binomial random variables, Stanford University CA Dept of Statistics, 1993.

[5] S. Brin and L. Page. The anatomy of a large-scale hypertextual web search engine. WWW, 1998.

[6] K.S. Candan and W.S. Li, Using random walks for mining web document associations. PAKDD'00, pp.37–46, 2000.

[7] K.S. Candan, J. Grant, and V.S.Subrahmanian, A Unified Treatment of Null Values Using Constraints, Information Sciences, 98 (1-4) (1997), pp. 99–156

[8] H. Cao, K.S. Candan, and M.L. Sapino. Skynets: Searching for Minimum Trees in Graphs with Incomparable Edge Weights. CIKM'11, 2011.

[9] S. Chakrabarti. Dynamic personalized pagerank in entity-relation graphs. WWW'07, 571–580, 2007.

[10] J.B. Collins and S.T. Smith. Network Discovery For Uncertain Graphs. Fusion'14, 2014.

[11] C. De Kerchove, L. Ninove, and P. Van Dooren. Maximizing pagerank via outlinks. Linear Algebra and its Applications, 429(5):1254–1276, 2008.

[12] L. Du, C. Li, H. Chen, L. Tan, and Y. Zhang. Probabilistic simrank computation over uncertain graphs. Information Sciences. 295:521–535, 2015.

[13] H. Ishii and R. Tempo. Computing the pagerank variation for fragile web data. SICE Journal of Control, Measurement, and System Integration, 2(1):1–9, 2009.

[14] G. Jeh and J. Widom. SimRank: A Measure of Structural-Context Similarity. SIGKDD'02, pages 538–543, 2002.

[15] G. Karypis and V. Kumar. A fast and high quality multilevel scheme for partitioning irregular graphs. SIAM Journal on Scientific Computing, 1998.

[16] A. Khan, F. Bonchi, A. Gionis, and F. Gullo. Fast Reliability Search in Uncertain Graphs. EDBT'14, 2014.

[17] A. Khan and L. Chen. On Uncertain Graphs Modeling and Queries. VLDB'15, pp. 2042–2043, 2015.

[18] J.H. Kim, K.S. Candan, M.Luisa. Sapino. Locality-sensitive and Re-use Promoting Personalized PageRank computations. Knowl. Inf. Syst. 47(2): 261-299 (2016)

[19] J.H. Kim. Efficient Node Proximity and Node Significance Computations in Graphs. PhD Thesis. Arizona State University, 2017.

[20] R.-H. Li, J.X. Yu, R. Mao, and T. Jin. Efficient and Accurate Query Evaluation on Uncertain Graphs via Recursive Stratified Sampling. ICDE'14, 2014.

[21] J. Leskovec and A. Krevl. SNAP Datasets: Stanford Large Network Dataset Collection. http://snap.stanford.edu/data. 2014.

[22] P. Lofgren. Efficient Algorithms for Personalized PageRank. PhD Thesis, Stanford University. 2015.

[23] X. Niu, L. Li, and K. Xu. Digrank: Using global degree to facilitate ranking in an incomplete graph. CIKM'11, pp 2297–2300. 2011.

[24] D.L. Nowell and J. Kleinberg. The Link Prediction Problem for Social Networks. CIKM'03, 2003.

[25] W. W. Piegorsch and G. Casella. Erratum: inverting a sum of matrices. SIAM review, 32(3):470, 1990.

[26] M. Potamias, F. Bonchi, A. Gionis, and G. Kollios. K-nearest neighbors in uncertain graphs. VLDB'10, 3(1-2):997–1008, 2010.

[27] K. Shin, J. Jung, L. Sael, and U Kang. BEAR: Block Elimination Approach for Random Walk with Restart on Large Graphs. SIGMOD'15, 2015.

[28] H. Tong, C. Faloutsos, and J.-Y. Pan. Fast random walk with restart and its applications. ICDM, pp. 613–622, 2006.

[29] Y. Yuan, L. Chen, G. Wang. Efficiently Answering Probability Threshold-Based Shortest Path Queries over Uncertain Graphs, DASFAA'10, 2010.

[30] Y. Yuan, G. Wang, H. Wang, and L. Chen. Efficient Subgraph Search over Large Uncertain Graphs. PVLDB, 4(11), 2011.

Adapting Markov Decision Process for Search Result Diversification

Long Xia, Jun Xu*, Yanyan Lan, Jiafeng Guo, Wei Zeng, Xueqi Cheng
CAS Key Lab of Network Data Science and Technology,
Institute of Computing Technology, Chinese Academy of Sciences
{xialong,zengwei}@software.ict.ac.cn, {junxu,lanyanyan,guojiafeng,cxq}@ict.ac.cn

ABSTRACT

In this paper we address the issue of learning diverse ranking models for search result diversification. Typical methods treat the problem of constructing a diverse ranking as a process of sequential document selection. At each ranking position, the document that can provide the largest amount of additional information to the users is selected, because the search users usually browse the documents in a top-down manner. Thus, to select an optimal document for a position, it is critical for a diverse ranking model to capture the utility of information the user have perceived from the preceding documents. Existing methods usually calculate the ranking scores (e.g., the marginal relevance) directly based on the query and the selected documents, with heuristic rules or handcrafted features. The utility the user perceived at each of the ranks, however, is not explicitly modeled. In this paper, we present a novel diverse ranking model on the basis of continuous state Markov decision process (MDP) in which the user perceived utility is modeled as a part of the MDP state. Our model, referred to as MDP-DIV, sequentially takes the actions of selecting one document according to current state, and then updates the state for the chosen of the next action. The transition of the states are modeled in a recurrent manner and the model parameters are learned with policy gradient. Experimental results based on the TREC benchmarks showed that MDP-DIV can significantly outperform the state-of-the-art baselines.

KEYWORDS

learning to rank; search result diversification; Markov decision process

ACM Reference format:
Long Xia, Jun Xu*, Yanyan Lan, Jiafeng Guo, Wei Zeng, Xueqi Cheng. 2017. Adapting Markov Decision Process
for Search Result Diversification. In *Proceedings of SIGIR17, August 7–11, 2017, Shinjuku, Tokyo, Japan, ,* 10 pages.
DOI: http://dx.doi.org/10.1145/3077136.3080775

* Corresponding author: Jun Xu.

SIGIR17, August 7–11, 2017, Shinjuku, Tokyo, Japan
© 2017 ACM. ISBN 978-1-4503-5022-8/17/08...$15.00.
DOI: http://dx.doi.org/10.1145/3077136.3080775

1 INTRODUCTION

In many information retrieval tasks, one important goal involves providing search results that covers a wide range of topics for a search query, called search result diversification [1]. One of the key problems in search result diversification is ranking, specifically, how to develop a ranking model that can sort documents based on their relevance to the given query as well as the novelty of the information in the documents.

Typical approaches to search result diversification, including the heuristic approaches and the learning approaches, treat the process of constructing a diverse ranking as a problem of sequential document selection. At each ranking position, the additional amount of information (utility) a document can provide is estimated, on the basis of the user query and the documents ranked ahead. The document that can provide maximal additional utility is selected. The sequential document selection matches well with the user activity of browsing the search results: search users usually browse the search results in a top-down manner. Thus, to accurately select the document at each of the positions, it is critical for a diverse ranking algorithm to model the utility of information the users have already perceived from the preceding documents.

Several methods for diverse ranking have been developed and applied to document retrieval. Different criteria are adopted in these methods to estimate the new utility a candidate document can provide. For example, in the representative heuristic approach of maximal marginal relevance (MMR) [2], the marginal relevance, which is defined as a sum of the query-document relevance and the maximal document distance, is used as the utility. In xQuAD [20], another widely used diverse ranking model, the utility is defined so as to explicitly account for the relationship between documents retrieved for the original query and the possible aspects underlying this query, in the form of sub-queries. In recent years, machine learning methods have been proposed and applied to search result diversification [18, 24–27, 31]. Typical diverse learning models, including the relational learning to rank (R-LTR) [31] and its variations [24–26], define the utilities as the linear combinations of the relevance features and the novelty features.

All the existing methods on diverse ranking [2, 20, 31] are designed to estimate the utility of a candidate document directly based on the user query and the preceding documents, calculated either by the carefully designed heuristics (e.g., the scoring functions in MMR and xQuAD) or as a linear combination of the handcrafted relevance features and novelty features (e.g., the scoring function in R-LTR). The utility perceived by the users from the preceding documents, however, is not explicitly modeled and fully utilized.

In this paper we propose to formalize the construction of a diverse ranking as a process of sequential decision making, which can be modeled with a continuous state Markov decision process (MDP). The new diverse ranking model, referred to as MDP-DIV, model the user perceived utility of information as a part of its MDP state. Specifically, in MDP-DIV, a document ranking with M positions is considered as a sequence of M discrete time steps where each time step corresponds to a ranking position. The ranking of documents, thus, is formalized as a sequence of M decisions and each action corresponds to selecting one document from the candidate set. At each time step, the agent receives the environment's state, which models the user's dynamic state on the perceived utility, starting from the first ranking position. Based on the received state, the agent chooses an action. One time step later, as a consequence of the action, the search users perceive some additional utility from the new selected document, and the system transit to a new state. The transition function, which maps old state and the selected document to a new state, is implemented in a recurrent manner. At each time step, the chosen of the action depends on a policy, which is a function maps from the current state to a probability distribution of selecting each actions.

Reinforcement learning is employed to train the model parameters. Given a set of labeled queries, at each time step, the agent can receive a numerical action-dependent reward which can be defined upon the diversity evaluation measures. The policy gradient algorithm of REINFORCE [22] is adopted to adjust the model parameters so that expected long-term discounted rewards in terms of the diversity evaluation measure is maximized. In the testing phase, the system fully trusts the learned policy. Given a query and the associated documents, the action with the maximal probability is selected at each ranking position.

Advantages of the proposed model include: 1) explicitly modeling the dynamic state on the user perceived utility of information in diverse ranking learning, which unifies the relevance and novelty and can be utilized as the criterion for selecting documents; 2) ability to conduct diverse ranking learning in an end-to-end manner, achieving a diverse ranking model with no need of handcrafting features; 3) ability to learn a ranking model towards to a diversity evaluation measure, via involving the measure in the training.

To evaluate the effectiveness of MDP-DIV, we conducted experiments on the basis of TREC benchmark datasets. The experimental results showed that MDP-DIV can significantly outperform the state-of-the-art diverse ranking approaches including the heuristic methods of MMR, xQuAD, and the learning methods of R-LTR, PAMM, and PAMM-NTN. We analyzed the results and showed that MDP-DIV improved the performances through 1) optimizing the diversity evaluation measures in training, 2) modeling the dynamic user state on the perceived utility, and 3) utilizing both the immediate rewards and the long-term returns in training phase.

2 RELATED WORK

2.1 Search result diversification

It is a common practice to formalize the construction of a diverse ranking list in search as a process of sequential document selection. This is based on the observation that in diverse ranking the additional utility a document can provide depends on not only the document itself but also the preceding documents. Different models designed different criteria for estimating the utility the search users can perceive from a candidate document. Following the idea, Carbonell and Goldstein [2] proposed the maximal marginal relevance criterion to guide the selection of the documents. At each iteration, the document with the highest marginal relevance score is selected, where the score is a linear combination of the query-document relevance and the maximum distance of the document to the documents in current result set, in other words, novelty. The marginal relevance score is then updated in the next iteration as the number of documents in the result set increases by one. Based on MMR, Guo and Sanner [7] proposed the probabilistic latent MMR model. xQuAD [19] directly models different aspects underlying the original query in the form of sub-queries, and estimates the utility as the relevance of the retrieved documents to each identified sub-query. PM-2 [5] treats the problem of finding a diverse search result as finding a proportional representation for the document ranking. Hu et al. [9] proposed a utility function that explicitly leverages the hierarchical intents of queries and selects the documents that maximize diversity in the hierarchical structure. Evaluation methods have also developed based on the intent hierarchies [23]. He et al. [8] proposed to combine the implicit and explicit topic representations for constructing better diverse rankings. Gollapudi and Sharma [6] proposed an axiomatic approach to result diversification.

Machine learning techniques, which automatically learn the ranking models from the human labeled data, have been applied to construct diverse ranking models. Most of learning approaches still adopt sequential document selection as the basic framework, and the additional utility a candidate document can provide is usually modeled as a sum of the relevance score and the novelty score. For example, Zhu et al. [31], Xia et al. [24], and Xu et al. [26] employed a set of handcrafted relevance features and novelty features to calculate the relevance score and the novelty score, respectively. Both of the scores are defined as linear combinations of the features. Xia et al.[25] proposed to model the novelty score with the deep learning model of neural tensor networks. SVM-DIV [18] propose to construct a diverse ranking with the diversity criterion only. Structured output learning [11] and deep learning models [15] have also been employed to address the problem of learning diverse rankings.

Existing methods calculates the ranking scores directly based on the query and the selected documents, with the heuristic rules or the ranking features. Though it is a critical issue for constructing optimal diverse rankings, the dynamic utility the search user perceived from the preceding documents is still not explicitly modeled and fully utilized in current diverse ranking methods.

2.2 MDP for information retrieval

In this paper we employ MDP for constructing diverse ranking model, which has been widely used in variant IR applications. For example, in [13], a win-win search framework based on partially observed Markov decision process (POMDP) is proposed to model session search as a dual-agent stochastic game. In the model, the state of the search users are encoded as a four hidden decision making states. In [30], the log-based document re-ranking is also modeled as a POMDP to improve the re-ranking performances. MDP is also used for building recommender systems. For example, [21] designed an MDP-based recommendation model for taking both the long-term effects of each recommendation and the expected value of each recommendation into account. Besides the MDP, researchers also employed the bandits model for constructing diverse ranking [18] and optimizing IR system [28].

Recent advances in deep learning makes it possible to incorporate deep learning methods with sequential decision making. In the literature of vision, Mnih et al. [16] attempts to implement attentional processing in a deep learning framework. Lu and Yang[12] proposes POMDP-Rec, a neural-optimized POMDP algorithm, for building a collaborative filtering recommender system.

Though MDP has been applied to various information retrieval tasks, applying it to learning to rank and search result diversification is hard. The difficulties lie in how to formalize diverse ranking under the MDP framework and how to convert the human labels to the supervision information that can be utilized by MDP. In this paper, we propose to formulate the diverse ranking learning as a problem of learning an MDP model.

3 MARKOV DECISION PROCESS

In the paper, we employ continuous state MDP[17, 22], a widely used sequential decision making model, for learning the diverse ranking. An MDP is composed by states, actions, rewards, policy, and transitions, and represented by a tuple $\langle S, A, T, R, \pi\rangle$:

States S is a set of states. For instance, in this paper we define the state as a tuple consisting of preceding document ranking, candidate documents, and the utility the user perceived from the preceding documents.

Actions A is a discrete set of actions that an agent can take. The actions available may depend on the state s, denoted as $A(s)$.

Transition T is the state transition function $s_{t+1} = T(s_t, a_t)$ which specifies a function which maps a state s_t into a new state s_{t+1} in response to the action selected a_t.

Reward $r = R(s, a)$ is the immediate reward, also known as reinforcement. It gives the immediate reward of taking action a at state s.

Policy $\pi(a|s)$ describes the behaviors of an agent, which is a probability distribution over the possible actions. π is usually optimized to decide how to move around in the state space to optimize the long term return.

The agent and environment interact at each of a sequence of discrete time steps, $t = 0, 1, 2, \cdots$. At each time step t the agent receives some representation of the environment's state, $s_t \in S$, and on that basis selects an action $a_t \in A(s_t)$, where $A(s_t)$ is the set of actions available in state s_t. One time step later, in part as a consequence of its action, the agent receives a numerical reward, $r_{t+1} \in \mathbb{R}$ and finds itself in a new state $s_{t+1} = T(s_t, a_t)$. Figure 1 illustrates the agent-environment interaction in MDP.

4 MDP FORMULATION OF DIVERSE RANKING

In this paper, we employ the continuous state MDP to model the construction of the diverse ranking.

4.1 The basic model

Suppose we are given a query $\mathbf{q}$, which is associated with a set of retrieved documents $X = \{\mathbf{x}_1, \cdots, \mathbf{x}_M\} \subseteq \mathcal{X}$, where both the

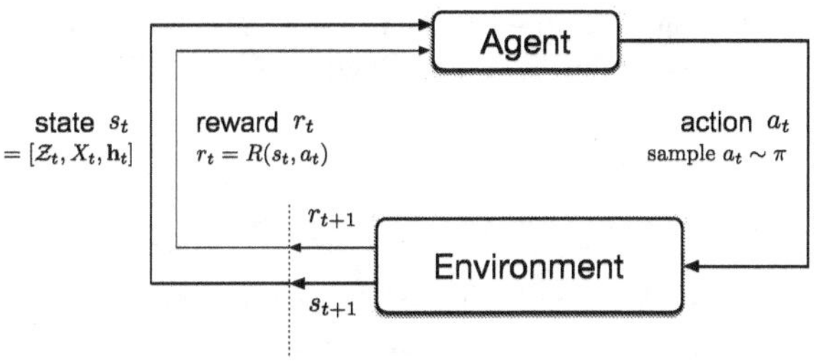

Figure 1: The agent-environment interaction in MDP.

query $\mathbf{q}$ and the documents $\mathbf{x}_i$ are represented as L-dimensional preliminary representations, i.e., the vectors learned by the doc2vec model [10], and $\mathcal{X}$ is the set of all possible documents. The goal of diverse ranking is to construct a model that can rank the documents so that the top ranked documents cover a wide range of subtopics for a search query.

Supervised learning approaches can be used to construct the model. Suppose we are given N labeled training queries $\{(q^{(n)}, X^{(n)}, J^{(n)})\}_{n=1}^N$, where $J^{(n)}$ denotes the human labels on the documents, in the form of a binary matrix. $J^{(n)}(i,j) = 1$ if document $\mathbf{x}_i^{(n)}$ contains the j-th subtopic of $q^{(n)}$ and 0 otherwise[1]. The learning of a diverse ranking model, thus, can be considered as the learning the parameters in an MDP model in which each time step corresponds to a ranking position. The states, actions, rewards, transitions, and policy of the MDP are set as:

States S: We design the state at time step t as a triple $s_t = [Z_t, X_t, \mathbf{h}_t]$, where $Z_t = \{\mathbf{x}_{(n)}\}_{n=1}^t$ is the sequence of t preceding documents, where $\mathbf{x}_{(n)}$ is the document ranked at position n. Note that we define $Z_0 = \emptyset$ is a empty sequence; $X_t \in 2^{\mathcal{X}}$ is the set of candidate documents; $\mathbf{h}_t \in \mathbb{R}^K$ is a vector that encodes the user perceived utility from preceding documents in Z_t, as well as the information need based on $\mathbf{q}$.

At the beginning ($t = 0$), the state is initialized as $s_0 = [Z_0 = \emptyset, X_0 = X, \mathbf{h}_0]$: Z_0 is initialized as an empty sequence $\emptyset$, the candidate set X_0 contains all of the M documents in X, and $\mathbf{h}_0$ is initialized as the user's initial information needs, implemented with a nonlinear transformation of the query:

$$\mathbf{h}_0 = \sigma(\mathbf{V}_q \mathbf{q}), \tag{1}$$

where $\mathbf{q} \in \mathbb{R}^L$ is the preliminary representation of the user issued query, $\mathbf{V}_q \in \mathbb{R}^{K \times L}$ is the transformation matrix, and $\sigma(\mathbf{x})$ is the nonlinear sigmoid function applied to each of the entries:

$$\sigma(\mathbf{x}) = \sigma(\langle x_1, \cdots, x_K\rangle) = \left\langle \frac{1}{1+e^{-x_1}}, \cdots, \frac{1}{1+e^{-x_K}} \right\rangle.$$

Actions A: At each time step t, the $A(s_t)$ is the set of actions the agent can choose, each corresponds to selecting a document from X_t. That is, the action at the time step t, $a_t \in A(s_t)$ selects a document $\mathbf{x}_{m(a_t)} \in X_t$ for the ranking position $t+1$, where $m(a_t)$ is the index of the document selected by a_t.

[1] Some datasets also use graded judgements. In this paper, we assume that all labels are binary.

Transition T: The transition function $T : S{\times}A \longrightarrow S$ also consists of three parts, as shown in the following Equation (2):

$$\begin{aligned} s_{t+1} &= T(s_t, a_t) \\ &= T([\mathcal{Z}_t, X_t, \mathbf{h}_t], a_t) \\ &= \left[\mathcal{Z}_t \oplus \{\mathbf{x}_{m(a_t)}\}, X_t \setminus \{\mathbf{x}_{m(a_t)}\}, \sigma(\mathbf{V}\mathbf{x}_{m(a_t)} + \mathbf{W}\mathbf{h}_t)\right], \end{aligned} \tag{2}$$

where $\oplus$ concatenates the old sequence $\mathcal{Z}_t$ with $\mathbf{x}_{m(a_t)}$, $\mathbf{V} \in \mathbb{R}^{K \times L}$ is the document-state transformation matrix, and $\mathbf{W} \in \mathbb{R}^{K \times K}$ is the state-state transformation matrix. At each time step t, based on state s_t the system chooses an action a_t. Then, the system moves to time step $t + 1$ and the system transits to a new state s_{t+1}: First, the system appends the selected document to the end of $\mathcal{Z}_t$, generating a new document sequence; Second, the selected document at step t is removed from the candidate set: $X_{t+1} = X_t \setminus \{\mathbf{x}_{m(a_t)}\}$. Thus, the number of actions the agent can choose at step $t + 1$ is reduced by one. Third, the information from the user's last state and the selected document are combined together to form a new user state.

Note that in the initialization of $\mathbf{h}$, the parameter $\mathbf{V}_q$ is used for transforming the query to state. In the state transformation, another parameter $\mathbf{V}$ is used for transforming the selected document to state. The setting is based on the consideration that they have different goals: $\mathbf{V}_q$ is for transforming the query q which represents the information needs of the search users; $\mathbf{V}$ is for transforming the documents $\mathbf{x}$ which contain the utility that can be perceived by the users for fulfilling the information needs.

Also note that though the state transition function is implemented in a recurrent fashion, they have striking difference with recurrent neural networks (RNN): in MDP-DIV the input at time step t depends on the output (action) at the time step $t - 1$.

Reward R: The reward can be considered as an evaluation of the quality of the selected document. In search result diversification, the diversity evaluation measures are used to evaluate the quality of a ranking. Most of these measures are calculated in a sequential manner. Thus, it is natural to define the reward function on the basis of the diversity evaluation measures. For example, based on the diversity evaluation measure of α-DCG, we can define the reward function as the promotion of α-DCG caused by choosing the action a_t:

$$R_{\alpha\text{-DCG}}(s_t, a_t) = \alpha\text{-DCG}[t + 1] - \alpha\text{-DCG}[t],$$

where α-DCG$[t]$ is the discounted cumulative gain [4] at the t-th position, and the α-DCG value at the rank 0 is defined as zero: α-DCG$[0] = 0$. [2]

Similarly, on the basis of diversity evaluation measure of S-recall [29], we can also define another reward which is the promotion of S-recall by the action:

$$R_{\text{S-recall}}(s_t, a_t) = \text{S-recall}[t + 1] - \text{S-recall}[t],$$

where S-recall$[t]$ is the S-recall value at the t-th position, and S-recall$[0] = 0$.

Since the training algorithm learns the model parameters under the supervision of the rewards, defining the rewards according to a diversity evaluation measure can guide the training process to achieve an optimal model in terms of that evaluation measure.

[2]The calculation of reward is based on the document sequence $\mathcal{Z}_t$ in s_t, the selected documents $\mathbf{x}_{m(a_t)}$, and the relevance labels of these documents. Here we assume that the state s_t also contains the document labels in the training phase.

Policy $\pi(a|s)$: The policy $\pi : A \times S \longrightarrow [0, 1]$ defines the probability of selecting each action. Given current state $s_t = [\mathcal{Z}_t, X_t, \mathbf{h}_t]$ and a possible action a_t, the policy π is defined as a normalized soft-max function whose input is the bilinear product of the utility and the selected document:

$$\pi(a_t | [\mathcal{Z}_t, X_t, \mathbf{h}_t]) = \frac{\exp\left\{\mathbf{x}_{m(a_t)}^T \mathbf{U}\mathbf{h}_t\right\}}{Z}, \tag{3}$$

where $\mathbf{U} \in \mathbb{R}^{L \times K}$ is the parameter in the bilinear product and Z is the normalization factor:

$$Z = \sum_{a \in A(s_t)} \exp\left\{\mathbf{x}_{m(a)}^T \mathbf{U}\mathbf{h}_t\right\}.$$

Construction of a diverse ranking for the queries in the training data can be formalized as: given a user query q, a set of M candidate documents X, and the corresponding human labels J, the system state is initialized as $s_0 = [\mathcal{Z}_0 = \emptyset, X_0 = X, \mathbf{h}_0 = \sigma(\mathbf{V}_q \mathbf{q})]$. Then, at each of the time steps $t = 0, \cdots, M-1$, the agent receives the state $s_t = [\mathcal{Z}_t, X_t, \mathbf{h}_t]$, chooses an action a_t which selects the document $\mathbf{x}_{m(a_t)}$ from the candidate set, and places it to the rank $t+1$. Moving to the next step $t + 1$, the state becomes $s_{t+1} = [\mathcal{Z}_{t+1}, X_{t+1}, \mathbf{h}_{t+1}]$. On the basis of the human labels J for the query, the agent receives immediate reward $r_{t+1} = R([\mathcal{Z}_t, X_t, \mathbf{h}_t], a_t)$, which could be used as supervision for training the model parameters. The process is repeated until the candidate set becomes empty.

Note that in online ranking/testing phase, there is no reward available because the queries are unlabeled. To construct a diverse ranking, we fully trust the learned policy and choose the action with maximal probability at each time step.

Next, we will discuss the off-line training algorithm and online ranking algorithm.

4.2 Learning with policy gradient

The model has parameters $\boldsymbol{\Theta} = \{\mathbf{V}_q, \mathbf{U}, \mathbf{V}, \mathbf{W}\}$ to learn. Inspired by the REINFORCE [22] algorithm of policy gradient, we devised a novel algorithm which can learn the parameters toward the diversity evaluation measure. The algorithm is referred as MDP-DIV and shown in Algorithm 1. The Algorithm 2 shows the procedure of sampling an episode for Algorithm 1.

The basic idea of Algorithm 1 is updating the parameters via Monte-Carlo stochastic gradient ascent. At each iteration, an episode (consisting a sequence of M states, actions, and rewards) is sampled according to current policy. Then, at each time step t of the sampled episode, the model parameters are adjusted according to the gradients of the parameters $\nabla_{\boldsymbol{\Theta}} \log \pi(a_t | s_t; \boldsymbol{\Theta})$, scaled by the step size η, discount rate γ^t, and the long-term return G_t, where G_t is defined as the discounted sum of the rewards from position t:

$$G_t = \sum_{k=0}^{M-1-t} \gamma^k r_{t+k+1}, \tag{4}$$

where $M = |X|$ is the number documents in the candidate set. Note that if $\gamma = 1$, G_0 is exactly the evaluation measure calculated at the final rank of the document list, i.e., α-DCG@M or S-recall@M. Intuitively, the setting of G_t let the parameters move most in the directions so that the favor actions can yield the highest return.

Algorithm 1 MDP-DIV learning

Input: Labeled training set $D = \{(\mathbf{q}^{(n)}, X^{(n)}, J^{(n)})\}_{n=1}^{N}$, learning rate η, discount factor γ, and reward function R

Output: $\Theta = \{\mathbf{V}_q, \mathbf{U}, \mathbf{V}, \mathbf{W}\}$

```
Initialize Θ = {V_q, U, V, W} ← random values in [−1, 1]
repeat
    for all (q, X, J) ∈ D do
        (s_0, a_0, r_1, ···, s_{M−1}, a_{M−1}, r_M) ← SampleEpisode(Θ, q, X, J, R) {Algorithm (2), and M = |X|}
        for t = 0 to M − 1 do
            G_t ← Σ_{k=0}^{M−1−t} γ^k r_{t+k+1} {Equation (4)}
            Θ ← Θ + ηγ^t G_t ∇_Θ log π(a_t|s_t; Θ) {Equation (5)}
        end for
    end for
until converge
return Θ
```

Algorithm 2 SampleEpisode

Input: Parameters $\Theta = \{\mathbf{V}_q, \mathbf{U}, \mathbf{V}, \mathbf{W}\}$, q, X, J, and R

Output: An episode

```
Initialize s ← [∅, X, σ(V_q q)]{Equation (1)}
M ← |X|
E = (){empty episode}
for t = 0 to M − 1 do
    A ← A(s) {Possible actions according to X in state s}
    for all a ∈ A do
        P(a) ← π(a|s; Θ)
    end for
    Sample an action â ∈ A, according to P
    r ← R(s, â){Calculation on the basis of J}
    Append (s, â, r) to the tail of E
    [Z, X, h] ← s
    s ← [Z ⊕ {x_{m(â)}}, X \ {x_{m(â)}}, σ(V x_{m(â)} + W h)]
end for
return E = (s_0, a_0, r_1, ···, s_{M−1}, a_{M−1}, r_M)
```

The gradient of MDP-DIV at time step t is $\nabla_\Theta \log \pi(a_t|s_t; \Theta)$, which the direction that most increase the probability of repeating the action a_t on future visits to state s_t, and is defined as

$$\nabla_\Theta \log \pi(a_t|s_t;\Theta) = \nabla_\Theta f(a_t|s_t) - \frac{\sum_{a\in A_t} \nabla_\Theta f(a|s_t) \exp\{f(a|s_t)\}}{\sum_{a\in A_t} \exp\{f(a|s_t)\}}, \tag{5}$$

where $f(a|s_t) = \mathbf{x}_{m(a)}^T(\mathbf{U}\mathbf{h}_t)$, and $\nabla_\Theta f(a|s_t) = \{\nabla_\mathbf{U} f(a|s_t), \nabla_{\mathbf{V}_q} f(a|s_t), \nabla_\mathbf{V} f(a|s_t), \nabla_\mathbf{W} f(a|s_t)\}$, where

$$\nabla_\mathbf{U} f(a|s_t) = \mathbf{x}_{m(a)}\mathbf{h}_t^T.$$

As for $\nabla_{\mathbf{V}_q} f(a|s_t)$, $\nabla_\mathbf{V} f(a|s_t)$, and $\nabla_\mathbf{W} f(a|s_t)$, they can be calculated in a similar way:

$$\begin{aligned}\nabla_{\mathbf{V}_q} f(a|s_t) &= \left(\nabla_{\mathbf{V}_q}\mathbf{h}_t\right)\mathbf{U}^T\mathbf{x}_{m(a)},\\ \nabla_\mathbf{V} f(a|s_t) &= (\nabla_\mathbf{V}\mathbf{h}_t)\,\mathbf{U}^T\mathbf{x}_{m(a)},\\ \nabla_\mathbf{W} f(a|s_t) &= (\nabla_\mathbf{W}\mathbf{h}_t)\,\mathbf{U}^T\mathbf{x}_{m(a)},\end{aligned}$$

where $\nabla_{\mathbf{V}_q}\mathbf{h}_t$, $\nabla_\mathbf{V}\mathbf{h}_t$, and $\nabla_\mathbf{W}\mathbf{h}_t$ can be calculated recursively:

$$\begin{aligned}\nabla_{\mathbf{V}_q}\mathbf{h}_t &= \nabla_{\mathbf{V}_q}\sigma(\mathbf{V}\mathbf{x}_{m(a_{t-1})} + \mathbf{W}\mathbf{h}_{t-1})\\ &= \mathrm{diag}(\mathbf{h}_t \circ (\mathbf{1} - \mathbf{h}_t))\left(\nabla_{\mathbf{V}_q}(\mathbf{W}\mathbf{h}_{t-1})\right)\\ &= \mathrm{diag}(\mathbf{h}_t \circ (\mathbf{1} - \mathbf{h}_t))\left(\nabla_{\mathbf{V}_q}\mathbf{h}_{t-1}\right)\mathbf{W}^T,\end{aligned}$$

where $\mathbf{1}$ is an K-dimensional vector of ones, operator "$\circ$" denotes the element-wise vector product, operator "diag" generates an $K\times K$ diagonal matrix according to the input vector, and $\nabla_{\mathbf{V}_q}\mathbf{h}_{t-1}$ can be further unrolled in a similar way. At $t = 0$, $\nabla_{\mathbf{V}_q}\mathbf{h}_0$ is:

$$\nabla_{\mathbf{V}_q}\mathbf{h}_0 = \nabla_{\mathbf{V}_q}\sigma(\mathbf{V}_q\mathbf{q}) = \mathrm{diag}(\mathbf{h}_0 \circ (\mathbf{1} - \mathbf{h}_0))\mathbf{I}_{K,L,K,L}\mathbf{q},$$

where $\mathbf{I}_{K,L,K,L} \in \mathbb{R}^{K\times L\times K\times L}$ is an identity tensor.

$$\begin{aligned}\nabla_\mathbf{V}\mathbf{h}_t &= \nabla_\mathbf{V}\sigma(\mathbf{V}\mathbf{x}_{m(a_{t-1})} + \mathbf{W}\mathbf{h}_{t-1})\\ &= \mathrm{diag}(\mathbf{h}_t \circ (\mathbf{1} - \mathbf{h}_t))\left(\nabla_\mathbf{V}(\mathbf{V}\mathbf{x}_{m(a_{t-1})} + \mathbf{W}\mathbf{h}_{t-1})\right)\\ &= \mathrm{diag}(\mathbf{h}_t \circ (\mathbf{1} - \mathbf{h}_t))\left(\mathbf{I}_{K,L,K,L}\mathbf{x}_{m(a_{t-1})} + (\nabla_\mathbf{V}\mathbf{h}_{t-1})\,\mathbf{W}^T\right),\end{aligned}$$

where $\nabla_\mathbf{V}\mathbf{h}_{t-1}$ can be unrolled in a similar way. At $t = 0$, $\nabla_\mathbf{V}\mathbf{h}_0$ is:

$$\nabla_\mathbf{V}\mathbf{h}_0 = \nabla_\mathbf{V}\sigma(\mathbf{V}_q\mathbf{q}) = \mathbf{0}_{K,L,1,K},$$

where $\mathbf{0}_{K,L,1,K} \in \mathbb{R}^{K\times L\times 1\times K}$ is a tensor of zeros.

$$\begin{aligned}\nabla_\mathbf{W}\mathbf{h}_t &= \nabla_\mathbf{W}\sigma(\mathbf{V}\mathbf{x}_{m(a_{t-1})} + \mathbf{W}\mathbf{h}_{t-1})\\ &= \mathrm{diag}(\mathbf{h}_t \circ (\mathbf{1} - \mathbf{h}_t))\left(\nabla_\mathbf{W}(\mathbf{V}\mathbf{x}_{m(a_{t-1})} + \mathbf{W}\mathbf{h}_{t-1})\right)\\ &= \mathrm{diag}(\mathbf{h}_t \circ (\mathbf{1} - \mathbf{h}_t))\left(\mathbf{I}_{K,K,K,K}\mathbf{h}_{t-1} + (\nabla_\mathbf{W}\mathbf{h}_{t-1})\,\mathbf{W}^T\right),\end{aligned}$$

where $\mathbf{I}_{K,K,K,K} \in \mathbb{R}^{K\times K\times K\times K}$ is an identity tensor, and $\nabla_\mathbf{W}\mathbf{h}_{t-1}$ can be unrolled in a similar way. At $t = 0$, $\nabla_\mathbf{W}\mathbf{h}_0$ is:

$$\nabla_\mathbf{W}\mathbf{h}_0 = \nabla_\mathbf{W}\sigma(\mathbf{V}_q\mathbf{q}) = \mathbf{0}_{K,K,1,K},$$

where $\mathbf{0}_{K,K,1,K} \in \mathbb{R}^{K\times K\times 1\times K}$ is a tensor of zeros.

Compared with conventional REINFORCE algorithm, MDP-DIV is based on a modified MDP model in which the user state of perceived utility is initialized with query and modeled in a recurrent manner. Thus, in the training phase, MDP-DIV needs to estimate the policy function, as well as the functions for state initialization and state transition. In [16], similar idea was presented for extracting information from images. In this paper we adapt the model for the task of search result diversification.

4.3 Online ranking

In the online ranking, the ranking system receives a user query q and the associated documents $X = \{\mathbf{x}_1, \cdots, \mathbf{x}_M\}$. Since there exists no human label for calculating the immediate rewards, the system fully relies on the learned policy π for generating the diverse ranking, as shown in Algorithm 3. After initializing with q, the algorithm makes a sequence of greedy decisions: at each step the action with the maximal probability is chosen (line 5 of Alglrithm 3), and the action in return update the state for choosing the next action (line 7 and line 8 of Algorithm 3).

The time complexity of the online ranking algorithm is of $O\left(\min\{KL^2, LK^2\}\frac{M(2+M)}{4} + (M-1)(K^2+KL)\right)$ per query. The first

Algorithm 3 MDP-DIV online ranking

Input: Parameters $\boldsymbol{\Theta} = \{\mathbf{V}_q, \mathbf{U}, \mathbf{V}, \mathbf{W}\}$, query q, documents X
Output: Permutation of documents τ
Initialize $s \leftarrow [\emptyset, X, \sigma(\mathbf{V}_q \mathbf{q})]$ {Equation (1)}
$M \leftarrow |X|$
for $t = 0$ **to** $M - 1$ **do**
  $A \leftarrow A(s)$ {Possible actions according to X in state s}
  $\hat{a} \leftarrow \arg\max_{a \in A} \pi(a|s; \boldsymbol{\Theta})$ {Choosing most possible action}
  $\tau[t+1] \leftarrow m(\hat{a})$ {Document $\mathbf{x}_{m(\hat{a})}$ is ranked at $t+1$}
  $[\mathcal{Z}, X, \mathbf{h}] \leftarrow s$
  $s \leftarrow [\mathcal{Z} \oplus \{\mathbf{x}_{m(\hat{a})}\}, X \setminus \{\mathbf{x}_{m(\hat{a})}\}, \sigma(\mathbf{V}\mathbf{x}_{m(\hat{a})} + \mathbf{W}\mathbf{h})]$
end for
return τ

part corresponds to calculating the policy for all of the possible actions at each iteration and the second part corresponds to updating the state for the next iteration. The term $\min\{KL^2, LK^2\}$ is for calculating the matrix multiplication $\mathbf{x}_{m(a_t)}^T U \mathbf{h}_t$ in the policy with different ways. In most cases L is larger than K. Please note that the online ranking algorithm actually runs $M - 1$ iterations for ranking M documents, because at the last iteration $A(s_{M-1})$ contains only one action. Usually, K and L are not very large, e.g, we set $K = 5$ and $L = 100$ in our experiments. Thus, the online ranking algorithm is efficient if the candidate set is not very large. In our experiments, on average it takes about 20 milliseconds for ranking about 200 documents, on a server with 24GB memory and two Intel Xeon E5410 2.33GHz Quad-Core processors. Note that in the analysis the time for document embedding is not taken into consideration as the document embeddings can be calculated offline.

4.4 Theoretical analysis

The learning phase of MDP-DIV tries to optimize general diversity evaluation measures with reinforcement learning. The measures can be α-DCG and S-recall, or any other measures that can be calculated at each of the ranking position. We explain why this is the case.

In the training, Monte-Carlo stochastic gradient ascent is used to conduct the optimization. Given a query q in the training set, we want to maximize the value V, which is the expected return of the query:

$$\max_{\boldsymbol{\Theta}} V(\mathbf{q}) = \mathbb{E}_\pi G_0,$$

where G_0 is the discounted sum of the rewards, starting from position 0, as defined in Equation (4). Please note G_0 is the diversity evaluation measure if $\gamma = 1$. Thus, maximizing $V(\mathbf{q})$ is actually maximizing the expected diversity evaluation measure for the query.

According to the policy gradient theorem presented in [22], chapter 13, the gradient of the performance metric with respect to the parameters $\boldsymbol{\Theta}$ on each query can be calculated as

$$\nabla_{\boldsymbol{\Theta}} V(\boldsymbol{\Theta}) = \mathbb{E}_{s \sim \rho, a \sim \pi} Q^\pi(s, a) \nabla_{\boldsymbol{\Theta}} \pi(a|s),$$

where ρ is the discounted state distribution given a query q and model parameters, which is defined as:

$$\rho(s|\mathbf{q}; \boldsymbol{\Theta}) = \sum_{t=1}^{\infty} \gamma^{t-1} p(s_0 \rightarrow s, t|\mathbf{q}_n; \boldsymbol{\Theta}),$$

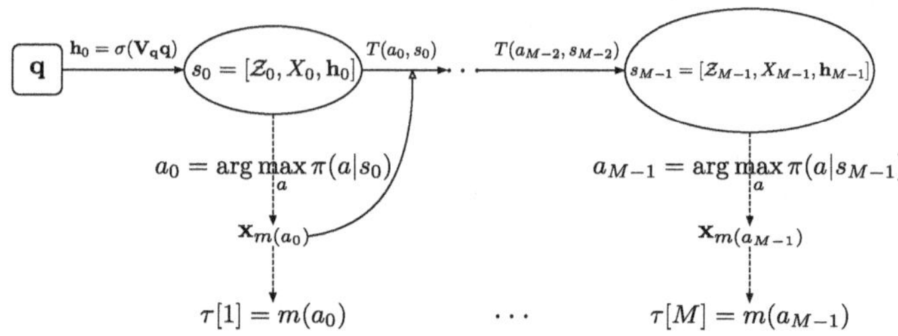

Figure 2: Online document ranking in MDP-DIV.

where $p(s_0 \rightarrow s, t|\mathbf{q}_n; \boldsymbol{\Theta})$ is the probability of transitioning from the initial state s_0 given the query q in t steps [22]. $Q^\pi(s, a)$ is the expected return starting from s, taking the action a and thereafter following the policy π:

$$Q^\pi(s, a) = \mathbb{E}_\pi[G_t | s_t = s, a_t = a].$$

Monte-Carlo method is used to estimate the gradient. Specifically, given a sampled episode $s_0, a_0, r_1, \cdots, s_{M-1}, a_{M-1}, r_M$ and a specific time step t, the gradient can be estimated as [22]

$$\begin{aligned}
\widehat{\nabla_{\boldsymbol{\Theta}} V(\boldsymbol{\Theta})} &\overset{\text{sample}}{=} \gamma^t \sum_{a \in A(s_t)} \nabla_{\boldsymbol{\Theta}} \pi(a|s_t) Q^\pi(s_t, a) \\
&= \gamma^t \sum_{a \in A(s_t)} \pi(a|s_t) \cdot \left(Q^\pi(s_t, a) \frac{\nabla_{\boldsymbol{\Theta}} \pi(a|s_t)}{\pi(a|s_t)} \right) \\
&\overset{\text{sample}}{=} \gamma^t Q^\pi(s_t, a_t) \frac{\nabla_{\boldsymbol{\Theta}} \pi(a_t|s_t)}{\pi(a_t|s_t)} \\
&\overset{\text{sample}}{=} \gamma^t G_t \nabla_{\boldsymbol{\Theta}} \log \pi(a_t|s_t).
\end{aligned}$$

The first $\overset{\text{sample}}{=}$ replaces s by its sample s_t, which is sampled according to ρ; the second $\overset{\text{sample}}{=}$ replaces a by its sample a_t, which is sampled according to π; and the third $\overset{\text{sample}}{=}$ replaces the thereafter decision process guided by π with the sampled episode. Note that $\mathbb{E}_\pi[G_t|s_t, a_t] = Q^\pi(s_t, a_t)$ and $\nabla_{\boldsymbol{\Theta}} \log \pi(a_t|s_t) = \frac{\nabla_{\boldsymbol{\Theta}} \pi(a_t|s_t)}{\pi(a_t|s_t)}$.

We can see that the updating rule in Algorithm 1 exactly follows the estimated gradients presented above. Thus, we can conclude MDP-DIV tries to optimize general diversity evaluation measures with Monte-Carlo stochastic gradient ascent when $\gamma = 1$.

4.5 Advantages

MDP-DIV provides an elegant approach to modeling user's dynamic state on the perceived utility during the browsing of the diverse ranking results. More importantly, it is a method that can be justified from the theoretical viewpoint, as discussed above. In addition, MDP-DIV has several other advantages when compared with the existing diverse ranking learning methods such as SVM-DIV, R-LTR and PAMM etc.

First, MDP-DIV can conduct an end-to-end learning of the diverse ranking model, which achieves a model with no need of handcrafting relevance features and novelty features. The inputs to the ranking model are the preliminary representations of the queries and the documents, e.g., the distributed representations learned by the doc2vec model. In contrast, all existing diverse ranking learning methods heavily depend on the handcrafted relevance features and/or novelty features. It has been widely observed that high quality features are critical for constructing diverse ranking, while designing the features, especially designing the novelty features, is very difficult in real applications [25]. MDP-DIV solves the issue via learning a ranking model that needs only the preliminary representations of the queries and the documents.

Second, MDP-DIV utilizes both the immediate rewards and the long-term returns as the supervision information during its training. Specifically, given an episode, the parameters are updated after receiving each of the immediate rewards (line 5-8 of Algorithm 1). Meanwhile, the updating rule also utilizes the long-term return G_t, which accumulates all of the future rewards (line 6-7 of Algorithm 1), to re-scale the step size. In contrast, existing methods that directly optimize evaluation measures are only based on a evaluation measure calculated at a fixed position [24, 26] on the basis of whole ranking. Our empirical analysis in Section 5.3.2 also showed that training with both the rewards and the returns can achieve better ranking accuracies.

Third, MDP-DIV makes use of a unified criterion, the additional utility a search user can perceive, for selecting documents at each iteration. In contrast, the criterion adopted by most existing methods, e.g., the marginal relevance, consists of two individual factors: the relevance and the novelty. Heuristic diverse ranking model xQuAD tried to replace these two factors with "the relevance to the underlying sub-queries", which has shown to be more reasonable and effective. In this paper, we also showed that under the MDP framework, the document selection criterion can be unified to "the perceived utility", which has shown to be simple in concept and be powerful in the real applications.

5 EXPERIMENTS

We conducted experiments to test the performances of MDP-DIV using a combination of four TREC benchmark datasets: TREC 2009 Web Track (WT2009), TREC 2010 Web Track (WT2010), TREC 2011 Web Track (WT2011), and TREC 2012 Web Track (WT2012).

5.1 Experimental settings

The training of MDP-DIV model need lots of labeled queries because it has a large number of parameters. In experiments, for effective training of the model parameters, we combined four TREC datasets, achieving a new dataset with 200 queries, and in total about 45,000 labeled documents. Each query includes several subtopics identified by the TREC assessors. The document relevance labels are made at the subtopic level and the labels are binary[3].

All the experiments were carried out on the ClueWeb09 Category B data collection[4], which is comprised of 50 million English web documents. Porter stemming, tokenization, and stop-words removal (using the INQUERY list) were applied to the documents as preprocessing. For each query, the initial ranking is generated by Query-likelihood language model[14]. We conducted 5-fold cross-validation experiments. We randomly split the queries into five even subsets. At each fold, three subsets were used for training, one was used for validation, and one was used for testing. The results reported were the average over the five trials.

[3]WT2011 has graded judgements. In this paper we treat them as binary.

[4]http://boston.lti.cs.cmu.edu/data/clueweb09

The TREC official evaluation metrics for the diversity task were used in the experiments, including the ERR-IA [3] and α-NDCG [4]. They measure the diversity of a result list by explicitly rewarding diversity and penalizing redundancy observed at every rank. Following the default settings in official TREC evaluation program, the parameter α in these evaluation measures are set to 0.5. We also used traditional diversity measures of subtopic recall (denoted as "S-recall") [29]. All of the measures are computed over the top-k search results (k = 5 and k = 10).

We compared MDP-DIV with several state-of-the-arts baselines in search result diversification, including the heuristic methods:

MMR [2]: a heuristic approach in which the document is selected according to maximal marginal relevance.

xQuAD [19]: a representative approach which explicitly models different aspects underlying the original query in the form of subqueries.

PM-2 [5]: a method of optimizing proportionality for search result diversification.

We also compared MDP-DIV with the learning methods:

SVM-DIV [27]: a learning approach which utilizes structural SVMs to optimize the subtopic coverage.

R-LTR [31]: a state-of-the-art learning approach developed in the relational learning to rank framework. Following the practice in [31], we used the results of R-LTR$_{\text{min}}$ in which the relation function was defined as the minimal distance of the candidate document to the selected documents

PAMM [24]: another learning algorithm under R-LTR framework. PAMM directly optimizes diversity evaluation measure using structured Perceptron. Following the practice in [24], we configured the PAMM algorithm to directly optimize α-NDCG@10 in our experiments, and set the number of sampled positive rankings per query $\tau^+ = 5$ and the number of sampled negative rankings per query $\tau^- = 20$.

NTN-DIV: a learning approach which automatically learns novelty features based on neural tensor networks. Following the practice in [25], we configured the learning of NTN-DIV algorithm to directly optimize α-NDCG@10 and the number of tensor slices is 7.

MDP-DIV and the baseline of NTN-DIV need preliminary representations of the queries and the documents as their inputs. In the experiments, we used the query vector and document vector generated by the doc2vec [10] to represent the document. Doc2vec model was trained on all of the documents in Web Track dataset and the number of vector dimensions were set to 100. For training the model, we used the distributed bag of words (DBOW) model[5]. The learning rate is set to 0.025 and the window size is set to 8.

The MDP-DIV also has some parameters. The reward function in MDP-DIV was set as either $R_{\alpha\text{-DCG}}$ or $R_{\text{S-recall}}$, denoted as MDP-DIV(α-DCG) and MDP-DIV(S-recall), respectively. In all of the experiments, the learning rate η is tuned on the basis of the validation set. We set the discounting parameter $\gamma = 1$, which means that the return is the undiscounted sum of the future rewards, which makes the long term return in Equation (4) becomes $G_t = \sum_{k=0}^{M-1-t} r_{t+k+1}$. It makes the training algorithm optimizes the diversity evaluation measure of α-DCG and S-recall.

[5]http://radimrehurek.com/gensim/tutorial.html

5.2 Experimental results

Table 1 reports the performances of our approach and all of the baseline methods in terms of the six diversity performance metrics, including α-NDCG@5, α-NDCG@10, S-recall@5, S-recall@10, ERR-IA@5, and ERR-IA@10. Boldface indicates the highest score among all runs. From the results we can see that, in terms of the six diversity evaluation metrics, both MDP-DIV(α-DCG) and MDP-DIV(S-recall) outperformed all of the baseline methods, including the heuristic method of MMR, xQuAD, PM-2 and learning methods of R-LTR, PAMM(α-NDCG), and NTN-DIV(α-NDCG). We conducted significance testing (t-test) on the improvements of our approaches over the best baseline NTN-DIV(α-NDCG). The results indicate that the improvements are significant (p-value < 0.05), in terms of all of the evaluation measures.

Comparing the results of the MDP-DIV(α-DCG) and MDP-DIV(S-recall), we can see that MDP-DIV(α-DCG) trained with α-DCG (setting α-DCG as reward function) performed better in terms of α-NDCG@5 and α-NDCG@10. Similarly, MDP-DIV(S-recall) trained with S-recall (setting S-recall as reward function) performed better in terms of S-recall@5 and S-recall@10. The results indicate that MDP-DIV can indeed enhance diverse ranking performance in terms of a measure by using the measure as reward function in training[6]. The result agrees well with the theoretical analysis shown in Section 4.4.

5.3 Discussion

We conducted experiments to show the reasons that MDP-DIV outperformed the baselines, using the results of MDP-DIV(α-DCG) on one trial of the cross validation as examples.

5.3.1 Effects of modeling user perceived utility. We analyzed how the user state on the perceived utility effects the selection of documents in MDP-DIV. Specifically, based on the trained MDP-DIV model, we tracked the online ranking process for query number 93 "ambiguous", which contains five subtopics. Figure 3 shows the details of the first three document selection steps, including the transition of the user dynamic state $\mathbf{h}_i$, the ranking score $f(a_t|s_t) = \mathbf{x}^T_{m(a_t)}\mathbf{U}\mathbf{h}_t$ for each of the actions[7], and the constructed document ranking. Due to the space limitation, we only showed the five top ranked documents $d_1, \cdots, d_5$, corresponding to the documents of enwp03-28-04544, en0007-80-16124, en0094-80-42411, en0006-08-03878, and en0010-24-38000 in the Clueweb09 collection, respectively. The subtopics covered by each of the documents are shown in the square brackets.

From Figure 3, we can see that $\mathbf{h}_t$ was updated after choosing each action, indicating the changes of the user state after perceiving the utility provided by the selected document. At step 0, the selected document d_2 covered subtopics 3 and 5. At step 1, as the consequence of the action the user state was updated, and the ranking score of d_4 (with the covered subtopic 5) was suppressed from 0.46 to 0.35, while the ranking scores of the other three documents (d_1, d_3, and d_5, with uncovered subtopics) were promoted. The results indicate that the user state $\mathbf{h}_1$ captured the utility provided by d_2, which made the ranking model focusing on documents that can provide the largest amount of new information. As the result, d_5, which contains two new subtopics 1 and 4, was selected at step 1. Similarly, at step 2 state vector $\mathbf{h}_2$ captured the utility provided by d_2 and d_5 and making the model to select d_1, which contains a new subtopic 2. In contrast, the ranking scores for d_3 and d_4, whose subtopics had been covered by the preceding documents, were suppressed. The phenomenon clearly indicates MDP-DIV can effectively capture the user perceived utility of information in its state, and utilize it for generating diverse rankings.

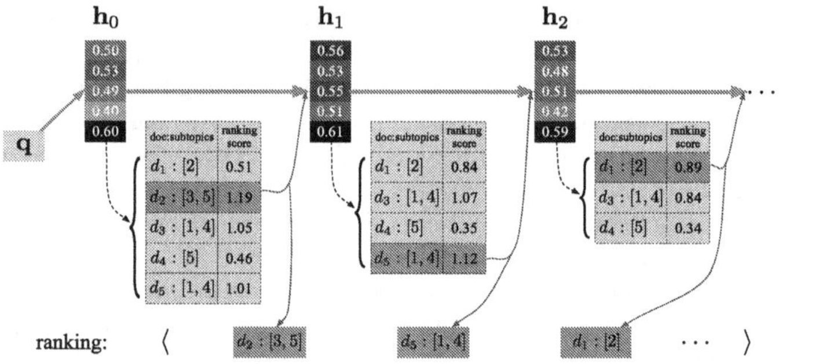

Figure 3: The online ranking process for query number 93.

5.3.2 Effects of using immediate rewards in training. One advantage of MDP-DIV is that it has the ability of utilizing the immediate rewards as the supervision in training, which makes the training more effective and efficient. We tried to verify the effectiveness and efficiency of using the immediate rewards in the training phase. Specifically, we modified the training Algorithm 1 so that the model parameters were updated only at the end of an episode (i.e., setting the iteration variable t in the line 5 of Algorithm 1 starts from M). In this way, the modified algorithm only utilizes the long term return of the whole episode for training, denoted as "MDP-DIV(ReturnOnly)". Figure 4 shows the performance curves of MDP-DIV(α-DCG) and MDP-DIV(ReturnOnly) trained with α-DCG, on the test data of one trail in the cross validation. The performances of other baseline methods on the same cross validation trail are also shown in the figure.

From the results, we can see that MDP-DIV(α-DCG) outperformed the MDP-DIV(ReturnOnly) in terms of both convergency rate and the converged performances. The result indicates that utilizing the immediate rewards in MDP-DIV(α-DCG) leads to an effective and efficient training algorithm. Note that in contrast, most existing learning approaches to diverse ranking, including R-LTR, PAMM, and NTN-DIV, can only utilize the accumulated information on the whole ranking as supervision in their training phase. For example, R-LTR uses the likelihood of the whole document rankings, and PAMM uses the predefined evaluation measure calculated based on the whole ranking. The experimental results showed one reason why MDP-DIV(α-DCG) can outperform these baselines.

We also noticed that the converged MDP-DIV(ReturnOnly) model still outperformed the baseline methods including SVM-DIV, R-LTR, PAMM, and NTN-DIV, indicating that modeling the user's dynamic state on the perceived utility with MDP is effective.

[6] Here we consider α-NDCG and α-DCG as "one" measure as the only difference between them is the normalization factor.

[7] In the online ranking, the selection of actions can be implemented as directly based on the ranking scores instead of based on the probabilities $\pi(a_t|s_t)$.

Table 1: Performance comparison of all methods on TREC web track datasets.

Method	α-NDCG@5	α-NDCG@10	S-recall@5	S-recall@10	ERR-IA@5	ERR-IA@10
MMR	0.2753	0.2979	0.4388	0.5151	0.2005	0.2309
xQuAD	0.3165	0.3941	0.4933	0.6043	0.2314	0.2890
PM-2	0.3047	0.3730	0.4910	0.6012	0.2298	0.2814
SVM-DIV	0.3030	0.3699	0.5122	0.6230	0.2268	0.2726
R-LTR	0.3498	0.4132	0.5397	0.6511	0.2521	0.3011
PAMM(α-NDCG)	0.3712	0.4327	0.5561	0.6612	0.2619	0.3029
NTN-DIV(α-NDCG)	0.3962	0.4577	0.5817	0.6872	0.2773	0.3285
MDP-DIV(S-recall)	0.4156	0.4734	**0.6123**	**0.7155**	0.2963	0.3477
MDP-DIV(α-DCG)	**0.4189**	**0.4762**	0.6102	0.7117	**0.2988**	**0.3494**

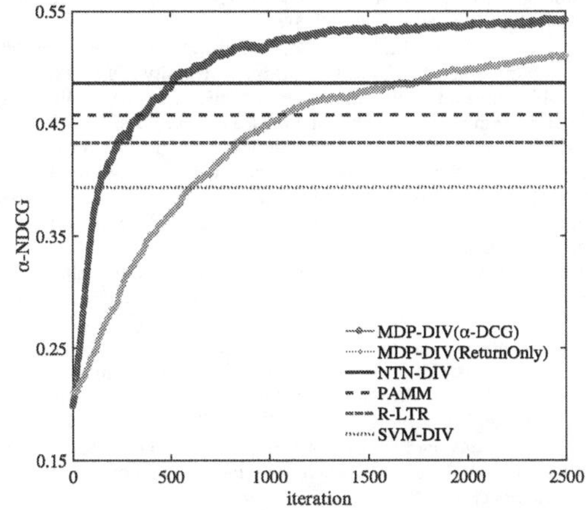

Figure 4: The performance curves on the test data for MDP-DIV(α-DCG), and the modified MDP-DIV(α-DCG) in which the training only involves the long-term returns. The performances of other baselines are shown as horizontal lines.

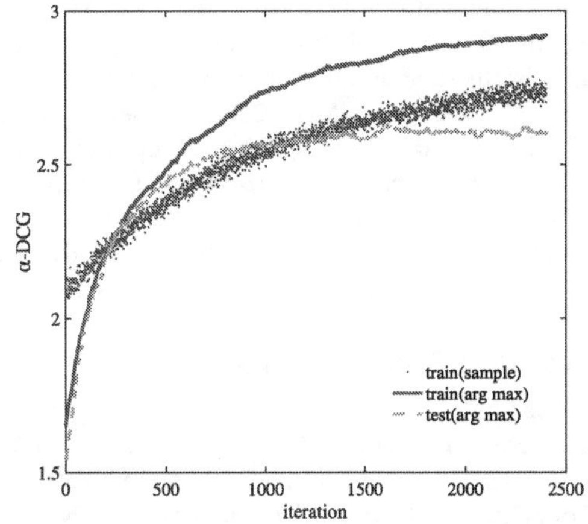

Figure 5: The performance curves in terms of α-DCG on the training data ("train(arg max)") and the test data ("test(arg max)"). The average performances of the sampled rankings over all training queries are also shown ("train(sample)").

5.3.3 *Analysis of convergence and online ranking criterion.* We conducted experiments to test whether the ranking accuracy in terms of the evaluation measure can be continuously improved, as the training of MDP-DIV goes on.

Specifically, we tested the MDP-DIV(α-DCG) models generated at each of the training iteration in one trail of the cross validation. The performances in terms of α-DCG at the last position of the whole document ranking is reported. For each model, the average performances over all of the training queries (or the testing queries) are reported. Figure 5 shows the performance curves on the training data (solid red line and denoted as "train(arg max)") and on the test data (dashed yellow line and denoted as "test(arg max)"). For these two curves, the document rankings for the queries are generated by the online ranking Algorithm 3. The document rankings can also be generated through sampling during the training, via the episode sampling Algorithm 2. The average performances of the sampled rankings for all the training queries are also shown in the figure (blue dots and denoted as "train(sample)").

From the results shown in Figure 5, we can see that on both of the training set and test set, the ranking accuracies of MDP-DIV(α-DCG) steadily improves, as the training goes on. The experimental results also showed that the ranking accuracies of the sampled rankings (by Algorithm 2) has an obvious trend of steadily improving with some random noise, as the training goes on.

Comparing the sampled rankings ("train(sample)") and the ranking generated by the online ranking algorithm ("train(arg max"), we can see that at the beginning of the training phase, the sampled rankings can achieve better α-DCG values than the rankings generated by the online ranking algorithm, on the basis of the training queries. As the training went on and after about 200 iterations, the online ranking algorithm outperformed the sampling method, and the trend remains to the end of the training. The phenomenon was repeated in other experiments. We analyzed the reasons. The online ranking algorithm (Algorithm 3) fully trusts the learned ranking model when generating the document ranking, i.e., $\hat{a} \leftarrow \arg\max_{a \in A} \pi(a|s; \Theta)$. In contrast, the sampled rankings are generated according to the same ranking model while with some randomness. At the beginning of the training phase, the model parameters are far from their optimal values. In many cases, fully trusting the policy leads to bad decisions and generating rankings with low performances. The sampling method, in contrast, may make better decisions due to the random natural of sampling. As the training goes on, the model parameters gradually converge to nearly optimal values. Fully trusting the learned policy has the advantages of achieving stable and (nearly) optimal decisions in most cases. The sampling method, however, hurts from unstable results due to the random noise. The results clearly indicate that, fully trusting the learned model (as that of in Algorithm 3) in the online ranking phase is a good criterion, given the model is well trained.

6 CONCLUSION AND FUTURE WORK

In this paper we have proposed a novel approach to learning diverse ranking model for search result diversification, referred to as MDP-DIV. In contrast to existing methods, MDP-DIV explicitly models the dynamic utility the search users perceived during the browsing of the ranking result. The dynamic utility is modeled with a continuous state MDP and the model parameters are estimated with reinforcement learning. MDP-DIV offers several advantages: no need for handcrafting ranking features, optimizing diversity evaluation measures in training, utilizing both immediate rewards and long-term returns as supervision, and high accuracy in ranking. Experimental results based on the TREC benchmark datasets show that MDP-DIV can significantly outperform the baseline methods.

7 ACKNOWLEDGEMENTS

The work was funded by the National Key R&D Program of China under Grant No. 2016QY02D0405, 973 Program of China under Grant No. 2014CB340401 and 2012CB316303, the National Natural Science Foundation of China (NSFC) under Grants No. 61232010, 61472401, 61433014, 61425016, and 61203298, the Key Research Program of the CAS under Grant No. KGZD-EW-T03-2, and the Youth Innovation Promotion Association CAS under Grants No. 20144310 and 2016102.

REFERENCES

[1] Rakesh Agrawal, Sreenivas Gollapudi, Alan Halverson, and Samuel Ieong. 2009. Diversifying Search Results. In *Proceedings of the Second ACM International Conference on Web Search and Data Mining (WSDM '09)*. ACM, New York, NY, USA, 5–14.

[2] Jaime Carbonell and Jade Goldstein. 1998. The Use of MMR, Diversity-based Reranking for Reordering Documents and Producing Summaries. In *Proceedings of the 21st Annual International ACM SIGIR Conference on Research and Development in Information Retrieval (SIGIR '98)*. ACM, New York, NY, USA, 335–336.

[3] Olivier Chapelle, Shihao Ji, Ciya Liao, Emre Velipasaoglu, Larry Lai, and Su-Lin Wu. 2011. Intent-based Diversification of Web Search Results: Metrics and Algorithms. *Inf. Retr.* 14, 6 (Dec. 2011), 572–592. DOI: http://dx.doi.org/10.1007/s10791-011-9167-7

[4] Charles L.A. Clarke, Maheedhar Kolla, Gordon V. Cormack, Olga Vechtomova, Azin Ashkan, Stefan Büttcher, and Ian MacKinnon. 2008. Novelty and Diversity in Information Retrieval Evaluation. In *Proceedings of the 31st Annual International ACM SIGIR Conference on Research and Development in Information Retrieval (SIGIR '08)*. ACM, New York, NY, USA, 659–666.

[5] Van Dang and W. Bruce Croft. 2012. Diversity by Proportionality: An Election-based Approach to Search Result Diversification. In *Proceedings of the 35th International ACM SIGIR Conference on Research and Development in Information Retrieval (SIGIR '12)*. ACM, New York, NY, USA, 65–74.

[6] Sreenivas Gollapudi and Aneesh Sharma. 2009. An Axiomatic Approach for Result Diversification. In *Proceedings of the 18th International Conference on World Wide Web (WWW '09)*. 381–390.

[7] Shengbo Guo and Scott Sanner. 2010. Probabilistic Latent Maximal Marginal Relevance. In *Proceedings of the 33rd International ACM SIGIR Conference on Research and Development in Information Retrieval (SIGIR '10)*. ACM, New York, NY, USA, 833–834.

[8] Jiyin He, Vera Hollink, and Arjen de Vries. 2012. Combining Implicit and Explicit Topic Representations for Result Diversification. In *Proceedings of the 35th International ACM SIGIR Conference on Research and Development in Information Retrieval (SIGIR '12)*. ACM, New York, NY, USA, 851–860.

[9] Sha Hu, Zhicheng Dou, Xiaojie Wang, Tetsuya Sakai, and Ji-Rong Wen. 2015. Search Result Diversification Based on Hierarchical Intents. In *Proceedings of the 24th ACM International on Conference on Information and Knowledge Management (CIKM '15)*. ACM, New York, NY, USA, 63–72.

[10] Quoc V. Le and Tomas Mikolov. 2014. Distributed Representations of Sentences and Documents. In *Proceedings of the 31th International Conference on Machine Learning, ICML 2014, Beijing, China, 21-26 June 2014*. 1188–1196. http://jmlr.org/proceedings/papers/v32/le14.html

[11] Liangda Li, Ke Zhou, Gui-Rong Xue, Hongyuan Zha, and Yong Yu. 2009. Enhancing Diversity, Coverage and Balance for Summarization Through Structure Learning. In *Proceedings of the 18th International Conference on World Wide Web (WWW '09)*. ACM, New York, NY, USA, 71–80.

[12] Zhongqi Lu and Qiang Yang. 2016. Partially Observable Markov Decision Process for Recommender Systems. *CoRR* abs/1608.07793 (2016).

[13] Jiyun Luo, Sicong Zhang, and Hui Yang. 2014. Win-win Search: Dual-agent Stochastic Game in Session Search. In *Proceedings of the 37th International ACM SIGIR Conference on Research & Development in Information Retrieval (SIGIR '14)*. ACM, New York, NY, USA, 587–596.

[14] Christopher D. Manning, Prabhakar Raghavan, and Hinrich Schütze. 2008. *Introduction to Information Retrieval.* Cambridge University Press, NY, USA.

[15] Lilyana Mihalkova and Raymond Mooney. 2009. Learning to Disambiguate Search Queries from Short Sessions. In *Machine Learning and Knowledge Discovery in Databases*. Lecture Notes in Computer Science, Vol. 5782. Springer.

[16] Volodymyr Mnih, Nicolas Heess, Alex Graves, and Koray Kavukcuoglu. 2014. Recurrent Models of Visual Attention. In *Proceedings of the 27th International Conference on Neural Information Processing Systems (NIPS'14)*. MIT Press, Cambridge, MA, USA, 2204–2212.

[17] Martin L. Puterman. 2008. *Markov Decision Processes.* John Wiley & Sons, Inc.

[18] Filip Radlinski, Robert Kleinberg, and Thorsten Joachims. 2008. Learning Diverse Rankings with Multi-armed Bandits. In *Proceedings of the 25th International Conference on Machine Learning (ICML '08)*. ACM, New York, NY, USA, 784–791.

[19] Rodrygo L.T. Santos, Craig Macdonald, and Iadh Ounis. 2010. Exploiting Query Reformulations for Web Search Result Diversification. In *Proceedings of the 19th International Conference on World Wide Web (WWW '10)*. 881–890.

[20] Rodrygo L. T. Santos, Jie Peng, Craig Macdonald, and Iadh Ounis. 2010. *Explicit Search Result Diversification through Sub-queries.* Springer Berlin Heidelberg, Berlin, Heidelberg, 87–99.

[21] Guy Shani, David Heckerman, and Ronen I. Brafman. 2005. An MDP-Based Recommender System. *J. Mach. Learn. Res.* 6 (Dec. 2005), 1265–1295.

[22] Richard S. Sutton and Andrew G. Barto. 2016. *Reinforcement Learning: An Introduction* (2nd ed.). MIT Press.

[23] Xiaojie Wang, Zhicheng Dou, Tetsuya Sakai, and Ji-Rong Wen. 2016. Evaluating Search Result Diversity Using Intent Hierarchies. In *Proceedings of the 39th International ACM SIGIR Conference on Research and Development in Information Retrieval (SIGIR '16)*. ACM, New York, NY, USA, 415–424.

[24] Long Xia, Jun Xu, Yanyan Lan, Jiafeng Guo, and Xueqi Cheng. 2015. Learning Maximal Marginal Relevance Model via Directly Optimizing Diversity Evaluation Measures. In *Proceedings of the 38th International ACM SIGIR Conference on Research and Development in Information Retrieval (SIGIR '15)*. 113–122.

[25] Long Xia, Jun Xu, Yanyan Lan, Jiafeng Guo, and Xueqi Cheng. 2016. Modeling Document Novelty with Neural Tensor Network for Search Result Diversification. In *Proceedings of the 39th International ACM SIGIR Conference on Research and Development in Information Retrieval (SIGIR '16)*. 395–404.

[26] Jun Xu, Long Xia, Yanyan Lan, Jiafeng Guo, and Xueqi Cheng. 2017. Directly Optimize Diversity Evaluation Measures: A New Approach to Search Result Diversification. *ACM Trans. Intell. Syst. Technol.* 8, 3, Article 41 (Jan. 2017), 26 pages.

[27] Yisong Yue and Thorsten Joachims. 2008. Predicting Diverse Subsets Using Structural SVMs. In *Proceedings of the 25th International Conference on Machine Learning (ICML '08)*. ACM, New York, NY, USA, 1224–1231.

[28] Yisong Yue and Thorsten Joachims. 2009. Interactively Optimizing Information Retrieval Systems As a Dueling Bandits Problem. In *Proceedings of the 26th Annual International Conference on Machine Learning (ICML '09)*. ACM, New York, NY, USA, 1201–1208.

[29] Cheng Xiang Zhai, William W. Cohen, and John Lafferty. 2003. Beyond Independent Relevance: Methods and Evaluation Metrics for Subtopic Retrieval. In *Proceedings of the 26th Annual International ACM SIGIR Conference on Research and Development in Informaion Retrieval (SIGIR '03)*. 10–17.

[30] Sicong Zhang, Jiyun Luo, and Hui Yang. 2014. A POMDP Model for Content-free Document Re-ranking. In *Proceedings of the 37th International ACM SIGIR Conference on Research & Development in Information Retrieval (SIGIR '14)*. ACM, New York, NY, USA, 1139–1142.

[31] Yadong Zhu, Yanyan Lan, Jiafeng Guo, Xueqi Cheng, and Shuzi Niu. 2014. Learning for Search Result Diversification. In *Proceedings of the 37th International ACM SIGIR Conference on Research & Development in Information Retrieval (SIGIR '14)*. ACM, New York, NY, USA, 293–302.

Learning to Diversify Search Results via Subtopic Attention

Zhengbao Jiang[1,2], Ji-Rong Wen[1,2,3], Zhicheng Dou[1,2],
Wayne Xin Zhao[1,2], Jian-Yun Nie[4], Ming Yue[1,2]
[1]School of Information, Renmin University of China
[2]Beijing Key Laboratory of Big Data Management and Analysis Methods, China
[3]Key Laboratory of Data Engineering and Knowledge Engineering, MOE, China
[4]DIRO, Université de Montréal, Québec
rucjzb@163.com, jirong.wen@gmail.com, dou@ruc.edu.cn,
batmanfly@gmail.com, nie@iro.umontreal.ca, yomin@ruc.edu.cn

ABSTRACT

Search result diversification aims to retrieve diverse results to satisfy as many different information needs as possible. Supervised methods have been proposed recently to learn ranking functions and they have been shown to produce superior results to unsupervised methods. However, these methods use implicit approaches based on the principle of Maximal Marginal Relevance (MMR). In this paper, we propose a learning framework for explicit result diversification where subtopics are explicitly modeled. Based on the information contained in the sequence of selected documents, we use attention mechanism to capture the subtopics to be focused on while selecting the next document, which naturally fits our task of document selection for diversification. The framework is implemented using recurrent neural networks and max-pooling which combine distributed representations and traditional relevance features. Our experiments show that the proposed method significantly outperforms all the existing methods.

KEYWORDS

search result diversification; subtopics; attention

1 INTRODUCTION

In real search scenario, queries issued by users are usually ambiguous or multi-faceted. In addition to being relevant to the query, the retrieved documents are expected to be as diverse as possible in order to cover different information needs. For example, when users issue "apple", the underlying intents could be the IT company or the fruit. The retrieved documents should cover both topics to increase the chance to satisfy users with different information needs.

Traditional approaches to search result diversification are usually unsupervised and adopt manually defined functions with empirically tuned parameters. Depending on whether the underlying intents (or subtopics) are explicitly modeled, they can be categorized into implicit and explicit approaches [28]. Implicit approaches [6] do not model intents explicitly. They emphasize novelty, i.e. the following document should be "different" from the former ones based on some similarity measures. Instead, explicit approaches [1, 12, 13, 16, 27, 35] model intents (or subtopics) explicitly. They aim to improve intent coverage, i.e. the following document should cover the intents not satisfied by previous ones. Intents or subtopics can be determined by techniques such as query reformulation [2, 14, 34, 38] and query clustering based on query logs and other types of information. Existing studies showed that explicit approaches have better performance [12, 13, 16, 27, 35] than implicit approaches due to several reasons: on the one hand, they provide a more natural way to handle subtopics than implicit approaches; on the other hand, their ranking functions are closer to the diversity evaluation metrics which are mostly based on explicit subtopics. Furthermore, most similarity measures used in the implicit approaches, e.g., those based on language model or vector space model, are determined globally on the whole documents, regardless of possible search intents. This might be problematic for search result diversification: two documents could contain similar words and considered globally similar, but this similar part may be unrelated to underlying search intents.

To avoid heuristic and handcrafted functions and parameters, a new family of research work using supervised learning is proposed. They try to learn a ranking function automatically. Their major focus lies in the modeling of diversity, including structural prediction [36], rewarding functions for novel contents [39], measure-based direct optimization [32], and neural network based method [33]. Regardless of diversity modeling and optimization methods, all these solutions inherit the spirit of MMR which is an implicit approach and do not take intents into consideration. Although the learning methods may result in a better similarity measure, they are hindered by the gap between reducing document redundancy and improving intent coverage. They suffer from similar problems with implicit unsupervised approaches. Without modeling subtopics explicitly, they can't directly improve intent coverage. Hence, there is a need to incorporate explicit subtopic modeling into supervised diversification methods.

To address the above issue, we propose to model subtopics in a general supervised learning framework. Our framework combines the strengths of both explicit unsupervised approaches and (implicit) supervised approaches. First, subtopics are explicitly modeled, allowing us to improve intent coverage in a proactive way. Second, it automatically learns the diversification ranking function, and is able to capture complex interaction among documents and

SIGIR'17, August 7–11, 2017, Shinjuku, Tokyo, Japan

ACM ISBN 978-1-4503-5022-8/17/08...$15.00
DOI: http://dx.doi.org/10.1145/3077136.3080805

Table 1: Subtopic relevance example.

doc\subtopic	i_1	i_2	i_3
d_1	√	√	×
d_2	√	√	×
d_3	×	×	√
d_4	×	√	×

subtopics. We call this framework Document Sequence with Subtopic Attention (DSSA). More specifically, to select the next document, we first model the sequence of selected documents in order to capture their contents as well as their relationship with the subtopics. Then based on the information contained by previous documents, attention mechanism is used to determine the under-covered subtopics to which we have to pay attention in selecting the next document. Attention mechanism has been successfully used to deal with various problems in image understanding [24] and NLP [3, 21]. This mechanism corresponds well to the document selection problem in search result diversification: attention on subtopics changes along with the addition of a document in the result list. For example. Assume that we have 3 subtopics and 4 documents whose relevance judgments are shown in Table 1. Given that we have selected d_1 and d_2, which cover subtopics i_1 and i_2, the attention for next choice should incline to i_3 which is not covered, thus d_3 is a better choice than d_4 at this position. We will show that the DSSA framework is general enough to cover the ideas of previous unsupervised explicit methods.

We then propose a specific implementation of DSSA using recurrent neural networks (RNN) and max-pooling to leverage both distributed representations and traditional relevance features, which we call DSSA-RNNMP. Experimental results on TREC Web Track data show that our method outperforms the existing methods significantly. To our knowledge, this is the first time that a supervised learning framework with attention mechanism is used to model subtopics explicitly for search result diversification.

2 RELATED WORK

2.1 Implicit Diversification Approaches

The basic assumption of implicit diversification approaches is that dissimilar documents are more likely to satisfy different information needs. The most representative approach is MMR [6]:

$$S_{\mathrm{MMR}}(q,d,C) = (1-\lambda)S^{\mathrm{rel}}(d,q) - \lambda \max_{d_j \in C} S^{\mathrm{div}}(d,d_j), \qquad (1)$$

where S^{rel} and S^{div} model document d's relevance to the query q and its similarity to a selected documents d_j respectively. To gain high ranking score, a document should not only be relevant, but also be dissimilar from the selected documents. The definition of measures for relevance and document similarity is crucial, which is done manually in this approach.

Recently, machine learning methods have been leveraged to learn score functions. Yue and Joachims [36] proposed SVM-DIV which uses structural SVM to learn to identify a document subset with maximum word coverage. However, word coverage may be different from intent coverage. Optimizing the former may not necessarily lead to optimizing the latter. Similar to MMR, Zhu et al. [39] proposed relational learning-to-rank model (R-LTR) which learns to score a document based on both relevance and novelty automatically, in order to maximize the probability of optimal rankings. Based on R-LTR score function, Xia et al. [32] proposed a perceptron algorithm using measures as margins (PAMM) to directly optimize evaluation metrics by enlarging the score margin of positive and negative rankings. They further proposed to use a neural tensor network (NTN) [33] to measure document similarity automatically from document representations, which avoids the burden to define handcrafted diversity features.

Table 2: Categorization of diversification approaches.

	unsupervised	supervised
implicit	MMR	SVM-DIV, R-LTR, PAMM, NTN
explicit	IA-Select, xQuAD, PM2, TxQuAD, TPM2, HxQuAD, HPM2, 0-1 MSKP	**DSSA** (our approach)

The above supervised approaches are shown to outperform the unsupervised counterparts. However, they are all implicit approaches without using subtopics. In this paper, we propose a learning-based explicit approach which models subtopics explicitly.

2.2 Explicit Diversification Approaches

Explicit approaches model subtopics underlying a query, aiming at returning documents covering as many subtopics as possible. These approaches leverage external resources to explicitly represent information needs in subtopics. IA-Select [1] uses classified topical categories based on ODP taxonomy. xQuAD [27] is a probabilistic framework that uses query reformulations as intent representations. PM2 [13] tackles search result diversification problem from the perspective of proportionality. TxQuAD and TPM2 [12] represent intents by terms and transform intent coverage to term coverage. Hu et al. [16] proposed to use a hierarchical structure for subtopics instead of a flat list, which copes with the inherent interaction among subtopics. Two specific models, namely HxQuAD and HPM2, were proposed using hierarchical structure. Yu et al. [35] formulated diversification task as a 0-1 multiple subtopic knapsacks (0-1 MSKP) problem where documents are chosen like filling up multiple subtopic knapsacks. To tackle this NP-hard problem, max-sum belief propagation is used.

As summarized in Table 2, all existing explicit approaches are unsupervised and the functions and parameters are defined heuristically. In this paper, we use supervised learning to model the interaction among documents and subtopics simultaneously.

2.3 RNN with Attention Mechanism

RNN can capture the interdependency between elements in a sequence. Attention mechanism, which is usually built on RNN, mimics human attention behavior focusing on different local region of the object (an image, a sentence, etc) at different times. In computer vision, Google DeepMind [24] used RNN with attention to extract information from an image by adaptively selecting a sequence of the most informative regions instead of the whole image. In NLP, attention mechanism is typically used in neural machine translation (NMT). Traditional encoder-decoder models encode the source sentence into a fixed-length vector from which the target sentence is decoded. Such fixed-length vector may not be powerful enough to reflect all the information of the source sentence. An attention-based model [3] was proposed to automatically pay unequal and varied attention to source words during decoding process. In particular, to decide the next target word, not only the fixed-length vector, but also the hidden states corresponding to source words relevant to the target word are used. Luong et al. [21] generalized the idea and proposed two classes of attention mechanism, namely global and local approaches. In this paper, attention mechanism is used on subtopics, which guides the model to emphasize different intents at different positions.

In the following section, we will first propose a general framework, then instantiate it with a specific implementation.

3 DOCUMENT SEQUENCE WITH SUBTOPIC ATTENTION FRAMEWORK

Given a query set Q, a document set $\mathcal{D}_q$ and a subtopic set $\mathcal{I}_q$ for each query $q \in Q$, the goal of explicit methods is to learn a ranking function $f(q, \mathcal{D}_q, \mathcal{I}_q)$ which is expected to output a ranking of documents in $\mathcal{D}_q$ that is both *relevant* and *diverse*. The loss function could be written in the following general form:

$$\sum_{q \in Q} L(f(q, \mathcal{D}_q, \mathcal{I}_q), \mathcal{Y}_q), \tag{2}$$

where L measures the quality gap between the ranking outputted by f and the best ranking $\mathcal{Y}_q$. Different from traditional retrieval tasks, diversity has to be considered in the ranking and evaluation process. Theoretically, diversity ranking is NP-hard [1, 7]. Hence, a common strategy is to make greedy selections [6, 27]: at the t-th position, we assume that $t-1$ documents have been selected and formed a document sequence C_{t-1}. The task is to select a locally optimal document d_t from the remaining candidate documents based on a score function $S(q, d_t, C_{t-1}, \mathcal{I}_q)$. Note that implicit supervised methods correspond to the case where $\mathcal{I}_q$ is an empty set.

To motivate our approach, we start with the ideas of the unsupervised explicit approaches, which can be formulated as the following general form:

$$\begin{aligned} &S_{\text{unsupervised}}(q, d_t, C_{t-1}, \mathcal{I}_q) = \\ &(1-\lambda)S^{\text{rel}}(d_t, q) + && \Rightarrow \text{relevance} \\ &\lambda \sum_{i_k \in \mathcal{I}_q} S^{\text{div}}(d_t, i_k) \underbrace{A(C_{t-1}, \mathcal{I}_q)_k}_{\text{subtopic weights}}, && \Rightarrow \text{diversity} \end{aligned} \tag{3}$$

where $i_k \in \mathcal{I}_q$ is the k-th subtopic of q and S^{rel} and S^{div} calculate document d_t's relevance to a query and to a subtopic respectively. The essence of diversity lies in the function A which calculates the weights for subtopics $\mathcal{I}_q$ based on previous document sequence C_{t-1}. For xQuAD, $A(C_{t-1}, \mathcal{I}_q)_k = P(i_k|q) \prod_{d_j \in C_{t-1}} (1 - P(d_j|i_k))$ where $P(i_k|q)$ is the initial importance of subtopic i_k, $P(d_j|i_k)$ is the probability that d_j is relevant to i_k. The weight of a subtopic is determined by the likelihood that previous documents are not relevant to this subtopic. PM2 mimics seats allocation of competing political parties to adjust subtopic weights after each selection, i.e. $A(C_{t-1}, \mathcal{I}_q)$ is estimated according to the difference between the subtopic's distributions in C_{t-1} and in $\mathcal{I}_q$. All these methods don't model the selected documents as a sequence. In addition, the functions and parameters are heuristically defined, which may not best fit the final goal.

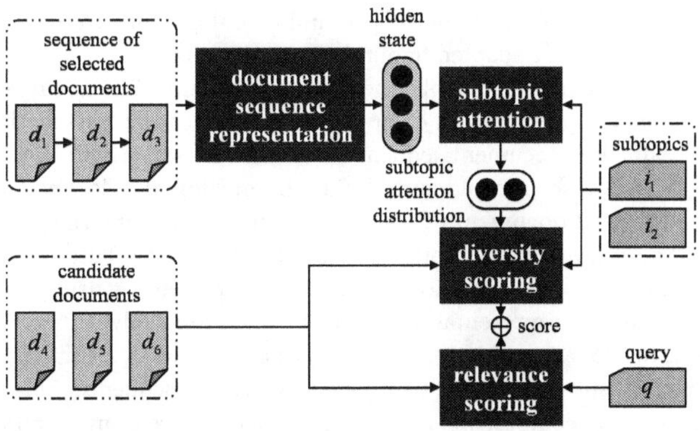

Figure 1: Illustration of DSSA framework.

Table 3: Notations in DSSA.

Notation	Definition
r, d_t	a ranking, the t-th document.
q, i_k	the query, the k-th subtopic.
$\boldsymbol{v}_{d_t}$	representation of the document at the t-th position.
$\boldsymbol{v}_q$	representation of the query.
$\boldsymbol{v}_{i_k}$	representation of the k-th subtopic.
$\boldsymbol{h}_t$	hidden state of previous t documents.
$a_{t,k}$	attention on the k-th subtopic at the t-th position. $\sum_{k=1}^{K} a_{t,k} = 1, a_{t,k} \in [0, 1]$ where K is the number of subtopics. A large value means that this subtopic is less satisfied by previous $t-1$ documents and thus needs more attention at the t-th position.
s_{d_t}	the final score of the document at the t-th position.

To tackle the above problems, we extend Equation (3) to the following general learning framework:

$$\begin{aligned} &S_{\text{DSSA}}(q, d_t, C_{t-1}, \mathcal{I}_q) = s_{d_t} = \\ &(1-\lambda)\mathcal{S}^{\text{rel}}(\boldsymbol{v}_{d_t}, \boldsymbol{v}_q) + && \Rightarrow \text{relevance} \\ &\lambda \mathcal{S}^{\text{div}}\Big(\boldsymbol{v}_{d_t}, \boldsymbol{v}_{i_{(\cdot)}}, \underbrace{\mathcal{A}\Big(\mathcal{H}([\boldsymbol{v}_{d_1}, \ldots, \boldsymbol{v}_{d_{t-1}}]), \boldsymbol{v}_{i_{(\cdot)}}\Big)}_{\text{subtopic attention}}\Big), && \Rightarrow \text{diversity} \end{aligned} \tag{4}$$

where documents, queries, and subtopics are denoted by their representations, as explained in Table 3. In this paper, we focus on learning a ranking function only and assume that these representations are given and will not be modified. There are three main components, namely (1) **document sequence representation** component $\mathcal{H}$, (2) **subtopic attention** component $\mathcal{A}$, and (3) **scoring** component $\mathcal{S}^{\text{rel}}$ and $\mathcal{S}^{\text{div}}$, which are also illustrated in Figure 1. This framework is inspired from the attention models used in image understanding [24] and neural machine translation [3, 21], however adapted to our diversification task.

Next, we briefly describe the three components. The document sequence representation component $\mathcal{H}$ encodes the information contained in document sequence C_{t-1} into a fixed-length hidden state $\boldsymbol{h}_{t-1}$, which could consider the interaction and dependency among these documents. $\boldsymbol{h}_{t-1}$ could be viewed as a comprehensive and high-level representation of C_{t-1}. The subtopic attention $\boldsymbol{a}_{t,(\cdot)}$ is calculated by the subtopic attention component $\mathcal{A}$ using $\boldsymbol{h}_{t-1}$ and subtopic representations $\boldsymbol{v}_{i_{(\cdot)}}$. The attention evolves from the first to the last ranking position, driving the model to emphasize different subtopics based on previous document sequence. Finally, the scoring components $\mathcal{S}^{\text{rel}}$ and $\mathcal{S}^{\text{div}}$ calculate relevance and diversity scores respectively. Notice that $\mathcal{S}^{\text{div}}$ is not limited to be a weighted sum over all subtopics as Equation (3). It can incorporate more complex interaction among subtopics.

The essence of this framework can be summarized as follows. Along with the selection of more documents, we encode the information of previous document sequence, and the attention mechanism will monitor the degree of satisfaction for each subtopic. High scores are assigned to the documents relevant to less covered subtopics. Finally, multiple subtopics would be well covered by adaptively learning the attention. In this way, our framework builds an intuitive approach to explicitly model subtopics. We name the framework **Document Sequence with Subtopic Attention (DSSA)**. DSSA is a unified architecture that takes both relevance and diversity into consideration, and diversity is achieved by modeling the interaction among documents and subtopics.

4 RESULT DIVERSIFICATION USING DSSA

In this section, we instantiate DSSA to a concrete form and articulate the training and prediction algorithms. The main idea of DSSA is to dynamically capture accumulative relevance information of previous document sequence, so as to calculate subtopic attention. Inspired by the recent progress on sequence data modeling, we adapt RNN to capture the information of previous document sequence based on distributed representations of documents. However, the effectiveness of distributed representation heavily depends on a large amount of training data. Typically, the representation is built automatically using the data to optimize an objective function [17]. We do not have such large data and we can only use unsupervised methods (e.g. doc2vec) to create representation, of which the effectiveness could be suboptimal. Indeed, our preliminary experiments using only the distributed representation created by unsupervised methods yield low effectiveness. To compensate this weakness, we also use traditional relevance features such as BM25 score, which are proven useful, to calculate subtopic attention and final score. Such a combination of distributed representations and features has been used in several previous works [29, 33]. In addition to RNN, we also adopt the way using max-pooling [33], which has been shown effective, to implement subtopic attention mechanism. We call this model DSSA-RNNMP (DSSA model using RNN and Max-Pooling), as illustrated in Figure 2. In addition, we also propose a list-pairwise approach for optimization, which is different from the existing studies.

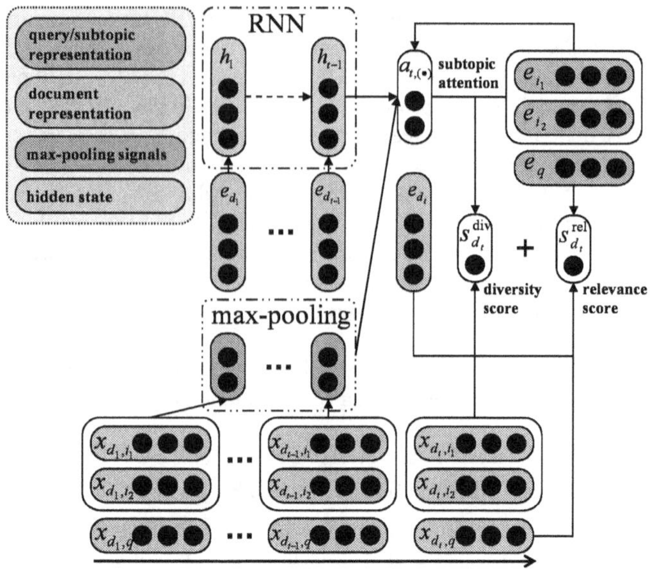

Figure 2: Architecture of DSSA-RNNMP. Previous $t-1$ documents are encoded into $\boldsymbol{h}_{t-1}$ from distributed representations $\boldsymbol{e}_{d_1}, \ldots, \boldsymbol{e}_{d_{t-1}}$. Attention on the k-th subtopic $a_{t,k}$ is then calculated based on (1) hidden state $\boldsymbol{h}_{t-1}$ and subtopic representation $\boldsymbol{e}_{i_k}$ (2) max-pooling on relevance features $\boldsymbol{x}_{d_1,i_k}, \ldots, \boldsymbol{x}_{d_{t-1},i_k}$.

Table 4: Parameters in DSSA-RNNMP.

Notation	Definition
$\boldsymbol{W}^n, \boldsymbol{b}^n$	parameters of RNN with vanilla cell.
$\boldsymbol{W}^a, \boldsymbol{w}^p$	parameters used in subtopic attention.
$\boldsymbol{W}^s, \boldsymbol{w}^r$	parameters used in scoring.

4.1 A Neural Network Implementation

We first describe the constitution of representations, namely $\boldsymbol{v}_{d_t}$, $\boldsymbol{v}_q$, and $\boldsymbol{v}_{i_k}$, then elaborate how we implement **document sequence representation**, **subtopic attention**, and **scoring** components. The parameters to be learned are listed in Table 4.

$\boldsymbol{v}_{d_t}$: the representation of a document is composed of two parts: distributed representations and relevance features. Distributed representation can be constructed in different ways. In this paper, we consider three methods: SVD, LDA [4], and doc2vec [18]. Relevance features are those used in traditional IR, such as BM25 score etc. Suppose that we have a distributed representation of size E_d, K subtopics, and R relevance features, the total size of $\boldsymbol{v}_{d_t}$ would be $E_d + R + KR$. We use $\boldsymbol{e}_{d_t} \in \mathbb{R}^{E_d}$, $\boldsymbol{x}_{d_t,q}$ and $\boldsymbol{x}_{d_t,i_k} \in \mathbb{R}^R$ to denote distributed representation, relevance features for a query and a subtopic respectively.

$\boldsymbol{v}_q$, $\boldsymbol{v}_{i_k}$: we first retrieve top Z documents using some basic retrieval model (such as BM25). These documents are concatenated as a pseudo document, then similar to $\boldsymbol{e}_{d_t}$, a distributed representation of size E_q is generated. For consistency, we also use $\boldsymbol{e}_q$ and $\boldsymbol{e}_{i_k} \in \mathbb{R}^{E_q}$ to represent these representations.

4.1.1 Document Sequence Representation. $\mathcal{H}$ is instantiated using RNN to encode the information of previous document sequence. Several types of RNN cell can be used, ranging from the simple vanilla cell, GRU cell [9], to LSTM cell [15]. For simplicity, we only show the vanilla cell here. At the t-th position, we derive the (accumulative) document sequence representation as follows:

$$\boldsymbol{h}_t = \tanh(\boldsymbol{W}^n[\boldsymbol{h}_{t-1}; \boldsymbol{e}_{d_t}] + \boldsymbol{b}^n), \quad (5)$$

where $\boldsymbol{W}^n \in \mathbb{R}^{U\times(U+E_d)}$ (U is the size of the hidden state), $\boldsymbol{b}^n \in \mathbb{R}^U$ and [;] is a concatenation. The cell transforms previous hidden layer $\boldsymbol{h}_{t-1}$ and current document distributed representation $\boldsymbol{e}_{d_t}$ to another space, where a bias $\boldsymbol{b}^n$ is added and a non-linear activation (i.e. tanh) then happens, producing the next hidden layer $\boldsymbol{h}_t$. $\boldsymbol{h}_0$ is initialized as a vector of zeros. The vanilla cell can be easily replaced by GRU and LSTM cells, whose results will be report in Section 6.2.

4.1.2 Subtopic Attention. By looking at $\boldsymbol{h}_{t-1}$ which stores the information of previous $t-1$ documents and $\boldsymbol{e}_{i_{(\cdot)}}$ which represents the meaning of each subtopic, we are capable of discovering which intents are not satisfied and thus need to be emphasized at the t-th position. To capture this idea, we use $\mathcal{A}'(\boldsymbol{h}_{t-1}, \boldsymbol{e}_{i_k})$ to measure the (unnormalized) importance of the k-th subtopic at the t-th position, which could be implemented in many ways. We consider the following two ways similar to [21]:

$$\mathcal{A}'(\boldsymbol{h}_{t-1}, \boldsymbol{e}_{i_k}) = \begin{cases} \boldsymbol{h}_{t-1}^{\mathsf{T}} \boldsymbol{W}^a \boldsymbol{e}_{i_k}, & \text{(general)} \\ -\boldsymbol{h}_{t-1}^{\mathsf{T}} \cdot \boldsymbol{e}_{i_k}, & \text{(dot)} \end{cases} \quad (6)$$

where $\boldsymbol{W}^a \in \mathbb{R}^{U\times E_q}$. The "general" operation uses bilinear tensor product to relate two vectors multiplicatively through its nonlinearity [30]. The "dot" product requires both vectors to be in the same space. Similar $\boldsymbol{h}_{t-1}$ and $\boldsymbol{e}_{i_k}$ mean that previous documents are likely to satisfy this subtopic, and thus a lower attention score will be attributed to it. The above way mainly relies on distributed representations, which may not always be effective, especially under limited data.

Hence, we further leverage relevance features to enhance the subtopic attention. $\boldsymbol{x}_{d_t,i_k}$ directly reflects the degree of satisfaction for a subtopic-document pair and is combined linearly using $\boldsymbol{w}^p$ to form an explicit signal. To derive the accumulative information of the document sequence, we adopt commonly used max-pooling to select the most significant signal from previous documents:

$$\mathcal{A}''(\boldsymbol{x}_{d_1,i_k}, ..., \boldsymbol{x}_{d_{t-1},i_k}) = \max([\boldsymbol{x}_{d_1,i_k}^{\mathsf{T}} \cdot \boldsymbol{w}^p, ..., \boldsymbol{x}_{d_{t-1},i_k}^{\mathsf{T}} \cdot \boldsymbol{w}^p]), \quad (7)$$

where $\mathcal{A}''(\boldsymbol{x}_{d_1,i_k}, ..., \boldsymbol{x}_{d_{t-1},i_k})$ measures the degree of satisfaction of the k-th subtopic based on relevance features through max-pooling. Lower value indicates that the previous documents are more likely to be relevant to this subtopic. Note that if we view the signals produced by max-pooling (i.e. the vectors in "max-pooling" section of Figure 2) as a part of the general hidden states, our concrete implementation fit in DSSA framework.

We adopt an addictive way to integrate both parts and then use softmax to produce (normalized) attention distribution:

$$\begin{aligned} a'_{t,k} &= \mathcal{A}'(\boldsymbol{h}_{t-1}, \boldsymbol{e}_{i_k}) + \mathcal{A}''(\boldsymbol{x}_{d_1,i_k}, ..., \boldsymbol{x}_{d_{t-1},i_k}), \\ a_{t,k} &= \frac{w_{i_k} \exp(a'_{t,k})}{\sum_{j=1}^{K} w_{i_j} \exp(a'_{t,j})} \quad (w_{i_j} \geq 0, \forall j). \end{aligned} \quad (8)$$

softmax is modified to include the initial subtopic importance w_{i_k}, which encodes our intuition that an important subtopic is more likely to gain attention than unimportant ones.

4.1.3 Scoring. The final score consists of relevance score $s_{d_t}^{\text{rel}}$ and diversity score $s_{d_t}^{\text{div}}$, which are combined by a coefficient λ:

$$s_{d_t} = (1-\lambda)s_{d_t}^{\text{rel}} + \lambda s_{d_t}^{\text{div}} \quad (0 \leq \lambda \leq 1). \quad (9)$$

The relevance score and diversity score are calculated as follows:

$$\begin{aligned} s_{d_t}^{\text{rel}} &= \mathcal{S}'(\boldsymbol{e}_{d_t}, \boldsymbol{e}_q) + \boldsymbol{x}_{d_t,q}^{\mathsf{T}} \cdot \boldsymbol{w}^r, \\ s_{d_t}^{\text{div}} &= \boldsymbol{a}_{t,(\cdot)}^{\mathsf{T}} \cdot \begin{bmatrix} \mathcal{S}'(\boldsymbol{e}_{d_t}, \boldsymbol{e}_{i_1}) + \boldsymbol{x}_{d_t,i_1}^{\mathsf{T}} \cdot \boldsymbol{w}^r \\ \vdots \\ \mathcal{S}'(\boldsymbol{e}_{d_t}, \boldsymbol{e}_{i_K}) + \boldsymbol{x}_{d_t,i_K}^{\mathsf{T}} \cdot \boldsymbol{w}^r \end{bmatrix}, \end{aligned} \quad (10)$$

where $\boldsymbol{w}^r \in \mathbb{R}^R$ and $\boldsymbol{a}_{t,(\cdot)}$ is the attention derived from subtopic attention component. The diversity score is calculated as a weighted combination of the document's relevance to each subtopic by attention distribution. We use the same way to calculate document's relevance to a query and to its subtopics using both distributional representations and relevance features, although different ways can be used. Specifically, d_t's relevance to a query q (or a subtopic i_k) is calculated based on both the similarity between two distributed representations $\mathcal{S}'(\boldsymbol{e}_{d_t}, \boldsymbol{e}_q)$ (or $\mathcal{S}'(\boldsymbol{e}_{d_t}, \boldsymbol{e}_{i_k})$) and relevance features $\boldsymbol{x}_{d_t,q}$ (or $\boldsymbol{x}_{d_t,i_k}$). $\mathcal{S}'$ intends to produce a matching score between two representations and $\boldsymbol{w}^r$ linearly combines features. Similar to $\mathcal{A}'$, $\mathcal{S}'$ could also be implemented as:

$$\mathcal{S}'(\boldsymbol{e}_{d_t}, \boldsymbol{e}_{i_k}) = \begin{cases} \boldsymbol{e}_{d_t}^{\mathsf{T}} \boldsymbol{W}^s \boldsymbol{e}_{i_k}, & \text{(general)} \\ \boldsymbol{e}_{d_t}^{\mathsf{T}} \cdot \boldsymbol{e}_{i_k}, & \text{(dot)} \end{cases} \quad (11)$$

where $\boldsymbol{W}^s \in \mathbb{R}^{E_d\times E_q}$. Then the score of a ranking r is calculated by summing up all the $|r|$ documents' scores:

$$s_r = \sum_{t=1}^{|r|} s_{d_t}. \quad (12)$$

Vector interaction operations $\mathcal{A}'$ and $\mathcal{S}'$ could be implemented using more complex models, such as multilayer perceptron (MLP), to model the interaction between two vectors more accurately. We could also use convolutional neural network (CNN) instead of RNN to model the interaction among a sequence of documents and encode their information. We deliberately choose to use simple mechanisms in this implementation in order to show that the general framework is capable of capturing the essence of diversification even without complex operations. More complex implementations will be examined in future work.

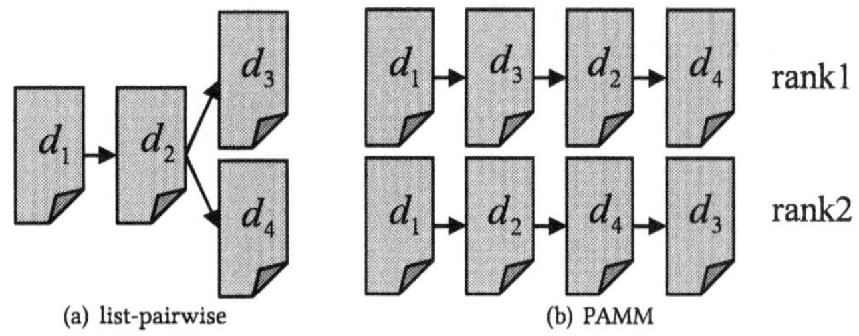

Figure 3: Pair sample examples of (a) list-pairwise and (b) PAMM. Both samples are positive.

4.2 A List-pairwise Approach for Optimization

Liu [19] classifies LTR approaches into three categories: pointwise, pairwise, and listwise. Search result diversification is naturally a listwise problem because the score of a document depends on the previous documents. Take Table 1 as an example, under no previous documents, d_2 is better than d_3 because d_2 covers one more subtopic (subtopics are of equal weight). However, given that we have selected d_1, which is similar to d_2 while dissimilar to d_3, d_3 becomes superior because it provides additional information.

4.2.1 List-pairwise Training. We propose a list-pairwise training approach. We call it list-pairwise because a sample in our algorithm consists of a pair of rankings (r_1, r_2): r_1 and r_2 are totally identical except the last document. The sample can be written as (C, d^1, d^2), where C is the shared previous document sequence. The pairwise preference ground-truth is generated based on an evaluation metric M, such as α-nDCG. If $M(r_1) > M(r_2)$, it is positive, otherwise it is negative. Our approach is similar to pairwise approaches because it aims to compare a pair of documents, but this is done within some context. Similarly to pairwise, the loss function can be defined as binary classification logarithmic loss:

$$L_{\text{list-pairwise}} = \sum_{q \in Q} \sum_{o \in O_q} w^{(o)} \left(y^{(o)} \log \left(P(r_1^{(o)}, r_2^{(o)}) \right) + (1 - y^{(o)}) \log \left(1 - P(r_1^{(o)}, r_2^{(o)}) \right) \right), \tag{13}$$

where O_q is all the pair samples of query q, $y^{(o)} = 1$ indicates positive and 0 for negative, and $P(r_1^{(o)}, r_2^{(o)})$ is the probability of being positive calculated by $\frac{1}{1+\exp(s_{r_2^{(o)}} - s_{r_1^{(o)}})}$. To enhance effectiveness, we weight pairs with $w^{(o)} = |M(r_1^{(o)}) - M(r_2^{(o)})|$, which means that the bigger the metric score gap, the more important the pair.

Because DSSA calculates document d's score s_d^C based on previous document C, we could also use Maximum Likelihood Estimation (MLE) or PAMM to optimize our model. We use Plackett-Luce model [22] to estimate the probability of a ranking r:

$$P(r) = \prod_{i=1}^{|r|} \frac{\exp(s_{d_i}^{r[:i-1]})}{\sum_{j=i}^{|r|} \exp(s_{d_j}^{r[:i-1]})}, \tag{14}$$

where $r[:i-1]$ means the top $i-1$ documents of ranking r. Then the loss functions could be written as:

$$L_{\text{MLE}} = \sum_{q \in Q} -\log(P(r_q^+)), \tag{15}$$

Algorithm 1 A List-pairwise Approach For Optimization

procedure LIST-PAIRWISE TRAINING
  input: loss function L, learning rate r, epochs V, query set Q, document set $\mathcal{D}$, evaluation metric M, random permutation count N
  output: DSSA with trained parameters θ
  initialize θ
  for i from 1 to V **do**
    for batch $b \in$ GetSamples($Q, \mathcal{D}, M, N$) **do**
      $g \leftarrow$ GetGradient($L(b, \theta)$)
      $\theta \leftarrow \theta - rg$
  return DSSA$_\theta$

procedure GETSAMPLES
  input: query set Q, document set $\mathcal{D}_q$ for each query q, evaluation metric M, random permutation count N
  output: a set of ranking pairs with weight and preference $\{(q^{(1)}, C^{(1)}, d_1^{(1)}, d_2^{(1)}, w^{(1)}, y^{(1)}), (q^{(2)}, C^{(2)}, d_1^{(2)}, d_2^{(2)}, w^{(2)}, y^{(2)}), \ldots\}$
  include: GetPerms($\mathcal{D}_q, l, N, M$) return a best ranking (under metric M) and N random permutations of length l. GetPairs($q, \mathcal{D}_q, C, M$) samples pairs of documents (d_1, d_2) from $\mathcal{D}_q \setminus C$ under context C if and only if they lead to different metric scores. Let $r_1 \leftarrow [C, d_1]$, $r_2 \leftarrow [C, d_2]$, $w = |M(r_1) - M(r_2)|$ and $y = [\![M(r_1) > M(r_2)]\!]$.
  $\mathcal{R} \leftarrow \emptyset$
  for query q in Q **do**
    for l from 0 to $|\mathcal{D}_q| - 1$ **do**
      for perm C in GetPerms($\mathcal{D}_q, l, N, M$) **do**
        $\mathcal{R} \leftarrow \mathcal{R} \cup$ GetPairs($q, \mathcal{D}_q, C, M$)
  return $\mathcal{R}$

$$L_{\text{PAMM}} = \sum_{q \in Q} \sum_{r_q^+, r_q^-} [\![P(r_q^+) - P(r_q^-) \leq M(r_q^+) - M(r_q^-)]\!], \tag{16}$$

where $[\![\text{condition}]\!]$ is 1 if the condition is satisfied, 0 otherwise, MLE maximizes the probability of positive rankings, and PAMM enlarges the probability margin between positive and negative rankings according to an evaluation metric. For MLE, the number of best rankings is usually small if we only have hundreds of queries, which may not be enough to train adequately the parameters. PAMM uses preferences between very different rankings that are not comparable (see Figure 3(b)). In contrast, list-pairwise method only allows the last document to be different (Figure 3(a)). This corresponds better to the decision-making situation in which we have to choose a document under a given context. It is expected that such a pair sample allows us to better train the ranking function. Experiments will show that our approach works better.

As shown in Figure 2, our architecture is a unified neural network and the attention function is continuous, so the gradient of the loss function can be backpropagated directly to train the model. We use mini-batch gradient descent to facilitate training process.

Unfortunately, it is impossible to acquire all the list-pairwise samples, which has in total $|\mathcal{D}_q|!$ ($|\mathcal{D}_q|$ is the number of candidate documents) different permutations. So we develop a sampling strategy similar to negative sampling [23] as described in Algorithm 1: for each query q, we sample a large number of pairs of rankings, whose length ranges from 1 to $|\mathcal{D}_q|$. We first obtain some contexts C from both best rankings and randomly sampled negative rankings (rankings that are not optimal). Then under each C, a pair of documents (d^1, d^2) are sampled from the remaining documents $\mathcal{D}_q \setminus C$ if and only if they lead to different metric scores.

4.2.2 Prediction. In prediction stage, for each query, we sequentially and greedily choose the document with the highest score and append it to the ranking list. Specifically, the first document is selected under initial subtopic importance from the whole candidate set $\mathcal{D}_q$. Once the top $t-1$ documents have been selected (i.e. $|C| = t-1$), we feed each document in $\mathcal{D}_q \setminus C$ into DSSA at the t-th position one by one and choose the one with the highest s_{d_t}. This process continues until all the documents in $\mathcal{D}_q$ are ranked.

4.2.3 Time Complexities. The training time complexity with vanilla cell and "general" operation is $O(V \cdot |Q| \cdot \Gamma \cdot |\mathcal{D}_q| \cdot \Theta)$ where V is the number of iterations, $|Q|$ is the number of training queries, $\Gamma = N \cdot |\mathcal{D}_q|^2$ is the number of sampled pairs where N is the number of random permutations, $|\mathcal{D}_q|$ is the number of candidate documents, and Θ is the complexity for each position:

$$\Theta = \underbrace{U(U+E_d)}_{\text{document sequence representation}} + \underbrace{KUE_q + KR}_{\text{subtopic attention}} + \underbrace{KE_dE_q + KR}_{\text{scoring}}, \quad (17)$$

where the dominating terms are KUE_q and KE_dE_q which are proportional to the number of subtopics K. How to efficiently handle a large number of subtopics is our future work. The prediction complexity is $O(|\mathcal{D}_q|^2\Theta)$ for each query. We can limit $|\mathcal{D}_q|$ to a small number (say 50), so the prediction time can be reasonable.

5 EXPERIMENTAL SETTINGS

5.1 Data Collections

We use the same dataset as [16] which consists of Web Track dataset from TREC 2009 to 2012. There are 198 queries (query #95 and #100 are dropped because no diversity judgments are made for them), each of which includes 3 to 8 subtopics identified by TREC assessors. The relevance rating is given in a binary form at subtopic level. All experiments are conducted on ClueWeb09 [5] collection.

We use query suggestions of Google search engine as subtopics, which are released by Hu et al. [16] on their website[1]. For DSSA, we only use the first level subtopics and leave the exploration of hierarchical subtopics to future work. Following the existing work [16], we simply use uniform weights for these subtopics.

5.2 Evaluation Metrics

We use ERR-IA [8], α-nDCG [10], and NRBP [11], which are official diversity evaluation metrics used in Web Track. They measure the diversity by explicitly rewarding novelty and penalizing redundancy. D♯-measures [26], the primary metric used in NTCIR Intent [25] and IMine task [20], is also included. In addition, we also use traditional diversity measures Precision-IA (denoted as Pre-IA) [1] and Subtopic Recall (denoted as S-rec) [37]. Consistent with existing works [32, 33, 39] and TREC Web Track, all these metrics are computed on top 20 results of a ranking. We use two-tailed paired t-test to conduct significance testing with p-value < 0.05.

[1]hierarchical search result diversification: http://www.playbigdata.com/dou/hdiv

Table 5: Relevance features. Each of the first 3 features is applied to body, anchor, title, URL, and the whole documents.

Name	Description	#Features
TF-IDF	the TF-IDF model	5
BM25	BM25 with default parameters	5
LMIR	LMIR with Dirichlet smoothing	5
PageRank	PageRank score	1
#inlinks	number of inlinks	1
#outlinks	number of outlinks	1

Table 6: Diversity features. Each feature is extracted over a pair of documents.

Name	Description
subtopic diversity	euclidean distance based on SVD
text diversity	cosine-based distance on term vector
title diversity	text diversity on title
anchor text diversity	text diversity on anchor
link-based diversity	link similarity of document pair
URL-based diversity	URL similarity of document pair

5.3 Baseline Models

We compare DSSA[2] to various unsupervised and supervised diversification methods. The non-diversified baseline is denoted as **Lemur**. We use **xQuAD** [27], **PM2** [13], **TxQuAD**, **TPM2** [12], **HxQuAD**, and **HPM2** [16] as our unsupervised baselines. We use **ListMLE** [31], **R-LTR** [39], **PAMM** [32], and **NTN** [33] as our supervised baselines. Top 20 results of Lemur are used to train supervised methods. Top 50 (i.e. $|\mathcal{D}_q|$) results of Lemur are used for diversity re-ranking. To construct the representation of a query or a subtopic, we use the top 20 (Z) documents. We use 5-fold cross validation to tune the parameters in all experiments based on α-nDCG@20, which is one of the most widely used metrics. A brief introduction to these baselines is as follows:

Lemur. We use the same non-diversified results as [16] for fair comparison. They are produced by language model and retrieved using the Lemur service[3] of which the spams are filtered. These results are released by Hu et al. [16] on the website[1].

ListMLE. ListMLE is a representative listwise LTR method without considering diversity.

xQuAD, PM2, TxQuAD, TPM2, HxQuAD, and HPM2. These are competitive unsupervised explicit diversification methods, as introduced in Section 2.2. All these methods use λ to control the importance of relevance and diversity. HxQuAD and HPM2 use an additional parameter α to control the weight of each layer of the hierarchical structure. Both λ and α are tuned using cross validation. They all require a prior relevance function to fulfill diversification re-ranking. Following [39], we use ListMLE.

R-LTR, PAMM, and NTN. For PAMM, we use α-nDCG@20 as the optimization metric. We optimize NTN based on both R-LTR and PAMM, denoted as R-LTR-NTN and PAMM-NTN respectively.

[2]data and code available at: http://www.playbigdata.com/dou/DSSA/

[3]Lemur service: http://boston.lti.cs.cmu.edu/Services/clueweb09_batch/

To achieve optimal results, for R-LTR and PAMM, we tune the relational function $h_S(R)$ from minimal, maximal, and average. For PAMM, we tune the number of positive rankings τ^+ and negative rankings τ^- per query. For NTN, the number of tensor slices is tuned from 1 to 10. LDA is used to generate distributed representations of size 100 for NTN and DSSA. For all these supervised methods, the learning rate r is tuned from 10^{-7} to 10^{-1}. For DSSA, we have different settings possible. In our first set of results, we will use "general" as the implementation of vector interaction operations $\mathcal{A}'$ and $\mathcal{S}'$, LSTM with hidden size of 50 as the cell of RNN. We set random permutation count as 10 in list-pairwise sampling. Similarly, λ of DSSA is tuned by cross validation. We also test the impact of different model settings and permutation counts on performance in Section 6.2 and Section 6.3 respectively.

Similar to [39], we implement 18 relevance features and 6 diversity features, as listed in Table 5 and 6 respectively. We collect the candidate and retrieved documents of all queries and subtopics to generate the distributed representations.

6 EXPERIMENTAL RESULTS

6.1 Overall Results

The overall results are shown in Table 7. We find that DSSA significantly outperforms all implicit and explicit baselines, including both unsupervised and supervised. The improvements are statistically significant (two-tailed paired t-test) for all metrics, except S-rec. The results clearly show the superiority of DSSA.

(1) DSSA vs. unsupervised explicit methods. **DSSA outperforms unsupervised explicit methods (xQuAD, PM2, TxQuAD, TPM2, HxQuAD, and HPM2) on all the measures.** The relative improvement over HxQuAD and HPM2, the best unsupervised explicit approaches, is up to 8.3% and 8.6% respectively in terms of α-nDCG. This comparison shows the great advantage of using supervised method for learning the ranking function.

(2) DSSA vs. supervised implicit methods. **DSSA also outperforms supervised implicit methods (R-LTR, PAMM, R-LTR-NTN, and PAMM-NTN) by quite large margins.** The improvement over R-LTR-NTN and PAMM-NTN, the best supervised implicit approaches is up to 9.9% and 9.4% respectively on α-nDCG. This result demonstrates the utility of taking into account subtopics explicitly in supervised approaches. The improvements are similar to those observed between explicit approaches and implicit approaches in unsupervised framework [12, 13, 16, 27]. The combination of the two observations suggests that explicit modeling of subtopics can improve result diversification, whether it is in a supervised or unsupervised framework.

6.2 Effects of Different Settings

We conduct experiments with different settings of DSSA to investigate whether the performance is sensitive to these settings. Different aspects of settings are listed follow. For simplicity, when investigating the impact of each aspect, we keep other aspects the same as the settings specified in Section 5.3.

(1) Representation generation methods: SVD, LDA, and doc2vec with window size of 5.
(2) Implementation of vector interaction operations $\mathcal{A}'$ and $\mathcal{S}'$: "general" and "dot".

Table 7: Performance comparison of all methods. The best result is in bold. Statistically significant differences between DSSA and baselines are marked with various symbols. ★ indicates significant improvement over all baselines.

Methods	ERR-IA	α-nDCG	NRBP	D♯-nDCG	Pre-IA	S-rec
Lemur①	.271	.369	.232	.424	.153	.621
ListMLE❶	.287	.387	.249	.430	.157	.619
xQuAD②	.317	.413	.284	.437	.161	.622
TxQuAD③	.308	.410	.272	.441	.155	.634
HxQuAD④	.326	.421	.294	.441	.158	.629
PM2⑤	.306	.411	.267	.450	.169	.643
TPM2⑥	.291	.399	.250	.443	.161	.639
HPM2⑦	.317	.420	.279	.455	.172	.645
R-LTR❷	.303	.403	.267	.441	.164	.631
PAMM❸	.309	.411	.271	.450	.168	.643
R-LTR-NTN❹	.312	.415	.275	.451	.166	.644
PAMM-NTN❺	.311	.417	.272	.457	.170	.648
DSSA	**.356**★	**.456**★	**.326**★	**.473**★	**.185**★	**.649**①②❶

Table 8: Effects of different settings.

Methods	ERR-IA	α-nDCG	NRBP	D♯-nDCG	Pre-IA	S-rec
SVD	.348	.450	.315	.470	.184	.646
LDA	.356	.456	.326	.473	.185	.649
doc2vec	.351	.452	.318	.471	.184	.646
general	.356	.456	.326	.473	.185	.649
dot	.347	.450	.314	.470	.184	.647
vanilla	.354	.454	.322	.471	.184	.649
GRU	.357	.457	.326	.473	.185	.649
LSTM	.356	.456	.326	.473	.185	.649
DSSA-RNN	.342	.445	.306	.466	.172	.657
DSSA-RNNMP	.356	.456	.326	.473	.185	.649

(3) RNN cell: vanilla, GRU, and LSTM cell.
(4) Dimensionality: we test several representative settings on the size of distributed representations E_d and E_q, the size of hidden state U as (25, 10), (50, 25), (100, 50), (200, 100).
(5) Max-pooling: we experiment without using max-pooling (denoted as DSSA-RNN) in subtopic attention component.

The results are reported in Table 8. We can observe that DSSA does not heavily rely on specific settings. As for different representation generation methods, LDA has slightly better results. doc2vec could have been more appropriate if we had large datasets with more queries. The "general" operation yields slightly better results. A possible reason is that it is bilinear and thus is more powerful than "dot" to model the interaction. GRU and LSTM cells yield slightly better results than vanilla cell because of their ability of modeling long-term dependency. The difference is however small. This may be due to that with a limited number of training data, a model is unable to take advantage of its higher complexity to capture the fine-grained subtlety. Results with different size of distributed representation and hidden state shown in Figure 4(a) also

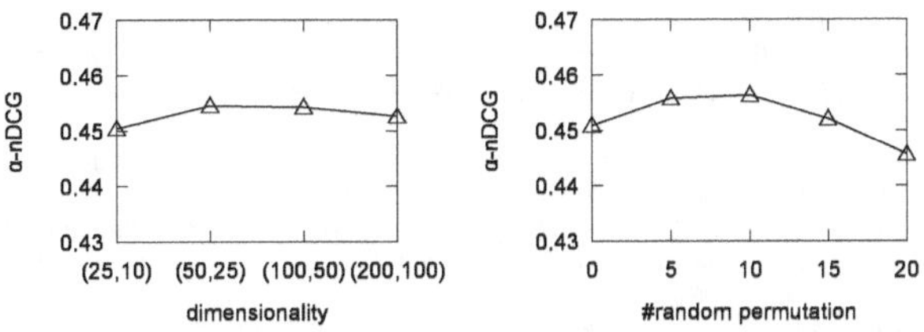

(a) α-nDCG *w.r.t.* different size (b) α-nDCG *w.r.t.* different random permutation count

Figure 4: Performance tendency of different settings.

Table 9: Effects of different optimization methods.

Methods	ERR-IA	α-nDCG	NRBP	D♯-nDCG	Pre-IA	S-rec
MLE	.349	.446	.315	.462	.176	.644
PAMM	.348	.445	.315	.463	.175	.644
list-pairwise	.356	.456	.326	.473	.185	.649

indicate no strong correlation between performance and settings. α-nDCG remains above 0.45 using different sizes. The best performance is achieved using 100-dimensional representation and 50-dimensional hidden state. This suggests that high dimensionality may result in overfitting. Without using max-pooling, α-nDCG drops to 0.445, which demonstrates the usefulness of using max-pooling to enhance subtopic attention. The small differences between different settings suggest that DSSA is a stable and robust framework. Note that we use both distributed representations and relevance features, which are complementary to each other. This may be one of the reasons of the stability.

6.3 Effects of Different Optimization Methods

Results in Table 9 shows that list-pairwise is more effective than MLE and PAMM. This confirms our earlier intuition that list-pairwise optimization corresponds better to the situation of diversification ranking than the two other methods. Note that even using MLE or PAMM as optimization methods, DSSA could also achieve state-of-the-art performances, which confirms the effectiveness of our explicit learning framework from another perspective.

We vary the number of random permutations used in list-pairwise sampling from 0 to 20 to investigate its effect. As depicted in Figure 4(b), the performance does not heavily rely it. The best performance is achieved around 10. More permutations lead to lower effectiveness, which could be explained by model overfitting.

6.4 Visualization and Discussion

We visualize the ranking results of DSSA and the variation of subtopic attention to better understand why DSSA performs well.

We show the top 5 ranking results of query #58 and #182 in Figure 5 to illustrate why DSSA outperforms implicit learning methods. We choose PAMM-NTN as comparison method, which is the best existing learning method. In Figure 5, white means relevant and black means irrelevant. For query #58, DSSA ranks a document relevant to subtopics i_3 and i_4 first and a document relevant to i_1 and i_2 at the second position, while the first two documents of PAMM-NTN cover the same subtopics. Note that there is no

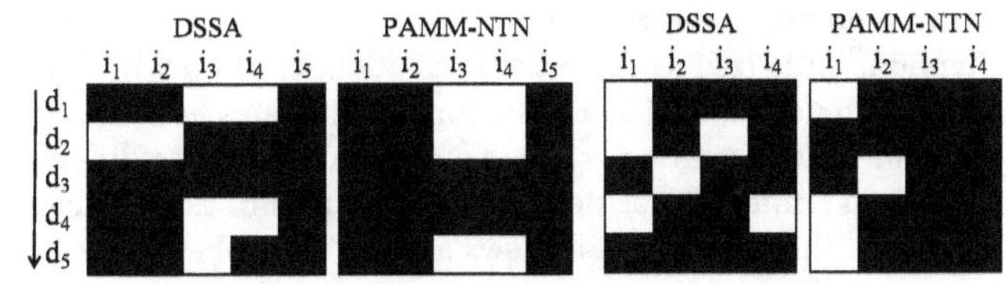

(a) ranking of query #58 (b) ranking of query #182

Figure 5: Case study for DSSA and PAMM-NTN. White means relevant and black means irrelevant.

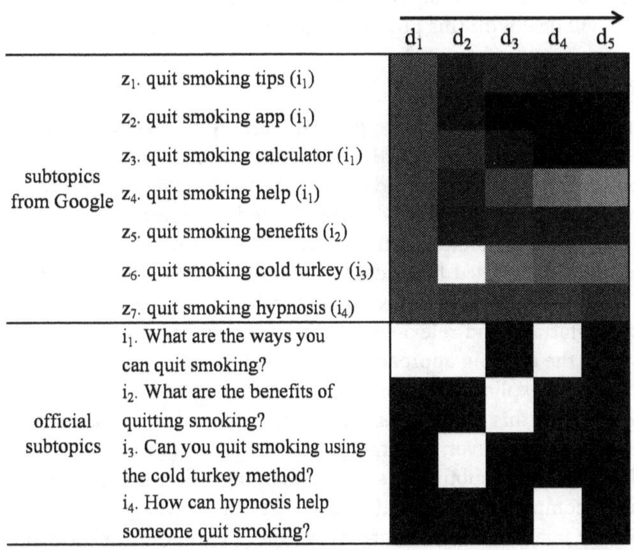

Figure 6: Subtopic attention variation of query #182. The top part is attention and the bottom part is relevance judgment.

document covering i_5 in the candidate set. For query #182, DSSA successively chooses documents that cover i_1, i_3, i_2, and i_4. One additional intent is satisfied at every position. PAMM-NTN, however, just covers i_1 and i_2 by top 5 documents, which is obviously not optimal. We see that the unequal and varied subtopic attention is capable of discovering unsatisfied subtopics at different positions, which eventually leads to more subtopic coverage.

To study attention mechanism, we further visualize the variation of subtopic attention of top 5 documents of query #182, namely "quit smoking", which has 4 official subtopics (i_1 to i_4), as shown in Figure 6. The top part is subtopic attention variation and the bottom part is relevance judgment. For attention part, the darker the cell is, the lower the attention (weight) on this subtopic is. Note that we actually leverage query suggestions of Google (z_1 to z_7) to serve as subtopics, which do not match official ones exactly. We manually align subtopics mined from Google to official ones. At the beginning, all the subtopics have equal attention. The first selected document d_1 is relevant to i_1, i.e. to the Goggle subtopics z_1, z_2, z_3 and z_4. We see that the attention to these latter decreases at second position. Then the document d_2 is selected, which is relevant to uncovered i_3. We see that the attention to the corresponding z_6 begins to diminish from the third position. d_3 and d_4 satisfy additional i_2 and i_4 respectively, which leads to the reduction of attention on z_5 and z_7 at the following position. The subtopic attention, initialized as uniform distribution, ends up with more emphasis on z_4, z_6, and z_7. This example illustrates how the unequal and varied attention drives the model to emphasize different subtopics at different positions, which is crucial in explicit diversification. This example also shows a potential problem inherent for any method using automatically discovered subtopics: those topics may be different from the ones defined by human assessors. Equal distribution is assumed on all the subtopics z_i. However, this implies an unequal distribution among the manually defined subtopics (more emphasis is put on i_1). Assuming an equal distribution at the beginning may not necessarily be the best approach. We will deal with this problem in our future work.

7 CONCLUSIONS

In this paper, we propose a general learning framework DSSA to model subtopics explicitly for search result diversification. Based on the sequence of selected documents, unequal and varied subtopic attention is calculated, driving the model to emphasize different subtopics at different positions. This is the first time that attention mechanism is used to model the process. We further instantiate DSSA using RNN and max-pooling to handle both distributed representations and relevance features, which outperforms significantly the existing approaches. The results confirm that modeling subtopics explicitly in a learning framework is beneficial and effective and this also avoids heuristically defined functions and parameters. However, accurately modeling the interaction among documents and subtopics is still challenging. There are many other more complex implementations besides our particular way, which will be investigated in future work. The proposed model contains a number of parameters to be learned. This requires a large number of training data. Collecting more training data to fully unlock the potential of the model is another direction. Finally, this work only deals with the learning of a ranking function, assuming that document and query representations have already been created. In practice, learning these representation is another interesting aspect, which could be incorporated into our framework, provided with sufficient training data.

ACKNOWLEDGMENTS

Zhicheng Dou is the corresponding author. This work was funded by the National Natural Science Foundation of China under Grant No. 61502501 and 61502502, the National Key Basic Research Program (973 Program) of China under Grant No. 2014CB340403, and the Beijing Natural Science Foundation under Grant No. 4162032.

REFERENCES

[1] Rakesh Agrawal, Sreenivas Gollapudi, Alan Halverson, and Samuel Ieong. 2009. Diversifying Search Results. In *WSDM*.

[2] Ricardo A. Baeza-Yates, Carlos A. Hurtado, and Marcelo Mendoza. 2004. Query Recommendation Using Query Logs in Search Engines. In *Current Trends in Database Technology EDBT 2004 Workshops*.

[3] Dzmitry Bahdanau, Kyunghyun Cho, and Yoshua Bengio. 2014. Neural Machine Translation by Jointly Learning to Align and Translate. *CoRR* abs/1409.0473 (2014).

[4] David M. Blei, Andrew Y. Ng, and Michael I. Jordan. 2003. Latent Dirichlet Allocation. *Journal of Machine Learning Research* 3 (2003).

[5] Jamie Callan, Mark Hoy, Changkuk Yoo, and Le Zhao. 2009. Clueweb09 data set. http://boston.lti.cs.cmu.edu/Data/clueweb09/. (2009).

[6] Jaime Carbonell and Jade Goldstein. 1998. The Use of MMR, Diversity-based Reranking for Reordering Documents and Producing Summaries. In *SIGIR*.

[7] Ben Carterette. 2009. An Analysis of NP-Completeness in Novelty and Diversity Ranking. In *ICTIR*.

[8] Olivier Chapelle, Donald Metlzer, Ya Zhang, and Pierre Grinspan. 2009. Expected Reciprocal Rank for Graded Relevance. In *CIKM*.

[9] Junyoung Chung, Çaglar Gülçehre, KyungHyun Cho, and Yoshua Bengio. 2014. Empirical Evaluation of Gated Recurrent Neural Networks on Sequence Modeling. *CoRR* abs/1412.3555 (2014).

[10] Charles L.A. Clarke, Maheedhar Kolla, Gordon V. Cormack, Olga Vechtomova, Azin Ashkan, Stefan Büttcher, and Ian MacKinnon. 2008. Novelty and Diversity in Information Retrieval Evaluation. In *SIGIR*.

[11] Charles L. A. Clarke, Maheedhar Kolla, and Olga Vechtomova. 2009. An Effectiveness Measure for Ambiguous and Underspecified Queries. In *ICTIR*.

[12] Van Dang and Bruce W. Croft. 2013. Term Level Search Result Diversification. In *SIGIR*.

[13] Van Dang and W. Bruce Croft. 2012. Diversity by Proportionality: An Election-based Approach to Search Result Diversification. In *SIGIR*.

[14] Amac Herdagdelen, Massimiliano Ciaramita, Daniel Mahler, Maria Holmqvist, Keith Hall, Stefan Riezler, and Enrique Alfonseca. 2010. Generalized Syntactic and Semantic Models of Query Reformulation. In *SIGIR*.

[15] Sepp Hochreiter and Jürgen Schmidhuber. 1997. Long Short-Term Memory. *Neural Computation* 9, 8 (1997).

[16] Sha Hu, Zhicheng Dou, Xiaojie Wang, Tetsuya Sakai, and Ji-Rong Wen. 2015. Search Result Diversification Based on Hierarchical Intents. In *CIKM*.

[17] Po-Sen Huang, Xiaodong He, Jianfeng Gao, Li Deng, Alex Acero, and Larry P. Heck. 2013. Learning deep structured semantic models for web search using clickthrough data. In *CIKM*.

[18] Quoc V. Le and Tomas Mikolov. 2014. Distributed Representations of Sentences and Documents. In *ICML*.

[19] Tie-Yan Liu. 2009. Learning to rank for information retrieval. *Foundations and Trends in Information Retrieval* 3, 3 (2009).

[20] Yiqun Liu, Ruihua Song, Min Zhang, Zhicheng Dou, Takehiro Yamamoto, Makoto P Kato, Hiroaki Ohshima, and Ke Zhou. 2014. Overview of the NTCIR-11 IMine Task.. In *NTCIR*. Citeseer.

[21] Thang Luong, Hieu Pham, and Christopher D. Manning. 2015. Effective Approaches to Attention-based Neural Machine Translation. In *EMNLP*.

[22] John I Marden. 1996. *Analyzing and modeling rank data*. CRC Press.

[23] Tomas Mikolov, Ilya Sutskever, Kai Chen, Gregory S. Corrado, and Jeffrey Dean. 2013. Distributed Representations of Words and Phrases and their Compositionality. In *NIPS*.

[24] Volodymyr Mnih, Nicolas Heess, Alex Graves, and Koray Kavukcuoglu. 2014. Recurrent Models of Visual Attention. In *NIPS*.

[25] Tetsuya Sakai, Zhicheng Dou, Takehiro Yamamoto, Yiqun Liu, Min Zhang, Ruihua Song, MP Kato, and M Iwata. 2013. Overview of the NTCIR-10 INTENT-2 Task.. In *NTCIR*.

[26] Tetsuya Sakai and Ruihua Song. 2011. Evaluating Diversified Search Results Using Per-intent Graded Relevance. In *SIGIR*.

[27] Rodrygo L.T. Santos, Craig Macdonald, and Iadh Ounis. 2010. Exploiting Query Reformulations for Web Search Result Diversification. In *WWW*.

[28] Rodrygo L.T. Santos, Craig Macdonald, Iadh Ounis, and others. 2015. Search result diversification. *Foundations and Trends® in Information Retrieval* (2015).

[29] Aliaksei Severyn and Alessandro Moschitti. 2015. Learning to Rank Short Text Pairs with Convolutional Deep Neural Networks. In *SIGIR*.

[30] Richard Socher, Danqi Chen, Christopher D. Manning, and Andrew Y. Ng. 2013. Reasoning With Neural Tensor Networks for Knowledge Base Completion. In *NIPS*.

[31] Fen Xia, Tie-Yan Liu, Jue Wang, Wensheng Zhang, and Hang Li. 2008. Listwise Approach to Learning to Rank: Theory and Algorithm. In *ICML*.

[32] Long Xia, Jun Xu, Yanyan Lan, Jiafeng Guo, and Xueqi Cheng. 2015. Learning Maximal Marginal Relevance Model via Directly Optimizing Diversity Evaluation Measures. In *SIGIR*.

[33] Long Xia, Jun Xu, Yanyan Lan, Jiafeng Guo, and Xueqi Cheng. 2016. Modeling Document Novelty with Neural Tensor Network for Search Result Diversification. In *SIGIR*.

[34] Jeonghee Yi and Farzin Maghoul. 2009. Query Clustering Using Click-through Graph. In *WWW*.

[35] Hai-Tao Yu and Fuji Ren. 2014. Search Result Diversification via Filling Up Multiple Knapsacks. In *CIKM*.

[36] Yisong Yue and Thorsten Joachims. 2008. Predicting Diverse Subsets Using Structural SVMs. In *ICML*.

[37] Cheng Xiang Zhai, William W. Cohen, and John Lafferty. 2003. Beyond Independent Relevance: Methods and Evaluation Metrics for Subtopic Retrieval. In *SIGIR*.

[38] Zhiyong Zhang and Olfa Nasraoui. 2006. Mining Search Engine Query Logs for Query Recommendation. In *WWW*.

[39] Yadong Zhu, Yanyan Lan, Jiafeng Guo, Xueqi Cheng, and Shuzi Niu. 2014. Learning for Search Result Diversification. In *SIGIR*.

Retrieval Algorithms Optimized for Human Learning

Rohail Syed
School of Information
University of Michigan
105 S. State St.,
Ann Arbor, Michigan 48109
rmsyed@umich.edu

Kevyn Collins-Thompson
School of Information
University of Michigan
105 S. State St.,
Ann Arbor, Michigan 48109
kevynct@umich.edu

ABSTRACT

While search technology is widely used for learning-oriented information needs, the results provided by popular services such as Web search engines are optimized primarily for generic relevance, not effective learning outcomes. As a result, the typical information trail that a user must follow while searching to achieve a learning goal may be an inefficient one involving unnecessarily easy or difficult content, or material that is irrelevant to actual learning progress relative to a user's existing knowledge. We address this problem by introducing a novel theoretical framework, algorithms, and empirical analysis of an information retrieval model that is optimized for learning outcomes instead of generic relevance. We do this by formulating an optimization problem that incorporates a cognitive learning model into a retrieval objective, and then give an algorithm for an efficient approximate solution to find the search results that represent the best 'training set' for a human learner. Our model can personalize results for an individual user's learning goals, as well as account for the effort required to achieve those goals for a given set of retrieval results. We investigate the effectiveness and efficiency of our retrieval framework relative to a commercial search engine baseline ('Google') through a crowdsourced user study involving a vocabulary learning task, and demonstrate the effectiveness of personalized results from our model on word learning outcomes.

KEYWORDS

Retrieval Models and Ranking; Intrinsic diversity; Assessment of learning in search

1 INTRODUCTION

Considerable research attention has focused on how computer-based learning can supplement traditional classroom learning environments [15]. As a supplement to traditional forms of learning, a computerized approach via technology such as intelligent tutoring systems (ITS) offers numerous benefits in the form of personalized instruction, modern and up-to-date educational material and the comfort of self-paced learning [15]. However, with all these benefits come a number of challenges. A computational teaching approach must somehow represent the state of a student's knowledge, and then, as in traditional classroom instruction, infer the knowledge required for students to progress in the curriculum to a certain goal. In particular, the right learning resources must be selected for each student that enables them to learn material effectively and efficiently, enabling them to do well in future assessments on the material.

At the same time, Web search is now a key information source that learners use to obtain their own resources for many education-related tasks [1]. Algorithms have been developed to enhance Web search for learners by providing intrinsically diverse results for topic exploration [17] or by personalizing results so that they are at an appropriate level of reading difficulty [5]. However, all of these previous retrieval methods used algorithms trained to optimize relevance, not learning, and their evaluations similarly focused on improvements in generic relevance, not actual learning outcomes.

In this study, we bring together these two fields of research to develop and evaluate the first retrieval framework that attempts to optimize directly for learning gains. We do this by first developing a theoretical model that casts information retrieval as the search for a optimal 'training set' of documents that optimize a utility function that is the composition of a computational model of learning with a relevance-based objective function. While this results in a difficult optimization problem, inspired by developments in *machine teaching* [22] we give an approximate, efficient algorithm to solve the retrieval problem that finds document sets that are personalized for the prior knowledge of individual learners, cover all constituent aspects of a topic, and optimize the learning gains of the student on future tests for that topic. Our model also naturally incorporates the notion of effort as a key component of the retrieval objective. We evaluate our approach with an empirical study that examines both the effectiveness and efficiency of learning outcomes on a vocabulary learning task. In effect, we show how to build a search engine that optimizes retrieval utility as seen through the 'lens' of human cognition.

2 RELATED WORK

Our work brings together three different research areas: core retrieval algorithms and evaluation metrics, search engine support for learning, and intelligent tutoring systems.

Core retrieval algorithms and evaluation metrics. The vast majority of research on retrieval algorithm optimization and evaluation has assumed metrics based on generic relevance. In contrast, we believe that ours is the first study to develop theoretical models and retrieval algorithms that explicitly optimize results for an educational goal as a key retrieval objective. Researchers have recognized the importance of going beyond traditional retrieval evaluation measures to consider user progress over time [19] as well as degree of effort [21], but little, if any, of that work has involved modeling or assessing human learning.

SIGIR '17, August 07-11, 2017, Shinjuku, Tokyo, Japan

ACM ISBN 978-1-4503-5022-8/17/08...$15.00
https://doi.org/10.1145/3077136.3080835

Prior work on understanding users' information needs has categorized the types of web search queries users issue as being navigational, transactional or informational [9][4]. Of particular interest here are the informational queries, whose intent is characterized as "to acquire some information assumed to be present on one or more web pages" [4]. Their study found that such queries account for the most queries of the three categories. A later study using the same search engine and breaking the taxonomy down to a finer granularity found similar results [18]. The study more specifically found that the predominant type of informational queries were undirected informational queries, characterized as: "I want to learn anything/everything about my topic. A query for topic X might be interpreted as 'tell me about X.'" [18]. Studies have shown that a majority of queries are in fact informational [9][4] and that many search sessions involve multiple queries [15]. This finding has been consistent across multiple popular search engines [9][1]. The focus in this paper is on queries that a student issues that are meant to explore a topic and are intrinsically diverse (ID) [16]. [17]. Such queries represent a specific topic of interest but their underspecified nature allows for retrieval of multiple sub-topics, or knowledge components. We formulate a strategy that estimates these sub-topics beforehand and provides the student a re-ranked set of documents that optimally teaches them about the topic by effectively covering of the sub-topics.

Search engine support for learning. Exploring new topic areas and learning important domain vocabulary is one popular instance of learning tasks that have been identified in search [1]. Because search engines are a primary conduit of educational information for learners, a number of studies have focused on understanding and supporting learning tasks in search, particularly on the Web. A study by Eickhoff et al. [10] investigated learning behaviors of Web search users, but used only indirect evidence via implicit indicators derived from Web search logs, rather than direct assessment of users. That study also did not develop or assess new retrieval algorithms that could be adapted to improve learning outcomes. Collins-Thompson et al. [5] explored how reading difficulty – a component of user effort – could be effective as a personalized ranking feature, but did not optimize, or assess its effectiveness, for actual learning tasks or outcomes.

While Raman et al. [17] demonstrate the effectiveness of an intrinsically diverse search ranking relative to a baseline in terms of standard IR measures, their study did not assess how well an intrinsically diverse ranking helped users learn. Therefore, subsequent work by Collins-Thompson et al. [6] implemented the intrinsic diversity algorithm formulated in [17] and evaluated improvements to learning in terms of low and high levels of cognitive complexity, as specified by the revised Bloom's taxonomy [12]. While the study in [6] did evaluate the learning gains offered by an intrinsically diverse search engine, they did not specifically develop a re-ranking objective to optimize for learning purposes, as we do here. We build on this prior work by modifying the objective function initially specified by Raman et al. to incorporate an emphasis on better learning effectiveness, and by exploring a modified variant of the ID algorithm in the context of a vocabulary learning task.

Intelligent tutoring systems. Prior studies have demonstrated that personalized traditional education can yield enormous gains in learning [3]. However, personalized instruction can be both expensive and difficult to scale, motivating the exploration of effective automated approaches, typically through the development of intelligent tutoring systems. Corbett [7] showed that existing intelligent systems can already get quite close to the improvement offered by personalized human tutors but so far there has been little evidence that this generalizes to learning any topic with a vast unstructured set of resources (e.g. learning through Web searches). Pirolli et al. [15] demonstrate an ITS model that yields highly significant learning gains and can strongly predict a learner's future performance on test questions. In their system, the tutor model manually decides which documents would be best for a learner to read for the given set of test questions. The expert model automatically decides which documents most closely provide answers to the test question. Their system makes the assumption that the test questions selected accurately test knowledge of subject J and that the knowledge needed to answer these questions can be represented in some finite quantitative form. We make these same assumptions in our model. Our study is primarily different from [15] in that our focus is on investigating how information retrieval (IR) algorithms can be directly optimized to improve a student's learning. In contrast, in [15], learners could find and choose the documents themselves and the choice of search algorithm was not controlled: while learners could use the tutor's recommendations, they were not required to.

3 LEARNING-OPTIMIZED RETRIEVAL MODELS

In a typical intelligent tutoring system, a student wants to learn about some subject J and the system delivers resources that optimally teach subject J. As in traditional education, the learner's performance would be measured by how well they perform on a test that covers knowledge of subject J. Given a set of test questions and an estimate of the user's current knowledge state, an effective system would be able to select a set of teaching resources that updated the learner's knowledge state so that they maximized their expected score on a future test. This individualized set of teaching resources would also be selected to minimize the effort required to obtain this optimal score. The objective of the ideal ITS system is then twofold: (1) to develop an expert model that can accurately determine the knowledge required to answer a set of test questions and (2) to develop a tutor model that can retrieve an optimal set of personalized resources.

In this paper we describe both elements, but focus on the retrieval algorithm needed for an effective tutor model. Mathematically, we start by defining a high-level retrieval objective inspired by recent work in *machine teaching* [22], which finds optimal training sets for a given learning algorithm. Our overall goal here is to find a set of documents $\mathcal{D}$ that maximizes a user's utility U, which is defined in terms of their learning outcome $H(\mathcal{D})$ while minimizing the effort $E(\mathcal{D})$ associated with the retrieved document set. This high-level objective is

$$\arg\max_{\mathcal{D}} U(\mathcal{D}) \quad = H(\mathcal{D}) - \lambda E(\mathcal{D}) \tag{1}$$

where the parameter λ controls the tradeoff between learning outcome and effort. In this framework, there are many possible ways to define learning outcomes $H(\cdot)$ and effort $E(\cdot)$, some of which we discuss later.

In general, given the combinatorially large number of potential document sets $\mathcal{D}$, solving Eq. 1 quickly enough for real users requires us to approximate this problem. To do this, we build on an

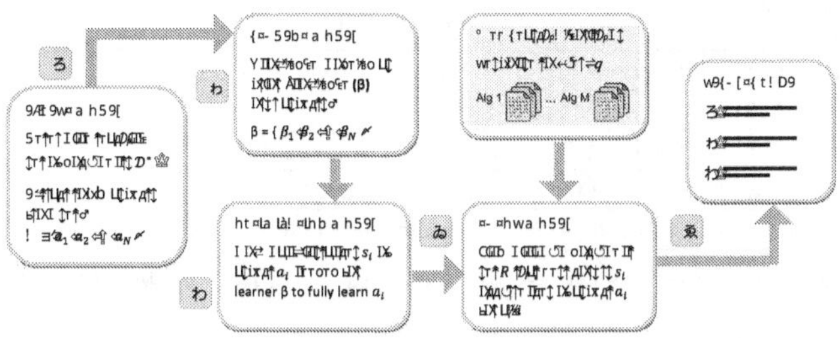

Figure 1: High-level learning-optimized retrieval process

approach described by Zhu [22], in which we proceed in two steps. First, we find a set of optimal sufficient statistics S that maximizes the combined learning and effort objective, which any candidate document set to be considered should satisfy. Second, we obtain a pool of candidate documents using an existing retrieval framework, and select a subset of them that approximately satisfies the desired sufficient statistics S.

To solve the first step, finding optimal sufficient statistics S, we solve an adjusted form of Eq. 1, but in terms of S

$$\arg\max_{S} U(S) = H(S) - \lambda E(S) \quad (2)$$

We show how to derive specific definitions for $H(\cdot)$ and $E(\cdot)$ in Sec. 3.1 and Sec. 3.2, using assumptions based on simple computational learning models from cognitive psychology, culminating in the complete specific form of the objective in Eq. 5 in Section 3.2. We solve the second step, using the optimal S from the first step to select documents for the tutor model, in Sec. 3.3. As part of developing this retrieval model, we now walk through the various stages of our learning-optimized retrieval process as shown in Figure 1.

3.1 Retrieval Components

While human learning is a rich, complex phenomenon whose goals can be categorized into a multi-level hierarchy [2], in this paper we focus on one of the lower-level form of learning task and outcome: *vocabulary learning*, since it is a key precursor to other higher-level learning activities and has relatively more straightforward and well-understood assessment measures. We also make a number of simplifying assumptions to make the retrieval model tractable.

We must first choose a knowledge representation for the vocabulary learning process. We assume the widely-used *knowledge-tracing model*, implemented so that knowledge of a subject area J is modeled in the form of a weighted multinomial distribution over knowledge aspects A_k. For example, in learning about the subject of 'igneous rocks' might involve learning about aspects that include their formation, location, and so on. For vocabulary learning, we assume these aspects correspond to K specific technical keywords.

Then, we can say that the knowledge to answer test question T_k is a function of how many units of relevant information the student has seen and the relative importance of that increase in knowledge. As a student only needs to read a finite amount of information about J to achieve mastery of the subject, we compute a target distribution $S = \{S_1, \ldots, S_K\}$ of how many examples of each of the K aspects the student needs to read in context for their learning to be considered complete. (We explain in Section 3.2.1 how these S_k are estimated.)

Expert Model. The expert model, (Step 1 of Figure 1), is responsible for curating the set of documents $\mathcal{D}^*$ that best represents the knowledge aspects A_k of the subject. In this process, the expert will generate a frequency multinomial of the A_k keywords given by the bag-of-words contents of $\mathcal{D}^*$. We define this target distribution to be our aspect weights W.

While any number of possible algorithms could be used in this process, we focus on using a term frequency measure weighted by the log of a global corpus frequency.[1] Specifically, in constructing W, we first represent $\mathcal{D}^*$ as a bag-of-words model and determine the important keywords in the document set by considering the term frequencies normalized by their log total occurrences from a large corpus. This approach will give us vocabulary words that the student likely hasn't learned yet and which occur frequently in $\mathcal{D}^*$. To avoid getting keywords that may be rare but not topically relevant, we weighted these values by their word2vec [14] similarity to the first term in the base query q. Specifically, for each unique word T_i in the bag-of-words of $\mathcal{D}^*$ we determine the important words by the score:

$$Score(T_i) = \frac{TF_i}{\log Total_i} \cdot word2vec(T_i, q)$$

We next extract the top K highest-scored keywords and generate W as the maximum likelihood estimation of these keywords' TF values[2]. Specifically, for $i = 1, 2, \ldots K$:

$$W_i = TF_i \cdot \left(\sum_{j=1}^{K} TF_j \right)^{-1}$$

For example, for the subject "igneous rocks" and $K = 5$, we get the distribution `W={'igneous':0.302, 'magma':0.178, 'felsic':0.057, 'mafic':0.069, 'rocks':0.394}`. Table 1 shows the top 5 keywords out of $K = 10$ for five different topics along with their corresponding weights.

Let us now consider the fact that different students may have different learning rates and different background knowledge. To avoid offering suboptimal reading resources, we must account for these differences by defining a *student model*.

Student model. The student model (Step 2 of Figure 1), represents the knowledge state of the student who is learning about subject J. To find documents that teach the student, we can simply find the set of documents that minimally reaches the required set of counts S. However, this approach ignores: (1) the fact that document length or keyword coverage is not necessarily indicative of topical relevance or quality and (2) different students may already know about certain aspects of J and their time would be better spent learning the aspects that they don't know.

We assume that we can measure a student's learning outcome in terms their performance on a test on the given subject, so that we can assess learning by measuring a learner's performance on a set of K test questions $T = \{T_k\}$ on those aspects (keywords). We code the learner's responses via the set Y of binomial variables Y_k such that:

$$Y_k = \begin{Bmatrix} 1 & \text{student answered } T_k \text{ correctly} \\ 0 & \text{otherwise} \end{Bmatrix}$$

[1] We used the British National Corpus (BNC)

[2] Words that were semantically the same as an earlier ranked word (word2vec similarity > 0.3) but with different tense/form were removed. Example: 'rock', 'rocks'

Topic	Keyword 1	Keyword 2	Keyword 3	Keyword 4	Keyword 5
Igneous rock	rocks (.308)	igneous (.236)	magma (.139)	minerals (.081)	basalt (.056)
Tundra	tundra (.346)	arctic (.211)	plants (.127)	permafrost (.088)	soils (.075)
Phrenology	phrenology (.382)	brain (.164)	skull (.103)	science (.079)	perception (.073)
Pottery	pottery (.517)	clay (.145)	pots (.105)	potters (.061)	ceramic (.057)
Synapse	neurons (.385)	electrical (.169)	axon (.100)	synapse (.077)	membrane (.069)

Table 1: Top 5 (out of 10) selected keywords for five topics, sorted by descending keyword weights W_i. The keywords to be learned range from easy ('rock') to technical ('permafrost').

We also make the assumptions that the student is a Bayesian learner and has no memory loss (post-reading knowledge is never less than pre-reading knowledge). We further assume that reading an instance of keyword A_k will monotonically increase the student's knowledge of that aspect (Step 3 of Figure 1). As such, we define the student's prior knowledge β to be a vector of how many instances of each keyword we expect them to have read before being provided $\mathcal{D}$. Then, we have:

$$\beta = \{\beta_1, \beta_2, \ldots, \beta_K\}$$

We assume the widely-used *item response theory* (IRT) model [11] as our cognitive learning model that defines the probability of a correct response Y_k on test T as a logistic function of user and item parameters:

$$P(Y_k = 1 \mid U, W_k, \beta_k, L_k, S_k) = \left(1 + e^{-f(U, W_k, \beta_k, L_k, S_k(\mathcal{D}))}\right)^{-1}$$

Here, the IRT model parameters are:

- U - The user's individual learning rate. This is defined such that the faster a student can learn, the less resources they will require to complete their understanding of J. In this study, we assume a fixed U for all users.
- W_k - The weight given to term k where W is the weight multinomial defined in the Expert model. Terms with higher weight assigned are more important for the student to learn and hence are assigned higher number of S_k.
- β_k - The student's prior knowledge of keyword k, measured by the number of instances of k the student has already seen before being provided the document set $\mathcal{D}$.
- L_k - A parameter that quantifies the ease of learning for keyword k.
- $S_k(\mathcal{D})$ - The target instances of keyword k the student sees in document set $\mathcal{D}$.

Now we define the function $f(\cdot)$ to be the log weighted sum of the total instances of the keyword the student has learned (prior knowledge + post-reading knowledge):

$$f(U, W_k, \beta_k, L_k, S_k(\mathcal{D})) = \log\left((\beta_k + S_k) \cdot W_k \cdot L_k \cdot U\right)$$

With these operational settings, we can then more specifically define the expected learning for the kth term as:

$$P(Y_k = 1 \mid U, W_k, \beta_k, L_k, S_k) = \left(1 + e^{-\log((\beta_k + S_k) \cdot W_k \cdot L_k \cdot U)}\right)^{-1}$$

3.2 Optimization model

We are now ready to define the learning outcome and effort components of Eq. 2 to obtain our final optimization problem for finding the optimal sufficient statistics $S = \{S_k\}$.

3.2.1 Learning objective. Prior to providing the document set, we assume that we already know the user's learning rate U, the weights multinomial W and the learner's prior knowledge of the topic β. Then, our objective is to find the total instances of each aspect keyword the student *still* needs to read in order to have learned the subject. Aggregating across all K aspect terms, we can now define the learning outcome part of the objective $H(S)$ in Eq. 2.

$$H(S) = \sum_{k=1}^{K} \left(1 + e^{-\log((\beta_k + S_k \cdot W_k \cdot U))}\right)^{-1} \tag{3}$$

3.2.2 Effort objective. There are two types of effort we could attempt to quantify in the $E(\mathcal{D})$ term of Eq. 1 for a given document set $\mathcal{D}$ (and thus for the proxy objective for S in Eq. 2). First, we could define the effort (or cost) involved on the part of the search engine in obtaining $\mathcal{D}$, e.g. from content access fees, retrieval latency, or other factors. Second, we could define the effort involved on the part of the user in reading and understanding $\mathcal{D}$. In this paper we focus only on the latter, i.e. the user's effort, as the most relevant factor for our study, but future systems could easily capture both types in our model.

Various studies (e.g. [21]) have explored user effort factors associated with processing retrieved documents. For example, depending on the specific application, we might define $E(\mathcal{D})$ as a function of the vocabulary difficulty levels of all words in the documents [5]. For simplicity, in this study we simply define $E(\mathcal{D})$ in terms of the total amount of subject reading a student has to do, i.e. the total count of keywords S_k in the document set $\mathcal{D}$. The tradeoff parameter, λ, sets the (possibly student-specific) preference for less or more reading material as a tradeoff against learning utility. In this study, we keep the effort tradeoff parameter λ constant[3] but in future work, we will investigate how student-specific penalties can change learning outcomes. So we can express effort in terms of total keywords as:

$$E(S) = \sum_{k=1}^{K} S_k \tag{4}$$

3.2.3 Combined objective. Combining the learning and effort functions as in Eq. 2 gives us the final optimization problem for obtaining the desired keyword counts $S = \{S_k\}$:

$$\begin{aligned} &\arg\max_S H(S) - \lambda E(S) \\ &= \arg\max_S \sum_{k=1}^{K} \left(1 + e^{-\log((\beta_k + S_k) \cdot W_k \cdot L_k \cdot U)}\right)^{-1} - \lambda \sum_{k=1}^{K} S_k \end{aligned} \tag{5}$$

[3]The parameter λ was set to 0.0060 based on simulated resultant S_k values. We have similarly kept the keyword weights W as uniform to avoid confounding variables in our experiment design.

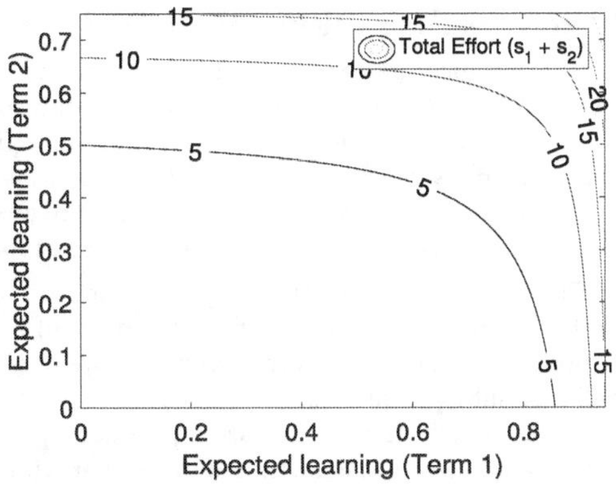

Figure 2: Possible tradeoffs in expected learning for each of two keywords (Term 1, Term 2) in a topic. Isolines show points of constant effort (total keyword instances read). Expected learning for each keyword is based on the logistic IRT definition above. (Ease of learning parameters for each keyword are set to $L_1 = 1.2$ and $L_2 = 0.2$ respectively.)

Note that without an effort penalty, we could simply maximize the learning utility by training the user with an unlimited number of documents, so effort plays an important role as a 'soft' constraint in the overall optimization problem. This particular instance of the problem can be solved using standard nonlinear optimization techniques to obtain the S_k values[4].

Figure 2 illustrates a simple instance of this optimization problem that shows the learning/effort tradeoff based on a topic with two keywords, using the sigmoid objective above. For a fixed total number of keywords to be read (shown by the isolines with total effort of 5, 10, 15, etc), there is a opportunity cost: for every additional unit assigned to one keyword, there also may be an expected potential loss in knowledge caused by *not* assigning the user's attention to the other keyword. In general these tradeoffs will also be affected by the ease of learning L_k for the kth keyword such that words that are easier to learn will result in a higher expected learning for the same total units assigned. For example, Fig. 2 shows that for a total effort of reading $S_1 + S_2 = 5$ keyword instances, to get the same expected learning for both keywords (i.e. the point that intersects the line $y = x$), we would assign $S_1 = \frac{1}{1.4}$ and $S_2 = \frac{6}{1.4}$ to get an expected learning outcome (probability of a correct test result) of 0.461 for both keywords.

3.3 Final retrieval stage: tutor model

Once the student model has determined how many instances of each target word the student must read (Step 3 of Figure 1), the last step is to design a retrieval algorithm that finds a set of Web documents that best covers these S optimal target word instances. Because users are learning the expert keywords solely from exposure to them in context, the quality and diversity of these contexts is important for learning. Thus, it is important to use a retrieval approach that finds documents that show the target keywords being used in a diverse set of contextually relevant contexts for a given topic. Toward this goal, we chose intrinsically diverse ranking [17] as our retrieval framework, because of its ability to jointly identify key subtopics along with the subtopics' most relevant documents.

[4]The general form of this objective is a sum-of-sigmoids, which for more sophisticated models may require sigmoidal optimization methods.

Tutor model. The tutor model decides what is the best set of documents $\mathcal{D}$ to provide the student to learn from (Step 4 of Figure 1). The tutor will first need to choose a retrieval algorithm to fetch a ranked list of candidate documents. In particular, as we will show in this section, our optimization objective very closely matches that used by [17] in their objective function. Next, the tutor will initiate with an empty set of documents $\mathcal{D}$ and will then greedily add candidate documents from the ranked list we retrieved. The stopping criteria for adding documents is determined by the cumulative keywords count in the bag-of-words of $\mathcal{D}$, given as vector $C_{\mathcal{D}}$. We will keep adding documents to $\mathcal{D}$ (Step 5 of Figure 1) until the following condition is reached:

$$C_{\mathcal{D}k} \geq S_k \quad k = 1, \ldots, K$$

In developing our choice of document retrieval algorithm, we required that it must incorporate: (1) a measure of document relevance to both the base query q and the subtopic queries q_i (that is, $Rel(d|q)$ and $Rel(d|q_i)$ respectively); (2) a measure η to avoid selecting redundant documents; (3) and a measure ϵ to maximize keyword density so that the student is provided with concise but relevant material.

We note that the intrinsic diversity objective developed by Raman et al. [17] meets most of these criteria and our generalization of it in [20] meets all the criteria with the objective:

$$\arg\max_{\mathcal{D}} \sum_{i=1}^{|\mathcal{D}|} Rel(d_i|q) \cdot Rel(d_i|q_i) \cdot e^{\delta \eta_i} \cdot e^{\alpha \epsilon_i} \tag{6}$$

Our generalization of this objective function differs from that proposed in [17] in two ways. Firstly, the η_i term that we use incorporates a measure of document novelty which the function by Raman et al. [17] did not.

Secondly, in our generalization, we add the ϵ_i term which is defined as the contribution document d_i offers in terms of how much closer it brings the student towards the required keyword counts S. We measure the contribution in terms of the keyword density of the document - that is, the useful keywords this document offers normalized by the total words the student has to read in this document. By normalizing the contribution, our algorithm will prefer documents that cover the content in less overall text.

We note that the implementation of the intrinsic diversity algorithm in [17] is essentially a special case of (6) where $\epsilon_i = 0$. A higher value of α gives a ranking that prioritizes finishing the reading in as few total words possible. This ensures the student expends the least possible effort but comes with the tradeoff of quality of the documents the student gets.

A recent study evaluated the learning gains using a similar objective function and showed that for several topics, putting the entire emphasis on the ϵ_i term (by setting $\alpha = \infty$) resulted in the highest learning gains per word read [20]. As they state in their study, a more rigorous method for selecting α values to test is needed and will be an area of future work.

While we have considered factors of relevance, document length and keyword coverage, we have not yet considered the reading difficulty of the given document. In particular, given two documents d_1 and d_2 that are identical in the above measures but differ in their vocabulary levels (one may be for a more expert audience and the other for a novice audience), we want to choose the document that is easier for the participant to learn from. So we normalize the keyword coverage instead by the *weighted* document length where for word w_k, we have Age-of-Acquisition readability score r_k. We get these scores from the study by Kuperman et al. [13].

Specifically, let $C_{\mathcal{D}}$ represent the cumulative keyword counts the student has seen so far and C_R represent the keywords frequency distribution of d_i. we have:

$$\epsilon_i = \left(\sum_{k=1}^{|d_i|} r_k \right)^{-1} \sum_{j=1}^{K} \begin{cases} C_{Rj} & C_{Rj} + C_{\mathcal{D}j} \leq S_j \\ \max(0, S_j - C_{\mathcal{D}j}) & \text{else} \end{cases} \tag{7}$$

The α variable in the objective function (Equation 6) controls how much importance we give to optimizing for keyword density versus intrinsic diversity. While we assume values of α are chosen manually, an automated approach to finding the optimal α is a natural next step for future work.

Algorithm 1 gives the final retrieval process which takes as input the vector S and a set of candidate documents D_i for each subtopic query where $D = \{D_i\}$. It then iteratively determines the candidate document that best improves the objective function (6), adding it to $\mathcal{D}$. All Web search queries issued in any part of this study were issued through the Google Search API[5] and we collected the top 70 links from each query as candidate documents.

Algorithm 1 IntrinsicTeacher algorithm that ranks documents for the vocabulary learning task. First developed in [20].

Input: D_i as Google search results for subtopic query q_i for all Q
C_{dk} given as vector of keyword counts in document $d_k \in D_i$.
$C_{\mathcal{D}}$ given as cumulative keyword counts for aspect $j \in A$ covered in $\mathcal{D}$.
S given as total required keyword counts for aspect $j \in A$.
Output: $\mathcal{D}$ given as output document set.

$\mathcal{D} \leftarrow \emptyset$
$C_{\mathcal{D}j} \leftarrow 0 \ \forall j \in C_{\mathcal{D}}$
while $\exists C_{\mathcal{D}j} : C_{\mathcal{D}j} < S_j$ **do** ▷ exit when all $C_{\mathcal{D}j} \geq S_j$
  $bestS \leftarrow 0$
  $bestD \leftarrow \emptyset$
  $C_D \leftarrow \emptyset$
  for all $q_i \in Q$ **do**
    for all $d_k \in D_i, d_k \notin \mathcal{D}$ **do**
      $docS \leftarrow Rel(d_k|q) \cdot Rel(d_k|q_i) \cdot e^{\beta \eta_i} \cdot e^{\alpha \epsilon_k}$
      if $docS > bestS$ **then**
        $bestS \leftarrow docS$
        $bestD \leftarrow d_k$ ▷ document with highest $bestS$
        $C_D \leftarrow C_{dk}$
      end if
    end for
  end for
  $\mathcal{D} \leftarrow \mathcal{D} \cup bestD$ ▷ append $bestD$ to output $\mathcal{D}$
  for all $C_{\mathcal{D}j} \in C_{\mathcal{D}}$ **do**
    $C_{\mathcal{D}j} \leftarrow C_{\mathcal{D}j} + C_{Dj}$ ▷ update keyword counts in $\mathcal{D}$
  end for
end while
return $\mathcal{D}$

[5]Queries used U.S. English, default API settings, and originated from Ann Arbor, MI.

3.4 Search results ranking algorithm

As discussed, the algorithm we use has the objective function given by Equation 6. While Raman et al. did a post-hoc study and were able to use historical search log data for capturing subtopic query signals, the same does not apply in a cold-start situation (where we have no input signals from the user besides for the query they issue). We operationalize each of the objective terms as follows:

(1) q - The base search query is the topic the user specifies they want to search for. To help narrow the intent of the query, we prefix the topic with "Introduction to ". We don't do this prefix for subtopic queries.
(2) q_i - A subtopic query for the base topic query q. In our implementation, we determine the set of these queries Q using the Wikipedia article corresponding to q. From the article, we extract the main subtopic headers and prefix them with q to generate the set of subtopic queries. We omit headers that are not related to the topic (e.g. "see also", "references", "further reading").
(3) $Rel(d_i|q)$ - The relevance of a document d_i for the base query q is given by its reciprocal rank in the commercial Web SERP results for q. That is, if d_i is ranked at position P, its relevance for q is given as $\frac{1}{P}$.
(4) $Rel(d_i|q_i)$ - Operationalized the same as $Rel(d_i|q)$ where the relevance is given by the reciprocal rank of d_i in the SERP page returned by the commercial search engine in response to subtopic query q_i.
(5) $\eta_i = \lambda\,[\cos(\text{snip}(q_i), \text{snip}(q))] - (1-\lambda) \max_{j<i} \left[\cos(d_i, d_j)\right]$
where $\cos(a, b)$ is the cosine similarity of a and b, $\text{snip}(x)$ is the bag of words representation of the top 10 snippets returned by query x and λ is a control parameter in the range [0,1] to let us decide how much importance we want to give to maintaining subtopic query relevance as opposed to maintaining document novelty.

We intend to refine our subtopic extraction methods to generalize beyond those available in Wikipedia topics in future work.

4 USER STUDY

To evaluate the learning effectiveness and efficiency of our model, we conducted a crowdsourced user study, focusing on the following research questions:

RQ 1. Does learning-optimized retrieval framework offer higher learning effectiveness or efficiency compared to traditional retrieval results of a baseline commercial Web search engine?
RQ 2. Do personalized search results that account for a user's prior knowledge improve learning effectiveness or efficiency?
RQ 3. How do learning effectiveness and efficiency vary across different topics (information needs) in different domains?

To explore these questions, we ran a crowdsourced user study that was based on a vocabulary learning task: learning the meaning of K target keywords by reading them in context. Participants first completed a multiple-choice pre-test to assess their existing knowledge of the keywords. Then, based on the condition they were assigned, they were instructed to read through a set of documents containing the keywords to be learned. Last, they completed an immediate post-test to assess their updated keyword knowledge.

For information needs, we developed a set of ten topics that were selected from top-level categories of the Open Directory Project to cover a range of areas, each having distinctive technical/expert vocabulary: Igneous rocks (geology), Tundra (environmental science), Cytoplasm (biology), Bioluminescence (biology), Phrenology (pseudo-science), Pottery (crafts), Cooking (food), Synapse (neuroscience), Refraction (optics) and Phenology (temporal phenomena).

We created one crowdsource job per topic, and for each topic job, each participant was randomly[6] assigned to one of three conditions:

(1) Commercial Web search baseline ('Web'). The participant was simply provided the top Web search results for the topic. Documents were only added until the same stopping criteria in Algorithm 1 was met.
(2) Non-personalized learning-optimized retrieval (α_N). The participant was provided a document set retrieved through the objective function described earlier with α parameter set to ∞. The $\alpha = \infty$ condition simply means that the keyword density ϵ_i term becomes the only factor in the ID retrieval objective.
(3) Personalized learning-optimized retrieval (α_P). The participant was provided a document set retrieved as defined above but with personalized S_k values calculated based on their prior knowledge β, computed from their pre-test scores.

Note that for all conditions, we truncated the retrieved document set to a maximum of 10 documents, so as to not overwhelm the participants and to reflect typical search environments where users see 10 documents on the first SERP page.

The pre- and post- vocabulary tests consisted of a series of multiple-choice questions, with one question for each of the K keywords. Both the pre- and post-test used identical questions, where we measured the participants' learning gain by the post-minus pre- scores[7]. To assess a participant's prior knowledge β, we looked at their pre-test answers for each of the K keywords. If they answered correctly for keyword k, that keyword was assigned a β_k value of 100 and a value of 0 otherwise. As the α_N condition is not personalized, we assume everyone has the same beginners prior knowledge (all $\beta_k = 0$). For the personalized condition, we used the optimized β vector (K-dimensional vector of student's prior knowledge of aspects A_k) when computing result lists. For non-personalized results, we set all the β values to 0. For the personalized condition, we pre-computed all possible sets of document/links that could be generated given different β_k values. As each question had two possible states (correct or incorrect), there were 2^K possible retrieved document sets. Thi study used $K = 10$, resulting in 1024 possible document sets for the α_P condition. Thus, we were able to provide participants in the α_P condition personalized document sets in real-time.

We used the Crowdflower platform for this study. Participants were offered US$0.04 per page (the equivalent of US$3.20/hr) for completing the tasks. For quality control, in addition to Crowdflower's proprietary mechanisms and 'gold standard' questions, we limited the participant pool to users from the U.S. and Canada, given the vocabulary-centric nature of the task and reliance on English reading skills. We also offered the tasks only to workers in the highest quality (level 3) pool, and only kept responses from those workers who spent at least four minutes on the task. Participants who scored perfectly on the pre-test were also omitted because, as per our model, they would theoretically have no room for improvement.

Measure	Web	α_N	α_P	p-value
Absolute Learning Gains	1.721	1.831	**1.982**	p=.046*
Learning Gain Per 1000 Words	0.109	0.252	**0.347**	p<.001!
Realized Potential Learning	0.384	0.425	**0.471**	p=.008†
Time Per Word	12.007	29.176	**35.022**	p<.001!
Signif. codes: 0 '!' 0.001 '†' 0.01 '*' 0.05 '·' 0.1 ' ' 1				

Table 2: Aggregated averages of key learning-related measures. Bold values are maximum across conditions. (All tables use same significance codes and bold meaning.)

The particular set of documents[8] shown to each participant was based on which α condition they were assigned. We gathered data for 40 participants per condition per topic, resulting in a total of 120 participants per topic and 1200 participants overall. After excluding those who didn't pass the initial training questions, those who didn't complete the full task and those who spent less than four minutes on the entire task, we ended up with 863 total participants. Further description of the experiment design, along with screenshots, can be found in an earlier study [20].

5 RESULTS

Overall, our analysis showed that different choices of document retrieval algorithms were in fact associated with differences in learning, as measured by both absolute and normalized gains from pre-test to post-test. In the following analysis, all tests for statistical differences across the three conditions were done using the Kruskal-Wallis test[9]. The following analysis will focus on assessing how the averages for the three conditions we tested varied across different measures of learning outcomes. In particular, we use the following measures of learning effectiveness and efficiency.

Absolute Learning Gains: The number of keywords where post-test score was higher than pre-test. Measures learning effectiveness.

Realized Potential Learning: Absolute learning gains normalized by maximum possible improvement. For example, if two students had an absolute learning gain of 2, but one student had pre-test score of 8/10 and the other had 3/10, the realized potential learning for the first is 2/2 but for the second is 2/7.

Learning Gains per Word Read: Absolute learning gains normalized by how many words a participant had to read to achieve their learning gain. Measures learning efficiency. (Table results reported in terms of learning gains per 1000 words.)

Time Per Word: Total time spent on reading documents normalized by total words contained in those documents. Measures how much attention users are focusing on what they read.

5.1 Absolute Learning Gains

We first analyze the data aggregated across all topics to get an overall view of how each condition performed (Table 2). We see

[6]Participants were sorted into conditions based on Crowdflower's random assignment to tasks.

[7]In measuring 'learning gain', we assume no memory loss so the learning gain is always no less than zero.

[8]To avoid multimedia confounds, we only allowed Web documents that contain only text and, at most, supplementary pictures.

[9]While ANOVA analysis and bootstrapped ANOVA also yielded nearly the same results reported, we used this test instead as we found evidence that the data for various measures of learning had strongly non-normal distributions.

	Learning Gain			Learning Gain/Word		
Topic	**Web**	α_N	α_P	**Web**	α_N	α_P
Igneous rock	1.769	2.533	2.364	0.081	0.118	**0.255***
Tundra	2.115	1.655	2.231	0.108	0.233	**0.266***
Cytoplasm	1.567	1.577	1.758	0.044	0.068	**0.178†**
Biolumin.	1.929	1.808	1.567	0.102	0.266	**0.406!**
Phrenology	1.156	1.424	**2.097†**	0.065	0.155	**0.360!**
Phenology	1.222	**2.036***	2.033	0.132	0.281	**0.316!**
Synapse	2.071	2.233	2.267	0.036	0.084	**0.142†**
Pottery	2.156	1.710	1.600	0.101	0.417	**0.611!**
Cooking	1.407	1.471	1.957	0.049	**0.293!**	0.110
Refraction	1.824	1.957	2.107	0.135	0.207	**0.230·**

Table 3: Absolute learning gains (left) and learning gains normalized per 1000 words (right) averaged across different conditions and topics.

Topic	**Web**	α_N	α_P	**p-value**
Igneous rock	0.390	0.557	**0.584**	p=.067·
Tundra	0.386	0.355	0.319	p=.667
Cytoplasm	0.283	0.350	0.390	p=.367
Bioluminescence	0.416	0.358	0.393	p=.633
Phrenology	0.325	0.402	**0.617**	p=.003†
Phenology	0.379	**0.602**	0.580	p=.066·
Synapse	0.410	0.463	0.492	p=.597
Pottery	0.480	0.454	0.454	p=.936
Cooking	0.498	0.350	**0.601**	p=.053·
Refraction	0.302	0.346	0.311	p=.707

Table 4: Averaged realized potential learning gains across different conditions. Bold values indicate maximums.

that for all measures, the differences are statistically significant and that the α_P (personalized) condition always performs the best with the α_N (non-personalized) condition always performing second best. At the aggregate level, these findings already show that RQ1 and RQ2 are both supported. However, we need to look deeper to investigate RQ3, the consistency of the findings across topics.

We analyzed overall, or absolute, learning gains (sum of learning gains for all K keywords) across the three conditions. We found that two out of the ten topics ('Phrenology' and 'Phenology') showed significantly different mean learning gains when compared with the three conditions. (Table 3). In both of these two topics, however, the mean learning gain in the α_P condition was almost double that of the commercial search baseline.

5.2 Realized Potential Learning Gains

While assessing absolute learning gains estimates how much a participant learned, it does not capture how well each student's *potential* learning gains were realized. A learning gain of 2 with a pre-test score of 8/10 is more significant that the same gain with a pre-test score of 3/10. Therefore, we also look at how much each student learned, relative to how much they *could* have learned. We calculate this by normalizing learning gains by (K - pre-test score). We show these results in Table 4.

We see that one topic has a statistically significant gain ($p < 0.05$) in realized potential learning, with the α_P condition giving almost twice the performance of the commercial Web search baseline. These results lend support to RQ1 and RQ2, i.e. that the $\alpha = \infty$ condition does in fact give some improvement for both actual learning gains and realized potential learning. In general, the α_P condition almost always had a consistently larger (though not always statistically significant) gain across all topics.

5.3 Learning Gains per Word Read

While both learning gains and realized potential learning measured the effectiveness of each of the three conditions, we also wanted to assess the *efficiency* of each algorithm. We define learning efficiency as the learning gains per unit effort spent. As per our model, we defined effort to be the total words read - we make the assumption that participants read the full documents they were provided - so we will evaluate learning gains per word read[10]. This measure incorporates effort such that, for two students scoring the same absolute gain, the one who achieved this gain with less effort (reading less text) is rewarded more.

Analysis of the three conditions shows a very strong and consistent trend of the α_P condition offering the best learning gains per word read and with very strong statistical significance ($p<.01$ for seven out of ten topics) (Table 3). In particular, for each topic, the α_P condition offers an average 3.55 times improvement in learning gains per word read over the Web (commercial search) baseline. The α_N condition offers a 2.63 times improvement. These results suggest that even without personalization, the $\alpha = \infty$ condition offers significantly more efficient learning gains for the participants compared to the Web baseline. These results lend further support to both RQ1 and RQ2 along with RQ3 where normalized learning gains were found to be consistently better in the $\alpha = \infty$ condition compared to the baseline and were almost consistently better in the personalized condition versus non-personalized.

5.4 Learning Gains per Unit Time

Considered as a single variable, learning gains per unit time spent reading was associated with significant differences across conditions for only two topics at the ($p<.05$) level. To understand this further, we split learning gains ΔL per unit time into two subfactors using the following decomposition:

$$\frac{\Delta L}{Time} = \frac{\Delta L}{Words} \times \frac{Words}{Time} = \frac{\Delta L}{Words} / \frac{Time}{Words}$$

The relationship of these two subfactors is visualized in Figure 3, with $\frac{Time}{Words}$ on the x-axis and $\frac{\Delta L}{Words}$ on the y-axis. As the plot makes evident, there is a positive correlation ($r=.374$, $p<.001$) between these two subfactors. Moreover, while the slope of this approximately linear relationship (which is exactly $\frac{\Delta L}{Time}$, learning per unit time), is relatively stable across conditions – as the initial analysis showed – there are in fact very different tradeoff regimes for user efficiency that lead to similar learning gains per unit time, across the three retrieval conditions. For example, the Web baseline is largely characterized by having the lowest average reading time per word as well as lowest learning gain per word (7/10 topics). In contrast, the personalized α_P condition is characterized by typically having the highest learning gain per 1000 words (8/10 topics).

[10]For simplicity in presenting these findings, we show the means multiplied by 1000 (Learning gains per 1000 words)

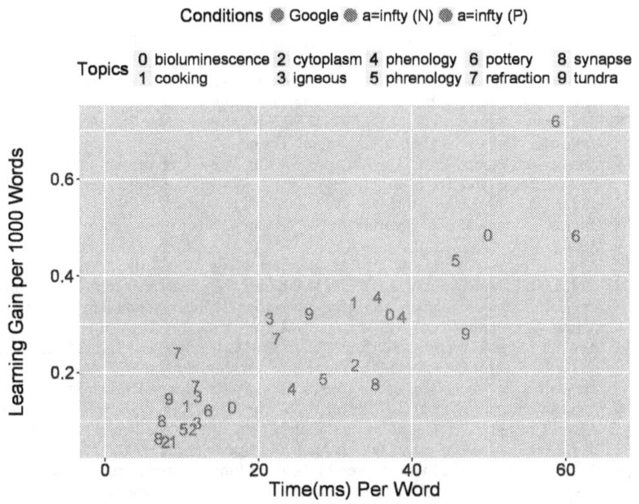

Figure 3: Learning gains per word generally increases with reading time per word. $\alpha = \infty$ (N) is the non-personalized condition and $\alpha = \infty$ (P) is the personalized condition.

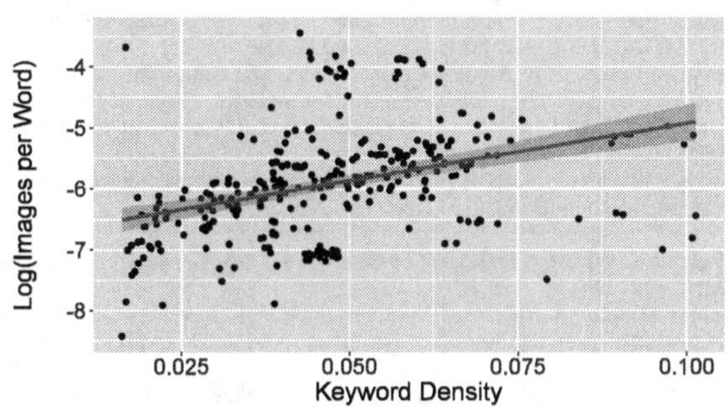

Figure 4: Image coverage increases with keyword density. Each data point represents a unique document set shown to a study participant.

5.5 Image Coverage

To gain more insight into why pages with increased keyword density might contribute to more efficient and effective learning, we investigated additional properties of the page content that might be correlated with keyword density. We found that while few result documents made use of multimedia such as animations, audio or video, some used images to supplement the text. Thus, the *picture superiority effect* [8], in which people tend to remember things better when they see pictures rather than words, could be relevant. We examined whether there was a relationship between image coverage – defined as total images divided by total words – and keyword density. We determined the number of relevant images manually for each page, excluding irrelevant images such as navigation icons and advertisements. We found that pages with higher keyword density did indeed tend to have increased image coverage. On average, participants saw 1.5, 4.8 and 3.9 images per 1000 words, for the Web, α_N, and α_P conditions respectively. Thus, participants in either of the two $\alpha = \infty$ conditions saw almost three times as many images per word as those in the Web commercial search baseline. We observe informally that pages using a higher density of keywords tend to be those that give an overview of topic for instructional purposes, and thus are more likely to be supplemented with images by the author. The keyword density of the document set a participant read did indeed show a linear relationship to the log of the image coverage. Fig. 4 shows a linear correlation between these measures (r=.37, p<.001)[11]. We intend to investigate this phenomenon and other content properties that may interact with learning in future work.

5.6 Operational ranking features

The retrieval process described above uses a multi-stage custom pipeline. Here we investigate whether we can use our findings to generate new ranking features for use in a standard retrieval framework, such as a learning-to-rank algorithm, while giving result sets comparable to the full pipeline. Specifically, we look at approximations to the keyword contribution density ϵ_i (corresponding to document d_i). For example, we can replace the original ϵ_i term with a version that does not require computation of the set of required keyword counts (s_k):

$$\epsilon_i^* = \left(\sum_{k=1}^{|d_i|} r_k \right)^{-1} \sum_{j=1}^{K} C_{R_j} \cdot f(C_{\mathcal{D}_j}, C_{R_j})$$

where C_R is the keyword counts in d_i and $f(C_{\mathcal{D}_j}, C_{R_j})$ is a function that decays the contribution of keyword j in the new document as a function of the new document's coverage of j and the coverage in all previous documents. Here, we propose the decay function

$$f(C_{\mathcal{D}_j}, C_{R_j}) = \left(C_{\mathcal{D}_j} + C_{R_j} \right)^{-\gamma}.$$

This offers an approximation to the full objective in Equation 7 by down-weighting the contribution of keywords the user has likely already seen many times and is thus unlikely to benefit more from. The γ parameter controls how fast the contribution of a given keyword will decay, which is related to the effort penalty λ in the full model[12]. For the personalized condition, the keyword contribution of terms the student already knows is set to zero.

With this approximation, we computed the set overlap (number of elements in the intersection) between equal numbers of documents retrieved using the original ϵ_i score, and the approximate ϵ_i^* score, averaging the overlap across topics (and in the personalization case, all personalized retrieval sets). We found that the approximate ϵ^* approach produced an average set overlap of 71.0% with the non-personalized document sets and a set overlap of 61.8% for the personalized document sets. Setting the decay function to a constant (1) results in a further drop to an average of 45.3% and 43.3% document sets overlap respectively. For comparison, the average set overlap between the Web condition document set and the personalized document set was only 6.4%. This suggests that at least some of the effect of our general approach could be incorporated into standard ranking frameworks using decay-controlled keyword density as an easily-computed feature.

[11] Documents with no images were omitted from the log calculation.

[12] The value $\gamma = 1.5$ yielded the best set overlap with documents produced via Eq. 7 and tested over all topics.

6 DISCUSSION

This study represents a first step in a new research direction in which computational models of human cognition are incorporated directly into the objective functions used to optimize retrieval. In a more general view, in our model the search engine becomes a mechanism for effectively choosing content that will update a user's cognitive state from a prior knowledge state, toward a goal state. Beyond supporting more sophisticated forms of learning, this could also suggest personalized mechanisms for addressing some kinds of algorithmic bias in search results, or helping users with reading disabilities. We made a number of simplifying assumptions that future work could seek to enhance and extend.

Our approach is also suited for applications that could be integrated with existing search engines. For example, query intent detection in search engines could be used to find queries focused on learning, and to trigger use of the keyword density parameter as a ranking feature for those queries. Using the heuristic approximation discussed above, this would be straightforward to accomplish and could yield increased learning benefits for users.

Our empirical results show evidence that most of our research questions were successfully answered by the empirical analysis, with RQ1 and RQ2 being supported and RQ3 being partially supported. However, we also note a few limitations to the current study. First, this study only assesses vocabulary learning, which covers only one level of cognitive complexity per Bloom's taxonomy [12]. More complex objectives and document representations may be able to capture the more subtle cues needed for higher-level learning tasks such as drawing correct analogies, or synthesizing multiple points of evidence. Second, we focused on the text content of pages, filtering out any images, video, or other non-text content. While we did provide an analysis of image coverage, the contribution of video in particular would be interesting to study. Third, our reliance on Wikipedia to mine subtopics limits our topics to those with an adequate Wikipedia entry: exploring methods for finding appropriate subtopics for arbitrary queries is a topic for future work.

7 CONCLUSION

We introduced a novel retrieval framework for optimizing search results for a learning-oriented objective by composing simple computational models of word learning with an intrinsically diverse ranking objective. We ran a crowdsourced user study to assess human learning gains on a vocabulary learning task using this framework, comparing the effectiveness and efficiency of personalized and non-personalized retrieval with a strong commercial search baseline. Across the topics that we tested, our personalized retrieval algorithm did in fact offer statistically significant overall learning gains per word read, for both absolute and realized potential learning scores. We did not extensively tune the parameters used in our models, so further gains may be possible with more exploration of the model and parameter spaces.

Acknowledgements. We thank the anonymous reviewers for their comments. This work was supported in part by the Michigan Institute for Data Science (MIDAS), and by the Institute of Education Sciences, U.S. Department of Education, through Grant R305A140647 to the University of Michigan. The opinions expressed are those of the authors and do not represent views of the Institute or the U.S. Department of Education.

REFERENCES

[1] Peter Bailey, Liwei Chen, Scott Grosenick, Li Jiang, Yan Li, Paul Reinholdtsen, Charles Salada, Haidong Wang, and Sandy Wong. 2012. User task understanding: a web search engine perspective. In *NII Shonan Meeting on Whole-Session Evaluation of Interactive Information Retrieval Systems, Kanagawa, Japan.*

[2] Benjamin S Bloom. 1956. *Taxonomy of educational objectives: The classification of educational goals.* New York, Longmans, Green.

[3] Benjamin S Bloom. 1984. The 2 sigma problem: The search for methods of group instruction as effective as one-to-one tutoring. *Educational Researcher* 13, 6 (1984), 4–16.

[4] Andrei Broder. 2002. A Taxonomy of Web Search. *SIGIR Forum* 36, 2 (Sept. 2002), 3–10.

[5] Kevyn Collins-Thompson, Paul N. Bennett, Ryen W. White, Sebastian de la Chica, and David Sontag. 2011. Personalizing Web Search Results by Reading Level. In *Proceedings of the 20th ACM International Conference on Information and Knowledge Management (CIKM '11).* ACM, New York, NY, USA, 403–412.

[6] Kevyn Collins-Thompson, Soo Young Rieh, Carl C. Haynes, and Rohail Syed. 2016. Assessing Learning Outcomes in Web Search: A Comparison of Tasks and Query Strategies. In *Proceedings of the 2016 ACM on Conference on Human Information Interaction and Retrieval (CHIIR '16).* ACM, New York, NY, USA, 163–172.

[7] Albert Corbett. 2001. Cognitive computer tutors: Solving the two-sigma problem. In *International Conference on User Modeling.* Springer, 137–147.

[8] Antonella De Angeli, Lynne Coventry, Graham Johnson, and Karen Renaud. 2005. Is a picture really worth a thousand words? Exploring the feasibility of graphical authentication systems. *International Journal of Human-Computer Studies* 63, 1 (2005), 128–152.

[9] Sergio Duarte Torres, Djoerd Hiemstra, and Pavel Serdyukov. 2010. An Analysis of Queries Intended to Search Information for Children. In *Proceedings of the Third Symposium on Information Interaction in Context (IIiX '10).* ACM, New York, NY, USA, 235–244.

[10] Carsten Eickhoff, Jaime Teevan, Ryen White, and Susan Dumais. 2014. Lessons from the Journey: A Query Log Analysis of Within-session Learning. In *Proceedings of the 7th ACM International Conference on Web Search and Data Mining (WSDM '14).* ACM, New York, NY, USA, 223–232.

[11] Brian W Junker. 1999. Some statistical models and computational methods that may be useful for cognitively-relevant assessment. *Prepared for the National Research Council Committee on the Foundations of Assessment. Retrieved April* 2 (1999), 81.

[12] David R Krathwohl. 2002. A revision of Bloom's taxonomy: An overview. *Theory into Practice* 41, 4 (2002), 212–218.

[13] Victor Kuperman, Hans Stadthagen-Gonzalez, and Marc Brysbaert. 2012. Age-of-acquisition ratings for 30,000 English words. *Behavior Research Methods* 44, 4 (2012), 978–990.

[14] Tomas Mikolov, Kai Chen, Greg Corrado, and Jeffrey Dean. 2013. Efficient estimation of word representations in vector space. *arXiv preprint arXiv:1301.3781* (2013).

[15] Peter Pirolli and Sanjay Kairam. 2013. A knowledge-tracing model of learning from a social tagging system. *User Modeling and User-Adapted Interaction* 23, 2-3 (2013), 139–168.

[16] Filip Radlinski and Susan Dumais. 2006. Improving Personalized Web Search Using Result Diversification. In *Proceedings of the 29th Annual International ACM SIGIR Conference on Research and Development in Information Retrieval (SIGIR '06).* ACM, New York, NY, USA, 691–692.

[17] Karthik Raman, Paul N Bennett, and Kevyn Collins-Thompson. 2014. Understanding intrinsic diversity in web search: Improving whole-session relevance. *ACM Transactions on Information Systems (TOIS)* 32, 4 (2014), 20.

[18] Daniel E Rose and Danny Levinson. 2004. Understanding User Goals in Web Search. In *Proceedings of the 13th International Conference on World Wide Web (WWW '04).* ACM, New York, NY, USA, 13–19.

[19] Mark D. Smucker and Charles L.A. Clarke. 2012. Time-based Calibration of Effectiveness Measures. In *Proceedings of the 35th International ACM SIGIR Conference on Research and Development in Information Retrieval (SIGIR '12).* ACM, New York, NY, USA, 95–104.

[20] Rohail Syed and Kevyn Collins-Thompson. 2017. Optimizing search results for human learning goals. *Information Retrieval Journal* (2017), 1–18.

[21] Emine Yilmaz, Manisha Verma, Nick Craswell, Filip Radlinski, and Peter Bailey. 2014. Relevance and Effort: An Analysis of Document Utility. In *Proceedings of the 23rd ACM International Conference on Conference on Information and Knowledge Management (CIKM '14).* ACM, New York, NY, USA, 91–100.

[22] Xiaojin Zhu. 2013. Machine teaching for bayesian learners in the exponential family. In *Advances in Neural Information Processing Systems.* 1905–1913.

Content Recommendation for Viral Social Influence

Sergei Ivanov
Skoltech

Konstantinos Theocharidis
University of Peloponnese & IMIS, Athena R.I.C.

Manolis Terrovitis*
IMIS, Athena R.I.C.

Panagiotis Karras
Aalborg University

ABSTRACT

How do we create content that will become viral in a whole network after we share it with friends or followers? Significant research activity has been dedicated to the problem of strategically selecting a *seed set* of initial adopters so as to maximize a meme's spread in a network. This line of work assumes that the success of such a campaign depends solely on the choice of a *tunable* seed set of adopters, while the way users perceive the propagated meme is *fixed*. Yet, in many real-world settings, the opposite holds: a meme's propagation depends on users' perceptions of its *tunable* characteristics, while the set of initiators is *fixed*.

In this paper, we address the natural problem that arises in such circumstances: Suggest content, expressed as a limited set of *attributes*, for a creative promotion campaign that starts out from a given seed set of initiators, so as to maximize its expected spread over a social network. To our knowledge, no previous work addresses this problem. Wefi nd that the problem is NP-hard and inapproximable. As a tight approximation guarantee is not admissible, we design an efficient heuristic, Explore-Update, as well as a conventional Greedy solution. Our experimental evaluation demonstrates that Explore-Update selects near-optimal attribute sets with real data, achieves 30% higher spread than baselines, and runs an order of magnitude faster than the Greedy solution.

ACM Reference format:
Sergei Ivanov, Konstantinos Theocharidis, Manolis Terrovitis[1], and Panagiotis Karras. 2017. Content Recommendation for Viral Social Influence. In *Proceedings of SIGIR '17, August 7–11, 2017, Shinjuku, Tokyo, Japan, ,* 10 pages.
DOI: 10.1145/3077136.3080788

1 INTRODUCTION

Online networking offers opportunities for new types of marketing. A prime example of such a new marketing technique is viral marketing, whereby organizations run promotion campaigns through word-of-mouth effects within online social networks. The *influence maximization* (IM) problem [26], studied intensively during the last decade, aims tofi nd well-chosen *seed nodes* from which to launch such campaigns so as to achieve good results.

Recent works [17, 18] have focused on the parameters that define the popularity of a post, campaign, idea, or *meme* within a network. Such works were thefi rst to study the question of how commercial brand posts engage online social network users, drawing from the theory of Uses & Gratifications [25]; they examine post parameters such as *content type* (e.g., entertaining, informational), *media type* (e.g., vivid, interactive), *posting time* (e.g., workday, peak hours) and *valence of comments* (e.g., positive, negative). Interestingly, such studies have reached some ambivalent conclusions; for instance, [18] ascertains that entertaining content decreases the number of "likes", while [17] claims the exact opposite.

Concurrent research has studied the problem of *viral product design* [3, 6], which calls for engineering products by incorporating viral attributes so as to generate peer-to-peer influence that encourages adoption within a network. Aral and Walker [3] study the question of viral attribute selection under randomized trials only; Barbieri and Bonchi [6] allude to the same problem as a complement to the standard IM problem of selecting a set of seed nodes that maximizes influence, but do not investigate it as a stand-alone problem in its own right. Conceptually, both these works pertain to attributes attached to products; they do not investigate the more general problem of choosing content, out of a set of eligible options, for any kind of *meme* spreading in a network, so as to make it viral.

In this paper, we introduce and study the problem of selecting content that characterizes any type of *meme*, so as to maximize its expected spread through a network, starting out from afi xed set of initial adopters. For instance, an advertisement post may feature aspects such as *topics*, *people*, *locations* and *abstract themes*. We are particularly interested in those content aspects that are associated with specific *online social network pages*; we denote such aspects as **content attributes**. Fittingly, online social network users themselves are associated with such non-personal network pages: they express their preferences for specific brands, topics of interest, public persons, hobbies, or locations by subscribing to or "liking" such pages. Thereby, an attribute's popularity can be gauged via its number of subscribers or page "likes". For our purposes, we denote the pages that a user subscribes to or "likes" as **user attributes**. We contend that, the more content and user attributes overlap, the more likely that user is to propagate that post. We envisage an organization that aims to achieve high viral effect of a campaign initiated from itsfi xed set of subscribers. For example, assume *FlyFast* airways wants to launch a promotion campaign in social media. *FlyFast* already has a social network presence, and its page has a subscribers' set S fixed at a given moment, while it faces constraints related to its budget and people's attention span. In their design, *FlyFast* consultants are interested to identify a set of k content attributes, out of a universe of eligible, mutually compatible options, that will maximize the expected network spread

[1]This author was supported by the IMIS research project KAMε.

SIGIR '17, August 7–11, 2017, Shinjuku, Tokyo, Japan

978-1-4503-5022-8/17/08...$15.00
DOI: 10.1145/3077136.3080788

of a post starting out from its subscribers' set S. Assume that, for $k = 4$, the optimal attribute set is {*"Best travel Accessories", "Airline food guide", "Hipster Europe", "Backpacker tips"*}. Guided by this knowledge, *FlyFast* can infuse its post with complementary content that appeals to users interested in those topics, e.g., promotions to backpackers, references to its hipster audience, and highlights on its food quality. Thereby, it can maximize its promotion's reach.

To our knowledge, we are the first to study the influence maximization problem in which the seed is *given* and post content is *sought*. Our related contributions are as follows:

Problem Setting We motivate the influence maximization problem in settings where the set of initial adopters is fixed, or even a single point of origin, and the content of a propagated meme can be tuned. We formulate the concept of *digital influence* as a special case of social influence.

Propagation Model We devise a *content-aware* propagation model, whereby the probability of influence across edges depends on content. We show that, with this model: (i) the problem of choosing content attributes that maximize influence is NP-hard; (ii) the spread function is not submodular, hence no submodularity-based approximation algorithm applies; and (iii) it is NP-hard to approximate the optimal solution within a factor of $n^{1-\varepsilon}$ for $\varepsilon > 0$.

Algorithm We design a fast algorithm, *Explore-Update*, which achieves higher influence spread than baselines; its effectiveness is based on the iterative estimation of the marginal spread achieved by each attribute, while its efficiency is gained by limiting such computations only to nodes within a probability-based distance threshold θ and attributes potentially affecting such nodes.

Experiments We compare Explore-Update to two baselines and show that it always achieves better propagation results, while it is significantly faster than a naïve Greedy approach; we calculate the optimal solution on a reduced dataset with a small universe of attributes, showing Explore-Update can achieve optimality; last, we demonstrate the scalability of Explore-Update on seed set size.

2 MOTIVATION AND BACKGROUND

We start our discussion drawing from cognitive science and marketing, paving the way for our problem definition.

2.1 Idea Habitats

An *idea habitat* [8] is the set of environmental cues that make people think about an idea and pass it along. Regardless of how well an idea is encoded, it will persist and spread only if the environment cues people to retrieve it regularly. In other words, even if an idea *can* be easily recalled, if it is only rarely cued by the environment, it may remain rare and be forgotten. It follows that, for an idea to spread, it should be not only well encoded and easily recalled, but also regularly retrieved. Promotion campaigns aim to assist the spread of any meme in the same way as idea habitats assist the spread of ideas. For instance, assume that *FlyFast* food is good and therefore memorable. Still, without a viral promotion, *FlyFast* will miss the spotlight, letting other airlines gain public attention.

2.2 Digital Influence

Social influence is defined based on peer behavior [1], so as to distinguish it from confounding factors [2, 19, 21, 29].

Definition 1. ***Social Influence*** *expresses the extent to which the behavior of one's peers changes the utility one expects to receive from engaging in a certain behavior, and hence the likelihood that one will engage in that behavior.*

This definition can be used to make an argument that, if we understand how behaviors spread from person to person, our society will be able to promote agreeable behaviors, such as physical exercise and financial responsibility, and limit disagreeable ones, such as violence and dirty needle sharing. By this definition, peer behaviors may relate to awareness, persuasiveness, imitation and social learning [1]. We propose that *digital influence* can be seen as a case of awareness-related social influence, defined as follows:

Definition 2. ***Digital Influence*** *expresses the extent to which the content of a commercial digital posting changes the support one wants to provide to that posting, and thus the likelihood that one will propagate it.*

In online social networks, posts are propagated from user to user by means of actions such as *like*, *share*, or *repost* [5]. Without loss of generality, we group all these actions under the *like* action. What matters is whether users endorse and promote a post further by making it visible to their friends and followers. In our setting, we emphasize the importance of earning *likes* from users at large.

Nowadays, as online social network users are exposed to a plethora of posts, we can safely assume that they become selective on what they *like*. Therefore, a brand that fails to issue likable posts via its social network pages is unlikely to spread awareness of its activities and products. In the same vein, a brand that can estimate how viral a post will be and create appropriate digital content, stands good chances to succeed. We argue that such estimation can be based on the digital influence of content associated with a meme; this observation brings us to the topic of *influence maximization*.

2.3 Influence Maximization

The classic Influence Maximization (IM) problem, formulated by Kempe et al. [26], has been intensively studied over the last decade. Recently, the focus has shifted to providing realistic definitions to the concept of *influence spread*. Barbieri et al. [7] proposed the *Topic-Aware Influence Cascade* (TIC) and *Topic-Aware Linear Threshold* (TLT) models, which are extensions of the IC and LT models [26].

Classic Influence Maximization. The first solutions to the IM problem were proposed by Domingos and Richardson [20, 31], yet had no guarantees on influence spread. Then, Kempe et al. [26] formulated the problem based on the Independent Cascade and Linear Threshold propagation models, proved its NP-hardness, and proposed a greedy algorithm with a $(1 - 1/e - \epsilon)$ approximation guarantee. Subsequent works investigated efficiency and scalability questions, either with heuristics [13, 14, 16] or preserving an approximation guarantee [9, 15, 22, 27, 32].

Topic-Aware Influence Maximization. Barbieri et al. [7] were the first to look at social influence taking content characteristics into consideration. They proposed methods that learn propagation model parameters such as topic-aware influence strength from a query log of past propagation traces, and verified experimentally that a larger influence spread can be engendered when taking item characteristics into consideration via their Topic-Aware Influence Maximization (TIM) models.

Aslay et al. [4] studied online TIM queries; the incentive for this online scenario is that many independent advertisers wish to instantly detect the k most influential users for advertising purposes; each advertisement contains a different set of keywords and hence induces a new probabilistic graph creating a separate TIM instance; the authors proposed an offline-online solution, INFLEX, based on an index used to identify similarities among a new and log TIM queries; pre-computed solutions for log queries are aggregated online so as to provide an approximate solution for a TIM query.

The online TIM problem is also studied in [10, 12]. Chen et al. [12] studied topic-aware influence results on two real networks and utilized the derived properties to form three preprocessing-based algorithms, of which MIS is the best; its main difference from INFLEX is that, in MIS, pre-computed seed sets are based on each separate topic rather than on a mixture of topics from different log queries. Chen et al. [10] utilized the maximum influence arborescence (MIA) model [13] to achieve high influence spread with a theoretical guarantee. The core idea is to utilize upper- and lower-bounding techniques, so that an exact marginal influence is computed only for the most promising nodes. This work provides the state-of-the-art solution for the online TIM problem [4].

Recently, Li et al. [28] proposed a variation on the online TIM problem, namely the alternative problem of Keyword-Based Targeted Influence Maximization (KB-TIM). By KB-TIM, each user is associated with a weighted vector of preferences for distinct keywords, which stand for topics. This vector can be generated by applying topic modeling techniques [23] on aggregated user social activities, such as posts, likes, etc. An advertisement then achieves an impact determined by its own topic-oriented keywords. The KB-TIM problem aims to maximize an advertisement's impact, expressed in terms of its spread to target users relevant to its keywords. The solution in [28] draws from previous work in [32], with the main difference being that, while in [32] θ users in a sampled Reverse Reachable (RR) set [9] are counted without prejudice, in [28] these sampled users are accounted in terms of exerted advertisement impact; [28] also employs two indexing methods to precompute RR sets for different keywords, so as to obtain RR sets associated with the query keywords on thefl y. Nevertheless, results in [28] are not compared to those in [10].

Our work differs drastically from all aforementioned works: rather than aiming to detect an influential set of users given a post's content attributes, we are interested tofi nd viral content attributes themselves, given a set of initial adopting users, so as to form an influential post. The aforementioned works do not examine what kind of posts would be most promising or powerful given all topics in the network. Besides, the topic-aware approach is based on general topical terms, like music, soccer, cars, etc., ignoring the high variation among different specimens within such terms. In contrast, we search for specific attributes that can form posts successful in terms of influence spread.

Influence Maximization with VPD. Aral and Walker [3] investigated the problem of viral product design under randomized trials focusing on product features like personalized referrals and broadcast notifications. Thereafter, Barbieri and Bonchi [6] studied the problem of influence maximization *in conjunction with* that of viral product design, aiming to detect a combination of seed nodes and product attributes that maximize influence in a network. The proposed solutions are generic methods named *Local Update* and *Genetic Update*; the former is a greedy algorithm allowing for both addition and removal of attributes at each greedy iteration; the latter is a brute-force method that randomly selects a subset of all attributes. By contrast, we investigate the problem of content selection for a post (not a product) as a stand-alone problem in its own right and study its distinctive characteristics.

2.4 Distinctiveness

We emphasize three distinct elements of this work.

Problem Formulation While our model takes into consideration the influence with regard to a post exercised by users themselves, we seek to maximize the influence exercised by the appeal and quality of a post's content within a network. To the best of our knowledge, we are thefi rst to define this problem, which is distinct from, and cannot be treated by methods aiming at, user selection.

Nature of Attributes In related works, attributes are configured as *general topics*; for example, Barbieri and Bonchi [6] assign *tags*, conceived of as general topics, to the role of product attributes. By contrast, in our problem formulation and in our experimental study, an attribute corresponds to a topic of interest *identifiable via a non-personal social network page.* Thus, even a page on an abstract theme (e.g., *Psychology of Relations*) is a possible attribute in our setting: it has a specific commercial value (4,719,837 followers) that differentiates it from other pages on similar topics.

Use of Tags The type of content attributes we investigate can hardly be articulated via tagging. Tags express highly idiosyncratic user impressions, focusing on arbitrary aspects of content; they are volatile as descriptors of content, whereas we need a stable ground truth to represent content. For example, a video post may relate to several specific topics of interest, yet it would be hard to identify these via user tagging. In consequence, past tagging does not offer valuable information in our problem setting.

3 PROBLEM STATEMENT

From the preceding discussion, we conclude that any brand would gain by maximizing the expected effectiveness of its product promotion campaigns within an online social network. We assume that there exists a certain set of *subscribers* to the brand's social network page, and a promotion campaign aims to influence the maximum number of *non-subscribers*; as we discussed, such users are associated with topics expressing their interests.

3.1 Content-Aware Cascade Model

We model an online social network as a directed graph $G = (V, E)$, where $V = \{v_1, v_2, ..., v_n\}$ is a set of nodes, each of which corresponds to an individual user, and $E \subset V \times V$ is a set of directed edges representing social relations among users. Each node v has a set of associated attributes $F_v = \{f_v^1, f_v^2, \ldots\}$, from a universe Φ, that define user preferences; we identify these attributes as the non-personal network pages a user expresses interest in. A meme propagated through the network is associated with a set of attributes $F = \{f_{p_1}, f_{p_2}, \ldots, f_{p_K}\} \subseteq \Phi$; these content attributes, along with the user attributes F_v associated with the targeted node v, affect the probability of its propagation across a network edge e_{uv}.

Accordingly, we define the *Content-Aware Cascade* model (CAC) as a variant of the Independent Cascade model (IC), in which edge propagation probabilities depend on content and user attributes. A CAC diffusion process unfolds in steps, starting from an initial seed set of activated nodes. A node u activated at time step t has a single chance to activate its out-neighbors. The process is incremental, as nodes can alternate only from inactive to active states; the diffusion ends when there is no newly activated node at a given step. At any step, a newly activated node u activates its out-neighbor v with probability $p(u, v)$ equal to:

$$\begin{aligned} p_{uv} &= b_{uv} + q_{uv} \cdot h_{uv}(F_v, F), \quad b_{uv}, q_{uv} \in [0, 1] \\ h_{uv}(F_v, F) &= \min \left\{ \frac{1-b_{uv}}{q_{uv}}, |F_v \cap F| \right\} \end{aligned} \tag{1}$$

where b_{uv} is a *base probability* on an edge and q_{uv} a *marginal probability* that indicates how much the probability on an edge increases for each selected attribute in F matching a preference of node v, as indicated by the transition function $h_{uv}(F_v, F)$, with a sanity bound of $\frac{1-b_{uv}}{q_{uv}}$. We emphasize that the marginal probability q_{uv} distinguishes among different user links, albeit not among different attributes for a given link; a more complex model could distinguish among different attributes, or even define a probability distribution function over the set of all attributes [7], to be learned by historical logs. We choose to relegate the problem of defining and learning such probability distribution functions to future work, and now study the problem under the modeling assumption that each attribute has the same independent effect on the probability function. Nevertheless, our simplified model forms a special case of any more complex model in which each attribute would have a different effect on the probability function; i.e., in this special case, such effects are rendered equal. Therefore, our subsequent hardness and inapproximability results hold for any such more complex model as well. Furthermore, parameters q_{uv} and b_{uv} can be obtained from past data, as in [7]; in our setting, we assume that such parameters have been obtained in advance.

Given a seed set S of subscribers, for every set of attributes F, we can obtain the total number of activated nodes after running several trials of the diffusion process from S [26]. The *expected* number of activated nodes for a given seed set S and a selected set of attributes F is called *influence spread*, denoted as $\sigma(F|S)$, or, as S isfi xed in our problem, just $\sigma(F)$. Thus, $\sigma(F)$ is the *expected* spread of the diffusion, which we can calculate using live-edge instances of the graph (i.e., instances of activated-only edges [26]) as:

$$\sigma(F) = \sum_{X} Prob[X] \cdot \sigma_X(F) \tag{2}$$

where $\sigma_X(F)$ is the influence spread in live-edge instance X.

3.2 Content-Aware Influence Maximization

We define the CAIM problem as follows:

PROBLEM1. *Given a directed graph $G = (V, E)$, where each node v is associated with user attributes $F_v = \{f_v^1, f_v^2, \ldots\}$ from a universe of eligible attributes Φ, a seed set of adopter nodes S, quantities q_{uv}, b_{uv} for each edge $e_{uv} \in E$, and a transition function $h_{uv}(F_v, F) = \min \left\{ \frac{1-b_{uv}}{q_{uv}}, |F_v \cap F| \right\}$ for edge probabilities, select a set of k attributes $F \subset \Phi$ that maximizes the spread $\sigma(F|S)$ of a diffusion process with content attributes F starting from S.*

CAIM is a novel problem that aims tofi nd out how one can maximize the benefits of a network promotion campaign with given points of departure. The motivation derives from the fact that, in the real world, brands want to exploit their own social network pages for marketing purposes. Instead of targeting the most influential initiators for a promotion, as in classical IM, one can judiciously invest in the creation of a post with lucrative content, underfi xed initiators, guided by the content attributes provided by the CAIM solution. As promotions can be formed with a wide variety of content attributes, each possible attribute set F corresponds to a different probabilistic graph, on which we can compute the influence spread of the seed set S; the attribute set F that achieves maximum spread constitutes the CAIM solution. We emphasize that, due to the drastic difference between classical IM and CAIM in the way influence spread is achieved, *the solutions to these two problems cannot be qualitatively compared against each other.*

4 HARDNESS AND INAPPROXIMABILITY

We now show the hardness of the CAIM problem and study the properties of influence spread function $\sigma(F)$. To calculate $\sigma(F)$, we first calculate edge probabilities with respect to the selected content attributes F and then estimate the expected spread on the graph starting from the given set of subscribed nodes S.

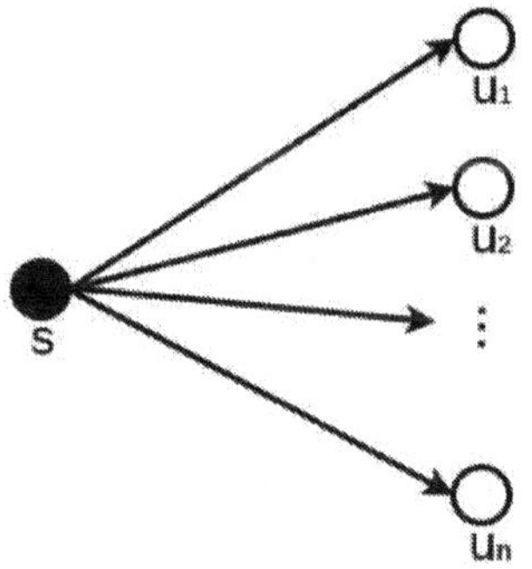

Figure 1: A graph instance demonstrating that the CAIM problem is NP-hard.

THEOREM4.1. *The CAIM problem with the Content-Aware Cascade model is NP-hard.*

PROOF. Consider an instance of the NP-complete SETC OVER problem, defined by a collection of subsets $S_1, S_2, \ldots, S_m$, a universe of elements $U = \{u_1, u_2, \ldots, u_n\}$ and an integer k. We are asked whether there are k sets that will cover all elements in U. We show that SETC OVER can be reduced to a *trivial* instance of CAIM as follows: We construct a bipartite graph with one activated node on the left side that connects to n nodes on the right side, as shown in Figure 1. We map each member u_i of universe U to a node on the right side and add an attribute f_j to set F_{u_i} if u_i belongs to subset S_j. We set $b_{uv} = 0$ and $q_{uv} = 1$ for all edges $(u, v) \in E$, i.e., a node v is influenced if at least one of its user attributes is selected. In this trivialized version of CAIM, the spread can be computed deterministically; there is no need for expected spread computations. Then, an algorithm that could optimally solve this trivial instance of CAIM, among others, would decide any instance of SETC OVER: if we can target all nodes in the CAIM instance using k attributes, we can in effect cover all elements in U using k subsets in SetCover. Otherwise, if the optimal spread in CAIM does not reach all nodes, it follows that there is no set of k subsets that covers all elements in SetCover. Thus, by reduction from Set Cover, CAIM is at least as hard as any problem in NP. □

By Theorem 4.1, there is no polynomial-time algorithm tofind an optimal set of attributes F, unless P=NP. We now proceed to study the properties of the influence spread function $\sigma(F)$.

A function $\sigma(F)$ is *submodular* if it follows a *diminishing returns* rule: the marginal gain from adding an element to a set F is at most as high as the marginal gain from adding the same element to a subset of F. That is, $\sigma(F_1 \cup \{f\}) - \sigma(F_1) \geq \sigma(F_2 \cup \{f\}) - \sigma(F_2)$, where $F_1 \subset F_2 \subset \Phi$, for any $f \in \Phi$.

We call a transition function $h_{uv}(F_v, F)$ *monotonic* on F if, for subsets of attributes $F_1 \subset F_2 \subset \Phi$, it holds that $h_{uv}(F_v, F_1) \leq h_{uv}(F_v, F_2)$, for any node v. If the transition function is not monotonic, then the influence spread function is neither monotonic, nor submodular, because selecting more attributes may reduce probabilities $p(u, v)$ and thereby reduce the total influence spread. We assume that attributes have nonnegative effects on users, rendering the transition function $h_{uv}(\cdot)$ monotonic: edge probabilities can only increase if we add attributes to F, i.e. $h_{uv}(F_v, F) \leq h_{uv}(F_v, F+\{f\})$ for any $f \in \Phi$ and $v \in G$; hence $\sigma(F)$ is monotonic. We now examine whether $\sigma(F)$ is also submodular. This turns out to not be the case, even for a monotonic and submodular transition function, as the following counterexample demonstrates.

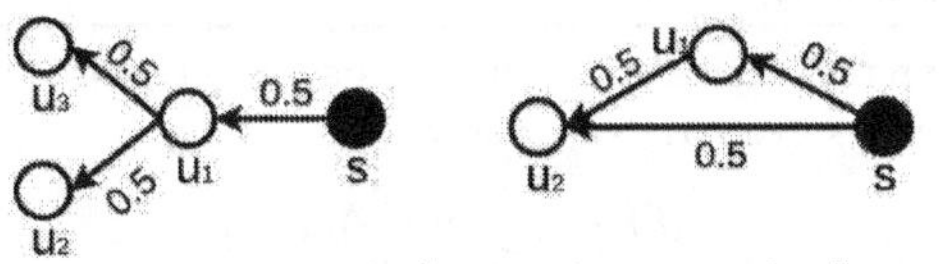

Figure 2: Increasing & decreasing marginal returns

Example 4.2. Consider the graph on the left-hand side in Figure 2, with a universe of attributes $\Phi = \{A, B, C\}$, sets of preferred attributes for each node be $F_{v_1} = \{A\}$ and $F_{v_2} = F_{v_3} = \{A, B, C\}$, $b_{uv} = 0.5$, $q_{uv} = \frac{1}{2|F_v|}$ on all edges, and one active node s. Then, consider two subsets of attributes $F_1 = \emptyset$, $F_2 = \{B, C\}$, where $F_1 \subset F_2$, and a attribute $f = A \in \Phi \setminus F_2$. The achieved spreads for each attributes subset, and the respective marginal gains obtained after adding attribute f to subsets F_1 and F_2, are calculated as follows. For subset attribute F_1 selected, we have:

$$p_{sv_1} = \tfrac{1}{2}, \quad p_{v_1v_2} = p_{v_1v_3} = \tfrac{1}{2}$$
$$\sigma(F_1) = \tfrac{1}{2} + 2\tfrac{1}{4} = 1$$

whereas when $f = A$ is added to F_1, we get:

$$p_{sv_1} = 1, \quad p_{v_1v_2} = p_{v_1v_3} = \tfrac{2}{3}$$
$$\sigma(F_1 + \{A\}) = 1 + 2 \cdot \tfrac{2}{3} = \tfrac{7}{3}$$

Hence $\Delta_1 = \sigma(F_1 + \{A\}) - \sigma(F_1) = \frac{7}{3} - 1 = \frac{4}{3}$. Similarly, for F_2 selected, we have:

$$p_{sv_1} = \tfrac{1}{2}, \quad p_{v_1v_2} = p_{v_1v_3} = \tfrac{5}{6}$$
$$\sigma(F_2) = \tfrac{1}{2} + 2 \cdot \tfrac{5}{12} = \tfrac{4}{3}$$

while when $f = A$ is added to F_2, we get:

$$p_{sv_1} = 1, \quad p_{v_1v_2} = p_{v_1v_3} = 1$$
$$\sigma(F_2 + \{A\}) = 3$$

Hence $\Delta_2 = \sigma(F_2 + \{A\}) - \sigma(F_2) = 3 - \frac{4}{3} = \frac{5}{3}$. Since $\Delta_2 > \Delta_1$, the submodularity of $\sigma(F)$ does not hold.

Given this negative result, the influence function $\sigma(F)$ might have an *increasing returns* property (supermodularity), whereby it would hold that $\sigma(F_1 \cup \{f\}) - \sigma(F_1) \leq \sigma(F_2 \cup \{f\}) - \sigma(F_2)$, for $F_1 \subset F_2 \subset \Phi$ and any attribute $f \in \Phi$. The following counterexample shows that this property does not hold either.

Example 4.3. Consider the graph on the right-hand side in Figure 2, with a universe of attributes $\Phi = \{A, B\}$, sets of preferred attributes per node $F_{v_1} = \{A, B\}$ and $F_{v_2} = \{A\}$, $b_{uv} = 0.5$ and $q_{uv} = \frac{1}{2|F_v|}$ on all edges, and one active node s. Consider two subsets of attributes $F_1 = \emptyset$ and $F_2 = \{B\}$. Then, for subset attribute F_1 selected, we have:

$$p_{sv_1} = \tfrac{1}{2}, \quad p_{sv_2} = p_{v_1v_2} = \tfrac{1}{2}$$
$$\sigma(F_1) = \tfrac{1}{2} + \left(1 - \left(1 - \tfrac{1}{4}\right)\tfrac{1}{2}\right) = \tfrac{9}{8}$$

whereas when $f = A$ is added to F_1 we get:

$$p_{sv_1} = \tfrac{3}{4}, \quad p_{sv_2} = p_{v_1v_2} = 1$$
$$\sigma(F_1 + \{A\}) = \tfrac{3}{4} + 1 = \tfrac{7}{4}$$

Hence $\Delta_1 = \sigma(F_1 + \{A\}) - \sigma(F_1) = \frac{7}{4} - \frac{9}{8} = \frac{5}{8}$. Similarly, for F_2 selected, we have:

$$p_{sv_1} = \tfrac{3}{4}, \quad p_{sv_2} = p_{v_1v_2} = \tfrac{1}{2}$$
$$\sigma(F_2) = \tfrac{3}{4} + \left(1 - \left(1 - \tfrac{3}{8}\right)\tfrac{1}{2}\right) = \tfrac{23}{16}$$

while when $f = A$ is added to F_2 we get:

$$p_{s,v_1} = 1, \quad p_{v_1v_2} = p_{v_1v_2} = 1$$
$$\sigma(F_2 + \{A\}) = 2$$

Hence $\Delta_2 = \sigma(F_2 + \{A\}) - \sigma(F_2) = 2 - \frac{23}{16} = \frac{9}{16}$. Since $\Delta_1 > \Delta_2$, the influence function $\sigma(F)$ is not supermodular either.

Eventually, we have established the following:

Theorem4.4. *The spread function $\sigma(F)$ with a probability transition function $h_{uv}(F_v, F) = \min\left\{\frac{1-b_{uv}}{q_{uv}}, |F_v \cap F|\right\}$ is neither submodular nor supermodular.*

By Theorem 4.4, it follows that we cannot use a greedy algorithm with an approximation guarantee based on submodularity, as in [26]. Moreover, in the following we show that it is NP-hard to approximate the optimal solution to CAIM.

Theorem4.5. *It is NP-hard to approximate the optimal solution to the CAIM problem with the Content-Aware Cascade model within a factor $n^{1-\varepsilon}$ for any $\varepsilon > 0$.*

Proof. Consider an instance of the SetCover problem, in which we need to decide whether we can cover all elements of a universe $U = \{u_1, u_2, \ldots, u_n\}$ by selecting at most k subsets out of a collection of $S_1, S_2, \ldots, S_m \subset U$.

We then construct a graph G for the CAIM problem with a single subscriber node s and nodes $u_1, u_2, \ldots, u_n$ corresponding to elements in U, connected so that u_{i-1} points towards u_i for all $i = 2 \ldots n$, and s is connected to u_1, and, for every subset S_j an element u_i belongs to, we add a attribute f_j to the preferred attributes of u_i. Next, for some integer c we add $\eta = n^c - n - 1$ more nodes $x_1, x_2, \ldots, x_\eta$ such that u_n has outgoing edges to them and each x_i has the same preferred attributes as u_n. Graph G, shown in Figure 3, has $N = n^c$ nodes. We set $b_{uv} = 0$ and $q_{uv} = 1$ for all edges, so that an edge becomes active if at least one of the attributes associated with its target node is selected. Then, if it is possible to select k subsets that cover all elements of universe U, we can also have $N = n^c$ activated nodes. Conversely, if there is no selection of k subsets that covers all U, then there is at least one node u_i that does not get activated, precluding influence spread to nodes $x_1, x_2, \ldots, x_\eta$. We can then only target at most n out of n^c nodes, a fraction of $n^{1-c} = N^{\frac{1}{c}-1}$. Thus, if we had a polynomial-time algorithm that approximated the optimal solution to CAIM within a factor of $N^{1-\varepsilon}$ for any $\varepsilon > 0$, then it would suffice to set $c = \left\lceil \frac{1}{\varepsilon} \right\rceil$ and use that algorithm so as to decisively distinguish between a case that accepts a solution activating all N nodes and one that does not, and thereby also decide SetCover. Thus, by reduction from SetCover, we have shown that it is NP-hard to approximate the optimal solution to CAIM within a reasonable factor. □

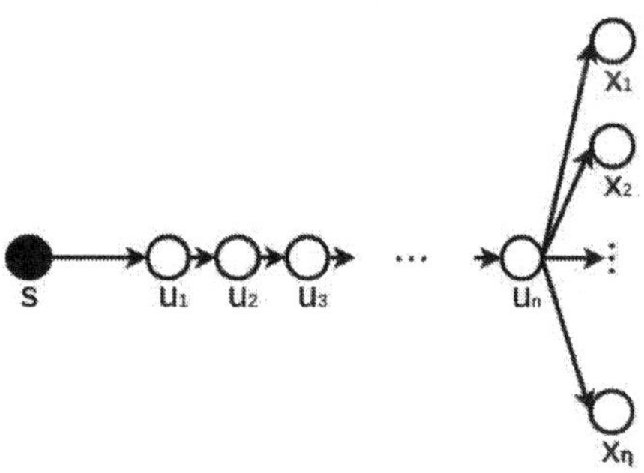

Figure 3: A graph instance demonstrating that it is NP-hard to approximate the optimal solution to the CAIM problem.

5 THE EXPLORE-UPDATE ALGORITHM

As it is NP-hard to approximate the CAIM solution within a factor of $n^{1-\varepsilon}$ with the Content-Aware Cascade model, we proceed to design heuristic solutions therefor. We structure our exposition as follows: we first present a simple, yet time-consuming greedy heuristic; then, through a sequence of simplifying assumptions, we will generate a much more efficient algorithm called Explore-Update.

Algorithm 1: Greedy(G, S, k)

```
F = ∅;
while |F| < k do
    for every f ∈ Φ \ F do
        calculate σ(F + {f}) using Monte Carlo simulations
    F = F ∪ argmax_f {σ(F + {f})}
return F
```

Our first proposal is a baseline greedy algorithm that selects the attribute of highest marginal gain to add at each iteration, shown in Algorithm 1. This is an adaptation of the *Local Update* algorithm in [6] to our problem. Intuitively, it is reasonable to greedily select the locally best attribute in each iteration, especially for small values of k. This kind of algorithm has been shown to achieve better quality than others in classical Influence Maximization [11, 13, 27].

Though simple and effective, Algorithm 1 is inefficient due to its calculation of influence spread by MC simulations. In a manner reminiscent of [13], we can improve efficiency by considering *maximum influence paths* between nodes and the seed set. We call a path $P_{max} = \langle u = u_0, u_1, u_2, \ldots, v = u_m \rangle$ between vertices $u \in S$ and $v \in G$ *maximum influence path* (MIP) if this path is the most probable among all paths between u and v: $P_{max} = \text{argmax}_P \prod_{i=0}^{m-1} prob(u_i, u_{i+1})$. Under the *simplifying assumption* that influence is propagated only through MIPs, we can estimate influence spread in polynomial time as follows: For a threshold θ and a node v, we build a tree structure called *in-arborescence* $A_{in}(v)$, which includes all MIPs of probability higher than θ from any node to v: $A_{in}(v) = \{\mathsf{MIP}(u,v) \mid prob(\mathsf{MIP}(u,v)) > \theta, u \in G\}$. Then, given a node u, the seed set S, and an arborescence $A_{in}(v)$, Algorithm 2 recursively estimates the probability that u is activated in $A_{in}(v)$, i.e., its *activation probability* $ap(u, A_{in}(v))$.

Algorithm 2: calculateAP(u, $A_{in}(v)$, S)

```
if u ∈ S then
    ap(u, A_in(v)) = 1
else if u has no in-neighbors in A_in(v) then
    ap(u, A_in(v)) = 0
else
    ap(u, A_in(v)) = 1 − ∏_{ω∈N_in(u)} (1 − ap(ω, A_in(v)) prob(ω, u))
return ap(u, A_in(v))
```

Based on these calculations, for all nodes $u \in G$, we can calculate the influence spread $\sigma(F)$ as follows:

$$\sigma(F) = \sum_{u \in G} ap(u, A_{in}(u)) \tag{3}$$

We can then employ Equation (3) so as to estimate influence spread in Algorithm 1, in lieu of MC simulations, deriving Algorithm 3; at each iteration, we compute the in-arborescence of node u for a given threshold θ by converting each probability p_e on an edge e to $-\log p_e$ and employing an efficient implementation of Dijkstra's algorithm. If computing an arborescence takes time t, then Lines 4-6 take nt and the total time is $O(k|\Phi|nt)$.

Algorithm 3: Arb(G, S, θ, k)

```
1 F = ∅;
2 while |F| < k do
3     for every f ∈ Φ \ F do
4         for every u ∈ G do
5             compute A_in(u) with threshold θ
6             ap(u, A_in(u)) = calculateAP(u, A_in(u), S)
7         calculate σ(F + f) = Σ_{u∈G} ap(u, A_in(u))
8     F = F ∪ argmax_f {σ(F + {f})}
9 return F
```

We further reduce the runtime of Algorithm 3 by eschewing redundant iterations of the loops over nodes u and attributes f. First, we limit the calculation of in-arborescences and activation probabilities only to nodes whose in-arborescence under threshold θ reaches at least one node in S; only such nodes can yield non-zero estimated activation probability. To find out these nodes, we compute the out-arborescence of all nodes in S, $A_{out}(S)$, consisting of all MIPs of probability higher than θ from a node $v \in S$ to other nodes in G. Nodes in $A_{out}(S)$ yield non-zero activation probability estimates. Yet the set of paths in $A_{out}(S)$ may contain directed loops, hence we cannot apply a recursive algorithm like Algorithm 2 directly on $A_{out}(S)$; we still need to obtain the in-arborescence $A_{in}(u)$ of each $u \in A_{out}(S)$; we do so while building $A_{out}(S)$, by adding $\mathsf{MIP}(v, u)$ to $A_{in}(u)$ for each $u \in A_{out}(v)$. Algorithm 4 illustrates this Explore process.

Algorithm 4: Explore(G, F, S, θ)

```
A_out(S) = ∅
A_in(u) = ∅ for every u in G
for every v ∈ S do
  | compute A_out(v) for given θ and F
  | update A_in(u) for each u ∈ A_out(v)
return {A_in(u) ≠ ∅| for u ∈ G}
```

Then we can calculate influence spread $\sigma(F)$ using the union of such in-arborescences, A_{in}, by Algorithm 5.

Algorithm 5: Update(A_{in}, S)

```
for every u ∈ A_in do
  | ap(u) = CalculateAP(u, A_in(u), S)
σ(F) = Σ_{u∈A_in} ap(u)
return σ(F)
```

Second, we limit the calculation of marginal gain in Algorithm 3 only to those attributes that can affect the influence spread. We call an edge in G *participating*, if at least one of its endpoints are in $A_{out}(S)$. Figure 4 presents a graph for a seed set S (and selected attributes set F) in the green area; the yellow area includes nodes in $A_{out}(S)$; the set of participating edges Π is shown in solid and dotted lines; dotted edges have only one endpoint in $A_{out}(S)$; non-participating edges are shown in dashed lines, in the gray area.

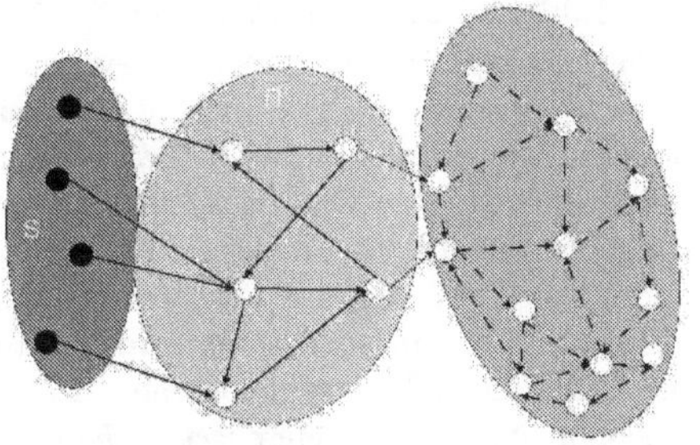

Figure 4: Participating and non-participating edges

Non-participating edges cannot increase influence spread, regardless whether their probability is increased; only participating edges have such potential. We limit the attributes Algorithm 3 considers based on this observation. Let $E(f)$ be the set of edges that include attribute f among their preferred attributes, hence their probability is affected when adding f to F. Then, at any iteration, if *none* of the edges in $E(f)$ is a participating edge, i.e., $E(f) \cap \Pi = \emptyset$, then attribute f need not be examined as a candidate to be added to F; it bears no effect to influence function $\sigma(F + \{f\})$.

Putting together our enhancements to Algorithm 3, we design the polynomial-time Explore-Update algorithm (Algorithm 6). In a nutshell, at each iteration, this Explore-Update algorithm selects the hitherto unselected attribute f affecting participating edges that brings about the largest increase of influence spread, using the Explore procedure for calculating in-arborescences and the Update procedure for calculating influence spread, while updating the set of participating edges Π at each iteration and using it to determine which attributes need to be examined at the next iteration.

Algorithm 6: Explore-Update(G, S, k, θ)

```
F = ∅
A_in = Explore(G, F, S, θ)
Π = {(u, v) ∈ G|u ∈ A_in or v ∈ A_in}
while |F| < k do
  | for f ∈ Φ \ F do
  |   | if E(f) ∩ Π ≠ ∅ then
  |   |   | A_in = Explore(G, F + {f}, S, θ)
  |   |   | Π_f = {(u, v) ∈ G|u ∈ A_in or v ∈ A_in}
  |   |   | σ(F + {f}) = Update(A_in, S)
  | f_max = argmax_f {σ(F + {f})}
  | F = F ∪ f_max
  | Π = Π_{f_max}
return F
```

Let the time complexity to calculate an out-arborescence for node in S be $t_{out\theta}$, then the Explore procedure takes $|S|t_{out\theta}$ and the Update procedure takes $O(n_{in\theta}n_{out\theta})$ time, where $n_{in\theta}$ is the number of nodes in in-arborescences, and $n_{out\theta}$ is the number of nodes in out-arborescence of S. Therefore, if we perform κ calculations of A_{in} per iteration, the total runtime is $O(k\kappa(|S|t_{out\theta} + n_{in\theta}n_{out\theta}))$. In effect, the Explore-Update algorithm is expected to perform well when the size of arborescences is small, and the number of updates κ per iteration is smaller than $|\Phi|$. As propagation probabilities on edges are usually small in real networks, the size of arborescences is indeed expected to be small. The number of updates depends on the structure of the network. In a large-diameter network where multiple hops are required to reach most nodes from S via a MIP, there is a good chance to reduce the number of computations significantly. We investigate this matter experimentally in the following.

6 EXPERIMENTAL STUDY

In this section we present a comprehensive experimental study on the Greedy and Explore-Update algorithms we have introduced. All experiments were run on a 32GB Intel Core i5-2450M CPU machine @ 2.50GHz, while algorithms were implemented[2] in C++.

As there is no previous work on the CAIM problem, we compare to basic baselines. Still, as we discussed, the previous work that comes closest to our problem is that by Barbieri and Bonchi [6]; yet that work solves primarily the problem of selecting a set of seed nodes, and secondarily a set of product attributes, so as to maximize product influence in a network. The best-performing algorithm for updating an attribute set in [6], *Local Update*, performs one addition or removal of an attribute to/from the current attribute set at each iteration; in effect, our Greedy algorithm can be considered as an adaptation of *Local Update* to our problem, where only additions of attributes are needed. Therefore, to the extent that a comparison to [6] is possible, *we conduct it via the comparison to the Greedy algorithm itself.* Another method for updating an attribute set proposed in [6], *Generic Update*, is a hard-to-tune genetic algorithm, which may lead to an unpredictable number of output attributes. Besides, as the experimental study in [6] shows, *Genetic Update* offers no qualitative advantage while it is much slower than *Local Update*, which is already by far the most time-consuming algorithm in our study. Therefore, we do not consider a genetic algorithm in our experimental study.

[2]Documentation and code is available at https://github.com/nd7141/Explore-Update

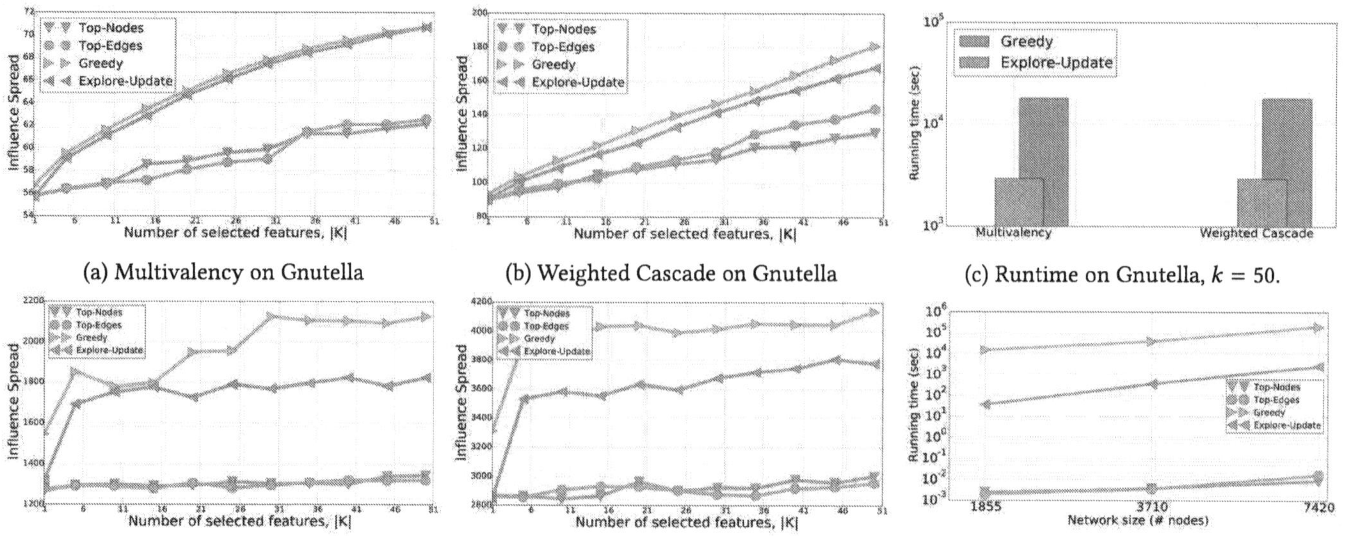

(a) Multivalency on Gnutella (b) Weighted Cascade on Gnutella (c) Runtime on Gnutella, $k = 50$.

(d) Multivalency on VK (e) Weighted Cascade on VK (f) Runtime on VK with Multivalency, $k = 20$.

Figure 5: Influence spread and runtime results.

Diffusion models. In the Content-Aware Cascade model the probability on edge (u, v) is a linear function of product and base probabilities q_{uv} and b_{uv}. To assign these probabilities we use two techniques prevalent in previous work [13].

- Weighted Cascade model: probability $\frac{1}{d_v}$ is assigned to edge (u, v), where d_v is the in-degree of node v. We use this model for the sake of compatibility with previous works, even while it may fit less to our problem setting.
- Multivalency model: the probability for edge (u, v) is drawn uniformly at random from a set of probabilities. We choose that set to be $[0.02, 0.04, 0.08]$.

We calculate b_{uv} for every edge (u, v), and set $q_{uv} = \frac{b_{uv}}{|F_v|}$.

Algorithms. We compare the Explore-Update algorithm under different threshold θ values to three other algorithms:

- **Greedy** This is Algorithm 1 in this paper, which is effectively an adaptation of *Local Update*, the best algorithm in [6]. A similar algorithm has been used extensively in the context of the Influence Maximization problem, and always demonstrated top performance in terms of spread, while being slower than other heuristics [11]; it requires specifying the number of Monte-Carlo simulations to calculate influence spread, as we do in the following.
- **Top-Nodes** This algorithm measures each attribute's frequency among node preferences and selects the k most frequent ones.
- **Top-Edges** This algorithm assigns to each edge $e = (u, v)$ the attribute preferences of node v, F_v, and select the k most frequent attributes across all edges.
- **Brute-Force** This algorithm finds all possible sets of attributes of size k, computes each one's influence spread using Monte-Carlo simulations, and opts for the best. Because the solution space is exponential, we use this method on reduced datasets.

Dataset	Gnutella	VK
Nodes	10,876	7,420
Edges	39,994	57,638
Average Clustering Coefficient	0.0062	0.28
Number of Triangles	934	168,284
Diameter	9	16
Attributes/Seed sets	151	3,882
Default Seed Size	34	15

Table 1: Data characteristics

Datasets. We run experiments in two real-world networks. The first network is a peer-to-peer file sharing directed network Gnutella[3], where nodes represent hosts and edges represent connections between the Gnutella hosts. Our second network is extracted by crawling the social network VK[4]; nodes are users and edges are friendships among them. Statistics are presented in Table 1.

Attribute assignment and seed selection. We utilize one general and one ad-hoc method for attribute preference assignment. In Gnutella, to assign an attribute preferences set F_v to node v, we find the block partitioning that minimizes the description length of the network by stochastic blockmodel ensemble; this technique is used to discover the block structure of empirical networks and results to block memberships for each node [24, 30]. We allow nodes to have overlapping memberships to different blocks. Each block β_i is associated with a distinct attribute f_i. The attribute preference set of a node v_j, F_{v_j} is the set of attributes of the blocks v_j belongs to. The returned partitioning consists of 151 blocks; the default seed set S is one of the blocks, of size 34. For VK, the data comes along with annotations of *groups* and *pages*, which allow us to derive both node attributes and seed sets. A *group* or *page* is a community of users that share content with each other and communicate about a topic of interest (e.g., football clubs or TV series). We use these group memberships to derive both node attributes and seed sets, consistently to our motivation. There are 3882 such groups; the default seed size is 15. Unless otherwise indicated, in our experiments we use the default seeds.

[3] https://snap.stanford.edu/data/p2p-Gnutella04.html
[4] https://vk.com/

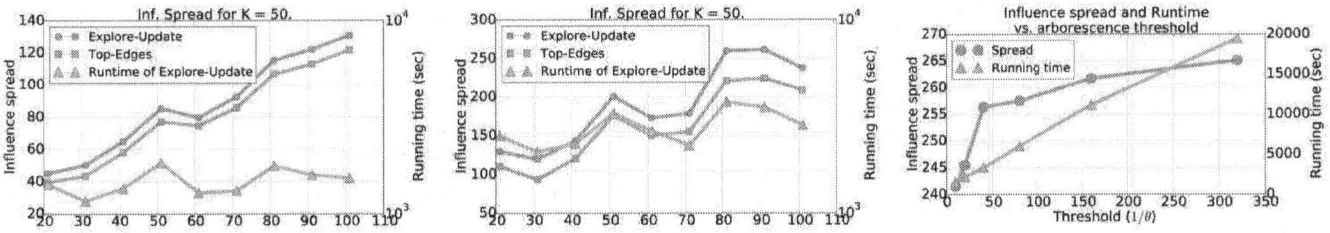

(a) vs. seed set size, MV (b) vs. seed set size, WC (c) vs. θ

Figure 6: Influence and runtime vs. seed set size and θ on Gnutella.

6.1 Influence spread

Figures 5(a-b) present our results on competing algorithms' influence spread[5] on the Gnutella network, varying number of selected attributes k from 1 to 51. We used 10000 MC simulations for Greedy, and $\theta = 1/320$ for Explore-Update. We observe that Explore-Update arrives just 1% and 5% below the performance of Greedy with the Multivalency and Weighted Cascade model, respectively. On the other hand, the Top-Edges and Top-Nodes algorithms reach only 88% and 85% of the spread of Explore-Update. Figures 5(d-e) present influence spread in VK network. Now Greedy used with just 500 Monte-Carlo simulations comfortably achieves 15%, 37%, and 48% higher spread than Explore-Update with $\theta = 1/40$, Top-Nodes, and Top-Edges, respectively, in MV model. The picture is similar with the WC model, where Greedy achieves spread 9%, 38%, 40% higher than Explore-Update, Top-Nodes, and Top-Edges. Overall, our results confirm that Explore-Update achieves high influence spread for networks where the local neighborhood of the seed set has structure amenable to long distance arborescences.

6.2 Runtime

We now compare algorithms in terms of runtime. Figure 5(c) presents the results with Gnutella for $k = 50$; Explore-Update ($\theta = 1/320$) runs an order of magnitude faster than Greedy (10000 simulations); Top-Edges and Top-Nodes output a selected set in less than a second, hence we do not include them. Next, we investigate how the algorithms scale with increasing network size. We extract subnetworks of VK consisting of 1855, 3710, and 7420 nodes of the original network (i.e., 1/4, 1/2, and full network) and proportional edge density to the full network. In all cases, we compute the runtime on a seed set S of size 15, with the Multivalency model for $k = 20$, for Greedy (10000 simulations), Explore-Update ($\theta = 1/40$), and the Top-Edges and Top-Nodes heuristics. Figure 5(f) shows that runtime scales linearly in network size in all cases. Moreover, we ascertain that while Explore-Update fares no better than Greedy in terms of influence spread, it is much faster.

6.3 Effect of Seed Size

We now test the performance of Explore-Update for different sizes of the seed set S. We select different seed sets from size 21 (minimal size for the current block partition) to 101 with step 10 on Gnutella. Figure 6(a-b) presents the influence spread for Explore-Update and Top-Edges for $k = 50$, as well as the runtime of Explore-Update, whereas Greedy is orders of magnitude slower for this setup, and Top-Nodes performs worse than Top-Edges. We note that Explore-Update always achieves better influence spread than Top-Edges. Interestingly, influence spread and runtime do not always grow with $|S|$. This is explicable by the fact that different seed sets induce different local structures.

6.4 Effect of θ

Next, we study the effect of the θ threshold, which controls the size of arborescences and thereby the influence spread achievable from seed set S. Figure 6(c) presents the influence spread and runtime with the Gnutella network for θ in $\{\frac{1}{10}, \frac{1}{20}, \ldots, \frac{1}{320}\}$, with the WC model for $k = 50$. The runtime of Explore-Update grows linearly in the inverse threshold θ, while influence spread grows logarithmically in it. A good tradeoff between quality and runtime is found at the knee point in the influence spread curve for $\theta = \frac{1}{40}$.

6.5 Comparison to the Optimal Solution

By Theorem 4.5, we proved it is NP-hard to approximate the optimal solution to CAIM. Now, we compare the results of heuristics to the optimal solution obtained by brute force; we reduce the total number of attributes to 16 and use a reduced Gnutella network by selecting 2K nodes, yielding similar degree distribution properties to the original. Figure 7 shows the influence spread results, with the Multivalency model, for a random seed set of size 10. Remarkably, Explore-Updatefi nds the optimal set of attributes with varying k.

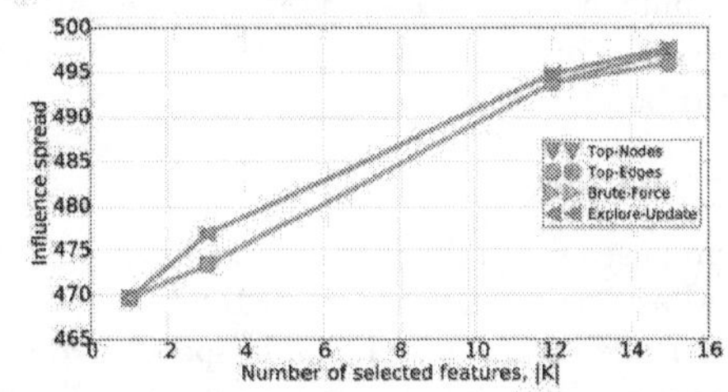

Figure 7: Influence spread on reduced network.

Next, we select $k = 10$, yielding $\binom{16}{10} = 8008$ possible attribute sets, and calculate, with a new random seed set of size 428, the *rank* of each algorithm's solution among all possible attribute sets: for each attribute set, we compute its influence spread using 10000 MC simulations; we sort sets by their spread values, and identify the rank of the solution returned by each heuristic. Table 2 presents those ranks. Explore-Update selects the optimal solution, while Greedy with 500 parsimonious MC simulations yields thefi fth best attribute set. The selected attribute sets differ from each other in 2 out of 10 attributes. We obtained similar results for other values of k, with Explore-Update always returning the optimal attribute set.

[5] We use 10000 Monte-Carlo simulations to compute thefi nal spread of all solutions.

Algorithm	Rank	Spread
Explore-Update	1	34.592
Greedy	5	34.114
Top-Edges	113	33.592
Top-Nodes	113	33.592
...		
–	8008	27.82

Table 2: Algorithm ranking w.r.t. optimal solution.

6.6 Real-World Examples

Last, we looked into the actual results - seed sets and selected attribute sets of our experiments, with special attention to the VK data set with the multivalency model, and inspected our results. One interesting observation was that those attributes that are liked by seed set users were rarely among the ones selected in thefinal solution; this fact indicates that our problem makes good practical sense, while a straightforward naive solution of sticking to what is liked by seed nodes does not yield good results. Nevertheless, selected attributes exhibited a remote, yet unpredictable, resemblance to the attributes liked by seed set nodes. For example, with a group titled "La vie et l'amour" as seed, the selected attributes in our VK network sample included "Home Comfort | Design | Interior Design | Style". With "Psychology of Relations" as seed, the selected attribute set included "Philosophy of Life". Such analogies between seed set and selected attributes, while retrospectively intuitive, would not be derived otherwise; they depend on the way nodes of diverse interests interact within the overall network structure. Such results vindicate our problem motivation.

We also checked how result sets change when we vary k. For example, we select 100 out of 431,374 subscribers of "Esoterica YOGA MEDITATION" as seed set. With $k = 3$, the selected attributes are {"MODA", "La vie et l'amour", "Blog for Men"}. As "Esoterica YOGA MEDITATION" targets primarily women, results such as "MODA" and "La vie et l'amour" are unsurprising. Nevertheless, interestingly, both E-U and Greedy also return "Blog for Men" as a selected attribute, whereas the simple Top-Nodes and Top-Edges heuristics do not. This result shows that our algorithm can select nontrivial attributes.

7 CONCLUSION

This paper proposed the problem of content-aware influence maximization (CAIM). The goal is to select k attributes that characterize a propagated meme's content, such that its spread across a network fromfi xed points of departure is maximized, whereby different attribute sets yield different propagation probabilities across network edges. To our knowledge, there is no previous work on this problem. We formulated a content-aware cascade model and showed that the problem is NP-hard and inapproximable, while the influence function is neither submodular, nor supermodular. We developed an efficient algorithm for CAIM using bounded local arborescences to calculate influence spread. Our experimental study demonstrates that this Explore-Update algorithm selects topics sets that achieve high spread and is orders of magnitude faster than a conventional Greedy solution resembling algorithms developed for related problems. We also provide evidence that our E-U algorithm can achieve the optimal solution when the number of selected topics is small. In the future, we plan to study other propagation models and investigate the parallelization of Explore-Update.

REFERENCES

[1] S. Aral. 2011. Commentaty-Identifying social influence: A comment on opinion leadership and social contagion in new product diffusion. *Marketing Science* 30, 2 (2011), 217–223.

[2] S. Aral, L. Muchnik, and A. Sundararajan. 2009. Distinguishing influence-based contagion from homophily-driven diffusion in dynamic networks. *Proc. of the National Academy of Sciences of the U.S.A.* 106, 51 (2009), 21544–21549.

[3] S. Aral and D. Walker. 2011. Creating social contagion through viral product design: A randomized trial of peer influence in networks. *Management Science* 57, 9 (2011), 1623–1639.

[4] C. Aslay, N. Barbieri, F. Bonchi, and R. A. Baeza-Yates. 2014. Online topic-aware influence maximization queries. In *EDBT.*

[5] C. Aslay, W. Lu, F. Bonchi, A. Goyal, and Laks V.S. Lakshmanan. 2015. Viral marketing meets social advertising: Ad allocation with minimum regret. *Proc. VLDB Endow.* 8, 7 (2015), 814–825.

[6] N. Barbieri and F. Bonchi. 2014. Influence maximization with viral product design. In *SDM.*

[7] N. Barbieri, F. Bonchi, and G. Manco. 2012. Topic-aware social influence propagation models. In *ICDM.*

[8] J. A. Berger and C. Heath. 2005. Idea Habitats: How the prevalence of environmental cues influences the success of ideas. *Cognitive Science* 29, 2 (2005), 195–221.

[9] C. Borgs, M. Brautbar, J. T. Chayes, and B. Lucier. 2014. Maximizing social influence in nearly optimal time. In *SODA.*

[10] S. Chen, J. Fan, G. Li, J. Feng, K.-L. Tan, and J. Tang. 2015. Online topic-aware influence maximization. *Proc. VLDB Endow.* 8, 6 (2015), 666–677.

[11] Wei Chen, Laks V. S. Lakshmanan, and Carlos Castillo. 2013. *Information and Influence Propagation in Social Networks.* Morgan & Claypool Publishers.

[12] W. Chen, T. Lin, and C. Yang. 2014. Efficient topic-aware influence maximization using preprocessing. *CoRR* abs/1403.0057 (2014).

[13] W. Chen, C. Wang, and Y. Wang. 2010. Scalable influence maximization for prevalent viral marketing in large-scale social networks. In *KDD.*

[14] W. Chen, Y. Yuan, and L. Zhang. 2010. Scalable influence maximization in social networks under the linear threshold model. In *ICDM.*

[15] Y. -C. Chen, W. -C. Peng, and S. -Y. Lee. 2012. Efficient algorithms for influence maximization in social networks. *Knowl. Inf. Syst.* 33, 3 (2012), 577–601.

[16] S. Cheng, H. Shen, J. Huang, W. Chen, and X. Cheng. 2014. IMRank: influence maximization viafi nding self-consistent ranking. In *SIGIR.*

[17] I. P. Cvijikj and F. Michahelles. 2013. Online engagement factors on Facebook brand pages. *Social Network Analysis and Mining* 3, 4 (2013), 843–861.

[18] L. de Vries, S. Gensler, and Peter S.H. Leeflang. 2012. Popularity of brand posts on brand fan pages: An Investigation of the Effects of Social Media Marketing. *Journal of Interactive Marketing* 26, 2 (2012), 83–91.

[19] C. Van den Bulte and G. L. Lilien. 2001. Medical innovation revisited: Social contagion versus marketing effort. *Am. J. Sociol.* 106, 5 (2001), 1409–1435.

[20] P. Domingos and M. Richardson. 2001. Mining the network value of customers. In *KDD.*

[21] D. Godes and D. Mayzlin. 2004. Using online conversations to study word-of-mouth communication. *Marketing Science* 23, 4 (2004), 545–560.

[22] A. Goyal, F. Bonchi, and L. V. S. Lakshmanan. 2011. A data-based approach to social influence maximization. *PVLDB* 5, 1 (2011), 73–84.

[23] L. Hong and B. D. Davison. 2010. Empirical study of topic modeling in twitter. In *SOMA.*

[24] Brian Karrer and M. E. J. Newman. 2011. Stochastic blockmodels and community structure in networks. *Phys. Rev. E* 83 (Jan 2011), 016107. Issue 1.

[25] E. Katz. 1959. Mass communications research and the study of popular culture: An editorial note on a possible future of this journal. *Studies in Public Communication* 2 (1959), 1–6.

[26] D. Kempe, J. Kleinberg, and E. Tardos. 2003. Maximizing the spread of influence through a social network. In *KDD.*

[27] J. Leskovec, A. Krause, C. Guestrin, C. Faloutsos, J. M. VanBriesen, and N. S. Glance. 2007. Cost-effective outbreak detection in networks. In *KDD.*

[28] Y. Li, D. Zhang, and K.-L. Tan. 2015. Real-time targeted influence maximization for online advertisements. *Proc. VLDB Endow.* 8, 10 (2015), 1070–1081.

[29] C. F. Manski. 1993. Identification of endogenous social effects: The reflection problem. *The Review of Economic Studies* 60, 3 (1993), 531–542.

[30] Tiago P. Peixoto. 2015. Model Selection and Hypothesis Testing for Large-Scale Network Models with Overlapping Groups. *Phys. Rev. X* 5 (2015), 20. Issue 1.

[31] M. Richardson and P. Domingos. 2002. Mining knowledge-sharing sites for viral marketing. In *KDD.*

[32] Y. Tang, X. Xiao, and Y. Shi. 2014. Influence maximization: near-optimal time complexity meets practical efficiency. In *SIGMOD.*

Exploiting Food Choice Biases for Healthier Recipe Recommendation

David Elsweiler*
University of Regensburg
Germany
david@elsweiler.co.uk

Christoph Trattner*
MODUL University Vienna
Austria
christoph.trattner@modul.ac.at

Morgan Harvey
Northumbria University
The United Kingdom
morgan.harvey@northumbria.ac.uk

ABSTRACT

By incorporating healthiness into the food recommendation / ranking process we have the potential to improve the eating habits of a growing number of people who use the Internet as a source of food inspiration. In this paper, using insights gained from various data sources, we explore the feasibility of substituting meals that would typically be recommended to users with similar, healthier dishes. First, by analysing a recipe collection sourced from Allrecipes.com, we quantify the potential for finding replacement recipes, which are comparable but have different nutritional characteristics and are nevertheless highly rated by users. Building on this, we present two controlled user studies (n=107, n=111) investigating how people perceive and select recipes. We show participants are unable to reliably identify which recipe contains most fat due to their answers being biased by lack of information, misleading cues and limited nutritional knowledge on their part. By applying machine learning techniques to predict the preferred recipes, good performance can be achieved using low-level image features and recipe meta-data as predictors. Despite not being able to consciously determine which of two recipes contains most fat, on average, participants select the recipe with the most fat as their preference. The importance of image features reveals that recipe choices are often visually driven. A final user study (n=138) investigates to what extent the predictive models can be used to select recipe replacements such that users can be "nudged" towards choosing healthier recipes. Our findings have important implications for online food systems.

KEYWORDS

Food RecSys; human decision making; behavioural change; information behaviour

1 INTRODUCTION

Search and recommendation systems play an increasingly important role in the way people choose what they eat: Internet recipe portals are a popular source of food inspiration [8, 20] and often allow users to rate, and receive suggestions of, recipes. People search for recipes in a variety of ways for many different purposes [8, 42] and a relatively large proportion of web search queries are related to food or lead to the visit of a food-related website [39]. As such, systems which provide access to online recipes or make personalised recommendations have been touted as a means to help people nourish themselves more healthily [14, 17]. Nevertheless, despite offering access to healthy content [34], analyses of the systems being used in practice indicate that they tend to promote unhealthy meals [35]. Metrics such as recipe ratings, recipe bookmark frequency and the sentiment scores of recipe comments all tend to correlate positively with recipes that are high in fat, sugar and calorie content [34]. In other words, the recipes consumed most frequently and judged most favourably by users are typically the least healthy. Moreover, when common recommender algorithms are tested on recipe data, it is found that their recommendations are, on average, unhealthier than those rated positively by users themselves [34]. Thus, food access and recommendation systems, by themselves - at least in their current form - are no magic bullet for promoting healthy nutrition and may even serve to increase the likelihood that users will make poor nutritional choices.

Deciding what food one should eat is a complex, multi-faceted process, influenced by many biological, personal and socio-economic factors [5]. Moreover, a large body of evidence demonstrates that the food choices people make can be subtly manipulated with biases and cues, such as the default choice (status quo bias [41]) and the people present when the choice is made (social dependence [38]). Recent work has shown user behaviour with search and recommendation systems to be similarly susceptible to manipulation via psychological and system biases [40]. We bridge these domains by investigating the process of choosing foods via search and recommendation systems. Combining insights gained from analyses of recipes sourced from the large online food portal Allrecipes.com, naturalistic behavioural data detailing how users interact with these recipes, as well as the results of a series of controlled experiments, we seek to understand the processes involved in choosing a recipe online. Furthermore, we use what we learn to establish whether it is possible to algorithmically select recipes to 'nudge' users towards healthier choices.

Our experiments are conceived based on a scenario in which the user has a particular type of dish in mind (e.g. a "stir fry", "cheesy pasta" or "onion soup"), and is searching for a suitable recipe - a scenario naturalistic data show to be commonplace [8] and for which systems have been designed to support [37]. The driving motivation behind our work is to investigate the possibility of replacing meals recommender algorithms predict users will like with healthier versions of similar recipes.

More specifically we address the following research questions:

*Both authors contributed equally to this work.

SIGIR '17, August 07-11, 2017, Shinjuku, Tokyo, Japan

DOI: http://dx.doi.org/10.1145/3077136.3080826

- RQ1: To what extent is it possible, using typical online recipe databases, to replace unhealthy versions of recipes with similar recipes with healthier nutritional properties?
- RQ2: To what extent are users able to distinguish between healthy and unhealthy versions of recipes?
- RQ3: How does the information available influence the estimates made?
- RQ4: What biases are involved in the selection of online recipes?
- RQ5: To what extent can these biases be exploited to influence online recipe selections?

Outline. After motivating our contribution in Section 2 by highlighting relevant related work in the areas of food recommendation, food decision-making and biases in human behaviour, Section 3 introduces the data set used as the basis for experiments. The first set of analyses, presented in Section 4 studies the potential for identifying replacement recipes within the data set. In Sections 5.1 and 5.2 we turn to the processes involved in perceiving and choosing recipes, showing by experiment that fat content is poorly estimated by users, but that recipe preference can be predicted. In Section 6 we describe a user study which investigates whether we can use what we have learned to nudge users towards less fatty choices. Finally, in Sections 7 and 8 we discuss the significance of our findings and present our conclusions.

2 RELATED WORK

Food Recommenders. Work in food recommender systems has typically focused on rating prediction, utilising recipe content [14, 33] and contextual information [17] to minimise prediction error. Harvey et al. [17] showed that one important contextual factor for recipe recommendation is the users themselves: a small group explicitly preferred healthier food, while the majority tended to prefer less healthy alternatives. Recent work has tried to incorporate healthiness into the recommendation process by substituting ingredients [33], incorporating calorie counts [16], and generating food plans [12]. Elsweiler et al. and Trattner et al. identified the need for a trade-off between recommending recipes that will be appreciated by users and recipes that can be considered healthy using quantifiable metrics [13, 34]. Experiments show that the trade-off can be improved to some extent using post-filtering [34], but little is yet known regarding how such algorithmic approaches may influence the food decisions people make [35] and whether users will accept the healthier alternatives proffered.

Food Choice. People typically make around 200 food choices every day [38]. Choosing which food to eat is a complex process influenced by a number of context factors at biological, personal, situational, social and socio-economic levels [5]. Choosing food can be cognitively challenging, particularly when the number of options is large [32], leading to decisions often being driven by primal instinct and heavily influenced by simple stimuli, such as colour [7].

Neuroscience research has revealed food choices to be guided by competing behavioural controllers [9]. *Pavlovian control* induces pre-programmed responses when exposed to specific stimuli; *Habitual control* offers more flexible responses based on the previous history of rewards; and *Goal-directed control* allows decisions to reflect goals, such as weight loss. The evidence suggests that environmental factors, such as time constraints and marketing campaigns, which induce cognitive load, lead to dominance of the Pavlovian controller [28]. Thus, modern busy lifestyles, where people have limited time and attention resources and are bombarded with advertising designed to appeal to sensory instincts, mean that making healthy food choices is naturally difficult for many, a consequence that has been linked to problems such as obesity [28]. Compounding this, research shows [10] that foods that are high in calories and fat are the most palatable but are also the least satiating, meaning that we often choose such foods due to their appetising nature but must eat an excessive quantity of them to feel full.

Biases in Decision Making. It is generally accepted that, precisely because of limited cognitive resources, people often base their decisions on heuristics rather than a rational differentiation between avaiable options [19]. While heuristics can work quite well, the choices people make of what to eat can be biased in countless ways. For example, people make poor decisions when stimulated (e.g. when hungry and surrounded by the sights and smells of calorie rich food) [38] or when emotional [24] or stressed [26]. People adapt their behaviour to their social context: obese individuals are more likely to be friends with other obese individuals [6] and people consume more when they eat in groups, rather than alone [38].

Debate exists as to whether it is more effective or ethically appropriate to 'nudge', where biases are exploited to change behaviour, or 'boost', where people are supplied with information so that they can take more informed and, hopefully, better choices. With food this debate resolves around efforts such food-labelling [11] versus, for example, the language used to describe food products, where positive adjectives, for instance, make people more likely to accept a recommendation [15]. Both approaches have been applied to search and recommenders. Educational approaches, such as in [3] or [25] can be considered to be examples of boosting, whereas query suggestions and manipulating the search box size [4] are nudges. What is lacking in the literature, however, is an understanding of how boosts and nudges can be applied to food choices from search and recommender systems and whether such approaches can lead to any real behavioural change.

In summary, previous work has highlighted a trade-off between recommending users meals they will find appealing and those that are healthy. One approach to optimising this trade-off would be to substitute meals that would typically be recommended to users (as in [14, 17]) with similar but healthier dishes. For this strategy to be successful, however, a number of prerequisites need to be fulfilled: 1) recipes need to exist that are sufficiently similar in style and content, but different in health properties. 2) there needs to be potential in the human decision-making process to allow for the selection of healthier dishes, if available. That is, people need to be unable to tell the difference between the healthy and unhealthy versions of meals, if their preferences are so influenced, or other factors need to be identified that can outweigh healthiness in the decision process. 3) It must be possible to select replacement dishes that are more attractive to users than the original suggestions. The remainder of this paper addresses exactly these points.

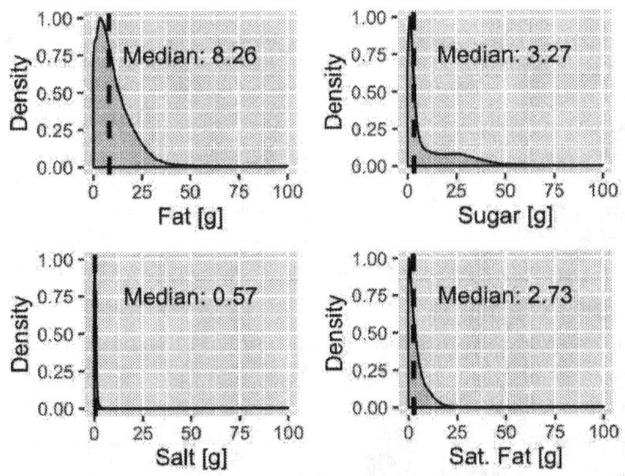

Figure 1: Density plots and medians for fat, sugar, salt and sat. fat content per 100g in the recipes of Allrecipe.com.

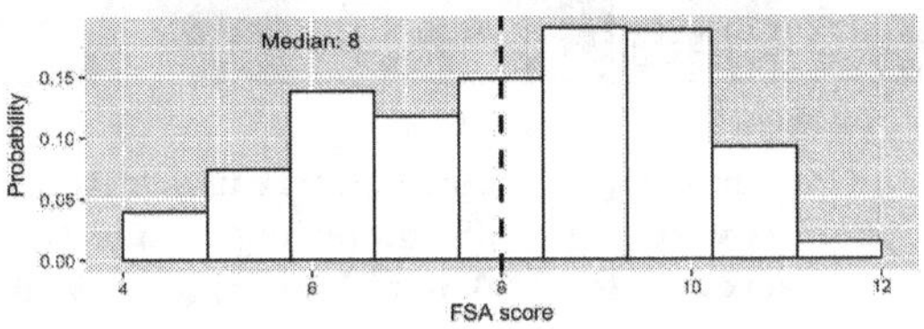

Figure 2: FSA score distribution (Probability: 1=100%).

3 DATASET

To address our research aims we obtained recipe and nutritional data from the Web by implementing a standard Web crawler. Between the 20th and 24th of July 2015, the crawler collected 242,113 recipes published between the years 2000 and 2015 on the Allrecipes.com website. We focus only on recipes published on the main site and ignore personal recipes, which are often incomplete and do not provide nutrition information. The primary reason for choosing Allrecipes.com was that, at the time of writing, it claims to be the world's largest food-focused social network and mantains a community of 40 million users from 24 countries accessing 3 billion recipes annually [2]. For our analysis, we relied only on those recipes for which all ingredients were present in the Allrecipes.com food database (out of 242,113 originally crawled recipes 58,263 had nutrition information available). We chose to focus on "fat", "saturated fat", "sugar" and "sodium" (measured in 100g per recipe) because they allow us to determine the healthiness of a recipe according to international standards introduced in 2007 by The Food Standards Agency (FSA) [1]. Following the procedure described in [18], for each meal we calculated the nutritional content per portion by dividing the total content by the number of portions in the meal. This allowed a so-called FSA health score to be calculated which measures, on a discrete scale, the extent to which a recipe is healthy or unhealthy [1]. The FSA front of package labelling system [1] relates to 4 macro-nutrients (sugar, sodium, fat and saturated fat). The scale is green (healthy), amber and red (unhealthy) and seeks to provide a clear and understandable indication of how healthful the product is. As in [30] we first assign an integer value to each colour (green=1, amber=2 and red=3) then sum the scores for each macronutrient resulting in a final range from 4 (very healthy) to 12 (very unhealthy). This metric, referred to as the "FSA score", provides a proxy for the healthiness of recipes. Figures 1 and 2, which plot the distributions of FSA scores, fat, saturated fat, sugar and salt for the dataset, reveal that the collection does contain recipes considered healthy according to these dimensions, but that the majority of recipes are indeed unhealthy.

Table 1: Overall probability of finding similar recipe pairs with 4 different thresholds (Probability: 1=100%).

Sim*	≥ 0.2	≥ 0.4	≥ 0.6	≥ 0.8
Probability	.051	.021	.007	.002

Note: * Cosine Similarity.

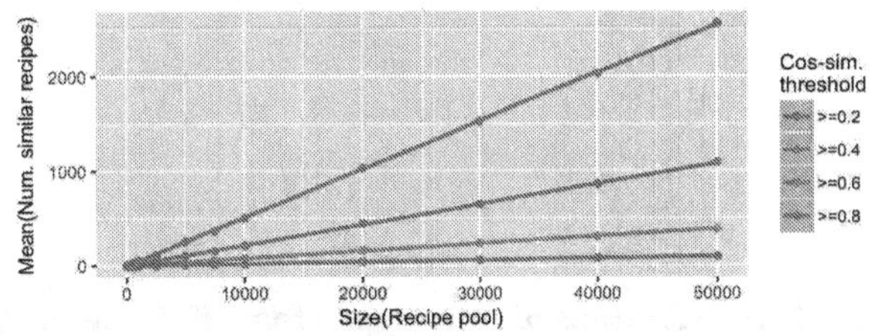

Figure 3: Recipe pool size vs mean number of similar recipes available for 4 different cosine similarity cut-off values.

4 RQ1: FINDING SUITABLE REPLACEMENTS

To realise our goal of replacing recipes with healthier alternatives, we must first establish if and when it is possible to find suitable replacements in the collection. We address this in three stages: First, following a method similar to [33], we establish recipe pairs based on their pairwise similarities; second, after such pairs have been established, we look at the distribution of various health properties across pairs to determine to what extent healthier replacements can be found. Finally, since replacements are unlikely to be accepted if the overall ratings are poorer than the original, we consider the rating distributions within pairs.

Table 1 shows the results of our first analysis, which examines the availability of similar recipes in the entire Allrecipes.com collection. We examined several similarity metrics, but report the cosine similarity as it was the metric used by [33], a standard reference from the literature[1,2]. The table shows how the probability of finding a similar recipe changes when the cosine similarity threshold is varied. For a given recipe, there are typically far fewer similar recipes than dissimilar ones, however some similar recipes do tend to exist. In particular, for a cosine similarity threshold of ≥ 0.2[3], there is a 5.1% probability of finding a partner recipe, while for a stricter threshold of ≥ 0.8 this reduces to 0.2%. In other words, with the recipe pool of 58,263 we have, out of 3.4 billion possible pairs approximately 6.8 million of these will have a similarity of 0.8 or higher. This means that each recipe will have an average of 116 potential replacements.

To understand the relationship between collection size and the probability of finding suitable replacements, we repeated the above

[1] There is a high correlation between cosine similarity and Jaccard coefficient (ρ=0.87) suggesting 1) ingredient quantities are not very important and 2) similar results would be expected regardless of the distance metric applied.

[2] Vector elements (ingredients) were weighted by the proportion of the recipe they represent. We experimented with various other weighting schemes but these produced pairs poorer results.

[3] The value used by [33], which we feel is not strong enough for our aims and thus report other threshold values.

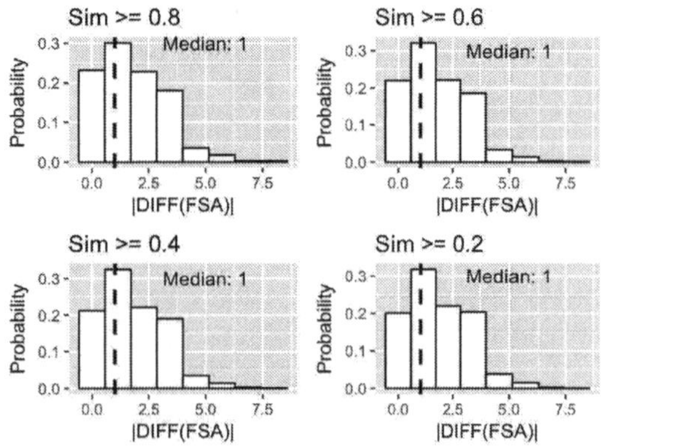

Figure 4: Distributions of recipe pairs for difference in FSA healthiness score and different sim. thresholds (Probability: 1=100%).

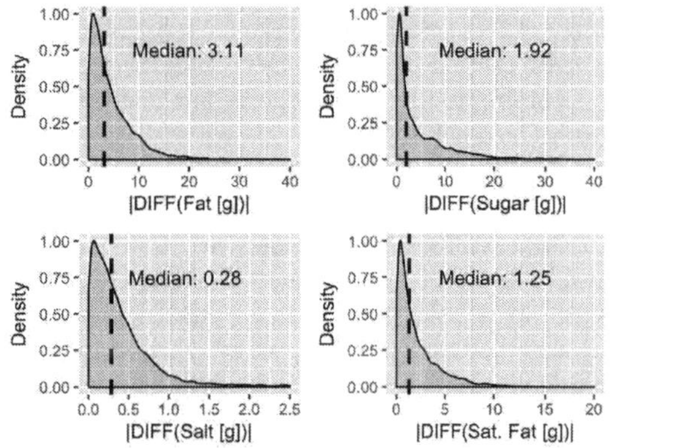

Figure 5: Density plots for recipe pairs for difference in fat, sat. fat, sugar and salt and with $sim \geq 0.8$.

procedure using recipe pools of various sizes drawn randomly from the full collection. To obtain statistically valid results, for each recipe pool we ran a boot-strap procedure with 1000 iterations.

The results of this experiment reveal that the relationship between pool size and number of similar recipes is linear, i.e., the larger the pool of recipes, the larger the number of similar recipes from which we can choose. The slope of the model is determined by the similarity threshold - the lower the threshold, the more similar recipes are available. For example, with a pool containing 100 recipes, we can expect to find on average 0.18 recipes with $sim \geq 0.8$, 0.78 for $sim \geq 0.6$, 2.2 for $sim \geq 0.4$ and 5.2 for $sim \geq 0.2$. A larger pool of 1000 recipes yields an average of 1.8 recipes with $sim \geq 0.8$ and so on. These results indicate that at least 555 recipes are required to find one similar recipe using a threshold 0.8 or higher and thus, even for relatively small recipe pools, it is typically possible to find very similar replacement recipes.

Next, we consider the relative healthiness of recipes and the extent to which we can find similar recipes that also exhibit very different nutritional properties. Figure 4 shows the results of experiments that explore the probability of finding similar recipes with different thresholds and with minimal differences in their FSA healthiness scores. Regardless of the similarity threshold chosen, the median difference in the FSA scores between the recipe pairs is 1, meaning that half of all the pairs differ in terms of FSA score by more than this. The 75th percentile is 2 for similarity thresholds

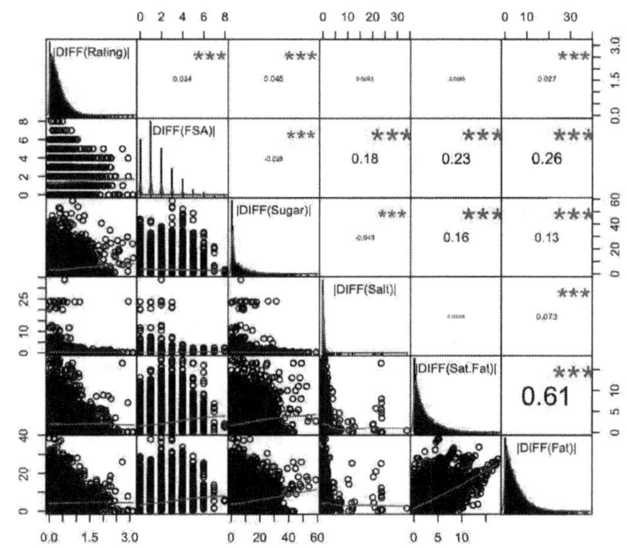

Figure 6: Correlation (spearman) matrix incl. distributions for recipe pairs with $sim \geq 0.8$ comparing ratings to macro-nutritional facts and the FSA health score ($^{*}p < 0.05$, $^{**}p < 0.01$, $^{***}p < 0.001$).

(≥ 0.4, ≥ 0.6, *and* ≥ 0.8) and 3 for $sim \geq 0.2$. As such, given a target recipe, it is feasible to find a number of alternative recipes that are similar in terms of content, but quite different in terms of nutrition. Figure 5 explores this relationship further on a macro-nutrient level, demonstrating that it is also possible to find recipe pairs that have quite different fat, sugar, salt and saturated fat levels. The plots also demonstrate that fat is the macro-nutrient with the greatest average difference in grams (Md=3.11)[4]. The tail of the distribution is also thick, suggesting it is easier to find similar pairs with very great difference in fat (g) than in the case of, for example, sugar.

Finally, we turn our attention to ratings. Figure 6 depicts a correlation matrix computed using only recipe pairs with a cosine similarity ≥ 0.8. The plot reveals a very slight correlation between user feedback in the form of ratings and the FSA score-based estimates of a recipe's healthiness (ρ=0.03), fat (ρ=0.03) etc. This contrasts with much stronger correlations between ratings and nutritional properties we reported in [34], where analysed the same data set, but did not restrict the analyses to similar pairs. We interpret this to mean that it is possible to find pairs of similar recipes where rating is not determined by healthiness. A further encouraging discovery with respect to our goals is provided by the distribution of rating divergence for recipe pairs with sim ≥ 0.8 (see top row in Figure 6), which shows that similar recipes have similar ratings (density peaks at zero).

In this section we have considered three properties of recipe pairs to establish whether it is possible to find appropriate healthy equivalents and have shown that, given a large enough pool, healthier recipes can typically be found. We have shown it is possible to

[4]In terms of Reference Intakes (RIs) based on a 2,000kCal daily diet, it is advised not to exceed 70g of fat, 20g sat. fat, 90g of sugar and 6g of salt [1]. As such, for the avg. portion size of 135.6g in our collection, 3.11g of fat difference amounts to $(3.11/70) * 135.6 = 6\%$ of daily recommended fat intake. For sugar this is $(1.92/90) * 135.6 = 2.9\%$, for salt $(0.28/6) * 135.6 = 6.32\%$ and for sat. fat. $(1.25/20) * 135.6 = 8.5\%$. Hence in respect to RIs the largest change can be made regarding sat. fats.

Table 2: A selection of recipe pairs.

French Crepes	Basic Crepes
Asparagus Soup in Seconds	Cream of Fresh Asparagus Soup II
Florentine Stuffed Chicken	Mom's Mozzarella Chicken for Drew
Ranch Crispy Chicken	Marinated Ranch Broiled Chicken
Buttermilk Coleslaw	Restaurant-Style Coleslaw I
French Toast I	Peanut Butter French Toast
French Onion Soup II	Lance's French Onion Soup

find similar recipes with different health characteristics and that these health characteristics are, in turn, only loosely correlated with rating. In sum, our analyses suggest replacing recipes with similar, healthy and comparably or better rated recipes is feasible.

5 INVESTIGATING PERCEPTION OF RECIPES

Now that we are satisfied that suitable replacement candidates can be found, we turn our attention to the decision processes involved in accepting recommendations. We wish to understand which informational cues are used to make these decisions and how the cues used relate, not only to a person's ability to correctly identify the healthiest recipe, but also to the choice of which recipe they select to eat. To this end we perform two experiments, both of which follow the same basic experimental design:

Basic Design. Participants were presented with a series of 10 recipe pairs, chosen randomly from a pool of 50 pairs in total. These were selected algorithmically such that recipes in the pair were very similar (similarity ≥ 0.8), but were different in fat content (one of the recipes contained at least twice the fat content of the other). A selection of example pairs is shown in Table 2.

Participants were questioned about each pair in a random order and, in each case, the two recipes were presented side-by-side. For each pair participants were asked 1) which recipe they found most appealing, 2) which they believed to contain the most fat, and 3) which piece of information most informed their opinion of relative fat content.

We questioned participants on a specific macro-nutritional property rather than asking them which recipe was "healthiest" because "health" is an ambiguous, subjective and multi-dimensional concept and, therefore, open to interpretation. We chose fat because our analyses above indicate that replacement recipes (i.e. similar recipes with lower fat content) would be plentiful. Future work will repeat our experiments with other macro-nutrient components.

The information presented for each recipe varied over the two studies: In the first study participants were shown only the recipe title as presented on Allrecipes.com and the first image available for the recipe on the site. Many recipes have several user-contributed images available, but we chose the first because this is the main one used for recommendation and search presentation on the website. In the second study, in addition to the title and image, participants were also provided ingredient lists for both recipes. The idea of having two studies with varying informational cues was to establish how much information was required and if extra cues can change the outcome.

Participants. 107 undergraduate information science students (64.5% male) took part in the first experiment. The students reported eating home cooked meals regularly (median= 5 days per week, IQR =2). The frequency with which they reported using online recipe websites varied. The distribution was spread uniformly over the categories "on a weekly or daily basis","on a monthly basis", "roughly every 3 months" and "hardly ever". The sample included 13 vegetarians, 3 vegans, and 6 pescatarians. On a 5-point Likert scale from "cooking is torture" to "I love cooking", the median value was 4 (IQR=1). When choosing a meal, the majority of participants perceived taste to be the most important criteria. However, some participants reported that the healthiness of the meal or the tastes of fellow diners were also important criteria.

A second group of 111 undergraduate information science students (59.5% male) participated in the follow-up experiment. The second group reported cooking at home in a very similar distribution to the first, perceived the cooking experience similarly (median=4) and also generally thought that taste was most important when choosing food, however they were less likely to use recipe websites on a daily basis. Among the participants, perception of the cooking experience was a significant predictor of preference towards healthy food (R^2=0.05, p=0.013,). There were 12 vegetarians, 2 vegans and 8 pescatarians.

Overall these groups represent convenience samples from a relatively homogeneous population of well-educated individuals primarily aged between 18-28. That being said the sample is diverse in terms of food preferences, priorities regarding the food they choose, the enjoyment of the cooking process, as well as the frequency with which online recipe sites are used, which we argue makes a good starting point to investigate our research questions.

5.1 RQs 2 & 3: Judging fat content

Participants in the first study were only able to correctly identify the recipe containing the most fat in 51.1% of cases, which is not significantly better than random (χ^2 = 0.61, df = 1, p = 0.43). A Krippendorff's alpha value of 0.101 moreover suggests little agreement among the participants. Unsurprisingly, in the second study, where participants were also provided with the ingredients list to make their judgements, the fattiest dish was correctly identified more often (in 56.7% of cases), which, despite being significantly better than random (χ^2 = 21.4, df = 1, df = 1, p < 0.001), is still hardly reliable. The Krippendorff's alpha value 0.116 is also slightly higher than without the ingredients list, but the agreement across participants is still only considered slight according to [23] .

In the first study, the participants reported mostly relying on the images to make their decision (71.9% of the time the image was the decisive cue) rather than the title. However, when one examines the success rate when different cues are used it seems that the cue used relates to the performance. Using the image resulted in a 50.4% success rate compared to 53.2% with the title. In the second study, decisions were often taken with the ingredients list as the decisive cue (in 52.7% of cases) compared to the image (37.4%) and title (10.0%). A Krippendorff's alpha value of 0.181 again indicates only slight agreement across participants. The ingredients list was associated with the highest accuracy (62.5% of estimates were correct) compared to the image (49.5%) and title (53.0%). A chi-square test confirms a relationship between the cue used and accuracy rate (χ^2 = 18.509, df = 2, p<0.01).

Figure 7: Example of a misleading image cue.

To investigate the extent to which cues can inform or mislead we divide pairs into groups along two dimensions: *agreement / little agreement* (with respect to the best cue on which to base judgments) and *high / low success-rate* (regarding the extent to which judgements were correct). Cue agreement across users was established at the level of recipe pair by calculating Shannon entropy for each pair. To avoid zeros we smoothed the probabilities by allocating 0.01% of the probability evenly across cues. Across the pairs there was considerable difference in the agreement (median = 1.24, IQR=0.34). The pair with the highest agreement had an entropy score of 0.81 and for this pair ingredients list was chosen 9 times, the image 3 times and the title was unused. The pair with the max entropy score (1.56) was rated 8 times, with 2 participants naming image as the primary cue, 3 the ingredients and 3 the title.

When the participants agreed on the best cue (i.e. entropy < median), the success rate was 60.8%, significantly better than 52.2% when there was poor agreement (χ^2 = 8.693, df = 1, p< 0.01). This means that typically, when participants agreed on the best cue, it tended to be a reliable indicator. This was not always the case however. Manually examining the cases where agreement was high and accuracy low allowed us, in some cases, to understand why the participants misjudged the fat content. Poor quality and misleading photographs were one source of bias. Pair 47 (shown in Figure 7) is a good example of how images can lead to incorrect judgements. The image for the dish with most fat (left) is misleading because it contains vegetables, which are not actually present in the recipe. The recipe on the right is similarly biased but in the opposite direction. The photographed accompaniment is cheesy pasta (again, not in the recipe). In the image the chicken looks as if it were deep-fried, whereas in the recipe it is actually baked, which reduces the fat content. Moreover, the plate in the recipe image (right) looks to feature what look like traces of fat, which may have influenced judgements. Examining the other user uploaded images for the same recipes suggests to us that if these were shown the participant estimates may have been very different.

Recipe titles can be similarly deceptive. For example, in the case of pair 38 ("Simple Red Sauce with Pasta","Holy Smoked Bacon and Mushroom Penne"), one third of the participants who incorrectly judged the first recipe to contain least fat, did so on the basis of the title, presumably associating "smoked bacon" with high fat content.

The title was not always informative of the fat content, which explains the infrequency with which it is cited as the best cue. However, in some cases (e.g. pair 8: "Banana Nut Bread III","Lower Fat Banana Bread II"), the title contained an obvious clue. In this case, only 57.9% of participants cited the title as the determining factor and 31.6% actually answered incorrectly. Amongst the participants who answered incorrectly was 1 participant who cited the title as his cue, but obviously doubted the veracity of its content.

In cases where the ingredients list was used as a cue and often incorrectly estimated revealed limited nutritional knowledge amongst some participants. It seemed, for example, that some participants were unaware that the fat content of red meats is higher than in white meats. In other words it was not only misleading cues, such as image or title biases, which led to incorrect judgements. Limited knowledge appears to be another factor.

In the demographic questionnaire, some participants cited the healthiness of the meals as being an important factor in their food choices. We split the sample into two groups. Those who rated the importance of healthiness below the median (n=27) and those who rated the importance >median (n=36). The healthy group seemed to be better at judging the fattier meal (58.1% vs 52.5%), but the difference is not significant (χ^2 = 1.7862, df = 1, p = 0.1814).

Summary. In summary, judging the fat content of online recipes is challenging: we observed poor accuracy in judgements and little agreement across participants. Even people who described health as being a priority when they choose a meal, were not significantly better than those who do not at judging which recipe contained most fat. Our analyses reveal different explanations for this: *lack of information* (the titles and images did not always provide the information necessary to judge), *lack of knowledge* to interpret the ingredient list correctly, and *misleading cues* - in many cases certain cues led users to falsely estimate the fat content of recipes.

5.2 RQ 4: Biases influencing selections

In the previous section, we showed that users find it hard to determine the fat content of a recipe and that certain cues (image of a recipe, recipe title or ingredient lists) can bias their interpretation. At first glance, this is a puzzling discovery as it does not fit well with the evidence from the literature suggesting that people, in the main, prefer fatty, calorie-rich recipes. In this section we focus on user preferences; concretely we investigate cues and biases influencing recipe selection using the data collected in the studies described above, as well as the naturalistic data set from Allrecipes.com. The main empirical contribution in this section is formulated as a prediction task, whereby we attempt to algorithmically estimate which of two recipes a user will prefer.

We take a machine learning approach to understand how various factors influenced the decision to choose one recipe over another. The prediction task is set up as follows: given a recipe pair (a, b), where recipes have a similarity $\geq$ 0.8, predict whether recipe(a) will be selected over recipe(b). Hence, in the prediction data set, each observation consists of a set of predictor variables or features that represent information about two recipes, and the response variable is a binary indicator with value "true" in the case when a was selected over b and the value "false" when b was selected over a. This is the setup previously employed in [33].

Feature Engineering. We selected 76 features relating to the three types of cues (recipe title, recipe image and recipe ingredients) investigated in the previous sections. Furthermore, we selected 20 additional features relating to the nutritional content of a recipe as well as its popularity and the extent to which it is appreciated on Allrecipes.com. Below we briefly summarise these features and their corresponding sets:

- **Title:** For the title feature set, we derived 27 features. Four were simple text metrics, e.g. length in words and characters and text entropy [27]. We also measured the sentiment of the title and counted the words appearing in the Oxford English Dictionary. The remaining title features refer to POS-tags[5], e.g. number of Adjectives, Nouns, etc..
- **Image:** For the image feature set we derived 5 features capturing image sharpness, brightness, colorfulness, contrast and entropy. These features have been successfully used in the past to determine the attractiveness of Flickr images [31].
- **Ingredients:** We also created a set of simple features based on the ingredients used in a recipe, e.g. number of ingredients, number of words and chars, equivalent to those for the title [6].
- **Popularity & Appreciation:** We used popularity indicators such as number of ratings and bookmarks as well as appreciation measures, e.g. average rating and sentiment (via comments) provided by users in Allrecipes.com as a predictor.
- **Nutrition:** Finally, we derived features based on nutritional facts of the recipes as features. These include: the number of calories, fat, saturated fat, sodium and sugar per 100g contained in a recipe and the FSA health score.

Feature Selection & Classification Setup. The classification experiment was conducted with the help of the Weka[7] machine learning suite and R. Classifiers employed for the experiment were Random Forest, Logistic Regression and Naive Bayes. The evaluation protocol employed was 10-fold cross-validation. The order of recipe combinations (i.e. which is A and which is B) was rotated to ensure balanced classes. Throughout our experiments, we use feature selection methods to reduce the feature dimensionality and to ensure the models estimated were as robust and interpretable as possible. The discriminative power of features was measured using Information Gain (IG), which weights features according to their correlation with class attribute (=user preference) based on entropy. For the purpose of our study, we used IG to determine the top-10 features in each of the prediction experiments conducted (see Table 3).

Prediction Results. Table 3 presents the main results of the prediction experiments. The results are organised in 4 sections, reflecting different training and testing data sets. The first two sections report the results using data from studies 1 and 2, respectively. The third section presents the results of the same experiments using pairs generated from a sample of 10,000 recipes drawn randomly from the subset of the Allrecipes.com pool, which had been rated by at least 10 users. We use the highest average rating as provided by the users in Allrecipes.com, as a proxy for user choice [8]. A fourth section reports the performance of models trained on the Allrecipes.com sample, while predicting the choices made in studies 1 and 2.

Table 3: Results of the prediction experiment.

	Accuracy			
Feature Set	Rand.For.	Logistic	Naive Bay.	Num. Feat.
Study 1 (Instances = 1102)				
Title	49.18%	48.63%	49.36%	54
Image	**64.25%**	**58.43%**	**60.16%**	10
Ingredients	62.25%	57.89%	55.71%	12
Nutr.	**64.25%**	58.25%	54.99%	12
Pop. & Appr	64.15%	55.53%	57.89%	8
Best (Top-10)	64.24%	60.61%	60.79%	10
All	64.33%	63.06%	63.52%	96
Study 2 (Instances = 1181)				
Title	48.43%	48.09%	49.87%	54
Image	**66.21%**	**61.64%**	**59.61%**	10
Ingredients	64.35%	60.96%	53.51%	12
Nutr.	65.96%	58.59%	54.19%	12
Pop. & Appr	65.96%	59.52%	58.59%	8
Best (Top-10)	66.04%	64.86%	61.05%	10
All	66.04%	64.86%	61.05%	96
Random Sample - Avg. Rating (Instances = 14,568)				
Title	62.95%	56.80%	54.60%	96
Image	**77.12%**	53.13%	52.83%	10
Ingredients	57.83%	52.42%	52.24%	12
Nutr.	75.41%	53.93%	52.79%	12
Pop. & Appr*	77.05%	**71.84%**	**69.54%**	6
Best (Top-10)	79.79%	71.29%	67.90%	10
All	84.78%	72.57%	65.95%	136
Random Sample (train) / Study 1 & 2 (test)				
Study1 (top-10)	**56.98%**	55.35%	52.54%	10
Study2 (top-10)	58.34%	**59.94%**	57.15%	10
Study1 (images)	**54.08%**	53.90%	49.63%	10
Study2 (images)	55.54%	**57.15%**	56.56%	10

Note: * Ratings were excluded.

Examining the results for studies 1 and 2 shows that comparable performance was achieved in the studies with the best performance (approx. 64-66%) being achieved by the random forest classifier. The strongest feature set was the image set, which outperformed the popularity / appreciation feature set for all three classifiers employed, although the differences are small. Unsurprisingly the title features, which we know from the user studies are not always informative, perform rather poorly.

Better performance was achieved all round when the same experiments were performed using the data from the Allrecipes.com random sample. This may simply be because more training data was available. Using all of the features available resulted in 84.78% being achieved; with the top 10 features this reduces to 79.79%. Again the image features provide solid predictive power by themselves and, as in the first two studies, when applying a random forest with these features alone, the best performance of all individual sets is achieved (77.12% accuracy). The title features seem to

[5]POS-tags were calculated with the popular Stanford NLP tagger see: http://nlp.stanford.edu/software/tagger.shtml. As title strings are short, we employed the GATE english pos-tagger model, see: https://gate.ac.uk/wiki/twitter-postagger.html

[6]We also experimented with words as features for both title and ingredients. However, since the number of words for recipe titles and ingredients in study 1 and 2 only cover a very small fraction of total words in the corpus, we decided to not train our model on these as we felt it would limit our chances of estimating a generalisable model

[7]http://www.cs.waikato.ac.nz/ml/weka/

[8]We also ran the same experiments using both number of ratings and bookmarks, as well as average sentiment as a proxy. Due to space limitations, we only present the results of the rating indicator. However, all experiments showed the similar performance and useful features.

Table 4: Top-10 features in each of the the 3 studies according to Information Gain (IG).

	Study 1		Study 2		Rand. Sample (rating)	
Rank	IG	Feature	IG	Feature	IG	Feature
1	.0933	IMG:contrast1	.0743	NUT:fat1	.1018	POP:sent2
2	.0829	IMG:brightness1	.0634	IMG:contrast2	.1016	POP:sent1
3	.0719	IMG:entropy1	.0573	IMG:colorfullness1	.0679	IMG:colorfullness1
4	.0707	POP:rating2	.0568	NUT:cal1	.0609	NUT:fat2
5	.0703	IMG:entropy2	.0542	NUT:satfat1	.0605	NUT:cal1
6	.065	POP:sent2	.0512	NUT:fat2	.0562	POP:book1
7	.0612	POP:book2	.0484	NUT:salt2	.0549	POP:book2
8	.0568	NUT:cal2	.0454	IMG:entropy1	.0430	IMG:sharpness1
9	.0551	IMG:colorfullness2	.0417	ING:charCount2	.0361	POP:ratings2
10	.055	POP:ratings1	.0390	IMG:entropy2	.0344	NUT:satfat2

do better in naturalistic environments, with the models trained on these features consistently outperforming the ingredient models on this data set. Table 4 lists the top 10 features for each data set estimated with IG. This shows that the image features are amongst the most important regardless of data set; the nutritional features help most in the second study, whereas for the Allrecipes.com sample the most discriminative features are spread across the popularity, nutritional and image sets.

To illustrate why the image features work so well, in Figure 8 we present the images associated with a series of recipe pairs. A model trained only on image features judged one recipe (top) from the pair to be particularly likely to be chosen while the other (bottom) was judged to be particularly unlikely to be chosen. In our subjective opinion, the top images are more attractive, particularly in the case of the 4 left-most examples. The 3 right-most examples are, in our opinion, less clear. We test the persuasive power of images selected by this model more thoroughly in Section 6.

As a final experiment we trained models using: 1) only the top-10 features; and 2) only image-related features) on the Allrecipes.com sample and tested how effective these models are at predicting the choices made by participants in the two user studies. The results (shown in the bottom section of Table 3), demonstrate that a maximum performance of 56.98% and 59.94% accuracy can be achieved with the top-10 features model for studies 1 and 2, respectively. Slightly poorer performance (54.08% and 57.15%) was achieved by the image feature models. In other words, significantly better than random[9] prediction performance can be achieved using only features, such as low-level image properties and general popularity indicators, trained on a data set with completely different users, collected in a different way. This despite knowing nothing about the individual preferences of the users. We view this as a strong indicator of the predictive power of the features and the robustness of the models.

In this section we have shown that when selecting recipes, user decisions are influenced by numerous cues. Despite not being consciously able to differentiate the fat content of recipes (see Section 5.1), users tended to, on average, select the recipe with the most fat content from the recipe pairs. Other good indicators included popularity metrics - it seems users in the main prefer recipes popular with other users - and low-level image properties, indicating that recipe choices are often visually driven.

[9] χ^2 tests show all the results to be significant, p<0.01.

6 RQ 5: NUDGING HEALTHIER CHOICES

The results presented above suggest the prerequisites for nudging we set out at the end of Section 2 can be met: replacement pairs exist (see Section 4), as does doubt in estimating fat content (see Section 5.1). We have also identified strong cues regarding the recipes people prefer (see Section 5.2). This section describes a final experiment, which determines if we can utilise what we have learned to realise the nudging of healthier recipes in practice.

The final study repeats the basic design reported above with participants choosing recipes from displayed pairs. In this case, however, pairs were selected using the models reported in the previous section to test to what extent it is possible to nudge people towards meals with significantly lower fat content. Thus, in this study participants are only required to indicate their recipe preference and were not required to make any explicit judgement with respect to the nutritional content of the meals. As in the previous experiments, a pool of 50 recipe pairs were chosen. We wanted to test to what extent it is possible to nudge people towards meals with significantly lower fat content, therefore we first restricted pairs to those in the top 30% in terms of difference in fat. From this subset we selected 25 pairs for which the random forest top-10 model trained on the Allrecipes.com sample predicted that the recipe with lowest fat content would be selected. Similarly, we choose 25 pairs where the random forest image-based model, trained on the Allrecipes.com sample, predicted the least fatty recipe would be selected. Further criteria for the selections were that 1) the pairs had to be comparable i.e. human users would consider them to be replacements for each other and 2) the same recipes did not feature repeatedly in the pairs.

138 participants, this time a more heterogeneous sample recruited via email lists and social media marketing, selected from 16 pairs. Based on a coin flip it was decided whether the next pair would be drawn randomly from top-10-model pairs or image-model pairs, thus a similar number of pairs were judged for each model.

The difference in fat content was similar for pairs selected by different models (top10: median Δfat =8.38g/100g, IQR=2.26; image: median Δfat = 8.34g/100g, IQR= 3.72). This represents a median nudge of 16.1% of the daily recommended fat intake for the avg. 2000kcal diet (see footnote 3). However, the certainty in prediction was significantly higher for the top-10 model (top10: median Δprediction = 0.82, IQR =0.08; image: median Δprediction = 0.70, IQR= 0.22).

Of the 134 participants who took part, 56% (n=75) were male and 78 reported their occupation. The most commonly stated occupation (n=40) was student, but others included historians, bar managers, lawyers and educators. Most participants (n=79) were between the ages of 18 and 24 and only 14 stated that they were older than 44. Similarly to the previous groups, participants reported eating home cooked meals regularly (median=5 days per week, IQR=3) and there were 14 vegetarians, 3 vegans and 10 pescatarians. Most rated taste as the most important factor when choosing what to eat, although many also stated that the healthiness of a recipes and social factors are important to them. As with previous groups, the median response to the 5-point Likert scale from "cooking is torture" to "I love cooking" was a 4 (IQR=1), indicating that most enjoyed cooking.

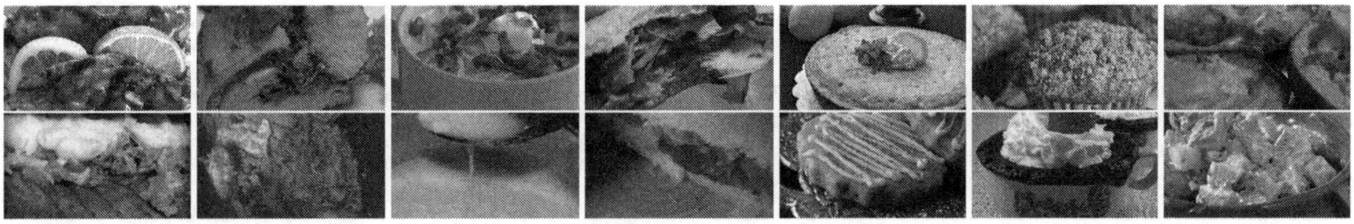

Figure 8: Example images from recipes a model trained on image-features predicts would be selected (top row) vs would not be selected (bottom row). The recipes are considered comparable (i.e. sim≥0.8).

Overall, in 62.2% of cases, the participants chose the recipe in the pair with the least fat, that is, the model predicted correctly. This is significantly better than random (χ^2 = 129.9, df = 1, p < 0.01) and the opposite of typical trends - people, as we know, generally choose recipes with most fat, demonstrating that we are indeed able to algorithmically "nudge" people and influence their food choices. In terms of the two competing models, the image model was able to predict the choice 65.2% of the time, outperforming the top-10 features model, which was correct in 59.3% of cases. Although both models individually were significantly better than random, the image-based model significantly outperforms the top-10 model (z=2.72, p < 0.01). This contrasts with the performance achieved in Section 5.2, where the top-10 model performed best.

It seems that the vegetarians were harder to sway - considering only the results from vegetarians, the percentage of correct predictions lowers to 56.4% over all pairs. With vegetarians removed, the accuracy of our methods increases to 62.8%, which is significantly better (p<0.05). The image-based model still works well for vegetarians (correct in 65.1% of cases), but the top-10 model performs very poorly and is correct only 48.7 % of the time. One plausible explanation is that for non-vegetarian recipes, these participants simply chose the best quality image. Meat-eaters, on the other hand it seems, can be nudged for such dishes using other cues.

In this section, we have demonstrated empirically that by selecting replacement recipes based on the predictive models trained in Section 5.2, we can tempt users into selecting the recipe containing the least fat.

7 SUMMARY & DISCUSSION

The main findings with respect to our RQs are summarised as follows:

- RQ1: The analyses in Section 4 show that, at least in the case of one extremely popular online recipe collection, it is possible to replace recipes with similar, healthy and comparably or better-rated alternatives.
- RQ2: Preference for fatty foods seems to be an implicit one as participants cannot tell the difference when asked, but typically select the fattier one as their preference.
- RQ3: Perception of fat content can be influenced by the information available and, in some cases, misleading cues (image or title) can bias and result in a false impression.
- RQ4: User preferences are predictable: several features can be useful predictors, however, the utility of low-level image features was consistent. We initially found this surprising, but perhaps we should not have - this is, after all, the pavlovian control in action.
- RQ5: We can exploit the biases to nudge people towards choosing the option with least fat. The high performance of the model trained only on image features shows how visually driven online food choices can be. Indeed, our approach shows that we can manipulate recommendations such that the pavlovian controller - the source of many unhealthy food decisions - can actually lead to choosing recipes containing less fat.

Taken together our results show that when a user is given a selection of two comparable recipes, we can select a pair such that the user is "nudged" towards the least fatty of the two. This is an extremely powerful finding and could potentially have far-reaching consequences. It does not mean, however, that the user is happy with the choice made nor that the recipe would actually be cooked and eaten in practice. Future research is needed to complement this work by experimenting in different settings, for example, in the context of SERPs. We are currently planning such studies and intend to measure additional outcomes, including user satisfaction with end choices.

Another limitation of this work is that the recipe pairs as we derived them are ignorant of individual user preferences. We are able to make accurate predictions in most cases, but any predictions may be undone because a user is allergic to eggs, does not particularly like broccoli or even icing on a cake. We believe that significant performance improvements could be achieved if we account for user preferences and future work will explore this in greater depth.

The lack of personalisation in our study also means that in some cases neither of the two recipes in a pair will have appealed to the participant. As discussed above, for instance, in some cases, vegetarians were required to choose from two meat-based dishes, which would be unlikely under normal circumstances. The fact that the image-based model performed better for non-meat eating participants suggests vegetarians' choices in these cases were perhaps even more strongly biased by the image than for two dishes they might actually consider eating. For example, they may have chosen one recipe because the image contained vegetables or salad or perhaps the image simply showed good lighting or presentation.

Our work, despite offering a new way of incorporating healthiness into the food recommendation problem, has only scratched the surface in terms of understanding how people make food choices online and how these choices can be influenced by search or recommendation systems. We are currently planning a series of studies to research this further, including eye-tracking studies to investigate how user behaviour changes when different information (e.g. nutritional information, food labels, recipe descriptions) are shown in different ways.

Our investigations of user perception and selection were restricted to the influence of fat content. While not all fats are unhealthy and low-fat does not necessarily mean healthy, current guidelines advise cutting down on all fats and replacing saturated fat with some unsaturated fat[10]. We plan on repeating our studies for other nutritional properties, such as sugar, carbohydrates and calories, to determine if similar effects can be achieved. We will also test if we can nudge to increase a nutritional element: can we nudge people to increase fibre or protein, for instance?

There are many other ways in which healthier recommendations could be achieved. The nutritional properties of recipes can be changed either by substituting individual ingredients [33] or simply by reducing the portion sizes. It would be interesting to study what kind of effects can be achieved with this approach. Finally, it is well known that cultural differences exist with respect to food choice and indeed the role food has in everyday life [29, 36]. We have begun to investigate whether or not the trends reported here are repeated in data collected from recipe websites from different countries. Our preliminary investigations with the German-based food portal Kochbar.de [21, 22] seem to indicate that many are.

8 CONCLUSIONS

This work combines insights from a broad range of empirical tools - analyses of online recipes, analysis of naturalistic behavioural data regarding how users interact with these recipes, as well as a series of controlled online experiments - to determine the feasibility of replacing online recipes with healthier equivalents. The results show that, despite (or perhaps even due to) the complexity of human food choices, the recommendation process can be manipulated through nudging such that a particular, "healthier" recipe will be chosen more often than would be expected by chance alone. This research provides the groundwork for the development of more sophisticated nudging techniques to build systems that help people to choose healthier meals whilst enjoying those choices even more.

REFERENCES

[1] 2007. FSA nutrient and food based guidelines for UK institutions. available at http://www.food.gov.uk/sites/default/files/multimedia/pdfs/nutrientinstitution.pdf. Last accessed on 20.6.2016. (2007).

[2] 2016. Allrecipe.com Press report. available at http://press.allrecipes.com/. Last accessed on 20.6.2016. (2016).

[3] Scott Bateman, Jaime Teevan, and Ryen W White. 2012. The search dashboard: how reflection and comparison impact search behavior. In *Proc. of SIGCHI'12*. ACM, 1785–1794.

[4] Nicholas J Belkin, Diane Kelly, G Kim, J-Y Kim, H-J Lee, Gheorghe Muresan, M-C Tang, X-J Yuan, and Colleen Cool. 2003. Query length in interactive information retrieval. In *Proc. of SIGIR'03*. ACM, 205–212.

[5] F Bellisle. 2005. The determinants of food choice. *EUFIC Review* 17, April (2005), 1–8.

[6] Nicholas A Christakis and James H Fowler. 2007. The spread of obesity in a large social network over 32 years. *New England journal of medicine* 357, 4 (2007), 370–379.

[7] Fergus M Clydesdale. 1993. Color as a factor in food choice. *Critical Reviews in Food Science & Nutrition* 33, 1 (1993), 83–101.

[8] Sally Jo Cunningham and David Bainbridge. 2013. An analysis of cooking queries: Implications for supporting leisure cooking. (2013).

[9] Nathaniel D Daw and John P O'Doherty. 2013. Multiple systems for value learning. *Neuroeconomics: Decision Making, and the Brain,* (2013).

[10] Adam Drewnowski. 1998. Energy density, palatability, and satiety: implications for weight control. *Nutrition reviews* 56, 12 (1998), 347–353.

[10] http://www.nhs.uk/Livewell/Goodfood/Pages/Fat.aspx

[11] Andreas C Drichoutis, Panagiotis Lazaridis, and Rodolfo M Nayga Jr. 2006. Consumers' use of nutritional labels: a review of research studies and issues. *Academy of marketing science review* 2006 (2006), 1.

[12] David Elsweiler and Morgan Harvey. Towards automatic meal plan recommendations for balanced nutrition. In *Proc. of RecSys'15*. ACM, 313–316.

[13] David Elsweiler, Morgan Harvey, Bernd Ludwig, and Alan Said. Bringing the "healthy" into Food Recommenders. In *Proc. of 2nd International Workshop on Decision Making and Recommender Systems, Bolzano, Italy, October 22-23*. 33–36.

[14] Jill Freyne and Shlomo Berkovsky. 2010. Intelligent food planning: personalized recipe recommendation. In *Proc. of IUI'10*. ACM, 321–324.

[15] Lorenzo Gatti, Marco Guerini, Oliviero Stock, and Carlo Strapparava. 2014. Sentiment variations in text for persuasion technology. In *International Conference on Persuasive Technology*. Springer, 106–117.

[16] Mouzhi Ge, Francesco Ricci, and David Massimo. Health-aware Food Recommender System. In *Proc. of RecSys '15*. 333–334.

[17] Morgan Harvey, Bernd Ludwig, and David Elsweiler. 2013. You are what you eat: Learning user tastes for rating prediction. In *Proc. of SPIRE'13*. Springer, 153–164.

[18] Simon Howard, Jean Adams, Martin White, and others. 2012. Nutritional content of supermarket ready meals and recipes by television chefs in the United Kingdom: cross sectional study. *BMJ* 345 (2012).

[19] Daniel Kahneman. 2011. *Thinking, fast and slow*. Macmillan.

[20] Marian Knopp. 2011. Information needs, preferences, and behaviors of home cooks. *Library and Information Research* 35, 109 (2011), 40–54.

[21] Tomasz Kusmierczyk, Christoph Trattner, and Kjetil Nørvåg. Temporal Patterns in Online Food Innovation. In *Proc. of WWW'15 Companion*.

[22] Tomasz Kusmierczyk, Christoph Trattner, and Kjetil Nørvåg. Temporality in online food recipe consumption and production. In *Proc. of WWW'15*.

[23] J Richard Landis and Gary G Koch. 1977. The measurement of observer agreement for categorical data. *biometrics* (1977), 159–174.

[24] Michael Macht. 2008. How emotions affect eating: a five-way model. *Appetite* 50, 1 (2008), 1–11.

[25] Neema Moraveji, Daniel Russell, Jacob Bien, and David Mease. 2011. Measuring improvement in user search performance resulting from optimal search tips. In *Proc. of SIGIR'11*. ACM, 355–364.

[26] Georgina Oliver, Jane Wardle, and E Leigh Gibson. 2000. Stress and Food Choice: A Laboratory Study. *Psychosomatic Medicine* 62 (2000), 853–865.

[27] Emily Pitler and Ani Nenkova. 2008. Revisiting Readability: A Unified Framework for Predicting Text Quality. In *Proc. of EMNLP'08*. Association for Computational Linguistics, Stroudsburg, PA, USA, 186–195.

[28] Antonio Rangel. 2013. Regulation of dietary choice by the decision-making circuitry. *Nature neuroscience* 16, 12 (2013), 1717–1724.

[29] Paul Rozin, Claude Fischler, Sumio Imada, Allison Sarubin, and Amy Wrzesniewski. 1999. Attitudes to food and the role of food in life in the USA, Japan, Flemish Belgium and France: Possible implications for the diet–health debate. *Appetite* 33, 2 (1999), 163–180.

[30] Gary Sacks, Mike Rayner, and Boyd Swinburn. 2009. Impact of front-of-pack traffic-light,nutrition labelling on consumer food purchases in the UK. *Health promotion international* 24, 4 (2009), 344–352.

[31] Jose San Pedro and Stefan Siersdorfer. 2009. Ranking and Classifying Attractiveness of Photos in Folksonomies. In *Proc. of WWW'09*. ACM, New York, NY, USA, 771–780.

[32] Benjamin Scheibehenne, Rainer Greifeneder, and Peter M Todd. 2010. Can there ever be too many options? A meta-analytic review of choice overload. *Journal of Consumer Research* 37, 3 (2010), 409–425.

[33] Chun-Yuen Teng, Yu-Ru Lin, and Lada A. Adamic. Recipe Recommendation Using Ingredient Networks. In *Proc. of WebSci'12*. 298–307.

[34] Christoph Trattner and David Elsweiler. 2017. Investigating the Healthiness of Internet-Sourced Recipes: Implications for Meal Planning and Recommender Systems. In *Proc. of WWW'17*. ACM.

[35] Christoph Trattner, David Elsweiler, and Simon Howard. 2017. Estimating the Healthiness of Internet Recipes: A Cross-sectional Study. *Frontiers in Public Health* 5 (2017), 16. DOI: http://dx.doi.org/10.3389/fpubh.2017.00016

[36] Viet Phu Tu, Dominique Valentin, Florence Husson, and Catherine Dacremont. 2010. Cultural differences in food description and preference: Contrasting Vietnamese and French panellists on soy yogurts. *Food Quality and Preference* 21, 6 (2010), 602–610.

[37] Youri van Pinxteren, Gijs Geleijnse, and Paul Kamsteeg. 2011. Deriving a recipe similarity measure for recommending healthful meals. In *Proc. of IUI'11*. ACM, 105–114.

[38] Brian Wansink. 2006. *Mindless eating*. Bantam Books.

[39] Robert West, Ryen W White, and Eric Horvitz. From cookies to cooks: Insights on dietary patterns via analysis of web usage logs. In *Proc. of WWW'13*. 1399–1410.

[40] Ryen White. 2013. Beliefs and biases in web search. In *Proc. of SIGIR'13*. ACM, 3–12.

[41] Jessica Wisdom, Julie S Downs, and George Loewenstein. 2010. Promoting healthy choices: Information versus convenience. *American Economic Journal: Applied Economics* 2, 2 (2010), 164–178.

[42] Michiko Yasukawa, Fernando Diaz, Gregory Druck, and Nobu Tsukada. 2014. Overview of the NTCIR-11 Cooking Recipe Search Task.. In *NTCIR*.

Embedding Factorization Models for Jointly Recommending Items and User Generated Lists

Da Cao[1,2], Liqiang Nie[3], Xiangnan He[4], Xiaochi Wei[5], Shunzhi Zhu[2,*], Tat-Seng Chua[4]
[1]Department of Automation, Xiamen University
[2]College of Computer and Information Engineering, Xiamen University of Technology
[3]School of Computer Science and Technology, Shandong University
[4]School of Computing, National University of Singapore
[5]School of Computer Science, Beijing Institute of Technology
{caoda0721, nieliqiang, xiangnanhe, xcwei.bit}@gmail.com; szzhu@xmut.edu.cn; dcscts@nus.edu.sg

ABSTRACT

Existing recommender algorithms mainly focused on recommending individual items by utilizing user-item interactions. However, little attention has been paid to recommend user generated lists (*e.g.*, playlists and booklists). On one hand, user generated lists contain rich signal about item co-occurrence, as items within a list are usually gathered based on a specific theme. On the other hand, a user's preference over a list also indicate her preference over items within the list. We believe that 1) if the rich relevance signal within user generated lists can be properly leveraged, an enhanced recommendation for individual items can be provided, and 2) if user-item and user-list interactions are properly utilized, and the relationship between a list and its contained items is discovered, the performance of user-item and user-list recommendations can be mutually reinforced.

Towards this end, we devise embedding factorization models, which extend traditional factorization method by incorporating item-item (item-item-list) co-occurrence with embedding-based algorithms. Specifically, we employ factorization model to capture users' preferences over items and lists, and utilize embedding-based models to discover the co-occurrence information among items and lists. The gap between the two types of models is bridged by sharing items' latent factors. Remarkably, our proposed framework is capable of solving the new-item cold-start problem, where items have never been consumed by users but exist in user generated lists. Overall performance comparisons and micro-level analyses demonstrate the promising performance of our proposed approaches.

CCS CONCEPTS

•Information systems → Recommender systems; •Human-centered computing → Collaborative filtering;

SIGIR'17, August 7-11, 2017, Shinjuku, Tokyo, Japan.
© 2017 ACM. 978-1-4503-4887-4/17/08...$15.00
DOI: http://dx.doi.org/10.1145/3077136.3080779

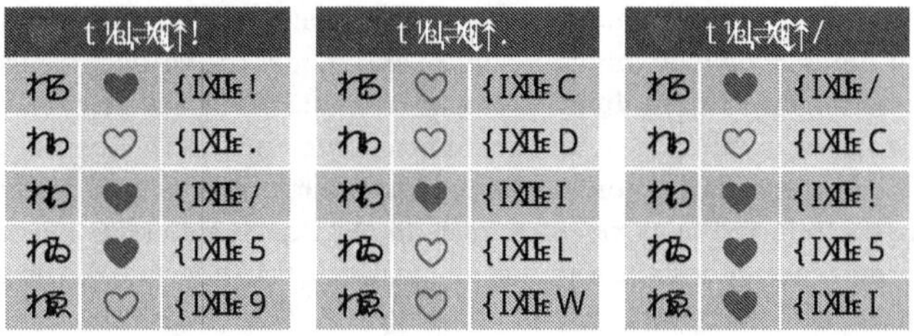

Figure 1: The illustrations of 1) a user's preference over lists; 2) the user's preference over items within lists; and 3) relationships among items and lists.

KEYWORDS

Recommender Systems, Factorization Model, Embedding-based Model, Cold-start Problem, Co-occurrence Information

1 INTRODUCTION

Recommender systems have received great attention in recent years owing to their ability in mitigating the information overload problem. In the light of this, recommender systems have been widely applied in multiple domains such as music [6, 7], image [4, 5], restaurant [14], and mobile app [3, 21, 22]. Existing studies on recommender systems mainly focused on recommending individual and independent items to users, and arousing several derived research topics such as cold-start problem [2], implicit feedback [1, 13], context-aware [11, 27], deep learning [35], and efficient hashing [30, 37]. However, traditional recommender systems are specifically designed for optimizing user-item interactions and are not optimized for some complex circumstances such as recommending user generated lists, which are very popular in various real-world scenarios such as lists of songs created by listeners on Netease[1], lists of books created by readers on GoodReads[2], and lists of products created by shoppers on Amazon[3].

User generated lists are created by users and are exposed to the public by default. Beyond the traditional searching process for isolated items, the list service offers a new way for users to explore their desired group of items. Figure 1 illustrates a user's

* Corresponding author.
[1]https://music.163.com
[2]https://www.goodreads.com
[3]https://www.amazon.com

preference over lists and their contained items in the domain of music. The items are manually grouped into a list according to a specific theme, which indicates the co-occurrence feature among items. Meanwhile, as the list is composed of several items, the preference over a list somehow signal one's preference over the contained items. Therefore, if users' preferences over items and lists are properly utilized and the relationship between the list and its items is discovered, the recommendation performance of user-item and user-list can be mutually reinforced.

Despite its value and significance, jointly recommending user generated lists and their contained items remains in its infancy due to the following challenges: 1) Unlike the traditional item-independent view, items within a list are gathered together based on a common theme, which provides rich signal about the correlation of items. However, how to capture and model the co-occurrence relationship among items is a non-trivial task. 2) The cold-start problem is much heavier for item recommendation since there are numerous items only exist in lists but are never consumed by users (referred to as *new-item cold-start*). Thus how to leverage co-occurrence information among items from lists to alleviate the new-item cold-start problem is of great interest. 3) A user's preference over a list also manifests her preference over items within the list, and vice versa. Therefore, how to devise an unified framework to reinforce the recommendation performance of both user-item and user-list is a valuable research issue. In summary, to better serve users with a quality recommendation service, it is highly desirable to develop techniques that comprehensively consider the co-occurrence information among items, new-item cold-start problem, and joint recommendation of items and lists.

To tackle these problems, we devise embedding factorization models, which jointly factorize user-item (user-item-list) interaction matrix and item-item (item-item-list) co-occurrence matrix, where the co-occurrence matrix is derived from embedding-based algorithms. In the first stage, we utilize lists as side-information to harvest the item co-occurrence relationship. The co-occurrence information among items is obtained by using word embedding method, whereby items are correlated within a fixed-length window. Furthermore, user-item interaction matrix and item-item co-occurrence matrix are factorized at the same time. As a byproduct, the new-item cold-start problem can be solved. In the second stage, we incorporate the list as a word into the item-item co-occurrence matrix, and refer the newly created matrix as item-item-list co-occurrence matrix. Moreover, user-item interaction matrix, user-list interaction matrix, and item-item-list co-occurrence matrix are factorized within a unified framework. Thus, the recommendation performance of user-item and user-list can be mutually enhanced. By conducting experiments on our constructed real-world datasets, we demonstrate that our proposed approaches yield significant gains as compared with other state-of-the-art methods.

Our contributions are summarized as follows:

- We explore the promising yet challenging problem of recommending user generated lists and their contained items. To the best of our knowledge, this is the first work that attempts to solve this problem by reinforcing recommendation approach with embedding-based algorithms.
- We present embedding factorization models that jointly factorize user-item (user-item-list) interaction matrix and item-item (item-item-list) co-occurrence matrix. The new-item cold-start problem can be well addressed, and the user-item and user-list recommendation performance can be mutually enhanced.
- Extensive experiments performed on our self-collected datasets demonstrate the effectiveness of our proposed approaches. Meanwhile, we have released the datasets and our implementation to facilitate the research community for further exploration[4].

2 RELATED WORK

The development of recommender systems has long been divided into two directions, namely, rating prediction and item recommendation. Rating prediction on explicit feedback has dominated the research community in the early stage of recommender systems, primarily due to its simplicity on model optimization and evaluation (as only observer data need to be considered [15, 16, 35]). However, in real-world scenarios, interactions between users and items are always in an implicit form, such as purchasing products and listening music. Obviously, due to the one-class nature of implicit data, rating prediction is no longer suitable, and the research trends turn to item recommendation task. Various ranking algorithms were designed to model implicit datasets, among which Bayesian personalized ranking (BPR) [26] is a typical work. BPR optimizes ranking performance through a general pair-wise ranking function. Meanwhile, users' preferences over items are inferred by utilizing a negative sampling strategy. Other commonly used item recommendation frameworks include point-wise regression [1, 40] and graph-based models [12, 33].

The aforementioned item recommendation techniques have indeed improved the recommendation performance over individual items. However, in practice, users are often exposed to a set of items and the items are not independent. Along this line, a framework for recommending relevant and diverse items was proposed [29], which explicitly takes the coverage of user's interests into account. Another curiosity-based work was introduced [38], which combines relevance and curiosity in the recommendation process. Except for the work considering the correlation among items, recommending a list of several items instead of isolated items is another remarkable direction. In [41], the authors defined the concept of bundle recommendation, in which a bundle refers to a set of items that users consider or consume together under a specific circumstance (*e.g.*, limit total price, contextual influence, and product compatibility or consistency). The work of [28] aims to recommend a list of items to users by optimizing the list's click-trough rate. Although these work recommends a list of items to users, users' explicit preferences over lists are ignored. The closest work to ours is [24], in which users' previous interactions with both lists and individual items are considered simultaneously. The relationship between the list and its contained items is built based on a linear combination. Distinct from previous work, we treat a list as a sentence and items within the list as words. We then resort to word embedding algorithms to explore the list recommendation problem from such a new perspective.

[4] https://listrec.wixsite.com/efms

Word embedding models have gained great success in natural language processing tasks, where words or phrases are mapped to vectors of real numbers. As a seminal method for word embedding, word2vec [25] is able to capture a large number of precise syntactic and semantic word relationships. It has been shown that the word2vec (skip-gram) is equivalent to perform implicit matrix factorization [19]. As an extension to word2vec, paragraph2vec [18] is later introduced, in which paragraph refers to variable-length pieces of texts (*e.g.,* sentences, paragraphs, and documents). It is a two-step model, where word vectors and paragraph vectors are obtained in the first and second phase, respectively. Inspired by paragraph2vec, hierarchical neural language models [8] are proposed by designing joint training models to obtain word vectors and paragraph vectors simultaneously.

There have been some efforts to tailor word embedding algorithms for delivering effective recommendation. Grbovic *et al.* [10] developed prod2vec models, in which a product is treated as a word and the list of a user's consumed products is regarded as a sentence. The recommendation is conducted by computing the distance between the new product (word) and the list of user's consumed products (sentence). To further enhance the performance of prod2vec, Vasile *et al.* [32] proposed to inject item metadata into the prod2vec to regularize the item embedding. By utilizing the skip-gram word2vec model and a pair-wise ranking loss, Liu *et al.* [23] devised a two-step strategy to explore the context of locations for personalized location recommendation. A co-factorization model, CoFactor [20], was presented, which jointly decomposes the user-item interaction matrix and the item-item co-occurrence matrix by sharing items' latent factors. CoFactor is inspired by the word2vec model which can be interpreted as factorizing the word co-occurrence matrix. Word embedding algorithms have shown great ability in enhancing the recommendation performance for individual items. This work is orthogonal to the above mentioned work, as we exploit the embedding-based techniques to tackle the list recommendation task, which to our knowledge, has never been explored before.

3 PRELIMINARIES

We first introduce the Bayesian-based ranking model, BPR, which is designed for optimizing users' preferences over pair-wise samples (*i.e.,* positive sample against negative or missing sample). We then describe how the skip-gram word2vec model is translated into factorizing a word-context matrix. Finally, the hierarchical neural language model is introduced, which is devised for representing sentences and their contained words.

3.1 Bayesian Personalized Ranking

BPR is a latent factor-based algorithm [26]. In BPR, each user u is represented as a latent factor $\mathbf{w}_u$, and each item i is denoted as a latent factor $\mathbf{h}_i$. The predicted rating on item i by user u is represented as $\hat{x}_{ui}$ and is generated by the inner product of the corresponding user latent factor and item latent factor, *i.e.,* $\mathbf{w}_u \cdot \mathbf{h}_i$. The optimization criterion for BPR consists of a Bayesian analysis and the prior probability for the model parameters, which is represented as,

$$\begin{aligned}\mathcal{L}_{\text{BPR}} &= \ln p(\boldsymbol{\Theta}|>_u) \\ &= \ln p(>_u|\boldsymbol{\Theta})p(\boldsymbol{\Theta}) \\ &= \ln \prod_{(u,i,j)\in\mathcal{D}_B} \sigma(\hat{x}_{uij})p(\boldsymbol{\Theta}) \\ &= \sum_{(u,i,j)\in\mathcal{D}_B} \ln\sigma(\hat{x}_{uij}) + \ln p(\boldsymbol{\Theta}) \\ &= \sum_{(u,i,j)\in\mathcal{D}_B} \ln\sigma(\hat{x}_{uij}) - \lambda_{\boldsymbol{\Theta}}||\boldsymbol{\Theta}||, \end{aligned} \tag{1}$$

where $>_u$ denotes the desired latent preference structure for the user u; $\hat{x}_{uij} = \hat{x}_{ui} - \hat{x}_{uj}$; the observed subset $\mathcal{D}_B$ of $>_u$ is used as training data; $\sigma = \frac{1}{1+e^{-x}}$ is the logistic sigmoid function; $\boldsymbol{\Theta}$ denotes all parameters (latent factors of users and items); and $\lambda_{\boldsymbol{\Theta}}$ is the model specific regularization parameter. BPR is suitable for matrix factorization (MF) [16] and k-nearest-neighbor (KNN) [15]. When it comes to MF, the problem of predicting $\hat{x}_{ui}$ can be seen as the task of estimating a matrix $\mathbf{X} : U \times I$. The estimation of $\mathbf{X}$ is approximated by the matrix product of two low-rank matrices $\mathbf{W} : |U| \times k$ and $\mathbf{H} : |I| \times k$,

$$\hat{\mathbf{X}} := \mathbf{W}\mathbf{H}^t, \tag{2}$$

where k is the dimensionality of the approximation. Meanwhile, the prediction formula can be written as,

$$\hat{x}_{ui} =< \mathbf{w}_u, \mathbf{h}_i >= \sum_{f=1}^{k} w_{uf} \cdot h_{if}. \tag{3}$$

To optimize the criteria of BPR, a stochastic gradient descent algorithm, LEARNBPR, is proposed which is based on bootstrap sampling of training triples. The model parameters for matrix factorization are $\boldsymbol{\Theta} = (\mathbf{W}, \mathbf{H})$. The optimization with LEARNBPR only lies on $\frac{\partial \hat{x}_{uij}}{\partial \theta}$.

3.2 Word Embedding as Matrix Factorization

The skip-gram word2vec model [25] is a simplified neural language model without any non-linear hidden layers. A log-linear classifier is used to predict the surrounding words within a certain distance based on the current one. To be precise, the object of the skip-gram model is to maximize the log-likelihood,

$$\mathcal{L}_{\text{SG}} = \sum_{t=1}^{T} \log \mathbb{P}(w_{t-c} : w_{t+c}|w_t), \tag{4}$$

where w_t is the tth word in the sequence, and $w_{t-c} : w_{t+c}$ represents successive words $(w_{t-c}, w_{t-c+1}, ..., w_{t+c})$ that act as the context to the word w_t. Several sophisticated implementations are designed for the skip-gram model, such as negative sampling and hierarchical softmax.

Levy and Goldberg [19] demonstrated that the skip-gram with negative-sampling word2vec model is implicitly factorizing a word-context matrix, whose cells are the pointwise mutual information (PMI) of the respective word and context pairs, shifted by a global constant. Given a training corpus $\mathcal{D}$ and a word i, several words are selected as the context words for word i according to a specific strategy (*e.g.,* the neighboring words falling in the fix-sized windows

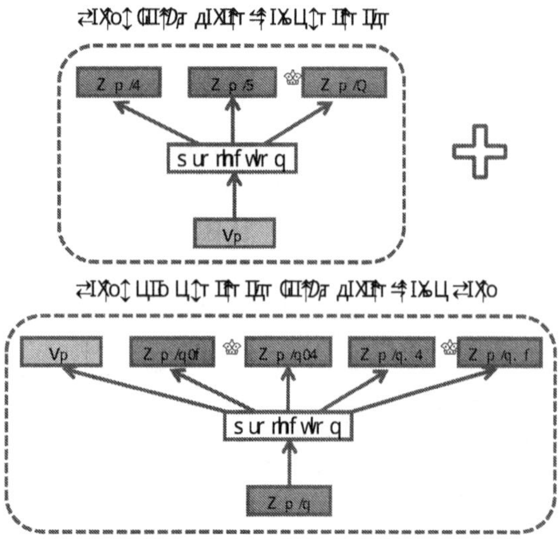

Figure 2: The visualization of the embedding model for sentences and their contained words.

centered at word i). The number of times that a context word j appears in the word i's context is denoted as $\#(i,j)$. PMI between a word i and its context j is defined as,

$$\mathrm{PMI}(i,j) = \log \frac{\#(i,j) \cdot \mathcal{D}}{\#(i) \cdot \#(j)}, \tag{5}$$

where $\#(i) = \sum_j \#(i,j)$, $\#(j) = \sum_i \#(i,j)$, and $\mathcal{D} = \sum_{ij} \#(i,j)$. Levy and Goldberg [19] further proposed to perform word embedding by spectral dimensionality reduction (*e.g.*, singular value decomposition) on the (sparse) shifted positive PMI (SPPMI) matrix,

$$\mathrm{SPPMI}(i,j) = \max\{\mathrm{PMI}(i,j) - \log h, 0\}, \tag{6}$$

where h is a hyperparameter that controls the density of the SPPMI matrix.

3.3 Embedding Model for Sentences

As an extension of the skip-gram word2vec model in Eq. (4), Le and Mikolov [18] proposed the paragraph2vec model to obtain the paragraph representation, which utilizes a two-phase strategy. Hierarchical neural language models [8, 10] were further presented to jointly represent sentences and their contained words. The training dataset is derived from the set of sentences $\mathcal{G}$, which comprised of sentences s_m and their contained sequential words $s_m = (w_{m1}, w_{m2}, \ldots, w_{mN})$, where N denotes the sentence length. As illustrated in [8], both skip-gram and continuous bag-of-word models can be used in any level of the hierarchy. We thus resort to utilize skip-gram in all levels of the hierarchy in order to make it consistent with Section 3.2. The architecture of such model is illustrated in Figure 2. The objective of the hierarchical model is to maximize the log-likelihood of the streaming data,

$$\begin{aligned}\mathcal{L}_{\mathrm{HM}} = \sum_{g \in \mathcal{G}} \Big(\sum_{w_{mn} \in s_m} & \log \mathbb{P}(w_{m,n-c} : w_{m,n+c}, s_m | w_{mn}) \\ & + \sum_{s_m \in g} (\log \mathbb{P}(w_{m1} : w_{mN} | s_m)),\end{aligned} \tag{7}$$

where c is the length of the training context for word sequences.

4 OUR PROPOSED APPROACHES

In this section, we present our embedding factorization models for jointly recommending user generated lists and their contained items. In the first stage, user generated lists are employed as side-information to correlate items within them. Meanwhile, the new-item cold-start problem can be solved, in which items exist in lists but are new to users. In the second stage, both user-item interactions and user-list interactions are considered, user generated lists and their contained items are recommended simultaneously.

4.1 Utilizing Lists as Side-Information

4.1.1 Exploring the Item Co-occurrence. Given the sparse user-item interaction matrix $\mathbf{X} \in \mathbb{R}^{U \times I}$ from U users and I items, where I items are from L lists, BPR decomposes it into the product of user and item latent factors. User generated lists are considered as side-information, which means users' preferences over lists are ignored in this stage but lists are utilized to correlate items within them. Let $\mathbf{M} \in \mathbb{R}_+^{I \times J}$ be the co-occurrence SPPMI matrix, where I represents the number of items in lists and J represents the number of context items[5]. The lists are divided into shorter segments of sequences according to the fixed-length window size c. $m_{ij} \in \mathbf{M}$ is computed according to Eq. (5) and Eq. (6). $\mathbf{M}$ is factorized into two low-rank matrices $\mathrm{H} : |I| \times k$ and $\mathrm{C} : |J| \times k$,

$$\hat{\mathbf{M}} := \mathrm{HC}^t, \tag{8}$$

where k is the dimensionality of the approximation. The task of the recommendation is to provide the user with a personalized total ranking $>_u$ of all items I, sorted according to the likelihood that the user will be interested in each of them.

Both BPR and word2vec's equivalent matrix factorization are latent factor-based methods. The main difference is that the former factorizes user-item interaction matrix to capture users' preferences over items, while the latter factorizes item-item co-occurrence matrix to obtain the co-occurrence relationship among items. Items' latent factors are shared across these two models. Therefore, we propose a joint learning model to seamlessly sew them up,

$$\begin{aligned}\mathcal{L}_{\mathrm{EFM-Side}} = & \sum_{(u,i,j) \in \mathcal{D}_T} \ln \sigma(\hat{x}_{uij}) \\ & + \lambda_s \sum_{(i,j,t) \in \mathcal{D}_S} \ln \sigma(\hat{m}_{ijt}) - \lambda_{\Theta} ||\Theta||,\end{aligned} \tag{9}$$

where $\mathcal{D}_T$ is the training corpus for the user-item entry $\hat{x}_{ui}$; $\mathcal{D}_S$ is the training corpus for the item-item entry $\hat{m}_{ij}$; λ_s balances the performance between BPR and word2vec's equivalent matrix factorization. This is the embedding factorization model by utilizing lists as side-information (denoted as EFM-Side). In fact, several co-training models (*e.g.*, collective matrix factorization [31] and multi-relational matrix factorization [17]) have been proposed, which co-factorize multiple matrices in the context of relational learning. We can regard EPM-Side as a special case of MR-BPR [17], which builds the co-occurrence relationship among items.

[5]In fact, the set of items in lists and the set of context items are the same.

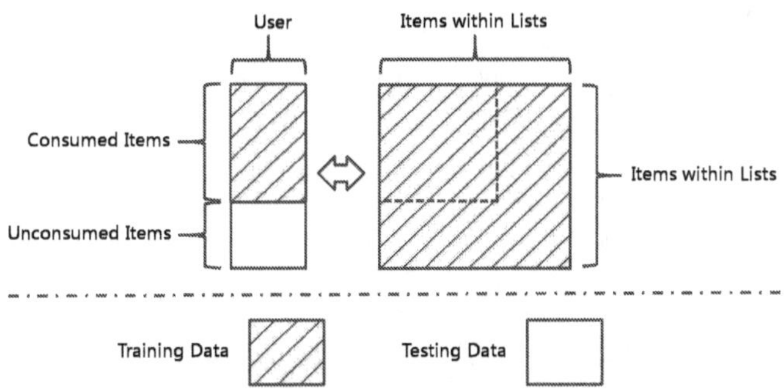

Figure 3: The illustration of the new-item cold-start problem, where cold-start items only exist in lists and are never consumed by users.

4.1.2 New-Item Cold-Start Problem. Apart from utilizing list as side-information to boost recommendation performance, we expect the new-item cold-start problem to be solved as well. In the new-item cold-start scenario, the task is to recommend the items that only exist in lists but are totally fresh to users. Figure 3 visualizes the new-item cold-start problem. The latent factors for users' consumed items are finely learnt from user-item interactions. For unconsumed items, their latent factors are adjusted by factorizing item-item co-occurrence matrix. Therefore, users' preferences over unconsumed items are estimated from the inner products of users' latent factors and the unconsumed items' latent factors. It is worth noting that in addition to the new-item cold-start problem, EFM-Side can also well handle warm-start scenarios where the initial few user-item interactions become available.

4.2 Jointly Recommending Items and Lists

Suppose we have U users, I items, and L lists, where I items are from L lists. Beside the sparse user-item interaction matrix $\mathbf{X} \in \mathbb{R}^{U \times I}$, the sparse user-list interaction matrix $\mathrm{Y} \in \mathbb{R}^{U \times L}$ is also available. As we know, the sentence embedding model is an extension to skip-gram word2vec, word2vec's equivalent matrix factorization can thus naturally expand to the embedding model for sentences. In Figure 2, the sentence is regarded as a word token to be embedded into the word2vec model. Regarding the concept of window size, the lists are further divided into shorter segments of sequences with the length of c. The sentence is appeared in the context of each word within it, and each word within the sentence is also appeared in the context of the sentence. Therefore, the co-occurrence SPPMI matrix $\mathbf{M} \in \mathbb{R}_+^{I \times J}$ is further extended to $\mathbf{R} \in \mathbb{R}_+^{|I'| \times |J'|}$, where $|I'|$ represents the number of items and lists, and $|J'|$ represents the number of context items and lists. Obviously, $|I'| = |J'| = |I| + |J|$. The elements in $\mathbf{R}$ are computed according to Eq. (5) and Eq. (6). Hence, we propose a joint learning model to enhance the recommendation performance of both item and list,

$$\mathcal{L}_{\text{EFM-Joint}} = \sum_{(u,i,j)\in\mathcal{D}_T} \ln\sigma(\hat{x}_{uij}) + \sum_{(u,i,j)\in\mathcal{D}_L} \ln\sigma(\hat{y}_{uij}) + \lambda_r \sum_{(i,j,t)\in\mathcal{D}_R} \ln\sigma(\hat{r}_{ijt}) - \lambda_{\Theta}||\Theta||, \tag{10}$$

Algorithm 1: The Optimization for EFM-Side

Random initialize $\mathbf{\Theta}$;
repeat
  `// Factorize user-item interaction matrix`
  repeat
    Draw $(\mathbf{w}_u, \mathbf{h}_i, \mathbf{h}_j)$ from $\mathcal{D}_T$;
    $\Theta \leftarrow \Theta + \mu\left(\frac{e^{-\hat{x}_{uij}}}{1+e^{-\hat{x}_{uij}}} \cdot \frac{\partial \hat{x}_{uij}}{\partial\Theta} + \lambda_\Theta \cdot \Theta\right)$;
  until *convergence*;
  `// Factorize item-item co-occurrence matrix`
  repeat
    Draw $(\mathbf{h}_i, \mathbf{c}_j, \mathbf{c}_t)$ from $\mathcal{D}_S$;
    $\Theta \leftarrow \Theta + \mu\left(\lambda_s \frac{e^{-\hat{m}_{ijt}}}{1+e^{-\hat{m}_{ijt}}} \cdot \frac{\partial \hat{m}_{ijt}}{\partial\Theta} + \lambda_\Theta \cdot \Theta\right)$;
  until *convergence*;
until *convergence or max-iteration has been reached*;

where $\mathcal{D}_T$ is the training corpus for the user-item entry $\hat{x}_{ui}$; $\mathcal{D}_L$ is the training corpus for the user-list entry $\hat{y}_{ui}$; $\mathcal{D}_R$ is the training corpus for the item-item-list entry $\hat{r}_{ij}$; and λ_r balances the performance between BPR and the embedding model for sentences' equivalent factorization model. This is the embedding factorization model which jointly recommends lists and their contained items (denoted as EFM-Joint).

4.3 Solutions

4.3.1 Optimization for EFM-Side. The optimization procedure for the loss function in Eq. (9) can be realized via the stochastic gradient descent (SGD) strategy. A sophisticated SGD strategy algorithm, called LEARNBPR, is proposed [26], which only considers user-item interactions. As an extension to BPR, EFM-Side further takes the item co-occurrence into account. We inherit the multi-relational SGD strategy proposed in [17] to realize our designed framework. Specifically, the optimization procedure is conducted alternatively with respect to $\mathcal{D}_T$ and $\mathcal{D}_S$. At each iteration of $\mathcal{D}_T$ and $\mathcal{D}_S$, a training instance is randomly sampled, and a gradient descent step for all related parameters regarding the loss of the training instance is performed. Algorithm 1 details the procedure. The derivative of the loss function presented in Eq. (9) is:

$$\frac{\partial \mathcal{L}_{\text{EFM-Side}}(\hat{x}_{uij})}{\partial\Theta} = \frac{-e^{-\hat{x}_{uij}}}{1+e^{-\hat{x}_{uij}}} \cdot \frac{\partial \hat{x}_{uij}}{\partial\Theta} - \lambda_\Theta \cdot \Theta, \tag{11}$$

$$\frac{\partial \mathcal{L}_{\text{EFM-Side}}(\hat{m}_{ijt})}{\partial\Theta} = \lambda_s \frac{-e^{-\hat{m}_{ijt}}}{1+e^{-\hat{m}_{ijt}}} \cdot \frac{\partial \hat{m}_{ijt}}{\partial\Theta} - \lambda_\Theta \cdot \Theta. \tag{12}$$

The derivatives of $\hat{x}_{uij}$ and $\hat{m}_{ijt}$ are,

$$\frac{\partial \hat{x}_{uij}}{\partial\Theta} = \begin{cases} \mathbf{h}_{if} - \mathbf{h}_{jf} & if \quad \theta = \mathbf{w}_{uf}, \\ \mathbf{w}_{uf} & if \quad \theta = \mathbf{h}_{if}, \\ -\mathbf{w}_{uf} & if \quad \theta = \mathbf{h}_{jf}, \\ 0 & else \end{cases} \tag{13}$$

$$\frac{\partial \hat{m}_{ijt}}{\partial\Theta} = \begin{cases} \mathbf{c}_{jf} - \mathbf{c}_{tf} & if \quad \theta = \mathbf{h}_{if}, \\ \mathbf{h}_{if} & if \quad \theta = \mathbf{c}_{jf}, \\ -\mathbf{h}_{if} & if \quad \theta = \mathbf{c}_{tf}, \\ 0 & else \end{cases} \tag{14}$$

Table 1: Statistics of the evaluation datasets.

Dataset	User-song interaction#	User-list interaction#	User#	Song#	Playlist#	User-song density	User-list density
User-Song	1, 128, 065	0	18, 528	123, 628	22, 864	0.05%	0
User-Song-Playlist	1, 128, 065	528, 128	18, 528	123, 628	22, 864	0.05%	0.12%

Algorithm 2: The Optimization for EFM-Joint

Random initialize $\boldsymbol{\Theta}$;
repeat
  `// Factorize user-item interaction matrix`
  repeat
    Draw $(\mathbf{w}_u, \mathbf{h}_i, \mathbf{h}_j)$ from $\mathcal{D}_T$;
    $\Theta \leftarrow \Theta + \mu\left(\frac{e^{-\hat{x}_{uij}}}{1+e^{-\hat{x}_{uij}}} \cdot \frac{\partial \hat{x}_{uij}}{\partial \Theta} + \lambda_\Theta \cdot \Theta\right)$;
  until *convergence*;
  `// Factorize user-list interaction matrix`
  repeat
    Draw $(\mathbf{w}_u, \mathbf{h}_i, \mathbf{h}_j)$ from $\mathcal{D}_L$;
    $\Theta \leftarrow \Theta + \mu\left(\frac{e^{-\hat{y}_{uij}}}{1+e^{-\hat{y}_{uij}}} \cdot \frac{\partial \hat{y}_{uij}}{\partial \Theta} + \lambda_\Theta \cdot \Theta\right)$;
  until *convergence*;
  `// Factorize item-item-list co-occurrence matrix`
  repeat
    Draw $(\mathbf{h}_i, \mathbf{c}_j, \mathbf{c}_t)$ from $\mathcal{D}_R$;
    $\Theta \leftarrow \Theta + \mu\left(\lambda_r \frac{e^{-\hat{r}_{ijt}}}{1+e^{-\hat{r}_{ijt}}} \cdot \frac{\partial \hat{r}_{ijt}}{\partial \Theta} + \lambda_\Theta \cdot \Theta\right)$;
  until *convergence*;
until *convergence or max-iteration has been reached*;

where f denotes the fth latent feature of the corresponding latent factor. We alternatively factorize user-item interaction matrix and item-item co-occurrence matrix until convergence or the maximum number of iterations is reached. The optimization procedure applies to the new-item cold-start problem as well.

4.3.2 Optimization for EFM-Joint. The optimization procedure for EFM-Joint is similar to the one illustrated in Section 4.3.1. The main difference is that the user-list interaction matrix is considered and the co-occurrence matrix is reconstructed which takes the list into account. We thus still resort to conduct SGD optimization alternatively with respect to $\mathcal{D}_T$, $\mathcal{D}_L$, and $\mathcal{D}_R$. Algorithm 2 details the detailed procedure. The derivative of the loss function presented in Eq. (10) is,

$$\frac{\partial \mathcal{L}_{\text{EFM-Joint}}(\hat{x}_{uij})}{\partial \Theta} = \frac{-e^{-\hat{x}_{uij}}}{1+e^{-\hat{x}_{uij}}} \cdot \frac{\partial \hat{x}_{uij}}{\partial \Theta} - \lambda_\Theta \cdot \Theta, \tag{15}$$

$$\frac{\partial \mathcal{L}_{\text{EFM-Joint}}(\hat{y}_{uij})}{\partial \Theta} = \frac{-e^{-\hat{y}_{uij}}}{1+e^{-\hat{y}_{uij}}} \cdot \frac{\partial \hat{y}_{uij}}{\partial \Theta} - \lambda_\Theta \cdot \Theta, \tag{16}$$

$$\frac{\partial \mathcal{L}_{\text{EFM-Joint}}(\hat{r}_{ijt})}{\partial \Theta} = \lambda_r \frac{-e^{-\hat{r}_{ijt}}}{1+e^{-\hat{r}_{ijt}}} \cdot \frac{\partial \hat{r}_{ijt}}{\partial \Theta} - \lambda_\Theta \cdot \Theta. \tag{17}$$

The derivatives of $\hat{x}_{uij}$, $\hat{y}_{uij}$, and $\hat{r}_{ijt}$ are,

$$\frac{\partial \hat{x}_{uij}}{\partial \Theta} = \begin{cases} \mathbf{h}_{if} - \mathbf{h}_{jf} & if \quad \theta = \mathbf{w}_{uf}, \\ \mathbf{w}_{uf} & if \quad \theta = \mathbf{h}_{if}, \\ -\mathbf{w}_{uf} & if \quad \theta = \mathbf{h}_{jf}, \\ 0 & else \end{cases} \tag{18}$$

$$\frac{\partial \hat{y}_{uij}}{\partial \Theta} = \begin{cases} \mathbf{h}_{if} - \mathbf{h}_{jf} & if \quad \theta = \mathbf{w}_{uf}, \\ \mathbf{w}_{uf} & if \quad \theta = \mathbf{h}_{if}, \\ -\mathbf{w}_{uf} & if \quad \theta = \mathbf{h}_{jf}, \\ 0 & else \end{cases} \tag{19}$$

$$\frac{\partial \hat{r}_{ijt}}{\partial \Theta} = \begin{cases} \mathbf{c}_{jf} - \mathbf{c}_{tf} & if \quad \theta = \mathbf{h}_{if}, \\ \mathbf{h}_{if} & if \quad \theta = \mathbf{c}_{jf}, \\ -\mathbf{h}_{if} & if \quad \theta = \mathbf{c}_{tf}, \\ 0 & else \end{cases} \tag{20}$$

where f also denotes the fth latent feature of the corresponding latent factor. The factorizations for user-item interaction matrix, user-list interaction matrix, and item-item-list co-occurrence matrix are alternatively conducted until convergence or max-iteration has been reached.

5 EXPERIMENTS

In this section, we conduct extensive experiments on our self-collected datasets to answer the following five research questions:

RQ1 How does our designed EFM-Side approach perform as compared with other state-of-the-art competitors?

RQ2 How does EFM-Side perform in handling the new-item cold-start problem?

RQ3 Does EFM-Side consistently outperform other algorithms with respect to items with differenct scale of ratings?

RQ4 How is the recommendation performance of user-item and user-list under the EFM-Joint framework?

RQ5 Are the items within a list equally important? Is EFM-Joint able to find the most representative item within a list?

5.1 Experimental Settings

5.1.1 Datasets Construction. We constructed the dataset by crawling data from Netease Cloud Music, which enables consumers to select their desired independent songs or user generated playlists via entering keywords or browsing from genres. We further processed the dataset by retaining playlists possessing at least 10 songs, songs appearing at least in 5 playlists, and users consuming at least 10 songs and 10 playlists. Based on these criteria, we ultimately obtained 18, 528 users, 123, 628 songs, 22, 864 playlists, 1, 128, 065 user-song interactions, and 528, 128 user-playlist interactions. In the experiments of evaluating EFM-Side, user-playlist interactions were erased and we denoted this dataset as User-Song. Meanwhile, in the experiments on EFM-Joint, user-playlist interactions were considered and we denoted this dataset as User-Song-Playlist. Statistics of these two datasets are summarized in Table 1.

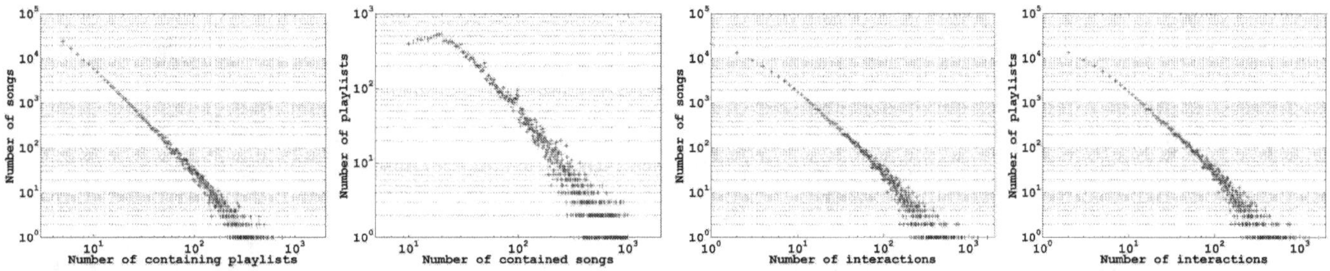

(a) Song-playlist. (b) Playlist-song. (c) Song-interaction. (d) Playlist-interaction.

Figure 4: Dataset statistics w.r.t. song and playlist.

To gain insights into the data with respect to songs and playlists, we performed some statistical analysis. We plotted the song and playlist distributions with respect to the number of containing playlists and the number of contained songs in Figure 4a and 4b (log-log plot), respectively. As we can see, both songs and playlists show a long-tail distribution — most songs appeared in few playlists, and only a small proportion of playlists have many songs. The distributions of songs and playlists with different scales of interactions are revealed in Figure 4c and 4d, which also show a long-tail distribution. This is consistent with most recommendation benchmarks, such as the Nexflix [15] and Yelp [14] datasets, and highlights the sparsity challenge faced by recommender systems.

In our experiments, we used two different strategies to generate the training, validation, and testing sets for different evaluation settings. 1) In the overall performance comparisons for EFM-Side and EFM-Joint, the original User-Song and User-Song-Playlist datasets were divided into three disjoint sets respectively, with 80%, 10%, and 10% randomly selected interactions for training, validation and testing, respectively. 2) In the new-item cold-start problem handling, 80% of songs were randomly selected and their corresponding user-song interactions were utilized for training, 10% of songs were randomly selected and their user-song interactions were used for validation, and the remaining 10% of songs and their user-song interactions were used for testing.

5.1.2 Evaluation Metrics. As practical recommender systems usually generate a ranked list of items for a given user, we evaluate the ranking performance. AUC [26], the area under the ROC curve, is a commonly used metric for evaluating the quality of a ranking list. Let the disjoint training and testing sets be $\mathcal{S}_{\text{train}}$ and $\mathcal{S}_{\text{test}}$, respectively. The average AUC can be computed as,

$$\text{AUC} = \frac{1}{|U|}\sum_{u}\frac{1}{|E(u)|}\sum_{(i,j)\in E(u)}\delta(\hat{x}_{ui} > \hat{x}_{uj}), \tag{21}$$

where $\delta(\hat{x}_{ui} > \hat{x}_{uj})$ is an indicator function which returns 1 if $\hat{x}_{ui} > \hat{x}_{uj}$ is true, and 0 otherwise. The evaluation pair for each user u is,

$$E(u) := \{(i,j)|(u,i) \in \mathcal{S}_{\text{test}} \wedge (u,j) \notin (\mathcal{S}_{\text{test}} \cup \mathcal{S}_{\text{train}})\}. \tag{22}$$

A higher value of AUC indicates better performance for ranking performance. The floor of AUC from random guess is 0.5 and the best result is 1.

5.1.3 Baseline Methods. To justify the effectiveness of our proposed EFM-Side and EFM-Joint methods, we compared with the following state-of-the-art algorithms.

BPR [26]. This is a sampling-based algorithm that optimizes the pair-wise ranking between observed instances and sampled negative instances. It optimizes parameters by SGD, and is used in the experiments for benchmarking the overall performance of both EFM-Side and EFM-Joint.

BPR-map [9]. This is a two-step model, where the latent factors for the entities in the auxiliary domain are obtained in the first step and the latent factors for other entities in the target domain are acquired in the second step. It is mainly designed for mitigating the cold-start issue in the target domain. It would be used in the experiment for new-item cold-start problem.

LIRE [24]. This method considers users' previous interactions with both individual items and user generated lists. It weights items within lists based on both position of items and personalized list consumption pattern. It also applies the BPR framework for optimization, and is a strong competitor in jointly recommending lists and their contained items.

CoFactor [20]. This is a joint learning model that combines recommendation algorithm with word embedding model. The co-occurrence relationships among items (lists) are discovered from users' consumed sequential items (lists). It would be deployed in overall performance comparisons for both EFM-Side and EFM-Joint.

All hyper-parameters and learning rates of aforementioned approaches were carefully tuned on the validation set by grid search. We repeated every experiment for 5 times to report the average results. We also conducted the paired two-sample t-test based on the 5 times experiment results. We used Python for our algorithm implementations. All the experiments were conducted over a server equipped with Intel(R) Core(TM) i7-6700 CPU at 4.00 GHz on 32G RAM, 8 cores and 64-bit Windows 7 operating system.

5.2 Individual Items Recommendation (RQ1)

To demonstrate the overall effectiveness of our proposed EFM-Side as introduced in Section 5.1.3, we compared the EFM-Side with state-of-the-art item recommendation approaches BRP and CoFactor. Users' interactions with lists were ignored in this stage. EFM-Side acquires the co-occurrence relationships among items from user generated lists, while CoFactor obtains them from user consumed item sequences.

Table 2: Overall performance comparison under the EFM-Side framework.

Methods	k=10		k=20	
	AUC	p-value	AUC	p-value
BPR	0.9101 ± 0.002	3.49*e*-10	0.9149 ± 0.003	2.86*e*-10
CoFactor	0.9226 ± 0.003	5.09*e*-09	0.9221 ± 0.004	9.95*e*-10
EFM-Side	**0.9357 ± 0.004**	–	**0.9418 ± 0.003**	–

Table 3: Models comparison in handling the new-item cold-start problem.

Methods	k=10		k=20	
	AUC	p-value	AUC	p-value
Random	0.4902 ± 0.002	1.14*e*-14	0.5019 ± 0.002	8.35*e*-15
BPR-map	0.7729 ± 0.003	8.30*e*-12	0.7777 ± 0.003	2.25*e*-12
EFM-Side	**0.8381 ± 0.004**	–	**0.8680 ± 0.003**	–

Experimental results are shown in Table 2. We have the following observations: 1) Our EFM-Side achieves the AUC of 0.9357 and 0.9418 when $k = 10$ and $k = 20$, respectively. It shows substatial improvements over BPR, CoFactor of 2.81%, 1.42% when $k = 10$, and 2.94%, 2.14% when $k = 20$. All the p-values between our model and each of the baselines are much smaller than 0.05, indicating that the improvements are statistically significant. This validates that the accuracy of EFM-Side can be strengthened through harvesting co-occurrence relationships among items from user generated lists. 2) The performance of CoFactor is superior to that of BPR. CoFactor does not take advantage of any extra information, but the co-occurrence relationships among items can still be uncovered from user consumed item sequences. The cost is some additional computation. 3) EFM-Side achieves preferable results as compared with CoFactor, which illustrates that the co-occurrence relationships among items generated from user generated lists are more useful as compared with that of user consumed item lists.

5.3 New-Item Cold-Start Problem (RQ2)

As introduced in Section 4.1.2, the new-item cold-start problem refers to recommend items that are never consumed by users but exist in user generated lists. We compared the performance of EFM-Side with that of 1) Random and 2) BPR-map. Random is the worst result for ranking performance, which randomly selects items for recommendation. For the new-item cold-start scenario, if we know nothing about the new items, the random guess is the most reasonable results. BPR-map utilizes a two-step strategy to cope with the cold-start problem. In the first step of BPR-map, the latent factors of items are obtained by factorizing the item-item co-occurrence matrix. In the second step, user personalized ranking are optimized by fixing item latent factors, which are obtained in the first stage, and adjusting user latent factors.

Results are displayed in Table 3. We observed: 1) EFM-Side achieves the AUC of 0.8381 and 0.8680 when $k = 10$ and $k = 20$, respectively, which gains improvements over Random, BPR-map at 70.97%, 8.43% when $k = 10$, and 72.94%, 11.61% when $k = 20$. The paired two-sample t-test also supports the conclusion of significant improvements. Experimental results demonstrate the effectiveness

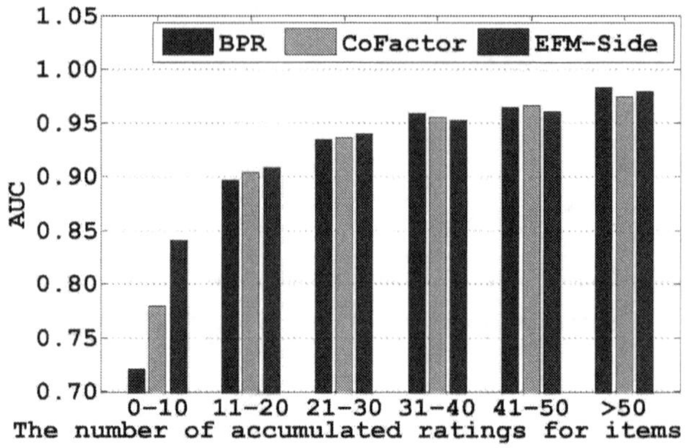

Figure 5: Micro-analysis w.r.t. items with different scale of accumulated ratings.

of EFM-Side in handling the new-item cold-start problem. 2) The random guess for the new-item cold-start scenario is around 0.5 with respect to AUC. In fact, the performance of both BPR-map and EFM-Side significantly exceeds the bottom line, which illustrates the effectiveness of these methods in handling the new-item cold-start problem. 3) EFM-Side consistently outperforms BPR-map with respect to different sizes of latent factors. The main difference between BPR-map and EFM-Side is that BPR-map utilizes a two-step process while EFM-Side employs a joint learning strategy. The latent factors separately obtained from the factorization of item-item co-occurrence matrix and the factorization of user-item interaction matrix belong to two different spaces. EFM-Side connects these two different semantic spaces by sharing common item latent factors, which obviously outperforms the suboptimal two-step approach.

5.4 Performance Analysis w.r.t. Items (RQ3)

The data sparsity problem is extremely serious as revealed in Figure 4c. Moreover, we know EFM-Side overall outperforms other algorithms from the results illustrated in Section 5.2, but we are not sure whether EFM-Side is consistently superior to other competitors with respect to items with different scales of accumulated ratings. In order to answer this question, we further disposed the results obtained in Section 5.2 by selecting items whose number of training ratings is located in specific range (*i.e.*, 1-10, 11-20, ..., > 50).

The performance of various methods is shown in Figure 5. We have the following observations: 1) EFM-Side outperforms BPR and CoFactor for sparse items (*i.e.*, accumulated ratings of 1-10, 11-20, and 21-30). EFM-Side considers the co-occurrence information among items, which has a great effect on alleviating the data sparsity problem when the item has only a few ratings. 2) With the increasing of the number of training ratings for items, the performance of BPR, CoFactor, and EFM-Side is getting closer. This is because that when enough ratings are obtained for the items, the latent factors of items can be well learnt even without co-occurrence information among items.

Table 4: Overall performance comparison under the EFM-Joint framework w.r.t. item recommendation.

Methods	k=10		k=20	
	AUC	p-value	AUC	p-value
BPR	0.9104 ± 0.003	4.30*e*-10	0.9175 ± 0.002	3.49*e*-10
LIRE	0.9194 ± 0.003	2.73*e*-09	0.9218 ± 0.004	7.28*e*-10
CoFactor	0.9231 ± 0.004	8.28*e*-09	0.9245 ± 0.003	1.25*e*-09
EFM-Joint	**0.9347 ± 0.003**	–	**0.9431 ± 0.003**	–

Table 5: Overall performance comparison under the EFM-Joint framework w.r.t. list recommendation.

Methods	k=10		k=20	
	AUC	p-value	AUC	p-value
BPR	0.8593 ± 0.002	9.56*e*-10	0.8729 ± 0.003	2.07*e*-09
LIRE	0.8675 ± 0.004	8.00*e*-09	0.8818 ± 0.003	4.73*e*-08
CoFactor	0.8605 ± 0.003	1.22*e*-09	0.8738 ± 0.004	2.59*e*-09
EFM-Joint	**0.8792 ± 0.003**	–	**0.8893 ± 0.004**	–

5.5 Jointly Recommend Items and Lists (RQ4)

In the EFM-Joint framework, the recommendation performance of items and lists can be mutually reinforced. We compared the performance of EFM-Joint with other state-of-the-art algorithms: 1) BPR; 2) LIRE; and 3) CoFactor. LIRE treats the list as a combination of items, and user preferences over items and lists are mutually reinforced. CoFactor discovers the co-occurrence among items and lists from users' interactions with both items and lists.

The comparison results are illustrated in Table 4 and Table 5. We can observe that: 1) Regarding to the item recommendation performance, EFM-Joint achieves the AUC of 0.9347 and 0.9431 when $k = 10$ and $k = 20$, which gains improvements over BPR, LIRE, CoFactor at 2.67%, 1.66%, 1.26% when $k = 10$, and 2.79%, 2.31%, 2.01% when $k = 20$. When it comes to the list recommendation, EFM-Joint obtains the AUC of 0.8792 and 0.8893 when $k = 10$ and $k = 20$, which shows improvements over BPR, LIRE, CoFactor at 2.32%, 1.35%, 2.17% when $k = 10$, and 1.88%, 0.85%, 1.77% when $k = 20$. The improvements are statistically significant. EFM-Joint consistently outperforms other competitors in the recommendation performance of both item and list, which demonstrates the effectiveness of our proposed joint learning framework. 2) LIRE beats CoFactor in the list recommendation, but lags behind in the item recommendation. LIRE is able to utilize the relationship between a list and its contained items. The recommendation performance of item can strengthen that of list. This is why LIRE outperforms CoFactor in the list recommendation. However, the co-occurrence relationships among items are ignored in LIRE, but are incorporated in CoFactor. This is why CoFactor outperforms LIRE in the item recommendation. 3) The recommendation performance of BPR and CoFactor in the list recommendation are quite similar. User's consumption process over items always show sequential feature, but the sequential feature is not that much obvious in the list consumption process (a user always consumes the list individually). The co-occurrence relationships among lists is not that much significant. This is why CoFactor does not show great improvement over BPR.

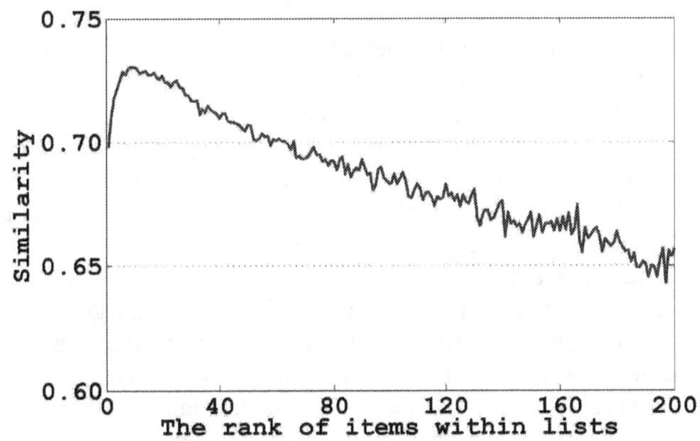

Figure 6: The similarity between the list and its contained items.

5.6 Importance of Items within A List (RQ5)

As discussed in word embedding algorithms [18, 25], the syntactic analogies and the semantic analogies of words and sentences can be found by computing the cosine distance among them. Once we have obtained the embedding representations of both items and lists, we can compute the similarity (the similarity is equal to 1 - distance) between a list and its contained words. In our datasets, we only know the rank of each item within a list, but we are not sure whether the items within a list are equally important. To answer this question, we explored the similarity between the embedding representation of a list and the embedding representations of its contained items. If the similarity between a list and an item is relatively high, it shows the item is relatively representative and important for the list.

In our datasets, the minimum and maximum length of lists is 10 and 996, respectively. The average length of lists is 77.8. Figure 6 shows the average similarity results between lists and their top 200 ranked items. As can be seen, the similarity increases first and then decreases, and reaches its maximum when the rank of item is around 10. This finding is relatively novel. First of all, the most representative item within a list is not ranked in the top of the list but in around the 10th position. It is mainly because when a user browses a list, his/her attention concentrates on items around the 10th position and then decides whether to favour the list. Meanwhile, the similarity between the list and its contained items gradually decreases when the rank of item increases beyond 10. This is mainly because the user's attention gradually faded with the increasing rank of items within the list.

6 CONCLUSION AND FUTURE WORK

This paper presents novel embedding factorization models for jointly recommending user generated lists and their contained items. Our methods nicely combine factorization models and embedding-based algorithms. Particularly, EFM-Side employs the list as side-information to discover the co-occurrence relationships among items. As a byproduct, it is capable of solving the new-item cold-start problem, where items are not yet consumed by users but exist in lists. By utilizing user interactions with item and list simultaneously, the recommendation performance of user-item and user-list can be mutually reinforced under the EFM-Joint framework. To validate the effectiveness of our proposed approaches, we constructed two benchmark datasets. Experiment results over these two datasets have demonstrated the effectiveness of our work. We also performed micro-analysis to show whether the items within a list are equally important, and whether EFM-Joint is able to find the most representative item in a list.

In future, we plan to extend our work in the following three directions: 1) Modeling the sequential feature in user generated sequential behaviors. Although the sequential behavior is ignored in user generated lists, sequential feature is extremely important in some real-world scenarios (*e.g.*, music listening behavior and visiting tourist attractions). 2) Realizing the item and list recommendation in an online setting [14, 39]. Users' personal interests evolve over time, so do the content of user generated lists and their contained items. As it is computationally prohibitive to retrain a recommender model online, it would be helpful to utilize users' reviews to capture the dynamic changes in an online learning manner. 3) Modeling multi-modal data. The current social web has been overwhelmed with user-generated images and videos. With recent advances on image understanding [34, 36], it is interesting to develop semantic list recommendation methods for multi-media objects.

7 ACKNOWLEDGMENTS

This work is supported by the National Natural Science Foundation of China (No. 61672442 and No. 61373147), and the Science and Technology Planning Project of Fujian Province (No. 2016Y0079). This work is also supported by NExT research centre, which is supported by the National Research Foundation, Prime Ministers office, Singapore under its IRC@SG Funding Initiative.

REFERENCES

[1] Immanuel Bayer, Xiangnan He, Bhargav Kanagal, and Steffen Rendle. 2017. A Generic Coordinate Descent Framework for Learning from Implicit Feedback. In *WWW*. ACM.

[2] Da Cao, Xiangnan He, Liqiang Nie, Xiaochi Wei, Xia Hu, Shunxiang Wu, and Tat-Seng Chua. 2017. Cross-Platform App Recommendation by Jointly Modeling Ratings and Texts. *ACM Transactions on Information Systems* (2017).

[3] Da Cao, Liqiang Nie, Xiangnan He, Xiaochi Wei, Jialie Shen, Shunxiang Wu, and Tat-Seng Chua. 2016. Version-sensitive mobile App recommendation. *Information Science* 381 (2016), 161–175.

[4] Jingyuan Chen, Hanwang Zhang, Xiangnan He, Liqiang Nie, Wei Liu, and Tat-Seng Chua. 2017. Attentive Collaborative Filtering: Multimedia Recommendation with Feature- and Item-level Attention. In *SIGIR*. ACM.

[5] Tao Chen, Xiangnan He, and Min-Yen Kan. 2016. Context-aware Image Tweet Modelling and Recommendation. In *MM*. ACM, 1018–1027.

[6] Zhiyong Cheng and Jialie Shen. 2016. On effective location-aware music recommendation. *ACM Transactions on Information Systems* 34, 2 (2016), 13.

[7] Zhiyong Cheng, Jialie Shen, and Steven CH Hoi. 2016. On Effective Personalized Music Retrieval by Exploring Online User Behaviors. In *SIGIR*. ACM, 125–134.

[8] Nemanja Djuric, Hao Wu, Vladan Radosavljevic, Mihajlo Grbovic, and Narayan Bhamidipati. 2015. Hierarchical neural language models for joint representation of streaming documents and their content. In *WWW*. ACM, 248–255.

[9] Zeno Gantner, Lucas Drumond, Christoph Freudenthaler, Steffen Rendle, and Lars Schmidt-Thieme. 2010. Learning attribute-to-feature mappings for cold-start recommendations. In *ICDM*. IEEE, 176–185.

[10] Mihajlo Grbovic, Vladan Radosavljevic, Nemanja Djuric, Narayan Bhamidipati, Jaikit Savla, Varun Bhagwan, and Doug Sharp. 2015. E-commerce in Your Inbox: Product Recommendations at Scale. In *SIGKDD*. ACM, 1809–1818.

[11] Xiangnan He and Tat-Seng Chua. 2017. Neural Factorization Machines for Predictive Analytics. In *SIGIR*. ACM.

[12] Xiangnan He, Ming Gao, Min-Yen Kan, and Dingxian Wang. 2017. BiRank: Towards Ranking on Bipartite Graphs. *IEEE Transactions on Knowledge and Data Engineering* 29, 1 (2017), 57–71.

[13] Xiangnan He, Lizi Liao, Hanwang Zhang, Liqiang Nie, Xia Hu, and Tat-Seng Chua. 2017. Neural Collaborative Filtering. In *WWW*. ACM.

[14] Xiangnan He, Hanwang Zhang, Min-Yen Kan, and Tat-Seng Chua. 2016. Fast matrix factorization for online recommendation with implicit feedback. In *SIGIR*. ACM, 549–558.

[15] Yehuda Koren. 2008. Factorization meets the neighborhood: a multifaceted collaborative filtering model. In *SIGKDD*. ACM, 426–434.

[16] Yehuda Koren, Robert Bell, Chris Volinsky, and others. 2009. Matrix factorization techniques for recommender systems. *Computer* 42, 8 (2009), 30–37.

[17] Artus Krohn-Grimberghe, Lucas Drumond, Christoph Freudenthaler, and Lars Schmidt-Thieme. 2012. Multi-relational matrix factorization using bayesian personalized ranking for social network data. In *WSDM*. ACM, 173–182.

[18] Quoc V Le and Tomas Mikolov. 2014. Distributed Representations of Sentences and Documents. In *ICML*. ACM, 1188–1196.

[19] Omer Levy and Yoav Goldberg. Neural word embedding as implicit matrix factorization. In *NIPS*.

[20] Dawen Liang, Jaan Altosaar, Laurent Charlin, and David M Blei. 2016. Factorization Meets the Item Embedding: Regularizing Matrix Factorization with Item Co-occurrence. In *RecSys*. ACM, 59–66.

[21] Jovian Lin, Kazunari Sugiyama, Min-Yen Kan, and Tat-Seng Chua. 2013. Addressing cold-start in app recommendation: latent user models constructed from twitter followers. In *SIGIR*. ACM, 283–292.

[22] Jovian Lin, Kazunari Sugiyama, Min-Yen Kan, and Tat-Seng Chua. 2014. New and improved: modeling versions to improve app recommendation. In *SIGIR*. ACM, 647–656.

[23] Xin Liu, Yong Liu, and Xiaoli Li. 2016. Exploring the Context of Locations for Personalized Location Recommendations. In *IJCAI*. AAAI Press, 1188–1194.

[24] Yidan Liu, Min Xie, and Laks VS Lakshmanan. 2014. Recommending user generated item lists. In *RecSys*. ACM, 185–192.

[25] Tomas Mikolov, Ilya Sutskever, Kai Chen, Greg S Corrado, and Jeff Dean. 2013. Distributed representations of words and phrases and their compositionality. In *NIPS*. MIT, 3111–3119.

[26] Steffen Rendle, Christoph Freudenthaler, Zeno Gantner, and Lars Schmidt-Thieme. 2009. BPR: Bayesian personalized ranking from implicit feedback. In *UAI*. AUAI, 452–461.

[27] Steffen Rendle, Zeno Gantner, Christoph Freudenthaler, and Lars Schmidt-Thieme. 2011. Fast context-aware recommendations with factorization machines. In *SIGIR*. ACM, 635–644.

[28] Oren Sar Shalom, Noam Koenigstein, Ulrich Paquet, and Hastagiri P Vanchinathan. 2016. Beyond Collaborative Filtering: The List Recommendation Problem. In *WWW*. ACM, 63–72.

[29] Chaofeng Sha, Xiaowei Wu, and Junyu Niu. 2016. A Framework for Recommending Relevant and Diverse Items. In *IJCAI*. AAAI Press, 3868–3874.

[30] Fumin Shen, Wei Liu, Shaoting Zhang, Yang Yang, and Heng Tao Shen. 2015. Learning binary codes for maximum inner product search. In *ICCV*. IEEE, 4148–4156.

[31] Ajit P Singh and Geoffrey J Gordon. 2008. Relational learning via collective matrix factorization. In *SIGKDD*. ACM, 650–658.

[32] Flavian Vasile, Elena Smirnova, and Alexis Conneau. 2016. Meta-Prod2Vec: Product Embeddings Using Side-Information for Recommendation. In *RecSys*. ACM, 225–232.

[33] Meng Wang, Weijie Fu, Shijie Hao, Hengchang Liu, and Xindong Wu. 2017. Learning on Big Graph: Label Inference and Regularization with Anchor Hierarchy. *IEEE Transactions on Knowledge and Data Engineering* 29, 5 (2017), 1101–1114.

[34] Meng Wang, Xueliang Liu, and Xindong Wu. 2015. Visual Classification by l1-Hypergraph Modeling. *IEEE Transactions on Knowledge and Data Engineering* 27, 9 (2015), 2564–2574.

[35] Suhang Wang, Jiliang Tang, Yilin Wang, and Huan Liu. 2015. Exploring Implicit Hierarchical Structures for Recommender Systems. In *IJCAI*. AAAI Press, 1813–1819.

[36] Hanwang Zhang, Xindi Shang, Huanbo Luan, Meng Wang, and Tat-Seng Chua. 2016. Learning from collective intelligence: Feature learning using social images and tags. *ACM Transactions on Multimedia Computing, Communications, and Applications* 13, 1 (2016), 1.

[37] Hanwang Zhang, Fumin Shen, Wei Liu, Xiangnan He, Huanbo Luan, and Tat-Seng Chua. 2016. Discrete collaborative filtering. In *SIGIR*. ACM, 325–334.

[38] Pengfei Zhao and Dik Lun Lee. 2016. How Much Novelty is Relevant? It Depends on Your Curiosity. In *SIGIR*. ACM, 315–324.

[39] Zhou Zhao, Hanqing Lu, Deng Cai, Xiaofei He, and Yueting Zhuang. 2016. User Preference Learning for Online Social Recommendation. *IEEE Transactions on Knowledge and Data Engineering* 28, 9 (2016), 2522–2534.

[40] Zhou Zhao, Ruihua Song, Xing Xie, Xiaofei He, and Yueting Zhuang. 2015. Mobile Query Recommendation via Tensor Function Learning.. In *IJCAI*, Vol. 15. AAAI Press, 4084–4090.

[41] Tao Zhu, Patrick Harrington, Junjun Li, and Lei Tang. 2014. Bundle recommendation in ecommerce. In *SIGIR*. ACM, 657–666.

Classification by Retrieval: Binarizing Data and Classifiers

Fumin Shen[1], Yadong Mu[2], Yang Yang[1], Wei Liu[3], Li Liu[4], Jingkuan Song[1], Heng Tao Shen[1*]
[1]Center for Future Media and School of Computer Science and Engineering, University of Electronic Science and Technology of China [2] Institute of Computer Science and Technology, Peking University
[3]Tencent AI Lab [4]Malong Technologies Co., Ltd

ABSTRACT

This paper proposes a generic formulation that significantly expedites the training and deployment of image classification models, particularly under the scenarios of many image categories and high feature dimensions. As the core idea, our method represents both the images and learned classifiers using binary hash codes, which are simultaneously learned from the training data. Classifying an image thereby reduces to retrieving its nearest class codes in the Hamming space.

Specifically, we formulate multiclass image classification as an optimization problem over binary variables. The optimization alternatingly proceeds over the binary classifiers and image hash codes. Profiting from the special property of binary codes, we show that the sub-problems can be efficiently solved through either a binary quadratic program (BQP) or a linear program. In particular, for attacking the BQP problem, we propose a novel bit-flipping procedure which enjoys high efficacy and a local optimality guarantee. Our formulation supports a large family of empirical loss functions and is, in specific, instantiated by exponential and linear losses. Comprehensive evaluations are conducted on several representative image benchmarks. The experiments consistently exhibit reduced computational and memory complexities of model training and deployment, without sacrificing classification accuracy.

CCS CONCEPTS

•Information systems →*Similarity measures;* **•Computing methodologies** →*Supervised learning by classification;*

KEYWORDS

Hashing; binary codes; classification; retrieval

ACM Reference format:
Fumin Shen[1], Yadong Mu[2], Yang Yang[1], Wei Liu[3], Li Liu[4], Jingkuan Song[1], Heng Tao Shen[1*]. 2017. Classification by Retrieval: Binarizing Data and Classifiers. In *Proceedings of SIGIR'17, August 7–11, 2017, Shinjuku, Tokyo, Japan,* 10 pages.
DOI: http://dx.doi.org/10.1145/3077136.3080767

*Corresponding author: Heng Tao Shen

DOI: http://dx.doi.org/10.1145/3077136.3080767

1 INTRODUCTION

In recent years, large-scale visual recognition problem has attracted tremendous research enthusiasm from both academia and industry owing to the explosive increase in data size and feature dimensionality [42–44]. Classifying an image into thousands of categories often entails heavy computations by using a conventional classifier, exemplified by k nearest neighbor (k-NN) and support vector machines (SVM), on a commodity computer. For the image recognition problem with many categories, the computational and memory overhead primarily stems from the large number of classifiers to be learned. The complexities can be high at the stages of both training and deploying these classifiers. Considering a classification task with C different classes and D-dimensional feature representation, even the simplest linear models are comprised of $D \times C$ parameters. As an inspiring example to our work in this paper, the ImageNet dataset [7] contains annotated images from 21,841 classes in total. When experimenting with some state-of-the-art visual features (*e.g.*, 4096-dimensional deep neural networks feature), a huge number of 80 million parameters need to be learned and stored, which clearly indicates slow training and low efficacy at the deployment phase. Real-world applications (such as industrial image search engine) often require a near-real-time response. The conventional ways of training multi-class image classifiers thus have much space to be improved.

Compact binary hash codes [9] have demonstrated notable empirical success in facilitating large-scale similarity-based image search, referred to as image hashing in the literature. In a typical setting of supervised learning, the hash codes are optimized to ensure smaller Hamming distances between images of the same semantic kind. In practice, image hashing techniques have been widely utilized owing to its low memory footprint and guaranteed scalability to large data.

Though the hashing techniques for image search has been a well-explored research area, its application on large-scale optimization still remains a nascent topic in the fields of machine learning and computer vision. Intuitively, one can harness the hash codes for the image classification task through naive methods such as k-NN voting. Both the training and testing images are indexed with identical hashing functions. A new image is categorized by the majority semantic label within the hashing bucket where it is projected into. However, since the hash codes are initially optimized for image search purpose, such a naive scheme does not guarantee high accuracy for image recognition.

The most relevant works to ours are approximately solving non-linear kernel SVM via hashing-based data representation [19, 20, 27]. These methods first designate a set of hashing functions that transform the original features into binary codes. The original non-linear kernels (*e.g.*, RBF kernel) are theoretically proved to be approximated by the inner product between binary hash bits. Prominent advantages of such a treatment are two-folds: the required hash bits only weakly hinge on the original feature dimensionality, and meanwhile the non-linear optimization problem is converted into a linear alternative. As a major drawback, these works still rely on the regular real-valued based classifiers upon the binary features. Though it enables the direct application of linear solvers, the potential advantage of binary codes is not fully utilized.

Our work is a non-trivial extension of the aforementioned line of research. We further elevate the efficacy of classification models by binarizing both the features and the weights of classifiers. In other words, our goal is to develop a generic multi-class classification framework. The classifier weights and image codes are simultaneously learned. Importantly, both of them are represented by binary hash bits. This way the classification problem is transformed to an equivalent and simpler operation, namely searching the minimal Hamming distance between the query and the C binary weight vectors. This can be extremely fast by using the built-in XOR and POPCOUNT operations in modern CPUs. We implement this idea by formulating the problem of minimizing the empirical classification error with purely binary variables. The overview of the proposed method is illustrated in Figure 2.

The major technical contributions of this work are summarized as below:

(1) We define a novel problem by binarizing both classifiers and image features and simultaneously learning them in a unified formulation. The prominent goal is to accelerate large-scale image recognition. Our work represents an unexplored research direction, namely extending hashing techniques from fast image search to the new topic of hashing-accelerated image classification.
(2) An efficient solver is proposed for the binary optimization problem. We decouple two groups of binary variables (image codes and binary classifier weights) and adopt an alternating-minimizing style procedure. Particularly, we show that the sub-problems are in the form of either binary quadratic program (BQP) or linear program. An efficient bit-flipping scheme is designed for the BQP sub-problem. Profiting from the special traits of binary variables, we are able to specify the local optimality condition of the BQP.
(3) Our formulation supports a large family of empirical loss functions and is here instantiated by exponential/linear losses. In our quantitative evaluations, both variants are compared with key competing algorithms, particularly a highly-optimized implementation of the SVM algorithm known as LibLinear [8]. Our proposed method demonstrates significant superiority in terms of train/test CPU time and classification accuracy, as briefly depicted by Figure 1.

We also discuss a sparse binary coding model, which will further reduce the computational and memory cost of our method when applied to high-dimensional images.

The rest of this paper is organized as follows. After discussing the related literature in Section 2, we present the details of our proposed model in Section 3. Section 4 shows the experimental results of our method, followed by the conclusions of this work in Section 5.

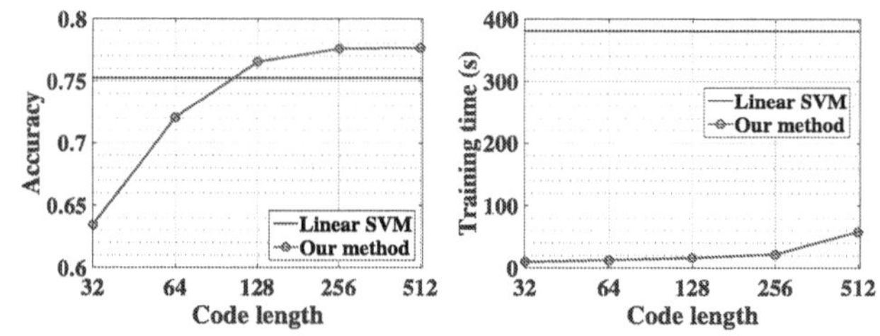

(a) Classification accuracy. (b) Training complexity.

Figure 1: Comparison of our method with the LibLinear implementation of Linear SVM for classification on the SUN dataset with 108K images from 397 scene categories. By coding both the image feature and learned classifiers with a small number of hash bits, our method achieves better results than Linear SVM, even with much smaller model training complexity.

2 RELATED WORK

Let us first review the related works which strongly motivate ours. They can be roughly cast into two categories:

2.1 Hashing for fast image search and beyond

Learning compact hash codes [41, 46] recently becomes a hot research topic in information retrieval [9, 28] and computer vision [2, 51]. The proliferation of digital photography has made billion-scale image collections a reality, and efficiently searching a similar image to the query is a critical operation in such image collections.

The seminal work of LSH [9] sheds a light on fast image search with theoretic guarantee. In a typical pipeline of hash code based image search [40, 48], a set of hashing functions are generated either in an unsupervised manner or learned by perfectly separating similar / dissimilar data pairs on the training set. The recent studies on the former category, unsupervised hashing, are more focused on the learning based methods. That is, different from the random LSH algorithm, these methods, a.k.a, *learning to hash* try to learn hash functions from the provided training data, which is shown to achieve promising performance with much more compact codes. Representative methods in this category include Spectral Hashing (SH [46]), Iterative Quantization (ITQ [10]), Manhattan Hashing [16], Anchor Graph Hashing (AGH [26]), Inductive Manifold Hashing (IMH [36, 37]), Discrete Graph Hashing (DGH [24]), *etc.*.

The latter category is known as supervised hashing since it often judges the similarity of two samples according to their semantic labels. For an unseen image, it finds the most similar images in the database by efficiently comparing the corresponding hash codes. It can be accomplished in sub-linear time using hash buckets [9]. Representative methods in this line include Binary Reconstructive Embedding (BRE [18]), Minimal Loss Hashing (MLH [30]), Semi-supervised Hashing (SSH [40]), LDA hashing [2], Kernel-Based Supervised Hashing (KSH [25]), CCA based Iterative Quantization (CCA-ITQ [10]), FastHash [21], Latent Factor Hashing (LFH [54]), Supervised Discrete Hashing (SDH [35]), Zero-shot Hashing (ZSH [50]), Discrete Semantic Ranking Hashing (DSeRH [23]) *etc.*. Recently, Shen *et al.*, [38] present a simple discrete optimization method which can substantially improve the performance of existing hashing methods.

The success of hashing technique is indeed beyond fast image search. For example, Dean et al. [6] used hash tables to accelerate the dot-product convolutional kernel operator in large-scale object detection, achieving a speed-up of approximately 20,000 times when evaluating 100,000 deformable-part models. Recently, the hashing technique was successfully applied to sketch-based image retrieval [22], action recognition [31, 32], image classification [52]. The hashing technique has been recently applied to collaborative filtering based recommendation systems [53, 55]. Particularly, the proposed model in this work can also be potentially applied to the closely related matrix factorization [3, 14], tag prediction [29, 45] and collaborative filtering [12, 13] problem.

2.2 Hashing for large-scale optimization

Noting the Hamming distance is capable of faithfully preserve data similarity, it becomes a natural thought to extend it for approximating non-linear kernels. Optimizing with non-linear kernels generally require more space to store the entire kernel matrix, which prohibits its scalability to large data. Real vectors based explicit feature mapping [39] partially remedies above issue, approximating kernel functions by the inner product between real vectors. However, they typically require high dimension towards an accurate approximation, and is thus beyond the scope of most practitioners. A more recent strand of research instead approximates non-linear kernel with binary bits, of which the prime examples can be found in [19, 20, 27]. In particular, Mu et al. developed a random subspace projection which transforms original data into compact hash bits. The inner product of hash code essentially plays the role of kernel functions. Consequently, the non-linear kernel SVM as their problem of interest can be converted into a linear SVM and resorts to efficient linear solvers like LibLinear [8].

The philosophy underlying all aforementioned works can be summarized as binarizing the features and harnessing the compactness of binary code. We here argue that the potential of hashing technique in the context of large-scale classification has not been fully explored yet. Related research is still in its embryonic stage. For example, a recent work by Shen et al. [35] proposed a Supervised Discrete Hashing (SDH) method under the assumption that good hash codes were optimal for linear classification. However, similar to other methods, SDH still classified the learned binary codes by real-valued weights. Thus the test efficiency for binary codes is still not improved compared to real-valued features.

The work [45] shared a similar idea with ours, which encoded both images and tags into binary codes for fast image tagging. However, [45] aimed to reconstruct the observed tags by the similarity estimated from the binary codes, which was very different our method which is formulated in binary codes classification. A related work is [34], which learned two sets of asymmetric binary codes to reconstructed the similarity by feature inner products. Recently, a few work [4, 15, 33] proposed to accelerate deep neural networks using binary weights and activations.

After surveying related literature, we are motivated to advocate in this paper the extreme binary learning model, wherein both image features and classifiers shall be represented by binary bits. This way the learned models get rid of real-valued weight vectors and can fully benefit from high-optimized hash bit operators such as XOR.

3 THE PROPOSED MODEL

Suppose that we have generated a set of binary codes $\mathbf{B} = \{\mathbf{b}_i\}_{i=1}^n \in \{-1, 1\}^{r\times n}$, where $\mathbf{b}_i$ is the r-bit binary code for original data $\mathbf{x}_i$ from the training set $\mathbf{X} = \{\mathbf{x}_i\}_{i=1}^n$. For simplicity, we assume a linear hash function

$$\mathbf{b} = \text{sgn}(\mathbf{P}^\top \mathbf{x}), \tag{1}$$

where $\mathbf{P} \in \mathbb{R}^{d\times r}$. In the context of linear classification, the binary codes $\mathbf{b}$ is classified according to the maximum of the score vector

$$\mathbf{W}^\top \mathbf{b} = [\mathbf{w}_1^\top \mathbf{b}, \cdots, \mathbf{w}_C^\top \mathbf{b}]^\top, \tag{2}$$

where $\mathbf{w}_c \in \{-1, 1\}^r$ is the binary parameter vector for class $c \in [1, \cdots, C]$. Taking advantage of the binary nature of both $\mathbf{w}_c$ and $\mathbf{b}$, the inner product $\mathbf{w}_c^\top \mathbf{b}$ can be efficiently computed by $r - 2\mathbb{D}_\mathbb{H}(\mathbf{w}_c, \mathbf{b})$, where $\mathbb{D}_\mathbb{H}(\cdot, \cdot)$ is the Hamming distance. Thereby the standard classification problem is transformed to searching the minimum from C Hamming distances (or equivalently the maximum of binary code inner products).

Following above intuition, this paper proposes a multi-class classification framework, simultaneously learning the binary feature codes and classifier. Suppose $\mathbf{b}_i$ is the binary code of sample $\mathbf{x}_i$ and it shall be categorized as class c_i. Ideally, it expects the smallest Hamming distance (or largest inner product) to $\mathbf{w}_{c_i}$, in comparison with other classifier $\mathbf{w}_c$, $c \neq c_i$. An intuitive way of achieving this is through optimizing the inter-class "margin". Formally, we can minimize the loss $\ell\big(-(\mathbf{w}_{c_i}^\top \mathbf{b}_i - \mathbf{w}_c^\top \mathbf{b}_i)\big)$, $\forall c$, where $\ell(\cdot)$ is a generic loss function. We re-formulate multi-class classification problem as below:

$$\begin{aligned} \min_{\mathbf{W},\mathbf{B},\mathbf{P}} \quad & \sum_{i=1}^{n}\sum_{c=1}^{C} \ell\big(-(\mathbf{w}_{c_i}^\top \mathbf{b}_i - \mathbf{w}_c^\top \mathbf{b}_i)\big) \\ \text{s.t.} \quad & \mathbf{b}_i = \text{sgn}(\mathbf{P}^\top \mathbf{x}_i),\ \forall i,\ \mathbf{w}_c \in \{-1,1\}^r,\ \forall c. \end{aligned} \tag{3}$$

We instantiate $\ell(\cdot)$ with the exponential loss (Section 3.1) and linear loss (Section 3.2). In fact, the loss function in Problem (3) can be broadly defined. Any proper loss function $\ell(\cdot)$ can be applied as long as it is monotonically increasing.

3.1 Learning with exponential loss

Using the exponential loss function, we have the following formulation:

$$\min_{\mathbf{W},\mathbf{B},\mathbf{P}} \sum_{i=1}^{n}\sum_{c=1}^{C} \exp\left[-(\mathbf{w}_{c_i}^\top \mathbf{b}_i - \mathbf{w}_c^\top \mathbf{b}_i)\right] \tag{4}$$

$$\begin{aligned} \text{s.t. } & \mathbf{b}_i = \text{sgn}(\mathbf{P}^\top \mathbf{x}_i),\ \forall i, \\ & \mathbf{w}_c \in \{-1,1\}^r,\ \forall c. \end{aligned} \tag{5}$$

We tackle problem (4) by alternatingly solving the sub-problems with $\mathbf{W}$, $\mathbf{B}$ and $\mathbf{P}$, respectively.

Learning binary classification weights. Assume $\mathbf{B}$ is known. We iteratively update $\mathbf{W}$ row by row, i.e., one bit each time for $\mathbf{w}_c, c = 1, \cdots, C$, while keep all other $r-1$ bits fixed. Let $\mathbf{w}(k)$ denote the k-th entry of $\mathbf{w}$ and $\mathbf{w}(\backslash k)$ the vector which zeros its k-th element. We then have

$$\exp(\mathbf{w}^\top \mathbf{b}) = \exp\left[\mathbf{w}(\backslash k)^\top \mathbf{b}\right] \cdot \exp\left[\mathbf{w}(k)\mathbf{b}(k)\right]. \tag{6}$$

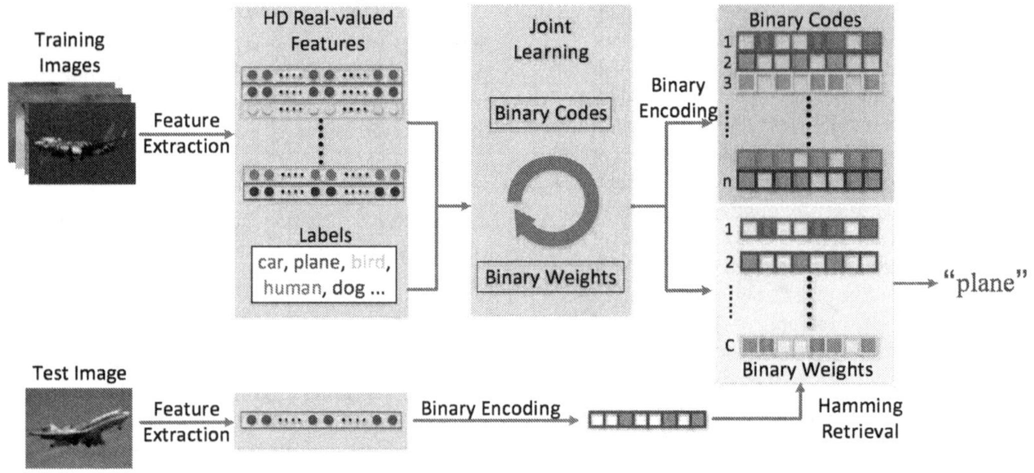

Figure 2: Overview of the proposed method. Both training images and classifiers are encoded by compact binary codes, and classifying a test image is thereby conducted by searching its neareast class codes by Hamming distances.

Denoting $u = \frac{e^{-1}+e^{1}}{2}$ and $v = \frac{e^{-1}-e^{1}}{2}$, it can be verified that

$$\exp\left[\mathbf{w}(k)\mathbf{b}(k)\right] = u - v \cdot \mathbf{b}(k)\mathbf{w}(k). \tag{7}$$

Equation (7) clearly shows the exponential function of the product of two binary bits equals to a linear function of the product. By applying (6) and (7), we write the loss term in (4) as:

$$\begin{aligned}&\exp\left[-(\mathbf{w}_{c_i}^\top \mathbf{b}_i - \mathbf{w}_c^\top \mathbf{b}_i)\right] \\ =&\gamma_{ick} \cdot \left[u - v \cdot \mathbf{b}_i(k)\mathbf{w}_c(k))\right] \cdot \left[u + v \cdot \mathbf{b}_i(k)\mathbf{w}_{c_i}(k))\right],\end{aligned} \tag{8}$$

where the constant $\gamma_{ick} = \exp\left[\left(\mathbf{w}_c(\backslash k) - \mathbf{w}_{c_i}(\backslash k)\right)^\top \mathbf{b}_i\right]$.

After merging terms with the same orders, optimizing problem (4) with regard to $\mathbf{w}^k = [\mathbf{w}_1(k); \cdots; \mathbf{w}_C(k)]$ becomes

$$\mathbf{w}^k \leftarrow \arg\min_{\mathbf{w}^k} \frac{1}{2}(\mathbf{w}^k)^\top \mathbf{H}^k \mathbf{w}^k + (\mathbf{w}^k)^\top \mathbf{g}^k, \tag{9}$$

where

$$\begin{aligned}\mathbf{H}^k &= -2v^2 \mathbf{Y}\Gamma^k, \\ \mathbf{g}^k &= uv\mathbf{Y}(\mathbf{b}^k \odot \Gamma \mathbf{1}) - uv\Gamma^\top \mathbf{b}^k.\end{aligned} \tag{10}$$

Here $\Gamma^k \in \mathbb{R}^{n \times C}$ includes its entries γ_{ick}, $\mathbf{b}^k$ is the n-dimension vector including the k_{th} binary bits of training data. $\mathbf{Y} \in \mathbb{R}^{C \times n}$ is the label matrix whose entry y_{ci} at coordinate (c, i) equals to 1 if sample $\mathbf{x}_i$ belongs to class c and 0 otherwise. $\odot$ denotes the element-wise product. $\mathbf{1}$ is the vector with all ones.

Problem (9) is a binary quadratic program (BQP) and can be efficiently solved by a sequential bit flipping operation. A local optimum can be guaranteed. We solve problem (9) by investigating the local optimality condition. Intuitively, for any local optimum, flipping any of its hash bits will not decrease the objective value of problem (9). Let $\mathbf{H}_{*,c}$, $\mathbf{H}_{c,*}$ denote the column or row vector indexed by c respectively. $\mathbf{g}(c)$ and $\mathbf{w}(c)$ represents the c_{th} element of $\mathbf{g}$ and $\mathbf{w}$, respectively. In problem (9), collecting all terms pertaining to $\mathbf{w}(c)$ obtains

$$f(\mathbf{w}^k(c)) = \frac{1}{2}\left(\mathbf{H}_{*,c}^{k\top} + \mathbf{H}_{c,*}^k\right)\mathbf{w}^k \cdot \mathbf{w}^k(c) + \mathbf{g}^k(c) \cdot \mathbf{w}^k(c).$$

Algorithm 1 Sequential bit flipping

```
while local optimality condition does not hold do
    Calculate the bit-flipping gain Δ_{w(c)→-w(c)} for c = 1, ..., C;
    Select ĉ = arg min_c Δ_{w(c)→-w(c)} and Δ_min = min_c Δ_{w(k)→-w(c)};
    if Δ_min < 0 then
        Set w(c) ← -w(c);
    else
        Exit;
    end if
end while
```

By flipping $\mathbf{w}(c)$, the gain of the objective function of problem (9) is

$$\Delta_{\mathbf{w}^k(c)\to-\mathbf{w}^k(c)} = f(-\mathbf{w}^k(c)) - f(\mathbf{w}^k(c)). \tag{11}$$

Regarding the local optimality condition of problem (9), we have the observation below:

Proposition 3.1. ***(Local optimality condition)**: Let $\mathbf{w}^*$ be a solution of problem (9). $\mathbf{w}^*$ is a local optimum when the condition $\Delta_{\mathbf{w}(c)\to-\mathbf{w}(c)} \geq 0$ holds for $c = 1, \ldots, C$.*

Proof. The conclusion holds by a simple application of proof of contradiction. Recall that $\mathbf{w}$ is a binary vector. Flipping any bit of $\mathbf{w}$ will incur a specific change of the objective function as described by $\Delta_{\mathbf{w}(i)\to-\mathbf{w}(i)}$. When the changes incurred by all these flipping operations are all non-negative, $\mathbf{w}^*$ is supposed to be locally optimal. Otherwise, we can flip the bit with negative $\Delta_{\mathbf{w}(i)\to-\mathbf{w}(i)}$ to further optimize the objective function. □

With the above analysis, we summarize our algorithm for updating the C-bit $\mathbf{w}^k$ as in Algorithm 1.

Binary code learning. With $\mathbf{W}$ fixed, we have the following problem

$$\min_{\mathbf{B},\mathbf{P}} \sum_{i=1}^{n}\sum_{c=1}^{C} \exp\left[-(\mathbf{w}_{c_i}^\top \mathbf{b}_i - \mathbf{w}_c^\top \mathbf{b}_i)\right] \quad (12)$$
$$\text{s.t. } \mathbf{b}_i = \operatorname{sgn}(\mathbf{P}^\top \mathbf{x}_i),\ \forall i,\ \mathbf{w}_c \in \{-1,1\}^r,\ \forall c.$$

Technically, we could reformulate this constrained problem into a joint learning problem regularized by the fidelity between binary codes and hash function outputs, as in [35]. However, in practice, we find this solution does not improve the performance than the two-step method: first learning binary codes followed by learning the hash prediction matrix. In this work, we adopt the two-step method.

Similar to the optimization procedure for $\mathbf{W}$, we solve for $\mathbf{B}$ by a coordinate descent scheme. In particular, at each iteration, all the rest $r-1$ hash bits are fixed except for the k-th hash bit $\mathbf{b}^k = [\mathbf{b}_1(k); \cdots; \mathbf{b}_n(k)]$. Let $\mathbf{b}_i(\backslash k)$ denote the vector which zeros its k-th element $\mathbf{b}_i(k)$. We rewrite equation (8) w.r.t $\mathbf{b}_i(k)$ as

$$\begin{aligned}&\exp\left[-(\mathbf{w}_{c_i}^\top \mathbf{b}_i - \mathbf{w}_c^\top \mathbf{b}_i)\right] \\ =&z_{ick} \cdot \exp\left[(\mathbf{w}_c(k) - \mathbf{w}_{c_i}(k))\mathbf{b}_i(k)\right]\end{aligned} \quad (13)$$

where $z_{ick} = \exp\left[(\mathbf{w}_c - \mathbf{w}_{c_i})^\top \mathbf{b}_i(\backslash k)\right]$.

Denote $u' = \frac{e^{-2}+e^2}{2}$, $v' = \frac{e^{-2}-e^2}{2}$. Similar as (7), we have

$$\begin{aligned}&\exp\left[(\mathbf{w}_c(k) - \mathbf{w}_{c_i}(k))\mathbf{b}_i(k)\right] \\ =&\begin{cases} 0, & \mathbf{w}_{c_i}(k) = \mathbf{w}_c(k) \\ u' + v' \cdot \mathbf{b}_i(k), & \mathbf{w}_{c_i}(k) = 1, \mathbf{w}_c(k) = -1 \\ u' - v' \cdot \mathbf{b}_i(k), & \mathbf{w}_{c_i}(k) = -1, \mathbf{w}_c(k) = 1. \end{cases}\end{aligned}$$

We can see that, the non-linear exponential loss term becomes either a constant or linear function with regard to $\mathbf{b}_i(k)$.

Let matrix $\mathbf{Z}^k \in \mathbb{R}^{n\times C}$ include its entry at the coordinate (i,c) as z_{ick} if $\mathbf{w}_{c_i}(k) = 1, \mathbf{w}_c(k) = -1$ and 0 otherwise; similarly let matrix $\bar{\mathbf{Z}}^k \in \mathbb{R}^{n\times C}$ include its entry at the coordinate (i,c) as z_{ick} if $\mathbf{w}_{c_i}(k) = -1, \mathbf{w}_c(k) = 1$ and 0 otherwise. Then the loss in (4) can be written as w.r.t $\mathbf{b}^k$

$$\begin{aligned}&\sum_{i=1}^{n}\sum_{c=1}^{C} \exp\left[-(\mathbf{w}_{c_i}^\top \mathbf{b}_i - \mathbf{w}_c^\top \mathbf{b}_i)\right] \quad (14) \\ =&\sum_{i=1}^{n}\sum_{c=1}^{C} \mathbf{Z}^k(i,c) \cdot (u' + v'\mathbf{b}_i(k)) + \bar{\mathbf{Z}}^k(i,c) \cdot (u' - v'\mathbf{b}_i(k)) \\ =&\sum_{i=1}^{n} \mathbf{z}^k(i) \cdot (u' + v'\mathbf{b}_i(k)) + \bar{\mathbf{z}}^k(i) \cdot (u' - v'\mathbf{b}_i(k)),\end{aligned}$$

where $\mathbf{z}^k(i) = \sum_{c=1}^{C} \mathbf{Z}^k(i,c)$ and $\bar{\mathbf{z}}^k(i) = \sum_{c=1}^{C} \bar{\mathbf{Z}}^k(i,c)$.

Then we have the following optimization problem

$$\min_{\mathbf{b}^k} v'(\mathbf{z}^k - \bar{\mathbf{z}}^k)^\top \mathbf{b}^k, \quad \text{s.t. } \mathbf{b}^k \in \{-1,1\}^r, \quad (15)$$

which has a optimal solution

$$\mathbf{b}^k = -\operatorname{sgn}(v'(\mathbf{z}^k - \bar{\mathbf{z}}^k)). \quad (16)$$

Figure 3 shows the objective value as a function of the bit updating iteration number. As can be seen, with the proposed coordinate descent optimizing procedure for both $\mathbf{W}$ and $\mathbf{B}$, the object value consistently decreases as updating the hash bits in each subproblem. The optimization for the original problem (4) typically

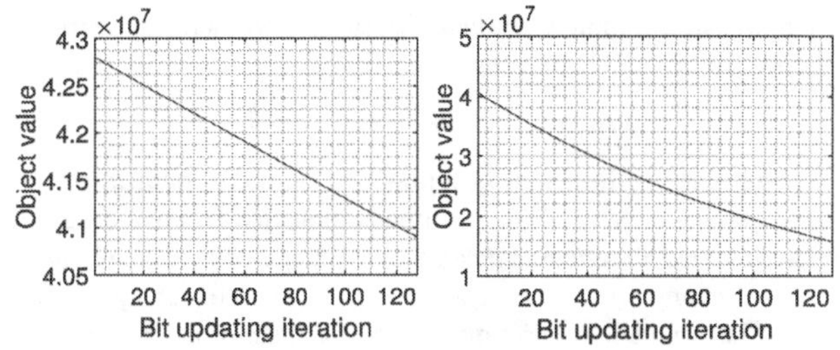

(a) Updating W. (b) Updating B.

Figure 3: Object value as a function of bit updating iteration k in optimizing W and B on the dataset of SUN397.

converges in less than 3 iterations of alternatively optimizing $\mathbf{W}$ and $\mathbf{B}$.

3.2 Learning with the linear loss

In this section, we instantiate our model with the simple linear loss:

$$\min_{\mathbf{W},\mathbf{B},\mathbf{P}} \sum_{i=1}^{n}\sum_{c=1}^{C}(\mathbf{w}_c^\top \mathbf{b}_i - \mathbf{w}_{c_i}^\top \mathbf{b}_i) \quad (17)$$
$$\text{s.t.} \quad \mathbf{b}_i = \operatorname{sgn}(\mathbf{P}^\top \mathbf{x}_i),\ \forall i,\ \mathbf{w}_c \in \{-1,1\}^r,\ \forall c.$$

Similar as with the exponential loss, we tackle problem (17) by alternatively solving the sub-problems regarding to $\mathbf{W}$, $\mathbf{B}$ and $\mathbf{P}$, respectively. We write problem (17) as w.r.t. $\mathbf{W}$,

$$\min_{\mathbf{W}} \sum_{i=1}^{n}\sum_{c=1}^{C}(\mathbf{w}_c^\top \mathbf{b}_i - \mathbf{w}_{c_i}^\top \mathbf{b}_i) \quad (18)$$
$$\text{s.t.} \quad \mathbf{w}_c \in \{-1,1\}^r, \forall c.$$

Collecting all terms with $\mathbf{w}_c$, $\forall c$, problem (18) writes

$$\min_{\mathbf{W}} \mathbf{w}_c^\top\Big(\sum_{i=1}^{n} \mathbf{b}_i - C\sum_{i=1,c_i=c}^{n} \mathbf{b}_i\Big) \quad (19)$$
$$\text{s.t.} \quad \mathbf{w}_c \in \{-1,1\}^r,$$

which has optimal solution

$$\mathbf{w}_c = \operatorname{sgn}\Big(C\sum_{i=1,c_i=c}^{n} \mathbf{b}_i - \sum_{i=1}^{n} \mathbf{b}_i\Big). \quad (20)$$

For the sub-problem regarding to $\mathbf{B}$, we first let matrix $\mathbf{W}^o$ of size $r \times n$ include its i_{th} column as $\mathbf{w}_i^o = \sum_{c=1}^{C} \mathbf{w}_c - C\mathbf{w}_{c_i}$. Problem (18) writes w.r.t. $\mathbf{B}$ as

$$\min_{\mathbf{B}} \operatorname{trace}(\mathbf{W}^{o\top}\mathbf{B}), \quad \text{s.t. } \mathbf{B} \in \{-1,1\}^{r\times n}.$$

$\mathbf{B}$ can be efficiently computed by $-\operatorname{sgn}(\mathbf{W}^o)$. It is clear that, both of the two sub-problems associated with $\mathbf{B}$ and $\mathbf{W}$ have closed-form solutions, which significantly reduces the computation overhead of classifier training and code learning.

3.3 Binary code prediction

With the binary codes $\mathbf{B}$ for training data $\mathbf{X}$ obtained, the hash function $h(\mathbf{x}) = \operatorname{sgn}(\mathbf{P}^\top \mathbf{x})$ is obtained by solving a simple linear regression system

$$\mathbf{P} = (\mathbf{X}^\top \mathbf{X})^{-1}\mathbf{X}^\top \mathbf{B}. \quad (21)$$

Then for a new sample $\mathbf{x}$, the classification is conducted by searching the minimum of C Hamming distances:

$$c^* = \arg\min_c \{\mathbb{D}_{\mathbb{H}}\big(\mathbf{w}_c, h(\mathbf{x})\big)\},\ c = 1, \cdots, C. \tag{22}$$

The binary coding step occupies the main computation in the testing stage, which is $O(dr)$ in time complexity. In some cases, the image feature dimensions d can be very large or the code length r need to be long for satisfying performance. Then the computational cost of binary code prediction and storage cost of the projection $\mathbf{P}$ should not be neglected. This motivates us to devise a sparse model, where most entries of the hash projection matrix $\mathbf{P}$ are zeros. That is, we solve the following ℓ_0 problem:

$$\min_{\mathbf{P}} ||\mathbf{P}^\top\mathbf{X} - \mathbf{B}||^2 \quad \text{s.t.}\ ||\mathbf{P}||_0 \le s, \tag{23}$$

where $||\cdot||_0$ denotes the ℓ_0 norm and t is the number of nonzero entries of $\mathbf{P}$. Problem (23) has been well known as the sparse representation problem, and exactly solving it can be NP-hard due to the involvement of nonconvex and nonsmooth ℓ_0 norm. The typical solution can be attained by relaxing the ℓ_0 norm to the convex ℓ_1, which is much easier to slove while still admitting the sparsity of resultant model [47]. In this work, however, we choose to solve the ℓ_0 problem since the nonzero number (and thus the computation and memory costs) can be exactly controlled.

Inspired by the recent advance of the proximal optimization method [1], we solve problem (23) by the following iterative procedure. First let us introduce the sparse projection operator:

$$T_s(\mathbf{U}) = \arg\min_{\mathbf{V}} \left\{||\mathbf{U} - \mathbf{V}||^2 : ||\mathbf{V}||_0 \le s\right\}. \tag{24}$$

It can be easily observed that the sparse projection operator selects exactly the first s largest elements (in absolute value) of $\mathbf{U}$ and set all other elements zeros. For convenience, let us denote the loss in (23) by $\mathcal{L}(\mathbf{P})$. According to [1], problem (23) can be solved by the proximal alternating linearization minimization (PALM) algorithm, that is, at the tth iteration, $\mathbf{P}$ is updated by

$$\mathbf{P}^{(t)} = T_s\Big(\mathbf{P}^{(t-1)} - \frac{1}{\gamma_t}\nabla\mathcal{L}(\mathbf{P})\Big), \tag{25}$$

where $\nabla\mathcal{L}(\mathbf{P}) = \mathbf{X}\mathbf{X}^\top\mathbf{P} - \mathbf{X}\mathbf{B}^\top$. The sequence of parameters γ_t is chosen such that γ_t is greater than the Lipschitz modulis of the loss function $\mathcal{L}$, which is $||\mathbf{X}\mathbf{X}^\top||_{\text{fro}}$ here. With this updating procedure, the generated sequence of $\mathbf{P}$ will globally converge to a critical point [1]. The reader is referred to [1] for the details of the PALM algorithm. The work [48] also proposed a sparse projection model for binary coding, which was however derived very differently. Another difference is the work [48] focuses on image retrieval while our method focuses on the classification task.

3.4 Discussion

As mentioned above, the proposed method classifies a new sample $\mathbf{x}$ by first computing its binary codes ($\text{sgn}(\mathbf{P}^\top\mathbf{x})$) and retrieving its nearest neighbor from $\{\mathbf{w}_c\}_{c=1}^C$. Taking advantage of extremely fast bit operations (XOR and POPCOUNT), the computation consumed by the second step can be mostly ignored. In fact, the computational burden of our proposed method in the testing phase mainly comes from projecting a feature vector onto the matrix $\mathbf{P}$, which costs $O(dr)$ in time. With the sparse model, the time complexity can be reduced to $O(D)$ with $D << dr$ the number of nonzero elements in $\mathbf{P}$. For conventional linear classifiers (*e.g.*, linear SVM), the time complexity for classifying a test sample is $O(dC)$.

It is clear that the proposed method is not always relatively more efficient, especially when the number of classes is small. However, we note that our method is more suitable for accelerating large-scale classification problems with a large number of classes. The time complexity does not change much with different numbers of classes. In this sense, our proposed method can be more reasonably treated as a classification method with nearly constant time complexity at test time, insensitive to the number of classes. In addition, we will show in the experiments that the proposed method has lower training complexity even with a small number of classes, as justified in Table 1.

Another advantage of our method is it significantly reduce the storage cost by converting high-dimensional real-valued features and classification models to compact binary codes. Differently, previous hashing algorithms fail to take advantage of the binary nature of obtained hash codes (still treated as real-valued features) when applied for classification.

4 EXPERIMENTS

In this section, we conduct comprehensive evaluations to validate the efficacy of our proposed method in terms of both classification accuracy and computational efficiency.

4.1 Datasets

Three large-scale datasets: SUN397 [49], ImageNet [7] and Caltech-256[2] are used in our experiments.

SUN397 [49] contains about 108K images from 397 scene categories, where each image is represented by a 1,600-dimensional feature vector extracted by PCA from 12,288-dimensional Deep Convolutional Activation Features [11]. We use a subset of this dataset including 42 categories with each containing more than 500 images; 100 images are sampled uniformly randomly from each category to form a test set of 4,200 images. As a subset of **ImageNet** [7], the large dataset ILSVRC 2012 contains over 1.2 million images of totally 1,000 categories. We form the evaluation database by the 100 largest classes with total 128K images from the training set, and 50,000 images from the validation set as the test set. We use the 4096-dimensional features extracted by the convolution neural networks (CNN) model [17]. The **Caltech-256** dataset contains 256 object categories including over 30K images. Similarly, we extract the 4096-dimensional CNN features by the model in [17]. For this dataset, we use half of the images in each category as training data and the other half as the test set.

4.2 Compared methods and evaluation metrics

The proposed method with both exponential loss (denoted by Ours-Exponential) and linear loss (denoted by Ours-Linear) are evaluated. The binary code prediction is conducted with (21) by default. We will evaluate the sparse model (23) in Section 4.5. The proposed methods are compared with two popular linear classifiers: one-vs-all linear SVM (OVA-SVM) and multi-class SVM (Multi-SVM [5]), both of which are implemented using the LibLinear software

[2]http://www.vision.caltech.edu/Image_Datasets/Caltech256/.

Table 1: Comparative results in terms of test accuracy (%), training and testing time (seconds). Experiments are conducted on a standard PC with a quad-core Intel CPU and 32GB RAM. For LSH, CCA-ITQ, SDH and our methods, 128 bits are used. OVA-SVM and Multi-SVM is performed with LibLinear, where the best accuracies are reported with parameter c chosen from {1e-3, 1e-2, 1e-1, 1, 1e1, 1e2, 1e3}.

Method	SUN397			ImageNet			Caltech-256		
	acc (%)	train time	test time	acc (%)	train time	test time	acc (%)	train time	test time
OVA-SVM	**77.39**	818.87	1.55e-5	**79.84**	151.02	1.15e-5	**73.31**	47.37	2.70e-4
Multi-SVM	75.28	380.94	1.01e-5	79.48	93.12	1.21e-5	73.25	38.54	2.58e-4
LSH	54.11	417.42	7.75e-6	58.16	107.41	1.32e-5	51.07	15.16	2.78e-5
CCA-ITQ	69.33	452.34	8.78e-6	76.30	142.95	1.25e-5	65.14	15.12	2.86e-5
KSH	59.67	2805.50	5.19e-5	74.38	11217.71	4.96e-5	57.85	2854.31	7.39e-5
FastHash	48.17	3144.80	1.20e-3	72.66	371.65	7.75e-4	55.51	522.71	6.58e-4
SDH	72.56	2522.33	7.43e-6	76.64	1102.21	1.43e-5	**66.90**	132.56	2.83e-5
Ours-Exponential	75.44	772.11	**3.67e-6**	**79.04**	245.14	**6.54e-6**	65.52	69.31	**1.31e-5**
Ours-Linear	**76.56**	**16.45**	**3.86e-6**	77.88	**35.16**	**6.86e-6**	65.48	**11.94**	**1.35e-5**

package [8]. For these two methods, we tune the parameter c from the range [1e-3, 1e3] and the best results are reported. Note that during classification, both the features and classifiers are continuous for the SVM algorithms, which is different from our methods. We also compare our methods against several state-of-the-art binary code learning methods including Locality Sensitive Hashing (LSH) implemented by signed random projections, CCA-ITQ [10], KSH [25], FastHash [21] and SDH [35]. Due to the expensive training of KSH and FastHash, we randomly select 5K and 10K samples, respectively, from training data for learning these two models. All available training data are used for learning for other methods. The classification results of these hashing methods are obtained by performing the multi-class linear SVM over the predicted binary codes by the corresponding hash functions. We use the public codes and suggested parameters of these methods from the authors.

We extensively evaluate these compared methods in terms of classification accuracy, computation efficiency (training time and testing time) and storage memory overhead.

4.3 Accuracy and computational efficiency

In this part, we extensively evaluate the proposed two methods with the compared algorithms in classification accuracy and computation time. We set the code length to 128 for our method and the hashing algorithms LSH, CCA-ITQ, KSH, FastHash and SDH.

The main results on SUN397, ImageNet and Caltech-256 are reported in Table 1. Between the algorithms with different loss functions of our proposed model, we can see that the method with the exponential loss performs slightly better than that with the linear loss, while the latter one benefits from a much more efficient training. This is not surprising because Ours-Linear solves two alternating sub-problems both with closed-form solutions. In the following experiments, we use the linear method for its high efficiency.

Compared to other methods, the results in Table 1 clearly show that, our methods achieve very competitive classification accuracies with the full-precision linear SVMs on SUN397 and ImageNet. For example, our method obtains 76.56% accuracy on SUN397 which is better Multi-SVM by 1.28%. While OVA-SVM achieves slightly better results than our method, the training and testing time cost are much higher. On the Caltech-256 dataset, our methods with 128 bits (together with other hashing algorithms) do not perform as well as SVM, which may be because the code length is too short to encode enough information. Figure 5 depicts the impacts of code lengths on the performance of our algorithm.

In the meanwhile, even being constrained to learning binary classification weights, our methods obtain noticeably better results than the state-of-the-art hashing algorithms. Specifically, Ours-Exponential outperforms the best results obtained the hashing algorithms by 2.88%, 2.4% on SUN397 and ImageNet , respectively. On Caltech-256, our two algorithms attain very competitive accuracies with CCA-ITQ and SDH which are much higher than those by LSH, KSH and FastHash.

In terms of training time, we can see that our method with the linear loss runs way faster than all other methods on all the evaluated three datasets. In particular, on SUN397, Ours-Linear is 50× and 23× faster than the LibLinear implementations of one-vs-all SVM and multi-class SVM. Compared with the hashing algorithm, our method runs over 28× faster than the fastest LSH followed by Liblinear. For the testing time, the benefit of binary dimension reduction for our methods and other three hashing algorithms is clearly shown on the SUN397 dataset with a large number of categories. Our methods require less testing time than the hashing based classification methods, due to the extremely fast classification implemented by searching in the Hamming space.

We also evaluate the compared methods with different code lengths, where the detailed results on SUN397, ImageNet and Caltech-256 are shown in Figure 4. From Figure 4, it is clear that with a relatively small number of bits (*e.g.*, 256 bits), our method can achieve close classification performance to or even better than the real-valued linear SVM with real-valued features. We can also observe that our method consistently outperforms other hashing algorithms by noticeable gaps at all code lengths on SUN397. On the ImageNet dataset, our method achieves marginally better results than SDH and CCA-ITQ, while better than KSH and the random

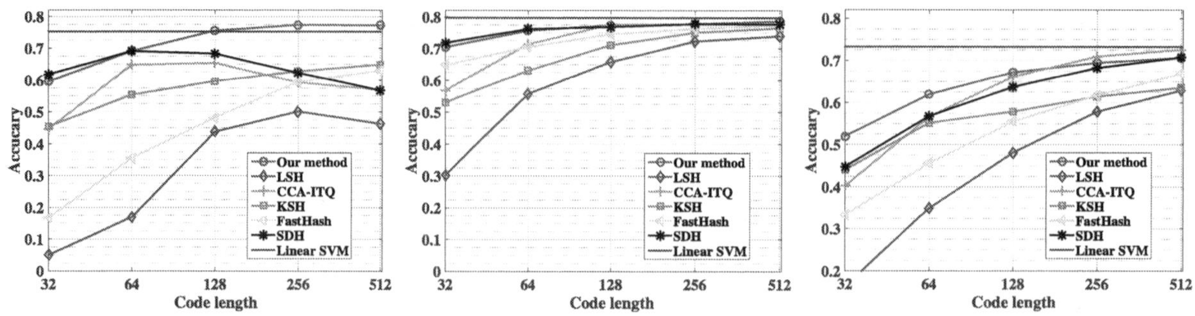

(a) SUN397 (b) ImageNet (c) Caltech-256

Figure 4: Comparative results of different methods in classification accuracy on SUN397 and ImageNet with code length from 32 to 512.

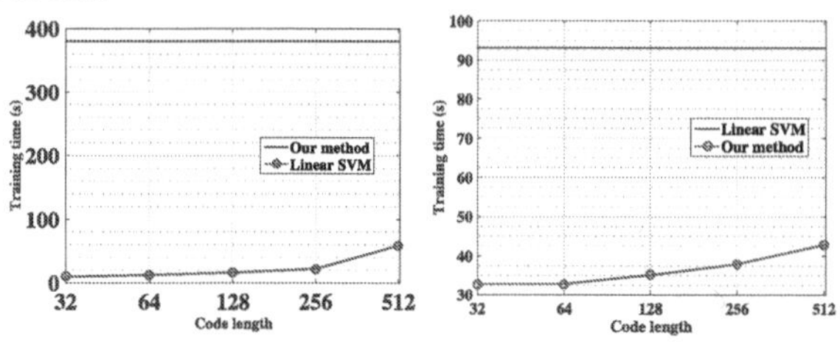

(a) SUN397 (b) ImageNet

Figure 5: Comparative results of our method and linear SVM in training time on SUN397 and ImageNet with code length from 32 to 512.

Table 2: Memory overhead (MB) to store the image features and classification model using Linear SVM and our method (128-bit). Note that, for our method, the trained model includes the real-valued hashing matrix (P) and the binary classification weight matrix W.

Dataset	Image features		Classification model	
	Real-valued	Binary	Linear SVM	Ours
ImageNet	3943.91	24.37	30.86	9.92
SUN397	1283.83	2.01	4.79	1.54
Caltech-256	157.04	0.97	7.89	3.95

LSH algorithm. For the Caltech-256 dataset, our method outperforms all of the compared hashing algorithms with less than 128 bits while CCA-ITQ achieves slightly better accuracies with long code lengths. However, we note that the results by ITQ are obtained by additionally learning a full-precision SVM on ITQ codes while our method classifies the generated binary codes by binary weights.

Figure 5 demonstrates the consumed training time by our method and Linear SVM by the Liblinear solver on two large-scale datasets. The computation efficiency advantage of our method is clearly shown. Our method has a nearly linear training time complexity with the code length, which can facilitate its potential applications in high-dimensional binary vector learning.

4.4 Storage cost

In this subsection, we analyze the storage cost of the image features (real-valued and binary codes) and also the running memory overhead of storing the classification model. For our method, the trained model includes the real-valued hash function matrix (P) and the binary classification weight matrix. The results are reported in Table 2. It is clearly shown that our approach requires much less memory than Linear SVM for storing both the image features and classification models. Taking the ImageNet for example, Linear SVM needs over 150 times more space than our method for the dataset and over 3 times more space for the classification models.

4.5 Evaluation of the sparse model

As discussed above, the image features or the target binary codes dimensionality can be very large, which will make the hash code prediction be expensive in both computation and storage of the hash model. To alleviate this problem, we develop a sparse model in Section 3.3. In this subsection, we evaluate the impact of the sparsity of the hash model P on the classification performance. Figure 6 demonstrates the accuracy vs. non-sparsity (the number of nonzeros in P over dr) of our method with various code lengths on SUN397, ImageNet and Caltech-256.

We can observe from Figure 6 that the accuracies are consistently improved with the increasing ratio of nonzeros in the hash model. However, the performance becomes stable when the non-sparsity is larger than 0.1 or 0.2 with a long code length being used on all these three datasets. This may provide a way for the trade-off between the performance and computation/memory cost.

5 CONCLUSIONS

This work proposed a novel classification framework, by which classification is equivalently transformed to searching the nearest binary weight code in the Hamming space. Different from previous methods, both the feature and classifier weight vectors are simultaneously learned with binary hash codes. Our framework can accommodate a large family of empirical loss functions, and we especially studied the representative exponential and linear losses. For the two sub-problems regarding the binary classifier and image hash codes, a binary quadratic program (BQP) and a linear program are formulated, respectively. In particular, for the BQP problem, a

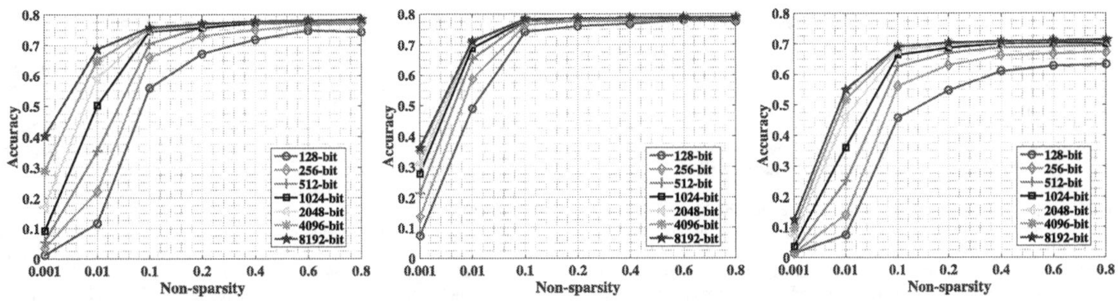

(a) SUN397 (b) ImageNet (c) Caltech-256

Figure 6: Classification accuracy vs. non-sparity of P of the proposed sparse model on SUN397, ImageNet and Caltech-256 with various code lengths.

novel bit-flipping procedure which enjoys high efficacy and the local optimality guarantee was developed. A significant computation overhead reduction in model training and deployment is obtained by our method, while without sacrificing the classification accuracy. We also discussed a sparse binary coding model, which provides a practical way to further reduce the computational and memory costs.

ACKNOWLEDGMENTS

This work was supported in part by the National Natural Science Foundation of China under Project 61502081, Project 61572108, Project 61673299 and Project 61632007, in part by the Fundamental Research Funds for the Central Universities under Project ZYGX2014Z007.

REFERENCES

[1] Jérôme Bolte, Shoham Sabach, and Marc Teboulle. 2014. Proximal alternating linearized minimization for nonconvex and nonsmooth problems. *Mathematical Programming* 146, 1-2 (2014), 459–494.

[2] M. M. Bronstein and P. Fua. 2012. LDAHash: Improved Matching with Smaller Descriptors. *IEEE Trans. Pattern Anal. Mach. Intell.* 34, 1 (2012), 66–78.

[3] Da Cao, Liqiang Nie, Xiangnan He, Xiaochi Wei, Shunzhi Zhu, Shunxiang Wu, and Tat-Seng Chua. 2017. Embedding Factorization Models for Jointly Recommending User Generated Lists and Their Contained Items. In *Proc. SIGIR.*

[4] Matthieu Courbariaux, Yoshua Bengio, and Jean-Pierre David. 2015. Binaryconnect: Training deep neural networks with binary weights during propagations. In *Proc. NIPS.* 3123–3131.

[5] Koby Crammer and Yoram Singer. 2002. On the algorithmic implementation of multiclass kernel-based vector machines. *J. Mach. Learn. Res.* 2 (2002), 265–292.

[6] Thomas Dean, Mark A. Ruzon, Mark Segal, Jonathon Shlens, Sudheendra Vijayanarasimhan, and Jay Yagnik. 2013. Fast, Accurate Detection of 100,000 Object Classes on a Single Machine. In *Proc. CVPR.* 1814–1821.

[7] Jia Deng, Wei Dong, Richard Socher, Li-Jia Li, Kai Li, and Li Fei-Fei. 2009. Imagenet: A large-scale hierarchical image database. In *Proc. CVPR.* 248–255.

[8] R.E. Fan, K.W. Chang, C.J. Hsieh, X.R. Wang, and C.J. Lin. 2008. LIBLINEAR: A library for large linear classification. *J. Mach. Learn. Res.* 9 (2008), 1871–1874.

[9] Aristides Gionis, Piotr Indyk, and Rajeev Motwani. 1999. Similarity search in high dimensions via hashing. In *Proc. VLDB.* 518–529.

[10] Yunchao Gong, Svetlana Lazebnik, Albert Gordo, and Florent Perronnin. 2013. Iterative quantization: A procrustean approach to learning binary codes for large-scale image retrieval. *IEEE Trans. Pattern Anal. Mach. Intell.* 35, 12 (2013), 2916–2929.

[11] Yunchao Gong, Liwei Wang, Ruiqi Guo, and Svetlana Lazebnik. 2014. Multi-scale orderless pooling of deep convolutional activation features. In *Proc. ECCV.* Springer, 392–407.

[12] Xiangnan He, Ming Gao, Min-Yen Kan, Yiqun Liu, and Kazunari Sugiyama. 2014. Predicting the popularity of web 2.0 items based on user comments. In *Proc. SIGIR.* 233–242.

[13] Xiangnan He, Lizi Liao, Hanwang Zhang, Liqiang Nie, Xia Hu, and Tat-Seng Chua. 2017. Neural Collaborative Filtering. In *Proc. WWW.*

[14] Xiangnan He, Hanwang Zhang, Min-Yen Kan, and Tat-Seng Chua. 2016. Fast matrix factorization for online recommendation with implicit feedback. In *Proc. SIGIR.* 549–558.

[15] Itay Hubara, Matthieu Courbariaux, Daniel Soudry, Ran El-Yaniv, and Yoshua Bengio. 2016. Binarized neural networks. In *Proc. NIPS.* 4107–4115.

[16] Weihao Kong, Wu-Jun Li, and Minyi Guo. 2012. Manhattan Hashing for Large-scale Image Retrieval. In *Proc. SIGIR.* 45–54.

[17] Alex Krizhevsky, Ilya Sutskever, and Geoffrey E Hinton. 2012. Imagenet classification with deep convolutional neural networks. In *Proc. NIPS.* 1097–1105.

[18] B. Kulis and T. Darrell. 2009. Learning to hash with binary reconstructive embeddings. In *Proc. NIPS.* 1042–1050.

[19] Ping Li, Gennady Samorodnitsk, and John Hopcroft. 2013. Sign Cauchy projections and Chi-square kernel. In *Proc. NIPS.* 2571–2579.

[20] Ping Li, Anshumali Shrivastava, Joshua L Moore, and Arnd C König. 2011. Hashing algorithms for large-scale learning. In *Proc. NIPS.* 2672–2680.

[21] Guosheng Lin, Chunhua Shen, Qinfeng Shi, Anton van den Hengel, and David Suter. 2014. Fast supervised hashing with decision trees for high-dimensional data. In *Proc. CVPR.* 1971–1978.

[22] Li Liu, Fumin Shen, Yuming Shen, Xianglong Liu, and Ling Shao. 2017. Deep Sketch Hashing: Fast Free-hand Sketch-Based Image Retrieval. In *Proc. CVPR.*

[23] Li Liu, Mengyang Yu, Fumin Shen, and Ling Shao. 2017. Discretely Coding Semantic Rank Orders for Image Hashing. In *Proc. CVPR.*

[24] Wei Liu, Cun Mu, Sanjiv Kumar, and Shih-Fu Chang. 2014. Discrete Graph Hashing. In *Proc. NIPS.* 3419–3427.

[25] Wei Liu, Jun Wang, Rongrong Ji, Yu-Gang Jiang, and Shih-Fu Chang. 2012. Supervised hashing with kernels. In *Proc. CVPR.* 2074–2081.

[26] Wei Liu, Jun Wang, Sanjiv Kumar, and Shih-Fu Chang. 2011. Hashing with Graphs. In *Proc. ICML.* 1-8.

[27] Yadong Mu, Gang Hua, Wei Fan, and Shih-Fu Chang. 2014. Hash-SVM: Scalable Kernel Machines for Large-Scale Visual Classification. In *Proc. CVPR.* 979–986.

[28] Liqiang Nie, Meng Wang, Zheng-Jun Zha, and Tat-Seng Chua. 2012. Oracle in image search: A content-based approach to performance prediction. *ACM Trans. Inf. Syst.* 30, 2 (2012), 13.

[29] Liqiang Nie, Yi-Liang Zhao, Xiangyu Wang, Jialie Shen, and Tat-Seng Chua. 2014. Learning to recommend descriptive tags for questions in social forums. *ACM Trans. Inf. Syst.* 32, 1 (2014), 5.

[30] Mohammad Norouzi and David M Blei. 2011. Minimal loss hashing for compact binary codes. In *Proc. ICML.* 353–360.

[31] Jie Qin, Li Liu, Ling Shao, Bingbing Ni, Chen Chen, Fumin Shen, and Yunhong Wang. 2017. Binary Coding for Partial Action Analysis with Limited Observation Ratios. In *Proc. CVPR.*

[32] Jie Qin, Li Liu, Ling Shao, Fumin Shen, Bingbing Ni, Jiaxin Chen, and Yunhong Wang. 2017. Zero-Shot Action Recognition with Error-Correcting Output Codes. In *Proc. CVPR.*

[33] Mohammad Rastegari, Vicente Ordonez, Joseph Redmon, and Ali Farhadi. 2016. Xnor-net: Imagenet classification using binary convolutional neural networks. In *Proc. ECCV.* Springer, 525–542.

[34] Fumin Shen, Wei Liu, Shaoting Zhang, Yang Yang, and Heng Tao Shen. 2015. Learning Binary Codes for Maximum Inner Product Search. In *Proc. ICCV.* 4148–4156.

[35] Fumin Shen, Chunhua Shen, Wei Liu, and Heng Tao Shen. 2015. Supervised Discrete Hashing. In *Proc. CVPR.* 37–45.

[36] Fumin Shen, Chunhua Shen, Qinfeng Shi, Anton van den Hengel, and Zhenmin Tang. 2013. Inductive Hashing on Manifolds. In *Proc. CVPR.* 1562–1569.

[37] Fumin Shen, Chunhua Shen, Qinfeng Shi, Anton van den Hengel, Zhenmin Tang, and Heng Tao Shen. 2015. Hashing on Nonlinear Manifolds. *IEEE Trans. Image Proc.* 24, 6 (2015), 1839–1851.

[38] Fumin Shen, Xiang Zhou, Yang Yang, Jingkuan Song, Heng Tao Shen, and Dacheng Tao. 2016. A Fast Optimization Method for General Binary Code Learning. *IEEE Transactions on Image Processing* 25, 12 (2016), 5610–5621.

[39] Andrea Vedaldi and Andrew Zisserman. 2012. Efficient additive kernels via explicit feature maps. *IEEE Trans. Pattern Anal. Mach. Intell.* 34, 3 (2012), 480–492.

[40] Jun Wang, Sanjiv Kumar, and Shih-Fu Chang. 2012. Semi-Supervised Hashing for Large Scale Search. *IEEE Trans. Pattern Anal. Mach. Intell.* 34, 12 (2012), 2393–2406.

[41] Jingdong Wang, Ting Zhang, Jingkuan Song, Nicu Sebe, and Heng Tao Shen. 2017. A survey on learning to hash. *IEEE Trans. Pattern Anal. Mach. Intell.* PP (2017).

[42] M. Wang, W. Fu, S. Hao, H. Liu, and X. Wu. 2017. Learning on Big Graph: Label Inference and Regularization with Anchor Hierarchy. *IEEE Trans. Know. Data Engin.* 29, 5 (2017), 1101–1114.

[43] Meng Wang, Weijie Fu, Shijie Hao, Dacheng Tao, and Xindong Wu. 2016. Scalable semi-supervised learning by efficient anchor graph regularization. *IEEE Trans. Know. Data Engin.* 28, 7 (2016), 1864–1877.

[44] Meng Wang, Xueliang Liu, and Xindong Wu. 2015. Visual Classification by ℓ_1-Hypergraph Modeling. *IEEE Trans. Know. Data Engin.* 27, 9 (2015), 2564–2574.

[45] Qifan Wang, Bin Shen, Shumiao Wang, Liang Li, and Luo Si. 2014. Binary codes embedding for fast image tagging with incomplete labels. In *Proc. ECCV*. Springer, 425–439.

[46] Yair Weiss, Antonio Torralba, and Robert Fergus. 2008. Spectral Hashing. In *Proc. NIPS*. 1753–fi?!1760.

[47] John Wright, Allen Y Yang, Arvind Ganesh, S Shankar Sastry, and Yi Ma. 2009. Robust face recognition via sparse representation. *IEEE Trans. Pattern Anal. Mach. Intell.* 31, 2 (2009), 210–227.

[48] Yan Xia, Kaiming He, Pushmeet Kohli, and Jian Sun. 2015. Sparse Projections for High-Dimensional Binary Codes. In *Proc. CVPR*. 3332–3339.

[49] Jianxiong Xiao, James Hays, Krista A Ehinger, Aude Oliva, and Antonio Torralba. 2010. Sun database: Large-scale scene recognition from abbey to zoo. In *Proc. CVPR*. 3485–3492.

[50] Yang Yang, Yadan Luo, Weilun Chen, Fumin Shen, Jie Shao, and Heng Tao Shen. 2016. Zero-Shot Hashing via Transferring Supervised Knowledge. In *ACM Multimedia*. 1286–1295.

[51] Yang Yang, Fumin Shen, Heng Tao Shen, Hanxi Li, and Xuelong Li. 2015. Robust discrete spectral hashing for large-scale image semantic indexing. *IEEE Trans. Big Data* 1, 4 (2015), 162–171.

[52] Yang Yang, Hanwang Zhang, Mingxing Zhang, Fumin Shen, and Xuelong Li. 2015. Visual coding in a semantic hierarchy. In *ACM Multimedia*. 59–68.

[53] Hanwang Zhang, Fumin Shen, Wei Liu, Xiangnan He, Huanbo Luan, and Tat-Seng Chua. 2016. Discrete Collaborative Filtering. In *Proc. SIGIR*. 325–334.

[54] Peichao Zhang, Wei Zhang, Wu-Jun Li, and Minyi Guo. 2014. Supervised Hashing with Latent Factor Models. In *Proc. SIGIR*. 173–182.

[55] Ke Zhou and Hongyuan Zha. 2012. Learning Binary Codes for Collaborative Filtering. In *Proc. KDD*. 498–506.

BitFunnel: Revisiting Signatures for Search

Bob Goodwin, Microsoft
Michael Hopcroft, Microsoft
Dan Luu, Microsoft
Alex Clemmer, Heptio
Mihaela Curmei, Microsoft
Sameh Elnikety, Microsoft
Yuxiong He, Microsoft

ABSTRACT

Since the mid-90s there has been a widely-held belief that signature files are inferior to inverted files for text indexing. In recent years the Bing search engine has developed and deployed an index based on bit-sliced signatures. This index, known as BitFunnel, replaced an existing production system based on an inverted index. The driving factor behind the shift away from the inverted index was operational cost savings. This paper describes algorithmic innovations and changes in the cloud computing landscape that led us to reconsider and eventually field a technology that was once considered unusable. The BitFunnel algorithm directly addresses four fundamental limitations in bit-sliced block signatures. At the same time, our mapping of the algorithm onto a cluster offers opportunities to avoid other costs associated with signatures. We show these innovations yield a significant efficiency gain versus classic bit-sliced signatures and then compare BitFunnel with Partitioned Elias-Fano Indexes, MG4J, and Lucene.

CCS CONCEPTS

• **Information systems** → **Search engine indexing**; *Probabilistic retrieval models; Distributed retrieval*; • **Theory of computation** → Bloom filters and hashing;

KEYWORDS

Signature Files; Search Engines; Inverted Indexes; Intersection; Bitvector; Bloom Filters; Bit-Sliced Signatures; Query Processing

1 INTRODUCTION

Commercial search engines [2, 5, 19, 24] traditionally employ inverted indexes. In this work, we show how to use signatures, or bit-strings based on Bloom filters [1], in a large-scale commercial search engine for better performance. Prior work comparing inverted files to signature files established that inverted files outperformed signature files by almost every criterion [28]. However, recent software and hardware trends (e.g., large Web corpora with of billions of documents, large main memory systems) motivated us to reconsider signature files.

In our signature-based approach, known as BitFunnel, we use a Bloom filter to represent the set of terms in each document as a fixed sequence of bits called a *signature*. Bloom filters are reasonably space efficient and allow for fast set membership, forming the basis for query processing.

Using this approach, however, poses four major challenges. First, determining the matches for a single term requires examining one signature for each document in the corpus. This involves considerably more CPU and memory cycles than the equivalent operation on an inverted index. Second, term frequency follows a Zipfian distribution, implying that signatures must be long to yield an acceptable false positive rate when searching for the rarest terms. Third, the size of web documents varies substantially, implying that signatures must be long to accommodate the longest documents. Fourth, the configuration of signature-based schemes is not a well-understood problem.

We develop a set of techniques to address these challenges: (1) we introduce *higher rank rows* to reduce query execution time; (2) we employ *frequency-conscious signatures* to reduce the memory footprint; (3) we shard the corpus to reduce the variability in document size; (4) we develop a cost model for system performance; and (5) we use this model to formulate a constrained optimization to configure the system for efficiency.

These techniques are used in the Microsoft Bing search engine, which has been running in production for the last four years on thousands of servers. Compared to an earlier production search engine based on inverted lists that it replaced, BitFunnel improved server query capacity by a factor of 10.

2 BACKGROUND AND PRIOR WORK

We focus on the problem of identifying those documents in a corpus that match a conjunctive query of keywords. We call this the *Matching Problem*.

Let corpus $\mathbb{C}$ be a set of documents, each of which consists of a set of text terms:

$$\mathbb{C} = \{\text{documents } D\}$$
$$D = \{\text{terms } t\}$$

Define query Q as a set of text terms:

$$Q = \{\text{terms } t\}$$

SIGIR '17, August 07-11, 2017, Shinjuku, Tokyo, Japan

ACM ISBN 978-1-4503-5022-8/17/08...$15.00
https://doi.org/10.1145/3077136.3080789

Query Q is said to match document D when every term $t \in Q$ is also an element of D. This happens when $Q \subseteq D$ or $Q = Q \cap D$. Define match set M as the set of documents matching Q:

$$M = \{D \in \mathbb{C} \mid Q = D \cap Q\}$$

The goal of the Matching Problem is to identify the match set M, given corpus $\mathbb{C}$ and query Q.

In Sections 2.2-2.4 we examine conservative probabilistic algorithms that never miss a match, but might falsely report matches. The goal for these algorithms is to identify a conservative filter set M'

$$M \subseteq M' \subseteq \mathbb{C}$$

where the false positive set $F = M' \setminus M$ is small.

2.1 Inverted Indexes

Perhaps the most common approach to the *Matching Problem* is the *inverted index* [4, 11]. This approach maintains a mapping from each term in the lexicon to the the set of documents containing the term. In other words,

$$Postings(t) = \{D \in \mathbb{C} \mid t \in D\}$$

With this approach, M can be formed by intersecting the posting sets associated with the terms in the query:

$$M = \bigcap_{t \in Q} Postings(t)$$

In practice, the posting sets are usually sorted, allowing fast intersection. They also draw on a large bag of tricks [4, 20] to compress and decompress posting sets [17, 23] while improving intersection time [6, 7]. This is a rich area with ongoing research into novel data structures such as treaps [16] and semi-bitvectors [13].

Inverted indexes find the exact match set, M, every time. Signature-based approaches [8–10, 15, 25], on the other hand, use probabilistic algorithms, based on superimposed coding [1, 21, 22] and newer approaches, like TopSig [12] to identify a conservative filter set M'. BitFunnel is based on classical bit-sliced signatures which are, in turn, based on bit-string signatures.

2.2 Bit-String Signatures

The key idea is that each document in the corpus is represented by its *signature*. In BitFunnel, the signature is essentially the sequence of bits that make up a Bloom filter representing the set of terms in the document. In constructing the Bloom filter, each term in the document is hashed to a few bit positions, each of which is set to 1.

Let n denote the number of bit positions in the Bloom filter. Define $H(n, t)$ as a function that returns the set of bit positions in the range $[0..n)$ corresponding to the hashes of term t. Define $\vec{s_t}$, the signature of term t, as the bit-vector of length-n where bit position i is set to 1 iff $i \in H(n, t)$. We can then define the signature of document D as the logical-or of the signatures of its terms:

$$\vec{s_D} = \bigcup_{t \in D} \vec{s_t}$$

In a similar manner, we can define the signature of query Q as the logical-or of the signatures of its terms:

$$\vec{s_Q} = \bigcup_{t \in Q} \vec{s_t}$$

Document D is said to be a member of M' when

$$\vec{s_Q} \cap \vec{s_D} = \vec{s_Q}$$

Given the signatures of the documents in the corpus, one can easily compute M' by identifying those documents whose signatures match the query's signature:

$$M' = \{D \in \mathbb{C} \mid \vec{s_Q} \cap \vec{s_D} = \vec{s_Q}\}$$

Here's the pseudocode to search a corpus for documents matching a query:

$M' = \emptyset$
for all $D \in \mathbb{C}$ **do**
  if $\vec{s_D} \cap \vec{s_Q} = \vec{s_Q}$ **then**
    $M' = M' \cup \{D\}$
  end if
end for

Bit-string signatures are elegant, but their uniform encoding of terms, independent of frequency, leads to poor memory utilization. Section 4.2 explains how BitFunnel uses *Frequency Conscious Signatures* to improve memory efficiency in signatures.

2.3 Bit-Sliced Signatures

If all of the signatures have the same length and share a common hashing scheme, $H(n, t)$, one can achieve significant performance gains by using a bit-sliced arrangement [9, 26, 27]. This approach transposes signature vectors from rows to columns in order to allow multiple documents to be searched simultaneously while eliminating the bit masks and shifting necessary to perform Boolean operations on individual bits.

Suppose we have a corpus $C = \{A..P\}$ and a query Q. The matrix in Figure 1 shows these documents and the query encoded as bit-sliced signatures. Each document corresponds to a column which holds its 16-bit signature. Each row corresponds to a bit position in the document signature.

In this example the signature for document B has bit positions 2, 5, 9, and 13 set. The signature for the query Q has bit positions 2, 5, and 9 set. Therefore, document B will match the query. It turns out that document F also matches the query.

With the bit-sliced layout, we need only inspect the rows corresponding to bit positions in Q that are set. These rows, which we call the query's rows, are shaded in Figure 1 and isolated in Figure 2. Each bit position in the query's rows corresponds to a document. The document matches if its bit position is set in all of the query's rows. We determine which documents match by intersecting the query's rows and looking for set bits. In Figure 2, columns B and F are the only columns without zeros. Therefore documents B and F are the only matches.

Here's the bit-sliced algorithm:

$\vec{a} = \sim 0$
for all i where $\vec{s_Q}[i] == 1$ **do**
  $\vec{a} = \vec{a}$ & $\vec{row_i}$
end for
$M' = \{i \mid \vec{a}[i] \neq 0\}$

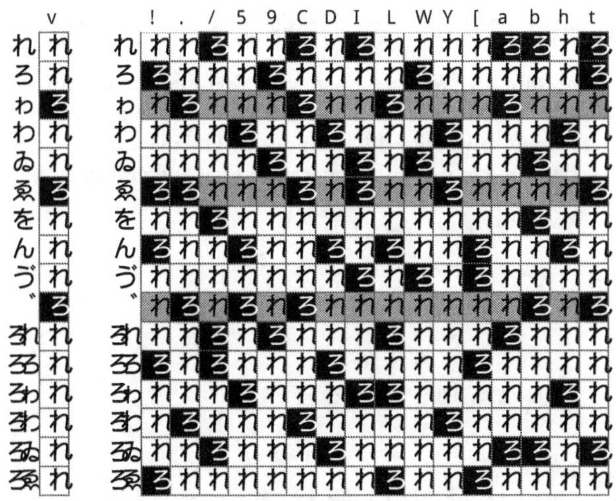

Figure 1: Layout with bit-sliced signatures, in which each column is a document signature. Q is the signature of the query.

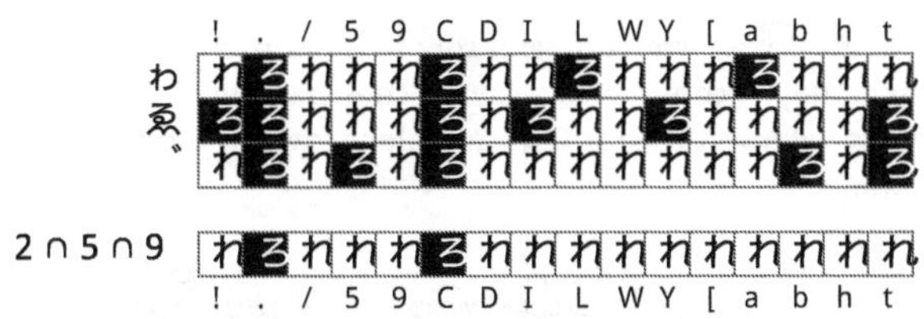

Figure 2: Bit-sliced signature layout. Rows 2, 5, and 9 yield documents *B* and *F*.

2.4 Bit-Sliced Blocked Signatures

While bit-sliced signatures offer a significant performance advantage over bit-string signatures, they still suffer from poor performance when searching for rare terms. The problem is that every document's bit position must be scanned, even in the case where only a handful of documents actually match.

The idea behind blocked signatures [14] is to create shorter rows by assigning multiple documents to each column in the signature matrix. The number of documents that share a column is called the *blocking factor*. Shorter rows improve performance because they can be scanned more quickly, but they introduce noise which increases the false positive rate.

Prior to BitFunnel, bit-sliced block signatures were used primarily as a single-level index into a set of bit-string signature files on disk. At the time the main concern with this approach was reducing the probability of an *unsuccessful block match* which occurred when a column signature matched the query but none of the documents contained all the terms in the query. Suppose, for example, a column held two documents, one containing the word "dog" and the other containing the word "cat". This column would match the query {*"dog"*, *"cat"*} even though neither document contains both terms. At least one paper proposed a solution to the problem of unsuccessful block matches [14], however [28] argued that blocking increases complexity while offering little benefit. In Section 4.1, we introduce *Higher Rank Rows* to address these problems.

3 THE BITFUNNEL SYSTEM

For the past 4 years, BitFunnel has powered Bing's fresh index of recently crawled documents. During this time the system, which runs on thousands of machines, spread across several data centers, has processed the entire query load sent to Bing.

3.1 Architectural Overview

Bing maintains multiple, georeplicated copies of the web index, each of which is sharded across a cluster of BitFunnel nodes. Figure 3 shows a single cluster. Queries are distributed, round robin, across the cluster. A node, upon receiving a query, parses it into an abstract syntax tree, rewrites the tree into an execution plan and then compiles the plan locally before broadcasting the compiled plan to the rest of the cluster. The nodes in the cluster run the compiled plan in parallel, returning results to the planning node for aggregation. These results are then passed on to other systems that score the matching documents and generate captions to display on the search results web page.

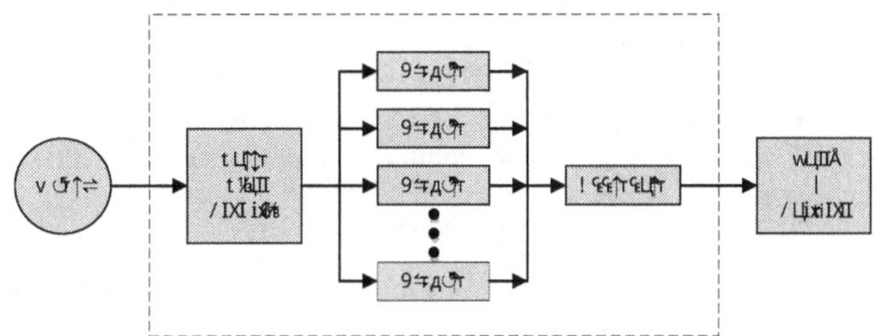

Figure 3: BitFunnel cluster.

3.2 The Cost of False Positives

One criticism specific to the signature file approach is the introduction of false positives into the result set. For scenarios like database queries where the identifying exact match set is the goal, the cost of filtering out the false positives can be prohibitive. In the case of web search, the cost of filtering out false positives is negligible. To see why, it is important to understand that the goal of web search is not to find documents matching Boolean expressions of keywords – rather it is to find the documents that best match the user's intent when issuing a query. In Bing, we employ a ranking system that, given a document and a query, will generate a score predicting how well the document matches the user's intent for the query. This system relies on many signals beyond keywords and to some extent its inner workings are opaque to us because it is configured by machine learning.

If we had unlimited resources, we could process each query by submitting every single document in the corpus to our ranking oracle and then return the top-n ranked documents. Since we don't have unlimited resources, we insert inexpensive filters upstream of the oracle to discard documents that the oracle would score low. The filters are designed to reject, with high probability, those documents that score low while never rejecting documents that score high. BitFunnel is such a filter.

In this context, the performance of BitFunnel is judged by its impact on the end-to-end system. BitFunnel wins when its time savings in the Boolean matching phase is greater than the time the oracle spends scoring false positives.

We turn our attention now to a single BitFunnel node to describe the techniques that enable fast query processing.

4 BITFUNNEL INNOVATIONS

In this section, we describe three innovations that address speed and space problems associated with bit-string and bit-sliced signatures.

4.1 Higher Rank Rows

BitFunnel generalizes the idea of blocking so that each term simultaneously hashes to multiple bit-sliced signatures with different blocking factors. The key to making this approach work is the ability to efficiently intersect rows with different blocking factors.

4.1.1 Mapping Columns Across Ranks. In BitFunnel, we restrict blocking factors to be powers of 2. We define a concept of row *rank*, where a row of rank $r \geq 0$ has a blocking factor of 2^r.

The BitFunnel blocking scheme is specific to the size of the machine word used for the bit-slice operations. Let w be the $\log_2$ of the number of bits in a machine word, so for example, a 64-bit processor would have $w = 6$. Then the document in column i_0 at rank 0 will be associated with column i_r at rank r as follows:

$$i_r = \frac{i_0}{2^{r+w}} + (i_0 \bmod 2^r) \quad (1)$$

Figure 4 gives a small example for a 4-bit machine word ($w = 2$) and ranks 0, 1, and 2. We can see that position 4 at rank 1 is associated with documents $\{4, 12\}$ while position 0 at rank 2 is associated with documents $\{0, 4, 8, 12\}$.

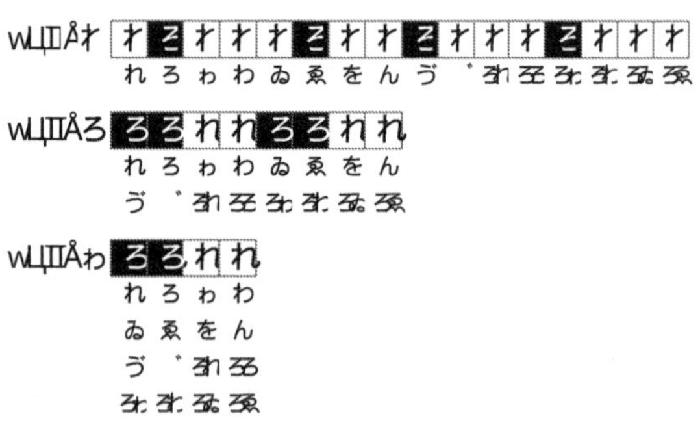

Figure 4: Forming higher rank equivalents of a single row.

Note that higher rank rows will, in general, magnify the bit density of their lower rank equivalents. This is because the value of each bit at a higher rank is the logical-or of multiple bits at a lower rank. In order to maintain a constant bit density of d across all signatures in BitFunnel, we must use longer signatures at higher ranks. Therefore, a single row at rank 0 will translate into multiple shorter rows at a higher rank. In most cases, a rank zero row and its higher rank equivalents will consume roughly the same amount of memory. We will derive an expression for the memory consumption in higher rank rows in Section 5.4.

Now suppose we have a query, Q, that maps to the three rows shown in Figure 5. To evaluate the query, we need some way of intersecting rows with different ranks. The mapping in Equation (1) is designed to make this operation easy and efficient.

Figure 5: Intersecting different rows with different ranks.

Logically we convert each row to its *rank-0 equivalent* by concatenating 2^r copies of the row as shown in Figure 6. Then we are free to intersect the rank-0 equivalent rows to produce the result vector.

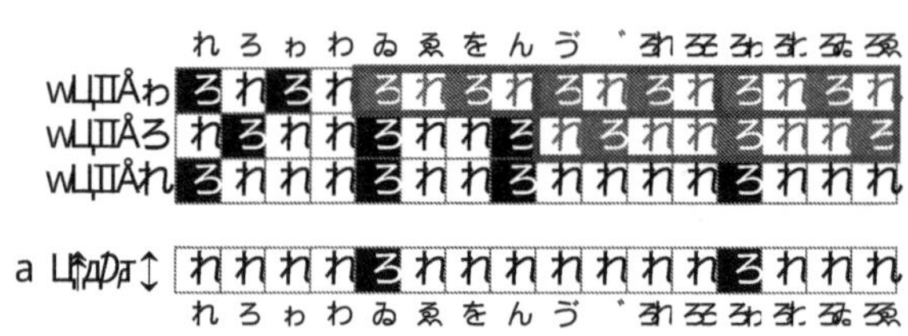

Figure 6: Rank-0 equivalent rows.

4.1.2 Optimizing Higher Rank Row Intersection. At a logical level, our approach is to intersect rank-0 equivalent rows. Were we to generate rank-0 equivalents for intersection, we would lose all of the performance gains that come from scanning shorter rows at higher ranks. Mapping (1) was structured specifically to provide opportunities to reuse intermediate results at every rank. As an example, in Figure 6, bits [0..3] of the rank 2 row need only be read once, even though they will be used for positions [4..7], [8..11], and [12..15]. Similarly, the intersection of the first two rows in positions [0..3] will be computed once and used again for positions [8..11]. We will leverage this insight in Section 5.3 where we derive an expression for the expected number of operations required to combine a set of rows with different ranks.

In BitFunnel, each term in a query maps to a set of rows that may include higher rank rows.

4.2 Frequency Conscious Signatures

We saw in Section 2.2 how Bloom filter signatures can be used to encode the set of terms in a document. One shortcoming with this approach is inefficient memory usage when terms in the lexicon have widely varying frequencies in the corpus.

The problem stems from the fact that, in its classical formulation [1], the Bloom filter is configured with an integer constant, k, which represents the number of hashes for each term[1]. This value of k is the same for all terms in lexicon L. In other words

$$|H(n,t)| = k, \ \forall_{t \in L}$$

To get an intuition for the problem of the one-size-fits-all k, it helps to think of the quantity of false positives in terms of signal-to-noise ratio. Let's consider a single set membership test for $t \in D$. In the context of the test, define the signal s to be the probability that term t is actually a member of document D. This is just the frequency of t in the corpus.

Define noise α to be the probability that the Bloom filter will incorrectly report t as a member. Assume the Bloom filter has been configured to have an average bit density of d. Since d is the fraction of the bits expected to be set, we can treat it as the probability that a random bit is set. A set membership test involves probing k bit positions. If all k probes find bits that are set to one, the algorithm will report a match. Therefore the noise is just the probability that k probes all hit ones when $t \notin D$:

$$\alpha = (1-s)d^k$$

The signal-to-noise ratio ϕ is then

$$\phi = \frac{s}{(1-s)d^k}$$

We can rearrange this and take the ceiling to get an expression for k as a function of d, s, and ϕ:

$$k = \left\lceil log_d \left(\frac{s}{(1-s)\phi} \right) \right\rceil$$

This is the minimum value of k that will ensure a signal-to-noise ratio of at least ϕ. The main take away is that k increases as s decreases. In other words, rare terms require more hashes to ensure a given signal-to-noise level. The following table shows values of k without the ceiling, for select values of s when $d = 0.1$ and $\phi = 10$:

signal (s)	hashes (k)
0.1	1.954242509
0.01	2.995635195
0.001	3.999565488
0.0001	4.999956568
0.00001	5.999995657

Now consider a Bloom filter that stores a typical document from the Gov2 corpus[2]. If we were to configure the Bloom filter with $k = 2$ we could just barely maintain a signal-to-noise ratio of 10 when testing for the term "picture" which appears with frequency 0.1. To test for the term "rotisserie", which appears with frequency 0.0001, we would need $k = 5$ to drive the noise down to a tenth of the signal.

With classical Bloom filters, one must configure for the rarest term in the lexicon, even though the vast majority of common terms could be stored more efficiently. Recent work in Weighted Bloom Filters [3] shows that it is possible to adjust the number of hash functions on a term-by-term basis within the same Bloom filter.

BitFunnel applies these ideas to reduce memory usage and determine the number of rows needed for each term.

4.3 Sharding by Document Length

Bit-sliced signatures have another one-size-fits-all problem resulting from the requirement that all of the document signatures have the same configuration (i.e. their bit lengths, n, must all be the same, and they must all use the same hashing scheme $H(n, t)$).

The problem is that real world documents vary greatly in length. In Wikipedia, for example, the shortest documents have just a handful of unique terms while the longest ones may have many thousands of terms. The dynamic range of document lengths on the internet is even higher because of files containing DNA sequences, phone numbers, and GUIDs. To avoid overfilling our Bloom filters and generating excessive false positives, it is necessary to configure the Bloom filters for the longest document expected, even if such a document is very rare. Unfortunately, such a configuration would waste enough memory as to offset all of the other benefits of the bit-sliced arrangement.

A workaround [28] suggested in the late 90s was to shard the index into pieces containing documents with similar lengths. This approach was rejected at the time because, on a single machine, the introduction of length sharding would multiply the number of disk seeks by the number of shards.

This concern is not a factor when the index is many times larger than the capacity of a single machine. As soon as the index is sharded across a large cluster, one must pay for the overhead of sharding. At this point sharding by document length costs the same as sharding by any arbitrary factor.

Even on a single machine, the cost of length sharding is greatly reduced on modern hardware where the index can be stored in RAM or on SSD because the access cost is dominated by fixed-sized block transfers (512-bit cache line for RAM, 4096 byte block for SSD), rather than hard disk seeks.

In BitFunnel, we partition the corpus according to the number of unique terms in each document such that each instance of BitFunnel manages a shard in which documents have similar sizes.

5 PERFORMANCE MODEL AND OPTIMIZATION

Signature-based approaches have historically been hard to configure because of a large number of design parameters that impact performance [10, 26, 28]. In this section we present an algorithm that optimizes the BitFunnel configuration, given a desired signal-to-noise ratio. The algorithm performs a constrained optimization, over relevant configuration parameters, of a cost function that expresses the system efficiency as DQ, the product of the corpus size D and query processing rate Q. The configuration parameters include the mapping from terms with various frequencies to their corresponding number of rows at each rank. The constraint is a lower limit on the allowable signal-to-noise ratio, ϕ.

In order to develop the cost function and constraint, we derive expressions for the signal-to-noise ratio, query processing speed, and memory consumption in BitFunnel. We then combine these

[1] In Bloom's original paper [1] this constant was the letter d; more contemporary descriptions [3] use the letter k.

[2] Term frequencies are from Corpus D described in Section 6.

expressions into a cost function and constraint used by the algorithm that identifies an optimized set of blocking factors and hash functions for each equivalence class of terms, based on frequency in the lexicon.

5.1 Prerequisites

Before deriving these fundamental equations, we discuss the impact of row rank on bit densities and noise. We then characterize two different components of noise in rank-0 equivalent rows. This will form the basis for the noise, speed, and storage equations in Sections 5.2, 5.3, and 5.4.

5.1.1 Signal in a Higher Rank Row. Because each bit in a higher rank row corresponds to multiple documents, the bit density contributed by a single term will nearly always be greater in higher rank rows. We can see this in Figure 4 where densities in the rank-0 row and its rank 1 equivalent are $\frac{4}{16}$ and $\frac{8}{16}$, respectively.

Let s_0 denote the signal in a rank-0 row and s_r denote the signal at rank r. We can express s_r as a function of s_0 and r. The probability that a bit at rank r is set due to signal is the probability that at least one of the 2^r corresponding rank-0 bits is signal. This is just one minus the probability that all of the 2^r rank-0 bits are zero:

$$s_r = 1 - (1 - s_0)^{2^r} \quad (2)$$

5.1.2 Noise in a Rank-0 Equivalent Row. Processing a query in BitFunnel is logically equivalent to intersecting the rank-0 equivalents of each row associated with the query. Converting a rank-r row to its rank-0 equivalent increases noise. The intuition behind this is simple — each bit set in a rank-r row means that at least one of 2^r documents is a match. It could be one document or all 2^r — we can't tell and this is the source of higher noise.

Let's look at a simple example. Suppose we have a corpus of 16 documents and would like to search for a term that happens to appear in documents 4 and 8. We hash our term to find its corresponding rows, and we get the set of rows $R = \{R_2, R_1, R_0\}$ with ranks 2, 1, and 0, respectively. We define the signal, s_0 as the fraction of the bit positions at rank-0 corresponding to a match. In the case of a term that appears in only 2 documents, $s_0 = \frac{2}{16}$. In Figure 7, the green squares labeled 'S' correspond to the signal.

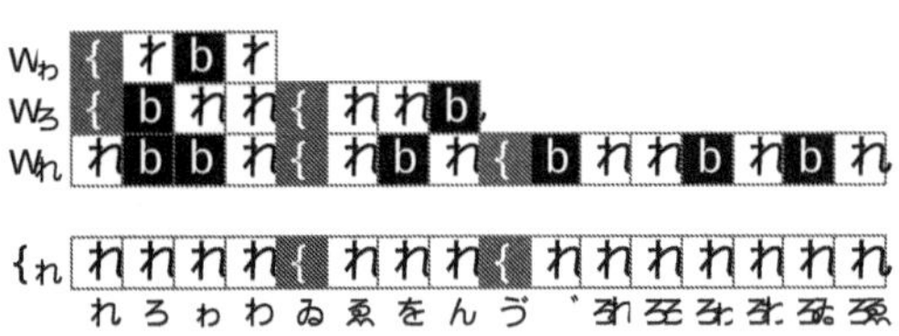

Figure 7: A term maps to three rows with different ranks. Since a row is shared with other terms, it contains signal and noise bits but has constant bit density.

R_2 has one signal bit, so its signal is $\frac{1}{4} = \frac{4}{16}$. We've arbitrarily added one noise bit, marked with an 'N' and shaded black. This bit is contributed from another term that also maps to R_2. The density of R_2 is $\frac{2}{4} = \frac{8}{16}$.

Row R_1 has two signal bits and two arbitrary noise bits so its signal is $\frac{2}{8} = \frac{4}{16}$ and its density is $\frac{4}{8} = \frac{8}{16}$.

Finally, in row R_0, the signal is equal to s_0 because each signal bit maps directly to a single document. As with the other rows, R_0 contains random noise bits from other terms, yielding $\frac{8}{16}$ density.

To process our query, we intersect the rank-0 equivalents of rows R_2 and R_1 with R_0. Figure 8 shows how the process of creating rank-0 equivalents increases noise.

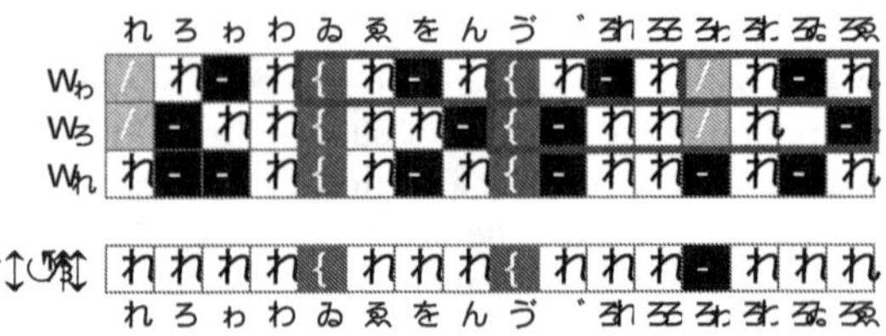

Figure 8: Noise in rank-0 equivalent rows.

Continuing with our example, the signal bit from position 0 in R_2 maps to bit positions 0, 4, 8, and 12 at rank 0. Of these four positions, only positions 4 and 8 correspond to signal bits. The others are noise bits introduced by the construction of the rank-0 equivalent, and they are colored yellow and marked with the letter 'C'. In a similar manner, R_2 bit position 2 introduces noise in rank-0 positions 2, 6, 10, and 14. These bits are colored black and marked with the letter 'U'. In the case of R_2, we went from a rank-2 row with $\frac{1}{4}$ signal and $\frac{1}{4}$ noise to a rank-0 row with $\frac{2}{16}$ signal and $\frac{6}{16}$ noise. The noise increase is entirely due to the signal bits in R_2. In contrast, the noise bits in R_2 contribute their same density without amplification, and therefore do not increase noise in the rank-0 equivalent row.

Now let's look at the rank-0 equivalent of R_1. We go from a rank-1 row with $\frac{2}{8}$ signal and $\frac{2}{8}$ noise to a rank-0 row with $\frac{2}{16}$ signal and $\frac{6}{16}$ noise. As with R_2, the noise increase is due entirely to signal in rank-1 row.

5.1.3 Correlated and Uncorrelated Noise. We turn to computing the noise resulting from the intersection of a set of the rows. The noise in any rank-0 row is the difference between the row's density and the signal s_0. If row R has density d, then its rank-0 equivalent has density d because it consists of the concatenation of 2^r copies of the R. Therefore, the noise in R's rank-0 equivalent is $d - s_0$.

Noise is made up of two components, one which is correlated and one which is not. In Figure 8, uncorrelated noise bits are shaded black while correlated noise bits are colored yellow. Row intersections are very effective at reducing uncorrelated noise, but they have less impact on correlated noise.

To better illustrate this, let's look at a simple, but extreme example. Suppose our query matches documents 2 and 13 and consists of the three rank-1 rows depicted in Figure 9. In the rank-0 equivalent

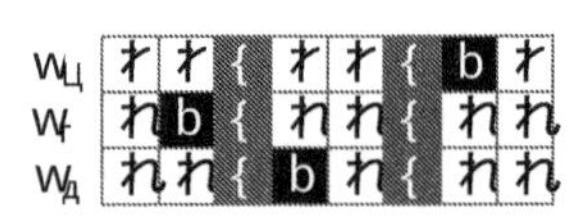

Figure 9: Three rank-2 rows.

rows, shown in Figure 10, noise has two components: correlated and

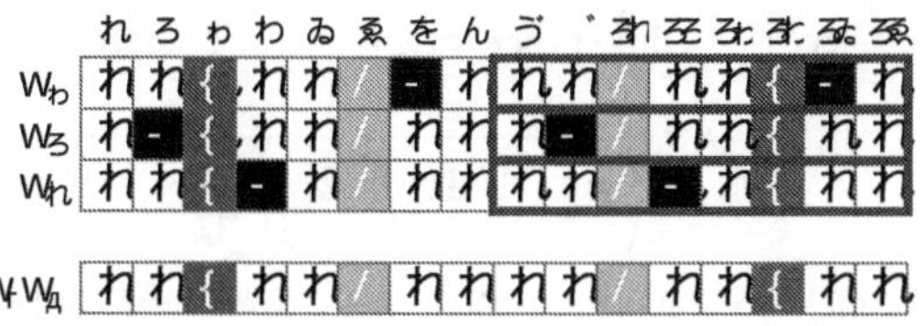

Figure 10: Correlated and uncorrelated noise in rank-0 equivalent rows.

uncorrelated. The uncorrelated noise, shown in black and marked with the letter 'U', is completely eliminated in three row intersections, but the correlated noise, shown in yellow and marked with the letter 'C' remains at the same level despite the intersections.

Effectively managing the impact of higher rank rows requires an understanding of the correlated noise in rank-0 equivalent rows. In the following we derive expressions for noise components.

Let n_r denote noise in a rank-r row R and n_0 denote noise in its rank-0 equivalent. We express n_0 as a function of r, s_0, and n_r. Row R will contribute n_r density due to noise already in R and s_r in density due to signal in R. A portion of the density in s_r corresponds to bonified signal. The remaining density is correlated noise introduced by the conversion to rank-0. Thus we compute noise at rank-0 by subtracting s_0 from the density contributed by R:

$$n_0 = n_r + s_r - s_0$$

To compute the correlated noise, we subtract n_r from n_0 and substitute $s_r = 1 - (1 - s_0)^{2^r}$:

$$n_0 - n_r = s_r - s_0 = 1 - (1 - s_0)^{2^r} - s_0 \tag{3}$$

Note that the number of correlated noise bits in a rank-0 equivalent is a function of the original rank. The higher the row rank, the greather the contribution in correlated noise to its rank-0 equivalent. Also, correlated noise remaining after intersecting a set of rank-0 equivalents is the correlated noise of the lowest rank row in the set. The other correlated noise is converted to uncorrelated noise.

It is important to note that the correlated noise bits in a lower rank equivalent always form a subset of the correlated noise bits in a higher rank equivalent. Our equations for noise and speed in Sections 5.2 and 5.3 make use of this fact.

5.2 Signal-to-Noise Ratio

We're now ready to write expressions for the noise components after a sequence of row intersections. For this derivation, we will perform the intersections in order from high rank to low rank. We will start with an accumulator, a, which has an initial bit density of 1.0 and then intersect in each row in turn.

Let a_i denote the total noise in the accumulator at the end of iteration i. Let c_i and u_i denote the amount of correlated and uncorrelated noise, respectively, on iteration i and let r_i denote the rank. The first iteration is effectively loading the first row into the accumulator so, $u_1 = n_1$. The correlated noise in the accumulator is always equal to the correlated noise in the last row intersected, so

$$c_i = 1 - (1 - s_0)^{2^{r_i}} - s_0$$

Since the rows are ordered by non-increasing rank, subsequent rows will never have more correlated noise. In the case where the rank decreases, the amount of correlated noise will decrease. When this happens, some of the correlated noise in the accumulator will become uncorrelated noise, moving forward. This new amount of uncorrelated noise in the accumulator will then be multiplied by the current row's total noise density n_{i+1}:

$$u_{i+1} = (u_i + c_i - c_{i+1})n_{i+1}$$

At any given point, the total accumulator noise a_i is just the sum of the correlated and uncorrelated noise:

$$a_i = c_i + u_i$$

The signal-to-noise ratio, ϕ, on iteration i is then

$$\phi_i = \frac{s_0}{a_i} = \frac{s_0}{c_i + u_i} \tag{4}$$

5.3 Query Execution Time

When modelling running time, we use the number of machine word accesses of unique memory addresses as our proxy for time. On a real computer, row intersections are typically performed in chunks that match the machine register size. As an example, if the machine register size is 64 bits, and the rank-0 rows are 256 bits long, a pairwise row intersection would require 4 register-sized logical-and operations. When intersecting a set of rows, the outer loop is typically over the register-sized chunks in each row and the inner loop is over the set of rows.

This ordering of the loops is desirable because intermediate results of row intersections can reside in the accumulator instead of being written to memory. In many cases, the accumulator will become zero in the inner loop before all of the rows have been examined. Since additional intersections cannot change the result, it is possible to break out of the inner loop at this point.

In practice, breaking out of the inner loop offers a significant performance improvement. To quantify this impact, we'll focus on the innermost loop which intersects a set of n machine words that reside in memory. Our goal is to write an expression for the expected number of machine words loaded from memory.

If we know the probability that a bit remains set after intersecting the first n rows, we can derive a formula for the expected number of machine words accessed when intersecting a set of rows.

Let N be a random variable denoting the machine words intersected and define $P_{BZ}(N > i)$ to be the probability that a random bit in the accumulator is zero after iteration i. $P_{BZ}(N > i)$ is the probability that the bit was not set by noise and not set by signal:

$$P_{BZ}(N > i) = 1 - s_0 - a_i$$

Define $P_A(N > i)$ to be the probability that at least one bit in the accumulator remains set after i intersections If b denotes the number of bits in a machine word then

$$P_A(N > i) = 1 - (P_{BZ}(N > i))^b$$

If we were to actually perform intersections on the rank-0 equivalent rows, the expected number of machine words accessed during one iteration of the outer loop would be

$$\mathbb{E}(N) = \sum_{i=1}^{n} P_A(N > i) = \sum_{i=1}^{n} 1 - (1 - s_0 - a_i)^b$$

As we saw in Section 4.1.2, the mapping of columns across ranks is structured in such a way that intermediate results from higher rank intersections can be reused. Since each rank-0 equivalent is just the concatenation of 2^r copies of a rank-r original, we need only load the accumulator once for each of the 2^r machine word positions in the rank-0 equivalent. This reduces the number of machine words accessed in each row by a factor of 2^{r_i}:

$$\mathbb{E}(N) = \sum_{i=1}^{n} \frac{1 - (1 - s_0 - a_i)^b}{2^{r_i}} \tag{5}$$

A similar approach can be used to model block devices like CPU cache and SSD block transfers, but it is somewhat more involved than substituting a different value for b.

5.4 Space Consumption

We express memory consumption as the number of bits per document required to store a term. Suppose we have a corpus, $\mathbb{C}$, with target bit density, d, and we wish to store a term with signal, s_0, in some row, q, that has rank r.

Since the corpus has $|\mathbb{C}|$ documents, row q must have $|\mathbb{C}|2^{-r}$ bit positions. Equation (2) shows that a term with frequency s_0 will set s_r of these bits. Therefore the term contributes $b_1 = s_r|\mathbb{C}|2^{-r}$ set bits to row q. Let b_0 denote the number of zero bits in row q. By definition,

$$d = \frac{b_1}{b_1 + b_0}$$

Rearranging, we get

$$b_0 = \frac{b_1}{d} - b_1$$

Therefore, the total number of bits required in row q to maintain density of d with a signal of s_0 is

$$b_0 + b_1 = \frac{b_1}{d} = \frac{s_r|\mathbb{C}|}{d2^r}$$

Dividing by the corpus size $|\mathbb{C}|$ gives the number of bits per document signature:

$$\frac{s_r}{d2^r}$$

For a set of rows, Q, the total memory consumption per document is therefore

$$\sum_{q \in Q} \frac{s_r(q)}{d2^r} \tag{6}$$

5.5 Choosing Term Configurations

Given expressions for signal-to-noise ratio, machine word reads, and storage consumed, we can now develop an approach for identifying the optimal row configuration for each term. The problem is a constrained optimization over a cost function parameterized by speed and space. Our constraint is that the signal-to-noise ratio, ϕ, must exceed some fixed threshold. The cost function is proportional to DQ, the product of the number of documents per unit storage and the number of queries processed per unit of compute.

D is inversely proportional to the amount of storage required per document. Q is inversely proportional to the number of machine words accessed while processing a query. Therefore

$$DQ \propto \frac{1}{\left(\sum_{i=1}^{n} \frac{1-(1-s_0-a_i)^b}{2^{r_i}}\right)\left(\sum_{q \in Q} \frac{s_r(q)}{d}\right)} \tag{7}$$

Given the small number of possible row configurations, it is easy to enumerate all configurations and choose the one with the highest DQ where ϕ exceeds the signal-to-noise threshold. For example, when considering configurations of 0 to 9 rows at each of seven ranks from 0 to 6, we need to examine 10^7 configurations for each s_0 value. If we group s_0 values into, say, 100 buckets correspondiong to IDF values from 0.1 to 10.0 in 0.1 increments, the entire optimization involves 10^9 evaluations of Equation 7. A modern multi-core processor can perform this optimization in a matter of seconds.

6 EXPERIMENATAL EVALUATION

Our experiments are based on the TREC Gov2 corpus. Apache Tikka[3] was used to extract terms, which were then converted to lower case, but not stemmed. Since BitFunnel shards its index by document term count, we selected five representative shards for our tests. Shard A has relatively short documents with term counts ranging from 64 to 127. Shards B, C, D and E have progressively larger documents.

Table 1: Corpora.

	A	B	C	D	E
Min terms	64	128	256	1,024	2,048
Max terms	127	255	511	2,047	4,095
Documents (M)	5.870	7.545	3.726	0.494	0.157
Total terms (M)	4.181	6.524	6.647	10.109	9.697
Postings (M)	563	1,411	1,268	687	432
Matches/query	1,115	3,561	5,124	3,728	3,688
Input text (GB)	6.85	25.48	21.02	22.89	20.26

Our query log is based the TREC 2006 Efficiency Topics. We removed punctuations from each query and then filtered out those queries that contained terms not in the corpus.[4] The resulting query log contains about 98k queries.

BitFunnel was implemented in C++14 and compiled with GCC 5.4.1 with the highest optimization level. Experiments were performed on a 4.0GHz 4-core i7-6700 with 32GB of 3.2GHz DDR4 RAM with Ubuntu 14.04 LTS on Windows Subsystem for Linux. BitFunnel was configured with lower bound signal-to-noise ratio $\phi = 10$.

The source code to replicate our experiments is available at http://bitfunnel.org/sigir2017.

6.1 Match Time vs. Quadwords

In Section 5.3 we developed a model for the number of machine words of row data accessed while processing a query. To verify that our model has predictive power, we examined the relationship between row intersection time and the number of quadwords accessed. Since BitFunnel has a significant per-match overhead that

[3] https://tika.apache.org/

[4] This filtering was necessary because the Partitioned Elias-Fano index we used requires all query terms be in the index.

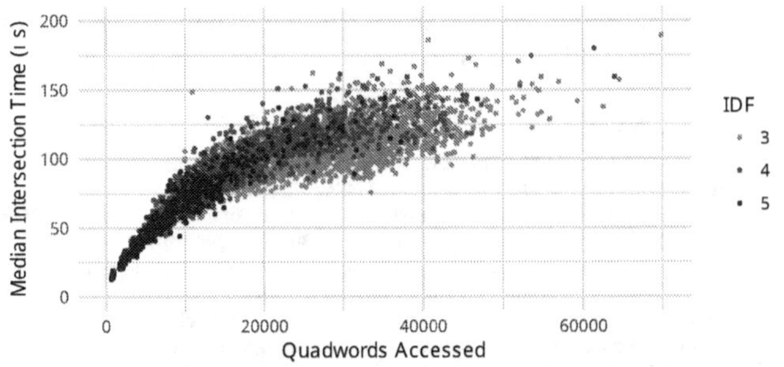

Figure 11: Intersection time increases with quadwords.

is not part of the row intersection cost model, we modified the code to perform row intersections, but not report matches. A sample of 5000 queries with $IDF > 3$ were chosen, at random, from our TREC query log, and these queries were run, single-threaded, against corpus D. To control for system variances not in the model, we ran each query 10 times and recorded the median row intersection time. The scatterplot in Figure 11 shows that row intersection time tends to grow as the number of quadwords increases. The correlation is more pronounced at higher IDF values.

6.2 Impact of Frequency Conscious Signatures and Higher Rank Rows

This experiment compares the time and space characteristics of (a) bit-sliced signatures configured with classical Bloom filters (BSS); (b) the same, but with Frequency Conscious Signatures as described in Section 4.2 (BSS-FC); and (c) Higher Ranked Rows as described in Section 4.1 and optimized per Section 5.5 (BTFNL).[5]

Table 2 examines Corpus D, comparing the three configurations at each of 5 bit densities. The DQ values measure overall system efficiency, expressed as the ratio of QPS to Bits/Posting. We use DQ because it is inversely proportional to the number of servers required, given a particular corpus and a desired QPS

Table 2: Impact of BitFunnel Innovations.

Treatment	Density	Bits/Posting	kQPS	DQ
BSS	0.05	80.0	14.0	175
BSS	0.10	50.0	11.3	225
BSS	0.15	46.7	9.1	194
BSS	0.20	40.0	8.2	204
BSS	0.25	36.0	6.9	191
BSS-FC	0.05	23.4	29.5	1,263
BSS-FC	0.10	16.8	25.5	1,515
BSS-FC	0.15	14.7	24.0	1,632
BSS-FC	0.20	13.1	21.4	1,634
BSS-FC	0.25	12.6	19.4	1,547
BTFNL	0.05	22.1	65.2	2,954
BTFNL	0.10	16.0	57.7	3,595
BTFNL	0.15	13.7	57.0	4,163
BTFNL	0.20	12.5	46.7	3,746
BTFNL	0.25	11.9	41.6	3,510

[5]The BSS Bloom filter targeted $\phi = 0.1$ for terms with IDF 4. The BSS-FC and BTFNL configurations set $\phi = 0.1$ for all terms, regardless of frequency.

Frequency consciousness reduces storage consumption while increasing speed. For example, at $d = 0.15$, the BSS configuration uses 46.7 bits per posting while the BSS-FC configuration uses only 14.7. This 3.2x reduction in storage is achieved while yielding a 2.6x increase in speed. The intuition behind the improvement is that frequency consciousness allows each term to have the right number of rows. With classical Bloom filters, every term has the same number of rows, meaning that more common terms get excess rows as a side effect of providing sufficient rows to ensure the target signal-to-noise level for rare terms.

Higher Rank Rows mainly impact speed. For example, when $d = 0.15$, BSS-FC runs at 24K queries per second, while BTFNL runs at 57.0K, a 2.4x improvement. The intuition behind the speed up is that higher rank rows can be scanned more quickly than rank-0 rows. Generally speaking, processing a rank-r row involves scanning $\frac{1}{2^r}$ of the quadwords necessary to process a rank-0 row.

The DQ column captures the tradeoff between space and speed. BSS-FC has a DQ of 1,632, while BTFNL has a DQ of 4,163, a 2.6x improvement. Combining frequency consciousness with higher rank rows yields a 21x improvement over that BSS DQ of 194.

We found that a density of 0.15 yielded the best DQ for Corpora B, C, and D, while A and E performed best at 0.05 and 0.20, respectively.

6.3 Comparison with Contemporary Indexes

The version of BitFunnel used by Bing includes a forward index with term frequencies used for BM25F ranking. Because this ranking code was not available to us at the time we designed our experiment, we limited our comparison to conjunctive boolean matching.

Our primary comparison system was Partitioned Elias-Fano or PEF[23]. This system is considered state-of-the-art, has excellent performance, and, like BitFunnel, is implemented in C++. We also compared with MG4J's Java implementation of PEF[6]. This implementation was the second fastest system in the SIGIR 2015 RIGOR workshop[18]. Our final comparison was with Lucene[7], a popular Java-based search engine that outperformed MG4J at the RIGOR workshop, in an apples-to-apples comparison using BM25F.

Each of these systems was configured to use a memory-mapped index that was non-positional, with scoring disabled. In this configuration, PEF and MG4J pay no runtime penalty associated with term frequencies because the frequencies are stored in a separate data structure that is never consulted. It is unclear whether Lucene pays a cost associated with stepping past term frequency values.

For each system we used 8 threads to process the entire 98k query log twice, back-to-back, measuring performance on the second pass. This ensured that relevant portions of the index were paged in, as they would be under continuous production load.

We can see from Table 3 that BitFunnel is faster than PEF in all cases, but sometimes this comes at a significant cost, for example in Corpus A, BitFunnel uses 5x as many bits per posting while yielding a false positive rate of 1.62%. Across the 5 corpora, MG4J is slower than PEF, as expected since it implements the same algorithm, but in Java. MG4J is faster than Lucene in all but Corpus C.

BitFunnel's overall performance relative to PEF improves as document lengths increase. It first surpasses PEF in Corpus C, where it

[6]http://mg4j.di.unimi.it/
[7]https://lucene.apache.org/

shows 3.2x the QPS of PEF while using only 2.6x the space. Examining DQ, the ratio of QPS to bits-per-posting, we see that BitFunnel outperforms PEF by factors of 1.3, 3.1, and 4.2 in Corpora C, D, and E, respectively, while PEF outperforms BitFunnel by factors of 3.4 and 1.6 in Corpora A and B.

Table 3: Query Processing Performance.

		BitFunnel	PEF	MG4J	Lucene
A	QPS	21,427	14,675	6,866	6,310
	False positives (%)	1.62	0.00	0.00	0.00
	Bits per posting	38.43	7.64	7.85	–
	DQ	558	1,921	875	–
B	QPS	8,674	5,049	3,636	3,011
	False positives (%)	4.32	0.00	0.00	0.00
	Bits per posting	20.72	7.33	7.59	–
	DQ	419	689	479	–
C	QPS	12,722	3,959	3,096	4,120
	False positives (%)	3.88	0.00	0.00	0.00
	Bits per posting	16.91	6.63	6.88	–
	DQ	752	598	450	–
D	QPS	57,014	8,268	5,900	3,632
	False positives (%)	2.43	0.00	0.00	0.00
	Bits per posting	13.69	6.25	6.28	–
	DQ	4,163	1,322	939	–
E	QPS	105,782	13,151	7,349	4,991
	False positives (%)	2.64	0.00	0.00	0.00
	Bits per posting	11.69	6.15	6.15	–
	DQ	9,047	2,139	1,195	–

These results are consistent with the interpretation that the biggest factor in BitFunnel performance is row length, which is directly proportional to the number of documents in the corpus. As document lengths increase and the corpus size drops, BitFunnel performance improves relative to PEF.

It is unclear from these results, the extent to which BitFunnel's performance gains are the result of a careful implementation versus actual algorithmic gains. We can see from PEF vs MG4J that choice of implementation language can have a significant impact on performance. Since BitFunnel compiles each query into x64 machine code, it is likely that some of BitFunnel's gains come from highly optimized query code.

7 CONCLUSION

This work revisits bit-sliced signatures and describes their use in a commercial search engine, which previously used inverted files. Signature-based approaches introduce several challenges and we develop a set of techniques to reduce the memory footprint and to process queries quickly. Furthermore, we derive a performance model that allows expressing the system configuration as an optimization problem. We evaluate the key techniques behind BitFunnel experimentally, and we provide the source code publicly to accelerate advances in this area.

8 ACKNOWLEDGMENTS

We thank the following colleagues for their contributions to BitFunnel: Andrija Antonijevic, Tanj Bennett, Denis Deyneko, Utkarsh Jain, and Fan Wang. We also thank the anonymous reviewers for their feedback which led to an improved experimental section.

REFERENCES

[1] Burton H Bloom. 1970. Space/time trade-offs in hash coding with allowable errors. *Commun. ACM* 13, 7 (1970), 422–426.
[2] Sergey Brin and Lawrence Page. 1998. The Anatomy of a Large-Scale Hypertextual Web Search Engine. *Computer Networks* 30, 1-7 (1998), 107–117.
[3] Jehoshua Bruck, Jie Gao, and Anxiao Jiang. 2006. Weighted bloom filter. In *2006 IEEE International Symposium on Information Theory*. IEEE.
[4] Stefan Büttcher, Charles LA Clarke, and Gordon V Cormack. 2016. *Information retrieval: Implementing and evaluating search engines*. Mit Press.
[5] Berkant Barla Cambazoglu and Ricardo A. Baeza-Yates. 2015. *Scalability Challenges in Web Search Engines*. Morgan & Claypool Publishers.
[6] J Shane Culpepper and Alistair Moffat. 2010. Efficient set intersection for inverted indexing. *ACM Transactions on Information Systems (TOIS)* 29, 1 (2010), 1.
[7] Bolin Ding and Arnd Christian König. 2011. Fast set intersection in memory. *Proceedings of the VLDB Endowment* 4, 4 (2011), 255–266.
[8] Chris Faloutsos. 1985. Access methods for text. *ACM Computing Surveys (CSUR)* 17, 1 (1985), 49–74.
[9] Christos Faloutsos. 1992. Information retrieval: data structures and algorithms. Prentice Hall PTR, 44–65.
[10] Christos Faloutsos and Stavros Christodoulakis. 1985. Design of a Signature File Method that Accounts for Non-Uniform Occurrence and Query Frequencies.. In *VLDB*. 165–170.
[11] Edward Fox, Donna Harman, w. Lee, and Ricardo Baeza-Yates. 1992. Information retrieval: data structures and algorithms. Prentice Hall PTR, 28–43.
[12] Shlomo Geva and Christopher M De Vries. 2011. Topsig: Topology preserving document signatures. In *Proceedings of the 20th ACM international conference on Information and knowledge management*. ACM, 333–338.
[13] Andrew Kane and Frank Wm Tompa. 2014. Skewed partial bitvectors for list intersection. In *Proceedings of the 37th international ACM SIGIR conference on Research & development in information retrieval*. ACM, 263–272.
[14] A Kent, Ron Sacks-Davis, and Kotagiri Ramamohanarao. 1990. A signature file scheme based on multiple organizations for indexing very large text databases. *Journal of the American Society for Information Science* 41, 7 (1990), 508.
[15] Donald E Knuth. 1998. *The Art of Computer Programming, Vol. 3, Sorting and Searching* (2nd ed.). Vol. 3. Addison-Wesley, 567–573.
[16] Roberto Konow, Gonzalo Navarro, Charles LA Clarke, and Alejandro López-Ortíz. 2013. Faster and smaller inverted indices with treaps. In *Proceedings of the 36th international ACM SIGIR conference on Research and development in information retrieval*. ACM, 193–202.
[17] Daniel Lemire and Leonid Boytsov. 2015. Decoding billions of integers per second through vectorization. *Software: Practice and Experience* 45, 1 (2015), 1–29.
[18] Jimmy Lin, Matt Crane, Andrew Trotman, Jamie Callan, Ishan Chattopadhyaya, John Foley, Grant Ingersoll, Craig Macdonald, and Sebastiano Vigna. 2016. Toward reproducible baselines: The open-source ir reproducibility challenge. In *European Conference on Information Retrieval*. Springer, 408–420.
[19] Sergey Melnik, Sriram Raghavan, Beverly Yang, and Hector Garcia-Molina. 2001. Building a distributed full-text index for the Web. In *Proceedings of the Tenth International World Wide Web Conference, WWW 10, Hong Kong, China, May 1-5, 2001*. 396–406.
[20] Alistair Moffat and Justin Zobel. 1996. Self-indexing inverted files for fast text retrieval. *ACM Transactions on Information Systems (TOIS)* 14, 4 (1996), 349–379.
[21] Calvin N Mooers. 1948. *Application of random codes to the gathering of statistical information*. Ph.D. Dissertation. Massachusetts Institute of Technology.
[22] Calvin N Mooers. 1951. Zatocoding applied to mechanical organization of knowledge. *American documentation* 2, 1 (1951), 20–32.
[23] Giuseppe Ottaviano and Rossano Venturini. 2014. Partitioned elias-fano indexes. In *Proceedings of the 37th international ACM SIGIR conference on Research & development in information retrieval*. ACM, 273–282.
[24] Knut Magne Risvik, Trishul M. Chilimbi, Henry Tan, Karthik Kalyanaraman, and Chris Anderson. 2013. Maguro, a system for indexing and searching over very large text collections. In *Sixth ACM International Conference on Web Search and Data Mining, WSDM 2013, Rome, Italy, February 4-8, 2013*. 727–736.
[25] Charles S Roberts. 1979. Partial-match retrieval via the method of superimposed codes. *Proc. IEEE* 67, 12 (1979), 1624–1642.
[26] Ron Sacks-Davis, A Kent, and Kotagiri Ramamohanarao. 1987. Multikey access methods based on superimposed coding techniques. *ACM Transactions on Database Systems (TODS)* 12, 4 (1987), 655–696.
[27] Harry KT Wong, Hsiu-Fen Liu, Frank Olken, Doron Rotem, and Linda Wong. 1985. Bit Transposed Files.. In *VLDB*, Vol. 85. Citeseer, 448–457.
[28] Justin Zobel, Alistair Moffat, and Kotagiri Ramamohanarao. 1998. Inverted files versus signature files for text indexing. *ACM Transactions on Database Systems (TODS)* 23, 4 (1998), 453–490.

Efficient Data Structures for Massive N-Gram Datasets

Giulio Ermanno Pibiri
University of Pisa *and* ISTI-CNR
Pisa, Italy
giulio.pibiri@di.unipi.it

Rossano Venturini
University of Pisa *and* ISTI-CNR
Pisa, Italy
rossano.venturini@unipi.it

ABSTRACT

The efficient indexing of large and sparse N-gram datasets is crucial in several applications in Information Retrieval, Natural Language Processing and Machine Learning. Because of the stringent efficiency requirements, dealing with billions of N-grams poses the challenge of introducing a compressed representation that preserves the query processing speed.

In this paper we study the problem of reducing the space required by the representation of such datasets, maintaining the capability of looking up for a given N-gram within micro seconds. For this purpose we describe compressed, exact and lossless data structures that achieve, at the same time, high space reductions and no time degradation with respect to state-of-the-art software packages. In particular, we present a trie data structure in which each word following a context of fixed length k, i.e., its preceding k words, is encoded as an integer whose value is proportional to the number of words that follow such context. Since the number of words following a given context is typically very small in natural languages, we are able to lower the space of representation to compression levels that were never achieved before. Despite the significant savings in space, we show that our technique introduces a negligible penalty at query time.

CCS CONCEPTS

•Information systems → Data compression; Language models; Information extraction;

KEYWORDS

Performance, Data Compression, Elias-Fano, Language Models

1 INTRODUCTION

N-grams are widely adopted for many vital tasks in Information Retrieval, Natural Language Processing and Machine Learning, such as: auto-completion in search engines, spelling correction, similarity search, identification of duplicated documents in databases, automatic speech recognition and machine translation [10, 19, 21, 25, 26, 34]. As an example, query auto-completion is one of the key features that any modern search engine offers to help users formulate their queries. The objective is to predict the query by saving keystrokes: this is implemented by reporting the top-k most frequently-searched N-grams that follow the words typed by the user [2, 25, 26]. The identification of such patterns is possible by traversing a data structure that stores the N-grams as seen by previous user searches. Given the number of users served by large-scale search engines and the high query rates, it is of utmost importance that such data structure traversals are carried out in a handful of microseconds [2, 10, 21, 25, 26]. Another noticeable example is spelling correction in text editors and web search. In their basic formulation, N-gram spelling correction techniques work by looking up every N-gram in the input string in a pre-built data structure in order to assess their existence or return a statistic, e.g., a frequency count, to guide the correction [23]. If the N-gram is not found in the data structure it is marked as a misspelled pattern: in such case correction happens by suggesting the most frequent word that follows the pattern with the longest matching history [10, 21, 23].

At the core of all the mentioned applications lies an efficient data structure mapping N-grams to their associated satellite data, e.g., a frequency count representing the number of occurrences of the N-gram or probability and backoff weights for word-predicting computations [17, 31]. The data structure efficiency should be both in time and space, because modern string search and machine translation systems make very frequent queries over databases containing several billion N-grams that often do not fit in internal memory [10, 21].

While several solutions have been proposed for the indexing and retrieval of N-grams, either based on tries [15] or hashing [24], their practicality is actually limited because of some important inefficiencies that we discuss now. Context information, such as the fact that *relatively few* words may follow a given context, is not currently exploited to achieve better compression ratios. When query processing speed is the main concern, space efficiency is almost completely neglected by not compressing the data structure using sophisticated encoding techniques [17]. Space reductions are usually achieved by lossy quantization of satellite values and/or randomized approaches with false positive allowed [35]. The most space-efficient and lossless proposals still employ binary search over the compressed representation to lookup for a N-gram: this results in a severe inefficiency during query processing because of the lack of a compression strategy with a fast random access operation [31]. To support random access, current methods leverage on block-wise compression with expensive decompression of a block every time an element of the block has to be retrieved. Even hashing schemes, adopted for their constant-time access capabilities, result sub-optimal for static corpora as long as open addressing with linear probing is used [17, 31].

Because a solution that is compact, fast and lossless at the same time is still missing, the aim of this paper is that of addressing the

SIGIR '17, August 07-11, 2017, Shinjuku, Tokyo, Japan
© 2017 ACM. 978-1-4503-5022-8/17/08...$15.00
DOI: http://dx.doi.org/10.1145/3077136.3080798

aforementioned problems by introducing compressed data structures that, despite their space efficiency, support efficient random access to the satellite N-gram values.

Our contributions. We list here our main contributions.

(1) We introduce a compressed trie data structure in which each level of the trie is modeled as a monotone integer sequence that we encode with *Elias-Fano* [12, 13] as to efficiently support random access operations and successor queries over the compressed sequence. Our hashing approach leverages on minimal perfect hash in order to use tables of size *equal* to the number of stored patterns per level, with one random access to retrieve the relative N-gram information.
(2) We describe a technique for lowering the space usage of the trie data structure, by reducing the magnitude of the integers that form its monotone sequences. Our technique is based on the observation that *few* distinct words follow a predefined context, in *any* natural language. In particular, each word following a context of fixed length k, i.e., its preceding k words, is encoded as an integer whose value is proportional to the number of words that follow such context.
(3) We present an extensive experimental analysis that shows our technique offers a significantly better compression with respect to the plain Elias-Fano trie, while only introducing a slight penalty at query processing time. Compared to the state-of-the-art proposals, our data structures outperform all of them for space usage, *without* compromising their time performance. More precisely, the most space-efficient proposals, which are both quantized and lossy, are no better than our trie data structure and up to 5 times slower. Conversely, we are as fast as the fastest competitor, but also retain an advantage of up to 65% in absolute space.

2 RELATED WORK

Two different data structures are mostly used to store large and sparse N-grams language models: trie [15] and hashing [24].

A trie is a tree devised for efficient indexing and search of string dictionaries. The common prefixes shared by the strings are represented once to achieve compact storage. This property makes this data structure useful for storing the N-gram strings in compressed space. In this case, each constituent word of a N-gram is associated a node in the trie and different N-grams correspond to different root-to-leaf paths. These paths must be traversed to resolve a query, which retrieves the string itself or an associated satellite value, e.g., a frequency count. Conceptually, a trie implementation has to store a triplet for any node: the associated word, satellite value and a pointer to each child node. As N is typically very small and each node has many children, tries are of short height and dense. Therefore, these are implemented as a collection of sorted arrays: for each level of the trie, a separate array is built to contain all the triplets for that level, sorted by the words. In this implementation, a pair of adjacent pointers indicates the sub-array listing all the children for a word, which can be inspected by binary search.

Hashing is another way to implement associative arrays: for each value of N a separate hash table stores all grams of order N. At the location indicated by the hash function the following information is stored: a fingerprint value to lower the probability of a false positive and the satellite data for the N-gram. This data structure permits to access the specified N-gram data in expected $O(1)$. Open addressing with linear probing is usually preferred over chaining for its better locality of accesses.

Tries are usually designed for space-efficiency as the formed sorted arrays are highly compressible. However, retrieval for the value of a N-gram involves $O(N)$ searches in the constituent arrays. Conversely, hashing is designed for speed but sacrifices space-efficiency since keys, along with their fingerprint values, are randomly distributed and, therefore, incompressible. Moreover, hashing is a randomized solution, i.e., there is a non-null probability of retrieving a frequency count for a N-gram *not* really belonging to the indexed corpus (false positive). Such probability equals $2^{-\delta}$, where δ indicates the number of bits dedicated to the fingerprint values: larger values of δ yield a smaller probability of false positive but also increase the space of the data structure. We now review how these two different data structural approaches have been used in the literature to implement the state-of-the-art solutions.

The paper by Pauls and Klein [31] proposes trie-based data structures in which the nodes are represented via sorted arrays or with hash tables with linear probing. The trie sorted arrays are compressed using a variable-length block encoding: a configurable radix $r = 2^k$ is chosen and the number of digits d to represents a number in base r is written in unary. The representation then terminates with the d digits, each of which requires exactly k bits. To preserve the property of looking up a record by binary search, each sorted array is divided into blocks of 128 bytes. The encoding is used to compress words, pointers and the positions that frequency counts take in a unique-value array that collect all distinct counts. The hash-based variant is likely to be faster than the sorted array variant, but requires extra table allocation space to avoid excessive collisions.

Heafield [17] improves the sorted array trie implementation with some optimizations. The keys in the arrays are replaced by their hashes and sorted, so that these are uniformly distributed over their ranges. Now lookup time for a record is reduced to $O(\log \log n)$ with high probability by using *interpolation* search [11]. Pointers are compressed using the integer compressor devised in [32]. Values can also be quantized using the *binning* method [14] that sorts the values, divides them into equally-sized bins and then elects the average value of the bin as the representative of the bin. The number of chosen quantization bits directly controls the number of created bins and, hence, the trade-off between space and accuracy.

Talbot and Osborne [35] use Bloom filters [4] with lossy quantization of frequency counts to achieve small memory footprint. In particular, the raw frequency count $f(g)$ of gram g is quantized using a logarithmic codebook, i.e., $\widetilde{f}(g) = 1 + \log_b f(g)$. The scale is determined by the base b of the logarithm: in the implementation b is set to $2^{1/v}$, where v is the quantization range used by the model, e.g., $v = 8$. Given the quantized count $\widetilde{f}(g)$ of gram g, a Bloom filter is trained by entering composite events into the filter, represented by g with an appended integer value j, which is incremented from 1 to $\widetilde{f}(g)$. Then at query time, to retrieve $\widetilde{f}(g)$, the filter is queried with a 1 appended to g. This event is hashed using the k hash functions of the filter: if all of them test positive, then the count is incremented and the process repeated. The procedure terminates as soon as any of the k hash functions hits a 0 and the previous count is reported. This procedure avoids a space requirement for the counts proportional to the number of grams in the corpus because only the codebook needs to be stored.

The use of the succinct encoding LOUDS [20] is advocated in [37] to implicitly represent the trie nodes. In particular, the pointers for a trie of m nodes are encoded using a bitvector of $2m + 1$ bits. Bit-level searches on such bitvector allow forward/backward navigation of the trie structure. Words and frequency counts are compressed using Variable-Byte encoding [33], with an additional bitvector used to indicate the boundaries of such byte sequences as to support random access to each element.

Because of the importance of strings as one of the most common computerized kind of information, the problem of representing trie-based storage for string dictionaries is among one of the most studied in computer science, with many and different solutions available [9, 18, 29]. Given the properties that N-gram datasets exhibit, generic trie implementations are not suitable for their efficient treatment. However, comparing with the performance of such implementations gives useful insights about the performance gap with respect to a general solution. We mention Marisa [38] as the best and practical general-purpose trie implementation. The core idea is to use Patricia [28] tries to recursively represent the nodes of a Patricia trie. This clearly comes with a space/time trade off.

3 ELIAS-FANO TRIES

In this section we introduce our main result: a compressed trie data structure, based on the *Elias-Fano* representation [12, 13] of monotone integer sequences for its efficient random access and search operations. As we will see, the constant-time random access of Elias-Fano makes it the right choice for the encoding of the sorted-array trie levels, given that we fundamentally need to randomly access the sub-array pointed to by a pair of pointers. Such pair is retrieved in constant time too. Now every access performed by binary search takes $O(1)$ *without* requiring any block decompression, differently from currently employed strategies [31].

We also describe a novel technique to lower the memory footprint of the trie levels by losslessly reducing the entity of their constituent integers. This reduction is achieved by mapping a word ID *conditionally* to its context of fixed length k, i.e., its k preceding words.

3.1 Core data structure

As it is standard, a unique integer ID is assigned to each distinct token (uni-gram) to form the vocabulary V of the indexed corpus. Uni-grams are indexed using a hash data structure that stores for each gram its ID in order to retrieve it when needed in $O(1)$. If we sort the N-grams following the token-ID order, we have that all the successors of gram $w_1^{N-1} = w_1, \ldots, w_{N-1}$, i.e., all grams whose prefix is w_1^{N-1}, form a strictly increasing integer sequence. For example, suppose we have the uni-grams ⟨a, b, c, d⟩, which are assigned IDs ⟨0, 1, 2, 3⟩ respectively. Now consider the bi-grams ⟨aa, ac, bb, bc, bd, ca, cd, db, dd⟩ sorted by IDs. The sequence of the successors of a, referred to as the *range* of a, is ⟨a, c⟩, i.e., ⟨0, 2⟩; the sequence of the successors of b, is ⟨b, c, d⟩, i.e., ⟨1, 2, 3⟩ and so on. Concatenating the ranges, we obtain the integer sequence ⟨0, 2, 1, 2, 3, 0, 3, 1, 3⟩. In order to distinguish the successors of a gram from others, we also maintain where each range begins in a monotone integer sequence of pointers. In our example, the sequence of pointers is ⟨0, 2, 5, 7, 9⟩ (we also store a final dummy pointer to be able to obtain the last range length by taking the difference between the last and previous pointer). The ID assigned to a uni-gram is also used as the position at which we read the uni-gram pointer in the uni-grams pointer sequence. Therefore, apart from uni-grams, each level of the trie has to store two integer sequences: one for the representation of the gram-IDs, the other for the pointers.

Among the many integer compressors available in the literature [33], we choose Elias-Fano, which has been recently applied to inverted index compression showing an excellent time/space trade off [30, 36]. We now briefly describe this elegant integer encoding.

Elias-Fano. Given a monotonically increasing sequence $S(n, u)$ of n positive integers upper-bounded by u, i.e., $S[i-1] \leq S[i]$, for any $1 \leq i < n$ with $S[n-1] \leq u$, we write each $S[i]$ in binary using $\lceil \log u \rceil$ bits. Each binary representation is then split into two parts: a *high* part consisting in the first $\lceil \log n \rceil$ most significant bits that we call *high bits* and a *low* part consisting in the other $\ell = \lfloor \log \frac{u}{n} \rfloor$ bits that we similarly call *low bits*. Let us call h_i and ℓ_i the values of high and low bits of $S[i]$ respectively. The Elias-Fano representation of S is given by the encoding of the high and low parts. The array $L = [\ell_0, \ldots, \ell_{n-1}]$ is stored in fixed-width and represents the encoding of the low parts. Concerning the high bits, we represent them in *negated unary* using a bit vector of $n + u/2^{\ell} \leq 2n$ bits as follows. We start from a 0-valued bit vector H and we set the bit in position $h_i + i$, $\forall i \in [0, n)$. The effect is that now the k-th unary integer m of H indicates that m integers of S have high bits equal to k. Finally the Elias-Fano representation of S is given by the concatenation of H and L and takes, overall, $\mathsf{EF}(S(n, u)) = n\lceil \log \frac{u}{n} \rceil + 2n$ bits.

Despite its simplicity, it is possible to randomly access an integer from a sequence compressed with Elias-Fano *without* decompressing it. The operation is supported using an auxiliary data structure that is built on bit vector H, able to efficiently answer $\mathsf{Select}_1(i)$ queries, that return the position in H of the i-th 1 bit. This auxiliary data structure is *succinct* in the sense that it is negligibly small compared to $\mathsf{EF}(S(n, u))$, requiring only $o(n)$ additional bits [8, 36]. Using the Select_1 primitive, it is possible to implement $\mathsf{Access}(i)$, which returns $S[i]$ for any $1 \leq i < n$, in constant time.

Gram-ID sequences and pointers. While the sequences of pointers are monotonically increasing by construction and, therefore, immediately Elias-Fano encodable, the gram-ID sequences could not. However, a gram-ID sequence can be transformed into a monotone one, though not strictly increasing, by taking range-wise prefix sums: to the values of a range we sum the last prefix sum (initially equal to 0). Then, our exemplar sequence becomes ⟨0, 2, 3, 4, 5, 5, 8, 9, 11⟩. The last prefix sum is initially 0, therefore the range of a remains the same, i.e., ⟨0, 2⟩. Now the last prefix sum is 2, so we sum 2 to the values in the range of b, yielding ⟨3, 4, 5⟩, and so on. In particular, if we sort the vocabulary IDs in decreasing order of occurrence, we make small IDs appear more often than large ones and this is highly beneficial for the growth of the universe u and, hence, for Elias-Fano whose space occupancy critically depends on it. We emphasize this point again: for each uni-gram in the vocabulary we count the number of times it appears in all gram-ID sequences. Notice that the number of occurrences of a N-gram can be different than its frequency count as reported in the indexed corpus. The reason is that such corpora often do not include the N-grams appearing less than a predefined frequency threshold.

Frequency counts. To represent the frequency counts, we use the unique-value array technique, i.e., each count is represented by its *rank* in an array, one for each separate value of N, that collects all distinct frequency counts. The reason for this is that the distribution of the frequency counts is extremely skewed (see Table 2), i.e., relatively few N-grams are very frequent while most of them appear only a few times. Now each level of the trie, besides the sequences of gram-IDs and pointers, has also to store the sequence made by all the frequency count ranks. Unfortunately, this sequence of ranks is not monotone, yet it follows the aforementioned highly repetitive distribution. Therefore, we assigned to each count rank a codeword of variable length. As similarly done for the gram-IDs, by assigning smaller codewords to more repetitive count ranks, we have most ranks encoded with just a few bits. More specifically, starting from $k = 1$, we first assign all the 2^k codewords of length k before increasing k by 1 and repeating the process until all count ranks have been considered. Therefore, we first assign codewords 0 and 1, then codewords 00, 01, and so on. All codewords are then concatenated one after the other in a bitvector B. Following [16], to the i-th value we give codeword $c = i + 2 - 2^{\ell_c}$, where $\ell_c = \lfloor \log(i + 2) \rfloor$ is the number of bits dedicated to the codeword. From codeword c and its length ℓ_c in bits, we can retrieve i by taking the inverse of the previous formula, i.e., $i = c - 2 + 2^{\ell_c}$. Besides the bitvector for the codewords themselves, we also need to know where each codeword begins and ends. We can use another bitvector for this purpose, say L, that stores a 1 for the starting position of every codeword. A small additional data structure built on L allows efficient computation of Select_1, which we use to retrieve ℓ_c. In fact, $b = \text{Select}_1(i)$ gives us the starting position of the i-th codeword. Its length is easily computed by scanning L upward from position b until we hit the next 1, say in position e. Finally $\ell_c = e - b$ and $c = B[b, e - 1]$.

In conclusion, each level i of the trie stores three sequences: the gram-ID sequence G_i, the pointer sequence P_i and the count ranks sequence R_i. Two exceptions are represented by uni-grams and maximum-order grams, for which gram-ID and pointer sequences are missing respectively.

Lookup. We now describe how to retrieve the frequency count given a gram w_1^m. We first perform m vocabulary lookups to map the gram tokens into its constituent IDs. We write these IDs into an array $W[1, m]$. This preliminary query-mapping step takes $O(m)$. Now, the search procedure basically has to locate $W[i]$ in the i-th level of the trie. Refer to Figure 1, which shows a pictorial representation of a trie of order 3. If $m = 1$, then our search terminates: at the position $k_1 = W[1]$ we read the rank $r_1 = R_1[k_1]$ to finally access $C_1[r_1]$. If, instead, m is greater than 1, the position

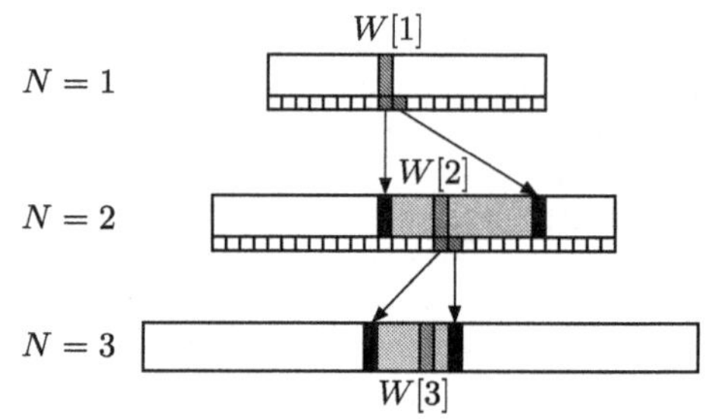

Figure 1: Search for the tri-gram $W[1, 3]$ in a trie data structure of order 3. The light gray shaded area indicates the range of IDs that follow a given gram and its is delimited by the black IDs pointed to by the pointers represented as blue squares.

k_1 is used to retrieve the pair of pointers $\langle P_1[k_1], P_1[k_1 + 1] \rangle$ in constant time, which delimits the range of IDs in which we have to search for $W[2]$ in the second level of the trie. This range is inspected by binary search, taking $O(\log(P_1[k_1 + 1] - P_1[k_1]))$ as each access to an Elias-Fano-encoded sequence is performed in constant time. Let k_2 be the position at which $W[2]$ is found in the range. Again, if $m = 2$, the search terminates by accessing $C_2[r_2]$ where r_2 is the rank $R_2[k_2]$. If m is greater than 2, we fetch the pair $\langle P_2[k_2], P_2[k_2 + 1] \rangle$ to continue the search of $W[3]$ in the third level of the trie, and so on. This search step is repeated for $m - 1$ times in total, to finally return the count $C_m[r_m]$ of w_1^m.

3.2 Context-based identifier remapping

In this subsection we describe a technique that lowers the space occupancy of the gram-ID sequences that constitute, as we have seen, the core of the trie data structure. The high level idea is to map a word w occurring after context w_1^k to an integer whose value is proportional to the number of words that *follow* the context w_1^k, and *not* proportional to the whole vocabulary size $|V|$. Specifically, w is mapped to the position it occupies within its siblings, i.e., all the words following the gram w_1^k. We call this technique *context-based remapping* as each ID is mapped to the position it takes relative to a context. As we will see in the experimental Section 5, the dataset vocabulary can contain several million tokens, whereas the number of words that naturally occur after another is typically very small. Even in the case of stopwords, such as "the" or "are", the number of words that can follow is far less than the whole number of distinct words for any N-gram dataset. This ultimately means that the remapped integers forming the gram-ID sequences of the trie will be much smaller than the original ones, which can indeed range from 0 to $|V| - 1$. Lowering the values of the integers clearly helps in reducing the memory footprint of the levels of the trie because *any* integer compressor takes advantage of encoding smaller integers, since fewer bits are needed for their representation [27, 30]. In our case the gram-ID sequences are encoded with Elias-Fano: from Section 3.1 we know that Elias-Fano spends $\lceil \log \frac{u}{n} \rceil + 2$ bits per integer, thus a number of bits proportional to the average gap between the integers. Remapping the integers as explained can *critically* reduce the universe u of representation, thus lowering the average gap of the sequence.

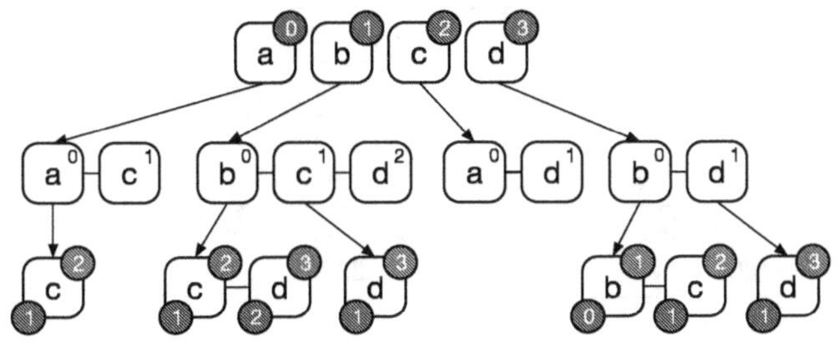

Figure 2: Example of a trie of order 3. Vocabulary IDs are represented in dark grey while level-3 IDs in red. The blue IDs are derived by applying a context-based remapping with context length 1.

To better understand the power of the idea, we consider now a concrete example. We continue the example from Section 3.1, extended to contain the tri-grams depicted in Figure 2. The Figure shows a trie model of order 3. The gray IDs are the vocabulary IDs and the red ones are the last token IDs of the tri-grams as assigned by the vocabulary. We now explain how the remapped IDs, represented in blue, are derived by the model using our technique with a context of length 1. Consider the tri-gram bcd. The default ID of d is 3. We now rewrite this ID as the position that d takes within the successors of the word preceding it, i.e., c (context 1). As we can see in the Figure, d appears in position 1 within the successors of c, therefore its new ID will be 1. Another example: take dbb. The default ID of b is 1, but it occurs in position 0 within the successors of its parent b, therefore its new ID is 0. As it is clear, the first two levels of the trie act as a *mapper* structure which is used to map the vocabulary ID of the last token of a tri-gram into its new ID. At query time, this mapper structure is used to retrieve the mapped ID that is finally searched in the third level of the trie. Therefore, notice that the technique takes full advantage of the N-gram model represented by the trie structure itself in that it does *not* need any redundancy to retrieve the remapped ID.

We observe that this strategy allows a great deal of flexibility, in that we can choose the length of the context. The example in Figure 2 illustrates how to map tri-grams using a context of length 1: this is clearly the only one possible as the first two levels of the trie must be used to retrieve the mapped ID at query time. However, if we have a gram of order 4, i.e., w_1^4, we can choose to map w_4 as the position it takes within the successors of w_3 (context length 1) or within the successors of w_2w_3 (context length 2). In general, with a gram of order $N \geq 2$ we can choose between $N-2$ distinct context lengths k, i.e., $1 \leq k \leq N-2$. This also means that, when using context length k, we have the first $k+1$ levels of the trie acting as the mapper structure and, hence, must be kept un-mapped. Clearly, the greater the context length we use, the smaller the remapped integers will be. The proper context length to use should take into account the characteristics of the N-gram dataset, in particular the number of grams per order.

To support our discussion, we present some real numbers regarding the effect of the context-based remapping on the average gap of the gram-ID sequences of Europarl, one of the datasets used in the experiments. As uni-grams and bi-grams must be kept un-mapped as explained, we report the statistics for the trie of order 5 built from the N-grams of the dataset. The average gap $\frac{u}{n}$ of the sequences of order $N \geq 3$ are respectively, without remapping: 2404, 2782 and 2920. With our technique, using a context of length 1, we obtain the following average gaps instead: 213, 480 and 646, i.e., an average reduction of 7.2 (up to 11.3 on tri-grams). With a context of length 2 we obtain: 48 and 101 for 4– and 5-grams respectively, i.e., an average reduction of 43.4 (up to 58 on 4-grams).

Lookup. The context-based remapping comes with an overhead at query time as the search algorithm described in Section 3.1 must map the default vocabulary ID to its remapped ID, before it can be searched in the proper gram sequence. If the remapping strategy is applied with a context of length k, it involves $k(N-k-1)$ additional searches. As an example, by looking at Figure 2, before searching the mapped ID 1 of d for the tri-gram bcd, we have to map the vocabulary ID of d, i.e., 3, to 1. For this task, we search 3 within the successors of c. As 3 is found in position 1, we now know that we have to search for 1 within the successors of bc. On the one hand, the context-based remapping will assign smaller IDs as the length of the context rises, on the other hand it will also spend more time at query processing. In conclusion, we have a space/time trade-off that we explore with an extensive experimental analysis in Section 5.

4 HASHING

Since the indexed N-gram corpus is static, we obtain a *full* hash utilization by resorting to Minimal Perfect Hash (MPH). We indexed all grams of the same order N into a separate MPH table T_N, each with its own MPH function h_N. This introduces a twofold advantage over the linear probing approach used in the literature [17, 31]: use a hash table of size *equal* to the exact number of grams per order (no extra space allocation is required) and avoid the linear probing search phase by requiring one single access to the required hash location. We use the implementation, publicly available at https://github.com/ot/emphf, of MPH as described in [3], which requires 2.61 bits per key on average. At the hash location for a N-gram we store: its 8-byte hash key as to have a false positive probability of 2^{-64} (4-byte hash keys are supported as well) and the position of the frequency count in the unique-value array C_N which keeps all distinct frequency counts for order N. As already motivated, these unique-value arrays, one for each different order of N, are negligibly small compared to the number of grams themselves and act as a direct map from the position of the count to its value. Although these unique values could be sorted and compressed, we do not perform any space optimization as these are too few to yield any improvement but we store them uncompressed and byte-aligned, in order to favor lookup time. We also use this hash approach to implement the vocabulary of the previously introduced trie data structure.

Lookup. Given N-gram g we compute the position $p = h_N(g)$ in the relevant table T_N, then we access the count rank r stored at position p and finally retrieve the count value $C_N[r]$.

		Europarl		YahooV2		GoogleV2	
		bpg	μs × query	bpg	μs × query	bpg	μs × query
	EF	1.97	1.28	2.17	1.60	2.13	2.09
	PEF	1.87 (−4.99%)	1.35 (+5.93%)	1.91 (−12.03%)	1.73 (+8.00%)	1.52 (−28.60%)	1.91 (−8.79%)
CONTEXT-BASED ID REMAPPING $k = 1$	EF	1.67 (−15.30%)	1.58 (+23.86%)	1.89 (−12.92%)	2.05 (+28.07%)	1.91 (−10.24%)	3.03 (+44.61%)
CONTEXT-BASED ID REMAPPING $k = 1$	PEF	1.53 (−22.36%)	1.61 (+25.89%)	1.63 (−24.91%)	2.16 (+35.22%)	1.31 (−38.71%)	2.30 (+9.88%)
CONTEXT-BASED ID REMAPPING $k = 2$	EF	1.46 (−25.62%)	1.60 (+25.17%)	1.68 (−22.32%)	2.08 (+30.23%)	—	—
CONTEXT-BASED ID REMAPPING $k = 2$	PEF	1.28 (−34.87%)	1.64 (+28.12%)	1.38 (−36.15%)	2.15 (+34.81%)	—	—

Table 1: Average bytes per gram (bpg) and average Lookup time per query in micro seconds.

5 EXPERIMENTS

We performed our experiments on the following standard datasets: Europarl, which consists in all unpruned N-grams extracted from the english Europarl parallel corpus [22]; YahooV2 [1] and GoogleV2 as the last English version of Web1T [5]. Each dataset comprises all N-grams for $1 \leq N \leq 5$ and associated frequency counts. Table 2 shows the basic statistics of the datasets.

N	Europarl n	Europarl m	YahooV2 n	YahooV2 m	GoogleV2 n	GoogleV2 m
1	304 579	4518	3 475 482	23 785	24 357 349	246 490
2	5 192 260	4663	53 844 927	31 711	665 752 080	722 966
3	18 908 249	2975	187 639 522	19 856	7 384 478 110	683 653
4	33 862 651	1744	287 562 409	10 761	1 642 783 634	133 491
5	43 160 518	1032	295 701 337	6167	1 413 870 914	104 025
Total	101 428 257	7147	828 223 677	45 285	11 131 242 087	1 073 473
gzip bpg	6.98		6.45		6.20	

Table 2: Number of N-grams per order (n); distinct frequency counts (m); and gzip average bytes per gram (bpg) for the datasets used in the experiments.

Compared Indexes. We compare the performance of our data structures against the following software packages that use the approaches introduced in Section 2.

- BerkeleyLM implements two trie data structures based on sorted arrays and hash tables to represent the nodes of the trie [31]. Java implementation available at: https://github.com/adampauls/berkeleylm.
- Expgram makes use of the LOUDS succinct encoding [20] to implicitly represent the trie structure and compresses frequency counts using Variable-Byte encoding [37]. C++ implementation available at: https://github.com/tarowatanabe/expgram.
- KenLM implements a trie with interpolation search and a hashing with linear probing [17]. C++ implementation available at: http://kheafield.com/code/kenlm.
- Marisa is a general-purposes string dictionary implementation in which Patricia tries are recursively used to represent the nodes of a Patricia trie [38]. C++ implementation available at: https://github.com/s-yata/marisa-trie.
- RandLM employs Bloom filters with lossy quantization of frequency counts to attain to low memory footprint [35]. C++ implementation available at: https://sourceforge.net/projects/randlm.

Experimental setup. All experiments have been performed on a machine with 16 Intel Xeon E5-2630 v3 cores (32 threads) clocked at 2.4 Ghz, with 193 GBs of RAM, running Linux 3.13.0, 64 bits. Our implementation is in standard C++11 and freely available at https://github.com/jermp/tongrams. The code was compiled with gcc 5.4.1, using the highest optimization settings.

The data structures were saved to disk after construction, and loaded into main memory to be queried. To test the speed of lookup queries, we use a query set of 5 million random N-grams for YahooV2 and GoogleV2 and of 0.5 million for Europarl. In order to smooth the effect of fluctuations during measurements, we repeat each experiment five times and consider the mean. All query algorithms were run on a single core.

5.1 Elias-Fano Tries

Gram-ID sequences. Table 1 shows the average number of bytes per gram including the cost of pointers, and lookup speed per query. The first two rows refers to the trie data structure described in Section 3.1, when the sorted arrays are encoded with Elias-Fano (EF) and partitioned Elias-Fano (PEF) [30]. Subsequent rows indicate the space gains obtained by applying the context-based remapping strategy using EF and PEF for contexts of lengths respectively 1 and 2. In particular, for GoogleV2 we use a context of length 1, as the number of tri-grams roughly takes 66% of the whole number of N-grams in the dataset, thus it would make little sense to optimize only the space of 4- and 5-grams.

As expected, partitioning the gram sequences using PEF yields a better space occupancy. However, though the paper by Ottaviano and Venturini [30] describes a dynamic programming algorithm that finds the partitioning able of minimizing the space occupancy of a monotone sequence, we instead adopt a *uniform* partitioning strategy. Partitioning the sequence uniformly has several advantages over variable-length partitions for our setting. As we have seen in Section 3.1, trie searches are carried out by performing a preliminary random access to the endpoints of the range pointed to by a pointer pair. Then a search in the range follows to determine the position of the gram-ID. Partitioning the sequence by variable-length blocks introduces an additional search over the sequence of partition endpoints to determine the proper block in which the search must continue. While this preliminary search only introduces a minor overhead in query processing for inverted index queries [30] (as it has to be performed once and successive accesses are only directed to forward positions of the sequence), it is instead the major bottleneck when random access operations are very frequent as in our case. By resorting on uniform partitions, we eliminate this first search and the cost of representation for the variable-length sizes. To speed up queries even further, we also keep the upper bounds of the blocks uncompressed and bit-aligned. We use partitions of 64 integers for bi-gram sequences, and of 128 for all other orders, i.e., for $N \geq 3$. Shrinking the size of blocks has the potential of speeding-up searches over plain Elias-Fano because a successor query has to be resolved over an interval potentially much smaller than a range length (number of successors of a gram). However, excessively reducing the block size will ruin the advantage in space reduction. We use 64-integer blocks for bi-gram sequences because these must be searched several times during the query-mapping phase when the context-based remapping is adopted. In conclusion, as we can see by the second row of Table 1, this sequence organization brings a negligible overhead in query processing speed (less than 8% on Europarl and YahooV2), while maintaining a noticeable space reduction (up to 29% on GoogleV2).

Concerning the efficacy of the context-based remapping, we have that remapping the gram IDs with a context of length $k = 1$ is already able of reducing the space of the sequences by ≈13% on average when sequences are encoded with Elias-Fano, with respect to the EF cost. If we consider a context of length $k = 2$ we *double* the gain, allowing for more than 28% of space reduction *without* affecting the lookup time with respect to the case $k = 1$. As a first conclusion, when space efficiency is the main concern, it is always convenient to apply the remapping strategy with a context of length 2. The gain of the strategy is even more evident with PEF: this is no surprise as the encoder can better exploit the reduced IDs by encoding all the integers belonging to a block with a universe relative to the block and not to the whole sequence. This results in a space reduction of more than 36% on average and up to 39% on GoogleV2. However, as explained in Section 3, the remapping strategy comes with a penalty at query time as we have to map an ID before it can be searched in the proper gram sequence. On average, we found that 30% more time is spent with respect to the Elias-Fano baseline. Notice that PEF does *not* introduce any time degradation with respect to EF with context-based remapping: it is actually faster on GoogleV2.

Frequency counts. For the representation of frequency counts we compare three different encoding schemes: the first one refers to the strategy described in Section 3 that assigns variable-length codewords (CW) to the ranks of the counts and keeps track of codewords length using a binary vector (BV), the other two schemes transform the sequence of count ranks into a non-decreasing sequence by taking its prefix sums (PF) and then applies EF or PEF. Table 3 shows the average number of bytes per count for these different strategies. The reported space also includes the space for the storage of the arrays containing the distinct counts for each order of N. As already pointed out, these take a negligible amount of space because the distribution of frequency counts is highly repetitive (see Table 2). The percentages of PS + EF and PS + PEF are done with respect to the first row CW + BV.

The time for retrieving a count was pretty much the same for all the three techniques. Prefix-summing the sequence and apply EF does not bring any advantage over the codeword assignment technique because its space is practically the same on Europarl but it is actually larger on both YahooV2 (by up to 32%) and GoogleV2. These two reasons together place the codeword assignment technique in net advantage over EF. PEF, instead, offers a better space occupancy of more than 16% on Europarl and 10% on GoogleV2. Therefore, in the following we assume this representation for frequency counts, except for YahooV2, where we adopt CW + BV.

	Europarl	YahooV2	GoogleV2
CW + BV	0.36	0.47	1.46
PS + EF	0.35 (−1.59%)	0.62 (+32.46%)	1.59 (+9.17%)
PS + PEF	0.30 (−16.65%)	0.51 (+8.67%)	1.30 (−11.03%)
VLBC	0.76 (+155.63%)	0.79 (+55.86%)	1.32 (+1.44%)
PLAIN	1.63 (+444.74%)	2.00 (+294.17%)	2.63 (+102.43%)
VByte + BV	3.21 (+975.40%)	3.32 (+554.66%)	—

Table 3: Average bytes per count (bpc).

We also report the space occupancy for the counts representation of BerkeleyLM and Expgram which, differently from all other competitors, can also be used to index frequency counts. BerkeleyLM COMPRESSED variant uses the variable-length block coding (VLBC) explained in Section 2 to compress count ranks, whereas the HASH variant stores uncompressed count ranks, referred to as PLAIN in the table, using the minimum number of bits necessary for their representation (see Table 2). Expgram, instead, does not store count ranks but directly compress the counts themselves using Variable-Byte encoding with an additional binary vector as to be able of randomly accessing the counts sequence. The available RAM of our test machine (192 GBs) was not sufficient to successfully build Expgram on GoogleV2. The same holds for KenLM and Marisa, as we are going to see in the next Section. Therefore, we report its space for Europarl and YahooV2. We first observe that rank-encoding schemes are far more advantageous than compressing the counts themselves, as done by Expgram. Moreover, none of the these techniques beats the three ones we previously introduced, except for the BerkeleyLM COMPRESSED variant which is ≈10% smaller on GoogleV2 with respect to CW + BV. However, notice that this gap is completely closed as soon as we adopt the combination PS + PEF.

Before concluding the subsection, we use the analysis to fix two different trie data structures that respectively privilege space efficiency and query time: we call them PEF-RTrie and PEF-Trie. For the PEF-RTrie variant we use PEF for representing the gram-ID sequences; PEF for the counts on Europarl and GoogleV2 but CW + BV for YahooV2. We also use the maximum applicable context length for the context-based remapping technique, i.e., 2 for Europarl and YahooV2; 1 for GoogleV2. For the PEF-Trie variant we choose a data structure using PEF for representing gram-ID sequences and the codeword assignment technique for the counts, without remapping. The corresponding size breakdowns are shown in Figures 3c and 3d respectively. Pointer sequences take very little space for both data structures, while most of the difference lies, not surprisingly, in space of the gram-ID sequences. The timing

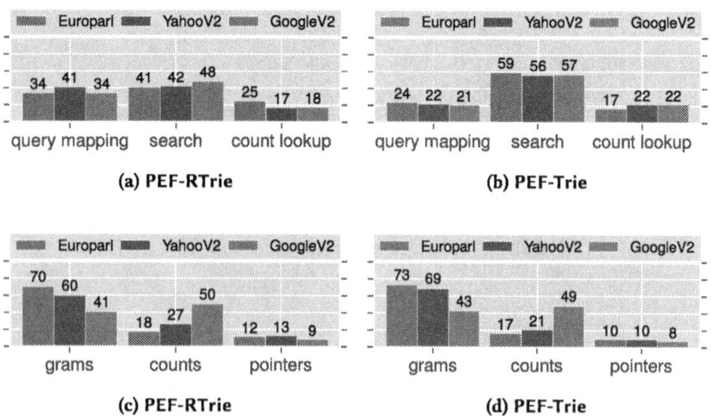

(a) PEF-RTrie (b) PEF-Trie (c) PEF-RTrie (d) PEF-Trie

Figure 3: Trie data structures timing (a-b) and size (c-d) breakdowns in percentage on the tested datasets.

breakdowns in Figures 3a and 3b clearly highlight, instead, how the context-based remapping technique rises the time we spend in the query-mapping phase, during which the IDs are mapped to their reduced IDs.

5.2 Hashing

We build our MPH tables using 8-byte hash keys, as to yield a false positive rate of 2^{-64}. For each different value of N we store the distinct count values in an array, uncompressed and byte-aligned using 4 bytes per distinct count on Europarl and YahooV2; 8 bytes on GoogleV2.

For all the three datasets, the number of bytes per gram, including also the cost of the hash function itself (0.33 bytes per gram) is 8.33. The number of bytes per count is given by the sum of the cost for the ranks and the distinct counts themselves and is equal to 1.41, 1.74 and 2.43 for Europarl, YahooV2 and GoogleV2 respectively. Not surprisingly, the majority of space is taken by the hash keys: clients willing to reduce this memory impact can use 4-byte hash keys instead, at the price of a higher false positive rate (2^{-32}). Therefore, it is worth observing that spending additional effort in trying to lower the space occupancy of the counts only results in poor improvements as we pay for the high cost of the hash keys.

The constant-time access capability of hashing makes gram lookup extremely fast, by requiring on average $\frac{1}{3}$ of a micro second per lookup (exact numbers are reported in Table 4). In particular, all the time is spent in computing the hash function itself and access the relative table location: the final count lookup is totally negligible.

5.3 Overall comparison

In this subsection we compare the performance of our selected trie-based solutions, PEF-RTrie and PEF-Trie, as well as our minimal perfect hash approach against the competitors introduced at the beginning of the section. The results of the comparison are shown in Table 4, where we report the space taken by the representation of the gram-ID sequences and lookup time per query in micro seconds. For the trie data structures, the reported space also includes the cost of representation for the pointers. We compare the space of representation for the N-grams excluding their associated information because this varies according to the chosen implementation: for example, KenLM can only store probability and backoffs, whereas BerkeleyLM can be used to store either counts or probabilities. For those competitors storing frequency counts, we already discussed their count representation in subsection 5.1. Expgram, KenLM and Marisa require too much memory for the building of their data structures on GoogleV2, therefore we mark as empty their entry in the table for this dataset.

Except for the last two rows of the table in which we compare the performance of our MPH table against KenLM probing (P.), we write for each competitor two percentages indicating its score against our selected trie data structures PEF-Trie and PEF-RTrie, respectively. Let us now examine each row one by one. In the following, unless explicitly indicated, numbers refer to average values over the different datasets.

BerkeleyLM COMPRESSED (C.) variant results ≈21% larger than our PEF-RTrie implementation and slower by more than 70%. It gains, instead, an advantage of roughly 9% over our PEF-Trie data structure, but it is also more than 2 times slower. The HASH variant uses hash tables with linear probing to represent the nodes of the trie. Therefore, we test it with a small extra space factor of 3% for table allocation (H.3) and with 50% (H.50), which is also used as the default value in the implementation, as to obtain different time/space trade-offs. Clearly the space occupancy of both hash variants do not compete with the ones of our proposals as these are from 3 to 7 times larger, but the $O(1)$-lookup capabilities of hashing makes it faster than a sorted array trie implementation: while this is no surprise, notice that our PEF-Trie data structure is anyway competitive as it is actually faster on GoogleV2.

Expgram is ≈13.5% larger than PEF-Trie and also 2 and 5 times slower on Europarl and YahooV2 respectively. Our PEF-RTrie data structure retains an advantage in space of 60% and it is still significantly faster: of about 72% on Europarl and 4.3 times on YahooV2.

KenLM is the fastest trie language model implementation in the literature. As we can see, our PEF-Trie variant retains 70% of its space with a negligible penalty at query time. Compared to PEF-RTrie, it results a little faster, i.e., ≈15%, but also 2.3 and 2.5 times larger on Europarl and YahooV2 respectively.

We also tested the performance of Marisa even though it is not a trie optimized for language models as to understand how our data structures compare against a general-purpose string dictionary implementation. We outperform Marisa in both space and time: compared to PEF-RTrie, it is 2.7 times larger and 38% slower; with respect to PEF-Trie it is more than 90% larger and 70% slower.

RandLM is designed for small memory footprint and returns approximated frequency counts when queried. We build its data structures using the default setting recommended in the documentation: 8 bits for frequency count quantization and 8 bits per value as to yield a false positive rate of $\frac{1}{256}$. While being from 2.3 to 5 times slower than our exact and lossless approach, it is quite compact because the quantized frequency counts are recomputed on the fly using the procedure described in Section 2. Therefore, while its space occupancy results even larger with respect to our grams representation by 61%, it is still no better than the whole space of our PEF-RTrie data structure. With respect to the whole

	Europarl		YahooV2		GoogleV2	
	bpg	$\mu s \times$ query	bpg	$\mu s \times$ query	bpg	$\mu s \times$ query
PEF-Trie	1.87	1.35	1.91	1.73	1.52	1.91
PEF-RTrie	1.28	1.64	1.38	2.15	1.31	2.30
BerkeleyLM C.	1.70 (−8.89%) (+32.90%)	2.83 (+108.88%) (+72.70%)	1.69 (−11.41%) (+22.04%)	3.48 (+101.84%) (+61.70%)	1.45 (−4.87%) (+10.83%)	4.13 (+116.57%) (+79.76%)
BerkeleyLM H.3	6.70 (+258.81%) (+423.40%)	0.97 (−28.46%) (−40.85%)	7.82 (+310.38%) (+465.36%)	1.13 (−34.35%) (−47.41%)	9.24 (+507.79%) (+608.07%)	2.18 (+13.95%) (−5.42%)
BerkeleyLM H.50	7.96 (+326.03%) (+521.45%)	0.97 (−28.49%) (−40.88%)	9.37 (+391.32%) (+576.87%)	0.96 (−44.27%) (−55.35%)	—	—
Expgram	2.06 (+10.18%) (+60.73%)	2.80 (+106.61%) (+70.82%)	2.24 (+17.36%) (+61.68%)	9.23 (+435.33%) (+328.87%)	—	—
KenLM T.	2.99 (+60.11%) (+133.56%)	1.28 (−5.47%) (−21.84%)	3.44 (+80.39%) (+148.52%)	1.94 (+12.32%) (−10.01%)	—	—
Marisa	3.61 (+93.09%) (+181.66%)	2.06 (+52.00%) (+25.67%)	3.81 (+99.60%) (+174.98%)	3.24 (+87.96%) (+50.58%)	—	—
RandLM	1.81 (−3.06%) (+41.41%)	4.39 (+224.20%) (+168.04%)	2.02 (+6.18%) (+46.29%)	5.08 (+194.35%) (+135.82%)	2.60 (+70.73%) (+98.90%)	9.25 (+384.54%) (+302.19%)
MPH	8.33	0.26	8.33	0.32	8.33	0.37
KenLM P.3	9.40 (+12.87%)	0.43 (+62.60%)	9.41 (+13.03%)	0.38 (+20.08%)	—	—
KenLM P.50	16.91 (+103.11%)	0.31 (+16.83%)	16.92 (+103.25%)	0.34 (+7.84%)	—	—

Table 4: Average bytes per gram (bpg) and average Lookup time per query in micro seconds.

space of PEF-Trie, it retains instead an advantage of ≈15.6%. This space advantage is, however, compensated by a loss in precision and a much higher query time (up to 5 times slower on GoogleV2).

The last two rows of Table 4 regard the performance of our MPH table with respect to KenLM PROBING. As similarly done for BerkeleyLM H., we also test the PROBING data structure with 3% (P.3) and 50% (P.50) extra space allocation factor for the tables. While being larger as expected, the KenLM implementation makes use of expensive hash key recombinations that yields a slower random access capability with respect to our minimal perfect hashing approach.

Perplexity. Besides the efficient indexing of frequency counts, our data structures can also be used to map N-grams to language model probabilities and backoffs. As done by KenLM, we also use the binning method [14] to quantize probabilities and backoffs, but allowing any quantization bits ranging from 2 to 32. Uni-grams values are stored unquantized to favor query speed: as vocabulary size is typically very small compared to the number of total N-grams, this has a minimal impact on the space of the data structure. Our trie implementation is *reversed* as to permit a more efficient computation of sentence-level probabilities, with a *stateful* scoring function that carries its state on from a query to the next as similarly done by KenLM and BerkeleyLM.

For the perplexity benchmark we used the query dataset, publicly available at http://www.statmt.org/lm-benchmark, that contains 306 688 sentences, for a total of 7 790 011 tokens [6]. We used Expgram utilities to build modified Kneser-Ney [7] 5-gram language models from the counts of Europarl and YahooV2 that have an OOV (out of vocabulary) rate of, respectively, 16% and 1.82% on the test query file. As Expgram only builds quantized models using 8 quantization bits for both probabilities and backoffs, we also use this number of quantization bits for our tries and KenLM trie.

	Europarl		YahooV2	
	bpg	$\mu s \times$ query	bpg	$\mu s \times$ query
PEF-Trie	3.48	0.25	3.64	0.38
PEF-RTrie	2.91	0.28	3.06	0.43
BerkeleyLM C.	6.50 (+87.03%) (+123.47%)	1.19 (+371.79%) (+322.22%)	6.39 (+75.72%) (+109.21%)	1.08 (+187.45%) (+152.17%)
BerkeleyLM H.3	9.36 (+169.17%) (+221.61%)	0.84 (+233.63%) (+198.58%)	8.75 (+140.41%) (+186.23%)	0.74 (+95.77%) (+71.75%)
BerkeleyLM H.50	12.31 (+254.00%) (+322.97%)	0.35 (+39.00%) (+24.39%)	12.01 (+230.05%) (+292.95%)	0.30 (−19.39%) (−29.28%)
Expgram	4.15 (+19.33%) (+42.59%)	3.83 (+1424.87%) (+1264.67%)	5.80 (+59.41%) (+89.79%)	14.05 (+3637.90%) (+3179.16%)
KenLM T.	4.58 (+31.80%) (+57.48%)	0.23 (−8.00%) (−17.66%)	5.04 (+38.53%) (+64.93%)	0.39 (+4.57%) (−8.26%)
RandLM	4.01 (+15.42%) (+37.90%)	6.48 (+2477.95%) (+2207.12%)	3.86 (+6.03%) (+26.24%)	6.25 (+1561.20%) (+1357.33%)
MPH	9.92	0.15	9.94	0.24
KenLM P.3	14.77 (+48.90%)	0.32 (+106.38%)	14.84 (+49.24%)	0.30 (+24.82%)
KenLM P.50	21.48 (+116.59%)	0.10 (−36.37%)	21.57 (+116.89%)	0.15 (−40.16%)

Table 5: Perplexity benchmark results reporting average number of bytes per gram (bpg) and micro seconds per query using modified Kneser-Ney 5-gram language models built from Europarl and YahooV2 counts.

For all data structures, BerkeleyLM truncates the mantissa of floating-point values to 24 bits and then stores indices to distinct probabilities and backoffs. RandLM was build, as already said, with the default parameters recommended in the documentation.

Table 5 shows the results of the benchmark. As we can see, the PEF-Trie data structure is as fast as the KenLM trie while being more than 30% more compact on average; the PEF-RTrie variant *doubles* the space gains with negligible loss in query processing speed (≈13% slower). We instead significantly outperform all other competitors in both space and time, including the BerkeleyLM H.3 variant. In particular, notice that we are also smaller than RandLM which is randomized and, therefore, less accurate. The query time of BerkeleyLM H.50 is smaller on YahooV2; however, it also uses from 3 up to 4 times the space of our tries.

The last two rows of the table are dedicated to the comparison of our MPH table with KenLM PROBING. While our data structure stores quantized probabilities and backoffs, KenLM stores uncompressed values for all orders of N. We found out that storing unquantized values results in indistinguishable differences in perplexity while unnecessarily increasing the space of the data structure, as it is apparent in the results. The expensive hash key recombinations necessary for random access are avoided during perplexity computation for the left-to-right nature of the query access pattern. This makes, not surprisingly, a linear probing implementation actually faster, by 38% on average, than a minimal perfect hash approach when a large multiplicative factor is used for tables allocation (P.50). The price to pay is the double of the space. On the other hand, the P.3 variant is larger (by 50%) and slower (by 60% on average).

6 CONCLUSION AND FUTURE WORK

We have presented highly compact and fast indexes for N-grams datasets that achieve substantial performance improvements over state-of-the-art approaches. Our trie data structure represents each level of the trie with Elias-Fano, preserving the query processing speed of the fastest implementation in the literature. We have also described how to reduce its memory footprint by introducing a context-based remapping for vocabulary tokens. This technique offers, on average, an additional 28% of space reduction with a context of length 1 and 35% with a context of length 2, with only a slight penalty at query processing speed.

Some interesting research problems naturally arise from the ideas described in the paper. We mention some of them. Is the frequency-based assignment of vocabulary tokens optimal for Elias-Fano? An interesting, yet hard, research problem could focus on devising an ID-assignment strategy with proven guarantees of optimality for Elias-Fano and for our context-based remapping technique. Additional efforts could also be spent on making trie searches even faster, e.g., by exploiting SIMD processor special instructions.

ACKNOWLEDGMENTS

This work was partially supported by the EU H2020 Program under the scheme INFRAIA-1-2014-2015: *Research Infrastructures*, grant agreement #654024 *SoBigData: Social Mining & Big Data Ecosystem* and by the *Pegaso* Project, POR FSE 2014-2020.

REFERENCES

[1] 2006. Yahoo! N-Grams, version 2.0. http://webscope.sandbox.yahoo.com/catalog.php?datatype=l.
[2] Ziv Bar-Yossef and Naama Kraus. 2011. Context-sensitive query auto-completion. In *WWW*. 107–116.
[3] Djamal Belazzougui, Paolo Boldi, Giuseppe Ottaviano, Rossano Venturini, and Sebastiano Vigna. 2014. Cache-oblivious peeling of random hypergraphs. In *DCC*. 352–361.
[4] Burton H. Bloom. 1970. Space/time trade-offs in hash coding with allowable errors. In *Communications of the ACM*. 422–426.
[5] Thorsten Brantz and Alex Franz. 2006. The Google Web 1T 5-Gram Corpus. http://storage.googleapis.com/books/ngrams/books/datasetsv2.html. In *Linguistic Data Consortium, Philadelphia, PA, Technical Report LDC2006T13.*
[6] Ciprian Chelba, Tomas Mikolov, Mike Schuster, Qi Ge, Thorsten Brants, Phillipp Koehn, and Tony Robinson. 2014. One billion word benchmark for measuring progress in statistical language modeling. In *INTERSPEECH*. 2635–2639.
[7] Stanley F. Chen and Joshua Goodman. 1996. An empirical study of smoothing techniques for language modeling. In *ACL*. 310–318.
[8] David Clark. 1996. *Compact Pat Trees*. Ph.D. Dissertation. University of Waterloo.
[9] David R. Clark and J. Ian Munro. 1996. Efficient suffix trees on secondary storage. In *SODA*. 383–391.
[10] Bruce Croft, Donald Metzler, and Trevor Strohman. 2009. *Search Engines: Information Retrieval in Practice* (1st ed.). Addison-Wesley Publishing Company.
[11] Erik D. Demaine, Thouis Jones, and Mihai Pătraşcu. 2004. Interpolation search for non-independent data. In *SODA*. 529–530.
[12] Peter Elias. 1974. Efficient Storage and Retrieval by Content and Address of Static Files. In *JACM*. 246–260.
[13] Robert Mario Fano. 1971. On the number of bits required to implement an associative memory. In *Memorandum 61, Computer Structures Group, MIT.*
[14] Marcello Federico and Nicola Bertoldi. 2006. How many bits are needed to store probabilities for phrase-based translation?. In *WMT*. 94–101.
[15] Edward Fredkin. 1960. Trie memory. In *Communications of the ACM*. 490–499.
[16] Kimmo Fredriksson and Fedor Nikitin. 2007. Simple compression code supporting random access and fast string matching. In *WEA*. 203–216.
[17] Kenneth Heafield. 2011. KenLM: Faster and smaller language model queries. In *WMT*. 187–197.
[18] Steffen Heinz, Justin Zobel, and Hugh E. Williams. 2002. Burst tries: a fast, efficient data structure for string keys. In *TOIS*. ACM, 192–223.
[19] Samuel Huston, Alistair Moffat, and W. Bruce Croft. 2011. Efficient indexing of repeated n-grams. In *WSDM*. 127–136.
[20] Guy Jacobson. 1989. Space-efficient Static Trees and Graphs. In *FOCS*. 549–554.
[21] Dan Jurafsky and James H. Martin. 2014. *Speech and language processing*. Pearson.
[22] Philipp Koehn. 2005. Europarl: A parallel corpus for statistical machine translation. http://www.statmt.org/europarl. In *MT summit*. 79–86.
[23] Karen Kukich. 1992. Techniques for automatically correcting words in text. In *CSUR*. 377–439.
[24] Ted G. Lewis and Curtis R. Cook. 1988. Hashing for dynamic and static internal tables. In *Computer*. 45–56.
[25] Bhaskar Mitra and Nick Craswell. 2015. Query auto-completion for rare prefixes. In *CIKM*. 1755–1758.
[26] Bhaskar Mitra, Milad Shokouhi, Filip Radlinski, and Katja Hofmann. 2014. On user interactions with query auto-completion. In *SIGIR*. 1055–1058.
[27] Alistair Moffat and Lang Stuiver. 2000. Binary Interpolative Coding for Effective Index Compression. In *IRJ*. 25–47.
[28] Donald R. Morrison. 1968. PATRICIA: practical algorithm to retrieve information coded in alphanumeric. In *JACM*. 514–534.
[29] Gonzalo Navarro, Ricardo A. Baeza-Yates, Erkki Sutinen, and Jorma Tarhio. 2001. Indexing methods for approximate string matching. In *IEEE Data Eng. Bull.* 19–27.
[30] Giuseppe Ottaviano and Rossano Venturini. 2014. Partitioned Elias-Fano Indexes. In *SIGIR*. 273–282.
[31] Adam Pauls and Dan Klein. 2011. Faster and Smaller N-gram Language Models. In *ACL*. 258–267.
[32] Bhiksha Raj and Ed Whittaker. 2003. Lossless Compression of Language Model Structure and Word Identifiers. In *ICASSP*. 388–391.
[33] David Salomon. 2007. *Variable-length Codes for Data Compression*. Springer.
[34] Jangwon Seo and W. Bruce Croft. 2008. Local text reuse detection. In *SIGIR*. 571–578.
[35] David Talbot and Miles Osborne. 2007. Randomised language modelling for statistical machine translation. In *ACL*. 512–519.
[36] Sebastiano Vigna. 2013. Quasi-succinct indices. In *WSDM*. 83–92.
[37] Taro Watanabe, Hajime Tsukada, and Hideki Isozaki. 2009. A succinct n-gram language model. In *IJCNLP*. 341–344.
[38] Susumu Yata. 2011. Prefix/Patricia trie dictionary compression by nesting Prefix/Patricia tries. In *NLP*.

Faster BlockMax WAND with Variable-sized Blocks

Antonio Mallia
University of Pisa, Italy
a.mallia@studenti.unipi.it

Giuseppe Ottaviano*
ISTI-CNR, Italy
giuseppe.ottaviano@isti.cnr.it

Elia Porciani
University of Pisa, Italy
e.porciani1@studenti.unipi.it

Nicola Tonellotto
ISTI-CNR, Italy
nicola.tonellotto@isti.cnr.it

Rossano Venturini
University of Pisa, Italy
rossano.venturini@unipi.it

ABSTRACT

Query processing is one of the main bottlenecks in large-scale search engines. Retrieving the top k most relevant documents for a given query can be extremely expensive, as it involves scoring large amounts of documents. Several *dynamic pruning* techniques have been introduced in the literature to tackle this problem, such as BlockMaxWAND, which splits the inverted index into constant-sized blocks and stores the maximum document-term scores per block; this information can be used during query execution to safely skip low-score documents, producing many-fold speedups over exhaustive methods.

We introduce a refinement for BlockMaxWAND that uses variable-sized blocks, rather than constant-sized. We set up the problem of deciding the block partitioning as an optimization problem which maximizes how accurately the block upper bounds represent the underlying scores, and describe an efficient algorithm to find an approximate solution, with provable approximation guarantees. Through an extensive experimental analysis we show that our method significantly outperforms the state of the art roughly by a factor 2×. We also introduce a compressed data structure to represent the additional block information, providing a compression ratio of roughly 50%, while incurring only a small speed degradation, no more than 10% with respect to its uncompressed counterpart.

1 INTRODUCTION

Web Search Engines [6, 19] manage an ever-growing amount of Web documents to answer user queries as fast as possible. To keep up with such a tremendous growth, a focus on efficiency is crucial. Query processing is one of the hardest challenges a search engine has to deal with, since its workload grows with both data size and query load. Although hardware is getting less expensive and more powerful every day, the size of the Web and the number of searches is growing at an even faster rate.

Query processing in search engines is a fairly complex process; queries in a huge collection of documents may return a large set of results, but users are often interested the most relevant documents, usually a small number (historically, the *ten blue links*). The relevance of a document can be arbitrarily expensive to compute, which makes it prohibitive to evaluate all the documents that match the queried terms; query processing is thus usually divided in multiple phases. In the first phase, the query is evaluated over an inverted index data structure [3, 29] using a simple scoring function, producing a medium-sized set of candidate documents, namely the top k scored; these candidates are then re-ranked using more complex algorithms to produce the final set of documents shown to the user.

In this work we focus on improving the efficiency of the first query processing phase, which is responsible for a significant fraction of the overall work. In such phase, the scoring function is usually a weighted sum of per-term scores over the terms in the document that match the query, where the weights are a function of the query, and the scores a function of the occurrences of the term in the document. An example of such a scoring function is the widely used BM25 [24].

An obvious way to compute the top k scored documents is to retrieve all the documents that match at least one query term using the inverted index, and compute the score on all the retrieved documents. Since exhaustive methods like this can be very expensive for large collections, several *dynamic pruning* techniques have been proposed in the last few years. Dynamic pruning makes use of the inverted index, augmented with additional data structures, to skip documents during iteration that cannot reach a sufficient score to enter the top k. Thus, the final result is the same as exhaustive evaluation, but obtained with significantly less work. These techniques include MaxScore [30], WAND [4], and BlockMaxWAND (BMW) [10].

We focus our attention on the WAND family of techniques. WAND augments the posting list of each term with the *maximum score* of that term among all documents in the list. While processing the query by iterating on the posting lists of its terms, it maintains the top k scores among the documents evaluated so far; to enter the top k, a new document needs to have score larger than the current k-th score, which we call the *threshold*. WAND maintains the posting list iterators sorted by current docid; at every step, it adds up the maximum scores of the lists in increasing order, until the threshold is reached. It can be seen that the current docid of the first list that exceeds the threshold is the first docid that can reach a score higher than the threshold, so the other iterators can safely skip all the documents up to that docid.

The core principle is that if we can upper-bound the score of a range of docids, and that upper bound is lower than the threshold,

*Author currently at Facebook, USA.

SIGIR'17, August 7–11, 2017, Shinjuku, Tokyo, Japan

ISBN 978-1-4503-5022-8/17/08...$15.00.
DOI: http://dx.doi.org/10.1145/3077136.3080780

then the whole range can be safely skipped. As such, WAND computes the upper bounds of document by using the maximum score of the terms appearing in the document. Nevertheless, it should be clear that the pruning effectiveness is highly dependent on the accuracy of the upper bound: the more precise the upper bound, the more docids we can skip, and, thus, the faster the query processing.

BMW improves the accuracy of the upper bounds by splitting the posting lists into constant-sized blocks of postings, and storing the maximum score per block, rather than per list only. This way, the upper bound of a document is the sum of the maximum score of the blocks in which it may belong to. This approach gives more precise upper bounds because the scores of the blocks are usually much smaller than the maximum in their lists. Experiments confirm this intuition, and, indeed, BMW significantly outperforms WAND [10].

However, the coarse partitioning strategy of BMW does not take into consideration regularities or variances of the scores that may occur in the posting lists and their blocks. As an example, consider a posting with a very high score surrounded by postings with much lower scores. This posting alone is responsible for a high inaccuracy in the upper bounds of all its neighbors in the same block. Our main observation is that *the use of variable-sized blocks would allow to better adapt to the distribution of the scores in the posting list.* The benefits of variable-sized blocks are apparent in the simple example above, where it is sufficient to isolate the highly-scored posting in its own block to improve the upper bounds of several other postings, stored in different blocks. More formally, for a block of postings we define the *block error* as the sum of the individual posting errors, i.e., the sum of the differences between the block maximum score and the actual score of the posting. Our goal is to find a block partitioning minimizing the sum of block errors among all blocks in the partitioning. Clearly, this corresponds to minimizing the average block error. Naïvely, the minimum cost partitioning would correspond to blocks containing only a single posting. However, if the blocks are too small, the average skip at query time will be short and, thus, this solution does not carry out any benefit. In this work we introduce the problem of finding a partition of posting lists into variable-sized blocks such that the the sum of block errors is minimized, subject to a constraint on the number of blocks of the partition. Then, we will show that an approximately optimal partition can be computed efficiently. Experiments on standard datasets show that our Variable BMW (VBMW) significantly outperforms BMW and the other state-of-the-art strategies.

Our Contributions. We list here our main contributions.

(1) We introduce the problem of optimally partitioning the posting lists into variable-sized blocks to minimize the average block error, subject to a constraint on the number of blocks. We then propose a practical optimization algorithm which produces an approximately optimal solution in almost linear time. We remark that existing solutions for this optimization problem run in at least quadratic time, and, thus, they are unfeasible in a practical setting. Experiments show that this approach is able to reduce the average score error up to 40%, confirming the importance of optimally partitioning posting list into variable-sized blocks.
(2) We propose a compression scheme for the block data structures, compressing the block boundary docids with Elias-Fano and quantizing the block max scores, obtaining a maximum reduction of space usage w.r.t. the uncompressed data structures of roughly 50%, while incurring only a small speed degradation, no more than 10% with respect to its uncompressed counterpart.
(3) We provide an extensive experimental evaluation to compare our strategy with the state of the art on standard datasets of Web pages and queries. Results show that VBMW outperforms the state-of-the-art BMW by a factor of roughly 2×.

2 BACKGROUND AND RELATED WORK

In the following we will provide some background on index organization and query processing in search engines. We will also summarize and discuss the state-of-the-art query processing strategies with a particular focus on the current most efficient strategy, namely BlockMaxWAND, leveraging block-based score upper bound approximations.

Index Organization. Given a collection $\mathcal{D}$ of documents, each document is identified by a non-negative integer called a *document identifier*, or *docid*. A *posting list* is associated to each *term* appearing in the collection, containing the list of the docids of all the documents in which the term occurs. The collection of the posting lists for all the terms is called the *inverted index* of $\mathcal{D}$, while the set of the terms is usually referred to as the *dictionary*. Posting lists typically contain additional information about each document, such as the number of occurrences of the term in the document, and the set of positions where the term occurs [5, 19, 32].

The docids in a posting list can be sorted in increasing order, which enables the use of efficient compression algorithms and document-at-a-time query processing. This is the most common approach in large-scale search engines (see for example [8]). Alternatively, the posting lists can be frequency-sorted [30] or impact-sorted [2], still providing a good compression rates as well as good query processing speed. However, there is no evidence of such index layouts in common use within commercial search engines [21].

Inverted index compression is essential to make efficient use of the memory hierarchy, thus maximizing query processing speed. Posting list compression boils down to the problem of representing sequences of integers for both docids and frequencies. Representing such sequences of integers in compressed space is a fundamental problem, studied since the 1950s with applications going beyond inverted indexes. A classical solution is to compute the differences of consecutive docids (deltas), and encode them with uniquely-decodable variable length binary codes; examples are unary codes, Elias Gamma/Delta codes, and Golomb/Rice codes [25]. More recent approaches encode simultaneously blocks of integers in order to improve both compression ratio and decoding speed. The underlying idea is to partition the sequence of integers into blocks of fixed or variable length and to encode each block separately with different strategies (see e.g., [17, 22, 28] and references therein).

More recently, the *Elias-Fano* representation of monotone sequences [11, 12] has been applied to inverted index compression [31], showing excellent query performance thanks to its efficient random access and search operations. However, it fails to exploit the local clustering that inverted lists usually exhibit, namely the presence of long subsequences of close identifiers. Recently, Ottaviano and Venturini [23] described a new representation based on partitioning the list into chunks and encoding both the chunks and their endpoints with Elias-Fano, hence forming a two-level data structure. This partitioning enables the encoding to better adapt to the local statistics of the chunk, thus exploiting clustering and improving compression. They also showed how to minimize the space occupancy of this representation by setting up the partitioning as an instance of an optimization problem, for which they present a linear time algorithm that is guaranteed to find a solution at most $(1 + \epsilon)$ times larger than the optimal one, for any given $\epsilon \in (0, 1)$. In the following we will use a variation of their algorithm.

Query Processing. In *Boolean retrieval* a query, expressed as a (multi-)set of terms, can be processed in conjunctive (AND) or disjunctive (OR) modes, retrieving the documents that contain respectively all the terms or at least one of them. Top-k *ranked retrieval*, instead, retrieves the k highest scored documents in the collection, where the *relevance score* is a function of the query-document pair. Since it can be assumed that a document which does not contain any query term has score 0, ranked retrieval can be implemented by evaluating the query in disjunctive mode, and scoring the results. We call this algorithm RankedOR.

In this work we focus on *linear* scoring functions, i.e., where the score of a query-document pair can be expressed as follows:

$$s(q, d) = \sum_{t \in q \cap d} w_t s_{t,d}$$

where the w_t are query-dependent weights for each query term, and the $s_{t,d}$ are scores for each term-document pair. Such scores are usually a monotonic function of the occurrences of the term in the document, which can be stored in the posting list alongside the docid (usually referred to as the *term frequency*).

It can be easily seen that the widely used BM25 relevance score [24] can be cast in this framework. In BM25, the weights w_t are derived from t's inverse document frequency (IDF) to distinguish between common (low value) and uncommon (high value) words, and the scores $s_{t,d}$ are a smoothly saturated function of the term frequency. In all our experiments we will use BM25 as the scoring function.

The classical query processing strategies to match documents to a query fall in two categories: in a term-at-a-time (TAAT) strategy, the posting lists of the query terms are processed one at a time, accumulating the score of each document in a separate data structure. In a document-at-a-time (DAAT) strategy, the query term postings lists are processed simultaneously keeping them aligned by docid. In DAAT processing the score of each document is fully computed considering the contributions of all query terms before moving to the next document, thus no auxiliary per-document data structures are necessary. We will focus on the DAAT strategy as it is is more amenable to dynamic pruning techniques.

Solving scored ranked queries exhaustively with DAAT can be very inefficient. Various techniques to enhance retrieval efficiency have been proposed, by dynamically pruning docids that are unlikely to be retrieved. Among them, the most popular are MaxScore [30] and WAND [4]. Both strategies augment the index by storing for each term its maximum score contribution, thus allowing to skip large segments of posting lists if they only contain terms whose sum of maximum scores is smaller than the scores of the top k documents found up to that point.

The alignment of the posting lists during MaxScore and WAND processing can be achieved by means of the $\text{NextGEQ}_t(d)$ operator, which returns the smallest docid in the posting list t that is greater than or equal to d. This operator can significantly improve the posting list traversal speed during query processing, by skipping large amounts of irrelevant docids. The Elias-Fano compression scheme provides an efficient implementation of the $\text{NextGEQ}_t(d)$ operator, which is crucial to obtain the typical subsecond response times of Web search engines.

Both MaxScore and WAND rely on upper-bounding the contribution that each term can give to the overall document score, allowing to skip whole ranges of docids [18].

However, both employ a *global* per-term upper bound, that is, the maximum score $s_{t,d}$ among all documents d which contain the term t. Such maximum score could be significantly larger than the typical score contribution of that term, in fact limiting the opportunities to skip large amounts of documents. For example, a single outlier for an otherwise low-score term can make it impossible to skip any document that contains that term.

To tackle this problem, Ding and Suel [10] propose to augment the inverted index data structures with additional information to store more accurate upper bounds: at indexing time each posting list is split into consecutive blocks of constant size, e.g., 128 postings per block. For each block the score upper bound is computed and stored, together with largest docid of each block.

These *local* term upper bounds can then be exploited by adapting existing algorithms such as MaxScore and WAND to make use of the additional information. The first of such algorithms is Block-MaxWAND (BMW) [10]. The authors report an average speedup of BMW against WAND of 2.78 – 3.04. Experiments in [9] report a speedup of ~3.00 and ~1.25 of BMW with respect to WAND and MaxScore, respectively. Several versions of Block-Max MaxScore (BMM), the MaxScore variant for block-max indexes, have been proposed in [7, 9, 26]. In [9], the authors implementation of BMM is 1.25 times slower than BMW on average.

3 VARIABLE BLOCK-MAX WAND

As mentioned in the previous section, BMW leverages per-block upper bound information to skip whole blocks of docids during query processing (we refer to the original paper [10] for a detailed description of the algorithm). The performance of the algorithm highly depends on the size of the blocks: if the blocks are too large, the likelihood of having at least one large value in each block increases, causing the upper bounds to be loose. If they are too small, the average skip will be short. In both cases, the pruning effectiveness may reduce significantly. A sweet spot can thus be determined experimentally.

The constant-sized block partitioning of BMW does not take into consideration regularities or variances of the scores that may occur in the posting lists and their blocks. The use of variable-sized blocks allows to better adapt to the distribution of the scores in the posting list.

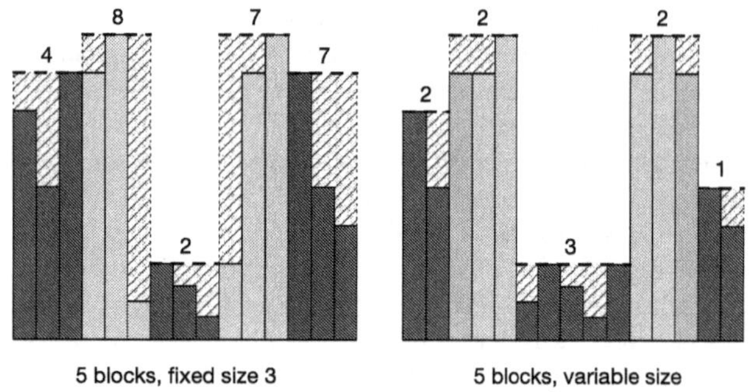

Figure 1: Block errors in constant (left) and variable (right) block partitioning.

The improvement with this kind of partitioning is apparent from the example in Figure 1. The figure shows a sequence of scores partitioned in constant-sized blocks and in variable-sized blocks. We define the *error* as the sum of the differences between each value and its block's upper bound, the shaded area in the figure. This example shows that a variable-sized partitioning can produce a much lower error, e.g., 28 in constant-sized partitioning (with blocks of length 3) versus 10 in variable-sized partitioning.

Problem definition. To give a more formal definition, for a partitioning of the sequence of scores in a posting list of n postings let $\mathcal{B}$ be the set of its blocks. Each block $B \in \mathcal{B}$ is a sequence of consecutive postings in the posting list. We use $b = |\mathcal{B}|$ and $|B|$ to denote the number of blocks of the partition and the number of postings in B, respectively. The term-document scores are defined above as $s_{t,d}$; however, since in the following we will work on one posting list at a time, we can drop the t, so s_d will denote the sequence of scores for each document d in the posting list.

We define the *error* of a partitioning $\mathcal{B}$ as follows:

$$\sum_{B \in \mathcal{B}} \left(|B| \max_{d \in B} s_d - \sum_{d \in B} s_d \right). \tag{1}$$

Here for each block of postings we are accounting for the the sum of its individual posting errors, i.e., the sum of the differences between the block maximum score and the score of the posting.

To simplify the formula above we can notice that the right-hand side of the subtraction can be taken out of the sum, since the blocks form a partition of the list, and the resulting term does not depend on $\mathcal{B}$. Thus, minimizing the error is equivalent to minimizing the following formula, which represents the perimeter of the envelope, for a given number of blocks $b = |\mathcal{B}|$:

$$\sum_{B \in \mathcal{B}} |B| \max_{d \in B} s_d. \tag{2}$$

Our goal is to find a block partitioning that minimizes the sum of block errors among all blocks in the partitioning. Naïvely, the minimum cost partitioning would correspond to blocks containing only a single posting. Since this solution clearly does not carry out any benefit, we fix the number of blocks in the partition to be b. As we will show in Section 5 minimizing the error can significantly improve BMW performance over constant-sized blocks.

Existing solutions. The problem of finding a partition that minimizes Equation (2) subject to a constraint b on the number of its blocks can be solved with a standard approach based on dynamic programming. The basic idea is to fill a $b \times n$ matrix M where entry $M[i][j]$ stores the minimum error to partition the posting list up to position j with i blocks. This matrix can be filled top-down from left to right. The entry $M[i][j]$ is computed by trying to place the jth posting in the optimal solutions that uses $i-1$ blocks. Unfortunately, the time complexity of this solution is $\Theta(bn^2)$, which is $\Theta(n^3)$ since, given that the average block size n/b is small (e.g., 32–128), thus, the interesting values of b are $\Theta(n)$. This algorithm is clearly unfeasible because n can easily be in the range of millions.

This optimization problem is similar in nature to the well-studied problem of computing optimal histograms (see again Figure 1). The complexity of finding the best histogram with a given number of bars is the same as above. Several approximate solutions have been presented. Halim et al. [16] describe several solutions and introduce an algorithm that has good experimental performance but no theoretical guarantees. All such solutions are polynomial either in n or in b. Some have complexity $O(nb)$. Guha et al. [15] introduce a $(1+\epsilon)$ approximation with $O(n + b^3 \log n + b^2/\epsilon)$ time. While these techniques can be useful in cases where b is small, in our case $b = \Theta(n)$, which makes these algorithms unfeasible for us. Furthermore, the definition of the objective function in these works is different from ours, as it minimizes the variance rather than the sum of the differences.

Our solution. We first present a practical and efficient algorithm with weaker theoretical guarantees regarding the optimal solution than what would be expected. Indeed, fixed the required number of blocks b and an approximation parameter ϵ, with $0 < \epsilon < 1$, the algorithm finds a partition with $b' \le b$ blocks whose cost is at most a factor $1+\epsilon$ larger than the cost of the optimal partition with b' edges. This algorithm runs in $O(n \log_{1+\epsilon} \frac{1}{\epsilon} \log(Un/b))$ time, where U is the largest cost of any block. The weakness is due to the fact that there is no guarantee on how much b' is close to the requested number of blocks b. Even with this theoretical gap, in all our experiments the algorithm identified a solution with a number of blocks very close to the desired one. In the last part of the section, we will fill this gap by showing how to refine the solution to always identify a $1+\epsilon$ approximated optimal solution with exactly b edges.

The first solution is a variation of the approximate dynamic programming algorithm introduced by Ottaviano and Venturini [23] to optimize the partitioning of Elias-Fano indexes.

It is convenient to look at the problem as a shortest path problem over a directed acyclic graph (DAG). The nodes of the graph correspond to the postings in the list; the edges connect each ordered pair $i < j$ of nodes, and represent the possible blocks in the partition. The cost $c(i,j)$ associated to the edge is thus $(j-i)\max_{i \le d < j} s_d$.

In this graph, denoted as G, each path represents a possible partitioning, and the cost of the path is equal to the cost of the partitioning as defined in (2). Thus, our problem reduces to an instance of *constrained shortest path* on this graph, that is, finding the shortest path with a given number of edges [13, 20].

We can compute the constrained shortest path with an approach similar to the one in [1, 13, 20]. The idea is to reduce the problem to a standard, unconstrained shortest path by using Lagrangian relaxation: adding a fixed cost $\lambda \geq 0$ to every edge. We denote the relaxed graph as G_λ. By varying λ, the shortest path in G_λ will have a different number of edges: if $\lambda = 0$, the solution is the path of $n-1$ edges of length one; at the limit $\lambda = +\infty$, the solution is a single edge of length n. It can be shown that, for any given λ, if the shortest path in G_λ has ℓ edges, then that path is an optimal ℓ-constrained shortest path in G. Thus, our goal is to find the value of λ that give $\ell = b$ edges. However, notice that not every b can be found this way, but in practice we can get close enough. Thus, our algorithm performs a binary search to find the value of λ that gives a shortest path with b' edges, with b' close enough to b. Each step of the binary search requires a shortest-path computation.

Each of these shortest-path computations can be solved in $O(|V|+|E|)$, where V are the vertices of G_λ and E the edges; for our problem, unfortunately, this is $\Theta(n^2)$, which is still unfeasible. We can however exploit two properties of our cost function to apply the algorithm in [23] and obtain a linear-time approximate solution for a given value of λ. These properties are *monotonicity* and *quasi-subadditivity*. The monotonicity property is stated as follows.

Property 1. *(Monotonicity) A function $f : V \times V \mapsto \mathbb{R}$ is said* monotone *if for each pair of values $i, j \in V$ the following holds:*

- $f(i, j+1) \geq f(i, j)$,
- $f(i-1, j) \geq f(i, j)$.

It is easy to verify that our cost function $c(i, j)$ satisfies Property 1, because if a block B is contained in a block B', then it follows immediately from the definition that the cost of B' is greater than the cost of B. Monotonicity allows us to perform a first pruning of G_λ: for any given approximation parameter $\alpha \in (0, 1]$, we define G^1_λ as the graph with the same nodes as G_λ, and all the edges (i, j) of G_λ that satisfy at least one of the following conditions.

(1) There exists an integer h such that

$$c(i,j) \leq \lambda(1+\alpha)^h < c(i, j+1)$$

(2) (i, j) is the last outgoing edge from i.

The number of edges in G^1_λ is $n \log_{1+\alpha}(\frac{U}{\lambda})$ where U is the maximum cost of an edge (which is equal to $n \max_d s_d$).

We denote as π_{G_λ} the shortest path of the graph G_λ and extend c to denote the cost of a path. It can be shown that $c(\pi_{G^1_\lambda}) \leq (1+\alpha)c(\pi_{G_\lambda})$, that is, the optimal solution in G^1_λ is a $(1+\alpha)$ approximation of the optimal solution in G_λ; see [14] for the proof. The complexity to find the shortest path decreases from $O(n^2)$ to $O(n \log_{1+\alpha}(\frac{U}{\lambda}))$. This would be already applicable in many practical scenarios, but it depends on the value U of the maximum score. We can further refine the algorithm in order to decrease the complexity and drop the dependency on U by adding an extra approximation function $(1+\beta)$ for any given approximation parameter $\beta \in (0, 1]$, by leveraging the quasi-subadditivity property.

Property 2. *(Quasi-subadditivity) A function $f : V \times V \mapsto \mathbb{R}$ is said* λ-quasi-subadditive *if for any i, k and $j \in V$, with $0 \leq i < l < j < |V|$ the following holds:*

$$f(i,k) + f(k,j) \leq f(i,j) + \lambda.$$

It is again immediate to show that $c(i, j)$ satisfies Property 2: splitting a block at any point can only lower the upper bound in the two resulting sub-blocks, so the only extra cost is the additional λ of the new edge.

This property allows us to prune from G^1_λ all the edges with cost higher than $L = \lambda + \frac{2\lambda}{\beta}$; we call the resulting graph G^2_λ. The new graph has $O(n \log_{1+\alpha} \frac{1}{\beta}) = \Theta(n)$ edges, thus shortest paths can be computed in linear time. It can be shown (see [23]) that this pruning incurs an extra $(1+\beta)$ approximation; the overall approximation factor is thus $(1+\alpha)(1+\beta)$, which is $1+\epsilon$ for any $\epsilon \in (0, 1]$ by appropriately fixing $\alpha = \beta = \frac{\epsilon}{3}$.

Clearly it is not feasible to materialize the graph G_λ and prune it to obtain G^2_λ, since the dominating cost would still be the initial quadratic phase. It is however possible to visit the graph G^2_λ without constructing it explicitly, as described in [23].

By using the above algorithm, every shortest path computation requires $O(n \log_{1+\epsilon} \frac{1}{\epsilon}) = \Theta(n)$ time and linear space.

Since we are binary searching on λ, the number of required shortest path computations depends on the range of possible values of λ. It is easy to see that $\lambda \geq 0$. Indeed, the shortest path in G_0 has the largest possible number of edges, $n-1$ and the smallest possible cost. We now prove that the shortest path in G_λ with $\lambda > Un/(b-1)$ has less than b edges, where U is the largest cost on G. Thus, in the binary search we can restrict our attention to integer values of λ in $[0, Un/(b-1)]$. The proof is as follows. Consider the optimal path with one edge in G, and let O_1 be its cost. By monotonicity, we know that $O_1 = U$. Let O_b be the cost of the best path with b edges in G. For any λ, the cost of these two paths in G_λ are $O_1 + \lambda$ and $O_b + b\lambda$. Observe that if $\lambda > Un/b$, the former path has a cost which is smaller than the cost of the latter. This means that we do not need to explore values of λ larger than $Un/(b-1)$ when we are looking for a path with b edges. Thus, the first phase of the algorithm needs $O(\log(Un/b))$ shortest path computations to find the target value of λ. Thus, if we restrict our search to integer values of λ, the number of shortest path computations is $O(\log(Un/b))$.

We can refine the above solution to find a provable good approximation of the shortest path with *exactly* b edges. The refinement uses the result in [13]. Theorem 4.1 in [13] states that, given a DAG G with integer costs which satisfy the monotonicity property, we can compute an additive approximation of the constrained shortest path of G. More precisely, we can compute a path with b edges such that its cost is at most $O_b + U$, where O_b is the cost of an optimal path with b edges and U is the largest cost on G. The algorithms works in two phases. In the first phase, it reduces the problem to a standard, unconstrained shortest path by using Lagrangian relaxation as we have done in our first solution. Thus, the first phase binary searches for the value of λ for which the shortest path on G_λ with the least number of edges has at most b edges, while the one with the most edges has at least b edges. If one of these two paths has exactly b edges, this is guaranteed to be an optimal solution and we are done. Otherwise, we start the second phase of the algorithm. The second phase is called *path-swapping* and its goal is to combine these two paths to find a path with b edges whose cost is worse than the optimal one by at most an additive term A, which equals the largest cost in the graph. We refer to [1] and [13] for more details.

We cannot immediately apply the above optimization algorithm because of two important issues. In the following we will introduce and solve both of them.

The first issue is that the above optimization algorithm assumes that the costs in G are integers, while in our case are not. The idea is to obtain a new graph with integer costs by rescaling and rounding the original costs of G. More precisely, we can obtain a new graph by replacing any cost $c(i, j)$ with $\lceil c(i, j)/\delta \rceil$, where $\delta \in (0, 1]$ is an approximation parameter. We can prove that this operation slightly affects the cost of the optimal path. Indeed, let O_b the cost of the shortest path with b edges in G, the shortest path on the new graph as cost $\tilde{O}_b$ which is $O_b \leq \tilde{O}_b \leq O_b + \delta b$. Due to space limitations, we defer the proof of this inequality to the journal version of the paper. Even if in general we cannot bound the additive approximation δb in terms of O_b, in practice the approximation is negligible because O_b is much larger that δb. Notice that this approximation increases U to $\frac{U}{\delta}$.

The second issue to address is the fact that additive approximation term A in the result of [13] is the largest edge cost U. In our problem this additive approximation term is the cost of the edge from 1 to n, which equals the cost of the worst possible path. This means that the obtained approximation would be trivial. However, we observe that, due to the approach of the previous paragraph, the largest cost on the approximated graph G^2_λ is $L = \lambda + \frac{2\lambda}{\beta}$ and we know that $\lambda \leq Un/b$. Thus, the additive approximation term A is $O(\frac{Un}{b\beta})$, which is negligible in practice.

Thus, we obtained the following theorem.

THEOREM 3.1. *Given a sequence of scores $S[1, n]$ and a fixed number of blocks b, we can compute a partition of S into b blocks whose cost is at most $(1+\epsilon)O_b + O(\frac{Un}{b\epsilon}) + \delta b$ in $O(n \log_{1+\epsilon} \frac{1}{\epsilon} \log(\frac{Un}{b\delta\epsilon}))$ time and linear space, where O_b is the cost of the optimal partition with b blocks, $U = \sum_{i=1}^{n} S[i]$, and $\epsilon, \delta \in (0, 1]$ are the two approximation parameters.*

4 REPRESENTING THE UPPER BOUNDS

BlockMaxWAND is required to store additional information about the block upper bounds. This additional information must be stored together with the traditional inverted index data structures, and while these upper bounds can improve the time efficiency of query processing, they introduce a serious space overhead problem.

The additional information required by BlockMaxWAND can be seen as two aligned sequences: the sequence of block boundaries, that is, the largest docid in each block, and the score upper bound for each block.

In the original implementation, the sequences are stored uncompressed, using constant-width encodings (for example, 32-bit integers for the boundaries and 32-bit floats for the upper bounds), and are usually interleaved to favor cache locality. We can however use more efficient encodings to reduce the space overhead.

First, we observe that the sequence of block boundaries is monotonic, so it can be efficiently represented with Elias-Fano. In addition to saving space, Elias-Fano provides an efficient NextGEQ operation that can be used to quickly locate the block containing the current docid at query execution time.

Second, as far as the upper bounds are concerned, we can reduce space use by *approximating* their value. The only requirement to preserve the correctness of the algorithm is that each approximate value is an upper bound for all the scores in its block. Thus, we can use the following quantization. First, we partition the score space into fixed size buckets. Any score is represented with the identifier of its bucket. Let us assume that the score space is $[0, U]$ and that we partition it into w buckets. Then, instead of storing a block upper bound with value $s \in [0, U]$, we store the identifier i such that $\frac{iU}{w} < s \leq \frac{(i+1)U}{w}$. At query time, the actual score s will be approximated with the largest possible value in its bucket, i.e., $\frac{(i+1)U}{w}$. Clearly, the representation of any score requires $\lfloor \log w + 1 \rfloor$ bits, a large space saving with respect to the 32 bits of the float representation. Obviously, the value of w can be chosen to trade off the space usage and the quality of the approximation.

A simple optimization to speed up access is to interleave the two sequences, by modifying of the Elias-Fano data structure. Elias-Fano stores a monotonic sequence by splitting each value into its ℓ *low bits*, and the remaining *high bits*. The value of ℓ a constant for the sequence. While the high bits are encoded with variable-length, the low bits are encoded verbatim in exactly ℓ bits per element, thus the low bits of the i-th element are at the position $i\ell$ of the low bitvector. We can then interleave the low bits and the quantized score by using a bitvector of $(\ell + w)$-bit entries, so that when the block is located, its quantized upper bound is already in cache.

5 EXPERIMENTAL RESULTS

In this section we analyze the performance of VBMW with an extensive experimental evaluation in a realistic and reproducible setting, using state-of-the-art baselines, standard benchmark text collections, and a large query log.

Testing details. All the algorithms are implemented in C++11 and compiled with GCC 5.4.0 with the highest optimization settings. The tests are performed on a machine with 8 Intel Core i7-4770K Haswell cores clocked at 3.50GHz, with 32GiB RAM, running Linux 4.4.0. The indexes are saved to disk after construction, and memory-mapped to be queried, so that there are no hidden space costs due to loading of additional data structures in memory. Before timing the queries we ensure that the required posting lists are fully loaded in memory. All timings are measured taking the results with minimum value of five independent runs. All times are reported in milliseconds.

The source code is available at https://github.com/rossanoventurini/Variable-BMW for the reader interested in further implementation details or in replicating the experiments.

Datasets. We performed our experiments on the following standard datasets.

- ClueWeb09 is the ClueWeb 2009 TREC Category B collection, consisting of 50 million English web pages crawled between January and February 2009.
- Gov2 is the TREC 2004 Terabyte Track test collection, consisting of 25 million .gov sites crawled in early 2004; the documents are truncated to 256 kB.

For each document in the collection the body text was extracted using Apache Tika[1], the words lowercased and stemmed using the

[1] http://tika.apache.org

Table 1: Basic statistics for the test collections

	ClueWeb09	Gov2
Documents	50,131,015	24,622,347
Terms	92,094,694	35,636,425
Postings	15,857,983,641	5,742,630,292

Porter2 stemmer; no stopwords were removed. The docids were assigned according to the lexicographic order of their URLs [27]. Table 1 reports the basic statistics for the two collections. If not differently specified, the inverted index is compressed by using partitioned Elias-Fano (PEF) [23] in the ds2i library[2].

Queries. To evaluate the speed of query processing we use Trec05 and Trec06 Efficiency Track topics, drawing only queries whose terms are all in the collection dictionary and having more than 128 postings. These queries are, respectively, the 90% and 96% of the total Trec05 and Trec06 queries for the Gov2 collection and the 96% and 98% of the total Trec05 and Trec06 queries for the ClueWeb09 collection. From those sets of queries we randomly select 1 000 queries for each length.

Processing strategies. To test the performance on query strategies that make use of the docids and the occurrence frequencies we perform BM25 top 10 queries using 5 different algorithms: RankedOR, which scores the results of a disjunctive query, WAND [4], MaxScore [30], BlockMaxWAND (BMW) [10], and the proposed Variable BMW (VBMW) in its uncompressed and compressed variants.

We use BMW_x to indicate that the *fixed* block size in BMW is x postings, while we use $VBMW_x$ to indicate that the *average* block size in VBMW is x postings. The compressed version of VBMW as described in Section 4 is denoted as $C\text{-}VBMW_x$.

Validating our BMW implementation. We implemented our version of BMW because the source code of the original implementation was not available. To test the validity of our implementation we compared its average query time with the ones reported in [10]. We replicated their original setting by using the same dataset (Gov2), by compressing postings with the same algorithm (PForDelta), by using queries from the same collections (Trec05 and Trec06), and by using BMW_{64}. However, since we are using a different faster machine, we cannot directly compare query times, but, instead, we compare the improving factors with respect to RankedOR, which is an easy-to-implement baseline.

Table 2 shows the query times reported in the original paper (top) and the ones obtained with our implementation (bottom). Results show that the two implementations are comparable, with ours which is generally faster. For example, it is faster by a factor larger than 2.4 on queries with more than three terms in Trec06.

The effect of the block size in BMW. Although the most commonly used block sizes for BMW are 64 and 128, a more careful experimental evaluation shows that the best performance in terms of query time is obtained with a block size of 40 postings.

Table 3 shows the average query time of BMW with respect to Trec05 and Trec06 on both Gov2 and ClueWeb09, by varying the

[2]https://github.com/ot/ds2i

Table 2: Query times (in ms) of RankedOR and BMW_{64} on Gov2 with queries in Trec05 and Trec06 as reported by Ding and Suel [10] (top) and the ones obtained with our implementation (bottom), for different query lengths.

	Number of query terms				
	2	3	4	5	6+
Trec05 (from [10])					
RankedOR	62.1 (x17.7)	238.9 (x18.8)	515.2 (x20.4)	778.3 (x25.9)	1,501.4 (x14.4)
BMW_{64}	3.5	12.7	25.2	30.0	104.0
Trec06 (from [10])					
RankedOR	60.0 (x14.7)	159.2 (x13.8)	261.4 (x7.8)	376.0 (x6.9)	646.4 (x5.7)
BMW_{64}	4.1	11.5	33.6	54.5	114.2
Trec05					
RankedOR	15.5 (x13.2)	51.3 (x17.3)	100.3 (x22.6)	158.0 (x22.7)	275.1 (x17.3)
BMW_{64}	1.2	3.0	4.5	7.0	15.9
Trec06					
RankedOR	15.5 (x14.7)	57.6 (x16.9)	117.6 (x19.7)	178.0 (x18.5)	311.2 (x13.8)
BMW_{64}	1.1	3.4	6.0	9.6	22.5

block size. We select the block size in the set $\{32, 40, 48, 64, 96, 128\}$. It is clear that in all cases, the best average query time is achieved with blocks size 40. BMW_{40} is 10% faster, on average, than BMW_{128}.

Table 3 also reports the space usage of the (uncompressed) additional information stored by BMW, namely the largest score in the block (as float) and the last posting in the block (as unsigned int). Posting lists with fewer postings than the block size do not store any additional information. The size of the inverted index of the Gov2 and ClueWeb09 collections (compressed with PEF) is 4.32 GiB and 14.84 GiB respectively. Thus, the space of the additional information required by BMW is not negligible, since it ranges between 15% and 42% of the compressed inverted index space on both Gov2 and ClueWeb09. As we will see later, this space usage can be reduced significantly by compressing the additional information.

The effect of the block size in VBMW. Now, we proceed by analyzing the behavior of VBMW. Instead of adopting the more sophisticated approximation approach detailed in Section 3, we use the simpler optimization algorithm which has no theoretical guarantees on the final number of blocks. Thus, we cannot choose an exact block size for our partitioning but we binary search for the λ in the parameter space that gives an average block size close to the values in $\{32, 40, 48, 64, 96, 128\}$.

Table 4 reports the average block sizes and score errors for different block sizes w.r.t. BMW and VBMW on Gov2 and ClueWeb09, and optimal values for the Lagrangian relaxation parameter λ. Note that for BMW, the average block size is not perfectly identical to the desired block size due to the length of the last block in the posting lists, which may be smaller than the desired block size. Our optimization algorithm is able to find an average block size for VBMW within 3% of the average block size for BMW. Thus, the weaker optimization algorithm of Section 3 suffices in practice to obtain the desired average block sizes. More importantly, the

Table 3: Space usage of the additional data required by BMW and average query times with queries in Trec05 and Trec06 on Gov2 and ClueWeb09, by varying the block size.

	Block size					
	32	40	48	64	96	128
Additional space (GiB)						
Gov2	1.83	1.55	1.38	1.15	0.92	**0.85**
ClueWeb09	5.04	4.14	3.62	3.04	2.40	**2.24**
Query time (ms) on Trec05						
Gov2	**3.6**	**3.6**	3.7	3.8	3.9	4.2
ClueWeb09	12.8	**12.6**	**12.6**	12.8	13.3	13.9
Query time (ms) on Trec06						
Gov2	8.3	**8.2**	8.3	8.5	8.9	9.2
ClueWeb09	**26.4**	**26.3**	26.5	27.0	28.0	29.4

Table 4: Average block sizes and score errors for different block sizes w.r.t. BMW and VBMW on Gov2 and ClueWeb09, and optimal values for the Lagrangian relaxation parameter.

		Block Size					
		32	40	48	64	96	128
Gov2							
Average Block Size	BMW	31.94	39.90	47.87	63.74	95.35	127.14
	VBMW	31.32	39.63	47.09	63.60	98.40	126.30
Average Score Error	BMW	1.47	1.55	1.61	1.70	1.83	1.92
	VBMW	0.82	0.91	0.98	1.09	1.26	1.35
λ	VBMW	12.0	15.2	18.0	24.0	35.1	45.9
ClueWeb09							
Average Block Size	BMW	31.96	39.94	47.91	63.83	95.65	127.29
	VBMW	30.24	39.54	48.03	63.29	97.43	127.72
Average Score Error	BMW	1.94	2.05	2.15	2.29	2.49	2.63
	VBMW	1.20	1.34	1.45	1.60	1.83	1.98
λ	VBMW	16.0	21.0	25.5	33.4	50.3	64.5

average score error for VBMW is sensibly smaller than the average score error for BMW, with a reduction ranging from 40% for small blocks up to 25% for large blocks. This confirms the importance of partitioning the posting lists with variable-sized blocks.

In Table 5 we can see that VBMW reaches the best average query times with approximatively 32 – 40 elements per block, similar to the best block size for BMW reported in Table 3, i.e., 40 postings per block. As shown in Figure 2, the trade-off in choosing this block size w.r.t. average query time is that we use more space to store block information, as reported in Table 3.

The effect of compression in VBMW. Figure 2 shows how the choice of w affects both query time and space usage of C-VBMW when the average number of blocks is fixed to 40 elements. We fixed the number of buckets w to quantize the scores to the powers

Table 5: Average query times of VBMW with queries in Trec05 and Trec06 on Gov2 and ClueWeb09, by varying the block size.

	Block size					
	32	40	48	64	96	128
Query time (ms) on Trec05						
Gov2	**2.1**	**2.1**	**2.1**	2.2	2.5	2.8
ClueWeb09	**7.2**	**7.2**	7.4	8.1	9.7	11.0
Query time (ms) on Trec06						
Gov2	**4.6**	4.7	4.8	5.3	6.1	6.9
ClueWeb09	**14.7**	15.2	16.1	17.8	21.2	23.7

of two from 32 to 512 and we reported the query time and the space of the additional information on both datasets with both set of queries. For comparison, we also plot the results of the plain version of VBMW by varying the average size of the blocks.

The first conclusion is that the compression approach is very effective. Indeed, C-VBMW improves space usage by roughly a factor 2 with respect to VBMW_{40}. We also notice that the compression approach is more effective than simply increasing the block size in the uncompressed VBMW. Indeed, for example, C-VBMW with $w = 32$ uses almost the same space as VBMW_{128} but is faster by 20% – 40%.

The second conclusion is that compression does not decrease query time which actually sometimes even improves. For example, C-VBMW with $w = 512$ and $w = 256$ is faster that its uncompressed version (VBMW_{40}) on both datasets with Trec05. This effect may be the results to a better cache usage resulting from the smaller size of additional information in C-VBMW.

We observe that there are small differences (less than 10%) in efficiency between the different values of w. Thus, for the next experiments we will fix w to 512 to obtain the best time efficiency.

Overall comparison. To carefully evaluate the performance of C-VBMW w.r.t. other processing strategies, we measured the query times of different query processing algorithms for different query lengths, from 2 terms queries to more than 5 terms queries, as well as the overall average processing times and the space use of any required additional data structure with respect the whole inverted indexes represented with PEF.

In Table 6, next to each timing is reported in parenthesis the relative speedup of C-VBMW_{40} with respect to this strategy. Table 6 also reports, in GiB, the additional space usage required by the different query processing strategies. Next to each size measure is reported in parenthesis the relative percentage against the data structures used to compress posting lists storing docids and frequencies only, as used by RankedOR.

Not very surprisingly, RankedOR is always at least 34 times slower than C-VBMW_{40}, while both MaxScore and WAND are from 1.4 to 11 times slower than C-VBMW_{40}. The maximum speedup of C-VBMW_{40} is achieved with queries of two terms where it ranges from 6.5 to 11. Space usage of MaxScore and WAND plainly store the score upper bounds for each term using the 4% – 5% of the inverted index.

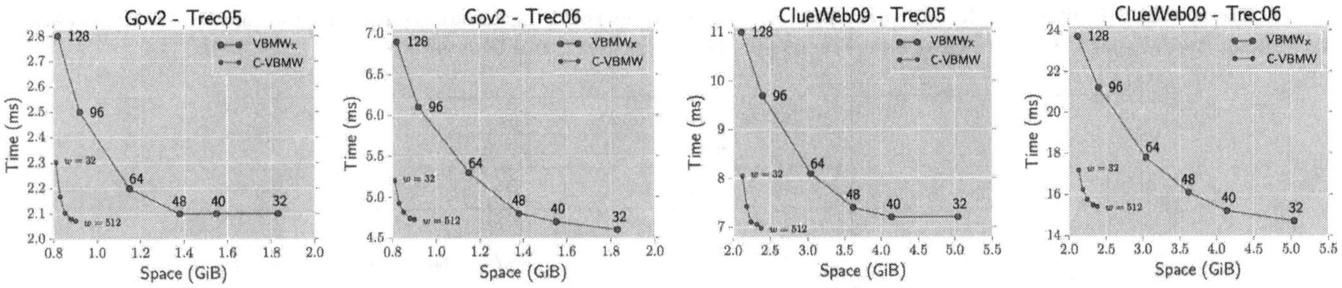

Figure 2: Space consumed vs. average query times of VBMW with different block sizes and C-VBMW with block size 40 by varying w for 32 to 512 with queries in Trec05 and Trec06 on Gov2 and ClueWeb09.

All block-based strategies report a minimal variance of query times among different query lengths. For both the most common block size (128 postings per block) and the most efficient one (40 postings per block), VBMW strategies process queries faster than BMW strategies, with the same space occupancies. The corresponding compressed versions, C-VBMW$_{128}$ and C-VBMW$_{40}$, sensibly reduce the space occupancies (by 6% and 17% respectively) but while C-VBMW$_{128}$ never processes queries faster than the corresponding uncompressed VBMW$_{128}$, C-VBMW$_{40}$ does not show relevant performance losses with respect to VBMW$_{128}$, but exhibits some cache-dependent benefits for short queries.

With respect to the current state-of-the-art processing strategy BMW$_{128}$, our best strategy in terms of query times is C-VBMW$_{40}$, able to improve the average query time by a factor of roughly 2×, effectively halving the query processing times for all query lengths, with a relative 3% – 5% gain in space occupancy. If space occupancy is the main concern, our best strategy is C-VBMW$_{128}$, able to reduce the space by a relative 30% against BMW$_{128}$, while still boosting the query times by a factor of roughly 1.5×.

6 CONCLUSIONS

We introduced Variable BMW, a new query processing strategy built on top of BlockMaxWAND. Our strategy uses variable-sized blocks, rather than constant-sized. We formulated the problem of partitioning the posting lists of a inverted index into variable-sized blocks to minimize the average block error, subject to a constraint on the number of blocks, and described an efficient algorithm to find an approximate solution, with provable approximation guarantees. We also introduced a compressed data structure to represent the additional block information. Variable BMW significantly improves the query processing times, by a factor of roughly 2× w.r.t. the best state-of-the-art competitor. Our new compression scheme for the block data structures, compressing the block boundary docids with Elias-Fano and quantizing the block max score, provides a maximum reduction of space usage w.r.t. the uncompressed data structures of roughly 50%, while incurring only a small speed degradation, no more than 10% with respect to its uncompressed counterpart.

Future work will focus on exploring the different space-time trade-offs that can be obtained by varying the quantization scheme exploited in the compression of the additional data structures.

ACKNOWLEDGMENTS

This work was partially supported by the EU H2020 Program under the scheme INFRAIA-1-2014-2015: *Research Infrastructures*, grant agreement #654024 *SoBigData: Social Mining & Big Data Ecosystem.*

REFERENCES

[1] Alok Aggarwal, Baruch Schieber, and Takeshi Tokuyama. 1994. Finding a Minimum-Weight k-Link Path Graphs with the Concae Monge Property and Applications. *Discrete & Computational Geometry* 12 (1994), 263–280.

[2] Vo Ngoc Anh, Owen de Kretser, and Alistair Moffat. 2001. Vector-space ranking with effective early termination. In *SIGIR.* 35–42.

[3] Nima Asadi and Jimmy Lin. 2013. Effectiveness/Efficiency Tradeoffs for Candidate Generation in Multi-stage Retrieval Architectures. In *SIGIR.* 997–1000.

[4] Andrei Z. Broder, David Carmel, Michael Herscovici, Aya Soffer, and Jason Y. Zien. 2003. Efficient query evaluation using a two-level retrieval process. In *CIKM.* 426–434.

[5] Stefan Büttcher, Charles L.A. Clarke, and Gordon V. Cormack. 2010. *Information retrieval: implementing and evaluating search engines.* MIT Press.

[6] Stefan Büttcher and Charles L. A. Clarke. 2007. Index compression is good, especially for random access. In *CIKM.* 761–770.

[7] Kaushik Chakrabarti, Surajit Chaudhuri, and Venkatesh Ganti. 2011. Interval-based Pruning for Top-k Processing over Compressed Lists. In *ICDE.* 709–720.

[8] Jeffrey Dean. 2009. Challenges in building large-scale information retrieval systems: invited talk. In *WSDM.*

[9] Constantinos Dimopoulos, Sergey Nepomnyachiy, and Torsten Suel. 2013. Optimizing Top-k Document Retrieval Strategies for Block-max Indexes. In *WSDM.* 113–122.

[10] Shuai Ding and Torsten Suel. 2011. Faster top-k document retrieval using block-max indexes. In *SIGIR.* 993–1002.

[11] Peter Elias. 1974. Efficient Storage and Retrieval by Content and Address of Static Files. *J. ACM* 21, 2 (1974), 246–260.

[12] Robert M. Fano. 1971. On the number of bits required to implement an associative memory. *Memorandum 61, Computer Structures Group, MIT, Cambridge, MA* (1971).

[13] Andrea Farruggia, Paolo Ferragina, Antonio Frangioni, and Rossano Venturini. 2014. Bicriteria data compression. In *SODA.* 1582–1595.

[14] Paolo Ferragina, Igor Nitto, and Rossano Venturini. 2011. On Optimally Partitioning a Text to Improve Its Compression. *Algorithmica* 61, 1 (2011), 51–74.

[15] Sudipto Guha, Nick Koudas, and Kyuseok Shim. 2006. Approximation and Streaming Algorithms for Histogram Construction Problems. *ACM Trans. Database Syst.* 31, 1 (2006), 396–438.

[16] Felix Halim, Panagiotis Karras, and Roland H.C. Yap. 2009. Fast and Effective Histogram Construction. In *CIKM.* 1167–1176.

[17] Daniel Lemire and Leonid Boytsov. 2015. Decoding Billions of Integers Per Second Through Vectorization. *Softw. Pract. Exper.* 45, 1 (2015), 1–29.

[18] Craig Macdonald, Iadh Ounis, and Nicola Tonellotto. 2011. Upper-bound approximations for dynamic pruning. *ACM Trans. Inf. Syst.* 29, 4 (2011), 17.

[19] Christopher D. Manning, Prabhakar Raghavan, and Hinrich Schütze. 2008. *Introduction to Information Retrieval.* Cambridge University Press.

[20] Kurt Mehlhorn and Mark Ziegelmann. 2000. Resource Constrained Shortest Paths. In *ESA.* 326–337.

[21] Alistair Moffat, William Webber, Justin Zobel, and Ricardo Baeza-Yates. 2007. A pipelined architecture for distributed text query evaluation. *Inf. Retr.* 10, 3 (2007), 205–231.

[22] Giuseppe Ottaviano, Nicola Tonellotto, and Rossano Venturini. 2015. Optimal Space-time Tradeoffs for Inverted Indexes. In *WSDM.* 47–56.

[23] Giuseppe Ottaviano and Rossano Venturini. 2014. Partitioned Elias-Fano Indexes. In *SIGIR.* 273–282.

Table 6: Query times (in ms) of different query processing strategies for different query lengths, average query times (Avg, in ms) and additional space (Space, in GiB) w.r.t. Trec05 and Trec06 on Gov2 and ClueWeb09.

	Number of query terms					Avg	Space
	2	3	4	5	6+		
Gov2 Trec05							
RankedOR	23.6 (x32.89)	76.5 (x44.39)	147.9 (x59.74)	235.4 (x60.47)	418.7 (x50.18)	106.7 (x50.88)	0.00
WAND	5.1 (x7.11)	5.9 (x3.43)	7.0 (x2.82)	8.8 (x2.27)	17.8 (x2.13)	7.0 (x3.36)	0.22 (5%)
MaxScore	4.7 (x6.61)	6.0 (x3.45)	7.1 (x2.86)	9.2 (x2.37)	14.2 (x1.70)	6.6 (x3.14)	0.22 (5%)
BMW_{40}	1.2 (x1.62)	2.9 (x1.65)	4.3 (x1.72)	6.7 (x1.72)	14.8 (x1.78)	3.6 (x1.74)	1.55 (36%)
$VBMW_{40}$	0.8 (x1.10)	1.7 (x1.01)	2.4 (x0.97)	3.8 (x0.97)	8.1 (x0.97)	2.1 (x1.00)	1.55 (36%)
C-$VBMW_{40}$	0.7	1.7	2.5	3.9	8.3	2.1	0.82 (19%)
BMW_{128}	1.4 (x1.99)	3.5 (x2.01)	4.8 (x1.93)	7.2 (x1.85)	15.9 (x1.90)	4.2 (x1.98)	0.85 (20%)
$VBMW_{128}$	1.0 (x1.42)	2.4 (x1.40)	3.2 (x1.30)	4.9 (x1.26)	10.7 (x1.28)	2.8 (x1.34)	0.85 (20%)
C-$VBMW_{128}$	1.1 (x1.53)	2.5 (x1.47)	3.4 (x1.37)	5.1 (x1.32)	11.3 (x1.36)	3.0 (x1.42)	0.58 (13%)
Gov2 Trec06							
RankedOR	23.1 (x34.72)	83.3 (x42.20)	169.1 (x52.34)	261.3 (x52.20)	470.7 (x37.56)	212.0 (x44.41)	0.00
WAND	4.7 (x7.12)	8.0 (x4.06)	9.3 (x2.86)	12.4 (x2.47)	26.3 (x2.10)	12.9 (x2.69)	0.22 (5%)
MaxScore	4.5 (x6.78)	7.8 (x3.97)	9.2 (x2.83)	11.7 (x2.34)	19.4 (x1.55)	11.3 (x2.37)	0.22 (5%)
BMW_{40}	1.1 (x1.58)	3.2 (x1.62)	5.5 (x1.70)	8.7 (x1.74)	22.1 (x1.76)	8.2 (x1.73)	1.55 (36%)
$VBMW_{40}$	0.8 (x1.12)	2.0 (x1.02)	3.2 (x0.98)	4.9 (x0.98)	12.3 (x0.98)	4.7 (x0.98)	1.55 (36%)
C-$VBMW_{40}$	0.7	2.0	3.2	5.0	12.5	4.8	0.82 (19%)
BMW_{128}	1.2 (x1.88)	3.9 (x1.98)	6.5 (x2.01)	10.1 (x2.03)	23.8 (x1.90)	9.2 (x1.93)	0.85 (20%)
$VBMW_{128}$	0.9 (x1.39)	3.1 (x1.56)	4.7 (x1.45)	7.3 (x1.46)	17.3 (x1.38)	6.9 (x1.43)	0.85 (20%)
C-$VBMW_{128}$	1.0 (x1.48)	3.2 (x1.64)	4.8 (x1.50)	7.6 (x1.52)	18.4 (x1.47)	7.2 (x1.51)	0.58 (13%)
ClueWeb09 Trec05							
RankedOR	77.9 (x36.01)	228.3 (x42.15)	429.3 (x55.20)	659.7 (x50.14)	1,214.0 (x41.72)	312.6 (x43.76)	0.00
WAND	23.8 (x10.98)	29.2 (x5.40)	25.7 (x3.31)	29.1 (x2.21)	57.1 (x1.96)	28.7 (x4.01)	0.53 (4%)
MaxScore	19.3 (x8.91)	22.9 (x4.23)	22.7 (x2.92)	28.1 (x2.14)	42.2 (x1.45)	23.4 (x3.28)	0.53 (4%)
BMW_{40}	4.2 (x1.93)	10.2 (x1.89)	14.7 (x1.89)	22.5 (x1.71)	49.7 (x1.71)	12.6 (x1.76)	4.14 (28%)
$VBMW_{40}$	2.7 (x1.23)	5.7 (x1.06)	7.8 (x1.01)	12.7 (x0.96)	27.8 (x0.96)	7.2 (x1.01)	4.14 (28%)
C-$VBMW_{40}$	2.2	5.4	7.8	13.2	29.1	7.1	2.12 (14%)
BMW_{128}	3.9 (x1.80)	11.2 (x2.06)	16.3 (x2.10)	25.6 (x1.94)	54.0 (x1.85)	13.9 (x1.94)	2.24 (15%)
$VBMW_{128}$	3.1 (x1.43)	8.9 (x1.63)	12.0 (x1.55)	19.2 (x1.46)	42.2 (x1.45)	11.0 (x1.54)	2.24 (15%)
C-$VBMW_{128}$	3.3 (x1.53)	9.6 (x1.77)	12.8 (x1.65)	20.4 (x1.55)	45.4 (x1.56)	12.0 (x1.67)	1.48 (10%)
ClueWeb09 Trec06							
RankedOR	60.6 (x33.63)	215.9 (x37.04)	439.1 (x41.46)	686.5 (x40.57)	1,270.5 (x32.81)	542.5 (x34.56)	0.00
WAND	14.2 (x7.86)	23.1 (x3.96)	27.3 (x2.58)	37.3 (x2.20)	73.8 (x1.91)	37.2 (x2.37)	0.53 (4%)
MaxScore	12.7 (x7.04)	21.3 (x3.66)	27.1 (x2.56)	33.9 (x2.00)	55.0 (x1.42)	32.3 (x2.06)	0.53 (4%)
BMW_{40}	3.2 (x1.77)	10.0 (x1.72)	17.5 (x1.65)	28.1 (x1.66)	65.9 (x1.70)	26.3 (x1.68)	4.14 (28%)
$VBMW_{40}$	2.1 (x1.15)	6.0 (x1.02)	10.3 (x0.97)	16.2 (x0.96)	37.0 (x0.96)	15.2 (x0.96)	4.14 (28%)
C-$VBMW_{40}$	1.8	5.8	10.6	16.9	38.7	15.7	2.12 (14%)
BMW_{128}	3.6 (x1.99)	12.0 (x2.06)	20.9 (x1.97)	32.5 (x1.92)	71.0 (x1.83)	29.4 (x1.87)	2.24 (15%)
$VBMW_{128}$	2.7 (x1.49)	10.0 (x1.71)	16.8 (x1.58)	25.9 (x1.53)	56.6 (x1.46)	23.6 (x1.50)	2.24 (15%)
C-$VBMW_{128}$	2.9 (x1.59)	10.6 (x1.83)	18.0 (x1.69)	28.0 (x1.65)	61.0 (x1.58)	25.2 (x1.60)	1.48 (10%)

[24] Stephen E. Robertson and Karen S. Jones. 1976. Relevance weighting of search terms. *Journal of the Am. Soc. for Information science* 27, 3 (1976), 129–146.

[25] David Salomon. 2007. *Variable-length Codes for Data Compression*. Springer.

[26] Dongdong Shan, Shuai Ding, Jing He, Hongfei Yan, and Xiaoming Li. 2012. Optimized Top-k Processing with Global Page Scores on Block-max Indexes. In *WSDM*. 423–432.

[27] Fabrizio Silvestri. 2007. Sorting Out the Document Identifier Assignment Problem. In *ECIR*. 101–112.

[28] Fabrizio Silvestri and Rossano Venturini. 2010. VSEncoding: Efficient Coding and Fast Decoding of Integer Lists via Dynamic Programming. In *CIKM*. 35–42.

[29] Nicola Tonellotto, Craig Macdonald, and Iadh Ounis. 2013. Efficient and Effective Retrieval Using Selective Pruning. In *WSDM*. 63–72.

[30] Howard Turtle and James Flood. 1995. Query evaluation: Strategies and optimizations. *Information Processing & Management* 31, 6 (1995), 831–850.

[31] Sebastiano Vigna. 2013. Quasi-succinct indices. In *WSDM*. 83–92.

[32] Justin Zobel and Alistair Moffat. 2006. Inverted files for text search engines. *ACM Comput. Surv.* 38, 2 (2006).

LoSHa: A General Framework for Scalable Locality Sensitive Hashing

Jinfeng Li, James Cheng, Fan Yang, Yuzhen Huang, Yunjian Zhao, Xiao Yan, Ruihao Zhao
Department of Computer Science and Engineering
The Chinese University of Hong Kong
{jfli,jcheng,fyang,yzhuang,yjzhao,xyan,rhzhao}@cse.cuhk.edu.hk

ABSTRACT

Locality Sensitive Hashing (LSH) algorithms are widely adopted to index similar items in high dimensional space for approximate nearest neighbor search. As the volume of real-world datasets keeps growing, it has become necessary to develop distributed LSH solutions. Implementing a distributed LSH algorithm from scratch requires high development costs, thus most existing solutions are developed on general-purpose platforms such as Hadoop and Spark. However, we argue that these platforms are both hard to use for programming LSH algorithms and inefficient for LSH computation. We propose LoSHa, a distributed computing framework that reduces the development cost by designing a tailor-made, general programming interface and achieves high efficiency by exploring LSH-specific system implementation and optimizations. We show that many LSH algorithms can be easily expressed in LoSHa's API. We evaluate LoSHa and also compare with general-purpose platforms on the same LSH algorithms. Our results show that LoSHa's performance can be an order of magnitude faster, while the implementations on LoSHa are even more intuitive and require few lines of code.

1 INTRODUCTION

Nearest neighbor (*NN*) search, which finds items similar to a given query item, serves as the foundation of numerous applications such as entity resolution, de-duplication, sequence matching, recommendation, similar item retrieval, and event detection. However, many indexing methods for NN search are inefficient when data dimensionality increases, and eventually perform even worse than brute-force linear scans [20]. Unfortunately, many types of data in real world, including texts, images, audios, DNA sequences, etc., are expressed and processed as high dimensional vectors.

To find similar items in high dimensional space, recent solutions focus on finding *approximate nearest neighbors* (*ANN*), for which *Locality Sensitive Hashing* (*LSH*[1]) [13] is widely recognized as the most effective method [20, 31]. The idea of LSH is that, by using carefully designed hash functions, similar items are hashed to the same bucket with higher probability and one only needs to check a small number of buckets for items similar to a query. LSH can be implemented on relational databases and has sub-linear querying time complexity regardless of the distribution of data/queries [31]. Due to its outstanding query performance and favorable characteristics, LSH algorithms have been extensively studied [7, 8, 12, 14, 19, 31, 32, 36]. There are also numerous applications of LSH in computer vision, machine learning, data mining and database. Due to its significance, LSH is cited as one of the two pieces of "Breakthrough Research" (the other one being MapReduce) by the 50th Anniversary issue of Communications of the ACM.

As we will discuss in Section 2.2.1, LSH algorithms are either *single-probing* or *multi-probing*. Query processing with single-probing LSH is simple but requires hundreds of hash tables in order to achieve good accuracy [30], which results in high memory and CPU usage. LSH algorithms developed in the early days, such as MinHash [2], SimHash [3] and E2LSH [5], belong to this category. In recent years, multi-probing LSH algorithms were proposed to reduce the number of hash tables [7, 12, 20, 24, 29, 31, 36], but the tradeoff is that query processing also becomes more complicated.

LSH is usually used to handle large-scale data (e.g., billions of images [29] or tweets [30]), for which distributed LSH has become necessary (to address the resource limitation of a single machine). However, implementing *distributed multi-probing LSH* is challenging due to the following two main reasons.

First, query processing with multi-probing LSH is complicated to be distributed. In fact, existing multi-probing LSH algorithms mainly adopt external-memory implementations [7, 12, 20, 29, 31, 36], which however have limited query throughput and long delay due to the computing capacity of a single machine.

Second, there is a lack of a general programming framework to implement LSH algorithms on existing general-purpose distributed frameworks such as Hadoop and Spark. While there are works such as Pregel [25] and PowerGraph [10] provide a general programming framework for graph processing [23], and parameter servers [15] for machine learning, there is no such framework for LSH implementations. For this reason, most of the distributed solutions [1, 18, 21, 22, 27, 28, 30] are single-probing LSH only, whose query processing is simple and easy to implement.

To address the above problems, we set out to design a general platform, called **LoSHa**, for LSH workloads with tailor-made abstractions and user-friendly APIs. LoSHa offers a simple `query-answer` programming paradigm (resembling map-reduce) so that users can express different types of LSH algorithms (especially multi-probing LSH) easily and concisely, while implementation details such as

[1]In this paper, LSH refers a broad class of algorithms [14, 32] and will be discussed in Section 2.

SIGIR '17, August 07-11, 2017, Shinjuku, Tokyo, Japan

ACM ISBN 978-1-4503-5022-8/17/08...$15.00
http://dx.doi.org/10.1145/3077136.3080800

defining complicated dataflow, choosing/implementing different operators (e.g., joins, de-duplication), workload distribution, and fault tolerance, are all shielded from users.

We implemented LoSHa as a subsystem upon a general-purpose platform (i.e., Husky [16, 33, 34]) to demonstrate its feasibility. We explored LSH specific data layout and system optimizations, and evaluated LoSHa on large real datasets, including 1 billion tweets and 1 billion image descriptors. Our results show that LoSHa is over an order of magnitude faster than existing LSH implementations [1, 28] on Spark and Hadoop, and can handle 10 times larger datasets with the same computing resources.

2 BACKGROUND

In this section, we give the background of LSH and highlight the challenges of making LSH applications distributed.

2.1 Notion and Notations of LSH

Indyk and Motwani [13] introduced the notion of LSH as follows.

Definition 2.1. Let $B(q, r)$ denote a ball centered at a point q with radius r. A hash function family $\mathcal{H} = \{h : R^d \rightarrow U\}$ is (r_1, r_2, p_1, p_2)-sensitive, if given any $q, o \in R^d$,

(1) if $o \in B(q, r_1)$, then $Pr_{\mathcal{H}}[h(o) = h(q)] \geq p_1$;
(2) if $o \notin B(q, r_2)$, then $Pr_{\mathcal{H}}[h(o) = h(q)] \leq p_2$.

A useful LSH family should satisfy inequality $r_1 < r_2$ and $p_1 > p_2$. For any d-dimensional point $o \in R^d$, a single hash function $h \in \mathcal{H}$ can hash o to a value $v \in U$. Two similar points with distance less than or equal to r_1 have a high probability of at least p_1 to be hashed to the same value, while two dissimilar points with distance larger than r_2 have a low probability of at most p_2 to be hashed to the same value. Some common LSH families include *min-wise permutation* for Jaccard distance [2], *random projection* for angular distance [3], and 2-*stable projection* for Euclidean distance [5], also known as *MinHash*, *SimHash*, and *E2LSH*, respectively.

Intuitively, a hash value $v \in U$ represents a bucket that contains similar items (i.e., points). We denote the probability of two items being hashed to the same value as the *to-same-bucket* probability. To improve the accuracy of LSH, multiple hash tables are generated, and multiple hash values are concatenated and used as a whole for each hash table. Specifically, $L \geq 1$ hash tables, i.e., $G_1, G_2, \ldots, G_L$, are generated. For each hash table, $k \geq 1$ randomly chosen hash functions, $(h_1, h_2, \ldots, h_k)$, are used, and the k hash values of an item o are concatenated to form a *signature*, $G(o) = (h_1(o), h_2(o), \ldots, h_k(o))$. In other words, L signatures, i.e., $G_1(o), G_2(o), \ldots, G_L(o)$, are obtained for the item o. The purpose of using k hash functions and L hash tables is to enlarge the gap of to-same-bucket probability between similar items and dissimilar items [27].

LSH is typically conducted in two phases. The first phase is *pre-processing*, which inserts data items into the hash tables. LSH projects each d-dimensional data item into a k-dimensional vector, i.e., a k-dimensional signature $G_i(o)$, and inserts the item into the corresponding bucket in hash table G_i, for $1 \leq i \leq L$, where $G_i(o)$ is the bucket ID. The second phase is *querying*. Given a *query item* q, we first obtain L bucket IDs for q in the same way as for a data item. Then, data items in the same bucket as q (called *candidate answers*) in each hash table are evaluated to obtain the final answer (e.g., items within a given distance from q). LSH achieves sub-linear querying complexity [13, 31] (as only candidate answers are evaluated) and hence is attractive in practice.

2.2 The State-of-the-art LSH

We first categorize existing LSH algorithms and then analyze the difficulties of implementing them on existing distributed frameworks.

2.2.1 LSH Algorithms. Querying by LSH was originally designed to probe a single bucket (i.e., the bucket q is hashed to) in each of the L hash tables. We name this querying method as *single-probing LSH* and typical examples include MinHash [2], SimHash [3] and E2LSH [5]. Single-probing LSH is simple [1, 18, 21, 22, 27, 28], but it suffers from two weaknesses. First, single-probing LSH is sensitive to r_1 and r_2, but the distance from a query to its nearest neighbor could be any number in practice. To guarantee a high recall (i.e., most of the query answer are found in the set of candidate answers), a large number of hash tables have to be generated [24, 31], which consumes a large amount of memory and incurs high deduplication overhead to remove duplicate candidate answers from the L buckets. For example, 780 hash tables are created in PLSH [30]. Second, single-probing LSH has poor recall if k is large (e.g., 64 or 128) [14, 19]. Thus, it is not applicable to most algorithms [14, 32] that learn hash functions from data and map each item to a hash code of long bits for better precision [19].

To address the weaknesses of single-probing LSH, many *multi-probing LSH* algorithms have been proposed [7, 12, 20, 24, 29, 31, 36]. The main idea is that, if similar items are not in the same bucket as q, they are likely in other buckets in the hash table that are "nearby" q's bucket because *the hashing is locality sensitive.* If we can compute new signatures corresponding to these "nearby" buckets, we can probe multiple buckets in the same hash table to improve the recall. As a result, multi-probing significantly reduces the number of hash tables [7, 12, 20, 24, 36] and effectively improves the recall when k is large [19, 32].

2.2.2 Distributed LSH. Although there are many LSH algorithms, no one can dominate others in all aspects (e.g., precision, recall and efficiency) [14, 26, 32]. And one common problem they have is the handling of large-scale data (e.g., billion-scale tweets or images), for which the typical solution is by distributed computing. To reduce the development cost, general-purpose distributed frameworks are normally used and most of distributed LSH solutions were developed on Hadoop and Spark. However, these distributed solutions are mostly single-probing LSH [1, 18, 21, 22, 27, 28] and suffer from the problems presented in Section 2.2.1. In addition, it is also challenging to implement distributed multi-probing LSH on Hadoop and Spark, due to the following two main factors.

First, to program multi-probing LSH, users need to define a complicated dataflow consisting of many steps. Each step involve multiple operations, and users have to carefully select suitable operators (e.g., which join operator to use) and consider many other implementation details (e.g., how to avoid unnecessary recomputation by data caching on Spark). It is easy to make a wrong choice in some steps, leading to an inefficient or even incorrect

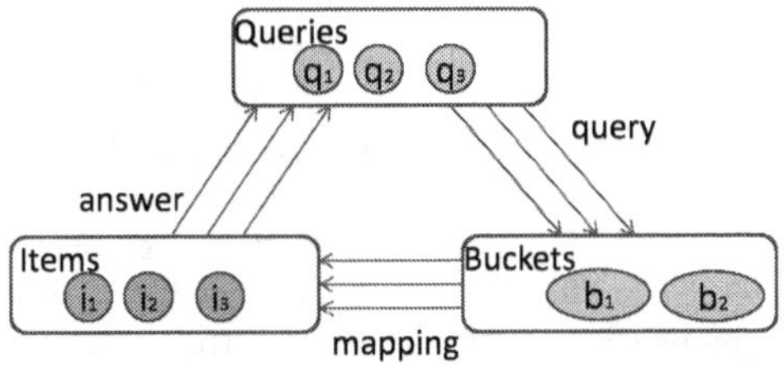

Figure 1: Query processing in LoSHa

implementation, much debugging and performance tuning efforts. To address these problems, we design higher-level abstractions and user-friendly APIs in Section 3, and demonstrate with examples in Section 4 how to implement multi-probing LSH algorithms.

Second, existing general-purpose platforms are not optimized for LSH. For example, in the LSH implementation on these platforms, queries and items are joined on signatures, which means that L copies of items and queries need to be shuffled and sent over the network, leading to high network traffic and enormous memory consumption. Furthermore, the execution strategies of their operators (e.g., join) are not best fit for LSH workloads. To give efficient implementations, users need to do the optimizations by themselves. In Section 5, we explore LSH-specific optimizations so that users are off-loaded from these difficult tasks.

3 LOSHA PROGRAMMING FRAMEWORK

A practical distributed computing framework must provide an easy-to-use programming interface in order to lower the development cost. One well-known example is MapReduce [6], which offers a simple programming interface for easy implementation of many distributed algorithms for data processing. Similarly, for scalable LSH computation, the most important first step is to design a unified programming model and a simple API. However, this is challenging because there are hundreds of LSH algorithms and many of them are complicated to implement, especially parallelizing them. We present the details of the LoSHa programming model in this section.

3.1 Overall Framework

LoSHa uses three data abstractions, `Query`, `Bucket`, and `Item`, to model input queries, buckets, and items, respectively. LoSHa first pre-processes data items to create a set of `Item` objects. It also creates a set of `Bucket` objects, where each `Bucket` object has a bucket ID, `bId`, and all `Item` objects having a signature equal to `bId` belong to this `Bucket` object. Queries are also processed similarly as items to create a set of `Query` objects.

Query processing in LoSHa requires users to specify the querying logic in two user-defined functions, `query` and `answer`. Figure 1 shows the flow of query processing, described as follows. LoSHa processes LSH queries iteratively. In each iteration, each `Query` object calls the `query` function to find a set of *potential buckets* that contain candidate items, and sends a message `QueryMsg` to each potential bucket, where `QueryMsg` contains the content of the query (and any other information required to evaluate the query). When a `Bucket` object receives a `QueryMsg` message, it forwards the message to its `Item` objects. When an `Item` object receives a `QueryMsg` message, it calls the `answer` function to evaluate the query (e.g., calculate the distance between the query and itself), and sends the results (as an `AnswerMsg` message) back to the `Query` object. Then in the next iteration, each `Query` object decides whether the query evaluation is completed or should continue based on the results received from the candidate `Item` objects.

Listing 1 Query API in LoSHa

```
template<typename Id,
    typename Content,
    typename QueryMsg = IdContent<Id, Content>,
    typename AnswerMsg = std::pair<Id, float>>
class Query
  :public IdContent<Id, Content>{
public:
  virtual void query(Factory<Id, Content>& fty);

  const IdContent<Id, Content>& getQuery();

  const std::vector<AnswerMsg>& getAnswerMsg();

  void sendToBucket(Sig& bId, QueryMsg& msg);

  void setFinished();
};
```

Iterative processing allows multi-probing LSH to be easily implemented; while for conventional single-probing LSH, we simply run just one iteration. LoSHa hides the complicated dataflow in the iterative process from users. The underlying system also optimizes key operations such as join and de-duplication, and automatically handles workload distribution and fault tolerance.

3.2 Application Programming Interface

In LoSHa, `Query`, `Bucket` and `Item` objects and their related operations are implemented by the respective `Query`, `Bucket` and `Item` classes in LoSHa's API. To program with LoSHa, users only need to subclass the `Query` and `Item` classes, and overload the `query` and `answer` functions.

The APIs for `Query` and `Item` are shown in Listings 1 and 2. Users specify four template arguments, `Id`, `Content`, `QueryMsg` and `AnswerMsg`. LoSHa expresses a query or an item by an `(Id, Content)` pair, denoted by `IdContent`, where `Id` is the type of the ID of the query/item and is used to locate the query/item, and `Content` is the type of the content of the query/item. LoSHa stores `Content` in a vector. The i-th element can be either the value of the i-th feature of the query/item (i.e., dense vector), or a (pos, v) pair representing the value v of the pos-th feature (i.e., sparse vector). The messages sent out by a query and an item are of type `QueryMsg` and `AnswerMsg`, respectively. For example, `QueryMsg` can be the query itself, i.e., `IdContent`, or just the query ID. An `AnswerMsg` message sent by an item is usually an `(Id, dist)` pair, where `Id` is the item ID and `dist` is the distance between the query and the item. A `Query` or `Item` object may also contain user-defined fields to carry any information useful for query processing.

Query API. Users implement the `query` function to specify the operations to be performed by a `Query` object (see an example in Listing 3). The `Query` class provides a number of built-in functions, and the `query` function may use `getQuery` to obtain a query's `IdContent`, use `getAnswerMsg` to collect messages sent by candidate items, and use `setFinished` to finish the evaluation of a query when the query predicate is satisfied. Signatures of a query

Listing 2 Item API in LoSHa

```
template<typename Id,
    typename Content,
    typename QueryMsg = IdContent<Id, Content>,
    typename AnswerMsg = std::pair<Id, float>>
class Item
  :public IdContent<Id, Content>{
public:
  virtual void answer(Factory<Id, Content>& fty);

  const IdContent<Id, Content>& getItem();

  const std::vector<QueryMsg>& getQueryMsg();

  void sendToQuery(Id& qId, AnswerMsg& msg);
};
```

Listing 3 Single-probing LSH in LoSHa

```
class LSHQuery : public Query<int, float>{
public:
  void query(Factory<int, float>& fty){
    //obtain buckets (i.e., signatures) to probe
    for(auto& bId : fty.calSigs(*this))
      sendToBucket(bId, this->getQuery());
  }
};
class LSHItem : public Item<int, float>{
public:
  void answer(Factory<int, float>& fty){
    //get messages to evaluate
    for(auto& q: getQueryMsg()){
      float dist = fty.calDist(q, *this);
      //output qualified items
    }
  }
};
```

can be calculated by functions provided in the Factory API (to be presented shortly). Each signature corresponds to one bucket ID, which is of type Sig (a k dimensional vector in LoSHa by default), and sendToBucket uses the ID to send messages to the bucket.

Item API. Users may use getQueryMsg in the Item class to collect messages forwarded to the item by Bucket objects, and then specifies in the answer function how to process the messages to evaluate the query (e.g., calculate the distance between the item and the query). The results are then sent via an AnswerMsg message to the corresponding Query object by sendToQuery.

Factory API. Many types of metric spaces are defined for different LSH applications. A different metric space requires a different distance calculation and signature computation. The Factory API allows three user-defined functions to be overloaded. Users can overload the calDist function to calculate the distance between two points in the given metric space, and the calSigs function to compute the signatures for a given point. Some LSHs (e.g., E2LSH [5]) first project an item to a real value and then round it to an integer to obtain the final hash value for the item. Rounding loses proximity information, which is useful for designing some multi-probing LSH strategy. Thus, we provide another function, calProjs, for users to obtain the un-rounded projected real values of a query or an item.

LoSHa supports a Factory library which includes many common metrics such as Hamming distance, Jaccard distance, Euclidean distance, Angular distance, etc. For a wide range of LSH algorithms, users may simply call functions for their applications using any of these metrics, and focus on the design of the querying logic. Users may also implement their own Factory functions for a new metric.

An example. We illustrate how to program with LoSHa's API by implementing a single-probing LSH algorithm, as shown in Listing 3. The query function calls calSigs of the Factory class to compute the signatures of a query, i.e., the IDs of the potential buckets to be probed, and then calls sendToBucket to send the QueryMsg message to each potential bucket. The QueryMsg message is just the query itself in this application.

The answer function simply checks each QueryMsg message forwarded to an item by its bucket, and calls the calDist function of the Factory class to calculate the distance between the item and the query in QueryMsg. The qualified answers are then written to the output.

The single-probing LSH implementation is simple. For multi-probing LSH, we only need to specify the multi-probing strategy in the query function, which we discuss in the following subsection, while in the answer function we simply use sendToQuery to send the results back to the query (instead of writing to the output).

3.3 Multi-probing LSH Strategies

Many multi-probing LSH algorithms have been proposed for various application scenarios [7, 20, 29, 31]. In order to provide a general programming framework for LSH implementations, we identify common patterns in these algorithms. Specifically, in the first iteration, we probe buckets as in single-probing. If the query predicate is not satisfied (e.g., less than K similar items are found), new signatures (i.e., new bucket IDs) are generated according to a multi-probing strategy, and we continue probing these new potential buckets in the next iteration. To demonstrate our framework can support multiple probings well, we adopt two strategies in the experiments and present them below.

Candidate expansion using similar items. The main idea of this strategy is that similar items are more likely to be clustered together. Assume o is a similar item of q returned in the current iteration from the l-th hash table, where $1 \le l \le L$. For each o, the query function computes a set of potential buckets (for the next iteration) with IDs equal to $G_1(o), \dots, G_{l-1}(o), G_{l+1}(o), \dots, G_L(o)$. Since o is returned from the bucket with ID $G_l(o)$ in the l-th hash table, we do not probe this bucket again to avoid duplicate probing. This strategy is good for radius-based search (i.e., return neighbors within a specific distance) as shown in Section 6.2.

Adjusted signatures. Many LSH algorithm [19, 20, 24] will first hash a point to a real value, then truncate it to an integer. The truncation may lose some proximity information between two points. For example, an E2LSH function [5] may hash two point q and o to values 1.001 and 0.999, which are then truncated to 1 and 0, respectively. Although the difference between q and o is only 0.002, it is enlarged by the truncation to 1. Such loss can be dismissed by adjusting the hash value of q from 1 to 0, and the idea has been used to design multi-probing LSH strategies in [24]. We implement the idea in LoSHa as follows. Let $r_i(q)$ be the real value that is truncated to give $h_i(q)$, where $1 \le i \le k$. We first calculate $d_i(q) = r_i(q) - h_i(q)$, sort $d_i(q)$ for $1 \le i \le k$ in ascending order of their values, and keep the sorted list in q's data field. Then, in the i-th iteration after the first iteration, if the query predicate is

Listing 4 Bucket API in LoSHa

```
template<typename Id,
         typename Content,
         typename QueryMsg,
         typename AnswerMsg>
class Bucket{
public:
  virtual void mapping(Factory<Id, Content>& fty);

  const std::vector<QueryMsg>& getQueryMsg();

  void sendToQuery(Id& qId, AnswerMsg& msg);
};
```

not satisfied, let $d_j(q)$ be the i-th value in the sorted list, the query function computes a new potential bucket ID by adjusting the j-th hash value in q's signature. This strategy significantly improves the quality of returned answers for k-nearest-neighbor search as reported in Section 6.4.

3.4 Support for Non-Querying Applications

Some applications of LSH do not require a querying process. For example, for overlapping clustering applied in Google News [4], we can implement it in MapReduce by first computing the signatures of the items in mappers and then distributing the items to reducers based on their L signatures. Each reducer then simply outputs the items distributed to it, labeling them as in the same cluster. Although LoSHa is a framework designed for query processing, we show that LoSHa can also handle such a non-querying workload as easily as MapReduce using the Bucket API given in Listing 4.

We consider each item as a query so that Query acts as Mapper and the query function acts as the map function, while the Item class is simply not used here. We also subclass the Bucket class, which acts as Reducer, and the mapping function of Bucket acts as the reduce function. In addition, our framework also supports efficient implementation of iterative algorithms which are expensive when implemented on the MapReduce framework.

4 APPLICATIONS

In this section, we illustrate how to implement two advanced multi-probing LSH algorithms in LoSHa's framework.

4.1 Multi-Probing PLSH in LoSHa

PLSH [30] is the fastest distributed LSH implementation for angular distance, but it is single-probing LSH and requires a large number of hash tables. We implement the LSH algorithm of PLSH with a multi-probing strategy to reduce the number of hash tables. We denote our implementation as *multi-probing PLSH (MPLSH)*.

Implementing the query function for multi-probing LSH consists of three main steps: *(1) collecting candidates from the previous iteration, (2) deciding whether to finish querying, (3) computing a new set of potential bucket IDs for the next iteration.* In Listing 5, the query function performs the above three steps as follows. First, it collects the candidate items sent from the previous iteration, if any, into a container *cands*. Then, the candidate items in *cands* are used to check whether the query predicate is satisfied (e.g., top K answers have been found), and to decide whether to finish or continue the query evaluation (note that users should output the query results

Listing 5 Multi-probing PLSH in LoSHa

```
class MPLSHQuery
  : public Query<int, Content, QueryMsg, int>{
public:
  virtual void query(Factory<int, Content>& fty){
    //collect candidates into cands
    for(auto& item : getAnswerMsg() )
      cands.insert(item);
    auto finished = ... //decide whether to stop
    if(finished) setFinished();
    //calculate new buckets(signatures) to probe
    auto newSigs = ... //calculate new signatures
    for(auto& bId : newSigs)
      sendToBucket(bId, this->getQuery());
  }
};
class MPLSHItem
  : public Item<int, Content, QueryMsg, int>{
public:
  void answer(Factory<int, Content> &fty){
    for(auto& q: getQueryMsg()){
      float dist = fty.calDist(q, *this);
      if(dist <= 0.9) sendToQuery(q.id, this->id);
    }
  }
};
```

before calling setFinished). If the query predicate is not satisfied yet, a new set of signatures is then calculated (e.g., using a probing strategy described in Section 3.3) and sendToBucket is called to initiate probing the potential buckets for the next iteration.

The answer function is much simpler. We only need to calculate the distance between a candidate item and a query using a standard angular distance calculation function in the Factory class, and calls sendToQuery to send the qualified candidates (e.g., items having an angle smaller than 0.9 from the query) to the query.

4.2 Parallelizing C2LSH with LoSHa

The problem of c-ANN [7] returns a data item o for a query q, such that $d(o, q) \leq c \cdot d(o^*, q)$, where o^* is the exact NN of q, $d(o, q)$ and $d(o^*, q)$ denote the distance between o and q, and between o^* and q. Many multi-probing LSH solutions have been proposed for this problem, but most are external-memory algorithms [7, 20, 29, 31, 36]. With our framework, we can easily implement a parallel version of these multi-probing LSH algorithms, which utilizes the aggregate memory of a cluster instead of resorting to the external memory of a single machine. We illustrate by converting C2LSH [7], one of the most efficient single-core multi-probing external-memory LSH algorithms, into a distributed LSH algorithm with LoSHa.

C2LSH works in Euclidean distance with E2LSH [5] as the hash function family. Only one hash function is used to compute each signature, i.e., $k = 1$, and hence we simply use $h(.)$ for $G(.)$. The query function probes bucket $h(q)$ in the first iteration, and then in the $(i + 1)$-th iteration (for $i > 0$), buckets with ID bId satisfying $\lfloor bId/(c^i) \rfloor = \lfloor h(q)/(c^i) \rfloor$ are probed. In the i-th iteration, the query function calls setFinished if it has collected more than K candidates whose distance to q is less than or equal to c^i, or more than $(K + \beta n)$ candidates are returned, where β is a user-defined percentage of false positives that are allowed and n is the total number of items. In C2LSH, an item o is considered as a candidate only if it collides with q in more than θ probed buckets. Thus, in the answer function, the collision count of an item with each query is maintained (as the data field of the item). If the count is larger than θ for a query q, the item will be sent to q.

Readers may refer to [7] for theoretical guarantees. We remark that the implementation of C2LSH on LoSHa takes about 200 lines of code, while the code of [7] has over 3,000 lines in order to handle large datasets.

5 SYSTEM IMPLEMENTATION

We now present the implementation details of LoSHa.

5.1 System Architecture

LoSHa is designed to run on a shared-nothing cluster with a typical master-worker architecture. The master mainly performs progress checking and coordination on the workers. Each machine in the cluster may run multiple workers, which perform the LSH computation on data.

A LoSHa program proceeds in iterations, where each iteration consists of three steps: `query`, `mapping`, and `answer`. A worker is processed by one thread. While all workers run in parallel, each worker executes in sequence the `query`, `mapping`, and `answer` functions for the sets of queries, buckets, and items that are distributed to the worker. Workers communicate with each other by message passing, and each worker maintains W message buffers, where W is the number of workers in the cluster. For messages to be sent to workers in the same machine, they can be referred without actual payload copy and network communication.

5.2 Data Layout

Data items and queries are stored as `Item` and `Query` objects in LoSHa. LoSHa generates L signatures for each item, using the `calSigs` function of the `Factory` class. Then, a `Bucket` object is created for each distinct signature (which is the ID of the bucket), and for all `Item` objects that have this signature, their item IDs are stored with this `Bucket` object. The `Item`, `Bucket` and `Query` objects are partitioned and distributed among workers by random hashing on their IDs.

LSH computation often requires to deliver messages to the receiving objects by their IDs. This can be implemented by hash join, but it incurs a higher overhead due to random access. We pre-sort objects in each worker by their IDs, and then sort messages by their target object IDs (if not sorted already) and hence the join requires only a linear scan. This allows better data locality and prefetching to improve performance. However, new queries keep coming in and there may also be new items inserted. To avoid incurring high cost in maintaining the pre-sorted order of the objects, we assign the ID of each new `Item`/`Query` object in increasing order as follows: worker i assigns the j-th new object with ID $(i + j * W)$. In this way, we can simply append the new object to the end of the pre-sorted array without re-ordering.

LoSHa's data layout also allows it to implement an efficient two-level join that maps queries first to potential buckets and then to candidate items. In contrast, existing LSH implementations in MapReduce framework require expensive joins on queries and items, which have higher CPU and memory usage, and also higher data transmission cost among the workers, as verified by our experiments.

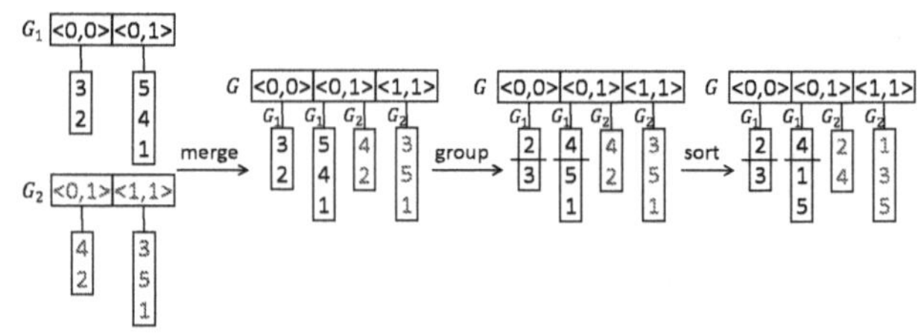

Figure 2: Bucket compression

5.3 Bucket Compression

Each item generates L signatures, and each signature corresponds to a bucket in a hash table. Suppose that each hash table has B distinct signatures on average. This requires $O(LBk)$ space for keeping the bucket objects and thus the memory consumption is high, because both L and B are large. For example, PLSH [30] uses $L = 780$ hash tables and $B = O(2^k)$ where $k = 16$. Note that PLSH is designed for SimHash, where each of the k hash values in a signature is boolean, and B can be much larger for other LSH families [5, 7, 12, 24, 29, 31] where each hash value is an integer.

We found that we can actually reduce the $O(LBk)$ space to $O(Bk)$ space by compressing the buckets with the same signature across the L hash tables. Such a compression is effective based on our observation that the size of the union of the sets of signatures of the L hash tables is cB, where c is usually a small constant. Thus, we can just use one hash table with cB distinct signatures, and keep all the item IDs with the same signature across the L hash tables in one single location. As illustrated in Figure 2, we compress the buckets with the same signature (i.e., $< 0, 1 >$) in the two hash tables G_1 and G_2 into a single bucket in G. Then, we are able to apply further optimizations as follows.

For each list of item IDs kept in a bucket, we first group them by the workers where the real items are stored, and then sort each group. For example, if we have two workers and an item with ID x is stored in worker $x\%2$, then the item IDs in Figure 2 are divided into two groups (i.e., even and odd) and then sorted. This new bucket structure has the following advantages. First, messages sent to multiple `Bucket` objects with the same signature are now sent to a single `Bucket` object. Second, to forward messages to items, we do not need to locate the items by hashing their IDs one by one, as the items are already grouped by their worker IDs and so we can simply forward the messages to their worker. Third, when their worker receives the messages (from multiple workers), we only need to merge them by the target item IDs which are already sorted (thus avoiding sorting during query processing).

5.4 Message Reduction

One major source of messages is the `QueryMsg` messages sent from each `Query` object to its potential buckets and then forwarded to all the items in each potential bucket. Since the `answer` function may calculate the distance between a query and a candidate item, the `QueryMsg` message should contain the query itself (i.e., a high dimensional vector) and thus sending `QueryMsg` messages many times through the network is expensive. To address this problem, we broadcast the query (together with other information needed for its evaluation) to each machine in the cluster, and only send query IDs in `QueryMsg`. Thus, when a worker executes the `answer` function on an item, it simply retrieves the corresponding query from the local machine. This significantly reduces the communication cost especially for multi-probing LSH.

Sending query IDs in QueryMsg and item IDs in AnswerMsg can be still costly since a large number of messages can be created in each step in an iteration. Combiner is a standard technique used to reduce the number of messages [6, 25]. To allow more message reduction, we implement a machine-level combiner. For the same QueryMsg message that is sent to multiple buckets in multiple workers, if these workers are in the same physical machine, LoSHa only sends a single QueryMsg message (together with the set of bucket IDs) to the machine. After reaching the remote machine, a thread is used to deliver the QueryMsg message to the corresponding buckets in each worker in this machine. In addition, all messages sent to the same machine are grouped together and sent in batches to make better use of network bandwidth.

In the mapping step in each iteration, however, we implement a two-level combiner because up to L copies of the same QueryMsg message can be forwarded to the same item, i.e., the item appears in all the L buckets to which the QueryMsg message is sent. We first combine the same QueryMsg messages sent to the same item at the worker level, and then we further combine the messages for the same item at the machine level. Finally, we combine the same QueryMsg messages that are sent to multiple items in multiple workers in the same target machine.

5.5 De-duplication

De-duplication is one of key issues in LSH implementations, as the same query can be mapped to the same item up to L times. In addition, after the query has been evaluated against an item in an iteration, multi-probing may generate new potential bucket IDs in any subsequent iterations such that the same item may appear again in some of these new potential buckets, meaning that the query would be evaluated against the item again if de-duplication is not performed.

De-duplication is mainly done by using a hash set, tree index, or bit vector [30]. In LoSHa, most duplicate copies of the same QueryMsg message sent to the same item have already been eliminated by the two-level combiner described in Section 5.4, and the number of multiple copies of the same QueryMsg message sent to the item from different machines is usually very small. Thus, it is efficient to simply use a hash set to do the de-duplication.

LoSHa also differs from existing work in that we take an flexible approach to decide where de-duplication should be handled. The evaluation of a query against an item (e.g., distance calculation) can be expensive for some applications (e.g., each data item is a dense high dimensional vector), while it is cheap for other applications. If the evaluation is expensive, then de-duplication is performed by an Item object: the item inserts the received QueryMsg messages into a hash set, which removes all duplicate copies. However, keeping a hash set for each item may consume much memory and incur extra cost of deleting old queries. Thus, if the evaluation is not expensive, de-duplication is better performed by a Query object: we allow duplicate copies of a query to be evaluated against an item, but insert duplicate AnswerMsg messages received by the Query object into a hash set, so that duplicate qualified items will be removed and not included in the final answer.

Table 1: Datasets

Dataset	Item#	Dim#	Entry#
SIFT1B	1,000,000,000	128	128
Tweets1B	1,050,000,000	500,000	avg 7.5
Glove2.2M	2,196,017	300	300

5.6 Online Processing and Fault Handling

LoSHa handles online queries and fault tolerance as follows.

Online queries. LoSHa is able to accept queries in real time. New queries will be read into a buffer in LoSHa. A greedy strategy can be used here such that each worker processes approximately the same number of queries. We adopt the mini-batch model as in PLSH [30], where a worker buffers new queries and starts their evaluation in the next iteration. Thus, new queries do not have to wait until all existing queries finish their evaluation.

Fault tolerance. Fault tolerance in LoSHa is by writing a copy of the item and bucket layout in each machine to HDFS. Usually we do infrequent batch-updates and hence we can re-write the entire copy of the item and bucket layout to HDFS each time. If the updates are frequent, we may apply checkpointing periodically. Query evaluation results are not backed up and we simply re-run the queries since the evaluation cost for a query is low.

6 EXPERIMENTAL EVALUATION

We evaluated LoSHa, by comparing with specific LSH implementations on existing general-purpose platforms and a highly optimized system [30] for SimHash. We also assessed the effectiveness of various optimizations in LoSHa and tested its scalability. LoSHa was implemented in C++ and will be made open source on http://www.husky-project.com/.

Setup. We ran the experiments on a cluster of 20 machines connected by a Broadcom's BCM5720 Gigabit Ethernet Controller. Each machine has two 6-core 2.0GHz Intel Xeon E5-2620 processors, 48GB DDR3-1,333 RAM, and a 600GB SATA disk (6Gb/s, 10k rpm, 64MB cache). CentOS 6.5 with 2.6.32 linux kernel and Java 1.8.0 are installed on each machine. We used Hadoop 2.6.0 and Spark 1.6.1. For Hadoop, we set the number of containers to 11 per machine (i.e., one for each core) and each is allocated 4GB RAM, and leave 1 core and 4GB RAM for other operations. For Spark, we set 4 workers per machine, and each worker is assigned 3 cores and 11GB RAM. We ran Spark on its standalone mode.For LoSHa, we used 12 cores per machine.

Datasets. We used three real datasets. For dense vectors, we used the largest publicly available dataset for ANN search, denoted by SIFT1B, which contains 1 billion SIFT image descriptors from http://corpus-texmex.irisa.fr/. We also used another dataset, denoted by Glove2.2M, which contains about 2.2 million vector representations for words obtained from http://nlp.stanford.edu/projects/glove/ (Common Crawl: 840B tokens, 2.2M vocab, cased, 300d vectors). For sparse vectors, we crawled 1.05 billion tweets from Twitter, denoted by Tweets1B. Table 1 lists the number of items (Item#), the number of dimensions of each item vector (Dim#), and the number of non-empty entries in each vector (Entry#).

For each dataset, we randomly selected 1,000 items as queries and removed these items from the datasets. Each query finds the top 10 ANNs of the query (unless otherwise specified).

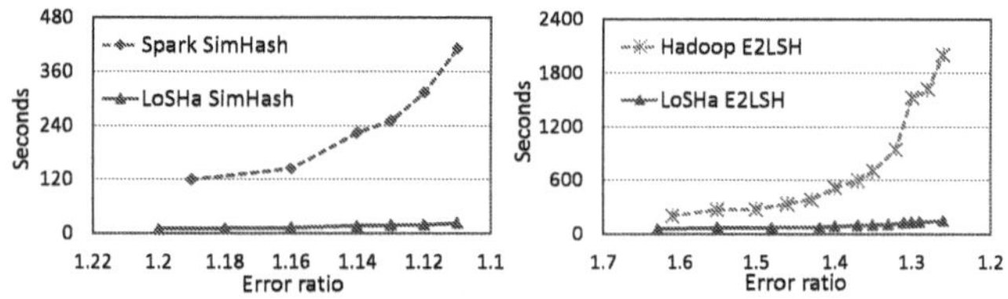

(a) **SimHash on** `Glove2.2M` (b) **E2LSH on** `SIFT0.1B`

Figure 3: Overall running time vs. Error ratio

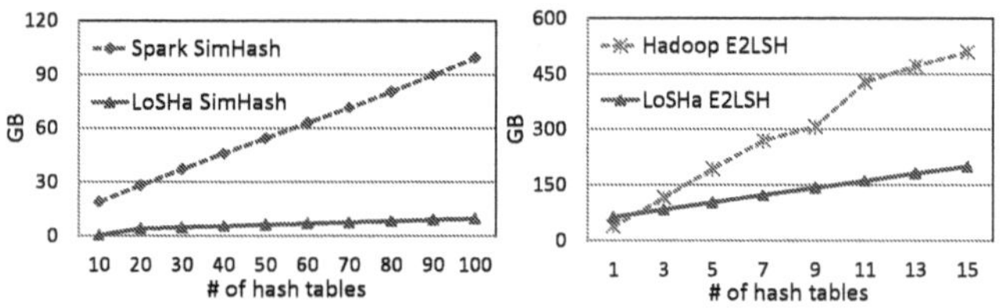

(a) **SimHash on** `Glove2.2M` (b) **E2LSH on** `SIFT0.1B`

Figure 4: Network traffic vs. Number of hash tables

Quality measure. Given a query set Q, let $o_1, o_2, \ldots, o_K$ be the top K ANNs returned by an LSH algorithm and $o_1^*, o_2^*, ..., o_K^*$ be the exact top K NNs. Let $d(o, q)$ denote the distance between o and q. *Error ratio*, $ER = (1/(|Q|K)) \sum_{q \in Q} \sum_{i=1}^{K} (d(o_i, q)/d(o_i^*, q))$, is widely used in existing work [7, 9, 20, 29, 31, 36] to measure the quality of their algorithm. A smaller error ratio means better quality of results, and an error ratio of 1 means that the exact results are found. But for single-probing LSH algorithms, there is no guarantee that K answers will be found. Thus, for those algorithms, we only used the number of answers returned to calculate the error ratio, and removed the query from Q if no answer was returned.

6.1 Comparison with LSH on Spark/Hadoop

We first compared LoSHa with specific LSH implementations on Spark and Hadoop. On Spark, SoundCloud implemented SimHash [3], which is used in production [28] and the most popular LSH implementation on Spark. We denote it by *Spark SimHash* and compared it with our implementation of SimHash on LoSHa, denoted by *LoSHa SimHash*. On Hadoop, we used the *Hadoop E2LSH* implementation provided by the authors of [1] and compared it with our implementation of E2LSH [5] on LoSHa, denoted by *LoSHa E2LSH*. Spark SimHash and Hadoop E2LSH have more than 800 and 1500 lines of Scala/Java code, respectively, while both LoSHa SimHash and LoSHa E2LSH have about 100 lines of C++ code.

Since both Spark SimHash and Hadoop E2LSH are slow and require a lot of computing resources to process large datasets, we could only test them on smaller datasets. SimHash is designed for angular distance and is used for querying text data, and thus we used the `Glove2.2M` dataset. We set $k = 20$ as normally used by Spark SimHash, and varied L from 10 to 100. E2LSH is for Euclidean space and thus we used it to query the SIFT image descriptor dataset. However, `SIFT1B` is too large for Hadoop E2LSH and thus we only used 0.1 billion items, denoted by `SIFT0.1B`. We set $k = 20$ and varied L from 1 to 15 (note that the running time of Hadoop E2LSH increases dramatically for larger L).

We report the overall running time of the four implementations in Figure 3. As we increase L, i.e., the number of hash tables, the running time also increases but the error ratio decreases. However, the running time of LoSHa increases much slower than Spark SimHash and Hadoop E2LSH. LoSHa SimHash attains an error ratio of 1.11 in 22.6 seconds, while Spark SimHash requires 411.6 seconds. LoSHa E2LSH attains an error ratio of 1.26 in 145.3 seconds, while Hadoop E2LSH uses 2,005.9 seconds.

The superior performance of LoSHa over the Spark/Hadoop implementations is mainly brought by our LSH-specific system implementation such as fine-grained data access and fast joins enabled by the data layout. In contrast, the Spark/Hadoop implementations follow the simple logic that joins queries and items by signatures (as discussed in Section 2.2.2), which incurs high network communication cost. As shown in Figure 4, LoSHa has significantly less network traffic (i.e., the total volume of messages sent over the network) than Spark/Hadoop, which verify the effectiveness of our LSH-specific system implementation. Note that Spark or Hadoop implementations may be made more efficient, but it will require non-trivial programming efforts from users. A better way could be to implement LoSHa upon Spark and Haoop, so that users need not worry about LSH-specific optimization details. Implementing the LoSHa framework upon Spark/Haoop, however, is not the objective of our work, which we leave as future work.

In Section 6.3, we will also compare LoSHa with the C++ MapReduce implementation as we examine in details the effectiveness of the optimization techniques in LoSHa.

6.2 Comparison with PLSH

This experiment compared LoSHa with PLSH [30], a highly optimized distributed implementation of SimHash [3]. Unfortunately, we could not obtain the code of PLSH to repeat their experiments. We could only try to mimic their experiments on LoSHa. We summarize our results in Figure 5.

PLSH achieved a recall of 92% by building 780 hash tables for processing 1 billion tweets, which requires 6.4TB RAM in 100 machines. If we use SimHash, we can generate at most 55 hash tables with the total 0.96TB of memory in our cluster, thus giving a poor recall of 27.4% only. Thus, we implemented the multi-probing version of SimHash (denoted as multi-probing SimHash) using the "Candidate expansion using similar items" strategy in Section 3.3, which improves the recall from 27.4% to 86.8% with only 55 hash tables. We further measured the average querying time of multi-probing SimHash, which is 1.86ms (vs. 1.42ms of PLSH). The result is significant since LoSHa can process the same-scale data and achieve performance not much worse than PLSH which uses significantly more computing resources (i.e., RAM and CPU).

We emphasize that PLSH is a specific system highly optimized for SimHash only, while LoSHa is a general framework for implementing different types of LSH algorithms and thus it is expected that LoSHa has poorer performance than PLSH for SimHash. In fact, it is the multi-probing strategy that helps LoSHa to achieve high performance using much less resources than PLSH. Therefore, it is necessary for a system to be user-friendly for implementing multi-probing algorithms. Note that our implementation of multi-probing SimHash has about 100 lines of effective code only, but it is definitely non-trivial to implement PLSH [30]. Thus, we believe that

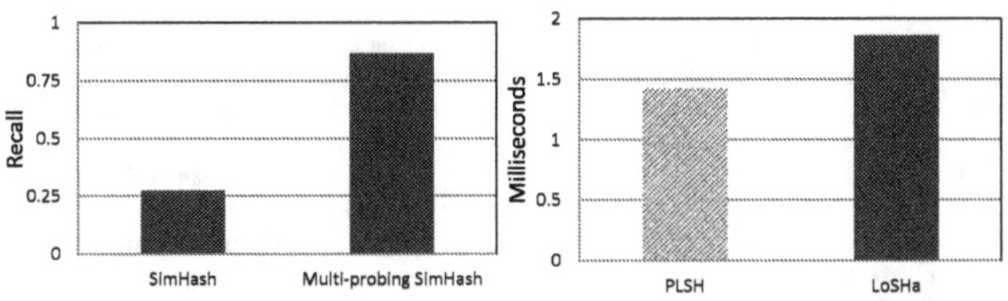

(a) Recall (b) Average querying time

Figure 5: Performance of multi-probing LoSHa

Table 2: Effectiveness of optimizations in LoSHa

	Glove2.2M		Tweets0.21B	
	Querying time	Network traffic	Querying time	Network traffic
LoSHa	0.52s	0.140GB	30.21s	20.13GB
No de-duplication	0.48s	0.143GB	82.38s	74.98GB
No message reduction	3.09s	4.95GB	282.29s	526.95GB
MapReduce LoSHa	187.61s	355.34GB	failed	failed

the abstraction, API and LSH-specific implementation of LoSHa can help promote multi-probing LSH on existing distributed platforms.

6.3 Effects of Optimization Techniques

We now examine the effectiveness of the various optimizations implemented in LoSHa. To do that, we created four versions of LoSHa: (1) LoSHa with all optimizations enabled, (2) LoSHa without performing de-duplication, (3) LoSHa by disabling the message reduction techniques (i.e., query broadcasting and various combiners), and (4) LoSHa by applying MapReduce (in C++) instead of the two-level join.

We first tested the performance of the four versions of LoSHa running SimHash on Glove2.2M, with $k = 20$ and $L = 100$. We also tested on a larger dataset, Tweets0.21B, by processing 0.21 billion tweets from Tweets1B, i.e., each machine processes 10.5 million tweets. As Tweets0.21B is too large for single-probing SimHash to work, we used the multi-probing SimHash, with $k = 16$ and $L = 55$. We report the time and network traffic for processing 1,000 queries in Table 2. We discuss the effects of different optimizations as follows.

Effect of de-duplication. By disabling de-duplication, the querying time of LoSHa for Glove2.2M is even reduced from 0.52s to 0.48s. This is because word vectors in Glove2.2M are relatively different from each other and thus the amount of duplicate processing is small, as verified by the similar volumes of network traffic measured for LoSHa and LoSHa without de-duplication. Note that duplicate copies may also be already removed by the two-level combiner in LoSHa (see details in Sections 5.4 and 5.5). On the other hand, de-duplication itself incurs overhead and thus the overall time may be even reduced without de-duplication. For the tweets dataset, however, disabling de-duplication significantly degrades the performance and query processing is almost 3 times slower. This is because many tweets are highly similar and thus the amount

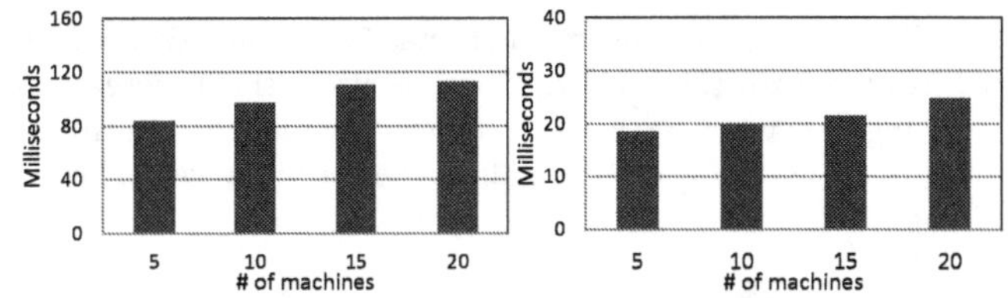

(a) M-SimHash on Tweets1B (b) M-E2LSH on SIFT1B

Figure 6: Average query time vs. Number of machines

of duplicate processing is much larger. In addition, we use multi-probing for Tweets0.21B, and hence duplicate candidates make queries probe more buckets in subsequent iterations. Thus, the volume of network traffic is also significantly increased from 20.13GB to 74.98GB when de-duplication is disabled in LoSHa.

Effect of message reduction. The importance of the message reduction techniques is obvious as disabling them immediately increases the network traffic by 35 times for Glove2.2M and 26 times for Tweets0.21B. As a result, communication cost dominates the total querying cost and thus the overall query performance is also severely degraded.

Effect of two-level join. LoSHa's data layout, which enables the two-level join for query processing, is the most critical optimization. When we replace the two-level join with a Map-Reduce procedure, a large number of messages are transmitted over the network and the processing time is also severely increased. Note that both machine-level combiner and de-duplication are already enabled. For Tweets0.21B, the system ran out of the (48 x 20)GB of aggregate memory in the cluster. Note that the Map-Reduce procedure is essentially a hash join between queries and items on their signatures, but it generates much more messages than the two-level join employed with LoSHa's data layout.

6.4 Scalability

We tested the scalability of LoSHa with the two billion-scale datasets, Tweets1B and SIFT1B. We varied the number of machines from 5 to 20, while fixing the number of data items per machine to 50 million.

For querying the tweets, we ran multi-probing SimHash (denoted by *M-SimHash*), with $k = 16$ and $L = 55$, as in Section 6.2. We report the average querying time for processing 1,000 queries in Figure 6a, which shows a gentle slowdown in query processing when the number of machines increases. Since the number of data items increases in the same rate as the increase in the number of machines, the small increase in querying time is reasonable as more data are transmitted through the network and also more coordination among workers is needed. We observed that there was no obvious straggler during the whole process and thus the slowdown is more likely to be caused by communication, for which a faster network (e.g., Infiniband instead of Gigabit Ethernet) will help reduce the slowdown.

We ran LoSHa E2LSH to query the SIFT data and used $k = 20$ as in Section 6.1. However, we could use at most 3 hash tables because the number of items is increased to 50 million per machine (note that unlike a tweet, a SIFT item is a dense vector). The error ratio is

1.72. Thus, we implemented multi-probing E2LSH on LoSHa, which reduces the error ratio to 1.23. There is also a small increase in querying time when we increase the number of machines from 5 to 20, as shown in Figure 6b, for the same reason as we explained for Figure 6a.

7 RELATED WORK

LSH [13] has been extensively studied and various hash function families for different metrics have been developed, such as l_p distance [5], angular distance [3], Jaccard distance [2], and so on. Since single-probing [1, 18, 21, 22, 27, 28] requires a large number of hash tables and cannot scale to handle large datasets, many multi-probing LSH algorithms have been proposed to use fewer hash tables and yet achieve comparable quality of results [7, 12, 20, 24, 29, 31, 36]. However, they are single-core algorithms and many still rely on external memory to handle large datasets.

Recently more distributed LSH algorithms have been developed to handle larger datasets. PLSH [30] is a highly optimized LSH implementation for distributed SimHash [3], but the development cost of such a system tailor-made only for one specific LSH algorithm is too high for general applications. Most existing distributed LSH algorithms were implemented on general-purpose platforms such as Hadoop [1, 18, 21], Spark [22, 28], and distributed hash tables [11]. However, these general-purpose platforms are not designed for solving domain-specific problems and thus the LSH implementations on these platforms are also inefficient.

For solving problems in a particular domain, quite a number of domain-specific systems, such as Parameter Server [17], PowerGraph [10] and LFTF [35], etc., have been developed, with which one can easily implement different types of distributed machine learning and graph analytics algorithms in one framework. However, we are not aware of any work on the development of a general framework that allows efficient and scalable implementation of all kinds of LSH algorithms.

8 CONCLUSIONS

We presented LoSHa, which offers a general, unified programming framework and a user-friendly API for easy implementation of a wide range of LSH algorithms. We explored various LSH-specific system implementation and optimizations to enable scalable LSH computation. Our experiments on billion-scale datasets verified the efficiency, scalability, and quality of results obtained by LoSHa's implementations of a number of popular LSH algorithms. We believe that LoSHa can benefit many applications of LSH as it can significantly lower the development cost and achieve high performance. Such a general framework for LSH can also lead to the development of more efficient distributed algorithms for new LSH applications.

Ack. This work was partially supported by Grants (CUHK 14206715 & 14222816) from the Hong Kong RGC, ITF 6904079, and Grant 3132821 funded by the Research Committee of CUHK.

REFERENCES

[1] B. Bahmani, A. Goel, and R. Shinde. Efficient distributed locality sensitive hashing. In *CIKM*, pages 2174–2178, 2012.
[2] A. Z. Broder, M. Charikar, A. M. Frieze, and M. Mitzenmacher. Min-wise independent permutations (extended abstract). In *STOC*, pages 327–336, 1998.
[3] M. Charikar. Similarity estimation techniques from rounding algorithms. In *STOC*, pages 380–388, 2002.
[4] A. Das, M. Datar, A. Garg, and S. Rajaram. Google news personalization: scalable online collaborative filtering. In *WWW*, pages 271–280, 2007.
[5] M. Datar, N. Immorlica, P. Indyk, and V. S. Mirrokni. Locality-sensitive hashing scheme based on p-stable distributions. In *SCG*, pages 253–262, 2004.
[6] J. Dean and S. Ghemawat. Mapreduce: Simplified data processing on large clusters. In *OSDI*, pages 137–150, 2004.
[7] J. Gan, J. Feng, Q. Fang, and W. Ng. Locality-sensitive hashing scheme based on dynamic collision counting. In *SIGMOD*, pages 541–552, 2012.
[8] J. Gao, H. V. Jagadish, W. Lu, and B. C. Ooi. DSH: data sensitive hashing for high-dimensional k-nnsearch. In *SIGMOD*, pages 1127–1138, 2014.
[9] A. Gionis, P. Indyk, and R. Motwani. Similarity search in high dimensions via hashing. In *VLDB*, pages 518–529, 1999.
[10] J. E. Gonzalez, Y. Low, H. Gu, D. Bickson, and C. Guestrin. Powergraph: Distributed graph-parallel computation on natural graphs. In *OSDI*, pages 17–30, 2012.
[11] P. Haghani, S. Michel, and K. Aberer. Distributed similarity search in high dimensions using locality sensitive hashing. In *EDBT*, pages 744–755, 2009.
[12] Q. Huang, J. Feng, Y. Zhang, Q. Fang, and W. Ng. Query-aware locality-sensitive hashing for approximate nearest neighbor search. In *PVLDB*, volume 9, pages 1–12, 2015.
[13] P. Indyk and R. Motwani. Approximate nearest neighbors: Towards removing the curse of dimensionality. In *STOC*, pages 604–613, 1998.
[14] Learning to Hash. http://cs.nju.edu.cn/lwj/l2h.html. 2017.
[15] S. Lee, J. K. Kim, X. Zheng, Q. Ho, G. A. Gibson, and E. P. Xing. On model parallelization and scheduling strategies for distributed machine learning. In *NIPS*, pages 2834–2842, 2014.
[16] J. Li, J. Cheng, Y. Zhao, F. Yang, Y. Huang, H. Chen, and R. Zhao. A comparison of general-purpose distributed systems for data processing. In *IEEE BigData*, pages 378–383, 2016.
[17] M. Li, D. G. Andersen, J. W. Park, A. J. Smola, A. Ahmed, V. Josifovski, J. Long, E. J. Shekita, and B. Su. Scaling distributed machine learning with the parameter server. In *OSDI*, pages 583–598, 2014.
[18] LikeLike. https://github.com/takahi-i/likelike. 2017.
[19] W. Liu, J. Wang, S. Kumar, and S. Chang. Hashing with graphs. In *ICML*, pages 1–8, 2011.
[20] Y. Liu, J. Cui, Z. Huang, H. Li, and H. T. Shen. SK-LSH: an efficient index structure for approximate nearest neighbor search. In *PVLDB*, volume 7, pages 745–756, 2014.
[21] LSH-Hadoop. https://github.com/lancenorskog/lsh-hadoop. 2017.
[22] LSH-Spark. https://github.com/marufaytekin/lsh-spark. 2017.
[23] Y. Lu, J. Cheng, D. Yan, and H. Wu. Large-scale distributed graph computing systems: An experimental evaluation. In *PVLDB*, volume 8, pages 281–292, 2014.
[24] Q. Lv, W. Josephson, Z. Wang, M. Charikar, and K. Li. Multi-probe LSH: efficient indexing for high-dimensional similarity search. In *VLDB*, pages 950–961, 2007.
[25] G. Malewicz, M. H. Austern, A. J. C. Bik, J. C. Dehnert, I. Horn, N. Leiser, and G. Czajkowski. Pregel: a system for large-scale graph processing. In *SIGMOD*, pages 135–146, 2010.
[26] L. Paulevé, H. Jégou, and L. Amsaleg. Locality sensitive hashing: A comparison of hash function types and querying mechanisms. In *Pattern Recognition Letters*, volume 31, pages 1348–1358, 2010.
[27] A. Rajaraman, J. D. Ullman, J. D. Ullman, and J. D. Ullman. *Mining of massive datasets*, volume 1. 2012.
[28] SoundCloud-LSH. https://github.com/soundcloud/cosine-lsh-join-spark. 2017.
[29] Y. Sun, W. Wang, J. Qin, Y. Zhang, and X. Lin. SRS: solving c-approximate nearest neighbor queries in high dimensional euclidean space with a tiny index. In *PVLDB*, volume 8, pages 1–12, 2014.
[30] N. Sundaram, A. Turmukhametova, N. Satish, T. Mostak, P. Indyk, S. Madden, and P. Dubey. Streaming similarity search over one billion tweets using parallel locality-sensitive hashing. In *PVLDB*, volume 6, pages 1930–1941, 2013.
[31] Y. Tao, K. Yi, C. Sheng, and P. Kalnis. Quality and efficiency in high dimensional nearest neighbor search. In *SIGMOD*, pages 563–576, 2009.
[32] J. Wang, H. T. Shen, J. Song, and J. Ji. Hashing for similarity search: A survey. In *CoRR*, volume abs/1408.2927, 2014.
[33] F. Yang, Y. Huang, Y. Zhao, J. Li, G. Jiang, and J. Cheng. The best of both worlds: Big data programming with both productivity and performance. In *SIGMOD*, pages 1619–1622, 2017.
[34] F. Yang, J. Li, and J. Cheng. Husky: Towards a more efficient and expressive distributed computing framework. In *PVLDB*, volume 9, pages 420–431, 2016.
[35] F. Yang, F. Shang, Y. Huang, J. Cheng, J. Li, Y. Zhao, and R. Zhao. LFTF: A framework for efficient tensor analytics at scale. In *PVLDB*, volume 10, pages 745–756, 2017.
[36] Y. Zheng, Q. Guo, A. K. Tung, and S. Wu. Lazylsh: Approximate nearest neighbor search for multiple distance functions with a single index. In *SIGMOD*, 2016.

Learning a Hierarchical Embedding Model for Personalized Product Search

Qingyao Ai[1], Yongfeng Zhang[1], Keping Bi[1], Xu Chen[2], W. Bruce Croft[1]
[1]College of Information and Computer Sciences, University of Massachusetts Amherst
Amherst, MA, USA 01003-9264
{aiqy,yongfeng,kbi,croft}@cs.umass.edu
[2]School of Software, Tsinghua University
Beijing, China 100084
xu-ch14@mails.tsinghua.edu.cn

ABSTRACT

Product search is an important part of online shopping. In contrast to many search tasks, the objectives of product search are not confined to retrieving relevant products. Instead, it focuses on finding items that satisfy the needs of individuals and lead to a user purchase. The unique characteristics of product search make search personalization essential for both customers and e-shopping companies. Purchase behavior is highly personal in online shopping and users often provide rich feedback about their decisions (e.g. product reviews). However, the severe mismatch found in the language of queries, products and users make traditional retrieval models based on bag-of-words assumptions less suitable for personalization in product search. In this paper, we propose a hierarchical embedding model to learn semantic representations for entities (i.e. words, products, users and queries) from different levels with their associated language data. Our contributions are three-fold: (1) our work is one of the initial studies on personalized product search; (2) our hierarchical embedding model is the first latent space model that jointly learns distributed representations for queries, products and users with a deep neural network; (3) each component of our network is designed as a generative model so that the whole structure is explainable and extendable. Following the methodology of previous studies, we constructed personalized product search benchmarks with Amazon product data. Experiments show that our hierarchical embedding model significantly outperforms existing product search baselines on multiple benchmark datasets.

KEYWORDS

Product Search, Personalization, Latent Space Model, Representation Learning

1 INTRODUCTION

Product search represents a special retrieval scenario where users submit queries to retrieve products from a search engine. The most direct application of product search is online shopping. E-shopping has become an important part of our lives today. About 8% (more than 300 billion dollars) of U.S. retail sales came from e-commerce and 71% of U.S. customers shopped online in 2015[1]. In a typical e-shopping scenario, users express their needs through queries submitted to a product search engine and explore the retrieved results to find items of interest (e.g., search on Amazon.com). Therefore, the quality of product search directly affects both user satisfaction with online shopping and the profits of e-commerce companies.

In contrast to traditional ad-hoc retrieval tasks, the concept of relevance can be highly personal in product search. Ad-hoc retrieval tasks, such as web search, focus on retrieving documents that satisfy a user's information need, which is usually related to the query topic. Although personalization is important in web search, it is not as fundamental as it is in product search since users actually want to purchase items from the result list, which is a more personal behavior. On the one hand, while multiple items could be topic-related with a user's query, only a few are actually purchased and different individuals have different opinions even on the same product (such as music CDs). Product search without considering users' differences will not satisfy the needs of all customers. On the other hand, personalization has explicit benefits for e-commerce companies as it potentially increases the chance of users to see the products that they are likely to buy. Retrieving relevant products is less important than finding potential items for purchase because the latter brings direct profits to sellers. Even a small improvement on personalized product search could be worth millions of dollars.

Personalization in product search has both potentials and pitfalls. Users of e-shopping websites often provide rich feedback about their purchases. The reviews written by customers provide information about both product properties and user preferences, which give the search engine more opportunities to learn and understand each individual. Using the review text, however, is not trivial because of the the significant vocabulary mismatch between the language of queries, products and users [30]. For example, the words used in reviews of a TV may not be found in the descriptions of a camera. Without capturing their semantic meanings, user reviews cannot provide useful information for personalized product search on a new query.

The main focus of this paper is to tackle the problem of personalized product search based on language data (i.e. words and reviews). Despite its importance in e-commerce, personalized product search has not been extensively studied so far. To the best of our knowledge, previous work focuses on product recommendation

SIGIR '17, August 07-11, 2017, Shinjuku, Tokyo, Japan

DOI: http://dx.doi.org/10.1145/3077136.3080813

[1]https://www.readycloud.com/info/ecommerce-statistics-all-retailers-should-know

in a non-search scenario [18, 19] or general product search without personalization [30]. To fill this gap, we propose a hierarchical embedding model specifically designed for personalized product search. Inspired by recent progress in distributed representation learning [2, 15], we construct a deep neural network and jointly learn latent representations for queries, products and users. Our hierarchical embedding model has three merits. First, it is a vector space model that represents queries, products and users with latent representations. The vocabulary mismatch problems in personalized product search can be effectively alleviated by conducting product retrieval in our latent semantic space. Second, our model is intentionally designed as a generative model. The likelihood of observed user-query-item triples can be directly inferred with their distributed representations, which makes the whole framework explainable and extendable. Last, our model is trained with stochastic gradient decent, which is efficient for training on GPUs and deployment in real systems. Following the methodology proposed by Gysel et al. [30], we constructed personalized product search benchmarks on Amazon product data and conducted empirical experiments to evaluate the effectiveness of our model. Our hierarchical embedding model significantly outperforms baselines including unigram-based retrieval models and the state-of-the-art latent space model for product retrieval. This demonstrates the potential of personalization with language data in product search.

2 RELATED WORK

There are three lines of research that are directly related to our work: product search, search personalization, and latent space models for information retrieval.

2.1 Product Search

The search function is important for exploring and finding products [14]. Most of the basic product information (i.e. brands, types and categories) can be structured and stored with relational databases. Considerable work has been done on searching products based on their structured aspects [17]. Despite their important applications in e-commerce, searching with structured data is not enough to satisfy the needs of e-shopping users. First, queries of product search users are often in natural language and are hard to structure. Duan et al. [10] noticed that, while languages like SQL are effective for querying structured databases, people tend not to use them in practice because they are difficult to learn. They [9, 10] propose a probabilistic mixture model to analyze product search logs from attribute levels and extend product databases with language modeling approaches to enable conditional search on specifications. Duan et al. [8] also tried to learn query representations for structured product data. Second, there is a gap between the language of product descriptions and free-form user queries. Nurmi et al. [23] reported that users' shopping lists often differ from the product information maintained by retailers. They designed a grocery retrieval system to directly retrieve products using the shopping lists written in natural language. Gysel et al. [30] also noticed the vocabulary mismatch problem existing in product search and introduced a latent vector space model that maps queries and products into a hidden semantic space for product retrieval. These studies are important steps toward language-based product search, but they ignore the effect of users in online shopping and only use the topic relevance between queries and products as their measurement of retrieval quality. In this paper, we focus on personalizing product search for each individual and use the actual purchase behavior as our gold standard.

2.2 Search Personalization

To the best of our knowledge, there are two types of personalized search: search on a personal collections (e.g. email search [6, 24]), and search on a general corpus with personalized result lists (e.g. web search [11, 22, 29]). The product search discussed in this paper is more related to studies on the latter since product collections are equally accessible for most users. In web search, research on personalization focuses on constructing user models with user-specific contents (i.e. queries), behaviors (i.e. click, clicked pages), contexts (i.e. location, time) and uses them to refine the ranked list produced by a global retrieval model [11]. Agichtein et al. [1] studied the clicks of users and introduced a behavior model to measure user preferences with the features extracted from queries, web pages and click-through logs. Teevan et al. [29] measure the ambiguity of web queries and propose a ranking model that incorporates personalizations with different strengths on different queries. In this paper, we focus on a different search scenario where users provide explicit feedback (product reviews) on some search results. To the best of our knowledge, our work is the first study that uses deep neural networks to learn user models from language data for personalized product search.

2.3 Latent Space Models

Latent space models have been widely studied for information retrieval. The basic idea of latent space models is to project both queries and documents into a high dimensional semantic space so that we can directly match their conceptual meanings and avoid vocabulary mismatch problems. Deerwester et al. [7] introduced Latent Semantic Indexing (LSI) and constructed latent vectors for words and documents by factorizing the corpus matrix of term frequency with singular value decomposition (SVD). Hofmanm[13] and Blei et al. [4] proposed pLSI and LDA by assuming that words are sampled from a fixed number of topics and documents are topic distributions. More recently, distributed representation learning with deep neural networks has attracted more attentions. Mikolov et al. [20] proposed a word2vec model which can efficiently learn high quality word embeddings on a large corpus. Le and Mikolov [15] constructed paragraph vector models to simultaneously learn distributed representations for words and documents. It has been shown that the paragraph vector model with distributed bag-of-words assumption (PV-DBOW) implicitly factorizes a tf-icf matrix and constructs a language model that is effective for semantic matching in information retrieval [2]. Inspired by these studies, we design a hierarchical embedding model to jointly learn distributed representations of words, queries, products and users for personalized product search.

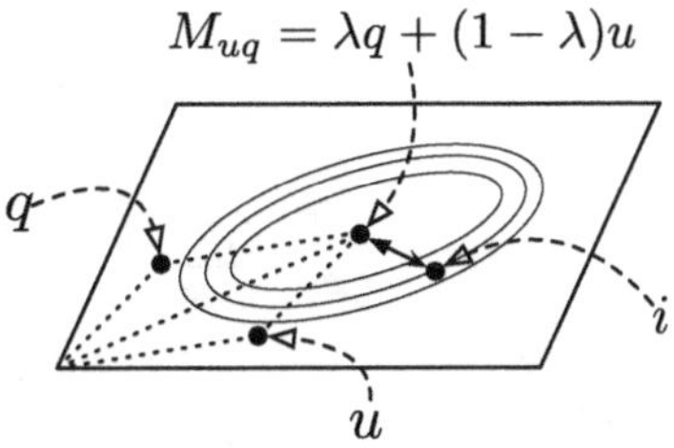

Figure 1: Personalized product search in a latent space with query q, user u, personalized search model M_{uq} and item i.

3 HIERARCHICAL EMBEDDING MODEL FOR PERSONALIZED PRODUCT SEARCH

In this section, we discuss how we tackle the problem of personalized product search with our hierarchical embedding model. In our model, queries, users and items are projected into a single latent space so that their relationships can be directly measured by their similarities. We propose a unified framework which jointly learns different level embeddings through maximizing the likelihood of purchased user-item pair given corresponding queries.

3.1 Personalized Product Search in Latent Semantic Space

For personalized product search, we consider two important factors when designing our retrieval model. The first is *query intent*, which determines whether an item is relevant to a query in general. The second is *user preference*, which decides whether an item satisfies the special need of a particular user. Although the preference of a user may vary depending on the intent of a query, it is unrealistic to construct query-dependent user models because we do not have adequate training data for each user-query pair. For simplicity, we assume that user preferences are independent from query intents and build query-independent user models for personalized product search.

To conduct product search in semantic space and to balance the profit and risk of personalization, we project both queries and users into a single latent space and explicitly control their weights in personalized product search model. Inspired by the design of word embedding models [20, 21], we design the latent representations of queries and users to have good compositionality so that the personalized search model could be directly computed as the linear combination of query models and user models. Formally, suppose that the query intent of a query q in semantic space is represented with a vector $\boldsymbol{q} \in \mathbb{R}^{\alpha}$ and the user preference of a user u is represented with $\boldsymbol{u} \in \mathbb{R}^{\alpha}$, we define the personalized search model for (u, q) as:

$$\boldsymbol{M_{uq}} = \lambda \boldsymbol{q} + (1-\lambda)\boldsymbol{u} \tag{1}$$

where λ is a hyper-parameter that controls the weight of query model $\boldsymbol{q}$ and user model $\boldsymbol{u}$.

We search products with $\boldsymbol{M_{uq}}$ following the framework of vector space retrieval models. Vector space models measure the relevance of query-document pair with the similarity of their vector representations. Similarly, we rank items according to the similarity between their latent representations and $\boldsymbol{M_{uq}}$. Let $\boldsymbol{i} \in \mathbb{R}^{\alpha}$ be the latent representation of item i, then the score of i with model M_{uq} can be computed as:

$$Score(i|u,q) = f(\boldsymbol{i}, \boldsymbol{M_{uq}}) = f(\boldsymbol{i}, \lambda\boldsymbol{q} + (1-\lambda)\boldsymbol{u}) \tag{2}$$

where f is a similarity function predefined for the latent space of queries, users and items. An illustration of our personalized product search in vector space is shown in Figure 1. The similarity function f in latent space models can be arbitrarily designed in many forms. In our experiments, we tried both cosine similarity and dot product (the sum of element-wise multiplications). We observed that cosine similarity yielded better performance in most cases.

3.2 Hierarchical Embedding Model

We now describe our hierarchical embedding model for personalized product search in detail. In our model, queries, users and items are represented with their associated text data. We define language models for users and items based on their distributed representations and assume that items are generated from a personalized search model constructed with query and user embeddings. We jointly learn embeddings for words, queries, users and items with this hierarchical structure by directly maximizing the likelihood of observed query-user-item triples.

The overall structure of our hierarchical embedding model is shown in Figure 2. Our model can be broadly separated into three parts. The first part of our model maps words to their corresponding word embeddings and constructs distributed representations for users and items by requiring them to predict the words from their associated reviews (R_u and R_i). The second part of our model builds query embeddings with query keywords and function ϕ. Finally, the third part of our model fine-tunes the representations of queries, users and items by requiring the composition of query and user embeddings – the personalized search model M_{uq} – to predict the purchased item. Given this structure, we can directly compute the likelihood of a query-user-item triple and train our model by maximizing the log likelihood of training data.

Embedding-based User/Item Language Model. Inspired by the paragraph vector models [15], we learn the distributed representations for users and items by constructing language models with word embeddings. Formally, given $\boldsymbol{e} \in \mathbb{R}^{\alpha}$ as the latent representation of an entity (which could be either a user or an item) and $\boldsymbol{w} \in \mathbb{R}^{\alpha}$ as the embedding of a word w, the probability that w is generated from the language model of e is defined as:

$$P(w|e) = \frac{\exp(\boldsymbol{w} \cdot \boldsymbol{e})}{\sum_{w' \in V_w} \exp(\boldsymbol{w'} \cdot \boldsymbol{e})} \tag{3}$$

where V_w is the corpus vocabulary and $P(w|e)$ is computed as a softmax over $\boldsymbol{e}$ and $\boldsymbol{w}$. For simplicity, we assume that words can be generated by user models and item models independently.

The use of embedding-based language models have two merits. First, through matching with distributed representations, the embedding-based language model alleviates the problem of vocabulary mismatch. It can directly measure the semantic similarity between words and entities in latent space. Second, the construction of embedding-based language models requires no priori knowledge about the corpus's topic distribution (e.g., the topic number in LDA [4]). It can automatically cluster entities based on the characteristics of input data.

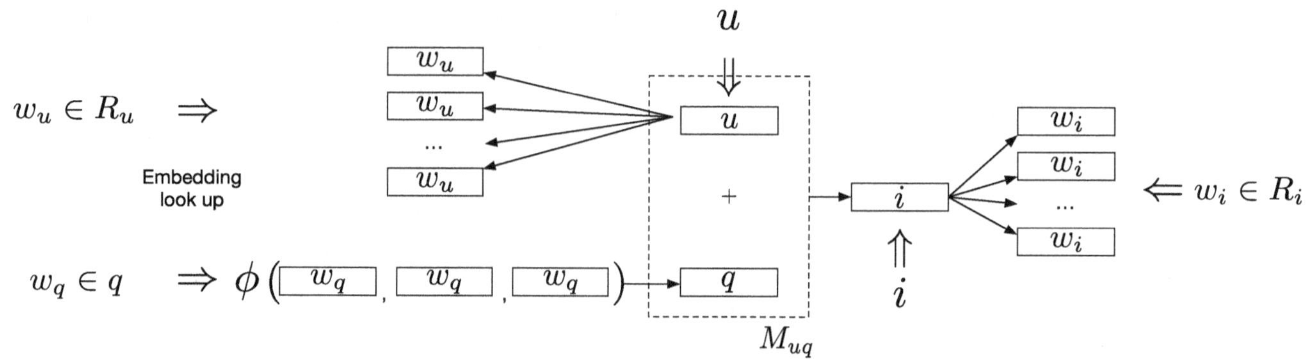

Figure 2: The structure of our hierarchical embedding model for personalized product search. R_u, R_i denote the sets of reviews for user u and item i; w_u, w_i, w_q denote the words in R_u, R_i and query q; and M_{uq} is the personalized search model constructed with query models and user models.

Query Embeddings. As the number of possible queries is very large, query embeddings learned off-line cannot be generalized in practice. Therefore, to construct distributed representations for queries on the fly, we define a projection function ϕ for queries and use the embeddings of query words as its inputs:

$$\boldsymbol{q} = \phi(\{w_q | w_q \in q\}) \tag{4}$$

Previous studies have proposed several methods to combine word embeddings to form a query embedding. The most simplest way is to aggregate and average the embeddings of query words directly [31], which can be formulated as:

$$\phi(\{w_q | w_q \in q\}) = \frac{\sum_{w_q \in q} \boldsymbol{w_q}}{|q|} \tag{5}$$

where $|q|$ is the length of query q. An extension of this method is to add a non-linear projection layer over the average word embeddings and form a new embedding vector [30]:

$$\phi(\{w_q | w_q \in q\}) = \tanh(W \cdot \frac{\sum_{w_q \in q} \boldsymbol{w_q}}{|q|} + b) \tag{6}$$

where $W \in \mathbb{R}^{\alpha \times \alpha}$ and $b \in \mathbb{R}^{\alpha}$ are parameters learned on a separate training set. Further, a more complex model that considers query structures is to sequentially input the query words into a recurrent neural network (RNN) and use the final network state as the latent query representation [25]:

$$\begin{aligned} \boldsymbol{o_t} &= (1 - \boldsymbol{a_t}) \odot \boldsymbol{o_{t-1}} + \boldsymbol{a_t} \odot \boldsymbol{s_t} \\ \boldsymbol{a_t} &= \sigma(W_a^{w} \boldsymbol{w_q^t} + W_a^{s} \boldsymbol{o_{t-1}}) \\ \boldsymbol{r_t} &= \sigma(W_r^{w} \boldsymbol{w_q^t} + W_r^{s} \boldsymbol{o_{t-1}}) \\ \boldsymbol{s_t} &= \tanh\left(W^{w} \boldsymbol{w_q^t} + W^{s}(\boldsymbol{r_t} \odot \boldsymbol{o_{t-1}})\right) \end{aligned} \tag{7}$$

where $\boldsymbol{s_t} \in \mathbb{R}^{\alpha}$ is the state vector on t step, w_q^t is the tth word in query q, $\odot$ is the element-wise product, $\sigma(x) = \frac{1}{1+e^{-x}}$ is a sigmoid function and $W^x, W^s, W_a^x, W_a^s, W_r^x, W_r^s \in \mathbb{R}^{\alpha \times \alpha}$ are parameters in the RNN with Gated Recurrent Unit [5]. The $\phi(\{w_q | w_q \in q\})$, namely the embedding of q, is equal to the final network state $\boldsymbol{s_{|q|}}$.

As far as we know, there is no query embedding method that satisfies the needs of all search scenarios. For example, the mean vector of word embeddings works well on short queries while the recurrent network performs better on long queries with complex linguistic structures. In our experiments, we explored all the methods above to identify the most effective model for query embedding in personalized product search.

Item Generation Model. To fine tune the embeddings of queries, users and items, we further construct an generative model for items that requires user embeddings and query embeddings to predict the items related to them. For users, related items are those purchased by the user; for queries, related items are those relevant to the query. The probability that an item is generated from a user model and a query model together is computed with their embedding representations and a softmax function:

$$P(i|u,q) = Score(i|u,q) = \frac{\exp\left(\boldsymbol{i} \cdot (\lambda \boldsymbol{q} + (1-\lambda)\boldsymbol{u})\right)}{\sum_{i' \in V_i} \exp\left(\boldsymbol{i'} \cdot (\lambda \boldsymbol{q} + (1-\lambda)\boldsymbol{u})\right)} \tag{8}$$

where V_i is the set of all possible items and λ is the weight of query model in the final ranking function (Equation 2).

The design of the item generation model aims to regularize the representations of users, queries and items so that relevant query-item pairs and preferable user-item pairs have high similarity in the final embedding space. Also, it forms a hierarchical structure that connects the learning of embeddings from different levels. With it, we can directly compute the likelihood of observed user-query-item triples in our hierarchical embedding model.

3.3 Joint Learning Framework

As mentioned previously, we learn the distributed representations of queries, users and items in our hierarchical embedding model by maximizing the likelihood of observed user-query-item triples. Let R_u and R_i be the sets of product reviews that are associated with user u and item i respectively, then the log likelihood of observing a query-user-item triple with corresponding reviews in our model can be computed as

$$\mathcal{L}(R_u, R_i, u, i, q) = \log P(R_u, R_i, u, i, q) \tag{9}$$

In our model, words in R_i are generated by the language model of i and words in R_u are generated by the language model of u. Thus, R_i is independent of u, q, R_u while R_u is independent of i, q, R_i.

Because we assume that user preferences and query intents are independent in personalized product search, we have the following:

$$\begin{aligned}\mathcal{L}(R_u, R_i, u, i, q) &= \log\Big(P(R_i, i|u, q)P(R_u, u, q)\Big) \\ &= \log\Big(P(R_i|i)P(i|u, q)P(R_u|u)P(u)P(q)\Big) \\ &= \log\Big(P(i|u, q)P(u)P(q)\prod_{w_i \in R_i} P(w_i|i)\prod_{w_u \in R_u} P(w_u|u)\Big) \\ &= \log P(i|u, q) + \sum_{w_i \in R_i}\log P(w_i|i) + \sum_{w_u \in R_u}\log P(w_u|u)\end{aligned} \tag{10}$$

where $P(u)$ and $P(q)$ are predefined as uniform distributions, which could be ignored in the computation of log likelihood. Therefore, the log likelihood of a query-user-item triple is actually the sum of log likelihood for the user language model, the item language model and the item generation model.

Directly computing the log likelihood of a query-user-item triple, however, is not practical due to the softmax function used in our hierarchical embedding model (Equation 3&8). For efficient training, we adopt a negative sampling strategy to approximate the softmax function in our model. Negative sampling was first proposed by Mikolov et al. [20] and has been extensively used in machine learning and information retrieval [2, 15]. It has been shown to be effective for approximating softmax functions and factorizing the mutual information matrix of two related entities [16]. The basic idea of negative sampling is to sample data from the corpus with a predefined distribution and form negative samples to approximate the denominator of softmax functions. In our model, the negative samples for language models are the words randomly sampled from the corpus. The log likelihood of a user model or an item model with negative sampling is:

$$\begin{aligned}\log P(w_i|i) &= \log\sigma(\boldsymbol{w_i}\cdot\boldsymbol{i}) + k\cdot\mathbb{E}_{w'\sim P_w}[\log\sigma(-\boldsymbol{w'}\cdot\boldsymbol{i})] \\ \log P(w_u|u) &= \log\sigma(\boldsymbol{w_u}\cdot\boldsymbol{u}) + k\cdot\mathbb{E}_{w'\sim P_w}[\log\sigma(-\boldsymbol{w'}\cdot\boldsymbol{u})]\end{aligned} \tag{11}$$

where k is the number of negative samples and P_w is a noise distribution for words. In our experiments, we define P_w as the unigram distribution raised to the 3/4rd power [20]. Similarly, we compute the log likelihood of our item generation model by conducting negative sampling on items:

$$\begin{aligned}\log P(i|u, q) &= \log\sigma\Big(\boldsymbol{i}\cdot(\lambda\boldsymbol{q} + (1-\lambda)\boldsymbol{u})\Big) \\ &\quad + k\cdot\mathbb{E}_{i'\sim P_i}\Big[\log\sigma\Big(-\boldsymbol{i'}\cdot(\lambda\boldsymbol{q} + (1-\lambda)\boldsymbol{u})\Big)\Big]\end{aligned} \tag{12}$$

where P_i is the uniform noise distribution for items.

We use stochastic gradient descent to learn the parameters of our hierarchical embedding model. All embeddings are trained simultaneously with this joint learning framework. Also, similar to previous studies [2, 30], we add L2 regularizations on the distributed representations of words, users and items. The final optimization goal is:

$$\begin{aligned}\mathcal{L}' &= \sum_{u,i,q}\mathcal{L}(R_u, R_i, u, i, q) + \gamma\Big(\sum_{w\in V_w}\boldsymbol{w}^2 + \sum_{u\in V_u}\boldsymbol{u}^2 + \sum_{i\in V_i}\boldsymbol{i}^2\Big) \\ &= \sum_{u,i,q}\Bigg(\sum_{w_i\in R_i}\Big(\log\sigma(\boldsymbol{w_i}\cdot\boldsymbol{i}) + k\cdot\mathbb{E}_{w'\sim P_w}[\log\sigma(-\boldsymbol{w'}\cdot\boldsymbol{i})]\Big) \\ &\quad + \sum_{w_u\in R_u}\Big(\log\sigma(\boldsymbol{w_u}\cdot\boldsymbol{u}) + k\cdot\mathbb{E}_{w'\sim P_w}[\log\sigma(-\boldsymbol{w'})\cdot\boldsymbol{u})]\Big) \\ &\quad + \log\sigma\Big(\boldsymbol{i}\cdot(\lambda\boldsymbol{q} + (1-\lambda)\boldsymbol{u})\Big) \\ &\quad + k\cdot\mathbb{E}_{i'\sim P_i}\Big[\log\sigma\Big(-\boldsymbol{i'}\cdot(\lambda\boldsymbol{q} + (1-\lambda)\boldsymbol{u})\Big)\Big]\Bigg) \\ &\quad + \gamma\Big(\sum_{w\in V_w}\boldsymbol{w}^2 + \sum_{u\in V_u}\boldsymbol{u}^2 + \sum_{i\in V_i}\boldsymbol{i}^2\Big)\end{aligned} \tag{13}$$

where γ is the strength of L2 regularization; V_w, V_u and V_i are the set of all possible words, users and items respectively.

4 EXPERIMENTAL SETUP

In this section, we introduce our experimental settings for personalized product search. We describe how to extract search queries from product corpus and give details about our data partitions. We also describe the baseline methods used in our experiments and the training settings for our model.

4.1 Datasets

We used the Amazon product dataset[2] as our experiment corpus. This dataset is a well-known benchmark for product recommendation. It includes millions of customers and products as well as rich metadata such as reviews, product descriptions and product categories. In our experiments, we used four subsets from the Amazon product dataset, which are *Electronics, Kindle Store, CDs & Vinyl* and *Cell Phones & Accessories*. The first three are large-scale datasets that cover three common types of products (electronic devices, books and music). The last one is a small dataset which is used to test our models in situations where text data are limited. Specifically, we use the 5-core data provided by McAuley et al. [18] where each user and each item has at least 5 associated reviews. In these datasets, a user has to purchase an item before writing a review for it. Therefore, we extract purchase user-item pairs directly based on user reviews. The objective of personalized product search in our experiments is to find items that are both relevant to the query and purchased by the user.

4.2 Query Extraction

As far as we know, there is no publicly available dataset that contains search queries for product search. Previous studies in e-shopping has described directed product search as users search for "a producer's name, a brand or a set of terms which described the category of the product" [27]. Therefore, a common query-extraction method for product search research is to extract queries from the category information of each product.

Following the paradigm used by Gysel et al. [30], we extract the search queries for each item with a three-step process. First, we

[2] http://jmcauley.ucsd.edu/data/amazon/

Table 1: Statistics for the 5-core data for *Electronics, Kindle Store, CDs & Vinyl* and *Cell Phones & Accessories* [18].

	Electronics	*Kindle Store*	*CDs & Vinyl*	*Cell Phones & Accessories*
Corpus				
Number of reviews	1,689,188	982,618	1,097,591	194,439
Review length	118.27±158.12	112.21±129.52	174.57±177.05	93.50±131.65
Number of items	63,001	61,934	64,443	10,429
Review per item	26.81±75.82	15.87±21.42	17.03±28.15	18.64±34.24
Number of users	192,403	68,223	75,258	27,879
Review per user	8.78±8.26	14.40±24.61	14.58±39.13	6.97±4.55
Queries				
Number of queries	989	4,603	694	165
Query length	6.40±1.64	7.07±1.89	5.71±1.62	5.93±1.57
Queries per item	1.02±0.23	5.08±2.04	4.04±1.92	1.11±0.38
Queries per user	8.13±5.84	35.65±37.48	21.75±16.53	4.95±2.60
Train/Test				
Number of reviews	1,275,432/413,756	720,006/262,612	804,090/293,501	150,048/44,391
Number of queries	904/85	3313/1290	534/160	134/31
Number of user-query pairs	1,204,928/5,505	1,490,349/232,668	1,287,214/45,490	114,177/665
Relevant items per pairs	1.12±0.48/1.01±0.09	1.87±3.30/1.48±1.94	2.57±6.59/1.30±1.19	1.52±1.13/1.00±0.05

Table 2: Example queries extracted following the paradigm proposed by Gysel et al. [30] from Amazon product data.

Electronics:
– video games playstation accessory kit
– software operate system microsoft window
Kindle Store:
– store kindle ebook cookbook food wine bake dessert
– books health fitness weight loss diet
CDs & Vinyl:
– musical instrument general accessory sheet music folder
– digital music hard rock thrash speed metal
Cell Phones & Accessories:
– cell phone accessory international charger
– cell phone accessory case sleeve

extract category information for each item from the metadata of products. Then, we concatenate the terms from a single hierarchy of categories to form a topic string. Final, stopwords and duplicate words are removed from the topic string and we use it as a query for the corresponding item. To ensure the quality of extracted queries, we ignore the category hierarchies with only one level as those categories are usually non-descriptive for items (e.g. "CDs & Vinyl"). Also, we try to maintain more terms from the sub-categories by removing duplicate words sequentially from the first level to the last level (e.g. *Camera, Photo → Digital Camera Lenses* would be converted to "photo digital camera lenses"). Some example queries are shown in Table 2.

For personalized product search, we construct user-query pairs by linking user-item pairs with each item's queries. If a user purchased an item, the pairing of this user with any query associated with the item are valid user-query pairs. Only the items that are purchased by the user and belong to the query are considered as relevant to the user-query pair. For simplicity, we do not conduct any filtering or initial retrieval in our experiments and use all possible items within each dataset as the candidate items for each query. Therefore, the relevant items for each user-query pair are very sparse and the personalized product search settings in our experiments are difficult by nature. More statistics about the subsets of Amazon product data are shown in Table 1.

4.3 Evaluation Methodology

We partitioned each dataset into a training set and a test set according to the following instructions. First, we randomly hide 30% of reviews for each user from the training process. User-item pairs from those reviews are used to represent purchase behaviors in the test data. Second, we randomly select 30% queries as the initial test query set. After that, if all queries of a training item are in the test query set, we randomly select one query and put it back to the training query set. Therefore, each item has at least one query in the training data. Finally, we match all test queries with users to form the final test data. The basic intuition of our setting is to ensure that every query and query-user-item triple in the test set is new and unobserved in the training process. Although the number of queries is limited, we have adequate user-query pairs due to the large number of users. The statistics for data partitions in each Amazon dataset are also shown in Table 1.

For each user-query pair, we compute evaluation metrics based on the top 100 items retrieved by each model. The ranking metrics we used are mean average precision (MAP), mean reciprocal rank (MRR) and normalized discounted cumulative gain (NDCG). Reciprocal rank is the precision on the rank of the first relevant result, which is actually the inversed rank value for the first user purchase in the retrieved items. In other words, MRR indicates the expected number of items that a user needs to explore before finding the "right" product. NDCG is a common metric for multi-label ranking problems. Although we only have binary labels in our settings of personalized product search, the value of NDCG shows how good the ranking is compared to the optimal ranked list. In our experiments, we compute NDCG at 10.

4.4 Baselines

For model evaluation, we used three types of baselines: the query likelihood model [26] (namely the standard language modeling approach), an extended query likelihood with user models, and the latent semantic entity model [30]. The first two are retrieval models based on bag-of-words representations and the last one is a state-of-the-art latent space model for product search.

Query Likelihood Model. The query likelihood model (QL) is a language modeling approach proposed by Ponte and Croft [26]. It is an unigram model that ranks documents based on the log likelihood of query words in the document's language models. Given a query Q, the probability that Q is generated from a document D is computed as

$$P_{QL}(Q|D) = \sum_{w \in Q} tf_{w,Q} \log \frac{tf_{w,D} + \mu P(w|C)}{|D| + \mu} \tag{14}$$

where $tf_{w,D}$ is the frequency of word w in D, $|D|$ is the length of D, μ is a parameter for Dirichlet smoothing and $P(w|C)$ is a background language model computed as the frequency of w divided by the total number of terms in the corpus C. In our experiments, the document for an item is constructed with the item's reviews. The value of μ are tuned around the average length of each document in the training data (from 1000 to 3000).

Extended Query Likelihood with User Models. The original QL model is not a personalized retrieval model, so we extended it to consider the effect of users in personalized product search. Based on similar assumptions, we define a user-query likelihood model (UQL) that ranks documents according to both the likelihood of query words and the words associated with each user. Formally, let U be the set of words written by a user u, then the likelihood of user-query pair (U, Q) in document model D is

$$P_{UQL}(U, Q|D) = \lambda P_{QL}(Q|D) + (1 - \lambda) P_{QL}(U|D) \tag{15}$$

Similar to Equation 2, we use λ to control the weights of U in retrieval. We tuned λ from 0.0 to 1.0 and show the results in Section 5.1&5.2. To improve efficiency, we removed stop words and used fifty of the most frequent words in U to compute $P_{UQL}(U, Q|D)$.

Latent Semantic Entity. The latent semantic entity model (LSE) proposed by Gysel et al. [30] is a latent space model specifically designed for product search. LSE learns item representations with their associated text data. Specifically, it extracts n-grams from the reviews of an item and projects them into a latent entity space with their word embeddings:

$$f_E(s) = \tanh(W_E \cdot (\frac{1}{|s|} \sum_{w \in s} \boldsymbol{w}) + b) \tag{16}$$

where $|s|$ is the length of a n-gram s, $\boldsymbol{w} \in \mathbb{R}^{\alpha}$ is the word embedding of word w, $f_E(s) \in \mathbb{R}^{\beta}$ is the representation of s in the latent entity space, and $W_E \in \mathbb{R}^{\alpha \times \beta}$, $b \in \mathbb{R}^{\beta}$ are parameters learned in the training process. LSE constructs distributed representation $\boldsymbol{e}$ for item e by maximizing the similarity between e and its n-grams in the latent entity space. Similarly to our hierarchical model, LSE uses negative sampling to define its loss function. However, our model approximates item embeddings by sampling negative words for each item while LSE approximates n-gram representations by sampling negative items for each n-gram. From the perspective of a generative model, the basic assumption of LSE is that each n-gram is a potential query that could generate the corresponding item. Therefore, LSE can directly use Equation 16 to compute the latent representations of queries and do product search by ranking items with their similarities to the query embedding. For simplicity, we set equal sizes for word embeddings and item embeddings ($\alpha = \beta$) in LSE and tuned them from 100 to 500. The best embedding size is 400 for *Electronics*, 300 for *Kindle Store*, 500 for *CDs & Vinyl* and 400 for *Cell Phones & Accessories*.

4.5 Model Training

Both LSE and our models are trained on a Nvidia Titan X GPU with 20 epochs. We set the initial learning rate as 0.5 and gradually decreased it to 0.0 in the training process. We used stochastic gradient decent with batch size 64 and clipped the global norm of parameter gradients with 5 to avoid unstable gradient updates. To speed up training on large datasets (*Electronics, Kindle Store* and *CDs & Vinyl*), we subsampled words with probability $10^4 \cdot cf_w/|C|$ where cf_w is the corpus frequency of word w and $|C|$ is the length of the corpus. For LSE and our models, we set negative sampling number as 5 and tuned L2 regularization strength γ from 0.0 to 0.005. We tuned the weight of query model λ (Equation 2&15) from 0.0 to 1.0 and tested embedding size from 100 to 500. The effect of λ and embedding size are shown in Section 5.2&5.3. The training of LSE and our models (except HEM_{RNN}) usually takes 7-8 hours to finish 20 epoch (about 100k words per second) on our largest dataset (*Electronics*). The source code can be found in the link below[3].

5 RESULTS AND DISCUSSION

Now we report our results on personalized product search benchmarks. We first show the overall retrieval performance of our hierarchical embedding models and baselines on different Amazon product datasets. Then we discuss the effect of user models in personalized product search. After that, we analyze the parameter sensitivity of embedding size in our models.

5.1 Retrieval Performance

Table 3 shows the overall results of baselines and our models on the personalized product search benchmarks of Amazon data *Electronics, Kindle Store, CDs & Vinyl* and *Cell Phones & Accessories*. In the Table 3, QL represents the query likelihood model [26]; UQL represents the extended query likelihood with user models; LSE represents the model of Latent Semantic Entity [30], and HEM denotes our hierarchical embedding models with ϕ function as mean vector (*mean*, Equation 5), projected mean (*pm*, Equation 6) and recurrent neural network (*RNN*, Equation 7). We conducted significant tests over QL, UQL and LSE for all models. All metrics reported in Table 3 are computed based on user purchases, which means that the personalized product search task is difficult by nature and even a small improvement could potentially lead to large profits for e-shopping companies.

[3]https://ciir.cs.umass.edu/downloads/HEM/

Table 3: Comparison of baselines and our hierarchical embedding models on the Amazon product search datasets. MAP and MRR are computed with top 100 items while NDCG is computed with top 10 items. $*$, $+$ and $\ddagger$ denote significant differences to QL, UQL and LSE in Fisher randomization test [28] with $p \leq 0.01$. The best performance is highlighted in boldface.

	Electronics			*Kindle Store*			*CDs & Vinyl*			*Cell Phones & Accessories*		
Model	MAP	MRR	NDCG	MAP	MRR	NDCG	MAP	MRR	NDCG	MAP	MRR	NDCG
QL	$0.289^{\dagger}$	$0.289^{\dagger}$	$0.316^{\dagger}$	$0.011^{\dagger}$	$0.012^{\dagger}$	$0.013^{\dagger}$	0.009	0.011	0.010	0.081	0.081	0.092
UQL	$0.289^{\dagger}$	$0.289^{\dagger}$	$0.316^{\dagger}$	$0.014^{*\dagger}$	$0.016^{*\dagger}$	$0.019^{*\dagger}$	0.018^{*}	0.021^{*}	0.021^{*}	0.081	0.081	0.092
LSE	0.233	0.234	0.239	0.006	0.007	0.007	0.018^{*}	0.022^{*}	0.020^{*}	0.098^{*+}	0.098^{*+}	0.084
HEM_{mean}	0.071	0.071	0.091	$0.015^{*+\dagger}$	$0.019^{*+\dagger}$	$0.018^{*\dagger}$	$0.029^{*+\dagger}$	$0.035^{*+\dagger}$	$0.034^{*+\dagger}$	0.047	0.047	0.053
HEM_{pm}	$\mathbf{0.308}^{*+\dagger}$	$\mathbf{0.309}^{*+\dagger}$	$\mathbf{0.329}^{\dagger}$	$0.029^{*+\dagger}$	$0.035^{*+\dagger}$	$0.033^{*+\dagger}$	$\mathbf{0.034}^{*+\dagger}$	$\mathbf{0.040}^{*+\dagger}$	$\mathbf{0.040}^{*+\dagger}$	$\mathbf{0.124}^{*+}$	$\mathbf{0.124}^{*+}$	$\mathbf{0.153}^{*+\dagger}$
HEM_{RNN}	0.198	0.198	0.214	$\mathbf{0.033}^{*+\dagger}$	$\mathbf{0.039}^{*+\dagger}$	$\mathbf{0.038}^{*+\dagger}$	$0.023^{*+\dagger}$	$0.027^{*+\dagger}$	$0.026^{*+\dagger}$	0.053	0.053	0.071

As shown in Table 3, the overall performance of baselines and our models varies considerably on different product datasets. According to the results for baseline models (QL, UQL and LSE), *Electronics* and *Cell Phones & Accessories* are "easy" datasets while *Kindle Store* and *CDs & Vinyl* are "hard" datasets. Empirically, there are multiple reasons that make *Electronics* and *Cell Phones & Accessories* much easier then *Kindle Store* and *CDs & Vinyl* in personalized product search. From the perspective of data content, *Kindle Store* and *CDs & Vinyl* contain items about books and music while *Electronics* and *Cell Phones & Accessories* consist of items about electronic devices. The tastes of books and music are more personal and difficult to capture compared to electronic devices. Also, the average reviews per item in *Kindle Store* and *CDs & Vinyl* are lower (15.87 and 17.03) than those in *Electronics* and *Cell Phones & Accessories* (26.81 and 18.64), which makes the modeling of items less adequate in both baselines and our models. From the perspective of queries, most items in *Electronics* and *Cell Phones & Accessories* are related only to 1 query while items in *Kindle Store* and *CDs & Vinyl* are related to 4 or 5 queries on average. For each user, there are more items that belong to the same queries but haven't been purchased in *Kindle Store* and *CDs & Vinyl*. The language for queries in *Electronics* and *Cell Phones & Accessories* showed high correlations with the language for user purchases. For example, the MAP of QL is much higher on *Electronics* and *Cell Phones & Accessories* (0.289 and 0.081) than it is on *Kindle Store* and *CDs & Vinyl* (0.011 and 0.008).

The relative performance of unigram models (QL and UQL) compared to latent space models (LSE, HEM) also varies on different datasets. On "easy" datasets such as *Electronics* and *Cell Phones and Accessories*, the performance of QL and UQL is comparable or better than the latent space baseline (LSE) and some variations of our hierarchical embedding models (HEM_{mean} and HEM_{RNN}). On difficult datasets like *Kindle Store* and *CDs & Vinyl*, however, vocabulary mismatch problems are more severe and unigram models are significantly worse than latent space models. Overall, our best model (HEM_{pm}) outperformed QL and UQL on all four datasets. The improvement of MAP over QL and UQL is 0.019 (7%) on *Electronics*, 0.018 (164%) and 0.015 (107%) on *Kindle Store*, 0.026 (325%) and 0.016 (89%) on *CDs & Vinyl*, and 0.043 (53%) on *Cell Phones and Accessories*. These results indicate that exact keyword matching is not enough to predict user purchases in product search. In many cases, the semantic relationships between queries, users and products considerably affect the purchase decisions of users.

Compared to LSE, we notice that the HEM models indeed produce better results on the tasks of personalized product search. Our best model (HEM_{pm}) outperformed LSE on MAP for 0.075 (32%) on *Electronics*, 0.023 (383%) on *Kindle Store*, 0.016 (89%) on *CDs & Vinyl* and 0.026 (27%) on *Cell Phones & Accessories*. There are two potential reasons for the good performance of our models. First, compared to LSE, our models explicitly construct user models with user's reviews. Purchase is a personal behavior and user models enable us to retrieve products according the preference of each individual. Second, our models are designed based on more general assumptions for queries, users and items. In LSE, each n-gram is considered as a potential query. Gysel et al. [30] conducted negative sampling by sampling items for each n-gram, which basically assumes that items are generated from models of n-grams. In contrast, we assume that words are generated from the models of items and items are generated from both query models and user models. We believe that items are more complex concepts and should be placed at a higher level than basic semantic units like words and n-grams.

The main differences between the variations of our hierarchical embedding models in Table 3 are their ϕ functions for query embedding. According to our experiments, HEM_{pm} is the most effective and robust model while HEM_{mean} is the worst one. Previous studies [31, 32] have shown that, despite the good compositionality of word embeddings, aggregating word embeddings directly to form query embeddings for information retrieval is not promising. In our experiments, we observed inferior performance for HEM_{mean} in Table 3. After adding a non-linear projection layer over the average word embeddings, however, our HEM_{pm} obtained significantly better results on almost all datasets. This indicates that the relation between queries and words is non-linear in semantic space. Also, we notice that the performance of the projected mean (*pm*) on three of our datasets is even better than RNN, which is considered to be a complex and powerful neural network in general. One possible reason is that the queries used in our personalized product search benchmarks are mostly keyword-based queries. As discussed in previous studies [12, 30], keyword-based queries in document retrieval and entity retrieval tend to be simple in structure and do not have complicated compositional meanings. Therefore, using neural networks as complex as RNN in our hierarchical embedding models brings little benefit to the process of query modeling and potentially increases the risk of model over-fitting.

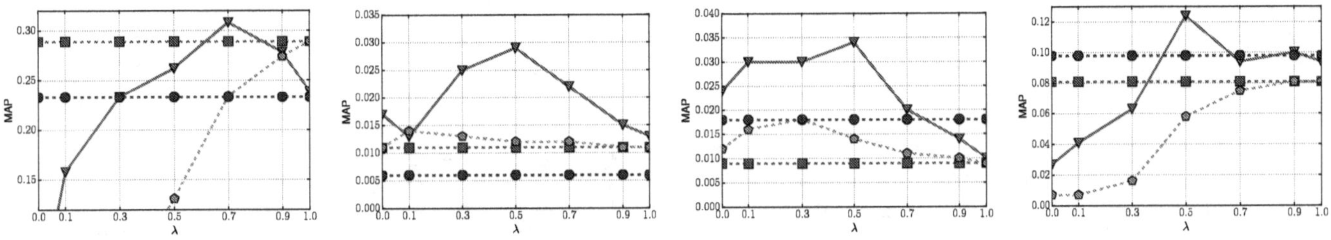

(a) *Electronics* (b) *Kindle Store* (c) *CDs & Vinyl* (d) *Cell Phones & Accessories*

Figure 3: The performance of HEM_{pm} and baselines on the Amazon personalized product search benchmark datasets with different query model weight λ. The red solid line with triangles represents the numbers of HEM_{pm}; the blue, green and cyan dashed lines with circles, squares and pentagons are results for LSE, QL and UQL respectively.

5.2 Personalization Weight

In our hierarchical embedding models, we define a hyper-parameter λ to control the weight of user models in personalized product search. To analyze the effect of personalization in our models, we plot the MAP value of baselines and HEM_{pm} with respect to λ in Figure 3. When λ is equal to 1.0, our model purely relies on query models to retrieve items for all users; when λ is equal to 0.0, our model only uses user models to find items for each individual.

As we can see in Figure 3, the optimal performance of our hierarchical embedding models is a tradeoff between query relevance and user preference. The personalized search model of the hierarchical embedding model is the linear composition of query models (query embeddings) and user models (user embeddings). When we do not consider queries in personalized product search ($\lambda = 0.0$), HEM_{pm} ranks items purely based on the preference of users and had poor performance on all datasets. When we conducted product search without personalization ($\lambda = 1.0$), HEM_{pm} obtained fair results on *Electronics* and *Cell Phones & Accessories* but still performed worse than our best models. The best value of λ for HEM_{pm} is 0.7 on *Electronics*, 0.5 on *Kindle Store*, *CDs & Vinyl* and *Cell Phones & Accessories*. As λ increased from 0.0 to 1.0, the performance of UQL increased in the beginning and decreased after 0.1 on *Kindle Store* and 0.3 *CDs & Vinyl*. On *Electronics* and *Cell Phones & Accessories*, however, the best UQL is the UQL with $\lambda = 1.0$, which is actually a QL model without using user reviews.

As discussed previously, the types of products not only influence the difficulty of product search but also affect the usefulness of personalization. According to our experiments, the needs of personalization on books (*Kindle Store*) and music (*CDs & Vinyl*) are higher than those on electronic devices (*Electronics*). Also, because each item belongs to one query in *Electronics* and *Cell Phones & Accessories* on average, the test queries are strong filters for items by themselves, which partially explains why using only the query models ($\lambda = 1.0$) still produced good results on these datasets.

5.3 Embedding Size

To analyze the effect of embedding sizes and potentially provide guides for future studies, we show the results of our hierarchical embedding models with different embedding sizes in Figure 4. The horizontal axes represent the size of embedding vectors for queries, users and items in our experiments.

Similar to personalization weights, we observed that the needs of high dimensional embedding vectors vary on different datasets. On *Cell Phones & Accessories* and *Kindle Store*, HEM_{pm} with embedding size 100 obtained the best performance on MAP. Higher embedding sizes brought no improvement but higher training cost and overfitting risks on these datasets. On *Electronics* and *CDs & Vinyl*, we observed better performance of HEM_{pm} with embedding size larger than 100. The best embedding sizes for *Electronics* and *CDs & Vinyl* are 400 and 300. Overall, the performance of HEM_{pm} are robust to the change of embedding sizes and outperformed the baseline models in most cases.

Arora et al. [3] conducted both empirical and theoretical analyses on word embedding models and argued that low dimension vectors (i.e. 300 dimensions) were already enough to encode the information needed by many natural language processing tasks. Because our models incorporate more complicated relationships between queries, users and items, larger embedding sizes could potentially lead to better performance in personalized product search. Nonetheless, we suggest starting with relatively low dimensional vectors and increasing embedding sizes latter if necessary.

6 CONCLUSION AND FUTURE WORK

In this paper, we introduce a hierarchical embedding model for personalized product search. Our model is a latent space retrieval model which projects queries, users and items into a semantic space and conducts product retrieval according to the semantic similarity between items and the composition of query and user models (the personalized search model). We design our neural embedding model in a generative way so that the distributed representations of queries, users, and items can be learned through optimizing the likelihood of observed query-user-item triples. Our results showed that our model significantly outperformed the state-of-the-art baselines on Amazon benchmarks and indicate that personalization with review text is fruitful for product search.

In our experiments, the performance of personalized product search and the importance of user models vary considerably from one dataset to another. We explained this phenomenon empirically according to the general statistics of different datasets such as the number of reviews per item, the number of queries per items etc., but more quantitative analyses are still required if we want to understand each dataset in detail. Those analyses would provide

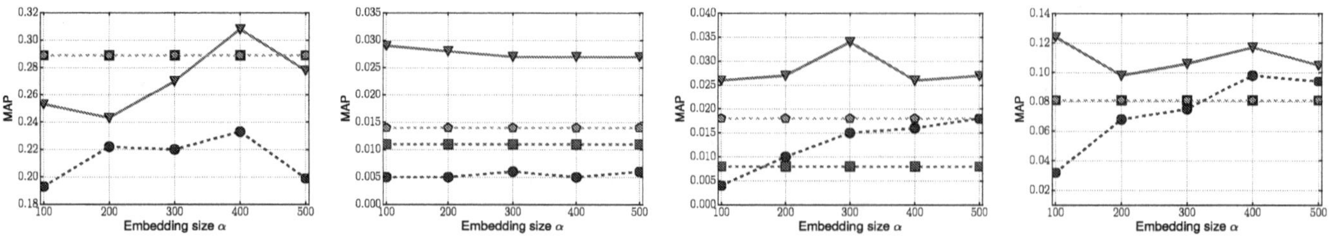

(a) *Electronics* (b) *Kindle Store* (c) *CDs & Vinyl* (d) *Cell Phones & Accessories*

Figure 4: The performance of HEM$_{pm}$ and baselines on the Amazon personalized product search benchmark datasets with different embedding size α. The red solid line with triangles represents the numbers of HEM$_{pm}$; the blue, green and cyan dashed lines with circles, squares and pentagons are results for LSE, QL and UQL respectively.

important guidelines for system design in e-shopping websites. Also, in our work, we only explored the potential of language data in personalized product search. In e-shopping websites, however, there is other user feedback that we haven't used, such as clicks, ratings and frequently asked questions (FAQ). How to effectively combine information from different resources for personalized product search remains to be an open question. We believe that studies in this direction would have great potential and real influence on e-commerce in the future.

7 ACKNOWLEDGMENTS

This work was supported in part by the Center for Intelligent Information Retrieval and in part by NSF IIS-1160894. Any opinions, findings and conclusions or recommendations expressed in this material are those of the authors and do not necessarily reflect those of the sponsor.

REFERENCES

[1] Eugene Agichtein, Eric Brill, Susan Dumais, and Robert Ragno. 2006. Learning user interaction models for predicting web search result preferences. In *Proceedings of the 29th ACM SIGIR*. ACM, 3–10.

[2] Qingyao Ai, Liu Yang, Jiafeng Guo, and W Bruce Croft. 2016. Analysis of the paragraph vector model for information retrieval. In *Proceedings of the ACM ICTIR'16*. ACM, 133–142.

[3] Sanjeev Arora, Yuanzhi Li, Yingyu Liang, Tengyu Ma, and Andrej Risteski. 2015. Rand-walk: A latent variable model approach to word embeddings. *arXiv preprint arXiv:1502.03520* (2015).

[4] David M Blei, Andrew Y Ng, and Michael I Jordan. 2003. Latent dirichlet allocation. *Journal of machine Learning research* 3, Jan (2003), 993–1022.

[5] Kyunghyun Cho, Bart Van Merriënboer, Caglar Gulcehre, Dzmitry Bahdanau, Fethi Bougares, Holger Schwenk, and Yoshua Bengio. 2014. Learning phrase representations using RNN encoder-decoder for statistical machine translation. *arXiv preprint arXiv:1406.1078* (2014).

[6] Nick Craswell, Hugo Zaragoza, and Stephen Robertson. 2005. Microsoft Cambridge at TREC 14: Enterprise Track.. In *TREC*.

[7] Scott Deerwester, Susan T Dumais, George W Furnas, Thomas K Landauer, and Richard Harshman. 1990. Indexing by latent semantic analysis. *Journal of the American society for information science* 41, 6 (1990), 391.

[8] Huizhong Duan and ChengXiang Zhai. 2015. Mining Coordinated Intent Representation for Entity Search and Recommendation. In *Proceedings of the 24th ACM CIKM*. ACM, 333–342.

[9] Huizhong Duan, ChengXiang Zhai, Jinxing Cheng, and Abhishek Gattani. 2013. A probabilistic mixture model for mining and analyzing product search log. In *Proceedings of the 22nd ACM CIKM*. ACM, 2179–2188.

[10] Huizhong Duan, ChengXiang Zhai, Jinxing Cheng, and Abhishek Gattani. 2013. Supporting keyword search in product database: a probabilistic approach. *Proceedings of the VLDB Endowment* 6, 14 (2013), 1786–1797.

[11] Susan T Dumais. 2014. Personalized Search: Potential and Pitfalls.. In *NTCIR*.

[12] Jiafeng Guo, Yixing Fan, Qingyao Ai, and W Bruce Croft. 2016. A deep relevance matching model for ad-hoc retrieval. In *Proceedings of the 25th ACM CIKM*. ACM, 55–64.

[13] Thomas Hofmann. 1999. Probabilistic latent semantic indexing. In *Proceedings of the 22nd ACM SIGIR*. ACM, 50–57.

[14] Bernard J Jansen and Paulo R Molina. 2006. The effectiveness of Web search engines for retrieving relevant ecommerce links. *Information Processing & Management* 42, 4 (2006), 1075–1098.

[15] Quoc V Le and Tomas Mikolov. 2014. Distributed Representations of Sentences and Documents.. In *ICML*, Vol. 14. 1188–1196.

[16] Omer Levy and Yoav Goldberg. 2014. Neural word embedding as implicit matrix factorization. In *Advances in neural information processing systems*. 2177–2185.

[17] Soon Chong Johnson Lim, Ying Liu, and Wing Bun Lee. 2010. Multi-facet product information search and retrieval using semantically annotated product family ontology. *Information Processing & Management* 46, 4 (2010), 479–493.

[18] Julian McAuley, Rahul Pandey, and Jure Leskovec. 2015. Inferring networks of substitutable and complementary products. In *Proceedings of the 21th ACM SIGKDD*. ACM, 785–794.

[19] Julian McAuley, Christopher Targett, Qinfeng Shi, and Anton van den Hengel. 2015. Image-based recommendations on styles and substitutes. In *Proceedings of the 38th ACM SIGIR*. ACM, 43–52.

[20] Tomas Mikolov, Kai Chen, Greg Corrado, and Jeffrey Dean. 2013. Efficient estimation of word representations in vector space. *arXiv preprint arXiv:1301.3781* (2013).

[21] Tomas Mikolov, Ilya Sutskever, Kai Chen, Greg S Corrado, and Jeff Dean. 2013. Distributed representations of words and phrases and their compositionality. In *Advances in neural information processing systems*. 3111–3119.

[22] Meredith Ringel Morris, Jaime Teevan, and Steve Bush. 2008. Enhancing collaborative web search with personalization: groupization, smart splitting, and group hit-highlighting. In *Proceedings of the 2008 ACM conference on Computer supported cooperative work*. ACM, 481–484.

[23] Petteri Nurmi, Eemil Lagerspetz, Wray Buntine, Patrik Floréen, and Joonas Kukkonen. 2008. Product retrieval for grocery stores. In *Proceedings of the 31st ACM SIGIR*. ACM, 781–782.

[24] Paul Ogilvie and Jamie Callan. 2005. Experiments with Language Models for Known-Item Finding of E-mail Messages.. In *TREC*.

[25] Hamid Palangi, Li Deng, Yelong Shen, Jianfeng Gao, Xiaodong He, Jianshu Chen, Xinying Song, and Rabab Ward. 2016. Deep sentence embedding using long short-term memory networks: Analysis and application to information retrieval. *IEEE/ACM Transactions on ASLP* 24, 4 (2016), 694–707.

[26] Jay M Ponte and W Bruce Croft. 1998. A language modeling approach to information retrieval. In *Proceedings of the 21st ACM SIGIR*. ACM, 275–281.

[27] Jennifer Rowley. 2000. Product search in e-shopping: a review and research propositions. *Journal of consumer marketing* 17, 1 (2000), 20–35.

[28] Mark D Smucker, James Allan, and Ben Carterette. 2007. A comparison of statistical significance tests for information retrieval evaluation. In *Proceedings of the sixteenth ACM CIKM*. ACM, 623–632.

[29] Jaime Teevan, Susan T Dumais, and Daniel J Liebling. 2008. To personalize or not to personalize: modeling queries with variation in user intent. In *Proceedings of the 31st ACM SIGIR*. ACM, 163–170.

[30] Christophe Van Gysel, Maarten de Rijke, and Evangelos Kanoulas. 2016. Learning latent vector spaces for product search. In *Proceedings of the 25th ACM CIKM*. ACM, 165–174.

[31] Ivan Vulić and Marie-Francine Moens. 2015. Monolingual and cross-lingual information retrieval models based on (bilingual) word embeddings. In *Proceedings of the 38th ACM SIGIR*. ACM, 363–372.

[32] Hamed Zamani and W Bruce Croft. 2016. Estimating embedding vectors for queries. In *Proceedings of the ACM ICTIR'16*. ACM, 123–132.

Exploring User-Specific Information in Music Retrieval

Zhiyong Cheng
National University of Singapore
jason.zy.cheng@gmail.com

Jialie Shen*
Northumbria University, UK
jerry.shen@northumbria.ac.uk

Liqiang Nie
Shandong University, China
nieliqiang@gmail.com

Tat-Seng Chua
National University of Singapore
chuats@comp.nus.edu.sg

Mohan Kankanhalli
National University of Singapore
mohan@comp.nus.edu.sg

ABSTRACT

With the advancement of mobile computing technology and cloud-based streaming music service, user-centered music retrieval has become increasingly important. User-specific information has a fundamental impact on personal music preferences and interests. However, existing research pays little attention to the modeling and integration of user-specific information in music retrieval algorithms/models to facilitate music search. In this paper, we propose a novel model, named User-Information-Aware Music Interest Topic (UIA-MIT) model. The model is able to effectively capture the influence of user-specific information on music preferences, and further associate users' music preferences and search terms under the same latent space. Based on this model, a user information aware retrieval system is developed, which can search and re-rank the results based on age- and/or gender-specific music preferences. A comprehensive experimental study demonstrates that our methods can significantly improve the search accuracy over existing text-based music retrieval methods.

CCS CONCEPTS

•**Information systems → Information retrieval; Music retrieval;** Retrieval models and ranking;

KEYWORDS

Semantic music retrieval, user demographic information, re-ranking, topic model

ACM Reference format:
Zhiyong Cheng, Jialie Shen, Liqiang Nie, Tat-Seng Chua, and Mohan Kankanhalli. 2017. Exploring User-Specific Information in Music Retrieval. In *Proceedings of SIGIR'17, August 7–11, 2017, Shinjuku, Tokyo, Japan,* , 10 pages.
DOI: http://dx.doi.org/10.1145/3077136.3080772

*Jialie Shen is corresponding author

SIGIR'17, August 7–11, 2017, Shinjuku, Tokyo, Japan
© 2017 ACM. 978-1-4503-5022-8/17/08...$15.00
DOI: http://dx.doi.org/10.1145/3077136.3080772

1 INTRODUCTION

With the rapid development of mobile computing technology and cloud-based streaming music service, smart devices have become the most popular platforms to consume music daily. Based on Nelsen's Music 360 2015 report[1] , 44% of US music listeners use smartphones to listen to music on a daily basis. Smartphones are typically designed for personal use and it is easy to obtain personal information from smartphones, which can be used in personalized applications to achieve better user experiences when developing personalized applications. With the rapidly growing trend in music consumption with smartphones, there has been an increasing interest in studying user-centered music retrieval [11, 25, 33, 34, 36]. Techniques to support effective user-centered music search are gaining its importance due to its wide range of potential applications [7, 25, 36]. Based on this technology, intelligent music search or recommendation systems can be developed to automatically cater to users' personal music needs.

Text-based music retrieval, as one of the most popular music search paradigms, typically requires users to provide a few text keywords as queries to describe their music information needs [20, 24, 27, 41]. Most previous research efforts in music retrieval have been devoted to the development of retrieval/recommendation algorithms [5, 11, 21, 27], effective music representations [23, 24, 31, 42], similarity measurement [6, 12, 38, 45, 48], and automatic music annotation [1, 3, 13, 26, 28, 37, 40, 41, 46]. However, the effects of user-specific information in music retrieval has not been well studied [25, 33, 34]. User-specific information or user background, such as *age, gender, social status, growing-up environment, culture background, etc.,* has great impact on users' long-term music interests. This hypothesis has received strong support in prior research studies [8, 22, 43]. Due to its great impact, given the same query, users with different backgrounds might expect different search results [11]. For example, given a query "*pop, sad*", the retrieved songs expected by a 40-year-old male could be very different from those favored by a 20-year-old female.

In this study, we develop a text-based music retrieval system, which can effectively leverage user-specific information to improve the search performance. The key challenges on effectively integrating user-specific information in music retrieval include: (1) how to model the influence of user-specific

[1] http://www.nielsen.com/us/en/insights/reports/2015/music-360-2015-highlights.html

information on music preferences; and (2) how to associate the influence with search queries and songs. To tackle these two challenges, a novel topic model named User Information Aware Music Interest Topic (UIA-MIT) is proposed. UIA-MIT can explicitly model the music preferences of different types of user-specific information. In this model, the music preferences affected by different factors (i.e., age and gender) are represented by probabilistic distributions on a set of latent topics. These latent topics are in turn probabilistic distributions of songs and terms (song's annotations or tags). Therefore, songs, terms, and music preferences (influenced by age and gender) can be associated by latent topics. Based on the UIA-MIT model, we develop a probabilistic text-based music retrieval method, which can effectively exploit user information to improve the search results. In our context, *user-specific information* refers to the *user related information* or *user backgrounds* which have been proven to have great impact on a user's long-term music interests, such as *age*, *gender*, and *country* [8, 22, 43].

In order to evaluate the performance of our proposed method, extensive experiments and comprehensive comparisons over different methods have been conducted on two retrieval tasks: ad-hoc search and re-ranking. The experimental results demonstrate that users' age and/or gender information play an important role on search performance improvement, which indicates the importance of utilizing user-specific information in real music retrieval system development. To the best of our knowledge, our work is the first attempt on designing advanced music retrieval methods to leverage user-specific information in retrieval. In summary, the main contributions of this work include:

- This is the first attempt to explore the incorporation of user-specific information in music retrieval algorithms for search accuracy improvement.
- We propose a UIA-MIT model, which can explicitly model the music preferences affected by different types of user information. Furthermore, based on the model, a text-based music retrieval method is developed to effectively utilize user-specific information for improving the search accuracy.
- We construct two test collections and empirically evaluate the performance of the proposed retrieval method and compare it with a set of baselines. The experimental results demonstrate significant performance improvement.

The remainder of this paper is organized as follows: Section 2 gives a brief overview of related work; Section 3 detailedly describes the proposed UIA-MIT model and retrieval method; Section 4 introduces the experimental datasets and configurations; and Section 5 reports the experimental results and main findings. Finally, Section 6 concludes the paper.

2 RELATED WORKS

In this following, we review the research directions which are closely related to this paper, including text-based music retrieval, the use of user information in music retrieval and recommender systems, and related topic models.

2.1 Text-based Music Retrieval

As one of the most popular music search paradigms, text-based retrieval system is built on the top of mature text retrieval techniques and typically requires users to provide a few text keywords as queries to describe their music information needs [20, 24, 27, 41]. Its search performance heavily relies on the meta-information (e.g., artist and title) and well-defined categorized information (e.g., genre and instrument). In many cases, users would also like to describe their current contexts, such as *emotions* and *occasions*, with the expectation that the music search engine return a playlist with suitable songs [19]. To support the search of such semantic queries, one needs to annotate songs with a rich vocabulary of music terms. However, human annotation is very expensive in terms of both time and labor, and thus it is unlikely to scale with the growth in the amount of recorded songs. To deal with this problem, many automated methods have been proposed to automatically annotate songs with music related concepts by learning the correlation between music acoustic contents and the semantic terms based on a well-annotated music collection. Most automated systems generate a vector of tag weights when annotating a new song for music retrieval [26]. An early work in this direction is described in [41]. They formalized the audio annotation and retrieval as a supervised multi-class labeling task. The dataset CAL500 they created in this study became a standard test collection for subsequent works [1, 13, 26, 28, 42, 44].

With the rapid development of social music websites, songs are annotated with user-contributed social tags, which provides an alternative way to navigate and search songs (e.g., Last.fm). Social tags have no constraints on the use of text and provide a rich vocabulary, which covers most terms used to describe songs. Extensive research efforts have been devoted to developing tag-based music search systems [24]. However, the user-provided tags are known to be noisy, incomplete and subjective [24], which limits the search performance of tag-based methods. Consequently, many works consider the combination of tags and acoustic similarity to improve the search performance [21, 24, 27].

2.2 User Information in Music Retrieval

In recent years, researchers have realized and advocated the importance of incorporating information about user into music information search and discovery [25, 33, 34, 36]. Previous work has shown that user information can be used to improve music recommendation [8, 43]. In [29], user demographic information was taken into a fuzzy system for context inference using Bayesian network. In [15], user information was used to infer user's mood, which is then used to match with the mood of songs predicted based on music content. [35] studied the influence of user information (e.g., age, gender, and country) on the task of artist recommendation. Although the use of user information in recommender systems is widespread, little effort has been devoted to the exploration of user information in music retrieval. Furthermore, previous studies have not explicitly modeled the music preferences of different ages and genders in recommendation. In this work, we propose a user-information aware music interests discovery model to capture the music preferences of different ages and genders, and develop a music retrieval framework to use age and/or gender information in music retrieval.

2.3 Topic Models in Music Retrieval

Topic models, such as pLSA [17] and LDA [4], were originally proposed to discover the underlying *themes* or *latent topics* for a large scale collection of text documents. In these models, latent topics are discovered by mining co-occurrence patterns of words in documents that exhibit similar patterns. By treating *users* as *documents* and *items* as *words*, topic models have been applied to discover user's latent interests [18, 30]. In the domain of music information retrieval and recommendation, several previous studies adapted the topic models to capture user's music interests [9, 11, 16, 47]. [47] used the three-way aspect model to discover user music interests in recommendation. [9] extended the three-away aspect model to incorporate both location context and global music trends for location-aware personalized music recommendation. User's local music preference is captured by the co-occurrence of songs in users' music profiles and the co-occurrence of music contents among songs. In [10], a location-aware topic model was proposed to discover the music preferences of different venue types. [16] proposed a variant of LDA to discover user's interests via the combination of co-occurrence of songs in the same user's playlist and co-occurrence of tags in the same song. In [11], a dual-layer music preference topic model was developed to characterize the correlation among users, songs, and search terms for personalized music retrieval.

3 OUR APPROACH

In general, users with similar demographics have more similar music interests than users with different demographics. For example, users in the same age or gender have more similar music interests [2, 22]. To model the influence of such user-specific factors, we propose a User Information Aware Music Interest Topic (UIA-MIT) model. In this model, a set of latent topics (i.e., K topics) are discovered based on the records of users' favorite tracks. Each latent topic represents one type/style of music or a *music interest dimension.* As users' music interests are influenced by different factors. UIA-MIT is designed to capture the influence of different factors on music interests. For example, what are the *general music interests* of users in *a certain age range or gender*; or in other words, the *likelihood* of each type of songs preferred by the users with regard to their ages and genders. In this model, a user's latent music interest is expressed as a mixture of multiple latent topic distributions. Each latent topic distribution represents a certain music interest which is dependent on a user-specific factor (e.g., age). Therefore, the mixture of multiple latent topic distributions in this model represents the music interests of a user, as the result of collective effects of different factors.

Table 1: Notations and their definitions

Notation	Definition
u, s	user, and song, respectively
c, a, g	country, age, and gender category
s_v, s_w	song, audio word, and text word
D	corpus, $(u, a, g, s, \boldsymbol{s_w}, \boldsymbol{s_v}) \in D$
$\|D_u\|$	number of songs in the u's music profile
$\mathcal{U}$, $\mathcal{S}$	user set and song set in the corpus
U, S	total number of users and songs in the corpus
$\mathcal{W}$, $\mathcal{V}$	text and audio word vocabulary, respectively
W, V	text and audio vocabulary size, respecitvely
$\mathcal{A}$, $\mathcal{G}$	age category set and gender category set
A, G	number of age and gender groups, respectively
K	total number of latent topics
y	indicator variable: decide z generated from θ_u, θ_a, or θ_g
$\boldsymbol{\lambda}$	mixing weight vector
$\boldsymbol{\alpha}, \boldsymbol{\beta}, \boldsymbol{\gamma}$	Dirichlet priors
$\boldsymbol{\theta_u}, \boldsymbol{\theta_a}, \boldsymbol{\theta_g}$	music preference of user u, age group a, and gender group g, respectively
$\boldsymbol{\phi_s}$, $\boldsymbol{\phi_v}$, $\boldsymbol{\phi_w}$	multinomial distributions over songs $\mathcal{S}$, audio words $\mathcal{V}$ and text words $\mathcal{W}$

3.1 Preliminaries

For ease of understanding and presentation, we first introduce some key concepts and notations. Table 1 lists the notations used in this paper.

Dataset The dataset D in our model consists of a set of records, with each record comprising a user, user information (i.e., age and gender), song, and song's content (i.e., tags and audio words), that is, $(u, a, g, s, \boldsymbol{s_w}, \boldsymbol{s_v}) \in D$, where $u \in \mathcal{U}$, $s \in \mathcal{S}$, $a \in \mathcal{A}$, $g \in \mathcal{G}$, $s_w \in \mathcal{W}$, and $s_v \in \mathcal{V}$. [2] One piece of record in the dataset is a user u of age a and gender g who loves a song s with tags $\boldsymbol{s_w}$ and audio content $\boldsymbol{s_v}$: $D_{usc} = \{(u, a, g, s, w, v) : w \in \boldsymbol{s_w}, v \in \boldsymbol{s_v}\}$.

Audio Word An audio word is a representative short frame (e.g., 0.5s in our implementation) of audio stream in a music corpus [11]. Audio words are used to represent the audio content of a song as a "bag-of-audio-words" document.

Latent Topic A latent topic z, or *topic* for short, in a song collection $\mathcal{S}$ is a probabilistic distribution over songs, i.e., $\{P(s|\boldsymbol{\phi_s}) : s \in \mathcal{S}\}$. Similarly, a topic in a text word corpus $\mathcal{W}$ is a probabilistic distribution over text words, i.e., $\{P(w|\boldsymbol{\phi_w}) : w \in \mathcal{W}\}$. A topic in an audio word corpus $\mathcal{V}$ is a probabilistic distribution over audio words, i.e., $\{P(v|\boldsymbol{\phi_v}) : v \in \mathcal{V}\}$.

User's Music Interest UIA-MIT models users' music interest as the mixture of three latent topic distributions (see Eq. 1): (1) $\boldsymbol{\theta_u}$: the music preferences as a collective result based on the influence of all other factors (e.g., personality) besides age and gender , (2) $\boldsymbol{\theta_a}$: age-based music preference, denoting *the music preferences of a certain age range a* or *the general music preferences of users in age range a*, and (3) $\boldsymbol{\theta_g}$:

[2] In the paper, unless otherwise specified, notations in bold style denote matrices or vectors, and the ones in normal style denote scalars.

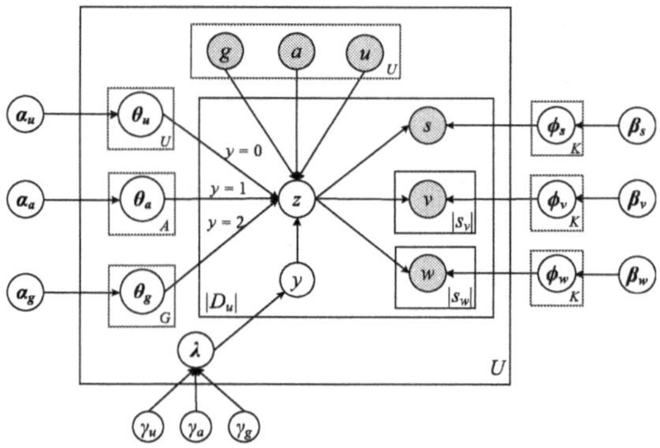

Figure 1: The graphical representation of the UIA-MIT model.

gender-based music preference, denoting *music preferences of male or female.*

3.2 UIA-MIT Model

3.2.1 Model Description. The graphical representation of the model is shown in Fig. 1, in which *age* and *gender* are considered. UIA-MIT explicitly models the music preferences of ages ($\boldsymbol{\theta_a}$) and genders ($\boldsymbol{\theta_g}$). The music preference, as a result of all other factors (excluding age and gender, such as user's personality and country), is modeled as a single probabilistic distribution of latent topics, denoted as user's personal music interest ($\boldsymbol{\theta_u}$). Notice that the UIA-MIT model can be easily extended to model the music preference of other individual factors (e.g., *country*).

From the generation perspective, the model mimics the music selection process by considering the user's music interest, age-based music preference, and gender-based music preference in a unified manner. Given a user with age a and gender g, the likelihood the user u selecting a music track is dependent on the music preferences of user age and gender as well as his/her personal music interest:

$$P(s|u,a,g,\boldsymbol{\theta_u},\boldsymbol{\theta_a},\boldsymbol{\theta_g},\boldsymbol{\phi_w},\boldsymbol{\phi_v},\boldsymbol{\phi_s}) = \lambda_u P(s|u,\boldsymbol{\theta_u},\boldsymbol{\phi_w},\boldsymbol{\phi_v},\boldsymbol{\phi_s}) + \lambda_a P(s|a,\boldsymbol{\theta_a},\boldsymbol{\phi_w},\boldsymbol{\phi_v},\boldsymbol{\phi_s}) + \lambda_g P(s|g,\boldsymbol{\theta_g},\boldsymbol{\phi_w},\boldsymbol{\phi_v},\boldsymbol{\phi_s}) \quad (1)$$

where $P(s|u,\boldsymbol{\theta_u},\boldsymbol{\phi_w},\boldsymbol{\phi_v},\boldsymbol{\phi_s})$ is the probability that song s is generated according to the personal music interest of user u, denoted as $\boldsymbol{\theta_u}$; $P(s|a,\boldsymbol{\theta_a},\boldsymbol{\phi_w},\boldsymbol{\phi_v},\boldsymbol{\phi_s})$ and $P(s|g,\boldsymbol{\theta_g},\boldsymbol{\phi_w},\boldsymbol{\phi_v},\boldsymbol{\phi_s})$ denote the probability that song s is generated according to the age music preference of a and gender music preference of g, denoted as $\boldsymbol{\theta_a}$ and $\boldsymbol{\theta_g}$ respectively. $\boldsymbol{\lambda} = \{\lambda_u, \lambda_a, \lambda_g : \lambda_u + \lambda_a + \lambda_g = 1\}$ is a categorial distribution, which controls the selection motivation of song s. That is, when selecting song s, it is possible that user u selects it according to his/her own music interests $\boldsymbol{\theta_u}$ with probability λ_u, or according to the age-based music preference $\boldsymbol{\theta_a}$ with probability λ_a, or according to the gender-based music preference $\boldsymbol{\theta_g}$ with probability λ_g. Note that $\boldsymbol{\lambda}$ is a group-dependent parameter, as users in different groups have different tendency to select music from different aspects. For example, from the training results, female users are more likely to select music tracks according to the general music preferences (namely, mainstreaming music) than male users.

The generation process of UIA-MIT is shown in Algorithm 1. Intuitively, UIA-MIT models user's music interests as the combination of the general music preferences according to certain user-specific information (age and gender here) and user's distinct music interests (affecting by user's personality, etc.). The general music preferences of certain user-specific information can be applied in music-related service.

Collapsed Gibbs sampling [14] is used to estimate the parameters in the topic model. Due to space limitation, we omit the description of parameter estimation in the paper.

Algorithm 1: Generation Process of UIA-MIT

for *each topic* $k = 1, ..., K$ **do**
  Draw $\boldsymbol{\phi_{k,s}} \sim Dir(\cdot|\boldsymbol{\beta_s})$;
  Draw $\boldsymbol{\phi_{k,w}} \sim Dir(\cdot|\boldsymbol{\beta_w})$;
  Draw $\boldsymbol{\phi_{k,v}} \sim Dir(\cdot|\boldsymbol{\beta_v})$;
for *each user* $u \in \mathcal{U}$ **do**
  Draw $\boldsymbol{\theta_u} \sim Dir(\cdot|\boldsymbol{\alpha_u})$;
for *each age range* $a \in \mathcal{A}$ **do**
  Draw $\boldsymbol{\theta_a} \sim Dir(\cdot|\boldsymbol{\alpha_a})$;
for *each gender* $g \in \mathcal{G}$ **do**
  Draw $\boldsymbol{\theta_g} \sim Dir(\cdot|\boldsymbol{\alpha_g})$;
for *each user* $u \in \mathcal{U}$ *with age* $a \in \mathcal{A}$ *and gender* $g \in \mathcal{G}$ **do**
  for *each song* $s \in D_u$ **do**
    Toss a coin according to categorical distribution $y_s \sim Dir(\gamma_u, \gamma_a, \gamma_g)$;
    if $y_s == 0$ **then**
      Draw $z_s \sim Multi(\boldsymbol{\theta_u})$ according to the music interest of user u;
    if $y_s == 1$ **then**
      Draw $z_s \sim Multi(\boldsymbol{\theta_a})$ according to the music preference of age a;
    if $y_s == 2$ **then**
      Draw $z_s \sim Multi(\boldsymbol{\theta_g})$ according to the music preference of gender g;
    After the sampling of the topic $z_s = k$, draw song $s \sim Multi(\boldsymbol{\theta_{k,s}})$;
    for *each word* $w \in s_w$ **do**
      Draw $w \sim Multi(\boldsymbol{\phi_{k,w}})$;
    for *each audio word* $v \in s_v$ **do**
      Draw $v \sim Multi(\boldsymbol{\phi_{k,v}})$;

3.3 Retrieval Method

Given a query q, UIA-MIT can be used to estimate $P(s|q)$ with the consideration of user's age and gender. In music retrieval, songs are then ranked in the descending order of $P(s|q)$ and the top results are returned to the user. Specifically, for a query $q = \{w_1, w_2.., w_n\}$ of user u with age a and gender g, the conditional probability $P(s|q)$ could be computed with estimated parameters $\boldsymbol{\Theta} = \{\boldsymbol{\theta_u}, \boldsymbol{\theta_a}, \boldsymbol{\theta_g}\}$ and $\boldsymbol{\Phi} = \{\boldsymbol{\phi_s}, \boldsymbol{\phi_w}\}$. For the simplicity of presentation, we use $P(s|q,\cdot)$ to denote $P(s|q,u,a,g,\boldsymbol{\Theta},\boldsymbol{\Phi})$ in the following.

$$P(s|q,\cdot) = \prod_{i=1}^{n} P(w_i|s,u,a,g,\boldsymbol{\Theta},\boldsymbol{\Phi}) P(s|u,a,g,\boldsymbol{\Theta},\boldsymbol{\phi_s}) \quad (2)$$

where query terms in q are assumed to be independent. $P(s|u, a, g, \boldsymbol{\Theta}, \boldsymbol{\phi_s})$ is computed as:

$$P(s|u, a, g, \boldsymbol{\Theta}, \boldsymbol{\phi_s}) = \sum_{k=1}^{K} P(s|z = k, \boldsymbol{\phi_s}) P(z = k|u, a, g, \boldsymbol{\Theta})$$
$$= \sum_{k=1}^{K} \phi_{k,s} \cdot (\lambda_u \theta_{u,k} + \lambda_a \theta_{a,k} + \lambda_g \theta_{g,k}) \tag{3}$$

According to Bayes rule and the graphical representation of the UIA-MIT model, $P(w_i|s, u, a, g, \boldsymbol{\Theta}, \boldsymbol{\Phi})$ is estimated as:

$$P(w_i|s, \cdot) = \sum_{k=1}^{K} P(w_i|z = k, \boldsymbol{\phi_w}) \frac{P(s, z_k|u, a, g, \boldsymbol{\Theta}, \boldsymbol{\phi_s})}{P(s|u, a, g, \boldsymbol{\Theta}, \boldsymbol{\phi_s})}$$
$$= \sum_{k=1}^{K} \phi_{k,w_i} \cdot \frac{\phi_{k,s} \cdot (\lambda_u \theta_{u,k} + \lambda_a \theta_{a,k} + \lambda_g \theta_{g,k})}{\sum_{k=1}^{K} \phi_{k,s} \cdot (\lambda_u \theta_{u,k} + \lambda_a \theta_{a,k} + \lambda_g \theta_{g,k})} \tag{4}$$

Based on Eq. 3 and Eq. 4, Eq. 2 becomes

$$P(s|q, \cdot) = \prod_{i=1}^{n} \sum_{k=1}^{K} \phi_{k,w_i} \cdot \phi_{k,s} \cdot (\lambda_u \theta_{u,k} + \lambda_a \theta_{a,k} + \lambda_g \theta_{g,k}) \tag{5}$$

Typically, when $\boldsymbol{\theta_u}$ of a particular user u is known, Eq. 5 can be used for personalized music search. However, for a new user to the system, $\boldsymbol{\theta_u}$ is unknown, while his/her age/gender information is relatively easier to be found. In such cases, we normalize λ_a and λ_g to $\lambda_a + \lambda_g = 1$, and the following equation is used for retrieval:

$$P(s|q, a, g, \boldsymbol{\Theta}, \boldsymbol{\Phi}) = \prod_{i=1}^{n} \sum_{k=1}^{K} \phi_{k,w_i} \cdot \phi_{k,s} \cdot (\lambda_a \theta_{a,k} + \lambda_g \theta_{g,k}) \tag{6}$$

If either age or gender information is available, only the corresponding music preferences will be used (namely, set $\lambda_a = 1$ or $\lambda_g = 1$ in the equation). Intuitively, $\phi_{k,w_i} \cdot \phi_{k,s}$ evaluates the similarity of the song s with respect to query q in the music dimension k in the music interest space, and $\lambda_a \theta_{a,k} + \lambda_g \theta_{g,k}$ estimates the music preferences with respect to age range a and gender g in the music dimension k. Thus it can be seen as that the model re-weights the original query in different music dimensions based on user's age and gender information. Given a new users with only age and/or gender information, our system can be used to search songs based on Eq. 6. Accordingly, the exploitation of age and gender (i.e., Eq. 6) can alleviate the cold-start problem in personalized music retrieval, in which user's music preference is unknown.

4 EXPERIMENTAL CONFIGURATION

We conduct a comprehensive experimental study to investigate the performance of our methods on two music retrieval tasks: *ad-hoc* and *re-rank*. The experiments mainly answer the following research questions:

RQ1 What is the performance of UIA-MIT based retrieval methods on ad-hoc search with the use of age and/or gender information as compared to other text-based music retrieval methods? (See Sect. 5.1.1)

RQ2 Whether the use of user-specific information (i.e., age and gender information in our study) for re-ranking can improve the music search performance? If so, how much can be improved by using age and/or gender information? (See Sect. 5.1.2 and Sect. 5.2)

RQ3 Whether the UIA-MIT model can be extended to model the music preference of other user information, such as country? (See Sect. 5.2)

RQ4 What are the impact of different types of user information on user's music preference, such as age, gender and country information? (See Sect. 5.3)

To answer these questions, we constructed two test collections to conduct experiments. In our experiments, test collections are split into a training set and a testing set. The training set is used to train the UIA-MIT model. User-specific information and users' favorite songs are used in the training stage. In the testing stage, only user-specific information is used in retrieval. The information of favorite songs are only used in the result evaluation. It is similar to the cold-start problem in personalized search, where user's personal preferences are unknown.

4.1 Datasets

To evaluate the search accuracy of retrieval systems with respect to query users, a great challenge is how to obtain the ground truth of the test queries with respect to the corresponding query users. In our retrieval task, given a query q of a user with certain information, a relevant song should not only be relevant to the query but also loved by the users with such information. We developed two test collections by crawling user information from Last.fm. Thousands of queries and corresponding ground truth are generated for testing. The dataset will be released for the repeatability of the experiments and other related studies.[3]

User Profile Dataset We construct a dataset with users' demographic information and their favorite music tracks from Last.fm. The dataset is collected in the following procedures. 160 recent active users were randomly selected from Last.fm[4]. The friends of these users and the friends of their friends were also collected with their demographic information, including age, gender, country. In total, 90,036 users were collected. Users who provide both age and gender information were retained. As the number of users with age under 16 or above 54 years old is small, we removed these users and only focused on studying the influence of ages between 16 to 54. Finally, the dataset remains 45,334 users. Users' favorite tracks were collected using Last.fm public API "User.getLovedTracks", and a 30-second audio stream of each song was downloaded from 7digital[5]. By removing users with less than 10 favorite songs and songs preferred by less than 10 users, there are 29,412 users (15,826 males and 13,586 females) and 15,323 songs in the final dataset. The social tags of these songs were

[3]Experimental datasets are accessible in:https://www.dropbox.com/sh/eue9it0lqlpzo7q/AAAe-v2MS0KYln5qSpSgPQQna?dl=0.
[4]Accessed http://www.last.fm/community/users/active on Mar 3, 2015.
[5]https://www.7digital.com/

collected from Last.fm using API "Track.getTopTags". The social tags of songs from Last.fm are used in the topic model training and the tag-based music retrieval method (see the TAG method in Section 4.2). We denote the dataset as D for ease of presentation.

Retrieval Test Collection 1 (TC1) To judge the relevance of songs with respect to queries, it is necessary to label the songs in the dataset with query concepts. CAL10K [39] is a labeled song collection. The annotations are used as ground truth in pervious text-based music retrieval research [27]. This dataset contains 10,870 songs from 4,597 different artists. The label vocabulary is composed of 137 "genre" tags and 416 "acoustic" tags. The number of tags of songs varies from 2 to 25 tags. The song tags are mined from the Pandora Web sites. The annotations in Pandora are contributed by music experts and are considered highly objective [39]. 2,839 songs in D are contained in the CAL10K. These songs are used as retrieval dataset in TC1. In experiments, we categorized the users into 7 age groups, as shown in Table 2. Thus, there are 14 user groups (7 age groups $\times$ 2 gender groups) in total.

Table 2: Number of users in each age group in Test Collection 1.

Group	0	1	2	3	4	5	6
Age	16-20	21-25	26-30	31-35	36-40	41-45	46-54
#Users	9,003	12,820	4,941	1,482	595	324	247

Retrieval Test Collection 2 (TC2) Due to the limited size of the well-labeled songs, TC1 contains only 2,839 songs in the retrieval stage, which is relatively small. TC1 can be used to to test the performance of the proposed retrieval methods by leveraging age and gender information. To examine the performance of our methods in large datasets and demonstrate the extendability of UIA-MIT to other user information ("*country*" here), we constructed TC2. TC2 uses social tags as annotations in relevance judgement. 26,468 users in D have age, gender, and country information. These users are from 179 different countries. With the age, gender, and country information, we categorize users into groups based on {age, gender, country}, e.g., 16-20_male_US. The top 30 user groups with the most number of users are used in experiments to examine the performance of our methods. These groups are shown in Table 3. By removing users with less than 10 favorite songs and songs liked by less than 10 users, TC2 has 14,715 users and 1, 0197 songs.

Query Set In experiments, we use a combination of k distinct terms as queries. Following the methodology in [27, 41], queries composed by $k = \{1, 2, 3\}$ terms are used. The method described in [27] is used to construct the query set. In TC1, all the terms in CAL10K dataset are treated as 1-term query candidates; and for 2-term and 3-term queries, all the term combinations are considered as candidates. In TC2, social tags are used to generate the queries. We first filtered the tags which appear less than 10 times in the dataset, and removed the tags which express personal interests in the song, such as "favorite", "great", "favor", "excellent", etc. After

Table 3: Number of users in different groups in Test Collection 2.

Country	Male			Female		
	16-20	21-25	26-30	16-20	21-25	26-30
Brazil	1605	1320	253	1665	809	156
Poland	179	270	83	472	401	98
Russia	83	269	109	184	314	92
UK	186	416	223	198	364	120
US	539	1360	684	457	1273	533

tokenizing the tags of each song into terms, all the terms are treated as candidates. For 2-term and 3-term queries, all the term combinations which appear in a song are treated as candidates. Next, query candidates with less than 10 relevant songs in the ground truth of all user groups were removed. For the 3-term query in TC2, we retain a random sample of 3,000 queries as [27]. Table 4 summarizes the number of queries in TC1 and TC2. Notice that the queries are the same for each group. Table 5 shows some query examples.

Table 4: Number of queries in TC1 and TC2.

Test Collection	# 1-Term	# 2-Term	# 3-Term
TC1	33	122	542
TC2	79	1691	3000

Table 5: Few examples for each type of queries.

1-Term Query	2-Term Query	3-Term Query
aggressive	aggressive, guitar	aggressive, angry, guitar
angry	aggressive, rock	angry, guitar, rock
breathy	bass, tonality	drums, angry, guitar
country	blues, guitar	guitar, aggressive, angry
danceable	country, guitar	guitar, pop, romantic

Ground Truth As the query is evaluated with respect to different user groups (i.e., age and gender groups), a relevant song with respect to a query should (1) contains all the query terms in the annotations (in the CAL10K dataset for TC1) or social tags (for TC2); and (2) be loved by at least 10 users in this user group. The second criterion is to guarantee that the relevant song is loved by users in a user group (i.e., with a certain age and gender). Based on the criteria, the relevant songs in the retrieval datasets of TC1 and TC2 are labeled. Notice that for each query, the numbers of relevant songs in different groups are different.

4.2 Experimental Setup

In our experiments, users were split into two sets for two-fold cross-validation: one set (users with their favorite tracks) is used for model training, and the other set is used to create the query set and generate the corresponding ground truth. The dataset is split in the way to guarantee each set has approximately equal number of users in the two sets. In the result presentation, the presented results are the average performance of the two sets. For the training of UIA-MIT, the corpus is formulated into three types of documents:

User-Song Document It represents a user's music profile. For each user, a user-song document is generated based on his/her favorite songs. The document is the concatenation of all the songs preferred by the users.

Song-Text Word Document This document represents the semantic content of a song. Songs' tags from Last.fm are used to form their text documents. In our implementation, tags that appeared less than 10 songs are filtered. The remaining tags of a song are concatenated and tokenized with a standard stop-list to form its text document.

Song-Audio Word Document This document represents the audio content of a song, namely, the audio words used in the UIA-MIT model. The audio contents of one song are represented by "bag-of-audio-words" document. An audio word is a representative short frame of audio stream (e.g., 0.5 second) in a music corpus. For each song, a 30-second audio track downloaded from 7digital is used to generate its "bag-of-audio-word" document. We follow the method described in [11] to generate the song-audio word documents.

4.2.1 Baselines.

- **TAG** In this method, the social tags of each song in Last.fm are used as the text description for retrieval. The standard tf-idf weighting scheme is used to compute the similarity between query and songs with the standard cosine distance in the Vector Space Model [32].
- **WLC** The first result returned by TAG is used as the seed for a content-based music retrieval (CBMR) method. Then the score of the TAG method and CBMR method are linearly combined together to generate the final search results. This method is implemented as described in [11].
- **PAR** This method is proposed in [21]. It incorporates audio similarity into an already existing ranking. In our experiments, the results of tag-based method (TAG) are used as the initial ranking list. In the implementation, we followed the details reported in the referred paper.
- **GBR** This method is proposed in [27]. It is a graph-based ranking method, which combines both tag and acoustic similarity in a probabilistic graph-based representation for music retrieval. In our implementation, we followed the details reported in the referred paper.
- **Music Popularity Based Re-ranking (MPR)** This method re-ranks the top (e.g., 100) songs returned by other retrieval methods according to the popularity of these songs in each user group. The popularity score is computed as:

$$POP(s) = \frac{N(s,a,g)}{N(a,g)} \tag{7}$$

  where $N(s,a,g)$ is the number of users in group (a,g) favoring song s, and $N(a,g)$ is the total number of the users in group (a,g).
- **Group User Music Representation (GUMR)** For each group, we aggregate the social tags of songs loved by the users in this group to form a music representation document for the group. For a given query q of user u in age a and gender g, the similarity score is computed as:

$$Sim(q,s,a,g) = w \cdot TAG(q,s) + (1-w) \cdot Sim(s,a,g) \tag{8}$$

  in which $TAG(q,s)$ is the cosine similarity between the song s and q using TAG method, and $Sim(s,a,g)$ is the similarity between user group preference and the song s using cosine distance with the standard tf-idf weighting scheme (based on song's text document and the group's music document). The combination weight is tuned in experiments.

The following methods are the variants of the proposed method, which simulate the scenarios when partial user information is available, and study the improvements of using such information individually or together in retrieval.

- **A-MIT**: only considering age information in UIA-MIT;
- **G-MIT**: only considering gender information in UIA-MIT;
- **C-MIT**: only considering country information in UIA-MIT (only tested in TC2);
- **AG-MIT**: considering both age and gender information in UIA-MIT.
- **AGC-MIT**: considering age, gender, and country information in UIA-MIT (only used in TC 2).

To the best of our knowledge, we have not found any music search methods using such information in retrieval. MPR and GUMR are two heuristic methods on utilizing age and gender information. Notice that if these methods can also improve the search accuracy, it further demonstrates the importance of considering user-specific information in music retrieval. In the above methods, PAR and MPR are reranking methods and thus are compared in the re-ranking task (Sect. 5.2). Other methods are compared in the ad-hoc search task (Sect. 5.1).

4.2.2 Metrics. Precision at k (**P@k**) and Mean Average Precision (**MAP**) are used as evaluation metrics. As the top search results are more important, we report P@10 and MAP@10 in experimental results.

4.2.3 Parameter Setting. In our implementation, the hyperparameters in the topic model are turned in a wide range of values. In the UIA-MIT model, without prior knowledge about the topic distributions of users in different ages and genders, we set $\boldsymbol{\alpha_u}$, $\boldsymbol{\alpha_a}$ and $\boldsymbol{\alpha_g}$ to be symmetric. For simplicity, we set them to be the same and tune them in the range of $\alpha = \alpha_u = \alpha_a = \alpha_g \in \{0.01, 0.05, 0.1, 1.0, 5.0\}$. Similarly, β_w, β_v and β_s are also set to be symmetric and tuned in similar manners: $\beta = \beta_w = \beta_v = \beta_s \in \{0.01, 0.05, 0.10, 0.15, 0.20, 0.25\}$. The values of γ_u, γ_a and γ_g bias the tendency of choosing music according to user's personal, age or gender music preferences. We would like the tendency to be learned from the data, thus γ_u, γ_a, γ_g are all set to 1. In Gibbs sampling for the training of topic models, 100 sampling iterations were run as burn-in iterations and then 50 sampling iterations with a gap of 10 were taken to obtain the final results. In

Table 6: Comparison of retrieval performance on TC1

Method	1-Term Query		2-Term Query		3-Term Query	
	P@10	MAP	P@10	MAP	P@10	MAP
TAG	.164	.134	.054	.041	.022	.014
WLC	.178	.142	.058	.051	.022	.023
GBR	.248	.267	.136	.147	.122	.125
GUMR	.133	.115	.030	.026	.015	.012
G-MIT	.276	.283	.139	.155	.116	.134
A-MIT	.250	.259	.135	.151	.111	.128
AG-MIT	**.339***	**.335***	**.177***	**.184***	**.149***	**.166***

the result presentation in Sect. 5, the reported results are based on the parameters with the best results.

5 EXPERIMENTAL RESULTS

In all the reported results, the symbol (*) after a numeric value denotes significant differences ($p < 0.05$, a two-tailed paired t-test) with the corresponding second best measurement. In our experiments, for each user group (i.e., male users between 16-20 years old), all the 1-term, 2-term and 3-term queries are used for retrieval and evaluation. All the results presented are the average values over all user groups in each test collection.

5.1 Performance on TC1

5.1.1 Retrieval Performance. Retrieval results of the proposed methods using age and/or gender information with the baselines are reported in Table 6. From the table, we observe that: First, for the three types of queries, it is obvious that queries with more terms is more difficult for all methods. As can be seen, the proposed method using age and gender information (AG-MIT) outperforms all the other methods over all types of queries. Besides, A-MIT and G-MIT methods obtain comparable or better performance over the GBR method, which shows the best performance besides our proposed methods. The results demonstrate the effectiveness of the proposed retrieval methods.

Second, compared to the TAG method which only uses text information in retrieval, WLC and GBR that use both text and acoustic features obtain better performance. WLC uses a linearly combination of similarities based on TAG and acoustic features. It can only slightly improve the search performance. Notice that the WLC uses the first search results of TAG as acoustic query, the search accuracy of TAG thus affects the improvement of the WLC method. GBR method explore both text and acoustic information by discovering and using the intrinsic correlation between the semantics of terms and the acoustic contents. It obtain much better results than the TAG method.

Third, it can be seen that the G-MIT and A-MIT methods can improve the search performance over the GBR method for 1-term query. The AG-MIT method can further improve the performance for 1-term, 2-term, and 3-term queries. The effects of using age or gender information in retrieval are comparable, and the gender information seems to be slightly more effective than age information. The performance of the AG-MIT method is obviously better than the G-MIT and A-MIT methods, indicating that the use of both age and gender information together is more effective than using them individually. The results of GUMR are quite poor, because of the simple method on modeling user's music preferences with age and gender information.

5.1.2 Re-ranking Performance. This section presents the re-ranking performance based on the top 100 results of different retrieval methods (i.e., TAG, WLC, and GBR). The results are reported in Table 7. In the table, the row starting with "-" shows the performance obtained by the corresponding baseline methods. Overall, the results are improved greatly and significantly by the re-ranking methods, even for 2- and 3-term queries whose initial results are very poor. An interesting finding is that the initial results of the TAG method is worse than the WLC method, however, the TAG method can obtain much better re-ranking results than the WLC method by all re-ranking methods. The results indicate that the WLC method can obtain better search results in top positions (e.g., top 10 results), while it reduces the number of relevant results in a longer list (i.e. top 100 results).

The effectiveness of the re-ranking methods based on the proposed models can be observed by comparing our methods (A-MIT, G-MIT, or AG-MIT) with the PAR method. The improvements of our methods are much greater than that of the PAR method. Notice that the UIA-MIT model explores the relevance between queries (semantic concepts or tags) and songs in a latent music interest space, which is discovered based on the music preferences of a large number of listeners. In other words, the method leverages the collaborative knowledge of crowds to estimate the relevance between query concepts and songs , or the music preference of general users on songs with respect to query concepts. The external knowledge is complementary to the information used by the TAG, WLG, or GBR methods, which compute the relevance between the query and song only based on the contents. Consequently, using the estimated relevance between query and song based on the UIA-MIT model for re-ranking can significantly improve the search performance.

The benefits of utilizing user information in music retrieval can be well demonstrated by the MPR method, which can improve the search performance greatly using a heuristic method - re-ranking the songs according to their popularity in user groups. For the 1-term query on $P@10$, the relative improvement by MPR achieves more than 133% and 43% over the TAG and GBR methods, respectively. The improvement over 2-term and 3-term queries is even larger. G-MIT and A-MIT methods obtain much better results than the MPR method. The AG-MIT method can further improve the performance. Notice that improvements achieved by A-MIT, G-MIT and AG-MIT are contributed by both the learned associations between query and songs and the

Table 7: Comparison of re-ranking performance on TC1

Method	1-Term Query						2-Term Query						3-Term Query					
	TAG		WLC		GBR		TAG		WLC		GBR		TAG		WLC		GBR	
	P@10	MAP	P@10	MAP	P@10	MAP	P@10	MAP	P@10	MAP	P@10	MAP	P@10	MAP	P@10	MAP	P@10	MAP
-	.164	.134	.178	.142	.248	.267	.054	.041	.058	.051	.136	.147	.022	.014	.022	.023	.112	.125
PAR	.233	.249	.086	.074	.330	.309	.099	.116	.036	.035	.197	.199	.068	.078	.022	.023	.182	.175
MPR	.383	.409	.185	.148	.355	.347	.237	.257	.063	.069	.241	.257	.184	.204	.039	.042	.206	.223
G-MIT	.460	.470	.197	.223	.439	.450	.260	.278	.069	.079	.263	.268	.191	.209	.048	**.053**	.215	.230
A-MIT	.444	.470	.195	.221	.431	.434	.254	.277	.077	.086	.273	.285	.192	.211	.045	.046	.215	.233
AG-MIT	**.479***	**.495**	**.228***	**.242**	**.444***	**.463***	**.267**	**.294***	**.087***	**.091***	**.285***	**.287**	**.200**	**.225***	**.053**	.048	**.226**	**.246***

Table 8: Comparison of re-ranking performance on TC2 based on the results of TAG

Method	1-Term Query		2-Term Query		3-Term Query	
	P@10	MAP	P@10	MAP	P@10	MAP
TAG	.122	.120	.042	.020	.022	.017
MPR	.216	.277	.135	.138	.103	.106
A-MIT	.240	.318	.146	.182	.103	.106
G-MIT	.228	.304	.135	.158	.104	.108
C-MIT	.244	.318	.144	.181	.104	.107
AG-MIT	.252	.330	.144	.176	.104	.108
AGC-MIT	**.375***	**.505***	**.160**	**.199***	**.105**	**.110**

captured age and gender music preferences in UIA-MIT. The relative improvement of the AG-MIT for the 1-term query on $P@10$ achieves more than 192% and 79% over the TAG and GBR methods, respectively. UIA-MIT captures the age music preference and gender music preference together and achieves consistent and better improvement over A-MIT and G-MIT. It shows that the influence of age and gender are correlated in affecting users' music interests. Thus, it is not optimal to use age-based music preference and gender-based music preference individually.

5.2 Performance on TC2

Similar results can be observed in TC2 for both ad-hoc and re-ranking tasks. Due to space limitation, we only present the performance of re-ranking performance based on TAG, because from the experimental results on TC1: (1) using our method in re-ranking can greatly improve the search results; and (2) re-ranking performance based on TAG are comparable or better than the performance based on WLC and GBR. Table 8 presents the re-ranking results of different methods on TC2. The second row shows the search results of TAG method, and 3 - 9 rows show the re-ranking results of different methods. From the table, it can be observed that user's country information (C-MIT) can also be used to improve the performance. AGC-MIT obtains the best performance, demonstrating that the UIA-MIT model can be easily extended to include other types of user information and the utilization of more types of user information can obtain better performance.

Table 9: Mean values of λ in the UIA-MIT model

Test Collection	Male Groups			Female Groups		
	λ_a	λ_g	λ_c	λ_a	λ_g	λ_c
TC1	.119	.170	-	.149	.217	-
TC2	.089	.137	.183	.143	.179	.185

5.3 Impact of Different User Information

In the UIA-MIT model, λ_u, λ_a, and λ_g control the contributions of users' unique music interests and general music interests of age and gender in music selection. Thus, the values of these parameters show the relative importance of different types of user information in users' music preferences. Table 9 shows the mean values of λ_a, λ_g, and λ_c of male and female groups in two test collections. λ_c is a similar parameter as λ_a, controlling the weight of the general music interest of users in different countries. Notice that UIA-MIT in TC1 has not considered country information. The values of those three parameters vary greatly across different user groups, indicating that those three factors are inter-correlated to affect users' music preferences. Overall, the differences of three parameters between male and female groups are more obviously (comparing to different age or country groups). In the table, we show the values of three parameters in male groups and female groups separately. Some interesting observations can be found on the global level: (1) users' personal music interests ($\boldsymbol{\theta_u}$) dominate the music selection, as $\lambda_u > 0.5$[6]; (2) the value of λ_c is greater than those of λ_g and λ_a, indicating that the effects of country on music selection is larger than age and gender; (2) the value of λ_g is slightly larger than that of λ_a, indicating that gender has more impact on the music preferences than age.

6 CONCLUSION

In this paper, we proposed a novel User-Information-Aware Music Interest Topic (UIA-MIT) model to discover the latent music interest space of general users and capture the music preferences of users in different ages and genders. Based on the proposed model, a music retrieval method is developed for text-based music retrieval, which can effectively incorporate user information to improve the search results. Extensive experiments were conducted to demonstrate the effectiveness of exploiting user's age and gender information

[6] $\lambda_u = 1 - \lambda_a - \lambda_g$ in TC1 or $\lambda_u = 1 - \lambda_a - \lambda_g - \lambda_c$ in TC2

in music retrieval. The results demonstrate the importance and potential of utilizing user-specific information in music retrieval systems. We hope this work can shed light on the direction of developing user-centric music retrieval systems and motivate more research efforts in this area.

ACKNOWLEDGMENTS

This research is supported by the National Research Foundation, Prime Minister's Office, Singapore under its International Research Centre in Singapore Funding Initiative.

REFERENCES

[1] L. Barrington, M. Yazdani, D. Turnbull, and G. RG Lanckriet. 2008. Combining feature kernels for semantic music retrieval. In *ISMIR*.

[2] P. Berkers. 2012. Gendered scrobbling: Listening behaviour of young adults on Last.fm. *Interactions: Studies in Communication & Culture* 2, 3 (2012), 279–296.

[3] T. Bertin-Mahieux, D. Eck, F. Maillet, and P. Lamere. 2008. Autotagger: A model for predicting social tags from acoustic features on large music databases. *Journal of New Music Research* 37, 2 (2008), 115–135.

[4] D. Blei, A. Ng, and M. Jordan. 2003. Latent dirichlet allocation. *J. Mach. Learn. Res.* 3 (2003), 993–1022.

[5] J. Bu, S. Tan, C. Chen, C. Wang, H. Wu, L. Zhang, and X. He. 2010. Music recommendation by unified hypergraph: combining social media information and music content. In *ACM MM*.

[6] M. Casey, C. Rhodes, and M. Slaney. 2008. Analysis of minimum distances in high-dimensional musical spaces. *IEEE Trans. Audio, Speech, Language Process.* 16, 5 (2008), 1015–1028.

[7] M. A Casey, R. Veltkamp, M. Goto, M. Leman, C. Rhodes, and M. Slaney. 2008. Content-based music information retrieval: Current directions and future challenges. *Proc. IEEE* 96, 4 (2008), 668–696.

[8] Òscar Celma. 2010. Music Recommendation. In *Music Recommendation and Discovery*, Òscar Celma (Ed.). Springer, Chapter 3, 43–86.

[9] Z. Cheng and J. Shen. 2014. Just-for-me: An adaptive personalization system for location-aware social music recommendation. In *ACM ICMR*.

[10] Z. Cheng and J. Shen. 2016. On effective location-aware music recommendation. *ACM Trans. Inf. Syst.* 34, 2 (2016), 13.

[11] Z. Cheng, J. Shen, and S. CH Hoi. 2016. On effective personalized music retrieval by exploring online user behaviors. In *ACM SIGIR*.

[12] J S. Downie. 2008. The music information retrieval evaluation exchange (2005-2007): A window into music information retrieval research. *Acoustical Science and Technology* 29, 4 (2008), 247–255.

[13] K. Ellis, E. Coviello, A. B. Chan, and G. RG Lanckriet. 2013. A bag of systems representation for music auto-tagging. *IEEE Trans. Audio, Speech, Language Process.* 21, 12 (2013), 2554–2569.

[14] T. L Griffiths and M. Steyvers. 2004. Finding scientific topics. *PNAS* 101, Suppl 1 (2004), 5228–5235.

[15] B.-J. Han, S. Rho, S. Jun, and E. Hwang. 2010. Music emotion classification and context-based music recommendation. *Multimed. Tools Appl.* 47, 3 (2010), 433–460.

[16] N. Hariri, B. Mobasher, and R. Burke. 2013. Personalized text-based music retrieval. In *Workshops at AAAI Conference on Artificial Intelligence*.

[17] T. Hofmann. 1999. Probabilistic latent semantic indexing. In *ACM SIGIR*.

[18] T. Hofmann and J. Puzicha. 1999. Latent class models for collaborative filtering. In *IJCAI*.

[19] J.-Y. Kim and N. J Belkin. 2002. Categories of music description and search terms and phrases used by non-music experts. In *ISMIR*.

[20] P. Knees, T. Pohle, M. Schedl, D. Schnitzer, and K. Seyerlehner. 2008. A document-centered approach to a natural language music search engine. In *ECIR*.

[21] P. Knees, T. Pohle, M. Schedl, D. Schnitzer, K. Seyerlehner, and G. Widmer. 2009. Augmenting text-based music retrieval with audio similarity. In *ISMIR*.

[22] A. LeBlanc, Y. Jin, L. Stamou, and J. McCrary. 1999. Effect of age, country, and gender on music listening preferences. *Bull. Counc. Res. Music Educ.* 141 (1999), 72–76.

[23] M. Levy and M. Sandler. 2008. Learning latent semantic models for music from social tags. *J. New Music Res.* 37, 2 (2008), 137–150.

[24] M. Levy and M. Sandler. 2009. Music information retrieval using social tags and audio. *IEEE Trans. Multimed.* 11, 3 (2009), 383–395.

[25] C. Liem, M. Müller, D. Eck, G. Tzanetakis, and A. Hanjalic. 2011. The need for music information retrieval with user-centered and multimodal strategies. In *ACM workshop on Music Information Retrieval with User-centered and Multimodal Strategies*.

[26] R. Miotto and G. Lanckriet. 2012. A generative context model for semantic music annotation and retrieval. *IEEE Trans. Audio, Speech, and Language Process.* 20, 4 (2012), 1096–1108.

[27] R. Miotto and N. Orio. 2012. A probabilistic model to combine tags and acoustic similarity for music retrieval. *ACM Trans. Inf. Syst.* 30, 2 (2012), 8.

[28] J. Nam, J. Herrera, M. Slaney, and J. O. Smith. 2012. Learning sparse feature representations for music annotation and retrieval. In *ISMIR*.

[29] H.-S. Park, J.-O. Yoo, and S.-B. Cho. 2006. A context-aware music recommendation system using fuzzy bayesian networks with utility theory. In *FSKD*.

[30] A. Popescul, D. Pennock, and S. Lawrence. 2001. Probabilistic models for unified collaborative and content-based recommendation in sparse-data environments. In *UAI*.

[31] M. Riley, E. Heinen, and J. Ghosh. 2008. A text retrieval approach to content-based audio retrieval. In *ACM SIGIR*.

[32] G. Salton, A. Wong, and C.-S. Yang. 1975. A vector space model for automatic indexing. *Commun. ACM* 18, 11 (1975), 613–620.

[33] M. Schedl and A. Flexer. 2012. Putting the user in the center of music information retrieval. In *ISMIR*.

[34] M. Schedl, A. Flexer, and J. Urbano. 2013. The neglected user in music information retrieval research. *J. Intell. Inf. Syst.* 41, 3 (2013), 523–539.

[35] M. Schedl, D. Hauger, K. Farrahi, and M. Tkalčič. 2015. On the influence ofuser characteristics on music recommendation algorithms. In *ECIR*.

[36] M. Schedl, S. Stober, E. Gómez, N. Orio, and C. CS Liem. 2012. User-aware music retrieval. *Multimod. Music Process.* 3 (2012), 135–156.

[37] J. Shen, W. Meng, S. Yan, H. Pang, and X. Hua. 2010. Effective music tagging through advanced statistical modeling. In *ACM SIGIR*.

[38] J. Shen, H. Pang, M. Wang, and S. Yan. 2012. Modeling concept dynamics for large scale music search. In *ACM SIGIR*.

[39] D. Tingle, Y. E Kim, and D. Turnbull. 2010. Exploring automatic music annotation with acoustically-objective tags. In *ISMIR*.

[40] D. Turnbull, L. Barrington, D. Torres, and G. Lanckriet. 2008. Semantic annotation and retrieval of music and sound effects. *IEEE Trans. Audio, Speech, Language Process.* 16, 2 (2008), 467–476.

[41] D. Turnbull, L. Barrington, D. Torres, and G. RG Lanckriet. 2007. Towards musical query-by-semantic-description using the cal500 data set. In *ACM SIGIR*.

[42] D. R Turnbull, L. Barrington, G. Lanckriet, and M. Yazdani. 2009. Combining audio content and social context for semantic music discovery. In *ACM SIGIR*.

[43] A. L Uitdenbogerd and R. Schyndel. 2002. A review of factors affecting music recommender success. In *ISMIR*.

[44] J.-C. Wang, Y.-C. Shih, M.-S. Wu, H.-M. Wang, and S.-K. Jeng. 2011. Colorizing tags in tag cloud: a novel query-by-tag music search system. In *ACM MM*.

[45] M. Wang, W. Fu, S. Hao, D. Tao, and X. Wu. 2016. Scalable semi-supervised learning by efficient anchor graph regularization. *IEEE Trans. Knowledge Data Eng.* 28, 7 (2016), 1864–1877.

[46] M. Wang, X. Liu, and X. Wu. 2015. Visual Classification by ell_1-Hypergraph Modeling. *IEEE Trans. Knowledge Data Eng.* 27, 9 (2015), 2564–2574.

[47] K. Yoshii, M. Goto, K. Komatani, T. Ogata, and H. G Okuno. 2008. An efficient hybrid music recommender system using an incrementally trainable probabilistic generative model. *IEEE Trans. Audio, Speech, Language Process.* 16, 2 (2008), 435–447.

[48] B. Zhang, J. Shen, Q. Xiang, and Y. Wang. 2009. CompositeMap: a novel framework for music similarity measure. In *ACM SIGIR*.

The Utility and Privacy Effects of a Click

Rachid Guerraoui
EPFL
rachid.guerraoui@epfl.ch

Anne-Marie Kermarrec
Inria
Anne-Marie.kermarrec@inria.fr

Mahsa Taziki
EPFL
mahsa.taziki@epfl.ch

ABSTRACT

Recommenders are becoming one of the main ways to navigate the Internet. They recommend appropriate items to users based on their *clicks*, i.e., *likes*, *ratings*, *purchases*, etc. These clicks are key to providing relevant recommendations and, in this sense, have a significant *utility*. Since clicks reflect the preferences of users, they also raise *privacy* concerns. At first glance, there seems to be an inherent trade-off between the utility and privacy effects of a click. Nevertheless, a closer look reveals that the situation is more subtle: some clicks do improve utility without compromising privacy, whereas others decrease utility while hampering privacy.

In this paper, for the first time, we propose a way to quantify the exact utility and privacy effects of each user click. More specifically, we show how to compute the privacy effect (*disclosure risk*) of a click using an *information-theoretic* approach, as well as its *utility*, using a *commonality-based* approach. We determine precisely when utility and privacy are antagonist and when they are not. To illustrate our metrics, we apply them to recommendation traces from Movielens and Jester datasets. We show, for instance, that, considering the Movielens dataset, 5.94% of the clicks improve the recommender utility without loss of privacy, whereas 16.43% of the clicks induce a high privacy risk without any utility gain.

An appealing application of our metrics is what we call a *click-advisor*, a visual user-aware clicking platform that helps users decide whether it is actually worth clicking on an item or not (after evaluating its potential utility and privacy effects using our techniques). Using a *game-theoretic* approach, we evaluate several user clicking strategies. We highlight in particular what we define as a *smart* strategy, leading to a Nash equilibrium, where every user reaches the maximum possible privacy while preserving the average overall recommender utility for all users (with respect to the case where user clicks are based solely on their genuine preferences, i.e., without consulting the click-advisor).

1 INTRODUCTION

The growth of data available online makes it difficult for individuals to extract information relevant to their interests. *Recommenders* do the job for them: they build profiles [35] representing user interests, and recommend items to users based on those profiles [23], typically using *collaborative filtering* (CF) schemes [38].

The profiles of users are derived from their *clicks*, e.g., their ratings in terms of *likes* (or *dislikes*) [35], their purchases, the pages they spend time on, etc. On the one hand, the clicks have an important effect on the recommender *utility* for a user. On the other hand, clicks may also *disclose private information* about users [34].[1] At first glance, a user might face a dilemma: *To click or not to click?* The click could improve the utility of a recommender for that specific user, yet might also disclose private information. But is there really always a trade-off between utility and privacy?

Consider as a first illustration, the case of Alice, a user who clicks on "Game of thrones". By doing so, Alice improves utility by helping the recommender find similar users to her. Assuming indeed that a large number of users have watched "Game of thrones", Alice's click makes her also less distinguishable among those users (than before she clicked). This click improves her privacy. There is no trade-off in this case between utility and privacy. If Alice instead had clicked on an esoteric movie, she would have revealed a lot. A curious user (an attacker), knowing through the item profiles that only one user liked that esoteric movie, could eventually deduce the entire profile of Alice. (The curious user could, through a KNN attack, create fake profiles containing the esoteric movie and would be recommended the entire profile of Alice.). The motivation of this work is to determine exactly when a click induces a trade-off and when it does not, by precisely quantifying the effects of every click on both utility and privacy.

In this paper, we compute the effect of a click on utility by introducing the notion of *commonality* of a user profile, i.e., representing through a number how close the taste of a user is to that of other users (which helps a recommender suggest relevant items that are likely to match the user's preferences). This notion captures *precision*, the classical well-known measure of the quality of recommenders [32]. Whereas the idea of precision has been so far considered as an empirical measure of the utility of a recommender for all the users, we compute commonality, theoretically, and for every individual user (in a user-centric manner).[2] The difference between the commonality of a user profile, before and after the click, is what we define as the *utility* of the click.

We compute the privacy effect of a click through the concept of *disclosure degree* of a user profile, using an *information-theoretic* approach. The disclosure degree corresponds to the amount of information stored in a user profile, also known as *entropy* [15]. Roughly speaking, the larger the amount of information in a user profile, the higher the disclosure degree of the user profile. If the disclosure degree of a user profile is low, then the user is not easily distinguishable from others. We capture the *disclosure risk* of a click, and hence its privacy effect, as the difference between the

SIGIR '17, August 07-11, 2017, Shinjuku, Tokyo, Japan

978-1-4503-5022-8/17/08...$15.00
DOI: http://dx.doi.org/10.1145/3077136.3080783

[1]This is without even considering the recommender itself as a threat, but only other curious users who could deduce other profiles through what is recommended to them.
[2]It is important to note at this point that two user profiles might be very different, and yet might have the same commonality, basically meaning that they could be recommended the same *number* of relevant items but not necessarily the same items.

	i_1	i_2	i_3	i_4
u_1	✓	$\mathbb{A}$	✓	
u_2			✓	✓
u_3		✗	**B**	✓
u_4	✓		$\mathbb{C}$	✗

Table 1: Clicks of Users

disclosure degree of a user profile before and after the click. Interestingly, we prove that after user u's click on item i, the disclosure degree of u is never increased by the clicks of other users on i.[3]

To illustrate our notions of utility and privacy effects of the clicks beyond Alice's example above, consider the example depicted in Table 1, involving 4 items and 4 users. (We will use this example throughout the paper.) A bold style (resp. an outlined style) depicts a like (resp. dislike) click on an item in the corresponding (user) row and (item) column, respectively. The check-marks and cross-marks represent the clicks already performed by the users and the capital letters represent the following three clicks that could be performed by the users:

$\mathbb{A}$ denotes a click by u_1 to dislike i_2. $\mathbb{A}$ improves the recommender utility for u_1 as $\mathbb{A}$ indicates that the preference of u_1 is close to that of u_3. Hence, the recommender can suggest relevant items to u_1 after $\mathbb{A}$ (e.g., i_4). However, $\mathbb{A}$ compromises the privacy for u_1 in the sense that u_1 becomes more distinguishable among other users after $\mathbb{A}$. Indeed, the group of users who dislike i_2 after $\mathbb{A}$ (u_1 and u_3) is smaller than the group of users who did not click on i_2 before $\mathbb{A}$ (u_1, u_2 and u_4); $\mathbb{A}$ induces a utility-privacy trade-off.

B denotes a click to like i_3 by u_3. **B** improves the privacy for u_3 in the sense that after this click, by knowing the preference of u_3 for i_3, u_3 becomes indistinguishable from a group of other users who liked i_3 (this group consists of two users out of the total of three users, other than u_3). Moreover, **B** helps the recommender find relevant items to u_3 because i_3 is similar to i_4 and i_1, and user u_3 has not clicked on i_1 yet; the recommender can now propose i_1 to u_3. Hence, **B** improves both utility and privacy for u_3.

$\mathbb{C}$ is a click by u_4 to dislike i_3 that neither improves privacy for u_4 nor helps the recommender suggest relevant items to u_4; before $\mathbb{C}$, the recommender could figure out that the preference of u_4 is close to u_1 (neither to u_2 nor u_3). However, $\mathbb{C}$ indicates that the preference of u_4 toward i_3 is also opposite to u_1. Hence, $\mathbb{C}$ does not improve the recommender utility for u_4; worst, $\mathbb{C}$ compromises the privacy for u_4.

Clearly, this example contradicts the traditional belief [29] of an inherent trade-off between utility and privacy, meaning that a user necessarily improves recommendation utility at the expense of compromising privacy (or vice versa). There are clicks that improve utility without decreasing privacy and, at the other extreme, there are clicks that hamper privacy without improving utility.

An interesting application of our work is what we call the *click-advisor*, a virtual platform enabling users to decide whether or not to actually click on an item. The process behind a click-advisor is as follows: a user (a) *pre-clicks* on an item, (b) gets a quick feedback (in constant time, i.e. $O(1)$, as shwon in the paper) on the utility and privacy effects of that pre-click and then (c) decides to *confirm*, *cancel*, or even *change* the pre-click.

We use a game-theoretic approach to explore several user clicking strategies. For example, a user may follow a *careful* strategy to confirm a pre-click iff the pre-click does not hamper privacy without improving utility (and to cancel the pre-click otherwise). We highlight in particular a Nash equilibrium strategy, which we call *smart*. If all users follow the smart strategy, they minimize their disclosure degrees (maximize their privacy) while ensuring that the expected value of the overall recommender utility for all users remains the same as the case without consulting the click-advisor.

We illustrate our notions of utility and disclosure risk of a click as well as the effects of various clicking strategies through experiments on real datasets from Movielens [2] and Jester [19]. We show that our notion of commonality of a user profile indeed conveys the classical concept of *precision* of a recommender [32], restricted to a user profile. We also show for instance that, according to Movielens, 5.23% of the clicks improve utility without loss of privacy–at the other extreme, 16.48% of clicks induce a high privacy risk without a utility gain. Finally, we also show that the smart clicking strategy does not impact utility (while maximizing privacy).

The rest of the paper is organized as follows. In Section 2 and Section 3, we define and show how to compute the effects of a click on utility and privacy, respectively. Section 4 discusses the relation between utility and privacy, and introduces our notion of a click-advisor. Section 5 analyzes several clicking strategies based on a game-theoretic approach. We report on our measurements with datasets from Movielens and Jester in Section 6. Section 7 discusses related work and Section 8 concludes the paper with remarks about future work. For space limitations, we defer some algorithms and discussions about the click-advisor as well as the proofs of our theorems and lemmas to a companion technical report [1].

2 UTILITY

2.1 Recommender Model

We consider a general model of a CF recommender scheme [23]. The set of user clicks is modeled as a matrix, denoted by E. The profile of user u, denoted by $\mathcal{U}$, corresponds to a row of E. Each column of E is related to an item. For the sake of presentation simplicity, but without loss of generality, we model each click as a like/dislike action.[4] The result of user u clicking on item i is either a "like" or a "dislike", represented by 1 and -1 in the corresponding cell of E, $e(u, i)$, respectively. Also, we mark 0 in $e(u, i)$ if user u has not clicked on item i.

We denote by M the size of the set of items and by N the number of users. A user profile, $\mathcal{U} \in \{-1, 0, 1\}^M$, is a vector of size M, in which the cell corresponding to item i is $e(u, i)$:

$$e(u, i) = \begin{cases} 1 & u \text{ has clicked on } i \text{ and likes it;} \\ 0 & u \text{ has not clicked on } i; \\ -1 & u \text{ has clicked on } i \text{ and dislikes it.} \end{cases}$$

For each item i, we denote by $N_{Like}(i)$ and $N_{Dislike}(i)$ the number of users who like and dislike i, respectively. The *item profile*

[3]Three remarks are in order here. First, our notion of disclosure degree is a privacy measure of a user profile, unlike k-anonymity [39] and differential privacy [12], which are privacy measures of a dataset and an algorithm, respectively. In Section 6, we show the extend to which our notion of disclosure degree is correlated to differential privacy and k-anonymity. Second, (just like commonality) the disclosure degree of a user profile depends on other profiles. The fact that Bob is the only one to click on his esoteric movie is what make his disclosure degree high. Third, a low disclosure degree conveys a protection against possible attacks of curious users, but not against a recommender, which is trusted.

[4]This can model binary as well as non-binary types of rating: a low rating as a dislike, and a high rating as a like.

Notations	
Items	The set of all items in the system
Users	The set of all users in the system
E	A recommender dataset
u	A user
$\mathcal{U}$	A user profile
i	An item
$\mathcal{I}$	An item profile
I	The set of all item profiles
M	The number of items in the system
N	The number of users in the system
$N_{Like}(i)$	The number of users who like item i
$N_{Dislike}(i)$	The number of users who dislike item i
$N_{NotClicked}(i)$	The number of users who have not clicked on item i
$Clicked(u)$	The set of items clicked by user u
U	A random created user profile based on the information in item profiles

Table 2: Notation Table

Item	Item Profile			Popularity	Preferability
	N_{Like}	$N_{Dislike}$	$N_{NotClicked}$		
i_1	2	0	2	0.5	0.5
i_2	0	1	3	0.25	-0.25
i_3	2	0	2	0.5	0.5
i_4	2	1	1	0.75	0.25

Table 3: Profiles, Popularity and Preferability of Items in Table 1

of i, denoted by $\mathcal{I}$, contains $N_{Like}(i)$, $N_{Dislike}(i)$ as well as the number of users who have not clicked on i yet, $N_{NotClicked}(i)$.[5] Although user profiles are *private*, item profiles are typically *public*[6] (e.g., in IMDb and Movielens). Table 2 summarizes the notations we use in the paper.

2.2 Commonality of a User Profile

To define our notion of *commonality* of a user profile (or simply, of a user), we first go through the concepts of *popularity* and *preferability* of items.

Definition 1. (Popularity)

$$popularity(i) = \frac{N_{Like}(i) + N_{Dislike}(i)}{N}.$$

Definition 2. (Preferability, i.e., average of preferences of users toward an item)

$$preferability(i) = \frac{N_{Like}(i) - N_{Dislike}(i)}{N}.$$

The item profiles as well as popularity and preferability of items in Table 1 are represented in Table 3.

Definition 3. (Mainstream preference) The mainstream preference of users for item i, denoted by $m(i)$, is computed as $popularity(i) \cdot preferability(i)$. For all items managed by a recommender, the mainstream preference of users is stored in a vector of size M in which the corresponding cell to item i is $m(i)$. We denote the mainstream vector by $m \in [-1, 1]^M$.

We now introduce the concept of commonality of user u, (with respect to other users) denoted by *commonality(u)*. Roughly speaking, we capture by a number, how close the user profile $\mathcal{U}$ is to other users profiles in the system in general.

[5]In other words, an item profile, $\mathcal{I}$, includes the average rating of i as well as the number of users who like/dislike i.

[6]Item profiles (the average rating, the percentages of users who have used/purchased an item, etc) play an important role in convincing a user to actually purchase an item.

	i_1	i_2	i_3	i_4	Commonality
u_1	✓		✓		$0.5 \times 0.5 + 0 + 0.5 \times 0.5 + 0 = 0.5$
u_2			✓	✓	$0 + 0 + 0.5 \times 0.5 + 0.75 \times 0.25 = 0.4375$
u_3		✗		✓	$0 - 0.25 \times (-0.25) + 0 + 0.75 \times 0.25 = 0.25$
u_4	✓			✗	$0.5 \times 0.5 + 0 + 0 - 0.75 \times 0.25 = 0.0625$

Table 4: Commonalities of Users in Table 1

Definition 4. (Commonality)

$$commonality(u) = \sum_{i \in I} popularity(i) \cdot preferability(i) \cdot e(u, i).$$

Remark 1. $commonality(u) = \mathcal{U} \cdot m^T$.

Remark 2. Basically, the commonality of a user represents how close the direction of the vector $\mathcal{U}$ is to the direction of the mainstream vector, m, by relatively computing the cosine of the angle between vector $\mathcal{U}$ and vector m.

The commonalities of the users in Table 1 are computed in Table 4 using Table 3 and Definition 4. As all the users clicked on exactly two items in Table 1, Table 4 shows that commonality is not proportional to the number of user clicks. Instead, commonality is a weighted function of user clicks based on how well the clicks help the recommender connect users (or items) to suggest them new items. For instance, the commonality of u_1 is higher than the commonality of u_4, therefore the recommender should provide more accurate recommendations to u_1 than to u_4. In Section 6, we emprically show that the commonality captures the quality of not only SVD-based recommenders but also KNN-based ones. [7]

2.3 Utility of a Click

The utility of a click by user u is the difference between $commonality(u)$ before and after that click. To distinguish both cases, we use the prime notation for the latter: $commonality'(u)$ denotes u's commonality after the click.

Definition 5. (Utility of a click by user u)

$$\Delta commonality(u) = commonality'(u) - commonality(u).$$

3 PRIVACY

We define the notion of *disclosure degree* of a user profile (or simply, of a user) based on the classical concept of *entropy* in information theory [15]. Basically, the disclosure degree of user u, which we denote by δ_u, corresponds to the amount of information that item profiles contain about u.[8] Remember that our goal here is to protect users from other (curious) users. We assume that the recommender, which stores all the user and item profiles, is trusted.

3.1 Disclosure Degree of a User Profile

We address the situation where an intruder (i.e., a curious user), given public item profiles (I), tries to disclose information about user profiles with a disclosure probabilistic model. The considered privacy disclosure conveys the intruder's ability to uniquely identify a user using this probabilistic model [3]. One could interpret the disclosure degree of u as the number of bits of information that the intruder has gained in order to uniquely identify u, given I.

The disclosure probabilistic model determines the probabilities that users have clicked on items; these probabilities are assigned by the intruder to a district random user profile, U. Let U have the

[7]The commonality of a user profile can be further specified for a CF recommender based on a factorization method with latent factors.

[8]We exclude users without any click from our study as those have no privacy concern.

User	Commonality	Disclosure Degree
u_1	0.5	$-\log(0.50 \times 0.75 \times 0.50 \times 0.25) = 1.329$
u_2	0.4375	$-\log(0.50 \times 0.75 \times 0.50 \times 0.50) = 1.028$
u_3	0.25	$-\log(0.50 \times 0.25 \times 0.50 \times 0.50) = 1.505$
u_4	0.0625	$-\log(0.50 \times 0.75 \times 0.50 \times 0.25) = 1.329$

Table 5: Disclosure Degrees of Users in Table 1

conditional disclosure probability function $Q(\mathcal{U}) = Pr(U = \mathcal{U}|I)$, in which $\mathcal{U}$ represents each possible user profile in the system. For a given disclosure probability distribution, the concept of disclosure degree provides a measure of the information (entropy in information theory) about user profile $\mathcal{U}$ stored in I. In this case, we denote by $\delta_u = H(\mathcal{U})$ the entropy of the user profile given the public item profiles, what we call the disclosure degree.

Naturally, the lower $Q(\mathcal{U}) = Pr(U = \mathcal{U}|I)$, the more unique user profile $\mathcal{U}$ is (the higher δ_u). When the interests of user u are determined by click on an item by u, most of the time, this click decreases $Pr(U = \mathcal{U}|I)$ and compromises the privacy for u. In other words, after a click, the user usually provides more information in the system and makes it hard for the recommender to hide this information (we show however this is not always the case).

To compute the disclosure degree of a user profile, we compute the probability of a click on an item i in U as follows:

$$E_i = \begin{cases} 1 & \text{with probability } \frac{N_{Like}(i)}{N} \\ & (U \text{ likes } i); \\ 0 & \text{with probability } 1 - \frac{N_{Like}(i)+N_{Dislike}(i)}{N} \\ & (U \text{ does not click on } i); \\ -1 & \text{with probability } \frac{N_{Dislike}(i)}{N} \\ & (U \text{ dislikes } i). \end{cases}$$

The following remark highlights the distribution of our disclosure probabilistic model for each possible user profile given I.

Remark 3. For any possible user profile $\mathcal{U}$:

$$Q(\mathcal{U}) = Pr(U = \mathcal{U}|I) = \prod_{i \in Items} Pr(E_i = e(u, i)).$$

We use the above disclosure model to define δ_u, the disclosure degree of user u:

Definition 6. (Disclosure degree)

$$\delta_u = -\log(Pr(U = \mathcal{U}|I)).$$

Note that δ_u captures the amount of information about a user profile stored in the public item profiles. In Section 6, we simulate a KNN attack [6] to illustrate the protection level of different users with different disclosure degrees. We show how accurately an intruder can disclose information about users with different disclosure degrees. The following remark highlights how to precisely compute δ_u. Later, we use Remark 4 to compute the privacy effect of a click by user u.

Remark 4. $\delta_u = -\sum_{i \in Items} \log(Pr(E_i = e(u, i)))$.

The disclosure degrees of the users in Table 1 are computed in Table 5 using Definition 6. The commonality and disclosure degree[9] of each user are shown in the corresponding columns in Table 5. Despite the fact that u_4 has a higher disclosure degree than u_2, the recommender can provide better recommendations to u_2 than to u_4 because the commonality of u_2 is higher than that of u_4. This shows that a higher disclosure degree does not necessarily

[9]A user with high disclosure degree has a low level of privacy.

	$\Delta commonality(u) > 0$	$\Delta commonality(u) < 0$
$\Delta\delta_u > 0$	Trade-off	Dangerous/Deleterious
$\Delta\delta_u < 0$	Safe	Trade-off

Table 6: Conditions for Each Click Zone

lead to a better utility. Actually, not only does the click of u_4 on i_4 compromise u_4's privacy but neither does it help her get good recommendations.

3.2 Disclosure Risk of a Click

We fix a user u for whom we compute the effect of a click on privacy. We denote the difference of the disclosure degree of user u before and after the click by $\Delta\delta_u$ which can be expressed as the disclosure risk of the click.

Definition 7. (Disclosure risk of a click by user u)

$$\Delta\delta_u = \delta'_u - \delta_u.$$

Note that a click with a positive disclosure risk compromises the privacy for a user. The larger the absolute value of the disclosure risk of a click, the greater the privacy effect of that click. The following remarks can then be easily derived:

Remark 5. Whenever u clicks on i, the disclosure degree of u does not increase over time by clicks of other users on i

Remark 5 basically says that the disclosure risk of a click on i by u is actually an upper bound of all changes in the disclosure degree of u corresponding to item i after the time of the click.

4 CLICK-ADVISOR

In traditional recommenders, when a user clicks on an item, the information about that click is directly propagated to the system. We propose to leverage our utility and privacy metrics to build a user-aware clicking tool: the *click-advisor*. After getting a new recommendation, a user *pre-clicks* on the item and previews the utility and privacy effects of the pre-click through the click-advisor. Based on the click-advisor feedback, the user finalizes the decision on whether to click or not.

We categorize the clicks into four different zones depending on the sign of utility and privacy effects of the click as well as its reverse[10]:

- Safe zone: improves both utility and privacy.
- Trade-off zone: induces a utility-privacy trade-off.
- Dangerous zone: compromises both utility and privacy but the reverse of the click improves privacy.[11]
- Deleterious zone: Both the click and its reverse compromise utility as well as privacy.

In Section 6, we show that, besides trade-off clicks, safe, deleterious and dangerous clicks indeed exist in real-world datasets. Table 6 describes the corresponding zones for all possible cases for the disclosure risk and utility of a click. Note that there are two cases in which the clicks induce a trade-off: clicks with positive utility and positive disclosure risk, as well as clicks with negative utility and negative disclosure risk. To distinguish deleterious and dangerous zones for a click, we compute the disclosure risk of the reverse of the click, $\Delta\delta^*(u)$. If $\Delta\delta^*(u) > 0$, the click is in a deleterious zone, otherwise, it is in a dangerous zone.

Table 7 shows the utility effect ($\Delta commonality$) and privacy effect ($\Delta\delta$) of each of the following clicks. The zone of a click is

[10]The reverse of a like click is a dislike click and vice versa.

[11]Note that the reverse of the click always compromises the utility for the user as it is not based on the real preferences of that user.

	i_1	i_2	i_3	i_4	Click	$\Delta commonality$	$\Delta\delta$	$\Delta\delta^*$
u_1	✓	○	✓		D^1_2	0.25	0.176	0.477
u_2		○	✓	✓	L^2_2	0	0.477	0.176
u_3		✗	○	✓	L^3_3	0.5625	-0.176	0.301
u_4	✓		○	✗	D^4_3	-0.1875	0.301	-0.176

Table 7: The Effects of Clicks

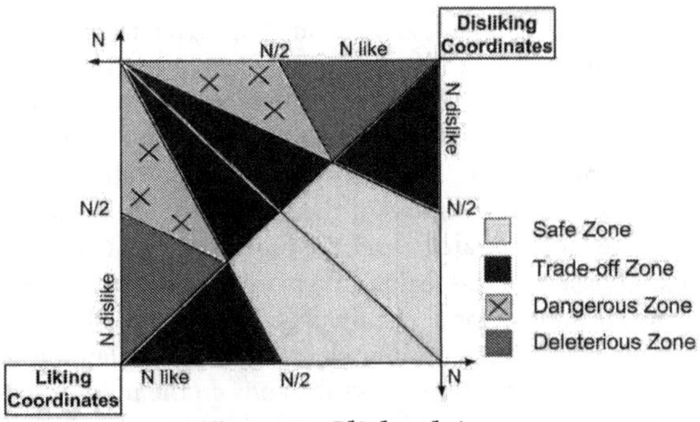

Figure 1: Click-advisor

determined by the sign of the utility and disclosure risk of that click as described in Table 6:

D^1_2 (the dislike click on i_2 by u_1): has a positive utility and a positive disclosure risk. Hence, D^1_2 is in the trade-off zone.

L^2_2 (the like click on i_2 by u_2): has a negative effect on the recommender utility for u_2. Moreover, not only L^2_2 has a positive disclosure risk but the reverse of L^2_2 also does. Hence, changing L^2_2 does not improve the privacy for u_2; L^2_2 is in a deleterious zone.

L^3_3 (the like click on i_3 by u_3): has a positive utility and a negative disclosure risk. L^3_3 thus improves both utility and privacy for u_3 and is thus a safe click.

D^4_3 (the dislike click on i_3 by u_4): compromises both utility and privacy for u_4; D^4_3 is an unsafe click for u_4. However, considering the reverse of D^4_3, even though changing D^4_3 decreases the recommender utility for u_4, the reverse of D^4_3 improves the privacy for u_4 ($\Delta\delta^*$), as shown in Table 7. That makes D^4_3 a dangerous click so u_4 may prefer to change this click.

The following theorem determines the exact signs of $\Delta\delta_u$, $\Delta\delta^*(u)$ and $\Delta commonality(u)$.

Theorem 1. When user u clicks on item i', the sign of the changes in commonality(u) and δ_u are as follows:

$$sgn(\Delta\delta_u) = sgn(2 - 3popularity(i) - e(u,i') \cdot preferability(i)),$$
$$sgn(\Delta commonality(u)) = sgn(e(u,i') \cdot preferability(i)),$$
$$sgn(\Delta\delta^*(u)) = sgn(2 - 3popularity(i) + e(u,i') \cdot preferability(i)).$$

Figure 1 represents the zones in the click-advisor in general. At any point in time the click-advisor of a user represents the zones as well as the points corresponding to all pre-clicks of the user. A pre-click is presented as a point in one of the zones based on the privacy and utility effects of a click and its reverse using Theorem 1 (which we prove in our technical report [1]) and Table 6. The location of a pre-click is defined by the corresponding coordinates based on whether the pre-click is a like or dislike. For example, to locate the corresponding point to a click on item i in order to like it, we use the liking coordinates.

Furthermore, the place of a pre-click in the click-advisor represents the amount of disclosure risk and utility of that pre-click and can be computed in $O(1)$ as shown in Algorithm 1. At the time

Algorithm 1 : Computations of Commonality and Disclosure Degree in $O(M)$ and Computation of the Utility and Privacy Effects and Updates after a Click in $O(1)$

procedure GETCOMMONALITY
    $commonality \leftarrow 0$.
    $\delta[u] \leftarrow 0$.
    for i : *Items* **do**
        if u likes i **then**
            $commonality \leftarrow commonality + m[i]$.
            $\delta[u] \leftarrow \delta[u] - \log(Pr(E_i = 1))$.
        else
            if u dislikes i **then**
                $commonality \leftarrow commonality - m[i]$.
                $\delta[u] \leftarrow \delta[u] - \log(Pr(E_i = -1))$.
            else
                $\delta[u] \leftarrow \delta[u] - \log(Pr(E_i = 0))$.
    return $(commonality, \delta[u])$;
procedure UPDATECLICK
    $m[i] \leftarrow m[i] + \Delta m[i]$.
    $\forall r \in \{-1, 0, 1\} : Pr(E_i = r) \leftarrow Pr(E_i = r) + \Delta Pr(E_i = r)$.

of a click on item i, Algorithm 1 only computes and updates $m[i]$, $Pr(E_i = 1)$, $Pr(E_i = 0)$ and $Pr(E_i = -1)$ in a constant time to be employed by the click-advisor. Also, Algorithm 1 computes the commonality (using Remark 1) and the disclosure degree (using Remark 4) of a user profile, linearly in the number of items.

The click-advisor solely uses the public item information to locate the pre-clicks of a users. Hence, the click-advisor can be implemented in the user-end to inform users about the utility and privacy effects of their pre-clicks without introducing any new privacy risks for the users. It is important to note here that the click-adviosr is not a privacy-preserving platform, but rather the visually informative one. More discussion about the click-advisor is available in our companion technical report [1]. For example, we show that safe pre-clicks never end up being in a dangerous or deleterious zone in the future because of the clicks of other users.

5 THE CLICKING GAME

To analyze the behavior of the users, we model the act of clicking as a game, which we call the *clicking game*. The players of this game are the users of the system (providing recommendations as well as a click-advisor) who want to maximize a *reward function*, described in the following, for each click.

5.1 Reward Function

The reward function is denoted by ϕ : *Users* $\rightarrow \mathcal{R}$. Without loss of generality, we assume that $\forall u \in$ *Users*, $\phi(u) = 0$ at the beginning. A click by user u with utility and privacy effects $\alpha = \Delta commonality(u)$ and $\beta = -\Delta\delta_u$ modifies $\phi(u)$ as follows:

$$\phi(u) \leftarrow \phi(u) + f(\alpha, \beta),$$

in which function $f : \mathcal{R}^2 \rightarrow \mathcal{R}$ has the following properties:

1. f is an increasing function over α.
2. f has the single crossing property over $\max(\alpha, \beta)$.

Property 1 of f implies that the higher the recommender utility for a user, the bigger the reward function for that user. The single crossing property (defined in [4]) merely defines the sign of f. More precisely, Property 2 means that the sign of $\max(\alpha, \beta)$ is the same as the sign of $f(\alpha, \beta)$. Property 2 of f implies the following naturally desired sub-properties for $\phi(u)$:

2a. If user u cancels a click, $\phi(u)$ remains the same.

2b. Compromising utility and privacy by a click of user u leads to decreasing $\phi(u)$ (because of a negative $f(\alpha, \beta)$).

Upon getting a new recommendation, a user pre-clicks on the item and consults the click-advisor for the effects of that pre-click. Then, the user chooses the desired action on the pre-click in order to maximize the reward function through the clicking game.

5.2 User Actions

Consider N users, playing the clicking game. If a pre-click of a user is in a safe or trade-off zone, then either the privacy or the utility improves for that user after confirming that pre-click. However, confirming a pre-click in either a dangerous or a deleterious zone compromises both utility and privacy. The user may then decide to change or cancel a deleterious or dangerous pre-click. Basically, we can consider three possible actions for the user:

- Confirm: When the click follows the initial preference of the user (i.e., the user confirms the pre-click), the utility and disclosure risk of the click are the same as what we computed in Theorems 1 and 2, respectively.
- Change (for better privacy): The user decides to change the pre-clicks (i.e., clicking to dislike an item instead of clicking to like it) to improve privacy. In this case, the disclosure risk of the click is the same as what is computed in Theorem 2. However, the utility of the click would change from what we measured in Theorem 1 because this click is not the real preference of the user, but actually the opposite to it. So, the utility of the click is the opposite of the utility computed in Theorem 1.[12]
- Cancel: In this case, the user decides not to click on an item to preserve privacy. By canceling a pre-click on the item, a user preserves privacy (which is the opposite of what is calculated based on Theorem 2 assuming the pre-click was confirmed) at the expense of missing a potential utility. With the same approach, the lost utility is what the user would get with the assumption (of confirming the pre-click) in Theorem 1.

5.3 User Strategies

After being recommended a new item, a user considers one of the above actions to gain the maximum possible reward over time. There are various possible user clicking strategies. We highlight few of them here.

- Basic: A user always confirms the pre-click based on her preference. In this strategy, the click-advisor is ignored.
- Careful: The user only cancels a pre-click in a dangerous or deleterious zone. Otherwise, the user confirms it.
- Smart: The user always confirms a pre-click in a safe or trade-off zone, cancels the deleterious pre-click and reverses the pre-click in a dangerous zone.

The following theorem says that the smart strategy leads to a Nash equilibrium in the clicking game.

[12]Note that the utility of a recommender for users depends on the real preferences of users. Hence, the action of changing a pre-click by a user always decreases the recommender utility for that user.

Theorem 2. All users playing smart is a Nash equilibrium, i.e., playing the smart strategy maximizes the reward function ϕ for a user u, if every user other than u plays smart.

Lemma 1. If all users play smart, for item i:
(i) If preferability(i) < 0, all users clicking on i disliked it.
(ii) If preferability(i) > 0, all users clicking on i liked it.

The proofs of Theorem 2 and Lemma 1 are given in our technical report [1]. From Lemma 1, we can conclude that playing the smart strategy by all users guarantees the maximum possible privacy for all users. However, it can hamper the recommender utility for users. We consider the sum of commonality for all users as an overall recommender utility. In the following, we compare the effect of the smart strategy and the basic strategy (the strategy of clicking based on the real preferences of users) on the overall recommender utility for users. By playing the smart strategy, the users may change some of their clicks. If all users play the smart strategy, the changes of the clicks depends on the initial clicks on items. In that case, we compute the average of the overall recommender utility for users for all possible initial clicks on items (in order to compare with the overall recommender utility for users playing the basic strategy in Theorem 3). The set of all possible initial clicks on all items is denoted by C. For user u who is playing the smart strategy and a possible $c \in C$, $commonality_{Smart(c)}(u)$ represents the commonality of the real profile of u when all users play the smart strategy and the initial clicks on items is c.

The following theorem says that the expected value of the average of the commonalities of the users in the case where they all play the smart strategy is the same as the case where all users play the basic strategy (users click on items based on their real preferences).

Theorem 3.

$$\sum_{u \in Users} commonality_{Basic}(u) = \mathbb{E}\Big(\sum_{u \in Users} commonality_{Smart(c)}(u)\Big).$$

In other words, Theorem 3 (which we prove in our technical report [1]) says that the overall average of the recommender utility for all users playing the smart strategy is the same as the case where users click on items based on their real preferences. However, with regard to privacy, the smart strategy provides better privacy compared to the basic strategy.

6 EXPERIMENTAL EVALUATION

We evaluate the utility and privacy metrics, as well as their application to build a click-advisor, on two real-world datasets: the Movielens 100K [2] and Jester [19] datasets. Movielens (ML) consists of 100,000 ratings given by 943 users over 1682 movies. Jester involves the clicks of 24,983 users on 100 items [10]. (As Jester does not provide timestamps, we perform the time-based evaluations for Movielens only).

6.1 Commonality as a Utility Measure

We first show here empirically that the notion of commonality of a user profile indeed expresses the quality of a recommender for that user. We more specifically highlight the positive linear correlation between commonality and the classical notion of precision [32].

We measure the precision of a recommender for each user as follows: we divide the dataset into a training set and a test set. We put each rating from the original dataset into the test set with

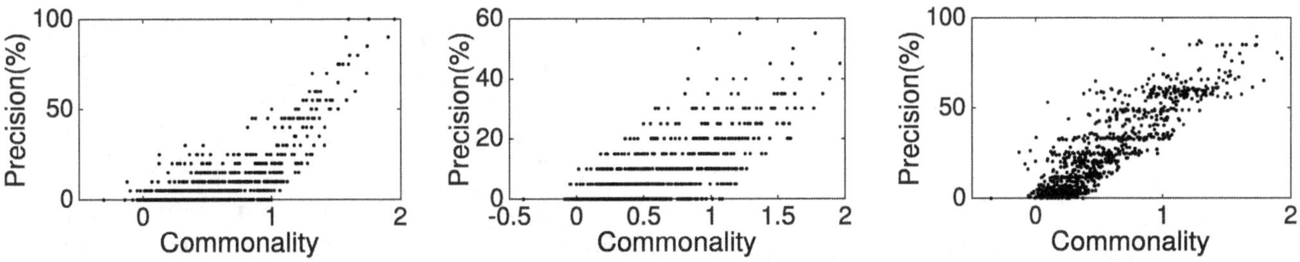

(a) Matrix Reconstruction as in [36] (b) SVD-based Neighborhood as in [24] (c) K Nearest Neighbors as in [38]

Figure 2: The Relation between Commonality and Precision in Movielens for Different Recommenders

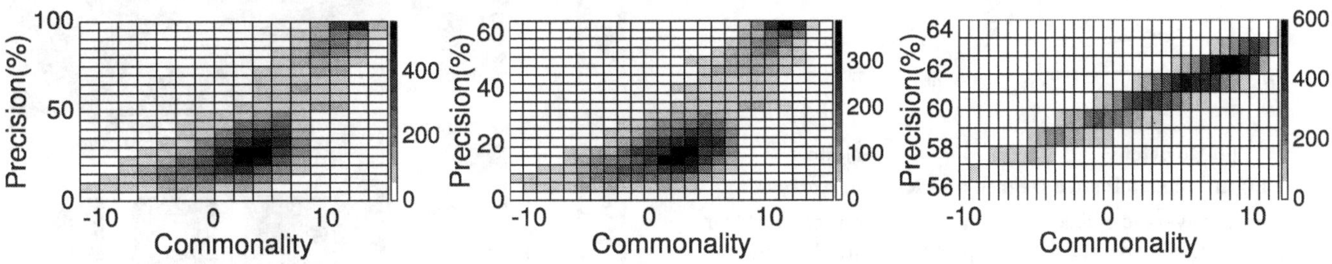

(a) Matrix Reconstruction as in [36] (b) SVD-based Neighborhood as in [24] (c) K Nearest Neighbors as in [38]

Figure 3: The Relation between Commonality and Precision in Jester for Different Recommenders

probability 20% and *hide* all the ratings in the test set from the training set. For a user u, we put $N_u = 0.2 \cdot |Clicked(u)|$ and determine the top-N_u recommendations for u based on state-of-the-art recommender algorithms, namely a KNN (K Nearest Neighbors) algorithm [38], a matrix reconstruction approach [36] and a SVD-based recommender leveraging neighborhood [24].

Precision is measured in terms of standard classification accuracy metrics (CAM) [32]. More precisely, we evaluate how well a recommender can predict the context of the test set of a user u using each of the mentioned algorithms on the training set. We compare the top-N_u recommendations for user u with the hidden part of user profile u (test set). We compute *Precision(u)* as the classification accuracy metric used on top-N_u recommenders computed in [10]. *Precision(u)* is then the ratio of the number of relevant recommended items to the total number of recommended items to user u. Actually, $Precision(u)$ computes the recommendation quality for u.

We report here on our results for both Movielens and Jester. As conveyed in Figures 2a and 2b, the commonality and precision follow a linear fashion in Movielens for a SVD-based recommenders using matrix reconstruction and neighborhood approaches. Mathematically evaluated, the correlation between commonality and precision is 0.6557 for SVD-based recommender using matrix reconstruction and the correlation increases to 0.6838 for a SVD-based recommender leveraging neighborhood. For Jester, because of the massive number of users, the direct correlation between commonality and precision in Jester for SVD-based recommenders is presented using pseudocolor plots in Figures 3a and 3b. Hence, the color of each block represents the number of users in it. (A darker color of a block means more number of users in that block.) For KNN recommender, Figures 2c and 3c depict a direct proportionality (more precisely, linear for both Movielens and Jester) between the commonality of a user profile and the precision of KNN recommender for the corresponding user. This basically means that users with high commonality get high precision for their recommendations in contrast to users with low commonality.

6.2 Disclosure Degree as a Privacy Measure

In this section, we use the Movielens and Jester datasets to show the extend to which our notion of disclosure degree (defined for each user profile) captures other well-known privacy concepts such as differential privacy [12, 31] (defined for algorithms) and k-anonymity [39, 8] (defined for datasets).

6.2.1 Differential Privacy. This guarantees that the presence or absence of a record in a dataset will not significantly affect the final output of the algorithm [12]. In the following, we study the disclosure degree as a privacy parameter of user profiles, and determine the relation between differential privacy and disclosure degree. We employ the approach proposed in [31] to provide differential privacy to recommenders by adding different levels of Laplacian noise to the Movielens dataset. Each noisy dataset corresponds to a level of differential privacy. Figure 4 represents the average of the disclosure degrees of user profiles in each of these noisy datasets. We observe that the users in a dataset with a high level of noise (i.e., a low ϵ) have smaller disclosure degrees in average compared to users in a dataset with a low level of noise. Intuitively, the presence (or absence) of a rare click (i.e., with high disclosure risk) highly affects the output of the recommender compared to the presence (or absence) of a regular expected click.

6.2.2 K-anonymity. F. Casino et. al. applied the concept of k-anonymity to collaborative filtering [8]. Figure 5 represents the average of disclosure degrees of user profiles in Movielens as well as Jester with different levels of k-anonymity. As depicted in Figure 5, increasing k (i.e., stronger anonymity for users) results in

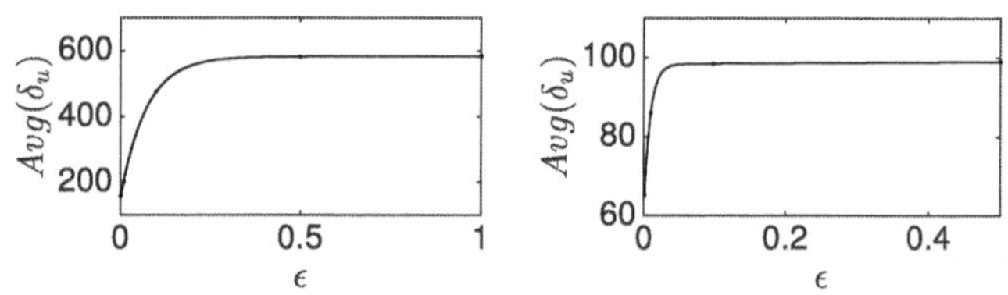

(a) Movielens (b) Jester

Figure 4: Disclosure Degree and Differential Privacy

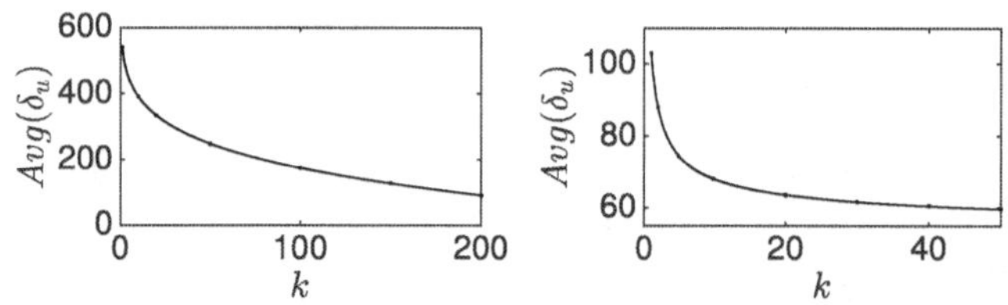

(a) Movielens (b) Jester

Figure 5: Disclosure Degree and K-anonymity

decreasing the average of disclosure degrees of user profiles.[13] Our concept of disclosure degree of a user profile captures how unique a user profile is in the system. Intuitively, the higher the disclosure degree of a user profile, the more distinguishable the user is among others (the higher the risk of identifying the corresponding user among all the users in the system).

6.2.3 KNN Attack. We consider here the KNN attack described in [6]. An attacker creates K fake profiles with some auxiliary information about a target user u_T and requests for recommendations. In the simple case of a KNN recommender, the K nearest neighbors of a fake profile are u_T and $K-1$ other fake profiles. When a fake profile gets a new item as a recommendation, this likely comes from the items which are already clicked by u_T. The reason is that the only items clicked by the K nearest neighbors of a fake profile which are not included in that fake profile are the items in the profile of u_T. Upon a recommendation for any of the fake profiles, all the fake profiles click on the recommended item in order to add the new recommended item to their profiles and be updated to get further information about u_T. The attack is performed through several iterations. In each iteration, the attacker accumulates new information about u_T. To figure out the relation between the disclosure degree of a user profile and the accuracy of the information an attacker can disclose about that user profile, we trigger this KNN attack for the users with different disclosure degrees in Movielens and Jester.

For this simulation, we consider the Movielens as well as the Jester dataset. We consider an attacker simulating a KNN attack to disclose information about a given target user. We denote the disclosure degree of the target user by δ_{u_T}. We illustrate the accuracy and the amount of extracted information (*%EI*) by the attacker about different target users with different disclosure degrees.

For our simulations, we put $K = 10$. Table 8 shows how accurate information an attacker can disclose by simulating the attack for users with different disclosure degrees after 10 iterations. Table 8

[13] As k anonymity is a privacy parameter for a dataset, not for a user profile, to compare k-anonymity and disclosure degree, we use the average disclosure degrees of all user profiles as an overall privacy measure for users.

Dataset	u_T	Auxiliary Information	δ_{u_T}	*%EI*	Accuracy
MLV	3	[1, 2, 3]	235.09	7.33	97.14
MLV	86	[1, 2, 3]	191.66	13.00	80.00
MLV	200	[1, 2, 3]	118.07	15.33	65.71
Jester	7	[0, 3, 6, 7, 5]	118.57	8.24	98.00
Jester	62	[1, 3, 4, 5, 0]	93.21	11.63	85.71
Jester	303	[5, 6, 7, 9, 10]	70.23	20.91	65.71

Table 8: Result of a KNN Attack for Jester and Movielens after 5 Iterations

(a) Pre-clicks (b) Click-advisor

Figure 6: An Screen-shot of the Implemented Click-advisor

shows that the higher the disclosure degree of a user, the more accurate the information disclosed by the attacker about that user.

We show that our notion of disclosure degree is compatible with state-of-the-art privacy metrics (i.e., k-anonymity and differential privacy). To illustrate the disclosure degree further, we show that a user with low disclosure degree is more resistant to a KNN attack, than another user with high disclosure degree. It is important to notice though that our concept of disclosure degree is independent of any particular attack. Also, remember that an attacker here has only access to the output of a recommender, not an (anonymized) version of the dataset. Therefore, de-anonymization attacks cannot be applied in this case.

6.3 Click Zones

We compute the utility and privacy effects as well as the zones of the clicks in Movielens, as discussed in Sections 2 and 3 and 4. (Jester does not provide timestamps.) We observe that most of the clicks (77.63%) induce a trade-off between utility and privacy. Yet, there are clicks which do not induce a utility-privacy trade-off: others are safe (5.94%), dangerous (2.00%) and deleterious (14.43%).

6.4 Click-advisor

We implemented the click-advisor for a SVD-based neighborhood recommender (as in [24]) using the Movielens dataset. Figure 6 represents a screen-shot of our click-advisor. At the beginning, three recommended items are provided to a user. The genuine pre-clicks (like or dislike) of a user on the recommended items are shown in Figure 6a. In Figure 6b, the zone of each pre-click (shown as grey circles) corresponds to the utility and privacy effects of that

	Confirm	Change	Cancel	Ask Me
Safe	100 %	0%	0%	0%
Trade-off	96.97 %	0 %	0 %	3.03 %
Dangerous	3.03 %	39.4 %	30.30 %	6.07 %
Deleterious	3.03 %	0 %	93.94 %	3.03 %

Table 9: The Preferred Default Action in the Click-advisor by the Participants in the Survey

Strategy	Smart	Careful	Basic
Precision(%)	27.02	24.63	28.87
Accuracy of a KNN Attack (%)	55.67	60.53	82.12

Table 10: Recommender Precision and KNN Attack Accuracy for Different User Strategies

pre-click on the user profile. Consulting the click-advisor, the user would decide an action for each pre-click.

The link to our click-advisor as well as a survey to gather the opinions of users on the click-advisor were distributed. More than 95% of respondents agreed that the click-advisor increases their confidence in clicking and their trust to click on more items. Also, we asked about the preferred default strategy in the survey. Table 9 represents the percentage of the respondents who prefer a default action (corresponding to a column) in the case of each types of a click (corresponding to a row). As shown in Table 9, the users chose the presented strategies as their default strategy as follows: Basic (3.03%), Careful (30.30%), and Smart (39.4%). The rest of respondents (6.06%) preferred to be asked as default for some types of clicks. Knowing that the Smart strategy is a Nash equilibrium, we can advertise the Smart strategy as the default strategy. However, the users may adopt their actions as they prefer.

6.5 Clicking Strategies

Section 5 discusses different user strategies for the clicking game. We consider here the *basic*, *careful*, and *smart* strategies and apply each of them to the Movielens dataset. Based on the timestamps in Movielens[14], we consider a click as a pre-click and place the pre-click of the user in the click-advisor instantaneously. Based on the position of the pre-click and the user strategy, we apply an action to the pre-click (confirm, cancel or change). Applying the same strategy to all the users, we create a new updated dataset and compute the precision of the recommender for this updated dataset. Table 10 shows the precision of the recommender applying each of the strategies to all the users. As predicted by Theorem 5, the precision is almost the same for the basic and smart strategies.

We also apply the KNN attack to the updated datasets for each user strategies. We consider the KNN attack with auxiliary information as what described in Section 6.2.3 for Movielens. For this experiment, we average the accuracy of the KNN attack over all the cases in which every single user is the target user. Table 10 shows that the users become more resistant to the KNN attack as they choose the Smart strategy over the Careful and Basic ones. [15]

7 RELATED WORK

CF recommenders. Although it has been shown that CF recommenders perform well, they have some limitations for sparse datasets [38]. Sarwar, et. al. applied Singular Value Decomposition (SVD) to reduce the dimensionality of sparse datasets of collaborative filtering recommenders [36]. Recently, many collaborative filtering recommenders used matrix factorization methods to cope with the sparsity of data, items correlations and dynamic recommendation domains [26, 24, 25, 28]. Our utility and privacy measures are compatible with matrix factorization-based CF recommenders as well as neighborhood-based ones.

Privacy in IR and recommenders. Privacy risks of user posts in online communities were studied in [5] for textual contents, unlike this paper which studies the privacy risks of a single click. Moreover, several papers proposed privacy-preserving methods in the context of recommenders [33, 30, 22]. Perturbative methods were proposed in [33], where users submit perturbed ratings to the recommender. However, even showing perturbed interest in a certain item may also disclose the preferences of users. For example, the perturbed rating of a user on a comedy movie still highlights the interest of the user in watching comedy movies. Furthermore, some works [17, 21] indicate that the use of randomized data distortion techniques might not able to preserve privacy. Regarding the use of cryptographic techniques, Canny proposed a method that enables a group of users to calculate a public aggregate of their profiles without revealing them on an individual basis [41, 7]. The major downside of this method is, however, the assumption of an acceptable number of users is online and willing to participate in the protocol. None of these privacy preserving approaches measured the privacy effect of a single click in a recommender (which we do in this paper).

Differential privacy. The notion of differential privacy was introduced by Dwork in the context of databases [12] and later adapted to recommender *algorithms* [31, 20, 16]. In contrast, our concept of disclosure degree studies the privacy for a specific user regardless of the recommender algorithm. While in differential privacy the recommendations are considered the only observation of an intruder, we take into account the public item profiles as another source of available information for the intruder (unlike differential privacy, we seek to assign a privacy parameter to each user profile in the system, regardless of the recommender algorithm).

A noise addition technique was described in [31] to apply differential privacy to recommenders. In Section 6, we analyze the relation between (a) the different levels of additional noise to dataset as a differential privacy approach in [31] and (b) the disclosure degree of users in the obfuscated datasets with different ϵ. We empirically show that the higher the level of noise in an obfuscated dataset (higher differential privacy), the lower the disclosure degrees of users in average.

K-anonymity. The concept of k-anonymity as a privacy protection method, was first formulated in [39], and recently applied to collaborative filtering recommenders in [8]. In Section 6, we compare the disclosure degree of users in different obfuscated datasets for different k, and we show that the average disclosure degree of users in a dataset actually captures the level of anonymity of that recommender dataset.

Degree of anonymity. Chaum introduced the notion of anonymity set in order to model the security of Dining Cryptographers' networks in [9]. Serjantov and Danezis raised some issues about anonymity sets [37]. For example, anonymity sets do not take into account the risk of inferring some sensitive attributes of

[14]The absence of timestamps makes this simulation impossible in Jester.

[15]A higher accuracy of a KNN attack means the users are less resistant to that attack.

the users in a set. To address these issues, a general measure to quantify the degree of anonymity for message passing was proposed in [37, 11]. Both papers independently proposed the use of entropy as the basis for formally measuring anonymity. The anonymity degree provided by the system quantifies the amount of information the system is leaking. We apply the idea of computing the amount of information stored in a user profile as a privacy parameter (disclosure degree) in the context of recommender datasets.

Disclosure risk. In the literature, disclosure risk measures have been classified as measures for record re-identification or confidential value disclosure [27, 14]. The latter focuses on measuring the risk of compromising a confidential value of a particular individual while the former focuses on measuring the risk of inferring the identity of an individual. In both cases, the disclosure risk measures may be applied to the database as a whole, or to individual records.

Alfalayleh and Brankovic measured the disclosure risk based on entropy [3]. However, if we use the same approach as in [3] to compute the disclosure risk of a user profile, we would get the same result for all users. Indeed, that approach provides a general metric for all users while our measure of disclosure degree is a specified metric for a user profile.

Recommender utility. The utility of recommenders has been measured differently in [18, 10, 13]. These measures, empirically evaluate the global quality of recommenders. In contrast, our commonality measure predicts the quality of recommenders for a user based on the user profile and an actual click. In Section 6, we show that commonality and precision indeed have a positive correlation.

Privacy-utility relation. The utility-privacy trade-off in databases was studied by Sankar et. al. in [29]. Their utility parameter is not applicable to recommenders for it computes the rate-distortion [40] of the database, which is related to the input of the recommender, not to the quality of its output. As we show in this paper, in the case of clicks in recommenders, there is not always a trade-off between utility and privacy.

8 CONCLUDING REMARKS

This paper is the first to precisely quantify the effects of a user click both in terms of utility and privacy in the context of recommenders. We show that all clicks do not have the same effect, neither in terms of privacy nor in terms of utility. In contrast to a common belief, we also show that there is not always a trade-off between utility and privacy. We introduce the idea of a click-advisor, which makes users aware of the effects of their clicks. Consulting the click-advisor, users can formulate their own informed clicks. Considering a reward function for the users in a clicking game, we highlight in particular a smart clicking strategy that leads to a Nash equilibrium. We prove that if all users follow this strategy, their privacy improves without compromising the average overall recommender utility (compared to the case where users do not use the click-advisor).

Our utility and privacy metrics could be further extended to latent factors of users and items in a SVD-based recommender. It would also be interesting to incorporate a recommender that optimizes the utility and privacy for all users solving a linear optimization problem for their commonalities and disclosure degrees.

Acknowledgements. This work has been supported in part by the European ERC Grant 339539 - AOC.

REFERENCES

[1] The utility and privacy effects of a click (technical report), 2017. http://go.epfl.ch/clickadvisor-technical-report.

[2] M. 100K. Movielens dataset, 2003.

[3] M. Alfalayleh and L. Brankovic. Quantifying privacy: A novel entropy-based measure of disclosure risk. In *IWOCA*, 2015.

[4] S. Athey. Monotone comparative statics under uncertainty. *QJE*, 2002.

[5] J. A. Biega, K. P. Gummadi, I. Mele, D. Milchevski, C. Tryfonopoulos, and G. Weikum. R-susceptibility: An ir-centric approach to assessing privacy risks for users in online communities. In *SIGIR*, 2016.

[6] J. A. Cal, A. Kilzer, A. Narayanan, E. W. Felten, and V. Shmatikov. You might also like: Privacy risks of collaborative filtering. In *S&P*, 2011.

[7] J. Canny. Collaborative filtering with privacy. In *S&P*, 2002.

[8] F. Casinoa, J. Domingo-Ferrerb, C. Patsakisc, D. Puigb, and A. Solanasa. A k-anonymous approach to privacy preserving collaborative filtering. *JCSS*, 2015.

[9] D. Chaum. The dining cryptographers problem: Unconditional sender and recipient untraceability. *JCRYPTOL*, 1988.

[10] P. Cremonesi, Y. Koren, and R. Turrin. Performance of recommender algorithms on top-n recommendation tasks. *RecSys*, 2010.

[11] C. Diaz, S. Seys, J. Claessens, and B. Preneel. Towards measuring anonymity. In *PET*, 2003.

[12] C. Dwork. Differential privacy. In *ICALP*, 2006.

[13] M. Ge, C. Delgado-Battenfeld, and D. Jannach. Beyond accuracy: evaluating recommender systems by coverage and serendipity. *RecSys*, 2010.

[14] D. L. George T. Duncan. Disclosure-limited data dissemination. *JASA*, 1986.

[15] R. M. Gray. *Entropy and information theory*. Springer, 2011.

[16] R. Guerraoui, A. Kermarrec, R. Patra, and M. Taziki. D2p: distance-based differential privacy in recommenders. *VLDB*, 2015.

[17] Z. Huang, W. Du, and B. Chen. Deriving private information from randomized data. In *SIGMOD*, 2005.

[18] M. Z. Islam, P. Barnaghi, and L. Brankovic. Measuring data quality: Predictive accuracy vs. similarity of decision trees. In *ICCIT*, 2003.

[19] Jester. Online joke recommender system, 2001.

[20] Z. Jorgensen, T. Yu, and G. Cormode. Conservative or liberal? personalized differential privacy. In *ICDE*, 2015.

[21] H. Kargupta, S. Datta, Q. Wang, and K. Sivakumar. On the privacy preserving properties of random data perturbation techniques. In *ICDM*, 2003.

[22] S. Katzenbeisser and M. Petkovic. Privacy-preserving recommendation systems for consumer healthcare services. *ARES*, 2008.

[23] J. A. Konstan and J. Riedl. Recommender systems: from algorithms to user experience. *UMUAI*, 2012.

[24] Y. Koren. Factorization meets the neighborhood: A multifaceted collaborative filtering model. In *KDD*, 2008.

[25] Y. Koren, R. Bell, and C. Volinsky. Matrix factorization techniques for recommender systems. *Computer*, 2009.

[26] D. kumar Bokde, S. Girase, and D. Mukhopadhyay. Role of matrix factorization model in collaborative filtering algorithm: A survey. *IJAFRC*, 2015.

[27] D. Lambert. Measures of disclosure risk and harm. *JOS*, 1993.

[28] S. Li, A. Karatzoglou, and C. Gentile. Collaborative filtering bandits. In *SIGIR*, 2016.

[29] L.Sankar, S. Rajagopalan, and H. Poor. Utility-privacy tradeoffs in databases: An information-theoretic approach. *IFS*, 2013.

[30] Y. Luo, J. Le, and H. Chen. A privacy-preserving book recommendation model based on multi-agent. *WCSE*, 2009.

[31] F. McSherry and I. Mironov. Differentially private recommender systems: Building privacy into the netflix prize contenders. In *KDD*, 2009.

[32] Y. K. P. Cremonesi and R. Turrin. Performance of recommender algorithms on top-n recommendation tasks. *RecSys*, 2010.

[33] H. Polat and W. Du. Privacy-preserving collaborative filtering using randomized perturbation techniques. *ICDM*, 2003.

[34] N. Ramakrishnan, B. J. Keller, B. J. Mirza, A. Y. Grama, and G. Karypis. Privacy risks in recommender systems. *Internet Computing*, 2001.

[35] A. M. Rashid, I. Albert, D. Cosley, S. K. Lam, S. M. McNee, J. A. Konstan, and J. Riedl. Getting to know you: learning new user preferences in recommender systems. In *IUI*, pages 127–134, 2002.

[36] B. M. Sarwar, G. Karypis, J. A. Konstan, and J. T. Riedl. Application of dimensionality reduction in recommender system – a case study. In *ACM WEBKDD Workshop*, 2000.

[37] A. Serjantov and G. Danezis. Towards an information theoretic metric for anonymity. In *PET*, 2002.

[38] X. Su and T. M. Khoshgoftaar. A survey of collaborative filtering techniques. *AAI*, 2009.

[39] L. Sweeney. K-anonymity: a model for protecting privacy. *IJUFKS*, 2002.

[40] E. Tuncel, P. Koulgi, and K. Rose. Rate-distortion approach to databases: storage and content-based retrieval. *IT*, 2004.

[41] J. Canny. Collaborative filtering with privacy via factor analysis. In *SIGIR*, 2002.

Privacy through Solidarity: A User-Utility-Preserving Framework to Counter Profiling

Asia J. Biega
Max Planck Institute for Informatics
Saarland Informatics Campus
jbiega@mpi-inf.mpg.de

Rishiraj Saha Roy
Max Planck Institute for Informatics
Saarland Informatics Campus
rishiraj@mpi-inf.mpg.de

Gerhard Weikum
Max Planck Institute for Informatics
Saarland Informatics Campus
weikum@mpi-inf.mpg.de

ABSTRACT

Online service providers gather vast amounts of data to build user profiles. Such profiles improve service quality through personalization, but may also intrude on user privacy and incur discrimination risks. In this work, we propose a framework which leverages solidarity in a large community to scramble user interaction histories. While this is beneficial for anti-profiling, the potential downside is that individual user utility, in terms of the quality of search results or recommendations, may severely degrade. To reconcile privacy and user utility and control their trade-off, we develop quantitative models for these dimensions and effective strategies for assigning user interactions to Mediator Accounts. We demonstrate the viability of our framework by experiments in two different application areas (search and recommender systems), using two large datasets.

KEYWORDS

Anti-Profiling, Privacy, User Utility, Personalization, Mediator Accounts, Profile Scrambling, Search Engines, Recommender Systems

1 INTRODUCTION

Motivation: Users are profiled and targeted in virtually every aspect of their digital lives: when searching, browsing, shopping, or posting on social media. The gathered information is used by service providers to personalize search results, customize ads, provide differential pricing, and more [19, 42]. Since such practices can greatly intrude on an individual's privacy, the goal of our research is to devise a mechanism to *counter* such extensive *profiling.*

A careful user can largely preserve her privacy by taking measures like anonymizing communication or using online services only in a non-linkable manner (for instance, by changing accounts or pseudonyms on a regular basis). However, this comes at the cost of greatly reducing utility, both for the service providers and the user. On the one hand, the service provider will miss out on learning from the same user's long-term behavior, which may result in less effective systems. This issue of system-level utility has been studied in the past research on privacy [20, 23]. On the other hand, the individual user will experience degraded service quality, such as poor search results, as the service provider would not understand the user's interests and intentions. This notion of user-level utility has not been extensively explored in prior work. Our paper formalizes the *trade-off* between a user's *profiling privacy* and her *individual utility.*

State of the art and its limitations: Research in privacy has primarily addressed the disclosure of critical properties in data publishing [5, 7, 13]. Common techniques include coarsening the data so that different users become indistinguishable (e.g., k-anonymity [41], l-diversity [26], and t-closeness [25]), or perturbing the answers of an algorithm so that the absence or presence of any record does not significantly influence the output – the principle of differential privacy [11]. These methods consider notions of utility that reflect a system-level error in an analytical task, such as classification. In contrast, our goal is to prevent detailed profiling and targeting while keeping the *individual user utility* as high as possible, for example, in terms of the quality of personalized search results or product recommendations.

For privacy-preserving search, many approaches have been proposed based on *query obfuscation* [14, 33]. In these solutions, queries are generalized to hide their actual intentions, or additional dummy queries are generated to prevent accurate profiling. Both techniques come at the cost of largely reducing user utility. Similar obfuscation-based techniques have been explored for recommenders [17, 27]. However, none of the prior work addressed the trade-off between privacy and user utility in a quantitative manner. A few methods [8, 33] have considered an entire user community as a means for query obfuscation. This idea is related to our approach in this paper – we generalize it and make it applicable in the context of anti-profiling.

Approach and contribution: Our approach to reconcile privacy and user utility builds on the following observation: service providers often do not need a complete and accurate user profile to return personalized results. Thus, in accordance with the need-to-know principle, we assign user requests to *Mediator Accounts* (MA) mimicking real users, such that (i) individual user profiles are scrambled across MAs to counter profiling, while (ii) coherent fragments of a user's profile are kept intact in the MAs to keep user utility high. We call this paradigm *privacy through solidarity.* Specifically, MAs are constructed by *split-merge assignment* strategies: splitting the interaction history of a user and merging pieces of different users together. Mediator Accounts are meant as an intermediate layer between users and the service provider, so that the provider *only sees MAs* instead of the real users.

Ideas along these lines have been around in the prior literature [15, 34–36, 44], but the formalization of the privacy - user-utility trade-off has never been worked out. In particular, to make

SIGIR '17, August 07-11, 2017, Shinjuku, Tokyo, Japan

DOI: http://dx.doi.org/10.1145/3077136.3080830

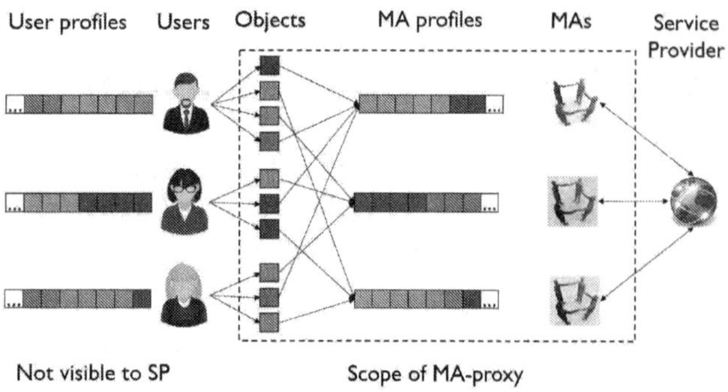

Figure 1: Overview of the MA framework.

this idea viable, one needs to devise quantitative measures for the effects of Mediator Accounts on privacy and utility. In addition, a strategy is needed for assigning user requests to such accounts. The simplest approach of uniform randomization would be ideal for privacy but could prove disastrous for user utility. This paper addresses these challenges within a framework of Mediator Accounts. Our ideas are general enough to be applied to search engines, recommender systems, and other online services where personalization is based on the user interaction history. Our salient **contributions** are:

- a model with measures for quantifying the trade-off between profiling privacy and user utility;
- the Mediator Accounts framework together with strategies for assigning user interactions to MAs;
- comprehensive experiments with two large datasets: search logs derived from the StackExchange Q&A community, and Amazon product ratings.

2 FRAMEWORK OVERVIEW

2.1 Architecture

The architecture of the Mediator Accounts framework is shown in Fig. 1. It consists of three parties: users, a service provider (SP), and a Mediator Accounts proxy (MA-proxy). A *user profile* consists of a set of *objects*, such as queries, product ratings or other forms of user interactions with the SP. Instead of issuing objects directly to the SP, users pass them on to the MA-proxy together with some context information. The goal of the MA-proxy is to redistribute the incoming objects on to mediator profiles mimicking real users. The MA-proxy assigns each incoming object to a Mediator Account offering the right context for the current object and user, and issues the object to the SP from the chosen MA. Upon receiving a response (for example, a result page or a product recommendation) from the SP, the MA-proxy passes it back to the user. When an interaction is over, the MA-proxy discards all linking information about the original user and the object and remembers only the association between the mediator account and the object. As a result, the original user profiles are scrambled across multiple MAs, and each MA consists of data from multiple users.

2.2 Incentives of participating parties

Users. The goal of a user participating in an MA system is to be able to get high-quality personalized results, while not letting any online provider (neither SPs nor the MA-proxy) keep her interaction history and link it to her as an individual. The MA-proxy has the user interaction history scrambled across multiple accounts, and no links between the objects and the real users are stored.

Users of anonymous services that do not offer topical personalization, such as the DuckDuckGo, Startpage or Qwant search engines, may be open to trading off some privacy for enhanced results through the MA framework.

Non-profiling service providers. The incentive of a non-profiling service provider would be to enhance personalization in the results, without compromising on the non-profiling principle.

Profiling service providers. A big question is whether profiling service providers would allow a third-party like an MA-proxy to mediate between them and the users. While examples of such third-parties already exist (the Startpage search engine uses Google as a source of search results), we believe that (i) an MA-proxy being able to group objects into realistic profiles that yield similar analytics results for the SP, and (ii) an MA-proxy being able to attract privacy-wary users who would not otherwise use the profiling SP, would be viable incentives for an SP not to block an MA service.

MA-proxy. An MA-proxy could be set up by individuals, or cooperatives of non-profiling SPs (to provide personalization without accumulating real user profiles), or by non-governmental organizations that promote online privacy. The Electronic Frontier Foundation is such an organization – a non-profit organization that has built privacy-preserving solutions like Privacy Badger.

2.3 Trusted and adversarial parties

MA-proxy. Users opting for an MA service would need to trust that it scrambles their profiles across mediator accounts, and discards the original profiles as well as any identifying information once an interaction (a single request or a session) is complete. A standard approach to gain such trust would be to make the MA solution open-source, enabling the code to be vetted by the community. A real implementation of an MA framework would have to take into account secure end-to-end communication channels between users and SPs via the MA-proxy. These issues may be resolved using encryption and security techniques (e.g., secure browser, onion routing, etc.), and are outside the scope of this paper.

Provider. The service provider is not exactly distrusted, but there have been cases where user-related information has been leaked or passed on beyond the original intentions – by sabotage, acquisition by other companies, or enforcement by government agencies. By detaching users from profiles and limiting their accuracy, the potential damage is bounded.

Other risks might result from service providers displaying privacy-sensitive personalized ads, such as ads related to pregnancy or health issues, especially when observed by others on a user's screen. The architecture would allow an MA-proxy to support filtering ads and adjusting them to users' topical interest. Such a configuration has indeed been found to be a preferable ad-serving setup in a user study [1]. Ad filtering, however, is orthogonal to this research.

Third parties. Profiling companies that operate outside the user-provider connections are considered untrusted. The same holds for agglomerates of providers that aggregate and exchange user data. A conceivable attack could be to guess a user's attribute (e.g., whether she is pregnant) by combining (i) observations on the MAs and (ii) observations on a set of accounts in a social network, using statistical inference methods. The MA framework aims to keep such risks low by breaking observable associations between MAs and real users, and limiting the profiling accuracy of the split-merge superpositions of different users that cannot be easily disentangled.

3 ASSIGNMENT MODEL

The core of the MA framework is an algorithm for assigning user objects to Mediator Accounts. To guide it on the privacy-utility trade-offs and to assess the quality of the output, we need measures for quantifying the effect of an assignment on privacy and user utility. This section presents such measures, and the algorithm for object assignment based on the split-merge concept.

3.1 Concepts and notation

We use the following notations:

- A set U of users $u_1 \dots u_p$.
- A set O of objects $o_1 \dots o_s$ issued by users; the objects are treated as unique even if they represent the same content. For instance, a query `folk music` issued by user u_i is treated as an object distinct from the same query issued by u_j. Analogously, a product rating for a book (`Folk Music History`, 3.0) by u_i is distinct from the rating by u_j for the same book, irrespective of the rating value.
- A set M of mediator accounts $m_1 \dots m_t$ to which objects are assigned by the MA-proxy.

We reserve the symbols i,j,k for subscripts of users, objects, and MAs. If user u_i issues object o_j, we write $o_j \in u_i$. Similarly, if o_j is assigned to MA m_k, we write $o_j \in m_k$.
Assignments. An *assignment* of objects on to MAs can be denoted as an $s \times t$ matrix A of 0-1 values, where $A_{ij} = 1$ means that o_i is assigned to m_j. If we think of the Cartesian product $O \times M$ as a bipartite graph, then the assignment can be conceptualized as a subgraph $S \subseteq O \times M$ where each node of type O has exactly one edge with one of the M nodes.

3.2 Objective

In a real application, an MA-proxy has to assign objects to accounts in an online manner, one object at a time as input arrives. In this paper, we focus on analyzing the model and assignments in an offline setting, although the algorithm we devise can be applied in both offline and online scenarios. The offline case is useful for two reasons. First, it is a foundation for understanding the underlying privacy-utility trade-offs. Second, performing offline assignment on a set of initial user profiles can address the cold-start problem that a new MA-proxy would face. Using the notation from Sec. 3.1, the *MA offline assignment problem* can be defined as follows:

- Given a set of objects O belonging to a set of users U, and the set of mediator accounts M, compute an assignment matrix A that optimizes a desired objective function for the privacy-utility trade-off.

The *MA online assignment problem* is:

- Given an assignment A of past user objects to MAs and a newly arriving object o of user u, find the best MA to which o should be assigned with regard to a desired goal for the privacy-utility trade-off.

3.3 Measuring privacy gain

An ideal situation from the perspective of privacy is when the objects from a user profile are spread across MAs uniformly at random – this minimizes the object-level similarity of any MA to the original profile. We thus measure privacy as the entropy of the user distribution over MAs, formalizing these notions as follows.
Entropy. We introduce for each user u_i an *MA-per-user vector* $\vec{mu}_i \in (\mathcal{N}_0)^t$ with one counter (≥ 0) per MA, written as $\vec{mu}_i = \langle x_{i1} \dots x_{ij} \dots x_{it} \rangle$ where x_{ij} is the number of objects by user u_i in account m_j (such that $\sum_{j=1}^{t} x_{ij} = |u_i|$). We can cast this into an *MA-per-user probability distribution* $\Phi_i = \langle \phi_{i1} \dots \phi_{ij} \dots \phi_{it} \rangle$ by setting $\phi_{ij} = x_{ij}/|u_i|$ followed by smoothing (e.g., Laplace smoothing) so that $\phi_{ij} > 0$ for each j and $\sum_{j=1}^{t} \phi_{ij} = 1$.

The degree of u_i's profile fragmentation can be captured by the entropy of the distribution Φ_i. We can define the *MA-per-user entropy* as a measure of *privacy gain* (gain over having each user exhibit her full individual profile):

$$privacy\text{-}gain(u_i) = H_i = -\sum_{j=1}^{t} \phi_{ij} \log \phi_{ij} \quad (1)$$

This quantifies the spread of the user's objects across accounts. The higher the entropy value, the higher the gain in profiling privacy.
Profile overlap. If a use-case requires a more user-interpretable measure of privacy, an alternative is to minimize the *maximum profile overlap*. For a user u_i, this measure can be expressed as:

$$O_i = \max_{j=1}^{t} \frac{|\{o \in u_i \cap m_j\}|}{|u_i|} \quad (2)$$

This measure of overlap can directly tell a user how much "error" could be made by an adversary, who assumes one of the MAs is the user's profile. The optimum for this measure, as with entropy, is achieved when the objects are uniformly spread across accounts. Thus, in the following, we use entropy as our privacy measure, and leave maximum profile overlap as a design alternative.

3.4 Measuring user utility loss

User utility loss measures to what extent an object o_k of user u_i is placed *out of context* by mapping it to account m_j. We define a real-valued function $sim(\cdot,\cdot)$ to measure the coherence of user and MA profiles: $sim(o_i,o_j) \in [0,1]$ is a symmetric measure of the relatedness between objects represented by o_i and o_j. In practice, different notions of relatedness can be used, based on object properties or usage. In settings where labels for topics or categories are available, we can set $sim(o_i,o_j) = 1$ if o_i and o_j are issued by the same user and have the same topic/category label, and 0 otherwise. Generally, we assume that sim measures are normalized with values between 0 and 1.

The objects of user u_i form a *context*, typically with high pairwise relatedness among the objects. When considering sets of objects as a whole (rather than time-ordered sequences of object posts), we can measure the *normalized context coherence* of an object o_k in the profile of user u_i by:

$$coh(o_k, u_i) = \frac{\sum_{o_l \in u_i, k \neq l} sim(o_k, o_l)}{|u_i| - 1} \quad (3)$$

When o_k is placed in MA m_j, we analogously define:

$$coh(o_k, m_j) = \frac{\sum_{o_l \in m_j, k \neq l} sim(o_k, o_l)}{|m_j| - 1} \quad (4)$$

The utility loss of u_i in a given MA assignment is then measured as an average coherence loss over all user objects:

$$utility\text{-}loss(u_i) = \frac{\sum_{o_k \in u_i} [coh(o_k, u_i) - coh(o_k, m_j)]}{|u_i|} \quad (5)$$

where m_j is the account containing o_k in the given assignment.

The normalization helps to account for varying sizes of user profiles. As a result, coherence values are always between 0 and 1, and utility loss is normalized to take values between −1 and 1. Note that our utility measure assumes that the context coherence can increase if an object is assigned to an MA with more similar objects. Coherence increase will result in negative utility loss.

3.5 Assignment algorithms

The role of an assignment algorithm is to scramble user objects across accounts so as to satisfy a desired privacy-utility tradeoff or optimize a corresponding objective function. In this paper, we experiment with a number of assignment algorithms and study their output quality.

3.5.1 Optimal assignment (Offline). The trade-off can be expressed as a joint non-linear optimization problem as follows:

$$\max_{A} \min_{u} [\alpha \cdot privacy\_gain(u) - (1 - \alpha) \cdot utility\_loss(u)] \quad (6)$$

Alternatively, one could optimize one of the two measures with a constraint on the other. Solving this problem exactly, however, is computationally expensive. If we use the less complex overlap privacy measure, we could cast the problem into a Quadratic Integer Program. However, this would have millions ($|M| \cdot |O|$) of variables; so it would remain intractable in practice. We thus do not pursue this direction in this paper and instead consider a number of heuristics. The following are also suitable for the *online case*.

3.5.2 Profiling-tradeoff assignment. We aim to approximate the combined objective function as follows. Let o be an object we want to assign to one of the accounts m_j. If we want to optimize for privacy (i.e., entropy), we should choose an MA at random from a uniform distribution over MAs:

$$P_{priv}(m_j|o) = \frac{1}{|M|} \quad (7)$$

If we want to optimize for utility, we could choose an MA that offers the best coherence:

$$P_{util}(m_j|o) = \begin{cases} 1, & \text{if } m_j = m_{max} \\ 0, & \text{otherwise} \end{cases} \quad (8)$$

where $m_{max} = \arg\max_{m_k} coh(o, m_k)$.

Let α be a parameter that controls the trade-off between privacy and utility. We sample an MA according to the distribution:

$$P(m_j|o) = \alpha \cdot P_{priv}(m_j|o) + (1 - \alpha) \cdot P_{util}(m_j|o) \quad (9)$$

In the offline case, we may choose an arbitrary order of objects to feed into this assignment heuristic. In the online case, we process objects ordered by the timestamps in which they are issued to the MA-proxy. It is also worth noting that in an online setting users could choose different α for each object, deciding that some should be assigned randomly, and some with the best possible context.

3.5.3 Random assignment. In this assignment, objects are assigned to accounts uniformly at random. This is a special case of the Profiling-tradeoff algorithm with $\alpha = 1$. This assignment maximizes privacy.

3.5.4 Coherent assignment. Personalization is usually based on semantically coherent parts of user profiles. If we retain such coherent fragments of a profile within the accounts, individual utility should be preserved better than in a completely random assignment. The mode in which we assign an object to the account that offers the best coherence is a special case of the Profiling-tradeoff algorithm, in which we set $\alpha = 0$. We refer to this method as Coherent. This assignment explicitly aims for the best utility only, yet some privacy is gained as chunks of user profiles get assigned to MAs randomly.

4 MA IN SEARCH SYSTEMS

By analyzing query-and-click logs, search engines can customize results to individual users. Such user profiling, however, may reveal a detailed picture of a person's life, posing potential privacy risks. At the same time, personalization of a single query is often based on only a subset of a user's history. Thus, as a first use case, we apply the MA framework in a search engine setting, scrambling the query histories of different users across accounts.

4.1 Framework elements

In the search scenario, the elements of the framework described in Sec. 3 are instantiated as follows. The objects are *keyword queries*, and user profiles consist of sets (or sequences) of queries, possibly with timestamps. Accounts contain re-assigned queries of different users. Object similarity can be understood as topical similarity between queries, with topics being either explicit such as categories or classifier labels, or latent, based on embeddings. As a query is characterized by a set (or weight vector) of topics, the similarity can be computed, for instance, using (weighted) Jaccard overlap or vector cosine. The service provider in this setting is a search engine, which, upon receiving a query from a given user profile, returns a ranked list of documents personalized for that user. User utility is measured by the quality of the result list.

4.2 Service provider model

The ability of the MA framework to preserve utility while splitting user profiles across accounts depends on a retrieval model for ranking query answers. We use the language-model-based retrieval technique [10], as described below.

Let $o \in u$ be a query of user u consisting of a number of words $w \in o$, and D be the document collection. The model retrieves the results in two steps. First, it fetches a set of top-k documents $D_o \subseteq D$, each document $d \in D$ being scored by the query-likelihood model with Dirichlet smoothing (parameter μ_D [10]):

$$score(o,d) = \log P(o|d) = \sum_{w \in o} \log \left(\frac{tf_{w,d} + \mu_D \cdot P(w|D)}{|V_d| + \mu_D} \right) \quad (10)$$

where $tf_{w,d}$ is the count of w in d, $P(w|D)$ is the probability that w occurs in D, and $|V_d|$ is the count of all words in d. For every user u, we compute a personalization score as the log-probability of the document d being generated from the user language model using Dirichlet smoothing with parameter μ_U, where U is the set of all users (or equivalently, the collection of their search histories):

$$score(d,u) = \log P(d|u) = \sum_{w \in d} \log \left(\frac{tf_{w,u} + \mu_U \cdot P(w|d)}{|V_u| + \mu_U} \right) \quad (11)$$

where $tf_{w,u}$ is the count of w in the search history of u, $P(w|d)$ is the probability that w occurs in d, and $|V_u|$ is the count of all words in the search history of u.

In the second step, documents $d \in D_o$ are re-ranked using a linear combination of the two scores:

$$score_u(o,d) = \gamma \cdot score(o,d) + (1 - \gamma) \cdot score(d,u) \quad (12)$$

In practice, γ would be set to a low value to put more importance on personalization.

When we use the MA framework, the computations are similar. The notion of a user is simply replaced by an account m. The personalization stage is adjusted as follows: we compute $score(d,m)$ using $P(d|m)$, which in turn is computed using $tf_{w,m}$, μ_M and $|V_m|$ with Eq. 11. Definitions of these quantities are analogous to their user counterparts.

5 MA IN RECOMMENDER SYSTEMS

Recommendation platforms like online shops, movie review forums, and music streaming sites, aggregate user interaction histories over time. As in the search setting, there is a direct correlation between the accuracy and completeness of user profiles and the quality of the obtained recommendations. Thus, as a second use case, we apply the MA framework to recommender systems.

5.1 Framework elements

Users of a recommendation platform rate different *items* like movies, books, and hotels. These *item-rating pairs* are the *objects* in the *profile* of a user. An item belongs to a set of *categories* (e.g., movie genres) from a taxonomy defined by the service provider. The *object similarity function* can be defined by topical similarity using such categories or tags. Additionally or alternatively, similarity can consider the ownership of objects, that is, whether two ratings are by the same user or different ones.

User utility here refers to the quality of recommendations. Rating predictions for items unseen by a user are made based on the past ratings of that user, as well as ratings of similar items by similar users. Thus, scrambling a user's ratings across accounts, if not done in a principled fashion, can potentially destroy user-item preference patterns, and hence degrade the quality of rating prediction.

5.2 Service provider model

A widely deployed rating prediction algorithm is *collaborative filtering* (CF) [22], which has been used by providers like Netflix, Amazon and Google [49]. In this model, the values of user-item ratings are stored as a matrix, where rows represent users, and columns represent items. CF maps both users and items into a low dimensional (latent) space using matrix factorization, such that user-item interactions (ratings) are modeled as inner products in that space, $\hat{r}(u_i, o_k) = \boldsymbol{q_{o_k}}^T \boldsymbol{p_{u_i}}$, where $\boldsymbol{p_{u_i}} \in \mathbb{R}^f$ and $\boldsymbol{q_{o_k}} \in \mathbb{R}^f$ are vector representations of the user u_i and item o_k in the latent space with dimensionality f. CF avoids overfitting by adding a regularization term to the objective function of the matrix factorization. To learn the low-dimensional vectors ($\boldsymbol{p_{u_i}}$ and $\boldsymbol{q_{o_k}}$), the system minimizes the regularized squared error on the set of known ratings (Eq. 13) [22]:

$$\min_{q^*,p^*} \sum_{(u_i,o_k) \in R} (r(u_i,o_k) - \boldsymbol{q_{o_k}}^T \boldsymbol{p_{u_i}})^2 + \lambda(||\boldsymbol{q_{o_k}}||^2 + ||\boldsymbol{p_{u_i}}||^2) \quad (13)$$

where R is the set of (u_i, o_k) pairs for which $r(u_i, o_k)$ is known (the training set of gold ratings), and λ is the regularization parameter. The trained model can then be used to predict ratings for unseen (user, item) pairs using the expression for $\hat{r}(u_i, o_k)$.

In the MA framework, the service provider no longer predicts the ratings for users, but for mediator accounts. Specifically, it learns a CF model from the MA-ratings data (triples of MA-id, item-id, rating), and then makes predictions for the unseen (m_j, o_k) pairs. As the ratings of an individual user are spread across different MAs, we need a method for *propagating the predicted ratings* from the MAs back to the individual users. Assume that we need to predict the rating $\hat{r}(u_i, o_k)$ when the MAs are present. Under a given assignment, u_i's items are split across MAs $\{m_j \in M\}$ with a distribution $\boldsymbol{\Phi_i}$ (Sec. 3.3), where the fraction of u_i's mass in some m_j is given by ϕ_{ij}. We assume that the MA-proxy has access to the predicted ratings $\hat{r}(m_j, o_k)$ from the service provider. We compute the propagated rating $\hat{r}^m(u_i, o_k)$ as the weighted sum of $\hat{r}(m_j, o_k)$:

$$\hat{r}^m(u_i, o_k) = \sum_{j=1}^{|M|} \phi_{ij} \hat{r}(m_j, o_k) \quad (14)$$

6 EXPERIMENTS ON SEARCH

6.1 Experimental setup

6.1.1 Dataset. For lack of publicly available query logs with user profiles, we created a query log and a document collection using the data from the Stack Exchange Q&A community (dump as of 13-06-2016). We excluded the large software subforums from outside the Stack Exchange web domain (such as StackOverflow), as they would dominate and drastically reduce the topical diversity. The final dataset consists of ca. $6M$ posts of type 'Question' or 'Answer' in 142 diverse subforums (e.g., Astronomy, Security, Christianity, Politics, Parenting, and Travel).

Document collection. We use all posts of type 'Answer' as our collection. The resulting corpus contains $3.9M$ documents.

User query histories. We construct a query log from posts of type 'Question', as these reflect users' information needs. Each question is cast into a keyword query selecting the top-l question words with the highest TF-IDF scores, where l is a random integer between 1 and 5. We consider only users with at least 150 questions, which yields a total of 975 users and 253K queries. Each query is assigned a topical label, used for object similarity. We set this label to the *subforum* where the original question was posted.

6.1.2 Service provider. For reproducible experiments, we base our search engine model on the open-source IR system Indri [40]. Indri ranks query answers based on state-of-the-art statistical language models with Dirichlet smoothing [10]. We use Indri to retrieve the top-100 results for every query from the entire corpus, and implement user-personalized re-ranking ourselves (see Sec. 4.2). We compute per-user language models from the original questions to tackle sparsity. The Dirichlet smoothing parameter is set to the average document length (56 words), and γ is set to 0.1.

6.1.3 Empirical measures.
Privacy Gain. The model entropy reflects how scrambled the user profiles are. Yet from the perspective of a profiling adversary it is rather the distribution over semantic topics that matters. Empirically, a proper way to measure privacy then is to compare the original topic distribution per user against the topic distributions of the MAs. The minimum KL-divergence between pairs of these distributions signifies the privacy level:

$$emp\!-\!priv\!-\!gain(u_i) = \min_{m_j \in M} D_{KL}(P^{u_i} \parallel Q^{m_j}) \quad (15)$$

where P^{u_i} and Q^{m_j} refer to the user and MA profile distributions over topics with add-one Laplace smoothing. We use subforums as explicit labels for topics.
Utility Loss. Rankings of documents d for a query are derived from $score_u(o,d)$ and $score_m(o,d)$ (Eq. 12), respectively, where the former refers to the query being issued by user u and the latter to the query being issued by the mediator account m (see Sec. 4.2). We quantify the empirical utility loss as the divergence between the two rankings. We compute two measures: the loss in Kendall's Tau over the top-100 document rankings: $1 - KTau@100$ (as the personalization step considers the top-100 documents), and the loss in Jaccard similarity coefficient over the first 20 ranking positions: $1 - Jaccard@20$ (as end-users typically care only about a short prefix of ranked results). For each user, we average these scores over all queries.

6.1.4 Assignment methods.
Object similarity. We set $sim(o_i, o_j) = 1$ if both o_i and o_j belong to the same user and to the same topic, and 0 otherwise. During the assignment, this measure helps to keep related parts of a user profile together.
Assignment algorithms. We run the Profiling-Tradeoff algorithm varying α between 0 and 1 with a 0.1 increment, and setting the number of MAs to be the number of users (975). With the chosen object similarity, the special case of $\alpha = 0$, i.e. the Coherent assignment, results in splitting user profiles into subforum chunks and assigning each chunk to a randomly chosen account.

6.2 Results and insights

Aggregate trends. Table 1 presents the results on the model measures and empirical measures for different values of the assignment trade-off parameter, macro-averaged over users. Recall that $\alpha = 0.0$ and $\alpha = 1.0$ correspond to the special cases of Coherent and Random assignments, respectively. These results need to be contrasted with the baseline, denoted *Original* in the table, where each original user forms exactly one account (i.e., no scrambling at all). Compared to the baseline, all numbers are statistically significant by

Table 1: Search results with trade-off parameter α for the model (M) and empirical (E) measures.

α	M-Priv-Gain (Entropy)	M-Util-Loss (Coherence Loss)	E-Priv-Gain (Min. KL-div.)	E-Util-Loss (1 - KTau@100)
Original	0.000	0.000	0.000	0.000
0.0 (Coh)	1.180	0.178	0.320	0.170
0.2	2.208	0.293	0.319	0.203
0.4	3.130	0.389	0.346	0.228
0.6	3.975	0.463	0.389	0.246
0.8	4.731	0.515	0.494	0.260
1.0 (Rand)	5.287	0.535	0.863	0.266

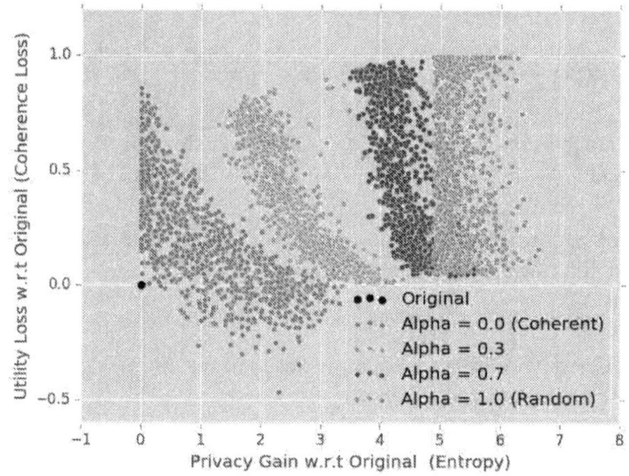

Figure 2: Model measures per user (search).

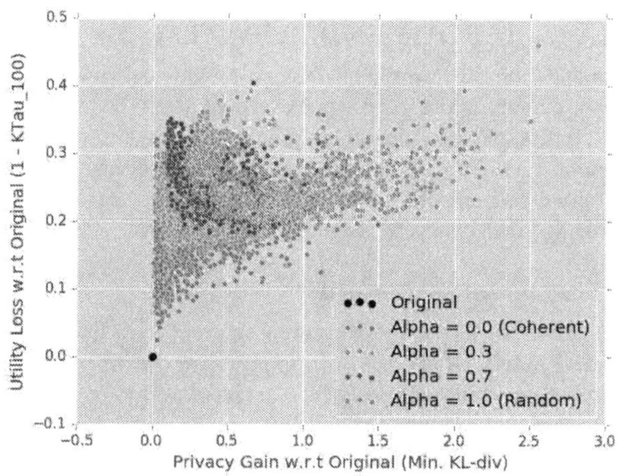

Figure 3: Empirical measures per user (search).

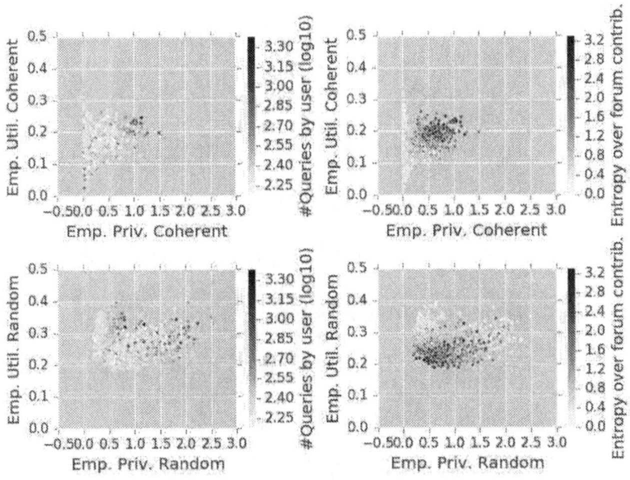

Figure 4: Effect of profile size and diversity (search).

paired t-tests with $p < 0.01$. For empirical utility loss, we report Kendall's Tau; the results for the Jaccard coefficient are similar.

The results show that the Profiling-Tradeoff assignments improve privacy over the *Original* baseline (the topical KL-div. between original users and MAs is increased) while keeping the utility loss low. This is largely true regardless of the exact choice of α. So the MA framework provides a fairly robust solution to reconciling privacy and utility, supporting the observation that high-quality topical personalization does not require complete user profiles.

With the α increasing, assignments become more random, so the privacy increases and utility is reduced (but with a low gradient). In this regard, the empirical measures reflect the expected behavior according to the model measures well.

Results per user. Figs. 2 and 3 show privacy and utility values of each user, for the model and empirical measures, respectively. Different colors represent different assignments, and each dot represents a user, with measures averaged over the user's queries. We have several observations:

- Higher privacy gain is correlated with higher utility loss. The Original assignment maps each user to the origin (0 utility loss, but also 0 privacy gain). No assignment reaches the bottom-right area of the chart – which would be an ideal.
- Varying α not only tunes the privacy-utility tradeoff at the community aggregate level, but also affects the variance over individual user scores. This suggests that we should further explore choosing α on an individual per-user basis (which is easily feasible in our framework, but is not studied in this paper).
- Even the Random assignment ($\alpha = 1.0$) keeps utility reasonably high. This is due to the fact that random MAs – sampled from queries in the community – end up being averaged rather than random profiles.
- Some users achieve high privacy gains without losing hardly any utility, and vice versa. We investigate this further below.

Effect of profile size and diversity. We analyze how different user profile characteristics affect the assignment results. Figure 4 presents the empirical trade-offs for the Coherent (top row) and Random (bottom row) assignments, where each dot is a user and the dot color represents (i) the logarithm of the number of queries in the user profile (left column), or (ii) the diversity of the profile measured by the entropy of the distribution of queries across topics (right column). We make the following observations:

- Users with more queries (darker dots) in the Coherent assignment clearly gain privacy at the cost of losing utility, whereas for the smaller profiles (lighter dots), the trade-off is not as pronounced. In the Random assignment this trade-off is less pronounced irrespective of the size of the profile.
- In the right column, one can see the lighter dots (profiles with little diversity) moving from the bottom-left for the Coherent assignment (little privacy gain, little utility loss) to the top-right for the Random assignment (higher privacy gain, higher utility loss). This suggests that our framework does not offer much help to the users with uniform and focused interests. This is an inherent limitation, regardless of which privacy protection is chosen. Such homogeneous users cannot hide their specific interests, unless they give up on personalization utility.
- Our split-merge assignments offer good results for users with high diversity. As suggested by the darker dots, the Coherent assignment leads to a lower utility loss and higher privacy gain for users with diverse profiles, when compared to the Random assignment. This is because such users have more independent and internally coherent chunks that can be split without affecting utility. This class of users is exactly where the right balance of utility and privacy matters most, and where we can indeed reconcile the two dimensions to a fair degree.

7 EXPERIMENTS ON RECOMMENDERS

7.1 Experimental setup

7.1.1 Dataset. We use the Amazon product rating data collected by Mukherjee et al. [30] which contains user-item ratings, along with review text and metadata. We extract (user, item, rating) triples from this data with associated timestamps, and restrict product type to `music`, one of the most frequent product types. We identify active users who rated between 50 and 1000 items. Within `music` there are 22 categories, as defined by Amazon: `rock`, `jazz`, `country`, etc. An item is originally associated with 2.12 categories on average, but we assign it uniquely to *one* category by selecting the most frequent category. The final data had 1,719 users, 72,464 items and 197,215 ratings (ratings are between 1 and 5).

7.1.2 Service provider. We used a parallelized implementation of a collaborative filtering model based on matrix factorization: ALS-WR [22, 49]. This is available in Apache Spark (https://goo.gl/X33DN9, Accessed 23 Jan 2017), and widely used. The model has three parameters – number of latent features f, the regularization parameter λ, and the number of iterations n_i to run. f was set to 22, which is the number of categories in the data. λ and n_i were learnt to be 0.3 and 10 respectively, using grid search on a separate development set of $60K$ ratings.

Table 2: Recommender results with parameter α for the model (M) and empirical (E) measures.

α	M-Priv-Gain (Entropy)	M-Util-Loss (Coh. Loss)	E-Priv-Gain (Min. KL-Div.)	E-Util-Loss (MSE)
Original	0.000	0.000	0.000	0.000
0.0 (Coh)	0.826	0.094	0.073	0.501
0.2	1.778	0.086	0.064	0.576
0.4	2.573	0.106	0.075	0.623
0.6	3.339	0.122	0.093	0.664
0.8	4.009	0.133	0.130	0.689
1.0 (Rand)	4.495	0.137	0.262	0.690

7.1.3 *Empirical measures.*

Privacy Gain. We use the same measure of per-user empirical privacy as in the search scenario, which is the KL-divergence between the topical distributions representing the user profile and the "closest" MA profile (Eq. 15). The distributions are computed over the 22 Amazon Music categories (with add-one Laplace smoothing).
Utility Loss. Empirical utility for user u_i is measured in terms of mean squared error (MSE). MSE is computed for $R_{u_i}^{test}$, where the system needs to generate recommendations for each of 40 given items, for each user u_i. These test cases are not part of the training data. The error is computed between predictions made by the user model and the model propagated through the MAs, i.e., $\hat{r}(u_i, o_k)$ and $\hat{r}^m(u_i, o_k)$ (Sec. 5.2). We thus have in Eq. 16:

$$emp\text{-}util\text{-}loss(u_i) = \frac{\sum_{y=1}^{|R_{u_i}^{test}|}(\hat{r_y}(u_i, o_k) - \hat{r_y}^m(u_i, o_k))^2}{|R_{u_i}^{test}|} \quad (16)$$

The set of 40 unseen items for a user to make predictions on is picked at random from the set of 72,464 items. Our complete test set thus contained 68,760 (= 1,719 × 40) (user, item) pairs.

Under the MA model, each user-item rating prediction requires multiple MA-item predictions. For the assignment methods presented, we had to make up to 7.5M predictions in total from the MA model, for the 68,760 test ratings. However, with the parallelized Spark implementation, this took only a few minutes on a single machine with 8 GB RAM.

7.1.4 *Assignment methods.*

We create 1,719 MA profiles, equal to the number of users. The object similarity is set to 1 if two objects belong to the same user and the same category, and 0 otherwise. The tradeoff parameter α was varied from 0.0 through 1.0 in steps of 0.1. Rating timestamps were used to determine the order of object assignments.

7.2 Results and insights

Aggregate trends. Table 2 shows how the model and empirical measures of privacy and utility vary with tradeoff parameter α. Each value is an average over all 1719 users. $\alpha = 0.0$ and 1.0 correspond to Coherent and Random assignments respectively. *Original* again denotes the baseline where each original user forms her own account. Note that *higher values for the privacy measures* of entropy and KL-divergence indicate better privacy gain, and *lower values for the utility measures* of coherence loss and MSE imply better user utility loss.

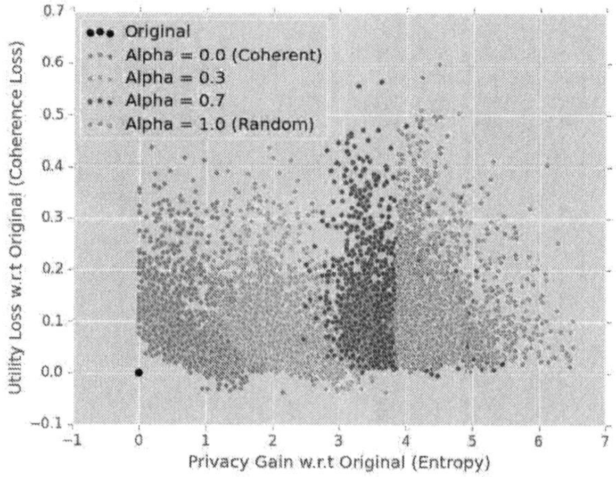

Figure 5: Model measures per user (recommenders).

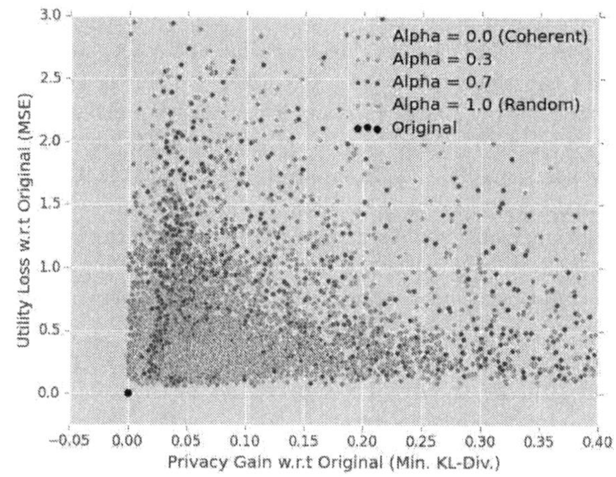

Figure 6: Empirical measures per user (recommenders).

The major insight here is the following. For the *Coherent assignment*, we observe good empirical utility (a very low MSE of 0.501), while providing a substantial improvement in empirical privacy (0.073 from 0). Thus, this assignment is a good candidate for practical deployment. Generally, the Profiling-Tradeoff assignment works well for all α, demonstrating the robustness of our approach.

The trends in empirical privacy and utility mimic those of the model measures. As α is increased from 0.0 to 1.0, there is gradual improvement in empirical privacy and a monotonic degradation in user utility, both with low gradients.

Results per user. Figs. 5 and 6 visualize privacy versus utility for model and empirical measures, where each point denotes an individual user. Different colors represent different tradeoff settings, as shown in the legend. There are two notable observations:

- Users form different clusters in the privacy-utility space as α is varied. The clusters are softer (more overlapping) in the empirical case than in the model. This shows that analytically

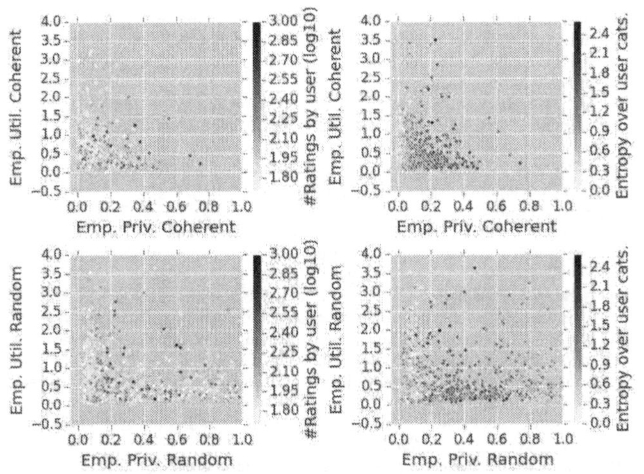

Figure 7: Effect of profile size and diversity (recommenders).

predicting these tradeoff statistics is not easy; hence our experimental approach.

- Fig. 6 indicates that, for the Coherent assignment, a fraction of users have both *high privacy gain* and *low utility loss* (the brown dots in the lower right area of the chart), while most users exhibit the expected privacy-utility tradeoff. This suggests further optimizations by tuning assignment parameters for each individual user separately.

Effect of profile size and diversity. As in the search setting, we report on the variation of the empirical measures with respect to changes in user profile size (number of items rated) and diversity (entropy of the distribution of item categories in the user profile) in Fig. 7. The two plots on the left refer to size and the ones on the right to diversity. The upper and lower plots correspond to the Coherent and Random assignments, respectively. We observe:

- Users with diverse interests do well on both dimensions (more dark dots towards lower right), and thus benefit the most from our framework. This represents a significant fraction of all users, as seen by the numerous dark dots in the diversity graphs.
- A higher profile size yields lower utility loss, for the Coherent assignment. So while a bigger profile typically entails better prediction accuracy (our measure of empirical utility), we can see that this is true only if related parts of the user profile are preserved in the MAs. This comes at the cost of somewhat reduced privacy gains. However, the Coherent assignment does fairly well in both dimensions. For Random assignment, profile size does not have a notable effect on privacy, and utility is often completely lost.
- Overall, users with larger profiles *and* varied interests have the best chance of preserving utility while having substantial privacy gains under the Coherent assignment. Thus, we can derive guidelines for tuning α (Table 2): α may be kept high in the beginning for objects of all users, and it may gradually be decreased when users show diversity in their interests as their profiles grow bigger (cf. Sec. 3.5.2).

8 RELATED WORK

Grouping for privacy: The idea of masking the traces of individual users by combining them into groups has been around since the *Crowds* proposal by [35]. However, this early work solely focused on anonymity of web-server requests. [31] devised an abstract framework for group privacy over obfuscated databases, but did not address utility. For search engines specifically, [21] proposed a notion of query bundles as an implicit grouping of users, but focused on countering de-anonymization in the presence of so-called vanity queries. The short paper [50] sketches a preliminary approach where semantically similar queries by different users are grouped for enhancing privacy. Aggregation of users' website-specific privacy preferences through a centralized server [47], can also be perceived as a type of *privacy through solidarity*. The principle of solidarity has moreover been explored through a game-theoretic framework over recommender systems [18].

Tracking and profiling: A good body of work investigates to what extent and how users are tracked by third parties in web browsers [24, 29, 47], or through mobile apps [28]. These are primarily empirical studies with an emphasis on identifying the tracking mechanisms. The interactions with service providers, where users log in and leave extensive traces, have been largely disregarded. In contrast, our framework helps counter both tracking and individual profiling by detaching users from online accounts.

To reduce the scale of profiling, a model called stochastic privacy has been proposed to selectively sample user profiles for use by personalizing algorithms [39]. To counter profiling by search engines in particular, [45] has proposed to issue queries anonymously, but provide the engine with a coarse topical profile for answer quality. On the tracking front, the Non-Tracking Web Analytics system reconciles users' need of privacy and online providers' need of accurate analytics [3]. Although these various works address the privacy-utility trade-off, no explicit control mechanism has been proposed for user utility.

Privacy-preserving IR: The intersection of privacy and IR has received some attention in the past years [46]. One of the key problems studied in the field is that of post-hoc log sanitization for data publishing [9, 16, 48]. Online sanitization, on the other hand, aims at proactively perturbing and blurring user profiles. Techniques along these lines typically include query broadening or dummy query generation (e.g., [4, 33, 37, 43]). It has also been proposed to perturb user profiles by making users swap queries and execute them on behalf of each other [34]. Very few of these prior works consider the adverse impact that obfuscation has on utility, and the usual focus is on the utility of single query results. To the best of our knowledge, none of them focuses on personalization utility or offers quantitative measures for the trade-off.

Another privacy concept studied in IR is that of exposure. Recently, the notions of R-Susceptibility and topical sensitivity have been proposed to quantify user exposure in sensitive contexts within a given community [6].

Privacy-preserving data mining: There is a vast body of literature on preserving privacy in mining data for rules and patterns and learning classifiers and clustering models [2, 12]. In this context, utility is measured from the provider's perspective, typically an error measure of the mining task at hand (e.g., classification error)

[5]. In the specific context of recommender systems, rating prediction accuracy [27, 32] and category aggregates [38] are typically used as proxies for utility. Techniques for user profile perturbation have also been studied for utility-preserving differentially-private recommeders [17].

9 CONCLUSIONS

We presented Mediator Accounts (MAs): a framework to counter user profiling while preserving individual user utility as much as possible. The framework enables decoupling users from accounts, making direct targeting impossible, and profile reconstruction or de-anonymization much harder. At the same time, users are still able to benefit from personalization by service providers. The versatility of the framework has been demonstrated in two different application scenarios. While our model allows for flexible trade-offs between privacy and utility, a key question in our two empirical studies has been to understand how well the MAs can preserve the utility in terms of high-quality search results and recommendations. The experiments show that the split-merge approach with Coherent assignment improves the privacy, while incurring little user utility loss. These benefits are most pronounced for users with larger profiles (i.e., more activity) and higher diversity of interests.

Open issues for future work include practical deployment, handling of other personalization features, and exploring the options for tuning assignments and framework parameters to the specific needs of individual users. On top of that, analyzing the three-dimensional trade-off between user privacy, user utility and the traditional service provider utility could help ensure that the resulting mediator profiles are a useful source for user analytics, making an MA proxy a tolerable component of the online landscape.

Finally, we would hope that the MA proposal stirs up the investigation of how the need-to-know principle could be implemented in case of personalized online services.

Acknowledgements. We would like to thank Subhabrata Mukherjee from MPII for useful discussions at various stages of this work.

REFERENCES

[1] L. Agarwal, N. Shrivastava, S. Jaiswal, and S. Panjwani. Do Not Embarrass: Re-examining User Concerns for Online Tracking and Advertising. In *SOUPS '13*.

[2] C. Aggarwal. *Data mining: The textbook*. Springer, 2015.

[3] I. E. Akkus, R. Chen, M. Hardt, P. Francis, and J. Gehrke. Non-tracking web analytics. In *CCS '12*.

[4] E. Balsa, C. Troncoso, and C. Diaz. Ob-pws: Obfuscation-based private web search. In *S&P '12*.

[5] E. Bertino, D. Lin, and W. Jiang. A survey of quantification of privacy preserving data mining algorithms. In *Privacy-preserving data mining '08*.

[6] J. A. Biega, K. P. Gummadi, I. Mele, D. Milchevski, C. Tryfonopoulos, and G. Weikum. R-Susceptibility: An IR-centric approach to assessing privacy risks for users in online communities. In *SIGIR '16*.

[7] B.-C. Chen, D. Kifer, K. LeFevre, and A. Machanavajjhala. Privacy preserving data publishing. *Foundations and Trends in Databases '09*.

[8] G. Chen, H. Bai, L. Shou, K. Chen, and Y. Gao. UPS: efficient privacy protection in personalized web search. In *SIGIR '11*.

[9] A. Cooper. A survey of query log privacy-enhancing techniques from a policy perspective. *TWeb '08*.

[10] W. B. Croft, D. Metzler, and T. Strohmann. *Search engines*. Pearson Education, Inc., 2010.

[11] C. Dwork. Differential Privacy: A Survey of Results. In *TAMC '08*.

[12] L. Fan, L. Bonomi, L. Xiong, and V. Sunderam. Monitoring Web browsing behavior with differential privacy. In *WWW '14*.

[13] B. C. M. Fung, K. Wang, R. Chen, and P. S. Yu. Privacy-preserving Data Publishing: A Survey of Recent Developments. *ACM Computing Surveys '10*.

[14] A. Gervais, R. Shokri, A. Singla, S. Capkun, and V. Lenders. Quantifying web-search privacy. In *CCS '14*.

[15] M. T. Goodrich, M. Mitzenmacher, O. Ohrimenko, and R. Tamassia. Privacy-preserving group data access via stateless oblivious RAM simulation. In *SODA '12*.

[16] M. Götz, A. Machanavajjhala, G. Wang, X. Xiao, and J. Gehrke. Publishing search logs: A comparative study of privacy guarantees. *TKDE '14*.

[17] R. Guerraoui, A.-M. Kermarrec, R. Patra, and M. Taziki. D2P: distance-based differential privacy in recommenders. *VLDB '15*.

[18] M. Halkidi and I. Koutsopoulos. A game theoretic framework for data privacy preservation in recommender systems. In *ECML PKDD'11*.

[19] A. Hannak, P. Sapiezynski, A. Molavi Kakhki, B. Krishnamurthy, D. Lazer, A. Mislove, and C. Wilson. Measuring personalization of web search. In *WWW '13*.

[20] X. He, A. Machanavajjhala, and B. Ding. Blowfish privacy: Tuning privacy-utility trade-offs using policies. In *SIGMOD '14*.

[21] R. Jones, R. Kumar, B. Pang, and A. Tomkins. Vanity fair: Privacy in querylog bundles. In *CIKM '08*.

[22] Y. Koren, R. Bell, and C. Volinsky. Matrix factorization techniques for recommender systems. *IEEE Computer '09*.

[23] A. Krause and E. Horvitz. A utility-theoretic approach to privacy in online services. *JAIR '10*.

[24] A. Lerner, A. K. Simpson, T. Kohno, and F. Roesner. Internet jones and the raiders of the lost trackers: An archaeological study of web tracking from 1996 to 2016. In *USENIX Security '16*.

[25] N. Li, T. Li, and S. Venkatasubramanian. t-closeness: Privacy beyond k-anonymity and l-diversity. *ICDE '07*.

[26] A. Machanavajjhala, D. Kifer, J. Gehrke, and M. Venkitasubramaniam. l-diversity: Privacy beyond k-anonymity. *TKDD '07*.

[27] F. McSherry and I. Mironov. Differentially private recommender systems: Building privacy into the Netflix prize contenders. In *KDD '09*.

[28] W. Meng, R. Ding, S. P. Chung, S. Han, and W. Lee. The Price of Free: Privacy Leakage in Personalized Mobile In-App Ads. In *NDSS '16*.

[29] W. Meng, B. Lee, X. Xing, and W. Lee. TrackMeOrNot: Enabling Flexible Control on Web Tracking. In *WWW '16*.

[30] A. Mukherjee, B. Liu, and N. Glance. Spotting fake reviewer groups in consumer reviews. In *WWW '12*.

[31] A. Narayanan and V. Shmatikov. Obfuscated databases and group privacy. In *CCS '05*.

[32] V. Nikolaenko, S. Ioannidis, U. Weinsberg, M. Joye, N. Taft, and D. Boneh. Privacy-preserving matrix factorization. In *CCS '13*.

[33] S. T. Peddinti and N. Saxena. Web search query privacy: Evaluating query obfuscation and anonymizing networks. *JCS '14*.

[34] D. Rebollo-Monedero, J. Forne, and J. Domingo-Ferrer. Query profile obfuscation by means of optimal query exchange between users. *TDSC '12*.

[35] M. K. Reiter and A. D. Rubin. Crowds: Anonymity for Web transactions. *TISSEC '98*.

[36] N. Santos, A. Mislove, M. Dischinger, and K. Gummadi. Anonymity in the personalized web. In *NSDI Posters '08*, 2008.

[37] X. Shen, B. Tan, and C. Zhai. Privacy protection in personalized search. In *SIGIR Forum '07*.

[38] Y. Shen and H. Jin. Epicrec: Towards practical differentially private framework for personalized recommendation. In *CCS '16*.

[39] A. Singla, E. Horvitz, E. Kamar, and R. White. Stochastic privacy. In *AAAI '14*.

[40] T. Strohman, D. Metzler, H. Turtle, and W. B. Croft. Indri: A language model-based search engine for complex queries. In *International Conference on Intelligent Analysis '05*.

[41] L. Sweeney. k-anonymity: A model for protecting privacy. *International Journal of Uncertainty, Fuzziness and Knowledge-Based Systems '02*.

[42] J. Teevan, S. T. Dumais, and E. Horvitz. Personalizing search via automated analysis of interests and activities. In *SIGIR '05*.

[43] P. Wang and C. V. Ravishankar. On masking topical intent in keyword search. In *ICDE '14*.

[44] Y. Xu, K. Wang, G. Yang, and A. W. Fu. Online anonymity for personalized web services. In *CIKM '09*.

[45] Y. Xu, K. Wang, B. Zhang, and Z. Chen. Privacy-enhancing personalized web search. In *WWW '07*.

[46] H. Yang, I. Soboroff, L. Xiong, C. L. Clarke, and S. L. Garfinkel. Privacy-Preserving IR 2016: Differential Privacy, Search, and Social Media. In *SIGIR '16*.

[47] Z. Yu, S. Macbeth, K. Modi, and J. M. Pujol. Tracking the trackers. In *WWW '16*.

[48] S. Zhang, G. H. Yang, and L. Singh. Anonymizing query logs by differential privacy. In *SIGIR'16*.

[49] Y. Zhou, D. Wilkinson, R. Schreiber, and R. Pan. Large-scale parallel collaborative filtering for the Netflix prize. In *AAIM '08*.

[50] Y. Zhu, L. Xiong, and C. Verdery. Anonymizing user profiles for personalized web search. In *WWW '10*.

Joint Learning of Response Ranking and Next Utterance Suggestion in Human-Computer Conversation System

Rui Yan[†,♮]
[†]Institute of Computer Science and Technology
Peking University
Beijing 100871, China
ruiyan@pku.edu.cn

Dongyan Zhao[†,♮]
[†]Institute of Computer Science and Technology
Peking University
Beijing 100871, China
zhaody@pku.edu.cn

Weinan E[♮]
[♮]Beijing Institute of Big Data Research
Peking University
Beijing 100871, China
weinan@math.pku.edu.cn

ABSTRACT

Conversation systems are of growing importance since they enable an easy interaction interface between humans and computers: using natural languages. To build a conversation system with adequate intelligence is challenging, and requires abundant resources including an acquisition of big data and interdisciplinary techniques, such as information retrieval and natural language processing. Along with the prosperity of Web 2.0, the massive data available greatly facilitate data-driven methods such as deep learning for human-computer conversation systems. Owing to the diversity of Web resources, a retrieval-based conversation system will come up with at least some results from the immense repository for any user inputs. Given a human issued message, i.e., query, a traditional conversation system would provide a response after adequate training and learning of how to respond. In this paper, we propose a new task for conversation systems: joint learning of response ranking featured with next utterance suggestion. We assume that the new conversation mode is more proactive and keeps user engaging. We examine the assumption in experiments. Besides, to address the joint learning task, we propose a novel Dual-LSTM Chain Model to couple response ranking and next utterance suggestion simultaneously. From the experimental results, we demonstrate the usefulness of the proposed task and the effectiveness of the proposed model.

CCS CONCEPTS

•**Information systems** → **Retrieval models and ranking; Web applications;** *Users and interactive retrieval;*

KEYWORDS

Response ranking; next utterance suggestion; neural networks; joint learning; conversation system

SIGIR'17, August 07-11, 2017, Shinjuku, Tokyo, Japan
© 2017 ACM. 978-1-4503-5022-8/17/08...$15.00
DOI: http://dx.doi.org/10.1145/3077136.3080843

1 INTRODUCTION

People talk to each other every day. Generally speaking, having conversations in natural languages is one of the basic ways to communicate. Since computers become a powerful tool and closely connected partner to humans, people expect that we give orders and have conversations with computers using natural languages. Such a communication interface is simple, easy, straightforward, and more importantly, human-like. For years, human-computer conversation systems have gained much attention for their functional, social, and entertainment roles in real-world applications.

To launch a human-computer conversation system is inevitably difficult and challenging. It is a hardcore problem which involves interdisciplinary techniques such as information retrieval, natural language processing, and advanced artificial intelligence. The task requires comprehensive semantics analysis to understand human utterances. The system needs to respond accordingly, either by organizing terms and tokens to synthesize new responses (i.e., generation-based conversation), or finding existed responses which are deemed appropriate to reply (i.e., retrieval-based conversation). People work hard on how to maintain relevant, meaningful and user-engaging conversations between human and computer.

Along with the prosperity of Web 2.0, people get used to having conversations which are publicly available on the websites, such as Bulletin Board System (BBS) forums, social media (e.g., *Facebook*, *Twitter*) and community question-answering platforms (e.g., *Baidu Zhidao*, *Yahoo! Answers*). These resources provide a unique opportunity to build a massive collection of naturally occurring conversations. The big data propel a fast development of retrieval-based techniques for conversation studies in the open domain. The merit is that owing to the diversity on the Web, the system will be able to retrieve at least some results for any user inputs, and can be trained to flow naturalistic conversations by learning from large volumes of human-to-human conversations. In this paper, we focus on research in the retrieval-based human-computer conversation system in the open domain.

Over time, notable accomplishments in conversation systems have been achieved with tremendous efforts devoted. People have developed a well-defined paradigm and deploy it into most of existed conversation systems: given a human utterance as the *query*, the computer returns a *response*. The standard procedure presumes that humans take the role to lead a conversation.

An interesting thought comes to our mind. Since query suggestion has been demonstrated to be helpful for classic information retrieval, and a search-based conversation system applies the retrieval paradigm, what if we introduce a *proactive* conversation mode with "response ranking" as well as "next utterance suggestion"? Query suggestion brings information outside of a particular user's scope and provides what others might search given the entire dataset, leading to better search experiences. So can we expect the utterance suggestion could improve the conversation experiences?

We believe the answer is yes. There are several advantages for a proactive human-computer conversation mode featured with next utterance suggestion. One typical situation is that the system predicts something that the user is going to express (similarly as query suggestion might do). In this scenario, the user just needs to click the suggestion and it becomes more convenient to talk. Moreover, conversations in the open domain generally do not limit to only one ground truth response, and people keep an open mind in chit-chat. By taking next utterance suggestions, users are able to continue a conversation about new contents that they might not originally intend to talk about. Thirdly, one more critical issue is that there can be "stalemates" during a human-computer conversation [14]. A passive conversation system cannot break the stalemates but a proactive one can, by suggesting appropriate next utterances to say. Due to manifold reasons, we expect better human-computer conversation experiences in the new proactive conversation mode.

We have two questions to answer: 1) does the proposed new conversation task really work? 2) If the task works, how to formulate the problem and design a model to solve it?

We briefly formulate the new task. Given a query q, the conversation system provides a pair of response and suggestion (r,s). r is to respond q, while s is to suggest how the conversation continues given r. In contrast to the traditional passive conversation style, the system now provides additional information to attract more user engagement, which is a "proactive" conversation style. The new mode is featured with next utterance suggestion and response ranking, simultaneously.

We can decompose the task into several subtasks. The most straightforward method is to find an appropriate response given the query, and then to find a good suggestion given the response in the same way. However, we will show that the simple solution does not work. For one thing, the suggestion is not guaranteed to be relevant to the query; moreover, if a response diverges from the query, a suggestion based on the response would become meaningless.

To this end, we propose a dual recurrent neural network chains with Long-Short Term Memory (LSTM) units for the new conversation task, namely Dual-LSTM Chain Model (*Dual-LSTM*). The model formulates two matching chains for *query-response* and *response-suggestion* separately, and couples the dual chains in an end-to-end joint learning manner. The information across the words is propagated through chains, and both chains are tangled to fuse input information via a unified way, which is a novel insight.

We conduct extensive experiments in a variety of human-computer conversation setups and evaluation metrics in terms of p@1, MAP, nDCG and MRR. We run experiments against several rival algorithms to answer the two questions that we brought up previously: is the task useful and is the model effective? The results are positive.

To sum up, we have several contributions as follows:

• To the best of our knowledge, we are the first to systematically investigate the proactive conversation mode with next utterance suggestion. The joint learning problem and our task formulation are novel[1].

• To solve the joint learning problem, we propose a novel Dual-LSTM Chain Model based on the recurrent neural networks. The proposed model simultaneously matches a query with a pair of response and suggestion as the next utterance.

• We conduct extensive experiments to investigate whether the proactive conversation mode is useful, and to examine the effectiveness of the Dual-LSTM model. By studying the phenomenon of the system equipped with the new conversation mode, we have some interesting discoveries.

The rest of the paper is organized as follows. We start by reviewing related work in Section 2. We introduce the task statement in Section 3. In Section 4, we describe our proposed model. We devise experimental setups and evaluations against a variety of baselines and discuss results in Section 5. We draw conclusions in Section 6.

2 RELATED WORK

For decades, researchers work on human-computer conversation systems. In early days, people generally focus on conversation systems established by rules or templates [30, 34]. The idea is simple and such methods require no data or few data for training, while instead require a great many human efforts to create enough handcraft rules or templates to run the system. To build rule-based systems is costly. Yet a conversation goes out of scope easily. People begin to pay more attention to data-driven methods.

From human-driven conversation systems to data-driven conversation systems, the need for a much bigger amount of data is substantially increasing. Nowadays, with the prosperity of social media (such as microblogs), forums and other Web 2.0 resources, people have conversations with each other on the Internet, publicly. It is feasible to collect a very large amount of human-to-human conversation data [33].

With massive data available, it is intuitive to build a retrieval-based conversation system as information retrieval techniques are developing fast. Given a user utterance as a query, the system searches for candidate responses by certain matching metrics. Leuski *et al.* build systems to select the most suitable response to the query from the question-answer pairs using a statistical language model as cross-lingual information retrieval [8]. The database consisting of a number of question-answer pairs is a key to success [9].

[1] Google works on utterance assistance in Allo and Gmail system with a vision of "responding without typing". So basically, the technique only produces a candidate response (w/o a next utterance). Our problem formulation with *response-suggestion* pairs is quite different.

Researchers propose to augment the database with question-answer pairs retrieved from plain texts [2, 19].

Another way to build a conversation system is to use language generation techniques. Higashinaka *et al.* propose to combine language template generation with the search-based methods [3]. Ritter *et al.* have investigated the feasibility of conducting short text conversation by using statistical machine translation (SMT) techniques, learning from millions of naturally occurring conversation data in Twitter [21]. In these approaches, a response is generated from a model, not retrieved from a repository, and thus it cannot be guaranteed to be a legitimate natural language text [42].

In recent years, deep neural networks (DNNs, also known as *deep learning*) have made a significant improvement. DNNs are highly automated learning machines; they can extract underlying abstract features of data automatically by exploring multiple layers of non-linear transformation [1]. Prevailing DNNs for sentence-level modeling include convolutional neural networks (CNNs) and recurrent neural networks (RNNs). In CNNs, we have a fixed-size sliding window to capture local patterns of successive words [7], whereas RNNs keep one or a few hidden states, and collect information along the word sequence in an iterative fashion [39]. Due to a well-known problem of gradient vanishing/explosion in vanilla RNN, Long-Short Term Memory (LSTM) and Gated Recurrent Unit (GRU) are proposed to address the issue [20, 28].

With the help of deep learning techniques, generation-based conversation systems are greatly advanced. In general, the conversation system applies the sequence-to-sequence generation manner [28]. A neural responding machine is proposed for single-turn conversation [24]. Soon, the conversation is extended into multi-turns, with plain contexts [26] and hierarchical contexts [23, 29]. Researchers gradually introduce various elements into conversation generation, such as diversity [12], persona [13], topic [38], knowledge [40] and additional contents [18].

Needless to say, retrieval-based conversation systems are also greatly advanced using neural networks. A series of information retrieval-based methods are applied to short-text conversations using microblog data, either for single-turn conversation [6, 11, 15] or multi-turn conversation [42, 43, 45]. Basically, these methods model sentences using convolutional [4, 15] or recurrent [20, 31] units to construct abstractive representations. Many matching metrics are proposed for retrieval using deep neural networks. Palangi *et al.* have proposed sentence matching based on vector similarities [20]. A recursive schema is later introduced for incremental sentence modeling [31, 32]. Usually, sentences are compared in a pairwise matching style via word-by-word matchings, known as sentence pair modeling [4, 41]. The chain-based matching is also demonstrated to be useful, where the first sentence's information is available when modeling the second one [10, 22]. In this paper, we use the chain-based matching with recurrent units. Auxiliary information such as topics [37], knowledge [36], and contents [14] can also be incorporated for better retrieval. Although not all of these methods are originally designed for conversation, they are very effective for short-text matching tasks in general. We include some of them as strong baselines in the experimental setups.

In this paper, we propose a new conversation task of response ranking and next utterance suggestion. The difference compared with related work is quite clear. The mentioned studies basically rank responses by certain matching metrics. Most traditional human-computer conversations are passive: the computers need only to respond. No content will be suggested to continue the conversation. Here in the new conversation mode, the computers become proactive to suggest next utterances when deemed appropriate. We investigate the new conversation task and evaluate its usefulness in the application scenario. Secondly, we propose a Dual-LSTM Chain Model to couple the joint learning task in this paper, which is also a novel insight.

3 TASK STATEMENT

3.1 Problem Formulation

The new conversation task contains two hops of retrieval. Given a query q from the human, the computer would retrieve several candidate responses r to respond. For each r, the system will retrieve a bunch of candidate suggestions s as next utterances. The two-hop process is illustrated in Figure 1. After the two hops of retrieval, we have one query to several responses, and each response is followed by several suggestions. We formulate them as triples, each as $\{q,r,s\}$.

For each triple of $\{q, r, s\}$, we feed them into the proposed neural network framework for sentence representation learning and semantics matching. The ranking score $\mathcal{F}(.)$ is a learned function from all evidences through an end-to-end learning. The best matched r and s will be output in pairs as an appropriate response and a next utterance suggestion. In contrast to a traditional conversation formulation as $r^\star = \text{argmax}_r\ \mathcal{F}(r|q)$, we formulate the joint learning task for a proactive conversation system as follows:

$$(r, s)^\star = \underset{r,s}{\text{argmax}}\ \mathcal{F}\big((r, s)|q\big) \quad (1)$$

We decompose the joint learning task into subtasks, and then analyze the major technical issues for each of them.

Subtask 1 (RESPONSE RANKING.) *Given a user issued query* $\boldsymbol{q}$*, we retrieve several candidate responses* $\boldsymbol{r}$ *from the conversational dataset* $\mathcal{D}$*. We learn to match* $\boldsymbol{r}$ *with* $\boldsymbol{q}$*.*

It is undoubted that the relevance between the query and the response is a key issue to the joint learning task. If a selected response is not related to the query, the entire task might become meaningless. Subtask 1 aims at modeling the semantic correlation between the query and the response. Here we apply an LSTM chain to characterize the semantic relevance and to measure whether a response is appropriate.

Subtask 2 (SUGGESTION RANKING.) *Given a candidate response* $\boldsymbol{r}$*, we retrieve several candidate suggestions* $\boldsymbol{s}$ *from the conversation dataset* $\mathcal{D}$*. We learn to match* $\boldsymbol{s}$ *with* $\boldsymbol{r}$*.*

Another key issue for the task is the relevance between the (selected) suggestion and the (selected) response. Intuitively, if the suggestion is not related to the response, the task would make less sense. This subtask characterizes the semantic matching between a response and a suggestion. We can apply another LSTM chain to model the relevance then decide how likely to give a suggestion as the next utterance.

Yet, these two LSTM chains should not be isolated. Since the choice of the first chain (a response) and the choice of the second chain (a suggestion) are provided as a pair, both components need to be somehow coupled together. Moreover, since part of the first chain is also part of the second chain, the first LSTM chain can have a positive impact (when appropriately matched), or negative penalty (when mismatched), on the second LSTM chain. In other words, the second LSTM chain will be influenced by an external "memory" from the first LSTM chain and the memory is a soft gating mechanism for the information propagation.

Subtask 3 (JOINT COUPLED LEARNING.) *Given the candidate responses* $\boldsymbol{r}$ *and suggestions* $\boldsymbol{s}$*, we learn to couple them together so as to rank a pair of* $(\boldsymbol{r}, \boldsymbol{s})$ *given* $\boldsymbol{q}$.

From subtasks 1 and 2, we can measure the correlations between a query and a response, as well as a response and a suggestion. Neither of the matching result will be output in isolation: they are further coupled through deep neural networks and we obtain a final ranking score for (r,s) pairs.

We believe that training such an end-to-end model to minimize a single objective function, and with minimum reliance on hand-crafted features, will yield superior performance in the long run. We introduce the Dual-LSTM Chain Model by taking into account of the 1) query-response relevance, 2) response-suggestion relevance, and 3) the joint learning. We will elaborate the components in Section 4.

3.2 System Pipeline

We briefly describe the system pipeline and data flow. Roughly, we have an off-line process and an online process.

Off-line Process. As mentioned, people now interactively have conversations with each other on the Internet, which provides a huge thesaurus of conversational data. Therefore we are able to collect sufficient human-to-human conversation data taken from the Web. Users post *messages* visible to the public, and then receive *replies*. Such conversations do not occur in strict real-time style but they are literally real human conversations which last for one turn or more. We collect the conversational data ($\mathcal{D}$), stored as "virtual documents" (d), each virtual document as d=($message$,$reply$) and $\mathcal{D}=\{d_i\}_{i=1}^{|\mathcal{D}|}$. The whole corpus is formatted in an inverted index prepared off-line. Besides, we train the matching model off-line to learn human conversations from the data.

Online Process. After taking in a user-issued *query*, we apply a standard retrieval process via keyword search from $\mathcal{D}$. To be more specific, we search for a *message* using the *query*, and returns the *reply* as the *response* to output, as shown in Figure 1(a). Similarly, we search for a *suggestion* given a candidate *response* using the same conversation repository $\mathcal{D}$, shown in Figure 1(b). For more details of how to retrieve responses from a conversational database, interested readers may refer to more elaborations in [42, 43]. The two-hop of retrieval returns a list of potentially relevant *responses* and *suggestions* out of the corpus given the *query*. We feed them into the learned matching model.

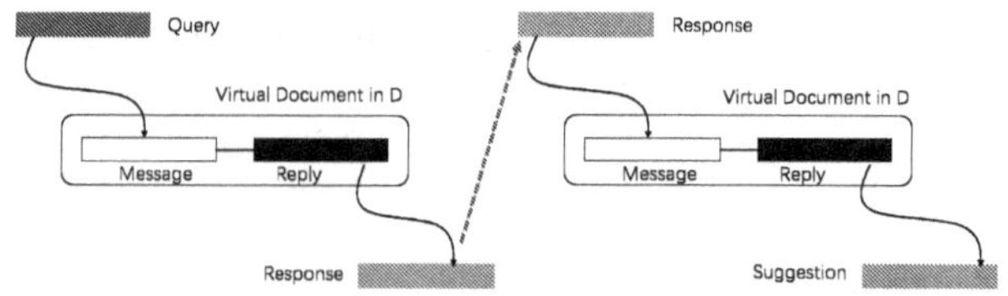

(a) 1st-hop Retrieval **(b) 2nd-hop Retrieval**

Figure 1: Two hops of retrieval to get *responses* and *suggestions* from the virtual documents given a *query*. In general, the retrieval process is to search for the *message* part and to return the *reply* part.

4 DUAL-LSTM CHAIN MODEL

To learn the representation and matching is the core component in the retrieval-based conversation system. We establish a joint learning framework. Two LSTM chains combine the ranking evidences and determine the match of a response-suggestion pair to a query. All ranking evidences are integrated together through the proposed Dual-LSTM Chain Model shown in Figure 2.

4.1 LSTM Chain

To be self-contained, we first give a quick overview of word embedding and the neural network structures.

4.1.1 Word Embeddings. In text-related models, a word generally acts as an atomic unit; thus, the internal relation between similar words might lose. A typical approach is to map a discrete word to a dense, low-dimensional, real-valued vector, called an *embedding* [17]. Each dimension in the vector captures some (anonymous) aspect of underlying word meanings. This process is known as vectorization. Given enough data, word embeddings can make highly accurate guesses about the meaning of a particular word. Embeddings can equivalently be viewed that a word is first represented as a one-hot vector and multiplied by a look-up table [17].

In our model, we first vectorize all words using their embeddings, which serve as the foundation of our deep neural networks. Word embeddings are initialized randomly, and then tuned during training as part of model parameters.

4.1.2 LSTM Networks. We use the recurrent neural networks (RNNs) with LSTM units to propagate information along the word sequence. RNNs keep a hidden state vector, which changes according to the input at each time step.

LSTM is an advanced type of RNN by further using memory cells and gates to learn long term dependencies within a sequence to address gradient vanishing or explosion problems [20, 28]. LSTM maintains a memory cell that updates and exposes its content only when deemed necessary. LSTM models are defined as follows: given a sequence of inputs, an

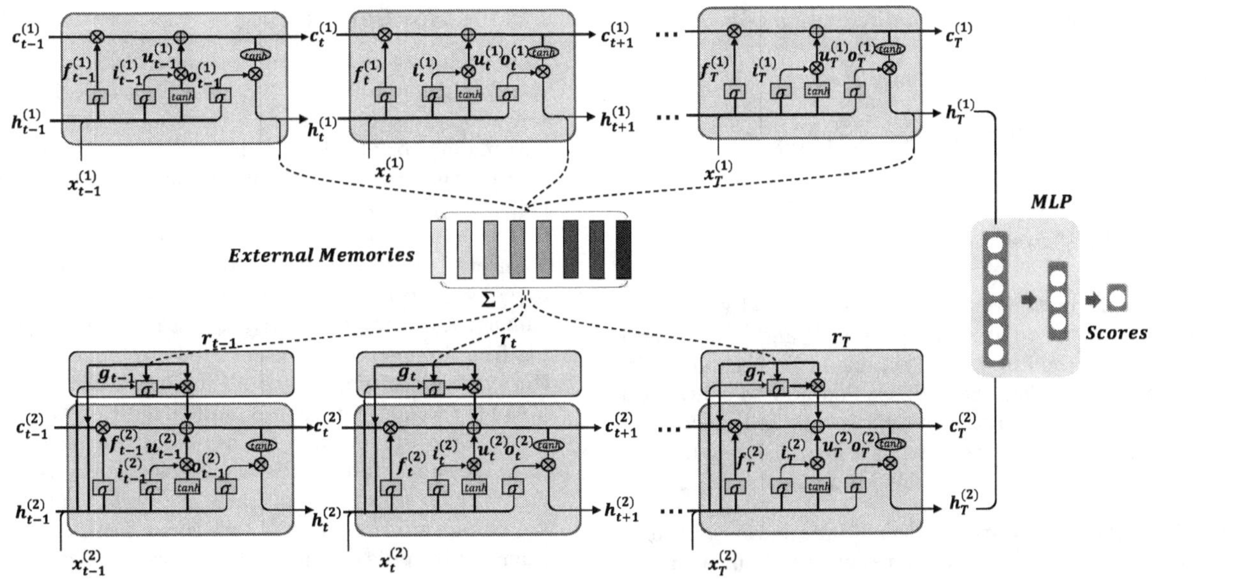

Figure 2: Dual-LSTM Chain Model with the first LSTM chain to characterize *query-response* and the second LSTM chain to characterize *response-suggestion*. The two LSTM chains are coupled by an external memory states and a multi-layer perceptron (MLP).

LSTM associates each position with *input, forget,* and *output gates,* denoted as $\mathbf{i}_t$, $\mathbf{f}_t$, and $\mathbf{o}_t$ respectively. The vector $\mathbf{c}_t$ is used to additively modify the memory contents. Given an input sentence $\mathbf{x} = \{\mathbf{x}_0, \mathbf{x}_1, \ldots, \mathbf{x}_T\}$, where $\mathbf{x}_t$ is the vector of word embedding for individual token (i.e., a word) at position t in the sentence. LSTM outputs a representation $\mathbf{h}_t$ by combining $\mathbf{h}_{t-1}$ and $\mathbf{x}_t$ for position t, given by

$$\begin{bmatrix} \mathbf{i}_t^{(1)} \\ \mathbf{f}_t^{(1)} \\ \mathbf{o}_t^{(1)} \end{bmatrix} = \begin{bmatrix} \sigma \\ \sigma \\ \sigma \end{bmatrix} (W \cdot \left[\ \mathbf{h}_{t-1}^{(1)}, \mathbf{x}_t^{(1)} \ \right] + \mathbf{b}) \tag{2}$$

$$\mathbf{u}_t^{(1)} = \tanh(W \cdot \left[\mathbf{h}_{t-1}^{(1)}, \mathbf{x}_t^{(1)}\right] + \mathbf{b}) \tag{3}$$

$$\mathbf{c}_t^{(1)} = \mathbf{f}_t^{(1)} \odot \mathbf{c}_{t-1}^{(1)} + \mathbf{i}_t^{(1)} \odot \mathbf{u}_t^{(1)} \tag{4}$$

$$\mathbf{h}_t^{(1)} = \mathbf{o}_t^{(1)} \odot \tanh(\mathbf{c}_t^{(1)}) \tag{5}$$

where $\mathbf{b}$ indicate the bias and $\odot$ denotes element-wise multiplication. $\sigma(\cdot) = \frac{1}{1+e^{-\cdot}}$ is a known as a sigmoid function. Intuitively, the forget gate controls the amount of which each unit of the memory cell is erased, the input gate controls how much each unit is updated, and the output gate controls the exposure of the memory state, which is stored in the internal memory cell.

For a pairwise matching, two sentences are matched via a transformation of an affinity matrix through parameters trained and learned from the network. In this paper, we use the chain-based matching through information propagated in the LSTM sequence. Such a method has been proved effective for matching and alignments [10, 22].

In this way, we obtain a series of state $\{\mathbf{h}_t^{(1)}\}$ with a superscript $^{(1)}$ from the first LSTM chain, and the final hidden state $\mathbf{h}_T^{(1)}$ which indicates the information from the query and response. As indicated in Section 3.1, the hidden states $\{\mathbf{h}_t^{(1)}\}$ will be utilized to characterize the other LSTM chain. We take the output vector $\mathbf{h}_T^{(1)}$ as a feature representation and feed it to a feed-forward neural work for future integration and optimization. The gradients are computed using the back-propagation algorithm [35].

4.2 Dual-LSTM Chain

We incorporate another LSTM chain for response-suggestion matching. The gist is similar to the first LSTM chain. Additionally, the first LSTM chain has an impact by propagating information through a soft gating mechanism on the second LSTM chain. We will first explain the external "memory" from the first LSTM chain. We formulate a relevance vector through a gating cell into the neural network units in the second LSTM chain so as to control information fusion.

4.2.1 External Memories. We use external memories constructed by history hidden states $\{\mathbf{h}_t^{(1)}\}$ from the first LSTM chain between the query and the response, which is:

$$\mathrm{M} = \{\mathbf{h}_1^{(1)}, \mathbf{h}_2^{(1)}, \ldots, \mathbf{h}_T^{(1)}\}$$

where $\mathbf{h}_t^{(1)}$ is the hidden state at time t emitted by the first LSTM chain. The memory blocks M are used to store the external information for matching. Hence, the history information can be read from the memory block. We denote a relevance vector (denoted as $\mathbf{r}$) from external memories as $\mathbf{r}_i$, which can be computed by soft attention mechanisms:

$$\mathbf{r}_i = \sum_{1}^{T} \alpha_{ij} \mathbf{h}_j^{(1)} \tag{6}$$

where α represents the attention distribution over the external memory states M.

The attention signal can be calculated as:

$$\alpha_{ij} = \text{Softmax}(\phi(\mathbf{h}_j^{(1)}, \mathbf{x}_i^{(2)}, \mathbf{h}_{i-1}^{(2)})) \quad (7)$$

where

$$\phi(\mathbf{h}_j^{(1)}, \mathbf{x}_i^{(2)}, \mathbf{h}_{i-1}^{(2)}) = \mathbf{v}^T \tanh(W \cdot \left[\mathbf{h}_j^{(1)}, \mathbf{x}_i^{(2)}, \mathbf{h}_{i-1}^{(2)}\right] + \mathbf{b}) \quad (8)$$

W are weight matrices, $\mathbf{v}$ is weight vector and $\mathbf{v}^T$ denotes its transpose. Here we use superscripts $^{(1)}$ and $^{(2)}$ to denote the vectors from the first LSTM chain and the second LSTM chain respectively. The score is based on how to control the information fusion from the query-response relevance. The attention schema is parametrized as a neural network which is jointly trained with all the other components [22, 24].

4.2.2 Gating Cell. With additional information of the external memory blocks, we have more evidence to measure the relevance between a response and a suggestion. The information from the first LSTM sequence is maintained and passed along for further judgments of the second LSTM chain. Our motivation is to propagate "reliable" relevance evidence from the first LSTM chain to measure the second one. To this end, we design a gating cell to read relevance memories into the second LSTM chain.

The gating cell is to control the information fusion into the second LSTM chain: relevance evidence can pass through the gate and irrelevant evidence shall not. In this way, the semantic relevance from the first chain implicitly performs as the clue for the selection of the second chain. Starting from the original vectors, at each time step the cell decides the alignment with the first LSTM chain, and decides what information should be retained for future time steps and discards the others. This cell plays the role of gating relevant information fusion, and the semantic clues can be integrated into the second LSTM chain smoothly.

We add a new gating cell, and the relevance information is incorporated into the LSTM units. The cells read the relevance vector, and decides whether or how to use the external memory from the first LSTM chain into the second one.

$$\begin{bmatrix} \mathbf{i}_t^{(2)} \\ \mathbf{f}_t^{(2)} \\ \mathbf{o}_t^{(2)} \\ \mathbf{g}_t \end{bmatrix} = \begin{bmatrix} \sigma \\ \sigma \\ \sigma \\ \sigma \end{bmatrix} (W \cdot \left[\ \mathbf{h}_{t-1}^{(2)}, \mathbf{x}_t^{(2)}, \mathbf{r}_t\ \right] + \mathbf{b}) \quad (9)$$

$$\mathbf{u}_t^{(2)} = \tanh(W \cdot \left[\mathbf{h}_{t-1}^{(2)}, \mathbf{x}_t^{(2)}, \mathbf{r}_t\right] + \mathbf{b}) \quad (10)$$

$$\mathbf{c}_t^{(2)} = \mathbf{f}_t^{(2)} \odot \mathbf{c}_{t-1}^{(2)} + \mathbf{i}_t^{(2)} \odot \mathbf{u}_t^{(2)} + \mathbf{g}_t \odot \mathbf{r}_t \quad (11)$$

$$\mathbf{h}_t^{(2)} = \mathbf{o}_t^{(2)} \odot \tanh(\mathbf{c}_t^{(2)}) \quad (12)$$

After updating the new LSTM units, the hidden state of $\mathbf{h}_T^{(2)}$ will be passed as the output of the second LSTM chain.

4.3 Coupled Chains

Now we have two final states denoted as $\mathbf{h}_T^{(1)}$ and $\mathbf{h}_T^{(2)}$ from the Dual-LSTM chains. We concatenate both vector representations together, and feed the concatenated vector to an ensuing network for further information mixing. Vector concatenation for matching is also applied in various studies like [44], which is effective yet of low complexity order.

The joint vector is then passed through a 3-layer, fully-connected, feed-forward neural network, also known as *multi-layer perceptron* (MLP) [1], which allows rich interactions. The network enables to extract features automatically, starting from lower-level representations to higher-level ones, till the system provides an overall judgment of the appropriateness for the query, response, and suggestion triple.

We have two options to formulate the task-specific output. We can formulate the whole task as a ranking problem. For ranking tasks, the outputs are scalar matching scores. We can also formulate the task as a classification problem, when the outputs are the probabilities of the different classes, which are computed by the softmax function on the matching vectors. In this paper, we use the first formulation of a ranking problem. A single neuron outputs the matching score of both components. As mentioned, $\mathcal{F}((r,s)|q)$ is in $\mathbb{R}$; the final scoring neuron is essentially a linear regression.

Here we apply hinge loss to train the proposed network. Given a triple of positive sample (q, r^+, s^+) in the training set, we randomly sample a negative instance r^- and/or s^-. The objective is to maximize the scores of positive samples while minimizing that of the negative samples. Concretely, we would like the score of positive samples $\mathcal{F}(+)$ to be as least the score of negative samples $\mathcal{F}(-)$ plus a margin Δ. Thus, the training objective is to

$$\underset{\theta}{\text{minimize}} \sum \max\{0, \Delta + \mathcal{F}(+) - \mathcal{F}(-)\} + \lambda\|\theta\|_2^2 \quad (13)$$

where we add an ℓ_2 penalty with coefficient λ for all the parameters θ which are weight and bias values optimized by the network from all ranking evidences.

As our model is (almost) everywhere differentiable, the parameters of the networks are optimized with stochastic gradient descent using the back prorogation algorithm to compute the gradients. The gradients can be propagated all the way back through coupling, matching, and individual sentence modeling. In this way, heterogeneous information can be incorporated organically with our model under the unified deep framework. According to the objective function to optimize in Equation (13), it is sufficient to learn the model by computing the gradients with respect to the model parameters. The computation for these gradients can be decomposed using chain rules.

4.4 Model Variants

Our proposed model has some natural connections to existed neural network models for conversation tasks. We add some more discussions about the model variants.

Model Degeneration. We have two LSTM chains to feed into the MLP function. If we just omit the semantic matching which comes from the second LSTM chain, the model degenerates to a traditional matching method for the standard human-computer conversation without next utterance suggestion. In other words, a model for the standard human-computer conversation is part of our proposed model.

Another degeneration is that we separate the proposed model into two isolated LSTM chains without any coupling structures. We use the first chain to match a *query* and a *response*, and use the second chain to match a *response* and a *suggestion*. The model degenerates into a Chain-LSTM model [10], which is the most intuitive way to tackle the proactive conversation mode with response ranking and next utterance suggestion. Although not coupled, two isolated chains still provide two ranking lists for either responses or suggestions. We include the model in experimental analysis.

Model Extension. There are two typical scenarios for conversations: single-turn conversation and multi-turn conversation with "context" information from a session [42, 43]. Since the proactive conversation mode with response ranking and next utterance suggestion is quite a new study, we start from the basic single-turn conversation scenario to verify its usefulness: the matching is measured among a triple of a *query*, a *response* and *suggestion*.

It is exciting to see that with small extensions, the proposed model will be compatible with the multi-turn conversation scenario. We can encode the contexts into the first LSTM chain as people generally do [23, 26]. The information from the first LSTM chain can still be propagated to the second LSTM chain, the Dual-LSTM model can be used for multi-turn conversation scenarios. We leave further investigations as our future work.

5 EXPERIMENTS AND EVALUATION

The objectives of our experiments are 1) to examine whether the new proactive mode with a next utterance suggestion is useful in human-computer conversation systems, and 2) to verify the effectiveness the Dual-LSTM model for the task.

5.1 Dataset

We use the data which contain a large number of human conversations crawled from open Web, where the users publish a message visible to the public, and then receive a bunch of subsequent replies to their utterances. We conducted data filtering and cleaning procedures by removing extremely short utterances and those of low linguistic quality.

We constructed another conversation dataset of 1,606,583 samples to train the proposed model, 357,018 for validation, and 11,097 for testing. It is important that the dataset for learning does not overlap with the data for retrieval: we strictly comply with the machine learning regime. For each training and validation sample, we randomly chose inappropriate responses and/or suggestions to obtain a negative sample. Validation was based on the model accuracy.

5.2 Hyperparameters

We use 128-dimensional word embeddings, and they were initialized randomly and learned during training. As our dataset is in Chinese, we performed standard Chinese word segmentation. We maintained a vocabulary of 177,044 phrases by choosing those with more than 2 occurrences.

The LSTM units have 128 hidden units for each dimension. We used stochastic gradient descent (with a mini-batch size of 100) for optimization, gradient computed by standard back propagation. Initial learning rate was set to 0.8, and a multiplicative learning rate decay was applied. The above parameters were chosen empirically. We used the validation set for early stopping.

During the experiments, a suggestion will be provided when the matching score of the triple exceeds a threshold (empirically set as 0.9 in this study). Otherwise, we still use the traditional conversation mode since we do not provide suggestions all the time with low confidence.

5.3 Evaluation

For evaluation, we need to examine the effectiveness of the new conversation task and the proposed Dual-LSTM model.

We need to demonstrate the proposed Dual-LSTM method is effective for the task. To this end, we evaluate the appropriateness of the response and the suggestion given a particular query. Since we can automatically construct training/testing sets, we evaluate based on 11,097 test cases. We hire annotators on a crowdsourcing platform to judge the appropriateness of top-10 ranked response and suggestion pairs from different methods for each test case. Each sample was judged by annotators via majority voting based on *appropriateness*. "1" denotes appropriateness and "0" indicates otherwise.

The evaluation design consists two parts: the evaluation interfaces are shown in Figure 3. The annotator will first be shown two sentences s_1 and s_2. They are asked whether the s_2 is good to respond s_1. In this way, we obtain the matching results for either *query-response* (recorded as Type I evaluation results) or *response-suggestion* (denoted as Type II evaluation results). We keep the appropriate pairs when s_1 is the query and s_2 is a response. Next s_3 is added into the evaluation, and annotators are asked to judge whether s_3 is appropriate given both s_1 and s_2. We know whether s_3 is a good suggestion given s_1 and s_2 (denoted as Type III evaluation). Other triples are annotated as inappropriate.

Given the ranking lists with scores, we evaluated the performance in terms of precision@1 (p@1), mean average precision (MAP) [27], and normalized discounted cumulative gain (nDCG) [5]. Since the system outputs the highest ranked results, p@1 is the precision at the 1st position, and should be the most natural way to indicate the fraction of suitable result among the top-1 triple retrieved. We also provide the top-10 ranking list for all test queries using nDCG and MAP, which test the potential for a system to provide more than one appropriate triples. We aimed at selecting as many

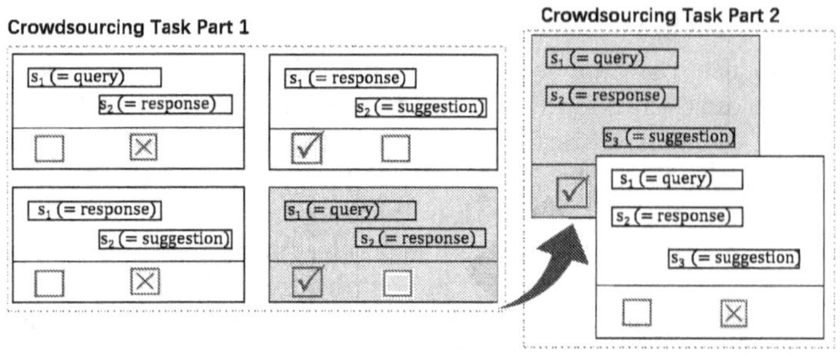

Figure 3: Interfaces for crowdsourcing evaluations. In Crowdsourcing Task 1, annotators are asked to judge whether a second sentence s_2 is appropriate to the first sentence s_1. Next we filter the results from Task 1, and keep the samples when s_1 is a test *query* and appropriateness judged as *yes* for Task 2. In Task 2, annotators judge whether the third sentence s_3 is appropriate given the matched s_1 and s_2.

appropriate candidates as possible into the top-10 list and rewarding methods that return suitable triples on the top.

Formally, the metrics are computed as follows.

$$\text{nDCG@i} = \frac{1}{|\mathcal{T}|}\sum_{q\in\mathcal{T}}\frac{1}{Z}\sum_{i=1}^{k}\frac{2^{\psi_i}-1}{\log(1+i)}$$

where $\mathcal{T}$ indicates the testing query set, k denotes the top-k position in the ranking list, and Z is a normalization factor obtained from a perfect ranking. ψ_i is the relevance score for the i-th candidate reply in the ranking list (i.e., 1: appropriate, 0: inappropriate).

MAP is computed by

$$\text{MAP} = \frac{1}{|\mathcal{T}|}\sum_{q\in\mathcal{T}}\frac{1}{N_q}\sum_{i=1}^{k}P_i \times \psi_i$$

Here N_q is the number of appropriate candidates selected, and P_i is the precision at i-th position.

Since we use real triplets collected from multi-turn human-human conversations for testing, we also have the human result added in the ranked list after matching. We include the Mean Reciprocal Rank (MRR) evaluation computed as:

$$\text{MRR} = \frac{1}{|\mathcal{T}|}\sum_{q\in\mathcal{T}}\frac{1}{rank(q)}$$

where $rank(q)$ is the position of the human result from the real triplet within the candidate ranking list.

Unlike MAP and nDCG, which examine the ranks of appropriate candidates, Mean Reciprocal Rank (MRR) focuses on evaluating the capability of retrieval systems to find (perhaps) the best result which means the positive triples created by humans in our dataset. MRR is useful but does not test the full capability because there can be multiple appropriate utterances to continue a conversation.

5.4 Competing Algorithms

We include several algorithms as baselines to compare. Since our proposed approach is technically a retrieval method, we mainly focus on retrieval-based conversation system. For fairness we use the same pre-processing procedure and the same data for all algorithms. Given a query, the systems return matched responses and suggestions accordingly.

- *Okapi BM25.* We include the standard retrieval technique to rank candidates. For each utterance, we retrieve the most relevant results using BM25 model [16].
- *ARC-II.* There are many convolutional kernel based sentence matching method [4, 15]. The ARC-II approach is a typical neural network based method with convolutionary layers which construct sentence representations and produce the final matching scores via a MLP layer [4].
- *LSTM-RNN.* A sentence is encoded as a vector representation by the last hidden state from an LSTM-RNN sequence. Two sentences are matched by cosine similarity in pairs [20].
- *MV-LSTM.* MV-LSTM is a deep architecture for word-to-word matching of two sentences with multiple positional sentence representations by LSTM sequences [31].
- *Chain-LSTM.* The Chain-LSTM indicates another matching style. When concatenated as a chain, the first sentence helps to model the second one. The information from both sentences interweaves sentence modeling and matching [10].
- *Dual-LSTM.* We propose the Dual-LSTM Chain Model based on several novel insights: two matchings are modeled by two LSTM chains, and the dual chains are coupled by joint learning through deep neural networks. We have some model variants and we discuss the analysis in Section 5.6.

5.5 Overall Performance

We conduct the appropriateness evaluation to see the performance of all methods. We have three types of results from the crowdsourcing evaluations. We measure the appropriateness between a query and a response (Type I), the appropriateness between a response and a suggestion (Type II), and most importantly, the appropriateness between a query and a (response, suggestion) pair (Type III). For baselines, they do not have the coupling component, thus we adapt two separate matchings for *query-response* and *response-suggestion*. The results are shown in three rows in Table 1.

Okapi BM25 represents the standard keyword-based retrieval method. The performance for BM25 is moderate, not surprising. In general, BM25 only utilizes the shallow representation of individual terms, while it is less capable to capture the deep semantics inside sentences.

Deep learning systems are demonstrated to have stronger capabilities to learn the abstractive representation [1, 7, 25]. The deep learning algorithm groups clearly outperform the shallow learning method. Measuring the interactions of each and every terms from the two sentences at every position can be ascribed as a classic matching style, either as a convolutional baseline *ARC-II*, or recurrent baseline *MV-LSTM*. Word-to-word matching in every position is better than the

Table 1: Appropriateness results of Type I, II, and III evaluations. Bold fonts indicate the acceptance of improvement hypothesis for the *joint learning* task (shown in gray rows) by Wilcoxon test at a significance level of 0.01. nDCG means nDCG@10.

Model	p@1	MAP	nDCG	MRR	
Okapi BM25	0.272	0.253	0.302	0.169	I
	0.259	0.226	0.284	0.156	II
	0.138	0.126	0.187	0.091	III
ARC-II	0.394	0.294	0.421	0.232	I
	0.387	0.291	0.415	0.217	II
	0.255	0.201	0.278	0.142	III
LSTM-RNN	0.338	0.283	0.371	0.228	I
	0.351	0.300	0.366	0.237	II
	0.206	0.195	0.233	0.128	III
MV-LSTM	0.435	0.322	0.409	0.308	I
	0.410	0.313	0.414	0.301	II
	0.269	0.251	0.267	0.168	III
Chain-LSTM	0.416	0.328	0.429	0.301	I
	0.422	0.316	0.410	0.307	II
	0.261	0.246	0.298	0.183	III
Dual-LSTM	0.431	0.339	0.441	0.312	I
	0.442	0.326	0.437	0.319	II
	0.425	**0.315**	**0.419**	**0.303**	III

matching from a single position (i.e., *LSTM-RNN*), which concurs the observation in [31].

The single *Chain-LSTM* method is regarded as another matching regime, and is demonstrated to be useful in other matching tasks such as entailment [22]. We have similar observations. The MRR score indicates that this method is good at capturing information flows through a conversation.

For all baselines, shallow or deep, pairwise or single-chain matching, responses and suggestions are isolated. There is no guarantee for baselines to couple both components in order to avoid conversation divergence from the query. Our proposed method performs well for Type I and II tasks, and it combines two isolated components together and shows an overwhelming improvement in Type III task. It is as expected: the information from the first match should be used to keep a response and the following suggestion in line.

5.6 Discussions

Now we have validated that our proposed model is good to tackle the task. Next we will take a closer look at the components, the structure and different model variants for more analysis and discussions.

5.6.1 Analysis. We have two LSTM chains, and we check the model with different components and variants. For the Dual-LTSM family, the first variant is to degenerate the full model into two isolated LSTM chains, which is exactly the Chain-LSTM model included in the baselines. We omit this variant due to strict page limits. We also degenerate the model by removing 1) the gating cell with external memories

Table 2: Component analysis for model variants.

Model	p@1	MAP	nDCG	MRR	
-MLP	0.422	0.326	0.432	0.304	I
	0.425	0.320	0.428	0.310	II
	0.271	0.248	0.313	0.216	III
-Cell	0.426	0.333	0.438	0.308	I
	0.430	0.331	0.422	0.317	II
	0.392	0.299	0.401	0.289	III
Dual-LSTM	0.431	0.339	0.441	0.312	I
	0.442	0.326	0.437	0.319	II
	0.425	0.315	0.419	0.303	III

and 2) the coupling MLP layer, separately. We observe that performance drops compared to the full Dual-LSTM model. The results are shown in Table 2.

This phenomenon indicates both coupling designs are useful for the joint learning task. The performance drops when we remove the gating cell, which explains that cells are used as soft attention from external memories. The performance drops even more when we remove the MLP layer, since the MLP layer directly mingles information from two chains together. We also have an interesting observation that compared with the Chain-LSTM method, the model variant with an MLP layer (i.e., *-Cell*) performs better even for the response ranking subtask. We assume that seeing the information from the "future" conversations helps ranking, which is another justification for the proactive conversation mode.

6 CONCLUSION

In this paper, we propose a novel conversation mode between humans and computers, featured with both response ranking and next utterance suggestion.

We propose a joint learning model for the new conversation task. Since we have two components of responses and suggestions to rank, we formulate a Dual-LSTM Chain Model to characterize each component and couple them together with deep neural networks. We examine the effect of the proposed model against a series of baselines. Our method consistently outperforms the baselines in terms of p@1, MAP, nDCG, and MRR. We also investigate experiments to analyze different components in Dual-LSTM.

To sum up, our contributions are that 1) we propose a new conversation paradigm, 2) a novel joint learning model, and 3) to verify the usefulness of the task and the model. This work opens to several interesting directions of future studies, such as next utterance suggestions for multi-turn conversations with session contexts available. We leave the idea as the future work for further investigations.

ACKNOWLEDGMENTS

We thank the reviewers for their insightful comments. This research is partially supported by 863 Grant No. 2015AA015403,

NSFC Grant No. 61672058, and by Key Laboratory of Science, Technology and Standard in Press Industry (Key Laboratory of Intelligent Press Media Technology).

REFERENCES

[1] Yoshua Bengio. 2009. Learning deep architectures for AI. *Foundations and Trends in Machine Learning* 2, 1 (2009), 1–127.

[2] Gao Cong, Long Wang, Chin-Yew Lin, Young-In Song, and Yueheng Sun. 2008. Finding Question-answer Pairs from Online Forums. In *SIGIR*. 467–474.

[3] Ryuichiro Higashinaka, Kenji Imamura, Toyomi Meguro, Chiaki Miyazaki, Nozomi Kobayashi, Hiroaki Sugiyama, Toru Hirano, Toshiro Makino, and Yoshihiro Matsuo. 2014. Towards an open domain conversational system fully based on natural language processing. In *COLING*.

[4] Baotian Hu, Zhengdong Lu, Hang Li, and Qingcai Chen. 2014. Convolutional neural network architectures for matching natural language sentences. In *NIPS*. 2042–2050.

[5] Kalervo Järvelin and Jaana Kekäläinen. 2002. Cumulated Gain-based Evaluation of IR Techniques. *ACM Trans. Inf. Syst.* 20, 4 (2002), 422–446.

[6] Zongcheng Ji, Zhengdong Lu, and Hang Li. 2014. An Information Retrieval Approach to Short Text Conversation. *CoRR* abs/1408.6988 (2014).

[7] Nal Kalchbrenner, Edward Grefenstette, and Phil Blunsom. 2014. A convolutional neural network for modelling sentences. *arXiv preprint arXiv:1404.2188* (2014).

[8] Anton Leuski, Ronakkumar Patel, David Traum, and Brandon Kennedy. 2009. Building effective question answering characters. In *SIGDIAL*. 18–27.

[9] Anton Leuski and David Traum. 2011. NPCEditor: Creating virtual human dialogue using information retrieval techniques. *AI Magazine* 32, 2 (2011), 42–56.

[10] Chaozhuo Li, Yu Wu, Wei Wu, Chen Xing, Zhoujun Li, and Ming Zhou. 2016. Detecting Context Dependent Messages in a Conversational Environment. In *COLING'16*. 1990–1999.

[11] Hang Li and Jun Xu. 2014. Semantic matching in search. *Foundations and Trends in Information Retrieval* 8 (2014), 89.

[12] Jiwei Li, Michel Galley, Chris Brockett, Jianfeng Gao, and Bill Dolan. 2016. A Diversity-Promoting Objective Function for Neural Conversation Models. In *NAACL'16*. 110–119.

[13] Jiwei Li, Michel Galley, Chris Brockett, Jianfeng Gao, and Bill Dolan. 2016. A Persona-Based Neural Conversation Model. In *ACL'16*. 994–1003.

[14] Xiang Li, Lili Mou, Rui Yan, and Ming Zhang. 2016. Stalemate-Breaker: A Proactive Content-Introducing Approach to Automatic Human-Computer Conversation. In *IJCAI'16*. 2845–2851.

[15] Zhengdong Lu and Hang Li. 2013. A Deep Architecture for Matching Short Texts. In *NIPS*. 1367–1375.

[16] Christopher D Manning, Prabhakar Raghavan, and Hinrich Schütze. 2008. *Introduction to Information Retrieval*. Vol. 1.

[17] Tomas Mikolov, Kai Chen, Greg Corrado, and Jeffrey Dean. 2013. Efficient estimation of word representations in vector space. *arXiv preprint arXiv:1301.3781* (2013).

[18] Lili Mou, Yiping Song, Rui Yan, Ge Li, Lu Zhang, and Zhi Jin. 2016. Sequence to backward and forward sequences: A content-introducing approach to generative short-text conversation. In *COLING'16*. 3349–3358.

[19] Elnaz Nouri, Ron Artstein, Anton Leuski, and David R Traum. 2011. Augmenting Conversational Characters with Generated Question-Answer Pairs. In *AAAI Fall Symposium: Question Generation*.

[20] Hamid Palangi, Li Deng, Yelong Shen, Jianfeng Gao, Xiaodong He, Jianshu Chen, Xinying Song, and Rabab Ward. 2015. Deep Sentence Embedding Using the Long Short Term Memory Network: Analysis and Application to Information Retrieval. *arXiv preprint arXiv:1502.06922* (2015).

[21] Alan Ritter, Colin Cherry, and William B. Dolan. 2011. Data-driven Response Generation in Social Media. In *EMNLP'11*. 583–593.

[22] Tim Rocktäschel, Edward Grefenstette, Karl Moritz Hermann, Tomáš Kočiskỳ, and Phil Blunsom. 2016. Reasoning about Entailment with Neural Attention. In *ICLR*.

[23] Iulian V Serban, Alessandro Sordoni, Yoshua Bengio, Aaron Courville, and Joelle Pineau. 2016. Building End-To-End Dialogue Systems Using Generative Hierarchical Neural Network Models. In *AAAI'16*. 3776–3783.

[24] Lifeng Shang, Zhengdong Lu, and Hang Li. 2015. Neural Responding Machine for Short-Text Conversation. In *ACL-IJCNLP'15*. 1577–1586.

[25] Richard Socher, Jeffrey Pennington, Eric H Huang, Andrew Y Ng, and Christopher D Manning. 2011. Semi-supervised recursive autoencoders for predicting sentiment distributions. In *EMNLP'11*. 151–161.

[26] Alessandro Sordoni, Michel Galley, Michael Auli, Chris Brockett, Yangfeng Ji, Margaret Mitchell, Jian-Yun Nie, Jianfeng Gao, and Bill Dolan. 2015. A Neural Network Approach to Context-Sensitive Generation of Conversational Responses. In *NAACL'15*. 196–205.

[27] Hiroaki Sugiyama, Toyomi Meguro, Ryuichiro Higashinaka, and Yasuhiro Minami. 2013. Open-domain Utterance Generation for Conversational Dialogue Systems using Web-scale Dependency Structures. In *SIGDIAL*. 334–338.

[28] Ilya Sutskever, Oriol Vinyals, and Quoc VV Le. 2014. Sequence to sequence learning with neural networks. In *NIPS'14*. 3104–3112.

[29] Zhiliang Tian, Rui Yan, Lili Mou, Yiping Song, Yansong Feng, and Dongyan Zhao. 2017. How to Make Contexts More Useful? An Empirical Study to Context-Aware Neural Conversation Models. In *ACL'17*.

[30] Marilyn A. Walker, Rebecca Passonneau, and Julie E. Boland. 2001. Quantitative and Qualitative Evaluation of Darpa Communicator Spoken Dialogue Systems. In *ACL*. 515–522.

[31] Shengxian Wan, Yanyan Lan, Jiafeng Guo, Jun Xu, Liang Pang, and Xueqi Cheng. 2016. A Deep Architecture for Semantic Matching with Multiple Positional Sentence Representations. In *AAAI'16*. 2835–2841.

[32] Shengxian Wan, Yanyan Lan, Jun Xu, Jiafeng Guo, Liang Pang, and Xueqi Cheng. 2016. Match-SRNN: Modeling the Recursive Matching Structure with Spatial RNN. In *IJCAI'16*. 2922–2928.

[33] Hao Wang, Zhengdong Lu, Hang Li, and Enhong Chen. 2013. A Dataset for Research on Short-Text Conversations.. In *EMNLP*.

[34] Jason Williams, Antoine Raux, Deepak Ramachandran, and Alan Black. 2013. The dialog state tracking challenge. In *SIGDIAL*. 404–413.

[35] Ronald J Williams and Jing Peng. 1990. An efficient gradient-based algorithm for on-line training of recurrent network trajectories. *Neural computation* 2, 4 (1990), 490–501.

[36] Yu Wu, Wei Wu, Zhoujun Li, and Ming Zhou. 2016. Knowledge Enhanced Hybrid Neural Network for Text Matching. *arXiv preprint arXiv:1611.04684* (2016).

[37] Yu Wu, Wei Wu, Zhoujun Li, and Ming Zhou. 2016. Topic Augmented Neural Network for Short Text Conversation. *arXiv preprint arXiv:1605.00090* (2016).

[38] Chen Xing, Wei Wu, Yu Wu, Jie Liu, Yalou Huang, Ming Zhou, and Wei-Ying Ma. 2016. Topic Augmented Neural Response Generation with a Joint Attention Mechanism. *arXiv preprint arXiv:1606.08340* (2016).

[39] Yan Xu, Lili Mou, Ge Li, Yunchuan Chen, Hao Peng, and Zhi Jin. 2015. Classifying relations via long short term memory networks along shortest dependency paths. In *EMNLP'15*. 1785–1794.

[40] Zhen Xu, Bingquan Liu, Baoxun Wang, Chengjie Sun, and Xiaolong Wang. 2016. Incorporating Loose-Structured Knowledge into LSTM with Recall Gate for Conversation Modeling. *arXiv preprint arXiv:1605.05110* (2016).

[41] Rui Yan, Liang Kong, Congrui Huang, Xiaojun Wan, Xiaoming Li, and Yan Zhang. 2011. Timeline Generation Through Evolutionary Trans-temporal Summarization. In *EMNLP'11*. 433–443.

[42] Rui Yan, Yiping Song, and Hua Wu. 2016. Learning to respond with deep neural networks for retrieval-based human-computer conversation system. In *SIGIR'16*. 55–64.

[43] Rui Yan, Yiping Song, Xiangyang Zhou, and Hua Wu. 2016. Shall I Be Your Chat Companion?: Towards an Online Human-Computer Conversation System. In *CIKM'16*. 649–658.

[44] Biao Zhang, Jinsong Su, Deyi Xiong, Yaojie Lu, Hong Duan, and Junfeng Yao. 2015. Shallow Convolutional Neural Network for Implicit Discourse Relation Recognition. In *EMNLP'15*. 2230–2235.

[45] Xiangyang Zhou, Daxiang Dong, Hua Wu, Shiqi Zhao, Dianhai Yu, Hao Tian, Xuan Liu, and Rui Yan. 2016. Multi-view response selection for human-computer conversation. In *EMNLP'16*. 372–381.

Learning to Rank Question Answer Pairs with Holographic Dual LSTM Architecture

Yi Tay
Nanyang Technological University
ytay017@e.ntu.edu.sg

Minh C. Phan
Nanyang Technological University
phan0005@e.ntu.edu.sg

Luu Anh Tuan
Institute for Infocomm Research
at.luu@i2r.a-star.edu.sg

Siu Cheung Hui
Nanyang Technological University
asschui@ntu.edu.sg

ABSTRACT

We describe a new deep learning architecture for learning to rank question answer pairs. Our approach extends the long short-term memory (LSTM) network with holographic composition to model the relationship between question and answer representations. As opposed to the neural tensor layer that has been adopted recently, the holographic composition provides the benefits of scalable and rich representational learning approach without incurring huge parameter costs. Overall, we present Holographic Dual LSTM (HD-LSTM), a unified architecture for both deep sentence modeling and semantic matching. Essentially, our model is trained end-to-end whereby the parameters of the LSTM are optimized in a way that best explains the correlation between question and answer representations. In addition, our proposed deep learning architecture requires no extensive feature engineering. Via extensive experiments, we show that HD-LSTM outperforms many other neural architectures on two popular benchmark QA datasets. Empirical studies confirm the effectiveness of holographic composition over the neural tensor layer.

KEYWORDS

Deep Learning, Long Short-Term Memory, Learning to Rank, Question Answering

1 INTRODUCTION

Learning to rank techniques are central to many web-based question answering (QA) systems such as factoid-based QA or community-based QA (CQA). In these applications, questions are matched against an extensive database to find the most relevant answer. Essentially, this is highly related to many search and information retrieval tasks such as traditional document retrieval and text matching. However, a key difference is that questions and answers are often much shorter compared to full-fledged documents whereby the problem of lexical chasm [1, 8, 32] becomes more prevalent. As such, this makes the already difficult task of designing features for questions and answers even harder. Furthermore, traditional approaches often involve extensive handcrafted features and domain expertise which can be laborious and expensive. In addition, constructing features from textual clues [24, 27, 33, 36] such as lexical and syntactic features is difficult and provide limited benefits. Overall, the challenges of learn-to-rank QA systems are two-fold. First, feature representations of questions and answers have to be learned or designed. Second, a similarity function has to be defined to match questions to answers.

Recently, deep learning architectures have been an extremely popular choice for learning distributed representations of words, sentences or documents [11, 14]. Generally, this is known as representational learning whereby low dimensional vectors are learned for words or documents via neural networks such as the convolutional neural networks (CNN), recurrent neural network (RNN) or standard feed-forward multi-layer perceptron (MLP). This has widespread applications in the field of NLP and IR such as semantic text matching [20, 25], relation detection [10], language modeling [14] and question answering [18, 20]. Essentially, the attractiveness of these models stem from the fact that features are learned in deep learning architectures in an end-to-end fashion and often require little or no human involvement. Furthermore, the performance of these models are often spectacular.

Additionally and recently, it has also been fashionable to model the relationship between vectors via tensor layers [18, 25, 30]. A recent work, the convolutional neural tensor network (CNTN) [18] demonstrates impressive results on community-based question answering. In their work, a convolutional neural network is used to learn representations for questions and answers while a tensor layer is used to model the relationship between the representations using an additional tensor parameter. This is powerful because the tensor layer models multiple views of dyadic interactions between question and answer pairs which enables rich representational learning. Overall, the CNTN is a unified architecture that learns representations and performs matching in an end-to-end fashion.

However, the use of a tensor layer may not be implication free. Firstly, adding a tensor layer severely increases the number of parameters which naturally and inevitably increases the risk of overfitting. Secondly, this significantly increases computational and memory cost of the overall network. Thirdly, the inclusion of a tensor layer also *indirectly* restricts the expressiveness of the QA representations since increasing the parameters of the QA representations would easily incur memory and computational costs of quadratic scale at the tensor layer.

SIGIR '17, August 07-11, 2017, Shinjuku, Tokyo, Japan

DOI: http://dx.doi.org/10.1145/3077136.3080790

In lieu of the above mentioned weaknesses, we propose an alternative to the tensor layer. For the first time, we adopt holographic composition to model the relationship between question and answer embeddings. Our approach is largely based on holographic models of associative memory and employs circular correlation to learn the relationship between QA pairs. The prime contributions of our paper can be summarized as follows:

- For the first time, we adopt holographic composition for modeling the interaction between representations of QA pairs. Unlike the tensor layer, our compositional approach is essentially parameterless, memory efficient and scalable. Furthermore, our approach also enables rich representational learning by employing circular correlation.
- As a whole, we present a novel deep learning architecture, HD-LSTM (Holographic Dual LSTM) for learning to rank QA pairs. Our model is a unified architecture similar to [18]. However, instead of the CNN, we use multi-layered long short-term memory neural networks to learn representations for questions and answers. Similar to other deep learning models, our approach does not require extensive feature engineering or domain knowledge.
- We provide extensive experimental evidence of the effectiveness of our model on both factoid question answering and community-based question answering. Our proposed approach outperforms many other neural architectures on TREC QA task and on the Yahoo CQA dataset.

2 RELATED WORK

Our work is concerned with ranking question and answer pairs to select the most suitable answer for each question. Across the rich history of IR research, techniques for doing so have been primarily focused on lexical and syntactic feature-dependent approaches. These techniques include the Tree Edit Distance (TED) model [5], Support Vector Machines (SVMs) with tree kernels [21] and linear chain Conditional Random Fields (CRFs) [33] with features from the TED model. However, apart from relying heavily on handcrafted features such as cumbersome parse trees, these approaches have limited performance and have been shown to be outclassed by modern deep learning approaches such as convolutional neural networks [20, 35].

The key intuition behind deep learning architectures is to learn low-dimensional representations of words, documents or sentences which can be used as input features. For example, Yu et al. [35] employed a convolutional neural network for feature learning of QA pairs and subsequently applied logistic regression for prediction. Despite its simplicity, the performance of Yu et al. has already surpassed all traditional approaches [5, 21, 27–29]. Another attractive quality of deep learning architectures is that features can be learned in an end-to-end fashion. Severyn et al. [20] demonstrated a unified architecture that trains a convolutional neural network together with a multi-layer perceptron. In short, features are learned while the parameters of the network are optimized for the task at hand.

In the architectures of Severyn et al. [20] and Yu et al. [35], representations of questions and answers are learned separately and concatenated for prediction at the end. Qiu et al. [18] introduced a tensor layer to model the relationship between question and answer representations. The tensor layer can be seen as a compositional technique to learn the relationship between two vectors and was adapted from the neural tensor network (NTN) by Socher et al. [22, 23]. The NTN was originally incepted in the field of NLP for semantic parsing and used as a compositional operator in recursive neural tensor networks (RNTN) [23] and also relational learning on knowledge bases [22]. It has also recently seen adoption for modeling document novelty in [30]. The tensor layer models multiple dyadic interactions between two vectors via an additional tensor parameter. This suggests rich representational learning that is useful for matching text pairs.

Additionally, recurrent neural networks such as the long short-term memory (LSTM) networks are also widely popular for learning sentence representations and has seen wide adoption in a variety of NLP tasks. Without an exception, LSTM networks are also widely adopted in QA [12, 25, 26]. The usage of grid-wise similarity matrices within neural architectures are also recently very fashionable and have seen wide adoption[1] in QA tasks [4, 15, 25] to model the interactions between QA pairs. For example, in the MV-LSTM [25], all positional hidden states from both LSTMs are being matched grid-wise using a variety of similarity scoring functions followed by a max-pooling layer. On the other hand, the works of [31] are concerned with learning grid-wise attentions. On a side note, it is good to note that, grid-wise matching, though highly competitive, naturally incurs a prohibitive computational cost of quadratic scale.

As seen in many recent works, the tensor layer is highly popular to model relationship between two vectors [18, 25]. However, a tensor layer adds a significant amount of parameters to the network causing implications in terms of runtime, memory, risk of overfitting as well as an inevitable restriction of flexibility in designing representations for questions and answers. Specifically, increasing the dimensionality of the LSTM or CNN output by x would incur a parameter cost of x^2 in the tensor layer which can be non-ideal especially in terms of scalability. As an alternative to the tensor layer, our novel deep learning architecture adopts the circular correlation of vectors to model the interactions between question and answer representations. The circular correlation of vectors, along with circular convolution, are typically used in Holography to store and retrieve information [3, 17] and are also known as correlation-convolution (holographic-like) memories. Due to its connections with holographic models of associative memories [17], we refer to our model as Holographic Dual LSTM. It is good to note that a similar but fundamentally different work [16] also used holography inspired operations *within* recurrent neural networks. However, our work is the first work to incorporate holographic representational learning for QA embeddings.

In addition, holographic composition [17] can also be interpreted as compressed tensor product which also enables rich representational learning **without** severely increasing the number of parameters of the network. In this case, the parameters of the network are learned in a way that best explains the correlation between questions and answers. In the same domain where the neural tensor network was incepted, holographic embeddings of knowledge graphs [13], demonstrates the effectiveness of holographic composition in the task of relational learning on knowledge bases. As

[1] Notably, our proposed holographic composition can also be used for grid-wise matching.

a whole, we propose a novel deep learning architecture based on long short-term memory neural networks while using holographic composition to model the interactions between QA embeddings, this enables rich representational learning with improved flexibility and scalability. The outcome is a highly performant end-to-end deep learning architecture for learning to rank for QA applications.

3 PRELIMINARIES

In this section, we introduce the background for the remainder of the paper. Namely, we formally give the problem definition and introduce fundamental deep learning models required to understand the remainder of the paper.

3.1 Problem Statement and Approach

The task of supervised learning to rank can be typically regarded as a binary classification problem. Given a set of questions $q_i \in Q$, the task is to rank a list of candidate answers $a_i \in A$. Specifically, we try to learn a function $f(q,a)$ that outputs a relevancy score $f(q,a) \in [0,1]$ for each question answer pair. This score is then used to rank a list of possible candidates. Typically, there are three different ways for supervised text ranking, namely, pairwise, pointwise and listwise. Pairwise considers maximizing the margin between positive and negative question-answer pairs with an objective function such as the hinge loss. Pointwise considers each pair, positive or negative, individually. On the other hand, listwise considers a question and all candidate answers as a training instance. Naturally, pairwise and listwise are much harder to train, implement and take a longer time due to having to process more instances. Therefore, in this work, we mainly consider a pointwise approach when designing our deep learning model.

3.2 Long short-term Memory (LSTM)

First, we introduce the Long Short-Term Memory (LSTM) [6]. LSTMs are a type of recurrent neural network that are capable of learning long term dependencies across sequences. Given an input sentence $S = (x_o, x_1 ..., x_n)$, the LSTM returns a sentence embedding h_t for position t with the following equations:

$$i_t = \sigma(W_i x_t + U_i h_{t-1} + b_i)$$
$$f_t = \sigma(W_f x_t + U_f h_{t-1} + b_f)$$
$$c_t = f_t c_{t-1} + i_t \, tanh(W_c x_t + U_c h_{t-1} + b_c)$$
$$o_t = \sigma(W_o x_t + U_o h_{t-1} + b_o)$$
$$h_t = o_t \, tanh(c_t)$$

where x_t and h_t are the input vectors at time t. W_*, b_*, U_* are the parameters of the LSTM network and $* = \{o, i, f, u, c\}$. σ is the sigmoid function and c_t is the cell state. For the sake of brevity, we omit the technical details of LSTM which can be found in many related works. The output of this layer is a sequence of hidden vectors $\mathbf{H} \in \mathbb{R}^{L \times d}$ where L is the maximum sequence length and d is the dimensional size of LSTM. It is also possible to stack layers of LSTMs on top of one another which form multi-layered LSTMs which we will adopt in our approach.

3.3 Neural Tensor Network

The Neural Tensor Network [22, 23] is a parameterized composition technique that learns the relationships between two vectors. The scoring function between two vectors are defined as follows:

$$s_t(\vec{q}, \vec{a}) = u^T f(\vec{q}^{\,T} M^{[1:r]} \vec{a} + V[\vec{q}, \vec{a}] + b) \quad (1)$$

where f is a non-linear function such as $tanh$ applied element wise. $M^{[1:r]} \in \mathbb{R}^{n \times n \times r}$ is a tensor (3d matrix). For each slice of the tensor M, each bilinear tensor product $\vec{q}^{\,T} M_r \, \vec{a}$ returns a scalar value to form a r dimensional vector. The other parameters are the standard form of a neural network. We can clearly see that the NTN enables rich representational learning of embedding pairs by using a large number of parameters.

4 OUR DEEP LEARNING MODEL

In this section, we introduce Holographic Dual LSTM for representational learning and ranking of short text pairs. In our model, we use a pair of *multi-layered* LSTMs denoted Q-LSTM and A-LSTM. First, the LSTMs learn sentence representations of question and answer pairs and subsequently holographic composition is employed to model the similarity between the outputs of Q-LSTM and A-LSTM. Finally, we pass the network through a fully connected hidden layer and perform binary classification. This is all done in an end-to-end fashion. Figure 1 shows the overall architecture.

4.1 Learning QA Representations

Our model accepts two sequences of indices (one for question and the other for answer) and a one-hot encoded ground truth for training. These sequence of indices are first passed through a look-up layer. At this layer, each index is converted into a low-dimensional vector representation. The parameters of this layer are $W \in \mathbb{R}^{|V| \times n}$ where V is the size of the vocabulary and n is the dimensionality of the word embeddings. Even though these word embeddings can be learned from the training process of our model, i.e., end-to-end, we do not do so since learning word embeddings often require an extremely large corpus like Wikipedia. Therefore, we initialize W with pretrained SkipGram [11] embeddings which is aligned with the works of [20, 35]. Next, these embeddings from question and answer sequences are fed into Q-LSTM and A-LSTM respectively. Subsequently, the last hidden output from Q-LSTM and A-LSTM are taken to be the final representation for question and answer respectively.

4.2 Holographic Matching of QA pairs

The QA embeddings learned from LSTM are then passed into what we call the holographic layer. In this section, we introduce our novel compositional deep learning model for modeling the relationship between q and a. We denote $q \circ a$ as a compositional operator applied to vectors q and a. We employ the *circular correlation* of vectors to learn relationships between question and answer embeddings.

$$q \circ a = q \star a \quad (2)$$

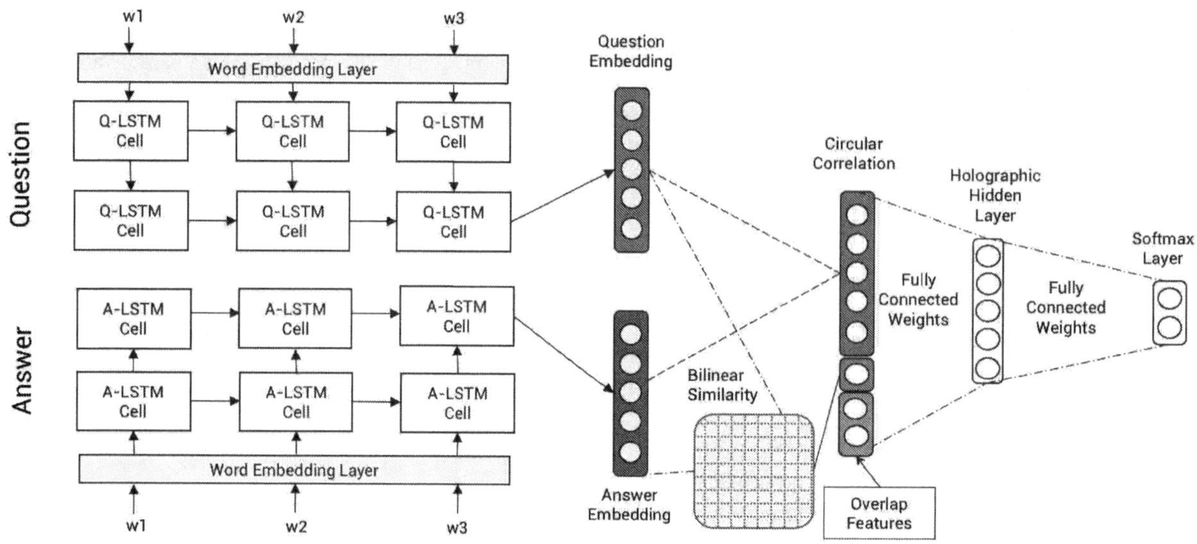

Figure 1: Holographic Dual LSTM Deep Learning Model for Ranking of QA Pairs

where $\star : \mathbb{R}^d \times \mathbb{R}^d \rightarrow \mathbb{R}^d$ denotes the circular correlation operator[2].

$$[q \star a]_k = \sum_{i=0}^{d-1} q_i \, a_{(k+i) \bmod d} \tag{3}$$

Circular correlation can be computed as follows:

$$q \star a = \mathcal{F}^{-1}(\overline{\mathcal{F}(q)} \odot \mathcal{F}(a)) \tag{4}$$

where $\mathcal{F}(.)$ and $\mathcal{F}^{-1}(.)$ are the *fast Fourier transform* (FFT) and *inverse fast Fourier transform.* $\overline{\mathcal{F}(q)}$ denotes the complex conjugate of $\mathcal{F}(q)$. $\odot$ is element-wise (or Hadamard) product. Additionally, circular correlation can be viewed as a compressed tensor product [13]. In the tensor product $[q \otimes a]_{ij} = q_i a_j$ a separate element is used to store each pairwise multiplication or interaction between q and a. In circular correlation, each element of the composed vector is a sum of multiplicative interactions over a fixed summation pattern between q and a. Figure 2 describes this process where the circular arrows depict the summation process in which vector $\vec{c}$ is the result of composing $\vec{q}$ and $\vec{a}$ with circular correlation.

One key advantage of this composition method is that there are no increase in parameters. The fact that the composed vector remains at the same length of its constituent vectors is an extremely attractive quality of our proposed model. In the case where question and answer representations are of different dimensions, we can simply zero-pad the vectors to make them the same length. As circular correlation uses summation patterns, it is still possible to compose them without much implications. However, for this paper we consider that $\vec{q}$ and $\vec{a}$ to have the same dimensions.

4.3 Holographic Hidden Layer

Subsequently, a fully connected hidden layer follows our compositional operator which forms the holographic layer.

$$h_{out} = \sigma(W_h . [q \star a] + b_h) \tag{5}$$

[2]For Holographic Composition, we use zero-indexed vectors for notational convenience.

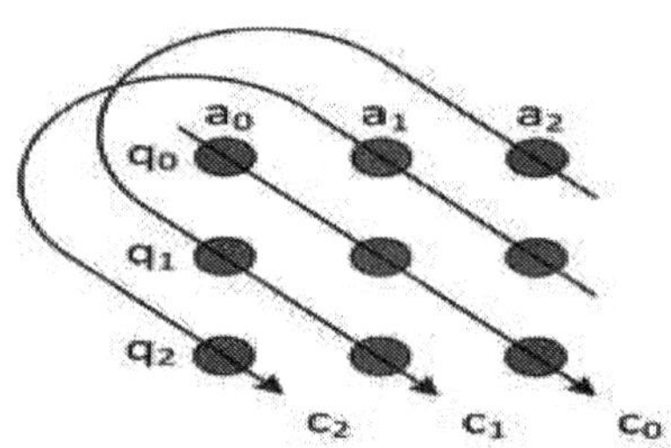

Figure 2: Circular Correlation as Compressed Tensor Product, Circular Arrows denote Summation Process, Adapted from Plate (1995) [17].

where w_h and b_h are parameters of the hidden layer and σ is a non-linear activation function like *tanh*. Traditionally, most models [7, 20] use the composition operator of concatenation, denoted $\oplus$ to combine the vectors of questions and answers. $\oplus : \mathbb{R}^{d_1} \times \mathbb{R}^{d_2} \rightarrow \mathbb{R}^{d_1+d_2}$ simply appends one vector after another to form a vector of their lengths combined. Obviously, concatenation does not consider the relationship between latent features of QA embeddings. Thus, the relationship has to be learned from the parameters of the deep learning model, i.e., the subsequent hidden layer. In summary, the fully connected dense layer that maps $[q \star a]$ to h_{out} forms the holographic hidden layer of our network.

Incorporating Additional Features Following the works of [2, 20], it is also possible (though optional) to incorporate additional features. First, we include an additional similarity measure in our model between QA embeddings. Namely, this similarity is known as the bilinear similarity which can be defined as:

$$sim(q, a) = \vec{q}^{\,T} M \vec{a} \tag{6}$$

where $M \in \mathbb{R}^{n \times n}$ is a similarity matrix between vectors $q \in \mathbb{R}^n$ and $a \in \mathbb{R}^n$. The bilinear similarity is a parameterized approach where M is an additional parameter of the network. The output of $sim(q, a)$ is a scalar value that is concatenated with $[q \star a]$. We experimented with concatenation at h_{out} but empirically found it to perform worse. It is also possible to include other manual features. For example, in [20], word overlap features X_{feat} were included before the hidden layers at the join layer. The rationale for doing so is as follows: First, it is difficult to encode features like word overlap into deep learning architectures [20, 35]. Secondly, word overlap features are relatively easy and trivial to implement and incorporate. As such, we are able to do the same with our model. Thus, when using external features, the inputs to the holographic hidden layer becomes a vector $[[q \star a], sim(q, a), X_{feat}]$.

4.4 Softmax Layer

The output from the holographic hidden layer is then passed into a fully connected softmax layer which introduces another two parameters W_f and b_f.

$$p = softmax(W_f . h_{out} + b_f) \tag{7}$$

where θ_k is the weight vector of the kth class and x is the final vector representation of question and answer after passing through all the layers in the network.

4.5 Training and Optimization

Finally, we describe the optimization and training procedure of our network. Our network minimizes the cross-entropy loss function as follows:

$$L = -\sum_{i=1}^{N} [y_i \log a_i + (1 - y_i) \log(1 - a_i)] + \lambda \|\theta\|_2^2 \tag{8}$$

where a is the output of the softmax layer. θ contains all the parameters of the network and $\lambda\|\theta\|_2^2$ is the L2 regularization. The parameters of the network can be updated by Stochastic Gradient Descent (SGD). In our network, we mainly employ the Adam [9] optimizer.

5 DISCUSSION

In this section, we discuss and highlight some of the interesting and advantageous properties of our proposed approach.

5.1 Complexity Analysis

To better understand the merits of our proposed approach, we study the computational and memory complexity of our model with respect to the alternatives like the tensor layer.

Operator	#Parameters	Complexity
Tensor Product $\otimes$	d^2	$O(d^2)$
Concatenation $\oplus$	$2d$	$O(d)$
Circular Correlation $\star$	d	$O(d \log d)$

Table 1: Complexity Comparison between Compositional Operators

First, Table 1 shows the parameter cost and complexity for the three different compositional operators. This assumes a simple example where $q, a \in \mathbb{R}^d$ and a vector of the same dimensionality as

Network	#Parameters	$d/h/k$	On TREC
NTN	$d^2k + 2dk + 2k$	640 / 0 / 5	2.1M
Ours	$2dh + 4h$	640 / 64 / 0	41.2K

Table 2: Memory Complexity Comparison between Tensor Layer and Holographic Layer

Network	Complexity
NTN	$O(d^2k + 2dk + 2k)$
Ours	$O(2dh + 4h + d \log d)$

Table 3: Complexity Comparison between Tensor Layer and Holographic Layer

$q \circ a$ is used to map the composed vector into a scalar value. Clearly, the cost of a simple tensor layer is of quadratic scale which makes it difficult to scale with large d. Concatenation, on the other hand, doubles the length of composed vectors and increases the memory cost by a factor of two. Finally, we see that the parameter cost of circular correlation that we employ is only d. As such, there can be significantly less parameters in the subsequent layers. Finally, the computational complexity of circular correlation is also relatively low at $d \log d$. Next, we compare the complexity of our network and the NTN. To enable direct comparison, we exclude any additional features at the holographic hidden layer of our network and include the subsequent softmax layer. Finally, the overall network and similarity between q and a can be modeled as follows:

$$s_h(\vec{q}, \vec{a}) = softmax(W_f^T f(W_h^T [\vec{q} \star \vec{a}] + b_h) + b_f) \tag{9}$$

where $W_h \in \mathbb{R}^{d \times r}$ is parameters at the holographic hidden layer following the composition operation, b_h is the scalar bias at the hidden layer, $W_f \in \mathbb{R}^{r \times 2}$ converts the output at the hidden layer to a 2-class classification problem and $q, a \in \mathbb{R}^d$ where d is the dimension size of the LSTM. $f(.)$ is a non-linear activation function. Note that since we consider use a softmax layer at the output, our final output $s(q, a)$ is a vector of 2 dimensions. Similarly, in the traditional tensor layer described in Equation (1), we are able to simply adapt the vector u to become a weight matrix of $u \in \mathbb{R}^{k \times 2}$ where k is the number of slices of tensors.

In Table 2 and Table 3, we compare the differences between the tensor layer and our holographic layer with respect to the number of parameters and computational complexity respectively. Note that d is the dimensionality of QA embeddings, h is the size of the hidden layer and k is the number of tensor slices. To facilitate easier comparison, we do not include complexity from learning QA representations, computing bias and activation functions but only matrix and vector operations. From Table 2, it is clear and evident that our approach does not require as much parameters as the NTN. We also report the optimal dimensions of the QA embeddings and hidden layer size on TREC QA. We see that our model only requires $41.2k$ parameters[3] as opposed to $2.1M$ parameters with the NTN. As such, we see that when optimal parameters required for sentence modeling is high, the cost on the subsequent matching

[3] We exclude word embedding and LSTM parameters in this comparison

layer becomes impractical. The problem of quadratic scale is also reflected in computational complexity. Thus, from a theoretical point of view, the holographic composition can be seen as a memory efficient and faster alternative to the neural tensor network layer.

5.2 Associative Holographic Memories

Holographic models of associative memories employ a series of convolutions and correlations to store and retrieve item pairs. This is sometimes referred to as convolution-correlation (holographic-like) memories [17]. At this point, it is apt to introduce circular convolution: $* : \mathbb{R}^d \times \mathbb{R}^d \rightarrow \mathbb{R}^d$ which is closely related to circular correlation.

$$[q * a]_k = \sum_{i=0}^{d-1} q_i \, a_{(k-i) \bmod d} \tag{10}$$

In holographic associative memory models, association of vector pairs can be encoded via correlation and then decoded with circular convolution. The relationship between correlation and convolution is as follows:

$$q \star a = \tilde{q} * a \tag{11}$$

where $\tilde{q}$ is the approximate inverse of q such that $q_i = q_{(-i \bmod d)}$. Typically, the encoding-decoding[4] process is done via Hebbian learning in associative memory models. However, in our case, our model is holographic in the sense that correlation-convolution memories are learned implicitly via back-propagation. For example, let h be the input to the hidden layer h_{out}, the gradients at a can be represented as:

$$\frac{\partial E}{\partial a_i} = \sum_k \frac{\partial E}{\partial h_j} q_{(k-j \bmod d)} \tag{12}$$

The gradient at a_i according to Equation (12) [16] is equivalent to correlating h with the approximate inverse of q. Recall that correlating with the inverse is equivalent to circular convolution. As such, this establishes the relation of our model to holographic memories. Since our main point is to illustrate these connections, we omit the entire back-propagation derivation due to the lack of space. Finally, we describe and summarize the overall advantages of employing a holographic layer in our deep architecture for learning to rank question answer pairs.

- Unlike circular convolution, circular correlation is non-commutative, i.e., $q \star a \neq a \star q$. This is useful as most applications of text matching are non-symmetric. For example, questions to answers or queries to documents are not symmetric in nature. As such, we utilize correlation as the encoding operation and allow the network to decode via circular convolution while learning parameters.
- The first index of the circular correlation composed vector $[q \star a]_0$ is the dot product of q and a. This is extremely helpful since question answer matching requires a measure of similarity.
- The computational complexity of FFT is $O(d \log d)$ which makes it an efficient composition.

[4]Ideally, that the euclidean norm of q and a should be ≈ 1. However, our preliminary experiments showed that adding a normalization layer did not improve the performance.

- Our composition does not increase the dimensionality of its constituent vectors, i.e, the composition of $\vec{q} \star \vec{a}$ preserves its dimensionality. On the other hand, concatenation doubles the parameter cost at the subsequent hidden layers. Furthermore, the relationship between question and answer embeddings have to be learned by the hidden layer.
- The association of two vectors, namely question and answer vectors are modeled end-to-end in the network. Via back-propagation, the network learns parameters that best explains this correlation via gradient descent.

Here it is good to note that the original holographic reduced representations [17] used convolution to encode and correlation to decode. However, this can be done vice versa as well [13].

6 EMPIRICAL EVALUATION ON TREC QA

We evaluate our model on the TREC QA task of answer sentence selection on factoid based QA.

6.1 Experiment Setup

In this section, we introduce the dataset, evaluation procedure, metrics and compared baselines used in this experiment.

6.1.1 Dataset. In this task, we use the benchmark dataset provided by Wang et al. [29]. This dataset was collected from TREC QA tracks 8-13. In this task of factoid QA, questions are generally factual based questions such as *"What is the monetary value of the Nobel Peace Prize in 1989?""*. In this dataset, we are provided with **two** training sets, namely, TRAIN and TRAIN-ALL. TRAIN consists of QA pairs that have been manually judged and annotated. TRAIN-ALL is a automatically judged dataset of QA pairs and contains a larger number of QA pairs. TRAIN-ALL, being a larger dataset, also contains more noise. Nevertheless, both datasets enable the comparison of all models with respect to availability and volume of training samples. Additionally, we are also provided with a development set for parameter tuning. The results of both training sets, development set and testing set are reported in Table 4. Finally, it is good to note that the maximum number of tokens for questions and answers are 11 and 38 respectively and the length of the vocabulary $|V| = 16468$.

Data	# Questions	# QA pairs	% Correct
TRAIN-ALL	1229	53417	12
TRAIN	94	4718	7.4
DEV	82	1148	9.3
TEST	100	1517	18.7

Table 4: Dataset Statistics for TREC QA Dataset

6.1.2 Evaluation Procedure and Metrics. Following the experimental procedure in [20], we report the results of all models in two settings. In the first setting, we measure the representational learning ability of all deep learning models without the aid of external features. Conversely, in the second setting, we include an additional feature vector $X_{feat} \in \mathbb{R}^4$ containing the count of word overlaps (ordinary and *idf* weighted) between question-answer pairs by considering inclusion and dis-inclusion of stop-words. Finally, the official evaluation metrics of MAP (Mean Average Precision) and MRR (Mean Reciprocal Rank) are used as our evaluation metrics.

MRR is defined as $\frac{1}{|q|}\sum_{q=1}^{|Q|}\frac{1}{rank(q)}$ where *rank(q)* is the rank of the first correct answer. MAP is defined as $\frac{1}{Q}\sum_{q=1}^{Q}AvgP(q)$. The MAP is the average precision across all queries $q_i \in Q$. For evaluation, we use the official `trec_eval` script.

6.1.3 Algorithms Compared. Aside from comparison with all published state-of-the-art methods, we also evaluate our model against other deep learning architectures. Since the deep learning models compared in [20] are based on Convolutional Neural Networks, we additionally compare our model with MV-LSTM [25] and a simple LSTM baseline in our experimental evaluation. The following lists the major and popular deep learning based models for direct comparison with our model. Model names with * indicate that we implemented the model ourselves.

- **CNN + Logistic Regression (Yu et al.)** This is the model introduced in [35]. Representations of questions and answers are learned by a convolutional neural network. Subsequently, logistic regression over the learned features is used to score QA pairs. We report two settings, namely Unigram and Bigram which are also reported in their work.
- **CNN*** We implemented a CNN model following the architecture and hyperparameters of [20]. This model includes a bilinear similarity feature while concatenating two CNN encoded sentence representations. Unlike Yu et al.'s model, this work ranks QA pairs using an end-to-end architecture.
- **CNTN*** We implemented a neural tensor network layer to performing matching of question and answer representations encoded by convolutional neural networks. This is similar to [18] but adopts the CNN architecture and hyperparameters of Severyn et al. [20]. For the tensor layer, we use $k = 5$ where k is the number of slices of the tensor.
- **LSTM*** We consider both single layer and multi-layered LSTMs as our baselines. These baseline models do not specially model the relationships between questions and answers. Instead, a concatenation operation is used to combine the QA embeddings in which the relationships between the two vectors are modeled by the hidden layer.
- **MV-LSTM* (Wan et al.)** This model, introduced in [25], considers matching of multiple positional embeddings and subsequently applying max-pooling of *top-k* interactions. For scalability reasons, we only consider the bilinear similarity setting for this model. We consider this sufficient for three reasons. First, it is reported in [25] that the performance benefits of tensor over bilinear is minimal. Second, it is extremely expensive computationally even when considering a bilinear similarity let alone the tensor similarity. Third, the comparison with this model mainly aims to investigate the effectiveness of multiple positional embeddings.
- **NTN-LSTM*** We consider a Neural Tensor Network + LSTM architecture instead of the CNTN to enable fairer comparison with our LSTM based model. In this model, we replace the holographic layer in HD-LSTM with a NTN layer which forms the major comparison in this paper. For the tensor layer, similar to the CNTN, we use $k = 5$ where k is the number of slices of the tensor.
- **HD-LSTM* (Ours)** Holographic Dual LSTMS is the model architecture introduced in this paper. In our HD-LSTM model, the QA representations are merged with Holographic Composition.

6.1.4 Implementation Details and Hyperparameters. We implemented all deep learning architectures ourselves with the exception of Yu et al. [35] which we directly report the results. To facilitate fair comparison, we implement the exact architecture of the CNN model from Severyn et al. [20] ourselves using the same evaluation procedure and optimizer. All hyperparameters were tuned on the development set using extensive grid search. We trained all models using the Adam [9] optimizer with an initial learning rate of 10^{-5} for LSTM models and 10^{-2} for CNN models[5] and minimized the same cross entropy loss in a point-wise fashion. We applied gradient clipping of 1.0 of the norm for all LSTM models.

With the exception of the single-layered LSTM and MV-LSTM, all LSTM-based models use a single-direction and multi-layered setting. The input sequences are all padded with zero vectors to the max length for questions and answers separately. The dimensionality of the LSTM models are tuned in multiples of 128 in the range of $[128, 640]$ for `TRAIN` and amongst $\{512, 1024\}$ for `TRAIN-ALL` in lieu of the larger dataset. Here it is good to note that the final feature vector of the model in Severyn et al is ≈ 1000. The number of LSTM layers are tuned from a range of $2-4$ and batch size is fixed to 256 for all LSTM based models. The hidden layer size for all LSTM models are amongst $\{32, 64, 128, 256, 512\}$. For regularization and preventing over-fitting, we apply a dropout of $d = 0.5$ and set the regularization hyperparameter $\lambda = 0.00001$. For MV-LSTM, we followed the configuration setting as stated in [25]. We used the pretrained word embeddings [20] of 50 dimensions trained on Wikipedia and AQUAINT corpus. The word embedding layer is set to non-trainable in lieu of the small dataset. We trained all models for a maximum of 30 epochs with early stopping, i.e., if the MAP score does not increase after 5 epochs. We take MAP scores on the development set at every epoch and save the parameters of the network for the top three models on the development set. We report the best test score from the saved models. All experiments were conducted on a Linux machine with a single Nvidia GTX1070 GPU (8GB RAM).

6.2 Experimental Results

This section shows the experimental results on the TREC QA answer sentence selection task. Table 5 shows the result of all deep learning architectures in four different configurations, i.e., different training sets (TRAIN vs TRAIN-ALL) and different feature settings (with and without additional features). Overall, we see that HD-LSTM outperforms all other deep learning models. The relative ranking of each deep learning architecture is in concert with our intuitions. Using a tensor layer for matching improves performance over their base models which is aligned with the results of [18]. However, we see that HD-LSTM outperforms NTN-LSTM by a significant margin across all datasets and settings despite being more efficient. This shows the effectiveness of holographic composition for rich representational learning of QA pairs despite having less parameters. Additionally, the average increase over the baseline multi-layered

[5] This learning rate works best for CNN models with Adam

	Setting 1 (raw)				Setting 2 (with extra features)				All	
	TRAIN		TRAIN-ALL		TRAIN		TRAIN-ALL		Average	
Model	MAP	MRR	MAP	MRR	MAP	MRR	MAP	MRR	MAP	MRR
CNN + LR (unigram)	0.5387	0.6284	0.5470	0.6329	0.6889	0.7727	0.6934	0.7677	0.6170	0.6982
CNN + LR (bigram)	0.5476	0.6437	0.5693	0.6613	0.7058	0.7846	0.7113	0.7846	0.6335	0.7186
LSTM (1 layer)	0.5731	0.6056	0.6204	0.6685	0.6406	0.7494	0.6782	0.7604	0.6280	0.6960
LSTM	0.6093	0.6821	0.5975	0.6533	0.7007	0.7777	0.7350	0.8064	0.6606	0.7299
CNN	0.5994	0.6584	0.6691	0.6880	0.7000	0.7469	0.7216	0.7899	0.6725	0.7208
CNTN	0.6154	0.6701	0.6580	0.6978	0.7045	0.7562	0.7278	0.7831	0.6764	0.7268
MV-LSTM	0.6307	0.6675	0.6488	0.6824	0.7327	0.7940	0.7077	0.7821	0.6800	0.7315
NTN-LSTM	0.6274	0.6831	0.6340	0.6772	0.7225	0.7904	0.7364	0.8009	0.6800	0.7379
HD-LSTM	**0.6404**	**0.7123**	**0.6744**	**0.7511**	**0.7520**	**0.8146**	**0.7499**	**0.8153**	**0.7042**	**0.7733**

Table 5: Experimental Results of all Deep Learning Architectures on TREC QA Dataset. Best result is in boldface.

LSTM are 4% and 5% in terms of MAP and MRR respectively which can be considered significant. We also note that there is quite significant improvement with using multi-layered LSTMs over a single layered LSTM. The performance of MV-LSTM is competitively similar to NTN-LSTM in this task. However, it is good to note that MV-LSTM takes $\approx 30s$ per epoch at the bilinear setting as opposed to our model's $\approx 0.1s$ epoch with the same LSTM configurations and settings and on the same machine and GPU. On the other hand, we see that the baseline LSTM models perform worse than CNN based models whereby a single layer LSTM performs poorly and does almost as poor as CNN with logistic regression from Yu et al. [35]. However, the NTN-LSTM and MV-LSTM perform better than the CNTN. It is good to note that our CNN model implementation achieves slightly worst results as compared to [20] because model parameters are saved at the batch level in their work while we evaluate at an epoch level instead. Nevertheless, the performance is quite similar.

Finally, Table 6 shows the results of all published models including non deep learning systems. Evidently, deep learning has significantly outperformed traditional methods in this task. It is also good to note that HD-LSTM outperforms **all** models (both deep learning and non-deep learning) even with the smaller TRAIN dataset. We find this result remarkable.

Model	MAP	MRR
Wang et al. (2007) [29]	0.6029	0.6852
Heilman and Smith (2010) [5]	0.6091	0.6917
Wang and Manning (2010) [28]	0.5951	0.6951
Yao (2013) [33]	0.6307	0.7477
Severyn & Moschitti (2013) [21]	0.6781	0.7358
Yih et al. (2013) [34]	0.7092	0.7700
Yu et al. (2014) [35]	0.7113	0.7846
Severyn et al. (2015) [20]	0.7459	0.8078
HD-LSTM TRAIN	**0.7520**	0.8146
HD-LSTM TRAIN-ALL	0.7499	**0.8153**

Table 6: Performance Comparison of all Published Models on TREC QA Dataset.

7 EMPIRICAL EVALUATION ON COMMUNITY-BASED QA

In this experiment, we consider the task of community-based question answering (CQA). We use the Yahoo QA Dataset[6] for this purpose. The objectives of this experiment are two-fold. First, we provide more experimental evidence of the QA ranking capabilities of our model. Second, we test all models on the Yahoo QA dataset which can be considered as a large web-scale dataset with a diverse range of topics which additionally includes informal social language.

7.1 Experimental Setup

We describe the dataset used, evaluation metrics and implementation details

	# QA Pairs	# Correct
TRAIN	253440	50688
DEV	31680	6336
TEST	31680	6336

Table 7: Dataset Statistics of Yahoo QA Dataset.

7.1.1 Dataset. The dataset we use is the Yahoo QA Dataset containing 142,627 questions and answers. We select QA pairs containing questions and best answers of length 5-50 tokens after filtering away non-alphanumeric characters. As such, we obtain 63, 360 QA pairs in the end. The total vocabulary size $|V|$ of this dataset is 116,900. We construct negative samples for each question by sampling 4 samples from the top 1000 hits obtained via *Lucene*[7] search. The overall statistics of the constructed dataset is shown in Table 7. In general, we can consider Yahoo to be a much larger dataset over TREC QA. Furthermore, in CQA, the questions and answers are generally of longer length.

7.1.2 Baselines and Implementation Details. For this experiment, our comparison against competitors are similar to the first experiment. Specifically, we compare our model with LSTM (baseline), MV-LSTM (Bilinear) and NTN-LSTM for LSTM-based deep learning models along with CNN and CNTN. In addition, we include the popular Okapi BM25 benchmark [19] as an indicator of the

[6] http://webscope.sandbox.yahoo.com/catalog.php?datatype=l&did=10
[7] http://lucene.apache.org/core/

difficulty of the test set. Note that our experimental results would be naturally different from [25] due to different train/test/dev splits and variations in the negative sampling process. The implementation details for LSTM based deep learning models are the same as Section 6.1.4. However, due to scalability reasons and the requirement of processing significantly much more QA pairs, we limit the dimensions of the LSTM and hidden layer to be 50. The number of layers of the LSTM is also set to 1. For all models, we only consider a single direction LSTM. The other hyperparameters, including the choice of pretrained word embeddings, dropout and regularization are the same unless stated otherwise.

7.1.3 Evaluation Metrics. For this experiment we use the same metrics as [25], namely the Precision@1 and MRR. P@1 can be defined as $\frac{1}{N}\sum_{i=1}^{N}\delta(r(A^{+})=1)$ where δ is the indicator function and A^{+} is the ground truth. For the sake of brevity, we do not restate MRR as it is already defined in Section 6.1.2. Note that we only consider the ranking of the ground truth amongst all the negative samples for a given question.

7.2 Experimental Results

Table 8 shows the results of the experiments on Yahoo QA Dataset. We show that HD-LSTM achieves state-of-the-art performance on the Yahoo QA Dataset. First, we notice that the performance of Okapi BM25 model is only marginal compared to random guessing. This signifies that the testing set is indeed a difficult one.

Model	P@1	MRR
Random Guess	0.2000	0.4570
Okapi BM-25	0.2250	0.4927
CNN	0.4125	0.6323
CNTN	0.4654	0.6687
LSTM	0.4875	0.6829
NTN-LSTM	0.5448	0.7309
HD-LSTM	**0.5569**	**0.7347**

Table 8: Experimental Results on Yahoo QA Dataset.

Unfortunately, we were not able to obtain any results with MV-LSTM due to computational restrictions. Specifically, each training instance involves 5000 matching computations to be made. Hence, each epoch takes easily ≈ 3 hours even with GPUs. Hence, from the perspective of practical applications, we can safely eliminate the MV-LSTM as an alternative. Once again, we see the trend that tensor layer improves results over their base models similar to the earlier evaluation on the TREC QA task. However, unlike the TREC datasets, the NTN-LSTM performs significantly better than the baseline LSTM probably due to the larger dataset. On the other hand, we also observe that the LSTM performs better compared to CNN on this dataset similar to the results reported in [25]. Finally, our HD-LSTM performs the best and outperforms the NTN-LSTM despite having less parameters and being more efficient as discussed in our complexity analysis section earlier.

8 ANALYSIS OF HYPERPARAMETERS

In this section, we discuss some important observations in our experiments. such as hidden layer size on our model. In particular, we investigate the HD-LSTM, NTN-LSTM and the baseline LSTM. Due to the lack of space, we only report the hyperparameter tuning process of the TREC QA task specifically with respect to the MAP metric.

8.1 Effect of Embedding Dimension

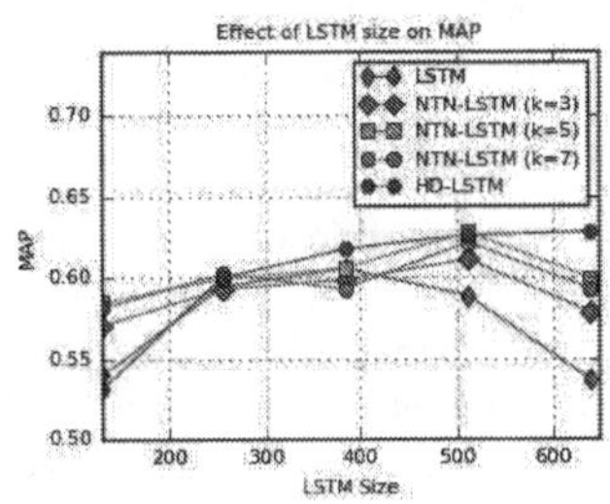

Figure 3: Effect of QA Embedding Size (LSTM Dimensions).

Figure 3 shows the influence of the size of the QA embedding on MAP performance on TREC `TRAIN` dataset. We investigate the NTN-LSTM at three different k levels (the number of tensor slices). We see that NTN-LSTM outperforms LSTM and HD-LSTM when the dimensionality of QA embeddings are small. This is because the introduction of extra parameters of quadratic scale at the tensor layer helps the NTN-LSTM fit the data. However, when increasing the dimensions of the sentence embedding, HD-LSTM starts to steadily outperform the NTN-LSTM. Furthermore, we note that at higher LSTM dimensions, i.e., 640, there is a steep decline in the performance of the NTN-LSTM probably due to overfitting. Overall, the performance of the baseline LSTM cannot be compared to both the HD-LSTM and NTN-LSTM. Evidently, the method used to model the relationship between the embedding of text pairs is crucial and has implications on the entire network. We see that the holographic composition allows more representational freedom in the LSTM by allowing it to have larger dimensions of text representations without possible implications.

8.2 Effect of Hidden Layer Size

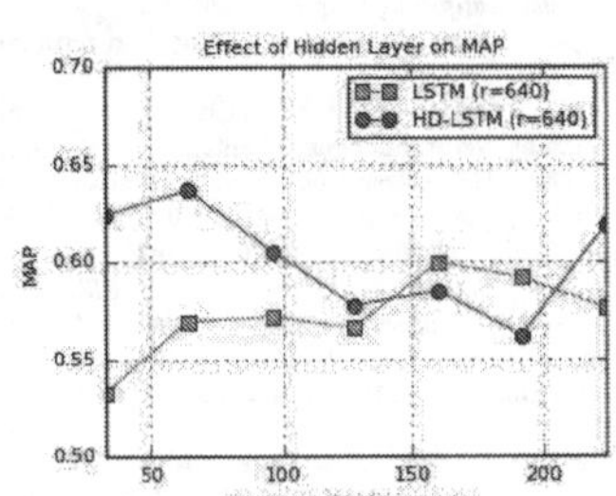

Figure 4: Effect of the Size of Hidden Layer on MAP.

The number of nodes at the hidden layer is an important hyperparameter in our experiments due to its close proximity and direct interaction with the composition between question and answer embeddings. Note that the hidden layer size is directly related to the number of parameters of the model. In this section, we aim to study the influence of the size of the hidden layer with respect to the LSTM and HD-LSTM. Note that we are unable to directly compare with the NTN-LSTM as the tensor M in the NTN layer acts like a hidden layer. Figure 4 shows the effect of the number of hidden nodes. Evidently, we see that a smaller hidden layer size benefits the HD-LSTM. On the other hand, the performance of LSTM is only decent above a certain threshold of hidden layer size. This is in concert with our understandings of the interactions of the parameters with the composition layer. Our model requires less parameters to model the relationship between text pairs because the correlation between question and answer embeddings is modeled via holographic composition. We see that our model achieves good results even with a smaller hidden layer, i.e., 64. Contrarily, LSTM requires more parameters to model the relationship between the text embeddings. We see that HD-LSTM with a small hidden layer produces the best results.

9 CONCLUSION

We proposed a novel deep learning architecture based on holographic associative memories for learning to rank QA pairs. The circular correlation of vectors has attractive qualities such as memory efficiency and rich representational learning. Additionally, we overcome the problem of scaling QA representations while keeping the compositional parameters low which is prevalent in models that adopt a tensor layer. We also outperform many variants of deep learning architectures including the NTN-LSTM and CNTN in the task of learning to rank for question answering applications.

REFERENCES

[1] Adam L. Berger, Rich Caruana, David Cohn, Dayne Freitag, and Vibhu O. Mittal. 2000. Bridging the lexical chasm: statistical approaches to answer-finding. In *SIGIR*. 192–199. DOI: http://dx.doi.org/10.1145/345508.345576

[2] Antoine Bordes, Jason Weston, and Nicolas Usunier. 2014. Open Question Answering with Weakly Supervised Embedding Models. In *Machine Learning and Knowledge Discovery in Databases - European Conference, ECML PKDD 2014, Nancy, France, September 15-19, 2014. Proceedings, Part I.* 165–180. DOI: http://dx.doi.org/10.1007/978-3-662-44848-9_11

[3] D. Gabor. 1969. Associative Holographic Memories. *IBM J. Res. Dev.* 13, 2 (March 1969), 156–159. DOI: http://dx.doi.org/10.1147/rd.132.0156

[4] Hua He, Kevin Gimpel, and Jimmy J Lin. Multi-Perspective Sentence Similarity Modeling with Convolutional Neural Networks.

[5] Michael Heilman and Noah A. Smith. 2010. Tree Edit Models for Recognizing Textual Entailments, Paraphrases, and Answers to Questions. In *Human Language Technologies: Conference of the North American Chapter of the Association of Computational Linguistics, Proceedings, June 2-4, 2010, Los Angeles, California, USA.* 1011–1019.

[6] Sepp Hochreiter and Jürgen Schmidhuber. 1997. Long short-term memory. *Neural computation* 9, 8 (1997), 1735–1780.

[7] Baotian Hu, Zhengdong Lu, Hang Li, and Qingcai Chen. 2014. Convolutional Neural Network Architectures for Matching Natural Language Sentences. In *Advances in Neural Information Processing Systems 27: Annual Conference on Neural Information Processing Systems 2014, December 8-13 2014, Montreal, Quebec, Canada.* 2042–2050.

[8] Jiwoon Jeon, W. Bruce Croft, and Joon Ho Lee. 2005. Finding similar questions in large question and answer archives. In *Proceedings of the 2005 ACM CIKM International Conference on Information and Knowledge Management, Bremen, Germany, October 31 - November 5, 2005.* 84–90. DOI: http://dx.doi.org/10.1145/1099554.1099572

[9] Diederik P. Kingma and Jimmy Ba. 2014. Adam: A Method for Stochastic Optimization. *CoRR* abs/1412.6980 (2014).

[10] Anh Tuan Luu, Yi Tay, Siu Cheung Hui, and See-Kiong Ng. 2016. Learning Term Embeddings for Taxonomic Relation Identification Using Dynamic Weighting Neural Network. In *Proceedings of the 2016 Conference on Empirical Methods in Natural Language Processing, EMNLP 2016, Austin, Texas, USA, November 1-4, 2016.* 403–413.

[11] Tomas Mikolov, Ilya Sutskever, Kai Chen, Gregory S. Corrado, and Jeffrey Dean. 2013. Distributed Representations of Words and Phrases and their Compositionality. In *Advances in Neural Information Processing Systems 26: 27th Annual Conference on Neural Information Processing Systems 2013. Proceedings of a meeting held December 5-8, 2013, Lake Tahoe, Nevada, United States.* 3111–3119.

[12] Jonas Mueller and Aditya Thyagarajan. 2016. Siamese Recurrent Architectures for Learning Sentence Similarity. In *Proceedings of the Thirtieth AAAI Conference on Artificial Intelligence, February 12-17, 2016, Phoenix, Arizona, USA.* 2786–2792.

[13] Maximilian Nickel, Lorenzo Rosasco, and Tomaso A. Poggio. 2016. Holographic Embeddings of Knowledge Graphs. In *Proceedings of the Thirtieth AAAI Conference on Artificial Intelligence, February 12-17, 2016, Phoenix, Arizona, USA.* 1955–1961.

[14] Hamid Palangi, Li Deng, Yelong Shen, Jianfeng Gao, Xiaodong He, Jianshu Chen, Xinying Song, and Rabab K. Ward. 2016. Deep Sentence Embedding Using Long Short-Term Memory Networks: Analysis and Application to Information Retrieval. *IEEE/ACM Trans. Audio, Speech & Language Processing* 24, 4 (2016), 694–707. DOI: http://dx.doi.org/10.1109/TASLP.2016.2520371

[15] Ankur P. Parikh, Oscar Täckström, Dipanjan Das, and Jakob Uszkoreit. 2016. A Decomposable Attention Model for Natural Language Inference. In *Proceedings of the 2016 Conference on Empirical Methods in Natural Language Processing, EMNLP 2016, Austin, Texas, USA, November 1-4, 2016.* 2249–2255.

[16] Tony Plate. 1992. Holographic Recurrent Networks. In *Advances in Neural Information Processing Systems 5, [NIPS Conference, Denver, Colorado, USA, November 30 - December 3, 1992].* 34–41.

[17] Tony A. Plate. 1995. Holographic reduced representations. *IEEE Trans. Neural Networks* 6, 3 (1995), 623–641. DOI: http://dx.doi.org/10.1109/72.377968

[18] Xipeng Qiu and Xuanjing Huang. 2015. Convolutional Neural Tensor Network Architecture for Community-Based Question Answering. In *Proceedings of the Twenty-Fourth International Joint Conference on Artificial Intelligence, IJCAI 2015, Buenos Aires, Argentina, July 25-31, 2015.* 1305–1311.

[19] Stephen E. Robertson, Steve Walker, Susan Jones, Micheline Hancock-Beaulieu, and Mike Gatford. 1994. Okapi at TREC-3. In *Proceedings of The Third Text REtrieval Conference, TREC 1994, Gaithersburg, Maryland, USA, November 2-4, 1994.* 109–126.

[20] Aliaksei Severyn and Alessandro Moschitti. 2015. Learning to Rank Short Text Pairs with Convolutional Deep Neural Networks. In *Proceedings of the 38th International ACM SIGIR Conference on Research and Development in Information Retrieval, Santiago, Chile, August 9-13, 2015.* 373–382. DOI: http://dx.doi.org/10.1145/2766462.2767738

[21] Aliaksei Severyn, Alessandro Moschitti, Manos Tsagkias, Richard Berendsen, and Maarten de Rijke. 2014. A syntax-aware re-ranker for microblog retrieval. In *The 37th International ACM SIGIR Conference on Research and Development in Information Retrieval, SIGIR '14, Gold Coast , QLD, Australia - July 06 - 11, 2014.* 1067–1070. DOI: http://dx.doi.org/10.1145/2600428.2609511

[22] Richard Socher, Danqi Chen, Christopher D. Manning, and Andrew Y. Ng. 2013. Reasoning With Neural Tensor Networks for Knowledge Base Completion. In *Advances in Neural Information Processing Systems 26: 27th Annual Conference on Neural Information Processing Systems 2013. Proceedings of a meeting held December 5-8, 2013, Lake Tahoe, Nevada, United States.* 926–934.

[23] Richard Socher, Alex Perelygin, Jean Y Wu, Jason Chuang, Christopher D Manning, Andrew Y Ng, and Christopher Potts. 2013. Recursive deep models for semantic compositionality over a sentiment treebank. Citeseer.

[24] Mihai Surdeanu, Massimiliano Ciaramita, and Hugo Zaragoza. 2011. Learning to Rank Answers to Non-Factoid Questions from Web Collections. *Computational Linguistics* 37, 2 (2011), 351–383. DOI: http://dx.doi.org/10.1162/COLI_a_00051

[25] Shengxian Wan, Yanyan Lan, Jiafeng Guo, Jun Xu, Liang Pang, and Xueqi Cheng. 2016. A Deep Architecture for Semantic Matching with Multiple Positional Sentence Representations. In *Proceedings of the Thirtieth AAAI Conference on Artificial Intelligence, February 12-17, 2016, Phoenix, Arizona, USA.* 2835–2841.

[26] Di Wang and Eric Nyberg. 2015. A Long Short-Term Memory Model for Answer Sentence Selection in Question Answering. In *Proceedings of the 53rd Annual Meeting of the Association for Computational Linguistics and the 7th International Joint Conference on Natural Language Processing of the Asian Federation of Natural Language Processing, ACL 2015, July 26-31, 2015, Beijing, China, Volume 2: Short Papers.* 707–712.

[27] Kai Wang, Zhaoyan Ming, and Tat-Seng Chua. 2009. A syntactic tree matching approach to finding similar questions in community-based qa services. In *Proceedings of the 32nd Annual International ACM SIGIR Conference on Research and Development in Information Retrieval, SIGIR 2009, Boston, MA, USA, July 19-23, 2009.* 187–194. DOI: http://dx.doi.org/10.1145/1571941.1571975

[28] Mengqiu Wang and Christopher D. Manning. 2010. Probabilistic Tree-Edit Models with Structured Latent Variables for Textual Entailment and Question Answering. In *COLING 2010, 23rd International Conference on Computational Linguistics, Proceedings of the Conference, 23-27 August 2010, Beijing, China.* 1164–1172.

[29] Mengqiu Wang, Noah A. Smith, and Teruko Mitamura. 2007. What is the Jeopardy Model? A Quasi-Synchronous Grammar for QA. In *EMNLP-CoNLL 2007, Proceedings of the 2007 Joint Conference on Empirical Methods in Natural Language Processing and Computational Natural Language Learning, June 28-30, 2007, Prague, Czech Republic.* 22–32.

[30] Long Xia, Jun Xu, Yanyan Lan, Jiafeng Guo, and Xueqi Cheng. 2016. Modeling Document Novelty with Neural Tensor Network for Search Result Diversification. In *Proceedings of the 39th International ACM SIGIR conference on Research and Development in Information Retrieval, SIGIR 2016, Pisa, Italy, July 17-21, 2016.* 395–404. DOI: http://dx.doi.org/10.1145/2911451.2911498

[31] Caiming Xiong, Victor Zhong, and Richard Socher. 2016. Dynamic Coattention Networks For Question Answering. *CoRR* abs/1611.01604 (2016).

[32] Xiaobing Xue, Jiwoon Jeon, and W. Bruce Croft. 2008. Retrieval models for question and answer archives. In *Proceedings of the 31st Annual International ACM SIGIR Conference on Research and Development in Information Retrieval, SIGIR 2008, Singapore, July 20-24, 2008.* 475–482. DOI: http://dx.doi.org/10.1145/1390334.1390416

[33] Xuchen Yao, Benjamin Van Durme, Chris Callison-Burch, and Peter Clark. 2013. Answer Extraction as Sequence Tagging with Tree Edit Distance. In *Human Language Technologies: Conference of the North American Chapter of the Association of Computational Linguistics, Proceedings, June 9-14, 2013, Westin Peachtree Plaza Hotel, Atlanta, Georgia, USA.* 858–867.

[34] Wen-tau Yih, Ming-Wei Chang, Christopher Meek, and Andrzej Pastusiak. 2013. Question Answering Using Enhanced Lexical Semantic Models. In *Proceedings of the 51st Annual Meeting of the Association for Computational Linguistics, ACL 2013, 4-9 August 2013, Sofia, Bulgaria, Volume 1: Long Papers.* 1744–1753.

[35] Lei Yu, Karl Moritz Hermann, Phil Blunsom, and Stephen Pulman. 2014. Deep Learning for Answer Sentence Selection. *CoRR* abs/1412.1632 (2014).

[36] Guangyou Zhou, Li Cai, Jun Zhao, and Kang Liu. 2011. Phrase-Based Translation Model for Question Retrieval in Community Question Answer Archives. In *The 49th Annual Meeting of the Association for Computational Linguistics: Human Language Technologies, Proceedings of the Conference, 19-24 June, 2011, Portland, Oregon, USA.* 653–662.

Incomplete Follow-up Question Resolution using Retrieval based Sequence to Sequence Learning

Vineet Kumar
IBM Research Labs, India
New Delhi
vineeku6@in.ibm.com

Sachindra Joshi
IBM Research Labs, India
New Delhi
jsachind@in.ibm.com

ABSTRACT

Intelligent personal assistants (IPAs) and interactive question answering (IQA) systems frequently encounter incomplete follow-up questions. The incomplete follow-up questions only make sense when seen in conjunction with the conversation context: the previous question and answer. Thus, IQA and IPA systems need to utilize the conversation context in order to handle the incomplete follow-up questions and generate an appropriate response. In this work, we present a *retrieval* based sequence to sequence learning system that can generate the complete (or intended) question for an incomplete follow-up question (given the conversation context). We can train our system using only a small labeled dataset (with only a few thousand conversations), by decomposing the original problem into two simpler and independent problems. The first problem focuses solely on selecting the candidate complete questions from a library of question templates (built offline using the small labeled conversations dataset). In the second problem, we re-rank the selected candidate questions using a neural language model (trained on millions of unlabelled questions independently). Our system can achieve a BLEU score of 42.91, as compared to 29.11 using an existing *generation* based approach. We further demonstrate the utility of our system as a plug-in module to an existing QA pipeline. Our system when added as a plug-in module, enables Siri to achieve an improvement of 131.57% in answering incomplete follow-up questions.

CCS CONCEPTS

•**Information systems → Query reformulation;**

KEYWORDS

retrieval based sequence to sequence learning; follow-up question resolution; query reformulation; intelligent personal assistants; interactive question answering

SIGIR '17, August 07-11, 2017, Shinjuku, Tokyo, Japan
© 2017 ACM. 978-1-4503-5022-8/17/08...$15.00
DOI: http://dx.doi.org/10.1145/3077136.3080801

1 INTRODUCTION

Intelligent Personal Assistants (IPAs) such as Siri[1], Cortana [11], Duer [49] and Allo[2] provide a rich and easy to use interface for human-computer interaction. IPAs provide many functionalities, for instance calendar and time management [33], making recommendations [29, 43] and task completion such as emailing, texting and application invocation [3]. Another core functionality offered by an IPA is general question answering (QA) [24, 37], which enables a user to ask questions such as "Who is the president of USA?". Once the system generates a response, users generally ask a follow-up question such as "and South Africa?", or "When did he?". The follow-up questions are often incomplete (when seen individually), terse [7] and refer to the entities and concepts mentioned either in the previous question, the previous answer or both. The follow-up questions make complete sense only in conjunction with the conversation context: the previous question and the previous answer.

Table 1 lists a few plausible follow-up questions. Note, how (a) & (b) need information only from the previous question $Q1$, while (c) & (d) require the previous answer $A1$, whereas (e) & (f) need both $Q1$ and $A1$ to understand the intended meaning of the incomplete question $Q2$. Also, note that (a) & (b) require completion of a missing part of the question (Ellipsis [30]), whereas (c) & (d) require pronoun references (Anaphora) to be resolved, and (e) & (f) require both ellipsis and anaphora. Thus, in order for an IPA and IQA system to generate an appropriate response for an incomplete follow-up question, it is necessary to utilize and select relevant information from the conversation context.

Table 1: A few plausible incomplete follow-up questions a user may ask after system generates the response $A1$, and the corresponding intended complete questions. (a) & (b) only require the previous complete question $Q1$, and need Ellipsis to resolve; (c) & (d) need only the previous answer $A1$, and need to handle Anaphora; (e) & (f) need both $Q1$ and $A1$, and need to handle both ellipsis and anaphora.

	Q/A	Utterance	Intended Utterance
	$Q1$	Who is the president of USA?	
	$A1$	Donald Trump	
(a)	$Q2$	and South Africa?	Who is the president of South Africa?
(b)	$Q2$	and defence secretary?	Who is the defence secretary of USA?
(c)	$Q2$	Who is he married to?	Who is Donald Trump married to?
(d)	$Q2$	When was he born?	When was Donald Trump born?
(e)	$Q2$	When?	When did Donald Trump become the president?
(f)	$Q2$	When did he?	When did Donald Trump become the president?

[1]http://www.apple.com/ios/siri/
[2]https://allo.google.com/

In this work, we present a *retrieval* based sequence to sequence learning system to handle incomplete follow-up questions. Our system can generate the complete (intended) question for an incomplete follow-up question, given the previous (complete) question and the previous answer. We approach this problem as a machine translation task, where the source text is the conversation context (the previous question $Q1$ and the previous answer $A1$) and an incomplete follow-up question $Q2$ (left half of Table 1), and the target text is the complete (or intended) follow-up question $R1$ (right half of Table 1).

A key challenge to approach the problem of question completion as machine translation is the paucity of labeled parallel corpus. Recently, Kumar & Joshi [25] proposed a *generation* based sequence to sequence learning approach for small datasets. They propose a syntactic sequence model, which focuses on the simpler problem of learning linguistic and syntactic patterns from questions. The trained syntactic sequence model is then used to generate a candidate question template, which can be trivially converted to a candidate question using a fixed symbol map. Generation based seq2seq approaches typically need huge parallel corpus [54]. Retrieval based models can alleviate this issue as they select from a pool of candidates which are grammatically well-formed and correct. Kanan et al. [21] recently proposed SmartReply, a retrieval based sequence to sequence learning system to generate responses for short e-mails. Inspired by their method, and the fact that there is paucity of data for a generation based approach to learn both patterns and a grammatically and semantically correct question, we use a *retrieval* based approach.

Retrieval based approach however comes with its own set of challenges [21]. One challenge for our question completion task, is the lack of labeled data, and thus lack of candidate questions. We address this problem by transforming original candidate questions to syntactic templates. Another challenge is the huge amount of computation time required at runtime to select the candidate questions. Though the syntactic transformations for candidates can be done offline by creating a library of question templates, we still need to select candidate questions at runtime, by computing probability of each candidate. We address this issue by reducing the number of comparisons required by using a prefix tree based approach.

Retrieval based approach itself helps us attain a BLEU score of 41.28 when compared to 29.11 with an existing generation based approach. It is important to note that although syntactic transformation of a question enables us to learn syntactic patterns, essential information to select a grammatically correct candidate is lost. We address this issue by using a neural language model which can be trained on a huge corpus with millions of unlabelled questions, to re-rank the selected candidates by the retrieval based syntactic sequence model, which enables us to boost the BLEU score to 42.91.

More concretely, we decompose the original problem of generating a complete question for an incomplete follow-up question given the conversation context, into two simpler and independent problems. For the first problem, we train a syntactic sequence model to select candidate question templates from a library of question templates generated offline. The syntactic sequence model can be trained using only a small labeled corpus of thousand conversations. The second problem re-ranks the selected candidate questions using a trained neural language model. The neural language model can be trained independently on huge questions corpus with millions of (unlabelled) questions.

Our system can be added as a plug-in module to an existing QA system pipeline, enabling it to handle incomplete follow-up questions. Our system when added as a plug-in module, enables Siri to achieve an improvement of 131.57% in answering incomplete follow-up questions.

Our key contributions can be summarized as follows:

- We present a *retrieval* based system that returns a complete question for an incomplete follow-up question, given the conversation context: the previous question and the previous answer. Our system achieves a BLEU score of 42.91 as compared to 29.11 obtained using an existing *generation* based approach.
- We decompose the original problem of question resolution into two simpler and independent problems. The first problem focuses on selecting candidate question templates using syntactic and linguistic patterns seen in the data.
- The second problem focuses on re-ranking candidate questions using a neural language model which can be trained independently on millions of unlabelled questions.
- Our system can be added as a plug-in module to an existing IPA or IQA system. Our system enables Siri to answer 88 incomplete follow-up questions as compared to 38 follow-up questions on an evaluation set of 100 questions. We release this dataset[3] to further research in IPA and IQA systems.

The rest of the paper is organized as follows. In Section 2, we discuss related work in interactive QA systems, dialogue systems and sequence to sequence learning. Section 3 presents the background necessary to understand our system. We describe our system in detail in Section 4, and discuss the experimental setup including the dataset in Section 5. Finally, we present quantitative, qualitative, language modeling improvements and comparison with Siri results in Section 6, and conclude in Section 7.

2 RELATED WORK

2.1 Interactive QA systems

In the past, a variety of approaches have been tried to handle incomplete follow-up questions for interactive QA systems. One set of work focuses on *rewriting* or resolving the incomplete follow-up question. An early system that can handle follow-up questions using resolution approach is RITS-QA [14]. Their approach requires identification of three key components in a complete question, such as "Who is the president of America?": topic presentation ('the president'), adjective expression ('of America') and the inquiring part ('who is') to resolve an incomplete follow-up question. This work was followed by a rule-based approach [13] to determine what information was missing in a follow-up question, and using word co-occurrence statistics and dictionary to resolve pronouns. There have been other efforts [28, 40, 48] which perform *rewriting* of an incomplete follow-up question by first explicitly identifying key components in previous questions and answers, and using word

[3]https://github.com/vineetm/siri-incomplete-questions

saliency statistics. Our system on the other hand does not need any explicit component identification in the complete or follow-up question, and is completely data driven.

Another set of work does not generate a complete follow-up question, but uses a keyword based approach [19], or changes the semantic representation of a question using the context [15, 39]. Another approach directly attempts to answer the follow-up question, by searching the Top-N documents that were used to generate the previous answer [6]. All of these approaches require modifying an existing QA pipeline. Our system on the other hand can be used as a plug-in module enabling an existing QA system to handle incomplete follow-up questions by generating the complete intended question.

Raghu et. al [38] presented a completely data driven approach to handle follow-up questions. However, their system can handle follow-up questions that only depend on the previous question. Thus their approach cannot handle Table 1(c) - (e).

2.2 Dialogue Systems

In dialogue systems, context is important for spoken language understanding (SLU) [47]. SLU system identifies three key components for an utterance: domain, intent and semantic slots. For example for an utterance 'I want a pizza with mushrooms and onions', the domain could be 'Food', the intent 'OrderPizza', and semantic slots would be pizza-toppings 'mushrooms' and 'onions'. Recent work [8, 42] shows that using the domain, intent and slots identified in the previous utterances can help improve slot filling and domain and intent classification or dialogue state tracking [50] for an utterance. Our system is different, as we look at a subset of utterances (follow-up questions), and we do not need to identify any key components. Our system can directly generate the intended utterance (complete follow-up question) by leveraging the conversation context (the previous question and the previous answer), and is completely data driven.

2.3 Sequence to Sequence Learning

Sequence to sequence learning [46] has been applied to a variety of applications including statistical machine translation [4, 45], language modeling [31, 32, 53], paraphrase generation [16, 36], semantic slot filling [26], image caption generation [20, 22, 51] among many others. Sequence to sequence learning has also been applied in dialogue systems for user modeling [2, 41, 52]. The closest application to our work is using a sequence to sequence model to generate a complete question [25]. However, their approach uses a *generation* based approach and is thus limited in learning to output correct questions from a small labeled corpus. We address the challenge of paucity of labeled data by using a *retrieval* based approach to learn syntactic patterns for complete questions. We further use a huge corpus of unlabelled questions to train a language model, to re-score candidates selected by the retrieval model. A retrieval based model related to our work is SmartReply [21]. However, SmartReply address the problem of generating a short email response, and does not have the issue of lack of labeled corpora.

Recently, Zoph et al. [54] proposed a novel method to train seq2seq models for low-resource languages. They propose training the seq2seq model on a resource rich language pair, and then re-training the model by keeping some parameters fixed on low resource language pair. However, it is not clear to us how this approach can be applied to the task of complete question generation from an incomplete follow-up question.

3 BACKGROUND

3.1 Sequence to Sequence Models

Sequence to sequence learning (seq2seq) [46] is a powerful framework to generate a sequence of output tokens given a sequence of input tokens. Seq2seq networks are trained on parallel corpus of data. Seq2seq uses a Recurrent Neural Network (RNN) based encoder decoder network. RNN encoder is used to compress the entire input sequence into a fixed length vector, called context vector. RNN decoder is then initialised with the context vector to generate a probability distribution over output tokens. The probability distribution is then used to sample an output token. The sampled output token, along with the context vector and RNN decoder's hidden state is used to generate a new probability distribution over output tokens. The entire process is repeated until a special end-of-sequence (EOS) token is sampled.

It is worth highlighting that RNN suffers form the problem of vanishing gradient problem [17]. This problem is addressed by using either a long short-term memory (LSTM) [18] or a gated recurrent unit (GRU) [9] cell. RNN also suffers from the problem of exploding gradients, and that is addressed by clipping the value of gradients [35].

One of the most successful applications of sequence to sequence learning is statistical machine translation [4, 46]. However, these models are trained on huge parallel corpus (of order of millions of data points). Obtaining a parallel corpus of this magnitude for question completion, is extremely hard, as the data has to be created manually. Thus, one needs to simplify the problem of sequence to sequence learning, by learning abstractions from data [25].

Seq2seq networks can be used to generate an output sequence of tokens given an input sequence of tokens. Seq2seq networks can also be used to compute the probability of output sequence given an input sequence $P(y_1, y_2, y_3, \cdots, y_{T_y} | x_1, x_2, x_3, \cdots, x_{T_x})$, where y_i represents an output token, x_j represents an input token, T_x represents length of input sequence and T_y the length of output sequence.

3.2 Syntactic Sequence Model

Seq2seq models have a large number of parameters, which can make training difficult for small datasets [25, 54]. This problem can be alleviated by reducing the size of vocabulary. Kumar et. al [25] recently proposed a syntactic sequence model which can be trained on small datasets, by focusing on simpler problem of learning linguistic or syntactic patterns in the data. Their approach restricts vocabulary size by assigning new symbols to out-of-vocabulary (OOV) words based on its position in the sequence, and reusing the symbols across training data. Table 2 depicts a conversation after OOV words are replaced by unknown (UNK) symbol and the corresponding source and target sequence. Note how such a model would learn only to reproduce $Q1$. Table 3 depicts how a syntactic sequence model can preserve linguistic information in a conversation, even with a restricted vocabulary.

3.3 Recurrent neural network based Language Model

Recurrent neural network (RNN) [10] based language model [31, 32] can be used to compute the probability of a word $x(t)$ at position (or time) t, given all the previous words $x(t-1), x(t-2), \cdots x(1)$ in a sentence. A word is further represented using a vector $w(t)$. The network also has a hidden state $s(t)$ and an output layer $y(t)$. Probability of a word $x(t)$, given the previous words is computed as follows:

$$a(t) = w(t) + s(t-1) \tag{1}$$

$$s_j(t) = f(\sum_i a_i(t)u_{ji}) \tag{2}$$

$$y_k(t) = g(\sum_j s_j(t)v_{kj}) \tag{3}$$

where $f(z)$ is the sigmoid function:

$$f(z) = \frac{1}{1+e^{-z}} \tag{4}$$

and g(z) is the softmax function:

$$g(z_m) = \frac{e^{z_m}}{\sum_k e^{z_k}} \tag{5}$$

Table 2: Utterances after replacing all out of vocabulary words with same symbol *UNK*.

	Utterance	Replaced Utterance
$Q1$	What is the capital of India?	What is the UNK of UNK?
$A1$	Delhi	UNK
$Q2$	and USA?	and UNK?
$R1$	What is the capital of USA?	What is the UNK of UNK?

Source:	What is the UNK of UNK? EOS UNK EOS and UNK?
Target:	What is the UNK of UNK?

4 SYSTEM DESCRIPTION

In this section, we describe our complete end-to-end system to handle incomplete follow-up question given conversation context. Figure 1 gives a high level description. The offline component works with two corpus: a labeled conversations corpus (Section 5.1), and an unlabelled corpus of questions. The labeled conversations corpus is used to train the syntactic sequence model (Section 3.2). The training corpus from the labeled conversation corpus is also used to create an offline library of candidate question templates after performing syntactic transformations. The unlabelled question corpus used to train a neural language model (Section 3.3).

The online component handles an incomplete follow-up question, by returning a ranked list of candidate questions. Conversation context (the previous question $Q1$ and the previous answer $A1$) along with the incomplete follow-up question $Q2$ is fed to syntactic transformation unit. This converts the input to a source sequence (Table 3) along with a symbol map. The source sequence is fed to candidate selection module, which uses a trained syntactic sequence model to select candidate question templates from an offline template library. The candidate templates are then converted to complete questions by replacing symbols from the symbol map. Finally, the trained language model is used to re-rank candidate questions and return the final list. We now describe each sub-component in detail.

Table 3: Utterances in the left side of Table 2, after replacing each OOV word with a new symbol, which corresponds to its position in the sequence.

	Utterance	Replaced Utterance
$Q1$	What is the capital of India?	What is the UNK1 of UNK2?
$A1$	Delhi	UNK3
$Q2$	and USA?	and UNK4?
$R1$	What is the capital of USA?	What is the UNK1 of UNK4?

Source:	What is the UNK1 of UNK2? EOS UNK3 EOS and UNK4?
Target:	What is the UNK1 of UNK4?

Symbol	Value
UNK1	capital
UNK2	India
UNK3	Delhi
UNK4	USA

4.1 Offline Question Template Library

We use a labeled conversation corpus (Section 5.1), which contains the previous complete question $Q1$, the previous answer $A1$, the incomplete follow-up question $Q2$ and the corresponding resolved complete question $R1$ to create a question template library offline. We use transformations to replace all out-of-vocabulary (OOV) words with new symbols, and then use the transformed complete questions $R1$ from the training split as templates.

In this work, we only experimented with syntactic transformations, where a new symbol is assigned based on its position in the sequence. It is worth noting that there are many other possible methods: one can create semantic abstractions as specified in semantic sequence model [25], or an entity, or part of speech based abstraction. Syntactic transformations allow us to look at an abstraction of the original data, and thus enables us to generalize even using a small dataset. For example, there are 6420 resolved questions $R1$ in our training data, but after syntactic transformation, this number is reduced to 5451 templates. This shows, that syntactic transformations already enable us to find patterns in complete questions.

4.2 Candidate Question Template Selector

At run time, candidate question template selector uses a trained syntactic sequence model to return a list of candidate question templates. A naive implementation would require to compute probability of each candidate given the source sequence. For example, in our specific case this would require 5451 probability computations for each incomplete follow-up question. This makes the run-time selection of candidate question templates slow. We address this challenge by using a prefix-tree based approach. Figure 2 depicts

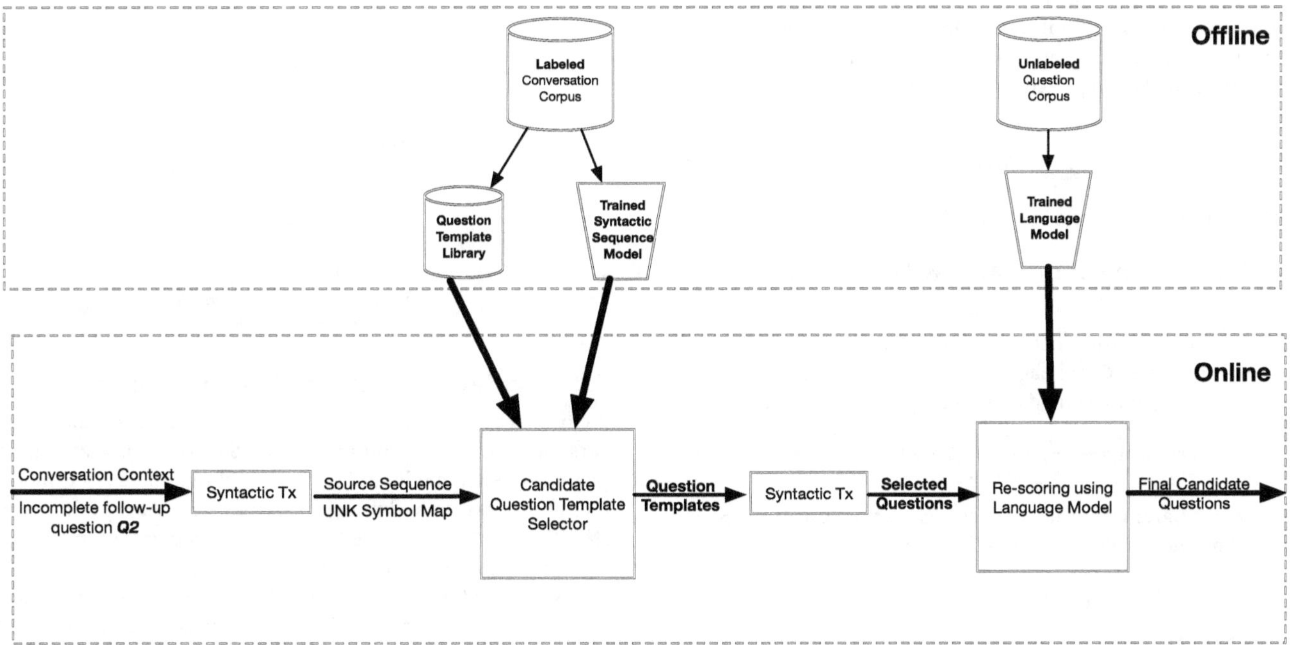

Figure 1: System description

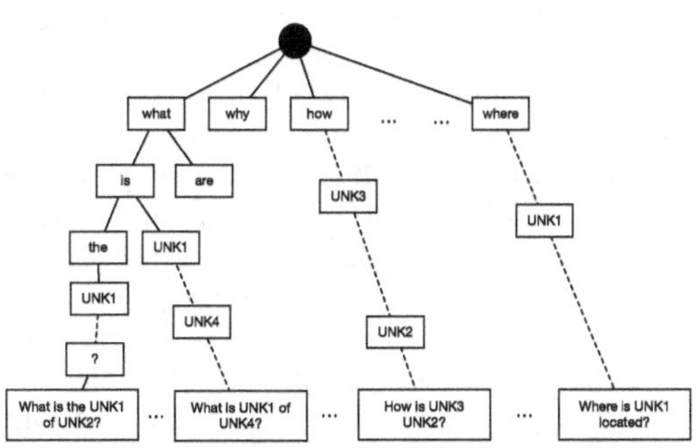

Figure 2: Prefix tree for syntactic question templates. Nodes at the first level denote start of a question template The leaves denote all the question templates.

a sample prefix tree for a library of question templates built using syntactic transformations. The very first level of tree represents the start of a candidate question template such as 'why', 'how' and 'is'. The subsequent level represents the second token in a candidate question, and finally the leaves represent the candidate question templates.

For a given incomplete question, first a source sequence is generated using syntactic transformation (Table 3). We use the prefix tree at runtime, by using a beam search based approach, with a window size *ws*. We initialize a priority queue (highest probability node first) with the root of the prefix tree. We then de queue the first entry (in this case the root node), and add all its children to the queue after computing the probability of the prefix given the source sequence. At this stage we prune the queue to only keep Top-*ws* nodes. We repeat the process, till we are only left with the leaf nodes, and return the list of selected question templates. Note that the window size *ws*, represents a tradeoff between time required and accuracy obtained. A small window size would discard most of candidate questions early, but would do quick computations. A large window size would be more accurate, but would have more computation requirements. Section 6.2 gives more details on how the window size is selected.

A seq2seq model can be used to compute the probability of a target sequence $y_1, y_2, \cdots, y_{T_y}$, given an input sequence $x_1, x_2, \cdots, x_{T_x}$. We compute the seq2seq score (*ss*) by computing the average probability of an output token, as follows:

$$ss = \frac{1}{T_y}\sum_{i=1}^{T_y} Pr(y_i|x_1, x_2, \cdots x_{T_x}, y_1, \cdots y_{i-1}) \tag{6}$$

A candidate template question can then be converted trivially to a candidate question, by replacing all the new symbols UNK_i using the symbol map.

4.3 Language Model for probability computation

We use a RNN based language model to compute the language score *ls* for a question. Probability of a question can be computed as follows:

$$Pr(x_1, x_2, \cdots, x_t) = \prod_i Pr(x_i|x_1, x_2, \cdots x_{i-1}) \tag{7}$$

However, Equation 7 favours short questions over long questions. For our purposes of computing a grammatically correct question, we are more concerned if each token selected has a high probability. We compute the language score ls for a question as follows:

$$ls = \frac{1}{t}\sum_{i=1}^{t} Pr(x_i|x_1, x_2, \cdots x_{i-1}) \quad (8)$$

where $Pr(x_i|x_1, x_2, \cdots x_{i-1})$ is computed using Equation 3.

4.4 Re-ranking candidates with Language Model

Seq2Seq model returns a list of k candidates. For each candidate, seq2seq score (ss) and language model score (ls) is computed. The final score $score_i$ for a candidate i is computed as follows:

$$score_i = \lambda * \frac{ss_i}{max_{j=1}^{k} ss_j} + (1-\lambda) * \frac{ls_i}{max_{j=1}^{k} ls_j} \quad (9)$$

where λ is a parameter that is learnt using the best BLEU Score obtained on the development data for k candidates.

5 EXPERIMENTS

5.1 Dataset

For all our experiments, we use the question completion dataset [38] which has 7220 labeled conversations. Each labeled conversation has four parts: a previous complete question $Q1$, a previous answer $A1$, an incomplete follow-up question $Q2$ and the corresponding intended complete question $R1$. Table 4 lists a few examples from the dataset.

Table 4: Sample conversations from the dataset

$Q1$	What is a native animal of Ireland?
$A1$	Hedgehog
$Q2$	What about Australia?
$R1$	What is a native animal of Australia?
$Q1$	Where does a white faced saki live?
$A1$	Suriname
$Q2$	What does it eat?
$R1$	What does a white faced saki eat?
$Q1$	Where are Porsche made?
$A1$	Germany
$Q2$	and when was the first?
$R1$	When was the first Porsche produced?

This dataset was created using Amazon Mechanical Turk[4] (AMT), by giving users question answer pairs ($Q1, A1$) and asking them to generate follow-up questions $Q2$. Users were also asked to generate the complete question $R1$.

For our experiments, we randomly split the dataset into training, development and test set. Table 5 lists a few details of the dataset, where $|V|$ refers to the number of unique tokens seen in the training data. We use the resolved questions $R1$ from the training set to create an offline library of question templates (Section 4.1).

[4]https://www.mturk.com

Table 5: Dataset statistics

Conversations	7220
Train	6420
Dev	400
Test	400
$\|V\|$	11759
$\|V\|$ (With Phrases)	13938
Words (Train)	157K
Words (Dev)	9893
Words (Test)	9853

5.2 Syntactic Sequence Model Training

We train a syntactic sequence model (Section 3.2) on the 6420 conversations from the training dataset (Section 5.1). Training a syntactic sequence model differs from a standard seq2seq model in its pre processing and post processing step. As a pre processing step, the vocabulary is fixed, and for each conversation all the out-of-vocabulary (OOV) tokens are assigned a new unknown symbol (UNK_i) according to its position in the sequence. As a post processing step, all the new unknown symbols are replaced by their original tokens using the symbol map. Table 3 gives an instance of a conversation after replacement with unknown symbols and the corresponding symbol map. Another important difference from a standard machine translation based seq2seq network, is that we use the same vocabulary for both source and target, as we are dealing with the same language (English), and more importantly tokens in source and target mean the same thing.

We use a recurrent neural network (RNN) [10] based encoder decoder network with gated recurrent unit (GRU) [9] as our seq2seq model. Adam [23] with default recommended parameters $\beta1 = 0.9, \beta_2 = 0.999, \epsilon = 10^{-8}$ is used as the optimization algorithm. We extend an open source implementation [5] of a machine translation model based on tensorflow [1] to train our seq2seq models.

As we are only interested in learning syntactic and linguistic patterns, we restrict our vocabulary to use only stop words. We include all the question keywords such as 'what', 'when' and 'why' in our stopword list. All our models are trained with a vocabulary size of 159, which includes tokens for new unknown symbols (UNK_i). We select all other hyper-parameters such as the embedding size (128), number of hidden units (128) and number of layers (1) that returns the highest BLEU score on Top-100 candidates (Section 4.2) for the development set. For all our experiments, we lowercase the text and use NLTK tokenizer [5] to generate tokens. We further convert the tokens to phrases using textblob [27]. For BLEU score computation we convert the phrases back to their constituent tokens.

5.3 Language Model Training

We train a RNN based language model as described in Section 3.3 using questions from knowitall dataset [12]. This dataset has about 30M questions (questions.txt). We restrict it to only questions that begin with question keywords (such as 'why', 'when and 'how'), which reduces the number of questions to 24M questions. We further randomize this dataset, and train the neural language model

[5]https://github.com/tensorflow/models/tree/master/tutorials/rnn/translate

on 2M questions. We use Long Short Term Memory (LSTM) [18] units, and apply dropout to train our networks [53]. We train our language model by applying dropout to LSTM We use an open source implementation[6] based on tensorflow [1] by using the default parameters specified in LargeConfig.

6 RESULTS

6.1 Evaluation using BLEU

As described in Section 4, our system returns Top-k candidate questions for an incomplete follow-up question (and the conversation context). We evaluate our system using BLEU [34]. We use the standard BLEU evaluation script [7], which computes and reports the exponential average of BLEU-1, BLEU-2, BLEU-3 and BLEU-4 scores. We measure BLEU by comparing each of k candidates against the *gold* resolved question, and report the highest BLEU score returned by a candidate. Thus, if Top-4 candidates have BLEU scores of 13.45, 40.34, 70.89 and 34.89, we report the BLEU as 70.89 when considering $k = 4$, and 40.34 when considering $k = 2$.

Table 6 reports the BLEU scores on a held out test set of 400 conversations. When we only select the top candidate ($k = 1$) returned by the retrieval based syntactic sequence model, we achieve a BLEU score of 41.28, as compared to 29.11 reported in our previous *generation* based approach [25]. After re-ranking the Top-100 candidates returned by the system with a trained language model (Section 4.4), and selecting the top ($k = 1$) candidate, we see further improvements and our final system can achieve a BLEU score of 42.91.

Figure 3 depicts BLEU scores attained by retrieval based model and the final system (when candidates are re-ranked using language model). As expected, we obtain higher BLEU scores when the number of candidates k increases. Re-ranking with language model helps further. It is also interesting to note that as k increases, the boost provided by the language model decreases. This can be explained by the fact, that with large k, the candidates selected by the language model are already present in Top-k candidates. Thus, the highest BLEU score does not change. Table 7 lists a few concrete examples where re-scoring with a trained neural language model helps. Finally, in Table 8 we highlight the candidate questions returned by our system.

Table 6: BLEU Score on Test Set

Model	BLEU
Baseline RNN (Kumar & Joshi) [25]	18.54
Syntactic Sequence (Kumar & Joshi) [25]	29.11
Our approach: Retrieval Model	**41.28**
Our approach: Retrieval Model + LM	**42.91**

6.2 Window size *ws* selection of prefix tree

In Section 4.2 we described how candidate question templates are selected from an offline question template library. Figure 4 depicts the total time taken for selecting 100 candidates for 10 incomplete follow-up questions from the development set. We select $ws = 8$, as the window size, as after this BLEU score increases marginally, though time taken increases considerably.

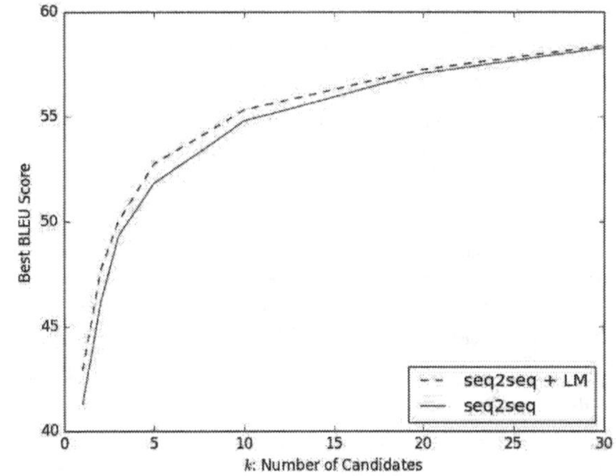

Figure 3: BLEU Scores

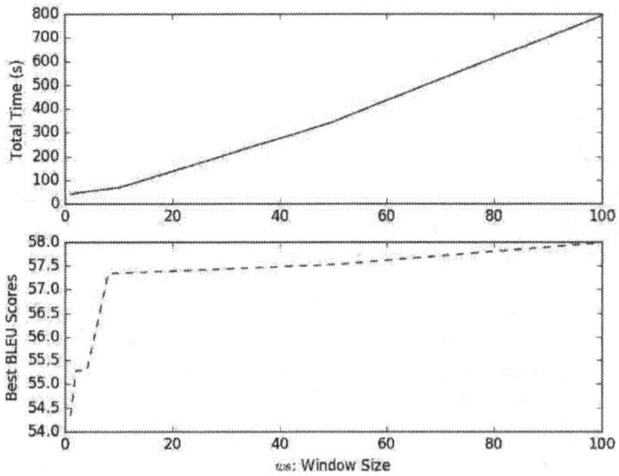

Figure 4: Total time taken and the best BLEU score for 10 incomplete follow-up questions from the development set over 100 candidates.

6.3 Comparison with Siri

Our system can generate the complete question for an incomplete follow-up question given the conversation context. This can be of value to an IPA such as Siri, as it can now process the generated complete question directly, without changing its existing pipeline. In this section, we demonstrate how our system, when added as a plug-in module enables Siri to answer more follow-up questions. In order to asses the utility of our system, we create a follow-up question dataset of 100 incomplete questions, along with the gold resolved questions. We only select questions which can be directly answered by Siri (and remove questions which return only a web

[6] https://github.com/tensorflow/models/tree/master/tutorials/rnn/ptb

[7] https://github.com/moses-smt/mosesdecoder/blob/master/scripts/generic/multi-bleu.perl

Table 7: Language Model helps in reordering seq2seq candidates

		Utterance	Seq2seq Retrieval Model	Seq2seq Retrieval Model + LM
(a)	$Q1$	Who is the chief of Indian army navy and air force?	who is the chief of indian army navy and charge ?	is president pranab mukherjee in charge of anything else ?
	$A1$	President Pranab Mukherjee	is president pranab mukherjee chief in air force a charge number ?	is president pranab mukherjee chief in air force a charge numb
	$Q2$	Is he in charge of anything else?	is president pranab mukherjee in charge of anything else ?	who is the chief of indian army navy and charge ?
	$Gold$	Is President Pranab Mukherjee in charge of anything else besides the indian military?		
(b)	$Q1$	What sport is the most common cause of eye injuries in US?	what sport is the knee injuries most common in eye injuries ?	what sport is the most common cause of knee injuries in us ?
	$A1$	baseball	what sport is the most knee injuries cause of eye injuries in us ?	what sport is the knee injuries most common in eye injuries ?
	$Q2$	knee injuries?	what sport is the most common cause of knee injuries in us ?	what sport is the most knee injuries cause of eye injuries in us
	$Gold$	What sport is the most common cause of knee injuries in the US ?		
(c)	$Q1$	type of joints used in squats?	what type of joints used in push-ups ?	what type of joints are used in push-ups ?
	$A1$	knee	type of joints used in push-ups ?	what type of joints used in push-ups ?
	$Q2$	and in push-ups ?	what type of joints are used in push-ups ?	type of joints used in push-ups ?
	$Gold$	type of joints used in push-ups ?		
(d)	$Q1$	in which sport was wally lewis a champion ?	how many goals did rugby score ?	how many goals did wally score ?
	$A1$	rugby	how many goals did wally score ?	how many goals did rugby score ?
	$Q2$	and how many goals did he score ?		
	$Gold$	and how many goals did wally lewis score ?		
(e)	$Q1$	a fuel that is burnt to form water. it is expensive and difficult to transport. what is it ?	why is hydrogen UNK to UNK ?	why is hydrogen difficult to transport ?
			why are hydrogen burnt to form ?	why is hydrogen UNK to UNK ?
	$A1$	hydrogen	why is hydrogen difficult to transport ?	why are hydrogen burnt to form ?
	$Q2$	Why is it difficult to transport?		
	$Gold$	Why is hydrogen difficult to transport?		
(f)	$Q1$	What are some of Maryland's major highways ?	what are some maryland in new york?	what are some of new york 's major highways ?
	$A1$	U.S. route 10	what are some maryland major highways in new york ?	what are some maryland in new york?
	$Q2$	how about in New York?	what are some of maryland 's new york ?	what are some maryland major highways in new york ?
	$Gold$	What are some of New York 's major highways ?	what are some of new york 's major highways ?	what are some of maryland 's new york ?

search). All the experiments were done on 14 Jan 2017 on iPhone 6S with iOS v10.2 (14C92). The dataset[8] is created as follows:

- We start with question answer pairs from the Question Answer dataset [44]. This dataset contains about 4000 question pairs. We eliminate all the questions which have a 'yes/no' answer.
- We further eliminate all the questions that cannot be answered directly by Siri. Thus, we do not consider questions that return a web search, as it is hard to check if the question is answered correctly.
- We further add questions from the list of documented questions that Siri can answer [9].
- We create incomplete follow-up questions for the remaining questions, by referring to the entities and concepts mentioned in the conversation.

Table 10 shows that our system enables Siri to answer 88 incomplete follow-up questions as compared to 38 questions, thus enabling Siri to achieve an improvement of 131.57%. We first ask Siri the complete question $Q1$, followed by the incomplete question $Q2$, and note the response generated by Siri. We then ask Siri the resolved *gold* question $R1$. We assume Siri has correctly answered the follow-up question if the response generated by $R1$ is same as $Q2$. Table 9 depicts a few example of Ellipsis follow-up questions, and how our system can enable Siri to answer them.

7 CONCLUSION

IPA and IQA systems frequently encounter incomplete follow-up questions which require the conversation context (previous question and answer) to make complete sense. In order to generate an appropriate response, IPA and IQA systems need to handle incomplete follow-up questions. In this paper, we present a *retrieval* based sequence to sequence learning system, that can return a compete question for an incomplete follow-up question (given conversation context). As there is paucity of labeled conversation data, we decompose the original problem into two simpler and independent problems. The first problem used a small labeled conversation corpus to select candidate questions. The second problem uses a trained neural language model (which can be trained on millions of unlabelled questions) to re-rank candidate questions, and thus return grammatically well-formed questions. Our system can achieve a BLEU score of 42.19, as compared to 29.11 reported by an existing *generation* based approach. We further demonstrate how our system can be added as a plug-in module to an existing IPA, such as SIRI and enable it to handle more follow-up questions.

As future work, we plan to experiment with retrieval models that look at other abstractions such as entities and concepts, and use an ensemble model to combine them.

[8] https://github.com/vineetm/siri-incomplete-questions

[9] http://www.apple.com/ios/siri/

Table 8: Candidate questions generated by our system for some incomplete follow-up questions

		Utterance	Gold Question ($R1$)	Candidate Question(s)
(a)	$Q1$ $A1$ $Q2$	What is the abbreviated form of the month of April ? apr and for the month of September?	and what is the abbreviated form of the month of september?	what is the abbreviated form of the month of september ?
(b)	$Q1$ $A1$ $Q2$	what kind of gelatin is used in haricot strawberry cream gummies ? beef what kind of sweetener?	what kind of sweetener is used in haricot strawberry cream gummies?	what kind of sweetener is used in haricot strawberry cream gummies ?
(c)	$Q1$ $A1$ $Q2$	What is food refuse? waste What are the consequences ?	what are the consequences of food refuse ?	what are the consequences of food refuse ? what are the consequences of UNK waste ?
(d)	$Q1$ $A1$ $Q2$	Who desired to westernize Russia? Mikhail Gorbachev in what year?	In what year did Gorbachev desire to westernize russia ?	in what year did mikhail gorbachev UNK westernize russia ?
(e)	$Q1$ $A1$ $Q2$	Who was the mayor before Rob Ford ? David Miller and before him?	Who was the mayor before David Miller?	who was the mayor in UNK ? who was the mayor before david miller ?
(f)	$Q1$ $A1$ $Q2$	minimum age to be a US representative ? 25 to be a senator?	minimum age to be a senator ?	minimum age to be a us senator ?
(g)	$Q1$ $A1$ $Q2$	Who is the inventor of the ac-130 ? lockheed when was that?	when did lockheed invent the ac-130 ?	when was the inventor of the ac-130 ? when was lockheed the inventor of ac-130 ?
(h)	$Q1$ $A1$ $Q2$	What year did the US troops leave Vietnam? 1973 and how long did that war last ?	How long did the Vietnam war last?	how long did 1973 war last ? how long did vietnam war last ?
(i)	$Q1$ $A1$ $Q2$	Who is the fastest man in the world? Usain Bolt how fast did he run ?	How fast did Usain Bolt run?	how fast did usain bolt run ?
(j)	$Q1$ $A1$ $Q2$	Who is considered the father of the US Constitution? James Madison Who was he?	Who was James Madison?	who is considered the father of the us james madison ? who was james madison ? who is james madison the father of the us constitution ?
(k)	$Q1$ $A1$ $Q2$	the capital of new zealand ? wellington what is it's population?	what is the population of wellington, new zealand?	what is new zealand 's population ? what is the new zealand 's population ? what is wellington 's population ?

Table 9: Follow-up questions resolution comparison with Siri

$Q1$	$Q2$	R1	Siri Response	With our system
How many miles in 5 kilometres ?	and 15 kilometres?		✓	✓
	and 15 ?	How many miles in 15 kilometres?	X	✓
When did Yuan Shikai die?	Where did he die?		✓	✓
	where?	Where did Yuan Shikai die?	X	✓
What is the square root of 64?	and cube root?	What is the cube root of 64?	X	✓
Who is the president of India?	how about prime minister?		✓	✓
	and prime minister?	Who is the prime minister of India?	X	✓

Table 10: Follow-up questions correctly answered by Siri. If the response generated for a follow-up question $Q2$ (after asking Siri $Q1$) is same as the response generated by $R1$, we assume Siri has correctly answered the follow-up question.

System	Correctly Answered
Baseline	38/100
Our System	88/100

REFERENCES

[1] Martın Abadi, Ashish Agarwal, Paul Barham, Eugene Brevdo, Zhifeng Chen, Craig Citro, Greg S Corrado, Andy Davis, Jeffrey Dean, Matthieu Devin, and others. 2016. Tensorflow: Large-scale machine learning on heterogeneous distributed systems. *arXiv preprint arXiv:1603.04467* (2016).

[2] Layla El Asri, Jing He, and Kaheer Suleman. 2016. A Sequence-to-Sequence Model for User Simulation in Spoken Dialogue Systems. *CoRR* abs/1607.00070 (2016).

[3] Amos Azaria, Jayant Krishnamurthy, and Tom M. Mitchell. 2016. Instructable Intelligent Personal Agent. In *AAAI*.

[4] Dzmitry Bahdanau, Kyunghyun Cho, and Yoshua Bengio. 2014. Neural Machine Translation by Jointly Learning to Align and Translate. *CoRR* abs/1409.0473 (2014).

[5] Steven Bird. 2006. NLTK: the natural language toolkit. In *Proceedings of the COLING/ACL on Interactive presentation sessions*. Association for Computational Linguistics, 69–72.

[6] Marco De Boni and Suresh Manandhar. 2005. Implementing clarification dialogues in open domain question answering. *Natural Language Engineering* 11 (2005), 343–361.

[7] Jaime G Carbonell. 1983. Discourse pragmatics and ellipsis resolution in task-oriented natural language interfaces. In *Proceedings of the 21st annual meeting on Association for Computational Linguistics*. Association for Computational Linguistics, 164–168.
[8] Yun-Nung Chen, Dilek Hakkani-Tür, Gokhan Tur, Jianfeng Gao, and Li Deng. 2016. End-to-end memory networks with knowledge carryover for multi-turn spoken language understanding. In *Proceedings of Interspeech*.
[9] Junyoung Chung, Caglar Gülçehre, Kyunghyun Cho, and Yoshua Bengio. 2015. Gated feedback recurrent neural networks. *CoRR, abs/1502.02367* (2015).
[10] Jeffrey L. Elman. 1990. Finding Structure in Time. *Cognitive Science* 14 (1990), 179–211.
[11] Emad Elwany. 2014. Enhancing Cortana User Experience Using Machine Learning.
[12] Oren Etzioni, Michael Cafarella, Doug Downey, Stanley Kok, Ana-Maria Popescu, Tal Shaked, Stephen Soderland, Daniel S Weld, and Alexander Yates. 2004. Web-scale information extraction in knowitall:(preliminary results). In *Proceedings of the 13th international conference on World Wide Web*. ACM, 100–110.
[13] Junichi Fukumoto. 2006. Answering questions of Information Access Dialogue (IAD) task using ellipsis handling of follow-up questions. In *Proceedings of the Interactive Question Answering Workshop at HLT-NAACL 2006*. Association for Computational Linguistics, 41–48.
[14] Junichi Fukumoto, Tatsuhiro Niwa, Makoto Itoigawa, and Megumi Matsuda. 2004. RitsQA: List answer detection and context task with ellipses handling. In *Working notes of the Fourth NTCIR Workshop Meeting, Okyo, Japan*. 310–314.
[15] Olivier Galibert, Gabriel Illouz, and Sophie Rosset. 2005. Ritel: an open-domain, human-computer dialog system. In *INTERSPEECH*.
[16] Sadid A Hasan, Bo Liu, Joey Liu, Ashequl Qadir, Kathy Lee, Vivek Datla, Aaditya Prakash, and Oladimeji Farri. 2016. Neural Clinical Paraphrase Generation with Attention.
[17] Sepp Hochreiter. 1998. The vanishing gradient problem during learning recurrent neural nets and problem solutions. *International Journal of Uncertainty, Fuzziness and Knowledge-Based Systems* 6, 02 (1998), 107–116.
[18] Sepp Hochreiter and Jürgen Schmidhuber. 1997. Long short-term memory. *Neural computation* 9, 8 (1997), 1735–1780.
[19] Kentaro Inui, Akiko Yamashita, and Yuji Matsumoto. 2003. Dialogue Management for Language-based Information Seeking.
[20] Xu Jia, Efstratios Gavves, Basura Fernando, and Tinne Tuytelaars. 2015. Guiding the Long-Short Term Memory Model for Image Caption Generation. In *ICCV*.
[21] Anjuli Kannan, Karol Kurach, Sujith Ravi, Tobias Kaufmann, Andrew Tomkins, Balint Miklos, Greg Corrado, László Lukács, Marina Ganea, Peter Young, and others. 2016. Smart Reply: Automated Response Suggestion for Email. In *Proceedings of the ACM SIGKDD Conference on Knowledge Discovery and Data Mining (KDD)*, Vol. 36. 495–503.
[22] Andrej Karpathy and Li Fei-Fei. 2015. Deep visual-semantic alignments for generating image descriptions. In *CVPR*.
[23] Diederik Kingma and Jimmy Ba. 2014. Adam: A method for stochastic optimization. *arXiv preprint arXiv:1412.6980* (2014).
[24] Natalia Konstantinova and Constantin Orasan. 2012. Interactive question answering. (2012).
[25] Vineet Kumar and Sachindra Joshi. 2016. Non-sentential Question Resolution using Sequence to Sequence Learning. In *COLING*.
[26] Gakuto Kurata, Bing Xiang, Bowen Zhou, and Mo Yu. 2016. Leveraging Sentence-level Information with Encoder LSTM for Semantic Slot Filling. In *EMNLP*.
[27] Steven Loria. 2014. TextBlob: simplified text processing. *Secondary TextBlob: Simplified Text Processing* (2014).
[28] Megumi Matsuda and Jun-ichi Fukumoto. 2005. Answering Questions of IAD Task using Reference Resolution of Follow-up Questions.. In *NTCIR*. Citeseer.
[29] Yoichi Matsuyama, Arjun Bhardwaj, Ran Zhao, Oscar Romeo, Sushma Akoju, and Justine Cassell. 2016. Socially-Aware Animated Intelligent Personal Assistant Agent. In *SIGDIAL Conference*.
[30] Jason Merchant. 2001. *The syntax of silence: Sluicing, islands, and the theory of ellipsis*. Oxford University Press on Demand.
[31] Tomas Mikolov, Anoop Deoras, Daniel Povey, Lukás Burget, and Jan Cernocký. 2011. Strategies for training large scale neural network language models. In *ASRU*.
[32] Tomas Mikolov, Martin Karafiát, Lukás Burget, Jan Cernocký, and Sanjeev Khudanpur. 2010. Recurrent neural network based language model. In *INTERSPEECH*.
[33] Karen L. Myers, Pauline M. Berry, Jim Blythe, Ken Conley, Melinda T. Gervasio, Deborah L. McGuinness, David N. Morley, Avi Pfeffer, Martha E. Pollack, and Milind Tambe. 2007. An Intelligent Personal Assistant for Task and Time Management. *AI Magazine* 28 (2007), 47–61.
[34] Kishore Papineni, Salim Roukos, Todd Ward, and Wei-Jing Zhu. 2002. BLEU: a method for automatic evaluation of machine translation. In *Proceedings of the 40th annual meeting on association for computational linguistics*. Association for Computational Linguistics, 311–318.
[35] Razvan Pascanu, Tomas Mikolov, and Yoshua Bengio. 2013. On the difficulty of training recurrent neural networks. *ICML (3)* 28 (2013), 1310–1318.
[36] Aaditya Prakash, Sadid A. Hasan, Kathy Lee, Vivek Datla, Ashequl Qadir, Joey Liu, and Oladimeji Farri. 2016. Neural Paraphrase Generation with Stacked Residual LSTM Networks. In *COLING*.
[37] Silvia Quarteroni and Suresh Manandhar. 2009. Designing an interactive open-domain question answering system. *Natural Language Engineering* 15, 01 (2009), 73–95.
[38] Dinesh Raghu, Sathish Indurthi, Jitendra Ajmera, and Sachindra Joshi. 2015. A Statistical Approach for Non-Sentential Utterance Resolution for Interactive QA System. In *16th Annual Meeting of the Special Interest Group on Discourse and Dialogue*. 335.
[39] Norbert Reithinger, Simon Bergweiler, Ralf Engel, Gerd Herzog, Norbert Pfleger, Massimo Romanelli, and Daniel Sonntag. 2005. A look under the hood: design and development of the first SmartWeb system demonstrator. In *ICMI*.
[40] Boris Van Schooten and Rieks Op Den Akker. 2010. Vidiam: Corpus-based Development of a Dialogue Manager for Multimodal Question Answering.
[41] Louis Shao, Stephan Gouws, Denny Britz, Anna Goldie, Brian Strope, and Ray Kurzweil. 2017. Generating Long and Diverse Responses with Neural Conversation Models.
[42] Yangyang Shi, Kaisheng Yao, Hu Chen, Yi-Cheng Pan, Mei-Yuh Hwang, and Baolin Peng. 2015. Contextual spoken language understanding using recurrent neural networks. In *ICASSP*.
[43] Max Sklar. 2016. Marsbot: Building a Personal Assistant. In *RecSys*.
[44] Noah A Smith, Michael Heilman, and Rebecca Hwa. 2008. Question generation as a competitive undergraduate course project. In *Proceedings of the NSF Workshop on the Question Generation Shared Task and Evaluation Challenge*.
[45] Jinsong Su, Zhixing Tan, Deyi Xiong, and Yang Liu. 2016. Lattice-Based Recurrent Neural Network Encoders for Neural Machine Translation. *CoRR* abs/1609.07730 (2016).
[46] Ilya Sutskever, Oriol Vinyals, and Quoc V Le. 2014. Sequence to sequence learning with neural networks. In *Advances in neural information processing systems*. 3104–3112.
[47] Gökhan Tür, Ye-Yi Wang, and Dilek Z. Hakkani-Tür. 2014. Understanding Spoken Language. In *Computing Handbook, 3rd ed.*
[48] Boris W. van Schooten, Rieks op den Akker, Sophie Rosset, Olivier Galibert, Aurélien Max, and Gabriel Illouz. 2009. Follow-up question handling in the IMIX and Ritel systems: A comparative study. *Natural Language Engineering* 15 (2009), 97–118.
[49] Haifeng Wang. 2016. Duer: Intelligent Personal Assistant. In *CIKM*.
[50] Jason D Williams, Pascal Poupart, and Steve Young. 2005. Factored Partially Observable Markov Decision Processes for Dialogue Management.
[51] Kelvin Xu, Jimmy Ba, Jamie Ryan Kiros, Kyunghyun Cho, Aaron C. Courville, Ruslan Salakhutdinov, Richard S. Zemel, and Yoshua Bengio. 2015. Show, Attend and Tell: Neural Image Caption Generation with Visual Attention. In *ICML*.
[52] Rui Yan, Yiping Song, and Hua Wu. 2016. Learning to Respond with Deep Neural Networks for Retrieval-Based Human-Computer Conversation System. In *SIGIR*.
[53] Wojciech Zaremba, Ilya Sutskever, and Oriol Vinyals. 2014. Recurrent Neural Network Regularization. *CoRR* abs/1409.2329 (2014).
[54] Barret Zoph, Deniz Yuret, Jonathan May, and Kevin Knight. 2016. Transfer Learning for Low-Resource Neural Machine Translation. In *EMNLP*.

Modelling Information Needs in Collaborative Search Conversations

Sosuke Shiga
Graduate School of Library, Information and Media Studies, University of Tsukuba
s1521619@u.tsukuba.ac.jp

Hideo Joho*
Research Center for Knowledge Communities, University of Tsukuba
hideo@slis.tsukuba.ac.jp

Roi Blanco
School of Computer Science and Information Technology, RMIT University
rblanco@udc.es

Johanne R. Trippas
School of Computer Science and Information Technology, RMIT University
johanne.trippas@rmit.edu.au

Mark Sanderson
School of Computer Science and Information Technology, RMIT University
mark.sanderson@rmit.edu.au

ABSTRACT

The increase of voice-based interaction has changed the way people seek information, making search more *conversational*. Development of effective conversational approaches to search requires better understanding of how people express information needs in dialogue. This paper describes the creation and examination of over 32K spoken utterances collected during 34 hours of collaborative search tasks. The contribution of this work is three-fold. First, we propose a model of conversational information needs (CINs) based on a synthesis of relevant theories in Information Seeking and Retrieval. Second, we show several behavioural patterns of CINs based on the proposed model. Third, we identify effective feature groups that may be useful for detecting CINs categories from conversations. This paper concludes with a discussion of how these findings can facilitate advance of conversational search applications.

CCS CONCEPTS

•**Information systems → Information retrieval;** *Query representation; Collaborative search;*

KEYWORDS

Conversation, Information Needs, Collaborative Search

ACM Reference format:

Sosuke Shiga, Hideo Joho, Roi Blanco, Johanne R. Trippas, and Mark Sanderson. 2017. Modelling Information Needs in Collaborative Search Conversations. In *Proceedings of SIGIR '17, August 07-11, 2017, Shinjuku, Tokyo, Japan,* 10 pages.
DOI: 10.1145/3077136.3080787

*Corresponding author. This work was carried out while the second author was visiting RMIT University.

SIGIR '17, August 07-11, 2017, Shinjuku, Tokyo, Japan
© 2017 ACM. 978-1-4503-5022-8/17/08...$15.00
DOI: 10.1145/3077136.3080787

1 INTRODUCTION

Verbal conversation used to be an integral part of the searching process when users were required to explain their information needs to an intermediary (e.g. librarian) who operated a catalogue system to find relevant records in a database. When the intermediary was replaced by search engines, textual queries and clicks on ten blue links became the conversation between users and search applications. In the last few years, however, verbal communication between users and search applications has increased due to the advance of automatic speech recognition (ASR) technologies, and the availability of voice-based applications and devices such as Amazon Echo and Google Home.

The increase of voice-based interaction has changed the way people seek information. A major search engine reports that 20% of mobile queries in the US are now submitted using voice (Google [9]). A study also shows that voice queries have different attributes from conventional written queries (Guy [13]). These findings highlight the importance of research on speech oriented interaction in Information Retrieval (IR) and related fields. Kiseleva, et al. [23]'s study also demonstrates that ASR enables mining from spoken interaction data to expand the capability of search applications to offer intelligent assistance.

One promising direction suggested by these studies is that search interaction are becoming more *conversational*. We are no longer limited to short underspecified text strings to predict information needs behind queries. This also means that searchable content could potentially be any spoken word that is recorded: a resource much larger than the Web (Oard [35]). This paper aims to contribute to such a direction by providing insights into the behaviour of information needs expressed in conversations, which we call *conversational information needs* (CINs) in this paper.

This paper sets the following research questions to gain better understanding of how people express a broad range of information needs in conversations of collaborative search tasks.

- RQ1: How can we model information needs expressed in conversations of collaborative search tasks?
- RQ2: What are the characteristics of CINs?
- RQ3: What features are effective at detecting CINs?

The contributions of this paper are as follows. First, we propose a model of CINs based on a synthesis of relevant theories in Information Seeking and Retrieval (ISR). Second, we show several behavioural patterns of CINs using spoken dialogue data we built from approximately 34 hours of recordings of collaborative search tasks. Third, we identify effective feature groups that can be useful for detecting CIN categories from conversations. Finally, this paper discusses how these findings can facilitate the advancement of conversational search applications.

It should be noted that we do not consider the accuracy of ASR or dialogue analyses systems in this work (Jiang, et al. [21]). Instead, we used professionally transcribed data and manually annotated information to exclude the effect of system inaccuracies in our research. It should also be noted that all experiments were carried out in Japanese, and thus, the descriptions and findings in this paper are translations from the original language. We discuss the implication of this limitation in Section 6.

The rest of the paper is structured as follows. Section 2 reviews studies related to this work. Section 3 proposes a model of CINs. Section 4 describes the conversation dataset we built for this study. Section 5 presents the results of analyses that examined the behavioural patterns of CINs and their prediction. Section 6 discusses the major findings, implications on the design of conversational search applications, and limitations of our findings. Section 7 concludes the paper with future directions.

2 RELATED WORK

2.1 Conversations in Information Seeking & Retrieval Research

Research on conversations is not new in ISR. Well known models such as Taylor's taxonomy of information needs [39] and Kuhlthau's Information Searching Process (ISP) model [24] were based on analyses of conversations between librarians and users, or between students in group work. Qualitative analyses of conversations during ISR led researchers to develop conceptual models that help describe complex searching behaviours.

Other studies have focused on discourse aspects of conversations. For example, Belkin, et al. [3] proposed a coding scheme to annotate conversations between librarians and users to better understand the design of expert systems. Their scheme showed that one can extract a range of contextual information from dialogues, including the description, states, modes of problems at hand, user models, search strategies, and search interactions. Later, Belkin, et al. [4] introduced a concept of scripts that described functions of dialogues, and applied them to the design of interactive IR system. Yuan and Belkin [20] also applied a dialogue structure to design an interactive IR system, allowing them to study users' search tactics in detail. A recent study by Trippas, et al. [40] proposed an annotation scheme of conversational search tasks in a context of speech-only interactions.

The increase of interest in collaborative search since mid 2000 led to some quantitative analyses of conversations during search (Morris and Teevan [33] and Hansen, et al. [15]) . For example, Shah and González-Ibáñez [37] classified textual collaborative search chats into the six stages of the ISP model, and visualised the progression of ISP stages during collaborative search tasks. Imazu, et al. [16] also manually classified utterances during collaborative search into search-oriented and task-oriented utterances, suggesting that utterances can be a useful resource to mine contextual information about underlying tasks. Foster [12] performed discourse analysis on talks in group work to examine the relationship between the function of talk and information seeking activities.

These studies suggest that collaborative search conversations can be a promising source to mine contexts of search. However, existing studies remain either conceptual, small-scale, or use text chat data. This paper examines over 32K spoken utterances from 34 collaborative search sessions, which were manually annotated[1].

2.2 Relevant Models of Information Needs

This section reviews theories, models, and findings that can help us investigate information needs expressed in conversations.

Information need has many definitions and conceptualisations in the literature (e.g., [2, 7, 8, 39]). In this paper, we adapt the one defined by Case [7][2]: "An *information need* is a recognition that your knowledge is inadequate to satisfy a goal that you have" (p. 5), since it serves as a good starting point in our discussion. As the definition implies, information needs emerge inside a user's head and are not immediately observable (Wilson [41]). A recent work by Moshfeghi, et al. [34] tackles this issue by analysing brain activities. Analysis of conversations during collaborative work has advantages since many information needs are naturally verbalised during the task, and they can be captured and examined without expensive equipment such as an fMRI.

Taylor's taxonomy of information needs [39] helps us conceptualise differences between perceived needs and queries. Taylor's model consists of four levels of information needs: *Visceral Needs*, *Conscious Needs*, *Formalised Needs*, and *Compromised Needs*. *Visceral Needs* are defined as a "vague sort of dissatisfaction" including nonverbal expressions. *Conscious Needs* are defined as an "ambiguous and rambling statement" of the needs, which may eventually evolve to *Formalised Needs*, which are a "qualified and rational" statement of the need. However, as query log analyses show (Jansen, et al. [19]), users often submit a short and underspecified query to search engines, which can be classified as *Compromised Needs* in Taylor's model. On the other hand, a Formalised Need can be seen as a question submitted to community-based QA sites or speech-oriented search applications.

Brystörm and Järvelin [6] state that the types of information searchers seek can vary over time in complex tasks. They include *problem information* (i.e., requirement of a task at hand), *domain information* (i.e., topical information about the task), and *problem solving information* (i.e., information regarding solutions). Furthermore, Hansen [14] and Ingwersen and Järvelin [17] emphasise the importance of distinguishing task levels such as *work task* (main task) and *search task* (sub tasks) to elicit contextual factors of a given information need. The significance of contextual factors to determine relevance of information objects is also recognised by Saracevic's stratified model of IR interaction [36].

[1] Although we are currently unable to release the dataset due to lack of explicit consent from participants, a project to develop a shareable English dataset is already in progress based on the methodology presented in this paper.

[2] Case [7] is a good place to learn more about various discussions on information needs.

Finally, McGareth's circumplex model of group tasks [11] informs that resolving group members' interest, preference, and opinion is a crucial step in successful collaborative work. This suggests that conversational information needs can be directed towards users themself, in addition to tasks at hand. In Section 3, we discuss how to operationalise these variables to investigate a broad range of information needs expressed in the conversations of a collaborative search task.

2.3 Spoken Dialogue Systems and Dialogue Acts

Finally, we briefly discuss the research on Spoken Dialogue Systems (SDS), which allows for interaction with computer-based applications such as expert systems or databases by spoken natural language (McTear [28]). For example, some SDS were designed to provide travel information or allow users to book trains or flights [27]. However, many of these SDS were based on a finite state-based or frame-based dialogue control which guides the user through a specified dialogue. This suggests that we might need a different approach to conversational search applications, supporting diverse domains, modes, scenarios, and levels of information needs expressed by search engine users.

Nevertheless, studies of broad dialogues offer promising features to better model information needs in conversations. One such example are Dialogue Acts. Dialogue Acts are communicative functions of dialogue segments [5], such as *request*, *inform*, *question*, *suggestion*, and *offer*. The scope and taxonomy of Dialogue Acts are wide and complex, with many different markup schemes available. In this work, we examine a relevant part of the Dialogue Acts' taxonomy defined by ISO 24617-2 [18] since it is the outcome of synthesising major annotation schemes. Another relevant concept, which is rarely examined in IR, is *turn-taking*. Dialogues can be divided into segments called turns. In one turn a single speaker has control over the dialogue and can produce several spoken segments (Khouzaimi, et al. [22]). Analysis of turn-taking structures allows researchers to examine, for example, how smooth the switches between two speakers were. In this work, we incorporate a simplified statistic of turn-taking phenomena as a feature to detect information needs from dialogue.

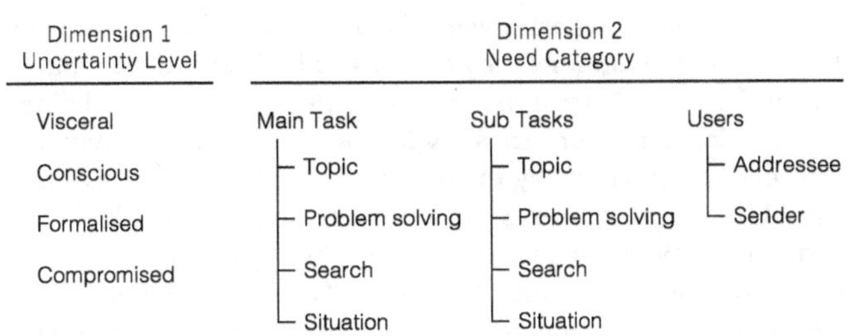

Figure 1: Proposed model of conversational information needs (CINs), consisting of two dimensions: Uncertainty level and need category.

3 PROPOSED MODEL OF CONVERSATIONAL INFORMATION NEEDS (CINS)

Having surveyed the relevant ISR models in literature, we propose to use two dimensions to describe conversational information needs: uncertainty level and need category (See Figure 1). The rest of this section discusses these two dimensions in detail.

3.1 Dimension 1: Uncertainty Level

The first dimension of our proposed model is about the level of uncertainty expressed by collaborative work conversations. Conversations allow us to mine information needs with multiple levels of uncertainty, which is difficult with conventional resources. The conceptual definitions of the uncertainty level are based on the taxonomy proposed by Taylor [39] (see Section 2.2). What we need are operational definitions of these levels. Based on the implications from Kuhlthau's ISP model [24], Belkin, et al.'s ASK [2], and Dialogue Act ISO [18], we devise a set of quantifiable operational definitions to the uncertainty levels as follows.

Regarding *Visceral Needs* ($L1$), we propose to explore negative expressions in conversations such as negation, rejection, disagreement, frustration, and hesitation. Affective states described in the ISP model seem to be appropriate to be considered at this high level of uncertainty in information needs. As for *Conscious Needs* ($L2$), we propose to focus on expressions related to lack of knowledge as informed by ASK and other models. For *Formalised Needs* ($L3$), we propose to take advantage of questions in conversations, since it offered clear and explicit expressions of information needs. This was also informed by the concept of information needs used in the Dialogue Act taxonomy. Finally, for *Compromised Needs* ($L4$), we propose to use actual queries submitted to search applications.

It should be noted that in this work, we focus on Conscious Needs ($L2$) and Formalised Needs ($L3$) since their potential impact on determining people's information needs from conversation is considered to be large. Investigation on Visceral Needs ($L1$) and cross examination with Compromised Needs ($L4$) are equally interesting, but are left to future work.

3.2 Dimension 2: Need Category

While the first dimension of our proposed CIN model was designed to quantify the level of uncertainty expressed in the conversations, the second dimension is designed to shape the types of information needs expressed by users. We devise ten categories stemming from the implications of studies such as Saracevic's relevance model [36], Belkin, et al.'s discourse analyses [3], Brystörm and Järvelin's task complexity [6], and McGrath's model of group tasks [p.14, 11].

The definition and sample utterances of the ten information need categories are shown in Table 1. The top level is divided into three groups: *Main task*, *Sub tasks*, and *Users*. In this work, the main task was travel planning, while sub tasks included finding interesting places to visit at a destination, comparing flight schedules, making a decision on hotels to stay in, and other smaller tasks that needed to be completed to achieve the main task. The main task and sub tasks categories have the common second level of needs on *Topic*, *Problem solving*, *Search*, and *Situation*. The user category has the second level of needs on *Addressee* (partner) and *Sender* (speaker).

The next section describes how we operationalised these variables using conversation data and their annotations.

4 CONVERSATION DATA

This section describes the development and annotation process for our spoken conversation corpus.

4.1 Data Collection

Conversations of collaborative work were collected by a laboratory-based user study[3]. The detail of the study is as follows.

4.1.1 Participants. A total of 34 pairs of participants was recruited for the study at University of Tsukuba. A call for participation was distributed via selected institution mailing lists, lab websites, and subsequent snowballing methods. People were asked to apply as a pair with someone who would be comfortable to perform collaborative work. Suitable applicants were recruited on a first-come first-serve manner. Of the 68 participants, 30 were female and 38 were male. All participants were in the age group of 18 to 24 years old. The academic background of participants varied from Computer Science and Information Science to Engineering, Social Science, and Humanities and Arts.

4.1.2 Collaborative Task. Each pair was asked to perform a travel planning task, one of the most common collaborative tasks performed with search (Morris, [31]). It is a highly information intensive task with many decisions to make based on outcomes of searching. It is also an engaging and familiar task to participants, which was essential to collect natural rich conversations in this work. Furthermore, a travel planning task has successfully been used by collaborative search studies (e.g., Morris and Horvitz [32], Aizenbud-Reshef, et al. [1], Arif, et al. [30]).

In our setting, participant pairs were given 60 minutes to make a travel plan for a 3-4 day trip in Japan with mutual friends. The destination of the trip was decided by participants. Before starting, a budget was set to a reasonable price to ensure realistic decisions were made during the task. We imposed two restrictions in the experiment. First, participants were not allowed to select a pre-defined package tour for the whole schedule. Second, all decisions had to be discussed and agreed between partners. In addition, participants were asked to decide initial roles of operating a shared PC (see below for experimental apparatus), and of writing down a travel plan. They were allowed to switch the roles any time.

4.1.3 Experimental Apparatus. Participants were given a PC, an sheet of A3 paper for writing a travel plan, and pens. Conversations were recorded during the task by a microphone on the table. The PC logged the transaction of operations, however, the focus of this paper is on the conversation between participants. Consequently, close examination of search logs is left to future work.

4.1.4 Protocol. Each experiment was carried out as follows. 1) Participants were given an information sheet to explain the aim and design of the experiment. 2) After a consent form was signed, an entry questionnaire was administered to gather demographic and background information about collaborative work and travel planning. 3) Next, the task of travel planning was introduced with a sample travel plan, and restrictions (see Section 4.1.2) were explained. 4) After a question answering session regarding the task design, participants started to perform the task and conversations and PC operations were recorded. 5) After the task was completed (or 60 minutes were gone), participants were asked to fill in an exit questionnaire to capture general feedback on the task and experiment. An experimenter was in the lab to address any technical issues.

[3]Ethics approval was obtained from University of Tsukuba.

4.2 Segmentation and Annotations

4.2.1 Segmentation. Approximately 34 hours of recordings of collaborative task conversations were first transcribed by a professional service. Transcription included a speaker ID, timestamp, and filler annotations. Then, transcribed conversations were manually segmented into utterances based on guidelines provided by Bunt, et al. [5]. In particular, we adapted the concept of *functional segments*, which is defined as "functionally relevant minimal stretches of communicative behaviour" [p.2549, 5], since they gave us a fine granularity to investigate the characteristics of information needs expressed in conversations. After the initial segmentation by the first author, a random sample of segmentations was examined by another author to ensure consistency in the process. As a result, 32,950 utterances were identified in the dataset, which formed the basis of our analyses.

4.2.2 Annotations. We used a crowdsourcing service[4] to annotate the segmented utterances with ten categories of conversational information needs as described in Section 3. The procedure was as follows. Each utterance was presented to a crowd worker who was also shown the previous and subsequent utterance as context. The annotation interface also provided, as instructions, the information shown in Table 1: the label, definition, and sample of ten information need categories. Crowd workers were then asked to select one of the ten need labels or choose the option "None of them".

We obtained three independent annotations for every dialogue in our dataset, and took a majority vote to assign the final label. When three votes disagreed on a category, we assigned them to "Others", along with those judged as "None of them". All crowd workers had to pass a labelling screening test with a score of > 80%, before they annotated our dataset. We also manually validated the credibility of annotations and removed those that were given by poor quality workers (approx. 20%).

Dialogue act categories were also labelled in the corpus using Dialogue Act definitions provided by ISO [18]. The ISO definition was written in a formal manner: e.g. the *question* act is defined as "A dialogue act performed by Sender, *S*, in order to obtain the information, described by the semantic content, which *S* assumes the addressee, *A*, posses; *S* puts pressure on *A* to provide this information". We rephrased the definitions slightly to ensure that crowd workers understood the scope of each act category. Since we focused on a subset of dialogue acts, only one label was selected per utterance based on a majority voting manner. The resulting distribution of dialogue acts is shown in Table 2. As can be seen, nearly half the dialogues in our dataset were categorised as the *Inform* act (45.0%), followed by *Question* (13.4%) and *Suggestion* (13.2%).

[4]https://lancers.jp/ Accessed: 24/01/2017.

Table 1: Definition and sample utterances of the proposed information need category. *L2* **and** *L3* **indicates** ***Conscious Needs*** **(expressing lack of knowledge) and** ***Formalised Needs*** **(expressing explicit questions), respectively.**

Label	Definition	Sample utterance(s)
Main Task		
Topic	Needs of topical knowledge of a main task	*How much time do we have for our trip? (L3)*
Problem Solving	Needs of knowledge about solving a problem of a main task	*I don't know how I should describe this in the plan sheet. (L2)*
Search	Needs of knowledge about search of a main task	*I can't bookmark this page. (L2)*
Situation	Needs of knowledge about a current situation of a main task	*How much have we spent so far? (L3)*
Sub Tasks		
Topic	Needs of topical knowledge of sub tasks	*I have no idea about interesting places in [location]. (L2)*
Problem Solving	Needs of knowledge about solving a problem of sub tasks	*What's the best way to visit [location]? (L3)*
Search	Needs of knowledge about search of sub tasks	*Hmm. I can't see access information on this page. (L2)*
Situation	Needs of knowledge about a current situation of sub tasks	*Have we checked the price of the entry fee? (L3)*
Users		
Addressee	Needs about a partner's opinions, preferences, and knowledge	*Have you been to [location]? (L3)*
Sender	Needs about a speaker's opinions, preferences, and knowledge	*Ah, the spelling doesn't come out. (L2)*

Table 2: Distribution of dialogue acts (DA).

	N	%
Inform	14,832	45.0
Question	4,412	13.4
Suggestion	4,362	13.2
Offer	548	1.7
Request	471	1.4
Others	8,325	25.3
Total	32,950	100.0

Table 3: Features used to detect CINs.

Category	Features
Temporal	Utterance Sequential ID (Sequential ID)
Dialogue	Dialogue Acts (except Question), Speaker IDs, Turn Ratio
Semantic	Word Embeddings (200 dimensions)
Linguistic	Entities, Filler, Interjection, Mark, Adjective, Post-positions, Auxiliary, Conjunction, Prefix, Verb, Adverb, Noun, Abdominal, Punctuation
Statistic	Characters, Words, Inverse Term Frequency (ITF)

Close examination of temporal patterns of dialogue acts in our dataset shows that the frequency of Dialogue Acts expressed by a pair of participants varies during the collaborative task. Some parts have frequent turns while other parts have a single user dominating the conversations. These observations suggest that mining dialogue acts, speaker IDs, and temporal aspects will be important signals to understand conversational information needs, which will be discussed in the next section in more detail.

Utterances were then categorised into *Concious Needs* or *Formalised Needs* (Uncertainty level dimension in the proposed CIN model) based on a simple rule as follows. If an utterance had one of the ten need category labels and the *Question* dialogue act label, then the utterance was categorised to a Formalised Need, since a question regarding one of the ten needs was explicitly asked. If an utterance had one of the ten need category labels and one of the dialogue act labels except *Question* and *Non Act*, then the utterance was categorised as a Conscious Need, since it expressed a lack of knowledge on an aspect of the task but the expression was not quite as explicit.

In addition to manual annotations, we used the Cloud Natural Language API[5] offered by Google to annotate Part of Speech (POS) and other linguistic tags and entities in utterances.

[5]https://cloud.google.com/natural-language/ Accessed: 14/01/2017.

4.3 Features

Finally, we developed and organised a set of features that were used to train and predict conversational information need categories. We used a Random Forest classifier, which is able to detect interdependencies between covariate features. We were able to estimate the importance of each feature based on its overall contribution to the final predictive model, dependent on every other feature used as a covariate. The features used in our study are summarised in Table 3. To better understand the effectiveness of features, we categorised them into five groups:

Temporal group represents temporal aspects of dialogues such as their sequential IDs;

Dialogue group includes features representing dialogue acts, speaker IDs, and turn ratio. The turn ratio was the number of utterance switches that occurred between two users divided by the sliding window size of *N* (*N* was arbitrarily set to 5 in our study). This was designed to quantify the frequency of exchanges of ideas between users;

Semantic group has word embeddings of non-functional words in utterances. We used the embedding vectors[6] (200 dimensions) trained by the entire Japanese Wikipedia corpus (as of 01/11/2016) using `word2vec`[7] [29];

Linguistic group consists of POS tags and entity annotations.

[6]http://www.cl.ecei.tohoku.ac.jp/~m-suzuki/jawiki_vector/ Accessed: 14/01/2017.
[7]https://code.google.com/archive/p/word2vec/ Accessed: 14/01/2017.

Table 4: Distribution of CINs (*L*2 and *L*3).

	N	%
Conscious Needs (*L*2)	2,410	7.3
Formalised Needs (*L*3)	3,072	9.3
Others	27,468	83.3
Total	32,950	100.0

Table 5: Distribution of Conscious Needs (*L*2) and Formalised Needs (*L*3) Categories.

		*L*2		*L*3	
		N	%	*N*	%
Main Task		179	7.4	233	7.6
	Topic	80	3.3	113	3.7
	Problem Solving	62	2.6	48	1.6
	Search	19	0.8	7	0.2
	Situation	18	0.7	65	2.1
Sub Tasks		1,224	50.8	1,988	64.7
	Topic	723	30.0	1,556	50.7
	Problem Solving	147	6.1	188	6.1
	Search	340	14.1	212	6.9
	Situation	14	0.6	32	1.0
Users		1,007	41.8	851	27.7
	Addressee	797	33.1	790	25.7
	Sender	210	8.7	61	2.0
Total		2,410	100.0	3,072	100.0

They are represented as a proportion of their frequency of occurrence in the total number of words in an utterance; and

Statistical group includes length of utterances both in characters and words, and inverse term frequency (ITF), which is calculated as $ITF = \log \frac{n_i}{N_i}$, where i represents an utterance sequence ID, n_i is a frequency of occurrence of term n at i, and N_i is a total number of frequency of occurrence of all terms at i. ITF of an utterance was the average of all terms in the utterance. The score will be high when an utterance has more new or infrequent terms, while the score will be low when an utterance consists of only highly repeated terms.

5 DATA ANALYSIS

We present the results of data analysis performed on the annotated conversation corpus described in Section 4. We begin by looking at some descriptive data of the corpus, followed by temporal analysis, state transition analysis, and finally, feature analysis for prediction.

5.1 Descriptive Analysis

The distribution of CINs based on the two dimensions of the proposed model is shown in Tables 4 and 5, respectively. These tables inform us about several aspects regarding the characteristics of conversational information needs. Table 4 shows that just under 17% of utterances in collaborative work includes expressions of information needs: 7.3% as Conscious Needs (*L*2) and 9.3% as Formalised Needs (*L*3).

The breakdown of need related utterances in Table 5 shows that the largest proportion of such utterances comes from conversations on sub tasks, both in Conscious Needs (*L*2) and Formalised Needs (*L*3). Similarly, many utterances were devoted to express needs of users at both levels. However, Conscious Needs (*L*2) include more dialogues on users while Formalised Needs (*L*3) include more dialogues on sub tasks. Under the main task and sub tasks, utterances on needs related to *Topic* were commonly the largest proportion at both levels.

5.2 Temporal Analysis

Figure 2(a) shows the progression of information needs over the collaborative task. For every participant pair, all utterances were divided into 25 bins, where Bin 1 indicates the beginning of the task and Bin 25 the end. For each bin, the proportion of utterances that were annotated as Conscious Needs (*L*2), Formalised Needs (*L*3), and others was calculated; the figure shows the average of 34 pairs.

Figure 2(a) shows that the proportion of utterances that express information needs (*L*2 + *L*3) is approximately 15-20% across the bins. We can observe a slight decrease in need related utterances towards the end of the bins. Pearson's coefficient shows that the proportion of Conscious Needs (*L*2) has a significant large negative correlation ($r = -.54, p \leq .001$) with the Bin IDs, suggesting that expressions of lack of knowledge slowly degrade as the collaborative task progresses. Conversely, the proportion of other dialogues has a significant medium level positive correlation ($r = .45, p \leq .02$) with the Bin IDs.

Figure 2(b) shows the progression of utterances that were annotated as Conscious Needs (*L*2). The figure shows that the proportion of needs related to the main task was larger at the beginning (e.g., confirming task requirements) and end of the task (e.g., validating the travel plan created) than the middle parts. On the other hand, the proportion of needs related to sub tasks and users remains at a similar level although they vary across the bins. No significant correlation was observed between the Conscious Needs categories and Bin IDs.

Figure 2(c) shows the same data as Figure 2(b) but for Formalised Needs (*L*3). The figure shows that Formalised Needs have a similar pattern to Conscious Needs on the main task related utterances. However, the proportion of sub task related information needs is larger than the other two categories of dialogues, which is different from Conscious Needs. Pearson's coefficient shows that the proportion of information needs related to users has a significant medium level of negative correlation ($r = -.46, p \leq .02$) with Bin IDs, suggesting that participants' explicit enquiries on each other slowly degrades towards the end of task.

5.3 State Transition Analysis

Figure 3 shows state transfer diagrams of utterances and information needs. Figure 3(a) depicts transitions between Conscious Needs utterances, Formalised Needs utterances, and others. A large proportion of utterances was transferred from need categories to

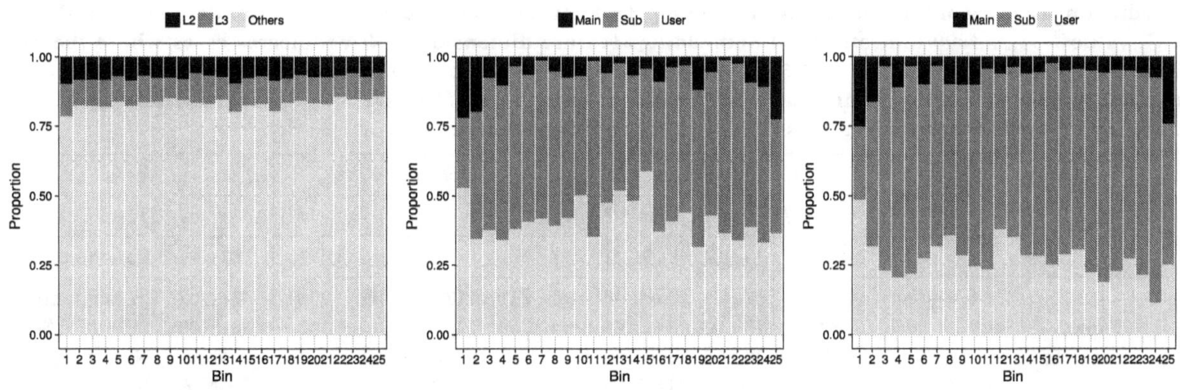

(a) All Dialogues (b) Conscious Needs ($L2$) (c) Formalised Needs ($L3$)

Figure 2: Progression of information needs over the collaborative task. Figure 2(a) shows that the proportion of utterances expressing information needs is approximately 15-20% across the bins. Figure 2(b) shows that the proportion of Conscious Needs ($L2$) related to the main task is larger at the beginning and end of the task. The proportion of needs related to sub tasks and users varies over the bins but remains similar size. Figure 2(c) shows that the proportion of Formalised Needs ($L3$) related to the main task is larger at the beginning and end of the task. Compared to the Conscious Needs, the proportion of sub task related needs is larger than the other two categories of utterances.

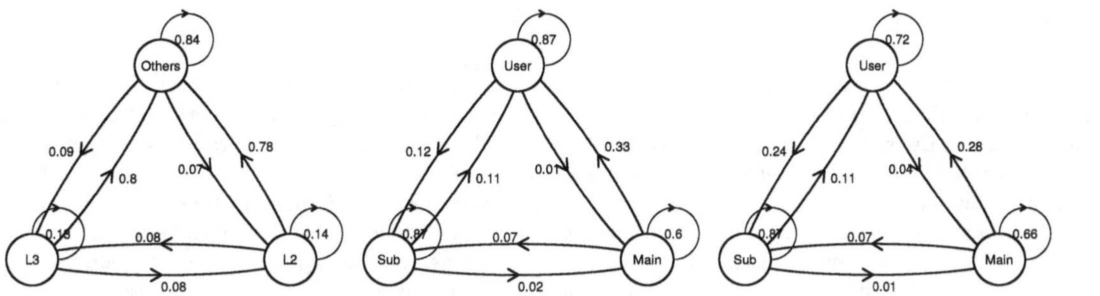

(a) All Dialogues (b) Conscious needs ($L2$) (c) Formalised needs ($L3$)

Figure 3: State transfer diagram of dialogues. Figure 3(a) shows that conversations between users do not necessarily progress from Conscious Needs to Formalised Needs directly, but via other dialogues. Figure 3(b) and 3(c) show that dialogues between users do not necessarily progress from main-task needs to sub task needs directly, but via needs regarding users.

the *Other* category, rather than directly transferring between the two levels of needs.

Figure 3(b) and 3(c) show the transition of the main task related needs, sub task related needs, and user related needs into Conscious Needs ($L2$) and Formalised Needs ($L3$), respectively. Note that the *Others* category were not included in these diagrams. The figures show that there exists a relatively high probability of self-state transition in all need categories, suggesting that utterances on a similar group of needs can continue in conversations. This is common in Conscious Needs ($L2$) and Formalised Needs ($L3$).

Another finding is that we observed little direct transition between *Main Task* and *Sub Tasks*. Instead, a common route of transition was via needs on *Users*. This suggests that it was common to express needs to a participants' partner or to themselves before moving on to a different subtask. This trend is stronger in Conscious Needs ($L2$) than Formalised Needs ($L3$).

5.4 Effective Features to Predict CINs

The final part of the analysis aimed to identify effective features to predict the ten information need categories.

5.4.1 Setup. We tested several algorithms, including Naïve Bayes, SVM, and Random Forest. However, we only report the outcomes of Random Forest, since it provided an overall best performance among them without requiring a large amount of training data. In addition, Mean Decrease Gini (MDG) values were obtained to rank features based on its importance to categorisation, and thus, identify effective features to predict needs related utterances. We used R's *randomForest* package[8] (Liaw and Wiener [25]).

The results of Random Forest and three best features are shown in Table 6, where we assume that the prediction of need categories is performed in a tree structure. In other words, the top level

[8]https://cran.r-project.org/web/packages/randomForest/ Accessed: 14/01/2017.

Table 6: Prediction accuracy of information needs and top 3 effective features determined by Random Forest's Mean Decrease Gini (MDG) values. f1 ... f200 indicate Word Embeddings feature dimensions. N/A indicates cases where the sample size was considered too small to examine ($N \leq 50$). Numbers in parentheses are the actual size of positive samples used in the experiment due to down-sampling requirement. Accuracy is a mean value of 20 iterations of experiments with 95% confidence interval. One sample t-test shows that all results are statistically significance ($p \leq .001$).

		Conscious Needs (*L2*)			Formalised Needs (*L3*)		
		N	Accuracy	Top 3 Features	*N*	Accuracy	Top 3 Features
All		2,410	.73±.01	f151, f17, f97	3,072	.82±.01	Punctuation, f34, f187
Main Task		179	.67±.03	Sequential ID, ITF, f117	233	.72±.02	f3, Sequential ID, f117
	Topic	80	.78±.03	ITF, Sequential ID, f130	113	.81±.03	f130, ITF, Sequential ID
	Problem Solving	62	.72±.05	f70, f50, f124	48	N/A	N/A
	Search	19	N/A	N/A	7	N/A	N/A
	Situation	18	N/A	N/A	65	.78±.04	Sequential ID, ITF, f185
Sub Tasks		1,224 (1,186)	.75±.01	DA, f149, f19	1,988 (1,084)	.74±.01	f52, f149, ITF
	Topic	723 (501)	.73±.02	f111, f191, f13	1,556 (432)	.73±.01	f111, f81, f129
	Problem Solving	147	.60±.02	f81, f86, f28	188	.77±.02	f81, f129, f111
	Search	340	.71±.02	f123, f197, f101	212	.73±.02	f101, f197, f85
	Situation	14	N/A	N/A	32	N/A	N/A
Users		1007	.75±.01	DA, f149, f11	851	.75±.01	f11, f149, f97
	Addressee	797 (210)	.84±.02	Punctuation, DA, f11	790 (61)	.74±.04	f11, f156, f196
	Sender	210	.85±.02	Punctuation, DA, f196	61	.73±.04	f11, f156, f196

classification of *Conscious Needs*, *Formalised Needs*, and *Others* is first performed. Then, within the *Conscious Needs* data, we classify *Main Task*, *Sub Tasks*, and *Users*, individually. Finally, within the *Main Task*, we further classify *Topic*, *Problem Solving*, *Search*, and *Situation* in a similar manner.

In all cases, the prediction was a binary judgement so that we can determine the prediction power of our features for each need category. For a given number of positive utterance samples of a particular need category (e.g., *Topic* of *Main Task*), we sampled the same number of negative samples. Then, a training set and testing set were divided into a 4:1 ratio. The training set was further divided for repeated sampling to determine optimal parameters of Random Forests. In the case where a sufficient number of either positive or negative samples was not available, we performed down-sampling. The numbers in parentheses in Table 6 are the actual size of positive samples used in the experiment. We also removed those categories with fewer than 50 positive samples from the analysis, since the sample size was considered to be too small to examine.

Since the division of training and testing sets involves random sampling, we repeated all experiments 20 times. Therefore, the accuracy in the tables were a mean of the 20 iterations, and the top 3 features were those most frequently selected features in 20 iterations. We ran one sample t-test on the 20 iterations, and all results were found to be statistically significant at $p \leq .001$.

5.4.2 Results. First, the classifier was able to indentify most categories with over 70% accuracy, suggesting that Random Forests were able to model the characteristics of needs related dialogues using our feature sets. Second, some need categories were easier than others to predict. For example, *Addressee* and *Sender* of *Users* in Conscious Needs (*L2*), and *Topic* of *Main Task* in Formalised Needs (*L3*) achieved over 80% of accuracy.

We gained insights into effective features too. For example, word embeddings (denoted as f1 ... f200 in the tables) were generally found to be useful for prediction, suggesting that the semantic features are effective at identifying a range of need categories in conversations. Formalised Needs (*L3*) seem to benefit from the semantic features more than Conscious Needs (*L2*). Dialogue features such as dialogue acts was also found to be useful for many categories of needs. In particular, user related utterances in Conscious Needs benefited from dialogue act information, along with linguistic features such as punctuation. Temporal features such as Dialogue sequence ID and statical features such as ITF were also found in several categories to be useful. For example, *Topic* and *Problem Solving* of *Main Task* (*L2*), and *Situation* of *Sub Tasks* (*L3*) were well categorised by these feature groups.

6 DISCUSSION

This work explored ways to model information needs that are expressed in collaborative search conversations. A spoken dialogue corpus was created and annotated to facilitate the study. Compared to past work, the corpus had several novel aspects. First, it is a transcription of spoken dialogues rather than text messages, which were the focus of past work [37]. Second, the annotations of information needs and a subset of dialogue acts were manually added to all utterances in the corpus. Third, the scale of the corpus was larger than most (if not all) dialogue-based studies in ISR. This section discusses the insight obtained from the study.

6.1 Major Findings

We had three research questions to address in this paper. The following discusses our findings on the three research questions, respectively.

6.1.1 RQ1: Modelling Conversational Information Needs (CINs). In the modelling of CINs, we proposed to use a two-dimensional structure which consisted of uncertainty levels and need categories, based on a synthesis of information seeking behaviour models. Although our operationalisation was limited to Conscious Needs and Formalised Needs, the proposed model was found to be useful for shaping behaviour patterns of CINs, and to determine effective features to predict CINs.

6.1.2 RQ2: Behavioural patterns of CINs. Analyses of 32K annotated utterances based on the proposed CIN model allowed us to obtain the following insights into the behaviour of conversational information needs in our dataset.

First, approximately 17% of utterances were found to express Conscious Needs (7.3%) or Formalised Needs (9.3%) in a collaborative search task. This means that one can increase the opportunity to gain information regarding users' needs by 80% if we extend our scope of information needs from Formalised Needs, which are explicit questions, to Conscious Needs, which are the expression of a lack of knowledge. Whether the additional 80% of signals can extend the range of user needs or not is yet to be determined. Nevertheless, it would seem that conversations in collaborative search can be a promising source to mine the information needs of searchers, which might not be expressed by conventional querying behaviour (e.g., Jansen, et al. [19], Guy [13]).

We also obtained some basic findings of such CINs: 1) The proportion of CINs in utterances slowly degrades as the task progresses but not in a drastic manner; 2) A large proportion of CINs consists of needs related to sub tasks and users, searchers discuss sub task related needs more than user related needs at Formalised Needs level; 3) The proportion of CINs on the main task (travel planning in this study) increases at the beginning and end of the task. The findings suggest that properties such as task development, uncertainty level, need category, and distinction of main task and sub task all play an important role in the modelling of CINs.

Second, the transition between utterances and CINs provided the following insights. 1) Direct transition between Conscious Needs and Formalised Needs is rare in conversations, and often takes place via other types of utterances. This suggests that further investigation on non-CIN utterances is still important to fully leverage conversations for mining searchers' needs. 2) Direct transition between the main task and sub tasks is also rare in conversations. Needs regarding users are often expressed to bridge the transition between the main task and sub tasks.

6.1.3 RQ3: Effective Features to Predict CINs. Here, we examined effective features to learn and predict CINs in conversations. We applied a Random Forests classifier to investigate the performance of five groups of features such as temporal, dialogue, semantic, linguistic, and statistical features.

Our results show that the semantic features based on word embeddings, partly due to their large dimensions, were the most highly ranked features to predict a range of information need categories both in Conscious Needs and Formalised Needs. Dialogue features such as Dialogue Acts, statistical features such as inverse term frequency, and temporal features such as dialogue sequence ID were also useful for several categories of information needs. On the other hand, our implementation of turn-taking phenomena was found to be too simplistic to be effective.

6.2 Implications on the Design of Conversational Search Applications

We demonstrated the effectiveness of word embeddings in predicting a range of CIN categories. This is promising since, unlike Formalized Needs, expressions of Conscious Needs (i.e., lack of knowledge) are unlikely to have clear question forms. Exploring more sophisticated representations of semantic features (e.g. domain specific word embeddings [10]) is likely to further improve CIN category prediction. Techniques such as question mining (e.g., Margolis and Ostendorf [26]) should improve the performance of detection in Formalised Needs.

Dialogue Acts were one of the more expensive features to obtain as they required manual annotations to ensure high accuracy. However, Dialogue Acts were often found to be effective features to detect CINs, therefore, advances in automatic detection of such Acts [38] will significantly impact the development of conversational search applications. Punctuations were artefacts of the transcription process in our investigation. However, given that they were effective features to identify some categories of CINs, developing a method to label punctuations on speech data might be worthwhile.

Finally, our study suggests that careful monitoring of task stages and users' progress through those stages is important for the accurate detection of information need categories from conversations. The proportion of categories varies over time and the stage of tasks. Features that capture temporal aspects were also found to be useful for detecting CINs. This echoes the findings from literature on single-person searches (e.g., Byström and Järvelin [6]), but in the context of conversational collaborative search.

6.3 Limitations

We examined one type of main collaborative task. Other tasks, which require different types of information or decision making should be studied to gain a more comprehensive view of CINs. In particular, the effectiveness of word embeddings for other CIN types is yet to be determined. In addition, our participants and conversation data were based on a particular age group in one organisation in one country. Cultural effects on our findings are left to future work.

7 CONCLUSION AND FUTURE WORK

Advances in ASR accuracy are resulting in significant opportunities and challenges in IR to make search more *conversational*. A deeper understanding of how people express a broad range of information needs in conversations can facilitate the development of conversational search applications. This paper examined over 32K spoken utterances collected during approximately 34 hours of a collaborative search task, based on a proposed model of CINs. The model consisted of two dimensions: uncertainty level and need category.

Our analyses elicited some key behavioural patterns of CINs such as the ratio of CINs in conversations, changes of CINs frequency over task development, and frequent transition to user related needs. Analyses with Random Forest classifiers also identified a range of features – such as semantic features, dialogue features, and temporal features – that are useful for detecting utterances that contain CINs in our dataset. The implications of our findings on the design of conversational search applications include the elicitation of effective features and opportunities for the development of new technologies to determine stages and progress of complex collaborative search tasks.

As for future work, close examination of query log data will allow us to better understand the impact of spoken dialogues on information searching behaviour. One might want to predict or formulate queries from conversations, or develop click models using conversation data. Expanding the scope of analysis to Visceral Needs ($L1$) using other speech features is also planned future work. More sophisticated techniques such as localised word embeddings [10] and advanced turn-taking phenomena [22] may be a promising direction to improve the detection of CINs. Finally, one could investigate the impact of languages and cultures on the behaviour of CINs.

ACKNOWLEDGMENTS

Authors thank to anonymous reviewers for their constructive comments to improve this paper. The work was supported in part by Microsoft Research Asia under MSR CORE-12 Project, Australian Research Council Projects (LP130100563 and LP150100252), Real Thing Entertainment Pty Ltd, and finally, SEEK Ltd. Any opinions, findings, and conclusions described here are the authors and do not necessarily reflect those of the sponsors.

REFERENCES

[1] Netta Aizenbud-Reshef, Artem Barger, Ido Guy, Yael Dubinsky, and Shiri Kremer-Davidson. 2012. Bon Voyage: Social Travel Planning in the Enterprise. In *Proceedings of CSCW 2012.* 819–828. DOI: http://dx.doi.org/10.1145/2145204.2145326

[2] N.J. Belkin, R.N. Oddy, and H.M. Brooks. 1982. Ask for Information Retrieval: Part I. Background and Theory. *Journal of Documentation* 38, 2 (1982), 61–71. DOI: http://dx.doi.org/10.1108/eb026722

[3] N. J. Belkin, H. M. Brooks, and P. J. Daniels. 1987. Knowledge Elicitation Using Discourse Analysis. *International Journal of Man-Machine Studies* 27, 2 (1987), 127–144. DOI: http://dx.doi.org/10.1016/S0020-7373(87)80047-0

[4] Nicholas J. Belkin, Colleen Cool, Adelheit Stein, and Ulrich Thiel. 1995. Cases, Scripts, and Information-Seeking Strategies: On the Design of Interactive Information Retrieval Systems. *Expert Systems with Applications* 9 (1995), 379–395.

[5] Harry Bunt, Jan Alexandersson, Jean Carletta, Jae-Woong Choe, Alex Chengyu Fang, Koiti Hasida, Kiyong Lee, Volha Petukhova, Andrei Popescu-Belis, Laurent Romary, Claudia Soria, and David Traum. 2010. Towards an ISO Standard for Dialogue Act Annotation. In *Proceedings of LREC 2010.*

[6] Katriina Byström and Kalervo Järvelin. 1995. Task complexity affects information seeking and use. *Information Processing and Management* 31, 2 (1995), 191 – 213.

[7] Donald Case. 2012. *Looking for Information: A Survey of Research on Information Seeking, Needs and Behavior* (3rd ed.). Emerald Group Publishing. 491 pages.

[8] Brenda Dervin. 1983. Information as a user construct: The relevance of perceived information needs to synthesis and interpretation. In *Knowledge Structure and Use: Implications for Synthesis and Interpretation.* 155–183.

[9] Google Developers. 2016. Google I/O 2016 - Keynote. (2016). https://www.youtube.com/watch?v=862r3XS2YB0 Online. Accessed: 23/01/2017.

[10] Fernando Diaz, Bhaskar Mitra, and Nick Craswell. 2016. Query Expansion with Locally-Trained Word Embeddings. In *Proceedings of ACL 2016.* 367–377. http://aclweb.org/anthology/P/P16/P16-1035.pdf

[11] Donelson R. Forsyth. 2005. *Group Dynamics* (international student ed.). Thomson Wadsworth. 640 pages.

[12] Jonathan Foster. 2009. Understanding interaction in information seeking and use as a discourse: A dialogic approach. *Journal of Documentation* 65, 1 (2009), 83–105. DOI: http://dx.doi.org/10.1108/00220410910926130

[13] Ido Guy. 2016. Searching by Talking: Analysis of Voice Queries on Mobile Web Search. In *Proceedings of SIGIR 2016.* 35–44. DOI: http://dx.doi.org/10.1145/2911451.2911525

[14] Preben Hansen. 1999. User interface design for IR interaction. a task-oriented approach. In *Proceedings of CoLIS 3.* 191–205.

[15] P. Hansen, C. Shah, and C.P. Klas. 2015. *Collaborative Information Seeking: Best Practices, New Domains and New Thoughts.* Springer International Publishing.

[16] Marika Imazu, Shin'ichi Nakayama, and Hideo Joho. 2011. Effect of Explicit Roles on Collaborative Search in Travel Planning Task. In *Proceedings of AIRS 2011.* 205–214. DOI: http://dx.doi.org/10.1007/978-3-642-25631-8_19

[17] Peter Ingwersen and Kalervo Järvelin. 2006. *The turn: Integration of information seeking and retrieval in context.* Springer. 448 pages.

[18] ISO 24617-2:2012 2012. *Language resource management – Semantic annotation framework (SemAF) – Part 2: Dialogue acts.* Standard. International Organization for Standardization, Geneva, CH. 104 pages.

[19] Bernard J. Jansen, Amanda Spink, and Tefko Saracevic. 2000. Real life, real users, and real needs: a study and analysis of user queries on the web. *Information Processing and Management* 36, 2 (2000), 207–227.

[20] Xiaojun (Jenny) Yuan and Nicholas J. Belkin. 2014. Applying an information-seeking dialogue model in an interactive information retrieval system. *Journal of Documentation* 70, 5 (2014), 829–855. DOI: http://dx.doi.org/10.1108/jd-06-2013-0079

[21] Jiepu Jiang, Wei Jeng, and Daqing He. 2013. How do users respond to voice input errors?: lexical and phonetic query reformulation in voice search. In *Proceedings of SIGIR 2013.* 143–152.

[22] Hatim Khouzaimi, Romain Laroche, and Fabrice Lefevre. 2015. Turn-taking phenomena in incremental dialogue systems. In *Proceedings of EMNLP 2015.* 1890–1895. DOI: http://dx.doi.org/10.18653/v1/D15-1216

[23] Julia Kiseleva, Kyle Williams, Ahmed Hassan Awadallah, Aidan C. Crook, Imed Zitouni, and Tasos Anastasakos. 2016. Predicting User Satisfaction with Intelligent Assistants. In *Proceedings of SIGIR 2016.* 45–54. DOI: http://dx.doi.org/10.1145/2911451.2911521

[24] Carol C. Kuhlthau. 1991. Inside the search process: Information seeking from the user's perspective. *Journal of the American Society for Information Science* 42, 5 (1991), 361–371.

[25] Andy Liaw and Matthew Wiener. 2002. Classification and Regression by randomForest. *R News* 2, 3 (2002), 18–22. http://CRAN.R-project.org/doc/Rnews/

[26] Anna Margolis and Mari Ostendorf. 2011. Question detection in spoken conversations using textual conversations. In *Proceedings of ACL 2011.* 118–124.

[27] Michael McTear, Zoraida Callejas, and David Griol. 2016. *The conversational interface.* Springer.

[28] Michael F McTear. 2002. Spoken dialogue technology: enabling the conversational user interface. *ACM Computing Surveys (CSUR)* 34, 1 (2002), 90–169.

[29] Tomas Mikolov, Ilya Sutskever, Kai Chen, Gregory S. Corrado, and Jeffrey Dean. 2013. Distributed Representations of Words and Phrases and their Compositionality. In *Proceedings of NIPS 2013.* 3111–3119.

[30] Abu Shamim Mohammad Arif, Jia Tina Du, and Ivan Lee. 2015. Understanding tourists' collaborative information retrieval behavior to inform design. *Journal of the Association for Information Science and Technology* 66, 11 (2015), 2285–2303. DOI: http://dx.doi.org/10.1002/asi.23319

[31] Meredith Ringel Morris. 2013. Collaborative Search Revisited. In *Proceedings of CSCW 2013.* 1181–1192. DOI: http://dx.doi.org/10.1145/2441776.2441910

[32] Meredith Ringel Morris and Eric Horvitz. 2007. SearchTogether: An Interface for Collaborative Web Search. In *Proceedings of UIST 2007.* 3–12. DOI: http://dx.doi.org/10.1145/1294211.1294215

[33] Meredith Ringel Morris and Jaime Teevan. 2009. Collaborative web search: Who, what, where, when, and why. *Synthesis Lectures on Information Concepts, Retrieval, and Services* 1, 1 (2009), 1–99.

[34] Yashar Moshfeghi, Peter Triantafillou, and Frank E. Pollick. 2016. Understanding Information Need: An fMRI Study. In *Proceedings of SIGIR 2016.* 335–344. DOI: http://dx.doi.org/10.1145/2911451.2911534

[35] Douglas W. Oard. 2008. Unlocking the Potential of the Spoken Word. *Science* 321, 5897 (2008), 1787–1788. DOI: http://dx.doi.org/10.1126/science.1157353

[36] Tefko. Saracevic. 1997. The stratified model of information retrieval interaction: Extension and applications. In *Proceedings of the American Society for Information Science,* Vol. 34. 313–327.

[37] Chirag Shah and Roberto González-Ibáñez. 2010. Exploring Information Seeking Processes in Collaborative Search Tasks. In *Proceedings of ASIS&T 2010.* 60:1–60:10.

[38] Andreas Stolcke, Noah Coccaro, Rebecca Bates, Paul Taylor, Carol Van Ess-Dykema, Klaus Ries, Elizabeth Shriberg, Daniel Jurafsky, Rachel Martin, and Marie Meteer. 2000. Dialogue Act Modeling for Automatic Tagging and Recognition of Conversational Speech. *Computational Linguistics* 26, 3 (2000), 339–373. DOI: http://dx.doi.org/10.1162/089120100561737

[39] Robert S. Taylor. 1962. The process of asking questions. *American Documentation* 13, 4 (1962), 391–396. DOI: http://dx.doi.org/10.1002/asi.5090130405

[40] Johanne R Trippas, Damiano Spina, Lawrence Cavedon, and Mark Sanderson. 2017. How Do People Interact in Conversational Speech-Only Search Tasks: A Preliminary Analysis. In *Proceedings of CHIIR 2017.* ACM, 325–328.

[41] Tom D. Wilson. 1981. On User Studies and Information Needs. *Journal of Documentation* 37, 1 (Jan 1981), 3–15. DOI: http://dx.doi.org/10.1108/eb026702

Author Index

NOTES

NOTES

www.ingramcontent.com/pod-product-compliance
Lightning Source LLC
LaVergne TN
LVHW080107011026
849160LV00013B/1045
* 9 7 8 1 4 5 0 3 5 6 6 8 8 *